Pediatric Otolaryngology

VOLUME 1

Pediatric Otolaryngology

VOLUME 1

Fourth Edition

Charles D. Bluestone, MD
Eberly Professor of Pediatric Otolaryngology
University of Pittsburgh School of Medicine
Director, Department of Pediatric Otolaryngology
Children's Hospital of Pittsburgh
Pittsburgh, Pennsylvania

Sylvan E. Stool, MD
Professor of Pediatrics and Otolaryngology
University of Colorado School of Medicine
Attending Physician
The Children's Hospital of Denver
Denver, Colorado

Cuneyt M. Alper, MD
Associate Professor of Otolaryngology
University of Pittsburgh School of Medicine
Department of Pediatric Otolaryngology
Children's Hospital of Pittsburgh
Pittsburgh, Pennsylvania

Ellis M. Arjmand, MD, PhD
Assistant Professor of Otolaryngology
University of Pittsburgh School of Medicine
Department of Pediatric Otolaryngology
Children's Hospital of Pittsburgh
Pittsburgh, Pennsylvania

Margaretha L. Casselbrant, MD, PhD
Professor of Otolaryngology
University of Pittsburgh School of Medicine
Director of Clinical Research and Education
Department of Pediatric Otolaryngology
Children's Hospital of Pittsburgh
Pittsburgh, Pennsylvania

Joseph E. Dohar, MD
Associate Professor of Otolaryngology
University of Pittsburgh School of Medicine
Department of Pediatric Otolaryngology
Children's Hospital of Pittsburgh
Pittsburgh, Pennsylvania

Robert F. Yellon, MD
Assistant Professor of Otolaryngology
University of Pittsburgh School of Medicine
Co-director and Director of Clinical Services
Department of Pediatric Otolaryngology
Children's Hospital of Pittsburgh
Pittsburgh, Pennsylvania

SAUNDERS
An Imprint of Elsevier Science
Philadelphia   London   New York   St. Louis   Sydney   Toronto

SAUNDERS
An Imprint of Elsevier Science

The Curtis Center
Independence Square West
Philadelphia, Pennsylvania 19106

Volume 1: Part no. 9997619838
Volume 2: Part no. 9997619846
PEDIATRIC OTOLARYNGOLOGY   Two-Volume Set: ISBN 0–7216–9197–8

Notice

Surgery/Otolaryngology is an ever-changing field. Standard safety precautions must be followed, but as new research and clinical experience broaden our knowledge, changes in treatment and drug therapy may become necessary or appropriate. Readers are advised to check the most current product information provided by the manfacturer of each drug to be administered to verify the recommended dose, the method and duration of administration, and the contraindications. It is the responsibility of the treating physician, relying on experience and knowledge of the patient, to determine dosages and the best treatment for each individual patient. Neither the Publisher nor the editor assumes any liability for any injury and/or damage to persons or property arising from this publication.

The Publisher

Library of Congress Cataloging-in-Publication Data

Pediatric otolaryngology / [edited by] Charles D. Bluestone . . . [et al.].—4th ed.
  p. ; cm.
    Includes bibliographical references and index.
    ISBN 0–7216–9197–8
  1. Pediatric otolaryngology. I. Bluestone, Charles D.
    [DNLM: 1. Otorhinolaryngologic Diseases—Infant—Child. WV 140 P37087 2002]
    RF47.C4 P38 2002
618.92′09751—dc21

                  2001049400

Acquisitions Editor: Stephanie Donley
Developmental Editor: Melissa Dudlick
Project Manager: Jennifer Ehlers
Book Designer: Gene Harris

PI/MVY

Printed in the United States of America.

Last digit is the print number: 9 8 7 6 5 4 3 2 1

*We dedicate this book
to our families, teachers, colleagues, house staff, and students,
but especially to our young patients and their families,
whom we hope will benefit from the information
contained in these volumes.*

Contributors

Gregory C. Allen, M.D.
Assistant Professor, Department of Otolaryngology—Head and Neck Surgery, University of Colorado Health Sciences Center; Attending Physician, Department of Pediatric Otolaryngology, The Children's Hospital, Denver, Colorado
Evolution of Pediatric Otolaryngology

Cuneyt M. Alper, M.D.
Associate Professor of Otolaryngology, University of Pittsburgh School of Medicine; Staff Otolaryngologist, Children's Hospital of Pittsburgh, Department of Pediatric Otolaryngology, Pittsburgh, Pennsylvania
Inflammatory Disease of the Mouth and Pharynx
Burns and Acquired Strictures of the Esophagus
Methods of Examination

Jack B. Anon, M.D.
Clinical Professor, University of Pittsburgh, Pittsburgh, Pennsylvania
Embryology and Anatomy of the Paranasal Sinuses

Ellis M. Arjmand, M.D., Ph.D.
Assistant Professor of Otolaryngology, University of Pittsburgh School of Medicine; Attending Otolaryngologist, Children's Hospital of Pittsburgh, Pittsburgh, Pennsylvania
Congenital Inner Ear Anomalies

Yasser Armanazi, D.M.D.
Associate Professor of Pediatric Dentistry, Case Western Reserve University, Cleveland, Ohio
Dental and Gingival Disorders

L'Tanya J. Bailey, D.D.S., M.S.
Department of Orthodontics, University of North Carolina School of Dentistry, Chapel Hill, North Carolina
Orthodontic Problems in Children

Roberto L. Barretto, M.D.
Fellow in Pediatric Otolaryngology, Children's Memorial Hospital, Feinberg School of Medicine at Northwestern University, Chicago, Illinois
Injuries of the Mouth, Pharynx, and Esophagus

Paul W. Bauer, M.D.
Assistant Professor, Department of Otolaryngology—Head and Neck Surgery, Children's Medical Center of Dallas, University of Texas Southwestern Medical Center, Dallas, Texas
Neck Masses

Nancy M. Bauman, M.D.
Associate Professor, University of Iowa College of Medicine; University of Iowa Hospitals, Iowa City, Iowa
Diseases of the Labyrinthine Capsule

Walter M. Belenky
Chief, Department of Pediatric Otolaryngology, Children's Hospital of Michigan, Detroit, Michigan
Nasal Obstruction and Rhinorrhea

Erica C. Bennett, M.D.
Assistant Professor of Clinical Otolaryngology—Head and Neck Surgery, University of Southern California Keck School of Medicine; Attending Physician, Division of Otolaryngology, Children's Hospital of Los Angeles, Los Angeles, California
Congenital Malformations of the Trachea and Bronchi
Thyroid

Fred H. Bess, Ph.D.
Professor and Chair, Vanderbilt University School of Medicine, Nashville, Tennesee
Amplification Selection for Children with Hearing Impairment

F. Owen Black, M.D.
Chief, Good Samaritan Hospital and Medical Center, Portland, Oregon
Tinnitus in Children

Charles D. Bluestone, M.D.
Eberly Professor of Pediatric Otolaryngology, University of Pittsburgh School of Medicine; Director, Department of Pediatric Otolaryngology, Children's Hospital of Pittsburgh, Pittsburgh, Pennsylvania
Methods of Examination: Clinical Examination
Otitis Media and Eustachian Tube Dysfunction
Intratemporal Complications and Sequelae of Otitis Media
Intracranial Complications of Otitis Media and Mastoiditis

William E. Bolger, M.D., F.A.C.S.
Associate Professor, Department of Otorhinolaryngology/
Head and Neck Surgery, University of Pennsylvania
School of Medicine; Chief, Division of Rhinology,
Department of Otorhinolaryngology/Head and Neck
Surgery, University of Pennsylvania Health System,
Philadelphia, Pennsylvania
Imaging of the Paranasal Sinuses in Pediatric Patients with
  Special Considerations for Endoscopic Sinus Surgery

J. Arturo Bonilla, M.D.
Pediatric Ear, Nose, and Throat Department, Institute of
South Texas, San Antonio, Texas
Surgical Management of Microtia and Congenital Aural Atresia

Jerry Bouquot, D.D.S., M.S.
Director of Research, The Maxillofacial Center for
Diagnostics and Research, Morgantown, West Virginia
Dental and Gingival Disorders

Charles M. Bower, M.D.
Associate Professor, Department of Otolaryngology,
Arkansas Children's Hospital, Little Rock, Arkansas
Diseases of the Salivary Glands

Amy C. Brenski, M.D.
Assistant Professor, University of Texas, Southwestern
Medical School; Medical Staff, Children's Medical Center
of Dallas, Dallas, Texas
Congenital Inner Ear Anomalies

Patrick E. Brookhouser, M.D., F.A.C.S.
Department of Otolaryngology, Boystown National
Research Hospital, Omaha, Nebraska
Diseases of the Inner Ear and Sensorineural Hearing Loss

Thomas C. Calcaterra, M.D.
Professor, Head and Neck Surgery, UCLA School of
Medicine, Los Angeles, California
Orbital Swellings

Thomas F. Campbell, Ph.D.
Director of Department of Audiology and
Communication Disorders, University of Pittsburgh
School of Medicine, Pittsburgh, Pennsylvania
Disorders of Language, Phonology, Fluency, and Voice:
  Indicators for Referral

Joseph A. Carcillo, M.D.
Associate Director, Pediatric Intensive Care Unit,
Children's Hospital of Pittsburgh, Pittsburgh,
Pennsylvania
Intensive Care Management of Infection-Related Acute Upper
  Airway Obstruction in Children

Stephen P. Cass, M.D., M.P.H.
Associate Professor, Department of Otolaryngology,
University of Colorado, Denver, Colorado
Tumors of the Ear and Temporal Bone

Maragaretha L. Casselbrant, M.D., Ph.D.
Professor of Otolaryngology, University of Pittsburgh;
Director, Clinical Research and Education, Children's
Hospital, Pittsburgh, Pennsylvania
Vestibular Evaluation
Balance Disorders
Methods of Examination

Kenny H. Chan, M.D.
Professor, Department of Otolaryngology–Head and
Neck Surgery, University of Colorado Health Sciences
Center; Chair, Department of Pediatric Otolaryngology,
The Children's Hospital, Denver, Colorado
Pediatric Otolaryngology: A Psychosocial Perspective

Kay Chang, M.D.
Menlo Park, California
Idiopathic Conditions of the Mouth and Pharynx

Jack L. Cluckman, M.D.
Professor and Chairman, University of Cincinnati College
of Medicine, Cincinnati, Ohio
Inflammatory Disease of the Mouth and Pharynx

Paul G. Comber, M.D., Ph.D.
Assistant Professor of Pediatrics, Albany Medical College;
Assistant Professor, Children's Hospital at Albany Medical
Center, Pediatric Pulmonary, Albany, New York
Infections of the Lower Respiratory Tract

George H. Conner, M.D.
Professor Emeritus of Surgery, Division of
Otolaryngology, Pennsylvania State University School of
Medicine, Hershey, Pennsylvania
Idiopathic Conditions of the Mouth and Pharynx

Cheryl S. Cotter, M.D.
Pediatric Otolaryngologist, Arnold Palmer Hospital for
Children and Women, Orlando, Florida
Obstructive Sleep Disorders

Robin T. Cotton, M.D.
Professor, Otolaryngology–Head and Neck Surgery,
University of Cincinnati Medical Center; Director,
Pediatric Otolaryngology, Cincinnati Children's Hospital
Medical Center, Cincinnati, Ohio
Gastroesophageal Reflux Disease
Stridor and Airway Obstruction
Management and Prevention of Subglottic Stenosis in Infants
  and Children
Velopharyngeal Insufficiency

Wade Cressman, M.D.
Clinical Assistant Professor, Department of
Otolaryngology, Head and Neck Surgery, University of
South Florida, Tampa, Florida; All Children's Hospital,
St. Petersburg, Florida
Nasal Physiology

William S. Crysdale, M.D.
Professor, University of Toronto; Senior Staff,
Department of Otolaryngology, Hospital for Sick
Children, Toronto, Ontario, Canada
The Management of Drooling

Marvin C. Culbertson, Jr., M.D.
Retired Clinical Professor, Department of Otolaryngology,
University of Texas Southwestern Medical Center, Dallas,
Texas
Epistaxis

Michael J. Cunningham, M.D.
Associate Professor, Department of Otology and
Laryngology, Harvard Medical School; Surgeon,
Department of Otolaryngology, Massachusetts Eye and
Ear Infirmary, Boston, Massachusetts
Malignant Tumors of the Head and Neck

Hugh Curtin, M.D.
Professor of Radiology, Harvard Medical School;
Professor of Radiology, The Massachusetts Eye & Ear
Infirmary, Boston, Massachusetts
Methods of Examination: Radiologic Aspects

David H. Darrow, M.D., D.D.S.
Associate Professor of Otolaryngology–Head and Neck
Surgery and Pediatrics, Eastern Virginia Medical School;
Attending Physician, Otolaryngology–Head and Neck
Surgery and Pediatrics, Children's Hospital of the King's
Daughters, Norfolk, Virginia
Foreign Bodies of the Larynx, Trachea, and Bronchi

Albert R. De Chicchis, Ph.D.
Associate Professor, Department of Communication
Science and Disorders, University of Georgia School of
Medicine, Athens, Georgia
Amplification Selection for Children with Hearing Impairment

Douglas D. Dedo, M.D.
Assistant Clinical Professor of Otolaryngology–Head and
Neck Surgery, University of Miami Medical School,
Miami, Florida
Neurogenic Diseases of the Larynx

Herbert H. Dedo, M.D.
Professor of Otolaryngology–Head and Neck Surgery,
University of California Medical School–Berkeley,
California
Neurogenic Diseases of the Larynx

Craig S. Derkay, M.D.
Professor, Otolaryngology and Pediatrics, Eastern Virginia
Medical School; Director, Pediatric Otolaryngology,
Children's Hospital of the King's Daughters, ENT
Department, Norfolk, Virginia
Physiology of the Mouth, Pharynx, and Esophagus
Dysphagia

**Joseph E. Dohar, M.D., M.S., F.A.A.P.,
F.A.C.S.**
Associate Professor of Otolaryngology, University of
Pittsburgh School of Medicine, University of Pittsburgh,
Pittsburgh, Pennsylvania
Otorrhea

Jay N. Dolitsky, M.D.
Assistant Professor of Otolaryngology, New York Medical
College, Valhalla, New York; Director of Pediatric
Otolaryngology, The New York Eye and Ear Infirmary,
New York, New York
Otalgia

Christine A. Dollaghan, Ph.D.
Professor of Communication Science and Disorders,
University of Pittsburgh, Pittsburgh, Pennsylvania
Disorders of Language, Phonology, Fluency, and Voice in
  Children: Indicators for Referral

Terry L. Donat, M.D.
Clinical Assistant Professor, Loyola University, Stritch
School of Medicine, Maywood, Illinois
Injuries of the Mouth, Pharynx, and Esophagus

John D. Durrant, Ph.D.
Professor of Communication Science and Disorders;
Otolaryngology; Rehabilitation Science, and Technology,
University of Pittsburgh, Pittsburgh, Pennsylvania
Physical and Physiologic Bases of Hearing

Robin A. Dyleski, M.D.
Department of Otolaryngology, Arkansas Children's
Hospital, Little Rock, Arkansas
Diseases of the Salivary Glands

Hamdy El-Hakim, F.R.C.S. Ed
Fellow, Hospital For Sick Children, Toronto, Ontario;
Senior Specialist Registrar, Aberdeen Royal Infirmary,
Aberdeen, Scotland
Hoarseness

Jose N. Fayad, M.D.
Injuries of the Ear and Temporal Bone

Jonathan D. Finder, M.D.
Assistant Professor of Pediatrics, University of Pittsburgh;
Pediatric Pulmonologist, Children's Hospital of
Pittsburgh, Pittsburgh, Pennsylvania
Noninfectious Disorders of the Lower Respiratory Tract

Philip Fireman, M.D.
Professor of Pediatrics and Medicine, University of
Pittsburgh School of Medicine; Children's Hospital,
Pittsburgh, Pennsylvania
Allergic Rhinitis

Jacob Friedberg, M.D.
Professor, University of Toronto; Otolaryngologist-in-
Chief, Hospital for Sick Children, Toronto, Ontario
Hoarseness

Joseph M. Furman, M.D., Ph.D.
Professor, Departments of Otolaryngology, Neurology,
and Bioengineering, University of Pittsburgh, Pittsburgh,
Pennsylvania
Vestibular Evaluation
Balance Disorders

Mark E. Gerber, M.D.
Assistant Professor, Northwestern University Medical
School; Division of Pediatric Otolaryngology, Childrens
Memorial Hospital, Chicago, Illinois
Congenital Laryngeal Anomalies

Chantal M. Giguère, M.D.
Pediatric Otolaryngology Fellow, University of Iowa
College of Medicine; Pediatric Otolaryngology Fellow,
University of Iowa Hospitals, Iowa City, Iowa
Diseases of the Labyrinthine Capsule

Edward Goldson, M.D.
Professor, Department of Pediatrics, The University of
Colorado Health Sciences Center; Staff Pediatrician, The
Children's Hospital, Denver, Colorado
Pediatric Otolaryngology: A Psychosocial Perspective

Nira A. Goldstein, M.D.
Assistant Professor of Otolaryngology, State University of
New York Downstate Medical Center; Attending
Physician, University Hospital of Brooklyn, Long Island
College Hospital, Kings County Hospital Center,
Brooklyn, New York
Embryology and Anatomy of the Mouth, Pharynx, and
    Esophagus

Carlos Gonzales, M.D.
Pediatric Otolaryngologist, Cirugia de Cabeza y Cuello en
Ninos, Santurce, Puerto Rico
Tumors of the Mouth and Pharynx

Christopher B. Gordon, M.D.
Principles and Methods of Management

Steven D. Gray, M.D.
Professor, Otolaryngology–Head and Neck Surgery,
University of Utah, Salt Lake City, Utah
Congenital Malformations of the Mouth and Pharynx
Voice

Kenneth M. Grundfast, M.D.
Department of Otolaryngology, Boston Medical Center,
Roxbury, Massachusetts
Hearing Loss

Joseph Haddad, Jr., M.D.
Associate Professor of Clinical Otolaryngology–Head and
Neck Surgery and Vice Chairman of Otolaryngology/Head
and Neck Surgery, Columbia University College of
Physicians and Surgeons, New York, New York
Methods of Examination

Steven D. Handler, M.D.
Professor, Department of Otorhinolaryngology–Head and
Neck Surgery, University of Pennsylvania School of
Medicine; Associate Director, Division of Otolaryngology,
The Children's Hospital of Philadelphia, Philadelphia,
Pennsylvania
Methods of Examination

Christopher J. Hartnick, M.D.
Department of Otolaryngology, Massachusetts Eye and
Ear Infirmary, Harvard Medical School, Boston,
Massachusetts
Stridor and Airway Obstruction

Michael S. Haupert, D.O.
Department of Pediatric Otolaryngology, Children's
Hospital of Michigan, Detroit, Michigan
Nasal Obstruction and Rhinorrhea

Gerald B. Healy, M.D.
Professor of Otology and Laryngology, Harvard Medical
School; Otolaryngologist-in-Chief, Childrens Hospital,
Boston, Massachusetts
Methods of Examination

Arthur S. Hengerer, M.D.
University of Rochester Medical Center; Professor and
Chair, Division of Otolaryngology, and Acting Chair,
Department of Surgery, Strong Memorial Hospital,
Rochester, New York
Congenital Malformations of the Nose and Paranasal Sinuses
Complications of Nasal and Sinus Infections

Angel W. Hernandez, M.D.
Staff Child Neurologist/Epileptologist, Cook Children's
Medical Center, Department of Neurology, Fort Worth,
Texas
Neurologic Disorders of the Mouth, Pharynx, and Esophagus

Keiko Hirose, M.D.
Cleveland Clinic Foundation, Cleveland, Ohio
Embryology and Developmental Anatomy of the Ear

Barry E. Hirsch, M.D.
Professor, Department of Otolaryngology, University of
Pittsburgh, Pittsburgh, Pennsylvania
Diseases of the External Ear

Lauren D. Holinger, M.D.
Professor of Otolaryngology, Department of
Otolaryngology–Head and Neck Surgery, Northwestern
University; Head, Division of Pediatric Otolaryngology,
Children's Memorial Hospital, Chicago, Illinois
Congenital Laryngeal Anomalies
Congenital Malformations of the Trachea and Bronchi
Foreign Bodies of the Larynx, Trachea, and Bronchi

Andrew J. Hotaling, M.D.
Professor, Department of Otolaryngology–Head and
Neck Surgery and Pediatrics, Loyola University Medical
Center, Maywood, Illinois
Functional Abnormalities of the Esophagus
Cough

Patricia A. Hughes, D.O.
Albany Medical College, Albany Medical School;
Associate Professor of Pediatrics, Section of Pediatric
Infectious Disease, Childrens Hospital at Albany Medical
College, Albany, New York
Infections of the Lower Respiratory Tract

Dennis J. Hurwitz, M.D.
Clinical Professor of Surgery, University of Pittsburgh
School of Medicine, Pittsburgh, Pennsylvania
Principles and Methods of Management
Pediatric Plastic Surgery of the Head and Neck

Barbara Hymer, D.D.S.
Program Director, The Children's Hospital; Clinical
Instructor, University of Colorado School of Dentistry,
Denver, Colorado
Postnatal Craniofacial Growth and Development

Glenn Isaacson, M.D.
Professor and Chairman, Department of Otolaryngology–
Head and Neck Surgery, Temple University School of
Medicine; Chief, Pediatric Otolaryngology, Temple
University Children's Medical Center, Philadelphia,
Pennsylvania
Developmental Anatomy and Physiology of the Larynx,
 Trachea, and Esophagus

Bruce W. Jafek, M.D.
Professor, Department of Otolaryngology, University of
Colorado School of Medicine, Denver, Colorado
Injuries of the Neck

Ivo P. Janecka, M.D.
Professor of Surgery, Harvard Medical School; Director
of Skull Base International, Children's Hospital, Boston,
Massachusetts
Pediatric Skull Base Surgery

D. Richard Kang, M.D.
Assistant Clinical Professor of Surgery, Uniformed
Services University of Health Services; Director, Hearing
Center, Childrens Hospital of San Diego, San Diego,
California
Tumors of the Larynx, Trachea, and Bronchi

Siloo B. Kapadia, M.D.
Director of Surgical Pathology, Milton S. Hershey
Medical Center, Hershey, Pennsylvania
Pediatric Skull Base Surgery

David E. Karas, M.D.
University of Medicine and Dentistry of New Jersey,
Newark, New Jersey
Otolaryngologic Manifestations of HIV Infection in Children

Collin S. Karmody, M.D.
New England Medical Center, Boston, Massachusetts
Developmental Anomalies of the Neck

Sandeep Kathju, M.D., Ph.D.
Attending Surgeon, Allegheny General Hospital,
Pittsburgh, Pennsylvania
Pediatric Plastic Surgery of the Head and Neck

Ken Kazahaya, M.D.
Assistant Professor, Department of Otorhinolaryngology/
Head and Neck Surgery, University of Pennsylvania,
School of Medicine; Attending Surgeon, Division of
Pediatric Otolaryngology, Children's Hospital of
Philadelphia, Philadelphia, Pennsylvania
Imaging of the Paranasal Sinuses in Pediatric Patients with
 Special Considerations for Endoscopic Sinus Surgery

Peggy E. Kelly, M.D.
Department of Pediatric Otolaryngology, Children's
Hospital, Denver, Colorado
Injuries of the Neck

Margaret A. Kenna, M.D.
Associate Professor of Otology and Laryngology, Harvard
Medical School; Associate in Otolaryngology, Children's
Hospital–Boston, Boston, Massachusetts
Embryology and Developmental Anatomy of the Ear
Sore Throat in Children: Diagnosis and Management

Karen Iler Kirk, Ph.D.
Associate Professor, Department of Otolaryngology,
Indiana University School of Medicine, Indianapolis,
Indiana
Cochlear Implants in Children

Jerome O. Klein, M.D.
Professor of Pediatrics, Boston University School of
Medicine, Boston, Massachusetts
Methods of Examination: Clinical Examination
Otitis Media and Eustachian Tube Dysfunction
Intratemporal Complications and Sequelae of Otitis Media
Intracranial Complications of Otitis Media and Mastoiditis

Darrell Alexander Klotz, M.D.
Chief Resident, Division of Otolaryngology, University of
Rochester School of Medicine; Strong Memorial Hospital,
Rochester, New York
Complications of Nasal and Sinus Infections

Martha L. Lepow, M.D.
Albany Medical College, Albany Medical School;
Professor of Pediatrics, Head, Section of Infectious
Disease, Children's Hospital at Albany Medical College,
Albany, New York
Infections of the Lower Respiratory Tract

David J. Lilly, Ph.D.
Director of Audiology, Good Samaritan Hospital and
Medical Center, Portland, Oregon
Tinnitus in Children

Frank Lucente, M.D.
Professor, SUNY HSCB; Chairman, Long Island College
Hospital, Brooklyn, New York
Facial Pain and Headache

Rodney P. Lusk, M.D.
Division Director, Pediatric Otolaryngology, St. Louis
Children's Hospital; Professor, Washington University, St.
Louis, Missouri
Surgical Management of Chronic Rhinosinusitis
Neck Masses

John Maddalozzo, M.D.
Assistant Professor, Northwestern University Medical
School; Attending Physician, Children's Memorial
Hospital, Chicago, Illinois
Thyroid

Bruce R. Maddern, M.D., F.A.C.S., F.A.A.P.
Courtesy Assistant Professor of Pediatrics, University of
Florida; Chief of Surgery and Otolaryngology, Wolfson
Childrens Hospital, Jacksonville, Florida
Obstructive Sleep Disorders

David N. Madgy, D.O.
Associate Chief, Department of Pediatric Otolaryngology,
Children's Hospital of Michigan, Detroit, Michigan
Nasal Obstruction and Rhinorrhea

Anthony E. Magit, M.D.
Associate Clinical Professor of Pediatrics and Surgery,
University of California, San Diego School of Medicine;
Vice Chairman, Department of Otolaryngology, Children's
Hospital and Health Center, San Diego, California
Tumors of the Nose, Paranasal Sinuses, and Nasopharynx

Robert H. Maisel, M.D.
Professor, Department of OTO-HNS, University of
Minnesota School of Medicine; Chief, Department of
OTO-HNS, Hennepin County Medical Center,
Minneapolis, Minnesota
Injuries of the Mouth, Pharynx, and Esophagus

Scott C. Manning, M.D.
Professor, Department of Otolaryngology, University of
Washington; Chief, Pediatric Otolaryngology, Children's
Hospital and Regional Medical Center, Seattle,
Washington
Epistaxis
Foreign Bodies of the Pharynx and Esophagus

Charles Margozian, M.D.
Associate Professor of Anesthesia, Harvard Medical
School, Boston, Massachusetts
Pediatric Skull Base Surgery

Brian S. Martin, D.M.D.
Clinical Associate Professor, University of Pittsburgh
School of Dental Medicine, Pittsburgh, Pennsylvania
Dental and Gingival Disorders

Mark Marunick, D.D.S., M.S.
Associate Professor and Director of Maxillofacial
Prosthetics, Wayne State University School of Medicine,
Detroit, Michigan
Injuries of the Mouth, Pharynx, and Esophagus

Robert H. Mathog, M.D.
Professor and Chairman, Department of OTO-HNS,
Wayne State University School of Medicine, Detroit,
Michigan
Injuries of the Mouth, Pharynx, and Esophagus

Mark May, M.D.
Clinical Professor, University of Pittsburgh, Pittsburgh,
Pennsylvania
Facial Paralysis in Children

William F. McGuirt, Jr., M.D.
Associate Professor, Department of Otolaryngology, Wake
Forest University Medical Center, Winston Salem, North
Carolina
Injuries of the Ear and Temporal Bone

Arlen D. Meyers, M.D., M.B.A.
Professor, Department of Otolaryngology, University of
Colorado School of Medicine, Denver, Colorado
Aspiration

Makoto Miura, M.D., D. Med. Sc.
Director, Department of Otolaryngology, Toyooka
Hospital, Toyooka City, Japan
Congenital Anomalies of the External and Middle Ears

Richard T. Miyamoto, M.D.
Arilla Spence DeVault Professor and Chairman, Indiana
University Medical School, Department of
Otolaryngology, Riley Hospital, Indianapolis, Indiana
Cochlear Implants in Children

Stephen E. Morrow, M.D.
Fellow, University of North Carolina, Chapel Hill, North
Carolina
Congenital Malformations of the Esophagus

George T. Moynihan, M.D.
Resident, Loyola University Medical Center, Maywood,
Illinois
Cough

Harlan R. Muntz, M.D.
Professor Otolaryngology–Head and Neck Surgery,
University of Utah; Pediatric Otolaryngology, Primary
Children's Medical Center, Salt Lake City, Utah
Congenital Malformations of the Mouth and Pharynx

Don K. Nakayama, M.D.
Chief, Department of Pediatric Surgery, University of
North Carolina, Chapel Hill, North Carolina
Congenital Malformations of the Esophagus

M. M. Nazif, D.D.S., M.D.S.
Director, Dental Services and Dental Residency Program,
Department of Pediatric Dentistry, Children's Hospital of
Pittsburgh, Pittsburgh, Pennsylvania
Dental and Gingival Disorders

Robert Niclerio, M.D.
Chairman, Division of Otolaryngology, Head and Neck
Surgery, University of Chicago, Chicago, Illinois
Nasal Physiology

Robert J. Nozza, Ph.D.
Professor, Department of Otolaryngology—Head and
Neck Surgery, Temple University School of Medicine;
Director of Audiology, Temple University Hospital and
Temple University Children's Medical Center,
Philadelphia, Pennsylvania
The Assessment of Hearing and Middle-Ear Function in
  Children

Michael J. Painter, M.D.
Professor of Neurology and Pediatrics, University of
Pittsburgh School of Medicine; Chief of Division of Child
Neurology, Children's Hospital of Pittsburgh, Pittsburgh,
Pennsylvania
Neurologic Disorders of the Mouth, Pharynx, and Esophagus

Jack L. Paradise, M.D.
Professor of Pediatrics, Family Medicine and Clinical
Epidemiology, and Otolaryngology, University of
Pittsburgh School of Medicine; Pediatrician, Children's
Hospital of Pittsburgh, Pittsburgh, Pennsylvania
Primary Care of Infants and Children with Cleft Palate
Tonsillectomy and Adenoidectomy

Saroj K. Parida, M.D., M.R.C.P.
Assistant Professor, University of Pittsburgh Medical
School, Pittsburgh, Pennsylvania
Respiratory Disorders of the Newborn

Sanjay R. Parikh, M.D.
Instructor in Otolaryngology, Albert Einstein College of
Medicine; Director, Pediatric Otolaryngology, Montefiore
Children's Hospital, Bronx, New York
Sore Throat in Children: Diagnosis and Management

Simon C. Parisier, M.D.
Clinical Professor, Cornell University Medical College,
New York, New York
Injuries of the Ear and Temporal Bone

Susan E. Pearson, M.D.
Children's National Medical Center, Washington, D.C.
Injuries to the Lower Respiratory Tract

Joseph F.A. Petrone, D.D.S., M.S.D.
Assistant Professor and Director, Advanced Education
Program in Orthodontia and Dentofacial Orthopedics,
University of Pittsburgh School of Dental Medicine,
Pittsburgh, Pennsylvania
Postnatal Craniofacial Growth and Development

Robert L. Pincus, M.D.
Associate Professor Otolaryngology, New York Medical
College; Director, New York Otolaryngology Group, New
York, New York
Facial Pain and Headache

Randall L. Plant, M.D.
Assistant Professor, Department of Otolaryngology–Head
and Neck Surgery, Eastern Virginia Medical School,
Norfolk, Virginia
Physiology of the Mouth, Pharynx, and Esophagus
Dysphagia

Avrum N. Pollock, M.D.
Assistant Professor of Radiology, University of Pittsburgh
School of Medicine; Assistant Professor of Radiology,
Children's Hospital of Pittsburgh, Pittsburgh,
Pennsylvania
Methods of Examination: Radiologic Aspects

J. Christopher Post, M.D., Ph.D.
Professor Otolaryngology, MCP Hahnemann School of
Medicine, Philadelphia; Director, Pediatric
Otolaryngology, and Medical Director, Center for
Genomic Sciences, Allegheny General Hospital,
Pittsburgh, Pennsylvania
Phylogenetic Aspects and Embryology
Molecular Biology in Pediatric Otolaryngology

William P. Potsic, M.D.
Professor, Department of Otorhinolaryngology–Head and
Neck Surgery, University of Pennsylvania School of
Medicine; Director, Division of Otolaryngology, The
Children's Hospital of Philadelphia, Philadelphia,
Pennsylvania
Methods of Examination

Seth M. Pransky, M.D.
Assistant Professor, Division of Otolaryngology, University
of California–San Diego; Director, Pediatric
Otolaryngology, Children's Specialists, San Diego
Children's Hospital, San Diego, California
Tumors of the Larynx, Trachea, and Bronchi

Sheila R. Pratt, Ph.D.
Assistant Professor of Communication Science and
Disorders, University of Pittsburgh, Pittsburgh,
Pennsylvania
Behavioral Intervention and Education of Children with Hearing
  Loss

Reza Rahbar, D.M.D., M.D.
Assistant Professor of Otology and Laryngology, Harvard
Medical School; Childrens Hospital, Boston,
Massachusetts
Methods of Examination

Don S. Respler, M.D.
Clinical Assistant Professor, University of Medicine and
Dentistry of New Jersey, Hackensack, New Jersey
Otolaryngologic Manifestations of HIV Infection in Children

James S. Reilly, M.D.
Chairman, Department of Surgery, Alfred L. Dupont
Hospital for Children, Wilmington, Delaware
Perilymphatic Fistulas in Infants and Children

Mark A. Richardson, M.D., M.B.A.
Professor and Chair of Otolaryngology/Head and Neck
Surgery, Oregon Health and Science University, Portland,
Oregon
The Neck: Embryology and Anatomy

Todd A. Ricketts, Ph.D.
Assistant Professor, Vanderbilt University; Director, Dan
Maddox Hearing Aid Research Laboratory, Vanderbilt
Bill Wilkerson Center, Nashville, Tennessee
Amplification Selection for Children with Hearing Impairment

Keith H. Riding, M.D.
Clinical Professor, B.C. Children's Hospital, Vancouver,
British Columbia, Canada
Burns and Acquired Strictures of the Esophagus

Frank L. Rimell, M.D.
Assistant Professor, University of Minnesota Medical
School; Director, Pediatric Otolaryngology, University of
Minnesota, Minneapolis, Minnesota
Injuries to the Lower Respiratory Tract

Michael Rontal, M.D.
Clinical Professor, University of Michigan, Ann Arbor,
Michigan; Attending Staff, WM Beaumont Hospital,
Royal Oak, Michigan
Embryology and Anatomy of the Paranasal Sinuses

Richard M. Rosenfeld, M.D., M.P.H.
Professor of Clinical Otolaryngology, SUNY Downstate
Medical Center; Director of Pediatric Otolaryngology,
Long Island College Hospital and University, Hospital of
Brooklyn, Brooklyn, New York
Cervical Adenopathy

Michael J. Rutter, F.R.A.C.S.
Assistant Professor, Department of Pediatric
Otolaryngology, Children's Hospital Medical Center,
Cincinnati, Ohio
Management and Prevention of Subglottic Stenosis in Infants
  and Children

Isamu Sando, M.D., D.Med.Sc.
Emeritus Professor, Department of Otolaryngology,
University of Pittsburgh, Pittsburgh, Pennsylvania
Congenital Anomalies of the External and Middle Ears

Barry M. Schaitkin, M.D.
Associate Professor of Otolaryngology, University of
Pittsburgh; Director, Facial Paralysis Center, UPMC
Shadyside, Pittsburgh, Pennsylvania
Facial Paralysis in Children

Rachel Schreiber, M.D.
Fellow, University of Pittsburgh Medical Center,
Pittsburgh, Pennsylvania
Allergic Rhinitis

Daniel M. Schwartz, Ph.D.
President, Neurophysiology Associates, Merion Station,
Pennsylvania
Amplification Selection for Children with Hearing Impairment

Nancy Sculerati, M.D.
Associate Professor, New York University Medical Center,
New York, New York
Foreign Bodies of the Nose

Andrew M. Shapiro, M.D.
Clinical Assistant Professor of Surgery, Penn State
University College of Medicine, Hershey, Pennsylvania
Facial Paralysis in Children
Injuries of the Nose, Facial Bones, and Paranasal Sinuses

Nina L. Shapiro, M.D.
Assistant Professor, Pediatric Otolaryngology, UCLA
School of Medicine, Los Angeles, California
Orbital Swellings

James Sidman, M.D.
Clinical Associate Professor of Otolaryngology, University
of Minnesota Medical School; Chief Otolaryngology,
Children's Hospital, Minneapolis, Minnesota
Injuries to the Lower Respiratory Tract

Kathleen C. Y. Sie, M.D.
Associate Professor, Children's Hospital and Regional
Medical Center, Seattle, Washington
The Neck: Embryology and Anatomy

Laura N. Sinai, M.D.
Pediatrician, Erdenheim Pediatrics, Philadelphia,
Pennsylvania
Oropharyngeal Manifestations of Systemic Disease

Nicole F. Siparsky, M.D.
Washington Hospital Center, Washington, DC
Hearing Loss

Marshall E. Smith, M.D.
Department of Surgery, Division of Otolaryngology,
University of Utah School of Medicine, Salt Lake City,
Utah
Voice

Richard J.H. Smith, M.D.
Professor, University of Iowa College of Medicine;
Professor and Vice Chairman, University of Iowa
Hospitals and Clinics, Iowa City, Iowa
Diseases of the Labyrinthine Capsule

Sylvan E. Stool, M.D.
Professor of Pediatrics and Otolaryngology, University of
Colorado School of Medicine; Attending Physician, The
Childrens Hospital of Denver, Denver, Colorado
Phylogenetic Aspects and Embryology
Postnatal Craniofacial Growth and Development
Evolution of Pediatric Otolaryngology
Foreign Bodies of the Pharynx and Esophagus

R. Casey Strahan, M.D.
Resident, University of Colorado School of Medicine,
Denver, Colorado
Aspiration

Anne Marie Tharpe, Ph.D.
Amplification Selection for Children with Hearing Impairment

Scott W. Thompson, M.D.
Adjunct Assistant Professor, Department of
Communication Sciences and Disorders, School of Public
Health, University of South Carolina; Physician, Midland
Ear, Nose, and Throat Clinic, Columbia, South Carolina
Congenital Anomalies of the External and Middle Ears

Lawrence W.C. Tom, M.D.
Associate Professor, Department of Otorhinolaryngology–
Head and Neck Surgery, University of Pennsylvania
School of Medicine; Associate Surgeon, Division of
Otolaryngology, The Children's Hospital of Philadelphia,
Philadelphia, Pennsylvania
Methods of Examination

Sharon M. Tomaski, M.D.
Pediatric Otolaryngologist, Children's Ear, Head and
Neck Associates, Denver, Colorado
Embryology and Anatomy of the Mouth, Pharynx, and
  Esophagus

Richard B. Towbin, M.D.
Professor of Radiology, University of Pennsylvania;
Professor of Radiology, Children's Hospital of
Philadelphia, Philadelphia, Pennsylvania
Methods of Examination: Radiologic Aspects

Carol-Ann Trotman, B.D.S., M.A., M.S.
University of North Carolina, Chapel Hill, North Carolina
Orthodontic Problems in Children

**Anne Chun-Hui Tsai, M.D., M.Sc., F.A.A.P.,
F.A.C.M.G.**
Assistant Professor, University of Colorado Health
Science Center; Attending Physician and Clinical
Geneticist, The Children's Hospital, Denver, Colorado
Phylogenetic Aspects and Embryology
Genetics, Syndromology, and Craniofacial Anomalies

Atul M. Vaidya, M.D.
Physician, Department of Otolaryngology, Loyola
University Medical Center, Maywood, Illinois
Functional Abnormalities of the Esophagus

Stephanie E. Vallee
Senior Genetic Counselor, University of Colorado Health
Sciences Center, Denver, Colorado
Genetics, Syndromology, and Craniofacial Anomalies

Ryan L. Van De Graaff, M.D.
Resident, University of Colorado Health Sciences Center,
Denver, Colorado
Tumors of the Ear and Temporal Bone

Katherine W.L. Vig, B.D.S., M.S., D.Orth.
Professor and Chair of Orthodontic Department, Section
of Orthodonticis, College of Dentistry, Ohio State Health
Sciences Center; Section Chief of Orthodontic Services,
Childrens Hospital, Columbus, Ohio
Postnatal Craniofacial Growth and Development

Ellen R. Wald, M.D.
Professor of Pediatrics and Otolaryngology, University of
Pittsburgh School of Medicine; Chief, Division of Allergy,
Immunology, and Infections Diseases, Children's Hospital
of Pittsburgh, Pittsburgh, Pennsylvania
Rhinitis and Acute and Chronic Sinusitis

Donald W. Warren, D.D.S., M.A., Ph.D.
Kenen Professor and Director, University of North
Carolina Craniofacial Center, Chapel Hill, North Carolina
Orthodontic Problems in Children

Peter C. Weber, M.D., M.B.A.
Professor and Program Director, Cleveland Clinic,
Cleveland, Ohio
Perilymphatic Fistulas in Infants and Children

Richard O. Wein, M.D.
Physician, Otolaryngology–Head and Neck Surgery,
University of Rochester Medical Center, Rochester, New
York
Congenital Malformations of the Nose and Paranasal Sinuses

Jay A. Werkhaven, M.D.
Associate Professor, Department of Otolaryngology,
Vanderbilt University Medical Center, Nashville,
Tennessee
Laser Surgery

Ralph F. Wetmore, M.D.
Surgeon, Department of Otolaryngology, Children's
Hospital of Philadelphia, Philadelphia, Pennsylvania
Tracheotomy

Susan L. Whitney, Ph.D.
Assistant Professor in Physical Therapy and
Otolaryngology, University of Pittsburgh; Director of
Outpatient Vestibular Physical Therapy, Centers for
Rehabilitation Services, Pittsburgh, Pennsylvania
Vestibular Evaluation

Kenneth R. Whittemore, Jr., M.D.
Resident in Otology and Laryngology, Harvard Medical
School; Resident in Otolaryngology, Massachusetts Eye
and Ear Infirmary, Boston, Massachusetts
Malignant Tumors of the Head and Neck

J. Paul Willging, M.D.
Associate Professor Otolaryngology–Head and Neck
Surgery, University of Cincinnati Medical Center and
Children's Hospital Medical Center, Cincinnati, Ohio
Velopharyngeal Insufficiency

Robert E. Wood, Ph.D., M.D.
Professor of Pediatrics and Otolaryngology, Department
of Pulmonary Medicine, Children's Hospital Medical
Center, Cincinnati, Ohio
Physiology of the Larynx, Airways, and Lungs

J. Scott Yaruss, Ph.D.
Assistant Professor, Communication Science and
Disorders; Clinical Research Consultant, Children's
Hospital of Pittsburgh, Pittsburgh, Pennsylvania
Disorders of Language, Phonology, Fluency, and Voice in
    Children: Indicators for Referral

Robert F. Yellon, M.D.
Assistant Professor of Otolaryngology, University of
Pittsburgh School of Medicine; Co-Director Director of
Clinical Services, Children's Hospital of Pittsburgh,
Pittsburgh, Pennsylvania
Gastroesophageal Reflux Disease
Surgical Management of Microtia and Congenital Aural Atresia
Head and Neck Space Infections
Management and Prevention of Subgottic Stenosis in Infants
    and Children
Head and Neck Space Infections

S. James Zinreich, M.D.
Johns Hopkins University, Baltimore, Maryland
Embryology and Anatomy of the Paranasal Sinuses

Preface

We are delighted to edit and contribute to this fourth edition of *Pediatric Otolaryngology*. There have been dramatic advances in almost all aspects of ear, nose, and throat diseases and disorders in infants and children since publication of the first edition in 1983, and we are pleased that the subsequent editions of this text have kept pace during the same period; the scope of the text also includes diseases and disorders of the tracheobronchial tree and esophagus. Not only have there been improvements in the nonsurgical and surgical management of patients, but we have seen a relative explosion in our knowledge base of these conditions. Over this time, chapters such as those devoted to molecular biology, genetics, otolaryngic manifestations of HIV infections, cochlear implants, skull base surgery, imaging of the paranasal sinuses, and gastroesophageal reflux have been added. Not only does the current edition include completely updated chapters and approximately 20% new authors, but we have added new chapters on thyroid disease, surgical correction of external and middle ear anomalies, and balance disorders. We have also included a section on the history of pediatric otolaryngology. As in previous editions, we critiqued all the chapters in the third edition, which aided in updating, revising, and adding new chapters. As in the past three editions, we have continued to include several chapters early in each section that present the differential diagnoses of the common presenting signs and symptoms, so that the reader can then turn to a more comprehensive review of the condition in the appropriate chapter; cross-referencing is used extensively to facilitate this process. We have made no attempt to include detailed chapters on pediatric diseases, such as diabetes and asthma, that may affect children with ear, nose, and throat diseases, because these topics are adequately addressed in current textbooks of pediatrics.

The text is written for all health care professionals who provide health care for infants and children, which includes, but is not limited to, otolaryngologists, pediatricians, family physicians, allergists, speech pathologists, audiologists, house staff, and students. It is not intended for only the pediatric otolaryngologist, who primarily concentrates on special problems or special children, or both, in special institutions, but for all others who encounter children with these problems.

We are pleased and thankful for the hard work and critical evaluation our new co-editors, Drs. Alper, Arjmand, Casselbrant, Dohar, and Yellon, have provided for this fourth edition. As editors, we hope that the health care of infants and children will be improved by those professionals who use this book as a reference in this new century.

Charles D. Bluestone, MD
Sylvan E. Stool, MD

Acknowledgments

The editors wish to acknowledge the distinguished and dedicated authors who contributed chapters to these volumes, without whom there would not be a fourth edition. We also want to acknowledge Deborah Hepple for her dedication and commitment to the coordination and collation of the manuscripts and for her kind but persistent reminders to our authors to adhere to our production schedule. Thanks also goes to Maria B. Bluestone in Pittsburgh, who provided expert and invaluable editorial aid for several of the chapters, to our capable editors at Saunders in Philadelphia, Stephanie Donley and Melissa Dudlick, and to our designer, Gene Harris. As in the past three volumes, Jon Coulter provided valuable photographic support for this edition.

In any effort as time-consuming as this, the authors' families and colleagues must provide support—and ours have made this task easier by their understanding and encouragement.

Contents

VOLUME 2

SECTION III

The Nose, Paranasal Sinuses, Face,
and Orbit 861

Craniofacial Growth, Development, and Malformations

Phylogenetic Aspects and Embryology

Anne Chun-Hui Tsai, M.D., M.Sc., F.A.A.P., F.A.C.M.G., Sylvan E. Stool, M.D., and J. Christopher Post, M.D., Ph.D.

It is appropriate that the first chapter of a text on pediatric otolaryngology be devoted to the broad subject of the development of the craniofacial complex. This is the major region involved in diseases of the ears, nose, and throat and serves as the entryway to the air and food passages. The more we know about the embryology, growth, and development of the face and about the various factors involved in normal variations and anomalies of this region, the better will be our understanding of the many otorhinolaryngologic disorders affecting infants and children.

The first region that the clinician and, indeed, the layperson inspect on encountering another person is the face. An impression of the face and an evaluation of the facial type and facial expression are usually made instantly. After this, the general body type and posture are noted, and the degree of interpersonal communication is ascertained. DeMyer[22] states:

One glance at the patient's face may settle the diagnostic issue, an Augenblick, or eyeblink diagnosis, in which the clinician immediately knows what syndrome the patient has. I am neither describing nor advocating a hasty, careless snap judgment, I am merely pointing out that the clinician, utilizing the pattern recognition attributes of his own brain, sometimes can diagnose abnormal faces with the speed and certainty with which he distinguishes the faces of family and friends.

On the basis of certain facial features, the clinician may decide that a recognizable syndrome associates the patient with a group of similar patients more than it does with the individual's own family. Therefore, the face and the cranial configuration contribute immeasurably to the total, or gestalt, diagnosis.

Any observer can appreciate that there is great variation in the appearance of the normal face. In addition, there are certain characteristics that we associate with facial types almost on an instinctive basis. These variations and expectations in facial types can be appreciated by examining Figure 1–1, which is a sketch of a group of white children from the same grammar school class. The variations in facial configuration are obvious: there are round, oval, and triangular faces. Individual characteristics of the eyes and the nose also show tremendous variation. A diagnosis of an abnormality that is based on facial configuration may be difficult to make unless the observer knows the hereditary background of the individual, although some abnormalities, such as Down syndrome, are expressed in similar facial features regardless of the child's origin. Thus, although we recognize great variations in facial type as being normal, we also instinctively recognize other features as being abnormal in a particular individual on the basis of our ability to assess facial patterns in the context of age, race, and hereditary background.

The human craniofacial complex is a result of at least 500 million years of progressive development.[5] These structures, which developed in the anterior portion of an

FIGURE 1–1. Children from a sixth-grade class. Note the variation of facial types, even though all the children are the same age and race.

ancestral organism, were designed to obtain and maintain first contact with the environment. The pattern that developed in the invertebrates was continued in the vertebrates, and according to Krogman,[59] there can be no doubt that the craniofacial complex from its beginning was a multistructured, highly integrated, diversely systematized center for almost every life need of the organism. In the development of the craniofacial complex in the human embryo and the fetus, the form and functions that have evolved for many millions of years take shape in fantastically rapid sequence. Those structures that required many millions of years of natural selection to evolve may form in minutes or hours in a human. This is especially true in the embryonic stages of development and is the reason that any interference with these processes in the early embryonic stages may have catastrophic consequences in the developing human. The embryogenesis of the craniofacial complex is indeed an amazing phenomenon; form and function must relate to each other with an almost unbelievable precision and at exactly the right points in time. To appreciate the structures and the physiologic processes that the physician interested in diseases of the ears, nose, and throat so frequently sees go awry, we begin this text with an abbreviated review of the normal development of the human head.

Although this text is organized into sections on the basis of organ systems and although each section has a discussion of the most important embryologic and developmental anatomy of that particular organ system, of necessity, there is some duplication and lack of continuity in this method of presentation. Therefore, this section is primarily concerned with the cranium, base of the skull,

face, and eyes and concentrates on the broad concepts involved in the development of these structures.

Since many of the advances in embryology of interest to the physician involved with craniofacial anomalies have occurred because of a better understanding of subcellular events, these events are presented. A general overview of the structure of the human face is presented first, followed by a discussion of the cellular and molecular events that lead to the facial configuration. This method of presentation parallels the way in which the clinician usually views patients with anomalies of this region.

Plan of the Human Face

In humans, the assumption of an upright posture has been associated with a number of anatomic developments (Fig. 1–2A).[28] With enlargement of the brain, especially of the frontal region, and the concomitant rotation of the eyes to the midline, there has been a relative decrease in the intraorbital distance in humans compared with that in lower mammals (Fig. 1–2B). The result is a smaller region at the root of the nose and a shortening of the muzzle, or snout. Thus, humans have close-set eyes and short, narrow noses that do not interfere with binocular vision.

The growth of the frontal lobes and other evolutionary changes have resulted in flexure of the cranial base (Fig. 1–2C), making the face appear to hang from the base of the skull. Other less obvious changes have occurred, such as rotation of the olfactory bulbs and nerves, so that the nasal region in humans has a vertical orientation and most of its important functional components are housed

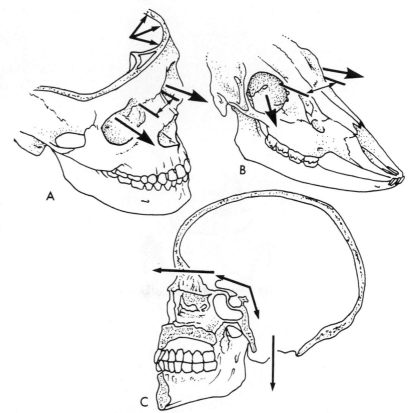

FIGURE 1–2. *A*, Drawing of the human face demonstrating an enlargement of the frontal lobes and rotation of the orbit, resulting in a narrow nasal root, in contrast to that of a lower animal *(B)*. *C*, Flexure of the cranial base results in an alteration of facial orientation. (Modified from Enlow D. Handbook of Facial Growth. Philadelphia, WB Saunders, 1975.)

within the face. This placement of the face within the flexure of the cranial base may be of some clinical significance; any condition that affects the cranial base may have some secondary effects on the airway and, ultimately, on the speech mechanisms (Chap. 102).

Prenatal Development of the Face

The development of the face from midembryonic through midfetal life is illustrated in Figure 1–3. The embryo at about 3 to 4 weeks of age is illustrated in Figure 1–3*A*. At this stage, the embryo does not have a face, the head is composed of a brain covered with a membrane, and the anterior neuropore is still present. The eyes, which are represented by optic vesicles, are on the lateral aspects of the head, as in fish, and the future mouth is represented by a stomodeum. The nasal pits develop only in the latter part of this period of embryonic growth. At the embryonic age of 5 to 6 weeks (Fig. 1–3*B*), the general shape of the face has begun to develop. The frontonasal process is prominent; the nasal pits are forming laterally; and with the increase in size of the first and second branchial arches, there is a suggestion of a mouth. In the subsequent weeks of embryonic life (Fig. 1–3*C*), the structures that we associate with the human face— jaws, nose, eyes, ears, and mouth—take on human configurations.[4]

During this period of rapid growth and expansion, there is also tremendous *differential* growth. Thus, the development of a human baby is not merely the enlargement or rearrangement of a previous form but, by differential growth, the development of a new configuration.

This is a concept that has been difficult for students to comprehend, perhaps because of the tendency for different stages of embryonic development to be illustrated with drawings of equal size. These illustrating techniques have been used because minute structures are difficult to demonstrate without magnification, but it is important to try to view human embryologic development in perspective to appreciate both its similarities to phylogenetic development and its unique course in humans.

The embryonic period ends at about 8 weeks, when the embryo has achieved sufficient size and form so that facial characteristics can be recognized and photographed at actual size (Fig. 1–3*D*). At this stage of late embryonic or early fetal development, the facial features are characterized by the appearance of hypertelorism; during subsequent growth, it will appear as though the eyes are moving closer together. This is not happening, however; the eyes continue to move farther apart, but the remainder of the face is growing at a much more rapid rate, and thus it appears that the eyes are moving closer together. Hypertelorism is actually decreasing as a result of differential development. These observations may be of importance in understanding some of the craniofacial syndromes in which hypertelorism is a prominent feature.

The rapid growth and change in configuration, not only of the face but also of the extremities and body, continue during the next few months (Fig. 1–3*E*). The fetus has facial features that are easily recognized and construed as human. The ears, nasal alae, and lips are well developed, and the head constitutes a large portion of the body mass—a relationship that exists at birth and gradually changes during extrauterine life.

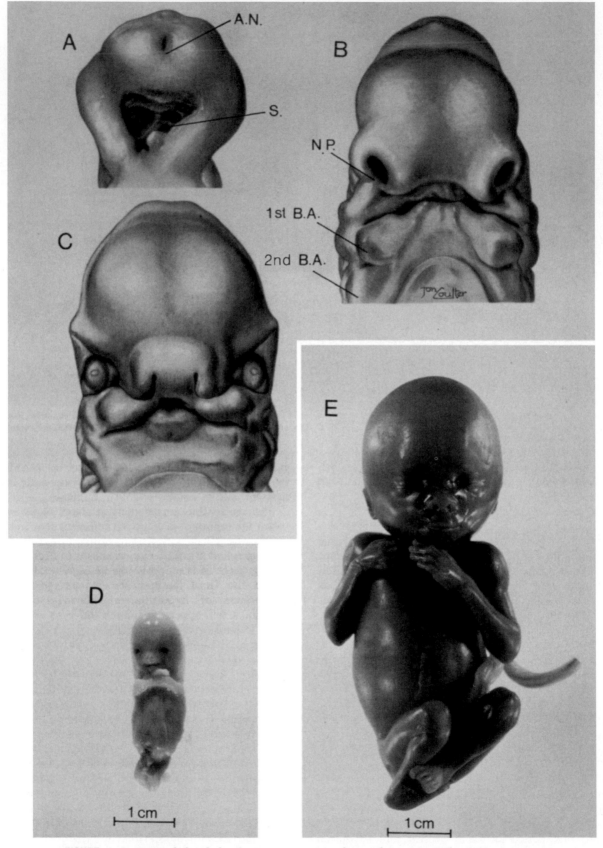

FIGURE 1–3. Prenatal facial development. *A,* An embryo of 3 to 4 weeks. A.N., anterior neuropore; S., stomodeum. *B,* An embryo of 5 to 6 weeks. N.P., nasal pit; 1st B.A., first branchial arch; 2nd B.A., second branchial arch. *C,* An embryo of 7 to 8 weeks. *D,* A fetus of 8 to 9 weeks. *E,* A fetus of 3 to 4 months. (Fetal specimens are from the Krause Collection, the Cleft Palate Center, University of Pittsburgh.)

The concept of differential growth is vital to the comprehension of both prenatal and postnatal development. Although this concept is difficult to grasp when the student must view development of structures of different ages magnified to the same size and when illustrations are in two dimensions, it is important to visualize the process in three dimensions *and* in the fourth dimension—time.

Formation of the Craniofacial Complex

The structures and the factors that form the craniofacial complex have been the subject of investigation by embryologists for many years, and their study has involved use of a number of sophisticated, time-consuming techniques.[105] Among the most interesting studies has been the research of Johnston[53] into the development and migration of cells in the neural crest. These cells are initially composed of ectoderm found at the junction of the neural plate and surface ectoderm; Figure 1–4A shows the neural crest cells forming around the anterior neuropore. It has been shown that the face of amphibians, as well as that of mammals, develops as a consequence of massive cell migrations and the interactions of loosely organized embryonic tissue. In most of the body, this embryonic tissue is derived from mesoderm; however, in the craniofacial complex, neural crest cells give rise to a large variety of connective and nervous tissues of the skull, face, and branchial arches. Therefore, this ectodermal tissue constitutes the majority of the pluripotential tissue of the face. The sequence of events after the initial formation of the neural crest cells is illustrated in Figure 1–4B. The differentiation, proliferation, and migration of those cells are critical in the formation of the face.

Migration occurs at different rates. For instance, the cells that form the frontonasal process are derived from the forebrain fold, and their migration is relatively short as they pass into the nasal region. However, the cells that form the mesenchyme of the maxillary processes have a considerably longer distance to migrate, since they must move into the branchial arches, where they surround the corelike mesodermal muscle plates.[59] In Figure 1–4C, the ultimate distribution of neural crest cells from the frontonasal process and from the branchial arches is illustrated. Since this mesenchymal tissue contributes the majority of the soft tissues and bone to the face, failure of proliferation or migration may be responsible for a number of abnormalities, such as orofacial clefts.[104] An illustration of a severe facial abnormality due to failure of migration is illustrated in Figure 1–4D. Less severe clefts of the lip, the palate, or both may also develop. In some cases, such as with severe holoprosencephaly, not only are mesodermal tissues involved, but central nervous system abnormalities occur as well.[22]

Divisions of the Human Face

From the foregoing, it can be seen that the human face may be divided embryologically (Fig. 1–4C). The median facial structures arise from the frontonasal processes, and the lateral structures arise from the branchial arches. This dual embryonic origin provides a basis for dividing the face into three *vertical* segments. The central segment, primarily the frontonasal process, includes the nose and the central portion of the upper lip. The two lateral segments that arise from the branchial arches may be called the otomaxillomandibular segments.[22] For convenience of description, the face can also be divided into three almost equal *horizontal* planes. The upper or frontal horizontal segment derives solely from the frontonasal process. The middle or maxillary segment derives from the maxillary process of the first branchial arch, and the prolabium originates from the frontonasal process. The third horizontal segment, the lower or mandibular segment, comes from the mandibular process of the first branchial arch.[22]

Prenatal Craniofacial Skeletal Components

The craniofacial skeleton provides support and protection for the human's most vital functions. Conceptually, it is a region with two divisions: that which is involved with the central nervous system, the *neurocranium*; and that which is involved with respiration and mastication, the *visceral cranium*. It consists of four components: cranial base, cranial vault, nasomaxillary complex, and mandible.

The skeletal structures originate spontaneously from two types of bone. One type of bone is first formed in cartilage, and the other is derived from membrane. In general, the bones of the skull that represent the earliest phylogenetic structures are first formed as cartilage, which subsequently ossifies; the more recently developed craniofacial structures are derived from membranous bone.

The components and structures of the fetal craniofacial complex are illustrated in Figures 1–5 through 1–8. Figure 1–5 is a parasagittal section through the cranial base and the facial structures. The cranial base is cartilaginous and provides a floor for the calvaria and a roof for the face.[15] The nasal space and nasopharynx are part of the airway system. Although the airway is not functional in the fetus, alterations of the cranial base during fetal life may affect its subsequent development. Figure 1–6 shows the cartilaginous continuity of the cranial base and nasal septum as well as the arrangement of the fetal facial bones and teeth around the cartilaginous nasal capsule. The nasal septum is attached to the cranial base and the palate and thus constitutes a large portion of the skeletal structure in the fetal midface. Although there is much difference of opinion on this subject, growth of craniofacial cartilage is considered by some to be of prime importance in facial development.[64]

As mentioned, the craniofacial skeletal complex is composed of bones of different embryonic origins. Figure 1–7 shows the bones of cartilaginous origin (dark stipple) and those of membranous origin (light stipple); cartilage that is of branchial arch origin is indicated by solid black. In general, the base of the skull and the sphenoid, petrosal, and ethmoid bones are of cartilaginous origin. Growth of the cartilage of the cranial base occurs primarily at the cartilaginous synchondroses until cartilage is replaced by bone; thereafter, growth is at the periosteal margins. Most of the cranial and facial bones are membranous,

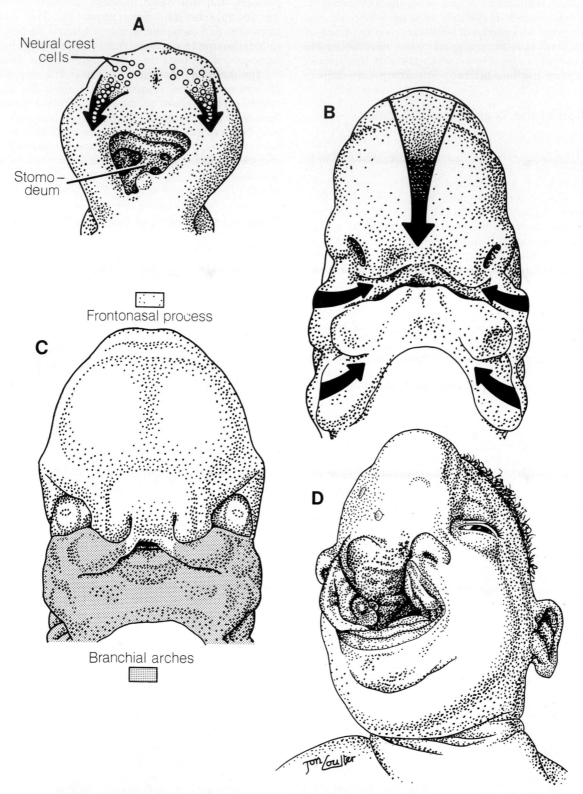

FIGURE 1–4. Formation of the craniofacial complex. *A,* An embryo of 3 to 4 weeks showing development and beginning migration of neural crest cells. *B,* Migration of neural crest cells to the forebrain and the branchial arches. *C,* Contributions to the face of the frontonasal process and branchial arches. *D,* Deformity caused by failure of neural crest cell migration.

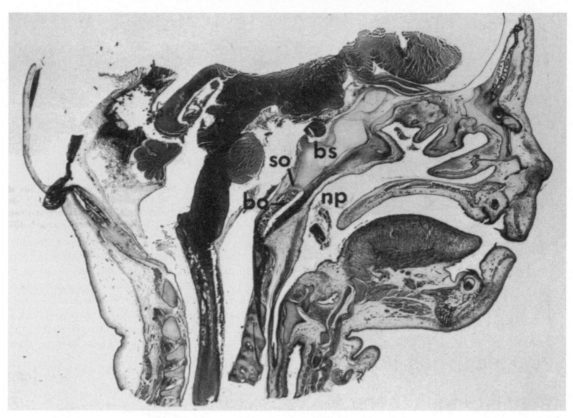

FIGURE 1–5. Photomicrograph of a parasagittal section of a 15-week-old fetal head. bo, basiocciput; bs, basisphenoid cartilage; np, nasopharynx; so, spheno-occipital synchondrosis. (From the Krause Collection, the Cleft Palate Center, University of Pittsburgh.)

and growth takes place primarily at the margins of these bones. The major facial bones are formed from numerous ossification centers, which subsequently produce single bones in later fetal life. The importance of understanding the dual embryonic origin of the skeleton is that many diseases that affect the craniofacial complex may be manifested because of their influence on particular types of bone. For example, achondroplasia, which affects bones of cartilaginous origin, usually results in a characteristic alteration of facial configuration. The formation of membranous and endochondral bones and remodeling of bone are discussed and illustrated in Chapter 2.

The sequential development of the fetal skeleton has been studied extensively by radiographic methods.[58] However, it is anticipated that newer imaging techniques, such as magnetic resonance imaging, will provide better visualization of the relationship of the various tissues and improve our understanding of craniofacial morphogenesis.[48, 71, 87] Figure 1–8 illustrates the definition of the structures that may be obtained by this technique. In addition, ultrasonography is a method of in vivo study that has achieved wide clinical use.[77] This technique permits prenatal study not only of structure but also of function. Figure 1–9 illustrates some of the information that may be obtained. These studies confirm many of the observations made by Hooker and Humphrey on prenatal activity[42, 45] (Fig. 1–10).

Development of Craniofacial Arteries, Muscles, and Nerves

Figure 1–11 illustrates the development of the cranium, arteries, nerves, and muscles during embryonic and early fetal life. The characteristics of these structures are discussed in their respective sections because their growth and development are interrelated.

Arteries

Figure 1–11A shows that the early arterial supply to the head consists primarily of the dorsal aorta and an arch with a small branch coming from it, which is the primitive internal carotid artery. The future musculature consists of mesenchymal tissue in the first and second branchial arches, which are just beginning to form. As the head begins to grow and the embryo starts to develop a face, the internal carotid artery increases in both size and length, and the aortic arches begin to develop. Each of the branchial arches contains not only an artery but also a nerve and a core of mesodermal tissue. Figure 1–11B shows an embryo of about 6 weeks, when the first and second aortic arches and their arteries have formed. As the face continues to develop, these vessels ultimately disappear. It must be appreciated that at this stage, the embryo is still small, and these vessels are correspond-

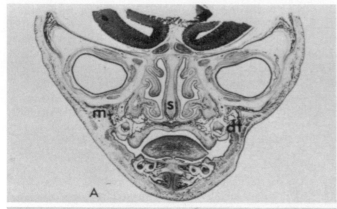

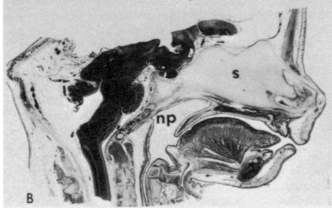

FIGURE 1–6. *A,* Coronal section of a 15-week-old fetal head. *B,* Sagittal section of a 15-week-old fetal head. dt, deciduous tooth germ; m, maxillary bone center; np, nasopharynx; s, nasal septum.

ingly tiny. In fact, the vessels themselves are responding to the needs of the tissue surrounding them; with further growth, their anastomosis will ultimately come from another source. The internal carotid artery at this stage has increased in size, and the facial muscles are beginning to develop in a laminar fashion. One group of muscles develops a lamina that grows posteriorly, and the other group of muscles comes from a lamina that extends anteriorly.

The nerves are beginning to develop as outgrowths of the central nervous system. The skull base forms, and foramina exist where bone forms *around* any preexisting soft tissue (blood vessels or nerves). The fifth cranial nerve (trigeminal), which ultimately supplies sensation to the face, is really a combination of three nerves with ophthalmic, mandibular, and maxillary divisions and a division to the muscles of mastication. The seventh cranial nerve, which is the nerve supply to the second branchial arch, has also begun its development.

By the time the embryo has facial characteristics that appear more human (Fig. 1–11C), the blood supply to the face and cranium has developed the pattern that persists into fetal and postnatal life. The third aortic arch is connected to the embryonic dorsal aorta. This arch becomes a common carotid artery, from which the external carotid artery develops to provide the major blood supply for the face. In general, these vessels have a rec-

ognizable pattern, but there is tremendous variation in their sites of origin and in the anastomosis between the internal and external carotid arteries. Figure 1–11D illustrates the formation of the arterial supply. Note the disappearance of the first and second aortic arches; the persistence of the third arch, which becomes the common carotid; and the disappearance of the dorsal aorta between the third and fourth arches, which on the left will become the aorta.

Muscles

By the end of embryonic life, the facial musculature has become well developed and has migrated extensively superiorly into the craniofacial region. Figure 1–11E shows the muscles contributed by the various laminae.[35] The first branchial arch contributes the muscles that lie beneath the musculature of the second branchial arch and, in general, have a different orientation. These muscles include the temporal, masseter, pterygoid, mylohyoid, and anterior belly of the digastric as well as the tensor muscle of the velum palatinum and the tensor muscle of the tympanum.

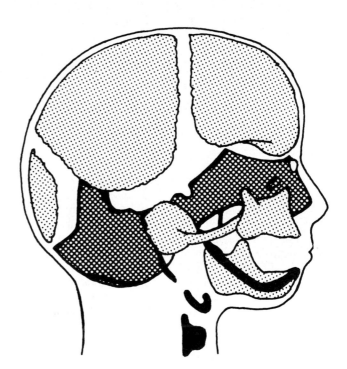

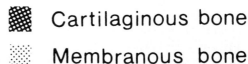 Cartilaginous bone

Membranous bone

FIGURE 1–7. Schematic illustration of the components of the fetal craniofacial complex of membranous origin (light stipple) and cartilaginous origin (dark stipple). The cartilage of branchial arch origin is indicated in black. (Redrawn from Stewart R. Genetic factors in craniofacial morphogenesis. In Stewart R, Prescott G [eds]. Oral Facial Genetics. St Louis, CV Mosby, 1976.)

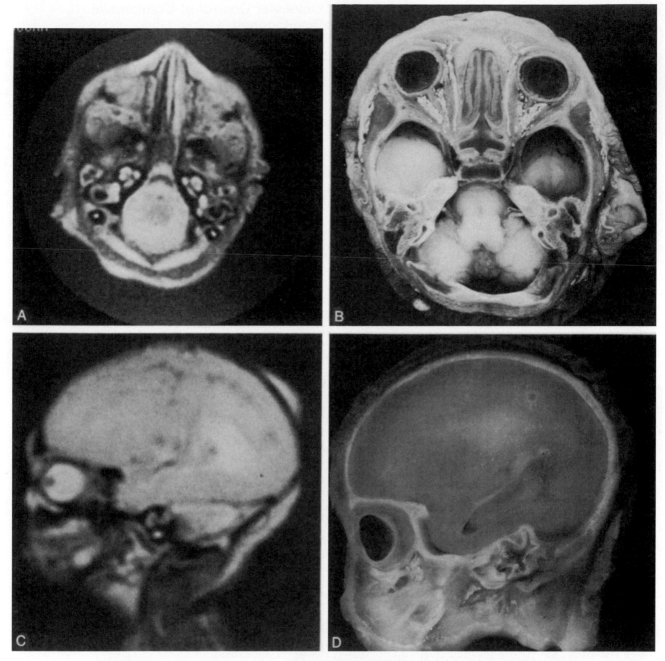

FIGURE 1–8. *A,* Transverse magnetic resonance image (T_2-weighted) of a 24-week-old aborted fetus at the level of the orbital floors and inner and middle ears. *B,* Transverse section through the fetal head at the level of the orbits (28 weeks of gestation). *C,* Sagittal magnetic resonance image of the fetal head (T_2-weighted). *D,* Sagittal section of the fetal head (24 weeks of gestation). (*B* from Isaacson G, Mintz MC, Crelin ES. Atlas of Fetal Sectional Anatomy. New York, Springer-Verlag, 1986. *C* from Isaacson G, Mintz MC. Magnetic resonance image of the fetal temporal bone. Laryngoscope 96:1343, 1986. *D* reprinted with permission from Prenatal visualization of the inner ear, by G Isaacson and MC Mintz. Journal of Ultrasound in Medicine, Vol 5, pp 409–410. Copyright 1986 by the American Institute of Ultrasound in Medicine.)

Nerves

The nerve supply to the muscles of the face has been described by Gasser[35] and is discussed in detail by him in May's book[73] on the facial nerve. These cranial nerves are mixed nerves, having autonomic, sensory, and motor components. By the time the fetus has reached 37 mm crown-rump length, all of the peripheral branches of the facial nerve are identifiable.

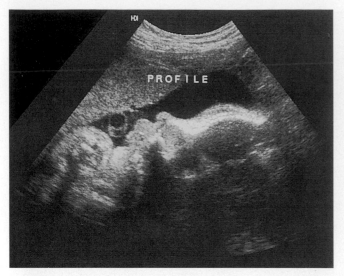

FIGURE 1–9. Ultrasound demonstration of the profile of a fetal face and a fetal ear at 31 to 32 weeks of gestation. (Courtesy of Dr. D.L. Shea, Lady Minto Gulf Island Hospital, B.C., Canada, and Mr. Sander Keil.)

Molecular Control of Craniofacial Development

The subject of embryology is complex, running the gamut from a descriptive chronology of events that transpire during prenatal life to details of genetic types and mutations and how they affect the individual proteins and nucleic acids that are part of the molecular biology of the embryo.[77] The transformation of a fertilized egg into a baby is a remarkable orchestration of cell migration, cell differentiation, programmed cell death, and differential growth. The information that controls this incredibly complex process is encoded in the DNA. Since each cell in the body contains the entire genome, the control of the expression of the different genes in the DNA is crucial to the differentiation of the developing organism. Thus, an understanding of the control of DNA is central to the understanding of morphogenesis.

Molecular Biology and Morphogenesis

As one traces human development back through the fetal and the embryonic periods in an attempt to understand

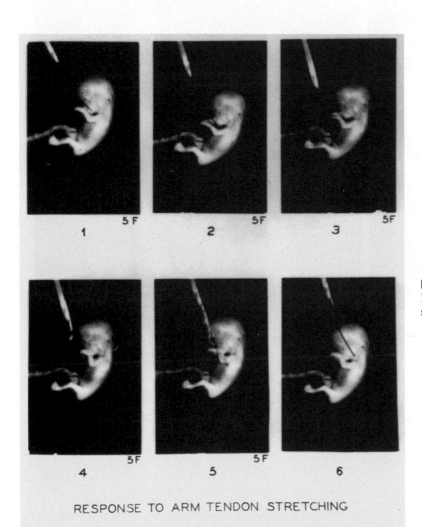

RESPONSE TO ARM TENDON STRETCHING

PROBABLE MENSTRUAL AGE — 9.5 WEEKS

FIGURE 1–10. Photograph of the original work of Davenport Hooker showing fetal response to tactile stimulation.

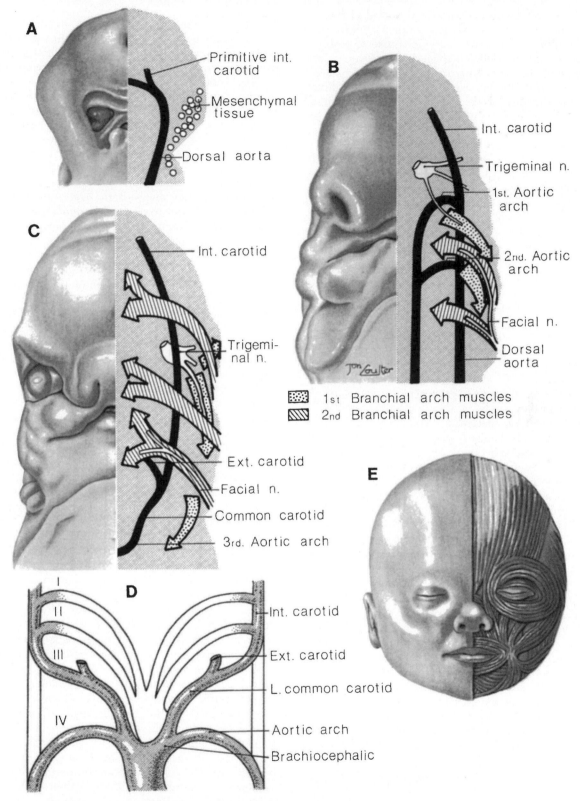

FIGURE 1–11. Development of the craniofacial arteries, muscles, and nerves. *A,* A 3- to 4-week-old embryo. *B,* A 5- to 6-week-old embryo. *C,* A 7- to 8-week-old embryo. *D,* The fate of the aortic arches (shaded vessels persist). (After Avery T. Developmental Anatomy, 7th ed. Philadelphia, WB Saunders, 1974.) *E,* Distribution of the facial musculature in the 15-week-old fetus. (After Gasser R. The development of the facial nerve in man. Ann Otol Rhinol Laryngol 76:37, 1961.)

the errors that produce disease, it becomes clear that many of the answers lie deeper—at the level of the cell and its genetic machinery. In one simple organism, it is possible to observe the developmental course of each cell of the embryo at the 500-cell stage and discover its role in determining the structure of the mature creature.[21] What controls the internal order of these cells and directs them as the organism develops into a complete animal? This is a fundamental question, the answers to which are beginning to unfold.

The molecular control of this orchestrated sequence of development is beginning to be understood. One of the most surprising findings has been the discovery that many diverse organisms use essentially the same genes to control development. This similarity across species is known as conservation. Developmental control genes are highly conserved; sequence homology is noted in *Drosophila melanogaster* (fruit flies), *Caenorhabditis elegans* (a roundworm), *Xenopus laevis* (a South African clawed frog), mice, and humans. This conservation across widely diverse species suggests that once an effective method of control was developed, new body shapes could be produced more easily by modifications of the method than by development of completely new strategies. This conservation is even more amazing when one recognizes that the invertebrates and vertebrates diverged 500 to 700 million years ago.

The plan that determines the major regions of the body is established early in the developing embryo. A critical determination that must be made is axis delineation or polarity. Mechanisms that determine the anteroposterior axis, the dorsoventral axis, and left-right symmetry operate early in embryonic development and have been the subject of intense investigation.[74]

The transmission and control of patterning data are complex, and the signal transduction system is modulated at all points. Establishment of the three layers (ectoderm, mesoderm, and endoderm) and the subsequent subdivision of the layers and tissue differentiation are under genetic and epigenetic control. Developmental control genes, peptide growth factors, and cytoskeletal elements are important in this process of establishing and coordinating sequential boundary formation. The regulatory mechanisms may act in a cascade fashion, such that a homeobox gene product (see later) regulates a peptide growth factor in the mesoderm, which in turn activates another homeobox gene in the neural ectoderm. Concentration gradients also control development in that different concentrations of the signaling molecule produce differing cell fates. The state of the responding cell is also important; receptor expression patterns and ligand affinities vary at different times throughout embryogenesis.

Developmental Gene Clusters

The molecular control of embryogenesis is achieved by a complex series of genes that are expressed in distinct spatial and temporal patterns in the developing embryo.[117] These molecules can be classified into several groups: transcription factors, signaling molecules, and receptors.[16]

Transcription Factors

The transcription factor genes act as master switches, turning other genes on and off, and thus provide genetic control of morphologic development. These genes are activated in an orderly sequence and encode nuclear DNA binding proteins that exert either positive or negative transcriptional control on other genes. These proteins act by high-affinity, site-specific binding to cognate DNA binding sites. The first family of control genes identified is called homeobox genes, or *HOX* genes. Other families include *PAX*, *POU*, and zinc finger (see later).

HOX genes are highly conserved genes that direct morphogenesis in many different species. Elements of the molecular cascade involved in head development have been deduced from work in *Drosophila*[32] and mice. Mutations in these various control genes have been shown to cause abnormal morphogenic phenotypes, some with human parallels (see later). A mutation in a gene called *Antennapedia* could, for example, cause a fly to have extra legs growing where its antennae should be. This type of mutation, in which a body part is replaced with a structure normally found elsewhere on the body, is called a homeotic mutation. Each gene involved in homeotic mutations has been shown to have a region that is highly conserved among the different genes. This conserved region is called the homeobox.

The homeobox region of each *HOX* gene encodes a sequence of amino acids that is known as the homeodomain. The homeodomain recognizes and binds to specific DNA sequences in the genes regulated by the *HOX* genes. This binding of the homeodomain protein either activates or suppresses the regulated gene's transcription and thus ultimately regulates the expression of the regulated gene's protein product. Homeodomain proteins differ greatly from one another except in the region of the homeodomain; these differences give each protein its specific activity. Since these proteins are active in the cell's nucleus (where they control transcription of DNA), they are known as nuclear proteins.

While the *HOX* genes are present in all cells of the developing embryo, the genes are expressed in discrete bands along the anteroposterior axis. *HOX* genes are arranged in clusters on separate chromosomes in the same order in which they are expressed along the developing anteroposterior body axis.[23] This agreement between the order of the genes along the chromosome and the rostrocaudal expression location is termed colinearity. Colinearity is important because it is involved in control of gene expression and in the establishment of anteroposterior body axis of the embryo. The different *HOX* genes are sequentially activated from the 3′ end of the chromosome to the 5′ end, with the gene located most 5′ end expressed last. *HOX* genes are also important in limb development; concentration gradients of their protein products control cellular position.

Vertebrates have four separate homeobox complexes arranged in 13 paralogous groups. Each cluster contains at least nine separate genes. In mice, homeobox genes are designated *Hox*; in humans, *HOX* gene clusters are designated by the capital letters *HOX*. The four separate groups were originally named HOX-1, 2, 3, and 4 and

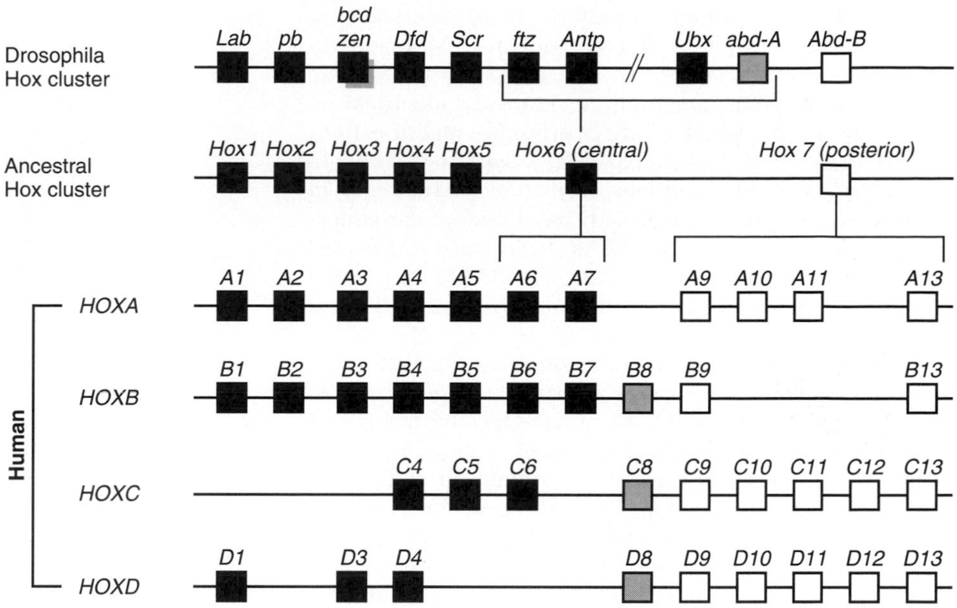

FIGURE 1–12. Comparison of mouse and human homeobox complexes. (Modified from Veraksa A, et al. Developmental patterning genes and their conserved functions from model organism to humans. Mol Genet Metab 69:85, 2000.)

subsequently changed to *HOXA, B, C,* and *D.* Figure 1–12 lists the comparison of mouse and human homeobox complexes and the contrast of the old and new terminology.[99, 111]

Studies of mice have begun to reveal the role of specific homeobox genes in development. The overexpression of the *Hoxa7* gene in transgenic mice produced craniofacial abnormalities consisting of open eyes at birth, nonfused pinnae, and cleft palate.[7] These abnormalities suggest that the mesenchyme derived from migrating neural crest cells is deficient and that overexpression of the *Hoxa7* gene may disrupt this migration. Mice homozygous for a disrupted *Hoxa3* gene develop a phenotype similar to DiGeorge syndrome; affected mice are athymic and aparathyroid and exhibit many pharyngeal, cardiac, and craniofacial abnormalities.[18] Mice homozygous for a disrupted *Hox1* gene were found to have delayed hindbrain neural tube closure, absence of cranial nerves and ganglia, and malformed inner ears and bones of the skull.[8, 69]

As *HOX* genes have a fundamental role in the specification of craniofacial structures, investigations into *HOX* genes provide a molecular means of examining the mechanisms in head development.[46] Mutations in HOX genes or mutations in the genes they control may be responsible for human genetic abnormalities, especially those of early embryonic or fetal development.[66]

Another group of developmental genes are known as paired-box genes *(PAX). PAX* genes were initially identified in *Drosophila* as being involved in segmentation during embryonic development. The initial gene in the fly was known as paired and contained a DNA sequence known as the paired box. All PAX proteins contain a paired domain of 128 amino acids, which binds to DNA. Various members of the group also contain entire or partial homeobox domains. The *PAX* genes family consists of nine known members, which have important roles in many aspects of mammalian development. Table 1–1 summarizes the members of *PAX* genes, the location, and known effects of mutants.[30, 118]

Malformations in both mice and humans are associated

TABLE 1–1. Summary of the Members of the *PAX* Gene Family

Gene	Chromosomal Localization—	Sites of Expression	Mutants		
	Human			**Mouse**	**Human**
PAX1	20p11	Sclerotome, perivertebral mesenchyme	*Undulated (un)*		
PAX9	14q12 -q13	Sclerotome, perivertebral mesenchyme			
PAX2	10p25	Urogenital, CNS	KO: no kidneys		Ocular-renal syndromes
PAX5	9p13	Pro-B cells, CNS	KO: no B cells		
PAX8	2q12 -q14	Thyroid, kidney, CNS			
PAX3	2q35	Dermomyotome, neural crest, muscle, CNS	*Splotch (sp)*		Waardenburg
PAX7	1p36	Dermomyotome, neural crest, muscle, CNS	KO: cranial neural crest defects		Rhabdomyosarcoma
PAX4	7q32	(Pseudogene?)			
PAX6	11p13	Eye, pancreas, CNS	*Small eye (Sey)*		Aniridia

CNS, central nervous system.
Modified from Wehr R, Gruss P. Pax and vertebrate development. Int J Dev Biol 40:369, 1996.

with mutations in various paired-box genes. Mutations in mice Pax genes result in Splotch mutant.[29] Mutations in *PAX3* have been associated with Waardenburg syndrome (see later). A point mutation in *Pax* was identified in undulated mice, which have vertebral malformations along the entire rostral-caudal axis, suggesting a role in mammalian vertebral column formation.[7] Mutations in *Pax6* cause mice to be born with nasal and ocular abnormalities, and mutations in *PAX6* have been associated with aniridia in humans. *PAX2* and *PAX8* have been shown to be expressed in Wilms tumor, an embryonal renal neoplasm.[107]

POU gene family gets its acronym from the first genes identified, namely, *PIT1*, a gene expressed specifically in the pituitary; *OCT1* and *OCT2*, a transcription factor that binds to octamer on DNA; and *Unc86*, a gene expressed in nematode. Genes in this family contain, in addition to a homeobox, a region coding 75 amino acids that binds to DNA through a helix-loop-helix structure.[94] Expression of POU genes differs from that of *HOX* genes both temporally and spatially. Several POU domain genes are expressed earlier in embryogenesis than *HOX* genes. POU domain proteins are expressed in the forebrain, whereas HOX genes are expressed in the hindbrain. POU domains and homeodomains also interact with DNA in different fashions; thus, POU domain proteins form a functionally distinct class of regulatory proteins. POU genes have been divided into five classes (*POU1* to *POU5*) and appear to be particularly important in the development of the central nervous system.

Zinc finger genes encode a class of proteins that bind to DNA and control its transcription. These proteins contain small looplike units known as fingers. Cystine and histidine units are bounded by zinc ions to cause the polypeptide chain to pucker into finger-like structures. These fingers can be inserted into specific regions in the DNA helix by arginine-guanine hydrogen bonds. *GLI3*, a zinc finger gene, when disrupted can cause Greig cephalopolysyndactyly (see later).

Signaling Molecules

Signal molecules leave the cells that produce them and exert their effects on other cells, which may be neighboring cells or cells located at greater distances. Many signaling molecules are peptide growth factors that mediate interactions such as inductions between groups of cells in embryogenesis. The *transforming growth factor-beta (TGF-beta)* and *fibroblast growth factor (FGF)* families are two well-known examples of this group. The *hedgehog* proteins are another newly discovered example. When the signaling molecules form complexes with the receptors, they set off a cascade of events in a signal transduction pathway that transmits the molecular signals to the nucleus of the responding cells.[93] Other examples include JAGGED1, patched, CREB-binding protein, GLI3, FGFR1, CASK, treacle, and FGFR2.[33]

The TGF-beta superfamily consists of a large number of molecules, up to 30 genes. They have a wide variety of roles during embryogenesis and postnatal life, including cell differentiation, motility, organization, and death.[124] This superfamily can be grouped into general classes (Fig.

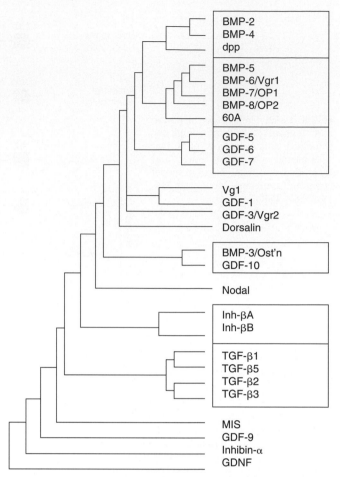

FIGURE 1–13. TGF-beta family comprises distinct factors that can be arranged into clusters (boxes) of related isoforms. BMP-3 is also called osteogenin. (Modified from Massagué J. TGF-β signal transduction. Annu Rev Biochem 67:753, 1994.)

1–13). This superfamily TGF-beta can inhibit proliferation of different cell lines and the so-called transforming activity resulting from secondary effects on matrix production and synthesis of other growth factors. Moreover, they participate in information processing for the basic body plan; stimulate the formation of cartilage, bone, and sex organ; suppress epithelial cell growth; and have a role in wound repair and regulation of important immune and endocrine functions. TGF-beta has an important role in cranial suture regulation,[95] i.e., maintaining the patency and closure of sutures at the proper time through interactions with other molecules, and it is said to have a secondary role in premature craniosynostosis.[20]

Members of the FGF family (FGF-1 to FGF-9) similarly fulfill various functions in embryogenesis, ranging from stimulations of mesenchymal cell proliferation to induction of elongation of the limb bud to stimulation of capillary growth to proliferation and survival of certain neurons.[119]

One of the most influential families of signaling molecules is the hedgehog protein. Sonic hedgehog plays a vital part as a chief secretory product produced by various organizing centers in the embryo. The sonic hedgehog undergoes proteolytic autocleavage and results in a 19-

kDa N-terminal peptide and a 27-kDa C-terminal peptide. The N-terminal binds covalently to cholesterol during proteolytic processing. After binding with a receptor molecule in the target cell, the sonic hedgehog signal stimulates the target cells to produce new gene products or to undergo new pathways of differentiation.[93] To date, three forms of hedgehog—sonic, Indian, and desert-derived—from three different genes have been described in mammals.

Receptors

The signaling molecules must interact with receptors to exert an effect on responding cells. Most receptors are located on the cell surface while some are intracellular, such as those for lipid-soluble molecules, e.g., steroid, retinoids, and thyroid hormone. Cell surface receptors are composed of three domains: extracellular, transmembrane, and cytoplasmic. Extracellular domains contain a binding site for the ligand, which when bound effects a conformational change in the cytoplasmic domain of the receptor molecule. Cell surface receptors are of the following main types: those with intrinsic protein kinase activity and those that use a second-messenger system to activate cytoplasmic protein kinases. An example of the first type is the family of receptors of FGFs (FGFRs), in which the cytoplasmic domain contains tyrosine kinase activity, and the receptors for the TGF-beta superfamily, in which the cytoplasmic domain contains serine/theronine kinase activity. In the second type of cell receptors, the receptors are activated by being bound with a ligand such as neurotransmitter, peptide hormone, and growth factor, but a series of intermediate steps is required to activate cytoplasmic protein kinase. Mutations in the FGFRs can result in craniofacial malformations and many skeletal dysplasias (see later).

Molecules and Morphology

The interaction between developmental control genes and other control systems is beginning to be delineated, with implications important for understanding human abnormalities. Retinoic acid controls development by acting as a patterning agent, or morphogen. Retinoic acid is a human teratogen but also has a role in normal development. Retinoic acid establishes a concentration gradient, particularly in limbs, and conveys positioning information to the cells. HOX genes have been shown to be sequentially activated by retinoic acid,[103] and administration to embryos through the maternal bloodstream can cause altered expression of HOX genes.[57] Retinoic acid has also been shown to stimulate the regeneration of auditory hair cells in mammals.[65] Organ of Corti explants from 3-day-old rats were exposed to neomycin, which destroyed the hair cells. Retinoic acid was then administered to the cell culture, and hair cell growth was noted. This stimulation of growth by retinoic acid did not occur if a mitosis-blocking agent, cytosine arabinoside, was added along with the retinoic acid.

Neural crest cell migration is controlled, in part, by a group of glycoproteins known as integrins. Integrins mediate interactions between neural crest cells and the surrounding extracellular matrix. When antisense oligonucleotides are used to block synthesis of integrin subunits, neural crest cell attachment to extracellular matrix components is perturbed.[61] Use of these types of molecular probes offers insights into neural crest cell migration and differentiation.

While neural crest cell migration has long been appreciated, other classes of cells are being identified. Neural plate cells, myoblasts, angioblasts, and placode-derived cells also migrate, either independently or in concert with other cells.[83] Advances in immunocytochemistry, in situ hybridization transgenic reporter genes, explantation experiments, and molecular probes all are providing insights into the way that genetic information is transformed into specific tissues and organs.

The Molecular Basis of Specific Craniofacial Syndromes

Waardenburg Syndrome

Waardenburg syndrome is an autosomal dominant disorder characterized by sensorineural hearing loss, dystopia canthorum, and pigmentary disturbances such as heterochromia iridis and white forelocks. Waardenburg syndrome is divided into type I (WS1) with dystopia canthorum and type II (WS2) without dystopia canthorum. Type III (WS3), with dystopia canthorum and limb abnormalities, also known as Klein-Waardenburg syndrome, and type IV (WS4), with Hirschsprung disease, also known as Waardenburg-Shah syndrome,[100] have also been described. WS1 and WS3 are due to mutations in the PAX3 gene[6, 43, 76, 78] on 2q35. Some WS2 cases (WS2A) are associated with mutations in the microphthalmia-associated transcription factor (MITF) gene on 3p14.1-p12,[62, 108] while other families of WS2 (WS2B) were mapped to 1p21-p13.3.[63] The WS4 phenotype can result from mutations in the endothelin-B receptor gene (EDNRB) on 13q22,[3, 89] in the gene for its ligand, endothelin-3 (EDN3) on 20q13.2-13.3,[26, 37] or in the SOX10 gene on 22q13.[47, 109] The mouse model of WS1 was known to be splotch.[2, 32] The splotch mouse was shown to have mutations in Pax3.[30] PAX3 is expressed in the dorsal neuroepithelium, the craniofacial mesectoderm, and the limb mesenchyme, which are the precursors of the tissues defective in Waardenburg syndrome. Waardenburg syndrome is an example of genetic heterogeneity, in which mutations in different genes can produce the similar phenotype. An interaction among SOX10, PAX3, and MITF has been demonstrated.[11] A cascade reaction was also proposed among PAX3, MITF, SOX10, EDNRB, and EDB3.[106] Such an epistatic relationship might explain why when these genes are altered, a variable range of auditory-pigmentary-neural crest changes results, as seen in different types of Waardenburg syndromes.

Greig Cephalopolysyndactyly

Greig cephalopolysyndactyly, an autosomal dominant syndrome that affects limb and craniofacial development, was originally mapped to 7p12-13 by the demonstration of tight linkage to the epidermal growth factor receptor gene *(EGFR)*.[13] Vortkamp et al.[113] have shown that a zinc finger gene, *GLI3*, mapped to 7p13, right next to *EGFR*, is interrupted by chromosomal translocations in patients with Greig cephalopolysyndactyly. These investigators advanced the hypothesis that mutations disrupting normal *GLI3* expression may have a causative role. Subsequent analyses of additional 24 cases confirm *GLI3* being the causative gene.[55] *GLI3* is homologous to the *Drosophila cubitus interruptus* (ci) gene product (CI), which shows transcriptional activation or repression activity and subcellular localization and regulates the patched *(PTC)*, gooseberry *(GSB)*, sonic hedgehog *(SHH)*, and decapentaplegic *(DPP)* genes.[102, 114] *GLI3* gene is one of the GLI-Kruppel family *(GLIN)* of human genes, which are amplified in certain glioblastomas.[96] However, instead of relating to glioma or other forms of neoplasia,[112] *GLI3* is important in the control of craniofacial and limb development. *GLI3* is a good example of one gene's causing many diseases. To date, in addition to Greig cephalopolysyndactyly, mutations in the *GLI3* gene had been identified in Pallister-Hall syndrome (a neonatally lethal malformation syndrome of hypothalamic hamartoblastoma, postaxial polydactyly, and imperforate anus). Some cases were associated with laryngeal cleft, abnormal lung lobation, renal agenesis or dysplasia, short fourth metacarpals, nail dysplasia, multiple buccal frenula, hypoadrenalism, microphallus, congenital heart defect, and intrauterine growth retardation.[10, 19, 39, 56] Postaxial polydactyly type A/B is an autosomal trait characterized by an extra digit in the ulnar and/or fibular side of the extremities. In type A, the extra digit is rather well formed and articulates with the fifth or an extra metacarpal; in type B, the extra digit is not well formed and is frequently in the form of a skin tag.[90, 91] The *GLI3* gene had been identified in Pallister-Hall syndrome and postaxial polydactyl type A/B. It was proposed that all phenotypes associated with *GLI3* mutations be called *GLI3* morphopathies, since the phenotypic borders of the resulting syndromes are not well defined and there is no apparent genotype-phenotype correlation.[91]

Craniosynostosis Syndromes

Craniosynostosis, Boston Type

The gene for Boston-type craniosynostosis was the first to be identified as causing craniosynostosis syndrome. In 1993, Warman et al. described a five-generation family with a novel craniosynostosis syndrome. In addition to their craniosynostosis, some affected individuals also have short first metatarsals, headaches, seizures, myopia, and visual deficits, but none was consistently associated with a specific craniofacial anomaly.[116] The gene *MSX2* (OMIN 123101), mapped to chromosome 5q,[84, 93] is an *HOX* gene whose role in normal craniofacial development is to regulate apoptosis of the neural crest cell–derived tissue from which much of the craniofacial region develops. This role has been supported by the identification of *MSX2* transcripts in osteoblasts adjacent to the calvarial sutures during mouse embryonic and postnatal development.[50, 68] A missense mutation P148H was detected in all affected family members.[70] Transgenic mice with same mutation or overexpression of *MSX2* also showed craniosynostosis.[68] This is clearly a rare syndrome, as this original family represents the only reported example of Boston-type craniosynostosis.

Fibroblast Growth Factor Receptors Mutations

Fibroblast Growth Factor Receptor-2—Mutations in Crouzon, Pfeiffer, Apert, Jackson-Weiss, and Other Syndromes

The *FGFR* genes are a family of four tyrosine kinase receptors that rest on cell surfaces and function to bind FGF, family signaling molecules that function to regulate cell proliferation, differentiation, and migration through various complex pathways. They are important in angiogenesis, wound healing, limb development, and malignant transformation. FGFs binds to FGFRs in a nonspecific manner, as any FGF can bind to the FGFR.[72, 79] FGFR mutations are hypermorphic, causing the gene product to perform its normal function excessively. Research has suggested that the exact mechanism of the hypermorphic effect is different for different types of mutations that have been reported in the FGFR craniosynostosis syndromes.[120]

Crouzon Syndrome. The gene for Crouzon syndrome (CS) was the next to be identified. CS is an autosomal dominant condition characterized by premature craniosynostosis, hypoplastic maxilla, shallow orbits with proptosis, and external auditory canal atresia. As many as 50% of patients with CS have hearing loss, both conductive and sensorineural. Otitis media with effusion is prevalent owing to eustachian tube dysfunction and malformation; thus, myringotomy and tube placement may be necessary to optimize hearing. Abnormalities in the organs of communication and hearing loss combine to challenge CS sufferers with various communicative disorders. Language development, acquisition of voice, and articulation skills are put at risk by the dysmorphogenesis of oral and pharyngeal structures.[85] CS has been mapped to the long arm of chromosome 10.[86] This mapping work was quickly followed by the discovery that mutations in the *FGFR2* gene were associated with some cases of CS.[92] Two lines of reasoning led to this discovery. *FGFR2* had been shown to map to 10q2526, and *FGFR2* gene products were expressed in murine embryogenesis, particularly in the frontal bones, maxilla, and mandible. Several of the point mutations noted substituted a tyrosine for a cysteine within the third immunoglobulin domain, presumably affecting the *FGFR2* ability to bind its ligands. Ligand binding is necessary for dimerization of the receptor, which in turn activates the intracellular tyrosine kinase domains.

Pfeiffer, Apert, and Jackson-Weiss Syndromes. Mutations in *FGFR2* have also been associated with three other craniosynostosis syndromes: Jackson-Weiss,[49] Apert,[121] and Pfeiffer.[60, 97] Patients with Jackson-Weiss syndrome differ from patients with CS in that the hands and feet are normal in patients with CS whereas those with Jackson-Weiss syndrome can have various foot deformities. Patients with Apert syndrome have syndactyly of the hands and feet. Pfeiffer syndrome is another craniosynostosis syndrome, characterized by premature cranial fusion, broad thumbs, and toe abnormalities. Of great interest is the fact that identical mutations in the *FGFR2* gene can cause both Pfeiffer syndrome and CS.[97] Mutations in FGFR1[81] have also been associated with Pfeiffer syndrome.

Thus, investigations to date have shown the following: Mutations in the same gene can cause four different clinical syndromes, mutations in different genes can cause the same syndrome, and identical mutations in the same gene can cause separate syndromes. The last observation implies that other genetic factors must be involved. The roles of the fibroblast growth factor receptors and ligands in human craniofacial development and overall skeletal morphogenesis have become the subject of intense investigation.

Other FGFR2 Mutations. The syndrome most recently shown to be caused by an *FGFR2* mutation is Beare-Stevenson cutis gyrata syndrome (OMIM 123790). This is a rare syndrome (fewer than 10 cases reported) in which affected individuals have a craniofacial appearance similar to the other *FGFR2* craniosynostosis syndromes and variable limb and other skeletal findings.[12] All patients to date are severely intellectually compromised. The syndrome is distinguished by its cutaneous findings, which include widespread cutis gyrata, acanthosis nigricans, skin tags, a prominent umbilical stump, and accessory nipples. Genital anomalies, such as bifid scrotum, prominent labial raphe, and rugated labia majora, are seen as well. Przylepa et al.[88] demonstrated two different *FGFR2* mutations in three sporadic cases of Beare-Stevenson syndrome.

FGFR3 and Craniosynostosis

FGFR3 mutations were initially described in dwarfism syndromes—achondroplasia, hypochondroplasia, and thanatophoric dysplasia. However, Meyers et al.[75] found a mutation in which alanine was substituted for glutamic acid at amino acid 391 in patients with a crouzonoid phenotype, acanthosis nigricans, and cementomas of the jaws.

The *FGFR3* coronal synostosis syndrome (Muenke-type craniosynostosis)[9, 80] is one of the most common human mutations known. It is frequently familial, often with a markedly variable phenotype, even within a single family. The mutation was first identified in a series of individuals and families with syndromic coronal craniosynostosis, including some who had been previously labeled as having Pfeiffer, Jackson-Weiss, and Saethre-Chotzen syndromes. This mutation (Pro252Arg) is analogous to the one that was described in *FGFR1* (Pfeiffer syndrome) and *FGFR2* (Apert syndrome). Subsequent studies have shown that this mutation can be found in patients with isolated unicoronal or bicoronal synostosis,[38] isolated macrocephaly,[40] and isolated sensorineural hearing loss.[41]

Saethre-Chotzen Syndrome

Saethre-Chotzen syndrome is an autosomal dominant acrocraniosynostotic syndrome characterized by craniosynostosis, low frontal hairline, facial asymmetry, brachydactyly, clinodactyly, and syndactyly. It has been mapped to chromosome 7p.[14] The gene, called *TWIST* (OMIM 601622), contains a basic helix-loop-helix domain, a motif commonly seen in DNA binding proteins, suggesting that *TWIST* functions as a transcription factor. Studies have shown that *TWIST* is required for normal cranial neural tube closure in mice, but its exact role in suture biology is yet to be defined. *TWIST* may be involved upstream in the same pathway as the FGFRs, possibly regulating their expression. *TWIST* mutations in patients with Saethre-Chotzen syndrome cause premature termination of the protein, suggesting that Saethre-Chotzen is caused by haploinsufficiency of *TWIST*.[27, 44] A significant proportion of patients with Saethre-Chotzen syndrome had deletions in 7p21.1 that encompass the *TWIST* gene; these could be detected by fluorescent in situ hybridization.[52] Studies on stability, dimerization capacities, and subcellular distribution of three types of *TWIST* mutant revealed that at least two distinct mechanisms account for loss of *TWIST* protein function in patients with Saethre-Chotzen syndrome—namely, protein degradation and subcellular mislocalization.[27, 84]

Treacher Collins Syndrome

Treacher Collins syndrome is an autosomal dominant craniofacial disorder characterized by facial bone hypoplasia, abnormal pinnae and ossicles, downward-slanting palpebral fissures with notching of the lower eyelids, and cleft palate. The gene *TCOF1* and the gene product TREACLE have been cloned and are located on 5q32-33.[24, 82, 110] The gene is widely expressed in various embryonic and adult tissues of the mouse. Peak levels of expression in the developing embryo were observed at the edges of the neural folds immediately before fusion and in the developing branchial arches at the time of critical morphogenetic events.[25] The exact role for this gene in the development of the craniofacial complex is not completely understood. However, TREACLE is believed to be involved in nucleolar-cytoplasmic transport.[122] One hypothesis is that the defective protein impairs the nucleolar trafficking that is critically required during craniofacial development, but others emphasize a nuclear phosphoration[54] role for TREACLE since appropriate kinase activity in branchial arches I and II coincides with peak expression of TREACLE.

Cleft Lip and Palate

Congenital structural anomalies of the lip and/or palate affect approximately 1 in 1000 live births. The frequent occurrence and the extensive psychologic, surgical, speech, and dental involvement emphasize the importance of understanding the underlying causes. The clefting appears to result from failure of mesenchymal cell migration or mesenchymal cell transformation at the point of fusion. It can present as a component of many congenital anomaly syndromes or as a single gene disorder, and it may have teratogenic origins. The nonsyndromic forms are the most common and are likely due to secondary gene-environment interactions. Advances in both molecular and quantitative approaches have begun to identify the genes responsible for the rare syndromic forms of cleft and have also identified both candidate genes and loci for the more common and complex nonsyndromic variants.

Specific alleles of TGF-alpha have been shown to be associated with nonsyndromic cleft palate.[1, 101] Related environmental factors include nutritional deprivation; phenytoin, valproic acid, thalidomide, alcohol, and dioxin are recognized teratogens that cause clefts.[34, 115, 123] The exposures may disrupt the metabolic pathway that has a role in the development of cleft lip and palate. *MSX1, TGFB3, RARA,* and *ARNT2* were proposed to be contributing genes for causing cleft lip and palate.[17, 51, 67] Van der Woude syndrome, a mendelian condition with nonsyndromic cleft lip and palate, was mapped to 1p36. Identification of this disease is likely to make great contribution to the understanding of other genes and pathways that play a part in the development of cleft lip and palate (Chap. 55).[98]

Conclusion

Progress in identifying the mechanisms of control of human facial development has been accelerated by advances in molecular genetics. Identification of the genes responsible is a crucial step toward the ultimate understanding of the development of the face. Mapping and identification of the genes associated with craniofacial abnormalities will eventually elucidate the biochemical and molecular mechanisms that control development of the human face. Knowledge of the molecular mechanisms of human craniofacial anomalies may suggest approaches for their amelioration, correction, and ultimate prevention.

Acknowledgments

We would like to thank Pei-Wen Chiang, Felicia Davis, Tina Combs, and Maria L. Soto for their invaluable contribution to this chapter.

SELECTED READINGS

Ayala F. The mechanisms of evolution. Sci Am 239:56, 1978.
> *This well-illustrated article explains the concepts of molecular biology as related to evolution. The entire issue is devoted to evolution.*

Burdi A. Biological forces which shape the human mid-face before birth. In McNamara J (ed). Craniofacial Growth Series, Monograph 6. Ann Arbor, MI, Center for Human Growth and Development, University of Michigan, 1976.
> *This comprehensive article relates molecular biology to embryonic and fetal growth.*

Cohen MM Jr, Maclean RE. Craniosynostosis Diagnosis, Evaluation and Management, 2nd ed. Oxford, NY, Oxford University Press, 2000.

Enlow D. Essentials of Facial Growth. Philadelphia, WB Saunders, 1996.
> *This book is written primarily in atlas style and illustrates craniofacial growth from embryonic to adult life.*

Isaacson G. Atlas of Fetal Sectional Anatomy. New York, Springer-Verlag, 1986.
> *An excellent atlas of fetal sectional anatomy, this book correlates gross, magnetic resonance imaging, and ultrasound findings.*

May M. The Facial Nerve, 2nd ed. New York, Thieme Medical Publishers, 2000.
> *An outstanding review of the anatomy, physiology, and disease states of the facial nerve.*

Moore KL. Before We Are Born: Basic Embryology and Birth Defects, 2nd ed. Philadelphia, WB Saunders, 1998.
> *A clinically oriented embryology text that is well illustrated.*

Robin NH. Molecular genetic advances in understanding craniosynostosis. Plast Reconstr Surg 103:1060, 1999.
> *A good review of the common craniosynostosis syndromes.*

Stewart R. Genetic factors in craniofacial morphogenesis. In Stewart R, Prescott G (eds). Oral Facial Genetics. St Louis, CV Mosby, 1976.
> *This comprehensive text with extensive references describes the genetic aspects of craniofacial abnormalities and gives other extensive descriptions of oral abnormalities.*

REFERENCES

1. Ardinger HH, Buetow KH, Bell GI, et al. Association of the genetic variation of the transforming growth factor-alpha gene with cleft lip and palate. Am J Hum Genet 45:348, 1989.
2. Asher J, Friedman T. Mouse and hamster mutants as models for Waardenburg syndromes in humans. J Med Genet 27:618, 1990.
3. Attie T, Till M, Pelet A, et al. Mutation of the endothelin-receptor B gene in Waardenburg-Hirschsprung disease. Hum Mol Genet 4:2407, 1995.
4. Avery T. Developmental Anatomy, 7th ed. Philadelphia, WB Saunders, 1974.
5. Ayala F. The mechanisms of evolution. Sci Am 239:56, 1978.
6. Baldwin CT, Hoth CF, Amos JA, et al. An exonic mutation in the *HuP2* paired domain gene causes Waardenburg's syndrome. Nature 355:637, 1992.
7. Balling R, Deutsch U, Gruss P. *Undulated,* a mutation affecting the development of the mouse skeleton, has a point mutation in the paired box of Pax 1. Cell 55:531, 1988.
8. Balling R, Mutter G, Gruss P, Kessel M. Craniofacial abnormalities induced by ectopic expression of the homeobox gene *HOX1.1* in transgenic mice. Cell 58:337, 1989.
9. Bellus FA, Gaudenz K, Zackai EH, et al. Identical mutations in three different fibroblast growth factor receptor genes in autosomal dominant craniosynostosis syndromes. Nat Genet 14:174, 1996.
10. Biesecker LG, Abbott M, Allen J, et al. Report from the workshop on Pallister-Hall syndrome and related phenotypes. Am J Med Genet 65:76, 1996.
11. Bondurand N, Pingault V, Goerich DE, et al. Interaction among *SOX10, PAX3,* and *MITF,* three genes altered in Waardenburg syndrome. Hum Mol Genet 9:1907, 2000.
12. Bratanic B, Praprotnik M, Novosel-Sever M. Congenital craniofacial dysostosis and cutis gyratum: the Beare-Stevenson syndrome. Eur J Pediatr 153:184, 1994.
13. Brueton J, Huson SM, Winter RM, Williamson R. The chromosomal localisation of a developmental gene in man. Direct DNA analysis demonstrates that Greig cephalopolysyndactyly (*GCPS*) maps to 7p13. Am J Med Genet 31:799, 1988.
14. Brueton LA, van Herwerden L, Chotai KA, Winter RM. The mapping of a gene for craniosynostosis: evidence for linkage of the Saethre-Chotzen syndrome to distal chromosome 7p. J Med Genet 29:681, 1992.
15. Burdi AR. Early development of the human basicranium: morphogenic basicranium: morphogenic controls, growth patterns and relations. In Bosma JF (ed). NIH Symposium on Development of the Basicranium. Washington, DC, U.S. Government Printing Office, 1977, pp 81-92.

16. Carlson BM. Human Embryology & Developmental Biology, 2nd ed. St Louis, CV Mosby, 1999.

17. Chenevix-Trench G, Jones K, Green AC, et al. Cleft lip with or without cleft palate: association with transforming growth factor alpha and retinoic acid receptor loci. Am J Hum Genet 51:1377, 1992.

18. Chisaka O, Capecchi MR. Regionally restricted developmental defects resulting from targeted disruption of the mouse homeobox gene Hox 1.5. Nature 350:473, 1991.

19. Clarren SK, Alvord EC Jr, Hall JG, et al. Congenital hypothalamic hamartoblastoma, hypopituitarism, imperforate anus, and postaxial polydactyly—a new syndrome? Part II: neuropathological considerations. Am J Med Genet 7:75, 1980.

20. Cohen MM Jr. Transforming growth factors and the fibroblast growth factors and their receptors: role in sutural biology and craniosynostosis. J Bone Miner Res 12:322, 1997.

21. Darnell J, Lodish H, Baltimore D. Molecular Cell Biology. New York, Scientific American Books, 1986, pp 985–1033.

22. DeMyer W. Median facial malformations and their implications for brain malformations. In Bergsma D (ed). Morphogenesis and Malformation of Face and Brain. New York, Alan R Liss, 1975, pp 155–181.

23. De Robertis EM, Oliver G, Wright CVE. Homeobox genes and the vertebrate body plan. Sci Am 263:46, 1990.

24. Dixon MJ, Dixon J, Houseal T, et al. Narrowing the position of the Treacher Collins syndrome locus to a small interval between three new microsatellite markers at 5q32-33.1. Am J Hum Genet 52:907, 1993.

25. Dixon J, Hovanes K, Shiang R, et al. Sequence analysis, identification of evolutionary conserved motifs and expression analysis of murine tcof1 provide further evidence for a potential function for the gene and its human homologue, TCOF1. Hum Mol Genet 6:727, 1997.

26. Edery P, Attie T, Amiel J, et al. Mutation of the endothelin-3 gene in the Waardenburg-Hirschsprung disease (Shah-Waardenburg syndrome). Nat Genet 12:442, 1996.

27. El Ghouzzi, V, Le Merrer M, Perrin-Schmitt F, et al. Mutations of the TWIST gene in the Saethre-Chotzen syndrome. Nat Genet 15:42, 1997.

28. Enlow D. Handbook of Facial Growth. Philadelphia, WB Saunders, 1975.

29. Epstein DJ, Vekemans M, Gruss P. Splotch (Sp²ʰ), a mutation affecting development of the mouse neural tube, shows a deletion within the paired domain of Pax3. Cell 67:767, 1991.

30. Epstein JA, Li J, Lang D, et al. Migration of cardiac neural crest cells in Splotch embryos. Development 127:1869, 2000.

31. Finkelstein R, Perrimon N. The molecular genetics of head development in Drosophila melanogaster. Development 112:899, 1991.

32. Foy C, Newton V, Wellesley D, et al. Assignment of the locus for Waardenburg syndrome Type I to human chromosome 2q37 and possible homology to the Splotch mouse. Am J Hum Genet 46:1017, 1990.

33. Francis-West P, Ladher R, Barlow A, et al. Signalling interactions during facial development. Mech Dev 75:3, 1998.

34. Garcia AM, Fletcher T, Benavides FG, et al. Parental agricultural work and selected congenital malformations. Am J Epidemiol 149:64, 1999.

35. Gasser R. The development of the facial nerve in man. Ann Otol Rhinol Laryngol 76:37, 1961.

36. Ghouzzi V, Legeai-Mallet L, Aresta S, et al. Saethre-Chotzen mutations cause TWIST protein degradation or impaired nuclear location. Hum Mol Genet 9:813, 2000.

37. Gopal Rao VVN, Loffler C, Hansmann I. The gene for the novel vasoactive peptide endothelin 3 (EDN3) is localized to human chromosome 20q13.2-qter. Genomics 10:840, 1991.

38. Gripp F-W, McDonald-McGinn DM, Gaudenz K, et al. Identification of a genetic cause for isolated unilateral coronal synostosis: a unique mutation in the fibroblast growth factor receptor 3. J Pediatr 132:714, 1998.

39. Hall JG, Pallister PD, Clarren SK, et al. Congenital hypothalamic hamartoblastoma, hypopituitarism, imperforate anus, and postaxial polydactyly—a new syndrome? Part I: clinical, causal, and pathogenetic considerations. Am J Med Genet 7:47, 1980.

40. Hollway GE, Phillips HA, Ades LC, et al. Localization of craniosynostosis Adelaide type to 4p16. Hum Mol Genet 4:681, 1995.

41. Hollway GE, Suthers GK, Battese KM, et al. Deafness due to Pro 250 Arg mutation of FGFR3. Lancet 351:887, 1998.

42. Hooker D. Fetal behavior. Association for Research in Nervous and Mental Disease XIX. Interrelationship of Mind and Body. Baltimore, Williams & Wilkins, 1939, pp 237–243.

43. Hoth CF, Milunsky A, Lipsky N, et al. Mutations in the paired domain of the human PAX3 gene causes Klein-Waardenburg syndrome (WSIII) as well as Waardenburg syndrome Type I (WSI). Am J Hum Genet 52:455, 1993.

44. Howard TD, Paznekas WA, Green ED, et al. Mutations in TWIST, a basic helix-loop-helix transcription factor, in Saethre-Chotzen syndrome. Nat Genet 15:36, 1997.

45. Humphrey T. Reflex activity in the oral and facial area of the human fetus. In Bosma J (ed). Second Symposium on Oral Sensation and Perception. Springfield, IL, Charles C Thomas, 1970.

46. Hunt P, Krumlauf R. Deciphering the HOX code: clues to patterning branchial regions of the head. Cell 66:1075, 1991.

47. Inoue K, Tanabe Y, Lupski JR. Myelin deficiencies in both the central and the peripheral nervous systems associated with a SOX10 mutation. Ann Neurol 46:313, 1999.

48. Isaacson G. Atlas of Fetal Sectional Anatomy. New York, Springer-Verlag, 1986.

49. Jabs EW, Li X, Scott AF, et al. Jackson-Weiss and Crouzon syndromes are allelic with mutations in fibroblast growth factor receptor 2. Nat Genet 8:275, 1994.

50. Jabs EW, Muller U, Li X, et al. A mutation in the homeodomain of the human MSX2 gene in a family affected with autosomal dominant craniosynostosis. Cell 75:443, 1993.

51. Jain S, Maltepe E, Lu MM, et al. Expression of ARNT, ARNT2, HIF1 alpha, HIF2 alpha and Ah receptor mRNAs in the developing mouse. Mech Dev 73:117, 1998.

52. Johnson D, Horsley SW, Moloney DM, et al. A comprehensive screen for TWIST mutations in patients with craniosynostosis identifies a new microdeletion syndrome of chromosome band 7p21.1. Am J Hum Genet 63:1282, 1998.

53. Johnston MC. The neural crest in abnormalities of the face and brain. Birth Defects 11:1, 1975.

54. Jones NC, Farlie PG, Minichiello J, et al. Detection of an appropriate kinase activity in branchial arches I and II that coincides with peak expression of the Treacher Collins syndrome gene product, treacle. Hum Mol Genet 8:2239, 1999.

55. Kalff-Suske M, Wild A, Topp J, et al. Point mutations throughout the GLI3 gene cause Greig cephalopolysyndactyly syndrome. Hum Mol Genet 8:1769, 1999.

56. Kang S, Graham JM Jr, Olney AH, et al. GL13 frameshift mutations cause autosomal dominant Pallister-Hall syndrome. Nat Genet 15:266, 1997.

57. Kessel M, Gruss P. Homeotic transformations of murine vertebrae and concomitant alterations of the HOX codes induced by retinoic acid. Cell 67:89, 1991.

58. Kier S. Fetal skull. In Newton T, Potts D (eds). Radiology of the Skull and Brain, Vol 1. St Louis, CV Mosby, 1971.

59. Krogman W. Craniofacial growth and development: an appraisal. Yearb Phys Anthropol 18:31, 1974.

60. Lajeunie E, Ma HW, Bonaventure J, et al. FGFR2 mutations in Pfeiffer syndrome. Nat Genet 9:108, 1995.

61. Lallier T, Bronner-Fraser M. Inhibition of neural crest cell attachment by integrin antisense oligonucleotides. Science 259:692, 1993.

62. Lalwani AK, Attaie A, Randolph FT, et al. Point mutation in the MITF gene causing Waardenburg syndrome type II in a three-generation Indian family. Am J Med Genet 80:406, 1998.

63. Lalwani AK, Baldwin CT, Morell R, et al. A locus for Waardenburg syndrome type II maps to chromosome 1p13.3-p21 (abstract). Am J Hum Genet 55(suppl):A14, 1994.

64. Latham R. An appraisal of the early maxillary growth mechanism. In McNamara J (ed). Craniofacial Growth Series, Monograph 6. Ann Arbor, MI, Center for Human Growth and Development, University of Michigan, 1976.

65. Lefebvre PP, Malgrange B, Staecker H, et al. Retinoic acid stimulates regeneration of mammalian auditory hair cells. Science 260:692, 1993.

66. Lewis EB. Clusters of master control genes regulate the development of higher organisms. JAMA 267:1524, 1992.

67. Lidral AC, Romitti PA, Basart AM, et al. Association of MSX1 and

TGFB3 with nonsyndromic clefting in human. Am J Hum Genet 63:557, 1998.

68. Liu YH, Kundu R, Wu L, et al. Premature suture closure and ectopic cranial bone in mice expressing Msx2 transgenes in the developing skull. Natl Acad Sci U S A 92:6137, 1995.

69. Lufkin T, Dierich A, LeMeur M, et al. Disruption of the *Hox1.6* homeobox gene results in defects in a region corresponding to its rostral domain of expression. Cell 66:1105, 1991.

70. Ma L, Golden S, Wu L, et al. The molecular basis of Boston-type craniosynostosis: the Pro 148-to-His mutation in the N-terminal arm of the *MSX2* homeodomain stabilizes DNA binding with altering nucleotide sequence preferences. Hum Mol Genet 5:1915, 1996.

71. Maue-Dickson W, Trefler M. Image quality in computerized and conventional tomography in the assessment of craniofacial anomalies. SPIE 127:353, 1977.

72. Mason IJ. The ins and outs of fibroblast growth factors. Cell 78:547, 1994.

73. May M. The Facial Nerve. New York, Thieme Medical Publishers, 1986.

74. Melton DA. Pattern formation during animal development. Science 252:234, 1991.

75. Meyers GA, Orlow SJ, Munro IR, et al. Fibroblast growth factor receptor 3 (FGFR3) transmembrane mutation in Crouzon syndrome with acanthosis nigricans. Nat Genet 11:462, 1995.

76. Milunsky A, Lipsky N, Sheffer R, et al. A mutation in the Waardenburg syndrome (WS-I) gene in a family with 'WS-III' (abstract). Am J Hum Genet 51(suppl):A222, 1992.

77. Moore KL. The Developing Human, 5th ed. Philadelphia, WB Saunders, 1999.

78. Morell R, Friedman T, Moeljopawiro S, et al. A frameshift mutation in the HuP2 paired domain of the probable human homolog of murine *Pax3* is responsible for Waardenburg syndrome type 1 in an Indonesian family. Hum Mol Genet 1:243, 1992.

79. Muenke M, Schell U. Fibroblast-growth-factor receptor mutations in human skeletal disorders. Trends Genet 11:308, 1995.

80. Muenke M, Gripp KW, McDonald-McGinn DM, et al. A unique point mutation in the fibroblast growth factor receptor 3 gene (*FGFR3*) defines a new craniosynostosis syndrome. Am J Hum Genet 60:555, 1997.

81. Muenke M, Schell U, Hehr A, et al. A common mutation in the fibroblast growth factor receptor 1 gene in Pfeiffer syndrome. Nat Genet 8:269, 1994.

82. Muller U, Warman ML, Mulliken JB, Weber JL. Assignment of a gene locus involved in craniosynostosis to chromosome 5qter. Hum Mol Genet 2:119, 1993.

83. Noden DM. Vertebrate craniofacial development: the relations between ontogenetic process and morphological outcome. Brain Behav Evol 38:190, 1991.

84. Online Mendelian Inheritance in Man, OMIM (TM). Center for Medical Genetics, Johns Hopkins University (Baltimore, MD.) National Center for Biotechnology Information, National Library of Medicine (Bethesda, MD), 2000. World Wide Web URL: http://www.ncbi.nlm.nih.gov/omim/

85. Peterson-Falzone SJ, Pruzansky S, Parris PJ, Laffer JL. Nasopharyngeal dysmorphology in the syndromes of Apert and Crouzon. Cleft Palate J 18:237, 1981.

86. Preston RA, Post JC, Keats BJB, et al. A gene for Crouzon craniofacial dysostosis maps to the long arm of chromosome 10. Nat Genet 7:149, 1994.

87. Prewitt J. Prospective medical advances in computerized tomography. In Bosma J (ed). Development of the Basicranium. NIH Publication 789. Washington, DC, U.S. Department of Health, Education, and Welfare, 1976.

88. Przylepa KA, Paznekas W, Zhang M, et al. Fibroblast growth factor receptor 2 mutations in Beare-Stevenson cutis gyrata syndrome. Nat Genet 13:492, 1996.

89. Puffenberger EG, Hosoda K, Washington SS, et al. A missense mutation of the endothelin-B receptor gene in multigenic Hirschsprung's disease. Cell 79:1257, 1994.

90. Radhakrishna U, Blouin J-L, Mehenni H, et al. Mapping one form of autosomal dominant postaxial polydactyly type A to chromosome 7p15-q11.23 by linkage analysis. Am J Hum Genet 60:597, 1997.

91. Radhakrishna U, Bornholdt D, Scott HS, et al. The phenotypic spectrum of *GLI3* morphopathies includes autosomal dominant preaxial polydactyly type-IV and postaxial polydactyly type-A/B: no phenotype prediction from the position of *GLI3* mutations. Am J Hum Genet 65:645, 1999.

92. Reardon W, Winter RM, Rutland P, et al. Mutations in the fibroblast growth factor receptor 2 gene cause Crouzon syndrome. Nat Genet 8:98, 1994.

93. Roberts DJ: Sonic hedgehog is an endodermal signal inducing *Bmp-4* and *Hox* genes during induction and regionalization of the chick hindgut. Development 121:3163, 1995.

94. Rosenfeld MG. *POU* domain transcription factors: powerful developmental regulators. Genes Dev 5:897, 1991.

95. Roth DA, Longaker MT, McCarthy JG, et al. Studies in cranial suture biology. J Bone Miner Res 12:311, 1997.

96. Ruppert JM, Kinzler KW, Wong AJ, et al. The *GLI*-Kruppel family of human genes. Mol Cell Biol 8:3104, 1988.

97. Rutland P, Pulleyn LJ, Reardon W, et al. Identical mutations in the *FGFR2* gene cause both Pfeiffer and Crouzon syndrome phenotypes. Nat Genet 9:173, 1995.

98. Schutte BC, Murray JC. The many faces and factors of orofacial clefts. Hum Mol Gen 8(10):1853, 1999.

99. Scott MP: Vertebrate homeobox nomenclature. Cell 71:551, 1992.

100. Shah KN, Dalal SJ, Desai MP, et al. White forelock, pigmentary disorder of irides, and long segment Hirschsprung disease: possible variant of Waardenburg syndrome. J Pediatr 99:432, 1981.

101. Shiang R, Lidral AC, Ardinger HH, et al. Association of transforming growth factor alpha gene polymorphisms with nonsyndromic cleft palate only (CPO). Am J Hum Genet 53:836, 1993.

102. Shin SH, Kogerman P, Lindstrom E, et al. *GLI3* mutations in human disorders mimic *Drosophila cubitus interruptus* protein functions and localization. Proc Natl Acad Sci USA 96:2880, 1999.

103. Simeone A, Acampora D, Nigro V, et al. Differential regulation by retinoic acid of the homeobox genes of the four *HOX* loci in human embryonal carcinoma cells. Mech Dev 33:215, 1991.

104. Stark R. Embryology of cleft palate. In Converse J (ed). Reconstructive Plastic Surgery. Philadelphia, WB Saunders, 1977, pp 1941–1949.

105. Stewart R. Genetic factors in craniofacial morphogenesis. In Stewart R, Prescott G (eds). Oral Facial Genetics. St Louis, CV Mosby, 1976, pp 46–66.

106. Tachibana M. A cascade of genes related to Waardenburg syndrome. J Invest Dermatol Symp Proc 4:126, 1999.

107. Tagge EP, Hanson P, Re GG, et al. Paired box gene expression in Wilms tumor. J Pediatr Surg 29:134, 1994.

108. Tassabehji M, Newton VE, Read AP. Waardenburg syndrome type 2 caused by mutations in the human microphthalmia (*MITF*) gene. Nat Genet 8:251, 1994.

109. Touraine RL, Attie-Bitach T, Manceau E, et al. Neurological phenotype in Waardenburg syndrome type 4 correlates with novel SOX10 truncating mutations and expression in developing brain. Am J Hum Genet 66:1496, 2000.

110. Treacher Collins Syndrome Collaborative Group: Positional cloning of a gene involved in the pathogenesis of Treacher Collins syndrome. Nat Genet 12:130, 1996.

111. Veraksa A, Del Campo M, McGinnis W. Developmental patterning genes and their conserved functions: from model organisms to humans. Mol Genet Metab 69:85, 2000.

112. Vogelstein B. Personal communication. Baltimore, MD, 5/9/1994 adopted from OMIM.

113. Vortkamp A, Gessler M, Grzeschik KH. *GL13* zincfinger gene interrupted by translocations in Greig syndrome families. Nature 352(6335):539, 1991.

114. Wang B, Fallon JF, Beachy PA. Hedgehog-regulated processing of Gli3 produces an anterior/posterior repressor gradient in the developing vertebrate limb. Cell 100:423, 2000.

115. Warkany J, Nelson RC, Schraffenberger E. Congenital malformations induced in rats by maternal nutritional deficiency. Am J Dis Child 65:882, 1943.

116. Warman ML, Mulliken JB, Hayward PG, et al. Newly recognized autosomal dominant craniosynostotic syndrome. Am J Med Genet 46:444, 1993.

117. Watson JD, Hopkins NH, Roberts JW, et al. Molecular Biology of the Gene, 4th ed. Menlo Park, CA, Benjamin/Cummings Publishing, 1987, pp 65–94, 606–618.

118. Weir R, Gruss P. Pax and vertebrate development. Int J Dev Biol 40:369, 1996.

119. Wilkie AOM. Functions of the FGFs and their receptors. Curr Biol 5:500, 1995.

120. Wilkie AOM. Craniosynostosis: genes and mechanisms. Hum Mol Genet 6:1647, 1997.

121. Wilkie AOM, Slaney SF, Oldridge M, et al. Apert syndrome results from localized mutations of *FGFR2* and is allelic with Crouzon syndrome. Nat Genet 9:165, 1995.

122. Wise CA, Chiang LC, Paznekas WA, et al. *TCOF1* gene encodes a putative nucleolar phosphoprotein that exhibits mutations in Treacher Collins syndrome throughout its coding region. Proc Natl Acad Sci USA 94:3110, 1997.

123. Wyszynski DF, Beaty TH. Review of the role of potential teratogens in the origin of human nonsyndromic oral clefts. Teratology 53:309, 1996.

124. Yamaguchi A. Regulation of the differentiation pathway of skeletal mesenchymal cells in the cell lines by TGF-β superfamily. Semin Cell Biol 6:165, 1995.

2

Postnatal Craniofacial Growth and Development

Sylvan E. Stool, M.D., Katherine W. L. Vig, B.D.S., M.S., D. Orth.,
Joseph F. A. Petrone, D.D.S., M.S.D., and Barbara Hymer, D.D.S.

Growth implies an increase in dimension and mass, whereas *development* implies a progression to more adult characteristics. In this chapter, we first describe the appearance of the soft tissues of the human head and then examine the underlying skeletal components, to relate the development of these components to some of the basic principles and concepts of cartilage and bone growth. The infant face rarely projects an image of the adult configuration. Conversely, it is usually impossible to attempt to identify an adult by examination of his or her "baby pictures." The face of the infant or child is not a miniature of an adult face but has definite proportions different from those of the adult. The changes that take place during maturation are part of a differential growth process. In general, newborns, regardless of their ethnic backgrounds, resemble each other more than each one does his or her parents. The different proportions of infant and adult faces have been studied extensively by artists and anthropologists and are appreciated almost instinctively by the layperson.[23, 33] These changes in facial configuration and proportions are illustrated in Figure 2–1.

The infant has a very prominent forehead because of the early development of the cerebral hemispheres in relation to the face. About 90% of the child's facial height is achieved by 5 years of age, whereas 90% of the facial width is attained by 2 years of age. Thus, the young child's head appears round.

The face of the infant is diminutive compared with the calvaria. As seen in Figure 2–1, the proportion of facial mass to cranial mass, viewed laterally, is 1 to 3. Subsequent growth in childhood alters this proportion so that the ratio becomes about 1 to 2.5, whereas in adolescents and adults the proportion becomes 1 to 2. However, if this proportion does not change as described, the adult is frequently referred to as having a "baby face." In addition, because the soft tissues of the face include fat, the external appearance does not necessarily reflect the underlying musculoskeletal structure of the face. Thus, the underlying proportions may change, but the general outline of the adult face may still appear childlike. The infant face has a "flat" configuration, which changes during adolescence when sharper angles develop as a result of orbital, mandibular, and nasal growth. The maxilla and mandible grow to accommodate the primary dentition (20

teeth), followed by the permanent dentition (32 teeth) (see Fig. 2–7). The chin of the infant is almost nonexistent, but it is usually a prominent structure in adults as a result of mandibular growth and development. The cheekbones are notable in adults because of loss of baby fat and rotation of the skeletal components. The ears of infants appear to be very low-set because the head in general is more ovoid than elongated; the ears appear to "rise" with growth because of the increase in the vertical dimension of the lower facial height. The configuration of the ear remains the same throughout life, although its mass increases.

The most prominent facial features, the relationship of which has become characteristic of human faces, are the nose and the eyes. The nose of the infant has a distinctive pug appearance. It is diminutive and remains so throughout most of childhood. During adolescence and later, especially in males, there is an increase in length, breadth, and protrusion of the nose, which is related to the increase in airway requirements at this age and is accompanied by a similar increase in the size of the internal airway. The growth of the face can more easily be explained if a subordinate position is given to the craniofacial skeleton, while a leading role is designated to the soft tissues and the functional components that play a part in the activities of the face. In these, the maintenance of the airway is predominant.[39] Humans are the only animals with a truly external nose, and this particularly human trait is subject to many variations, depending in part on ethnic background.

The relationship between vertical dentofacial morphology and respiration in adolescents has been studied by Fields and colleagues,[19] who compared normal and long-faced subjects aged 11 to 17 years. Both morphologic and contemporary respirometric techniques were used for the two groups and resulted in no significant differences being found in airway impairment, although different oronasal breathing modes were present.

The eyes of infants appear to be wide-set with a very prominent inner canthal fold, giving an appearance of hypertelorism because of the lack of vertical dimension of the face. If the infant's face is bisected horizontally, the eyes are located in the inferior half of the face. During childhood the eyes appear to move upward, but in fact

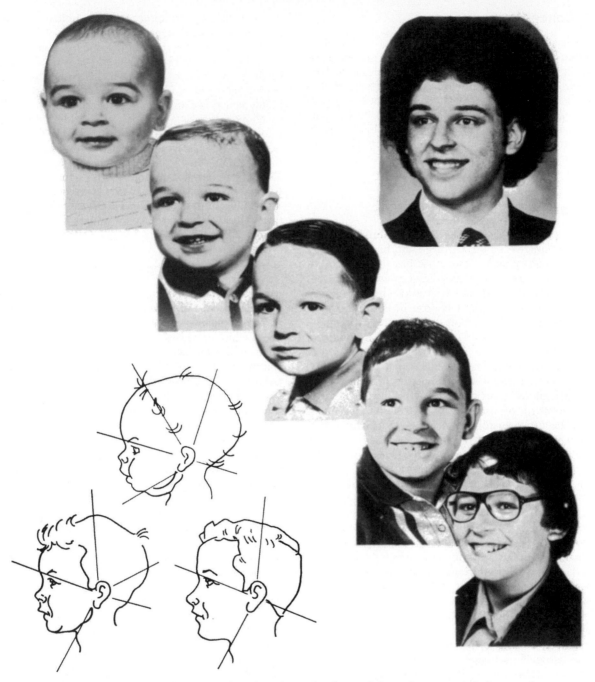

FIGURE 2–1. Postnatal growth of a white boy. The diagonal from the *upper left* downward shows the boy at ages 6 months, 2 years, 4 years, 8 years, and 12 years; the photograph in the *upper right* corner is the same child at 18 years. Drawings in the *lower left* show the changes in proportion of face mass to cranial mass. In the infant, it is 1 to 3; during childhood, it gradually changes to 1 to 2.5. From adolescence through adult life, it is 1 to 2.

the lower half of the face grows more than the upper half, so the maxilla and mandible become more prominent. In older children, the eyes are placed midway in the face. In adolescence, with further growth and development of the lower half of the face relative to the upper half, the eyes finally appear to be just above the dividing line. This adult configuration is the result of differential growth of facial components. The same principle may be used to explain why in adults the eyes are less prominent than they appear to be in children: with growth of the supraorbital rim during adolescence, less of the eye is exposed.

Even though somatic growth is measured by height and weight recordings during childhood and adolescence, there is no reason to assume that it terminates at adulthood. A study conducted by Behrents[3] as an extension of the Bolton-Brush longitudinal growth studies revealed continuing growth of the craniofacial complex throughout all age levels, similar in direction to adolescent alterations but of lesser magnitude and rate.[2]

Growth Concepts

As Pierce et al[41] state, "Parallel evaluation of the cranium and of other parts of the skeleton is at the present time the basis for the clinical distinction of generalized skeletal disorders from cranial abnormalities." Therefore, to understand the normal morphologic changes that occur with growth, as well as craniofacial abnormalities, it is important to describe some basic concepts of skeletal growth: bone formation, remodeling, and displacement. The information presented in the following section can be studied more fully in references 16, 37, 44, 48, and 54.

Bone Formation

Humans possess an endoskeleton that is fabricated from specialized connective tissue: cartilage and bone. Cartilage is a special, tough, pliable tissue that has the capacity to form in regions that experience direct pressure; it does not always calcify and does not necessarily have a surface membrane. Its most important feature in the craniofacial complex is its ability to function as a precursor or model for bone. The characteristics of bone are hardness and rigidity and the possession of a surface membrane, or periosteum. It is a complex substance that is viewed by the chemist as a compound of protein, polysaccharide, mineral, and cellular constituents. To the histologist, it is a tissue composed of osteogenic cells and intracellular matrix. To the gross anatomist, it is an organ with vascular and nerve supplies.

The cells of cartilage and bone are derived from fetal mesenchymal tissue, which has a fairly uniform and undifferentiated appearance. These cells differentiate into chondroblasts and osteoblasts. Osteoblasts secrete a matrix that mineralizes and surrounds and encases them; they mature into osteocytes. Multinucleated giant cells called *osteoclasts*, which are known to destroy mineralized bone, also develop. They do not act on uncalcified bone—a fact of some importance in certain dysplasias—but they play an important role in the process of destruction and deposition that results in bone formation. A more detailed description of these cells and factors affecting their function can be found in references 9 and 11.

Bone always forms in preexisting connective tissue. When this tissue is cartilage, the process is called *endochondral ossification*; when it is noncartilaginous, it is called *intramembranous ossification*. The sequence of events is illustrated in Figure 2–2. Regulation of bone formation is further discussed by Raisz and Kream.[42]

Membranous bone in the skull forms as a layer of mesenchyme with foci of condensation. These areas of condensation begin to ossify, and the process extends until the areas meet to form suture lines. Craniosynostosis will result if premature closure of sutures in the cranium occurs. This condition is described thoroughly by Cohen.[12]

Endochondral ossification is a more complex process that is easier to visualize in the tubular bones. The mesenchyme condenses and then undergoes chondrification. This forms a precise model for future bone surrounded by a limiting membrane. Formation of a periosteal collar is followed by development of a primitive marrow cavity and an ossification center, which forms at the end of the bone. It is possible to identify four distinct segments in the tubular bone. The epiphysis is covered by an articular cartilage in tubular bones and includes the ossification center. The physis, or growth plate, is a very narrow but highly active region that consists of four zones, all related to chondrogenesis. The metaphysis is a zone where the transformation, or change of growing cartilage into bone, takes place. Growth in length is achieved primarily through the activities of cells in the metaphysis. This is also an important region in the remodeling process. Eventually, when growth ceases, the physis will undergo ossification and disappear. The diaphysis is the shaft of the bone.

Remodeling and Displacement

In the craniofacial complex, growth and development depend on two separate but interrelated processes: displacement, which involves motion between bones, and remodeling, which involves a change in the configuration of the bone while displacement is occurring. Bone grows by a continuous process of deposition and resorption. This is not a uniform process throughout the entire bone but is a differential growth process. If this were not so, the adult skeleton would be the same as the fetal configuration. The mechanism by which these two different but complementary functions are achieved is influenced by a number of factors, such as stress on the surface and various nutritional, hormonal, and genetic influences. The biodynamics have been studied for years and are still undergoing conceptual changes.[8]

In the simplest terms, bone growth occurs when bone is both deposited by osteoblastic activity and resorbed during osteoclastic activity. At any given point in time during the growth process, entire regions of a bone may be found to be undergoing localized deposition or resorption. These areas undergoing change are known as growth fields, and the entire surface of a growing bone may be composed of such localized fields, the cumulative effects of which provide for increase in bone size and change in shape.[17]

In long bones, this concept is fairly easy to visualize. Growth of long bones is best described by the "V principle."[16] Growth at the metaphysis (Fig. 2–3) involves endochondral bone formation, which effectively separates or displaces the epiphysis from the diaphysis. Remodeling of the wider metaphysis into a narrower diaphysis requires depository endosteal growth fields and resorptive periosteal fields in the area of the narrowing metaphysis. The pattern of growth can then be described as an expanding V, as shown in Figure 2–6. Anything that interferes with this process will result in an abnormal configuration. In the tubular bones, this concept is fairly easy to visualize. For a bone to increase in length and retain its normal shape, it is necessary to add and subtract bone. This is illustrated in Figure 2–3.

The craniofacial region is a much more complex area, and perhaps the process of bone growth in this region

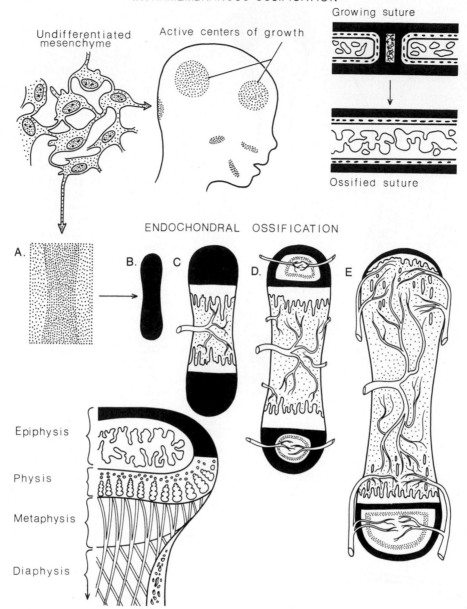

INTRAMEMBRANOUS OSSIFICATION

Undifferentiated mesenchyme

Active centers of growth

Growing suture

Ossified suture

ENDOCHONDRAL OSSIFICATION

Epiphysis

Physis

Metaphysis

Diaphysis

FIGURE 2–2. Mechanism of formation of the two types of bone found in the skull. Undifferentiated mesenchyme is the precursor of both. *Intramembranous ossification:* mesenchyme condenses to form centers of growth, which enlarge until they meet to form a suture. Growth proceeds at these sutures and remains active until the stimulus is removed and the suture ossifies. *Endochondral ossification: A,* Endochondral bone formation also begins with condensation. *B,* Cartilage anlage is formed. *C,* Vascular mesenchyme forms a primary marrow, and a periosteal collar forms. *D,* Ossification centers develop at the extremities, resulting in the four segments illustrated in the *lower left. E,* Eventually the bone is completely ossified and the segmental differences disappear. The segments of a typical long bone are shown in the *lower left. Epiphysis:* a secondary ossification center covered with cartilage. *Physis:* the cartilage growth plate. *Metaphysis:* the segment in which cartilage is transformed to bone by endochondral bone formation. *Diaphysis:* the shaft separating the growing ends. (Redrawn in part from Williams et al, 1969, and Rubin, 1964.)

can best be visualized by describing the technique by which an artist working with clay might construct a bowl, using coils. A basic hollow form is constructed, to which clay is added superficially. The edges may be smoothed to achieve a pleasing configuration. To keep the wall thickness uniform, it may be necessary to remove (subtract) some clay from the inner surface of the bowl (resorption). If a change in the configuration is desired, it can be

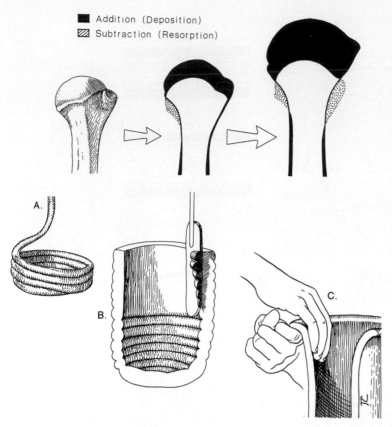

■ Addition (Deposition)
▨ Subtraction (Resorption)

FIGURE 2–3. The concept of remodeling is illustrated. To prevent distortion of growing bone, there is osteoclastic cutback at the metaphysis. An example is this tubular bone, in which there is addition (deposition) at the epiphysis and subtraction (resorption) at the metaphysis. The concepts involved in skeletal growth and development are illustrated using the analogy of the ancient coil technique of clay construction. The initial step is formation by deposition (addition) (*A*); during this process, there is concomitant removal, resorption (subtraction), resulting in differential growth (*B*). The final configuration is achieved by these two processes as well as an additional one, displacement (*C*).

accomplished by applying pressure on the inner surface (displacement) and modeling the outer surface. Although this simple explanation is of some help in understanding the mechanics of bone formation, it does not explain why these events occur in humans.

For the clinician, it is important to realize that bone formation begins in the fetus and undergoes constant changes throughout life. This twofold process is important

not only in the formation of craniofacial structures but also in the growth of other bones. In a series of investigations utilizing both cross-sectional and longitudinal material, Israel[27-30] came to the conclusion that, with aging, the cranial skeleton and vertebrae basically gain in all dimensions studied.

The effects of abnormal bone formation can well be illustrated in human skull growth (Fig. 2–4). In achon-

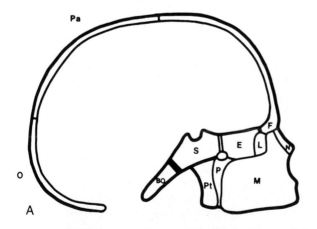

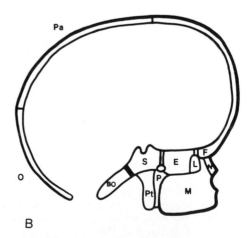

FIGURE 2–4. *A,* Normal skull: the bones of the calvaria, cranial base, and upper face. The position of the spheno-occipital synchondrosis is shown in heavy black in the cranial base. M, maxilla; N, nasal bone; F, frontal bone; L, lacrimal bone; E, ethmoid; P, vertical plate of the palatine bone; S, body of the sphenoid; Pt, pterygoid plate; O, occipital; BO, basioccipital; Pa, parietal. (Note: Any relative forward growth of the anterior cranial base will carry the upper facial region with it into a more anterior position.) *B,* Achondroplastic skull. Note the shortened skull base, sunken bridge of the nose, and general reduction in the development and size of the facial region.

droplasia, all bone forming from cartilage (having a cartilaginous precursor) is abnormal, including the chondrocranium. This results in a shortened skull base, a flattened palate, a sunken bridge to the nose, and a general reduction in the development and size of the facial region (Fig. 2–4B).[50] The growth of the calvaria, which does not rely on ossification of cartilage for growth, is unhindered.

A certain group of disorders are affected by alterations in membranous bone formation. For instance, a craniometaphyseal abnormality involves alterations of the remodeling process, which are best understood by examination of the extremities. Some systemic diseases, such as hemolytic and iron deficiency anemias, may first be recognized in the cranium. Obviously, complete diagnosis of some cranial abnormalities necessitates evaluation of the remainder of the skeleton.

Postnatal Skeletal Growth

The external features and some of the basic concepts of bone growth of the craniofacial complex have been discussed. We will now examine the changes that occur in the skeleton. Skeletal growth is more readily assessed and easier to document than soft tissue growth, because it is subject to radiographic examination and physical measurements.[14, 43] These methods yield good estimates of skeletal proportions. Because of the availability of these tools, skeletal growth parameters have come to be widely used as indices for general growth evaluation. Skeletal age is one of the biologic ages used to ascertain the normality of growth and development. Usually, this is evaluated not only with cephalometric radiography but also by examination of the extremities, most commonly the wrist.

The skull is a complex structure formed from many component bones that articulate along an intricate network of sutures. The final location of each bone is determined by a composite of many different localized growth processes as well as regional changes. Figure 2–5A presents frontal views of the skulls of a newborn, a child, and an adult; Figure 2–5B shows three-quarter views; Figure 2–5C shows these same skulls with the infant and the child enlarged to the same size as the adult so that the vertical dimensions are equal. This provides a graphic means of illustrating changes in proportion.

Growth and development of the craniofacial complex will be discussed as involving the cranium, mandible, and nasomaxillary complex. The bones that make up the cranium must be considered in two parts—the calvaria (roof) and the basicranium (floor)—because distinctly different circumstances and modes of growth are involved for each.

Cranium

Calvaria

The calvaria is constructed from the frontal and parietal bones and portions of the temporal, occipital, and sphenoid bones. At birth, the bones are separated by six fontanelles bridged by fibrous tissue. The anterior fontanelle is the last to close, at about 18 months. As seen in Figure 2–5C, the skull of an infant is almost round. Sullivan[50] makes the following comparison: the curvature of the surface of a large sphere is less than that of a small sphere. The adult calvaria is larger than the infant's and shows a corresponding reduction in curvature (Fig. 2–5D).

At birth, the brain weighs about half as much as the adult brain, and by ages 5 to 8 years it attains 90% of its adult weight. In conjunction with the expansion of the underlying hemispheres, the bones of the skull base are carried outward; they do not grow in an ectocranial dimension by their own depository and resorptive activity. As the bones are all displaced circumferentially, tension fields are established in the sutural membranes; this is believed to trigger (directly or indirectly) the progressive deposition of new bone by the sutures.[18] This enlarges the perimeter of each bone.

Basicranium

The basicranium is a particularly fascinating region that has been the subject of much investigation.[6] Phylogenetically, it is the oldest skeletal component; anatomically, it has been considered the cornerstone of craniofacial growth. The basicranium is formed from the basal part of the occipital, the sphenoid, the petrous part of the temporal, and the ethmoid bones. It is primarily composed of bones formed by the ossification of cartilage precursors. Synchondroses, in addition to sutures, are present in the cranial base. They represent regional adaptation to the pressure-located areas of the growing cranium.[35] In the case of the spheno-occipital synchondrosis, ossification takes place on both the sphenoidal and the occipital faces of the cartilage. (This is in contrast to ossification in the epiphyseal cartilage of a long bone, which occurs on only one surface.)

Investigators are not agreed on the exact role of cartilage in craniofacial development.[1, 31] The spheno-occipital synchondrosis has been presumed to represent the primary growth site of the basicranium. This assumption has been the subject of much controversy, and whether the synchondrosis acts as a primary growth center or not, it must not be regarded as the only mechanism participating in cranial base growth, although it continues active growth until 18 to 20 years of age. The anterior cranial base stabilizes in early childhood with the closure of the sphenoethmoidal synostosis. This provides a convenient area of superimposition for comparing longitudinal cephalometric records of craniofacial growth. Additionally, future growth of the maxillary complex will be affected by early closure of the sphenoethmoidal synostosis, as occurs in the craniosynostoses. This results in varying degrees of sagittal and vertical maxillary deficiency.[7]

It is difficult to visualize the basicranium from the anterior view. Figure 2–6, which is a tangential view of the inferior aspect of the skull, reveals that the nasomaxillary complex covers the anterior portion, beneath the anterior cranial fossa. The posterior portion of the cranial base provides the roof of the nasopharynx. In Figure 2–6, the shape of this region has been traced on three skulls from different age groups. In the infant, this line is relatively flat, but with growth and development it assumes a more

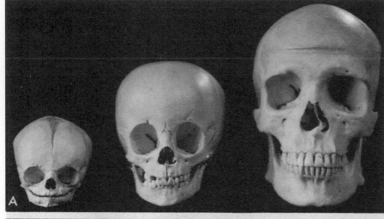
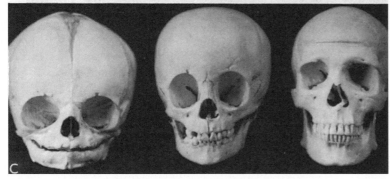

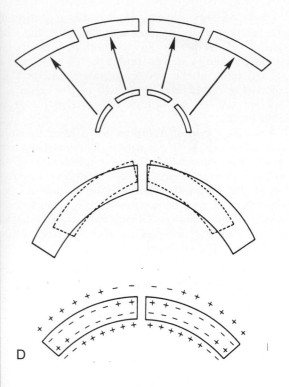

FIGURE 2–5. Skulls of a newborn, a child, and an adult illustrate skeletal changes during growth and development. *A,* Frontal view. *B,* Three-quarter view. *C,* The newborn and the child skulls have been enlarged to the same size as the adult skull to demonstrate the changes in proportion with growth. *D,* The outward displacement of the bones of the calvaria *(top)* is accompanied by changes in their regional curvatures *(middle).* Ectocranial and endocranial periosteal surfaces *(bottom)* are predominantly depository (+), and endosteal surfaces are resorptive (−). However, localized changes in surface contours are produced by opposite combinations, particularly in areas near sutural junctions. (Adapted from Enlow DH. Facial Growth, 3rd ed. Philadelphia, WB Saunders, 1990, p 99.)

curved appearance in the child. This is due not only to increased depth, which results from remodeling of the palate, but also to the flexure of the basicranium. These changes provide an enlarged nasal airway to meet the requirements of gas exchange and speech resonance in the adult.

For the otolaryngologist, this region is important for several reasons. Many bone dysplasias affecting the skeleton may also affect the cranial base. As major nerves and vessels passing through foramina in the basicranium become involved, classic symptomatology results. One such example is osteopetrosis and facial palsy, which is thoroughly discussed by Hamersma and May.[21] Also, the size of the nasopharyngeal airway is in part determined by the configuration of the basicranium, and this has an effect on respiration and middle ear function because of the dynamics of airflow. Finally, the ear may also be affected as the osseous eustachian tube passes through the cranial

base, and the muscles that control the cartilaginous portion of the tube originate from it.

Mandible

The human mandible is a membrane bone that forms in close association with Meckel's cartilage, the first branchial arch cartilage. At birth, the bone is in two parts joined in the midline by the symphysis mandibularis, which closes by the end of the first year of life. The mandible is unusual in having a secondary growth cartilage under the surface of the articular condyle.[50]

In studying craniofacial growth, it is often helpful to recognize that the bones of the face grow in a pattern balanced among its parts. Growth (increase in size or change in location) of one bone or portion of bone must be met with a congruent change in other bony parts of

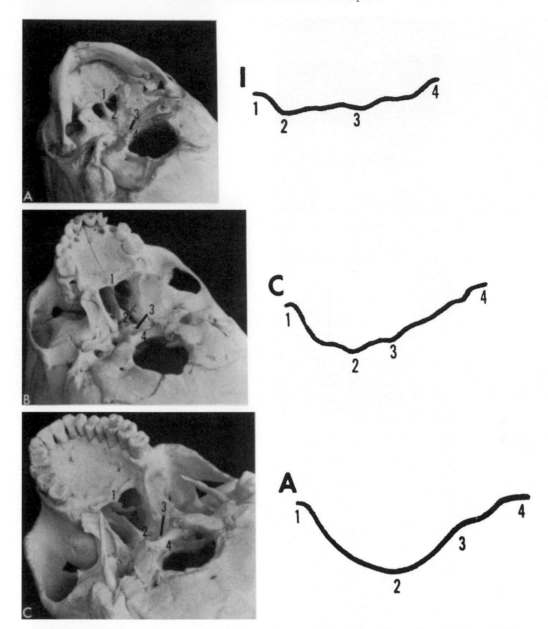

FIGURE 2–6. Tangential views of the inferior aspect of the skulls of an infant (I) *(A)*, a child (C) *(B)*, and an adult (A) *(C)*. All illustrate the change in configuration of the nasopharynx. The anatomic landmarks indicated are the posterior nasal spine (1); the junction of the vomer with the base of the skull (2); the spheno-occipital synchondrosis (3); and the edge of the foramen magnum (4). The change in size and configuration of the posterior choanae and the nasal airway with age can be appreciated.

the face if an imbalance in the overall pattern of growth is to be avoided. Enlow[16] identifies particular areas of the facial skeleton that fit into this unique part-counterpart pattern. For example, the anterior cranial fossa, the palate, and the corpus of the mandible are considered to be counterparts of the bony maxillary arch. Growth changes occurring in any one of these parts must be accompanied by congruent changes in each of the others if the existing relationships are to be preserved. As the maxillary dental arch lengthens, so must the corpus of the mandible for the normal relationship between them to be preserved. The mandibular ramus and the middle cranial fossa are

also considered to be counterparts. Growth of the middle cranial fossa must be matched by changes in the ramus, which again serve to maintain a balanced pattern of facial growth.

The condyle grows in whatever direction and to whatever extent it must to provide a functional occlusal position for the dental arch. Although controversy still exists, many investigators currently hold that the condylar cartilage may not perform an actual primary role in mandibular growth and development, but rather that it is an important adaptive site of growth.[16] In a study regarding shape change in the mandible during adolescence, Dib-

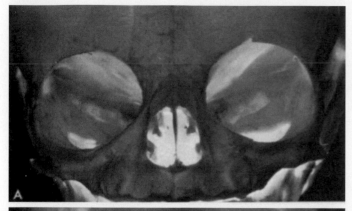

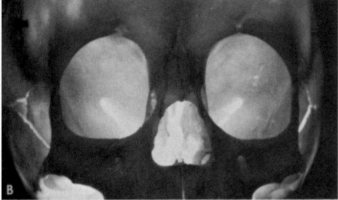

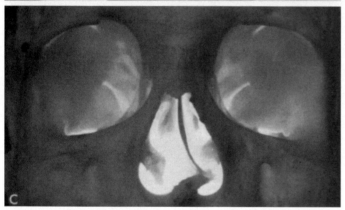

FIGURE 2–7. Skulls of a newborn (*A*), a child (*B*), and an adult (*C*) that have been transilluminated to emphasize the change in the relationship of the floor of the orbit to the floor of the nose. In the newborn and the child, there is little separation. In the adult, however, the distance increases because of downward growth and displacement of the floor of the nose and upward growth of the floor of the orbit.

bets et al[13] found further support for the theories that postulate local control factors for mandibular growth. They noted that the growth process of the mandible does not always proceed at a uniform rate for corpus and ramus, concluding that the growing mandible may favor either at any specific time.

Nasomaxillary Complex

The nasomaxillary complex consists of the nasal, lacrimal, maxillary, zygomatic, palatine, and pterygoid bones and the vomer. It can be seen that this regional complex is closely related to the anterior segment of the cranium formed by the frontal, ethmoid, and sphenoid bones (see Fig. 2–4A). Any relative forward growth of the anterior cranial base will carry the upper facial region with it into a more anterior position. Development of the nasomaxillary complex has been the subject of extensive investiga-

tion.[34] Although long ago it was observed that growth of these structures occurs downward and forward, the mechanism of such growth has been the subject of debate. The problem has been that it is difficult to design studies in which the variables are effectively controlled.[15] In addition, this is a complex anatomic region that is difficult to visualize from one perspective. Growth in this region occurs in both the horizontal and the vertical planes, and different segments grow at varying rates. This can be appreciated by examining Figure 2–7, which shows the change in configuration and relationship of the orbits and the nasal apertures with age in the skulls of a newborn, a child, and an adult. All have been transilluminated so that the changes in density of the bone and the outline of the nasal apertures are more apparent.

The remodeling changes that take place in the orbit are very complex because many bones are involved, each of which undergoes different amounts of growth and dis-

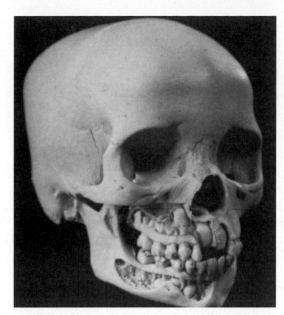

FIGURE 2–8. Skull of a child that demonstrates mixed dentition. The multitiered battery of teeth is partially responsible for the increase in the vertical and horizontal dimensions of the jaws with increasing age.

placement. One of the most marked changes is the difference in the relationship of the floor of the nose to the floor of the orbit. In newborns, the two structures are almost level; in children, there is some separation. In adults, however, there is a marked change due to the downward displacement of the entire maxilla. This change is more complex, as the floor of the orbit is displaced superiorly and the floor of the nose is displaced inferiorly. The change in the bony septum with age is rather dramatic. In the newborn, the septum appears straight, and in the adult skull, shown in Figure 2–7C, there is marked septal deviation, a common finding. It is interesting that the breadth of the nasal bridge does not increase noticeably from early childhood to adulthood, although the shape of the nasal aperture changes from almost circular to pear-shaped—a characteristic that shows marked racial variation.

The biomechanical force for displacement of the nasomaxillary complex is the subject of much controversy. According to Scott,[46] it is due to the expansion of the nasal septum, whereas Latham[32] believes that it is due to traction on the septopremaxillary ligaments. Early principles noted by van der Klaauw[52] were strengthened and advanced by Moss[36, 38] as the "functional matrix" theory, which proposes that the genetic determinants of skeletal growth do not reside within the actual bony part itself. That is, the pacemakers of the displacement and the bony remodeling processes are found in the surrounding soft tissue parts. It is important to understand that the functional matrix concept describes essentially what happens during displacement and remodeling but is not intended to explain how this growth happens or what the regulating processes actually are at the tissue and cellular levels.

Another factor that influences the nasomaxillary complex is dentition. There is little evidence in the newborn's jaw of the dental structures that will develop. However,

Figure 2–8, which shows the maxilla and mandible of a child, reveals a palisade of multitiered primary and permanent teeth in many stages of development.[16] The growth and development of teeth and related dental architecture have been studied extensively, and methods of evaluation and modalities of treatment of these structures are discussed in Chapters 58 and 59. Early surgical intervention necessitates care in placing the osteotomy cuts to avoid interrupting the developing succedaneous teeth, as the distances between the orbit and the alveolar ridge are shallow.

The development of the craniofacial skeleton has been investigated widely by means of standardized cephalometric radiographs. Currently, work is being completed at Children's Hospital of Pittsburgh employing this technique to explore relationships between upper airway obstruction and craniofacial growth. Cephalometric studies have also been undertaken to examine sexual dimorphism in the craniofacial complex. Ingerslev and Solow[26] found that the cranium was, on the average, smaller in the female than in the male group except for the nasal bone, the foramen magnum, and the inner orbital distance. The female group showed a more prominent frontal bone and a less prominent nasal bone than the male group. Bibby[5] noted that the patterns of craniofacial morphology in males and females appear to be identical except in posterior facial height. In addition, the male skulls were 8.5% larger than the female skulls.

Many factors have been shown to affect craniofacial growth and development.[22, 45, 47, 51, 53] A detailed description of each is not given here, but Figure 2–9 provides an overall view of both the general growth factors and the local factors postulated to influence craniofacial growth. In strong contrast to the many factors known to influence general growth, little information is available concerning the local control mechanisms that guide the growth of the bones and the development of the craniofacial skeleton. Much is known of what happens, but little is known about *how* it happens.

Functions of the Human Craniofacial Complex

In these first two chapters, we have discussed prenatal and postnatal development and have alluded to some of the many functions of the craniofacial complex: respiration, olfaction, speech, digestion, hearing, balance, vision, and neural integration. The tissue components of this complex can be classified as skeletal tissue, soft tissue, and functional spaces (nasopharyngeal and oropharyngeal). Only a brief discussion of these functions can be undertaken here, but since the musculature is intimately related to skeletal development, it will be discussed in more detail.

Eye

One of the most salient elements of human evolution has been the development of vision as a dominant sense. It was this sense that enabled primitive humans to survive as a species and to develop our present state of technology. The development of binocular vision enabled hu-

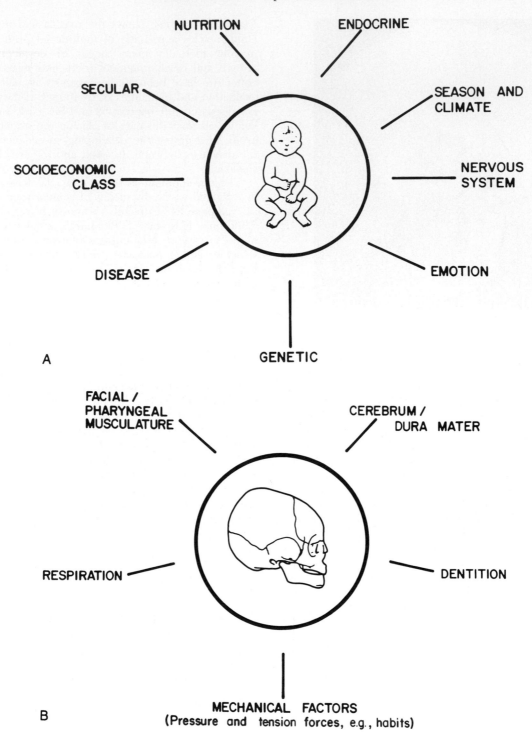

FIGURE 2–9. *A,* General factors affecting growth and development. *B,* Local factors postulated to affect craniofacial growth.

mans to evolve a system of eye-hand coordination that their increased cerebral function can utilize.

Ear

The ear has the dual functions of hearing and balance. The balance mechanism is of earlier phylogenetic development and is represented by paired organs that are connected to the brain. Hearing is a person's most impor-

tant contact with the environment, for without adequate hearing, speech and communication may not develop (see Chap. 9).

Nose

The sense of smell, which is of such importance in the lower animals, is one of the less important basic functions in humans. However, the conditioning of inhaled air and

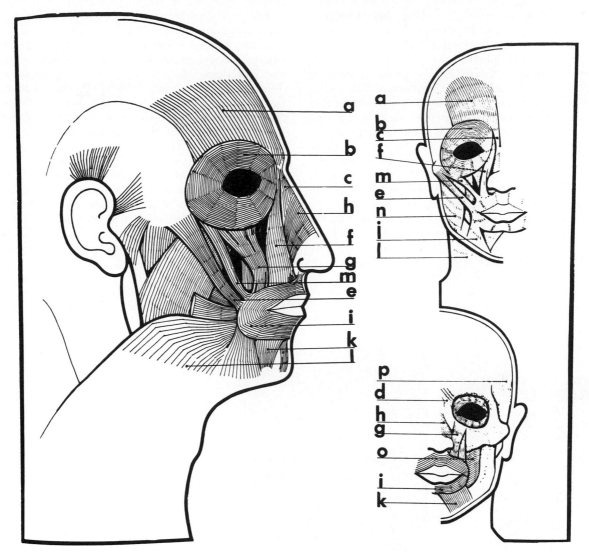

FIGURE 2–10. The distribution of the facial muscles and the complexity of this musculature are illustrated. The muscles originate in laminar form and segment into specific muscles, as described by Gasser (1967): a, frontalis; b, orbicularis oculi; c, procerus; d, corrugator; e, zygomaticus major; f, levator labii superioris et alae nasi; g, levator labii; h, compressor naris; i, orbicularis oris; j, depressor anguli oris; k, depressor labii inferioris; l, platysma; m, zygomaticus minor; n, masseter nonexpressive; o, buccinator nonexpressive; p, temporal nonexpressive.

the provision of a nasal airway are two important functions of the nose in respiration (see Chap. 34).

Mouth

As the initial portion of the digestive tract, the mouth has a vital function, and although it may be temporarily bypassed by artificial means, the ultimate growth and development of the organism will be affected if the anatomy of this area is altered (see Chap. 51).

Speech, which utilizes both the air and food passages, is a relatively recent phylogenetic function. For humans, however, speech is one of the major achievements and represents the most important means of communication and expression. The neuromuscular functions of the craniofacial complex are concerned with both the aesthetic and the expressive functions of the face. The human face covers a highly complicated skeletal framework with extremely flexible and expressive soft tissue. It is capable of an amazing number of motions and has the ability to convey emotion. Since the face is not covered, even slight facial deformities may be difficult to conceal and can seriously affect the appearance, and thus the interpersonal relationships, of a child. This was expressed beautifully by Charles Bell in 1821[4]:

The human countenance performs many functions—in it are combined the organs of mastication, of breathing, of natural voice and speech, and of expression. These motions are performed directly by the will; here also are seen signs of emotions, over which we have but a very limited or imperfect control; the face serves for the lowest animal enjoyment, and partakes of the highest and most refined emotions.

Figure 2–10 illustrates the distribution of the facial

34   Craniofacial Growth, Development, and Malformations

musculature and demonstrates the relationship of the various facial muscle masses. Facial movements that occur during fetal life were described by Hooker[24] and discussed in detail by Humphrey.[25]

At birth, the infant's musculature is primarily involved with the functions of suckling and swallowing. The airway is maintained, and there are primitive facial reflexes that provide some expression. Experiments have shown that there are responses to taste such as sweet and sour.[49] Early postnatal facial expressions are largely imitations, but most of the facial muscles are used for mandibular stabilization and airway functions. During subsequent postnatal growth and development, the facial neuromusculature undergoes tremendous changes. According to Enlow,[16] more study has been given to the growth of the craniofacial skeleton than to the growth of the neuromusculature. One reason is that it is much more difficult to study the neuromusculature of the face than it is to study its bone structures; consequently, we know less about the facial and jaw muscles (and are less certain of what we do know) than we do about bones and teeth.

During the early periods of embryonic growth, an intimate functional relationship exists between the muscles and the bones to which they are attached. Obviously, when the bones grow, the muscles also must change their size and shape. As a consequence, the muscles occupy different positions, and there is constant adjustment in the attachments of muscles to the skeleton. For instance, changes in the vertical dimensions of the skull will result in a reorientation of the angles at the musculo-osseous junctions.

The influence of the facial musculature on skeletal growth depends on the region involved. Since the most powerful of the facial muscles are involved with mastication, the influence of musculature on the dentition and especially on the mandible will be considerable. Muscles of the airway and food passages compete for influence with the tongue, one of the most powerful muscles of the head.

As a final comment on postnatal craniofacial growth and development, just as the embryo begins as an undifferentiated cell mass, so the newborn appears with an

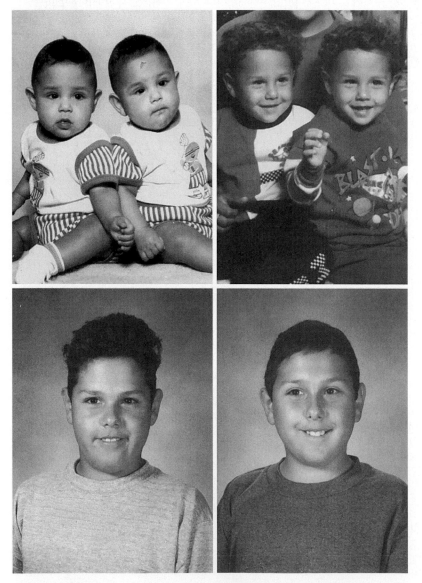

Figure 2–11. These series of pictures show identical twins at 6 months, 2½ years, and 8 years of age. Both underwent an adenotonsillectomy at age 3½ years. The child on the right developed nasopharyngeal stenosis and complete nasal obstruction. Adenoid facies is clearly evident in the child on the right.

undifferentiated craniofacial complex. Because of differential growth, highly developed individual characteristics will appear as the newborn matures. In the skeleton, osteoblastic and osteoclastic activity leads to bone deposition, resorption, and displacement. The stimuli for alterations in skeletal development are both genetic and environmental, and it is a balance of these two factors that is responsible for the ultimate craniofacial configuration.

Research in craniofacial growth has led to the realization that the mechanisms controlling the growth processes in the face are complex, interrelated, and interdependent. Models of facial growth have evolved from those based on strict genetic predetermination to new paradigms that view the craniofacial complex as highly adaptive and under both local and epigenetic control mechanisms.[10] Growth of the mandible alone is seen to be modulated by a highly complex cybernetic system[40] involving both local and peripheral feedback mechanisms and hormonal and central nervous system influences. The functions of the craniofacial complex, the most characteristic of which in humans are binocular vision (so important in eye-hand coordination), speech, and an infinite variety of facial expressions, have evolved over millions of years. It is understandable that we should desire to know more about this very important area of development, but it is also obvious why study of the craniofacial complex involves deep concentration and unusual effort to yield results.

There are numerous theories regarding facial growth, ranging from intrinsic genetic factors controlling the mechanisms of growth to functional or environmental determinants. General concepts or paradigms have shifted with new knowledge and changing frameworks of reference, so that currently a combination of genetic and environmental or functional determinants predominates our understanding of an epigenetic paradigm. Figure 2–11 demonstrates this concept. The development of current concepts in facial growth and development as they relate to craniofacial biology has been reviewed by Carlson.[10]

SELECTED REFERENCES

Dorst JP. Changes of the skull during childhood. In Newton TH, Potts DG (eds). Radiology of the Skull and Brain, Vol 1. St Louis, CV Mosby, 1971, pp 118–131.

   This is a concise description of skeletal growth during childhood. It also discusses some cranial abnormalities.

Enlow DH. Handbook of Craniofacial Growth, 3rd ed. Philadelphia, WB Saunders, 1990.

   This well-organized text illustrates the various growth concepts and also includes an extensive bibliography.

Proffit WR. Contemporary Orthodontics, 2nd ed. St Louis, Mosby–Yearbook, 1993.

   This is an excellent source for understanding postnatal growth.

Rubin P. Dynamic Classification of Bone Dysplasias. Chicago, Yearbook, 1964.

   This book describes some of the anomalies of the craniofacial complex and also discusses the growth mechanisms by which they occur.

Sullivan PG. Skull, jaw, and teeth growth patterns. In Falkner F, Tanner JM (eds). Human Growth, Vol 2. Postnatal Growth. New York, Plenum Press, 1986, pp 243–268.

This well-written chapter discusses in detail the differential growth of the skull and jaw.

REFERENCES

1. Babula WJ, Smiley GR, Dixon AD. The role of the cartilaginous nasal septum. Am J Orthod 58:250, 1970.
2. Bassett AH. The biophysical approach to craniofacial morphogenesis. Acta Morphol Neerl Scand 10:71, 1972.
3. Behrents RG. Growth in the aging craniofacial skeleton. In Craniofacial Growth Series, Monograph No. 17. Ann Arbor, MI, Center for Human Growth and Development, University of Michigan, 1985.
4. Bell C. The nervous system of the human body. Papers delivered to the Royal Society on the Subject of the Nerves. Stereotyped by Duff Green, for the Register and Library of Medical and Chirurgical Science, 1833.
5. Bibby RE. A cephalometric study of sexual dimorphism. Am J Orthod 76:256, 1979.
6. Bosma J (ed). Symposium on the Development of the Basicranium (NIH Publication No. 76-989). Bethesda, MD, US Dept of Health, Education and Welfare, 1976.
7. Burdi A, Vig KWL, Reynold R. The craniosynostoses: etiopathogenesis and clinical implications. In Hunter WS, Carlson DS (eds). Essays in Honor of Robert E Moyers. In Craniofacial Growth Series, Vol 24. Ann Arbor, MI, Center for Human Growth and Development, University of Michigan, 1991, pp 227–249.
8. Burr A. Orthopedic principles of skeletal growth, modeling and remodeling. In Carlson DS, Goldstern SA (eds). Bone Biodynamics in Orthodontic and Orthopedic Treatment. Craniofacial Growth Series, Monograph No. 27. Ann Arbor, MI, Center for Human Growth and Development, University of Michigan, 1992, pp 15–50.
9. Canalis E. The hormonal and local regulation of bone formation. Endocrin Rev 4:62, 1983.
10. Carlson D. Craniofacial biology as "normal science." In Johnston LE (ed). New Vistas in Orthodontics. Philadelphia, Lea & Febiger, 1985, pp 12–37.
11. Centrella M, Canalis E. Local regulators of skeletal growth: a perspective. Endocr Rev 6:544, 1985.
12. Cohen MM. Craniosynostosis: Diagnosis, Evaluation, and Management. New York, Raven Press, 1986.
13. Dibbets JM, deBruin R, Van der Weele L. Shape change in the mandible during adolescence. In Craniofacial Growth Series, Monograph No. 20. Ann Arbor, MI, Center for Human Growth and Development, University of Michigan, 1987, pp 69–85.
14. Dorst JP. Changes of the skull during childhood. In Newton TH, Potts DG (eds). Radiology of the Skull and Brain, Vol I. St Louis, CV Mosby, 1971.
15. Enlow DH. Growth and the problem of the local antral mechanism. Am J Anat 178:2, 1973.
16. Enlow DH. Handbook of Craniofacial Growth. Philadelphia, WB Saunders, 1990.
17. Enlow DH. Normal craniofacial growth. In Cohen MM (ed). Craniosynostosis: Diagnosis, Evaluation, and Management. New York, Raven Press, 1986, pp 131–156.
18. Enlow DH. Postnatal facial growth. In Forrester DJ, Wagner ML, Fleming J (eds). Pediatric Dental Medicine. Philadelphia, Lea & Febiger, 1981, pp 40–54.
19. Fields HW, Warren DW, Black K, Phillips CH. Relationship between vertical dentofacial morphology and respiration in adolescents. Orthod Dentofac Orthop 99:147, 1991.
20. Gasser RF. The development of the facial muscles in man. Am J Anat 120:357, 1967.
21. Hamersma H, May M. Osteopetrosis and facial palsy. In May M (ed). The Facial Nerve. New York, Thieme, 1986, pp 469–483.
22. Harris JE, Kowalski CJ, Watnick SS. Genetic factors in the shape of the craniofacial complex. Angle Orthod 43:107, 1973.
23. Hogarth B. Drawing the Human Head, 9th ed. New York, Watson Guptill, 1965.
24. Hooker D. Fetal behavior. In Association for Research in Nervous and Mental Disease. XIX. Interrelationship of Mind and Body. Baltimore, Williams & Wilkins, 1939, pp 237–243.

25. Humphrey T. Reflex activity in the oral and facial area of the human fetus. In Bosma J (ed). Second Symposium on Oral Sensation and Perception. Springfield, IL, Charles C Thomas, 1970.
26. Ingerslev CH, Solow B. Sex differences in craniofacial morphology. Acta Odontol Scand 33:85, 1975.
27. Israel H. Age factor and the pattern of change in craniofacial structures. Am J Phys Anthropol 39:111, 1973.
28. Israel H. Continuing growth in the human cranial skeleton. Arch Oral Biol 13:133, 1968.
29. Israel H. The dichotomous pattern of craniofacial expansion during aging. Am J Phys Anthropol 47:47, 1977.
30. Israel H. Loss of bone and remodeling-redistribution in the craniofacial skeleton with age. Fed Proc 26:1723, 1967.
31. Koski K. Mechanisms of craniofacial skeletal growth. In Barrer HG (ed). Orthodontics: The State of the Art. Philadelphia, University of Pennsylvania Press, 1981, pp 209–222.
32. Latham RA. Maxillary development and growth: the septomaxillary ligament. J Anat 107:471, 1970.
33. Ligett J. The Human Face. London, Constable & Co, 1974.
34. McNamara J. Factors affecting the growth of the midface. In Craniofacial Growth Series, Monograph No. 6. Ann Arbor, MI, Center for Human Growth and Development, University of Michigan, 1976.
35. Michejda M. The role of basicranial synchondroses in flexure processes and ontogenetic development of the skull base. Am J Phys Anthropol 37:143, 1972.
36. Moss ML. The functional matrix. In Kraus BS, Riedel RA (eds). Vistas in Orthodontics. Philadelphia, Lea & Febiger, 1962, pp 85–98.
37. Moss ML. The primacy of functional matrices in one facial growth. Dent Pract Dent Rec 19:65, 1968.
38. Moss ML. The role of the nasal septal cartilage in midfacial growth. Craniofacial Growth Series, Monograph No. 6. Ann Arbor, MI, Center for Human Growth and Development, University of Michigan, 1976, pp 169–204.
39. Moss ML, Salentijn L. The primary role of functional matrices in facial growth. Am J Orthod 55:566, 1969.
40. Petrovic AG. Postnatal growth of bone: a perspective of current trends, new approaches and innovations. In Dixon AB, Sarnot BB (eds). Factors and Mechanisms Influencing Bone Growth: Progress in Clinical and Biological Research. New York, H Liss, 1982.
41. Pierce RH, Mainen MW, Bosma JF. The Cranium of the Newborn Infant (NIH DHEW Publication No. 76-788). Bethesda, MD, US Dept of Health, Education and Welfare, 1977.
42. Raisz L, Kream B. Regulation of bone formation. N Engl J Med 309:83, 1983.
43. Riolo M, Moyers R, McNamara J, Hunter W. An Atlas of Craniofacial Growth: Cephalometric Standards from the University School Growth Study, The University of Michigan. Craniofacial Growth Series, Monograph No. 2. Ann Arbor, MI, Center for Human Growth and Development, University of Michigan, 1974.
44. Rubin P. The Dynamic Classification of Bone Dysplasias. Chicago, Year Book, 1964.
45. Schumaker GH. Factors influencing craniofacial growth. In Dixon AD, Sarnat BG (eds). Normal and Abnormal Bone Growth: Basic and Clinical Research. New York, Alan R. Liss, 1985, pp 3–22.
46. Scott JA. The cartilage of the nasal septum. Br Dent J 95:37, 1953.
47. Sinclair D. Human Growth after Birth, 4th ed. Oxford, Oxford University Press, 1985, pp 148–169.
48. Sokoloff L, Bland J. The Musculoskeletal System. Baltimore, Williams & Wilkins, 1975.
49. Steiner J. The gustofacial response: observations on normal and anencephalic infants. In Bosma J (ed). Oral Sensation and Perception (NIH DHEW Publication No. 73–546). Bethesda, MD, US Dept of Health, Education, and Welfare, 1973.
50. Sullivan PG. Skull, jaw, and teeth growth patterns. In Falkner F, Tanner JM (eds). Human Growth, Vol 2. Postnatal Growth. New York, Plenum Press, 1986, pp 243–268.
51. Susanne C. Developmental genetics of man. In Johnston FE, Roche AF, Susanne C (eds). Human Physical Growth and Maturation: Methodologies and Factors. New York, Plenum Press, 1980, pp 221–242.
52. van der Klaauw CJ. Size and position of the functional components of the skull. Arch Neerl Zool 9:1, 1948.
53. van Limborgh J. The role of genetic and local environmental factors in the control of postnatal craniofacial morphogenesis. Acta Morphol Neerl Scand 10:37, 1972.
54. Williams PL, Wendell Smith CP, Treadgold S, et al. Basic Human Embryology, 2nd ed. Philadelphia, JB Lippincott, 1969.

3

Genetics, Syndromology, and Craniofacial Anomalies

Anne Chun-Hui Tsai, M.D., M.Sc., F.A.A.P., F.A.C.M.G. and Stephanie E. Vallee, M.S.

Understanding the role of genetics in the diagnosis of craniofacial anomalies requires a knowledge of several topics in human genetics. This chapter reviews these subjects, which include the fundamental issues in human medical genetics (e.g., chromosomes, genes, inheritance patterns, genetics terminology, pedigrees). Furthermore, the chapter provides an approach to genetics syndromology. These topics are further illustrated with examples of the more common genetic diagnoses. This chapter serves as a key with which to explore the modern literature regarding genetics and craniofacial anomalies.

Genetics

The word *genetic* is derived from the Greek root *gen-* ("to become or grow into something"). Two related terms, *congenital* and *familial*, usually arise when discussing characteristics or traits of an individual. Congenital refers to a trait that is present at birth, while familial indicates that the trait appears in more than one family member. However, neither term clearly defines a trait as genetic. Intrauterine infection is congenital, but not genetic; horizontal transmission of the hepatitis B virus is familial, but not genetic. One can have a genetic disorder, such as phenylketonuria, without a family history of this disorder.

More precisely, genetic disease should be defined as a disease resulting from a change or variation in genetic material. This change may be inherited or result from a new mutation in an affected person. Genetic disorders can be categorized into the following classic groups: chromosomal anomalies, single-gene disorders, and multifactorial disorders.

Chromosomal Anomalies

All humans typically have 46 chromosomes, present in 23 pairs. One member of each chromosome pair is inherited from parents at the time of conception. The first 22 pairs of chromosomes are called *autosomes*, which are the same in males and females. The last pair of chromosomes are the *sex chromosomes*, so named for their involvement in gender determination. Typically, males have one X and one Y chromosome while females have two X chromosomes. The centromere separates the chromosome into

two arms. The short arm of the chromosome, called the *p arm* (petite), and the *long arm*, or *q arm* (named because Q is the next alphabetical letter) are used in describing chromosomal locations. Each arm is further subdivided into numbered bands that are visible using different staining techniques. The use of named chromosome arms and bands allows for universal communication of chromosome description. Details of the banding system and nomenclature can be found in ISCN.[15] Figure 3–1 demonstrates normal karyotypes for males and females.

Chromosome anomalies occur in 0.4% of all live births. They are a prevalent cause of mental retardation and congenital anomalies or birth defects. Chromosome anomalies are present in a much higher frequency among spontaneous abortions and stillbirths. Abnormalities of the chromosome number and structure, fragile sites, chromosome breakage, and mosaicism are examples of some chromosomal anomalies.

Abnormalities of Chromosomal Number

When a human cell has 23 chromosomes, such as human ovum or sperm, it is in the *haploid state (n)*. After conception, in cells other than the reproductive cells, 46 chromosomes are present in the *diploid state (2n)*. Any number that is an exact multiple of the haploid number, e.g., 46 (2n), 69 (3n), and 92 (4n), is called *euploid*. *Polyploid cells* are those that contain any number other than the usual diploid number of chromosomes. Polyploid conceptions are usually not viable except in *mosaic state*, with the presence of more than one cell line in the body (mosaicism is discussed later). Cells deviating from the multiple of the haploid number are called *aneuploid*, meaning not euploid and indicating an extra chromosome. *Trisomy*, an example of an euploid, is the presence of three of a particular chromosome rather than two. Trisomy is the most common numerical chromosome anomaly in humans. Table 3–1 summarizes the most common autosomal trisomies. *Monosomies*, the presence of only one member of a chromosome pair, may be complete or partial. Complete monosomies may result from nondisjunction or anaphase lag. All complete autosomal monosomies appear to be lethal early in development and only survive in mosaic forms. Sex chromosome monosomy, however, can be viable.

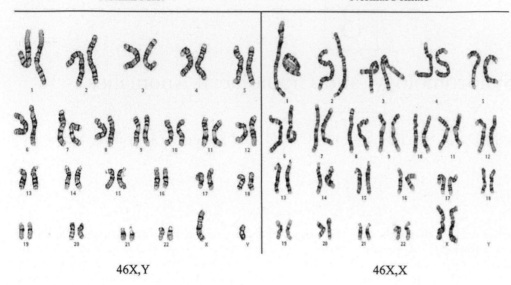

FIGURE 3–1. Normal human chromosomes. (Courtesy of Billie Carstens at Colorado Cytogenetics Lab, UCHSC.)

Abnormalities of Chromosomal Structure

There are many different types of structural chromosome anomalies, which are briefly described. Furthermore, standard cytogenetic nomenclature and classic clinical examples are provided. Please refer to Figure 3–3 for an ideogram of these chromosomal anomalies.

Deletions (del). (See Fig. 3–3A.) A deletion is an absence of normal chromosomal material; deletions can be

terminal (removing an end of a chromosome) or interstitial (within a chromosome). The missing part is described using the code del, followed by the number of the involved chromosome in parentheses, followed by a description of the missing region of that chromosome, also in parentheses: e.g., 46,XX,del(1)(p36.3). This nomenclature describes the loss of genetic material of band 36.3 of the short arm of chromosome 1. Figure 3–2 shows a child with 1p36.3 deletion. Other deletions result in clini-

TABLE 3–1. Common Autosomal Trisomies

Feature	Trisomy 21	Trisomy 18	Trisomy 13	Trisomy 8 Mosaicism
Eponym	Down syndrome	Edward syndrome	Patau syndrome	
Liveborn incidence	1:800	1:8000	1:15,000	
Tone	Hypotonia	Hypertonia	Hypo- or hypertonia	Variable
Cranium/brain	Mild microcephaly, flat occiput, three fontanels	Microcephaly, prominent occiput	Microcephaly, sloping forehead, occipital scalp defects, holoprosencephaly	High prominent forehead
Eyes	Up-slanting, epicanthal folds; speckled iris (Brushfield spots)	Small palpebral fissures, corneal opacity	Micro-ophthalmia, hypotelorism, iris coloboma, retinal dysplasia	
Ears	Small, low-set, overfolded upper helices	Low-set, malformed	Low-set, malformed	Low-set
Facial features	Protruding tongue, large cheeks, low flat nasal bridge	Small mouth, micrognathia	Cleft lip and palate	Long face, wide upturned nose, thick everted lower-lip micro-retrognathia, high arched/cleft palate
Skeletal	Clinodactyly 5th digit, gap between toes 1 and 2, excess nuchal skin, short stature	Clenched hand, absent 5th finger distal crease, hypoplastic nails, short stature, thin ribs	Postaxial polydactyly, hypoconvex fingernails, clenched hand	Absent patella or osteoarticular anomalies
Cardiac defect	40%	60%	80%	
Survival	Long-term	90% die within first year	80% die within first year	
Other features	Large fontanel, thick nuchal folds, single palmar creases	Rocker-bottom feet, polycystic kidneys, dermatoglyphic arch pattern	Genital anomalies, polycystic kidneys, increased nuclear projections in neutrophils	Myelodysplasia

Modified from Jones KL (ed). Pediatric Secrets, 2nd ed. Philadelphia, Hanley & Belfus, 1997.

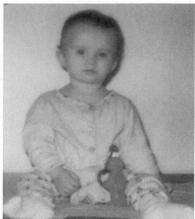

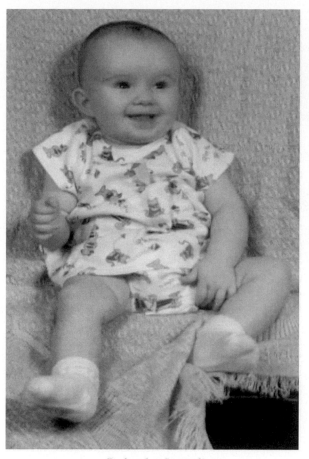

FIGURE 3–2. Chromosome 1p36.3 deletion syndrome (note prominent forehead and deep-set eyes).

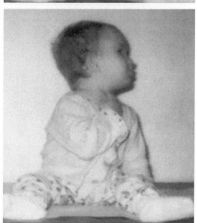

Proband at 8 months

Proband at 21 months

cally recognizable conditions associated with mental handicaps and characteristic facial features. Wolf-Hirschhorn syndrome, del(4p), produces an unusual face with "Greek helmet"; cri-du-chat syndrome, del(5p), causes the infant to produce an unusual high-pitched cry.

Duplication (dup). (See Fig. 3–3B.) Duplication is the presence of an extra copy of a chromosomal segment, which can be *tandem* (genetic material present in the original direction) or *inverted* (genetic material present in the opposite direction). A duplication of chromosome 22q11 causes cat-eye syndrome, resulting in iris coloboma and anal or ear anomalies, or both.

Inversions (inv). (See Fig. 3–3C.) An inversion is an intrachromosomal rearrangement such that the rearranged section of the chromosome is inverted. Inversions can be *paracentric* (not involving the centromere) or *pericentric* (involving the centromere).

Ring chromosomes (r). (See Fig. 3–3D.) A ring chromosome is a deletion of the normal telomeres (and possibly other subtelomeric sequences) with subsequent fusion of both ends to form a circular chromosome. Ring chromosome anomalies often cause growth retardation and mental handicap.

Translocations (trans). (See Fig. 3–3E.) A translocation is an interchromosomal rearrangement of genetic material. These may be *balanced* (the cell has a normal content of genetic material arranged in a structurally abnormal way) or *unbalanced* (the cell has gained or lost genetic material because of chromosomal interchange). Translocations may further be described as *reciprocal* (exchange of genetic material between two nonhomologous chromosomes) or *robertsonian* (fusion of two acrocentric chromosomes).

Insertions (ins). An insertion is breakage at two points within a chromosome into which another piece of chromosomal material is incorporated. This requires three breakpoints and may occur between two chromosomes or within the same chromosome. The phenotype depends on the origin of the inserted materials.

Microdeletion. Microdeletion is also known as *contiguous gene syndrome*. Microdeletions arise via the loss of genes that are adjacent to each other on a chromosome. Table 3–2 summarizes some common microdeletion syndromes. This type of deletion is too small to be detected by traditional cytogenetic methods, including high-resolution karyotyping, and usually requires a specialized molecular cytogenetic method—fluorescence in situ hybridization, or FISH—to detect it. The presence of two visible fluorescent lights represents binding of the FISH probe to both copies of chromosomal region 22q11. This finding is diagnostic of a microdeletion at this chromosomal locus, confirming a diagnosis of velo-cardio-facial syndrome.

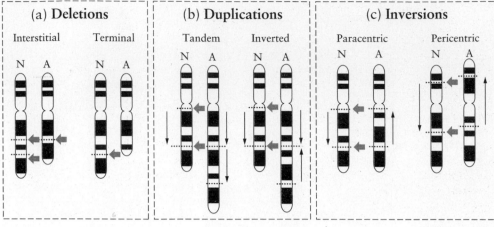

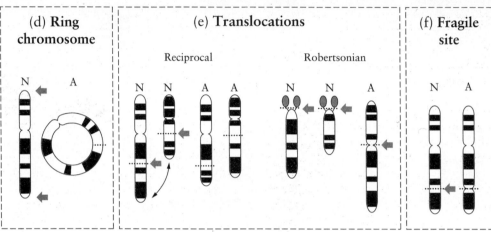

FIGURE 3–3. Structural chromosomal anomalies. (From Medical Genetics 1992.)

TABLE 3–2. Common Human Microdeletion Syndromes

Disorder	Clinical Features	Microdeletion
Williams syndrome	Unusual face, aortic stenosis, joint laxity, mental disability, cocktail personality	7q11 (elastin gene)
Langer-Giedion syndrome	Unusual face, cartilaginous exostoses, mental disability	8q23-q24
Beckwith-Wiedemann syndrome	Large size, omphalocele, hypoglycemia	11p11-p15 Dup (p15) also
Wilms tumor-aniridia-genital defects-retardation (WAGR) syndrome	Iris, genital defects, Wilms tumor, mental disability	11p13 (WT-1 Wilms tumor gene)
Prader-Willi syndrome	Unusual face, early hypotonia, feeding difficulty, later morbid obesity	15q11 pat; (some are ? point mutation)
Angelman syndrome	Unusual face with prominent jaw, seizures, mental disability	15q11 mat
Rubinstein-Taybi syndrome	Unusual face with broad thumbs, mental disability	16p13.3
Smith-Magenis syndrome	Unusual face, aberrant behaviors, mental disability, sleep difficulty	17p11
Hereditary neuropathy with predisposition to pressure palsies	Peripheral nerve dysfunction	17p11 (PMP 22 gene) Dup (17p11) causes CMT disease
Miller-Dieker syndrome	Hypotonia, lissencephaly (smooth brain), mental disability	17p13 (LIS-1 gene)
Alagille syndrome	Unusual face, pulmonary artery stenosis, vertebral anomalies, cholestatic liver disease	20p11-p12 (some have point mutation of JAG gene)
Shprintzen/DiGeorge syndrome	Unusually long face with palatal and speech defects, immune or genital defects	22q11
Duchenne muscular dystrophy, CGD, RP, McLeod phenotype	Muscle weakness, immune dysfunction, vision problems	XP21 (dystrophin gene, others)

CGD, chronic granulomatous disease; RP, retinitis pigmentosa; PMP, peripheral myelin protein; CMT, Charcot-Marie-Tooth; LIS, lissencephaly; JAG, jagged Alagille gene.

TABLE 3–3. Most Common Sex Chromosome Disorders

	47,XXY (Klinefelter Syndrome)	47,XYY	47,XXX	45,X (Turner Syndrome)
Frequency of live births	1/2000	1/2000	1/2000	1/8000
Maternal age association	Yes	No	Yes	No
Phenotype	Tall, eunuchoid habitus, underdeveloped secondary sexual characteristics, gynecomastia	Tall, severe acne, indistinguishable from normal males	Tall, indistinguishable from normal females	Short stature, web neck, shield chest, pedal edema at birth, coarctation of the aorta
IQ and behavior	80–100, behavioral problems	90–110, behavioral problems, aggressive behavior	90–110; behavioral problems	Mildly deficient to normal intelligence, spatial-perceptual difficulties
Reproductive function	Extremely rare	Common	Common	Extremely rare
Gonads	Hypoplastic testes, Leydig cell hyperplasia, Sertoli cell hypoplasia, seminiferous tubule dysgenesis, few spermatogenic precursors	Normal-sized testes, normal testicular histology	Normal-sized ovaries, normal ovarian histology	Streak ovaries with deficient follicles, 5%–10% have Y-chromosomal material and are at risk for gonadoblastoma; a careful screening for Y chromosome should be performed

Modified from Donnenfeld AE, et al. Common chromosome disorders detected prenatally. Postgrad Obstet Gynecol 6:5, 1986.

Sex Chromosomal Anomalies

Abnormalities involving sex chromosomes, including aneuploidy and mosaicism, are relatively common in the general population. Table 3–3 summarizes the most common sex chromosome anomalies and their clinical features.

Fragile Sites

Fragile sites are defined as regions of chromosomes that show a tendency toward separation, breakage, or attenuation under particular growth conditions. Examples are 2q13, 6p23, 9q32, 12q13, 20p11, and Xq27. Some fragile sites are related to malformation syndromes, others to cancer formation. The classic example of the fragile X chromosome site, Xq27, is now known to be due to allelic expansion of a CGG trinucleotide repeat. Fragile X syndrome is characterized by a long face, prominent jaw, prominent ears, autistic tendency, mental retardation, and speech delay. It is the most common single-gene disorder causing mental retardation in males. In 50% of patients with fragile X syndrome, a fragile site on the X chromosome can be induced by growing the cells in a medium depleted of folic acid. While identification of a fragile site at Xq27 was previously the diagnostic standard for fragile X syndrome, this form of clinical testing has been re-

TABLE 3–4. Common Chromosomal Breakage Syndromes

Syndrome	Clinical Features	Gen	Cytogenetic	Cancers
Ataxia telangiectasia	Progressive cerebellar ataxia, oculocutaneous telangiectasia, immunodeficiency	AR	Gaps, breaks, pseudo-diploid clones with rearrangements of chromosomes 7 and 14	Lymphomas, lymphocytic leukemia
Bloom syndrome	Gestational dwarfism, photosensitive telangiectatic erythroderma, long face, malar hypoplasia	AR	Excessive sister chromatid exchanges, breaks and rearrangements	Nonlymphocytic leukemias
Fanconi anemia	Radial malformations, progressive pancytopenia, hyperpigmentation, poor growth	AR	Chromatid breaks and gaps, mitomycin sensitivity	Leukemia, hepatocellular carcinoma, squamous cell carcinoma
Incontinentia pigmenti	Marbled skin pigmentation, eye malformations, heart, teeth, and skeleton defects	XL	Gaps, rearrangements in lymphocytes	Acute myelogenous leukemia, pheochromocytoma
Werner syndrome	Premature aging, scleropoikiloderma, juvenile cataracts, short stature with thin limbs and stocky trunk	AR	Variegated translocation mosaicism	Sarcomas, meningiomas
Xeroderma pigmentosum	Photosensitivity, neurologic deficits	AR	UV and UV mimetic sensitivity, no spontaneous chromosome instability	Basal cell carcinoma, squamous cell carcinoma

AR, autosomal recessive; XL, X-linked.
Adapted from Thurmon TF. A Comprehensive Primer on Medical Genetics. New York, Parthenon, 1999, p 112.

placed by the molecular study of the number of CGG repeats of the FMR1 gene.

Chromosomal Breakage Syndromes

Several recessive disorders are associated with breakage and rearrangement of chromosomes. The breaks may be spontaneous or they can be induced by a variety of mitogens and radiation. Such examples include some types of Fanconi pancytopenia syndrome, Bloom syndrome, incontinentia pigmenti, Werner syndrome, and ataxia telangiectasia (Table 3–4). These syndromes have specific clinical presentations about which chromosome breakage does not provide an explanation of the disorder; rather, these presentations are part of the phenotype.

Mosaicism

Mosaicism refers to the presence of two different cell lines in one individual. These varying cell lines are derived from a single fertilized egg. Studies of chorionic villus sampling tissue show that at least 2% of all conceptions are mosaic for chromosomal anomalies at or before 10 weeks' gestation. A zygote may start out as a viable or nonviable trisomy, but "chromosome rescue" may result in the additional chromosome being lost during mitosis. If a normal cell line develops, the fetus may survive and the original trisomic cell line may be present in some percentage or it may be lost. Mosaicism can be difficult to document through routine clinical cytogenetic analysis. While peripheral cell lines are the most obtainable tissues, they represent only one type of tissue that may be affected by mosaicism. Mosaicism also may be present in some tissues but not in others. Clinical presentations associated with mosaicism can vary widely. Body asymmetry, linear patchy skin, and hyper- and hypopigmentation can occur with chromosomal mosaicism (e.g., hypomelanosis of Ito).

Single-Gene Disorders

Mendelian Principles

Traditionally, autosomal single gene disorders follow the principles explained by Mendel's observations, summarized in Figure 3–4. The inheritance of genetic traits through generations relies on segregation and independent assortment. *Segregation* is the process through which our gene pairs are separated during gamete formation. Each gamete receives only one copy of each of our genes (alleles). Figure 3–4 shows the two alleles, A1 and A2, segregating into two separate gametes. *Independent assortment* refers to the idea that the segregation of different alleles occurs independently. The diagram shows two separate genes, A and B, and their respective alleles segregating independently of one another. This assumes that the genes are distant from one another on the same chromosome or are located on two different chromosomes. Neighboring genes may not segregate independently.

Mendelian Disorders

Victor McKusick's catalog, *Mendelian Inheritance in Man*, lists more than 10,000 entries in which the mode of inheritance is presumed to be autosomal dominant, autosomal recessive, X-linked dominant, X-linked recessive, and Y-linked. Single genes at specific loci on one or a pair of chromosomes cause these disorders. Understanding the terminology of inheritance is helpful in approaching mendelian disorders. Inheritance patterns can usually be explained by analysis of the pedigree and the pattern of transmission in the family, identification of a specific condition, and knowledge of that condition's mode of inheritance.

Terminology

Several terms are important in understanding heredity patterns. These are listed below:

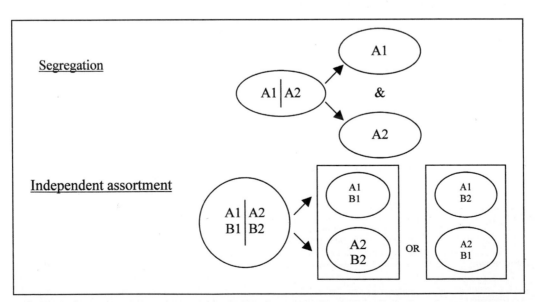

FIGURE 3–4. Mendel's principles. (Adapted from Aylsworth AS. Genetics Review Course. ACMG, 1999.)

(a)

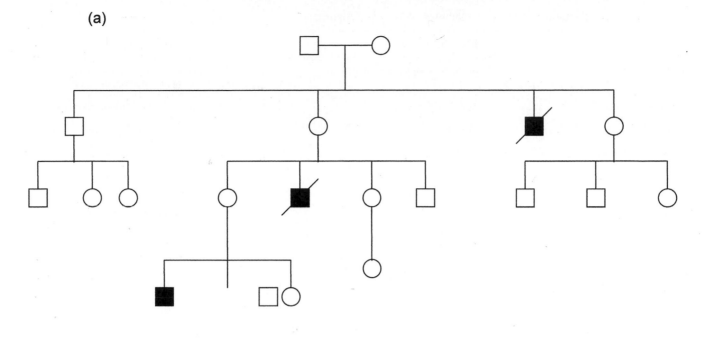

(b)

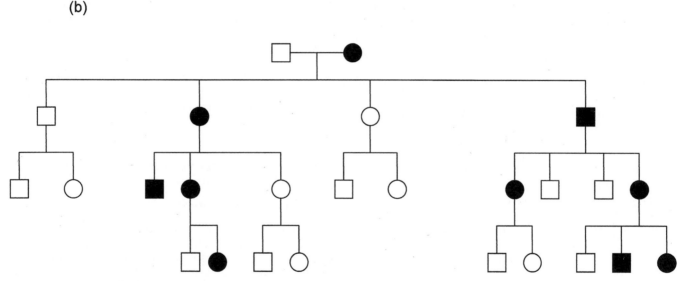

FIGURE 3–8. Example pedigree of X-linked recessive. *A,* X-linked recessive. *B,* X-linked dominant.

the other hand, female carriers of X-linked disorders are usually functionally mosaic. Because most females have two X chromosomes, they can have two cell populations—one carrying the normal X chromosome gene and the other carrying the altered gene. *X inactivation,* a process through which one X chromosome is "turned off" during early embryologic development, is completed for dosage compensation. As a result of X inactivation, both male and female carriers have only one X chromosome active in each cell. This process is typically random; therefore, female carriers of X-linked disorders may exhibit skewed X inactivation. By chance, a female carrier

may have more normal X chromosomes inactivated and display some symptoms of an X-linked disorder, either clinically or biochemically.

A male affected with an X-linked recessive disorder transmits the nonworking gene to all of his daughters, who receive his only X chromosome, and to none of his sons, who receive his Y chromosome. Affected men in a family are related through women in the family; male-to-male transmission never occurs. A typical pedigree of an X-linked recessive condition is shown in Figure 3–8A, and common examples of X-linked recessive syndromes are listed in Table 3–7.

TABLE 3-7. Clinical Features in Selected Examples of X-Linked Disorders

Disease	Gene Localization	Incidence	Clinical Findings
Hemophilia A	Xq28 (large gene; many mutations)	1 : 10,000	Prolonged bleeding; bruising; joint and muscle hemorrhages; deficiency of factor VIII
Alport syndrome	Xq21.3-q22	1 : 10,000	Renal failure, sensorineural hearing loss
Norrie disease	Xp11.4	Rare	Pseudoglioma, hypogonadism, mental retardation, microcephaly
Fragile X syndrome	Xq27.3	1 in 2000	Mental retardation, long face, prominent jaw and ears, autistic tendencies, macro-orchidism
DMD	Xp21.2	1 in 3500	Progressive muscle weakness, calf pseudohypertrophy, mild mental retardation, onset >6 years, cardiomyopathy
X-ALD	Xq28	Rare	Peroxisomal disorder resulting in accumulation of very-long-chain fatty acids in white matter and adrenal gland, eventual neurologic symptoms and Addison disease
Otopalatodigital syndrome, type 1	Xq28	1 : 10,000	Hearing loss, digital anomalies, cleft palate

X-linked dominant disorders may be equally expressed in females and males since only one genetic change is needed to cause the condition. The presence of a second functioning copy of the gene on a female's other X chromosome does not affect the severity of the condition. As our ability to detect manifestations in female carriers of X-linked recessive conditions improves, the distinction between X-linked dominant and recessive blurs. Pedigrees of X-linked dominant disorders demonstrate that affected women have affected children of both sexes while affected men have affected daughters and no affected sons.

Some X-linked dominant disorders appear to be lethal to males and are only found in females. Examples are Rett syndrome (early normal development followed by regression to severe mental retardation and seizures), Aicardi syndrome (agenesis of the corpus callosum, severe seizures, hemivertebrae, and chorioretinal abnormalities), Goltz syndrome (focal dermal hypoplasia, finger and hand anomalies, hypodontia, and colobomas), and incontinentia pigmenti (abnormalities of the hair, teeth, nails, and skin, including several stages of cutaneous changes: perinatal inflammatory vesicles, verrucous patches, distinctive hyperpigmentation, and dermal scarring). Typical pedigrees are presented in Figure 3–8B.

Y-Linked Inheritance

Also known as *holandric inheritance,* conditions attributable to Y-linked inheritance are caused by genes on the Y chromosome. These conditions are relatively rare, with only about 40 entries listed in McKusick's catalog. Male-to-male transmission occurs in this category, with all sons of affected males being affected and no daughters or females being affected. Figure 3–9 shows a typical Y-linked inheritance pedigree. Table 3–8 shows several examples of genes and conditions caused by genes on the Y chromosome.

Variations and Exceptions to Traditional Mendelian Inheritance Patterns

Mitochondrial Inheritance

Mitochondria, the energy producers in cells, have their own genetic material separate from the DNA in the cell's nucleus. These organelles are located in the ovum at the time of conception. Sperm cells do not contribute mitochondria to zygotes. All mitochondrial genes are therefore inherited only from the mother. These genes are passed

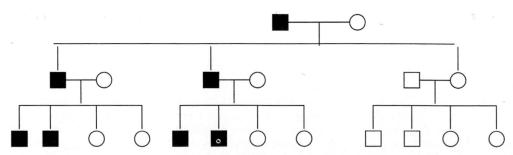

FIGURE 3–9. Example of Y-linked pedigree.

TABLE 3–8. Y-Linked Genes/Phenotypes (Male-to-Male Transmission Only)

Gene	Gene Name	Clinical Features
AZF2	Azoospermia factor 2	Azoospermia, oligospermia
Unknown	N/A	Retinitis pigmentosa
AZF1	Azoospermia factor 1	Non-obstructive azoospermia/oligospermia
GBY	Gonadoblastoma	Phenotypic females with dysgenetic gonads, gonadoblastoma risk
Unknown	N/A	Long hairs on ear helix
GCY	Y-chromosome–influenced growth control	Involved in determination of stature
SRY	Sex-determining region, Y	Involved in sex determination in mammals
TSPY	Testis-specific protein, Y-encoded	Possibly related to spermatogonial proliferation, found in cytoplasm of spermatogonia, found in early forms of seminomatous testicular tumors

down from mothers to all of their children, and conditions caused by mutations within the mitochondrial genome are commonly described as following a *maternal inheritance* pattern. For a classic pedigree representing mitochondrial inheritance, see Figure 3–10 and, for clinical examples, see Table 3–9. Please note that mitochondrial diseases are not equivalent to mitochondrial inheritance. Some of the enzymes on mitochondria, or that are required in mitochondria to produce energy, are made by the nuclear genes. The examples of the nuclear genes include the individual subunits of the OXPHOS enzyme, complex I and PDH E1-α.

Imprinting

Imprinting describes the process in which genetic material is expressed differently, depending on the parent of origin. Conditions affected by imprinting may involve either a maternal or a paternal imprinting effect, in which individuals express only their paternal or maternal copy of specific genes, respectively. Maternal imprinting implies that the maternal copy of the gene is not expressed, and paternal imprinting results in no expression of the paternal copy of the gene. Mutations in these genes may have no effect if inherited from the parent whose gene is imprinted, or turned off. Table 3–10 shows the common diseases with the imprinting mechanism, and Figure 3–11 shows classic clinical examples of maternal

genomic imprinting. Prader-Willi syndrome, which is maternally imprinted, means that the mother's allele is inactive, while the paternal allele is turned off in Angelman syndrome.

Uniparental Disomy

Uniparental disomy (UPD), literally meaning "one parent, two chromosomes," describes a situation in which both copies of one chromosome or chromosomal region are derived from a single parent, rather than typical biparental inheritance. UPD may be *isodisomic* if two copies of the same homolog are present or *heterodisomic* when one copy of each parental homolog is present. This phenomenon was only recently discovered in humans and can arise in a number of ways. An originally trisomic pregnancy may "rescue" itself by removing one copy of the extra chromosome. If the embryo is left with two chromosomes from the same parent, UPD of that chromosome results. UPD can also arise after the conception of a monosomic pregnancy following nondisjunction. A monosomic cell may result in UPD if the monosomic chromosome replicates itself. Table 3–10 lists the relationship of imprinting and UPD in several genetic syndromes. Referring to the conditions highlighted in Table 3–10, UPD plays a role in disorders with imprinting. Prader-Willi syndrome can be the result of UPD of the maternal chromosome 15, Angelman syndrome the result of UPD of the paternal

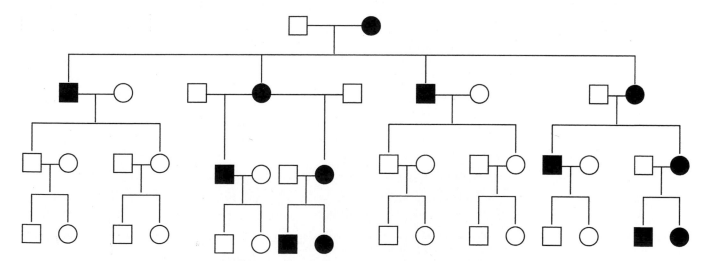

FIGURE 3–10. Pedigree of mitochondrial inheritance.

TABLE 3-9. Common Mitochondrial Disorders of Mitochondrial Inheritance

Disorder	Clinical Features
Kearns-Sayre syndrome	External ophthalmoplegia, retinal degeneration, elevated cerebrospinal fluid protein, cardiac conduction defect
Leber hereditary optic neuropathy	Early-onset progressive optic atrophy
Mitochondrial encephalopathy, lactic acidosis, stroke	Short stature, sensorineural deafness, encephalomyopathy, lactic acidosis, strokelike episodes
Myoclonic epilepsy and ragged red fibers	Myoclonic epilepsy, myopathy, ragged red muscle fibers, lipomas
Neuropathy, ataxia, retinitis pigmentosa	Neuropathy, ataxia, retinitis pigmentosa

chromosome 15, and Beckwith-Wiedemann the result of UPD of the paternal allele.

Dynamic Mutations and Anticipation

Expression of some autosomal dominant disorders appears to become more severe or to have an earlier age of onset with each succeeding generation, or both. For a number of years, this phenomenon—called *anticipation*—was attributed to biased ascertainment of patients. It is easy to see that in studying conditions with a wide range of intrafamilial expressivity, one is much more likely to ascertain families in whom symptoms are more severe (or started earlier) in current generations than families in which the condition was much more severe in ancestors and milder in the current generation. Figure 3-12 demonstrates the historical observation of anticipation in several genetic diseases. While bias of ascertainment may be a correct explanation for apparent anticipation in many dominant conditions, *some* conditions have been identified in which the feature has a molecular basis. In these conditions, the phenotype actually can become more severe or have earlier onset with succeeding generations, or both. In these disorders showing "true anticipation," a region of the gene is unstable because of a region of repeated trinucleotides. Normally, small numbers of such repeats are stable while a moderate number

of repeats (the critical number varies with the disorder) lead to instability of the sequence, causing a large number of repeats and disrupted gene function in subsequent generations. Examples are given in Table 3-11.

Phenocopy

Phenocopy is defined as an environmentally produced phenotype that mimics a genetic phenotype. Children with intrauterine exposure of retinoids can present with ear anomaly, heart defect, and 3rd and 4th pharyngeal pouch involvement, as occurs in DiGeorge syndrome. In such a scenario, prenatal exposure to retinoids can produce a phenocopy of DiGeorge syndrome. Apparent dominant transmission of a multiple congenital anomaly/mental retardation syndrome due to familial alcoholism and multiple affected generations may also have this effect. For example, sporadic or environmentally caused asthma, cancer, obesity, hypertension, psychosis, and alcoholism in families may appear to represent a monogenic predisposing gene.

Multifactorial Disorders

Multifactorial disorders are those caused by multiple factors, both genetic and environmental. These disorders may recur in families but do not show particular inheritance patterns in the pedigree. Because these conditions are more common, epidemiologic studies have allowed estimation of empirical recurrence risks for individual defects. Some multifactorial traits, such as tall and short stature, are merely variations of normal; others, such as neural tube defects and congenital heart disease, are thought to exhibit a threshold effect. This threshold may vary by the sex of the affected individual, the severity of the defect, the number of family members affected, and other factors. Another group of multifactorial disorders includes those diseases common to adult life, such as diabetes mellitus, hypertension, common psychiatric disorders, and many forms of cancer and coronary artery disease. Major genetic factors are undeniable in several of these diseases, but environmental risk factors are also important and contributory.

Common multifactorial birth defects are listed in Table 3-12 along with the approximate recurrence risks for first-degree relatives (siblings, additional children). Many

TABLE 3-10. Common Syndromes Associated with Imprinting

Syndrome	Clinical Features	Comment
Prader-Willi syndrome	Neonatal hypotonia, feeding difficulties, failure to thrive; eventual hyperphagia, central obesity; almond-shaped eyes, hypogonadism, mild–moderate mental retardation	Two thirds of cases are caused by deletion of paternal 15q11q13 and one fifth of cases by uniparental disomy of maternal chromosome 15
Angelman syndrome	Seizure disorder, gait ataxia/tremulous limbs, microcephaly, mental retardation, severe speech impairment, inappropriate laughter	Most cases are caused by deletion of maternal 15q11q13, with only 3% caused by uniparental disomy of paternal chromosome 15
Beckwith-Wiedemann syndrome	Overgrowth disorder, umbilical hernia/omphalocele, macroglossia, hemihypertrophy, earlobe creases, Wilms tumor	Half of cases are caused by paternal duplication of 11p15, and one fourth are caused by uniparental disomy paternal allele

tance is presumed, although no specific gene has been confirmed.

Cervico-Oculo-Acoustic Syndrome (Wildervanck Syndrome). *Facies/HEENT:* Facial asymmetry with short neck and low hairline, preauricular skin tags and pits, Duane anomaly, and sensorineural conductive/mixed hearing loss. Additional features include Klippel-Feil anomaly, Sprengel deformity, and mental retardation. The genetic cause is unknown; all reported cases have been sporadic.

Coffin-Lowry Syndrome. *Facies/HEENT:* Coarse facial features, down-slanting palpebral fissures, maxillary hypoplasia, mild hypertelorism, prominent brow, short and broad nose with thick alae nasi and septum, anteverted nares, large mouth with thick everted lower lip, prominent ears, hypodontia, and malocclusion. Additional findings include mild to moderate postnatal growth deficiency, severe mental retardation, pectus deformities, vertebral defects, large hands, tapering fingers, ligament laxity. Mutations in the RSK2 on Xp22.2 can cause this syndrome, which is inherited as an X-linked dominant pattern. The RSK2 gene is part of a gene family implicated in cell-cycle regulation through the mitogen-activated protein kinase cascade.

Costello Syndrome. *Facies/HEENT:* Macrocephaly, coarse facial features, low-set ears with thick lobes, epicanthic folds, strabismus, thick lips, depressed nasal bridge, curly hair. Additional findings include postnatal growth deficiency; mental retardation; thin and deep-set nails; dark skin pigmentation; deep plantar and palmar creases; short neck; tight Achilles tendons; papillomas in the perioral, nasal, and anal regions; and hypertrophic cardiomyopathy. Autosomal recessive and dominant inheritance have been hypothesized. No specific genes have been identified.

Ectrodactyly-Ectodermal Dysplasia-Clefting Syndrome. *Facies/HEENT:* Blue irides; blepharophimosis; defects of the lacrimal duct system; cleft lip with or without cleft palate; partial anodontia; and light-colored, sparse, thin, wiry hair. Additional findings include fair, thin skin with mild hyperkeratosis, hypotrichosis, hypohidrosis, hypoplastic nipples, variable defects in the midportion of the hands and feet from syndactyly to ectrodactyly, and genitourinary defects in about 50% of patients. Autosomal dominant inheritance with variable expressivity is implied, with linkage to 7q11.2-q21.3.

Floating Harbor Syndrome. *Facies/HEENT:* Triangular facies with broad, bulbous nose with prominent nasal bridge and wide columella, short smooth philtrum, wide mouth with thin lips, prominent eyes in infancy, deep-set appearing eyes later, posteriorly rotated ears, short neck, and low posterior hairline. Additional findings include being small for gestational age with dramatic postnatal growth deficiency and delayed bone age, brachydactyly, clinodactyly, and mild mental retardation with significant speech delay and normal motor development. All cases have been sporadic, and a new mutation of autosomal dominant inheritance is presumed.

Fraser Syndrome (Cryptophthalmos). *Facies/HEENT:* Bilateral cryptophthalmos, unusual eyebrows, hypoplastic notched nares, ear anomalies with atresia of the external auditory canal, and cupped ears. Additional findings include mental retardation in 50% of patients, partial cutaneous syndactyly, incompletely developed genitalia, laryngeal stenosis/atresia, and renal hypoplasia/agenesis. Autosomal recessive inheritance has been documented, although no specific genes have been identified.

Frontonasal Dysplasia Sequence. *Facies/HEENT:* Ocular hypertelorism, lateral displacement of inner canthi, widow's peak, anterior cranium bifidum occultum defect, and varied nasal defects, ranging from notched broad nasal tip to completely divided nostrils with median cleft lip. This condition, occurring sporadically, is a primary defect in midface development.

Kabuki Syndrome. *Facies/HEENT:* Long palpebral fissures with everted lateral lower eyelids, ptosis, arched eyebrows, epicanthic folds, large protuberant ears, and cleft palate. Additional findings include cardiac defects in up to 50% of patients, postnatal growth deficiency, mild to moderate mental retardation, clinodactyly, and persistent fetal finger pads. This syndrome is reportedly sporadic, with new dominant mutations possible. Some families follow an X-linked inheritance.

Langer-Giedion Syndrome (Tricho-Rhino-Phalangeal Syndrome, Type II). *Facies/HEENT:* Microcephaly, large protruding ears, heavy eyebrows, deep-set eyes, large bulbous nose with thickened alae nasi and septum, simple philtrum, thin upper lip, and sparse scalp hair. Additional findings include postnatal mild growth deficiency, mild to severe mental retardation, loose skin in infancy, cone-shaped epiphyses, and multiple exostoses of the long bones. This condition is a contiguous gene disorder due to loss of the TRPS1 and EXT1 genes at 8q24.11-q24.13. FISH testing for the EXT1 gene is clinically available.

Larsen Syndrome. *Facies/HEENT:* Flat facies, depressed nasal bridge, prominent forehead, hypertelorism, and cleft palate. Additional findings include multiple congenital joint dislocations, long nontapering fingers with short fingernails, and dysraphism. Autosomal dominant inheritance is most likely, although autosomal recessive inheritance has been suggested. The dominant locus has been linked to 3p21.1-p14.1. Genetic testing is not clinically available.

Marshall Syndrome. *Facies/HEENT:* Short depressed nose with flat nasal bridge and anteverted nares, large-appearing eyes, cataracts, myopia, flat midface, and prominent, protruding upper incisors. Additional findings include short stature, sensorineural deafness, calvarial thickening, and spondyloepiphyseal abnormalities. Autosomal dominant inheritance and linkage to 1q21 have been reported.

Miller Syndrome (Postaxial Acrofacial Dysostosis). *Facies/HEENT:* Malar hypoplasia, sometimes with vertical bony cleft; down-slanting palpebral fissures; colobomata of the eyelids; ectropion; micrognathia; cleft lip or palate, or both; and hypoplastic cup-shaped ears. Additional findings include absence of fifth digits on all limbs and accessory nipples. Autosomal recessive inheritance is likely because of familial recurrences. This syndrome presents with Treacher Collins–like facial features with postaxial limb anomalies.

Moebius Sequence. *Facies/HEENT:* Congenital sixth and seventh nerve palsy. This condition is typically sporadic and is likely to involve several genetic factors.

Nager Syndrome (Nager Acrofacial Dysostosis). *Facies/ HEENT:* Malar hypoplasia, down-slanting palpebral fissures, high nasal bridge, partial to total absence of lower eyelashes, low-set posteriorly rotated ears, atresia of external auditory canal, and cleft palate. Additional findings include radial limb hypoplasia, conductive hearing loss, and normal development and cognition. Nager syndrome is also a Treacher Collins–like syndrome but is associated with preaxial limb deficiency. New dominant mutations are probably responsible for this condition. Localization to chromosomal locus 9q32 has been accomplished through correlation with structural chromosome abnormalities.

Noonan Syndrome. *Facies/HEENT:* Webbing of the neck, down-slanting palpebral fissures, ptosis, hypertelorism, low-set ears, and low posterior hairline. Additional findings include short stature, shield chest, pectus excavatum, cryptorchidism, and pulmonic stenosis; one third of patients have bleeding diatheses. Autosomal dominant inheritance occurs, and clinical genetic testing is not available. Genetic linkage to 12q24 has been shown.

Oculodentodigital Syndrome. *Facies/HEENT:* Microphthalmos; short palpebral fissures; epicanthic folds; tooth enamel hypoplasia; thin, hypoplastic alae nasi with small nares; poor-growing, sparse hair; and mandible with wide alveolar ridge. Additional findings include syndactyly of 4th and 5th fingers and 3rd and 4th toes and broad tubular bones. Inheritance is autosomal dominant with variable expression and many new mutations. Genetic linkage analysis has mapped locus to 6q22-q24.

Opitz G/BBB Syndrome. *Facies/HEENT:* Hypertelorism, broad flat nasal bridge with anteverted nostrils, cleft lip with or without cleft palate, posteriorly rotated ears, and micrognathia. Additional findings include mild to moderate mental retardation, hypospadias, cryptorchidism, hernias, and other midline defects (including swallowing/ feeding and breathing problems). X-linked recessive and autosomal dominant inheritance has been identified. The X-linked gene, MID1, has been implicated, although clinical diagnostic testing is not available. Some cases of Opitz G/BBB syndrome have been attributed to deletions of chromosome region 22q11, for which testing is offered.

Oral-Facial-Digital Syndrome, Type I. *Facies/HEENT:* Oral frenula and clefts, hypoplastic nasal alae, lateral displacement of inner canthi, median cleft lip, cleft palate, and bifid tongue. Additional findings include digital asymmetry, variable mental retardation, and adult polycystic kidney disease. X-linked dominance with male lethality is present. The CXORF5 gene at Xp22.2-p22.3 has been implicated. No genetic testing is currently available.

Oral-Facial-Digital Syndrome, Type II (Mohr Syndrome). *Facies/HEENT:* Cleft tongue, low nasal bridge with lateral displacement of the inner canthi, broad nasal tip, and midline partial cleft palate. Additional findings include conductive hearing loss, partial reduplication of the hallux and first metatarsal, bilateral postaxial polydactyly of the hands, and bilateral polysyndactyly of the feet. Autosomal recessive inheritance has been reported.

Oto-Palatal-Digital Syndrome, Type I. *Facies/HEENT:* Cleft palate, frontal and occipital prominence, thick frontal bone, thick base of skull, hypertelorism, and small nose and mouth. Additional findings include moderate conductive deafness, broad distal digits with short nails, small trunk, pectus excavatum, small stature, and mental deficiency. This X-linked disorder, linked to Xq28, has intermediate expression in carrier females. No genetic testing is clinically available.

Oto-Palatal-Digital Syndrome, Type II. *Facies/HEENT:* Prominent forehead, late closure of fontanelles, microcephaly, low-set malformed ears, down-slanting palpebral fissures, flat nasal bridge, small mouth, micrognathia, and cleft palate. Additional findings include flexed overlapping finger; short broad thumbs and great toes; small thorax; bowing of radius, ulna, femur, and tibia; flattened vertebral bodies; and conductive hearing loss. This X-linked disorder has mild expression in carrier females. No specific genetic cause has been identified.

Robinow (Fetal Face) Syndrome. *Facies/HEENT:* Hypertelorism, prominent eyes, frontal bossing, down-slanting palpebral fissures, small upturned nose, long philtrum, triangular mouth with down-turned angles, crowded teeth, and posteriorly rotated ears. Additional features include short forearms, small hands, clinodactyly, hemivertebrae of thoracic spine, genital hypoplasia, and moderately short stature. Autosomal dominant and recessive inheritance have been suggested, and no testing is offered.

Rubinstein-Taybi Syndrome. *Facies/HEENT:* Microcephaly, frontal bossing, delayed fontanelle closure, down-slanting palpebral fissures, hypoplastic maxilla with narrow palate, small mouth, beaked nose, low-set malformed ears, heavy high-arched eyebrows, and long eyelashes. Additional features include mental retardation, broad thumbs and toes, speech difficulties, unsteady gait, cryptorchidism, and hirsutism. In a minority of cases, this contiguous gene deletion syndrome can be confirmed by FISH testing for 16p13.3. Point mutations within the cAMP-regulated enhancer-binding protein gene have also been detected. While FISH testing is clinically available, direct mutation analysis is not currently offered.

Seckel Syndrome. *Facies/HEENT:* Severe microcephaly, prominent nose, receding forehead, low-set malformed ears, and relatively large eyes with down-slanting palpebral fissures. Additional features include marked pre- and postnatal growth deficiency and mental retardation. Autosomal recessive inheritance has been discussed, with linkage to 3q22.1-q24. No clinical testing is offered.

Shprintzen Syndrome (22q11 Deletion Syndrome). *Facies/HEENT:* High-arched/cleft palate, velopharyngeal incompetence, prominent nose with square nasal root, retrognathia, and microcephaly. Additional features include mild cognitive impairment, postnatal onset short stature, conductive hearing loss, slender hands and fingers, cardiac defects in up to 85% of patients, and increased incidence of adult psychiatric diagnoses. Inheritance is autosomal dominant with FISH-positive 22q11 deletion. This contiguous gene syndrome has inter- and intrafamilial variability, and diagnostic testing is widely available.

Smith-Lemli-Opitz Syndrome. *Facies/HEENT:* Microcephaly with narrow frontal area, low-set, rotated ears, ptosis, epicanthic folds, broad nasal tip with anteverted nares, and micrognathia. Additional features include syndactyly of the 2nd and 3rd toes, hypospadias, cryptorchidism, failure to thrive, and moderate to severe mental retardation. This autosomal recessively inherited disorder of cholesterol metabolism causes decreased 7-dehydrocholesterol levels in plasma. Genetic testing for mutations within the sterol Δ-7-reductase gene (DHCR7, chromosomal locus 11q12-q13) is clinically available.

Stickler Syndrome. *Facies/HEENT:* Flat facies, depressed nasal bridge, midface hypoplasia, clefts or hard/soft palate, bifid uvula, sensorineural and conductive deafness, dental anomalies, myopia, retinal detachments, and cataracts. Additional features include spondyloepiphyseal dysplasia, hyperextensibility, arthropathy, hypotonia, and mitral valve prolapse. This dominantly inherited disorder is due to mutations within the COL2A1, COL11A1, and COL11A2 collagen genes. Genetic sequencing of these genes is available clinically.

Tricho-Rhino-Phalangeal Syndrome, Type I. *Facies/HEENT:* Pear-shaped bulbous nose; prominent long philtrum; narrow palate; large prominent ears; small carious teeth; sparse, thin hair; and relative hypopigmentation. Additional features include mild growth deficiency, thin nails, epiphyseal coning, and short 4th and 5th metacarpals and metatarsals. Autosomal dominant inheritance with an occasional FISH-positive deletion of 8q24.12 (EXT1 gene) has been documented. This form of testing is currently offered.

Townes-Brock Syndrome. *Facies/HEENT:* Auricular anomalies including overfolded ears, preauricular skin tags, and some evidence of hemifacial microsomia. Additional features include thumb anomalies, anal defects, and renal anomalies. Autosomal dominant inheritance with high variability is due to mutations within the sal-like 1 (SALL1) gene. Clinical genetic testing for these mutations is not available.

Van der Woude Syndrome. *Facies/HEENT:* Lower-lip pits; cleft lip or cleft palate, or both; and missing central/lateral incisors, canines, bicuspids, or any combination thereof. This dominantly inherited condition is linked to 1q32 and exhibits incomplete penetrance and high variability. No diagnostic genetic testing is clinically available.

Williams Syndrome. *Facies/HEENT:* Prominent lips with open mouth, hoarse voice, medial eyebrow flare, periorbital fullness, blue eyes with stellate irides, anteverted nares, and long philtrum. Additional features include cardiovascular anomalies; growth deficiency; mild to moderate mental retardation; friendly, cocktail-party personality; renal anomalies; colic; and hypercalcemia. This contiguous gene deletion syndrome involves the elastin gene and other neighboring genes at 7q11.2. Microdeletions of the elastin gene are diagnostic (detected through FISH testing, which is widely available).

REFERENCES

1. Aase JM. Diagnostic Dysmorphology. New York, Plenum, 1990.
2. Aase JM. Dysmorphologic diagnosis for the pediatric practitioner. Pediatr Clin North Am 39:135, 1992.
3. Arthur S. Aylsworth Genetics Review Course. ACMG, 1999.
4. Bennett RJ, Steinhaus KA, Uhrich SB, et al. Recommendations for standardized human pedigree nomenclature. Pedigree Standardization Task Force of the National Society of Genetic Counselors. Am J Hum Genet 56:745, 1995.
5. Curry CM. An approach to clinical genetics. In Rudolph's Fundamentals of Pediatrics, 2nd ed. Norwalk, Appleton & Lange, 1999, pp 147–180.
6. Donnenfeld AE, et al. Common chromosome disorders detected prenatally. Postgrad Obstet Gynecol 6:5, 1986.
7. Gorlin RJ, Cohen MM Jr, Levin S. Syndromes of the Head and Neck, 3rd ed. New York, Oxford University Press, 1990.
8. Graham JM. Clinical approach to human structural defects. Semin Perinatol 15:2, 1991.
9. Graham JM (ed). Smith's Recognizable Patterns of Human Deformation, 2nd ed. Philadelphia, WB Saunders, 1988.
10. Hall JG, Froster-Iskenius UG, Allanson JE. Handbook of Normal Physical Measurements. Oxford, Oxford Medical, 1989,
11. Harper PS. Practical Genetic Counseling, 5th ed. Boston, Butterworth Heinemann, 1998.
12. Jones KL (ed). Smith's Recognizable Patterns of Human Malformation, 5th ed. Philadelphia, WB Saunders, 1997.
13. Leppig KA, Werler MM, Cann CI, et al. Predictive value of minor anomalies: I. Association with major malformations. J Pediatr 110: 531, 1987.
14. McKusick VA. Mendelian Inheritance in Man, internet version: http://www3.ncbi.nlm.nih.gov/omim.
15. Mitelman F (ed). An International System for Human Cytogenetic Nomenclature. Basel, S Karger, 1995.
16. Saul RA, Skinner SA, Stevenson RE, et al. Growth References from Conception to Adulthood. Proceedings of the Greenwood Genetic Center. Greenwood, SC, Greenwood Genetic Center, 1998.
17. Thurmon TF. A Comprehensive Primer on Medical Genetics. New York, Parthenon, 1999, p 112.
18. Zackai EH, et al. In Polin RA, Ditmar MF (eds). Pediatric Secrets, 2nd ed. Philadelphia, Hanley & Belfus, 1997.

4

Evolution of Pediatric Otolaryngology

Gregory C. Allen, M.D., and Sylvan B. Stool, M.D.

Pediatric otolaryngology did not develop in a vacuum, nor did any of the pioneers of this specialty learn their trade in isolation. Sir Isaac Newton said, "If I have seen further it is by standing on the shoulders of giants." It is true: we all stand on the shoulders of those who came before. The history of pediatric otolaryngology is intertwined with the history of otolaryngology, pediatrics, and children's hospitals in general. The organized specialty of otolaryngology as we know it today is in its infancy. Laryngology, rhinology, and otology all developed as separate medical specialties during the second half of the 18th century. Otolaryngology, although one of this country's earliest recognized specialties, was frequently associated with ophthalmology. The American Academy of Ophthalmology and Otolaryngology, founded in 1896, did not formally separate into two distinct societies until 1979.

Pediatric otolaryngology, although long part of the practice of the general otolaryngologist, was not truly born until a few men began to base their practices in the country's newly developing children's hospitals. In addition, the new technologies and therapeutic interventions of the second half of the 19th century led several pioneering specialists to develop pediatric otolaryngology as a separate subspecialty, largely without forethought. Many of the disorders cared for by the pediatric otolaryngologist are due to improved survival of premature infants and children with congenital malformations. A significant number of the infants and children we care for today would have died of their primary disease processes just 50 years ago. Charles D. Bluestone routinely tells those interested in fellowship training at the Children's Hospital in Pittsburgh, "We take care of special problems or special children, or both, in a special institution." Pediatric surgery paved the way for pediatric surgical subspecialists, and this history has been recounted by the former Surgeon General, C. Everett Koop.[5]

Parallel to the development of pediatric otolaryngology, many other pediatric subspecialties began to emerge: genetics, neonatology, and pediatric divisions of critical care medicine, anesthesiology, pulmonary medicine, gastroenterology, ophthalmology, emergency medicine, and radiology all had strikingly similar beginnings. They were born out of a need for specialists with the expertise and interest to treat infants and children. Although some of these specialties competed with the otolaryngology for patients and procedures, this competitive spirit spurred on the technological and therapeutic advances in the field. In addition, the overall atmosphere of the children's hospital and focused desire to treat children, our most vulnerable society members, led to friendlier competition and collaboration.

It is this combination of pioneers, new technologies and therapeutics, pediatric subspecialization, and the rise of institutions and organizations committed to the care of children that laid the foundation for and stimulated the genesis of pediatric otolaryngology. This review of the history of pediatric otolaryngology is not intended to be all-encompassing, and some important figures are not discussed and landmark technologies not mentioned.

People

Those who have experienced very little first-hand learn most of what they know about the history of pediatric otolaryngology from listening to the stories of others and from reading. It is amazing how events and details fall into place. Many of the contemporary giants in the field, despite their tremendous impact on pediatric otolaryngology, happened into the specialty much by accident. Those who pursued this direction with more intention seemed to be in the right place at the right time. Indeed, many of the giants that made this history are still in the right place at the right time, practicing and actively contributing.

Joseph O'Dwyer, an obstetrician from New York, published his method of intubation in the New York Medical Journal in 1885 (Fig. 4–1). His article was titled "Two Cases of Croup Treated by Tubage of the Glottis."[9] In 1886, he published a series of 50 cases treated with endotracheal intubation; 86% of his subjects were less than 6 years old. Although his published mortality rate of 70% is quite dismal by today's standards, it was certainly an improvement over the almost certain death from the disease alone. His development of a set of tubes of various size for his technique undoubtedly saved the lives of many children (Figs. 4–2, 4–3). In the late 1800s, the problem of diphtheria was becoming increasingly widespread. Denver physician John Elsner described it as fever, headache, and malaise followed by a progressive sore throat. Examination of the child's throat revealed a characteristic "false membrane" that was often black.

FIGURE 4–1. Joseph O'Dwyer, M.D. (Courtesy of Sylvan E. Stool, M.D., Denver, CO.)

The odor of the breath becomes fetid or even gangrenous. The breathing becomes greatly oppressed . . . the patient passes into a semi-asphyxiated state, face livid, looks anxious and frightened, eyes stare widely, forehead clammy, and extremities cold. At each recurrence of the dyspnea the attack is more severe.[4]

The Chicago physician Frank Waxham dedicated himself to learning the new technique of intubation, and after months of practice on cadavers he began to practice the technique on "street urchins whom he hired for the purpose" and then on his own children (Fig. 4–4). Because many of his patients with diphtheria had advanced disease, many of them died, and the death was often attributed to the intubation. Dr. Waxham often had to flee the physical assault of angry parents who followed him in the poorer districts of Chicago. The AMA launched an investigation of the practice, which it eventually enthusiastically supported. In 1893, Dr. Waxham and his wife moved to Denver to seek relief from her tuberculosis, and in 1894 he presented his experience with more than 500 cases treated with intubation.[14] In 1894, Emil von Behring introduced diphtheria antitoxin, which decreased the disease's severity in many cases, but it did not disappear. In 1906, in Colorado, diphtheria made a surprise comeback, and in that year alone there were 122 disease-related deaths. Dr. Waxham attributed the resurgence to the fact that antitoxin was not readily available to poorer populations. Before the state legislature, he argued that surely a state that could afford $65,000 to gild the capital dome with gold and "preserve game animals" could afford $5000 to save the lives of its children. The legislature agreed, but Governor Shafroth pocketed the bill by saying, "He could not understand why the State of Colorado should furnish free antitoxin to the people any more than free horses and carriages to physicians."[10] Diphtheria continued to be a significant pediatric airway problem not only in the West but throughout the country until the introduction of toxoid and active immunization in the 1920s.

The concept of a surgical specialty devoted to ear, nose, and throat problems in infants and children gradually evolved, and not only in North America. One of the first physicians to develop this subspecialty was Jan Gabriel Danielewicz of Poland. He was born in 1903 and, after completing his studies, decided to dedicate himself to the treatment of young patients. He was aware of the differences of laryngologic problems in children; he organized a pediatric laryngology ward that he ran for 12 years. In 1953, he became head of the Institute of the Mother and Child in Warsaw. In 1959, the Minister of Health Care made pediatric otolaryngology a separate

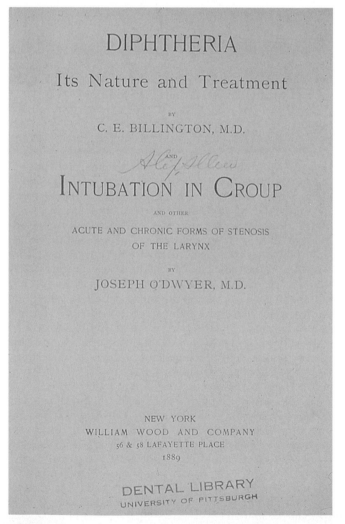

DIPHTHERIA

Its Nature and Treatment

BY

C. E. BILLINGTON, M.D.

AND

Alex Allen

INTUBATION IN CROUP

AND OTHER

ACUTE AND CHRONIC FORMS OF STENOSIS
OF THE LARYNX

BY

JOSEPH O'DWYER, M.D.

NEW YORK
WILLIAM WOOD AND COMPANY
56 & 58 LAFAYETTE PLACE
1889

DENTAL LIBRARY
UNIVERSITY OF PITTSBURGH

FIGURE 4–2. Book written by Joseph O'Dwyer, M.D.

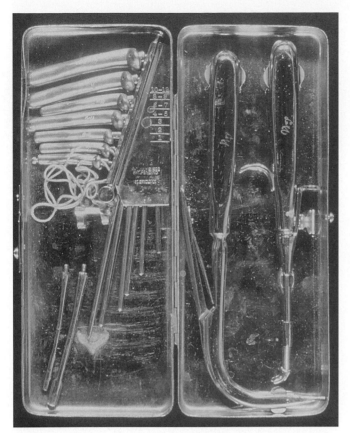

FIGURE 4–3. Tubes used for intubation by Frank Waxham, M.D. (Courtesy of Sylvan E. Stool, M.D., Denver, CO. Donated by Herman Laff, M.D.)

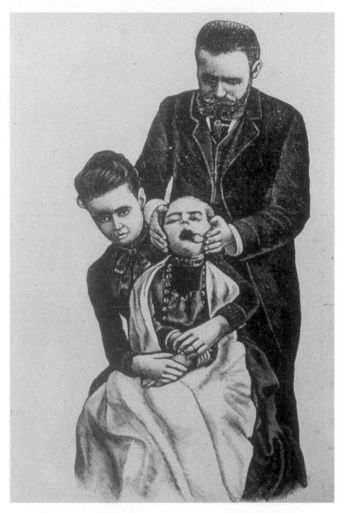

FIGURE 4–4. Frank Waxham, M.D., demonstrating intubation of the larynx with O'Dwyer tubes.

medical specialty with its own examining board. Dr. Danielewicz had a very active practice with an office run out of his family's apartment (Fig. 4–5). His son remembers his parents having the children wait in the stairwell outside the apartment for hours just to have a chance to be treated. In 1974, Dr. Danielewicz organized the first Panel of Pediatric Otolaryngology at the International Congress in Venice (Fig. 4–6). An afternoon was devoted primarily to airway problems, which provided for a lively and often heated discussion. This afternoon also was an opportunity for those interested primarily in children to affiliate and led to the formation of other societies. Dr. Danielewicz trained many laryngologists and received many awards, but because he was an independent thinker and was at odds with the authority of the day he was never granted professorship. Professors Kossowaska and Chmielik continued his work at the Warsaw University Medical School (Professor Mieczyslaw Chmielik and Dr. and Mrs. Pawel Danielewicz, personal communication, June 1999).

With the development and mass production of antibiotics in the years following World War II, interest in otolaryngology began to decline. Many considered it a dead specialty, and young physicians were discouraged from considering it. On opposite poles of the United States, at Children's Medical Center in Boston and the Children's Hospital of Los Angeles, young otolaryngologists working with pediatric patients began to realize that

children had otolaryngologic problems that required special expertise. Many consider Seymore Cohen of Los Angeles and Charles Ferguson of Boston to be the first pediatric otolaryngologists in North America. Dr. Ferguson and his colleague Carlyle Flake worked full-time at

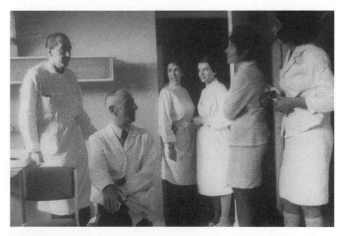

FIGURE 4–5. Dr. Jan Gabriel Danielewicz in his clinic in Warsaw, Poland.

FIGURE 4–6. Dr. Jan Gabriel Danielewicz at the International Congress in Venice.

the Children's Medical Center and had wards dedicated to the treatment of croup and operating rooms on the same floor as their offices. Dr. Ferguson was involved in many national meetings and societies, but he claimed that there was "very little interest in the formation of organizations devoted to Pediatric Otolaryngology."[12] Little did he know, but the persons he was training would be the ones to reap the benefits of his work. These young energetic physicians with a vision for the future would be the ones responsible for starting the organizations and training programs we have today in pediatric otolaryngology.

Born in 1912 in Chicago as one of triplet brothers, Seymore Cohen and his brothers attended the University of Chicago for undergraduate education. All three eventually entered medical school at the University of Illinois, Eli and Seymore immediately and Harold after obtaining his PhD. Seymore and Eli interned at Los Angeles County Hospital in 1942 until receiving orders for World War II. After choosing an otolaryngology residency program in Los Angeles over Chicago "because the weather was better," Seymore Cohen began training in otolaryngology on January 1, 1944. Because of the war, he was the only trainee for the entire first year; despite cross-coverage with the ophthalmology resident, he was still on call every night. He recounts many vivid stories from those years of training. Polio, tuberculosis, and diphtheria were rampant, and during this time critical care of the respiratory tract began. In one year alone he did over 700 tracheotomies, most at the bedside with only a gooseneck lamp for illumination. He attributes the skills he learned to being "trained by the masters." Howard House was on the medical staff, and not only was he an excellent otologist but, in speaking of his endoscopic skills, Dr. Cohen said, "He was a very, very good endoscopist . . . the man, no matter what he does, he's good!" After residency, Dr. Cohen entered practice with his mentor Victor Goodhill. In 1949, when Dr. Goodhill limited his practice to otology, Dr. Cohen opened his own practice. His keen interest in pediatric care was stimulated; he noted how so many children regressed developmentally after surgery and suffered from nightmares. He thought that every child should be prepared for surgery on a level that they could comprehend.

Borrowing a strainer from his kitchen at home, he began to show the children who came to his office how they would fall asleep using ether. He was also almost dismissed from the medical staff at many hospitals because he insisted that mothers stay with their children in the hospital postoperatively. He said, "The child's needs were not covered by the adult physician," and by 1954 he was seeing very few adults. Over the next few years he developed strong, long-distance consultative relationships with Sylvan Stool and Blair Fearon. These three pioneers shared their ideas not only on clinical care but on the development of the specialty. When recently commenting on the role of pediatric otolaryngology, Dr. Cohen remarked:

The pediatric otolaryngologist is not just a tonsil remover. He's not just a man who performs myringotomies; he should have a concept of the whole child and his problems. What you do to a child is with him for many, many years. That is the quality of a pediatric otolaryngologist—that he has the ability to choose the proper treatment because of his knowledge of what the disease entity will be in the future. We all make bad judgments, but the most expert people make the fewest. (Videotape interview with Seymore Cohen by K. Grundfast and S.E. Stool at the Broadmore Hotel, Colorado Springs, CO, 1989.)

After a 2-year rotating internship and residency in general practice, Sylvan Stool responded to an advertisement in the *Journal of the American Medical Association* and went to the Children's Orthopedic Hospital in Seattle to be a fellow in pediatric surgery. When it was not possible to get further training in surgery, he decided to go into pediatrics. After the Korean War, he received an appointment as an unpaid fellow in the outpatient department at the Children's Medical Center in Boston. In 1953, at the request of Charles Janeway, a professor of pediatrics, Dr. Stool covered the otolaryngology service for a resident who came down with hepatitis. This position allowed him to work closely with Drs. Ferguson and Flake and to stay in the house officers' quarters and eat two free meals a day. After leaving Boston, Dr. Stool went to Denver General Hospital and practiced pediatrics; in the outpatient department, he started an informal ENT clinic.

He realized that he needed further formal instruction. When Victor Hillyard was appointed to the University Hospital, Dr. Stool asked Dr. Hillyard about training. Dr. Hillyard immediately offered him a residency position because he had a conditional approval and no other candidates. Following his residency, in 1963, Dr. Stool received an inquiry from the Children's Hospital of Philadelphia to help establish a rehabilitation center with Mary Ames to serve children with multiple defects. Philadelphia presented a much different and difficult-to-understand atmosphere from that of the West. The Easterners seemed much more set in their ways and tended to be resistant to changing established medical fields. For instance, only the Jackson-trained bronchoesophagologists performed endoscopy. The concept of an age-related specialist in otolaryngology was difficult for the community to accept. After a few years, the training programs in the city recognized there were opportunities in pediatrics, and their residents requested rotations at the Children's

Hospital. Dr. Stool realized that unless pediatric otolaryngology achieved academic recognition and the ability to train fellows, it could never be established as a specialty. Because this recognition seemed impossible to achieve in Philadelphia, he accepted an offer from Eugene Myers and Charles Bluestone to join them in Pittsburgh in 1975. The hospital funded a fellow for 1 year, and in 1985 the National Institutes of Health made it possible to fund a fellow for the second year through a training grant.[12]

Having trained with Paul Holinger, Kenneth Johnston, and Richard Buckingham, among others, at the University of Illinois Research and Educational Hospital and the Illinois Eye and Ear Infirmary in Chicago, Charles Bluestone returned to his hometown of Pittsburgh in 1964 after 2 years with the United States Air Force. During his years as a private practitioner, he was Clinical Associate Professor of Otolaryngology at the University of Pittsburgh School of Medicine and Chief of the Otolaryngology Service at Children's Hospital of Pittsburgh. In 1972, Dr. Bluestone left private practice and moved to Boston, where he became the first full-time Director of the Otolaryngology Department at Boston City Hospital. In 1974, a somewhat reluctant Gerald B. Healy, who was much more interested in head and neck oncology than pediatric otolaryngology at this time, joined him. In 1975, Dr. Bluestone returned to his hometown, Pittsburgh, to become the first full-time Director of the Department of Pediatric Otolaryngology at Children's Hospital of Pittsburgh and Professor of Otolaryngology at the University of Pittsburgh School of Medicine (Charles D. Bluestone, personal communication, June 1999). The fellowship program begun by Drs. Bluestone and Stool in 1975 has trained over 50 pediatric otolaryngologists to date and has been funded by the National Institutes of Health since 1985; in 1997, the fellowship received approval by the Residency Review Committee. When reflecting on the opportunity to take over the clinical otolaryngology service at the Children's Hospital of Pittsburgh, Dr. Bluestone stated, "At that time, I did not even think of limiting my practice to children." A mentor from his residency had told him, "Don't do it Charley, a children's hospital is a dead end."[7] Fortunately for Dr. Bluestone and for all of us, this prophecy was incorrect; pediatric otolaryngology, children's hospitals, and those who work in them have continued to thrive.

After the departure of Dr. Bluestone, Gerald B. Healy became chief of otolaryngology at Boston City Hospital. In 1976, he moved across town to Boston Children's Hospital and in 1979 became Chief of Pediatric Otolaryngology at that institution. Because no formal otolaryngology service had existed for several years, tremendous work was done to update facilities and services. Modern concepts of pediatric otology, head and neck surgery, and bronchoesophagology were introduced, and for the first time laser surgery of the upper airway was performed in the pediatric population. After the otolaryngology service was moved to the main operating room, one of the first cases was the excision of a large lingual thyroid. If the general surgeons were shocked to learn that no blood transfusions had been arranged ahead of time, they were even more amazed when the procedure was completed via a transoral approach by CO_2 laser with virtually no

blood loss. Dr. Healy's efforts led to otolaryngology becoming one of the premiere services in the hospital, and with his strong research and clinical background, he soon became a dominant figure in the treatment of all types of head and neck disorders in children in Boston and the surrounding area. He has authored over 150 peer-reviewed publications, and he and his colleagues have trained over 30 pediatric otolaryngologists (Gerald B. Healy, personal communication, June 1999).

During the rapid rise in the incidence of neonatal subglottic stenosis of the late 1960s and early 1970s, Robin T. Cotton found himself as a resident under Dr. Blair Fearon at the University of Toronto. They noted that because of growth concerns, surgeons were generally reluctant to operate on the pediatric larynx and trachea. In 1972, with funding supplied by the Medical Research Council of Canada, Drs. Fearon and Cotton used infant monkeys to begin what would become a new era of pediatric airway reconstruction.

In 1971, Dr. Cotton arrived in Cincinnati to interview for a head and neck fellowship with Dr. Shumrick. Upon finishing the fellowship in 1973, Dr. Cotton convinced Dr. Shumrick to allow him to head the Otolaryngology Service at Children's Hospital Medical Center. He never left. Captivated by his basic science and early clinical work in Toronto, he became increasingly aware of the airway problems of infants who were graduating from the neonatal intensive care unit (Robin T. Cotton, personal communication, June 1999). In 1980, Dr. Cotton published his experience with the anterior cricoid split as an adjunct to aid extubation in premature neonates in whom multiple attempts had failed.[3] A year later, he published his 5-year experience with laryngotracheal reconstruction for subglottic stenosis.[2] In the years since, he has continued to refine his treatment of congenital and acquired upper-airway obstruction, and to date he has published more than 100 peer-reviewed publications on basic science research and clinical treatment. In addition, the fellowship program in pediatric otolaryngology that he and his colleagues started in 1977 has trained over 40 of this country's best pediatric airway surgeons.

Scientific and Technologic Advances

There is no questioning the influence of scientific and technological advances on the development and maturation of pediatric otolaryngology. Without antibiotics, vaccines, mechanical ventilators, the rod-lens telescope, computed tomography, and countless other therapies and devices, many of the children and disorders treated by pediatric otolaryngologists would not be around.

In Philadelphia, Jack Downs and others started a pediatric intensive care unit in a small ward adjacent to the operating rooms. This and similar units came into being in the early 1960s, when improved mechanical ventilation and monitoring equipment became available. Shortly thereafter, because no one specialty had all the necessary skills, team management and pediatric critical care medicine was born. In 1965, McDonald and Stocks published their article "Prolonged Nasotracheal Intubation," recommending intubation over tracheotomy for mechanical ventilation of neonates.[8] Because of their expertise in managing the airway, pediatric otolaryngologists became integral members of the critical care team as the incidence of subglottic stenosis continued to rise. The in-house presence of the pediatric otolaryngologist continued to grow throughout children's hospitals in this country.

Endoscopy of the upper aerodigestive tract in general has a long and complicated history. This development has been meticulously and eloquently recounted by Dr. Bernard Marsh of Baltimore in his Centennial Series Article for *Otolaryngology—Head and Neck Surgery* entitled "Historic Development of Bronchoesophagology."[7] No single development or technology has had greater impact on pediatric endoscopy than that of Harold H. Hopkins and Karl Storz in 1959 and 1960. Hopkins, a physicist-professor at the University of Reading in England, made and patented a unique rod-lens optical system. No one in England was interested, and Americans did not approve because it was invented elsewhere. Meanwhile, Storz, of Tuttlingen, Germany, realized that a fiberoptic viewing system he had seen at a congress in Holland in 1960 could also be used for the efficient transport of light to the distal end of a telescope. In 1965, after Hopkins presented his rod-lens optical system at a photographic exhibition in Köln, Germany, he was contacted by Storz, who recognized the potential of combining the two technologies: the rod-lens system for viewing and the fiberoptic light cable for illumination. Unlike previous systems, which used small lenses, the rod-lens system used a series of glass rods to provide better resolution, increased contrast, greater brightness, a wider viewing angle, and a smaller diameter; the fiberoptic light transmission provided for brighter and, more importantly, more reliable distal illumination. The new endoscopes were introduced into pediatric bronchoscopy in Germany in about 1968, and successful application to urology was reported in 1969.[6]

Dr. Stool first became aware of the instruments in 1972 when Dr. Koop, who was then Chief of Surgery at The Children's Hospital of Philadelphia, told Dr. Stool that he had ordered a set of the instruments. Dr. Koop had become aware of the instruments because of his involvement as the editor of *Pediatric Surgery*. The instruments arrived in Philadelphia with no instructions and many parts. With a little experimentation, they learned to assemble the instrument and thus embarked on a whole new era of pediatric endoscopy. Soon the development of teaching adapters turned the first assistant from a head-holder to an active assistant in the entire procedure. Subsequent development of endoscopic forceps revolutionized foreign-body removal and other therapeutic interventions. Cooler and brighter light sources led first to still photographic documentation and then to 16-mm motion pictures.[12] Today, video and digital image-capturing techniques are the standard and play a tremendous role in student and resident education. Many times I (GCA) have heard my coauthor (SES) remark, "The telescopes and cameras of today make endoscopy easy. Anybody can remove a foreign body and look like a technical master. You should have been around when we were changing that little bulb on the end of the Jackson bronchoscope three or four times during a case" as a prelude to another of his countless stories.

Institutions and Societies

Construction of institutions committed only to the treatment of children had a profound impact not only on pediatrics but on all pediatric subspecialties, including pediatric otolaryngology. Pediatrics was initially an age-related specialty of internal medicine. Institutions that had their beginnings as orphanages later became distinct medical facilities. The physicians treating children in these institutions soon began to attract private patients. Medical staff membership paid nothing, but it did provide a means to effectively study disease and bolster the physician's reputation in the community. One of the first institutions of this type in the United States was the Children's Hospital of Philadelphia, founded in 1855. Burton Alexander Randall documented the development of pediatric otolaryngology at this hospital in his personal memoirs.[13]

Ferguson and Flake had realized the need for organized societies devoted to pediatric otolaryngology, but because of their busy clinical practices they were unable to generate adequate interest. In 1965, a notice was posted at the American Academy of Pediatrics meeting in Las Vegas that invited all who were interested in pediatric otolaryngology to attend a cocktail party. About 20 physicians and audiologists responded, and this was followed by an interdisciplinary group, which met in the Atlanta airport in 1967. This group was then named the Society for Ear, Nose, and Throat Advances in Children (SENTAC). A constitution and bylaws were written, and Robert Ruben was elected as the first president. In 1977, a group of 20 physicians convened a study session in Pittsburgh. The outcome of this meeting was the formation of the Otolaryngology and Bronchoesophagologic Section of the American Academy of Pediatrics, and Dr. Bluestone was elected the first chairman (Fig. 4–7). Some members of the study group also felt the need for a group that not only confined their practices to infants and children but also had academic interests. The initial meeting of the American Society of Pediatric Otolaryngology (ASPO) was held in 1985 in Bermuda, and Dr. Seymore Cohen was elected the first president.[1]

Subsequently, ASPO has joined with other subspecialty societies to become part of the Combined Otolaryngology Spring Meeting (COSM). These societies have fostered research collaborations, promoted pediatric otolaryngology as a true subspecialty, and guided the training of future pediatric otolaryngologists.

In 1996, the Residency Review Committee of the American Council on Graduate Medical Education (ACGME) began reviewing fellowship programs that had applied for approval; at the time of this writing, four programs (Pittsburgh, Cincinnati, Iowa, and Baylor) have been approved. These four programs offer the only ACGME-approved residency training programs in pediatric otolaryngology, consisting of clinical and research experience of at least 2 years following general otolaryngology training. This ensures standards of knowledge, training, and experience among newly trained pediatric otolaryngologists.

The history of pediatric otolaryngology is inseparable from the history of medicine in general. Advancing medi-

FIGURE 4–7. Initial 1977 meeting of 20 pediatric otolaryngologists in Pittsburgh. The outcome of this meeting was the formation of the Otolaryngology and Bronchoesophagologic Section of the American Academy of Pediatrics.

cal technology and improved childhood survival inspired pioneering physicians with a vision for the future to branch out and develop the specialty of pediatric otolaryngology. Institutions and organizations committed to research, uncompromised clinical care, and training have provided a firm foundation for the future growth and development of the specialty.

ACKNOWLEDGMENTS

We would like to thank Charles D. Bluestone, MD, Gerald B. Healy, MD, Robin T. Cotton, MD, Seymore Cohen, MD, Professor Mieczyslaw Chmielik, and Dr. and Mrs. Pawel Danielewicz for their personal comments that made the preparation of this manuscript possible.

REFERENCES

1. Bluestone CD. Pediatric Otolaryngology: past, present, future. Arch Otolarygol Head Neck Surg 121:505, 1995.
2. Cotton RT, Evans IN. Laryngotracheal reconstruction in children: five-year follow-up. Ann Otol Rhinol Laryngol 90:516, 1981.
3. Cotton RT, Seid AB. Management of the extubation problem in the premature child. Anterior cricoid split as an alternative to tracheotomy. Ann Otol Rhinol Laryngol 89:508, 1980.
4. Eisner J. Diphtheria. Denver Medical Times 6:65, 1886.
5. Koop CE. Pediatric surgery: the long road to recognition. Pediatrics 92:618, 1993.
6. Linder TE, Simmen D, Stool SE. Revolutionary inventions in the 20th century. The history of endoscopy. Arch Otolaryngol Head Neck Surg 123:1161, 1997.
7. Marsh BR. Historic development of bronchoesophagology. Otolaryngol Head Neck Surg 114:689, 1996.
8. McDonald LH, Stocks JG. Prolonged nasotracheal intubation. Br J Anaesth 37:161, 1965.
9. O'Dwyer JP. Two cases of croup treated by tubage of the glottis. N Y Med J 42:145, 1885.
10. Shikes RH. Rocky Mountain Medicine: Doctors, Drugs, and Disease in Early Colorado. Boulder, Colorado, Johnson Publishing Company, 1986.
11. Stool SE. A brief history of pediatric otolaryngology. Otolaryngol Head Neck Surg 115:278, 1996.
12. Stool SE. Evolution of pediatric otolaryngology. Pediatr Clin North Am 36:1363, 1989.
13. Stool SE, Kemper M, Kemper B. The compleat otolaryngologist: Burton Alexander Randall. Laryngoscope 94:16, 1984.
14. Waxham FE. Report of five hundred cases of intubation of the larynx. Trans Colorado State Med Soc 26:105, 1894.

5

Molecular Biology in Pediatric Otolaryngology

J. Christopher Post, M.D., Ph.D.

We practice medicine in the age of information. The collection, processing, storage, and dissemination of information have revolutionized our society. This revolution has been extended to the realm of biology and medicine by molecular biology. Molecular biology is the study of the flow of information through the cell. This information determines the destiny of the cell and controls the cell's activities. Distortion of the information leads to the dysfunction or death of the cell. All of this information is stored in the DNA, where it must be packaged not only for easy accessibility but to fit in a small space. Almost every cell in the body contains all of the information necessary to make any other cell. Thus, the control of information expression, both temporally and spatially, is of extreme importance.

The sequencing of the human genome was one of the seminal advances in science and has given researchers a blueprint for mankind. We are now in a postgenomic era, where the task is now to understand the normal and abnormal function of each gene in the cell. One of the surprises of the Human Genome Project is that the number of human genes, originally thought to number 100,000, is now thought to be around 30,000. It has become clear that human proteins come in multiple variant forms, which is due to alternative splicing of the mRNA. The recognition of this variation has led to the study of the complete protein set of organisms, or proteomics.

Health care practitioners caring for children with otolaryngologic problems must deal with infections, cancer, inherited hearing loss, and congenital malformations. The diagnosis and treatment of these diseases are in the process of being changed by advances made in molecular biology. Molecular-based diagnostic and therapeutic advances are becoming part of the armamentarium of the pediatric otolaryngologic caregiver. To provide the best possible care for our patients, it is incumbent on us to have a familiarity with the concepts underlying these advances. We must become as adept at genetic counseling as we are at surgery. However, the speed of the advances in the field and the proliferation of specialized terminology make it difficult for the practitioner to obtain this familiarity (see Table 5–1 and Glossary).

This chapter begins by covering the underlying concepts of molecular biology and reviews the tenets of classical genetics. As most of the advances in molecular biology have been technique driven, current molecular techniques are briefly described. The molecular aspects of specific areas of interest to practitioners in the field of pediatric otolaryngology are then covered, including hearing and speech, congenital syndromes, infectious disease, cancer, and physiology. The principles of gene therapy are delineated, and the ethical challenges and the issues of counseling and patient management presented by molecular advances are discussed. Definitions of terms used in molecular biology are found at the end of the chapter. The reader desiring a more in-depth treatment of the basic concepts of molecular biology and genetics is referred to several excellent texts listed in the Selected References at the end of the chapter.

An Introduction to Molecular Biology

We wish to suggest a structure for the salt of deoxyribose nucleic acid (D.N.A.). This structure has novel features which are of considerable biological interest.[86]

Thus began probably the most famous paper in the field of molecular biology. Since the seminal paper by Watson and Crick proposing a structure for DNA, tremendous advances have been made in our understanding of life's most important molecule. DNA is a high-molecular-weight polymer that exists as two single strands wound together in a double helix. Each strand consists of a linear array of four different nucleotides. Each nucleotide is made up of three components: a five-carbon sugar (deoxyribose), a phosphate group, and a base. The nucleotides, adenine (A), guanine (G), thymine (T), and cytosine (C), are covalently linked. The two strands are held together with hydrogen bonds, such that A binds with T, and C binds with G. Because of this specificity in base pairing, when the nucleotide sequence of one strand is known, the nucleotide sequence of the second strand may be deduced. The two strands are thus referred to as complementary. When the two strands separate, each strand can act as a template to form two new daughter DNA molecules. Enzymes that link the nucleotides together to form a strand are called polymerases, because of the polymeric nature of the resulting molecule.

The majority of DNA is contained in the nucleus, while protein synthesis occurs in the cytoplasm on small

TABLE 5–1. Timeline of Genetic Discoveries

1900 Drosophila used in early gene studies
1953 Watson and Crick determine the structure of DNA
1975 Southern blotting developed (DNA)
1977 Northern blotting developed (RNA)
1981 Western blotting developed (protein)
1985 Cloning of ancient Egyptian mummy DNA
1986 PCR developed
1989 Identification of the cystic fibrosis gene, the first gene isolated strictly by positional cloning
1990 First gene therapy
1990 Herman, the first transgenic bull, has a gene for human lactoferrin
1990 Human Genome Project launched
1991 First transgenic dairy cows
1991 DNA testing of tissue from Abraham Lincoln
1992 Discovery of the gene for Waardenburg syndrome type 1
1992 Mapping of DFNA1
1994 Mapping of DFNB1
1997 Discovery of gene mutated in DFNA1
1997 Dolly the sheep, first mammal cloned from adult cells
1997 Discovery of connexin 26
1998 Sequencing the entire genome of a multicellular organism, the nematode worm *Caenorhabditis elegans*
1999 First reported death of a gene therapy patient
1999 Thomas Jefferson paternity case
2000 Tetra, the first cloned monkey
2000 Sequencing the entire genome of *Drosophila melanogaster*
2000 Discovery of the first dominant modifier gene, DFNM1
2000 Sequencing the human genome
2001 ANDi, the first genetically modified nonhuman primate.

organelles called ribosomes; thus, the information coded for in the DNA sequences of nucleotides has to be transferred to the ribosomes. This information is transmitted in the form of mRNA (messenger ribonucleic acid). This is the central dogma of molecular biology, that information flows from DNA to RNA to proteins. RNA differs from DNA in several respects. The sugar in the RNA nucleotide is ribose instead of deoxyribose. RNA is single stranded and contains a unique base, uracil (U), instead of thymine. Like thymine, uracil specifically forms base pairs with adenine. Enzymes that make RNA are called RNA polymerases and also require DNA templates.

A gene is a segment of DNA that encodes for a specific mRNA. Human genes can range in length from several hundred base pairs to several million. In a process known as transcription, mRNA is made from the DNA. The two strands of DNA separate, and one strand acts as a template for the synthesis of a complementary RNA molecule, a primary gene transcript. By convention, the transcribed DNA strand is known as the "antisense" strand. Because the mRNA transcribed is complementary to the antisense strand, the mRNA has the same nucleotide sequence as the "sense" DNA strand. Genes represent approximately 10% of human DNA. The other 90% of DNA does not encode for proteins and does not have an apparent function. This has led to the labeling of this DNA as "junk" DNA. However, this DNA may help maintain the structure of chromosomes and control the function of genes.

As noted previously, each cell contains all of the DNA necessary to encode the entire organism. However, only a small fraction of genes are used to make any given cell, whether it is a hair cell in the cochlea or a mucosal cell.

Additionally, differing sets of genes are used in a developing cell as compared to a mature cell. Thus, exquisite control of transcription is maintained, both temporally and spatially, by regulatory sequences that surround the coding region. There are many different types of regulatory sequences. Promoter sequences initiate transcription by signaling the RNA polymerase. These promoters can be regulated, in turn, by cofactors. Enhancing sequences control transcription by controlling the condensation of the chromatin, which is the DNA and its associated proteins. Opening up the chromatin can expose DNA sequences for transcription, while closing it can make the DNA unavailable for transcription.

After the RNA is transcribed, it is modified by a process known as splicing. Portions of the RNA sequences are cut out and discarded; these are known as intervening sequences, or introns. The remaining sequences of the RNA are known as exons. These exons are spliced together to form the mature mRNA molecule. Splicing is another way of regulating the flow of information through the cell, in that the primary transcription product of one gene can be spliced together in different ways to form differing mRNAs and, thus, different proteins.

The informational content of the RNA is specified by the nucleotide sequence. The information is coded in three-nucleotide-long sequences called codons. These codons encode for the amino acid sequences that make up specific polypeptides and proteins. Other codons specify chain termination (stop codons). The order of the three nucleotides is of critical importance. Since each of the three positions can have one of four combinations (A, U, C, or G), there are $4 \times 4 \times 4 = 64$ possible codons. Sixty-one of the codons code for amino acids, and three codons (UAA, UAG, UGA) are stop codons. As there are only 20 proteins coded for, it can be seen that the genetic code is redundant, i.e., several different codons can code for one amino acid. Thus, for example, the amino acid valine can be coded for by GUU, GUC, GUA, or GUG. The mRNA goes through the nuclear membrane to the ribosomes, the location of protein synthesis. The process of making a specific polypeptide chain from a molecule of mRNA is known as translation, the translation of the nucleic code into the protein code.

The DNA in one human cell is approximately 1 meter long and contains approximately 3 billion base pairs. The packaging arrangements to fit this length of DNA into a cell that is 10^{-5} m in diameter while still allowing access for transcription and replication are extraordinary. DNA is wrapped around a group of proteins called histones, much like thread is wrapped around a spool. This combination of DNA and histones is called a nucleosome. Nucleosomes wrap into higher order structures, which form a chromosome. Each chromosome consists of a single piece of double-stranded DNA and contains 50 million to 400 million base pairs of DNA. Chromosomes are of different sizes and have characteristic shapes and staining patterns (the karyotype) that can best be recognized during the metaphase of the cell cycle.

Humans have 22 matching (homologous) pairs of chromosomes and 2 sex chromosomes, for a total of 46 chromosomes. The 22 matching pairs are known as autosomes; one member of each pair is inherited from the mother, and the other member is inherited from the father. Genes come in pairs; thus, one copy is maternally inherited and the other copy is paternally inherited. One sex chromosome is inherited from the mother and is always an X chromosome; the other sex chromosome is inherited from the father and can be either an X or a Y. A female has two X chromosomes, and a male has one X chromosome and one Y chromosome.

Autosomal dominant (AD) diseases are those that are caused by a single copy of a mutant gene. Autosomal dominant inheritance is characterized by a vertical mode of inheritance, i.e., there are multiple, consecutive generations with affected members. A child of an affected parent has a 50% chance of being affected. Males and females are affected in equal proportions. Crouzon syndrome is an example of an autosomal dominant inherited disease.

If two copies of a mutant gene are required to manifest the disease, the disease is said to be autosomal recessive (AR). Autosomal recessive inheritance is characterized by a horizontal mode of inheritance, i.e,. most generations in a pedigree do not have affected members. A person carrying one copy of the mutated gene is phenotypically normal and is termed a carrier. For a child to be affected, both parents must be carriers, with each child having a 25% chance of being affected. Males and females are affected in equal proportions. Cystic fibrosis is an example of an autosomal recessive inherited disease.

Disease-causing genes on the X chromosome most commonly affect males, as males possess a single X chromosome and are phenotypically affected with any mutation. Each son of a carrier mother has a 50% chance of being affected, and each daughter of a carrier mother has a 50% chance of being a carrier. Pedigrees are characterized by the lack of male-to-male transmission, as a father can pass only a Y chromosome to his son.

Molecular Techniques

The Polymerase Chain Reaction

The polymerase chain reaction (PCR) is an extraordinarily sensitive and specific primer-dependent enzymatic DNA amplification method.[64] The power of the PCR lies in its ability to make, in just a few hours, a billion exact copies of a specific DNA segment. This is obviously of great practical use, for as one or two copies of DNA are difficult to work with and detect, a billion copies are much easier. This automated process can produce in a few hours what previously required months or years of painstaking labor. The DNA region of interest is known as the target DNA, which can be a specific region of DNA from any species. The DNA does not have to be purified before it is amplified; thus, the PCR has a great advantage over protein-based analysis systems. DNA is a stable molecule and can be amplified from pathologic specimens or from archival (e.g., temporal bones; see later) or paleontologic specimens. The PCR has found application not only in the fields of molecular genetics and infectious diseases but also in areas such as forensics and anthropology as well.

PCR requires the use of primers, which are short sequences of DNA that flank the target area, and a thermostabile DNA polymerase that was originally isolated from *Thermus aquaticus*, a bacterium that thrives in hot springs in Yellowstone National Park. This polymerase, known as *Taq*, is remarkable in that it is stable at temperatures that ordinarily denature proteins. In an automated machine called a thermocycler, the primers, *Taq* polymerase, and target DNA combine to produce an exponential increase of target DNA molecules.

The amplified DNA target can then be detected in a number of ways, including staining with ethidium bromide, hybridization with a radioactive-labeled oligonucleotide probe, or by fluorescent-labeled tags. RNA can also be amplified by first converting the RNA to DNA by use of an enzyme known as reverse transcriptase. This process is known as reverse-transcriptase PCR (RT-PCR). The DNA generated is then used as the target for PCR. RT-PCR is used to detect the presence of RNA viruses or mRNA.

Gene Mapping

Why is it important to map and find genes? Finding the gene responsible for a particular disease can lead to a better understanding of the pathophysiologic mechanism of the disorder. Elucidation of the molecular disorder underlying a particular illness is a powerful approach to further our understanding of disease. In addition, carrier detection and prenatal diagnosis become possible. Finally, gene therapy, which requires an exact knowledge of the gene and its function, is becoming a component of the clinician's armamentarium.

A gene associated with a specific phenotype can be found by several approaches. One approach is to recognize the underlying protein defect of a specific disease and then to find the gene that encodes for that protein. This approach, known as functional cloning, has several limitations: the protein defect must be known; the protein must be available in sufficient quantities; and the protein must be able to be purified to ensure that the amino acid sequence generated is the desired sequence. These conditions limit the widespread applicability of functional cloning.

Another approach is positional cloning, or mapping. In this approach, a gene can be isolated without any specific knowledge of the gene's protein product or the specific pathophysiologic defect of the disease. The majority of genes are now mapped by positional cloning. Mapping a gene is entirely dependent on the careful ascertainment of affected families or individuals and offers a rich opportunity for effective collaboration between clinicians and laboratory scientists. The mapping of many genes important to pediatric otolaryngology, including those for Waardenburg and Crouzon syndromes and for pediatric gastroesophageal reflux, and of the majority of non-syndromic deafness genes, began with the observations of astute clinicians.[27, 28, 36, 58]

Positional cloning is also dependent upon the availability of suitable genetic markers and genetic maps. Markers are specific points whose location in the genome is known, analogous to milepost signs along an interstate highway. Maps depict the order in which genes and genetic markers appear along a chromosome. There are several different types of maps. Physical maps determine the actual distances between genes on a chromosome; genetic linkage maps are based on the frequency with which genetic markers are coinherited. The Human Genome Project has greatly increased the number of markers available and provided exquisitely detailed maps of the human genome.

Mapping a gene is analogous to looking for an individual somewhere in the world. The first step is to determine in what country (chromosome) the person is located. The next is to determine the state or province (chromosomal region). These steps are performed by using linkage analysis, which compares, down through the generations, the inheritance of the desired gene with the inheritance of DNA markers of known chromosomal location. If a specific marker and the disease gene are on separate chromosomes, they assort randomly during meiosis and are not inherited together. If a specific marker and the gene of interest are present on the same chromosome, they are inherited together throughout the generations unless recombination occurs. Recombination is the process whereby portions of homologous chromosomes break off and recombine with each other, resulting in the exchange of genetic material. The closer together the marker and the disease gene are on the chromosome, the less likely it is that recombination will occur. The frequency of recombination can be measured, and the genetic distance between the marker and the disease locus is calculated. In a manner analogous to the statistical analysis of data using p values, the chance of a particular marker being inherited with the trait of interest is evaluated by a statistical technique known as a LOD (for logarithm of the odds) score. LOD scores greater than 3 are generally accepted as evidence that the gene and marker are co-inherited.

Many different types of markers have been used in mapping strategies, but the ones commonly used now are microsatellites, which are repetitive DNA elements interspersed throughout the human genome, and single nucleotide polymorphisms (SNPs, pronounced "snips"). SNPs are single base changes interspersed throughout the genome, generally without any functional significance. Use of these markers means that the area of interest can be narrowed from the 3 billion base pairs of the human genome to a few million base pairs, i.e., our search for a person has been narrowed down to one city.

Gene Identification

Once the specific chromosomal location of a gene has been determined, various techniques can be used to further narrow the region of interest, identify the actual gene of interest, and determine the mutations that cause disease (finding the person). Fine-structure genetic mapping, chromosome "walking" and "jumping," and exon-trapping are all techniques that can further define the

region that contains the gene. Known genes that are in the area of interest can be examined for mutations (the "candidate gene" approach). The DNA between two flanking markers can be cloned and analyzed for expressed sequences in that region. Searching electronic databases for information (research performed *in silico*, also known as data mining) to find genes in the chromosomal region of interest has become an increasingly important tool.

A powerful technique for identifying genes of interest is constructing a pull-down library. In this approach, genes that are expressed in the tissue of interest (e.g., the cochlea for deafness genes) are hybridized to DNA sequences in the chromosomal region of interest identified through positional cloning. Genes thus identified become very likely candidates for actually being the desired gene. ESTs are expressed sequence tags or complementary DNAs (cDNAs) that are made from mRNA being expressed in a tissue of interest, such as the cochlea.[68] Hybridizing ESTs to DNA from the region of interest is a method to quickly identify candidate genes.

Functional Genomics

Advances in gene technology have allowed the investigation of the entire panoply of genes that are expressed under a given physiologic condition (the expressome). The identification of this set of genes provides powerful insight into development, differentiation, regeneration, and plasticity, and it reveals gene regulation events involved in disease progression and also identifies potential targets for therapeutics. This work is the province of functional genomics. Several techniques exist to identify whole groups of genes simultaneously, including differential display and microarrays. Differential display is a PCR-based approach that compares the expression of genes under two separate physiologic conditions. Using differential display to examine gene expression on the chick basilar papilla before and after noise trauma, genes that are induced by noise can be identified and their role in the cascade of events following noise trauma determined.[41a]

Microarrays are one of the latest breakthroughs in molecular genetics and allow the monitoring of the expression of thousands of genes simultaneously. While the technology has been variously described as DNA chip, DNA microarray, gene chip, and biochip, the basic concept is that an array is an orderly arrangement of samples that provides a method for matching known and unknown nucleic acid samples with each other based on the base-pairing rules described above. To make an array, short lengths of DNA from known and unknown genes are immobilized on a glass or nylon substrate. This "spotting" of oligonucleotides is generally done under robotic control, and the precise location of each sequence is known. Arrays can be made from oligonucleotides from specific organs (e.g., the cochlea) or from a specific chromosome. The immobilized array is exposed to samples of DNA or RNA, complementary sequences hybridize to each other, and fluorescent or other detection technologies are used to detect this hybridization. Literally thousands of reactions can occur simultaneously. One of the main challenges of this technology is the data analysis, which generally requires advanced bioinformatics systems.

Polygenic Diseases

While many human diseases result from mutations in a single gene, other diseases, such as otitis media (vide infra), hypertension, and obesity, result from the interaction of multiple genes together with environmental factors. In these diseases, several genes can contribute in an incremental fashion toward the development of overt disease. Additionally, the identification of large, extended pedigrees is problematic. Traditional mapping strategies cannot readily be applied to find these genes, so other techniques are being developed to identify these quantitative (polygenic) trait loci. These approaches involve the use of affected and unaffected sibling pairs, microarray technology, mapping with SNPs, and advanced computational techniques.

These diseases affect large numbers of patients and thus are attractive targets for pharmaceutical companies to develop therapies. Information obtained from gene discovery is being used to identify potential new drug targets in a process known as pharmacogenetics. Current pharmaceutical research focuses on identifying metabolic pathways associated with disease and developing pharmaceutical agents to manipulate these pathways. Results can often be disappointing because metabolic pathways are complex. Identifying the gene or genes responsible for the disease and developing strategies to correct that defect offer the potential for a whole array of new therapies.

Discovering genes can lead to many benefits: diagnostics; replacement of defective genes by use of different vectors; development of therapeutic antisense oligonucleotides; recombinant DNA production of therapeutic proteins; and assay systems to discover new molecules with pharmaceutical potential. While funding for the initial discoveries of the molecular revolution came from the National Institutes of Health, other government organizations, and philanthropic foundations, the application of this technology to medicine is becoming more and more the province of the biotechnology industry.

Recombinant DNA Technology

Several systems have been developed to manipulate and clone (copy) specific DNA sequences of interest. These systems are the basis of recombinant DNA technology, which is the combining of DNA derived from several different sources. Plasmids are small, autonomously replicating, bacterial DNA molecules. DNA sequences of interest (generally less than 10 kilobases) can be inserted into plasmids, which are then introduced into a suitable colony of bacteria. The bacteria are grown and the plasmids replicate, generating many copies of the DNA fragment of interest. To isolate the colonies of bacteria that have successfully incorporated the plasmids, the DNA sequence of interest is generally linked to another gene that confers antibiotic resistance. When the bacteria are grown

in the presence of the antibiotic, only those bacteria that carry plasmids that have successfully integrated the sequence of interest will grow. Conversely, the integrated DNA can be inserted into the gene that codes for beta-galactosidase, and the colonies of bacteria are screened by a color assay. Cosmids are plasmid vectors that can carry up to 45 kilobases of DNA. Yeast artificial chromosomes (YACs) are another way of handling large pieces of DNA. Yeast can carry up to a million base pairs (one megabase) of foreign DNA without disruption to their own operations and readily make multiple copies of introduced DNA.

Libraries of human chromosomes can be generated by cutting human chromosomes into pieces and splicing them into the various vectors. These libraries consist of all the different clones of the genome. Probes, which are specific, labeled strands of DNA that can complementarily bind to the DNA region of interest, can be used to determine the location of the specific sequence of interest. These probes allow a library to be screened for the specific clone among all the other clones. A contig map consists of a set of overlapping segments of DNA that completely cover the region of interest.

Fluorescence In Situ Hybridization

Fluorescence in situ hybridization (FISH) is a molecularly based cytogenetic technique to visualize unique DNA sequences, chromosomal rearrangements or deletions, or entire chromosomes. This is accomplished by hybridizing fluorescent-labeled probes to the DNA of interest. FISH has been successfully used to diagnose syndromes such as Prader-Willi syndrome and Angelman syndrome and can detect chromosomal deletions associated with disease.

Transgenic Mice

To study genes at the level of the whole organism, a gene can be inserted into the developing organism by microinjection or retrovirus vectors. The foreign DNA is incorporated into the germline of the embryo and is inherited as a mendelian trait in subsequent generations. Thus, the phenotypic effects of the gene can be studied for several generations. This introduced gene is known as a trans gene; thus, the resulting organism is a transgenic organism. YACs can be used to insert not only the gene of interest but also the promoters and other DNA sequences that regulate the gene's expression. Transgenic mice provide model systems for study of gene regulation and gene expression and have provided important information in the study of human genetic disease, particularly in the study of genes associated with deafness.

Hereditary Deafness

The progress that has been made in determining the molecular basis of hereditary deafness has been extraordinary. A determined effort by a group of talented investigators to understand the causes of deafness has begun to identify the large number of genes that are involved in hearing, which, when mutated, cause deafness.[91] These initial findings have already caused a rethinking of certain aspects of cochlear pathology.[71] Progress in this field is extremely rapid. An excellent source of up-to-date information is the Hereditary Hearing Loss homepage (http://www.uia.ac.be/dnalab/hhh) maintained by Drs. Guy van Camp and Richard Smith.

Syndromic deafness is defined as deafness that appears in association with other recognizable signs that together form a syndrome, e.g., Waardenburg syndrome, which is characterized by sensorineural hearing loss, heterochromia iridis, dystopia canthorum, and pigmentary abnormalities. Thus, patients with syndromic deafness are easier to categorize in the sense that the other clinical features provide guidance in assigning the patient a particular diagnosis. Approximately 70% of hereditary deafness is nonsyndromic, such that deafness is present without any other clinical abnormality. Patients with nonsyndromic deafness are much more difficult to classify, as there is no current method to separate those individuals who are phenotypically similar (i.e., deaf) and genetically different. Approximately 70% to 85% of nonsyndromic deafness is inherited in an autosomal recessive fashion; therefore, relatively few individuals in a given family will be affected by deafness. Autosomal recessive nonsyndromic deafness genes have mostly been localized using single consanguineous families.[92] Other challenges to mapping recessive genes include the fact that deaf individuals generally preferentially marry other deaf individuals; thus, a given pedigree may have a high degree of genetic heterogeneity. Finally, deafness resulting from environmental conditions or infections may be impossible to distinguish from deafness of genetic etiology.

Autosomal Dominant Hereditary Hearing Loss

Over 20 autosomal dominant loci have been mapped, and 10 of these genes have been cloned. These genes encode for transcription factors, extracellular matrix components, ion channels, cytoskeletal components, and unknown functions. Most of the hearing loss associated with dominantly inherited genes is a postlingual hearing loss that is progressive in nature.[78] As the genes associated with dominant hearing loss have been mapped, they have been assigned numbers. Thus, DFNA1 denotes a deafness gene (DFN) that is dominant (A) and was the first one to be mapped.

Autosomal Recessive Hereditary Hearing Loss

At least 30 genes for nonsyndromic autosomal recessive hereditary hearing loss have been localized, and at least 6 genes have been cloned. The genes encode a variety of proteins, including ion channels, extracellular matrix components, cytoskeletal components, proteases, and synaptic vesicular trafficking.[73] A surprising discovery has been that mutations in one gene, GJB2, accounts for up to 50% of autosomal recessive hearing impairment[52] (see later). Most of these genes cause hearing loss that is nonprogressive, severe to profound, and prelingual. Autosomal recessive genes are also identified according to the sequence of mapping; thus, DFNB1 is a deafness gene

(DFN) that is recessive (B) and was the first deafness recessive gene to be mapped. A modifier gene, DFNM1, has been mapped that suppresses deafness in some individuals with DFNB26.[61]

Molecular Analysis of Temporal Bone Specimens

Archived temporal bones have proved a rich resource for molecular analysis. With the discovery that DNA could be amplified from preserved temporal bones,[80] the molecular pathology of many auditory, vestibular, and facial nerve disorders has been explored. A variety of disease processes have been investigated by DNA amplification from temporal bone specimens. Since Bell palsy, vestibular neuritis, and sudden hearing loss are thought to be due to viral reactivation in temporal ganglia, temporal bones have been examined for the presence of herpes simplex type 1 with the finding that in all temporal bones examined, HSV-1–specific DNA was detected.[5, 66] However, yields were lower from suboptimally stored specimens,[6] suggesting that preservation techniques that optimize nucleic acid recovery should be standardized in temporal bone banks if the maximal amount of information is to be gleaned. Temporal bones from patients with Ramsay Hunt syndrome supported amplification of varicella-zoster viral DNA from the geniculate ganglion of two patients with facial paralysis and cutaneous manifestations, and from the inner ear of a patient with sudden hearing loss. No varicella DNA was identified in temporal bone specimens from five patients with Bell palsy and 10 patients without otologic disease.[81]

DNA amplification has revealed the presence of measles virus in temporal bones from patients with otosclerosis[47] and demonstrated that temporal bones from patients with presbycusis have a higher percentage of mitochondrial DNA mutations associated with aging than do controls.[1, 20] RNA can also be recovered from archived celloidin-embedded temporal bones, a development that will expand the usefulness of this technique.[51]

Connexin 26

GJB2 encodes a gap junction protein, connexin 26 (Cx26). Connexins join together in groups of six to form connexons. Connexons from adjoining cells align in the extracellular space to form a channel that connects the intracellular space. These intracellular gap junctions are needed for potassium circulation between the cells, which is important during sound transduction. The most common connexin mutation is a deletion of a guanine within the stretch of six guanines between nucleotide position 30 and 35 of the cDNA (known either as 30delG or 35delG) that results in a frameshift and a premature stop codon. This mutation can readily be detected in a reliable and inexpensive fashion.[7]

Temporal bone analysis of a patient with congenital severe-to-profound deafness and a Cx26 mutation revealed no neural degeneration, a good population of spiral ganglion cells, near total degeneration of hair cells, a detached and rolled-up tectorial membrane, agenesis of the stria vascularis, and a cyst in the scala media. The preservation of the spiral ganglion neurons suggests that cochlear implantation would be very successful in patients with Cx26 mutations.[30] This does indeed appear to be the case, in that children with Cx26 deafness who receive early cochlear implantation develop excellent language skills, markedly better than unimplanted children and implanted children with other types of deafness.[23]

Usher Syndrome

Usher syndrome (US) is the most common cause of deafness and blindness and is the cause of 50% of the cases of combined deafness and blindness in the United States. US, an autosomal recessive disorder characterized by deafness and retinitis pigmentosa, is divided into three types. Patients with US type 1 lack vestibular function, are profoundly deaf, and have retinal degeneration beginning in childhood. Type 2 patients have normal vestibular function, a lesser degree of hearing loss, and later onset of retinal degeneration. Type 3 patients have progressive hearing loss and a variable age of onset of retinal degeneration. US is an example of a heterogeneous disorder, as at least 10 distinct genetic loci are associated with the three clinical types.

Several genes that cause Usher syndrome have been identified. *MYO7A* encodes for myosin VIIa, a member of the myosin motor proteins that move on actin filaments in the cytoplasm, and mutations in *MYO7A* can cause USH type 1, USH type 3, and surprisingly, recessive (*DFNB2*) and dominant (*DFNA11*) nonsyndromic hearing loss.[33] *Usherin* is the gene responsible for US type 2A. This gene encodes a protein that may be involved in the basal lamina, extracellular matrix, or in cell-cell adhesion.[89] US type 1C is caused by mutations in harmonin, a protein expressed in hair cells.[79] US type 1D and *DFNB12* are caused by mutations in a cadherin-like gene, *CDH23*.[3] Other myosin-encoding genes, *VI* and *XV*, are associated with hearing loss in the mouse mutant Snell's waltzer, and *DFNB3*, respectively.[21] A non-muscle myosin heavy chain gene, *MYH9*, is mutated in *DFNA17*.[38]

Waardenburg Syndrome

Waardenburg syndrome (WS) is an example of an auditory-pigmentary syndrome, which is caused by the absence of melanocytes from the skin, hair, eyes, and the stria vascularis of the cochlea. WS is an autosomal dominant disorder characterized by sensorineural hearing loss and pigmentary abnormalities, including heterochromia iridis, and it represents one of the most common forms of hereditary deafness. The spectrum of WS has expanded and the division WS into various types has been somewhat controversial. Type I is associated with dystopia canthorum (widely spaced medial canthi), whereas patients with type II have normally spaced canthi. WS type III is similar to type I but is also characterized by musculoskeletal abnormalities. WS type IV is also known as Shah-Waardenburg syndrome with Hirschsprung disease.

The various forms of WS result from the abnormal development of structures derived from the embryonic neural crest, a process that is controlled by a variety of genes. Type I and type III result from loss-of-function mutations in a gene known as *PAX3*, which is a DNA-binding protein expressed during development that regulates the expression of other genes.[26, 75] Type II is associated with mutations in microphthalmia associated transcription factor (*MITF*) gene, and type IV can be caused by mutations in the genes for *SOX10*, a transcription factor.[40] The various types of WS are interrelated, as *MITF* is regulated by *SOX10* and *PAX3*.[57]

Waardenburg syndrome is a good example of a disease with little or no genotype-phenotype correlation in terms of hearing loss. This means that a certain gene mutation does not result in a certain phenotype, even within families. Thus, even when a mutation is detected, it is impossible to predict the ultimate phenotype (i.e., how hearing-impaired the patient will be), although there is a suggestion that some *PAX3* mutations are more closely associated with pigmentary changes.[12] A lack of genotype-phenotype correlation makes the task of genetic counseling more difficult and also suggests that there are other genes or nongenetic factors that are responsible for the ultimate phenotype.

Pendred Syndrome

Pendred syndrome is characterized by sensorineural hearing loss and hypothyroidism and may account for up to 7.5% of all childhood deafness. After the mapping of Pendred syndrome to chromosome 7q22-31.1, the causative gene, *PDS*, was identified.[19] *PDS* encodes a transmembrane protein known as pendrin, which functions as a transporter of chloride and iodide.[67]

Mitochondrial Deafness

Mitochondria are cell organelles involved in energy production and are believed to have originally been bacteria-like organisms that developed a symbiotic relationship with eukaryotic cells. While most of the DNA in a cell is in the nucleus (nDNA), the mitochondria contain DNA (mtDNA) that has several interesting characteristics. The mtDNA is a circular, double-stranded molecule within the mitochondrial matrix that contains 16,569 base pairs. This DNA encodes for some of the proteins involved in oxidative phosphorylation and for some mitochondrial tRNA. Because sperm carry few mitochondria, mtDNA is almost completely inherited maternally. Therefore, characteristics or diseases that result from mutations in the mtDNA are transmitted maternally. The mtDNA genes also mutate at a much higher rate than nDNA genes. These two characteristics combine to make mtDNA important in studies that examine human migration patterns, such as the spread of American Indians across the Bering Strait, through North America, and into South America.

Each cell can contain thousands of copies of mtDNA, both normal and mutant genomes. This condition is known as heteroplasmia. The mitochondria are randomly distributed with mitosis or meiosis; thus, the proportion of normal or mutant mtDNAs can drift toward a predominance of one or another (homoplasmia). The clinical expression of disease can depend on the ratio of normal to abnormal mitochondria present in each cell (a threshold phenomenon). Mitochondrially inherited diseases generally include neurologic and muscular abnormalities, although hearing impairment can also be seen. Mitochondrial diseases could well lend themselves to gene therapy.[13]

Families have been described in China and Japan that maternally inherit a susceptibility to aminoglycoside-induced hearing loss. Deafness develops in members of these families after a much shorter duration of exposure to aminoglycosides, compared with nonfamily members. As aminoglycosides function by interacting with bacterial ribosomes, mitochondrial ribosomal RNA (rRNA) genes were good candidate genes to examine for mutations that might be associated with this susceptibility to aminoglycoside-induced hearing loss. Sequencing these genes revealed a consistent mutation that was found in these families and not in 278 control individuals.[59] The mutation is an A to G substitution at position 1555 in the 12S rRNA gene. This mutation is in a highly conserved region of the rRNA that binds aminoglycosides.

This same mutation was noted in an Arab-Israeli family with maternally inherited deafness not associated with aminoglycoside administration. Thus, it appears that at least two events are necessary for the development of deafness in these pedigrees: the inheritance of the mitochondrial rRNA mutation, and either the administration of an aminoglycoside or the interaction of a cochlea-specific ribosomal subunit with the rRNA mutation. The combination of these two events would perturb the translational ability of the mitochondrial ribosome, leading to hearing loss. Other mitochondrial mutations leading to hearing loss have also been reported.[77] Why these mutations preferentially affect the inner ear, despite being present in mitochondria throughout the body, is unknown.

Animal Models

Strategies other than family mapping studies have been developed for the study of hereditary deafness. One major effort involves mapping and cloning the genes involved in auditory physiology and hearing impairment in the mouse model. The mouse has long been a useful experimental model for studying many different aspects of human disease, and this usefulness has been extended to the genomic level. The human and mouse genomes are approximately the same size and share many genes in common. A large number of mouse mutants have been described, including mice with middle ear defects, peripheral and central neural defects, neuroepithelial defects, and cochleo-saccular and morphogenic inner ear defects.[70] Differing strains of mice show varying susceptibility to noise-induced hearing loss and age-related hearing loss.[11, 18]

Once mouse deafness genes are identified, the considerable sequence homology between the mouse and human genome is exploited to discover genes responsible for human deafness. As an example of this strategy, the gene responsible for deafness in a mouse model known as shaker-1 (so named for the hyperactivity, head tossing, and circling due to vestibular dysfunction) was identified as encoding for an unconventional myosin, myosin VII.[22] This gene was in a homologous human region that had been previously identified by mapping studies as being the location for Usher syndrome type 1B. Thus, the murine gene became a good candidate gene for human US type 1B because the phenotype (deafness and vestibular dysfunction) and the location in both the murine and human genome were the same. The myosin VIIA from patients with US type 1B was sequenced, and mutations in affected persons were found that would result in the absence of a functional protein, demonstrating that US type 1B most likely results from a primary cytoskeletal defect.[87]

The problem of transducing airborne sound waves into sensory input is an ancient one; thus, an understanding of strategies developed by lower organisms to solve this problem should provide insight into the molecular basis of auditory mechanosensation in human systems. To this end a variety of mechanotransduction systems are studied in other organisms, including *Caenorhabditis elegans*. Insects use mechanosensory transducers, known as chordotonal organs, which are developmentally related to vertebrate auditory hair cells. An insect model that has provided insights into human hearing is *Drosophila melanogaster*, the fruit fly.[83] During courtship, males produce a courtship song to attract females, but the song, when played to other males, induces courtship among groups of males. This stylized behavior can be exploited as a mutagenesis screen for mutations that disrupt the auditory response, i.e., males that do not respond to the courtship song could have mutations in the genes that are responsible for the mechanotransduction of sound waves into neural impulses. Advantages of this mutagenesis screen include the ability to induce point mutations in the *Drosophila* genome, the very brief generational cycle of the fruit fly, and the thorough knowledge of the *Drosophila* genome sequence. Using this approach, several genes important in hearing have been identified, including *beethoven*, which may be a candidate gene for human hearing loss.[14a]

Zebra fish (*Brachydanio rerio*) have also proved to be a useful model for the identification and characterization of genes important for human hereditary deafness. Zebra fish possess two mechanosensory organs, the inner ear, involved in audition and equilibrium, and a lateral line, involved in the detection of water movement. Zebra fish are useful as they are a vertebrate model with a very short generational time and are relatively transparent during early development, which allows for examination of their mechanosensory organs. A specific zebra fish mutant known as *mariner* has been shown to have mutations in the gene encoding for Myosin VIIa, the same gene that is mutated in US type 1B, *DFNB2* and *DFNA11*.[17] Zebra fish have also been useful in studying the expression patterns of *eya1*, which is the homologue of the human gene *EYA-1*, the gene mutated in branchio-otorenal syndrome.[63] These findings illustrate the striking conservation of these genes throughout vertebrate evolution.

Molecular Advances in Other Diseases

Pediatric Gastroesophageal Reflux

Pediatric gastroesophageal reflux (GER) is an excellent example of a common disease that has recently been shown to have a genetic basis. Using DNA from families with multiple affected members, a gene for severe GER was mapped to chromosome 13q14.[27] A candidate gene encoding a serotinin receptor was shown in an article published in 2000 not to be the gene for pediatric GER.[28]

Neurofibromatosis

The neurofibromatoses are autosomally dominant conditions important to pediatric otolaryngology. Neurofibromatosis type 1 (NF1) is characterized by peripheral nerve tumors, café au lait spots, optic nerve gliomas, and bone abnormalities and has a frequency of 1 in 3000 individuals. NF1 is caused by mutations in neurofibromin, which appears to be involved in modulating a signal transduction pathway. Disruption of this pathway can lead to tumor formation.

Neurofibromatosis type 2 (NF2) is an autosomal dominant disease characterized by the development of bilateral vestibular schwannomas (acoustic neuromas) and other schwannomas and meningiomas of the cranial nerves and nerve roots. NF2 affects about 1 in 37,000 individuals. Members of families at risk for the development of these benign tumors are currently screened by a combination of auditory testing and magnetic resonance imaging. Screening for this disease is important because the tumors are generally asymptomatic when small. As the morbidity of surgical removal increases with tumor size, early detection allows a better surgical outcome. The gene, named *merlin* (for moesin, ezrin, radixinlike gene), appears to be a tumor suppressor gene that functions as a cytoskeleton mediator.[62] A point mutation in the *merlin* coding sequence has been identified that was consistently present in affected members of a large family with NF2 and not present in unaffected members or unrelated individuals.[43] By searching for this mutation in at-risk individuals in this family, expensive and time-consuming testing could be avoided in those individuals with negative test responses for the mutation. These types of screening programs allow the conservation of expensive medical resources, reduce psychological burdens, and improve medical care for affected family members.

Other Genetic Diseases

Many other diseases, syndromes, and physiologic processes of interest to pediatric otolaryngologists are under investigation at the molecular level. A partial list includes Jervell and Lange-Nielsen syndrome, von Willebrand disease, Treacher Collins syndrome, Crouzon syndrome, Saethre-Chotzen syndrome, Aarskog syndrome, acrofrontofacial nasal dysostosis, Stickler syndrome, Beckwith-Wiedemann syndrome, branchio-otorenal syndrome, olfaction, language disorders, atopy, malignant hyperthermia, otosclerosis, and Meniere disease. Interestingly, absolute pitch, which is a behavioral trait defined as the ability to identify the pitch of tones in the absence of a reference pitch, appears to aggregate in families. Absolute pitch may well be a model to investigate gene and environmental interactions in the development of complex human behaviors.[2] Molecular techniques are also contributing to our understanding of the fundamental mechanisms of vestibular function.[82]

Infectious Disease

The Role of the Polymerase Chain Reaction in Microbial Diagnosis

Tremendous advances in molecular biologic knowledge and techniques are transforming the study of human disease. The study of infectious diseases has been profoundly altered by the advent of the PCR.[56] It has been shown to be superior to conventional cultural and serologic techniques in many circumstances, particularly when it is applied to the identification of viral pathogens. The diagnostic potential of PCR and RT-PCR–based amplification schemes has been repeatedly documented for numerous viral families in a multitude of clinical settings. PCR has been used to diagnose infections in almost all tissues and body fluids, and assays have been developed for a host of infectious agents.[15]

Otitis Media

While otitis media (OM) is the most common primary diagnosis made by pediatric practitioners in the United States for children younger than 15 years of age, a poor understanding of the etiology and pathogenesis of this disease has hampered the development of rational therapeutic approaches. Multiple infectious agents are implicated in OM, but a complete understanding of the pathogenic cascade has been impeded by the inherent limitations of conventional culturing methods that are inadequate for the elucidation of fastidious pathogens. The PCR and other molecular techniques are beginning to be used to further our understanding of otitis media, particularly otitis media with effusion (OME). The majority of culture-negative OME specimens support amplification of either *Haemophilus influenzae, Moraxella catarrhalis,* or *Streptococcus pneumoniae* DNA,[55] and culture-negative, DNA-positive specimens have metabolically active *H. influenzae* as demonstrated by the amplification of bacterial-specific mRNA.[60] PCR has been used to demonstrate the presence of influenza virus and *S. pneumoniae* in culturally sterile, induced OM.[4]

The association of antecedent viral infection with OM has long been clinically recognized,[24] but studies attempting to characterize the viral infections have been hampered by the low yield and the technical difficulty of viral culture techniques.[27] The PCR has been shown to be superior to culture in the detection of viral nucleic acid in OME specimens.[50a, 54] The most common viruses isolated include adenovirus, parainfluenza virus, influenza virus, respiratory syncytial virus, and rhinovirus.

The Genetics of Infectious Disease Susceptibility, Including Otitis Media

Although a thoughtful consideration of the great plagues of mankind suggests that there is an inherent "innate-susceptibility" and a "natural resistance" to infectious disease, physicians are not accustomed to thinking about the influence of genes on the susceptibility to infectious disease, particularly common diseases such as OM. There is a growing body of evidence that the host genome can influence the susceptibility to, and the severity of, viral, bacterial, parasitic, and fungal infectious diseases.[42] These diseases include malaria, mycobacterial infections, meningococcus, and acquired immune deficiency syndrome (AIDS).[35] The progression of human immunodeficieny virus type 1 (HIV-1) infection has been shown to be significantly altered by variation in human leukocyte antigen (HLA) genes and circulating chemokine molecules and their cell-surface receptors (CCR).[32] Individuals homozygous for a particular *CCR5* allele are strongly protected against HIV infection and the development of AIDS.[41, 65] Additionally, mutations in the gene responsible for cystic fibrosis have been shown to be associated with a predisposition to chronic rhinosinusitis in adults.[85] Defining the genes that influence susceptibility to infectious pathogens and disease progression can provide insights into pathogenesis and identify new targets for prophylactic and therapeutic interventions.[25]

An exciting development in the study of OM has been the demonstration that susceptibility to OM can be inherited. In a prospective, blinded, longitudinal comparative study of monozygotic and dizygotic twins and triplets, Casselbrant and colleagues[7a] conclusively demonstrated that OM in children has a strong heritable component. This work provides a strong scientific foundation for the elucidation of the genetic factors that control susceptibility to OM and to other infectious diseases. While it is doubtful that there is a single "otitis media" gene, modern technology will allow the identification of the genes that confer susceptibility to otitis. Susceptibility to OM will, no doubt, be an example of a complex disease, i.e., a disease determined by the interplay of a variety of genes.[16]

Recurrent Respiratory Papillomatosis

Recurrent respiratory papillomatosis (RRP) is the result of infection with human papillomavirus (HPV). Papillomatosis can be difficult to treat successfully and has a predilection for recurrence. The PCR has been used to identify a number of HPV types associated with RRP,[53] to amplify HPV DNA from the smoke plume resulting from the treatment of RRP with the carbon dioxide laser,[31] and to demonstrate the low likelihood of horizontal transmission between patients and siblings or other family members.[72]

Cancer

Cancer is a genomic process that is the result of a series of DNA mutations culminating in clinical disease. The molecular mechanisms of cancer pathogenesis are becoming clearer, particularly as microarray technology is applied to the study of tumorigenesis.[46] Programmed cell death, or apoptosis, is increasingly recognized as important in the normal development of an organism. Loss of control of this tightly regulated process underlies a variety of disease states, including neoplasia.[50] Cell growth is regulated, in part, by proto-oncogenes and tumor suppressor genes. Proto-oncogenes can mutate into oncogenes that force the growth of tumor cells. Inactivation of tumor suppressor genes leads to a loss of cell growth control. Loss of cell growth regulation is central to the development of malignant disease.

One tumor suppressor gene in particular, *p53,* has been the subject of intensive study. Families with the Li-Fraumeni syndrome have sarcomas, breast cancer, and other cancers at an early age. Children with Li-Fraumeni syndrome are at risk for the development of rhabdomyosarcomas. This syndrome results from the inheritance of a mutant *p53* gene. Research protocols that deliver *p53* by adenovirus to head and neck cancer patients are now under way to determine its role as a surgical adjuvant.[8]

Characterization of the molecular events that lead to cancer will allow the detection of a predisposition to cancer, so that screening resources can be concentrated on those patients at high risk and provide an opportunity for early intervention. Eventually, gene therapy will allow the replacement of defective oncogenes and tumor suppressor genes by functional genes. Other genes that are potential targets for gene therapy include cytokine genes, genes coding for immunostimulation, and genes encoding bacterial and viral pro-drug–activating enzymes, also known as suicide genes.[84] Gene therapy will join the traditional cancer treatments of surgical resection, radiation therapy, and chemotherapy.

Gene Therapy

Gene therapy is a revolutionary new approach for treating disease. Gene therapy is moving from the research laboratories to the bedside and carries the promise of curing a host of diseases for which there currently is only symptomatic treatment. Initial hyperbole as to the promise of gene therapy has given way to the realization that true progress will be incremental and will be based on a solid understanding of the basic science behind the therapy. Progress in gene therapy has been slowed by the lack of knowledge of the genetic components of disease, the complexity of developing effective vectors and active agents as therapies, and the need for testing to ensure safety.[14]

Gene therapy can broadly be defined as the introduction of nucleic acids (either DNA or RNA) into the cells of a patient for the amelioration of disease. Successful gene therapy requires the identification of the affected gene, the determination of the appropriate tissue or organ system to be treated, and an effective delivery system for the new gene. Successful gene transfer systems would transfer the new gene only into the desired cell at an efficiency that would make the transfer clinically relevant. Once the new gene has been successfully integrated into the target cell or tissue, the desired protein product should be produced in sufficient quantities to be clinically important. The cell type chosen for modification should be capable of long-term production of the gene product. The delivery system chosen will vary, depending on the target tissue as well as the biologic and biochemical characteristics of the underlying disease. Of particular importance is whether the target tissue consists of dividing or nondividing cells, because many viral vectors cannot transfer nucleic acids into nondividing, postmitotic cells.

Many different gene transfer systems have been devised and can be divided into physical and viral methods. Physical gene transfer methods consist of direct injection of plasmid DNA into muscle tissue, liposome-mediated gene transfer, and receptor-mediated gene transfer. Viruses have been introducing nucleic acids into cells for millions of years and thus are attractive for use as gene vectors. They can achieve high percentages of infections in cell populations and can often do so without killing the target cell. Current viruses being considered as vectors for gene therapy include retroviruses, adenoviruses, herpesviruses, and adeno-associated virus. The specific virus chosen depends on several factors, including the target tissue, whether the target cell is actively dividing or is postmitotic, and viral cytotoxic effects.

In ex vivo approaches, the genome of the target cell is modified outside of the patient, and the target cell is then administered to the patient. In vivo approaches involve directly introducing the gene into the patient, with subsequent modification of the target cell.

Gene therapy has been increasingly applied to the inner ear.[39] The first biologic response of an inner ear tissue to transduction by a gene therapy vector expressing a therapeutic gene has been demonstrated in vitro.[77a] A reporter gene has been introduced into the cochlea of guinea pigs by a viral vector known as adeno-associated virus.[37] Gene transfer to the middle ear by recombinant adenovirus vectors has been demonstrated in the guinea pig model.[49]

Regulation of Gene Therapy

The control and regulation of gene therapy is the responsibility of several federal agencies. The Recombinant DNA Advisory Committee of the National Institutes of Health is responsible for the overseeing of gene therapy protocols that have received federal funding or are performed at institutions that receive federal funds. This committee encourages scientific evaluation and broad public discussion of the ethical and social issues involved. The Food and Drug Administration is responsible for the development of safe and effective biologic products and as such has developed a regulatory framework and technical standards for gene therapy products.[34]

The Human Genome Project

In what will surely rank as one of the greatest achievements of humanity, a working draft of the human genome has been produced. The product of a competitive effort between the publicly funded international consortium Human Genome Project (HGP) and privately funded Celera Genomics, the sequencing of the human genome was an ambitious, large-scale collaborative effort to map and sequence the human genome and to determine the location of the initially estimated 100,000 (since revised to 30,000) human genes. The effort to map the human genome formally began as a cooperative effort between the National Institutes of Health (NIH) and the Department of Energy (DOE) in 1990. The DOE, which was primarily concerned with the production of nuclear weapons, needed to find a new mission after the end of the Cold War. The DOE had long studied DNA structure because of its interest in monitoring genetic damage from radiation; additionally, the organization had expertise in large-scale projects. Another of the project's goals was to analyze the DNA from several non-human organisms to provide comparative DNA information for help in understanding the human genome. These organisms include *Haemophilus influenzae*, *Drosophila*, and *Caenorhabditis elegans*.

One of the biggest challenges of the HGP was to develop inexpensive new technologies for the determination of DNA sequence information. The optimization of current strategies through automation and increased data throughput and the development of completely new strategies were two approaches undertaken to develop improved sequencing technology.

One of the challenges of the HGP was to develop systems to manage the vast amount of data generated by the project. The information from sequencing the human genome fills the equivalent of 14 sets of the *Encyclopaedia Britannica*. A joint task force on information technology was established between the NIH and the DOE to coordinate the findings of the program. Several computerized databases have been developed to maintain the DNA sequence information, including GenBank, a database managed by the National Center for Biotechnology Information, National Library of Medicine, National Institutes of Health, and the European Molecular Biology Laboratory Data Library. The Genome Data Base at Johns Hopkins University is a central database of mapped genes and the international repository for mapping information. The Online Mendelian Inheritance in Man catalogues gene assignments to specific human chromosomes.

Ethics, Counseling, and Management of Patients

Ethical Concerns

Medical research, particularly in children, raises complex moral, legal, and social issues, and advances in molecular genetics have placed a renewed emphasis on conducting research in an ethical fashion.[48] While it is the responsibility of the individual researcher to conduct investigations in an ethical fashion, all members of the research and clinical community bear the responsibility to ensure that our patients are treated in a humane and ethical fashion. Abuses in the past such as the Nazi physician "medical" experiments conducted on concentration camp internees, the Tuskegee Study, where physicians from the Public Health Service withheld treatment for syphilis from African American men in order to determine the long-term consequences of the disease, and radiation experiments on prisoners, military personnel, and cancer patients have shown the need for the ethical conduct of research. Principles and Guidelines such as the "Belmont Report" contain the ethical principles on which the federal regulations for protection of human subjects are based. The basic principles of ethical research are respect for persons, beneficence, and justice. Particular vigilance must be exercised in conducting research on "vulnerable populations" such as children, which is a population commonly used in genetic research. Additional concerns are raised when researchers have financial interests in the research that they are conducting.[45] Institutional Review Boards (IRBs) are charged with the responsibility of determining whether a proposed research protocol meets the appropriate ethical standards.

A desire to keep ethical and moral issues central to the HGP prompted the National Center for Human Genome Research, National Institutes of Health, to fund the Ethical, Legal and Social Issues (ELSI) Program. Some of the questions that are addressed are: 1) Will effective legislative solutions to genetic discrimination be found?; 2) Who will decide when genetic tests are ready?; and 3) Can health care providers and the public become genetically literate in time?[9]

The ELSI program has, as one of its activities, funded a series of interdisciplinary conferences organized by the American Association for the Advancement of Science Directorate for Science and Policy Programs.[69] These conferences have focused on ethical issues of genetic testing, including the ethical and legal aspects of large-pedigree research. Large-pedigree research raises multiple ethical issues as information generated from studied individuals can potentially affect family members not included in the study. Whether informed consent should be obtained from every family member who is included in a pedigree database and whether permission to publish the pedigree should be obtained from every family member if the family could be identified from the pedigree are potential issues in this type of research. Researchers and IRBs that review genetic-based protocols need to consider not only these ethical issues but also issues concerning therapeutic interventions at the genetic level. Particularly problematic is research into germ-line therapy. Germ-line therapy, as opposed to somatic cell therapy, affects future generations, and the ethical questions raised by this type of therapy are particularly difficult.[44, 74]

An example of the sort of ethical questions that pediatric otolaryngologists currently face include the request from a family of a deaf child to test the unaffected siblings to see whether or not they are carriers. Approximately one third of deaf children born to normal-hearing parents have mutations in Cx26, and two thirds of normal-hearing siblings will be carriers of mutant Cx26 genes. Well-intentioned families will request that the nor-

mal-hearing siblings be tested to determine whether they carry a copy of the mutant allele. While on the surface this seems to be a reasonable request, current recommendations are that asymptomatic children not be tested for carrier status, as this information is only useful to them in the context of reproductive decisions that they will be making as adults. As an adult, they have the right to not know their carrier status; thus, decisions concerning carrier status should be left to the child when he or she becomes an adult, rather than be made by the parents.[10]

The potential for great good to come from genetic research as well as the potential for abuse of genetic information has been recognized. The Council of International Organizations of Medical Sciences has issued a statement concerning genetics, ethics, and human values entitled The Declaration of Inuyama. In this statement, the council declares that efforts to map the human genome are worthwhile, especially as the knowledge revealed will be used for human betterment. It stresses the responsibility of individual researchers and physicians to act in an ethical manner and to ensure that developing countries also receive the benefits of the new technology.

Abuse of genetic information could lead to a restriction of personal freedom and an increase in the control a government could exert over its citizens. Potential abuses of genetic information include refusal of insurance coverage, employment discrimination, and adverse social and personal consequences.[88] Insurance companies would be interested in identifying people with a genetic predisposition to a disease that would prove costly to treat. The identification of people as carriers of sickle cell trait has led to social ostracism.[90] Governments must make decisions about the regulation of genetic tests and how the information produced will be used as well as decide how access to these tests and counseling will be provided. Unfortunately, genetic discrimination has already occurred on a large scale. The eugenics movement in England and the United States spawned such abuses as involuntary sterilization of mentally retarded individuals.

Patients, families, health care professionals, society, and government will all be affected by the ongoing revolution in molecular biology. We have a tremendous opportunity to improve the welfare of our patients and to profoundly increase our knowledge of human biology; but it is only through continual education, thoughtful discussion, and careful attention to ethical issues that the full benefits of this revolution can be realized.[29, 76]

Counseling and Management of Patients

Advances in molecular genetics have resulted in genetic testing becoming an option for deaf individuals and their families. Families are very interested in obtaining this information as evidenced by the fact that in a survey of normal hearing parents with one or more deaf children, 96% of the families recorded a positive attitude toward genetic testing for deafness. However, 98% of the families incorrectly estimated the recurrence risk of deafness and misunderstood the concept of inheritance. These results clearly illustrate that affected families are very interested in genetic testing, but will need a great deal of genetic counseling in order to use the information correctly.[3a]

Presymptomatic DNA-based diagnosis is becoming possible for a growing number of diseases. Identification of patients at genetic risk for development of these diseases allows increased surveillance, with the hope that detection of the disease in its earliest symptomatic state will increase the chances of cure. Examples of diseases that clearly illustrate the benefits of genetic-based presymptomatic diagnosis are retinoblastoma and breast cancer. Identification of patients at risk for the disease allows for the opportunity for increased surveillance, with attendant increases in survival.

As our knowledge of genetic diseases increases and gene therapy becomes more widespread, genetic counseling becomes of even greater importance. Who is going to provide this counseling? The number of trained genetic counselors is small, so that much of the counseling and follow-up will be performed by people without formal training in the area. Pediatric otolaryngologists will increasingly become a source of information for these families.

Effective counseling can take place only after a patient and family understand the implications of the molecular diagnosis and are offered effective ways to act on the diagnosis. Initially, presymptomatic disease diagnosis will almost always be possible before effective therapies are designed. Ensuring that genetic tests have the requisite sensitivity and specificity, controlling access to and preventing discrimination because of test results, ensuring that testing is made available to all patients, and helping patients understand the test results are all challenges to be faced.

Genetic counseling for hereditary deafness has a unique set of concerns. Deafness is regarded by some members of the deaf community, social scientists, and linguists not as a disease or as a condition that requires treatment but rather as one aspect of a separate culture. The deaf community has unique language, beliefs, social customs, and values. Members of this community may have goals to be achieved different from genetic counseling and do not necessarily view being deaf as a condition that requires treatment.[3]

Conclusions

We are entering the Golden Age of Biology. Understanding the information basis of an organism reveals operational principles and allows us to understand exactly how an organism can function. Sequencing entire genomes has shown that we have a distance to go before this understanding is complete, as at least half of the sequenced genes have no known function. Microarray technology is moving us from the "one gene, one experiment" approach toward a total understanding of the interactions of thousands of genes simultaneously. With the sequencing of the human genome, we are now entering the postgenomic era. Progress in understanding human disease will accelerate at a rate previously unimaginable. This progress will be an iterative, interconnected process involving clinical family studies, molecular and proteomic-based investigations, bioinformatics, and animal models, resulting in improved diagnostics and better patient care.

The Art of War, written by Sun Tzu over 2400 years ago, is the oldest military treatise in the world. In this work, Sun Tzu emphasizes that ultimate success is predicated upon obtaining information regarding your opponent. So is it true in defeating disease. Advances in genomics are laying bare the secrets of disease, and will lead to cures currently unimaginable.

This Golden Age will bring with it huge challenges for scientists, clinicians, society, and families. There will no doubt be cloned humans very shortly. Single-cell DNA amplification techniques are being used to select healthy embryos prior to implantation. The creation of a transgenic rhesus monkey bearing a gene from a fluorescent jellyfish created much more than a monkey that could glow in the dark. It is the first demonstration that primates can be genetically modified through germ cell engineering. Using this type of technology, faulty genes will be replaced in humans. But who is to say exactly what constitutes a faulty gene?

Finally, discoveries in genetics are demonstrating that we are far more similar to each other than we are different from each other. As more is learned about genes and their functions, it is becoming clear that all organisms use essentially the same genetic pathways, whether it be for developmental organization, mechanical signal transduction, or wound healing. The difference between the genes of a chimpanzee and a human is less than 2%. Humans are 99.9% identical, with fewer than 200,000 base pairs (of 3 billion) being different between any two individuals.

GLOSSARY

Allele. An allele is the particular form of a gene. If a person has one normal allele on one chromosome, and the allele on the homologous chromosome is different, that person is said to be heterozygous.

CA repeat. A specific DNA polymorphism useful in linkage studies and in DNA "fingerprinting" for forensic use.

Carrier. A person who carries a mutated gene but is not phenotypically affected. The term is used in conjunction with autosomal recessive and X-linked disorders.

Congenital. Congenital means that the condition is present at birth. Not all deafness that is present at birth is hereditary. For example, infants born to mothers who had been infected with rubella during their pregnancy were often born deaf, with their deafness secondary to infection, not genes. Thus, these rubella babies had congenital deafness that was not hereditary.

Contig. Clones must be placed in the correct order for reconstruction of the original DNA sequence of interest. These reassembled contiguous stretches of DNA are called contigs.

Cosmid. Specially designed vectors that can carry DNA clones up to 45,000 base pairs in length.

Exon. That portion of the RNA that remains after the processing of transcribed DNA into mRNA.

Expression. The degree to which physical findings are manifested in an individual with a mutated gene.

Fluorescence in situ hybridization. A technique that allows the visualization of chromosomal deletions or additions.

Functional genomics. Understanding how genes work together to control biologic processes.

Gene. A segment of DNA that encodes for a specific mRNA.

Genetic heterogeneity. The concept that different mutations, possibly in different genes, can cause identical phenotypes. Autosomal recessive, nonsyndromic hearing loss is one of the best examples of a genetically heterogenic disorder.

Genotype. The genetic information of an organism.

Genotype-phenotype correlation. A disease with high genotype-phenotype correlation means that a certain genetic mutation will always result in the same physical manifestations. Genetic counseling is easier in these cases, as the resulting physiology can be predicted with some degree of certainty. A low genotype-phenotype correlation, on the other hand, means that a certain gene mutation does not result in a predictable pathology, even within families. Thus, even when a mutation is detected, it is impossible to predict the ultimate phenotype (e.g., how hearing-impaired the patient will be), which makes the task of genetic counseling more difficult.

Hereditary. Caused by the expression of a gene.

Heteroplasmia. Mixtures of normal and mutant mitochondrial DNA (mtDNA) in a cell.

Homologous chromosomes. Each member of a chromosome pair is generally identical in size and shape.

Homoplasmia. The predominance in a cell of one form of mtDNA, either normal or mutant.

Homozygote. A person with two identical alleles for a particular gene; each allele is on a homologous chromosome.

Imprinting. The concept that which parent passes on a mutated gene influences the expression of the mutated gene.

Intron. That portion of the RNA that is spliced out and discarded during the processing of transcribed DNA into mRNA.

Karyotype. The characteristic shapes and staining patterns of an organism's chromosomes that can best be recognized during the metaphase of the cell cycle.

Marker. A point in the genome whose specific location is known, analogous to a mile marker on an interstate highway. Markers are essential to positional cloning.

PCR. The polymerase chain reaction is an automated technique that can make billions of exact copies of a single DNA fragment in just a few hours.

Penetrance. Whether or not an individual with a mutation manifests any physical findings associated with that mutation. Penetrance is an all-or-none phenomenon.

Phenotype. The observable characteristics of an organism.

Plasmid. Small circular molecules of DNA that can be used as vectors for cloning foreign DNA.

Positional cloning. The process of finding the chromosomal location of a gene without any a priori knowledge of its location, structure or function.

Postlingual hearing loss. Hearing loss that begins after the onset of speech. Postlingual hearing loss is much more common than prelingual, with 10% of the population affected by age 60 and 50% by age 80.

Prelingual hearing loss. Hearing loss that begins before the onset of speech. About one child in a thousand is born with prelingual hearing loss.

Proteomics. The study of the complete protein sets of organisms. Proteomics arose from the recognition that multiple variant proteins can be made from a single DNA sequence. These multiple variants result from the various splicing strategies used to assemble mRNAs.

Replication. The copying of one DNA into two DNA just before a single cell divides into two cells.

Restriction enzyme. Bacterial enzymes that recognize and cleave DNA at specific nucleotide sequence sites.

Sequencing. Identifying the order of bases in a segment of DNA.

Syntenic. Genes that have been mapped to the same chromosome.

Syndrome. A set of abnormalities that are recognizable because other patients have the same or similar sets of abnormalities. Patients affected with a syndrome resemble each other more than they resemble their nonaffected siblings. Not all syndromes are genetically based; rather some are due to exogenous factors, e.g., fetal alcohol syndrome.

Transcription. The synthesis of single-stranded RNA from double-stranded DNA.

Transgenic. An animal that carries a foreign gene in its genome.

Translation. The synthesis of an amino acid sequence from its mRNA template. In this process, the information of nucleic acids is *translated* into a protein.

Yeast artificial chromosome. Yeast artificial chromosomes (YACs) are a method of handling up to a million base pairs of DNA. YACs readily make multiple copies of introduced DNA.

SELECTED REFERENCES

Gelehrter TD, Collins FS, Ginsburg D. Principles of Medical Genetics, 2nd ed. Baltimore, Lippincott Williams & Wilkins, 1998.

> *A clear, concise explanation of modern medical genetics, designed for the clinician with little experience in the field.*

Lewin B. Genes VII. New York, Oxford University Press, 2000.

> *An up-to-date, concise textbook that presents the subject of genes based on the molecular properties of the eukaryotic gene itself.*

Van Camp G, Smith RH. Hereditary Hearing Loss Homepage—(http://www.uia.ac.be/dnalab/hhh).

> *This is a constantly updated site with a wealth of information regarding the progress being made in deafness gene mapping and discovery.*

REFERENCES

1. Bai U, Seidman MD, Hinojosa R, Quirk WS. Mitochondrial DNA deletions associated with aging and possibly presbycusis: a human archival temporal bone study. Am J Otol 18:449, 1997.
2. Baharloo S, Service SK, Risch N, et al. Familial aggregation of absolute pitch. Am J Hum Genet 67:755, 2000.

3. Bork JM, Peters LM, Riazuddin S, et al. Usher syndrome 1D and nonsyndromic autosomal recessive deafness DFNB12 are caused by allelic mutations of the novel cadherin-like gene CDH23. Am J Hum Genet 68:26, 2001.

3a. Brunger JW, Matthews AL, Smith RH, Robin NH. Genetic testing and genetic counseling for deafness: the future is here. Laryngoscope 111(4 Pt 1):715, 2001.

4. Buchman CA, Doyle WJ, Skoner DP, et al. Influenza A virus-induced acute otitis media. J Infect Dis 172:1348, 1995.

5. Burgess RC, Michaels L, Bale JF Jr, Smith RJ. Polymerase chain reaction amplification of herpes simplex viral DNA from the geniculate ganglion of a patient with Bell's palsy. Ann Otol Rhinol Laryngol 103:775, 1994.

6. Carreno M, Ona M, Melon S, et al. Amplification of herpes simplex virus type 1 DNA in human geniculate ganglia from formalin-fixed, nonembedded temporal bones. Otolaryngol Head Neck Surg 123:508, 2000.

7. Casademont I, Chevrier D, Denoyelle F, et al. A simple and reliable method for the detection of the 30delG mutation of the CX26 gene. Mol Cell Probes 14(3):149, 2000.

7a. Casselbrant ML, Mandel EM, Fall PA, et al. The heritability of otitis media: a twin and triplet study. JAMA 282(22):2125, 1999.

8. Clayman GL. The current status of gene therapy. Semin Oncol 27:39, 2000.

9. Collins F. Keynote Scientific Address. American Academy of Otolaryngology-Head and Neck Surgery Annual Meeting, Washington, DC, Sept. 2000.

10. Davis DS. Discovery of children's carrier status for recessive genetic disease: some ethical issues. Genet Test 2:323, 1998.

11. Davis RR, Cheever ML, Krieg EF, Erway LC. Quantitative measure of genetic differences in susceptibility to noise-induced hearing loss in two strains of mice. Hear Res 134:9, 1999.

12. DeStefano AL, Cupples LA, Arnos KS, et al. Correlation between Waardenburg syndrome phenotype and genotype in a population of individuals with identified PAX3 mutations. Hum Genet 102:499, 1998.

13. DeGrey AD. Mitochondrial gene therapy: an arena for the biomedical use of inteins. Trends Biotechnol 18:394, 2000.

14. Dyer MR, Herrling PL. Progress and potential for gene-based medicines. Mol Ther 1:213, 2000.

14a. Eberl DF, Duyk GM, Perrimon N. A genetic screen for mutations that disrupt an auditory response in Drosophila melanogaster. Proc Natl Acad Sci U S A 94(26):14837, 1997.

15. Ehrlich GD, Greenburg SJ. PCR-Based Clinical Diagnostics in Infectious Disease. Boston, Blackwell Scientific Publications, 1994.

16. Ehrlich GD, Post JC. Susceptibility to otitis media. Strong evidence that genetics plays a role. JAMA 282:2167, 1999.

17. Ernest S, Rauch GJ, Haffter P, et al. Mariner is defective in myosin VIIA: a zebrafish model for human hereditary deafness. Hum Mol Genet 9(14):2189, 2000.

18. Erway LC, Shiau YW, Davis RR Krieg EF. Genetics of age-related hearing loss in mice. III. Susceptibility of inbred and F1 hybrid strains to noise-induced hearing loss. Hear Res 93:181, 1996.

19. Everett LA, Glaser B, Beck JC, et al. Pendred syndrome is caused by mutations in the putative sulfate transport gene (PDS). Nat Genet 17:411, 1997.

20. Fischel-Ghodsian N, Bykhovskaya Y, Taylor K, et al. Temporal bone analysis of patients with presbycusis reveals high frequency of mitochondrial mutations. Hear Res 110:147, 1997.

21. Freidman TB, Sellers JR, Avraham KB. Unconventional myosins and the genetics of hearing loss. Am J Med Genet 89:147, 1999.

22. Gibson F, Walsh J, Mburu P, et al. A type VII myosin encoded by the mouse deafness gene shaker-1. Nature 374:62, 1995.

23. Green GE, Scott DA, McDonald JM, et al. Performance outcomes after cochlear implantation for GJB2-related deafness. American Society of Pediatric Otolaryngology, 15th Annual Meeting, May 2000, Orlando, FL.

24. Heikkinen T, Chonmaitree T. Viral-bacterial synergy in otitis media: implications for management. Curr Infect Dis Rep. 2:154, 2000.

25. Hill AV. Genetics and genomics of infectious disease susceptibility. Br Med Bull 55:401, 1999.

26. Hoth CF, Milunsky A, Lipsky N, et al. Mutations in the paired domain of the human PAX3 gene cause Klein-Waardenburg syndrome (WSIII) as well as Waardenburg syndrome type I (WSI). Am J Hum Genet 52:455, 1993.

27. Hu FZ, Preston RA, Post JC, et al. Mapping of a gene for severe pediatric gastroesophageal reflux to chromosome 13q14. JAMA 284:325, 2000.

28. Hu FZ, Post JC, Johnson S, et al. Refined localization of a gene for pediatric gastroesophageal reflux makes HTR2A an unlikely candidate gene. Hum Genet 107:519, 2000.

29. Juengst ET. Caught in the middle again: professional ethical considerations in genetic testing for health risks. Genet Test 1:189, 1997.

30. Jun AI, McGuirt WT, Hinojosa R, et al. Temporal bone histopathology in connexin 26-related hearing loss. Laryngoscope 110:269, 2000.

31. Kashima HK, Kesis T, Mounts P, et al. Polymerase chain reaction identification of human papillomavirus DNA in CO2 laser plume from recurrent respiratory papillomatosis. Otolaryngol Head Neck Surg 104:191, 1991.

32. Kaslow PA, McNicholl JM. Genetic determinants of HIV-1 infection and its manifestations. Proc Assoc Am Physicians 111:299, 1999.

33. Keats BJ, Corey DP. The usher syndromes. Am J Med Genet 89:158, 1999.

34. Kessler DA, Siegel JP, Noguchi PD, et al. Regulation of somatic cell therapy and gene therapy by the Food and Drug Administration. N Engl J Med 329:1169, 1993.

35. Kwiatkowski D. Genetic dissection of the molecular pathogenesis of severe infection. Intensive Care Med 26:S89, 2000.

36. Lalwani AK, Grundfast KM. A role for the otolaryngologist in identification and discovery of genetic disorders and chromosomal abnormalities. Arch Otolaryngol Head Neck Surg 119:1074, 1993.

37. Lalwani AK, Walsh BJ, Reilly PG, et al. Development of in vivo gene therapy for hearing disorders: introduction of adeno-associated virus into the cochlea of the guinea pig. Gene Ther 3:588, 1996.

38. Lalwani AK, Mhatre AN. Cochlear gene therapy. Adv Otorhinolaryngol 56:275, 2000.

39. Lalwani AK, Goldstein JA, Kelley MJ, et al. Human nonsyndromic hereditary deafness DFNA17 is due to a mutation in nonmuscle myosin MYH9. Am J Hum Genet 67:1121, 2000.

40. Lee M, Goodall J, Verastegui C, et al. Direct regulation of the Microphthalmia promoter by Sox10 links Waardenburg-Shah syndrome (WS4)-associated hypopigmentation and deafness to WS2. J Biol Chem 275(48):37978, 2000.

41. Liu R, Paxton WA, Choe S, et al. Homozygous defect in HIV-1 cereceptor accounts for resistance of some multiply-exposed individuals to HIV-1 infection. Cell 86:367, 1996.

41a. Lomax MI, Huang L, Cho Y, et al. Differential display and gene arrays to examine auditory plasticity. Hear Res 147(1–2):293, 2000.

42. McNicholl JM, Cuenco KT. Host genes and infectious diseases. HIV, other pathogens, and a public health perspective. Am J Prev Med 16:141, 1999.

43. MacCollin M, Mohney T, Trofatter J, et al. DNA diagnosis of neurofibromatosis 2. Altered coding sequence of the merlin tumor suppressor in an extended pedigree. JAMA 270:2316, 1993.

44. Marshall E. Medical ethics. Moratorium urged on germ line gene therapy. Science 289:2023, 2000.

45. Marshall E. Gene therapy's web of corporate connections. Science 288:954, 2000.

46. Marx J. Medicine. DNA arrays reveal cancer in its many forms. Science 289:1670, 2000.

47. McKenna MJ, Kristiansen AG, Haines J. Polymerase chain reaction amplification of a measles virus sequence from human temporal bone sections with active otosclerosis. Am J Otol 17:827, 1996.

48. Meslin EM. Of clones, stem cells, and children: issues and challenges in human research ethics. J Womens Health Gend Based Med 9:831, 2000.

49. Mondain M, Restituito S, Vincenti V, et al. Adenovirus-mediated in vivo gene transfer in guinea pig middle ear mucosa. Human Gene Ther 9:1217, 1998.

50. Mostafapour SP, Hockenbery DM, Rubel EW. Life and death in otolaryngology: mechanisms of apoptosis and its role in the pathology and treatment of disease. Arch Otolaryngol Head Neck Surg 125:729, 1999.

50a. Moyse E, Lyon M, Cordier G, et al. Viral RNA in middle ear mucosa and exudates in patients with chronic otitis media with effusion. Arch Otolaryngol Head Neck Surg 126(9):1105, 2000.

51. Ohtani F, Furuta Y, Iino Y, et al. Amplification of RNA from archival human temporal bone sections. Laryngoscope 109:617, 1999.

52. Orzan E, Polli R, Martella M, et al. Molecular genetics applied to clinical practice: the Cx26 hearing impairment. Br J Audiol 33:291, 1999.
53. Penaloza-Plascencia M, Montoya-Fuentes H, Flores-Martinez SE, et al. Molecular identification of 7 human papillomavirus types in recurrent respiratory papillomatosis. Arch Otolaryngol Head Neck Surg 126:1119, 2000.
54. Pitkaranta A, Jero J, Arruda E, et al. Polymerase chain reaction-based detection of rhinovirus, respiratory syncytial virus and coronavirus in otitis media with effusion. J Pediatr 133:390, 1998.
55. Post JC, Preston RA, Aul JJ, et al. Molecular analysis of bacterial pathogens in otitis media with effusion. JAMA 273(20):1598, 1995.
56. Post JC, Ehrlich GD. The impact of the polymerase chain reaction in clinical medicine. JAMA 283:1544, 2000.
57. Potterf SB, Furumura M, Dunn KJ, et al. Transcription factor hierarchy in Waardenburg syndrome: regulation of MITF expression by SOX10 and PAX3. Hum Genet 107:1, 2000.
58. Preston RA, Post JC, Keats BJ, et al. A gene for Crouzon craniofacial dysostosis maps to the long arm of chromosome 10. Nat Genet 7:149, 1994.
59. Prezant TR, Agapian JV, Bohlman C, et al. Mitochondrial ribosomal RNA mutation associated with both antibioticinduced and nonsyndromic deafness. Nature Genetics 4:289, 1993.
60. Rayner MG, Zhang Y, Gorry MC, et al. Evidence of bacterial metabolic activity in culture-negative otitis media with effusion. JAMA 279:296, 1998.
61. Riazuddin S, Castelein CM, Ahmed ZM, et al. Dominant modifier DFNM1 suppresses recessive deafness DFNB26. Nat Genet 26:431, 2000.
62. Rouleau GA, Merel P, Lutchman M, et al. Alteration in a new gene encoding a putative membrane organizing protein causes neurofibromatosis type 2. Nature 363:515, 1993.
63. Sahly I, Andermann P, Petit C. The zebrafish eya1 gene and its expression pattern during embryogenesis. Dev Genes Evol 209:399, 1999.
64. Saiki R, Gelfand DH, Stoffel S, et al. Primerdirected enzymatic amplification of DNA with a thermostable DNA polymerase. Science 230:1350, 1988.
65. Samson M, Libert F, Doranz BJ, et al. Resistance to HIV-1 infection in caucasian individuals bearing mutant alleles of the CCR-5 chemokine receptor gene. Nature 382(6593):722, 1996.
66. Schultz P, Arbusow V, Strupp M, et al. Highly variable distribution of HSV-1-specific DNA in human geniculate, vestibular and spiral ganglia. Neurosci Lett 252:139, 1998.
67. Scott DA, Wang R, Kreman TM, et al. The pendred syndrome gene encodes a chloride-iodide transport protein. Nat Genet 21:440, 1999.
68. Skvorak AB, Weng Z, Yee AJ, et al. Human cochlear expressed sequence tags provide insight into cochlear gene expression and identify candidate genes for deafness. Hum Mol Genet 8:439, 1999.
69. Smith RM. AAAS conference explores ethical aspects of large pedigree genetic research. JAMA 267:2158, 1992.
70. Steel KP. Inherited hearing defects in mice. Annu Rev Genet 29:675, 1995.
71. Steel KP. Deafness genes: expressions of surprise. Trends Genet 15:207, 1999
72. Sun JD, Weatherly RA, Koopmann CF Jr, Carey TE. Mucosal swabs detect HPV in laryngeal papillomatosis patients but not family members. Int J Pediatr Otorhinolaryngol 53:95, 2000.
73. Sundstrom RA, Van Laer L, Van Camp G, Smith RJ. Autosomal recessive nonsyndromic hearing loss. Am J Med Genet 89:123, 1999.
74. Szebik I, Glass KC. Ethical issues of human germ-cell therapy: A presentation for public discussion. Acad Med 76:32, 2001.
75. Tassabehji M, Read AP, Newton VE, et al. Waardenburg's syndrome patients have mutations in the human homologue of the Pax3 paired box gene. Nature 355:635, 1992.
76. Thomas SM. Genomics: the implications for ethics and education. Br Med Bull 55:429, 1999.
77. Van Camp G, Smith RH. Maternally inherited hearing impairment. Clin Genet 57:409, 2000.
77a. Van de Water TR, Staecker H, Halterman MW, Federoff HJ. Gene therapy in the inner ear. Mechanisms and clinical implications. Ann NY Acad Sci 884:345, 1999.
78. Van Laer L, McGuirt WT, Yang T, et al. Autosomal dominant nonsyndromic hearing impairment. Am J Med Genet 89:167, 1999.
79. Verpy E, Leibovici M, Zwaenepoel I, et al. A defect in harmonin, a PDZ domain-containing protein expressed in the inner ear senssory hair cells, underlies usher syndrome type 1C. Nat Genet 26:51, 2000.
80. Wackym PA, Chen CT, Kerner MM, Bell TS. Characterization of DNA extracted from archival celloidin-embedded human temporal bone sections. Am J Otol 16:14, 1995.
81. Wackym PA. Molecular temporal bone pathology: II. Ramsey Hunt syndrome (herpes zoster oticus). Laryngoscope 107:1165, 1997.
82. Wackym PA, Balaban CD. Molecules, motion and man. Otolaryngol Head Neck Surg 118:S16, 1998.
83. Walker RG, Willingham AT, Zuker CS. A Drosophila mechanosensory transduction channel. Science 287:2229, 2000.
84. Walther W, Stein U. Therapeutic genes for cancer gene therapy. Mol Biotechnol 13:21, 1999.
85. Wang X, Moylan B, Leopold DA, et al. Mutation in the gene responsible for cystic fibrosis and predisposition to chronic rhinosinusitis in the general population. JAMA, 284:1814, 2000.
86. Watson JD, Crick FHC. Molecular structure of nucleic acids: a structure for deoxyribose nucleic acid. Nature 171:737, 1953.
87. Weil D, Blanchard S, Kaplan J, et al. Defective myosin VIIA gene responsible for Usher Syndrome type 1B. Nature 374:60, 1995.
88. Weinberg JM. Breaking bonds: discrimination in the genetic revolution. JAMA 268:1767, 1992.
89. Weston MD, Eudy JD, Fujita S, et al. Genomic structure and identification of novel mutations in usherin, the gene responsible for Usher syndrome type IIa. Am J Hum Genet 66:1199, 1999.
90. Wilfond BS, Fost N. The cystic fibrosis gene: medical and social implications for heterozygote detection. JAMA 263:2777, 1990.
91. Willems PJ. Mechanisms of Disease: Genetic Causes of Hearing Loss. NEJM. 342:1101, 2000.
92. Zbar RI, Ramesh A, Srisailapathy CR, et al. Passage to India: the search for genes causing autosomal recessive nonsymdromic hearing loss. Otolaryngol Head Neck Surg 118:333, 1998.

6

Principles and Methods of Management

Christopher B. Gordon, M.D., and Dennis J. Hurwitz, M.D., F.A.C.S.

The surgery of craniofacial malformations is an evolving discipline that includes a variety of dental, medical, surgical, and other specialized procedures. Each anomaly must be thoroughly analyzed through meticulous physical examination, advanced imaging techniques, and often extensive surgical exposure. Complex relationships between soft tissue and bone must be appreciated, and the effect of repositioning one or the other needs to be anticipated. Osseous correction involves the isolation of bone segments by osteotomies: alteration of the position of bone in space and fixation by wires or plates and screws, or manipulation of undesirable contours by shaving, burring, or staggering incomplete osteotomies. Soft tissue alignment, coordinated with underlying osseous procedures, is the movement of skin, fat, muscle, and mucous membranes from a nearby or distant location to achieve a desirable correction of the deformity. Surgical exposure of the craniofacial skeleton and the raising of soft tissue flaps should not injure nearby vital structures. A conscientious effort is made to avoid direct cerebral and ocular injuries, fistulas, infections, and inadequate correction of the deformity.

As this surgery is performed primarily in children, the dynamics of growth must be understood and anticipated in the timing and execution of the operations. Successful rehabilitation is more likely when the treatment is performed by an experienced and active craniofacial team. Most of the surgical groups have been developed from an existing cleft palate team by the addition of neurosurgical and ophthalmologic surgeons.

Historical Perspective

Craniofacial surgery has its origins in ancient history. From the Trojan War chronicle of Homer to the first report of Crouzon in 1912, the study of anomalies of the head and neck was largely descriptive. Recently, it has been discovered that both the ancient Inca and Maya employed craniotomy techniques to "correct" a variety of ailments. Craniofacial anomalies are described in pre-Colombian writings, and there is evidence that the Maya revered persons with certain craniofacial anomalies as divine.[138] The earliest description of reduction and fixation of facial fractures dates back more than two millennia to the *Corpus Hippocraticum,* which advocated closed re-

duction, interdental wiring, and external bandaging of mandible fractures.[2] There was little innovation for the next 2000 years.

Guillaume of Saliceto, a 13th century Italian, described a method of intermaxillary fixation and external splinting for treatment of a variety of facial fractures.[174] These methods remained in use until the middle of the 19th century. J. Rhea Barton, a Philadelphian, reintroduced the external bandaging method of treatment of mandible fractures that remained in use until the Civil War.[9] Thomas Bryan Gunning first described the use of molded rubber splints in treating mandible fractures. Similar splints are still used today for the treatment of edentulous mandible fractures.[62] The next major innovation came with the work of Edward Hartley Angle, who advocated the use of fracture bands and intermaxillary fixation for fracture treatment in the early 20th century. He single-handedly launched the specialty of orthodontia. His work made modern orthognathic surgery possible.[4]

The understanding of maxillary fractures remained primitive until Rene Le Fort described the three major fracture patterns of the maxilla. His famous cadaver experiments provided the anatomic basis for subsequent open reduction and internal fixation techniques.[86] Limited strip craniectomies for craniosynostosis were advocated in 1921,[110] and Longacre popularized onlay rib grafting to the midface to camouflage the stigmata of Crouzon syndrome in the 1940s.[42] Sir Harold D. Gillies was probably the first to make the leap from the primary treatment of facial fractures to secondary osteotomy and mobilization of malreduced segments based on radiographs and dental models. He also used bone grafts to stabilize the segments, laying the groundwork for the treatment of congenital anomalies.[50] Reed O. Dingman was performing similar work in the United States in the late 1940s, using bone grafts to stabilize Le Fort I and II segments.[36]

Gillies again published the first description of a craniofacial advancement for a congenital problem. The procedure was performed in 1942 on a patient who had either Crouzon or Pfeiffer syndrome. After establishing that intracranial hypertension was not problematic (despite the radiographic description of the "beaten-silver" markings of what is today called *thumbprinting*), a Le Fort III osteotomy was performed, the segment was advanced, and fixation was maintained with a plaster helmet and

83

elastic traction. No bone grafts were used, and the entire segment relapsed.[51] Gillies himself recognized that bone grafts would have maintained the advancement, an observation that was not lost on his assistant, Hugo Obwegeser. He went on to systematize and popularize orthognathic surgery, employing the same basic techniques to permit correction of midface and mandibular deformities.[159]

Paul Tessier spent a significant amount of time in England and was familiar with the Gillies operation. Tessier was subsequently posted to the Hopital Foch, where he was presented with a number of patients with Crouzon syndrome. After extensive cadaver dissection, then an unprecedented process in France, Tessier developed the operations that would form the basis of modern craniofacial surgery. His bicoronal approach to the anterior cranial base, combined with a pterygomaxillary disjunction and interpositional bone grafting, served as the launching pad for the specialty of craniofacial surgery.[157]

Spectrum of Anomalies

Craniofacial surgery has been subsequently defined as surgery of the craniofacial skeleton that involves degloving the orbits to provide access to or advancement of the anterior cranial base or upper maxilla and orbits. To qualify as a craniofacial operation, at least one orbit must be entirely stripped of soft tissue except for the attachments of the nasolacrimal apparatus at the point of entry of the optic nerve. In practice, most congenital anomalies that involve the craniofacial skeleton are lumped together under this heading. The specialty has grown to embrace tumor surgery, orbital reconstruction, craniosynostosis, and the treatment of facial fractures.[60, 75, 143, 171] The treatment of the craniofacial dysostoses, Apert and Crouzon syndromes, has served as the model for the growth of the specialty.[54] Indeed, progress in the treatment of these disorders propelled many of the early advances in the specialty. Other diseases that fall under the mantle of craniofacial syndromes include Treacher Collins syndrome, hemifacial microsomia, craniosynostosis, orbital hypertelorism, and rare craniofacial clefts.

Craniosynostosis

Perhaps the most straightforward craniofacial anomalies that are amenable to craniofacial techniques are the craniosynostoses. Craniosynostosis is defined as abnormal early closure of one or more of the sutures of the calvarium. Unlike the sutures of the facial skeleton, which remain patent throughout life, the cranial sutures close predictably, from anterior to posterior and from inferolateral to superomedial.[115] The metopic suture is the first to close, with fusion typically beginning at 2 years and ending by 3 years. In up to 10% of patients, the metopic suture may remain patent through adulthood.[117] In 1851, Virchow described an inhibition of growth perpendicular to a synostosed suture.[165] The subsequent growth of the remaining open sutures causes abnormal skull growth.

Early or asymmetrical closure of the coronal or lambdoidal sutures may cause a skull deformity known as *plagiocephaly,* with characteristic findings. Plagiocephaly is a generic cranial vault asymmetry that may be caused by both intrinsic (*craniosynostotic*) and extrinsic (*deformational*) factors. The term is derived from the Greek *plagios* ("slanted or crooked") and *kephale* ("head"). It is important to distinguish between deformational and synostotic plagiocephaly. The former is the most common form of cranial vault anomaly, occurring in up to 25% of newborns.[64] It has become increasingly common in light of current American Academy of Pediatrics guidelines for parents, which recommend supine positioning to avoid sudden infant death syndrome.[1, 79] Early presentation of deformational plagiocephaly relates to compressive forces during delivery or from engagement of the cranial vault with the maternal pelvis. Severity of deformity correlates with early pelvic engagement. The most common plagiocephaly is left anterior deformational plagiocephaly, which relates to the most common pelvic "lie" of left occipital anterior position. Other factors that influence deformational plagiocephaly include multiple pregnancies, oligohydramnios, and abnormal lie.[63]

Unilateral coronal suture synostosis is the most common nondeformational plagiocephaly, occurring in approximately 1 in 10,000 births. Up to 80% of cases occur in females. The affected side assumes a classic shape: the forehead is flattened, the eyebrow is elevated, the ear rotates anterosuperiorly, and the nose and chin may deviate to the opposite side. There is contralateral bossing of the frontal bones and opposite forehead. Ordinarily, the stenosis begins at the pterion and progresses medially. Torticollis is associated with this abnormality in up to 14% of children, most commonly on the contralateral side. When viewed from above, the head has a rhomboid shape. Radiographically, the affected orbit assumes a characteristic shape known as a *harlequin orbit*.[95] Most cases are nonsyndromic. Recently, however, the role of the fibroblast growth factor (FGF) family of genes in craniosynostosis has been investigated. The FGF3 gene has several point mutations, which cause only isolated coronal synostosis without other facial malformations. Single-suture synostosis is associated with a low incidence of increased intracranial pressure (ICP). The risk increases dramatically with multiple-suture synostosis, which can be successfully treated with a variety of surgical methods.

Unilateral lambdoidal suture synostosis is a rare phenomenon, accounting for only 3% to 5% of all craniosynostoses, and is frequently confused with posterior positional plagiocephaly.[14] It nearly always presents at birth, as the deformity begins in utero. The condition presents with ipsilateral posterior flattening and ipsilateral occipitomastoid bulging. The ipsilateral ear is posteriorly displaced. The fused suture is frequently either palpable or visible. Contralateral frontoparietal bossing is also common. The vertex view gives the impression of a trapezoid. The indications for surgery and vault-remodeling procedures are similar to those for anterior plagiocephaly. The morbidity of posterior vault remodeling may be higher than anterior vault procedures, and mild posterior deformity is often left untreated as this area is readily camouflaged with hair.

Nonsynostotic plagiocephaly is a self-limited deformity that frequently improves spontaneously. Careful positioning of the sleeping infant on the prominent portions of the skull is often adequate to improve the deformity to the point that it is of no social consequence. Typically, improvement occurs once the child begins to walk and spends less time supine. More severe deformational plagiocephaly is often amenable to orthopedic treatment with molding helmets, provided the intervention occurs early enough (typically by age 6 months).[162] These nonsurgical treatments are cumbersome, are somewhat costly, and require multiple sessions of refitting to permit maximal remodeling of the cranial vault. Nonetheless, they are an option that should be explained to parents. Surgery should be considered only in severe deformational plagiocephaly in which the social impact is profound.[123] The deformity is amenable to a variety of surgical techniques, none of which has been demonstrated to produce superior results.

Scaphocephaly (keel skull) is caused by premature closure of the sagittal suture. This is the most common craniosynostosis, with current estimates of prevalence at 1 in 5000 births. There is a male predilection of nearly 3:1, and there is a small familial risk estimated at 5% to 10%. It accounts for nearly 50% of all craniosynostoses. There is a palpable midline ridge in most cases, accompanied by a characteristic dolichocephalic shape, bitemporal narrowing, and frontal/occipital bossing. When viewed from the side, the cranial vault is elongated. The deformity often presents at birth and then progresses. Surgical techniques range from simple suture release to total cranial vault remodeling.[96] Successful correction of both elevated ICP and deformity are attained by a variety of methods.

Lane[83] and Lannelongue[84] simultaneously described strip craniectomy as a treatment for craniosynostosis (Fig. 6–1). The high incidence of recurrent deformity and intracranial hypertension from early reossification led to the Tessier-inspired treatment, which is the most common approach today. Hoffman and Mohr created the lateral canthal advancement procedure in which a limited unilateral release of the retruded forehead and upper orbit provided limited correction.[66] Whitaker et al,[172] Marchac,[98] and others proposed more extensive mobilization of the entire fronto-orbital complex and the orbital barre with improved results. Barone, Ortiz-Monasterio, and Vicari espoused a return to strip craniectomy techniques, using endoscopic techniques to minimize morbidity and subsequent molding helmet use to achieve successful correction of both plagiocephaly and scaphocephaly. Long-term outcomes remain to be seen.[8]

Premature fusion of the metopic suture leads to a wedge-shaped frontal deformity known as *trigonocephaly*. There is a characteristic frontal ridge with bitemporal narrowing and hypotelorism. The standard treatment is currently fronto-orbital advancement with frontal remodeling and orbital barre advancement. Metopic synostosis has been less amenable to minimally invasive techniques because of the early and extensive bone growth along the anterior skull base.

Losken and associates studied unilateral coronal synostosis in a syndromic rabbit model and applied distraction techniques to correct the underlying skull anomalies.[114] Another innovation involves the use of absorbable fixation to minimize hardware-induced growth impairment. Current problems relate to partial recurrence of the deformities, and it is common to perform secondary procedures to correct bitemporal narrowing and forehead irregularity.

In certain cases, premature fusion of the coronal, lambdoid, and metopic sutures en masse leads to a "clo-

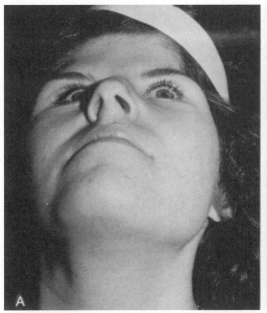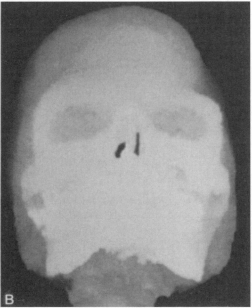

FIGURE 6–1. *A*, This teenaged girl had bicoronal synostosis that failed to respond to extended strip craniectomy in infancy. *B*, Computed tomographic scan. In addition to deep supraorbital and temporal depressions, which are more extensive on the left side than on the right side, she has marked asymmetry of the orbits. The right orbit is much wider than the left, with the lateral orbital rim being 50% wider on the right than on the left. The nasal bone deviation to the right is well visualized.

verleaf skull," often called the *kleeblattschädel deformity*. In severe forms, all cranial sutures may be fused. While this may occur spontaneously, it is most often associated with a syndromic diagnosis, including Pfeiffer syndrome, thanatophoric dysplasia, camptomelic dysplasia, achondroplasia, and rarely Crouzon syndrome.[131]

Syndromic Craniosynostosis

Crouzon syndrome is a common form of craniofacial dysostosis. It is usually inherited in an autosomal dominant pattern with variable penetrance. It is characterized by coronal suture synostosis with occasional multiple-suture involvement, midface hypoplasia with exorbitism, and commonly elevated ICP. Without treatment, papilledema, blindness, and decreased cognitive function are predictable sequelae. Hydrocephalus is present in 5% to 20% of patients, perhaps as a consequence of decreased venous outflow from the cranial base. The vault deformity is typically brachycephaly with bicoronal synostosis. Less commonly, other sutures are affected. Other anomalies include choanal atresia, high-arched palate with or without cleft, and multiple anomalies of the external auditory canal, eustachian tube, and external ears. Conductive hearing loss is also common, occurring in up to 55% of patients. Up to 15% of patients have atretic external auditory canals. Obstructive sleep apnea from midface impingement on the nasopharynx and cranial base kyphosis is a constant feature, varying with the degree of deformity. Severe early deformity often leads to tracheostomy in the infant, in whom obstructed nasal breathing is more physiologically problematic. Uncorrected, it can lead to cor pulmonale and even death. Mild cases may only manifest as obligate mouth breathing.

Early treatments focused on camouflage of the periorbital deformity.[130] Longacre popularized the use of split rib grafts to the midface before the quantum leap of Tessier.[94, 104, 167] Today, treatment typically involves a simultaneous bicoronal suture release and anterior cranial vault remodeling/advancement as a first step. Subsequently, midface advancement with Le Fort III osteotomy and fixation is carried out in the early school years.[145] Early facial advancement was fraught with a high rate of relapse.[172] Distraction techniques may permit earlier intervention with less relapse (see later discussion of distraction); several groups are investigating endoscopic approaches to the deformity.

Apert syndrome is a rare condition similar to Crouzon syndrome, in which there is bicoronal synostosis with turribrachycephaly, midface hypoplasia, orbital hypertelorism, complex polysyndactyly of both hands and feet, and acne vulgaris. Apert syndrome is also known as acrocephalosyndactyly type I. The incidence is estimated at 16 in 1,000,000 live births. Additional findings are synostosis of the spheno-occipital, sphenovomerine, and vomero-maxilary sutures. This aggressive synostosis commonly leads to elevated ICP and developmental delay. Optic nerve atrophy secondary to the accompanying papilledema is common. Other features include deafness secondary to chronic otitis, cleft palate, strabismus, and palpebral pto-

sis. The midface is profoundly hypoplastic in all dimensions, and there is a characteristic V-shaped anterior open bite with a class III malocclusion. The incidence of cleft soft palate is 30%. Severe dental crowding is the rule, and delayed dental eruption makes orthopedic and orthodontic management more complicated. Single mutations in FGF2 account for nearly all cases, and it is thought that most cases represent new mutations. Advanced paternal age has been described as a risk factor for a new mutation.[45]

The profound nature of the synostosis and progression of central nervous system symptoms in Apert syndrome necessitate a more aggressive surgical treatment. Recurrence of increased ICP and facial deformity leads to more frequent reoperation. Tessier developed a new surgical philosophy for the treatment of Apert syndrome that included modifications of the basic Gillies craniofacial disjunction, an intracranial and extracranial approach through the bicoronal incision, and multiple iliac crest bone grafts, both as onlay grafts and as wedges at the osteotomy sites.[25–27, 30, 152, 156, 158] Ortiz Monasterio subsequently described a monobloc osteotomy, advancing the forehead, orbits, and midface as a single unit for the correction of Crouzon syndrome.[128, 175] Van der Meulen described a modification of this technique, including in his plan a wedge osteotomy between the orbits to remove a portion of the ethmoids and the nasal bones to simultaneously correct the orbital hypertelorism.[163]

Tessier returned to this technique and a developed a procedure that is now known as *facial bipartition*. Subsequently, Tessier introduced the use of split calvarial bone grafts, which has become the standard technique for stabilization of craniofacial advancements.[155] The discrepancy between the orbital and lower maxillary retrusion necessitates a subsequent procedure for correction of the occlusion after dental maturation, typically at the Le Fort I level. Typical ancillary procedures include sliding genioplasty, nasal onlay grafts, and orthodontia. Management of the hands and feet is carried out by a pediatric hand surgeon. The incidence of strabismus also is significant, which can necessitate concomitant procedures to prevent amblyopia.

Other less common craniosynostosis syndromes include Saethre-Chotzen syndrome, Jackson-Weiss syndrome, Baller Gerhold syndrome, and Carpenter syndrome. There are numerous other anomalies in which craniosynostosis occurs, although less consistently than in the previously described syndromes.

Saethre-Chotzen syndrome is characterized by bilateral coronal suture synostosis, brachycephaly, variable midface hypoplasia, low-set hairline, cleft palate, strabismus, digital anomalies, and occasional mental retardation, presumably through intracranial hypertension. The cranial vault anomaly is often manifested as acro- or brachycephaly, with a characteristic flat forehead. Radiographically, additional findings of an enlarged sella turcica and widened sagittal sutures are common. Lid ptosis and lacrimal anomalies are frequent, as is medial canthal displacement. Interestingly, the lateral canthi are usually normal. Skeletal anomalies are common but are not pathognomonic. As the craniofacial anomalies are inconstant, Saethre-

Chotzen syndrome is more commonly misdiagnosed than other craniofacial syndromes. Again, advanced paternal age has been implicated as a risk factor.[46]

Pfeiffer syndrome is divided into three types. *Type I* involves craniosynostosis, wide thumbs and great toes, brachydactyly with or without syndactyly, and maxillary hypoplasia. *Type II* presents with cloverleaf skull and elbow ankylosis. *Type III* demonstrates a non-cloverleaf pansynostosis with extreme exorbitism and multiple visceral anomalies. These include malrotation and "prunebelly." Types II and III are often fatal. The cranial anomalies include acrobrachycephaly with bilateral coronal suture synostosis up to pansynostosis. The midface is comparable to that with Crouzon deformity. Other skeletal anomalies are less common, but the surgeon should rule out cervical fusion before attempting cranial vault correction in the infant with Pfeiffer syndrome. Inheritance is autosomal dominant in the classic description, but types II and III most often represent new mutations. This syndrome encompasses a variety of mutations in both FGF1 and FGF2 subgroups of the FGF genes and may be reclassified into several separate syndromes as molecular techniques identify variants.

Baller Gerhold syndrome presents with craniosynostosis, radial limb hypoplasia, gastrointestinal and genitourinary anomalies, cardiac anomalies, and central nervous system defects.

Carpenter syndrome is synostosis accompanied by deafness, retardation, and multiple limb anomalies with brachysyndactyly, most commonly. Obesity and cardiac anomalies are also common. This condition is also known as *acrocephalopolysyndactyly type II*. The cranial vault anomaly begins with sagittal synostosis, progressing to the lambdoidals and finally to the coronal sutures. Asymmetry and severe deformity are common. Hypertelorism or hypotelorism may occur, along with shallow orbits, proptosis, antimongolian slant, ptosis, and papilledema. Skeletal anomalies include varus foot deformity, genu valga, preaxial polydactyly, camptodactyly, and clinodactyly. Cardiac anomalies present in up to 50% of patients and include ventricular septal defect, patent ductus arteriosus, pulmonary stenosis, and tetralogy of Fallot. Abdominal wall anomalies and hypogonadism are also reported. Interestingly, mental retardation is thought to be independent of the elevated ICP. Carpenter syndrome is inherited as an autosomal recessive trait with widely variable penetrance, but there are many new cases.[46]

Treacher Collins syndrome, or *mandibulofacial dysostosis*, is a craniofacial syndrome first described by Berry in 1889.[10] It was Treacher Collins who provided the classic description that gained wide acceptance as a syndrome.[47, 161] The syndrome is often described as a form of Tessier-type clefts, with variable clefting of type 6 to 8 bilaterally. The anomaly is further associated with bilateral lower lid colobomata, absent medial lower lashes, malar hypoplasia, and bilateral microtia. Micrognathia is typical. Approximately 30% to 40% of patients have a palatal cleft. Mental retardation is not normally associated with the anomaly. The conductive hearing loss is typically treated with bone-conduction hearing aids with success.

The genetic basis of the disease is a defect in the Treacle gene on chromosome 5q. The molecular basis for the syndrome remains unknown. It is inherited in an autosomal dominant pattern with variable expression, and the rate of new cases is estimated to be as high as 60% in persons with the genetic defect.

Treatment remains controversial, and results vary widely. The most common repair often consists of Z plasties across the lower lid, myocutaneous flaps from the upper lid to reconstruct the lower lid, and canthopexy (Fig. 6–2). The treatment of the hypoplastic malars is also controversial.[137] A wide variety of materials has been

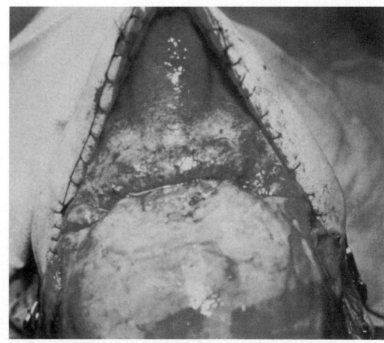

FIGURE 6–2. Coronal incision showing subperiosteal dissection to base of nose and exposing upper portions of both orbits.

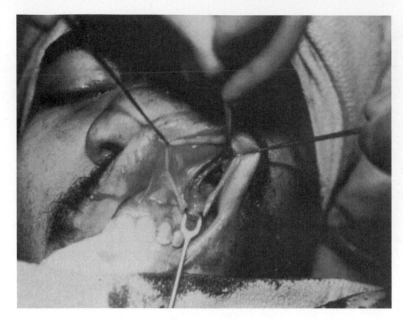

FIGURE 6–3. Buccal sulcus incision for exposure of lower face.

used to reconstruct the zygomas, including split- and full-thickness calvarial bone[176] (both pedicled[71, 108] and free), rib grafts, and temporoparietal or pericranial flaps. No single method has proven entirely satisfactory. The mandible has been treated with both orthognathic procedures and distraction osteogenesis.[126] With the most severe cases, distraction appears to be the treatment of choice.

Nager syndrome, also called *preaxial acrofacial dysostosis,* is characterized by severe malar hypoplasia, nasomaxillary hypoplasia, cleft palate, micrognathia, radial preaxial limb anomalies (often with absence of thumbs), and multiple external-ear anomalies. Even patients without cleft frequently have velopharyngeal insufficiency. Conductive hearing loss is inconsistent. The facial deformity is often compared with the Treacher Collins anomaly, with downward slanting lids, lower-lid colobomata, strabismus, and lagophthalmos. Occasionally, genitourinary anomalies occur, with both external genital and internal anomalies from minor cysts and duplications up to renal agenesis. Uncommonly, craniosynostosis is associated. Other anomalies include multiple skeletal deformities of limbs, spine, and pelvis. Intelligence is usually normal. Inheritance has been attributed to both autosomal dominant and recessive patterns but is most frequently sporadic. The treatment is similar to that of Treacher Collins syndrome.

Orbital Hypertelorism[40, 87, 164, 166]

Frontonasal dysplasia is a rare syndrome that has been described as a Tessier 0-14 cleft. The features include orbital hypertelorism, cranium bifidum occultum, and bifid nose, upper lip, and palate. This condition can occur sporadically or in conjunction with craniofrontonasal dysplasia, ophthalmofrontonasal dysplasia, and Greig cephalopolysyndactyly syndromes. The cranial vault may manifest coronal suture synostosis, and there is nearly always telecanthus and hypertelorism. Concomitant strabismus and the so-called V-syndrome are common. Other anomalies

can include colobomata of any ocular or lid structure, epibulbar dermoids, blepharophimosis, and microphthalmia. Any midline facial anomaly merits central nervous system evaluation. Agenesis of the corpus callosum occurs in up to 30% of patients. Encephalocele, meningocele, hydrocephalus, and Dandy-Walker anomaly can also occur with the syndrome. Typically, treatment is with a combined intracranial and extracranial approach, treating the hypertelorism at the same time as addressing the encephalocele that frequently occurs (Fig. 6–3). The results are often excellent, and relapse is uncommon (Fig. 6–4). A problematic aspect of the treatment sequence is the transnasal canthopexy, which is prone to recidivism, necessitating repeat canthopexy in the teen years. For severe cases, the "open roof" approach through the facial midline has gained favor.[13, 31, 53, 151, 153, 154, 160]

Oculo-Auriculo-Vertebral Spectrum: Microtia to Goldenhar Syndrome

The oculo-auriculo-vertebral spectrum of malformations comprises a wide variety of clinical deformities, ranging from simple microtia to full-blown Goldenhar syndrome. The phenotypic variation is wide, but the typical features of more severe cases include microtia, micrognathia, cervical spine anomalies, epibulbar dermoid cysts, and renal anomalies. Less commonly, cardiovascular anomalies are present, ranging from ventricular septal defect to monotruncal anomalies. Pulmonary anomalies can also occur, with tracheoesophageal fistulas, abnormal lobation, and even pulmonary agenesis on the affected side. Some authors think that preauricular tags merit inclusion into the spectrum. The oculo-auriculo-vertebral spectrum is the second most common craniofacial anomaly after cleft lip and palate. Incidence estimates range from 0.15% to 0.3% of live births. Goldenhar syndrome accounts for approximately 5% to 10% of total cases. There is no distinct pattern of heredity. Some authors report autosomal dominant, autosomal recessive, and sporadic occur-

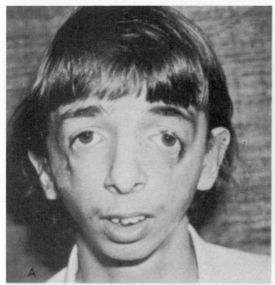
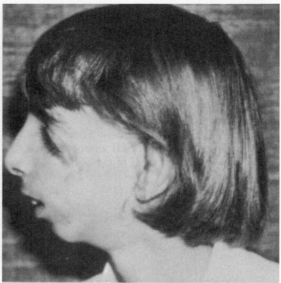

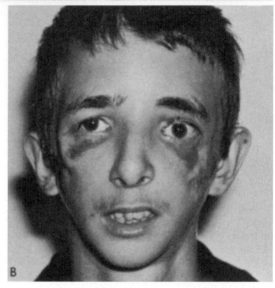

FIGURE 6–4. *A*, Preoperative full-face and profile views of patient with Treacher Collins syndrome showing pseudocolobomata, extreme zygomatic hypoplasia, and hypoplasia of the chin. *B*, Postoperative view showing correction of colobomata, zygomatic hypoplasia, and chin deficiency. The zygomatic hypoplasia was corrected with onlay grafts, the chin deformity with a combination of sliding genioplasty and onlay grafts.

rence. There is clearly a mild genetic propensity, with "nonaffected" members of a pedigree exhibiting increased incidence of mild external-ear malformations. Other possible causes include chromosomal defects, teratogens, and hemorrhage of the stapedial artery in utero.

Pruzansky developed the classification scheme that has been most commonly used to describe the mandibular deformity. In *type I* deformities, the mandibular ramus and condyle are present, but hypoplastic. *Type IIa* involves malformed condyles, and *type IIb* describes absence of a satisfactory articulation. *Type III* describes complete absence of the vertical ramus. This scheme seems to best aid in treatment planning.

Other significant craniofacial anomalies include temporal bone anomalies up to absence of the external auditory canal and severely deformed ossicles, facial nerve palsy, cranial vault anomalies, zygomatic hypoplasia, wide variation in maxillary deformity, cleft lip or palate (or both), and profound soft tissue hypoplasia of the affected side, which can present the most difficult aspect of the reconstruction. Cranial base anomalies and cervical spine fu-

sions can render correction of torticollis impossible. Infrequently, the anomaly may be bilateral.

Correction depends greatly on the degree of deformity. Mild cases can be approached with orthodontia, onlay bone grafts, and otoplasty (Fig. 6–5). Classic orthognathic procedures can adequately treat moderate deformities. Currently, distraction osteogenesis has found favor, and most authors agree that the soft tissue expansion afforded by gradual distraction is preferable to other techniques. Grade III deformities have been traditionally addressed by rib grafts with condylar reconstruction. Results have varied, with both undergrowth and overgrowth of grafts reported. Ankylosis is also a common and difficult complication to remedy. Anecdotal reports of distraction on grade III mandibles are surfacing. The rapid proliferation of tissue-engineering techniques may ultimately address the difficult soft tissue problems with tissue-engineered fat. In the meantime, authors have reported microvascular soft tissue transfer and serial fat injection with adequate results.[23, 24, 29, 93, 107, 119, 122]

Ear reconstruction is also problematic and prone to

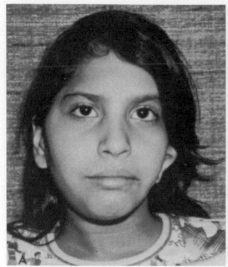

FIGURE 6–5. *A*, Preoperative view of patient with left hemifacial microsomia. *B*, Postoperative view of same patient after onlay grafts to zygoma, dermal graft, and lateral canthopexy on the left. (From Whitaker LA. Evaluation and treatment of upper facial asymmetry. In Whitaker LA, Randall P [eds]. Symposium on Reconstruction of Jaw Deformity. St Louis, CV Mosby, 1978.)

complications. In expert hands, total auricular reconstruction with rib cartilage, utilizing the method of either Brent[11] or Nagata,[125] produces outstanding results, but there are notable failures, with many aesthetically inadequate results despite meticulous surgical technique. Alloplastic materials have been employed, but despite exciting aesthetic results, infrequent but catastrophic exposure and infection have prevented their wide acceptance.[141] Osseointegrated implants and removable prosthesis placement provide excellent results as well.[148] Tissue engineering has tantalized us with reports of engineered total auricular cartilage frameworks, but no human trials have been reported to date. The ideal method for ear reconstruction remains elusive.

Planning Craniofacial Reconstruction

The major craniofacial anomalies can be considered as a group for the purposes of general operative planning. Because the majority of these anomalies are structural, rather than functional or physiologic, the craniofacial surgeon has the luxury of being able to base surgical correction on standards of facial structure and function. These standards have been widely published and used for everything from anthropologic studies to orthognathic surgery planning. In many cases, the surgeon can refer to tables that outline cephalometric norms, compare clinical preoperative measurements to these tables, and have a surgical "blueprint" plan prior to entering the operating room.[52, 168]

Physical examination is the first stage of evaluation of symmetry and form, keeping in mind the basis of the underlying anomaly. If the syndrome presents with abnormalities in soft tissue envelope, nasal form, or auricular structure, symmetry should be the dominant principle of the surgical plan. The eye is exquisitely sensitive to asymmetry, and any variation from the ideal is noticeable. The

anterior hairline should be more or less horizontal, and the brows should be on the same plane and approximately parallel to the palpebral fissure. Racial characteristics can deviate from these general principles, especially in the canthal insertions. The medial and lateral canthal tendons can be moved up to several millimeters in the coronal plane to affect the ethnic character of the eye. Often, the lateral canthus is located slightly higher than the medial canthus, and this should be studied prior to surgery. The ear is another structure in which there are many variations in acceptable form, but generally, the superior pole of the auricle should be located approximately at the level of the brow when viewed from the anterior aspect.

Bony movements predictably affect soft tissue correction. Measurements between the craniofacial bony landmarks serve as the bases for these movements.[12] As previously mentioned, any asymmetry or abnormality in the appearance of the eyelids and globes is obvious. Even untrained observers are sensitive to small deviations from the norm, and anthropomorphic traits are commonly (and cruelly) ascribed to variations in these structures. The characteristics that make the face uniquely human and attractive do not have to be disturbed by much to become disfiguring and dehumanizing. The interpupillary distance is therefore one of the keys to orbitocranial surgery. Because of strabismus, this distance can vary and is often considered a range. The normal range is 58 to 71 mm in adults. Medial intercanthal distance is obtained by using calipers to locate the medial vertex of the palpebral fissures. This soft tissue measurement represents the final result of the bony correction. Orbital bony shifts are performed to correct this value, but the interorbital bony distance as based on computed tomography is often used to calculate bony cuts. The normal medial intercanthal distance is usually 5 to 8 mm more than the interorbital bony distance.

Orbital volume and its affect on globe and lid position can be measured in a variety of ways. The simplest way to determine abnormal globe position is the hand-held Luedde exophthalmometer. It measures the distance from the lateral orbital rim to the corneal surface. The normal range is 12 to 16 mm. The difference between the measured values and the norm represents the soft tissue correction. If the orbital bones relate abnormally to the lateral orbital rim, compensations have to be calculated and based on planned movements to leave the soft tissue attachments in an appropriate position. An example would be the complex three-dimensional movements needed to correct the Apert anomaly. The upper face is commonly split, a medial wedge of bone is removed, the lateral orbits are differentially advanced more than the medial structures, and the nasal pyramid is advanced simultaneously with the midface. Obviously, final lateral orbital location is based on a complex bony plan.

The medial intercanthal distance and the direct exophthalmetric reading can be used to accurately estimate orbital shifts if the planned movements are more straightforward. These two measurements are often all that is needed in simple plagiocephaly correction, and intraoperative measurement of symmetry and position guides the final correction.

Bitemporal distance is also important, although it does not require such strict adherence to norms. The zygomatic arch and malar eminence projection are also considered, but these too vary widely even within ethnic groups. Prominence of the zygomas is essential to the normal "drape" of the soft tissues. These are often hypoplastic in craniofacial syndromes. In mandibulofacial dysostosis, they may be absent entirely. Reconstruction of these structures is one of the most challenging problems in craniofacial surgery. The complex shape of the zygoma, along with its substantial bony volume and intimate relation with the eyelids and origins of muscles of facial expression and mastication, makes its reconstruction very complex. Bone grafts, whether free or pedicled to pericranium, must be tailored to the defect in three dimensions, placed accurately in space, and related correctly to the external auditory canal, orbit, and soft tissue, avoiding impingement on the masseter.

Preoperative photography is essential to surgical planning. Photographs give a fixed point of reference for soft tissue and bone shifts. Anthropometric analysis can be accurately derived from photographs, and emerging technologies may soon permit three-dimensional modeling based only on digital photograph capture. The soft tissue goals that have been accurately based on cephalograms in simple orthognathic movements may be extrapolated to the more intricate movements in craniofacial surgery. These photographs are used in conjunction with dental models, radiographs, and databases of soft tissue results after bony movements to plan surgical strategies.[43]

Dental models are essential to planning any facial movements that will affect occlusion. Sub-millimeter discrepancies are often noticeable to patients, and malocclusion after surgery can lead to trismus, temporomandibular joint problems, and the need for corrective orthodontia. Therefore, it is common to base bony movement on occlusion and alter non-occlusal bone movements to accommodate the occlusion. Small movements in the jaws drastically affect soft tissues around the midface and lips. All dental-arch movements affect the final aesthetic quality of the reconstruction. Recently, computed tomography of dental radiographs has been used to perform model surgery on the computer. Perhaps the 40-year era of orthognathic surgery based on plaster models will soon give way to a fully computerized surgical plan.

Posteroanterior and lateral cephalograms are the standard in dentofacial analysis. They permit reproducible measurement of the skeleton and subsequent reconstruction. Often, the decision to perform an intracranial procedure such as a monoblock advancement, or an extracranial movement such as a Le Fort III osteotomy, is based on the cephalometric analysis.

Computed tomography is the current state of the art in bony imaging. Computed tomography is a precise tool that can provide critical information about the three-dimensional relationship between structures, information that is not available in plain films. Three-dimensional reconstructed images of the bones and soft tissues allow the surgeon to view the craniofacial structures as if they were a prepared dry skeleton. This is of incalculable value in understanding skeletal relationships. These images present the surgeon with a visual summary of the data from the axial images in a form that is easily understood. They are not merely a convenience or aid for the surgeon but are an invaluable tool that should be obtained in every major craniofacial case.

Craniofacial surgery affects so many different systems that it is important that the patient be treated by an experienced team. Typically, teams include plastic surgeons, maxillofacial surgeons, otolaryngologists, orthodontists, speech pathologists, audiologists, geneticists, ophthalmologists, and neurosurgeons. Nonclinicians on the team can include social workers, team coordinators, and dental technicians. Anesthesia issues can be complex; many centers have a specialized difficult airway team to handle these cases with the otolaryngologists. Tracheostomies are being performed less frequently as techniques in intubation become more sophisticated. In severe micrognathia, tracheostomy provides the safest airway, but mandibular distraction techniques may permit avoidance of tracheostomies even in neonates.[58] Postoperatively, surgical intensive care is becoming more routine. Familiarity with the treatment of these patients is shortening stays in the intensive care unit, lowering the incidence of unrecognized complications and standardizing treatment parameters. Surgical intensivists often help in the postoperative management, lessening the workload for the busy surgical team.

Surgical Methods

Preoperatively, the patient is prepared for a craniofacial procedure in increasingly standardized fashion.[33, 121] Blood products are typed and cross-matched, often from donor-directed sources, and reserved. Inhalational agents are used to partially induce anesthesia prior to invasive procedures to minimize patient stress. Endotracheal intubation is carried out, frequently with flexible endoscopic control.

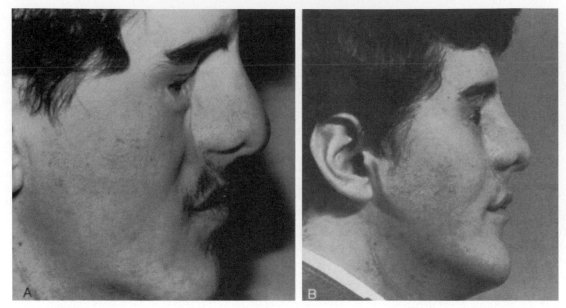

FIGURE 6–6. *A,* This young man, with bilateral oblique facial cleft, has severe maxillomalar retrusion despite a prior Le Fort I advancement osteotomy and recession of the mandible. In addition, he has congenital anophthalmic orbit on the right. *B,* The postoperative view shows the result after a superficial temporal artery full-thickness parietal bone graft, which has maintained its projection owing to its enhanced vascularity.

The endotracheal tube is often wired or sutured into place. A neurosurgical headrest is often used to permit access to the cranial vault. The patient is protected with silicone-gel pads as needed to avoid decubiti. Preoperative antibiotics are started. Steroids are often administered to assist in control of edema. Invasive monitoring lines are started, typically a central venous catheter, arterial line, esophageal temperature probe, and sometimes lumbar drains to aid management of cerebrospinal fluid. A Foley catheter is placed, and oximetry and capnometry are initiated. Presurgical shaving is becoming less common and is not routine in our institution. Surgical approaches are injected with diluted epinephrine solutions to minimize blood loss. Finally, surgical preparation is meticulously performed. The patient is then ready for the procedure.

Surgical Exposures

The basic surgical exposure for craniofacial procedures is the coronal incision (Fig. 6–6). This incision is carried out from the superior tragal notch on one side to the contralateral side, crossing over the vertex of the skull. Many surgeons "jog" the incision slightly posteriorly above the ear to permit hair to fall across the healed scar, camouflaging the most visible portion of the incision. Others employ multiple V or S plasties for similar advantage. The scalp flap and forehead are then elevated in a subgaleal plane until the supraorbital region is reached. There, a subperiosteal approach is initiated, and the supraorbital nerves are visualized. If necessary, a 2-mm osteotome is used to liberate the nerves from the supraorbital foramen to permit the flap to turn completely without avulsing the nerves. Excellent visualization of the

upper face and midface is afforded, and the orbits and nasal bones can be osteotomized and reduced and fixation can be applied from this vantage.[65, 70] Some surgeons perform a transconjunctival approach to the orbital floor, while others osteotomize a portion of the orbit blindly while retracting the periorbital contents. Previous scars may be used for surgical access, but visible facial incisions are to be avoided. Only in severe hypertelorism is a dorsal nasal incision frequently necessary to remove redundant soft tissue. In several centers, cranial-vault procedures are routinely performed with the endoscope. Combining cranial-vault osteotomies with orbital osteotomies presents unique challenges, and no reports of completely endoscopic craniofacial advancements have yet been published. That is the next surgical challenge.

The lower face, below the zygomas, is approached either through transconjunctival incisions or through the superior buccal sulcus (Fig. 6–7). A cuff of mucosa and buccinator is left to be sewn during closure, and the midface is degloved in a subperiosteal plane. This permits access to the inferior orbital and malar areas. This approach is useful for midface osteotomies, such as the Le Fort I, II, and III procedures. The intraoral portion of the procedure should be avoided, if possible, because the theoretical risk of infection from oral flora increases. Nonetheless, infections remain thankfully rare.

Extracranial Corrections

The simplest craniofacial procedures involve adding to areas of deficient bone stock. This can be as simple as a cranioplasty for contour deformity or as complex as a pedicled calvarial graft for a Treacher Collins malar reconstruction. Currently, a variety of materials are avail-

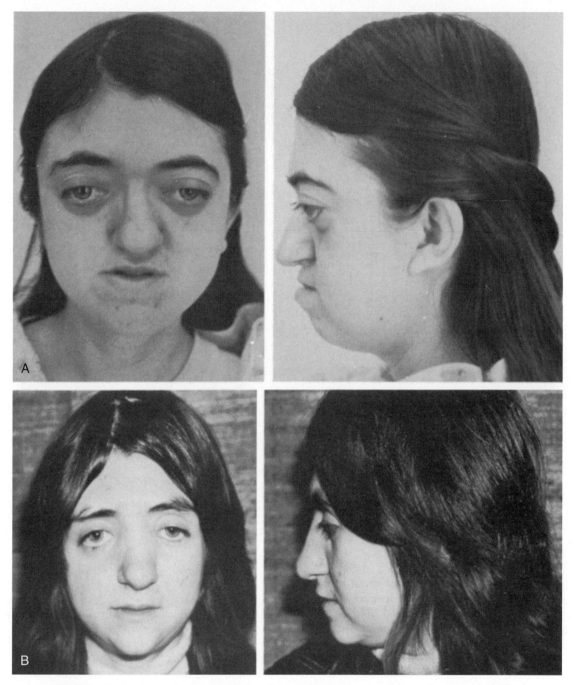

FIGURE 6–7. *A*, Preoperative views of patient with Crouzon syndrome showing exorbitism, nasal deformity, and zygomaticomaxillary hypoplasia. *B*, Postoperative views showing deformities corrected after Le Fort III midface advancement.

Illustration continued on following page

able for this purpose, but most surgeons have favored autogenous material.

The most common donor sites for bone grafts have been the ribs, calvaria, and iliac crest. Up to four ribs can be harvested without concern for flail chest by leaving a central strut and harvesting on either side. In very young patients, the ribs have been reported to regenerate if harvested subperiosteally. Typically, a 4- to 5-cm inframammary incision is made, and the ribs are dissected out in a subperiosteal plane in 8- to 15-cm segments, de-

pending on the size of the patient. Subsequent re-harvest of the same rib segments has been reported.[92]

An alternative site for autogenous bone harvest is the iliac crest. The ileum has the advantage of providing more bone stock that is especially rich in cancellous bone. Disadvantages include more donor-site morbidity, including pain, scarring, hernia, and growth disturbance. The thickness of the iliac crest permits the surgeon more freedom to sculpt the grafts to fit the recipient site and optimize contact between the graft and recipient bed.

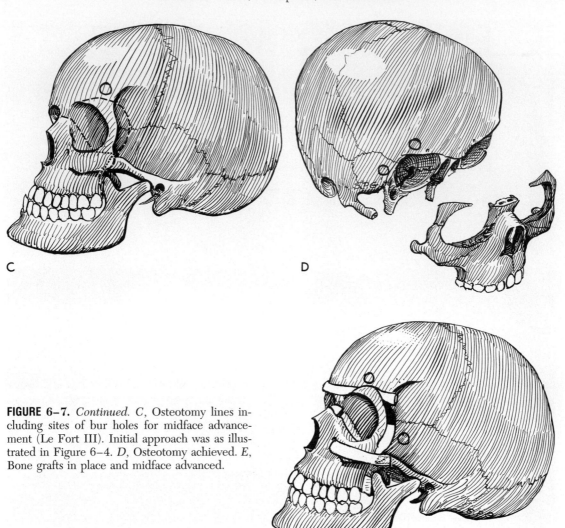

FIGURE 6–7. *Continued. C,* Osteotomy lines including sites of bur holes for midface advancement (Le Fort III). Initial approach was as illustrated in Figure 6–4. *D,* Osteotomy achieved. *E,* Bone grafts in place and midface advanced.

Cancellous bone is also useful in areas of marginal vascularity, where there may be an advantage compared with cortical bone. Nonetheless, the resorption of bone grafts is unpredictable and is one of the major hurdles still faced by the surgeon.

The bone grafts are tailored to the appropriate size and shape and fixed into place. Traditional wire osteosynthesis has the advantage of speed and ease of use, low cost, and familiarity. More complex shapes are often fixed with miniplates and screws. Titanium is the standard plate material, but more and more surgeons are turning to absorbable plating systems in younger patients to avoid subsequent growth restriction and migration. In patients with Treacher Collins syndrome, multiple split rib grafts are typically used in the malar region, and a single or double is used later across the lateral orbit. The reconstruction in hemifacial microsomia is similar but is usually unilateral.[28]

With care, large segments of split- or full-thickness temporoparietal bone can be harvested in a single block (Fig. 6–8). The donor sites of full-thickness grafts can be reconstructed with alloplastic materials ranging from methylmethacrylate to hydroxyapatite, as well as cadaveric allograft or split grafts from other areas. These membranous bone grafts have been reported to undergo less resorption than endochondral bone grafts but have the disadvantage of being more brittle and prone to fracture during contouring. Bone thickness also plays a part in selection of graft site. Calvarial bone is much thinner than iliac crest. In highly selective situations, such as in the case of the Treacher Collins syndrome with bony and soft tissue deficiency of the zygomaticomaxillary complex, vascularized parietal bone grafts transferred to the face on a pedicle of the superficial temporal artery may result in permanent improvement.[32, 71, 109]

Free autogenous bone grafts, with occasional need for pedicled grafts, are the current standard for bone augmentation. A variety of alloplastic materials—including porous polypropylene, ceramic, irradiated cadaveric bone, and PTFE—have been used for secondary augmentation of the craniofacial skeleton. None has found universal acceptance.

Osteototomies and en bloc movements of segments of facial bone are sometimes performed extracranially. In

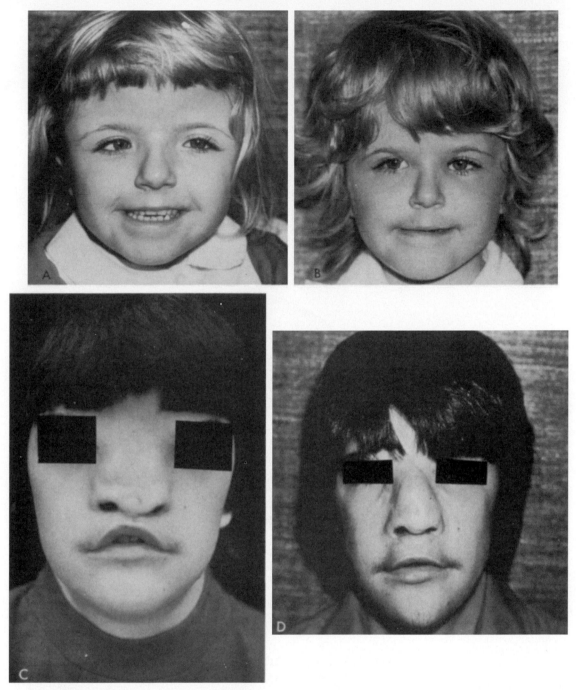

FIGURE 6–8. *A,* Patient with craniofacial dysostosis, forehead deformity, and orbital hypertelorism. *B,* Postoperative view showing correction of orbital hypertelorism and reshaping of forehead intracranially. *C,* Preoperative view of patient with orbital hypertelorism, nasal deformity, and extremely short upper lip. *D,* Postoperative view showing correction of orbital hypertelorism, correction of nasal deformity, and lengthening of lip.

Illustration continued on following page

particular, the modified Le Fort III osteotomy has been typically performed as an extracranial procedure (Fig. 6–9). Advancement of the zygomaticomaxillary complex has also been performed in this way. The segments of interest are osteotomized, mobilized, and placed in their desired position. Rigid fixation and bone grafting is used to hold the segments in place. Relapse is common be-

cause of the paucity of bone stock behind these segments. Cranial distraction procedures hold the promise of generating fracture callus behind the advancing segments, and these procedures probably represent the current state of the art in subcranial advancements. Eventually, the technical complexities of distraction will probably permit more sophisticated multisegmental movements. Postoper-

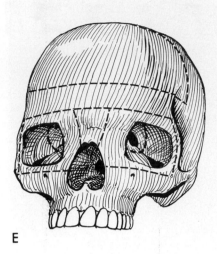

E

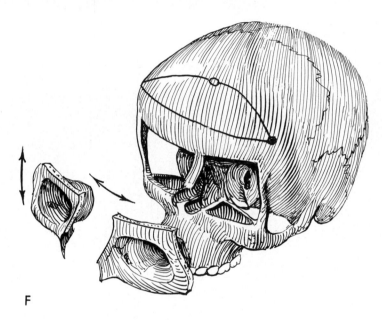

F

FIGURE 6–8. *Continued.* *E*, Basic osteotomy sites for orbital shifts used with variations in the two patients. Full craniotomy was necessary for brain protection. *F*, Orbits mobilized. *G*, Orbits in place with bone grafts. (*A* and *B* from Whitaker LA, Broennle AM, Kerr LP, Herlich A. Improvements in craniofacial reconstruction: methods evolved in 235 consecutive patients. Plast Reconstr Surg 65:561, 1980.)

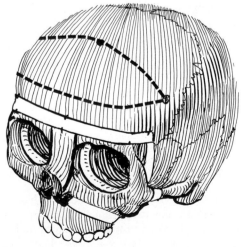

G

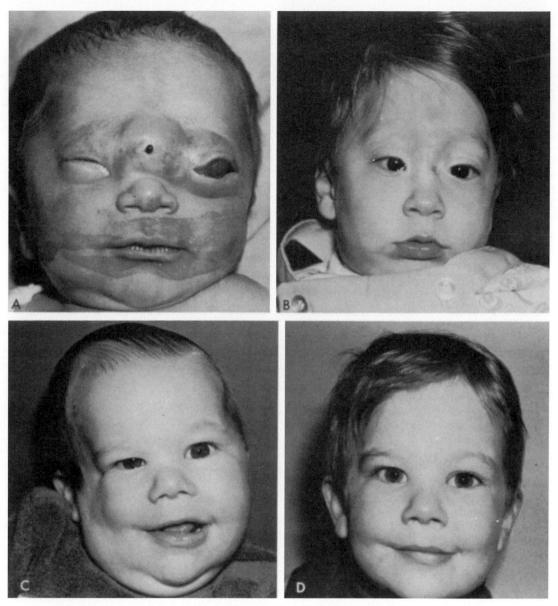

FIGURE 6–9. *A,* Preoperative view of patient with encephalocele and orbital hypertelorism. *B,* Postoperative view of same patient. *C,* Preoperative view of patient with isolated craniostenosis. *D,* Postoperative view of same patient. (*A* and *B* from Whitaker LA, Broennle AM, Kerr LP, Herlich A. Improvements in craniofacial reconstruction: methods evolved in 235 consecutive patients. Plast Reconstr Surg 65:561, 1980. *C* and *D* from Whitaker LA, Schut L, Kerr LP. Early surgery for isolated craniofacial dysostosis. Plast Reconstr Surg 60:575, 1977.)

ative intermaxillary fixation or elastic traction, or both, are used to maintain the correction.

Limited Intracranial Approaches with En Bloc Movements

Limited intracranial approaches involve limited bifrontal craniotomy via bur-hole trephination and removal of the frontal bones to permit retraction of the frontal lobes and cranial base osteotomies. These approaches are performed most frequently for the extended Le Fort III osteotomy to protect the brain or for the Le Fort II osteotomy, in which visualization of the crista galli and

anterior cranial base is desirable. These segments are fixed with miniplates and intermaxillary wires or elastics. Careful presurgical planning must be coordinated with the orthodontist to avoid postoperative malocclusion.[48, 67, 74, 127]

Intracranial Procedures

The most complex craniofacial procedures require a combined intracranial and extracranial approach. The access needed to completely osteotomize and mobilize the orbits and midface in units typically requires a bifrontal craniotomy. The neurosurgeon removes the frontal bones, exposing the orbital roof, the cribriform plate, and the crista galli; the craniofacial surgeon mobilizes the facial and cranial base structures. Approaching the cranial base from an intracranial vantage enhances visibility and protection of the brain and sagittal sinus.

Typically, the neurosurgeon makes multiple bur holes in the frontoparietal region. A bifrontal craniotomy is then carried out. This is usually performed with a craniotome, which consists of a side-cutting, high-speed bur and a footplate designed to displace the dura mater during the cuts. The bur holes are dissected carefully, bleeding bone is waxed, and the dura and sagittal sinus are protected during removal of the frontal bones. After the neurosurgeon has completed the craniotomy, the frontal lobes, and sometimes the temporal lobes, are retracted; communicating veins are bipolar-electrocoagulated; and the orbits are osteotomized. This is performed with sagittal saws, burs, and osteotomes. The bicoronal flap is easily retracted, permitting direct visualization of the orbit both intracranially and from within the orbital cavity itself. Thus, the periorbita and globes are protected with malleable retractors.

In orbital hypertelorism, a segment of bone is removed from between the orbits in the area of the glabella. The ethmoid air cells are removed, the olfactory nerves are protected, and the orbits are infractured medially. Similarly, with maxillary osteotomies, the orbit may be mobilized as a single unit and moved in any desired direction. The intraorbital cuts are usually performed through the thin bone nearer the orbital apex, and the orbits are plated into position. If advancement is substantial, as in Crouzon and Apert syndrome to correct exorbitism, bone grafting is frequently needed.[169] In selected cases wherein the deformity lends itself to the technique, the orbit and midface can be mobilized in a single unit, or *monoblock*.[128] This technique is readily combined with the facial bipartition procedure for the correction of exorbitism, hypertelorism, and midface retrusion as occurs in Apert syndrome. Historically, this procedure has been criticized for frequent infections due to the communication between the sinus and the intracranial cavity. Perhaps with the advent of distraction osteogenesis, the early callus may isolate the two anatomic areas, permitting a renaissance of the technique. In the meantime, any substantial bony gaps left after advancement of the segments should be bone-grafted with split rib or cranial bone and the segments rigidly fixed. The cranial bones may be further contoured and bent to achieve an adequate frontal and temporal contour.[69, 120]

Preventive Surgery

Surgery in the first year of life is an exciting clinical arena in craniofacial surgery. It is particularly applicable to the upper face and cranium, an area where the surgery permits the growing brain to mold and shape the bony segments to mimic normal growth. The brain nearly triples in volume during the first year of life, and the ocular globes follow a similar growth pattern. After age 3 months, the soft tissue dissection required for a craniofacial procedure becomes technically easier and the bones are easily cut and manipulated. The bones are not rigid enough to maintain their shape for more complex cranial vault–reshaping procedures, but safety can be maintained by taking advantage of this early brain growth, simple strip craniectomies, orbital advancements, and the less severe hypertelorism corrections. After the surgical correction, the bony vault and orbital structures should theoretically follow normal growth curves under the influence of the developing brain and globes. In addition to the technical advantages of early correction, cranial bone grafts are easily obtained and integrate well. Endoscopic procedures may supplant some of these simple cranial vault operations, but complex procedures that require correction in multiple dimensions remain beyond current technology.[38, 39, 49, 73, 91, 170, 173]

Results

Ancillary Procedures

The facial appearance is to a great extent controlled by the bony skeleton. Fine-tuning of major bony reconstruction is supplemented by soft tissue refinements. Additional procedures are often required to attain the best possible aesthetic results. These procedures include lateral canthopexies with hypertelorism, mandibulofacial dysostosis, and craniofacial dysostosis. Along with medial orbital shifts, nasolacrimal apparatus instrumentation or drainage procedures, or both, are frequently needed. Osteoplasty and cranioplasty is a common method of enhancing soft tissue contour. Medial canthal webbing associated with syndromal development is camouflaged with canthoplasty. Brow position may be modified either with asymmetrical flap tailoring upon closure or with endoscopic techniques borrowed from the aesthetic surgery armamentarium. Nasal soft tissue procedures are frequently required, especially in hypertelorism and midface retrusion, in which nasal development is impaired. These procedures may be performed in conjunction with the bony procedures. External-ear and lip reconstruction may be required, and these usually are performed at a separate surgical stage. Mandibular and maxillary orthognathic procedures are commonly required and are usually performed in the mid-teen years. Combining jaw procedures with midface osteotomies and upper-facial movements may create an unstable framework prone to relapse, so these are best left to subsequent procedures.

A clever and useful modification of the facial bipartition procedure introduced by Van der Meulen and championed by Caronni is the placement of the vertex of facial rotation at the anterior nasal spine. When the hemifacial segments are rotated, the palate is expanded transversely as the orbits are impacted. Thus, lower facial and occlusive goals are addressed simultaneously with the bony upper- and midface procedure.

Problems and Complications

The invasive and large-scale nature of these surgeries makes them hazardous. Worldwide, the mortality rate has been estimated at approximately 1.5%. Death has been attributed to intracranial swelling associated with length of surgery, brain damage during osteotomy, intracranial infection, and hemorrhage. Blindness is a thankfully rare complication, associated with correction of severe hypertelorism. Neglected intracranial hypertension with its associated bleeding, papilledema, and increased surgical difficulty has also contributed to perioperative visual loss.

Infection has been the most frequent major complication in this type of surgery, with one large series reporting a nearly 7% infection rate.[169] The risk of infection associated with intracranial procedures is slightly increased when the oral cavity is entered, but overall, the infection rate has been uniform for intra- and extracranial procedures. Through use of the routines outlined previously, the infection rate in our institution falls below the national average.

Temporary palsy of cranial nerves is not uncommon and can involve the sixth nerve and the frontal branch of the seventh nerve. Areas of hypoesthesia in the distribution of the fifth nerve are frequent but typically resolve rapidly as is typical of neuropraxia injuries.

Canthal drift is another problematic area. After medial or upward repositioning of the lateral canthus, there is frequent relapse of the canthal tendon. Telecanthus after orbital mobilization for hypertelorism is minimized by preliminary dissection of the medial canthal ligaments. External compression-type splints have fallen out of favor and can cause skin necrosis in the canthal area. Direct deep suturing of the skin of the medial canthal region to the repositioned nasal and orbital bones has minimized the occurrence of drift, but revision surgery is frequently needed.

Growth patterns after surgery in craniofacial dysostosis are unpredictable. Extensive fronto-orbital mobilization as performed in correction of Apert syndrome is usually accompanied by some recurrence of the original deformity. The growth potential of the involved bones has been implicated in this problem. The cranial bones once mobilized do not grow normally, as is logical in an anomaly based on growth factor receptor. Reoperation is usually necessary in the school years and sometimes in the teens. In older patients, the soft tissues are often so poorly adaptable that adequate re-drape and contraction may not occur, with unsatisfactory aesthetic results.

Strabismus is a frequent problem in orbital procedures. It is usually self-limiting but may lead to strabismus surgery in a small number of patients. In many cases, strabismus may be improved after orbital procedures.

Velopharyngeal insufficiency is an infrequent complication of midface advancement. Theoretically, any cleft palate patient in whom the midface is advanced is at risk for velopharyngeal insufficiency, but clinically this problem is insignificant.

Bony resorption is a common and probably underestimated problem. Bone grafts take unpredictably, and advanced segments likely undergo some degree of resorption. Current thinking suggests that en bloc movements are less prone to resorption when soft tissue stripping is minimal. The same concept is applied to distraction osteogenesis, and bone growth can be spectacular, achieving centimeters of new growth in a few weeks of distraction.

Similarly, drastic soft tissue movements have been associated with disappointing ultimate results, but some application has been found for tissue expansion in the face. Nasal reconstruction, in particular, has benefited from this technique. Silicone reservoirs are placed subcutaneously and slowly filled by percutaneously injecting a port every week or so. Studies have shown actual hyperplasia of soft tissue rather than simple stretching of the skin. Through the avoidance of Z plasty and large rotational flaps, scars may be placed in less conspicuous locations. Again, proponents of distraction osteogenesis point to the better aesthetic results with slow elongation of soft tissues.[116, 129]

Growth seems to progress more or less normally in the upper face after craniofacial procedures. Early midface surgery, in contrast, has been criticized for profound diminution of midface growth. Therefore, midface osteotomies have been reserved for patients in whom there is a compelling social aspect to the deformity that would outweigh the predictable consequences of early surgery.[78, 81]

Recovery is prolonged with craniofacial procedures as postoperative edema and airway concerns make intubation a standard sequence for the early postoperative period. Swelling around the eyes and mouth make communication difficult. Younger patients seem to tolerate this situation better than teens, in whom the inability to speak can provoke anxiety. Facial swelling persists for weeks, and many patients opt to defer return to normal activities until the face appears more normal. Patients are counseled that up to 1 year can be required to see all of the subtle changes that occur after surgery.

Timing of Surgery

The planning of the surgical rehabilitation with a major craniofacial anomaly ideally begins when the patient is born. The decisions regarding timing of the surgery must balance the psychosocial needs of the patient with the technical limitations of surgery and the ultimate growth potential of the repositioned facial structures. The maxilla may be repositioned to achieve ideal facial appearance, but if subsequent growth is deficient, the surgical goal is thwarted.

The release of coronal synostosis is typically carried out by fronto-orbital advancement at about age 6 months, when the cranial bones are firm enough to be effectively remodeled and retain the new shape, yet it is not too late to take advantage of subsequent brain growth.[102] Treatment has been more successful with asymmetrical deformities than with symmetrical ones. Many surgeons have strong feelings that bilateral fronto-orbital advancement for plagiocephaly yields superior results. Control of the late remodeling caused by frontal sinus development on the unoperated side by bilateral orbital barre advancement gives a more stable long-term result. Surgery undertaken early in infancy with bilateral fronto-orbital advancement should include reconstruction of the temporal and lateral orbital structures with cranial bone so that subsequent procedures can be accomplished with stable bone stock. Craniectomized bone is fragile, brittle, and difficult to contour.

In general, the rare infant with Crouzon or Apert syndrome who has a compromised airway, impending visual loss, or feeding problems can be temporized with tracheostomy, feeding tube, and tarsorrhaphy. Intracranial hypertension is an absolute indication for cranial-vault expansion in these children. Life-threatening hemorrhage and poor stability have characterized the results of early frontofacial advancements advocated by some groups. In contrast, early results of cranial-vault distraction have been promising. Advantages include more stability, less bone resorption, and more normal growth curves. Long-term results will tell if these advantages hold up.

Muhlbauer et al demonstrated the reliability of early monobloc advancement in young infants.[118] Marchac and Renier[97] advocated early craniofacial approaches for the most severe deformities. Severe midfacial retrusion, particularly when complicated by nasopharyngeal obstruction, globe exposure, corneal ulceration, and possible social impact, may prompt an early Le Fort III advancement at approximately age 3 years. Again, distraction procedures are being visited earlier in an attempt to prevent some of these sequelae. Typically, the Le Fort III procedure is overcorrected at about 5 years; with luck, there is no need for reoperation in the teen years. The stability of the maxilla and vertical growth of the midfacial segment was demonstrated in 12 children younger than 7 years who were observed for 5 years after surgery.[103] If not performed early for the previously discussed reasons, midface advancement is probably best left until facial growth is complete.

The stability of the standard bipartition operations for orbital hypertelorism is good, and even with septal resection, facial growth is minimally reduced. Mulliken and Kaban agreed that growth is minimally affected but were disappointed with early relapse associated with more aggressive orbital translocations.[119] Nasal grafts were resorbed excessively when combined with these procedures.

Malar and maxillary reconstruction in Treacher Collins syndrome has proven to be disappointing as there is predictable resorption of bone grafts. Pedicled temporal fascial flaps have corrected some of this resorption, showing normal growth. Nonetheless, the aesthetic results with all techniques have been mixed. Perhaps tissue engineering will provide the impetus for acceptable, reliable midface reconstruction in these patients.

As mentioned, hemifacial microsomia is an area in which distraction techniques have supplanted traditional techniques. Consensus opinions suggest that bone grafting should be employed only in severe Pruzansky grade III anomalies. The results of soft tissue envelope correction with distraction are unequaled by previous techniques. Extrapolation from this less complex hypoplasia to other craniofacial deformities is ongoing.

The psychosocial development of the child with a craniofacial anomaly is critical. Pertschuk and Whitaker[133] demonstrated that if left uncorrected, "craniofacial malformations are associated in adolescence and childhood with measurable disturbances in mood, self-concept, and socialization. Individuals are typically able to perform well enough to avoid psychiatric intervention; however, relative to the general population, these patients are at a distinct psychosocial disadvantage." Improved appearance through corrective surgery in children has been shown to improve or enhance psychosocial development. No such improvement has been reliably demonstrated in adults. Therefore, craniofacial surgery remains intimately related to childhood, and the rewards of a satisfactory reconstruction in a young child more than compensate for all of the effort and worry that go along with major surgery in children.

Distraction Osteogenesis

Since the third edition of *Pediatric Otolaryngology*, remodeling of facial bones by surgical distraction has rapidly developed into a major clinical tool and source for investigation. A comprehensive discussion follows.

Distraction osteogenesis is a surgical and mechanical process that results in gradual bone lengthening. It was first described by Alexander Codivilla nearly a century ago for the treatment of shortened limbs.[15] This concept was reintroduced by Ilizarov as a means of treating posttraumatic defects of the long bones. His system standardized a method for osteotomy and gradual distraction of the endochondral bones and paved the way for the application of these techniques in the craniofacial skeleton.[72]

Snyder and colleagues first published a report of mandibular lengthening in a canine model in 1973.[147] McCarthy adapted this work to humans and published the first human cases of mandibular distraction in 1992, ushering in the era of craniofacial distraction.[107] Shortly thereafter, Molina and Ortiz-Monasterio presented a large series of cases demonstrating the clinical application of these concepts in syndromic patients.[113] Work in this field has since exploded, with reports of distraction on virtually all of the bones of the craniofacial skeleton, both for reconstruction of syndromic deformities and for treatment of acquired bony defects.[150]

Currently, distraction has become the standard of care for treatment of many types of congenital deformity and has become increasingly more common in adult surgery.[18] Major areas of interest in distraction include mandibular lengthening, repair of segmental mandibular and maxillary defects, alveolar augmentation for dental rehabilitation, midface advancement, and combined craniofacial advancement. The bewildering variety of devices available and the rapidly changing technology of distraction highlights the intense interest in this field.

Mandibular Distraction

There are many indications for elongation of the mandible, the most common being correction of congenital deformity. In addition to improving appearance, there are added benefits to mandibular advancement. Sagittal split osteotomy and mandibular advancement with screw fixation has been used for many years to improve the patency of the upper airway. This technique is effective in the treatment of obstructive sleep apnea in adults.[5]

In the skeletally immature patient, the position of the tooth buds and difficulty in safely performing osteotomy has limited acceptance of mandibular surgery. In addition, these procedures have been reported to cause significant growth disturbance in children. Some groups have reported enhanced skeletal growth using orthopedic techniques without osteotomy in mild cases. In severe cases, however, this method has been inadequate to improve the airway.[68, 100] Therefore, in severe cases of micrognathia, treatment has included tracheostomy, continuous positive-pressure ventilation, tonsillectomy with adenoidectomy, and hyoid suspension. In addition, severe obstructive sleep apnea is known to be associated with gastroesophageal reflux.[20] This may require long-term medical treatment with or without Nissen fundoplication and may negatively affect pulmonary function. In addition, children with chronic apnea may be prone to right-sided heart failure, developmental and growth disturbance, and even intellectual impairment. Children whose severe obstructive sleep apnea requires tracheostomy may require years of enteral feeding and tracheostomy care prior to attaining sufficient mandibular growth for decannulation.[44] The impact of long-term tracheostomy on oromotor development, speech, and social interaction cannot be overstated. The costs associated with treatment of long-term tracheostomy, reflux, and associated disorders are significant. Therefore, a safe alternative for early mandibular advancement has long been sought.

The advent of distraction osteogenesis has shown that mandibular distraction can reduce the need for conventional airway procedures with restoration of mandibular morphology. The design of mandibular angle or ramus osteotomies permits the surgeon to leave the floor-of-mouth musculature attached to the mandible. Advancement of the mandibular body carries this soft tissue forward, improving glossoptosis and prolapse of the epiglottis into the airway. How much bony advancement is required, how much relapse is to be expected, and how this surgery will affect subsequent mandibular growth are all questions that must be answered before this becomes routine treatment of sleep apnea.

Mandibular distractors come in many designs, but these may be conveniently divided into internal and external types. The earliest and most commonly used devices are external distractors. These typically consist of articulating threaded bars that support pins that enter the mandible percutaneously. A screw or nut is turned, causing the pins to distract the two ends of the osteotomized bone apart. The gap is filled with bone callus, which matures into bone over a period of weeks to months. In their simplest form, these are single vector devices, elongating the mandible in a single direction. The multivector devices permit much more sophisticated management of the direction of bone growth, with adjustments for varus/valgus, angulation, and vertical and sagittal advancement. Growth of the mandible may be guided during distraction to more closely resemble the normal mandible morphology (Fig. 6–10).

Internal mandibular distractors are miniaturized versions of the external devices and are designed to be buried in the soft tissue around the site of the osteotomy. They are most commonly placed in a subperiosteal position along the buccal cortex of the mandibular ramus and body. Osteotomies similar to those used with external devices are performed, and an activation arm or cable is brought out through either a cervical tunnel or intraorally through the buccal mucosa. Internal devices are more difficult to place but have some theoretical advantages

over the external devices. First, the scarring caused by pin tracking is eliminated, although some devices are activated percutaneously. Next, mechanical efficiency is improved because forces are transmitted directly to the bone rather than through long pins, which may flex and not distract linearly. The internal devices may also have the advantage of being more readily accepted by parents and children. The engineering challenges presented by the internal designs are formidable, and many surgeons think that this technology is not yet as mature and predictable as the external variety of distractors.

Since McCarthy's first reports, distraction has rapidly supplanted conventional techniques in the treatment of congenital micrognathia. There are many pediatric micrognathia syndromes, but virtually all of them are amenable to treatment with distraction. The common thread among most of these techniques is the use of an osteotomy near the mandibular angle. In older children, either a modified sagittal split technique or a partial corticotomy must be used to avoid damage to the inferior alveolar nerve. In neonates, the nerve enters the mandible mesial to the mandibular ramus, permitting a full osteotomy with little risk to the nerve.[57, 113]

The most common congenital cause of micrognathia is hemifacial microsomia, a part of the oculo-auriculo-vertebral spectrum of deformities. In addition to cervical, renal, and other anomalies, there is a hypoplasia of the mandibular ramus and condyle. Severe cases involve microtia, global soft tissue hypoplasia of the first and second branchial arch structures (often with facial nerve palsy), and progressive deformity related to maxillary growth compensation. Pruzansky described the grading system that is most commonly used (described earlier). The previous treatment involved conventional orthognathic procedures for types I and II, with costochondral grafting to the mandibular ramus for type III.[77] This technique was fraught with problems, including scarring, resorption, overgrowth, and donor-site morbidity.

The most common current treatment method for this condition is external, multivector, mandibular distraction (Fig. 6–11). Typically, the surgeon places four threaded pins percutaneously through the mandible adjacent to the site of planned osteotomy. Then, an intraoral incision is used to dissect the mandibular angle region in a subperiosteal plane. The osteotomy is performed, avoiding the inferior alveolar nerve and the teeth and tooth buds. The distraction rates range from 1 to 3 mm/day, with younger patients tolerating more rapid distraction. There is no consensus about timing of the procedures, but the trend is toward earlier surgery. Complications include scarring, inadequate distraction, open-bite generation, device loosening, and potential nerve and dental injury. In cases of extreme asymmetry, some authors advocate bilateral osteotomy to minimize remodeling forces on the contralateral temporomandibular joint and to better treat facial scoliosis. There are many other published techniques for distraction with these patients, the details of which are beyond the scope of this text.

The Pierre Robin sequence consists of micrognathia, glossoptosis with airway obstruction, and cleft palate. There is a wide spectrum of deformity, but severe cases often require tracheostomy, lip–tongue adhesion, and

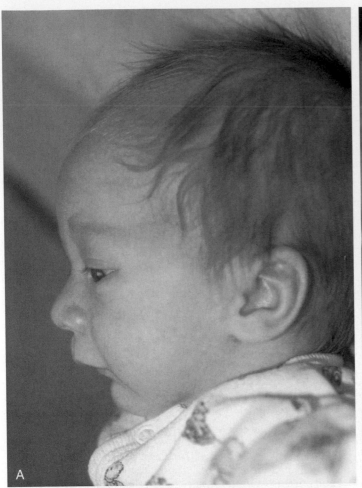

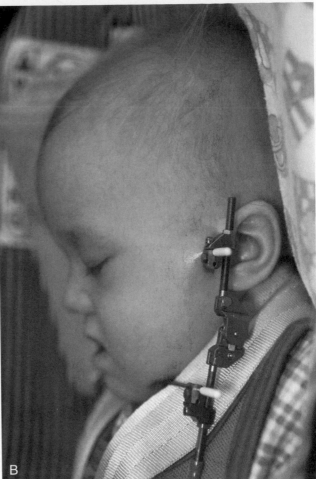

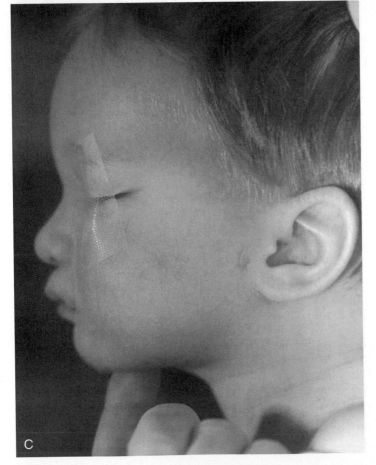

FIGURE 6–10. *A*, Infant with micrognathia causing airway obstruction. *B*, Left side of multivectored bilateral mandibular distraction set, near completion of advancement with the use of transmandibular pins. *C*, Appearance after removal of the distraction device and manipulation of the mandible to close the cross bite.

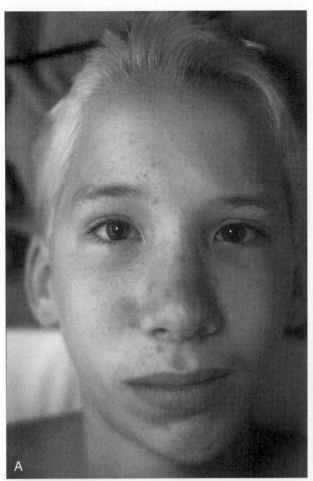

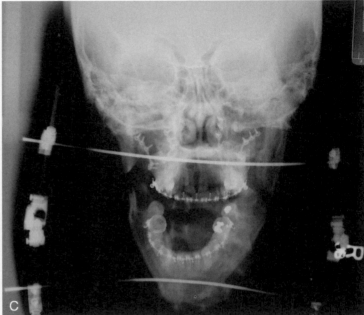

FIGURE 6–11. *A,* Teenager with type I Pruzansky left hemifacial microsomia with marked deviation of the chin to the left, rise to left labial commissure, and lateral cross bite. *B,* Complete correction of the deformity, after mandibular distraction. *C,* Anteroposterior cephalogram during distraction, showing callus and pin placement.

prolonged vigilance for sleep apnea. Distraction has revolutionized the treatment of these infants. Multiple authors have published preliminary reports describing effective treatment of micrognathia by distraction osteogenesis.[19, 21, 76, 142] Rapid distraction sequences of up to 4 mm/day have been presented, permitting the use of endotracheal intubation as a temporizing measure in conjunction with rapid distraction. After several days of distraction, the infants can usually be safely extubated and nasogastric or orogastric feeding continued until the device is removed.[35]

At the University of Pittsburgh, a protocol is in place for evaluation of the neonate or infant with micrognathia. First, cephalography and three-dimensional computed tomography are performed to permit surgical planning. Then, sleep studies and pH probing are performed to evaluate the degree of obstructive sleep apnea and reflux. The otolaryngologist performs panendoscopy to rule out other causes of airway obstruction. If pH probe data are unavailable, esophageal biopsy is performed. Once upper-airway obstruction secondary to glossoptosis has been confirmed, the craniofacial surgeon places a single-vector distractor.

Both internal and external devices have been used, but we prefer external devices for ease of care and the ability to distract up to 75 mm, which is impossible with the smaller internal devices (Fig. 6–12). In addition, there are relatively few sites in which to safely place pins. In neonates, bone stock is often insufficient to safely place the four screws used in multivector devices. In addition, many authors have described rapid device loosening secondary to bony resorption around the threaded screws or pins that fix the distractor to the mandible. For this reason, we have opted for a single-vector distraction with two transfacial pins. After distraction, the callus is molded into the appropriate shape for maintenance of closed bite and normal occlusion. The advantages of this technique relate to neonatal mandibular anatomy.

The anatomy of the neonatal mandible is unique in several ways. First, there is a "window" in the bone in the anterior mandible just distal to the canine tooth bud. This permits the anterior pin to be placed with minimal risk to the nerve and tooth buds. There is no lingula per se, and the inferior alveolar nerve courses through the soft tissue of the cheek, entering the mandible just mesial and medial to the retromolar area of the mandibular angle. There is no true condyle, only a rounded terminal end of the ramus. Additionally, the ramus is anterior to the ca-

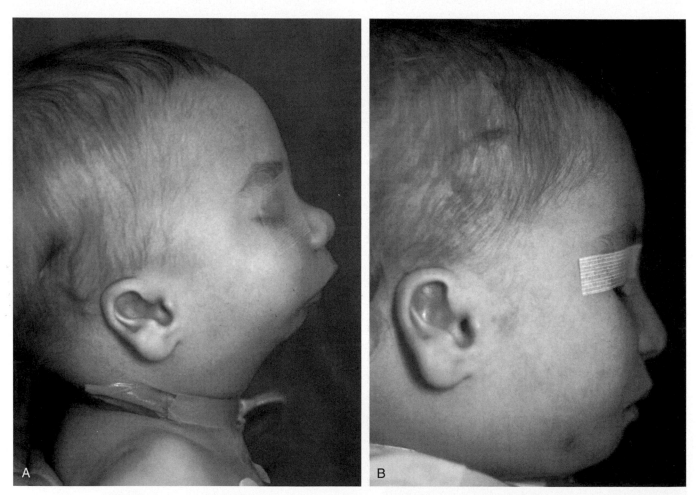

FIGURE 6–12. *A,* Neonate with Nager acrofacial dysostosis with a tracheostomy in place because of obstructed airway. *B,* Appearance after removal of the distractor and prior to decannulation.

rotid and soft palatal musculature. Therefore, this anatomy is suited to a two-pin technique in which long pins completely traverse the mandibular rami and the menton.

A small diameter (5/64 inch) Steinman pin is placed inferior to the tooth buds and just posterior to the mental nerve in the anterior mandible. In the posterior site, we prefer a transpharyngeal pin. This pin is placed percutaneously as high along the mandibular ramus as is practical. This technique has several advantages. Neonatal bone is so soft that threaded screws typically loosen prior to completion of the distraction sequence. With this technique, the device may slide back and forth as the pins loosen but it cannot come dislodged. The screw-borne devices that do not traverse the face bilaterally with a single pin often fall out, requiring repeat osteotomy and pin placement. The wide spacing of the pins permits soft tissue stretch with minimal pin-track scarring. In fact, scar revision is rarely needed in these patients.

The osteotomy is performed at the mandibular angle, in a gentle sagittal orientation, as close to the entry of the neurovascular bundle and first molar tooth bud as is practical. This is performed through an oral buccal sulcus incision under direct vision. In addition, the use of long transfacial flexible pins permits the recognition of premature consolidation when increased pin flexion and discomfort is observed. Subsequent blind reosteotomy through the mesial callus may then be performed with knowledge of the nerve position to permit up to 60 mm of distraction in cases of severe micrognathia. In over 40 patients undergoing mandibular distraction who were younger than 1 year, all but five patients either avoided tracheostomy or were successfully decannulated. There were no open bites, which is a common complication of the conventional multivector technique. Furthermore, scarring was minimal.[55]

After approximately 3 to 5 days of intubation in severe cases, repeat endoscopy is used to document improvement of the airway. The child can usually be extubated at this time and is observed in the intensive care unit until no further apneas or bradycardias are observed. Overcorrection of the micrognathia is performed to allow for a planned degree of relapse, followed by device removal after confirmation of normal airway. We perform callus manipulation at this time, allowing correction of the open bite, which is a by-product of single-vector distraction. The soft callus permits the child's natural sucking and chewing motion to maintain a closed bite with normal intermaxillary relationships until the callus matures over the next several weeks. Finally, repeat imaging studies are performed to demonstrate the stability of the bony regenerate. Lateral cephalograms are also useful to observe the epiglottis and tongue base and to follow mandibular growth over time. Repeat sleep studies are helpful in confirming the correction of more subtle airway obstruction.

There are dozens of other syndromic and nonsyndromic micrognathias, but the basic techniques described here apply equally to the majority of these patients as well. Patients who have ankylosis of the temporomandibular joint have been successfully treated with a combination of condylectomy and subsequent distraction of the remaining ramus back toward the condylar fossa.[105] First described by McCarthy, this technique relies on the interposition of soft tissue between the neocondyle and the skull base to minimize the risk of reankylosis. Long-term follow-up will determine whether this method is comparable to standard techniques for treatment of this difficult problem. An interesting subset of patients are those in whom previous techniques have failed. There are numerous reports of successful distraction in patients who have previously undergone surgery. The correct placement of osteotomies and the timing of intermaxillary fixation and consolidation are controversial, but these techniques have been impressive in the salvage of previous surgical failures (see Fig. 6–4).

Many groups have reported successful correction of large mandibular defects after tumor extirpation and segmental mandibular loss after trauma using bone-transport techniques.[101] These are essentially distractors that are affixed to the mandible on both sides of a segmental defect, with a chassis to transport a small bony segment across the gap. Once the defect is bridged, the patient is taken back to surgery for final osteosynthesis and removal of the device. This technique has been used to correct gaps of up to two thirds of the anterior mandible. An advantage is that this method does not require a lengthy microsurgical procedure and is better tolerated by critically ill patients. Of course, in the setting of exposure of vital structures of the neck, the free tissue transfer provides immediate coverage. The indications for this technique are being developed in several centers. Another advantage is that the vertical bone stock of a distracted mandible is typically more amenable to rehabilitation with implants. The fibula, which is the standard of care for treatment of segmental mandibular defects today, is narrow, making the placement of implants more likely to lead to failure of the bone–implant interface secondary to mechanical stress on the implant. Distracted bone is usually as wide as the donor bone, thereby providing a more robust bed for implant therapy.

In the pursuit of oral rehabilitation, several authors have reported small series of vertical distraction of fibular free flaps to augment the quantity of bone used to support dental implants after reconstruction for cancer.[146] The consensus seems to be that external transport devices combined with osteotomies and distraction techniques are a viable alternative to microsurgical reconstruction of the mandible. Whether this is applicable to irradiated fields, to elderly patients, and in the setting of potential local recurrence of tumor remains to be determined.

Cranial and Midface Distraction

The idea that the midface can be advanced with traction predates the current surgical approaches by a century. Fractures of the midface have been treated with this technique for decades. Delaire and associates popularized the use of a reverse-pull headgear to orthopedically advance the midface without osteotomies. This device, commonly called a *Delaire mask*, has become a mainstay in orthodontia and was one of the earliest appliances used to surgically distract the midface.[34, 149] Tessier himself devised a neurosurgical halo-type appliance to provide a means of applying traction to the midface for use in conjunction with single-stage advancements of the bony midface. Several investigators have begun to study midface advancement in animal models.[139, 140] It was not until Polley and Figueroa reintroduced this concept with their "RED" device that this technique was routinely applied to distract the midface.[136]

The indications for midface distraction are myriad but include postcleft midface deficiency, syndromic midface deficiency (e.g., Crouzon and Apert syndromes), and skeletal malocclusion that is not amenable to conventional orthognathic techniques. The Le Fort I segment becomes unstable when advanced more than 10 to 12 mm by conventional plate and screw fixation. Even with bone grafting, these movements are unpredictable. Vertical elongation of the maxilla has been very unpredictable, and authors have used interpositional corticocancellous grafts, coralline hydroxyapatite, and other methods to attempt to stabilize the Le Fort I segment during descent.[144] Distraction osteogenesis has been thought to be more stable in these movements, although still not without a tendency toward relapse.[3, 61] The Le Fort III segment has been traditionally regarded as among the most prone to relapse of midface advancement osteotomies. Multiple authors have hailed distraction as the answer to the relapse problem with this otherwise versatile procedure.[80]

The monobloc procedure, in which the orbitofrontal barre and midface are advanced together, was introduced by Ortiz Monasterio. It has been criticized for a tendency toward infection due to the presence of dead space adjacent to the ethmoid sinuses and cranial base. Blood loss, relapse, and technical difficulty also have limited its widespread acceptance. This procedure has been used in conjunction with facial bipartition to treat hypertelorism.[17] Several authors have returned to the monobloc with distraction and have reported outstanding results with little of the previously associated morbidity.[16, 22, 111, 124, 135] Some authors are even performing distraction of multiply osteotomized midfaces, fixing the segments prior to distraction or differentially distracting the segments simultaneously. Upper-facial osteotomies and large advancements often cause relative enophthalmos, ectropion or lid distortion, compressive lacrimal obstruction, and transient diplopia. Therefore, ancillary procedures to correct these problems are commonly required.

Our preferred method for midface advancement combines a Le Fort III or monobloc distraction with a subsequent return to surgery for removal of hardware, canthal procedures, rhinoplasty to address the substantial change in nasal morphology associated with these advances, and a "finishing" Le Fort I osteotomy, which may be distracted or fixated depending on cephalometric analysis. This hybrid treatment plan is well suited for the treatment of Crouzon syndrome. Le Fort III distraction followed by a finishing LeFort I procedure permits the surgeon to attain occlusal and aesthetic goals that are difficult to accomplish with single osteotomies.

Midfacial advancement for Crouzon syndrome has focused on the upper face, but occlusal considerations often compromise aesthetic goals. Multilevel midfacial osteotomies, advancement, and simultaneous rigid fixation have been fraught with relapse and instability. Midfacial distraction at the Le Fort III and monobloc level has found favor because of superior stability and less relapse.[6] Simultaneous multilevel distraction has been difficult to predictably control. An alternative is the "stairstep" procedure, which is a hybrid of a distracted upper-facial osteotomy with a conventional or distracted lower-facial osteotomy.

Nine patients with Crouzon syndrome have been treated with this method at the University of Pittsburgh. The patients underwent either monobloc or Le Fort III distraction with an internal distractor system. Once upper-facial harmony was attained, a finishing Le Fort I osteotomy was performed at the time of distractor removal to correct malocclusion independently of upper-facial structural goals.[56] Various additional procedures were added to this regimen to enhance aesthetic results, including orbital contouring, canthopexy, genioplasty, rhinoplasty, and midface suspension. Stable predictable advancement was attained with midface distraction in all patients. Exophthalmos, elevated ICP, and upper-facial hypoplasia were corrected in the monobloc group. Complications included seroma, transient frontal branch palsy, and pneumonia. There were no surgical failures. One patient with severe preoperative trismus had transiently worsened symptoms. Cephalometric analysis reveals superior aesthetic results compared with traditional craniofacial advancement. Upper midface distraction followed by finishing Le Fort I osteotomy combines the stability of distraction with the predictability of orthognathic surgery. Future work will focus on minimally invasive approaches to these large procedures.[88]

Interestingly, after advancement and descent of the midface to correct exorbitism and restore normal midface morphology, the mandible is often relatively deficient compared with the new midfacial position. There is a common tendency toward limitation of mandibular opening related to the clockwise rotation of the occlusal plane. Therefore, several groups now advocate mandibular advancement as a part of treatment of the craniofacial dysostoses.

The external halo-type midface distractors consist of a pin-borne arch, similar to a neurosurgical halo device, which is affixed to the cranial bones. From this base, a variety of cantilevered arms may protrude, permitting either elastic or wire traction to be applied to the midface. Many authors prefer to apply the forces to a palatal splint, which is fixed to the teeth with orthodontic bands. This technique has numerous variants, and a common approach is to combine plate and screw fixation with wires, which percutaneously attach to the malar or nasal spine area to augment the palatal fixation. These devices provide a powerful method for advancing the maxilla and upper facial bones. Disadvantages include difficulty in controlling distraction vectors, cumbersome hardware, patient compliance issues, and unpredictable relapse, especially in the vertical dimension.

Many devices are being used internally for midface advancement (Fig. 6–13). Typically, these consist of plate and screw baseplates, which are affixed to the midface

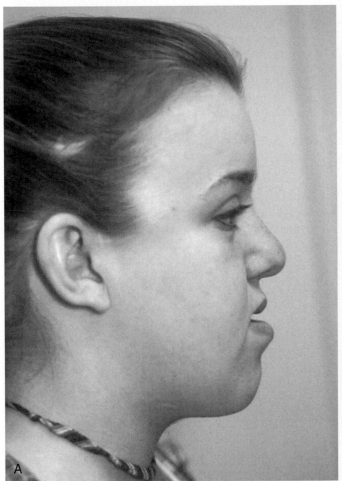

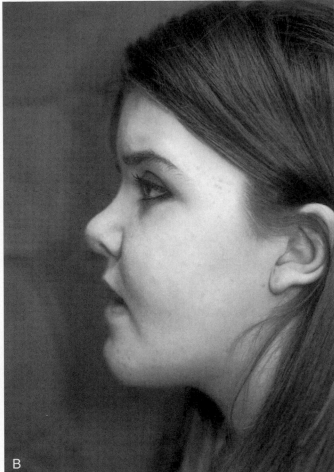

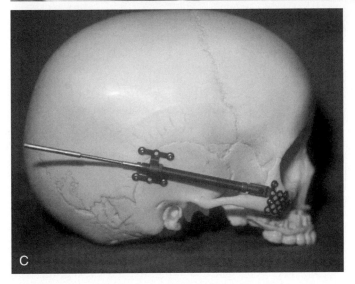

FIGURE 6–13. *A,* Midface and lower orbital retrusion in 16-year-old patient with Crouzon syndrome who underwent successful monoblock frontofacial advancement at age 8 years. *B,* Appearance after stair-step osteotomies and a distracted Le Fort III procedure followed by a finishing Le Fort I procedure, genioplasty, canthopexy, and costochondral bone graft to the nasal dorsum. *C,* Mock-up of the internal midfacial distractor on a plastic skull.

and cranial base in a subperiosteal plane. The distractor runs along the lateral orbit toward the mastoid. The distraction screw is typically a flexible cable or an articulated universal joint–type axle, which exits the scalp through a stab wound. The specifics of the distraction are similar to those of other rigid external distractors. The disadvantages of these devices include the need for extensive dissection to place the devices, the need for general anes-

thesia to remove the devices, infection of the dead space around the distractor, displacement of the plates, fracture across the malar region, and eyelid distortion during distraction.

Several groups have investigated the possibility of treating isolated cranial-vault anomalies with distraction techniques. Lauritzen and collaborators have even used metallic springs as completely submerged internal devices for enlarging the cranial vault. Guerrero has a substantial series of infants with plagiocephaly who have been treated with unilateral vault osteotomies and internal distractors. Early results of several investigators are promising.[37, 82, 85, 132] The complexities of cranial-vault distraction clearly require the engineering of more sophisticated internal devices. Given current advances in endoscopic cranial-vault surgery, the future treatment of choice may very well involve endoscopic osteotomies and minimally invasive placement of cranial-vault distractors.

Palatal Distraction

Cleft lip and palate surgery is replete with groups who have attempted to combine elements of the various surgeries into a single procedure. Problems with subsequent growth impairment led several pioneers to abandon early palatal surgery. Currently, the standard of care is rotation-advancement lip repair at approximately age 4 months, followed by palatoplasty at 1 year. The alveolar cleft is then bone-grafted in mixed dentition; rhinoplasty and orthognathic procedures may be necessary in the teen years.

With this approach, the fear is that diminished facial growth may accompany early palatal surgery. This fear leads to multiple surgeries, leaving parts of the pathology to be fixed in later stages for technical reasons that have nothing to do with the ultimate surgical goals. The ongoing lack of bony continuity creates stability problems that in turn generate complex orthopedic and orthodontic problems that stretch into adulthood. Many of these teens still require orthognathic surgery after such conscientious care as infants. What was lacking was a way to control the bony defect and not compromise the soft tissue surgery or skeletal relationships to achieve bony cleft closure.

With distraction techniques, some of these issues may be resolved.[7, 34, 89, 90] Classically, lip closure is performed at age 2 to 4 months, but the alveolus is left to mold. Some teams use lip adhesion or external traction to accomplish this; others use a Latham device to align the cleft segments. Arch widening, orthodontia, and bone grafting are carried out in mixed dentition. If early palate surgery could be performed without diminution of facial growth, this staged approach could be simplified.

Skoog proposed primary periosteoplasty in 1965. Millard went on to integrate early alveolar surgery and orthopedic treatment. Cutting and others have elaborated on this concept with gingivoperiosteoplasty. What these techniques all have in common is the collapse of the cleft segments, followed by bone generation using whatever method the surgeon prefers, then further orthopedic movements to restore architecture of the arch. Later, bone grafting, dental, and orthodontic treatments may be necessary, up to and including orthognathic surgery because of inadequacy of the bony arch.

Distraction cheiloplasty is a technique that permits regeneration of the cleft segment with distraction. By taking advantage of the collapse of the segments, bony contact is achieved.[59] By using a bone graft to generate a large bony callus, the cleft site serves as a *bone bank* rather than a defect. The graft callus is distracted primarily to, in effect, "grow" a new cleft segment and bridge the gap. Overcorrecting the arch prevents segment collapse, permitting early and more normal dental eruption, and allows the tongue to mold the alveolus during infancy. Indeed, the lip, palate, and nasal surgery are all performed simultaneously and are made easier by the intentional preliminary collapse of the segments.

This natural collapse avoids the wide dissections and vomerine flaps that may retard facial growth. The soft tissues are then subjected to a slow elongation analogous to that in other distractions, which mimics the growth process. No complex flaps or extensive undermining are necessary to achieve closure.

This method was studied prospectively by our group at the Hospital Infantil de Mexico:

1. Pretreatment evaluation consists of three-dimensional computed tomography, posteroanterior and lateral cephalometry, periapical palatal views, and dental casts and models with facial bow and bite registration for subsequent model surgery.
2. Model surgery is based on typical relationships of superior and inferior arches. The segments are mobilized as they swing through the arc of rotation of the planned collapse and expansion. A final overcorrection is planned to correct cross-bite and provide additional facial convexity and posteroanterior projection of maxilla.
3. A modified Latham device is fabricated for the collapse phase using acrylic splints, buttons, trihelical posterior axes to guide segment rotation, and elastic chains. Transverse and anteroposterior chains are typically used to position the minor segment, which is often malpositioned as well as rotated. The screw is embedded with the correct number of turns set to reach planned expansion at the limits of the screw movements.
4. Collapse phase: the patient uses the appliance 24 hours a day, fixed to the palate with denture adhesive, and weekly visits guide the collapse until segmental contact is achieved.
5. Surgery consists of palatoplasty using alveolar "unwinding" flaps much like the prolabial flaps that Cutting uses in his lip repair. Rib grafting is used to fill the still rather large inverted pyramidal defect in the alveolus and nasal floor. Lip repair is a modified Millard technique. Palatoplasty is performed. Primary cleft lip rhinoplasty (McComb) is performed. A nasal conformer is used.
6. The bone graft is integrated for 1 month, with weekly periapical radiography, until graft integration becomes evident.
7. A fixed palatal distractor, consisting of acrylic splints fixed to the palate with miniscrews, is fabricated and applied, avoiding greater palatine vessels and tooth buds.
8. Distraction phase: parents perform screw activation, 0.5 mm daily. This is continued until the limits of the distractor are reached.

9. Consolidation phase: the fixed appliance is used for 1 month without activation to permit bone maturation.
10. The apparatus is removed in the office.
11. Post-treatment evaluation consists of three-dimensional computed tomography, posteroanterior and lateral films, dental casts and models, bone scanning, and clinical evaluation of dentition and arches.

Forty infants between ages 4 and 10 months were enrolled in the protocol and underwent treatment. One left the protocol for cardiac surgery. There were 16 unilateral and 3 bilateral clefts. The other 20 patients underwent standard cleft repairs. Complications were minor.

Findings

1. Segmental collapse occurred rapidly between 1 and 3 months' duration. There were no failures of the collapse phase.
2. Underestimation of defect by clinician: even with the alveolar segments in contact, computed tomography revealed large defects of 2 to 3 cm in diameter. This necessitated a more aggressive bone graft than initially had been anticipated.
3. Lip, nose, and palate surgery was technically difficult to perform at the same time.
4. Time in the operating room was longer (mean, 3.5 hours).
5. There were no failures of bone graft or palatoplasty and no dehiscences of lips.
6. Lip and nasal aesthetics were excellent, comparable to standard techniques.
7. Callus distraction was rapid and robust, and there was ample clinical and radiographic evidence of new bone growth.

This technique is reproducible, with low morbidity. It generates new bone in the alveolar cleft and reconstructs the arch to final form in one procedure. This integrates all of the elements of cleft lip and palate repair into a single cohesive treatment utilizing skeletal distraction. This method is a feasible alternative to conventional techniques.

There is excitement about the possibility of using distraction osteogenesis to improve velopharyngeal performance and avoid secondary procedures in the treatment of cleft palate.[99] Several groups have used intraoral distractors to elongate the hard palate in the anteroposterior direction in an effort to make up for deficient velar soft tissue.[112] Long-term evaluation of velopharyngeal function will be critical to determine the role of these new technologies.

In summary, distraction osteogenesis techniques represent a major advance in the management of craniofacial deformities and have begun to supplant conventional osteotomies in many applications. These techniques have the potential to revolutionize craniofacial surgery, much as the concepts of Tessier did with the treatment of craniosynostosis.

REFERENCES

1. AAP Task Force on Infant Positioning and SIDS. Positioning and SIDS. Pediatrics 89:1120, 1992.
2. Adams F. The Genuine Works of Hippocrates. Baltimore, Williams & Wilkins, 1939.
3. Altuna G, Walker DA, Freeman E. Surgically assisted rapid orthodontic lengthening of the maxilla in primates—a pilot study. Am J Orthod Dentofacial Orthop. 107:531, 1995.
4. Angle EH. The Angle system of treating fractures of the maxillary bones. Br J Dent Sci 33:484, 1890.
5. Aragon SB. Surgical management for snoring and sleep apnea [review]. Dent Clin North Am 45:867, 2001.
6. Arnaud E, Marchac D, Renier D. Distraction osteogenesis with double internal devices combined with early frontal facial advancement for the correction of facial craniosynostosis. Report of clinical cases [in French]. Ann Chir Plast Esthet 46:268, 2001.
7. Ascherman JA, Marin VP, Rogers L, Prisant N. Palatal distraction in a canine cleft palate model. Plast Reconstr Surg 105:1687, 2000.
8. ASPS Annual Meeting, Los Angeles, 2000.
9. Barton JR. Systemic bandage for fracture of the lower jaw. Am Med Rec 2:153, 1819.
10. Berry GA. Note on a congenital defect (?coloboma) of the lower lid. R Lond Hosp Rep 12:255, 1889.
11. Brent B. Auricular repair with autogenous rib cartilage grafts: two decades of experience with 600 cases. Plast Reconstr Surg 90:355, 1992.
12. Cameron J. Interorbital width, new cranial dimension. Am J Phys Anthropol 15:509, 1931.
13. Caronni EP. Facial bipartition in hypertelorism. Cleft Palate J 23(Suppl):19, 1986.
14. Centers for Disease Control. Cluster of Craniosynostosis—Colorado, Public Health Service publication No. EPI-83-58-2. Atlanta, Division of Birth Defects and Developmental Disabilities, Center for Environmental Health and Injury Control, 1987.
15. Codivilla A. On the means of lengthening in the lower limbs, the muscles and tissues which are shortened through deformity. Am J Orthop Surg 2:353, 1905.
16. Cohen SR, Boydston W, Burstein FD, Hudgins R. Monobloc distraction osteogenesis during infancy: report of a case and presentation of a new device. Plast Reconstr Surg 101:1919, 1998.
17. Cohen SR, Boydston W, Hudgins R, Burstein FD. Monobloc and facial bipartition distraction with internal devices. J Craniofac Surg 10:244, 1999.
18. Cohen SR, Burstein FD, Williams JK. The role of distraction osteogenesis in the management of craniofacial disorders [review]. Ann Acad Med Singapore 28:728, 1999.
19. Cohen SR, Burstein FD, Williams JK. The role of distraction osteogenesis in the management of craniofacial disorders. Ann Acad Med Singapore 28:728, 1999.
20. Cohen SR, Simms C, Burstein FD, Thomsen J. Alternatives to tracheostomy in infants and children with obstructive sleep apnea. J Pediatr Surg 34:182, 1999.
21. Cohen SR, Simms C, Burstein FD. Mandibular distraction osteogenesis in the treatment of upper airway obstruction in children with craniofacial deformities. Plast Reconstr Surg 101:312, 1998.
22. Cohen SR. Craniofacial distraction with a modular internal distraction system: evolution of design and surgical techniques. Plast Reconstr Surg 103:1592, 1999.
23. Converse JM, Coccaro PJ, Wood-Smith D. Corrective treatment of skeletal asymmetry in hemifacial microsomia. Plast Reconstr Surg 51:268, 1973.
24. Converse JM, Horowitz SL, Coccaro PJ, Wood-Smith D. Corrective treatment of skeletal asymmetry in hemifacial microsomia. Plast Reconstr Surg 52:221, 1973.
25. Converse JM, McCarthy JG, Wood-Smith D. Orbital hypertelorism: pathogenesis, associated faciocerebral anomalies and surgical correction. Plast Reconstr Surg 56:389, 1975.
26. Converse JM, Ransohof Mathews ES, et al. Ocular hypertelorism. Plast Reconstr Surg 45:1, 1970.
27. Converse JM, Wood Smith D, McCarthy JG. Report on a series of 50 craniofacial operations. Plast Reconstr Surg 55:283, 1975.

28. Converse JM, Wood-Smith D, McCarthy JG, Coccaro PJ. Craniofacial surgery. Clin Plast Surg 1:499, 1974.
29. Converse JM, Wood-Smith D, McCarthy JG, et al. Bilateral facial microsomia. Plast Reconstr Surg 54:413, 1974.
30. Converse JM, Wood-Smith D. An atlas and classification of midfacial facial osteotomies. In Transactions of the Fifth International Congress of Plastic and Reconstructive Surgery. Melbourne, Butterworth, 1971, p 931.
31. Currarino G, Silverman FN. Orbital hypertelorism, arhinencephaly and trogonocephaly. Radiology 74:206, 1960.
32. Cutting CB, McCarthy JG, Berenstein A. The blood supply of the upper craniofacial skeleton. The search for composite grafts. Plast Reconstr Surg 74:603, 1984.
33. Davies DW, Munro IR. The anesthetic management and intraoperative care of patients undergoing major facial osteotomies. Plast Reconstr Surg 55:50, 1975.
34. Delaire JP, Verdon J, Lumineau A, et al: Quelques resultants des tractions extra-orales appui fronto-mentonier dans de tractment orthopédique des malformations maxillomandibulaires de Class III et des sequelles osseuses des fente labio-maxillaires. Rev Stomatol Chir Maxillofac 73:633, 1972.
35. Denny AD, Talisman R, Hanson PR, Recinos RF. Mandibular distraction osteogenesis in very young patients to correct airway obstruction. Plast Reconstr Surg 108:302, 2001.
36. Dingman RO. Surgery of Facial Fractures. Philadelphia, WB Saunders, 1963.
37. do Amaral CM, Di Domizio G, Tiziani V, et al. Gradual bone distraction in craniosynostosis. Preliminary results in seven cases. Scand J Plast Reconstr Surg Hand Surg 31:25, 1997.
38. Edgerton MT, Jane JA, Bern FA, Fuller JC. Feasibility of craniofacial osteotomies in infants and young children. Scand J Plast Reconstr Surg 8:164, 1974.
39. Edgerton MT, Jane JA, Berry F. Craniofacial osteotomies and reconstructions in infants and young children. Plast Reconstr Surg 54:13, 1974.
40. Edgerton MT, Udvarhely GB, Knox DL. The surgical correction of ocular hypertelorism. Ann Surg 172:3, 1970.
41. Edgerton MT, Udvarhely GB, Knox DL. The surgical correction of ocular hypertelorism. Ann Surg 172:3, 1970.
42. Faber HK, Towne EB. Early craniectomy as a preventive measure in oxycephaly and allied conditions, with special reference to the prevention of blindness. Am J Med Sci 173:701, 1927.
43. Farkas LG, Munro IR (eds). Anthropomorphic Facial Proportions in Medicine. Springfield, IL, Charles C Thomas, 1987.
44. Figueroa A, Glupker TJ, et al: Mandible, tongue, and airway in Pierre Robin sequence: a longitudinal cephalometric study. Cleft Palate Craniofac J 28:4, 1991.
45. Fink SC, Hardesty RA. Craniofacial syndromes. In Bentz ML (ed). Pediatric Plastic Surgery. Stamford, CT, Appleton & Lange, 1998.
46. Fink SC, Hardesty RA. Craniofacial syndromes. In Bentz ML (ed). Pediatric Plastic Surgery. Stamford, CT, Appleton & Lange, 1998.
47. Franceschetti A. Craniofacial dysostoses. In Symposium of Surgical and Medical Management of Congenital Anomalies of the eye. New Orleans Academy of Ophthalmology, 16th Symposium. St Louis, CV Mosby, 1968, p 77.
48. Freihofer HP. Results after midface osteotomies. J Maxillofac Surg 1:30, 1973.
49. Freihofer HP. Kieferorthopadische operationen im jugendalter—ja oder nein? Vortrag Dtsch Ges Kiefer Gesichtschir (Hamburg) 1974.
50. Gillies HD, Harrison SH. Operative correction by osteotomy of recessed malar maxillary compound in a case of oxycephaly. Br J Plast Surg 3:123, 1950.
51. Gillies HD, Millard DR Jr. The Principles and Art of Plastic Surgery. Boston, Little Brown, 1955.
52. Gonzales-Ulloa M. Quantitative principles in cosmetic surgery of the face (profileplasty). Plast Reconstr Surg 29:186, 1962.
53. Gonzales-Ulloa M. Quantum method for the appreciation of the morphology of the face. Plast Reconstr Surg 34:241, 1964.
54. Goodman RM, Gorlin RJ. Atlas of the Face in Genetic Disorders, 2nd ed. St Louis, CV Mosby, 1977.
55. Gordon CB, et al. Submitted for publication.
56. Gordon CB, Heil BV, Chang T, et al. 3rd International Congress on Cranial and Facial Bone Distraction Processes, Paris, June 14–16, 2001.
57. Gordon CB, Heil BV, Chang T, et al. Stairstep Midfacial Distraction in Crouzon Syndrome. In press.
58. Gordon CB, Ortiz-Monasterio F, et al. Airway management in mandibular distraction: is tracheostomy necessary? J Craniofacial Surg (In press)
59. Gordon CB, Reyna Rodriguez XP, Ochoa Lopez Diaz E, et al. Distraction cheiloplasty. J Plast Reconstr Surg, In Press.
60. Gruss JS, Bubak PJ, Egbert MA. Craniofacial fractures, algorithms to optimize results. Clin Plast Surg 19:195. 1992.
61. Guerrero CA. Maxillary intraoral distraction osteogenesis. In Arnaud E, Diner PA (eds). Proceedings of 3rd International Congress on Cranial and Facial Bone Distraction Processes, Paris, June 14–16, 2001. Bologna, Monduzzi Editore, 2001, pp 381–387.
62. Gunning TB. The treatment of lower jaw by interdental splints. N Y Med J 3:433, 1866.
63. Haberkern CM, Smith DW, Jones KL. The "breech-head" and its relevance. Am J Dis Child 133:154, 1979.
64. Hansen M, Mulliken JB. Frontal plagiocephaly: diagnosis and treatment. Clin Plast Surg 21:543, 1994.
65. Hobar PC. Method of rigid fixation. Clin Plast Surg 19:31, 1992.
66. Hoffman HJ, Mohr G. Lateral canthal advancement of the supraorbital margin: a new technique in the treatment of coronal synostosis. J Neurosurg 45:376, 1976.
67. Hogemann KE, Willmar K. On LeFort III osteotomy for Crouzon's disease in children. Scand J Plast Reconstr Surg 8:169, 1974.
68. Huertas D, Ghafari J. New posteroanterior cephalometric norms: a comparison with craniofacial measures of children treated with palatal expansion. Angle Orthod 71:285, 2001.
69. Hurwitz DJ, Pang D, Albright AL. Creation of a dome in the surgery of craniosynostosis. In Caronni EP (ed). Craniofacial Surgery 3. Bologna, Monduzzi Editore, 1991, p 315.
70. Hurwitz DJ. Indications for use of a microsystem for internal fixation in craniofacial surgery. J Craniofac Surg 1:35, 1990.
71. Hurwitz DJ. The long term results of pedicled calvarial bone grafts to the midface. J Craniofac Surg 4:237, 1994.
72. Ilizarov GA, Devyatov AA, Keamerin VK. Plastic reconstruction of longitudinal bone defects by means of compression and subsequent distraction. Acta Chir Plast 122:32.
73. Ingraham FD, Alexander E Jr, Matson DD. Clinical studies in craniosynostosis: analysis of 50 cases and description of a method of surgical treatment. Surgery 24:518, 1948.
74. Jabaley ME, Edgerton MT. Surgical correction of congenital midface retrusion in the presence of mandibular protrusion. Plast Reconstr Surg 44:1, 1969.
75. Jones WD III, Whitaker LA, Murtagh F. Applications of reconstructive craniofacial techniques to acute upper facial trauma. J Trauma 17:339, 1977.
76. Judge B, Hamlar D, Rimell FL. Mandibular distraction osteogenesis in a neonate. Arch Otolaryngol Head Neck Surg 125:1029, 1999.
77. Kaban LB, Moses MH, Mulliken JB. Surgical correction of hemifacial microsomia in the growing child. Plast Reconstr Surg 82:9, 1988.
78. Kahan LB, Conover M, Mulliken JB. Midface position after LeFort III advancement. A long term study. Cleft Palate J 23(Suppl): 75, 1986.
79. Kane AA, Mitchell LE, Craven KP, et al. Observations on a recent increase in plagiocephaly without synostosis. Pediatrics 97:6, 1996.
80. Ko EW, Figueroa AA, Guyette TW, et al. Velopharyngeal changes after maxillary advancement in cleft patients with distraction osteogenesis using a rigid external distraction device: a 1-year cephalometric follow-up. J Craniofac Surg 10:312, 1999.
81. Kreiborg S, Aduss H. Pre- and postsurgical facial growth in patients with Crouzon's and Apert's syndrome. Cleft Palate J 23:78, 1986.
82. Lalikos JF, Tschakaloff A, Mooney MP, et al. Internal calvarial bone distraction in rabbits with experimental coronal suture immobilization: effects of overdistraction. Plast Reconstr Surg 96:689, 1995.
83. Lane LC. Pioneer craniectomy for relief of mental imbecility due to premature sutural closure and microcephalus. JAMA 18:49, 1892.
84. Lannelongue M. De la craniectomie dans la microcephalie. Compte Rendu Academ Sci 110:1382, 1890.
85. Lauritzen C, Sugawara Y, Kocabalkan O, Olsson R. Spring medi-

ated dynamic craniofacial reshaping. Case report. Scand J Plast Reconstr Surg Hand Surg 32:331, 1998.

86. LeFort R. Etude experimental sur les fractures de la machoire superieur. Rev Chir Paris 23:280, 1901.

87. Lejoyeux E, Tulasne JF, Tessier PL. Maxillary growth following total septal resection in correction of orbital hypertelorism. Cleft Palate J 23(Suppl):27, 1986.

88. Levine JP, Rowe NM, Bradley JP, et al. The combination of endoscopy and distraction osteogenesis in the development of a canine midface advancement model. J Craniofac Surg 9:423, 1998.

89. Liu C, Song R, Song Y. Sutural expansion osteogenesis for management of the bony-tissue defect in cleft palate repair: experimental studies in dogs. Plast Reconstr Surg 105:2012, 2000.

90. Liu C, Song R, Song Y. Suture distraction osteogenesis for closure of cleft palate in the dog: long-term effect and its influence on facial growth [in Chinese]. Zhonghua Zheng Xing Wai Ke Za Zhi 16:357, 2000.

91. Longacre JJ, DeStefano A, Holmstrand KE. The early versus the late reconstruction of congenital hypoplasia of the facial skeleton and skull. Plast Reconstr Surg 27:489, 1961.

92. Longacre JJ, DeStefano GA. Reconstruction of extensive defects of the skull with split rib grafts. Plast Reconstr Surg 19:186, 1957.

93. Longacre JJ, Stevens GA, Holmstrand KE. The surgical management of first and second branchial arch syndrome. Plast Reconstr Surg 31:507, 1963.

94. Longacre JJ. The early reconstruction of congenital hypoplasia of the facial skeleton and skull: surgical management of facial deformation secondary to craniosynostosis. In Longacre JJ (ed). Craniofacial Anomalies: Pathogenesis and Repair. Philadelphia, JB Lippincott, 1968, p 151.

95. Losken HW. Craniosynostosis. In Bentz ML (ed). Pediatric Plastic Surgery. Stamford, Appleton & Lange, 1997.

96. Losken HW. Craniosynostosis. In Bentz ML (ed). Pediatric Plastic Surgery. Stamford, Appleton & Lange, 1997.

97. Marchac D, Renier D. Treatment of craniosynostosis in infancy. Clin Plast Surg 14:61, 1987.

98. Marchac D. Radical forehead remodelling for cranio-stenosis. Plast Reconst Surg 61:823, 1978.

99. Matteini C, Mommaerts MY. Posterior transpalatal distraction with pterygoid disjunction: a short-term model study. Am J Orthod Dentofacial Orthop 120:498, 2001.

100. Mattick CR, Chadwick SM, Morton ME. Mandibular advancement using an intra-oral osteogenic distraction technique: a report of three clinical cases. J Orthod 28:105, 2001.

101. Maull DJ. Review of devices for distraction osteogenesis of the craniofacial complex. Semin Orthod 5:64, 1999.

102. McCarthy JG, Karp NS, Latrenta GS, Thorne CHM. The effect of early fronto-orbital advancement in frontal sinus development and forehead aesthetics. Plast Reconstr Surg 86:1078, 1990.

103. McCarthy JG, La Trenta GS, Breibart AS, Zide BM. Hypertelorism correction in the young child. Plast Reconstr Surg 86:214, 1990.

104. McCarthy JG, La Trenta GS, Breibart AS, et al. The Le Fort III advancement osteotomy in the child under 7 years of age. Plast Reconstr Surg 86:633, 1990.

105. McCarthy JG, personal communication.

106. McCarthy JG, Schreiber J, Karp N, et al. Lengthening of the human mandible by gradual distraction. Plast Reconstr Surg 89:1, 1992.

107. McCarthy JG, Schreiber J, Karp N, et al. Lengthening the human mandible by gradual distraction. Plast Reconstr Surg 89:1, 1992.

108. McCarthy JG, Zide BM. The spectrum of calvarial bone grafting: introduction of the vascularized calvarial bone flap. Plast Reconstr Surg 74:10, 1984.

109. McCarthy JG, Zide BM. The spectrum of calvarial bone grafting: introduction of the vascularized calvarial bone flap. Plast Reconstr Surg 74:10, 1984.

110. Mehner A. Beitrage zu den Augenveranderungen bei der Schadeldeformitat des sog. Turmschadels mit besonderer Berucksichtigung des Rontgenbildes. Klin Monatsbl Augenheilkd 61:204, 1921.

111. Meling TR, Tveten S, Due-Tonnessen BJ, et al. Monobloc and midface distraction osteogenesis in pediatric patients with severe syndromal craniosynostosis. Pediatr Neurosurg 33:89, 2000.

112. Molina F, Felemovicius J. Distraction of the bony palate and its effects on velopharyngeal competence. Presented at the Annual Meeting of the American Society of Plastic and Reconstructive Surgery, Boston, October, 1998.

113. Molina F, Ortiz Monasterio F. Mandibular elongation and remodeling by distraction: a farewell to major osteotomies. Plast Reconstr Surg 96:4, 1995.

114. Mooney MP, Losken HW, Siegel MI, et al. Development of a strain of rebbits with congenital simple nonsyndromic coronal suture synostosis: II. Somatic and craniofacial growth patterns. Cleft Palate Craniofac J 31:8, 1994.

115. Mooney MP, Losken HW, Tschakaloff A, et al. Congenital bilateral coronal suture synostosis in a rabbit and comparisons with experimental models. Cleft Palate Craniofac J 30:121, 1993.

116. Moore MH, Trott JA, David DJ. Soft tissue expansion in the management of the rare craniofacial clefts. Br J Plast Surg 45:155, 1992.

117. Moss ML. The pathogenesis of premature cranial synostosis in man. Acta Anat (Basel) 37:351, 1959.

118. Muhlbauer W, Anderl H, Ramatschi P, et al. Radical treatment of craniofacial anomalies in infancy and the use of miniplates in craniofacial surgery. Clin Plast Surg 14:101, 1987.

119. Mulliken JB, Kaban LB. Analysis and treatment hemifacial microsomia in childhood. Clin Plast Surg 14:91, 1986.

120. Munro IR. Cranial vault reshaping. Presented at the Second International Conference on the Diagnosis and Treatment of Craniofacial Anomalies, New York, 1976.

121. Munro IR. Orbito-cranio-facial surgery: the team approach. Plast Reconstr Surg 55:170, 1975.

122. Munro IR. Treatment of craniofacial microsomia. Clin Plast Surg 14:77, 1986.

123. Murray JE, Swanson LT. Midface osteotomy and advancement for craniostenosis. Plast Reconstr Surg 41:299, 1968.

124. Nadal E, Dogliotti PL, Rodriguez JC, Zuccaro G. Craniofacial distraction osteogenesis en bloc. J Craniofac Surg 11:246, 2000.

125. Nagata S. A new method of total reconstruction of the auricle for microtia. Plast Reconst Surg 92:187, 1993.

126. Obwegeser H. Correction of skeletal anomalies of otomandibular dysostosis. J Maxillofac Surg 2:73, 1974.

127. Obwegeser H. Surgical correction of small or retrodisplaced maxillae. Plast Reconstr Surg 43:351, 1969.

128. Ortiz-Monasterio F, Fuente de Campo A, Carrillo A. Advancement of the orbits and face in one piece, combined with frontal repositioning for the correction of Crouzon's deformities. Plast Reconstr Surg 61:507, 1978.

129. Ortiz-Monasterio F, Glassman RD, Soto JL. Simultaneous soft tissue expansion and craniofacial surgery. In Caronni EP (ed). Craniofacial Surgery 3. Bologna, Monduzzi Editore, 1991, p 251.

130. Pagnell A. The use and behavior of bone grafts to the deformed facial skeleton. In Transactions of the Second International Congress of Plastic Surgery. Edinburgh, Livingstone, 1960.

131. Persing JA, Edgerton MT, Jane JA. Scientific Foundation and Surgical Treatment of Craniosynostosis. Baltimore, Williams & Wilkins, 1989.

132. Persing JA, Morgan EP, Cronin AJ, Wolcott WP. Skull base expansion: craniofacial effects. Plast Reconstr Surg 87:1028, 1991.

133. Pertschuk MJ, Whitaker LA. Psychosocial considerations in craniofacial deformity. Clin Plast Surg 14:163, 1986.

134. Pinto PX, Mommaerts MY, Wreakes G, Jacobs WV. Immediate postexpansion changes following the use of the transpalatal distractor. J Oral Maxillofac Surg 59:994, 2001.

135. Polley JW, Figueroa AA, Charbel FT, et al. Monobloc craniomaxillofacial distraction osteogenesis in a newborn with severe craniofacial synostosis: a preliminary report. J Craniofac Surg 6:421, 1995.

136. Polley JW, Figueroa AA. Management of severe maxillary deficiency in childhood and adolescent through distraction osteogenesis with an external, adjustable, rigid distraction device. J Craniofac Surg 181, 1997.

137. Posnick JC, Goldstein JA, Waitzmann AA. Surgical correction of the Treacher Collins malar deficiency: quantitative CT scan analysis of long term results. Plast Reconstr Surg 92:12, 1993.

138. Poswillo D. The pathogenesis of the Treacher Collins syndrome (mandibulofacial dysostosis). Br J Oral Surg 13:1, 1975.

139. Rachmiel A, Jackson IT, Potparic Z, Laufer D. Midface advancement in sheep by gradual distraction: a 1-year follow-up study. J Oral Maxillofac Surg 53:525, 1995.

140. Rachmiel A, Potparic Z, Jackson IT, et al. Midface advancement by gradual distraction. Br J Plast Surg 46:201, 1993.
141. Reinisch J, personal communication.
142. Rodriguez JC, Dogliotti P. Mandibular distraction in glossoptosis-micrognathic association: preliminary report. J Craniofac Surg 9:127, 1998.
143. Rohrich RJ, Hollier LH, Watumull D. Optimizing the management of orbitozygomatic fractures. Clin Plast Surg 19:149, 1992.
144. Rosen HM. Porous block hydroxyapatite as an interpositional bone graft substitute in orthognathic surgery. Plast Reconstr Surg 183:985, 1989.
145. Salyer KE, Munro IR, Whitaker LA, et al. Difficulties and problems to be solved in the approach to craniofacial malformations. Birth Defects 11:315, 1975.
146. Siciliano S, Lengele B, Reycherm H. Distraction osteogenesis of a fibula free flap used for mandibular reconstruction: a preliminary report. J Craniomaxillofac Surg 26:386, 2000.
147. Snyder CC, Levine GA, Swanson HM, et al. Mandibular lengthening by gradual distraction. Plast Reconstr Surg 51:506, 1973.
148. Sotereanos G, personal communication.
149. Staffenberg DA, Wood RJ, McCarthy JG, et al. Midface distraction advancement in the canine without osteotomies. Ann Plast Surg 34:512, 1995.
150. Swennen G, Schliephake H, Dempf R, et al. Craniofacial distraction osteogenesis: a review of the literature: Part 1. Clinical studies [review]. Int J Oral Maxillofac Surg 30:89, 2001.
151. Tessier P. Anatomical classification of facial, craniofacial and laterofacial clefts. J Maxillofac Surg 4:69, 1976.
152. Tessier P. Craniofacial surgery in syndromic craniosynostosis. In Cohen MM (ed). Craniostenosis: Diagnosis, Evaluations and Management. New York, Raven Press, pp 312–411.
153. Tessier P. Experiences in the treatment of orbital hypertelorism. Plast Reconstr Surg 53:1, 1974.
154. Tessier P. Orbital hypertelorism 1. Successive surgical attempts, material and methods, causes and mechanisms. Scand J Plast Reconstr Surg 6:135, 1972.
155. Tessier P. Orbitocranial surgery. In Transactions of the Fifth International Congress of Plastic and Reconstructive Surgery. Melbourne, Butterworth, 1971, p 903.
156. Tessier P. Relationship of craniostenoses to craniofacial dysostoses, and to faciostenoses. Plast Reconstr Surg 48:224, 1971.
157. Tessier P. The definitive treatment of the severe facial deformities of craniofacial dysostoses. Crouzon's and Apert's diseases. Plast Reconstr Surg 48:419, 1971.
158. Tessier P. Total osteotomy of the middle third of the face for faciostenosis or for sequelae of Le Fort III fractures. Plast Reconstr Surg 48:533, 1971.
159. Trauner R, Obwegeser H. The surgical correction of mandibular prognathism and retrognathia with consideration of genioplasty: Part I. Oral Surg 10:677, 1957.
160. Trautman RC, Converse JM, Smith B. Plastic and Reconstructive Surgery of the Eye and Adnexa. Washington, DC, Butterworths, 1962.
161. Treacher-Collins E. Cases with symmetrical congenital notches in the outer part of each lid and defective development of the malar bones. Trans Ophthalmol Soc U K 20:190, 1960.
162. Turk AE, McCarthy JG, Thorne CHM, et al. The "back to sleep" campaign and deformational plagiocephaly: is there cause for concern? J Craniofac Surg 7:12, 1996.
163. Van der Meulen JC. Medial faciotomy. Br J Plast Surg 32:339, 1979.
164. Van der Meulen JC. Surgery related to the correction of hypertelorism. Plast Reconstr Surg 71:1, 1983.
165. Virchow R. Uber den Crentinismus, namentlich in Franken, uber pathologische Schadelformen. Wurzburg Verh Phys Med Gesellsch 2:230, 1851.
166. Webster JP, Deming EG. Surgical treatment of bifid nose. Plast Reconstr Surg 6:1, 1950.
167. Whitaker LA, Bartlett SP. The craniofacial dysostoses: guidelines for management of the symmetric and asymmetric deformities. Clin Plast Surg 14:73, 1987.
168. Whitaker LA, LaRossa D, Randall P. Structural goals in craniofacial surgery. Cleft Palate J 12:23, 1975.
169. Whitaker LA, Munro IR, Jackson IT, Salyer KE. Problems in craniofacial surgery. J Maxillofac Surg 4:131, 1976.
170. Whitaker LA, Randall P. The developing field of craniofacial surgery. Pediatrics 54:571, 1974.
171. Whitaker LA, Schaffer D. Severe traumatic oculo-orbital displacement: diagnosis and treatment. Plast Reconstr Surg 59:352, 1977.
172. Whitaker LA, Schut L, Kerr LP. Early surgery for isolated craniofacial dysostosis. Plast Reconstr Surg 91:977, 1997.
173. Whitaker LA, Schut L, Randall P. Craniofacial surgery: present and future. Ann Surg 184:558, 1976.
174. William of Saliceto. Praexos Totos Mediciniae. Venice, 1975.
175. Wolfe SA, Morrison G, Page LK, Berkoxvitz S. The monoblock frontofacial advancement: do the pluses outweigh the minuses? Plast Reconstr Surg 91:977, 1993.
176. Zins JE, Whitaker LA. Membranous vs. endochondral bone autografts: implications for craniofacial reconstruction. Surg Forum 30:521, 1979.

7

Otolaryngologic Manifestations of HIV Infection in Children

David E. Karas, M.D., and Don S. Respler, M.D.

In the decade during which human immunodeficiency virus (HIV) came to be recognized, HIV infection and the acquired immunodeficiency syndrome (AIDS) became a threat to children worldwide. Initial reports of pediatric AIDS were few and limited to children of women infected with HIV or who received contaminated blood products. The first group associated with HIV infection and AIDS was homosexual men. As the infection spread to illicit drug abusers, the heterosexual population—including a large number of childbearing women—became infected from either unprotected contact with an infected person or a contaminated needle. These women then transmitted HIV infections to their offspring. Fortunately, advances in medical therapy have dramatically decreased transmission rates. Additionally, medical therapy, particularly in the developed nations, has transformed AIDS from a life-threatening illness to a chronic disease.

Historical Background and Classification

AIDS traces its short history back to early 1981, when five young homosexual men in Los Angeles were hospitalized with *Pneumocystis carinii* pneumonia (PCP), a rare infection in healthy young persons.[6] Soon after, the Centers for Disease Control (CDC) reported unusually high numbers of Kaposi sarcoma among sexually active homosexual men in New York.[7] By July 1982, 216 cases of this new syndrome were identified; 84% involved homosexual men, 9% intravenous drug abusers, and 5% women. Of the 216 patients, 88 (41%) had died from the sequelae of this disease. In that same month, three cases were reported among hemophiliacs receiving concentrated blood-clotting factors.[8] This strongly suggested "the possible transmission of an agent through blood products."

In May 1983, the first reports of pediatric AIDS appeared in the literature.[45] These reports found that pediatric AIDS occurred where there were high numbers of adult cases, specifically in families of patients with AIDS. Initial reports suggested that children living in high-risk households were susceptible to AIDS and that sexual contact, drug abuse, or exposure to blood products might not be necessary for disease transmission. It was later found that perinatal transmission was responsible.

In September 1982, the CDC defined the criteria for a case definition of AIDS.[9] These included one or more of the following 12 opportunistic infections: (1) atypical mycobacteriosis (disseminated), (2) esophageal candidiasis, (3) cytomegalovirus (CMV) infection (pulmonary, gastrointestinal, or central nervous system), (4) cryptococcosis (meningeal or disseminated), (5) cryptosporidiosis, (6) herpes simplex virus (HSV) infection (chronic mucocutaneous or disseminated), (7) Kaposi sarcoma in a patient younger than 60 years, (8) papovavirus infection (progressive multifocal encephalopathy), (9) PCP, (10) primary lymphoma limited to the brain, (11) strongyloidiasis (pulmonary, central nervous system, or disseminated), and (12) toxoplasmosis (encephalitis or disseminated) (Table 7–1).

In 1985[10] and again in late 1987,[13] the CDC revised the criteria for case definition of AIDS. These revisions were partly due to the availability of tests to confirm infection with the HIV virus. The new definition was divided into three categories: (1) when no laboratory evidence for the presence of HIV infection was available, (2) when laboratory evidence corroborated the existence of HIV infection, and (3) when laboratory evidence suggested that HIV infection was not present.

The first part was essentially the same as the 1982 definition, except it clearly delineated what other causes of immunodeficiency would preclude a diagnosis of AIDS even if one or more of the listed opportunistic diseases were identified. In the second category, when the HIV test result was positive, an additional 12 infections or disease states, if diagnosed definitively, would fulfill the criteria for a case definition of AIDS. These indicator diseases included (1) recurrent/multiple bacterial infections in a patient younger than 13 years (except otitis media and superficial skin or mucosal abscesses or infections), (2) coccidioidomycosis (disseminated), (3) HIV encephalopathy, (4) histoplasmosis (disseminated), (5) isosporiasis with diarrhea persisting for more than 1 month, (6) Kaposi sarcoma at any age, (7) lymphoma of the brain (primary) at any age, (8) other non-Hodgkin lymphoma of B-cell origin or unknown histologic type, (9) atypical mycobacterial disease (disseminated), (10) extrapulmonary tuberculosis, (11) *Salmonella* (nontyphoid) septicemia (re-

TABLE 7–1. Some Opportunistic Infections Associated with AIDS and HIV Infection

---

Pneumocystis carinii pneumonia
Candida albicans infection (bronchial, esophageal, or pulmonary)
Cryptococcus neoformans infection (extrapulmonary)
Disseminated toxoplasmosis (after age 1 month)
Disseminated *Mycobacterium tuberculosis* infection
Disseminated *Mycobacterium* species infection (*M. avium-intracellulare* or *M. kansasii*)
Disseminated histoplasmosis
Chronic isosporiasis
Chronic cryptosporidiosis
Extraintestinal strongyloidiasis
Coccidioides immitis infection (extrapulmonary)
Cytomegalovirus infection outside of liver, spleen, and lymph node (after age 1 month)
Nocardiosis
Progressive multifocal leukoencephalopathy

From Handcock WJ, McIntosh K. Pediatric infections with the human immunodeficiency virus. Otolaryngol Clin North Am 22:639, 1989.

current), and (12) HIV wasting syndrome. The second category also provided for some manifestations that were diagnosed presumptively. The third category was for patients in whom the test response for HIV infection was negative but who had severe immunodeficiency without any other apparent cause. These specific manifestations included a definitive diagnosis of PCP or any of the diseases from the second category with a CD4$^+$ lymphocyte count of less than 400/mm^3.

In December 1992, the CDC published its expanded AIDS surveillance case definition, which would take effect in 1993.[15] The expanded AIDS surveillance case definition now includes all HIV-infected persons with CD4$^+$ lymphocyte counts below 200 cells/mL or a CD4$^+$ percentage less than 14. The new case definition also added three more clinical conditions: pulmonary tuberculosis, recurrent pneumonia, and invasive cervical carcinoma. This expanded definition requires laboratory confirmation of HIV infection in addition to any of the CD4$^+$ lymphocyte or clinical criteria mentioned.

In May 1986, the CDC introduced a classification system that categorized HIV infection (at that time human T-cell lymphotropic virus or lymphadenopathy-associated virus) into four mutually exclusive groups designated I to IV.[11] Group I included patients with transient signs and symptoms occurring during acute infection. Group II included patients with antibody-positive seroconversion with no symptoms that would otherwise categorize them into group III or IV. Group III included patients with a persistent generalized lymphadenopathy who did not have any of the manifestations that would place them in group IV. Patients who had some manifestation that placed them in group IV would not subsequently be placed back into group II or III when the manifestation resolved. Group IV infection was reserved for patients with many of the signs and symptoms usually associated with AIDS and HIV infection. This group was divided into five subgroups, one of which had additional categories contained within it. All patients with AIDS would be classified into group IV, but not all group IV patients had AIDS.

In December 1992, the CDC published the 1993 Revised Classification System for HIV Infection and Expanded Surveillance Case Definition for AIDS Among Adolescents and Adults.[15] The revised system divided the classification into two broad categories, CD4$^+$ T-lymphocyte categories and clinical categories. The CD4$^+$ T-lymphocyte categories are divided into three categories on the basis of CD4$^+$ T-lymphocyte counts: *category 1*, 500 cells/mL and above; *category 2*, 200 to 499 cells/mL; and *category 3*, less than 200 cells/mL. The lowest accurate, but not necessarily the most recent, CD4$^+$ T-lymphocyte count is used in this classification.

There are also three clinical categories designated A, B, and C. *Category A* essentially includes groups I to III from the 1986 classification with no evidence of the conditions listed in category B or C. *Category B* consists of symptomatic conditions in an HIV-infected adolescent or adult that are not included in clinical category C and that meet at least one of the following criteria: the conditions are attributed to HIV infection or are indicative of a defect in cell-mediated immunity, or the conditions are considered by physicians to have a clinical course or to require management that is complicated by HIV infection. Some of these conditions include, but are not limited to, (1) bacillary angiomatosis, (2) oropharyngeal candidiasis, (3) vulvovaginal candidiasis that is persistent, frequent, or poorly responsive to therapy, (4) cervical dysplasia (moderate or severe)/cervical carcinoma in situ, (5) constitutional symptoms, such as fever (38.5°C) or diarrhea lasting more than 1 month, (6) hairy leukoplakia (oral), (7) herpes zoster (shingles) involving at least two distinct episodes or more than one dermatome, (8) idiopathic thrombocytopenic purpura, (9) listeriosis, (10) pelvic inflammatory disease, particularly if complicated by tubo-ovarian abscess, and (11) peripheral neuropathy. Once patients have been diagnosed with a condition that places them in category B, they remain in category B even when that condition has resolved. *Category C* includes the clinical conditions listed in the AIDS surveillance case definition. Once a category C condition has occurred, a patient remains in that category.

In April 1987, the CDC adopted a separate classification system for HIV infection in children younger than 13 years.[12] Furthermore, since newborn infants could have a positive HIV antibody test response from maternal antibody acquired passively in utero without actually having HIV infection, children required a specific definition for HIV infection; this was divided into two categories, one for children younger than 15 months and the other for older children. HIV infection was defined by one or more of the following criteria: (1) identification of virus in blood or tissues, (2) presence of HIV antibody (positive screening test result plus confirmatory test), or (3) symptoms meeting the CDC case definition for AIDS. The second criteria was modified for infants and children younger than 15 months: in addition to the presence of HIV antibody, there would have to be evidence of both cellular and humoral immune deficiency and one or more of the categories from class P2. *Class P2* is the category for symptomatic infection in the official classification of HIV infection in children younger than 13 years.

The classification of HIV infection in children younger

than 13 years is divided into three broad categories: (1) indeterminate infection, (2) asymptomatic infection, and (3) symptomatic infection. Indeterminate infection *(P0)* corresponds to those infants and children up to 15 months old who have antibody to HIV indicating exposure to a mother who is infected but are not known to harbor the virus themselves. Asymptomatic infection *(P1)* is reserved for children who fulfill one of the definition criteria for HIV infection but at present show no symptoms of disease. Finally, symptomatic infection *(P2)* includes children who not only fulfill one of the definition criteria but also have at some time had symptoms associated with HIV infection. Once children have entered class P2, they are not reassigned to class P1 if signs or symptoms resolve (Table 7–2).

Three immunologic categories (Table 7–3) were established to categorize children less than 13 years old. This system was revised in 1994 when the CDC revised its classification system for HIV infection in children by the severity of immunosuppression attributable to HIV infection. CD4$^+$ T-lymphocyte depletion is a major consequence of HIV infection and is responsible for many of the severe manifestations of HIV infection in adults. For this reason, CD4$^+$ counts are used in the adult HIV classification system.[11] However, several findings complicate the use of CD4$^+$ counts of assessing immunosuppression resulting from HIV infection in children. Normal CD4$^+$ counts are higher in infants and young children than in adults and decline over the first few years of life.[12-16] In addition, children may develop opportunistic infections at higher CD4$^+$ levels than in adults.[17-19] Although data are insufficient to correlate CD4$^+$ levels with disease progressions at all age groups, low age-specific CD4$^+$ counts appear to correlate with conditions associated with immunosuppression in children.[12, 17, 20, 21] Therefore, despite these complications, classification based on age-specific CD4$^+$ levels appears to be useful for describing the immunologic status of HIV-infected children.

Fewer data are available on age-specific values for the CD4$^+$ T-lymphocyte percentage of total lymphocytes than for absolute counts. However, the CD4$^+$ T-lymphocyte percent shows less measurement variability than the absolute count.[22] To establish the age-specific values of the CD4$^+$ percentage that correlate with the CD4$^+$ count thresholds, the CDC compiled data from selected clinical projects in the United States and Europe. The data included CD4$^+$ counts exceeding 9000, with the corre-

TABLE 7–2. Summary of the Classification of HIV Infection in Children Younger than 13 Years

Class P0. Indeterminate infection
Class P1. Asymptomatic infection
  Subclass A. Normal immune function
  Subclass B. Abnormal immune function
  Subclass C. Immune function not tested
Class P2. Symptomatic infection
  Subclass A. Nonspecific findings
  Subclass B. Progressive neurologic disease
  Subclass C. Lymphoid interstitial pneumonitis
  Subclass D. Secondary infectious diseases
Category D1. Specified secondary infectious diseases listed in CDC surveillance case definition for AIDS
Category D2. Recurrent serious bacterial infections
Category D3. Other specified secondary infectious diseases
  Subclass E. Secondary cancers
    Category E1. Specified secondary cancers listed in CDC surveillance definition of AIDS
    Category E2. Other cancers possibly secondary to HIV infection
  Subclass F. Other diseases possibly due to HIV infection

sponding CD4$^+$ percentage determinations, from both HIV-infected and uninfected children older than 13 years. Nonparametric repression modeling was used to establish the CD4$^+$ count percentage boundaries that best correlated with the CD4$^+$ count boundaries in the classifications system.

The immunologic category classification (Table 7–4) is based on either the CD4$^+$ T-lymphocyte count or the CD4$^+$ percentage of total lymphocytes. If both the CD4$^+$ count and the CD4$^+$ percentage indicate different classification categories, the child should be classified into the more severe category. Repeat follow-up CD4$^+$ values that result in a change in classification should be confirmed by a second determination. Values thought to be in error should not be used. A child should not be reclassified to a less severe category regardless of subsequent CD4$^+$ determinations.

Children infected with HIV or perinatally exposed to HIV may be classified into one of four mutually exclusive clinical categories based on signs, symptoms, or diagnoses related to HIV infection (Table 7–5). As with the immunologic categories, the clinical categories have been defined to provide a staging classification (e.g., the prognosis for children in the second category would be less favorable than for those in the first category).

Category N, not symptomatic, includes children with

TABLE 7–3. Pediatric HIV Classification*

	Clinical Categories			
Immunologic Categories	*N: No Signs/Symptoms*	*A: Mild Signs/Symptoms*	*B:† Moderate Signs/Symptoms*	*C:† Severe Signs/Symptoms*
1: No evidence of suppression	N1	A1	B1	C1
2: Evidence of moderate suppression	N2	A2	B2	C2
3: Severe suppression	N3	A3	B3	C3

* Children whose HIV infection status is not confirmed are classified by using the above grid with a letter E (for perinatally exposed) placed before the appropriate classification code (e.g., EN2).
† Both category C and lymphoid interstitial pneumonitis in category B are reportable to state and local health departments as acquired immunodeficiency syndrome.
From CDC 1994 revised classification system for HIV infection in children less than 13 years of age. MMWR 43:1, 1994.

TABLE 7–4. Immunologic Categories Based on Age-Specific CD4+ T-Lymphocyte Counts and Percent of Total Lymphocytes

	Age of Child					
	<12 Months		*1–5 Years*		*6–12 Years*	
Immunologic Categories	μL	(%)	μL	(%)	μL	(%)
1: No evidence of suppression	≥1500	(≥25)	≥1000	(≥25)	≥500	(≥25)
2: Evidence of moderate suppression	750–1499	(15–24)	500–999	(15–24)	200–499	(15–24)
3: Severe suppression	<750	(<15)	<500	(<15)	<200	(<15)

From CDC 1994 revised classification system for HIV infection in children less than 13 years of age. MMWR 43:1, 1994.

no signs or symptoms considered to be the result of HIV infection or with only one of the conditions listed in *category A,* mildly symptomatic. Category N was separated from category A partly because of the substantial amount of time that can elapse before a child manifests the signs or symptoms defined in *category B,* moderately symptomatic. Also, more staging information can be obtained during this early stage of disease by separating categories N and A. In addition, for children who have uncertain HIV-infection status *(prefix E),* categories N and A may help to distinguish those children who are more likely to be infected with HIV[23] (i.e., children in category EA may be more likely to be infected than children in category EN).

Category B includes all children with signs and symptoms thought to be caused by HIV infection but not specifically outlined under category A or category C, severely symptomatic, The conditions listed in Table 7–5 are examples only: any other HIV-related conditions not included in category A or C should be included in category B. Anemia, thrombocytopenia, and lymphopenia have defined thresholds in the new classification system.[23]

Category C includes all AIDS-defining conditions except lymphoid interstitial pneumonitis (LIP) (Table 7–6).

TABLE 7–5. Clinical Categories for Children with HIV Infection

CATEGORY N: NOT SYMPTOMATIC
Children who have no signs or symptoms considered to be the result of HIV infection or who have only one of the conditions listed in category A.

CATEGORY A: MILDLY SYMPTOMATIC
Children with two or more of the conditions listed below but none of the conditions listed in categories B and C.
- Lymphadenopathy (≥0.5 cm at more than two sites; bilateral = one site)
- Hepatomegaly
- Splenomegaly
- Dermatitis
- Parotitis
- Recurrent or persistent upper respiratory infection, sinusitis, or otitis media

CATEGORY B: MODERATELY SYMPTOMATIC
Children who have symptomatic conditions other than those listed for category A or C that are attributed to HIV infection. Examples of conditions in clinical category B include but are not limited to:
- Anemia (<8 g/dL), neutropenia (<1000/mm³), or thrombocytopenia (<100,000/mm³) persisting ≥30 days
- Bacterial meningitis, pneumonia, or sepsis (single episode)
- Candidiasis, oropharyngeal (thrush), persisting (>2 months) in children >6 months of age
- Cardiomyopathy
- Cytomegalovirus infection, with onset before 1 month of age
- Diarrhea, recurrent or chronic
- Hepatitis
- Herpes simplex virus (HSV) stomatitis, recurrent (more than two episodes within 1 year)
- HSV bronchitis, pneumonitis, or esophagitis with onset before 1 month of age
- Herpes zoster (shingles) involving at least two distinct episodes or more than one dermatome
- Leiomyosarcoma
- Lymphoid interstitial pneumonia or pulmonary lymphoid hyperplasia complex
- Nephropathy
- Nocardiosis
- Persistent fever (lasting >1 month)
- Toxoplasmosis, onset before 1 month of age
- Varicella, disseminated (complicated chickenpox)

CATEGORY C: SEVERELY SYMPTOMATIC
Children who have any condition listed in the 1987 surveillance case definition for acquired immunodeficiency syndrome, with the exception of LIP (see Table 7–6).

From CDC 1994 revised classification system for HIV infection in children less than 13 years of age. MMWR 43:1, 1994.

Several reports indicate that the prognosis for children with LIP is substantially better than that for children who have other AIDS-defining conditions.[21, 24, 25] Thus, LIP has been separated from the other AIDS-defining conditions in category C and placed in category B.

Signs and symptoms related to causes other than HIV

TABLE 7–6. Conditions Included in Clinical Category C for Children Infected with HIV

CATEGORY C: SEVERELY SYMPTOMATIC
- Serious bacterial infections, multiple or recurrent (i.e., any combination of at least two culture-confirmed infections within a 2-year period), of the following types: septicemia, pneumonia, meningitis, bone or joint infection, or abscess of an internal organ or body cavity (excluding otitis media, superficial skin or mucosal abscesses, and indwelling catheter–related infections)
- Candidiasis, esophageal or pulmonary (bronchi, trachea, lungs)
- Coccidioidomycosis, disseminated (at site other than or in addition to lungs or cervical or hilar lymph nodes)
- Cryptococcosis, extrapulmonary
- Cryptosporidiosis or isosporiasis with diarrhea persisting >1 month
- Cytomegalovirus disease with onset of symptoms at age >1 month (at a site other than liver, spleen, or lymph nodes)
- Encephalopathy (at least one of the following progressive findings present for at least 2 months in the absence of a concurrent illness other than HIV infection that could explain the findings): a) failure to attain or loss of developmental milestones or loss of intellectual ability, verified by standard developmental scale or neuropsychological tests; b) impaired brain growth or acquired microcephaly demonstrated by head circumference measurements or brain atrophy demonstrated by computed tomography or magnetic resonance imaging (serial imaging is required for children <2 years of age); c) acquired symmetric motor deficit manifested by two or more of the following: paresis, pathologic reflexes, ataxia, or gait disturbance
- Herpes simplex virus infection causing a mucocutaneous ulcer that persists for >1 month; or bronchitis, pneumonitis, or esophagitis for any duration affecting a child >1 month of age
- Histoplasmosis, disseminated (at a site other than or in addition to lungs or cervical or hilar lymph nodes)
- Kaposi sarcoma
- Lymphoma, primary, in brain
- Lymphoma, small, noncleaved cell (Burkitt), or immunoblastic or large cell lymphoma of B-cell or unknown immunologic phenotype
- *Mycobacterium tuberculosis,* disseminated or extrapulmonary
- *Mycobacterium,* other species or unidentified species, disseminated (at a site other than or in addition to lungs, skin, or cervical or hilar lymph nodes)
- *Mycobacterium avium* complex or *Mycobacterium kansasii,* disseminated (at a site other than or in addition to lungs, skin, or cervical or hilar lymph nodes)
- *Pneumocystis carinii* pneumonia
- Progressive multifocal leukoencephalopathy
- *Salmonella* (nontyphoid) septicemia, recurrent
- Toxoplasmosis of the brain with onset at >1 month of age
- Wasting syndrome in the absence of a concurrent illness other than HIV infection that could explain the following findings: a) persistent weight loss >10% of baseline OR b) downward crossing of at least two of the following percentile lines on the weight-for-age chart (e.g., 95th, 75th, 50th, 25th, 5th) in a child ≥1 year of age OR c) <5th percentile on weight-for-height chart on two consecutive measurements, ≥30 days apart PLUS a) chronic diarrhea (i.e., at least two loose stools per day for ≥30 days) OR b) documented fever (for ≥30 days, intermittent or constant)

From CDC 1994 revised classification system for HIV infection in children less than 13 years of age. MMWR 43:1, 1994.

infection (e.g., inflammatory or drug-related causes) should not be used to classify children. For example, a child with drug-related hepatitis or anemia should not be classified in category B solely because these conditions may be associated with HIV infection. In contrast, a child with anemia or hepatitis should be classified in category B when the condition is thought to be related to HIV infection. The criteria for diagnosing some conditions and determining whether a child's signs, symptoms, or diagnoses are related to HIV infection may not be clear in all cases and therefore may require the judgment of the clinicians and researchers using the classification system.

Categories in the 1987 pediatric HIV classification system can be translated into categories in the 1994 system in most cases (Table 7–6). Class P0 is now designated by the prefix *E*, and class P1 is now class N. Children previously classified as P2A are now classified in more than one category, reflecting the different prognoses for children with different conditions included in the P2A category (e.g., children who have wasting syndrome have a worse prognosis than children with lymphadenopathy).

Epidemiology

The epidemiology of HIV infection has changed dramatically in recent years. Since the recognition that zidovudine (ZDV) therapy significantly reduced the risk of perinatal transmission of HIV infection, there has been a concomitant drop in transmission rates. A number of studies have shown that ZDV effectively lowered perinatal transmission rates from the range of 25% to 30% to approximately 5%. This discovery, considered the first major breakthrough in the prevention of HIV transmission, has been rapidly accepted and implemented by both pregnant mothers and health care workers.

HIV infection in children accounts for a small proportion of the total number of cases in the United States. However, in 1997, HIV was the 11th leading cause of death in children 1 to 4 years old. As of June 30, 1998, 8596 cases of pediatric AIDS (birth to 13 years) have been reported to the CDC for 49 states, Puerto Rico, and the U.S. Virgin Islands.[44]

These numbers provide only a portion of the entire story. The figures quoted are for those with AIDS, the most severe manifestation of HIV infection, and do not represent the total number of children with HIV infection in whom AIDS is yet to develop. AIDS is a distinct entity that requires certain diagnostic criteria as put forth by the CDC. The estimated number of children with HIV infection is currently around 2000.[18]

The geographic distribution of AIDS cases clearly indicates that this disease is predominantly found in metropolitan areas with populations greater than 500,000.[16, 17] Fifty-eight percent of all cases were reported from only four states: New York (26%), Florida (16%), New Jersey (9%), and California (7%). In addition to geographic differences, there are obvious race and ethnic predilections. Black children account for approximately 15% of the total population of children in the United States but for 58% of pediatric AIDS cases. Only 9% of children in the

United States are Hispanic, but almost 23% of pediatric AIDS cases occur among Hispanics. The prevalence of AIDS in Native Americans and Asian/Pacific Islanders is exceedingly small.[18]

The numbers above are encouraging considering how many patients were infected in the early 1990s and the projections from that time. The nationwide figures have leveled off in recent years, largely because of control of perinatal transmission. Although incidence figures are decreasing in the United States, the world in general tells an entirely different story. HIV infection has reached epidemic proportions. The latest figures reveal that in 1997, 600,000 children were infected worldwide. It is currently estimated that 1.1 million children are living with HIV infection, almost 90% of whom live in sub-Saharan Africa and the developing nations in southeast Asia.[67] Most of these children were infected by perinatal transmission or breast-feeding. These figures are devastating and provide a real challenge to the international health care community.

It is now well known that there are four ways to become infected with HIV: (1) intimate contact with someone infected with HIV, (2) intravenous drug abuse with the use of a contaminated needle or syringe, (3) maternal transmission to the fetus in utero or to the neonate at delivery, and (4) transfusion of infected blood or blood products. Children in the United States have acquired HIV infection primarily through the last two routes. The majority of these cases are by maternal transmission, which accounts for 91% of pediatric AIDS cases. This is significantly different from the adolescent group. In this group, boys and girls differ in their relative exposure categories as well as in the probability of contracting disease. In adolescent boys (13 to 19 years), the most common cause of all reported cases is transfusion of blood or blood products (49%); the overwhelming majority of these patients have hemophilia or a coagulation disorder. In adolescent girls, the most common risk behavior is heterosexual contact (54%), and the majority of these contacts are with a drug abuser. In adolescent groups, boys are more than twice as likely to be infected as girls; this appears to be due to the greater frequency of coagulation disorders in boys. However, the frequency of AIDS cases from infected blood products should presumably decrease with a safer blood supply.

Pathophysiology

The etiologic agent for AIDS is HIV. This was formerly called *human T-cell lymphotropic virus III* or *lymphadenopathy-associated virus,* indicating its predilection for T-cells and in particular the CD4 receptor commonly found on the helper/inducer T-lymphocytes. The HIV virus is a retrovirus; like all retroviruses, it is able to convert its own single-stranded RNA into double-stranded DNA to allow incorporation into the host's genome. The structure of the virus is generally divided into two broad subunits, the *envelope* and the *core.*

The envelope consists of a lipid bilayer that is of host-cell origin. A glycoprotein, gp160, is embedded in the lipid bilayer of the envelope.[72] This gp160 glycoprotein can be enzymatically cleaved into the two major envelope glycoproteins, gp41 and gp120. The gp41 glycoprotein is the transmembrane portion of gp160 and is responsible for anchoring gp120 to the virion. The gp120 glycoprotein protrudes from the surface of the virus and functions as the binding site to the host cell. It is now known that when gp120 comes in contact with host-cell CD4 receptors, this glycoprotein is responsible for the high-affinity binding. Also found in the envelope are membrane proteins derived from the host that remain after virion synthesis.

The viral core is composed of two main portions, the nucleocapsid and the enzymes contained within it. The nucleocapsid is synthesized as a single precursor protein of 53 kD and subsequently cleaved by HIV-1 protease into four proteins: p7, p9, p17, and p24. The p17 protein is found immediately adjacent to the inner surface of the lipid bilayer of the envelope. The p24 protein, the primary protein of the nucleocapsid, is found within the p17 protein and surrounds the RNA and enzymes. The two strands of RNA, the p7 and p9 proteins that are intimately associated with the RNA, and the enzymes compose the core of the nucleocapsid. The enzymes are reverse transcriptase (probably the most important), ribonuclease, integrase, and viral protease.

Once HIV infection has occurred, its spread within the body is similar to that of other viruses. The cell cycle of HIV begins with contact of the virus with a receptive host cell, usually a helper T-lymphocyte or other cell bearing CD4 surface receptors (monocytes, macrophages, and central nervous system dendritic cells). After the gp120 glycoprotein of the virus binds with the CD4 receptor of the host cell, the virus is internalized by the host cell. Viral RNA then directs DNA synthesis, which is catalyzed by the enzyme reverse transcriptase. This process is the target of the medications presently used to combat HIV infection. These medications, namely, zidovudine (formerly called azidothymidine [AZT]) and didanosine, function through the inhibition of viral reverse transcriptase.

The virus then incorporates the newly created DNA into the host-cell DNA. The virus is called a *provirus* at this stage, and the host cell has been permanently infected with HIV. After this, the virus, or provirus, enters a latent phase in which there appears to be no further viral activity. This latency usually corresponds with a clinically quiescent stage of disease. However, as the cells duplicate, so does the virus that has been incorporated into the cell's genome. In addition, these cells infected with latent virus appear to have functional impairment of their response to antigenic stimulation. Even uninfected CD4+ cells have been found to be impaired by a disturbance of the normal cell-to-cell interaction that usually occurs between these cells.

This provirus form remains latent until some as yet unknown activation factor causes expression of these genes that have been embedded in the cell genome. Some evidence indicates that HSV or CMV infection may be involved in HIV stimulation.[72] Once this activation has occurred, the cell begins to produce new HIV particles at the direction of the previously incorporated provirus. This process takes place with the use of host-cell enzymes and machinery, ultimately resulting in cell lysis and release of a relatively large number of HIV particles. These newly synthesized viruses are then free to infect other cells with CD4 surface receptors.

Since monocytes and macrophages also have CD4 surface receptors, they are also susceptible to infection by HIV. However, these cells have relatively fewer CD4 surface receptors and become infected at a slower rate than helper T-lymphocytes do. These cells are also more likely to produce viral particles by intracytoplasmic vacuoles, where viral particles bud off from the cell surface. In these situations, the host cell is not destroyed but continues to produce HIV. The fact that the virus is contained within these intracytoplasmic vacuoles may protect the virus from any possible immunotherapy or chemotherapy. This reservoir of infection may become important in the development of new agents to combat the disease.

As HIV infection progresses, more CD4 receptor cells become involved, especially helper T-lymphocytes. The result is not only a decreased number of these CD4+ cells but also abnormal function of the ones that are present.[49] The helper T-cell is at the center of a complex system that coordinates the entire immune response. Therefore, a disturbance of helper T-cell function may have profound effects on the entire immune system. In children with developing immune systems, it is not clear how these defects alter the development of these immune systems. CD4+ cell counts are presently obtained as a laboratory marker to observe progression of disease. These numbers have become important because the CD4+ count appears to correlate with particular types of clinical manifestations of disease. Since helper T-cells orchestrate the body's immune response, HIV infection causes noticeable qualitative effects on B-lymphocyte, natural killer, and cytotoxic T-cell functions.

Diagnosis

There are three broad groups of testing for HIV infection: antibody testing, antigen testing, and viral culture. It seems obvious that the best way to test for the presence of a virus would be to test for the virus itself (i.e., viral culture) or at least a component of the virus (i.e., antigen testing). Instead, antibody testing, although imperfect, provides relatively accurate and reliable results. The test most often used in the United States for diagnosis of HIV infection is the enzyme-linked immunosorbent assay (ELISA), usually confirmed with a Western blot analysis. Both of these tests have sensitivities and specificities that exceed 99% if performed properly with approved materials.[1]

The method of testing for HIV antibody is with an ELISA. If the response is positive, it is reported as "initially reactive"; if it is negative, it is reported as "nonreactive." In either situation, the ELISA is repeated. If both test results are negative, the report states "negative for HIV antibodies" and no further tests are performed. If both test results are positive for the presence of HIV antibodies, the report states "repeatedly reactive for HIV antibodies" and additional testing is performed. If the two test results disagree, a third ELISA is performed that

decides the outcome of ELISA testing. If two of the ELISA test results are positive, a Western blot analysis is used for confirmation.

This type of antibody testing works relatively well in almost all age groups. As stated, it is both sensitive and specific for presence of antibody, which in most situations correlates well with HIV infection. However, in young children, this type of testing presents several problems. The antibody tested for is immunoglobulin G, which can cross the placenta; if the mother is infected with HIV, maternal HIV antibody can be detected in the infant's serum up to the age of 15 to 18 months. Therefore, children younger than this age who have HIV antibodies in their serum may or may not actually be infected with HIV. These children require either a re-test at a later age or some other measure of HIV infection.

The most commonly performed test in children younger than 2 years is the DNA polymerase chain reaction (PCR) test. In this test, DNA strands are amplified and then hybridization is attempted with a radiolabeled marker. This test has been found to be extremely sensitive and specific for HIV infection. PCR testing is sometimes performed simultaneously with ELISA antibody testing in older high-risk populations.

Another problem encountered in testing young children is that a significant number of infants who are actually infected with HIV do not produce detectable levels of antibody and test "negative for HIV antibodies." This phenomenon is thought to be due to B-lymphocyte dysfunction secondary to HIV infection. This is an additional reason that PCR testing is preferred. This situation of B-lymphocyte dysfunction causing negative results to antibody testing may also occur in adults and adolescents in the later stages of infection, when circulating antibody levels are low. Antibody test results also are falsely negative in persons infected with HIV but who have not produced antibodies to the virus; this is the "window period" before seroconversion has taken place. Other situations can cause a false-negative report. These include immunosuppressive therapy, transfusions, and heat inactivation.[40]

Clinical Manifestations

Otitis Media

HIV infection is a disease process characterized by recurrent infections. Otitis media is already the most common infection in non-immunocompromised children after upper respiratory infections. Otitis media in children with AIDS may be even more common and more difficult to eradicate. This increased prevalence may be due not only to the fact that these children are more difficult to treat successfully but also to the host's failure to prevent initial infection. One study indicated that children with HIV infection were not more likely to experience acute otitis media, but those who did have one episode of acute otitis media were more likely to suffer a recurrence than were normal children.[54] This may indicate that these children are predisposed to chronic otitis media as well. However, for the most part, otitis media can be expected to respond relatively well to the usual therapeutic regimen.

Otitis in these children is etiologically similar to otitis in those who are not immunocompromised; however, infected children have additional abnormalities that may increase their likelihood of contracting disease. The patient's underlying immunocompromised status may prevent the host from mounting an adequate response to foreign antigenic stimulation. Eustachian-tube dysfunction appears more common in AIDS populations. This may be due to recurrent upper respiratory infections, adenoidal hypertrophy causing obstruction, or HIV infection itself. Some authors have indicated that that allergies might be more common in the HIV-infected population.[61] This assertion is supported by the fact that immunoglobulin E levels have been found to be elevated in HIV-infected patients.

The bacteriology of otitis media in HIV-infected children does not appear to be significantly different from that of otitis media in uninfected children. Some reports have noted a higher frequency of *Staphylococcus, Pseudomonas,* and *Candida* infections as well as a greater variety of microbes not usually associated with middle-ear infections.

Initial treatment does not differ significantly from that of otitis media in those not affected by HIV infection. Amoxicillin is still the drug of choice for initial therapy in HIV-infected children with otitis media. Failure of initial medical therapy may be due to the presence of organisms that produce β-lactamase, such as *Haemophilus influenzae* and *Moraxella catarrhalis.* For these patients, treatment with an antibiotic that is effective against these organisms is required, such as amoxicillin-clavulanate. Tympanocentesis is indicated for severe pain, complications, and persistent acute otitis media and when an unusual organism is suspected. When otitis media is refractory to all medical therapy, myringotomy and tube placement, with or without adenoidectomy, are usually required. When the patient requires surgical intervention for treatment of refractory otitis media, intraoperative cultures of middle-ear fluid are indicated. This information may help detect unusual organisms, such as *Mycobacterium tuberculosis* or *Nocardia asteroides,* which have been found in the middle-ear fluid of patients with AIDS. (See Chapters 23 and 24.)

Sinusitis

It is known that HIV infection is accompanied by an increase in bacterial infections, and in this respect, sinusitis is similar to otitis media. Several studies of adults have indicated that the prevalence of sinusitis in this HIV-infected population is anywhere from 12% to 68%.[56] The literature contains little information on sinusitis in HIV-infected children, so much of the information is extrapolated from adults. These patients, similar to patients not infected with HIV, are susceptible to the entire spectrum of sinonasal disease from mucosal thickening in an isolated sinus to pansinusitis. Many of the same reasons for increased prevalence of otitis media are true for sinusitis, except that we are concerned with obstruction of the sinus ostia instead of obstruction of the eustachian tube. Some of these reasons include decreased immune surveillance to primary infection, recurrent upper respiratory infections, HIV infection itself, and possible increased allergic response in this population. One study demonstrated that the correlation between immunoglobulin E levels and severity of sinusitis was significant in HIV-infected adults.[61] Other studies noted that the best correlate with the occurrence of sinusitis in this population was a decreasing CD4+ count.[28, 71]

Once again, the bacteriology is similar to the situation for otitis media. The most common organisms are those normally associated with sinusitis in the non–HIV-infected population. These are predominantly *Streptococcus pneumoniae, H. influenzae, M. catarrhalis,* and anaerobes. Again, unusual pathogens such as *Legionella pneumophila, Pseudomonas aeruginosa,*[20] and *Pneumocystis carinii* are found with increased frequency in HIV-infected patients.[29] Fungal sinusitis associated with HIV infection is reported in the literature, but it is unclear whether the frequency of fungal sinusitis is increased in this population.[66]

The clinical manifestations of acute sinusitis are no different from what would be expected in the general population. The most common presenting signs and symptoms are fevers, headaches, mucopurulent nasal discharge, cough, and upper respiratory symptoms. These clinical symptoms are almost always sufficient for diagnosis. Further diagnostic procedures, such as computed tomographic scans, are reserved for patients in whom medical therapy has failed, who experience complications of sinusitis, or who are being considered for surgical intervention (Fig. 7–1).

Treatment consists of the standard combination of oral antibiotics, decongestants, and mucolytics. Initial antibiotic treatment is usually amoxicillin or erythromycin-sulfisoxazole for a minimum of 3 weeks. Amoxicillin-clavulanate and cephalosporins are usually reserved for patients unresponsive to primary treatment. The significance of decongestants and mucolytics cannot be overemphasized in these patients. Decongestants should be used both systemically and topically; however, topical treatment should not exceed 3 days. A double-blind, randomized study by Wawrose et al[68] comparing high-dose guaifenesin with placebo found a significant difference in nasal congestion and thinner secretions among the group taking guaifenesin. Surgical therapies for sinusitis in children are not addressed in the literature. At present, these approaches have been reserved for patients with complications or in whom aggressive medical therapy has failed. For the latter group, the preferred approach has been a nasal antral widow for culture and irrigation. The experience with endoscopic sinus surgery in HIV-infected children is exceedingly small, and it is unclear whether there is any benefit to such an approach. (See Chapters 41 and 43.)

Cervical Lymphadenopathy

Lymphadenopathy is common within the course of pediatric AIDS treatment. Cervical lymphadenopathy develops relatively early in the progression of pediatric HIV infections.[21, 69] The HIV lymphadenopathy syndrome is charac-

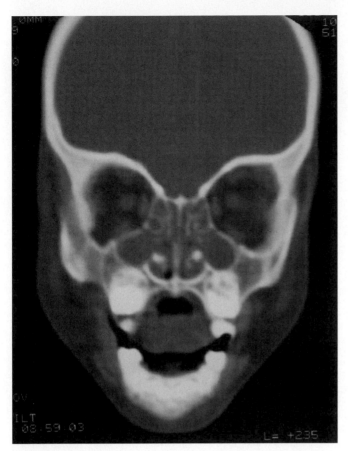

FIGURE 7–1. Coronal computed tomographic scan of a 3-year-old patient with pansinusitis.

pathogens. Such infections are common in cervical lymphadenopathy and include staphylococcal infections, mycobacterial tuberculosis, atypical tuberculosis, toxoplasmosis, *Pneumocystis* infection, and fungal infections such as cryptococcosis, histoplasmosis, and coccidioidomycosis. Atypical tuberculosis is common in pediatric AIDS in the cervical region; the most common organism is *Mycobacterium avium* complex (MAC). Skin testing (using purified protein derivative [PPD]) is useful for *M. tuberculosis,* although this type of testing is not useful with MAC. MAC responds poorly to traditional anti-tuberculin antimicrobial agents. Newer antimicrobial agents, such as clofazimine and ciprofloxacin, have proved to be somewhat effective against these resistant strains.[38] However, ciprofloxacin is not approved for use in children younger than 16 years.

Parotid Enlargement

Gradual and persistent parotid enlargement, which occurs in approximately 30% of children with AIDS, is usually bilateral and commonly arises early in the course of pediatric AIDS.[69] This is due to either lymphocytic infiltration of the parotid lymph nodes or lymphoepithelial cyst formation, most likely secondary to lymphoepithelial infiltration and obstruction of the salivary ducts.[42, 59] These parotid lymphoepithelial cysts are unique to HIV infection, and their presence necessitates HIV testing. Progressive parotid swelling for months with minimal tenderness can be the first presentation of HIV infection (Fig. 7–2). Transient elevations of amylase occasionally accompany the onset of cyst formation, although gradual or persistent parotid enlargement usually leads to normal amylase lev-

terized by enlarged lymph nodes in two or more extra-inguinal sites lasting at least 3 months. This type of lymphadenopathy is typically symmetrical; regularly shaped, soft nodes are not adherent to underlying structures. The lymph nodes enlarge and regress without any apparent cause during the course of the disease. Observation is most advisable unless these nodes have an atypical appearance, are unilateral, are very enlarged, grow rapidly, or cause pain necessitating a specific diagnosis. (See Chapters 95 and 97.)

The location of HIV cervical lymphadenopathy most often includes posterior cervical triangle, preauricular and postauricular, submandibular, submental, supraclavicular, and anterior cervical regions.[42] Histopathologic examination of these nodes most commonly reveals florid reactive follicular hyperplasia with the presence of multinucleated giant cells. These findings are not exclusive to HIV infection; they also are present in other forms of viral lymphadenitis. Another pattern occurring in progression of pediatric HIV cases is called *lymphocyte depletion*. This pattern shows washed-out lymph nodes with few or no follicles and a lack of small lymphocytes. Two different patterns of lymphocyte depletion also occur in the thymus.[37] Lymphocyte depletion is associated with the rapid progression to AIDS with poor overall prognosis and correlates with a decline in the CD4+ count.[42]

The hallmark of AIDS is opportunistic infection as well as increased frequency of the common bacterial

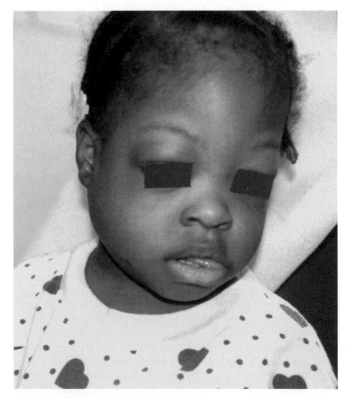

FIGURE 7–2. A 20-month-old child with parotid enlargement.

els.[19, 21] These cysts can enlarge and regress in size for several years and can become quite enlarged (>4 cm). The pathologic features include diffuse lymphoid hyperplasia, reactive hypervascularity, and identification of HIV antigen in lymphoid cells with dendritic and cytoplasmic processes. These lymphoepithelial cysts are surrounded by squamous epithelium, and myoepithelial islands occur in some cases.[59] Computed tomography reveals multiple thin-walled cystic masses within the parotid gland, often with bilateral involvement. Magnetic resonance imaging shows the cyst to have low intensity T_1-weighted images with high-intensity T_2-weighted images.[42]

Lymphoepithelial cysts lead a benign course and have little impact on the patient's overall prognosis. The diagnosis can usually be confirmed by imaging studies as well as fine-needle aspiration biopsy. Aspiration alone provides only temporary improvement, and repeated procedures are needed to provide sustained decompression. Sclerosing agents such as tetracycline injected into these cysts after aspiration have been somewhat successful in preliminary studies and offer an alternative to parotidectomy.[21, 42] The role of surgery for these patients is limited to cases with diagnostic uncertainty or large deforming lesions unresponsive to other treatments. (See Chapter 63.)

Adenotonsillar Hypertrophy

Lymphadenopathy, common in HIV-infected patients, can involve Waldeyer's ring. Although this lymphoid hyperplasia is generally asymptomatic, the adenotonsillar hypertrophy can cause upper-airway obstruction. Recurrent adenotonsillar hypertrophy in these children may cause obstructive sleep apnea symptoms, which have been successfully treated with adenotonsillectomy.[21, 42] (See Chapter 59.)

Oral and Esophageal Candidiasis

Oral candidiasis is the most common fungal infection in children.[43] It not only is common in children infected with HIV but also frequently occurs in children born to drug-abusing mothers in whom the test result for HIV infection is negative. Furthermore, oral candidiasis may occur in as many as 5% to 7% of otherwise normal, healthy infants, presumably because of immature immunologic defense mechanisms.[57] The accepted prevalence figures for oral candidal infections in HIV-infected children are approximately 38%, and up to 75% of HIV-infected children may be affected at some point during the clinical course of their disease.[43]

The etiologic agent of most candidal infections is the fungus *Candida albicans,* although other *Candida* species are sometimes isolated, such as *C. glabrata* and *C. tropicalis.*[57] Oral candidiasis manifests as four known distinct clinical variants of candidal infection: (1) pseudomembranous, (2) erythematous (atrophic), (3) hyperplastic, and (4) angular cheilitis.[24] The pseudomembranous and erythematous variants are the most common. The pseudomembranous variant is characterized by the presence of soft, light-yellowish, creamy plaques that may be removed by wiping a gauze swab firmly over the areas covered by the plaques. This usually reveals a bright-red, slightly bleeding surface. Pseudomembranous candidiasis may in-

volve any part of the oral mucosa but most frequently involves the dorsum of the tongue. Atrophic candidiasis, more commonly called *erythematous candidiasis,* usually appears as a red lesion varying in intensity from pink to bright red. The most common locations are on the palate and dorsum of the tongue, which may appear as depapillated areas. This form, while common in adults, may occur less frequently in children; however, this finding may be due to under-reporting. The hyperplastic variant is most common bilaterally on the buccal mucosa as whitish yellow plaques that are not easily removed by scraping the surface. These lesions can be confused with hairy leukoplakia. Since candidal hyphae can be obtained from the superficial epithelium of hairy leukoplakia lesions, only close histopathologic examination revealing koilocytes (found in hairy leukoplakia) distinguishes the two lesions. Angular cheilitis is characterized by cracked red fissures at the oral commissures. This entity has many other causes and may not indicate candidal infection at all. These other causes should also be considered before therapy is initiated.

Initial treatment for oral candidiasis in children consists of good oral hygiene and topical antifungal drugs, such as nystatin or clotrimazole. A nystatin suspension, which requires prolonged contact with the oral mucosa, is usually not tolerated well by infants but is tolerated well by most older children. Older children may also be given clotrimazole troches, which are sucked on and may be more convenient than the nystatin suspension, even though both are given five times per day. More severe cases require systemic therapy with oral ketoconazole or intravenous amphotericin B.

Esophageal candidiasis is found in approximately 20% of pediatric AIDS cases. Since esophageal candidiasis is one of the surveillance case definitions for AIDS, all HIV-infected children in whom candidal esophagitis is diagnosed have AIDS. The most common clinical finding is dysphagia, although diagnosis depends on barium-swallow examination or fiberoptic endoscopy (Fig. 7–3). If left untreated, these lesions can result in stricture formation.[19] Candidal infections can involve any other area of the upper aerodigestive tract, including the pharynx, larynx, and even nasopharynx. Treatment is similar to that for oral candidiasis, except that systemic therapy is more often required. For infections that involve areas such as the nasopharynx, topical therapy is not effective; topical agents do not contact these surfaces.

Mycobacterial Diseases

Tuberculosis has made a resurgence in the United States in both children and adults. The reasons for this are probably multifactorial, including (1) the current epidemic of HIV infection, (2) the decline of public health services, and (3) the increase in immigration of people from countries with a high prevalence of tuberculosis.[64] HIV infection in the population at large increases the frequency of tuberculosis in HIV-infected children as follows: (1) adults infected with HIV may transmit the infectious agent to these children and (2) HIV-infected children appear to be at high risk for progression from

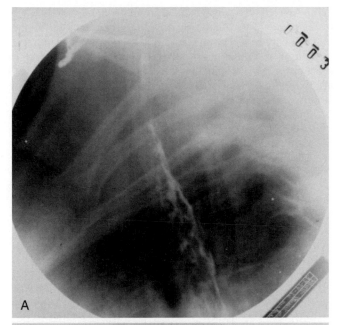

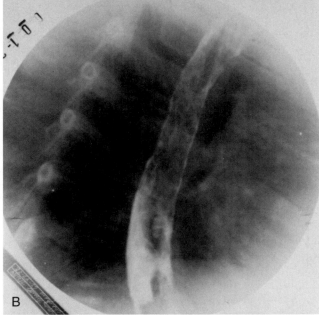

FIGURE 7–3. A and B, Barium swallow study of a 2-year-old child with esophageal candidiasis. Note the shaggy or cobblestone appearance of the mucosal outline. (Courtesy of Dr. Marquis, Children's Hospital of New Jersey.)

asymptomatic infection with *M. tuberculosis* to clinically evident disease.

Tuberculosis is usually acquired differently in HIV-infected children than in HIV-positive adults. Adults usually acquire asymptomatic *M. tuberculosis* infection when they are immunocompetent, when the infection remains controlled, and subsequently experience active disease when they become immunodeficient from HIV infection.[4] Children, on the other hand, usually have active tuberculosis during their primary *M. tuberculosis* infection since they are already immunocompromised.[39] Pulmonary and extrapulmonary forms of disease are evident in both chil-

dren and adults infected with HIV.[60] However, initial presentations in children may be more unusual than in adults. Extrapulmonary tuberculosis is not reported frequently in the literature in children with AIDS but, when present, is often found in the lymph nodes. Treatment of pulmonary tuberculosis usually includes isoniazid and rifampin; if infection is extrapulmonary, a third agent, such as pyrazinamide or streptomycin, is frequently added.

Other nontuberculous mycobacteria are also encountered in the pediatric HIV population. The most common of these is MAC, which apparently has minimal virulence in the immunocompetent host.[33] In HIV-infected patients, MAC may be responsible for focal infections in the esophagus (or gastrointestinal tract), pneumonia, or more commonly, disseminated disease. The most common clinical presentations include persistent fever, night sweats, weight loss, anemia, and gastrointestinal complaints.[35] These symptoms are frequently associated with primary HIV infection, which makes diagnosis difficult. Diagnosis can be made by culture of the organism from any involved site, especially blood, a lymph-node biopsy specimen, bone marrow, or liver. At present, no adequate therapy exists; as mentioned, some authors have reported limited success with clofazimine and ciprofloxacin.

Pneumonia

Pulmonary disease in pediatric HIV infection accounts for a significant amount of morbidity associated with AIDS. The two major contributors to pulmonary disease suffered by these children are PCP and LIP. Other insults to the lung include *M. tuberculosis*, CMV, MAC, and a variety of other viral and bacterial agents.

P. carinii is a small, ubiquitous protozoan (although some have made valid arguments for its classification as a fungus), which is thought to be spread by water droplet.[58] Between 40% and 65% of children with AIDS have PCP. The disease is characterized by fever, nonproductive cough, tachypnea, and a diffuse interstitial pattern on the chest radiograph. Diagnosis is confirmed when characteristic cysts are obtained from sputum induced from an older child or bronchoalveolar lavage. Treatment is with trimethoprim-sulfamethoxazole (TMP-SMX); pentamidine is reserved for those unable to tolerate TMP-SMX. Pancreatitis, hypoglycemia, and renal failure are common with pentamidine therapy; therefore, pentamidine should be used only if true sensitivity to TMP-SMX exists.[5]

PCP in children with HIV infection is associated with a high degree of morbidity and mortality. PCP prophylaxis is instituted in an attempt to avoid these complications of infection. The current recommendations for prophylaxis are for children 1 to 11 months old with CD4$^+$ counts under 1500 cells/mm^3, for children 12 to 23 months old with CD4$^+$ counts under 750 cells/mm^3, for children 2 to 5 years old with CD4$^+$ counts under 500 cells/mm^3, and for children at least 6 years old with CD4$^+$ counts under 200 cells/mm^3.[70] Since the normal percentage of CD4$^+$ cells does not change with age, any child whose CD4$^+$ percentage drops below 20% should receive PCP prophylaxis (Table 7–7). The drug of choice for prophylaxis is oral TMP-SMX given three times per

TABLE 7–7. CD4+ Lymphocyte Values for the Initiation of Antiretroviral Therapy and *Pneumocystis carinii* Pneumonia (PCP) Prophylaxis

	Criteria for Antiretroviral Therapy	Criteria for PCP Prophylaxis
CD4+ (%)		
<1 yr	<30	<20
1–2 yr	<25	<20
>2 yr	<20	<20
CD4+ (cells/mm³)		
<1 yr	<1700	<1500
1–2 yr	<1000	<750
2–5 yr	<750	<500
>6 yr	<500	<200

From Working Group on Antiretroviral Therapy: National Pediatric HIV Resource Center. Antiretroviral therapy and medical management of the human immunodeficiency virus–infected child. Pediatr Infect Dis 12:515, 1993.

week on consecutive days. Alternative therapy includes aerosol pentamidine, oral dapsone, and parenteral pentamidine.

Other measures of prophylaxis are undertaken routinely to prevent a variety of infectious diseases to which the HIV-infected child is likely to be more susceptible. Intravenous immune globulin (IVIG) has been used in HIV-infected children for several years now. A number of studies have suggested that these monthly treatments may decrease the frequency of bacterial infections and hospitalizations but have not been shown to prolong survival.[70] Although it is not clear who should receive IVIG, recommendations are for HIV-infected children who show any evidence of humoral immune defects or who have had two or more serious infections in less than 1 year.

LIP is a disease process characterized by a diffuse infiltration of the pulmonary interstitium with lymphocytes and plasma cells. LIP is much more common in children than in adults and is in fact an AIDS-defining condition only in children younger than 13 years. The incidence figures for LIP range from 30% to 50% of children perinatally infected with HIV.[53] The cause of this disease is unknown, but a number of theories exist. Among these theories are that HIV itself is responsible, that the Epstein-Barr virus (EBV) is responsible, or that both are. The disease usually presents as a chronic progressive interstitial lung disease with an insidious development of cough and digital clubbing in the second to third year of life. The clinical course of this disease is frequently accompanied by generalized lymphadenopathy and salivary gland enlargement. Chest radiography may reveal hyperinflation or a reticular or reticulonodular pattern with or without patchy infiltrates. Lung biopsy is the only definitive diagnostic procedure. Treatment depends on the severity of the disease but is predominantly supportive with bronchodilators and oxygen; steroids are sometimes used.

Malignant Neoplasm

Compared with adults, the incidence of cancer in the pediatric AIDS population remains relatively small. However, it has been suggested that as children with this syndrome continue to live longer with improved medical care, the frequency of cancer in this population is likely to increase. This belief stems from the established fact that cancer and immune system function are related. Although other malignant neoplasms have been reported, the most common cancers associated with pediatric AIDS are lymphomas and Kaposi sarcoma (Table 7–8). (See Chapters 46, 64, 89, and 100.)

Lymphomas are the most common malignant lesion associated with AIDS in children. Primary lymphoma of the brain and non-Hodgkin lymphomas of B-cell origin are the predominant lymphomas in HIV-infected children. There appears to be a general B-lymphocyte activation evidenced not only by the increased frequency of these lymphomas but also by increased levels of circulating immunoglobulins and B-cells. These facts are generally attributed to the depressed suppressor T-cell function; however, some evidence indicates primary B-cell stimulation by HIV infection.[5]

Kaposi sarcoma is the most common malignant neoplasm associated with AIDS in adults; in children, this cancer is relatively uncommon.[22] Even among adults, the majority of patients with AIDS and Kaposi sarcoma are homosexual men with mucocutaneous sequelae of this disease. In children, the most common manifestation of this disease appears to be lymphadenopathy. Some evidence suggests that children infected with HIV postnatally are more likely to have the mucocutaneous form of Kaposi sarcoma.[51] Some studies have also implicated a second independently transmitted infectious agent. This agent may be more efficiently transmitted by homosexual behavior than by other risk behaviors and may account for its predominance in this population. However, this does not explain the different manifestations of the disease in the different groups. Speculation as to the nature of this agent has provided several reports that have suggested both CMV and human papillomavirus (HPV) as possible etiologic agents for the development of Kaposi sarcoma against the background of HIV infection.[2, 36, 48] Diagnosis is usually suggested by inspection and confirmed by biopsy in the mucocutaneous or the lymphadenopathic form of the disease. Treatment consists of a combination of surgery, radiation therapy, and intralesional and systemic therapy with single or multiple chemotherapeutic drugs. Local therapy is preferred for regional disease, whereas systemic therapy is preferred for widespread disease.

Oral Hairy Leukoplakia

Oral hairy leukoplakia was first described in HIV-infected homosexual men by Greenspan et al in 1984.[31] Since then, it has been rarely reported in children. Clinically,

TABLE 7–8. Secondary Cancers Associated with AIDS and HIV Infection

Kaposi sarcoma
Primary lymphoma of brain
B-cell non-Hodgkin lymphoma

From Handcock WJ, McIntosh K. Pediatric infections with the human immunodeficiency virus. Otolaryngol Clin North Am 22:639, 1989.

oral hairy leukoplakia appears as a white thickening of mucosa, usually of the lateral border of the tongue. On histologic examination, this condition is characterized by parakeratosis of varying thickness, acanthosis, minimal submucosal inflammatory cell infiltrate, and frequent association with candidiasis.[26] The cause is thought to be opportunistic infection by EBV. It has even been suggested that hairy leukoplakia could be a latent form of EBV infection. Diagnosis is confirmed by biopsy or in situ hybridization of scrapings from suspected lesions that have undergone cytospin. Treatment is with acyclovir or its analog desciclovir, which is of questionable long-term efficacy. The literature contains some reports of the use of ganciclovir and tretinoin (RetinA), separately, with some success.[30] (See Chapter 64.)

Other Viral Infections

The viruses most responsible for disease in HIV-infected children are the herpesvirus group and HPV. The herpesvirus group includes HSV-1 and HSV-2, EBV, CMV, and varicella-zoster virus (VZV). The herpesvirus group lesions, while found in both adults and children, are frequently more severe in children. This may be due to the fact that the disease is usually a manifestation of previous infection during a period of immunocompetence in adults, who then experience a form of latent disease secondary to immunodeficient status. In children, the disease may be a manifestation of previous infection but is usually a product of primary infection, and as such the immune system has no previous antibodies directed toward these pathogens. Even if this is a latent form of disease, since most children acquire HIV perinatally, it usually represents previous infection during a period of immunodeficiency.

HSV-1 and HSV-2, similar to all herpesviruses, are large, enveloped DNA viruses that frequently infect immunocompetent hosts. The clinical presentation in orolabial disease is usually an acute cluster of painful lesions appearing on the gingiva and palate. These ulcerating vesicles spread in the next several days to involve the mouth, lips, and surrounding skin. Fever is not unusual in children. Treatment is with oral acyclovir; intravenous acyclovir is reserved for cases that prevent adequate oral intake, for visceral disease, or for disseminated disease. For acyclovir-resistant HSV infections documented by cultures, intravenous foscarnet (trisodium phosphonoformate hexahydrate) is used.[25]

VZV infection may be primary, chickenpox, or a reactivation of previous infection known as herpes zoster. Chronic, severe, persistent VZV infection is a relatively common finding in children with HIV infection, who are thought to be the largest group of VZV-susceptible immunodeficient children in the world.[38] In infants, widespread cutaneous lesions appear and may persist for months, frequently becoming superinfected with bacteria. These lesions sometimes present as orofacial lesions, but vesicles may appear anywhere on the body. The clinical appearance is usually sufficient for diagnosis, but uncertainty can be resolved with a Tzanck smear. Treatment for exposure or symptomatic disease is aggressive because

untreated disease is at substantial risk for dissemination, with resulting significant morbidity and mortality. Treatment is with varicella-zoster immune globulin or intravenous γ-globulin (if no varicella-zoster immune globulin) is available within 96 hours of exposure. Active infection is treated with acyclovir intravenously or orally, depending on the severity of disease. Herpes zoster is not common in young children, but with head and neck lesions it is commonly in the distribution of the trigeminal nerve. Ramsay Hunt syndrome is identified in some of these patients. Depending on the degree of involvement, acyclovir may be beneficial in herpes zoster treatment.

CMV is a common pathogen in children with symptomatic HIV infection, with an incidence as high as 45% in one study.[27] Primary head and neck manifestations have not been described, but CMV may cause pneumonia requiring treatment with ganciclovir, a toxic drug that has only limited efficacy in CMV pneumonia. EBV has been linked to lymphoproliferative disorders and B-cell lymphomas. EBV is also associated with oral hairy leukoplakia as discussed elsewhere in this chapter.

HPVs are small, nonenveloped DNA viruses that are commonly associated with a variety of warts and papillomas on the skin and mucous membranes in humans. More than 60 genotypically distinct subtypes are known to cause disease in humans. HPV-5 has been reported with flat cutaneous warts involving the face and body in HIV-infected children.[55] Similar oral warts have been described in association with HIV infection; however, there are no reports of more aggressive laryngeal papilloma in HIV-infected children.

Other Lesions Associated with HIV Infection

The otolaryngologist may encounter a host of other problems associated with HIV infection. These include neurologic, dermatologic, and other otorhinolaryngologic insults that these patients are more likely to experience because of their underlying immunodeficiency.[62] Among the neurologic symptoms that may be encountered by the otolaryngologist are infectious focal encephalitides, diffuse encephalitides, meningitides, cranial nerve neuropathies, and a variety of other neuromuscular disorders.[47] Dermatologic conditions include bacillary angiomatosis, molluscum contagiosum, seborrheic dermatitis, and drug reactions.[3] Head and neck manifestations that have been described are sensorineural hearing loss, vertigo, facial nerve paralysis,[41] and allergic rhinitis. Other sequelae of concern to the otolaryngologist are the bleeding problems encountered by many of these children because of thrombocytopenia and possible abnormalities of platelet function. It is not unusual for these children to have recurrent episodes of epistaxis or other mucosal bleeding.

Antiretroviral Treatment

At present there are 13 drugs within three antiretroviral classes. Ten of these drugs have pediatric indications for HIV infection. This is a significant improvement from only a few years ago, when there were only three antiretroviral drugs. The first two classes of drugs target the reverse transcriptase enzyme—nucleoside reverse transcriptase inhibitors (NRTIs) and non-nucleoside reverse transcriptase inhibitors (NNRTIs). The third class, protease inhibitors, target the viral protease enzyme.

The most commonly used drug, ZDV (an NRTI), was approved by the Food and Drug Administration for use in children in 1989. It was the first drug approved for use in HIV infection. It currently has widespread use in prevention of perinatal transmission and primary therapy.

In clinical trials of ZDV, children were found to have reduced cerebrospinal fluid levels of p24 antigen, negative viral cultures of cerebrospinal fluid when they had previously been positive, and an immediate increase in CD4+ cell counts that later subsided to levels above baseline.[46] Clinically, children were found to have a decrease in the severity of opportunistic infections, weight gain, and improvement of cognitive function on formal neuropsychological testing.[32] The disadvantages in the use of ZDV are primarily hematologic. Some protocols have revealed hematologic toxic effects in as many as 61% of children. Anemia was found in 26% and neutropenia in 48% of children in the study protocol. These high percentages of adverse reactions frequently require dose reductions and holidays.

Didanosine (ddI) is an approved antiretroviral agent for use in children who are "ZDV-intolerant."[70] The initial trials of ddI in children revealed a sustained increase in CD4+ cell counts, a decrease in p24 antigen levels, and a possible improvement of neurodevelopmental status. The advantage of ddI is lack of hematologic side effects that are encountered with ZDV, and long-term administration appears to be well tolerated in children. However, approximately 5% of children had pancreatitis, and a similar percentage had retinal depigmentation that was not associated with any visual impairment. Peripheral neuropathy is a side effect of both ddI and zalcitabine, an NRTI used uncommonly in children.

Lamivudine and stavudine are two newer NRTIs that are relatively well tolerated. Their potency is thought to be as good as or better than the older agents in this class. Abacavir is the newest agent and is particularly promising in combination therapy for patients who have not been treated previously with retroviral agents.

It is recommended that immunizations follow the usual schedule for any child, with some notable exceptions. The inactivated poliovirus vaccine is used instead of the usual oral poliovirus vaccine, which contains the live virus. In addition, the pneumococcal and influenza vaccines are included in the standard prophylactic regimen for the HIV-infected child.[70]

Precautions for the Otolaryngologist

In 1989, the CDC formally introduced the guidelines for universal precautions that should be followed for preventing the spread of HIV.[14] These guidelines were put forth as an attempt to reduce the risk of transmission of HIV or any infectious agent to health care workers. These guidelines were revised several years ago and renamed *standard precautions*. The following is a list of the general guidelines for standard precautions.[34, 45, 52, 65]

- Hand washing continues to be the most important means of preventing the transmission of infectious agents. This should be done before and after examining patients, even when gloves are worn.
- Gloves should be worn during office examinations, especially since the routine examination usually causes contact with body fluids. Gloves should be removed immediately after the examination is completed. Special care should be taken not to handle other objects or surfaces once gloves have been contaminated. Double-gloving for surgical procedures is also recommended.
- Gowns are necessary only when performing procedures or treating patients in situations wherein clothes are likely to be soiled (e.g., epistaxis).
- Masks are generally not necessary outside of the operating room, except for prolonged close contact with a patient who is likely to cough frequently.
- Eye protection should be worn if there is any risk of aerosolization or splashing of body fluids.
- Proper handling of sharp objects is extremely important. Needles should not be recapped before disposal.
- Contaminated materials should be disposed of in appropriate containers, and all instruments should be cleaned and disinfected before reuse.
- Postexposure prophylactic drug regimens are recommended for exposures that have a recognizable transmission risk. Basic exposures should be treated with an appropriate dose of ZDV or ZDV plus lamivudine for 4 weeks. With expanded exposures, indinavir, nelfinavir, or ritonavir is also added for a 4-week period.

SELECTED READINGS

Burroughs MH, Edelson PJ. Medical care of the HIV-infected child. Pediatr Clin North Am 38:45, 1991.
General summary of HIV-related disease in children with appropriate therapy.
Chanock SJ, McIntosh K. Pediatric infection with the human immunodeficiency virus: issues for the otorhinolaryngologist. Otolaryngol Clin North Am 22:637, 1989.
Review of head and neck manifestations of pediatric HIV disease.
Osguthorpe JD. Occupational human immunodeficiency virus exposure: risks to the health care worker. Otolaryngol Clin North Am 25:1341, 1992.
Thorough review of universal precautions and guidelines for handling and disposing of infected materials. Also a review of appropriate treatment for the exposed health care worker.
Pizzo PA, Wilfert CM (eds). Pediatric AIDS. Baltimore, Williams & Wilkins, 1991.
Comprehensive text covering all facets of pediatric AIDS.
Rogers M. HIV/AIDS in infants, children, and adolescents. Pediatr Clin North Am 47:1, 2000.
Sooy CD. Otolaryngologic manifestations. In Cohen PT, Sande MA, Volberding PA (eds). The AIDS Knowledge Base: A Textbook on HIV Disease from the University of California, San Francisco General Hospital. Waltham, MA, Medical Publishing Group, 1990, section 5.12.1.
A reference text for the entire spectrum of HIV-related diseases, directed primarily toward adults.
Working Group on Antiviral Therapy: National Pediatric HIV Resource Center. Antiretroviral therapy of the human immunodeficiency virus-infected child. Pediatr Infect Dis J 12:513, 1993.
The latest recommendations for antiretroviral treatment of HIV-

infected children as agreed on by the leading experts in the field.

Zurlo JJ. Human immunodeficiency virus: basic concepts of infection and host response. Otolaryngol Clin North Am 25:1159, 1992.

Good review of basic science of the human immunodeficiency virus and host response to infection.

REFERENCES

1. Alcamo IE. AIDS: The Biological Basis. Dubuque, IA, Wm C Brown Communications, 1993.
2. Baum LG, Vinters HV. Lymphadenopathic Kaposi's sarcoma in a pediatric patient with acquired immune deficiency syndrome. Pediatr Pathol 9:459, 1989.
3. Berger TG. Dermatologic findings in the head and neck in human immunodeficiency virus-infected persons. Otolaryngol Clin North Am 25:1227, 1992.
4. Braun MM, Cauthen G. Relationship of the human immunodeficiency virus epidemic to pediatric tuberculosis and bacillus Calmette-Guérin immunization. Pediatr Infect Dis J 11:220, 1992.
5. Burroughs MH, Edelson PJ. Medical care of the HIV-infected child. Pediatr Clin North Am 38:45, 1991.
6. Centers for Disease Control. *Pneumocystis carinii* pneumonia—Los Angeles. MMWR 30:250, 1981.
7. Centers for Disease Control. Kaposi's sarcoma and *Pneumocystis carinii* pneumonia—New York City and California. MMWR 30:305, 1981.
8. Centers for Disease Control. *Pneumocystis carinii* pneumonia among persons with hemophilia A. MMWR 31:365, 1982.
9. Centers for Disease Control. Update on the acquired immunodeficiency syndrome (AIDS)-United States. MMWR 31:507, 1982.
10. Centers for Disease Control. Current trends: revision of the case definition of acquired immunodeficiency syndrome for national reporting. MMWR 34:373, 1985.
11. Centers for Disease Control. Classification system for human T-cell lymphotrophic virus type III/lymphadenopathy-associated virus infections. MMWR 35:334, 1986.
12. Centers for Disease Control. Classification system for human immunodeficiency virus in children under 13 years of age. MMWR 36:225, 1987.
13. Centers for Disease Control. Revision of the CDC surveillance case definition for the acquired immunodeficiency syndrome. MMWR 36:51, 1987.
14. Centers for Disease Control. Guidelines for prevention of human immunodeficiency virus and hepatitis B virus to health care and public safety workers. MMWR 38(Suppl 6):3, 1989.
15. Centers for Disease Control. 1993 Revised classification system for HIV infection and expanded surveillance case definition for AIDS among adolescents and adults. MMWR 41:1, 1992.
16. Centers for Disease Control. HIV/AIDS surveillance report. MMWR February:1, 1993.
17. Centers for Disease Control. HIV/AIDS surveillance report. 5:9, 1993.
18. Centers for Disease Control and Prevention. HIV/AIDS surveillance report. 11:1, 1999.
19. Chanock SJ, McIntosh K. Pediatric infection with the human immunodeficiency virus: issues for the otorhinolaryngologist. Otolaryngol Clin North Am 22:637, 1989.
20. Cheung SW, Lee KC, Cha I. Orbitocerebral complications of *Pseudomonas* sinusitis. Laryngoscope 102:1385, 1992.
21. Chow JH, Stern JC, Kaul A. Head and neck manifestations of the acquired immunodeficiency syndrome in children. Ear Nose Throat J 69:416, 1990.
22. Connor E, Boccon-Gibod L, Joshi V. Cutaneous acquired immunodeficiency syndrome-associated Kaposi's sarcoma in pediatric patients. Arch Dermatol 126:791, 1990.
23. Connor EM, Sperling RS, Gelber R, et al. Reduction of maternal-infant transmission of human immunodeficiency virus type 1 with zidovudine treatment. N Engl J Med 331:1173, 1994.
24. Dichtel WJ. Oral manifestations of human immunodeficiency virus infection. Otolaryngol Clin North Am 25:1211, 1992.

25. Eversole LR. Viral infections of the head and neck among HIV-seropositive patients. Oral Surg Oral Med Oral Pathol 73:155, 1992.
26. Fernandez JF, Benito C, Lizaldez EB, et al. Oral hairy leukoplakia: a histopathologic study of 32 cases. Am J Dermatopathol 12:571, 1990.
27. Frenkel LD, Gaur S, Tsolia M, et al. Cytomegalovirus in children with AIDS. Rev Infect Dis 12:S820, 1990.
28. Godofsky EW, Zinreich J, Armstrong M, et al. Sinusitis in HIV-infected patients: a clinical and radiographic review. Am J Med 93:163, 1992.
29. Grant A, Shoenberg MV, Grant HR, et al. Paranasal sinus disease in HIV antibody positive patients. Genitourin Med 69:208, 1993.
30. Greenspan D, Greenspan JS. Significance of oral hairy leukoplakia. Oral Surg Oral Med Oral Pathol 73:151, 1992.
31. Greenspan D, Greenspan JS, Conant M, et al. Oral "hairy" leucoplakia in homosexuals: evidence of association with both papillomavirus and a herpesgroup virus. Lancet 2:831, 1984.
32. Grubman S, Conviser R, Oleske J. HIV infection in infants, children, and adolescents. In Wormser GP (ed). AIDS and Other Manifestations of HIV Infection, 2nd ed. New York, Raven Press, 1992, p 201.
33. Horsburgh CR. *Mycobacterium avium* complex infection in the acquired immunodeficiency syndrome. N Engl J Med 324:1332, 1991.
34. Hospital Infection Control Practices Advisory Committee. Guideline for isolation precautions in hospitals. J Infect Control Hosp Epidemiol 17:53, 1996.
35. Hoyt L, Oleske J, Holland B. Nontuberculous mycobacteria in children with acquired immunodeficiency syndrome. Pediatr Infect Dis J 11:354, 1992.
36. Huang YQ, Li JJ, Rush MG. HPV16-related DNA sequences in Kaposi's sarcoma. Lancet 339:515, 1992.
37. Joshi V. Pathology of childhood AIDS. Pediatr Clin North Am 38:97, 1991.
38. Jura E, Chadwick EG, Josephs SH, et al. Varicella-zoster virus infections in children infected with human immunodeficiency virus. Pediatr Infect Dis J 8:586, 1989.
39. Khouri YF, Mastrucci MT, Hutto C. *Mycobacterium* tuberculosis in children with human immunodeficiency virus type 1 infection. Pediatr Infect Dis J 11:950, 1992.
40. Krasinski K, Borkowsky W. Laboratory diagnosis of HIV infection. Pediatr Clin North Am 38:17, 1991.
41. Lalwani AK, Sooy CD. Otologic and neurotologic manifestations of acquired immunodeficiency syndrome. Otolaryngol Clin North Am 25:1183, 1992.
42. Lee KC, Cheung SW. Evaluation of the neck mass in human immunodeficiency virus–infected persons. Otolaryngol Clin North Am 25:1287, 1992.
43. Leggott PJ. Oral manifestations of HIV infection in children. Oral Surg Oral Med Oral Pathol 73:187, 1992.
44. Lindegren ML, Steinberg S, Byers R. Epidemiology of HIV/AIDS in children. Pediatr Clin North Am 47:1, 2000.
45. Lucente FE. Impact of the acquired immunodeficiency syndrome epidemic on the practice of laryngology. Ann Otol Rhinol Laryngol Suppl 161:1, 1993.
46. McKinney RE. Antiviral therapy for human immunodeficiency virus infection in children. Pediatr Clin North Am 38:133, 1991.
47. Mehta P, Kula RW. Neurologic manifestations of human immunodeficiency virus infection. Otolaryngol Clin North Am 25:1249, 1992.
48. Nickoloff BJ, Huang YQ, Li JJ. Immunohistochemical detection of papillomavirus antigens in Kaposi's sarcoma. Lancet 339:548, 1992.
49. Noel GJ. Host defense abnormalities associated with HIV infection. Pediatr Clin North Am 38:37, 1991.
50. Oleske J, Minnefor A, Cooper R, et al. Immune deficiency syndrome in children. JAMA 249:2345, 1983.
51. Orlow SJ, Cooper D, Petrea S. AIDS-associated Kaposi's sarcoma in Romanian children. J Am Acad Dermatol 28:449, 1993.
52. Osguthorpe JD. Occupational human immunodeficiency virus exposure: risks to the health care worker. Otolaryngol Clin North Am 25:1341, 1992.
53. Pitt J. Lymphocytic interstitial pneumonia. Pediatr Clin North Am 38:89, 1991.
54. Principi N, Marchisio P, Tornaghi R, et al. Acute otitis media in human immunodeficiency virus–infected children. Pediatrics 88:566, 1991.

55. Prose NS, Knebel-Doeberitz CV, Miller S, et al. Widespread flat warts associated with human papillomavirus type 5: a cutaneous manifestation of human immunodeficiency virus infection. Am Acad Dermatol 23:978, 1990.
56. Rubin JS, Honigberg R. Sinusitis in patients with the acquired immunodeficiency syndrome. Ear Nose Throat J 69:460, 1990.
57. Samaranayake LP. Oral mycoses in HIV infection. Oral Surg Oral Med Oral Pathol 73:171, 1992.
58. Saunders-Laufer D, Debruin W, Edelson PJ. *Pneumocystis carinii* pneumonia in HIV-infected children. Pediatr Clin North Am 38:69, 1991.
59. Seifert G. Tumour-like lesions of the salivary glands, the new WHO classification. Pathol Res Pract 188:836, 1992.
60. Slutsker L, Castro KG, Ward JW. Epidemiology of extrapulmonary tuberculosis among persons with AIDS in the United States. Clin Infect Dis 16:513, 1993.
61. Small CB, Kaufman A, Armenaka M. Sinusitis and atopy in human immunodeficiency virus infection. J Infect Dis 167:283, 1993.
62. Sooy CD. Otolaryngologic manifestations. In Cohen PT, Sande MA, Volberding PA (eds). The AIDS Knowledge Base: A Textbook on HIV Disease from the University of California, San Francisco General Hospital. Waltham, MA, Medical Publishing Group, 1990, section 5.12.1.
63. Sperling RS, Shapiro DE, Coombs RW, et al. Maternal viral load, zidovudine treatment, and the risk of transmission of human immunodeficiency virus type 1 from mother to infant. N Engl J Med 335:1621, 1996.
64. Starke JR, Jacobs RF, Jereb J. Resurgence of tuberculosis in children. Pediatrics 120:839, 1992.
65. Tami TA, Lee KC. Manifestations of the acquired immunodeficiency syndrome. In Bailey BJ (ed). Head and Neck Surgery—Otolaryngology. Philadelphia, JB Lippincott, 1993, p 774.
66. Tami TA, Wawrose SF. Diseases of the nose and paranasal sinuses in the human immunodeficiency virus infected population. Otolaryngol Clin North Am 25:1199, 1992.
67. UNAIDS/WHO: Joint United Nations programme on HIV/AIDS (UNAIDS), World Health Organization. Report on the global HIV/AIDS epidemic. June 1998.
68. Wawrose SF, Tami TA, Amoils CP. The role of guaifenesin in the treatment of sinonasal disease in patients infected with the human immunodeficiency virus (HIV). Laryngoscope 102:1225, 1992.
69. Williams MA. Head and neck findings in pediatric acquired immunodeficiency syndrome. Laryngoscope 97:713, 1987.
70. Working Group on Antiviral Therapy: National Pediatric HIV Resource Center. Antiretroviral therapy of the human immunodeficiency virus–infected child. Pediatr Infect Dis J 12:513, 1993.
71. Zurlo JJ. Human immunodeficiency virus: basic concepts of infection and host response. Otolaryngol Clin North Am 25:1159, 1992.
72. Zurlo JJ, Feurstein IM, Lebovics R, et al. Sinusitis in HIV-1 infection. Am J Med 93:157, 1992.

The Ear and Related Structures

8

Embryology and Developmental Anatomy of the Ear

Margaret A. Kenna, M.D., and Keiko Hirose, M.D.

To understand normal variations in anatomy, as well as congenital and acquired ear disease, one must know the embryology of the ear. A basic understanding of the developmental anatomy of the otic capsule and the branchial arch system is necessary to comprehend the overall embryology of the ear. Anatomically, the ear is divided into the *external ear,* the *middle ear,* and the *inner ear.* The middle ear and the inner ear develop in the lateroinferior portion of the skull called the *temporal bone.* There is some disagreement among authors about the exact timing of different developmental events; the timing of such events given here is an attempt to represent the most current consensus. (See also Chapters 20, 23, and 26.)

External Ear

The external ear is divided into the pinna, or auricle, and the external auditory canal (EAC). During the fourth week of gestation, the pinna begins development from first (mandibular) and second (hyoid) branchial arch mesoderm surrounding the first branchial cleft.

During the fifth and sixth weeks of gestation, this mesoderm gives rise to six outgrowths, the hillocks of His, that condense and fuse by the third month to form the pinna. The first three hillocks derive from the mandibular arch, the second three from the hyoid arch. There is controversy over the exact adult structures that form from these hillocks. One view asserts that the tragus is derived from the first arch consisting of the first three hillocks of His, while the rest of the pinna, with the exception of the concha, is derived from the second arch, consisting of the second three hillocks.[41] A second, more widely accepted theory is that the first hillock gives rise

to the tragus, the second forms the crus of the helix, the third forms the majority of the helix, the fourth becomes the antihelix, the fifth produces the antitragus, and the sixth gives rise to the lower helix and lobule.[32] The concha is derived from ectoderm from the first branchial groove. Initially, the developing pinna is located caudal to the mandibular area, but by the 20th fetal week, as the mandible grows and develops, the pinna migrates cephalad to attain the adult configuration and location (Fig. 8–1A, B). In a child 4 to 5 years old, the pinna is approximately 80% of the adult size; in a 9-year-old child, the pinna has attained complete adult size. In a newborn, the cartilage of the pinna is soft and pliable, with relatively more chondrocytes and an immature matrix. In a 9-year-old child, the cartilage is firmer and histologically mature. The darwinian tubercle, which corresponds to the tip of the pinna in lower animals, appears at roughly 6 months of gestation.[16]

The postnatal anatomy of the pinna is shown in Figure 8–1C–E. Anteriorly the skin is firmly adherent to the elastic cartilage of the pinna, with an absence of subcutaneous tissue, while posteriorly the skin is separated from the cartilage by a distinct subcutaneous layer. The lobule is devoid of cartilage and contains only fibrous tissue and fat. Three extrinsic muscles (the anterior, superior, and posterior auricular muscles) attach the pinna to the scalp and the skull. These muscles, when well developed, can move the auricle as a whole. In humans, there are several intrinsic auricular muscles that are indistinguishable grossly and are functionally insignificant.

The EAC develops from the first branchial groove between the mandibular and hyoid arches. At 4 to 5 weeks of gestation, a solid core of epithelial cells, derived from

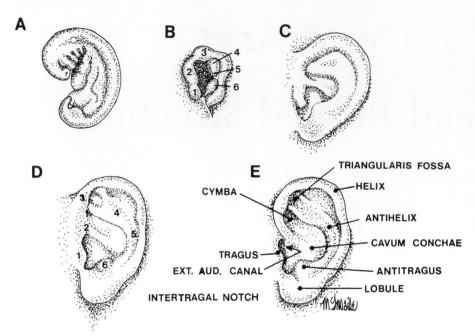

FIGURE 8–1. Auricular development and anatomy. *A,* Fetus (5 mm); branchial arch development is evident. *B,* First and second branchial arches in an 11-mm fetus. Six hillocks are present; hillocks 1, 2, and 3 are from the first (mandibular) arch; hillocks 4, 5, and 6 are from the second (hyoid) arch. *C,* Newborn auricle: adult configuration but smaller. *D,* Auricle, fully developed, showing the hillocks' relationship to anatomy. *E,* Auricle fully developed, showing anatomic parts. (Adapted from Anson BJ, Donaldson A. Surgical Anatomy of the Temporal Bone and Ear, 2nd ed. Philadelphia, WB Saunders, 1973, p 31.)[3]

the ectoderm of the first groove, comes into contact with the endoderm of the first pharyngeal pouch in the area of the tympanic ring. Then, mesoderm grows between the ectoderm and the endoderm and the contact is disrupted. At 8 weeks, the cavum conchae (first branchial groove) deepens, forming a funnel-shaped tube, the primary meatus, that becomes surrounded by cartilage and eventually becomes the fibrocartilaginous portion of the adult EAC, composing the outer one third of the ear canal. During the ninth week of gestation, the groove deepens, grows toward the middle ear, and comes into contact with the

epithelium of the first pharyngeal pouch. A solid epidermal plug extends inward from the primary meatus to the primitive tympanic cavity, forming the meatal plate.

Next, mesenchyme forms between epithelial cells of the tympanic cavity and the meatal plate to become the fibrous layer of the tympanic membrane (TM), and at 9 weeks this is surrounded by the four membrane bone ossification centers of the tympanic ring.[16] Figure 8–2 demonstrates this complicated process in the mouse embryo (in which these events occur earlier in gestation than in humans), while Figure 8–3 demonstrates the hu-

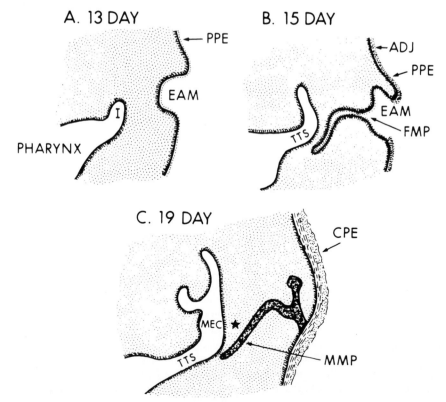

FIGURE 8–2. Diagram of the development of the external auditory meatus and meatal plate in *(A)* 13-day-old, *(B)* 15-day-old, and *(C)* 19-day-old mouse embryos. Initially (13th day), the epidermal histology of the adjacent, non-otic skin (ADJ) is the same as that lining the external auditory meatus (EAM) and over the presumptive pinnal tissues (PPE). By the 15th day, the tubotympanic sulcus (TTS) has grown dorsally from the pharyngeal pouch (I); the sulcus' endodermal lining approaches the presumptive meatal plate (FMP). The lumen of the latter may still be patent distally, but its epidermis, like that of the meatus, bears only a single layer of superficial peridermal cells, while that of the pinna (PPE) and the adjacent skin now have several layers of peridermal cells. By 19 days, the lumen of the external meatus and the enlarged meatal plate (MMP) have become completely occluded. The epidermis of the pinna and the adjacent skin show the first signs of cornification beneath the multi-layered periderm, while the meatal plate appears as a simple plate but is in fact two younger epiderms lying en face. The star indicates the approximate location of the presumptive tympanic tissues, which lie between the meatal plate and the developing middle ear cavity (MEC). CPE, cornified peridermal epithelium.

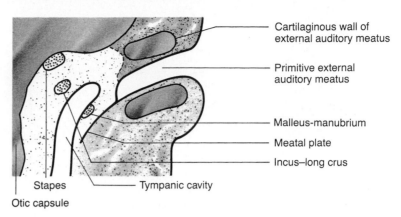

FIGURE 8–3. Development of the meatus and meatal plate in relation to tympanic cavity at 9 weeks' gestation. (Redrawn from English GM [ed]. Otolaryngology, vol I. Diseases of the Ear and Hearing. Philadelphia, JB Lippincott, 1988, p 12.)

man anatomy at 9 weeks of gestation. During the 21st fetal week, the cord of epithelial cells begins to resorb, forming a canal. By the 28th week, the deepest cells of the ectodermal plug remain, forming the superficial layer of the TM. The medial two thirds of the EAC is derived from the new ectodermal tube and becomes the bony portion of the canal.[32, 37] If the resorption process stops prematurely, an atretic or very stenotic membranous canal may result, with a more normally developed bony ear canal, TM, and middle and inner ear.

At birth, the EAC is not ossified, except for the tympanic ring, and is not of adult size. Ossification is completed by the second year of life, and adult size is reached by age 9 years. After ossification, the lateral one third of the ear canal is cartilaginous; the medial two thirds is bony. The skin of the cartilaginous portion contains hair follicles and sebaceous and ceruminous glands.

The intrinsic and extrinsic auricular muscles are innervated by the seventh cranial (facial) nerve. The nerve supply to the medial portion of the EAC is from the auriculotemporal (mandibular branch of the trigeminal) nerve. The nerve supply to the posterior ear canal and the area around the TM proceeds from Arnold's nerve, the only cutaneous branch of the vagus (tenth cranial) nerve. Arterial supply to both the pinna and the EAC is from the superficial temporal and posterior auricular arteries.[8]

Tympanic Membrane

The TM develops from structures associated with both the external ear and the middle ear. At 4 to 5 weeks of gestation, the primitive TM is represented by the area of contact between the ectodermal meatal forming the external auditory meatus (first branchial groove) and the lateral end of the endodermal tubotympanic recess (first pharyngeal pouch). At 8 weeks, mesodermal tissue grows between the first pharyngeal pouch and the first branchial groove. The mesoderm thins out in the area of the meatal plate and becomes the fibrous layer of the TM. The fibrous layer consists of outer radial fibers and inner circular fibers. At 21 weeks, the epidermal plug (ectodermal cord) begins to resorb, forming the EAC. The most medial portion of this plug becomes the lateral layer of the TM. The completed TM has three layers:

- An outer epithelial layer, from ectoderm of the first branchial groove
- A middle fibrous layer, from the mesoderm in between the first groove and the first pouch
- An inner mucosal layer, derived from endoderm of the tympanic cavity, derived in turn from the first pharyngeal pouch

The TM inserts into the tympanic ring, which is formed during the ninth week of gestation, from four membrane ossification centers. These centers fuse and grow rapidly; the development of the tympanic ring is nearly complete by 16 weeks, with maximal growth in diameter attained in the term fetus.[9] The ring is deficient at the superior cranial aspect, the notch of Rivinus. During the first postnatal year, the tympanic ring extends laterally, completing the formation of the bony EAC, the sheath of the styloid process, and the nonarticular part of the glenoid fossa. By the end of the first postnatal year, two prominences found on the ventral portion of the ring have grown and fused, dividing the previous space into the adult EAC and the inferior foramen of Huschke. This foramen, except in rare instances of agenesis, closes with continuing growth of bone.

At birth, the TM is almost adult-sized and is nearly horizontal; however, it becomes more vertical with development of the EAC.[2] The mature TM consists of two parts, the pars tensa and the pars flaccida. The pars flaccida is located superiorly, over the notch of Rivinus and the epitympanum, and is composed of only a lateral squamous and a medial mucosal layer. The pars tensa, constituting most of the TM, overlies the middle ear and is composed of all three layers: squamous, fibrous, and mucosal (Fig. 8–4). Laterally, innervation to the TM is the same as that to the EAC. Medially, innervation is supplied by the tympanic branch of the ninth nerve. Laterally, the blood supply is from the deep auricular branch of the internal maxillary artery, whereas medially it is supplied by the stylomastoid branch of the posterior auricular artery and the anterior tympanic branch of the internal maxillary artery.

Middle Ear

The middle ear consists of the TM, the tympanic cavity, three ossicles, two muscles, several tendons, and the eus-

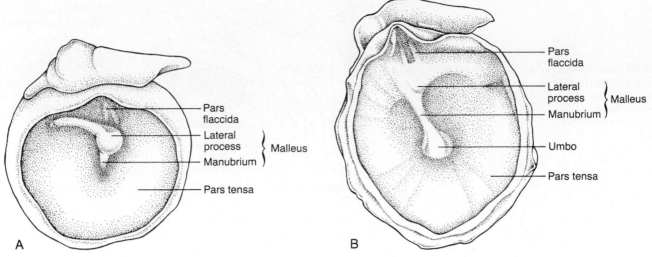

FIGURE 8–4. Tympanic membrane development. *A,* Newborn: the tympanic membrane is almost horizontal. The lateral process of the malleus is most prominent. The pars flaccida is thicker and more vascular. *B,* Adult: the tympanic membrane is more vertical. The lateral process of the malleus is less prominent. The manubrium of the malleus is more vertical. The pars flaccida appears less vascular.

tachian tube. Connection to the mastoid bone is via the aditus ad antrum from the middle ear. The eustachian tube connects the middle ear to the nasopharynx.

During the third week of gestation, expansion of the first (and, according to some sources, the second) pharyngeal pouch, lined with endoderm, forms the tubotympanic recess. During weeks 4 to 6, expansion is progressive; this expansion begins at the inferior aspect of the definitive tympanic cavity and progresses by invading the adjacent, loosely organized mesenchyme.[16] At week 7, constriction of the midportion of the recess by the second branchial arch leads to the formation of the eustachian tube (medially) and the tympanic cavity (laterally). The terminal end of the first pharyngeal pouch divides into four sacci: anticus, posticus, superior, and medius, which progressively expand to pneumatize the middle ear and epitympanum. These four sacs become distinct anatomic areas. The saccus anticus becomes the anterior pouch of Tröltsch. The saccus medius develops into the epitympanum and petrous area. The saccus superior becomes the posterior pouch of Tröltsch, the inferior incudal space, and part of the mastoid. The saccus posterior becomes the round window, the oval window, and the sinus tympani. This expansion of the sacci also envelops the ossicles and lines the tympanomastoid compartment; the junction of two sacci gives rise to mucosal folds that transmit blood vessels.

At about week 18 of gestation, the epitympanum, which leads into the antrum and the mastoid, forms from an extension of the tympanic cavity. During the development of the tympanic cavity, differentiation of mesenchymal tissue above, medial to, and posterior to the tympanic cavity produces the ossicles, muscles, and tendons of the middle ear. Eventually, these structures extend into the cavity and are covered by the epithelial lining of the cavity, derived from the end of the first pharyngeal pouch.[32]

There are two middle-ear muscles. The tensor tympani and its tendon are derived from mesoderm of the first branchial arch; innervation is by the mandibular branch of the trigeminal nerve. This muscle is contained in a bony semicanal above the eustachian tube and attaches via the tendon to the manubrium of the malleus. The stapedius muscle is derived from mesoderm of the second arch and is innervated by the seventh cranial nerve. This muscle originates from the pyramidal eminence and inserts via its tendon onto the neck of the stapes.

The roof of the tympanic cavity, the tegmen tympani, is formed laterally by an extension of the otic capsule and medially by fibrous tissue. This roof becomes ossified at the beginning of the 23rd week of gestation. The anterior epitympanic wall and part of the lateral tympanic cavity are formed from the tympanic process of the squamous portion of the temporal bone.[2] One view holds that the main part of the floor of the middle ear is formed from an offshoot of the petrous pyramid; another view theorizes that the floor of the middle ear arises from a separate bone formed between the pyramid and the tympanic ring.

During development, the tympanic cavity is filled with mucoid mesenchymal tissue. Beginning in the third month of gestation, this tissue becomes looser and vacuolated, allowing expansion of the tympanic cavity. During this expansion, the ossicles, muscles, and tendons become wrapped with tympanic cavity epithelium (Fig. 8–5). It may take 1 year, or even longer, for all mesenchymal tissue to resorb, and remnants of embryonic connective tissue may be evident as strands of tissue draped over the oval and round window in the adult.

By the 30th week of gestation, expansion of the tympanic cavity is complete, followed 4 weeks later by complete expansion of the epitympanum. Pneumatization starts at approximately the 30th week and is nearly complete at birth. Many factors, including heredity, environ-

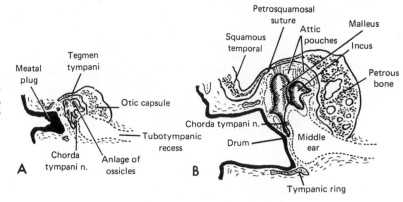

FIGURE 8–5. *A* and *B*, Expansion of the middle ear. (From Anson BJ, Davies J. Embryology of the ear. In Paparella MM, Shumrick DA [eds]. Otolaryngology, vol I, 2nd ed. Philadelphia, WB Saunders, 1980, p 11.)

ment, nutrition, infection, and adequate ventilation, may play a role in the marked variability of temporal bone pneumatization.[37]

Ossicles

There are three middle-ear ossicles: the malleus, the incus, and the stapes. They are formed from the mesenchyme of the mandibular and the hyoid arches and from the otic capsule (stapes only). Specifically, the head of the malleus, and the short crus and body of the incus, arise from the mandibular arch. The manubrium of the malleus, the long process of the incus, and the head, neck, crura, and tympanic surface of the footplate of the stapes arise from the hyoid arch. The medial surface of the stapedial footplate and the annular stapedial ligament arise from the otic capsule.

At 4.5 weeks of gestation, the mesenchyme of the second arch forms the blastema, which is then divided by the seventh nerve into the stapes, interhyale, and laterohyale. The stapes ring forms around the stapedial artery during weeks 5 to 6, and otic capsule mesenchyme appears, forming the medial footplate and the annular ligament. At 8.5 weeks, the incudostapedial joint forms. During the tenth week, the shape of the stapes changes from that of a ring to that of a stirrup. The interhyale forms the stapedius muscle and tendon, and the laterohyale becomes the posterior wall of the middle ear. The laterohyale also joins with the otic capsule to partially form the anterior wall of the facial canal and the bone of the stapedial pyramid.

All three ossicles begin to develop during the fourth to sixth fetal weeks. During the next 3 to 4 weeks, the mesenchyme develops into cartilaginous models of the ossicles. The models for the incus and the malleus grow to adult size by 15 weeks; the model for the stapes reaches full size by 18 weeks. The incus and the malleus (which start as a single mass) separate, and the malleoincudal joint is formed at 8 to 9 weeks. Ossification of the malleus and the incus begins at 15 weeks and appears first at the long process of the incus. Remodeling of the bone of the incus and the malleus continues throughout postfetal life. Ossification of the stapes begins at week 18. The fetal bone of the stapes undergoes no remodeling during postfetal life. At birth, all the ossicles are of adult size and shape. When the mesenchyme resorbs and the ossicles are free, the endodermal epithelium of the tym-

panic cavity connects the ossicles to the cavity wall in a mesentery-like manner. The supporting ossicular ligaments develop in these epithelial connections (Fig. 8–6).[2, 32, 37] Figure 8–7 shows the overall fate of the first and second branchial arches, with reference to the ossicles and surrounding structures.

Tympanic Antrum, Mastoid Air Cells, and Related Spaces

The antrum is usually the largest and, in poorly pneumatized mastoids, often the only identifiable air cell in the mastoid air cell system. The antrum appears as a lateral extension of the epitympanum at 21 to 22 weeks. The lumen of the antrum is well developed by the 34th week, and its pneumatization is complete during the first year of life.

In the adult, nearly all parts of the temporal bone are extensively pneumatized, including the zygoma, squama, petrous apex, and jugular wall areas. Air cell formation is usually completed during postfetal life but may continue into old age. Pneumatization of the petrous pyramid, which is highly variable, begins at approximately the 28th fetal week, whereas pneumatization of the mastoid air cells starts at the 33rd week. The mastoid itself is formed when the bone of the antrum and the tympanic plate expand, with air cells formed by the extension of epithelium from the antrum into the developing mastoid bone area. In the infant, the antrum is nearly adult-sized, and the bulge of the lateral semicircular canal is visible in the antrum's floor. The pattern of mastoid pneumatization is generally symmetrical; however, individuals show much variation. The mastoid process appears at age 1 year. The various forms of otitis media are often associated with poorly pneumatized mastoids; however, the cause-and-effect relationship between these two findings is controversial. Currently, it is thought that mastoid air cell development can be hindered by early and repeated middle-ear disease.[30, 39] Heredity might also play a role in the extent of mastoid pneumatization.

Temporal Bone

There are four parts to the adult temporal bone: petrous, squamous, tympanic, and mastoid; however, only the petrous, squamous, and tympanic parts have formed at birth.

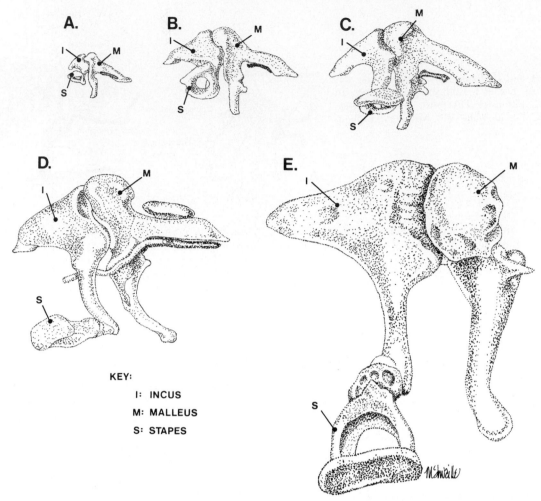

KEY:

I: INCUS

M: MALLEUS

S: STAPES

FIGURE 8–6. Ossicular development. *A,* Fetus at 2 months: the cartilaginous ossicles are recognizable. *B,* Fetus at 3 months. *C,* Fetus at 4 months: attaining adult configuration but cartilaginous. *D,* Fetus at 6 months: adult configuration and size; ossification begins. *E,* Adult ossicles. (Adapted from Anson BJ, Davies J. Developmental anatomy of the ear. In Paparella MM, Shumrick DA [eds]. Otolaryngology, vol I, 2nd ed. Philadelphia, WB Saunders, 1980, p 8.)

The squamous and tympanic portions form by membranous bone development. The squamous portion begins to develop at approximately week 8, the tympanic during weeks 9 to 10. The petrous portion is formed from cartilage (endochondral bone) of the periotic capsule, with ossification starting in the sixth month. All portions of the temporal bone, except the petrous, continue to develop in postfetal life. The mastoid bone develops primarily after birth, with a mastoid process evident by the age of 1 year and well developed by age 3 years. Mastoid development is mainly lateral and posterior to the antrum. After birth, the styloid process is formed from ossification of the mesoderm in the upper part of the second arch.

At birth, the middle-ear cavity is approximately adult-sized, as are the oval and round windows and the TM. The malleus, incus, and stapes reach adult size by the sixth month of gestation. At birth, the eustachian tube is about 1.7 cm long, about half as long as in the adult. It is fairly horizontal, with the pharyngeal opening at the level of the hard palate. With growth, the tube angles down-

ward, with the opening at the level of the inferior nasal turbinate by age 6 years.

During the newborn period and infancy, the lateral surface of the temporal bone differs from that in the adult. There is no bony ear canal, except superiorly, and no mastoid process. The facial nerve is very superficial as it emerges from the stylomastoid foramen behind the TM, and the nerve can be injured by obstetric forceps or the usual posterior auricular incision used in mastoid surgery.[16]

The lateral surface anatomy of the temporal bone is important surgically. In postnatal life, the spine of Henle marks the posterosuperior aspect of the external ear canal and the antrum is usually found medial to the spine. In the infant, the bone over the antrum is cribriform, allowing infection to extend subperiosteally, with posterior auricular edema, erythema, and abscess formation. The temporal line, the inferior margin of the temporal muscle, marks the approximate level of the middle fossa. The bony external canal has two suture lines: the tympano-

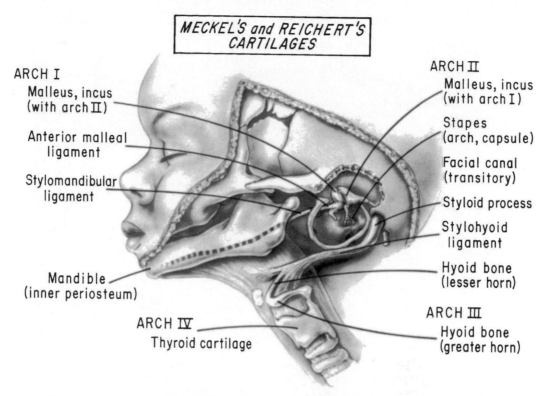

FIGURE 8–7. Structures derived from the branchial arch system. The diagram shows the contributions to adult anatomy of the head and neck from Meckel's and Reichert's cartilages: the first (mandibular) and second (hyoid) arches, respectively. These are listed with the drawing of an infant head.

mastoid posteriorly and the tympanosquamous superiorly. The surgeon uses these suture lines as landmarks when making incisions in the EAC. The mandibular fossa, involved in articulation of the condyle of the mandible, is a concavity on the inferior surface of the squamous part of the temporal bone (Fig. 8–8).

Facial Nerve

The facial nerve (seventh cranial nerve) is the nerve of the second branchial arch. At the end of the third gestational week, a collection of cells, the acousticofacial ganglion (also called the *crest* or *primordium*) can be identified as an aggregation of neural crest cells dorsolateral to the rhombencephalon and rostral to the otic placode. By the end of the fourth week, the facial and acoustic portions of the primordium have become more distinct. The facial division extends ventrally to a thickened area of surface ectoderm, the epibranchial placode, located on the upper surface of the second branchial arch. During the fifth week, the neuroblasts of the geniculate ganglion appear in the facial portion of the primordium, where the placode and the neural crest cells are contiguous. Next, the distal portion of the primordium divides equally, with one portion going caudally into the second-arch mesenchyme and eventually becoming the main facial nerve trunk. The other division extends rostrally into the first arch and becomes the chorda tympani nerve (at 5 weeks). The terminal branches of the chorda tympani end in the same region that the lingual nerve (termination of a

branch of the mandibular nerve) ends in; there, the two nerves unite just proximal to the submandibular ganglion by the end of the seventh week.[12, 32, 37]

A 1994 study by Gasser et al[13] notes that the formation of the ear and associated facial nerve can be divided into three developmental time periods: (1) the *blastemal phase,* in which ear structures are surrounded by mesenchyme, (2) the *cartilaginous phase,* during which the mesenchyme transforms into the cartilaginous otic capsule, and (3) an *osseous phase,* with bone replacing cartilage. These authors suggest that the course of the facial nerve is well established during the blastemal phase and is essentially set by the end of the embryonic period (57 days).

The facial motor nucleus develops separately from the acousticofacial primordium and is derived from neuroblasts in the upper portion of the rhombencephalon. The motor nuclei of the sixth and seventh cranial nerves develop in close proximity in the pons, which explains the involvement of both the sixth and seventh nerves in the congenital Moëbius syndrome as well as findings in other neoplastic, inflammatory, and vascular disorders.

The sensory nervus intermedius develops from the geniculate ganglion at 7 weeks of gestation and extends to the brain stem between the motor root of the seventh and eighth nerves. The greater superficial petrosal nerve, the second branch of the seventh nerve to develop, comes from the most ventral part of the geniculate ganglion at about 5 weeks. The branch to the stapedius muscle develops at about 8 weeks, and geniculate gan-

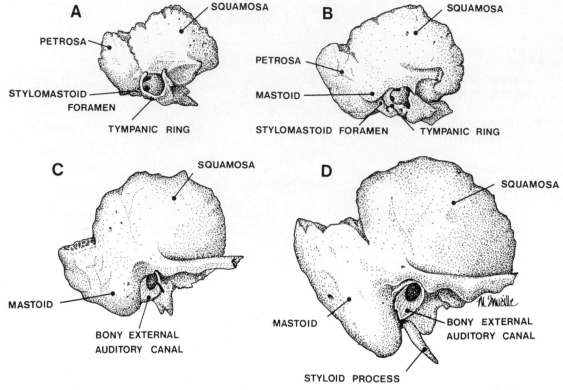

FIGURE 8–8. Lateral temporal bone development. *A,* Newborn: the petrous, squamous, and tympanic portions are present; the mastoid portion is not developed. The stylomastoid foramen (exit of the facial nerve) is just behind the tympanic ring. *B,* Infant, 1.5 years old: mastoid development is under way. The stylomastoid foramen can still be exposed and is not covered by the mastoid process. The tympanic ring is ossifying. *C,* Child, 5 years: the mastoid process is well developed and covers the stylomastoid foramen. The tympanic ring has completely ossified, and the entire bony external auditory canal is osseous. *D,* Adult: normal anatomy.

glion development is completed by week 15. This separate development of the sensory and motor parts of the seventh nerve allows patients with congenital facial paralysis to retain sensation and taste.

The seventh nerve is located in the facial canal, which develops as a sulcus on the lateral aspect of the otic capsule by the eighth fetal week. The future canal is still cartilaginous and contains the stapedius muscle, the facial nerve, and blood vessels. Closure of the canal is nearly complete by the seventh month.

At birth, facial-nerve development is complete. The fully developed facial nerve originates from the facial nucleus, leaving the brain stem at the inferior border of the pons between the olive and the inferior cerebellar peduncle. The nerve enters the internal acoustic meatus (internal auditory canal) accompanied by the nervus intermedius and travels in a bony canal, the fallopian canal, laterally to the geniculate ganglion. The greater and lesser superficial petrosal nerves diverge at this point, and the remainder of the facial nerve turns posteriorly and traverses the middle ear, still in the bony canal. The facial nerve lies just above the oval-window niche and, at the pyramidal eminence, turns again to take a vertical, or mastoid, course. There, the nerve is located just lateral and inferior to the lateral semicircular canal, finally exit-

ing from the stylomastoid foramen at the anterior end of the digastric groove. The chorda tympani nerve leaves the facial nerve in the vertical mastoid portion, passing in its own canal to the posterior iter. There the chorda tympani nerve passes lateral to the long process of the incus and medial to the malleus handle to the anterior iter, entering the anterior petrotympanic fissure (canal of Huguier) to leave the middle ear.[27] In as many as 55% of cases, the bony facial canal is found to be dehiscent in part of its course, most commonly in the horizontal portion.[4, 12] Gerhardt and Otto[14] have suggested that the course of the facial nerve in the middle ear influences the development of the ossicles, including malformations. For example, if the facial nerve overlies the footplate, the stapes may be malformed or even atretic.

The completed adult form of the middle ear has several important spaces and landmarks. The canal of Huguier, already mentioned, is in the anterior middle ear and contains the chorda tympani nerve. The ponticulus is the bony ridge between the oval window and the sinus tympani; the subiculum is the bony ridge between the round-window niche and the sinus tympani. The sinus tympani is bounded medially by the bony labyrinth, laterally by the pyramidal eminence, superiorly by the lateral semicircular canal and ponticulus, inferiorly by the subiculum and the jugular wall, and posteriorly by the posterior semicircular canal. The facial recess is bounded medially by the facial nerve, laterally by the bony tympanic annulus and chorda tympani, and superiorly by the short process of the incus. When middle-ear cholesteatoma is present, both the facial recess and the sinus tympani can be involved; cholesteatoma can be difficult to detect and remove from these areas. On the anterior medial wall of the middle ear is the cochleariform process, the curved end of the tensor tympani semicanal; in revision mastoid surgery, this may be one of the few safe remaining landmarks.

Inner Ear

The inner ear is in the petrous portion of the temporal bone and consists of a membranous labyrinth inside a bony labyrinth. At birth, it is adult in size and configuration except for changes in the periosteal layer of the bony labyrinth and continued postfetal growth of the endolymphatic sac and duct.

Membranous Labyrinth

The adult membranous labyrinth consists of the utricle, saccule, semicircular ducts, endolymphatic sac and duct, and cochlear duct. It is housed in the bony labyrinth, contains endolymph, and is bathed by perilymph.

The membranous labyrinth develops from surface ectoderm at the end of the third week of gestation. An area of plaquelike thickening appears on the lateral aspect of the neural fold dorsal to the first branchial groove and in close relation to the hindbrain (rhombencephalon). During the fourth week, the placode invaginates to become the auditory pit and then the auditory vesicle (otocyst). During this process, the placode becomes surrounded by mesenchyme that will become the cartilaginous capsule of the otocyst (otic capsule).[26] The auditory vesicle becomes divided into two pouches by three folds: the ventral

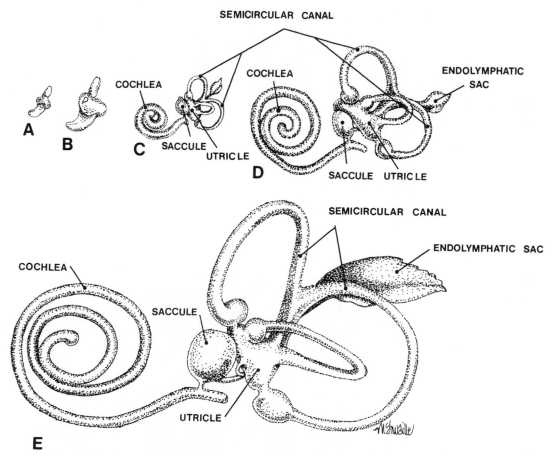

FIGURE 8–9. Development of the membranous labyrinth. *A*, Fetus at 5 weeks: development of ventral (cochlear) and dorsal (vestibular) pouches. *B*, Fetus at 6 weeks: rapid growth. *C*, Fetus at 2.5 months: adult structures easily recognizable. The cochlea has attained its 2.5 turns; the semicircular canals, utricle, saccule, and endolymphatic sac and duct are well developed. *D*, Fetus at 6 months: membranous labyrinth development is complete, except that the endolymphatic sac and duct continue to grow during infancy. *E*, Adult: fully developed labyrinth. (Adapted from Anson BJ, Davies J. In Paparella MM, Shumrick DA [eds]. Otolaryngology, vol I, 2nd ed. Philadelphia, WB Saunders, 1980, p 14. After Bast TH, Anson BJ. The Temporal Bone and Ear. Springfield, IL, Charles C Thomas, 1949.)

(cochlear, pars inferior) pouch will form the saccule and the cochlear duct, and the dorsal component (vestibular, pars superior) will give rise to the utricle, the semicircular ducts, and the endolymphatic duct. As differentiation of the membranous labyrinth progresses, the adult configuration is recognizable by 10 weeks of fetal life, and the membranous labyrinth without the end organ is complete by 6 months of fetal life (Fig. 8–9). However, the endolymphatic sac and duct continue to grow after birth in conjunction with the rest of the temporal bone and with the enlargement of the posterior cranial fossa.

Utricle and Saccule

The utricle and the saccule are otolithic organs. The utricle is sensitive to linear acceleration, but the function of the saccule in humans is unclear. The utricle is derived from the dorsal (vestibular) pouch of the auditory vesicle, while the saccule comes from the ventral (cochlear) pouch. The utricle, saccule, and endolymphatic duct begin to develop at about week 6 of gestation and achieve adult configuration by week 8. The ductus reuniens, which connects the saccule to the cochlear duct, forms at about 7 weeks. A Y-shaped duct connects the utricle to the saccule and is composed of the utriculoendolymphatic duct and the sacculoendolymphatic duct.

Neuroepithelial cells develop in the maculae of the saccule and the utricle and the cristae ampullaris of the semicircular canals (Fig. 8–10). By week 11 of gestation, development of this neuroepithelium and the supporting cells is complete. These areas of sensory epithelium secrete a gelatinous substance that becomes the otolithic membranes of the cristae. This gelatinous substance contains rhombic crystals of calcium carbonate called *otoconia*. The macula of the saccule lies in the vertical plane on the medial wall, whereas the macula of the utricle lies on the anterolateral wall, perpendicular to the saccular macula. The primary receptor cells in the maculae are types I and II hair cells (Fig. 8–11). Cilia from these sensory cells extend upward into the otolithic membrane, which contains the otoconia. The hair cells are surrounded by columnar supporting cells.

The utricle and the saccule are both contained in the vestibule of the inner ear. The utricle is ovoid and flattened, with a rounded end that occupies the elliptic recess of the posterosuperior vestibule. The semicircular canals open into its posterior wall, and the utriculosaccular duct opens into it anteriorly. The saccule, smaller and rounded, is in the anteroinferior portion of the vestibule, near the oval window footplate, and connects to the cochlea via the ductus reuniens. The utricle connects posteriorly with the semicircular canals and anteriorly with the saccular and endolymphatic ducts.[8]

Endolymphatic Duct and Sac

The endolymphatic duct and sac develop from the dorsal component of the otocyst at about 6 weeks of gestation, and growth continues in postfetal life. The fully developed duct lies mainly in the vestibular aqueduct, is surrounded by perilymph and periotic tissue, and is connected to the utriculosaccular duct. At its distal end lies the endolymphatic sac, in a fossa on the posterior portion of the petrous temporal bone. The duct's two main functions are endolymph absorption and pressure equalization between the cerebrospinal fluid and the endolymphatic systems.

Semicircular Canals

During week 6 of gestation, the semicircular canals begin to develop from the dorsal component of the otic vesicle.

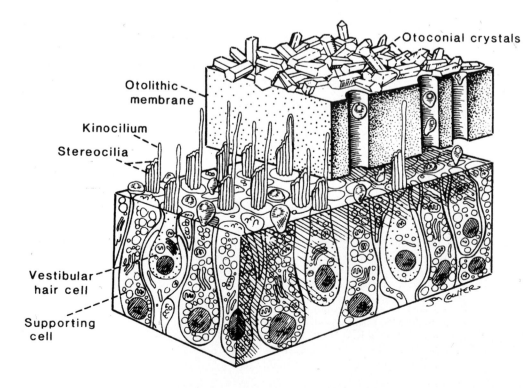

Otoconial crystals

Otolithic membrane

Kinocilium

Stereocilia

Vestibular hair cell

Supporting cell

FIGURE 8–10. Otolithic membrane and hair cells of utricular macula. The vestibular hair cells are mechanotransducers that convert linear acceleration and static tilt into electrical impulses carried along the eighth nerve. The stereocilia on the apical surface of the hair cells are embedded in a gelatinous matrix that contains otolithic crystals on the surface. (From Furman JM, Cass SP. Balance Disorders: A Case-Study Approach. Philadelphia, FA Davis, 1996, p 6.)

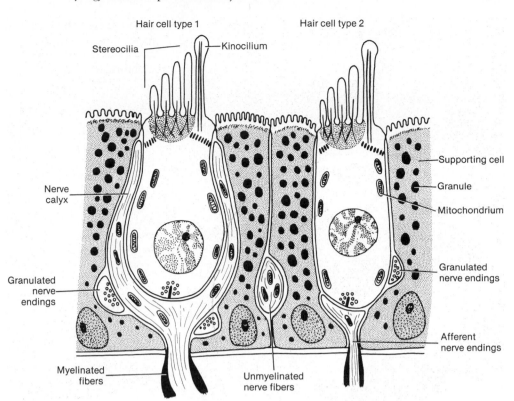

FIGURE 8–11. Type I and type II hair cells. Both type I and type II hair cells are found in the vestibular organs. The type I hair cell is more flask-shaped and has a cuplike contact with the afferent nerve fiber. The efferent terminals form synapses with the afferent terminals, but not directly on the type I hair cell itself. The type II hair cell is more elongated and thin and has both afferent and efferent terminals, which directly contact the basolateral surface of the hair cell. (From Schwarz DWF. Physiology of the vestibular system. In Cummings CW, Fredrickson JM, Harker LA, et al [eds]. Otolaryngology—Head and Neck Surgery, vol IV. St Louis, CV Mosby, 1986, p 2681.)

The superior canal develops first, followed by the posterior and then the lateral canals. During week 7, a ridgelike structure, the crista ampullaris, composed of neuroepithelial cells, develops at the dilated, or ampullary, end of each semicircular duct. The ampullated end of each canal opens into the utricle, while the nonampullated end of the posterior and superior canals fuse to form the common crus, which opens into the middle portion of the utricle. The nonampullated end of the lateral duct opens separately into the utricle. By week 11, the neuroepithelium and supporting cells of the cristae are complete. The superior semicircular duct reaches maximal growth by week 19, followed by the posterior canal. The lateral canal reaches maximal growth by the 22nd week. Like the macula, the cristae contain both type I and type II hair cells with cilia that extend upward into the cupula. The cupula is a gelatinous mass of mucopolysaccharides within a keratin framework and forms a partition across the ampulla (Fig. 8–12).

Cochlear Duct and Organ of Corti

During the sixth week of gestation, the cochlear duct develops from the ventral (saccular) pouch of the auditory vesicle. At week 7, one turn of the cochlea is formed, and by week 8 the entire 2.5 to 2.75 turns have been completed. The narrow tube connecting the cochlear duct to the saccule is called the *ductus reuniens.*

The organ of Corti arises in the wall of the cochlear duct. The epithelium in the area of the future organ of Corti differentiates into two ridges of tall columnar cells that extend the entire length of the cochlear duct. The cells of these ridges secrete a gelatinous substance that becomes the tectorial membrane.

The larger inner ridge becomes the spiral limbus, and the outer smaller ridge becomes the organ of Corti. At the 22nd week of gestation, this outer ridge develops inner and outer hair cells, pillar cells, and Hensen cells. Differentiation of the inner and outer ridges begins at the basal turn of the cochlear duct and spreads to the apex. At week 8, the stria vascularis begins to develop in the external wall of the cochlear duct; it is well developed by week 20. The organ of Corti completes its development during the fifth month of gestation, with the tunnel of Corti and the spaces of Nuel being formed at the 26th week.

The organ of Corti contains the sensory epithelium for hearing, which consists of hair cells and supporting cells. The afferent fibers of the auditory (eighth) nerve and the efferent fibers of the olivocochlear bundle enter the organ of Corti from beneath the basilar membrane and innervate the hair cells. The sensory cells are of two types, the inner and the outer hair cells, so named because of the cells' relative proximity to the tunnel of Corti (located medially in the spiral cochlea). Each cell has a stereocilia bundle extending from its apical surface, and each cell surface contains a small region without the presence of a cuticular plate that indicates where a kinocilium was located during development. The supporting cells are known as Deiters, Hensen, Claudius, and Boettcher cells, the inner border cells, the inner phalangeal cells, the inner and outer pillar cells, and the outer sulcus cells (Fig. 8–13). In the adult, the cochlear duct extends from the cochlear recess of the vestibule and ends in a blind pouch, the cupular cecum, at the apex. At its basal end, the small ductus reuniens communicates with the saccule.

In the completed state, the cochlear duct is triangular

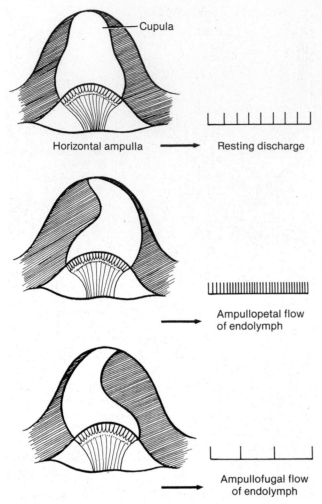

FIGURE 8–12. Crista ampullaris, cupula, and ampullary nerve. The crista ampullaris is an enlarged portion of the end of each semicircular canal where the hair cells that encode angular acceleration are located. Within the crista of each semicircular canal, there is a cupula, or a membrane that deforms when there is acceleration in the plane of the semicircular canal. This deformation of the membrane stimulates the hair cell, and the nerve firing rate changes to account for the angular acceleration in the given plane. (From Schwarz DWF. Physiology of the vestibular system. In Cummings CW, Fredrickson JM, Harker LA, et al [eds]. Otolaryngology—Head and Neck Surgery, vol IV. St Louis, CV Mosby, 1986, p 2681.)

and divides the bony cochlear canal into three separate compartments: the scala media (cochlear duct); the scala vestibuli, adjoining the Reisslner membrane; and the scala tympani, adjacent to the basilar membrane. The scala media contains endolymph, and both the scala tympani and the scala vestibuli contain perilymph. The floor of the cochlear duct is the basilar membrane, and the roof is the Reisslner membrane, which extends from the vestibular crest of the spiral ligament to the spiral limbus and divides the scala media from the scala vestibuli. The Reisslner membrane has two layers: a single layer of connective cells that faces the scala vestibuli and a single layer of epithelial cells that faces the scala media. These two layers of cells are joined by tight junctions, which prevent the free mixing of perilymph and endolymph,

although selective transport does occur.[21] The basilar membrane is suspended between the spiral limbus and the spiral ligament. The organ of Corti overlies the basilar membrane.

Audiovestibular Nerve

It is currently thought that the cells that form the eighth-nerve ganglion are derived from the otic vesicle. During the fourth week of gestation, these cells migrate between the epithelium and basement membrane of the otic vesicle and form the auditory ganglion. The eighth-nerve ganglion then divides into a superior part (pars superior) and an inferior part (pars inferior). The pars superior gives rise to the superior (utricular) branch of the vestibular nerve, which supplies the utricular macula and the cristae ampullaris of the lateral and superior semicircular canals. The pars inferior becomes the inferior portion of the vestibular nerve (supplying the saccular macula and the crista of the posterior semicircular canal) and the cochlear nerve (supplying the organ of Corti). The nerve cells in the cochlear and vestibular nerve ganglia are unusual in that they remain bipolar throughout life, the central processes terminating in the brain stem and the peripheral processes terminating in the sensory areas of the developing inner ear.[32, 37]

Bony Labyrinth, or Otic Capsule

The bony labyrinth encloses the membranous labyrinth and consists of the cochlea, three semicircular canals, the vestibule, and the perilymphatic spaces. Development of the bony labyrinth occurs in three stages. The first stage involves condensation of mesenchyme around the developing membranous labyrinth during the fourth to sixth weeks of gestation. Areas marking the location of the internal auditory canal, the entrance of the eighth nerve, and the developing endolymphatic duct can be identified at this point. Precartilage formation begins and continues during weeks 6 and 7, when true cartilage formation begins. In the areas where the membranous semicircular duct is expanding, dedifferentiation of cartilage and precartilage allows for growth while redifferentiation into cartilage is found in the trailing edge areas of membranous labyrinth growth (i.e., where expansion has stopped). The process continues until the membranous labyrinth attains adult size in midterm. The perichondrium of the otic capsule appears at week 12.

The second stage in otic capsule development involves the formation of perilymphatic spaces. The vestibule, enclosing the utricle, the saccule, and part of the cochlear duct, begins to develop at week 8, followed by development of the scala tympani during weeks 8 to 9. The scala tympani begins under the round window, and the scala vestibuli starts slightly later as an outpouching of the vestibule, near the oval window. The growth and development of the scalae closely follow that of the cochlear duct, and the scalae attain adult size by 16 weeks. The perilymphatic spaces around the semicircular ducts begin to develop after the scalae, the one around the lateral semicircular duct being the most developed.

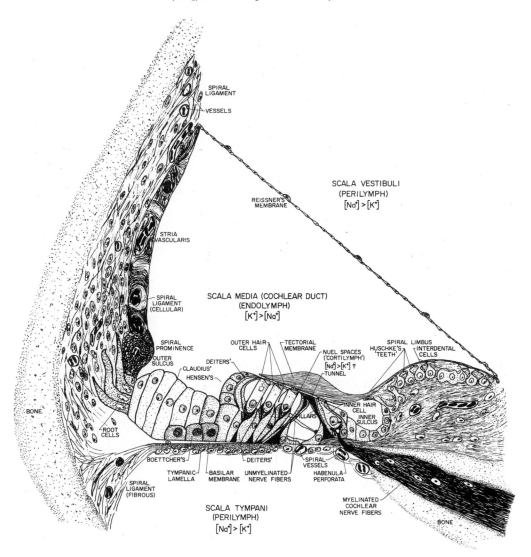

FIGURE 8–13. Transverse midmodiolar view of the cochlear duct (guinea pig, basal turn). (From Hawkins JE. Hearing: anatomy and acoustics. In Best CH, Taylor WB [eds]. Physiological Basis of Medical Practice, 8th ed. Baltimore, Williams & Wilkins, 1966.)

There are four projections from the perilymphatic space: the perilymphatic (periotic) duct, the fossula post fenestram, the fissula ante fenestram, and an unnamed projection around the endolymphatic duct. The fissula traverses the bony partition between the inner and the middle ear anterior to the oval window and is thought to provide an overflow channel for perilymph. The perilymphatic duct runs in a canal through the petrous bone and connects the scala tympani with the subarachnoid space. The fossula post fenestram is located posterior to the oval window and is found in only about two thirds of embryos.

The third stage of otic capsule development involves ossification. This begins at about the 15th fetal week, from 14 centers, and forms the petrous part of the temporal bone. Calcification in the 14 centers precedes ossification. By the 23rd week, all the centers have fused to form a complete bony capsule. Ossification of the inner ear does not occur until each portion has attained adult size. In the adult, the bony capsule has three layers: (1) an outer layer of perichondral (periosteal) bone, (2) a

middle layer of intrachondral and endochondral bone, and (3) an inner layer of internal perichondrial bone. In the adult, the middle and inner layers can still be identified. In the region of the fissula ante fenestram, the middle layer is considered a favored site for development of otosclerosis.

Variations and Anomalies

The otologic surgeon must be prepared to encounter and recognize many possible variations and anomalies (Fig. 8–14). The causes of these variations may be multifactorial but certainly include genetic and environmental influences. Environmental factors may include prenatal infection or exposure to teratogens, as well as other poorly defined environmental effects. The definition of a normal variation versus an anomaly may be arguable, but in any case, they are uncommon and can cause severe problems for the patient and the surgeon. Some of the more com-

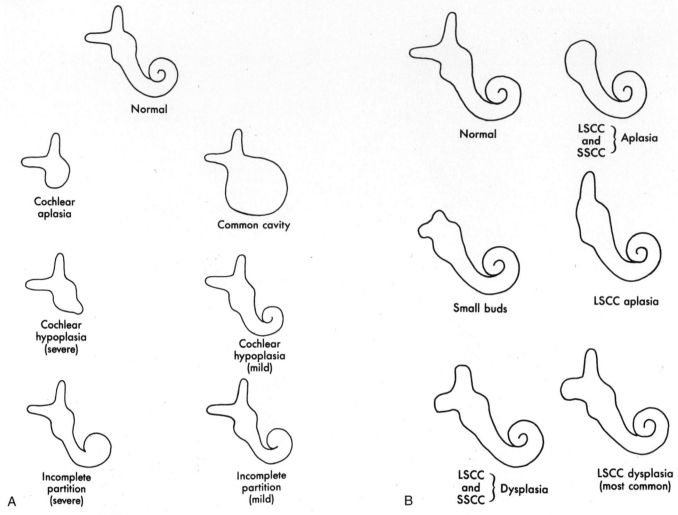

FIGURE 8–14. Congenital malformations of the otic capsule, cochlea, and semicircular canals. *A*, Cochlear malformations range from mild to severe abnormalities in the cochlear partition, to a common cavity, to total cochlear aplasia. *B*, The abnormalities of the semicircular canals are similarly graded from isolated enlargement of the lateral semicircular canal manifested by mild dilatation to significant dysplasia in all three semicircular canals with rudimentary bud formations. LSCC, lateral semicircular canal; SSCC, superior semicircular canal. (From Jackler RK, Luxford WM, House WF. Congenital malformations of the inner ear: a classification based on embryogenesis. Laryngoscope 97:2, 1987.)

mon variations include persistence of the stapedial artery, a high-riding jugular bulb, a dehiscent facial nerve, and congenital perilymphatic fistula. A persistent stapedial artery may tether the developing carotid artery so that it courses through the middle ear more laterally and posteriorly than it would ordinarily. In addition, incomplete pneumatization of the epitympanum may lead to fixation of the head of the malleus. (See also Chapter 20.)

Many congenital anomalies can occur as an isolated defect without an associated syndrome. However, over half of the commonly observed anomalies of the ear are associated with other abnormalities, often composing a recognizable syndrome.[5] Some authors have extensively studied various otologic anomalies associated with other diseases and have attempted to classify them by etiology.[23, 24] Conditions that can be seen as isolated traits include microtia, preauricular skin tags, preauricular pits,

branchial cleft sinuses, anomalies of the ossicles, aberrant facial nerve, high-riding jugular bulb, anomalous carotid artery, and absence of the round window (Table 8–1).[35]

A number of classification systems for anomalies of the external and middle ear have been devised to account for the extent and severity of the malformation. One of these systems is described in Table 8–2. This classification was produced by Cremers and colleagues and combines features of the external ear, the ear canal, and the middle ear, separating them into type I, IIA, IIB, and III. Another classification system developed by Jahrsdoerfer et al is designed to predict the likelihood of success for middle-ear reconstruction and surgical hearing rehabilitation by using a scoring system for each of the following structures: stapes, oval window, middle-ear space, facial nerve, malleus and incus complex, mastoid pneumatization, incudostapedial joint, round window, and appearance of the

TABLE 8–1. Distribution of All External Ear and Branchial Cleft Malformations

Malformation	Number	Rate per 10,000*
Preauricular sinus	446	83.74
Preauricular tags	91	17.09
Microtia	16	3.00
Other malformed pinna†	61	11.45
Branchial cleft sinus	12	2.25

* Based on a total NCPP population size of 53,257. Bilateral cases of any given malformation were counted as one for purposes of incidence calculations.

† Includes all other cases of malformed pinna. With the exception of microtia, the diagnostic labels and/or descriptions of the anomalies were not sufficiently clear to make certain the precise nosologic category.

From Gorlin RJ. Morphogenesis and malformation of the ear. Birth Defects 16:304, 1980.

external ear (Table 8–3).[20] Surgical restoration of hearing is considered very favorable with a score of 8 to 10 points and unfavorable with a score below 6.

Isolated malformations of the external ear and canal are visible in approximately 1% of newborn infants; a hearing loss can be documented in 9.3% of these children.[6] Isolated anomalies of the branchial arches are much less common, with an incidence of 0.02%.[28] Syndromes of the first and second branchial arches, such as Treacher Collins or the oculoauriculovertebral syndrome, are accompanied by anomalies of these arches, including microtia, atresia or stenosis of the external ear canal, absent TM with an associated atresia plate, ossicular anomalies, and aberrant shape or volume of the middle ear and mastoid. The facial nerve may be hypoplastic (especially in oculoauriculovertebral syndrome) or displaced anatomically. The branchio-otorenal (Melnick-Frasier) syndrome is characterized by preauricular sinuses, cysts or fistulas of the second branchial arch, renal anomalies, and sensorineural hearing loss as prominent features.

Structural abnormalities of the inner ear have been classified in various ways. Jackler et al have proposed a classification system derived from the embryologic stage at which development was arrested.[19] This classification incorporates various different anomalies that have been described in the past (Table 8–4). The Michel type is the most severe and consists of complete labyrinthine aplasia.

TABLE 8–2. Classification of External- and Middle-Ear Malformations

Type	Location	Malformation
I	External canal	Lateral bony atresia
	Tympanic membrane	Normal
	Middle ear	Normal
IIA	External canal	Fistular or medial bony atresia
IIB	External canal	Complete atresia
III	Pinna	Severely malformed or absent
	External canal	Absent
	Tympanic membrane	Small or absent
	Ossicles	Rudimentary or absent
	Mastoid	Non-pneumatized

Adapted from Cremers CWRJ, Oudenhoven JMTM, Marres EHMA. Congenital aural atresia: a new subclassification and surgical management. Clin Otolaryngol 19:199, 1984.

TABLE 8–3. Grading System of Candidacy for Congenital Aural Atresia Surgery

Variable	Points
Stapes present	2
Oval window open	1
Facial nerve	1
Middle-ear space	1
Mastoid pneumatization	1
Malleus/incus complex	1
Incudostapedial connection	1
Round window	1
Appearance of external ear	1
Total points	10

Interpretation of Rating for Surgery

Rating	Type of Candidate
10	Excellent
9	Very good
8	Good
7	Fair
6	Marginal
5	Poor

Adapted from Jahrsdoerfer RA, Yeakley JW, Aguilar EA, et al. Grading system for the selection of patients with congenital aural atresia. Am J Otol 13:6, 1992.

The Mondini type results in development of a small cochlea with an incomplete or absent interscalar septum and either normal or malformed semicircular canals. This type is sometimes called an *incomplete partition*. The Bing-Siebenmann malformation is underdevelopment of the membranous labyrinth with a well-formed bony otic capsule. The Scheibe type of anomaly is a malformation isolated to the membranous portion of the organ of Corti and sacculus.

In some cases, perilymphatic fistula is a congenital

TABLE 8–4. Grading System of Candidacy for Congenital Aural Atresia Surgery

With an Absent or Malformed Cochlea:

1. *Complete labyrinthine aplasia (Michel):* no inner-ear development
2. *Cochlear aplasia:* no cochlea, semicircular canals and vestibule are normal or malformed
3. *Cochlear hypoplasia:* small cochlear bud, normal or malformed semicircular canals and vestibule
4. *Incomplete partition of cochlea (Mondini):* small cochlea with incomplete or no interscalar septum, normal or malformed vestibule and semicircular canals
5. *Common cavity (Cock):* cochlea and vestibule form a common cavity without internal architecture; normal or malformed semicircular canals

With a Normal Cochlea:

1. *Vestibule-lateral semicircular canal dysplasia:* enlarged vestibule with a short dilated lateral semicircular canal; remaining semicircular canals are normal
2. Enlarged vestibular aqueduct; accompanied by normal semicircular canals, normal or enlarged vestibule

Adapted from Jackler RK, Luxford WM, House WF. Congenital malformations of the inner ear: a classification based on embryogenesis. Laryngoscope 97:2, 1987.

anomaly. It has been commonly associated with Mondini-type dysplasia and may be due to coexisting fistulas in the oval window and the fundus of the modiolus.[36] Other anatomic areas that have been identified histopathologically with clinical signs and symptoms of perilymphatic fistula include a patent fissula ante fenestram and a patent fissure between the round window and posterior canal ampulla.[22] (See Chapter 21.)

Large vestibular aqueduct syndrome is a relatively common congenital anomaly that is associated with progressive or fluctuating hearing loss. Hearing loss may occur spontaneously or may be associated with even mild head trauma. In patients with large vestibular aqueducts, hearing is often normal at birth but declines progressively during the first and second decades of life. The diagnosis of large vestibular aqueduct syndrome is based on high-resolution computed tomography of the temporal bone. This anomaly of the vestibular aqueduct can be associated with other bony anomalies of the labyrinth such as a Mondini-type dysplasia. This condition also occurs in conjunction with congenital stapes fixation and perilymphatic gusher. However, in a considerable number of cases, large vestibular aqueduct syndrome may occur as an isolated anomaly. An endolymphatic-to-subarachnoid shunt was used in an attempt to preserve hearing.[18] This technique proved to be unsuccessful and resulted in immediate postoperative hearing loss in more than half of subjects. As a result, endolymphatic shunt is not recommended for these patients. Early studies have demonstrated that endolymphatic sac obliteration may slow the progressive decline of hearing.[40] However, no definitive treatment, aside from avoidance of any type of head trauma, has been established for these patients, and deafness may eventually result despite attempts to improve or stabilize hearing. Cochlear implantation has been used successfully in these patients after hearing loss has become profound.

Congenital cholesteatoma is a well-described entity of unclear origin. The most commonly held theory invokes the role of an epidermoid formation, which normally occurs during the course of development. This epidermoid formation consists of a collection of stratified squamous cells that occurs between 10 and 33 weeks of gestation in the anterosuperior portion of the middle ear, adjacent to the TM. Ordinarily, the epidermoid formation undergoes involution at 33 weeks' gestation. However, it is thought that in cases of congenital cholesteatoma, this epidermoid formation persists and starts to create keratin.[25, 29]

Despite the popularity of this theory, epidermoid rests have been observed in postmortem temporal bones of both third-trimester fetuses and children as old as 10 years without signs of keratinization or growth. Other theories for the possible embryologic origin of congenital cholesteatomas include squamous metaplasia of cuboidal epithelium of the middle ear, resulting in keratin formation in the mesotympanum[34]; entrance of squamous epithelium into the middle ear through a marginal perforation[33]; ectodermal implants between the fusion planes of the first and second branchial arches[31]; and residual amniotic-fluid squamous debris that floats into the mesotympanum and takes root.

Conclusions

The embryology and developmental anatomy of the ear are complex, but an understanding of them can help explain many congenital anomalies. Depending on the time of gestation in which the abnormalities occurred, anomalies of the outer ear (pinna, EAC) and the middle ear may or may not be related to anomalies of the inner ear. Sophisticated evaluation of audiologic function (brain stem evoked responses and otoacoustic emissions) as well as radiographic evaluation of the middle and inner ear (computed tomography and magnetic resonance imaging) allow comprehensive investigation of these structures in young children and infants.

SELECTED READINGS

Anson BJ, Davies J, Duckert LG. Embryology of the ear. In Paparella MM, Shumrick DA, Gluckman JL, Meyerhoff WL (eds). Otolaryngology, 3rd ed. Philadelphia, WB Saunders, 1991, pp 3–22.
Gasser RF. The development of the facial nerve in man. Ann Otol Rhinol Laryngol 76:37, 1967.
Pearson AA. Developmental anatomy of the ear. In English GM (ed). Otolaryngology, revised ed. New York, Harper Medical, 1988, pp 1–68.

REFERENCES

1. Anson BJ, Davies J. Embryology of the ear. In Paparella M, Shumrick DA (eds). Otolaryngology, vol I, 2nd ed. Philadelphia, WB Saunders, 1980, pp 8–11.
2. Anson BJ, Davies J, Duckert LG. Embryology of the ear. In Paparella MM, Shumrick DA, Gluckman JL, Meyerhoff WL (eds). Otolaryngology, vol I. Philadelphia, WB Saunders, 1991, pp 3–22.
3. Anson BJ, Donaldson JA. Surgical Anatomy of the Temporal Bone and Ear, 2nd ed. Philadelphia, WB Saunders, 1973.
4. Baxter A. Dehiscence of the fallopian canal: an anatomical study. J Laryngol Otol 85:587, 1971.
5. Bergstrom L. Assessment and consequence of malformation of the middle ear. Birth Defects 16:217, 1980.
6. Bodurtha J, Nance WE. Genetics of hearing loss. In Alberti PW, Ruben RJ (eds). Otologic Medicine and Surgery. New York, Churchill-Livingstone, 1988, pp 831–854.
7. Cremers CWRJ, Oudenhoven JMTM, Marres EHMA. Congenital aural atresia: a new subclassification and surgical management. Clin Otolaryngol 19:199, 1984.
8. Donaldson JA, Duckert LG. Anatomy of the ear. In Paparella MM, Shumrick DA, Gluckman JL, Meyerhoff WL (eds). Otolaryngology, vol II. Philadelphia, WB Saunders, 1991, pp 23–58.
9. Donaldson JA, Lambert PM, Duckert LG, Rubel EW. The ear: developmental anatomy. In Donaldson JA, Anson BJ (eds). Surgical Anatomy of the Temporal Bone, 4th ed. New York: Raven Press, 1992, pp 19–142.
10. English G. Otolaryngology. New York: Harper Medical, 1988.
11. Furman JM, Cass SP. Balance disorders: A Case-Study Approach. Philadelphia, FA Davis, 1996.
12. Gasser RF. The development of the facial nerve in man. Ann Otol Rhinol Laryngol 76:37, 1967.
13. Gasser RF, Shigihara S, Shimada K. Three-dimensional development of the facial nerve path through the ear region in human embryos. Ann Otol Rhinol Laryngol 103:395, 1994.
14. Gerhardt JJ, Otto HD. The infratemporal course of the facial nerve and its influence on the development of the ossicular chain. Acta Otolaryngol (Stockh) 91:567, 1981.
15. Gorlin RJ. Morphogenesis and malformation of the ear. Birth Defects 16:1, 1980.

16. Gulya AJ. Developmental anatomy of the ear. In Glasscock ME, Shambough GE, Johnson GD (eds). Surgery of the Ear. Philadelphia, WB Saunders, 1990, pp 5–33.
17. Hawkins JE. Hearing: anatomy and acoustics. In Best C, Taylor WB (eds). Physiological Basis of Medical Practice, 8th ed. Baltimore: Williams & Wilkins, 1966.
18. Jackler RK, Cruz ADL. The large vestibular aqueduct syndrome. Laryngoscope 99:1238, 1989.
19. Jackler RK, Luxford WM, House WF. Congenital malformations of the inner ear: a classification based on embryogenesis. Laryngoscope 97:2, 1987.
20. Jahrsdoerfer RA, Yeakley JW, Aguilar EA, et al. Grading system for the selection of patients with congenital aural atresia. Am J Otol 13: 6, 1992.
21. Johnson LG. Reissner's membrane in the human cochlea. Ann Otol Rhinol Laryngol 80:425, 1971.
22. Kohut RI, Hinojosa R, Budetti JA. Perilymphatic fistula: a histopathological study. Ann Otol Rhinol Laryngol 95:466, 1986.
23. Konigsmark BW. Pathology of hereditary deafness. N Engl J Med 281: , 1969.
24. Konigsmark BW, Gorlin RJ. Genetic and Metabolic Deafness. Philadelphia, WB Saunders, 1976.
25. Levenson MJ, Michaels L, Parisier SC, Juarbe C. Congenital cholesteatomas in children: an embryologic correlation. Laryngoscope 98: 949, 1988.
26. Li CW, McPhee J. Influences on the coiling of the cochlea. Ann Otol Rhinol Laryngol 88:280, 1979.
27. May M. Anatomy of the facial nerve for the clinician. In May M (ed). The Facial Nerve. New York, Thieme Medical, 1985, pp 21–62.
28. Melnick M. The etiology of external ear malformations and its relation to abnormalities of the middle ear, inner ear, and other organ systems. Birth Defects 16:303, 1980.
29. Michaels L. Origin of congenital cholesteatomas from a normally occurring epidermoid rest in the developing middle ear. Int J Pediatr Otorhinolaryngol 15:51, 1988.
30. Palva T, Palva A. Size of the human mastoid air cell system. Acta Otolaryngol (Stockh) 62:237, 1966.
31. Paparella MM, Rybak L. Congenital cholesteatoma. Otolaryngol Clin North Am 11:113, 1978.
32. Pearson AA. Developmental anatomy of the ear. In English GM (ed). Otolaryngology. New York, Harper Medical, 1988, pp 1–68.
33. Rudei L. Cholesteatoma forming in the middle ear in animal experiments. Acta Otolaryngol (Stockh) 50:233, 1959.
34. Sadé J, Babiacki A, Pinkus G. The metaplastic and congenital origin of cholesteatoma. Acta Otolaryngol (Stockh) 96:119, 1983.
35. Sando I, Shibahara Y, Wood RP. Congenital anomalies of the external and middle ear. In Bluestone CD, Stool SE (eds). Pediatric Otolaryngology. Philadelphia, WB Saunders, 1990, pp 271–304.
36. Schuknecht IIF. Mondini dysplasia: a clinical and pathological study. Ann Otol Rhinol Laryngol 89(Suppl 65):1, 1980.
37. Schuknecht HF, Gulya AJ. Phylogeny and embryology. In Schuknecht H, Gulya A (eds). Anatomy of the Temporal Bone with Surgical Implications. Philadelphia, Lea & Febiger, 1986, pp 235–273.
38. Schwarz DWF. Physiology of the vestibular system. In Cummings CW, Fredrickson JM, Harker LA, et al (eds). Otolaryngology—Head and Neck Surgery, vol IV. St Louis, CV Mosby, 1986, pp 2679–2721.
39. Tos M, Stangerup SE, Hvid G. Mastoid pneumatization: evidence of the environmental theory. Arch Otolaryngol Head Neck Surg 110: 502, 1984.
40. Wilson DF, Hodgson RS, Talbot JM. Endolymphatic sac obliteration for large vestibular aqueduct syndrome. Am J Otol 18:101, 1997.
41. Wood-Jones F, Wen IC. The development of the external ear. J Anat 68:525, 1934.

9

Physical and Physiologic Bases of Hearing

John D. Durrant, Ph.D.

The Auditory Response Area and Basic Auditory Abilities

Sound is a form of energy created by a vibratory source, such as the vibrating prongs of a tuning fork, that causes molecules of the substance of the medium, such as air, to be displaced to and fro. Therefore, as the source vibrates, it alternately compresses and rarefies the particles of the surrounding medium, creating local alterations of pressure. These changes are minute. For instance, at sound pressures in air capable of causing pain to the ear, the steady-pressure equivalent amounts to only about 0.1 atmospheres, whereas the minimum sound pressure detectable by the normal human ear is one ten-millionth of this value. This illustrates the exquisite sensitivity of the auditory system and its impressive dynamic range—approximately $10^{14}:1$ in acoustic intensity (in the vicinity of 1000 Hz). It is the purpose of this brief introduction to review basic quantities of sound, the physical domain of normal hearing, and (other) basic capacities of the human auditory system.

The quantification of sound actually requires two measures. The first is its magnitude, measured in units of acoustic intensity (w/m^2) or, more practically, sound pressure in units of pascals (1 pa = 1 newton/m^2). The minimal detectable sound is approximately 20 μpa (that is, 2 x 10^{-5} pascals or newtons/m^2). It is the magnitude of sound that primarily determines one's sense of loudness. The other measure in question is frequency, the primary determinant of pitch. The unit of measure is cycles-per-second, or hertz (Hz), the reciprocal of period, which is the time expended in completing one cycle of a given frequency component. It is important to realize that sounds such as those produced by the familiar tuning fork are relatively simple, since they reflect oscillations at a single frequency. Most sounds in nature or the environment are typically more complicated in their frequency composition. Nevertheless, these sounds can be analyzed and represented in terms of their frequency components and the amplitude (i.e., peak magnitude of the sinusoid) and phase of each (i.e., starting point within the cycle). This is called spectrum analysis. Sounds of particular interest to humans, such as speech and music, not only have complex spectra, but their spectra also change rapidly over time. For the auditory system to analyze such sounds, it must be able to perform some form of spectrum analysis and to do so at rather high rates. The spectrum of the sound stimulus determines not only the loudness and pitch of a given sound but also perceived sound qualities such as timbre. It is this ability of the auditory system to analyze complex sounds that permits one to distinguish among musical instruments even when they play the same note (i.e., identical pitch).

The auditory response area, shown in Figure 9–1A, is a map of the physical domain of normal hearing. The dynamic range was noted earlier, but this is truly a two-dimensional space, apropos the primary measures of sound—magnitude and frequency. The conventional practice is to determine and plot the magnitude measure against frequency in log-log coordinates. Consequently, frequency appears on the abscissa with logarithmic scaling. This places 1000 Hz at approximately the middle of the human auditory response area. The unit of measure of sound pressure is the decibel (dB), which itself is a logarithmic number. The use of decibels, rather than units of sound pressure directly, is favored by virtue of the inherent compression of the regular, linear number scale, making very small and very large numbers more manageable. The dynamic range, for example, translates from $10^{14}:1$ into a range of 0 to 140 dB. The only catch is that the decibel is equal to 20 times the log of a pressure ratio, so a reference quantity is required. The generally accepted reference for sound pressure level (SPL) is 20 μPa.

The lower boundary of the auditory response area is defined by the threshold of hearing—the smallest sound pressure detectable with consistency. It has been speculated that hearing sensitivity is limited only by the "noise floor" formed by random bombardment of particles of the medium or fluid within the inner ear (e.g., brownian movement or thermal noise). For humans, however, such noise appears to be some 20 dB below the limits of hearing for even the most sensitive normal-hearing individuals.[50]

The upper limit is no less remarkable, but for much different reasons. It is an expression of the limit of physiologically appropriate stimulation of the auditory system. Sounds approaching 140 dB SPL are brutally loud and uncomfortable, if not painful, and permanent damage to the hearing organ is imminent at such levels, even for the

A

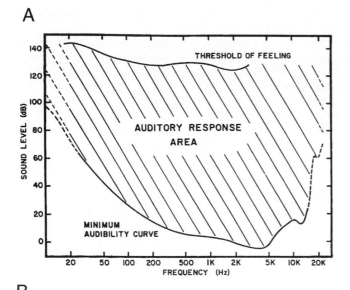

B

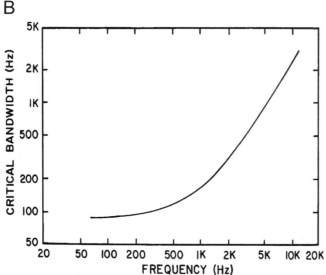

FIGURE 9–1. *A,* The auditory response area. The minimum audibility curve is based on data of Robinson and Dadson (1956). The extreme low and high frequency portions of the curve (*broken line*) have been extended based on data of Yeowart and Evans (1974) and Corso (1967), respectively. The curve representing the threshold-of-feeling curve is based on data of Wegel (1932). *B,* The critical bandwidth as a function of frequency at the center of the band. (After Zwicker E, Flottrop G, Stevens SS. Critical bandwidth in loudness summation. J Acoust Soc Am 29:548, 1957.)

most brief exposure. Damage to the ear from brief, intense exposures to sound is called *acoustic trauma*. Even well below 140 dB, there are warning signs that the ear's limit of tolerance is close. Exposures to sounds of just 90 dB SPL (A-scale weighting) can cause permanent damage to the hearing organ if sustained for hours per day, nonstop, day after day. Indeed, this is the level that the National Institute of Occupational Safety and Health has stipulated as the maximum daily noise dose permissible for workers without the use of hearing protection.[146] Higher levels of sound exposure are safe only for progressively shorter durations of exposure. Other signs of over-

stimulation may include the perceptions of aural fullness, distortion, and tinnitus (typically experienced as ringing in the ears).

Returning to the limits of hearing sensitivity, the values measured are seen to be unequal across frequency, so the boundary formed is called the minimum audibility curve (see Fig. 9–1A).[124] This curve thus delimits hearing along the frequency axis as well. While the auditory system is quite sensitive over a mid-range of frequencies, sensitivity suffers increasingly at the extremes above and below. What exactly the lower and upper limits of hearing are, however, is a matter of definition and is species-dependent. For humans, the usable frequency range is fairly well centered on the spectrum of speech, although the entire hearing frequency range is not required for the reproduction or reception of speech (i.e., with adequate intelligibility). For instance, the telephone is engineered to reproduce sound only over the range of about 300 to 3000 Hz, representing a much narrower bandwidth than the pass-band of the normal human auditory system. The range from 20 to 20,000 Hz is generally accepted as the nominal useful bandwidth of human hearing, although auditory responses to sound are demonstrable significantly below[169] and above this range.[19, 20] Still, outside of the band of 20 to 20,000 Hz, rather high SPLs are required to just reach threshold and may cause distortion[161] or be devoid of a clear sense of pitch.[20]

Another important basic ability is detection of changes in the parameters of the sound, or *discrimination* among different sounds. This capacity for discrimination even between complex sounds of similar spectra, such as the spoken words [bit] and [pit], is a testimonial to the superb engineering of the human auditory system. The psychophysical measure called *difference limen* provides an indication of the basic differential sensitivity of the auditory system. The difference limen for intensity is, serendipitously, about 1 dB,[60] which amounts to a 12% change in intensity—less than 1% of the dynamic range. The difference limen for frequency is approximately 0.2%,[166] meaning that with training and careful listening, one should be able to distinguish between a tone of 1000 Hz and 1002 Hz. However, these specifications of differential sensitivity, particularly the difference limen for frequency, are valid only for the central region of the auditory response area. Decreased discrimination ability is observed at the extremes of the frequency range or as the limits of hearing sensitivity are approached.[83]

The stated difference limen for frequency also does not realistically characterize the limits of the frequency-resolution of the auditory system for sounds more complex than simple tones or simultaneously occurring sounds in general. For instance, if the 1000 Hz and 1002 Hz tones in the example were presented simultaneously, two tones would not be perceived. Rather, a single tone, i.e., one pitch (related to the average of the two frequencies) would be heard but its loudness would wax and wane, or "beat," two times per second (at the difference frequency of 2 Hz).[159]

There are other perceptual attributes that reflect the inability of the auditory system to resolve closely spaced spectral components of complex sounds,[115] a limit known as the *critical bandwidth*.[134, 173] Like the frequency difference limen, the critical bandwidth varies across frequency (Fig. 9–1*B*), and critical bands influence the loudness of complex sounds or how loudness grows as sounds are added together. Within a critical band, the loudness, for example, depends primarily on the total sound energy, whereas the loudness of sound whose spectral components extend beyond a single critical band also depends on how many critical bands are spanned. Beyond one critical band, loudness itself summates. For instance, speech presented at the same overall SPL as a single pure tone will sound louder than the tone. This is why patients who fake or otherwise demonstrate nonorganic losses of hearing rarely escape the attentive clinician, given their thresholds for both pure tones and speech. Hearing sensitivity for speech will be remarkably better than expected from the tonal audiogram. Such patients tend to set an internal loudness reference, but less intensity is needed to reach this criterion for speech due to loudness summation across the critical bands. The frequency range of hearing spans over 25 critical bands. This may seem like a much more coarse resolution than anticipated from the difference limen, but the limits of these bands are not fixed. Furthermore, the auditory system processes information from the critical bands nearly simultaneously and continuously ("on the fly"), providing the bases for an efficient continuous spectrum analysis. Temporal information within the channels also is not ignored. Indeed, what makes the auditory system such an impressive instrument is that it achieves good frequency resolution without sacrificing temporal resolution. It is by virtue of these properties that this system is capable of carrying out spectrum analysis in real time and, thereby, providing the free-running speech-communication enjoyed by humans.

With these basic concepts of how well the auditory system functions in hand, how the system works now can be considered. Perhaps surprisingly, many of the abilities described and their limits are determined by or depend greatly upon events in the auditory periphery. This is where sound energy is transduced into electrochemical events leading to neural impulses transmissible within the acoustic nerve and the brain. It also is the peripheral system that is accessible to noninvasive medical examination and the most accessible to therapeutic and surgical treatment. Therefore, much attention is given here to the peripheral auditory system and its workings.

Routing of Sound Energy to the Cochlea: The Outer and Middle Ear Transformers

The overall role of the outer and middle ears in hearing is straightforward enough: They serve to collect sound energy and funnel it to the inner ear. These are physical functions that cannot be appreciated fully, however, without consideration of the basic acoustic and mechanical principles underlying this functional role. Considering the anatomy of the ear of various submammalian species (e.g., frogs, lizards, birds), the outer ear at first seems expendable, and, indeed, it is the middle ear that makes the more substantial contribution to auditory capabilities.

It is thus fitting to start more medially with this description of physiologic acoustics.

One can appreciate the function of the middle ear by considering the problem of transmitting sound energy from one medium to another. The classic example is what happens when sound waves in air encounter water. Under the most ideal circumstances (i.e., plane wave propagation with a zero angle of incidence), only 0.1% of the energy will be transmitted; 99.9% will be reflected. This represents a 30 dB loss of sound energy from air to water. [Note: 0.1% = 0.001, representing a ratio of 1000: 1; 10 log(1000/1) = 10 log(10^3) = 10 x 3 = 30 dB.] Given that the organ of Corti is housed in the fluid-filled cochlea, it is clear that optimal hearing sensitivity will not be possible via direct transmission of sound from air to cochlea.

It is well known from physics that the transfer of sound or vibratory energy from one medium or vibratory system to another is optimal only when the media or systems involved are matched in terms of their impedances. Impedance is a form of opposition to vibratory motion that arises from the combined mass (or density), elasticity, and friction of a medium or system. Mathematically, impedance is a complex number, meaning that it has both magnitude and phase. It is not necessary to delve into such details. The essential, all-important concept here, again, is that the most efficient power transfer occurs only when impedances are matched. This is true in electrical, mechanical, and acoustic systems. For example, the output impedance of a high-fidelity ("hi-fi") amplifier must be matched to the input impedance of the loudspeaker to achieve the widest frequency response with the greatest power transfer. Because not all amplifiers have output impedances that match the input impedance of a given loudspeaker, a transformer is often used to match the impedances. So too does the middle-ear mechanism serve as a transformer to match the impedance of air to that of the cochlear input—the oval window.

The classic description of the elements of the middle ear is illustrated in Figure 9–2. Here the middle ear is modeled as a system of plates or pistons and levers. The analysis of this system has been described extensively by various writers[22, 36, 176] and is presented only conceptually here. The most obvious transformation, and indeed the largest component (numerically) of the transformation, is the large area ratio of the tympanic membrane and the stapes footplate. As with the diaphragm of a loudspeaker, not all of the surface of the eardrum is free to vibrate; but even allowing for this factor, the ratio is relatively large—approximately 13:1. Thus, the force of a sound wave acting over the eardrum-piston is funneled to the much smaller footplate area, yielding sound pressure amplification (since pressure equals force divided by area). There is an additional force amplification through the leverage of the ossicular chain system amounting to about 1.3:1. The total pressure amplification amounts to 13 x 1.3 = 17, which can be represented in decibels, equaling about 25 dB.

At first glance, this number seems to offer the sort of match that was needed, if the air-to-water analogy were

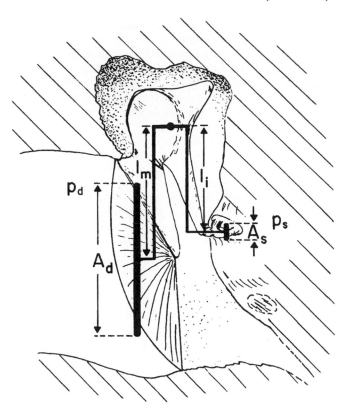

FIGURE 9–2. Components of the middle ear transformer, viewed as a system of two pistons connected by a folded lever. A, area; p, sound pressure; l, length. Subscripts: d, eardrum; m, manubrium of the malleus; i, long crus of the incus; s, stapes footplate. (Inspired by drawing of Zwislocki JJ, 1965.)

valid. However, the input impedance of the cochlea does not appear to be as great as that of water,[175] thus limiting the validity of the air-to-water analogy. Additionally, pressure amplification is not the only consideration. For instance, tremendous pressure might be generated by a given system. Yet, if no motion results, work (in the physical sense) has not been accomplished, and no power transfer will occur. Therefore, a more comprehensive analysis requires consideration of both sound pressure and velocity transformations that, in turn, are reflected in the impedance transformation through the system. Results of such analyses have been surprisingly pessimistic, suggesting the human middle ear system to be only about 60% efficient, or "worth" about 13 dB. However, although of great heuristic value, holograms of the tympanic membrane in motion suggest the classic piston model to be, at the very least, an oversimplification.[152]

Another aspect of the mechanics of the middle ear that has been questioned is the proper model for the impedance of the stapes footplate.[74] That the middle ear transformer could be considerably more efficient, indeed, may be argued from clinical experience. The fenestration operation—predecessor of stapes mobilization surgery, wherein the eardrum is essentially connected directly to a surgically formed window in the osseous labyrinth—at times was found to yield improvements in hearing approaching 25 dB.[30]

Whatever the true impedance transformation of the middle ear, there is yet another value of the middle ear, one that is even less easily quantified but is conceptually easy to appreciate. Were it not for the middle-ear transformer, the round window would not be protected. Sound waves that would otherwise reach both windows are prevented from so doing, and, in turn, phase cancellation within the cochlea is averted. Such an effect can be appreciated by a simple demonstration with a tuning fork. The fork is struck and set into vibration and then held near one ear. Rotating the vibrating fork, one finds that the intensity of the sound varies. The lowest amplitude is observed with the tuning fork broadside to the side of the head. Sound waves are excited by each vibrating prong but destructively interfere—cancel one another—between the prongs. While the principle of "protection of the round window" has guided creative reconstructive surgeries in cases in which the tympanic membrane and most of the ossicular chain have been lost, total cancellation cannot actually result in the ear, at least not at all frequencies. The two windows simply do not lie in the same plane. The complete absence of the tympanic membrane and ossicular chain, or simply disruption of the ossicular chain, can cause hearing losses only up to about 60 dB. This magnitude of loss still is not as severe as it would be with total phase cancellation.[108]

Conductive hearing losses up to 60 dB, on the other hand, are themselves perplexing and beg the question of how hearing losses caused by middle ear diseases, malformations, disarticulations, or other pathologic lesions can exceed even the most liberal estimate of the numeric worth of the middle ear. Losses of more than 25 dB indeed are common. The answer is that, as implied by the previous paragraph, the worth of the middle ear mechanism does not rest entirely on the transformer ratio. Furthermore, pathologic changes can cause the system to work even less efficiently than having no middle ear transformer at all. Consider the case of the atretic ear. Patients with such a condition demonstrate air conduction hearing losses on the order of 50 dB. Coincidentally, when unilaterally deaf subjects are tested under earphones, transcranial conduction is observed to occur at 40 to 70 dB. These values largely reflect the air-to-skull impedance mismatch (although in the latter example there is some acoustic leakage under the earphone cushion that adds to the crossover). It is not difficult to imagine that as the outer or middle ear pathologic condition worsens, a specific acousticomechanical pathway into the inner ear is lost. The physical problem then is no longer the one confronting nature in the evolution of the hearing mechanism, that is the air-to-cochlea mismatch. Now, energy can reach the inner ear only by bone vibration, which, in turn, is governed by the air-to-skull mismatch.

In the final analysis, even the most pessimistic estimates of the worth of the middle ear by physical-systems standards make it appear quite efficient overall. Yet this efficiency is not realized without a price: Its efficiency is limited across frequency. In other words, the middle ear filters sound, efficiently transferring sound energy (again) only over the midfrequency range of hearing. The middle-ear mechanism becomes increasingly inefficient at the

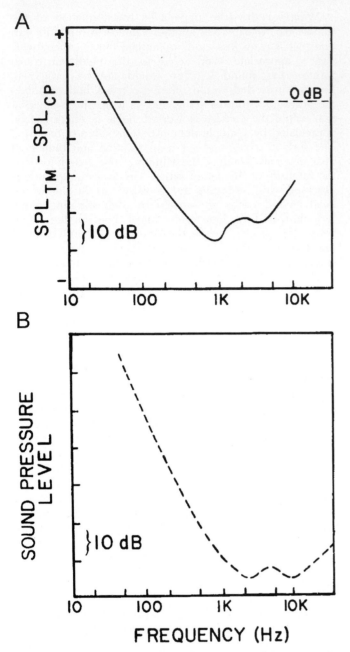

FIGURE 9–3. Comparison of sound pressure gradient across the cochlear partition (A) and behavioral thresholds (minimum audibility curve) (B) in the cat. CP, cochlear partition; SPL, sound pressure level; TM, tympanic membrane. (Part A based on data of Nedzelnitsky, 1974; part B based on Dallos' adaptation, 1973, of data from Miller et al, 1963.)

extremes of the hearing range, as was demonstrated by the minimum audibility curve (see Fig. 9–1). This point is further demonstrated by the graphs in Figure 9–3, wherein the sound pressure transformation between the eardrum and the cochlea yields a derived sensitivity curve remarkably similar to the minimum audibility curve. In short, the overall shape of the minimum audibility curve, and therefore the frequency limits of hearing, are ostensibly determined by the transfer characteristics of the middle ear.[22] That is not to say that, for example, the cochlea

of a bat would work in the elephant, or vice versa. Certainly, the inner and middle ears have evolved symbiotically, and it is the structures and mechanics of the organ of Corti that determine the overall sensitivity of the ear. The point is, rather, that the mechanical efficiency and response-versus-frequency characteristics reflected by the minimum audibility curve are largely determined by the middle ear transformer.

The middle ear impedance and response characteristics, however, are not entirely static but are subject to slight changes, even under normal operation. First, there is the effect of changes in air pressure that can push or pull on the eardrum and effectively alter the stiffness of the middle ear. (This is done purposefully in tympanometry.) These pressure changes are relieved by opening the eustachian tube during swallowing, for example. Second, and more interesting from a physiologic acoustics point of view, are changes caused by activation of the acoustic reflex (alternatively referred to as the *middle-ear muscle reflex* or *stapedius reflex*, the latter term reflecting the dominance of the stapedius muscle when the reflex is elicited by sound). The acoustic reflex can be monitored by observing the change in the input impedance (primarily increased stiffness) during intense sound stimulation. Clinically, acoustic reflex measurement is accomplished using an immittance test instrument, the electroacoustic "bridge," as used in tympanometry.

Perhaps the most commonly assumed role of the reflex is that of protecting the inner ear from overstimulation. Given that the activation of the reflex does reduce the transmission of sound through the middle ear, some protection is likely via this mechanism. However, this protection is also limited to the low frequencies, where the increased stiffening of the ossicular chain is most effective.[97, 98] The reflex also seems too sluggish to protect the ear from impulsive sounds,[141] and it probably adapts too much to offer protection against relatively constant noises.[151] Furthermore, it is not clear why such a protective mechanism would have evolved in the first place, since noise pollution is a relatively modern phenomenon and is clearly man-made. Still, the acoustic reflex provides the central auditory system a means of controlling the input to the brain at the periphery, even if limited. Furthermore, the contribution of the musculature does not rest entirely on activation. The muscles also cause damping (a form of friction), which, in turn, helps to smooth out peaks and valleys in the natural frequency response of the system, i.e., due to resonances and antiresonances.[140] Another role of the reflex is revealed by the fact that it is activated just before and during vocalization; the reflex thus attenuates one's own voice.[5]

Despite the pervasive influence of the middle ear on hearing, the outer ear is not acoustically transparent. Just as would be the case with a microphone, one cannot place the middle ear transformer at the end of a tube (some 2.5 cm long) in a dense sphere with a convoluted flange at the opening and not expect acoustic consequences. Indeed, the outer ear plays a substantial role in matching the mechanics of the ear to the air medium outside, amplifying sound in ways that are important to the particular species. Both the head and the auricle or pinna act as acoustic baffles, meaning that they will reflect some of the sound wave, which then will interfere with the incident sound wave. This creates nuances in the spectrum of sound reaching the eardrum that are azimuth-dependent, creating cues for the localization of sounds of different elevations, as well as front-back sound location. By virtue of its small size, these effects are restricted to frequencies above 4 kHz, that is, short-wavelength sounds.[10, 137, 139] Therefore, although somewhat small and immobile in humans, the auricle is not vestigial.

The head itself, nevertheless, forms the much larger and more significant baffle, causing essentially constructive interference for sounds from sources nearest an ear or casting a sound shadow on the opposite ear. The importance of this effect in sound localization will be considered momentarily. First, completing the outer-ear acoustic system, the tube-like external auditory meatus is seen to resonate, in effect, by virtue of the formation of standing waves. This is the same phenomenon that occurs when one blows over the mouth of an open test tube to produce a tone. The ear canal thus acts acoustically like a pipe with one end closed; the first mode of this tube (or so-called resonant frequency of the ear canal) occurs around 3400 Hz.[165] The combined acoustics of the head and auricle baffle effects and the ear canal resonance contribute as much as 20 dB sound pressure amplification at the eardrum in the 2000 to 5000 Hz region.[139] Comparison of the graphs in panels A and B of Figure 9–3, although based upon data from cats, shows how there would be a progressive decrease in sensitivity above about 1000 Hz if sound energy were fed directly to the tympanic membrane, as with a free-standing microphone. Instead, hearing continues to be fairly sensitive for more than two octaves above this level. In humans, these acoustic effects facilitate the reception of consonant sounds particularly. This is important because consonants have much less energy than vowels. Unfortunately, it may be this same amplification that (at least in part) predisposes the 4000 Hz region of hearing to damage from noise exposure.[128, 151]

Lastly, the placement of the ears on opposite sides of the head enhances one's ability to locate sounds from side to side. It is for sounds of relatively short wavelengths, compared with the diameter of the head (roughly above 1000 Hz), that the baffle effect of the near ear and shadowing of the far ear occur. For relatively long-wavelength sounds (roughly below 1000 Hz), sound bends or diffracts around the head, yet the separation of the two ears creates time delays between the arrival of sound at the two ears. Interaural intensity and time differences are thus the cues for the localization of sound differing in position horizontally. The substantial separation of the two ears in humans provides for excellent sound localization ability over a broad frequency range. However, the seemingly peerless localization ability of humans is not due to acoustics alone but also reflects on more medial and central structures that can faithfully encode, preserve, and ultimately decode the acoustic cues.[49] The first step in this chain of events is the critical function of absorbing and encoding the energy of the physical stimulus, namely the fundamental function of all sensory systems.

The Role and Function of Hair Cells

As described in the previous section, the purpose of the outer and middle ears is to efficiently transfer sound energy from air to the fluid-filled inner ear. The role of the cochlea and many of the structures of the hearing organ is to couple this vibratory energy, delivered to the oval window by the stapes footplate, to the hair cells, the sensory transduction cells of hearing (and balance). To appreciate the mechanisms and events involved, it is worthwhile to consider first just what it takes to stimulate hair cells in general. All sensory systems employing hair cells are similar in overall design and constitute a class of mechanoreceptor; the basic role of mechanoreceptors, as their name implies, is to transduce mechanical force into electrochemical energy.

Stimulating the Generic Hair-Cell Mechanoreceptor

For many years, understanding of the workings of the cochlear hair cell was limited to a combination of theory, observations of the extracellularly recorded gross electrical potentials of the cochlea, and extra- and intracellular recordings from hair cells of the lateral line organs (found, for example, on the skin of fishes and frogs[42]). Observations on lateral-line hair cells were supplemented by observations on vestibular hair cells.[39] The hair cells of these two systems have both stereocilia and a single kinocilium. As illustrated by Figure 9–4, the kinocilium provides a clear morphologic signpost that indicates the preferred direction of deflection of the sensory hairs for excitation of the associated sensory neuron. Back-and-forth deflection of the hair bundle along the axis defined by the kinocilium leads to alternating depolarization and hyperpolarization of the cell. Displacement of the hairs from side to side is ineffective. The fact that both excitation and inhibition are reflected in the pattern of discharges in the sensory neuron reflects an important aspect of neural encoding in vestibular and auditory systems alike. The vast majority of neurons in these systems exhibit some level of spontaneous activity, often 20 or more spikes per second. In the auditory system, this spontaneous activity is random over time and, even in the absence of sound stimulation, most primary auditory neurons are active.[41, 70] This characteristic reflects, in part, the keen mechanical sensitivity of the hair cell receptors. Indeed, neurons with a higher spontaneous rate tend to exhibit the greater sensitivity.[41] (More on this point follows.) Having a relatively high spontaneous activity also substantially influences how sound stimuli are encoded and processed by the central nervous system.

The model of hair cell transduction that has guided research in this area for years is that of the late Hallowel Davis.[29] Davis postulated that the bending of the sensory hairs depolarizes (and alternately hyperpolarizes) the hair-cell membrane by altering the membrane resistance. The hair-cell membrane appears to be "leaky," so that there is a small but constant amount of ionic current flow across the cell membrane. This leakage current is presumably the stimulus for the spontaneous background activity in the associated nerve fiber. Deflection of the hairs in the

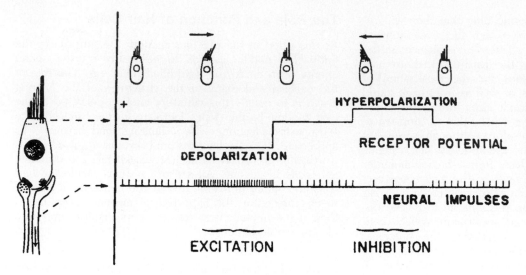

FIGURE 9–4. Relationship of discharge rate of action potentials in the afferent neuron connected to the hair cell in response to different directions of shearing of the hairs. (Adapted from Flock A. Transducing mechanisms in lateral line canal organ receptors. Cold Spring Harbor Symp Quant Biol 30:133, 1965.)

excitatory direction then increases the current flow and causes increased release of transmitter substance at the base of the hair cell (Fig. 9–5).[44] Only over the past couple of decades, however, have the underlying membrane biophysics begun to be understood.[25, 55] Suffice it to say, these details largely represent elaborations of the Davis model, the major tenet of which has reasonably withstood the test of time.[150]

A pivotal component of Davis' theory, specific to the cochlear model of hair cells, was the suggested role of the endolymphatic potential (EP)—the resting potential measured within scala media and generated by the stria vascularis.[147] The EP is viewed as providing an extra force for driving current through the hair cell.[29] Visualizing the EP and the resting membrane potential of the hair cells as batteries, these batteries are wired in series; this essentially doubles the transmembrane potential. The fact that the EP is found in an extracellular space that, additionally, is filled with a high concentration of potassium represents an intriguing physiologic phenomenon and gives rise to a long-standing "chicken and egg" argument: Is the EP a byproduct of the biochemical mechanisms needed to create the high potassium (and low sodium) concentration or vice versa? There is no question, nevertheless, that the presence of a normal EP is requisite for a completely normally functioning hearing organ, as reflected by EP-dependent changes in the cochlear electrical potentials discussed subsequently.[54]

Stimulating Cochlear Hair Cells

Cochlear hair cells have no kinocilia. Still, there are compelling anatomic signs and electrophysiologic evidence that they too are directionally sensitive. A clear morphologic indicator is the pattern of the stereocilia atop the outer hair cells. Maximally excitatory displacements are in the direction of the tallest hairs, which, coincidentally, is toward the base of the characteristic W pattern of the hairs, pointing radially away from the modiolus. The cochlear receptor cells thus appear to be stimulated optimally by radial deflections of their hairs (Fig. 9–6). The most interesting morphologic finding in recent years sup-

porting this notion is provided by the demonstration of a system of fine linkages between successive rows of stereocilia, called *tip links*.[111, 112] There also are cross-links, oriented horizontally (with respect to the hair-bearing surface of the cell); they are believed to stiffen the hair bundle. Tip links, however, are nearly vertically oriented but slant radially (since successive rows of hairs are taller) and are believed to be significant components in the molecular-level transduction process. They appear to act as ionic gates, regulating current flow into the hair cell (as predicted, in effect, by the Davis model). These molecular ionic gates thus have been localized to the tips of the stereocilia.[56]

The problem of stimulating cochlear hair cells is how to cause bending of the hairs (back-and-forth motion) via vibration, an up-and-down motion of the body of the hearing organ. A plausible solution to this puzzle is suggested by Figure 9–6 and relies heavily on the structural relation between the tectorial membrane and the body of the hearing organ.[130] The former pivots effectively at the lip of the internal sulcus, whereas the organ of Corti, supported by the basilar membrane, effectively pivots at or near its attachment to the osseous spiral lamina. Since the two pivot points are displaced in space, up-and-down motion of the organ creates a radial shear between them. Therefore, the geometry of the hearing organ is a critical part of its design.

The stereocilia have been shown to be stiff normally,[43] and, as illustrated in Figure 9–6, the tallest hairs of the outer hair cells clearly impale the underbelly of the tectorial membrane.[57] It thus is fairly clear that coupling between the tectorial membrane and the stereocilia is relatively tight,[84] so the shearing displacements created by the up-and-down motion of the basilar membrane will lead to radial deflection of the hairs. Indeed, these structural factors apparently figure into the entire scheme of the mechanics of the cochlear partition (as discussed later).

The mode of displacement of the stereocilia of the inner hair cells is less obvious and more controversial, beginning with the issue of whether the hairs of inner hair cells are as tightly coupled to the tectorial membrane as those of the outer hair cells. The consensus is that hairs of inner hair cells, at most, just touch the tectorial membrane. But even if these stereocilia are free-standing, it is probable that they would be displaced by the virtual flow of fluid created in the channel between the tectorial membrane and the surface of the organ, which, in turn, would be alternately compressed by the up-and-down-to-shearing-motion transformation.[130] Therefore, the hairs of outer hair cells should be stimulated more directly by basilar membrane displacements, whereas velocity of the basilar membrane theoretically is the effective input of the inner hair cells.[26] Actually, both velocity and displacement responses have been proposed based on electrophysiologic recording from inner hair cells.[176] Neverthe-

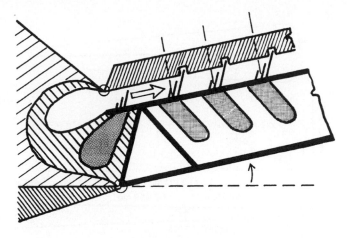

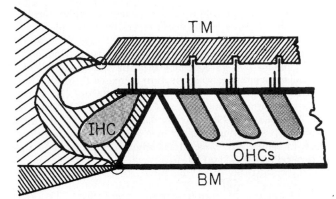

FIGURE 9–6. Schematic representation of the organ of Corti illustrating how shearing displacements of the stereocilia can result from displacement of the basilar membrane. BM, basilar membrane; IHC, inner hair cell; OHCs, outer hair cells; TM, tectorial membrane. (Adapted from Ryan A, Dallos P. Physiology of the cochlea. In Northern JL (ed). Hearing Disorders, 2nd ed. Boston, Little, Brown, 1984, pp 253–266.)

less, the difference in degree of coupling suggests different roles for the two types of hair cells in the mammalian hearing organ. An even more compelling case for such dichotomous roles is made in the section to follow.

Motion of the Basilar Membrane: Cochlear Macromechanics versus Micromechanics

The entire cochlear partition, that is, the Reisner membrane, the organ of Corti, the basilar membrane, and the fluid contained in the cochlear duct, actually move together in response to fluid displacement caused by motion of the stapes. The basis of this motion is illustrated in Figure 9–7A, revealed by the classic experiments of the late Nobel laureate, George von Bekesy,[3] and verified more recently by researchers using highly sophisticated measurement techniques.[120] Noteworthy here is the fact that stapes displacement does not lead to bulk fluid displacement via the helicotrema, except for low-frequency vibrations or static displacements of the stapes.[21] An inward displacement of the stapes thus displaces principally perilymph in scala vestibuli, which pushes down on the cochlear partition, displacing fluid in scala tympani, thus

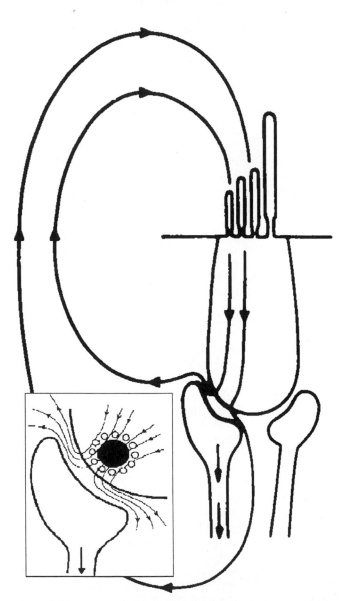

FIGURE 9–5. Schematic representation of excitatory current flow through the hair cell (*left*) and (*inset*) mechanism of chemical transmission between the hair cell and the afferent nerve ending (*right*). (Adapted from Flock A, Jorgensen M, Russell I. The physiology of individual hair cells and their synapses. In Moller AR (ed). Basic Mechanisms in Hearing. New York, Academic Press, 1973, pp 273–306.)

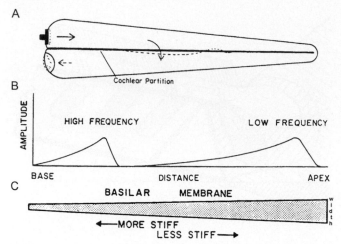

FIGURE 9–7. *A,* Illustration of the manner in which displacement of the stapes leads to displacement of the cochlear partition (the basilar membrane, in particular). *B and C,* Peak displacement of the traveling wave at different frequencies of the sound stimulus and its dependence on the stiffness gradient of the basilar membrane, which in turn increases in width toward the apex. (Based on drawings and data of Bekesy GV. Experiments in Hearing. Translated and edited by EG Wever. New York, McGraw-Hill, 1960; also on data of Rhode WS. An investigation of postmortem cochlear mechanics using the Mössbauer effect. In Moller AR. Basic Mechanisms in Hearing. New York, Academic Press, 1973, pp 39–63.)

pushing out on the round window membrane. The opposite series of events occurs in response to a pull on the stapes. In this manner, the round window membrane vibrates sympathetically with vibration of the stapes.[3]

In Figure 9–7A, the cochlea is uncoiled for illustrative purposes, and the cochlear partition is represented as a single membrane, the mechanics of which are determined extensively (in fact) by the properties of the basilar membrane. Interestingly, a displacement of the cochlear partition, or basilar membrane, to a push on the stapes does not lead to uniform displacement along its entire length. The displacement of the cochlea is regional because of the peculiar wave motion that is excited along the basilar membrane, called the *traveling wave.* The most familiar example of traveling waves are waves observed at the seaside. In the cochlea, the traveling waves build up from the basalward aspect of the basilar membrane and crest as they progress apicalward at or near a place uniquely related to the frequency of the vibration of the stapes. It is at this place that, over several cycles of vibration, the overall maximum displacement will occur and beyond which vibration of the partition decays quickly (Fig. 9–7B), since the basilar membrane is critically damped. It is in this way that frequency is transformed into a place code of excitation. That the central auditory system actually uses this frequency-to-place transformation is considered in a later discussion; in any event, this mechanism provides for efficient coupling of vibratory energy delivered by the stapes to the hearing organ over a broad range of frequencies.

How traveling waves occur is rather involved, but the primary mechanical parameter that governs their behavior is well-established and described simply. As shown by

Figure 9–7C, it is the gradient of stiffness along the basilar membrane that primarily determines the frequency-to-place transformation. Toward the base, the basilar membrane becomes more stiff, whereas it is less stiff near the apex. This change in stiffness, in turn, is due to the change in width radially of the membrane—narrower toward the base and wider toward the apex (Fig. 9–7C). The gradient of stiffness along the entire length of the basilar membrane amounts to about 100:1. Of course, there are many other aspects of the structure of the cochlea and organ of Corti that contribute to the detailed mechanical events of the cochlea. These may include such microstructural features as the change in the number and lengths of the stereocilia, angle of orientation of the W pattern, and the tectorial membrane–stereocilia interface from base to apex.[84]

Based on Bekesy's historic observations, it had been estimated that, at just detectable levels of sound, displacement of the basilar membrane must be on the order of the diameter of the hydrogen atom, if not less. It is difficult to conceive of such minute displacements, let alone how they could be translated into any significant movement of the stereocilia, but linearity had been assumed in the calculation. Evidence of nonlinearities in the auditory system abound in the literature, however, and the nonlinearity of basilar membrane displacement has since become firmly established.[61, 121] This nonlinearity is compressive: proportionally less output (displacement) occurs with increasing input (SPL at the tympanic membrane). Even more intriguing was the ultimate realization that this nonlinearity is an essential characteristic of sound transduction by the hair cells themselves and the discovery of the specific, if not peculiar, role of the outer hair cells. It is the outer hair cells to which the exquisite sensitivity of hearing is now attributed.[24, 25] The outer hair cells appear to serve more as effectors, or motor cells, than receptor cells, serving thus a motoric function.

Actin is recognized as an essential component in muscle cells and their contractile ability, suggesting a similar role in hair cells.[149] This protein is prominent in the structure of hair cells, including the fibrous-like structure of the stereocilia that makes them stiff and nearly brittle.[43] Truly one of the most exciting observations in hearing science since Bekesy's observations was the demonstration and subsequent confirmation that isolated outer hair cells react to an applied electric field by changing in length.[6, 28] Given again the tight coupling of the tectorial membrane to the stereocilia and the inherent stiffness of the latter, the outer hair cells appear to facilitate the vibration of the organ by actively adding energy to this motion. The general principle[24] is that the driving voltage is the outer hair cell's own receptor potentials, which, in turn, activate motor units distributed throughout the outer hair cell's skin, providing positive feedback to the motion of the basilar membrane. This is not unlike how a child being pushed in a swing can facilitate his own motion by pulling and pushing on the rope and kicking out in proper timing with the motion first imparted by his playmate. The child in the swing thus can go faster and higher if he is not just along for the ride. It is clear that outer hair cells are not just along for the ride.

All the engineering invested into this system by evolution was not just for exquisite sensitivity (outer hair cell motoric response) and wide dynamic range (compressive nonlinearity), however. It also was dedicated to selective response to sounds of different frequencies, thereby permitting the system to more precisely represent the frequency content of even the most complex sounds (like speech) and even at low levels of stimulation. The following sections are dedicated to exploring, first, the extent to which peripheral encoding is passed along and within the central auditory system and, second, what further processing might be implicated.

Neural Encoding of the Sound Stimulus and Basic Auditory Information Processing

Frequency

The links between the hair cell receptors and the central auditory system are, naturally, the primary auditory neurons that richly innervate the organ of Corti. The response of an individual neuron can be examined using microelectrodes. Much as one can determine the minimum audibility curve, the response area of an individual primary auditory neuron can be determined.[70] As illustrated in Figure 9–8A, the SPL at which a criterion increase in spike discharge rate (above the spontaneous rate) occurs is measured versus the frequency of stimulation. This minimum audibility curve for neurons is called a tuning function, and, as seen in Figure 9–8A, it has a sharp minimum or "peak" of sensitivity at one frequency—the characteristic frequency (CF). The value of the CF depends on the place of origin of the neuron along the basilar membrane. In other words, nerve fibers originating from more basalward regions will have higher CFs, and those from more apical regions will have lower CFs. It is evident from the tuning function that, while primary auditory neurons are quite selective in their sensitivity, they are not discretely sensitive to a single frequency. Also, the roll-off in sensitivity is much steeper for frequencies above than for frequencies below CF, particularly once the SPL has been increased around 40 dB above that at which CF occurs.

The question that baffled researchers for many years is whether the observed pattern of the tuning function and the degree of frequency selectivity represented by the "tip" region of the tuning function around CF is attributable completely to the cochlear hydromechanical events described earlier, or whether additional filtering is needed between the receptor and nerve cells The answer, as illustrated in Figure 9–8B, is now known to be the former; the peripheral mechanical events provide all the selectivity necessary to account for the tuning curves of primary auditory neurons.[69, 129] Since tuning curves derived from psychoacoustic measures[172] show little increase in selectivity over the tuning functions of primary auditory fibers, it appears that the cochlear mechanics account for the frequency discrimination ability of the auditory system. However, as will be discussed further, some central processing is required for pitch perception and, in general, the processing of complex sounds, such as those created by musical instruments and speech. This is be-

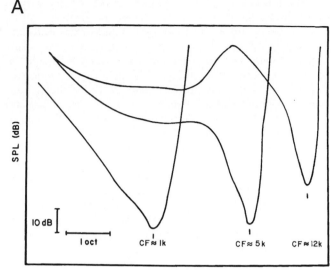

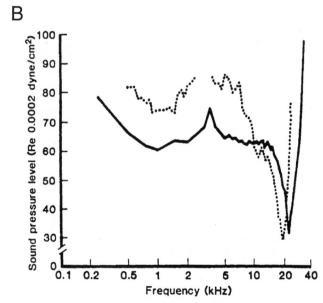

FIGURE 9–8. *A*, Tuning functions illustrating the frequency response of primary auditory neurons (in this case, from a cat). (Based on data of Kiang and Moxon, 1974, as presented by Zwicker, 1974.) *B*, Comparison of tuning functions for the response of the basilar membrane versus a first-order neuron. The solid line is a plot of the sound pressure level required for 3 x 10^{-8} cm basilar membrane displacement at the point of observation in the base of the cat cochlea. The *dashed line* is a single-unit tuning function (obtained in a different animal and in another laboratory by M.C. Liberman); the data shown are from a unit whose characteristic frequency is near that at which the minimum of the mechanical tuning function occurs. (From Khana, SM, Leonard DG. Basilar membrane tuning in the cat cochlea. Science 215:305, 1982.)

cause, for complex sounds, there are correspondingly complex patterns of motion of the basilar membrane arising from overlapping traveling waves excited by the spectral components of the given sound.[65] This creates a correspondingly more complex task for the auditory system than, say, differentiating between discrete tones of different frequency, one presented after the other (i.e., as typical of the classic psychophysical paradigm for determining the frequency difference limen, discussed in the introductory section of this chapter). Nevertheless, if in fact place is the primary cue for frequency encoding, it should be possible to reconstruct the overall pattern of motion of the basilar membrane from activity recorded from neurons throughout the acoustic nerve. Through tedious and meticulous electrophysiologic experiments, such demonstrations indeed can be, and have been, made.[109]

Since the auditory neurons leave the hearing organ in an orderly fashion, the frequency-to-place code is also expected to be reflected in the organization of the central nuclei to which the primary fibers radiate. This organizational scheme, known as tonotopic organization, also has been demonstrated for all major nuclei of the central pathways and the primary auditory cortex.[8, 94, 155] As illustrated schematically in Figure 9–9, this is demonstrated by the systematic progression in CFs of neurons encountered as a recording microelectrode is advanced along an appropriate axis. It is as if the cochlea were mapped along this axis. Since there are multiple nuclei (starting with the dorsal and ventral cochlear nuclei) or major subdivisions of nuclei (for example the posterior and anterior ventral cochlear nuclei), there are actually multiple maps at most, if not all, levels of the ascending of the auditory pathway.

The pervasiveness of tonotopic organization in the auditory system bespeaks the importance of the place code in the encoding and processing of frequency information. Yet it is most certainly not the only cue. The auditory neurons show considerable ability to encode temporal features of the stimulus. As expected from basic neurophysiology, however, individual neurons are capable of

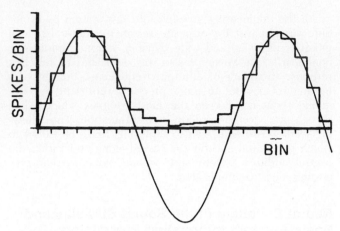

FIGURE 9–10. Periodicity in the pattern of neural discharges reflected by a histogram of the spikes occurring in each time bin over the period observed. (Based on Brugge et al, 1969.)

following each cycle of the stimulus in a one-to-one fashion for only relatively low frequencies. Even the notion of volleying, once believed to be the mechanism for overcoming this limitation,[160] is oversimplified. A more statistical concept is necessary to describe the temporal pattern of discharges, as illustrated in Figure 9–10. Recalling that auditory neurons typically discharge spontaneously and randomly in the absence of external sound stimulation, it is shown here that the probability of discharge at any time reflects the stimulus waveform.[7, 126] This is remarkably different than any scheme, such as volley theory, that supposes precise triggering of discharges during a cycle of stimulation. The "probabilistic pattern" of synchrony is robust, and, in this sense, auditory neurons appear to be able to "synchronize" to the periodicity of the stimulus up to frequencies of about 5000 Hz. Not only is this information available to be extracted by the central system, to provide, for example, a sense of fundamental pitch for complex tones, it is also available for other temporal discrimination–based tasks. One of the most important such functions is binaural sound localization, to which the discussion alluded earlier. For now, it is sufficient to acknowledge that the auditory system is indeed capable of impressively high-frequency and high-speed temporal encoding, as expected of any system capable of encoding and processing of such complex stimuli as speech, particularly in real time.

Intensity

The intensity of the sound is important too, of course, and must be encoded for neural transmission within and for further processing by the central auditory system. At the first level of encoding, the auditory system works like most sensory systems. As illustrated in Figure 9–11A, intensity is translated into rate of spike discharge,[72] so the more intense the stimulus, the more vigorous the rate of discharge of the auditory neuron. There are limits, however. First, the stimulus must be sufficiently strong to cause a significant increase in discharges above the background (spontaneous) rate. A possible exception is at relatively low frequencies, wherein synchronous firing of the

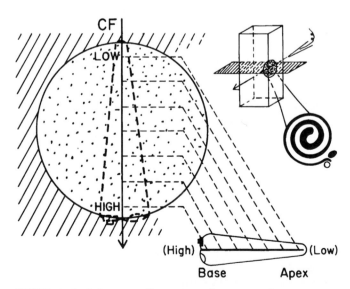

FIGURE 9–9. Schematic illustration of tonotopical organization of a nucleus along the brain stem auditory pathway. A tonal map of the cochlea is projected effectively onto this hypothetical auditory nucleus by virtue of the orderly connection between it and the hair cells along the basilar membrane. Thus, an electrode traversing the path indicated by the arrow records activity from neurons, the characteristic frequencies (CF) of which systematically vary from low to high.

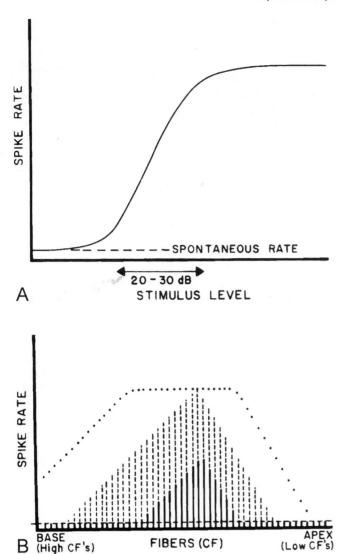

FIGURE 9–11. *A,* Graph of typical spike rate versus intensity function for a first-order neuron monitored at the characteristic frequency. (Based on data from Kiang, 1968.) *B,* Hypothetical histogram of spike rate for an array of fibers. (Modified after Whitfield IC. Electrophysiology of the central auditory pathway. Br Med Bull 12:105, 1956.) The activity of these fibers is shown at only a few sound levels. The *dotted line* denotes saturation of fibers whose characteristic frequencies are near that of the stimulus (i.e., originating near the peak of the traveling wave excited along the basilar membrane).

neurons is most robust; it may be sufficient in this case for there to be only a significant increase in the degree of synchronization without a net increase in discharge rate.[126]

The other limit is that the discharge rate ultimately saturates. At CF for neurons responsible for the most sensitive hearing (i.e., high spontaneous rate fibers), this typically occurs at only 20 to 30 dB above the spontaneous rate. Off CF, this limit moves up to 40 dB or more.[131] The saturation effect raises an interesting question. If the dynamic range of the individual neuron near CF is a mere 20 to 40 dB, how is it that the dynamic range of the auditory system is on the order of 140 dB? The dynamic-range puzzle remains a debated issue. A

workable, although not infallible, solution derives from the idea of off-frequency listening of the neurons, as implied earlier. Therefore, as intensity of the sound increases, a spread of excitation occurs (Fig. 9–11B). Looking across many neurons, the central auditory system thus sees continued growth in the total density of neural discharges, even after neurons tuned to or near the stimulus have saturated.[163] Indeed, the notion of spread of excitation accounts well, for example, for how one tone masks the detection of another.[158] This is known as *spread of masking*.

Listening off-frequency, on the other hand, does not appear to be necessary for intensity discrimination, since nearly the same difference limens are obtained in the presence of stop-band noise,[154] that is, a masker with energy above and below (but not within) the desired frequency range. The density-of-discharge code also does not necessarily address, and indeed may complicate, the problem of preservation of the spectral features of speech and other complex stimuli. There are, nevertheless, low spontaneous rate fibers that have very wide dynamic ranges. Still, it seems likely that the central system must decompress the input from the periphery.[167] The central system perhaps can set some rules for weighing activity from different neurons (based on synchrony of discharges, for example), thereby preserving spectral features in the neural code.[132, 171] Furthermore, there are central neurons, at least in the cortex in primates, that show sharp tuning characteristics for intensity, much as most neurons show selectivity for frequency.[110]

Other Aspects of Central Auditory Processing

Functional Overview of Human Central Auditory Pathways

To some extent, how the central nervous system processes information is suggested by the "wiring" of the central pathways. Much of what is known about the central auditory pathways, as in other parts of the system, draws heavily on experiments in animals, but interspecies differences can be significant. Nevertheless, the detailed wiring of the human central auditory pathways is becoming much better understood.[102] It is beyond the scope of coverage here to delve into a detailed discussion of the neuroanatomy of the central auditory pathways and functions performed at various levels of the central system. A basic flow chart for the human system, on the other hand, can be described for the on-response of neurons to presentation of a simple stimulus such as the acoustic click (a brief broad-band sound, like that produced by the snap of the fingers). This is the stimulus typically used during clinical tests of the auditory brain stem response (see subsequent discussion). The major forward flow of information through the brain stem to produce such a basic response of the system is shown in Figure 9–12. The pathway involving the majority of ascending neurons, as classically described, appears to be crossed (via the trapezoid body and dorsal stria) but tends to bypass the superior olivary complex. Interestingly, only the less populous uncrossed pathway and an even less populated

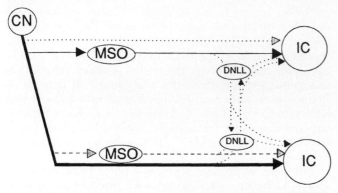

FIGURE 9–12. Schematic of the human brain stem auditory pathways, for input from one ear, as presumably involved in the onset response to an acoustic click. Relative neuronal populations of the primary and secondary crossed and uncrossed pathways are signified by line density. CN, cochlear nuclei; DNLL, dorsal nucleus of the lateral lemnisci; IC, inferior colliculus; MSO, medial superior olive. (Inspired by drawings by Moore, 1987.)

crossed pathway incorporate the superior olivary complex as a kind of way station.

A peculiar feature of the human system is the complexity of the nuclei of the lateral lemnisci. On each side are actually several nuclei, although only the dorsal nucleus seems to be involved in audition. Decussation also occurs at this level. Finally, the inferior colliculi appear to be mandatory synapses for all ascending fibers in the lateral lemnisci. The inferior colliculi thus receive terminations of second-, third-, and perhaps fourth-order neurons. The auditory system thus has robust representation of each ear on both sides of the brain and ample opportunities for crossover of information from one side of the brain stem to the other.

Central Monaural Processing

With the entry of the acoustic nerve into the brain stem, there immediately begins, in effect, a multiplication of the primary auditory neurons. Therefore, as noted earlier, multiple tonotopical maps of the cochlea can be found throughout the auditory system. This may seem redundant, but there also appears to be increased specialization of the response patterns of auditory neurons at the level of the cochlear nuclei and higher centers. Whereas discharge patterns are pretty much the same from one primary neuron to the next, no fewer than five different patterns of discharge have been identified within the cochlear nucleus complex.[71] As suggested by Figure 9–13, these different patterns may be linked to the different morphologic cell types, although the association of discharge pattern with cell morphology may not be exactly as shown, nor as simple. Still, the observed variations in discharge patterns represent one mechanism of feature detection by central auditory neurons. For instance, the discharge pattern of some neurons reflects selective response to stimulus onset (see cell #4 in Fig. 9–13), while others demonstrate varying patterns of response after onset (compare cells #1, 2, 3, and 5, with #1 being primary-like). More centrally, neurons may be

found to be more sensitive to, say, frequency modulation than to the mere onset of the stimulus. Therefore, central neurons appear to be dedicated more to the detection of particular features of the stimulus.[64, 145] Additionally, the circuitry of the central system is elaborated, as manifested by the multiplicity of ordering of neurons in the ascending pathways, branching of ascending fibers, and the formation of feedback loops.

The idea of feedback suggests the presence of a substantial descending or efferent auditory pathway,[51] as is the case. However, it is the lowest part of the system, the olivocochlear system, that is best known.[46, 156] The central system thus possesses, at the very least, some capacity for varying its input sensitivity, namely at the level of the hair cells. Again, there is also the middle-ear muscle reflex system, subserving a similar function, albeit on essentially opposite ends of the dynamic range (and perhaps with different contributions according to frequency region). The two systems are speculated to work symbiotically to improve signal-to-noise ratio,[82] and there is growing support for the notion of a protective role for the efferent system.[86] Although there remains much controversy about the detailed functioning of the descending system, there is no lack of experimental evidence that this system can be activated and, once activated, does something. Direct tetanic electrical stimulation of the efferents, for instance, causes substantial suppression of cochlear-nerve action potentials, particularly at lower levels of stimulation.[76] This is gratifying, since this is the end of the dynamic range over which the outer hair cells operate (without saturation), and it is the outer hair cells that receive direct efferent innervation.[156]

There has long been suspicion that the efferent system could influence frequency discrimination ability via changes in peripheral frequency tuning. However, some of the most compelling recent findings, from a study of single-unit tuning functions in cats with surgically induced cochlear de-efferentation, failed to support such expectations.[81] Continued interest in the auditory efferents, nevertheless, has been stimulated by investigations of otoacoustic emissions; as discussed later, these "echoes" from the inner ear are an expression of an active micromechanical process of the cochlea, attributed to the outer hair cells.[67] The otoacoustic emissions have been found to be suppressed at least somewhat by contralateral stimulation,[18] suggesting involvement of efferent pathways. Although this effect is not nearly as robust as the effects of electrical stimulation, frequency-specific effects and equivalent decibel shifts in otoacoustic emission input-output functions under contralateral suppression suggest that efferent influence may be significant. Clear experimental evidence of a substantial contribution of the efferents to auditory processing, specifically in humans and in everyday listening situations, is still lacking.[135] Yet there are potential clinical interests for tests of efferent function.[153]

Binaural Sound Processing

A truly impressive aspect of central auditory processing is binaural sound localization. Although the majority ascend-

A

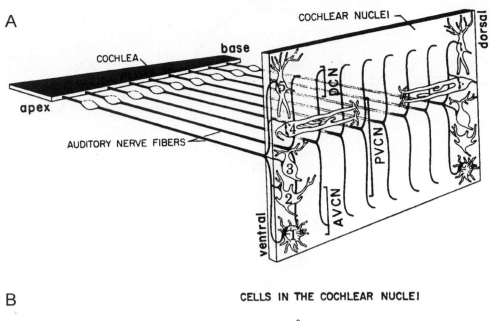

B

CELLS IN THE COCHLEAR NUCLEI

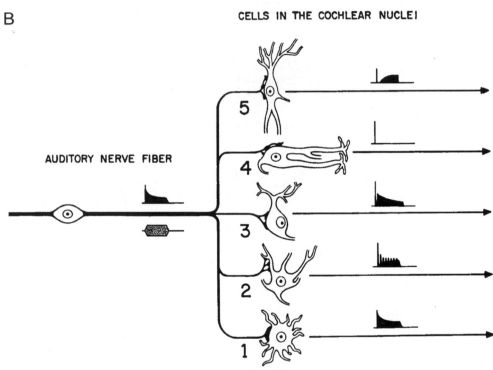

FIGURE 9–13. *A,* Schematic representation of connections between the peripheral auditory system and the cochlear nuclei. AVCN, anterior ventral cochlear nucleus; DCN, dorsal cochlear nucleus; PVCN, posterior ventral cochlear nuclei. Some of the complexity of the morphology of the second-order neurons is indicated (five different types of neurons illustrated). *B,* Possible relation between cell types and discharge patterns as reflected in post-stimulus time histograms. Response types are as follows: 1, primary-like; 2, "chopper"; 3, primary-like with notch; 4, "on"; and 5, "pauser." (From Kiang NY-S. Stimulus representation in the discharge patterns of auditory neurons. In Eagles EL. The Nervous System. Vol. 3: Human Communication and Its Disorders. New York, Raven Press, 1975, pp 81–96.)

ing auditory pathway is crossed, the ipsilateral ascending pathway is substantial.[52] With decussation of fibers at several levels of the central system, it is clear that there must be considerable interaction of information from the two ears. Nerve-cell specialization or "wiring" also is encountered that facilitates the comparator functions underlying binaural processing.[13, 14, 40, 59, 89, 103, 127] There are neurons at the levels of the superior olive and the inferior colliculus, for example, that receive inputs from both ears and may be excited by binaural stimuli while being inhibited by monaural stimuli. Interestingly, there is evidence that the cochlear nuclei may also play a role in binaural processing, namely via descending pathway connections from the superior olivary complex or by virtue of inherent properties of neurons of the dorsal cochlear nucleus, or

both. This neural circuitry may help to suppress echoes that could degrade precision of sound localization.[62]

Although the functional anatomy may be rather involved, the basic cues for binaural sound localization[96, 105] are evident, as in effect suggested earlier in this chapter. To elaborate, these cues are more easily appreciated from observations on the related phenomenon of binaural lateralization.[114] Lateralization is generally demonstrated via presentation of a sound to the two ears individually, namely via earphones. Despite this discrete mode of stimulating the two ears, the impression is that the sounds are fused and that this fused image is located somewhere inside the head between the two ears. (The sound image is generally externalized with loud-speaker presentation.) This is essentially the same paradigm used by the physi-

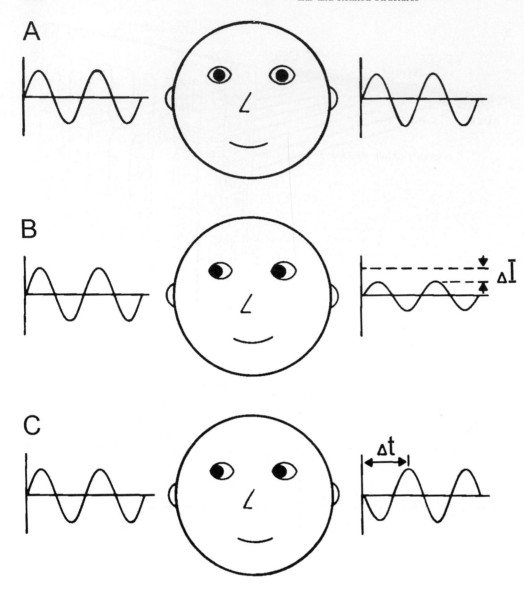

FIGURE 9–14. Illustration of the binaural lateralization of the sound image obtained when the same frequency tone is presented via earphones at the same intensity and time/phase (*A*), at different intensities (ΔI) (*B*), and at different times/phases (Δt) (*C*) to the two ears.

cian performing the Weber test with the tuning fork: The patient is asked to determine from which side of the head the sound seems to come. Normally, the tuning fork applied somewhere to the skull at midline stimulates the two ears at the same intensity, frequency, and phase. As illustrated in Figure 9–14, this condition leads to the perception of a single sound coming from the center of the head. With either a larger amplitude or leading phase (or earlier arrival in time) of the sound to one ear, the sound image is lateralized toward that ear. A pathologic lesion in one ear can have the same effect, hence the perception of lateralization during the Weber test. The binaural system is quite sensitive to interaural time and intensity disparities.

In a person listening to sounds from the environment, similar disparities are created, again, by the separation of the two ears and acoustic effects of the outer ear and head. As noted earlier and illustrated by Figure 9–15A, the time and intensity cues each serve different frequency ranges in sound localization.[96] To iterate, at lower frequencies, the diameter of the head is less than the wavelengths of the sound waves, so diffraction occurs,[75] scat-

tering the sound wave around the head. Consequently, intensity of the sound at the two ears is not appreciably different, regardless of which way the head is turned (re: direction of the sound source). Nevertheless, it takes longer for the sound to reach the ear farthest from the sound source, so a temporal disparity is created. With increasing frequency, the synchrony of discharge of auditory neurons diminishes, but then diffraction no longer occurs (Fig. 9–15B). Now, the head shadows the ear farthest from the sound source—an intensity disparity is created. For complex sounds (typical of environmental sounds), temporal cues are actually available even for sounds with predominantly high-frequency energy, namely by virtue of interaural delays in the envelopes of amplitude modulations of these sounds.[170] Such amplitude modulations are well represented in the temporal code.[99]

This is not to say that sound localization is entirely dependent on binaural processing. Monaural localization is possible but is much less precise. Monaural localization is, in part, an adaptation of intensity discrimination and takes advantage of the head shadow effect. Monaural localization may also take advantage of mechanisms under-

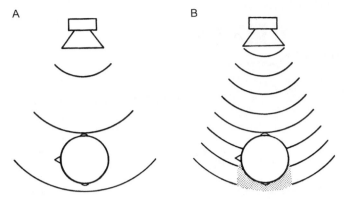

FIGURE 9–15. Simplified representation of the acoustic effects of the head on sound waves with wavelengths greater than the head diameter (*A*), wherein diffraction occurs, and sound waves with shorter wavelengths (*B*), wherein the head casts a "shadow."

lying the auditory system's ability to localize sounds at different elevations, even in the midsagittal plane. Here the auricle (again) makes a special contribution.[10] Its convolutions apparently create subtle changes in the high-frequency sound spectrum as the sound source is raised or lowered or the head is tilted. The importance of the mobility of the head also must not be underestimated in sound localization; the head may be turned to null out binaural differences, to allow the listener to "zero in" on a sound.

The emphasis here on binaural sound localization, furthermore, is not meant to imply that binaural processing is singularly dedicated to this function. Binaural processing also facilitates the detection and discrimination of sounds in a background of noise,[91] as well as selective attention.[15] Indeed, one of the most common complaints of unilaterally hearing impaired individuals and in hearing impaired individuals who wear only one hearing aid is difficulty in understanding speech in noisy places, at meetings, or in other situations in which there are competing messages.

Cortical Processing

Much, if not all, of the processing discussed can be and is likely to be accomplished at the brain stem level of the central auditory system. Indeed, several of the basic auditory abilities appear to be attributable to subcortical processing. It has been shown, for example, that auditory decorticate animals are capable of detecting the presence of sound and changes in intensity, frequency, and location of sound.[12, 14, 53, 88, 105] So impressive are the capabilities of brain stem auditory processing that one may wonder just what, if any, of the auditory abilities require cortical processing. There is, of course, no doubt of the necessity of cortical processing for cognition and deciphering speech information which, in turn, doubtlessly requires more than the primary auditory cortex, per se. Additionally, auditory decorticate animals have been found to be incapable of distinguishing between tonal patterns (wherein the same tones are included in the different patterns presented), discriminating changes in sound duration,

and, in general, discriminating between stimulus conditions that involve no net change in neural activity.[105] Although such animals show amazing abilities to compensate, they appear not to truly localize sound in space. This requires an internal map of auditory space,[77] which is apparently relegated to the cortex.[4]

The neuroanatomic and neurophysiologic bases for cortical auditory processing are many, but the gross manifestations are tonotopical organization over the surface of the primary auditory cortex[94, 125, 168] and perhaps columnar organization through different layers.[1, 45, 58, 66] The former is perhaps a mere byproduct of the orderly arrangement of neurons in the ascending pathway. Still, this system should serve to pre-sort information according to frequency. Columnar organization, which is known better in other sensory systems, is perhaps the basis for the more advanced processing for which the cortex is responsible. At the cortex, one also expects even further specialization in the response of the neurons, and it is through the layers of the cortex that the morphologic variants in the cells and the intracellular circuits are found that would be expected, intuitively, to be required for this advanced processing.

Objective Assessment of Auditory Function: Physiologic-Acoustic Bases

Throughout this overview of the auditory system, great reliance has been placed on information obtained from single-unit recordings in infrahuman species, that is, bioelectrical recordings made utilizing microelectrodes capable of picking up activity from just outside or even inside single cells. However, there are also a number of gross or compound potentials that can be recorded in the auditory system; one of these, the endolymphatic potential, was already mentioned. There are also various stimulus-related potentials. Much more surprising is the appearance of weak, but readily measurable, echo-like sounds appearing in the ear canal but originating from the cochlea. These sound-evoked responses represent the activity of many cells (receptor or neural) and have provided valuable indices of end-organ, eighth-nerve, and central pathway activation for basic research of auditory function. Most have also proven to be recordable, at least to some extent, in humans and to have clinical utility. Details of such clinical applications and methods are presented in other chapters of this text; presented here are underlying principles of the phenomena and such applications and methods.

Electrocochleography

The stimulus-related electrical potentials of the organ of Corti and the acoustic nerve make up the electric response whose recorded waveform has been called the electrocochleogram. First, there are two cochlear potentials that arise from hair-cell receptor potentials, cochlear microphonics (CM), and summating potentials,[22] as shown in Fig. 9–16. The CM has a waveform that mimics the waveform of the sound stimulus. Therefore, if the stimulus is a tone burst, the CM will appear as a sinusoidal

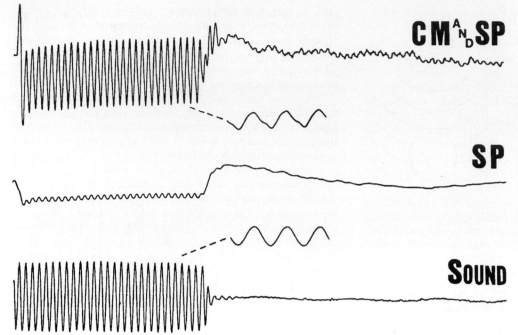

FIGURE 9–16. Tracings from recordings of the cochlear microphonic (CM) and summating potential (SP) along with the output of the monitoring microphone (SOUND). *Insets* show details of tracings via an expanded time-base. (From Durrant JD [1981]. Auditory physiology and an auditory physiologist's view of tinnitus. J Laryngol Otol Suppl 4:21, 1981.)

pulse. However, the CM waveform will often appear to be offset; the zero axis will be displaced above or below the baseline of the recording (Fig. 9–16). If the CM is stripped away via low-pass filtering or averaging with phase cancellation, this offset can be isolated. This is the summating potential—a direct current pulse in response to tone bursts. The CM and summating potential are products of mechanoelectrical transduction of the hair cells, with the summating potential being a direct mani-

festation of the hair cells' characteristic nonlinearity.[22] A small component of the summating potential also may arise from the dendrites of the primary auditory neurons, reflecting generator potentials.[23] The CM and summating potential are recordable in the cochlear fluid spaces, on the round window, and at remote extracochlear sites (such as on the eardrum), so they are clearly extracellular manifestations of the unit receptor potentials of many stimulated cells. The unit potentials, in turn, are distrib-

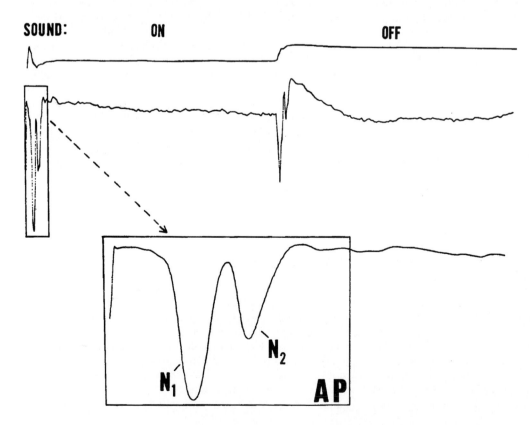

FIGURE 9–17. Recording of the whole-nerve action potential (AP). *Inset*: time-base expanded to illustrate major component waves of the action potential (N_1 and N_2). The top trace is actually the summating potential, used here to indicate exactly when the stimulus has been turned on and off at the level of the hair-cell transducer (thus eliminating inherent time delays due to propagation of sound down the ear canal and of the traveling wave in the cochlea). (From Durrant JD. Auditory physiology and an auditory physiologist's view of tinnitus. J Laryngol Otol Suppl 4:21, 1981.)

uted through the elaborate electroanatomy of the cochlea. The genesis of these grossly recorded potentials thus is somewhat complex, yet they provide useful indices of the hydromechanical events of the cochlea and the integrity of the hair cells.[22, 31]

The other component of the electrocochleogram is the whole-nerve action potential. This is the compound action potential of the acoustic nerve in response to the onset and, to a lesser degree, off-set of a sound stimulus, as shown in Figure 9–17. Although primary auditory neurons discharge repeatedly in the presence of sound, it is at the onset of sound that they respond most vigorously (see Fig. 9–13) and to which discharges are most synchronized. In general, compound nerve action potentials are proportional to the number of neurons activated.[63] Although tone-bursts and other means of stimulation can be used to derive frequency-specific information from the action potential,[27] the most robust responses tend to be obtained with the broad-spectrum transient known as the *click* (again, a sound similar to that produced by a snap of the fingers). Nevertheless, the action potential tends to represent excitation with a bias toward the basalward fiber populations where synchronization is best.[71] The action potential, then, provides an indication of the pattern of excitation of the auditory neurons. Like the cochlear receptor potentials, the action potential also can be recorded from inside or outside of the cochlea.

Recording the action potential and other components of the electrocochleogram at extracochlear sites accessible clinically requires appropriate electrodes, methods, and signal processing using computer-based signal averaging. For greatest sensitivity, the transtympanic method is preferred,[2] whereby a needle electrode is pushed through the eardrum with its tip resting on the promontory. However, this method generally requires local anesthesia or, in children and some adults, general anesthesia. On the other hand, with an acceptable loss of sensitivity for most purposes, it is possible to obtain electrocochleograms of reasonable quality from the surface of the tympanic membrane[144] or the surface of the skin of the external auditory meatus.[16] However, the farther away from the eardrum, the poorer the sensitivity and quality of the recording, since the signal diminishes systematically with distance from the cochlea while the noise level is essentially independent of site. The action potential also is reasonably prominent (at least in normally hearing subjects or subjects with only mild hearing loss) in surface recordings, namely from the ear lobe or mastoid, and represents the front end of the auditory brain stem response, to be discussed momentarily. The choice among the various methods is a matter of what information is being sought and cost-benefit considerations (i.e., the need to know) versus potential risks, should sedation or anesthesia be required.

Otoacoustic Emissions

In a study of distortion in the ear, Bekesy[3] demonstrated more than half a century ago that some sound energy must be emitted from the cochlea back into the external meatus. At about the same time, Gold[67] suggested an active model of hair cell transduction that would lead to the feedback of sound from the inner ear. It is only relatively recently, however, that otoacoustic emissions (OAEs) actually have been demonstrated.[67] They now have been studied extensively[118] and have gained extensive clinical interest for purposes of objective assessment of peripheral sensitivity.[85, 123] Although not an electrophysiologic response per se, OAE measurement is an evoked response method and objective test of auditory function, providing clear signs of the reaction of the hearing organ to sound. The OAEs are intriguing in particular as they appear to reflect the excitation of an active micromechanical process, now recognized as the motile response of outer hair cells discussed earlier. That the OAEs really do come from the interior of the cochlea is suggested by several factors: (1) the acoustic response has a latency and persists beyond mere reflections off the eardrum; (2) OAEs are vulnerable to adverse metabolic conditions; (3) they are absent in cases of partial or complete cochlear deafness (and in dummy/test cavities simulating the volume of the ear canal); (4) they grow nonlinearly with stimulus level.

The OAEs are measured using miniature transducers for sound generation and measurement in the ear canal, together with computer signal processing techniques similar to the measurement of evoked electrical responses. Figure 9–18 illustrates the click-evoked OAE (one of several OAE measures available). Although the click stimulus facilitates observation of the cochlear echo and is a useful clinical and screening test paradigm, OAEs can be elicited by brief tone bursts as well as continuous sounds (the latter being known as *stimulus frequency emissions*). Distortion products in the OAE, as implied by Bekesy's observations, also can be recorded. Two frequency primaries are presented, f_1 and f_2. The component of broadest research and clinical interest currently is the cubic distortion product whose frequency is equal to $2f_1 - f_2$. The keen interest in this particular distortion product OAE is attributable to two facts: the cubic distortion product tends to be the most robust overall and it is pervasive in other auditory measures (e.g., the easiest product to hear out in psychoacoustic experiments).

An even more intriguing OAE from a theoretical perspective, although of little apparent clinical value, is the spontaneous OAE. These are OAEs that occur in the absence of external stimulation. Many normally hearing adults and most newborns produce measurable spontaneous OAEs, and they may appear at one to five or more frequencies, although they are typically found in the midrange of hearing (namely, where the middle ear is most efficient).

Far-Field and Cortical Evoked Potentials

The excitation of the whole-nerve action potential by an abrupt sound actually initiates a series of electrical waves reflecting a relatively long-lasting response of the nervous system.[113] Within the first few milliseconds or so after stimulus onset, the action potentials of the primary auditory neurons are triggered and propagate through the nerve trunk to the cochlear nuclei. Since the nerve trunk

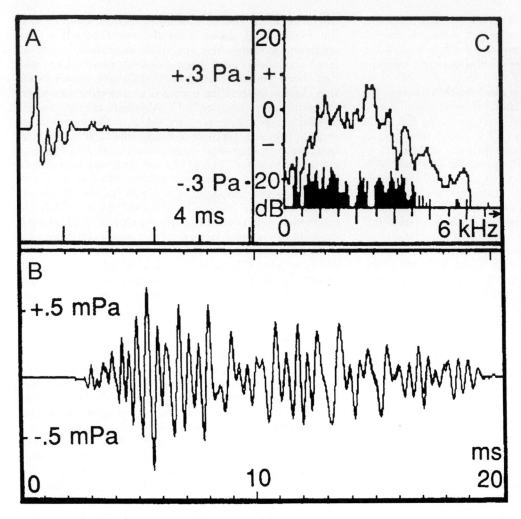

FIGURE 9–18. Transient evoked otoacoustic emission recording obtained in an ear of a 7.5-year-old girl with entirely normal hearing (specifically, pure-tone audiometric thresholds of 5 dB hearing level or better). *A*, Amplitude scale set to permit examination of the input (click) stimulus; the stimulus was 83 dB sound pressure level (peak equivalent). *B*, Time window extended, sensitivity increased, and initial 4 msec of trace zeroed (blanking out input stimulus) to favor detailed inspection of the otoacoustic emission itself; there are actually two tracings overlaid, demonstrating the outstanding reproducibility of the response in this subject. (The stimulus was presented in the nonlinear mode, a paradigm that ensures negligible contribution of stimulus artifact). *C*, Spectra of the response versus background noise (*black area*), demonstrating the excellent signal-to-noise ratio in this case. (Data courtesy of Diane Sabo, Ph.D., University of Pittsburgh, Pittsburgh, Pennsylvania.)

is insulated well (electrically) within the internal auditory meatus, the electrical manifestations of this initial bioelectrical activity, as seen from surface electrodes, are two waves—one essentially from the distal end and the other from the proximal end of the nerve.[100] Then the second and higher order neurons are excited. From here, the picture gets increasingly cloudy and controversial as to which structures, specifically, are most responsible for which bumps in the waveform of the potential. At least three, but perhaps four or five, waves are presumed to arise sequentially from generators in the brain stem auditory pathways,[9, 101] with waves III through V reflecting activity from the brain stem at levels from the cochlear nuclei to the inferior colliculus.[37, 102] Therefore, whereas the time difference between the occurrence of the first and third waves reflects peripheral propagation of action potentials, the interval between the third and fifth waves reflects transmission through the pontine-level pathways.

The components of the electrocochleogram and the above-mentioned brain stem potentials constitute the class of auditory evoked potentials known as short-latency potentials, or the fast components. The whole-nerve action potential and brain stem potentials thus collectively constitute the auditory brain stem response (ABR), which occurs approximately within the first 10 msec of stimulus onset (depending on the intensity and spectrum of the stimulus, maturation, and other factors). As more time is permitted between stimuli, still other potentials emerge. The time window of approximately 10 to 50 msec contains the middle latency response (Fig. 9–19). The components of the middle latency response arise from higher auditory brain stem centers and primary auditory cortex.[113] Lastly, there are the long-latency potentials, which are cortical in origin.[119] The P_1-N_2 components demarcate what has traditionally been called the auditory evoked potential, but the long-latency responses include still other components, such as the mismatch negativity, cognitive potential (or P300), contingent negative variation, sustained, and steady-state potentials. The long-latency potentials presumably reflect activity of much more than primary auditory cortex and appear to reflect discriminatory, cognitive, and integrative processing.[116, 133] All of these potentials can be recorded from common electrodes placed on the surface of the scalp (for instance, one electrode on the mastoid and the other at the vertex). Analysis filter and time windows, recording montage, and stimulus parameters or paradigms are varied to emphasize one class of potentials or response components over the other. The shortest latency potentials are the smallest and require the most stimulus repetitions to achieve enough signal-to-noise enhancement via signal averaging to extract them from the background noise. Here too, which

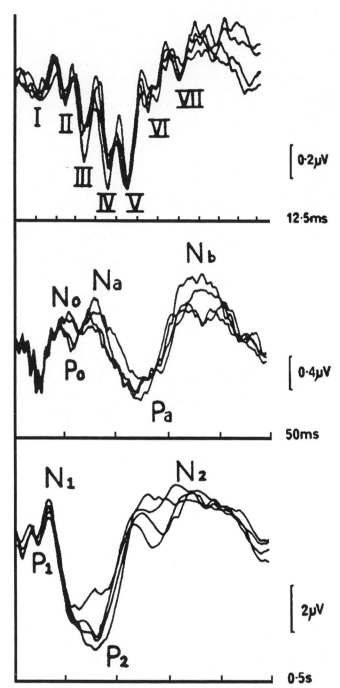

FIGURE 9–19. Components of the auditory evoked response recorded with scalp electrodes from a human subject, elicited by an acoustic click (presented 60 dB above the subject's behaviorally determined threshold). Tracings obtained in four different trials are overlaid to demonstrate repeatability of the responses. *Top*, Short-latency or brain stem components. *Middle*, Middle latency components. *Bottom*, Late or long-latency (cortical) components. Major wavelets are labelled according to convention. Note: vertex-positive voltages are plotted in the downward direction, for consistency between tracings here and in Figure 9–18; this is opposite to the most popular convention but is merely a matter of how the electrodes are connected to the recording amplifier. (From Picton TW, Hillyard SA, Krausz HI, Galambos R. Human auditory evoked potentials. I: Evaluation of components. EEG Clin Neurophysiol 36:179, 1974.)

potentials are recorded and the techniques used are matters of what information is desired and the need to know. Additionally, since the long-latency potentials can be quite sensitive to level of arousal, and even state of attention,[136] the clinical application of these potentials tends to be more restricted than that of the shorter-latency potentials, which, in turn, are relatively unaffected by level of arousal (from comatose to awake and alert) or by most sedatives or anesthesias, particularly the eighth nerve and brain stem components.

Fundamentals of Clinical Utility

Nearly all auditory evoked potentials (with suitable recording and processing methods) are traceable to or near the limits of hearing, as determined by conventional audiometry (namely, using behavioral methods), making them of keen interest for objective audiometry. Further interest derives from their inherent value in assessment of neurologic integrity. Starting from the top and working down the auditory pathways, the long-latency or cortical auditory evoked potentials have been known for decades and, indeed, have commanded interest from otologists, neurologists, audiologists, psychologists, and psychiatrists. However, interests in the long-latency responses waned considerably among otolaryngologists and audiologists during the 1970s, the period of research and development of short-latency potential measurement using surface-recording methods. Nevertheless, the P300 has attracted interest back to the long-latency time frame and, more recently, much excitement has developed regarding a component that occurs just before the P300, known as the mismatched negativity. Like the P300, the mismatched negativity is demonstrated by comparing averages involving epochs recorded with infrequently versus frequently occurring stimuli. The mismatched negativity, however, can be elicited in inattentive subjects and holds promise as the basis for objective assessment of central auditory function in pediatric as well as adult subjects, particularly precognitive discrimination processing of complex stimuli such as speech.[79, 80]

The middle latency responses also have grown in interest and may be used singly or in conjunction with ABR evaluations. These potentials may provide the basis for a more comprehensive analysis of auditory function (than ABR alone) since, at least, some components of the middle latency response appear to arise from the primary auditory cortex. The middle latency response also is attractive for objective audiometry as an adjunct to ABR-based testing. The middle latency response exhibits reasonably good responsivity to low-frequency stimuli,[78, 93] whereas ABRs elicited by low-frequency stimuli are much less robust.

By far the greatest interest in evoked potentials for otologic, neurotologic, and audiologic clinical applications, nevertheless, has been focused on the ABR.[34, 38, 48] Within a decade of the first description of the ABR in the literature, ABR evaluations became a routine offering of audiology clinics, otology and neurology practices, and electroencephalography laboratories. Evaluations of the ABR have proven valuable in several areas:

- Determination of the integrity of the auditory nerve and brain stem to detect and distinguish between cochlear and retrocochlear lesions (site-of-lesion testing)

- Screening for possible hearing defects in newborns

- Estimating hearing thresholds in pediatric and other difficult-to-test patients

- Intraoperative monitoring during otologic or neurosurgery

- Screening/monitoring brain stem function in critically ill or comatose patients, including evaluations of brain death

While the ABR is a sensitive indicator of auditory nerve and brain stem pathologic conditions[47, 138, 142] and while it indeed can be used to estimate hearing sensitivity,[92] ABR evaluations are not tests of hearing per se. Objective audiometry thus should not be viewed as equivalent to or a replacement for behavioral audiometry. The stimuli often used are brief transients, such as clicks and tone pips (perhaps of 3 msec duration or less), unlike the relative long-duration tone bursts used in audiometry. More importantly, a normal ABR finding does not guarantee hearing, and not all normally hearing subjects have normal ABR findings. The ABR certainly reflects some aspects of auditory processing but is not necessarily dependent on the same neural events that are essential for perception or the auditory capabilities discussed earlier.[48] Indeed, as a compound neural potential, the ABR merely reflects the most robust and the most redundant feature of auditory neuronal response—stimulus onset (as noted earlier).

During the early development of the ABR evaluation as a clinical tool, clinical electrocochleography also was vying for acceptance as a routine test procedure. Although interest in electrocochleography has waxed and waned in the United States, noninvasive electrocochleography is certainly a useful supplement to the ABR evaluation, to improve the pick-up of the auditory nerve component.[33] Additionally, the summating potential is known to be especially sensitive to cochlear hydrops or Meniere disease[17] and may be useful in the assessment of fistulas.[11] Auditory neuropathy,[143] in effect, has given electrocochleography another surge of clinical interest, as it may be useful in more clearly defining this recently described cause. On the other hand, combined OAE and ABR testing is helpful in the evaluation of many such cases or suspected cases, as well as other retrocochlear lesions,[122] and is technically less demanding.

The OAEs, again, are quite sensitive to pathologic lesions of the organ of Corti and are yet another evoked response traceable to the limits of hearing. So, the level of clinical interest that OAEs now command is well justified. All methods of OAE measurement are viable candidates for applications in newborn screening, but current interests remain focused on transient and distortion-product OAE testing. The evoked OAE methods also permit the acquisition of frequency-specific information, suggesting audiometric-like applications. This is a perceived strength of distortion product OAE assessment, in particular.

The analysis of distortion product OAEs naturally produces an audiometric graph commonly called the DP-gram (Fig. 9–20). Unfortunately, recent clinical research has not boded well for hearing loss prediction based on OAE measurement. The major limitation of OAE measurement for purposes of objective audiometry lies in the fundamental fact that outer hair cells are the generators of OAEs (Trautwain, et al. 199); outer hair cells account for only the first 40 dB or so of the dynamic range of hearing, as alluded to earlier. Consequently, for the quantitative assessment of cochlear impairment, the test is inherently limited to hearing losses of merely subclinical and mild degrees, although mere detection of more severe losses is clearly possible. For hearing screening, therefore, this limitation is not a problem.

A global problem, however, is the limited usable frequency range. This limitation is due, first, to the noise floor of the analysis, which rises systematically with decreasing frequency, typically obscuring the response starting somewhere below 1 kHz (see Fig. 9–20). Lastly, since OAEs truly are sounds conducted out of the inner ear, the status of the middle ear is an important and

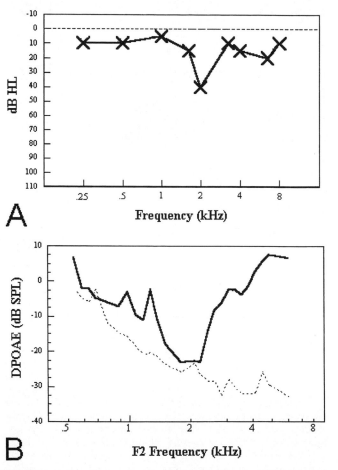

FIGURE 9–20. Audiogram (A), demonstrating a mild, punctate cochlear loss, and corresponding DP-gram (B), demonstrating the excellent sensitivity of otoacoustic emissions to such fine hearing losses. *Solid line*, distortion product otoacoustic emission $(2f_1 - f_2)$; *dotted line*, noise floor of recording $(f_2/f_1 = 1.2, P_2 = P_1 = 65$ dB sound pressure level).

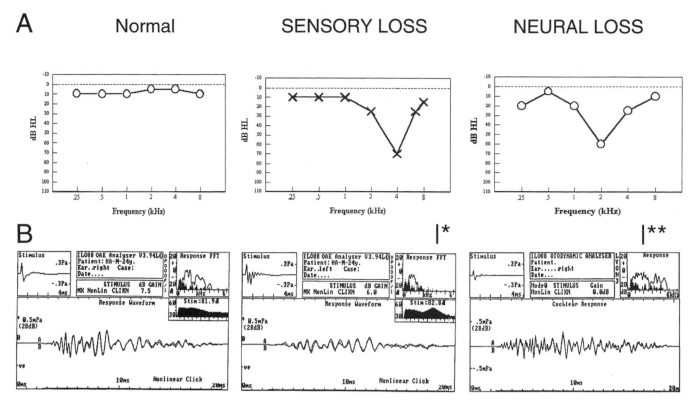

FIGURE 9–21. Audiograms (*A*) and click-evoked otoacoustic emission results (*B*) for right (normal) and left (sensory loss) ears in a case of unilateral acoustic trauma and for a case of acoustic tumor of the right ear (neural loss). In the sensory loss case, the spectrum (response window) shows no measurable emission in the frequency region of the hearing loss,* in contrast to the neural loss case, which shows robust emissions in the vicinity of the hearing loss.** (Nonlinear click mode data courtesy of Lionel Collet, M.D., Ph.D., Claude Bernard University, Lyon, France.)

potentially confounding variable.[87] For purposes of screening auditory pathologic conditions, this too is not necessarily a limitation, but it is likely to account for some false-positive findings in newborn screening, i.e., relative to the true incidence of congenital sensorineural hearing losses.

Nevertheless, OAE assessment has received wide interest and endorsement for newborn screening and other clinical applications. Screening of OAEs is generally considered to be a more efficient test than ABR screening, an important consideration for universal newborn screening. Large-scale studies have recently been completed and are providing information by which practical programs may be implemented.[90, 117] Screening OAEs in older children, for purposes of school screenings, is also being considered.[107]

Finally, OAE testing certainly can be useful in qualitatively corroborating hearing loss, particularly in the differential diagnosis of peripheral versus central disorders, as alluded to earlier.[122] This is illustrated by clinical data presented in Figure 9–21, which serve also to summarize various points discussed in foregoing paragraphs. Here, click-evoked transient OAEs recorded in the normal ear of a patient and in the opposite ear present a 4-kHz noise notch audiometrically. This is most certainly a case of end-organ pathology (definite history of acoustic trauma). In contrast are the OAE findings in one ear of

another patient with a similarly notched audiogram, although occurring an octave lower. This case proved to be one of retrocochlear lesion due to an acoustic tumor. The lattermost findings, however, are entirely typical of the effects of acoustic tumors, which can involve concurrent end-organ and eighth-nerve pathologic lesions, since such tumors may compress both the nerve and the cochlear blood supply.[35, 148] Nevertheless, OAE testing paired with electrophysiologic methods can be extremely valuable in teasing out the relative contributions of sensory and neural components of hearing loss.[122] Here, the inherent frequency specificity of the DP-gram is particularly useful. In addition to the obvious importance of detecting and confirming central pathologic conditions, it is important to confirm the peripheral component. This is a matter not only of differential diagnosis and medical treatment or other management vis-a-vis the central lesion but also of medical treatment and nonmedical therapeutic approaches relevant to the end-organ or more peripheral component of the hearing loss, such as hearing-aid fitting.

In summary, it is now technically feasible to record objective indicators of auditory function at essentially any level of the auditory system using noninvasive techniques. Otoacoustic emissions provide yet another measure of auditory function, particularly the most sensitive side of the auditory response area. Together with emittance test methods—tests of middle ear function—the clinician has at his or her disposal an incredible armamentarium of objective test methods. Such tests can be employed to supplement information from more traditional tests or to provide an indication of the functional status of the auditory system when more traditional methods are unsuccessful or simply not applicable. Modern technology and accompanying computer economics have made these test procedures broadly accessible, nearly fool-proof, and, therefore, alluring. Such methods must be applied with a solid foundation of knowledge of auditory function, however; the overall goal of this chapter was to provide such background. Only with sufficient understanding of the workings of the auditory system can inappropriate test use and interpretation be avoided.

Acknowledgment

The author wishes to express his appreciation to his friend and associate, Jean H. Lovrinic, Ph.D., for her helpful comments and criticisms of this chapter in earlier editions. Revision of this chapter for the current edition was supported in part by the Claude Bernard University and the Rhone-Alps Region, Lyon, France.

SELECTED REFERENCES

Durrant JD, Lovrinic JH. Bases of Hearing Science, 3rd ed. Baltimore, Williams & Wilkins, 1995.

> *Comprehensive introductory text providing not only more depth of coverage of physiologic acoustics and psychoacoustics, as summarized herein, but also underlying fundamentals from physics/acoustics and neurophysiology.*

Geisler CD. From Sound to Synapse. New York, Oxford University Press, 1998.

> *In-depth treatise on the physiology of hearing, particularly the initial stages of encoding from outer ear to brain stem, including a thorough but user-friendly treatment of the concept of nonlinearity and its importance in auditory processing.*

Haggard MP, Evans EF (eds). Hearing. Br Med Bull 43:775, 1987.

> *Collection of brief but information-packed reviews of topics in hearing, nearly half of which deal specifically with physiologic acoustics. Although now more than a decade old, the articles in this publication reflect the revolution of knowledge forming the basis of current understanding of auditory function.*

REFERENCES

1. Abeles M, Goldstein MH Jr. Functional architecture in cat primary auditory cortex: columnar organization and organization according to depth. J Neurophysiol 33:172, 1970.
2. Aran JM, Portmann M. Electrocochleography in adults and children: electrophysiological study of the peripheral receptor. Audiology 11:77, 1972.
3. von Bekesy G. Experiments in Hearing. Translated and edited by Wever EG. New York, McGraw Hill, 1960.
4. Benson DA, Hienz RD, Goldstein MH. Single-unit activity in the auditory cortex of monkeys actively localizing sound sources: spatial tuning and behavioral dependency. Brain Res 219:249, 1981.
5. Borg E, Zakrisson JE. The activity of the stapedius muscle in man during vocalization. Acta Otolaryngol (Stockh) 79:325, 1975.
6. Brownell WE, Bader CR, Bertrand D, de Ribaupierre Y. Evoked mechanical responses of isolated cochlear outer hair cells. Science 227:194, 1985.
7. Brugge JF, Anderson DJ, Hind JE, Rose JE. Time structure of discharges in single auditory nerve fibers of the squirrel monkey in response to complex periodic sounds. J Neurophysiol 32:386, 1969.
8. Brugge JF, Geisler CD. Auditory mechanisms of the lower brainstem. Annu Rev Neurosci 1:363, 1978.
9. Buchwald JS, Huang CM. Farfield acoustic response: origins in the cat. Science 189:382, 1975.
10. Butler RA, Helwig CC. The spatial attributes of stimulus frequency in the median sagittal plane and their role in sound localization. Am J Otolaryngol 4:165, 1983.
11. Campbell KC, Parnes L. Electrocochleographic recordings in chronic and healed perilymphatic fistula. J Otolaryngol 21:213, 1992.
12. Canford JL. Auditory cortex lesions and interaural intensity and phase-angle discrimination in cats. J Neurophysiol 42:1518, 1979.
13. Casseday JH, Covey E. Central auditory pathways in directional hearing. In Yost WA, Gourevitch G (eds). Directional Hearing. New York, Springer-Verlag, 1987, p 109.
14. Casseday JH, Neff WD. Auditory localization: role of auditory pathways in brain stem of the cat. J Neurophysiol 38:842, 1975.
15. Cherry C. Two ears-but one world. In Rosenblith WA (ed). Sensory Communication. Cambridge, MA, MIT Press, 1959, p 99.
16. Coats AC. On electrocochleographic electrode design. J Acoust Soc Am 56:708, 1974.
17. Coats AC. The summating potential and Meniere's disease. Arch Otolaryngol 107:199, 1981.
18. Collet L, Kemp DT, Veuillet E, et al. Effect of contralateral auditory stimuli on active cochlear micromechanical properties in human subjects. Hear Res 43:251, 1990.
19. Corso JF. The Experimental Psychology of Sensory Behavior. New York, Holt, Rinehart & Winston, 1967, p 280.
20. Corso JF, Levine M. Pitch discrimination at high frequencies by air and bone conduction. Am J Psychol 78:557, 1965.
21. Dallos P. Low-frequency auditory characteristics: species dependence. J Acoust Soc Am 48:489, 1970.
22. Dallos P. The Auditory Periphery: Biophysics and Physiology. New York, Academic Press, 1973.
23. Dallos P. Cochlear physiology. Annu Rev Psychol 32:153, 1981.
24. Dallos P. The active cochlea. J Neurosci 12:4575, 1992.
25. Dallos P. Overview: Cochlear neurobiology. In Dallos P, Popper AN, Fay RR (eds). The Cochlea. New York, Springer, 1996, p 1.
26. Dallos P, Billone MC, Durrant JD, et al. Cochlear inner and outer hair cells: functional differences. Science 177:356, 1972.
27. Dallos P, Cheatham MA. Compound action potential (AP) tuning curves. J Acoust Soc Am 59:591, 1976.
28. Dallos P, Evans BN, Hallworth R. Nature of the motor element in electrokinetic shape changes of cochlear outer hair cells. Nature 350:155, 1991.
29. Davis H. A model for transducer action in the cochlea. Cold Spring Harb Symp Quant Biol 30:181, 1965.
30. Davis H, Walsh TE. The limits of improvement of hearing following the fenestration operation. Laryngoscope 60:273, 1950.
31. Durrant JD. Comments on the effects of overstimulation on microphonic sensitivity. J Acoust Soc Am 66:597, 1979.
32. Durrant JD. Auditory physiology and an auditory physiologist's view of tinnitus. J Laryngol Otol Suppl 4:21, 1981.
33. Durrant JD. Combined ECochGABR versus conventional ABR recordings. Semin Hear 7:289, 1986.
34. Durrant JD, Ferraro JA. Short-latency auditory evoked potential: electrocochleography and auditory brainstem response. In Musiek FE, Rintelmann WF (eds). Contemporary Perspectives in Hearing Assessment. Boston, Allyn and Bacon, 1999, p 197.
35. Durrant JD, Kamerer DB, Chen DA. Combined OAE and ABR studies in acoustic tumor patients. In Hoehmann D (ed). ECoG, OAE and Intraoperative Monitoring: Proceedings of the First International Conference. Amsterdam, Kugler Publications, 1993, p 1.
36. Durrant JD, Lovrinic JH. Bases of Hearing Science, 3rd ed. Baltimore, Williams & Wilkins, 1995.
37. Durrant JD, Martin WH, Hirsch B, Schwegler J. 3CLT ABR analyses in a human subject with unilateral extirpation of the inferior colliculus. Hear Res 72:99, 1994.
38. Durrant JD, Wolf KE. Auditory evoked potentials: basic aspects. In

Rintelmann WF (ed). Hearing Assessment, 2nd ed. Austin, TX, ProEd, 1991, p 321.

39. Duvall AJ, Flock A, Wersall J. The ultrastructure of the sensory hairs and associated organelles of the cochlear inner hair cell with reference to directional sensitivity. J Cell Biol 29:497, 1966.

40. Erulkar SD. Comparative aspects of spatial localization of sound. Physiol Rev 52:238, 1972.

41. Evans EF, Palmer AR. Relationship between the dynamic range of cochlear nerve fibers and their spontaneous activity. Exp Brain Res 40:115, 1980.

42. Flock A. Transducing mechanisms in the lateral line canal organ receptors. Cold Spring Harb Symp Quant Biol 30:133, 1965.

43. Flock A, Cheung HC. Actin filaments in sensory hairs of inner ear receptor cells. J Cell Biol 75:339, 1977.

44. Flock A, Jorgensen M, Russell I. The physiology of individual hair cells and their synapses. In Moller AR (ed). Basic Mechanisms in Hearing. New York, Academic Press, 1973, p 273.

45. Galaburda A, Sanides F. Cytoarchitectonic organization of the human auditory cortex. J Comp Neurol 190:597, 1980.

46. Galambos R. Neural mechanisms in audition. Laryngoscope 68:388, 1958.

47. Glattke TJ. Short-Latency Auditory Evoked Potentials. Baltimore, University Park Press, 1983.

48. Goldstein R, Aldrich WM. Evoked Potential Audiometry. Boston, Allyn and Bacon, 1999.

49. Gourevitch G. Binaural hearing in land mammals. In Yost WA, Gourevitch G (eds). Directional Hearing. New York, Springer-Verlag, 1987, p 226.

50. Green DM. An Introduction to Hearing. Hillsdale, NJ, Lawrence Erlbaum Associates, 1976.

51. Harrison JM, Howe ME. Anatomy of the afferent auditory nervous system of mammals. In Keidel WD, Neff WD (eds). Handbook of Sensory Physiology, Vol V/1. Anatomy Physiology (Ear). Berlin, Springer-Verlag, 1974, p 183.

52. Harrison JM, Howe ME. Anatomy of the descending auditory system (mammalian). In Keidel WD, Neff WD (eds). Handbook of Sensory Physiology, Vol V/1. Anatomy Physiology (Ear). Berlin, Springer-Verlag, 1974, p 363.

53. Heffner H. Effect of auditory cortex ablation on localization and discrimination of brief sounds, J Neurophysiol 41:963, 1978.

54. Honrubia V, Ward PH. Dependence of the cochlear microphonics and the summating potential on the endocochlear potential. J Acoust Soc Am 46:388, 1969.

55. Hudspeth AJ. The cellular basis of hearing: the biophysics of hair cells. Science 230:745, 1985.

56. Hudspeth AJ. The ionic channels of a vertebrate hair cell. Hear Res 22:21, 1986.

57. Hunter-Duvar IM. Electron microscopic assessment of the cochlea. Acta Otolaryngol Suppl (Stockh) 351:2, 1978.

58. Imig TJ, Reale RA, Brugge JF. The auditory cortex: patterns of corticocortical projections related to physiological maps in the cat. In Woolsey CN (ed). Cortical Sensory Organization, Vol 3. Multiple Auditory Areas. Clifton, NJ, Humana Press, 1982, p 1.

59. Irving R, Harrison JM. The superior olivary complex and audition: a comparative study. J Comp Neurol 130:77, 1967.

60. Jesteadt W, Wier CC, Green DM. Intensity discrimination as a function of frequency and sensation level. J Acoust Soc Am 61:169, 1977.

61. Johnstone BM, Patuzzi R, Yates GK. Basilar membrane measurements and the travelling wave. Hear Res 22:147, 1986.

62. Kaltenbach JA, Meleca RJ, Falzarano PR, et al. Forward masking properties of neurons in the dorsal cochlear nucleus: possible role in the process of echo suppression. Hear Res 67:35, 1993.

63. Katz B. Nerve, Muscle, and Synapse. New York, McGraw-Hill, 1966.

64. Keidel WD. Information processing in higher parts of the auditory pathway. In Zwicker E, Terhardt E (eds). Facts and Models in Hearing. New York, Springer-Verlag, 1974, p 216.

65. Keidel WD. Neurophysiological requirements for implanted cochlear prostheses. Audiology 19:105, 1980.

66. Kelly JP, Wong D. Laminar connections of the cat's auditory cortex. Brain Res 212:1, 1981.

67. Kemp DT. Stimulated acoustic emissions from within the human auditory system. J Acoust Soc Am 64:1386, 1978.

68. Kemp DT. Developments in cochlear mechanics and techniques for noninvasive evaluation. Adv Audiol 5:27, 1988.

69. Khanna SM, Leonard DGB. Basilar membrane tuning in the cat cochlea. Science 215:305, 1982.

70. Kiang NYS. Discharge Patterns of Single Fibers in the Cat's Auditory Nerve. Cambridge, MA, MIT Press, 1965.

71. Kiang NYS. Stimulus representation in the discharge patterns of auditory neurons. In Eagles EL (ed). The Nervous System, Vol 3. Human Communication and Its Disorders. New York, Raven Press, 1975, p 81.

72. Kiang NYS. A survey of recent developments in the study of auditory physiology. Ann Otol 77:656, 1968.

73. Kiang NYS, Moxon EC. Tails of tuning curves of auditory-nerve fibers. J Acoust Soc Am 55:620, 1974.

74. Killion MC, Dallos P. Impedance matching by the combined effects of the outer and middle ear. J Acoust Soc Am 66:599, 1979.

75. Kinsler LE, Frey AR. Fundamentals of Acoustics. New York, John Wiley, 1962.

76. Klinke R, Galley N. Efferent innervation of vestibular and auditory receptors. Physiol Rev 54:316, 1974.

77. Knudsen EI, Konishi M. A neural map of auditory space in the owl. Science 200:795, 1978.

78. Kraus N, McGee T. Clinical implications of primary and nonprimary pathway contributions to the middle latency response generating system. Ear Hear 14:36, 1993.

79. Kraus N, McGee T, Carrell T, et al. Speech-evoked cortical potentials in children. J Am Acad Audiol 4:238, 1993.

80. Kraus N, McGee T, Sharma A, et al. Mismatch negativity event-related potential elicited by speech stimuli. Ear Hear 13:158, 1992.

81. Liberman MC. Effects of chronic cochlear deefferentation on auditory nerve response. Hear Res 49:209, 1990.

82. Liberman MC, Guinan JJ. Feedback control of the auditory periphery: anti-masking effects of middle ear muscles vs. olivocochlear efferents. J Commun Disord 31:471, 1998.

83. Licklider JCR. Basic correlates of the auditory stimulus. In Stevens SS (ed). Handbook of Experimental Psychology. New York, John Wiley, 1951, p 985.

84. Lim DJ. Cochlear micromechanics in understanding otoacoustic emission. Scand Audiol Suppl 25:17, 1986.

85. Lonsbury-Martin BL, Whitehead ML, Martin GK. Clinical applications of otoacoustic emissions. J Speech Hear Res 34:964, 1991.

86. Maison SF, Liberman MC. Predicting vulnerability to acoustic injury with a noninvasive assay of olivocochlear reflex strength. J Neurosci 20:4701, 2000.

87. Margolis RH, Trine MB. Influence of middle-ear disease on otoacoustic emissions. In Robinette MS, Glattke TJ (eds). Otoacoustic Emissions: Clinical Applications. 1997, p 130.

88. Massopust LC, Wolin L, Frost V. Frequency discrimination thresholds following auditory cortex ablations in the monkey. J Aud Res 11:227, 1971.

89. Masterson RB, Glendenning KK, Nudo RJ. Anatomical pathways subserving the contralateral representation of a sound source. In Gatehouse RW (ed). Localization of Sound: Theory and Applications. Groton, CT, Amphora Press, 1982, p 113.

90. Maxon AB, White KR, Culpepper B, Vohr BR. Maintaining acceptably low referral rates in TEOAE-based newborn hearing screening programs. J Commun Disord 30:457, 1997.

91. McFadden D. Masking-level differences determined with and without interaural disparities in masker intensity. J Acoust Soc Am 44:212, 1968.

92. McGee TJ, Clemis JB. The approximation of audiometric thresholds by auditory brain stem responses. Otolaryngol Head Neck Surg 88:295, 1980.

93. Mendel MI, Wolf KE. Clinical applications of the middle latency responses. Audiol J Cont Educ 8:141, 1983.

94. Merzenich MM, Knight PL, Roth GL. Representation of cochlea within primary auditory cortex in the cat. J Neurophysiol 38:231, 1975.

95. Miller JD, Watson CS, Covell WP. Deafening effects of noise on the cat. Acta Otolaryngol Suppl (Stockh) 176:1, 1963.

96. Mills AW. Auditory localization. In Tobias JV (ed). Foundations of Modern Auditory Theory, Vol 1. New York, Academic Press, 1972, p 303.

97. Moller AR. An experimental study of the acoustic impedance of

the middle ear and its transmission properties. Acta Otolaryngol (Stockh) 60:129, 1965.

98. Moller AR. The middle ear. In Tobias JV (ed). Foundations of Modern Auditory Theory, Vol 2. New York, Academic Press, 1972, p 135.

99. Moller AR. Coding of amplitude modulated sounds in the cochlear nucleus of the rat. In Moller AR (ed). Mechanisms in Hearing. New York, Academic Press, 1973, p 593.

100. Moller AR, Jannetta PJ. Comparison between intracranially recorded potentials from the human auditory nerve and scalp recorded auditory brainstem responses (ABR). Scand Audiol 11:33, 1982.

101. Moller AR, Jannetta PJ, Bennett M, Moller MB. Intracranially recorded responses from the human auditory nerve: new insights into the origin of brainstem evoked potentials (BSEP). Electroencephalogr Clin Neurophysiol 52:18, 1981.

102. Moore JK. The human auditory brain stem as a generator of auditory evoked potentials. Hearing Res 29:33, 1987.

103. Moushegian G, Stillman RD, Rupert AL. Characteristic delays in superior olive and inferior colliculus. In Sachs MB (ed). Physiology of the Auditory System: A Workshop. Baltimore, National Educational Consultants, 1971, p 245.

104. Nedzelnitsky V. Measurement of sound pressure in the cochleae of anesthetized cats. In Zwicker E, Terhardt E (eds). Facts and Models in Hearing. New York, Springer-Verlag, 1974, p 45.

105. Neff WD. Neural mechanisms of auditory discrimination. In Rosenblight WA (ed). Sensory Communication. Cambridge, MA, MIT Press, 1959, p 259.

106. Neff WD. Localization and lateralization of sound in space. In DeReuck AVS, Knight J (eds). Hearing Mechanisms in Vertebrates. Boston, Little, Brown, 1968, p 207.

107. Nozza RJ, Sabo DL, Mandel EM. A role for otoacoustic emissions in screening for hearing impairment and middle ear disorders in school-age children. Ear Hear 18:227, 1997.

108. Peake WT, Rosowski JJ, Lynch TJ III. Middle-ear transmission: acoustic versus ossicular coupling in cat and human. Hear Res 57: 245, 1992.

109. Pfeiffer RR, Kim DO. Cochlear nerve fiber responses: distribution along the cochlear partition, J Acoust Soc Am 58:867, 1975.

110. Pfingst BE, O'Connor TA. Characteristics of neurons in auditory cortex of monkeys performing a simple auditory task. J Neurophysiol 45:16, 1981.

111. Pickles JO, Corey DP. Mechanoelectrical transduction by hair cells. Trends Neurosci 15:254, 1992.

112. Pickles JO, Comis SD, Osborne MP. Crosslinks between stereocilia in the guinea pig organ of Corti, and their possible relation to sensory transduction. Hear Res 15:103, 1984.

113. Picton TW, Hillyard SA, Krausz HI, Galambos R. Human auditory evoked potentials. I. Evaluation of components. Electroencephalogr Clin Neurophysiol 36:179, 1974.

114. Plenge G. On the differences between localization and lateralization. J Acoust Soc Am 56:944, 1974.

115. Plomp R. Old and new data on tone perception. In Neff WD (ed). Contributions to Sensory Physiology, Vol 5. New York, Academic Press, 1971, p 179.

116. Polich JM, Starr A. Middle, late, and long latency auditory evoked potentials. In Moore EJ (ed). Bases of Auditory Brain-Stem Evoked Responses. New York, Grune & Stratton, 1983, p 345.

117. Prieve B, Dalzell L, Berg A, et al. The New York State universal newborn hearing screening demonstration project: outpatient outcome measures. Ear Hear 21:104, 2000.

118. Probst R. Otoacoustic emissions: an overview. In Pfaltz CR (ed). New Aspects of Cochlear Mechanics and Inner Ear Pathophysiology. Basel, Karger, 1990, p 1.

119. Reneau JP, Hnatiow GZ. Evoked Response Audiometry: A Topical and Historical Review. Baltimore, University Park Press, 1975.

120. Rhode WS. Basilar membrane motion: results of Mössbauer measurements. Scand Audiol Suppl 25:7, 1986.

121. Rhode WS. An investigation of postmortem cochlear mechanics using the Mössbauer effect. In Moller AR (ed). Basic Mechanisms in Hearing. New York, Academic Press, 1973, p 39.

122. Robinette MS, Durrant JD. Contributions of evoked otoacoustic emissions in differential diagnosis of retrocochlear disorders. In Robinette MS, Glattke TJ (eds). Otoacoustic Emissions: Clinical Applications. New York, Thieme, 1997, p 205.

123. Robinette MS, Glattke TJ (eds). Otoacoustic Emissions: Clinical Applications, 2nd ed. New York, Thieme, 2002.

124. Robinson DW, Dadson RS. A redetermination of the equal loudness relations for pure tones. Br J Appl Phys 7:166, 1956.

125. Romani GL, Williamson SJ, Kaufman L. Tonotopic organization of the human auditory cortex. Science 216:1339, 1982.

126. Rose JE, Brugge JF, Anderson DJ, Hind JE. Phase-locked response to low-frequency tones in single auditory nerve fibers of the squirrel monkey. J Neurophysiol 30:769, 1967.

127. Rose JE, Gross NB, Geisler CD, Hind JE. Some neural mechanisms in the inferior colliculus of the cat which may be relevant to localization of a sound source. J Neurophysiol 29:288, 1966.

128. Rosowski JJ. The effects of external and middle ear filtering on auditory threshold and noise induced hearing loss. J Acoust Soc Am 90:124, 1991.

129. Russell IJ, Sellick PM. Tuning properties of cochlear hair cells. Nature 267:858, 1977.

130. Ryan A, Dallos P. Physiology of the cochlea. In Northern JL (ed). Hearing Disorders, 2nd ed. Boston, Little, Brown, 1984, p 253.

131. Sachs MB, Abbas PJ. Rate versus level functions for auditory-nerve fibers in cats: tone-burst stimuli. J Acoust Soc Am 56:1835, 1974.

132. Sachs MB, Young ED. Encoding of steady-state vowels in the auditory nerve: representation in terms of discharge rate. J Acoust Soc Am 66:470, 1979.

133. Sams M, Paavilainen P, Alho K, Naatanen R. Auditory frequency discrimination and event-related potentials. EEG Clin Neurophysiol 62:437, 1985.

134. Scharf B. Critical bands. In Tobias JV (ed). Foundations of Modern Auditory Theory, Vol 1. New York, Academic Press, 1970, p 159.

135. Scharf B, Magnan J, Chays A. On the role of the olivocochlear bundle in hearing: 16 case studies. Hear Res 103:101,1997.

136. Schwent VL, Hillyard SA, Galambos R. Selective attention and the auditory vertex potential. I. Effects of stimulus delivery rate. Electroencephalogr Clin Neurophysiol 40:604, 1976.

137. Searle CL, Braida LD, Cuddy DR, Davis MF. Binaural pinna disparity: another auditory localization cue. J Acoust Soc Am 57: 448, 1975.

138. Selters WA, Brackmann DE. Acoustic tumor detection with brain stem electric response audiometry. Arch Otolaryngol 103:181, 1977.

139. Shaw EAG. The external ear. In Keidel WD, Neff WD (eds). Handbook of Sensory Physiology, Vol V/1. Auditory System: Anatomy, Physiology (Ear). Berlin, Springer-Verlag, 1974, p 455.

140. Simmons FB. Perceptual theories of middle ear muscle function. Ann Otol Rhinol Laryngol 73:724, 1964.

141. Solomon G, Starr A. Electromyography of middle ear muscles in man during motor activities. Acta Neurol Scand 39:161, 1963.

142. Starr A, Achor LJ. Auditory brain stem responses in neurological disease. Arch Neurol 32:761, 1975.

143. Starr A, Picton TW, Sininger Y, et al: Auditory neuropathy. Brain 119:741, 1996.

144. Stypulkowski PH, Staller SJ. Clinical evaluation of a new ECocG recording electrode. Ear Hear 8:304, 1987.

145. Suga N. Feature detection in the cochlear nucleus, inferior colliculus, and auditory cortex. In Sachs MB (ed). Physiology of the Auditory System: A Workshop. Baltimore, National Educational Consultants, 1971, p 197.

146. Sutter AH. Hearing conservation. In Berger EH, Ward WD, Morrill JC, Royster LH (eds). Noise and Hearing Conservation Manual. Akron, OH, American Industrial Hygiene Association, 1986, p 1.

147. Tasaki I, Spyropoulos CS. Stria vascularis as source of endocochlear potential. J Neurophysiol 22:149, 1959.

148. Telischi FF, Roth J, Stagner BB, et al. Pattern of evoked otoacoustic emissions associated with acoustic neuromas. Laryngoscope 105: 675, 1995.

149. Tilney LG, Derosier DJ, Mulroy MJ. The organization of actin filaments in the stereocilia of cochlear hair cells. J Cell Biol 86:244, 1980.

150. Tonndorf J, Davis D. 1961 revisited: signal transmission in the cochlear hair cell nerve junction. Arch Otolaryngol 101:528, 1975.

151. Tonndorf J. Relationship between the transmission characteristics of the conductive system and noise-induced hearing loss. In Hen-

derson D, Hamernik RP, Dosanjh DS, Mills JH (eds). Effects of Noise on Hearing. New York, Raven Press, 1976, p 159.

152. Tonndorf J, Khanna SM. The role of the tympanic membrane in middle ear transmission. Ann Otolaryngol 79:743, 1970.

153. Veuillet E, Khalfa S, Collet L. Clinical relevance of medial efferent auditory pathways. Scand Audiol 51:53, 1999.

154. Viemeister NF. Auditory intensity discrimination at high frequencies in the presence of noise. Science 221:1206, 1983.

155. Walzl EM. Representation of the cochlea in the cerebral cortex. Laryngoscope 57:778, 1947.

156. Warr WB, Guinan JJ. Efferent innervation of the organ of Corti: two separate systems. Brain Res 173:152, 1979.

157. Wegel RL. Physical data and physiology of excitation of the auditory nerve. Ann Otol Rhinol Laryngol 41:740, 1932.

158. Wegel RL, Lane CE. The auditory masking of one pure tone by another and its probable relation to the dynamics of the inner ear. Physiol Rev 23:266, 1924.

159. Wever EG. Beats and related phenomena resulting from the simultaneous sounding of two tones. Psychol Rev 36:402, 1929.

160. Wever EG. Theory of Hearing. New York, Dover Publications, 1949.

161. Wever EG, Bray CM. The perception of low tones and the resonance volley theory. J Psychol 3:101, 1937.

162. Wever EG, Lawrence M. Physiological Acoustics. Princeton, Princeton University Press, 1954.

163. Whitfield IC. The Auditory Pathway. Baltimore, Williams & Wilkins, 1967.

164. Whitfield IC. Coding in the auditory nervous system. Nature 213:756, 1967.

165. Wiener FM, Ross DA. The pressure distribution in the auditory canal in a progressive sound field. J Acoust Soc Am 18:401, 1946.

166. Wier CC, Jesteadt W, Green DM. Frequency discrimination as a function of frequency and sensation level. J Acoust Soc Am 61:178, 1977.

167. Winter IM, Robertson D, Yates GK. Diversity of characteristic frequency rate-intensity functions in guinea pig auditory nerve fibres. Hear Res 45:191, 1990.

168. Woolsey CN. Tonotopic organization of the auditory cortex. In Sachs MB (ed). Physiology of the Auditory System: A Workshop. Baltimore, National Educational Consultants, 1971, p 271.

169. Yeowart NS, Evans MJ. Thresholds of audibility for very low frequency pure tones. J Acoust Soc Am 55:814, 1974.

170. Yost WA, Hafter ER. Lateralization. In Yost WA, Gourevitch G (eds). Directional Hearing. New York, Springer-Verlag, 1987, p 49.

171. Young ED, Sachs MB. Representation of steady-state vowels in the temporal aspects of the discharge patterns of populations of auditory-nerve fibers. J Acoust Soc Am 66:1381, 1979.

172. Zwicker E. On a psychoacoustical equivalent of tuning curves. In Zwicker E, Terhardt E (eds). Facts and Models in Hearing. New York, Springer-Verlag, 1974, p 132.

173. Zwicker E, Flottrop G, Stevens SS. Critical bandwidth in loudness summation. J Acoust Soc Am 29:548, 1957.

174. Zwislocki JJ. Analysis of some auditory characteristics. In Luce R, Bush R, Galanter E (eds). Handbook of Mathematical Psychology, Vol 3. New York, John Wiley, 1965, p 1.

175. Zwislocki JJ. The role of the external and middle ear in sound transmission. In Eagles EL (ed). The Nervous System, Vol 3. Human Communication and Its Disorders. New York, Raven Press, 1975, p 45.

176. Zwislocki JJ, Sokolich WG. Velocity and displacement in auditory-nerve fibers. Science 182:64, 1973.

10

Methods of Examination: Clinical Examination

Charles D. Bluestone, M.D., and Jerome O. Klein, M.D.

The diagnosis of middle-ear disease, when inflammation is present, can usually be made by obtaining the pertinent medical history and performing a physical examination that includes *pneumatic otoscopy*. (Chapter 23 provides a detailed discussion of the diagnosis of middle-ear disease.) Although less common than the inflammatory disorders, congenital, traumatic, and neoplastic problems are also important (Chaps. 20, 29, 30). In addition to these two important examination methods, evaluation of the child's hearing and middle-ear function (Chap. 11) and assessment of the vestibular system (Chap. 13) may also be indicated.

Signs and Symptoms

Nine prominent signs and symptoms are primarily associated with diseases of the ear and temporal bone. *Otalgia* is most commonly associated with inflammation of the external and middle ear but may also be of nonaural origin. In most cases, otalgia not associated with otitis media can be identified as referred pain due to discomfort with swallowing (tonsillitis), nasal obstruction, or pain in the throat (pharyngitis), but any lesion in the areas of the trigeminal, facial, glossopharyngeal, vagal, great auricular, or lesser occipital nerve supply can result in earache[19] and include lesions in the temporomandibular joint, the teeth, or the pharynx. In young infants, pulling at the ear or general irritability, especially when associated with fever, may be the only sign of ear pain (Chap. 14).

Purulent *otorrhea* is a sign of otitis externa, otitis media with perforation of the tympanic membrane, or both. Bloody discharge may be associated with acute or chronic inflammation, trauma, or neoplasm. A clear drainage may be indicative of a perforation of the drum with a serous middle-ear effusion or cerebrospinal fluid otorrhea draining through a defect in the external auditory canal or through the tympanic membrane from the middle ear (Chap. 15).

Hearing loss is a symptom that may be the result of disease of either the external or the middle ear (conductive hearing loss) or the result of a pathologic condition in the inner ear, retrocochlea, or central auditory pathways (sensorineural hearing loss) (Chap. 26). (Physical abnormalities and associated syndromes related to hearing loss are described in detail in Chapter 16.)

Swelling about the ear is most commonly the result of inflammation (e.g., external otitis, perichondritis, or mastoiditis), trauma (e.g., hematoma), or on rare occasions, neoplasm.

Vertigo is not a common complaint in children but is present more often than was once thought. The most common cause is eustachian tube–middle ear–mastoid disease,[10, 15, 17] but vertigo may also be due to labyrinthitis; perilymphatic fistula between the inner and middle ear resulting from a congenital defect, trauma, or cholesteatoma; vestibular neuronitis; benign paroxysmal positional vertigo; Meniere disease; or disease of the central nervous system. Older children may describe a feeling of spinning or turning, whereas younger children may not be able to verbalize the symptom but manifest the dysequilibrium by falling, stumbling, or "clumsiness." Unidirectional horizontal jerk *nystagmus*, usually associated with vertigo, is vestibular in origin (Chap. 17).

Tinnitus is another symptom that children infrequently describe but is commonly present, especially in patients with eustachian tube–middle ear disease or conductive or sensorineural hearing loss (Chap. 18).

Facial paralysis is an infrequent but frightening condition for both child and parents. When it is due to disease within the temporal bone in children, it most commonly occurs as a complication of acute or chronic otitis media; however, facial paralysis may also be idiopathic (Bell palsy) or the result of temporal bone fracture or neoplasm; on rare occasions, it is due to herpes zoster oticus (Chap. 19).

Purulent *conjunctivitis* can be associated with acute otitis media. The conjunctivae are infected, there is tearing or purulent discharge, and in some children there is concurrent ear pain.[4] Simultaneous cultures of conjunctivae and middle-ear exudates reveal nontypable *Haemophilus influenzae* in almost all cases.[5]

Other signs and symptoms of conditions that may be associated with ear disease may also be present, such as symptoms of upper respiratory allergy associated with otitis media (Chaps. 23 and 47). *Fever* is a relatively poor predictor of otitis media, but when associated with other signs and symptoms, such as otalgia, it can be a good predictor.[24]

Physical Examination

Aside from the history, the most useful method for diagnosing ear disease is a physical examination that includes pneumatic otoscopy. Adequate examination of the entire child, with special attention to the head and neck, can lead to the identification of a condition that may predispose to or be associated with ear disease. The appearance of the child's face and the character of his or her speech may be important clues to the possibility of an abnormal middle ear. Many craniofacial anomalies, such as mandibulofacial dysostosis (Treacher Collins syndrome) and trisomy 21 (Down syndrome), are associated with an increased incidence of ear disease (Chap. 4). Mouth breathing and hyponasality may indicate intra- or postnasal obstruction, while hypernasality is a sign of velopharyngeal incompetence. Examination of the oropharyngeal cavity may uncover an overt cleft palate or a submucous cleft (Fig. 10–1), both of which predispose the infant to otitis media with effusion.[26, 33] Although a bifid uvula has been associated with an increased incidence of middle-ear disease,[34] more recent studies fail to corroborate this finding.[14, 30] An examination of the child's head and neck may also reveal posterior nasal or pharyngeal inflammation and discharge. Other pathologic conditions of the nose, such as polyposis, severe deviation of the nasal septum, or a nasopharyngeal tumor, may also be associated with otitis media (Chaps. 23 and 33).

Examination of the ear itself is the most critical part of the clinician's assessment of the patient, but it must be performed systematically. The auricle, periauricular area, and external auditory meatus should be examined first; all too frequently these areas are overlooked in the physician's haste to make a diagnosis by otoscopic examination, but the presence or absence of signs of infection in these areas may aid later in the differential diagnosis or evaluation of complications of ear disease. For instance, external otitis may result from acute otitis media with discharge, or inflammation of the postauricular area may be indicative of periostitis or a subperiosteal abscess that has extended from the mastoid air cells (Chap. 24). Palpation of these areas will determine whether tenderness is present; exquisite pain on palpation of the tragus would indicate acute diffuse external otitis (Chap. 22).

After examination of the external ear and canal, the clinician may proceed to the most important part of the physical assessment, the otoscopic examination.

Otoscopic Examination

Positioning the Patient for Examination

The position of the patient for otoscopy depends on the patient's age and ability to cooperate, the clinical setting, and the preference of the examiner. Otoscopic evaluation of an infant is best performed on an examining table. The presence of a parent or assistant is necessary to restrain the baby, as undue movement usually prevents an adequate evaluation (Fig. 10–2). Some clinicians prefer to place infants prone on the table, whereas others prefer them to be supine. Use of the examining table is also desirable for older infants who are uncooperative or when a tympanocentesis or myringotomy is performed without general anesthesia. Figure 10–3 shows that infants and young children who are only apprehensive and not struggling actively can be evaluated adequately while sitting on the parent's lap. When necessary, the child may be restrained firmly on an adult's lap if the parent holds the child's wrists over the abdomen with one hand and holds the child's head against the adult's chest with the other hand. If necessary, the child's legs can be held between the adult's thighs. Some infants can be examined by placing their head on the parent's knee (Fig. 10–4). Cooperative children sitting in a chair or on the edge of an examination table can usually be evaluated successfully. The examiner should hold the otoscope with the hand or finger placed firmly against the child's head or face, so that the otoscope will move with the head rather than cause trauma (pain) to the ear canal if the child moves suddenly (Fig. 10–5). Pulling up and out on the pinna will usually straighten the ear canal enough to allow expo-

FIGURE 10–1. Bifid uvula, widening attenuation of the median raphe of the soft palate, and a V-shaped midline notch, rather than a smooth curve, are diagnostic of a submucous cleft palate.

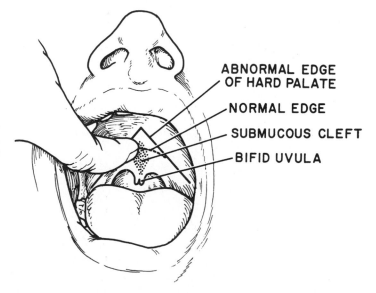

ABNORMAL EDGE OF HARD PALATE

NORMAL EDGE

SUBMUCOUS CLEFT

BIFID UVULA

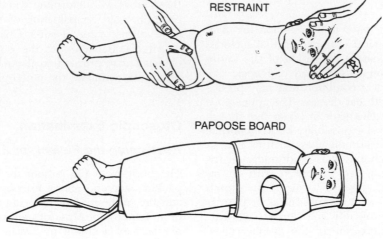

FIGURE 10–2. Methods of restraining an infant for examination and for procedures such as tympanocentesis or myringotomy. (From Bluestone CD, Klein JO. Otitis Media in Infants and Children, 3rd ed. Philadelphia, WB Saunders, 2001.)

sure of the tympanic membrane. In young infants the tragus must be moved forward and out of the way.

Removal of Cerumen

Before adequate visualization of the external canal and tympanic membrane can be obtained, all obstructing cerumen must be removed from the canal. Many children with acute otitis media have moderate to large accumulations of cerumen in the ear canal. For optimal visualization of the tympanic membrane, mechanical removal was necessary in approximately one third of 279 patients observed by Schwartz and colleagues.[31] The necessity for cerumen removal was inversely proportional to age, with more than half of cerumen removal procedures per-

formed in infants under 1 year of age. Removal of cerumen can usually be accomplished by use of an otoscope with a surgical head and a wire loop or a blunt cerumen curette (Fig. 10–6), or by irrigating the ear canal *gently* with warm water delivered through a dental irrigator (Water Pik) (Fig. 10–7). Tympanic membrane perforations and ossicular disruption have been reported after oral jet irrigation, indicating the need for caution and use only at a low-power setting.[13] Instillation of hydrogen peroxide (3% solution) in the ear canal for 2 to 3 minutes softens cerumen and may facilitate removal with subsequent irrigation. Carbamide peroxide in glycerol (Debrox) can be used in the ear canal prior to irrigation. But some commercial preparations such as triethanolamine polypep-

FIGURE 10–3. Method of restraining a child for examination of the ear.

FIGURE 10–4. Method of positioning a baby for otoscopic examination.

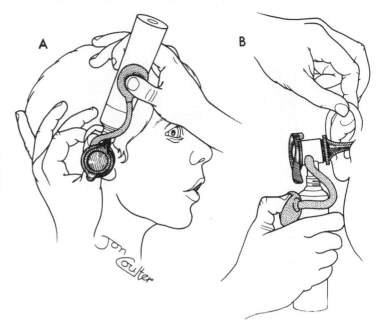

FIGURE 10–5. Methods of positioning an otoscope to enhance visualization and minimize the risk that head movement will result in trauma to the ear canal. Both of the otoscopist's hands can be used (*A*), or when the child is cooperative, a finger touching the child's cheek is sufficient (*B*).

tide oleate-condensate (Cerumenex) have been reported to cause dermatitis of the external canal. These materials may be of value if used infrequently and under the physician's supervision.

Otoscope

For proper assessment of the tympanic membrane and its mobility, a pneumatic otoscope in which the diagnostic head has an adequate seal should be used.[11] The quality of the otoscopic examination is limited by deficiencies in the designs of commercially available otoscopes. The speculum employed should have the largest lumen that can comfortably fit in the child's cartilaginous external auditory meatus. If the speculum is too small, adequate

visualization may be impaired and the speculum may touch the bony canal, which can be painful. In most models, an airtight seal is usually not possible because of a leak of air within the otoscope head or between the stiff ear speculum and the external auditory canal, although leaks at the latter location can be stopped by cutting a small section of rubber tubing and slipping it over the tip of the ear speculum (Fig. 10–8).

Many otolaryngologists prefer to use a Bruening or Siegle otoscope with the magnifying lens. Both of these instruments allow for excellent assessment of drum mobility because they have an almost airtight seal. A head mirror and lamp or a headlight (Fig. 10–9) is necessary to provide light for the examination. But the use of a head mirror or even a headlight for examination of the

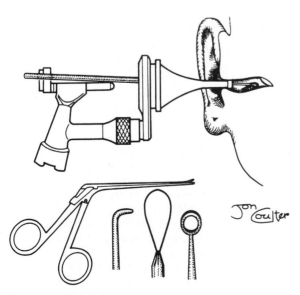

FIGURE 10–6. Method of removing cerumen from the external ear canal, employing the surgical head attached to the otoscope, and instruments that can be used.

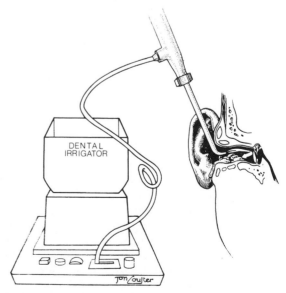

FIGURE 10–7. Irrigation of the external canal with a dental irrigator to remove cerumen.

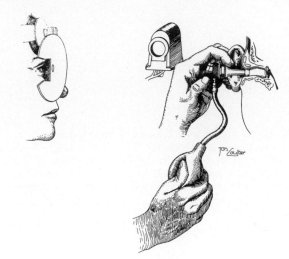

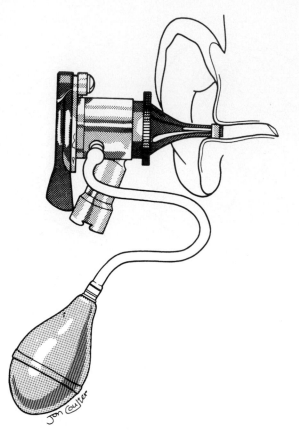

FIGURE 10–8. Pneumatic otoscope with a rubber tip on the end of the ear speculum to provide a better seal in the external auditory canal.

FIGURE 10–9. Observation of eardrum mobility with the Bruening otoscope with magnifying lens. The light source is from a lamp reflected off a head mirror.

tympanic membrane of an infant or child is usually not feasible, unless the child is effectively restrained, and when strained, the traditional otoscope or more accurately, the otomicroscope, is preferred.

Examination of Tympanic Membrane

Inspection of the tympanic membrane should include evaluation of its *position, color, degree of translucency,* and *mobility.* Assessment of the light reflex is of limited value because it does not indicate the status of the middle ear in the evaluation of tympanic membrane–middle ear disorders. Clinical otoscopic examinations compare favorably with histologic temporal bone specimens.[29]

Positions of the Tympanic Membrane

The positions of the tympanic membrane when the middle ear is aerated and when effusion is present are illustrated in Figure 10–10.

The normal eardrum should be in the neutral position, with the short process of the malleus visible but not prominent through the membrane.

Mild retraction of the tympanic membrane usually indicates negative middle-ear pressure, an effusion, or both. The short process of the malleus and the posterior mallear fold are prominent, and the manubrium of the malleus appears to be foreshortened.

Severe retraction of the tympanic membrane is characterized by a prominent posterior mallear fold and short process of the malleus and a severely foreshortened manubrium. The tympanic membrane may be severely retracted, presumably owing to high negative pressure in association with a middle-ear effusion.

Fullness of the tympanic membrane is apparent initially in the posterosuperior portion of the pars tensa and pars flaccida, because these two areas are the most highly compliant parts of the tympanic membrane.[22] The short process of the malleus is commonly obscured. The fullness is caused by increased air pressure, effusion, or both within the middle ear. When bulging of the entire tympanic membrane occurs, the malleus is usually obscured, which occurs when the middle ear–mastoid system is filled with an effusion.

Appearance of the Tympanic Membrane

The normal tympanic membrane has a ground-glass appearance; a blue or yellow color usually indicates a middle-ear effusion seen through a translucent tympanic membrane. A red tympanic membrane alone may not be indicative of a pathologic condition, because the blood vessels of the drum head may be engorged as the result of the patient's crying, sneezing, or nose blowing. It is critical to distinguish between translucency and opacification of the eardrum to identify a middle-ear effusion. The normal tympanic membrane should be translucent, and the observer should be able to look through the drum and visualize the middle-ear landmarks (the incudostapedial joint promontory, the round window niche, and frequently the chorda tympani nerve) (Fig. 10–11). If a middle-ear effusion is present medial to a translucent drum, an air-fluid level or bubbles of air admixed with the liquid may be visible (Fig. 10–12). An air-fluid level or bubbles can be differentiated from scarring of the tympanic membrane by altering the position of the head while observing the drum with the otoscope (if fluid is

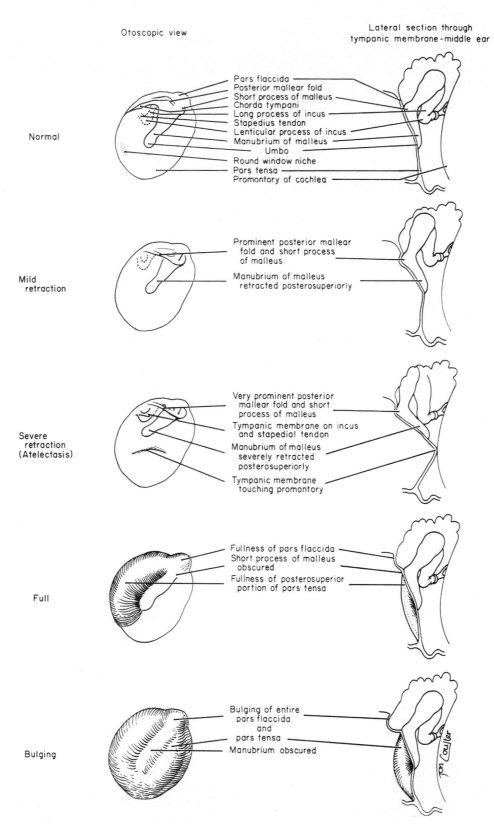

FIGURE 10–10. Otoscopic view compared with a lateral section through the tympanic membrane and middle ear to demonstrate the various positions of the drum with their respective anatomic landmarks (see text).

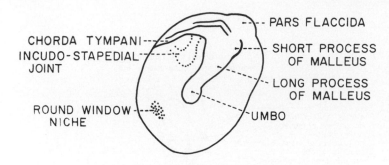

CHORDA TYMPANI
INCUDO-STAPEDIAL
JOINT

PARS FLACCIDA
SHORT PROCESS
OF MALLEUS
LONG PROCESS
OF MALLEUS

ROUND WINDOW
NICHE

UMBO

FIGURE 10–11. Diagrammatic view of the tympanic membrane depicting important landmarks that can usually be visualized with the otoscope.

present, the air-fluid level will shift in relation to gravity) or by seeing movement of the fluid during pneumatic otoscopy. The line frequently seen when a severely retracted membrane touches the cochlear promontory will disappear (the drum will pull away from the promontory) if sufficient negative pressure can be applied with the pneumatic otoscope. Inability to visualize the middle-ear structures indicates opacification of the drum, which is usually the result of thickening of the tympanic membrane, an effusion, or both.

A bright light is necessary for accurate otoscopy. Barriga and colleagues[1] surveyed otoscopes in physicians' offices and hospital clinics and found that many were inadequately maintained. A light output of 100 footcandles or more was optimal for clinical otoscopy. Replacement of the bulb rather than of the battery was more likely to restore adequate light to the units with poor performance.[1] Otoscope batteries should be replaced frequently so that the ability of the examiner to look "through" the tympanic membrane will not be impaired. The electric otoscope is better than the battery type. A halogen bulb

with greater than or equal to 100 footcandles is currently recommended.[28]

Mobility of the Tympanic Membrane

Abnormalities of the tympanic membrane and the middle ear are reflected in the pattern of tympanic membrane mobility when first positive and then negative pressure is applied to the external auditory canal with the pneumatic otoscope.[2, 3, 12] As shown in Figure 10–13, this is achieved by first applying *slight* pressure on the rubber

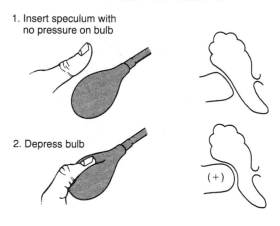

TO OBTAIN POSITIVE PRESSURE:

1. Insert speculum with no pressure on bulb

2. Depress bulb

(+)

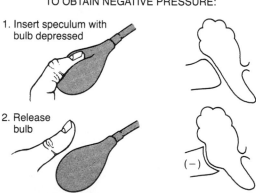

TO OBTAIN NEGATIVE PRESSURE:

1. Insert speculum with bulb depressed

2. Release bulb

(−)

FIGURE 10–13. Pressure applied to the rubber bulb attached to the pneumatic otoscope will deflect the normal tympanic membrane inward with applied positive pressure and outward with applied negative pressure if the middle-ear pressure is ambient. The movement of the eardrum is proportionate to the degree of pressure exerted on the bulb until the tympanic membrane has reached its limit of compliance.

RETRACTED

AIR/FLUID LEVEL

BUBBLES IN
FLUID

Jon Coulter

FIGURE 10–12. Three examples of otoscopic findings (right ear).

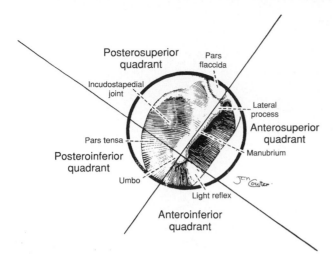

FIGURE 10–14. The four quadrants of a right tympanic membrane.

bulb (positive pressure) and then, after momentarily breaking the seal, releasing the bulb (negative pressure).

When the tympanic membrane and middle ear are normal, forceful application of positive and negative pressure (i.e., deeply depressing and releasing the thumb on the rubber bulb) can be painful to the child, since the tympanic membrane is overdistended. If the tympanic membrane does not move when slight pressure is applied, more pressure is applied.

The presence of effusion, high negative pressure, or both within the middle ear can markedly dampen the movements of the eardrum. When the middle-ear pressure is ambient, the normal tympanic membrane moves inward with slight positive pressure in the ear canal and outward toward the examiner with slight negative pressure. The motion observed is proportionate to the applied pressure and is best visualized in the posterosuperior quadrant of the tympanic membrane (Fig. 10–14). If a two-layered membrane or an atrophic scar (due to a

healed perforation) is present, mobility of the tympanic membrane can also be assessed more readily by observing the movement of the flaccid area.

The movement of the tympanic membrane to the applied pressure from the rubber bulb attached to the otoscope can determine, in general, whether there is relatively normal pressure within the middle ear, negative or positive pressure, or a possible effusion. Figure 10–15 shows a simple relationship between the pressure applied by the pneumatic otoscope and the response of that applied positive and negative pressure to the movement medial (in) and lateral (out) of the tympanic membrane. Figure 10–16 shows a more specific relationship between mobility of the tympanic membrane, as measured by pneumatic otoscopy, and the middle-ear contents and pressure. Figure 10–16, Frame 1, shows the normal tympanic membrane when the middle ear contains only air at ambient pressure. A hypermobile eardrum (Frame 2) is seen most frequently in children whose membranes are atrophic or flaccid. The mobility of the tympanic membrane is greater than normal (the drum is said to be highly compliant) if the drum moves when even slight positive or negative external canal pressure is applied; if the drum moves equally well to both applied positive and negative pressures, the middle-ear pressure is approximately ambient. However, if the tympanic membrane is hypermobile to applied negative pressure but immobile when positive pressure is applied, the tympanic membrane is flaccid and negative pressure is present within the middle ear.

A middle-ear effusion is rarely present when the tympanic membrane is hypermobile, even though high negative middle-ear pressure is present. A thickened tympanic membrane (caused by inflammation, scarring, or both) or a partly effusion-filled middle ear (in which middle-ear air pressure is ambient) shows decreased mobility to applied pressures, both positive and negative (Frame 3).

Normal middle-ear pressure is reflected by the neutral position of the tympanic membrane as well as by its

		Response to applied negative pressure	
		Yes	No
Response to applied positive pressure	Yes	Normal ME pressure	Positive ME pressure
	No	Negative ME pressure	ME effusion, or very high ME pressure, or both

FIGURE 10–15. Middle-ear (ME) pressure as determined by the response of the tympanic membrane when positive and negative pressures are applied with the pneumatic otoscope. If the tympanic membrane moves medial (in) to applied positive pressure and lateral (out) to applied negative pressure, ME pressure is within relatively normal limits. If the eardrum moves on applied positive pressure, but not when negative pressure is applied, positive pressure is within the ME (with or without effusion). If the drum moves on applied negative pressure, but not when positive pressure is applied, negative pressure is within the ME (with or without effusion). If the tympanic membrane fails to move after application of positive and negative pressure, effusion is present in the ME, or there is very high negative ME pressure, or both are present.

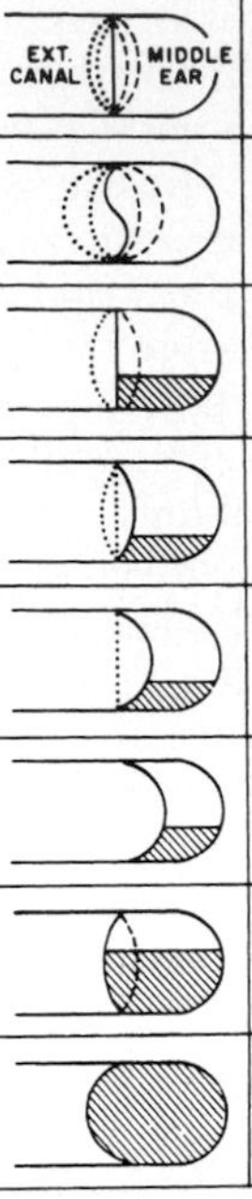

	EARDRUM POSITION*		EARDRUM POSITIVE PRESSURE▽		EARDRUM NEGATIVE PRESSURE		MIDDLE EAR CONTENTS	MIDDLE EAR PRESSURE
			LOW	HIGH	LOW	HIGH		
1.	NEUTRAL		1+	2+	1+	2+	AIR	AMBIENT
2.	NEUTRAL		2+	3+	2+	3+	AIR	AMBIENT
3.	NEUTRAL		0	1+	0	1+	AIR OR AIR AND EFFUSION	AMBIENT
4.	RETRACTED		0	0	1+	2+	AIR OR AIR AND EFFUSION	LOW NEGATIVE
5.	RETRACTED		0	0	0	1+	AIR OR EFFUSION AND AIR	HIGH NEGATIVE
6.	RETRACTED		0	0	0	0	AIR OR EFFUSION OR BOTH	VERY HIGH NEGATIVE OR INDETERMINATE
7.	FULL		0	1+	0	0	AIR AND EFFUSION	POSITIVE OR INDETERMINATE
8.	BULGING		0	0	0	0	EFFUSION	POSITIVE OR INDETERMINATE

* POSITION OF EARDRUM:
— AT REST; - - - POSITIVE PRESSURE APPLIED (BULB COMPRESSED);
··· NEGATIVE PRESSURE APPLIED (RELEASE BULB)

† DEGREE OF TYMPANIC MEMBRANE MOVEMENT AS VISUALIZED THROUGH THE OTOSCOPE; 0 = NONE, 1+ = SLIGHT, 2+ = MODERATE, 3+ = EXCESSIVE

▽ COMPRESSION OF BULB EXERTS POSITIVE PRESSURE ; RELEASE OF A COMPRESSED BULB INDUCES NEGATIVE PRESSURE

FIGURE 10–16. Pneumatic otoscopic findings related to middle-ear contents and pressure (see text).

response to both positive and negative pressures in each of the previous examples (Frames 1 to 3). In other cases the eardrum may be retracted, usually because negative middle-ear pressure is present (Frames 4 to 6). The compliant membrane is maximally retracted by even moderate negative middle-ear pressure and hence cannot visibly be deflected inward further with applied positive pressure in the ear canal. However, negative pressure produced by releasing the rubber bulb of the otoscope will cause a return of the eardrum toward the neutral position if a negative pressure equivalent to that in the middle ear can be created by releasing the rubber bulb (Frame 4), a condition that occurs when air, with or without an effusion, is present in the middle ear. When middle-ear pressure is even lower, there may be only slight outward mobility of the tympanic membrane (Frame 5) because of the limited negative pressure that can be exerted through the otoscopes currently available. If the eardrum is severely retracted with extremely high negative middle-ear pressure, if middle-ear effusion is present, or if both occur, the examiner is not able to produce significant outward movement (Frame 6).

The tympanic membrane that exhibits fullness (Frame 7) will move to applied positive pressure but not to applied negative pressure if the pressure within the middle ear is positive and if air, with or without an effusion, is present. In such an instance the tympanic membrane is stretched laterally to the point of maximal compliance and will not visibly move outward any farther to the applied negative pressure, but it will move inward to applied positive pressure as long as some air is present within the middle ear–mastoid air cell system. When this system is filled with an effusion and little or no air is present, the mobility of the bulging tympanic membrane (Frame 8) is severely decreased or absent to both applied positive and negative pressure. Gates,[16] using these principles, compared the sensitivity, specificity, and predictive value of pneumatic otoscopy and tympanometry in the detection of middle-ear effusion. As the skill of the otoscopist increases, the reliance on tympanometry in the diagnosis of effusion should decrease.

Figure 10–17 shows examples of common conditions of the middle ear as assessed with the otoscope, in which position, color, degree of translucency, and mobility of the tympanic membrane are diagnostic aids.

Figure 10–18 depicts the pneumotoscopic method used to determine whether a line that is visualized on the lower portion of the tympanic membrane is (1) the tympanic membrane touching the promontory, (2) an effusion level, or (3) a scar within the tympanic membrane. When the tympanic membrane is severely retracted and no middle-ear effusion is present, the tympanic membrane may touch the promontory, and a line can be seen through the membrane. However, if the tympanic membrane can be pulled laterally when negative pressure is applied with the pneumatic otoscope, the line will disappear, since the membrane is no longer touching the promontory (Fig. 10–18A). A line that is due to a fluid

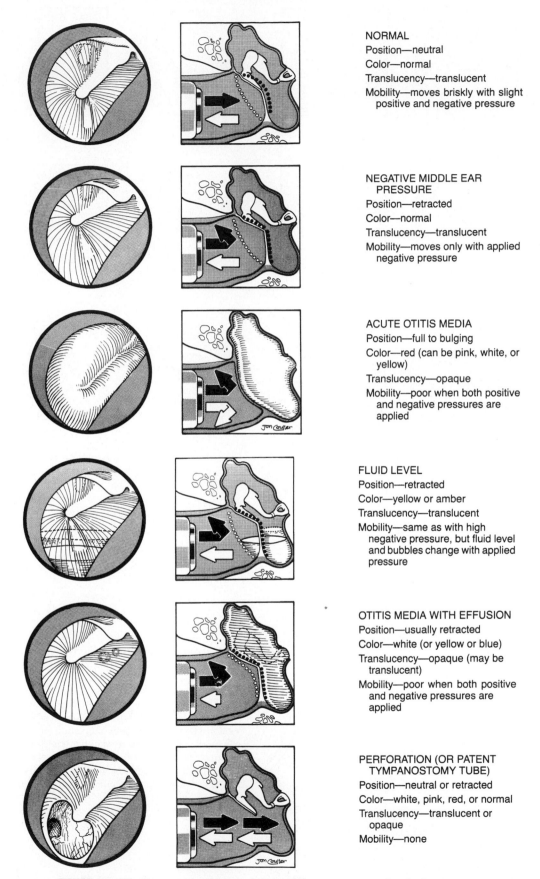

NORMAL
Position—neutral
Color—normal
Translucency—translucent
Mobility—moves briskly with slight positive and negative pressure

NEGATIVE MIDDLE EAR PRESSURE
Position—retracted
Color—normal
Translucency—translucent
Mobility—moves only with applied negative pressure

ACUTE OTITIS MEDIA
Position—full to bulging
Color—red (can be pink, white, or yellow)
Translucency—opaque
Mobility—poor when both positive and negative pressures are applied

FLUID LEVEL
Position—retracted
Color—yellow or amber
Translucency—translucent
Mobility—same as with high negative pressure, but fluid level and bubbles change with applied pressure

OTITIS MEDIA WITH EFFUSION
Position—usually retracted
Color—white (or yellow or blue)
Translucency—opaque (may be translucent)
Mobility—poor when both positive and negative pressures are applied

PERFORATION (OR PATENT TYMPANOSTOMY TUBE)
Position—neutral or retracted
Color—white, pink, red, or normal
Translucency—translucent or opaque
Mobility—none

FIGURE 10–17. Common conditions of the middle ear as assessed with the otoscope.

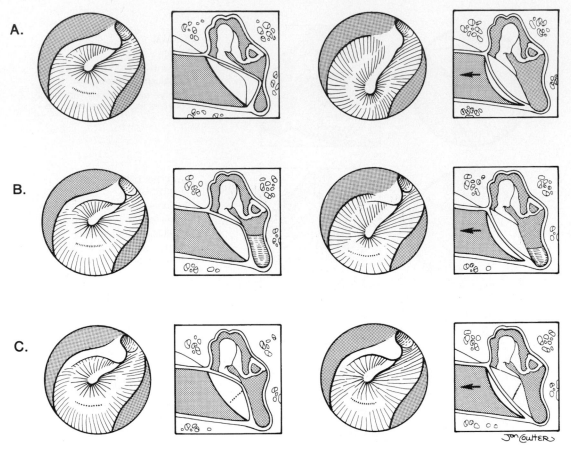

FIGURE 10–18. Diagnostic significance of changing relative pressure and marks on the tympanic membrane. *A*, Tympanic membrane touching promontory. *B*, Fluid level. *C*, Scar in tympanic membrane (see text).

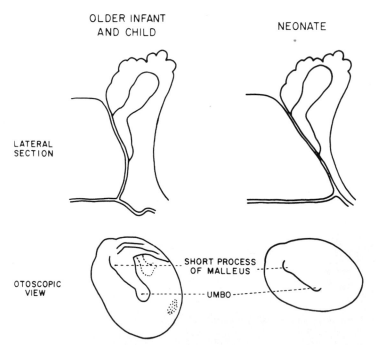

OLDER INFANT
AND CHILD

NEONATE

LATERAL
SECTION

OTOSCOPIC
VIEW

SHORT PROCESS
OF MALLEUS

UMBO

FIGURE 10–19. Comparison of the tympanic membrane of an older infant or a child with that of a neonate. The lateral section shows the greater angulation of the neonate's external canal with regard to the tympanic membrane. The appearance of the eardrums and canals on otoscopy is depicted in the lower drawings; the neonate appears to have a smaller tympanic membrane because of angulation of the eardrum.

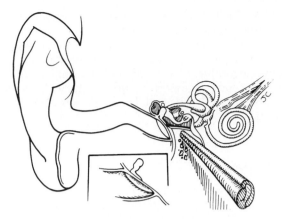

FIGURE 10–20. The position of the tympanic membrane in the child is more vertical than it is in the neonate.

level will move (1) up when positive pressure is applied, since the middle-ear cavity is made smaller; and (2) down when negative pressure is applied, since the middle-ear cavity is made larger (Fig. 10–18*B*). If the line is a scar, it will stay in the same place on the tympanic membrane when positive and negative pressures are applied (Fig. 10–18*C*).

Otoscopy in the Newborn Infant

The tympanic membrane of the neonate is in a position different from that of the older infant and child; if this is not kept in mind, the examiner may perceive the eardrum to be smaller and retracted because in the neonate the tympanic membrane appears to be as wide as it is in older children but not as high (Fig. 10–19). Figure 10–20 shows that this perception is due to the more horizontal position of the neonatal eardrum, which frequently makes it difficult for the examiner to distinguish the pars flaccida of the tympanic membrane from the skin of the wall of the deep superior external canal.

In the first 2 days of life, the ear canal is filled with vernix caseosa, but this material is readily removed with a small curette or suction tube. Low-birth-weight infants (less than 1200 g) have external canals that may be so narrow as not to permit entry of the 2-mm diameter speculum. The canal walls of the young infant are pliable and tend to expand and collapse with insufflation during pneumatic otoscopy. Because of the pliability of the canal walls, it may be necessary to advance the speculum farther into the canal than would be the case in an older child. The tympanic membrane often appears thickened and opaque during the first few days. In many infants the membrane is in an extreme oblique position, with the superior aspect proximal to the observer (see Fig. 10–19). The tympanic membrane and the superior canal wall may appear to lie almost in the same plane, so that it is often difficult to distinguish the point where the canal ends and the pars flaccida begins. The inferior canal wall bulges loosely over the inferior position of the tympanic membrane and moves with positive pressure, simulating the movement of the tympanic membrane. The examiner must distinguish between the movement of the canal walls and that of the membrane. The following should be

considered to differentiate the movement of these structures: vessels are seen within the tympanic membrane but not in the skin of the ear canal; the tympanic membrane moves during crying or respiration; and, inferiorly, the wall of the external canal and the tympanic membrane lie at an acute angle. By 1 month of age the tympanic membrane has assumed an oblique position, one with which the examiner is familiar in the older child. During the first few weeks of life, however, examination of the ear requires patience and careful appraisal of the structures of the external canal and the tympanic membrane.

Accuracy, Validation Techniques, and Interexaminer Reliability of Otoscopy

Otoscopy is subjective and thus is usually an imprecise method of assessing the condition of the tympanic membrane and middle ear. Many clinicians still do not use a pneumatic otoscope, and few have been trained adequately to make a correct diagnosis. The primary reason for this lack of proper education is the method of teaching employed. Because otoscopy involves a monocular assessment of the tympanic membrane, the teacher cannot verify that the student actually visualized the anatomic features that led to the diagnosis. An otoscope with a second viewing port is available (Fig. 10–21). Teacher and student can make observations together, and student errors can be corrected immediately. One of the most effective means of education currently available is the correlation of the otoscopic findings with those obtained by an otomicroscope that has an observer tube for the student. In this manner the instructor can point out the critical landmarks and can demonstrate tympanic mobility using the Bruening otoscope.

Assessment techniques can also be improved by correlating otoscopy findings with a tympanogram taken immediately after the otoscopic examination.[7] Lack of agreement between the otoscopic findings and tympanometry usually results in a second otoscopic examination, because

FIGURE 10–21. Teaching otoscope with sidearm viewer. (From Welch Allyn, New York.)

tympanometry is generally accurate in distinguishing between normal and abnormal tympanic membranes and middle ears (specifically, in the identification of middle-ear effusions). The presence or absence of negative pressure within the middle ear as measured by pneumatic otoscopy can be verified only by similar results on the tympanogram. Validation of the presence or absence of effusion as observed by otoscopy is best achieved by performing tympanocentesis or myringotomy immediately after the examination. When surgical opening of the tympanic membrane is indicated, preliminary otoscopy by several examiners is an effective way of teaching many students to evaluate the state of the middle ear.

In most studies of otitis media the disease has been identified by otoscopy; however, in many such studies no information has been offered to enable the reader to evaluate the ability of the otoscopist to make the diagnosis correctly. In an attempt to classify tympanometric patterns, Paradise and colleagues[27] validated the diagnosis of the otoscopist by performing a myringotomy shortly after the otoscopic examination. This method of validation was also used in studies of infants with cleft palates in which two otoscopists were involved.[25, 26] However, most other studies of otitis media have not reported validation of the diagnostic criteria, and when attempts have been made to determine interexaminer reliability in these studies, the results have been so poor as to suggest that the data reported are inaccurate. Jordan[20] reported the consistency of descriptions of middle-ear appearance by otologists. In assessing normality or abnormality of the tympanic membrane, the examiners agreed in only 60% of the observations in 10 children.

In the design of a study in which otoscopic examination is used to identify otitis media and related conditions, the diagnostic abilities of all otoscopists included in the study must be validated, and interexaminer reliability must be established. If the primary ear disorder being studied is the presence or absence of middle-ear effusion, each otoscopist should have a high degree of accuracy in identifying effusion. This can be achieved by performing otoscopy in a group of children immediately before tympanocentesis or myringotomy.[7] The sensitivity (total number of otoscopic diagnoses of middle-ear effusion present divided by the total myringotomy findings when middle-ear effusion is aspirated) and specificity (total number of otoscopic diagnoses of middle-ear effusion absent divided by the total myringotomy findings when middle-ear effusion is not aspirated) should be as high as possible. Interexaminer reliability can be tested by having all the otoscopists involved in the study independently make an otoscopic diagnosis before the tympanocentesis or myringotomy.[9]

From the Children's Hospital of Pittsburgh, Kaleida and Stool[21] reported an ongoing evaluation program of 30 clinicians, between 1980 and 1990, in their ability to diagnose middle-ear effusion compared with the findings at myringotomy. The arbitrary criteria for the lowest acceptable limits for sensitivity and specificity were 80% and 70%, respectively. A total of 4147 ears were assessed, and the mean sensitivity and mean specificity for the group were 87% and 74%, respectively. The investigators con-

cluded that a formal validation program should be used to determine otoscopic accuracy.

In studies such as the one by Mandel and coworkers,[23] the diagnosis of middle-ear effusion was based on a decision-tree algorithm[6] that combined the findings of a validated otoscopist, as described previously, with the results of tympanometry and middle-ear muscle reflex testing (Chap. 11).

Otomicroscopy

Many otolaryngologists use the otomicroscope to improve the accuracy of diagnosis of otitis media and related conditions. For the assessment of tympanic membrane mobility, the microscope, when used with the Bruening otoscope and nonmagnifying lens (Fig. 10–22), is superior to conventional otoscopes; this is because the microscope provides binocular vision (and therefore depth perception), a better light source, and greater magnification. Under most conditions, otomicroscopic examination is impractical and generally not necessary. However, when a diagnosis by otoscopy is in doubt, the otomicroscope is an invaluable diagnostic aid and frequently essential in arriving at the correct diagnosis (e.g., in differentiating a deep retraction pocket in the posterosuperior quadrant of the tympanic membrane from a cholesteatoma). In addition to the advantages offered by the otomicroscope for certain diagnostic problems, it is superior to the conventional otoscopes for minor surgical procedures such as tympano-

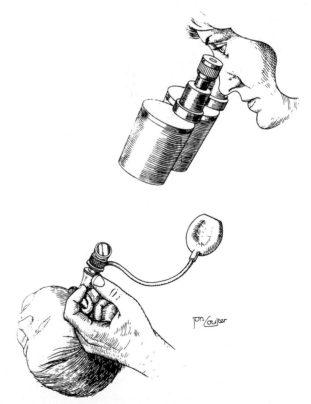

FIGURE 10–22. Precise assessment of tympanic membrane mobility employing the otomicroscope and a Bruening otoscope with a nonmagnifying lens.

centesis, because it allows for a more precise visualization of the field.

Even though several previous studies used the otomicroscopic examination as a validator for the presence or absence of middle-ear disease (otitis media with effusion), no study has reported on the sensitivity and specificity of the microscopic examination for detecting middle-ear effusion. It is purported to be superior to the standard otoscopic examination, but its superiority to tympanometry with otoscopy has not yet been shown. However, as a teaching device, the otomicroscope with an observer tube attachment is preferable to the currently available otoscope.

Whenever the otoscopic examination is unsatisfactory owing to inability to adequately visualize the tympanic membrane (e.g., in a narrow external canal or an uncooperative child), an examination under general anesthesia (EUA) of the ears employing the otomicroscope may be indicated in selected infants and children, such as those in whom a suppurative complication is suspected or is present.

Hearing Tests

Evaluation of hearing is discussed in detail in Chapter 11, but there are other tests of hearing available, such as tuning fork tests.

Tuning Fork Tests

Before the widespread availability of audiometric evaluation of hearing, tuning forks were an essential part of the physical examination of patients with a suspected hearing loss. In the modern era, many otolaryngologists have not included tuning fork tests as part of their routine examination of the ear and hearing. Sheehy and co-workers[32] advocate their continued use to validate the audiometric assessment, and Yung and Morris[35] believe that tuning forks are of value in screening for hearing loss. Their usefulness in children has been questioned, and they are considered by many to be unreliable in this age group. Capper and colleagues[8] compared the Rinne and Weber test responses to audiometric findings in 125 children and reported that about one third of tuning fork responses were incorrect, especially in children under 6 years of age. In older children and teenagers, tuning fork tests can be helpful in assessing hearing when audiometry is unavailable or unreliable or when serial evaluation of hearing is desired after an initial audiogram has been obtained. Examples of the latter situation would be following the course of otitis media or during the immediate postoperative period after middle-ear surgery.

The Weber test is performed by placing a tuning fork (usually 512 Hz) at the vertex or against the teeth and asking the child if the sound lateralizes to one ear or not. The Rinne test is performed by asking the child to compare the loudness level of the tuning fork applied to the mastoid bone and opposite the external auditory canal. (An extensive description of these and other tuning fork tests is provided by Glasscock and Shambaugh.[17])

FIGURE 10–23. A Bárány noisemaker.

Other Subjective Tests of Hearing

Although not ideal, tests of a child's ability to hear conversational and whispered speech can be helpful as an alternative to frequent periodic audiometric tests. An example of the usefulness of such testing is when the clinician wants to serially assess the hearing of a child who has a middle-ear effusion and a previously documented conductive hearing loss, as an aid in management decisions (e.g., watchful waiting versus surgical intervention), since the hearing loss may fluctuate.

When performing the testing, the clinician should present words that are familiar to the child, first at a conversational level and then in a whisper. The clinician should be behind the child on the side being tested, to prevent lip reading, while masking the opposite ear; gently rubbing a small sheet of paper over the ear not being tested is usually sufficient for masking. A child who fails to repeat words spoken at a conversational level will have about a 60-dB loss or greater, whereas if conversational speech is heard and whispered speech is not, the loss can be judged to be between 30 and 60 dB. These tests should not replace behavioral or nonbehavioral audiometric tests, because their reliability is questionable, especially in young children. However, these tests can be a cost-effective way of periodically assessing hearing after audiograms have been obtained.

When the findings of audiometry reveal that the child has no hearing in one ear (i.e., anacusis), the use of a Bárány noisemaker (Fig. 10–23) as a masking device may be helpful to further verify the loss. When the noisemaker is inserted into the hearing ear, the patient with an anacoustic ear will not be able to repeat words that are presented in a loud voice (e.g., shouted words).

SELECTED REFERENCES

Bluestone CD, Cantekin EI. Design factors in the characterization and identification of otitis media and certain related conditions. Ann Otol Rhinol Laryngol 88:13, 1979.

This article describes the way to arrive at a method to diagnose middle-ear effusion for research purposes.

Carlson LH, Stool SE. Diagnosis. In Rosenfeld RM, Bluestone CD, (eds). Evidence-Based Otitis Media. Hamilton, Canada, 1999, pp 105-116.

This text provides an up-to-date review of diagnostic techniques for diagnosis of otitis media.

Kaleida PH, Stool SE. Assessment of otoscopists' accuracy regarding middle-ear effusion. Otoscopic validation. Am J Dis Child 146:433, 1992.

This excellent article describes the methods of validation of otoscopy for clinical and research use.

Schwartz RH, Rodriguez WJ, McAvery W, et al. Cerumen removal: how necessary is it to diagnose acute otitis media? Am J Dis Child 157: 1064, 1983.

The authors present their method of removing cerumen in a clinical practice.

Sheehy JL, Gardner G, Hambley WM. Tuning fork tests in modern otology. Arch Otolaryngol Head Neck Surg 94:132, 1971.

This classic description of the use of tuning forks is recommended reading for all clinicians who evaluate the hearing of children.

REFERENCES

1. Barriga R, Schwartz RH, Hayden GF. Adequate illumination for otoscopy: variations due to power source, bulb, and head and speculum design. Am J Dis Child 140:1237, 1986.
2. Bluestone CD, Cantekin EI. Design factors in the characterization and identification of otitis media and certain related conditions. Ann Otol Rhinol Laryngol 88:13, 1979.
3. Bluestone CD, Shurin P. Middle-ear disease in children: pathogenesis, diagnosis and management. Pediatr Clin North Am 21:370, 1974.
4. Bodor FF. Conjunctivitis-otitis syndrome. Pediatrics 69:695, 1982.
5. Bodor FF, Marchant CD, Shurin PA, et al. Bacterial etiology of conjunctivitis-otitis media syndrome. Pediatrics 76:26, 1985.
6. Cantekin EI. Algorithm for diagnosis of otitis media with effusion. Ann Otol Rhinol Laryngol 92:6, 1983.
7. Cantekin EI, Bluestone CD, Fria TJ, et al. Identification of otitis media with effusion. Ann Otol Rhinol Laryngol 89:190, 1980.
8. Capper JWR, Slack RWT, Maw AR. Tuning fork tests in children. J Laryngol Otol 101:780, 1987.
9. Carlson LH, Stool SE. Diagnosis. In Rosenfeld RM, Bluestone CD. Evidence-Based Otitis Media. Hamilton, Canada, B.C. Decker, 1999, pp 105-116.
10. Casselbrant ML, Black FO, Nashner L, Panion R. Vestibular function assessment in children with otitis media with effusion. Ann Otol Rhinol Laryngol (Suppl) 92:46, 1983.
11. Cavanaugh RM Jr. Obtaining a seal with otic specula: must we rely on an air of uncertainty? Pediatrics 87:114, 1991.
12. Cavanaugh RM Jr. Quantitative pneumatic otoscopy in pediatric patients with normal and abnormal tympanic membrane mobility. In

Lim DJ, Bluestone CD, Klein JO, et al (eds). Recent Advances in Otitis Media—Proceedings of the Fifth International Symposium. Burlington, Ontario, Decker Publications, 1993, pp 39-40.
13. Dinsdale RC, Roland PS, Manning SC, Meyerhoff WL. Catastrophic otologic injury from oral jet irrigation of the external auditory canal. Laryngoscope 101:75, 1991.
14. Fischler RS, Todd NW, Feldman C. Lack of association of cleft uvula with otitis media in Apache Indian children. Am J Dis Child 141:866, 1987.
15. Gates GA. Vertigo in children. Ear Nose Throat J 59:358, 1980.
16. Gates GA. Differential otomanometry. Am J Otolaryngol 7:147, 1986.
17. Glasscock ME III, Shambaugh GE Jr. Surgery of the Ear, 4th ed. Philadelphia, WB Saunders, 1990.
18. Grace ARH, Pfleiderer AG. Disequilibrium and otitis media with effusion: what is the association? J Laryngol Otol 104:682, 1990.
19. Ingvarsson L. Acute otalgia in children—findings and diagnosis. Acta Pediatr Scand 71:705, 1982.
20. Jordan RE. Epidemiology of otitis media. In Glorig A, Gerwin KS (eds). Otitis Media. Proceedings of the National Conference, Gallier Hearing and Speech Center, Dallas, TX. Springfield, IL, Charles C Thomas, 1972, pp 31-35.
21. Kaleida PH, Stool SE. Assessment of otoscopists' accuracy regarding middle-ear effusion: otoscopic validation. Am J Dis Child 146:433, 1992.
22. Khanna SM, Tonndorf J. Tympanic membrane vibrations in cats studied by time-averaged holography. J Acoust Soc Am 51:1904, 1972.
23. Mandel EM, Rockette HE, Bluestone CD, et al. Efficacy of amoxicillin with and without decongestant-antihistamine for otitis media with effusion in children. N Engl J Med 316:432, 1987.
24. Medellin G, Roark R, Berman S. The usefulness of symptoms to identify otitis media. Arch Pediatr Adolesc Med 150:98, 1996.
25. Paradise JL, Bluestone CD. Early treatment of universal otitis media of infants with cleft palate. Pediatrics 53:48, 1974.
26. Paradise JL, Bluestone CD, Felder H. The universality of otitis media in fifty infants with cleft palate. Pediatrics 44:3542, 1969.
27. Paradise JL, Smith CG, Bluestone CD. Tympanometric detection of middle-ear effusion in infants and young children. Pediatrics 58:198, 1976.
28. Pelton SI. Otoscopy for the diagnosis of otitis media. Pediatr Infect Dis J 17:540, 1998.
29. Ruah CB, Barros E, Ruah S, et al. Paediatric otoscopy—clinical and histological correlation. J Laryngol Otol 106:307, 1992.
30. Schwartz RH, Hayden GF, Rodriguez WJ, et al. The bifid uvula: is it a marker for an otitis-prone child? Laryngoscope 95:1100, 1985.
31. Schwartz RH, Rodriguez WJ, McAveney W, et al. Cerumen removal: how necessary is it to diagnose acute otitis media? Am J Dis Child 137:1064, 1983.
32. Sheehy JL, Gardner G, Hambley WM. Tuning fork tests in modern otology. Arch Otolaryngol Head Neck Surg 94:132, 1971.
33. Stool SE, Randall P: Unexpected ear disease in infants with cleft palate. Cleft Palate J 4:99, 1967.
34. Taylor GD. The bifid uvula. Laryngoscope 82:771, 1972.
35. Yung MW, Morris TMD. Tuning fork tests in the diagnosis of serous otitis media. Br Med J 283:1576, 1981.

11

The Assessment of Hearing and Middle-Ear Function in Children

Robert J. Nozza, Ph.D.

From the time of birth, a child exists in a world of sensory experiences. The reception and perception of these experiences provide the framework for communication and other interactive links to the environment. Consequently, a decrement in sensory experience endangers the normal development of cognitive skills vital to the child's successful interaction with the environment. If a child has an undetected or unremediated sensory impairment in the months crucial to learning, a developmental lag results. This lag may prove to be irreversible, and the child may never realize his or her potential capabilities.

The long-term effects of hearing loss cannot be dismissed as trivial even when the impairment appears to be mild or transient. As a result, health care professionals are obligated to identify children with impaired hearing, to assess the nature and the extent of the impairment, and to manage the child's present and future environmental interactions in the context of the impairment. Further, audiologic data provide information to the practitioner that is critical to the diagnosis of diseases or defects of the ear and provide a way to monitor the effectiveness of management strategies. This chapter focuses on the procedures used to assess hearing in children. An excellent review of the medical evaluation of symptoms of hearing impairment and issues related to audiologic evaluation is provided in Chapter 16, and the philosophies and techniques for the habilitation or rehabilitation of children with impaired hearing are presented in Chapters 105 and 106. Physiology is discussed in Chapter 9.

To understand the auditory system and its function, one must understand the anatomy, physiology, and psychology of hearing. The development of this complex process is largely unknown, and the ability to assess it during development has limitations. However, it is during development that disordered hearing has its greatest impact, so the assessment of hearing in infants and children is one of the greatest challenges that faces audiologists. It is impossible to cover comprehensively material on the assessment of hearing and middle-ear function in children in one chapter; several of the topics provided as subheadings here have entire textbooks devoted to them. Therefore, this chapter cannot be the only resource in pediatric audiology used by the medical professional or student. It is at best a guide to some of the many possible avenues and approaches to the evaluation of the ear with respect to its primary purpose, which is the sensing and interpreting of meaningful acoustic information in the environment.

The methods for the assessment of hearing in children are either behavioral or physiologic. Behavioral methods of assessment include behavioral observation audiometry (BOA), conditioned orientation reflex (COR) audiometry, visual reinforcement audiometry (VRA), conditioned play audiometry, tangible reinforcement operant conditioning audiometry (TROCA), and conventional audiometry.

Electroacoustic immittance, otoacoustic emissions (OAEs), and auditory evoked potentials (AEPs) are the three most commonly used physiologic measures in pediatric auditory assessment. Such methods provide information regarding the integrity of the auditory system but do not directly assess the perceptual event that is called *hearing*.

Regardless of the assessment technique that is used, the examiner must interpret the behavioral or physiologic responses that are obtained and judge whether a given child's hearing is normal or impaired. However, the reliability and validity of this judgment do depend on the particular assessment technique that is used and the skill and experience of the observer. For this reason, a judgment of normal or impaired hearing, based on a single evaluation or a single technique, should be regarded with caution, and often a combination of several techniques and multiple evaluations over time is necessary to arrive at a valid assessment of hearing in the very young.

In addition, the age and developmental level of the child significantly influence the precision with which assessment information may be obtained. The nature of the auditory response is inherently gross and nonvolitional in the neonate and becomes more refined and voluntary as the child develops. However, the common belief that some children are too young to be evaluated properly is not true. Reasonably precise estimates of hearing are obtainable in most cases by objective measures of physiologic responses combined with behavioral tests. The methods used and their limitations are described in detail in the following sections.

Behavioral Methods of Assessment

Early in life, there is a change with age in the ability to respond to sound. The discussion that follows is therefore organized around appropriate tests for various age groups. The test methods described were designed, or evolved, to capitalize on response capabilities and proclivities at different stages of development. The age and the developmental level of a child dictate which behavioral assessment method is most likely to yield meaningful information.

Behavioral Observation Audiometry

Behavioral observation audiometry is a term used to describe procedures typically used for the assessment of auditory function in infants younger than approximately 6 months.[40] BOA is any procedure in which the examiner presents a stimulus sound and observes the associated behavioral response of the child. True BOA procedures do not incorporate conditioning procedures; rather, they rely on the observer's understanding of naturally occurring responses to auditory stimulation early in life and the conditions under which they most probably occur. Involuntary responses that often occur after sound stimulation in the young infant include eye blinks, eye widening, startle or Moro reflex, leg kicks, crying, and quieting. The more complex the spectrum of the sound (e.g., speech or noise as opposed to a tone) and the greater the intensity, the more likely it is that the infant will respond.[46] Also, an infant in a quiet or lightly sleeping state is more inclined to provide an involuntary response to sound than is an alert and active one, a crying and fussing one, or even one in a deep sleep. BOA is typically used as a screening procedure and can take place in the office setting or the audiology clinic.

In the office setting, the child typically is seated on the mother's lap, and the physician or examiner presents the stimulus to either side of the baby and observes the associated behavioral response. Simple noisemakers, such as rattles, squeak toys, Oriental bells, and crinkled onion-skin paper, are common stimulus devices in the office setting. These devices produce sounds composed of a broad range of frequencies of indeterminate relative intensities, and consequently their use provides only a gross qualitative estimate of hearing. There is a chance for false-positive judgments of impairment, especially if the infant's state during screening is not taken into account. A child who does not respond in the expected way must be referred for more extensive testing at a center devoted to pediatric hearing assessment. However, false-negative judgments of impairment are common and could be more serious. For example, a child with a significant high-frequency hearing loss may respond to a broad-frequency noisemaker in an apparently normal fashion. Children often behave as though responding to sound when there is a visual cue that prompts the response, or they may simply be moving randomly. Concomitant persistence of parental or grandparental concern about the hearing of such children should alert the physician to the need for referral for more extensive tests. A comprehensive discus-

sion of the use of noisemakers is presented by Northern and Downs,[168] and the reader intending to use these devices will profit from their suggestions.

In audiology centers concerned with the assessment of hearing in children, BOA is conducted in a manner different from the way in which it is performed in the office setting. The test environment is carefully controlled, and only calibrated stimuli are used. To avoid the unwanted influence of background sounds, the child is tested in a sound-treated test booth designed to attenuate ambient noise. To permit stimulation from either side, the child is situated (usually on the mother's lap or in a highchair) between two loudspeakers. Stimuli are presented through the loudspeakers by the audiologist from an adjoining control room with calibrated audiometric equipment.

When tones through loudspeakers are used, the tones are "warbled," which means they are electronically modulated in frequency to avoid standing waves in the test booth that would make stimulus intensity calibration impossible. Warbled tones with center frequencies of 500, 1000, 2000, and 4000 Hz are commonly used. Narrow bands of noise, with energy concentrated around the same frequencies, can be used as alternatives to warbled tone signals. Speech stimuli are also used and usually consist of the examiner's live voice, a recording of the parent's voice, or other recorded speech materials. The examiner is usually an experienced audiologist who observes the child through a window between the control room and the test booth. In some centers, two examiners conduct the test: one presents the stimuli from the control room, and the other, in the test booth, observes the child's responses.

The ability to elicit a response varies widely as a function of the stimulus used in a BOA procedure. Hoversten and Moncur[92] and Thompson and Thompson[241] observed large differences in responses to speech stimuli as opposed to noise or tones. Speech was a more powerful stimulus for both young and older infants. It is very important to add that knowledge of the loudness, the spectrum, and the time of onset of a stimulus in the BOA procedure can influence an observer's decision regarding the presence or absence of a response.[159, 255] This bias is increased in the office setting, where additional cues are available to the infant and there is less control over the stimulus. On the other hand, involuntary, reflexive responses such as those used in BOA are subject to habituation. Infant responses diminish rapidly to repetitive stimuli when there is no consequence (i.e., reinforcement) accompanying them. Wilson and Thompson[265] suggest that the response variability, observer bias, and response habituation inherent in BOA preclude its use as an assessment tool and that it should serve only as an initial screening procedure to determine levels for further testing.

BOA, then, is a term used to describe a technique whereby a child's behavioral response to a variety of stimulus sounds is observed. The procedure is most commonly used to evaluate neonates and infants younger than 6 months. The nature of the stimulus, the child's prestimulus activity, response habituation, and the unpredictable bias of the observer are factors that can weaken the reliability of the procedure as an assessment tool. BOA should be considered as a subjective screening procedure that serves best to detect only significant auditory impairment.[40]

Conditioned Orientation Reflex Audiometry or Visual Reinforcement Audiometry

COR and VRA also involve the presentation of a stimulus sound and the observation of the child's associated behavioral response. The response, a conditioned head turn toward the source of the sound, is rewarded with a visual stimulus such as a blinking light, an illuminated picture or toy, an animated toy located above the loudspeaker, or a computer/video display. The visual stimulus serves to strengthen the child's response to the sound, decrease the effects of response habituation, and increase the examiner's control of the child's responses. As such, the visual stimulus is referred to as the *visual reinforcer*.

Suzuki and Ogiba[232, 233] suggested a technique to condition the "orientation" or localization reflex in young infants, and many clinic personnel refer to the test as *conditioned orientation reflex audiometry*. However, as Wilson[263] points out, the technique can be taught to children who do not exhibit a spontaneous orientation reflex, and consequently the general term *visual reinforcement audiometry* is probably more appropriate. VRA is most successful for the assessment of infants 6 to 24 months old.

In the early COR and VRA approaches, a simple visual reinforcer, such as a blinking light or an illuminated toy, was used to reward localization responses. However, Moore and colleagues[161, 162] showed that a complex visual reinforcer (an animated toy) elicited a greater number of responses in normal 6- to 18-month-old infants than did a simple blinking light reward. In VRA, the infant is asked only to turn in one direction, but in COR, the infant must localize the sound and turn in the direction of the sound source. One advantage of the unilateral head-turn procedure is that the infant does not need to know where the sound is coming from to make the correct response. Also, because with earphones on the localization cue becomes a cue inside the head, infants sometimes have trouble making a turn right–turn left response. The unilateral response eliminates the requirement to localize the sound source.

In most applications of the VRA procedure, the infant sits facing forward on the lap of a parent or in a highchair in the sound room. The parent's role is to support the infant both physically and emotionally during the test but not to interact with the child in any way. An examiner sits with them, either directly in front of the infant or to one side, and uses soft and quiet toys to both attract the infant's attention and keep his or her gaze straight ahead. The examiner with the infant must vary the levels of activity and nature of the distraction toys to keep the infant's level of arousal appropriate for the VRA task. If the infant is lethargic and not very responsive, a more animated and active involvement of the examiner is required. If an infant is very active and excited, a calmer and more quieting approach is better. Because of differences between infants that relate to the age or developmental level of the infant, the time of day relative to naps and feeding, and individual personality characteristics, the examiner must be flexible and have a variety of maneuvers available to modify the infant's behavior as needed. This takes some experience to master. Sometimes, the examiner with the infant also serves as the observer to judge infant responses. Often, the examiner in the control room, who initiates the stimuli and activates the reinforcer, serves as the judge. In some cases, a system can be wired such that both examiners must agree that a response has occurred before the animated toy reinforcer is made available to the infant.[40]

In laboratory work using the VRA technique, computer-based systems are used to take over at least part of the decision making.[185] One such system was developed for use in the clinical setting: intelligent visual reinforcement audiometry (IVRA) (Intelligent Hearing Systems, Inc, Miami, Florida).[44, 45, 258, 259] With this system, certain features of the VRA protocol are program controlled, allowing the test to be run by a single examiner in the room with the infant, using a switch box interfaced with the computer.[44, 45, 258, 259]

With IVRA, matters such as the duration of each test stimulus presentation, duration of the reinforcer, and intensity of the signals are computer controlled. Intensity varies according to programmed decision rules, so a staircase tracking procedure is followed to estimate threshold. Also, blank or control trials are included on a quasi-random basis, preventing the examiner from ever being sure what, if anything, is presented to the infant and thereby reducing observer bias. In the sound-field application of VRA, the parent and the examiner in the room should be masked so they cannot hear what comes from the loudspeaker. When insert earphones are used, masking for the parent or examiner is not necessary.

Wilson and Thompson[265] cited the work of others[239, 264] to demonstrate that VRA with an animated toy reward yielded minimum response levels (MRLs) significantly lower than those obtained with conventional BOA and that the MRLs were not far removed from normal adult thresholds. More important, the range of stimulus intensities required to elicit a response was significantly smaller with the VRA procedure. The reduced variability for the normal ears using VRA makes discrimination of normal from impaired ears much more reliable and valid than with BOA.

Consequently, VRA is a particularly viable procedure for the assessment of auditory responses in infants as young as 6 months. This assessment tool is reliable, reduces variability among infants, and reflects MRLs in normal infants that approximate adult values. In addition, many young infants tolerate earphones, so ear-specific hearing measures can be made.[40] The insert earphone is particularly well suited for infant testing because it eliminates the need for the cumbersome and heavy headset used with the conventional earphone/supra-aural cushion combination and because the need for masking is reduced owing to the increased interaural attenuation of sound when using inserts.

Tangible Reinforcement Operant Conditioning Audiometry

TROCA uses tangible reinforcement such as candy, sugar-coated cereal, or other edibles to reward the child for pressing a bar when the stimulus is heard. A special apparatus dispenses the reward when the bar is pressed. TROCA is described by Lloyd and coworkers[132] as a technique applicable for use with severely retarded children. Subsequent studies[58, 263] have reported the usefulness of TROCA in obtaining auditory MRLs in infants. Fulton and colleagues[58] used earphones in their study and obtained thresholds at the standard audiometric test frequencies, but they were able to do so only in infants 12 months old or older. These same investigators found that an average of 11.4 test sessions were required for earphone testing.

In 1977, Wilson and Decker (as cited by Wilson[263]) used both TROCA and tangible reinforcement operant conditioning audiometry (the same technique using visual reinforcement instead of a tangible reward) to assess 7- to 20-month-old infants with warbled tone stimuli presented through loudspeakers. These investigators found that an average of four test sessions were required to establish MRLs. Of the infants younger than 12 months, 64% were successfully tested, whereas 84% of those 13 to 20 months of age were successfully evaluated.

Owing to the special equipment required and the inordinate amount of time necessary for accurate results, TROCA has not been used widely in clinical settings as a primary assessment procedure. However, the technique is quite promising as a tool for the assessment of difficult-to-test children, such as those who are severely mentally retarded or developmentally delayed.

Conditioned Play Audiometry

The behavioral assessment techniques discussed thus far are best applied to children younger than 3 years. At 2 years of age, a child can yield voluntary responses to sound that are premature prototypes of the adult response. Conventional audiometric techniques can be used, but they must be modified to be more interesting for the young child. This is accomplished by structuring the test situation in such a manner that the child can appropriately respond to stimuli by participating in a form of "play" activity. For this reason, the technique is often called *play audiometry*. It can be used to assess hearing levels for both speech and pure tone stimuli.

Play audiometry requires a considerable amount of flexibility and creativity on the part of the examiner. A play activity must be used that both interests the child and permits him or her to respond appropriately while "playing." A common approach is to use a series of colored disks of different sizes that are stacked on a peg. The child is instructed to hold a disk up to the ear and, when the "bell" or the "birdie" (i.e., the stimulus) comes on, to stack the disk onto the peg. With a short practice session, the child can be taught to respond appropriately as stimulus frequency and intensity are varied. This technique is ideal for the 2- to 5-year-old child but can also be helpful for the evaluation of chronologically older chil-

dren who are mentally retarded or emotionally disturbed.[12, 31] Of course, there is nothing sacred about a colored disk on a peg, and a variety of other activities can be, and have been, used successfully. However, the general principle underlying the technique remains the same.

Conventional Audiometry

The use of conventional audiometric techniques is traditionally reserved for the child aged 5 years or older, although there are some 3- and 4-year-olds who can be tested with conventional methods. Simply, the child is instructed to listen quietly for the test sound and to indicate when it is heard by raising a hand or even using a simple verbal response. The intensity is varied from trial to trial, depending on the response of the child during the previous trial. The lowest intensity at which at least 50% of the presentations are correctly detected is taken as the threshold estimate.

As with any behavioral test procedure that requires a voluntary response, VRA, conditioned play audiometry, and conventional hearing test methods require an experienced audiologist to obtain reliable and valid results. A number of pitfalls can arise in assuming that an infant or a young child understands the rules of our test procedures (or "games"). In testing children, false responses are common, so care must be taken when instructing or conditioning the child or interpreting the responses. Likewise, the child may fail to respond for many reasons. The audiologist must be armed with more than an understanding of the auditory system; strategies for assessment are based on an understanding of auditory behavior and auditory dysfunction, as well as audiologic test procedures, child development, and child behavior. Unlike passive examinations, behavioral audiometry requires considerable voluntary cooperation from the child over a substantial period. The test environment and the ability of the audiologist to interact with the child and caretaker or caretakers are critical to the success of the pediatric behavioral audiologic evaluation.

Bone-Conduction Testing and Masking

Bone-conduction testing and the use of masking are no less valuable in the identification, differential diagnosis, and management of hearing impairment in children than they are in adults. Responses to bone-conducted stimuli can be obtained in children through the use of most of the techniques previously described. Head-turn responses can even be elicited using bone-conducted stimuli and VRA. Calibration standards for bone-conducted signals on the heads of infants and children have not been established, but in infants the presence of an air-bone gap can be determined grossly using the bone-conduction oscillator. As with the fitting of earphones, infants sometimes object to wearing this oscillator, but it is always worth a try when there is a question about conductive versus sensorineural hearing loss (SNHL).

Masking to eliminate the participation of the nontest ear in either air- or bone-conduction testing is often necessary. A discussion of masking and masking techniques requires greater attention than is possible in this chapter, but the concept should not be ignored. The interested reader can consult Goldstein and Newman[63] for a review of masking considerations. As mentioned previously, the use of insert earphones when testing by air conduction reduces the need for masking because of the increase in interaural attenuation. Even with bone-conduction testing, masking with insert earphones rather than the cumbersome headphones is easier and probably less prone to error because the oscillator is more easily fit when there are no headphones with which to contend. It has been shown that if masking is required, infants can perform VRA under conditions of masking.[175, 176, 182, 184, 185] Infant masked thresholds are about 5 dB greater than those of adults, so we recommend using about 5 dB less masking than would be required for adults under the same circumstance. Children capable of performing play audiometry or TROCA should be able to perform with earphones and maskers without difficulty. It is important that the professionals who interpret hearing test results be aware of the possible crossover of stimuli to the nontest ear and the need for masking to produce a valid result. Likewise, in situations in which masking cannot be accomplished because the child is fatigued or uncooperative, the professional who interprets the results should use caution in drawing conclusions about the nature and the extent of hearing loss.

Speech Audiometry

Speech can be used as a stimulus in any of the procedures previously described. Speech awareness threshold, the lowest level at which a listener can reliably respond to the presence of speech, provides only limited information with respect to the nature and the degree of impairment. More meaningful information is obtained when the ability of the patient to recognize words can be assessed.

Speech Recognition Threshold

The speech recognition threshold (SRT) is a threshold for recognition of words that are entirely familiar to the listener. For older children and adults, *spondee words* (two-syllable words with equal stress on each syllable, such as baseball and airplane) are typically used. For younger children, the test is usually altered to accommodate the language level of the child being tested. Rather than asking the young child to repeat the words, a different response mode must be used. Young children are frequently reluctant to say words back to the audiologist or may have poor articulation, confounding the assessment of auditory skills with limitations in production. Alternative approaches include asking the child to point to pictures of familiar objects displayed on a table or to respond by pointing to a selection of objects or to body parts. For older children, simple verbal repetition is appropriate as a response.

The SRT is most often administered by the audiologist using live-voice presentation. However, commercial tapes are available, with calibrated lists of spondee words that can be used for greater reliability and validity in testing.

Individual ear SRTs provide a check on the threshold estimates made using more frequency-specific stimuli, such as pure tones, warbled tones, and narrow-band noises. The SRT typically is within 8 dB of the pure-tone average (PTA [average of thresholds at 500, 1000, and 2000 Hz; see later]) when it has been obtained reliably and can provide a check on the reliability of the pure-tone thresholds. However, a word of caution about the relationship between the PTA and the SRT is necessary. The correspondence between the two measures is quite good only when several criteria are met. First, the person being tested must respond in a reliable and consistent way. Second, the words used to estimate the SRT must be chosen from a large set of possible words rather than from a small set. The fewer words that are used, the greater is the chance that guessing will influence performance and improve the score. Third, and most important, the configuration and the type of hearing loss can influence the degree to which the SRT and the PTA correspond. The most common cause of discrepancy between the PTA and the SRT occurs in cases of sharply sloping high-frequency SNHL. In such a case, the PTA might be quite high because of elevated thresholds at 1000 or 2000 Hz. The SRT, on the other hand, may appear quite good because of the information available to the listener in the low frequencies of the speech sound. Again, a small closed set of words from which to choose and a reasonably careful listener can provide an SRT that is considerably better (lower) than the PTA. Conversely, the SRT can be considerably poorer than the PTA in cases of SNHL in which there is severe distortion. The listener may detect the words but may be unable to recognize what is being said. These possibilities should be considered carefully before a child is labeled "unreliable" or "inconsistent" on the basis of lack of agreement between the PTA and the SRT. (See below for testing of functional hearing loss.) Such possibilities also serve to alert one to the limitations of speech recognition testing alone as a means to identify and describe a hearing loss.

Word Intelligibility Testing

Word intelligibility testing, or *speech discrimination testing*, as it is sometimes called, serves a different purpose from that of the SRT. Monosyllabic words are presented to the child at a level well above the SRT or the PTA, such as 30- or 40-dB sensation level (SL [decibels above a given threshold, such as the SRT]). The word lists are commonly "phonetically balanced" so that an appropriate sampling of all phonemes in the language is represented. Lack of ability to recognize words, even when presented at levels well above threshold, provides important diagnostic information as well as information necessary to make a prognosis for rehabilitation. Performance versus intensity on word intelligibility tests, for example, can be useful in locating the site of the lesion that is producing the hearing loss, as well as in providing important information with respect to fitting and use of amplification.

Word intelligibility test scores are usually the percentage of words correctly understood at a given hearing level (HL [refers to normal hearing for a group of young adults]). Most lists used in intelligibility testing have 50 words, so each word represents 2 points. Sometimes half-lists can be used with good reliability, but then each word has a value of 4 points. Scoring is usually recorded simply as "correct" or "incorrect." Tests that use finer analyses of errors, such as phoneme omissions and replacements, are available but have not been used widely in the general clinical setting with children.

It is always important to be aware of the circumstances under which the word intelligibility test score was obtained. In isolation, the percentage of words correctly identified is virtually meaningless. Performance on the test depends very heavily on the intensity level at which the words are presented, the configuration of the hearing loss, the difficulty of the test words, the receptive vocabulary of the child being tested, and, perhaps, whether the words are presented as "live-voice" or using a professional recording. The audiologist reports on the audiogram, in addition to the score, the level of presentation, the test and the list used, and the manner of presentation, so that other professionals can interpret the result properly.

In many clinics, word intelligibility tests are presented routinely at 30- or 40-dB SL (re: SRT). Ordinarily, this level is adequate for the child to achieve maximal performance. However, in cases of SNHL with recruitment, 40-dB SL may be too great and may make it difficult for the child to achieve maximal performance. Again, the configuration of the loss influences the relationship between the SL of the words and the word intelligibility score. The child with a high-frequency hearing loss, for example, may have a low SRT, agreeing with some better low-frequency thresholds. In that case, presentation of words at 30- or 40-dB SL may not be sufficient to permit maximal performance on word intelligibility testing because high-frequency consonants may still be below threshold when presented at those SLs. A presentation level at which speech sounds are comfortably loud is sometimes used and is often a good way to achieve a maximal score with a single test. As a rule, a low discrimination score for a child with hearing loss should indicate to the audiologist that testing at other intensity levels should be done regardless of how the intensity level for the initial test was chosen. In no case should word intelligibility test scores be reported or interpreted without taking into account the presentation level, manner of presentation, and word list.

In some cases, hearing-aid evaluations in particular, word intelligibility lists may be presented in a sound field at intensity levels that more closely represent the levels of conversational speech, such as 50- to 60-dB HL. Performance can then be compared with intelligibility scores obtained monaurally under earphones at higher intensity levels relative to threshold. This information is useful in predicting potential performance with amplification. Thus, testing with hearing aids at conversational levels provides the audiologist with an index (albeit limited) of the benefit gained with specific amplifying devices. In addition, assessment can be made with noise or competing messages in the background to help define the ability of the child to use the hearing aid under less favorable listening conditions.

Children older than about 7 years can typically per-

form the word intelligibility test designed for adults (e.g., Central Institute for the Deaf [CID] W-22 word list[89]). There have also been a number of tests developed for word intelligibility testing in younger children. Haskins,[80] recognizing the need for a test better suited to the level of a child, developed a list of words considered to be within the vocabulary of kindergarten children. The phonetically balanced kindergarten (PBK) series[80] is commonly used today for children aged 4 to 7 years, vocabulary level permitting. Tests for even younger children have also been developed. The same problem that faces the audiologist in obtaining an SRT from a young child exists with respect to testing word intelligibility; that is, a response mode other than verbal repetition is required. This is particularly important when testing hearing-impaired children, who may have poor articulation.

Ross and Lerman,[205] addressing the need for a word intelligibility test suitable for hearing-impaired children, developed a test that uses a picture-pointing response. It is called the Word Intelligibility by Picture Identification (WIPI) test. The norms for this test were derived from a group of hearing-impaired youngsters, so it has greatest validity with that population. However, the WIPI works well with many young children in audiology clinics.

Elliott and Katz[48] developed a word intelligibility test suitable for a receptive language level of children as young as 3 years. Like the WIPI, it incorporates a picture-pointing response; thus, very young children can respond. The test, which was developed at Northwestern University and is called NU-CHIPS (Northwestern University Children's Perception of Speech), has good normative data and is fairly easy to administer.

Finally, Jerger and others[103, 104] developed the Pediatric Speech Intelligibility (PSI) test, which was designed to provide not only a useful word intelligibility test for young children but also a means of assessing central auditory processing. In this test, sentences or words in isolation are used. In addition, words and sentences can be presented in the presence of a competing message, either diotically or dichotically, to better assess central auditory function. The test also uses a picture-pointing task and has applications for children as young as 2 years.

Each of the aforementioned word intelligibility tests for children is available in tape-recorded lists. The audiologist is sometimes more successful, in the tests that permit it, with word lists that use monitored live-voice presentation. However, differences in voice characteristics from one tester to another, careless monitoring of vocal output, or both tend to weaken the reliability and validity of speech test results. With small children, the need for flexibility is great. Therefore, the objectivity and control provided by professionally recorded materials must sometimes be sacrificed, and methods more likely to produce results are used. The professional who must interpret speech results should be aware of the limitations inherent in live-voice, half-list tests and the increase in test-retest variability when testing is done by more than one audiologist.

It should also be noted that each test has its own characteristics with respect to performance as a function of age.[214] Audiologists should be able to interpret word intelligibility test scores appropriately if they are aware of the age-appropriate norms for the test used. A low score by a young child may be age appropriate if the test is designed for an older child. Therefore, the consumer of audiologic information should be aware of all the limitations of interpreting a test score in isolation.

The Audiogram and Hearing Loss

The audiogram is a graphic representation of a child's hearing thresholds for air- and bone-conducted pure-tone stimuli at octave frequencies from 250 to 8000 Hz.° The octave stimulus frequencies are represented on the audiogram abscissa, and stimulus intensities, in decibels referenced to hearing level (dB HL),[5] are shown on the ordinate. At each stimulus frequency, coded symbols are used to denote the threshold. An example of the audiogram form and coded symbols suggested by the American Speech-Language-Hearing Association (ASHA)[7] is shown (Fig. 11–1).

A child's air-conduction thresholds at the tested stimulus frequencies are connected with a solid line. Ordinarily, the thresholds for both ears are plotted on the same graph, but some clinicians prefer to use a separate graph for each ear.

The audiogram most often represents thresholds obtained through earphones. Thresholds obtained with warbled pure tones or narrow-band noise in the sound field (i.e., using loudspeakers) can be plotted using an S to denote "sound field," a W to denote "thresholds for the warbled tone," and an NBN to denote "narrow-band noise."

The audiogram indicates whether hearing is normal or impaired and, if hearing is impaired, the nature and degree of the hearing loss. Several guidelines can be used to retrieve this information from the audiogram. The decision as to whether certain results indicate normal or impaired hearing has been the subject of considerable

°Owing to equipment limitations, bone-conduction thresholds are not tested for an 8000-Hz stimulus.

disagreement among various clinicians and investigators, particularly in the context of hearing loss in children. It has been suggested that impairment begins when the PTA exceeds 25-dB HL,[5] but this is based on adult data. Northern and Downs[168] suggest that significant impairment begins when the average threshold exceeds 15-dB HL, and such children may benefit from trial amplification with a hearing aid. As a compromise, one may consider 20-dB HL as the limit of normal hearing, with impairment beginning when air-conducted sound thresholds exceed this level. However, this compromise may overlook significant conductive hearing loss.

Consequently, when the air- and bone-conduction thresholds of a given child are equal (or within 10 dB of each other) and 20-dB HL or better, hearing is within normal limits. When the audiogram reflects impaired hearing, the relative threshold of air and bone conduction will indicate the nature of the hearing loss: conductive, sensorineural, or mixed.

The audiogram of a child with a conductive hearing loss shows normal bone-conduction thresholds and elevated air-conduction thresholds (Fig. 11–2A). The exception to this general guideline would be a case in which air-conduction thresholds were within the 20-dB normal limit but the bone-conduction thresholds were at least 15 dB better. In other words, the bone-conduction scores could be −5- or 0-dB HL, and the air-conduction scores would be 15- or 20-dB HL. This, too, would be considered a conductive impairment owing to the significant air-bone "gap" of 15-dB or more.

The nature of the hearing loss is sensorineural when the audiogram shows both air- and bone-conduction thresholds to be elevated but within 10 dB of each other (see Fig. 11–2B). When both air- and bone-conduction thresholds are elevated but are separated by more than 10 dB, the hearing loss is mixed in nature (see Fig. 11–2C).

In addition to indicating the nature of the hearing impairment, if any, the audiogram suggests the degree of impairment based on the PTA, which is the average of

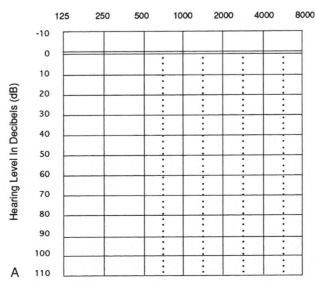

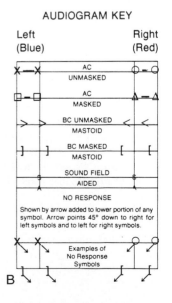

FIGURE 11–1. The audiogram (A) and the symbols (B) used to denote hearing thresholds in decibels of hearing level (re: ANSI, S3.6, 1996), as suggested by the American Speech-Language-Hearing Association.[7]

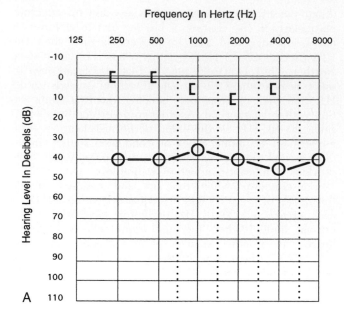

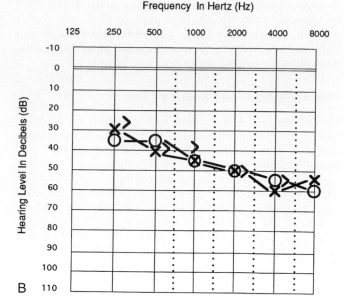

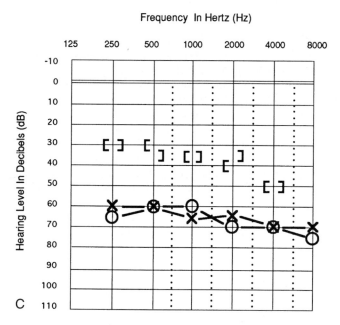

FIGURE 11-2. Sample audiograms showing three different types of hearing loss: *A*, conductive hearing loss (right ear); *B*, sensorineural hearing loss (bilateral); and *C*, mixed hearing loss (bilateral).

air-conduction thresholds at 500, 1000, and 2000 Hz. A preferable way of denoting the degree of hearing loss in a child is to rate the loss as mild, moderate, moderately severe, severe, or profound. The average hearing thresholds[5] often associated with these ratings are 21 to 40 dB (mild), 41 to 55 dB (moderate), 56 to 70 dB (moderately severe), 71 to 90 dB (severe), and 91 dB or greater (profound). Pediatric audiologists often consider thresholds greater than 15-dB HL as the beginning of impairment.[168]

Hence, the audiogram can describe the nature and degree of hearing impairment. This information, along with much more, is helpful in estimating the disability a child might realize. In this context, a description of the loss as either unilateral or bilateral is relevant. A bilateral

impairment has more serious implications than a unilateral loss. However, Bess and Tharpe[14, 238] and Matkin[149] independently concluded that children with even mild bilateral or unilateral hearing losses are educationally handicapped. Limited ability to hear optimally in the poor signal-to-noise ratios (SNRs) common in classrooms seems to be a major factor. An interesting discussion of the impact of unilateral versus bilateral impairment is presented in Chapter 105.

The effects of bilateral hearing impairment on a child's function depend in part on the degree of impairment, whether the impairment is conductive or sensorineural, and the age of onset. Also, the early identification of and intervention for hearing impairment are essential to minimize the effects of early hearing impairment on the child and the child's family. The more severe the hearing loss and the earlier the onset with respect to language acquisition, the more that factors other than the hearing loss influence the child's outcome. Factors such as parental involvement, intelligence, medical status, and multiple handicaps are at least as important to the ability of the severely hearing-impaired child to achieve academically and to learn language and speech as are the degree and configuration of the hearing loss.[21, 151, 158, 206]

Summary of Behavioral Assessment Techniques

The material presented thus far has shown that a variety of age-dependent behavioral techniques are available for the audiologic assessment of neonates, infants, and young children. Ordinarily, the techniques for neonates and infants up to about 6 months of age provide only qualitative information about the auditory function of the child in question (i.e., hearing screening), so clinicians rely more on physiologic tests in this age group. At about 6 months of age, quantitative threshold information, including frequency- and ear-specific thresholds, to air- and bone-conducted signals, is obtainable with VRA. By 3 years of age, most children can be assessed using conditioned play audiometric techniques that can provide complete audiometric data.

The various assessment techniques rely on a continuum of auditory responsivity, from gross auditory reflexes to refined voluntary responses. Certain techniques are better suited to the evaluation of behavior at opposite ends of this continuum, whereas other techniques (e.g., VRA and TROCA) can assess responsivity throughout the continuum. Through a knowledge of where on the continuum the child falls, the appropriate test can be used, and judgment as to whether the hearing is normal or impaired can be made on the basis of the appropriateness of the child's responses.

Physiologic Assessment Techniques

It can be difficult to obtain a reliable test of hearing in the pediatric patient when using behavioral test methods. Tests that do not require a behavioral response are helpful to the pediatric audiologist and otolaryngologist. The three physiologic assessment techniques most often used are acoustic immittance measures (admittance or impedance), OAEs, and AEPs. These tests are often considered objective because, rather than requiring a voluntary response from the patient, they take advantage of naturally occurring physiologic responses. However, the information obtained by such tests must still be interpreted by a human observer and is still susceptible to artifact and error. Therefore, the objectivity of such tests should be treated with a healthy skepticism. The behavioral audiogram remains the gold standard of hearing sensitivity, so physiologic test results are taken to supplement or provide information until the audiogram can be obtained. The primary goal of the ongoing audiologic assessment of a child with hearing impairment is to develop a reliable and valid audiogram.

Acoustic Immittance Measurements and Acoustic Reflectance

Immittance is a term used to describe the transfer of acoustic energy, whether measured in terms of acoustic *admittance* (flow of energy) or *acoustic impedance* (opposition to flow of energy). Admittance and impedance are reciprocals and so provide similar information in a different way. Clinical immittance measures, which are measures of either acoustic admittance or acoustic impedance at the tympanic membrane, provide information from which inferences about the integrity of the entire middle-ear system can be made. Immittance measures that are commonly used are *tympanometry* and the *acoustic reflex* (the activation of the stapedius muscle by sound). They can be used in adults as well as in children but are particularly valuable in children because they require little cooperation and no voluntary response from the patient. Also, there is a high prevalence of middle-ear disease among children, especially otitis media with effusion, that can be reliably identified and monitored using immittance measures.

To fully understand and interpret acoustic immittance test results, one should first have an understanding of the basic underlying physical principles. Only a brief introduction to some of the many and complex factors involved in acoustic immittance is presented here. The interested reader should consult the references for more comprehensive information on the development of acoustic immittance instruments and the principles of acoustic immittance testing.[15, 139, 143, 144, 194, 217, 248, 261]

Impedance Versus Admittance

Impedance

The opposition to the flow of acoustic energy that is attributable to mass and stiffness is called *reactance*. In reactance, energy is stored. The portion of reactance that is due to stiffness is called *negative*, or *compliant*, reactance; the part attributable to mass is called *positive*, or *mass*, reactance. *Resistance* is the portion of the impedance attributable to friction in the system, in which case energy is dissipated. If a system has stiffness and mass, the overall reactance will be the sum of the two reactances contributed. Because one component is negative (compliant) and the other is positive (mass), the absolute magnitude of the reactance is less than either one alone. The reactance and the resistance together determine the total impedance. However, because the reactance and the resistance are out of phase with each other, the combination of components requires the use of complex (real and imaginary) numbers, which, for simplicity's sake, are not discussed in this chapter. Mass reactance is proportional to frequency, and compliant reactance is inversely proportional to frequency; thus, their relative effects depend on the frequency of the driving force. Compliant reactance increases as frequency decreases. Mass reactance increases with increases in frequency. If a system has greater compliant reactance than mass reactance, it is called a *stiffness-controlled system*. If a system has greater mass reactance, it is called a *mass-controlled system*.

Admittance

The reciprocal of impedance is admittance. The terms used to describe the components of admittance are *susceptance* (the reciprocal of reactance) and *conductance* (the reciprocal of resistance). The reciprocal of negative (compliant) reactance is *positive susceptance, or compliance*. The reciprocal of positive (mass) reactance is *negative susceptance*.

Middle-Ear Immittance

The middle-ear system has all three elements of the mechanical systems previously described. There is stiffness provided by the tympanic membrane, the ossicular chain, and the volume of air in the middle ear. Mass is provided primarily by the ossicles. The resistance (or conductance) component comes primarily from the cochlea.

The basis for acoustic immittance testing in the auditory system is the ability to determine the input acoustic immittance of the middle-ear system at the tympanic membrane. This is done by introducing a controlled force (sound pressure in the form of a probe tone) into the ear canal and measuring the resulting sound pressure level (SPL). The degree to which the middle ear permits the flow of acoustic energy determines how much acoustic energy is reflected from the tympanic membrane and, as a result, how much can be measured in the ear canal. The SPL of the signal in the ear canal is proportional to the immittance in the system.[15] For a given force, the greater the flow of acoustic energy through the middle ear (greater admittance, less impedance), the lower is the overall SPL in the ear canal. The poorer the flow of acoustic energy through the middle ear (less admittance, greater impedance), the greater is the SPL in the ear canal.

Probe-Tone Effects

The normally functioning middle-ear system is a stiffness-controlled system when immittance is measured using a low-frequency probe tone (e.g., 226 Hz). For all practical purposes, the measure is one of compliant reactance (or compliance). For this reason, acoustic immittance measures using a low-frequency probe tone are often called measures of middle-ear compliance.

Some instruments incorporate a higher-frequency probe tone in addition to a tone around 226 Hz. Probe tones of 678 and 1000 Hz are closer to the resonant frequency of the middle ear and are less dominated by the stiffness in the system. A change in the stiffness of the middle ear resulting from a pathologic condition causes a greater proportional change in immittance with a high-frequency probe tone than with a low-frequency probe tone, making abnormalities easier to detect with the higher-frequency probe. This is true for pathologic conditions that increase stiffness (e.g., otosclerosis) as well as those that decrease stiffness (e.g., disarticulation of the

ossicles). In addition, the high-frequency probe tone is a more sensitive indicator of changes in mass, such as those that accompany cholesteatoma and adhesions.

Instrumentation

Instruments measure or report immittance values in different ways. Some use impedance values (Z) and some use admittance values (Y). Some also have circuitry that permits the separation of admittance into its susceptance (B) and conductance (G) components. Combined with low- and high-frequency probe tones, the capability to evaluate in detail the immittance characteristics of the middle-ear system is greatly enhanced when there is separation of the B and G components. Some characteristics of the abnormal middle-ear system can be obscured if one assumes that there is only a stiffness-controlled system and uses only a low-frequency probe tone.

In clinical immittance-measuring systems, the probe signal is introduced into the ear canal via a probe assembly and tip made to fit snugly into the ear canal. The assembly includes a driver, or transducer, to deliver the probe signal to the ear and a microphone used in the measurement of ear-canal SPL. The other important component of the delivery system is a pump that allows the tester to vary the pressure in the ear canal. When the probe assembly is fit hermetically into the ear canal with the soft tip, acoustic immittance of the ear canal and middle-ear system can be measured with different amounts of air pressure in the ear canal. That is, the air pressure in the ear canal can be increased or decreased with the pump, and changes in voltage at the earphone needed to maintain a constant SPL in the ear canal can be used to derive measures of immittance. The changes in immittance as a function of changing air pressure in the ear canal are plotted graphically as a tympanogram.

Tympanometry

Most clinical immittance instruments measure acoustic admittance rather than acoustic impedance, in large part because the measurement of admittance requires simpler circuitry and analysis. An admittance tympanogram is simply a plot of the admittance of the middle ear as a function of air pressure in the ear canal. Admittance of the middle ear is actually inferred from two measures: a measure of the admittance of the ear canal between the tip of the probe and the tympanic membrane, and a measure of the admittance of the entire system, from probe tip through the middle ear. The acoustic admittance of only the middle ear is estimated as the difference between these two measures.

The admittance of the ear canal is estimated by first sealing the ear canal with the probe tip and changing the ear-canal pressure to a very high (+200 or +400 daPa) pressure or to a very low (−400 daPa) pressure, thereby effectively stiffening the tympanic membrane so that it has, for all practical purposes, no compliance (i.e., zero admittance). In that case, all of the admittance measured at the probe is a result of the volume of air in the ear canal. When a probe tone around 226 Hz is used at

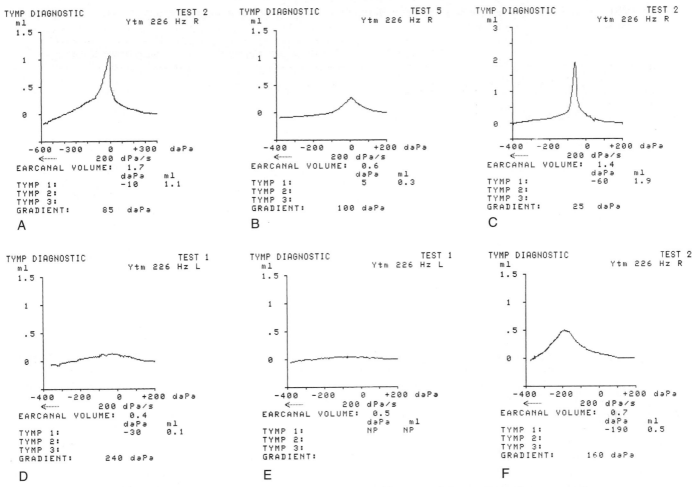

FIGURE 11–3. Admittance tympanograms. *A,* Normal-hearing adult ear. Equivalent ear-canal volume was estimated at +400 dPa, air pressure was swept positive-to-negative starting at +400 dPa, and a 226-Hz probe tone was used. (Tympanometric peak pressure = −10 dPa; peak admittance = 1.1 ms or mL; and gradient [measured as the tympanometric width] = 85 dPa.) *B,* Admittance tympanogram for a normal-hearing adult ear with low peak admittance (0.3 mL) according to norms for the instrumentation settings used but with tympanometric peak pressure and tympanometric width (gradient) within normal limits. *C,* Admittance tympanogram for an 11-year-old boy with mild low-frequency conductive hearing loss. Notice that peak admittance is abnormally high (1.9 mL), causing the scale on the ordinate to change from 0-to-1.5 mL to 0-to-3 mL. Tympanometric width (gradient) at 25 dPa is also abnormally small. *D,* Admittance tympanogram for an 11-month-old infant with otitis media with effusion. The tympanogram has a low, rounded shape, with peak admittance at 0.1 mL and tympanometric width (gradient) equal to 240 dPa. *E,* Admittance tympanogram for the left ear of a 12-month-old infant with otitis media with effusion. The lack of a discernible peak causes the instrument to record "NP" (no peak) for the admittance values. *F,* Admittance tympanogram for the right ear of the same infant with peak admittance and tympanometric width (gradient) within normal limits but with high negative tympanometric peak pressure (not an unusual finding in the contralateral ear of a child with unilateral otitis media with effusion).

atmospheric pressure, the acoustic admittance, in milli-Siemens (mS), of the ear canal is approximately equivalent to the volume (mL or cc) of air in the ear canal. The estimate of ear-canal volume has some clinical value and is discussed later. After the estimate of the ear-canal admittance, ear-canal air pressure is varied smoothly from the extreme starting pressure, toward ambient pressure (0 daPa), and then on to the opposite extreme. Most clinical tympanometric protocols start with high positive pressure, measure ear-canal admittance (i.e., equivalent ear-canal volume), and then sweep the pressure in a positive-to-

negative direction while continuously measuring admittance. For example, Figure 11–3A is a tympanogram from a normal adult ear. The ear-canal volume (1.7 mL) was estimated first and then the immittance system's air pump swept pressure from +400 to −600 daPa as admittance medial to the probe was monitored. The tympanogram plot reflects compensated admittance; that is, the admittance attributed to the ear canal is deducted from the dynamic admittance estimate so that the tympanogram reflects only the admittance of the middle ear. In a normally functioning middle ear, admittance increases as

TABLE 11–1. Mean Values and 90% Range for Normal Ears of Children Ages Approximately 3 Years Old and Older From Three Data Sets

	Nozza et al[180]*	Koebsell and Margolis[124]†	Margolis and Heller[142]‡
Ear-canal volume (mL)			
Mean	0.900	NA	0.74
SD	0.26		NA
5th to 95th percentiles	0.6–1.35		0.42–0.97
n	130		92
Peak admittance (mS)			
Mean	0.78	0.67	0.50
SD	0.31	0.22	0.19
5th to 95th percentiles	0.4–1.39	NA	0.22–0.81
n	130	60	92
Tympanometric width (daPa)			
Mean	104	124	100
SD	32	33	NA
5th to 95th percentiles	60–168	68–187	59–151
n	130	60	92

° +400 to −600 daPa; 3–16 years old. Equivalent volume estimated at +400 daPa.

† MAX/MIN method, +400 to −400 daPa; 2.8–5.8 years old. Equivalent volume estimated by using value of minimum tail of tympanogram, which was at −400 daPa for 43 subjects and at +400 daPa for 17 subjects.

‡ +200 to −300 daPa; 3.7–5.8 years old. Equivalent volume estimated at +200 daPa.

NA, not available from report.

ear-canal air pressure approaches ambient pressure. Peak admittance of the middle ear should occur in the vicinity of 0 daPa, although there is some range of normal values (usually +50 to −150 daPa for children). As air pressure goes further toward high negative pressure, admittance decreases and the result is the characteristic inverted V tympanogram shape.

Peak compensated admittance is the middle-ear admittance at the peak of the tympanogram (1.1 mL in Fig. 11–3A). Note that for this instrument, admittance using the 226-Hz probe tone is given in equivalent volume (mL) rather than in actual physical units of admittance (mS), which are equivalent for that frequency under normal atmospheric conditions. The ear-canal pressure at which peak compensated admittance occurs is called the *tympanometric peak pressure* (−10 daPa on the tympanogram in Fig. 11–3A). This is highly correlated with pressure in the middle ear, as the middle-ear admittance is usually greatest when the pressure difference between the ear canal and the middle ear is low or zero.[237] The tympanometric peak pressure may not necessarily reflect the actual air pressure condition of the middle ear but

still is of some clinical value with respect to tympanogram interpretation.

Tympanometric gradient is a measure that quantifies the rate of change in admittance around the peak of the tympanogram. Several ways of quantifying gradient have been suggested.[37] The method most favored at this time is known as *tympanometric width*; this is the horizontal distance (in daPa units) between the sides of the tympanogram at half the peak admittance. The more sharp the peak of the tympanogram, the smaller is the tympanometric width. An alternative gradient measure is a ratio of two values, a/b, derived from the tympanogram. The first (a) is the difference in admittance between the tympanogram peak and the admittance at which the tympanogram is 100 daPa wide, and the second (b) is peak admittance. When gradient is expressed as a ratio, the possible range of values is 0 to 1 and, in contrast to the tympanometric width, the more sharp is the peak of the tympanogram, the greater is the gradient value. Table 11–1 provides data on children 3 years old and older, with normal otoscopic examination, from several different studies. The protocols in the studies of the children differed in some

TABLE 11–2. Values for Peak Admittance and Tympanometric Width for Normal Ears of Children Approximately 6 Months to 3 Years Old

	Age (mo)						
	De Chicchis et al[36]			Roush et al[208]			
	6–11	12–23	24–35	6–12	13–18	19–24	25–30
Peak admittance (mS)							
Mean	0.32	0.34	0.47	0.39	0.41	0.48	0.52
SD	0.16	0.01	0.24	0.15	0.16	0.18	0.24
Tympanometric width (daPa)							
Mean	168	143	130	160	148	149	142
SD	57	37	33	54	42	43	44

ways that are known to affect the data; all three studies are presented, with information about the protocols used, so the values can be interpreted properly. Table 11–2 provides data on younger children and illustrates developmental change in the first years of life in tympanometric variables.

The tympanogram in Figure 11–3A is within the normal range for adults.[262] It provides gradient in the form of tympanometric width, which for this individual is 85 daPa.

Some characteristics of tympanograms are useful for making clinical diagnoses. In general, pathologic conditions that stiffen the middle-ear system reduce acoustic admittance and thereby produce tympanograms with low peak admittance values (Fig. 11–3B). Pathologies that loosen the middle-ear system increase acoustic admittance and thereby produce tympanograms with high peak admittance values (Fig. 11–3C). Note that the tympanogram in Figure 11–3C does not look radically different from the one in Figure 11–3A. However, careful attention should be paid to the y-axis (admittance), which has been rescaled to accommodate the abnormally high admittance peak (1.9 mL). This also changes the ratio of units on the x-axis to y-axis, so the relationships between admittance and pressure are different from those for the normal ear in Figure 11–3A. It is important to be aware of the potential for changes in scaling to occur and the impact that they have on the pattern of the tympanogram, even though the actual values for the immittance parameters are accurately represented in the numeric table below the tympanogram.

Otitis media with effusion tends to stiffen the middle-ear system, so peak admittance is reduced, but the tympanometric shape (i.e., gradient) also changes, becoming more rounded or even flat (Fig. 11–3D). Tympanometric width tends to increase as a middle-ear condition worsens and, usually, as effusion develops. Eventually, the peak is no longer detectable, and a tympanogram is considered to have "no peak," with no estimate of tympanometric peak pressure, peak admittance, or gradient (tympanometric width) provided (Fig. 11–3E). Figure 11–3F shows the tympanogram of the contralateral ear of that in Figure 11–3E and represents normal tympanometric width and peak admittance but high negative tympanometric peak pressure, a common finding in the contralateral ear of a child with unilateral otitis media with effusion.

In 1987, the American National Standards Institute (ANSI) published a standard for specifications for immittance instruments. The standard requires that instruments be designed to measure actual physical quantities of immittance (admittance or impedance). It also requires that for the range of admittance values commonly associated with normal adult ears, the admittance tympanogram should maintain an aspect ratio of 300 daPa (x-axis) to 1.0 mS (y-axis). Therefore, admittance tympanograms recorded on different instruments that meet the ANSI[4] standard should be comparable with each other. (However, it should be noted that in a study that compared tympanograms from different instruments on a panel of normal ears, some differences were found.[35]) It is important to note that instruments designed before the new

standard recorded impedance in arbitrary compliance units rather than in absolute physical quantities, and the ratio of air pressure to "compliance units" varied from subject to subject. With those earlier instruments, actual physical quantities (impedance) had to be computed on the basis of specific measurements apart from the tympanogram. The significance of this information is that a great deal of the history of interpretation of tympanograms for screening and diagnosis is tied to the early impedance instruments with arbitrary compliance units.[188, 190] Unfortunately, there is no way to directly compare the data from currently available instruments with those using the arbitrary units, so the use of pattern classification schemes developed based on previous methods of plotting tympanograms may not apply to the admittance tympanograms obtained with instruments that meet the current ANSI standard.

Tympanogram Classification by Pattern Identification

In the past, pattern classification schemes[96, 190] were used almost exclusively for tympanogram interpretation. The one most well known is that proposed by Jerger.[96] Because the system was developed using impedance meters with arbitrary compliance units, it is not quantitatively described. For Jerger type A, there is a peak that is within the normal range with respect to tympanometric peak pressure. Type A was subdivided into A_S (type A, shallow), which refers to a tympanogram with a peak within the normal range of tympanometric peak pressures but with low peak immittance, and type A_D (type A, deep), which refers to a tympanogram with a peak within the normal range of tympanometric peak pressures but with high peak immittance. Type B is the absence of a peak (i.e., a flat tympanogram). Type C has a peak, but it has high negative (outside the normal range) tympanometric peak pressure. Type A is considered normal. Type A_S is associated with a stiffening pathology and normal middle-ear pressure (e.g., otosclerosis), and type A_D is associated with a loosening pathology and normal middle-ear pressure (e.g., fracture or dislocation of ossicles). Type B is associated most commonly with middle-ear effusion; Type C is associated with eustachian tube dysfunction or other conditions that cause problems in equalization of pressure in the middle ear. Some have subdivided type C into type C_1 and type C_2 categories by arbitrarily dividing the range of possible tympanometric peak pressures at −100 and −200 daPa, so that a peak between −100 and −200 daPa is type C_1 and a peak beyond −200 daPa is type C_2.[137, 251]

The pattern classification scheme attributed to Jerger[96] and its variations are used widely in clinics. However, they have never been validated adequately, and given that the new instruments record tympanograms using the actual physical units rather than the arbitrary compliance units that were used for the original classifications, the validity of such schemes using current tympanograms is more uncertain. For example, different practitioners use different peak admittance values to differentiate between

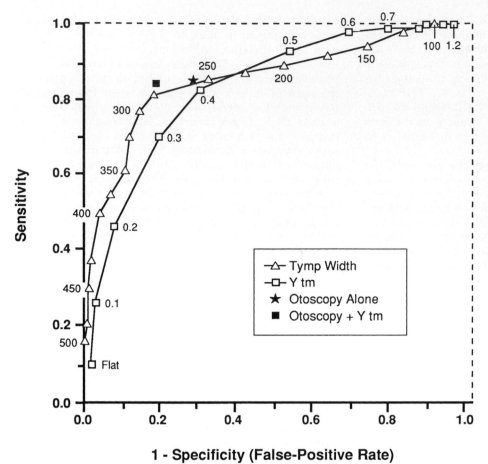

FIGURE 11–4. Receiver operating characteristic space with sensitivity and 1 − specificity (i.e., false-positive rate) of tympanometric width and peak admittance (Ytm) represented as curves with symbols at selected cut-off values. Also indicated are otoscopy results combined with the two tympanometric variables. (Modified from Nozza RS, Bluestone CD, Kardatzke D, Bachman RN. Identification of middle ear effusion by aural acoustic admittance and otoscopy. Ear Hear 15:310, 1994.)

the subcategories of type A or use different definitions of type B (e.g., does it represent no peak at all or some arbitrarily chosen low value of peak admittance?). In addition, the Jerger classification scheme does not take into account the shape (gradient) of the tympanogram, which carries valuable diagnostic information.[22, 124, 142, 180, 181, 190]

An alternative pattern classification scheme using Y, B, and G tympanograms was proposed by Vanhuyse and associates[249] and has been discussed by others.[76, 143, 144, 248] Variations in tympanogram shape can occur when admittance is separated into the susceptance (B) and conductance (G) components and when a higher-frequency probe tone is used. A detailed review of the categorization scheme is beyond the scope of this chapter, but the Vanhuyse model has added to the diagnostic power of immittance measures and is important to those with an interest in a more complex categorization of acoustic admittance measures.

Tympanogram Classification by Quantitative Analysis

With the absolute physical values of immittance provided by current tympanograms, there has been increased interest in using quantitative schemes for interpretation.[142, 178] With information on the normal range of values for different age groups (see Tables 11–1 and 11–2), interpretation of quantitative tympanograms is facilitated. We know that high peak admittance values can be an indica-

tion of middle-ear pathology that has reduced the stiffness of the middle-ear system or is a consequence of tympanic membrane abnormality. We can quantitatively identify ears that have low peak admittance that can result from increased stiffness such as accompanies otosclerosis or other middle-ear diseases. Abnormal middle-ear pressure may indicate eustachian tube dysfunction.

Identification of Middle-Ear Effusion

Tympanometry

In children, the most frequent application of tympanometry is for the diagnosis of middle-ear effusion. Nozza and colleagues[36, 180, 181] examined the relationship between the quantitative measures of admittance tympanograms and middle-ear effusion as diagnosed by surgeons at the time of myringotomy and tube placement and/or as diagnosed by a validated otoscopist. Using logistic regression analyses, the relative ability of various tympanometric measures, alone and in combination with each other, to discriminate between ears with and ears without effusion was determined. The two best immittance measures for identifying middle-ear effusion in ears of children scheduled for myringotomy and tube surgery (a chronic otitis media group) were tympanometric width and peak compensated admittance. Receiver operating characteristic (ROC) curves for the latter two measures, along with some other combined variables, indicate the relative sen-

TABLE 11–3. Sensitivity and Specificity of Tympanometric Width and Peak Admittance for Identification of Middle-Ear Effusion in Ears of School-Age Children Representative of the General Population

Variable	Criterion	Sensitivity (%) (n = 9)	Specificity (%) (n = 135)
Tympanometric width° (daPa)	>150	89	93
	>200	78	99
	>250	78	100
Peak admittance† (mmho)	≤0.1	67	100
	≤0.2	78	100
	≤0.3	78	98
	≤0.4	78	89

° From Nozza et al, 1994[181] (measures made on tympanometric data originally reported in Nozza et al, 1992[180]).
† From Nozza et al, 1992.[180]

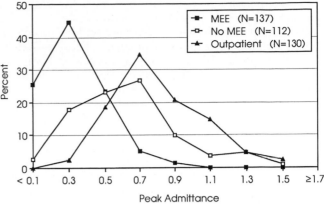

FIGURE 11–5. Distributions in percentage of ears for values of peak admittance for three groups of ears: those with middle-ear effusion (MEE) as determined by a surgeon from a group of children undergoing myringotomy and tube surgery (MEE group); those with no MEE from the children undergoing surgery (no MEE group); and those with no MEE from a group of children representative of the general population who entered the hospital as outpatients for services unrelated to their ears (outpatient group). (Data from Nozza RJ, Bluestone CD, Kardatzke D, Bachman RN. Towards the validation of aural acoustic immittance measures for diagnosis of middle ear effusion in children. Ear Hear 13:442, 1992.)

sitivity and specificity of the measures (Fig. 11–4). In these ears, the findings of the surgeons provided the gold standard for the presence or absence of effusion.

Depending on the population being evaluated, the criteria developed for ears of children with chronic or recurrent middle-ear disease may or may not be appropriate. For that reason, the sensitivity and specificity of criteria based on data from children more representative of the general population[180, 181] were also determined (Table 11–3). The specificity of the admittance variables is much lower for the group of children receiving tubes (see Fig. 11–4) than for the group representing the general population (Table 11–3). This is probably due to the greater overlap in the distributions of ears with and ears without effusion for the different admittance variables in children undergoing myringotomy and tube surgery. For example, the distributions of peak admittance for ears with effusion from the group receiving tubes, ears with no effusion from the group receiving tubes, and ears with no effusion from the group of children representing the normal population[181] are shown (Fig. 11–5). It is clear that there are three different distributions. The overlap between the distributions of the two sets of ears from the surgery group is great, limiting the extent to which any criterion is able to separate them well. The distribution for the ears with no effusion from the nonsurgery ears is much farther removed along the peak admittance continuum and therefore does not overlap with the ears with effusion from the surgery group. The effects of the population being tested and the diagnostic criterion used are illustrated by these data and discussed in other places.[177–179] There is no set of criteria that are universally satisfactory.

The combination of otoscopic diagnosis and tympanometric information has also been evaluated.[181] In the ears undergoing myringotomy and tube surgery, diagnostic decision criteria based on both acoustic immittance measures and the otoscopist's diagnosis could be found that improved performance a little. For example, in our study,[181] the otoscopist was highly experienced and had been validated against surgical findings. However, as is often the case, although the sensitivity of otoscopy was

good (85%), the specificity was low (71%). When the acoustic immittance data were taken into account, specificity could be improved with only a little sacrifice in sensitivity. For example, a decision criterion might be as follows. If the peak admittance is 0.1 or less, the ear is considered to have effusion; if the peak admittance is more than 0.6, the ear is considered to have no effusion; and if peak admittance is between 0.2 and 0.6, the otoscopic diagnosis rules. In our data set from children undergoing myringotomy and tube surgery, a group with chronic or recurrent middle-ear disease, sensitivity was 81% and specificity was 85%, a little better than either otoscopy or peak admittance alone (see Fig. 11–4). A variety of such combined decision criteria are described by Nozza and associates.[181]

Some investigators have recommended addition of the acoustic reflex in the immittance test battery for identification of middle-ear effusion. The role of the acoustic reflex in that context is discussed in the section on acoustic reflex.

Acoustic Reflectometry

An alternative method for the identification of middle-ear effusion uses a measurement called *acoustic reflectometry*. The acoustic reflectometer generates a sound in the ear canal and measures the sound energy reflected back from the tympanic membrane.[235] The instrument is hand-held and has a speculum-like tip that is put into the entrance of the ear canal. No hermetic seal is required, thus making the test desirable for use with children. The relationship between the known output of the device and the resultant sound in the ear canal provides diagnostic information. An early version of the instrument used only the sound pressure level in the ear canal in the diagnostic decision. Because of variability in performance,[127, 128, 235] a different way of analyzing the reflected sound was investigated. Combs[28] suggested that plotting out the reflectivity data on frequency by amplitude axes provided better diagnostic information than the scale of reflectivity. Combs[28] measured the angle of the spectral plot and determined that the angle holds more diagnostic information with respect to middle-ear effusion than the reflectivity (dB) scale. The current version of the instrument automatically determines the spectral angle and displays a number between 1 and 5 to indicate the likelihood of an effusion. This version of the instrument may provide better diagnostic information than did the original version and is getting some favorable response in primary care settings.[117, 118, 191, 201]

Diagnostic Value of Ear-Canal Volume Estimates

When a tympanogram is flat and has an abnormally high equivalent ear-canal volume measurement, it is often associated with an opening in the tympanic membrane. Tympanometry performed during follow-up of myringotomy and tube surgery often provides evidence of a functioning polyethylene tube in that way. Sometimes, visual inspection does not detect a small perforation or is insufficient to determine the status of a tube, so the tympanometric findings can be helpful. However, it is not always clear that a given ear-canal volume measurement is abnormally large. It has been reported that the volume of an ear with perforation in the tympanic membrane may be very near the limits of the normal range when the middle-ear mucosa is inflamed.[248p57] When there is a question, comparison with a normal contralateral ear is sometimes useful, because ear-canal volume is highly correlated between the ears of the same individual. If there is a large difference between the ears, an opening in one tympanic membrane is suspected. Also, previous tympanograms sometimes provide comparative data of value in making a diagnosis.

An abnormally small ear-canal volume can be evidence of poor probe fit in the ear canal or of an obstructed probe. Sometimes, in trying to obtain a hermetic seal, particularly with a hand-held probe, the tip may be pressed against the ear-canal wall and occlude the tip. Also, debris or cerumen from the ear canal can get into the probe. Wax in the probe may cause measurement errors of an unpredictable nature. One should always be certain that the probe assembly is free of wax or other materials so that valid admittance measures can be obtained.

Other Considerations

Some points should be borne in mind in performing tympanometry and interpreting tympanometric information. First, one should understand that the immittance of the system is measured at the plane of the tympanic membrane. If there are abnormalities of the tympanic membrane that cause it to have very high admittance, such as atrophic areas, the lower admittance of the rest of the system is obscured in the measurement. The high admittance of the tympanic membrane is recorded, and the remainder of the system does not reveal its ability to transfer acoustic energy.

Also, differences in instrumentation settings can cause differences in tympanometric configuration. The rate and direction of air-pressure changes, for example, can cause differences in peak pressure and amplitude from one instrument to the next.

Tympanometry With Infants

The use of tympanometry with infants younger than 6 months is controversial. Paradise and colleagues[190] found that impedance testing using a 226-Hz probe tone was not sensitive for identifying ears filled with fluid in young infants. Apparently, compliance of the ear-canal wall interferes with the recording of immittance at the tympanic membrane. Marchant and colleagues[138] reported success in identifying otitis media with effusion in young infants, using a 660-Hz probe tone and the susceptance (B) tympanogram. Peak admittance less than 0 mS correctly indicated effusion (as determined by myringotomy) in a high percentage of ears of young infants. On the other hand, Holte and colleagues,[91] in a study of multifrequency tympanometry in infants, found that infants younger than 4 months had middle-ear admittance different from that of adults. They found that the use of a 226-Hz probe tone resulted in the least variability and recommended use of the low-frequency probe tone for admittance testing in infants. The value of high-frequency probe tone tympanometry in newborns has gained attention.[202] Tympanograms of infants with middle-ear effusion are illustrated in Figure 11–6. Two ears are shown: one with middle-ear effusion and one with normal middle-ear function. The 226-Hz tympanograms both exhibited peak admittance values in the normal range. However, examination of the 1000-Hz tympanograms clearly reflects the difference between the ear with middle-ear effusion and the one with the normal middle-ear function. High-frequency probe tone tympanometry can be invaluable when performing follow-up rescreening and diagnostic evaluations of very young infants who have been screened as newborns. This is particularly important as universal newborn screening programs increase in numbers and increasing numbers of infants are referred for follow-up at very young ages (see Chapters 10 and 23).

Summary of Physiologic Assessment Techniques

Tympanometry is a graphic representation of tympanic membrane immittance when air pressure is varied in the ear canal. The tympanogram provides an estimate of acoustic immittance of the middle ear, middle-ear pressure, and how admittance changes under changing ear-canal pressure. The peak compensated acoustic immittance, tympanometric width (or gradient), and, in some cases, tympanometric peak pressure can be used to infer the status of the middle ear.

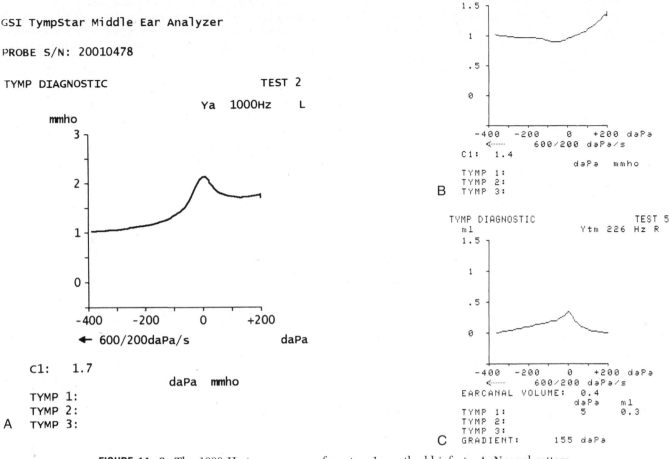

FIGURE 11–6. The 1000-Hz tympanograms from two 1-month-old infants. *A*, Normal pattern; a normal otoacoustic emission was measured in this ear. *B*, Abnormal pattern reflecting presumed middle-ear disorder. No otoacoustic emission was present. *C*, A 226-Hz tympanogram measured at the same time in the same ear as in *B*. The low-frequency pattern suggests normal middle-ear function, illustrating the potential false-negative finding using low-frequency probe tones in the ears of young infants.

Acoustic Middle-Ear Muscle Reflex

Acoustic immittance instrumentation can also be used to detect the contraction of the middle-ear muscles, the stapedius and tensor tympani, to intense sound stimulation. This contraction is called the *acoustic middle-ear muscle reflex,* or simply the *acoustic reflex.*[169]

The anatomy of the acoustic reflex arc is described in Chapter 9. The afferent portion of the arc, up to and including the superior olivary complex, is shared with the hearing mechanism. The efferent fibers of the acoustic reflex arc arise from brain stem neuronal connections between the olivary complex and the facial nerve nucleus for the stapedius muscle and between the olivary complex and the trigeminal nerve nucleus for the tensor tympani muscle.[95]

The acoustic immittance instrument indicates the status of the acoustic reflex in two ways: first, the reflex results in a stiffening of the ossicular chain and a concomitant change in immittance; second, because the reflex is bilateral to a unilateral stimulus (the muscles of both sides contract when one ear is stimulated), an intense stimulus can be delivered to one ear, and the probe tip of the immittance instrument inserted in the opposite ear can detect the change in immittance caused by the reflex.

When the immittance instrument is used to detect an acoustic reflex elicited by stimulating the opposite ear, the response is commonly called the *contralateral,* or *crossed,* acoustic reflex. Many acoustic immittance instruments have probe tips designed both to stimulate and to detect the acoustic reflex in the same ear; the reflex is elicited and its effect on immittance is detected in the same ear. Under these conditions, the response is called the *ipsilateral,* or *uncrossed,* acoustic reflex.

For clinical purposes, three acoustic reflex parameters are commonly considered: the reflex threshold intensity, its response amplitude decay in time, and the differential response to different types of sound stimuli. These features enable the examiner to make qualitative judgments about hearing, such as the type of impairment and the probable site of a lesion, as well as quantitative judgments, such as an estimation of the degree of hearing loss and hearing-aid effectiveness.

The threshold of the acoustic reflex is operationally defined as the minimal stimulus intensity required to produce a reliable change in monitored immittance. This minimal intensity, or *acoustic reflex threshold,* is typically specified in either dB HL or dB SL (referenced to the individual's behavioral hearing threshold for a given stimulus). For example, a reflex threshold of 85-dB HL for a 1000-Hz pure tone can also be expressed as 85-dB SL if the individual's hearing threshold for that stimulus is 0-dB HL. If the individual's hearing threshold for the same 1000-Hz pure tone is 30-dB HL, the reflex threshold of 85-dB HL can also be expressed as 55-dB SL. These relationships between SL and HL are important to an understanding of the acoustic reflex parameters.

In adults with normal hearing, the contralateral acoustic reflex threshold for pure tones of different frequencies is approximately 85 dB poorer than behavioral hearing thresholds (i.e., 85-dB SL). The range of effective stimulus intensities is 70- to 95-dB SL.[95, 96] Approximately 20-dB less intensity is required to elicit a reflex with a broad-band noise stimulus.[95, 221] Ipsilateral reflex thresholds are approximately 10 dB better than contralateral thresholds.[56, 156]

Age is an important factor that relates to the presence of the acoustic reflex and its threshold. In one school-age population of 1600 ears,[130] 13% had absent acoustic reflexes. In school-age children, the threshold is on the average 92-dB HL.[130] An adult with normal hearing has an average threshold of about 85-dB HL.[95, 96] On the other hand, only a small percentage of neonates exhibit an acoustic reflex when an impedance bridge with a 220-Hz probe-tone frequency is used to detect the response.[116, 153] However, some studies have shown that the acoustic reflex is measurable in infants when a high-frequency probe tone is used.[13, 88, 140, 154, 254] Early research suggested that when the acoustic reflex is present in infants and young children, its threshold is slightly higher than that found in adults.[95, 203] Average thresholds in neonates and infants approximated 95-dB HL in some studies.[116, 153] However, Hirsch and associates[88] reported ipsilateral acoustic reflex thresholds in newborns for a 2000-Hz tone at 78-dB SPL, and for a broad-band noise at 64-dB SPL, using a high-frequency probe tone (800 Hz), in the intensive care unit.

Various types of hearing impairment can influence the acoustic reflex. As Jerger and associates[100] point out, the influence on the acoustic reflex of sensorineural impairment of cochlear origin is complex, but in general, there is less difference between hearing and reflex thresholds. The reflex can occur at about the same absolute level as found in normal ears, but because of the elevated hearing threshold, ears with a sensorineural impairment apparently require less stimulus intensity above the hearing threshold to elicit the responses. Jerger and associates[101] reported that the likelihood of eliciting the acoustic reflex was significantly reduced when the degree of SNHL exceeded 80-dB HL.

The influence of middle-ear impairment and attendant conductive hearing loss on the reflex is not so straightforward, as a result of the mode of reflex stimulation. Recall that ipsilateral acoustic reflex tests stimulate and detect the response in the same ear through the immittance instrument probe-tip assembly. In an impaired middle ear, the impedance is already abnormally altered, and further changes in impedance due to middle-ear muscle contraction may not be observable; to be detectable, these changes may require elevated stimulus intensity levels.

It follows that ipsilateral acoustic reflex testing in an impaired middle ear most likely yields no response; if the response is present, the threshold of the response tends to be elevated. For that reason, the ipsilateral acoustic reflex has been used in acoustic immittance schemes for diagnosing middle-ear effusion. Cantekin and associates[23] incorporated the acoustic reflex into an algorithm that included tympanometric pattern classifications and otoscopy, with the reflex serving to disambiguate one pattern that was equivocal with respect to its relationship to middle-ear effusion. Silman and colleagues[219] have also suggested that the acoustic reflex, in combination with other immittance variables, assists in the diagnosis of middle-ear effusion. On the other hand, some research has shown that the acoustic reflex is often absent in ears with no middle-ear effusion and is responsible for a high false-positive rate when used as part of a diagnostic rule for middle-ear effusion. As a result, ASHA guidelines do not include acoustic reflex in the criteria for screening for middle-ear disease.

The other drawback to the use of the acoustic reflex for the diagnosis of a middle-ear condition is that the reflex depends not only on middle-ear function but also on hearing and on the integrity of portions of the central nervous system (CNS). Children with severe to profound hearing impairments do not exhibit acoustic reflexes, and children with CNS disorders may have abnormal acoustic reflexes, so the use of a scheme for the diagnosis of middle-ear effusion that incorporates the acoustic reflex can never be universally applied.

The influence of middle-ear impairment on the contralateral acoustic reflex may be somewhat harder to understand. The contralateral reflex will probably be absent if the middle ear with the probe-tip assembly is impaired or if the impaired middle ear with the stimulus earphone has a moderate to moderately severe conductive hearing loss.[97] The reason for the first situation is given in the previous paragraph. In the second situation, the conductive hearing loss necessitates reflex stimulus levels that may be beyond the output capabilities of the instrument. For these reasons, the contralateral acoustic reflex is generally absent in cases of bilateral middle-ear impairment. When the impairment is unilateral, the contralateral reflex will also be absent for both ears if the impaired ear has a moderate to moderately severe conductive hearing loss.

The acoustic reflex is useful in diagnosing lesions beyond the cochlea (at the eighth cranial nerve or brain stem level). Such lesions can result in either an absent or an elevated reflex or in a reflex response amplitude that rapidly decays in time to a continuous stimulus.[8, 19, 73, 99, 102, 218] Anderson and colleagues[8] first demonstrated that for tones of 500 and 1000 Hz, the acoustic reflex in patients with an eighth cranial nerve tumor tends to have a response amplitude that decays to half strength or less in less than 5 seconds of continuous pure-tone stimulation.

Jerger and associates[99] and Sheehy and Inzer[218] reported reflex findings in a larger series of such tumor cases and substantiated the clinical significance of reflex decay. However, these investigators found the reflex to be absent in most of the cases reviewed. In these studies, an abnormal reflex (absent or decaying) correctly identified 80% to 86% of such retrocochlear impairments. Greisen and Rasmussen[73] and Jerger and Jerger[102] demonstrated how the comparison of ipsilateral and contralateral reflexes can be used to identify eighth nerve and brain stem level impairments.

It should be apparent that the presence or absence of the acoustic reflex, its threshold, and the degree of response amplitude decay can suggest a variety of underlying pathologic conditions. Consequently, the acoustic reflex alone cannot pinpoint a specific pathologic condition. Reflex findings must be viewed in the context of the tympanometric and behavioral audiometric results to infer the nature of hearing impairment and the possible location of the underlying lesion.

An absent acoustic reflex or a significantly elevated acoustic reflex threshold is highly suggestive of an impairment at some level of the auditory system. If the tympanogram is also abnormal, the level of impairment is likely to be the middle ear. An absent or elevated reflex with a normal tympanogram usually suggests a sensorineural impairment of either cochlear or retrocochlear origin, depending on the degree of associated SNHL. The probability of retrocochlear involvement is increased when the reflex is absent or elevated, and the tympanometrically normal ear has an SNHL of less than 80-dB HL. When the associated SNHL is 80-dB HL or more, an absent or elevated reflex can suggest either severe cochlear damage or a retrocochlear lesion. If the reflex occurs at essentially normal levels (70- to 100-dB HL) and does not decay in a tympanometrically normal ear with less than 80-dB HL SNHL, a probable location of the lesion is the cochlea.

Certain children are unable or unwilling to yield reliable behavioral hearing test results. In these, the reflex and tympanogram can provide evidence that corroborates impressions of the child's suspected impairment. If both the reflex and the tympanogram are normal, the likelihood of an SNHL exceeding 80-dB HL is low. Although a small proportion of otherwise normal children do not have a recordable acoustic reflex, a child with absent reflexes and a normal tympanogram in both ears may have a severe SNHL. Consequently, when less-than-reliable behavioral hearing tests suggest an impairment, measurements of the reflex and a tympanogram recording can add credence to associated clinical impressions.

Niemeyer and Sesterhenn[167] first suggested that the difference between acoustic reflex thresholds for pure tones and broad-band noise could be used to estimate the degree of hearing loss. Ordinarily, the reflex threshold for broad-band noise is approximately 20 dB better than that for pure tones. Niemeyer and Sesterhenn observed that this difference was reduced in ears with SNHLs and that the reduction was systematically related to the degree of the sensorineural loss. Consequently, these authors concluded that the degree of loss could be predicted from the tone-noise difference in reflex thresholds.

The use of the acoustic reflex as a predictor of degree of hearing loss has been further investigated by several authors.[98, 100, 111, 141, 215, 250] In general, these investigations have shown that the tone-noise reflex threshold difference is best used to differentiate normal from impaired hearing but cannot accurately estimate the degree of associated hearing loss. An estimation of the degree of hearing loss may be effectively provided on the basis of the acoustic reflex threshold for broad-band noise, which tends to increase along with increased sensorineural impairment.[100, 111]

A number of investigators[38, 200, 223, 243] evaluated the use of the acoustic reflex in guiding the choice of an appropriate hearing aid. In this context, the reflex is most useful in pediatric and geriatric populations when behavioral indices of hearing ability are unavailable.

In these cases, the acoustic reflex can provide information about the most effective hearing-aid volume setting to avoid exceeding an individual's loudness discomfort level with a particular hearing aid. A more extensive discussion of this acoustic reflex application is given in Chapter 105. Because of the many variables involved and the lack of definitive experimental evidence, the use of the acoustic reflex in fitting hearing aids in children should be approached with caution.

Otoacoustic Emissions

In 1978, Kemp[119] described the measurement of sounds in the ear canal that were generated within the cochlea. These sounds, *cochlear emissions*, are generated as a nonlinear by-product of biomechanical activity within the cochlea, probably at the level of the outer hair cells. Although it was hypothesized many years ago that such an event occurred in the normal processing of sound, the technology, mainly miniature sensitive microphones and computerized signal analysis techniques, has now reached a level that permits measurement of these small acoustic events in the ear canal.

There are two major categories of OAEs: spontaneous and evoked. Evoked OAEs have the greatest potential for clinical application and are discussed in this chapter. Spontaneously occurring emissions have not yet been found to have great clinical significance in the pediatric patient, and so are not discussed further here. However, the interested reader can find information on spontaneous emissions, as well as more detailed information on all types of OAEs, in several publications.[3, 62, 170, 198]

There are three types of evoked OAEs: transient, distortion product, and stimulus frequency. Stimulus frequency emissions are technically difficult to measure and have not been studied extensively for clinical applications. Because of the relative technical advantage to measurement of transient evoked and distortion product OAEs, they have been studied more thoroughly with respect to clinical testing and are favored in the clinical environment. Otoacoustic emissions of all kinds are being studied extensively, and new data are becoming available at a rapid rate. Readers of a text such as this should pay particular attention to information in periodicals regarding OAEs to keep up with the rapidly changing and exciting developments in this area.

Measurement

Evoked OAEs require that a probe assembly, similar to that used for acoustic immittance tests, be fit into the ear canal.[39] In the OAE system, the probe includes a microphone for recording acoustic energy in the ear canal and a port, or ports, from which either one sound stimulus (for transient evoked) or two sound stimuli (for distortion product) are delivered. Typically, the sound source is built into the probe itself, but in some systems the sound source or sources are external earphone drivers that are connected to the probe via sound tubes. In general, the measurement of evoked OAEs requires that a stimulus be presented and that the acoustic events in the ear canal be monitored. For transient stimuli, the acoustic energy in the ear canal, including any OAEs, is measured in a time frame following the time it takes the energy produced by the transient stimulus to dissipate. For distortion product OAEs (DPOAEs), the emission is measured during the presentation of the stimuli, but it is frequency specific and is measured in a spectral region apart from the evoking stimuli. Because OAEs are very low in amplitude, the acoustic energy in the ear canal must be computer averaged to improve the SNR sufficiently to identify the response in the presence of the ambient ear-canal noise levels. With proper technique, evoked OAEs are measurable in virtually all normally functioning peripheral auditory systems.[120, 129, 133, 198] Test-retest reliability is also quite high.[51, 78] Evoked OAEs are simply measured, reliable, and objective and require simple patient preparation. As such, they have great potential for use as a clinical test.

Transient Evoked Otoacoustic Emissions

Transient evoked OAEs (TEOAEs) are broad-band emissions evoked using a transient stimulus such as a click or a tone burst.[122] For many years, ILO (Otodynamics Ltd, Hatfield, Herts, United Kingdom.) OAE systems were the only instruments available commercially for clinical testing using transient stimuli. Consequently, most of the data in the literature and virtually all clinical information were obtained using ILO systems. Default settings for the ILO88 system provide a "nonlinear" click stimulus (0.08-msec rectangular pulse) presented in four-stimuli groups. It is called a nonlinear click because in each group of four stimuli, three are presented at equal amplitude, and the fourth is presented at three times that amplitude and is inverted in polarity. With such a presentation of stimuli, the averaged response in the ear canal for each group of four is virtually free of stimulus artifact because, in a linear system (i.e., the ear canal), the inverted pulse effectively cancels the other three pulses in the averaged response. The remaining nonlinear acoustic response in the ear canal is a result of the cochlear emission. Because the emission occurs over some period of time after the stimulus, the acoustic response in the ear canal during the 20-msec period after each click is monitored. Responses to stimulus groups (i.e., the four-click packets) are averaged in the time domain and alternately stored in two separate buffers (designated A and B). In the ILO88 default mode, the responses to 260 of the stimulus packets, in each buffer, are required to complete the measurement. There is a noise-rejection system that defaults to a level of 47.3-dB SPL. Whenever the overall intensity level in the ear canal exceeds the noise-rejection intensity level, the system stops averaging responses until the noise level is again below 47.3-dB SPL. The default stimulus level is set to create a transient with a peak equivalent (pe) RMS pressure of 0.3 mPa (83.5-dB peSPL) in a 2-mL cavity. The default setting for the transient is expected to generate slightly greater stimulus intensity in the ear canals of young children, who have smaller ear canals than adults. Settings for these parameters are adjustable by the user. The stimulus-intensity level can be adjusted over a limited range and the noise-rejection level may be varied, even during the course of a measurement, using the ILO system. The system also provides a means of presenting a "linear" click and tone-burst stimuli in addition to the "nonlinear" click.

The transient stimulus has a broad-band spectrum. When the probe tip is properly fixed to the probe and the probe is seated properly in the ear canal, the spectrum is flat through about 4 or 5 kHz. In a normal ear, the TEOAE has a broad-band response that reflects, in general, the spectrum of the evoking stimulus. When tone bursts are used, evoked emissions are spectrally similar to the evoking stimulus (i.e., somewhat frequency specific) in ears with normal peripheral function.

A great deal of information is provided in the response output display of the ILO88 system (Fig. 11–7). The display of the TEOAE measurement includes the averaged time waveforms (buffers A and B) as measured in the ear canal, a display of the stimulus spectrum, a display of the response spectrum, the ear-canal noise level, the OAE response amplitude, and other information that is useful to interpretation. Figure 11–7 shows the TEOAE measurement for a 6-year-old girl with normal hearing and middle-ear function. A measure called *wave reproducibility,* which represents the correlation between the two independent measurements of the averaged waveform (A and B buffers) in the ear canal, is often used to determine the presence or absence of response. The system also provides a value of the overall emission amplitude (called *response*) and the estimated noise (the difference between the A and B waveforms) in the response. In addition, a Fourier analysis of the averaged waveforms is made to obtain the spectra of both the OAE and of the ear-canal noise, which can then be examined as SNR in a frequency-specific way. The software also provides frequency-specific measures of reproducibility (1 to 5 kHz).

In normal ears of children, a strong TEOAE response is typically found when the intensity of the transient stimulus is 80-dB peSPL or greater, but OAE amplitude tends to decrease with age.[196, 260] Spektor and colleagues[225] reported that the average OAE amplitude in children 4 to 10 years old with normal peripheral auditory function was 13.5-dB SPL. Nozza and associates[183] also reported a mean OAE amplitude of 13.3-dB SPL for children between 5 and 10 years old. Data reported by Prieve and colleagues[195, 196] are consistent with those values. In the latter three studies, the children were free of middle-ear disorder on otoscopic examination and had

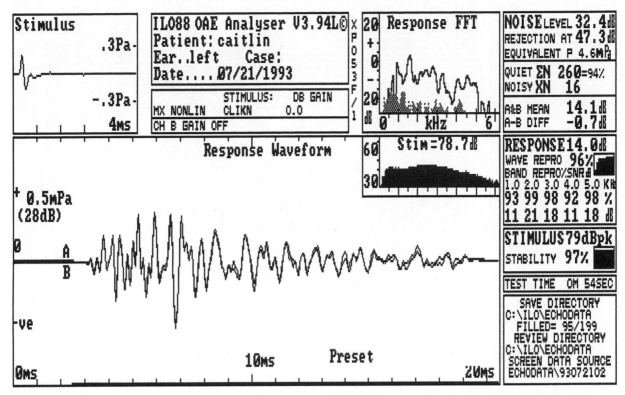

FIGURE 11–7. Output display of the transient evoked otoacoustic emission (OAE) test. The display is for a normal-hearing 6-year-old child. The upper left window ("Stimulus") displays stimulus waveform, which is helpful for assessing the fit of the probe. The top center window identifies the patient and the test ear, the date, and any other descriptive information that is added. To the right of the identification window is a window called "Response FFT," which has the spectrum of the background noise (*dark shaded region*) and the spectrum of the OAE (*clear outlined area*). Below the "Response FFT" is the "Stim" window, with the overall peak equivalent sound pressure level (peSPL) value and the spectrum of the stimulus as it is in the ear canal. The large window in the center ("Response Waveform") displays two separately averaged ear-canal response waveforms (overlaying each other); the time window is 0 to 20 msec, with the first 2.5 msec blanked out to eliminate recording of the stimulus. The column on the right has the average noise level in the ear canal during recording and the noise level at which responses would begin to be rejected (in dB SPL and in mPa). "Quiet Σ N 260 = 94%" is the user set automatic test termination number and the percentage that that number represents of all the test stimulus presentations. "Noisy XN 16" represents the number of stimulus presentations that occurred during times when ear-canal noise was above the noise-rejection level and therefore were not included in the averaged response. That is, the preset stopping number of 260 is 94% of all 276 (260 + 16) stimulus presentations. Also on the right is the OAE amplitude ("RESPONSE 14.0 dB") and the correlation ("wave reproducibility" 96%) between the 260 averaged responses in one storage buffer and the 260 averaged responses in the second storage buffer. The wave reproducibility (%) and the signal-to-noise ratio ("SNRdB") for narrow-band (i.e., frequency-specific) sections of the OAE are presented. "Stimulus 79dBpk" provides the amplitude of the stimulus in dB peSPL, agreeing with that in the "Stim" window, and a measure of "Stability," which, along with the histogram beside it, documents how well the stimulus waveform conformed, over the period of the test, to the waveform in the ear canal at the time the test was started. Finally, information is provided on the time it took to complete the test (54 seconds) and on storage and retrieval information.

normal hearing. We know also that young infants have even greater response amplitude (25- to 30-dB SPL) to the click stimulus (Fig. 11–8).

The greater the correlation (reproducibility) for the waveforms in buffers A and B, the greater confidence one has that an emission is present. Some suggest that a minimal wave reproducibility of 50% is required before a measurement can be accepted as a true response. The frequency-specific reproducibility and SNR measures are useful for identifying frequency-specific areas of emission. Various criteria have been applied, but at least a 3-dB SNR is required to accept a response for a given frequency band in most clinical applications. The response (the light-outlined area) is prominent relative to the noise (the dark-shaded area) when a response is present.

Using clicks between 80- and 86-dB peSPL, responses in children can typically be obtained in ears with no more than a mild hearing loss (about 30- to 35-dB HL).[79, 171, 260]

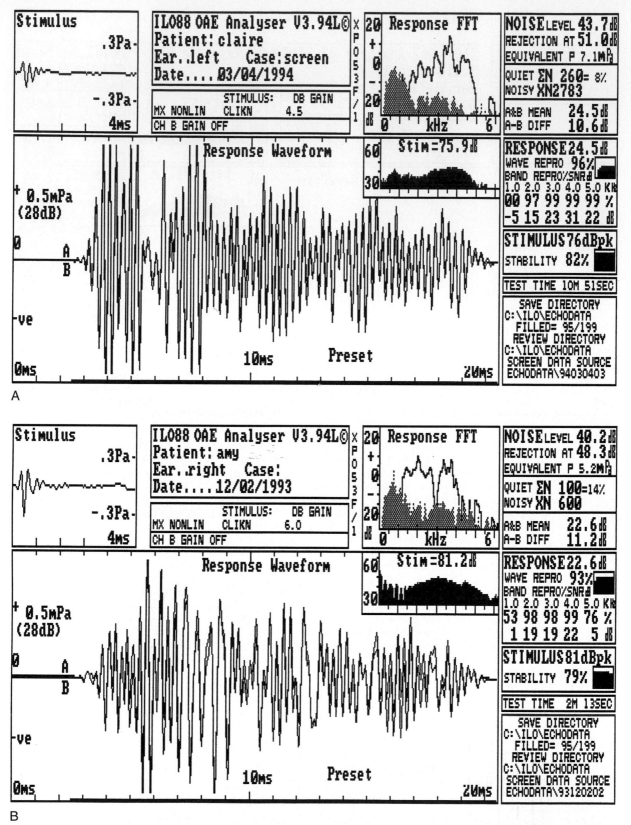

FIGURE 11–8. Transient evoked otoacoustic emissions of two 2-month-old infants with presumed normal hearing. Note that the amplitude of the waveforms and the shapes of the stimulus and response FFTs differ from those of the 6-year-old child in Figure 11–6. This is typical of infants, with greater amplitude and a slightly higher frequency response. *A,* Infant was in a light and restless sleep. To complete 260 stimulus group presentations, more than 3000 presentations were made; the test took nearly 11 minutes to complete. *B,* The infant was also restless, but the test was stopped after 100 presentations of the stimulus groups were made. With a strong response, it is not necessary to continue the test until all 260 (default number) stimulus group presentations are made. The latter test (*B*) took only 2 minutes 13 seconds.

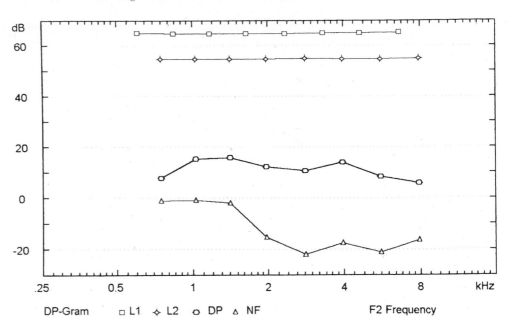

FIGURE 11–9. Distortion product otoacoustic emissions (DPOAEs), in decibels of sound pressure level (dB SPL) of a child with normal hearing. Circular symbols connected by solid lines represent DPOAEs generated using two primary tones. The stimulus tones were of unequal levels (f_1 = 65 dB SPL, f_2 = 55 dB SPL) with a frequency ratio (f_2/f_1) of 1.22 and are indicated at the top of the graph with the square and diamond symbols, respectively. The abscissa is the frequency of the second primary tone (f_2).

As such, OAEs are very useful for discriminating between ears with and ears without hearing loss. The potential of evoked OAEs for estimating threshold is the object of much research, but the data are not clear regarding the relationship between OAEs and thresholds. In general, there is a reduction in emission amplitude with decreasing intensity of the click stimulus, but it is not a linear change. The TEOAE saturates at about 70- or 80-dB peSPL in ears with normal peripheral hearing and middle-ear function. Because of the low-amplitude emission and the noise in the measuring environment (i.e., the ear canal), it is difficult to determine the lowest intensity level at which an emission can be elicited.

Distortion Product Otoacoustic Emissions

DPOAEs are frequency-specific OAEs that are a consequence of the nonlinear nature of the cochlea. When a sound signal composed of two pure tones close in frequency and intensity is presented, that signal is reliably transduced within the cochlea, but energy at frequencies not in the original signal is also produced. The frequencies of these intermodulation distortion products are predictable, coming at frequencies equivalent to $mf_1 - nf_2$, where f_1 is the lower-frequency component of the two-tone stimulus, f_2 is the higher-frequency component of the stimulus, and m and n are integers. The most common distortion product measured by DPOAE systems is the $2f_1 - f_2$ distortion product, because in most cases it has the greatest amplitude. Cochlear distortion products have been studied psychoacoustically for many years. The fact that distortion products can be measured objectively has helped provide an understanding of cochlear function as well as providing a potentially valuable clinical tool. Because the DPOAE is generated using two pure tones close in frequency, it has quite a frequency-specific origin.

Most investigators consider the stimulus frequency in a DPOAE measurement as the frequency of the second primary tone (i.e., f_2) or as the geometric mean of the two primary tones, because it is believed that the area of generation along the cochlear partition of the intermodulation distortion product is at, or just apical to, the place of the second primary tone. One advantage of the DPOAE relative to the transient evoked emission is that it can be used to estimate cochlear function at frequencies above those that can be assessed using the transient. With DPOAEs, test frequencies of 8 kHz, and sometimes as high as 10 kHz, can be assessed. Several instruments are commercially available for the measurement of DPOAEs.

Amplitudes of the DPOAEs are typically 40 to 70 dB below the levels of the primary tones. Lonsbury-Martin and associates[133] have shown that the average amplitude of DPOAE varies with frequency between about 1 and 5 kHz, with the lowest amplitudes in the 2- and 3-kHz regions and the highest amplitudes in the 1- and 4-kHz regions. The amplitude of the DPOAEs varies with the ratio between the two primary frequencies (f_2/f_1) and the difference between intensity levels of the two primaries (L_1/L_2). A primary frequency ratio of around 1.22 has been shown to produce DPOAEs with the greatest amplitude. A level difference of about 10 to 15 dB is commonly used, because in most cases, it optimizes the DPOAE amplitude.[61, 66, 67, 77, 82, 198]

DPOAEs are usually plotted as DP audiograms, or "DP-grams," with emission amplitude plotted as a function of frequency (Fig. 11–9). As many frequencies as are desired can be assessed, from one or two points per octave up to eight or more points per octave. The DP-gram typically includes an estimate of the noise in the ear canal in the region of the DP frequency at the time of the measurement. That is, amplitude of the response at the DP frequency is considered the DPOAE, and amplitude of the response in some frequency range surrounding the DP frequency is taken as an estimate of the noise level in the region of the DP frequency. Signal averaging techniques are used to increase the SNR in the measurement so the low-amplitude emission can be identified in the background noise.

As with the TEOAE, the DPOAE changes with age[197, 260] and has a nonlinear growth function. However, the DPOAE may be measurable with slightly greater degrees of hearing loss than the TEOAE. Because noise is a problem for DPOAE measurement, some investigators favor the use of the SNR (i.e., DP-to-noise ratio) rather than the absolute amplitude of the DPOAE to determine whether a response is present. Because OAEs are detected using an averaging technique, the duration of averaging time and the level of the background noise affect the DP-to-noise ratio. Most agree that to consider a DPOAE as present in the response, the amplitude at the DP frequency should be greater than the mean noise level for that frequency; some favor using as much as two standard deviations (usually about 5 or 6 dB) above the mean noise level before accepting a measurement as a response.

The OAE is also affected by nonauditory factors.[9] Gender differences have been reported, with women producing slightly greater emission amplitudes than men. At least one report revealed a difference between ears, with right ears producing greater emissions than left ears.[204] Some of these differences may be attributable to greater prevalence of spontaneous emissions, which, when present at a DP frequency, would add to the DPOAE measurement.

Clinical Use of Evoked Otoacoustic Emissions

Both TEOAE and DPOAE measurements are attractive clinical tests because they are quick, noninvasive, easy, reliable, and objective. The presence of an OAE within the normal range virtually ensures normal auditory function up to and including the outer hair cells in the cochlea. Because OAEs depend primarily on outer hair cell function and on the biomechanical properties of the cochlea, they are vulnerable to toxic and physical agents. As such, OAEs can be used to monitor the status of ears of individuals who are receiving medical therapies known to be ototoxic or are exposed to high levels of noise.

It is important to note that outer- or middle-ear disorder can prevent detection of an OAE in the ear canal, even in the presence of normal inner-ear function.[134, 145, 146, 189, 195] That is, failure to see a response on an OAE test could be due to outer-, middle-, or inner-ear abnormality, or a combination. It has been shown that experimentally induced abnormal ear-canal pressures can diminish or eliminate the emission in the ear canal.[163, 244] OAEs typically cannot be measured in most ears with middle-ear effusion. It has been shown, however, that a small percentage of ears with middle-ear effusion still produce emissions, at least in the 2- to 4-kHz range, so the sensitivity of OAEs for identification of middle-ear effusion is not perfect. It is also important to note that ears with polyethylene tubes in place typically produce OAEs, unless the tube is blocked with otorrhea (Fig. 11–10). After treatment, OAEs were again measured (Fig. 11–11).

Norton[171] suggests that an idea about the degree of hearing loss may be derived by using more than one intensity level when testing for TEOAEs. The presence of an emission at 80-dB peSPL in the absence of an emission at 70-dB peSPL may suggest a mild degree of hearing impairment, whereas strong responses at both intensity levels might provide stronger evidence of a normally functioning ear.

Frequency-specific data available from both the TEOAE and DPOAE tests can provide information on auditory function relative to frequency.[133, 135, 136, 166] For example, Figure 11–12 shows the evoked OAEs of an 11-year-old child with unusual audiometric configuration. In the right ear (Fig. 11–12A), there is a mild low-frequency conductive hearing loss and an abnormally high admittance tympanogram (see Fig. 11–3C). The transient evoked emission was absent (wave reproducibility of 34% and response below the noise floor). For the left ear (Fig. 11–12B), there is an unusual audiometric configuration (Fig. 11–12C), with islands of normal hearing between some evidence of SNHL. This child was being seen as part of a study of children with attention deficit disorder and hyperactivity and was somewhat unreliable during behavioral testing. However, a frequency analysis of the TEOAE was quite consistent with the behavioral results, revealing emissions in the frequency regions of normal hearing on the audiogram and absent response in regions of hearing loss. Figure 11–13 shows the DPOAE of a 5-year-old child with a unilateral 2-kHz notch SNHL.

Auditory Evoked Potentials

Many chapters and even texts have been devoted to AEPs, and some[34, 49, 52, 60, 75, 256] are quite thorough in their treatment of the topic. The monograph by Davis[33] is an additional excellent reference. The present chapter does not attempt to cover the entire area in as much depth but instead offers a brief description of component AEPs and how they are measured. Those responses that are particularly valuable in the evaluation of hearing in children are discussed more fully. Finally, a pragmatic approach is taken that identifies the children to whom the procedure is most applicable.

There are several component AEPs, and each component response occurs in a different time frame after stimulus onset. These components and their general time frames, which may overlap to some extent, include (1) the "cochlear" components (0 to 4 msec), (2) the "early" components (4 to 10 or 12 msec), (3) the "middle" components (8 to 50 or 80 msec), (4) the "long" components (50 to 300 msec), and (5) the "late" components (300 to 800 msec).[49] In addition, there is a category of responses called steady state evoked potentials. The steady state evoked potential is a brain potential evoked by amplitude modulation of a carrier frequency, which can be chosen to match audiometric test frequencies. The steady state evoked potential has been shown to be useful for predicting thresholds in adults and children when modulation rates between approximately 70 and 110 Hz are used.[109, 131, 192]

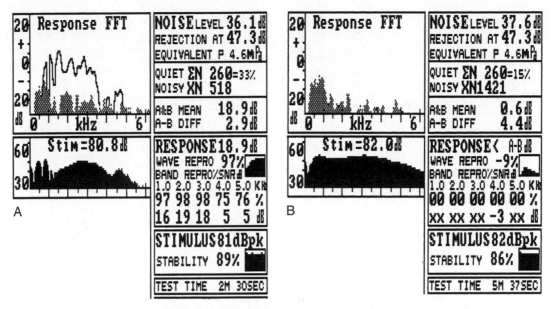

FIGURE 11–10. Evoked otoacoustic emissions of a 2-month-old infant with cleft palate, poly-ethylene tubes in place, and suspected hearing impairment. This infant failed an auditory brainstem response screening on two separate occasions at another facility shortly after birth. For the right ear *(A)*, there is a strong transient evoked otoacoustic emission, with slightly better reproducibility and frequency-specific signal-to-noise ratios up to 3 kHz than at 4 and 5 kHz. For the left ear *(B)*, no emission could be measured, and the ear was determined to have a blocked PE tube and middle-ear effusion.

Each of these components reflects electric activity from different anatomic levels in the auditory system; the earlier components are from peripheral and brain stem levels, and the latter components are from midbrain and cortical levels. Three miniature electrodes are used to record these responses. An *active* electrode is placed either in close proximity or in a favorable orientation to the neural generators responsible for the response component of interest. The *reference* electrode is placed on a site that is presumably "quiet" with respect to the component being measured. The third, or *ground*, electrode is placed on an indifferent site, usually the forehead or contralateral neck or mastoid process. The actual placement of active, reference, and ground electrodes varies with the component of interest.

The activity from the recording electrodes is then amplified, filtered, and analyzed by the AEP system. In essence, a computer serves to "average out" background electroencephalographic and myogenic activity, thereby enhancing the response associated with multiple stimulus presentations. The computer analysis is "triggered" at the onset of each stimulus and continues to include the time frame corresponding to the response component being measured.

Excessive muscle activity, as well as electric artifacts from the surrounding environment, or line current inadequacies, can obliterate an otherwise observable electric response. Consequently, the child must be relaxed or, preferably, asleep. In addition, the test environment must be conducive to accurate recordings; the environment must be void of nearby sources of electric artifacts, such as transformers or fluorescent light ballasts, and adequate line current grounding is essential.

In general, AEPs provide perhaps the best data for physiologic assessment of the responsivity of the auditory system in children. However, not all response components are equally useful. The validity of the long (50- to 300-msec) and late (300- to 800-msec) components for evaluating infants and children remains open to question,[125] although these components can provide useful clinical information in an older child who is awake, cooperative, and alert (however, such a child is not often referred for such testing). Usually, the child who is a candidate for AEP testing is either unable or unwilling to cooperate with conventional hearing tests.

With regard to the long component, the inherent degree of intersubject and intrasubject variability and of the variability due to the age and attentive state of the child can lead to significant clinical error.[11, 64, 199] In addition, if drugs are used to induce sleep in the child, the reliability of the long components is adversely influenced.[32, 222] According to Davis[33] and Kraus and associates,[125] the middle components show promise as tools for evaluating infants and children, but the clinical acceptance of these components has not been widespread.

Kraus and associates[125] report that middle latency responses (10 to 80 msec, in their view) can be used to obtain information in children on peripheral hearing, especially in the low frequencies, where the auditory brain stem response (ABR) is inadequate. In addition, the middle latency response is not as sensitive as the ABR to problems in neural synchrony. However, because sleep

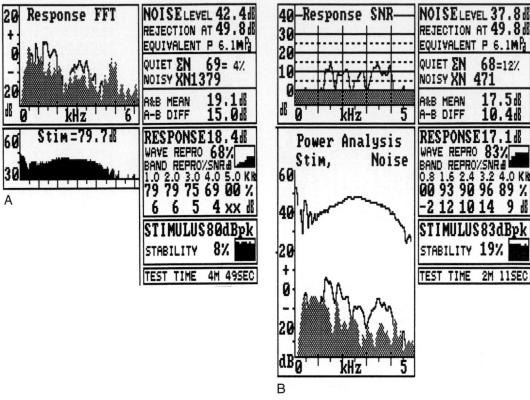

FIGURE 11–11. Transient evoked otoacoustic emissions (OAEs) for the left ear of the infant described in Figure 11–13 at 2 months later, after medical treatment for otitis media. Despite the infant failing to sleep, an abbreviated run (only 69 stimuli groups accepted) revealed evidence of a transient evoked OAE (A). The test was rerun using a feature called Quickscreen (B), which doubles the rate of presentation of the stimuli while sampling over a shorter (12 versus 20 msec) period. The Quickscreen function is especially good for screening newborns and other difficult-to-test populations. Despite the noise created by the awake infant and the small number of samples, clear evidence of a transient evoked OAE was obtained.

state is a critical variable in detecting a response, these authors recommend monitoring sleep state while recording auditory middle latency responses, so they can be interpreted properly.

The cochlear (0 to 4 msec) and early (4 to 12 msec) components are used as clinical measures for assessing peripheral hearing in children. The common names for these components are electrocochleography (ECochG) and ABR, respectively. The ABR is used widely and has found a place as part of the pediatric audiologic test battery almost everywhere.

Electrocochleography

These first components reflect cochlear and eighth cranial nerve activity; the latter is also known as the *whole-nerve action potential,* or simply the *eighth-nerve action potential.* The eighth-nerve action potential is the response of interest in the procedure.

ECochG requires that the active electrode be placed in close proximity to the neural generator of the response (the eighth cranial nerve). For this reason, the most effective active electrode placement is through the tympanic membrane and onto the promontory in the middle ear.[43, 75] Because this electrode placement requires a sur-

gical procedure and a general anesthetic in children, other less-invasive electrode placements have been tried. The ear canal appears to be a reasonable compromise location for the active electrode in ECochG.[26, 30, 47, 213, 266] The compromise involved, however, is that the response is an order of magnitude smaller at this location, and consequently response sensitivity and reliability are open to question. Ruth[210] and Ruth and Lambert[211] reported on successful tympanic membrane electrode placement.

ECochG with a promontory electrode has been demonstrated to be useful in establishing the validity of the behavioral audiogram[43] and in the detection of eighth cranial nerve impairments.[20, 187]

ECochG is very useful in cases of Meniere disease and when performing intraoperative monitoring of the peripheral auditory system.[210] The major limitation of ECochG as a tool for the evaluation of infants and children is the required surgical procedure for placement of the active electrode and the related use of general anesthesia. Ear-canal electrodes may be more appropriate with children, eliminating the need for anesthesia, if ECochG is needed. The availability of the ABR, which is noninvasive and requires at most a sedative to induce sleep, has prompted many clinicians to choose the ABR instead of ECochG for evaluating infants and children. In addition, the ABR reflects

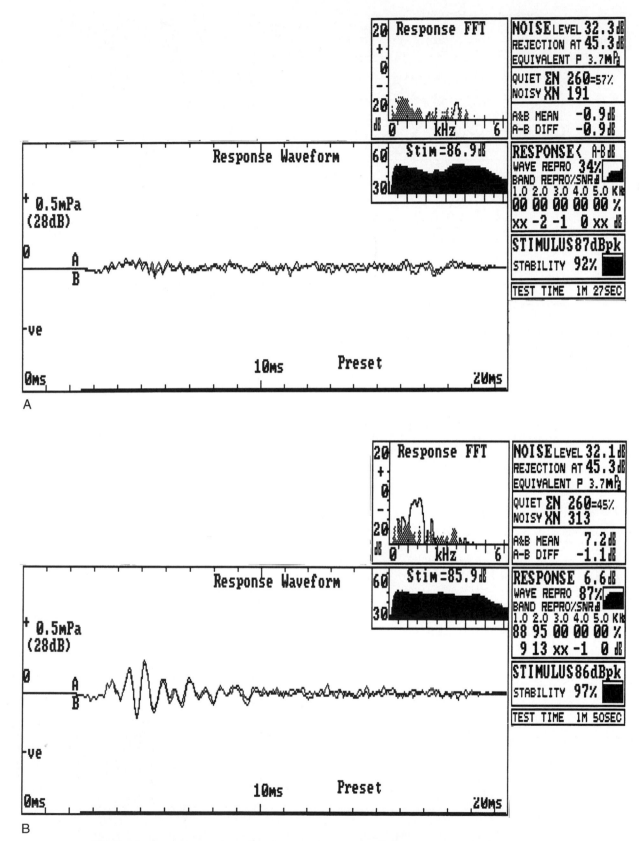

FIGURE 11–12. Transient evoked otoacoustic emissions for an 11-year-old child. *A,* Right ear, which had a mild conductive hearing loss and abnormally high admittance tympanogram (shown in Fig. 11–3*C*). Note that even with an 87-dB peak equivalent sound pressure level stimulus, a transient evoked emission cannot be measured. *B,* Left ear, which has mild sensorineural hearing loss of an unusual configuration.

Illustration continued on following page

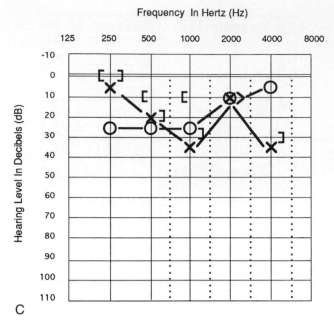

C

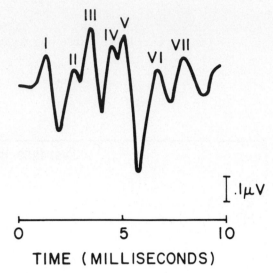

FIGURE 11–14. The auditory brain stem response for a young adult with normal hearing. Component waves are labeled I to VII.

FIGURE 11–12. *Continued (C)* with normal tympanometric findings. A frequency-specific analysis of the emission showed peak energy between 1 and 2 kHz, the region of improving hearing on the audiogram. Ear-canal noise below 1 kHz obscures a possible emission in that region.

activity not only of eighth cranial nerve fibers but also of central auditory centers. The principles and clinical application of ECochG are discussed elsewhere.[42, 43, 75, 209, 210]

Auditory Brain Stem Response

The evoked potentials recorded in the first 10 msec have been referred to as *brain stem evoked response, brain stem auditory evoked response,* or *auditory brain stem response* (ABR). ABR is used in this chapter. It consists

of five to seven vertex-positive° waves, labeled I to VII, that occur in the first 10 msec after stimulus onset (Fig. 11–14). The response was first reported by Sohmer and Feinmesser,[224] but the landmark articles in this area were by Jewett and colleagues.[105–108]

The neural generators of the ABR have been difficult to determine precisely. Moeller and Jannetta[157] discussed the complexity of establishing a relationship between ABR waves and specific regions of the ascending pathways using a far field recording method. Relating findings

---

°"Vertex-positive" refers to the condition in which the active electrode, on the vertex of the skull, is connected to the positive input of the preamplifier. The waves can also be referred to as "vertex-negative" if the active electrode is connected to the negative input of the preamplifier. The former situation, however, is becoming an accepted convention.

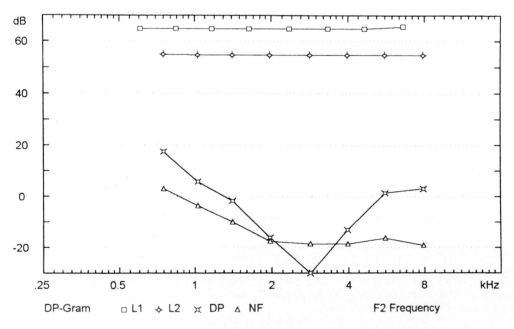

FIGURE 11–13. Distortion product otoacoustic emissions *(star)* of a child with an unusual notched sensorineural hearing loss in the 2- to 4-kHz range only in the left ear. Parameters were the same as in Figure 11–9.

in animals to those in humans also is not appropriate. Nevertheless, numerous carefully conducted studies led Müller and Jannetta to conclude the following regarding the relationship between neural generators and ABR waves. Wave I is associated with activity from the distal portion of the eighth nerve; wave II originates from the proximal portion of the eighth nerve; wave III is associated primarily with activity in neurons of the cochlear nucleus; and wave IV has its origin primarily from neurons of the superior olivary complex, although there probably are contributions from neurons at the level of the cochlear nucleus and the lateral lemniscus as well. In general, wave V receives contributions from both the lateral lemniscus and the inferior colliculus. Waves VI and VII are dominated by activity from the inferior colliculus. Müller and Jannetta caution that there are multiple generators for each of the ABR waves beyond wave III and that each generator beyond the cochlear nucleus contributes to more than one of the ABR waves. This latter view is echoed by Moore,[160] emphasizing the complexity of transmission through the CNS.

The electrode configuration for the ABR includes the active electrode on the vertex of the skull or the mid-forehead at the hairline and the reference and ground electrodes, respectively, on the ipsilateral and contralateral mastoid processes or earlobes. The ABR is a far field recording of minute electric discharges from multiple neurons. Therefore, the stimulus must be one that can cause simultaneous discharges of large numbers of the involved neurons. Stimuli with very rapid onset, such as clicks or tone bursts, must be used. It is unfortunate that the rapid onset required to create a measurable ABR also creates a spread of energy in the frequency domain, reducing the frequency specificity of the response. The responses to 1000 to 2000 clicks, filtered clicks, or brief, pure-tone bursts are typically averaged for each stimulus intensity that is used. The stimuli are presented at a rapid rate (10 to 30 per second). The length of time required for a test depends on such factors as the number of stimuli and intensity levels tested per ear, the rate of presentation, and the number of stimuli "averaged" per test. The total test duration can be 1 hour or more.

The deleterious effects of excessive muscle activity were mentioned earlier, and this factor is particularly pertinent to obtaining accurate ABR recordings. For this reason, a child must be completely relaxed, preferably asleep, for the procedure. Natural sleep can often be facilitated by feeding babies up to about 6 months of age immediately before the test. Often, children 7 years or older can lie quietly for the procedure. The ABR is not affected by sedation or general anesthesia. Infants and children between about 6 months and 6 or 7 years of age can be sedated to avoid problems related to muscle activity during testing. Rules for conscious sedation are recommended by associations such as the American Academy of Pediatrics, and each hospital has policies regarding sedation. Anyone undertaking sedated ABR testing should be familiar with guidelines and policies that apply. ABR testing can also be done in the operating room when a child is anesthetized for another procedure.

Investigations subsequent to early descriptions of the ABR have shown the response to be consistent between and within subjects and to be unchanged in awake and sleeping subjects. Of the five to seven waves that constitute the ABR, waves I, III, and V can be obtained consistently, whereas waves II and IV appear inconsistently between and within subjects. The latency (the time of occurrence after stimulus onset) of the various waves increases and wave amplitudes decrease, with reductions in stimulus intensity; at stimulus intensities close to behavioral hearing threshold, only wave V can be discerned (Fig. 11–15). These and other ABR properties have emerged from the extensive research efforts of a number of investigators, which have been adequately reviewed.[75]

There are developmental changes in the response morphology, wave amplitudes, and wave latencies of the ABR. Very early in life, only waves I, III, and V are evident, with wave I having a much greater amplitude than that of wave V. Over time, the relationship changes, with wave V becoming much more prominent than the other waves in the normal adult ABR. For the most part, changes in latency provide the most consistent index of development of the ABR. All ABR waves decrease in latency during early life. However, the rate of maturation of the various waves varies. Wave I has the shortest developmental time course, reaching adult latency value by about 2 to 3 months. Wave V has the longest course, reaching adult latency value sometime in the second year of life.[29, 84, 85, 212, 234] Wave III matures at a point in time between the ages at which waves I and V mature. Interwave latencies (I to III, III to V, and I to V) also show developmental change.

It is not clear what accounts for the developmental

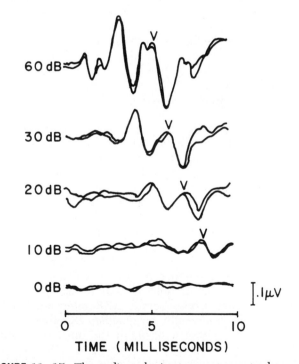

FIGURE 11–15. The auditory brain stem response to decreasing stimulus intensity. Each trace represents the averaged response to 1500 stimuli of the same intensity, and for the four lower traces, stimulus intensity was reduced by 10 dB. Note the reduction in amplitude and the increase in response time (latency) of wave V with decreased stimulus intensity.

change in ABR wave latency, but some mechanisms have been suggested, including maturation of the cochlea, increasing myelination of the central fibers, changes in transmission characteristics of the middle ear, increased synchrony, and greater synaptic efficiency.[84, 85]

The ABR is commonly used in two ways in the pediatric setting: first, as an audiometric test, providing information regarding the ability of the peripheral auditory system to transmit information to the auditory nerve and beyond; and second, in the differential diagnosis or monitoring of CNS pathologic conditions.[52, 70, 75]

For the audiometric approach, a search is conducted for the minimum stimulus intensity yielding an observable ABR.[54, 256] ABR thresholds using click stimuli are correlated best with behavioral hearing thresholds in the higher frequencies (1000 to 4000 Hz). The conventional ABR is unable to assess adequately responsivity to lower stimulus frequencies.[33] Efforts have been made to obtain more frequency-specific information using the ABR. Stapells and colleagues[226, 227] reviewed the various ways of altering the stimulus ensemble and the recording parameters to yield more frequency-specific information than is provided by using the predominantly high-frequency click stimulus. Filtering clicks and rapidly gating tones to make tone bursts are alternatives. Gorga and Thornton[69] showed that very frequency-specific stimuli can be generated using proper signal gating techniques. Use of the Blackman window,[186] a gating function, provides tone bursts with rapid onset and narrow-frequency bandwidth, suitable for eliciting frequency-specific ABR.

Many investigators have used a variety of masking techniques, including high-pass filtered noise masking, notched-noise masking, and pure-tone masking, to increase frequency specificity of the ABR. All these methods have some limitations in their ability to limit the response to the frequency desired or in their ability to generate a clear ABR. Although progress has been made, there still is no reliable and valid method for predicting the audiogram from low to high frequencies using the ABR.

Although one must be cognizant of the frequency-specificity limitations of the ABR used for audiometric purposes, it is also important to realize that the technique does not assess the perceptual event called *hearing*. The ABR reflects auditory neuronal electric responses that are adequately correlated to behavioral hearing thresholds, but a normal ABR suggests only that the auditory system, up to the midbrain level, is responsive to the stimulus used, and it does not guarantee the presence of normal hearing. Conversely, failure to elicit the ABR indicates an impairment of the system's synchronous response, but it does not prove that a child is deaf or has profoundly impaired hearing. Consequently, ABR interpretation for audiometric purposes must be qualified by other clinical assessment data, either available at the time or resulting from follow-up evaluations.

As an otoneurologic technique, the ABR may be used to infer the level of the auditory system—middle ear, cochlea, eighth cranial nerve, or brain stem—at which an impairment exists.[87] The latency of the ABR waves is the primary consideration in these applications. For middle-ear and cochlear impairments, wave latency as a function of stimulus intensity is important. Wave latencies at a fixed stimulus intensity provide the basis for the detection of eighth cranial nerve and brain stem impairments.

In cases of middle-ear impairment, the entire series of ABR waves is delayed in time by an amount commensurate with the degree of conductive hearing loss.[50, 57, 86] Typically, wave V latency as a function of decreasing stimulus intensity is used to detect such impairment, but other evidence[155] suggests that wave I latency provides a better index of middle-ear impairment.

The ABR in cases of cochlear impairment generally yields a steeper latency-intensity function. In other words, wave latencies are essentially normal at a high stimulus intensity but become excessively prolonged as stimulus intensity is decreased.[52, 193] Consequently, the characteristic ABR finding in cochlear impairment includes a normal I-to-V interwave latency in addition to the steep latency-intensity function. However, the problem is complicated by the fact that the slope or configuration of the hearing loss may influence results.

The ABR has also proved effective in detecting eighth cranial nerve impairment[25, 27, 216, 236, 242] and brain stem impairment.[228, 230, 231] In general, such impairments show an increased latency difference between waves I and V.

The ABR, then, is a series of positive waves occurring in the first 10 msec after stimulus onset that apparently reflect activity in successively higher levels of the auditory tract, up to, and perhaps including, lower midbrain centers. Within limits, the response can be used audiometrically to estimate hearing acuity, and it also has use for inferring at which level of the auditory system impairment might exist. The consistent nature of the ABR in both newborns and older children, and in both sleeping and awake subjects, makes the test a particularly useful tool for evaluating hearing in pediatric populations. However, it is important to remember that the ABR is evidence of synchronous neural firing and that, in some cases of CNS dysfunction, behavioral response to sound can be normal but no ABR can be recorded.

The ABR and other electric responses are extremely complex and difficult to interpret. A number of factors, including instrumentation design and settings, environment, and patient characteristics, may influence the quality of the recording. Testing and interpretation of electrophysiologic activity must be carried out by persons who are adequately trained; otherwise, there is the risk that unreliable and perhaps erroneous conclusions may affect patient care.

Referral Criteria for the Auditory Brain Stem Response

As stated earlier, the ABR has great advantages for evaluating the auditory system of young or uncooperative patients. It is a very stable phenomenon that is essentially free from the effects of state. The ABR can be measured in a patient who is awake, under sedation, or under anesthesia. Disadvantages include the fact that measurement of the ABR is not a test of hearing but rather of electric responses in the pathways of the eighth nerve and brain stem that occur as a result of auditory stimulation. In its most common application using the click stimulus, it also lacks frequency specificity.

Nevertheless, the ABR test has become an irreplaceable component of the audiologic test battery. It is not an assessment technique that should be applied to every patient in need of audiologic services. However, there are situations for which the ABR can provide information essential to identification, diagnosis, or management that could not be acquired in any other way. There are other situations in which the ABR supplements or corroborates other clinical or audiologic evidence.

Infants who should be referred for ABR testing include (1) newborns who have been referred from universal newborn hearing screening program follow-up rescreening protocols; (2) postmeningitic infants; (3) infants with recurrent acute otitis media, persistent otitis media with effusion, or both; (4) children with significant mental retardation, emotional disturbance, or both for whom ear-specific behavioral hearing testing is not possible; (5) children with suspected eighth nerve or brain stem disorders; (6) children with sudden-onset, fluctuating, progressive, or unilateral SNHL; (7) other difficult-to-test patients; (8) patients (especially infants) for whom ear-specific auditory responses are needed; and (9) those for whom confirmation of suspected auditory or CNS dysfunction is required.[70]

Early Identification and Intervention of Children With Hearing Impairment

The benefit of early identification and intervention of hearing impairment in infants and children is no longer in doubt. Clinical experience and research clearly demonstrate that the earlier a young child with hearing impairment is identified and is entered into an early intervention program, the better is the prognosis for speech and language development as well as for future academic achievement.[267, 268] This knowledge in combination with technology that makes screening for hearing loss quick, easy, and inexpensive has been instrumental in increasing support and generating initiatives for screening the hearing of all newborns.[1, 114, 115, 152, 165, 245, 246, 257] Many states (36 as of this writing) have passed legislation that mandates universal newborn hearing screening. Screening beyond the newborn period is also important, because some children acquire hearing loss or have late-onset or progressive hearing loss. Screening only in the newborn period should not cause clinicians to lose sight of the fact that children can have hearing impairment during childhood that would not have been present during a newborn hearing screening.

Universal Newborn Hearing Screening

The notion of universal newborn hearing screening has been a controversial one. The incidence of significant congenital hearing loss is low, about 3:1000 births in the general population. What has to be considered carefully is whether there is the ability to effectively screen all infants to identify a few in a cost-effective way. With the development of screening technologies such as the automated

ABR (AABR) and OAEs, many have concluded that it is now feasible to conduct universal newborn hearing screening efficiently and effectively.* In the past, newborn screening programs were limited to identification of newborns with risk indicators such as those provided in the Joint Committee on Infant Hearing position statements[112, 113] and to the application of hearing screening tests such as the ABR[53, 59] to only such children. Some programs involved the identification of those with risk indicators, who would be invited to have a diagnostic audiologic evaluation at a later time. In either case, it was determined that an unacceptably high number of infants with hearing loss were not being identified early and as a result were not given access to early intervention services and amplification devices that could help to minimize the impact of their hearing loss. The cost to society of serving children with congenital hearing loss who are identified late is great because such children require more special education services and therapies than do children who are identified early and receive early intervention services.

One of the questions of a specifically audiologic nature has been which measure of auditory function would best serve in universal newborn hearing screening applications. Many early newborn screening programs used diagnostic ABR systems, with click stimuli presented at one or two hearing levels and pass/refer criteria set based on the outcomes of those measures.[53, 59] Such programs typically were used for screening only those determined to be at risk, so the numbers of infants screened could be managed with that approach. However, universal screening programs involve numbers too great to make such a protocol practical. Instead, audiologists have turned to AABR systems and to OAEs. Each comes with advantages and disadvantages, ranging from the extent of the information provided to pass/refer rates to cost. Both ABR[74, 94, 229] and OAEs[17, 18, 110, 121, 123, 148, 172, 229, 269] have been the focus of much study and interest since the 1990s,[114, 115, 164, 165] including a federally funded consortium project that investigated the performance of ABR, TEOAEs, and DPOAEs in screening newborns. The project, comprehensively reported in a series of articles that composed the October 2000 issue of *Ear and Hearing* (Volume 21), was conducted at seven centers across the country and included more than 7000 newborns.[174] The recommendations of the investigators in that project were that ABR, TEOAEs, and DPOAEs all had sufficient performance characteristics to serve well in universal newborn hearing screening applications. This is consistent with data from clinical programs that used one or more of the technologies and reported acceptable performance.

The Rhode Island Hearing Assessment Program (RIHAP)[252, 253] was instrumental in demonstrating that TEOAEs could be used in a cost-effective way to screen all infants. The work done in that project gave impetus to the use of OAEs in well-baby nurseries as well as the neonatal intensive care units and helped persuade many that universal newborn hearing screening could become a reality.

Because of the development of almost universal access

---

*See references 41, 65, 68, 71, 74, 81, 83, 93, 94, 126, 164, 173, 174, 202.

to the Internet, a great deal of information on universal newborn hearing screening and related subjects is available on the Internet. For example, the Centers for Disease Control and Prevention National Center on Birth Defects and Developmental Disabilities has a Web site on their Early Hearing Detection and Intervention Program (www.cdc.gov/ncbdddd/ehdi). Web sites at the National Center for Hearing Assessment and Management (NCHAM) (www.infanthearing.org) and at the Marion Downs National Center (www.colorado.edu/slhs/mdnc/) provide a wealth of information regarding statewide screening programs, instrumentation, follow-up protocols, intervention, resources and information for parents and families, and more. Also, a number of states have Web pages specific to their statewide programs, including excellent information from Texas (www.tdh.state.tx.us/audio/audiology.htm), Georgia (http://health.state.ga.us/programs/unhs/index.shtml), Oregon (www.ohd.hr.state.or.us/pcah/hearing/welcome.htm2), and Virginia (www.vahealth.org/hearing/), among others. Each site has additional links, and new sites are added frequently. The American Academy of Audiology (AAA) (www.audiology.org) and ASHA (www.professional.asha.org/infant hearing/index.htm) also have helpful information and links to relevant sites.

Otoacoustic Emissions Screening

Despite the strong support and use of new technologies for screening, protocols from programs that use OAEs vary, and pass/refer criteria seem to be determined on a program-by-program basis. There is as yet no consensus on which frequencies to consider when screening and what response parameters should be considered. Some instruments that are designed specifically for screening have preset pass/refer criteria that are not modifiable by the person screening. The test is run and the response is analyzed against the criteria. If the criteria are met, the instrument reports a "pass"; if not, it reports a "refer." For this reason, it is critical that an audiologist with knowledge and experience in screening, in screening technologies, and in pediatric audiology be in a position of responsibility in any universal newborn hearing screening program because predetermined test criteria may or may not be appropriate for a given program.

TEOAEs. Criteria vary for "pass" and "refer" across programs using TEOAEs. The RIHAP reported that examination of the OAE-to-noise ratio in three frequency bands (1 to 2, 2 to 3, and 3 to 4 kHz) and declaration of a "pass" if the ratio was more than 3 dB in each of the bands resulted in good performance characteristics. Some programs use good responses in four of five or three of four frequency bands. Others might use different criteria for accepting a response depending on the frequency band. One such protocol is to use a 3-dB SNR at 1000 and 1500 Hz and a 6-dB SNR at 2000, 3000, and 4000 Hz, with good response at four of five frequencies to indicate a "pass." It is important for any professional with responsibility for such a program to closely monitor performance of the screening protocol that is used and to clearly understand the principles of screening. An understanding of how changes in criteria can affect not only pass and

refer outcomes but also sensitivity, specificity, and predictive ability of the protocol is critical. For example, a program with a referral rate that is considered too high may change criteria to reduce the referral rate. However, a simple reduction in referrals does not necessarily indicate that the protocol has been improved if it results in an unacceptable increase in false-negative outcomes.

DPOAEs. There are more data on newborn hearing screening protocols using TEOAEs than using DPOAEs. However, it is evident from the consortium study and from the clinical information in the literature that DPOAEs also can serve well in universal newborn screening programs.[65, 68, 71, 83, 129, 174, 197] The specific frequencies considered and the criteria for accepting a response vary from program to program with DPOAEs in the same way they do for TEOAEs. In newborn screening applications, the ability to measure an emission below 1500 Hz can be very difficult due to noise generated by the infant and the nursery environment. Many programs opt for screening only frequencies of 1500 or 2000 Hz and above because of the false-positive rates that result when lower frequencies are included.[68]

Automated Auditory Brain Stem Response

The AABR has been around for some time. The cost of a test using the AABR is greater than the cost for an OAE test. However, cost effectiveness is aided by the lower referral rates with AABR. The AABR screens infants using a click at 35-dB HL. When an infant passes the AABR, all except perhaps a mild hearing loss can be ruled out. One advantage of the AABR over OAEs is that it assesses not only the peripheral auditory system but also the lower brain stem response. This is unlike OAEs, which are a cochlear phenomenon and likely generated at the level of the outer hair cells.

Screening Protocols

Screening program protocols vary nearly as much as they vary in criteria used for "pass" and "refer." Many programs that use OAEs will rescreen before discharge those infants who do not pass an initial screening.[24] Because of problems with vernix in the ear canal and mesenchyme in the middle ear shortly after birth, OAE screening has a fairly high referral rate within the first 24 hours after birth. Sometimes, infants are screened within that time period because of discharge policies of the hospital. Rescreening before discharge can considerably reduce the over-referral rate, especially if the rescreening is done with AABR rather than with a second OAE measurement. An infant discharged from the hospital without passing the newborn screening will be referred for follow-up at about 2 to 4 weeks. Follow-up may be done in the hospital or in an audiology outpatient facility. Follow-up protocols vary, but one that is favored is to rescreen using OAEs if the nursery screening or screenings were conducted with OAEs only. At the age of 2 to 4 weeks, the vernix or mesenchyme often is no longer present to interfere with the OAE measurement, and a "pass" outcome is obtained. For infants who still do not pass the OAE rescreen, AABR is often used. It is also advisable to perform tympanometry with a high-frequency probe tone at this time. In our center, we use a 1000-Hz probe tone and compare the results with the norms published by Rhodes and colleagues.[202] The AABR has slightly better performance characteristics than the OAE (at possibly greater cost, as described earlier) and can tolerate a mild middle-ear disorder. If the infant passes the AABR with an abnormal 1000-Hz tympanogram, our recommendation to the parents is to see the pediatrician with attention to possible middle-ear disorder. If the infant does not pass the AABR, our recommendation depends on the tympanogram. If it is abnormal, we recommend medical examination of the middle ear before scheduling a diagnostic audiologic evaluation. If the tympanogram is within the normal range, we directly recommend a diagnostic audiologic evaluation.

For infants referred because they did not pass the AABR in the nursery, an OAE is performed and the AABR is repeated on rescreen at 2 to 4 weeks. Regardless of the nature of the original screening protocol, if an infant does not pass the AABR at the rescreening visit, he or she is scheduled for a diagnostic audiologic evaluation. The diagnostic audiologic evaluation is an ABR at a clinical pediatric audiology center. At that time, ABR thresholds to clicks and to frequency-specific signals should be obtained using both air- and bone-conducted stimuli. Follow-up diagnostic evaluations of infants who have not passed screenings and rescreenings should be done in a facility with appropriate instrumentation and with audiologists experienced in evaluation of infants using ABR with both click and frequency-specific stimuli.

Auditory Neuropathy

There has been increasing interest in a diagnostic category that has come to light with the advent of OAEs. Auditory neuropathy is a disorder found in infants and older persons who exhibit behaviors or other evidence of hearing loss, fail to generate an ABR, but have normal or near-normal OAEs. That is, at least to the level of the outer hair cells, the peripheral auditory system is functioning within a normal range. It is presumed that the auditory deficit is at the level of the inner hair cells or in the auditory nerve and beyond. This phenomenon was not discovered until OAEs gave clinicians a window into the cochlea, outer hair cells in particular, and allowed them to further isolate the site of the lesion. This is a phenomenon with a very low incidence and may be related to specific risk criteria in the young. For example, many infants demonstrating evidence of auditory neuropathy have a history of elevated bilirubin levels during the neonatal period.[220]

Older Infants and Young Children

Once infants leave the newborn nurseries, access to them for mass screening programs of any kind is limited. The Joint Committee on Infant Hearing[115] position statement includes suggestions for early identification of hearing impairment in infants up to 24 months of age. The high-risk indicators offered in this statement for the older infants are also listed in Table 11–4. Methods such as the ABR, OAE, and VRA are all available for screening in this age group. A computer-based VRA system has an algorithm (CAST [Classification of Audiograms by Sequential Testing]) for quick screening of infants behaviorally.[45]

Figure 11–16 shows the TEOAE for a 13-month-old infant with bilateral severe SNHL. This child was identified at the age of 13 months, 7 months after the mother began to express concern over the infant's responses to sound. The tests for both ears, including preparation of the infant, took less than 30 minutes. The child was immediately evaluated and found to have at least a severe SNHL. She is enrolled in an early intervention program and is wearing hearing aids bilaterally.

Special emphasis is placed on the value of parental/caregiver reports of abnormal auditory behavior or delayed development of speech and language in Joint Committee on Infant Hearing[114, 115] position statements. Primary care physicians need to be sensitive to the concerns of parents and to be aware themselves of signs of delayed auditory development.[150] After the newborn pe-

TABLE 11–4. Indicators Associated With Hearing Loss as Provided in the Joint Committee on Infant Hearing 2000 Position Statement

A. For use with neonates (birth–28 days) when universal screening is not available
  1. Illness or condition requiring admission of 48 hours or greater to a neonate intensive care unit
  2. Stigmata or other findings associated with a syndrome known to include a sensorineural and/or a conductive hearing loss
  3. Family history of permanent childhood sensorineural hearing loss
  4. Craniofacial anomalies, including those with morphologic abnormalities of pinna and ear canal
  5. In utero infection such as cytomegalovirus, rubella, syphilis, herpes, and toxoplasmosis
B. For use with infants (29 days–2 years). These risk indicators place an infant at risk for progressive or delayed-onset sensorineural hearing loss and/or conductive hearing loss.
  1. Parent/caregiver concern regarding hearing, speech, language, and/or developmental delay
  2. Family history of permanent childhood sensorineural hearing loss
  3. Stigmata or other findings associated with a syndrome known to include a sensorineural and/or a conductive hearing loss
  4. Postnatal infections associated with sensorineural hearing loss including bacterial meningitis
  5. In utero infection such as cytomegalovirus, rubella, syphilis, herpes, or toxoplasmosis
  6. Neonatal indicators—specifically, hyperbilirubinemia at a serum level requiring exchange transfusion, persistent pulmonary hypertension of the newborn associated with mechanical ventilation, and conditions requiring the use of extracorporeal membrane oxygenation (ECMO)
  7. Syndromes associated with progressive hearing loss such as neurofibromatosis, osteopetrosis, and Usher syndrome
  8. Neurodegenerative disorders, such as Hunter syndrome, or sensory motor neuropathies, such as Friedreich ataxia and Charcot-Marie-Tooth syndrome
  9. Head trauma
  10. Recurrent or persistent otitis media with effusion for at least 3 months

From Joint Committee on Infant Hearing. 2000 Position statement. Am J Audiol 9:9, 2000.

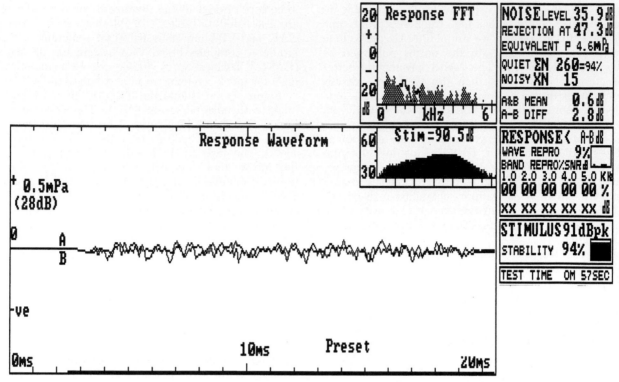

FIGURE 11–16. Transient evoked otoacoustic emission of a 13-month-old infant with severe sensorineural hearing impairment of unknown cause. The child sat awake on the parent's lap during testing. Even with a stimulus of 91 dB peak equivalent sound pressure level, no evidence of an emission can be seen.

riod, most infants and children with hearing impairment are first identified by a parent or caretaker. Unfortunately, the concerns of parents are sometimes minimized by primary care practitioners, largely because of the wide range of variability in normal development, because of a belief that hearing cannot be assessed adequately in the very young, or because of concerns over the cost of assessments. The consequence of delayed assessment of suspected hearing loss is delayed intervention, not only for the affected child but for the family as a whole.[10, 240] The impact on a family of a child with a disability such as hearing impairment is great but is complicated tremendously when parents (one or both parents) are treated as being overconcerned or foolish or are put off for many months by professionals. Parents are reliable reporters of their infant's development, and their concerns should be taken seriously. The information in this chapter is evidence that the means are available to obtain reliable, valid, ear-specific, and frequency-specific hearing data on infants. The cost of an audiologic evaluation is far outweighed by the benefit to the family of confirming (or ruling out) a serious disability, possibly helping to diagnose associated disabilities and beginning beneficial interventions for both infant and family. As has been stressed in legislation, such as the Education of the Handicapped Act and its reauthorizations and amendments, intervention for children with disabilities should be family centered rather than child centered. Independent of the degree to which one agrees with the success of intervention programs for particular classes of disabled individuals,

families have the right and need to know as much as possible, and as soon as possible, regarding the nature and extent of their child's disability if a successful outcome is to be achieved.

Screening Preschool and School-Age Children

Because preschool and school-age children can typically perform behavioral audiometric tasks, such as play audiometry or conventional audiometry, pure-tone hearing screening rather than OAE or ABR tests is usually employed.[207] ASHA guidelines for screening for hearing impairment and middle-ear disorders[6] recommend that for children 3 years old and above, pure-tone hearing screening be done at 20-dB HL at test frequencies of 0.5, 1, 2, and 4 kHz in each ear, using behavioral test methods. A screening failure occurs when a child fails to respond to any frequency in either ear. As with all audiometric tests, noise in the test environment can artificially elevate thresholds, so screening done outside sound-treated rooms must be done with an understanding of the potential pitfalls associated with poor environmental noise conditions.

The ASHA guidelines[6] also provide a suggested protocol for screening for middle-ear disease. The protocol has several components, including recent otologic history, visual inspection of the external auditory meatus and tympanic membrane, and acoustic immittance testing. The history taking is designed to learn, either from a parent/

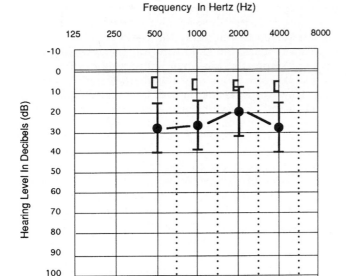

FIGURE 11–17. Mean audiometric thresholds (1 SD) of a group of children with otitis media with effusion. Many children with otitis media with effusion have hearing thresholds within the normal range. (Data from Fria TJ, Cantekin, EI, Eichler JA. Hearing acuity of children with otitis media with effusion. Arch Otolaryngol 111:10, 1989.)

caretaker or from the child, of any recent ear pain, drainage, or other related conditions that would signal the need for immediate medical referral. The visual inspection with an otoscope is designed to identify gross obstructions or defects in the external auditory meatus or gross abnormalities of the tympanic membrane that require immediate medical referral; it is not intended to be used for diagnosis of middle-ear disease.

The acoustic immittance battery is designed primarily to identify ears that are at risk for middle-ear effusion.[207] However, one component is designed to determine whether, in the presence of a flat tympanogram, the ear-canal volume is abnormally large. If so, an opening in the tympanic membrane is suspected that warrants medical referral unless the child is known to have polyethylene tubes in place. With respect to identification of middle-ear effusion, the need for the immittance test relates to the poor sensitivity of pure-tone hearing screening for that purpose. Figure 11–17 provides the mean (1 SD) hearing thresholds for children with middle-ear effusion.[55] The data reveal that many children with middle-ear effusion have hearing thresholds at or below (i.e., better than) the screening fence of 20-dB HL and as a result would not be identified by a hearing screening test alone.[55, 72]

Both AAA and ASHA have put forth guidelines[2, 6] regarding screening for middle-ear disease. Both groups have recommended the use of peak admittance and tympanometric width in the decision of whether to refer. Both protocols require referral on two tympanometric screenings separated by about 6 to 8 weeks because of the transient nature of middle-ear disease. With a single test, over-referral rates tend to be very high. Choosing cut-offs for screening tests is difficult. Factors that must

be considered are the population characteristics, the nature and definition of the disease to be identified, the test method, instrumentation parameter settings, and others.[177, 179] Also, in a protocol that calls for two tests, the prevalence of disease is different in the group requiring retest relative to the group initially screened. This may mean that two separate sets of criteria are necessary: one for the initial screening (overall population) and another for the group to be retested (subgroup at risk). Anyone who uses acoustic immittance screening tests should be aware of the effects of different factors on the performance of the test.[177]

Monitoring for Ototoxicity or Overexposure to Noise

Children with serious illnesses are sometimes placed on medications known to be ototoxic. Monitoring of the hearing of such children is an important function of the audiology service of medical centers at which they are treated. Sometimes, early identification of the effects of ototoxic medication can be determined by periodic hearing testing during the treatment period. A typical protocol requires that a child have a hearing test before initiation of the treatment, with regular follow-up as long as the treatment continues and then after completion of treatment. If evidence of SNHL is observed, usually a change in hearing of 10 dB or more at one or more frequencies, the managing physician should be notified and decisions are then made regarding the possibility of alternative treatment.

Hearing loss due to ototoxicity occurs in the high frequencies first, so it is important that a monitoring program examine these. DPOAE testing, which has capability to measure cochlear function in high frequencies, is used to monitor in cases of treatment with ototoxic medications. It is possible that DPOAEs are sensitive enough to suggest changes before they become clinically evident. Extra-high-frequency audiometry is now available with clinical audiometers, so it is possible to test at frequencies as high as 16 to 20 kHz in some cases. Normative data for the extra-high frequencies are limited, so centers that use this technique should develop their own norms. Also, it is important to understand that at the very highest frequencies (e.g., above 14 kHz), there is great variability in the measurement and very little dynamic range for the measurement of hearing loss. That is, the intensity levels required to reach thresholds in individuals with normal hearing are not very far below the maximum output possible from the instrumentation, thereby limiting clinical usefulness. Theoretically, the higher the frequencies that can be tested, the earlier potential ototoxicity can be detected.

Sometimes, there is resistance from personnel in oncology or pulmonology departments because there is no alternative to the ototoxic medication and it must be administered so the child may survive. A report from the audiologist that the hearing of a patient is being damaged is disheartening and frustrating to the managing physician because there is no choice in the matter. However, it is important to understand that audiologists are equipped not only to identify and diagnose hearing loss but also to work with children and families in the management of hearing impairment. Children who lose substantial amounts of hearing while hospitalized or while undergoing treatment become frightened, and their parents are perplexed. An audiologist can help the family understand what the child is going through and provide support, amplification, and strategies for preserving communication skills during what has to be a very unpleasant experience. The administration of an ototoxic drug may be necessary, but it is not necessary to have the child and family suffer the consequences of the drug without the help that is available.

Many children are exposed to loud noise. Some children shoot toy guns, ride loud motorbikes, listen to loud music through lightweight headsets, and so on. Hearing conservation efforts are critical so that young people do not permanently damage their hearing. Audiologic monitoring of children known to be exposed to high levels of noise is essential to prevent significant hearing loss. Professionals in the areas of otolaryngology, pediatrics, and audiology must continue educational efforts to ensure that children practice good hearing conservation in their daily activities.

Autonomic Responses

Over the years, the autonomic nervous system has been used for the assessment of hearing in difficult-to-test populations. In routine clinical practice, such measures, which include changes in respiration, heart rate, and electrodermal activity in the skin, have not gained great acceptance. The interested reader can consult Hogan[90] for a review of the autonomic correlates of audition.

Tests for Functional (Nonorganic) Hearing Loss

One of the problems that audiologists face in assessing hearing behaviorally is the identification of the child with functional, or nonorganic, hearing loss. Because much of the routine clinical assessment requires a voluntary behavioral response, clinicians must take precautions to make sure that a child is not exaggerating hearing loss. Children might wish to exhibit a hearing loss because of the secondary gains that accrue from added attention or because this may help explain other undesirable behaviors, such as poor performance in school or personality problems.[147] The consequences of falsely labeling a child as hearing impaired may appear in the form of parental distress, inappropriate management of the child, or reinforcement of the child's psychological difficulties, depending on the origin of the functional hearing loss.

Northern and Downs[168] point out that the child who exaggerates or invents hearing loss is most probably doing so for reasons that are important to him or her. The audiologist or other professional who encounters a suspected nonorganic hearing loss should consider whether the child has a psychological or emotional need that is being met by the consequences of a hearing loss. Therefore, it is necessary in such patients that the audiologist first assesses as accurately as possible the true status of the auditory system. Second, assistance in determining which needs of the child are being met by feigning hearing loss should be offered to the family.

In many cases, the child with functional hearing loss is suspected from the beginning. Observations of the child outside the test room may reveal exaggerated efforts to hear. However, observation may belie any hearing loss at all. The child's behavior may be very different once he or she is involved with the structured task of the hearing test. A competent pediatric audiologist will notice exaggerated efforts to hear the sound, inconsistencies on repeated attempts to obtain threshold for a given stimulus, widely different thresholds depending on the method used, and lack of correspondence between SRT and PTA (although the caution previously offered regarding the effect of hearing loss configuration on this relationship should be heeded when functional hearing loss is considered). Current test methods allow clinicians to virtually rule out hearing loss in normal-hearing individuals with so-called objective test measures. Immittance testing, especially the acoustic reflex, OAE, and ABR tests, can usually provide sufficient hard evidence to establish whether hearing is really impaired to the degree exhibited. These tests can be used to corroborate results and impressions from informal observation and behavioral testing.

There are behavioral assessment techniques that can be used in adults to obtain estimates of thresholds in patients who seem to be exaggerating. The use of such complicated tests in children is not common because of the lack of sophistication on their part in performing the tasks or in providing convincing performances on traditional testing. The Stenger test, which is beneficial in identifying functional hearing loss in patients with unilateral or asymmetric hearing loss, can be used in older children.

With small children, there often are large discrepancies in the results of routine tests, so the identification of nonorganicity is not difficult. Sometimes, young children can be instructed to say "yes" when they hear a tone and "no" when they do not. A youngster who is too immature to appreciate the stimulus-response contingency will respond "no" to the sounds that are heard but are below the selected minimal response level. Infants and children with unusual configurations of hearing loss can respond in atypical ways on standard tests. The trained pediatric audiologist must use experience and creativity, along with a test battery, to establish accurate and reliable estimates of hearing.

The Role of the Audiologist

This chapter has provided a description of the various techniques available for assessing hearing in infants and children. The reader should now have a basic understanding of the techniques for such assessment and an awareness of sources where more extensive discussion of a particular technique can be found. Throughout this chapter, it was emphasized that no one method of assessment is definitive and that accurate assessment involves the consideration of information provided by several tests of hearing used in combination. Although certain techniques can be used in isolation as screening tools in certain situations (e.g., BOA in the office setting), comprehensive assessment is based on the results of a combination of these tests.

The audiologist plays a multifaceted role in the assessment process; he or she must devise and implement an assessment strategy composed of procedures that are applicable to the child in question and must interpret the results in the context of the impairment that is suspected. The audiologist must also convey assessment results to the referral source and must provide suggestions that are meaningful for the management of the child. In concert with the referral source, the audiologist can also play an important role in interpreting the results to concerned family members and in counseling the family with regard to the impact an impairment may have on the child's future interaction with the environment from a social and an educational point of view.

The audiologist can serve as a valuable resource for the implementation of habilitative or rehabilitative plans for a hearing-impaired child. In addition, the audiologist is usually aware of the public and special school programs in the community that will play an active role in the child's education and is often responsible for ensuring that appropriate agencies provide necessary services. The audiologist maintains contact with such programs and agencies so that the long-term follow-up of a particular child is maintained even if family resources are limited.

In conclusion, the audiologist should be an active team member in the general pediatric assessment of any child, regardless of age. At the audiologist's disposal are the knowledge, experience, and techniques required to make a meaningful assessment of hearing in infants and children. In view of the importance of adequate hearing in infancy and childhood, health care professionals are obligated to give the assessment of hearing the high priority it deserves (see also Chapter 16).

Acknowledgments

The author would like to acknowledge the contribution of Thomas J. Fria, PhD, to this chapter. Dr. Fria wrote the chapter on hearing assessment in children in the first edition of this text. Although there have been substantial changes in methods for assessment of hearing in children since that time and the chapter has undergone three major revisions by the present author, much of the material contributed by Dr. Fria is still accurate and timely and remains as part of this chapter.

Having said that, the present author accepts full responsibility for the material included in the current chapter.

SELECTED REFERENCES

American Journal of Otology. Otoacoustic emissions. Am J Otol 15 (Suppl 1), 1994.
> *A collection of articles that summarize OAEs.*
American Speech-Language-Hearing Association. Competencies in auditory evoked potential measurement and clinical application. ASHA 19 (Suppl):23, 1999.
> *Association recommendation for competencies needed to perform AEP measurements.*
Bess FH (ed). Children With Hearing Impairment: Contemporary Trends. Nashville, Tennessee, Vanderbilt Bill Wilkerson Center Press, 1998. Proceedings of the Fourth International Symposium on Childhood Deafness, Kiawah Island, SC, October 1996.
> *These articles cover a wide range of topics ranging from early identification and screening to assessment of hearing and management of the hearing-impaired child.*
Bess FH (ed). Hearing Impairment in Children. Parkton, York Press, 1988. Proceedings of the Third International Symposium on Childhood Deafness, Nashville, Tenn, July 1986.
> *Contributed chapters cover three major areas: etiology/audiology disorders, identification and assessment, and management. Excellent up-to-date reviews make this an important reference to have.*
Fria TJ. The auditory brain stem response: background and clinical applications. Monogr Contemp Audiol 2:1, 1980.
> *A complete but not lengthy explanation of the fundamentals of the ABR. A good basic publication for reference.*
Goldstein R, Aldrich WM. Evoked Potential Audiometry: Fundamentals and Applications. Boston, Allyn and Bacon, 1999.
> *Designed as a text for graduate students preparing for careers in audiology, this publication has a great deal of useful information in a very readable form. It is not a multi-authored text, so is consistent in style and form throughout. Chapters range from instrumentation considerations, through the range of AEPs, to applications in screening, threshold assessment, and otoneurologic diagnostics.*
Gravel JS and Hood LJ. Pediatric audiological assessment. In Musiek FE, Rintelmann WF (eds). Contemporary Perspectives in Hearing Assessment. Boston, Allyn and Bacon, 1999, pp 305–326.
Hall JW. Handbook of Auditory Evoked Responses. Needham Heights, Mass, Allyn and Bacon, 1992.
> *A comprehensive, single-authored text on auditory evoked responses that is very complete in coverage and abundance of primary references. An excellent resource for those interested in or using evoked potentials in the clinical setting.*
Jacobsen JT. The Auditory Brain Stem Response. San Diego, College Hill Press, 1985.
> *Contributed chapters from many authors. Topics range from basic technical issues of the ABR, to neuroanatomy, to the clinical application of the ABR. An entire section is devoted to pediatric assessment.*
Jerger J (ed). Pediatric Audiology: Current Trends. San Diego, College Hill Press, 1984.
> *Contributed chapters from experts in pediatric audiology. Major topics include behavioral assessment, emittance, evoked potentials, hearing aid selection, and aural rehabilitation.*
Lonsbury-Martin BL, Martin GK, McCoy MJ, Whitehead ML. Testing otoacoustic emissions in newborns, infants, toddlers and children. In Gerber SE (ed). The Handbook of Pediatric Audiology. Washington, DC, Gallaudet Press, 1996, pp 173–205.
> *Good overview of the use of OAEs in the clinical evaluation of infants and children.*
Margolis RH, Shanks JE. Tympanometry. In Katz J (ed). Handbook of Clinical Audiology, 3rd ed. Baltimore, Williams & Wilkins, 1985, pp 438–475.
> *This short chapter provides a good explanation of the fundamentals of tympanometry. It includes the latest methods of interpreting tympanograms.*
Martin FN, Clark JG (eds). Hearing Care for Children. Boston, Allyn and Bacon, 1996.
> *Collection of chapters covering pediatric audiology, etiologies of hearing loss, identification and assessment, management and intervention, and more.*
Matkin ND, Roush J (eds). Infants and Toddlers With Hearing Loss. Parkton, Md, York Press, 1994.
> *Chapters contributed by experts on early intervention of hearing loss.*

Northern JL, Downs MP. Hearing in Children, 4th ed. Baltimore, Williams & Wilkins, 1991.

> *Fourth edition of a text covering all aspects of pediatric audiology. This book presents the viewpoints of two pediatric audiologists with a wealth of experience and knowledge. A valuable resource for anyone interested in hearing and hearing impairment in children.*

Robinette MS, Glattke TJ (eds). Otoacoustic Emissions: Clinical Applications. New York, Thieme, 1997.

> *Chapters contributed by experts in various applications of OAE testing. It covers basic underlying physiologic mechanisms believed to be responsible for OAEs, as well as normative and clinical data.*

Spivak LG (ed). Universal Newborn Hearing Screening. New York, Thieme, 1998.

> *Issues related to all aspects of universal newborn hearing screening are covered in this timely book.*

Van Camp KJ, Margolis RJ, Wilson RH, et al. Principles of Tympanometry. ASHA Monogr 24, 1986.

> *A monograph covering basic principles and clinical data in tympanometry. Despite the date of publication, there is excellent coverage of some of the more technical aspects of emittance.*

White KR, Behrens TR (guest eds). The Rhode Island Hearing Assessment Project: implications for universal newborn hearing screening. Semin Hear 14, 1993.

> *Articles related to a newborn hearing-screening project using transient evoked OAE and ABR tests. This project has gained national attention and is providing important information.*

White KR, Vohr BR, Maxon AB, et al. Screening of all newborns for hearing loss using transient evoked otoacoustic emissions. Int J Pediatr Otorhinolaryngol 29:203, 1994.

Wilber LA, Feldman AS. Acoustic Impedance and Admittance—The Measure of Middle Ear Function. Baltimore, Williams & Wilkins, 1976.

> *A complete text on the fundamentals of emittance testing. There are chapters on clinical application, including acoustic and nonacoustic stapedial reflex tests, and detailed information on the physics of the middle-ear system.*

REFERENCES

1. American Academy of Audiology. Early identification of hearing loss in infants and children (position statement). Audiology Today 2:8, 1988.
2. American Academy of Audiology. Identification of hearing loss and middle-ear dysfunction in preschool and school-age children (position statement). Audiology Today 9:21, 1997.
3. American Journal of Otology. Otoacoustic emissions. Am J Otol 15 (Suppl 1), 1994.
4. American National Standards Institute. American National Standard Specifications for Instruments to Measure Aural Acoustic Impedance and Admittance (Aural Acoustic Immittance). New York, ANSI, 1987, S3.39 (R1996).
5. American National Standards Institute. Standard Specifications for Audiometers. New York, ANSI, 1996, S3.6.
6. American Speech-Language-Hearing Association. Guidelines for Audiologic Screening. Rockville, Md, American Speech-Language-Hearing Association, 1997.
7. American Speech-Language-Hearing Association. Guidelines for audiometric symbols. ASHA 32 (Suppl 2):25, 1990.
8. Anderson H, Barr B, Wedenberg E. Early diagnosis of VIIIth nerve tumors by acoustic reflex tests. Acta Otolaryngol (Stockh) 263:232, 1970.
9. Baer J, Hall J III. Effects of nonpathologic factors on OAEs. Hear J 45:17, 1992.
10. Bailey DB Jr. Current issues in early intervention. In Bess FH, Hall JW (eds). Screening Children for Auditory Function. Nashville, Tenn, Bill Wilkerson Center Press, 1992, pp 385–398.
11. Barnet AB, Goodwin RS. Averaged evoked electroencephalographic responses to clicks in the human newborn. Electroencephalogr Clin Neurophysiol 18:441, 1965.
12. Barr B. Pure-tone audiometry for pre-school children. Acta Otolaryngol (Stockh) Suppl 121, 1955.
13. Bennett MJ, Weatherby LA. Newborn acoustic reflexes to noise and pure-tone signals. J Speech Hear Res 25:383, 1982.
14. Bess FH, Tharpe AM. Unilateral hearing impairment in children. Pediatrics 74:206, 1984.
15. Block MG, Wiley TL. Overview and basic principles of acoustic emittance. In Katz J (ed). Handbook of Clinical Audiology, 4th ed. Baltimore, Williams & Wilkins, 1994, pp 271–282.
16. Bluestone CD, Fria TJ, Arjona SK, et al. Controversies in screening for middle ear disease and hearing loss in children. Pediatrics 77:57, 1986.
17. Bonfils P, Dumont A, Marie P, et al. Evoked otoacoustic emissions in newborn hearing screening. Laryngoscope 100:186, 1990.
18. Bonfils P, Uziel A, Pujol R. Screening for auditory dysfunction in infants by evoked oto-acoustic emissions. Arch Otolaryngol Head Surg 114:887, 1988.
19. Bosatra A, Russolo M, Poli P. Modifications of the stapedius muscle reflex under spontaneous and experimental brain stem impairment. Acta Otolaryngol (Stockh) 80:61, 1975.
20. Brackman DE, Selters WA. Electrocochleography in Meniere's disease and acoustic neuromas. In Ruben RJ, Elberling C, Salomon G (eds). Electrocochleography. Baltimore, University Park Press, 1976, pp 315–330.
21. Brookhouser PE, Moeller MP. Choosing the appropriate habilitative track for the newly identified hearing-impaired child. Ann Otol Rhinol Laryngol 95:51, 1986.
22. Brooks DN. An objective method of detecting fluid in the middle ear. Int Audiol 7:280, 1968.
23. Cantekin EI, Bluestone CD, Fria TJ, et al. Identification of otitis media with effusion in children. Ann Otol Rhinol Laryngol 89 (Suppl 68):190, 1980.
24. Clemens C, Davis S. Minimizing false-positives in universal newborn hearing screening: a simple solution. Pediatrics 107:E29, 2001.
25. Clemis JD, McGee T. Brain stem electric response audiometry in the differential diagnosis of acoustic tumors. Laryngoscope 89:31, 1979.
26. Coats AC, Dickey JR. Non-surgical recording of human auditory nerve action potentials from the tympanic membrane. Ann Otol Rhinol Laryngol 29:844, 1970.
27. Coats AC, Martin JL. Nerve action potentials and brain stem evoked responses: effects of audiogram shape and lesion location. Arch Otolaryngol 103:605, 1977.
28. Combs JT. Predictive value of the angle of acoustic reflectometry. Pediatr Infect Dis J 10:214, 1991.
29. Cox LC. Infant assessment: developmental and age-related considerations. In Jacobson JT (ed). The Auditory Brainstem Response. San Diego, College Hill Press, 1985, pp 297–316.
30. Cullen JK, Ellis MS, Berlin CI, et al. Human acoustic nerve action potential recordings from the tympanic membrane without anesthesia. Acta Otolaryngol (Stockh) 74:15, 1972.
31. Darley FL (ed). Identification audiometry. Speech Hear Disord Suppl 9, 1961.
32. Davis H. Sedation of young children for evoked response audiometry (ERA): summary of a symposium. Audiology 12:55, 1973.
33. Davis H. Principles of electric response audiometry. Ann Otol Rhinol Laryngol 85 (Suppl):1, 1976.
34. Davis H, Owen JH. Auditory evoked potentials. In Owen JH, Davis H (eds). Evoked Potential Testing: Clinical Applications. New York, Grune & Stratton, 1985.
35. De Chicchis AR, Nozza RJ. Comparison of acoustic immittance measures obtained with different commercial instruments. J Am Acad Audiol 7:120, 1996.
36. De Chicchis AR, Todd NW, Nozza RJ. Developmental changes in aural acoustic admittance measurements. J Am Acad Audiol 11:97, 2000.
37. de Jonge R. Normal tympanometric gradient: a comparison of three methods. Audiology 25:299, 1986.
38. Denenberg LJ, Altshuler MW. The clinical relationship between acoustic reflexes and loudness perception. J Am Audiol Soc 2:79, 1976.
39. DeVries SM, Decker TN. Otoacoustic emissions: overview of measurement methodologies. Semin Hear 13:15, 1992.
40. Diefendorf AO, Gravel JS. Behavioral observation and visual rein-

forcement audiometry. In Gerber S (ed). Handbook of Pediatric Audiology. Washington, DC, Gallaudet University Press, 1996, pp 55–83.

41. Doyle KJ, Fujikawa S, Rogers P, Newman E. Comparison of newborn hearing screening by transient otoacoustic emissions and auditory brainstem response using ALGO-2. Int J Pediatr Otorhinolaryngol 43:207, 1998.

42. Durrant JD. Observations on combined noninvasive electrocochleography and auditory brainstem response recording. Semin Hear 7:289, 1986.

43. Eggermont JJ, Odenthal DW, Schmidt PH, et al. Electrocochleography: basic principles and clinical application. Acta Otolaryngol (Stockh) Suppl 316, 1974.

44. Eilers RE, Ozdamar O, Steffens ML, et al. Classification of audiograms by sequential testing: reliability and validity of an automated behavioral hearing-screening algorithm. J Am Acad Audiol 4:172, 1993.

45. Eilers RE, Widen JE, Urbano R, et al. Optimization of automated hearing test algorithms: a comparison of data from simulations and young children. Ear Hear 12:199, 1991.

46. Eisenberg RB. Auditory Competence in Early Life. Baltimore, University Park Press, 1976.

47. Elberling C. Action potentials along the cochlear partition recorded from the ear canal in man. Scand Audiol 3:13, 1974.

48. Elliott LL, Katz DR. Development of a New Children's Test of Speech Discrimination. St Louis, Auditec of St Louis, 1980.

49. Ferraro JA, Durrant JD. Auditory evoked potentials: overview and basic principles. In Katz J (ed). Handbook of Clinical Audiology, 4th ed. Baltimore, Williams & Wilkins, 1994, pp 317–338.

50. Finitzo-Hieber T, Friel-Patti S. Conductive hearing loss and the ABR. In Jacobson JT (ed). The Auditory Brainstem Response. San Diego, College Hill Press, 1985, pp 113–132.

51. Franklin D, McCoy M, Martin G, Lonsbury-Martin B. Test/retest reliability of distortion-product and transiently evoked otoacoustic emissions. Ear Hear 13:417, 1992.

52. Fria TJ. The auditory brain stem response: background and clinical applications. Monogr Contemp Audiol 2:1, 1980.

53. Fria TJ. Identification of congenital hearing loss with the auditory brainstem response. In Jacobson JT (ed). The Auditory Brainstem Response. San Diego, College Hill Press, 1985, pp 317–334.

54. Fria TJ. Threshold estimation with early latency auditory potentials. In Katz J (ed). Handbook of Clinical Audiology, 3rd ed. Baltimore, Williams & Wilkins, 1985, pp 549–564.

55. Fria TJ, Cantekin EI, Eichler JA. Hearing acuity of children with otitis media with effusion. Arch Otolaryngol 111:10, 1985.

56. Fria TJ, Leblanc J, Kristensen R, et al. Ipsilateral acoustic reflex stimulation in normal and sensorineural impaired ears: a preliminary report. Can J Otolaryngol 4:695, 1975.

57. Fria TJ, Sabo DL. Auditory brainstem responses in children with otitis media with effusion. Ann Otol Rhinol Laryngol 68:200, 1980.

58. Fulton RT, Gorzycki PA, Hull WL. Hearing assessment with young children. J Speech Hear Dis 40:397, 1975.

59. Galambos R, Wilson MJ, Silva PD. Identifying hearing loss in the intensive care nursery: a 20-year summary. J Am Acad Audiol 5:151, 1994.

60. Gardi JN, Mendel M. Evoked brainstem potentials. In Gerber SE (ed). Audiometry in Infancy. New York, Grune & Stratton, 1977, pp 205–246.

61. Gaskill SS, Brown AM. The behavior of the acoustic DP, 2f1-f2, from the human ear and its relation to auditory sensitivity. J Acoust Soc Am 88:821, 1990.

62. Glattke TJ, Kujawa SG. Otoacoustic emissions. J Am Acad Audiol 1:29, 1991.

63. Goldstein BA, Newman CW. Clinical masking: a decision-making process. In Katz J (ed). Handbook of Clinical Audiology, 4th ed. Baltimore, Williams & Wilkins, 1994, pp 109–131.

64. Goodhill V, Lowell EL, Lowell, MO. Computerized Objective Auditory Testing in Infancy. Washington, DC, Department of Health, Education, and Welfare, 1970, Final Report of Project DHEW H-181.

65. Gordts F, Naessens B, Mudde CA, Clement PA. Reference data for DPOAE in healthy newborns. Scand Audiol 29:79, 2000.

66. Gorga M, Neely S, Bergman B, et al. Otoacoustic emissions from normal-hearing and hearing-impaired subjects: distortion product responses. J Acoust Soc Am 93:2050, 1993.

67. Gorga M, Neely S, Ohlrich B, et al. From laboratory to clinic: a large-scale study of distortion product otoacoustic emissions in ears with normal hearing and ears with hearing loss. Ear Hear 18:440, 1997.

68. Gorga M, Norton S, Sininger Y, et al. Identification of neonatal hearing impairment: distortion product otoacoustic emissions during the perinatal period. Ear Hear 21:400, 2000.

69. Gorga MP, Thornton MP. The choice of stimuli for ABR measurements. Ear Hear 10:217, 1989.

70. Gould HJ, Mandel MI. Auditory evoked responses. In Gerber SE (ed). The Handbook of Pediatric Audiology. Washington, DC, Gallaudet University Press, 1996, pp 145–172.

71. Gravel J, Berg A, Bradley M, et al. New York State Universal Newborn Hearing Screening Demonstration Project: effects of screening protocol on inpatient outcome measures. Ear Hear 21:131, 2000.

72. Gravel, J, Nozza RJ. Hearing loss among children with otitis media with effusion. In Roberts J, Wallace I, Henderson F (eds). Otitis Media in Young Children: Medical, Developmental, and Educational Considerations. New York, Brookes, 1997, pp 63–92.

73. Greisen O, Rasmussen P. Stapedius muscle reflexes and otoneurological examinations in brain stem tumors. Acta Otolaryngol (Stockh) 70:66, 1970.

74. Hahn M, Lamprecht-Dinnesen A, Heinecke A, et al. Hearing screening in healthy newborns: feasibility of different methods with regard to test time. Int J Pediatr Otorhinolaryngol 5:83, 1999.

75. Hall JW. Handbook of Auditory Evoked Responses. Needham Heights, Mass, Allyn & Bacon, 1992.

76. Hall JW, Chandler D. Tympanometry in clinical audiology. In Katz J (ed). Handbook of Clinical Audiology, 4th ed. Baltimore, Williams & Wilkins, 1994, pp 283–299.

77. Harris FP, Lonsbury-Martin BL, Stagner BB, et al. Acoustic distortion products in humans: systematic changes in amplitude as a function of f2/f1 ratio. J Acoust Soc Am 85:220, 1989.

78. Harris FP, Probst R, Wenger R. Repeatability of transiently evoked otoacoustic emissions in normally hearing humans. Audiology 30:135, 1991.

79. Harrison W, Norton S. Characteristics of transient evoked otoacoustic emissions in normal-hearing and hearing-impaired children. Ear Hear 20:75, 1999.

80. Haskins H. A phonetically balanced test of speech discrimination for children. Master's thesis, Northwestern University, 1949.

81. Hatzopoulos S, Pelosi G, Petruccelli J, et al. Efficient otoacoustic emission protocols employed in a hospital-based neonatal screening program. Acta Otolaryngol 121:269, 2000.

82. Hauser R, Probst R. The influence of systematic primary-tone level variation L2-L1 on the DPOAE 1f1-f2 in normal human ears. J Acoust Soc Am 89:280, 1991.

83. Hayes D. Newborn hearing screening: selected experience in the United States. Scand Audiol Suppl 53:29, 2001.

84. Hecox K. Electrophysiological correlates of human auditory development. In Cohen LB, Salapatek PL (eds). Infant Perception From Sensation to Cognition, Vol 2. Perception of Space, Speech and Sound. New York, Academic Press, 1975.

85. Hecox K, Burkard R. Developmental dependencies of the human brainstem auditory evoked response. Ann N Y Acad Sci 388:538, 1982.

86. Hecox K, Galambos R. Brainstem auditory evoked responses in human infants and adults. Arch Otolaryngol 99:30, 1974.

87. Hecox KE. Neurologic application of the auditory brainstem response to the pediatric age group. In Jacobson JT (ed). The Auditory Brain Stem Response. San Diego, College Hill Press, 1985, pp 287–295.

88. Hirsch JE, Margolis RH, Rykken JR. Comparison of acoustic reflex and auditory brain stem response screening of high-risk infants. Ear Hear 13:181, 1992.

89. Hirsh IJ, Davis H, Silverman SR, et al. Development of materials for speech audiometry. J Speech Hear Disord 17:321, 1952.

90. Hogan DD. Autonomic correlates of audition. In Fulton RT, Lloyd LL (eds). Auditory Assessment of the Difficult-to-Test. Baltimore, Williams & Wilkins, 1975, pp 262–290.

91. Holte L, Margolis RH, Cavanaugh RM Jr. Developmental changes in multifrequency tympanograms. Audiology 30:1, 1991.

92. Hoversten GH, Moncur JP. Stimuli and intensity factors in testing infants. J Speech Hear Res 12:687, 1969.

93. Iley K, Addis R. Impact of technology choice on service provision for universal newborn hearing screening within a busy district hospital. J Perinatol 20 (8 pt 2):S122, 2000.

94. Jacobson JT, Jacobson CA, Spahr RC. Automated and conventional ABR screening techniques in high-risk infants. J Am Acad Audiol 1:187, 1990.

95. Jepsen O. Middle ear muscle reflexes in man. In Jerger J (ed). Modern Developments in Audiology. New York, Academic Press, 1963, pp 193–239.

96. Jerger J. Clinical experience with impedance audiometry. Arch Otolaryngol 92:311, 1970.

97. Jerger J, Anthony L, Jerger S, et al. Studies in impedance audiometry, III: middle ear disorders. Arch Otolaryngol 99:165, 1974.

98. Jerger J, Burney P, Mauldin L, et al. Predicting hearing loss from the acoustic reflex. J Speech Hear Disord 18:11, 1974.

99. Jerger J, Harford E, Clemis J, et al. The acoustic reflex in eighth nerve disorders. Arch Otolaryngol 99:409, 1974.

100. Jerger J, Hayes D, Anthony L, et al. Factors influencing prediction of hearing level from the acoustic reflex. Monogr Contemp Audiol 1:1, Minneapolis, Maico Hearing Instruments, Inc. 1978.

101. Jerger J, Jerger S, Mauldin L. Studies in impedance audiometry, I: normal and sensorineural ears. Arch Otolaryngol 96:513, 1972.

102. Jerger S, Jerger J. Diagnostic value of crossed vs. uncrossed acoustic reflexes: eighth nerve and brainstem disorders. Arch Otolaryngol 103:445, 1977.

103. Jerger S, Jerger J, Lewis S. Pediatric speech intelligibility test, II: effect of receptive language age and chronological age. Int J Pediatr Otorhinolaryngol 3:101, 1981.

104. Jerger S, Lewis S, Hawkins J, et al. Pediatric speech intelligibility test, I: generation of test materials. Int J Pediatr Otorhinolaryngol 2:217, 1980.

105. Jewett DL. Volume-conducted potentials in response to auditory stimuli as detected by averaging in the cat. Electroencephalogr Clin Neurophysiol 28:609, 1970.

106. Jewett DL, Romano MN. Neonatal development of auditory system potentials averaged from the scalp of the rat and cat. Brain Res 36:101, 1972.

107. Jewett DL, Romano MN, Williston JS. Human auditory evoked potentials: possible brainstem components detected on the scalp. Science 167:1517, 1970.

108. Jewett DL, Williston JS. Auditory evoked far fields averaged from the scalp of humans. Brain 94:681, 1971.

109. John MS, Lin OG, Boucher BL, Picton TW. Multiple auditory steady state response (MASTER): stimulus and recording parameters. Audiology 37:59, 1998.

110. Johnsen NJ, Bagi P, Elberling C. Evoked acoustic emissions from the human ear. Scand Audiol 12:17, 1983.

111. Johnsen NJ, Osterhammel D, Terkildsen K, et al. The white noise middle ear muscle reflex thresholds in patients with sensorineural hearing impairment. Scand Audiol 5:313, 1976.

112. Joint Committee on Infant Hearing. Position statement. ASHA 24:1017, 1982.

113. Joint Committee on Infant Hearing. 1990 Position statement. ASHA 33 (Suppl 5):3, 1991.

114. Joint Committee on Infant Hearing. 1994 Position statement. ASHA 36:38, 1994.

115. Joint Committee on Infant Hearing. 2000 Position statement. Am J Audiol 9:9, 2000.

116. Keith RW. Impedance audiometry with neonates. Arch Otolaryngol 97:465, 1993.

117. Kemaloglu Y, Beder L, Sener T, Goksu N. Tympanometry and acoustic reflectometry in ears with chronic retraction without effusion. Int J Pediatr Otorhinolaryngol 55:21, 2000.

118. Kemaloglu Y, Sener T, Beder L, et al. Predictive value of acoustic reflectometry (angle and reflectivity) and tympanometry. Int J Pediatr Otorhinolaryngol 48:137, 1999.

119. Kemp DT. Stimulated acoustic emissions from within the human auditory system. J Acoust Soc Am 64:1386, 1978.

120. Kemp DT, Bray P, Alexander L, Brown AM. Acoustic emission cochleography: practical aspects. Scand Audiol Scand 25:71, 1986.

121. Kemp DT, Ryan S. OAE tests in neonatal screening programs. Acta Otolaryngol Suppl 482:73, 1991.

122. Kemp DT, Ryan S, Bray P. A guide to the effective use of otoacoustic emission. Ear Hear 11:93, 1990.

123. Kemp DT, Ryan SM. The use of transient evoked otoacoustic emissions in neonatal hearing screening programs. Semin Hear 14:30, 1993.

124. Koebsell KA, Margolis RH. Tympanometric gradient measured from normal preschool children. Audiology 25:149, 1986.

125. Kraus N, Kileny P, McGee T. Middle latency auditory evoked potentials. In Katz J (ed). Handbook of Clinical Audiology, 4th ed. Baltimore, Williams & Wilkins, 1994, pp 387–402.

126. Lafreniere D, Smurzynski J, Jung M, et al. Otoacoustic emissions in full-term newborns at risk for hearing loss. Laryngoscope 103:1334, 1993.

127. Lampe RM, Schwartz RH. Diagnostic value of acoustic reflectometry in children with acute otitis media. Pediatr Infect Dis J 8:59, 1989.

128. Lampe RM, Weir MR, Spier J, Rhodes MF. Acoustic reflectometry in the detection of middle ear effusion. J Pediatr 76:75, 1985.

129. Lasky R, Perlman J, Hecox K. Distortion-product otoacoustic emissions in human newborns and adults. Ear Hear 13:430, 1992.

130. Liden G, Renvall U. Impedance audiometry for screening middle ear disease in school children. In Harford ER, Bess FH, Bluestone CD, et al (eds). Impedance Screening for Middle Ear Disease in Children. New York, Grune & Stratton, 1978, pp 197–206.

131. Lins OG, Picton TW, Boucher BL, et al. Frequency-specific audiometry using steady-state responses. Ear Hear 17:81, 1996.

132. Lloyd LL, Spradlin JE, Reed MJ. An operant audiometric procedure for difficult-to-test patients. J Speech Hear Disord 33:236, 1968.

133. Lonsbury-Martin BL, Harris FP, Stagner BB, et al. Distortion product emissions in humans, I: basic properties in normally hearing subjects. Ann Otol Rhinol Laryngol 99 (Suppl 147):3, 1990.

134. Lonsbury-Martin BL, Martin GK, McCoy MJ, Whitehead ML. Otoacoustic emissions testing in young children: middle-ear influences. Am J Otol 15 (Suppl 1):13, 1994.

135. Lonsbury-Martin BL, Martin GK, Probst R, Coats A. The clinical utility of distortion product otoacoustic emission. Ear Hear 11:144, 1990.

136. Lonsbury-Martin BL, McCoy MJ, Whitehead ML, Martin GK. Clinical testing of distortion-product otoacoustic emissions. Ear Hear 14:11, 1993.

137. Lous J. Three impedance screening programs on a cohort of seven-year-old children. Scand Audiol Suppl 17:60, 1983.

138. Marchant CD, McMillan PM, Shurin PA, et al. Objective diagnosis of otitis media in early infancy by tympanometry and ipsilateral acoustic reflex thresholds. J Pediatr 109:590, 1986.

139. Margolis RH. Fundamentals of acoustic immittance. In Popelka GR (ed). Hearing Assessment With the Acoustic Reflex. New York, Grune & Stratton, 1981, pp 117–143.

140. Margolis RH. Detection of hearing impairment with the acoustic stapedial reflex. Ear Hear 14:3, 1993.

141. Margolis RH, Fox CM. A comparison of three methods for predicting hearing loss from acoustic reflex thresholds. J Speech Hear Res 20:241, 1977.

142. Margolis RH, Heller JW. Screening tympanometry: criteria for medical referral. Audiology 26:197, 1987.

143. Margolis RH, Shanks JE. Tympanometry. In Katz J (ed). Handbook of Clinical Audiology, 3rd ed. Baltimore, Williams & Wilkins, 1985, pp 438–475.

144. Margolis RH, Shanks JE. Tympanometry: basic principles and clinical applications. In Rintelmann WF (ed). Hearing Assessment, 2nd ed. Austin, Tex, Pro-Ed, 1991, pp 179–245.

145. Margolis R, Trine M. Influence of middle-ear disease on otoacoustic emissions. In Robinette M, Glattke T (eds). Otoacoustic Emissions: Clinical Applications. New York, Thieme, 1997, pp 130–150.

146. Marshall L, Heller L, Westhusin L. Effect of negative middle-ear pressure on transient-evoked otoacoustic emissions. Ear Hear 18:218, 1997.

147. Martin FN. Pseudohypacusis. In Katz J (ed). Handbook of Clinical Audiology, 4th ed. Baltimore, Williams & Wilkins, 1994, pp 553–567.

148. Martin GK, Whitehead ML, Lonsbury-Martin BL. Potential of evoked otoacoustic emissions for infant hearing screening. Semin Hear 11:186, 1990.

149. Matkin ND. Diagnostic case study in pediatric audiology. Presented at the Annual Convention of the American Speech-Language-Hearing Association, Detroit, 1986.

150. Matkin ND. Early recognition and referral of hearing-impaired children. Pediatr Rev 6:151, 1984.
151. Matkin N. The challenge of providing family-centered services. In Bess F (ed). Children With Hearing Impairment: Contemporary Trends. Nashville, Tenn, Vanderbilt Bill Wilkerson Center Press, 1998, pp 299–304.
152. Mauk GW, Behrens TR. Historical, political, and technological context associated with early identification of hearing loss. Semin Hear 14:1, 1993.
153. McCandless GA, Allred PL. Tympanometry and emergence of the acoustic reflex infants. In Harford ER, Bess FH, Bluestone CD, et al (eds). Impedance Screening for Middle Ear Disease in Children. New York, Grune & Stratton, 1978, pp 57–68.
154. McMillan PM, Marchant CD, Shurin PA. Ipsilateral acoustic reflexes in infants. Ann Otol Rhinol Laryngol 94:145, 1985.
155. Mendelson T, Salamy A, Lenoir M, et al. Brainstem evoked potential findings in children with otitis media. Arch Otolaryngol 105:17, 1979.
156. Moeller AR. The sensitivity of contraction of the tympanic muscles in man. Ann Otol Rhinol Laryngol 71:86, 1962.
157. Moeller AR, Jannetta PJ. Neural generators of the auditory brainstem response. In Jacobson JT (ed). The Auditory Brainstem Response. San Diego, College Hill Press, 1985, pp 13–32.
158. Moeller P, Condon M. Family matters: making sense of complex choices. In Bess F (ed). Children With Hearing Impairment: Contemporary Trends. Nashville, Tenn, Vanderbilt Bill Wilkerson Center Press, 1998, pp 305–310.
159. Moncur JP. Judge reliability in infant testing. J Speech Hear Res 11:348, 1968.
160. Moore JK. The human auditory brainstem as a generator of auditory evoked potentials. Hear Res 29:33, 1987.
161. Moore JM, Thompson G, Thompson M. Auditory localization of infants as a function of reinforcement conditions. J Speech Hear Disord 40:29, 1975.
162. Moore JM, Wilson WR, Thompson G. Visual reinforcement of head-turn responses in infants under 12 months of age. J Speech Hear Disord 42:328, 1977.
163. Naeve SL, Margolis RH, Levine SC, Fournier EM. Effect of ear-canal air pressure on evoked otoacoustic emissions. J Acoust Soc Am 91:2091, 1992.
164. National Institute on Deafness and Other Communication Disorders. Recommendations of the NIDCD Working Group on Early Identification of Hearing Impairment on acceptable protocols for use in statewide universal newborn hearing screening programs. Bethesda, Md, NIDCD Clearing House, 1997.
165. National Institutes of Health. Early identification of hearing impairment in infants and young children. NIH Consensus Statement 11 (1), 1993.
166. Nelson D, Kimberly B. DPOAEs and auditory sensitivity in human ears with normal hearing and cochlear hearing loss. J Speech Hear Res 35:1142, 1992.
167. Niemeyer W, Sesterhenn G. Calculating the hearing threshold from the stapedius reflex threshold for different sound stimuli. Audiology 13:421, 1974.
168. Northern JL, Downs MP. Hearing in Children, 4th ed. Baltimore, Williams & Wilkins, 1991.
169. Northern JL, Gabbard SA. The acoustic reflex. In Katz J (ed). Handbook of Clinical Audiology, 4th ed. Baltimore, Williams & Wilkins, 1994, pp 300–316.
170. Norton SJ. Cochlear function and otoacoustic emissions. Semin Hear 13:1, 1992.
171. Norton SJ. Application of transient evoked otoacoustic emissions to pediatric populations. Ear Hear 14:64, 1993.
172. Norton SJ. Emerging role of evoked otoacoustic emissions in neonatal hearing screening. Am J Otol 15 (Suppl 1):4, 1994.
173. Norton S, Gorga M, Widen J, et al. Identification of neonatal hearing impairment: transient evoked otoacoustic emissions during the perinatal period. Ear Hear 21:425, 2000.
174. Norton S, Gorga M, Widen J, et al. Identification of neonatal hearing impairment: evaluation of transient evoked otoacoustic emission, distortion product otoacoustic emission, and auditory brain stem response test performance. Ear Hear 21:508, 2000.
175. Nozza RJ. The binaural masking level difference in infants and adults: developmental change in binaural hearing. Infant Behav Dev 10:105, 1987.
176. Nozza RJ. Estimating the contribution of nonsensory factors to infant-adult differences in behavioral thresholds. Hear Res 91:72, 1995.
177. Nozza RJ. Critical issues in acoustic immittance screening for middle-ear effusion. In Silman S (ed). Audiologic and Medical Profile of Middle-Ear Effusion: State-of-the-Art. Semin Hear 16:86, 1995.
178. Nozza R. Identification of otitis media. In Bess F (ed). Children with Hearing Impairment: Contemporary Trends. Nashville, Tenn, Vanderbilt Bill Wilkerson Center Press, 1998, pp 207–214.
179. Nozza RJ, Bluestone CD, Kardatzke D. Sensitivity, specificity, and predictive value of immittance measures in the identification of middle ear effusion. In Bess FH, Hall JW (eds). Screening Children for Auditory Function. Nashville, Tenn, Bill Wilkerson Center Press, 1992, pp 315–329.
180. Nozza RJ, Bluestone CD, Kardatzke D, Bachman RN. Towards the validation of aural acoustic immittance measures for diagnosis of middle ear effusion in children. Ear Hear 13:442, 1992.
181. Nozza RJ, Bluestone CD, Kardatzke D, Bachman RN. Identification of middle ear effusion by aural acoustic admittance and otoscopy. Ear Hear 15:310, 1994.
182. Nozza RJ, Henson AM. Unmasked thresholds and minimum masking in infants and adults: separating sensory from nonsensory contributions to infant-adult difference in behavioral thresholds. Ear Hear 20:483, 1999.
183. Nozza RJ, Sabo DL, Mandel EM. A role for otoacoustic emissions in screening for hearing impairment and middle ear disorders in school age children. Ear Hear 18:227, 1997.
184. Nozza RJ, Wagner ER, Crandell ME. Binaural release from masking for a speech sound in infants, preschoolers, and adults. J Speech Hear Res 31:212, 1988.
185. Nozza RJ, Wilson WR. Masked and unmasked pure-tone thresholds of infants and adults: development of auditory frequency selectivity and sensitivity. J Speech Hear Res 27:613, 1984.
186. Nuttal AH. Some windows with very good sidelobe behavior. IEEE Trans Acoust Speech Signal Proc 29:84, 1981.
187. Odenthal DW, Eggermont JJ. Electrocochleography study in Meniere's disease and pontine angle neurinoma. In Ruben RJ, Elberling C, Salomon G (eds). Electrocochleography. Baltimore, University Park Press, 1976, pp 331–352.
188. Orchik DJ, Morff R, Dunn JW. Middle ear status at myringotomy and its relationship to middle ear immittance measurements. Ear Hear 1:324, 1980.
189. Owens JJ, McCoy MJ, Lonsbury-Martin BL, Martin GK. Influence of otitis media on evoked otoacoustic emission in children. Semin Hear 13:53, 1992.
190. Paradise JL, Smith CG, Bluestone CD. Tympanometric detection of middle ear effusion in infants and young children. Pediatrics 58:198, 1976.
191. Pichichero M. Acute otitis media, part I: improving diagnostic accuracy. Am Fam Physician 61:2051, 2000.
192. Picton TW, Durieux-Smith A, Champagne SC, et al. Objective evaluation of aided thresholds using auditory steady-state responses. J Am Acad Audiol 9:315, 1998.
193. Picton TW, Woods DL, Baribeau-Braun J, et al. Evoked potential audiometry. J Otolaryngol 6:90, 1977.
194. Popelka GR. Acoustic immittance measures: terminology and instrumentation. Ear Hear 5:262, 1984.
195. Prieve BA. Otoacoustic emissions in infants and children: basic characteristics and clinical application. Semin Hear 13:37, 1992.
196. Prieve B, Fitzgerald T, Schulte L. Basic characteristics of click-evoked otoacoustic emissions in infants and children. J Acoust Soc Am 102 (pt 1):2860, 1997.
197. Prieve B, Fitzgerald T, Schulte L, Kemp D. Basic characteristics of distortion product otoacoustic emissions in infants and children. J Acoust Soc Am 102 (pt 1):2871, 1997.
198. Probst R. Otoacoustic emissions: an overview. Adv Otorhinolaryngol 44:1, 1990.
199. Rapin I, Bergman M. Auditory evoked responses in uncertain diagnosis. Arch Otolaryngol 90:307, 1969.
200. Rappaport BE, Tait CA. Acoustic reflex threshold measurement in hearing aid selection. Arch Otolaryngol 102:129, 1976.
201. Reingold S, Davis N, Plecque D, Kelly G. Acoustic reflectometry as an aid to the diagnosis of acute otitis media in children. Acad Emerg Med 8:439, 2001.
202. Rhodes MC, Margolis RH, Hirsch JE, Napp AP. Hearing screen-

ing in the newborn intensive care nursery: comparison of methods. Otolaryngol Head Neck Surg 120:799, 1999.

203. Robertson EO, Peterson JL, Lamb LE. Relative impedance measurements in young children. Arch Otolaryngol 88:162, 1968.

204. Robinette MS. Clinical observations with transient evoked otoacoustic emissions with adults. Semin Hear 13:23, 1992.

205. Ross M, Lerman J. A picture identification task for hearing-impaired children. J Speech Hear Res 13:44, 1970.

206. Roush J. Screening for Hearing Loss and Otitis Media in Children. San Diego, Singular, 2001.

207. Roush J. Strengthening family-professional relations: Advice from parents. In Matkin ND, Roush J (eds). Infants and Toddlers With Hearing Loss. Parkton, Md, York Press, 1994, pp 337–350.

208. Roush J, Bryant K, Mundy M, et al. Developmental changes in static admittance and tympanometric width in infants and toddlers. J Am Acad Audiol 6:334, 1995.

209. Ruben RJ, Elberling C, Salomon G. Electro-cochleography. Baltimore, University Park Press, 1976.

210. Ruth RA. Electrocochleography. In Katz J (ed). Handbook of Clinical Audiology, 4th ed. Baltimore, Williams & Wilkins, 1994, pp 339–350.

211. Ruth RA, Lambert PA. Electrocochleography: tympanic membrane versus promontory electrode. Presented at the 10th Biennial International Symposium of the International ERA Study Group, Charlottesville, Va, August 23–27, 1987.

212. Salamy A, McKean CM. Postnatal development of human brainstem potentials during the first year of life. Electroencephalogr Clin Neurophysiol 40:418, 1976.

213. Salomon G, Elberling G. Cochlear nerve potentials recorded from the ear canal in man. Acta Otolaryngol (Stockh) 71:319, 1971.

214. Sanderson-Leepa ME, Rintelmann WF. Articulation functions and test-retest performance of normal-hearing children on three speech discrimination tests: WIPI, PBK-50, and NU Auditory Test No. 6. J Speech Hear Disord 41:503, 1976.

215. Schwartz DM, Sanders J. Critical bandwidth and sensitivity prediction in the acoustic stapedial reflex. J Speech Hear Disord 41:244, 1976.

216. Selters WE, Brackmann DE. Acoustic tumor detection with brainstem electric response audiometry. Arch Otolaryngol 103:181, 1977.

217. Shanks JE. Tympanometry. Ear Hear 5:268, 1984.

218. Sheehy JL, Inzer BE. Acoustic reflex test in neuro-otologic diagnosis. Arch Otolaryngol 102:647, 1976.

219. Silman S, Silverman CA, Arick DS. Acoustic-immittance screening for detection of middle-ear effusion in children. J Am Acad Audiol 3:262, 1992.

220. Sininger Y, Starr A. Auditory Neuropathy: A New Perspective on Hearing Disorders. San Diego, Singular, 2001.

221. Skinner BK, Norris TW, Jirsa RE. Contralateral-ipsilateral acoustic reflex thresholds in preschool children. In Harford ER, Bess FH, Bluestone CD, et al (eds). Impedance Screening for Middle Ear Disease in Children. New York, Grune & Stratton, 1978, pp 161–170.

222. Skinner PH, Shimota J. A comparison of the effects of sedatives on the auditory evoked cortical response. J Am Audiol Soc 1:71, 1975.

223. Snow T, McCandless G. The use of impedance measures in hearing aid selection. Natl Hear Aid J 7:32, 1976.

224. Sohmer H, Feinmesser M. Cochlear action potentials recorded from the external ear in man. Ann Otol Rhinol Laryngol 76:427, 1967.

225. Spektor Z, Leonard G, Kim DO, et al. Otoacoustic emissions in normal and hearing-impaired children and normal adults. Laryngoscope 101:965, 1991.

226. Stapells DR, Oates P. Estimation of the pure tone audiogram by the auditory brainstem response: a review. Audiol Neurotol 2:257, 1997.

227. Stapells DR, Picton TW, Perez-Abalo M, et al. Frequency specificity in evoked potential audiometry. In Jacobson JT (ed). The Auditory Brainstem Response. San Diego, College Hill Press, 1985, pp 147–177.

228. Starr A, Achor LJ. Auditory brainstem responses in neurological disease. Arch Neurol 32:761, 1975.

229. Stevens JC, Webb HD, Smith MF, et al. A comparison of otoacoustic emissions and brain stem electric response audiometry in the normal newborn and babies admitted to a special care baby unit. Clin Phys Physiol Meas 8:95, 1987.

230. Stockard JJ, Rossiter US. Clinical and pathologic correlates of brainstem auditory response abnormalities. Neurology 27:316, 1977.

231. Stockard JJ, Stockard JE, Sharbrough FW. Detection and localization of occult lesions with brainstem auditory responses. Mayo Clin Proc 52:761, 1977.

232. Suzuki T, Ogiba Y. A technique of pure tone audiometry for children under three years of age: conditioned orientation reflex (COR) audiometry. Rev Laryngol 81:33, 1960.

233. Suzuki T, Ogiba Y. Conditioned orientation reflex audiometry. Arch Otolaryngol 74:192, 1961.

234. Teas DC, Klein AJ, Kramer SJ. An analysis of auditory brainstem responses in infants. Hear Res 7:19, 1982.

235. Teele DW, Teele J. Detection of middle ear effusion by acoustic reflectometry. J Pediatr 104:832, 1984.

236. Terkildsen K, Huis in't Veld F, Osterhammel P. Auditory brainstem responses in the diagnosis of cerebellopontine angle tumors. Scand Audiol 3:123, 1977.

237. Terkildsen K, Thomsen KA. The influence of pressure variations on the impedance of the human eardrum. J Laryngol Otol 73:409, 1959.

238. Tharpe A, Bess F. Minimal, progressive, and fluctuating hearing losses in children: characteristics, identification, and management. Pediatr Clin North Am 46:65, 1999.

239. Thompson G, Weber BA. Responses of infants and young children to behavioral observation audiometry (BOA). J Speech Hear Disord 39:140, 1974.

240. Thompson M. Birth to five: the important early years. In Bess FH, Hall JW (eds). Screening Children for Auditory Function. Nashville, Tenn, Bill Wilkerson Center Press, 1992, pp 399–434.

241. Thompson M, Thompson G. Responses of infants and young children as a function of auditory stimuli and test methods. J Speech Hear Res 15:699, 1972.

242. Thomsen J, Terkildsen K, Osterhammel P. Auditory brain stem responses in patients with acoustic neuromas. Scand Audiol 7:179, 1978.

243. Tonnison W. Measuring in-the-ear gain of hearing aids by the acoustic-reflex method. J Speech Hear Res 18:5, 1975.

244. Trine MB, Hirsch JE, Margolis RH. The effect of middle ear pressure on transient evoked otoacoustic emissions. Ear Hear 14:401, 1993.

245. US Department of Health and Human Services (HHS). Healthy People 2000: National Health and Disease Prevention Objectives. Washington, DC, US Public Health Service, 1990.

246. US Department of Health and Human Services. Healthy People 2010 (conference edition in two volumes). Washington, DC, US Public Health Service, January 2000.

247. Van Camp KJ, Creten WL. Principles of acoustic impedance and admittance. In Feldman AS, Wilber LA (eds). Acoustic Impedance and Admittance: The Measurement of Middle Ear Function. Baltimore, Williams & Wilkins, 1976, pp 300–334.

248. Van Camp KJ, Margolis RJ, Wilson RH, et al. Principles of tympanometry. ASHA Monogr 24, 1986.

249. Vanhuyse JJ, Creten WL, Van Camp KJ. On the W-notching of tympanogram. Scand Audiol 4:45, 1975.

250. Van Wagoner RS, Goodwine S. Clinical impressions of acoustic reflex measures in an adult population. Arch Otolaryngol 103:582, 1977.

251. Vaughan-Jones R, Mills RP. The Welch Allyn Audioscope and Microtymp: their accuracy and that of pneumatic otoscopy, tympanometry and pure tone audiometry as predictors of otitis media with effusion. J Laryngol Otol 106:600, 1992.

252. Vohr BR, Carty L, Moore P, Letourneau K. The Rhode Island Hearing Assessment Program: experience with statewide hearing screening (1993–1996). J Pediatr 133:353, 1998.

253. Vohr BR, White KR, Maxon AB, Johnson MJ. Factors affecting the interpretation of transient evoked otoacoustic emission results in neonatal hearing screening. Semin Hear 14:57, 1993.

254. Weatherby LA, Bennett MJ. The neonatal acoustic reflex. Scand Audiol 9:103, 1980.

255. Weber B. Validation of observer judgments in behavioral observation audiometry. J Speech Hear Disord 34:350, 1969.

256. Weber BA. Auditory brainstem response: threshold estimation and auditory screening. In Katz J (ed). Handbook of Clinical Audiology, 4th ed. Baltimore, Williams & Wilkins, 1994, pp 375–386.

257. White KR, Vohr BR, Maxon AB, et al. Screening of all newborns for hearing loss using transient evoked otoacoustic emissions. Int J Pediatr Otorhinolaryngol 29:203, 1994.

258. Widen JE. Behavioral screening of high-risk infants using visual reinforcement audiometry. Semin Hear 11:342, 1990.

259. Widen JE. Adding objectivity to infant behavioral audiometry. Ear Hear 14:49, 1993.

260. Widen JE. Evoked otoacoustic emissions in evaluating children. In Robinette MS, Glattke TJ (eds). Otoacoustic Emissions: Clinical Applications. New York, Thieme, 1997, pp 271–306.

261. Wilber LA, Feldman AS. Acoustic Impedance and Admittance—The Measure of Middle Ear Function. Baltimore, Williams & Wilkins, 1976.

262. Wiley TL, Oviatt DL, Block MG. Acoustic-immittance measures in normal ears. J Speech Hear Res 30:161, 1987.

263. Wilson WR. Behavioral assessment of auditory function in infants. In Minifie FD, Lloyd LL (eds). Communicative and Cognitive Abilities—Early Behavioral Assessment. Baltimore, University Park Press, 1978, pp 37–59.

264. Wilson WR, Moore JM, Thompson G. Sound field auditory thresholds of infants utilizing visual reinforcement audiometry (VRA). Presented at the Annual Convention of the American Speech and Hearing Association, Houston, November 1976.

265. Wilson WR, Thompson G. Behavioral audiometry. In Jerger J (ed). Pediatric Audiology: Current Trends. San Diego, College Hill Press, 1984, pp 1–44.

266. Yoshie N, Ohasi T, Suzuki T. Non-surgical recording of auditory nerve action potentials in man. Laryngoscope 77:76, 1967.

267. Yoshinaga-Itano C, Sedey A, Coulter D, Mehl A. Language of early and later identified children with hearing loss. Pediatrics 102:1161, 1998.

268. Yoshinaga-Itano C, Coulter D, Thomson V. The Colorado Newborn Hearing Screening Project: effects on speech and language development for children with hearing loss. J Perinatol 20 (8 pt 2):S132, 2000.

269. Zwicker E, Schorn K. Delayed evoked otoacoustic emissions—an ideal screening test for excluding hearing impairment in infants. Audiology 29:241, 1990.

12

Methods of Examination: Radiologic Aspects

Avrum N. Pollock, M.D., Hugh Curtin, M.D., and Richard B. Towbin, M.D.

Introduction

Cross-sectional imaging has evolved rapidly. Today, high-resolution and three-dimensional computed tomography (CT) scans can be performed in only a few minutes. Magnetic resonance imaging (MRI) is able to produce sophisticated images of the head and neck.

These advances have had a profound effect on imaging of the ear. Progress has at times been so rapid that textbook descriptions of imaging may be outdated by the time of, or shortly after, their publication. The descriptions found in this chapter are unlikely to be exceptions. It is our hope that the otolaryngologist, radiologist, and other physician groups will work together for judicious use of these diagnostic tools to provide the optimal imaging modality for the specific problem of the individual patient. In this chapter the imaging modalities most commonly used are described and specific points made regarding several common clinical situations.[33, 37, 44, 48, 49]

Imaging Modalities

Plain Film Radiography and Tomography

In the past, radiography and complex motion tomography were the mainstays of petrous bone imaging. Bone anatomy is well demonstrated by these techniques owing to the density differences of bone, air, and soft tissues. However, interpretive problems occur because of the superimposition of one structure on another and the lack of bony and soft tissue contrast. Consequently, CT has replaced plain film studies of the temporal bone because of the excellent anatomic detail and tissue contrast it provides. MRI has also become a diagnostic option in certain instances. Both techniques are discussed later in this chapter.

Although mostly no longer obtained, plain film examinations remain of value in selected instances. For example, the Stenver view is used for evaluation of cochlear implants. The metals used in implants sometimes create artifacts on CT and can give a distorted image, making the evaluation of anatomic relationships difficult. When this problem arises, plain films or tomography may still be used. The high density of metal allows good visualization of the prosthetic components on plain film when

needed. Oblique views may be obtained as required (Fig. 12–1).

Computed Tomography

The technical advancement that allowed CT to surpass plain film tomography for imaging of the temporal bone is the "bone algorithm." Currently several algorithms (soft tissue, bone) are available for displaying images, and the radiologist selects the appropriate algorithm for each case. The bone algorithm is preferred for imaging the petrous bone because it best displays bone by allowing the computer to remanipulate data to enhance margins between tissues with high attenuation differences. This best accentuates differences among bone, air, fluid, and soft tissue in any combination. The bone algorithm is not to be confused with the bone window of CT, which represents a display of a soft tissue algorithm at a wider range of density levels rather than a recalculation of the raw computed data (see Fig. 12–9). CT images obtained using the bone algorithm rival plain film tomography for spatial resolution and far surpass it in the ability to differentiate one tissue's attenuation from another. Advanced computed data manipulation also makes it possible to obtain multiple projections in CT through reformatting. For example, reformatting axial images gives reasonable (although not as detailed) coronal, sagittal, or oblique images without additional scan time or radiation (Figs. 12–2 and 12–3). However, resolution is best with the direct coronal or axial projections using 1.0- or 1.5-mm overlapping slices. These resultant high-resolution, thin-section images provide excellent anatomic detail of the temporal bone, including the facial nerve canal and the crura of the stapes (Fig. 12–4).

The choice of initial imaging plane (axial or coronal) is based on the indication for the study. In general, the axial plane is preferred for studying children with sensorineural hearing loss, possible anatomic anomalies, and trauma. Coronal imaging is selected for evaluation of conductive hearing loss, cholesteatoma, and destructive processes, including neoplasms. Coronal images may also be useful for evaluating infection and traumatic injury after neck and central nervous system (CNS) injuries have been excluded. Because petrous bone imaging and processing are time consuming, a single plane of imaging is preferred

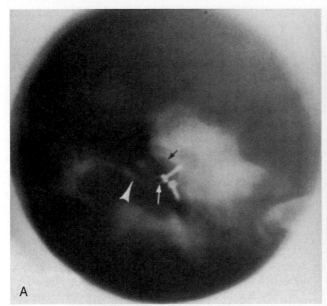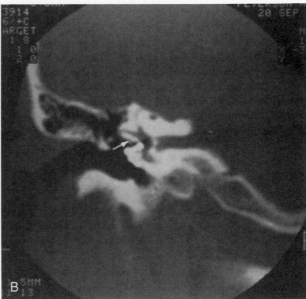

FIGURE 12–1. *A,* Pluridirectional tomogram of the right temporal bone, with stapedial prosthesis in place, shows excellent detail of the prostheses, including the small wires used to attach the prosthesis to an ossicle. The second prosthesis is seen adjacent to the promontory. The resolution is higher than on computed tomography (CT) (see *B*). Attachment wire indicated by white arrow. Facial nerve canal shown by black arrow. Arrowhead marks scutum. Note how the actual bony cortex of the facial nerve canal can be defined. *B,* CT of the same patient. The demonstration of the two prostheses is much less precise because of the high density of the metal. The position of the prostheses is much more precisely defined on the tomogram. Note also the less sharp image of the facial nerve canal *(white arrow)* compared with that on the tomogram.

whenever possible. However, there are often situations in which both axial and coronal planes are obtained. These include aural atresia and other processes in which good visualization of the facial nerve canal anatomy is needed. Complex conditions such as tumor (e.g., parameningeal rhabdomyosarcoma) or possible CNS extension of infection may also require axial and coronal imaging. Initial images are reviewed while the patient is still on the scanner table to determine whether another projection is needed for additional information. Unless a vascular abnormality, a tumor, or another enhancing lesion such as an intracranial abscess is suspected, studies are usually performed without intravenous contrast administration.

In our practice, patients under 6 years of age usually require sedation. Children under 1 year of age receive oral sedation, while those over 1 year receive intravenous medications. All children who are sedated are kept in NPO status for 8 hours for solids, 6 hours for formula, 4 hours for breast milk, and 2 hours for clear liquids before the study, and closely monitored by an experienced pediatric nurse using a pulse oximeter.

A variety of drugs can be used to sedate children. In our institution for children 1 year of age or less, we have found chloral hydrate, 50 to 100 mg/kg orally, to be effective. An initial dose of 50 to 75 mg/kg is given, and an additional 25 mg/kg if the child is still awake after 20 minutes. The maximal total chloral hydrate dose is 1 g or 100 mg/kg. Intravenous drugs are preferred for older children. We have been very successful with intravenous pentobarbital and fentanyl: an initial dose of 3 mg/kg of

pentobarbital is injected, and if the child is not asleep after 5 minutes, 1 μg/kg of fentanyl is given. Repeated doses of each are given as needed. Additionally, 0.05 mg/kg of Versed (midazolam) may be added as a third agent if need be, to supplement the effects of the other two agents (pentobarbital and fentanyl). Regardless of medication preference, it is important for the medical team to become familiar with the drug formulary.*

Magnetic Resonance Imaging

An extensive description of MRI is beyond the scope of this chapter, but several terms and ideas may be useful since they recur frequently in the discussions of this modality.

1. Almost all clinical imaging is currently done by stimulating hydrogen nuclei. MRI takes advantage of the fact that these hydrogen atoms can be stimulated by use of very specific radiofrequencies. These stimulated nuclei return a characteristic radiofrequency that is proportional to the strength of the magnetic field. Thus, an image can be produced by varying the magnetic field in an imaginary grid and pinpointing slightly different characteristic frequencies within that grid.

---

*These are not meant to be complete sedation guidelines. A more thorough review of sedation techniques is recommended for those imaging the very young patient.

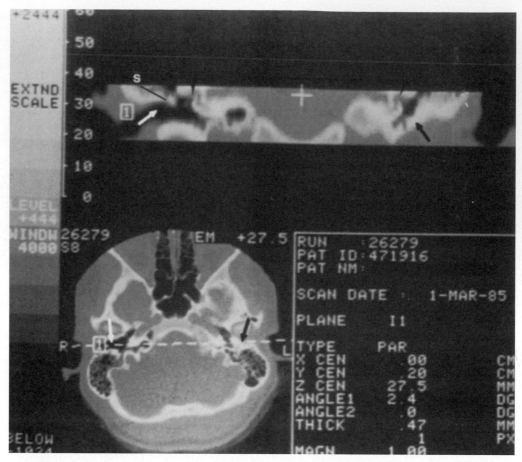

FIGURE 12–2. Coronal re-format. External auditory canal (EAC) atresia. Axial slices were initially done, and coronal re-format was performed by the computer. The EAC is seen on the normal side *(white arrow)* in both the axial and coronal re-formatted images. Note the atretic plate *(black arrow)* on the abnormal side, again in both axial and re-formatted images. Oval window indicated by arrowheads. S, scutum.

2. On most systems, signal is indicated by whiteness. The signal intensity (black, gray, or white) depends on the pulse sequences used and types of tissue being imaged. Generally, T_1-weighted images

FIGURE 12–3. Three-dimensional reconstruction of axial CT. c, cochlea; f, facial nerve canal; v, vestibule; s, superior semicircular canal (SCC); h, horizontal SCC; p, posterior SCC.

(T_1WI) are best for displaying anatomy, while proton density and T_2-weighted images (T_2WI) best demonstrate pathology.

3. Not all tissues return a detectable signal. Some tissues lack hydrogen atoms (air); others leave the imaging grid too rapidly to return a signal (flowing blood). Finally, the hydrogen atoms in dense fibrous tissue and compact bone are bound in a tight lattice work that prohibits effective signal generation and therefore does not return a signal. These areas of absent signal are termed *signal voids* and are responsible for one of the major limitations of MRI of the temporal bone.

Because air and bone each result in a signal void, the margin between them will not be imaged as in CT unless the bone contains marrow. For example, air cells within the mastoid portion of the temporal bone cannot be differentiated from cortical bone, and the entire region normally appears as a single signal void, as does the ossicular chain within a well-aerated middle-ear cavity. Obviously, this limits the evaluation of middle-ear anatomy. Conversely, normally fluid-filled structures (cochlea, semicircular canals [SCC]) and soft tissue structures (facial nerve) are visualized because they are surrounded by the

FIGURE 12-4. Axial CT of the right temporal bone. With use of 1.0-mm slice thickness and a bone algorithm, the crura of the stapes (*small white arrows*) can be seen.

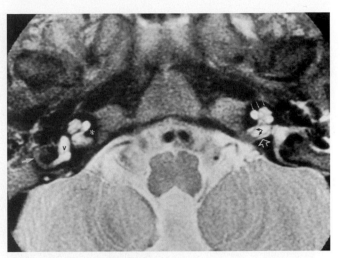

FIGURE 12-5. High-resolution fast spin echo magnetic resonance imaging (MRI) through the cochleas (TR 7000, TE 22, NEX2 slice thickness 3.0 mm). Note that the bone of the inner ear appears as a signal void (°) compared with the fluid-filled cochlea and SCC. The basal, middle, and apical turns of the cochlea are well demonstrated (*three small white arrows*). The internal auditory canal (IAC) (*open arrow*) contains cranial nerves (*small black arrows*). v, vestibule. The horizontal SCC is shown by the large white arrow.

signal void of bone (Fig. 12–5). Abnormal soft tissue or fluid collections such as tumors or inflammatory fluid are easily detected for the same reason. Intravenous injection of contrast medium (i.e., gadolinium) is used if tumor is suspected, since most tumors demonstrate abnormal enhancement.

In a comparison of CT and MRI, each has its advantages and disadvantages.

The advantages of MRI over CT include

1. No ionizing radiation.
2. The posterior fossa, temporal lobe, and craniocervical junction are better demonstrated.
3. Any imaging plane can be obtained: sagittal, coronal, and oblique views are obtained as easily as axial views.
4. Noninvasive vascular imaging (magnetic resonance angiography) allows evaluation of major arteries and veins (e.g., sigmoid sinus blood flow) (Fig. 12–6).

Negative aspects of MRI include

1. Its inability to distinguish air from cortical bone.
2. Longer examination time.
3. Higher cost.

Previously the minimal slice thickness of MRI was slightly greater than that of CT, and there was difficulty in obtaining contiguous images. This meant less imaging detail than with CT. These limitations are becoming less important with the use of thin-slice, high-resolution MRI and volumetric acquisitions (see Fig. 12–5).

Young patients usually require sedation for both CT and MRI.

Clinical Situations

Imaging studies of the temporal bone are most commonly ordered to evaluate acute and chronic infection, tumor, congenital anomalies, and trauma.[33, 37, 44, 48, 49]

Acute Infection

Thin-section, high-resolution, noncontrasted CT is the imaging test of choice for acute infection. With CT, even small amounts of fluid in the middle-ear and mastoid air cells are detectable (Fig. 12–7). Small bony erosions are easily demonstrated on direct coronal CT images, since this projection best demonstrates the scutum, tegmen tympani, and Prussak space. The axial projection is needed to evaluate complex or advanced disease and possible abnormalities of the facial nerve canal, and when the coronal projection cannot be obtained. CT is useful in assessing the integrity of the bony septa within the mas-

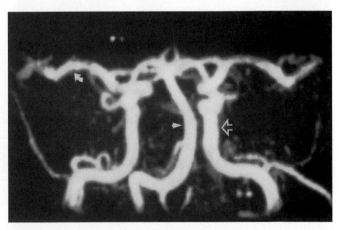

FIGURE 12-6. Magnetic resonance angiography (MRA) coronal projection. The blood flow through patent vessels is clearly demonstrated. The left internal carotid artery (*open arrow*), basilar artery (*arrowhead*), and right middle cerebral artery (*curved arrow*) are seen.

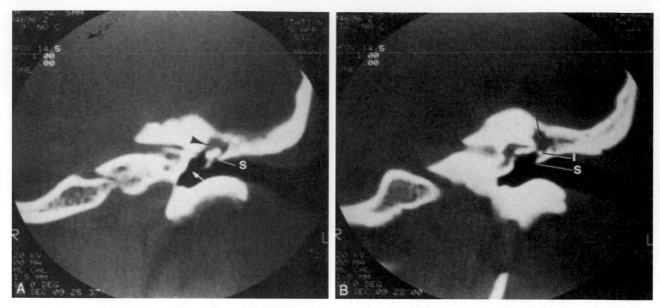

FIGURE 12–7. Atticoantral disease with blockage at the level of the isthmus. *A,* The lower left middle ear *(arrow)* is normal. However, the attic *(arrowhead)* is filled with fluid, which does not extend below the scutum (s). *B,* A slightly posterior slice shows the uneroded scutum (S) and the short process of the incus (I), with opacification of the upper attic and antrum *(arrow).*

toid and in evaluating the integrity of the overlying cortex and the surrounding soft tissues (Fig. 12–8).

MRI usually reveals abnormal fluid collections (demonstrated by bright signal where there should be none on T_2WI images) but is not able to detect subtle bony changes, for reasons previously discussed. Thus, MRI does not play a significant role in evaluating patients with simple inflammatory disease of the temporal bone.

When the middle ear and mastoid are being evaluated for acute infection, intravenous administration of contrast

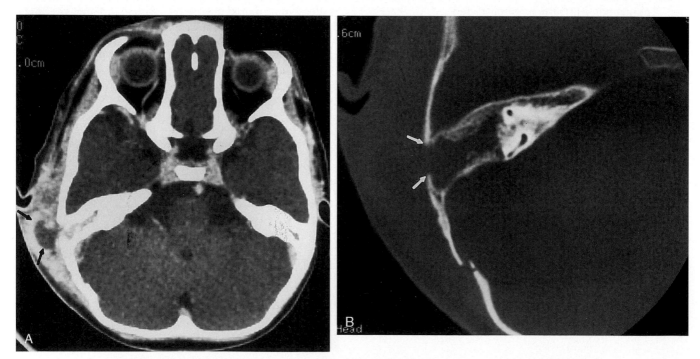

FIGURE 12–8. Coalescent mastoiditis/osteomyelitis. Axial contrast enhanced 1-mm thick CT images of the temporal bone imaged on soft tissue *(A)* and magnified bone windows *(B),* in a patient with clinical suspicion of mastoiditis, demonstrate opacification of the right mastoid with resorption of the bony septae and a soft tissue abscess *(black arrows)* contiguous with the site of bony breakthrough *(white arrows),* through the outer cortex (osteomyelitis).

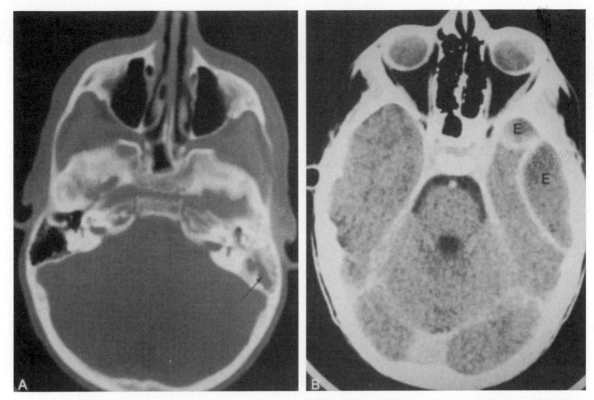

FIGURE 12–9. *A,* Axial bone window (not algorithm) shows fluid in the left mastoid *(arrow)* and in attic *(arrowhead)*. Compare with the opposite side. The bone is less distinct than would be expected in a bone algorithm. *B,* A slightly higher slice shows several loculations of epidural abscess (E). Note how they taper toward the calvarium.

material is not necessary unless an intracranial complication is suspected. Intravenous contrast is administered to detect extra-axial epidural or subdural abscess or intra-axial brain abscess (Fig. 12–9). An epidural abscess is suggested when a lenticular collection is noted adjacent to the calvarium. Associated bone destruction (osteomyelitis) is occasionally present. The dura enhances after contrast administration (Fig. 12–10). A common location of an otogenic epidural abscess is adjacent to the sigmoid sinus. The sigmoid sinus is intradural and is easily displaced medially and compressed. The blood flow may be slowed or obstructed. When occlusion occurs, the thrombus can propagate either proximally or distally. Thus, it is important to look for a filling defect in the jugular vein or transverse sinus (Fig. 12–11).

Determination of sigmoid sinus and jugular vein patency can be difficult with CT. The obstructed sigmoid sinus may be hard to distinguish from the adjacent epidural abscess (see Figs. 12–9 and 12–10). Both can be lucent with rim enhancement and can be located adjacent to the petrous bone. Sinus thrombosis is suggested by CT when an oval or round area of lower attenuation representing a filling defect extends into the jugular foramen or superiorly into the transverse sinus after bolus contrast injection (see Fig. 12–11).

Both CT and MRI have been used to evaluate suspected sigmoid sinus thrombosis. As discussed above, flowing blood within a vessel should appear as a distinct signal void on MRI. A vascular thrombus should appear (on T_1WI) as an abnormal signal of moderate intensity

where a signal void would normally be seen. A variable amount of surrounding bright signal representing a small amount of slow-flowing blood may be seen in a partially occluded vessel (see Fig. 12–11). Slow-flowing blood is delayed within the field of study long enough to return a characteristic signal. However, thrombus evaluation on MRI contains numerous pitfalls that can give false-positive results. A negative MRI picture (using gradient echo flow sensitive sequences, not just T_1WI) is very reliable for excluding thrombus (Figs. 12–12, 12–13).

On contrast-enhanced CT the normal sigmoid sinus is a well-defined homogenous structure of higher attenuation than surrounding brain. Thrombus in the vessel will appear to be of moderate attenuation similar to brain. This is best demonstrated after rapid bolus administration of intravenous contrast. A CT scan with this finding is a very reliable indication of the presence of thrombus.

At the same time, if abscess is present, MRI will demonstrate abnormal increased signal in the epidural space or brain on T_2WI and postcontrast T_1WI. The dura will be abnormally enhancing on postcontrast T_1WI.

Gradenigo Syndrome

A now uncommon complication of suppurative otitis media in the postantibiotic era is the clinical entity known as Gradenigo syndrome (Fig. 12–14). The classic clinical findings are that of a triad including petrous apicitis, ipsilateral abducens nerve palsy (CNVI), and deep

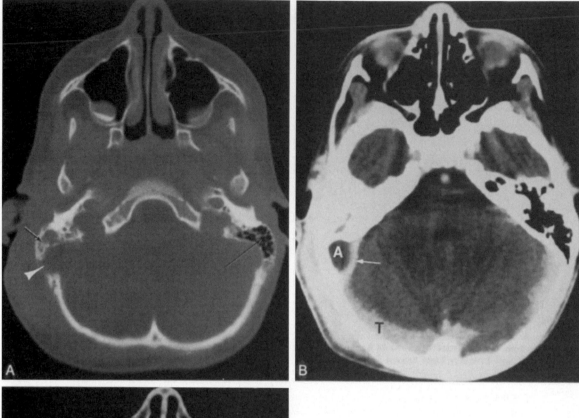

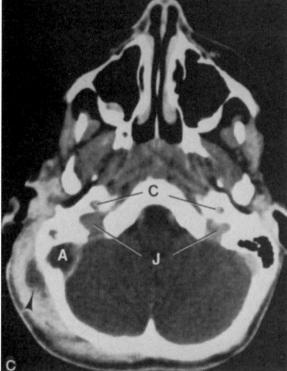

FIGURE 12-10. Patient with acute mastoiditis and epidural and superficial abscesses. *A,* Bone algorithm showing definite demineralization of the septations in the right mastoid *(shorter arrow)* and around the sigmoid sinus *(arrowhead).* Note the black density of air within the normal side *(longer arrow). B,* Soft tissue algorithm shows decreased attenuation (A) at the abscess collection. Again, the enhancement medial to the collection *(arrow)* could represent residual blood flow or enhancing dura. Note that this enhancement is of the same density as that of the transverse sinus (T). *C,* A slightly lower slice shows the abscess (A) in the region of the sigmoid sinus but also in the superficial soft tissue *(arrowhead).* Note that in this patient, the jugular bulb on the involved side is approximately the same as that on the normal side as well as approximately the same as the carotid arteries. This suggests that there is no jugular vein thrombosis. J, jugular bulbs; C, carotid arteries.

facial pain in the distribution of the trigeminal nerve (CNV).[10, 11, 13, 17, 26, 29, 30, 31] With adjacent dural inflammation, the cranial nerves involved can become inflamed such as is the case with the abducens nerve as it courses through the Dorello canal, under the petroclinoid ligament, or with the involvement of the Gasserian ganglion in the region of the Meckel cave, as is the case with the trigeminal nerve.

Cholesteatoma and Chronic Inflammatory Disease

In patients with cholesteatoma, CT is the examination of choice.[15, 43, 49, 52] Contrast enhancement is not needed unless there is concern regarding a concurrent intracranial pathologic condition. Cholesteatomas occur in two varieties, acquired and congenital.[15, 43, 49, 52] Approximately 98% of middle ear cholesteatomas are acquired. Congenital cholesteatomas will be discussed later in this chapter (see Fig. 12–42). Cholesteatomas are epidermal inclusion cysts, sacs lined by keratinizing stratified squamous epithelium that are trapped and left to grow within the middle ear cavity. Classically, cholesteatoma manifests as a soft tissue density mass in the middle-ear cavity with adjacent bone erosion Figs. 12–15, 12–16, 12–17). On CT there may be problems in differentiating a cholesteatoma from fluid or granulation tissue, as they are of the same soft tissue density. However, the radiologist can identify bone erosion (see Figs. 12–15, 12–16), and erosion of bone, especially the scutum, is presumptive evidence of cholesteatoma. Detection of erosion of the ossicles is less reliable: large erosions can be seen, but small erosions are difficult to exclude.

Coronal imaging is excellent for evaluating the facial nerve canal, tegmen, scutum, and lateral wall of the attic as well as the lateral aspect of the horizontal SCC (see Fig. 12–17). In the coronal projection the scutum can be carefully inspected along its inferior surface for erosion (Fig. 12–18). If more information regarding the horizontal SCC is desired, additional axial images will show it in its entirety on a single slice.

Dystrophic calcification, often referred to as tympanosclerosis, is considered a sequela of chronic inflammation and can be visualized on CT (Fig. 12–19). Labyrinthitis ossificans is an entity that is radiographically identifiable on both CT and MRI and is thought to be caused by several etiologies, divided into three main causes: meningogenic (from the meninges), tympanogenic (from the middle ear), and hematogenic (from the blood stream), all of which are thought to lead to suppurative labyrinthitis.[16, 19, 32, 50, 53] Labyrinthitis ossificans is thought to occur in three stages: The first stage is the acute stage, with bacteria and leukocytes being lodged within the perilymphatic spaces; this is followed by the fibrous stage, characterized by fibroblast proliferation; and finally by the ossification stage, the stage in which CT findings become evident. The ossification is thought to occur when undifferentiated mesenchymal cells in the endosteum, modiolus, and basilar membranes begin to proliferate, differentiate into fibroblasts, and subsequently into osteoblasts. The osteoblasts form the abnormal trabeculae within the labyrinthine spaces that are visible radiologically. With meningogenic labyrinthitis ossificans (Fig. 12–20), the type common in children, suppuraton is thought to spread to the inner ear along the subarachnoid spaces via the cochlear aqueduct and the internal auditory canal.

Lastly, it should not be forgotten that not all causes of hearing loss are reflected in findings seen within the temporal bone. Children with in utero infections of the toxoplasmosis/other infection/rubella/cytomegalovirus/herpes simplex (TORCH) variety (Fig. 12–21) have associated hearing loss and typical findings on CT of the brain of periventricular (circumventricular) calcifications.[37]

Tumors

CT and MRI are both valuable for determining the extent of a head and neck neoplasm. Tumors originating within the petrous bone are best examined by CT. CT best documents the extent of bone destruction and also defines the soft tissue component well. Initially, on MRI, the temporal bone was considered a poor subject for tumor evaluation because neither the cortical bone nor the air gave signal, and thus everything looked "black." However, as tumor replaces either cortical bone or air, one finds signal (brightness) where there should be none. Thus, one does indeed see the image of the actual tumor rather than the hole that the tumor makes. Another feature to evaluate on MRI is the fat in the petrous apex. Normally, fat is very bright on T_1WI and gray on T_2WI. As tumor replaces this fat, the brightness is replaced by the lower signal of the tumor, resulting in low signal on T_1WI and high signal on T_2WI. MRI also has the potential to differentiate tumor from fluid trapped in the mastoid. On T_2WI the signal of the tumor is usually less than that of the retained fluid, allowing the tumor to be distinguished from the trapped fluid.

On CT, when tumor extends into the neck, it obliterates soft tissue and fat planes and so is detectable (Fig. 12–22). Intracranial extension of the tumor is generally discernible by its mass effect and higher CT density compared with that of the cerebrospinal fluid. MRI is often helpful in imaging tumor extent both into the neck and intracranially, and is best at defining the intracranial extent of tumor. With the use of various sequences to optimize tissue contrast, tumor margins can be most easily seen.

Contrast agents should be used for tumor evaluation with both CT and MRI, as tumors usually demonstrate enhancement in both studies. This makes identification and differentiation from adjacent tissues easier. Gadolinium is a paramagnetic agent and currently the most common contrast medium used in MRI. Rhabdomyosarcoma (see Fig. 12–22) is the most common soft tissue sarcoma affecting children, and approximately 41% of these tumors occur in the head and neck region. Of the head and neck rhabdomyosarcomas, 8% occur within the temporal bone region.[45, 54, 56] Of the four cell subtypes that are observed (pleomorphic, alveolar, botryoid, and embryonal), embryonal cell is the most common subtype found in the head and neck region.

For evaluation of acoustic neuromas, contrast-enhanced MRI is the examination of choice. The tumor "lights up" on the relatively brief T_1WI, thus offering the hope of quicker and more cost-effective examinations. Acoustic neuromas (schwannomas) are rare but do occur occasionally in children with neurofibromatosis. Specifically, acoustic schwannomas, which occur bilaterally in neurofibromatosis type II (NFII), are well delineated on MRI as bilateral IAC enhancing masses (Fig. 12–23, 12–24, 12–25).[49] This is an autosomal dominant disorder, transmitted by chromosome 22, and is associated with multiple other CNS lesions including intracranial meningiomas, spinal cord ependymomas and nerve root Schwannomas, and spinal meningiomas.[37]

Langerhans cell histiocytosis (LCH), previously known

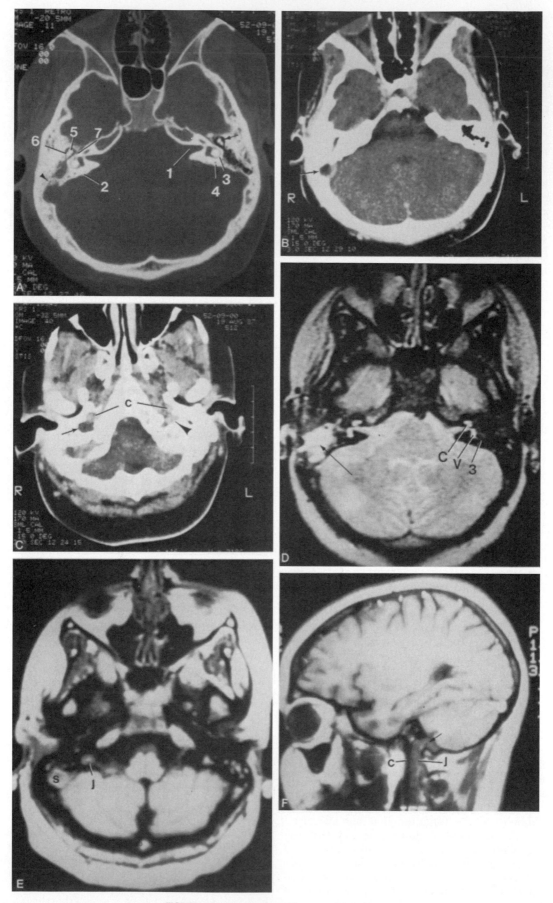

FIGURE 12-11 *See legend on opposite page*

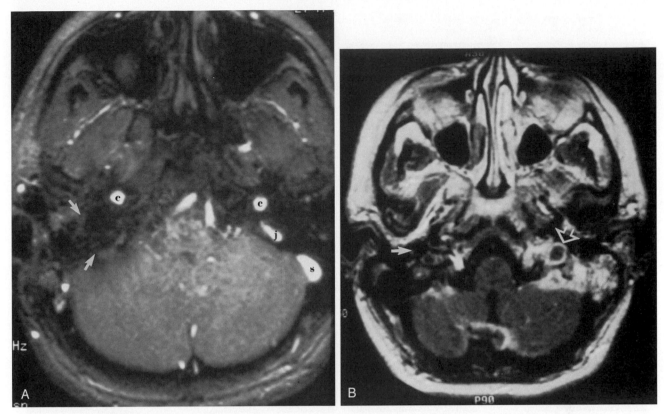

FIGURE 12–12. *A*, Absence of flow through the right jugular vein caused by obstruction due to glomus tumor *(small white arrows)* as seen on gradient echo flow sensitive MRI. Normal flow through carotid arteries (c), the left jugular vein (j), and the dural angle of the sigmoid sinus (s) is shown. *B*, Absence of flow void on postcontrast T₁WI spin echo MRI. The normal right jugular vein *(white arrow)* is seen as a signal void. The left jugular vein is filled with thrombus and shows a ring of peripheral enhancement *(open arrows)*.

as histiocytosis X (including the three entities, eosinophilic granuloma [EG], Letterer-Siwe disease, and Hand-Schüller-Christian disease), is known as the great mimicker in radiology, in that it has protean presentations and can occur within any soft tissue or bone within the body, including the temporal bone.[1, 2, 14, 35] This lesion is characterized pathologically by aggregates of proliferating histiocytes and other inflammatory cells. The temporal bone may be affected as a solitary site or as a part of multisystem disease, and may be involved in up to 60% of patients (range of 15% to 60%). Radiographically, osseous involvement is demonstrated by well-defined lytic (lucent) lesions replaced by soft tissue mass, with sharp borders and without surrounding reactive sclerosis (Fig. 12–26).

FIGURE 12–11. Patient with mastoiditis, epidural abscess, and jugular vein occlusion. *A*, Axial CT with bone algorithm shows opacification of the right attic and the antrum, with minimal demineralization of bone *(arrowhead)* next to the sinodural angle. Note the air within the attic *(short arrow)* on the opposite side. 1, IAC; 2, vestibular aqueduct; 3, horizontal SCC; 4, posterior SCC; 5, malleus; 6, incus; 7, facial nerve canal. *B*, Soft tissue algorithm shows lucency *(black arrow)* with some small enhancement medially that may represent on this image a small amount of residual flow or could be enhancement of the dura. *C*, A lower slice shows decreased density or attenuation in the vascular portion of the jugular foramen *(arrow)* compared with the normal side *(arrowhead)* or with the carotid arteries (C). This raises the possibility of a jugular vein thrombosis. *D*, Magnetic resonance scan with intermediate weighting. The bright signal in the mastoid *(arrow)* indicates retained secretions or fluid. Compare with the opposite side. Note that there is some signal from the vestibule (V) and cochlea (C), and part of the horizontal SCC (3) can be seen. *E*, On a lower slice, T₁-weighted image (T₁WI), there is a stronger signal in the sigmoid sinus (S) and the jugular vein (J) than is usually seen with rapidly flowing blood. (Caution: It must be noted that the jugular vein can have various appearances.) *F*, Sagittal T₁WI shows a definite difference in signal between the jugular vein (J) and the carotid artery (C). Note the curve of the jugular *(arrow)* passing toward the sigmoid sinus. Again, this suggests jugular vein thrombosis.

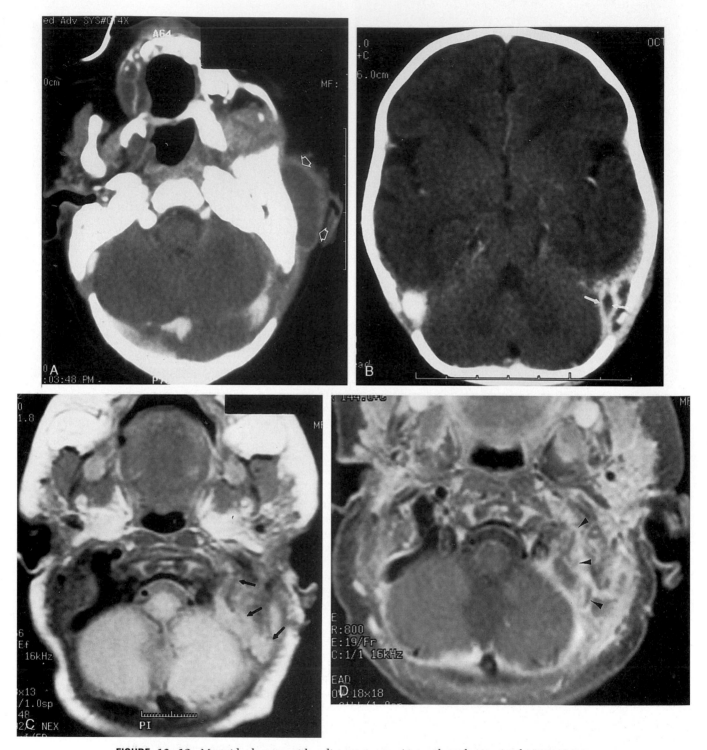

FIGURE 12–13. Mastoid abscess with adjacent venous/sinus thrombosis. Axial contrast enhanced 1-mm thick CT images of the temporal bone in a patient with clinical suspicion of mastoiditis, imaged on soft tissue windows *(A and B)* demonstrate a soft tissue abscess *(A)* *(open white arrows)* and a filling defect *(B)* *(white arrows)* in the adjacent transverse sinus. Axial proton density MRI *(C)* *(black arrows)*, and axial contrast enhanced MRI using fat saturation technique *(D)* *(black arrow heads)* at the level of the sigmoid sinus demonstrate the lack of flow void in the adjacent left dural venous sinus, confirmed on axial phased contrast magnetic resonance venogram *(E)* through the posterior fossa *(small white arrowheads)*.

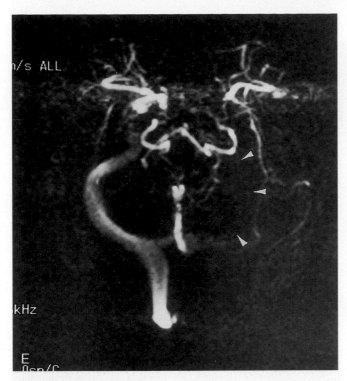

FIGURE 12–13 *Continued*

Due to its dense bony covering, the bony labyrinth is infrequently affected, but its involvement should be suspected if the patient has concomitant sensorineural hearing loss, as opposed to conductive hearing loss, which is not unexpected with infiltrative changes in the middle ear, ossicles, or external auditory canal.

Congenital Anomalies

CT remains the study of choice for evaluation of congenital anomalies of the external, middle, and inner ears.* The middle and external ears share a common embryologic origin, so it is not surprising that congenital malformations tend to involve both areas. Isolated middle-ear anomalies are possible, but congenital malformations of the inner ear are most often isolated because of a separate embryologic origin. Even with an obvious external-ear deformity, a detailed study of the middle and inner ears is necessary to exclude additional anomalies that may affect surgical planning. Congenital anomalies are not uncommon in children referred for hearing loss. However, CT results may still be normal in these patients if the cause lies in the neuroepithelium or sensory epithelium, since in these cases the bony labyrinth is normal.

To be considered normal, the cochlea must demonstrate the normal 2½ to 2¾ turns with an intact bony septum between the second and apical turns (Fig. 12–27). If this bony septum fails to develop, a Mondini malformation results. The CT appearance of the Mondini anomaly is a normal basal turn with the middle and apical turns replaced by a cystlike cavity (Figs. 12–28, 12–29). Usually this is an isolated anomaly, and the remainder of

---

*See Refs. 3–6, 8, 12, 18, 20, 22, 24, 27, 40, 51.

the ear is normal, but variants are possible. The cochlea is well seen on thin-section, high-resolution CT, and cochlear hypoplasia (microcochlea) and labyrinthine aplasia (Michel deformity) are easily identified (Fig. 12–30).

SCCs may be absent or demonstrate variable deformities that may be isolated or seen concomitantly with other anomalies (Figs. 12–31, 12–32). SCC anomalies include saclike malformations, small complete canals, or segmental dilatation; the saclike malformations are most common (Figs. 12–33, 12–34). The SCC most likely to be malformed is the lateral SCC.

The vestibular and cochlear aqueducts should be bilaterally symmetric. The normal vestibular aqueduct diameter should be equal to or smaller than the diameter of the posterior semicircular canal. Abnormal dilatation is best seen on axial images (Figs. 12–35, 12–36). The normal vestibular aqueduct is frequently not seen on CT. A rare but aggressive tumor can occur in the region of the vestibular aqueduct and is known as the endolymphatic sac tumor, which is a retrolabyrinthine adenomatous tumor arising from the site of the endolymphatic sac (Fig. 12–37).[24] The cochlear aqueduct can be visualized in nearly all axial CT examinations if 1.0- or 1.5-mm contiguous images are obtained. A normal diameter for the cochlear aqueduct has not been determined, but it should have a trumpet-like configuration that tapers rapidly from medial to lateral. The internal auditory canal (IAC) varies in size and length depending on patient size and age. There is a suggested association between an abnormally narrow IAC and sensorineural hearing loss. In addition, there is an association of an enlarged IAC with sensorineural hearing loss, known as X-linked sensorineural hearing loss, which is a chromosomal abnormality that causes perilymphatic hydrops due to fistulous connection between the IAC and the cochlea.[24] This syndrome is seen in young men with profound sensorineural or mixed hearing loss that is often progressive and may be associated with vestibular dysfunction. The imaging characteristic in X-linked sensorineural hearing loss is IAC enlargement that is often symmetric and bilateral, often associated with hypoplasia of the base of the cochlea. Other findings can include an enlarged vestibular aqueduct and a widened proximal facial nerve canal. Of greatest significance and importance in detecting this abnormality is its association with congenital stapes fixation and stapes gusher, or perilymphatic flooding.

Auricular and external auditory canal (EAC) abnormalities are fairly common. In EAC atresia the tympanic membrane is replaced by an atresia plate of variable thickness (Fig. 12–38). Associated malformations of the middle ear and ossicles are frequent. The most common anomaly is fusion of the malleus to the atresia plate (Fig. 12–39). Anterior migration of the mastoid portion of the facial nerve is usually seen with external- and middle-ear anomalies. Preoperative CT evaluation of EAC atresia is necessary to exclude concomitant congenital cholesteatoma and demonstrate any pathologic anatomy (Fig. 12–40). If an isolated middle-ear anomaly is present, the stapes is the ossicle most commonly involved, while the malleus is the least often involved. Ossicular anomalies may include absence, hypoplasia, or fixation to another middle-ear structure (Fig. 12–41).

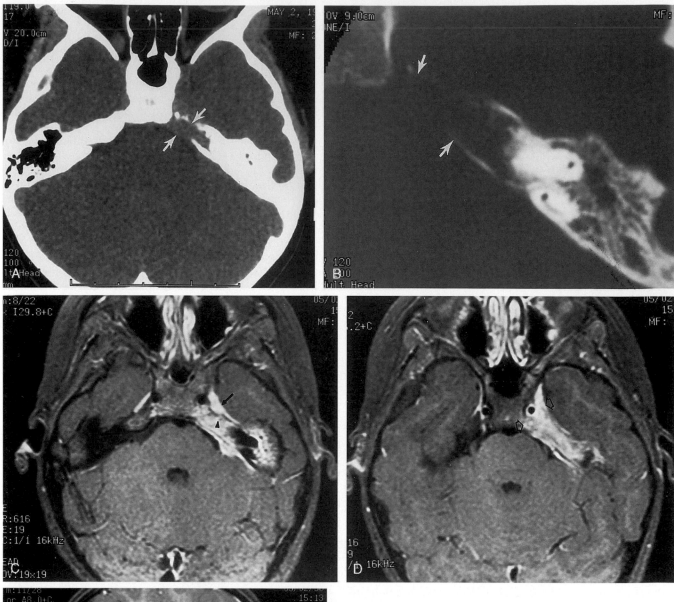

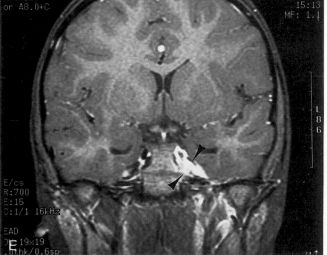

FIGURE 12–14. Gradenigo syndrome. Axial contrast enhanced 1-mm thick CT images of the left temporal bone imaged on soft tissue (*A*) and magnified bone windows (*B*), in a 6-year-old girl with headaches, nasal congestion, and left 6th nerve palsy demonstrate opacification of the left petrous apex with bony erosion (*white arrows*). Axial contrast enhanced T$_1$-weighted (T$_1$W) MRI using fat saturation technique at the level of the petrous apex (*C*) and cavernous sinus (*D*) as well as coronal images using the same parameters (*E*) demonstrate abnormal enhancement and opacification of the left petrous apex (*small black arrowhead*) and the adjacent dura (*black arrow*) (*C*), the cavernous sinus (*D*) (*open black arrows*), and Meckel cave (*E*) (*large black arrowheads*).

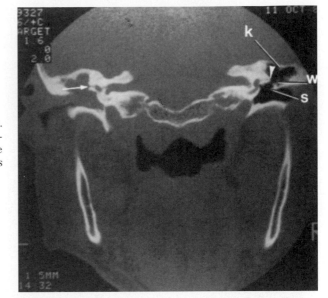

FIGURE 12–15. Coronal CT scan in a patient with cholesteatoma. Note the complete erosion of the right scutum and ossicles and erosion into the horizontal SCC *(arrow)*. Note the normal anatomy on the opposite side. s, scutum; w, lateral wall of the attic; k, Koerner's septum. The intact horizontal SCC is shown by the arrowhead.

Congenital cholesteatomas (epidermoid) are much less common than the acquired variety and are believed to arise from aberrant epithelial remnants or rests left at the time of closure of the neural groove, between the third and fifth week of fetal life.[43, 49] These lesions tend to occur in the anterosuperior middle ear, adjacent to the eustachian tube and the cochlear promontory (Fig. 12–42), and occur with an intact tympanic membrane, without history of perforation.

First branchial cleft cysts are classified as either type I or type II.[48] Type I cysts are purely related to the exter-

nal auditory canal, while the type II abnormality occurs primarily near the angle of the mandible, with the tract extending through the parotid gland toward the EAC (Fig. 12–43).

Isolated anomalies of the facial nerve do occur, but an altered course of the facial nerve canal is most often caused by incomplete formation of the temporal bone seen with middle- and inner-ear anomalies. If the cochlea is small or absent, there is anterior and medial displacement of the facial nerve canal (Fig. 12–44). Aberrant position is one of the two most common abnormalities of

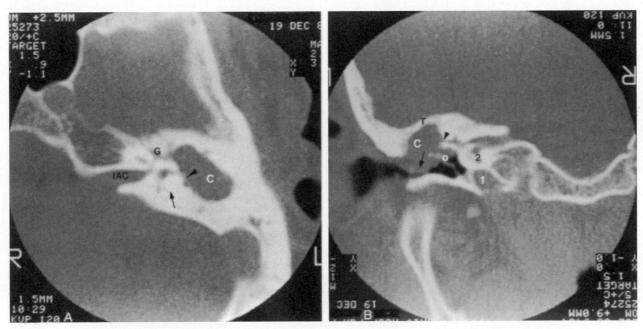

FIGURE 12–16. Axial slice of cholesteatoma. *A,* Cholesteatoma (C) fills the attic and the antrum. Note the defect *(arrowhead)* in the horizontal SCC. IAC, internal auditory canal; G, geniculate ganglion. The posterior limb of the horizontal SCC is indicated by the arrow. *B,* Coronal image of cholesteatoma. There is absence of the right scutum as the cholesteatoma (C) grows down into the EAC *(arrow)*. Again, there is erosion of the horizontal SCC *(arrowhead)*. The ossicle (O) is displaced. 1, carotid artery; 2, cochlea; T, tegmen.

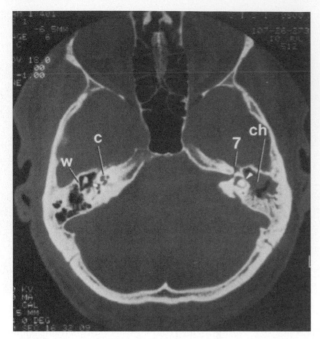

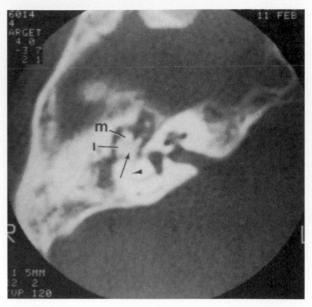

FIGURE 12–17. Cholesteatoma (ch) partially filling the left attic and eroding the anterolateral margin of the horizontal SCC *(arrowhead)*. Note the metallic density of a stapes prosthesis in the opposite oval window. w, lateral wall of the attic normal side; c, cochlea; 7, geniculate ganglion.

FIGURE 12–19. Tympanosclerosis and a chronic middle-ear inflammatory problem. Dense calcification *(arrow)* is shown between the right horizontal SCC and the incus. There is opacification of the attic and the antrum as well. The horizontal SCC is indicated by the arrowhead. i, incus; m, malleus.

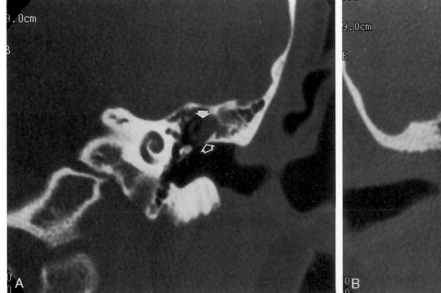

FIGURE 12–18. Acquired cholesteatoma. Coronal 1-mm thick noncontrasted CT images, imaged on bone windows, at the level of the middle ear in two patients with conductive hearing loss and cholesteatoma, early in the left temporal bone in patient 1 *(A)* and late in the right temporal bone of patient 2 *(B)*. Note the preservation of the scutum with early acquired cholesteatoma *(open white arrow)*, despite the epitympanic opacification *(solid white arrow)*, but the erosion of tegmen tympani *(small white arrows)* and the lateral semicircular canal *(black arrowhead)* with advanced cholesteatoma.

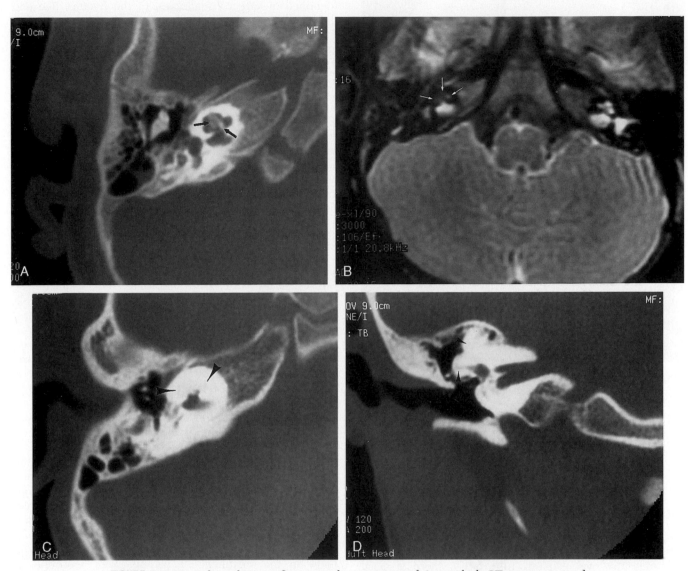

FIGURE 12–20. Labyrinthitis ossificans. Axial non-contrasted 1-mm thick CT images, imaged on bone windows *(A)* and axial FSE T$_2$-weighted images using fat saturation technique *(B)* at the level of the cochlea (modiolus), in a patient with postmeningitic sensorineural hearing loss, demonstrate the subtle early changes of right-sided labyrinthitis ossificans, with mild increase in density/attenuation of the cochlea on CT *(A)* *(small black arrows)* and fairly striking loss of T$_2$ signal (brightness) on MRI *(B)* *(small white arrows)* given the replacement of perilymph (with its high water content), by calcium, which appears dark on T$_2$-weighted images. MRI is more sensitive in detecting early changes of labrynthitis ossificans, but once advanced disease is detected on CT examination *(C, D)*, MRI is of no added benefit. Axial 1-mm *(C)* and coronal 1-mm *(D)* noncontrasted CT image on bone window, of the right temporal bone patient with postmeningitic sensorineural hearing loss with advanced labrynthitis ossificans, demonstrate dense calcification/ossification of the bony labyrinth, best seen in the cochlea on image C *(large black arrowheads)*, and the semicircular canals on image D *(small black arrowheads)*.

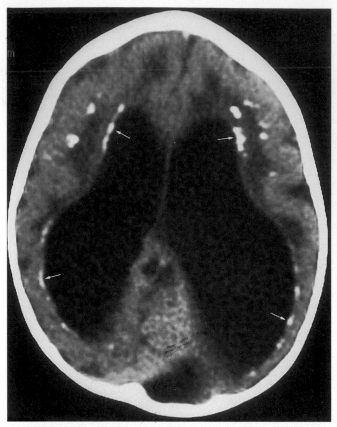

FIGURE 12–21. Cytomegalovirus (CMV) infection. Axial noncontrasted CT image of the head, imaged on soft tissue windows, at the level of the lateral ventricles in a 7-month-old girl with CMV exposure, demonstrates the typical periventricular calcifications (circumventricular), associated with CMV infection (*white arrows*).

the facial nerve (Fig. 12–45). The other is partial absence of the bony wall of the second portion of the facial nerve canal. Rarely, the facial nerve protrudes into the tympanic cavity, sometimes coming into contact with the stapes or obscuring the oval window. Also rarely, there is canal duplication.

Finally, the facial nerve canal is abnormally small in Möbius syndrome.

Identification of vascular variants and malformations is of utmost importance for preoperative planning. The most important but rarest anomaly is the aberrant internal carotid artery, which extends into the middle-ear cavity and on CT appears as a soft tissue mass along the promontory (Figs. 12–46, 12–47). Axial contrast-enhanced CT demonstrates a vascular "mass" continuous with the transverse portion of the carotid canal. A dehiscent jugular bulb may protrude into the middle-ear cavity and have soft tissue or "mass" density on CT, but will be seen to be continuous with jugular vein (Fig. 12–48). The appearance of vascular abnormalities is fairly characteristic on CT, as the expected course of the vessel is seen to be altered. If the diagnosis of dehiscent jugular bulb is problematic, contrast administration should be definitive.

Trauma

Trauma to the ear is also best evaluated by CT (Figs. 12–49 to 12–54).[21, 23, 28, 36, 42] Fractures are generally easily identified by direct visualization of the fracture line and fluid in adjacent air cells (see Figs. 12–49 and 12–51). Fractures through the septations of the mastoid are easily appreciated. Ossicular disruption can be defined (see Figs. 12–50 and 12–53). One must keep in mind that CT cannot completely exclude a fracture, especially a hairline undisplaced fracture. The fractures most often missed are those that are parallel to, or in the plane of, a CT slice rather than perpendicular to the slice. For instance, a vertical (superoinferior) fracture in the squamous temporal bone would be in the plane of a coronal slice and could be missed. Such a fracture would "cross" an axial slice and so should be apparent. CT also gives excellent visualization of the more vital intracranial structures in a traumatized patient.

Miscellaneous

Various bony dysplasias can be diagnosed and staged with CT, especially with bone algorithms. The characteristic density of fibrous dysplasia is slightly less dense than that of normal cortical bone.[7, 9, 38, 39, 55] Areas of soft tissue can be seen within, depending on the degree of mineralization (Fig. 12–55). Similarly, CT can demonstrate the demineralized bone of otosclerosis contrasted against the denser otic capsule (Fig. 12–56). Cochlear otosclerosis has a very characteristic appearance, with a lucency abutting the cochlear lumen. Although early changes can be missed, narrowing of the oval window and demineralization in the region of the fissula ante fenestram (just anterior to the oval window) can often be detected.

Although not a bone dysplasia, Chiari II malformation leads to a recognizable deformity within the temporal bone region due to the inability of the small posterior fossa to fully contain the cerebellar and brainstem structures.[37] Hence there is typical scalloping of the petrous apices, well delineated on CT of the head (Fig. 12–57).

Cochlear implants have become an important development in the treatment of patients with sensorineural hearing loss.[25, 34, 41, 46, 47] These can be visualized on CT examination (Fig. 12–58) with some degree of spray artifact, not a limitation present with conventional temporal bone radiographs.

Summary

The usefulness of plain films is now limited primarily to evaluation of cochlear prostheses. CT is now the study of choice for evaluation of trauma, congenital anomalies, acute and chronic inflammation, and tumor (Figs. 12–59, 12–60). (See Box 12–1 for definitions of the labels used in Figs. 12–59, 12–60, and 12–61.) However, if vascular compromise or intracranial extension of infection or tumor is suspected, MRI is extremely useful (it also provides excellent evaluation of nerves) (Fig. 12–61). MRI continues to advance rapidly, and its use in examinations of the temporal bone will no doubt continue to increase in the years to come.

Text continued on page 271

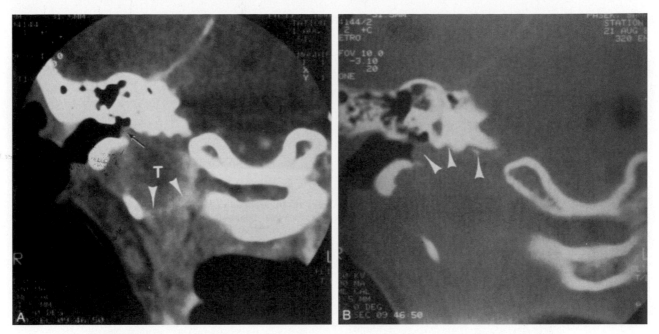

FIGURE 12–22. Rhabdomyosarcoma eroding up into the middle ear. *A,* Soft tissue algorithm shows the tumor (T) eroding bone extending into the right middle ear *(arrow).* Note that the lower margin of the tumor *(arrowheads)* can be defined, as it is contrasted against the normal fat planes beneath the skull base. *B,* Bone algorithm shows the erosion of the bone *(arrowheads),* but the lower margin of the lesion is less well defined.

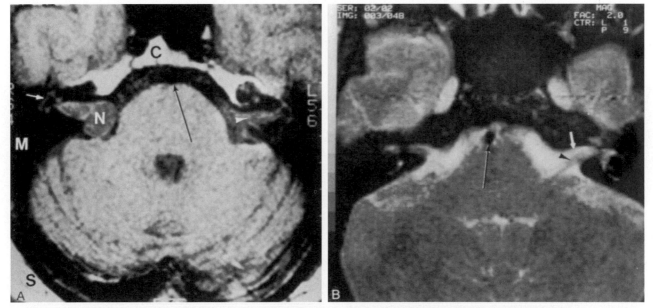

FIGURE 12–23. *A,* T$_1$-weighted image (short TR, short TE). Acoustic neuroma. The cerebrospinal fluid (CSF) is dark *(long arrow)* and can be seen entering the left IAC *(arrowhead).* The acoustic neuroma (N) fills the abnormal IAC and bulges into the cerebellopontine angle cistern. In the mastoid (M), neither bone nor air gives enough signal to be seen, so they cannot be differentiated. The fat in the subcutaneous area (S) as well as in the clivus (C) gives a very bright signal. The tumor produces an intermediate signal, and the facial nerve canal *(short white arrow)* has enough tissue to give an intermediate signal as well. *B,* Normal IAC T$_2$WI shows bright CSF contrasted against the nerves extending into the IAC canal. CSF in the IAC is indicated by the white arrow. Cranial nerves in the IAC are shown by the arrowhead. Note the signal void in the basilar artery *(black arrow).*

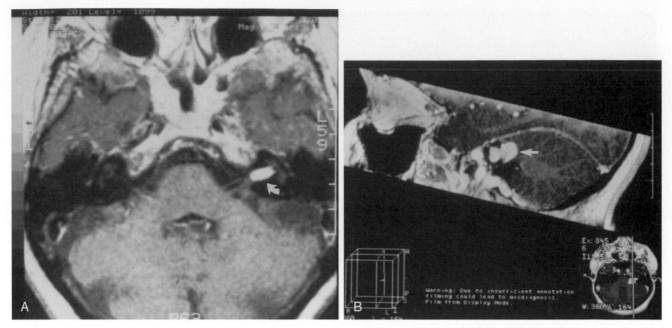

FIGURE 12–24. *A,* MRI, axial projection. The left-sided tumor (acoustic neuroma) is brightly enhanced after contrast administration *(arrow)*. *B,* Contrast enhanced re-formatted volume acquisition MRI through the temporal bone for acoustic neuroma. The tumor *(white arrow)* appears as a brightly enhancing mass.

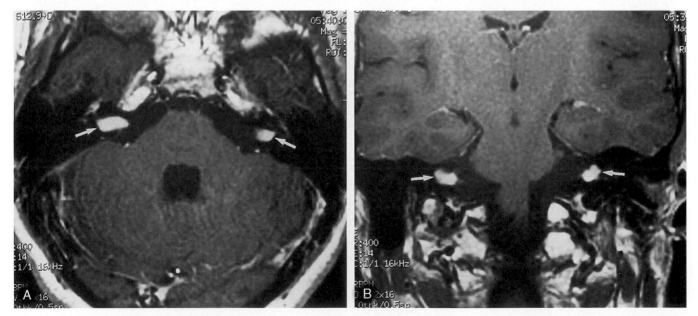

FIGURE 12–25. Bilateral acoustic neuromas/schwannomas. Axial *(A)* and coronal *(B)* T₁W gadolinium-enhanced images through the region of the IACs in a 17-year-old boy with neurofibromatosis type II demonstrate bilateral (right > left) enhancing masses in the expected location of the eighth cranial nerves *(white arrows)*.

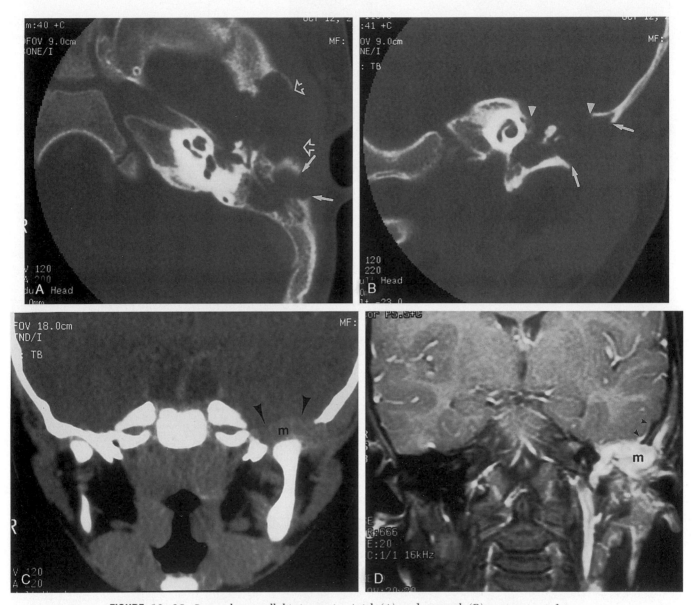

FIGURE 12–26. Langerhans cell histiocytosis. Axial *(A)* and coronal *(B)* postcontrast 1-mm thick CT images of the left temporal bone imaged on bone windows and coronal soft tissue windows *(C)*, as well as coronal T_1W post-gadolinium images using fat saturation technique *(D)*, in a 2-year-old with left ear mass and recurrent otitis media despite antibiotic therapy, demonstrate replacement of the majority of the mastoid bone by soft tissue with relative maintenance of the mastoid morphology. However, the lateral wall of the mastoid *(small white arrows)* and the lateral border of the middle cranial fossa *(A)* *(open arrows)* are disrupted *(A, B)*, as is the epitympanum *(B)* *(white arrowheads)*, with enhancing soft tissue mass (m) seen replacing the glenoid fossa *(C)* *(large black arrowheads)* abutting the undersurface of the temporal lobe *(D)*, with minimal thickening of the adjacent meninges *(small black arrowheads)*. The mandibular head appears to articulate with the dura of the middle cranial fossa.

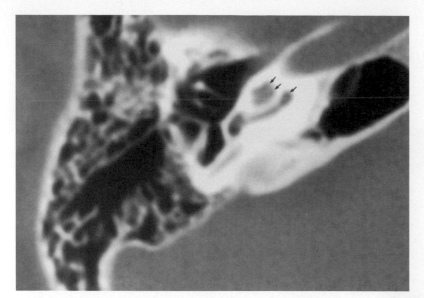

FIGURE 12–27. Axial CT. The normal turns of the right normal cochlea are well demonstrated (*small black arrows*) using 1.5-mm slice thickness and a bone algorithm.

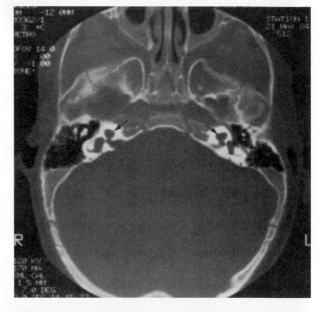

FIGURE 12–28. Mondini malformation. Note the cystic dilatation of the cochlea *(arrows)* bilaterally. (From Curtin HD. Congenital malformations of the ear. Otolaryngol Clin North Am 21:317, 1988.)

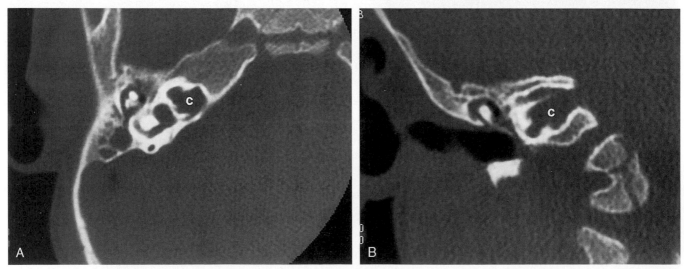

FIGURE 12–29. Mondini defect. Noncontrasted axial *(A)* and coronal *(B)* 1-mm thick CT images of the right temporal bone, imaged on bone windows, in a 2-year-old boy with bilateral sensorineural hearing loss (SNHL), demonstrate saccular dilatation of the cochlea with lack of the normal 2.5 turns (c).

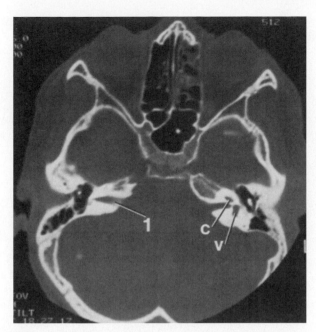

FIGURE 12–30. Michel deformity. Level of the IAC (1). No cochlea or vestibule is seen on the right side. V, vestibule on the normal side; C, cochlea. (From Curtin HD. Congenital malformations of the ear. Otolaryngol Clin North Am 21:317, 1988.)

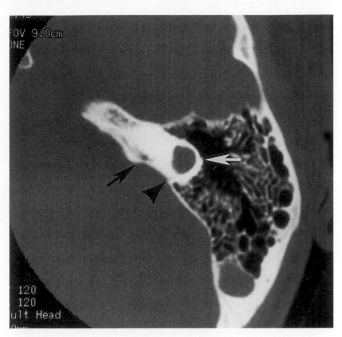

FIGURE 12–32. Aplasia of IAC, lateral, and posterior semicircular canals. Noncontrasted axial 1-mm thick CT images, imaged on bone windows at the expected level of the left IAC in a 17-year-old boy with left-sided hearing loss, demonstrate aplasia of the IAC *(large black arrow)* and both the lateral *(large white arrow)* and posterior semicircular canals *(black arrowhead)*.

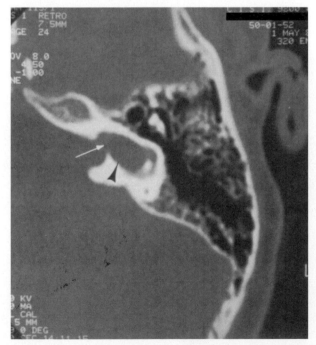

FIGURE 12–31. Severe deformity of the left cochlea and the vestibule. The IAC appears to communicate widely *(arrow)* with the vestibule and the cochlea, which are represented by a single large, dilated sac *(arrowhead)*. The ossicular chain is relatively normal.

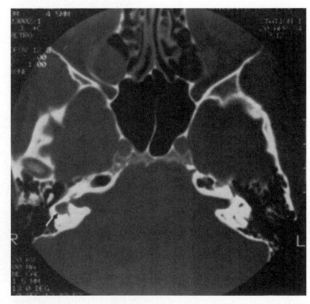

FIGURE 12–33. The right horizontal SCC *(arrow)* is represented by a cystic dilated remnant. (From Curtin HD. Congenital malformations of the ear. Otolaryngol Clin North Am 21:317, 1988.)

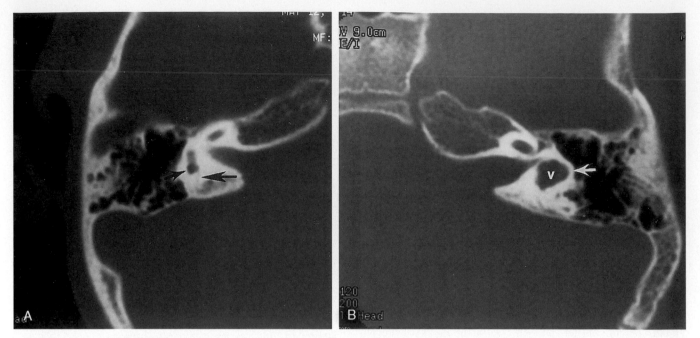

FIGURE 12–34. Vestibular and semicircular canal anomalies. Noncontrasted axial 1-mm thick CT images, imaged on bone windows, of the right *(A)* and left *(B)* temporal bones in two separate patients with SNHL. *A* demonstrates both vestibular *(small black arrow)* and semicircular canal hypoplasia *(large black arrow)*, whereas in *B* the vestibule is bulbous (v) and is associated with hypoplasia of the lateral semicircular canal *(white arrow)*.

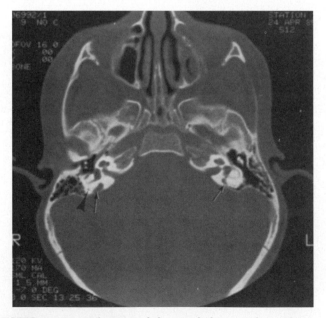

FIGURE 12–35. Dilatation of the vestibular aqueduct. The vestibular aqueducts *(arrows)* are larger than usual. Normal maximums are approximately the same as that of the posterior SCC *(arrowhead)*.

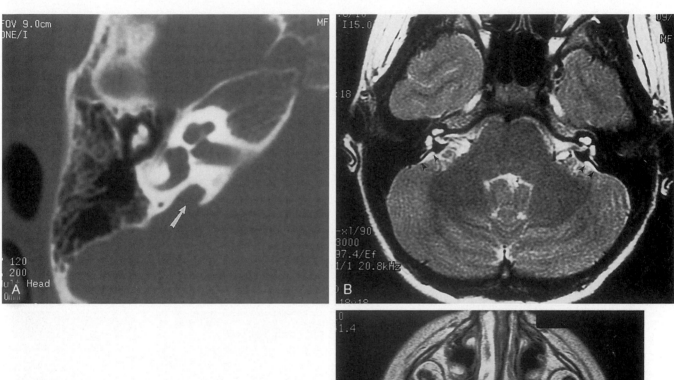

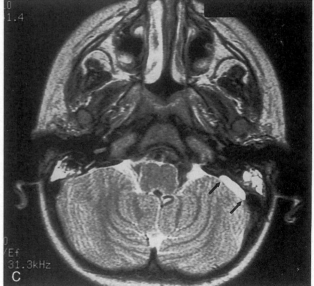

FIGURE 12–36. Enlarged vestibular aqueduct. Noncontrasted axial 1-mm thick CT image of the right temporal bone *(A)* imaged on bone windows, and high resolution T$_2$-weighted (T$_2$W) MRI at the level of the vestibular aqueducts *(B, C)* in three patients with SNHL. On CT *(A)*, the vestibular aqueduct (VA) *(white arrow)* is much larger than the adjacent semicircular canal. On MRI in patient 2, the vestibular aqueducts *(black arrowheads)* are mildly enlarged bilaterally, while in patient 3 *(C)*, the left VA *(black arrows)* is markedly enlarged.

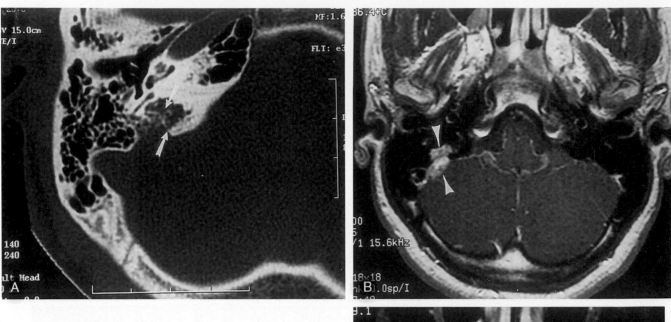

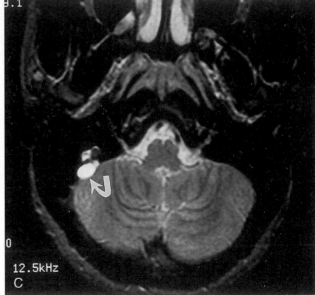

FIGURE 12–37. Endolymphatic sac tumor. Noncontrasted axial 1-mm thick CT image of the right temporal bone *(A)*, imaged on bone windows, and postcontrast T_1W *(B)* and axial T_2W images all in the same patient with SNHL demonstrate bony erosion *(A)* *(white arrows)* and an enhancing soft tissue mass *(B)* *(white arrowheads)* that is bright on T_2W images *(C)* *(curved white arrow)* in the expected location of the endolymphatic sac (posterior to the vestibular aqueduct).

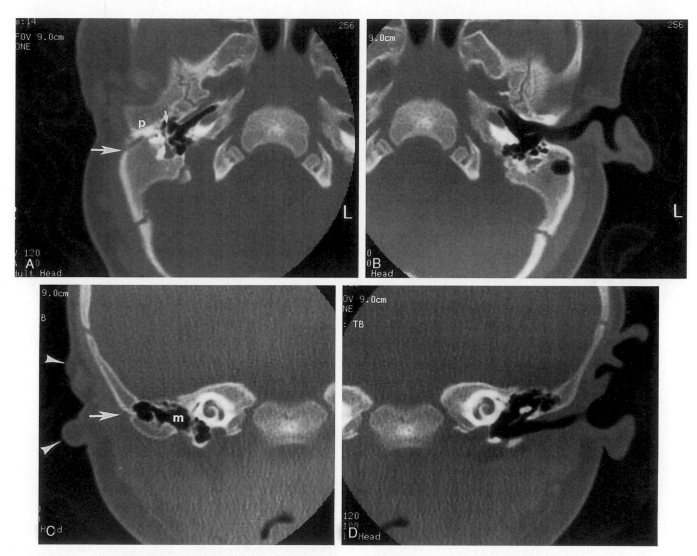

FIGURE 12–38. Aural atresia. Noncontrasted axial 1-mm thick (*A, B*) and coronal 1-mm thick CT images (*C, D*), imaged on bone windows, in a patient with right-sided conductive hearing loss (CHL) and microtia. *A* and *C* represent the affected right side, whereas *B* and *D* represent the normal left side for comparison. Note the absence of the right EAC (*large white arrow*), the small middle ear cavity (m), and the bony atresia plate (p) with adjacent mal-formed/fused ossicles (*small white arrow*) and an hypoplastic pinna (*white arrowheads*).

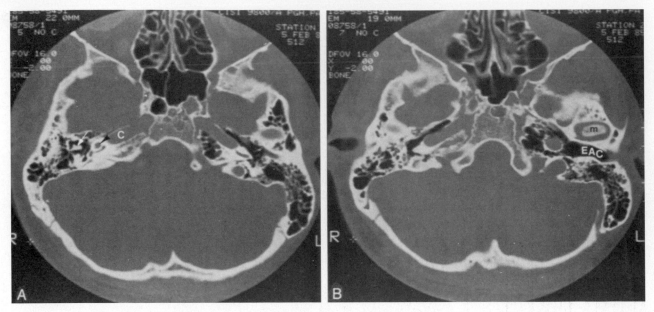

FIGURE 12–39. *A,* EAC atresia with fusion of the right ossicular chain. Note the fusion of the malleus and incus *(arrow).* The cochlea is normal. The bony separation between the second and apical turns *(arrowhead)* is the finding that essentially excludes a Mondini malformation of the cochlea. C, carotid canal. *B,* EAC atresia, lower slice than that shown in *A.* The normal EAC is contrasted with that on the opposite side. m, mandibular condyle. (From Curtin HD. Congenital malformations of the ear. Otolaryngol Clin North Am 21:317, 1988.)

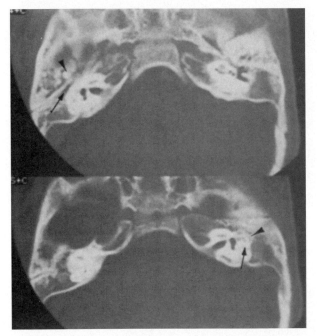

FIGURE 12–40. EAC atresia, with a very underdeveloped middle ear. Upper image shows very narrow right middle ear *(arrow),* with some minimal ossicular differentiation *(arrowhead).* On the lower image (actually more superior in the patient), bone *(arrowhead)* is immediately contiguous with the horizontal SCC *(arrowhead).* The very narrow middle ear may be filled with fluid or with tissue. (From Curtin HD. Congenital malformations of the ear. Otolaryngol Clin North Am 21:317, 1988.)

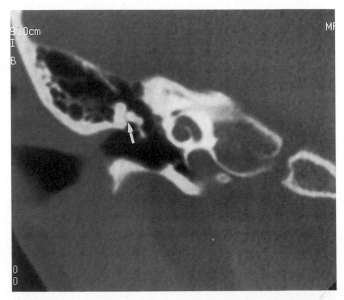

FIGURE 12–41. Ossicular-epitympanic fusion. Noncontrasted coronal 1-mm thick CT image, imaged on bone windows, of the right temporal bone demonstrates lateral fusion of the ossicles *(white arrow)* to the epitympanum, in a patient with CHL.

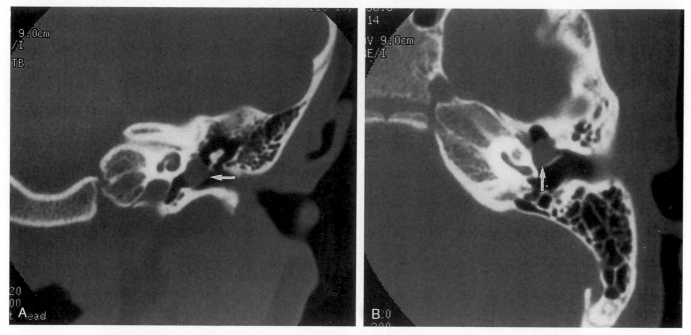

FIGURE 12–42. Congenital cholesteatoma (*A* and *B*). Noncontrasted coronal (*A*) and axial (*B*) 1-mm thick CT images of the left temporal bone at the level of the cochlear promontory, in a patient with CHL, demonstrate a rounded soft tissue mass (*white arrow*) remote from the Prussak space.

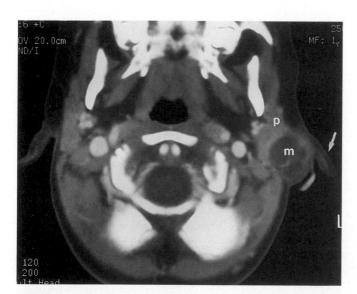

FIGURE 12–43. Type I branchial cleft cyst. Axial contrast-enhanced 5-mm thick CT image, imaged on soft tissue windows at the level of the left parotid gland, in a patient with a left-sided retroauricular mass, demonstrates an ovoid to rounded low attenuation mass (m) displacing the left parotid gland (p) anteriorly and medially, and the pinna (*white arrow*) anteriorly and laterally.

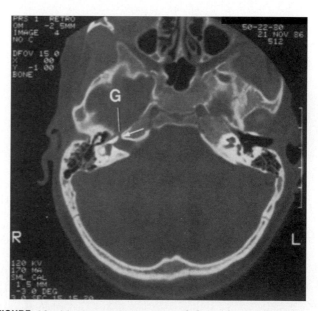

FIGURE 12–44. Anterior migration of the right facial nerve canal: bone algorithm. The facial nerve canal has migrated anteriorly and medially along the petrous apex. An inferior slice showed a very small cochlear remnant. G, geniculate ganglion. Arrow indicates the labyrinthine segment of the facial nerve canal. (From Curtin HD. Congenital malformations of the ear. Otolaryngol Clin North Am 21:317, 1988.)

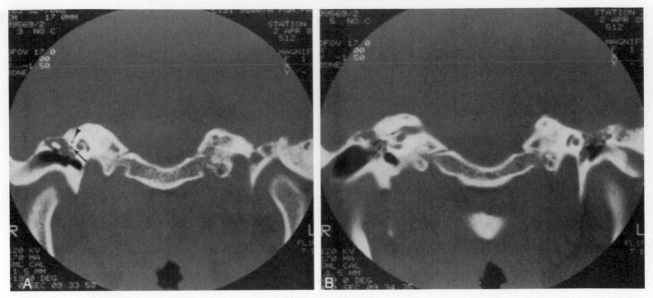

FIGURE 12–45. Coronal image. Inferior migration of the tympanic segment of the right facial nerve canal. *A*, The tympanic segment of the facial nerve canal *(arrow)* is much more inferior than usual. Normally, it is more lateral to the labyrinthine segment *(arrowhead)*. There is also opacification of the attic. *B*, A more posterior slice through the region of the oval window shows an indistinct density representing the facial nerve canal *(arrow)*. It is inferiorly displaced and very close to the oval window. No lucency is seen immediately beneath the horizontal canal in the normal location of the facial nerve *(arrowhead)*. (From Curtin HD. Congenital malformations of the ear. Otolaryngol Clin North Am 21:317, 1988.)

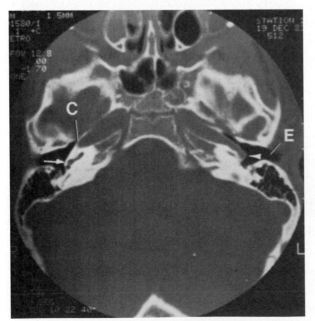

FIGURE 12–46. Aberrant left carotid artery. The left carotid artery extends more laterally than usual, extending out over the promontory, where it can be seen through the EAC. Compare its position with that on the normal, opposite side. Arrowhead indicates the lateral extent of the aberrant carotid. E, EAC. Arrow indicates the promontory. Note the intact bony wall of the carotid canal on the normal side (C). (From Curtin HD. Congenital malformations of the ear. Otolaryngol Clin North Am 21:317, 1988.)

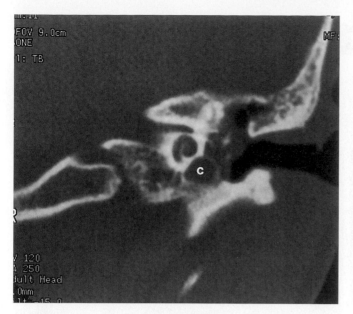

FIGURE 12–47. Aberrant left carotid artery. Noncontrasted coronal 1-mm thick CT image, imaged on bone windows, at the level of the left cochlea demonstrates a superiorly and laterally positioned carotid artery (C) in a patient with associated middle ear opacification.

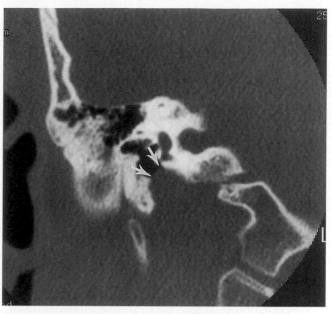

FIGURE 12–48. Dehiscent right jugular vein/bulb. Noncontrasted coronal 1-mm thick CT image, imaged on bone windows, at the level of the right vestibule, demonstrates absence of the bony covering *(white arrows)* of the right jugular bulb from the 9 o'clock to 11 o'clock positions.

FIGURE 12–49. Oblique longitudinal fracture of the right mastoid. The fracture line *(arrows)* can be partially seen. The path of the fracture is reflected by fluid and indistinctness of the septations. The facial nerve canal tympanic segment is shown (7).

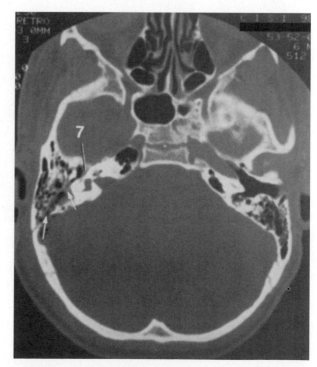

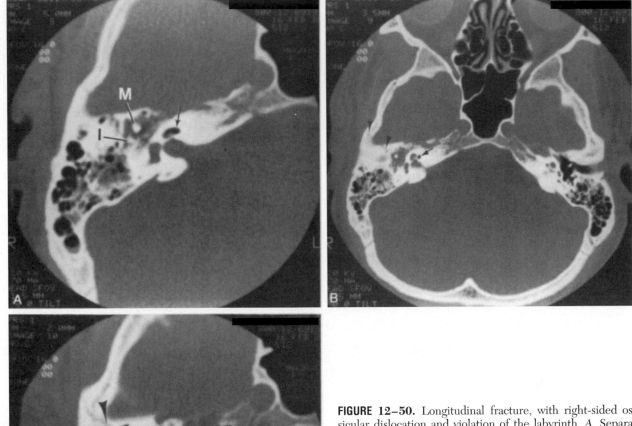

FIGURE 12–50. Longitudinal fracture, with right-sided ossicular dislocation and violation of the labyrinth. *A,* Separation of the malleus (M) and the incus (I). Note the air within the cochlea, which is much blacker than normal *(arrow). B,* Fracture line *(arrowheads).* Air in the cochlea is indicated by the arrow. *C,* Inferior slice. Fracture lines *(arrowheads).* The fracture line through the petrous portion, more medially, should not be confused with the cochlear aqueduct *(arrow),* which can be seen indistinctly slightly posteriorly.

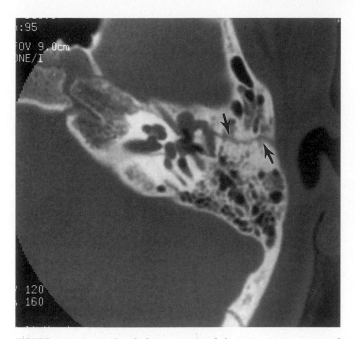

FIGURE 12–51. Left-sided transmastoid fracture. Noncontrasted axial 1-mm thick CT image, imaged on bone windows, at the level of the left incudomalleolar joint in a patient with head trauma, demonstrates a linear fracture *(black arrows)* extending into the middle ear cavity.

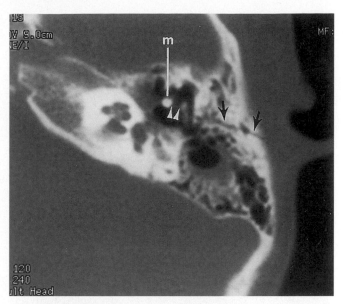

FIGURE 12–53. Left-sided transmastoid fracture with associated incudomalleolar dislocation. Noncontrasted axial 1-mm thick CT image, imaged on bone windows, at the level of the left incudomalleolar joint, in a patient with post-traumatic conductive hearing loss (CHL), demonstrates a transmastoid fracture *(black arrows)* extending into the middle ear cavity associated with disruption and diastasis *(white arrowheads)* of the incudomalleolar joint with separation of the malleus (m) from the incus.

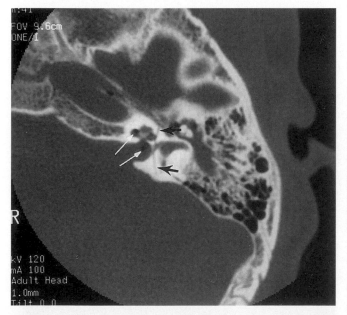

FIGURE 12–52. Left-sided temporal bone fracture crossing the inner ear. Noncontrasted axial 1-mm thick CT image, imaged on bone windows, at the level of the left cochlea, in a patient with post-traumatic SNHL, demonstrates a linear fracture *(black arrows)* extending anteriorly from the eustachian tube, and coursing posteriorly to skirt the lateral aspect of the cochlea, the lateral aspect of the IAC, and the medial aspect of the vestibule. Note the air/gas *(white arrows)* in the medial cochlea and lateral aspect of the IAC.

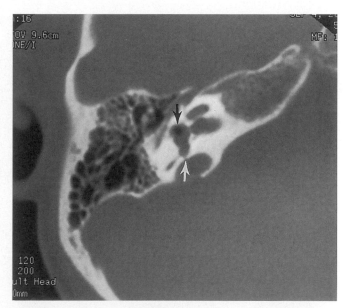

FIGURE 12–54. Right temporal bone fracture with inner ear involvement. Noncontrasted axial 1-mm thick CT image, imaged on bone windows, at the level of the right vestibule, in a patient with post-traumatic SNHL, demonstrates a fracture *(white arrow)* through the posterior vestibular region associated with gas/air *(black arrow)* within the vestibule.

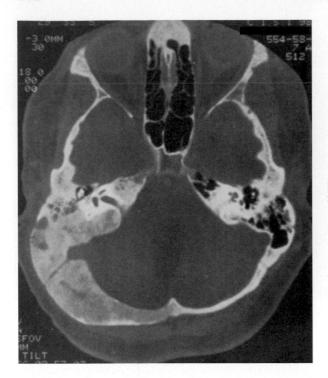

FIGURE 12–55. Fibrous dysplasia showing thickening of the right occipital and temporal bones, with intermediate mineralization.

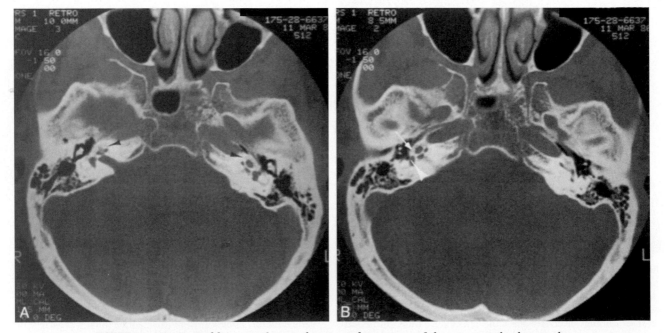

FIGURE 12–56. *A,* Cochlear otosclerosis showing indistinctness of the otic capsule close to the cochlea *(arrowheads). B,* A slightly inferior slice shows slight thickening of the bone, which is undermineralized *(arrow),* in the region of the fissula ante fenestram just anterior to the footplate of the stapes *(arrowhead).*

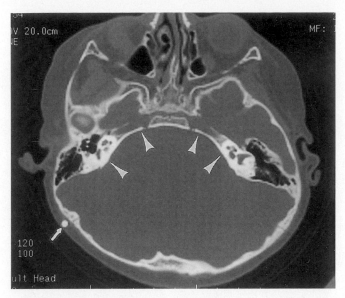

FIGURE 12–57. Scalloped petrous apices in a patient with Chiari II malformation. Noncontrasted axial 1-mm thick CT image, imaged on bone windows, at the level of the cochlea, in a patient with a Chiari II malformation. Note the scalloping and concave anterior appearance *(white arrowheads)* of the petrous bones, secondary to remodeling of the bone due to a small posterior fossa, unable to adequately accommodate the cerebellum and brain stem. Note also the ventricular peritoneal shunt catheter *(white arrow)* at the level of the right lambdoid suture, commonly present in these patients who are afflicted with communicating hydrocephalus secondary to obstruction of the CSF outflow at the level of the outlet foramina.

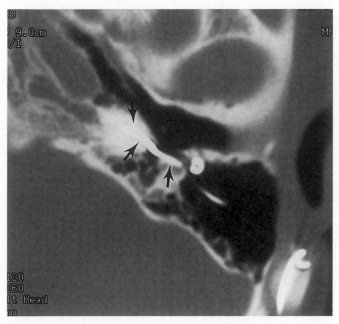

FIGURE 12–58. Left cochlear implant. Noncontrasted axial 1-mm thick CT image of the left temporal bone, imaged on bone windows, in a patient with left-sided SNHL, demonstrates a metallic density seen entering the cochlea *(black arrows)* at the level of its base turn.

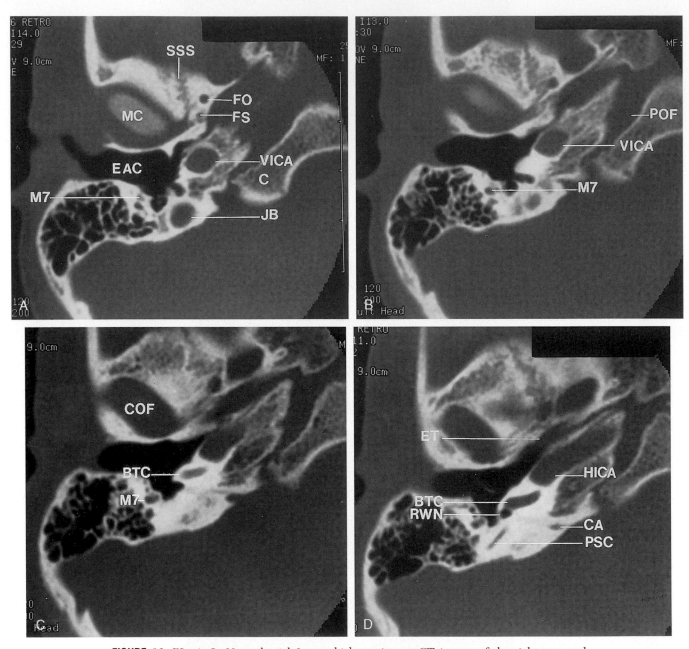

FIGURE 12–59. *A–L,* Normal axial 1-mm thick contiguous CT images of the right temporal bone, displayed sequentially from inferior to superior, from the level of the temporomandibular joint to the level of the superior semicircular canal. (See Box 12–1 for definitions of labels used to identify structures.)

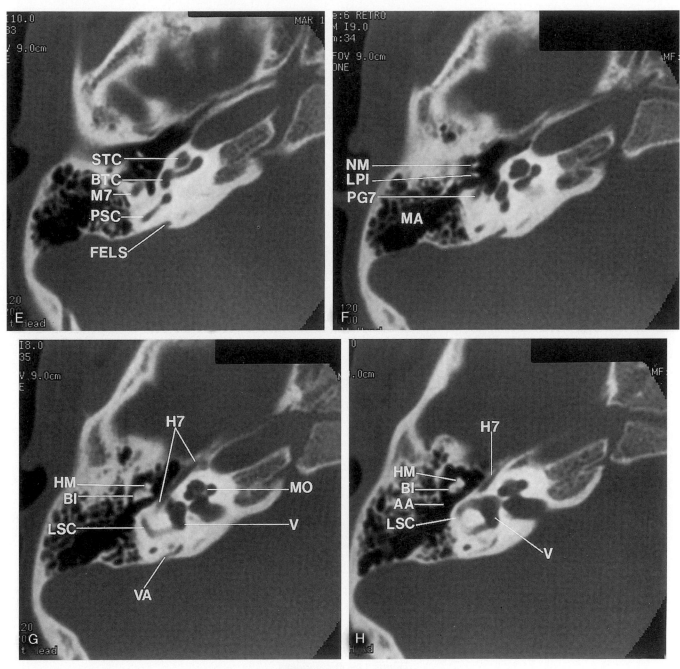

FIGURE 12–59 *Continued*

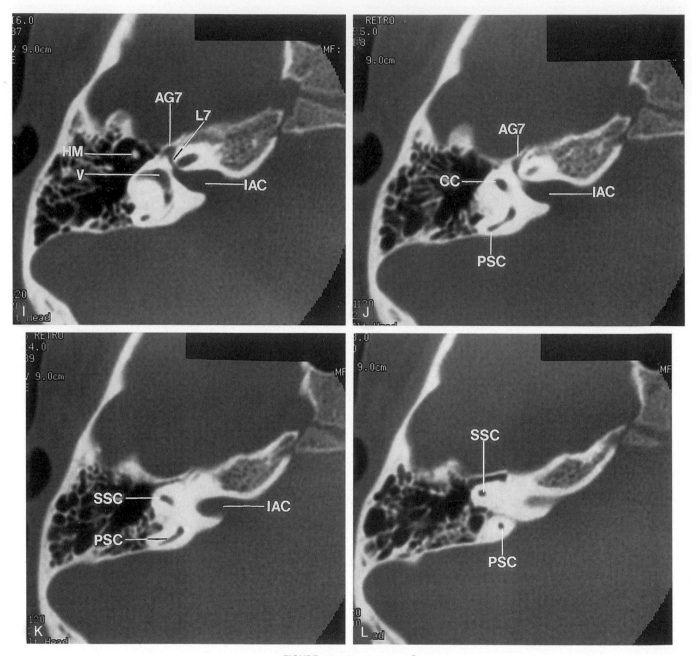

FIGURE 12–59 *Continued*

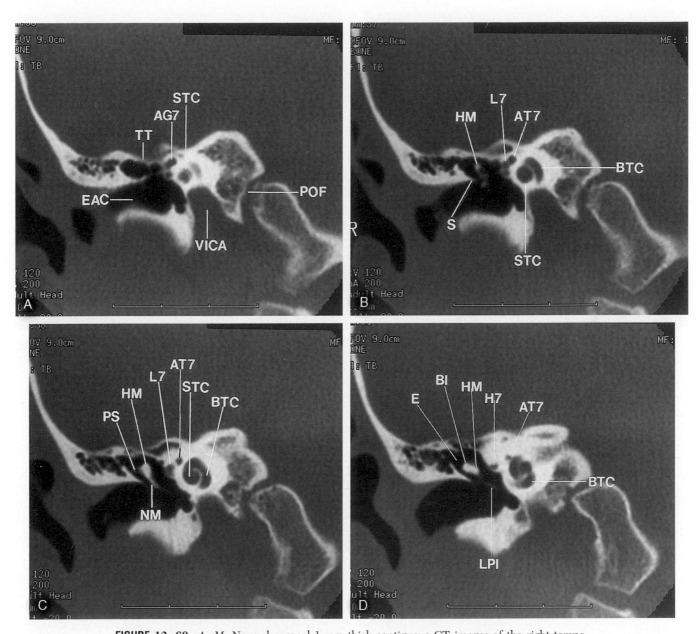

FIGURE 12–60. *A–M*, Normal coronal 1-mm thick contiguous CT images of the right temporal bone, displayed sequentially from anterior to posterior, from the level of the carotid artery to the jugular bulb. (See Box 12–1 for definitions of labels used to identify structures.)

Illustration continued on following page

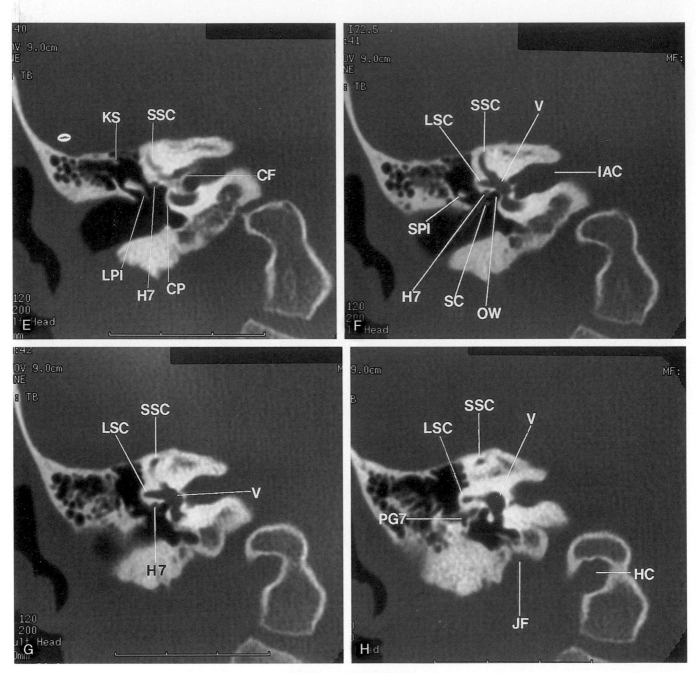

FIGURE 12–60 *Continued*

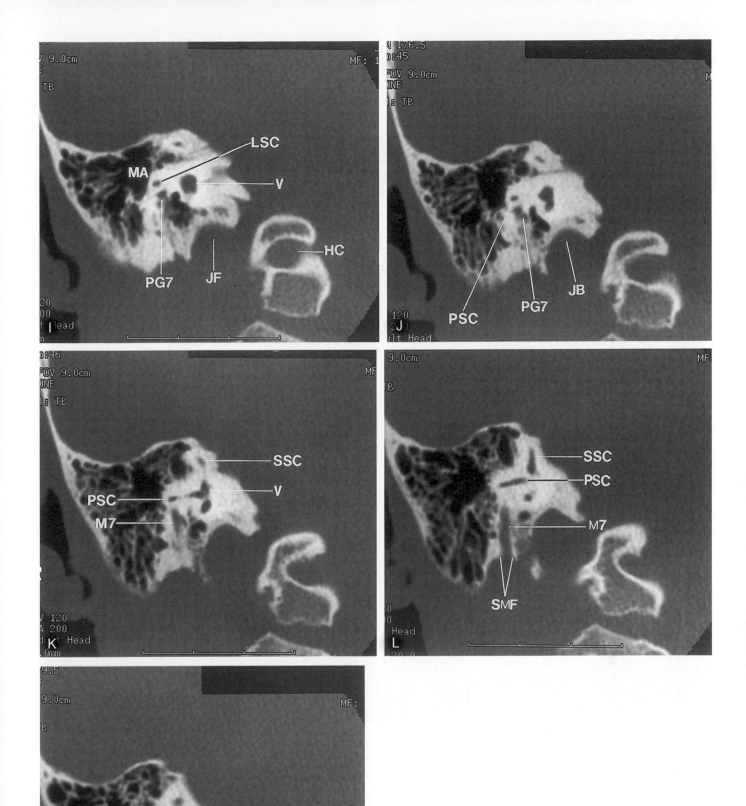

FIGURE 12–60 *Continued*

Box 12–1. Labels for Figures 12–59 to 12–61

AA	Aditus ad antrum
AG7	Anterior genu of facial nerve (geniculate ganglion segment)
AT7	Anterior tympanic segment of facial nerve
BI	Body of incus
BTC	Basal turn of cochlea
C	Clivus
CA	Cochlear aqueduct
CC	Common crus (common limb of semicircular canals)
CF	Crista falciformis
CN	Cranial nerve
COF	Condylar fossa
CP	Cochlear promontory (lateral cochlear wall projecting into middle ear cavity)
E	Epitympanum
EAC	External auditory canal
ET	Eustachian tube
FELS	Fovea for endolymphatic sac
FO	Foramen ovale
FS	Foramen spinosum
HC	Hypoglossal canal
HICA	Horizontal portion of petrous internal carotid artery
HM	Head of malleus
H7	Tympanic segment of facial nerve (horizontal segment)
IAC	Internal auditory canal
JB	Jugular bulb
JF	Jugular foramen

KS	Koerner's septum
LPI	Long process of incus
LSC	Lateral semicircular canal (horizontal semicircular canal)
L7	Labyrinthine segment of facial nerve
MA	Mastoid antrum
MC	Mandibular condyle
MO	Modiolus of cochlea
M7	Mastoid segment of facial nerve (descending segment)
NM	Neck of malleus
OW	Oval window
PG7	Posterior genu of facial nerve
POF	Petro-occipital fissure
PS	Lateral epitympanic recess (Prussak's space)
PSC	Posterior semicircular canal
RWN	Round window niche
S	Scutum
SC	Stapes crura
SMF	Stylomastoid foramen
SPI	Short process of incus
SSC	Superior semicircular canal
SSS	Sphenosquamosal suture
STC	Second turn cochlea
TT	Tegmen tympani ("roof" of the middle ear)
V	Vestibule
VA	Vestibular aqueduct (bony channel holding endolymphatic duct and part of sac)
VICA	Vertical portion of petrous internal carotid artery

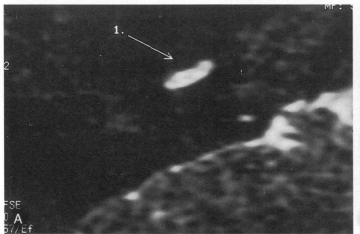

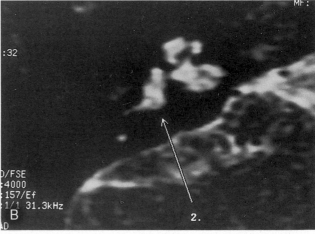

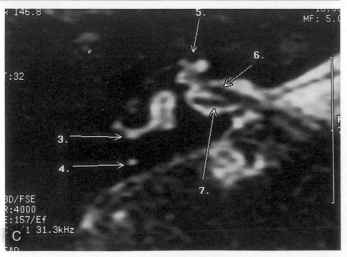

FIGURE 12–61. *A–C,* Normal thin high-resolution T$_2$-weighted axial MRI images of the right temporal bone displayed from inferior to superior, from the level of the base turn of the cochlea to the level of the superior semicircular canal. 1, BTC; 2, V; 3, LSC; 4, PSC; 5, STC; 6, CN VII; 7, CN VIII. (See Box 12–1 for definitions of labels used to identify structures.)

REFERENCES

1. Al-Ammar AY, Tewfik TL, Bond M, Schloss MD. Langerhans' cell histiocytosis: paediatric head and neck study. J Otolaryngol 28:266, 1999.
2. Angeli SI, Luxford WM, Lo WWM. Magnetic resonance imaging in the evaluation of Langerhans' cell histiocytosis of the temporal bone: case report. Otolaryngol Head Neck Surg 114:120, 1996.
3. Antonelli PJ, Varela AE, Mancuso AA. Diagnostic yield of high-resolution computed tomography for pediatric sensorineural hearing loss. Laryngoscope 109:1642, 1999.
4. Bamiou DE, Savy L, O'Mahoney C, et al. Unilateral sensorineural hearing loss and its aetiology in childhood: the contribution of computerised tomography in aetiological diagnosis and management. Int J Pediatr Otorhinolaryngol 51:91, 1999.
5. Bamiou DE, Sirimanna T. Temporal bone computed tomography findings in bilateral sensorineural hearing loss. Arch Dis Child 82:257, 2000.
6. Birman CS, Gibson WPR. Hearing loss associated with large internal auditory meatus: a report of five paediatric cases. J Laryngol Otol 113:1015, 1999.
7. Brown EW, Megerian CA, McKenna MJ, Weber A. Fibrous dysplasia of the temporal bone: imaging findings. AJR 164:679, 1995.
8. Calzolari F, Garani G, Sensi A, Martini A. Clinical and radiological evaluation in children with microtia. Br J Audiol 33:303, 1999.
9. Chinski A, Beider B, Cohen D. Fibrous dysplasia of the temporal bone. Int J Pediatr Otorhinolaryngol 47:275, 1999.
10. Chole RA, Donald PJ. Petrous apicitis clinical considerations. Ann Otol Rhinol Laryngol 92:544, 1983.
11. Chole RA. Petrous apicitis: surgical anatomy. Ann Otol Rhinol Laryngol 94:251, 1985.
12. Dahlen RT, Harnsberger HR, Gray SD, et al. Overlapping thin-section fast spin-echo MR of the large vestibular aqueduct syndrome. AJNR 18:67, 1997.
13. Davé AV, Diaz-Marchan PJ, Lee AG. Clinical and magnetic resonance imaging features of Gradenigo syndrome. Am J Ophthalmol 124:568, 1997.
14. Fernández-Latorre F, Menor-Serrano F, Alonso-Charterina S, Arenas-Jimenez J. Langerhans' cell histiocytosis of the temporal bone in pediatric patients: imaging and follow-up. AJR 174:217, 2000.
15. Garber LZ, Dort JC. Cholesteatoma: diagnosis and staging by CT scan. J Otolaryngol 23:121, 1994.
16. Green JD, Marion MS, Hinojosa R. Labyrinthitis ossificans: histopathologic consideration for cochlear implantation. Otolaryngol Head Neck Surg 104:320, 1991.
17. Hardjasudarma M, Edwards RL, Ganley JP, Aarstad RF. Magnetic resonance imaging features of Gradenigo's syndrome. Am J Otolaryngol 16:247, 1995.
18. Harnsberger HR, Dahlen RT, Shelton C, et al. Advanced techniques in magnetic resonance imaging in the evaluation of the large endolymphatic duct and sac syndrome. Laryngoscope 105:1037, 1995.
19. Hartnick CJ, Kim HY, Chute PM, Parisier SC. Preventing labyrinthitis ossificans: the role of steroids. Arch Otolaryngol Head Neck Surg 127:180, 2001.
20. Johnson J, Lalwani A. Sensorineural and conductive hearing loss associated with lateral semicircular canal malformation. Laryngoscope 110:1673, 2000.
21. Kou B, Macdonald R. Toronto's Hospital for Sick Children study of traumatic sudden sensorineural hearing loss. J Otolaryngol 27:64, 1998.
22. Lemmerling MM, Mancuso AA, Antonelli PJ, Kubilis PS. Normal modiolus: CT appearance in patients with a large vestibular aqueduct. Radiology 204:213, 1997.
23. Lourenco MTC, Yeakley JW, Ghorayeb BY. The "Y" sign of lateral dislocation of the incus. Am J Otol 16:387, 1995.
24. Lowe LH, Vezina LG. Sensorineural hearing loss in children. Radiographics 17:1079, 1997.
25. Luntz M, Balkany T, Hodges AV, Telischi FF. Cochlear implants in children with congenital inner ear malformations. Arch Otolaryngol Head Neck Surg 123:974, 1997.
26. Marianowski R, Rocton S, Ait-Amer JL, et al. Conservative management of Gradenigo syndrome in a child. Int J Pediatr Otorhinolaryngol 57:79, 2001.
27. Mayer TE, Brueckmann H, Siegert R, et al. High-resolution CT of the temporal bone in dysplasia of the auricle and external auditory canal. AJNR 18:53, 1997.
28. Meriot P, Veillon F, Garcia JF, et al. CT appearances of ossicular injuries. Radiographics 17:1445, 1997.
29. Minotti AM, Kountakis SE. Management of abducens palsy in patients with petrositis. Ann Otol Rhinol Laryngol 108:897, 1999.
30. Motamed M, Kalan A. Gradenigo's syndrome. Postgrad Med J 76:559, 2000.
31. Murakami T, Tsubaki J, Tahara Y, Nagashima T. Gradenigo's syndrome: CT and MRI findings. Pediatr Radiol 26:684, 1996.
32. Nadol JB, Hsu W. Histopathologic correlation of spiral ganglion cell count and new bone formation in the cochlea following meningogenic labyrinthitis and deafness. Ann Otol Rhinol Laryngol 100:712, 1991.
33. Naidich TP, Mann SS, Som PM. Imaging of the osseous, membranous, and perilymphatic labyrinths. Neuroimaging Clin N Am 10:23, 2000.
34. Nair SB, Abou-Elhamd A, Hawthorne M. A retrospective analysis of high resolution computed tomography in the assessment of cochlear implant patients. Clin Otolaryngol 25:55, 2000.
35. Nanduri VR, Pritchard J, Chong WK, et al. Labyrinthine involvement in Langerhans' cell histiocytosis. Int J Pediatr Otorhinolaryngol 46:109, 1998.
36. Nicol JW, Johnstone AJ. Temporal bone fractures in children: a review of 34 cases. J Accid Emerg Med 11:218, 1994.
37. Osborn AG. Diagnostic Neuroradiology. St Louis, Mosby, 1994.
38. Palacios E, Valvassori G. Fibrous dysplasia of the temporal bone. ENT—Ear Nose Throat J 78:414, 1999.
39. Papadakis CE, Skoulakis CE, Prokopakis EP, et al. Fibrous dysplasia of the temporal bone: report of a case and a review of its characteristics. ENT—Ear Nose Throat J 79:52, 2000.
40. Park AH, Kou B, Hotaling A, et al. Clinical course of pediatric congenital inner ear malformations. Laryngoscope 110:1715, 2000.
41. Phelps PD, Proops DW. Imaging for cochlear implants. J Laryngol Otol 113:21, 1999.
42. Resnick DK, Subach BR, Marion DW. The significance of carotid canal involvement in basilar cranial fracture. Neurosurgery 40:1177, 1997.
43. Robert Y, Carcasset S, Rocourt N, et al. Congenital cholesteatoma of the temporal bone: MR findings and comparison with CT. AJNR 16:755, 1995.
44. Robson CD, Robertson RL, Barnes PD. Imaging of pediatric temporal bone abnormalities. Neuroimaging Clin N Am 9:133, 1999.
45. Said H, Phang KS, Razi A, et al. Rhabdomyosarcoma of the middle ear and mastoid in children. J Laryngol Otol 102:614, 1988.
46. Seidman DA, Chute PM, Parisier S. Temporal bone imaging for cochlear implantation. Laryngoscope 104:562, 1994.
47. Shpizner BA, Holliday RA, Roland JT, et al. Postoperative imaging of the multichannel cochlear implant. AJNR 16:1517, 1995.
48. Som PM, Curtin HD. Head and Neck Imaging, 3rd ed. St Louis, Mosby, 1996.
49. Swartz JD, Harnsberger HR. Imaging of the Temporal Bone, 3rd ed. New York, Thieme Medical Publishers, 1998.
50. Swartz JD, Mandell DM, Faerber EN, et al. Labyrinthine ossification: etiologies and CT findings. Radiology 157:395, 1985.
51. Taskin Yücel O, Sarac S, Sennaroglu L. Imaging quiz case 3 [Radiology Forum]. Arch Otolaryngol 126:794, 2000.
52. Vanden Abeele D, Coen E, Parizel PM, Van De Heyning P. Can MRI replace a second look operation on cholesteatoma surgery? Acta Otolaryngol (Stockh) 119:555, 1999.
53. Weissman JL, Kamerer DB. Labyrinthitis ossificans. Am J Otolaryngol 14:363, 1993.
54. Wiatrak BJ, Pensak ML. Rhabdomyosarcoma of the ear and temporal bone. Laryngoscope 99:1188, 1989.
55. Xenellis J, Bibas A, Savy L, Maragoudakis P, et al. Monostotic fibrous dysplasia of the temporal bone. J Laryngol Otol 113:772, 1999.
56. Zampa V, Mascalchi M, Giordano GP, Bongini U, et al. Rhabdomyosarcoma of the petrous ridge. Acta Radiol 33:76, 1992.

13

Vestibular Evaluation

Joseph M. Furman, M.D., Ph.D., Margaretha L. Casselbrant, M.D., Ph.D., and
Susan L. Whitney, Ph.D.

Vertigo is defined in clinical practice as a subjective sensation of movement, such as spinning, turning, or whirling, of the patient or the surroundings. *Dizziness* is a nonspecific term used by patients to describe sensations of altered orientation to the environment that may or may not include vertigo.

While vertigo may be a symptom of a vestibular disorder in the pediatric population, patients react to and describe dizziness in different manners in relation to their age. For instance, young children cannot accurately relate symptoms of dizziness. Preschool children rarely complain of vertigo or dizziness but may feel clumsy or be perceived as such by family or teachers. Older children and adolescents are usually able to explain their symptoms well, with their explanations differing little from explanations of adults.

In any case, a vestibular abnormality should be suspected in a child who is observed to be clumsy, displays unprovoked fright, or who spontaneously clings to a parent. Sudden and recurrent bouts of unexplained nausea and vomiting also are suggestive of a vestibular abnormality.

Vertigo and dizziness are symptoms, not diagnoses. However, these symptoms may not indicate a vestibular loss, since balance is maintained through visual, proprioceptive, and vestibular signals. These three systems provide the information required for "good balance." Damage to any of these systems or an abnormality in the central nervous system (CNS) that coordinates impulses from these three sensory systems can cause symptoms.

In children as well as in adults, a careful history, physical examination, and laboratory testing can establish the cause of dizziness in most patients. In certain cases, parents are the sole source of information. It is important to allocate the time to fully investigate the medical history.

Physiologic Basis of Balance

When a hair cell is stimulated by rotation, translation, or change in orientation due to gravity, the firing rate in the eighth nerve fiber innervating that particular hair cell either increases or decreases. Movements that cause the stereocilia to bend toward the kinocilium result in a depolarization of the hair cell and cause the eighth nerve fiber to increase its firing rate, while movements that bend the stereocilia away from the kinocilium decrease the neural firing in the eighth nerve. The eighth nerve synapses in the vestibular nuclei, which consist of a superior, medial, lateral, and inferior divisions. In addition to the input from the labyrinth, the vestibular nuclei receive input from other sensory systems such as vision, somatic sensation, and audition. The sensory information is integrated and the output from the vestibular nuclei influence eye movements, truncal stability, and spatial orientation. (For anatomic description of the labyrinth, see Chapter 8.)

The vestibulo-ocular reflex is a mechanism by which a head movement automatically results in an eye movement that is equal and opposite to the head movement so that the visual axis of the eye stays on target, i.e., a leftward head movement is associated with a rightward eye movement and vice versa. The vestibulo-ocular reflex is mediated by a three-neuron arc that includes, for the horizontal system, the eighth cranial nerve, an interneuron from the vestibular nucleus to the abducens nucleus, and the motor neuron to the eye muscle. Even when the head is at rest, there are action potentials creating a "resting discharge" in each neuron in the vestibular portion of the eighth nerve. This resting discharge is unique in that it allows the neurons to sense motion in both the excitatory and the inhibitory direction by increasing and decreasing their firing rate, respectively.

Another feature of the vestibulo-ocular reflex is that the two vestibular nuclear complexes on each side of the brain stem cooperate with one another in such a way that, for the horizontal system, when one nucleus is excited, the other is inhibited. This reciprocal "push-pull" effect increases the sensitivity of the vestibulo-ocular reflex. The CNS responds to differences in neural activity between the two vestibular complexes. When there is no head movement, the neural activity, i.e., the resting discharge, is symmetrical in the two vestibular nuclei. The brain detects no differences in neural activity and concludes that the head is not moving (Fig. 13–1A). When the head moves, e.g., to the left, endolymph flow produces an excitatory response in the labyrinth on the side toward which the head moves, e.g., on the left, and an inhibitory response on the opposite side, e.g., on the

No Head Movement

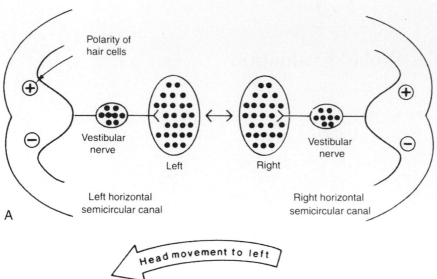

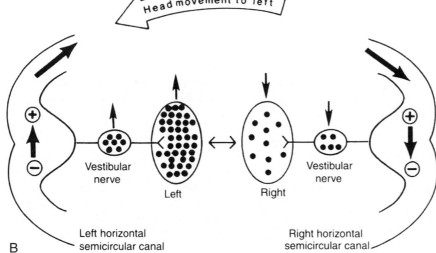

FIGURE 13–1. Schematic illustrations of the "push-pull" effect of the vestibular-ocular reflex: *A*, no head movement in healthy subject; *B*, head movement to the left in healthy subject; *C*, right acute peripheral vestibular injury.

Right Acute Peripheral Vestibular Injury

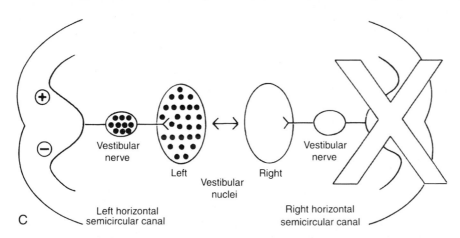

right. Thus, neural activity in the vestibular nerve and nuclei, e.g., on the left and right, increases and decreases, respectively (see Fig. 13–1B). The brain interprets this difference in neural activity between the two vestibular complexes as a head movement and generates appropriate

vestibulo-ocular and postural responses. This reciprocal push-pull balance between the two labyrinths is disrupted following labyrinthine injury.

An acute loss of peripheral vestibular function unilaterally, e.g., on the right, causes a loss of resting neural

Chronic Right Peripheral Vestibular Injury

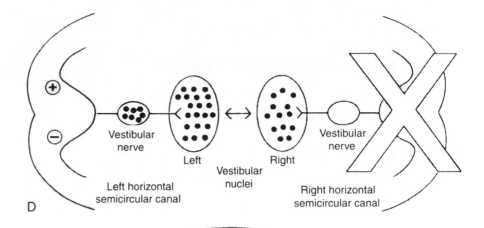

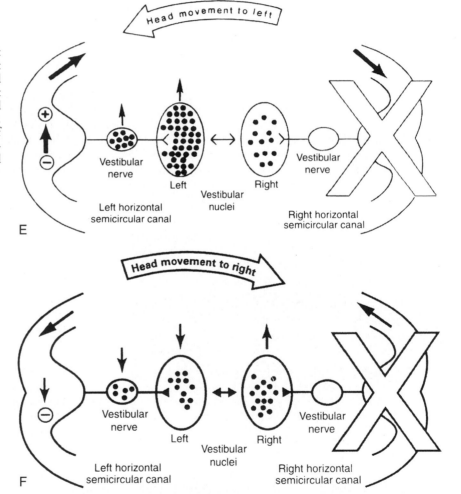

FIGURE 13–1. *Continued. D,* chronic right peripheral vestibular injury; *E,* chronic right peripheral vestibular injury during head movement to the left; and *F,* chronic right peripheral vestibular injury during head movement to the right. For details see text. (From Furman JM, Cass SP. Evaluation of dizzy patients. Slide lecture series. American Academy of Otolaryngology-Head and Neck Surgery Inc., 1994.)

discharge activity in that vestibular nerve and the ipsilateral nucleus (see Fig. 13–1C). Since the brain responds to differences between the two labyrinths, this will be interpreted by the brain as a rapid head movement toward the healthy labyrinth, e.g., toward the left. "Corrective" eye movements are produced toward the opposite side, resulting in nystagmus, with the slow component moving toward the abnormal side, e.g., the right, and with the quick components of nystagmus moving toward the healthy labyrinth, e.g., the left. Through compensatory mechanisms, the CNS restores the resting discharge activity within the deafferented vestibular nucleus, which reduces the asymmetry of neural activity within the bilateral vestibular nuclei and thus partially restores a functional vestibulo-ocular reflex (see Fig. 13–1D). Thus, during head movements with only one functional labyrinth, although neural activity within only one vestibular nerve is modulated both up and down, this activity causes both increases and decreases in vestibular nuclei activity (see Figs. 13–1E and F). A unilateral loss of vestibular function thus results in a reduction of sensitivity to vestibular stimuli (i.e., a reduced "gain" of the vestibulo-ocular reflex) and an asymmetric response.

Office Evaluation of Patients with Dizziness

At the initial visit, in addition to the chief complaint, a complete medical history that includes associated symptoms, past medical history, family history, and medication use is mandatory. A questionnaire sent to the patient before the initial assessment can be useful because it helps the patient or the parents to think about the child's dizziness before the assessment. The responses should be reviewed with the patient/parent at the initial visit.

After the interview, a complete physical examination should be performed, including pneumatic otoscopy and, if possible, otomicroscopy; a neurologic examination, with particular emphasis on the cranial nerves; and an examination of the eyes for spontaneous nystagmus with and without fixation and positional testing by using Frenzel goggles (Fig. 13–2) or video infrared goggles.

History

Chief Complaint. It is important that the child explain the symptoms in his or her own vocabulary and describe associated sensations such as headache, nausea, vomiting, or motion sickness. It might be helpful to relate the patient's symptoms to experiences such as being on a

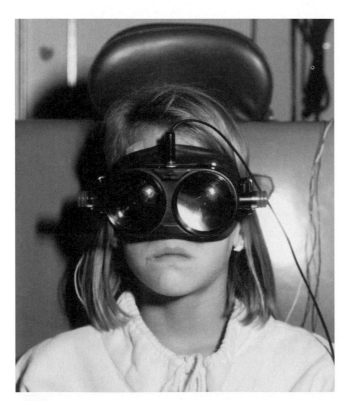

FIGURE 13–2. Frenzel glasses with magnifying lenses and built-in illumination to facilitate observation of the eye movement.

merry-go-round. It is important to establish the onset, duration, and frequency of dizziness episodes and to associate the episodes with certain activities.

Otologic Symptoms. To determine otologic symptoms, the clinician should inquire about the presence of hearing loss (sensorineural or conductive), its onset, evolution or progression, fluctuation and worsening, and improving or stable status. Does the patient have tinnitus or a feeling of fullness? Is the hearing loss bilateral or unilateral? Does the child have a history of otitis media? Is otorrhea present? Is the patient complaining of otalgia? Previous audiograms, if available, should be reviewed.

Neurologic Symptoms. To establish the presence of neurologic symptoms, the clinician should determine whether there have been instances of convulsions, altered mental status, weakness, numbness, disturbances of swallowing or taste, coughing, facial paralysis, or blurring and loss of vision.

Past Medical History. In establishing past medical history, the clinician should acquire information regarding pregnancy and delivery, e.g., history of birth trauma, anoxia at delivery, presence of infectious diseases, e.g., measles, mumps, or syphilis, and presence of CNS infections, including meningitis. Is there a history of administration of ototoxic medications in the neonatal period? Has the patient had diabetes, hypothyroidism or other endocrine or renal disease, eye disorders, epilepsy, noise exposure, or relevant previous surgeries?

Family History. In establishing the family history, the clinician should inquire in particular whether there is a family history of migraine, epilepsy, hearing loss or deafness, endocrine or renal disease, or neurofibromatosis.

Physical Examination

The physical examination of children requires time and patience. Gaining the child's confidence before starting the examination may help a great deal to get the most from a physical examination. This can be accomplished by explaining, in words the child can understand, what is going to be done and how it is going to be done, sometimes by offering a book, a toy, or even a reward to the child. General physical examination should include obtaining the patient's blood pressure with the patient sitting, standing, and lying down.

Ear examination should include pneumatic otoscopy or the use of an operating microscope. The nose, throat, and neck should also be evaluated as part of a complete physical examination.

Since vertigo in childhood can be a symptom of a neurologic abnormality, a complete neurologic evaluation with special attention to examination of the cranial nerves is appropriate. The optic nerve is tested by standard acuity, and both eyes are tested separately. The clinician checks for visual field defects and visualizes the fundi. The oculomotor, trochlear, and abducens nerves are tested by examining the pupils and extraocular motility. The trigeminal nerve is checked by testing sensations in the three peripheral divisions by stimulation of the forehead, cheek, and mental regions. The corneal reflex should be tested as well. Mastication function is examined by asking the patient to bite and observing the action of the temporalis and masseter muscles. The facial nerve is assessed by observing voluntary motion in all areas of the face and by evaluation of facial symmetry. The auditory nerve is tested by use of tuning forks. The glossopharyngeal nerve is tested by assessing sensation in the posterior third of the tongue and tonsillar pillars. The vagus nerve can be evaluated by assessing the gag reflex. The spinal accessory nerve is assessed by elevation of the shoulders and rotation of the head. The hypoglossal nerve is tested by asking the patient to protrude the tongue.

The child should also be observed when walking or running for incoordination of movements, i.e., ataxia. Dysmetria may be demonstrated by the finger-to-nose and heel-to-shin test. Additional abnormalities associated with cerebellar lesions can be assessed by evaluating the patient for dysdiadochokinesia, hypotonia, and decreased deep tendon reflexes.

Evaluation of Nystagmus

The eye movement examination can best be performed in the office through observation and by use of Frenzel goggles to look for the presence or absence of spontaneous nystagmus (see Fig. 13–2). Frenzel goggles are +20 lenses with internal illumination shining into the eyes. The advantages of Frenzel goggles are that they reduce visual fixation and magnify the size of the eye. An alternative to Frenzel goggles is the infrared video system.

Spontaneous and Gaze-Evoked Nystagmus

Spontaneous nystagmus is an involuntary, rhythmic movement of the eyes not induced by any external stimulation. Spontaneous nystagmus has two components: slow and fast (Fig. 13–3). Nystagmus is named by the fast component, which is easily identified. Spontaneous nystagmus is tested by having the patient look straight ahead. Gaze-evoked nystagmus is assessed by having the patient devi-

ate the eyes laterally (no greater than 30 degrees). Nystagmus observed at the extreme limits of gaze, i.e., greater than 30 degrees, is usually physiologic. Nystagmus is classified in terms of severity by the "degree" of nystagmus. *First-degree vestibular nystagmus* is present only when the eyes are looking toward the fast component. This is the weakest intensity of spontaneous nystagmus. *Second-degree nystagmus* is present when the eyes are looking straight ahead and on looking toward the fast component (Fig. 13–4). In *third-degree nystagmus*, the nystagmus is present when the eyes are looking away from the fast component and is therefore seen in all eye positions. This represents the strongest degree of spontaneous nystagmus.

Positional Nystagmus

Positional testing is performed with the use of maneuvers that may produce nystagmus or vertigo. Static positional nystagmus is assessed by placing the patient in each of the following six positions: sitting, supine, supine with the head turned to the right, supine with the head turned to the left, and right and left lateral positions. Frenzel goggles should be used in conducting the test. The nystagmus presents as soon as the patient assumes the position and persists for as long as the patient remains in the provocative position. Paroxysmal positional nystagmus, on the other hand, has a brief latency, fatigues on repeat provocations, is usually associated with vertigo, and is evaluated by the Dix-Hallpike maneuver. To perform the Dix-Hallpike maneuver, the patient is moved rapidly from the sitting position to a right or a left head-hanging position.

Perilymph Fistula Test

Perilymph fistula testing can be performed by pressing the tragus and thereby creating a positive pressure in the external auditory canal or by applying positive and negative pressure in the external ear canal with use of a

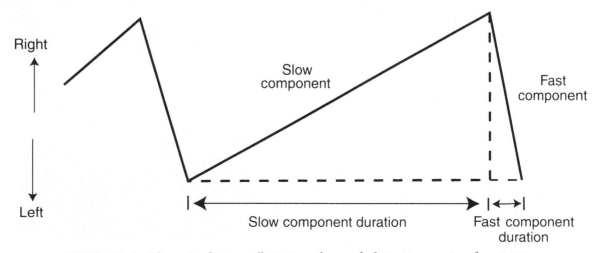

FIGURE 13–3. Schematic diagram illustrating slow and fast components of nystagmus. (Adapted from Jacobson GP, Newman CW, Quartet JM. Handbook of Balance Function Testing. St. Louis, Mosby–Year Book, 1993.)

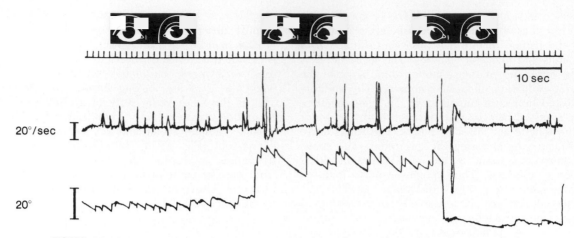

20°/sec

20°

FIGURE 13–4. A spontaneous nystagmus toward the right is increased by gaze toward the right and nearly abolished by gaze toward the left (second-degree nystagmus). (From Henriksson NG, Pfaltz CR, Torok N, Rubin W. A Synopsis of the Vestibular System: An Effort to Standardize Vestibular Conceptions, Tests, and Their Evaluation. Basel, Sandoz, 1972.)

politzer bag or a tympanometer while observing the patient's eyes behind Frenzel goggles. The fistula test response is positive if nystagmus and a sensation of dizziness are generated (see Chapters 21 and 24).

Motor Function Test

A child's motor performance changes with age and, as a result, no one motor performance tool is the gold standard across all developmental ages. Several reliable, valid tools are used to assess "balance" performance in children. The motor performance measures discussed herein include the *Peabody Development Motor Scale* (PDMS),[4] the *Bruininks-Oseretsky Test of Motor Proficiency* (BOTMP),[2] and the *Pediatric Clinical Test of Sensory Interaction for Balance* (P-CTSIB).

The Peabody Developmental Motor Scale

The PDMS was developed to screen, evaluate, and determine program planning for children and to identify gross and fine motor skills that are delayed or abnormal. The PDMS assesses developmental changes in children. Researchers have demonstrated the tool's construct, predictive, and concurrent validity; furthermore, it appears to be responsive to change over time. A component of the PDMS (the gross motor scale) is commonly used to assess motor performance. The gross motor scale includes assessment of reflexes, balance, nonlocomotor skills, locomotion, and the ability to grasp and move objects in the test environment. Raw scores, percentile scores, z-scores, and a developmental quotient can be obtained for each section and from the total gross motor battery. The tool was developed for use with children aged from birth to 7 years. The gross motor battery of the PDMS provides extensive information about the child's motor performance (Fig. 13–5), but it is time and energy intensive and requires a large, quiet space and equipment that is not typically found in an otolaryngology office.

The Bruininks-Oseretsky Test of Motor Proficiency

The BOTMP was developed for use in children from 4½ to 14½ years of age. It includes both gross and fine motor components. The BOTMP has more difficult balance items than the PDMS. The BOTMP balance subsection includes single leg stance on a solid surface, standing

FIGURE 13–5. A 4-year-old child attempts to skip as part of the Peabody Developmental Motor Scale.

FIGURE 13–6. *A*, A child standing on the medium-density foam with her eyes open (condition 4) and standing on the foam with the visual conflict dome (condition 5) (*B*). Both conditions are part of the Pediatric Clinical Test of Sensory Organization and Balance.

on a beam, standing on a beam with eyes closed, walking forward on a line, balance beam walking, tandem walking on a solid surface and on a beam, and stepping over a stick while on a balance beam. The complete battery also includes running speed, eight items of bilateral coordination, and strength. A standard score, percentile rank, and stanine are computed for the gross motor composite, fine motor composite, and the entire battery.

The BOTMP is generally the tool used after children become able to complete the PDMS gross motor items.

TABLE 13–1. Types of Sensory Inputs during the Six Testing Conditions Using the Clinical Test of Sensory Interaction for Balance

Testing Conditions	Sensory Inputs		
	Vision	*Somatosensory*	*Vestibular*
1. Eyes open, hard floor	+	+	+
2. Eyes closed, hard floor	−	+	+
3. Conflict dome, hard floor	−	+	+
4. Eyes open, foam floor	+	−	+
5. Eyes closed, foam floor	−	−	+
6. Conflict dome, foam floor	−	−	+

+, sensory input present; −, sensory input absent/distorted.

The BOTMP takes much less time and equipment than the PDMS; it also takes considerably less space.

The Pediatric Clinical Test of Sensory Integration and Balance

The P-CTSIB was developed as a modification of Shumay-Cook and Horak's balance test for adults.[8] It has been shown to have fair to good reliability in children. Children stand on medium-density foam (Fig. 13–6*A*) or with a visual conflict dome (see Fig. 13–6*B*) for 30 seconds. Body sway under six sensory conditions is determined with the malleoli touching and in tandem stance (heels and toes touching). The six sensory conditions are listed in Table 13–1. The P-CTSIB is an inexpensive method to replicate dynamic posturography in a clinical setting.

Audiologic Evaluation

Behavioral Audiometry

Behavioral testing that is appropriate for the patient's age is performed to assess whether there is a concomitant hearing loss and to help define the side of the lesion. The audiologic evaluation should also include, if possible, speech reception threshold and word recognition score, acoustic reflex, and tone decay. A tuning fork (512 Hz) should be used to confirm the audiometric findings. Masking is mandatory, specifically when there is a difference of hearing sensitivity between ears. The Bárány box is a useful tool for implementing office masking, or a piece of paper can be rubbed in the ear not tested. Tympanometry is performed to assess middle-ear status. (For detailed description, see Chapter 11.)

Auditory Brain Stem Response Audiometry

In cases of unilateral hearing loss and asymmetric hearing loss, the auditory brain stem response is extremely useful in the diagnostic evaluation process to determine the site of the lesion. The procedure is noninvasive and excellent for testing in small children and children who cannot cooperate on behavioral testing. Auditory brain stem testing may require sedation for small children.

Clicks are delivered through earphones and are monitored by signal averaging while the patient is relaxed or asleep. The waveform and latency are studied, and the waves are compared in both ears as well as with those of normal subjects. The latencies are the most sensitive indicator of disease. Tumors can result in increased latencies and prolonged waves I to V. (For detailed description, see Chapter 11.)

Additional Testing

After the initial office visit, with the completion of the medical history and the physical examination, the physician will have a basic understanding of the problem, classifying the disorder tentatively as nonvestibular, peripheral vestibular, or central vestibular disease. The physician determines whether further work-up is necessary to document and confirm the initial impression. Further tests may include vestibular testing, laboratory testing, and imaging.

Vestibular laboratory testing is recommended in any child with a history of dizziness in whom a thorough history and physical examination has not established a diagnosis, to differentiate between a peripheral or central vestibular lesion, and to identify side of lesion in a peripheral abnormality. Because children with severe sensorineural hearing loss may have vestibular abnormalities, vestibular laboratory testing is recommended.[7] This is especially important in infants and young children with delayed motor development.[9]

Laboratory testing is indicated when a nonvestibular condition such as metabolic abnormalities or blood dyscrasia is suspected of causing the "dizziness." Laboratory tests include complete blood count, serum glucose, thy-

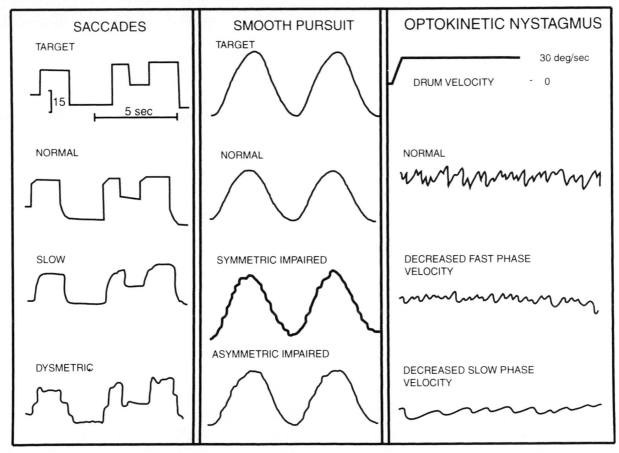

FIGURE 13–7. Examples of normal responses and abnormalities of the saccadic eye movement system, the pursuit system, and optokinetic nystagmus. (From Baloh RW. The Essentials of Neurotology. Philadelphia, FA Davis, 1984.)

roid function, triglyceride, and cholesterol determinations; fluorescent treponemal antibody absorption test; erythrocyte sedimentation rate; and rheumatoid factor, antinuclear antibody, and autoimmune studies when appropriate.

Imaging studies include computed tomography with or without contrast enhancement for the evaluation of bony structures of the temporal bone and middle ear. Computed tomography is performed to rule out any congenital malformations or bony abnormalities caused by infectious processes or a cholesteatoma eroding the bone or a temporal bone fracture. Magnetic resonance imaging with gadolinium injection is the most important test for ruling out a CNS lesion, cerebellopontine angle mass, posterior fossa disease, and craniovertebral abnormalities. (For detailed reading, see Chapter 12.)

Vestibular Laboratory Evaluation

Vestibular laboratory testing may be helpful in distinguishing a peripheral vestibular abnormality from a central vestibular abnormality. Also, vestibular laboratory testing may identify the side of lesion in a peripheral vestibular abnormality. In addition, it provides permanent documentation, and changes can be followed up by repeat testing.

Vestibular laboratory testing includes vestibulo-ocular and vestibulospinal tests. Both types of tests provide only an indirect measure of the function of the vestibular end organs, in that they rely on measures of motor response, i.e., eye movements or postural sway, resulting from vestibular sensory input.

Electronystagmography

Electronystagmography (ENG) or video-ENG is the laboratory diagnostic tool most commonly used to study patients with complaints of dizziness, vertigo, or imbalance. Eye movements are recorded with electro-oculography or infrared video goggles. The physiologic basis for electro-oculography is the corneal-retinal dipole potential. This is created by the metabolic activity of the retina, which causes the eye to act as a dipole oriented along the visual axis.

ENG/video-ENG includes ocular motor testing, positional testing, and caloric testing and provides a permanent record of the spontaneous nystagmus or induced nystagmus (positional or caloric) with objective measurement of the response. For electro-oculography, surface electrodes are placed either bitemporally to record the combined motion of the eyes or at the medial and lateral canthus of each eye to assess the eyes separately. For video-ENG, comfortable darkened or see-through goggles with an infrared camera are used. The ENG/video-ENG evaluation requires approximately 1 hour. Patients should not be allowed to take sedatives or vestibular suppressant medications that can alter the test results for 2 days before testing. Children and adolescents can tolerate the ENG/video-ENG examination readily, but patience, understanding, and cooperation between technician and child are the key to success.

Ocular Motor Testing

Ocular motor testing consists of several tests and is designed to evaluate the ocular motor system, i.e., neural motor output independent of the vestibular system (Fig. 13–7). Abnormalities in the ocular motor system may affect the vestibulo-ocular reflex and misleading conclusions can be drawn.

Saccade testing, which includes calibration of the equipment, is performed by having the patient look alternatively at two targets separated by 20 degrees. By convention, upward displacement of the pen indicates eye movement to the right, and downward movement represents eye movement to the left. More extensive testing of the integrity of the saccade system uses a computer-controlled sequence of target jumps. Saccade abnormalities are defined as overshooting the target (hypermetric saccades) and undershooting the target (hypometric saccades). Disorders in the saccadic system suggest a CNS abnormality.

A *search for nystagmus*, including spontaneous nystagmus and gaze-evoked nystagmus, is recorded with fixation and without fixation (closing the eyes or darkness) (Fig. 13–8) and by asking the patient to look 30 degrees to the right and left (see Fig. 13–4). Spontaneous nystagmus that is present in darkness without fixation and decreases or resolves with fixation suggests a peripheral vestibular disorder. However, spontaneous nystagmus that is present with fixation and does not significantly decrease with loss of fixation is most likely a CNS abnormality.

Sinusoidal pursuit tracking involves asking the patient to follow a moving target back and forth along a slow pendular path. Normal subjects can follow a target

Spontaneous Vestibular Nystagmus

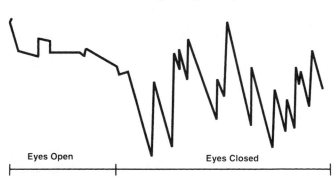

FIGURE 13–8. Recording of spontaneous nystagmus. Note that during eyes open (with fixation) the patient had almost no nystagmus, but during eyes open in the dark (without fixation) a latent vestibular nystagmus became manifest. Upward deflections denote rightward movement. (From Furman JM, Cass SP. Evaluation of dizzy patients. Slide lecture series. American Academy of Otolaryngology-Head and Neck Surgery Inc., 1994.)

smoothly without interruption. Abnormalities of pursuit tracking are caused by lesions in the CNS.

Optokinetic nystagmus is induced by a visual pattern (usually black and white vertical stripes) moving across the visual field. The test is performed at different speeds with the stripes moving in the clockwise and counter-clockwise directions. In children, the projection of animals or friendly figures may help them perform the same task successfully. Abnormalities include asymmetries or absence of responses. Abnormalities of the optokinetic system suggest a CNS abnormality.

Positional Testing

Positional testing includes both static and paroxysmal testing. *Static positional testing* includes sitting, supine, head left, head right, left lateral, and right lateral positions. Static positional nystagmus, contrary to paroxysmal nystagmus, presents as soon as the patient assumes the provocative position and persists for as long as the patient stays in that position. When static positional nystagmus is observed, it is important to assess the effect of visual fixation. Failure to suppress static positional nystagmus with visual fixation is suggestive of a CNS lesion. Static positional nystagmus is otherwise a nonspecific, nonlocalizing sign.

Paroxysmal positional testing includes moving rapidly from a sitting position to head-hanging right and head-hanging left positions (Dix-Hallpike's maneuver). During paroxysmal positional testing, the patient looks straight ahead with the eyes open behind darkened goggles while eye movements are recorded with ENG/video-ENG. Paroxysmal positional nystagmus is associated with vertigo, has a brief latency of 5 to 10 seconds, fatigues on repeat provocations, and is suggestive of a peripheral lesion.

Caloric Testing

Caloric testing is the mainstay of vestibular laboratory testing and produces nystagmus by thermal stimulation of the vestibular system. The advantage of caloric stimulation is that each labyrinth can be tested separately. Furthermore, it can also be performed in infants and young children. The patient is placed in a position so the horizontal semicircular canals lie in the vertical plane (head elevated 30 degrees). Caloric stimulation is thought to be based on a convection current in the horizontal semicircular canal induced by a thermal stimulus colder or warmer than body temperature in the external auditory canal. The gradient of temperature produces a change in the specific gravity of the endolymph in the horizontal semicircular canal, which causes a coupler deflection and a change in activity of the vestibular nerve. Cold irrigation produces a utriculofugal deflection (fast nystagmus component away from the ear); warm irrigation produces a utriculopedal displacement (fast nystagmus component toward the ear) (Fig. 13–9). There are several methods of producing a caloric stimulation.

Most caloric tests use direct water stimulation. This technique requires an intact eardrum and a patent and unblocked external auditory canal. In cases of eardrum

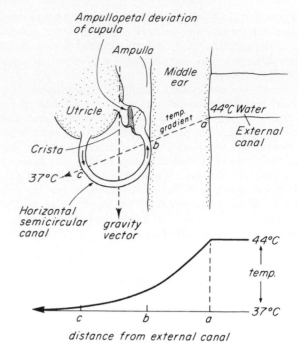

FIGURE 13–9. Mechanism of caloric stimulation of the horizontal semicircular canal (see text for details). (From Baloh RW, Hornbill V. Clinical Neurophysiology of the Vestibular System, 2nd ed. Philadelphia, FA Davis, 1990.)

perforation or tympanostomy tubes, air caloric or closed-loop water irrigation can be used to avoid contamination of the middle ear by water. Binaural bithermal caloric testing uses stimuli of 30°C and 44°C, and each canal is irrigated for 30 seconds with 250 mL of water. There is a rest period of 5 minutes between each irrigation. If there is no response to cold and warm irrigation, ice water irrigation should be performed. In children with bilateral vestibular loss, caloric responses are reduced or absent in both ears. However, caloric responses can be reduced or even absent with normal rotational responses in the same patient. This can be explained by the fact that caloric stimulation is nonphysiologic, whereas rotational stimulation is the natural stimulus to the labyrinth.

There are several different methods to measure the caloric response. These include peak slow-component velocity, nystagmus duration, and nystagmus frequency. The most common parameter used is the peak slow-component velocity, whose magnitude reflects the intensity of the vestibular response. Many vestibular laboratories have computerized systems that incorporate software to determine slow-component velocity and calculate vestibular paresis or hypofunction and directional preponderance. To compare the responsiveness of one ear to the other ear, it is established practice to use Jongkees' formula to compute a percent of "reduced vestibular response" (Eq. 13–1):

JONGKEES' FORMULA

Reduced Vestibular Response Formula:
$$\frac{(R30° + R44°) - (L30° + L44°)}{(R30° + R44° + L30° + L44°)} \times 100\%$$

Directional Preponderance Formula:

$$\frac{(R30° + L44°) - (R44 + L30°)}{(R30° + R44° + L30° + L44°)} \times 100\%$$

R = Right
L = Left

For many laboratories, normal limits are considered a reduced vestibular response of more than 24%. A *reduced vestibular response,* i.e., a vestibular paresis, suggests a peripheral vestibular lesion. *Directional preponderance,* i.e., more nystagmus beating in one direction than the other, is a nonlocalizing sign that is either central or peripheral.

Rotational Testing

Rotational stimulation, the natural stimulus to the semicircular canals, can create a nystagmic response. Bárány[1] described the use of a manual rotary chair to produce an observable nystagmus after cessation of rotation. This technique has been improved by use of computers and sophisticated hardware. Rotational testing has advantages and disadvantages. Advantages are as follows: (1) the rotation test causes less nausea than caloric stimulation, (2) the rotational stimulus is physiologic, (3) precise patterns of acceleration can be delivered, and (4) infants and young children can be tested because the child can sit on the parent's lap during testing. The main disadvantage is that rotation stimulates both labyrinths at the same time and thus it is impossible to identify the vestibular function of each labyrinth separately. Thus, the caloric response and the rotation test are complementary.

The rotation of the chair is produced by torque motors to control the stimulus precisely. Many different trajectories of rotation can be used for rotational testing. The most common trajectories are sinusoidal harmonic acceleration. Usually, rotation is in the horizontal plane, i.e., the chair is rotated about an earth vertical axis. For the semicircular canals to be brought into the horizontal plane to be maximally stimulated by the angular acceleration, the patient's head is tilted about 15 to 20 degrees forward (Fig. 13–10). Testing is performed in darkness to eliminate visual fixation. Electro-oculographic or video-ENG recordings are made of the eye movements induced by the rotation. The slow-component eye velocity is compared with chair velocity. Three parameters are derived from rotational testing: gain, phase, and symmetry.

Gain is a measure of the *magnitude* of the response (eye velocity) in relation to the stimulus (rotational chair velocity). Reduced gain indicates decreased vestibular sensitivity. Unilateral vestibular loss may not reduce gain less than normal. Thus, reduced gain usually indicates bilateral vestibular loss.

Phase describes the *timing* relationship between the stimulus (rotational chair velocity) and the response (eye velocity). If the eye movement is perfectly compensatory for the head movement, then the eye movement is 180 degrees out of phase with the head movement. This, by convention, is a zero phase lead. Perfectly compensatory eye movement (zero phase lead) usually occurs at higher

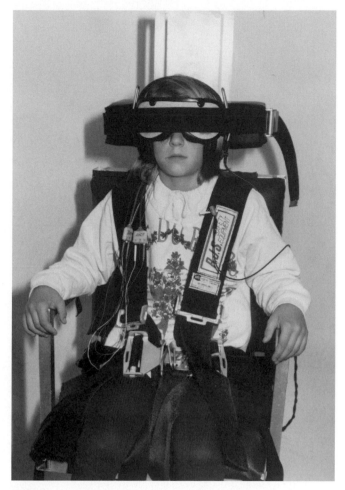

FIGURE 13–10. Rotational testing. The chair is rotating back and forth with the head tilted forward slightly; the testing is performed in darkness to avoid visual fixation.

frequencies (i.e., greater than 0.1 Hz). Large phase leads are present at low frequency (i.e., less than 0.05 Hz). Phase is a highly sensitive but nonspecific measure of vestibular system abnormalities. Phase changes with peripheral vestibular injury, and the changes are permanent. While phase is obtained from sinusoidal rotation, the *time constant,* a similar measure, is obtained from constant velocity rotation and describes how rapidly the vestibular nystagmus decays after an abrupt stop of the rotational chair. This is also a sensitive measure, but it is nonspecific.

Asymmetry of the response, i.e., directional preponderance, is derived by computing the difference between the velocity of the eye movement to right and left. The significance of asymmetry is similar to that of directional preponderance in the caloric evaluation, mainly a nonspecific sign.

Changes seen in gain, phase, and asymmetry do not indicate the site or the side of the lesion. However, rotational testing measures change in response to vestibular disease and can be used to monitor the patient's progress. Rotational testing, like many other tests in the vestibular laboratory, is helpful if it is used in relation to the results

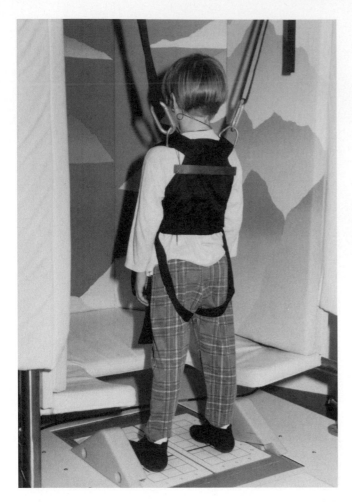

FIGURE 13–11. EquiTest system (NeuroCom International, Inc.) shows the child standing on the platform surrounded by a visual scene. A safety harness is attached to the child should loss of balance occur. The platform surface and visual surround are capable of moving independently or simultaneously. Pressure-sensing strain gauges beneath the platform surface detect the patient's sway by measuring vertical and horizontal forces applied to the surface.

EquiTest™ Conditions

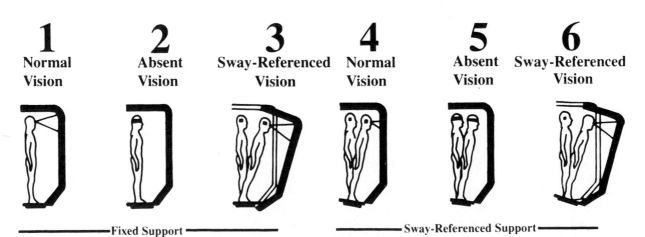

FIGURE 13–12. The six sensory testing conditions of the EquiTest posturography platform (From NeuroCom International, Inc., Clackman, Ore.)

of the entire neuro-otologic assessment rather than as an isolated test.

Dynamic Platform Posturography

As mentioned earlier, balance and posture are maintained by three sensory inputs: visual, proprioceptive, and vestibular. Platform posturography can be used to assess a patient's reliance on these sensory inputs as well as the motor responses generated to maintain proper equilibrium when the floor is moved. Computerized dynamic posturography is marketed commercially under the trade name EquiTest by NeuroCom International, Inc. (Fig. 13–11). Both the platform and the background move while the anteroposterior sway of the patient standing on the platform is monitored. Six different sensory conditions are used to test the patient's ability to use combinations of sensory inputs (Fig. 13–12). The six EquiTest conditions are comparable to the six sensory conditions described in Table 13–1.

The testing software supplied by NeuroCom allows two broad categories of tests: (1) recording of responses to small, brief movements of the support surface, either translations or rotations, and (2) recording of postural sway during various combinations of sensory inputs. These two types of tests have been called the *motor control tests* (formerly the movement coordination tests) and *sensory organization tests*. The motor control tests use a total of nine forward and nine backward translations of three different magnitudes. Also, five sequential platform rotations are delivered in the toes-up and then the toes-down direction. The forces generated during these maneuvers are analyzed by computer. The patient's responses are compared with responses from an age-appropriate group of normal subjects. The sensory organization

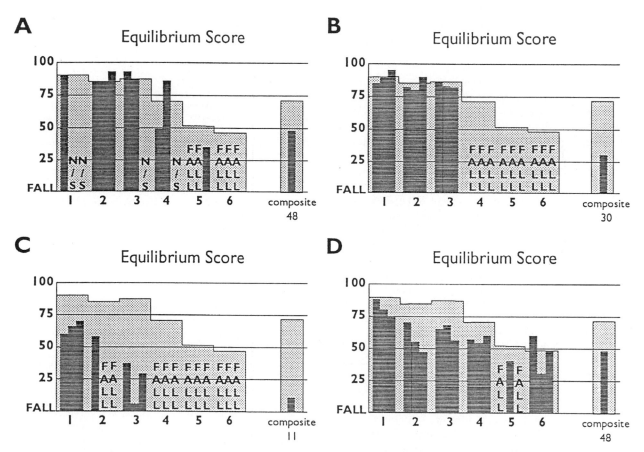

FIGURE 13–13. Patterns of abnormality on computerized dynamic platform posturography. Results shown were obtained by using the EquiTest system. The six sensory conditions refer to those shown in Table 13–1. The ordinate refers to peak-to-peak sway amplitude with 100 = 12 degrees of sway and 0 = a fall. *A,* Vestibular pattern. Note that the patient swayed excessively on conditions 5 and 6. *B,* Surface-dependent pattern. This pattern is also known as a combined visual-vestibular pattern. Note that the patient fell on conditions 4, 5, and 6, all of which are characterized by inaccurate somatosensory information because of a sway-referenced support surface. *C,* Severe pattern. Note the excessive sway on all conditions with a low composite score. *D,* Nonspecific pattern. Because sway on condition 6 was within normal limits while all other conditions were associated with excessive sway, this patient should be suspected of having produced an aphysiologic result, possibly on the basis of poor cooperation. (From Fuhrman JM. The role of posturography in the management of vestibular patients. Otolaryngol Head Neck Surg 112:8–15, 1995.)

test uses six sensory conditions described earlier. For the two conditions wherein the visual surround is *moving* (conditions 3 and 6) and for the three conditions wherein the platform is *moving* (conditions 4, 5, and 6), the movement of the visual surround or the platform is coupled to the sway of the patient in an attempt to "stabilize" the visual surround or platform rotations, thereby providing a nearly null or, at best, a distorted input from that sensation, i.e., vision or somatosensation, respectively. The sensory organization test is the portion of computerized dynamic posturography most useful in the assessment of patients with suspected vestibular disorders. By providing reduced or distorted sensory information from the visual system and somatosensory system, the sensory organization test forces patients to rely on their vestibular sensations to maintain upright balance. In this manner, conditions 5 and 6 assess how patients use vestibular information when it is the only available input providing reliable information.

Posturography and Vestibular Disorders—Results from the Medical Literature

Several authors have studied large populations of patients suspected of having vestibular disorders and noted, as would be expected from the design of the sensory organization test, that patients with ongoing vestibular disorders have abnormal postural sway during conditions 5 and 6. Various other patterns aside from the "5,6" pattern also have been discussed in the literature and are shown in Figure 13–13.

Figure 13–13A illustrates the typical 5,6 pattern seen in patients with acute vestibular imbalance. Another pattern, the "4,5,6" pattern (see Fig. 13–13B), has been labeled surface-dependent or combined visual-vestibular deficit. Patients with the 4,5,6 pattern are unable to stand when somatosensation is distorted despite having the opportunity for normal visual and vestibular inputs. Another pattern that has been described is that of a "severe" abnormality of postural sway (see Fig. 13–13C), wherein patients have great difficulty maintaining balance in all of the conditions. Figure 13–13D illustrates a nonspecific pattern. Another pattern that has been described is that of an "aphysiologic" response, wherein patients appear to do better on paradigms that logically should be more difficult.[6]

"Compensation" begins when patients are able to make use of information from a single labyrinth as adequate vestibular input to the ocular motor, spinal motor, and perceptual systems. The process of compensation depends on a patient's age, neurologic status generally, and his or her level of physical activity, specifically, activities that include combined visual, vestibular, and somatosensory inputs. Several studies have suggested that after successful compensation, posturography test results normalize and that patients lose their 5,6 pattern and may, in fact, have normal postural sway.[5] Fetter et al[3] observed the time course of recovery after unilateral peripheral vestibular injury with posturography. Some of their data suggest that 2 to 3 weeks after loss of unilateral peripheral vestibular function, most patients lose their 5,6 pattern. Thus, posturography, it has been suggested, can provide valuable information regarding the status of compensation for a peripheral vestibular deficit.

Summary

The most important part of the evaluation of the patient with vertigo and dizziness is obtaining a good medical history and a complete physical and neuro-otologic examination. Gaining maximal cooperation from each child should be attempted. Once all the information is available, the findings are analyzed by placing every result in perspective. Additional work-up required to confirm the diagnosis is then planned.

SELECTED REFERENCES

Baloh, JM, Halmagyi GM. Disorders of the Vestibular System. New York, Oxford University Press, 1996.
Baloh RW, Honrubia V. Clinical Neurophysiology of the Vestibular System, 2nd ed. Philadelphia, FA Davis, 1990.
Barber HO, Stockwell CW. Manual of Electronystagmography, 2nd ed. St Louis, CV Mosby, 1980.
Furman JM, Cass SP. Evaluation of Dizzy Patients. Slide lecture series. American Academy of Otolaryngology-Head and Neck Surgery, 1994.
Jacobson GP, Newman CW, Kartush JM. Handbook of Balance Function Testing. St Louis, Mosby–Year Book, 1993.
Leigh RJ, Zee DS. Neurology of Eye Movements, 3rd ed. Philadelphia, FA Davis, 1998.

REFERENCES

1. Bárány R. Physiologie und Pathologie des Bogengangsapparates beim Menschen. Vienna, Deuticke, 1907.
2. Bruininks RH. Bruininks-Oseretsky test of motor proficiency: examiners manual. Circle Pines, MN, American Guidance Services, 1978.
3. Fetter M, Diener H, Dichgans J. Recovery of postural control after an acute unilateral vestibular lesion in humans. J Vestib Res 1:373, 1991.
4. Folio M, Fewell R. Peabody Development Motor Scales and Activity Cards. Hingham, MA, DLM Teaching Resources, 1983.
5. Furman JM. Role of posturography in the management of vestibular patients. Otolaryngol Head Neck Surg 112:8, 1995.
6. Hamid M, Hughes G, Kinney S: Specificity and sensitivity of dynamic posturography: a retrospective analysis. Acta Otolaryngol Suppl (Stockh) 481:596, 1991.
7. Horak FB, Shumway-Cook A, Crowe TK, Black FO. Vestibular function and motor proficiency of children with impaired hearing or with learning disability and motor impairments. Dev Med Child Neurol 30:64, 1988.
8. Shumway-Cook A, Horak FB. Assessing the influence of sensory interaction of balance. Suggestion from the field. Phys Ther 66:1548, 1986.
9. Tsuzuku T, Kaga K. The relation between motor function development and vestibular function tests in four children with inner ear anomaly. Acta Otolaryngol Suppl (Stockh) 481:443, 1991.

14

Otalgia

Jay N. Dolitsky, M.D.

One of the most common symptoms occurring in childhood is the complaint of otalgia. This complaint can be a particularly distressing problem for parents because otalgia has many possible causes, many of which do not arise in the ear itself. The sensory innervation of the ear is such that sensations arising from a variety of areas in the head and neck can be felt in or about the ear. This is called *referred otalgia*. To find the source of an earache can be a challenge and generally requires obtaining a thorough history and performing a complete head and neck examination. This is particularly true when the symptoms are vague or the ear appears normal on physical examination. Otitis media and teething in the infant are examples of two common conditions that manifest with similar, if not identical, symptoms yet require very different management.

Depending on the age of the child and the nature of the disease process, otalgia may be expressed in a variety of ways. The infant or nonverbal child may rub or tug at the ear or may have a less directed symptom such as irritability, nocturnal awakening, or poor appetite. As the child ages and becomes increasingly verbal, a more directed complaint is elicited. The more localized the disease process is to the external or middle ear, the more likely a child is to complain of earache. Also, associated symptoms, such as hearing loss or imbalance, may help to localize the problem.

Otalgia in children should be divided into otologic (intrinsic) and non-otologic (extrinsic or referred) causes. It is also helpful to subdivide these causes by site of origin (Table 14–1).

Otologic Causes of Otalgia

External Ear

Pain of the external ear can be caused by a variety of disorders involving the skin or perichondrium of the pinna and external canal or the external layer of the tympanic membrane.

When otalgia is due to an abnormality of the external ear, the diagnosis can usually be made on physical examination. Associated symptoms, such as fullness, hearing loss, or discharge, may be present, depending on the nature of the particular disease. The more common causes of pain of the external ear, acute otitis externa, cerumen impaction, perichondritis, foreign body of the external auditory canal, myringitis, and folliculitis, are discussed individually.

Otitis Externa

Otitis externa is an inflammatory process of the external auditory canal that is usually caused by moisture or trauma. It is most commonly seen during the summer because of increased participation in swimming. For this reason, it is frequently referred to as "swimmer's ear." In addition to severe otalgia, the child usually complains of a clogging sensation in the ear, decreased hearing, and frequently aural discharge. On physical examination, the pinna and tragus are usually tender to movement. The external canal is usually swollen and erythematous. Frequently, debris or exudate lines the external canal and possibly covers the tympanic membrane. The nature of the exudate may vary with the type of infection. *Aspergillus niger* usually produces an exudate that looks somewhat cottonoid with tiny black dots at the surface. Bacterial otitis externa, of which the most common causative organism is *Pseudomonas aeruginosa*, has a more purulent exudate. The external or epithelial layer of the tympanic membrane, when visualized, may be erythematous because it is continuous with the skin of the external auditory canal. Treatment involves a thorough cleansing of the debris and instillation of acidic drops that may or may not contain an antibiotic. The newer drops contain quinolones, which are effective against both *P. aeruginosa* and *Staphylococcus aureus*. Unless there is extension of the inflammatory process beyond the external canal such that the pinna, preauricular area, and postauricular area are involved, antibiotics are not necessary. The patient must observe strict water precautions until the infection is completely clear and skin changes have returned to normal.

Cerumen Impaction

When cerumen is completely impacted in the external canal such that no air can get through to the tympanic

TABLE 14–1. Causes of Otalgia in Children

Intrinsic

I. External Ear

    A. External Otitis
    B. Cerumen impaction
    C. Foreign body
    D. Perichondritis
    E. Preauricular cyst or sinus
    F. Insects
    G. Myringitis
    H. Trauma
    I. Tumor

II. Middle Ear, Eustachian Tube, and Mastoid

    A. Barotrauma
    B. Middle-ear effusion
    C. Negative intratympanic pressure (eustachian tube dysfunction)
    D. Acute otitis media
    E. Mastoiditis
    F. Aditus block
    G. Complication of otitis media
    H. Tumor
    I. Eosinophilic granuloma
    J. Wegener granulomatosis

Extrinsic

I. Trigeminal Nerve IV

    A. Dental
    B. Jaw
    C. Temporomandibular joint
    D. Oral cavity (tongue)
    E. Infratemporal fossa tumors

II. Facial Nerve

    A. Bell palsy
    B. Tumors
    C. Herpes zoster

III. Glossopharyngeal Nerve

    A. Tonsil
    B. Oropharynx
    C. Nasopharynx

IV. Vagus Nerve

    A. Laryngopharynx
    B. Esophagus
    C. Gastroesophageal reflux
    D. Thyroid

V. Cervical Nerves

    A. Lymph nodes
    B. Cysts
    C. Cervical spine
    D. Neck infections

VI. Miscellaneous

    A. Migraine
    B. Neuralgias
    C. Paranasal sinuses
    D. Central nervous system
    E. Drug induced (mesalazine, sulfasalazine)
    F. Munchausen syndrome

membrane, the patient experiences a clogging sensation and a minor hearing loss. If the cerumen is impacted against the tympanic membrane, movement of the cerumen or the tympanic membrane causes pain. The cerumen must be cleaned out thoroughly and carefully so as not to traumatize the external canal or the tympanic membrane. If possible, it is recommended that the cerumen be removed with a suction or curette. Irrigation with water should be avoided because, if there is a perforation

or atrophy of the tympanic membrane or an infection of the external canal behind the cerumen, water will aggravate the situation (see Chap. 24).

Perichondritis

Infection or inflammation of the perichondrium of the pinna or external canal causes severe tenderness with movement or bending of the pinna. There is usually erythema of the pinna and possibly edema with subtle loss of contour. Perichondritis frequently has an antecedent history of minor trauma or insect bite. Treatment involves antimicrobial therapy (see Chap. 24).

Foreign Body

Occasionally, a child places a foreign body in the external auditory canal. Symptoms vary, depending on the nature of the foreign body, the size of the foreign body, and the duration that the foreign body has been present. An object that is completely obstructing the external auditory canal causes fullness and hearing loss. A sharp object may cause bleeding. A particularly dangerous foreign body is the lithium button battery. These batteries are extremely caustic and can cause extensive damage to the external auditory canal, tympanic membrane, and middle ear. They should be removed as expeditiously as possible.[3, 9] It may be necessary to remove a foreign body lodged in the external auditory canal under general anesthesia, and use of an operating microscope and an assortment of otologic instruments is recommended (see Chap. 24).

Myringitis

Inflammation of the tympanic membrane alone without infection or inflammation in the middle ear is termed *myringitis*. This causes severe otalgia and may be associated with minor hearing loss. The tympanic membrane is erythematous; however, there is no evidence of fluid in the middle ear. Frequently, bullae are seen on the surface of the tympanic membrane. The treatment is antimicrobial therapy (see Chap. 24). In an older, cooperative child, incising the bullae affords significant symptomatic relief.

Folliculitis

Inflammation of a hair follicle on the external third of the external auditory canal occasionally causes a localized, tender swelling. The symptoms are similar to those of acute otitis externa; however, on physical examination, there is no diffuse swelling or erythema of the external canal, and there is no discharge. A folliculitis is frequently missed on physical examination because the otoscope is inserted beyond the folliculitis on initial examination. It is therefore important to examine the external portion of the external auditory canal carefully in cases of otalgia, particularly when there are no other associated symptoms and there are no other findings on physical examination. A careful examination occasionally reveals a focal erythematous papule that is tender to palpation and elicits the same otalgia. This can best be treated with topical antibacterial ointment. If there is further extension of the folliculitis, systemic antibiotics may be necessary.

A variety of less common and dermatologic diseases can afflict the external ear and cause otalgia. These are discussed in Chapter 24.

Middle Ear and Mastoid

The most common cause of otalgia originating in the middle ear is otitis media. Depending on the type of otitis media, the symptoms vary. Other forms of eustachian tube dysfunction or inadequate ventilation of the middle ear and mastoid, whether they are inflammatory or neoplastic in nature, cause otalgia as well (see Chaps. 25 to 27).

Otitis Media

Acute otitis media can cause severe otalgia and is usually associated with fever, irritability, and hearing loss. On physical examination, the tympanic membrane is erythematous with increased vasculature and may be either retracted or bulging, with purulent fluid in the middle ear.

Otitis media with effusion or serous otitis media may be associated with discomfort and hearing loss but no overwhelming pain or fever. The tympanic membrane is usually dull and retracted on physical examination, with impaired mobility on insufflation.

Barotrauma

When a child has eustachian tube dysfunction, an acute decrease in the atmospheric pressure may induce trauma to the middle ear and tympanic membrane. When this occurs, the child has severe pain. This most commonly occurs during the descent of an airplane flight, in scuba diving, or when traveling in high altitudes.

Physical findings on otoscopy may include a retracted tympanic membrane, hemotympanum, erythema of the tympanic membrane, and middle-ear effusion.

Eustachian Tube Dysfunction

Children who suffer from chronic eustachian tube dysfunction with or without middle-ear effusion frequently complain of discomfort in the ear. This discomfort is often associated with "popping" or "clicking" and fullness. These symptoms may be exacerbated by an allergy, mild barotrauma, or upper respiratory infection. On otoscopy, the tympanic membrane is retracted; mobility is limited on positive insufflation, with the greater movement seen on release of the pneumatic insufflator.

Acute Mastoiditis

Children with acute mastoiditis present with otalgia and fever. On physical examination, the postauricular area is erythematous, and occasionally the pinna is protruding. In these situations, it is important to visualize the tympanic membrane, because severe cases of acute otitis externa can also manifest with postauricular erythema and protrusion of the pinna. In acute mastoiditis, the tympanic membrane is usually erythematous and possibly bulging. If there is breakdown of the bony partitions in the mastoid air cells, a condition known as *coalescent mastoiditis*, the posterior portion of the external auditory canal may be bulging as well. The combination of the protrusion of the pinna and bulging of the posterior external auditory canal is known as the "flagging and sagging" of acute coalescent mastoiditis. Mastoid x-ray examination or computed tomographic (CT) scan confirms the diagnosis. When the external auditory canal is diffusely swollen and the tympanic membrane appears clear, the diagnosis is most likely acute otitis externa. When the canal is swollen and visualization of the tympanic membrane is not possible, CT scan of the temporal bones is indicated to differentiate between the two disease processes.

Acute coalescent mastoiditis is a surgical emergency and is usually managed with tympanostomy tube insertion and "simple" mastoidectomy. Occasionally, the mastoid cortex breaks down because of coalescent mastoiditis, and a subperiosteal abscess may develop. A fluctuant, tender, erythematous swelling is then noted over the mastoid.

When a child complains of otalgia or postauricular pain despite a completely normal otoscopic examination, one should suspect aditus, or attic-antral, block. This is an obstruction of the communication between the middle ear and mastoid, such that the middle ear is ventilated but the mastoid is not. Confirmation of this diagnosis is made on CT scanning.

Complications of tympanomastoiditis can be intratemporal or intracranial. Intratemporal complications include facial nerve paralysis; labyrinthitis, which is usually associated with vertigo; and Gradenigo syndrome, also known as petrous apicitis. Gradenigo syndrome is a triad of retro-orbital pain, otorrhea, and diplopia. Intracranial complications include meningitis, lateral sinus thrombosis, and epidural, subdural, or brain abscesses. Children with intracranial complications usually appear toxic as well. Confirmation is made on CT or magnetic resonance imaging (MRI). Emergency management is required and is usually surgical. These diseases are discussed in further detail in Chapters 26 and 27.

Tumors of the ear and temporal bone are rare but include rhabdomyosarcoma, lymphoma, leukemic infiltration, eosinophilic granuloma, and Wegener granulomatosis. Manifestation usually includes otalgia and refractory otorrhea. Diagnosis is usually suggested by radiologic imaging and confirmed by pathologic examination.

Referred (Non-otologic) Otalgia

When a child complains of ear pain and there are absolutely no physical ear findings, one should consider the possibility of referred otalgia. This phenomenon occurs because the sensory innervation of the ear is derived from four cranial nerves—the trigeminal, facial, glossopharyngeal, and vagus—and two cervical nerves—the lesser occipital (C2) and great auricular (C2, C3). Sensations arising in other areas along the pathway of these nerves can cause pain to be experienced in the ear. It is therefore necessary to inspect other sites innervated by these nerves to determine whether they are the source of the otalgia.

The anatomy and function of each of these nerves are reviewed here to better understand their role in referring pain to the ear from other sites in the head and neck region.[7, 12, 15]

Trigeminal Nerve

The trigeminal or fifth cranial nerve divides into three major branches exiting the trigeminal ganglion, just proximal to the foramen ovale (Fig. 14–1). The ophthalmic branch provides sensation to the scalp and the upper portion of the face, including the periorbital areas and the forehead, and to portions of the nasal mucosa and mucosa of the paranasal sinuses. The maxillary division supplies sensation to the skin of the midportion of the face, including most of the nose and cheeks. It also innervates the mucous membrane of the nasopharynx; the upper portion of the oral cavity, including the palate, uvula, and upper teeth; and portions of the ethmoid and maxillary sinuses. The mandibular division supplies the skin of the lower third of the face as well as the mandible and the lower portion of the oral cavity, including the lower teeth, the tongue, and the floor of the mouth. The auriculotemporal branch of the mandibular division of the trigeminal nerve runs with the superficial temporal artery and vein and supplies sensation to the anterior portion of the pinna, the tragus, the superior and anterior aspects of the external auditory canal, and the anterior aspect of the tympanic membrane. It is thus understood that areas innervated by any of the three divisions of the trigeminal

nerve can refer sensations to the ear via the auriculotemporal nerve. The most common sites causing referred otalgia via this pathway are the teeth, the soft tissues of the oral cavity, the temporomandibular joint, the oropharynx, the nasopharynx, and the parotid gland.

Teeth

Probably the most common cause of otalgia in young children comes from the teeth. This may be caused by carious teeth, by inflammation of the gingivae, and most commonly by erupting teeth. As infants cut teeth, they frequently rub or pull at their ears, causing the parents to assume a problem with the ear. This is particularly confusing in a child with a history of otitis media because the child can be irritable and refuse to eat; furthermore, crying can cause hyperemic tympanic membrane. Additionally, such a child is generally uncooperative, making the examination more difficult. Parents and physicians may be misled by the child's history. In such a circumstance, the physician must instruct the parent on proper restraining technique to obtain an adequate look at the tympanic membrane, perform pneumatic otoscopy, and examine the oral cavity (see Chap. 58).

Temporomandibular Joint

Inflammation and pain of the temporomandibular joint (TMJ) is one of the most common causes of referred otalgia, particularly in older children and adults. Included in the structures that cause TMJ pain are the muscles of mastication and the ligaments associated with the TMJ. Irritation of the TMJ in children is usually caused by

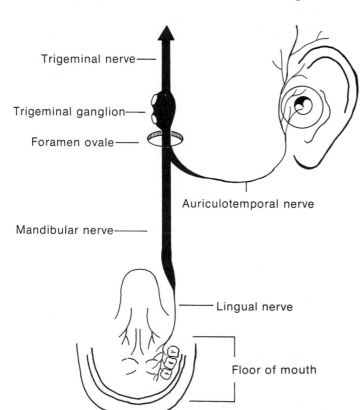

Trigeminal nerve——

Trigeminal ganglion——

Foramen ovale——

Auriculotemporal nerve

Mandibular nerve——

Lingual nerve

Floor of mouth

FIGURE 14–1. Referred otalgia mediated by the trigeminal nerve may be caused by intraoral disorders, such as carious teeth, impacted wisdom teeth, and a calculus in the duct of the submandibular salivary gland.

excessive use or abuse. This can occur in children who frequently clench their teeth because of anxiety or habit, or as a result of frequent gum chewing, malocclusion, or nighttime bruxism. Rarely, intrinsic disease such as rheumatoid arthritis can be present in the TMJ. Associated symptoms include tinnitus and headache. To confirm the diagnosis, one should carefully and gently palpate the TMJ externally by placing the fingers just anterior to the tragus and having the patient open and close the mouth. The patient will wince or complain of otalgia during attempted occlusion. It is also important to attempt to elicit pain in the pterygoid muscles by palpating intraorally between the zygomatic arch and the coronoid process of the mandible (see Chap. 59).

Oral Cavity

Careful inspection of all aspects of the oral cavity, including the tongue, floor of mouth, and palate, is important to look for traumatic lesions, aphthous ulcers, and other inflammatory lesions. Examination should include the intraoral openings of Stensen and Wharton ducts. (see Chaps. 60 and 63).

Paranasal Sinuses

Inflammatory processes of the paranasal sinuses can occasionally result in referred otalgia. One should fully assess the paranasal sinuses by careful nasal examination and palpation of the sinuses to elicit tenderness (see Chaps. 43 to 45).

Infratemporal Fossa Tumors

Out of 615 adults with ear pain and a normal ear examination, 18 were diagnosed as having malignant infratemporal fossae tumors. MRI with gadolinium is therefore recommended in such cases for early detection.[8] Although such pathology is rare in young children, one must maintain a certain level of suspicion in teenaged children, particularly when no diagnosis is found with persistent otalgia.

Facial Nerve

The facial or seventh cranial nerve is predominantly a motor nerve to the muscles of facial expression; however, there are sensory fibers of the facial nerve—the posterior auricular nerve and the nervus intermedius of Wrisberg—that innervate the skin overlying the lateral portion of the concha and anthelix as well as the posterior lobule and skin overlying the mastoid. A portion of the posterior wall of the external auditory canal and posterior portion of the tympanic membrane obtain sensory innervation from branches of the facial nerve. Diseases of the facial nerve may, therefore, cause referred otalgia.

The most common cause of referred otalgia associated with the facial nerve occurs in idiopathic facial paralysis, or Bell palsy, and patients frequently complain of otalgia several days before the onset of facial paralysis. The physical findings at the time are usually negative, although it

has been described that an inflamed chorda tympani can be seen just before the onset of Bell palsy.

Herpes zoster oticus, also known as Ramsay Hunt syndrome, is a condition of facial paralysis associated with a vesicular eruption along the sensory distribution of the facial nerve. Patients complain of otalgia in addition to facial nerve paralysis. Findings of vesicles along the concha or posterior canal wall confirm the diagnosis. The otalgia, however, may precede the eruption of vesicles and can last for weeks beyond the resolution of vesicles (see Chap. 19). The Hitselberger sign, hypesthesia of the posterior external canal postauricular, is associated with an acoustic neuroma and is mediated through this pathway.[15]

Glossopharyngeal Nerve

The glossopharyngeal (ninth cranial) nerve exits the skull through the jugular foramen along with the vagus and spinal accessory nerves (Fig. 14–2). It provides sensory innervation to the mucous membrane of the oropharynx, including the tonsillar region and the base of tongue. A branch of the glossopharyngeal nerve, or the Jacobson nerve, ascends from the glossopharyngeal ganglion to the middle ear and, with the caroticotympanic plexus of the internal carotid, forms the tympanic plexus on the promontory of the middle ear. This plexus supplies sensation to the middle ear mucosa, including the medial surface of the tympanic membrane, the eustachian tube, and the mastoid air cells.[4] Pain from the pharynx, particularly the

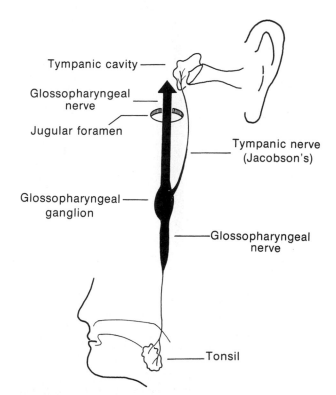

FIGURE 14–2. Referred otalgia mediated by the glossopharyngeal nerve may be caused by tonsillitis, peritonsillar abscess, or neural irritation after tonsillectomy.

tonsils, is a common cause of referred otalgia through this pathway.

Acute pharyngitis, tonsillitis, peritonsillitis, and peritonsillar abscess are common diseases that cause referred otalgia. Patients also frequently complain of otalgia after tonsillectomy. In these cases, the otalgia subsides when the pharynx heals. Lingual tonsillitis and foreign bodies, such as fish bones or chicken bones embedded in the base of the tongue or tonsillar area, are other common causes of referred otalgia. Tumors of the base of the tongue or tonsil are rare causes of referred otalgia in the pediatric population.

Vagus Nerve

The Arnold nerve, a branch of the vagus nerve that arises from the nodose ganglion outside the jugular foramen, provides sensation to the cavum conchalis, posterior and inferior aspect of the external auditory canal, and postero-inferior portion of the tympanic membrane (Fig. 14–3). The Arnold nerve is responsible for the cough reflex that occurs when the external auditory canal is manipulated. The main trunk of the vagus nerve goes on to provide sensation to the mucosa of the larynx, hypopharynx, trachea, esophagus, and thyroid gland.[2, 15] Pain originating in any of these sites can therefore refer sensation to the ear.

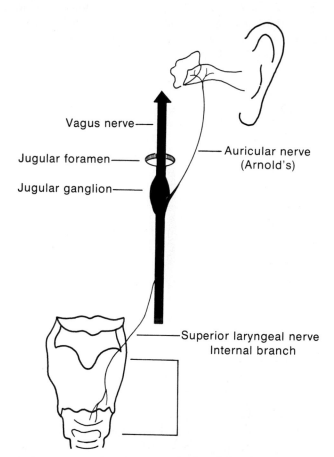

Vagus nerve

Jugular foramen

Jugular ganglion

Auricular nerve (Arnold's)

Superior laryngeal nerve Internal branch

FIGURE 14–3. Referred otalgia mediated by the vagus nerve may be caused by such laryngopharyngeal disorders as retropharyngeal abscess, epiglottitis, esophagitis around an impacted foreign body, and a sharp foreign body in the piriform sinus.

The lesser occipital (C2) and great auricular (C2, C3) nerves supply the skin overlying the mastoid area.

Laryngeal Disease

All forms of laryngitis can cause referred otalgia. Ear pain associated with hoarseness requires a thorough investigation of the larynx as well as of the ears. Laryngeal injuries or foreign bodies embedded in the larynx frequently cause pain radiating to the ear. Although rare in children, tumors of the larynx and hypopharynx cause referred otalgia (see Chaps. 87, 90, and 91).

Esophageal Disease

Foreign bodies embedded in the esophagus can refer pain via the vagus nerve. Gastroesophageal reflux has also been reported to cause otalgia (see Chaps. 69, 71, and 72).[3]

Gastroesophageal reflux has been described as a source of referred earache in the absence of any signs of inflammatory disease of the ears. Medical management relieves or decreases the symptoms.[5]

Thyroid Disease

Inflammatory diseases of the thyroid, such as subacute or de Quervain thyroiditis, frequently cause symptoms of sore throat and may cause referred otalgia. In fact, chronic thyroiditis in childhood is often misdiagnosed as pharyngitis. It is therefore important to palpate the thyroid gland to elicit tenderness in children with unexplained throat pain or ear pain. In subacute thyroiditis, the erythrocyte sedimentation rate is usually elevated. Treatment is with nonsteroidal anti-inflammatory agents (see Chap. 102). Acute bacterial thyroiditis with abscess formation has been reported to cause otalgia. Management with needle aspiration of the abscess and antimicrobial therapy resulted in resolution the thyroid disease and ear symptoms.[10]

Cervical Nerves

The posterior portion of the lateral surface of the pinna and the majority of the medial surface of the pinna derive sensation from the great auricular nerve, a sensory nerve made up of fibers from C2 and C3 of the cervical plexus. The skin overlying the mastoid region receives its innervation from the lesser occipital nerve, formed from fibers of C2. The great auricular and lesser occipital nerves overlap in contributing sensation on the upper medial portion of the pinna.[15] These cervical nerves are also responsible for sensory innervation of the skin and muscles of the neck and spine. Pain arising from the neck or the spine can therefore refer pain to the external portion of the ear.

A common cause of referred otalgia from the cervical plexus is cervical lymphadenitis, particularly of the lymph nodes in the occipital, mastoid, and upper jugular areas. Cysts and malformations of the lateral neck, such as branchial cleft anomalies, particularly when they are infected, can cause pain radiating to the ear. Deep neck infections, such as parapharyngeal abscesses that have overlying erythema and inflammation of the muscles and skin, can refer pain to the ear as well. Such patients occasionally present with a torticollis, with the head tilted toward the ipsilateral shoulder. Traumatic injury of the sternocleidomastoid muscle can also result in torticollis and referred otalgia.

Inflammation or injury of the cervical spine may cause discomfort of the neck and refer pain to the ear. This can be seen in patients who have cervical arthritis or traumatic injuries to the neck and spine. Grisel syndrome, or subluxation of the atlantoaxial joint, can follow upper respiratory tract infection or surgery in the head and neck. This condition can cause referred otalgia.

Neuralgias

A neuralgia is a condition in which one experiences sharp, lancinating pain along the distribution of a particular sensory nerve. This pain can often be elicited when a specific area known as a "trigger zone" is palpated.

Trigeminal neuralgia, or tic douloureux, has been described as recurrent episodes of severe pain along the distribution of the lower divisions of the trigeminal nerve. This condition can therefore cause otalgia. A similar situation can be seen when the glossopharyngeal nerve is stimulated by swallowing, causing severe pain in the pharynx that radiates to the ear. Sectioning of the tympanic plexus has been advocated for controlling the otalgia caused by glossopharyngeal neuralgia.

Sluder syndrome, also known as sphenopalatine neuralgia, is caused by triggering of the sphenopalatine ganglion with resultant severe, sharp pain in the region of the eye and nose. Again, pain in this area can radiate to the ear through the greater petrosal nerve to the geniculate ganglion.

Geniculate neuralgia originates from the geniculate ganglion or the nervus intermedius of Wrisberg (sensory fibers from the facial nerve). CT scan and MRI are useful tools to rule out a tumor or vascular malformation adjacent to the nerve.

Miscellaneous Causes of Otalgia

Eagle syndrome is a condition in which an elongated styloid process causes otalgia or sore throat, usually exacerbated by swallowing, yawning, or chewing. One may consider the diagnosis if pain can be elicited by palpation of the styloid process through the pharynx. X-ray films of the mastoid and styloid process confirm the diagnosis.

Carotidynia is a disorder of pain in the neck over the carotid bulb radiating to the ipsilateral ear. This is caused by inflammation of the sympathetic plexus overlying the carotid bulb and can be elicited by palpation of the carotid bulb. Treatment involves nonsteroidal anti-inflammatory agents.

Patients with migraine headaches may complain of otalgia. The drugs mesalazine and sulfasalazine have been reported to cause ear pain in a 46-year-old man with ulcerative colitis. The authors proposed the otalgia to be a headache variant and therefore of central origin.[13]

An 18-year-old woman with intrapetrous carotid artery aneurysm was reported to have presented with epistaxis and otalgia. Following myringotomy, MRI, and CT studies, the diagnosis was made on angiography.[1]

Munchausen syndrome was described in a 13-year-old boy who coerced his physicians into ordering several unnecessary tests and performing two mastoid surgeries by complaining of otalgia and by other deceptions.[6]

Approach to the Child with Otalgia or Suspected Otalgia

When faced with a child complaining of otalgia, one should obtain a thorough history of the complaint (Fig. 14–4). It is important to determine the nature of the ear pain, associated symptoms, such as hearing loss, otorrhea, and imbalance, and antecedent events. One should investigate previous otologic history, such as recurrent otitis media and ear surgery. Any regional symptoms, such as odynophagia, pain in the oral cavity, neck pain, or headache should be ascertained.

Physical examination should begin with a thorough examination of the ear, including examination of the pinna and periauricular areas, the external canal, and the tympanic membrane. One must take into account that a screaming, straining child will have a hyperemic tympanic membrane that may be unrelated to inflammation. As the child strains, a Valsalva effect may also occur, which can affect tympanic membrane mobility. For this reason, it is advisable to allay the child's fear of the examination before using the otoscope. This can often be accomplished by allowing the child to touch the otoscope with his or her hand before placing it in the ear. When cooperation by the child is unobtainable, proper restraint in a parent's lap or a papoose is necessary. If cerumen is obstructing or partially obstructing visualization of the tympanic membrane or limiting examination of the entire external auditory canal, it should be removed gently and carefully with use of an open otoscope or microscope. If no identifiable cause for the child's complaint can be found on otologic examination, one should carefully inspect the patient's scalp, periauricular area, nose, nasal cavities, sinuses, oral cavity, oropharynx, neck, temporomandibular joint, and, if possible, nasopharynx and larynx. Specific attention should be paid to the sites most likely to cause referred otalgia, such as the teeth, tongue, tonsils, TMJ, and thyroid gland ("the five Ts").

When an infant is suspected of having otalgia on the basis of rubbing or pulling at the ear, irritability, poor feeding, or awakening at night, a thorough physical examination is of the utmost importance because a first-person history is unobtainable. It is particularly important to carefully inspect the tympanic membrane. Many cases of erupting teeth or tonsillitis have been misdiagnosed as acute otitis media owing to inadequate examination of a squirming, crying child with resulting hyperemic, bulging tympanic membrane.

Following physical examination, other diagnostic tools can be used to aid in identifying the cause of an earache.

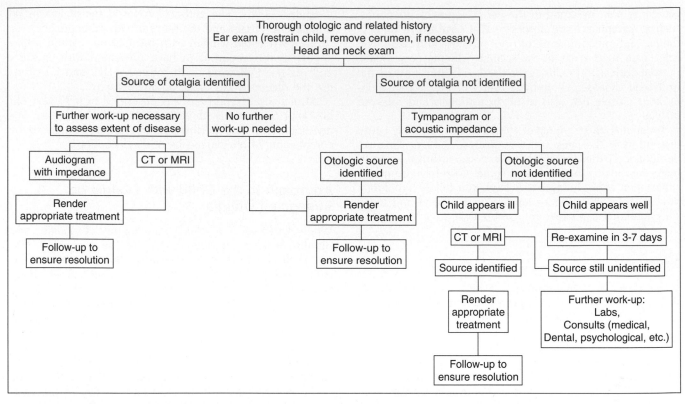

FIGURE 14–4. Management algorithm for child with otalgia or suspected otalgia.

Tympanometry is an objective means of assessing tympanic membrane mobility, which is affected by middle-ear pressure, fluid, and tympanic membrane integrity. The sensitivity and specificity of tympanometry in diagnosing acute otitis media range between 83% and 91% and between 63% and 93%, respectively.[11] It is the author's opinion that tympanometry is best used as an adjunct to, not in place of, a careful examination of the tympanic membrane; however, when visualization of the tympanic membrane is obstructed, tympanometry is useful alone.

Acoustic reflectometry measures middle-ear fluid by measuring reflection of sound waves off the tympanic membrane. The device used, unlike tympanometry, does not require a seal and is not affected by crying. Most studies conclude, however, that acoustic reflectometry adds little to a good history and physical examination in the acute setting.[11] Again, when visualization of the tympanic membrane is not practically possible, reflectometry is more helpful.

CT and MRI studies are useful in evaluating both otologic and referred or non-otologic causes of ear pain. When an otologic source is suspected, CT scan of the temporal bone may help in identifying the cause or in defining the extent of disease. Cholesteatoma, acute mastoiditis, and, less commonly, petrous apicitis or malignant neoplasms are examples of conditions in which radiographic imaging is helpful in forming a diagnosis and determining the degree of disease. Unsuspected non-otologic sources may be identified, such as intracranial abscesses and infratemporal fossa tumors. It is best to consult with a radiologist to help tailor the imaging examination for each patient.[14]

Conclusion

In the investigation of any medical complaint, there is no substitution for a thorough history and physical examination. Because of the rich sensory innervation of the external and middle ears, one should always be aware of the possibility of a non-otologic origin of ear pain. Nearly all otologic ear pain should manifest with some visible finding; therefore, when none is present, one must complete a thorough physical examination of the head and neck. One should keep in mind the common causes of referred otalgia but should not overlook the more esoteric causes when no other findings are evident. The use of imaging is recommended when earache persists despite a lack of findings.

REFERENCES

1. Banfield GK, Brasher PF, et al. Intrapetrous carotid artery aneurysm presenting as epistaxis and otalgia. J Laryngol Otol 109:865, 1995.
2. Blau JN. Ear pain referred by the vagus. BMJ 299:1569, 1989.
3. Capo JM, Lucente FE. Alkaline battery foreign bodies of the ear and nose. Arch Otolaryngol Head Neck Surg 112:562, 1986.
4. Cook JA, Irving RM. Role of tympanic neurectomy in otalgia. J Laryngol Otol 104:114, 1990.
5. Gibson Jr WS, Cochran W. Otalgia in infants—a manifestation of gastroesophageal reflux. Int J Pediatr Otorhinolaryngol 28:213, 1994.
6. Gilbert RW, Pierse PM, Mitchell DP. Cryptic otalgia: a case of Munchausen syndrome in a pediatric patient. J Laryngol Otol 16:4,1987.

7. Hollinshead WH. Anatomy for Surgeons, vol 1. The Head and Neck. New York, Harper & Row, 1982.

8. Leonetti JP, Li J, Smith PG. Otalgia. An isolated symptom of malignant infratemporal tumors. Am J Otol 19:496, 1998.

9. Skinner DW, Chiu P. The hazards of "button-sized" batteries as foreign bodies in the nose and ear. J Laryngol Otol 100:1315, 1986.

10. Stevenson J. Acute bacterial thyroiditis presenting as otalgia. J Laryngol Otol 105:788, 1991.

11. Stewart MH, Siff JE, Cydulka RK. Evaluation of the patient with sore throat, earache and sinusitis: an evidence based approach. Emerg Med Clin North Am 17:153, 1999.

12. Wazen JJ. Referred otalgia. Otolaryngol Clin North Am 22:1205, 1989.

13. Wareing M, Mitchell D. Drug induced otalgia due to mesalazine and sulphasalazine. J Laryngol Otol 110:466, 1996.

14. Weissman JL. A pain in the ear: the radiology of otalgia. Am J Neuroradiol 18:1641, 1997.

15. Yanagisawa K, Kveton JF. Referred otalgia. Am J Otolaryngol 13:323, 1992.

15

Otorrhea

Joseph E. Dohar, M.D., M.S.

Otorrhea refers to discharge from the ear of any etiology. Although the causes of otorrhea are legion, it is most commonly due to infection of one or more anatomic sites of the ear. Certain less common infectious and noninfectious etiologies of otorrhea are discussed in other chapters in this book.

The three most common infectious diseases that manifest, in part, with otorrhea are acute diffuse bacterial otitis externa (OE), acute otitis media in the presence of a tympanostomy tube, also referred to as tympanostomy tube otorrhea (TTO), and chronic suppurative otitis media (CSOM) in the presence of a chronic perforation of the tympanic membrane. Of these, OE is the most common; it is usually straightforward to diagnose and treat and is associated with only minimal otorrhea (see Chapter 24). Refer to Chapter 25 for a comprehensive review of the middle-ear infections that cause otorrhea.

This chapter aims to accomplish two objectives. First, it presents a symptom-oriented approach to the differential diagnosis of otorrhea in general and to the treatment of infectious otorrhea deriving from a middle-ear source. A problem-oriented algorithm serves as a summation and quick reference, as does a table listing a comprehensive differential diagnosis. Second, since the most recent and significant developments in the treatment of otorrhea have been in the development of new ototopical therapies, general concepts and recent developments related to ototopical therapy are detailed.

Features

Character of the Discharge

Although not specific, the character of the discharge may provide a clue to the etiology of the otorrhea. In general, there are four types of otorrhea: sanguineous, serous, mucoid, and purulent. "Watery" or serous drainage may suggest the presence of a cerebrospinal fluid leak, particularly if there are copious amounts of drainage. Furthermore, if an antecedent history of trauma is obtained, cerebrospinal fluid leak must be assumed until proven otherwise. Temporal bone imaging, radionucleotide scanning, or biochemical tests on the fluid itself for glucose determination or, more specifically, beta-2 transferrin should be considered.

"Bloody" or sanguineous discharge usually is associated with the finding of granulation tissue on otoscopic examination and often represents an exuberant mucosal inflammatory response to infection. One must be cautious, however, to consider noninfectious causes, in that bloody drainage may be a harbinger of a more serious process such as tumor. If it does not respond to treatment within a reasonable amount of time, further diagnostic testing should be performed (Fig. 15-1).

Odor

Pseudomonas aeruginosa, the most common bacterial cause of otorrhea, has a characteristic "sweet" odor. A foul-smelling odor, often found in drainage present for weeks rather than days, suggests a mixed infection including anaerobes.

Mucoid, purulent, and mucopurulent drainage are most suggestive of infection. Although mucoid effusion is commonly found at the time of tympanostomy tube placement when an effusion has been present chronically, it is rare in the setting of a nonintact tympanic membrane. The presence of white cells on Gram stain suggests nasopharyngeal pathogens.

Source of Drainage

From a diagnostic perspective, the most critical distinction to make when faced with a patient with a "draining ear" is whether the source of the otorrhea is from the external or middle ear. This is usually a straightforward distinction made on history and confirmed on physical examination with careful pneumatic otoscopy. In general, pain is the key symptom that aids in differentiating these. In external auditory canal (EAC) infections, pain is prominent, and tenderness on manipulation of the pinna is the key sign that corroborates the history. In rare cases in which history and physical examination alone are not adequate to differentiate an outer- from a middle-ear infection, computed tomography (CT) imaging of the temporal bone is useful. The usual scenario for which a CT scan is obtained is in the child with an OE that has become invasive and involves the periauricular soft tissue, leading to postauricular erythema, edema, and secondary protrusion of the lobule, signs often seen in acute coalescent

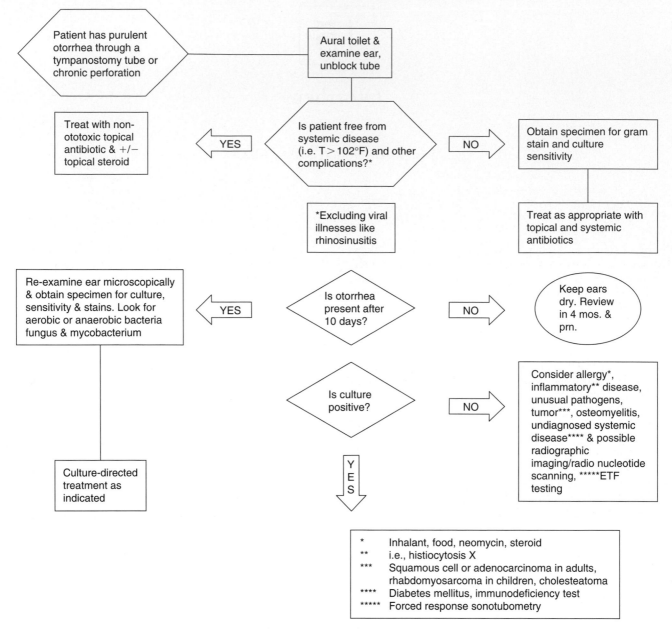

FIGURE 15–1. Diagnostic testing.

mastoiditis. The EAC is often too swollen and tender to permit adequate visualization of the eardrum, so CT imaging of the middle ear cleft air cell system almost always confirms the diagnosis.

Once the middle ear is determined to be the source of the infection, the next important factor that affects treatment choice is whether the patient manifests any systemic signs of illness (see Fig. 15-1). In children who manifest no systemic signs of illness, careful aural toilet should be performed and a non-ototoxic antibiotic should be empirically chosen. If, on the other hand, the person has systemic signs of infection such as temperature greater than 102°F, then a systemic antibiotic, usually

orally administered, may be added. However, it remains a common practice, mostly among primary care physicians, to treat these cases with a systemic agent only. Generally, the empirical choice of an oral antibiotic is one from the penicillin, cephalosporin, sulfa, or macrolide families indicated for otitis media with an intact eardrum. The problem with this approach is that *P. aeruginosa* is often the primary pathogen isolated in TTO. At present, there is no oral antibiotic indicated by the U. S. Food and Drug Administration with adequate activity against this organism. Clearly, then, especially in children, an ototopical agent must be used in all cases and the decision is whether, in addition, a systemic agent should be used.

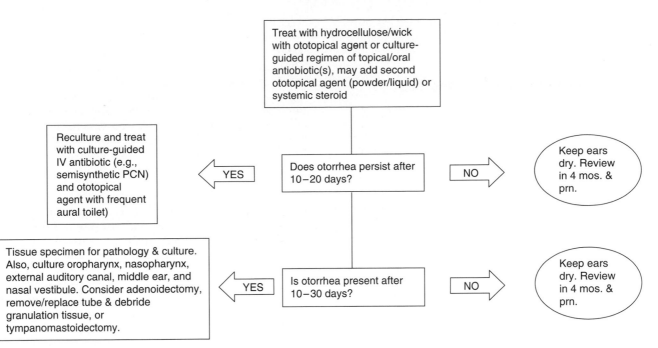

FIGURE 15–1. *Continued*

Topical versus Systemic Therapy

There are many advantages of using topical rather than systemic therapy. First, the medication is delivered *directly* to the target organ. By bypassing the systemic circulation, pharmacokinetic factors such as solubility, intestinal absorption, and hepatic first-pass effects do not affect ultimate tissue concentrations. Perhaps more importantly is that, unlike systemic antibiotics, topical antibiotics do not usually contribute to the development of community-acquired resistance.

Antibiotic resistance is the single most important modern day concern in the management of infectious disease. In 1982, the U.S. Food and Drug Administration stated that it "is unaware of any evidence that . . . topical antibiotics . . . have led to an increase in infection in the general population by resistant organisms. . . . The agency believes that if resistance were a problem . . . it would have been known by now."[22] This tenet on resistance and topical therapy holds for short-term use in the community as long as drug delivery is effective. This point was corroborated by a study done in Pittsburgh. Two hundred and thirty-one consecutive children seen at the outpatient otolaryngology clinic with draining ears from which *P. aeruginosa* was isolated were studied.[13] In these patients, the sensitivity to polymyxin B, one of the active ingredients in Cortisporin, which was commonly used in the community since the 1970s, was 99.6%. Only one strain of *P. aeruginosa* proved resistant to polymyxin B. The authors concluded that, despite widespread use of ototopical polymyxin B in their community for nearly three decades, resistance by *P. aeruginosa*, known to be quite facile in developing resistance strategies, had not developed. The same has been observed for topical skin antibiotics as well as topical eye drops.

Three reasons likely account for this finding. First, the concentrations of topical antibiotics so far exceeds the minimal inhibitory concentrations at the site of infection that eradication is more rapid and complete, thus obviating the emergence of treatment-related resistance. Second, in general, ototopical agents are used for relatively short treatment courses. Third, these infections are, by and large, community acquired in otherwise immunocompetent hosts. It is important to note that all five pathogens most commonly isolated from draining ears—*P. aeruginosa, Streptococcus pneumoniae, Staphylococcus aureus, Haemophilus influenzae,* and *M. catarrhalis*—are of major concern to the Centers for Disease Control and Prevention because of their propensity to develop resistance. All five pathogens must be covered empirically in the absence of a confirmatory culture because they can all be found in all ages from both acutely and chronically draining middle ears in the face of a nonintact tympanic eardrum. (For a detailed description of microbiology of OE, TTO, and CSOM, see Chapters 24 and 25.)

Resistance and pharmacokinetics are not the only advantages of topical therapy. The side effect profile of systemic agents far exceeds that of topical agents. The product label of any systemic antibiotic lists the incidence of such untoward effects as diarrhea, nausea, rash, vomiting, abdominal pain, and headache, among others. More significant are the far more severe side effects such as Stevens-Johnson syndrome, aplastic anemia, seizure, and anaphylaxis. With topical agents, only minor local irritative and allergic effects are commonly seen. A recent trial comparing the efficacy and safety of topical ofloxacin with those of amoxicillin/clavulanate found an incidence of 6% treatment-related side effects associated with the ototopical agent compared with 31% for the systemic agent.[16]

Last, on average, topical therapies cost anywhere from one half to one third that of a 10-day course of a branded, broad-spectrum oral agent. With third-party payers and the public increasingly more focused on economic issues, less expensive topical therapies should be used in place of systemic therapies where appropriate.

Formulation and Physical Properties Considerations

pH

Most traditional ototopical agents were formulated as acidic solutions and suspensions with an average pH of 3.45. According to the *Physician's Desk Reference*, for example, Cortisporin solution has a pH of 3.0. Although acidic concentrations were probably used in ototopical formulations to solubilize the steroid to varying degrees, two additional reasons have been offered to justify such pH. First, acetic acid is bactericidal to *P. aeruginosa*, the major pathogen isolated from otorrhea.[32] For example, VoSol (Denver Chemical Company), a 2% solution of acetic acid with 3% propylene glycol, is effective in the treatment of some discharging ears. Bactericidal activity of acetic acid and Burow's solution (glacial acetic acid and 13% aluminum acetate) has been shown against *S. aureus*, *Proteus mirabilis*, *Pseudomonas aeruginosa*, and *Staphylococcus pyogenes*.[32] Addition of aluminum to acetic acid to form aluminum acetate (Burow's solution) results in even greater inhibition of growth of these four organisms. An antibiotic effective in eradicating the significant pathogens at near neutral pH would theoretically be better tolerated in most instances.

The adverse effect of acid against *P. aeruginosa* is true for other pathogens as well. Some fungi are suppressed in vitro. The role of fungi in ear disease is debated and there is question as to whether they warrant specific treatment. On the one hand, fungi are known pathogens in other regions of the body. On the other hand, because the environment is humid, dark, and warm in a draining ear, conditions that ideally support the growth of fungi, their presence in aural drainage may only be as saprophytes and not as opportunistic primary pathogens. If this hypothesis is correct, simply drying up the ear is all that should be necessary to eliminate the fungi. Curiously, fungi are rarely isolated from TTO. One recent study found that fungi were isolated from TTO in only 2% of cases.[11] Given such a low incidence of fungi, even if they did participate in the primary pathogenesis, the disadvantages of pain and discomfort are enough reason to avoid the routine use of acidic preparations as antifungal agents. Besides, non-acidic topical alternatives exist for the treatment of fungal infections.

Second, the physiologic pH of the EAC is acidic. It has been hypothesized that restoring the pH of the EAC, which is often altered by otorrhea, is beneficial. To my knowledge, this hypothesis has never been proven. In conclusion, the disadvantages of using acidic preparations outweigh the advantages and, therefore, using more neutral preparations is prudent.

Viscosity

Viscosity is also important. The term *viscosity* is usually applied to liquids, and means, in a qualitative sense, the resistance that a liquid offers to flow. A liquid with a high viscosity such as molasses flows slowly, compared with water, which has a lower viscosity and flows much faster. The viscosity varies considerably between preparations and is significant because drug delivery is crucial. Resistance is not seen in ototopical anti-infectives (see earlier discussion). The key is that the drug must be *delivered effectively*. In general, this is the case with topical skin creams, ophthalmic preparations, and eardrops. In contrast, treatment-related resistance involving topical anti-infectives delivered to other sites, such as the lungs, has been reported.[4, 11, 17] Therefore, because the high surface tension at the orifice of the tympanostomy tube is one of the most critical factors that determines entry of the drops into the middle ear and because viscosity of the liquid is a variable directly related to surface tension and, more importantly, to velocity of flow, viscosity is clearly an important issue to consider when choosing an ear drop. In general, suspensions are more viscous than solutions. Because of pH issues, otic suspensions (which are usually less acidic) are more commonly used than their solution counterparts. Increasing viscosity of ototopical preparations not only negatively impacts drug delivery to the middle ear but also impairs the use of eardrops in conjunction with otowicks. Since the principle of otowicks relies on drug delivery via capillary action, solutions with all components solubilized would be expected to be absorbed and delivered most efficiently.

In general, the addition of a steroid and the pH of the solution directly affect viscosity. In order to solubilize or at least suspend the steroid, lower and more acidic pHs are necessary. Suspensions containing steroid, therefore, are generally more viscous and less acidic. Since increasing viscosity may have a negative impact on drug delivery and since the pH of such preparations are in the acidic range, one must carefully assess the need to add a steroid to ototopical preparations and be sure that the benefits outweigh the risks.

Topical Antibiotic Alone or Combined with a Steroid?

The need for a steroid in combination with an ototopical antibiotic has become a debated issue. The rationale for the inclusion of a steroid in ototopical preparations is theoretically sound. Steroids have known potent anti-inflammatory activity. Since ototopicals are most commonly used in conditions of the ear in which inflammation is a prominent component (most often as a result of infection), the inclusion of a steroid makes sense. The problem, however, is that conclusive supportive data on the benefits of topical steroids are lacking. One study by Gyde et al[17] compared the treatment of otorrhea with gentamicin alone or with a combination of colistin, neomycin, and hydrocortisone. The researchers believed that the steroid-antibiotic combination was more effective in relieving inflammation in a shorter period of time and that gentamicin alone appeared to be more effective in eradicating the infecting organisms. The sample size was small and the comparators were less than ideal. Combined gentamicin-steroid therapy was compared with placebo in a study of 163 patients with chronic otitis, and more clinical cures (52% vs. 30%) resulted with the combination treatment.[4]

A recent primate study found that, in cynomolgus monkeys with CSOM, treatment with topical ciprofloxacin effectively eradicated *P. aeruginosa* from the middle ear when compared with saline. However, there was no difference between the two groups in terms of the rate at which the otorrhea ceased.[11] This outcome may have been observed despite the eradication of the infecting organism if the inflammatory mucositis was inadequately treated. A second study using the same animal model found that antibiotic and steroid (tobramycin plus dexamethasone) resulted in more rapid resolution of otorrhea compared with antibiotic alone.[1] The rate of decrease in the otorrhea score was more rapid for groups given an antibiotic and, as stated, the addition of dexamethasone to the antibiotic hastened this decrease even more.

A recent clinical trial compared ciprofloxacin alone with ciprofloxacin plus hydrocortisone in the treatment of OE. A more rapid time course to resolution of pain (0.8 days) was seen when the steroid was added to fluoroquinolone as compared with treatment with fluoroquinolone alone.[28] In my opinion, this clinical trial is the best yet performed and provides the strongest data in support of the addition of a steroid to an anti-infective agent.

Yet, other clinical trials lead one to question the need for a combination steroid-antibiotic in all cases. Two randomized, evaluator-blind, multicenter, prospective clinical trials were performed, one in children aged 1 to 11 years and a second in patients 12 years or older.[21] The safety and efficacy of ototopical ofloxacin was compared with the safety and efficacy of Cortisporin (neomycin sulfate, polymyxin B sulfate, and hydrocortisone). The investigators found no statistically significant differences in clinical or microbiological and clinical cure rates. Further studies are warranted to aid in a final conclusion on this issue.

Many physicians erroneously believe that the addition of a steroid may help but "can't hurt." This is not entirely true. The 49th edition of the *Physician's Desk Reference* states, in a warning for Cortisporin regarding the steroid component, that "Since corticoids may inhibit the body's defense mechanism against infection, a concomitant antimicrobial drug may be used when this inhibition is considered to be clinically significant in a particular case."[26a] Furthermore, even though steroids are thought of as anti-inflammatory agents, the opposite can be observed, most likely as a result of a sensitization to the steroid itself. In a recent article by van Ginkel et al,[34] the authors said, "In spite of their intrinsic anti-inflammatory activity, topical steroids can also enhance the inflammation due to sensitization." In their study, 6 of 34 patients (18%) with chronic otorrhea (i.e., more than 3 months) treated with a steroid-containing ototopical agent had positive patch tests to steroids. This finding raises the possibility that patients with CSOM refractory to treatment with a steroid-containing topical agent are refractory, not because of failure to resolve the initial infection but because of allergic inflammation perpetuated by continued exposure to the steroid. Until better data are available, the best approach may be to treat with single-agent therapy unless it is thought that combination therapy is necessary in se-

lected cases (e.g., when there is an exuberant inflammatory response manifesting as obstructing granulation tissue). Then, addition of a steroid is warranted. Most of the currently available steroid-containing combination ototopical agents contain hydrocortisone as the anti-inflammatory agent. On a relative scale, hydrocortisone is a relatively weak steroid. If one believes that anti-inflammatory action is necessary, it makes better sense theoretically to use a more potent steroid than hydrocortisone.

How Many Antibiotics to Use?

Cortisporin, Pediotic, and Coly-Mycin, for example, are all ototopical preparations that contain more than one antibiotic. The rationale for the antibiotics combined in such preparations is not clear. Polymyxin B sulfate (10,000 units/mL), which is used in most topical ear preparations, is effective against *P. aeruginosa* and other gram-negative bacteria, including strains of *Escherichia*.[26b] Similarly, colistin sulfate also has bactericidal activity against most gram-negative organisms, notably *P. aeruginosa*, *E. coli*, and *Klebsiella* species.[26b] Neomycin sulfate is an aminoglycoside, again with primary bactericidal activity against gram-negative organisms and some activity against *S. aureus* as well. None of the antibiotic components of Cortisporin or Pediotic provide adequate coverage against *S. pneumoniae*.[26c] Yet, *S. pneumoniae* is one of the three most common pathogens isolated in TTO.[12] In a real-life situation, if a child has a draining ear, the physician is likely to treat it by empirically selecting an antibiotic. One that does not cover a primary potential pathogen would clearly not be a wise choice. In such a setting, Cortisporin would have to be combined with a systemic antibiotic, defeating the goal of using topical therapy alone. The U.S. Food and Drug Administration has become much more stringent and less likely to approve combination preparations unless a separate *significant* contribution of elements is shown. This approach is prudent because the side effect profile of combination drugs is expanded and the potential for toxicity increases, as does cost in most cases. Furthermore, it makes little sense to run the risk of sensitization to a compound that may be of benefit to the patient later in life if there is not a significant proven benefit for its inclusion in a combination drug. The newer quinolone agents, ofloxacin and ciprofloxacin, provide excellent coverage of all five common pathogens in TTO and appear microbiologically superior to older alternatives for this indication.

The last issue is whether dual therapy is needed to treat pseudomonal infections of the ear. This has been conventional teaching with other pseudomonal infections such as pneumonia, based on the rationale that the synergy resulting when two drugs with different modes of activity against pseudomonal species are used is crucial in preventing the emergence of treatment-induced resistance and in increasing ultimate cure rates. In part, this rationale may have led to the development of combination ototopical agents containing an aminoglycoside (e.g., neomycin) and a member of the polymyxin class of antibiotics (e.g., polymyxin B sulfate). The data on the treatment of pseudomonal infections of the ear have not indicated the need for dual therapy, either topically or systemically, for routine, uncomplicated cases. A recent study from Pittsburgh[14] revealed excellent in vitro susceptibility of aural isolates of *P. aeruginosa* to the semisynthetic penicillin. In children with CSOM refractory to outpatient management, single-agent intravenous therapy from this class of antibiotics has been the standard treatment, with excellent results. Ototopical fluoroquinolone antibiotics provide excellent coverage of all the major pathogens found in TTO. One recent study[12] found that microbiologic eradication by ofloxacin used topically eradicated 94% or more of *P. aeruginosa, H. influenzae, S. pneumoniae, S. aureus,* and *M. catarrhalis,* the five major pathogens isolated in TTO. In a second clinical trial studying the efficacy of ciprofloxacin in the treatment of OE, the eradication of the pathogens was equally impressive. Taking advantage of the impressive broad-spectrum coverage of this class of antibiotics is desirable and enables single-agent treatment of these infections.

Adverse Events with Ototopical Agents

Allergic Sensitization

The major disadvantage of products containing neomycin is its propensity to lead to sensitization. This manifests as allergic inflammation, most often of the skin of the EAC and pinna. Van Ginkel et al[34] stated that "Because of the high risk of sensitization, topical preparations containing neomycin . . . should not be used routinely." In patients with otitis that has been treated topically, neomycin is invariably the most important sensitizer.[15, 19, 27, 30, 31, 34] I believe that neomycin sensitization is vastly underestimated. When used in the EAC, the package insert of Cortisporin[26a] states that the manifestation of sensitization to neomycin is usually a low-grade reddening with swelling, dry scaling, and itching. Sensitization may manifest as failure to heal. As in nasal allergy, mucosa responds to allergic triggers with edema and drainage. In both skin and mucosa, the inflammatory manifestations of allergy and infection are clinically similar, if not indistinguishable.

Ototoxicity

Few subjects are greeted with more controversy and debate than the subject of ototoxicity to ototopical compounds. There is little question that reversible and irreversible ototoxicity and nephrotoxicity have long been recognized as a result of the systemic administration of aminoglycoside antibiotics.[35] What is less certain is whether such antibiotics, when applied topically to the middle ear, are significantly injurious to the cochlea and labyrinth. This concern has recently been further heightened by the fact that the treatment of Meniere disease may include topical gentamicin aimed at *purposely* destroying the labyrinth and, in a significant percentage of cases, results in loss of hearing as well.[25] It is generally believed that substances in a healthy middle ear can enter the inner ear by diffusion across the round window and the oval window.[5] Conclusive evidence to prove that ototoxicity can occur as a result of aminoglycosides used

topically in an infected ear does not exist. One of the primary problems in proving such causality is that sensorineural hearing loss can occur as a result of otitis media itself.[20] Determining whether the toxicity results from the primary disease or from its treatment is extraordinarily difficult. Several anecdotal reports suggest the latter.[23, 24, 33] Podoshin et al[29] found that, in patients with CSOM and comparable disease duration, those who received topical steroid alone ($n = 24$) had a mean sensorineural hearing loss of only 0.9 dB, as opposed to those who received a combination of topical dexamethasone, neomycin, and polymyxin B ($n = 124$), who had a mean sensorineural hearing loss of 6 dB. This difference was statistically significant ($p < .025$). The authors concluded that the potential for ototoxicity resulting from certain topical preparations should not be ignored. The American Academy of Otolaryngology-Head and Neck Surgery adopted a policy statement, #1420, on July 9, 1994, and reaffirmed on March 1, 1998, recognizing "the appropriateness of utilizing currently available topical preparations, including those containing aminoglycosides, in the treatment of external and middle ear disorders."[6] Although the incidence of ototoxicity resulting from the use of ototopical agents in the face of infection is rare, it most likely occurs. In a recent survey of otolaryngologists,[24] 3.4% of respondents indicated that they had witnessed *irreversible* inner ear damage following the use of anti-infective ototopical formulations. This does not include the instances of *reversible* toxicity or the instances of *unidentified* ototoxicity. There are several reasons why clinicians may not have identified such toxicity if and when it did occur. First, it may be reversible. This is significant especially in children. Second, those children at highest risk for TTO are either not walking or just beginning to walk. Even if a vestibular insult were to occur in the toddler, it may likely be written off to age-appropriate "clumsiness." Only recently have the labyrinthine effects as a result of chronic otitis media with effusion been recognized in this age group.[7, 8] Third, the ability to centrally compensate for a unilateral vestibular insult, especially in younger individuals, probably results in missed diagnoses as well. Fourth, if vestibular symptoms were to occur in a patient undergoing treatment for TTO with a topical aminoglycoside, those symptoms would conceivably be attributed to the disease and not to its treatment. Since only histopathologic examination of the temporal bones would distinguish between the two etiologies, such potential toxic effects go misdiagnosed. And fifth, if hearing loss occurs as a result of topical aminoglycosides in the middle ear, the highest frequencies are at greatest risk. Ultra high-frequency audiometry would be needed to detect the hearing loss, a test that is not routinely done. A recent consensus panel report[18] concluded "the availability of non-ototoxic ototopical antibiotics should lead to their consideration as first-line therapy for the treatment of uncomplicated CSOM and TTO." On the basis of what is currently known from both animal studies and clinical experience, ototoxicity may occur as a result of application of aminoglycosides, as well as certain vehicles and antiseptics to the middle ear. This is a rare event, especially when such agents are used in the setting of mucosal infection and inflammation for a limited duration of time and in restricted dosages. Furthermore, it is likely that the true incidence of such toxic outcomes has been underestimated and that safer alternatives should be used when possible.

Treatment

Once the middle ear is positively identified as the source of infection, good aural toilet must be performed. Since the microbiology is so predictable, it is reasonable to treat empirically and culture only treatment failures. Culture-directed treatment is best and is advised if the patient is seen 7 to 10 days later and the otorrhea persists or if systemic signs of illness manifest. Care should be taken to obtain the sample from the middle ear rather than from the EAC, because pathogens from the latter site may not represent those responsible for the middle-ear infection.[3]

Interpreting Culture Data when Applied to Topical Antimicrobial Therapy

One must be careful when interpreting culture results. Two recent trials highlight this point nicely. A first trial reported the overall clinical response rate and the pathogen sensitivity for ofloxacin-treated TTO to be completely independent of one another. An 88% and a 50% clinical cure rate were noted in those patients with sensitive and intermediate-resistant pathogens, respectively, as compared with 100% in those with resistant or acquired resistant pathogens (personal communication, Mindell Seidlin, M.D., Daiichi Pharmaceutical Corporation, 1999). Similarly, in patients under treatment for CSOM, patients with sensitive pathogens were cured 95% of the time as compared with those with intermediate, resistant, or acquired resistant pathogens who all had cure rates of 100%. Although the number of nonsensitive pathogens in the studies were small ($n = 18$) relative to the overall sample sizes of 131 and 156, it was nonetheless significant enough to demonstrate a lack of correlation between in vitro susceptibilities and clinical outcomes when topical therapies were used for treatment (personal communication, Mindell Seidlin, M.D., Daiichi Pharmaceutical Corporation, 1999).

So what accounts for this ostensible contradiction that cure rates were independent of pathogen susceptibility? The National Committee of Laboratory Standards (NCCLS) breakpoints used by standard microbiology laboratories are determined based on typical tissue antibiotic levels achieved with systemic administration of antibiotics. Ototopical concentrations are, on average, 1000-fold higher than that. One study revealed that, when 0.3% ofloxacin solution was administered in a single dose to patients with CSOM, serial sampling up to 2 hours afterward showed 388.8 to 2849.8 μg/mL at 30 minutes with the highest value being close to the concentration of the drug itself (3000 μg/mL).[26] This was in contrast to Bluestone and Klein's findings that middle-ear fluid levels of antibiotics after oral administration only ranged from 0.2 to 8.2 μg/mL at 0.5 to 2.5 hours after administration.[2] Since increasing concentration is one of the key strategies in overcoming resistance (thus, the latest recommenda-

tions to use 80 to 85 mg/kg of amoxicillin rather than 40 mg/kg to overcome the intermediate resistant pneumococcus), only in vitro data that adjusts for the substantially higher topical concentrations would be useful. At The Children's Hospital of Pittsburgh, this point was further substantiated when we retrospectively reviewed 23 positive cultures for methicillin-resistant S. aureus in 17 children from 1992 through 1996 seen in the outpatient department.[10] Follow-up by telephone contact revealed that by the third or fourth day of treatment when the culture and sensitivity data were available, the majority of cases of otorrhea had resolved, even though data suggested that the organism was resistant to the topical treatment empirically prescribed. Even the most frightening resistant organisms such as methicillin-resistant S. aureus can effectively be eradicated with topical treatment.

Troubleshooting

It is highly unlikely that a treatment failure is due to a "drug-bug" issue when using a broad-spectrum ototopical agent. Investigation of alternative reasons should ensue. Focus should be on ways to *enhance drug delivery*. I am convinced that failure to deliver the drug underlies most failures.

Topical drug delivery may be improved using several strategies. First, carefully perform aural toilet. Dry mopping and suctioning the EAC with or without antiseptic irrigation are both acceptable. Second, review with the parents the appropriate means of administering the ototopical agent. Be certain the caretaker is aware that the auricle must be retracted posteriorly and superiorly in order to straighten the EAC and provide a more linear path into the middle ear. Third, it is critical that, after the dose is administered, the tragus be pumped to exceed the surface tension of the tympanostomy tube. Fourth, although product labels vary regarding the recommended time that the patient should remain with the treated ear in the upright position, the longer the better, and an average of 5 to 10 minutes is recommended, especially in refractory cases. This is most important if one is dealing with a more highly resistant organism. Avoiding runoff and maintaining the concentration of the antibiotic above the higher minimum inhibitory concentration is critical in resolving the infection. Finally, the use of an otowick has been beneficial in refractory cases. Wicks are not only helpful in the case of OE associated with significant swelling of the EAC but also in refractory TTO. Fenestrated wicks are recommended in TTO to allow drainage while continuing to ventilate the middle ear. The precise mechanism underlying their effectiveness is unknown; however, suspected mechanisms include (1) improved delivery of the medication to the medial aspect of the ear canal and middle ear via capillary action, (2) "depot" delivery of the drug resulting from the retention of the medication by the wick, and (3) aural toilet by absorbing the otorrhea draining from the middle ear. Furthermore, the EAC is more easily sterilized with a wick in place, likely preventing reinfection of the middle ear from this source. Finally, solid, nonfenestrated wicks may carry the additional advantage of increasing the middle-ear pressure "cushion," possibly minimizing nasopharyngeal reflux of organisms via the eustachian tube. This may have a similar effect to removing the tube.

Allergy should be suspected in refractory cases. As stated earlier, sensitization to topical agents is a common cause of treatment failures. Skin sensitization manifests as erythema, edema, desquamation, otalgia, and pruritus, the same symptoms as OE. Similarly, mucosa reacts to allergens to which it is sensitive by producing drainage, the same principal sign as infection. In short, a failure to heal in either OE or otitis media may, in fact, represent a contact sensitization of the ototopical agent, most commonly seen with neomycin-containing products.

A systemic agent administered orally or, in cases in which infection persists beyond 3 to 6 weeks, intravenously may be needed to supplant ototopical therapy. Ultimately, tympanomastoid surgery, adenoidectomy, or removal of the tubes may be necessary to resolve the otorrhea.

Future Research

Because treatment-related resistance appears less likely to occur in response to ototopical agents and safe ototopical quinolones are available, topical chemoprophylaxis may be a possibility for the future. Presently, no agent is indicated to prevent recurrent OE, TTO, or CSOM. Such chemoprophylaxis may need to be delivered to not only the EAC but possibly also to the nasopharynx via a nasal application. The topical application of chemoprophylaxis to the nose in an attempt to reduce the bacterial load of the nasopharynx may hold exciting promise as a novel means of preventing recurrent acute otitis media. Such a strategy may not only be efficacious and safe but may also not have the disadvantage of treatment-related resistance.

Also warranting future study is CSOM and other chronic infectious diseases as what some investigators term a *biofilm disease*.[9] A biofilm is a complex organization of sessile bacteria that are living together in a mutualistic fashion. Biofilms can be composed of multiple bacterial species (both aerobic and anaerobic) living within distinct microenvironments. These bacteria are believed to be distinct from their planktonic forms (free-floating organisms), very resistant to antibiotics and host defense mechanisms, and difficult to isolate by routine culture techniques. Biofilm research is exciting and holds promise to greatly improve understanding and success in treating CSOM and several other chronic infectious diseases.

REFERENCES

1. Alper CM, Dohar JE, Gulhan M, et al. Treatment of chronic suppurative otitis media with topical tobramycin and dexamethasone. Arch Otolaryngol Head Neck Surg 126:165, 2000.
2. Bluestone CD, Klein J. Clinical practice guideline on otitis media with effusion in young children: strengths and weaknesses. Otolaryngol Head Neck Surg 112:507, 1995.
3. Brook I, Gober AE. Reliability of the microbiology of spontaneously draining acute otitis media in children. Pediatr Infect Dis J 19:571, 2000.
4. Browning GG, Gatehouse S, Calder IT. Medical management of active chronic otitis media: a controlled study. J Laryngol Otol 102:491–495, 1988.
5. Brummett RE, Harris RF, Lindgren JA. Detection of ototoxicity from drugs applied topically to the middle ear space. Laryngoscope 86:1177, 1976.
6. Bulletin. American Academy of Otolaryngology-Head and Neck Surgery. Alexandria, Va, 1998, pp 17–20.
7. Casselbrant ML, Furman JM, Rubenstein E, Mandel EM. Effect of otitis media on the vestibular system in children. Ann Otol Rhinol Laryngol 104:620, 1995.
8. Casselbrant ML, Redfern MS, Furman JM, et al. Visual-induced postural sway in children with and without otitis media. Ann Otol Rhinol Laryngol 107:401, 1998.
9. Costerson JW, Lewandowski Z, Caldwell DE, et al. Microbial biofilms. Ann Rev Microbiol 49:711, 1995.
10. Coticchia JM, Dohar JE, Sordes, M, et al. Children with methicillin-resistant *Staphylococcus aureus* (MRSA) otorrhea following tympanostomy tube insertion. 2001, in press.
11. Dohar JE, Alper CM, Rose EA, et al. Treatment of chronic suppurative otitis media with topical ciprofloxacin. Ann Otol Rhinol Otolaryngol 107:865, 1998.
12. Dohar JE, Garner, ET, Nielsen RW, et al. Topical ofloxacin treatment of otorrhea in children with tympanostomy tubes. Arch Otolaryngol Head Neck Surg 125:537, 1998.
13. Dohar JE, Kenna MA, Wadowsky RM. In vitro susceptibility of aural isolates of *P. aeruginosa* to commonly used ototopical antibiotics. Am J Otol 17:207, 1996.
14. Dohar JE, Kenna MA, Wadowsky RM. Therapeutic implications in the treatment of aural *P.* infections based on *in vitro* susceptibility patterns. Arch Otolaryngol Head Neck Surg 121:1022, 1995.
15. Fraki JE, Kalimo K, Tuohimaa P, Aantaa E. Contact allergy to various components of topical preparations for treatment of external otitis. Acta Otolaryngol 100:414, 1985.
16. Goldblatt EL, Dohar JE, Nozza RJ, et al. Topical ofloxacin versus systemic amoxicillin/clavulanate in purulent otorrhea in children with tympanostomy tubes. Int J Pediatr Otorhinolaryngol 15:91, 1998.
17. Gyde MC, Norris D, Kavalec EC. The weeping ear: clinical re-evaluation of treatment. J Int Med Res 10:333, 1982.
18. Hanley MT, Denneny JC, Holzer SS. Use of ototopical antibiotics in treating 3 common ear infections. Otolaryngol Head Neck Surg 122:934, 2000.
19. Holmes RC, Johns AN, Wilkinson JD, et al. Medicament contact dermatitis in patients with chronic inflammatory ear disease. J R Soc Med 75:27, 1982.
20. Hunter LL, Margolis RH, Rykken JR, et al. High frequency hearing loss associated with otitis media. Ear Hear 17:1, 1996.
21. Jones RN, Milazzo J, Seidlin M. Ofloxacin otic solution for treatment of otitis externa in children and adults. Arch Otolaryngol Head Neck Surg 123:1193, 1997.
22. Langford JH, Benrimoj SI. Clinical rationale for topical antimicrobial preparations. J Antimicrob Chemother 37:399, 1996.
23. Lelieve WC. Topical gentamicin-induced positional vertigo. Otolaryngol Head Neck Surg 93:553, 1985.
24. Lundy LB, Graham MD. Ototoxicity and ototopical medications: a survey of otolaryngologists. Am J Otol 14:141, 1993.
25. Monsell EM, Cass SP, Rybak LP. Therapeutic use of aminoglycosides in Meniere's disease. Otolaryngol Clin North Am 26:737, 1993.
26. Ohyama M, Furuta S, Uenok, et al. Ofloxacin otic solution in patients with otitis media: an analysis of drug concentrations. Arch Otolaryngol Head Neck Surg 125:337, 1999.
26a. Physician's Desk Reference, 49th ed. Montvale, NJ, Medical Economics Data Production, 1995.
26b. Physician's Desk Reference, 42nd ed. Montvale, NJ, Medical Economics Data Production, 1988.
26c. Physician's Desk Reference, 51st ed. Montvale, NJ, Medical Economics Data Production, 1997, pp 1076–1077.
27. Pigatto PD, Bigardi A, Legori A, et al. Allergic contact dermatitis prevalence in patients with otitis externa. Acta Derm Venereol 71:162, 1991.
28. Pistorius B, Shan M, Heyd A. Ciprofloxacin otic solution. Paper presented at the 37th Interscience Conference on Antimicrobial Agents and Chemotheraputics (ICAAC), Toronto, Canada. September 28 to October 1, 1997.
29. Podoshin L, Fradis M, David JB. Ototoxicity of ear drops in pa-

tients suffering from chronic otitis media. J Laryngol Otol 103:46, 1989.

30. Rasmussen PA. Otitis externa and allergic contact dermatitis. Acta Otolaryngol 77:344, 1974.

31. Smith IM, Keay DG, Buxton PK. Contact hypersensitivity in patients with chronic otitis externa. Clin Otolaryngol 15:155, 1990.

32. Thorp MA, Kruger J, Oliver S, et al. The antibacterial acidity of acetic acid and Burow's solution as topical otological preparations. J Laryngol Otol 112:925, 1998.

33. Tommerup B, Moller K. A case of profound hearing impairment following the prolonged use of framycetin ear drops. J Laryngol Otol 98:1135, 1984.

34. Van Ginkel CJ, Bruintjes TD, Huizing EH. Allergy due to topical medications in chronic otitis externa and chronic otitis media. Clin Otolaryngol 20:326, 1995.

35. Waisbren BA, Spink WW. Clinical appraisal of neomycin. Ann Intern Med 33:1099, 1950.

16

Hearing Loss

Kenneth M. Grundfast, M.D., and Nicole F. Siparsky, M.D.

At one time, the role of an otolaryngologist managing hearing loss in children was mostly limited to determining the child's hearing threshold, finding out whether a hearing aid might be beneficial, and referring the child for management to other professionals. Investigating the cause of the hearing loss might have been considered a pursuit largely of academic interest, superfluous in terms of the patient's management. In the past several decades, however, the entire approach to diagnosis and management of childhood hearing impairment has changed. As more is learned about the biologic basis for childhood hearing impairment and more can be done to assist even those children with the most profound hearing loss, the approach to diagnosis and management of childhood hearing loss is changing. Now, universal newborn hearing screening programs employing auditory brain stem response (ABR) and otoacoustic emissions testing (OAE) are likely to detect hearing impairment as early as possible in affected neonates.[61] Technologic advancements, including hearing aids and cochlear implants, are available to assist the hearing-impaired child in developing good language and communication skills. Furthermore, genetic testing can uncover gene mutations responsible for hearing impairment.

Much of a child's learning is dependent on information received from listening to speech and other sounds in the environment. As children grow and develop, they continually rely on their hearing as they acquire and refine their communicative skills, cognitive abilities, and skills in social interaction. As such, significant hearing impairment may affect many aspects of a child's development. Given the importance of hearing in the context of a child's overall development, a child suspected of having a hearing loss deserves thorough evaluation. To delay and temporize can be detrimental, whereas an evaluation that leads to a finding of normal hearing either may allay a parent's fears about possible deafness or may lead to the conclusion that there is dysfunction somewhere in the nervous system other than in the auditory portion.

Depending on the age of the child, an evaluation to determine whether manifest symptoms are due to hearing impairment can be difficult. There is an element of subjectivity inherent in the meaningful perception of auditory stimuli. Although inferences can be made from observing a child's response to auditory stimuli, only the child is actually aware of the type of information that is ultimately received from auditory stimuli. Younger children are less able than older children to describe in words any abnormalities in the perception of sound that they are experiencing or to cooperate for the behavioral audiologic tests that might confirm a suspected hearing impairment. However, objective, nonbehavioral audiologic testing allows the otolaryngologist to estimate the hearing ability of neonates, infants, and young children. Most importantly, neonatologists and pediatricians who are confronted with a parent's or someone else's concern that a baby may not be hearing normally must keep in mind this dictum:

No neonate, infant, or child is too young to have hearing tested when there is the suspicion that hearing may not be normal.

The Five Cs of Evaluation and Management

All children suspected of having hearing impairment must be fully evaluated either until hearing loss is confirmed and appropriately managed or until objective data prove that hearing is normal. Therefore, once hearing impairment is suspected, further assessment of hearing is mandatory. However, knowing where to begin an evaluation for the symptom of hearing loss may not always be easy. This chapter is organized using a convenient memory aid to assist those involved in the evaluation of children with hearing loss. The "Five Cs of Hearing Impairment" are used to recall the steps of evaluation and management of a child suspected or known to have hearing impairment. The complete process of evaluation and management can be subdivided into the following components:

1. Core information: Gather information; explore reasons that hearing loss is suspected.
2. Confirm hearing threshold: Use all appropriate test methods to determine the hearing threshold for each ear.
3. Characterize the hearing impairment: Determine whether the hearing impairment is conductive, sensorineural, or mixed.
4. Cause: Determine the cause of the hearing impairment.
5. Care: Provide appropriate care to assist the child in developing good communications skills despite the hearing impairment.

Clarifying Confusion

Definition of Hearing Loss

The American National Standards Institute defines *hearing loss* as the difference from the normal ability to detect sound relative to its established standards. Audiometric 0 corresponds to the average detection of sound at a range of signal frequencies, for example, 500 Hz, 1000 Hz, 2000 Hz, and so forth. Individuals generally are considered to have normal hearing if their ability to detect sound falls between 0 and 15 to 20 dB. Categories of hearing loss have been described and are used routinely by audiologists. Mild hearing loss is described as detection of sound within the 15 to 30 dB range, moderate hearing loss within 31 to 60 dB, severe hearing loss within 61 to 90 dB, and profound hearing loss at 91 dB or greater. Individuals with hearing losses in the mild, moderate, and even severe categories are more likely to be called "hard of hearing," while those with profound hearing loss are more likely to be called "deaf."[40]

Hearing loss in childhood can adversely affect communication, education, and the development of cognitive skills. Delays and disorders of communication can significantly affect speech perception and production as well as oral language reception and expression.[17] Social interactions, emotional development, and family functioning also can be affected when a child is hearing impaired.[46] With an understanding of the importance of these factors, comprehensive management of a child with hearing impairment should include early intervention. Hearing aids, speech therapy, and cochlear implantation should be considered when appropriate.

To facilitate early intervention, the Year 2000 Joint Committee on Infant Hearing (JCIH) has published guidelines for the early detection of hearing loss through federally mandated Universal Newborn Hearing Screening programs. These programs aim to identify a conductive or sensorineural loss averaging 30 to 40 dB or more in the speech recognition frequencies (500–4000 Hz) of a unilateral or bilateral nature using objective audiologic screening methods such as ABR and OAE.[61]

Hearing Loss versus Hearing Impairment

The terms *hearing loss* and *hearing impairment* are often used interchangeably. Clarifying these two terms, which really are not synonymous, can be helpful in the evaluation and management of children. Hearing loss describes a hearing deficit that is the result of a decline of hearing from normal or near-normal levels. Hearing loss conveys the notion that a patient's ability to hear was lost after birth. In contrast, hearing impairment describes a hearing deficit that is known to have been or is likely to have been present at birth. Hearing impairment conveys the concept that the child was born with impaired hearing.[40]

Hearing Impairment versus Deafness

Although many physicians make little effort to distinguish between the terms *deafness* and *hearing impairment*, it is helpful to think of deafness as the most severe type of hearing impairment. A hearing-impaired individual uses speech as his or her primary method of communication, despite the severity of his hearing impairment. In contrast, a *deaf* individual primarily uses sign language or depends on a cochlear implant for communication, despite his use of lip-reading and speech. Using the term "partial deafness" is confusing and, in fact, sometimes is considered distasteful by members of the Deaf community who believe that individuals are either deaf or not deaf.[40]

Congenital Hearing Impairment versus Hereditary Hearing Impairment

The terms *congenital hearing impairment* (CHI) and *hereditary hearing impairment* (HHI) are frequently used interchangeably and believed to be synonymous. However, the difference between congenital and hereditary hearing impairment is significant. CHI describes any hearing impairment that is present at birth. CHI may be due to a genetic mutation or a pathologic process that occurs during pregnancy or labor. Spontaneous or inherited mutations, as well as exposure to myriad pathogenic processes (e.g., maternal-fetal infection, hypoxemia, ototoxic agents, trauma), can result in CHI. For example, during the 1960s rubella epidemic, thousands of children were born deaf as a result of maternal-fetal infection. Similarly, babies born today with cytomegalovirus infection can have hearing impairment that is congenital but not hereditary.

Conversely, HHI is the result of a genetic mutation and can either be manifest at birth or develop later in life. Such a genetic mutation can occur spontaneously or be inherited. HHI present at birth is termed *congenital hereditary hearing impairment*, while HHI that develops later in life is termed *delayed-onset hereditary hearing impairment*. For example, one of the most common types of HHI is autosomal-dominant nonsyndromic delayed-onset progressive sensorineural hearing loss. In this genetic disorder, affected individuals are born with normal hearing. However, hearing thresholds begin to decline in the second decade of life. Depending on the severity of the disorder within a family, the hearing loss can progress rapidly and result in severe or profound loss by 50 years of age. In such cases, a history of similar hearing loss in several other family members helps to differentiate this hereditary disorder from autoimmune inner ear disorder. A large number of similarly affected family members further supports such a diagnosis.[40]

Syndromic versus Hereditary Hearing Impairment

Clinicians have a tendency to believe that a patient with a recognizable syndrome has a genetic disorder. However, the term *syndrome* means that an individual has a pattern or constellation of abnormalities that is recognizable and familiar, while the cause of a syndrome can be either genetic or exogenous factors. Common hearing impairment syndromes that are caused by gene mutations include Usher, Pendred, Waardenburg, and branchio-oto-renal syndromes. Syndromes that are not inherited or caused by a gene mutation include congenital rubella and Goldenhar syndromes. Also, it is important to remember that a gene mutation can occur spontaneously so that a child with a hearing impairment syndrome may have no affected relatives. For example, approximately half of the genetic mutations responsible for neurofibromatosis are spontaneous; that is, only half of individuals with neurofibromatosis inherit from a parent the gene mutation responsible for their hearing loss.[40]

Changing Epidemiology of Childhood Hearing Loss

Although much has been written about the epidemiology of childhood hearing impairment, the relative incidence of different causes of hearing impairment in children remains confusing. Various studies performed decades ago at schools for the deaf in the United States, Europe, and elsewhere yielded data that might have been accurate in the past. However, these data may no longer be relevant. Performed decades ago, many of these studies employed ill-defined parameters for the categorization of deaf or hearing-impaired children.[36] As such, it is difficult to determine the precise incidence and prevalence of the different causes of childhood hearing impairment from these studies. Estimates of the frequency of childhood hearing impairment include that of Wilson,[122] who estimated that there are 70 million people in the world with hearing loss greater than 55 dB. Additionally, Cohen and Gorlin estimated that there were between 2500 and 4500 profoundly deaf infants born in the United States in 1985.[6, 38]

Many epidemiologic studies in the United States and Europe suggest that at least one third of all cases of hearing impairment are hereditary. In fact, there is some evidence to suggest that half of congenital hearing impairment is hereditary.[40] Autosomal-recessive inheritance of HHI is acknowledged to be the most common pattern of inheritance. Although quoted rates vary slightly, as much as 77% to 85% of HHI is inherited in an autosomal-recessive pattern,[16] explaining the fact that about 90% of children with CHI have normally hearing parents. Autosomal-dominant inheritance is estimated to be the mode of inheritance in 15% to 23% of cases of HHI,[16] while X-linked inheritance is less frequently seen, resulting in 2% to 4% of the total number of cases of HHI. Mitochondrial inheritance of HHI is rare, responsible for less than 1% of cases. Interestingly, two thirds of cases of HHI are not associated with other findings and therefore are described as "nonsyndromic." Furthermore, HHI is not always manifest at birth; many types have a delayed onset and manifest in the second and third decades of life.

In about one third of cases of acquired (noncongenital) childhood hearing impairment, a cause for the malfunction in the auditory system can be identified with reasonable assurance.[38] However, the frequency of various identifiable causes of hearing impairment is dynamic rather than static. For example, during the era of the rubella epidemic in the 1960s, rubella was a leading cause of CHI. Similarly, just one decade ago, mumps and bacterial meningitis were leading causes of acquired sensorineural hearing loss. However, with the advent of the measles-mumps-rubella vaccine, the number of children developing acquired hearing loss due to mumps or bacterial meningitis is diminishing. On the other hand, today, cytomegalovirus infection is the leading infectious cause of congenital hearing impairment.[89]

The remaining one third of all cases of childhood hearing impairment that are not clearly hereditary and not obviously correlated with a specific causative factor can be described as *cryptogenic*. Much of what was previously considered cryptogenic is now understood to be hereditary, however. At present, less than 10% of the 200 or more genes thought to be responsible for hereditary hearing impairment have been identified.[40] As such, what is viewed today as cryptogenic hearing impairment may conceivably be understood at a future time to be hereditary. With further study and continued technologic advances in molecular biology, we may soon rely on genetic mutation detection and gene studies in a routine evaluation of hearing loss. In doing so, we will arrive at more accurate estimates of the true incidence of various types of childhood hearing impairment.

Even now, some commonly held notions about the epidemiology of childhood hearing impairment warrant reappraisal. For example, textbooks frequently state that the three most commonly occurring types of syndromic hereditary deafness are Pendred, Usher, and Jervell and Lange-Nielsen syndromes. Depending on how deafness is defined, this may or may not be a true statement. If deafness is defined as congenital, bilateral, profound hearing loss, then Pendred, Usher, and Jervell and Lange-Nielsen syndromes may be the most frequently *encountered* syndromic types of HHI. However, Goldenhar syndrome is the most commonly *occurring* syndrome. The three hearing impairment syndromes most likely to be encountered by a community-based primary care physician or otolaryngologist are Treacher-Collins, Waardenburg, and Usher syndromes. Furthermore, *nonsyndromic* HHI is far more common than syndromic HHI. There are more children who have unilateral and bilateral moderate or severe sensorineural or mixed conductive and sensorineural hearing loss than there are children born with bilateral profound sensorineural hearing impairment. Therefore, even though syndromes that include hearing impairment are interesting and worth knowing about, it is important to remember that for every one child with syndromic hearing impairment, there are two children without physical or other findings recognizable as a syndrome.

Acquiring Core Information

Acquiring core information includes obtaining a history (which includes gestational, perinatal, medical, surgical, and family history) and completing a thorough physical examination. Appropriate laboratory studies and genetic testing may provide additional useful information (see Diagnosis of Hereditary Hearing Impairment).

Gestational History

The infant born with impaired hearing, by definition, has congenital hearing impairment. In gathering information to determine the cause of a congenital impairment, the clinician will find it helpful to identify the factors that may have adversely affected fetal development of the cochlea or other parts of the auditory system. The human embryo is most susceptible to factors that can cause major morphologic abnormalities during the third to 10th weeks of gestation; until 20 weeks of gestation, certain physiologic defects and minor morphologic abnormalities may occur.[82] Prenatal infections, such as rubella, toxoplasmosis, influenza, cytomegalovirus infection, and syphilis, can cause changes in the embryo that will ultimately result in some form of hearing impairment.[7] For example, subclinical rubella infection in the mother can cause rubella embryopathy; this can occur even if the mother has had a previous attack of rubella, as immunity is not necessarily permanent[64] (see TORCHS section for more information).

Maternal ingestion of ototoxic or teratogenic medication may result in sensorineural, conductive, or mixed hearing loss. Teratogenic medications can damage the fetal auditory system (e.g., inner and outer hair cell damage), especially during the sixth and seventh weeks of gestation, resulting in sensorineural hearing loss. Ototoxic drugs potentially affect development of the auditory system (e.g., aplasia of the inner ear, organ of Corti dysplasia, middle ear anomalies and ossicular malformation, absence of cranial nerves VII and VIII, and a decreased number of ganglion cells), resulting in sensorineural, conductive, or mixed hearing loss.[102] Streptomycin (especially in the dihydro- form), quinine, and chloroquine damage neural elements in the developing ear of the embryo or fetus and thereby cause sensorineural hearing loss. In contrast, thalidomide embryopathy is due to a widespread involvement of the auditory apparatus, including the pinnae and osseous structures of the middle and inner ear.[68, 92, 105] Additionally, there have been reports of endocrine diseases of the mother, such as pseudohypoparathyroidism[53] or diabetes mellitus,[62, 66] that may predispose the fetus to congenital hearing loss. Thus, the prenatal history must be reviewed to identify any potential factor, infectious or otherwise, that may have had a deleterious effect on middle or inner ear development in utero.

Perinatal History

Certainly, the birth process and adaptation to extrauterine life can be stressful for the neonate. Intrauterine asphyxia and anoxia may lead to hearing impairment through toxic damage of the cochlear nuclei or inner ear hemorrhages.[31, 47] There is some evidence that the auditory system is selectively vulnerable to brief episodes of asphyxia at birth.[47] Early injury to brain stem auditory pathways can interfere with the development of normal auditory processing and can cause impaired language development. Kernicterus may also damage cochlear nuclei or other central auditory pathways.[52, 74] Although there is no definitive supportive evidence, it is logical to assume that events such as intrauterine hemorrhage, placenta previa, prolonged labor, forceps delivery, and possibly cesarean section may cause damage to the middle ear, inner ear, or central auditory pathways of the newborn.

To alert physicians to the increased risk of hearing impairment in certain infants, the JCIH has identified indicators or risk factors for hearing impairment in neonates and infants. The JCIH recommends, in their Year 2000 report, regular assessment of hearing every 6 months for 3 years for individuals with one or more of the following indicators:

1. Parent or caregiver concern about hearing impairment
2. Family history of childhood permanent sensorineural hearing loss
3. Syndromic findings associated with hearing impairment or eustachian tube dysfunction
4. In utero infection (e.g., TORCHS infection, influenza) or postnatal infection (e.g., bacterial meningitis)
5. Neonatal conditions including hyperbilirubinemia (requiring exchange transfusion), persistent pulmonary hypertension associated with mechanical ventilation, or use of extracorporeal membrane oxygenation
6. Admission to the neonatal intensive care unit for 48 hours or more
7. Head trauma
8. Acute, chronic, or recurrent otitis media for at least 3 months

Family History

Careful review of the family history provides information that can give clues to the cause and mode of inheritance of a newly diagnosed case of HHI. For example, when two or more siblings are affected and the parents and other relatives are not, recessive inheritance is probable. When boys but not girls in a family are affected, it may be difficult to differentiate X-linked hearing impairment from the autosomal variety. When the parents are consanguineous, it can be presumed that inheritance is autosomal-recessive, and this is true whether one or several children are affected. When one or more siblings are hearing impaired in addition to other relatives (such as parents, uncles, aunts, grandparents, or cousins), identification of a specific mode of inheritance may be extremely difficult. However, the presence of unilateral or mild bilateral sensorineural hearing loss in siblings, parents, or grandparents is suggestive of dominant inheritance. Familial conductive hearing loss that is not part of an obvious syndrome is likely to be inherited in an autosomal dominant or, more rarely, X-linked recessive manner. (No examples are known of conductive autosomal-recessive hearing impairment that is not part of a syndrome.) The most common type of dominant, clinically undifferentiated conductive hearing loss is otosclerosis, but this does not usually affect young children. In this way, characterizing a hearing impairment by mode of inheritance helps to narrow the differential diagnosis of hearing impairment.

Even if one is persistent in acquiring information about family members who had hearing impairment early in life, it may be difficult to construct a meaningful pedigree. Hearing impairment can be defined in social as well as biologic terms, and persons who are mildly or unilaterally affected may not consider themselves hearing impaired, or they may even be unaware of their hearing impairment. As audiometric test methods improve and as mandatory screening tests become more prevalent, children will be discovered who have significant sensorineural hearing impairment, although the same degree of hearing impairment in their parents or in previous generations may have remained undetected throughout life. In fact, it is not uncommon for such mild hearing loss in parents and other relatives to be identified for the first time during a family investigation initiated because a child failed to pass a school screening test.[36] When investigating a family's history of hearing impairment, the clinician may find the following specific questions helpful in eliciting useful family history:

1. Are there parents, siblings, or cousins with hearing impairment?
2. Are there any family members under the age of 30 years who have been diagnosed with hearing impairment or who wear a hearing aid?
3. Is there a family member with pigment abnormalities (such as a white forelock, premature grey hair, different colors within one eye, two different colored eyes, abnormal pigmentation of the skin, or unusual birthmarks)?
4. Are there any family members with eyes spaced widely apart?
5. Do any family members have blood or protein in the urine or kidney problems?
6. Are there any family members who have developed blindness or night-blindness?
7. Are there any family members with history of childhood fainting or loss-of-consciousness episodes or cardiac arrhythmias?

(For more information on HHI and genetic testing, see the Diagnosis of Hereditary Hearing Impairment and Genetics and Molecular Biology of Hearing Impairment sections.)

Physical Examination

Significant abnormalities detected during a physical examination may indicate that an observed hearing loss is part of a syndrome (Table 16–1). For example, certain eye and pigmentary abnormalities can provide clues to the presence of a syndrome. In Table 16–2, physical abnormalities that may suggest the presence of a syndrome are listed in a way that assists in making a diagnosis. Although many syndromes have an eponym, learning the generic name is more helpful in remembering the major components of the syndrome. For example, Goldenhar syndrome can also be described as hemifacial microsomy or oculoauriculovertebral spectrum. Remembering only the eponym does not help in remembering the components of the syndrome of this relatively common syndrome.[40]

In examining the ears, the size and shape of the pinnae and external auditory canals should be noted and compared to identify asymmetry. It is best to use a pneumatic otoscope to test eardrum mobility and to gain information about the presence or absence of fluid in the middle ear.[96]

Laboratory Studies

Although many otolaryngologists have attempted to develop a battery of tests[60] that might be helpful for diagnosis, there really is no specific set of standardized tests that has proved to be of exceptional diagnostic value in the assessment of all children with hearing losses.[6, 7, 60] Most often, an appropriately selected laboratory test will serve to confirm or negate a reasonable tentative diagnosis rather than to uncover a diagnosis previously completely unsuspected. The laboratory studies that may be helpful include those discussed in the following sections.

TORCHS Studies

As Universal Newborn Hearing Screening (UNHS) programs help to identify hearing impairment at an earlier age, otolaryngologists initially evaluating the hearing impaired will be responsible for determining the cause of newly discovered hearing impairment. Traditionally, the child newly identified with hearing impairment has been evaluated to investigate the possibility that the hearing impairment might have been caused by a perinatal viral or other infection. TORCHS is an acronym used to recall a group of congenital infections acquired by transplacental transmission during pregnancy: Toxoplasma gondii (TOxoplasmosis), rubivirus (Rubella), Cytomegalovirus, Herpes simplex virus, and treponema pallidum (Syphilis). Acquired in utero, each of these agents can potentially cause hearing impairment in the neonate or infant. TORCHS studies can help to determine retrospectively whether an intrauterine infection may have caused a hearing impairment.

Ideally, prenatal care would include TORCHS screening. To date, a plethora of data exist on cord blood and amniocentesis laboratory examinations designed to screen for infection or confirm suspicion of infection. Unfortunately, although many modalities are available for testing (e.g., polymerase chain reaction, enzyme-linked immunosorbent assay, Western blot test, culture), none are sufficiently sensitive or specific to warrant screening costs. Furthermore, the sensitivity and specificity of individual tests is not yet reliably high. Even combinations of tests fail to achieve reliable detection rates. Understandably, many mothers are not willing to undergo screening amniocentesis or cord blood sampling when the risk of complications from the procedure is greater than the risk of TORCHS infection.

The natural history of TORCHS complicates matters even more. Without reliable in utero detection through screening, clinicians will be relied on to detect congenital infection and have a low threshold for evaluation and management of subsequent hearing impairment. However, many infants with TORCHS go undetected, and, as

TABLE 16–1. Physical Abnormalities and Their Associated Hearing Impairment Syndromes

Examination	Abnormality	Disease or Syndrome	Hearing Impairment
Skull	Macrocephaly	Osteopetrosis (Albers-Schonberg disease)	PSN or PC
		Osteogenesis Imperfecta	PSN or PC
	Abnormal shape	Apert syndrome	CC
		Crouzon disease	CC, CSN, or both
		Craniostenosis	CC
		Craniometaphyseal dysplasia (Pyle disease)	CC, CSN, or both
		Cranial clefts	CC
		Osteitis deformans (Paget disease)	PSN or CC
	Failure of fontanelle to close	Cleidocranial dysostosis	CSN
Hair	White forelock	Waardenburg syndrome	CSN
	Low posterior hairline	Turner and Klippel-Feil syndromes	CC
	Twisted hair	Recessive pili torti	CSN
Face	Hemifacial atrophy	First branchial arch syndrome	CC
	Facial clefts		CC
	Leonine facies	Generalized cortical hyperostosis (van Buchem syndrome)	PSN
		Osteopetrosis	PSN or PC
	Dysplasia of supraorbital ridges	Frontometaphyseal dysplasia (Gorlin-Hart syndrome)	CSN and CC
	Prominence of frontal bone and coarse facial features	Hurler syndrome	CC
	Frontal bossing	Otopalatodigital syndrome	CC
	Narrow face in region of orbits and flattening of midface	Otofacial cervical syndrome	CC
	Flattened cheeks and coloboma of eyelids	Treacher-Collins syndrome	CC
	Facial paralysis	Mobius syndrome	CC
Eyes	Strabismus	Mobius syndrome	CC, CSN, or both
		Duane syndrome	CC
	Hypertelorism		CC
	Eyelid abnormalities		
	Coloboma of eyelids, slant, epicanthal fold, ptosis		CC and CSN
	Lateral displacement of medial canthi	Waardenburg syndrome	CSN
	Adherent	Cryptophthalmos	CC
	Microphthalmos		CSN
	Coloboma	CHARGE association	CSN
	Corneal dystrophy	Fehrs dystrophy	PSN
	Clouding or keratoconus		CC and CSN
	Epibulbar dermoids	Oculoauriculovertebral dysplasia (Goldenhar syndrome)	CC
	Blue sclera	Osteogenesis imperfecta (Ehlers-Danlos syndrome)	PSN or PC
	Iris heterochromia	Waardenburg syndrome	CSN
	Lens cataracts	Congenital rubella	CSN
	Fundus abnormalities	Usher syndrome	CSN, PSN
	Blindness	Norrie disease	PSN
		Primary testicular insufficiency	PSN
Ears	Pinna malformations		CC
	Atresia		CC and CSN
	Preauricular sinuses (dominant)		CSN
Nose	Saddle	Congenital Lues-Marshall syndrome	CSN
	Bifid	Medial facial cleft	CC
	Cleft lip, nose		CC
Mouth	Midline cleft lip	Orofaciodigital syndrome (Mohr II)	CC
	Microstomia	Otopalatodigital syndrome	CC
		Trisomy 18 syndrome	CSN, CC
Teeth	Pegged incisors	Congenital Lues syndrome	CSN or PSN
	Abnormal dentine	Osteogenesis imperfecta	PSN, PC, or both
	Coniform teeth and dominant onychodystrophy		CSN
	Abnormal dental crown morphology		CSN
Palate	Cleft palate	Otopalatodigital syndrome	CC
		Pierre Robin syndrome	CC, CSN, or both
		Other syndromes	CC
	Bifid uvula		CC

Table continued on following page

TABLE 16–1. **Physical Abnormalities and Their Associated Hearing Impairment Syndromes** *Continued*

Examination	Abnormality	Disease or Syndrome	Hearing Impairment
Neck	Goiter (recessive)	Pendred syndrome	CSN
	Goiter (recessive) and stippled epiphyses		CSN
	Short (torticollis)	Klippel-Feil syndrome	CC, CSN, or both
		Wildervanck syndrome	CC, CSN, or both
	Absent clavicles	Cleidocranial dysostosis	CC
	Narrowing of shoulders	Otofaciocervical syndrome	CC
	Webbing	Turner syndrome	CC, CSN, or both
Chest	Pigeon breast	Stippled epiphyses	CSN
		Trisomy 18 syndrome	CC, CSN, or both
		Marfan syndrome	CC, CSN, or both
Lungs	(none)		
Heart	Murmur	Ventricular septal defect with congenital rubella	CSN
	Murmur of congenital pulmonary stenosis	Lewis syndrome	CSN
	Murmur of mitral insufficiency	Forney syndrome	CC
Abdomen	Hepatomegaly	Wilson disease	CSN
Extremeties			
Hands	Knuckle pads and leukonychia		CC, CSN, or both
	Small fissured nails	Dominant onychodystrophy and coniform teeth	CSN
	Small fissured nails	Recessive onychodystrophy and strabismus	CSN
Hands and feet	Congenital flexion contractions of fingers and toes	"Hand-hearing" syndrome	CSN
	Clubfoot	Diastrophic dwarfism	CSN
	Split hand-foot	Wildervanck syndrome	CSN
	Flexion contracture of fingers	Hurler syndrome	CC
	Absent joint of fingers	Symphalangism and strabismus syndrome	CC
	Exaggerated space between thumb and index fingers	Otopalatodigital syndrome	CC
	Lobster-claw hands and feet	Cockayne syndrome	CC
	Stiff joints	Arthrogryposis	CC
Legs	Short lower legs	Absence of tibia	CSN
	Bowing of legs	Osteogenesis imperfecta	CC, CSN, or both
Arms	Limited elbow motion	Frontometaphyseal dysplasia	CSN
	Limited radial abduction of arm and hand	Madelung deformity	CC
Spine	Scoliosis		CC, CSN, or both
Stature	Achondroplasia		CSN
Skin	Albinism-dominant		CSN
	Small hyperpigmented lesion, especially head and neck	Dominant lentigines	CSN
	Hypopigmentation spots, especially head and arms	Hereditary piebaldness	CSN
	Keratitis, ichthyosis	KID syndrome	CSN
	Leopard-like spots of hypo- and hyperpigmentation	Sex-linked pigmentary abnormalities	CSN
	Ichthyosis of arms but not legs	Recessive atypical atopic dermatitis	CSN
	Inability to sweat	Dominant anhidrosis (ectodermal dysplasia)	CSN
	Xeroderma pigmentosum (with neurologic disease)	De Sanctis-Cacchione syndrome	CSN
	Urticaria, nephritis, and amyloidosis	Muckle-Wells syndrome	PSN
	Ota nevus		
	Neurofibromatosis	von Recklinghausen disease	PSN and CC
Neurologic			
Epilepsy	Photosensitive epilepsy	Hyperprolinemia type I (major part)	
		Hermann syndrome	PSN
	Progressive familial myoclonic epilepsy and progressive cerebral degeneration (minor part)	Unverricht disease	PSN

TABLE 16–1. Physical Abnormalities and Their Associated Hearing Impairment Syndromes *Continued*

Examination	Abnormality	Disease or Syndrome	Hearing Impairment
Mental status			
Retardation from birth	And ataxia and hypogonadism	Richards-Rundle syndrome	CSN
	And coarse facies, spine and digit bone changes	Hurler syndrome	
	And muscle wasting and recessive retinal detachment	Small syndrome	CSN
	And hyperprolinemia type I (minor part)	Shafer syndrome	
	And hereditary nephritis, epilepsy, diabetes	Hermann syndrome	PSN
	And retinitis pigmentosa, obesity, and polydactyly	Laurence-Moon-Biedl syndrome	CSN
	And retinal malformation	Norrie disease	PSN
	And homocystinuria (one case)		
Mental deterioration	And retinitis pigmentosa	Cockayne syndrome	PSN
	And myopia	Flynn-Aird syndrome	CSN
	And encephalopathy, subcortical	Schilder disease	
Motor abnormalities	Cerebral palsy		CSN
	Spasticity and optic atrophy	Opticocochleodentate degeneration	CSN
	Ataxia	Spinocerebellar degeneration (Friedreich ataxia)	PSN
		Richards-Rundle syndrome	CSN
		Hermann syndrome	PSN
		Vestibulocerebellar and retinitis pigmentosa (Hallgren syndrome)	CSN
		Hyperuricemia and renal insufficiency (dominant in Rosenberg Progressive ataxia)	PSN
	Childhood Huntington chorea (rare part)		CSN and PSN
Sensory neuropathy	Dominant sensory radicular neuropathy		PSN
Motor neuropathy	Polyneuropathy, ichthyosis, and retinitis pigmentosa	Refsum syndrome	PSN
	Peripheral neuropathy, skeletal anomalies, and dominant myopia	Flynn-Aird syndrome	CSN
	Familial polyneuropathy (resembling Charcot-Marie-Tooth disease) with nerve deafness seen with optic atrophy, nephritis, neurofibromatosis, achalasia		
	And mental deficiency and ataxia	Richards-Rundle syndrome	CSN
Myopathy	And growth failure and chronic lactic acidemia		
	Muscle wasting, retinal detachment, and mental retardation	Small syndrome	CSN
	Facioscapulohumeral dystrophy associated with nerve deafness		
Endocrine	Goiter	Pendred syndrome	CSN
	Hypogonadism and blindness		CSN
	Obesity and diabetes, retinal degeneration	Alstrom syndrome	CSN
	Obesity, polydactyly, and retinitis pigmentosa	Laurence-Moon-Biedl syndrome	CSN
Multiple physical changes		Trisomy 13–15 (Patau syndrome, Trisomy D1)	CSN and CC
No physical findings		Trisomy 18 (Trisomy E)	CSN and CC

CC, congenital conductive; CSN, congenital sensorineural; PC, progressive conductive; PSN, progressive sensorineural.
Modified from Jaffe BF. Hearing Loss in Children: A Comprehensive Text. Baltimore, University Park Press, 1977.

such, clinicians will likely refer these patients for otolaryngologic evaluation *after* the onset of hearing impairment of unknown origin.

With the implementation of universal newborn hearing screening, more patients with impaired hearing are expected to be identified at an earlier age and be referred for evaluation. These patients will likely represent the youngest patients that an otolaryngologist will evaluate for TORCHS-related hearing impairment. However, the onset of TORCHS-related hearing impairment may be delayed; patients who experience such a delay are likely to be missed by universal screening.

TABLE 16–2. Syndromic Diagnosis Scoring System

Findings	A	B	C	D	G	J	P	S	T	U	W	X
Premature gray hair, white forelock											2	
Branchial cleft cyst		2										
Unilateral mandibular hypoplasia					3							
Bilateral mandibular hypoplasia									1		1	
Macrostomia					1				1			
Goiter							4					
Pigmentary changes, vitiligo, depigmentation											1	
Skeletal abnormalities, enlargement of ankles, knees, wrists								3				
Pain or stiff joints								1				
Vertebral dysplasia					2							
EKG abnormalities, prolonged QT interval, syncopal episodes						4						
Stapes surgery, perilymph gusher												4
Chronic nephritis or renal insufficiency	1											
Hematuria	3											
Renal dysplasia or abnormal-shaped kidneys	2	2										
Downward-sloping palpebral fissures									2			
Stapes fixation					1				1			2
Marfanoid habitus								1				
Mental retardation										1		
SNHL without findings listed above			1	1								
Congenital SNHL		1	4			1	1	1		2	1	
Mixed hearing loss		1						1	1			1
Congenital hearing loss		1			1			1	1			1
Progressive hearing loss	1			4								
Vestibular hypofunction										1	1	1
Preauricular pits		2			1							
Deformed external ear, micotia		1			1				3			
Atretic canal					1				1			
Retinitis pigmentosa										3		

TABLE 16–2. Syndromic Diagnosis Scoring System *Continued*

Findings	A	B	C	D	G	J	P	S	T	U	W	X
Lenticonus, splenophakia, cortical cataracts	1							1				
Widely spaced medial canthorum, dystopia canthorum											1	
Confluent eyebrows (synophrys)											1	
Heterochromia											1	
Congenital/progressive myopia								2				
Retinal detachment								1				
Glaucoma and/or cataracts	1							1				
Coloboma					1				2			
Lateral cilia deficient to coloboma									1			
Flat midface, broad nasal root									1	1	1	
Unilateral facial paralysis					1							
Cleft lip or palate, high arch									1	1	1	
Patient's total score												

A, Alport syndrome; B, branchio-oto-renal (BOR) syndrome; C, dominant congenital sensorineural hearing loss; D, autosomal-dominant/nonsyndromic hearing loss; G, Goldenhar syndrome; J, Jervell and Lange-Nielson syndrome; P, Pendred syndrome; S, Stickler syndrome; T, Treacher-Collins syndrome; U, Usher syndrome; W, Waardenburg syndrome; X, X-linked mixed hearing loss with stapes gusher.

Today, with universal newborn hearing screening, an otolaryngologist will be called on to evaluate TORCHS-related hearing impairment in the earliest days of life. In evaluating young patients suspected of TORCHS-related hearing impairment, it is important to keep in mind the individual natural history of each infection. In many cases, a patient may require regular follow-up for detection and treatment of delayed-onset hearing impairment resulting from a TORCHS infection. When evaluating any neonate or infant, it is important to recognize that the *natural history of disease*, not the available tests, can make diagnosis difficult.

TORCHS Infections

Congenital Toxoplasmosis

Historically, infection with the protozoan *Toxoplasma gondii* was associated with the ingestion of food or water contaminated with animal feces or of raw or undercooked meat containing encysted organisms. The current risk factors most strongly predictive of acute infection in pregnant women were recently identified in a study of the population of six large European cities: eating undercooked meat (30–63%), contact with soil (6–17%), and travel outside of the United States, Canada, or Europe. Unlike in prior studies, however, contact with cats was not a risk factor. Investigators suggested that cat feces (which contains infectious cysts), not the cat itself (e.g.,

cat fur), is infectious; contact with infected soil or litter was noted as the source of infection.[18] Furthermore, tachyzoite-stage *T. gondii*, often present in unpasteurized milk and milk products, was thought previously to be destroyed by gastric juice during ingestion. However, recent evidence, which includes a case of acute toxoplasmosis in a breast-fed infant, suggests that ingested tachyzoites can cause infection.

Today, the time of infection and history of prior maternal *T. gondii* infection contribute to assessing the risk of *T. gondii* intrauterine infection. Mothers without prior exposure to *T. gondii* are at risk for transmitting a newly acquired (primary) infection across the placenta, potentially resulting in congenital toxoplasmosis. Primary maternal infections place the fetus at a higher risk of symptomatic infection, with transmission rates around 15 to 20%. Despite the type of infection (primary, secondary, or reactivation), transmission of *T. gondii* in early pregnancy is associated with the most severe congenital infection and sequelae in infancy. Those infections transmitted either late in pregnancy or in the presence of serologic protection (secondary or reactivation infection) often result in an asymptomatic clinical picture at birth with disease later in life. In one recent study, only 15% of infants with congenital toxoplasmosis had signs or symptoms of infection at birth. Unfortunately, a low infectious load results in negative early clinical and laboratory examination findings in 25% of congenital toxoplasmosis cases.[100] Monitoring of prenatal and postnatal maternal and infant sera still misses at least 50% to 85% of cases of congenital toxoplasmosis.

For this reason, the diagnostic testing standard for identifying congenital *T. gondii* infection is infant IgG seroconversion within the first 12 months of life, detected by serial enzyme-linked immunosorbent assay examinations of infant serum. The most reliable testing includes neonate (drawn within 4 weeks of life) and infant (drawn at 3-month intervals) serum enzyme-linked immunosorbent assay and Western blot test for immunoglobulin (Ig) A, IgM, and IgG.[101, 117] A fetus exposed to *T. gondii* in utero may have negative cord blood and amniocentesis laboratory findings, as well as negative clinical and laboratory findings at birth and in early life. Within the first 12 months of life, the infant will clear maternal IgG from its system and begin to produce its own. As such, an infant should demonstrate a *T. gondii*-specific IgG seroconversion within 12 months of life. An IgM response, suggesting acute infection in the neonate and infant, is difficult to detect, as the window of IgM production may be only several weeks. Nevertheless, maternal seroconversion (IgM, IgG) during pregnancy should raise suspicion of subclinical infection in the neonate or infant, warranting following for infant seroconversion. When choosing immunoglobulin analysis, the practitioner should keep in mind that IgA[28] and IgE[116] add marginally to improving the diagnosis of congenital toxoplasmosis. However, the short kinetics of IgE make it useful in precise dating, while early detection of persistent IgE levels is associated with a progressive course.

Treatment of congenital toxoplasmosis has not been well studied. In one study, no significant benefit from administration of antiparasitic treatment during pregnancy on positive serologic results was observed. Furthermore, there have been no reports of randomized clinical trials investigating the efficacy of current treatment regimens for congenital toxoplasmosis in the neonate or infant. In cases of seroconversion, treatment using agents such as sulfadiazine and pyrimethamine should be coordinated with the patient's pediatrician, as other sequelae of *T. gondii* infection must be followed (e.g., chorioretinitis, leading to blindness).

Congenital Rubella Syndrome

Congenital rubella syndrome is a clinical diagnosis that requires laboratory confirmation. Laboratory confirmation methods include serologic testing in either the infant or the mother as well as isolation of the rubivirus from an infant specimen.[14] In developing nations, rubella vaccination is infrequently a part of immunization programs. However, in mothers with a history of either vaccination or previous exposure, maternal and fetal or neonate infection may be subclinical and go undetected. As in other viral infections, rubivirus infection in the early first trimester can result in profound hearing loss, as there is no embryonic immunologic response to prevent virus spread. Deafness, retinopathy, and neurologic and cardiovascular changes occur when infection occurs prior to the first 16 weeks of gestation and are rare after this time, limited by the fetal immune response of the second trimester and

increased transfer of maternal IgG.[118] By the age of 3 years, as many as one half of children born to mothers with maternal symptomatic first-trimester rubella will have demonstrable hearing loss.

The chance of embryonic infection decreases in the second trimester but again increases later in the third trimester, possibly because of placental changes. As such, first- and third-trimester infections place the fetus at the greatest risk for hearing loss. The pathogenesis of congenital rubella syndrome remains unclear, although one popular theory suggests that rubivirus spreads through the vascular system, affecting the small blood vessels of the body, including the inner ear.[118]

Infants born with congenital rubella syndrome demonstrate elevated fetal serum IgM during the first few years of life in addition to clinical signs and symptoms of infection. In contrast, serial rubella titers of unaffected infants born to exposed mothers show a decline and disappearance of maternal rubella antibody at about 6 months of age, at which time the majority of maternal antibody detected in infant serum has been cleared. At 10 to 12 months of age, IgM and IgG titer determinations should be repeated. In congenital rubella syndrome, rubivirus may be cultured from serum as late as 3 years after birth despite the presence of rubella antibodies.[82] Persistent elevation of antibody titers in an infant without recognizable sequelae of infection is still highly suggestive of in utero infection. Quite possibly, the widespread use of rubella vaccine may aid in the late diagnosis of subclinical congenital rubella as a cause of hearing loss. About 19% of children with known congenital rubella have no demonstrable antibody titer by 5 years of age.[32] When these children are given the rubella vaccine, only 10% convert to seropositive. Although more work needs to be done in this area, the failure of a deaf or hearing-impaired child to develop antibodies after receiving the rubella vaccine may suggest that rubella could have been the cause of the hearing loss.[6]

Congenital Cytomegalovirus

Exposure to cytomegalovirus (CMV) can be demonstrated in about 80% of adults by serologic testing. As with varicella virus, CMV infections can reactivate, but the majority of CMV infections in adults are asymptomatic.[37] Maternal infection or reactivation of CMV infection in pregnancy places the fetus at risk for intrauterine infection and congenital cytomegalovirus infection (CCMVI).[15, 75] Primary maternal CMV infection places the fetus at the greatest risk for infectious sequelae and is transmitted (at a rate of 40%–50%[13]) more frequently than reactivation infection,[15, 75] which is transmitted 0.5% to 1% of the time. Overall, CMV infection is transmitted to 0.3% to 2.3% of newborns.[1, 48, 75, 106] In populations with low socioeconomic status, the prevalence of CCMVI is as high as 6.8%. However, in both types of transmission, severe neurologic sequelae are possible.

Currently, there are no CMV screening guidelines, even though approximately 2 infants are affected per 1000 live births. Using maternal serum anti-CMV IgM and IgG detection, pilot screening programs aim to identify maternal infection during routine prenatal screening.[48, 75] However, 90% of maternal infections are asymptomatic and go undetected without such programs. Furthermore, less than 20% of infected infants are symptomatic at birth.[34, 75, 106] Although the mortality rate in symptomatic infants reaches 30%, nearly all (>90%) of asymptomatic infants will develop neurologic sequelae, including deafness, making CMV the most common infectious cause of central nervous system damage today.[75]

With the widespread immunization of children against measles, mumps, and rubella, CCMVI has now become the leading infectious cause of sensorineural hearing loss in infants.[33, 89] The onset of sensorineural hearing loss may occur at birth or be delayed, and the hearing loss becomes progressively worse in nearly half of all patients with CCMVI. Approximately 3% to 6.5% of children with CCMVI who are older than 3 months will develop late-onset hearing loss.[34] By 1 year of age, approximately 17% of infants with CCMVI have demonstrable hearing impairment.[15] Prior to universal newborn hearing screening, only 14% of children with sensorineural hearing loss attributed to CCMVI were detected.[34] As universal newborn hearing screening becomes more prevalent, the early detection of sensorineural hearing loss attributed to CCMVI may increase. Risk factors for hearing loss, including suspicion of CMV infection, aminoglycoside use, and family history of hearing loss, may help in identifying candidates for serial audiologic evaluations, which are useful in the early detection of CCMVI-related sensorineural hearing loss in the first 3 years of life.

Patients with CCMVI are chronically infected. The kidney is a prominent site of virus replication,[75] and, as such, the fetus, neonate, and infant excrete CMV in the urine for years. For this reason, the gold standard for CMV diagnosis remains urine culture. However, CMV culture of other bodily fluids is available (e.g., blood, human milk), as is urinary CMV antigen detection (e.g., by enzyme-linked immunosorbent assay). In establishing a diagnosis of congenital infection, it is important to obtain neonate samples for culture within the first few weeks of life. After this time, positive cultures and antigen testing will strongly implicate, but not confirm, congenital infection in the neonate.

Sensorineural hearing loss and progressive sensorineural hearing loss can occur in children who are known to have had CMV urine excretion for a relatively short time. Virus is cleared from the blood in both symptomatic and subclinically infected infants.[98] As such, serum examinations are unreliable in confirming CMV infection. At times, the diagnosis of CMV is a difficult one to make, as testing is often complicated by virus latency, reactivation, and infection without disease.[97] Currently, no federally approved treatment for CCMVI exists, although results of clinical trials of ganciclovir for newborns are currently being analyzed. Women in contact with children who attend day care centers are at risk for maternal CMV infection; 25% of mothers acquire their CMV infection by this method of contact.[33] In summary, although CMV infection of pregnant mothers and newborn babies is relatively common, determining the extent to which CMV causes hearing impairment in children without obvious sequelae of CMV infection can be extremely difficult.

Congenital Herpes Simplex Virus Infection

Although TORCHS testing of infants newly diagnosed with hearing impairment has been traditional, the extent to which herpes simplex virus (HSV) actually causes congenital hearing impairment is not well known. Neonatal HSV is usually of the HSV-2 type. However, neonatal infections are rarely caused by in utero exposure. Despite the mode of transmission, signs of infection are present by 3 weeks of age in most (97%) neonates, with neurologic impairment and hearing loss seen in most cases of disseminated infection. Unfortunately, neonates with disseminated infection have a mortality rate of 85%. Skin lesions and scars are the more easily detected physical findings of in utero HSV-2 infection.[102] Confirmation of HSV infection transmitted either in utero or in delivery warrants suspicion of concomitant hearing impairment and evaluation with follow-up, as both types of transmission can be associated with hearing impairment.

Congenital Syphilis

The last national syphilis epidemic in the United States in the late 1980s was followed by a congenital syphilis epidemic in the early 1990s. Since then, national rates of congenital syphilis have declined from 1992 to 1998. However, rates of congenital syphilis in the southeastern United States and in minority racial or ethnic populations remain disproportionately high, despite impressive treatment success rates with penicillin. The risk of fetal transmission is estimated to be 70% to 100% for untreated early syphilis. Unlike other intrauterine infections, infection of the fetus is rare before the fourth month of gestation. The later the stage of syphilis in the mother, the lower the risk for transmission of infection.[5]

There are two forms of congenital syphilis. Rhinorrhea, hepatosplenomegaly, and failure to thrive herald the early form of congenital syphilis prior to 2 years of age.[5] Manifestations of the late form of congenital syphilis appear after 2 years of age and include neurologic sequelae, such as hearing loss. Although there is a spectrum of syphilis disease manifestation in the infant, the majority of infants who are infected with *Treponema pallidum* are asymptomatic at birth.[102] As such, clinicians rely mainly on laboratory studies to make the diagnosis of congenital syphilis. Although the Venereal Disease Research Laboratory (VDRL) test provides a good method for screening a population for syphilis, the VDRL test result may *not* be positive in children with congenital syphilis. Therefore, the fluorescent treponemal antibody absorption (FTA-ABS) test rather than the VDRL test must be performed when congenital syphilis is suspected. In many hospitals and clinics, samples that are VDRL-positive are automatically sent for FTA-ABS testing. However, many laboratories will not proceed to the FTA-ABS test until a VDRL test result is positive. When attempting to rule out congenital syphilis as the cause of a neonate's or infant's hearing impairment, one should note clearly that the FTA-ABS test, not the VDRL test, is *required*.

As with other congenital infections, antibodies detected in infant serum in the early months of life are usually maternal in origin, acquired passively through the placenta. In this situation, a comparison of neonate/infant and maternal IgM and IgG titers reveals positive titers in both individuals, with a relatively lower titer in the child. Acquired maternal antibody is cleared within 3 to 6 months of life. As such, infant titers should become negative within 6 to 12 months of life.

During this first year of life, the infant immune system matures and ultimately develops an IgM response to infection, if one is present. As such, negative IgM results do not exclude the possibility that infection is present until age 1 year. For this reason, maternal and infant serial titers, obtained every 3 months during the first year of life, are helpful in ruling out congenital syphilis.[5] Rising maternal titers over time, or IgM or IgG detection in the infant after 6 months of age, is suggestive of infection. In cases of infection, infant IgM is usually elevated (1–4 g/L; normal, <0.7 g/L); this supports a retrospective diagnosis of congenital syphilis.

Titers should be followed after treatment; post-treatment neonate or infant IgM titers should return to normal. When analyzing results in an immunocompromised mother and child, one should interpret negative results with caution, as the individual may be infectious but seronegative. Finally, despite treatment of late-stage congenital infection, titers may fluctuate for months to years, and the VDRL test result frequently remains positive in association with a positive FTA-ABS test result.[123]

The diagnosis of congenital syphilis is a tissue diagnosis.[5] A presumptive diagnosis can be made by dark field examination of lesions and by serologic assays. Penicillin remains the antibiotic of choice for the treatment of syphilis and congenital syphilis. Additionally, penicillin is the only agent proven to be effective in the treatment of congenital syphilis.[54] While benzathine penicillin G is useful, treatment failures have been associated with it; some clinicians avoid the benzathine-type penicillin for this reason.[5]

Urinalysis

Urinalysis is useful in detecting proteinuria, hematuria, or cellular casts. Urine findings may indicate that hearing impairment is part of a syndrome, such as Alport syndrome (hereditary nephritis and progressive sensorineural hearing loss) or Muckle-Wells syndrome (nephritis with recurrent urticaria and deafness). In such cases, a renal biopsy should be considered for the definitive diagnosis of nephritis. Because hearing loss can occur in children with mucopolysaccharide abnormalities, a urine screen for products of inborn errors in metabolism can be helpful if a metabolic or mucopolysaccharide abnormality is suspected.

Thyroid Function Tests

In approximately half of the cases of Pendred syndrome (congenital defective binding of iodine by the thyroid gland associated with sensorineural hearing loss), some abnormality of thyroid function can be detected. Initially, a thyroid-stimulating hormone assay is the first test ordered to look for abnormal thyroid function, although some clinicians still use the T4 uptake test as an initial screening tool. The perchlorate discharge test is still widely used in confirming iodine organification defects, and it is often helpful in confirming the suspicion of Pendred syndrome, as half of Pendred cases will be missed with a screening thyroid-stimulating hormone test. For patients strongly suspected of having Pendred syndrome, however, a molecular analysis is useful, since there are four recurrent mutations that account for 75% of the mutations seen in patients with Pendred syndrome.

Complete Blood Cell Count and Chemistry

A hereditary type of hearing impairment has been reported in association with macrothrombocytopenia. Additionally, blood glucose screening for diabetes can be helpful in identifying Alstrom syndrome (congenital sensorineural hearing loss with associated diabetes and retinal degeneration).

Electrocardiography

A prolonged QT interval or inverted, biphasic, or upright large T wave, when associated with syncopal episodes and congenital sensorineural hearing loss, is indicative of Jervell and Lange-Nielsen syndrome. Electrocardiographic abnormalities, such as increased PQ interval, nodal and auricular extrasystoles, and QRS complex alterations, are seen in about one third of children with Refsum syndrome (retinitis pigmentosa, hypertrophic peripheral neuropathy, and sensorineural hearing loss).[99] In some cases of Friedreich ataxia (ataxia, speech impairment, lateral curvature of the spinal column, peculiar swaying and irregular mannerisms, and paralysis of muscles, especially of the lower extremities), both sensorineural hearing loss and cardiomyopathy may be present.

Vestibular Function Tests

In evaluating the child with sensorineural hearing loss, the testing of vestibular function can be problematic. Depending on the age of the child, obtaining sufficient cooperation to complete test procedures can be difficult, and the acquisition of data that can be meaningfully interpreted is sometimes nearly impossible. However, when vestibular function is accurately assessed, analysis of the data can confirm that the labyrinth as well as the cochlea is affected by an underlying disorder. Tests of vestibular function appropriate for children include caloric tests, torsion swing, simple and computerized rotating chair studies, and electroposturography. Abnormal caloric responses have been found in children with cretinism,[19] Hallgren syndrome, Klippel-Feil malformation,[34, 36] onychodystrophy,[29] Pendred syndrome,[11] unilateral congenital deafness,[11] Waardenburg syndrome,[80] and cervico-oculoacoustic syndrome of Wildervanck,[11] as well as in 26 of 33 ears of children with various disorders reported by Valvassori et al.[114]

Children as young as 6 years of age may undergo electronystagmography. Electronystagmographic abnormalities have reportedly been detected along with con-

TABLE 16–3. Classification of Congenital Malformations of the Inner Ear

Cochlea	Congenital Malformation	Findings	
		Vestibule and Semicircular Canals (SCCs)	*Cochlea*
Absent or malformed	Complete labyrinthine aplasia	No inner ear development; also known as Michel deformity	None
	Cochlear aplasia	Normal or malformed	None
	Cochlear hypoplasia	Normal or malformed	Small bud
	Incomplete partition	Normal or malformed; incomplete or lack of interscalar septum	Small
	Common cavity	Normal or malformed SCCs; cochlea and vestibule form common cavity without architecture	Normal
Normal	Vestibule-lateral SCC dysplasia	Enlarged vestibule with short dilated lateral SCC; remaining SCCs are normal	Normal
	Enlarged vestibular aqueduct	Normal or enlarged vestibule; normal SCCs	Normal

Modified from Jackler RK, Luxford WM, House WF. Congenital malformations of the inner ear: a classification based on embryogenesis. Laryngoscope 97(3 Pt 2 Suppl 40):2, 1987.

genital deafness in three patients with familial hyperuricemia and ataxia.[104] In addition, electronystagmographic abnormalities were reported in one patient with rubella and central nervous system involvement.[7] Absent vestibular function was found in two rubella patients in whom electronystagmograms were obtained.[2] This suggests pathologic change more extensive than the classic cochleosaccular degeneration traditionally reported in cases of rubella. Results of vestibular function tests may help to differentiate Usher syndrome type 1 from Usher syndrome type 2. Children with Usher syndrome type 1 have congenital hearing impairment and absent vestibular function, whereas children with Usher syndrome type 2 usually are born with normal or near-normal hearing and normal vestibular function.

Other Tests

Additional tests, such as genetic testing, dermatoglyphics, electroretinography, amino acid screening, blood urea nitrogen determination, serum pyrophosphate determination, and uric acid assay, may be of diagnostic value in certain instances, especially in confirming the tentative diagnosis of a syndromic type of hearing impairment (see the section on genetic testing at the end of the chapter).

Radiographic and Imaging Studies

Although there is no single imaging study that is needed for diagnosis in all cases of childhood hearing impairment, some studies can be helpful. Since the information derived from an imaging study often does not change a plan of management, the dose of radiation to which an infant will be exposed should be considered in deciding if and when to request an imaging study for evaluation of the newborn or infant with hearing impairment.[93] The imaging studies that may help include the following: plain radiography, computed tomography (CT), magnetic resonance imaging (MRI), and magnetic resonance angiography. Plain radiographs provide little useful information and are inferior to CT in the evaluation of infants with hearing impairment. Therefore, CT and MRI are the primary techniques used to investigate the middle and inner ear and surrounding structures.

In 1987, Jackler et al[59] devised a classification system for congenital malformations of the inner ear. Until that time, most radiographic abnormalities were simply referred to as "Mondini deformity." Recognizing the need for more precise radiographic descriptions to aid in the diagnosis and management of a wide variety of inner ear anomalies, Jackler et al detailed a spectrum of cochlear malformations detectable by CT, including complete labyrinthine aplasia, common cavity (average size of cavity, 6.8 mm × 10.6 mm), cochlear aplasia, cochlear hypoplasia, and incomplete partition (average cochlear diameter, 5.6 mm in vertical dimension). Jackler et al also identified inner ear malformations that did not include the cochlea: vestibular malformations (most commonly involving the lateral semicircular canal), enlarged vestibular aqueducts (average diameter, 3.6 mm), and internal auditory canal abnormalities. See Table 16–3 for the classification criteria.

Of note, only 20% of cases of congenital sensorineural hearing loss were associated with CT abnormalities in the Jackler series. In their review, the most common cochlear deformity on CT scan was incomplete partition (55%); this finding is the radiographic counterpart of the histologic finding of Mondini dysplasia. The remaining 45% of radiographic findings included cochlear and noncochlear abnormalities. In general, the more severe the anomaly, the poorer the associated hearing.

The most common radiographic abnormality of the temporal bone in children with sensorineural hearing loss is an enlarged vestibular aqueduct. Other less commonly encountered temporal bone abnormalities that can be identified with imaging studies include cochlear dysplasias, such as the Mondini deformity (incomplete partition) or the Michel deformity (common cavity), and abnormalities of the internal auditory canal, such as variation in size or shape.

Computed Tomography

Since there usually is no need to intervene surgically when a neonate or infant is discovered to have hearing impairment, the request for a CT scan of the temporal bones usually can be deferred until the child reaches approximately 3 years of age or until such time that a CT scan might be needed in the planning for insertion of a cochlear implant. For children 3 years of age and older, there is a benefit to obtaining a CT scan to look for developmental abnormalities of the temporal bone that could help in understanding the cause of hearing loss.

A non–contrast-enhanced, high-resolution, axial and coronal, 1 mm to 1.5 mm section CT scan serves as the initial imaging study of choice in the evaluation of hearing loss in most children. Viewed on a wide window setting (4000 Hounsfield units), bone and bone abnormalities are most easily defined. CT remains the imaging modality of choice for examination of the ossicular chain anatomy and oval and round windows. Beginning at the level of the carotid canal, coronal CT sections illustrate middle and inner ear structures, including the malleus, vestibule, internal auditory meatus, stapes, and oval window. The lateral semicircular canal, pyramidal eminence, descending facial canal, posterior semicircular canal, and jugular fossa should also be examined. To evaluate the mastoid antrum and air cells, further sections may be needed. To image abscesses and other extracranial or intracranial complications of suppurative ear disease, contrast may be considered. Otherwise, the use of contrast is rarely indicated, because MRI is both readily available and more sensitive than CT in the evaluation of soft tissue structures.[93]

Magnetic Resonance Imaging

Although CT is the imaging study of choice in attempting to detect a developmental or morphologic abnormality of the inner ear, MRI is indicated in some cases. MRI traditionally has been better than the CT for imaging soft tissues, but new methods of using the MRI are beginning to yield images comparable to some of the CT images, and MRI is almost as useful as CT for evaluating such disorders as cochlear dysplasia and enlarged vestibular aqueduct.

Evaluation by MRI (with and without gadolinium) of a child with sensorineural hearing impairment should be considered to look for evidence of an acoustic tumor (vestibular schwannoma) if (1) the child experiences sudden or rapidly progressive sensorineural hearing loss and a disproportionately poor discrimination score in the affected ear, and (2) he or she has relatives diagnosed with neurofibromatosis type 2.

Postgadolinium T1-weighted enhancement on the MRI scan is the hallmark of viral labyrinthitis, while T2-weighted images are useful in detecting labyrinthine membranous obliteration and fibrosis, which leads to ossification. Normally, air and bone appear black on MRI, and the middle ear cannot be seen in the absence of middle-ear fluid. On T2-weighted sequences, the fluids of the labyrinth give high signal, and nerves, such as the facial nerve, can be seen. In contrast to CT, in which the bony facial canal can be seen, MRI allows visualization of the entire length of the facial nerve. In cases of documented acute hearing loss, hearing loss associated with deficits in cranial nerve function, or hearing loss associated with central nervous system involvement, MRI may be preferable to CT scan as the initial diagnostic imaging study.[93]

Recent experience suggests that a new imaging technique, fast spin echo MRI (FSE-MRI), may provide information equal to that obtained from the MRI scan done with gadolinium for assessment of children with sensorineural hearing loss. The advantages of the FSE-MRI are reduced study cost and duration. In many medical centers, the FSE-MRI can be obtained on demand rather than having to be scheduled in advance, and this often enables an otolaryngologist to have the imaging study done on the same day that a child with hearing impairment is being evaluated in the office for the first time. The T2-weighted FSE-MRI scan has been shown to be a highly sensitive screening tool for unilateral sensorineural hearing loss, providing the ability to detect a variety of lesions other than a vestibular schwannoma. In one study, investigators demonstrated that T2-weighted FSE-MRI provides a cost-effective, sensitive method of evaluating unilateral sensorineural hearing loss compared with gadolinium-enhanced T1-weighted images. Screening for inner ear lesions of the internal auditory canal and cerebellopontine angle with high-resolution T2-weighted FSE-MRI of the internal auditory canal reduced screening costs by 54%.[21, 22] Additionally, T2-weighted FSE-MRI was more sensitive in detecting a spectrum of cochlear and vestibular anomalies present in ears with large endolymphatic ducts syndrome, providing "exquisite characterization of large endolymphatic ducts syndrome and local anatomy, which is useful both in diagnosis and in surgical planning."[23]

With equally good sensitivity at a lower cost, and excellent detailing of internal auditory canal anatomy, FSE-MRI has replaced brain stem audiometry and rivals CT as a screening modality to evaluate most cases of suspected acoustic tumor in some practices.[108] However, enhancing agents may still aid in visualizing the cochlea, vestibule, and almost any inflammatory lesions or inflammatory conditions, including labyrinthitis.

Newer MRI techniques, including fat suppression and magnetic resonance angiography, are available as well. Fat suppression is useful in identifying lesions of the orbit or skull base where surrounding fat obscures lesions with its high signal. With fat signal suppression and contrast, such enhancing lesions are most likely detected. Magnetic resonance angiography is rapidly replacing conventional angiography as a noninvasive technique for evaluating nonlaminar flow in large and medium-sized arteries. Vascular pathologic lesions of smaller-sized vessels, such as those of tumors, are not seen as easily with this imaging method, which uses the physiologic signal of blood flow to image the vascular system.[93]

Common Radiographic Findings

Enlarged Vestibular Aqueduct

The most common radiographic abnormality of the temporal bone in children with sensorineural hearing loss of unknown cause is the enlarged vestibular aqueduct (EVA). In 1978, Valvassori and Clemis[113] described 50 cases of EVA in 3700 consecutive patients referred for tomograms of the temporal bones. Since then, Levenson et al,[76] Jackler and De La Cruz,[58] and Arcand et al[3] have reported EVA series, and the relationship between an

EVA and hearing loss has evolved into the large vestibular aqueduct syndrome.

Early studies found that a vestibular aqueduct was not seen or was appreciated only by a lucent line never exceeding 2 mm in diameter anywhere along its length. In ears with EVA, the mean external pore size of the vestibular aqueduct was 6.2 mm on the right side and 5.0 mm on the left. Serial audiogram analysis revealed a subset of children with EVA who experienced hearing loss immediately following minor head trauma, forceful blowing into a wind instrument, and traveling by airplane.[114] Today, patients with EVA commonly present with failure of school screening audiogram, speech development delay, speech deterioration, otitis media, or imbalance.

Usually, large vestibular aqueduct syndrome includes hearing loss that is bilateral and progressive in a step-wise manner, often beginning in childhood in association with an enlarged vestibular aqueduct as the sole radiographic finding. Some children with large vestibular aqueduct syndrome may be asymptomatic, referred for a hearing evaluation after failing a routine screening test. Others suffer a recognizable worsening in hearing triggered by minor head trauma. Often, parents who report that their child is exceedingly clumsy may be referred to an otolaryngologist to rule out a vestibular cause of imbalance and poor coordination. Adults with EVA may be referred to an otolaryngologist for evaluation of vertigo, varying in severity from mild to severe.[40, 123]

Recently, comparison of high-resolution FSE-MRI and CT in the detection of enlarged vestibular aqueduct showed excellent correlation. While CT was slightly more sensitive in detecting enlarged vestibular aqueducts, FSE-MRI was more sensitive in detecting other subtle soft tissue findings. As such, investigators believe that FSE-MRI of the inner ear is complementary to CT in studying patients with large vestibular aqueduct syndrome, as MRI better displays the soft tissue and fluid of the membranous labyrinth.[20, 50]

Mondini Malformation

The second most common imaging finding in children with sensorineural hearing loss is the Mondini malformation of the cochlea. The Mondini malformation results from intrauterine insult during the seventh week of gestation. Progressive, sometimes fluctuant deafness is the usual symptom for which a hearing evaluation is obtained. On imaging, a distal sac or common cavity accompanies a normal basal turn of the cochlea. Patients with a Mondini malformation are candidates for cochlear implantation because the basal turn is not enlarged, and, as such, does not place them at risk for a cerebrospinal fluid fistula.[93]

Perilymphatic Fistula

In contrast to the Mondini cochlear malformation, the widened basal turn seen in more severe cases of cochlear dysplasia is associated with common cavity lesions that connect with both the subarachnoid space (of the internal auditory meatus) and the perilymph-endolymph space, placing the patient at risk for cerebrospinal fluid fistulas,

perilymphatic fistulas (PLFs), and meningitis. Absence of or a defect in the stapes footplate may allow a pathologic connection between the inner ear and the external ear and nasopharynx, placing the patient at risk for recurrent meningitis, labyrinthitis, or both.[93]

Accounting for 6% of unexplained cases of sensorineural hearing loss, PLF may be present with (25–50%) or without other temporal bone findings or extracranial congenital anomalies, including a shortened cochlear coil, dilated semicircular canals, and a widened inner ear vestibule. While no specific temporal bone findings correlate with PLF, such ear anomalies may predispose a patient to PLF, as a patent cochlear aqueduct can transmit cerebrospinal fluid pressure changes to the inner ear via labyrinth window rupture. This occurs when force is exerted on inner ear membranes (e.g., Reissner membrane, basilar membrane, or tectorial membrane). Intracochlear membrane rupture allows for mixing of perilymph and endolymph, which may result in hearing loss and vestibular symptoms. Patients with PLF often present with fluctuating (and, less commonly, stable) sudden hearing loss or progressive worsening of hearing that is unilateral or bilateral. These patients frequently suffer from persistent unexplained imbalance as well.[91] They often experience a sudden profound hearing loss after minor head injury, the Valsalva maneuver, or barotraumas.[14, 40]

The hearing loss associated with PLF correlates with the site of cochlear rupture, resulting in 100 Hz holes, or 100 Hz hearing deficits. These 100 Hz holes are frequently missed on screening audiometry, and, as such, the use of 100 Hz incremental audiometry from 400 Hz to 1300 Hz is useful in detecting this hearing loss. The fistula test may be employed to detect PLF by applying positive pressure followed by negative pressure to the affected ear. A positive test result is obtained in a patient who startles and moves away from the pressure. (Electronystagmography can be used to document such a response.) Exploratory tympanotomy is indicated when the patient has a history of sudden sensorineural hearing loss after head trauma or barotrauma. The beta-2 transferrin analysis, once thought to be a promising diagnostic test for PLF, now is widely viewed as being of questionable diagnostic significance.[14, 40]

In male patients with mixed hearing loss, X-linked mixed hearing loss with stapes gusher must be considered as a possible diagnosis. In 1991, Phelps et al[94] described a radiographic finding associated with X-linked mixed hearing loss with stapes gusher. The abnormality described by Phelps is a characteristic bulbous internal auditory meatus (IAM) as an associated finding of a thin or deficient bony plate separating the subarachnoid space from the perilymphatic space in the IAM. This thin bony radiologic finding cannot be appreciated by measuring the IAM, as was the practice in past years, because the malformation is not in the IAM. Instead, the deficient bone is the radiographic diagnostic finding; it cannot be measured because it is curved and has an associated physiologic gap of the spiral ganglion, which is located in the modiolus. Instead, appreciation of the deficiency of bone separating coils of cochlea from the IAM is a qualitative one. In such cases, fistulas may develop between the subarachnoid space and the internal auditory canal, placing the patient at risk for perilymphatic hydrops and gusher on stapes manipulation. Interestingly, carrier females of X-linked hearing loss mutations tend to have slight hearing loss and radiographs that are usually normal.

In cases of X-linked mixed hearing loss with stapes gusher, an attempt to remove or mobilize a fixed stapes bone is likely to result in a sudden rush of perilymph fluid out of the vestibule of the inner ear, placing the patient at risk for profound hearing impairment. There is no need to induce a gusher to diagnose this disorder. Additionally, enlargement of the vestibular aqueduct, hypoplasia of the cochlear base, and widening of the proximal facial nerve canal may also be present.[40, 93]

Michel Deformity

Cochlear and vestibular aplasia are accompanied by profound hearing loss that is often bilateral. The result of arrested development of the labyrinth during the fourth week of gestation, the Michel deformity is an anatomic anomaly that is revealed on imaging studies as an absence of the inner ear structures. Cystic cavities and hypoplastic internal auditory canals may be present. The Michel deformity is notable for middle-ear cavity expansion in the absence of a cochlea. This feature distinguishes the Michel deformity from labyrinthitis obliterans-ossificans.[93]

Abnormal Internal Auditory Canal

In adults, abnormality of the size and shape of the internal auditory canal as seen on a CT scan can be diagnostic of a tumor (e.g., Schwannoma, acoustic neuroma) of the eighth cranial nerve. Although eighth nerve tumors can and do occur in children, the incidence of such tumors is extremely low. However, abnormalities of configuration of the internal auditory canal that can help in diagnosis may be detected in children with sensorineural hearing loss. For example, an enlarged, bulbous lateral aspect of the internal auditory canal is the hallmark imaging finding associated with X-linked profound sensorineural or mixed hearing loss in young men (see previous discussion). Less commonly, widening of the proximal facial canal, EVA, or widening of the cochlear base is present. If a tumor is suspected, the use of MRI should be considered for further evaluation.[93]

Stapes Ankylosis

Stapes ankylosis is the most common congenital abnormality responsible for conductive deafness. Congenital abnormalities of the stapes footplate can rarely be detected with radiographic imaging but might be suspected if there are abnormalities of the cochlea or dysplasia of the temporal bone. Since exploratory tympanotomy or middle ear endoscopy using a telescope are the only methods for confirming suspicion of stapes ankylosis, imaging studies could be considered superfluous in the patient's assessment.[93]

Age-Specific Tasks: The Neonate

The use of an age-specific, task-oriented approach in the evaluation of hearing loss in a neonate can make a seemingly awesome challenge manageable.

Confirm

Universal newborn hearing screening (UNHS) is rapidly being implemented in hospitals throughout the United States. Probably within the next decade, every baby born in a hospital in the United States will have a screening hearing test prior to hospital discharge. Despite the inherent value of UNHS, the notion that all babies should have their hearing tested has not been accepted readily by all professionals involved in the early detection of hearing impairment. For many years, experts have held diverse opinions about the best method for early identification of hearing impairment. Some experts have advocated hearing screening only for those infants who manifest certain "risk criteria" as the most cost-effective approach. One review demonstrated that one quarter of infants ultimately diagnosed with some type of hearing impairment did not manifest any of the risk criteria delineated in the 1982 Joint Committee on Infant Hearing Position Statement. Opponents of the risk-criteria–dependent selective screening method contended that the risk criteria were not sufficiently reliable as indicators and instead advocated for universal newborn hearing screening.

With improved methods of auditory brain stem response (ABR) and otoacoustic emissions (OAE) testing, the possibility of testing the hearing of all infants soon after birth became feasible and cost-effective. Those who had developed UNHS pilot programs reported a greater rate of detection with lower cost and lower false-positive rates compared with targeted screening. Additional reports demonstrated that the false-positive rate could be reduced to less than 1%, with only a small impact on the mother-infant relationship in the rare false-positive case.

In October 1999, The United States Congress passed the Newborn and Infant Hearing Screening and Intervention Act (formerly known as the Walsh Bill) in support of early hearing impairment detection, diagnosis, and intervention. However, this federal law did *not* require that newborn hearing screening programs be initiated nationwide, nor did the law appropriate federal funds to pay for newborn hearing screening programs. Instead, the federal legislation appropriated funding to the Center for Disease Control and the Health Resources Science Administration to collect data on the effectiveness of newborn hearing screening programs.

Today, individual states are responsible for developing and implementing their own programs. Each state has the option of passing legislation requiring UNHS and then appropriating state funds to support those newly initiated programs. Currently, 32 states have UNHS programs. At the time of this publication, laws in 32 states require UNHS, and 8 states have similar legislation pending. However, for those states that do screen hearing, follow-up rates as low as 50% have been reported.

Recognizing the need for a UNHS program, the Joint

Committee on Infant Hearing (JCIH) published practice guidelines and recommendations in October 2000. These recommendations were based on numerous studies that demonstrate both the deleterious effects of hearing loss on development and the benefits of early intervention for hearing loss that is mild to profound:

1. All infants have access to physiologic hearing screening by OAE and ABR.
2. Infants who fail the screen undergo medical evaluation to confirm hearing impairment by 3 months of age. Individuals demonstrating permanent unilateral or bilateral sensory or conductive hearing loss averaging 30 to 40 dB or more in the speech recognition frequency region (500–4000 Hz) fail the screen.
3. Multidisciplinary intervention is undertaken prior to 6 months of age for infants with confirmed hearing impairment.
4. Individuals who pass their newborn screen but demonstrate risk factors for neonatal (birth to 28 days of age) or delayed-onset (29 days to 2 years of age) auditory or speech or language disorder should receive ongoing surveillance. Neonatal risk factors include admission to the neonatal intensive care unit for more than 48 hours, syndromal findings, family history of hearing loss, craniofacial anomalies, and in utero infection. Risk factors for infants (age 28 days through 2 years of age) include parent or caregiver concern regarding hearing, speech, or language development, family history, syndromal findings, postnatal infection, in utero infection, neonatal indicators such as hyperbilirubinemia requiring exchange transfusion and persistent pulmonary hypertension associated with mechanical ventilation, syndromes associated with hearing impairment, neurodegenerative disorders, head trauma, and chronic or recurrent otitis media with effusion.
5. Infant and family privacy rights are guaranteed through informed choice and consent; results are confidential.
6. Quality control programs monitor results to ensure compliance, cost-efficacy, etc.[61]

Currently, some early intervention services for infants with hearing loss are funded by government agencies. Personal amplification, language development, speech training, and cochlear implants are examples of effective habilitation strategies that have been combined to achieve the best outcomes. Depending on the screening technology, however, infants with hearing that is less than 30 dB worse than normal hearing or with hearing impairment related to neural conduction disorders or auditory dyssynchrony (formerly known as auditory neuropathy) may not be detected. For these patients, as well as others that pass their initial screen, ongoing monitoring for the development of delayed auditory or communication skills is important. Infants who display such delays should be referred for audiologic evaluation to rule out hearing loss. Such monitoring should include both OAE and ABR, as some conditions, including auditory dyssynchrony, are not detected using OAE alone.

In the future, newborn hearing screening may include genetic testing as well. Test batteries of genetic markers may become cheaper and could be used in infants with a family history of hearing loss, syndromal findings, or other predictors of hearing loss. For these reasons, the otolaryngologist will need a solid understanding of the genetics and molecular biology of deafness to evaluate a new population of infant patients that will present for evaluation of hearing loss in the future. For example, almost half of inherited deafness is due to mutations in *GJB2*, which encodes connexin-26, a gap junction component, on chromosome 13. Similar in frequency to cystic fibrosis in European and American populations, the prevalence of connexin-26 deafness is the result of a long-standing tradition of intermarriage among members of the deaf community.

Today, mutations in the *GJB2* gene are the leading cause of moderate-to-profound congenital hereditary hearing impairment in the United States. For this reason, some clinicians have called for universal *GJB2* mutation screening, and several simple, inexpensive, reliable polymerase chain reaction screening tests have been designed. However, other clinicians suggest that further study is needed in larger populations to better identify the relationship between hearing loss and allele variants prior to establishing the use of this test, which only marginally improves the power of conventional screening at a significant cost.

It is logical to attempt to test the hearing ability of neonates soon after birth and before discharge from the hospital in which the neonate was born. In a sense, while neonates are still in the hospital, they are part of a captive population, whereas when they are discharged to their respective homes, it becomes more difficult to identify and test those children suspected of having hearing impairment. Thus, much attention has been focused on in-hospital hearing screening programs for neonates. Further evaluation is warranted for any newborn who fails the newborn screening test or has identifiable JCIH risk factors (see earlier discussion).

The first step is to confirm the impression that there is impairment of hearing and to assess the degree of hearing loss. Not long ago, it was nearly impossible to reliably test a neonate's hearing. Today, however, nonbehavioral (objective) tests such as ABR and OAE are available. Although these may not actually be tests of hearing, they are helpful indicators of significant functional impairment in the neural pathways serving the auditory system. As for quantifying hearing loss, it is virtually impossible to measure precise hearing thresholds in the neonate. Despite this, nonbehavioral tests can be used to estimate a relative magnitude of hearing impairment. That is, test results can be interpreted as being nearly normal, indicative of significant hearing impairment, or indicative of moderate to severe hearing impairment. Although such information may not be precise, it can be helpful in identifying newborn children who will need close follow-up, further evaluation, and possibly early hearing amplification.

Characterize

Unless there is obvious ear canal atresia or other aural deformity, it is extremely difficult to differentiate conductive and sensorineural hearing impairment in the neonate.

Observations made on ABR test patterns can be helpful. Delayed appearance of the first wave with normal interwave latencies may be indicative of a conductive-type hearing loss. Elevated thresholds without a delay in the appearance of the first wave and with normal interwave latencies indicate that sensorineural impairment is probable. When interwave latencies are abnormal, some central nervous system abnormality may be responsible for the hearing impairment. Again, these are helpful diagnostic indicators, but they are not as precise or reliable as a battery of sophisticated behavioral tests. However, in dealing with neonates, it is of primary importance to know whether a significant hearing impairment is present; characterization of the type of hearing loss is of secondary importance. After it has been established that a neonate has poor hearing, further testing and evaluation during the first 2 years of life will usually elicit the information that is needed to proceed with proper diagnosis and management.

Cause

Hearing impairment that is discovered during the neonatal period is most probably the result of some untoward circumstance that occurred during fetal development or at birth.

Hereditary Congenital Hearing Impairment

Hereditary factors need to be considered, and a detailed gestational, perinatal, and family history should be obtained. A thorough physical examination should reveal abnormalities characteristic of a syndrome with which hearing loss is associated. A urine sample tested for protein and inborn errors in metabolism may be helpful in diagnosing syndromes that include nephritis (e.g., Alport syndrome) or abnormalities of mucopolysaccharide metabolism. If thyroid enlargement is apparent, Pendred syndrome should be considered and thyroid function evaluated. If there is a family history of Usher syndrome or if the neonate appears to have eye abnormalities, electroretinography may be of diagnostic value. An electrocardiogram is rarely helpful, although the Jervell and Lange-Nielsen syndrome can be diagnosed early in life when profound congenital deafness is found in association with a prolonged QT interval. Routine mastoid films and temporal bone CT scan are probably not warranted in the evaluation of neonates with hearing impairment because radiographic findings will be of little value in formulating plans for management of the neonate with impaired hearing (see Acquiring Core Information and the sections on hereditary hearing impairment).

After information has been gathered and analyzed, it may be possible to discover the cause of a neonate's hearing impairment. Of course, to recognize syndromic types of hearing impairment, one must have some familiarity with the syndromes that include hearing loss. Syndromes that can include hearing impairment are listed in Tables 16-4, 16-5, and 16-6. While these tables can be helpful, advancements in computer technology and data storage have made easier the task of recognizing syndromes and interpreting the significance of physical findings. Software programs, such as Pictures Of Standard Syndromes and Undiagnosed Malformations (POSSUM), are now available on CD-ROM. POSSUM contains information on more than 1500 published syndromes and 1600 patients, with 22,000 illustrations of syndromes and affected patients. Also available on CD-ROM is the London Dysmorphology Database.

Even though it is possible to conceive of numerous factors that may cause hearing impairment in the neonate, it may be difficult to detect a specific cause in individual cases unless the neonate has a clear family pedigree of inherited hearing loss or unless there are obvious abnormalities characteristic of a nonmendelian malformation syndrome known to include morphologic or functional aberrations in the auditory system. Today, a genetics consult may be useful in cases of cryptogenic hearing impairment, as genetic testing for common mutations responsible for hearing impairment is available at many institutions. In addition, geneticists may recognize more subtle physical findings associated with a syndrome. However, the majority of cases of hereditary hearing impairment are nonsyndromic; as such, no associated findings will be identifiable.[46]

Nonhereditary Congenital Hearing Impairment

Some acquired neonatal conditions are associated with hearing impairment that is present at birth. Congenital TORCHS infections (toxoplasmosis, rubella, cytomegalovirus, herpes simplex virus, syphilis) can result in hearing impairment at birth. TORCHS studies are helpful in determining whether intrauterine infection may have been a causal factor (see Laboratory Studies section for details). Also of note are neonatal intensive care unit (NICU) graduates and neonates born to mothers who abuse alcohol or street drugs, both of whom are commonly at risk for hearing impairment.

Premature Birth and Neonatal Intensive Care Unit Admission

With advances in neonatal medicine, an increasing number of premature babies and ill neonates successfully graduate from the NICU, often with documented hearing loss. In many cases, hearing loss is the result of a synergism of ototoxic drugs and noise exposure (e.g., closing cabinet doors, adjusting the position of the bed), although there are potentially numerous events and exposures that may contribute either directly or indirectly to hearing impairment. For example, hypoxia (directly), hyperbilirubinemia (directly), and persistent pulmonary hypertension (indirectly by metabolic derangements and use of ototoxic diuretics) are commonly seen in NICU-admitted babies; such conditions place a neonate at risk for hearing impairment.[102] For this reason, the JCIH has drawn attention to these conditions by naming many of them as risk factors for infant hearing impairment.[61]

Drug-Dependent Neonates

For the last two decades, the prevalence of illicit drug consumption has risen steadily in the United States. Un-

TABLE 16–4. Skeletal and Cranial Defects Associated with Hearing Impairment

Syndrome	Inheritance	Characteristics	Sensorineural	Conductive	Mixed
			_____ Type of Hearing Loss _____		
Osteogenesis imperfecta	Recessive	Brittle bones, blue sclerae	X	X	X
Hurler syndrome	Recessive	Mental retardation, cloudy corneas, blindness, thick eyebrows, onset of skeletal deformities after first year of life	X	X	
Morquio disease	Recessive	Dwarfism, normal-sized head, long extremities, short trunk			
Otopalatodigital syndrome	Recessive	Frontal bossing, prominent occiput, ocular hypertelorism, antimongoloid slant of eyes, fishmouth, pseudowinged knobby scapulae, broad distal phalanges of hands and feet, cleft palate		X	
Albers-Schonberg syndrome	Recessive	Brittle bones, intermittent facial palsy, optic atrophy, hydrocephalus, ocular nystagmus, exophthalmos	X	X	X
Klippel-Feil syndrome	Recessive	Fused cervical vertebrae, low posterior hairline; spina bifida and external canal atresia may be present	X	X	X
Cervico-oculoacoustic syndrome	Recessive	Fused neck vertebrae, spina bifida occulta, abducens palsy of eye, possible radiographic evidence of underdevelopment of the cochlea or labyrinth	X		
Crouzon disease	Dominant	Synostosis of cranial sutures, shallow orbits with secondary proptosis (frog eyes), hypoplasia of maxilla with relative prognathism, parrot nose, possible atresia of external auditory canal	X	X (usually conductive)	X
Cleidocranial dysostosis	Dominant	Fontanelles fail to close, facial bones underdeveloped, high arched palate, absence of clavicles	X		
Treacher-Collins syndrome	Dominant	Malformations of malar and other facial bones, antimongoloid slant of eyes with notching of lids (colobomas), high palate, external auditory canal and pinna malformations, middle-ear ossicular abnormalities	X	X	
Pierre Robin syndrome	Dominant	Cleft palate, small mandible, glossoptosis; may have atresia of ear canal, microtia of pinnae, middle-ear anomalies, digital anomalies	X	X	
Apert syndrome	Dominant	Acrocephaly (tower skull), fused digits (lobster-claw hands), shallow orbits, underdeveloped maxillas, fixation of stapes footplate		X	
Achondroplasia	Dominant	Dwarfism with normal-sized trunk, large head and shortened extremities, saddle nose, and frontal mandibular bone protrusions	X	X°	X
Marfan syndrome	Dominant	Long spidery fingers, scoliosis, hammer toe, pigeon breast, dolichocephaly, low hairline, tall and thin body structure	X	X	X
Branchial anomalies (Karmody-Feingold)	Dominant	Cervical fistulas, malformed external ears, preauricular pits, preauricular appendages	X	X	X
Myositis ossificans	Dominant	Formation of true osseous tissue in skeletal muscles, microdactyly of great toes, shortened thumbs	X	X	X
Symphalangism	Dominant	Fusion of proximal and middle phalanges of fingers and toes giving characteristic "stiff finger and toe" appearance, prominence on medial and lateral sides of foot at level of navicular and fifth metatarsal bones		X	

° Due to middle-ear effusions.

Modified from Black FO, Bergstrom L, Downs M, et al. Congenital Deafness: A New Approach to Diagnosis Using a High Risk Register. Boulder, CO, Colorado Associated University Press, 1971.

derreporting[69] of maternal abuse of street drugs (e.g., heroin, cocaine, cannabis, amphetamines, barbiturates) during pregnancy has been well documented, and such abuse places many unidentified fetuses at risk for passive substance dependency. In utero, maternal withdrawal can inhibit fetal oxygenation, resulting in hypoxia and secondary auditory system injury. Alternatively, neonates born to substance-abusing mothers often enter the world with one or more drug dependencies from which they can develop withdrawal symptoms and secondary complications.[116] For example, postnatal withdrawal in the neonate may result in respiratory distress and secondary hypoxia, again placing the auditory system at risk for hypoxic injury. Substance abuse, such as cocaine abuse, often results in premature delivery[17] and concomitant NICU admission, placing the neonate at risk for the hearing loss-related complications of premature birth/NICU admission.

With increasing numbers of so-called cocaine babies born every year, as many as half of drug-associated births are now estimated to be cocaine-related. Cocaine-related pregnancy complications (e.g., abruptio placenta) as well as cocaine-related fetal maldevelopment (e.g., growth retardation, congenital malformations) ultimately contribute

TABLE 16–5. Eye Abnormalities Associated with Hearing Impairment

Syndrome	Inheritance	Characteristics	Type of Hearing Loss: Sensorineural	Conductive	Mixed
Usher syndrome	Recessive	Retinitis pigmentosa, vestibulocerebellar ataxia, mental retardation	X		
Cockayne syndrome	Recessive	Retinal atrophy, motor disturbances, mental retardation, dwarfism	X		
Alstrom syndrome	Recessive	Obesity, diabetes mellitus, retinal degeneration	X		
Hallgren syndrome	Recessive	Retinitis pigmentosa, vestibulocerebellar ataxia, nystagmus, mental retardation	X		
Laurence-Moon-Biedl-Bardet syndrome	Recessive	Retinitis pigmentosa, polydactyly, hypogenitalism, obesity, mental retardation	X		
Refsum syndrome (heredopathia atactica polyneuritiformis)	Recessive	Retinitis pigmentosa, cerebellar ataxia, polyneuritis, electrocardiographic abnormalities, ichthyosis-type skin disorder	X		
Duane syndrome	Recessive	Ocular palsy (congenital fibrous replacement of rectus muscle), auricular malformations, meatal atresia, cervical rib, torticollis, cervical spina bifida		X	
Mobius syndrome	Recessive	Facial diplegia; lateral or medial rectus palsy bilaterally; auricular malformation; micrognathia; absence of hands, feet, fingers, or toes; tongue paralysis; mental retardation	X	X	X

Modified from Black FO, Bergstrom L, Downs M, et al. Congenital Deafness: A New Approach to Diagnosis Using a High Risk Register. Boulder, CO, Colorado Associated University Press, 1971.

to the profound neurodevelopmental sequelae of maternal cocaine abuse during pregnancy.[17] The onset of neurosequelae varies from immediate to delayed (appearing in childhood).[116]

Animal models have been used to demonstrate aberrant central nervous system development associated with the administration of alcohol, nicotine, or cocaine, supporting the theory that fetal exposure to such substances may result in altered nervous system and auditory system development.[30] This may result in impaired hearing in the neonate, infant, preschool-age child, or school-age child. In one small study, however, ABRs performed on neonates born to opiate-addicted mothers did not demonstrate a significant risk for early-onset hearing loss.[39] Therefore, while a variety of street drugs have been associated with acute withdrawal during the neonatal period, the resulting altered neurodevelopment may include hearing impairment that is detected at birth or at a later date. In such cases, prevention of withdrawal symptoms is crucial during the neonatal period to prevent such nervous system insult.[116]

Fetal Alcohol Syndrome

Fetal alcohol syndrome (FAS), also known as fetal alcohol abuse syndrome, is a collection of physical anomalies and nervous system abnormalities associated with maternal alcohol consumption during pregnancy. This syndrome, which occurs in the United States at a rate of 2 newborns per 1000 live births, is remarkable for diffuse neurodevelopmental disorder, classically including growth retardation, craniofacial anomalies, and central nervous system dysfunction. Of note, development of the central nervous system, which includes auditory structures, depends largely on sensory input during the first 2 to 3 years of life. For this reason, impaired sensory function at an early age, as in FAS, can irreversibly affect speech, language,

TABLE 16–6. Pigmentary Abnormalities Associated with Hearing Impairment

Syndrome	Inheritance	Characteristics	Type of Hearing Loss: Sensorineural	Conductive	Mixed
Albinism-deafness syndrome	Recessive or X-linked	Fair skin and hair; absence of pigment in iris, sclera, and fundus	X		
	dominant	Fair skin, fine hair; eyes not affected (blue irides)	X		
Partial albinism or piebaldness	Dominant	Areas of skin depigmentation, light blue clumps of pigment throughout the retina, good vision	X		
Waardenburg syndrome	Dominant	Heterochromic irides, broad nasal root, thick eyebrows, lateral displacement of medial canthi, white forelock, dappling of skin	X		

Modified from Black FO, Bergstrom L, Downs M, et al. Congenital Deafness: A New Approach to Diagnosis Using a High Risk Register. Boulder, CO, Colorado Associated University Press, 1971.

and cognitive function. Church and Abel[17] have described four types of hearing disorders that result from prenatal alcohol exposure, one or more of which are present in nearly every infant with FAS. The hearing disorders associated with FAS include central hearing loss, auditory system maturation delay, sensorineural hearing loss, and conductive hearing loss with recurrent serous otitis media.

In FAS, hearing loss results from ethanol-induced auditory nervous system damage in utero. Central structures, including brain stem auditory nuclei and tracts, auditory cortex and radiations, and the corpus callosum, may be affected (e.g., by poor myelination and impaired synaptic efficiency). The result of such damage is a spectrum of hearing loss, from mild loss to profound deafness, which is associated with ABR findings indicative of neural transmission slowing. Some infants with FAS demonstrate delayed maturation of the auditory system, a marker of permanent central nervous system damage on ABR testing. Half of such infants develop delays in hearing, speech, and motor function.

Auditory end-organ damage due to intrauterine alcohol exposure includes the cochlea and auditory nerve, resulting in sensorineural hearing loss such as that seen in 27% to 29% of FAS cases reviewed in studies conducted at a threshold of 15 dB in Denver and Detroit. (A study conducted at 20 dB thresholds obtained a lower incidence of 7%.) In these studies, sensorineural hearing loss was rarely greater than 40 dB and was limited to high frequencies (>2000 Hz) in one half of cases, although some low-frequency loss or equivalent loss at all frequencies was observed. Animal studies in mice and rats suggests that such end-organ damage occurs at the inner and outer hair cell level in the embryo (e.g., cell death, missing hair cells, malformed stereocilia), although poor myelination of auditory nerve fibers may also contribute to hearing loss.

Lastly, intermittent conductive hearing loss secondary to recurrent serous otitis media may be seen in 75% to 93% of FAS cases. Eustachian tube dysfunction or malformation (e.g., tensor veli palatini deficiency, stenosis, tortuosity) and cleft palate are common in patients with FAS, placing them at risk for recurrent serous otitis media. However, FAS patients with cleft palate are nearly equally likely to develop otitis when compared with FAS patients without cleft palate (87.5% vs. 80%). Of note, the vestibular system may also be affected, although poor balance and coordination are more likely to be due to cerebellar insult, which is common and often present in the absence of identifiable vestibular dysfunction.[17]

Nearly every infant with FAS has an identifiable hearing disorder that can result in profound developmental delays or aggravate delays that result from central nervous system damage. For example, delays in language acquisition and expression (seen in one study in 86% of FAS cases) are probably caused by the combined effects of hearing and cognitive dysfunctions. Infants at risk for delays cannot be identified by physical examination findings: A higher number, a greater severity, or a particular type of craniofacial anomaly does not place the patient with FAS at an increased risk for hearing disorders. In fact, partial expression of the classic syndrome is most likely the result of the timing of exposure and not the severity of exposure. As such, clinicians must recognize the need for early multidisciplinary intervention for patients with FAS, to whom hearing amplification and appropriate services are of great value.

Furthermore, differentiating between truly congenital hearing loss (i.e., that present at birth) and acquired hearing loss is extremely difficult during the neonatal period. Fraser[35] has succinctly summarized the difficult task of determining the cause of neonatal hearing loss: "It is clear that the relationship between perinatal problems and subsequent deafness is an exceedingly complicated one and, while in some cases a specific circumstance, such as hemorrhage into the inner ears as a result of birth injury, the administration of ototoxic drugs, or kernicterus due to Rhesus incompatibility, may be identified as the proximate cause of hearing loss, in many others multiple factors must be taken into consideration; these may arise as a result of interaction between both genetic and environmental variables." Thus, it can be seen that finding the cause of hearing loss detected in a neonate may be a complex and difficult problem. Nonetheless, an attempt should be made to find the factors that are most likely to have caused an observed hearing impairment.

Care

Once it has been established that a neonate has impaired hearing, management must be planned. Otologic surgery is not warranted during the neonatal period, and usually the infant must be older than 2 months before fitting of a hearing aid can be considered. Early steps will have to be taken to assist the child with a congenital hearing loss to learn speech and language. It is most important to help the parents of a hearing-impaired child to understand and adjust to the different needs of their child.[111] In addition, if the family is indigent or without adequate medical insurance coverage, it will be necessary to involve appropriate agencies so that the family can continue to provide the medical care and special education that the child may require.

Age-Specific Tasks: The Infant

Confirm

If an infant passes a universal newborn hearing screening test, the parents are likely to assume that their infant has normal hearing until something worrisome arises. The parents of a baby born with significant binaural hearing impairment that has gone undetected during the newborn period are likely to become concerned when their baby is 6 to 12 months of age. Usually, a parent, grandparent, or child-care provider will make some kind of observation that raises suspicion of possible hearing impairment. The concern might begin with the observation that the baby appears not to respond in an appropriate way to sounds in the environment. A parent might report to a pediatrician that the infant does not appear to be startled by loud noises or awaken when a sibling in the same room is crying loudly. Parents may be concerned that the child of about 2 years is not speaking words while they remember that an older sibling was saying three-word phrases by the age of 18 months. If an infant has had meningitis or a severe infection that required the administration of potentially ototoxic medications, the astute pediatrician or family physician may want to have the infant's hearing evaluated.

Even if the clinician thinks that parents are overly impatient about their child's seeming delay in speech development or inappropriately anxious about their child's lack of response to sounds, an adequate assessment of hearing *must* be done in all cases. Performing rudimentary tests of hearing such as shaking a rattle or clapping hands near the baby are not appropriate ways to assess the hearing of a baby suspected of having hearing impairment. Furthermore, it is inadvisable to attempt to reassure the parents that concerns about their baby's hearing impairment are unfounded without having available results of appropriate objective tests of hearing. Therefore, when the parent, a physician, or anyone who knows an infant well becomes concerned about the infant's hearing ability, a full evaluation, including ABR and OAE testing, is warranted.

Between the ages of 2 months and 24 months, an infant progressively becomes easier to condition for play audiometry. Although hearing assessment in the neonate necessarily relies on nonbehavioral, objective test methods, including ABR and OAE, the use of behavioral hearing assessment techniques during infancy is a possibility. Although young babies cannot follow instructions sufficiently well to achieve accurate behavioral hearing testing results, infants become easier to test with the use of behavioral techniques as they grow older.

There is a subtle but significant difference between objective tests of hearing and behavioral hearing tests. ABR testing records the electrophysiologic response to sound stimuli, primarily of frequencies between 1000 Hz and 4000 Hz. An infant may have absent auditory evoked responses and still have usable hearing at frequencies lower than 1000 Hz. At about the age of 1 year, an infant develops the ability to localize sound, and this enables the use of visual reinforcement audiometry. Beyond the age of 1 year, development of the bony tympanic ring makes the ear canal less pliable and more rigid. This means that tympanometry can more readily be used to provide accurate information about physical properties of the eardrum and the middle ear.

A more detailed discussion of methods for audiometric testing in infants can be found elsewhere in this textbook. Although some audiologists may not have the requisite equipment or specific skills for testing infants, there usually is some nearby medical or audiologic testing facility where the necessary equipment and experienced audiologists are available. In summary, whenever there is a suspicion that an infant has a hearing impairment, it is imperative that the infant undergo the appropriate audiologic testing. There is no reason for delaying such tests until the later childhood years.

Characterize

Once it has been determined that an infant has hearing impairment, it is important to determine both the severity and the type of hearing loss. ABR testing, OAE testing, tympanometry, and acoustic reflex testing can be helpful in characterizing the type of hearing loss.

In considering the types of hearing loss that can be seen in infancy, conductive hearing loss due to otitis media with effusion deserves specific mention. When otitis media with effusion is discovered in the infant who has been referred for evaluation of hearing impairment, it should *not* be assumed that effusion in the middle ear is the only reason for the hearing loss. Audiologic tests should be obtained to determine whether a previously undetected sensorineural hearing loss is also present. Furthermore, if tympanostomy tubes are inserted as treatment for a chronic effusion, a repeat audiogram several weeks after myringotomy should be obtained when the middle ear is aerated (i.e., when no effusion is present). If it was possible to obtain an air-conduction and bone-conduction pure-tone audiogram before insertion of a tympanostomy tube, then a repeated audiogram after the tube insertion should reveal air-conduction thresholds that have returned to normal. If a conductive hearing loss persists after the insertion of a tympanostomy tube with aeration of the middle ear, the infant may have a congenital ossicular abnormality. If it was not possible to obtain an air-conduction and bone-conduction audiogram before insertion of the tympanostomy tube, then a persistent hearing loss after insertion of the tube may be entirely sensorineural or mixed, or the residual conductive loss may be associated with an ossicular abnormality. For example, a child with Down syndrome (trisomy 21) or Goldenhar syndrome who has conductive hearing loss after insertion of tympanostomy tubes might have a congenital ossicular abnormality.[4]

Combining an ABR test with myringotomy and insertion of tympanostomy tubes under general anesthesia can help to determine the extent to which an infant's hearing loss is conductive, sensorineural, or both. Comparing characteristics of the ABR pattern before and after the insertion of a tympanostomy tube gives clues that may aid in diagnosis. Although it may not always be possible to characterize an infant's hearing loss accurately, some attempt should be made to discover the type of hearing loss that is present. Certainly, the diagnostic possibilities and plans for management will vary according to the type of hearing impairment that is discovered.

Cause

Differentiating the commonly occurring conductive hearing loss associated with otitis media from the potentially more significant sensorineural hearing loss that may be present without associated symptoms in the infant is important. Conductive hearing loss resulting from otitis media with middle ear effusion is the most common type of hearing loss in children. However, although far less common than the hearing loss associated with otitis media, moderate or severe sensorineural hearing loss that is bilateral can have a significant adverse effect on a child's ability to learn speech. Diagnosis of otitis media is based on detecting characteristic otoscopic findings with additional confirmation from tympanometry (immittance testing) or reflectometry. Parents generally understand and expect that a child with fluid in his or her ears may experience hearing loss with an upper respiratory infection. However, when a child with fluid in the ears seems to have hearing loss that is more than mild and if that hearing loss persists for months, the child is likely to be referred to an otolaryngologist for further evaluation. Depending on the severity of a child's hearing loss and the frequency with which ear infections have occurred, insertion of tympanostomy tubes may be indicated. Primary care physicians and otolaryngologists should keep in mind this concept:

When a child with middle ear effusion in one or both ears has a pure tone average greater than 30 dB in the ear or ears with effusion, then there could be a previously undetected congenital sensorineural hearing loss in the involved ears.

Hearing loss discovered during infancy can be thought of as being either congenital or noncongenital (acquired). Quite obviously, the earliest detection of congenital hearing impairment is most likely to be achieved when a baby is born in a hospital that has a universal neonatal hearing screening program or a selective (risk-factor–based) hearing testing program. Babies with congenital hearing loss who were not identified as being hearing-impaired during the neonatal period are likely to have their hearing loss detected before reaching 3 years of age. The more severe the hearing impairment is in both ears, the more likely it is that the hearing impairment will be detected early.

In evaluating an infant with hearing loss, it is advisable to obtain copies of the medical record from the hospital where the infant was born. Notably, these records may include results of a newborn hearing screening test. In addition, hospital records can be reviewed to identify possible factors in the pathogenesis of hearing impairment, such as a history of excessive jaundice for a prolonged period, infection, or administration of ototoxic medications.

Next, it is helpful to question the parents carefully about how the suspicion of hearing loss arose. Some helpful questions follow:

1. Do you think that your child was born with normal hearing?
2. When did you first become suspicious that your infant has difficulty in hearing?
3. What gives you the impression that your child has a hearing loss?
4. Did your baby babble and coo? Has the babbling activity ceased? If so, when? What is the level of the infant's speech development?
5. Did meningitis, measles, a high fever, seizures, an exanthematous disease, a viral infection, or any other disorder immediately precede the noticeable hearing problem?
6. Has your child had frequent bouts of otitis media? If so, what characterized each episode, and how were they treated?
7. Are there any family members who were diagnosed with hearing loss or who were fitted for a hearing aid during childhood?

Answers to these questions may help determine whether the hearing loss is congenital and possibly hereditary or likely to have been acquired as a result of infection or some other factor. Often, the infant born with a severe hearing impairment will experiment with verbalization, making several speech sounds; then at about 8 months of age, lacking the reinforcement of hearing his or her voice and lacking the stimulation of hearing others speak, the infant eventually stops experimenting with speech. Thus, language development sometimes offers a clue about the time of onset of hearing impairment.

In contrast to the difficulty of uncovering the cause of congenital hearing loss, a more direct cause-and-effect relationship may be discernible in cases of infant hearing impairment. For example, in the past, bacterial meningitis has been a relatively common cause of sensorineural hearing impairment acquired after the perinatal period.[87, 110] Obviously, if an infant appeared to be developing speech normally and then hearing difficulty was noticed after the occurrence of bacterial meningitis, it can reasonably be assumed that meningitis was a factor in causing the hearing loss, especially if there was no suspicion of a hearing loss preceding the meningitis.

Although parents often recall and attribute causal significance to events such as a high fever, a viral syndrome, or some minor head trauma that seemed to immediately precede the realization that their child is hearing impaired, proving that such events contributed to the child's hearing loss is virtually impossible. Still, it is worthwhile to investigate what the parents *think* was the time of onset and cause of their infant's hearing loss. Understanding the parents' concept of the cause for their infant's hearing loss can be of help in counseling the parents and in mollifying the lingering sense of guilt that they may harbor. Further, it is worthwhile to collect whatever information seems relevant so that a retrospective analysis can be undertaken and relative probability of causality can be attributed to whatever events are believed by parents or others to have caused the hearing loss. After all, as the pathogenesis of childhood hearing loss is elucidated further in the years ahead, certain seemingly unrelated factors at the time of diagnosis may be found to play a causal role in hearing loss later on.

Physical examination contributes additional information that can be helpful in determining the cause of hearing loss. Subtle abnormalities that were not noticed at birth may become evident when the infant with a hearing loss undergoes a thorough examination. Special attention must be directed during the physical examination to the pinnae, preauricular skin, ear canals, eardrums, retinae, facial bones, and neck. In addition, to the extent possible, function of the cranial nerves should be tested. The size of the external-ear canal can be significant. Unilateral or bilateral ear canal stenosis can be associated with congenital middle-ear ossicular abnormalities with conductive hearing loss. Many of the laboratory studies suggested for the evaluation of the neonate are useful for evaluation of nonsyndromic infants with a hearing loss of unknown cause. Radiographic studies are usually not warranted during infancy unless the infant is a candidate for having cochlear implant.

As already mentioned, otitis media with effusion cannot always be assumed to be the sole cause of a confirmed significant hearing impairment. If it appears that genetic factors are not responsible for the hearing impairment, a hypothesis should be based on review of all collected information. In many cases, there will be no clear cause to explain the hearing loss discovered during infancy.

Care

When a significant hearing impairment is discovered during infancy, habilitative measures can be taken. If chronic bilateral otitis media with effusion is discovered, the hearing can be improved simply by aspirating the fluid and inserting tympanostomy tubes. Almost all infants born with cleft palate have abnormal eustachian tube function and a consequent tendency to develop recurrent or persistent otitis media with effusion. The palate deformity makes acquisition of speech difficult. Therefore, every attempt must be made to provide for the child with a cleft palate keen auditory acuity so that the child can hear clearly the subtleties of speech pronunciation that he or she will try so hard to imitate. Early insertion of tympanostomy tubes is advisable and may conveniently be done in conjunction with the first plastic surgery repair of a cleft lip deformity or as a brief surgical procedure for the infant born with an isolated cleft palate deformity.

When an infant without a craniofacial defect is found to have hearing impairment because of recurrent or chronic middle-ear effusions, the decision to perform a myringotomy with insertion of tympanostomy tubes should be based on the severity and duration of a measurable hearing loss and the persistence of the effusions despite medical therapy. In some instances, it will be advisable to insert tympanostomy tubes more as a means of diminishing a sizable conductive hearing loss than as a therapeutic measure aimed at reducing the frequency of middle-ear infections.

When all available evidence seems to indicate that there is a significant conductive hearing loss caused by a factor other than middle-ear effusion, therapeutic measures should be aimed at providing amplification of sound and assistance in learning speech. Surgical procedures to repair malformations or fixation of the ossicles and thereby improve hearing deficits are not usually undertaken during infancy. Rather, ossicular reconstruction of the congenitally malformed ear is better undertaken later in childhood.

If the hearing impairment is more sensorineural than conductive, the infant should undergo a complete developmental and neurologic evaluation. The infant discovered to have a moderate or severe sensorineural hearing impairment may also have one or more other previously undetected abnormalities. That is, the sensorineural hearing loss could be either an isolated problem or one among several congenital or acquired problems. If the hearing impairment is an isolated problem, early amplification with one or two hearing aids and speech training should be recommended. If the sensorineural hearing impairment is part of a constellation of problems, then the benefit to be derived from early hearing aid amplification will have to be considered in relation to the child's capabilities and other limitations. However, it is best not to consider an infant too young or unsuitable for a hearing aid until after the infant has been seen and evaluated by an audiologist skilled in the evaluation of infants.[119] In fact, in formulating a plan for the management of a severely hearing-impaired infant, it is best to make sure that a pediatrician, otolaryngologist, audiologist, and perhaps a social worker are involved initially and that each is kept informed of the infant's progress.

Hearing-impaired children can manifest delays in acquisition of speech and communicative skills even if an intensive preschool program is initiated by 3 years of age. Therefore, every attempt should be made to detect a child's hearing impairment as soon as possible. Parents can assist their hearing-impaired children to acquire speech and communication skills. Early intervention programs are widely available and are likely to be helpful to both the child and the parents. These programs guide parents in adapting to the changes that occur when a severely hearing-impaired child becomes part of a family.

Commonly, speech and hearing centers design programs to maximize the benefits of learning in the home in one of three ways. Some programs focus on the role of the parents in the home,[55] while others are designed to send specially trained teachers into the child's home on a regular basis to provide instruction to the parents. "Model home" programs have even been designed. The model home enables concurrent teaching of parents, audiologic assessment, and use of videotape and sophisticated audiovisual equipment to facilitate teaching of parents while closely monitoring the child's development.

In summary, the primary goals in the management of a severely hearing-impaired infant should be the acquisition of communicative skills and fostering a positive attitude toward learning. As the child develops during the infant years, the child's potential will become manifest. Some hearing-impaired children will show a remarkable ability to function nearly normally, whereas others will have difficulty in communicating. By the time a hearing-impaired child reaches 3 years of age, the parents and educators should be able to determine the educational mode that is best for the child. Essentially, the alternatives for education will be a school for the deaf, a special class in a regular public school, or an ordinary public school class. The more information that is gathered during the infant years regarding a child's capabilities, the more appropriate future educational programs are likely to be. Further, the earlier that special training is begun and the more sophisticated and intensive the training, the greater a child's chance will be for integration into a regular public school system. Early, aggressive, and appropriate intervention yields the best results.

Age-Specific Tasks: The Preschool-Age Child

The main difference between the preschool-age child and the infant is that a child 2 to 5 years of age is able to talk about and complain of difficulty hearing. Moreover, preschool-age children begin to become involved in group play and social interactions that depend in large part on having good hearing in both ears.

Confirm

It is becoming common for state and local health agencies to encourage or require screening hearing tests for nursery school children and children about to enter elementary school. As a result, increasing numbers of young children are being referred for otologic examination and confirmative audiologic testing. Of the children who fail screening tests, some actually have hearing impairment, whereas others do not. In each case, an attempt should be made to assess the validity and meaningfulness of the screening procedure with the following questions:

1. Was the screening test merely a tympanogram, or was it a pure-tone audiogram?
2. Was the screening test administered to several children simultaneously in a classroom, or was each child tested individually in a soundproof booth?
3. Did the child have an upper respiratory tract or ear infection at the time that the screening test was administered or within the week before the test?
4. Before the child's failing the screening test, was there any suspicion of his or her having abnormal hearing?
5. Is there a history of frequent acute or chronic otitis media with effusion?
6. Is there a family history of hearing loss beginning during the early childhood years?

With the information gained from the answers to these questions, it is possible to formulate an impression quickly regarding the validity and meaningfulness of the screening results. Pneumatic otoscopy can then be used to gain additional information about the status of the eardrum and the middle ear. Tuning fork tests may be helpful in older preschool-age children, but young children often find it difficult to comprehend the instructions they are given for comparing the relative loudness of tuning fork tones. Definitive confirmation of an apparent hearing loss consists of a complete air-conduction and bone-conduction pure-tone audiogram with the child in a sound-proof booth, assessment of speech reception thresholds, and possibly immittance testing (obtaining tympanograms).

Surprisingly often, repeated audiologic tests reveal normal hearing in a child who has been referred for having failed a screening test. There are several reasons for this. First, the screening examinations may have been performed where noise conditions were less than optimal and where children might have been easily distracted or tempted to trick the examiner. Second, the child may have had an upper respiratory tract infection accompanied by a transient otitis media with effusion at the time that the screening test was administered; such children may have normal hearing as soon as the infection resolves. Children with mild forms of eustachian tube dysfunction often tend to have an otitis media with effusion when they have an upper respiratory tract infection. Thus, a child who recently failed a hearing screening test and then appears to have normal hearing when a more complete audiogram is obtained may have borderline abnormal eustachian tube dysfunction. Third, parents and primary care physicians need to know that screening programs using only tympanometry are not testing hearing. Such programs are supposedly designed to identify children who have previously undiagnosed otitis media with effusion. Because the tympanogram is really measuring acoustic immittance rather than hearing, children with normal hearing and various eardrum or middle-ear pressure abnormalities are likely to be identified as "abnormal" and referred for further evaluation. Thus, when an abnormal tympanogram is the main reason for referral, obtaining a reliable air-conduction and bone-conduction audiogram along with speech reception thresholds should differentiate children with significant hearing problems from those who have innocuous types of tympanogram abnormalities.

Confirming that a preschool-age child does have a unilateral hearing impairment often raises a question that is difficult to answer: Is the hearing loss newly discovered, or has it developed recently? That is, could the hearing loss have been present since birth and gone undetected, or was the child born with normal hearing in both ears and now is beginning to lose hearing in one ear? Often, unless the child has previously undergone a screening hearing test that tested each ear separately, there may be no way to differentiate between newly developed and newly discovered unilateral hearing loss. Parents who are aware of some of the uncertainties in evaluation of their child with unilateral hearing impairment often have three questions that they want to have answered by a physician or a team of physicians:

1. What caused the hearing loss?
2. Will the hearing loss get worse?
3. What are the chances that my child will begin to lose hearing in the opposite ear, which seems now to be unaffected?

Providing meaningful answers to these questions can be difficult. Although there may be no definitive answers, some comments that may be helpful are provided in the following section.

Cause

When a child who is 3 to 5 years old is discovered to have a unilateral hearing loss, determining the cause of the hearing loss retrospectively is nearly impossible, unless certain factors are manifest in the history, physical examination findings, or radiographic examination findings. A prior history of having had mumps might suggest a viral cause of the hearing loss, but infection with the mumps virus is far less common now that most children are immunized against it early in life. If there is a history of an episode of vertigo and dysequilibrium that lasted for several days, then the hearing loss could be the result of viral infection or perilymph fistula. Slight facial asymmetry with even the most mild degree of mandibular hypoplasia on the affected side could indicate that the child's hearing loss is a component of a mild form of oculoauriculovertebral dysplasia (Goldenhar syndrome). The radiographic finding of an enlarged vestibular aqueduct (EVA) on the side ipsilateral to the hearing loss probably means that the hearing impairment is the result of an error in embryogenesis involving the temporal bone and related structures.

Stable, Fluctuating, or Progressive Hearing Loss

There is some information to suggest that certain audiogram configurations may be predictive of unstable or progressive hearing loss, while other audiogram configurations are believed to be more suggestive of a hearing loss that will be stable and not progress. However, there is not yet sufficient information available to predict the course of a child's hearing loss on the basis of an audiogram configuration. This being the case, well-meaning attempts to predict stability of a child's hearing loss to allay a parent's anxiety may be more harmful than helpful. Perhaps the best approach is simply to say that the hearing loss *could* worsen. The longer the hearing loss remains stable, the greater the likelihood that there will *not* be further hearing loss. In other words, in dealing with childhood sensorineural hearing loss, the past is helpful in predicting the future. Children with rapid or sudden-onset sensorineural hearing loss or well-documented fluctuation in hearing are more likely to have progression of the hearing loss than are children who have a hearing loss that remains stable for 2 years after initial detection.

Chances that the Unaffected Ear Will Become Affected

There is no way of predicting whether a hearing loss that initially presents as unilateral will continue to involve only one ear. Again, radiographic findings on CT scan can be helpful. If the child has a unilateral temporal bone abnormality such as EVA, Mondini malformation, or some other cochlear dysplasia that is ipsilateral to the hearing impairment, then involvement of the opposite ear in the future probably is not likely. However, if no radiographic abnormalities are seen on the CT scan, or temporal bone abnormalities are bilateral and symmetric, there is a reasonable chance for future hearing loss in the ear that at the time of initial evaluation has normal hearing. Unfortunately, such predictions cannot be based on firm data, since there are no longitudinal studies that provide information sufficient to accurately predict whether a unilateral hearing loss will eventually involve the opposite ear.

Characterize

When a preschool-age child's hearing impairment has been established, a variety of audiologic tests can be employed to determine the type of hearing loss that is present. At the age of approximately 2 years, it becomes possible to condition a child to respond to pure-tone signals. In addition, the normal 2-year-old child has developed some receptive and expressive language skills, enabling him or her to follow simple, explicit instructions. Both speech and pure-tone testing can be used. Children can be asked to identify familiar pictures as the loudness is varied for the words describing the pictures. Audiometers are available that route a speech signal to a bone vibrator so that a bone-conduction speech threshold can be obtained.

Although speech testing in younger children may differentiate conductive from sensorineural hearing loss, pure-tone testing is required to yield information about hearing ability at specific frequencies. An air-conduction and bone-conduction audiogram can usually be obtained when a child is able to be conditioned to respond to a pure-tone signal by dropping an object into a box, placing rings on a peg, or performing some other simple task. Further information about the type of hearing impairment can be gained with the ABR test. With a cooperative child, the ABR test can be done while the patient is awake. In children who are not cooperative, sedation or general anesthesia can be used. Tympanometry (sometimes referred to as immittance or impedance testing) can be useful in assessing the functional status of the eardrum and ossicular chain.

Thus, it should be possible to characterize a hearing impairment in the young child as being conductive, sensorineural, or mixed. From the test results, it might be difficult to distinguish a retrocochlear type of hearing loss from a sensorineural one. Analysis of the ABR test pattern, word recognition (discrimination) scores, and other clinical information should be helpful in making such a differentiation. Although retrocochlear lesions such as vestibular schwannomas (acoustic neuromas) are rarely seen in young children, they can occur in this age group.

Cause

Otitis media with effusion is the most common cause of conductive hearing loss in preschool-age children. Mild to moderate conductive hearing losses due to congenital ossicular chain abnormalities or congenital cholesteatoma may also be discovered in children of this age.

Children with congenital bilateral severe sensorineural hearing losses are usually identified before 2 years of age, but the hearing impairment may go unnoticed until the third year of life in some cases. When a bilateral moderate to severe sensorineural hearing loss is first discovered in a child between 2 and 3 years of age, the following question often arises: Was the child born with poor hearing or did his or her hearing progressively worsen in the first few years of life? A clue to the time of onset of the hearing loss lies in the child's ability to speak. Children who were born with little or no hearing ability usually have considerable difficulty in learning to speak, whereas those who could hear initially tend to have better speech. In general, the greater the difficulty a child experiences in pronouncing the "s" sound, the younger the onset of the child's hearing impairment.

Genetic factors may be the cause of the hearing impairment that was present at birth or developed in the first years of life. There are at least 16 types of hereditary hearing loss with no associated physical abnormalities.[71] In the early-onset type of inherited hearing loss, the auditory impairment can begin during the preschool years. The family pedigree, shape of the audiogram, severity of the hearing loss, and age at onset of hearing impairment help in differentiating one type of inherited hearing loss from another when there are no associated physical anomalies to aid in identifying a genetic or other etiologic factor.

Two thirds of cases of hereditary hearing impairment (HHI) are nonsyndromic, while the remaining third are syndromic. For many years, textbooks stated that the three most common types of syndromic HHI are Usher, Pendred, and Jervell and Lange-Nielsen syndromes. However, past epidemiology of HHI was based on surveys performed at schools for the deaf many years ago and is likely to be inaccurate today. In recent years, as methods for testing the hearing of children have improved and more has been learned about genetic disorders that include hearing loss, a different picture of the epidemiology of HHI has emerged. Although a definitive national statistical survey has not been undertaken to determine exactly which genetic disorders that include hearing impairment are most common, Goldenhar syndrome (oculoauriculovertebral dysplasia) is the most commonly *occurring* syndrome. The three most commonly *encountered* syndromes of HHI are Treacher-Collins syndrome (mandibulofacial dysostosis), Waardenburg syndrome, and Usher syndrome. (See Acquiring Core Information for more information on eliciting a family history of HHI and useful diagnostic testing.)

Although frequently requested as part of a "shotgun" approach to diagnosis, laboratory studies are unlikely to be helpful in the absence of clinical suspicion of a syndrome that includes a finding detectable by laboratory testing (e.g., electrocardiogram for detection of conduction abnormalities in Jervell and Lange-Nielsen syndrome). Requesting karyotyping is also usually not helpful, since almost all cases of HHI result from point mutations rather than deletions or chromosomal rearrangements that are detectable with cytogenetic evaluation. However, genetic mutation screening for common mutations associated with hearing impairment, such as the connexin-26 mutations, are well supported in the literature and should be considered. (For more information, see the section on genetic testing.)

If a genetic cause of the hearing impairment is suspected and findings on physical examination are not entirely normal, consultation with a clinical geneticist may help uncover a genetic disorder that otherwise would be inapparent through the detection of subtle abnormalities and focused genetic screening for common mutations. Similarly, consultation with an ophthalmologist, preferably a pediatric ophthalmologist with expertise in diagnosis of genetic disorders, may help detect related retinitis pigmentosa or any other eye abnormality that could lead to a diagnosis of syndromic HHI. Electroretinography is sometimes needed to confirm or rule out a diagnosis of retinitis pigmentosa, especially if there is evidence of recessive inheritance of hearing impairment in the family.

If it appears that hereditary factors are not responsible for the hearing loss, the search for an identifiable (acquired) etiologic factor begins with a careful prenatal and perinatal history. A history of meningitis or any other severe infection during infancy may be significant. If the child had been hospitalized for any reason, it is worthwhile to obtain the hospital records to see whether ototoxic medications were administered.

Care

Management of conductive hearing loss differs from the management of sensorineural hearing loss. Hearing impairments discovered in children of preschool age are usually conductive and tend to be less severe than sensorineural hearing impairments. There is no consensus on management of the child who has unilateral or bilateral middle-ear effusion with associated conductive hearing loss. Audiologists, educators, and medical practitioners hold variant opinions on the timing and the types of intervention that are warranted. Divergent opinions notwithstanding, it should be realized that impairment of hearing may adversely affect language development and cognitive function in young children.[49, 70] To avoid or minimize adverse effects, a child with middle-ear effusion and concomitant hearing loss should be seen frequently and should undergo sequential audiologic tests. If the child's hearing is significantly worse than normal (speech reception threshold greater than 20 dB in both ears) the majority of the time, measures to improve hearing should be considered.

Although decongestant medication is often prescribed to promote and quicken the resolution of otitis media with effusion, the efficacy of such medication for this purpose has never been scientifically proven. Tympanocentesis with aspiration of fluid from the middle-ear space can result in a quick resolution of the conductive hearing loss caused by a middle-ear effusion. Insertion of tympanostomy tubes is widely accepted as a method of ensuring that an aspirated middle-ear effusion will not recur. Although the efficacy of tympanostomy tubes in reducing the frequency of bouts of acute otitis media is controversial, myringotomy with insertion of tympanostomy tubes is one effective method of removing middle-ear effusion, preventing its recurrence, and eradicating the conductive hearing loss associated with the effusion.[36, 43, 78] If the use of tympanostomy tubes is deemed inappropriate, then a hearing aid might be helpful.

In contrast to the management of otitis media with effusion, the management of sensorineural or predominantly sensorineural mixed hearing losses is primarily directed toward finding optimal ways of coping with a given hearing impairment. When a significant sensorineural hearing loss is discovered in a preschool-age child, attention is focused on methods for enabling the child to develop communicative skills, and plans must be made for selecting an appropriate educational environment.

The preschool years are exceptionally important in a child's overall development. During this time, a child develops concept formation and methods for problem solving. A child's natural curiosity and eagerness to explore the environment make the preschool years most fertile for educational experiences. A child's earliest attempts to interact with others occur during this period constitute the experiences that form the child's impression of the world. Much of the learning experience of a preschool-age child is derived from activities at home with the family. As such, parental participation is of utmost importance in fostering optimal development for the hearing-impaired child.[26, 86]

Once a preschool-age child is diagnosed with moderate, severe, or profound hearing impairment, a comprehensive program should be undertaken to counsel and provide guidance and teaching for the parents. Emotional and psychological support is often warranted to help parents cope with the concept of having a handicapped child and to aid in resolving their feelings of guilt. Parents need to be taught how to maximally use a child's residual hearing for linguistic stimulation during play and other home activities. If the child has no residual hearing, the parent must learn new methods of communication to maximize the quality of the parent-child interaction. In addition, parents require factual information regarding sources for financial assistance, local and regional education centers for hearing-impaired children, and special nursery school programs suited for preschool-age hearing-impaired children. Parents should be made aware that special laws have lowered or eliminated the minimal age for enrollment in publicly funded special education programs.[25]

In 1975, Public Law 94-142 was passed, acknowledging and protecting the right of handicapped children to free public education. Under the provisions of PL 94-142, state and local education agencies were required to develop and administer suitable programs for these children. The age specifications of PL 94-142 varied for the different provisions of the law. An extremely important stipulation of PL 94-142 was the requirement that an individualized education program be prepared for each child identified as handicapped and that this plan be monitored and updated annually.[90] In a sense, the legislation virtually ensured that a hearing-handicapped child could attend a regular public school, provided that a suitable individualized educational program could be developed and annual evaluations indicated that the child was learning adequately.

In 1986, Public Law 99-457, covering education for the handicapped, was passed. There are three main sections to PL 99-457. Title I, often referred to as the "handicapped infants and toddlers section," established a discretionary program calling for states to create comprehensive systems for providing early intervention services to disabled infants from birth until their third birthday. Title II required states to provide free and appropriate public education and related services to disabled children older than 3 years of age by 1992. Effectively, this section of PL 99-457 replaced the earlier PL 94-142. Title III of PL 99-457 reauthorized discretionary programs, such as services for deaf-blind children. Physicians and other professionals who work with severely hearing-impaired infants and young children should be familiar with certain aspects of PL 99-457. The law represents the first federal government commitment to supporting disabled children with early intervention from the time of birth. Compared with PL 94-142, the more recent PL 99-457 is designed to foster better cooperation between health care professionals and educators and place a greater emphasis on needed services for the families of affected children.

Thus, the options for educating a child with significant hearing impairment have been expanded. As a result, the matter of selecting an appropriate educational setting has become somewhat controversial. In the past, severely hearing-impaired and deaf children attended *deaf schools*, separate schools that were specifically equipped and staffed to educate these children. However, some parents and educators are in favor of educating children with severe hearing impairments in the regular public school system. This concept of integrating hearing-impaired children and normal-hearing children is known as *mainstreaming*. Proponents of mainstreaming believe early integration allows a hearing-impaired child to cope with real-life situations at an earlier age. They believe that proper assistance and preparation will enable the hearing-impaired child to receive a solid education without having to attend a special school. Opponents of mainstreaming believe that the hearing-impaired child's total education and general sense of well-being may suffer when he is forced to try to learn from teachers who are not specifically trained in methods of educating the hearing-impaired.

There is probably no single best way of educating a severely hearing-impaired child. The child should be placed in the educational setting that best accommodates his or her capabilities and needs. However, in general, children born with severe hearing impairments or total deafness require more specialized types of training. When a severe hearing impairment is discovered late in the preschool years and the child has not yet developed communication skills, attempts to have the child attend a regular public school may be ill-advised. On the other hand, when a child's hearing impairment is discovered early, the child may develop receptive and expressive skills through specific habilitation that are sufficient to enable the child to attend classes with normally hearing children.

Thus, the most important aspect of management of a preschool-age child who has significant sensorineural hearing impairment is education. After an appropriate hearing aid has been provided, attention should be focused on development and preservation of language skills. The decision regarding where and how the child will receive an education is one that should be made with liberal advice from an audiologist, a psychologist, parents, educators, and others. A book written for parents of children newly diagnosed with deafness is *Choices in Deafness: A Parent's Guide*.[107] Additional services that are important in such cases are genetic counseling for parents and maintenance of otologic care for the hearing-impaired child. In cases of hereditary hearing impairment, parents usually welcome a discussion of hearing impairment in future offspring. Children who use hearing aids need frequent otologic and audiologic re-evaluation to ensure proper function of the hearing aid, proper earmold fit (that does not cause skin excoriation or ulceration), and detection of changes in hearing thresholds, and to uncover symptoms of intermittent middle-ear disorders that could superimpose a conductive hearing loss on the sensorineural impairment already present.

If a child has profound hearing impairment in both ears, then the child is considered deaf, and options for management must be evaluated carefully. First, the parents need to be informed of the results of the hearing evaluation, which confirms that the child has a profound hearing impairment. This news must be imparted with compassion, not hurriedly or in a setting that limits the parents' ability to speak privately with the audiologist or physician, as such news can be devastating. However, if one or both parents are deaf, they usually receive such news with less concern and fear. Once the parents understand that their child is deaf, there will be many questions to answer and many decisions to be made.

In providing advice to parents of a preschool-age deaf child, physicians need to know that there exist many viewpoints on how best to provide an education for the deaf child. Members of the Deaf culture advocate teaching the child sign language and having the child educated either at a nearby day school for the deaf or at a regional residential (state-supported) school for the deaf. On the other hand, proponents of the aural-oral approach advocate powerful hearing aids, perhaps a cochlear implant, and education for the child in a regular school either in a special program for the hearing impaired or, ultimately, in the mainstream regular classroom along with normal-hearing children.

Those who advocate for a particular approach tend to have great emotional investment in believing that the approach they advocate is the right one and, conversely, that other approaches are not in the best interest of the child. Despite the emotionally charged controversy and the strident debate that has continued for decades, there is not one correct approach that is applicable to all deaf children in all situations. The best way to advise parents who have just learned that their young preschool-age child is deaf is to provide as much information as possible, arrange for the parents to speak with other parents of a deaf child, and direct the parents to the many resources and support services available in the community and nationwide. Physicians and audiologists should know about the cochlear implant as an option and be able to refer parents of the child to one of the local or regional centers that has expertise not only with surgical insertion of the cochlear implant but also in providing the training necessary to achieve success with the cochlear implant in children.

An excellent source of information for families considering the advantages and disadvantages of a cochlear implant for their deaf child is the documentary film *Sound and Fury*. This extraordinary documentary, directed by Josh Aronson, tells the true and poignant story of Mr. and Mrs. Peter Artinian, both deaf, and their three children, who are deaf. One of the children, Heather, decides that she wants a cochlear implant. Peter is strongly opposed to a cochlear implant for Heather because he feels that his family is very much a part of the Deaf community and he views his daughter's desire to have the cochlear implant as a rejection of Deaf people and Deaf culture. On the other hand, Peter's normal-hearing brother, Chris, and Heather's normal-hearing aunt, Mari, are in favor of Heather getting the cochlear implant. This movie clearly shows the tension between two brothers, one deaf and one hearing, in regard to the perception of deafness and the benefits of having a cochlear implant. However, this movie provides information about more than the appropriateness of a cochlear implant. This superb documentary captures the lives of deaf individuals living in the United States as well as the profound impact a deaf child has on its family. If the film is not available in local video rental stores, parents can be directed to contact the producer, Public Policy Productions.*

Age-Specific Tasks: The School-Age Child

Confirm

Hearing screening tests are almost universally required by schools, either before enrollment or during the first school year. If a child fails the school screening test, school officials usually request that the child be evaluated by an audiologist, a medical practitioner, or both. Thus, large numbers of children are referred for a hearing evaluation after failing a school screening audiogram.

With such mandatory school screening programs and an increasing awareness of hearing problems in children, the likelihood of a school-age child's significant hearing impairment going undetected is diminishing. In fact, many school screening tests have a high sensitivity and only a moderately high specificity, ensuring that all children with significant hearing impairment are detected at the cost of pursuing further evaluation of some children with normal hearing.

Almost all school-age children are able to cooperate for some type of behavioral audiologic test. However, there are some children who are frightened by earphones or the soundproof booth or generally are uncooperative in other ways. Children who are difficult to test may have failed a screening procedure performed in a test situation where the time allotted, space, and personnel did not accommodate the child's special needs. Children with slightly lower than normal intelligence or those who are emotionally immature may not perform well on a screening hearing test; when the child is tested individually in more optimal surroundings, results may reveal that the child's hearing is not impaired.

When a child fails a screening hearing test but is found on later testing to have normal hearing, it is advisable to obtain additional information. A history of frequent otalgia and otitis media is likely to indicate that the child has some form of eustachian tube dysfunction with variations in middle-ear pressure and possibly intermittent otitis media with effusion. For example, at the time of a screening test, a child may have otitis media with effusion, which resolves without treatment prior to further evaluation and more definitive audiometric tests. When there is suspicion that variations in middle-ear pressure or effusion are causing intermittent hearing difficulty, it is best to have the child return for audiologic tests in 1 or 2 months and to instruct the parent to return with the child whenever it seems that the child is having difficulty hearing.

---

*Public Policy Productions: phone, 914-398-2119; fax, 914-398-2620; or website, ppptv@aol.com.

Children who appear to have difficulty learning in school should undergo hearing evaluation. Children who are having difficulty with reading may have subtle hearing deficits. Aware of the importance of auditory acuity in the learning process, many educators and specialists in developmental psychology are now referring children for hearing evaluation as part of a total evaluation for learning disability. In assessing these children, it is important to bear in mind that a child's ability to respond to pure-tone signals at normal threshold levels does not entirely rule out auditory pathway problems as a contributing factor in the learning disability. Thus, it may be necessary to obtain tests of central auditory processing. Moreover, children who seem to have difficulty hearing, especially children who manifest most of their hearing or listening problems in school, need to be evaluated for attention deficit disorders. Attention deficit disorders can mimic mild to moderate sensorineural hearing loss in a school-age child.[42]

Characterize

Most school-age children are able to cooperate for the behavioral and immittance tests that enable assessment of the severity and diagnosis of the type of hearing impairment that is present. Many of the tests used for adults are adapted for use with children. A pure-tone audiogram and speech reception thresholds can be obtained with conditioning and play audiometry. Simple word lists can be used to assess word recognition and to derive the discrimination score. As more attention is focused on learning disabilities, newer tests are being developed for assessing central auditory function in children. Thus, once it is confirmed that a school-age child has a hearing impairment, tests are available to characterize and quantify the hearing loss.

Hearing impairment that is newly discovered during the early school years will usually be conductive or of the mild sensorineural type. Children with more severe types of hearing impairment often have difficulty with language development, which usually leads to recognition of the hearing deficit before the child is of school age. On the other hand, children with unilateral moderate to severe sensorineural hearing losses may learn to speak without difficulty and appear to have normal hearing until the time that they enter school. A screening test may then uncover the hearing deficit, or difficulty in listening to the teacher may make the child aware of the hearing impairment.

Cause

Conductive Hearing Impairment

Most of the inherited forms of conductive hearing impairment are discovered before a child enters school. A large proportion of children whose hearing impairment develops during the school years have eustachian tube dysfunction or middle-ear disorders, such as effusion, negative pressure, or both. As a child who is susceptible to the development of otitis media with effusion ages, the ten-

dency to develop effusions usually diminishes, and hearing tends to improve. However, some children have sequelae of otitis media that adversely affect hearing. Children who have had chronic middle-ear effusions and numerous bouts of acute otitis media during early childhood can have, around the age of 5 to 8 years, any of the following: eardrum retraction, eardrum perforation, tympanosclerosis, erosion of portions of the ossicular chain, or even cholesteatoma. The lenticular process of the incus is the portion of the ossicular chain that is most vulnerable to damage from acute and chronic types of otitis media. Trauma must also be considered as an etiologic factor. School-age children may poke objects into the ear canal, causing damage to the eardrum, the ossicles, or even the inner ear. Blunt head trauma, as in an automobile accident, can cause dislocation of the ossicles and can result in a conductive hearing loss. Tumors involving the temporal bone are rare. Benign neoplasms such as osteomas or fibrous dysplasia can affect hearing, depending on the location of the lesion. Malignant lesions, such as rhabdomyosarcoma, may cause hearing loss when portions of the auditory system are destroyed.

Sensorineural Hearing Impairment

When a school-age child is discovered to have sensorineural hearing impairment, an attempt should be made to determine whether the hearing loss is stable or progressive, and an attempt should be made to discover the cause of the hearing loss. Even though sensorineural hearing impairment is not detected in the first 5 years of life, genetic factors cannot be excluded in attempting to discover the cause of such a hearing loss. There is a type of dominant, high-frequency, progressive sensorineural hearing loss that begins to appear after 5 years of age and rapidly worsens until the third decade.[57] Other types of inherited progressive sensorineural hearing losses with no associated anomalies follow[71]:

1. Autosomal-dominant, low-frequency hearing loss—onset of hearing loss can be in infancy, but progression is not usually seen until adulthood.
2. Autosomal-dominant, mid-frequency hearing loss—onset of hearing loss in childhood with early progression.
3. Autosomal-dominant, early-onset, progressive hearing loss—moderate to severe hearing loss by adolescence, considerable variation in expressivity.
4. Autosomal-recessive, early-onset neural hearing loss—onset early in childhood with progression to a plateau of marked severity by middle to late childhood.
5. X-linked, early-onset neural hearing loss—progressive deafness after attainment of speech.
6. X-linked, moderate hearing loss—slowly progressive hearing loss in males.

Nongenetic causes of sensorineural hearing loss in school-age children include infections, such as syphilis (congenital), meningitis, or mumps. Noise-induced trauma to the inner ear can be found in children who listen to rock music with loud volume, especially when earphones are used. (See Noise-Induced Hearing Loss in the Age-Specific Tasks: The Pre-Adolescent section.) Administration of ototoxic medications can cause sensorineural hearing loss. All of the aminoglycoside antibiotics can affect the inner ear. Dihydrostreptomycin and kanamycin mostly affect the auditory system, whereas streptomycin and gentamicin mostly affect the vestibular system. Neomycin affects both systems nearly equally. Diuretics, such as furosemide and ethacrynic acid, can affect hearing, and salicylates can cause a reversible type of hearing impairment. It has been reported that the intravenous administration of erythromycin lactobionate is associated with reversible sensorineural hearing loss.[63]

Perilymph Fistula

Fistulas can develop at the oval or round window membrane with leakage of perilymph fluid and associated sensorineural hearing impairment.[41] Usually, a child who has a perilymph fistula (PLF) has some history of barotrauma, blunt head trauma, or a predisposing condition such as a widely patent cochlear aqueduct or an anomaly involving the temporal bone. Classically, the patient with a PLF experiences a sudden onset of fluctuating hearing loss and ataxia. In the past, there were reports of patients with fluctuating and progressive sensorineural hearing loss who were found to have PLFs of the oval and round windows. Petroff et al hypothesized that "emerging perilymph fistula syndromes" occur in children whose congenital hearing impairment predisposes them to PLF. In such cases, the hearing impairment may be secondary to fistulas that have developed. Consistent with reports by other authors, Petroff et al believe that repair of a PLF is more likely to "stabilize" a progressive sensorineural hearing loss than to restore normal hearing.[55]

The otologic surgeon should view with some skepticism the claims that there is a large population of patients with many different types of fluctuating and progressive sensorineural hearing loss caused by PLF. A paucity of pathognomonic findings, the lack of reliable diagnostic studies, and the extreme subtlety of confirmatory intraoperative findings combine to make the ultimate diagnosis of PLF, in some ways, the artifactual self-fulfilling prophecy of a well-meaning otologic surgeon attempting to offer some hope and assistance to a child who is losing or has lost hearing in an affected ear. More scientific studies are needed to support or refute the notion that PLF is a commonly overlooked diagnosis responsible for progressive sensorineural hearing loss. Furthermore, even if PLF occurs more commonly than had previously been recognized in patients with progressive or fluctuating sensorineural hearing loss, well-designed randomized controlled studies have not yet been done to prove sufficiently that surgical intervention offers the patient any better chance for "stabilizing" or improving the hearing loss than observation alone.[44]

If the family history gives no clues to the cause of a hearing loss and if the child has no history of exposure to ototoxic agents that could have caused an observed sensorineural hearing loss, some diagnostic tests may help to discover an underlying cause for the hearing loss. (Refer to Laboratory Studies section for further testing information.)

A CT scan is indicated when the history, physical examination, and laboratory studies fail to reveal any specific diagnosis. The most common radiographic abnormality associated with sensorineural hearing loss detected during childhood is the widened vestibular aqueduct. (See Enlarged Vestibular Aqueduct in Acquiring Core Information section.) When a child presents with sensorineural hearing loss and poor word recognition (discrimination) in the involved ear, then acoustic neuroma should be considered and an MRI scan with gadolinium enhancement should be obtained. Although rare, acoustic neuromas do occur in children, especially in families with a history of neurofibromatosis type 2. When a PLF is suspected as the cause of the hearing loss, it is worthwhile to perform the fistula test as well as to obtain an electronystagmograph.

Finally, the diagnosis and management of a sudden or fluctuating sensorineural hearing loss differ from those of a stable or slowly progressive sensorineural loss. In general, otologists view sudden-onset and fluctuating hearing losses as potentially treatable disorders. Although there are numerous approaches to treatment of a patient with sudden hearing loss, no single therapeutic regimen is universally effective. Similarly, no single approach to the management of patients with fluctuating hearing losses has been shown to be optimal. Despite the lack of a proven therapeutic regimen, it is advisable to immediately pursue complete evaluation of any child who suddenly develops a sensorineural hearing loss or who has documented variations in sensorineural hearing.

Care

Management of the school-age child with a hearing loss depends on the type and severity of the hearing impairment. The discussion provided previously in this chapter concerning management of preschool-age children with middle-ear disorders also pertains to school-age children. However, while younger children are susceptible to development of otitis media, the incidence of middle-ear infection decreases as a child grows older. Hence, the child who has a history of frequent middle-ear infections with sequelae including impaired conductive hearing may be a candidate for tympanoplasty with ossicular reconstruction as an older child. Reconstructive otologic surgery is best undertaken whenever it appears that problems with otitis media and inadequate ventilation of the middle ear have subsided.

At one time, children with unilateral hearing impairment were thought to require minimal, if any, special care. Classically, advising "preferential seating" in school was all that was done for children with unilateral hearing loss, even if the hearing impairment was profound in the single involved ear. Reports now demonstrate that unilateral hearing impairment of varying severity can represent a significant handicap for a child.[9, 10, 67]

When a bilateral moderate to severe sensorineural

hearing loss develops during the school years, a hearing aid may be necessary. Sometimes, speech therapy is indicated to help avoid the deterioration of a child's ability to articulate and enunciate properly because of loss of auditory feedback.

Age-Specific Tasks: The Pre-Adolescent

Confirm

Preadolescence can be a turbulent time emotionally, with endocrinologic changes occurring and an increased sense of body awareness. In contrast to younger children, the preadolescent child is more likely to complain of difficulty in hearing rather than to have an unnoticed hearing deficit uncovered through screening testing. With younger children, the task of confirming a suspected hearing loss involves selection of an audiologic test procedure that will demonstrate the hearing deficit. A cooperative preadolescent child should be entirely capable of providing valid responses to air-conduction and bone-conduction pure-tone signals and to speech and word recognition (discrimination) testing. However, tests for nonorganic or functional types of hearing loss sometimes are needed in the process of evaluating the preadolescent child.

Another point to remember is that the preadolescent child may be subject to noise-induced temporary threshold shifts. With many children listening to portable radios using insert earphones or participating in rock bands, the possibility arises that a hearing loss may be induced by acoustic trauma. In confirming the presence of a hearing loss, consider that certain types of hearing impairment in this age group may be transient.

Characterize

Audiologic testing for a preadolescent child should be a relatively straightforward matter. Air-conduction and bone-conduction pure-tone audiograms with speech reception threshold tests are sufficient in most cases. Where retrocochlear pathologic change is suspected, discrimination tests and other sites-of-lesion audiologic tests may be warranted. When nonorganic hearing loss is suspected, acoustic reflex testing and such tests as the Stenger, Doerfler-Stewart, or delayed auditory feedback test may be indicated.

Cause

By the time they reach the preadolescent years, most children have outgrown troublesome middle-ear disorders. Ossicular damage or adhesive changes caused by early childhood middle-ear disease can cause conductive hearing loss that persists into a child's later years. Otospongiosis, an early form of otosclerosis, can cause conductive hearing loss in children approximately 11 to 14 years of age. Delayed-onset HHI may manifest for the first time in a preadolescent. Endolymphatic hydrops (Meniere disease) can account for a sensorineural hearing loss when it is associated with tinnitus and vertigo.[51, 81] Multiple sclerosis can cause transient sensorineural hear-

ing loss as well as vertigo during adolescence.[85] Inadequately treated or previously undiagnosed congenital syphilis can cause sensorineural hearing loss in late childhood. Acoustic trauma should also be considered as a possible cause of sensorineural hearing loss. Although the sensorineural hearing loss from bacterial meningitis is generally thought to be stable approximately 2 years after resolution of the meningitis, reports suggest that additional hearing loss can occur many years after the episode of meningitis.[109]

Noise-Induced Hearing Loss

Noise-induced hearing loss is a preventable type of hearing loss that predominantly affects preadolescents and adolescents. Noise-induced hearing loss is defined as thresholds of 15 dB at any or all of the higher frequencies (3000, 4000, 6000 Hz), with an improved threshold of at least 10 dB at 8000 Hz. This threshold pattern results in the classic notch-type audiogram configuration. Initially, temporary threshold shifts are observed following exposure to injurious sounds. With repeated exposure, temporary threshold shifts may progress to noise-induced hearing loss; the reversible anatomic changes of temporary threshold shifts (e.g., hair cell swelling or vascular spasm) may worsen and become permanent. However, injurious exposures may also result directly in acoustic trauma and hearing loss.

Classically, exposure to a sound louder than 140 dB for a short duration is capable of inducing changes that result in immediate, severe, permanent hearing loss. In cases such as this, hair cells swell and degenerate, while the organ of Corti may even be displaced from the basilar membrane. This phenomenon evolves into a nonspecific high-frequency hearing loss with continued exposure to loud sounds, and it is characterized by a loss of the notch in the audiogram configuration. For example, sound levels at rock concerts commonly reach 115 dB and are frequently the cause of temporary threshold shifts in adolescents. Music, machinery (e.g., snowmobiles, firearms, power tools), and explosives (e.g., firecrackers) are well-documented sources of injurious sounds in the literature. Of note, approximately 90% of cases of noise-induced hearing loss are seen in males, three quarters of which are identified prior to 16 years of age.[102]

When sensorineural hearing loss develops in late childhood and no cause is apparent, acoustic neuroma (vestibular schwannoma) must be considered, especially if the word recognition (discrimination) scores are significantly worse than what would be expected from the pure-tone average.

Other than serologic tests for syphilis, urinalysis, and CT of the temporal bones, special studies are not usually helpful in the evaluation of sensorineural hearing loss that occurs late in childhood. An electrocardiogram will probably be superfluous unless the patient has experienced syncopal episodes. Thyroid function tests, such as a screening thyroid-stimulating hormone test, will probably not be helpful unless the patient has a palpable, enlarged thyroid gland and a family history of goiter. When a child has had middle-ear disease early in childhood followed by a conductive hearing loss, temporal bone CT scan can be helpful in assessing the status of the ossicles or the location of a potential cholesteatoma. At times, CT can provide information that is helpful in choosing an operative approach or planning reconstruction of the middle ear. Finally, when there is a question of a retrocochlear pathologic condition or a demyelinating disorder, the ABR test can provide helpful information.

Care

Compared with the potentially devastating effect of hearing loss in early childhood, the hearing loss of later childhood tends to present fewer problems in management. By the time a child has reached the preadolescent years, language and communication skills are well developed. Although it is usually inadvisable to attempt ossicular reconstruction during a child's younger years, when otitis media with effusion is most prevalent, there is diminution of the tendency to develop otitis media during adolescence. Thus, it is reasonable to attempt otologic surgery that may improve certain conductive hearing deficits. For children who have a sensorineural loss late in childhood, hearing amplification, speech preservation/conservation training, and counseling are appropriate.

Hereditary Hearing Impairment

Diagnosis

In recent years, the gene mutations responsible for many of the common forms of HHI have been identified. Today, genetic testing is available to aid in diagnosis of many types of HHI. In the future, as childhood hearing loss from infection and various neonatal risk factors diminishes in prevalence, the proportion of cases of childhood hearing loss caused by hereditary factors is likely to increase compared with childhood hearing loss caused by other factors. As discoveries about HHI emerge, the following facts are worth remembering:

1. Most HHI is nonsyndromic. Therefore, there are more children with hereditary deafness who have no associated findings recognizable as a syndrome than there are children who have deafness as part of a syndrome.
2. Of all children with HHI, including both those with a syndrome and those without a syndrome, the predominant mendelian inheritance pattern is autosomal-recessive. In fact, for about 80% of children with HHI, the inheritance pattern is autosomal-recessive. Therefore, a child newly diagnosed with sensorineural hearing loss could have hereditary hearing impairment even if the parents, grandparents, and one or more siblings have normal hearing.
3. There is a degree of relativity in the ability of physicians to make the diagnosis of HHI. All physicians are not equally likely to elicit the bits of information that might lead to a diagnosis of nonsyndromic HHI. Furthermore, some physicians are more astute in finding the variations from normal anatomy on physical examination that might suggest the presence of a syndrome. In addition, the smaller the size of a child's family, the more difficult it can be to have pedigree data sufficient to rule in or rule out a genetic cause of hearing impairment. If a child is adopted, there may not be any information available to construct a useful pedigree.
4. In the past, the configuration of a child's audiogram was used as a clue to the cause of the hearing impairment. The U-shaped or "cookie bite" configuration with better hearing in the high and low frequencies and worse hearing in the mid-frequencies has been reported to suggest hereditary cause. Although this correlation between the U-shaped/cookie bite audiogram and hereditary cause of the hearing loss can be seen with some syndromic types of HHI, a report by Liu and Xu reveals that children with nonsyndromic hereditary hearing loss have audiogram configurations similar to those for hearing loss caused by factors other than gene defects. Nonetheless, the U-shape or cookie bite audiogram could be suggestive of hereditary hearing impairment.

Inheritance Patterns

Approximately half of all cases of congenital hearing impairment discovered during childhood are due to a gene mutation.[88] HHI can be the result of a gene inherited from one or both parents or the result of a spontaneous gene mutation. If the hearing impairment is the result of a gene inherited from one or both parents, then the mode of inheritance of the hearing impairment should be discernible and can be described as one of the classic mendelian inheritance patterns, which include autosomal-dominant, autosomal-recessive, X-linked, and mitochondrial.

Autosomal-recessive inheritance is the most common mode of transmission of HHI, accounting for approximately 75% to 88% of cases. When the hearing impairment is inherited as an autosomal-recessive trait, the parents of an affected child are likely to have normal or near-normal hearing, despite carrying a gene for hearing loss. Typically, there is a 25% chance that each child will inherit a maternal and paternal recessive mutation that results in HHI. The second most common form of inheritance of childhood HHI is autosomal-dominant, accounting for about 18% to 20% of all cases of HHI. The less common types of inheritance of HHI are X-linked (1% to 3%) and mitochondrial (<1%).

When visualized in a pedigree, autosomal-recessive inheritance is associated with a horizontal pattern of affected individuals: unaffected gene-carrying parents are followed by offspring, one quarter of whom are affected. In contrast to the horizontal pattern of autosomal-recessive inheritance, autosomal-dominant inheritance typically exhibits a vertical pattern of transmission, in which affected parents give birth to affected children, as each child inherits an abnormal gene responsible for dominant HHI. In X-linked inheritance, male offspring of carrier mothers are commonly affected, as they inherit a single X-chromosome from their mother. The most common type of HHI is X-linked recessive mixed hearing loss with stapes fixation, accounting for 75% of cases of HHI and

25% of cases of congenital hearing impairment (CHI). Rarely, inheritance of mutated mitochondrial genes results in HHI in all of the offspring of an affected mother. (Recall that all offspring inherit mitochondrial mutations from their mother, whose egg contributes the entire compliment of mitochondrial DNA to the zygote.) For example, susceptibility to aminoglycoside ototoxicity has been associated with a point mutation in a mitochondrial rRNA gene.

Although most childhood HHI is sensorineural, mixed hearing loss and conductive hearing loss can also be inherited. It is most important to remember that HHI does not have to be manifest or even detectable at birth. Some types of HHI have a delayed onset, such that hearing will be normal until the second or third decade of life.[103] In general, regardless of the time of onset of the hearing impairment, hearing loss that is inherited in a dominant manner tends to worsen progressively, whereas recessively inherited hearing loss usually remains stable.

Consider the likelihood of a child having hearing impairment caused by a gene defect, and keep the following in mind:

Autosomal-Dominant Hearing Impairment. These disorders can have variable penetrance and expression. If gene penetrance is low, parents and relatives of an affected child may possess the dominant gene but not manifest evidence of the expression of such a gene. Furthermore, even if a gene is penetrant, the gene expression might be extremely mild so that the physical findings are subtle and nearly inapparent.

Autosomal-Recessive Hearing Impairment. Family size can be a factor in determining whether a child's hearing impairment might be caused by a recessive gene. In contrast to the autosomal dominant pattern of inheritance (affected individuals in prior generations), parents and relatives carrying an autosomal-recessive gene mutation would not necessarily be expected to have hearing loss. The smaller the family is, the more difficult the process of confirming a tentative diagnosis of HHI. For example, the diagnosis of nonsyndromic HHI cannot be ruled out with assurance in an only child with severe sensorineural hearing loss who has few cousins, aunts, or uncles and whose parents have no family history of childhood hearing loss.

X-Linked Hearing Impairment. Both parents usually have normal hearing. Half of the males are affected, and half of the females have normal hearing but would be expected to be carriers of the abnormal gene. Affected males uncommonly produce affected offspring and themselves are the offspring of normal-hearing female carriers of the abnormal gene. However, all of the daughters of an affected male are carriers of the abnormal gene. In instances in which a female is hearing impaired, the female is the offspring of an affected father and a normal-hearing carrier mother. Such a situation often involves parents who are related (consanguineous). Examples of X-linked recessive hearing impairment include Alport syndrome, Norrie syndrome, and progressive mixed hearing loss with perilymphatic gusher. A temporal bone CT scan finding of a bulbous lateral aspect of the internal auditory canal with bony dehiscence of the base of the modiolus has been described by Phelps as being correlated with and highly suggestive of the X-linked recessive progressive mixed hearing loss with stapes gusher caused by a genetic defect localized to Xq13-Xq21.1.

Mitochondrial Hearing Impairment. This rare inheritance pattern is characterized by transmission of the hearing impairment trait from the mother to all sons and daughters. Only females transmit the mitochondrial gene mutations, as the egg contributes all mitochondria to the zygote during fertilization. However, diagnosis of this type of HHI may be difficult, since expression of mitochondrially inherited disorders varies considerably and not all of the children are affected. This variability in expression is explained by the fact that not all of a mother's mitochondria will necessarily have the mutation, and there may be nuclear genes that can mollify or lessen the effect of a mitochondrial gene defect.

Syndromic Hereditary Hearing Impairment

The most commonly occurring syndromes associated with HHI are Goldenhar, Treacher-Collins, Waardenburg, and Usher syndromes (see Tables 16–4 through 16–7).

Goldenhar Syndrome (Oculoauriculovertebral Spectrum, Hemifacial Microsomia)

Goldenhar syndrome, or oculoauriculovertebral spectrum, is a craniofacial malformation, usually unilateral, involving structures derived from the first and second branchial arches, especially the pinna, external-ear canal, and middle-ear ossicles. The incidence of oculoauriculovertebral spectrum is reported to be 1 per 5600 births, with a male-to-female ratio of at least 3:2.[38] The majority of cases are sporadic; there is no clearly discernible mendelian inheritance pattern, although there have been reports of oculoauriculovertebral spectrum occurring within families in an autosomal-dominant pattern. Marked facial asymmetry is present in 20% of cases, and some degree of facial asymmetry is seen in 65% of cases. On examination, one may observe hypoplasia with flattening of the malar eminence of the maxillary bone, the temporal bone, and the ascending ramus and condyle of the mandible on the affected side. Abnormality of the external ear may range from anotia to an amorphous mass of soft tissue displaced anteriorly and inferiorly to a mildly dysmorphic pinna that is almost imperceptibly smaller or different in shape compared with the opposite ear. The external auditory canal may be stenotic, tortuous, or atretic; preauricular skin tags or pits may also be present. In more than 50% of cases, there is some hearing loss, which is usually conductive, although it is sometimes of the mixed variety; stapes fixation may contribute to this loss. Abnormalities in position of the facial nerve as well as congenital facial paresis or paralysis are also seen.

TABLE 16–7. Syndromic Hearing Impairment Genes

Syndrome	Inheritance	Gene	Locus	Location	Study
Alport	XLR	COL4A5		Xq22	Barker et al, 1990
	AD	COL4A3		2q36-q37	Mochizuki et al, 1994
	AD	COL4A4		2q36-q37	Mochizuki et al, 1994
Branchi-oto-re-nal	AD	EYA1	BOR	8q13.3	Abdelhak et al, 1997
	AD	unknown	BOR2?	1q31	Kumar et al, 2000
Jervell and Lange Niel-sen	AR	KVLQT1	JLNS1	11p15.5	Neyroud et al, 1997
	AR	KCNE1	JLNS2	21q22.1-q22.2	Tyson et al, 1997; Schulze-Bahr et al, 1997
Norrie disease	XLR	Norrin	ND	Xp11.3	Berger et al, 1992; Chen et al, 1992
Pendred	AR	PDS	PDS	7q21-q34	Everett et al, 1997
Stickler	AD	COL2A1	STL1	12q13.11-q13.2	Williams et al, 1996
	AD	COL11A2	STL2	6p21.3	Vikkula et al, 1995
	AD	COL11A1	STL3	1p21	Richards et al, 1996
Treacher-Collins	AD	TCOF1	TCOF1	5q32-q33.1	Dixon et al, 1996
Usher	AR	unknown	USH1A	14q32	Kaplan et al, 1992
	AD	MYO7A	USH1B	11q13.5	Weil et al, 1995
		USH1C	USH1C	11p15.1	Smith et al, 1992; Verpy et al, 2000; Bitner-Glindzicz et al, 2000
		CDH23	USH1D	10q	Wayne et al, 1996
		unknown	USH1E	21q22.1-q22.2	Chaib et al, 1997
		unknown	USH1F	10	Wayne et al, 1997
		USH2A	USH2A	1q41	Kimberling et al, 1990; Eudy et al, 1998
		unknown	USH2B	3p23-24.2	Hmani et al, 1999
		unknown	USH2C	5q14.3-q21.3	Dahl et al, Molecular Biology of Hearing and Deafness 10/8/2000
		unknown	USH3	3q21-q25	Sankila et al, 1995
Waardenburg		PAX3	WS1	2q35	Tassabehji et al, 1992
		MITF	WS2	3p14.1-p12.3	Tassabehji et al, 1994
		PAX3	WS3	2q35	Hoth et al, 1993
		EDNRB	WS4	13q22	Attie et al, 1995
		EDN3	WS4	20q13.2-q13.3	Edery et al, 1996
		SOX10	WS4	22q13	Pingault et al, 1998

AD, autosomal dominant; AR, autosomal recessive; XLR, x-linked recessive.

Additional components of the syndrome include ocular abnormalities such as epibulbar dermoid (35%), blepharoptosis, coloboma (20%), and narrowed palpebral fissures; cervical spine and cranial base abnormalities (vertebral fusion, 35%); and renal abnormalities, such as renal agenesis, double ureter, crossed renal ectopia, and hydronephrosis. An external auditory canal that admits a speculum no larger than a size #3, while the opposite side accepts a larger speculum, is suspicious for oculoauriculovertebral spectrum. Patients with such a condition may benefit from external ear and ossicular reconstruction.[40]

Treacher-Collins Syndrome (Mandibulofacial Dysostosis)

The facial abnormalities associated with Treacher-Collins syndrome are bilateral and usually symmetric. Inheritance of the gene TCOF1 (5q32-q33.1) is in an autosomal-dominant manner, demonstrating variable expressivity. In patients with this syndrome, the face is narrow, the midface is small and constricted with depressed malar eminences (cheekbones), the palpebral fissures have a characteristic downward slant, and there is often a receding chin and down-turned mouth. The nose appears to be large because of the hypoplastic supraorbital rims and hypoplastic zygomas. In about 75% of cases, there is a coloboma in the outer third of the lower eyelid. External-ear anomalies range from anotia to amorphous soft tissue mass to microtia and cup-shaped pinna. Complete external auditory canal atresia, narrowing or agenesis of the middle-ear cleft, and hypoplastic and malpositioned facial nerve can be seen. Mild to moderate bilateral conductive hearing impairment (rarely with a sensorineural component) occurs in more than 55% of cases and is due to significant anatomic abnormalities involving the pinnae, middle-ear ossicles, cochlea, or vestibule.[38] Anatomic abnormalities of the stapes as well as stapes ankylosis and stenotic oval window can also be part of the syndrome.

In general, attempts to surgically create an external auditory canal and improve hearing in children with Treacher-Collins syndrome who have bilateral anotia with external auditory canal atresia, marked middle-ear anomalies, and maximal conductive hearing loss do not yield good, sustained hearing improvement. It is also difficult to achieve a significant hearing improvement with tympanoplasty and ossiculoplasty in these patients. Auditory rehabilitation with amplification is helpful.

Waardenburg Syndrome

Waardenburg syndrome is a pigmentary and integumentary system disorder believed to be responsible for 2% to 5% of all congenital hearing impairment. Waardenburg syndrome is inherited in an autosomal-dominant manner with high gene penetrance but significant variability in expression of the gene. Waardenburg syndrome types I (*PAX3* 2q35), II (*MITF* 3p14.1–p12.3), III (*PAX3* 2q35), and IV (*EDNRB* 13q22, *EDN3* 20q13.2-q13.3, *SOX10* 22q13) have been described.

Previous reports suggest that 20% of individuals with Waardenburg syndrome type I have hearing impairment, while 50% with type II Waardenburg syndrome have hearing impairment. The severity and progression of the unilateral or bilateral sensorineural hearing loss is highly variable within families and between affected families. A host of inner ear abnormalities, including absent or abnormal organ of Corti, strial atrophy, decreased cochlear neural population, and spiral ganglion atrophy may be present. In addition, type I Waardenburg syndrome is characterized by the presence of dystopia canthorum, a measurable and quantifiable lateral displacement of the medial canthi of the eyes. The maximal normal inner canthal distance in children up to 16 years of age is 34 mm; in adult women, it is 37 mm; and in adult men, it is 39 mm. Approximately 85% of individuals with Waardenburg syndrome have inner canthal separation measurements exceeding these distances; they are classified as having type I syndrome.

Individuals with type II Waardenburg syndrome do not have dystopia canthorum, but they do manifest some or all of the other findings, such as high broad nasal root, synophrys (confluent eyebrows), heterochromia iridis (eyes of two different colors or one eye with segments of a different color), hypoplastic blue irides (brilliant blue eyes), hypopigmented ocular fundi, white forelock, premature graying of the hair, partial albinism, hypoplastic nasal alae, smooth nasolabial frenulum, and mild to severe sensorineural hearing loss that can be unilateral or bilateral. Type III Waardenburg syndrome includes findings of types I and II in association with ptosis, various dactyly, and severe growth retardation. Type IV Waardenburg syndrome includes findings of type II with associated Hirschsprung disease.

Usher Syndrome

Usher syndrome is an autosomal-dominant disorder that is responsible for 3% to 10% of congenital deafness and is seen in nearly half of the deaf-blind population. Retinitis pigmentosa in the first two decades of life is seen in patients with all types of Usher syndrome, while a spectrum of hearing impairment and vestibular involvement is observed. Generally, type I Usher syndrome includes profound deafness at birth with severe balance disturbance. Such patients receive little or no benefit from hearing aids and primarily use sign language for communication. Type II Usher syndrome usually involves moderate to severe hearing impairment for which hearing aids are often helpful. Such patients commonly use speech to communicate, and they tend to perform well in the classroom. In cases of type III Usher syndrome, normal hearing worsens over time and progresses to deafness by adulthood without any balance disturbance. Early referral for electroretinography is helpful in diagnosing retinitis pigmentosa and in implementing appropriate intervention, such as early Braille teaching and hearing aids.

Genetics and Molecular Biology of Hearing Impairment

Growing Relative Incidence of Hereditary Hearing Impairment

In the last two decades, the relative incidence of acquired versus congenital hearing impairment has changed. The acquired types of hearing impairment have decreased in frequency, while the congenital and inherited types of hearing impairment have grown to account for a larger proportion of childhood hearing impairment.[88] In the United States, the increasing use of vaccination for *Haemophilus influenzae* type B and measles-mumps-rubella has resulted in a decreased frequency of hearing loss due to bacterial and viral infection. Federal and state laws that mandate the use of infant car seats, seat belts, and child bicycle helmets have helped to decrease the frequency of trauma to the temporal bone and concomitant hearing loss. Careful monitoring of peak and trough levels in infants receiving potentially ototoxic medications has helped to diminish hearing loss from ototoxicity. Therefore, the acquired causes of hearing loss are diminishing while the incidence of HHI is either remaining stable or increasing.

Until recently, only genes responsible for syndromic HHI had been identified. However, in the last 5 years, many genes that contribute to nonsyndromic HHI have been identified.[121] As of March 1999, at least 53 loci have been identified for nonsyndromic HHI.[112] Today, our understanding of the molecular biology of the auditory system continues to grow as scientists identify HHI genes. Therefore, the otolaryngologist should have a basic understanding of HHI and the molecular biology of the auditory system in order to employ new methods of genetic testing for diagnosis, treatment, and prevention of sensorineural hearing loss.

As we approach an era in medicine during which genetic testing will become increasingly available and useful, the otolaryngologist should learn about genetic tests helpful in the evaluation of children with hearing impairment. Additionally, he or she should remain informed of newly discovered gene mutations, new genetic tests that become available, and new treatments that are developed. In the future, individuals carrying a genetic mutation responsible for progressive hearing loss may be able to receive a sufficient amount of normal gene product to prevent auditory dysfunction. The Boys Town Research Registry for HHI* provides information on clinical and research issues to families, clinicians, and researchers interested in HHI and deafness. The Registry also collects information on new research and matches families with collaborating research projects. Other national and international resources for patients include the National Institutes of

---

*Research Registry for Hereditary Hearing Loss: deafgene. registry@boystown.org

Health's Deafness and Other Communication Disorders division† and the Royal National Institute for the Deaf.‡

Genetics and Molecular Biology of Hearing Impairment

Almost all of the genes implicated in hearing loss were identified within the last 10 years. Some of these genes encode related proteins, many of which are well studied. These include the connexin genes, the myosin genes, the POU genes, and the ion channel genes. In addition, a number of unrelated genes have been identified.[121] When considering genetic testing, one should keep in mind that options change daily with the advent of new tests and with the discovery of new genes. As such, the otolaryngologist should be familiar with the normal and pathologic molecular biology of hearing.

Connexins

The connexin gene family is made up of a group of genes that encode plasma membrane channel proteins of the alpha (A) and beta (B) types.[56] To form an intercellular channel for communication, two adjacent cells each contribute six connexin subunits. Intercellular exchange of small molecules and ions occurs through these channels in regions known as *gap junctions* (GJ), where connexin channels are concentrated. During sound transduction, potassium ions move in and out of stereocilia-containing hair cells, a process that is facilitated by gap junctions. Mutations in connexin can alter this process and affect hearing. In fact, impaired intercellular coupling due to abnormal gap junction assembly has been demonstrated in vitro.[79] To date, syndromal (e.g., X-linked Charcot-Marie-Tooth syndrome) and nonsyndromal (e.g., autosomal-dominant and autosomal-recessive) patterns of genetic hearing loss have been documented.[120, 121]

So far, at least four connexin genes have been identified, and a number of mutations have been characterized. Of all genetic mutations resulting in hearing loss, the prototype gene for study has been *GJB2*, the connexin-26 gene. Connexin-26 mutations have been identified and characterized worldwide, and the frequencies of mutations have been measured in many populations. For example, the deletion of a guanine molecule at position 30 in the connexin-26 gene *GJB2* is termed the *30delG* mutation. This mutation is responsible for most genetic hearing loss in Europe and is carried in the European-descended population at a frequency of 1% to 3%. A similar mutation, the *35delG*, is the leading cause of 40% to 70% of nonsyndromic autosomal-recessive deafness in the midwestern United States. Approximately 4% percent of Ashkenazi Jews carry a similar thymine mutation (*167delT*),[121] while the carrier rate for the most common *GJB2* mutation in Japan, *235delC*, is approximately 1%.[73] In Ghana,

several families in one village are known for their highly prevalent profound nonsyndromic hearing loss; recent mutation analysis revealed that 21 subjects in 11 families possessed the same homozygous mutation R143W (a tryptophan arginine exchange) in *GJB2*.[12]

In American schools for the deaf, investigators identified a variety of mutations. In this study, at least 16% to 34% of patients with profound hearing impairment of unknown cause were homozygotes or compound heterozygotes for *GJB2* mutations. Individuals with affected siblings demonstrated homozygous mutation rates that were nearly double (64%) the rate in patients without a known affected sibling. Finally, these investigators suggest that as much as 10% of the deaf population demonstrates auditory dyssynchrony (formerly known as auditory neuropathy) secondary to a form of retrograde neurologic degeneration, a process that may be induced by mechanical changes in the cochlea that results from absence or detachment of inner hair cells.[8]

To identify patients with common connexin mutations, screening tests, such as the 30delG and 35delG screens, have been designed and studied. Their utility, reliability, simplicity, efficiency, and cost-efficacy have been demonstrated, thereby supporting the use of genetic screening in the evaluation of hearing loss.*

Myosins

The myosin gene family is related to the superfamily of myosin genes expressed throughout the body. Several unconventional myosin genes expressed in the ear have been implicated in hereditary hearing loss (e.g., myosin VI, myosin VIIA, myosin XV genes). In the ear, myosins are necessary for stereocilia movement. In addition, they may facilitate vesicle transport in hair cells and may provide structural support in hair cells and their stereocilia. Autosomal recessive nonsyndromic hearing loss as well as syndromic hearing loss (e.g., Usher syndrome) have been described. Many mouse models have been used to study these mutations, including Snell's waltzer mice [Myo6(sv)], shaker 1 [Myo7(ash1)], and shaker 2 [Myo15(sh2)]. To date, the shaker mice mutations have led to the identification of mutations responsible for Usher syndrome 1B and nonsyndromic autosomal-recessive deafness.[65] Deafness due to stereocilia abnormalities has been demonstrated in such mice as well.[121]

POU Gene Products

Members of the POU gene family encode transcription factors, some of which are expressed in the inner and middle ear. *POU4F3* is uniquely expressed in hair cells, where it regulates the survival of the organ of Corti. *POU3F4* is expressed in the middle and inner ear, regulating bone maturation. In mouse models, mutations in *POU3F4* result in bony labyrinth and ossicle developmental abnormalities.[121]

†National Institute on Deafness and other Communication Disorders, National Institutes of Health Building 31, Room 3c-35, Bethesda, Maryland 20892

‡Royal National Institute for the Deaf, 105 Gower St., London WC1EAH, Great Britain

*For more information on connexin-26, visit the connexin-26 website: http://www.iro.es/cx26deaf.html.

TABLE 16–8. Autosomal-Recessive Nonsyndromic Hearing Impairment Genes

Gene	Locus	Location	Most Important Study
MYO7A	DFNB2	11q13.5	Guilford et al, 1994; Liu et al, 1997 Weil et al, 1997
MYO15	DFNB3	17p11.2	Friedman et al, 1995; Wang et al, 1998
PDS	DFNB4	7q31	Baldwin et al, 1995; Li et al, 1998
unknown	DFNB5	14q12	Fukushima et al, 1995
unknown	DFNB6	3p14-p21	Fukushima et al, 1995
unknown	DFNB7	9q13-q21	Jain et al, 1995
TMPRSS3	DFNB8	21q22.3	Veske et al, 1996; Scott et al, 2000
OTOF	DFNB9	2p22-p23	Chaib et al, 1996; Yashunga et al, 1999
TMPRSS3	DFNB10	21q22.3	Bonne-Tamir et al, 1996
unknown	DFNB11	9q13-q21	Scott et al, 1996
CHD23	DFNB12	10q21-q22	Chaib et al, 1996
unknown	DFNB13	7q34-q36	Mustapha et al, 1998
unknown	DFNB14	7q31	Mustapha et al, 1998
unknown	DFNB15	3q21-q25 19p13	Chen et al, 1997
unknown	DFNB16	15q21-q22	Campbell et al, 1997
unknown	DFNB17	7q31	Greinwald et al, 1998
unknown	DFNB18	11p14-p15.1	Jain et al, 1998
unknown	DFNB19	18p11	Green et al, Mol Bio of Hearing and Deafness Meeting (10/8–10/11/1998)
unknown	DFNB20	11q25-qter	Moynihan et al, 1999
TECTA	DFNB21	11q	Mustapha et al, 1999
reserved	DFNB22		
unknown	DFNB23	10p11.2-q21	Smith, unpublished
unknown	DFNB24	11q23	Smith, unpublished
unknown	DFNB25	4p15.3-q12	Smith, unpublished
unknown	DFNB26	4q2 modif 1q22-q23	Riazzuddin et al, 1999
reserved	DFNB27		
unknown	DFNB28	22q13	Walsh et al, 2000
CLDN14	DFNB29	21q22	Wilcox et al, 2000
unknown	DFNB30	10p	Avraham, King unpublished

Potassium Channels

The potassium channel gene superfamily includes genes that are expressed in the inner ear. In normal potassium trafficking, the *KCNQ4* gene product distributes potassium from hair cells into surrounding cells, while *KCNQ1* and *KCNE1* gene products secrete this newly distributed potassium into the endolymph. Mutations in these genes (i.e., *KCNQ4*, *KCNQ1*, and *KCNE1*) result in mutant potassium channels that are responsible for abnormal potassium traffic into and out of the cell. The abnormal electric potentials of the hair cells alter sound transduction and result in hearing loss. In humans, hearing loss and conduction abnormalities of the heart are seen in Jervell and Lange-Nielsen syndrome. In mice models, Ca^{2+} channel gene mutations cause a similar syndrome of deafness with sinoatrial node dysfunction.[95] Na-K-Cl cotransporter mutations have also been shown to cause deafness in mice.[24]

Autosomal-Recessive Hearing Impairment

Autosomal-recessive forms of deafness involve gene loci, *DFNB loci*, that have been mapped to multiple chromosomes (Table 16–8). Researchers continue to study these genes and the mechanisms by which genetic mutations result in hearing impairment. Recently, investigators demonstrated both dominant and recessive modes of inheritance of hearing impairment due to mutations in the same gene.[77, 84] For example, the DFNB1 locus on chromosome 13 is a major locus for recessive and dominant nonsyndromic deafness.[77] Mutations at this site are responsible for autosomal-recessive deafness in about 80% of Mediterranean families.[27] The frequency of one of the most common mutations at this site, the 35delG mutation, is estimated to be 1 in 51 in the overall European population and is estimated to be 1 in 35 in southern European communities.[27] These families possess a mutation in the connexin-26 gene, which encodes an integral membrane protein that contributes to cellular gap junctions (see discussion of connexins). Recycling of endolymphatic potassium ions during the transduction of audition depends on these junctions in epithelial and connective tissue cells. As such, expression of mutant connexin-26 in the cochlea can result in HHI. Recently, a novel mutation in this gene has been identified in the Japanese population (about 1 in 100), thereby further demonstrating the genetic heterogeneity that exists worldwide.[73] Similarly, mutations in a related gene encoding another connexin, connexin-31 (*GJB3*), have been implicated in both recessive and dominant nonsyndromic hearing loss in people in China.[77]

Autosomal-Dominant Hearing Impairment

Fifteen percent of cases of nonsyndromic HHI are inherited in an autosomal-dominant manner. Autosomal domi-

TABLE 16–9. Autosomal-Dominant Nonsyndromic Hearing Impairment Genes

Gene	Locus	Location	Most Important Study
HDIA1	DFNA1	5q31	Leon et al, 1992; Lynch et al, 1997
GJB3	DFNA2	1p34	Coucke et al, 1994; Xia et al, 1999;
KCNQ4	DFNA2	1p34	Kubisch et al, 1999
GJB2	DFNA3	13q12	Chaib et al, 1994; Denoyelle et al, 1998;
GJB6	DFNA3	13q12	Grifa et al, 1999
unknown	DFNA4	19q13	Chen et al, 1995
DFNA5	DFNA5	7p15	Van Camp et al, 1995; Van Laer et al, 1998
unknown	DFNA6	4p16.3	Lesperance et al, 1995
unknown	DFNA7	1q21-q23	Fagerheim et al, 1996
TECTA	DFNA8	11q22-q24	Kirschhofer et al, 1996; Verhoeven et al, 1998
COCH	DFNA9	14q12-q13	Manolis et al, 1996
EYA4	DFNA10	6q22-q23	O'Neill et al, 1996
MYO7A	DFNA11	11q12.3-q21	Tamagawa et al, 1996; Liu et al, 1997
TECTA	DFNA12	11q22-q24	Verhoeven et al, 1997 and 1998
COL11A2	DFNA13	6p21	Brown et al, 1997; McGuirt et al, 1999
unknown	DFNA14	4p16.3	Van Camp et al, 1999
POU4F3	DFNA15	5q31	Vahava et al, 1998
unknown	DFNA16	2q24	Fukushima et al, 1999
MYH9	DFNA17	22q	Lalwani et al, 1999
unknown	DFNA18	3q22	Boensch et al, 1998
unknown	DFNA19	10 (pericen)	Green et al, Mol Bio of Hearing and Deafness Meeting (10/8–10/11/1998)
unknown	DFNA20	17q25	Morell et al, 2000
reserved	DFNA21		
reserved	DFNA22		
unknown	DFNA23	14q21-q22	Salam et al, 1999 and 2000
unknown	DFNA24	4q	Hafner et al, 1999
unknown	DFNA25	12q21-q24	Greene et al, 1999
unknown	DFNA26	17q35	Yang et al, 2000
unknown	DFNA27	4q12	Fridell et al, 1999
unknown	DFNA28	8q22	Anderson et al, 1999
reserved	DFNA29		
unknown	DFNA30	15q26	Mangino et al, 1999
withdrawn	DFNA31		
unknown	DFNA32	11p15	Li et al, 2000
reserved	DFNA33		
	DFNA34	1q44	Kurima et al, 2000
reserved	DFNA35		
	DFNA36	9q13-q21	Kurima et al, 2000
	DFNA37	1p21	Talebizadeh et al, 2000
reserved	DFNA38		Young, King unpublished
unknown	DFNA39	4q21	Xiangyin Kong, unpublished

nant forms of deafness in humans involve *DFNA loci*, which are located on numerous chromosomes (Table 16–9). The functions of some of the genes that are associated with autosomal dominant nonsyndromic hearing impairment have yet to be determined. Others, such as those of the *GJB loci*, have been well studied, and mutations at these loci have been implicated in otologic as well as systemic disease.[72] Generally, this form of HHI is characterized by progressive hearing loss and less severe impairment. While autosomal-recessive forms of hearing loss are almost all due to cochlear defects, the autosomal-dominant forms of HHI often involve conductive or sensorineural defects. This has been demonstrated in a study of a family with dominant, progressive, low-frequency sensorineural hearing loss due to a mutation in *DFNA6* (4p16.3).[84] Recently, for example, mutation in *KCNQ4*, found in the DFNA2 locus, was implicated in a form of nonsyndromic dominant deafness by Kubisch et al. *KCNQ4* is normally expressed in the sensory outer hair cell of the cochlea. Mutant *KCNQ4* gene product alters the function of the potassium channels in these hair cells,

leading to hair cell dysfunction and concomitant hearing impairment.

X-Linked Hearing Impairment

The extreme genetic heterogeneity of hearing impairment contributes to the challenge of isolating and cloning genes responsible for HHI. Linkage analysis requires large individual families. X-linked forms account for only 1.7% of HHI. Most of the X-linked genes responsible for HHI have yet to be elucidated.

Nonsyndromic X-linked deafness is even more uncommon than syndromic X-linked deafness.[64] In the majority of pedigrees demonstrating nonsyndromic X-linked deafness, the hearing impairment is of prelingual onset and is characterized by one of two forms. X-linked stapes fixation with perilymphatic gusher and mixed hearing impairment has been localized to the DFN3 locus, which encodes the *POU3F4* transcription factor (see POU Gene Products).[120] X-linked forms of hearing impairment may also involve congenital sensorineural deafness.[77] Both

TABLE 16–10. Mitochondrial Hearing Impairment Genes

Gene	Mutation	Phenotype	Study
Syndromic			
tRNALeu(UUR)	3243A → G	MELAS and MIDD	Goto et al, 1990
			Ouweland et al, 1992
tRNALys	8344A → G	MERRF	Shoffner et al, 1990
	8356T → C	MERRF	Zeviani et al, 1993
	8296A → G	MIDD	Kameoka et al, 1998
tRNASer(UCN)	7512T → C	Progressive myoclonic epilepsy; ataxia, hearing impairment	Jaksch et al, 1998b
Several	Large deletions	KSS	Moraes et al, 1989
Several	Large deletion/duplication	MIDD	Ballinger et al, 1992
tRNAGlu	14708T → C	MIDD	Hao et al, 1995
Nonsyndromic			
12S rRNA	1555A → G	None proven	Prezant et al, 1993
			Usami et al, 1997
			Esteville et al, 1998
tRNASer(UCN)	7445A → G	Palmoplantar keratoderma	Reid et al, 1994
			Fischel-Ghodsian et al, 1995
			Sevior et al, 1998
	7472insC	Neurologic dysfunction, including ataxia, dysarthria and myoclonus	Tiranti et al, 1995
			Jaksch et al, 1998a
			Jaksch et al, 1998b
			Schuelke et al, 1998
			Verhoeven et al, 1999
	7510T → C	None reported	Hutchin et al, 1989
	7511T → C	None reported	Friedman et al, 1999
			Sue et al, 1999

KSS, Kearns-Sayre syndrome; MELAS, mitochondrial encephalopathy, lactic acidosis, and stroke-like episodes; MERRF, myoclonic epilepsy and ragged red fibers; MIDD, maternally inherited diabetes and deafness.

forms of nonsyndromic HHI have been linked to Xq13q21.2. Furthermore, some authors have identified an X-linked sensorineural hearing impairment associated with the Xp21.2 locus. The auditory impairment in affected males was congenital, bilateral, sensorineural, and profound, affecting all frequencies. Adult carrier females demonstrated bilateral, mild to moderate, high-frequency sensorineural hearing impairment of delayed onset, suggesting the involvement of genomic imprinting.

Mitochondrial Hearing Impairment

Mutations in mitochondrial DNA are transmitted from an affected mother to all of her offspring. (Recall that offspring solely inherit maternal mitochondria.) Systemic expression of mitochondrial genes results in mitochondrial hearing impairment as part of a syndrome of multiple organ system disease. However, a mitochondrial gene mutation may result in a spectrum of phenotypes, including nonsyndromic hearing loss.

Interestingly, no point mutations in genes encoding mitochondrial proteins have been identified to date. The majority of mitochondrial mutations are tRNA gene point mutations, rearrangements, deletions, and duplications (Table 16–10). Such mutations commonly result in syndromic hearing impairment. The most frequently observed diseases resulting from mitochondrial gene mutation are neuromuscular syndromes (e.g., Kearns-Sayre syndrome, myoclonic epilepsy and ragged red fibers syndrome, mitochondrial encephalopathy-lactic acidosis-stroke-like syndrome, and maternally inherited diabetes and deafness syndrome). Most mitochondrial syndromes have an onset in youth.

Less commonly, point mutations in tRNA and rRNA genes are implicated in nonsyndromic hearing impairment. Nonsyndromic mitochondrial hearing impairment syndromes have been identified in patients with mitochondrial rRNA and tRNA gene mutations. For example, the 1555AG 12S rRNA mutation has been identified in Spanish and Japanese populations at higher-than-average rates. The 1555AG mutation is responsible for nonsyndromic hearing impairment, while mutation carriers are at risk for aminoglycoside ototoxicity when exposed to normally safe levels of aminoglycosides. Through a theoretical mechanism similar to that involved in bacteria, the 1555AG mutation is thought to impart a secondary structure to the gene that has a greater susceptibility to aminoglycoside binding, thereby enhancing the toxicity of aminoglycoside at otherwise safe concentrations.

Choosing Genetic Tests

There is not yet a consensus among otolaryngologists, pediatricians, geneticists, audiologists, and others on when to request genetic testing or which tests to request in the evaluation of children with newly diagnosed hearing impairment. Nonetheless, there is enough information available about genes that cause hearing impairment to help guide the clinician in choosing when to request genetic testing.

First, use information obtained in the family history to decide whether there might be some discernible pattern to the inheritance of a hearing impairment and then consider the likelihood that the hearing impairment might be caused by one of the gene mutations that has been described. For example, if a child's siblings or cousins have hearing impairment without any dysmorphic features, then consider that the hearing impairment could be caused by a mutation in the connexin-26 gene. Connexin-26 gene mutations are among the most common types of genetic hearing impairment known to occur in the United States and other countries. Therefore, connexin-26 mutation testing should be considered. Second, if the mode of inheritance suggests that the mutation causing the hearing impairment is always coming from the mother in a family and never from the father, then consider that the genetic mutation might be in the mitochondrial genes rather than in the nuclear genes. That is, when a maternal pattern of transmission of nonsyndromic hearing impairment is detected, consider genetic testing to look for mitochondrial RNA mutations such as the 12S 1555AG. Finally, when findings on physical examination suggest that the child might have a syndrome, then consultation with a clinical geneticist should be requested. If there is a family history of cardiac arrhythmia or unexplained syncope, then an electrocardiogram should be obtained to look for the prolonged Q-T interval that would help to make a diagnosis of Jervell and Lange-Nielsen syndrome. If there is a family history of goiter, then a diagnosis of Pendred syndrome should be considered, and genetic testing for one of four mutations responsible for 75% of Pendred cases may be useful. If there is a family history of night blindness or progressive loss of visual acuity, then a diagnosis of Usher syndrome should be considered. If there is a family history of branchial cleft cysts, then branchio-oto-renal syndrome should be considered. Since the gene mutations causing all four of the aforementioned syndromes have been identified, most likely, within a few years, genetic tests will become readily available to confirm the suspicion that a child's hearing impairment is caused by a recognizable gene mutation.

Since new "hearing gene" mutations are being discovered rapidly and new genetic tests are becoming readily available, the otolaryngologist needs to gain access to the latest discoveries and the newest genetic tests being offered. There are many clinical laboratories that can test for mutations in the connexin-26 gene (see Connexins section). In addition, many laboratories soon will offer tests for mitochondrial tRNA and rRNA gene mutations, Pendred gene mutations (*PDS*), Stickler syndrome collagen gene mutations (*COL2A1,11A1, 11A2*), Treacher-Collins syndrome gene mutation (*TCOF1*), and Usher syndrome genes, which include a myosin gene (*USH 1C,2A; MYO7A*).

Ordering Tests

The appropriateness and availability of genetic testing is changing rapidly. An otolaryngologist who wants to look for a gene mutation as the cause of a child's hearing impairment likely will be able to find certain useful tests available through a local academic medical center or a commercial laboratory that offers specific genetic testing. Frequently, academic centers employ standard techniques and require either blood or buccal smear samples that are obtained using a kit provided by the laboratory. Outside of academic centers, kits can be obtained by mail, or standard techniques for sample collection (e.g., blood draw, buccal swab) can be employed. Until genetic testing becomes part of a set of diagnostic tests routinely available in most laboratories, the otolaryngologist should attempt to determine those applicable genetic tests that are available locally, their costs, and the procedures for collecting and sending specimens. Also, the practicing otolaryngologist should be aware that protocols used in some laboratories for mutation screening may be used *only* to detect one or two of the more common mutations for hearing impairment, while procedures used in other laboratories may involve gene sequencing if no mutation is identified in screening.

The safest and simplest method of obtaining patient DNA is by buccal swab. The buccal swab is a brush scraping of the buccal mucosa, which captures epithelial cells for DNA isolation. In prenatal testing, amniocentesis or cord blood may be employed in genetic testing. In newborn testing, a heel stick can be used to obtain blood. Organ or skin biopsy may even be required for some testing. In cases of familial disease, testing of pathologic specimens preserved in an archive may also be possible.

Finally, most academic centers provide a genetics consult service, which may be of great use in identifying subtle physical findings associated with a syndrome (for which genetic testing confirmation is available), recommending genetic testing centers, recommending genetic tests as they become available, and identifying mode of transmission. Academic centers frequently study kindreds and may offer free testing in exchange for consent for study of the entire family. Often, such services prove invaluable when genetic counseling is indicated.

SUMMARY

With the technologic advancements that have made feasible universal newborn hearing screening, identification and cloning of many of the genetic mutations that cause hereditary hearing impairment, and improvements in cochlear implants, the overall diagnosis and management of childhood hearing impairment is changing. Now, a child's hearing impairment can be detected early in life, and more can be done to help a hearing-impaired child than ever before. Therefore, although profound hearing impairment can be a devastating handicap for some children, there likely will be more options available in the future for early detection, early intervention, and possibly even prevention of some types of childhood hearing impairment.

WEB SITES

Connexin-26 Home Page: http://www.iro.es/cx26deaf.html
Research Registry for Hereditary Hearing Loss: deafgene.registry@boystown.org

Information on Genetic Testing: http://www.genetests.org
Hereditary Hearing Loss Home Page: http://dnalab-www.uia.ac.be/
Human Genetic Disease Database: http://www.tua.ac.il/~racheli/genedis/
    deafness/deafness/html

CONTACTS

National Institute on Deafness and other Communication Disorders
National Institute of Health Building 31, Room 3c-35
Bethesda, Maryland 20892
Royal National Institute for the Deaf
105 Gower St.
London WC1EAH
Great Britain

REFERENCES

1. Ahlfors K, Ivarsson SA, Harris S. Report on a long-term study of maternal and congenital cytomegalovirus infection in Sweden: review of prospective studies available in the literature. Scand J Infect Dis 31:443, 1999.
2. Alford BR. Rubella: la bete noire de la medecine. Laryngoscope 88:1623, 1968.
3. Arcand P, Desrosiers M, Dube J, et al. The large vestibular aqueduct syndrome and sensorineural hearing loss in the pediatric population. J Otolaryngol 20:247, 1991.
4. Balkany TJ, Downs MP, Jafek BW, et al. Hearing loss in Down's syndrome: a treatable handicap more common than generally recognized. Clin Pediatr 18:116, 1979.
5. Bennet M, Lynn A, Klein L, Balkowiec K. Congenital syphilis: subtle presentation of fulminant disease. J Am Acad Dermatol 36:351, 1997.
6. Bergstrom L, Stewart J. New concepts in congenital deafness. Otolaryngol Clin North Am 4:431, 1971.
7. Bergstrom L. Hearing loss in children. In Northern JL, Downs MP (eds). Hearing in Children. Baltimore, Williams & Wilkins, 1974.
8. Berlin, et al. The search for auditory neuropathy patients and connexin 26 mutations in deaf and hard-of-hearing people. Abst Assoc Res Otolaryngol Feb, 2000.
9. Bess FH, Tharpe AM. Unilateral hearing impairment in children. Pediatrics 74:206, 1984.
10. Bess FH. The minimally hearing-impaired child. Ear Hear 6:43, 1985.
11. Black FO, Bergstrom L, Downs M, et al. Congenital Deafness: A New Approach to Early Detection of Deafness Using a High Risk Register. Boulder, CO, Associated University Press, 1971.
12. Brobby. Connexin 26 R143W mutation associated with recessive nonsyndromic sensorineural hearing deafness in Africa. N Engl J Med 338:548, 1998.
13. Brown HL, Abernathy MP. Cytomegalovirus infection. Semin Perinatol 22:260, 1998.
14. Bullens D, Smets K, Vanhaesebrouck P. Congenital rubella syndrome after maternal reinfection. Clin Ped 39:113, 2000.
15. Casteels A, et al. Neonatal screening for congenital cytomegalovirus infections. J Perinatol Med 27:116, 1999.
16. Chung CS, Robinson OW, Morton NE. A note on deaf mutism. Ann Hum Genet 23:357, 1959.
17. Church A. Substance abuse in pregnancy: fetal alcohol syndrome—hearing, speech, language, and vestibular disorders. Obstet Gynecol Clin 25:85, 1998.
18. Cook AJ, et al. Sources of toxoplasma infection in pregnant women: European multicenter case-control study. BMJ 321:142, 2000.
19. Costa A, Cottino F, Mortara M, et al. Endemic cretinism in piedmont. Pam Med 6:250, 1964.
20. Dahlen RT, Harnsberger HR, Gray SD, et al. Overlapping thin-section fast spin-echo MR of the large vestibular aqueduct syndrome. AJNR Am Journal Neuroradiol 18:67, 1997.
21. Daniels RL, Shelton C, Harnsberger HR. Ultra high resolution nonenhanced fast spin echo magnetic resonance imaging: cost-effective screening for acoustic neuroma in patients with sudden sensorineural hearing loss. Otolaryngol Head Neck Surg 119:364, 1998.
22. Daniels RL, Swallow C, Shelton C, et al. Causes of unilateral sensorineural hearing loss screened by high-resolution fast spin echo magnetic resonance imaging: review of 1,070 consecutive cases. Am J Otol 21:173, 2000.
23. Davidson HC, Harnsberger HR, Lemmerling MM, et al. MR evaluation of vestibulocochlear anomalies associated with large endolymphatic duct and sac [see comments]. Am J Neuroradiol 20:1435, 1999.
24. Dixon, et al. Mutation of the Na-K-Cl co-transporter gene Slc2a2 results in deafness in mice. Hum Mol Genet 8:1579, 1999.
25. Ebenson A. Legal change for the handicapped through litigation. State-Federal Clearinghouse for Exceptional Children. Arlington, VA, The Council for Exceptional Children, 1963.
26. Erickson E. Childhood and Society. New York, WW Norton, 1963.
27. Estivill. High carrier frequency of the 35delG deafness mutation in European populations: genetic analysis consortium of GJB235delG. Eur J Hum Genet 8:19, 2000.
28. Faure, et al. Lack of value of specific IgA detection in the postnatal diagnosis of congenital toxoplasmosis. J Clin Lab Anal 13:27, 1999.
29. Feinmesser M, Zelig S. Congenital deafness associated with onychodystrophy. Arch Otolaryngol 74:507, 1961.
30. Ferriero DM, Dempsey DA. Impact of addictive and harmful substances on fetal brain development. Curr Opin Neurol 12:161, 1999.
31. Fisch L. The etiology of congenital deafness and audiometric patters. J Laryngol 69:479, 1955.
32. Florman AL, et al. Response to rubella vaccine among seronegative children with congenital rubella. First Plenary Session. Am Pediatr Soc Abstr May 1970.
33. Folwer KB, et al. Newborn hearing screening: will children with hearing loss caused by congenital cytomegalovirus infection be missed? J Pediatr 135:60, 1999.
34. Fowler SL. A light in the darkness: predicting outcomes for congenital cytomegalovirus infections. Pediatrics 137:4, 2000.
35. Fraser GR. The Causes of Profound Deafness in Childhood. Baltimore, Johns Hopkins University, 1976.
36. Gates GA, Wachtendorf C, Hearne EM, et al. Treatment of chronic otitis media with effusion: results of tympanostomy tubes. Am J Otolaryngol 6:249, 1985.
37. Gladwin M, Tratter B. Clinical Microbiology Made Ridiculously Simple, 2nd ed. New York, Medmaster, 1997.
38. Gorlin R, Toriello H, Cohen M. Hereditary Hearing Loss and Its Syndromes. Oxford, Oxford University Press, 1995.
39. Grimmer I, et al. Hearing in newborn infants of opiate-addicted mothers. Eur J Pediatr 158:653, 1999.
40. Grundfast, Josephson. Hereditary hearing loss. In Clinical Otology, 2nd ed. 1997, pp 269–287.
41. Grundfast K, Bluestone CD. Sudden or fluctuating hearing loss and vertigo in children due to perilymph fistula. Ann Otol Rhinol Laryngol 87:761, 1978.
42. Grundfast KM, Berkowitz R, Connors C, et al. Complete evaluation of the child identified as a poor listener. Int J Pediatr Otolaryngol 21:65, 1991.
43. Grundfast KM, Carney C. Ear Infections in Your Child. Hollywood, FL, Compact Books, 1987.
44. Grundfast KM. Progressive sensorineural hearing loss. In Harker L (ed). Otolaryngology—Head and Neck Surgery Clinics Update. St Louis, CV Mosby, 1988.
45. Grundfast, Atwood, Chuong. Genetics and molecular biology of deafness. Otolaryngol Clin North Am 32:1067, 1999.
46. Grundfast, Siparsky, Chuong. Genetics and molecular biology of deafness. Otolaryngol Clin North Am 33:1367, 2000.
47. Hall J. Cochlea and cochlear nuclei in asphyxia. Acta Otolaryngol Suppl (Stockh) 10:194, 1964.
48. Halwachs-Baumann, et al. Screening and diagnosis of congenital cytomegalovirus infection: a 5-year study. Scand J Infect Dis 32:137, 2000.
49. Hanson DG, Ulvestad RF. Otitis media and child development:

speech, language, and education. Ann Otol Rhinol Laryngol 88(Suppl 60):20, 1979.

50. Harnsberger HR, Dahlen RT, Shelton C, et al. Advanced techniques in magnetic resonance imaging in the evaluation of the large endolymphatic duct and sac syndrome. Laryngoscope 105:1037, 1995.

51. Hausler R, Toupet M, Guidetti G, et al. Meniere's disease in children. Am J Otolaryngol 8:187, 1987.

52. Haymaker, et al. Pathology of Kernicteric and Posticteric Encephalopathy: Kernicterus. Springfield, IL, Charles C Thomas, 1961, pp 22–230.

53. Hinojosa R. Pathohistological aural changes in the progeny of a mother with pseudohypoparathyroidism. Ann Otol Rhinol Laryngol 67:964, 1958.

54. Hollier LM, Cox SM. Syphilis. Semin Perinat 22:323, 1998.

55. Horton KB. Early intervention through parent training in sensorineural hearing loss in children. Otol Clin North Am 8:143, 1975.

56. Connexin-26 Home Page: Available at http://www.iro.es/cs26deat.html

57. Huizing EH, Van Bolhuis AH, Odenthal DW. Studies on progressive hereditary perceptive deafness in a family of 335 members. Acta Otolaryngol 61:35, 1966.

58. Jackler RK, De La Cruz A. The large vestibular aqueduct syndrome. Laryngoscope 99:1238, 1989.

59. Jackler RK, Luxford WM, House WF. Congenital malformations of the inner ear: a classification based on embryogenesis. Laryngoscope 97(3 Pt 2 Suppl 40):2, 1987.

60. Jaffe BF. Hearing Loss in Children: A Comprehensive Text. Baltimore, University Park Press, 1977.

61. Joint Committee on Infant Hearing. Year 2000 Position Statement: Principles and guidelines for early hearing detection and intervention programs. Pediatrics 106:798, 2000.

62. Jorgensen MB. Influence of maternal diabetes on the inner ear of the foetus. Acta Otolaryngol (Stockh) 53:49, 1961.

63. Karmody CS, Weinstein L. Reversible sensorineural hearing loss with intravenous erythromycin lactobinate. Ann Otol Rhinol Laryngol 87:761, 1978.

64. Karmody CS. Subclinical maternal rubella and congenital deafness. N Engl J Med 278:809, 1968.

65. Keats, et al. The usher syndromes. Am J Med Genet 89:158, 1999.

66. Kelemen G. Maternal diabetes. Changes in the hearing organ of the embryo: additional observation. Arch Otolaryngol 71:921, 1960.

67. Keller WD, Bundy RS. Effects of unilateral hearing loss upon educational achievement. Child Care Health Dev 6:93, 1980.

68. Kittel G, Saller K. Ohrmissbidungen in Beziechung zu Thalidomide. Z Laryngol Rhinol 43:469, 1964.

69. Klein J, Karaskov T, Koren G. Clinical applications of hair testing for drugs of abuse: the Canadian experience. Forens Sci Int 107:281, 2000.

70. Klein JO. Otitis media and the development of speech and language. Pediatr Infect Dis 3:389, 1984.

71. Konigsmark BW, Gorlin RJ. Genetic and Metabolic Deafness. Philadelphia, WB Saunders, 1976.

72. Krutovskikh, et al. Connexin gene mutations in human genetic diseases. Mut Res 462:197, 2000.

73. Kudo, et al. Novel mutation in the connexin-26 gene (GJB2) responsible for childhood deafness in the Japanese population. Am J Med Genet 90:141, 2000.

74. Kuriyama M, Konishi Y, Mikawa H. The effect of neonatal hyperbilirubinemia on the auditory brainstem response. Brain Dev 8:240, 1986.

75. Lazzarotto T, et al. Prenatal indicators of congenital cytomegalovirus infection. J Pediatr 137:90, 2000.

76. Levenson M, Parisier S, Jacobs M, et al. The large vestibular aqueduct syndrome in children. Arch Otolaryngol Head Neck Surg 115:54, 1989.

77. Liu, et al. Mutations in connexin31 underlie recessive as well as dominant nonsyndromic hearing loss. Hum Mol Gen 9(1):63–67, 2000.

78. Luxford WM, Sheehy JLK. Ventilation tubes: indications and complications. Am J Otol 5:468, 1984.

79. Martin, et al. Properties of connexin-26 gap junctional proteins derived from mutations associated with nonsyndromal hereditary deafness. Hum Mol Genet 8:2369, 1999.

80. Matalon R, Jacobson CB, Dorfman A. Prenatal diagnosis of the mucopolysaccharidoses by a chemical method. Am Pediatr Soc Abstr First Plenary Session, May 1970.

81. Meyeroff WL, Paparella MM, Shea D. Meniere's disease in children. Laryngoscope 88:1504, 1978.

82. Michaels RH. Immunologic aspects of congenital rubella. Pediatrics 43:339, 1969.

83. Moore KL. The Developing Human: Clinically Oriented Embryology. Philadelphia, WB Saunders, 1977.

84. Morle, et al. A novel C202F mutation in the connexin-26 gene (GJB2) associated with autosomal dominant isolated hearing loss. J of Med Genet 37:368, 2000.

85. Moteni R. Vertigo as a presenting symptom of multiple sclerosis in childhood. Am J Dis Child 131:553, 1977.

86. Mowrer OH. Learning Theory and Behavior. New York, John Wiley, 1960.

87. Nadol J. Hearing loss as a sequela of meningitis. Laryngoscope 88:739, 1978.

88. Nance WE, Sweeney A. Genetic factors in deafness of early life in sensorineural hearing loss in children: early detection and intervention. Otolaryngol Clin North Am 8:1, 1975.

89. Noyola, et al. Cytomegalovirus urinary excretion and long term outcome in children with congenital cytomegalovirus infection. Pediatr Infect Dis J 19:505, 2000.

90. Palfrey JS, Mervis RC, Butler JA. New directions in the evaluation and education of handicapped children. N Engl J Med 298:819, 1978.

91. Paparella. Interactive inner-ear, middle-ear disease, including perilymphatic fistula. Acta Otol Suppl 485:36, 1991.

92. Partsch J, Maurer H. Zur formalen Genese von Ohrmissbildungen bei der Thalidomide-Embriopathis. Arch Ohr Nas Ukelk Heilk 182:594, 1963.

93. Phelps, Vezina. Radiology of the temporal bone. In Lalwani, Grundfast (eds). Pediatric Otology and Neurotology. Philadelphia, Lippincott, 1998, pp 181–197.

94. Phelps P, Reardon W, Pembrey M, et al. X-linked deafness, stapes gushers and a distinctive defect of the inner ear. Neuroradiology 33:326, 1991.

95. Platzer, et al. Congenital deafness and sinoatrial node dysfunction in mice lacking class D L-type Ca2+ channels. Cell 102:89, 2000.

96. Pransky S, Grundfast KM. Pneumatic otoscopy. J Respir Dis 8:61, 1987.

97. Rawlinson WD. Broadsheet number 50: Diagnosis of human cytomegalovirus infection and disease. Pathology 31:109, 1999.

98. Revello, et al. Diagnostic and prognostic value of human cytomegalovirus load and IgM antibody in blood of congenitally infected newborns. J Clin Virol 14:57, 1999.

99. Richterich R, Van Mechelen P, Rossi E. Refsum's disease (heredopathia atactica polyneuritiformis). Am J Med 39:230, 1965.

100. Robert-Gangneux F, et al. Value of prenatal diagnosis and early postnatal diagnosis of congenital toxoplasmosis: retrospective. J Clin Micro 37:2893, 1999.

101. Robert-Gangneux, et al. Performance on Western blot assay to compare mother and newborn anti-toxoplasma antibodies for the early neonatal diagnosis. Eur J Clin Micro Infect Dis 18:648, 1999.

102. Roizen N. Etiology of hearing loss in children: nongenetic causes. Pediatr Clin North Am 46:49, 1999.

103. Rose SP, Conneally PM, Nance NE. Genetic analysis of childhood deafness. In Bess FH (ed). Childhood Deafness. New York, Grune & Stratton, 1976.

104. Rosenberg AL, Bergstrom L, Troost BT, et al. Hyperuricemia and neurologic deficits: a family study. N Engl J Med 282:992, 1970.

105. Rosendal T. Thalidomide and aplasia-hypoplasia of the otic labyrinth. Lancet 1:724, 1963.

106. Santos DV, et al. Congenital cytomegalovirus infection in a neonatal intensive care unit in Brazil evaluated by PCR and association with perinatal aspects. Rev Instit Med Trop 42:129, 2000.

107. Schwartz S. Choices in Deafness: A Parent's Guide. Kensington, MD, Woodbine House, 1987.

108. Shelton C, Harnsberger HR, Allen R, King B. Fast spin echo magnetic resonance imaging: clinical application in screening for acoustic neuroma. Otolaryngol Head Neck Surg 114:71, 1996.

109. Silkes ED, Chabot J. Progressive hearing loss following Haemophilus influenzae meningitis. Int J Pediatr Otolaryngol 9:249, 1985.

110. Teng YC, Liu JH, Hsu YH. Meningitis and deafness. Clin Med J 81:127, 1962.

111. Terry LL. Support of programs for the communicatively disadvantaged child: role of the private foundation. Ann Otol Rhinol Laryngol Suppl 89(pt2, suppl 74):5, 1980.

112. Tranebjaerg. Genetic causes of hearing loss: status and perspectives. Ugeskrift Laeger 162:3044, 2000.

113. Valvassori G, Clemis J. The large vestibular aqueduct syndrome. Laryngoscope 87:723, 1978.

114. Valvassori GE, Naunton RF, Lindsay RJ. Inner ear anomalies: clinical and histopathological considerations. Ann Otol Rhinol Laryngol 78:929, 1969.

115. Villena I, et al. Detection of specific immunoglobulin E during maternal, fetal, and congenital toxoplasmosis. J Clin Micro 37:3487, 1999.

116. Wagner CL, et al. The impact of prenatal drug exposure on the neonate. Obstet Gynecol Clin North Am 25:169, 1998.

117. Wallon M, et al. Diagnosis of congenital toxoplasmosis at birth: what is the value of testing for IgM and IgA? Eur J Pediatr 158:645, 1999.

118. Webster WS. Teratogen update: congenital rubella. Teratology 58:13, 1998.

119. Whetnall E, Fry DB. The Deaf Child. Springfield, IL, Charles C Thomas, 1964, pp 14–31.

120. White TW. Functional analysis of human cx26 mutations associated with deafness. Brain Res Rev 32:181, 2000.

121. Willems. Mechanisms of Disease: Genetic Causes of Hearing Loss. N Engl J Med 342:1101, 2000.

122. Wilson J. Deafness in developing countries: approaches to a global program of prevention. Scand Audiol Suppl 28:37, 1988.

123. Young H. Syphilis: serology. Dermatol Clin 16:691, 1998.

17

Balance Disorders*

Margaretha L. Casselbrant, M.D., Ph.D., and Joseph M. Furman, M.D., Ph.D.

Balance disorders in children may escape recognition because of the child's inability to describe the symptoms, the short duration of most "dizzy" episodes, overwhelming autonomic symptoms, or the mistaken idea that an episode of organic dizziness may be a manifestation of a behavioral disorder. Although dizziness can indicate a disorder of the vestibular system, it can also indicate an abnormality of other sensory systems or an abnormality in virtually any organ system. Since the etiology of balance disorders in children is multifactorial, the management depends on an accurate diagnosis. Disorders associated with dizziness in children can be divided into the following three broad categories: (1) acute nonrecurring spontaneous vertigo, (2) recurrent vertigo, and (3) nonvertiginous dizziness, dysequilibrium, and ataxia (Table 17–1).[53] The assessment of a "dizzy" child including history, physical examination, and vestibular laboratory testing is discussed in Chapter 13.

Discussion of Acute Nonrecurring Spontaneous Vertigo

Acute nonrecurring spontaneous vertigo is unusual in children. In an acute vestibular syndrome, the vertigo that is experienced by a patient is a result of the rapid loss of unilateral peripheral vestibular function, which disrupts the "push-pull" interaction of the two labyrinths (see Chap. 13). The rapid loss of peripheral vestibular function on one side causes a reduction in the normal baseline activity in the ipsilateral vestibular nerve. Since the brain responds to differences in activity between the two vestibular nuclear complexes, an acute unilateral loss of peripheral vestibular function is interpreted by the CNS as a continuous head movement. Thus, the patient experiences vertigo and exhibits nystagmus, with the fast component beating toward the contralateral ear. Additionally, the child may experience autonomic symptoms including nausea and vomiting. A process called "vestibular

compensation" begins immediately and the CNS "learns" to use the signal from one labyrinth as a sole source of vestibular input. This process of compensation depends on several factors, including a normal CNS, especially brain stem and cerebellar function, a significant amount of active eye, head, and body movements, and abstinence from vestibular suppressant medications.[16] Typically, children recover from an acute loss of unilateral peripheral vestibular function in a matter of days; some children may recover so quickly that it is scarcely known that they even had an acute vestibular episode at all.

Head Trauma

Head trauma can cause an acute episode of vertigo by abruptly affecting the vestibular end organ directly, i.e., a *labyrinthine concussion* as described in Case 1. Although several theories have been proposed, the mechanism of injury in labyrinthine concussion is poorly understood. Pressure waves transmitted directly to the labyrinth through the skull or intracranially via the cochlear aqueduct may cause rupture of the membranous labyrinth or damage to hair cells, hair bundles, or specialized structures in the ampulla or macula. The child usually recovers completely within a short period of time, but, on rare occasions, *benign paroxysmal positional vertigo* or *delayed endolymphatic hydrops* may develop. Benign paroxysmal positional vertigo is characterized by nystagmus and associated vertigo elicited by rapid changes in head position from upright to head hanging. It is thought to be caused by canalithiasis and can be treated with particle repositions.[25]

Other mechanisms of vertigo after head trauma include injury of the CNS, specifically, a *brain stem* or *cerebellar contusion,* or a *temporal bone fracture.* A temporal bone fracture may be longitudinal or transverse. A transverse fracture is the most common cause of vertigo caused by injury to the eighth nerve or the otic capsule. This type of fracture also causes a significant sensorineural hearing loss (see Chap. 29). Another diagnostic consideration for a patient with head trauma followed by vertigo or nonspecific dizziness is that of *perilymphatic fistula.*

---

*The case reports in this chapter are borrowed from Furman JM. Management of vertigo in children. In Bluestone C, Meyers E, Brackmann DE, Krause C (eds). Advances in Otolaryngology. Chicago, Mosby, 1969, pp 105–120, with permission.

TABLE 17–1. Comparison of Disorders Causing Childhood Dizziness

Disorders	Duration of Symptoms/ Episodes	Hearing	Vestibular Laboratory Abnormalities
Nonrecurrent Vertigo			
Vestibular neuritis	Days	Normal	Unilateral caloric reduction
Trauma—labyrinthine concussion	Days	Often impaired SNHL	Possible unilateral caloric reduction
Perilymphatic fistula	Variable	Often impaired SNHL	Possible unilateral caloric reduction
Recurrent Vertigo			
Meniere disease	Minutes to hours	Low-frequency SNHL	Unilateral caloric reduction
Migraine	Variable	Normal	Directional preponderance
Anxiety	Minutes	Normal	Directional preponderance
Seizure disorder	Seconds to minutes	Normal	Normal
Periodic ataxia	Hours to days	Normal	Normal
Nonvertiginous Dizziness			
Bilateral vestibular loss	Constant	Usually normal but may be impaired	Bilateral caloric reduction/reduced gain on rotation
Otitis media	Constant	Conductive	Abnormal posturography
Cerebellar lesions	Constant	Normal	Abnormal ocular motor testing

SNHL, sensorineural hearing loss.
Modified from Tusa RS, Saada AA, Niparaka JK. Dizziness in childhood. J Child Neurol 9:261, 1994.

Perilymphatic Fistula

Perilymphatic fistula is an anomalous connection between the inner ear and middle ear spaces and has been well documented in children.[52] Although perilymphatic fistula is usually associated with hearing loss, it can be associated with vertigo alone.[31] A perilymphatic fistula can be acquired or congenital. The congenital fistulas are associated with abnormalities in the temporal bone, particularly in the area of the stapes, but also in the round window area. Acquired perilymphatic fistulas are generally caused by trauma. Iatrogenic trauma, barotrauma, penetrating trauma, or head trauma may or may not be associated with a temporal bone fracture. Barotrauma can be either implosive or explosive as described by Goodhill et al.[30] Implosive barotrauma can occur during diving and flying or violent sneezing and coughing and is due to a sudden pressure change in the middle ear. The explosive mechanism is caused by a sudden increase in the spinal fluid pressure and, in susceptible individuals, may be induced by straining or any type of excessive exertion such as heavy lifting or sit-ups.

No symptoms are pathognomonic for a perilymphatic fistula. However, several features of the history are suggestive: (1) a history of hearing loss or vertigo after physical strain or stress, exposure to sudden alterations in environmental pressure (e.g., diving or flying), or marked alteration in middle-ear pressures (e.g., violent sneezing,

---

1. Acute Nonrecurring Spontaneous Vertigo

CASE 1. A 14-year-old girl was referred for evaluation of dizziness. Five days earlier, she was involved in a motor vehicle accident in which she struck the side of her head on the inside of the passenger compartment. The patient did not lose consciousness but did note some worsening of hearing on the right. After several days of a sensation of spinning, the patient was only symptomatic when making rapid head movements or trying to walk in dimly lit environments. There was no positional dizziness. A computed tomographic scan obtained shortly after the accident was normal. Coughing or sneezing did not exacerbate symptoms. Physical examination revealed that Weber's tests lateralized to the left. Rinne tests were positive bilaterally. Neurotologic examination revealed a low-amplitude, spontaneous, left-beating vestibular nystagmus behind Frenzel glasses. The patient had difficulty standing on a compliant foam surface with eyes closed. Vestibular testing revealed a 35% right-reduced vestibular response, a mild left-directional preponderance on rotational test ing, and a "vestibular pattern" on computerized dynamic posturography testing, i.e., the patient fell on those trials in which the platform was moving and either the eyes were closed or the visual surround was moving. Audiometric testing revealed a mild-to-moderate right-sided sensorineural hearing loss. Hearing in the left ear was normal.

Comment. This patient is likely to have sustained a labyrinthine concussion during the motor vehicle accident. Results of the patient's laboratory testing suggest a right peripheral ailment given the hearing loss and reduced vestibular response on caloric testing. The patient's abnormal rotational and posturography test results suggest incomplete central nervous system (CNS) compensation for the presumed peripheral vestibular ailment.

Differential Diagnosis. Labyrinthine concussion, brain stem or cerebellar contusion, temporal bone fracture, perilymphatic fistula, vestibular neuritis, and acute labyrinthitis.

laughing, or blowing a wind instrument), (2) a sensorineural hearing loss that is sudden or fluctuating, or both, (3) dizziness, which may be increased by postural change, or continuous poor balance or ataxia, and (4) a sensation of a "pop" in the ear followed by hearing loss or dizziness.

No test is specific for perilymphatic fistula, and the diagnosis may be difficult to make. Applying positive and negative pressures to the external ear canal may produce eye movements or nystagmus, which may indicate the presence of a fistula ("fistula test"). However, a negative response does not exclude a perilymphatic fistula. Fluctuating hearing loss also may indicate a perilymphatic fistula. An inner-ear or middle-ear anomaly such as a Mondini malformation or ossicular deformities demonstrated on a high-resolution computed tomography scan should heighten the clinical suspicion of a congenital perilymphatic fistula.[56]

The diagnosis and treatment of perilymphatic fistula consists of exploration of the middle ear and repair of the fistula by packing with temporalis fascia or muscle. At the time of surgery, fluid from the middle ear should be collected and sent for beta-2 transferrin testing, which is considered to be an objective test for the diagnosis of a perilymphatic fistula.[55]

Vestibular Neuritis

Vestibular neuritis is rarely seen in children younger than 10 years old. It should be considered when a viral syndrome is followed by symptoms suggestive of an acute unilateral peripheral vestibular loss, which is more common in children than in adults.[49] It presents with acute severe vertigo, nystagmus, nausea, and vomiting. The vertigo is worsened by head movements, and patients often prefer to lie down, usually with the affected ear up. There is no hearing loss or tinnitus. Vestibular laboratory testing indicates a unilateral reduced vestibular response to bithermal caloric testing. The symptoms resolve in children within a few days. Management is supportive and symptomatic with early ambulation. A short course of corticosteroids, such as prednisone, may shorten the duration of the illness, but no studies of its efficacy in children have been performed.

Labyrinthitis

The diagnosis of acute labyrinthitis should be used to indicate an inflammatory condition that affects the labyrinth and generally leads to both vestibular and auditory symptoms and signs. The etiology of serous (toxic) labyrinthitis is unknown, but bacterial toxins or other biochemical substances in middle-ear fluid are thought to be absorbed into the inner ear, usually through the round and oval windows. Symptoms may be mild with little or no sensorineural hearing loss and resolve spontaneously (see Otitis Media). In bacterial or suppurative labyrinthitis, there is an invasion of a bacterial infection into the labyrinth from the middle ear through preformed pathways that may be caused by chronic otitis media with cholesteatoma, a prior temporal bone fracture, or a con-

2. Recurrent Vertigo

CASE 2. A 13-year-old boy's chief complaint was dizziness of 4 months' duration occurring in episodes once or twice per week. The patient described a spinning sensation that lasted for several minutes associated with a feeling of imbalance and a tendency to fall. The patient noted that, if he disregarded these symptoms and continued his normal activities, he could become nauseated and on two occasions had actually vomited. The patient had no complaint of hearing loss or tinnitus and did not describe fullness in the ears. The patient's school performance was excellent, but there had been some recent difficulty in gym class and performance of extracurricular sports. The patient had a history of carsickness, especially when riding in the back seat of the car. The patient did not notice a particular association between dizziness episodes and diet. There was a strong family history of migraine headaches on the maternal side; the patient's mother and maternal aunt had throbbing headaches associated with photophobia, phonophobia, and nausea. Also, the patient's mother remembered having carsickness and avoiding amusement parks during her childhood. The patient's physical examination was normal, including general, neurologic, otologic, and neurotologic examinations. Vestibular laboratory testing revealed normal caloric responses and no positional nystagmus. Rotational testing revealed a left-directional preponderance. Audiometry was normal.

Comment. This patient's history, physical examination, and laboratory studies suggest an ongoing vestibulo-ocular imbalance without evidence for peripheral vestibular involvement. Moreover, there was no evidence of auditory system involvement or evidence for a structural abnormality of the CNS. Taken together, these findings make a diagnosis of benign paroxysmal vertigo of childhood, a migraine variant, most likely.

Differential Diagnosis. Meniere's disease, migraine (benign paroxysmal vertigo of childhood, basilar artery migraine), seizure disorder, anxiety disorder, and periodic ataxia syndrome.

genital bony abnormality. Alternatively, in patients with bacterial meningitis, there may be invasion of bacteria via the internal auditory canal or the cochlear aqueduct. The symptoms of suppurative labyrinthitis are severe, and the condition often results in loss of vestibular as well as auditory function on the affected side. Bacterial or suppurative labyrinthitis is a serious complication that requires immediate intravenous antimicrobial therapy and may require surgical intervention (see Chap. 24).

Discussion of Recurrent Vertigo

Recurrent vertigo in children can be a result of disease of the peripheral or central vestibular system. However, most recurrent vertigo in children is the result of a CNS disorder rather than a peripheral vestibular disorder (see Table 17–1).

Meniere's Disease

Meniere's disease, a syndrome presumably caused by endolymphatic hydrops, can occur spontaneously or as a delayed sequela of previous insult from trauma or viral infection. The disorder rarely occurs in children.[22, 34, 43] The disease is characterized by a complex of symptoms including dizziness, unilateral hearing loss, and unilateral tinnitus, which are usually preceded by a feeling of fullness in the affected ear. Symptoms vary among patients and may vary in the same patient over time. Some patients may have only hearing loss and tinnitus, whereas others may have only vestibular symptoms. The duration of the vertiginous episode may vary from half an hour to several hours, and episodes are frequently accompanied by autonomic symptoms such as pallor, perspiration, nausea, and vomiting. Between these acute episodes, adults and rarely children may have vague symptoms of dysequilibrium. The hearing loss in Meniere's disease is usually a low-frequency sensorineural loss that fluctuates, i.e., returns to normal between the attacks, during the early stages of the disease. Later, the hearing loss may progress to a flat sensorineural hearing loss that does not fluctuate. Children are more likely to recover auditory function than are adults. Meniere's disease can be bilateral. Also, with time, a reduction in the responsiveness of the involved peripheral vestibular system occurs. Management of endolymphatic hydrops in children includes reassurance and explanations of the condition to the parents in addition to salt restriction and a diuretic.[16] The need for surgical treatment is rare in children.

Migraine-Related Dizziness

Migraine is probably the most common cause of recurrent vertigo in children. Whereas migraine typically presents as headache in adults, other manifestations of migraine, including recurrent vertigo and dysequilibrium, are more common in children. Benign paroxysmal vertigo of childhood, which is likely to be of migrainous origin, as well as paroxysmal torticollis of infancy and basilar artery migraine, can present with recurrent vertigo in children. Nonvertiginous symptoms of vestibular dysfunction can also be related to migraine. Thus, the manifestations of migraine in childhood are quite varied, including episodic true vertigo, constant imbalance, movement-associated dysequilibrium, and space and motion discomfort (Table 17–2). Because of this highly varied presentation of symptoms, the diagnosis of migraine-related vestibulopathy requires an awareness of the potential vestibular manifestations of migraine, a meticulous history with specific inquiry into the occurrence of headache and other migraine-associated symptoms, and a careful family history. Ultimately, migraine-related dizziness remains a diagnosis of exclusion. Basser[5] described a particular variety of paroxysmal vertigo occurring in childhood with the cardinal symptom of vertigo in isolation, termed *benign paroxysmal verttigo of childhood*. There are no cochlear symp-

TABLE 17–2. Symptoms in Migraine-Related Dizziness (*n* = 100)

Movement-Associated Dysequilibrium, Light-Headedness, and Unsteadiness	79%
Seconds to minutes	14%
Hours	41%
Days to weeks	25%
Always	34%
True Vertigo	21%
Seconds	10%
Minutes	38%
Hours	52%

From Cass SP, Furman JM, Ankerstjerne J, et al. Migraine-related vestibulopathy. Ann Otol Rhinol Laryngol 106:182, 1997.

toms such as tinnitus and hearing loss. The age of onset is usually within the first 3 or 4 years of life but may occur later at age 7 or 8. The spells of vertigo are brief, usually less than 1 minute; they may last only seconds and rarely last more than a few minutes. During a severe attack, the child usually remains still and is unable to move, and frequently the child becomes limp. During a less severe attack the child may clutch on to something. There are no known precipitating factors and the attacks can occur sitting, standing, or lying. Pallor, nausea, sweating, and occasionally vomiting occur. Consciousness is not impaired and the child can recall the episode. There is no pain or headache associated with the attacks. Immediately after the attack, the child resumes normal activities. The interval between the attacks varies from weekly to every 6 months, with monthly to bimonthly episodes being the most common. The attacks usually cease spontaneously after a few years. Physical examination, including a neurologic evaluation, is normal, as is imaging of the skull and temporal bones. Basser[5] reported a moderate or complete canal paresis on caloric testing. However, the response to bithermal caloric testing has been found to be highly variable.[18, 23, 44] Other testing is normal. Children with benign paroxysmal vertigo of childhood often have a positive family history of migraine, and migraine headaches may develop in later years[37, 38] and may respond positively to antimigrainous treatment. The initial treatment of migraine in children is dietary restrictions of foods known to provoke migraine.[1] If unsuccessful, the next step is symptomatic treatment with a vestibular suppressant, such as meclizine, during episodes. If spells are frequent and especially if they impair school performance, use of a prophylactic antimigrainous agent, such as propranolol, should strongly be considered.[11]

Paroxysmal torticollis of infancy was first described by Snyder[50] and consists of episodes of head tilt, which may be associated with nausea, vomiting, pallor, and agitation. The torticollis may alternate from side to side. The episodes are brief and self-limiting and may recur for several months, but they usually resolve by age 2 to 3 years. Physical examination is normal aside from the torticollis. Nystagmus has not been reported. Paroxysmal torticollis of infancy and benign paroxysmal vertigo of childhood have been reported to occur in the same patient.[18, 46]

Bickerstaff[6] was the first to associate vertiginous symptoms preceding migraine with dysfunction of the brain

3. Nonvertiginous Dizziness, Dysequilibrium, Imbalance, and Ataxia

CASE 3. A 17-year-old female high school student complained of dizziness and dysequilibrium that was constant for several years. The patient noted that she had gait instability with veering both to the right and to the left. There was no true vertigo. Rather, the patient experienced light-headedness and dysequilibrium, especially when tipping her head back even while seated. Rapid head movements did not particularly bother the patient. There were no complaints of hearing loss or tinnitus. There was no significant past medical history. Family history was noncontributory.

General examination was normal. Neurologic examination revealed gaze-evoked nystagmus on left gaze, right gaze, and upward gaze. Oblique down and lateral gaze revealed an oblique-torsional nystagmus, i.e., downbeating nystagmus. The patient also had saccadic overshoot dysmetria both when looking to the right and to the left and abnormal ocular pursuit with "catch-up" saccades. The patient had no nystagmus in the primary position but, behind Frenzel glasses, demonstrated a spontaneous right-beating nystagmus. The remainder of the patient's cranial nerve examination was normal. There was normal strength and sensation. Coordination testing was normal. The patient had a widened base of her gait. Even though the Romberg test was negative, the patient had difficulty standing on a compliant foam surface. Otologic examination was normal. A magnetic resonance imaging scan revealed a Chiari malformation with the cerebellar tonsils approximately 5 mm below the foramen magnum with an obliterated ambient cistern.

Comment. This patient's history is extremely non-specific but does suggest a balance system disorder. The patient's symptoms cannot be definitively localized to either the central or peripheral vestibular system. However, the absence of vertigo and the absence of symptoms with rapid head movements suggest a central rather than a peripheral vestibular system abnormality. The worsening of the patient's symptoms when tipping her head back suggests the possibility of a posterior fossa abnormality. The patient's downbeating nystagmus clearly points to a caudal midline cerebellar lesion.

Differential Diagnosis. Bilateral peripheral vestibular loss, otitis media, motion sickness, CNS abnormalities (cerebellar vermian hypoplasia, posterior fossa tumors, Chiari malformations) anxiety disorders, side effects of medication, and systemic disorders.

stem and areas within the distribution of the basilar artery. The majority of his patients were adolescent girls in whom the symptoms often occurred premenstrually, but symptoms have also been described in preadolescent children[19, 27] and adults.[32, 39] The initial symptom in this entity, termed *basilar artery migraine,* is typically visual, consisting of either a total loss of vision or visual aberrations throughout both visual fields. This is usually followed by vertigo, ataxia of gait, dysarthria, and motor weakness often of a hemiparetic type. The headache that follows is usually occipital rather than hemicranial and lasts between 5 minutes and 1 hour. In addition, the patient may experience hearing loss, tinnitus, restlessness, or impairment of consciousness. Complete loss of consciousness occurs in some patients. Management of the patient is similar to that of other patients with migraine.

Seizure Disorders

Seizure disorders are often accompanied by some sense of dizziness and dysequilibrium, although seizures are not frequently associated with true vertigo. However, "tornado epilepsy" has been used to describe seizures that are associated with a sense of spinning that can mimic the symptoms of a peripheral vestibular ailment.[20] Treatment for seizures accompanied by dizziness is similar to treatment for other seizures that have an aura. The choice of anticonvulsant depends upon the particular type of seizure, e.g., simple partial vs. complex partial, and whether there is secondary generalization of the seizure.

Familial Periodic Ataxia

Familial periodic ataxia is a rare syndrome with autosomal dominant inheritance and is characterized by episodes of dizziness, dysequilibrium, and gait instability that may last for several hours. At least two types of the syndrome have been identified[21, 47] and genetic testing is available. These syndromes differ in the duration of the episodes of ataxia. Auditory symptoms are usually absent in these patients. Often, these patients experience migraine headaches. In adults, such patients may have a cerebellar syndrome comparable to that seen in patients with cerebellar degeneration. Treatment with acetazolamide has been shown to reduce the frequency and severity of attacks in some patients.[3]

Discussion of Nonvertiginous Dysequilibrium

Patients with both peripheral and central vestibular disorders can have nonvertiginous dysequilibrium, imbalance, and ataxia. Indeed, many disorders affecting the CNS are symptomatic in this way. Peripheral vestibular disorders that typically occur without vertigo and thus may mimic a central disorder include bilateral peripheral vestibular loss and otitis media. Numerous CNS abnormalities can be associated with nonvertiginous dizziness. Many of these abnormalities involve the cerebellum and include cerebellar hypoplasia, posterior fossa tumors, and Chiari malformations. Also, medication side effects should not be overlooked when evaluating a child with dizziness and dysequilibrium.

Bilateral Peripheral Vestibular Loss

Bilateral peripheral vestibular loss can be either congenital or acquired. The most common causes of acquired bilateral vestibular loss include meningitis, exposure to ototoxic medications, such as aminoglycoside antibiotics, and autoimmune disease of the inner ear. Congenital bilateral vestibular loss is often the result of an inner ear malformation. Some of these malformations affect only hearing, some affect only balance, and some affect both hearing and balance function. The most common inner-ear malformations include Mondini dysplasia, the enlarged vestibular aqueduct syndrome, *Scheibe aplasia,* and Usher syndrome (see Chap. 26). Regardless of etiology, bilateral vestibular loss, if severe, causes *Dandy syndrome,* which is characterized by two specific symptoms, oscillopsia (i.e., jumbling of the visual surround during head motion) and severe gait instability in darkness.[17] Children with bilateral vestibular loss often learn to use alternative sensory inputs such as vision and proprioception. Also, they modify strategies of eye movements. Environments that require vestibular function are extremely challenging for individuals with bilateral vestibular loss, such as ambulating in dimly lit spaces or trying to maintain stable vision during walking.

Otitis Media

Otitis media has been considered one of the most common diseases in infants and children. It often causes a mild-to-moderate conductive hearing loss that may delay speech development and may be associated with learning disabilities. In addition, eustachian tube dysfunction with and without middle ear effusion has been considered the most common cause of vestibular disturbances in children.[2, 8, 10, 24, 26, 42] Often parents report that children have started to walk or are less clumsy after tympanostomy tube insertion. However, only recently have studies been performed in children that confirm the anecdotal evidence that vestibular balance and motor function may deteriorate during an episode of middle-ear effusion.[12, 13, 15, 28, 29, 33, 36, 45] Also, children with otitis media may be more visually dependent[14] as a result of the deterioration of vestibular function causing excessive reliance on other nonvestibular sensory cues to maintain balance. Furthermore, placement of tympanostomy tubes in children with otitis media has been shown to improve balance.[13, 15, 28, 33, 45] In addition to postural control abnormalities, some studies have indicated that children with otitis media can have spontaneous and positional nystagmus,[28] which resolves after tympanostomy tube insertion. The pathophysiologic basis for the balance disturbance seen in children with otitis media is still unknown and further studies are required to determine the cause. Treatment includes medical or surgical interventions. Because the recurrence rate of middle-ear effusion is high after medical therapy,[40] insertion of tympanostomy tubes is the preferred treatment.

Motion Sickness

Motion sickness refers to pallor, diaphoresis, dizziness, nausea, and vomiting induced by passive motion, e.g., riding in a car, or by visual motion while standing still. The etiology of motion sickness is believed to be due to a sensory mismatch between vision and vestibular cues.[9]

Interestingly, motion sickness is more common in patients with migraine. In a study by Bille,[7] severe motion sickness was present in 49% of children with migraine compared with only 10% in control children; a later study by Barabas et al[4] showed similar results, with motion sickness occurring in 45% of children with migraine compared with 5% to 7% of control children.

Central Nervous System Disorders

Numerous CNS disorders cause dizziness, dysequilibrium, imbalance, and ataxia. In childhood, cerebellar abnormalities, such as cerebellar vermian hypoplasia, posterior fossa tumors, and Chiari malformation, are the most common disorders encountered. The clinical presentation of such patients may be confusing, because they are unlikely to have vertigo and may not display evidence of limb ataxia if their abnormalities affect solely midline cerebellar structures.

Chiari malformations consist of four (I to IV) congenital anomalies of the cerebellum and brain stem. Despite their common anatomic location, the four anomalies have distinct features. Types III and IV are rare. In type I Chiari malformation, there is caudal displacement of the cerebellar tonsils into the upper cervical spinal canal. Type I was previously diagnosed in older children or young adults due to late onset of symptoms, but since the advent of magnetic resonance imaging, the diagnosis is being made at an earlier age. The caudal midline cerebellum is typically affected, resulting in gait instability and vestibulo-ocular abnormalities in addition to other neurologic signs and symptoms (see Case 3). Type II is the more common lesion and usually manifests in the first few months of life. In type II malformation, the structures herniating through the foramen magnum include the cerebellar vermis, brain stem, and fourth ventricle. Type II malformation is often associated with myelomeningocele and multiple brain anomalies. Suboccipital decompression of the foramen magnum prevents further progression and may lead to improvement of neurologic symptoms.[48, 51]

The most common *posterior fossa tumors* in children are astrocytoma, medulloblastoma, ependymoma, and glioma. The clinical manifestations are largely those of increased intracranial pressure, except for the gliomas, because the majority of the tumors are in the midline structures where a mass lesion causes obstruction of cerebrospinal fluid circulation. In addition, tumors may also present with signs of unilateral cerebellar dysfunction, with symptoms such as hypotonia, intention tremor on the side of the lesion, nystagmus, and gait ataxia.

Acoustic neurinoma is a benign schwannoma arising from the eighth nerve and usually presents with unilateral sensorineural hearing loss and tinnitus. When large, these tumors can cause ataxia and dizziness. This tumor usually does not occur in children, except as part of *neurofibromatosis* type II. Neurofibromatosis is inherited as an autosomal dominant trait. Type I (von Recklinghausen's disease) is relatively common with the neurinomas occurring throughout the body, whereas neurofibromatosis type II, the central form with bilateral acoustic neurinoma occurring in 96% of patients, is less common.[41] The diagnosis of a posterior fossa tumor is best established using magnetic resonance imaging.

Drug-Induced Dizziness

Many drugs can cause dizziness in addition to the *ototoxicity* caused by aminoglycosides, especially gentamicin, which may cause oscillopsia. In the pediatric age group, phenytoin is used in the treatment of epilepsy but may produce dizziness and nystagmus as signs of intoxication. With this in mind, any child in whom dizziness develops while on a regular medication should be viewed as a possible case of iatrogenic dizziness.

Non-neurotologic Disorders

Another cause of dizziness in children is *psychiatric dizziness*, which usually occurs in children of school age. It may be associated with depression, adjustment reaction of adolescence, and behavior problems. Such children usually have normal vestibular and auditory testing, normal electroencephalogram, and normal imaging studies. When evaluating a child with dizziness, it is essential to determine whether the patient has an associated *anxiety disorder* either as the sole cause for their vertiginous complaints, as an accompaniment to an underlying balance system abnormality, or indirectly related to the dizziness, e.g., through a common brain stem ailment causing both dysequilibrium and an anxiety disorder. Treating anxiety disorders in children is challenging because of medication side effects. If the anxiety symptoms are severe, patients should be referred to a child psychiatrist.

Systemic disorders tend to cause vague light-headedness and dysequilibrium rather than vertigo or ataxia. Anemic states and hypoperfusion states such as vasovagal instability typically produce light-headedness, but not syncope. Congenital heart diseases and arrhythmia should also be considered as a cause of dizziness. Autonomic nervous system dysfunction may produce orthostatic hypotension. Thyroid disease, hypoglycemia, and Addison's disease are other disorders that may produce light-headedness.

Conclusion and Discussion of Hearing Loss

Disorders that cause vertigo in children vary with respect to one another in many ways. Table 17–1 indicates the time course of several of the disorders discussed earlier. Note that peripheral vestibular disorders rarely cause symptoms lasting more than a few minutes, although endolymphatic hydrops can cause symptoms lasting for hours. Migraine can cause symptoms lasting for virtually any duration. Table 17–1 also indicates the likelihood that hearing is affected. Numerous clinical studies have addressed the issue of balance and vestibular function in children with hearing loss. Although balance function is often impaired in children with otitis media, which is associated with a conductive hearing loss, most studies concerning balance and vestibular function in children with hearing loss have concerned children whose hearing

loss is sensorineural. These studies typically report children whose hearing loss could be attributed to a specific etiologic factor. Taken together, these studies suggest that vestibular function is impaired in children with sensorineural loss. A recent study addressed vestibular function in children with unilateral or bilateral mild-to-moderate sensorineural hearing loss that could not be attributed to a specific cause.[35] The study suggests that many children with sensorineural hearing loss of uncertain etiology have an associated vestibular system abnormality based upon laboratory testing, whether or not the children complain of dizziness. It is important to assess vestibular function in infants and young children with sensorineural hearing loss and delayed motor development because abnormalities in the vestibular system could be the cause of the delayed motor development.[54]

REFERENCES

1. American Council for Headache Education, Constantine LM, Scott. Migraine: The Complete Guide. New York, Dell Trade Paperback, 1994.
2. Balkany TJ, Finkel RS. The dizzy child. Ear Hear 7:138, 1986.
3. Baloh R, Winder A. Acetazolamide-responsive vestibulocerebellar syndrome; clinical and oculographic features. Neurology 41:429, 1991.
4. Barabas G Mathews WS, Ferrari M. Childhood migraine and motion sickness. Pediatrics 72:188, 1983.
5. Basser L. Benign paroxysmal vertigo of childhood. Brain 87:141, 1964.
6. Bickerstaff E. Basilar artery migraine. Lancet 1:15, 1961.
7. Bille BS. Migraine in school children. Acta Paediatr Scand 51:1, 1962.
8. Blayney AW, Colman BH. Dizziness in childhood. Clin Otolaryngol 9:77, 1984.
9. Brandt T, Daroff RB. The multisensory physiological and pathological vertigo syndromes. Ann Neurol 7:195, 1980.
10. Busis SN. Vertigo in children. Pediatr Ann 5:478, 1976.
11. Cass SP, Furman JM, Ankerstjerne J, et al. Migraine-related vestibulopathy. Ann Otol Rhinol Laryngol 106:182, 1997.
12. Casselbrant ML, Black FO, Nashner L, Panion R. Vestibular function assessment in children with otitis media. Ann Otol Rhinol Laryngol 107:46, 1983.
13. Casselbrant ML, Furman JM, Rubenstein E, Mandel EM. Effect of otitis media on the vestibular system in children. Ann Otol Rhinol Laryngol 104:620, 1995.
14. Casselbrant ML, Redfern MS, Furman JM, et al. Visual-induced postural sway in children with and without otitis media. Ann Otol Rhinol Laryngol 107:401, 1998.
15. Cohen H, Friedman EM, Lai D, et al. Balance in children with otitis media with effusion. Int J Pediatr Otorhinolaryngol 42:107, 1997.
16. Cyr DG, Rubin A. The evaluation of vestibular function in infants and young children. Insights 7:1, 1992.
17. Dandy WE. The surgical treatment of Meniere disease. Surg Gynecol Obstet 72:421, 1941.
18. Dunn DW, Snyder CH. Benign paroxysmal vertigo of childhood. Am J Dis Child 130:1099, 1976.
19. Eviatar L. Vestibular testing in basilar artery migraine. Ann Neurol 9:126, 1981.
20. Eviatar L, Eviatar A. Vertigo in children: differential diagnosis and treatment. Pediatrics 59:833, 1977.
21. Farmer TW, Mustian VM. Vestibulocerebellar ataxia. Arch Neurol 8:471, 1963.
22. Filipo R, Barbara M. Juvenile Meniere's disease. J Laryngol Otol 99:193, 1985.
23. Finkelhor BK, Harker LA. Benign paroxysmal vertigo of childhood. Laryngoscope 10:1161, 1987.

24. Fried MP. The evaluation of dizziness in children. Laryngoscope 90: 1548, 1980.

25. Furman JM, Cass SP. Benign paroxysmal positional vertigo. N Engl J Med 341:1590, 1999.

26. Gates GA. Vertigo in children. Ear Nose Throat J 59:44, 1980.

27. Golden GS, French JH. Basilar artery migraine in young children. Pediatrics 56:722, 1975.

28. Golz A. Westerman ST, Gilbert LM, et al. Effect of middle ear effusion on the vestibular labyrinth. J Laryngol Otol 105:987, 1991.

29. Golz A, Netzer A, Angel-Yeger B, et al. Effects of middle ear effusion on the vestibular system in children. Otolaryngol Head Neck Surg 119:695, 1998.

30. Goodhill V, Brockman SJ, Harris I, et al. Sudden deafness and labyrinthine window ruptures. Ann Otol Rhinol Laryngol 82:2, 1973.

31. Grundfast KM, Bluestone CD. Sudden or fluctuating hearing loss and vertigo in children due to perilymph fistula. Ann Otol Rhinol Laryngol 87:761, 1978.

32. Harker LA, Rassekh CH. Episodic vertigo in basilar artery migraine. Otolaryngol Head Neck Surg 96:239, 1987.

33. Hart MC, Nichol DS, Butler EM, Barin K. Childhood imbalance and chronic otitis media with effusion: effect of tympanostomy tube insertion on standardized tests of balance and locomotion. Laryngoscope 108:665, 1998.

34. Hausler R, Toupet M, Guidetti G, et al. Meniere's disease in children. Am J Otolaryngol 8:187, 1987.

35. Horak FB, Shumway-Cook A, Crowe TK, Black FO. Vestibular function and motor proficiency of children with impaired hearing or with learning disability and motor impairments. Dev Med Child Neurol 30:64, 1988.

36. Jones NS, Radomskij P, Prichard AJN, Snashall SE. Imbalance and chronic secretory otitis media in children: effect of myringotomy and insertion of ventilation tubes on body sway. Ann Otol Rhinol Laryngol 99:477, 1990.

37. Koehler, B. Benign paroxysmal vertigo of childhood: a migraine equivalent. Eur J Peadiatr 134:149, 1980.

38. Lanzi G, Ballotin U, Fazzi E, et al. Benign paroxysmal vertigo of childhood: a long-term follow-up. Cephalalgia 14:458,1994.

39. Love JT. Basilar artery migraine presenting as fluctuating hearing loss and vertigo. Otolaryngol Head Neck Surg 86:450, 1978.

40. Mandel EM, Rockette HE, Bluestone CD, et al. Efficacy of amoxicillin with and without decongestant-antihistamine for otitis media with effusion in children. N Engl J Med 316:432, 1987.

41. Martuza RL, Eldridge R. Neurofibromatosis 2 (bilateral acoustic neurofibromatosis). N Engl J Med 318:684, 1988.

42. Mercia FS. Vertigo due to obstruction of the eustachian tube. JAMA 118:1282, 1942.

43. Meyerhoff WL, Paparella MM, Shea D. Meniere's disease in children. Laryngoscope 88:1504, 1978.

44. Mira E, Piacentino G, Lanzi G, Balottin U. Benign paroxysmal vertigo in childhood, diagnostic significance of vestibular examination and headache provocation tests. Acta Otolaryngol Suppl(Stockh) 406:271, 1984.

45. Orlin MN, Effgen SK, Handler SD. Effect of otitis media with effusion on gross motor ability in preschool-aged children: preliminary findings. Pediatrics 99:334, 1997.

46. Parker W. Migraine and the vestibular system in childhood and adolescence. Am J Otol 10:364, 1989.

47. Parker HL. Periodic ataxia. Mayo Clin Proc 38:642, 1946.

48. Pollack IF, Kinnunen D, Albright AL. The effect of early craniocervical decompression on functional outcome in neonates and young infants with myelodysplasia and symptomatic Chiari II malformations: results from a prospective series. Neurosurgery 38:703, 1996.

49. Sekitani T, Imate Y, Noguchi T, et al. Vestibular neuronitis: epidemiological survey by questionnaire in Japan. Acta Otolaryngol Suppl (Stockh) 503:9, 1993.

50. Snyder CH. Paroxysmal torticollis in infancy. Am J Dis Child 117: 458, 1969.

51. Spooner JW, Baloh RW. Arnold Chiari malformation: improvement in eye movements after surgical treatment. Brain 104:51, 1981.

52. Supance JS, Bluestone CD. Perilymph fistulas in infants and children. Otolaryngol Head Neck Surg 91:663, 1983.

53. Tusa RJ, Saada AA, Niparka JK. Dizziness in childhood. J Child Neurol 9:261, 1994.

54. Tsuzuku T, Kaga K. The relation between motor function development and vestibular function tests in four children with inner ear anomaly. Acta Otolaryngol (Stockh) 481:443, 1991.

55. Weber PC, Kelly RH, Bluestone CD, Bassiouny M. β_2-transferrin confirms perilymphatic fistula in children. Otolaryngol Head Neck Surg 110:381, 1994.

56. Weissman JL, Weber PC, Bluestone CD. Congenital perilymphatic fistula: computed tomography appearance of middle ear and inner ear anomalies. Otol Head Neck Surg 110:243, 1994.

18

Tinnitus in Children

F. Owen Black, M.D., and David J. Lilly, Ph.D.

Why is it that the buzzing in the ears ceases if one makes a sound? Is it because the greater sound drives out the less?
    Hippocrates[52]

The term *tinnitus* refers to a variety of perceived sounds, usually of unknown origin. Tinnitus is a symptom, not a diagnosis or disease.[90] Most auditory perceptions and sensations classified as tinnitus are audible only to the patient (subjective tinnitus). Subjective tinnitus is defined as the perception of sound in the absence of a corresponding external auditory stimulus. Occasionally a clinician, using an unaided ear, may hear sounds also perceived by the patient (objective tinnitus). Auscultation[30, 58] and other sound amplification devices increase the probability of detection of objective tinnitus and often increase sound fidelity for better characterization of the tinnitus. Some clinicians have added additional modifiers to indicate whether the tinnitus fills the patient's head (tinnitus cerebri) or to indicate localization to one or both ears (tinnitus aurium).[17] Until a better understanding of the pathophysiology of tinnitus comes about, careful clinical documentation of auditory perceptions provides the major clues for diagnosis in those relatively few cases in which a definitive diagnosis can be made.

The problem of tinnitus in adults is reviewed systematically in most standard otolaryngology reference works and other reviews.[29, 120] In contrast, textbooks and monographs that focus on pediatric otorhinolaryngology,[62] hearing in children,[61, 98] and pediatric audiology[83] provide little information regarding the incidence, prevalence, etiology, evaluation, and management of tinnitus in children. The goals of this chapter are (1) to summarize work that addresses specifically the pathophysiology of tinnitus in children, and (2) to discuss diagnosis and treatment methods.

Classification

The classification by Evered and Lawrenson[21] has been modified to meet the needs of pediatric otolaryngologists. In contrast to adults, who often present with a primary complaint of tinnitus, children with normal hearing rarely complain of sounds not present in their environment unless they are specifically questioned about this. Consequently, the clinician must usually seek (or inquire about without leading the patient) a history of perceived sounds in order to elicit the presence of tinnitus in most children afflicted with this condition.

Classification by Described Characteristics

This classification is completely dependent on the child's ability to characterize tinnitus verbally. Obviously, its value is related directly to the age of the patient and to the level of language acquisition.[74] However, if the child can describe the "sounds" perceived in the ears or in the head, the classification can serve as a framework for the history.

Descriptive Classification

Ask the child to describe the sound or sounds perceived, first without suggestion, then by comparing the sound(s) heard with familiar sounds in the environment. How many different sounds does the child hear? Once the presence of tinnitus has been established, it is often helpful to ask the child to compare the sound(s) heard with sounds generated by the examiner (e.g., pure tones, noise makers, common toys, white and band-limited ["pink"] masking noise) in an attempt to approximate the acoustic characteristics of the tinnitus.

Subjective Classification

Subjective Assessment of Tinnitus Acoustic Parameters. It is important to establish the child's subjective assessment of the loudness of the tinnitus as a base line or "control." This information is useful for clinical documentation of tinnitus and should be obtained during the initial interview; before, during, and after any period of partial residual inhibition; and before and after efforts to suppress tinnitus. A seven-point rating scale, in which 0 indicates silence and 7 indicates a very loud sound, is recommended.[21] This concept is easier for children to grasp if the magnitude-estimation task is changed to one of magnitude production. Specifically, young children find it easier to slide a plastic ear along a horizontal continuum that has appropriate pictures or colors at each of the seven positions. If recruitment is present and the child is old enough, the patient's effective loudness level should also be determined.[84]

Each sound perceived, or at least the most troublesome sensations, should be classified with respect to the following factors:

Loudness. Is the sound faint (does not interfere with speech communication), moderately loud (interferes with speech communication), or very loud (prevents effective communication using speech)?

Pitch. Is the pitch of medium or high frequency? If the sound does not have a spontaneously discernible pitch, the child should be asked to compare the tinnitus with other familiar sounds in the environment that approximate pure tones (e.g., piano notes, two-tone doorbells, pitchforks). Does the pitch of the sound remain steady or does it change? If the tinnitus pitch changes, attempt to identify the circumstances, especially if the tinnitus is altered by physical exertion or barometric pressure changes.

Temporal Characteristics. Is the tinnitus continuous or intermittent? If intermittent, when does it occur and how long is it present? How long are the silent intervals? Does the sound pulsate in synchrony with respiration or with pulse rate? What causes the sound to occur, or what makes it worse? If the sound changes from time to time, does it change "by itself" or with movement, such as walking, running, jumping, lying down, getting up; with sounds in the environment; when eating? Is the tinnitus present only at night or in quiet surroundings? Loud tinnitus in a quiet bedroom where the usual environmental masking noise is absent is sometimes the source of fear of the dark.

Localization. Is the sound perceived to be in one ear only, in both ears, throughout the head, or "outside" the head? Children with subjective tinnitus almost invariably have difficulty answering this question.

Annoyance. Is the sound annoying to the child? If so, is the annoyance judged to be mild, moderate, or severe? Does the sound prevent the child from getting to sleep? Does it ever waken the child? What makes the sound tolerable or causes it to go away?

Affective (Psychological) Component. What nonphysical conditions exacerbate the tinnitus? What nonphysical conditions produce remission? Are any characteristics of the sound affected by stress or by relaxation? Are there secondary gains obtained by complaining of sounds no one else can perceive (rare in children)?

Effect of Environmental Noise. How do environmental sounds affect the tinnitus? Is the sound suppressed or absent, masked, unchanged, or worsened by environmental noise?

Classification According to Psychophysical Estimates of Perceived Sounds

Evered and Lawrenson[21] underscored the value of psychophysical measurements to characterize tinnitus. Pitch matching, loudness matching, and masking tests can be accomplished successfully by most children who give reliable responses during pure-tone audiometry, although the reliability and the accuracy of these measurements increase with the age of the child. Moreover, instruments for tinnitus evaluations in adults can often be used even with young children to help them with judgments of sound quality, depending on the patience and ingenuity of the examiner.

Each classification category that follows is labeled with the name of the recommended test. The procedure is then outlined briefly.

Quality Judgment of Tinnitus

Pure tones, narrow bands of noise, and broad-band noise are presented to establish an estimate of comfortable loudness level. The tinnitus is classified with respect to the external signal that has a similar quality (in decibels of sound pressure level [dB SPL]).

Pitch Matching of Tinnitus

If the tinnitus has a tonal quality, the frequency of an external pure tone or the center frequency of a noise band is varied systematically until the child obtains the closest match. The tinnitus is classified with respect to the external auditory signal that produces the closest match with respect to frequency. When this test is used with young children, it is often necessary to spend some time establishing the difference between pitch and loudness, which is difficult for some children (and some adults) to determine.

Relative Loudness of Tinnitus

The SPL (dynes/cm^2) of the signal identified during the pitch-matching test is adjusted systematically until the child reports that the loudness of the test signal approximates the loudness of the tinnitus. (Note: It is very important to determine the fundamental frequency [frequencies] of the perceived tinnitus before attempting this psychophysical task.) For classification purposes, the loudness of the child's tinnitus is reported in decibels SPL or in decibels relative to the threshold of the external test signal (dB sensation level [SL]).

Masking of Tinnitus

The SPL of the signal identified during the pitch-matching test is next increased until it covers completely (masks) the child's tinnitus. When possible, this test is repeated with a frequency-specific (e.g., 500 Hz—the subject's perceived fundamental frequency) tone and with white or pink (center frequency of perceived sound) noise. If the tinnitus can be masked, the characteristics of effective, external maskers are reported. Feldman[24] used the masking test results to establish a useful five-group classification scheme for tinnitus.

Test of Residual Inhibition of Perceived Tinnitus

The SPL of the most effective masker is increased in 10-dB increments until masking of the tinnitus is achieved. The masking signal is then turned on for 60 seconds. (Stimulus can be presented to one or both ears.) When the masker is turned off, the child is asked whether the tinnitus has changed, and if so, how. The child's response is recorded. If the tinnitus has disappeared, this response is labeled total residual inhibition. The child may report that the loudness of the tinnitus has decreased (partial residual inhibition) but has not gone away. The patient may also report that the tinnitus is unchanged or that perceived loudness has increased. The duration of total inhibition or partial inhibition should be measured from the cessation of the test signal, and recorded.

Classification by Anatomic Source of the Perceived Sound (Objective Tinnitus)

The traditional terms *objective* and *subjective* have been used to classify tinnitus in children.[75] This classification is valuable and is used extensively in clinical reports. This chapter expands this classification somewhat and takes the approach suggested by Evered and Lawrenson.[21] Specifically, the terms *peripheral, central, para-auditory*, and *unknown* are used to identify the putative structure or generation site for the tinnitus perceived by the child. These terms improve the resolution of anatomic and physiologic classification while using categories that are familiar to clinicians who deal with ear disease in children.

Peripheral Tinnitus

Peripheral tinnitus is defined as tinnitus arising from the middle ear, cochlea, or eighth nerve and subdivided into tinnitus associated with the classic types of hearing loss: conductive, sensorineural, and mixed, respectively.

Conductive Tinnitus. Tinnitus arising as a consequence of a conductive hearing loss in children is most commonly caused by middle-ear effusions,[18] acute and chronic otitis media,[106, 116] atelectasis,[7] chronic mastoiditis and cholesteatoma,[99] granulomatous diseases of the middle ear,[73] and fixation of the stapes[94] or the lateral ossicular chain.[9, 34] In some cases, especially if the tinnitus persists after resolution of the conductive hearing loss, the tinnitus may reflect cochlear involvement owing to the relative permeability of the round window membrane to toxic agents produced by inflammatory middle-ear diseases (Chap. 25).[108]

Impacted cerumen and foreign bodies lodged in the external auditory meatus are not uncommon findings in pediatric otologic practice. Especially if the foreign body remains in place for sufficient time for an external otitis to develop with swelling and occlusion of the external canal skin, a conductive hearing loss will result. When these problems produce conductive hearing losses, they also reduce the masking effects of environmental sounds. This attenuation of background noise can make tinnitus produced by sensorineural or by para-auditory structures distressingly loud to the patient. Obviously, a correct diagnosis and satisfactory resolution of the conductive hearing loss can reduce anxiety for the parents who have been listening to the child's complaints of "strange or funny noises" in the head. Under no circumstances should irrigation of the affected ear be used in an attempt to remove external canal-impacted cerumen or foreign bodies in these cases. Such efforts are highly likely to result in complications, including tympanic membrane perforations and/or sensorineural hearing loss. The proper treatment is removal of external canal-impacted cerumen or foreign bodies under direct vision using the operating microscope, followed by proper treatment of the comorbid external otitis.

Finally, obstruction of the external auditory meatus and many middle-ear disease processes produce an enhancement of hearing by bone conduction at low frequencies. This "occlusion effect"[6, 57, 125, 133] increases the perceived loudness of tinnitus generated by structures near the inner ear, particularly the middle ear, eustachian tube, and the temporomandibular joint.

Sensorineural Tinnitus. This is tinnitus associated with sensorineural pathology, with or without a hearing loss. It originates within the cochlear hair cells, possibly by the attachment of the hair cells to the tectorial membrane or by alterations in neurotransmitters, or within the neural auditory structures and connections.

Chapter 28 summarizes the primary congenital and postnatal conditions that produce sensorineural hearing impairment in children. A review of the literature suggests that tinnitus has been associated with virtually every one of these lesions and highlights at least 10 additional generalizations regarding tinnitus in children:

1. Children rarely have a primary complaint of tinnitus,[38, 75] although a sensation of tinnitus can be elicited by careful questioning. Afflicted patients often describe the tinnitus as "normal."
2. Although adult patients without measurable hearing loss may complain of tinnitus,[27, 40, 50, 115] the frequency and severity of the perceived tinnitus both are related directly to the magnitude of the average pure-tone hearing thresholds.[132] This same observation seems to hold for the pediatric population.[38, 95]

   The prevalence of tinnitus without some hearing impairment has been questioned.[87] The reduced frequency range and frequency resolution of most clinical audiometers can obscure a hearing problem that coexists with the tinnitus.[87] More specifically, pure-tone audiometry with children is normally accomplished at octave intervals from 250 to 8000 Hz. The onset of tinnitus, however, may signal the progression of disease at the basal end of the cochlea, where the effects on hearing are for frequencies beyond the range of the clinical audiometer. A common example involves the child who has received aminoglycosides[23] or other ototoxic agents, especially cisplatin. When questioned, the child may describe a high-pitched tinnitus; he or she may have a significant loss of hearing at 13,000 Hz but normal hearing at 8000 Hz and below (Chap. 26).[22]

Further, a child may have a focal cochlear lesion that produces tinnitus and a significant hearing loss for a restricted range of frequencies. If this range falls between two standard (octave) test frequencies, the audiogram will appear normal.[67, 135] These "notches" in the audiogram can be characterized best if the child is able to understand and perform the task required for sweep-frequency Békésy audiometry.[136]

In spite of aggressive public information campaigns, rock music, either live or from amplification systems, is a major cause of tinnitus and eventual hearing loss.[139] Yassi and co-workers in 1993 demonstrated that 81% of subjects showed a temporary threshold shift (TTS) of 10 dB or more 5 to 20 minutes after a rock concert, which persisted after 40 to 60 minutes in 76% of subjects. This is not a new finding. These data confirm that children and adolescents are at very high risk for traumatic hearing loss and tinnitus from exposure to rock music (Chap. 26).

3. The histopathologic characteristics of congenital sensorineural lesions can be categorized according to whether the osseous labyrinth and the cochlear neuroepithelia are normal or abnormal.[111] In general, sensorineural tinnitus is a less common complaint from a child with an abnormal bony labyrinth than it is from a hearing-impaired child whose bony labyrinth is normal but whose organ of Corti is presumably abnormal (Chap. 20).

4. It has been known for more than a century that some clinically useful drugs are also toxic to the auditory system, the vestibular system, or both systems.[97, 114] Since the 1940s,[113] however, there has been a proliferation of drugs that are potentially ototoxic. Review of the literature suggests that complaints of sensorineural tinnitus have been associated with the use of virtually all these agents. This observation holds for analgesics (salicylates), antimalarials (quinine), "loop" diuretics (furosemide, ethacrynic acid), metalloid compounds (mercurials, arsenicals), and antineoplastic drugs (e.g., cisplatin).[16, 45, 86] Most reports of tinnitus in children, however, have been associated with neonatal administration of antibacterial aminoglycosides (gentamicin, kanamycin) and polypeptide antibiotics (viomycin, vancomycin).[19, 20, 25, 140]

When a child complains of tinnitus, the clinician should question the parents carefully regarding the medications the child has taken. If indicated, an effort should also be made to secure records of drug therapy during neonatal or early childhood hospitalization. This information can be especially useful in the case of children with a history of neonatal intensive care.

5. For some children, the existence of tonal tinnitus may lead to pure-tone audiometric findings that are inconsistent.[39] This problem can be reduced,

however, if an ascending rather than a descending method is used to present the test tones.[38]

6. Some children report that hearing aids can suppress or mask their tinnitus.[39] This type of relief has been documented in adult patients. Approximately 50% of new hearing-aid wearers report partial or total relief from tinnitus.[112, 122] In contrast, a hearing aid that has excessive acoustic gain and inadequate limiting of its acoustic output can overstimulate structures on the child's organ of Corti, which may produce temporary or permanent loss of hearing and provoke or exacerbate sensorineural tinnitus (Chap. 107).[55, 59, 63, 70, 81, 109]

7. Most adults with acquired tinnitus describe a constant auditory sensation.[11, 46] In contrast, most children with congenital deafness report intermittent tinnitus.[38, 96]

8. "Perilymph" fistulas have been reported in all age groups. However, they are probably more common in the pediatric population than the literature would indicate because the history is invariably more difficult to obtain from a child. A moderately severe sensorineural hearing loss in a toddler, especially if fluctuant, may be assumed to be congenital. Vertiginous spells in young children may be diagnosed as a nonspecific disorder, e.g., benign paroxysmal vertigo of childhood. We have no doubt that some of these disorders are fistulas that could be treated.[101] With the following quotation, Parnes and McCabe[101] open their discussion of a retrospective study of perilymph fistulas in 16 children: "Symptoms and signs of cochleovestibular disease were observed in 26 ears of these 16 patients. For six of the children, radiologic studies revealed developmental abnormalities of the inner ear (Mondini dysplasia). A history of trauma was reported for six additional children. No discernible cause for the symptoms could be identified in the remaining four children. At exploratory tympanotomy, at least one perilymph fistula was found and repaired in at least one ear of each child. Preoperatively, 11 of the children (69 per cent) complained of tinnitus. Seven reported tinnitus following surgery."

The report of Parnes and McCabe[101] reinforces the clinical observation that, because of the variety and variability of signs and symptoms, perilymph fistulas can masquerade as many other inner-ear problems.[35, 48, 121, 123] Perilymph fistula is one of the few pediatric inner-ear disorders that can be confirmed and treated successfully at surgery. For this reason, it should be included in the differential diagnosis for any child with sensorineural tinnitus (Chaps. 21 and 24).

9. Sensorineural hearing impairment, vestibular dysfunction, and tinnitus often accompany the various stages of congenital luetic disease.[1, 26, 60, 66, 69] Steckelberg and McDonald[119] reported a complaint of tinnitus from 12 of 15 patients with congenital syphilis. Almost half of the patients in this series noted tinnitus at the onset of their ear disease.

These patients frequently used terms such as "roaring," "machine-like," and "waterfall" to describe the perceived sensation. The youngest patient in the group with congenital disease was 12 years old. The authors' experience in this area has led to the inclusion of the treponema-specific fluorescent treponemal antibody absorption (FTA-ABS) test when a child has tinnitus associated with a fluctuating or progressive low-frequency (or flat) sensorineural hearing loss, especially if this is associated with vertigo and/or ataxia (Chap. 26).

10. Tinnitus is a common complaint reported by 55% to 93% of all adult patients with acoustic neurilemomas and other neoplasms that invade the cerebellopontine angle.[14, 44, 53, 56, 78] Tumors of cranial nerve VIII, occurring either as primary neurilemomas or in association with neurofibromatosis (von Recklinghausen disease, neurofibromatosis type II), are rare in children. They should be considered in the differential diagnosis, however, if the child has a family history or stigmata of neurofibromatosis type I or II, or other evidence of retrocochlear ear disease (Chap. 30).[118]

Mixed Tinnitus. This occurs with a mixed hearing loss, i.e., the patient's hearing loss has both a conductive and a sensorineural component. A common mixed configuration in children involves a patient with serous middle-ear effusion (serous otitis media) who is also receiving aspirin. Salicylates have the potential for producing both a mild, temporary sensorineural hearing loss and tinnitus.[85, 88, 91, 93] The conductive hearing loss attenuates environmental masking sounds, making the tinnitus more intense.[75]

Central Tinnitus

Central tinnitus, like its audiologic counterpart, central auditory dysfunction, is encumbered by speculation, controversy, and inconclusive reports. There is little doubt that intracranial lesions that affect the central auditory nervous system can disrupt many aspects of auditory processing.[8, 64, 79] Moreover, these processing problems have been documented for children and for adults with normal hearing for pure tones.[12, 32, 33, 54, 72] It is difficult, however, to determine the prevalence of tinnitus within these groups. Although some investigators have documented the presence and type of tinnitus reported by their patients,[100] this information is missing in most studies that focus on central auditory and central vestibular disease. Accordingly, the authors reviewed 48 published case reports. When all patients with evidence of peripheral ear disease were excluded, as well as all patients on medication that might induce tinnitus,[76] tinnitus was a complaint for only about 16% of patients with intracranial lesions and evidence of central auditory or central vestibular dysfunction. This value is about one fifth of the 83% that House and Brackmann[56] reported for a series of 500 patients with acoustic neuromas.

Tinnitus is a potential side effect for hundreds of drugs.[103] This chapter does not address the reputed sensorineural or central mechanisms for these sources of

tinnitus in children, or the role of central tinnitus in cases in which there is an apparent sensorineural source. The preponderance of published evidence suggests that a central component may be associated with many forms of peripheral tinnitus. If this were not the case, (1) how could unilateral tinnitus be masked by signals presented at virtually the same level to *either* ear,[127] and (2) how could tinnitus persist for some patients after complete transection of cranial nerve VIII?[56] Human and animal research currently under way may ultimately provide answers to these questions. For the present, however, one must consider the possibility of a central component in all peripheral tinnitus. Finally, from the pediatric point of view, it is difficult to distinguish between central tinnitus and bilateral sensorineural tinnitus in small children, and children who, for various reasons, cannot perform the audiometric and psychophysical tests essential for characterization of their tinnitus.

Objective (Para-auditory) Tinnitus

Objective (para-auditory) tinnitus has also been called "extra-auditory"[21] and "nonauditory" tinnitus.[75] Objective tinnitus can arise from any normal or abnormal bodily function capable of generating motions in the frequency range of auditory function. The most common type in this group is tinnitus arising from transmission of normal or abnormal vascular pulsations to the cochlea. Although the sound stimulus producing the tinnitus is arising outside the auditory system, a defect within the auditory system (e.g., a conductive hearing loss) can exacerbate or cause the patient to perceive the normally masked sound, producing a tinnitus.

Tinnitus of vascular origin has been divided by some researchers into two categories[51]: (1) tinnitus caused by an anomaly within the arteries of the head and neck, and (2) essential tinnitus, which constitutes a category for which no reasonable explanation can be found. It is believed by many investigators, however, that the cause of this latter type of tinnitus can be explained by vibrations arising from turbulence within the venous structures of the head.[129]

Vascular Causes. The more common causes of vascular tinnitus are listed in Table 18–1. Some examples of the conditions are described, as well as the management of the conditions and the eventual outcome following treatment.[51] In most cases, according to Hentzer, the anoma-

TABLE 18–1. Causes of Vascular Tinnitus

Stenosis of carotid or other cerebral arteries
Arterial aneurysms
Arterial malformations
Arteriovenous malformations
Arteriosclerosis of basilar artery
Transmitted cardiac murmur
Inflammatory hyperemia of ear
Hemangioma of head and neck
Chemodectomas of head and neck

After Hentzer[51] and Glasscock et al.[31]

lies within the arterial system can be demonstrated by angiography. The advent of magnetic resonance imaging (MRI) makes angiography much safer.

Venous causes of tinnitus arising from the neck are usually associated with changes in head position. Turning the head away from the side of the tinnitus typically increases the intensity of the sound, possibly owing to some internal jugular vein compression by the ipsilateral sternocleidomastoid muscle. Occlusion of the involved vein will remove or markedly diminish the intensity (loudness) of the tinnitus.

Less common vascular causes have been described by Rossberg,[110] Wengraf,[131] Ward and associates,[129] and Tyler and Babin[126] and include:

1. Arteriovenous malformations between the branches of the occipital artery and the transverse sinus. These types of malformations are relatively more common in the posterior cranial fossa but may occur in the middle cranial fossa between the posterior branch of the middle meningeal artery and the greater petrosal sinus.
2. Abnormalities occurring between the internal maxillary artery and vein resulting from trauma or lesions in that region.
3. Cerebral or cervical angiomas and giant cell tumors of the mandible.
4. Nasopharyngeal angiofibromas. Arteriovenous fistulas often occur in these tumors, creating bruits.

Also of serious import are arteriovenous communications (fistulas) between the internal carotid artery and the cavernous sinus, which occur after head trauma (basilar skull fractures). The pulsatile tinnitus associated with these vascular fistulas may often be detected by both patient and physician. Palpation of the eye often reveals a thrill, and on auscultation a bruit may be heard (Table 18–2). Arteriovenous fistulas should be suspected in any child with tinnitus and an increased (widened) pulse pressure, regardless of the descriptive classification.

Essential (Idiopathic) Tinnitus. Tinnitus of unknown cause[37] is by far the most common type. As a minimum, the following criteria should be fulfilled before a diagnosis of essential tinnitus can be made. First, the tinnitus must be of sudden onset and must be unrelated to any demonstrable disease or injury. Second, the character of tinnitus can change in pitch and intensity. Essential tinnitus, however, should be persistent and unchanging for a year or more. Third, there should be pronounced lateralization, and any changes of the perceived sound should

not be synchronous with the arterial pulse or occur with changes in head or body position. The diagnosis of idiopathic tinnitus cannot be made until other causes, including increased intracranial pressure, pulsating exophthalmos, and abnormalities of extracranial arteries or veins, have been ruled out.

Myogenic Causes of Objective ("Nonauditory") Tinnitus. Tinnitus resulting from rhythmic contractions of the soft palate was first described by Politzer in 1878.[105] Since then, tinnitus of myogenic origin has been described by many others and has been classified according to the three main muscle groups affected[138]: soft palate, eustachian tube, and intratympanic muscles.

Palatal Myoclonus. Tinnitus arising from palatal myoclonus occurs as the result of involuntary rhythmic contractions of the soft palate and pharyngeal musculature, including the tensor veli palatini, levator veli palatini, salpingopharyngeus, and constrictor pharyngis superior muscles of the pharynx. These pathologic contractions commonly affect younger people and are associated with an audible clicking. The patient may volunteer the information that there are rhythmic contractions occurring somewhere in the oropharynx or oral cavity and that they are associated with a disturbing sound.

Examination of the mouth and pharynx in these cases reveals a rhythmically contracting pharyngeal musculature associated with an audible click that can be detected by the unaided ear or by using a Toynbee tube. The palatopharyngeal contractions may not be present with the mouth widely open, especially with tongue depression, and may have to be viewed endoscopically with the mouth closed. The abnormal rhythmic palatopharyngeal muscle contractions are usually continuous and persist during sleep.

No underlying cause can be determined for most cases of palatal myoclonus. However, there are many reports of this condition,[49, 77, 80, 124, 126] including a discussion of probable causes and the pathologic anatomy associated with it.[10] In 1886, Spencer[117] described "pharyngeal nystagmus" in a 12-year-old boy who had a tumor of the cerebellar vermis. Others have described the condition in association with cerebral and cerebellar pathologic changes.[41, 102] Pathologic correlation has been possible in other cases, and most of the lesions that were thought to have caused the condition were found in the pons, brain stem, and cerebellar regions.[36, 71, 128, 137] Lesions associated with palatal myoclonus have been located in a triangular area within the midbrain bounded by the red nucleus, the inferior olivary and accessory nuclei, and the contralateral dentate nucleus.[42, 43] Palatal myoclonus has also been associated with brain stem infarctions, multiple sclerosis, brain stem tumors, trauma, syphilis, malaria, and other degenerative processes. Thus, it appears that any destructive lesion within this anatomic triangle can result in palatopharyngeal myoclonus (Table 18–3).

Tinnitus Arising from Abnormal Contraction of Intratympanic Muscles. Intermittent tinnitus during recovery from facial paralysis due to facial nerve dysfunction has been reported.[130] The tinnitus typically occurred in associ-

TABLE 18–2. Diagnostic Criteria for Essential (Objective) Tinnitus

Sudden onset, related to other disease or injury
Persistence, unchanged for more than 1 year
Pronounced lateralization
Synchrony with pulse
Related to altered head position
No symptoms of increased intracranial pressure
No pulsation exophthalmos
No abnormalities of extracranial arteries
Normal cerebral angiogram

TABLE 18–3. Causes of Palatal Myoclonus

Moderate or severe cerebrovascular insufficiency
Myocardial infarction and diabetes
Progressive cerebellar degeneration of multiple sclerosis
Brain stem tumors
Trauma
Syphilis
Malaria
After surgical clipping or ligation of posteroinferior cerebellar
  artery
Familial tremor associated with palatal myoclonus
Cerebellar tumors
Idiopathic

ation with both voluntary and involuntary facial muscle contractions. The tinnitus in these eight cases was relieved by cutting the stapedial muscle tendon. Williams[134] described post-traumatic facial-nerve synkinesis to the stapedius muscle and the resultant tinnitus.

Rhythmic contractions of the tensor tympani are usually associated with palatal myoclonus. Among the many biologic factors considered to be related to this tinnitus produced mechanically in the middle ear are the following:

1. Propagation of noise produced by muscle contractions.
2. Periodic vibration of the tympanic membrane.
3. Stimulation of the tympanic plexus.
4. Temporal variation of inner-ear pressure or cochlear microphonic potentials.

Each of these was considered,[130] but a conclusion could not be reached concerning the genesis of the tinnitus.

Sounds Transmitted via the Eustachian Tube. Nasopharyngeal sounds may be transmitted via a patient's eustachian tube to the middle-ear space. The most common eustachian tube abnormality is persistent patency of the tube, which allows transmission of sounds produced by voice (autophonia), upper airway flow, and deglutition to the middle ear and cochlea. Eustachian tube patency occurs most commonly after rapid weight loss and is often a complaint of young female adolescents with eating disorders such as bulimia. Occasionally, vascular tumors, such as nasopharyngeal angiofibromas, may transmit sounds to the auditory system via the eustachian tube or via bone conduction. Any condition that causes atrophy of the eustachian tube or palatal muscles may result in patency (Chap. 23).

Nonauditory Objective Tinnitus. This may arise from crepitation in the temporomandibular joint (TMJ) (TMJ syndrome). Most young patients with this type of tinnitus also have bruxism.

Unknown

Unknown was the word selected to classify tinnitus when the probability of identifying correctly the putative structure or generation site "is assessed at 50 per cent or less."[21] In the authors' experience, this category is used more with young children than with adults because of problems associated with history taking, with describing the symptoms, and with psychophysical testing. It may also be necessary to use the unknown category when the psychological source of the tinnitus cannot be separated from the anatomic and physiologic sources.[28, 107]

Epidemiology

Definitive epidemiologic data on tinnitus are not currently available. Consequently, the prevalence and characteristics of tinnitus for most of the disease processes reviewed here are unknown or limited in scope. Nodar[95] was probably the first to study the prevalence of tinnitus in schoolchildren. He administered questionnaires during audiometric screening sessions to more than 2000 children ranging in age from 10 to 18 years over a period of 3 years. The presence of tinnitus was reported by 13.3% of those children who passed the audiometric screening and by 58.6% of those who failed. The more common responses to the question "When do you hear" these "noises in your ears?" were related to (1) time ("late at night"); (2) emotional stress; (3) physical stress; (4) noise exposure; (5) illness, "colds," or "headaches"; (6) frequency ("all the time" or "whenever it's quiet"); and (7) location ("in the library" or "in bed").

Graham surveyed 74 children ranging in age from 12 to 18 years whose hearing losses were severe enough to require the use of hearing aids. The main findings of this study follow:[38]

1. Sixty-four per cent of the children had tinnitus.
2. Only two children had continuous tinnitus; in all others it was intermittent.
3. In the small number (14) whose hearing loss was symmetric between the two ears and who used aids in only one ear, the tinnitus was equally prevalent in the aided and the unaided ears. Their tinnitus was not related to the use of amplification (hearing aids).
4. Tinnitus was more common in a child's better hearing ear.
5. The degree of annoyance was considered to be disturbing by 40% of the children.

These epidemiologic findings have been supported generally in all subsequent studies.[38, 39, 96]

Medical Diagnosis and Treatment

Definitive treatment is possible in most patients only when the source of an objective tinnitus can be identified and removed. Supportive care may help some patients. Addictive drugs should not be used to treat tinnitus in children, unless they have a terminal illness and the tinnitus is significantly altering the quality of life (e.g., preventing sleep). Education and prevention of environmental causes of hearing loss and tinnitus are the responsibility of parents, health care providers (especially family physicians and pediatricians), teachers (especially music and vocational teachers), promoters of rock concerts, and producers of electronic devices for sound amplification.[13]

Caution is advised when considering tympanotomy for middle-ear masses in patients with pulsatile tinnitus. A thorough neurovascular work-up, including a computed tomographic scan for integrity of temporal bone structures and three-dimensional "time-of-flight" MR angiography for evaluation of vascular structures, especially the internal carotid artery (for middle-ear carotid aneurysm), should be obtained before surgery.[15]

Summary

Because hearing loss is a common complaint in childhood, it is probable that the symptom of tinnitus is much more frequent in children than has previously been recognized, particularly because consciousness of body image is not fully developed at that age. The most common cause of intermittent, fluctuating tinnitus in children is seen during conductive hearing losses associated with purulent otitis media or with serous middle-ear effusions, especially if the child is taking aspirin. Continuous and persistent tinnitus is usually associated with loss of sensory or neural auditory function and may be associated with systemic nervous system diseases. If tinnitus is associated with nonauditory complaints or physical findings (e.g., a middle-ear mass), the critical path to diagnosis may be simplified considerably. When vertigo and hearing loss occur with tinnitus, the problem is most likely within or near the temporal bone. If involvement of other cranial nerves, headaches, or other systemic symptoms are present, a search for central nervous system or general system disease, respectively, should be instituted.

SELECTED REFERENCES

Hazell JWP. Tinnitus. Edinburgh, Churchill Livingstone, 1987, pp 1–207.

This current tinnitus handbook provides a clear summary of historical antecedents, theory, epidemiology, assessment, and drug therapy, together with surgical, nonsurgical, and psychological management. Although the focus is not pediatrics, the chapter by Graham includes references to all major reports on tinnitus in children, along with a concise review of assessment and management.

Hentzer E. Objective tinnitus of the vascular type. Acta Otolaryngol (Stockh) 66:273, 1968.

The author describes 24 cases of tinnitus of vascular origin and classifies them into two groups: those caused by arterial anomalies within the head and neck and those that probably arise within the venous system of the head and neck. He gives guidelines for the best form of treatment based on his extensive experience.

Shulman A. Proceedings of the Second International Tinnitus Seminar. J Laryngol Otol Suppl 9:1, 1984.

These seminar proceedings include contributions from 43 participants. In addition to the topics covered in the Hazell handbook (above), this compendium also addresses electric stimulation of the inner ear and additional techniques for objective evaluation, quantitative assessment, and measurement of tinnitus.

Tyler RS, Babin RW. Tinnitus. In Cummings CW, Harker LA (eds). Otolaryngology—Head and Neck Surgery, Vol IV. Ear and Skull Base. St Louis, Mosby, 1986, pp 3201–3217.

This work is the counterpart for adults of the present chapter. The terminology in the two chapters is similar, and both have been prepared by an otolaryngologist and an audiologist working together. The Tyler and Babin work provides good background for psychoacoustic measurements and electroacoustic measurements and their potential value in the characterization of tinnitus. Although some of the techniques described are not applicable to younger children, many of the sections on diagnosis, management, and surgery have value for all patients.

REFERENCES

1. Adams DA, Kerr AG, Smyth GDL, et al. Congenital syphilitic deafnessa further review. J Laryngol Otol 97:399, 1983.
2. Ahmmed AU, Mackenzie I, Das VK, et al. Audio-vestibular manifestations of Chiari malformation and outcome of surgical decompression: a case report. J Laryngol Otol 110:1060, 1996.
3. Aschendorff A, Pabst G, Klenzner T, Laszig R. Tinnitus in cochlear implant users: The Freiburg Experience. Int Tinnitus J 4:162, 1998.
4. Baguley DM, McFerran DJ. Tinnitus in childhood. Int J Pediatr Otorhinolaryngol 49:99, 1999.
5. Ben-David J, Podoshin L, Fradis M. Tinnitus in children—still a neglected problem. Int Tinnitus J 1:155, 1995.
6. Bing A. Ein neuer Stimmgabelversuch. Beitrag zur Differentialdiagnostik der Krankheiten des mechanischen Schallleitungs-und des nervösen Hörapparates. Wien Med Blatter 41:637, 1891.
7. Bluestone CD, Klein JO. Otitis media with effusion, atelectasis and eustachian tube dysfunction. In Bluestone CD, Stool SE (eds). Pediatric Otolaryngology, Vol 1. Philadelphia, WB Saunders, 1983, pp 356–512.
8. Bocca E, Calearo C. Central hearing processes. In Jerger J (ed). Modern Developments in Audiology. New York, Academic Press, 1963, pp 337–370.
9. Causse JR, Causse JB. Otospongiosis as a genetic disease. Am J Otol 5:211, 1984.
10. Chadwick DL, MacBeth R. Rhythmic palatal myoclonus. J Laryngol 67:301, 1953.
11. Coles RRA, Baskill JL, Sheldrake JB. Measurement and management of tinnitus. Part 1. Measurement. J Laryngol 98:1171, 1985.
12. Collard ME, Lesser RP, Luders H, et al. Four dichotic speech tests before and after temporal lobectomy. Ear Hear 7:363, 1986.
13. Consensus National Conference. Noise and Hearing Loss. JAMA 263:3185, 1990.
14. Cushing H. Tumors of the Nervus Acusticus and the Syndrome of the Cerebellopontine Angle. Philadelphia, WB Saunders, 1917, pp 153–154.
15. Davis WL, Harnsberger HR. MR angiography of an aberrant internal carotid artery. AJNR 12:1225, 1991.
16. DeBeukelaer MM, Travis LB, Dodge WF. Deafness and acute tubular necrosis following parenteral administration of neomycin. Am J Dis Child 121:250, 1971.
17. Douek E. Classification of tinnitus. Ciba Found Symp 85:4, 1981.
18. Draper WL. Secretory otitis media in children: a study of 540 children. Laryngoscope 77:636, 1967.
19. Eichenwald HF. Some observations on dosage and toxicity of kanamycin in premature and fullterm infants. Ann N Y Acad Sci 132:984, 1966.
20. Elfving R, Pettay O, Raivio M. A follow-up study on the cochlear, vestibular and renal function in children treated with gentamicin in the newborn period. Chemotherapy 18:141, 1973.
21. Evered D, Lawrenson G, eds. Tinnitus. Ciba Found Symp 85:300, 1981.
22. Fausti SA, Rappaport BZ, Schecter MA, et al. Detection of aminoglycoside ototoxicity by high-frequency auditory evaluation: selected case studies. Am J Otolaryngol 5:177, 1984.
23. Fee WE. Aminoglycoside ototoxicity in the human. Laryngoscope 90 Suppl. 24, 1980.
24. Feldman H. Homolateral and contralateral masking of tinnitus by noise bands and pure tones. Audiology 10:138, 1971.
25. Finitzo-Hieber T, McCracken GH Jr, Roeser RJ, et al. Ototoxicity in neonates treated with gentamicin and kanamycin: results of a four-year controlled follow-up study. Pediatrics 63:443, 1979.
26. Fiumara NJ, Lessell S. Manifestations of late congenital syphilis: an analysis of 271 patients. Arch Dermatol 102:78, 1970.
27. Fowler EP. Determining factors in tinnitus aurium. Laryngoscope 23:182, 1913.
28. Fowler EP, Fowler EP Jr. Somatopsychic and psychosomatic fac-

tors in tinnitus, deafness, and vertigo. Ann Otol Rhinol Laryngol 64:29, 1955.

29. George RN, Kemp S. A survey of New Zealanders with tinnitus. Br J Audiol 25:331, 1991.

30. Glanville JD, Coles RRA, Sullivan BM. A family with high-tonal objective tinnitus. J Laryngol Otol 85:1, 1971.

31. Glasscock ME, Dickins JRE, Jackson CG, et al. Vascular anomalies of the middle ear. Laryngoscope 90:77, 1980.

32. Goetzinger CP. The Rush Hughes test in auditory diagnosis. In Katz J (ed). Handbook of Clinical Audiology. Baltimore, Williams & Wilkins, 1972, pp 325–333.

33. Goldstein R, Goodman AC, King RB. Hearing and speech in infantile hemiplegia before and after left hemispherectomy. Neurology 6:869, 1956.

34. Goodhill V. Tinnitus. In Goodhill V (ed). Ear Diseases, Deafness and Dizziness. Hagerstown, MD, Harper & Row, 1979, pp 731–739.

35. Goodhill V. Leaking labyrinth lesions, deafness, tinnitus and dizziness. Ann Otol Rhinol Laryngol 90:99, 1981.

36. Graeffner A. Berl Klin Wschr 47:1081, 1910.

37. Graf W. Kraniala Blas Jud Nord Med 28:2499, 1952.

38. Graham JM. Tinnitus in hearing-impaired children. In Hazell JWP (ed). Tinnitus. Edinburgh, Churchill Livingstone, 1987, pp 131–143.

39. Graham JM, Butler J. Tinnitus in children. J Laryngol Otol Suppl 9:236, 1984.

40. Graham JT, Newby H. Acoustical characteristics of tinnitusan analysis. Arch Otolaryngol 75:162, 1962.

41. Grunwald L. Hyperkinetic disturbances of the pharynx. In Atlas and Epitome of Diseases of the Mouth, Pharynx and Nose, 2nd ed. Philadelphia, WB Saunders, 1903, p 186.

42. Guillain G, Mollaret P. Deux cas de myoclonies synchrones et rhythmées velo-pharyngolaryngo-oculo-diaphragmatiques. Rev Neurol (Paris) 2:545, 1931.

43. Guillain G, Mollaret P, Bertrand I. Sur la lesion responsable du syndrome myoclonique du troie cerebrae. Rev Neurol (Paris) 2:666, 1933.

44. Hambley WM, Gorshenin AN, House WF. The differential diagnosis of acoustic neuroma. Arch Otolaryngol 80:708, 1964.

45. Hawkins JE. Drug ototoxicity. In Keidel WD, Neff WD (eds). Handbook of Sensory Physiology, Vol 5. Berlin, Springer-Verlag, 1976, pp 707–748.

46. Hazell JWP. Patterns of tinnitus: medical and audiologic findings. J Laryngol Otol Suppl 4:39, 1981.

47. Hazell JWP. Tinnitus. Edinburgh, Churchill Livingstone, 1987.

48. Healy GB, Friedman JM, Strong MS. Vestibular and auditory findings of perilymph fistula: a review of 40 cases. Trans Am Acad Ophthalmol Otolaryngol 82:44, 1976.

49. Heller MF. Vibratory tinnitus and palatal myoclonus. Acta Otolaryngol (Stockh) 55:292, 1962.

50. Heller MF, Bergman M. Tinnitus aurium in normally hearing persons. Ann Otol Rhinol Laryngol 62:73, 1953.

51. Hentzer E. Objective tinnitus of the vascular type. Acta Otolaryngol (Stockh) 66:273, 1968.

52. Hippocrates. Book 32. Paragraph 961–A, c. 400 BC.

53. Hitselberger WE, House WF. Tumors of the cerebellopontine angle. Arch Otolaryngol 80:720, 1964.

54. Hodgson WR. Filtered speech tests. In Katz J (ed). Handbook of Clinical Audiology. Baltimore, Williams & Wilkins, 1972, pp 313–324.

55. Holmgren L. Can hearing be damaged by a hearing aid? Acta Otolaryngol (Stockh) 28:440, 1939.

56. House JW, Brackmann DE. Tinnitus: surgical treatment. Ciba Found Symp 85:204, 1981.

57. Huizing EH. Bone conduction, the influence of the middle ear. Acta Otolaryngol Suppl (Stockh) 155:1, 1960.

58. Huizing EH, Spoor A. An unusual type of tinnitus. Arch Otolaryngol 98:134, 1973.

59. Humes LE, Bess FH. Tutorial on the potential deterioration in hearing due to hearing aid usage. J Speech Hear Res 24:3, 1981.

60. Hungerbuhler JP, Regli F. Cochleovestibular involvement as the first sign of late syphilis. J Neurol 219:199, 1978.

61. Jaffe BF, ed. Hearing Loss in Children. Baltimore, University Park Press, 1977.

62. Jazbi B, ed. Symposium on pediatric otorhinolaryngology. Otolaryngol Clin North Am 10:1, 1977.

63. Jerger JF, Lewis N. Binaural hearing aids: are they dangerous for children? Arch Otolaryngol 101:480, 1975.

64. Jerger S, Jerger J. Auditory Disorders: A Manual for Clinical Evaluation. Boston, Little, Brown, 1981, pp 79–93.

65. Jero J, Salmi T. Palatal myoclonus and clicking tinnitus in a 12-year-old girl—case report. Acta Otolaryngol Suppl 543:61–62, 2000.

66. Karmody CS, Schuknecht HF. Deafness in congenital syphilis. Arch Otolaryngol 83:18, 1966.

67. Kemp DT. The evoked cochlear mechanical response and the auditory microstructureevidence for a new element in cochlear mechanics. Scand Audiol Suppl 9:35, 1979.

68. Kentish RC, Crocker SR, McKenna L. Children's experience of tinnitus: a preliminary survey of children presenting to a psychology department. Br J Audiol 34:335, 2000.

69. Kerr AG, Smyth GDL, Cinnamond MJ. Congenital syphilitic deafness. J Laryngol Otol 87:1, 1973.

70. Kinney CE. The further destruction of partially deafened children's hearing by the use of powerful hearing aids. Ann Otol Rhinol Laryngol 70:828, 1961.

71. Klein H. Neurol Zentrabl 26:245, 1907.

72. Korsan-Bengtsen M. Distorted speech audiometry. Acta Otolaryngol Suppl (Stockh) 310:7, 1973.

73. Lederer FL. Granulomas and other specific diseases of the ear and temporal bone. In Paparella MM, Shumrick DA (eds). Otolaryngology, Vol 2. Ear. Philadelphia, WB Saunders, 1973, pp 161–184.

74. Lenneberg EH. Biological Foundations of Language. New York, John Wiley, 1967.

75. Leonard G, Black FO, Schramm VL. Tinnitus in children. In Bluestone CD, Stool SE (eds). Pediatric Otolaryngology, Vol 1. Philadelphia, WB Saunders, 1983, pp 271–277.

76. Levin VA, Chamberlain MC, Prados MD, et al. Phase I–II study of eflornithine and mitoguazone combined in the treatment of recurrent primary brain tumors. Cancer Treat Rep 71:459, 1987.

77. Litman RS, Hausman SA. Bilateral palatal myoclonus. Laryngoscope 92:1187, 1982.

78. Lundborg T. Diagnostic problems concerning acoustic tumors. Acta Otolaryngol Suppl (Stockh) 99:28, 1952.

79. Lynn G, Benitez J, Eisenbrey A, et al. Neuroaudiological correlates in cerebral hemisphere lesions. Audiology 11:115, 1972.

80. MacKinnon DM. Objective tinnitus due to palatal myoclonus. J Laryngol 82:369, 1968.

81. Macrae JH, Farrant RH. The effect of hearing aid use on the residual hearing of children with sensorineural deafness. Ann Otol Rhinol Laryngol 74:409, 1965.

82. Malm J, Kristensen B, Carlberg B, et al. Clinical features and prognosis in young adults with infratentorial infarcts. Cerebrovasc Dis 9:282, 1999.

83. Martin FN, ed. Pediatric Audiology. Englewood Cliffs, NJ, Prentice-Hall, 1978.

84. Matsuhira T, Yamishita K, Yasuda M. Estimation of the loudness of tinnitus from matching tests. Br J Audiol 26:387, 1992.

85. McCabe PA, Dey FL. The effect of aspirin upon auditory sensitivity. Ann Otol Rhinol Laryngol 74:312, 1965.

86. McCracken GH, Nelson JD. Antimicrobial Therapy for Newborns. Practical Application of Pharmacology to Clinical Usage. New York, Grune & Stratton, 1977.

87. McFadden D. Tinnitus Facts, Theories and Treatments. Washington, National Academy Press, 1982, p 23.

88. McFadden D, Plattsmier HS. Aspirin can induce noise-induced temporary threshold shift. J Acoust Soc Am 71:S106, 1982.

89. Melcher JR, Sigalovsky IS, Guinan JJ Jr, Levine RA. Lateralized tinnitus studied with functional magnetic resonance imaging: abnormal inferior colliculus activation. J Neurophysiol 83:1058, 2000.

90. Mihail RC, Crowley JM, Walden BE, et al. The tricyclic trimipramine in the treatment of subjective tinnitus. Ann Otol Rhinol Laryngol 97:120, 1988.

91. Mongan E, Kelly P, Nies K, et al. Tinnitus as an indication of therapeutic serum salicylate levels. JAMA 226:142, 1973.

92. Muhlnickel W, Elbert T, Taub E, Flor H. Reorganization of auditory cortex in tinnitus. Proc Natl Acad Sci 95:10340, 1998.

93. Myers EN, Bernstein JM. Salicylate ototoxicity: a clinical and experimental study. Arch Otolaryngol 82:483, 1965.

94. Nager FR. Pathology of the labyrinthine capsule and its clinical significance. In Fowler EP Jr (ed). Medicine of the Ear. New York, Thomas Nelson, 1947, Chap. VII.

95. Nodar RH. Tinnitus aurium in school-age children: a survey. J Aud Res 12:133, 1972.

96. Nodar RH, LeZak MHW. Pediatric tinnitus (a thesis revisited). J Laryngol Otol Suppl 9:234, 1984.

97. North A. Two cases of poisoning by the oil of chenopodium. Am J Otol 2:197, 1890.

98. Northern JL, Downs MP. Hearing in Children, 4th ed. Baltimore, Williams & Wilkins, 1991.

99. Parisier SC, Chute PM, Kramer MS, et al. Tinnitus in patients with chronic mastoiditis and cholesteatoma. J Laryngol Otol Suppl 9:94, 1984.

100. Parker W, Decker RL, Richards NG. Auditory function and lesions of the pons. Arch Otolaryngol 87:228, 1968.

101. Parnes LS, McCabe BF. Perilymph fistula: an important cause of deafness and dizziness in children. Pediatrics 80:524, 1987.

102. Pfeiffer RA. Mschr Psychiat Neurol 45:96, 1919.

103. Physician's Desk Reference, 47th ed. Oradell, NJ, Medical Economics, 1993.

104. Podoshin L, Ben-David J, Teszler CB. Pediatric and geriatric tinnitus. Int Tinnitus J 3:101, 1997.

105. Politzer A. Lehrbuch der Ohren hal Kunde. Stuttgart, 1878.

106. Proctor B. Chronic otitis media and mastoiditis. In Paparella MM, Shumrick DA (eds). Otolaryngology, Vol 2. Ear. Philadelphia, WB Saunders, 1973, pp 121–160.

107. Reinhart JB. The psychiatric aspects of ear, nose and throat disorders. Pediatr Clin North Am 28:991, 1981.

108. Ronis M. Inflammatory ear disease and tinnitus. J Laryngol Otol Suppl 9:203, 1984.

109. Ross M, Lerman J. Hearing aid usage and its effect upon residual hearing. Arch Otolaryngol 86:639, 1967.

110. Rossberg G. Pulsierende Ohrerausche bei Anomalie der Arteria carotis und Arteria occipitalis externa. J Laryngol Rhinol 46:79, 1967.

111. Ruben RJ. Diseases of the inner ear and sensorineural deafness. In Bluestone CD, Stool SE (eds). Pediatric Otolaryngology, Vol 1. Philadelphia, WB Saunders, 1983, pp 577–604.

112. Saltzman M, Ersner M. A hearing aid for relief of tinnitus aurium. Laryngoscope 57:358, 1947.

113. Schatz A, Bugie E, Waksman SA. Streptomycin, a substance exhibiting antibiotic activity against gram-positive and gram-negative bacteria. Proc Soc Exp Biol Med 55:66, 1944.

114. Schwabach D. Uber bleibende Storungen im Gehororgan nach Chinin und Salicylgebrauch. Dtsch Med Wschr 10:163, 1884.

115. Seltzer A. The problems of tinnitus in the practice of otolaryngology. Laryngoscope 57:623, 1947.

116. Shambaugh GE, Quie PG. Acute otitis media and mastoiditis. In Paparella MM, Shumrick DA (eds). Otolaryngology, Vol 2. Ear. Philadelphia, WB Saunders, 1973, pp 113–120.

117. Spencer HR. Pharyngeal and laryngeal nystagmus. Lancet 2:702, 1886.

118. Stam JR. Tumors of the ear and temporal bone. In Bluestone CD, Stool SE (eds). Pediatric Otolaryngology, Vol 1. Philadelphia, WB Saunders, 1983, pp 637–644.

119. Steckelberg JM, McDonald TJ. Otologic involvement in late syphilis. Laryngoscope 94:753, 1984.

120. Stouffer JL, Tyler RS. Characterization of tinnitus by tinnitus patients. J Speech Hear Dis 55:439, 1990.

121. Supance JS, Bluestone CD. Perilymph fistulas in infants and children. Otolaryngol Head Neck Surg 91:663, 1983.

122. Surr RK, Montgomery AA, Mueller HG. Effect of amplification on tinnitus among new hearing aid users. Ear Hear 6:71, 1985.

123. Thompson JN, Kohut RI. Perilymph fistulae: variability of symptoms and results of surgery. Otolaryngol Head Neck Surg 87:898, 1979.

124. Toland AD, Porubsky ES, Coker NJ, et al. Velo-pharyngo-laryngeal myoclonus: evaluation of objective tinnitus and extrathoracic airway obstruction. Laryngoscope 94:691, 1984.

125. Tourtual C. Th. Die Sinne des Menschen in den Wechselseitigen Beziehungen ihres psychischen und organischen Lebens. Ein Beitrag zur physiologischen Aesthetit. Munster, Friedrich Regensberg, 1827.

126. Tyler RS, Babin RW. Tinnitus. In Cummings CW, Harker LA (eds). Otolaryngology—Head and Neck Surgery, Vol IV. Ear and Skull Base. St Louis, Mosby, 1986, pp 3201–3217.

127. Tyler RS, Conrad-Armes D. Masking of tinnitus compared to the masking of pure tones. J Speech Hear Res 27:106, 1984.

128. Van Bogaert I, Bertrand I. Sur les myoclonies associées synchrones et rhythmiques par lesionsen foyer du trone cérébrale. Rev Neurol (Paris) 1:203, 1928.

129. Ward PH, Babin R, Calcaterra TC, et al. Operative treatment of surgical lesions with objective tinnitus. Ann Otol Rhinol Laryngol 84:473, 1975.

130. Watanabe I, Kumagami H, Tsuda Y. Tinnitus due to abnormal contraction of stapedial muscle. Otorhinolaryngolica 36:217, 1974.

131. Wengraf C. A case of objective tinnitus. J Laryngol 81:143, 1967.

132. Weston TET. Presbycusisa clinic study. J Laryngol Otol 78:273, 1964.

133. Wheatstone C. Experiments on audition. Q J Sci Lit Art 67:67, 1827.

134. Williams JD. Unusual but treatable cause of fluctuating tinnitus. Ann Otol Rhinol Laryngol 89:239, 1980.

135. Wilson JP. Evidence for a cochlear origin for acoustic re-emissions, threshold fine-structure, tonal tinnitus. Hear Res 2:233, 1980.

136. Wilson JP. Otoacoustic emissions and tinnitus. Scand Audiol Suppl 25:109, 1986.

137. Wilson SAK. Cases of palato-laryngeal nystagmus. Brain 51:119, 1928.

138. Yamamoto T. Objective tinnitus. Otolaryngology (Tokyo) 30:708, 1958.

139. Yassi A, Pollock N, Tran N, Cheang M. Risks to hearing from a rock concert. Can Fam Physician 39:1045, 1993.

140. Yow MD, Tengg NE, Bangs J. The ototoxic effects of kanamycin sulfate in infants and children. J Pediatr 60:230, 1962.

19

Facial Paralysis in Children

Andrew M. Shapiro, M.D., Barry M. Schaitkin, M.D., and Mark May, M.D.

Because the most common cause of facial paralysis is a lesion within the temporal bone,[10] the otolaryngologist should best be able to handle problems of this nature. However, most clinicians have not had sufficient opportunities to deal with facial paralysis to accumulate a knowledgeable approach to these cases and must rely on scattered journal reports—frequently representing conflicting or controversial opinions on the subject—to formulate a plan of management.

This chapter presents the senior author's approach to facial paralysis, which has been developed during years of evaluating and treating this problem in 2350 patients. Of these patients, 537 were 18 years old or younger (Tables 19–1 and 19–2). With few exceptions, the patients had complete medical otoneurologic evaluations and were followed up for 6 months or longer.

Anatomy of the Facial Nerve

A fundamental knowledge of the anatomy of the seventh cranial nerve is essential for localizing the level of the lesion and is helpful in arriving at the diagnosis (Fig. 19–1; Table 19–3). Furthermore, locating the site of the lesion is critical for the surgical approach in instances of nerve compression by infection, neoplasms, or fractures.

In this discussion, the course of the facial nerve is conveniently divided into three segments: supranuclear, nuclear, and infranuclear. The infranuclear segment is further subdivided into the (1) cerebellopontine angle, (2) internal auditory canal, and (3) labyrinthine, tympanic, mastoid, and extracranial segments (see Fig. 19–1). Pathologic conditions at any particular level may be diagnosed by special tests, detailed in Figure 19–1.

Supranuclear Segment

In the cortex, the tracts to the upper face are crossed and uncrossed. The tracts to the lower face are crossed only; therefore, the forehead is bilaterally innervated, and a lesion in the facial area on one side of the cortex would spare the forehead. However, one must not rely solely on sparing of the forehead to differentiate supranuclear from infranuclear lesions, because sparing of the forehead or other parts of the face can occur with lesions involving a more distal portion of the nerve. In addition to an intact

upper face, characteristics of supranuclear lesions include facial tone, spontaneous facial expression, and loss of volitional facial movement. Most important, there are usually other neurologic signs of central nervous system involvement. The sparing of involuntary movement with supranuclear lesions is thought to be due to sparing of the extrapyramidal system, which is considered to be responsible for involuntary or emotional facial movement. With nuclear and infranuclear lesions, there is loss of both involuntary and voluntary movement.

Nuclear Segment

From its nucleus in the pons, the facial nerve begins a circuitous journey around the sixth nerve nucleus before emerging from the brain stem. Because of this relationship between the sixth and seventh cranial nerves, a lesion in the region of the pons that caused a facial paralysis of the peripheral type would most probably be accompanied by a sixth cranial nerve palsy and would result in inability to rotate the eye to the side of the facial paralysis.

Infranuclear Segment

Cerebellopontine Angle

At the cerebellopontine angle, the eighth cranial nerve joins the facial nerve and they enter the internal auditory canal together. Lesions in this area, including schwannomas of the facial nerve, are often associated with vestibular and cochlear deficits before clinical involvement of the facial nerve. Large lesions filling the cerebellopontine angle might compress other cranial nerves and cause deficits of the fifth cranial nerve and later the 9th, 10th, and 11th cranial nerves.

Internal Auditory Canal

The motor facial nerve and the intermediary nerve of Wrisberg are loosely joined together as they enter the internal auditory meatus with the acoustic nerve. The acoustic nerve enters the internal auditory canal inferiorly, while the facial nerve runs superiorly along the roof of the internal auditory canal. The intracranial segment of

TABLE 19–1. Causes of Facial Palsy in Children

Diagnosis		No. of Patients	%
Bell palsy		207	38.5
Atypical Bell palsy		5	0.9
Trauma		98	18.2
Surgical	16		
Iatrogenic	34		
Accidental	48		
Tumor		26	4.8
Malignant	2		
Benign	24		
Tumor suspect		1	0.2
Herpes zoster oticus		15	2.8
Infection		51	9.5
Birth		121	22.5
Birth trauma	14		
Developmental	107		
Central nervous system		2	0.4
Brain stem	1		
Cerebellum	0		
Cerebral	1		
Other		11	2.0
Totals		537	

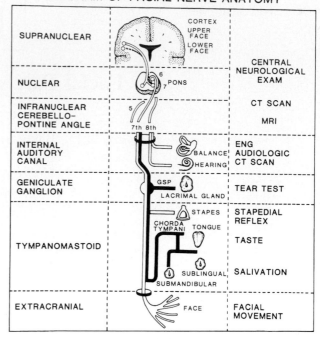

DIAGRAM OF FACIAL NERVE ANATOMY

FIGURE 19–1. The facial nerve may be divided into three segments for anatomic study: supranuclear, nuclear, and infranuclear. The infranuclear segments have been further divided, as shown in the left column. Each level can be identified by employing tests listed in the column on the right and signs detailed in Table 19–3. CT, computed tomography; MRI, magnetic resonance imaging; ENG, electronystagmography; GSP, greater superficial petrosal nerve.

the facial nerve from the brain stem to the fundus of the internal acoustic meatus is covered only by a thin layer of glia, which makes it vulnerable to any type of surgical manipulation but resistant to a slow process of stretching or compression. The facial nerve in this region can become elongated and spread out over the surface of a sizable but slow-growing vestibular nerve schwannoma without any gross evidence of facial weakness. Although facial nerve motor involvement is unusual to see in this instance, there is often evidence of such involvement in disruption of tearing, taste, and salivary flow owing to compression of the intermediary nerve.

Labyrinthine Segment

At the fundus of the internal auditory meatus, the facial nerve is physiologically "pressed" into the fallopian canal.

TABLE 19–2. Diagnosis of Pediatric Patients with Facial Paralysis due to Neoplasms

Tumor Type		No. of Patients
Benign		
	Schwannoma (VII)	4
	Acoustic neuroma	1
	Neurofibroma	2
	Glioma	2
	Granular cell myoblastoma	1
	Meningioma	2
	Arteriovenous malformation	1
	Osseus hemangioma	4
	Congenital cholesteatoma	3
	Other	4
Malignant		
	Lymphoma	1
	Medulloblastoma	1
	Total	26

The facial and intermediary nerves carry with them a continuation of the dura mater and periosteum from the internal acoustic meatus, and this dural continuation forms a well-defined and tough fibrous sheath that covers these nerves all the way to the terminal branches of the facial nerve in the face and neck. The portion of the facial nerve from its entrance into the fallopian canal to the geniculate ganglion is designated the *labyrinthine segment* because it runs between the cochlear and vestibular labyrinths. This segment lies beneath the middle fossa and is the shortest and narrowest part of the fallopian canal, averaging 5 mm in length and 0.68 mm in diameter.[19] Because this is the narrowest part of the facial canal, it is reasonable to suspect that this is the most vulnerable part of the facial nerve when there are inflammatory changes within the canal. The facial nerve in the labyrinthine segment is further jeopardized by any process that causes further limitation of this narrow space, because the blood supply to the nerve in this region is unique: this is the only segment of the facial nerve in which there are no anastomosing arterial arcades.[8]

The labyrinthine segment of the facial nerve includes the geniculate ganglion, from which arises the first branch of the facial nerve, the greater superficial petrosal nerve (Fig. 19–2). This nerve carries secretory motor fibers to the lacrimal gland. The second branch from the geniculate ganglion is a tiny thread that forms the lesser superficial petrosal nerve as it is joined by fibers of the tympanic

TABLE 19–3. Signs and Probable Diagnoses Resulting from Lesions of Facial Nerve at Various Levels as Detailed in Figure 19–1

Level	Signs	Diagnosis
Supranuclear		
Cortex Internal capsule	Tone and upper face intact, loss of volitional movement with intact spontaneous expression, slurred speech (tongue weakness), hemiparesis (arm greater than leg) on side of facial involvement	Lesion of motor cortex or lateral capsule on opposite side of facial involvement; paresis upper extremity (middle cerebral artery); paresis lower extremity (another cerebral artery)
Extrapyramidal	Increased salivary flow, spontaneous facial movement impaired, volitional facial movement intact	Tumor or vascular lesion of basal ganglion
Midbrain	Involvement of face and oculomotor roots—loss of pupillary reflexes, external strabismus, and oculomotor paresis on opposite side of facial paresis	Unilateral Weber syndrome (vascular lesion)
	Bilateral facial paresis with other cranial nerve deficits, emotional lability, hyperactive gag reflex, marked hyperreflexia associated with hypertension	Pseudobulbar palsy—associated with multiple infarcts
Nuclear		
Nuclear pons	Involvement of cranial nerves VII and VI on side of lesion, with gaze palsy on side of facial paresis; contralateral hemiparesis, ataxia, cerebellovestibular signs	Involvement of pons at level of cranial nerves VII and VI nuclei by pontine glioma, multiple sclerosis, encephalitis, infections, or poliomyelitis
	Cranial nerves VII and VI involved with other anomalies noted at birth	Congenital facial palsy, Möbius syndrome, and thalidomide toxicity
Infranuclear/Intracranial	Involvement of cranial nerve VII (decreased tearing and taste, stapes reflex decay, decreased discrimination), facial motor deficit (late sign)	Acoustic neuroma
Cerebellopontine angle	Cranial nerves VIII and VII involved in succession, beginning with facial pain or numbness; computed tomography (CT) scan shows pathologic change, enhanced with contrast	Meningioma
	Cranial nerves VII and VIII involved successively, beginning with facial twitching, appearance of erosion on temporal bone CT scan	Cholesteatoma arising in temporal bone
Skull base	Cranial nerves VII, VIII, IX, X, XI, and XII involved in succession; pulsatile tinnitus, purple-red pulsating mass noted bulging through tympanic membrane	Glomus jugulare tumor
	Same as above with cranial nerve involvement	Glomus jugulare tumor extending to petrous apex and involving middle fossa
	Conductive or sensorineural hearing loss, acute or recurrent Bell palsy, positive family history by skull radiography	Osteopetrosis
	Multiple cranial nerves involved in rapid succession	Carcinomatous meningitis, leukemia, Guillain-Barré syndrome, mononucleosis, diphtheria, tuberculosis, sarcoidosis
Infranuclear/Transtemporal Bone	Same as listed under Cerebellopontine angle	Same as listed under Cerebellopontine angle
Internal auditory canal	Ecchymoses around pinna and mastoid prominence (Battle sign); hemotympanum with sensorineural hearing loss by tuning fork (lateralizes to normal side); vertigo, nystagmus (fast component away from involved side); sudden, complete facial paralysis after head trauma	Fracture of temporal bone involving otic capsule
Geniculate ganglion	Dry eye, decreased taste, and decreased salivation; erosion of geniculate ganglion area or middle fossa as demonstrated by temporal bone imaging	Neurinoma, meningioma, cholesteatoma, ossifying hemangioma, arteriovenous malformation
	Pain, vesicles on pinna, dry eye, decreased taste and salivary flow; sensorineural hearing loss, nystagmus, vertigo, red chorda tympani nerve	Herpes zoster oticus (Ramsay Hunt syndrome)
	Same as above without vesicles and no cause can be found (keep in mind, if no recovery in 6 months, dealing with tumor at geniculate ganglion, which may require exploration for confirmation)	Bell palsy (viral inflammatory-immune disorder)
	Ecchymoses around pinna and mastoid (Battle sign), hemotympanum; conductive hearing loss by tuning fork (lateralizes to involved ear, bone greater than air), no vestibular involvement	Fracture of temporal bone sparing otic capsule; may be proximal or at geniculate ganglion (dry eye), or distal to geniculate ganglion (tears symmetric)

Table continued on following page

TABLE 19-3. Signs and Probable Diagnoses Resulting from Lesions of Facial Nerve at Various Levels as Detailed in Figure 19-1 *Continued*

Level	Signs	Diagnosis
Infranuclear/Transtemporal Bone		
Tympanomastoid segment	Involvement at this level characterized by decreased taste and salivation and loss of stapes reflex; tearing is normal; there is sudden onset of facial paralysis, which may be complete or incomplete and may progress to complete	
	Pain and vesicles present, red chorda tympani	Herpes zoster oticus
	Pain without vesicles, red chorda tympani	Bell palsy
	Red, bulging tympanic membrane, conductive hearing loss; usually a history of upper respiratory infection; lower face may be involved more than upper	Acute suppurative otitis media
	Foul drainage through perforated tympanic membrane; history of recurrent ear infection, drainage, and hearing loss	Chronic suppurative otitis media, most likely associated with cholesteatoma
	Pulsatile tinnitus, purple-red pulsatile mass noted through tympanic membrane	Glomus tympanicum or jugulare
	Recurrent facial paralysis, positive family history, facial edema, fissured tongue; may present with simultaneous bilateral facial paralysis	Melkersson-Rosenthal syndrome
Extracranial	Incomplete involvement of facial nerve (usually one or more major branches spared); hearing, balance, tearing, stapes reflex, taste, and salivary flow spared	Penetrating wound of face; postparotid surgery; malignancy of parotid, tonsil, or oronasopharynx
	Uveitis, salivary gland enlargement, fever	
Sites Variable	Facial paralysis, especially simultaneous bilateral facial paralysis with symmetrical ascending paralysis, decreased deep tendon reflexes, minimal sensory changes. Abnormal spinal fluid (protein and few cells, albuminocytologic dissociation)	Guillain-Barré syndrome

Gratitude is extended to Richard Kasden, M.D., for his assistance in developing this table. (Material relating to signs of facial nerve involvement in supranuclear and nuclear regions based on Crosby EC, De Jonge BR. Experimental and clinical studies of the central connections and central relations of the facial nerve. Ann Otol Rhinol Laryngol 72:735, 1963.)

plexus, contributed by the ninth cranial nerve. This nerve carries secretory fibers to the parotid gland.

Tympanic Segment

At the geniculate ganglion, the facial nerve makes a sharp angled turn backward, forming a knee, or genu, to enter the tympanic or horizontal portion of the fallopian canal. The proximal end of the tympanic portion is marked by the geniculate ganglion, from which point the facial nerve courses peripherally 3 to 5 mm, passing posterior to the cochleariform process and the tensor tympani tendon. The distal end of the tympanic segment of the facial nerve lies just above the pyramidal eminence, which houses the stapedius muscle. This segment is approximately 12 mm long. At the beginning of the tympanic segment, the fallopian canal forms a prominent, rounded eminence between the bony horizontal semicircular canal and the niche of the oval window. The tympanic wall of this part of the fallopian canal is thin and easily fractured. In addition, there are frequent dehiscences, allowing contact between the nerve and the tympanic mucoperiosteum. In some patients, the uncovered nerve is prolapsed into the oval window niche, partly or completely concealing the footplate of the stapes, and is therefore subject to trauma during stapes surgery. (The surgeon must look for this anomaly when there is a congenital deformity of the incus and stapes superstructure. It is also worthwhile to palpate the horizontal segment of the facial nerve in performing surgery of the middle ear or tympanomastoid to determine whether the nerve is covered by bone or whether there is a dehiscence in the fallopian canal.)

Just distal to the pyramidal eminence, the fallopian aqueduct makes another turn downward, the second genu. The second genu is another area where the facial nerve may be injured during mastoid surgery. The nerve emerges from the middle ear between the posterior canal wall and the horizontal semicircular canal, just beneath the short process of the incus. When there is chronic infection, in which granulation tissue is present, one must be careful not to confuse a pathologic dehiscence of the facial nerve in this region with a mound of granulation tissue. The best way to avoid this is to identify the nerve proximal and distal to the area that looks suspicious. The facial nerve gives off its third branch, the motor nerve, to the stapedius muscle at the distal end of the tympanic segment.

Mastoid Segment

The fallopian canal aqueduct proceeds vertically down the anterior wall of the mastoid process to the stylomastoid foramen. The distance from the second genu to the foramen averages 13 mm.

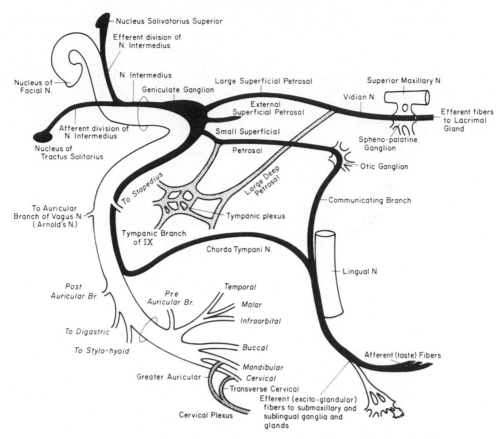

FIGURE 19–2. Diagram of facial nerve connections with other nerves. The facial nerve connects with the fifth cranial nerve through the large superficial and large deep petrosal nerves, which join the vidian nerve. The small petrosal passes through the otic ganglion. The chorda tympani joins the lingual nerve. The tympanic branch of the cranial nerve in the middle ear (Jacobson nerve) connects with the facial nerve. The auricular branch of the vagus (Arnold nerve) connects with the facial nerve. The cervical plexus connects with the peripheral branches of the facial nerve in the neck and lower face. (Modified from Warwick R, Williams PL. Gray's Anatomy, 36th ed. London, Churchill Livingstone, 1979.)

The chorda tympani nerve is the fourth branch of the facial nerve and its last sensory branch, thus becoming the terminal branch of the intermediary nerve. It usually arises from the distal third of the mastoid segment of the facial nerve, runs upward and anteriorly over the incus and under the malleus, and crosses the tympanic cavity through the petrotympanic fissure to join the lingual nerve. The chorda tympani nerve contains secretory motor fibers to the submaxillary and sublingual glands; it also contains sensory fibers from the anterior two thirds of the tongue (taste) and from the posterior wall of the external auditory meatus (pain, temperature, and touch).

Extracranial Segment

The facial nerve leaves the fallopian canal at the stylomastoid foramen, lateral to the styloid and vaginal processes. In newborns and in children up to 2 years of age, the facial nerve as it exits the skull is just deep to the subcutaneous tissue underlying the skin. After 2 years of age, as the mastoid tip and tympanic ring form, the facial nerve takes a deeper position up to 2 cm from the level of the skin.

Beyond the age of 2 years, the facial nerve is protected by the tympanic bone, the mastoid tip, the ascending ramus of the mandible, and the fascia between the parotid and cartilaginous external canal. In this region, there are branches from the occipital artery and a venous plexus, which account for brisk bleeding when this area is entered in the process of approaching the facial nerve. (Meticulous hemostasis during surgery can be achieved without injuring the facial nerve, which lies deep to these vessels, by employing a bipolar cautery.) As the nerve exits the stylomastoid foramen, nerve branches to the digastric and stylohyoid and postauricular muscles are given off. The seventh nerve communicates with branches from the 9th and 10th cranial nerves, as well as with the auriculotemporal branch of the fifth nerve. In addition, there are anastomoses between the great auricular and lesser occipital branches of the cervical plexus (see Fig. 19–2). After exiting the stylomastoid foramen, the facial nerve runs anteriorly for about 2 cm before bifurcating into an upper and lower division under the fascia of the masseter muscle.

In newborns and infants, the marginal mandibular nerve, which innervates the lower lip, courses over the mandible and is superficial and quite vulnerable to injury.

In adults, however, the nerve is up to 2 cm or more below the angle of the jaw.[60] The upper division of the facial nerve courses over the fascia covering the zygomatic arch and is anterior to the superficial temporal artery and vein. The branches to the midface cross superficial to the buccal compartment and run deep to the facial muscles. At this point, there is widespread intermingling of nerve fibers, with duplication of fibers innervating the same areas. This duplication allows for injuries in the periphery to recover by peripheral sprouting without any noticeable deficit. During surgery, it also allows for borrowing from the extra branches for cross-face reinnervation.

There are also free communications between the peripheral segments of each of the branches of the facial nerve with each of the divisions of the trigeminal nerve. This free intermingling between the fifth and seventh nerves has been proposed as a mechanism for spontaneous return of facial nerve function after unrepaired peripheral injuries to the nerve. Based on clinical and laboratory experiments, it is generally agreed that the only possible regenerative role of these anastomoses is to provide available roots for the facial nerve to regrow through aberrant and communicating pathways, eventually reaching the denervated facial muscles. There has been no evidence to support the fifth nerve nucleus and its axonal extensions as an alternative system for facial mimicking and expressive functions.

Pathophysiology of Injury and Classification of Facial Function Recovery

Sunderland[64] described five possible degrees of injury that a nerve fiber might undergo. Figure 19–3 and Table 19–4 show the pathologic changes that occur in the nerve and the anticipated responses of the nerve to electrical testing, as well as the type of recovery (House-Brackmann classification system[28]) expected with the various types of injuries. The range of electrical responses as well as recovery reflects the variations of degree of injury that might occur.

The five degrees of injury suggested by Sunderland describe the pathophysiologic events associated with all types of disorders that affect the facial nerve. The first three degrees of injury can occur with the viral inflammatory immune disorders, such as Bell palsy and herpes zoster cephalicus. The fourth and fifth degrees of injury occur when there is disruption of the nerve, as in transection, which might occur during surgery, as a result of a severe temporal bone fracture, or from a rapidly growing benign or malignant tumor.

In a first-degree injury, referred to as *neurapraxia*, a physiologic neural block is created by increased intraneural pressure. The nerve does not conduct an impulse across the site of compression, but it does respond to electrical stimulation applied distal to the lesion. If the compression is relieved, return of facial movement may begin immediately or within 3 weeks (Fig. 19–4).

A second-degree injury occurs if the compression is not relieved. The mechanism of injury is thought to be obstruction of venous drainage with increased intraneural pressure, further damming up of axoplasm with proximal and distal swelling, and eventual interruption of the flow of nutrients via the compressed arterioles. The result is loss of axons and myelin. If the process is reversed, there is complete recovery, although this recovery takes longer than with a first-degree injury, beginning in 3 weeks to 2 months, because it takes time for the degenerated axons to regenerate. If it is a pure second-degree injury, recovery is complete without any evidence of faulty regeneration. Because the lesions are rarely pure, second-degree injury usually has an element of third-degree injury, and therefore recovery is usually marred by some faulty regeneration. There may be slight blink lag, asymmetry with smiling, or subtle evidence of synkinesis.

The pathologic processes causing facial paralysis in patients with Bell palsy and herpes zoster cephalicus usually do not progress beyond first- or second-degree injury, which accounts for satisfactory recovery in most individuals.

A similar process is involved in facial paralysis resulting from acute suppurative otitis media, chronic otitis media associated with a cholesteatoma, slow-growing benign neoplasms, and temporal bone fractures. In each of these disorders, the nerve is usually not transected but rather is compressed. In acute otitis media and trauma, compression may be sudden or slowly progressive, evolving over 5 to 10 days, just as it is with Bell palsy and herpes zoster cephalicus. However, unlike the process that occurs within the latter two conditions, pressure in these other disorders is exerted on the nerve from without rather than from within the intraneural space; nevertheless, the results of compression of the nerve are the same. Eventually, axoplasm is dammed up and compression of venous drainage leads to further compression of the nerve, loss of axons, and eventual loss of endoneural tubes, which leads to third-degree injury.

Fourth- or fifth-degree injury results from partial or complete transection of the nerve. Spontaneous recovery should not be expected from fourth- or fifth-degree injury to the nerve; the best results are achieved by surgical nerve repair at the earliest possible moment after injury. Because most or all of the endoneural tubes have been disrupted, as well as the perineurium in fourth-degree injuries and the perineurium and epineurium in fifth-degree injuries, recovery even under ideal conditions is never as good as with the first three degrees of injury.

Electrophysiologic Testing

The challenge for the clinician who sees a patient with facial paralysis of recent onset is to determine whether the involved nerve is mildly compressed and is in a state of first-degree injury from which it will recover spontaneously, or whether there is initial second-degree injury that will proceed to third-degree injury and involve the entire nerve trunk if pressure is not relieved. Three electrical tests are useful clinically: (1) the maximal percutaneous excitability test or maximal stimulation test (MST), (2) the evoked electromyography (EEMG), (3) and electromyography (EMG). The first two tests are capable of detecting early or ensuing degeneration, i.e., within the first 2 weeks after the onset of paralysis. The last test is useful between 10 and 21 days following the onset of paralysis.

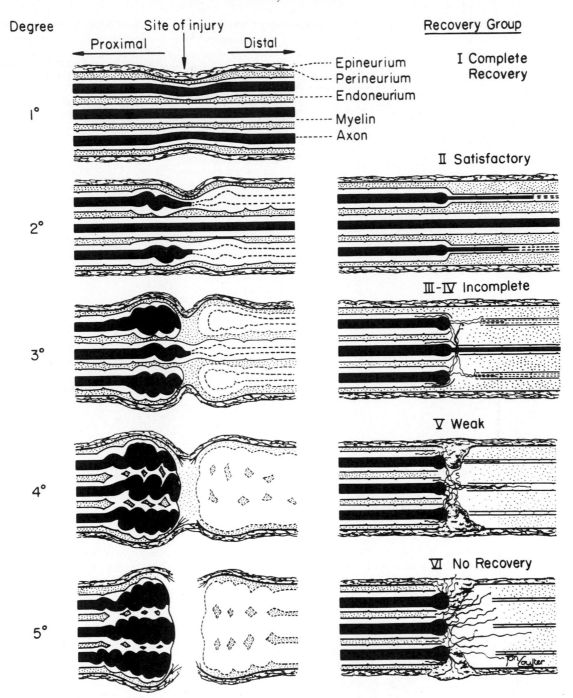

FIGURE 19–3. Facial nerve injuries may be classified[64] by the extent of the lesion from first degree (1°) to fifth degree (5°). First degree compression without loss of structure; recovery is complete. Second degree: axon degeneration; regeneration is appropriate and recovery is satisfactory. Third degree: loss of endoneural tubes; recovery is incomplete with synkinesis. Fourth degree: disruption of perineurium; recovery is poor. Fifth degree: complete disruption; no recovery. Recovery is classified[28] from grade I to grade VI. (From May M, ed. The Facial Nerve. New York, Thieme Medical Publishers, 1985, p 71.)

Electrical Tests

Maximal Stimulation Test

The MST is based on the fact that a motor nerve will conduct a response to an electrical stimulus applied distal to a lesion, even though the lesion blocks volitional movement, as long as the nerve is morphologically intact distal to the lesion (i.e., the injury is first degree). When the injury is second degree, causing damage to the axon, an increase in the intensity of the stimulus is required to cause a muscle twitch. If the myelin and axon distal to the lesion have degenerated, as with a third-degree injury, no conduction occurs no matter how intense the stimulus. A completely sectioned nerve may continue to

TABLE 19–4. Neuropathologic Findings and Spontaneous Recovery Correlated with Degree of Injury to Facial Nerve

Degree of Injury	Pathologic Findings	EEMG Response (% of Normal)	Neural Recovery	Clinical Recovery Begins	Spontaneous Recovery Result 1 Yr. Postinjury*
1	Compression, damming up of axoplasm; no morphologic changes (neurapraxia)	100	No morphologic changes noted	1–3 wk	Grade I Complete, without evidence of faulty regeneration
2	Compression persists; increased intraneural pressure; loss of axons but endoneurial tubes remain intact (axonotmesis)	11–25	Axons grow into intact, empty myelin tubes at a rate of 1 mm/day, which accounts for longer period for recovery in second-degree compared with first-degree injuries; less than complete recovery is due to some fibers with third-degree injury	3 wk to 2 mo	Fair (some noticeable difference with volitional or spontaneous movement), minimal evidence of faulty regeneration
3	Intraneural pressure increases; loss of myelin tubes (neurotmesis)	0–10	With loss of myelin tubes, new axons have opportunity to get mixed up and split, causing mouth movement with eye closure (synkinesis)	2–4 mo	Grades III–IV Moderate to poor (obvious incomplete recovery to crippling deformity) with moderate to marked complications (Fig. 19–6)
4	Above plus disruption of perineurium (partial transection)	0	In addition to problems caused by second- and third-degree injuries, axons are now blocked by scars, impairing regeneration	4–18 mo	Grade V Recovery poor, complications of faulty regeneration are not as noticeable because of marked facial weakness
5	Above plus disruption of epineurium (transection)	1	Complete disruption with scar-filled gap presents insurmountable barrier to regrowth and neuromuscular hook-up	None	Grade VI None

EEMG, evoked electromyography.
*Classification by Grades I to VI modified from House and Brackmann.[28]

conduct distal to the section for as long as 48 to 72 hours after the injury. For this reason, the MST has limited value until 48 to 72 hours after the onset of paralysis. In addition, MST is of value only as long as the nerve remains intact. After the nerve degenerates and response to electrical excitability is lost, the test is no longer useful. Duchenne,[16] who first suggested the excitability test, stated that, when excitability is lost after degeneration, it returns in only a minority of cases, even if there is recovery and return of volitional movement. Another limitation of this test is the need to compare the results of the involved side with those of the normal side, which acts as a control. Thus, in cases of recurrent palsy or alternating bilateral involvement, the test has limited value.

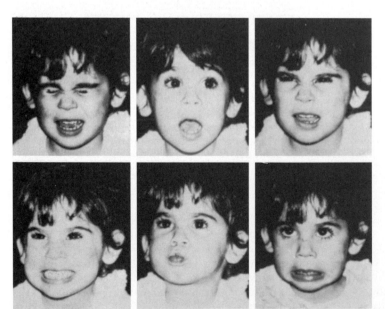

FIGURE 19–4. Example of evaluable facial movements elicited in a young child through play. Example of fair recovery 6 months after Bell palsy. Upper photographs suggest complete recovery. Lower photographs taken at the same time demonstrate incomplete recovery. This series of photographs highlights the importance of including pictures of facial movement that are exaggerated in order to give accurate evaluation.

The excitability test can be performed with any electrical stimulus in which the strength and duration can be varied. The Hilger nerve stimulator is especially designed to test the facial nerve. The test is performed by setting the intensity at 5 mA, or the highest setting tolerated by the patient without undue discomfort. An area of the patient's skin between the sideburns and the eyebrow and extending down over the cheek, jaw, and neck is wiped with electrode conduction paste. The stimulating probe is then passed slowly over this area. The responses over the forehead, eye, nose, mouth, lower lip, and neck are noted and recorded as equal, decreased, or absent on the involved side compared with those on the normal side. The test is repeated by stimulating the area of the stylomastoid foramen, between the mastoid tip and the ascending ramus. Because degeneration proceeds from proximal to distal, evidence of degeneration may be detected a day or two earlier by testing at the site where the facial nerve exits the temporal bone. The nerve is tested more peripherally to evaluate each major branch, which cannot be done by testing only in the area of the stylomastoid foramen.

Results of the MST, as described, were more reliable and became altered earlier than did those of the minimal percutaneous electrical stimulation test, which depends on looking for a 3.5-mA difference in excitability between the two sides.[41] The MST, although useful, was not completely accurate in predicting the patient's ultimate degree of recovery. When the response to maximal stimulation was equal, 12% of the patients had incomplete return of facial function; when the response to MST was decreased, 73% had incomplete return. The test was most accurate when MST was lost. In this case, all patients had incomplete return with marked evidence of faulty regeneration.[42]

The rationale for testing each major facial motor area supplied by the nerve is that certain fibers can be affected more than others, depending on the nature, location, and severity of the lesion. (The senior author has observed a first-degree injury in one part of the face and a third-degree injury in another part.) This has been noted in acute cases as well as during the phase of recovery. In acute involvement of the facial nerve, as with paralysis following trauma or infection, the electrical test ideally should be repeated daily until the response to MST becomes abnormal or return of volitional facial movement is noted.

Evoked Electromyography

EEMG is the recording of evoked summation potentials (SPs). This test was popularized and referred to by Fisch[19] as electroneurography. In principle, it is similar to the MST except that, instead of depending on the muscle twitch elicited, evoked SPs are recorded on a graph produced by a sophisticated electrodiagnostic apparatus, the direct recording electromyograph. The amount of degeneration is related to the difference in amplitude of the measured SPs on the normal and involved sides.

The great advantage of EEMG over the simple observation of facial movements as described under maximal stimulation is the precise quantitative assessment of the response available with EEMG.

Fisch[19] recommended surgical exposure of the intratemporal portion of the facial nerve (1) in traumatic lesions when the amplitude of the SP becomes reduced to 10% or less of that of the normal side within 6 days after the onset of the palsy; (2) in idiopathic (Bell) palsy as soon as the SP becomes reduced to 10% or less of that of the normal side within 2 weeks of onset of the palsy, or in the presence of a lesser reduction when inner-ear symptoms are present; and (3) in acute otitis media when there is a reduction to 10% or less despite paracentesis and antibiotic treatment.

Another potential outcome derived from the EEMG evaluation is the measurement of facial nerve latency, the time between the application of electrical stimulation to the trunk of the facial nerve and the start of the first compound muscle action potential. The facial nerve latency test (FNLT) is an objective measurement of nerve transmission, and can be performed within the first 24 hours. Danielides et al[14] found the FNLT provided accurate prognostic data in adults as well as children.

EEMG is a welcome contribution to help document accurately the electrical changes in an injured nerve; however, it has the same disadvantages as MST. Furthermore, waiting until the SPs become reduced to 10% of normal values may preclude intervention at an appropriate time to reverse nerve damage.

Electromyography

After degeneration occurs, EMG is indispensable as a measure of damage to the nerve. Acutely, the presence of a volitional motor unit action potential confirms an intact neural unit. Following denervation, the affected muscle, being hyperirritable, produces spontaneous electrical potentials referred to as *fibrillation potentials*. Usually, these fibrillation potentials do not appear until 10 to 21 days after degeneration occurs. Although the time delay is a major limitation in EMG application, EMG is the most reliable test to determine nerve degeneration because it samples motor unit activity. Furthermore, reappearance of motor unit potentials in acute facial palsies in which response to EEMG is absent indicates a deblocking phenomenon and, despite loss of response to EEMG, indicates that the acute process impairing nerve function is abating.

Imaging

Imaging often plays a role in the diagnostic evaluation of patients with facial paralysis. High-resolution computed tomography (CT) imaging of the temporal bone is essential in the evaluation of congenital facial paralysis associated with anomalies of the external or middle ear, following trauma, or in cases of acute and chronic otitis media with mastoiditis or cholesteatoma.

Gadolinium-enhanced magnetic resonance imaging demonstrated enhancement of the facial nerve in 6 of 14 children with idiopathic facial paralysis. Enhancement seemed to correlate with a protracted recovery time, although it failed to provide prognostic information regarding final outcome, which was uniformly good in the population reported. Interestingly, inflammatory sinus disease has commonly been noted on magnetic resonance imaging scans in patients with Bell palsy compared with a sample population imaged for other indications, although the significance of this finding has yet to be determined.[9]

Determining Prognosis

Prognostic evaluation of a particular case of facial paralysis must be based on the history of onset, the duration of palsy, and the completeness of the paralysis, in addition to electrical test results. The progression of paresis to complete paralysis over a period of 3 to 10 days is a poor prognostic sign. In 75% of patients with this type of history, degeneration with incomplete return of function developed.[39] The maintenance of some facial movement, or the early return of facial movement within the first 2 weeks of onset, indicates a favorable prognosis for spontaneous recovery despite the presence of abnormal prognostic indicators, such as abnormal electrical test results.

The most useful application of EEMG lies in predicting the outcome in acute facial paralysis. Studying the results of EEMG and evaluating the completeness of the palsy can predict the patient's prognosis for recovery of facial function with a high degree of accuracy. Ninety percent of patients will have a satisfactory recovery if the palsy is incomplete and response to EEMG remains greater than 10% of normal response beyond the first 14 days after onset. However, fewer than 50% of patients with a complete palsy and response to EEMG of 10% or less than that of the normal side within the first 14 days will achieve a satisfactory recovery. This latter group requires the greatest attention in terms of treatment directed toward improving the natural history of facial palsy and preventing complications of nerve degeneration. At the moment, surgical therapy, including treatment of compression of the meatal segment (the most proximal portion of the fallopian canal reached through a middle fossa approach), remains investigational (see Surgery). Patients who fall into the poor prognostic group can be advised that recovery of facial function may not occur for 2 to 4 months from the time of onset and are offered guidelines for eye care.

Diagnosis: General Principles

The patient and family confronted with facial paralysis generally have three fundamental concerns: (1) What caused the paralysis? (2) When can recovery be expected? (3) What can be done to bring about the most complete recovery at the earliest possible time? For the physician, these issues can be viewed as (1) diagnosis, (2) prognosis, and (3) therapy, and represent a logical approach to the management of patients with facial paralysis.

The diagnosis of facial paralysis in children, as in adults, can generally be made with a careful history taking, physical examination, and neuro-otologic evaluation. However, certain allowances must be made when a young child is first seen for evaluation. For instance, the child may be unable to relate historical factors such as alterations in sensation, hearing, balance, taste, or tear production, all of which may be helpful in determining a diagnosis. This information might be obtained by questioning the parents, but even the most concerned parents are not always accurate historians. However, parents can often provide useful information and must be questioned carefully regarding the time of onset of the asymmetric cry or whether tears formed on the involved side. It may be helpful to look at family photographs of the child to help determine the time of onset of weakness.

Evaluation of facial motor function is possible with children as young as 2 years of age who can mimic facial expressions. Although most require observation while spontaneous emotions are displayed, play therapy, tickling, and at times provocation of crying, such as might occur with electrophysiological testing, are useful in the evaluation of facial motor function and of tear production. Caution should be exercised, however, in determining the degree of deficit while examining a supine infant, since the loss of gravity effect in conjunction with the excellent muscle tone of the newborn may mask asymmetries in facial function.

The integrity of the chorda tympani cannot be reliably evaluated through taste testing in the young child. However, because the taste papillae in children are prominent, one may easily note by inspection if the papillae have atrophied on the involved side, which suggests that the chorda tympani nerve has been interrupted. Such a lesion may be located anywhere between the middle ear and the brain stem.

Auditory assessment can usually be made in even the youngest children by means of evoked auditory brain stem potentials. Vestibular function tests can be performed in cooperative children if necessary.

Electrical tests may be used if the stimulus is kept below the pain threshold. Usually young children tolerate a stimulus in the range of 2 to 3 mA. MST, EEMG, and EMG can be used in young children given sedation or general anesthesia (without neuromuscular relaxation).

Etiology

Congenital Facial Paralysis

The incidence of congenital facial paralysis has been estimated to be between 0.8 and 1.8 per 1000 births.[17, 26, 61] Facial paralysis in the neonate can be broadly classified into two categories. The first, *traumatic*, refers to injuries acquired as a result of intrauterine positioning or delivery. The second, *developmental*, implicates faulty embryogenesis as the cause of the paralysis. The distinction has important prognostic, therapeutic, and medicolegal implications. In general, developmental facial paralysis does not improve, whereas acquired paralysis improves spontaneously in up to 90% of affected infants. Furthermore, traumatic paralysis may require surgical intervention, whereas the developmental type presents no urgency.

The differentiation of traumatic from developmental paralysis is usually possible on the basis of an adequate history and physical examination (Table 19–5). CT scanning may also be of benefit. In difficult cases, electro-

TABLE 19–5. Facial Palsy at Birth: Differential Diagnosis

Characteristics of Congenital Causes	Method of Differentiation	Characteristics of Traumatic Causes
Illness in first trimester	History	Total paralysis at birth with some recovery noted subsequently
No recovery of facial function after birth		
Family history of facial and other anomalies		
Other anomalies, facial diplegia (bilateral palsy)	Physical examination	Hemotympanum, ecchymoses, tics, synkinesis
Anomalous (external, middle, or inner ear)	Radiography of temporal bone	Fracture
Response reduced or absent without change	MST	Normal at birth, then decreasing response may be lost
Reduced or absent response, no evidence of degeneration	EEMG	
	EMG	Normal at birth, then loss of spontaneous motor units and fibrillations 10–21 days later

EEMG, evoked electromyography; EMG, electromyography; MST, maximal stimulation test.

physiologic testing performed sequentially during the first days of life can often resolve this problem unequivocally. In developmental paralysis, results of facial nerve conduction studies are usually abnormal immediately at birth; with traumatic injuries, conduction studies are normal at birth and become abnormal 3 to 7 days later. Infants with congenital facial palsy of uncertain etiology should therefore undergo electrophysiologic testing performed sequentially starting 2 days after birth or sooner.

Traumatic

A significant proportion of congenital facial paralyses are acquired as the result of trauma; in some series, trauma was thought to be responsible for the vast majority.[17, 61] Parmalee suggested that intrauterine positioning may be responsible in some cases.[55] More commonly, these injuries occur in association with difficult and prolonged labor, classically in a primiparous mother with a large infant. It has been proposed that positioning of the infant head against the maternal sacrum during passage through the birth canal may produce a compressive injury to the nerve.[27] Subsequent studies have documented that most of these cases occur in association with forceps deliveries, but it remains uncertain whether forceps are directly responsible for the injury or simply indicative of the difficulty of the delivery.[17, 61]

Physical examination usually reveals unilateral facial weakness in association with signs of trauma, including hemotympanum and external ecchymosis or lacerations of the face or head. The site of injury may be the intracranial, intratemporal, or extratemporal portion of the nerve. Most cases appear to be the result of indentation of the thin bone of the fallopian canal, with subsequent compression injury to the underlying nerve.[47] Transection of the facial nerve as a consequence of birth trauma has not been documented. This may account for the excellent spontaneous recovery rates reported with these injuries (>90%[5]) and can be contrasted with the fractures encountered in adults, which are more likely to transect the nerve. Reports of surgical decompression for this condition are essentially anecdotal. Patients with very poor prognostic indicators may still make a complete spontaneous recovery. Surgical intervention should be considered only for infants who meet the following criteria: (1) complete unilateral paralysis at birth, (2) evidence of temporal

bone trauma on physical examination and fracture on CT scan, (3) electrophysiologic tests demonstrating loss of facial nerve function by 3 to 5 days after birth, and (4) no evidence of clinical or electrophysiologic function at 5 weeks of age. This period of observation minimizes the likelihood of unnecessary surgery while still allowing for satisfactory results if intervention is required.[6]

Developmental

The presence of other congenital anomalies, facial diplegia, or isolated palsy of the lower lip or upper face suggests an underlying developmental defect as the cause of the facial paralysis. Exploration of the facial nerve in such patients carries no benefit; the nerve generally tapers to a fibrous filament peripherally, making interposition grafting or decompression futile.[35] Furthermore, the coexisting abnormalities of the facial musculature generally preclude restoration of function via reinnervation alone.

Associated Anomalies

Most commonly, developmental facial paralysis is associated with other anomalies. In the senior author's series, the most common site was the maxilla, including defects such as cleft palate, hypoplastic maxilla, and duplication of the palate. Others have demonstrated a propensity for anomalies of the pinna and external auditory canal, ranging from mild defects to severe microtia and atresia.[7] Sensorineural hearing loss may be present, and auditory evoked brain stem testing should be performed uniformly in affected infants.

Möbius Syndrome

Möbius syndrome is a rare congenital disorder characterized by unilateral or bilateral facial palsy, often sparing the lower half of the face, as well as abducens palsy. Common associated findings include anomalies of the extremities in half of the patients, absence of the greater pectoral muscles, and involvement of other cranial nerves. The disease is often recognized in newborns, but if involvement is symmetrical, the diagnosis may be delayed. The cause of Möbius syndrome is unknown, and there is controversy over whether the primary defect is an agenesis of the facial nucleus or of the facial musculature.[35] A number of teratogens, in particular thalidomide, can cause anomalies similar to those found in Möbius syndrome.

Oculoauriculovertebral Syndrome

Oculoauriculovertebral syndrome constitutes a spectrum of diseases that includes hemifacial microsomia, Goldenhar syndrome, and a number of related disorders characterized by a unilateral malformation affecting first and second branchial arch derivatives. Affected patients display hypoplasia of the maxilla and mandible, microtia, and microstomia. The asymmetry may not be present at birth but usually becomes apparent with facial growth. There may be associated deformities of other organ systems, in particular the central nervous system. Goldenhar syndrome, found in approximately 10% of these patients, consists of the characteristic facial findings in addition to epibulbar dermoids and vertebral anomalies. Facial weakness occurs in approximately 10% to 20% of patients overall but is noted more commonly in the Goldenhar subset.[7, 24] Familial cases have been described but are rare.

Asymmetric Crying Facies

Also referred to as congenital unilateral lower lip palsy, this rather mild deformity tends to be one of the more common diagnoses in series of congenital facial paralysis,[30] with an estimated incidence of 1 in 120 to 1 in 160 newborns. Typically, the deformity is noted when the affected lower lip fails to depress with crying, because there is generally no functional deficit related to the paralysis. This syndrome is most notable for the fact that affected children frequently have associated birth defects. The most common of these affect the pinna, but cardiac anomalies (cardiofacial syndrome) are present in up to 10% of affected children and may be severe.[11]

Older Infants and Children

Bell Palsy

In the series of 300 patients younger than 18 years of age with facial paralysis (see Table 19–1), Bell palsy was the most common diagnosis, accounting for nearly 40% of cases.[37] Bell palsy is a diagnosis of exclusion that should be made only when no other cause for the paralysis can be found. As noted previously, the evaluation of a child with acute facial paralysis begins with a careful history and physical examination, with particular attention to the cranial nerves. Characteristically, the facial paralysis in Bell palsy evolves over 3 weeks or less. Slow progression over weeks to months, or the presence of twitching, should prompt further investigation. There should be no evidence of middle-ear disease, and the audiogram should be normal. Several factors may make the diagnosis of Bell palsy more likely: (1) an inflamed chorda tympani nerve, which is found in approximately 15% of patients,[34] (2) a positive family history, which is found in approximately

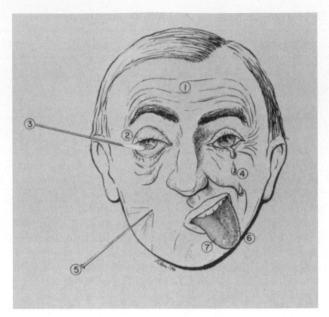

FIGURE 19–5. Misleading signs associated with Bell palsy: (1) intact forehead, (2) Horner syndrome (constricted pupil and ptosis of upper eyelid), (3) loss of corneal sensation, (4) tearing only on uninvolved side, (5) loss of skin sensation, (6) apparent tongue deviation, (7) loss of taste papillae. (Courtesy of Laryngoscope.)

10% of patients, and (3) a recent history of viral illness, usually with upper respiratory or gastrointestinal symptoms. Despite the emphasis on facial nerve involvement in Bell palsy, clinical findings suggest that the disease is actually a polyneuropathy (Fig 19–5). Associated complaints often include pain or diminished sensation over the ipsilateral face, head, ear, neck, or shoulder—signifying involvement of the fifth cranial nerve, as well as C2 and C3. Lingual nerve involvement may be suggested by hypesthesia of the ipsilateral tongue in up to 50% of patients. Dysacusis and diminished tearing are also common complaints.

The cause of Bell palsy remains enigmatic. The two most widely accepted etiologies are (1) new or reactivation of viral infection of the seventh nerve and (2) compression due to swelling of the nerve within the fallopian canal, perhaps secondary to (1). It has been specifically proposed that reactivation of latent herpes simplex virus (HSV) within the geniculate ganglion is the cause for most episodes of Bell palsy. Histopathologic evaluation of the nerve after the acute onset of facial palsy has revealed a variety of abnormalities, ranging from "degeneration," i.e., breakdown of myelin, to diffuse lymphocytic infiltration within the nerve—characteristics consistent with a viral etiology.[33] Thus far, electron microscopy has failed to identify viral particles.[54] However, HSV antigens have been identified in facial nerve epineural tissue obtained at the time of decompression,[50] while HSV DNA has been demonstrated by polymerase chain reaction within the endoneurial fluid of patients with Bell palsy, but not in control subjects.[51] An acute, reversible form of facial paralysis with histopathologic changes consistent

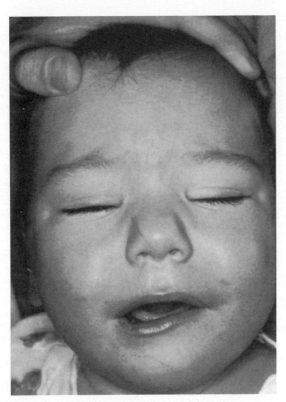

FIGURE 19–6. Palsy of the left lower lip associated with acute suppurative otitis media involving the left ear.

with Bell palsy developed in rabbits after injection of HSV into the stylomastoid foramen[31]; injection trauma could potentially produce similar results. Other investigators have found no evidence of inflammation in cases of acute facial palsy.[33] Engorgement of venous channels, which would be expected in a compression-type phenomenon, has rarely been described, but hemorrhage and bone resorption have been demonstrated.

The natural history of Bell palsy is usually spontaneous recovery, which is complete in 71% of patients and satisfactory in 84% (House-Brackmann grade I or II).[33, 56] Children, in general, have an excellent prognosis, with complete recovery in approximately 90%. In general, patients who do not progress to total paralysis can expect complete recovery. In the 60% to 70% of patients with total paralysis and EEMG amplitude less than 10% of normal, the outcome is significantly worse, with 50% to 75% of patients demonstrating House-Brackmann grade III or IV results. The time course of recovery is also prognostically significant. Recovery that begins before the third week is almost universally complete; recovery beginning between 3 weeks and 2 months is generally satisfactory. If recovery is delayed until 2 to 4 months, less than 30% of patients will achieve a House Brackmann grade I or II result.

Recurrence of Bell palsy is noted in 10% of patients, and in two thirds of cases the paralysis is contralateral. Ipsilateral facial paralysis is associated with tumors involving the facial nerve in approximately 10% of cases, most commonly facial neuromas. Diabetes has been found in approximately 30% of adult patients with recurrent palsy as opposed to 12% in nonrecurrent cases.[57]

Infection

Infections cause a relatively large proportion of cases of facial paralysis in children. In fact, if one considers Bell palsy, herpes zoster oticus, Guillain-Barré, and otitis media as a group, infection is the most common cause of facial paralysis in patients younger than 18 years of age.

Acute Otitis Media

Acute otitis media (Fig. 19–6) is a particularly common cause of facial paralysis in young children. Although classic signs of otitis media may be present, patients who have received antibiotic therapy may have few findings indicative of acute inflammation. Infection may penetrate the thin bone of the fallopian canal through direct erosion, congenital dehiscences, or the preformed pathways for the stapedius nerve, chorda tympani, and posterior tympanic artery.[65] Edema of the nerve within the bony confines of the canal leads to compression, diminished perfusion, and loss of function. Unlike Bell palsy, paralysis due to otitis media is not benign in nature, and an incomplete recovery was noted in more than 40% of the patients. The treatment for acute otitis media complicated by facial paralysis is myringotomy and culture-directed antibiotics. Despite such therapy, however, the disease may progress and further surgical therapy may be required.

Chronic Otitis Media

Facial paralysis from chronic otitis media is usually associated with middle-ear cholesteatoma directly compressing the nerve. Less frequently, the paralysis may be secondary to granulation tissue that has eroded through the fallopian canal. Removal of the cholesteatoma or granulations relieves the pressure and usually provides resolution. Because the pathophysiologic events in chronic infection are less acute, the results of early surgical decompression have been excellent.

Lyme Disease

Acute facial palsy is the most common focal neurologic manifestation of Lyme disease, a tick-borne disorder caused by the spirochete *Borrelia burgdorferi*. The disease was originally described in rural New England, but subsequent reports indicate a nearly worldwide distribution. After the tick bite, a characteristic expanding erythematous lesion known as *erythema chronicum migrans* occurs at the site of inoculation in 60% to 80% of patients. Within days to weeks, dissemination occurs and a variety of symptoms may be manifested, most commonly diffuse rashes, headache and neck stiffness, migratory joint pains, and severe fatigue. Unilateral or bilateral facial paralysis may also occur during this stage.[63] Lyme disease appears to be most common in children, and some series suggest that it may be the most common cause of pediatric facial paralysis within certain populations.[12] Treatment with appropriate antibiotics has generally been associated with an excellent prognosis for recovery.

Herpes Zoster Oticus

Also known as Ramsay Hunt syndrome, this disease accounts for approximately 3% to 12% of cases of facial paralysis. Findings include severe pain, small vesicles in the ear canal and pinna, and a rapidly progressing facial paralysis. Frequently, other cranial nerves are involved, most commonly the eighth nerve, so that hearing impairment and vertigo may be present. The diagnosis can usually be secured on the basis of the physical examination; increasing antibody titers or complement fixation tests can be confirmatory. Thirty percent to 50% of patients with Ramsay Hunt syndrome experience persistent weakness or mass movement.

Idiopathic Diseases

Kawasaki Disease

Kawasaki disease is a childhood disorder of undetermined cause and is defined by the presence of persistent high fever, erythema of the oral mucosa, cervical lymphadenitis, conjunctival infection, and upper and lower extremity edema and desquamation. Rare cases may be associated with peripheral neuropathies, including facial paralysis. The paralysis is typically transient, and full recovery can generally be expected.[29]

Melkersson-Rosenthal Syndrome

A pattern of relapsing, alternating facial paralysis; recurrent or persisting facial edema, commonly involving the lip; and fissured tongue is diagnostic of Melkersson-Rosenthal syndrome. Usually the disease becomes manifest in childhood. Although the cause is unknown, histologic evidence of noncaseating granulomas in involved tissues suggests a relationship with sarcoid. Most cases are sporadic, although a familial tendency has been described. Facial paralysis may be partial or complete, unilateral or bilateral, and may precede or follow the development of facial edema by months or years.[24]

Trauma

Temporal Bone Fractures

Mitchell and Stone reported the incidence of facial paralysis among 1015 children with head injuries over a 2-year period. Of the total, 71 patients had temporal bone fractures, and 21% of these had facial paralysis.[49] Temporal bone fractures are classified as longitudinal or transverse, although an individual fracture often has features of both. Longitudinal fractures account for approximately 90% of temporal bone fractures and usually course along the long axis of the petrous pyramid just lateral to the labyrinth, disrupting the tegmen and external auditory canal. These injuries may be associated with compression, contusion, or transection of the facial nerve at the geniculate ganglion, tympanic portion, or less commonly at the second genu in the mastoid segment. Associated findings typically include conductive hearing loss resulting from hemotympanum, ossicular chain disruption, and tears of the tympanic membrane. Less frequently, sensorineural hearing loss, vertigo, and nystagmus may be present with labyrinthine concussion or subluxation of the stapes into the oval window (see Chap. 29).

Transverse fractures are usually secondary to more severe head injuries and may be associated with facial paralysis in up to 50% of cases. Most of these patients suffer a fracture through the otic capsule, resulting in sensorineural deafness and vertigo.

Treatment of traumatic facial paralysis should be delayed until the patient's more serious injuries have been stabilized. Management depends on the onset and degree of paralysis, the results of daily electrical testing, and the demonstration of a fracture on CT scan. In paralysis of delayed onset, when any facial movement has been detected, one can be relatively certain that transection has not occurred.[48] However, it is important to note that children may maintain excellent facial tone and eye closure even with a transected nerve; the examination should be performed carefully to avoid unnecessary delay in treatment. In cases of immediate, complete paralysis, serial EEMGs should be obtained; if function remains greater than 10% of normal for 5 days, a satisfactory outcome is likely and the patient can be observed. Rapid deterioration of EEMG results over a 5-day period is an indication for surgical intervention. Exploration should be performed and the facial nerve decompressed from the meatal segment to the stylomastoid foramen; the CT scan may be useful in localizing the site of injury. The surgical approach depends on the status of the hearing. In patients with profound sensorineural hearing loss, a translabyrinthine route is most suitable. In patients with intact hearing, a combined transmastoid–middle fossa approach has been most commonly used, although we have found that complete decompression with hearing preservation can be obtained via a transtemporal–sub-middle fossa approach (Fig. 19–7).

The nerve sheath should be opened and the continuity of the nerve assured. Direct anastomosis or nerve grafting should be performed, depending on the extent of the injury. Surgery for traumatic facial paralysis is extremely challenging; in addition to complete decompression and microsurgical repair of the nerve, the surgeon must be prepared to repair tears of the tympanic membrane, ossicular disruptions, and cerebrospinal fluid leaks and harvest sural or cervical cutaneous nerve grafts.

Facial Wounds

Injuries to the extracranial segment of the facial nerve should be explored as soon as possible so that the distal segments can be stimulated and localized. Usually this can be performed up to 3 days after the injury. If the wound is clean, primary repair or interposition grafting should be performed. In contaminated wounds, the distal

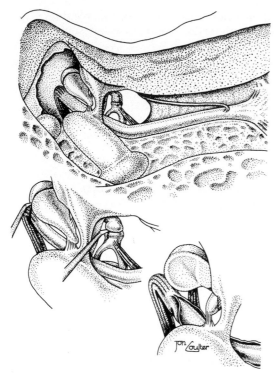

FIGURE 19–7. Transmastoid, extralabyrinthine, subtemporal approach to the right facial nerve can reach the labyrinthine segment while avoiding a middle fossa craniotomy. The top drawing illustrates posterior tympanotomy looking at the mastoid and tympanic segment of the facial nerve. The bottom two drawings show that by disarticulating the incus and rotating it forward with its attachment to the fossa incudis, the surgeon can reach the geniculate ganglion and labyrinthine segment of the facial nerve. The incus is replaced in its anatomic position at completion of the procedure.

segments should be tagged with clips or nonabsorbable sutures. The site should be drained and allowed to heal by secondary intention. The temptation to repair the nerve immediately should be resisted; the outcome is often less satisfactory, a result that generally does not become apparent until the ideal time to intervene has passed. Repair of the nerve can be accomplished within 3 weeks with essentially the same results achievable by immediate repair.

Iatrogenic

Otologic Surgery

Facial nerve injuries in otologic surgery may occur even in the most experienced hands. The most common site of injury is the second genu in the mastoid, followed by the narrow angle at the anterior epitympanum. The position of the nerve may be altered as a result of congenital anomalies, or distorted by chronic granulations, cholesteatoma, or tumor, thereby increasing the likelihood of injury. Positive identification of the nerve during all stages of surgery of the temporal bone or parotid is the best way to avoid such an injury. Anatomic landmarks that help to identify the facial nerve in the temporal bone have been described by Rulon and Hallberg[59] and by Glasscock.[23] Facial nerve monitoring may be a useful adjunct to surgical localization of the nerve but is not sufficient per se to ensure that the nerve will not be injured.

If a patient awakens from anesthesia with a facial paralysis when no injury was expected, a short period of observation (e.g., 2 hours) is reasonable to allow residual local anesthetic to dissipate. The mastoid dressing should be removed to ensure that the nerve is not compressed. If the nerve was clearly identified and uninjured during the surgery, there is no need for exploration. This is also the case if the nerve sheath was torn without injury to the nerve itself, and subsequent proximal and distal decompression performed.

If unexpected facial paralysis follows temporal bone surgery and the nerve was not identified, exploration of the nerve is mandatory. Despite the dogma that such situations require almost immediate intervention, it is often advantageous to plan to explore the nerve the following day. This waiting period allows for recovery from the associated stress and fatigue and provides time for discussion with the patient and family, and consultation with other physicians when appropriate. The nerve should be decompressed from several millimeters proximal to the site of injury to the stylomastoid foramen. If the sheath is frayed but the endoneural contents are grossly intact, decompression alone should suffice. If the nerve is transected, the ends should be freshened and repaired either primarily or with an interposition graft. The anticipated results can be predicted by the degree of injury (see Fig. 19–3 and Table 19–3). With an intact nerve, the injury may be of first- to third-degree severity; if the nerve is frayed or transected, the injury is usually at the fourth- to fifth-degree level (see Chap. 24).

Parotid Surgery

Surgery of the parotid gland in the young child is hazardous. The facial nerve fibers are extremely small and often require magnification for identification. The most common tumors in this area—hemangiomas and lymphangiomas—produce numerous finger-like projections that may envelop the facial nerve and make dissection difficult. These lesions should generally be managed conservatively (see Chap. 63).

If surgery in this region is necessary, great skill and experience is required to avoid nerve injury. Familiarity with the anatomic variations of the facial nerve in the young child is essential. The lack of development of the mastoid tip, the narrow tympanic ring, and the lack of subcutaneous tissue in young children place the main trunk just beneath the skin as it emerges from the temporal bone. In comparison with adults, the lower division of the facial nerve in young children runs very superficially over the angle of the mandible. The nerve may be injured at either of these sites even during the skin incision.

To avoid injury to the facial nerve during parotid surgery, the nerve must be clearly identified during the procedure and stimulated at the main trunk before the incision is closed. If movement of the entire face is produced, the nerve is intact; even if the patient awakens with a total paralysis, complete recovery can be expected and no further therapy is required. On the other hand, if any portion of the face does not respond to stimulation after the procedure, the branches should be followed to their termination in an effort to locate the site of injury. If the nerve appears intact, no further therapy is required. Branches that are severed should be repaired with a fascicular anastomosis in standard fashion with an interposition graft if necessary. Immediate repair should yield excellent results.[45]

Tumors

Although a rare cause of facial paralysis in children, tumors accounted for 6% of the patients in the senior author's series. A variety of lesions can cause facial paralysis, regardless of the rate of onset or the age of the patient (see Table 19–1). However, a tumor involving the facial nerve should be strongly considered in patients with any of the following: (1) facial paralysis that does not resolve after 6 months, (2) paralysis that progresses slowly beyond 3 weeks, (3) paralysis that recurs on the same side, (4) facial weakness preceded by twitching, or (5) facial paralysis associated with other neurologic signs.

In children, benign tumors cause facial paralysis more commonly than do malignancies. Tumors of the nerve sheath make up the greatest proportion, followed by vascular lesions. Malignant tumors generally produce a more rapid onset of paralysis. Leukemia involving the temporal bone may directly compress or infiltrate the facial nerve.[32] Rhabdomyosarcoma involving the head and neck may produce a variety of cranial neuropathies but most commonly involves the seventh nerve.[18] The intracranial facial nerve may be involved in brain tumors, particularly those arising infratentorially. Finally, metastasis from a variety of tumors, including Wilms tumors and neuroblastoma, has been reported to cause facial paralysis (see Chaps. 30, 46, and 100).

Patients with facial paralysis caused by tumors frequently have clinical features suggestive of an underlying neoplasm, yet they may experience a significant delay between the onset of symptoms and appropriate diagnosis and treatment. It cannot be overemphasized that all patients with facial nerve disorders should be carefully evaluated so that appropriate intervention can be instituted as rapidly as possible.

Systemic Diseases

Myotonic Dystrophy

Myotonic dystrophy is an autosomal dominant disease characterized by progressive muscle weakness, wasting, and variable degrees of mental impairment. Facial weakness is an early and consistent feature, and many patients have facial diplegia at birth.

Albers-Schönberg Disease

This familial disease is marked by increased density of bones and the absence of resorption of primary bone,

leading to compression of nerves. Blindness, deafness, and facial paralysis are common manifestations.

Hypertension

Facial paralysis with associated hypertension has been well described in children.[67] The pathologic event appears to be edema and hemorrhage into the facial nerve, and most cases appear to be reversible with management of the hypertension.

Management Issues in the Care of the Patient with Facial Paralysis

Because most patients with facial paralysis recover spontaneously, clinicians frequently approach this problem with no particular urgency. Occasionally, however, a patient is seen with a facial paralysis that represents an underlying life-threatening disorder; others may spend their lives with unnecessary deformity because treatment was not offered until death of the facial nerve was established by electrical tests. An example is facial paralysis resulting from cholesteatoma, in which denervation may occur by the second or third day, and decompression must be performed as rapidly as possible.

Mild cases of paralysis may go unnoticed by both patient and family, so that the significance of the lesion from a psychological perspective may be minimal. However, more marked deficits may be the focus of tremendous grief, even in the absence of significant functional disturbances. It is essential to provide the family with a realistic assessment of the expected degree of recovery and the therapeutic options available. It may be reassuring to tell them that almost all patients will experience some degree of recovery. Certain families may benefit from contact with appropriate support groups or psychological counseling.

Eye Care

In patients with congenital facial paralysis, ophthalmologic sequelae from facial paralysis are unlikely to develop, even though lacrimation may be decreased. On the other hand, acquired paralysis in older children necessitates the same meticulous eye care used in adults. This is particularly important in circumstances in which tear production is impaired, corneal anesthesia is present, or the patient lacks an adequate Bell phenomenon (e.g., BAD syndrome—absent Bell phenomenon, corneal anesthesia, and dry eye). Treatment is directed toward protecting the eye from exposure and drying. Frequent instillation of artificial tears during the day and a lubricating ophthalmic ointment at night is beneficial. A moisture chamber (Pro-Optics, Palatine, Ill) is also an effective means of protection, and under some circumstances a temporary tarsorrhaphy may be helpful. Closing the eye with tape or patching the eye is less effective and may be irritating. A small semicircle of tape on the upper eyelid may provide additional corneal protection by helping to overcome the pull of the superior levator muscle. Cases of acute facial paralysis with a favorable prognosis can be managed adequately by this conservative treatment, and eye care should be continued until the return of spontaneous eye closure.

If keratitis develops despite such measures, and in particular if the prospects for return of spontaneous function are poor, a variety of surgical techniques are available. The traditional management of such patients has consisted of tarsorrhaphy, which has generally provided satisfactory protection at the cost of function and cosmesis. However, reanimating the upper eyelid by placement of a gold weight or spring has proven to be a more attractive option.[36] In the case of the lower eyelid, excellent tone is generally maintained in children, and ectropion is rare. However, the lower eyelid may become lax with time, and lid-tightening procedures or placement of an auricular cartilage graft may be beneficial in rare cases.[43]

Medical Therapy

Without question, appropriate antimicrobial agents have an important role in the management of facial paralysis resulting from acute suppurative otitis media. In conjunction with myringotomy, antibiotics may provide rapid resolution of facial paralysis in these patients.

Glucocorticoids have been used extensively in the management of facial paralysis, particularly in Bell palsy and herpes zoster oticus. They have been reported to reduce pain, prevent denervation and progression to total paralysis, and improve both the duration and ultimate outcome of the paralysis.[1, 3, 57] Numerous articles have been published purporting to demonstrate the benefits of steroids, but in the vast majority of these articles, methodologic shortcomings compromise the conclusions.[44] Two comprehensive reviews of the literature, one a meta-analysis, emphasize these deficiencies.[58, 62] Only a few controlled studies have demonstrated a benefit of steroids over placebo. However, an equally well-designed study failed to show any significant difference.[40] No study has specifically demonstrated the benefit of glucocorticoid therapy in children, who in general have an excellent prognosis. The potential risks, in particular gastrointestinal hemorrhage and impaired immunity, are notable but rare in most series. Therapy is discouraged in patients with brittle diabetes, peptic ulcer disease, immunocompromise, or tuberculosis.

At this time, many physicians choose to treat idiopathic facial paralysis with steroids, although this practice remains controversial. Steroids probably reduce the likelihood of total paralysis and degeneration.[3] There is little role for steroids in patients who have not progressed to complete paralysis after 1 week. However, since early treatment seems to be necessary if any benefit is to be derived, all patients seen within the first week must theoretically receive treatment to maximize benefit.

The antiviral acyclovir has been proposed to treat both Ramsay Hunt syndrome and Bell palsy, based on the presumption that both processes are the result of herpesvirus infections.[15] Adour et al[2] compared the outcome of 99 patients with Bell palsy treated in a double-blind fashion with either prednisone/placebo or prednisone/acyclovir within 3 days after onset. Return to normal function occurred more frequently in the latter cohort (87% vs.

72%), and the incidence of denervation as measured by electrical testing was reduced. There was no statistical difference in the number of patients who progressed to complete paralysis or in the development of contracture with synkinesis. Interestingly, the results for the prednisone-only group were significantly worse than in the author's prior prednisone study, underscoring the variation in outcomes among different populations and the limitations of relatively small series.[2, 3] Valacyclovir is a new generation antiviral with fewer gastrointestinal side effects and improved absorption; no evidence of benefit for facial paralysis has been presented at this time. Furthermore, the benefit of antiviral therapy in children has not been specifically addressed.

Surgery

Facial Nerve Decompression

To prevent total degeneration, Fisch and Esslen suggested complete decompression (middle fossa plus transmastoid) in cases of complete facial paralysis if EEMG demonstrates 90% denervation.[21] Gantz et al[22] reported the results of a multi-institutional study evaluating early middle fossa decompression for patients in this poor prognostic category. Although the study was not randomized, a greater proportion of patients undergoing decompression had a satisfactory outcome (House-Brackmann grade I or II) compared with those who declined surgery. This approach is widely accepted in clinical practice. Anecdotal reports also support decompression for recurrent idiopathic paralysis. However, no randomized, stratified, controlled clinical trial with a sufficient number of patients has shown that surgical decompression of the facial nerve is effective in relieving facial paralysis resulting from any pathologic condition that has not interrupted the nerve. Furthermore, no study has specifically addressed the role of surgery in children. Thus, the benefit of surgery has not been definitively established for idiopathic (Bell) palsy, herpes zoster cephalicus, acute suppurative otitis media, necrotizing external otitis, or facial paralysis after iatrogenic or external temporal bone trauma. However, facial paralysis due to an ongoing process, such as chronic suppurative otitis media, can be relieved only by eradicating the primary process. In this case, surgery should be performed before electrical denervation to produce the most satisfactory recovery of facial function. Specifically, surgery must not be delayed if the palsy has progressed from incomplete to complete and if the response to EEMG is less than 25% of normal or is dropping precipitously after the third day following onset. There are also two situations in which surgery is absolutely indicated for facial nerve disorders: (1) to rule out or treat facial nerve transection and (2) to treat infiltration by tumor.

Rehabilitation of the Paralyzed Face

Patients with facial paralysis require an individualized approach to rehabilitation, taking into consideration the cause and duration of the paralysis as well as the functional and emotional needs of the patient. If it is likely that the paralysis will be long-standing, a variety of surgical techniques are available to improve cosmesis and function. Even under the best of circumstances, however, "normal" facial animation generally cannot be obtained with currently available methods, and it is essential that patients and families have realistic expectations before embarking on a surgical course.

The timing for such procedures varies with the clinical situation. Patients with a recent injury benefit from rapid reinnervation. Conversely, children with congenital paralysis or absence of suitable muscle may be best served by waiting until facial growth is completed. In general, the following hierarchy is appropriate in considering the rehabilitative options available to a patient:

1. Direct facial nerve anastomosis. If a sharp transection of the nerve has occurred as a result of surgery or trauma, debridement and direct anastomosis without tension should be performed as early as possible. Within 72 hours, the distal nerve stumps may be electrically stimulated, thereby aiding localization. If this is not possible, repair should be performed as early as feasible; studies indicate that repair can be performed with satisfactory results for a minimum of several months after the injury.[5] Results have generally been poor if repair is delayed for more than 1 year after injury, after which fibrosis of the distal nerve and atrophy of the facial muscles have occurred.

2. Interposition grafting. After blunt trauma or tumor extirpation, a significant length of the facial nerve may be damaged and may require resection. The resultant gap requires placement of a nerve graft; typically, a cervical cutaneous or sural nerve is used as the donor. Early repair results in the best outcome, independent of the need for graft placement.

3. Nerve transposition. Although restoring the continuity of the facial nerve provides superior results, other cranial nerves may be "hooked" to the distal facial nerve if the proximal portion of the facial nerve is unavailable. This technique requires intact facial musculature, making it inappropriate for most cases of developmental paralysis or paralysis of greater than 2 years' duration. Nerve transposition is especially useful after injury to the facial nerve at the brain stem. The phrenic, spinal accessory, contralateral facial, and hypoglossal nerves have been used for this purpose. Theoretically, the best results should be obtained with a cross-facial nerve graft, allowing appropriate segmental input to the facial musculature and permitting involuntary facial movement. The outcome of this surgery has been inconsistent, however, most likely because the prolonged period before reinnervation permits atrophy of the facial muscles. The most satisfying results have been achieved using the hypoglossal nerve; 90% of patients obtained symmetry and tone and 77% satisfactory motor function.[13] Despite these results, loss of motor innervation to the ipsilateral tongue has frequently been a source of significant morbidity. The hypoglossal-facial "jump-graft" technique reported by May and colleagues[46] has largely ameliorated this functional deficit and allows for the per-

formance of bilateral hypoglossal-facial anastomoses if necessary.

4. Microneurovascular free muscle transfer. The current state-of-the-art for patients with no restorable facial musculature is a free muscle transfer with neurovascular anastomosis. The largest experience has been with a two-stage procedure consisting of crossed facial nerve grafting, followed by muscle transfer after axons have reached the ipsilateral face. The gracilis muscle has been used most frequently for this procedure, although the flexor digitorum and serratus muscles have also been used. Results have been reported as "excellent" in 50% to 60% of patients.[4, 52] A more attractive option may be a one-stage procedure, with a hypoglossal-facial "jump-graft" used for neural input. Preliminary results with this procedure have been satisfactory. These procedures are technically challenging and require specialized training in microvascular surgery. The long-term results of such therapy, particularly in children, have not yet been assessed.

5. Pedicled temporal or masseter transpositions. The indications for these techniques are the same as described for microneurovascular free muscle transfer and have been successful in providing excellent tone and, with training, satisfactory voluntary movement. Most of the transposition procedures are appropriate for rehabilitation of the lower half of the face; the rehabilitative eye procedures described previously have provided excellent functional and cosmetic results in the upper face.

SELECTED REFERENCES

Schaitkin B, May M. Evaluation and management of facial nerve disorders. Curr Opin Otolaryngol Head Neck Surg 1:79, 1993.
>   *This brief review highlights the diagnostic approach to facial nerve disorders, focusing on the current literature on this topic.*

Silman J, Niparko J, Lee S, Kileny P. Prognostic value of the evoked and standard electromyography in acute facial paralysis. Otolaryngol Head Neck Surg 107:377, 1992.
>   *Although the debate over which Bell palsy patients should be operated on continues, this article suggests that additional patients can be excluded from the possibility of undergoing surgery. Supporting the work of Fisch and May, the combination of evoked electromyography and voluntary EMG was used to further predict positive outcome.*

REFERENCES

1. Adour K. Medical management of idiopathic (Bell's) palsy. Otolaryngol Clin North Am 24:663, 1991.
2. Adour K, Roboyianes J, Von Doersten P, et al. Bell's palsy treatment with acyclovir and prednisone compared with prednisone alone: a double blind, randomized, controlled trial. Ann Otol Rhinol Laryngol 105:371, 1996.
3. Adour K, Wingerd J, Bell D, et al. Prednisone treatment for idiopathic facial paralysis (Bell's palsy). N Engl J Med 287:1268, 1972.
4. Aviv J, Urken M. Management of the paralyzed face with microneurovascular free muscle transfer. Arch Otolaryngol Head Neck Surg 118:909, 1992.

5. Barrs D. Facial nerve trauma: optimal timing for repair. Laryngoscope 101:835, 1991.

6. Bergman I, May M, Wessel HB, Stool SE. Management of facial palsy caused by birth trauma. Laryngoscope 96:381, 1986.

7. Bergstrom L, Baker BB. Syndromes associated with congenital facial paralysis. Otolaryngol Head Neck Surg 89:336, 1981.

8. Blunt MJ. The possible role of vascular changes in the etiology of Bell's palsy. J Laryngol Otol 70:701, 1956.

9. Burgio D, Siddique S, Haupert M, Meleca R. Magnetic resonance imaging of the facial nerve in children with idiopathic facial paralysis. Otolaryngol Head Neck Surg 122:556, 2000.

10. Cawthorne T. Surgery of the temporal bone. Hunterian lecture. J Laryngol Otol 67:437, 1953.

11. Cayler GC. Cardiofacial syndrome. Congenital heart disease and facial weakness, a hitherto unrecognized association. Arch Dis Child 44:69, 1969.

12. Christen HJ, Bartlau N, Hanefield F, et al. Peripheral facial palsy in childhood—Lyme borreliosis to be suspected until proven otherwise. Acta Paediatr Scand 79:1219, 1990.

13. Conley J. Hypoglossal-facial anastomosis. In Brackman DE, ed. Neurological Surgery of the Ear and Skull Base. New York, Raven Press, 1982, pp 93–98.

14. Danielides V, Skevas A, Panagopoulos K, Kastanioudakis I. Value of the facial nerve latency test in the prognosis of childhood Bell's palsy. Childs Nerv Syst 8:126, 1992.

15. Dickins J, Smith J, Graham S. Herpes zoster oticus: treatment with intravenous acyclovir. Laryngoscope 98:776, 1988.

16. Duchenne GB. De I Electrisation Localise, 3rd ed. Paris, Bailliere, 1872, pp 864–870.

17. Falko NA, Erickson E. Facial nerve palsy in the newborn: incidence and outcome. Plast Reconstr Surg 85:1, 1990.

18. Feldman BA. Rhabdomyosarcoma of the head and neck. Laryngoscope 92:424, 1982.

19. Fisch U. Total facial nerve decompression and electroneurography. In Silverstein H, Norrell H, eds. Neurological Surgery of the Ear. Birmingham, Ala, Aesculapius Publishing, 1977.

20. Fisch U. Surgery for Bell's palsy. Arch Otolaryngol Head Neck Surg 107:1, 1981.

21. Fisch U, Esslen E. Total intratemporal exposure of the facial nerve; pathologic findings in Bell's palsy. Arch Otolaryngol Head Neck Surg 95:335, 1972.

22. Gantz BJ, Rubinstein JT, Gidley P, Woodworth GG. Surgical management of Bell's palsy. Laryngoscope 109:1177, 1999.

23. Glasscock ME. Unusual facial nerve problems. Some thoughts on identifying the nerve in the temporal bone. Laryngoscope 81:8669, 1971.

24. Gorlin RJ, Cohen MM, Levin LS. Syndromes of the Head and Neck, 3rd ed. Oxford, Oxford University Press, 1990, p 641.

25. Gorlin RJ, Cohen MM, Levin LS. Syndromes of the Head and Neck, 3rd ed. Oxford, Oxford University Press, 1990, p 611.

26. Harris LE, Stayura LA, Ramirez-Talavera PF, et al. Congenital and acquired abnormalities observed in live-born and stillborn neonates. Mayo Clin Proc 50:85, 1975.

27. Hepner WR Jr. Some observations on facial paresis in the newborn infant. Etiology and incidence. Pediatrics 8:494, 1951.

28. House JW, Brackmann DE. Facial nerve grading system. Otolaryngol Head Neck Surg 93:146, 1985.

29. Kleinman MB, Passo MH. Incomplete Kawasaki disease with facial nerve paralysis and coronary artery involvement. Pediatr Infect Dis J 7:301, 1988.

30. Kobiyashi T. Congenital unilateral lower lip palsy. Acta Otolaryngol 88:303, 1979.

31. Kumagami H. Experimental facial nerve paralysis. Arch Otolaryngol 95:305, 1972.

32. Lilleyman JS, Antoniou AG, Sugden PJ. Facial nerve palsy in acute leukemia. Scand J Hematol 22:87, 1979.

33. Liston S, Kleid S. Histopathology of Bell's palsy. Laryngoscope 99:23, 1989.

34. May M. Red chorda tympani nerve and Bell's palsy. Laryngoscope 84:1507, 1974.

35. May M. Disorders in the newborn and children. In May M (ed). The Facial Nerve. New York, Thieme, 1986, p 405.

36. May M. Gold weight and wire spring implants as alternatives to tarsorrhaphy. Arch Otolaryngol Head Neck Surg 113:656, 1987.

37. May M, Fria TJ, Blumenthal F, Curtin H. Facial paralysis in children: differential diagnosis. Otolaryngol Head Neck Surg 89:841, 1981.

38. May M, Hardin WB. Facial palsy: interpretation of neurologic findings. Laryngoscope 88:1352, 1978.

39. May M, Hardin WB, Sullivan J, et al. Natural history of Bell's palsy; the salivary flow test and other prognostic indicators. Laryngoscope 86:704, 1976.

40. May M, Hardin WB, Sullivan J, et al. The use of steroids in Bell's palsy: a prospective controlled study. Laryngoscope 86:1111, 1976.

41. May M, Harvey JE, Marovitz WF, et al. The prognostic accuracy of the maximal stimulation test compared with that of the nerve excitability test in Bell's palsy. Laryngoscope 81:931, 1971.

42. May M, Harvey JE, Marovitz WF, et al. The prognostic accuracy of the maximal stimulation test compared with that of the nerve excitability test in Bell's palsy. Laryngoscope 81:931, 1976.

43. May M, Hoffman DF, Buerger GF. Management of the paralyzed lower eyelid by implanting auricular cartilage. Arch Otolaryngol Head Neck Surg 116:786, 1990.

44. May M, Klein SR, Taylor FH. Idiopathic (Bell's) facial palsy: natural history defies steroid or surgical treatment. Laryngoscope 95:406, 1985.

45. May M, Sobol S, Mester SJ. Managing segmental facial nerve injuries by surgical repair. Laryngoscope 100:1062, 1990.

46. May M, Sobol S, Mester S. Hypoglossal-facial nerve interpositional-jump graft for facial reanimation without tongue atrophy. Otolaryngol Head Neck Surg 104:818, 1991.

47. McHugh HE, Sowden KA, Levitt MN. Facial paralysis and muscle agenesis in the newborn. Arch Otolaryngol 89:131, 1969.

48. McKennan KX, Chole RA. Facial paralysis in temporal bone trauma. Am J Otol 13:167, 1992.

49. Mitchell DP, Stone P. Temporal bone fracture in children. Can J Otolaryngol 2:156, 1973.

50. Mulkens SJ, Breeker JD, Schroder FP, et al. Bell's palsy: a viral disease? An experimental study. In Portmann M, ed. Facial Nerve. New York, NY, Masson Publishing, 1985, p 227.

51. Murakami S, Mizobuchi M, Nakashiro Y, et al. Bell palsy and herpes simplex virus: identification of viral DNA in endoneurial fluid and muscle. Ann Intern Med 124(pt 1):27, 1996.

52. O'Brien BM, Pederson WC, Khazanchi RK, et al. Results of management of facial palsy with microvascular free-muscle transfer. Plast Reconstr Surg 86:12, 1990.

53. Olsen PZ. Prediction of recovery in Bell's palsy. Acta Neurol 52(Suppl 6):1, 1975.

54. Palva T, Hortling L, Ylikoski J, Collan Y. Viral culture and electron microscopy of ganglion cells in Meniere's disease and Bell's palsy. Acta Otolaryngol (Stockh) 86:269, 1978.

55. Parmalee AH. Molding due to intra-uterine posture: facial paralysis probably due to such molding. Am J Dis Child 42:443, 1931.

56. Peitersen E. The natural history of Bell's palsy. Am J Otol 4:107, 1982.

57. Pitts D, Adour K, Hilsinger R. Recurrent Bell's palsy: analysis of 140 patients. Laryngoscope 98:535, 1988.

58. Ramsey M, Dersimonian R, Holtel M, Burgess L. Corticosteroid treatment for idiopathic facial nerve paralysis: a meta analysis. Laryngoscope 110:335, 2000.

59. Rulon JT, Hallberg OE. Operative injuries to the facial nerve. Explanation for its occurrence during operations on the temporal bone and suggestions for its prevention. Arch Otolaryngol Head Neck Surg 76:131, 1962.

60. Sammarco JG, Ryan RF, Longenecker CG. Anatomy of the facial nerve in fetuses and stillborn infants. Plast Reconstr Surg 37:566, 1966.

61. Smith JD, Crumley R, Harker L. Facial paralysis in the newborn. Otolaryngol Head Neck Surg 89:1021, 1981.

62. Stankiewicz JA. A review of the published data on steroids and idiopathic facial paralysis. Otolaryngol Head Neck Surg 97:481, 1987.

63. Steele AC. Lyme disease. N Engl J Med 321:586, 1989.

64. Sunderland S. Nerve and Nerve Injuries, 2nd ed. London, Churchill Livingstone, 1978, pp 88–89, 96–97, 133.

65. Tschiassny K. Facial palsy, when complicating a case of acute otitis media, indicative for immediate mastoid operation? Cincinnati J Med 25:262, 1944.

66. Uri N, Greenberg E, Meyer W, Kitzes-Cohen R. Herpes zoster oticus: treatment with acyclovir. Ann Otol Rhinol Laryngol 101:161, 1992.

67. Voorhees RL, Zeitzer LD, Ross M. Hypertension and associated peripheral facial paralysis. Laryngoscope 82:899, 1972.

20

Congenital Anomalies of the External and Middle Ears

Makoto Miura, M.D., D.Med.Sc., Isamu Sando, M.D., D.Med.Sc., and Scott Thompson, M.D.

We owe a great debt for our knowledge of congenital anomalies of the ear to the early students of otohistopathology and their successors. Guild, Nager, Rüedi, and Lindsay stand out in any list of distinguished investigators in temporal bone disease. At the time when much of their work was done, the surgical techniques for correction of middle ear anomalies did not exist. The period of rapid development of otosurgical techniques that began in the early 1950s has continued to the present. Although much of this work has been focused on the treatment of chronic infectious disease, an important result of such study has been the development of procedures applicable to the correction of middle ear anomalies.

From studying the temporal bones of patients who suffered from many varied diseases, we know that congenital anomalies of the ear may be caused by genetic (familial) factors, chromosomal alterations in utero, and maternal infectious diseases. Agents that are related to the production of congenital anomalies may have an effect either on genetic material or directly on the developing otocyst anlagen. In many cases, congenital anomalies are of unknown origin, but by comparing the nature and extent of the anomaly and the normal embryonic development of the ear, we can determine the point in gestation at which the insult occurred in some cases.

The clinician must be cognizant of the association of certain anomalies with others. When one congenital anomaly is found, others must be sought. The use of a high-risk register for deafness is helpful in this regard.

For the otologic surgeon, knowledge of the associated occurrence of structural anomalies is imperative. In dealing with anomalous ears, failure to realize that the presence of a normal fallopian canal detected on computed tomographic (CT) scan does not ensure that the facial nerve lies within the canal has resulted in many surgical disasters.

The purpose of this chapter is to make the physician aware of the possibility of encountering anomalies of the external and middle ears during examinations and surgery. To do this, the anomalies are reviewed and discussed by grouping them according to their etiology (Classification I) and the anatomic structures involved (Classification II).

Classification of Diseases with Anomalies of the External and Middle Ears by Their Etiologic Factors (Classification I)

The diseases associated with anomalies of the external and middle ears can be classified by their origins into seven divisions.

- Diseases of Unknown Etiology
- Diseases Associated with Chromosomal Abnormalities
- Diseases with Mendelian Inheritance Patterns
- Diseases Associated with Prenatal Infections
- Diseases of Maternal Drug Abuse
- Diseases of Iatrogenic Ototoxicity
- Diseases Associated with Environmental Factors

Each of these classifications is dealt with in turn. Although some diseases have more than one etiologic factor or more than one mode of hereditary transmission, only one representative description is selected for each disease in this chapter.

Table 20–1 is a list of the diseases by eponym and pathologic name to assist the reader.

Diseases of Unknown Etiology

1. Aberrant Facial Nerve[*16] (M)†

The etiology of an aberrant facial nerve is unknown. This condition is thought to be rare and present at birth. It may be observed alone.

---

*The asterisk before a reference number indicates the report in which the temporal bone histopathologic findings are described.

Some of the information listed for the diseases in Classifications I and II may not be annotated by the reference listed. Only one recent, representative reference was permitted for each category of disease and anatomic structural anomaly; selected papers with the latest literature review were added in some cases.

TABLE 20–1. Diseases with Anomalies of the External and Middle Ears Listed by Traditional Name and Pathologic Defect

Traditional Name	Pathologic Defect
4.° Wildervanck syndrome	Cervico-oculoacoustic syndrome
20. Goldenhar syndrome	Oculoauriculovertebral spectrum
24. Turner syndrome	Gonadal aplasia
25. Patau syndrome	Trisomy 13–15 syndrome
26. Edwards syndrome	Trisomy 18 syndrome
27. Down syndrome	Trisomy 21 syndrome
29. Wolf-Hirschhorn syndrome	4p-syndrome
31. Apert syndrome	Acrocephalosyndactyly Type I
32. Saethre-Chotzen syndrome	Acrocephalosyndactyly Type III
33. Pfeiffer syndrome	Acrocephalosyndactyly Type V
35. Townes-Brocks syndrome	Anus imperforate with hand, foot, and ear anomalies
36. Alagille syndrome	Arteriohepatic dysplasia
38. Klippel-Feil syndrome	Brevicollis
39. Say syndrome	Cleft palate, microcephaly, large ears, and short stature
40. Pierre Robin syndrome	Cleft palate, micrognathia, and glossoptosis
42. Beals syndrome	Congenital contractural arachnodactyly
43. Möbius syndrome	Congenital facial diplegia
45. Fanconi syndrome	Constitutional aplastic pancytopenia with multiple anomalies
46. Crouzon disease	Craniofacial dysostosis
47. Pyle disease	Craniometaphyseal dysplasia
52. Léri-Weill syndrome	Dyschondrosteosis
54. Beckwith-Wiedemann syndrome	Exomphalos-macroglossia-gigantism syndrome
55. Aarskog syndrome	Faciodigitogenital syndrome
56. Hurler syndrome	Gargoylism
59. Levy-Hollister syndrome	Lacrimoauriculodentodigital syndrome
62. Treacher Collins syndrome	Mandibulofacial dysostosis
67. Mohr syndrome	Orofaciodigital syndrome Type II
68. Melnick-Needles syndrome	Osteodysplasty
70. Albers-Schönberg disease	Osteopetrosis
72. Potter syndrome	Renal agenesis, bilateral
75. DiGeorge syndrome	Third and fourth pharyngeal pouch syndrome

°The number indicates the disease as it is listed in the classification system in the first section of this chapter.

Many anomalies of the facial nerve have been reported. The nerve may be displaced anteroinferiorly, with or without the fallopian canal, and pass through the middle ear on either side of the stapes. It may run in a canal on the promontory inferiorly from the geniculate ganglion. Also, the nerve may be seen to split into two or three branches that continue separately in the descending (mastoid) portion of the nerve; this condition is frequently associated with hypoplasia of the nerve. Stapes anomalies, atresia of the external auditory canal, malformations of the pinna, and other anomalies may be seen with anomalies of the facial nerve.

Cases of facial nerve aberrations produce no specific audiometric findings.

†The numbers of the classification represent the diseases as we have designated them in the text. The following notations are used throughout the chapter: D, autosomal dominant hereditary disease; R, autosomal recessive hereditary disease; X, X-linked hereditary disease; E, anomalies observed in the external ear; M, anomalies observed in the middle ear; I, anomalies observed in the inner ear; O, anomalies observed in other parts of the body.

2. Anomalies of Ossicles[*][37, 106] (E, M)

This is a disorder of unknown etiology that is present at birth, but autosomal dominant inheritance has been reported in some cases. Ossicular anomalies can frequently be observed alone or with external ear anomalies, such as microtia and meatal atresia, although they may occur as a feature of various syndromes.

Mallear anomalies include absence of the malleus, deformed mallear head, triple bony union of the mallear handle with the long process of the incus and head of the stapes, and bony fusion of the incudomalleal joint. Incudal anomalies include absence of the incus, bony fusion of the short process of the incus with the horizontal semicircular canal wall, shortening of the long process of the incus, malformed long process of the incus, absence of the incudostapedial joint, bony fusion of the incudostapedial joint, and fibrous union of the incudostapedial joint. Stapes anomalies include absence of the stapes, absence of the head and crura of the stapes, small or fetal form of the stapes, columella-type stapes, bony fusion of the stapes head to the promontory, and stapes footplate fixation.

The major anomalies of the middle ear associated with ossicular anomalies include facial nerve anomalies, absence of the stapedial muscle, stapedial tendon and pyramidal eminence, and bony elongation of the pyramidal eminence. In cases of a congenitally fixed stapes footplate, an abnormally patent cochlear aqueduct may be present, which results in a gusher of cerebrospinal fluid if the footplate is removed at surgery.

Audiometric testing of individuals with ossicular anomalies reveals a unilateral or bilateral, nonprogressive, moderate to severe, flat-type conductive or mixed hearing loss.

3. Anomalous Internal Carotid Artery in Middle Ear[163] (M)

This is a disorder of unknown origin. It is rare; six cases have been described (five in girls and one in a boy) and it is present at birth. The condition is usually unilateral.

The middle ear shows a vascular mass in the anterior or inferior portion of the tympanum behind the tympanic membrane. There are no associated anomalies.

Clinical findings include pulsatile tinnitus with a bruit heard in the external auditory canal. The carotid arteriogram shows a small internal carotid artery coming up through the hypotympanum, turning abruptly forward beneath the stapes and the fallopian canal to head toward the area of the eustachian tube. CT scans do not show a normal carotid canal, and indentations are seen on the promontory. A conductive or mixed type of hearing loss may be present.

This condition may be confused with an aneurysm of the carotid artery or a glomus jugulare tumor.

4. Cervico-oculoacoustic Syndrome (Wildervanck Syndrome[40, 42]) (E, M, I, O)

This syndrome consists of congenital sensorineural deafness, Klippel-Feil anomaly (fusion of cervical vertebrae), and Duane retraction syndrome (deficient abduction with retraction on adduction). An overwhelming majority of patients with this disorder are female (male-to-female ratio 7:75), which has led to the idea that the mode of inheritance is X-linked dominant with lethality in the male. Nevertheless, multifactorial inheritance is considered to be most likely at present.

Anomalies of the external ear include preauricular tags, posteriorly displaced pinnae, small and deformed ears, and hypoplasia or absence of the external auditory canal. Middle-ear anomalies that have been reported are rudimentary ossicles, fusion of the malleus and incus, absence of the stapes and oval window, fixation of the stapes, and ossified stapedius tendon.

Abnormal semicircular canals, underdeveloped bony labyrinth, and stenosis or bony septum within the internal auditory canal may be observed in the inner ear and temporal bone.

Other associated anomalies and clinical findings, except for Klippel-Feil anomaly and Duane retraction syndrome, include facial asymmetry, torticollis, epibulbar dermoids, cleft palate, and low posterior hairline.

Audiometric tests usually reveal unilateral or bilateral, moderate to severe sensorineural or mixed hearing loss. Abnormal vestibular response is also common.

5. Clover Leaf Skull Syndrome (E, M, O)[°131]

This is a rare disorder of unknown etiology characterized by a trilobed skull resulting from congenital hydrocephalus associated with intrauterine synostosis of the coronal and lambdoidal sutures. Other diagnostic features of this syndrome include exophthalmus, abnormalities of extremities, low-set ears, and beak-like nose.

External and middle ear anomalies include narrowed external auditory canal and thickened and malformed stapes.

6. Coloboma, Heart Anomaly, Choanal Atresia, Retardation, and Genital and Ear Anomalies (CHARGE Association)[25, 43, 48, °71, °72, 134, 143, °201] (E, M, I, O)

Most cases with this condition are sporadic, although autosomal dominant and autosomal recessive inheritances have been reported in some cases.

External ear anomalies range from small ears without malformation of the pinna to cup-shaped lop ears. Low-set short and wide cup-shaped ears with a triangular concha, discontinuity between the anthelix and antitragus, small or absent earlobes, and "snipped-off" portions of the helical fold can be typically observed. Anomalies of the middle ear that have been reported are absence of the stapes superstructure, foreshortened incus with its long process missing, misshaped footplate of the stapes, absent stapedius tendon and pyramidal process, and absence of oval and round windows.

Inner ear anomalies associated with this syndrome that have been reported are Mondini dysplasia of the pars inferior, absence of the semicircular canals, short cochlea, and hypoplasia of the vestibular sense organs and nerves.

Except for ear anomalies, CHARGE association is characterized by colobomas of the eye, congenital heart anomalies (tetralogy of Fallot, atrial or ventricular septal defect, patent ductus arteriosus), atresia of the choanae, short stature due to retarded growth, developmental delay, mental retardation, central nervous system anomalies, and genital hypoplasia. Other associated anomalies include facial palsy, cleft palate, gastroesophageal reflux, esophageal atresia with tracheoesophageal fistula, and renal abnormalities.

Deafness in CHARGE association is usually of mixed type with a characteristic "wedge"-shaped audiogram that shows a descending bone conduction curve intersecting at low frequencies with a flat curve for air conduction. The conductive hearing loss is considered to result from ossicular anomalies and middle-ear effusions due to serous otitis media, which is common in this syndrome. As to the sensorineural hearing loss, retrocochlear and cochlear lesions are suspected. Vestibular dysfunction has also been reported.

7. Congenital Absence of Round Window[78] (M)

This anomaly is of unknown origin and is rare. It is present at birth and can be observed alone. The audiometric configuration of round window closure by itself is indistinguishable from that observed with oval window closure; there is a nonprogressive, moderate, flat, conductive hearing loss.

8. Congenital Aural Atresia,[9, 45, *83, 94] (E, M, I, O)

Congenital aural atresia with anomalies of the external and middle ears is a relatively common malformation. The frequency of moderate to severe forms have been estimated as 1 to 5 in 20,000 live births. Most of the cases are isolated and sporadic, although some familial cases of microtia and aural atresia with autosomal dominant and autosomal recessive modes of transmission have been reported. This anomaly affects boys more than girls. Unilateral atresia is more common than bilateral atresia and affects the right ear more frequently than the left. Congenital aural atresia is usually combined with anomalies of the pinna and the middle ear, occasionally with the inner ear anomalies and the other general anomalies. According to severity, aural atresia is classified to the following three groups:

Group 1 (mild): Some portion of the external auditory canal, although hypoplastic, is present. The tympanic bone is hypoplastic, and the eardrum is smaller than normal. The tympanic cavity is of normal size or hypoplastic.

Group 2 (moderate): The external auditory canal is completely absent, the tympanic cavity as a rule is diminished in size and its content deformed in varying degrees. The "atresia plate" is either completely or partially osseous.

Group 3 (severe): The external ear canal is absent, the middle ear cavity is markedly hypoplastic or completely missing. The atresia is more commonly bony rather than membranous.

External ear anomalies associated with atresia are deformed ears, microtia, and anotia. Middle ear anomalies associated with atresia include a misshaped tympanic membrane, replacement of the tympanic membrane by a bony plate, absence of the malleus and incus, fused malleus and incus, misshaped malleus and incus, lack of an incudostapedial connection, absence of the stapes head and crura, deformed stapes and crura, stapes footplate fixation, anomalous course of the chorda tympani nerve, absence of the lesser superficial petrosal nerve, hypoplastic and displaced tensor tympani muscle, persistent stapedial artery, hypoplastic tympanic cavity, and absence of the tympanic cavity. Lateral and anterior displacement of the descending portion of the facial nerve is common in aural atresia.

Inner ear anomalies include all degrees of deformity of the cochlea, vestibule, semicircular canals, and internal auditory meatus. Associated conditions include epilepsy,

mental retardation, internal hydrocephalus, posterior choanal atresia, hemifacial microsomia, cleft palate, and musculoskeletal and genitourinary anomalies.

Audiometric testing shows the presence of a nonprogressive maximal conductive loss with variable degrees of sensorineural loss, including total absence of hearing.

9. Congenital Cholesteatoma of the Middle Ear (Epidermoid of Middle Ear[84]) (E, M)

This is a lesion of unknown origin that is usually acquired but is occasionally congenital (approximately 2% to 4% of all cholesteatomas). Congenital cholesteatoma is most often unilateral and rarely bilateral, and it may often be found in young children without a history of the long-standing infection that is usually associated with the growth of acquired cholesteatoma.

The findings in the middle ear include an epidermoid mass found behind an intact tympanic membrane. The ossicles and bony walls of the tympanum may be eroded by this growth. Occasionally, cholesteatoma has been described in connection with atresia, appearing behind an atretic bony plate, and also in association with cup ears or ossicular anomalies including hypoplasia of the long process of the incus or superstructure of the stapes.

CT scans reveal areas of bone erosion by cholesteatoma in the petrous pyramid and mastoid region. A conductive hearing loss may result from involvement of the tympanic membrane or ossicles.

10. Congenital Heart Disease[*51, 160] (M, I, O)

Congenital heart disease is of unknown origin but is frequently associated with trisomies 13–15, 18, and 21, although no regular relationship between the chromosomal and cardiac anomalies has yet been established. Any major congenital heart defect may be associated with ear anomalies. Findings are present at birth.

Anomalies of the external ear include dysplastic low-set ears, preauricular tags, and atresia or stenosis of the external auditory canal. Middle ear anomalies include a bulky incus, wide angle of the facial genu, persistence of the stapedial artery, high jugular bulb, dehiscence of the facial canal, and remnants of mesenchymal tissue present in the middle ear.

Observed anomalies of the inner ear include shortened cochlea, thickened trabecular bone at the cribriform base of the cochlea, absence of the helicotrema, patent utriculoendolymphatic valve, complete absence of all semicircular canals, and simple outpouching of the lateral semicircular canal.

Other associated anomalies include scleral dermoid, cleft of the soft palate, Meckel diverticulum, duodenal atresia, absence of the spleen, supernumerary pulmonary lobulation, and absence of the kidney.

11. Congenital Perilymph Fistula[195] (M, I)

Perilymph fistula is a condition in which there is an abnormal communication between the perilymphatic space of the inner ear and the middle ear space. Through this communication, the perilymphatic fluids pass into the middle ear from the inner ear. This fistula can be classified as either congenital or acquired. The congenital fistula can be associated with various middle or inner ear anomalies.

The sites of the fistulas are varied, but most can be seen in the oval window area. Associated middle-ear anomalies include a malformation of the stapes superstructure, a defect in the stapes footplate, abnormalities about the orientation and the shape of the round window, and a malformed incus.

As to the inner ear anomalies, congenital perilymph fistula has been described in association with the Mondini deformity, a wide cochlear aqueduct, an enlarged vestibular aqueduct, a deformity of the fundus of the internal auditory canal, and a defect of Hyrtl fissure.

Clinically, sensorineural hearing loss that is sometimes fluctuating, progressive, or of sudden onset, and tinnitus, vertigo, and recurrent meningitis can be seen.

12. Cornelia de Lange Syndrome[46, 101, °172, °203] (E, M, I, O)

This is a disorder of unknown etiology characterized by multiple physical malformations (including low birth weight, hirsutism, synophrys, micrognathia, microbrachycephaly, and limb malformations) and mental retardation. Middle-ear anomalies include the remaining mesenchyme, dehiscence of the facial canal, and loose curve of the facial nerve around the geniculate ganglion. Inner-ear anomalies include short cochlea, dislocated vestibule, and dislocated spiral ganglion cells. Severe hearing loss has been reported in several cases.

13. Cryptotia[179] (E)

Cryptotia is of unknown etiology and is present at birth. It may be observed alone. This anomaly is rare. The pinna demonstrates fusion of the superior portion with the scalp.

14. Herniation of Jugular Bulb[181] (M)

This is a disorder of unknown origin and unknown prevalence. The anomaly is present at birth as a jugular bulb in the middle ear, occurring just below the oval window through the dehiscent floor of the middle ear. There are no associated anomalies and no audiometric findings. There is no specific treatment.

15. Imperforate Oropharynx with Costovertebral and Auricular Anomalies[57] (E, O)

The etiology of this disorder is unknown. As the auricular anomalies, malformed and malpositioned ears (cupped, low-set, and posteriorly angulated ears) have been reported.

Other anomalies include atresia of the oropharynx, which may be interpreted as resulting from failure of the buccopharyngeal membrane to rupture, and costovertebral anomalies.

16. Internal Carotid Artery Aneurysm[180] (M)

This is a disorder of unknown etiology and unknown prevalence; however, it is rare. It presents as a pulsatile smooth mass in the anteroinferior portion of the tympanic cavity. There are no known associated anomalies. It is sometimes symptomatic, with the patient complaining of pulsatile tinnitus. The diagnosis is aided by carotid arteriograms with subtraction studies. No specific treatment is required.

17. Kabuki Make-up Syndrome (Niikawa-Kuroki Syndrome[144]) (E, O)

This is a disorder of unknown etiology characterized by postnatal dwarfism, mental retardation, and specific craniofacial and skeletal malformations. It is considered that this syndrome may be a nongenetic disorder because of the absence of familial occurrence and normal karyotype. Most of the patients reported are Japanese children.

Ear anomalies observed are large, protruding, posteriorly rotated, and low-set ears.

Other common associated malformations include peculiar facies (arched eyebrow sparse in the lateral halves, long eyelashes, long palpebral fissures with ectropion of the lower eyelids, and broad or depressed nasal tip), widely spaced teeth, cleft or high-arched palate, low posterior hairline, retrognathia, fifth finger clinodactyly, scoliosis, and dislocation of the hip joint. Other clinical features include mental retardation, progressive shortness of stature, and susceptibility to infection.

The hearing loss has been reported in several cases.

18. Macrotia[179] (E)

Macrotia is of unknown etiology and may be observed alone. This anomaly is uncommon. Associated anomalies are rare.

19. Microtia[128] (E, M)

Microtia occurs in newborn infants with a population frequency of 0.03%. This anomaly is always associated with stenosis or atresia of the external auditory canal and frequently with ossicular anomalies. Most of the cases with congenital microtia and aural atresia are isolated and sporadic, although some familial cases with autosomal dominant and autosomal recessive modes of transmission have been reported. According to the severity, microtia is generally divided into the following three groups:

Grade I: malformed pinnae with smaller size than normal, showing, however, most of the characteristic features of the pinna.

Grade II: rudimentary pinnae consisting of a low, oblong elevation, hook-formed at the cranial end corresponding to the helix.

Grade III: more defective pinnae showing only a part of a malformed lobule, with absence of the rest of the pinna.

20. Oculoauriculovertebral Spectrum (Goldenhar Syndrome)[17, 33, 47, 55, °129, 147 °170, °196] (E, M, I, O)

Although this is a disorder of unknown origin, it is possibly due to a vascular abnormality during fetal life. Most cases are sporadic, but the possibility of autosomal recessive or autosomal dominant inheritance has also been reported. This condition affects the development of primarily the first and second branchial arch derivatives. Asymmetric appearance of the ear and face is considered to be one of the characteristic symptoms.

The findings in the external and middle ears include preauricular tags, deformity of the pinna, atresia of the external auditory canal, malformation or absence of ossicles, hypoplasia of the oval window, hypoplasia of the facial nerve, absence of the chorda tympani nerve, absence of the stapedius muscle, absence of the tensor tympani muscle and straightened tensor tympani tendon running past the absent cochleariform process. The eustachian tube anomalies include widely opened cartilaginous portion of the eustachian tube lumen and absence of the lateral lamina of the eustachian cartilage.

Anomalies of the inner ear include dysplasia and shortening of the lateral and superior semicircular canals and narrowing and shortening of the internal auditory meatus.

Other anomalies include unilateral facial hypoplasia, dermoids, lipodermoids, lipomas of the eyes, colobomas of the upper eyelid, and vertebral abnormalities.

21. Otocephaly[°22, °82] (E, M, I, O)

This is a lethal malformation of the first and second branchial arches characterized by mandibular hypoplasia or aplasia, ventromedial displacement of the external ear, microstomia, and hypoplasia or aplasia of the tongue.

External ear anomalies include low-set ears and dislocated external auditory canal.

Middle-ear anomalies include malrotation of the middle-ear structures, malformed and malpositioned ossicles, abnormal course of the facial nerve, large dehiscence of the facial canal, absence of the chorda tympani nerve, and abnormal course of the internal carotid artery.

Inner ear anomalies include incompletely developed otic capsule and cochlear bony dehiscence.

Other anomalies include central nervous system deformities, pharyngeal stenosis, renal anomalies, congenital heart disease, cyclopia and anomalies of the extremities.

22. Stapedius Tendon Ossification[69] (M)

This is a rare anomaly in which a solid bony bar in place of the normal stapedius tendon (extending from the pyramidal eminence to the neck of the stapes) is observed. The presence of the bony bar causes fixation of the stapes, resulting in congenital conductive hearing loss.

23. VATER Syndrome[°167] (M, I, O)

This syndrome is of unknown origin, but the most probable possibility is a single primary defect in the germinal center of disk morphogenesis leading to disorganization of the primitive streak and thus migration of early caudal mesoderm.

Anomalies in the middle ear include hypoplasia of the facial nerve, chorda tympani nerve, and greater superficial petrosal nerve; marked reduction of cells in the geniculate ganglion; anteriorly curved superstructure of the stapes; and hypertrophic anterior annular ligament.

Observed anomalies of the inner ear include irregular course of the lateral semicircular canal and duct; superiorly positioned utricle; abnormally high location of the saccule; large endolymphatic sinus, duct, and sac; and reduction in the population of spiral ganglion cells.

Other anomalies and clinical findings include vertebral defects, anal atresia, tracheoesophageal fistula with esophageal atresia, renal defects, radial limb dysplasia, large fontanelles, cardiac defects, single umbilical artery, and genital anomalies.

Diseases Associated with Chromosomal Abnormalities

24. Gonadal Aplasia (Turner Syndrome)[184, 194] (E, M, O)

Turner syndrome is a chromosomal aberration; in approximately half of the cases, the patients are sex-chromatin negative with a chromosomal configuration of XO. Mosaicism, X-chromosome deletion, isochromosomes and rings, and Y-chromosome deletions are also identified as the chromosomal basis for the phenotype. The overall prevalence of Turner syndrome in the female population is estimated at 1 in 5000.

Anomalies of the external ear include low-set ears, cup ears, large lobes, abnormal fusion of the inferior and superior crus of the anthelix, loss of the triangular fossa, and overhanging helical fold. Poor development of the mastoid air cell system, developmental malformations of the ossicles, and Mondini-type deformity have been reported in some cases.

Other anomalies and clinical findings include short stature, sexual infantilism attributed to gonadal dysplasia (primary amenorrhea and lack of development of secondary sexual characteristics), short and thick neck with a low hairline, pterygium colli, mandibular hypoplasia, narrowing of the maxilla with a high-arched palate, epicanthic folds, ptosis of the upper eyelids, antimongoloid palpebral slant, and narrowing at the root of the nose. Renal malformations, congenital heart disease, and skeletal anomalies can also be observed.

In the patients with Turner syndrome, it has been reported that serous otitis media is common from early childhood and is usually persistent; chronic suppurative otitis media often ensues. These middle-ear diseases cause a conductive hearing loss and, subsequently, a progressive cochlear hearing loss that results in a mixed hearing loss. In several cases, an audiometrically specific midfrequency sensorineural hearing loss that progresses in teenage years has been described.

25. Trisomy 13–15 Syndrome (Patau Syndrome)[171, 109] (E, M, I, O)

Trisomy 13–15 is a chromosomal aberration in which the somatic cells have an extra chromosome in the 13–15 group. The lesions are present at birth. The prevalence of this syndrome is 0.45 per 1000 births.

Findings in the external and middle ears include low-set malformed ears, stenotic external auditory canal, small tympanic membrane, thick manubrium of the malleus, distorted incudostapedial joint, deformed stapes, small facial nerve, wide angle of the facial genu, absence of the stapedial muscle and tendon, persistence of the stapedial artery, dehiscence of the facial canal, absence of the pyramidal eminence, absence of the antrum, small antrum, and small mastoid.

Anomalies of the inner ear include distorted and shortened cochlea, absence of the hook portion of the cochlea, malformed apical turn of the cochlea, absence of the modiolus, underdevelopment of the modiolus, malformed Rosenthal canal, scala communis between apical and middle cochlea turns, scala communis between middle and basal cochlea turns, underdevelopment of the osseous spiral lamina, malformed scala vestibuli with moderately small space in the basal turn, displacement and encapsulation of the tectorial membrane, large and patent cochlear aqueduct, unusual shape of the macule of the utricle, shortened utriculoendolymphatic valve, direct communication between the utricle and saccule, partial absence of the lateral limb of the superior semicircular canal, partial absence of the membranous superior semicircular canal, wide bony lateral semicircular canal, large ampulla of the membranous lateral semicircular canal, nearly flat crista of the membranous lateral semicircular canal, narrow lumen of the bony posterior semicircular canal, short and straight endolymphatic duct, shallow and wide internal auditory canal, spiral ganglion cells serving the basal turn located in the fundus of the internal auditory canal, and singular nerve entering the otic capsule from the posterior fossa by a separate canal.

Individuals with trisomy 13–15 syndrome may have other associated anomalies: microcephaly, arrhinencephaly, multiple eye anomalies, hypertelorism, cleft lip and palate, ventricular septal defect, abnormal palm print, simian creases, and hyperconvexity of the nails.

The diagnosis is proved by the karyotype, which shows 47 chromosomes with an extra chromosome in the 13–15 group. It arises as a result of nondisjunction of the chromosomes.

26. Trisomy 18 Syndrome (Edwards Syndrome)[77, 168] (E, M, I, O)

The symptoms of trisomy 18 syndrome are due to the presence of an extra chromosome in the 16–18 group. The findings are present at birth. The prevalence is 0.23 to 2 per 1000 births. It appears to be more common in infants born of older mothers.

Anomalies of the external and middle ears include low-set deformed ears, atretic external auditory canals, flat tympanic membranes, deformed malleus and incus, mal-formed stapes of the columella type or of a fetal form, split tensor tympani muscle in separate bony canals, exposed stapedial muscle in the middle-ear cavity, absence of the stapedial tendon, underdevelopment of the facial nerve, abnormal course of the facial and chorda tympani nerves, and absence of the pyramidal eminence.

Anomalies of the inner ear include incompletely developed modiolus, scala communis between apical and middle turns, underdeveloped cystic stria vascularis, absence of the utriculoendolymphatic valve, large utricle, partial defect of the anterior semicircular canal and crista, absence of the posterior semicircular canal, partial defect of the lateral semicircular canal, flat and macula-like crista of the lateral semicircular canal, enlarged endolymphatic duct, and double singular nerve.

Other associated anomalies include ptosis of the eyelids; high-arched palate; micrognathia; flexion deformities, such as the index finger overlapping the third finger; and hypertrophy of the pancreatic tissue. These patients generally show failure to thrive, mental retardation, and hypertonicity and have a poor prognosis.

Audiometric testing shows a failure to respond to sound.

27. Trisomy 21 Syndrome (Down Syndrome)[14, 21, 75, 90, 178, 183] (E, M, I, O)

The trisomy 21 syndrome is due to a chromosomal aberration in which the somatic cells have an extra chromosome in the 21–22 group. The findings are present at birth. The prevalence is 0.1 to 1.0 per 1000 births.

The findings in the external ear are small, malformed, and low-set pinnae and stenosis of the external auditory canal. Middle ear anomalies that have been reported include remnant of mesenchymal tissue, large dehiscence of the facial canal, wide angle of the facial genu, slightly bulky malleus and incus with a moderate amount of bone marrow, deformed stapes, slightly distorted crura of the stapes, somewhat underdeveloped pyramidal eminence, high jugular bulb, and poor development of the mastoid air cells. As to the eustachian tube, it has been reported in a fetus with this syndrome that the lumen was small and narrow, or collapsed, especially in the area from the midcartilaginous portion to the tympanic portion, and that the lateral lamina of the tubal cartilage was smaller than normal.

Associated anomalies in the inner ear include shortened cochlea, decreased population of the spiral ganglion cells, absence of the utriculoendolymphatic valve, wide utricular space and semicircular canal, wide cochlear aqueduct, hypogenesis of the posterior semicircular canal, and enlarged bony posterior canal ampulla.

Other associated anomalies include hypertelorism; epicanthic fold; slanting eyes; strabismus; narrowing of the nasal space; impaired development of the paranasal sinuses; protruding tongue; high palate; flattening of the skull; and cardiovascular malformations, such as a ventricular or atrial septal defect, patent ductus arteriosus, and situs inversus. Moderate to severe mental retardation can also be present.

Audiometric tests show the presence of a sensorineural, mixed, or conductive hearing loss. In the children with this syndrome, it is well known that otitis media with effusion frequently occurs and that it has been described in association with many factors, including tubal malfunction that may be caused by the tubal anomalies mentioned before, recurrent upper respiratory tract infections, and structural anomalies of the nasopharynx. Such middle-ear disease can be the main cause of conductive hearing loss.

28. Trisomy 22 Syndrome[∘12, ∘130] (E, M, I, O)

Trisomy 22 syndrome is due to an extra chromosome, which is derived from two identical segments of chromosome 22 consisting of satellites, the entire short arm, the centromere, and a tiny piece of the long arm.

Findings in the external and middle ears include low-set ears, preauricular pits and tags, aural atresia, lack of pneumatization of the middle ear, large dehiscence of the facial canal, absence of the stapedius muscle, absence of the stapes and oval window, and bony closure of the round window niche. The eustachian tube anomalies include widely developed medial lamina of the eustachian tube cartilage, undeveloped lateral lamina of the eustachian tube cartilage and absence of attachment of the tensor veli palatini muscle to the eustachian tube cartilage.

Anomalies of the inner ear include shortened cochlea, incompletely developed modiolus, rudimentary osseous spiral lamina, hypoplastic saccule, and short and wide lateral semicircular canal.

Other associated anomalies include mild mental deficiency; mild hypertelorism; downslanting palpebral fissures; inferior coloboma of the iris, choroid, retina, or all three; micrognathia; cardiac defects; renal agenesis; and anal atresia.

29. 4p-Syndrome (Wolf-Hirschhorn Syndrome)[204] (E, O)

This syndrome results from deletion of the short arm of chromosome 4 and is characterized by severe psychomotor and growth retardation.

Anomalies of the external ear include low-set ears, poorly differentiated ("simple") cup-shaped ears, preauricular pits, and narrow external auditory canals.

Other manifestations include microcephaly, hypertelorism, strabismus, epicanthic folds, antimongoloid slant, cleft lip-palate, prominent glabella, beaked nose with a broad base, scalp defects, congenital heart malformations, cryptorchidism, hypospadias, and severe mental retardation. Seizures have been reported in 70% of the patients.

Diseases with Mendelian Inheritance Patterns

30. Achondroplasia (Chondrodystrophia Fetalis)[∘173] (D, M, I, O)

Achondroplasia is a hereditary dominant disorder with many sporadic cases and is probably the result of mutation. It is also seen as a recessive trait in rare instances. The onset of the anomalies occurs in fetal life. The disor-

der occurs in 1 of 10,000 newborn infants and 1 of 50,000 in the general population.

Anomalies of the middle ear associated with achondroplasia include fusion of the ossicles to the surrounding bony structures and the appearance of dense, thick trabeculae without islands of cartilage in the endochondral bone and periosteal bone.

Associated anomalies of the inner ear include a deformed cochlea and thickened intercochlear partitions. Other associated anomalies include dwarfism due to imperfect ossification within the cartilage of the long bones, which results in shortening of the extremities, with the proximal bones being more affected than the distal bones. Many of these patients die at birth or shortly thereafter.

The hearing loss associated with this disorder has been described as being either conductive or mixed.

31. Acrocephalosyndactyly Type I (Apert Syndrome)[∘114] (D, M, I, O)

This disorder is apparently transmitted as an autosomal dominant trait. It appears to be associated with a high mutation rate and has been related to increasing parental age. The malformation occurs in 1 in 100,000 to 1 in 160,000 live births, and the manifestations are present at birth.

There are no reports of external ear anomalies. The middle ear anomaly associated with this disorder is fixation of the stapedial footplate. Inner ear anomalies include a patent cochlear aqueduct, an enlarged internal auditory canal, and an unusually large subarcuate fossa that connects to the middle fossa dura.

Other associated anomalies reported include craniofacial dysostosis, brachiocephaly, hypertelorism, bilateral proptosis, saddle nose, high-arched palate, spina bifida, ankylosis of the joints, and syndactyly.

The audiometric findings are usually those of a flat conductive hearing loss, although a sensorineural component is suspected in some cases.

32. Acrocephalosyndactyly Type III (Saethre-Chotzen Syndrome)[1] (D, E, O)

This disorder is inherited as an autosomal dominant trait and is characterized by acrocephaly, asymmetry of the skull and face, and mild soft tissue syndactyly of hands and feet. As to the ear anomalies, small ears, low-set ears, an unusually prominent crus and anthelix, and small external auditory canals have been reported.

Other associated anomalies include parrot-beaked nose, deviation of the nasal septum, ptosis, strabismus, stenosis of the lacrimal duct, and high-arched palate.

33. Acrocephalosyndactyly Type V (Pfeiffer Syndrome)[38, 191] (D, M, O)

The mode of inheritance of this disorder is autosomal dominant. It is characterized by acrocephalosyndactyly with broad thumbs and broad big toes. Associated external and middle-ear anomalies that have been reported include stenotic external auditory canal, ankylosis of the stapes, fixation of the incus in the epitympanum, and hypoplastic tympanic cavity and mastoid.

Other characteristics include craniofacial dysostosis with acrobrachycephaly, hypertelorism, hypoplasia of the maxilla, high-arched palate, prominent mandible, dental abnormalities, and deformities of the first metatarsal and the first phalanx.

The degree of hearing loss varies from mild to severe. Many cases demonstrate conductive hearing loss.

34. Anencephaly[10, 63] (R, E, M, I, O)

This anomaly is a hereditary recessive disorder and consists of complete or incomplete absence of the forebrain and midbrain. Anencephaly accompanies acrania, which is described as holocrania or meroacrania on the basis of the degree of the osseous changes. The prevalence of this disease is 1 in 1000 births.

Anomalies of the external and middle ears include small stapes footplate, exposed facial nerve, hypoplasia of the intratympanic muscles, persistent stapedial artery, dehiscence of the facial canal, and small oval window.

Inner ear anomalies include shortened cochlea, underdeveloped modiolus, scala communis between middle and basal cochlea turns, communication between the bony lateral canal and the posterior canal, and unusually narrow or wide internal auditory canal.

Other associated anomalies reported are spina bifida and amelia.

35. Anus Imperforate with Hand, Foot, and Ear Anomalies (Townes-Brocks Syndrome)[107, 190] (D, E, M, O)

This is a hereditary autosomal dominant disorder characterized by anorectal malformations with hand, foot, and ear anomalies.

Anomalies of the external ear include satyr ears, cup-shaped ears, large ears, microtia, and overfolded superior helix. Preauricular tags, auricular pits, pretragal sinus, and cheek skin tags may also be observed. Ossicular malformations, narrowed oval window, and mixed hearing loss have been reported in one patient.

Anorectal malformations, which are the most common anomalies, include imperforate anus with or without fistula, covered anus, anal stenosis, anteriorly placed anus, and excess skin around the anus. Other associated anomalies include hand anomalies, such as preaxial hexadactyly and triphalangeal thumb, and foot, urorenal, and cardiac anomalies.

Hearing loss has been reported in about one third of the patients, and audiometric examinations usually demonstrate sensorineural hearing loss.

36. Arteriohepatic Dysplasia (Alagille Syndrome)[141] (D, E, M, I, O)

This disorder is characterized by intrahepatic cholestasis; cardiovascular, ocular, and vertebral anomalies; and facial dysmorphism. The inheritance pattern appears to be au-

tosomal dominant with variable expression and reduced penetrance.

The reported external ear anomaly is large ears with helices that are incompletely folded. Anomalies of the middle ear include bulky incus and stapes and immature interossicular joints.

Inner ear anomalies include dysplasia of the cochlea, partial or total absence of posterior and anterior semicircular canals, and absence or stenosis of the cochlear aqueduct.

Intrahepatic cholestasis is due to a paucity of intrahepatic bile ducts, and the most common cardiovascular anomaly is peripheral pulmonary artery stenosis. Other associated anomalies and clinical findings include characteristic facies consisting of prominent forehead, hypertelorism with deep-set eyes, small chin and saddle or straight nose, "butterfly-like" vertebrae, narrow interpedicular distance, posterior embryotoxon, and growth and mental retardation.

37. Branchio-otorenal Dysplasia (Branchio-otorenal Syndrome)[30, 56, 124] (D, E, M, I, O)

This disorder is inherited as an autosomal dominant trait and occurs at an approximate prevalence of 1 of 40,000 newborn infants. It is characterized by preauricular pits, auricular malformations, hearing loss, cervical fistulas or cysts, and renal abnormalities, but not all of these manifestations are always present.

Anomalies of the external ears include small ears, low-set ears, cup-shaped anteverted pinnae, and preauricular pits or fistulas. Main anomalies in the middle ear are malformation and fixation of the ossicles, including shortening of the manubrium of the malleus or of the long process of the incus, bulky malleus and incus, absence of the stapes, fixation of malleus and incus into the attic, dysplasia or fixation of the stapedial footplate, and lateral displacement of the ossicles. A small middle-ear cavity, absence of the oval window or the stapedial muscle tendon, abnormally large and deep oval window niche, and hypoplastic facial nerve with a large dehiscence of the bony canal may also be observed. The patients may have facial nerve paralysis.

Inner ear anomalies observed radiologically include dilated vestibule, small semicircular canals, saccular wide appearance of the lateral canal, hypoplasia of the cochlea, and dilatation of the endolymphatic duct. Histopathologic findings in the inner ear include lack of the ampulla and the crista in the lateral canal, termination of the posterior canal at a short distance from the ampulla, small cochlear cavity, dislocation and small populations of the spiral ganglion cells, and slightly deformed and partly atrophic stria vascularis.

Other possible associated anomalies include cervical fistulas or cysts, renal abnormalities, long narrow facies, stenosis or atresia of the lacrimal duct, and retrognathia. Cervical fistulas or cysts are generally situated below the level of the hyoid and just anterior to the sternocleidomastoid muscle. Renal abnormalities include malformations ranging in severity from mild renal hypoplasia to renal agenesis, distorted calyceal system, and abnormalities of position and rotation of the kidney. Severe renal dysplasia occurs in about 6% of the affected persons.

The hearing loss of varying severity is one of the constant findings and may be conductive (30%), sensorineural (20%), or mixed (50%). It may be present at birth or may develop during childhood or adolescence.

38. Brevicollis (Klippel-Feil Syndrome)[123, 139, 155, 198] (R, E, M, I, O)

Brevicollis is a hereditary disorder that appears to be due to a recessive gene, although the X-linked trait that is lethal in males or dominant inheritance is also suggested. This rare disease is characterized by fusion of several cervical vertebrae with associated pectoral girdle deformities. The cause of this disorder is considered to be faulty mesodermal differentiation at about the second month of gestation.

Anomalies of the external ear include low-set ears, microtia, presence of a preauricular appendage, and atresia or narrowing of the external auditory canal. Middle-ear anomalies include absence of ossicles, slitlike malleoincudal joint, short process of the incus fused to the floor of the attic, long process of the incus attached to the stapes by fibrous tissues without any sign of a lenticular process, elongated stapes with its anterior crus fused to the cochleariform process, fixation of the stapes to the oval window, and fistula of the stapes footplate. An abnormal course of the facial nerve may be observed.

Inner ear anomalies include rudimentary cochlea (a short, curved, single tube extending from the vestibule), rudimentary modiolus, dilated semicircular canals, wide communication between the saccule and the utricle, poorly developed and shallow internal auditory canal, internal auditory canal more superiorly positioned than normal, absence of statoacoustic nerve in the internal auditory canal, and vestigial inner ear.

Other associated anomalies include a congenital numeric reduction of the cervical vertebrae due to fusion of the vertebral bodies, spina bifida, and a Sprengel scapular deformity. There is a short, almost immobile neck with prominent soft tissue and the hairline extending down to the back.

Deafness is the second most common finding in this disorder and is of the sensorineural, conductive, or mixed type. The syndrome that comprises Klippel-Feil anomaly (fusion of cervical vertebrae), Duane retraction syndrome (deficient abduction with retraction on adduction), and congenital sensorineural hearing loss is known as cervicooculoacoustic syndrome or Wildervanck syndrome. An absence of vestibular function is also frequently observed.

39. Cleft Palate, Microcephaly, Large Ears, and Short Stature (Say Syndrome)[2] (D, E, O)

This syndrome has been reported in only two families thus far. The mode of inheritance is considered to be probably autosomal dominant.

Reported anomalies of the external ear are large pro-truding ears with a prominent anthelix, a poorly formed antitragus, and a notch on the superior helix.

Other associated anomalies and clinical findings include cleft palate, microcephaly, short stature, digital anomalies, proximal renal tubular acidosis with cystic renal dysplasia, and developmental delay.

40. Cleft Palate, Micrognathia, and Glossoptosis (Pierre Robin Syndrome)[73, 89] (D, E, M, I, O)

This is a hereditary disorder that may also result from an intrauterine insult in the first trimester. When hereditary, the syndrome is probably inherited as an autosomal dominant trait with variable penetrance. The prevalence is 1 in 30,000 live births. The findings are present at birth.

Anomalies of the external ear include cup ears and low-set ears. Anomalies of the middle ear include thickened stapes crura and footplate, small facial nerve, dehiscence of the facial canal, absence of the middle ear and extremely suppressed mastoid pneumatization.

Inner ear anomalies observed are a scala communis between the apical and middle cochlear turns, an underdeveloped modiolus, an abnormally narrow communication between the crus commune and the utricle, a superior dislocation of the crus commune and the posterior semicircular canal, and a small internal auditory canal.

Other associated findings include mental retardation, hydrocephalus, microcephaly, microphthalmia, myopia, congenital cataracts, esotropia, retinal detachment, sixth nerve palsy, Mobius syndrome, cleft palate, hypoplasia of the mandible, displacement of the tongue backward and downward, congenital heart anomalies, spina bifida, hip dislocation, syndactyly, and clubfoot.

Conductive hearing loss, especially attributable to otitis media with effusion, has been found to be associated with this disorder.

41. Cleidocranial Dysostosis[58] (D, E, M, O)

This is a hereditary autosomal dominant disorder. The findings are present at birth.

Anomalies of the external and middle ears include small pinna, atresia of the external auditory canal, narrow external auditory canal, small ossicles, absence of the manubrium of the malleus, absence of the long process of the incus, fixation of the stapes footplate, and small tympanic cavity.

Associated anomalies include aplasia of the clavicle, overdevelopment of the transverse diameter of the cranium, and retardation of ossification of the fontanelles.

Audiometric tests may reveal a sensorineural hearing loss.

42. Congenital Contractural Arachnodactyly (Beals Syndrome)[52, 154] (D, E, O)

This disorder is characterized by autosomal dominant inheritance, deformed pinnae, arachnodactyly, camptodactyly, and limited extension of the knees and elbows. The deformity of the pinnae is due to extra convolutions of the helix and has been described as "crumpled" ears.

43. Congenital Facial Diplegia (Möbius Syndrome)[99, 116, *165] (D, E, M, I, O)

This disorder may be either genetic or nongenetic in etiology; on a genetic basis, it appears to be of the autosomal dominant type. Parental consanguinity and the possibility of recessive inheritance have also been suggested. Most patients have no family history of the disease. It is rare. The main characteristic clinical findings associated with this syndrome are the inability to close the eyes and to suckle, which are due to bilateral congenital facial nerve paralysis.

Anomalies of the external ear include microtia and slight atresia of the external auditory canal. Some form of auricular malformation is seen in 15% of patients. Anomalies of the middle ear include an ossicular mass without a clearly identifiable stapes, oval window, or round window at surgical exploration and absence of the facial nerve.

Anomalies of the inner ear that have been observed radiologically include a dilated vestibule and canal system.

Other associated anomalies are absence of the abductors of the eye; aplasia of the brachial and thoracic muscles; anomalies of the extremities; and involvement of the cranial nerves, especially of the oculomotor, trigeminal, facial, and hypoglossal nerves.

On audiometric examination, deafness has been reported in 15% of individuals with this syndrome. Electromyographic studies show that motor unit activity in the facial and extraocular muscles is decreased.

44. Congenital Heart Disease, Deafness, and Skeletal Malformation[59] (D, E, M, O)

This disorder is inherited as an autosomal dominant trait. Its prevalence is unknown. Anomalies of the external and middle ear include a narrowed and oblique external auditory canal and fixation of the stapes footplate in the oval window.

Associated anomalies and clinical findings include fusion of the carpal and tarsal bones and mild to moderate mitral insufficiency. Audiometric tests show a moderate congenital conductive hearing loss.

45. Constitutional Aplastic Pancytopenia with Multiple Anomalies (Fanconi Syndrome)[76, 121] (R, E, M, O)

Fanconi syndrome consists of congenital abnormalities and aplastic anemia. This is a hereditary autosomal recessive disorder. External ear anomalies include atresia of the external ear. Anomalies of the middle ear include fixation of the stapedial footplate.

Inner ear anomalies include hypodevelopment of the hook portion of the cochlea and reduced overall length of the cochlear duct. Other associated anomalies include

skin pigmentation, skeletal deformities, renal anomalies, and mental retardation.

46. Craniofacial Dysostosis (Crouzon Disease)[36, *108, 153] (D, E, M, O)

Craniofacial dysostosis is a hereditary autosomal dominant disorder. It is a rare condition. This disease is characterized by premature craniosynostoses, midfacial hypoplasia with relative mandibular prognathism, ocular malformations, and aural malformations.

Anomalies of the external ear reported to be associated with this disease are rotated ears, low-set ears, atresia or stenosis of the external auditory canal, and microtia. Anomalies of the middle ear include absence of the tympanic membrane, ankylosis of the malleus to the outer wall of the epitympanum, deformed stapes with bony fusion to the promontory, distortion and narrowing of the middle-ear space, narrow round window niche, underdevelopment of the periosteal portion of the labyrinth, and greatly reduced periosteal layer of the petrous bone.

Other associated anomalies consist of craniosynostosis involving the coronal, sagittal, and lambdoid sutures with increased intracranial pressure, small maxillae, relative mandibular prognathism, exophthalmos, ocular hypertelorism, external strabismus, parrot-beaked nose, short upper lip, high-arched or cleft palate, stylohyoid ligament calcification, and cervical spine and elbow abnormalities.

Audiometric findings reveal that approximately one third of the patients with this syndrome have a hearing loss that is usually nonprogressive and conductive in nature. It is also suggested that the patients with Crouzon disease are at increased risk for acquired middle-ear diseases, such as otitis media with effusion and chronic otitis media, because of their eustachian tube dysfunction.

47. Craniometaphyseal Dysplasia (Pyle Disease)[108] (D, M, I, O)

This hereditary autosomal disorder is rare; some cases have appeared to be inherited as an autosomal recessive trait. The disorder becomes evident clinically in early childhood and is progressive.

Anomalies of the middle ear include encasement of the malleus in bone from the promontory, deformed incus fixed by bone to the promontory, stapes head in an oval window filled with bone, and enlargement of the chorda tympani nerve.

The inner ear anomaly most frequently observed is constriction of the internal auditory meatus.

Associated anomalies and clinical findings include hypertelorism, deformity of the nasal dorsum, saddle nose, prognathism, posterior choanal atresia, defective dentition, metaphyseal widening of the long bones, nystagmus, optic atrophy, seventh nerve palsy, narrowing of the nasal passage, obliteration of the paranasal sinus, and obstruction of the nasolacrimal duct.

Audiometric tests have shown a sensorineural, high-frequency sloping loss with an associated large conductive loss. No results of vestibular tests on such individuals have been reported.

48. Cryptophthalmos with Other Malformations (Cryptophthalmos-Syndactyly Syndrome)[189] (R, E, O)

This is a hereditary autosomal recessive disorder of cryptophthalmos associated with syndactyly; renal agenesis; genital anomalies; abnormalities of the nose, ears, and larynx; skeletal defects; and mental retardation. External ear anomalies include malformed or low-set ears, fusion of the superior margin of the helix to the scalp (cryptotia), microtia, and stenosis or atresia of the external auditory canals.

49. Dominant Proximal Symphalangia and Hearing Loss[192] (D, E, M, O)

This disease is inherited as an autosomal dominant trait with variable penetrance. Anomalies of the external and middle ear include stenotic external auditory meatus, elongated long process of the incus, and fusion of the stapes to the petrous bone.

Associated anomalies include symphalangia involving the proximal interphalangeal joints, most marked at the ulnar digits. Audiometric tests reveal a conductive hearing loss.

50. Duane Retraction Syndrome (Duane Syndrome)[146, 186] (D, E, M, O)

This syndrome involves autosomal dominant inheritance, but multifactorial or autosomal recessive inheritance is most likely in several cases. It is more frequent in girls. The pathogenesis of this disorder is still unknown, although congenital aberrant innervation of the lateral rectus muscle has been suggested as the cause in some reports.

Anomalies of the external ear include preauricular skin tags, malformed pinnae, microtia, and hypoplasia or atresia of the external auditory canal. Middle-ear anomalies reported are various malformations of the ossicles, such as fusion of the ossicles, lack of contact of the fused ossicles with the oval window, closure of the oval window by a thin membrane, and an ossicular mass that does not connect to the stapes.

Also seen in this disorder are limitation or absence of abduction, restriction of adduction, retraction of the globe on adduction, and narrowing of the palpebral fissure on adduction. The condition is usually unilateral and most often occurs on the left side. Other congenital ocular abnormalities include nystagmus, epibulbar dermoids, ptosis, and anisocoria. Besides these abnormalities, skeletal deformities (hemifacial microsomia, hypoplasia of extremities, thoracic scoliosis), congenital skin lesions such as hemangiomas, central nervous system disorders (hypotonia, convulsion), and genitourinary anomalies may be observed.

The hearing loss can be conductive, sensorineural, or mixed. The syndrome that comprises Duane retraction syndrome (deficient abduction with retraction on adduction), Klippel-Feil anomaly (fusion of cervical vertebrae), and congenital sensorineural hearing loss is known as cervico-oculoacoustic syndrome or Wildervanck syndrome.

51. Dubowitz Syndrome[91] (R, E, O)

This syndrome is inherited as an autosomal recessive trait and is characterized by psychomotor retardation, microcephaly, facial and skeletal anomalies, and eczema. Its common ear anomalies are large and prominent ears.

Facial abnormalities include long narrow faces, long slanting forehead, large and long nose, ptosis, blepharophimosis, and retromicrognathia. A high-pitched, hoarse voice seems to be a constant feature. Skeletal anomalies such as brachyclinodactyly of the fifth finger and syndactyly of the second and third toes, dental anomalies, and genital anomalies can be present. Various degrees of mental retardation and abnormal behavior, such as hyperactivity, can also be observed.

52. Dyschondrosteosis (Léri-Weill Syndrome, Madelung Deformity)[138] (D, E, M, O)

This is a hereditary autosomal dominant disorder characterized by short-limbed dwarfism of the mesomelic type and deformity of the distal radius and ulna and proximal carpal bones. The wrist deformity is often referred to as Madelung deformity, which is caused by failure of development of the distal radial epiphysis on its medial side.

External and middle ear anomalies associated with a conductive hearing loss, including narrow external auditory canal, absence of the malleus, small vestigial incus, and deformed stapes, have been reported.

53. Ectrodactyly, Ectodermal Dysplasia, and Cleft Lip-Palate (EEC Syndrome)[158, 159] (D, E, M, O)

This is an autosomal dominant syndrome characterized by ectrodactyly, ectodermal dysplasia, cleft lip-palate, and lacrimal duct abnormalities.

Anomalies of the external ear include large and protruding ears, a periauricular tag, a vertical crease at the junction of the helix with the antitragus, and an ovoid depression on the posterior rim of the helix. Middle-ear anomalies that have been reported are absence of the stapes and part of the incus and absence of the incus.

As a form of ectrodactyly, the split hand and foot or "lobster-claw" deformity, in which the central ray of the hand and foot are absent, can be present. Ectodermal dysplasia involves various skin abnormalities, trichodysplasia, dental anomalies, onychodysplasia, and dyshidrosis. Other manifestations include genitourinary anomalies, nipple anomalies, and mental retardation.

Conductive deafness is one of the common features of this syndrome, but sensorineural hearing loss and vestibular hypofunction have also been reported.

54. Exomphalos-Macroglossia-Gigantism Syndrome (Beckwith-Wiedemann Syndrome)[145] (D, E, M, O)

This syndrome is inherited as an autosomal dominant trait. Exomphalos, macroglossia, and gigantism as well as the external ear anomalies are cardinal signs of this disorder. Associated external ear anomalies are earlobe creases and posterior helical ear pits; as to the middle-ear anomaly, fixation of the stapes was revealed in some patients in whom conductive deafness was reported.

Other anomalies and clinical findings include facial nevus flammeus; midface hypoplasia; visceromegaly of the liver; kidney, spleen, and genitourinary anomalies; advanced bone age; and neonatal hypoglycemia.

55. Faciodigitogenital Syndrome (Aarskog Syndrome)[86] (X, E, O)

This syndrome is characterized by short stature and anomalies of the facies, digits, and genitalia. The mode of inheritance of this disorder is thought to be X-linked recessive. The external ear anomaly is typically a thick and down-turned superior helix.

Other facial abnormalities include a broad and round face, hypertelorism, ptosis, hypoplastic maxilla, and broad philtrum. Anomalies of hands, feet, and genitalia include brachydactyly, clinodactyly of the fifth fingers, interdigital skin webbing, simian crease, clubbing of toe, broad forefoot, shawl-form scrotum, cryptorchidism, and inguinal hernia.

56. Gargoylism (Hurler Syndrome)[*62, *103] (R, E, M, O)

Gargoylism is inherited as an autosomal recessive, sometimes X-linked disorder and was the first of the genetic mucopolysaccharidoses to be recognized. The clinical findings become manifest by 1 year of age.

The external ear anomaly usually included in this syndrome is low-set ears. Anomalies of the middle ear include absence of the incudomalleal joint, deformed stapes, fibrous tissue invasion into the otic capsule with the presence of "gargoyle cells," multiple bony outgrowths into the middle ear, small middle-ear space filled with mesenchymal tissue, obliteration of the oval window and round window areas by mesenchymal tissue, small mastoid antrum, poor development of the mastoid air cell system, and hypertrophy of the mucosa.

Other associated anomalies and clinical findings include dwarfism, hepatosplenomegaly, corneal clouding, and mental deficiency. These patients frequently have large, deformed heads with hypertelorism, prominent eyebrows, saddle nose, wide nostrils, long mouth, high palate, thick lips and tongue, widely spaced teeth, and prominent chin. Also seen are optic nerve atrophy, hypertrichosis, short neck, deformed thorax, lumbar kyphosis, prominent abdomen, hernia, limitation of joint movements, and broad hands with stubby fingers.

The diagnosis is made on the basis of the presence of mucopolysaccharides (dermatan sulfate and heparan sulfate) in the urine. These same substances may be seen in the tissues. In the autosomal recessive type, deafness is seen in 5.2% of individuals. In the X-linked recessive type, which is rare, deafness is seen in 43% of individuals.

57. Hallux Syndactyly-Ulnar Polydactyly-Abnormal Earlobe Syndrome[66] (D, E, O)

This disorder is inherited as an autosomal dominant trait. External ear anomalies associated with this syndrome include a deep horizontal groove or a nodule on the earlobe.

Other associated anomalies include webbed toes, partial toe syndactyly, and absence of the middle phalanx. Neither audiometric nor vestibular test results have been reported in such cases.

58. Knuckle Pads, Leukonychia, and Deafness[15] (D, M, O)

This disease is inherited as an autosomal dominant trait. The knuckle pad manifestation appears in childhood. Anomalies of the middle ear include absence of the ossicles and facial nerve, high jugular bulb, and absence of the facial canal.

Audiometric and vestibular examinations reveal sensorineural and mixed hearing losses and hypoactive vestibular responses.

59. Lacrimoauriculodentodigital Syndrome (Levy-Hollister Syndrome)[85, 113] (D, E, I, O)

This syndrome is inherited as an autosomal dominant trait. It is characterized by malformations of the lacrimal system, auricular anomalies, hearing loss, dental anomalies, and upper limb malformations. At least some of the manifestations are present at birth, but there is a great variation in phenotypic expression.

The most characteristic anomaly of the external ear is a simple cup-shaped ear with a short helix and undeveloped anthelix. Narrow external auditory canal and preauricular appendage have also been reported.

Middle-ear anomalies include ossicular deformity such as defect of the stapes head and absence of the oval window.

Inner ear anomalies include hypoplastic cochlea and modiolar deficiency.

Anomalies of the lacrimal system include nasolacrimal duct obstruction, hypoplasia or aplasia of the lacrimal puncta, and hypoplasia or aplasia of the lacrimal glands; epiphora or dry-eye symptoms may be observed. Dental anomalies include hypodontia, peg-shaped incisors, and enamel hypoplasia. Discoloration, excessive wear, and premature decay of the teeth frequently occur. Upper limb anomalies are the most common and variable and typically consist of a radial ray defect. Tapering of the thumb and clinodactyly of the fifth finger are frequently observed. Other possible associated anomalies include hypoplasia or aplasia of the major salivary glands, lower limb malformations, and renal anomalies that have been described in some cases.

The hearing loss is mainly of the mixed type with varying severity.

60. Larsen Syndrome[117] (R, M, O)

This syndrome is characterized by multiple joint dislocations and characteristic facial abnormalities. It is considered to be inherited as an autosomal recessive trait, although a dominant pattern of transmission has also been recognized in some cases.

As to the middle-ear anomalies, a bulbous lenticular process of the incus, incudostapedial joint laxity, and fixation of the stapes footplate have been reported in one case.

The specific skeletal abnormalities include anterior dislocation of the knee, dislocation of the hip and elbows, equinovarus or equinovalgus deformity of the feet, and nontapering cylindric fingers with spatulate thumbs. The facial abnormalities consist of hypertelorism, frontal bossing, and depressed nasal bridge.

The hearing loss is usually of the conductive type.

61. Lenz Microphthalmia[65] (X, E, O)

This is an X-linked dysmorphogenic syndrome of microphthalmia associated with multiple congenital malformations and clinical features, which are characterized by microcephaly, vertebral and dental anomalies, renal and urogenital abnormalities, digital defects, ear anomalies, and mental retardation. Anomalies of the external ear include "simple" pinnae with minimal convolutions and anteverted ears.

62. Mandibulofacial Dysostosis (Treacher Collins Syndrome)[28, 108, 148, 152, °169] (D, E, M, I, O)

Mandibulofacial dysostosis is a hereditary disorder of the first and second branchial arch and its derivatives. It is of dominant inheritance, but in 60% of cases it is secondary to a recent mutation. The cause of the abnormalities of this disease is probably deficient migration of the neural crest cells into the branchial arches.

Associated anomalies of the ear are predominantly observed in the external and middle ears. External ear anomalies include various auricular deformities and atresia or stenosis of the external auditory canal. Anomalies of the middle ear include replacement of the tympanic membrane by a bony plate and deformities of the malleus, incus, and stapes. Other anomalies are absence of the tensor tympani muscle, stapedius muscle, tendon of the stapedius muscle, pyramidal eminence, cochleariform process, and mastoid antrum. The facial nerve has been seen to course directly lateral in this disorder with no tympanic or mastoid portions. The chorda tympani and superficial petrosal nerves have also been reported to be absent. The epitympanum and sometimes the mesotympanum are said to be small, irregular, and filled with fibrous tissue. The attic and antrum usually have a slit-like appearance on coronal section tomograms.

Anomalies of the inner ear that have been observed include a huge cochlear aqueduct and a blind-pouch horizontal canal. However, the inner ear is considered to be essentially normal in most of the cases.

Other associated anomalies include an antimongoloid slant to the palpebral fissures, colobomas of the lower eyelids, absence of eyelashes medially, micrognathia, short palate, and hypoplasia of the malar bones and intraorbital rims. Cleft lip and cleft palate are sometimes present. Absence of the temporomandibular joint, abnormal temporal muscle, clinodactyly and sternal deformities have also been reported. The features of this syndrome are characteristically bilateral and symmetric.

The hearing loss is usually bilateral and conductive, ranging from moderate to severe, whether or not atresia of the external auditory canal is present, although unexplained sensorineural hearing loss has occasionally been reported. This conductive hearing loss is considered to be due to various deformities of the ossicular chain associated with a small cavity of the middle ear, especially of the epitympanum.

63. Mixed Deafness with Perilymph Gusher During Stapes Surgery[39, 137, 149] (X, M, I)

This is a hereditary X-linked recessive disorder characterized by perilymph gusher during stapes surgery, mixed hearing loss with a rapid progression of the sensorineural component, and markedly impaired vestibular function. Congenital fixation of the stapedial footplate was reported as a middle-ear anomaly associated with this disorder.

Inner ear anomalies that have been revealed radiologically include dilation of the lateral part of the internal acoustic canal, thin osseous separation between the lateral end of the internal acoustic canal and the vestibule/basal turn of the cochlea, widening of the labyrinthine portion of the facial canal, abnormal cochlea size, and dilated vestibule.

It is considered that pressure of the perilymphatic fluid is elevated by a wide communication between the perilymphatic space and the cerebrospinal fluid space along the internal auditory canal in patients with this disorder.

64. Mixed Hearing Loss, Low-Set Malformed Ears, and Mental Retardation[127] (R, E, M, O)

This rare disorder is inherited as an autosomal recessive trait. Anomalies of the external and middle ears are present at birth and include a low-set, malformed pinna; a single ossicle shaped like a malleus and placed posteriorly; absence of the incus, stapes superstructure, and footplate; and absence of the round window niche.

Associated anomalies and clinical findings include mental retardation, high-arched palate, systolic murmur, and small stature.

The hearing loss is mainly of the conductive type, with some sensorineural loss. Vestibular tests may be normal.

65. Noonan Syndrome (Pseudo-Turner Syndrome)[41, 126] (D, E, M, O)

The phenotypic spectrum of Noonan syndrome is similar to that of Turner syndrome, but the chromosomes show normal karyotype in most cases, and both boys and girls can be affected. Although various etiologic possibilities for this syndrome (autosomal dominant, autosomal recessive, X-linked dominant and multifactorial inheritance, and chromosomal aberration such as mosaicism) have been described, autosomal dominant inheritance is considered to be a slightly better possibility than the rest.

Ear anomalies include low-set and fleshy ears and prominence or folding of the upper transverse portion of the helix. Ossicular anomalies (absence of the long process of the incus and abnormal position of the stapes in relation to the malleus) have been reported in one case.

Other associated characteristics include short stature, pterygium colli, short neck, low nuchal hairline, high-arched palate, micrognathia, hypertelorism, epicanthus, antimongoloid palpebral slant, ptosis, cubitus valgus, cryptorchidism, cardiovascular anomalies such as pulmonary stenosis, and skeletal anomalies.

On audiometric examination, suspected congenital sensorineural loss and conductive hearing loss have been reported in association with this syndrome.

66. Odontotrichomelic Syndrome[61] (R, E, O)

This syndrome is thought to be inherited as an autosomal recessive trait. External ear anomalies associated with this syndrome are large and anteverted ears with incomplete folding of the helix and hypoplastic lobules. The upper crus of the anthelix and the rim of the helix form a broad plane lacking the normal scaphal depression.

Other associated anomalies include extensive deficiencies of the upper and lower limbs, hypotrichosis, abnormal dentition (small, conic, and widely spaced teeth; persistence of some deciduous teeth and absence of some permanent teeth), hypoplastic areolae and nipples, thin and dry skin, and dysplastic nails.

67. Orofaciodigital Syndrome Type II (Mohr Syndrome)[156] (R, M, O)

This is a hereditary autosomal recessive disorder. Its prevalence is unknown. Anomalies of the middle ear include blunting of the long process of the incus and absence of the incudostapedial joint.

Associated anomalies include facial deformities with widely spaced medial canthi; flat nasal ridge; high-arched palate; hypoplastic body of the mandible; lobulated tongue; and digital abnormalities, including polydactyly, syndactyly, and brachydactyly.

Audiometric tests reveal a conductive hearing loss.

68. Osteodysplasty (Melnick-Needles Syndrome)[176] (D, E, M, O)

This is a hereditary autosomal dominant disorder. The anomalies of the external ear include small and distorted pinnae and narrow external auditory canals. Anomalies of the middle ear include absence of a round window and mastoid sclerosis.

Other associated anomalies include late closure of fontanelles; dense base of skull; small facial bones with prominent eyes; full cheeks; lag in paranasal sinus development; small mandible; short upper arms; short distal phalanges; bowing radius and tibia; flaring of distal humerus, tibia, and fibula; and coxa valga.

69. Osteogenesis Imperfecta[∗18, ∗136, ∗175] (D, R, M, I, O)

Osteogenesis imperfecta is a hereditary disorder of connective tissue caused by a defect in type I collagen synthesis. The prevalence is 5 per 1000 live births, and there is no sex, racial, or ethnic predilection. According to the current classification, this disorder is divided into four major types. Type I osteogenesis imperfecta, the mildest form, is the classic syndrome dominantly inherited with distinctly blue sclerae. It is distinguished by non-deforming fractures that occur in childhood and cease after puberty, but the fracture may develop with trauma and in postmenopausal women. Type II, the most severe form, is almost always lethal and shows autosomal recessive inheritance. It is characterized by multiple fractures during intrauterine life and either stillbirth or neonatal death resulting from extreme bone fragility. Type III is less severe and is frequently compatible with life. It is characterized by severe short stature, moderate joint laxity, and progressive deformities of long bone and spine. The sclerae become progressively less blue with age. The mode of the inheritance is autosomal recessive. Type IV usually results in moderate long bone deformities and blue sclerae; lax joints and hearing impairment are less common. Both autosomal dominant and recessive modes of inheritance are recognized.

Anomalies of the middle ear include an abnormally shaped stapes head and crura (extremely thin crural arches, nonunion of the superstructure with the footplate); they may be delicate and are sometimes replaced by fibrous tissue. The remainder of the temporal bone may show areas of skeinlike bone throughout its structure. Otosclerosis commonly occurs in association with osteogenesis imperfecta and appears to have a more aggressive nature than when it occurs in isolation.

Other associated anomalies and clinical findings include blue sclerae, skein-like bone replacing lamellar bone throughout the body, multiple bone fractures, weak joints, prominence of the occiput, and abnormal tooth dentin with caries and dental fractures. Deformities such as kyphoscoliosis and pectus excavatum are common; internal hydrocephalus, nerve root compression, cardiovascular and platelet lesions, and thin and atrophic skin also occur with this syndrome.

The audiogram usually shows a conductive hearing loss, although a sensorineural loss may occur in the high frequencies. Conductive hearing loss in this disorder may be the result of osteogenesis imperfecta alone (deformities of the stapes), otosclerosis, or a combination of both.

70. Osteopetrosis (Albers-Schönberg Disease)[108] (D, R, M, O)

Osteopetrosis is a hereditary disorder characterized by increased skeletal density and abnormalities that occur from a failure of resorption of calcified cartilage and primitive bone and a subsequent interference with the formation of the adult bone. This disorder is roughly classified into two types, although several different classifications have been described by various authors. One is a benign dominant form, and the other is a malignant recessive form. In the benign form, the disorder is clinically detected later in life, usually in adolescence, and normal longevity may be expected. Malignant autosomal recessive osteopetrosis may be recognized at birth or even in utero. Affected infants may be stillborn or die in infancy or early childhood. The cause of death is usually a myelophthisic anemia, which results from bony obliteration of the mallow cavity or secondary infection.

Anomalies of the middle ear associated with malignant recessive osteopetrosis include a stapes of fetal form with an abnormal malleus and incus, persistence of the stapedial artery, small middle-ear space, lack of pneumatization of the antrum, and abnormally basophilic endochondral bone.

Associated deformities and clinical findings include macrocephaly, blindness due to optic nerve atrophy, absence of the paranasal sinuses, choanal atresia, facial paralysis, hepatosplenomegaly, bone fractures due to brittleness of the bones, and severe anemia.

The hearing impairment is a common finding in osteopetrosis and is of the conductive, sensorineural, or mixed type. However, moderate mixed hearing loss beginning in childhood is frequently recognized.

71. Otopalatodigital Syndrome[108, *177] (X, M, I, O)

This syndrome is inherited as an X-linked trait. The middle-ear anomalies associated with this syndrome include crudely shaped ossicles that resemble their fetal forms, fixed stapes, and no round window. Anomalies of the inner ear include a defect of the modiolus.

Associated deformities include characteristic facies consisting of frontal and occipital bossing, hypertelorism, broad nasal root, small mandible, and cleft palate. Mild dwarfism and skeletal abnormalities, including retardation of ossification in the carpal and tarsal centers, also occur. There are abnormalities of the hands with widely spaced first and second digits and a shortened first digit. Mental retardation may also be associated with this disease.

The hearing loss is of the conductive type.

72. Renal Agenesis, Bilateral (Potter Syndrome)[17, *20, *150, *166, 199] (D, E, M, I, O)

Although it has been reported that most cases of renal agenesis are sporadic and that its familial occurrence is relatively rare, study results suggest that autosomal dominant inheritance may be the major mode of transmission for this disorder. The frequency of bilateral renal agenesis has been considered to vary from 1 in 3000 to 1 in 9000 births.

Bilateral renal agenesis is frequently accompanied by anomalies in the external and middle ear, including low-set ears with deficient auricular cartilages, hypoplastic external auditory canal, malformed incus, fixation of the malleus and incus in the attic, absence of auditory ossicles, atresia of the oval window, large amount of residual mesenchyme, wide dehiscence of the fallopian canal, and abnormal course of the facial nerve.

Findings in the inner ear include hypoplasia of the basal turn of the cochlear membranous labyrinth.

Other associated anomalies and clinical findings include redundant and dehydrated skin, wide-set eyes, prominent fold arising at the inner canthus of each eye, parrot-beaked nose, receding chin, facial expression of an older infant, "no urine output," and bilateral absence of kidneys. The patient may have multiple malformations, including bilateral pulmonary hypoplasia, gastrointestinal malformations, genital organ abnormalities, single umbilical artery, and major deformities of the lower part of the body or of the lower limbs.

Anomalies of the face, limbs, lungs, and skin are regarded as secondary to compression as a result of oligohydramnios, whatever the cause, and they are not considered pathognomonic of renal agenesis.

73. Sickle Cell Disease[*133] (D, M, O)

Sickle cell disease is a hereditary dominant disorder. It is said that it affects 7% to 8% of African blacks. Anomalies of the middle ear include resorption of the body and long process of the incus and the head of the stapes.

Other associated anomalies include hemolytic anemia, extramedullary hematopoiesis, and hyperplastic bone marrow.

Audiometric tests may reveal a sensorineural hearing loss.

74. Thickened Ear Lobule and Incudostapedial Malunion[53] (D, E, M)

This is a hereditary dominant, non-X-linked autosomal anomaly of rare occurrence. It is present at birth.

Anomalies of the external and middle ears include hypertrophic and thickened ear lobule, malformation of the long process of the incus, absence of the lenticular process of the incus, presence of a fibrous connection from the stapes to the incus, and absence of the stapes head.

A conductive hearing loss should be present. No vestibular studies have been reported.

75. Third and Fourth Pharyngeal Pouch Syndrome (DiGeorge Syndrome, Partial DiGeorge Syndrome)[3, *4, *24, *140] (R, E, M, I, O)

This is a hereditary autosomal recessive defect. The anomalies are present at birth. The prevalence of this syndrome is low.

Anomalies of the external and middle ears include malformed, low-set pinna; atresia of the external auditory canal; absence of the malleus, incus, and stapes; small facial nerve; absence of the stapedial muscle; partial atresia of the tympanic cavity; and absence of the oval window.

Anomalies of the inner ear include absence of the apical portion of the modiolus, absence of the horizontal semicircular canal, and hypoplastic seventh and eighth cranial nerves.

Other anomalies include absence or hypoplasia of the thymus, abnormalities of the aortic arch, patent ductus arteriosus, agenesis of the thyroid, acrania, microcephaly, and micrognathia.

Diseases Associated with Prenatal Infections

76. Congenital Rubella Syndrome[70], [79] (M, I, O)

Maternal rubella is an infectious viral disorder. Its manifestations are present at birth.

Anomalies of the middle ear include a small area of malleus head fixation on one side; absence of the medial component of the posterior incudal ligament; anomalous stapes with a rudimentary thickened head, neck, crura, and footplate; cartilaginous fixation of the stapes footplate; and persistence of fetal mesenchymal tissue in the middle ear.

Associated features in the inner ear include depression of the Reissner membrane, cystic dilatation of the stria vascularis, rolling of the tectorial membrane into the inner sulcus, hair cell degeneration, spiral ganglion cell loss, and collapse of the saccular membrane with adherence to the saccular macula.

Other associated anomalies and clinical findings are mental retardation, microcephaly, microphthalmia, retinitis, congenital cataracts, thrombocytopenia, cardiovascular deformities, and deformities of the lower extremities. Confirmatory tests include the presence of fluorescent antibodies in the serum, serum hemagglutination, and positive viral cultures of the stool and throat.

Audiometric testing reveals sensorineural and conductive hearing losses.

77. Congenital Syphilis[102] (M, I, O)

Congenital syphilis is an infection of the fetus by *Treponema pallidum* that passes through the placenta. Symptoms may begin in childhood, but symptoms first develop in 50% of individuals between the ages of 25 and 35 years.

The middle-ear findings reported are thickening of the malleus as a result of bone hyperplasia, fusion of the malleolar head to the body of the incus, spongy appearance of the long process of the incus, and abnormalities of the stapes. Histopathologic examination of the temporal bones reveals primary osteitis with mononuclear leukocyte infiltration and obliterative endarteritis of the otic capsule with secondary labyrinthitis characterized by endolymphatic hydrops and degeneration of the membranous labyrinth end organs.

Other associated findings are perforated nasal septum, interstitial keratitis, and Hutchinson teeth.

Audiometric findings include a typical sensorineural type of hearing loss with a flat audiometric curve in 38% of the patients with congenital syphilis. The curve some-times shows a conductive component if the middle ear is involved. The onset of hearing loss in childhood is usually sudden, bilaterally symmetric, severe to profound, and unaccompanied by marked vestibular symptoms. In adults, deafness begins abruptly, and a partial, asymmetric, flat, sensorineural hearing loss is accompanied by episodes of vertigo. Tinnitus may be present. Treatment involves the administration of large doses of penicillin and steroids.

The diagnosis is made by the history and verifying tests, including serum and cerebrospinal fluid tests for syphilis. However, these tests are not always positive.

Diseases of Maternal Drug Abuse

78. Fetal Alcohol Syndrome[31], [32] (E, O)

Maternal abuse of ethanol during pregnancy can cause alterations in fetal growth and morphogenesis and may result in growth deficiency and various congenital anomalies. The phenotype of this syndrome is variable, depending on exposure dose, gestational timing, and individual differences in fetal and maternal vulnerability to ethanol. There is, however, a tendency for higher levels of ingestion or more frequent intake of alcohol to give rise to more seriously affected children. Anomalies of major organs have been reported in offspring of severe, chronic alcoholic mothers. The occurrence of the syndrome is between 1 and 2 per 1000 live births, but at least one third of the children born to chronic alcoholic mothers demonstrate some of the stigmata of fetal alcohol syndrome.

Major malformations and clinical findings associated with this syndrome are central nervous system dysfunction including mental retardation, microcephaly and behavioral abnormality, craniofacial anomalies, and prenatal and postnatal growth deficiencies. Ear anomalies that have been reported as one of the craniofacial anomalies include posteriorly rotated ears, low-set ears, lop ears, microtia, and poorly formed concha.

Other craniofacial anomalies and clinical findings include short palpebral fissures, epicanthus, ptosis, strabismus, myopia, small anteverted nares, flat nasal bridge, micrognathia, cleft palate, thin upper lip, and long and flat philtrum. Besides these findings, congenital heart defects, increased susceptibility to infection, and cutaneous lesions such as hemangiomas may be present.

Regarding hearing loss associated with fetal alcohol syndrome, conductive hearing loss due to recurrent serous otitis media, which is common in affected children, and bilateral sensorineural hearing loss have been reported.

Diseases of Iatrogenic Ototoxicity

79. Anticonvulsant Drug-Induced Malformations (Fetal Hydantoin Syndrome)[164] (E, M, I, O)

Anticonvulsant drugs including phenobarbital, phenytoin, mephobarbital, mephenytoin, and primidone may have a teratogenic effect. There is a possibility for infants born to mothers taking these drugs during pregnancy to have various malformations. The reported malformations and clinical findings include cleft lip and palate; craniofacial and skeletal anomalies; mental and growth retardation; and cardiovascular, gastrointestinal, and genitourinary malformations.

As to the ear anomalies, prominent, slightly malformed and low-set ears have been reported in some cases as one of the craniofacial malformations. In one report, middle and inner ear anomalies observed histopathologically included deformed ossicles, absence of the oval and the round window, cochlea and vestibule consisting of round chambers, absence of the common crus and the endolymphatic sac, deformed or absent cochlear ducts, and shortness or absence of the cochlear aqueduct and the endolymphatic duct.

80. Isotretinoin Syndrome[93, 96, 112] (E, M, I, O)

Isotretinoin (13-*cis*-retinoic acid), an oral synthetic vitamin A derivative, is efficacious in the treatment of severe recalcitrant cystic acne, but vitamin A and its derivatives have been experimentally known as major teratogens. Isotretinoin is considered to cause serious congenital malformations in about 25% of fetuses exposed in utero in the first trimester of pregnancy. Isotretinoin-induced anomalies include craniofacial, central nervous system, and cardiac malformations and abnormalities of thymic morphogenesis.

External ear anomalies include anotia, low-set microtia, macrotia, atresia or stenosis of the external auditory canal.

Middle-ear anomalies include anomalous ossicles, hypoplasia of the facial nerve, absence of the chorda tympani nerve and absence of the stapedius muscle.

Inner ear anomalies include anomalies of the membranous labyrinth in the vestibule, hypoplastic lateral semicircular canal, and large vestibular aqueduct and endolymphatic sac. The ear anomalies always occur bilaterally, but the severity is often asymmetric.

The craniofacial malformations except for ear anomalies include micrognathia, cleft palate, hypertelorism, and various deformities of the facial bones and calvarium. A flat and depressed nasal bridge is a common feature. The most common central nervous system malformation is hydrocephalus; microcephaly, megacisterna magna, and cerebellar hypoplasia or agenesis of the vermis may also be observed.

81. Thalidomide Ototoxicity[100] (E, M, I, O)

Thalidomide ototoxicity is an iatrogenic, drug-induced congenital disorder that occurs after the administration of thalidomide to a pregnant woman. The probability of malformation after exposure is unknown.

Twenty percent of the children suffering from thalidomide-induced anomalies show ear anomalies. Anomalies of the external and middle ear include deformed or absent pinna, complete or partial atresia of the external auditory canal, deformed tympanic membrane, fixed malleus, displaced long process of the incus, absence of the stapes, absence of the facial nerve and chorda tympani

nerve, persistence of the stapedial artery, slit-shaped tympanic cavity, and absence of the oval window.

Inner ear anomalies include aplasia of the inner ear and absence of the facial nerve and statoacoustic nerve in the internal auditory canal.

Associated anomalies include shortening, deformity, or absence of the long bones; capillary hemangiomas of the forehead, nose, and lips; colobomas; microphthalmia; congenital heart disease; intestinal atresia; and renal hypoplasia or agenesis.

Approximately 75% of the infants affected can be expected to have a moderate to profound sensorineural hearing loss, and 25% have a maximal conductive hearing loss. Absence of vestibular function has also been reported.

Diseases Associated with Environmental Factors

82. Endemic Cretinism[193] (M, I, O)

This disease is caused by environmental factors. Contrary to Pendred syndrome, perchlorate test results are negative in these individuals. Anomalies of the external and middle ears associated with endemic cretinism include plump ossicles, thickened periosteal parts of the stapes, small mastoid process, and thickened periosteal layers of the otic capsule.

Other anomalies include brachiocephalic cranium, brachydactyly with shortness of the thumb, and abnormal hip joint.

These individuals often have a hearing loss of mixed type.

Classification of External-Ear and Middle-Ear Anomalies by Their Involved Anatomic Structures (Classification II)

To enhance the reader's understanding of anomalies of the external and middle ears, the various kinds of anomalies that occur in the external and middle ears are classified according to the anatomic structures involved in the anomaly.

Congenital External-Ear Anomalies

A. Auricular Anomalies (4, 5, 12, 17–20, 24–27, 29, 32, 34–38, 40–43, 46, 48, 50, 51, 53–59, 61, 62, 64–66, 68, 72, 74, 75, 78–81)†

1. Auricular Anomalies in General (4–6, 8–10, 12, 13,

---

†Numbers in parentheses refer to the diseases listed in Classification I.

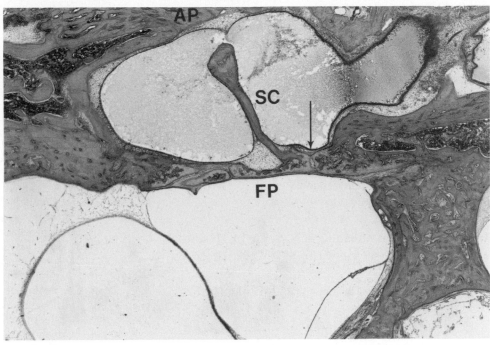

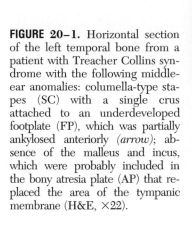

FIGURE 20–1. Horizontal section of the left temporal bone from a patient with Treacher Collins syndrome with the following middle-ear anomalies: columella-type stapes (SC) with a single crus attached to an underdeveloped footplate (FP), which was partially ankylosed anteriorly (*arrow*); absence of the malleus and incus, which were probably included in the bony atresia plate (AP) that replaced the area of the tympanic membrane (H&E, ×22).

15, 17–20, 24–27, 29, 32, 34–38, 40, 41, 43, 46, 48, 50, 51, 53, 56, 59, 61, 62, 64–66, 68, 75, 78–81)

   a. Absence of auricle—anotia[7]
   b. Superior portion of the auricle buried in the scalp-cryptotia, pocket ear[7]
   c. Double ear[7]
   d. Auricle smaller than normal—microtia[6]
   e. Auricle larger than normal—macrotia[7]
   f. Auricle standing away from the head at an angle greater than normal-bat ear, flaring ear, cup ear, protruding ear, prominent ear, projecting ear, dumbo ear[7]
   g. Auricle located on the upper anterior cervical region near the midline of the neck—synotia[22]
   h. Ear located on the cheek—melotia[7]
   i. Lack of aural ascent due to underdevelopment of the mandibular area—low-set ear[10]
   j. Other[7]

2. Lobular Anomalies (6, 24, 54, 57, 66, 74)
   a. Absence of lobule[7]
   b. Adherent lobule[7]
   c. Split lobule[7]
   d. Deep horizontal groove on the lobule[66]
   e. Hypertrophic and thickened lobule[53]
   f. Nodule on the lobule[66]

3. Helix Anomalies (35, 36, 42, 55, 59, 65, 66)
   a. Auricle folded forward and downward in varying degrees from above and behind—cat's ear[7]
   b. Helix with sharp angle on its tip portion—cercopithecoid ear[7]
   c. Narrowing of the upper third of the auricle because of a helical collapse—satyr ear[44]
   d. Small projection from the descending part of the helix—macacus ear[7]

4. Anthelix Anomalies (6, 24, 29, 32, 35, 55, 59, 61, 66, 78)

   a. Absence of anthelix[84]
   b. Poor development of the anthelix—lop ear[35]
   c. Anthelix protruding above a plane passing through the tragus and helix—Wildermuth ear[7]
   d. Enlarged portion of the anthelix connecting with the helix—Mozart ear[7]
   e. Crus extending from the helix to the cymbae—Stahl ear[7]

5. Tragus Anomaly (8)
   a. Rudimentary tragus[6]

6. Conchal Anomaly (78)
   a. Vertical cartilaginous ridge in the concha—crus cymbae[7]
   b. Hypotrophic concha with an overall narrow ear involving a lobule—devil's ear[44]

7. Appendage (4, 10, 35, 38, 50, 53)
   a. Numerous appendages—polyotia[7]
   b. Preauricular appendage[7]

8. Fistula (29, 35, 37, 53, 54)
   a. Colloaural fistula[7]
   b. Preauricular fistula[7]
   c. Postauricular fistula[7]
   d. Prehelical pit (preauricular pit)[125]
   e. Posterior helical ear pit[110]

B. External Auditory Meatus Anomalies (4, 5, 8–10, 19, 20, 24–29, 32–34, 38, 40, 41, 43–46, 48–50, 52, 59, 62, 68, 72, 75, 79, 80)

   a. *Atresia auris[6] (Fig. 20–1)
     i. Membranous atresia
     ii. Bony atresia

*The asterisk before an anomaly indicates that this particular anomaly has been reported histopathologically.

b. *Stenotic external auditory meatus[103]
c. *Short bony external auditory meatus[10]
d. Long bony external auditory meatus[182]

Congenital Middle-Ear Anomalies

A. Tympanic Membrane Anomalies (8, 9, 25, 26, 46, 62, 81)

a. *Tympanic membrane replaced by bony plate[169] (see Fig. 20–1)
b. Tympanic membrane replaced by fibrous tissue[174]
c. *Small tympanic membrane[26]
d. *Distorted tympanic membrane[168]

B. Ossicular Anomalies (2, 4, 6, 8–11, 19, 20, 23–28, 30, 31, 33–38, 40, 41, 43–47, 49, 50, 52–54, 56, 58–60, 62–65, 67, 69–77, 79–82)

1. Ossicular Anomalies in General (30, 37, 43, 50, 71, 72, 79, 80)
   a. *Remnant ossicle[34]
   b. *Fusion of three ossicles[88]
   c. Thickening of ossicles[27]
   d. Lateral displacement of ossicles[120]
2. Malleus Anomalies (2, 4, 8, 9, 20, 25–27, 37, 38, 41, 46, 47, 52, 58, 62, 64, 70–72, 75–77, 81, 82)
   a. Absence of
      i. *Malleus[162] (see Fig. 20–1)
      ii. Manubrium[81]
      iii. Lateral process[84]
      iv. Head[81]
   b. Bony fusion of
      i. *Mallear head to epitympanic wall[157]
      ii. Anterior mallear ligament to tympanic ring[122]
   c. Other anomalies
      i. *Displacement of malleus[161]

ii. Long manubrium[88]
iii. Shortening of manubrium[27]
iv. Cartilaginous fusion between malleus and Meckel cartilage[205]

3. Incus Anomalies (2, 4, 6, 8–11, 20, 25–27, 33, 36–38, 41, 47, 49, 52, 53, 56, 58, 60, 62, 64, 65, 67, 70–75, 77, 81, 82)
   a. Absence of
      i. *Incus[169] (see Fig. 20–1)
      ii. Long process[58]
      iii. *Lenticular process[123]
   b. Bony fusion of
      i. *Incus to malleus[6]
      ii. Incudomalleal joint[118]
      iii. *Short process to floor of aditus ad antrum[123]
      iv. Short process to horizontal canal wall[106]
   c. Other anomalies
      i. *Displacement of incus[161]
      ii. Shortening of short process[95]
      iii. Shortening of long process[118]
      iv. *Dislocation of long process[168]
      v. Resolution of body and long process[133]
4. Stapes Anomalies (2, 4–6, 8, 9, 11, 20, 23–28, 31, 33, 34, 36–38, 40, 41, 43–47, 49, 52–54, 56, 58–60, 62–65, 67, 69–77, 81, 82)
   a. Absence of
      i. Stapes[54]
      ii. *Incudostapedial joint[9]
      iii. *Head[9]
      iv. Superstructure[92]
      v. *Crus[10]
      vi. *Footplate[100]
   b. Rudimentary form of stapes
      i. *Columella-type stapes[104] (see Fig. 20–1)
      ii. *Doughnut-type stapes[88]
      iii. *Thickening of stapes[168] (Fig. 20–2)
      iv. *Two-layer footplate[115]

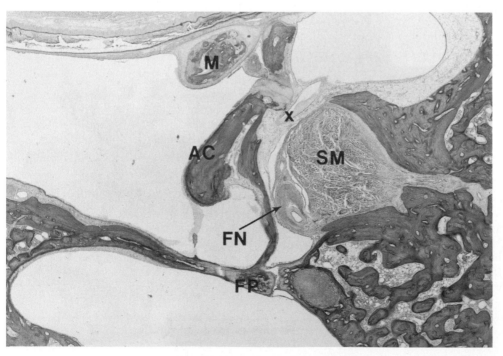

FIGURE 20–2. Horizontal section of the right temporal bone in a case of trisomy 18 syndrome showing several middle ear anomalies. An anterior crus of the stapes (AC) is thickened, and a huge stapedius muscle (SM) is exposed in the middle ear space, pushing an underdeveloped facial nerve (FN) medially. Note absence of the stapedius tendon and the pyramidal eminence (x) and large dehiscence of the facial nerve. FP, footplate of stapes; M, malleus (H&E, ×12).

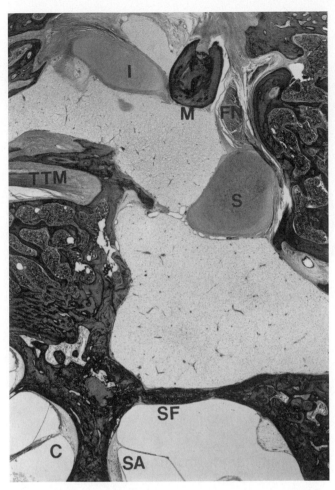

FIGURE 20–3. Horizontal section of the right temporal bone from a 6-month-old patient with Goldenhar syndrome showing anomalous bony and cartilaginous masses, presumably malleus (M), incus (I), and primordium of stapes (S). Note no connection between primitive stapes footplate (SF) and primordium of stapes and cartilaginous fusion of stapes footplate to the otic capsule. C, cochlea; FN, facial nerve; SA, saccule; TTM, tensor tympani muscle (H&E, ×18).

c. Bony fusion of
   i. Incudostapedial joint[87]
   ii. Head to promontory[88]
   iii. *Head to facial canal[6]
   iv. *Crus to cochleariform process[123]
   v. *Crus to oval window bony wall[9]
   vi. *Crus to promontory[100]
   vii. Crus to pyramidal eminence[27]
   viii. *Footplate to otic capsule[10]
d. Other anomalies
   i. Adherence of stapes to facial nerve[50]
   ii. *Fibrous connection of incudostapedial joint[123]
   iii. Displacement of incudostapedial joint[23]
   iv. *Resolution of head[133]
   v. Degeneration of crus into fibrous threads[142]
   vi. *Small bone on footplate[19]
   vii. *Cartilaginous primordium of the stapes[170] (Fig. 20–3)
   viii. *Cartilaginous fixation of footplate to the otic capsule[170] (see Fig. 20–3)

C. Nerve Anomalies (1, 8, 10, 20, 23, 25–27, 33, 37, 38, 40, 43, 47, 58, 62, 72, 75, 80, 81)

1. Facial Nerve Anomalies (1, 8, 10, 12, 20, 23, 25–27, 34, 37, 38, 40, 43, 47, 58, 62, 72, 75, 80, 81)
  a. *Absence[100]
  b. *Poor development[80, 105] (see Fig. 20–2)
  c. Abnormal course
    i. In general[98]
    ii. *Wide angle of facial genu[51]
    iii. *Runs laterally from geniculate ganglion and leaves temporal bone immediately[169] (Fig. 20–4)
    iv. Runs inferiorly from geniculate ganglion[29]
    v. *Runs more inferiorly than normal[3, 197, 200]
    vi. *Absence of second genu[168]
    vii. Lateral and anterior displacement of descending portion of facial nerve[45]
    viii. Facial nerve located medial to stapedial muscle[168] (see Fig. 20–2)
    ix. Bifurcation in the tympanic portion[74] (Fig. 20–5)
  d. Other
    i. *Exposed facial nerve[10]
2. Chorda Tympani Nerve Anomalies (8, 20, 23, 26, 47, 62, 80, 81)
  a. *Absence[169]
  b. Abnormal course
    i. *Runs out of temporal bone[6]
    ii. Runs from the area of the geniculate ganglion[60]
    iii. *Runs more vertically than normal[168]
    iv. Bifurcation[50]
  c. Other anomalies
    i. Enlargement[87]
    ii. Chorda tympani with bony sleeve at posterior edge of external auditory meatus[111]
3. Superficial Petrosal Nerve Anomalies (8, 23, 62)
  a. *Absence of greater superficial petrosal nerve[169]
  b. *Absence of lesser superficial petrosal nerve[6]

D. Intratympanic Muscle Anomalies (4, 6, 8, 20, 22, 25, 28, 34, 37, 62, 75)

1. Tensor Tympani Muscle and Tendon Anomalies (8, 20, 34, 62)
  a. Absence of muscle and tendon[169]
  b. Abnormal course
    i. Abnormal course without connection to cochleariform process and malleus[161]
    ii. Abnormal course without connection to cochleariform process[83]
    iii. *Split in muscle[109]
2. Stapedius Muscle and Tendon Anomalies (4, 6, 20, 22, 25, 26, 28, 34, 37, 62, 75, 80)
  a. *Absence of muscle and tendon[169]
  b. *Huge muscle exposed in the middle ear[168] (see Fig. 20–2)
  c. Two muscles[202]
  d. Absence of tendon[95] (see Fig. 20–2)
  e. Atrophy of tendon[185]
  f. Ossification of tendon[87]

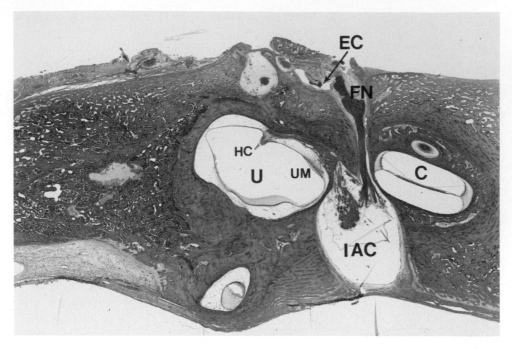

FIGURE 20–4. Horizontal section of the left temporal bone from a patient with Treacher Collins syndrome demonstrating an extremely small epitympanic cavity (EC) and abnormal course of the facial nerve (FN) directly from the internal auditory canal (IAC) to the outside of the temporal bone without any course in the middle-ear space. The utricle (U) is enlarged and contains the crista ampullaris of the horizontal canal (HC) as well as the utricular macula (UM). C, cochlea (H&E, ×4.5).

g. Tendon attached to lenticular process[92, 151]
h. Tendon attached to head or posterior crus[87]
3. Other Anomalies[25]
   a. *Supernumerary or ectopic muscles[49]

E. Vascular Anomalies (3, 8, 10, 14, 16, 25, 27, 34, 58, 70, 81)

1. Internal Carotid Artery Anomalies (3, 16)
   a. Existence in middle ear[67]
   b. Existence of aneurysm in the middle ear[181]
2. Stapedial Artery Anomaly (8, 10, 25, 34, 70, 81)

   a. *Persistence[5, 119, 132] (Fig. 20–6)
3. Jugular Bulb Anomalies (10, 14, 25, 27, 58)
   a. Herniation of jugular bulb into the middle ear[67]
   b. *High jugular bulb[51] (Fig. 20–7)

F. Tympanic Cavity Anomalies (6, 8–10, 12, 20, 25–27, 33, 34, 37, 38, 40, 41, 46, 56, 58, 62, 70, 72, 75, 81)

a. Absence of
   i. Tympanic cavity[64]
   ii. *Cochleariform process[169]

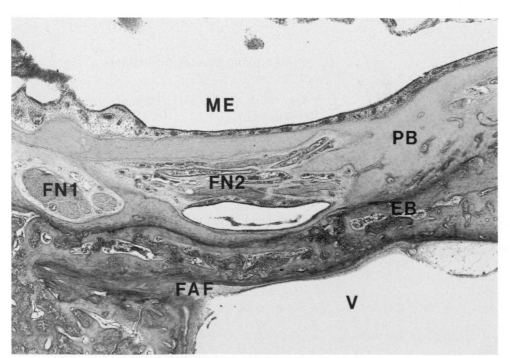

FIGURE 20–5. Horizontal section of the right temporal bone from a patient with choanal atresia showing absence of the oval window and abnormal course of the facial nerve. Note that a thick bony layer consisting of periosteal bone (PB) and endochondral bone (EB) occupies the area where the oval window should be. Facial nerve is bifurcated (FN1 and FN2), and the FN2 portion is crossing the oval window area. FAF, fissula ante fenestram; ME, middle ear; V, vestibule (H&E, ×37).

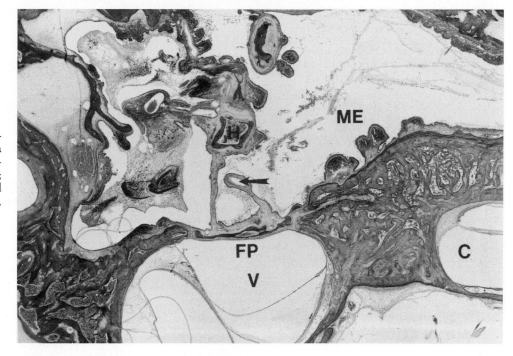

FIGURE 20–6. Persistent stapedial artery (*arrow*) observed in a patient with trisomy 13 syndrome. C, cochlea; V, vestibule; FP, footplate of stapes; H, head of stapes; ME, middle ear (H&E, ×15).

iii. *Facial canal[10]
iv. *Pyramidal eminence[168] (see Fig. 20–2)
b. Dehiscence of
   i. *Facial canal[10, 132, 187] (Fig. 20–8; see also Fig. 20–2)
   ii. Floor[181]
   iii. *Tegmen tympani[169]
c. Rudimentary form
   i. *Small tympanic cavity[100]
   ii. *Small tympanic cavity with fetal connective tissue[100]
d. *Bony mass in promontory[169]

e. Others
   i. *Congenital cholesteatoma[84]
   ii. *H-shaped tympanic cavity[161]
   iii. Large facial canal[54]

G. Window Anomalies (4, 6, 7, 11, 20, 28, 34, 35, 37, 43, 46, 50, 59, 64, 68, 71, 72, 75, 79, 81)

1. Oval Window Anomalies (4, 6, 20, 28, 34, 35, 37, 43, 50, 59, 72, 75, 79, 81)
  a. *Absence[74, 97, 100] (see Fig. 20–5)

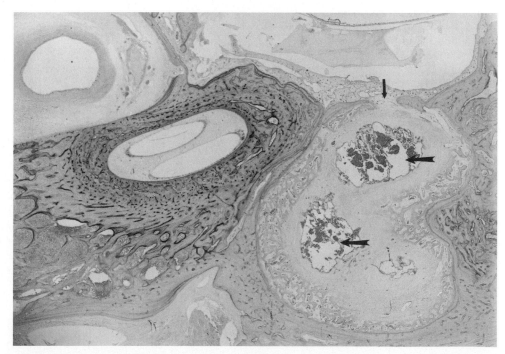

FIGURE 20–7. High jugular bulb (*large arrows*) accompanied by dehiscence (*small arrow*) of the medial bony wall of the tympanic cavity (H&E, ×11).

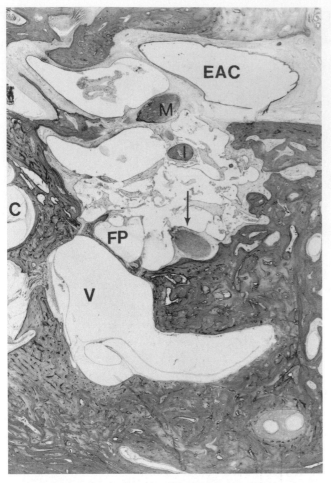

FIGURE 20–8. Severe dehiscences of the facial canal (*arrow*) in a patient with congenital heart anomalies. C, cochlea; EAC, external auditory canal; FP, footplate of stapes; I, incus; M, malleus; V, vestibule (H&E, ×10.5).

  b. *Calcification of annular ligament[44]
  c. *Filled with fetal connective tissue[103]
  d. Thin membranous window[116]
  e. *Small[169]
2. Round Window Anomalies (6, 7, 11, 28, 43, 46, 64, 68, 71, 79)
  a. Absence[88]
  b. Round window partitioned by bony bar[116]
  c. Displacement of round window[87]
  d. Absence of niche[87]
  e. Connective tissue obstruction of niche[162]
  f. Narrow niche[13]

H. Otic Capsule Anomalies (30, 46, 56, 69, 70, 77, 82)
  a. *Achondroplasia[173]
  b. *Fibrous resorption focus in two external layers due to gargoylism[103]
  c. *Osteitis due to syphilis[68]
  d. *Osteogenesis imperfecta[11]
  e. *Osteopetrosis[135]
  f. Thickened periosteal layer due to endemic cretinism[193]

  g. *Underdevelopment of periosteal layer due to craniofacial dysostosis[13]

I. Mastoid Anomalies (24, 25, 27, 28, 33, 40, 56, 62, 68, 82)

  a. *Absence of mastoid antrum[169]
  b. *Poor development of mastoid antrum[162]
  c. *Poor development of mastoid air cells[162]
  d. *Small mastoid process[162]

J. Eustachian Tube Anomalies (including its associated structures) (20, 27, 28)

  a. Absence[8]
  b. Abnormally narrow[6]
  c. Diverticula of eustachian tube (Von Kostanecki, 1887, quoted by Altmann[8])
  d. Congenital tumor (polyp) (Henke, 1924, quoted by Altmann[8])
  e. Collapsed lumen of the eustachian tube[178]
  f. *Maldeveloped eustachian tube cartilage[129, 130, 188] (Figs. 20–9 and 20–10)
  g. *Absence of attachment of the tensor veli palatini muscle to the eustachian tube cartilage[129, 130] (see Figs. 20–9 and 20–10)

Discussion

Anomalies of the external and middle ears are of major importance to both the patient and the otologist. When they are bilateral and associated with significant hearing loss from birth, they result in poor speech and language development or failure of such development. Children thus afflicted are sometimes mistakenly classified as mentally retarded and are needlessly condemned to a lifetime of institutionalization and intellectual deprivation. Also, cosmetic anomalies of the external ear may produce severe psychological trauma in children. Early correction of deformities is essential in ensuring normal development of speech and is also helpful to the psychological development of the patient who is affected by the anomaly. Correction of congenital anomalies represents a challenge to the surgical ingenuity of the otologist; but the fact that a hearing loss is frequently correctable by modern otomicrosurgical techniques should be encouraging to the patient, the family, and the otologist. As mentioned, surgical misadventures may result from encountering unexpected anatomic variations. However, even with anomalies of unknown origin, studies of the nature and extent of the anomaly and the normal embryonic development of the ear often provide the otologist with some clue as to the period of embryonic development during which the insult occurred and, thus, what other anomalies might be encountered during corrective surgery. To help such studies, a timetable of major developmental events related to the external and middle ears and the facial nerve is presented in Table 20–2.

From a review of the literature on this subject and from study of temporal bones, certain trends are evident.

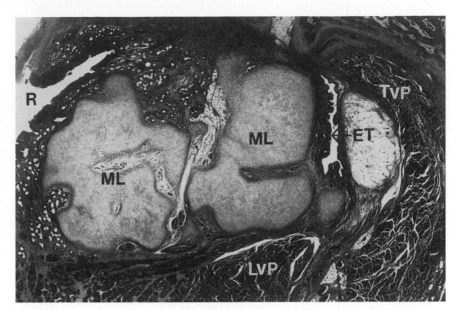

FIGURE 20–9. Vertical section of the mid-cartilaginous portion of the left eustachian tube (ET) in a patient with trisomy 22. Note that the lateral lamina (LL) of the ET cartilage is absent. In contrast, the medial lamina (ML) of the ET cartilage is widely developed, expanding to the site near Rosenmuller's fossa (R). The tensor veli palatini muscle (TVP) is not attached to the ET cartilage. LVP, levator veli palatini muscle (H&E, ×24).

1. Anomalies of the external and middle ears usually occur together to a variable extent because of their closely related embryonic development.
2. Anomalies of the external and middle ears that occur in the absence of other associated anomalies are usually of unknown origin and occur in the absence of any family history of anomalies.
3. Anomalies of the external and middle ears that occur with other anomalies are usually of known etiology or are associated with a positive family history.
4. Of the middle-ear anomalies that occur without other anomalies, those most frequently encountered include ossicular anomalies and anomalies of the facial nerve. There is a tendency for middle-ear anomalies to occur together, such as facial nerve and ossicular anomalies, especially those involving the stapes. This, of course, reflects their interdependent embryonic development.

5. In the case of anomalies of the external and middle ears associated with other anomalies, the association of branchial arch anomalies with anomalies of the external and middle ears is clear. Because of the small number of histopathologic reports available regarding the temporal bone, it is not yet possible to compile a comprehensive list of associated anomalies.
6. Routine audiometric testing does not provide any clue to the nature of the anomaly.

Some findings do provide us with diagnostic clues.

1. A positive family history of congenital malformations is important.
2. A maternal history of infectious disease during pregnancy and drug ingestion or exposure to ionizing radiation before or during pregnancy should be sought.

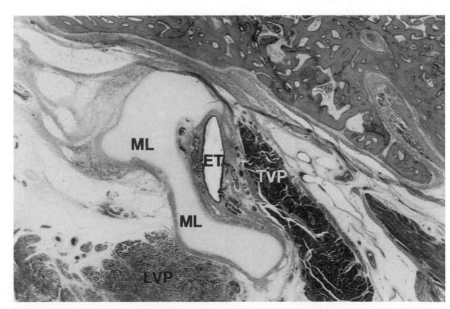

FIGURE 20–10. Vertical section of the mid-cartilaginous portion of the left eustachian tube (ET) in a patient with oculoauriculovertebral spectrum. Note that the ET lumen is primitive with few ridges of mucosal folds and rather patent than the normal slitlike luminal space. The medial lamina (ML) of the ET cartilage demonstrates its counterclockwise rotation. The lateral lamina of the ET cartilage is almost absent. The tensor veli palatini muscle (TVP) is not attached to the ET cartilage. LVP, levator veli palatini muscle (H&E, ×24).

3. A history of a nonprogressive, usually unilateral, conductive hearing loss present since birth suggests an anomaly of the external auditory meatus or ossicles, or both.

4. A history of delayed or absent speech development suggests a congenital hearing loss.

5. The presence of any other congenital anomalies makes a complete physical and audiometric examination imperative.

In studying suspected congenital anomalies of the external and middle ears, we would make the following suggestions.

1. A careful family history must be taken, with emphasis on congenital anomalies, ear infections, hearing aid use, and hearing loss.

2. The maternal history of drug ingestion, exposure to ionizing radiation, or use of chelating agents or antimetabolites before or during pregnancy as well as a history of infectious diseases, especially viral, during pregnancy is important.

3. For differential diagnosis, a history of postnatal in-

fections, perinatal trauma, or postnatal injury or surgery may provide information about the origin of the anomaly.

4. Roentgenologic studies by polytomography and CT scans may reveal anomalies of the external auditory meatus, middle ear, and inner ear.

5. The result of testing a child with an anomaly with tympanometry may make possible a differential diagnosis between ossicular fixation and ossicular discontinuity.

6. Chromosomal analysis may be helpful in making a differential diagnosis.

7. Surgical exploration, aided by radiographic findings, provides the only definitive diagnosis for, and also the treatment of, these conditions.

8. During surgery to correct conductive hearing losses of unknown origin, extreme care must be exercised to avoid injuring anatomic structures, such as the facial nerve, that may be in other than their usual locations in anomalous ears. A knowledge of embryology provides the surgeon with some information about where these structures are likely to

TABLE 20–2. Timetable of Major Developmental Events Related to the External Ear, Middle Ear, and Facial Nerve

| Fetal Week | External Ear | Middle Ear | | Facial Nerve |
		Auditory Ossicles	Others	
3rd			First pharyngeal pouch expands to form a tubotympanic recess.	AFP, a collection of neural crest cells, appears.
4th	Tissue of first and second branchial arches thickens.	Interbranchial bridge connecting mandibular and hyoid visceral bars appears.		
5th	Six hillocks are formed. Ectoderm of first branchial groove comes in contact with endoderm of first pharyngeal pouch.	Primordia of malleus and incus are formed. Primordium of stapes is formed.	Primitive tympanic membrane is formed between first branchial groove and first pharyngeal pouch.	AFP separates into facial and acoustic nerve. GG appears in facial portion of AFP. Chorda tympani nerve is identified. Greater superficial petrosal nerve arises from the most ventral part of GG.
6th	Six hillocks are transformed into two folds.	Stapes ring is formed around stapedial artery. Malleus and incus completely separate from hyoid visceral bars. Precartilage appears and forms in future ossicles and two visceral bars.		Facial nerve bends caudally at GG, and external benu is formed.
7th	Cartilage of pinna starts to develop.		Constriction of midportion of tubotympanic recess occurs and forms eustachian tube and tympanic cavity.	Nervus intermedius arises from GG. Chorda tympani and lingual nerve are joined.
8th	Cavitas conchae deepens to form a funnel-shaped tube, the primary meatus, which becomes outer third of EAM.		Lower half of tympanic cavity is formed.	Nerve to stapedius muscle is identified. Definitive relationships of intratemporal segment are mainly established. Five major peripheral subdivisions of facial nerve are formed.
9th	Meatal plate is formed	Malleoincudal and incudostapedia 1 joints are formed. Malleus and incus attain complete cartilaginous form.	Tympanic ring is formed. Three tissue layers are formed at tympanic membrane. Mesenchymal cells derived from interhyale aggregates to form stapedius muscle.	

TABLE 20–2. Timetable of Major Developmental Events Related to the External Ear, Middle Ear, and Facial Nerve *Continued*

Fetal Week	External Ear	Middle Ear		Facial Nerve
		Auditory Ossicles	*Others*	
10th		Stapes changes in shape from a ring to a stirrup.		
12th		Primordium of tensor tympani muscle is formed.		
15th		Malleus and incus reach adult size and begin to ossify.		Development of GG is complete.
16th			Development of tympanic ring is complete.	
18th		Stapes reaches adult size and begins to ossify.	Epitympanum is formed from extension of tympanic cavity.	
20th				Intratemporal segment begins to be enclosed by bone.
21st	Cord of epithelial cells begins to resolve to form a canal.			
22nd			Antrum appears as a lateral extension of epitympanum.	
23rd			Tegmen tympani begins to ossify.	
24th	Pinna attains adult shape.			
28th	Meatal plate is hollowed out to form inner two thirds of EAM.		Pneumatization of petrous pyramid starts.	Closure of facial canal is nearly complete.
30th			Expansion of tympanic cavity is complete, and its pneumatization starts.	
32nd		Ossification of malleus and incus is complete.		
33rd			Pneumatization of mastoid starts.	
34th			Expansion of epitympanum is complete, and its pneumatization starts.	
35th			Most of antrum is pneumatized.	
After birth	Ossification of EAM is complete by 2 years of age. Both pinna and EAM reach adult size at approximately 9 years of age.		Pneumatization of tympanic cavity is almost complete at birth. Most of mastoid air cells are developed after birth. Tympanic membrane is almost adult size at birth and changes relative position during first 2 years.	Extratemporal segment runs just under skin in newborn.

AFP, acousticofacial primordium; EAM, external auditory meatus; GG, geniculate ganglion.

be found when they are not in their normal locations.

An intensive campaign should be carried out to obtain the temporal bones from all patients with known anomalies of the ear, other associated anomalies, or conductive and sensorineural hearing loss of unknown origin so that histopathologic studies of the temporal bone can be done.

SELECTED REFERENCES

Konigsmark W, Gorlin RJ. Genetic and Metabolic Deafness. Philadelphia, WB Saunders, 1976.
This textbook is a valuable reference source for information on many types of hereditary hearing loss.
Schuknecht HF. Pathology of the Ear, 2nd ed. Philadelphia, Lea & Febiger, 1993.
This textbook should be extremely helpful to both researchers and clinicians who concern themselves with the function of hearing in association with anomalies of the external and middle ears.

REFERENCES

1. Aase JM, Smith DW. Facial asymmetry and abnormalities of palms and ears. A dominantly inherited developmental syndrome. J Pediatr 76:928, 1970.
2. Abu-Libdeh B, Fujimoto A, Ehinger M. Syndrome of cleft palate, microcephaly, large ears, and short statue. Am J Med Genet 45:358, 1993.
3. Adkins WY Jr, Gussen R. Oval window absence, bony closure of round window, and inner ear anomaly. Laryngoscope 84:1210, 1974.
4. Adkins WY Jr, Gussen R. Temporal bone findings in the third and fourth pharyngeal pouch (DiGeorge) syndrome. Arch Otolaryngol 100:206, 1974.
5. Altmann F. Anomalies of the internal carotid artery and its branches. Laryngoscope 58:313, 1947.
6. Altmann F. Problem of so-called congenital atresia of the ear. Arch Otolaryngol 50:759, 1949.
7. Altmann F. Malformations of the auricle and the external auditory meatus (a critical review). Arch Otolaryngol 54:115, 1951.
8. Altmann F. Malformations of the eustachian tube, the middle ear, and its appendages (a critical review). Arch Otolaryngol 54:241, 1951.

9. Altmann F. Congenital atresia of the ear in man and animals. Ann Otol Rhinol Laryngol 64:824, 1955.

10. Altmann F. The ear in severe malformations of the head. Arch Otolaryngol 66:7, 1957.

11. Altmann F. The temporal bone in osteogenesis imperfecta congenita. Arch Otolaryngol 75:486, 1962.

12. Arnold W, Schuknecht HF, von Voss H. Felsenbeinbefunde bei der Trisomie 22. Laryngol Rhinol Otol (Stutlg) 60:545, 1981.

13. Baldwin JL. Dysostosis craniofacialis of Crouzon. Laryngoscope 78:1660, 1968.

14. Balkany TJ, Mischke RE, Downs MP, et al. Ossicular abnormalities in Down's syndrome. Otolaryngol Head Neck Surg 87:372, 1979.

15. Bart RS, Pumphrey RE. Knuckle pads, leukonychia and deafness. A dominantly inherited syndrome. N Engl J Med 276:202, 1967.

16. Basek M. Anomalies of the facial nerve in normal temporal bones. Ann Otol Rhinol Laryngol 71:382, 1962.

17. Bergsma D. Birth defects compendium. In Bergsma D (ed). Birth Defects Compendium. New York, AR Liss, 1979.

18. Bergstrom L. Osteogenesis imperfecta. Otologic and maxillofacial aspects. Laryngoscope 87 (Suppl):6, 1977.

19. Bergstrom L, Hemenway WG, Sando I. Pathological changes in congenital deafness. Laryngoscope 82:1777, 1972.

20. Bhaya MH, Schaherm P, Morizono T, et al. Potter's syndrome: a temporal bone histopathological study. J Otolaryngol 22:195, 1993.

21. Bilgin H, Kasemsuwan L, Schachern PA, et al. Temporal bone study of Down's syndrome. Arch Otolaryngol Head Neck Surg 122:271, 1996.

22. Black FO, Myers EN, Rorke LB. Aplasia of the first and second branchial arches. Arch Otolaryngol 98:124, 1973.

23. Black FO, Sando I, Wagner JA, et al. Middle and inner ear abnormalities, 13–15 (D_1) trisomy. Arch Otolaryngol 93:615, 1971.

24. Black FO, Spanier SS, Kohut RI. Aural abnormalities in partial DiGeorge syndrome. Arch Otolaryngol 101:129, 1975.

25. Blake KD, Russel-Eggitt IM, Morgan DW, et al. Who's in CHARGE? Multidisciplinary management of patients with CHARGE association. Arch Dis Child 65:217, 1990.

26. Bordley JE, Hardy JMB. Laboratory and clinical observations on prenatal rubella. Ann Otol Rhinol Laryngol 78:917, 1969.

27. Buran DJ, Duvall AJ. The oto-palato-digital (OPD) syndrome. Arch Otolaryngol 85:394, 1967.

28. Cannistra C, Barbet JP, Houette A, et al. Mandibulo-facial dysostosis: compartion study of a neonate with mandibulo-facial dysostosis and a normal neonate. J Craniomaxillofac Surg 26:92, 1998.

29. Caparosa RJ, Klassen D. Congenital anomalies of the stapes and facial nerve. Arch Otolaryngol 83:420, 1966.

30. Chitayat D, Hodgkinson KA, Chen MF, et al. Branchio-oto-renal syndrome: further delineation of an underdiagnosed syndrome. Am J Med Genet 43:970, 1992.

31. Church MW, Gerkin KP. Hearing disorders in children with fetal alcohol syndrome: findings from case reports. Pediatrics 82:147, 1988.

32. Clarren SK, Smith DW. The fetal alcohol syndrome. N Engl J Med 198:1063, 1978.

33. Cohen Jr MM, Rollnick BR, Kaye CI. Oculoauriculovertebral spectrum: an updated critique. Cleft palate J 26:276, 1989.

34. Cohn M, Statloff J, Lindsay JR. Histiocytosis X (Letterer-Siwe disease) with involvement of the inner ear. Arch Otolaryngol 91:24, 1970.

35. Converse JM, Nigro A, Wilson FA, et al. A technique for surgical correction of lop ears. Plast Reconstr Surg 15:411, 1955.

36. Corey JP, Caldarelli DD, Gould HJ. Otopathology in cranial facial dysostosis. Am J Otol 8:14, 1987.

37. Cousins VC, Milton CM. Congenital ossicular abnormalities: a review of 68 cases. Am J Otol 9:76, 1988.

38. Cremers CWRJ. Hearing loss in Pfeiffer's syndrome. Int J Pediatr Otorhinolaryngol 3:343, 1981.

39. Cremers CWRJ, Hombergen GCHJ, Scaf JJ, et al. X-linked progressive mixed deafness with perilymphatic gusher during stapes surgery. Arch Otolaryngol 111:249, 1985.

40. Cremers CWRJ, Hoogland GA, Kuypers W. Hearing loss in the cervico-oculo-acoustic (Wildervanck) syndrome. Arch Otolaryngol 110:54, 1984.

41. Cremers CWRJ, van der Burgt CJAM. Hearing loss in Noonan syndrome. Int J Pediatr Otorhinolaryngol 23:81, 1992.

42. Cross HE, Pfaffenbach DD. Duane's retraction syndrome and associated congenital malformations. Am J Ophthalmol 73:442, 1972.

43. Davenport SL, Hefner MA, Mitchell JA. The spectrum of clinical features in CHARGE syndrome. Clin Genet 29:298, 1986.

44. Davis J. Aesthetic and reconstructive otoplasty. New York, Springer-Verlag, 1987.

45. De La Cruz A, Linthicum FH, Luxford WM. Congenital atresia of the external auditory canal. Laryngoscope 95:421, 1985.

46. De Lange C. Sur un type nouveau de degeneration(Typus Amstelodamenis). Arch Med Enf 36:713, 1933.

47. Dijkstra BKS. Goldenhar's syndrome, oculo-auricular malformation, in a Bantu girl. ORL 39:101, 1977.

48. Dhooge I, Lemmerling M, Lagache M, et al. Otological manifestation of CHARGE association. Ann Otol Rhinol Laryngol 107:935, 1998.

49. Druss JG. Supernumerary muscle of middle ear. Arch Otolaryngol 55:206, 1952.

50. Durcan DJ, Shea JJ, Sleeckx JP. Bifurcation of the facial nerve. Arch Otolaryngol 86:619, 1967.

51. Egami T, Sando I, Myers EN. Temporal bone anomalies associated with congenital heart disease. Ann Otol Rhinol Laryngol 88:72, 1979.

52. Epstein CJ, Graham CB, Hodgkin WE, et al. Hereditary dysplasia of bone with kyphoscoliosis, contractures, and abnormally shaped ears. J Pediatr 73:379, 1968.

53. Escher F, Hirt H. Dominant hereditary conductive deafness through lack of incus-stapes junction. Acta Otolaryngol (Stockh) 65:25, 1968.

54. Fernandez AO, Ronis ML. Congenital absence of the oval window. Laryngoscope 74:186, 1964.

55. Fisher SR, Farmer JC, Baylin G. Bilateral congenital absence of the stapes and cervical spine anomaly. Am J Otol 4:166, 1982.

56. Fitch N, Lindsay JR, Srolovitz H. The temporal bone in the preauricular pit, cervical fistula, hearing loss syndrome. Ann Otol 85:268, 1976.

57. Flannery DB. Syndrome of imperforate oropharynx with costovertebral and auricular anomalies. Am J Med Genet 32:189, 1989.

58. Føns M. Ear malformations in cleidocranial dysostosis. Acta Otolaryngol (Stockh) 67:483, 1969.

59. Forney WR, Robinson SJ, Pascoe DJ. Congenital heart disease, deafness, and skeletal malformations: a new syndrome? Pediatrics 68:14, 1966.

60. Fowler EP Jr. Variations in the temporal bone course of the facial nerve. Laryngoscope 71:937, 1961.

61. Freire-Maia N. A newly recognized genetic syndrome of tetramelic deficiencies, ectodermal dysplasia, deformed ears, and other abnormalities. Am J Hum Genet 22:370, 1970.

62. Friedmann I, Spellacy E, Crow J, et al. Histopathological studies of temporal bones in Hurler's disease [mucopolysaccharidosis (MPS) IH]. J Laryngol Otol 99:29, 1985.

63. Friedmann I, Wright JLW, Phelps PD. Temporal bone studies in anencephaly. J Laryngol Otol 94:929, 1980.

64. Gnanapragasam A. Bilateral symmetrical maldevelopment of the external ear and middle ear cleft with pharyngeal and soft palate defects. J Laryngol Otol 89:845, 1975.

65. Goldberg MF, McKusick VA. X-linked colobomatous microphthalmos and other congenital anomalies. A disorder resembling Lenz's dysmorphogenetic syndrome. Am J Ophthalmol 71:1128, 1971.

66. Goldberg MJ, Pashayan HM. Hallux syndactyly-ulnar polydactyly-abnormal ear lobes: a new syndrome. Birth Defects 12:255, 1976.

67. Goldman NC, Singleton GT, Holly EH. Aberrant internal carotid artery. Arch Otolaryngol 94:269, 1971.

68. Goodhill V. Syphilis of the ear: a histopathologic study. Ann Otol Rhinol Laryngol 48:676, 1939.

69. Grant WE, Grant WJ. Stapedius tendon ossification: a rare cause of congenital conductive hearing loss. J Laryngol Otol 105:763, 1991.

70. Gussen R. Middle and inner ear changes in congenital rubella. Am J Otolaryngol 2:314, 1981.

71. Guyot JP, Gacek RR, DiRaddo P. The temporal bone anomaly in CHARGE association. Arch Otolaryngol Head Neck Surg 113:321, 1987.

72. Haginomori SI, Sando I, Miura M, et al. Temporal bone histopathology in CHARGE association. Ann Otol Rhinol Laryngol (in press).

73. Handzic-Cuk J, Cuk V, Gluhinic M. Mastoid pneumatization and

aging in children with Pierre-Robin syndrome and in the cleft palate population out of syndrome. Eur Arch Otorhinolaryngol 256: 5, 1999.

74. Harada T, Black FO, Sando I, et al. Temporal bone histopathologic findings in congenital anomalies of the oval window. Otolaryngol Head Neck Surg 88:275, 1980.

75. Harada T, Sando I. Temporal bone histopathologic findings in Down's syndrome. Arch Otolaryngol 107:96, 1981.

76. Harada T, Sando I, Stool SE, et al. Temporal bone histopathologic features in Fanconi's anemia syndrome. Arch Otolaryngol 106:275, 1980.

77. Harada T, Takahara T, Ishii S. Three-dimensional reconstruction of the temporal bone from a case of E trisomy. Laryngoscope 103: 541, 1993.

78. Harrison WH, Shambaugh GE Jr, Derlacki EL. Congenital absence of the round window: case report with surgical reconstruction by cochlear fenestration. Laryngoscope 76:967, 1966.

79. Hemenway WG, Sando I, McChesney D. Temporal bone pathology following maternal rubella. Arch Klin Exp Ohr Nas Kehlk Heilk 193:287, 1969.

80. Henderson JL. The congenital facial diplegia syndrome: clinical features, pathology and aetiology. A review of sixty-one cases. Brain 62:381, 1939.

81. Herberts G. Otological observations on the "Treacher Collins syndrome." Acta Otolaryngol (Stockh) 54:457, 1962.

82. Hinojosa R, Green JD, Brecht K, et al. Otocephalus: histopathology and three-dimensional reconstruction. Otolaryngol Head Neck surg 114:44, 1996.

83. Hiraide F, Nomura Y, Nakamura K. Histopathology of atresia auris congenita. J Laryngol Otol 88:1249, 1974.

84. Hoenk BE, McCabe BF, Anson BJ. Cholesteatoma auris behind a bony atresia plate. Arch Otolaryngol 89:470, 1969.

85. Hollister DW, Klein SH, De Jager HJ, et al. The lacrimo-auriculo-dento-digital syndrome. J Pediatr 83:438, 1973.

86. Hoo JJ. The Aarskog (facio-digito-genital) syndrome. Clin Genet 16:269, 1979.

87. Hough JVD. Malformations and anatomical variations seen in the middle ear during the operation for mobilization of the stapes. Laryngoscope 68:1337, 1958.

88. Hough JVD. Congenital malformations of the middle ear. Arch Otolaryngol 78:335, 1963.

89. Igarashi M, Filippone MV, Alford BR. Temporal bone findings in Pierre Robin syndrome. Laryngoscope 86:1679, 1976.

90. Igarashi M, Takahasi M, Alford BR, et al. Inner ear morphology in Down syndrome. Acta Otolaryngol (Stockh) 83:175, 1977.

91. Ilyina HJ, Lurie IW. Dubowitz syndrome: possible evidence for a clinical subtype. Am J Med Genet 35:561, 1990.

92. Isenberg SF, Tubergen LB. An unusual congenital middle ear ossicular anomaly. Arch Otolaryngol 106:179, 1980.

93. Ishijima K, Sando I. Multiple temporal bone anomalies in isotretinoin syndrome: a temporal bone histopathologic case report. Arch Otolaryngol Head Neck Surg 125:1385, 1999.

94. Jafek BW, Nager GT, Strife J, et al. Congenital aural atresia: an analysis of 311 cases. ORL 80:588, 1975.

95. Jaffee IS. Congenital shoulder-neck-auditory anomalies. Laryngoscope 78:2119, 1968.

96. Jahn AF, Ganti K. Major auricular malformations due to Accutane (isotretinoin). Laryngoscope 97:832, 1987.

97. Jahrsdoerfer RA. Congenital absence of the oval window. Trans Am Acad Ophthalmol Otolaryngol 84:904, 1977.

98. Jahrsdoerfer RA. The facial nerve in congenital middle ear malformations. Laryngoscope 91:1217, 1981.

99. Jamal MN, Samara NS, Al-Lozi MTA. Moebius' syndrome: a report of two cases. J Laryngol Otol 102:350, 1988.

100. Jørgensen MB, Kristensen HK, Buch NH. Thalidomide-induced aplasia of the inner ear. J Laryngol Otol 78:1095, 1964.

101. Kaga K, Tamai F, kitazumi E, et al. Auditory brainstem responses in children with Cornelia de Lange syndrome. Int J Pediatr Otorhinolaryngol 31:137, 1995.

102. Karmody CS, Schuknecht HF. Deafness in congenital syphilis. Arch Otolaryngol 83:18, 1966.

103. Kelemen G. Hurler's syndrome and the hearing organ. J Laryngol Otol 80:791, 1966.

104. Kelemen G. Rubella and deafness. Arch Otolaryngol 83:520, 1966.

105. Kodama A, Sando I, Myers EN, et al. Severe middle ear anomaly with underdeveloped facial nerve. Arch Otolaryngol 108:93, 1982.

106. Koide Y, Kato I, Yamasaki H, et al. Congenital anomalies of the ossicles without deformities of the external ear. Jpn J Otol 70:1358, 1967.

107. König R, Schick U, Fuchs S. Townes-Brocks syndrome. Eur J Pediatr 150:100, 1990.

108. Konigsmark W, Gorlin RJ. Genetic and Metabolic Deafness. Philadelphia, WB Saunders, 1976.

109. Kos AO, Schuknecht HF, Singer JD. Temporal bone studies in 13–15 and 18 trisomy syndromes. Arch Otolaryngol 83:439, 1966.

110. Kosseff AL, Herrmann J, Opitz JM. The Wiedemann-Beckwith syndrome: genetic considerations and a diagnostic sign. Lancet 1: 844, 1972.

111. Kraus P, Ziv M. Incus fixation due to congenital anomaly of chorda tympani. Acta Otolaryngol (Stockh) 72:358, 1971.

112. Lammer EJ, Chen DT, Hoar RM, et al. Retinoic acid embryopathy. N Engl J Med 313:817, 1985.

113. Lemmerling MM, Vanzieleghem BD, Dhooge IJ, et al. The Lacrimo-Auriculo-Dento-Digital (LADD) syndrome: temporal bone CT findings. J Comput assist Tomogr 23:362, 1999.

114. Lindsay JR, Black FO, Donnelly WH. Acrocephalo-syndactyly (Apert's syndrome). Temporal bone findings. Ann Otol Rhinol Laryngol 84:174, 1975.

115. Lindsay JR, Sanders SH, Nager GT. Histopathologic observations in so-called congenital fixation of the stapedial footplate. Laryngoscope 70:1587, 1960.

116. Livingstone G, Delahunty JE. Malformation of the ear associated with congenital ophthalmic and other conditions. J Laryngol Otol 82:495, 1968.

117. Maack RW, Muntz HR. Ossicular abnormality in Larsen's syndrome: a case report. Am J Otolaryngol 12:51, 1991.

118. Maran AGD. Persistent stapedial artery. J Laryngol Otol 79:971, 1965.

119. Marion M, Hinojosa R, Khan AA. Persistence of the stapedial artery: a histopathologic study. Otolaryngol Head Neck Surg 93: 298, 1985.

120. Martini A, Comacchio F, Candiani F, et al. Branchio-oto-renal dysplasia and branchio-oto dysplasia: report of eight cases. Am J Otol 8:116, 1987.

121. McDonough SR. Fanconi anemia syndrome. Arch Otolaryngol 92: 284, 1970.

122. McGrew RN, Gregg JB. Anomalous fusion of the malleus to the tympanic ring. Ann Otol Rhinol Laryngol 80:138, 1971.

123. McLay K, Maran AGD. Deafness and the Klippel-Feil syndrome. J Laryngol Otol 83:175, 1969.

124. Melnick M, Bixler D, Nance WE, et al. Familial branchio-oto renal dysplasia: a new addition to the branchial arch syndromes. Clin Genet 9:25, 1976.

125. Melnick M, Bixler D, Silk K, et al. Autosomal dominant branchio-oto-renal dysplasia. Birth Defects 11:121, 1975.

126. Mendoz HMM, Opitz JM. Noonan syndrome: a review. Am J Med Genet 21:493, 1985.

127. Mengel MC, Konigsmark BW, Berlin CI, et al. Conductive hearing loss and malformed low-set ears, as a possible recessive syndrome. J Med Genet 6:14, 1969.

128. Meurman Y. Congenital microtia and meatal atresia. Observations and aspects of treatment. Arch Otolaryngol 66:443, 1957.

129. Miura M, Sando I, Takasaki K, et al. Histopathological study of temporal bone and eustachian tube in oculoauriculovertebral spectrum. Ann Otol Rhinol Laryngol 110:922, 2001.

130. Miura M, Sando I, Haginomori SI, et al. Histopathological study on temporal bone and eustachian tube in trisomy 22. Int J Pediatr Otorhinolaryngol 56:191, 2000.

131. Miyata H, Kato Y, Yoshimura M, et al. Temporal bone findings in cloverleaf skull syndrome. Acta Otolaryngol (Stockh) Suppl. 447: 105, 1988.

132. Moreano EH, Paparella MM, Zelterman D, et al. Prevalence of facial canal dehiscence and of persistent stapedial artery in the human middle ear: a report of 1000 temporal bones. Laryngoscope 104:309, 1994.

133. Morgenstein KM, Manace ED. Temporal bone histopathology in sickle cell disease. Laryngoscope 79:2172, 1969.

134. Murofushi T, Ouvrier RA, Parker GD, et al. Vestibular abnormalities in charge association. Ann Otol Rhinol Laryngol 106:129, 1997.

135. Myers EN, Stool SE. The temporal bone in osteopetrosis. Arch Otolaryngol 89:460, 1969.
136. Nager GT. Osteogenesis imperfecta of the temporal bone and its relation to otosclerosis. Ann Otol Rhinol Laryngol 97:585, 1988.
137. Nance WE, Stetleff R, McLedd A. X-linked deafness with congenital fixation of the stapedial footplate and perilymphatic gusher. Birth Defects 4:64, 1971.
138. Nassif S, Harboyan G. Madelung's deformity with conductive hearing loss. Arch Otolaryngol 91:175, 1970.
139. Ohtani I, Dubois CN. Aural abnormalities in Klippel-Feil syndrome. Am J Otol 6:468, 1985.
140. Ohtani I, Schuknecht HF. Temporal bone pathology in DiGeorge's syndrome. Ann Otol Rhinol Laryngol 93:220, 1984.
141. Okuno T, Takahashi H, Shibahara Y, et al. Temporal bone histopathologic findings in Alagille's syndrome. Arch Otolaryngol Head Neck Surg 116:217, 1990.
142. Opheim O. Loss of hearing following the syndrome of van der Hoeve-De Kleyn. Acta Otolaryngol (Stockh) 65:337, 1968.
143. Pagon RA, Graham JM Jr, Zonata J, et al. Coloboma, congenital heart disease, and choanal atresia with multiple anomalies: CHARGE association. J Pediatr 99:223, 1981.
144. PeBenito R, Ferretti C. Kabuki makeup syndrome (Niikawa-Kuroki syndrome) in a black child. Ann Ophthalmol 21:312, 1989.
145. Pettenati MJ, Haines JL, Higgins RR, et al. Wiedemann-Beckwith syndrome: presentation of clinical and cytogenic data on 22 new cases and review of the literature. Hum Genet 74:143, 1986.
146. Pfaffenbach DD, Cross HE, Kearns PK. Congenital anomalies in Duane's retraction syndrome. Arch Ophthalmol 88:635, 1972.
147. Phelps PD, Lloy GAS, Poswillo DE. The ear deformities in craniofacial microsomia and oculo-auriculo-vertebral dysplasia. J Laryngol Otol 97:995, 1983.
148. Phelps PD, Poswillo D, Lloy GAS. The ear deformity in mandibulofacial dysostosis (Treacher Collins syndrome). Clin Otolaryngol 6:15, 1981.
149. Phelps PD, Reardon W, Pembrey M, et al. X-linked deafness, stapes gusher and a distinctive defect of the inner ear. Neuroradiology 33:326, 1991.
150. Piza JE, Northrop CC, Eavey RD. Neonatal mesenchyme temporal bone study: typical receding pattern versus increase in Potter's sequence. Laryngoscope 106:856, 1996.
151. Pou JW. Congenital absence of the oval window. Laryngoscope 73:384, 1963.
152. Pron G, Galloway C, Armstrong D, et al. Ear malformation and hearing loss in patients with Treacher Collins syndrome. Cleft Palate Craniofac J 30:97, 1993.
153. Proudman TW, Moore MH, Abbott AH, et al. Noncraniofacial manifestations of Crouzon's disease. J Craniofac Surg 5:218, 1994.
154. Ramos Arroyo MA, Weaver DD, Beals RK. Congenital contractural arachnodactyly. Report of four additional families and review of literature. Clin Genet 27:570, 1985.
155. Richards SH, Gibbin KP. Recurrent meningitis due to congenital fistula of stapedial footplate. J Laryngol Otol 91:1063, 1977.
156. Rimoin DL, Edgerton MT. Genetic and clinical heterogeneity in the oral-facial-digital syndrome. J Pediatr 71:94, 1967.
157. Ritter FN. The histopathology of the congenital fixed malleus syndrome. Laryngoscope 81:1304, 1971.
158. Robinson GC, Wildervanck LS, Chiang TP. Ectrodactyly, ectodermal dysplasia, and cleft lip-palate syndrome. Its association with conductive hearing loss. J Pediatr 82:107, 1973.
159. Rodini ESO, Richieri-Costa A. EEC syndrome: report on 20 new patients, clinical and genetic considerations. Am J Med Genet 37:42, 1990.
160. Roizin H, Toren M, Berkenstadt M, et al. Congenital heart disease and external ear anomalies with hearing loss: a report of two new cases and a review of the literature. J Craniofac Genet Dev Biol 9:225, 1989.
161. Ruben RJ, Toriyama M, Dische MR, et al. External and middle ear malformations associated with mandibulo-facial dysostosis and renal abnormalities: a case report. Ann Otol Rhinol Laryngol 78:605, 1969.
162. Rüedi L. The surgical treatment of atresia auris congenita: a clinical and histological report. Laryngoscope 64:666, 1954.
163. Ruggles RL, Reed RC. Symposium on ear surgery. V. Treatment of aberrant carotid arteries in the middle ear: a report of two cases. Laryngoscope 82:1199, 1972.
164. Saad JJ, Schuknecht HF. Otologic manifestations of the hydantoin syndrome. Am J Otolaryngol 7:360, 1986.
165. Saito H, Kishimoto S, Furuta M. Temporal bone findings in a patient with Mobius syndrome. Ann Otol Rhinol Laryngol 90:80, 1981.
166. Saito R, Takata N, Matumoto N, et al. Anomalies of the auditory organ in Potter's syndrome. Arch Otolaryngol 108:484, 1982.
167. Sakai N, Igarashi M, Miller RH. Temporal bone findings in VATER syndrome. Arch Otolaryngol Head Neck Surg 112:416, 1986.
168. Sando I, Bergstrom L, Wood RP II, et al. Temporal bone findings in trisomy 18 syndrome. Arch Otolaryngol 91:552, 1970.
169. Sando I, Hemenway WG, Morgan WR. Histopathology of the temporal bones in mandibulofacial dysostosis (Treacher Collins syndrome). Trans Am Acad Ophthalmol Otol 72:913, 1968.
170. Sando I, Ikeda M. Temporal bone histopathological findings in oculo-auriculo-vertebral dysplasia (Goldenhar syndrome). Ann Otol Rhinol Laryngol 95:396, 1986.
171. Sando I, Leiberman A, Bergstrom L, et al. Temporal bone histopathological findings in trisomy 13 syndrome. Ann Otol Rhinol Laryngol 84 (Suppl):21, 1975.
172. Sasaki T, Kaga K, Ohira Y, et al. Temporal bone and brain stem histopathological findings in Cornelia de Lange syndrome. Int J Pediatr Otorhinolaryngol 36:195, 1996.
173. Schuknecht HF. Pathology of sensorineural deafness of genetic origin. In McConnell F, Ward PH (eds). Deafness in Childhood. Nashville, Vanderbilt University Press, 1967, pp 69–90.
174. Schuknecht HF. Pathology of the Ear. Cambridge, MA, Harvard University Press, 1974.
175. Schuknecht HF. Pathology of the Ear, 2nd ed. Philadelphia, Lea & Febiger, 1993.
176. Sellars SL, Beighton PH. Deafness in osteodysplasty of Melnick and Needles. Arch Otolaryngol 104:225, 1978.
177. Shi SR. Temporal bone findings in a case of otopalatodigital syndrome. Arch Otolaryngol 111:119, 1985.
178. Shibahara Y, Sando I. Congenital anomalies of the eustachian tube in Down syndrome. Ann Otol Rhinol Laryngol 98:543, 1989.
179. Silcox L. The ear. In Rubin A (ed). Handbook of Congenital Malformation. Philadelphia, WB Saunders, 1967, pp 229–247.
180. Stallings JO, McCabe BF. Congenital middle ear aneurysm of internal carotid. Arch Otolaryngol 90:39, 1969.
181. Steffen TN. Vascular anomalies of the middle ear. Laryngoscope 78:171, 1968.
182. Stratton HJM. Gonadal dysgenesis and the ears. J Laryngol Otol 79:343, 1965.
183. Strome M. Down's syndrome: a modern otorhinolaryngological perspective. Laryngoscope 91:1581, 1981.
184. Szpunar J, Rybak M. Middle ear disease in Turner's syndrome. Arch Otolaryngol 87:34, 1968.
185. Tabor JR. Absence of the oval window. Arch Otolaryngol 74:515, 1961.
186. Tachibana M, Hoshino A, Oshima W, et al. Duane's syndrome associated with crocodile tear and ear malformation. Arch Otolaryngol 110:761, 1984.
187. Takahashi H, Sando I. Facial canal dehiscence: histologic study and computer reconstruction. Ann Otol Rhinol Laryngol 101:925, 1992.
188. Takasaki K, Sando I, Balaban CD, et al. Postnatal development of eustachian tube cartilage. A study of normal and cleft palate cases. Int J pediatr Otorhinolaryngol 52:31, 2000.
189. Thomas IT, Frias JL, Felix V, et al. Isolated and syndromic cryptophthalmos. Am J Med Genet 25:85, 1986.
190. Townes PL, Brocks ER. Hereditary syndrome of imperforate anus with hand, foot, and ear anomalies. J Pediatr 81:321, 1972.
191. Vallino-Napoli LD. Audiologic and otologic characteristics of Pfeiffer syndrome. Cleft Palate Craniofac J 33:524, 1996.
192. Vase P, Prytz S, Pedersen PS. Congenital stapes fixation, symphalangism and syndactylia. Acta Otolaryngol (Stockh) 80:394, 1975.
193. Warkany J. Congenital Malformations: Notes and Comments. Chicago, Year Book, 1971, pp 401–416.
194. Watkin PM. Otological disease in Turner's syndrome. J Laryngol Otol 103:731, 1989.
195. Weber PC, Perez BA, Bluestone CD. Congenital perilymphatic fistula and associated middle ear abnormalities. Laryngoscope 103:160, 1993.
196. Wells MD, Phelps PD, Michaels L. Oculo-auriculo-vertebral dysplasia. A temporal bone study of a case of Goldenhar's syndrome. J Laryngol Otol 97:689, 1983.

197. Willis R. Conductive deafness due to malplacement of 7th nerve. J Otolaryngol 6:1, 1977.
198. Windle-Taylor P, Emery PJ, Phelps PD. Ear deformities associated with the Klippel-Feil syndrome. Ann Otol 90:210, 1981.
199. Winter JSD, Kohn G, Mellman WJ, et al. A familial syndrome of renal, genital and middle ear anomalies. J Pediatr 72:88, 1968.
200. Winther LK, Elbrønd O. Congenital anomaly of the facial nerve. J Laryngol Otol 91:349, 1977.
201. Wright CG, Brown OE, Meyerhoff WL, et al. Auditory and temporal bone abnormalities in CHARGE association. Ann Otol Rhinol Laryngol 95:480, 1986.
202. Wright JLW, Etholm B. Anomalies of the middle ear muscles. J Laryngol Otol 87:281, 1973.
203. Yamanobe S. Temporal bone findings in a case of Cornelia de Lange syndrome. Pract otol (Kyoto) Suppl 32:100, 1989 (in Japanese).
204. Zellweger H, Bardach J, Bordwell J, et al. The short arm deletion syndrome of chromosome 4 (4p-syndrome). Arch Otolaryngol 101:29, 1975.
205. Zonis RD. Meckel's cartilage remnant. Laryngoscope 79:2012, 1969.

21

Surgical Management of Microtia and Congenital Aural Atresia

J. Arturo Bonilla, M.D., and Robert F. Yellon, M.D.

Microtia is the most common major congenital anomaly of the external ear. Surgical management of microtia and congenital aural atresia remains among the most challenging problems in reconstructive surgery and otology. Surgery for microtia involves a delicate balance between the aesthetics of the auricular reconstruction and the limitations of blood supply to the local tissue flaps used for the reconstruction. The fine details of microtia reconstruction require the surgeon to have a complete understanding of the three-dimensional form of the auricle as well as sound surgical principles of soft tissue management and transfer. For microtia reconstruction, the preservation of adequate blood supply must always take precedence over cosmesis, to avoid complications. With technical advances in the reconstruction of the microtic ear, results have been dramatically improving in the hands of experienced ear reconstructive surgeons. For congenital aural atresia, the challenge arises from the altered anatomy and the absence of the usual surgical landmarks. Considerable skill and judgment are required to determine the actual surgical landmarks in cases of congenital aural atresia. Safety in preservation of hearing and the seventh cranial nerve must always take precedence over the desire to improve hearing. On the other hand, use of high-resolution computed tomography (CT) and seventh nerve electrophysiologic monitoring represent significant advances in increasing the safety of aural atresia reconstruction.

Special acknowledgement must be given to Burt Brent,[4] for his excellent work in the area of microtia reconstruction, and to Robert Jahrsdoerfer,[39] whose technique and results set the standard for congenital aural atresia repair. Many of the techniques described in this chapter are derived from the work of these surgeons.

Demographics and Associated Deformities

The incidence of microtia or congenital aural atresia has been reported to be 1 in 1000 to 1 in 5800 to 8000 births.[15] In a report on 1000 patients with microtia by Brent, 58% of cases were right-sided, 32% were left-sided, and 9% were bilateral. Sixty-three percent of the patients were male and 37% were female. Associated de-

formities were common and included facial asymmetry (36.5%), facial nerve weakness (15.2%), cleft lip or palate or both (4.3%), urogenital defects (4%), cardiovascular malformations (2.5%), and macrostomia (2.5%). Recurrence of microtia within the family occurred 4.9% of the time in the immediate family and 10.3% of the time when extended families were included.

Microtia may occur as a result of in utero tissue ischemia secondary to obliteration of the stapedial artery or actual hemorrhage into the local tissues.[20] Some studies have reported an increased trend in the prevalence at birth of auricular anomalies with maternal age.[10] Genetic studies have revealed several possible etiologic factors causing microtia, such as chromosomal aberrations, multifactorial inheritance, and both autosomal and recessive traits. Known teratogens associated with microtia include thalidomide, isotretinoin, vincristine, colchicine, and cadmium.[18, 23, 24, 30] Associated anomalies such as oculoauriculovertebral (Goldenhar) syndrome, or Treacher-Collins syndrome should be noted. Syndromes associated with microtia and aural atresia are listed in Table 21–1.

Classification of Microtia

Microtia is classified from less severe (grade I) to absence of the external ear (anotia) (grade IV), as follows:

Grade I: (Fig. 21–1) The pinna is malformed and smaller than normal. Most of the characteristics of the pinna, such as the helix, triangular fossa, and scaphae, are present with relatively good definition.

Grade II: (Fig. 21–2) The pinna is smaller and less developed than in grade I. The helix may or may not be fully developed. The triangular fossa, scaphae, and antihelix have much less definition.

Grade III: (Fig. 21–3) The pinna is essentially absent except for a vertical, sausage-shaped skin remnant. The superior aspect of this sausage-shaped skin remnant consists of underlying unorganized cartilage, and the inferior aspect of this remnant consists of a relatively well-formed lobule.

Grade IV (Anotia): (Fig. 21–4) There is total absence of the pinna.

TABLE 21–1. Diseases with Anomalies of the External and Middle Ears Listed by Pathologic Defect and Traditional Name

Pathologic Name	Eponym
4p–syndrome	Wolf-Hirschhorn syndrome
Acrocephalosyndactyly type I	Apert syndrome
Acrocephalosyndactyly type III	Saethre-Chotzen syndrome
Acrocephalosyndactyly type V	Pfeiffer syndrome
Anus imperforate with hand, foot, and ear anomalies	Townes-Brocks syndrome
Arteriohepatic dysplasia	Alagille syndrome
Brevicollis	Klippel-Feil syndrome
Cervico-oculoacoustic syndrome	Wildervanck syndrome
Cleft palate, microcephaly, large ears, and short stature	Say syndrome
Cleft palate, micrognathia, and glossoptosis	Pierre Robin syndrome
Congenital contractural arachnodactyly	Beals syndrome
Congenital facial diplegia	Möbius syndrome
Constitutional aplastic pancytopenia with multiple anomalies	Fanconi syndrome
Craniofacial dysostosis	Crouzon disease
Craniometaphyseal dysplasia	Pyle disease
Dyschondrosteosis	Léri-Weill syndrome
Exomphalos-macroglossia-gigantism syndrome	Beckwith-Wiedemann syndrome
Faciodigitogenital syndrome	Aarskog syndrome
Gargoylism	Hurler syndrome
Gonadal aplasia	Turner syndrome
Lacrimoauriculodentodigital syndrome	Levy-Hollister syndrome
Mandibulofacial dysostosis	Treacher-Collins syndrome
Oculoauriculovertebral dysplasia	Goldenhar syndrome
Orofaciodigital syndrome type II	Mohr syndrome
Osteodysplasty	Melnick-Needles syndrome
Osteopetrosis	Albers-Schönberg disease
Renal agenesis, bilateral	Potter syndrome
Third and fourth pharyngeal pouch syndrome	DiGeorge syndrome
Trisomy 13–15 syndrome	Patau syndrome
Trisomy 18 syndrome	Edwards syndrome
Trisomy 21 syndrome	Down syndrome

From Sando S, et al. Pediatric Otolaryngology, 3rd ed.

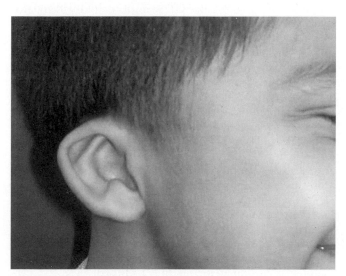

FIGURE 21–1. Grade I microtia.

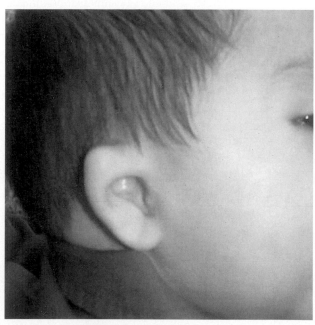

FIGURE 21–2. Grade II microtia.

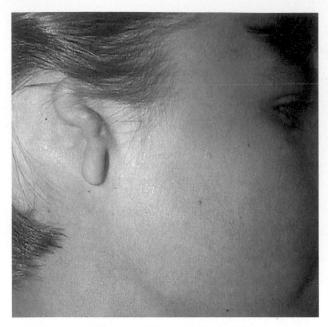

FIGURE 21–3. Grade III microtia.

Initial Evaluation

The ideal time to consult on a patient born with microtia and congenital aural atresia is soon after birth. Because this condition is rarely noticed prenatally, it is very traumatic for the parents. During the initial consultation, the ear reconstructive surgeon should initially reassure the parents, as well as outline the future management of their child's condition. The parents should be told that the two important factors are, first, maximizing the opportunity for good hearing and, second, cosmesis. Of course a thorough history should be obtained and physical examination performed, with special attention to the anomalous ear as well as the normal ear. A history of intrauterine exposure to teratogens should be sought.

Assuming that the microtia or atresia is the only developmental anomaly, the evaluation of the child's hearing status is mandatory. Auditory brain stem response testing

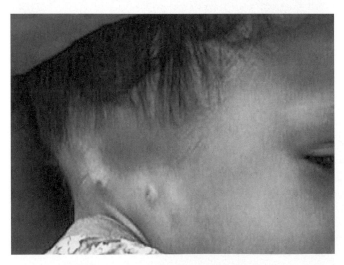

FIGURE 21–4. Grade IV microtia or anotia.

should be performed within the first 2 or 3 months of age, to document the hearing function in the normal ear and, if possible, the degree and type of hearing loss in the atretic ear. The bone conduction is usually, but not always, normal with aural atresia. Conductive hearing loss is usually maximal at 60 dB secondary to the lack of the external auditory canal as well as to ossicular fixation. For unilateral cases, no special intervention is needed other than preferential seating and close otologic follow-up for the normal ear. Speech is usually normal in the unilateral microtia/atresia patients. Frequent otologic evaluations are very important to rule out other possible problems, such as otitis media in the normal ear. A slightly lower threshold for tympanostomy tube placement should be considered in patients with recurrent acute otitis media and persistent otitis media to preserve hearing in the normal ear, since the anomalous ear usually has maximal conductive loss. For bilateral cases of microtia and congenital aural atresia, a bone conduction hearing aid is placed as soon as possible.

Computed tomography of the temporal bones, in both the axial and the coronal plane, is obtained when the child is several months old to evaluate the anatomy for possible reconstruction and to rule out the presence of possible cholesteatoma. The incidence of congenital cholesteatoma in aural atresia has been reported to be between 4% and 7%.[17, 29] Even if no surgery for the aural atresia is contemplated, an initial CT scan should be obtained as well as a repeat CT scan several years later. The repeat CT scan is important to rule out congenital cholesteatoma that enlarged but was not evident on the initial scan (Fig 21–5). Evidence of cholesteatoma or chronic suppurative otitis media that is refractory to intravenous antimicrobials is an indication for surgery even if the anatomy is unfavorable for a good hearing result. The parents should be counseled to look for the signs and symptoms of complications of cholesteatoma or chronic suppurative otitis media such as facial twitching, vertigo, a mass near the microtic vestige, or drainage.

Figure 21–6 shows the CT scan of a child with microtia/atresia who had staphylococcal chronic suppurative otitis media that was refractory to intravenous antimicrobial agents. The middle and inner ears were severely anomalous. The patient had CHARGE association, and the affected ear was anacoustic. He also had no seventh nerve function on that side. He was judged to not be a candidate for microtia reconstruction because of behavioral problems. He underwent radical mastoidectomy with temporalis muscle flap obliteration of the cavity. Interestingly, yellowish tissue removed during the procedure proved to be ectopic salivary gland. The patient has done well with no further otorrhea.

The parents should be counseled about the realistic expectations for both hearing and cosmesis. In general, they should be told that an auricle may be constructed that will look much better than the microtic vestige but that it will not look perfectly normal. Similarly, if the anatomy is favorable for hearing reconstruction, the parents are counseled that hearing may improve dramatically, but that the expectation of perfectly normal hearing is probably unrealistic. The parents should be informed that the overall plan for reconstruction of both the auricle

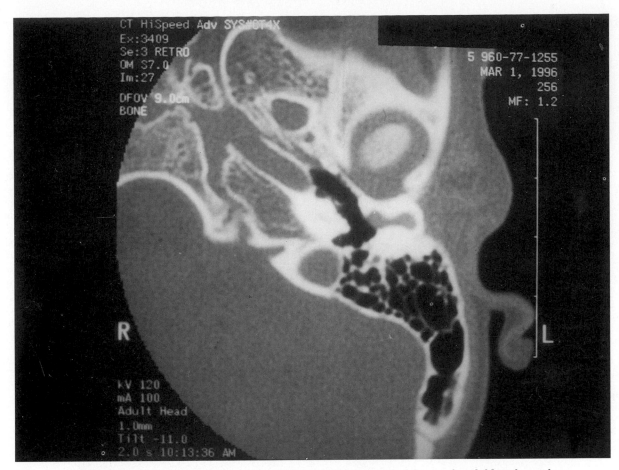

FIGURE 21–5. Axial computed tomography scan of left temporal bone of a child with aural atresia and congenital cholesteatoma. Note soft tissue density medial to atretic plate. The aural atresia and maximal conductive hearing were repaired. The final speech reception threshold was 10 dB.

and the aural atresia will require several staged surgeries and that revision surgery may be required to refine the results. Possible complications, which are discussed in the following sections, should be described. The child should be followed in the office at 6- to 12-month intervals.

Anatomy of the Ear

The anatomy of the external, middle, and inner ear should be well known to the reconstructive surgeon (Fig. 21–7). The important landmarks include the helix, helical crus, antihelix, crura of the antihelix, tragus, antitragus, scapha, triangular fossa, concha cymba, concha cavum, and lobule.

During the sixth week of gestation, the first and second arches give rise to six hillocks called the hillocks of His. The first three hillocks are derived from the first arch and the final three hillocks are derived from the second arch. These hillocks then fuse, forming the future ear. The structures of the adult ear corresponding to the hillocks are the tragus (first hillock), the helical crus (second hillock), the helix (third hillock), the antihelix (fourth and fifth hillocks), and the antitragus (sixth hillock).[1]

The primary blood supply to the external ear is via the superficial temporal artery and branches of the posterior auricular artery. The sensory innervation of the external ear is via the anterior and posterior branches of the greater auricular nerve.

The location and reference point of the ear must be well understood. The angle of the long axis of the ear approximates the angle of the nasal dorsum. The superior point of the ear is usually at the eyebrow level. In the average 5- to 7-year-old child, the helical crus is approximately 6.5 to 7 cm from the lateral canthus. The inferiormost aspect of the lobule on the microtic ear is usually 0.5 cm higher than on the normal side.

Psychology of Patients with Microtia or Atresia

Before the age of 3 to 4 years, there is usually little psychological impact on a child with a microtic ear. After this time, children usually begin to notice that their ears are different. It is essential that the parents treat the child as normal as any other child. Although it may not be obvious to the parents, children feel their anxiety. Parents who attempt to cover the ear tend to hinder the confidence of the child. The children with the lowest self-esteem tend to be the ones whose parents transmitted anxiety about the ear throughout their childhood. Patients whose ears have not been reconstructed as children have

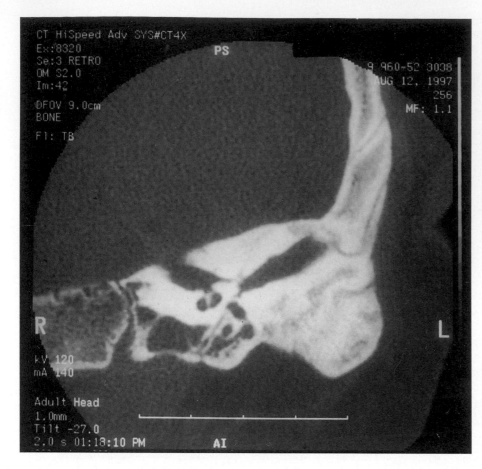

FIGURE 21–6. Coronal computed tomography scan of left temporal bone of a child with CHARGE association aural atresia, chronic staphylococcal suppurative otitis media, and an ectopic salivary gland. Note severe anomalies of the inner ear. The otorrhea did not resolve with intravenous antimicrobials. There was associated anacusis and no facial nerve function. Radical mastoidectomy with temporalis muscle flap obliteration was performed. Yellowish tissue removed from mastoid cavity proved to be an ectopic salivary gland.

to deal with the peer pressure of adolescence. During this time, "fitting in" with their peers is of much importance. Teenagers are particularly conscious of their looks and are very aware of their microtic ear. Although they tend to be more eager to undergo surgical reconstruction, their expectations tend to be more unrealistic.

Timing and Sequence of Surgeries for Microtia and Aural Atresia

Our preference is to begin auricular reconstruction at the age of 5 to 6 years. In a large child with bilateral microtia or atresia, reconstruction may begin at 4 to 5 years of age because the need for reconstruction of the auricle and for improved hearing is more pressing than with the unilateral anomaly. On the other hand, for a petite child with unilateral microtia or atresia, reconstruction can be deferred until a later age. If possible, it is desirable to complete reconstruction before the patient reaches the age of 7 years, so that the child can both benefit from the improved hearing and avoid the psychological trauma of ridicule from others and the altered self-image concerning the congenital anomaly. Various surgeons have recommended reconstruction to begin at a wide range of ages, from 2 to 9 years. Proponents for early reconstruction argue that psychological trauma is minimized and hearing function is improved with early intervention. Proponents

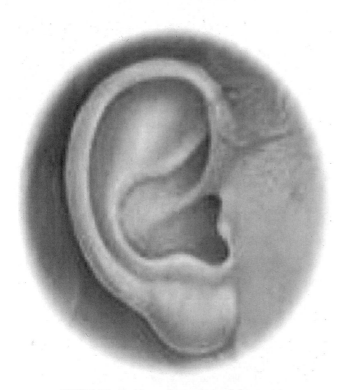

FIGURE 21–7. Normal anatomy of the auricle.

for later reconstruction argue that better cosmetic results are obtained when the available rib cartilage is larger to allow more detail and projection to be carved into the graft. Additionally, an older child will be more cooperative with dressing changes and postoperative management.

Although some otologists have reported series of aural atresia repairs without microtia repairs, we feel strongly that the auricle reconstruction should precede the aural atresia reconstruction. The best chances for auricle reconstruction occur when the skin and tissues of the surgical site have not been previously operated on. Previous operations may compromise the blood supply to the surgical site and may decrease the chances of successful cartilage graft implantation.

Not all surgeons should undertake auricular reconstruction. Considerable experience is required for flap design, elevation, and delicate tissue handling. Also of critical importance are the technical skills and artistic abilities required to sculpt a cartilage graft that is aesthetically appealing. Appropriate surgical training and practice carving auricles in soap, wood, or some other material is important prior to undertaking the actual procedure.

The presence of a low hairline that will bring undesirable hair-bearing skin to cover the top of the auricle is a problem that can be managed by preoperative laser hair removal or following microtia reconstruction by electrolysis or by replacing the hair-bearing skin with full-thickness skin grafts.[3, 4, 36] Yotsuyanagi et al[40] described the use of a regional postauricular flap as the first stage of microtia repair to allow excision of the low hair line with replacement by the flap.

For unilateral cases, the normal ear is used as a template for the cartilage graft. Radiographic film is used as the template material, as it can be sterilized for use in the surgical field. For bilateral cases, the ear of a volunteer is used as the template and the template is saved for use during the second auricular reconstruction. Aguillar[1] suggests using the mother's ear as the template for bilateral cases. The dimensions of the graft are carved approximately 3 mm smaller than the template to allow for the thickness of the overlying skin flaps after implantation. Photographic documentation of the initial anomaly, as well as before and after all stages of reconstruction, is important for improvement of results, for teaching, and for possible medicolegal situations.

The first stage is cartilage graft implantation. Prophylactic perioperative antimicrobial agents are administered for all stages of reconstruction. The synchondrosis of the sixth and seventh ribs and an additional portion of the seventh rib lateral to the synchondrosis are harvested via a curvilinear incision along the lower rib border (Fig. 21–8). This graft is used for the body of the auricular reconstruction. Portions of the eighth rib and floating ninth rib are also harvested and will be sculpted into the helix of the reconstructed auricle. The perichondrium is left on the cartilage. An additional wedge of cartilage from the more medial portion of the synchondrosis can be harvested and banked for later use to increase projection of the auricle during the third stage, which is elevation.[4] The rib cartilage harvest is performed on the side of the

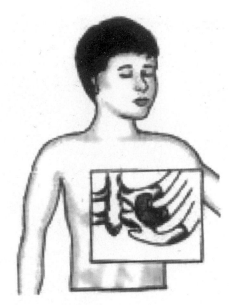

FIGURE 21–8. Rib harvest site. Cartilage for the body of the graft is harvested from the seventh rib and the synchondrosis of the sixth rib. Helix is harvested from the eighth and ninth ribs. The superior rim of the sixth rib is preserved to decrease the chances of chest wall deformity. A medial piece of cartilage may also be harvested and banked for later use.

body opposite the auricular reconstruction because the curve of the ribs is more favorable to increase projection of the auricle.

If cartilage is plentiful, as with an older child or adult, the auricular cartilage graft can be carved as a solid block (Fig. 21–9). If the amount of rib cartilage that is available is small, an open framework can be fashioned by suturing the helical rim to the body of the graft in a manner that allows the helix to bow out from the body (Fig. 21–10). Thus, spaces within the graft are acceptable when cartilage is scarce.

If the parietal pleura is violated during rib harvest, it can be closed over a rubber suction tube, which is removed during final chest incision closure while the anesthesiologist applies positive pressure ventilation. Persistent pneumothorax does not usually occur unless the visceral pleura of the lung is violated, and then a chest tube should be placed. A closed suction drain is usually placed after the parietal pleura and muscular layers are closed.

Scalpels, gouges, and rasps are used to sculpt the cartilage graft. Power tools are avoided because they increase trauma to the chondrocytes. To create the helix, the cartilage is thinned, and small, partial-thickness incisions can be made around the outside surface of the helical cartilage to help weaken its tendency to resist being placed in a curved position. Perichondrium is preserved whenever possible. The separate portions of the graft are sutured together with 4-0 clear nylon sutures. Care is taken to bury all sutures and knots away from the surface of the graft to decrease the chances of extrusion. Additional small pieces of cartilage that are sculpted appropriately can be stacked over parts of body or helix to increase lateral projection and detail (see Fig. 21–10). To increase

FIGURE 21-9. Auricular cartilage graft carved as a solid block from an older child who had a generous amount of donor rib cartilage.

lateral projection of the helix, the helix can be sutured to the body of the graft in a more lateral position instead of flush with its medial surface.[4]

If sufficient cartilage is available, the surgeon can create a tragus during the first stage of reconstruction by suturing a strut of cartilage from the bottom of the body of the graft in the area of the antitragus to the root of the helix. If sufficient cartilage is not available, the tragus can be created using the methods described later in the section on fourth-stage reconstruction.

In most cases of microtia, the auricular vestige is functionally and cosmetically useless. However, the skin overlying the auricular vestige is precious and is preserved for coverage of the cartilage graft. An incision is made anterior to the vestige, and the skin flap is carefully elevated in a plane just deep to the subdermal plexus. On one hand, it is important to have a thin skin flap to obtain maximal detail of the cartilage graft. On the other hand, it is critical to avoid disruption of the blood supply to the skin flap, which may lead to flap loss, cartilage graft exposure, infection, and ultimate loss of the cartilage graft. Therefore, whenever a decision is to be made between the two competing influences of the desire for a thin flap versus risking loss of critical blood supply and flap necrosis, preserving blood supply must be chosen.

The template is used to mark the position of the auricular graft. For the unilateral anomaly, the graft should be positioned at a vertical level equivalent with the normal ear. Additionally, care should be taken to place the auricular graft in an anterior to posterior position that is equal to the distance of the normal ear to the lateral canthus. When additional anomalies are present, such as hemifacial microsomia with significant facial asymmetry (Fig. 21-11), considerable judgment is required for the most optimal placement of the graft for the best aesthetic result. Finally, to simulate the normal axis of the auricle, it is important to place the auricular graft in approximately a 30-degree angle, with the position of the superior portion of the auricular reconstruction placed in a more posterior position than the inferior portion.

The microtic cartilage vestige is excised, preserving as much skin as is possible. Deep dissection should not be undertaken, to avoid possible injury to an aberrant seventh nerve. The skin flap is elevated beyond the marked position for the auricular graft to provide relaxation for the skin flap to cover the cartilage graft without tension. If tension is excessive and the skin flap blood supply is

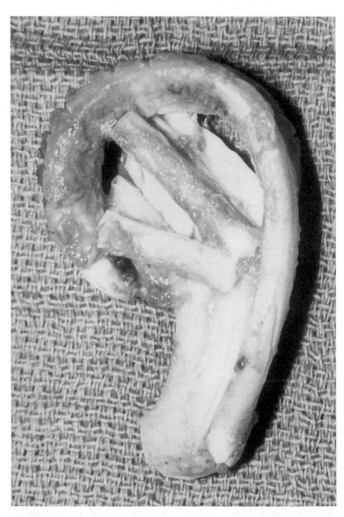

FIGURE 21-10. Cartilage graft created with mild deficiency of rib cartilage. Note how two additional pieces of cartilage were carved and beveled and then stacked on top of the body of the graft to increase projection and detail in the area of the superior and inferior crura. The helix was also allowed to bow out from the body to create a pleasing helical contour in areas where the cartilage of the body was insufficient (open framework).

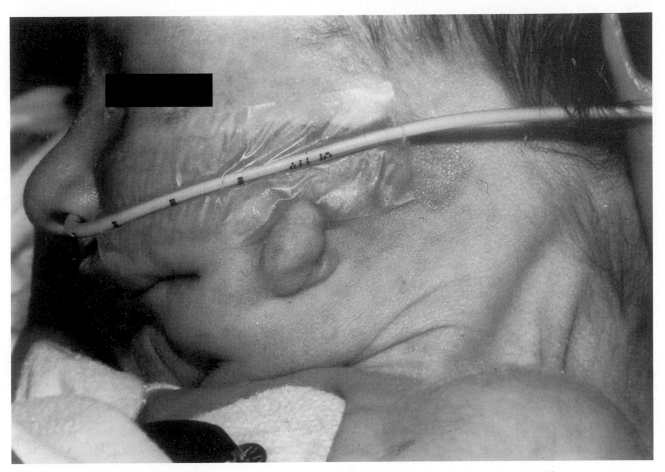

FIGURE 21–11. Severe microtia/aural atresia associated with oculoauriculovertebral (Goldenhar) syndrome. This child had significant mandibular hypoplasia with airway obstruction and required tracheotomy.

questionable, a full-thickness skin graft may be placed with an overlying bolster, to allow a minimal tension closure. Skin grafting is usually not necessary at this stage. Brent[4] described the use of an expandable catheter for acute tissue expansion to decrease skin tension when necessary.

After cartilage graft placement, two small suction drains are placed to remove blood and to better coapt the skin flaps to the auricular graft (Fig. 21–12). Using sutures to coapt the skin to the cartilage graft results in a greater chance of compromise of the blood supply and skin flap loss and is not recommended.[3] Vaseline gauze dipped in antibiotic ointment is packed into the nooks and crannies over the skin flap and cartilage graft. A sterile mastoid dressing is then applied. The drains are removed after 5 to 7 days when the drainage becomes minimal. Incentive spirometry is used to decrease the atelectasis that frequently occurs from pain and chest wall splinting at the rib harvest site.

At least 2 or 3 months are allowed between the various stages of auricular reconstruction to allow for adequate healing and vascularization of the flaps and grafts. If a lobule is present, it should be preserved at the time of auricular graft implantation and used for the second stage of the reconstruction. The lobule associated with a microtic auricle is usually positioned too far anterosupe-

riorly. The second stage of auricular reconstruction is essentially a Z-plasty with lobule rotation into a more posterior and inferior position (Fig. 21–13). The flaps of the Z-plasty are trimmed and beveled to achieve a smooth transition from the body of the reconstructed auricle to the lobule without unnatural excessive lateral projection of the lobule or extra skin folds. The lateral projection of the lobule can also be decreased by placement of a suture from skin on the medial side of the lobule portion of the Z-plasty to the soft tissue on the medial portion of the auricular cartilage graft, which rotates the lobule medially.

The third stage of auricular reconstruction is the elevation of the auricle, with creation of a postauricular sulcus using a split-thickness skin graft 0.017 inch in thickness (Fig. 21–14). The postauricular incision is made approximately 3 to 4 mm posterior and superior to the cartilage graft. The auricle is elevated in the plane just lateral to the temporalis fascia. Care is taken to leave the perichondrium and soft tissue attached to the cartilage graft and to avoid direct cartilage exposure, which may increase the chances of infection and decrease the chances of skin graft healing. The elevation is carried anteriorly as far as possible, but preservation of the blood supply to the anteriorly based flap of the reconstructed auricle must be given highest priority.

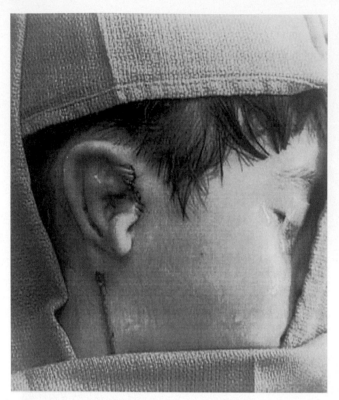

FIGURE 21–12. First-stage microtia repair. The majority of the skin of the microtic vestige was preserved. Note how the lobule is positioned too far anterosuperiorly. Note the small suction drain.

The scalp posterior and superior to the auricle is undermined and advanced so that the edge of the scalp incision lies medial to the cartilaginous auricle and thus the edge of the incision is hidden from the lateral view. This advancement of the scalp also decreases the size of the area that requires skin grafting. A split-thickness skin

graft is harvested from an inconspicuous site on the hip, buttocks, or medial surface of the upper arm. It is sutured into the exposed area on the medial surface of the auricular graft and to the defect anterior to the scalp advancement flap. The sutures for the skin graft are left long and a bolster is placed.

A variant of microtia is cryptotia. With cryptotia, the cartilaginous auricle, lobule, external auditory canal, and tympanic membrane are well formed, but the auricle never separated from the head and thus no postauricular sulcus is present. Repair of cryptotia is essentially the same as the auricular elevation stage of microtia repair. Yellon et al[11] described elevation of a cryptotic ear with advancement of the postauricular scalp and placement of a full-thickness skin graft (Fig. 21–15).

A common problem that occurs following the third-stage repair is formation of a postauricular scar that obliterates part of the postauricular sulcus and decreases lateral projection of the auricle. This problem can be managed in several ways. A simple method is to incise the postauricular scar and cover the raw area with a full-thickness skin graft. This method is the simplest but results in the least augmentation of the lateral projection of the auricle. The second method involves harvest of an additional wedge of cartilage at the initial time of rib harvest. The wedge is banked subcutaneously in the postauricular area or chest wall incision, or may be harvested at a later time. If the outer portion of the rib is harvested and the perichondrium is left intact, a warping of the cartilage will occur that provides a favorable curvature to the cartilage. This wedge-shaped graft is placed in the postauricular sulcus after incision of the scar or as part of the first-stage repair. The wedge is then covered with a postauricular occipitalis fascial advancement flap followed by a split-thickness skin graft.[4] An alternative is to use a temporoparietal fascia flap followed by split-thickness skin to cover the wedge. The temporoparietal flap and cartilage wedge are used as the preferred method of auricle

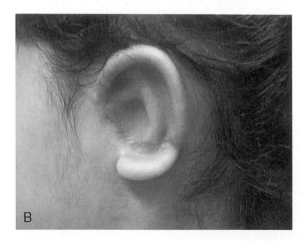

FIGURE 21–13. Second-stage microtia repair. *A*, Note how the lobule is positioned too far anterosuperiorly. Incisions for Z-plasty are marked. *B*, Completed Z-plasty with transposition of lobule. Note how the tissue of the lobule was trimmed to create a smooth transition from the lobule to the rest of the reconstructed auricle.

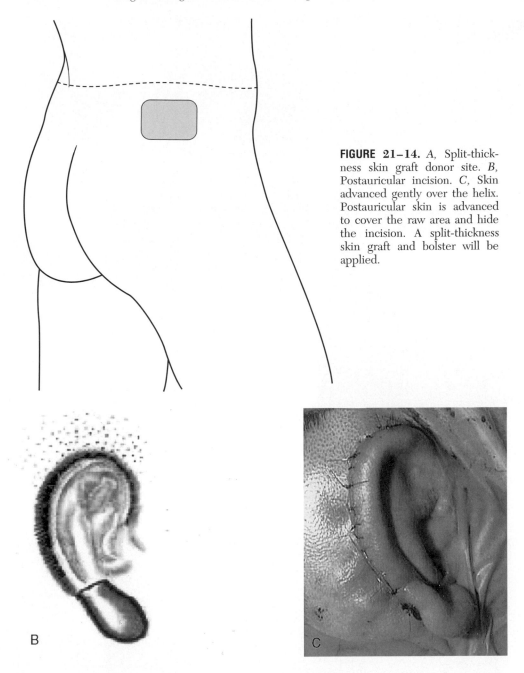

FIGURE 21–14. *A,* Split-thickness skin graft donor site. *B,* Postauricular incision. *C,* Skin advanced gently over the helix. Postauricular skin is advanced to cover the raw area and hide the incision. A split-thickness skin graft and bolster will be applied.

B

C

elevation by some authors.[21] There is less overall dissection with the postauricular occipitalis fascia flap than the temporoparietal flap, and if the former flap is used, the latter flap can be saved for salvage procedures.

A fourth method for reconstruction of a postauricular sulcus was described by Eavey.[9] Instead of advancing the hair-bearing scalp superior to the auricle in an inferior direction, Eavey excises a portion of this skin and replaces it with full-thickness skin. A second full-thickness skin graft is placed on the medial surface of the auricular cartilage graft.

If no lobule is present, there are two options. The first is to carve the lobule as part of the cartilage graft during the first stage. During the second stage, a Z-plasty can be performed during which the skin that should have contained the lobule (but is simply flat) is wrapped around

the medial and lateral portion of the cartilage graft that was carved to be the lobule. Alternatively, no second stage is performed and the lobule is created during the elevation of the reconstructed auricle, which is usually the third stage. In this situation, the elevation is carried more inferiorly and anteriorly to allow elevation of the part of the auricle that was carved as the lobule. Next, the tissues posterior and inferior to the lobule portion of the cartilage graft are advanced anterosuperiorly to lie medial to this portion of the cartilage graft. The skin covering the lobule portion of the cartilage graft is gently advanced over the cartilaginous lobule. If local skin coverage is inadequate, the usual split-thickness skin graft used for the third stage is extended to cover the exposed area on the medial surface of the cartilage graft.

For bilateral cases, the third stage should not be per-

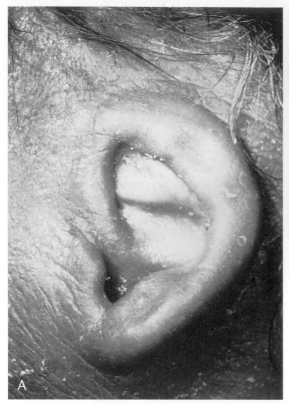

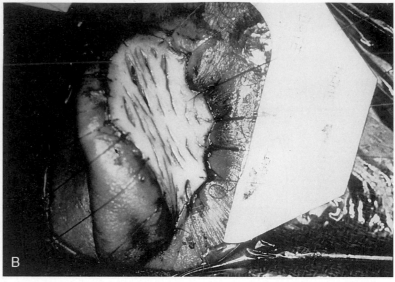

FIGURE 21–15. *A,* Auricle of a child with cryptotia associated with a genetic skin disorder (ichthyosis). Although well-formed, the auricle never separated from the head and is quite flat. *B,* Auricle of a child with cryptotia that was reconstructed by postauricular incision, scalp advancement, and full-thickness skin grafting. Note that the sutures that secured the skin graft are left long to allow the bolster to be tied in place.

formed on both sides simultaneously, to avoid necrosis of the postauricular split-thickness skin graft of the reconstruction on the first side while the surgeon performs the third-stage reconstruction on the second side (B. Brent, personal communication). For bilateral cases, however, the second stage or Z-plasty for lobule rotation can be done on both sides simultaneously, if the blood supply appears to be robust.

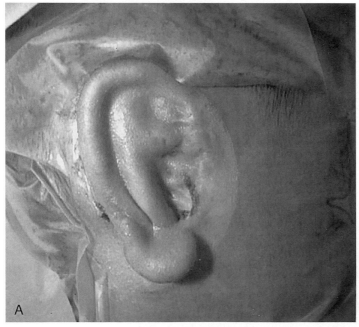

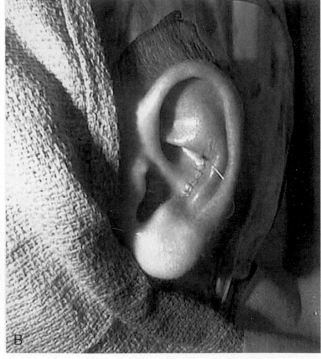

FIGURE 21–16. *A,* Tragal reconstruction. A J-shaped incision for the chondrocutaneous graft recipient site. *B,* Donor site of the chondrocutaneous graft from a normal auricle.

The fourth stage of auricular reconstruction involves creation of a tragus and the appearance of an external auditory meatus (Fig. 21–16). In cases in which there is sufficient cartilage, the tragus can be created during the first stage of reconstruction, as described earlier. If a tragus is not created during the first stage, then, ideally, tragal reconstruction can be combined with the definitive aural atresia reconstruction (Fig. 21–17). Two choices are available for the tragal reconstruction as a fourth-stage procedure. For unilateral cases, the tragus is fashioned from a chondrocutaneous composite flap that is harvested from the lateral aspect of the concha of the normal ear (see Fig. 21–16B). This procedure simultaneously provides a composite graft for the tragus and reduces the lateral projection of the normal ear to improve frontal symmetry.[3] A J-shaped incision (see Fig. 21–16A) is made on the reconstructed auricle, and the skin posterior to the incision is elevated. To create the appearance of a conchal bowl, soft tissue is excised deep to the elevated skin, but caution should be exercised because the seventh nerve may lie in a superficial, vulnerable position. The elevated skin is draped medially over the newly created conchal bowl. Next, the skin anterior to the J-shaped

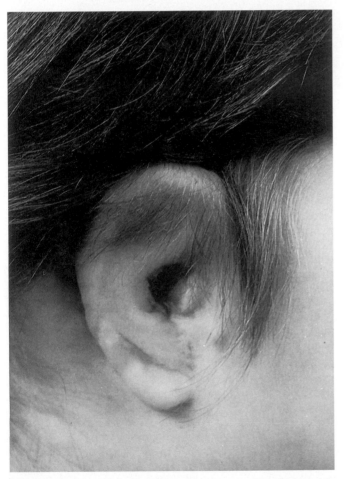

FIGURE 21–17. Final result for the right ear in a child who had bilateral microtia/atresia. Tragal reconstruction was performed at the time of aural atresia repair. An anteriorly based skin flap was used to create the tragus, cover the cartilage graft, and line the anterior portion of the meatus. Some hair removal will still be required on the superior aspect of the auricle.

incision is also elevated for a short distance. The chondrocutaneous graft is sutured into the area of the J-shaped incision with the graft oriented such that the skin of the composite graft lies in a posterior position and the cartilage lies in an anterior position. Additionally, the lateral aspect of the composite graft should be oriented posterior to the medial aspect of the graft. This orientation creates a situation in which the newly created tragus will cast a shadow that helps to create the illusion of a deep external auditory meatus (see Fig. 21–18D). Bolsters made of sterile dental roll are sutured into the concha and to both sides of the newly created tragus to maintain their position and prevent hematoma formation, which could cause skin flap or cartilage loss. Figure 21–18 depicts the four-stage microtia reconstruction technique from beginning to end.

The second choice for the fourth stage of the repair again involves creation of a conchal bowl and a tragus, but an anteriorly based skin flap is used.[32] This choice is usually used for bilateral cases of microtia when no composite graft can be harvested from a normal ear. In this situation, a U-shaped, anteriorly based skin flap is incised and elevated. The surgeon creates the conchal bowl by excising the soft tissue under the skin flap and placing a full-thickness skin graft. A small, rectangular cartilage graft ($6 \times 4 \times 2$ mm) to be used as the tragal cartilage graft is harvested from the larger auricular cartilage graft after the skin and soft tissue are elevated and preserved over the donor site. The cartilage that is harvested for the tragus is from the auricular cartilage graft at the posterior or inferior aspect of the newly created conchal bowl and has the secondary benefit of enlarging the concha. The soft tissues are closed over the exposed cartilage of the donor site.

To create the tragus, the small, rectangular cartilage graft is wrapped anteriorly and posteriorly with the anteriorly based skin flap that was elevated previously. Bolster sutures are placed to maintain the position of the "cartilage sandwich" of the newly created tragus. A bolster is also placed to hold the full-thickness skin graft of the concha in place.

Nagata[21] described a two-stage technique of microtia reconstruction in which he creates the main cartilaginous framework and the tragus and rotates the lobule during the primary procedure. In the second stage of reconstruction, which is elevation of the auricle, Nagata describes the placement of a postauricular wedge of cartilage that greatly increases lateral projection of the reconstructed auricle. The postauricular wedge of cartilage is covered by a temporoparietal fascia flap that is then covered by a skin graft. Advantages of this approach include increased lateral projection of the reconstructed auricle and decreased number of general anesthetic procedures needed. Disadvantages include the increased number of hours that the first procedure takes to complete and the planned use of the temporoparietal axial fascia flap that will then not be available for possible salvage procedures.

Park et al[25] described the variations of blood supply to the temporoparietal flap. Sixty-three percent of flaps were supplied by the usual superficial temporal artery and vein. Nine percent were supplied by the posterior auricular artery, and 3% by the occipital artery. The use

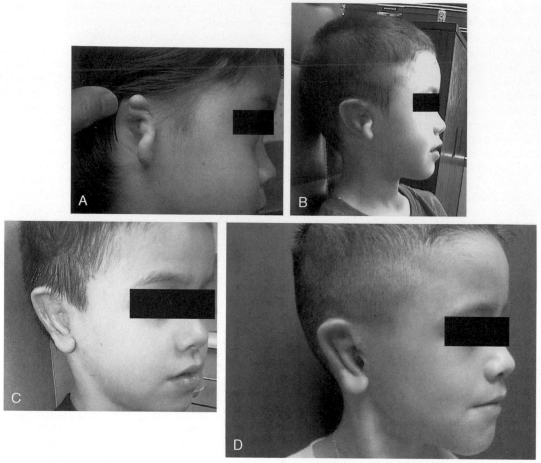

FIGURE 21–18. Four stages of microtia repair. *A,* Initial grade III microtia. *B,* Completed cartilage graft implantation. *C,* Completed lobule rotation and elevation of auricle. *D,* Completed reconstruction of tragus and conchal bowl.

of a Doppler device to identify the feeding vessels may prevent flap loss from transection of unusual feeder vessels.

Complications of Microtia Reconstruction

In microtia surgery, the limits of blood supply to the skin flap may be exceeded. If there are small areas of skin flap loss, they will usually heal with local care as well as topical and systemic antimicrobials. Moderate areas may require full-thickness skin grafting. Larger areas of skin loss require the addition of a viable blood supply from a local flap, such as a temporoparietal flap (Fig. 21–19) with full-thickness skin graft coverage.[25]

Infection of the operative site may be subtle. There may not be purulent discharge. Mild edema and erythema may be the only indicators. The management includes intravenous antimicrobials as well as insertion of small catheters under the skin flaps for irrigation with topical antimicrobials. Cultures should be taken to direct the antimicrobial coverage.

Hematomas can be drained with needle aspiration or open incision and placement of a gentle bolster or drain.

Care must be taken to avoid applying the bolster so tightly as to cause necrosis of the skin flap.

Postauricular scar formation is common following the elevation of the auricle with split-thickness skin grafting (third-stage microtia repair). Whether this scarring represents a true complication rather than a normal variant of wound healing is not clear. This scar typically forms at the junction of the upper two thirds and lower one third of the auricle. The scar partially obliterates the postauricular sulcus and decreases lateral projection of the reconstructed auricle. This common problem can be managed by several methods, as described in the section on the third stage of microtia repair. Nagata[22] has described the use of the innominate fascia flap as a possible source of blood supply for salvage procedures when the temporoparietal flap has been used previously.

Chest wall deformity may result from rib harvest. Preservation of the top rim of the sixth rib above the harvested synchondrosis can help to decrease the chances of chest wall deformity.[4] Eavey and Ryan[8] reported that preservation and retraction of the rectus abdominis muscle during rib harvest instead of division of this muscle decreases the pain and the possibility of chest wall deformity.

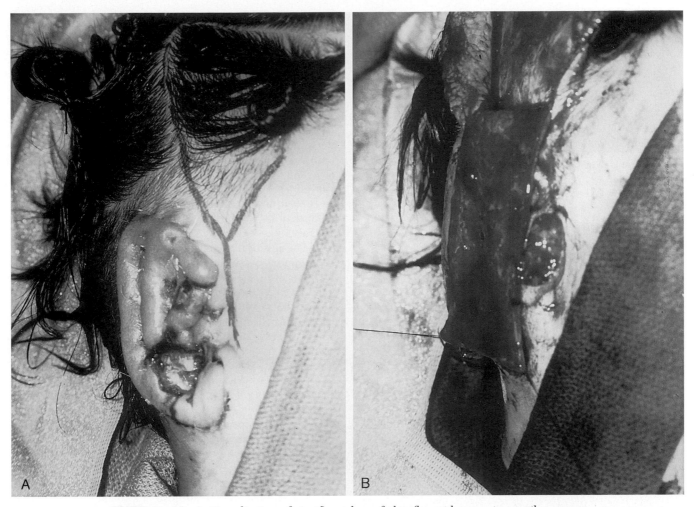

FIGURE 21–19. *A*, Complication of significant loss of skin flap with extensive cartilage exposure following the first stage of microtia repair by a surgeon other than the authors. Note the incision lines marked for temporoparietal flap. *B*, A salvage procedure was performed with a temporoparietal flap that was turned down and tunneled under the skin flap and then covered with full-thickness skin graft.

Alternatives to Microtia Reconstruction

In poor surgical candidates or those who wish to avoid surgery, a prosthetic ear can be used. The prosthesis can be anchored to the patient's skull with glue, or transcutaneous titanium osseointegrated implants can be used as anchors. The indications for placement of osseointegrated implants include patients who have undergone major cancer resection; those who have received radiation therapy; those with compromised local tissues, failed autogenous reconstruction, or significant additional craniofacial anomalies; those who represent a poor operative risk; and those with a preference, either their own or their family's, for a prosthesis.[37]

In the past, a silicon prosthesis was used by some surgeons instead of the cartilage graft for auricular reconstruction. The silicon prostheses had a higher rate of extrusion and have thus fallen out of favor.[33] Similarly, Medipore frameworks tend to extrude and become infected.[5, 35, 38] In the 1940s, Young[41] and Peer[26] attempted to create cartilaginous auricles from diced cartilage that was placed in Vitallium molds, which were then banked in the abdominal wall. The cartilage was harvested and implanted several months later. The results were often poor, with distortion of the implanted graft that was believed to be secondary to contracture of scar tissue.

New tissue engineering techniques have allowed auricle derived from bovine chondrocytes to be grown on the backs of mice.[6] These techniques have also been applied to human chondrocytes.[28] The tissue-engineered auricles are not yet available for human use but hold promise for the future.

Congenital Aural Atresia Reconstruction

Congenital aural atresia is usually associated with microtia, although there are occasional cases of congenital aural atresia associated with normal auricles. When both anomalies are present, congenital aural atresia reconstruction may be performed after tragal reconstruction has been completed or during the same procedure. Of course, it is desirable to do them simultaneously to decrease the number of general anesthetic procedures required.

TABLE 21–2. Grading System for Candidacy for Surgery for Congenital Aural Atresia

Parameter	Points
Stapes present	2
Oval window open	1
Middle ear space large and favorable	1
Facial nerve position favorable	1
Malleus-incus complex well formed	1
Mastoid well pneumatized	1
Incus and stapes connected	1
Round window visible and open	1
Appearance of external ear is normal	1
Total available points	10

The most important factor in decision making for reconstruction of congenital aural atresia is proper patient selection. Jahrsdoerfer et al[39] have devised a grading scale based on the CT appearance of the temporal bone and auricle to determine which patients are favorable candidates for aural atresia repair. High-resolution axial and coronal CT scans are required to assess the anatomy for aural atresia repair. Each of the factors, if favorable, receives 1 point. The presence of a favorable stapes is the one factor that receives 2 points (Table 21–2; Fig. 21–20). A total score of less than 6 indicates that the patient is not a surgical candidate, while a score of 6 or greater indicates that the patient may be considered as a candidate for aural atresia repair. The higher the number is on the grading scale, the more likely a good hearing result will be obtained.

Since the ultimate hearing result requires conduction of sound vibrations to the inner ear via the oval window, the presence of an open oval window and mobile stapes is most important. With congenital conductive hearing loss, even if a stapes is present, it may be fixed. Stapes fixation occurs in 4% of cases.[14] Therefore, the congenital ear surgeon must always be prepared to perform stapedectomy or stapedotomy during any aural atresia repair, and the family must be aware of the risks of stapedectomy and give consent for this possible portion of the procedure.

A well-pneumatized middle ear space is more favorable than a minimally pneumatized middle ear space, because there will be more room to work in the middle ear. The position of the facial nerve is a critical factor in determining candidacy for aural atresia repair. In a normal ear, the facial nerve will lie superior to the oval window in its horizontal portion. It will then turn inferiorly at the second genu to run through the mastoid cavity in its vertical portion. In congenital aural atresia, the seventh nerve may lie in a normal position. However, a common anomaly of the facial nerve in congenital aural atresia is that the facial nerve may totally or partially cover the oval window and stapes, obscuring the view and thus precluding a surgical approach to the window. Additionally, in the normal course of the facial nerve, the nerve makes approximately a 90-degree turn at the second genu. In congenital aural atresia, the facial nerve may make a more acute turn at the second genu and pass anteriorly instead of inferiorly. In this situation, the facial nerve crosses the middle ear and would be vulnerable to injury during a lateral surgical approach to the middle ear. With high-resolution CT, good patient selection, facial nerve monitoring, and excellent surgical technique, there should be no facial nerve injury.

In aural atresia, it is very common to have a fused malleus-incus complex. Additionally, it is very common to have the complex fixed to the bony atresia plate. It is most favorable when the malleus-incus complex is well formed and attached to the atresia plate in a limited area. It is also favorable when the CT scan shows a well-formed incus to stapes connection. It is not uncommon for the lenticular process to be absent, creating ossicular discontinuity. The presence of a round window is favorable because obliteration of the round window may impair energy transfer from the oval window into the inner ear. A normal auricle is given 1 point because, embryologically, it is formed earlier than the middle ear. A relatively normal auricle may indicate a lesser degree of deformity of the middle ear.

Other factors to consider include the position of the temporomandibular joint and the middle fossa dura. If the temporomandibular joint lies lateral to the middle ear cleft instead of in its usual anterior position, it will preclude a surgical approach. Similarly, if the middle fossa dura is in a low-lying position, it may limit access to the middle ear cleft.

Any anomaly of the inner ear, including vestibule, semicircular canals, or internal auditory canal, excludes

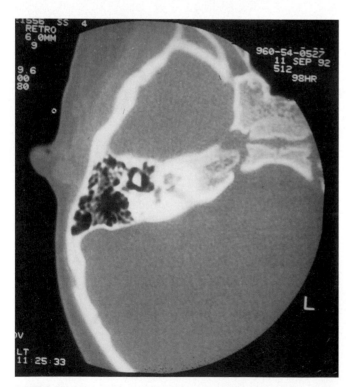

FIGURE 21–20. Axial computed tomography scan of the right temporal bone of a child with bilateral microtia/aural atresia. Note the well-pneumatized middle ear and mastoid cavity, well-formed malleus-incus complex, and the stapes present in the oval window.

the child from being a candidate for aural atresia repair because of an increased incidence of sensorineural hearing loss in this group.[39]

Another useful classification system that assists in developing an appreciation for the spectrum of severity of congenital anomalies of the external auditory canal and middle ear structures is the four-level grading system developed by Schuchtnecht.[29] The type A anomaly is meatal stenosis and is the mildest form. Embryologically, meatal stenosis occurs as a result of partial failure of canalization of the external auditory canal from the usual medial to lateral direction (Fig. 21–21A). There may be associated canal cholesteatoma as desquamated epithelium is trapped and builds up medial to the stenotic area.

The middle ear structures are usually normal or have only mild anomalies. Isolated meatal stenosis may be repaired, if severely narrow, via canaloplasty with drilling of the bony ear canal to widen it. Localized areas of bone exposure may be covered with a full-thickness skin graft. The type B anomaly is a more extensive external auditory canal stenosis.

Middle-ear anomalies are more common (Fig. 21–21B). Again, canaloplasty is performed if the narrowing is severe. Extensive and circumferential areas of exposed bone will require coverage with a split-thickness skin graft. Circumferential full-thickness skin grafts are too bulky and will narrow the canal. Type C anomalies have total aural atresia but relatively normal middle ear struc-

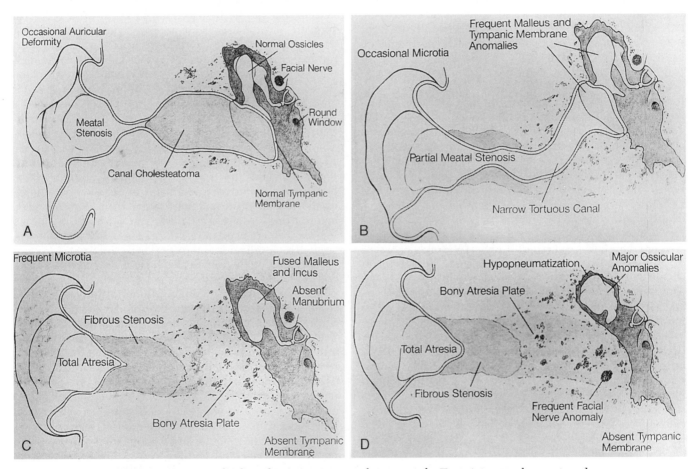

FIGURE 21–21. *A,* Schuchtnecht type A congenital ear anomaly. Type A is meatal stenosis and is the mildest form. Note the associated canal cholesteatoma. The middle-ear structures are usually normal or have only mild anomalies. Isolated meatal stenosis can be repaired, if severely narrow, via canaloplasty with drilling of the bony ear canal to widen it. Localized areas of bone exposure can be covered with a full-thickness skin graft. *B,* Schuchtnect type B congenital ear anomaly. The type B anomaly is a more extensive external auditory canal stenosis. Middle-ear anomalies are more common. Canaloplasty is performed if the narrowing is severe. Extensive and circumferential areas of exposed bone will require coverage with a split-thickness skin graft. Full-thickness skin is too bulky and will narrow the canal. *C,* Schuchtnect type C congenital ear anomaly. Type C anomalies have total aural atresia but relatively normal middle-ear structures and favorable pneumatization and facial nerve position. These ears are repaired by true aural atresia surgery as is described in the text. *D,* Schuchtnecht Type D congenital ear anomaly. Type D anomalies are the most severe. There is true aural atresia as well as poor pneumatization of the middle ear and major ossicular and facial nerve anomalies. Type D atresias may not be candidates for repair because of the severity of the anomalies.

tures and favorable pneumatization and facial nerve position (Fig. 21–21C). These ears are repaired by true aural atresia surgery, as described later. Type D anomalies are the most severe. There is true aural atresia as well as poor pneumatization of the middle ear and major ossicular, and facial nerve anomalies (Fig. 21–21D). Type D atresias may not be candidates for repair because of the severity of the anomalies.

For unilateral atresia, the selection criteria for surgical repair should be slightly more stringent than the criteria used for bilateral cases. In other words, since a child with unilateral atresia has a normal ear, there is less urgency to perform atresia repair for hearing purposes. For bilateral atresia cases, there is a greater need to perform surgical repair in an attempt to improve the hearing to a degree that will allow the child to no longer need the bone conduction hearing aid. This is especially true for boys who find the headband type of bone-conduction hearing aid to be cosmetically unacceptable. Atresia repair is more important in bilateral cases because of the overall greater degree of hearing loss. On the other hand, for unilateral cases, acquisition of binaural hearing and improved sound localization is also desirable.

For bilateral cases, it is reasonable to consider atresia repair as soon as the first three stages of microtia repair are completed, to provide the benefits of improved hearing at as early an age as is possible. For unilateral cases, the timing of atresia repair is controversial. Proponents of early atresia repair believe that acquisition of binaural hearing and sound localization at as early an age as possible is most beneficial for good surgical candidates operated on by skilled surgeons. Proponents of late atresia repair believe that the decision for aural atresia repair should be delayed until the patient is old enough (teenage years or early adulthood) to take part in the decision and is willing to accept the risks of potential facial nerve injury and sensorineural hearing loss.

In the case of bilateral aural atresia, the ear with the better hearing and more favorable anatomy is selected to operate on first. This decision is in contrast to the philosophy in traditional chronic ear surgery in that when bilateral hearing loss is present, the worse-hearing ear is operated on first. For bilateral aural atresia, the better hearing ear and ear with the most favorable anatomy is selected first because this selection maximizes the chances for a good hearing outcome, while minimizing the chances of complications. The better hearing ear would also be operated on in the case of a unilateral total aural atresia with a partial aural atresia or external auditory canal stenosis on the contralateral side. In this situation, maximal conductive hearing loss is found on the total aural atresia side and a lesser degree of conductive hearing loss is found on the partial aural atresia or stenosis side. It is less risky to operate on the ear with partial atresia or stenosis of the external auditory canal because the presence of any bony external canal provides an important surgical landmark that allows easier and less risky access to the middle ear than in the case of total bony aural atresia.

Prior to the definitive aural atresia reconstruction, prophylactic antimicrobials are administered. The reconstructed auricle is elevated via an incision in the postauricular sulcus. The auricle is elevated preferably in the plane of the temporalis fascia. Care is taken to leave the perichondrium attached to the auricular cartilage graft and to preserve the anterior blood supply to the graft. An incision is made through the temporalis fascia and soft tissue down to the bone over the mastoid cortex. The soft tissue is elevated off the bone until the landmarks of the zygomatic root and the temporomandibular joint are identified. There may be a pit or vestige of the tympanic bone that can be used as a landmark to begin drilling the external auditory canal.

In general, the more anterior and superior one drills, the safer it is because this is the least likely position for the facial nerve. Three-dimensional CT can be useful to define the surface topography of the temporal bone to help determine the best location to begin drilling.[16] Most surgeons favor the anterior approach described by Jahrsdoerfer.[15] Earlier surgeons such as Schuchtnecht performed aural atresia repair via a canal wall–down mastoidectomy approach.[29] The poorer hearing results and increased chances for mastoid cavity problems make this approach less desirable. De la Cruz et al[19] described a canal wall–up mastoidectomy approach in which a mastoidectomy is drilled first to identify the depth and position of the horizontal semicircular canal. The external auditory canal is then drilled with preservation of its posterior wall, and the previously identified position of the horizontal semicircular canal helps to anticipate the depth of the atresia plate and middle-ear cleft. This so-called anterior and posterior approach can be useful as an aid for less experienced atresia surgeons, but the anterior approach described by Jahrsdoerfer is preferred.[13]

The dura of the middle fossa is an excellent landmark and it should be identified but not exposed by excessive bone removal. Drilling continues until a thin bony atresia plate is identified. Entry into the middle ear via the attic is preferable. It must be remembered that the fused malleus-incus complex is usually attached to the bony atresia plate, and excessive drill energy may be transmitted to the ossicles during drilling on the atresia plate. Therefore, diamond burrs are used and the preferred technique is to thin the atresia plate to eggshell thickness and then remove it with picks and gentle curettage. It is quite common to find a small degree of high-frequency sensorineural hearing loss following aural atresia repair from transmitted drill energy, even when excellent technique is practiced.[12]

Fixation of the ossicles may occur at multiple sites, including the atresia plate, the attic, and the suspensory ligaments. If a fixated ossicle is mobilized, it is preferable, when possible, to remove significant bone surrounding the fixation site. When this bone is not removed, the growth of new bone and fibrosis often lead to recurrent fixation of the ossicles.

The full spectrum of ossiculoplasty techniques may be required, including stapedectomy.[31] Total or partial ossicular reconstruction prostheses may be required, and these should be covered with a small piece of cartilage harvested from the auricular cartilage graft, with care taken to preserve the perichondrium and close the donor site. It may not be possible to visualize the stapes and oval window without removing the malleus-incus complex. Visualization of the stapes and oval window is always preferable but not always possible without removal of the malleus-incus complex. At that point, a conservative decision can be made to leave the malleus-incus complex in situ and place the temporalis fascia graft that is used for creation of the tympanic membrane directly over the visualized, mobile ossicles, if the CT scan suggests a normal stapes, oval window, and connection between the incus and stapes (Fig. 21–22A).

If unacceptable conductive hearing loss persists, revision surgery can be performed, with removal of the malleus-incus complex and direct visualization of the stapes and oval window. The appropriate ossiculoplasty or stapes

surgery is then performed. If no stapes or oval window is found after a diligent search, the procedure should be aborted. The hearing results following the use of a total or partial ossicular reconstruction prosthesis may be less favorable than when the patients' own ossicles are used.[17] In the setting of aural atresia, fenestration of the horizontal semicircular canal has been associated with increased chances of sensorineural hearing loss and should be abandoned.[15]

The new external auditory canal and bony annulus should be widened as much as is possible, up to 15 mm in diameter. In practice, achieving 15 mm diameter is uncommon, since the widening of most external auditory

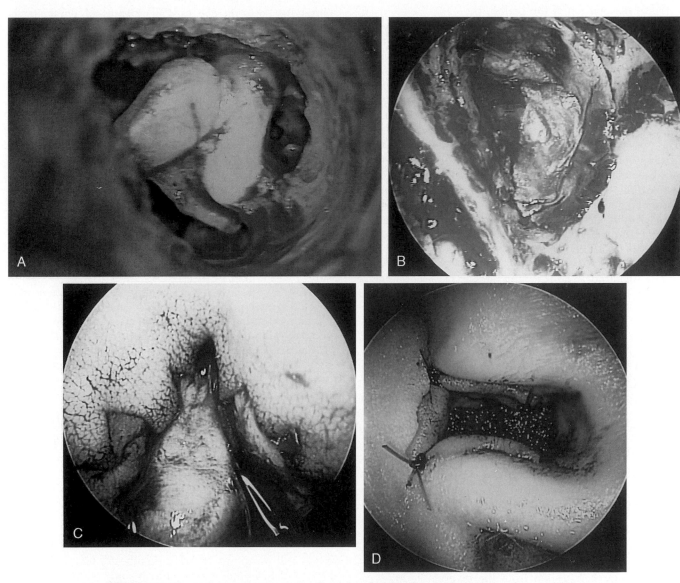

FIGURE 21–22. *A*, Intraoperative view of ossicles during congenital aural atresia repair. The bony atresia plate has been removed, and the fused malleus-incus complex is visible. The stapes is not well visualized in this view. *B*, Aural atresia repair. Temporalis fascia is placed over the ossicles to create a tympanic membrane. *C*, Aural atresia repair. A split-thickness skin graft is used to line the new external auditory canal. *D*, Anterior approach to aural atresia repair. A meatus has been created in the reconstructed auricle by excision of a core of tissue. The split-thickness skin graft is brought out through the meatus and sutured to the skin of the meatus.

canals will be limited by the dura, temporomandibular joint, facial nerve, or mastoid air cells. After grafting and scarring, it can be expected that most reconstructed external auditory canals will undergo some narrowing, especially at the meatus. A split-thickness skin graft harvested from the buttocks, thigh, or inner aspect of the upper arm is used to line the reconstructed external auditory canal. The temporalis fascia graft for the tympanic membrane is placed first (Fig. 21–22B), followed by placement of the split-thickness skin graft (Fig. 21–22C). A small disc of thick silastic sheeting is placed over the temporalis fascia graft and medial portion of the partially overlapping split-thickness skin graft to anchor these structures in a medial position and to prevent lateralization.[13] Packing is placed in the external auditory canal to stabilize the position of the grafts.

The surgeon creates an external auditory meatus by excising a disc of tissue from the appropriate location on the reconstructed auricle. The J-shaped incision discussed earlier for creation of the tragus can be used for unilateral cases of microtia. The chondrocutaneous composite graft from the otoplasty of the normal ear is used to create the tragus, as described earlier. The skin in the area of the meatus and concha is elevated and preserved. The soft tissue and cartilage deep to the area of the meatus and concha is excised sharply and a generously sized meatus is created. The tissue excised for creation of the external auditory meatus may need to be beveled to ensure a smooth transition to the bony external auditory canal. Additionally, the lateral portion of the external auditory canal may need to be beveled with a drill to create a smooth transition to the external auditory meatus. The previously elevated skin flap is rotated down into the external auditory meatus to line part of it. Partial lining of the new external auditory meatus with full-thickness skin flaps decreases the likelihood of stenosis in this area.

In cases of bilateral microtia or atresia, an anteriorly based skin flap is incised and elevated as described earlier for tragal reconstruction for microtia. Again, the soft tissue and cartilage deep to the area of the meatus and concha is excised sharply, and a generously sized meatus is created. A portion of cartilage is harvested from the auricular cartilage graft and the perichondrial tissue is closed over the graft donor site. This small rectangular cartilage graft is then covered anteriorly and posteriorly with the anteriorly based skin flap to create the tragus, as described earlier[32] (see Fig. 21–17). Any additional length of skin flap that remains after creation of the tragus is rotated medially into the external auditory meatus to line the anterior portion of the meatus to decrease the chances of meatal stenosis.

The reconstructed auricle is then replaced in its original position, but the position may have to be adjusted to create a smooth transition from the external auditory canal to the meatus. The split-thickness skin graft that was used to line the external auditory canal is then brought out through the external auditory meatus. The edges of the split-thickness skin graft from the external auditory canal are sutured to the edges of the skin from the meatus to line the remainder of the external auditory meatus (Fig. 21–22D). More packing is placed to stabilize the position of the grafts and flaps. The packing and silastic disc are removed 7 to 10 days postoperatively.

The reconstructed external auditory canal may not be self-cleaning and thus may require periodic débridement of desquamated epithelium.

Complications of Aural Atresia Surgery

Facial nerve injury is a known complication of aural atresia repair. It has been reported to occur in 1% to 7% of cases.[13, 17, 29] With high-resolution CT, careful patient selection, intraoperative facial nerve monitoring, and excellent surgical technique, facial nerve injury should not occur.

Significant sensorineural hearing loss has been reported to occur in 2% to 4% of cases of aural atresia repair.[13, 17, 29] It may occur from excessive transmission of drill energy to the ossicles during removal of the atresia plate. It may also occur as a known complication of stapes surgery during atresia repair.[13] Sensorineural hearing loss will frequently follow horizontal semicircular canal fenestration or labyrinthotomy, and therefore these procedures are not recommended. It is not unusual to have a small degree of insignificant high-frequency sensorineural hearing loss following atresia repair.[14]

Stenosis of the external auditory meatus may occur as a complication of infection or independently. This is the most common complication of aural atresia repair and most common reason for revision surgery.[17] This complication may occur in 18% to 20% of cases.[12, 17] Injection of triamcinolone into the meatus at the time of surgery or subsequently helps to decrease the degree of stenosis. The tympanic membrane may become lateralized and require revision surgery in up to 8% of cases.[17]

Once aural atresia repair is completed, the patient may develop recurrent acute otitis, otitis media with effusion, retraction pocket cholesteatoma, mastoiditis, chronic suppurative otitis media, tympanic membrane perforation, or any other disease or complication of the ear or ear surgery. Each of these complications or diseases should be managed in an appropriate manner.

Hearing Results for Aural Atresia Repair

For the anterior approach, the standard for aural atresia repair is to obtain minimal conductive hearing loss with a 25 dB or smaller hearing threshold in at least 75% of patients.[14] Chandrasekhar et al[7] reported an air-bone gap of 30 dB or less in 60% of their patients following atresia repair. The hearing results for canal wall–down atresia repair are less favorable. Schuchtnecht[29] reported that 50% of his patients had 30 dB or better hearing following canal wall–down procedures. Lambert[17] had longer follow-up of his aural atresia patients and reported that the hearing results may undergo some deterioration over time.

Alternatives for Aural Atresia Repair

The development of the osseointegrated implant as an anchor has allowed creation of the bone-anchored hearing aid. This device, which was developed in Sweden, has recently been approved for use in children at least 2 years of age.[27] This device may be useful for children with aural atresia repair who have unfavorable anatomy for reconstruction, or for children who are poor surgical candidates for a lengthy procedure for medical reasons. Pure tone averages improved by 37% and discrimination improved by 23% following bone-anchored hearing aid placement in 11 children older than 5 years of age.[2] In children, the procedure is usually performed in two stages. In adults, the procedure is usually performed in a single stage.

In the first stage for children, a scalp flap is raised in the postauricular area, and special low-torque drills are used to tap a hole for placement of the actual porous titanium osseointegrated implant. Although the hair over the implant is removed, the skin is left intact for 2 to 3 months. In the second portion of the procedure, a hole is cut through the skin flap to allow the implant to pass transcutaneously and an adapter is placed. A second healing period of 2 weeks is allowed before the bone-anchored hearing aid is attached to the adapter of the osseointegrated implant and activated. A recent report by van der Pouw et al[34] described improved sound localization and speech perception in a small series of children with bilateral aural atresia who underwent bilateral bone-anchored hearing aid placement.

The use of the bone-anchored hearing aid is preferable to the use of the bone-conduction hearing aid for older children. This is especially true for male patients, who find the traditional headband-like bone-conduction hearing aid cosmetically unacceptable, or for patients with local pain, skin irritation, or headaches from the bone-conduction hearing aid.

Conclusion

Surgical management of microtia and congenital aural atresia repair continue to be part of the most exciting, challenging, and rewarding area of reconstructive and otologic surgery. Attention to detail, careful planning, adequate training, and excellent judgment are required for the most favorable results. It is hoped that continued refinements in surgical technique and technology will allow even better results for these patients in the future.

REFERENCES

1. Aguilar F. Auricular reconstruction of congenital microtia. Laryngoscope 106:1, 1996.
2. Bejar Solar I, Rosete M, Madrazo M, et al. Percutaneous bone-anchored hearing aids at a pediatric institution. Otolaryngol Head Neck Surg 122:887, 2000.
3. Brent B. Auricular repair with autogenous rib cartilage grafts: two decades of experience with 600 cases. Plast Reconstr Surg 90:355, 1992.
4. Brent B. Technical advances in ear reconstruction with autogenous rib cartilage grafts: personal experience with 1200 cases. Plast Reconstr Surg 104:319, 1999.
5. Bresnick SD, Reinsch RF. Reconstructive techniques for salvage of the Medpore ear reconstruction. Presented at Ear Reconstruction '98: Choices for the Future, Chateau Lake Louise, Canada, March 5, 1998.
6. Cao Y, Vacanti P, Paige KT, et al. Transplantation of chondrocytes utilizing a polymer-cell construct to produce tissue-engineered cartilage in the shape of a human ear. Plast Reconstr Surg 100:297, 1997.
7. Chandrasekhar SS, De la Cruz A, Carrido E. Surgery of congenital aural atresia. Am J Otol 16:713, 1995.
8. Eavey RD, Ryan DP. Refinements in pediatric microtia reconstruction. Arch Otolaryngol Head Neck Surg 122:617, 1996.
9. Eavey RD. Microtia repair: creation of a functional postauricular sulcus. Otolaryngol Head Neck Surg 120:789, 1999.
10. Harris J, Kallen B, Robert E. The epidemiology of anotia and microtia. J Med Genet 33:809, 1996.
11. Ho S, Lee D, Yellon R. Cryptotia. Otolaryngol Head Neck Surg 123:339, 2000.
12. Jahrsdoerfer RA, Cole RR, Gray LC. Advances in congenital aural atresia. In Advances in Otolaryngology—Head and Neck Surgery. St. Louis, Mosby, 1991, pp 1–15.
13. Jahrsdoerfer RA, Hall JW. Congenital malformations of the ear. Am J Otol 7:267, 1986.
14. Jahrsdoerfer RA. External auditory canal atresia. In Lalwani AK, Grundfast KM (eds). Pediatric Otology and Neurotology. Philadelphia, Lippincott-Raven, 1998, pp 533–540.
15. Jahrsdoefer RA. Congenital atresia of the ear. Laryngoscope 88(suppl 13):1, 1978.
16. Jahrsdoerfer RA, Garcia E, Yeakley J, et al. Surface contour three dimensional imaging in congenital aural atresia. Arch Otolaryngol Head Neck Surg 119:95, 1993.
17. Lambert PR. Complications of surgery for congenital atresia. In Eisele DW (ed). Complications in Head and Neck Surgery. St. Louis, Mosby, 1993, pp 660–665.
18. Lammer EJ, Chen DJ, Hoar RM, et al. Retinotic acid embryopathy. N Engl J Med 313:837, 1985.
19. Malony TB, De la Cruz A. Surgical approaches to congenital atresia of the external auditory canal. Otolaryngol Head Neck Surg 103:991, 1990.
20. McKenzie J, Craig J. Mandibulo-facial dysostosis. Arch Dis Child 30:391, 1955.
21. Nagata S. A new method of total reconstruction of the auricle for microtia. Plast Reconstr Surg 92:187, 1993.
22. Nagata S. Secondary reconstruction for unfavorable microtia results utilizing temporoparietal and innominate fascia flaps. Plast Reconstr Surg 94:254, 1994.
23. Newman LM, Hendrickx AG. Fetal ear malformations induced by maternal ingestion of thalidomide in the bonnet monkey (Macaca radiata). Teratology 23:351, 1981.
24. Padmanabhan R. Abnormalities of the ear associated with exencephaly in mouse fetuses induced by maternal exposure to cadmium. Teratology 35:9, 1987.
25. Park C, Lew DH, Yoo WM. An analysis of 123 temporoparietal fascial flaps: anatomic and clinical considerations in total auricular reconstruction. Plast Reconstr Surg 104:1295, 1999.
26. Peer LA. Reconstruction of the auricle with diced cartilage grafts in a vitallium ear mold. Plast Reconstr Surg 3:653, 1948.
27. Powell RH, Burrell SP, Cooper HR, Proops DW. The Birmingham bone anchored hearing aid programme: pediatric experience and results. J Laryngol Otol 110(suppl 21):21, 1996.
28. Rodriguez A, Cao YL, Ibarra C, et al. Characteristics of cartilage engineered from human pediatric auricular cartilage. Plast Reconstr Surg 103:1111, 1999.
29. Schuchtnecht HG. Congenital aural atresia. Laryngoscope 99:908, 1989.
30. Sieber SM, Whang PJ, Botkin C, Knutsen T. Teratogenic and cytogenetic effects of some plant-derived antitumor agents (vincristine, colchicine, maytansine, VP-16-213 and VM-26) in mice. Teratology 18:31, 1978.
31. Shih L, Crabtree JA. Long-term surgical results for congenital aural atresia. Laryngoscope 103:1097, 1993.
32. Tanzer RC. Total reconstruction of the external ear. Plast Reconstr Surg 23:1, 1959.
33. Tanzer RC. Discussion of silastic framework complications. In Tanzer RC, Edgerton MT (eds). Symposium on Reconstruction of the Auricle. St Louis, Mosby, 1974, pp 87–88.
34. Van der Pouw KTM, Snik FM, Cremers WRJ. Audiometric results

of bilateral bone-anchored hearing aid application in patients with bilateral congenital aural atresia. Laryngoscope 108:548, 1998.

35. Wellisz T. Reconstruction of the burned external ear with a Medpor porous polyethylene pivoting helix framework. Plast Reconstr Surg 91:811, 1993.

36. Wheeland RG. Laser-assisted hair removal. Dermatol Clin 15:469, 1997.

37. Wilkes GH, Wolfaardt JF, Dent M. Osseointegrated alloplastic versus autogenous ear reconstruction: criteria for treatment selection. Plast Reconstr Surg 93:967 1994.

38. Williams JD, Romo T III, Sclafani AP, Cho H. Porous high-density polyethylene implants in auricular reconstruction. Arch Otolaryngol Head Neck Surg 123:578, 1997.

39. Yeakley J, Jahrsdoerfer RA. CT evaluation of congenital aural atresia: what the radiologist and surgeon need to know. J Comput Assist Tomogr 20:724, 1996.

40. Yotsuyanagi T, Yoloi K, Nihei Y, Sawada Y. Management of the hairline using a local flap in total reconstruction for microtia. Plast Reconstr Surg 104:41, 1999.

41. Young F. Cast and precast cartilage grafts: their use in the restoration of facial contour. Surgery 15:735, 1944.

22

Congenital Inner Ear Anomalies

Amy C. Brenski, M.D., and Ellis M. Arjmand, M.D., Ph.D.

Congenital anomalies of the labyrinth are frequently seen in association with sensorineural hearing loss (SNHL). Historically, abnormalities limited to the membranous labyrinth have been seen only on histopathologic sectioning of the temporal bone, but the widespread use of computed tomography (CT) for temporal bone imaging has led to the early clinical diagnosis of inner ear anomalies that have an osseous component. In some cases, the relationship between the structural abnormality and the auditory function is clearly established; in other cases, the clinical significance of the inner ear malformation is uncertain. While advances in magnetic resonance imaging (MRI) may allow for the accurate clinical diagnosis of membranous labyrinthine abnormalities, much work remains to be done in order to understand the clinical significance of the radiographic findings.

In this chapter, the classification of congenital labyrinthine anomalies is reviewed, as is the typical clinical presentation of each. The extensive recent literature on abnormalities of the vestibular aqueduct is reviewed in detail, and the implications of labyrinthine anomalies for cochlear implantation are presented.

Related information is contained in Chapters 8, 28, and 29.

The History of Classification

The classification of inner-ear anomalies has evolved over several centuries. The most renowned report of inner-ear abnormalities in a deaf patient is attributed to Mondini in 1791.[39] Alexander further described the abnormalities seen by Mondini histopathologically.[64] Knowledge of congenital anomalies from these early histologic studies is still used today, and specific abnormalities carry eponyms reflecting the names of the investigators who first described them.

In 1960, Ormerod published a comprehensive list of known inner-ear anomalies using the eponyms that reflect these early discoveries, and Omerod's work provides the basis for the method of classification of inner-ear anomalies that is widely used today.[40] This classification scheme and its variations are pervasive in the literature. However, some confusion arises because the eponyms do not necessarily reflect the actual anomaly as it was originally described. Considerable ambiguity exists in the literature regarding the definitions of these classic anomalies.

Schuknecht's historic histopathologic temporal bone study of abnormalities of the inner ear is an example of the reclassification of known anomalies. He separated the congenital labyrinthine anomalies into three groups: Scheibe, Mundini, and trisomy types. Various combined membranous and osseous dysplasias were grouped under the heading of "Mundini Dysplasia."[79] These included any hypoplasia of the cochlea with or without abnormalities of the vestibular labyrinth. He acknowledged the rare occurrences of the Alexander and Bing-Siebenmann isolated membranous abnormalities as previously described, but did not think them sufficiently frequent to be of great clinical importance. His landmark work has been widely cited.

Radiography provides another basis for the classification of abnormalities of the temporal bone. The development of tomography in the 1960s allowed for more detailed assessment of the temporal bone.[64] Studies using tomography by Phelps and Valvassori began to describe the incidence of bony congenital anomalies of the temporal bone. Early tomographic studies demonstrated that abnormalities of the semicircular canals were the most common finding.[45, 63, 92] Previous temporal bone histopathologic studies had been used to describe inner-ear anomalies, but the introduction of tomograms allowed for the clinical application of information regarding inner-ear abnormalities in the evaluation and management of individual patients.

The ability to define the structures of the inner ear was further refined with the development of CT. The widespread use of CT in the evaluation of patients with SNHL highlighted other temporal bone abnormalities and raised questions regarding causal relationships to hearing loss. Radiographically determined abnormalities of the internal auditory canal (IAC), vestibular aqueduct, and cochlear aqueduct have all been reported. Several authors report that enlargement of the vestibular aqueduct is the most common temporal bone abnormality.[45, 93] A detailed discussion of this subject is presented below.

Jackler et al[39] developed an embryologically based classification of labyrinthine anomalies in 1987. The classification of congenital malformations of the inner ear was established by defining points of arrest in temporal bone

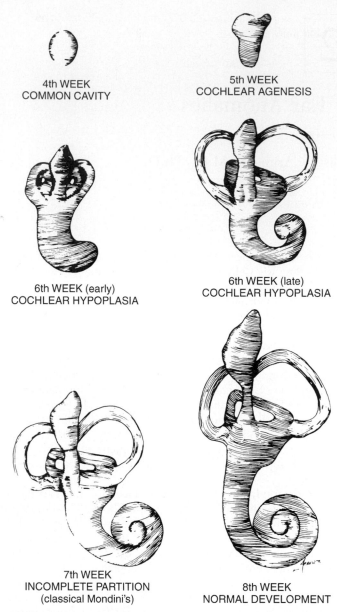

FIGURE 22–1. Embryogenesis of cochlear malformations. (From Jackler RK, Luxford WM, House WF. Congenital malformations of the inner ear: a classification based on embryogenesis. Laryngoscope 97[3 pt 2 Suppl 40]:2–14, 1987.)

classification of inner-ear anomalies. Other methods of classification reflect the same embryogenic pattern but with a larger number of specific categories. The other methods provide detailed information regarding associated anomalies, including middle-ear anomalies, but they are less conceptually organized and typically more cumbersome.[84]

Congenital Inner-Ear Anomalies

Anomalies of the inner ear are classified as either membranous or combined membranous and osseous. The characteristic anatomic findings and a summary of the typical functional level are provided. Vestibular and coch-

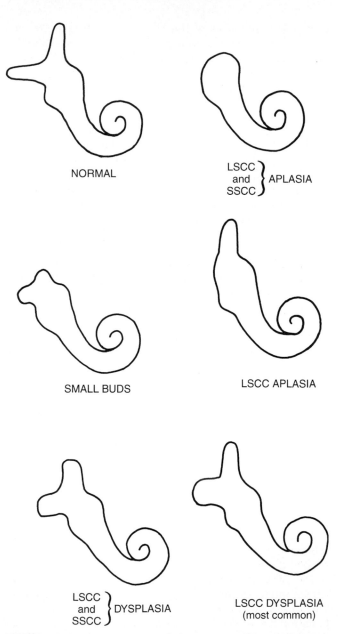

FIGURE 22–2. Malformations of the semi-circular canal. (From Jackler RK, Luxford WM, House WF. Congenital malformations of the inner ear: a classification based on embryogenesis. Laryngoscope 97 [3 pt 2 Suppl 40]:2–14, 1987.)

embryogenesis, based on information obtained from both histologic sections and radiographic imaging. Figure 22–1 shows the embryonic stages at which arrest occurs, and Figures 22–2 and 22–3 show the corresponding abnormalities. Both membranous and combined (membranous and osseous) anomalies are described. The classification system includes malformations with a cochlear abnormality, with or without associated vestibular abnormalities, and malformations with a normal cochlea (Table 22–1). This provides a method for classifying specific anomalies that do not fit well into one of the traditionally defined categories. For example, this system can be used to account for the many different presentations of the Mondini malformation.

This system has become a widely accepted method of

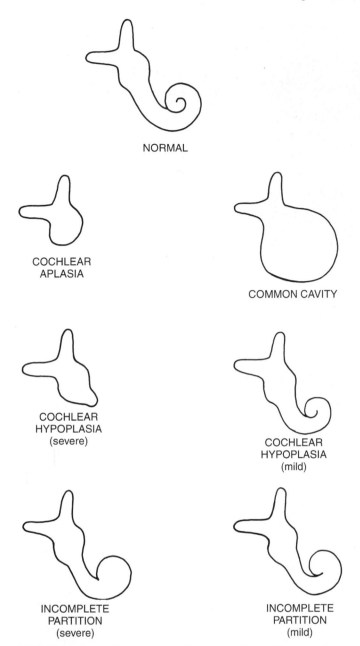

NORMAL

COCHLEAR
APLASIA

COMMON CAVITY

COCHLEAR
HYPOPLASIA
(severe)

COCHLEAR
HYPOPLASIA
(mild)

INCOMPLETE
PARTITION
(severe)

INCOMPLETE
PARTITION
(mild)

FIGURE 22–3. Malformations of the cochlear. (From Jackler RK, Luxford WM, House WF. Congenital malformations of the inner ear: a classification based on embryogenesis. Laryngoscope 97 [3 Pt 2 Suppl 40]:2–14, 1987.)

lear aqueduct abnormalities are discussed, as are implications for cochlear implantation.

Malformations of the Membranous Labyrinth

Complete Membranous Labyrinthine Dysplasia

Complete membranous labyrinthine dysplasia is a relatively rare defect, first described by Siebenmann and Bing in 1907. Complete aplasia or severe dysplasia of the entire membranous labyrinth is seen. The presentation is profound congenital SNHL. The osseous labyrinth is normal and has a normal appearance on CT scan. At this

TABLE 22–1. Classification of Congenital Malformations of the Inner Ear

Absent or Malformed Cochlea
Complete labyrinthine aplasia: no inner ear development
Cochlear aplasia: no cochlea; normal or malformed vestibule; semicircular canals
Cochlear hypoplasia: small cochlear bud, normal or malformed vestibule; semicircular canals
Incomplete partition: small cochlea with incomplete or no interscalar septum; normal or malformed vestibule; semicircular canals
Common cavity: cochlea and vestibule form a single cavity without internal architecture; normal or malformed semicircular canals
Normal Cochlea
Vestibule-lateral semicircular canal dysplasia: enlarged vestibule with a short, dilated lateral semicircular canal; remaining semicircular canals are normal
Enlarged vestibular aqueduct: accompanied by normal semicircular canals; normal or enlarged vestibule

time, the diagnosis can only be reliably made by histopathologic sectioning.

On microscopic examination, both the cochlear and vestibular portions of the membranous labyrinth are abnormal. A poorly differentiated organ of Corti is seen, with atrophy of the stria vascularis and frequently with collapse of the Reisner membrane.[20] The number of the spiral ganglion cell bodies is reduced, and degeneration of the cochlear nerve is seen. Vestibular findings may include degeneration of both saccular and macular maculae, and atrophy of cristae ampullaris and the Scarpa ganglion.[86] This anomaly has been described in association with retinitis pigmentosa and Usher syndrome.[20, 86, 94]

Limited Membranous Dysplasia

Cochleosaccular Dysplasia (Scheibe). Cochleosaccular dysplasia was first reported by Scheibe in 1892. Only the structures that originate from the pars inferioris, which develop later than those of the pars superioris, are affected.[78] Therefore, the utricle and semicircular canals are normal. Microscopic findings include atrophy of the stria vascularis, deformity of tectorial membrane and organ of Corti, and collapse of the Reisner membrane.[75] The wall of the saccule is also collapsed onto an atrophic and deformed sensory epithelium. The cochlear neurons, which develop independently of the intracochlear structures, are normal.[79]

This may be the most frequent labyrinthine anomaly in children with profound congenital SNHL. It has been described in association with several types of autosomal recessive hearing loss, including Jervell and Lange-Nielsen, Refsum, Waardenburg, and trisomy 18 syndromes.[71, 72, 86] It has also been associated with the acquired SNHL of congenital rubella.[75]

Cochlear Basal Turn Dysplasia. The first description of this anomaly of the membranous labyrinthine, which is isolated to the basal turn of the cochlear duct, has been attributed to Alexander, but the deformity initially reported by Alexander included osseous abnormalities as well as diffuse hypoplasia of portions of both the vestibu-

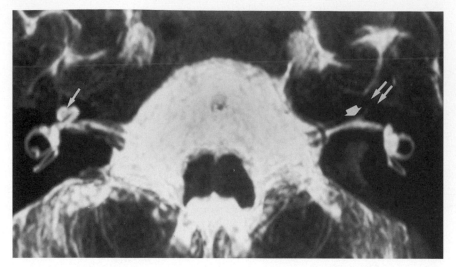

FIGURE 22–4. MRI, T$_2$-weighted 3-D fast spin echo (FSE) reconstruction of 0.8 mm axial slices of a child with congenital unilateral sensorineural hearing loss. Note small internal auditory canal and hypoplasia of cochlear nerve on left (fat arrow) and complete absence of cochlea (double arrow) as compared to normal right cochlea (single arrow).

lar and cochlear membranous labyrinth.[62, 64] However, the changes seen in the membranous labyrinth at the basal turn of the cochlea have been named for Alexander.

No bony abnormalities are present with this anomaly. Microscopic findings include incomplete differentiation of the organ of Corti and spiral ganglion cells in the region of the basal turn.[75] The characteristic audiometric finding is high-frequency SNHL.

Malformations of the Osseous and Membranous Labyrinth

Complete Labyrinthine Aplasia

Complete labyrinthine aplasia, also known as *Michel aplasia*, consists of complete aplasia of the osseous and membranous labyrinth. Although named for Michel, who described this anomaly in 1863, it was actually first described by Saissy in 1819.[79] Profound SNHL is seen. Because there is complete lack of development of labyrinthine structures, Michel aplasia has a characteristic radiographic appearance and is easily diagnosed by CT scan. The only abnormality that can mimic this severe anomaly radiographically is labyrinthitis ossificans. However, with labyrinthitis ossificans, the promontory remains

visible and convex in a normal-sized middle-ear space, whereas the area of the promontory is flat or concave and the middle-ear space is enlarged due to an absent cochlea in the aplastic ear.[25] Distinction between the two entities is an important consideration in the evaluation for cochlear implantation.

Michel aplasia has been seen in association with Klippel-Feil syndrome and in thalidomide embryopathy.[43, 63, 97]

Cochlear Abnormalities

Cochlear Aplasia. No cochlear structures are present in this rare anomaly. Vestibular structures are present but often demonstrate some deformity (Fig. 22–4). Profound SNHL is the clinical presentation.

Cochlear Hypoplasia. In cases of cochlear hypoplasia, the cochlear size and differentiation are variable, depending on the timing of the arrest of development. Usually the cochlea is a small, rounded structure lacking any turns or definition (Fig. 22–5). Auditory function depends on the presence and degree of differentiation of the neuroepithelial elements. Hearing may be better than predicted on the basis of cochlear appearance.

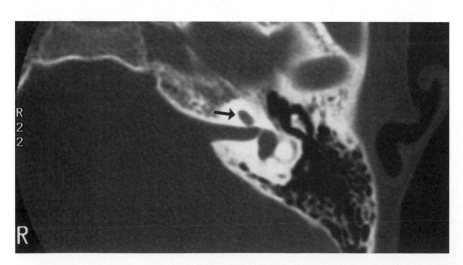

FIGURE 22–5. Axial CT, bone algorithm, demonstrates a small, bud-like, hypoplastic cochlea (arrow).

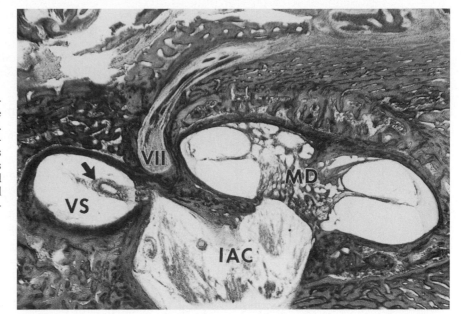

FIGURE 22–6. Mondini dysplasia: Histopathologic cross section of a temporal bone of an infant with CHARGE association. Note the single turn of the cochlea and deficient modiolus (MD). The vestibule (VS) is reduced in size and the utricle (arrow) is dysplastic. The facial nerve (VII) followed an aberrant course through the temporal bone and the middle ear. The internal auditory canal (IAC) is also shown.

Incomplete Partition. Carlo Mondini in 1791 originally described the incomplete partition of the cochlea: one and one half turns and lacking an apical turn and an interscalar septum, associated with deafness. His original description included associated enlargement of the vestibule and vestibular aqueduct. Over time, numerous variations of this deformity have come to be known as Mondini malformations. The same eponym has been used to describe a continuum of cochlear dysplasia with associated vestibular abnormalities.

These anomalies have been attributed to arrest in embryonic development in the seventh week (see Chap. 8). If the arrest of development happens earlier, the semicircular canals and vestibule are more likely to be involved. The severity of the cochlear malformation can range from the classic one and one half turns to subtle abnormalities of the interscalar septum in an otherwise normal-appearing cochlea (Figs. 22-6 and 22–7). The latter malformation is also known as an incomplete partition defect, accounting for more than 50% of all cochlear deformities.[39]

Valvassori further described the cochlear dysplasia when he recognized the "dwarf" cochlea seen on tomography. The vertical height of the cochlea, as seen on a tomogram, is reduced from 8 to 10 mm to 5 to 6 mm.[92] Valvassori subsequently described this abnormality in association with vestibular anomalies, such as the enlarged vestibular aqueduct.[91] Deficiencies of the modiolus are usually present, the diagnosis of which is limited by current CT imaging capabilities[4, 41] (Fig. 22–8A).

In general, the degree of osseous deformity reflects the degree of membranous malformation. However, variable degrees of membranous change can be seen at the microscopic level. The membranous deformity may extend to the vestibular structures to include semicircular canal deformity, a dilated vestibule, or both. Enlargement of the vestibular aqueduct and the endolymphatic sac and duct have also been described in association with Mondini malformations (see later discussion), typically when the cochlea is more severely affected.

The degree of hearing loss parallels the degree of membranous cochlear dysplasia, specifically, the level of development of the organ of Corti. A diminished number of ganglion cells may be present, which may affect the success of cochlear implantation. Changes affecting the organ of Corti or the spiral ganglion cells may not be reflected in the osseous labyrinth and, thus, may not be radiographically detectable.

Stapedial footplate anomalies are often present, and affected patients may be predisposed to recurrent meningitis and perilymphatic fistula.[80] The risk of recurrent meningitis is thought to be increased when the basal turn of the cochlea is enlarged.[65, 66] Anomalous inner ear anatomy should be suspected in cases of recurrent meningitis.

Syndromes associated with this group of Mondini malformations include Klippel-Feil, Wildervanck, Waardenburg, Pendred, and DiGeorge. Isolated Mondini malformations may be inherited in an autosomal dominant fashion. They have been associated with an enlarged vestibular aqueduct,[5, 91] and they have also been reported in cases of congenital cytomegalovirus infection.[12]

Common Cavity. With the common cavity deformity, the vestibular and cochlear structures communicate freely with one another in a large common space (Fig. 22-9). The common cavity was first described by Cock in 1838,[30, 64] and this malformation can be readily diagnosed by CT imaging. Common cavity deformities are often associated with severe to profound hearing loss resulting from the poorly differentiated membranous structures. Neuronal elements may be diminished, which may impact the efficacy of cochlear implantation.

Malformations of the Vestibular Labyrinth

Vestibule and Semicircular Canal Dysplasia. Abnormalities of the vestibular labyrinth most often involve the lateral semicircular canal, which develops earlier than the posterior and superior canals.[63] The dysplasia can range

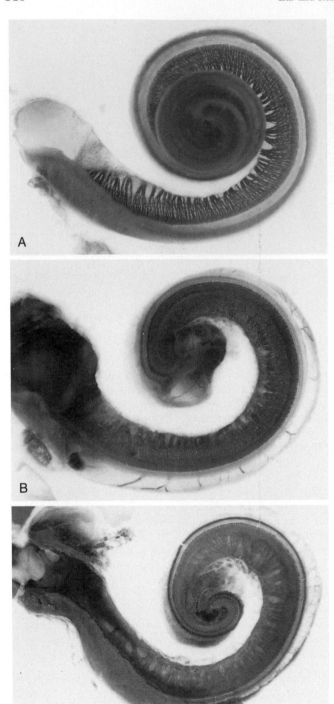

FIGURE 22–7. Cochlear microdissections, low power views. *A,* Normal cochlear duct; *B,* Cochlea of an infant with trisomy 21 illustrating Mondini dysplasia, diminished number of cochlear turns, and absent apical turn; *C,* Similar findings seen in this patient with CHARGE association.

from a slight dilation, to a broad cystic structure contiguous with the vestibule, to complete aplasia. Dilation of the vestibule is also a frequent finding. Affected patients have a range of vestibular symptoms, and many have reduced or absent vestibular responses when tested. However, vestibular testing has not regularly been per-

formed in most series, and the actual relationship between vestibular function and vestibular anomalies is not known.

Cochlear anomalies are often seen in patients with vestibular dysplasia.[74]

Other Abnormalities of the Temporal Bone

Large Vestibular Aqueduct

The vestibular aqueduct is the bony canal that contains the endolymphatic duct. The endolymphatic duct connects the endolymphatic sac to the vestibule. The endolymphatic sac, which lies adjacent to the posterior fossa dura, serves as a reservoir for endolymph and regulates the active exchange between the cerebrospinal fluid (CSF) and endolymph.[23, 42] The endolymphatic sac may have immunologic functions.[79]

Early in fetal development, the vestibular aqueduct runs parallel to the common crus. The vestibular aqueduct is directed downward during development, resulting in its mature inverted "J" shape. This process continues in the first few years of life. The vestibular aqueduct is generally considered enlarged if it measures greater than 1.5 mm in its greatest anterior-posterior dimension.[23, 93] However, some authors use a 2-mm measurement as the upper limit of normal.[5, 37, 61, 100] Enlargement of the vestibular aqueduct is currently thought to be the most common inner-ear abnormality[14, 45, 89] (Figs. 22–10 and 22–11).

In 1978, Valvassori and Clemis described a Meniere disease–like disorder consisting of fluctuating hearing loss and dizziness, associated with a large vestibular aqueduct (LVA), which they named the "large vestibular aqueduct syndrome" (LVAS).[93] Subsequently, this syndrome was described as presenting with a moderate to profound SNHL on the side of the LVA.[23] Levenson et al[42] then reported the isolated LVA in children with SNHL as a distinct clinical entity, more commonly seen than the Mondini malformation by 4:1. In contrast with previous reports, he found the hearing loss to be acquired during childhood rather than congenital. He also described a distinct down-sloping pattern (high-frequency SNHL) to the audiogram, which he attributed to reflux of hyperosmolar endolymphatic sac contents into the basal end of the cochlea from fluctuations in intracranial pressure.

This report established the isolated enlarged vestibular aqueduct, or the LVA, as a distinct clinical entity, leading to the commonly accepted definition of LVAS. However, some authors continue to use the term *LVAS* to describe any patient with an LVA[52]; others consider this abnormality to be included in the Mondini malformation continuum.[12, 91]

Jackler and De La Cruz[37] reported their findings in 1989 in a group of adult and pediatric patients with enlarged vestibular aqueduct. They found 94% bilaterality, a propensity for progression of SNHL with head trauma (65%), and a slight female preponderance. Nearly one third of their patients demonstrated a conductive component to their hearing loss. They also reported a significant deterioration of hearing following endolymphatic sac decompression and shunt surgery, and they recommended

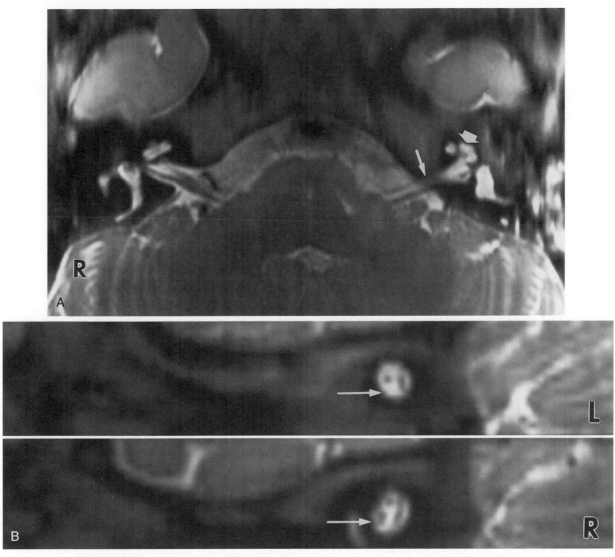

FIGURE 22–8. *A*, MR, T_2-weighted 3-D FSE 0.8 mm axial slice, of a 4-year-old with left sided sensorineural hearing loss. Note deficiency of modiolus in shortened cochlea (fat arrow). Compare narrow left IAC (thin arrow) with normal right side. *B*, MR oblique sagittal section shows cross section of IAC's of same patient. Compare normal cochlear nerve on right and severely hypoplastic cochlear nerve on left (arrows). R, right ear; L, left ear.

avoidance of this procedure in congenitally malformed ears.

Endolymphatic sac obliteration has been performed in patients with LVA, with results suggesting a stabilization of hearing in most patients. However, the follow-up period in the study was only 6 months.[98] Other investigators attempted to reproduce these results using a modification of the procedure and have failed to demonstrate any significant stabilizing effect on hearing. They caution that the procedure may actually exacerbate hearing loss and have abandoned endolymphatic sac occlusion in these patients until long-term follow-up results are available.[95, 96]

Several audiometric patterns have been reported in association with LVA, including down-sloping[23, 37, 42] and flat,[102] and no one pattern has been shown to predominate. There are also reports of patients with normal hearing and the incidental finding of LVA.[23] These patients may be predisposed to development of hearing loss,[102]

but the findings are inconclusive. There also does not appear to be a significant correlation between the size of the vestibular aqueduct and the degree of hearing loss or tendency to progress.[29, 96, 100, 102]

Both sudden SNHL and fluctuating SNHL have been described in the LVAS. In Jackler's study of 17 patients with LVA, fluctuating hearing was documented in only two patients. Long-term follow-up demonstrated a stepwise progression of SNHL in 65%, with an overall deterioration of 25 dB over a follow-up period of 6 years. Furthermore, sudden SNHL developed in two patients following relatively minor head trauma.[37] The authors doubted endolymphatic hydrops as the cause of progression of SNHL following trauma. Instead, the authors suggested that histologic evidence supported the idea that hearing loss developed as a result of a dysfunctional endolymphatic sac, which resulted in abnormal composition of endolymph.[37]

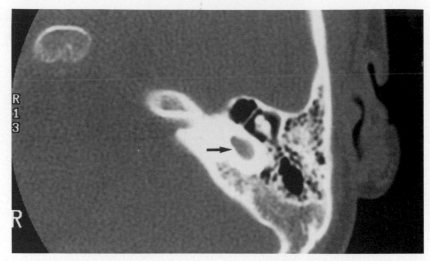

FIGURE 22–9. CT, axial view, showing a common cavity deformity. The cochlea is seen as a small outpouching of the dilated vestibule.

Other theories have been discussed to explain the mechanism of injury in LVA patients with progressive SNHL. One theory hypothesizes intrinsic membrane defects within the cochlea, leading to endocochlear fistulization with admixture of perilymph and endolymph.[33] Other investigators have recommended middle-ear exploration to rule out a perilymphatic fistula through a defect in the otic capsule (see Chap. 23), in which case a high incidence of associated middle-ear abnormalities have been reported.[15]

Several authors have independently reported a relationship between minor head trauma and sudden SNHL.[5, 76] Govaerts et al[29] described several cases of sudden SNHL associated with minor head trauma and noted a rate of progression of hearing loss in affected patients of 4 dB per year. The authors speculated that the hearing loss progresses with only partial recovery, thus leading to a gradually progressive SNHL. The authors caution that the changes are subtle and that progressive SNHL can be missed unless audiometric findings are reviewed with specific attention to the possibility of progressive SNHL.

Okumura[53] reported a 61% rate of sudden SNHL in a group of 13 patients with LVA. Interestingly, sudden SNHL was only seen in the patients with LVA and a normal cochlea. Sudden SNHL was not seen in any of the patients with associated cochlear anomalies, although some of these patients had slowly progressive SNHL. These authors attribute these findings to the irreversible effects of the LVA on a normal cochlea.

The studies reveal a tendency for progressive SNHL in patients with LVA. The risk appears to be increased with head trauma or sudden changes in barometric or intracranial pressure. However, the degree of risk to hearing with specific activities (e.g., contact sports, diving) is still undefined. One can advise a patient that there is believed to be a risk of hearing loss with activities that cause a sudden change in intracranial pressure, but the likelihood of further hearing loss with a particular activity cannot be given.

Several authors have noted a conductive component to the hearing loss seen in patients with LVAS, despite apparently normal middle-ear structures. Valvassori[91] proposed that increased perilymph or endolymph pressure from a widely patent vestibular aqueduct or endolymphatic duct resulted in dampening of the excursion of the stapes footplate. Other authors have confirmed the presence of a conductive component to hearing loss in their patients with LVAS, with some suggesting the finding of mixed hearing loss should be considered pathognomonic for the LVAS.[29, 37]

Only a few authors have reported on the vestibular function of patients with LVA. Of the original 160 patients of Valvassori and Clemis, three fourths of whom were children, only seven were reported to have vestibular symptoms, including loss of balance, rotary vertigo, and dizziness with nausea and vomiting. All of these patients had an isolated LVA. Vestibular testing was performed in 10 patients, and responses were absent or markedly diminished in eight.[91] Nearly one third of the patients described by Jackler et al complained of vertigo. However, only two patients underwent vestibular testing. Although one of these patients had no vestibular complaints, both were abnormal studies.

Two other studies have shown abnormal vestibular function in LVAS patients who do not have vestibular symptoms.[23, 35] One author described three patients with LVAS who experienced the Tullio sign (vertigo after exposure to loud noise), suggesting either a pathologic perilymphatic fistula or a lower threshold for sound to stimulate the vestibular system.[76]

Summary

Mondini originally described the LVA in great detail as part of the anomaly that carries his name. It is described in isolation as part of a clinical constellation of symptoms including hearing loss,[37, 42, 64] and it is discussed as part of the continuum of anomalies of inner-ear structures often referred to as the Mondini malformation.[12] Both isolated LVA and LVA with Mondini malformations have been

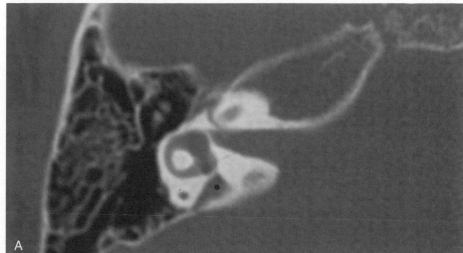

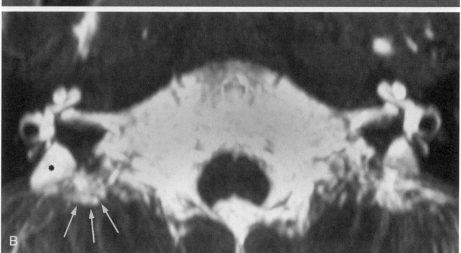

FIGURE 22–10. *A,* Axial CT of a 4-year-old female with bilateral sudden sensorineural hearing loss. Asterisk marks the large vestibular aqueduct. *B,* MR 3-D FSE reconstruction of same patient showing bilateral large vestibular aqueducts (asterisk) and markedly enlarged endolymphatic sacs (arrows).

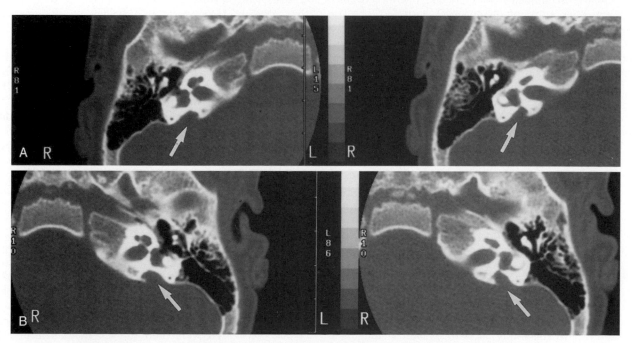

FIGURE 22–11. *A, B,* CT axial views right (R) and left (L), bilateral large vestibular aqueducts (arrow).

seen with various modes of inheritance and etiology: syndromic, nonsyndromic, hereditary, and acquired.[19, 31, 32] The isolated LVA is most often a sporadic mutation, but there are reports of familial occurrence of LVA, both as an isolated finding and in association with other inner-ear anomalies.[19, 32] Because LVA occurs within families, it may represent the variable phenotype of either autosomal recessive or X-linked recessive inheritance.[31, 32, 52, 89] Family members of affected individuals may be at risk and should be screened with audiometry and possibly CT scan.[52]

LVA has been reported in association with Pendred syndrome (PDS), both alone and with associated cochlear anomalies.[21] Up to 80% of patients with PDS have inner-ear anomalies.[69] Mutations in the PDS gene have been isolated to chromosome 7 in six families with LVA, without associated goiter or cochlear hypoplasia.[1, 2] The protein product of the PDS gene, pendrin, serves as an iodine and chloride transport system.[1, 24] The clinical manifestations of the PDS include euthyroid goiter and SNHL. PDS is diagnosed by an abnormal potassium perchlorate test, which demonstrates the defective organic binding of iodine in the thyroid gland. Variable phenotypes occur with autosomal recessive inheritance, including absence of goiter and the presence of a normal potassium perchlorate test, as in the case of the families discussed earlier. Screening for PDS gene mutations has been recommended by some investigators in all patients with the diagnosis of LVA.[1, 24, 26]

Enlarged Cochlear Aqueduct

The cochlear aqueduct is a bony canal containing the periotic or perilymphatic duct, which connects the subarachnoid space with the scala tympani.[57, 58] Its function may be related to the maintenance of fluid and pressure balance between the inner ear perilymph and the CSF.[28, 59] The cochlear aqueduct was first described by Du Verney in 1684, and it was first systematically measured in a temporal bone histologic study by Karlefors.[7, 8] Studies have provided differing descriptions of the anatomy of this structure, and the role an abnormal cochlear aqueduct might play in otologic pathology remains unclear.[38, 50, 56, 57]

A study by Gopen and Merchant of 101 temporal bone histologic specimens contained several important findings. The lumen of the cochlear aqueduct was found to have one of four forms: patent, occluded with soft tissue, occluded with bone, or atretic.[28] The lumen usually remains patent and is only partially filled with fibroconnective tissue. The lumen may be completely occluded with soft tissue, but this does not appear to be a normal consequence of aging as had been previously suggested.[28, 56, 99] The lumen may be completely occluded with bone, which does not appear to have any effect on the cochlear or vestibular function.[28] Or the lumen of the cochlear aqueduct may be truly atretic, appearing as a vestigial fibrous cord. The atretic cochlear aqueduct does not appear to be associated with a high jugular bulb, as was previously suggested.[68, 88] In this study, individuals with meningitis in whom labyrinthitis developed did not have unusually wide or patent cochlear aqueducts.[68]

It has been suggested that perilymphatic "gushers" seen at stapedectomy are associated with an enlarged cochlear aqueduct.[50] However, a model describing the physiology of the cochlear aqueduct showed that even the most patent cochlear aqueduct could not support the flows seen with a gusher,[28] and that the cochlear aqueduct probably has little impact on the dynamics of the ossicular chain, as was previously suggested.[51]

The actual function of the cochlear aqueduct is not precisely known. However, it appears to protect the inner-ear structures from fluctuations in intracranial pressure transmitted via the subarachnoid space. Other functions, such as an immunologic role or the regulation of perilymph composition and volume, have been suggested, but they have not been confirmed by histopathologic studies or models.[59] At this time, the relationship, if any, between cochlear aqueduct size and inner-ear pathology has not been defined.

Internal Auditory Canal

The relationship between IAC size and hearing loss has also been studied. The normal dimensions of the IAC have been evaluated in anatomic and histologic studies.[3, 54, 60] Radiographic studies were initially performed with both dried temporal bones and population polytomography.[16] In recent years, CT imaging has been used to determine normal dimensions of the IAC.[61] The dimensions of the IAC are fairly consistent from one study to another, although there is some variation as a function of the precise location from which the measurements are taken. For this reason, comparisons between studies can be difficult.

Both narrow and wide IACs have been reported to be associated with SNHL, but a comparison group of individuals with normal hearing has been included in only a few studies. In a study by McClay et al[46] comparing temporal bone CT scans in 247 children with normal hearing and those with SNHL, a narrow IAC was seen more often in children with SNHL than in those without. Of children with SNHL, a narrow IAC was present in 30% of those with a syndrome, compared with only 1.2% of those with nonsyndromic SNHL ($p < .0001$).[46]

The radiographic finding of a narrow IAC (2 mm or less in height) has been related to an absent or markedly hypoplastic vestibulocochlear nerve.[22, 81] However, evaluation of the eighth nerve should be by MRI, because a narrow IAC has been described in normal-hearing subjects and in those with an absent vestibulocochlear nerve.[18, 46, 81] Promontory stimulation testing and functional MRI of the auditory cortex to exclude the presence of nonvisualized small cochlear nerve fibers has been suggested.[18] Vestibular nerve aplasia or hypoplasia with a normal cochlear nerve has not been described; therefore, MRI demonstration of the absence or hypoplasia of the vestibulocochlear nerve might predict failure of a cochlear implant (see Figs. 22–8A and B).

An IAC larger than 8 mm in greatest dimension is generally considered wide, and it has been associated with SNHL.[61, 88] Both a wide IAC and bulbous-appearing IAC have been described in association with SNHL.[16, 60, 92] In

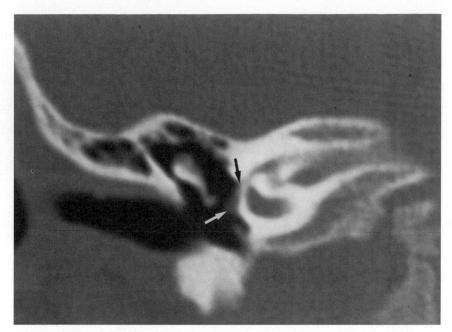

FIGURE 22–12. Coronal CT of a 3-year-old male with congenital mixed hearing loss. The oval window is absent adjacent to a dilated basal turn of the cochlea (black arrow). The facial nerve is displaced inferiorly and partially overlies the usual location of the oval window (white arrow).

particular, a bulbous IAC has been described in association with X-linked mixed hearing loss and stapes fixation,[27] which may indicate a high incidence of stapes gusher at stapedectomy.[49, 85] The risk has been shown to be higher in patients in whom the vestibule effaced the IAC, i.e., no bony separation is present between the basal turn of the cochlea and the lateral end of the IAC.[62] The theory holds that this allows for free flow between the subarachnoid space CSF and the perilymph in the cochlea.[67]

Associated Middle-Ear Anomalies

External and middle-ear anomalies are frequently associated with inner-ear anomalies (see Chap. 20). Ossicular malformations, particularly those of the stapes footplate and the round and oval windows, have been associated with perilymphatic fistulas and recurrent meningitis.[80] When round window or oval window anomalies are present in association with malformations of the inner ear, an abnormal connection may exist between the middle ear and CSF of the central nervous system.

The incidence of middle-ear anomalies in patients with inner-ear anomalies is not known. A histopathologic temporal bone study by Sando showed that 70 of 100 temporal bones examined had inner-ear malformations. Of these, approximately 85% had associated middle-ear anomalies.[73] The study included abnormalities of the tympanic membrane and cordae tympani as middle-ear abnormalities. The incidence of ossicular or oval and round window abnormalities only has been estimated to be as high as 50% by some authors.[70, 101]

The presence of an inner-ear malformation alone may predispose an individual to progressive SNHL, but one must be aware of the possibility of an associated middle-ear anomaly. Round window or oval window anomalies may increase the likelihood of progressive SNHL due to perilymphatic fistula, and affected patients may be at increased risk for development of meningitis. CT imaging remains the study of choice for evaluation of the middle ear (Fig. 22–12). When imaging studies are inconclusive, middle-ear exploration should be considered in patients with recurrent meningitis or mixed hearing loss.

Diagnosis

The evaluation of a child with sensorineural hearing loss remains an area of debate and uncertainty (see Chaps. 16 and 28). Even a thorough medical evaluation fails to reveal the etiology of SNHL in approximately 30% of children.[14] However, radiographic imaging provides useful diagnostic information in up to 30% of cases, representing a high diagnostic yield compared with other tests and procedures.[10, 14, 101] Radiographic imaging has generally only allowed for assessment of the bony labyrinth, but it is estimated that 90% of congenital sensorineural deafness is due to an isolated membranous labyrinthine defect.[40] Advances in MRI may lead to additional diagnostic information in these cases.

CT or MRI scanning should be considered for any child with sensorineural hearing loss, mixed hearing loss, or unexplained conductive hearing loss. CT scan has become a widely used diagnostic test in the evaluation of childhood SNHL, with an estimated diagnostic yield of 13% to 30%.[4, 10, 11, 14, 82, 101] However, the lack of normal-hearing subjects for comparison in these studies limits their broad clinical applicability, and studies of normal temporal bone imaging in children are rare. Pappas reviewed CT scans of adult and pediatric patients with SNHL that were read initially as normal and found that approximately three fourths had subtle abnormalities or borderline measurements of many structures.[61]

Refinement of three-dimensional CT reconstruction and advances in MR imaging techniques have already greatly improved our ability to image the temporal bone and inner ear. MRI has greatly enhanced visualization of the structures of the IAC. The importance of such information will grow in significance as imaging techniques are further developed.

Very little information is available regarding vestibular function in children with SNHL. Symptoms may be subtle or absent because of the slow progression, the central compensation, or both.[40] An obvious problem in obtaining data on vestibular function in affected children is the difficulty of performing vestibular testing in this population. However, normative data in a study of children with recurrent acute otitis media has recently been published,[17] and further study of vestibular function in children with SNHL is warranted.

Congenital Inner-Ear Anomalies and Cochlear Implantation

Children with inner-ear malformations were previously excluded from cochlear implant surgery for several reasons. The risk of meningitis was thought to be higher in these patients, and there was concern about damage to the electrode[9] or the spiral ganglion cells.[77] There was uncertainty about the efficacy of electrical stimulation of reduced number and abnormally positioned spiral ganglion cells,[55] and increased risk of facial nerve injury was also a concern.[36, 48]

Advances in imaging technology and increased experience with cochlear implantation in children with congenitally malformed ears has allowed surgeons to anticipate difficulties in implantation surgery, such as labyrinthitis ossificans, aberrant facial nerve anatomy, and anomalies associated with CSF leak. To date, children with congenital malformations have had comparable results to those of similar age and history of deafness and language, although there are indications that performance may be better in those with less severe anomalies.[6, 13, 34, 83, 87, 90]

MRI has greatly enhanced our ability to visualize the structures in the IAC.[22] Hypoplasia of the cochlear nerve has been reported in cases of cochlear hypoplasia,[18] which can lead to nonuse of the cochlear implant or facial nerve stimulation.[30] Oblique sagittal views allow cross-sectional analysis of the IAC (see Fig. 22–8B), which can help determine whether a patient has an adequate cochlear nerve present to allow for adequate electrical stimulation. This is a concern in patients with cochlear hypoplasia or common cavity malformation.

The number of neurons and spiral ganglion cells necessary for effective cochlear implant stimulation is not known. Early studies suggested that at least 10,000 spiral ganglion cells are required for speech discrimination, with at least 3000 of them being present in the apex of the cochlea.[55] However, given the different type of stimulation by a cochlear implant, fewer ganglion cells may be required. One report of a cochlear implant patient who perceived sound in life demonstrated only 3300 ganglion cells on histopathologic sections of the cochlea (Fig. 22–13).[44]

An increased incidence of perilymphatic fistula or CSF leak at the cochleostomy has been reported in association with inner-ear anomalies. It occurs more frequently with cochlear anomalies and abnormalities of the IAC,[83] and it has been reported in several series in association with the

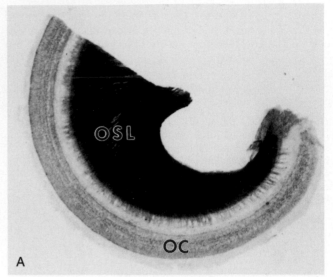

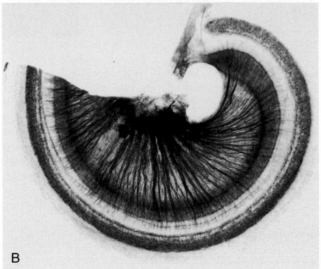

FIGURE 22–13. Cochlear microdissections showing the osseous spiral lamina (OSL) and organ of Corti (OC) at the apical turn. *A,* Normal cochlea; note darkly stained myelinated nerve fibers within the OSL; *B,* Cochlea of a child with multiple congenital anomalies and profound sensorineural hearing loss; note the markedly reduced number of cochlear nerve fibers, but nearly intact organ of Corti. (Micrographs, magnification 40×)

common cavity malformation.[83, 90] Patients who have increased perilymph flow at the time of cochleostomy are more likely to experience vestibular symptoms.[6, 13] The severity of the symptoms seems to be proportional to the amount of perilymph lost at the time of surgery, and the symptoms appear to be self-limited.[6] Studies that report no evidence of CSF leak or gusher do not include patients with common cavity malformations.[34, 87]

A modified surgical approach of a transmastoid labyrinthotomy has been proposed to improve access for controlling a perilymph leak rapidly and to avoid injury to an aberrant facial nerve.[47, 48] A 33% incidence of aberrant facial nerve has been reported in association with the common cavity deformity.[47] When necessary to prevent a CSF leak, the use of a postoperative lumbar drain has been recommended, and the use of a suction drain is discouraged.[47] Removal of the incus in the traditional transmastoid facial recess approach can also improve access to the cochleostomy and improve visualization of the facial nerve. Intraoperative facial nerve monitoring is essential in cases of congenital malformations.[83]

Further discussion of pediatric cochlear implantation can be found in Chapter 29.

Conclusion

Knowledge of the anatomy of the membranous labyrinth is critical to the otologic surgeon. As our ability to image these structures improves, we will obtain more information about individual patients. The clinical significance of various anomalies will become more apparent, and knowledge of the anomalies will likely influence decisions in the management of affected children.

Parents should be made aware of the potential increased risk of meningitis in a child with a congenitally malformed ear. It is likely that certain abnormalities, such as LVA and certain dilatations of the internal auditory meatus, are associated with increased risk for sudden sensorineural hearing loss or progression with head trauma. Recommendations for the avoidance of contact sports or barotrauma are probably prudent for these patients, although recommendations are not well defined. Affected children should undergo close surveillance for progression of hearing loss and speech development.

Early intervention is critical in a child who is at risk for progression to profound sensorineural hearing loss. Cochlear implant technology is advancing rapidly and special devices for congenitally malformed inner ears may improve our ability to assist these children. Vestibular testing should be used when possible, because this may shed light on the prognosis and natural history of certain malformations. Ultimately, this will allow us to better counsel parents and patients.

Acknowledgments

Tim Booth, M.D., Dallas Children's Hospital, Dallas, Texas

Charles G. Wright, Ph.D., Callier Center, University of Texas Southwestern Medical Center, Dallas, Texas

REFERENCES

1. Abe S, Usami S, Hoover DM, et al. Fluctuating sensorineural hearing loss associated with enlarged vestibular aqueduct maps to 7q31, the region containing the Pendred gene. Am J Med Genet 82(4):322, 1999.
2. Abe S, Usami S, Shinkawa H. Three familial cases of hearing loss associated with enlargement of the vestibular aqueduct. Ann Otol Rhinol Laryngol 106(12):1063, 1997.
3. Amjad AH, Scheer AA, Rosenthal J. Human internal auditory canal. Arch Otolaryngol 89(5):709, 1969.
4. Antonelli PJ, Nall AV, Lemmerling MM, et al. Hearing loss with cochlear modiolar defects and large vestibular aqueducts [see comments]. Am J Otol 19(3):306, 1998.
5. Arcand P, Desrosiers M, Dube J, Abela A. The large vestibular aqueduct syndrome and sensorineural hearing loss in the pediatric population. J Otolaryngol 20(4):247, 1991.
6. Au G, Gibson W. Cochlear implantation in children with large vestibular aqueduct syndrome. Am J Otol 20(2):183, 1999.
7. Bachor E, Byahatti S, Karmody CS. The cochlear aqueduct in pediatric temporal bones. Eur Arch Otorhinolaryngol Suppl 1(8):S34, 1997.
8. Bachor E, Byahatti S, Karmody CS. New aspects in the histopathology of the cochlear aqueduct in children. Am J Otol 20(5):612, 1999.
9. Balkany T, Hodges AV, Luntz M. Update on cochlear implantation. Otolaryngol Clin North Am 29(2):277, 1996.
10. Bamiou DE, MacArdle B, Bitner-Glindzicz M, Sirimanna T. Aetiological investigations of hearing loss in childhood: a review. Clin Otolaryngol 25(2):98, 2000.
11. Bamiou DE, Phelps P, Sirimanna T. Temporal bone computed tomography findings in bilateral sensorineural hearing loss. Arch Dis Child 82(3):257, 2000.
12. Bauman NM, Kirby-Keyser LJ, Dolan KD, et al. Mondini dysplasia and congenital cytomegalovirus infection. J Pediatr 124(1):71, 1994.
13. Bent JP 3rd, Chute P, Parisier SC. Cochlear implantation in children with enlarged vestibular aqueducts. Laryngoscope 109(7 Pt 1):1019, 1999.
14. Billings KR, Kenna MA. Causes of pediatric sensorineural hearing loss: yesterday and today [see comments]. Arch Otolaryngol Head Neck Surg 125(5):517, 1999.
15. Bluestone CD. Otitis media and congenital perilymphatic fistula as a cause of sensorineural hearing loss in children. Pediatr Infect Dis J 7(11 Suppl):S141, 1988.
16. Camp JDC, Earl IL. The significance of asymmetry of the pori acustici as an aid in the diagnosis of eighth nerve tumors. Am J Roentgenol Radium Ther 41(5):713, 1939.
17. Casselbrant ML, Furman JM, Mandel EM, et al. Past history of otitis media and balance in four-year-old children. Laryngoscope 110(5 Pt 1):773, 2000.
18. Casselman JW, Offeciers FE, Govaerts PJ, et al. Aplasia and hypoplasia of the vestibulocochlear nerve: diagnosis with MR imaging. Radiology 202(3):773, 1997.
19. Chan KH, Eelkema EA, Furman JM, Kamerer DB. Familial sensorineural hearing loss: a correlative study of audiologic, radiographic, and vestibular findings. Ann Otol Rhinol Laryngol 100(8):620, 1991.
20. Cremers CW, Delleman WJ. Usher's syndrome, temporal bone pathology. Int J Pediatr Otorhinolaryngol 16(1):23, 1988.
21. Cremers WR, Bolder C, Admiraal RJ, et al. Progressive sensorineural hearing loss and a widened vestibular aqueduct in Pendred syndrome. Arch Otolaryngol Head Neck Surg 124(5):501, 1998.
22. Ellul S, Shelton C, Davidson HC, Harnsberger HR. Preoperative cochlear implant imaging: is magnetic resonance imaging enough? Am J Otol 21(4):528, 2000.
23. Emmett JR. The large vestibular aqueduct syndrome. Am J Otol 6(5):387, 1985.
24. Everett LA, Glaser B, Beck JC, et al. Pendred syndrome is caused by mutations in a putative sulphate transporter gene (PDS). Nat Genet 17(4):411, 1997.
25. Fisher NA, Curtin HD. Radiology of congenital hearing loss. Otolaryngol Clin North Am 27(3):511, 1994.
26. Fugazzola L, Mannavola D, Cerutti N, et al. Molecular analysis of the Pendred's syndrome gene and magnetic resonance imaging studies of the inner ear are essential for the diagnosis of true Pendred's syndrome. J Clin Endocrinol Metab 85(7):2469, 2000.
27. Glasscock ME, Storper IS, Haynes DS, Bohrer PS. Stapedectomy in profound cochlear loss. Laryngoscope 106(7):831, 1996.
28. Gopen Q, Rosowski JJ, Merchant SN. Anatomy of the normal human cochlear aqueduct with functional implications. Hear Res 107(1-2):9, 1997.
29. Govaerts PJ, Casselman J, Daemers K, et al. Audiological findings in large vestibular aqueduct syndrome. Int J Pediatr Otorhinolaryngol 51(3):157, 1999.
30. Graham JM, Phelps PD, Michaels L. Congenital malformations of the ear and cochlear implantation in children: review and temporal bone report of common cavity. J Laryngol Otol Suppl 25:1, 2000.
31. Griffith AJ, Arts A, Downs C, et al. Familial large vestibular aqueduct syndrome. Laryngoscope 106(8):960, 1996.
32. Griffith AJ, Telian SA, Downs C, et al. Familial Mondini dysplasia. Laryngoscope 108(9):1368, 1998.
33. Gussen R. Sudden hearing loss associated with cochlear membrane

rupture. Two human temporal bone reports. Arch Otolaryngol 107(10):598, 1981.

34. Harker LA, Vanderheiden S, Veazey D, et al. Multichannel cochlear implantation in children with large vestibular aqueduct syndrome. Ann Otol Rhinol Laryngol Suppl 177:39, 1999.

35. Hill JH, Freint AJ, Mafee MF. Enlargement of the vestibular aqueduct. Am J Otolaryngol 5(6):411, 1984.

36. House JR, Luxford WM. Facial nerve injury in cochlear implantation [see comments]. Otolaryngol Head Neck Surg 109(6):1078, 1993.

37. Jackler RK, De La Cruz A. The large vestibular aqueduct syndrome. Laryngoscope 99(12):1238, discussion 1242, 1989.

38. Jackler RK, Hwang PH. Enlargement of the cochlear aqueduct: fact or fiction? Otolaryngol Head Neck Surg 109(1):14, 1993.

39. Jackler RK, Luxford WM, House WF. Congenital malformations of the inner ear: a classification based on embryogenesis. Laryngoscope 97(3 Pt 2; Suppl 40):2, 1987.

40. Lalwani AK, Grundfast KM. Pediatric Neurotology. Philadelphia: Lippincott-Raven, 1995.

41. Lemmerling MM, Mancuso AA, Antonelli PJ, Kubilis PS. Normal modiolus: CT appearance in patients with a large vestibular aqueduct. Radiology 204(1):213, 1997.

42. Levenson MJ, Parisier SC, Jacobs M, Edelstein DR. The large vestibular aqueduct syndrome in children. A review of 12 cases and the description of a new clinical entity. Arch Otolaryngol Head Neck Surg 115(1):54, 1989.

43. Lindsay JR. Inner ear pathology in congenital deafness. Otolaryngol Clin North Am 4(2):249, 1971.

44. Linthicum FH Jr, Fayad J, Otto S, et al. Inner ear morphologic changes resulting from cochlear implantation. Am J Otol 12(Suppl): 8, discussion 18, 1991.

45. Mafee MF, Charletta D, Kumar A, Belmont H. Large vestibular aqueduct and congenital sensorineural hearing loss. AJNR Am J Neuroradiol 13(2):805, 1992.

46. McClay JE, Tandy R, Grundfast K, Choi S, Vezina G, et al. Major and minor temporal bone abnormalities in children with and without sensorineural hearing loss. In American Society of Pediatric Otolaryngology Abstracts. Palm Desert, Calif, 1999.

47. McElveen JT Jr, Carrasco VN, Miyamoto RT, Linthicum FH Jr. Cochlear implantation in common cavity malformations using a transmastoid labyrinthotomy approach. Laryngoscope 107(8):1032, 1997.

48. Molter DW, Pate BR Jr, McElveen JT Jr. Cochlear implantation in the congenitally malformed ear. Otolaryngol Head Neck Surg 108(2):174, 1993.

49. Nance WE, Setleff R, McLeod A, et al. X-linked mixed deafness with congenital fixation of the stapedial footplate and perilymphatic gusher. Birth Defects Original Article Series 7(4):64, 1971.

50. Narcy P, Viala P, Sellier N, et al. Congenital perilymphatic fistula in children. Ann Otolaryngol Chir Cervicofac 106(7):449, 1989.

51. Nishihara S. Transmission of changes in the external ear atmospheric pressure to the perilymph. Nippon Jibiinkoka Gakkai Kaiho 93(5):707, 1990.

52. Nowak KC, Messner AH. Isolated large vestibular aqueduct syndrome in a family. Ann Otol Rhinol Laryngol 109(1):40, 2000.

53. Okumura T, Takahashi H, Honjo I, et al. Sensorineural hearing loss in patients with large vestibular aqueduct. Laryngoscope 105(3 Pt 1):289, discussion 293, 1995.

54. Olivares FP, Schuknecht HF. Width of the internal auditory canal. A histological study. Ann Otol Rhinol Laryngol 88(3 Pt 1):316, 1979.

55. Otte J, Schunknecht HF, Kerr AG. Ganglion cell populations in normal and pathological human cochleae. Implications for cochlear implantation. Laryngoscope 88(8 Pt 1):1231, 1978.

56. Palva T. Cochlear aqueduct in infants. Acta Otolaryngol 70(2):83, 1970.

57. Palva T, Dammert K. Human cochlear aqueduct. Acta Otolaryngol 246:5–57, 1969.

58. Palva T, Gussen R. Cochlear aqueduct. Arch Otolaryngol 91(5):493, 1970.

59. Palva T, Raunio V, Karma P, Ylikoski J. Fluid pathways in temporal bones. Acta Otolaryngol 87(3–4):310, 1979.

60. Papangelou L. Study of the human internal auditory canal in relation to age and sex. J Laryngol Otol 89(1):79, 1975.

61. Pappas DG, Simpson LC, McKenzie RA, Royal S. High-resolution

computed tomography: determination of the cause of pediatric sensorineural hearing loss. Laryngoscope 100(6):564, 1990.

62. Phelps PD. The basal turn of the cochlea. Br J Radiol 65(773):370, 1992.

63. Phelps PD. Congenital lesions of the inner ear, demonstrated by tomography. Arch Otolaryngol 100(1):11, 1974.

64. Phelps PD. Ear dysplasia after Mondini. J Laryngol Otol 108(6):461, 1994.

65. Phelps PD. Mondini and "pseudo Mondini" [editorial]. Clin Otolaryngol 15(2):99, 1990.

66. Phelps PD, Lloyd GA. Mondini dysplasia is not associated with meningitis and cerebrospinal fluid fistula [letter; comment]. Arch Otolaryngol Head Neck Surg 117(8):931, 1991.

67. Phelps PD, Reardon W, Pembrey M, et al. X-linked deafness, stapes gushers and a distinctive defect of the inner ear. Neuroradiology 33(4):326, 1991.

68. Rask-Andersen H, Stahle J, Wilbrand H. Human cochlear aqueduct and its accessory canals. Ann Otol Rhinol Laryngol Suppl 86(5 Pt 2; Suppl 42):1, 1977.

69. Reardon W, Bellman S, Phelps P, et al. Neuro-otological function in X-linked hearing loss: a multipedigree assessment and correlation with other clinical parameters. Acta Otolaryngol 113(6):706, 1993.

70. Roland PSMBF. Hearing Loss. New York: Thieme, 1997.

71. Sando I, Bergstrom L, Wood RP, Hemenway WG. Temporal bone findings in trisomy 18 syndrome. Arch Otolaryngol 91(6):552, 1970.

72. Sando I, Leiberman A, Bergstrom L, et al. Temporal bone histopathological findings in trisomy 13 syndrome. Ann Otol Rhinol Laryngol 84(4 Pt 2; Suppl 21):1, 1975.

73. Sando I, Shibahara Y, Takagi A, et al. Congenital middle and inner ear anomalies. Acta Otolaryngol Suppl 458:76, 1988.

74. Sando I, Shibahara Y, Takagi A, et al. Frequency and localization of congenital anomalies of the middle and inner ears: a human temporal bone histopathological study. Int J Pediatr Otorhinolaryngol 16(1):1, 1988.

75. Sando I, Takahara T, Ogawa A. Congenital anomalies of the inner ear. Ann Otol Rhinol Laryngol Suppl 112:110, 1984.

76. Schessel DA, Nedzelski JM. Presentation of large vestibular aqueduct syndrome to a dizziness unit. J Otolaryngol 21(4):265, 1992.

77. Schmidt JM. Cochlear neuronal populations in developmental defects of the inner ear. Implications for cochlear implantation. Acta Otolaryngol 99(1–2):14, 1985.

78. Schuknecht HF. Mondini dysplasia; a clinical and pathological study. Ann Otol Rhinol Laryngol Suppl 89(1 Pt 2):1, 1980.

79. Schuknecht HF. Pathology of the Ear, 2nd ed. Philadelphia: Lea and Febiger, 1993.

80. Schultz P, Stool S. Recurrent meningitis due to a congenital fistula through the stapes footplate. Am J Dis Child 120(6):553, 1970.

81. Shelton C, Luxford WM, Tonokawa LL, et al. The narrow internal auditory canal in children: a contraindication to cochlear implants. Otolaryngol Head Neck Surg 100(3):227, 1989.

82. Shusterman D, Handler SD, Marsh RR, et al. Usefulness of computed tomographic scan in the evaluation of sensorineural hearing loss in children. Arch Otolaryngol Head Neck Surg 118(5):501, 1992.

83. Slattery WH 3rd, Luxford WM. Cochlear implantation in the congenital malformed cochlea. Laryngoscope 105(11):1184, 1995.

84. Suehiro S, Sando I. Congenital anomalies of the inner ear: introducing a new classification of labyrinthine anomalies. Ann Otol Rhinol Laryngol Suppl 88(4 Pt 3; Suppl 59):1, 1979.

85. Szeremeta WK. Enlarged Internal Auditory Canals and Sensorineural Hearing Loss. In American Society of Pediatric Otolaryngology, May 12–14, Durango, Colo, 1995.

86. Takasaki K, Balaban CD, Sando I. Histopathologic findings of the inner ears with Alport, Usher and Waardenburg syndromes. Adv Otorhinolaryngol 56:218, 2000.

87. Temple RH, Ramsden RT, Axon PR, Saeed SR. The large vestibular aqueduct syndrome: the role of cochlear implantation in its management. Clin Otolaryngol 24(4):301, 1999.

88. Tomura N, Sashi R, Kobayashi M, et al. Normal variations of the temporal bone on high-resolution CT: their incidence and clinical significance [see comments]. Clin Radiol 50(3):144, 1995.

89. Tong KA, Harnsberger HR, Dahlen RT, et al. Large vestibular

aqueduct syndrome: a genetic disease? AJR Am J Roentgenol 168(4):1097, 1997.

90. Tucci DL, Telian SA, Zimmerman-Phillips S, et al. Cochlear implantation in patients with cochlear malformations. Arch Otolaryngol Head Neck Surg 121(8):833, 1995.

91. Valvassori GE. The large vestibular aqueduct and associated anomalies of the inner ear. Otolaryngol Clin North Am 16(1):95, 1983.

92. Valvassori GE. Radiologic diagnosis of neuro-otologic problems by tomography. Arch Otolaryngol 89(1):57, 1969.

93. Valvassori GE, Clemis JD. The large vestibular aqueduct syndrome. Laryngoscope 88 (5): 723–8, 1978.

94. Wagenaar M, Schuknecht H, Nadol J Jr, et al. Histopathologic features of the temporal bone in usher syndrome type I. Arch Otolaryngol Head Neck Surg 126(8):1018, 2000.

95. Welling DB, Martyn MD, Miles BA, et al. Endolymphatic sac occlusion for the enlarged vestibular aqueduct syndrome. Am J Otol 19(2):145, 1998.

96. Welling DB, Slater PW, Martyn MD, et al. Sensorineural hearing loss after occlusion of the enlarged vestibular aqueduct. Am J Otol 20(3):338, 1999.

97. West PD, Gholkar A, Ramsden RT. Wildervanck's syndrome—unilateral Mondini dysplasia identified by computed tomography. J Laryngol Otol 103(4):408, 1989.

98. Wilson DF, Hodgson RS, Talbot JM. Endolymphatic sac obliteration for large vestibular aqueduct syndrome. Am J Otol 18(1):1016, discussion 106, 1997.

99. Wlodyka J. Studies on cochlear aqueduct patency. Ann Otol Rhinol Laryngol 87(1 Pt 1):22, 1978.

100. Yetiser S, Kertmen M, Ozkaptan Y. Vestibular disturbance in patients with large vestibular aqueduct syndrome (LVAS). Acta Otolaryngol 119(6):641, 1999.

101. Zalzal GH, Shott SR, Towbin R, Cotton RT. Value of CT scan in the diagnosis of temporal bone diseases in children. Laryngoscope 96(1):27, 1986.

102. Zalzal GH, Tomaski SM, Vezina LG, et al. Enlarged vestibular aqueduct and sensorineural hearing loss in childhood. Arch Otolaryngol Head Neck Surg 121(1):23, 1995.

23

Perilymphatic Fistulas in Infants and Children

Peter C. Weber, M.D., and James S. Reilly, M.D.

Advances in modern understanding of genetics, better methods of infant hearing screens, and greater scrutiny of clinical and operative diagnoses have refined our knowledge of the causes of sensorineural hearing loss (SNHL) in infants and young children. Etiologies are either hereditary or acquired. Sometimes a hereditary cause may not be apparent, and the hearing loss is then termed *cryptogenic* pending further clinical observation and investigation.[1]

Perilymphatic fistulas (PLFs) are simply defined as an abnormal communication between the middle and inner ear. Congenital perilymphatic fistulas (PLFs) are abnormal leaks of perilymph (cerebrospinal fluid [CSF]) caused by a hereditary weakness or defect in the temporal bone, particularly in the region of the stapes footplate (the most common site being the fissula ante fenestram[51]). Congenital PLFs are associated usually with progressive, fluctuating, or sudden SNHL. Occasionally, vertigo may also be a symptom, either alone or with hearing impairment, but this is less likely.

The larger PLF leaks may be observable and persistent; the smaller PLF leaks may be occult or intermittent. Most hereditary PLFs cause hearing loss in the first decade of life and, if large, may be associated with recurrent meningitis.

Acquired PLFs are either related to external trauma, such as occurs in diving or head trauma, or to surgery within the temporal bone. "Spontaneously" occurring PLFs may occur from exertion that raises the pressures between the middle ear and the inner ear, e.g., sneezing, Valsalva maneuver, or heavy lifting.[28] However, spontaneous PLFs are controversial in their existence.[10] A hereditary underlying predisposition, such as microfissures of the oval window, may explain the rarity of these events to a population that is susceptible.[21]

Health care professionals may develop a better understanding of these hereditary and sometimes occult PLFs from a brief historical review of the patterns and associated symptoms.

Historical Perspective

The evolution of knowledge of hereditary PLF and of associated temporal bone defects, CSF leaks, meningitis, and deafness began a century ago, with the earliest description of a young girl with spontaneous CSF otorrhea.[9] The triad of gross CSF otorrhea, temporal bone abnormalities, and recurrent (later fatal) meningitis was later confirmed, again in a young child, in whom postmortem examination of the temporal bone revealed a large communication between the middle ear and the brain through a defect of the petrous apex.[7]

This existence of spontaneous, occult CSF leaks within the middle ear remained largely unreported for almost 40 years until a middle-ear exploration was undertaken to determine the cause of recurrent meningitis in a young deaf girl. The middle ear was grossly abnormal, with a malformed cochlea and semicircular canals. This child was the first to survive this condition, because a craniotomy was performed and the CSF leak sealed.[31] As this association of deafness, occult CSF leaks, and recurrent meningitis became more widely recognized, prompt middle-ear explorations were undertaken to successfully repair and correct this condition.[1]

Spontaneous decreases in hearing, without meningitis, were the next stage of enlightenment of occult PLF and resulted in stabilization of a progressive SNHL in both adults[43] and children.[14] Could these "leaks" be occurring every day in normal children with unexplained progressive SNHL? Is recurrent meningitis or gross CSF otorrhea still required to confirm the diagnosis?

Five children with fluctuating, progressive SNHL were confirmed by middle-ear surgery to have PLF, and, in three, hereditary malformations of ossification were the sole explanation.[15] The investigators challenged the rarity of this condition and postulated congenital PLF as a not uncommon hereditary defect in temporal bone structure.

There is a variety of temporal bone abnormalities associated with hereditary PLF. Previous generations of physicians relied solely on temporal bone specimens to define the leaks from the CSF pathway. Malformations of the round window, together with a large cyst of the cochlear or vestibular aqueduct, have been noted.

One report demonstrated a significant number of middle-ear anomalies (80%), particularly of the superstructure of the stapes (60%), when a congenital PLF was diagnosed (Fig. 23–1).[51] This same study demonstrated bilateral PLFs 30% of the time; in 17.5% of cases, the oval window and round window were positive for PLF (Fig. 23–2).

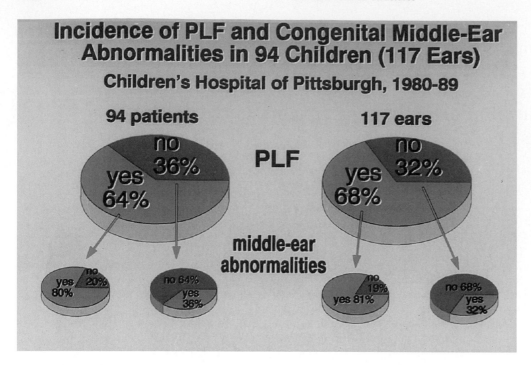

FIGURE 23–1. Demonstrates the relationship of middle ear abnormalities with congenital perilymphatic fistulas. (From Weber PC, Perez BA, Bluestone CD. Congenital perilymphatic fistula and associated middle ear abnormalities. Laryngoscope 103:160, 1993.)

The footplate is dependent on the otic capsule and the stapes to "jointly" form the annular ligament. Isolated defects in the second branchial arch–derived stapes may weaken the stapes footplate linkage and predispose the patient to leaks of PLF.[18]

Detailed radiologic examination of the temporal bone has provided clues to hidden temporal bone defects. Basal cysternography first demonstrated that radiopaque contrast material was able to pass from the internal auditory canal through the vestibule and into the middle ear preoperatively in a child with congenital PLF.[45] CT cisternography can still be used to detect congenital PLFs.[25] Polytomographic examination of the temporal bone visualized dysgenesis of the labyrinth and a Mondini-type de-

formity in cases of otitic meningitis.[2] The importance of radiographic demonstration of abnormal anatomy of the temporal bone as a critical marker for congenital PLF of children has been emphasized in several large studies.[33, 46, 53] A recent report demonstrated abnormal stapes and other ossicles.[53] However, round window anomalies are hard to see on CT scan.

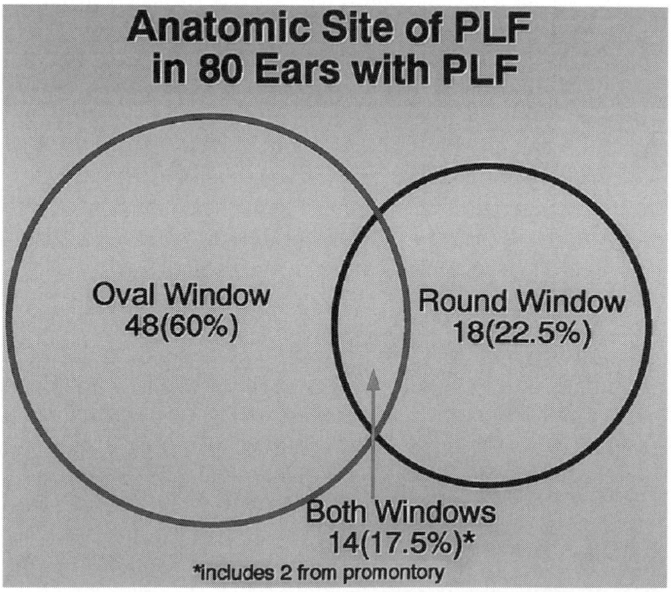

Inner-ear malformations (Mondini or enlarged vestibular or cochlear aqueducts) are associated with a congenital PLF 25% of the time as seen on CT scan.[53] Thus, 85% of congenital PLFs had one middle- or inner-ear abnormality in one study.[51] Another study demonstrated fluid collections, presumed CSF, as noted by CT scan in a child with unilateral, documented PLF.[54] Finally, magnetic resonance imaging with gadolinium enhancement has imaged experimentally induced PLFs in animal models[29] and in humans with unexplained sudden SNHL.[26]

However, unexplained fluctuations of hearing, particularly with documented progression of bilateral SNHL, should never be ignored. This type of hearing loss often merits exploratory tympanotomy to rule out hereditary PLF, even in the presence of "normal" temporal bone anatomy as observed on imaging studies. A study of 70 children with apparently "normal" temporal bones on CT examination and with SNHL demonstrated that 75% had minor but detectable abnormalities when measurements were obtained and closely compared with those of true normal subjects.[33] This further suggests that hereditary factors affect temporal bone morphology in both the first and second trimesters of intrauterine development.[34] A prospective study of 244 children with unexplained SNHL identified 15 children (6%) with PLF that could be explained only as a hereditary predisposition[37] (Fig. 23–3). In 75% of the children, deterioration of hearing was the primary symptom.[37] Hereditary hearing loss associated with PLF must be included in the differential diagnosis of unexplained SNHL in children (Fig. 23–4).

Anatomic Site of PLF in 80 Ears with PLF

Oval Window
48(60%)

Round Window
18(22.5%)

Both Windows
14(17.5%)*

*includes 2 from promontory

FIGURE 23–2. Demonstrates the site of PLF.

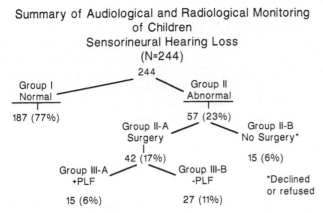

FIGURE 23–3. Distribution of children evaluated for unexplained sensorineural hearing loss demonstrating 15 children (6%) with perilymphatic fistula. (Modified from Reilly JS. Congenital perilymphatic fistula, a prospective study in infants and children. Laryngoscope 99:393–397, 1989.)

Evaluation

Infants and children who are suspected of having unexplained progression of hearing loss should be evaluated thoroughly. A complete birth and developmental history must be obtained. Questions must be directed toward any history of viral infections, particularly cytomegalovirus or bacterial infections, birth or head trauma, exposure to teratogens or ototoxic drugs, or prematurity. We regularly use a comprehensive questionnaire.

Physical examination is important. Any craniofacial anomalies must be noted and compared with known syndromes that have associated SNHL, including Waardenburg's and Treacher Collins.[16] Otitis media, eustachian tube dysfunction, or both may be present and must be treated and eliminated as a cause of any recent hearing change. Complete ophthalmologic examination is important to look for cataracts (rubella), widened interpupillary distances (Waardenburg type I), myopia (Stickler's), or retinal changes (Refsum's, Usher's, or Stickler's).

Complete audiologic evaluation includes conventional audiologic testing via both soundfield and headphone. In very young infants or in poorly cooperative children, serial auditory brain stem response (ABR) testing may be necessary to confirm deterioration in hearing. Otoacoustic emissions represent a new and promising screening technique that should be of great value if widely applied for neonatal hearing screens. Combined with ABR, it may detect frequency-specific cochlear hearing loss.[23] All previous audiologic test results should be obtained and thoroughly reviewed for documentation. Significant deterioration of hearing (greater than 20 dB in speech reception thresholds) is frequently seen to affect primarily one ear in children with PLF.

Young children may also be examined by a speech therapist to compare their level of language skills with that of normally hearing children. Good language acquisition suggests that near normal hearing was preserved during the first 2 years of life and that any deterioration of hearing may be of recent onset. This is helpful, since audiograms from early months of life may not be available.

Imaging of the temporal bone is the next critical step. CT scanning is currently the most useful technique. A thorough study, using thin (1.0 mm) sections obtained through both axial and coronal planes, is important. Bony detail is enhanced by proper windowing programs. The images must be carefully and critically evaluated by a skilled radiologist familiar with temporal bone anatomy. Malformations of the cochlea include loss of partitioning between interscalar septa (Mondini deformity) (Fig. 23–5). Development of a common cavity or complete aplasia (Michel deformity) can be seen in extreme cases. The vestibule or vestibular aqueduct may be enlarged, and the horizontal semicircular canal may be foreshortened and rudimentary.[32]

The internal auditory canal and enlarged cochlear aqueduct may be dilated and asymmetric. The latter must be larger than 2 mm at all points to be significant, because there is a wide range of normal for this structure.[19]

Use of 1.0-mm sections of CT imaging provides an opportunity to better assess the normality or abnormality of middle-ear structures; however, some middle-ear abnormalities, such as the round window, are still missed.[45] A review of a large series of children with documented SNHL and evaluation of the temporal bone by conventional polytome or CT scan illustrated a spectrum of malformations of the cochlea and semicircular canals. The authors were able to correlate the stage of labyrinthine development with the week of arrested embryogenesis of the temporal bone. Several abnormalities occur during

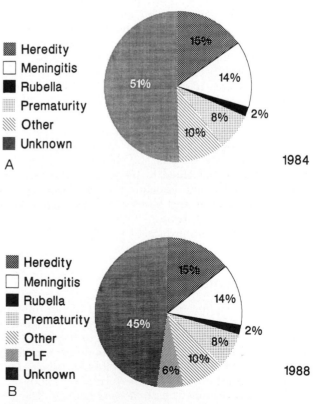

FIGURE 23–4. Distribution of causes of sensorineural hearing loss. (Modified from Schildroth A. Hearing impaired children under age 6. Am Ann Deaf 131:85–90, 1997.)

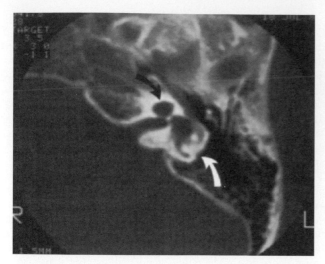

FIGURE 23–5. Computed tomographic scan in the axial plane demonstrating Mondini dysplasia. The black arrow shows the dilated cochlea; the white arrow, the enlarged vestibule.

the fourth week and more subtle changes during the seventh week (Fig. 23–6).[20]

Evaluation of vestibular function for vertigo or dysequilibrium has been useful in a few cases, generally only when a degenerative neurologic abnormality is the cause of the instability. The classic fistula test, a sweep of −400 mm H_2O to +400 mm H_2O pressure in the ear canal, and monitoring for eye movements with electrodes, has not been useful. However, the use of video goggles provides better visualization and results. The classic fistula test did not detect a leak in any of 15 PLF-affected children.[37] Platform posturography has been tested in clinical settings for PLF, but accuracy and correlation with surgical findings have not yet proved reliable, especially in children.[42] Electrocochleography, usually used in Meniere's disease, may be positive for PLFs as well. However, the transtympanic approach is not feasible for the awake child.[39]

After all testing has been completed, the information should be thoroughly reviewed by the physician and discussed with the audiologists and the child's family. The results should be explained to the family, who are often extremely anxious and hopeful. Careful follow-up and monitoring of speech and hearing are important. (Many children are screened, because PLF occurs in only about 1 in 20 children with unexplained SNHL.)

Clinical Presentation

Two different syndromes of congenital PLF are discernible.[36] The first involves young infants with bilateral congenital PLF whose hearing deteriorates in the first 2 to 3 years of life. This condition has frequently been misdiagnosed and labeled "congenital" when it is hereditary. Only ABR or otoacoustic emissions, performed promptly at a young age, can document early normal hearing. The second, more common syndrome occurs in children with unilateral hearing loss who experience deterioration of

hearing in the good ear over months to a year.[36] We agree with these findings.

The second type of syndrome is easier for the physician to diagnose and perhaps occurs more frequently. When a hereditary PLF is identified, the contralateral ear appears to be at risk in about one half[37] to less than one third[33] of the children. Unless the hearing remains normal in the good ear, surgery should be considered to rule out a bilateral PLF.

The degree of hearing loss experienced by the child with congenital PLF can vary. Mild hearing loss is present in 22% of children with PLF, and 14% of children have severe hearing losses. The hearing loss was asymmetric in about half of the children. No specific pattern of hearing impairment was regularly seen. However, a predominant low-frequency loss was occasionally observed in children with better hearing. Numerous children have been reported with serial decreases in hearing over periods of months to years before surgical identification and repair.[36, 52]

Vertigo and tinnitus are two symptoms that are more commonly elicited from adults with PLF but are rarely noted in children. Of 244 children evaluated, 27 (11%) exhibited vertigo or dysequilibrium.[37] More than half of these children (15 of 27) had vertigo as the sole complaint. Only two children with severe vertigo underwent middle-ear exploration and PLFs were not identified. In other series of children, PLFs were noted to be present with vertigo, which tended to improve after repair.[35, 41] In both of these studies, the children had a history of trauma as the probable cause,[41] which is more common in adults.[12, 13, 35]

Treatment

The treatment of persistent PLFs that are clinically suspected and associated with any symptoms (e.g., hearing loss, recurrent meningitis, vertigo, tinnitus, and fullness of the ear) consists of surgical control of the fistula. Most PLFs are controlled satisfactorily through a middle-ear exploration and packing of the fistula site. Temporalis fascia muscle[37] is used for packing, although some clinicians prefer laser graft site preparation combined with autologous fibrin glue "buttress"[3] or subcutaneous areolar tissue plus Avitene.[27] Fat alone is not a good choice of tissue.

The most common site of PLF is the oval window–stapes footplate (60%), followed by the round window (30%). Since abnormalities of the stapes superstructure are most common, a small, 90-degree angled pick is used to palpate the stapes crura and the obturator foramen.[51] Fibrous adhesions may be present and should be lysed to permit adequate inspection of the oval and round windows.[6]

Chemical analysis of PLF fluid has been suggested for confirmation of the diagnosis by free amino acid analysis[40] or electrophoresis detection of beta$_2$-transferrin, which is only found in CSF, vitreous lesion, and perilymph.[30, 47, 49, 50] However, problems do exist with the beta$_2$ test and it may not be as reliable as was once thought.[5, 8, 24, 44]

Radiographic appearance
(coronal plane)

Embryologic development (frontal view)

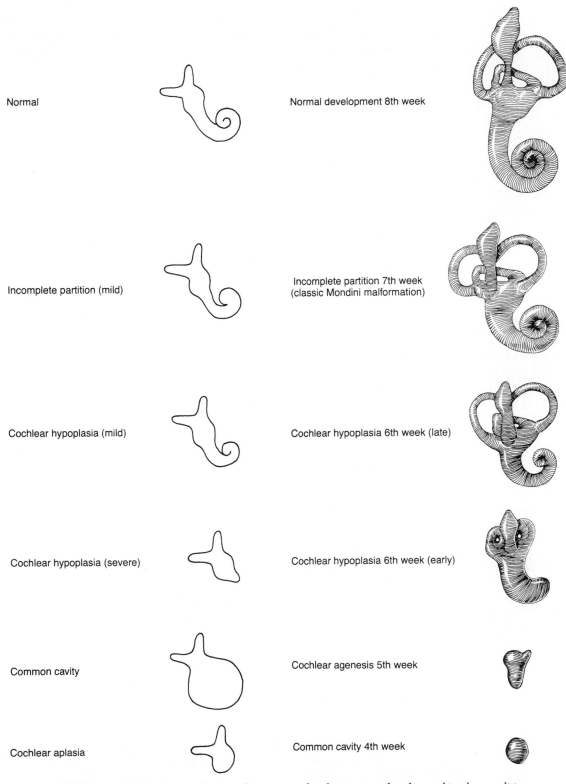

Normal

Normal development 8th week

Incomplete partition (mild)

Incomplete partition 7th week
(classic Mondini malformation)

Cochlear hypoplasia (mild)

Cochlear hypoplasia 6th week (late)

Cochlear hypoplasia (severe)

Cochlear hypoplasia 6th week (early)

Common cavity

Cochlear agenesis 5th week

Cochlear aplasia

Common cavity 4th week

FIGURE 23–6. Correlation of arrested inner ear development and radiographic abnormalities. (Adapted from Jackler RK, Luxford WM, House WF. Congenital malformations of the inner ear: a classification based on embryogenesis. Laryngoscope 97(Suppl 40):2, 1987.)

TABLE 23–1. Audiologic Follow-up of Children with Sensorineural Hearing Loss

	Presence of PLF				Absence of PLF			
	Better	Same	Worse	Number of Ears	Better	Same	Worse	Number of Ears
Supance and Bluestone, 1982	1 (5%)	19 (86%)	2 (9%)	22	1 (6%)	11 (73%)	2 (13%)	14
Pappas et al, 1988	1 (25%)	1 (25%)	2 (50%)	4	2 (6%)	20 (62%)	10 (31%)	32
Reilly, 1989°	5 (23%)	13 (59%)	3 (14%)	22	2 (6%)	24 (75%)	5 (16%)	32
TOTALS:	7 (15%)	33 (69%)	7 (15%)	48	5 (6%)	55 (71%)	17 (22%)	78

° Two ears with no follow up.
PLF, perilymphatic fistula.

Both of these tests take several hours to perform and are not quick enough for intraoperative diagnoses.[44] Fluorescein injection into the CSF before middle-ear surgery has not proved clinically useful.[4]

When the PLF results in copious and persistent CSF leaks despite middle-ear packing, a stapedectomy with placement of a prosthesis and tissue graft may be used. If there is no serviceable hearing, the vestibule may have to be packed completely to seal the leak. If all otologic methods are unsuccessful at stopping a significant leak, an exploratory craniotomy with lining of middle cranial fossa or posterior cranial fossa may be necessary if the site of the leak is detected radiographically.

Additional sites of temporal bone PLF have been reported, including petrosquamous suture, Hyrtl fissure, the epitympanic space, and the mastoid antrum. In most children, PLFs have been explored through the middle ear, and microfissures of the oval and round windows have become suspicious sites of leakage when associated with a progressive hearing loss.[17, 21]

Hearing Outcome

There remains some disagreement among otologists whether a PLF not identified at the time of surgery should be repaired.[11] In the most severe cases, recurrent meningitis must be controlled or eliminated. Unexplained or persistent vertigo seems to be improved also when the proper tissue repair of a PLF is achieved.[22]

Perhaps the most important outcome for children is stabilization and improvement of hearing. Sudden or progressive SNHL is a frightening symptom that brings children to medical attention. Isolated case reports have documented dramatic improvements in hearing in some cases, but this is generally not the result. Studies of PLF in children have provided audiologic follow-up[37] (Table 23–1). Although the numbers are small, they suggest that hearing is improved in approximately 15% of children.[48] Deterioration of hearing occurs less frequently in children with PLF (15%) than in children without PLF (22%). In approximately 70% of children, hearing remains stable. Weber and colleagues demonstrated stabilization or improvement in hearing in 93% of children.[48] One series reported approximately 48% improvement of hearing.[41] This dramatic result has not been observed in other studies.

Most investigators agree that the sooner the PLF is identified and repaired, the better is the chance of hearing improvement or stabilization.[41] The methods of each series vary, but the average age of detection of PLF in our children was 7.7 years of age.[51]

There may well be other multiple abnormalities of the cochlea in addition to window defects that may seriously impair hearing and prevent recovery. A study of 100 temporal bones of children with congenital anomalies showed numerous abnormalities of temporal bone structures in children that had not been previously recognized.[38] Cochlear anomalies were present in 44%, with 16 different types of deformities noted. Vestibular abnormalities were even more common. The vestibule was generally enlarged (18%) and the lateral semicircular canal was absent or foreshortened (100%).

Summary

Congenital PLFs are abnormalities of the temporal bone that occur in approximately 6% of children with unexplained, asymmetric SNHL. These leaks can be associated with fluctuating, progressive, or sudden hearing loss, vertigo, fullness of the ear, tinnitus, and even recurrent meningitis in severe cases. Repair of the fistula is essential and is generally accomplished by an exploratory tympanotomy and patching of both the oval and round windows. Hearing improvement can occur but should be expected in only approximately 15% of cases.

SELECTED REFERENCES

Weber PC, Perez BA, Bluestone CD. Congenital perilymphatic fistula and associated middle ear abnormalities. Laryngoscope 103:160, 1993.

The most complete and detailed review of congenital perilymphatic fistulas, including a review of theories of pathophysiology for use. It is important to read this article for a proper understanding of this complex condition.

Reilly, JS. Congenital perilymphatic fistula, a prospective study in infants and children. Laryngoscope 99:393, 1989.

The first series to look prospectively at a group of children with congenital PLF.

REFERENCES

1. Barr B, Wersall J. Cerebrospinal otorrhea with meningitis in congenital deafness. Arch Otolaryngol 81:26, 1965.

2. Biggers WP, Howell NN, Fischer ND, et al. Congenital ear anomalies associated with otic meningitis. Arch Otolaryngol 97:399, 1973.

3. Black FO, Pesznecker S, Norton T, et al. Surgical management of perilymphatic fistulas: a Portland experience. Am J Otol 13:254, 1992.

4. Bojrab DI, Bhansali SA. Fluorescein use in the detection of perilymphatic fistula: a study in cats. Otolaryngol Head Neck Surg 108:348, 1993.

5. Buchman CA, Luxford WM, Hirsch BE, et al. Beta-2 transferrin assay in the identification of perilymph. Am J Otol 20:174–178, 1999.

6. Calhoun KH, Strunk CL. Perilymph fistula. Arch Otolaryngol Head Neck Surg 118:693, 1992.

7. Canfield RB. Some conditions associated with the loss of cerebrospinal fluid. Ann Otol Rhinol Laryngol 22:604, 1913.

8. Delaroche O, Bordure P, Lippert E, Sagniez M. Perilymphatic detection by beta-2 transferrin immunoblocking assay—application to the diagnosis of perilymphatic fistula. Clin Chim Acta 245:93–104, 1996.

9. Escat E. Ecoulement spontane de liquide cephalorachidien parle-conduit auditif externe: fistule congenitale probable. Arch Int Laryngol 10:653, 1897.

10. Friedland DR, Wackym PA. A critical appraisal of spontaneous perilymphatic fistulas of the inner ear. Am J Otol 20:261–279, 1999.

11. Gibson WP. Spontaneous perilymphatic fistula: electrophysiologic findings in animal and man. Am J Otol 14:273, 1993.

12. Glasscock ME, Hart MJ, Rosdeutscher JD, Bhansali SA. Traumatic perilymphatic fistula: how long can symptoms persist? Am J Otol 113:333, 1992.

13. Glasscock ME, McKennan KX, Levine CC. Persistent traumatic perilymph fistulas. Laryngoscope 97:860, 1987.

14. Goodhill V, Harns I, Brockman SJ, et al. Sudden deafness and labyrinthine window ruptures: audiovestibular observations. Ann Otol Rhinol Laryngol 82:2, 1973.

15. Grundfast KM, Bluestone CD. Sudden or fluctuating hearing loss and vertigo in children due to perilymph fistula. Ann Otol Rhinol Laryngol 87:761, 1978.

16. Grundfast KM, Lalwani MD. Practical approach to diagnosis and management of hereditary hearing impairment. Ear Nose Throat J 71:479, 1992.

17. Harada T, Sando H, Myers EN. Microfissure in the oval window area. Ann Otol Rhinol Laryngol 90:174, 1981.

18. Hough JVD. Congenital malformations of the middle ear. Arch Otolaryngol 78:335, 1967.

19. Jackler RK, Hwang PH. Enlargement of the cochlear aqueduct: fact or fiction? Otolaryngol Head Neck Surg 109:14, 1993.

20. Jackler RK, Luxford WM, House WF. Congenital malformations of the inner ear: a classification based on embryogenesis. Laryngoscope 97(Suppl 40):2, 1987.

21. Kammerer DB, Sando I, Hirsch B, et al. Perilymph fistula resulting from microfissures. Am J Otol 8:849, 1987.

22. Kubo T, Kohno M, Naramura H, Itoh M. Clinical characteristics and hearing recovery in perilymphatic fistulas of different etiologies. Acta Otolaryngol (Stockh) 113:307, 1993.

23. Lafreniere D, Smurzynski J, Jung M, et al. Otoacoustic emissions in full-term newborns at risk for hearing loss. Laryngoscope 103:1334, 1993.

24. Levenson MJ, Desloge RB, Priser SC. Beta 2 transferrin: limitations of use as a clinical marker for perilymph. Laryngoscope 106:159–161, 1996.

25. Lovblad KO, Ozdoba C, Negri S. CT cisternography in congenital perilymphatic fistula of the inner ear. J Comput Assist Tomogr 19:797–799, 1995.

26. Mark AS, Fitzgerald D. Segmental enhancement of the cochlea on contrast-enhanced MR: correlation with the frequency of hearing loss and possible sign of perilymphatic fistula and autoimmune labyrinthitis. AJNR Am J Neuroradiol 14:991, 1993.

27. McCabe B, Seltzer S. Perilymphatic fistula. In Gates GA, ed. Current Therapy in Otolaryngology–Head and Neck Surgery, 5th ed. St Louis, CV Mosby, 1994.

28. Meyerhoff WL. Spontaneous perilymphatic fistula: myth or fact? Am J Otol 14:47, 1993.

29. Morris MS, Kil J, Carvin MJ. Magnetic resonance imaging of perilymphatic fistula. Laryngoscope 103:729, 1993.

30. Naiberg JB, Flemming E, Patterson M, Hawke M. The perilymphatic fistula: the end of an enigma? J Otolaryngol 19:260, 1990.

31. Nenzelius C. On spontaneous cerebrospinal otorrhea due to congenital malformations. Acta Otolaryngol (Stockh) 39:314, 1951.

32. Odrezin GT, Royal SA, Young DW, et al. High resolution computed tomography of the temporal bone in infants and children: a review. Int J Pediatr Otorhinolaryngol 19:15, 1990.

33. Pappas DG, Simpson LC, Godwin GH. Perilymphatic fistula in children with pre-existing sensorineural hearing loss. Laryngoscope 98:507, 1988.

34. Pappas DG, Simpson LC, McKenzie RA, Royal S. High resolution computed tomography: determination of the cause of pediatric sensorineural hearing loss. Laryngoscope 100:564, 1990.

35. Parell GJ, Becker GD. Results of surgical repair of inapparent perilymph fistulas. Otolaryngol Head Neck Surg 95:344, 1986.

36. Petroff MA, Simmons FB, Winzelbert J. Two emerging perilymph fistula syndromes in children. Laryngoscope 96:498, 1986.

37. Reilly JS. Congenital perilymphatic fistula, a prospective study in infants and children. Laryngoscope 99:393, 1989.

38. Sando I, Shigahara Y, Takagi A, et al. Frequency and localization of congenital anomalies of the middle ear and inner ears: a human temporal bone study. Int J Pediatr Otorhinolaryngol 16:1, 1988.

39. Sarsk D, Magnurson M. Transtympanic electrocochleography in the assessment of perilymphatic fistulas. Audiol Neurootol 2:391, 1997.

40. Schweitzer VG, Woodson BT, Mawhinney TD, et al. Free amino acid analysis of guinea pig perilymph: a possible clinical assay for the PLF enigma? Otolaryngol Head Neck Surg 103:981, 1990.

41. Seltzer S, McCabe B. Perilymph fistula: the Iowa experience. Laryngoscope 94:37, 1986.

42. Shepard NT, Telian SA, Niparko JK, et al. Platform pressure test in identification of perilymphatic fistula. Am J Otol 13:49, 1992.

43. Simmons FB. Theory of membrane breaks in sudden hearing loss. Arch Otolaryngol 88:41, 1968.

44. Skedros DG, Cass SP, Hirsch BE, Kelly RH. Beta-2 transferrin assay in clinical management of cerebral spinal fluid and perilymphatic fluid leaks. J Otolaryngol 22:541, 1993.

45. Stool SE, Leeds NE, Shuhnan K. The syndrome of congenital deafness and otitis meningitis diagnosis and management. J Pediatr 71:547, 1967.

46. Supance JS, Bluestone CD. Perilymph fistulas in infants and children. Otolaryngol Head Neck Surg 91:663, 1982.

47. Telian SA, Disular MJ, Sun Q, Andrews P. Biochemical maskers for identification of human perilymph. Abstr Am Otol Soc 131:39, 1998.

48. Weber PC, Bluestone CD, Perez B. Outcome of surgery for congenital perilymphatic fistulas. (Unpublished data.)

49. Weber PC, Bouissouny M, Kelly R, Bluestone CD. Beta-2 transferrin confirms perilymphatic fistula in children. Otolaryngol Head Neck Surg 110:381, 1994.

50. Weber PC, Kenna MA, Bluestone CD, Kelly RH. The correlation of beta-2 transferrin and middle ear anomalies in congenital perilymphatic fistulas. Am J Otol 16:277, 1995.

51. Weber PC, Perez BA, Bluestone CD. Congenital perilymphatic fistula and associated middle ear abnormalities. Laryngoscope 103:160, 1993.

52. Weider DJ. Treatment and management of perilymphatic fistula: a New Hampshire experience. Am J Otol 13:158, 1992.

53. Weissman JL, Weber PC, Bluestone CD. Congenital perilymphatic fistulas: CT appearance of middle ear and inner ear anomalies. Otolaryngol Head Neck Surg 111:243, 1994.

54. Zalzal GH, Shott SB, Towbin R, Cotton RT. Value of CT scan in the diagnosis of temporal bone diseases in children. Laryngoscope 96:27, 1986.

24

Diseases of the External Ear

Barry E. Hirsch, M.D.

The external auditory meatus is a unique anatomic structure in that it is the only skin-lined cul-de-sac in the body. The thin skin lining and pilosebaceous cerumen glands are often subject to inflammatory and infectious processes frequently seen in pediatric patients. A variety of other diseases that affect the skin and its appendages, perichondrium, cartilage, bone, and tympanic membrane must be recognized for appropriate management to be provided.

Anatomy

The external ear consists of the pinna and the cartilaginous and bony external auditory meatus. The shape of the flexible and pliable pinna is defined at infancy and maintains its overall configuration throughout life. In contrast, the relationship of the length of the cartilaginous to the bony external auditory meatus changes during early development. In infancy, the bony canal is not developed and consists only of the tympanic ring. Thus, the external auditory meatus is predominantly cartilaginous. The tympanic membrane is horizontally oriented, with the superior tympanic membrane being located more laterally. With development of the bony tympanic ring, the external auditory meatus takes on an S-shaped canal, approximately 2.5 cm in length, that is narrowed at the isthmus by convexity of the anterior and inferior bony walls. The lateral cartilaginous portion composes 33% to 40%; the remainder is the osseous canal. The tympanic membrane becomes vertically oriented but angled so that the anterior canal wall and tympanic membrane form a narrowed sulcus.

Squamous epithelium lines the entire external auditory meatus and lateral surface of the tympanic membrane. The skin lining the osseous portion of the external auditory meatus is approximately 0.2 mm thick and is void of germinal papilla and subcutaneous tissue. More laterally, the skin becomes thicker over the cartilaginous portion of the external auditory meatus. There is subcutaneous tissue containing hair follicles and sebaceous and ceruminous glands. The sebaceous glands, located more superficially in the dermis, empty into follicular canals that surround the hair shaft. The ceruminous glands are located deeper in the dermis. While the sebaceous glands secrete an oily material called *sebum*, the apocrine (ceru-

minous) glands secrete a milky opaque fatty fluid. Cerumen, or wax, is a mixture of secretions from the sebaceous and apocrine glands along with desquamated keratin epithelium from the stratum corneum. This forms a protective acidic lipid (wax) layer that inhibits maceration from water or sweat and pathogenic bacterial overgrowth. The deepest structure of the lateral external auditory meatus is composed of perichondrium and cartilage. In the anterior and inferior aspects of the cartilaginous wall are small horizontal clefts (fissures of Santorini) that communicate with the parotid gland. Through these areas, infection, inflammation, and tumors may spread to and from the parotid gland, preauricular soft tissue, and temporomandibular joint.

The blood supply to the pinna and lateral external canal is predominantly from the posterior auricular and superficial temporal branches of the external carotid artery. The more medial canal and lateral surface of the tympanic membrane are supplied by the deep auricular branch of the internal maxillary artery. Venous drainage is by the superficial temporal, mastoid, and posterior auricular veins to the external and internal jugular veins. Lymph channels drain into preauricular parotid nodes, superficial cervical nodes along the external jugular vein, posterior auricular nodes over the lateral surface of the mastoid, and superior deep cervical nodes.

Both cutaneous and cranial nerves supply sensory innervation through the external auditory meatus and pinna. The pinnae are innervated by cutaneous branches from the second and third cervical nerve roots by the lesser occipital and great auricular nerves. The inferior and posterior lateral external auditory meatus and concha are supplied by sensory branches from the cervical plexus (C2-3) and the facial (VII), glossopharyngeal (IX), and vagal (X) cranial nerves. The tympanic membrane and medial external auditory meatus are innervated by auriculotemporal branches of the trigeminal (V) nerve.

Similar to skin elsewhere on the body, the external auditory meatus has normal bacterial flora. Cultures from both normal children and adults show similar organisms. Ear canal cultures obtained from children with non-otologic problems showed 80% of the patients to have aerobic bacteria. The most common isolates were *Staphylococcus epidermidis* (albus), alpha-hemolytic streptococcus, diphtheroid species, and *Pseudomonas aeruginosa*. Anaerobic bacteria alone were identified in 3% of patients. These organisms were usually *Propionibacterium acnes* and *Peptococcus* species. In 17% of the cultures, there were both anaerobic and aerobic organisms.[4] In a similar control study, cultures obtained from adults yielded 56% of patients with aerobic bacteria. Again, the most common isolates were *S. epidermidis* and diphtheroid species. Infection of the external auditory meatus occurs from local trauma or breakdown of the natural defense mechanisms provided by cerumen and keratinized skin. Saprophytic or exogenous organisms become pathologic, causing localized or diffuse infections.

Infection of the pinna and external auditory canal is common. The external auditory meatus is a keratinized epithelium-lined blind sac subject to potential maceration and self-induced trauma. Environmental factors also predispose the ear canal to acute and chronic infections and inflammatory processes.

Cerumen Impaction

The external ear canal is normally self-cleaning. Epithelial migration from the tympanic membrane to the external auditory meatus carries cerumen to the lateral orifice. Focal collections of cerumen end their lateral migration in the hair follicles. Dry or inspissated cerumen may literally fall out of the ear or be removed with digital cleaning. Impaction of cerumen often results from self-manipulation of the ear. This is frequently due to the use of cotton-tipped applicators, when a bolus of cerumen is forced medially deeper into the osseous canal. Children may introduce rolled tissue paper or other foreign bodies into the ear canal, thus pushing cerumen deeper. In addition, children with congenital stenotic ear canals, such as patients with trisomy 21 anomalies, are susceptible to occlusion of their canals by cerumen.

Removal of cerumen may be accomplished in a variety of ways. When cerumen is identified during otoscopic examination, switching the diagnostic otoscopy head to an instrumentation scope facilitates removal. A small, firm plug can quickly be removed with an ear curette, loop, or spoon. Wet debris is removed with a thin cotton-tipped applicator or suction. Cerumen located more medially in the canal requires greater dexterity for removal. An operating microscope provides excellent illumination and binocular vision. Most children are cooperative sitting alone in an examination chair or on a parent's lap, or lying supine on the table. Supportive parental assistance can ease a child's apprehension. Allowing an anxious child to feel the suction on the hand and listen to its noise at the pinna may result in greater cooperation. Attempts at removal are made at the time of the initial evaluation. Cerumen that is impacted and inspissated may need to be hydrated and made more viscous. This is accomplished with over-the-counter preparations or simply with use of mineral oil or other oily otic preparations. Aural irrigation may also be used. Flushing the ears with warm tap water is also effective. The integrity of the tympanic membrane should be known or questioned before forceful introduction of water is undertaken. However, this method may be both emotionally and physically traumatic to an unco-

operative, fearful child. Establishing a rapport with the parent and child expedites initial and subsequent visits.

Keratosis Obturans

Keratosis obturans is a disorder of unknown etiology manifested by excessive buildup of dense keratinizing squamous epithelium in the medial external auditory canal. Patients experience a plugged, full sensation of the ears with subsequent conductive hearing loss as the thickened layer of debris accumulates. It is typically a bilateral process that can cause remodeling of the medial osseous canal. The debris often creates a cylindrical cast of the canal and tympanic membrane, which is evident upon removing the keratin mass. The underlying canal skin appears shiny, atrophic, and erythematous. It is unclear whether there is excess production and desquamation of epithelial cells or whether the lateral migration and self-cleaning are impeded. Keratosis obturans is more common in young and middle-aged patients.

Treatment for this disorder is often frustrating and repetitive. If the keratin cast is long-standing, removal can be difficult and painful. Frequent debridement in the office may be necessary. Reducing the frequency and degree of accumulation is the short-term goal. Topical preparations used by the author include steroid drops, mineral oil, acetic acid rinses, Diprosone with urea, and 5-fluorouracil. These agents reduce the rate of epithelial cell turnover, provide added viscosity to the keratin cast, and mechanically clean and dry the medial canal skin.

Acute External Otitis

Acute external otitis is a diffuse cellulitis of the external auditory meatus that may involve underlying structures, such as the conchal and tragal cartilages, along with the skin of the pinna and regional lymph nodes. Also termed *diffuse otitis externa* and "swimmer's ear," acute external otitis usually develops under the conditions of increased heat, humidity, water contamination, and localized trauma. The disease usually occurs in warmer climates and during summer months in more temperate locations. The cleanliness of the water does not appear to influence the likelihood of infection in that acute external otitis may occur after swimming in pools, lakes, rivers, or oceans. Other potential sources of water contamination include hot tubs, whirlpools, and pressurized ear irrigation for removal of cerumen. In immunocompetent hosts, some form of trauma is necessary to potentiate development of infection in the external auditory meatus. This may take the form of ear irrigations, hearing aid irritation or improper fit, earplugs or foam inserts for sound protection, use of cotton-tipped applicators or any other foreign object to "clean" or scratch the ear canal, or simply aggressive manipulation with one's finger. Cerumen has an acidic pH that limits bacterial and fungal growth and an oily, waxy composition that protects the underlying skin. Removal of protective cerumen predisposes the ear canal to maceration and bacterial or fungal overgrowth, allowing penetration into the underlying skin.

Patients with acute external otitis usually complain of

acute onset of unilateral ear pain, itching, and stuffiness. Significant edema incurs hearing loss. Pain may range from mild discomfort to severe, unrelenting pain requiring narcotic analgesics. Otalgia is often exacerbated by jaw movement with chewing, clenching, and, occasionally, talking. Progression of the infection yields ear drainage that becomes malodorous. Further manipulation of the ear aggravates the pain.

The diagnosis of acute external otitis is readily made on physical examination. Inspection of the conchal bowl and surrounding auricular skin may reveal erythema and swelling (inflammation) along with serous or purulent drainage coming from the external auditory meatus. In early stages of acute external otitis, the canal skin shows mild inflammation with erythema and minimal edema. Progression of the disease is demonstrated by increased skin edema and more profuse exudate. Palpable regional preauricular and postauricular adenopathy may be present. The infection is usually circumferential and diffuse, extending from the lateral meatus to the bony external auditory canal. Greater involvement encompasses the more medial canal and outer surface of the tympanic membrane. The keratinized epithelium is macerated and desquamated, filling the ear canal with wet ceruminous, epithelial, and exudative debris. Pulling the pinna posterosuperiorly to facilitate examination usually elicits complaints of pain, as does palpation of the tragus. Severe inflammation completely closes the ear canal, potentially creating a conductive hearing loss. Progression and extension of the infection involve the surrounding conchal bowl and periauricular skin with circumscribed cellulitis (Fig. 24–1).

Ideally, it is desirable to visualize the tympanic membrane, although this may be difficult with an obstructed ear canal. Cleaning of the ear canal is important for evaluation, diagnosis, and management. Removal of the exfoliated epithelium and purulent debris by suction permits inspection of the condition and facilitates treatment. The malodorous discharge, which appears as a greenish gray or creamy yellow exudate with a pungent odor, is usually due to *P. aeruginosa*. The second most common organism is *Staphylococcus aureus*.[8] Other organisms responsible for acute otitis externa include *S. epidermidis*, *Proteus* species, *Enterococcus faecalis*, and *Bacteroides fragilis*.[8, 21]

After removal of wet debris by suction, further gentle cleaning can be done with cotton-tipped applicators. Great care should be taken to minimize any further trauma to the canal. If the infection is recurrent or persistent, or if the patient is immunocompromised, bacterial and fungal cultures are obtained. The tympanic membrane should be visualized to determine whether the ear canal infection is secondary to acute otitis media with perforation and discharge or is a long-standing condition such as chronic otitis media with or without cholesteatoma. Acute external otitis due to either of these conditions warrants systemic antibiotics and disease-specific management.

Topical medication can be instilled once the ear canal is cleaned and dried. Frequently the ear canal is swollen and obstructed, which prohibits examination of the tympanic membrane and impedes instillation of ototopic

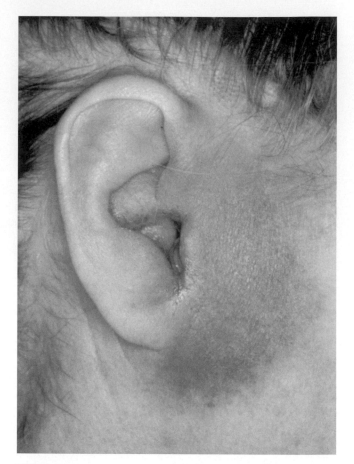

FIGURE 24–1. Severe acute external otitis and inflammatory obstruction of the ear canal with surrounding cellulitis.

medications. In this situation, a wick is necessary to facilitate medical treatment. A wick can be made from a variety of materials, including a strip of gauze, a cotton pledget, or an expandable sponge. Readily available tightly wound cotton is preferable in that the size (diameter and length) of the wick can be determined by the anatomy of the canal and degree of swelling.

The choice of medications available for treatment of acute external otitis is varied. Table 24–1 categorizes many of the commonly used preparations by their mechanism of action. In principle, it is desirable to reduce the inflammation and lower the canal pH to encourage reduction of swelling and eliminate the causative organism, respectively. The infection frequently responds to ear canal cleaning and the use of an acidic solution with steroid preparation, which demonstrates that bacteria-specific antimicrobial medications are not always mandatory. In a study by Lawrence et al,[17] the in vitro efficacy of available topical preparations against the usual organisms (bacteria and fungi) seen in otitis externa was illustrated. The results are outlined in Table 24–2.

A consensus panel report from the American Academy of Otolaryngology—Head and Neck Surgery Foundation emphasized that topical antibiotics alone constitute the first line of treatment for most patients. Non-ototoxic preparations should be used if the status of the tympanic membrane is unknown.[12] Commonly used ototopic prepa-

TABLE 24–1. Medications for Acute External Otitis

Organic Acids	Colistin
pH 3	Gentamicin
Acetic acid 2%	Neomycin
Benzoic acid	Ofloxacin
Boric acid	Oxytetracycline
Salicylic acid	Polymyxin B
Phenols and Alcohols	Sulfanilamide
Alcohol 95%	**Antifungals**
Chloroxylenol	Amphotericin B
Phenol	Clotrimazole
Thymol 1%	Fluorocytosine (5-FC)
General Antiseptics	Iodochlorhydroxyquin
m-Cresyl acetate 25%	Miconazole
Gentian violet 2%	Nystatin
Thimerosal 1:1000	**Anti-inflammatories**
Povidone-iodine 1%	Betamethasone
Burow solution (aluminum acetate)	Desonide
Antibiotics	Dexamethasone
Chloramphenicol	Hydrocortisone
Ciprofloxacin	Prednisolone

rations include 2% acetic acid with 1% hydrocortisone (VōSol HC); polymyxin B, neomycin sulfate, and hydrocortisone (Cortisporin); and tobramycin with dexamethasone (TobraDex). Recent otic formulations containing quinolones such as ciprofloxacin and ofloxacin include Cipro HC and Floxin, respectively. Drops are instilled directly onto the wick or in the ear canal two to four times daily for 7 to 10 days, depending on the preparation. If a wick was placed, patients or parents are instructed to remove it after 72 hours. A properly sized wick occasionally falls out, indicating partial resolution of canal edema.

Patients are instructed to refrain from further water contamination (swimming, unprotected showering), ear cleaning with cotton-tipped applicators, and use of headphones with ear inserts or a hearing aid. Extensive inflammation with periauricular cellulitis requires systemic antibiotics. Medication options, often based on culture results, include erythromycin, amoxicillin, cephalosporin, or clindamycin. The canal may need to be cleaned at the conclusion of therapy. Complete resolution can be confirmed with a follow-up visit in a few weeks.

Persistent inflammation despite the use of antibacterial preparations poses a diagnostic challenge. Preparations containing neomycin may induce an allergic contact dermatitis, which is manifested by increased itching and skin excoriation. Culture of the canal should be done in this situation and the drop formulation changed. Ophthalmic drops containing gentamicin and tobramycin are effective against *Pseudomonas* but usually do not elicit the same allergic reaction as neomycin. Solutions of chloramphenicol, sulfa-based preparations, and ciprofloxacin are also available. Additional astringent and antiseptic preparations that are effective include boric acid, alcohol, gentian violet, thimerosal (Merthiolate), *M*-cresyl acetate (Cresylate), and ichthammol.

The symptoms of aural pain, fullness, itchiness, and hearing loss are manifestations of other forms of acute external otitis. Bullous external otitis and myringitis are characterized by vesicles or bullae noted in the osseous portion of the external auditory meatus and on the tympanic membrane. Although these vesicles are frequently thought to be a manifestation of *Mycoplasma* infection, rupture can also yield *P. aeruginosa* on culture.[18] The ear canal typically has less edematous swelling, and thus a wick can be avoided. The same topical eardrops used for acute external otitis are effective in bullous myringitis. Evidence of middle-ear infection and bullae present on the tympanic membrane prompt treatment for otitis media with systemic antibiotics.

Other forms of acute diffuse otitis externa include erysipelas and herpes simplex infection, which usually involve only the pinna. Early manifestation of herpes zoster oticus (Ramsay Hunt syndrome) also shows symptoms of pain, aural fullness, and occasional itching. The early stage may show normal examination findings. Subsequent development of vesicles and blister formation confirms the diagnosis. Topical acyclovir ointment is available for painful skin lesions that fail to desiccate rapidly.

Chronic External Otitis

Patients with persistent symptoms of ear fullness, itchiness, and occasional discharge have chronic external otitis.

TABLE 24–2. In Vitro Antimicrobial Activity of 12 Otic Preparations

Agent	Candida sp.	Aspergillus sp.	Mucor sp.	Pseudomonas aeruginosa	Proteus vulgaris	Escherichia coli	Staphylococcus aureus
Aqueous Merthiolate	+4	+4	+4	+4	+4	+4	+4
Cresylate	+3	+4	+4	+2	+2	+3	+1
pH 3	+2	+3	+2	+4	+4	+4	+4
Nystatin	+4	+4	+4	0	0	0	0
Lotrimin	+4	+4	+4	±	0	0	+4
Amphotericin B	+3	+2	+3	0	0	0	0
Propylene glycol	+1	0	0	0	0	0	0
Thymol	+1	+1	+1	+1	+4	+2	+3
Gentian violet	+2	+3	+2	+1	+3	+3	+4
Coly-Mycin S	0	0	+4	+4	+4	+4	+4
Cortisporin	0	0	+3	+3	+4	+4	+4
Aerosporin	0	0	+3	+3	0	+4	0

From Lawrence TL, Ayers LW, Saunders WH. Drug therapy in otomycosis: an in vitro study. Laryngoscope 88:1755, 1978.

This may be the result of partially treated acute external otitis that is refractory because of ongoing predisposing factors. Again, heat, localized trauma, maceration from water, and high humidity maintain the milieu for persistent disease. It is necessary to break the cycle by eliminating the predisposing factors and treating the inflammation. Along with topical antibiotics, steroid preparations are most useful. Frequent cleaning of the ear canal with instillation of triamcinolone, dexamethasone, or other fluorinated steroid preparations in the form of topical creams, ointments, or drops can often reverse the itch-scratch cycle.

The differential diagnosis of unresponsive chronic otitis externa includes otomycosis, dermatomycosis, seborrheic dermatitis, psoriasis, contact eczematoid dermatitis, carcinoma of the ear canal, and dermatophytid reaction.[5] Rarely, prolonged disease causes the skin to take on permanent diffuse inflammatory changes (pachyderma) with narrowing of the external auditory meatus and blunting of the anterior and inferior tympanic sulcus. It may be necessary to perform a canaloplasty by removing the involved skin and reconstructing with a split-thickness skin graft.

Otomycosis

Acute fungal otitis externa or otomycosis describes a yeast or fungal infection of the external auditory meatus. This disorder is more common in tropical climates but certainly occurs under the same conditions as bacterial external otitis. This disorder is also common in patients with mastoid cavities and those who wear hearing aids with occlusive earmolds. Saprophytic fungi potentially residing in the ear canal include *Aspergillus, Candida albicans, Phycomycetes, Rhizopus, Actinomyces,* and *Penicillium.* Under certain conditions of increased heat, humidity, glucose concentration (diabetes), immunosuppression, or overuse of systemic or topical antibiotics and steroids, these saprophytic fungi can become pathogenic.

The onset of signs and symptoms of otomycosis is more insidious than that of bacterial otitis externa. Pain is not a predominant complaint. Symptoms of aural pruritus and fullness are more bothersome. Examination reveals mild inflammation and debris that may be wet or dry. The characteristic finding is isolated areas or a diffuse coating of macroscopically evident hyphae and mycelia. *Aspergillus niger* accounts for 90% of otomycosis infections, appearing as a wispy, cottony filamentous base sprinkled with a gray-black powdery covering. Thorough cleaning of the ear canal (or mastoid cavity) is necessary. This is accomplished with curettes, forceps, or suction. The canal is then wiped dry with a cotton applicator. Various methods are available to treat otomycosis. Acidification of the canal with acetic acid solution or aluminum sulfate–calcium acetate (Domeboro) effectively eliminates the organism. Additional preparations include thimerosal (Merthiolate), *M*-cresyl acetate (Cresylate), gentian violet, 5% clioquinol in boric acid powder (Vioform), clotrimazole, and antifungal creams such as nystatin and ketoconazole. In rare cases, local cellulitis develops that may be resistant to oral antibiotics. Oral itraconazole is an effective systemic antifungal agent.

Furunculosis

Furunculosis is an infection that occurs in the hair-bearing portion of the ear canal at the junction of the conchal and canal skin. Pain aggravated by chewing may occur with lesions on the anterior canal wall. Insertion of an ear speculum often elicits pain. Care must be taken not to bypass the lesion when the canal is examined. Swelling may occasionally be so severe as to limit visualization of the medial canal. This may be confused with acute otitis externa. However, obtaining a history of ear pain without drainage and seeing a dry ear canal with localized subcutaneous swelling suggest furunculosis.

The usual offending organisms are gram-positive cocci, particularly *S. aureus*. Localized lesions associated with mild swelling can be treated with an oral antistaphylococcal antibiotic, such as dicloxacillin, cephalosporins, erythromycin, other macrolides, or clindamycin.[13] If the lesion progresses and develops into an abscess, incision and drainage may be necessary. Injection with a local anesthetic may minimize some of the discomfort associated with this procedure if a deep abscess cavity is present. A wick can be made of iodinated gauze or a rubber band Penrose drain. A wick often falls out quickly, although short-term drainage is often effective. The use of a topical warm compress provides local relief and facilitates increased vascularity and healing.

Necrotizing (Malignant) External Otitis

Necrotizing external otitis was first reported by Meltzer and Kelemen[23] in 1959 as a case of pyocutaneous osteomyelitis of temporal bone resulting from *Bacillus pyocyaneus,* which is now known as *Pseudomonas aeruginosa.* The term *malignant external otitis* (MEO) was given by Chandler[7] in 1968 when he published a report of 13 patients with this infection. Other terms ascribed to this serious infection include progressive, fulminant, and invasive external otitis. Despite the reluctance to use the term *malignant,* physicians have come to understand that it is not a neoplastic disorder.[19] This invasive infectious process is more commonly seen in elderly diabetics or individuals with altered immune function. The systemic microangiopathy of diabetes along with poor glucose control impedes the immune response. Acute external otitis that is partially treated may smolder and become deeply seated in the canal skin at the bone-cartilage junction. The most common organism identified in patients with MEO is *P. aeruginosa.* The inciting factors leading to this severe infection are similar to those of acute external otitis, namely, water maceration, local trauma, and contamination with the offending organism. A common practice of ear irrigation for cerumen cleaning with use of water contaminated by *Pseudomonas* may be one of the causes of MEO. It was determined that 62% of patients with MEO had tap water aural irrigation within 2 weeks of the onset of symptoms.[29] Other potential causative events may be similarly minor. These include mild acute external otitis or self-inflicted limited trauma that could occur by use of cotton-tipped applicators. Rather than resolving with natural host defenses, the infection in susceptible individuals remains localized and progresses to diffuse involvement unless appropriate care is given.

Since the original description by Chandler, MEO has been reported in children as well. The first cases of MEO in children were recognized by Joachims[15] in 1976. A persistent external ear canal infection with subsequent facial paralysis in both a 2-year-old child with various medical problems and a 7-month-old with recurrent bronchopneumonia was recognized and treated. MEO has also been diagnosed in infants. Coser et al[9] reported MEO in two infants, age 5 and 6 months. They were considered to be in poor health, undernourished, and anemic. In one child, *Proteus mirabilis* was the causative agent.

In contrast to adults, most of the children with MEO do not have diabetes mellitus. However, they have all been found to be immunocompromised, which permits this opportunistic infection to be progressive and virulent. Disorders other than diabetes mellitus that have been associated with MEO in children include anemia, leukemia, malnutrition, solid tumors, Stevens-Johnson syndrome, immunoglobulin deficiency, and genetic agranulocytosis.[6, 14, 25] The pathogenesis of MEO in the adolescent mimics that in adults. These older children are usually otherwise healthy, but have juvenile-onset insulin-dependent diabetes.

The insidious virulence of *Pseudomonas* in an unchallenged host permits ingress of the organism into the soft tissues surrounding the ear canal, the bone of the tympanic ring and skull base, the parotid gland, the facial nerve, and the regional lymph nodes. Further extension may involve cranial nerves within the jugular foramen and hypoglossal canal. The infectious process can spread to the middle ear, sigmoid sinus, and intracranial space. Osteomyelitis may develop in the bone of the skull base, involving the contralateral side. Early in the disease, the epicenter of the infection is at the junction of the bony and cartilaginous external auditory meatus. However, in children, MEO usually involves the tympanic membrane and middle ear. It is theorized that the more medial location of the bone-cartilage junction in the infant and child accounts for earlier compromise of the facial nerve and associated mastoiditis.[14]

Diagnosis

In contrast to adults, younger children have limited development of the tympanic ring and mastoid. Thus, the radiographic diagnosis of MEO in children by computed tomography (CT) scan may be hampered if bone destruction is considered to be a primary diagnostic criterion. Soft tissue swelling and inflammation demonstrated by obliteration of fat planes beneath the temporal bone, parapharyngeal space, and infratemporal fossa into the nasopharynx are diagnostic of skull base involvement.

The diagnosis of MEO is based on the patient's history, physical examination findings, laboratory information, and the physician's heightened suspicion. Patients complain of aural pain, discharge, ear fullness, and, often, hearing loss. Unrelenting pain, especially at night, is suggestive of a deeply seated infection. Examination of the ear canal often shows inflammation and granulation tissue

at the bone-cartilage junction. More advanced disease may obstruct the examiner's view of the tympanic membrane and manifest inflammation in the pre- and infra-auricular areas. In contrast to the disease in adults, complete facial paralysis is an early presenting sign and often permanent in children.[14] Specimens for culture with sensitivity testing should be obtained from the ear canal. Debridement and biopsy of the pathologic tissue in the ear canal should be done to ensure that the process is one of inflammation and granulation tissue rather than malignant neoplasm. The infecting organism is almost always *P. aeruginosa*, although MEO due to *S. aureus*, *Aspergillus*, and *P. mirabilis* has been reported.[2, 8, 27] Laboratory investigations address glucose levels, complete blood count, and sedimentation rate along with hepatic and renal function. An elevated sedimentation rate is helpful not only in identifying an inflammatory state but also in monitoring therapy.

Radiographic and radionuclide scanning initially helps establish the diagnosis and extent of disease and provides the base line with which to compare future studies. CT imaging can identify not only bone erosion but changes in the soft tissue around the external auditory canal and skull base. The CT may also exclude progression and identify resolution of soft tissue changes in the inflammatory process.[30] Magnetic resonance imaging is a sensitive method for recognizing changes in soft tissue densities. This imaging would be useful in diagnosing skull osteomyelitis with infratemporal fossa and parapharyngeal space involvement. Magnetic resonance imaging may more readily determine sigmoid sinus thrombosis, especially if CT imaging with iodinated contrast enhancement is contraindicated. Coronal images are readily obtained on magnetic resonance imaging if the patient is unable to hyperextend the neck for CT positioning. However, CT scanning can determine changes in soft tissue inflammation, is less expensive than MRI, and is better able to delineate subtle cortical bone erosions of the external auditory meatus and skull base.

Technetium-99m radionuclide scanning provides a sensitive method for identifying osteoblastic activity present in osteomyelitis. This is a sensitive method for identifying bone involvement, but osteoneogenesis is a continuing process reflective of ongoing osteoblastic activity. Technetium scanning cannot be used to determine when treatment can be terminated because the enhanced activity may remain indefinitely.[26]

Gallium-67 citrate imaging is another sensitive method for identifying areas of active inflammation. Gallium binds to actively dividing cells, such as white blood cells or neoplastic tumor cells. Like technetium, gallium is sensitive in identifying infection and inflammation but has relatively poor anatomic resolution. Resolution of osteomyelitis and the inflammatory process presumably eliminates white blood cell activity. In contrast to the technetium scan, a normal gallium scan is considered to be important for determining the end point of therapy. However, numerous reports have documented recurrent or persistent disease in the face of a normal gallium study.[11, 16, 24]

Treatment of MEO in children is, in principle, similar to that in adults. Effective intravenous antipseudomonad antibiotic treatment is necessary. Surgery has a minor role in the management of MEO. Aggressive intervention has been advocated if, after 2 weeks of medical treatment, there was persistent granulation tissue in the external auditory canal, new onset of cranial neuropathies, or other signs or symptoms of active infection.[28] Biopsy examination of the ear canal early in the diagnostic determination is necessary to ascertain that malignant change is not present. Operative intervention is usually limited to surgical debridement of persistent granulation tissue, bony sequestra, abscess, and necrotic cartilage.[1]

Hospitalization, supportive care, frequent ear cleaning, debridement of devitalized tissue, and intravenous and topical antibiotic eardrops are the mainstay of management. Effective oral antipseudomonad antibiotics that are available for adults are not approved by the Food and Drug Administration for use in children. Combination intravenous antibiotic therapy consisting of an aminoglycoside and an antipseudomonad semisynthetic penicillin (such as carbenicillin, ticarcillin, or piperacillin) or an effective cephalosporin alone (ceftazidime or cefoperazone) is usually given. Newer antibiotics, such as imipenem and aztreonam, are also effective against *Pseudomonas* and may be useful for patients with allergy or organisms showing resistance to the previously mentioned drugs. Blood levels of aminoglycosides and audiometric thresholds should be monitored to avoid ototoxic effects. Similarly, serum creatinine and blood urea nitrogen levels are reflective of renal function. Treatment duration for adults is usually a minimum of 4 to 6 weeks. It has been shown that, if a clinical response is evident early, a 2- to 3-week course of antimicrobial therapy may suffice in children.[31] Hyperbaric oxygen therapy is an adjuvant method of treatment for recalcitrant, advanced, or recurrent MEO. This has been shown to be effective when the infectious process becomes refractory to appropriate antibiotic treatment.[10, 22]

In children, the subsequent healing of the external auditory canal, despite successful treatment of MEO, often entails cartilaginous deformities and cicatricial stenosis of the external auditory meatus.[7] Despite these problems of wound healing and the higher frequency of facial paralysis, mortality rate of MEO in children compared with that in adults is relatively low.[9]

Eczematous External Otitis

Eczema is a common dermatologic expressive form of atopic or seborrheic dermatitis. It is also associated with psoriasis, lupus erythematosus, neurodermatitis, sensitivity to topical medications, contact dermatitis, purulent otitis media, and infantile eczema.[3] The pinna and conchal bowl are often involved, with swelling of the soft tissue and lesions that are moist, erythematous, and pruritic. Fissuring, weeping, and inflammation are seen in the various niches and creases, particularly noted in the postauricular sulcus (Fig. 24–2). In the external auditory meatus, scaling, crusting, oozing, and vesicles may be evident. Aggravated trauma resulting from the intense pruritus or nervous self-inflicted manipulation may cause secondary infection. Both contact dermatitis and drug eruptions can manifest with findings similar to eczematous external oti-

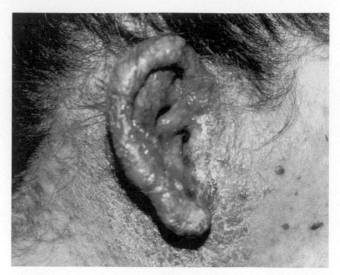

FIGURE 24–2. Diffuse eczematous cellulitis and otitis externa.

tis. Contact or chemical dermatitis refers to a local inflammatory reaction to specific offending agents or aural discharge. Some of the materials that are causative of contact dermatitis associated with purulent drainage include metals (especially nickel and chromium) present in earrings, rubber or plastic used for earmolds or earphones, solutions or sprays used for hair care, and insecticides or herbicides. Neomycin is the most common topical antibiotic incriminated in causing contact dermatitis. Other chemicals that may cause contact dermatitis include *m*-cresyl acetate and thimerosal. Allergic contact dermatitis may also occur from hypersensitivity to poison ivy.

Topical and sometimes systemic steroids are important in the initial management of this disorder. Topical astringents for acute oozing or weeping, such as Burow (aluminum sulfate–calcium acetate) solution, provide aural hygiene and symptomatic relief. Irritative chemicals, spray colognes, hair sprays, shampoos, and soaps should be eliminated. Minimizing inflammation and avoiding secondary infection may prevent subsequent scarring and potential stenosis of the external auditory meatus that may occur with persistent disease. The long-term use of fluorinated topical steroids may cause skin atrophy, so intermittent cautious use is advised. Consultation with a dermatologist in treating concomitant systemic lesions is often helpful.[20]

Perichondritis

Perichondritis of the ear represents a serious infection that may occur after surgical procedures of the ear or traumatic injuries to the pinna. Such insults include acupuncture to the pinna and ear jewelry placed higher in the scapha and helix. Piercing with contaminated equipment or improper hygiene predisposes the ear to perichondritis and cellulitis (Fig. 24–3). Extremes of temperature in the way of frostbite or burns often elicit perichondritis of the pinna. This may extend into the cartilaginous external auditory meatus. When infected, perichondritis may result in suppurative destruction of

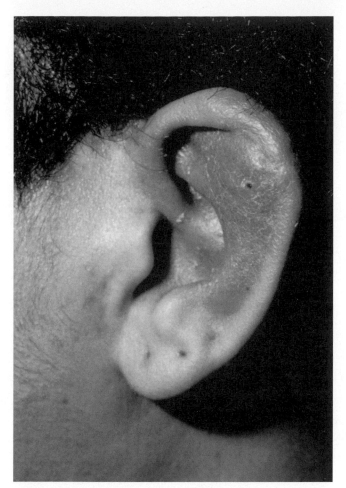

FIGURE 24–3. Auricular perichondritis due to ear piercing through scapha.

or strips of antibiotic-impregnated gauze is molded into the recesses of the pinna, and a mastoid dressing is applied. Frequent examination is necessary to ensure that reaccumulation of fluid has not occurred.

Relapsing Polychondritis

Relapsing polychondritis is considered a systemic, multifocal, autoimmune disorder characterized by inflammatory degeneration of various cartilage structures. These include the pinnae, ribs, and joints, and the nasal, laryngeal, tracheal, and eustachian tube cartilages. This disorder is unusual in young children but may be seen in late adolescence. Relapsing polychondritis is a rare disorder in children. It is predominantly seen in the fourth decade of life, affecting women slightly more often than men. It is presumed to be an autoimmune disorder, given its association with other connective diseases and nonspecific laboratory evidence of inflammation. Along with an elevated erythrocyte sedimentation rate and elevated titers of antinuclear antibody and rheumatoid factor, elevated liver enzymes and anemia are typically present.

The cartilage of the ear, nose, and various joints is most commonly affected. The pinna may become the first area to become involved and mimic perichondritis. Pain-

auricular cartilage, which subsequently results in a deformed (cauliflower) ear. Patients experience moderate to severe pain. Examination reveals significant inflammation, with erythema, induration, and edema over the affected areas. Of significance, the lobule of the ear is uninvolved because of the lack of cartilage. Infecting organisms are usually *P. aeruginosa* and *S. aureus*. If *Pseudomonas* is suspected, intravenous systemic antibiotics are necessary for the child. Separation of the perichondrium from cartilage with fluid collection may yield a fluctuant lesion. This can initially be managed by repeated aspiration. If reaccumulation continues to occur, the involved area should be incised, cultured, and drained.

Other forms of local trauma may also result in perichondritis. This typically takes the form of blunt trauma or a fall directly on the ear. Bleeding and hematoma may separate the perichondrium from the underlying cartilage. Cell lysis with partial absorption results in seroma formation. If this becomes secondarily infected, perichondritis again may develop. Wrestling and boxing are common forms of trauma in which an auricular hematoma, seroma, and potential perichondritis may occur (Fig. 24–4).

Treatment consists of aspiration or incision and drainage under sterile conditions. A sterile pressure dressing is necessary to minimize reaccumulation. A contoured pressure dressing of cotton balls moistened with mineral oil

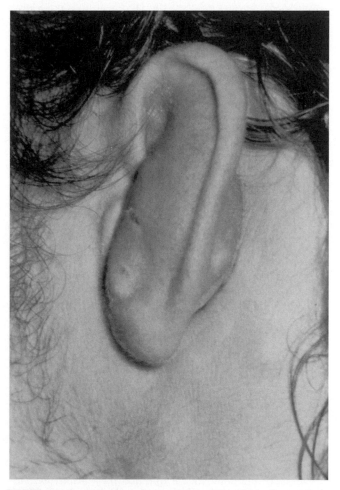

FIGURE 24–4. Auricular seroma and perichondritis due to wrestling injury.

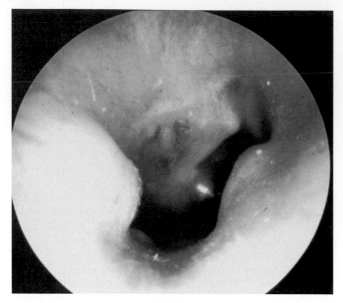

FIGURE 24–5. Moderate canal narrowing from exostosis of posterior and anterior bony walls.

ful erythematous swelling of the pinna is a common presenting sign. Involvement of the laryngeal arytenoid joints and tracheal cartilage gives rise to hoarseness and occasional dyspnea or airway obstruction. The diagnosis of relapsing polychondritis is made clinically; biopsy is reserved for when the diagnosis is in question or treatment management is ineffective. The histopathologic examination reveals perichondritis, chondritis, and chondrolysis with granulation tissue response. Subsequent reparative healing results in fibrous connective scarring. The mainstay of treatment is corticosteroids. Other effective agents include salicylates, indomethacin, cyclophosphamide (Cytoxan), dapsone, and other nonsteroidal anti-inflammatory medications.

Exostosis

Exostoses represent hyperplasia of the periosteum and underlying bone of the external auditory meatus. They are commonly seen in people who have frequently engaged in cold water swimming. Occasionally, patients will deny any such exposure, yet still manifest these bony overgrowths. The findings are often bilateral; multiple bony lesions appear as broad-based convex nodules just lateral to the tympanic annulus (Fig. 24–5). Unless there is impingement on the lateral process of the malleus, hearing loss is uncommon. However, cerumen entrapment may occur more readily after aggressive ear cleaning. Exostoses can be differentiated from osteomas. Osteomas are benign bony lesions of unknown origin composed of lamellar bone having an outer cortex with inner cancellous trabeculations. Osteomas are singular, unilateral lesions usually located at the tympanomastoid or tympanosquamous suture line and have a narrow base. Osteomas vary in size from a few millimeters to more than 2 cm.[32]

No intervention is usually necessary when exostoses or osteomas are identified. Cleaning of cerumen medial to the lesions may be necessary. Patients are instructed to avoid self-manipulation of their ears. If either lesion grows to obstruct the ear canal, then surgical intervention may be warranted. Osteomas, with a narrow pedicled base, can frequently be removed from the external auditory meatus with a curette. Larger lesions or exostoses that become obstructive may require a postauricular approach with elevation of skin flaps. A cutting or diamond bur removes the lesion and restores patency to the external auditory meatus. Split-thickness skin grafting is occasionally necessary over large denuded areas. Packing of the ear canal with antibiotic-impregnated Gelfoam or a silk rosebud pack is left for 10 days.

Keloid

Keloid formation represents a hypertrophic cutaneous scar that occurs in reaction to accidental or iatrogenic trauma. These injuries may occur with surgical incisions, insect bites, blunt trauma, ear piercing, or chronic inflammation such as in sebaceous cysts. They are typically painless, although pruritus is a common complaint.

Management of keloids is usually by surgical excision. Removal with sharp dissection is necessary. Keloids of the earlobe due to pierced ears are unique (Fig. 24–6). Typically, the keloid is located on the medial aspect of the lobule but has a connecting core along the tract to the lateral surface of the lobule. Resection of the keloid often leaves a through-and-through defect, with the lateral aspect of the fistula being a small irregular hole. The lateral defect is reapproximated with either fast-absorbing gut or nylon. The deeper and larger medial or posterior defect requires a two-layer closure. Before skin reapproximation, the subcutaneous tissues are injected with a steroid preparation, such as triamcinolone suspension. Postoperatively, a few weekly injections with the same steroid preparation may be necessary to minimize the reactive scar tissue response.

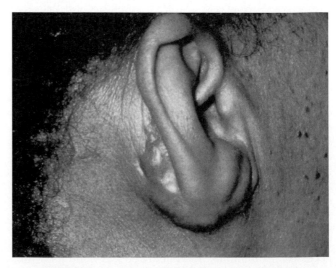

FIGURE 24–6. Keloid of lobule due to ear piercing.

Factitious Dermatitis

Self-inflicted injuries caused by the patient may be difficult to diagnose and manage. Ear lesions can be created by scratching, piercing, rubbing, burning, or applying caustic irritants to the skin. Findings can be unilateral or bilateral. This diagnosis needs to be one of exclusion. All other sources of infection or manifestations of systemic disease must be eliminated. Difficult or compulsive patients may not be forthcoming in response to the physician's clinical suspicions of self-mutilation. Under the pretense of applying a beneficial topical treatment, the physician may place an occlusive mastoid dressing to limit a patient's access to the ear. On rare occasions, hospitalization with observation may be necessary if factitious dermatitis is suspected and not successfully managed on an outpatient basis.

Summary

The pinna and external auditory meatus may be host to local infections, trauma, or tumors. The ear may also manifest systemic disease, such as relapsing polychondritis. A thorough knowledge of the anatomy and disease processes provides the necessary foundation for effective diagnosis and management of disorders affecting this area. This chapter reviews many of these relevant pathologic conditions.

SELECTED REFERENCES

Hirsch BE. Otogenic skull base osteomyelitis. In Jackler RK, Brackmann DE (eds). Neurotology. Chicago, Mosby–Year Book, 1994, pp 1157–1168.

This chapter provides a comprehensive review of malignant external otitis. Topics covered are etiology, staging, imaging, complications, and treatment.

Hirsch BE. Infections of the external ear. Am J Otolaryngol 13:145, 1992.

Along with discussions of bacterial and fungal infections, this article also provides a good discussion of herpes zoster oticus. The history, symptoms and signs, cytopathologic changes, and management are reviewed.

Hirsch BE. Antimicrobial therapy for external ear infections. In Johnson JT (ed). Antibiotic Therapy in Head and Neck Surgery. New York, Marcel Dekker, 1987.

The chapter reviews most of the medications available and used to treat infections of the pinna and external auditory meatus. The components of commonly used ototopical preparations are outlined.

Senturia BH, Marcus MD, Lucente FE. Diseases of the External Ear. New York, Grune & Stratton, 1980.

This textbook is devoted to disorders, infections, and tumors of the pinna and external auditory meatus. This is an excellent reference source.

REFERENCES

1. Babiatzki A, Sadeá J. Malignant external otitis. J Laryngol Otol 101:205, 1987.
2. Bayardelle P, Jolivet-Granger M, Larochelle D. Staphylococcal malignant external otitis. Can Med Assoc J 126:155, 1982.
3. Bergstrom LV. Diseases of the external ear. In Bluestone CD, Stool SE, eds. Pediatric Otolaryngology, vol 1. Philadelphia, WB Saunders, 1983, pp 605–613.
4. Brook I. Microbiological studies of the bacterial flora of the external auditory canal in children. Acta Otolaryngol (Stockh) 91:285, 1981.
5. Busch RF. Dermatophytid reaction and chronic otitis externa. Otolaryngol Head Neck Surg 118:420, 1998.
6. Castro R, Robinson R, Klein J, et al. Malignant external otitis and mastoiditis associated with an IgG-4 subclass deficiency in a child. Del Med J 62:1417, 1990.
7. Chandler JR. Malignant external otitis. Laryngoscope 78:1257, 1968.
8. Clark WB, Brook I, Bianki D, Thompson DH. Microbiology of otitis externa. Otolaryngol Head Neck Surg 116:23, 1997.
9. Coser PL, et al. Malignant external otitis in infants. Laryngoscope 90:312, 1980.
10. Davis JC, Gates GA, Lerner C, et al. Adjuvant hyperbaric oxygen in malignant external otitis. Arch Otolaryngol Head Neck Surg 118:89, 1992.
11. Gherini SG, Brachmann DE, Bradley WG. Magnetic resonance imaging and computerized tomography in malignant externa otitis. Laryngoscope 96:542, 1989.
12. Hannley MT, Denneny JC III. Consensus Panel Report: Use of ototopical antibiotics in treating 3 common ear diseases. Otolaryngol Head Neck Surg 122:934, 2000.
13. Hirsch BE. Infections of the external ear. Am J Otolaryngol 13:145, 1992.
14. Horn KL, Gherini S. Malignant external otitis of childhood. Am J Otol 2:402, 1981.
15. Joachims HZ. Malignant external otitis in children. Arch Otolaryngol 102:236, 1976.
16. Kraus DH, Rehm SJ, Kinney SE. The evolving treatment of necrotizing external otitis. Laryngoscope 9:934, 1988.
17. Lawrence TL, Ayers LW, Saunders WH. Drug therapy in otomycosis: an in vitro study. Laryngoscope 88:1755, 1978.
18. Linstrom CJ, Lucente FE. External otitis. In English GM (ed). Otolaryngology, vol 5. Philadelphia, JB Lippincott, 1990, pp 1–15.
19. Lucente FE, Parisier SC, Som PM, et al. Malignant external otitis: a dangerous misnomer? Otolaryngol Head Neck Surg 90:266, 1982.
20. Lucente FE, Parisier SC, Bojrab DI, Kamerer DB. Medical management of external ear disease. In Johnson JT, Derkay CS, Mandell-Brown MK, Newman RK (eds). Instructional Courses. St Louis, Mosby–Year Book, 1993, pp 373–380.
21. Ludman H. Mawson's Diseases of the Ear, 5th ed. Chicago, Year Book, 1989.
22. Mader JT, Love JT. Malignant external otitis cure with adjuvant hyperbaric oxygen therapy. Arch Otolaryngol Head Neck Surg 108:38, 1982.
23. Meltzer PE, Kelemen G. Pyocyaneus osteomyelitis of the temporal bone, mandible and zygoma. Laryngoscope 69:1300, 1959.
24. Mendelson MH, Myers BR, Hirschman SZ, et al. Treatment of invasive external otitis with cefsulodin. Rev Infect Dis 6:698, 1984.
25. Nir D, Nir T, Danino J, et al. Malignant external otitis in an infant. J Laryngol Otol 104:488, 1990.
26. Parisier S, Lucente F. Nuclear scanning in necrotizing progressive "malignant" external otitis. Laryngoscope 92:1016, 1982.
27. Phillips P, Bryce G, Shepherd J, et al. Invasive external otitis caused by *Aspergillus*. Rev Infect Dis 12:277, 1990.
28. Raines J, Schindler RA. The surgical management of recalcitrant malignant external otitis. Laryngoscope 90:369, 1980.
29. Rubin J, Kamerer DB, Yu VL, Wagener M. Aural irrigation with water: a potential pathogenic mechanism for inducing malignant external otitis? Ann Otol Rhinol Laryngol 99:117, 1990.
30. Rubin J, Curtin HD, Kamerer DB. Malignant external otitis: utility of CT in diagnosis and follow-up. Radiology 174:391, 1990.
31. Rubin J, Yu VL, Stool S. Malignant external otitis in children. J Pediatr 113:965, 1988.
32. Senturia BH, Marcus MD, Lucente FE. Diseases of the External Ear. New York, Grune & Stratton, 1980.

25

Otitis Media and Eustachian Tube Dysfunction

Charles D. Bluestone, M.D., and Jerome O. Klein, M.D.

Today, otitis media is the most frequent diagnosis recorded for infants and children who visit physicians because of illness. Children exhibit not only the signs and symptoms of the acute episode but also the sequelae of infection of the middle ear, most important of which is persistent effusion. There is a wealth of new information from otolaryngologists, pediatricians, epidemiologists, biochemists, microbiologists, immunologists, and physiologists that has increased understanding of the disease and its most appropriate management. This chapter summarizes the results of recent investigations, integrates this information with that available previously, assesses the current state of the art, and considers optimal choices for management of the various stages of otitis media.

In Table 25–1 we provide a "road map" (i.e., table of contents) for the main sections in this chapter that will aid the reader in finding specific information on the various aspects of otitis media and eustachian tube dysfunction. Also, at the beginning of the section on Management we have provided another, more detailed, "road map" which lists the headings and subheadings of this comprehensive section. Chapter 26 provides information on the intratemporal (extracranial) complications and sequelae of otitis media and related conditions, and Chapter 27 covers the intracranial complications of otitis media.

Definitions, Terminology, and Classification

Over the past 20 years, the scientific community interested in the clinical and research aspects of otitis media

TABLE 25–1. Road Map for This Chapter

have made a concerted effort to agree on the definitions and terminology of the disease.[998] Before that time, many terms existed to describe the inflammatory conditions of the middle ear, including *secretory otitis media*, *middle-ear catarrh*, and *suppurative otitis media*. This resulted in confusion and misunderstanding among clinicians who provided health care to infants and children with middle-ear disease. This confusion also impeded appropriate evaluation of studies reported in the literature, since interpreting results of investigations depends on precise definitions of the disease studied.

In addition, many of the terms were defined before the advent of modern otology, which gives us an opportunity to examine patients with the operating microscope in the ambulatory setting and at the time of otologic surgery. The more recent availability of radiologic imaging technology has also allowed us to visualize the contents of the temporal bone and the intracranial cavity in a way that the pioneers in otology could not.

There is now a broad consensus for using the terms *acute otitis media* and *otitis media with effusion*, but there is no consensus on how to *grade* these disease entities nor is there any agreement on the *classification*, *definitions of terms*, or *staging systems* used to describe the complications and sequelae of otitis media. (The grade of otitis media, and related diseases and disorders, relates to the severity of the condition, whereas a stage is a period or distinct phase in the course of otitis media or one of its complications or sequelae.) If available, such agreement would improve our ability to study the natural history of otitis media and to conduct and evaluate research in a more uniform manner from center to center and country to country. That, in turn, would result in more effective management of patients and allow us to achieve evidence-based information in the future.

The following terms, definitions, and classifications of otitis media and its complications and sequelae have been used in this chapter and in Chapters 26 and 27, and most have been used in international symposia, conferences, guidelines, and textbooks related to the disease.[130, 132, 141, 645, 646, 1069] Also, a recently convened research meeting of international experts reached consensus on the terminology that follows,[131] but the definitions of these terms await future deliberations.

Terminology and Definitions

The terms most commonly used in relation to otitis media are defined as follows:

Otitis media is an inflammation of the middle ear without reference to cause or pathogenesis.

Acute otitis media is the rapid onset of signs and symptoms, such as otalgia and fever, of acute infection within the middle ear.

Otitis media with effusion is an inflammation of the middle ear with a collection of liquid in the middle-ear space. The signs and symptoms of acute infection are absent and there is no perforation of the tympanic membrane.

Middle-ear effusion designates a liquid in the middle ear but not cause, pathogenesis, pathologic appearance, or duration. An effusion may be (1) serous: a thin, watery liquid; (2) mucoid: a thick, viscid, mucus-like liquid; (3) purulent: a pus-like liquid; or (4) a combination of these. An effusion can be the result of either acute otitis media or otitis media with effusion. The effusion can be of recent onset, acute, or more long-lasting, subacute, or chronic.

Persistent middle-ear effusion is an effusion that persists in the middle ear following an episode of acute otitis media.

Otorrhea is a discharge from the ear, originating at one or more of the following sites: the external auditory canal, middle ear, mastoid, inner ear, or intracranial cavity.

Classification

Table 25–2 presents a classification derived from our current knowledge of otitis media and its complications and sequelae. Terms used in this classification are defined in the following paragraphs.

Initially, otitis media is classified into *acute otitis media* and *otitis media with effusion*, and its related disorder, *eustachian tube dysfunction*. Complications and sequelae of otitis media are classified into *intratemporal* (extracra-

TABLE 25–2. Classification of Otitis Media and Its Complications and Sequelae

Acute otitis media	Labyrinthitis
Otitis media with effusion	Acute
Acute (short duration)	Serous
Subacute	Localized (circumscribed)
Chronic	Generalized
Eustachian tube dysfunction	Suppurative
Intratemporal (extracranial) complications and sequelae	Localized
Hearing loss	Generalized
Conductive	Chronic
Sensorineural	Labyrinthine sclerosis
Vestibular, balance, and motor dysfunctions	Facial paralysis
Perforation of tympanic membrane	Acute
Acute perforation	Chronic
Without otitis media	External otitis
With otitis media (acute otitis media with perforation)	Acute external otitis
Without otorrhea	Chronic external otitis
With otorrhea	Atelectasis of the middle ear
Chronic perforation	Localized
Without otitis media	Without retraction pocket
With otitis media	With retraction pocket
Acute otitis media	Generalized
Without otorrhea	Adhesive otitis media
With otorrhea	Cholesteatoma
Chronic otitis media (and mastoiditis) (chronic suppurative otitis media)	Without infection
Without otorrhea	With infection
With otorrhea	Acute
Mastoiditis	Without otorrhea
Acute	With otorrhea
Acute mastoiditis—without periosteitis/osteitis	Chronic (cholesteatoma with chronic suppurative otitis media)
Acute mastoiditis with periosteitis	Without otorrhea
Acute mastoiditis with osteitis	With otorrhea
Without subperiosteal abscess	Cholesterol granuloma
With subperiosteal abscess	Tympanosclerosis
Subacute	Ossicular discontinuity
Chronic	Ossicular fixation
Without chronic suppurative otitis media	Intracranial complications
With chronic suppurative otitis media	Meningitis
Petrositis	Extradural abscess
Acute	Subdural empyema
Chronic	Focal otitic encephalitis
	Brain abscess
	Dural sinus thrombosis
	Otitic hydrocephalus

From Bluestone CD, Klein JO. Otitis Media in Infants and Children, 3rd ed, Philadelphia, WB Saunders, 2001.

nial) complications and sequelae, which are those that occur within the temporal bone, and those that occur within the intracranial cavity (*intracranial* complications). Several conditions may be complications or sequelae not of otitis media but of a related condition. An example of this would be the presence of a retraction pocket of the tympanic membrane, in which a discontinuity of the ossicular chain occurs or an acquired cholesteatoma develops.[126, 127]

In Table 25–2, we have grouped the intratemporal complications and sequelae of otitis media and related disorders, such as the atelectasis of the middle ear with retraction pocket, followed by adhesive otitis media, and then cholesteatoma, since we believe cholesteatoma frequently progresses in this order. Also, the suppurative complications are grouped, such as mastoiditis, petrositis, labyrinthitis, and facial paralysis. The proposed staging systems for each of the complications and sequelae of otitis media are presented with each of these conditions in Chapters 26 and 27.

Acute Otitis Media

The rapid and short onset of signs and symptoms of inflammation in the middle ear is characteristic of *acute otitis media*. *Acute suppurative otitis media* or *purulent otitis media* are synonyms still used by some practitioners, but they are not recommended terms. One or more local or systemic signs are present: otalgia (or pulling of the ear in the young infant), otorrhea, fever, recent onset of irritability, anorexia, vomiting, and diarrhea. The tympanic membrane is full or bulging, is opaque, and has limited or no mobility to pneumatic otoscopy, all of which indicate middle-ear effusion. Erythema of the eardrum is an inconsistent finding. The acute onset of ear pain, fever, and a purulent discharge (otorrhea) through a perforation of the tympanic membrane (or tympanostomy tube) would also be evidence of acute otitis media. This is known as *acute otitis media with perforation*, a complication that is discussed later.

Grading of Severity

There may be some advantage to grading the severity of acute otitis media, since the outcome of treatment, or no treatment, may vary. Kaleida et al[558] graded acute otitis media in infants and children who were entered into a clinical trial of the efficacy of antibiotics or myringotomy or both in subjects who had acute *severe* otitis media. The efficacy of the antibiotic agent was compared to its placebo in subjects who were judged to have acute *nonsevere* otitis media. Enrollment criteria were based on an otalgia scoring system that took into account estimated parental anxiety and reliability and assigned 1, 3, or 12 points, respectively, for each hour of otalgia or apparent discomfort (in infants, ear pulling or irritability) rated as mild, moderate, or severe. An episode of acute otitis media was classified as severe if the subject's temperature had reached 39°C orally or 39.5°C rectally within the 24-hour period before presentation or if the child attained an otalgia point score equal to or greater than 12 points.

Episodes of acute otitis media not meeting these criteria were classified as *nonsevere* (see section on Management later in this chapter).

The following grading system can be used:

- *Acute severe otitis media*: presence of moderate to severe otalgia or fever equal to or higher than 39°C orally or 39.5°C rectally, or both
- *Acute nonsevere otitis media*: presence of mild otalgia and fever less than 39°C orally or 39.5°C rectally, or no fever

In the earliest stage of acute otitis media, only inflammation of the mucous membrane and tympanic membrane of the middle ear will be present without a middle-ear effusion, i.e., *acute otitis media without effusion*. Pneumatic otoscopy may reveal only myringitis in the appearance of the tympanic membrane in which there is usually erythema and opacification of the eardrum but relatively normal mobility in response to applied positive and negative pressure. Blebs or bullae may be present when the disease is acute, and positive pressure may be present within the middle ear; positive middle-ear pressure can be visualized with the pneumatic otoscope or identified by tympanometry. Children who have functioning tympanostomy tubes in place may present to their physician very early at the acute onset of fever and otalgia and with an erythematous tympanic membrane but no otorrhea.

Evidence for the existence of this type of otitis media, which may also be chronic, has been provided by the examination of histopathologic specimens of temporal bone.[827, 829] The absence of a middle-ear effusion when a tympanocentesis is performed in the presence of acute otitis media—the child is symptomatic and the tympanic membrane is thick and opaque—has provided clinical proof that this condition exists in certain cases, especially when pathogenic bacteria are isolated following irrigation and aspiration of the middle ear with nonbactericidal saline.

The term *persistent middle-ear effusion* can be used to describe asymptomatic middle-ear effusion persisting for weeks to months following the onset of acute otitis media. It should be defined, however, since this stage of acute otitis media is clinically and pathologically indistinguishable from otitis media with effusion (see next section). Otitis media with effusion is not preceded by a clinically evident episode of acute otitis media, whereas persistent middle-ear effusion continues following an attack of symptomatic acute otitis media. When middle-ear effusion persists for 3 months or longer after an attack of acute otitis media, it is considered to be chronic. Management at this stage is similar to management of chronic otitis media with effusion (see section on Management later in this chapter).

Otitis Media with Effusion

There are many synonyms for relatively asymptomatic effusion developing in the middle ear, such as *secretory otitis media*, *nonsuppurative otitis media*, or *serous otitis media*, but the most acceptable term is *otitis media with effusion*. Because the effusion may be serous (transudate), the term *secretory* may not be correct in all cases. Likewise, the term *nonsuppurative* may not be correct, as asymptomatic middle-ear effusion often contains bacteria[881, 914] and may even be purulent.[922] The term *serous otitis media* has been used if an amber or bluish effusion can be visualized through a translucent tympanic membrane, but this term is not recommended today. Also, the most frequent otoscopic finding is opacification of the tympanic membrane, which prevents assessment of the type of effusion (e.g., serous, mucoid, or purulent).

Pneumatic otoscopy frequently reveals either a retracted or a convex tympanic membrane with impaired mobility. Fullness or even bulging may be visualized in some patients. Also, an air-fluid level, bubbles, or both may be observed through a translucent tympanic membrane. The most important distinction between otitis media with effusion and acute otitis media is that the signs and symptoms of acute infection (e.g., otalgia and fever) are lacking in otitis media with effusion. Hearing loss is usually present in both conditions.

Grading of Severity and Duration

As with acute otitis media, there may be an advantage to grading otitis media with effusion according to severity, since natural history or effect of treatment, or both, may vary. One system proposes treating young children with chronic otitis media with effusion associated with bilateral hearing loss of 20 dB hearing threshold or worse in the better-hearing ear. Children who have better hearing or a unilateral effusion, or both, would be candidates for observation.[1069] An alternative grading method is to use a tympanometric pattern classification. For example, a flat pattern would be considered to be more severe than a pattern with any degree of gradient. Still another system could be grading according to otoscopic appearance. For example, a tympanic membrane that is completely opaque and immobile to pneumatic otoscopy would be considered to be more severe than a tympanic membrane that is translucent and mobile to pneumatic otoscopy, in which bubbles or an air-fluid level, or both, can be seen through the eardrum.

The following grading and staging system can be used. It distinguishes between mild, moderate, or severe based on one or more of the following: otoscopic appearance, tympanometric patterns, or hearing thresholds. Duration (not the severity) of the effusion is *acute* (less than 3 weeks), *subacute* (3 weeks to 3 months), or *chronic* (longer than 3 months). The full system describes cases as follows:

- Acute mild, moderate, or severe otitis media with effusion
- Subacute mild, moderate, or severe otitis media with effusion
- Chronic mild, moderate, or severe otitis media with effusion

Eustachian Tube Dysfunction

Eustachian tube dysfunction is a middle-ear disorder that can have symptoms similar to those of otitis media, such as hearing loss, otalgia, and tinnitus, but with no middle-ear effusion. The dysfunction may be related to a eustachian tube that is too closed (i.e., obstructed) or too open (i.e., patulous). The latter condition is most frequently associated with symptoms of autophony.

Grading of Severity and Duration

The severity of this condition can be graded into cases involving patients with mild, moderate, or severe symptoms. This is based on the frequency, duration, and severity of symptoms and the degree of disability caused by the symptoms, such as tinnitus, otalgia, autophony, dysequilibrium or vertigo, and hearing loss. The duration of this condition can be acute, subacute, or chronic (similar to the duration descriptions recommended for grading otitis media with effusion).

The following grading system can be used:

- Acute mild, moderate, or severe eustachian tube dysfunction
- Subacute mild, moderate, or severe eustachian tube dysfunction
- Chronic mild, moderate, or severe eustachian tube dysfunction

Intratemporal (Extracranial) Complications and Sequelae of Otitis Media

The following intratemporal complications and sequelae are classified into complications and sequelae. Some, however, may be both a complication and a sequela, such as hearing loss. Another disease or disorder that is concurrent with the otitis media is considered a *complication*, whereas a *sequela* of otitis media is a disease or disorder that follows, is a consequence of, or is caused by otitis media. Also, a complication or sequela may also cause another complication or sequela, e.g., a cholesteatoma may cause a facial paralysis (see Chap. 26).

Many of the complications and sequelae of otitis media can also be iatrogenic, such as those that may follow tympanostomy tube insertion, tympanoplasty, or tympanomastoidectomy. These can include tympanosclerosis, adhesive otitis media, ossicular discontinuity or fixation, or cholesteatoma, all of which in turn may cause conductive hearing loss.

Hearing Loss

Hearing loss is the most common complication and sequela of otitis media and can be *conductive, sensorineural*, or both. When conductive, the loss may be either transient or permanent. When sensorineural in origin, the impairment is usually permanent.

Conductive Hearing Loss. Fluctuating or persistent loss of hearing is present in most children who have middle-ear effusion due to acute otitis media or otitis media with effusion. The hearing loss can be either mild or moderate, with the maximum loss being no greater than 60 dB. However, the loss is usually between 15 and 40 dB. When due to otitis media with effusion, there is an average loss of 27 dB.[386] The hearing usually returns to normal thresholds when the middle-ear effusion resolves. Permanent conductive hearing loss can occur, however, as a result of recurrent acute or chronic inflammation due to adhesive otitis media or ossicular discontinuity or fixation. Negative pressure in the ear, in the absence of middle-ear effusion, can also be a cause of conductive hearing loss.[372] Patients with eustachian tube dysfunction and intermittent or persistent high negative pressure may have an associated conductive hearing impairment.

Although a debated subject, hearing loss caused by chronic and recurrent middle-ear effusions may be associated with delay or impairment of speech, language, and cognition in young children, which may or may not affect performance in school.[838, 1109]

Sensorineural Hearing Loss. Sensorineural hearing loss can be caused by otitis media or by one its complications or sequelae. The hearing loss can be mild, moderate, severe, or profound. Reversible sensorineural hearing impairment is generally attributed to the effect of increased tension and stiffness of the round window membrane. Permanent sensorineural hearing loss is most likely due to the spread of infection or products of inflammation through the round window membrane into the labyrinth,[541, 669, 764, 828] development of a perilymphatic fistula in the oval or round window,[443, 1085, 1179] or a suppurative complication such as labyrinthitis.

Perforation of the Tympanic Membrane

A perforation of the tympanic membrane can be acute or chronic; otitis media may or may or may not be present, and when otitis media is present, otorrhea may or may not be present. Classification of perforation should include the site, extent, and duration of the perforation, but no classification system exists that has received widespread acceptance.

A reasonable classification system related to site, extent, and duration is the following:

- *Site*: (1) Pars tensa: anterosuperior, anteroinferior, posterosuperior, or posteroinferior quadrant; (2) Pars flaccida
- *Extent*: Pars tensa: (1) limited to one quadrant (less than 25%); (2) involving two or more quadrants, but not total; (3) total perforation, i.e., all four quadrants
- *Duration*: (1) acute; (2) chronic

Acute Perforation. Perforation of the tympanic membrane, when acute, is most commonly associated with otitis media (with or without otorrhea) but may also occur without otitis media. Otorrhea indicates otitis media when there is a perforation.

Most commonly, acute perforations without otitis media occur following acute perforation *with* otitis media; the middle-ear inflammation resolves but the perforation persists. Such perforations will either spontaneously heal or progress to a chronic perforation. Although relatively uncommon compared to the above pathogenesis, a perforation of the tympanic membrane can occur in the absence of otitis media. This may result from penetrating trauma, as a complication of extreme changes in middle-ear pressures (e.g., barotrauma) or, more rarely, long-standing severe atelectasis.

One of the most common complications of acute otitis media is perforation of the tympanic membrane accompanied by acute drainage (otorrhea) through the defect. This is known as *acute otitis media with perforation*. Also, an acute perforation can be present in which there is otitis media but there is no evidence of otorrhea (see Table 25–2). Acute otitis media with perforation was more frequently encountered before the widespread use of antimicrobial therapy. It is still prevalent in developing countries where primary health care is inadequate.[133] An acute perforation can occur, however, as a complication of chronic otitis media with effusion, as reported in Australian Aboriginal people.[159]

When an attack of acute otitis media is complicated by a perforation (usually accompanied by otorrhea), one of four outcomes is possible: (1) resolution of the acute otitis media and healing of the tympanic membrane defect; (2) resolution of the acute otitis media, but the perforation becomes chronic; (3) the perforation and otitis media persist to become chronic (i.e., chronic suppurative otitis media); or (4) a suppurative complication of otitis media develops.

Chronic Perforation. Chronic perforation occurs when an acute perforation of the tympanic membrane fails to heal after 3 months. It may be present with or without otitis media; the former condition may or may not be associated with otorrhea. Some clinicians have termed chronic perforation that is without otorrhea as *"inactive" chronic suppurative otitis media* and a chronic perforation associated with otorrhea as *"active" chronic suppurative otitis media*.[175] This classification is not only confusing but is inappropriate in some cases, such as when there is a chronic perforation and the middle ear does not become infected. Inclusion of chronic perforations under the term *chronic otitis media* irrespective of the status of the middle ear should be avoided. The term is confusing and potentially misleading.

A chronic perforation that is not associated with either acute otitis media or chronic suppurative otitis media does not usually heal spontaneously. The middle ear is susceptible to acute otitis media, however, and subsequently to chronic suppurative otitis media when a perforation is present. This can result from contamination of the middle ear through the external auditory canal or by reflux of nasopharyngeal secretions into the middle ear (see subsequent discussion).

When a chronic perforation is associated with otitis media, the middle-ear (and mastoid) infection may be either acute or chronic. The mastoid gas cell system is invariably involved when the inflammatory process is chronic. Otorrhea may or may not be evident when either acute or chronic middle-ear infection is present.

When a chronic perforation is present and the middle ear becomes acutely infected, the disease is appropriately termed a *chronic perforation with acute otitis media*: otorrhea may or may not be present (see Table 25–2). The otitis media, with or without otorrhea, will have one of four possible outcomes: (1) acute otitis media occurs but resolves without progressing to the chronic stage; (2)

recurrent acute otitis media occurs but does not progress to the chronic stage; (3) acute otitis media persists into the chronic stage (i.e., *chronic suppurative otitis media*); or (4) recurrent acute otitis media and chronic suppurative otitis media occur periodically over time.[133]

Chronic perforation with chronic otitis, or more commonly, *chronic suppurative otitis media* is a stage of ear disease in which there is chronic inflammation of the middle-ear cleft (*middle-ear cleft* is a term frequently used for the middle ear, eustachian tube, and mastoid gas cells) and there is a chronic perforation of the tympanic membrane. Mastoiditis is invariably a part of the pathologic process. The condition has been called *chronic otitis media,* but this term can be confused with chronic otitis media with effusion, in which no perforation is present. It is also called *chronic suppurative otitis media and mastoiditis, chronic purulent otitis media,* and *chronic otomastoiditis.* The most descriptive term is *chronic otitis media with perforation, discharge, and mastoiditis,*[998] but this is not commonly used. When a cholesteatoma is also present, the term *cholesteatoma with chronic suppurative otitis media* is used; cholesteatoma can be present even if there is no acute or chronic otitis media.

Mastoiditis

Mastoiditis may or may not be a suppurative complication of otitis media, since both acute otitis media and otitis media with effusion can also involve the mastoid. Mastoiditis may be acute, subacute, or chronic. The following is a classification of the stages of this suppurative complication that has recently been revised based on an understanding of the pathogenesis and pathology and on the more recent availability of computed tomographic (CT) scans.[119]

Acute Mastoiditis

Acute mastoiditis can be staged as follows:

- Acute mastoiditis without periosteitis/osteitis
- Acute mastoiditis with periosteitis
- Acute mastoid osteitis

Acute mastoiditis-without periosteitis/osteitis is the natural extension and part of the pathologic process of acute middle-ear infection. No periosteitis or osteitis of the mastoid is present. Most likely, all patients with acute otitis media probably have extension of the middle-ear disease into the mastoid gas cell system, but this stage of acute mastoiditis is not strictly a complication of otitis media. It can nevertheless be misinterpreted as a complication of otitis media, especially when CT scans are obtained for other reasons during an episode of otitis media, e.g., following head trauma. Specific signs or symptoms of mastoid infection such as protrusion of the pinna, postauricular swelling, tenderness, pain, or erythema, are not present in this most common type of mastoiditis. This stage of mastoiditis can either resolve (most common) or progress into a true complication of otitis media, i.e., *acute mastoiditis with periosteitis.* This in turn can progress to *acute mastoid osteitis.*

Acute mastoiditis with periosteitis can develop when infection within the mastoid spreads to the periosteum covering the mastoid process. The route of infection from the mastoid cells to the periosteum is by venous channels, usually the mastoid emissary vein. This stage of acute mastoiditis should not be confused with the presence of a subperiosteal abscess. Acute mastoiditis with periosteitis is characterized by erythema, mild swelling, and tenderness in the postauricular area. The pinna may or may not be displaced inferiorly and anteriorly, with loss of the postauricular crease; sagging of the posterior external auditory canal is infrequently present.[419]

Acute mastoid osteitis has also been termed *acute "coalescent" mastoiditis* or *acute surgical mastoiditis* but the pathologic process is *osteitis.* When infection within the mastoid gas cell system progresses, rarefying osteitis can cause destruction of the bony trabeculae that separate the mastoid cells. The postauricular area is usually involved but mastoid osteitis can occur without evidence of postauricular involvement. The signs and symptoms are similar to those described above for acute mastoiditis with periosteitis; a *subperiosteal abscess* may or may not be present (see Table 25–2).

Subacute Mastoiditis

Although relatively uncommon, subacute mastoiditis may develop if an acute middle-ear and mastoid infection fails to totally resolve within the usual 10 to 14 days. This stage has also been termed *masked mastoiditis.* The classic signs and symptoms of acute mastoiditis such as pinna displacement, postauricular erythema, or subperiosteal abscess are usually absent but otalgia with postauricular pain and fever may be present. The diagnosis is made by CT scan. In this stage, the infection in the mastoid can progress into another intratemporal complication or even an intracranial complication.

Many cases of subacute mastoiditis occur in patients with persistent signs and symptoms of acute otitis media who, if initially administered antimicrobial treatment, are considered "treatment failures." When this condition occurs, tympanocentesis for diagnosis of the causative organism and myringotomy for drainage of the middle ear and mastoid in conjunction with culture-directed antimicrobial therapy will usually cure this condition without the need for mastoidectomy. If no middle-ear effusion is present the aditus-ad-antrum may be obstructed and the patient may require more aggressive management, such as mastoidectomy.

Chronic Mastoiditis

When the mastoid is chronically infected, it is usually due to *chronic suppurative otitis media* with a *chronic perforation* of the tympanic membrane. Chronic mastoiditis may also occur in the absence of chronic suppurative otitis media. Patients with relatively asymptomatic chronic otitis media with effusion frequently have some or all of the mastoid gas cell system involved in the chronic disease process. This is commonly visualized on CT scans of the temporal bones. Chronic infection may also be present in the mastoid, even in the absence of middle-ear disease due to obstruction of the aditus-ad-antrum; the otitis media resolved but the disease in the mastoid did not. Symptoms can include low-grade fever and chronic otalgia and tenderness over the mastoid process.

Petrositis

Infection from the middle ear and mastoid gas cells can spread into the petrosal gas cells of the mastoid apex, which is called *petrositis*, also termed *petrous apicitis* or *apical petrositis*. This suppurative complication may be either acute or chronic and may result from acute otitis media or chronic ear disease. When chronic infection is the cause, it is usually due to chronic suppurative otitis media or cholesteatoma, or both.

Labyrinthitis

When infection spreads from the middle ear or mastoid gas cells, or both, into the cochlear and vestibular apparatus, the resulting complication is termed *labyrinthitis*. The classification proposed by Schuknecht[982] is appropriate, describing the complication as either: *serous labyrinthitis* (also termed *toxic labyrinthitis*) or *suppurative labyrinthitis*. Labyrinthitis may also be due to meningitis, which may or may not be a complication of otitis media. Serous and suppurative labyrinthitis may be acute or chronic, or circumscribed or generalized, respectively. The end stage of chronic labyrinthitis is termed *labyrinthine sclerosis*.

Facial Paralysis

Facial paralysis caused by otitis media or one of its complications or sequelae may be either acute or chronic. It may result from acute otitis media or chronic middle-ear and mastoid disease, such as cholesteatoma or chronic suppurative otitis media, or both.[1007] The grading system of the degree of injury to the face proposed by House and Brackmann[506] is generally accepted and correlates with recovery but has been developed only for chronic facial paralysis, not acute.

External Otitis

Acute otitis media with perforation and otorrhea or chronic suppurative otitis media can cause an infection of the external auditory canal termed *external otitis*; also termed *infectious eczematoid external otitis*. An infection in the mastoid may also erode the bone of the ear canal or the postauricular area, resulting in dermatitis. The skin of the ear canal is erythematous, edematous, filled with purulent drainage, and yellow-crusted plaques may be present. The organisms involved are usually the same as those found in a middle-ear–mastoid infection but the flora of the external canal usually contribute to the infectious process.

Classification is based on duration as follows:

- *Acute external otitis:* duration of the external auditory canal infection is less than 3 months
- *Chronic external otitis:* duration of the external auditory canal infection is 3 or more months

Atelectasis of the Middle Ear

Atelectasis of the middle ear is a sequela of eustachian tube dysfunction. Retraction or collapse of the tympanic membrane is characteristic of the condition; the tympanic membrane is a component of the lateral wall of the middle ear. Collapse implies passivity (absence of high negative middle-ear pressure), whereas retraction implies active pulling inward of the tympanic membrane, usually from negative middle-ear pressure, due to eustachian tube dysfunction. Middle-ear effusion is usually absent in atelectasis. The condition may be acute or chronic, localized (with or without a *retraction pocket*) or generalized, and mild, moderate, or severe.

Sadé[963] has classified atelectasis based on the position of the tympanic membrane as follows:

- Stage 1: Slightly retracted
- Stage 2: Retracted onto the incus
- Stage 3: Retracted onto the promontory
- Stage 4: Adherent in the sinus tympani, with accumulation of keratin, i.e., cholesteatoma

This system does not provide mutually exclusive staging or include all anatomic sites or duration.

Atelectasis can be classified, graded, and staged based on extent and duration as follows.

Partial Atelectasis

Partial (localized) atelectasis of the tympanic membrane may or may not be a *retraction pocket,* since the depth of the retraction may be mild, moderate, or severe. When partial (with or without a retraction pocket), it may be found in one of the four quadrants of the pars tensa (anterosuperior, anteroinferior, posterosuperior, posteroinferior); in the pars flaccida; or in two or more of these anatomic sites. Localized atelectasis results from recurrent or chronic moderate to severe underpressures in the middle ear, which is in turn due to eustachian tube dysfunction.

Partial atelectasis without retraction pocket occurs when one or more but not all quadrants of the pars tensa is atelectatic. The atelectatic area can be mild, moderate, or severe and acute or chronic. When severe, a retraction pocket is usually present.

Partial atelectasis with retraction pocket is marked by a retraction pocket characterized by a localized area of atelectasis of the tympanic membrane. An indrawing of the membrane forms *borders* (an edge or margin), most frequently at the site of an osseous anatomic structure (e.g., the notch of Rivinus or scutum) or the malleus. The retraction pocket can be in one or more of the four quadrants of the pars tensa or in the pars flaccida and may be acute or chronic, or reversible or irreversible.

Sadé[962, 963] has classified posterosuperior retraction pockets according to the state of the pocket, as follows:

- Stage 1: Slightly retracted and self-cleansing
- Stage 2: Deeper and needing cleansing
- Stage 3: Deeper still and partly hidden, requiring excision
- Stage 4: So deep that the pocket can be removed only

by exposing the scutum and the rest of the framework (i.e., *retraction pocket cholesteatoma*)

This staging system is helpful but does not include duration, presence, or absence of adhesive changes—which relates to reversibility—or other sites.

Persistent and progressive partial atelectasis with retraction pocket can lead to sequelae commonly attributed to otitis media, such as hearing loss, ossicular chain discontinuity, and cholesteatoma.

The four stages of a retraction pocket can be subclassified as acute (less than 3 months' duration) or chronic (3 months' or longer duration). Key factors that affect the progression of a retraction pocket from stage 1 to 4 are (1) *relation to middle-ear structures*: does or does not *approximate* (touch) or is or is not *adherent* to (i.e., adhesive otitis media) an ossicle or ossicles (i.e., incus, incudostapedial joint, stapes, head of malleus, or incudomalleolar joint) or other middle-ear structure, such as promontory of the cochlea; (2) *expands with pressure*: entire pocket does or does not easily expand to the normal position when negative pressure is applied with a pneumatic otoscope or with the Bruening otoscope with a nonmagnifying lens under the otomicroscope, or when positive pressure is applied when the patient is anesthetized with nitrous oxide; (3) *extent visualized*: the entire pocket is visualized or parts are not seen even after pressure is applied. This is because the pocket extends beyond the visible portion of the middle-ear space (e.g., sinus tympani, facial recess, epitympanum, or medial to other parts of the tympanic membrane); and (4) retraction pocket is *self-cleansing and free of infection*: epithelial debris, crusting, or purulent material is or is not within the pocket.

Combining the above classifications, the following staging system can be used:

- Stage 1a. *Acute mild retraction pocket*: membrane of pocket neither approximates nor is adherent to any middle-ear structure and expands with pressure. The entire contents of the pocket are readily visible and the pocket is self-cleansing.
- Stage 1c. *Chronic mild retraction pocket*: same as Stage 1a but chronic.
- Stage 2a. *Acute moderate retraction pocket*: membrane of pocket is applied to one or more middle-ear structures but it is not adherent. The pocket expands with pressure, its extent can be visualized, and it is self-cleansing without infection.
- Stage 2c. *Chronic moderate retraction pocket*: same as stage 2a but chronic.
- Stage 3a. *Acute severe retraction pocket*: tympanic membrane is adherent to one or more middle-ear structures, its extent is visualized, and it is without infection. Cannot be expanded with pressure.
- Stage 3c. *Chronic severe retraction pocket*: same as stage 3a but chronic.
- Stage 4a. *Acute retraction pocket/cholesteatoma*: tympanic membrane is adherent to one or more middle-ear structures. Its extent cannot be visualized and it is not self-cleansing or free of infection.
- Stage 4c. *Chronic retraction pocket/cholesteatoma*: same as stage 4a but chronic.

Total (Generalized) Atelectasis

Total atelectasis may be acute (duration less than 3 months) or chronic (3 months or longer). It involves all four quadrants of the pars tensa, with or without involvement of the pars flaccida and can be staged as follows:

- Stage 1a. *Acute total mild atelectasis*: middle ear aerated.
- Stage 1c. *Chronic total mild atelectasis*: same as stage 1a but chronic.
- Stage 2a. *Acute total severe atelectasis*: middle ear not aerated (i.e., no apparent middle-ear space).
- Stage 2c. *Chronic total severe atelectasis*: same as stage 2a but chronic.

Adhesive Otitis Media

Adhesive otitis media is a result of healing following chronic inflammation of the middle ear and mastoid. The mucous membrane is thickened by proliferation of fibrous tissue, which frequently impairs movement of the ossicles, resulting in conductive hearing loss. The pathologic process is a proliferation of fibrous tissue within the middle ear and mastoid termed *fibrous sclerosis*.[982a] When cystic spaces are present, it is called *fibrocystic sclerosis*, and when there is new bone growth in the mastoid, it is termed *fibro-osseous sclerosis*.

In addition to fixation of the ossicles, adhesive otitis media may be the cause of ossicular discontinuity and conductive hearing loss due to rarefying ossicular osteitis, especially of the long process of the incus. Severe localized atelectasis (a retraction pocket) in the posterosuperior portion of the pars tensa of the tympanic membrane may cause adhesive changes to bind the tympanic membrane to the incus, stapes, and other surrounding middle-ear structures and cause resorption of the ossicles. The development of a cholesteatoma then becomes possible.

Adhesive otitis media can be staged as follows:

- Stage 1: Adhesive otitis media within the middle ear or mastoid, or both, with no functional deficit secondary to the adhesive changes (i.e., hearing loss). The middle ear remains aerated.
- Stage 2: Adhesive otitis media within the middle ear (with or without mastoid involvement) with mild hearing loss secondary to adhesive pathology. This may involve fixation or discontinuity, or both, of the ossicular chain (see Ossicular Discontinuity and Ossicular Fixation), or limit tympanic membrane compliance, or both. The middle ear remains aerated.
- Stage 3: Similar to stage 2 but with maximum conductive hearing loss secondary to ossicular pathology. No middle-ear space is present. Both conditions are due to extensive adhesive otitis media.

Cholesteatoma

Cholesteatoma occurs when keratinizing stratified squamous epithelium accumulates in the middle ear or other pneumatized portions of the temporal bone. The term *aural* distinguishes this type of cholesteatoma from a similar pathologic entity that occurs outside the temporal bone. *Acquired* distinguishes it as a sequela of otitis media or related conditions (e.g., retraction pocket of the tympanic membrane) distinct from aural congenital cholesteatomas. Even though this term is a misnomer—*keratoma* is more consistent with the pathologic appearance—cholesteatoma is in common usage and is thus accepted.[366]

Cholesteatoma can be classified as *congenital* or *acquired*.[376] Acquired cholesteatoma can be further subclassified as a sequela of otitis media (and certain related conditions) or as a result of implantation (iatrogenic or due to trauma). Otitis media may also be involved in the pathogenesis of congenital cholesteatoma. *Congenital cholesteatoma* is not a sequela of otitis media, whereas *acquired cholesteatoma* is. Despite a recent alternative acquired pathogenetic theory,[1132] classically, congenital cholesteatoma develops as a result of epithelial tissue within the temporal bone in the absence of a defect in the tympanic membrane. In contrast to this strict definition, an *aural acquired cholesteatoma* develops from a retraction pocket in the pars tensa or pars flaccida (see earlier description), migration of epithelium through a preexisting defect of the tympanic membrane (e.g., perforation), or, more rarely, metaplasia of the middle-ear–mastoid mucous membrane. A cholesteatoma may involve only the middle ear, only the mastoid, or both and may or may not extend beyond the temporal bone.

Cholesteatoma may or may not be associated with otitis media and mastoiditis, but when otitis media is present, the infection may be acute or chronic and otorrhea may or may not be present. The cholesteatoma may be a cyst-like structure with no signs of infection. A cholesteatoma that is present in association with chronic inflammation of the middle ear and mastoid is defined as *cholesteatoma with chronic suppurative otitis media*. Thus, cholesteatoma may or may not be associated with chronic suppurative otitis media. It is inappropriate to include cholesteatoma, lacking an associated infection such as chronic suppurative otitis media, under the term *chronic otitis media*.

Aural acquired cholesteatoma can be staged under the following categories according to presence and duration of otitis media or its absence:

- *Cholesteatoma without infection:* cholesteatoma that is not associated with infection within the cholesteatoma or in any other portion of the middle-ear cleft (can be further classified by its site and extent).
- *Cholesteatoma with infection:* the infection may be acute (with or without otorrhea) or chronic suppurative otitis media.

The following staging system can be used:

- Stage 1: Cholesteatoma confined to the middle ear (hypoepitympanum or mesoepitympanum), with no erosion of ossicular chain.
- Stage 2: Same as stage 1 but with erosion of one or more ossicles.
- Stage 3: Middle-ear and mastoid gas cell system involved without erosion of ossicles.
- Stage 4: Same as stage 3 but with erosion of one or more ossicles.
- Stage 5: Extensive cholesteatoma of the middle ear,

mastoid, and other portions of the temporal bone and not totally accessible to surgical removal (e.g., medial to labyrinth), with one or more ossicles involved. Fistula of the labyrinth may or may not be present.
- Stage 6: Same as stage 5, but cholesteatoma extends beyond the temporal bone.

Cholesterol Granuloma

Cholesterol granuloma is a relatively uncommon sequela of otitis media. It has often been termed *idiopathic hemotympanum,* but this term is a misnomer because there is no evidence of blood in the middle ear.[959] The blue appearance of the tympanic membrane is most likely due to the reflection of light from the thick liquid (granuloma) within the middle ear. The tissue is composed of chronic granulations with foreign body giant cells, foam cells, and cholesterol crystals within the middle ear or mastoid, or both.[751]

Staging cholesterol granuloma is based on the site and extent of the cholesterol granuloma as follows:

- Stage 1: Cholesterol granuloma localized to one portion of the mastoid gas cell system or middle ear.
- Stage 2: Cholesterol granuloma involving entire middle-ear cleft.

Tympanosclerosis

Tympanosclerosis is characterized by whitish plaques in the tympanic membrane and nodular deposits in the submucosal layers of the middle ear. The pathologic process occurs in the lamina propria in the tympanic membrane and affects the basement membrane within the middle ear. Hyalinization is followed in both sites by deposition of calcium and phosphate crystals. Conductive hearing loss may occur if the ossicles become embedded in the deposits. Tympanosclerosis is usually a sequela of chronic middle-ear disease (chronic otitis media with effusion or chronic suppurative otitis media) but is also associated with trauma, such as following tympanostomy tube insertion. Conductive hearing loss secondary to tympanosclerosis involving only the tympanic membrane is rare, although scarring of the eardrum at the site of tympanostomy tube insertion is common.[40, 612, 644]

Tympanosclerosis can be staged as follows:

- Stage 1: Tympanosclerosis is limited to the tympanic membrane (i.e., little or no involvement of the middle ear) and the hearing is unaffected, which is commonly termed *myringosclerosis*. This stage can be subclassified as follows:

   Stage 1–1: Tympanosclerosis is limited to one quadrant of the pars tensa.
   Stage 1–2: Tympanosclerosis is limited to two or more quadrants but tympanic membrane is not totally involved.
   Stage 1–3: Tympanic membrane is totally involved.
- Stage 2: Same as stage 1 (designate subclass), but hearing loss secondary to the tympanosclerosis is present.
- Stage 3: Tympanosclerosis involves the middle ear but with no hearing loss.

- Stage 4: Same as stage 3 but with hearing loss. This stage can be subclassified based on the ossicle or joint involved (see Ossicular Fixation).
- Stage 5: Tympanosclerosis involving the tympanic membrane (designate subclass) and middle ear but with no hearing loss.
- Stage 6: Extensive tympanosclerosis involves both the tympanic membrane (stage 1–3) and middle ear (designate ossicle or joint involved) with hearing loss.

Ossicular Discontinuity

Ossicular discontinuity, a sequela of otitis media and certain related conditions, is the result of rarefying osteitis caused by inflammation; a retraction pocket or cholesteatoma can also cause resorption of ossicles. The most commonly involved ossicle is the incus; its long process usually erodes, resulting in a disarticulation of the incudostapedial joint. The second most commonly eroded ossicle is the stapes; usually the crural arches are initially involved. The malleus may also become eroded, but not as commonly as the incus and stapes.

Ossicular discontinuity can be classified based on the site of pathologic lesion, as follows:

- Stapes crura
- Incudostapedial joint
- Incus
- Incudomalleolar joint
- Malleus

Ossicular Fixation

The ossicles can become fixed as a sequela of chronic middle-ear inflammation, usually by fibrous tissue caused by adhesive otitis media or tympanosclerosis, or both. Each of these has a staging system for extent and presence or absence of hearing loss. The ossicle itself or one or both of the joints (i.e., incudostapedial or incudomalleolar) may be fixed.

Ossicular fixation can be classified based on the site of pathologic lesion, as follows:

- Stapes footplate
- Incudostapedial joint
- Incus
- Incudomalleolar joint
- Malleus

Intracranial Complications of Otitis Media

There are seven intracranial suppurative complications of otitis media. These may be caused by an intratemporal complication such as mastoiditis or labyrinthitis, or one or more of the other complications of otitis media within the intracranial cavity.

Meningitis

Meningitis is an inflammation of the meninges, which, when a suppurative complication of otitis media or certain related conditions (e.g., labyrinthitis), is usually caused by a bacterium associated with infections of the middle ear or mastoid, or both. The infection may spread directly from the middle ear–mastoid through the dura and extend to the pia-arachnoid, causing generalized meningitis. Suppurative complications in an adjacent area, such as a subdural abscess, brain abscess, or lateral sinus thrombophlebitis, may also cause an inflammation of the meninges.

Extradural Abscess

Extradural abscess, also termed *epidural abscess*, is an infection that occurs between the dura of the brain and the cranial bone. It usually results from the destruction of bone adjacent to the dura by cholesteatoma or chronic suppurative otitis media, or both. This occurs when granulation tissue and purulent material collect between the lateral aspect of the dura and the adjacent temporal bone. Dural granulation tissue within a bony defect is much more common than an actual accumulation of pus. When an abscess is present, a dural sinus thrombosis or, less commonly, a subdural or brain abscess, may also be present.

Subdural Empyema

A *subdural empyema* occurs when purulent material collects within the potential space between the dura externally and the arachnoid membrane internally. Since the pus collects in a preformed space, it is correctly termed *empyema* rather than *abscess*. Subdural empyema may develop as a direct extension or, more rarely, by thrombophlebitis through venous channels.

Focal Otitic Encephalitis

Focal otitic encephalitis (also termed *cerebritis*) is a potential suppurative complication of acute otitis media, cholesteatoma, or chronic suppurative otitis media. It may also be a complication of one or more of the suppurative complications of these disorders, such as an extradural abscess or dural sinus thrombophlebitis, in which a focal area of the brain is edematous and inflamed. The signs and symptoms of this complication are similar to those associated with a brain abscess, but suppuration within the brain is not present.

Brain Abscess

Otogenic *brain abscess* is a potential intracranial suppurative complication of cholesteatoma or chronic suppurative otitis media, or both. It may also be caused by acute otitis media or acute mastoiditis. In addition, an intratemporal complication such as labyrinthitis or apical petrositis may be the focus, or the abscess may follow the development of an adjacent intracranial otogenic suppurative complication such as lateral sinus thrombophlebitis or meningitis.

Brain abscesses can be classified based on the following:

- *Site in the brain* (e.g., temporal lobe or cerebellum)

- *Number of lesions* (solitary or multiple)
- *Definition* (well-defined or ill-defined [*cerebritis*]). This is related to management and outcome.

Dural Sinus Thrombosis

Lateral and *sigmoid sinus thrombosis* or *thrombophlebitis* arises from inflammation in the adjacent mastoid. The superior and petrosal dural sinuses are also intimately associated with the temporal bone but are rarely affected. This suppurative complication can occur as a result of acute otitis media, an intratemporal complication (e.g., acute mastoiditis or apical petrositis), or another intracranial complication of otitis media.

Otitic Hydrocephalus

Otitic hydrocephalus describes a complication of otitis media in which there is increased intracranial pressure without abnormalities of cerebrospinal fluid. The pathogenesis of the syndrome is unknown, but since the ventricles are not dilated, the term *benign intracranial hypertension* also seems appropriate. The disease is usually associated with lateral sinus thrombosis.

Conclusions

This classification, which provides definitions, terminology, grading, and staging of otitis media and its complications and sequelae, makes it clear that the clinician or investigator must define the specific disease or disorder being managed or studied. Also, there is a critical need to establish universal consensus regarding the definitions, grading, and staging of many of these disease entities.

Epidemiology

Epidemiologic data about otitis media in infants and children provide information about risk features of children who have recurrent and severe disease, indicate temporal trends in incidence and severity of disease, and suggest a basis for methods of prevention and therapy. Longitudinal studies are a particularly rich source of information about otitis media. Among the longitudinal studies (in order of year of publication) of value are the Arctic Health Research Center study of middle-ear disease in Alaskan Inuit children[565, 915]; studies by two pediatricians, Virgil Howie and John Ploussard of Huntsville, Alabama, of the natural history of otitis media in children seen in their office practice[509, 512]; a prospective study of otitis media in 2565 children observed from birth by pediatricians in the Greater Boston area[1106]; studies by members of the Department of Pediatrics, University of North Carolina School of Medicine, of respiratory disease in children attending the Frank Porter Graham Child Development Center, a day-care project[484, 656, 972, 1223, 1224]; a prospective study of 2404 children born in Malmö, Sweden, in 1977[667]; studies of Finnish children and adults[897, 899]; a study of 210 Nashville children observed from birth to 2 years of age[1201]; studies of Pittsburgh-area infants during the first 2 years of life[211, 841]; a study of Australian aboriginal and nonaboriginal infants in the first year of life[159]; a study of otitis media with effusion from birth to 3 years in infants born in the Oxford area[496]; a study of Greenlandic children from birth to 8 years of age[500]; and a study of Minnesota infants observed from birth to 6 months of age.[266]

Meta-analysis of host and environmental risk factors for acute otitis media provides a summation of extensive epidemiologic data. Host factors that lead to increased risk include male sex and a member of the family with acute otitis media. Environmental factors include day care outside the home, parental smoking, use of a pacifier, and not being breast fed.[1147] Other risk features include race, altered host defenses and underlying disease, early occurrence of infection (early and often appears to be the rule), respiratory season, and environmental pollution. Each of these risk features is discussed in the following sections.

Historical Perspective

It is likely that humans have always had acute infection of the middle ear and its suppurative complications. Studies of 2600-year-old Egyptian mummies reveal perforations of the tympanic membrane and destruction of the mastoid.[673] Evidence of middle-ear disease was also apparent in skeletal material from a prehistoric Iranian population (1900 to 800 BC).[913] Before the introduction of antimicrobial agents, bacterial otitis media either resolved spontaneously (by central perforation of the tympanic membrane or evacuation of the middle-ear contents through the eustachian tube) or came to the attention of a physician, who drained the middle ear by means of myringotomy. Purulent otitis media was a frequent reason for hospital admission. In 1932, purulent otitis media accounted for 27% of all pediatric admissions to Bellevue Hospital.[50] Mastoiditis and intracranial complications were common. The introduction of sulfonamides in 1935 and subsequent antibacterial drugs limited the course of otitis media and reduced the incidence of suppurative complications. Otitis media in children from developing countries with limited access to medical care today resembles the disease seen in the United States and Western Europe before the era of chemotherapy.

Incidence of Otitis Media

Acute Otitis Media

National Survey Data

Otitis media is one of the most common infectious diseases of childhood. A survey of diagnoses made in office practices in the United States in 1990 by epidemiologists at the Centers for Disease Control (CDC) identified 24.5 million visits at which the principal diagnosis was otitis media.[979] For children younger than 15 years, otitis media was the most frequent diagnosis in office practices. Diagnoses of otitis media increased from 9.91 million visits in 1975 to 24.5 million visits in 1990 (Fig. 25–1). A survey of the frequency of infectious diseases during the first year of life in 246 Rochester, NY, children indicated that

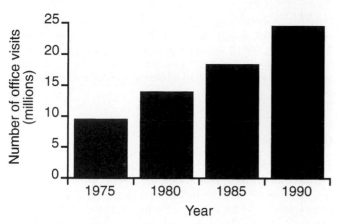

FIGURE 25–1. Office visits with a principal diagnosis of otitis media in the United States, 1975–1990. (Data from Shappert SM. Office visits for Otitis Media: United States, 1975–1990. Vital and Health Statistics of the Centers for Disease Control No. 214. Hyattsville, Maryland, National Center for Health Statistics, 1992, pp 1–18.)

otitis media was second only to the common cold as a cause of infectious illness.[495] Boston children had an average of 1.2 and 1.1 episodes of otitis media in the first and second years of life, respectively.[1106] Using a sample size of approximately 4.3 million children currently born in the United States each year, one can extrapolate from the Boston data that approximately 23.65 million episodes of acute otitis media occur each year in children from birth through the seventh year of life, a figure similar to the 24.5 million episodes identified by the CDC. The results of a survey of ambulatory surgery in the United States in 1994 included data on myringotomy with insertion of tube, tonsillectomy with or without adenoidectomy, and adenoidectomy without tonsillectomy. These results are listed in Table 25–3: myringotomy with insertion of tube was the most frequent ambulatory surgical procedure in children younger than 15 years of age (circumcision is more common but was not included in the survey).

Temporal Trends

Because of differences in definition and techniques of diagnosis of acute otitis media, incidence data are difficult to compare from time to time, unless the same observers are responsible. In addition, factors that could affect the diagnosis of otitis media may change over time, including changes in health care and reporting systems, access to and use of medical care, parent and physician awareness of the disease, and its importance. Nevertheless, a variety of studies suggest that in recent years there has been an increased number of diagnoses of otitis media (see Fig. 25–1), including a 250% increase from 1975 to 1990 identified in the CDC survey described before.[979] The increased use of antimicrobial agents, most of which are for otitis media, is discussed later. An increased number of operative procedures, including myringotomy and placement of ventilating tubes, was identified in Montreal children for only a 2-year period from 1981 to 1983.[258] The reasons for the apparent increase in diagnoses and courses of therapy are uncertain but may represent an increased awareness of the disease and perceived need for aggressive use of antimicrobial agents and operative procedures, an increase in exposure, as may occur with the large number of children in day care, or another unknown epidemiologic feature.

Antibiotic Use as an Indicator of Incidence of Otitis

Most use of oral antibiotics in the United States is for otitis media, and the number of prescriptions suggests the incidence of the disease and temporal trends in diagnoses. Investigators of the United States Food and Drug Administration (FDA) found that approximately half of the courses of antibiotics prescribed for children younger than 10 years in 1986 were administered for otitis media; 44.5 million courses were prescribed, and 42% of the prescriptions were for otitis media.[791] The number of prescriptions for anti-infectives represented 38% of all outpatient prescriptions.[790] An increase in antibiotic use was noted for the 10-year period, 1977 to 1986, of the survey for children younger than 3 years; 125 uses per 100,000 children in 1977 increased to 185 uses per 100,000 children in 1986.

A study of 222 children enrolled in the Primary Care Clinic at Johns Hopkins Hospitals from birth to 5 years of age identified amoxicillin as the most frequently prescribed medication (31.7%); long- and short-acting epinephrine was second (8%); parenteral penicillin for pneumonia and streptococcal infections was third (7.9%); oral nystatin was fourth (5.0%); and trimethoprim-sulfamethoxazole was fifth (4.8%). Otitis media accounted for 33% of all prescription medications.[382] In a study of 2253 Pittsburgh-area infants, the mean number of days of antimicrobial treatment for otitis media was 41.9 and 48.6 for the first and second years of life, respectively; infants

TABLE 25–3. National Survey of Ambulatory Surgery Procedures, 1994: Myringotomy with Insertion of Tube, Tonsillectomy and/or Adenoidectomy, and Adenoidectomy Only

Procedure	Number in Thousands			Age (yrs)	
	Total	Male	Female	<15	15–44
Myringotomy and Tube	579	340	239	556	14
Tonsillectomy and/or adenoidectomy	378	163	215	263	106
Adenoidectomy only	152	96	56	142	8

From Koszak LJ, Hall MF, Pokras R, Lawrence L. Ambulatory Surgery in the United States, 1994. From Vital and Health Statistics of the Centers for Disease Control/National Center for Health Statistics. Publication number 283. 1997, pp 1–15.

TABLE 25–4. Surgical Procedures for Children with Otitis Media*

| Age (yrs) | Number per 1000 child-years† | | |
	Tympanostomy Tubes	Adenoidectomy	Mastoidectomy
<1	15	0.35	0
1–2	62	4.3	0.3
2–3	61	12.9	0.9
3–6	44	29	0.6
6–13	29	26.4	3.4

* Enrolled in Colorado Medicaid program
† For children with otitis media surveyed over a 2-year period
From Byrns PJ, Bondy J, Glazner JE, Berman S. Utilization of services for otitis media by children enrolled in Medicaid. Arch Pediatr Adolesc Med 151:407, 1997.

received antimicrobial treatment for other reasons for a mean of only 1.9 and 4.1 days in the first and second years of life, respectively.[841]

The high attack rates of otitis media in the infant and toddler years is reflected also in the number of surgical procedures performed for otitis media. The national data for ambulatory surgery provide the rate of procedures for ventilating tubes, adenoidectomy, and mastoidectomy to 13 years of age (Table 25–4). These data are similar to those described by investigators in Pittsburgh[841] and Boston.[1116] The percentage of subjects undergoing tympanostomy tube operations was 1.8 and 4.2 in the first and second years of life, respectively, of Pittsburgh children. A similar proportion of Boston children also had placement of tubes: 1.5% and 5.7% among children with at least one episode of acute otitis media in the first and second years of life.[1116]

Utilization of Services for Otitis Media Based on Insurance Data

Berman and colleagues have used Colorado Medicaid data to track utilization of services for otitis media by children younger than 13 years[187] and otitis media–related outcomes, expenditures, and antibiotic prescribing patterns.[87] The utilization data for 1991 and 1992 included ambulatory visits for otitis media of 0.7 per child-year for all children enrolled in Medicaid and 2.8 visits for children with otitis media; drug fills were 0.5 per child-year for all children and 1.8 per child-year for children with otitis media; surgical procedures were 16.9 per 1000 child-years and 64 per 1000 child-years for children with otitis media. Surgical procedures by age from the Medicaid data are listed in Table 25–4.

Massachusetts children younger than 10 years of age enrolled by a large health insurance company in New England were surveyed for characteristics of the management of otitis media.[1116] Study subjects averaged 2.9 office visits for otitis media; among children younger than 2 years of age, one quarter had six or more visits for otitis media. Amoxicillin was prescribed as initial therapy in 56.6% of all episodes of acute otitis media, followed by cephalosporins (18.3%), trimethoprim-sulfamethoxazole

(12.3%), macrolides (6.4%), and amoxicillin-clavulanate (6.0%). Surgical procedures related to otitis media (the majority of which were myringotomy and insertion of tympanostomy tube) were performed on 3.8% of all study subjects, including 4.6% of children younger than 2 years of age.

Office Visits

The proportion of office visits of young children for otitis media was further elucidated by Teele et al[1108] (Table 25–5). Disease of the middle ear accounted for a large proportion of visits during the first 5 years of life, rising from 22.7% in the first year to approximately 40% in years 4 and 5. About one visit in three made for illness of any kind resulted in the diagnosis of middle-ear disease, approximately three quarters of all visits for follow-up of any illness were made for disease of the middle ear, and either acute otitis media or asymptomatic middle-ear effusion was diagnosed at 5% to 10% of all well-child visits. In the longitudinal study of Pittsburgh children, otitis media was responsible for a mean of 2.9 and 3.1 office visits during the first and second year, respectively.[841]

TABLE 25–5. Proportion of Visits Attributable to Disease of the Middle Ear in Children in Greater Boston (1975–1982)

Purpose of Visits*	Mean Number of Visits	Percentage of Visits for or with Middle-Ear Disease
First Year of Life (2176 child-years of observation)		
Illness	2.19	34.0
Follow-up illness	1.18	69.9
Well-baby visit	4.73	5.7
Totals	8.10	22.7
Second Year of Life (1720 child-years of observation)		
Illness	2.10	34.7
Follow-up illness	1.10	75.7
Well-baby visit	1.77	7.1
Totals	4.96	33.9
Third Year of Life (1317 child-years of observation)		
Illness	1.75	29.5
Follow-up illness	0.77	74.1
Well-baby visit	1.07	5.7
Totals	3.58	34.6
Fourth Year of Life (660 child-years of observation)		
Illness	1.84	35.4
Follow-up illness	1.00	76.6
Well-baby visit	0.71	9.6
Totals	3.55	41.8
Fifth Year of Life (529 child-years of observation)		
Illness	1.39	34.2
Follow-up illness	0.66	72.1
Well-baby visit	0.59	9.0
Totals	2.64	38.1

* According to patients.
From Teele DW, Klein JO, Rosner B, et al. Middle-ear disease and the practice of pediatrics: burden during the first five years of life. JAMA 249:1026, 1983. Copyright 1983, American Medical Association.

TABLE 25–6. Incidence of Acute Otitis Media in Boston Children*

Patient Age (mo)	Incidence (%)		
	0 Episodes	*1 or 2 Episodes*	*3 Episodes*
≤3	91	9	0
6	75	25	0
12	53	38	9
24	35	40	24
36	29	38	33

* 2565 children enrolled.
From Teele DW, Klein JO, Rosner B. Epidemiology of otitis media during the first seven years of life in children in greater Boston: a perspective, cohort study. J Infect Dis 160:83, 1989. Copyright 1989, The University of Chicago Press.

"Otitis-Prone" Child

The longitudinal studies suggest that by 3 years of age, children can be categorized into three groups of approximately equal size relative to acute infections of the middle ear. One group is free of ear infections; a second group may have occasional episodes of otitis; and a third group is otitis-prone, subject to repeated episodes of acute middle-ear infections. The definition of number of episodes to be identified as otitis-prone has varied among investigators, including three, four, or six episodes in various time periods.[10] Howie et al[512] identified in their office practice one in seven children who had more than six episodes of otitis media by their second birthday. The Boston study showed that 46% of children had three or more and 16% had six or more episodes of acute otitis media by 3 years of age[1106] (Table 25–6). The risk features should be assessed so that children who are otitis-prone can be identified as early as possible and managed aggressively with prophylactic methods.

Risk Features

Risk features for recurrent infections have been identified and include male gender, sibling history of recurrent otitis media, early occurrence of the infection, not being breast fed, being in group day care, and exposure to smoke in the household. These features are further discussed later.

Are "Otitis-Prone" Children More Susceptible to Other Infectious Diseases?

Children with defects of phagocyte function or humoral systems such as agammaglobulinemia or chronic granulomatous disease often have severe and recurrent episodes of acute otitis media as well as other suppurative diseases. The vast majority of children with severe and recurrent episodes of otitis do not have overt immune defects; but are they susceptible to other infectious diseases? Stenstrom and Ingvarsson[1064] compared the medical experience of 252 children with six or more episodes of acute otitis media with an age- and sex-matched control group. Children who were otitis-prone had significantly more diagnosed episodes of bronchopulmonary, gastrointestinal,

and urinary tract infections. Of the otitis-prone group, 8% had been hospitalized for pneumonia, contrasted with 2% in the control group. The otitis-prone children also had more visits to the orthopedic clinic than the control subjects. Whether the increased number of medical events in the otitis-prone group reflects a subtle immune deficiency or some generalized socioeconomic or environmental factor or excessive parental concern is uncertain. The increased number of medical events in the otitis-prone child does have important economic and psychological ramifications that warrant further study.

Persistent and Asymptomatic Middle-Ear Effusions

Persistence of Middle-Ear Effusion After Acute Otitis Media

The incidence or prevalence of otitis media with effusion that is apparently asymptomatic and unrecognized by parents (and therefore not brought to medical attention) has been the subject of many studies in the United States and in Scandinavia. Persistence of middle-ear effusion for weeks to months after the onset of acute otitis media was frequent in Boston children[1107]: 70% of children still had effusion at 2 weeks, 40% had effusion at 1 month, 20% had effusion at 2 months, and 10% had effusion at 3 months (Fig. 25–2). The means of periods of time spent with middle-ear effusion after the first, second, and third episode of acute otitis media were almost identical, ranging from 39 to 44 days. Age at time of diagnosis was inversely associated with duration of middle-ear effusion after first episodes of acute otitis media. Similar results of persistent middle-ear effusion after an episode of acute otitis media have been noted in studies from other centers (Table 26–7).

Because of the frequency of episodes of acute otitis media during the first years of life, the child may spend a significant proportion of these years of dynamic language development with effusion and associated hearing impairment. The prospective study of 2253 Pittsburgh children indicated that children had a mean of 20.4 and 16.6 days

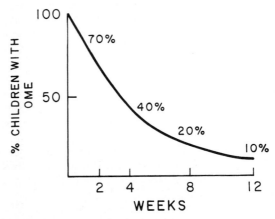

FIGURE 25–2. Persistence of middle ear effusion after onset of acute otitis media. (Modified from Teele DW, Klein JO, Rosner BA. Epidemiology of otitis media in children. Ann Otol Rhinol Laryngol 89:5, 1980.)

TABLE 25–7. Incidence of Persistent Middle-Ear Effusion After Initiating Antibiotic Treatment for Acute Otitis Media

Study	Antibiotics	Incidence of Middle-Ear Effusions After Treatment (%)				
		10 to 14 days	4 weeks	6 weeks	8 weeks	12 weeks
Puhakka et al[896]		58	29			
Teele et al[1107]	Ampicillin°	70	40		29	10
Thomsen et al., 1980		50	33			25
Schwartz et al[991]		50	23		12	8
Mandel et al[681]	Amoxicillin	56		33		
	Cefaclor	41	31			
Marchant et al., 1984a	Cefaclor	84	73			
	TMP-SMZ	85	67			
Odoi et al[803]	Cefaclor	72	48	29	7	
	Amoxicillin + clavulanic acid	70	44		13	5

° Ampicillin in all but a small number of children who received various alternative regimens.
TMP-SMZ, trimethoprim-sulfamethoxazole.
From Bluestone CD, Klein JO. Otitis Media in Infants and Children, 3rd ed, Philadelphia, WB Saunders, 2001.

with middle-ear effusion in the first and second years of life.[841]

Risk Features

Prolonged duration of middle-ear effusion in children has been associated with male gender, sibling history of ear infection, and not being breast fed[1106]; smoking in the household[342]; attendance in day care[268]; and even the use of pacifiers.[759] To determine risk for individual episodes of prolonged middle-ear effusion of 8 weeks or more, Daly et al[268] identified the following predictors: bilateral otitis media with effusion; duration of effusion for more than 2 weeks at enrollment; and day care attendance.

Middle-Ear Effusion in Healthy Children

Surveys of healthy children for the presence of middle-ear fluid have identified a high incidence of apparently asymptomatic middle-ear effusion.[369, 663, 883, 1044, 1136, 1138, 1139] All surveys used tympanometry to assess the status of the middle ear. The prevalence of effusion varied with age and the time of year. Incidence of effusion peaked during the second year of life and was more prevalent in winter than in summer months. Repeated examinations[663, 1044, 1139] revealed that the middle-ear fluid cleared spontaneously in most children within a few months. A survey of 2- to 5-year-old African-American children in day care revealed that time with middle ear effusion decreased progressively with increasing age: the mean proportion of examinations demonstrating bilateral effusion ranged from 12% between 24 and 30 months to 4% between 54 and 60 months of age.[1224]

In Pittsburgh children 2 to 6 years of age observed monthly for a 2-year period, approximately two thirds of the episodes of otitis media with effusion cleared within 1 month.[207] In many children, the duration of effusion may be as short as 1 or several days; a novel investigation of daily impedance screening of children 3 to 6 years of age in a day care center revealed that many children had tympanometric evidence of effusion (B curves) for 1 day only.[115] Some children, however, had fluid for 6 months or longer, and it was often seen first in one ear and then in the other on subsequent examinations. Thus, asymptomatic middle-ear effusion is relatively frequent in healthy children but usually resolves without medical or surgical intervention.

Age

Otitis media is a disease of infancy and early childhood. The peak age-specific attack rate occurs between 6 and 18 months of age. Children who have had little or no experience with otitis media by 3 years of age are unlikely to have subsequent severe or recurrent disease. The reasons for the occurrence of disease early in life are probably a result of maturing anatomic, physiologic, and immunologic factors, some of which are identifiable (change in skull configuration and vectors of eustachian tube, a development of protective antibodies to bacterial pathogens) but many of which are still to be defined.

Newborn Infants

In the newborn infant, otitis media may be an isolated infection or it may be associated with sepsis, pneumonia, or meningitis. There is a paucity of data about the incidence of otitis media in newborn infants. A partial explanation may be that otoscopy is not always a part of the examination of the neonate. The incidence of otitis media in newborn infants is uncertain. Otitis media with effusion was identified in 24 of 70 Cleveland infants (34%) recruited from normal newborn nurseries observed at or before 2 months of age. Approximately half of the children at 2 months of age with otitis media with effusion were asymptomatic.[696] Warren and Stool[1178] consecutively examined 127 infants whose birth weights were less than 2300 g and found 3 with infections of the middle ear (at 2, 7, and 26 days). Jaffe et al[535] examined 101 Navajo infants within 48 hours of birth and identified 18 with impaired mobility of the tympanic membrane. Balkany et al[52] identified effusion in the middle ears of 30% of 125 consecutively examined infants who were admitted to a neonatal intensive care unit. The clinical diagnosis was corroborated by aspiration of middle-ear fluid. Nasotracheal intubation for more than 7 days was correlated with presence of effusion. Pestalozza[861] observed 970 Italian newborn infants, 2 to 25 days of age, who were on the neonatal pathology ward; 205 infants (21.1%) were diagnosed as having otitis media by otoscopy, corroborated in two consecutive visits within 48 hours.

Low birth weight and prematurity are of uncertain importance as risk features for subsequent experience with otitis media. Neither studies of Boston children[1105] nor studies of Finnish children[9] identified low birth weight or prematurity as a factor of importance in children with serious and recurrent ear infections. An Australian study of very low birth weight infants (<1500 g), however, did identify significant differences in the incidence of otitis media and in conductive hearing loss for the first 5 years of life in infants of very low birth weight contrasted with infants of normal birth weight.[593] Based on longitudinal data acquired by the National Maternal and Infant Health Survey, Nalluswami et al[782] reported that very low birth weight infants were at increased risk of frequent otitis media in the first 3 years of life.

Infants and Toddlers

Otitis media is common in infants beyond the neonatal period (after 28 days of age). In the study of children in Boston, 9% had at least one episode of otitis media by 3 months of age, 25% had one or more episodes by 6 months of age, and 62.4% experienced otitis media by 12 months of age.[1105] The highest age-specific incidence for all episodes of acute otitis media (first and subsequent episodes) occurred between 6 and 13 months of age. Similar results were identified in Nashville children observed from birth; by 3 months of age, 7% had an episode of acute otitis media, and the peak incidence of middle-ear infection was 7 to 9 months of age.[1201] Of 3189 Finnish infants, 34.5% had one or more episodes of acute otitis media during their first year of life, 24.8% had one or two episodes, and 9.7% had three or more attacks.[581]

School-Age Children, Adolescents, and Adults

The incidence of otitis media declines with age after the first year of life, except for a limited reversal of the downward trend between 5 and 6 years of age, the time of entrance into school. Otitis media is less common in children 7 years of age and older. Although the incidence of acute otitis media is limited in adults, a survey by the National Disease and Therapeutic Index published in 1970 found that there are almost 4 million visits by adults each year to private physicians for this infection.[785] Approximately 20% of young Swedish adult men (20 to 30 years old) and 30% of older men (50 to 60 years old) had pathologic changes of the tympanic membrane; most with serious pathologic findings had histories of otitis and otorrhea of long duration.[953]

Age at First Episode and Recurrent Otitis Media

Age at first episode of acute otitis media is significantly associated with recurrent episodes. In the Boston study,[1105] the peak incidence for first episodes of acute otitis media occurred at 6 months of age. Age at first episode of acute otitis media was significantly and inversely associated with risk for one or more episodes of acute otitis media in the 12 months after initial diagnosis. Cleveland infants with onset of otitis media with effusion before 2 months of age had a mean of 3.5 total months of bilateral effusion, compared with 1.2 months for infants with later onset of the condition. Bilateral middle-ear effusion in these infants at 2 months of age was highly predictive of subsequent bilateral persistent otitis media with effusion (effusion for a continuous period of 3 months or longer).[696] Navajo infants with otitis media during the first months of life had more recurrences than did those infants free of disease early in life.[535] Alaskan Inuit children who had onset of disease during the first 2 years of life had many more middle-ear infections in later life than did children who escaped middle-ear infections early in life.[565] Howie and colleagues[512] noted that children with two or more episodes in the first year of life had twice as many subsequent episodes of otitis media than did children who had no or one episode in the first year.

The reasons that children with episodes of acute otitis media early in life are at risk for recurrent disease are uncertain. These children may have an anatomic defect such as cleft palate or submucous cleft, a less apparent physiologic disability as occurs with eustachian tube dysfunction, or an overt (agammaglobulinemia or chronic granulomatous disease) or subtle (immunoglobulin subclass deficiency) immunologic defect that predisposes to middle-ear infection. The early onset of infection highlights the underlying predisposing anatomic, physiologic, or immunologic deficit analogous to an infection of the urinary tract, leading to identification of the underlying anatomic or physiologic defect of the urinary tract.

Age and Duration of Middle-Ear Effusion

The age-specific incidence of otitis media with effusion parallels that of acute infection; the peak was at ages 6 to 13 months in Boston children[1105] and 10 to 12 months in Nashville children.[1201] Persistent effusions of the middle ear were more likely in young children. Pelton et al[851] found that approximately 50% of children 2 years of age or younger had effusions that lasted for 4 weeks or more after an episode of acute otitis media, whereas only 20% of children older than 2 years had effusions of this duration. Similar findings were noted in the Danish surveys of healthy children; middle-ear effusion and high negative pressure were more frequent in children 1 to 4 years of age than in children aged 7 years and older (Table 25–8).

Sex

As is true of most infections of infancy and childhood, males have a higher incidence of acute otitis media than

TABLE 25–8. Prevalence and Morbidity of Otitis Media with Effusion and High Negative Pressure in Danish Children, Newborn to 7 Years of Age

Study	Patient Age	Months of Evaluation	Presence of Negative Pressure (%)	Presence of Middle-Ear Effusions (%)
Poulsen and Tos[883]	2–4 days	Jan 1977	10.6	—
	3 months	Apr 1977	17.9	—
	6 months	Jul 1977	36.9	1.3
Tos et al, 1979	9 months	Oct 1978	48.3	4.2
	12 months	Jan 1978	46.6	13.1
Tos and Poulsen[1138]	2 years	Nov 1977	39.4	12.0
		Feb 1978	38.5	14.6
		May 1978	36.7	77.3
		Aug 1978	29.7	7.2
Fiellau-Nikolajsen, 1979	3 years	Jan 1978	27.4	9.8
		Aug 1978	22.1	8.2
Thomsen and Tos, 1981		Feb 1979	39.0	11.0
Tos et al, 1982	4 years	Feb 1979	48.6	14.2
		May 1979	47.4	11.3
		Aug 1979	51.2	10.2
		Nov 1979	53.8	14.4
		Feb 1980	56.2	18.1
Lous and Fiellau-Nikolajsen,[663]	7 years	Aug–Sep 1978	15.0	5.7
		Nov 1978–Apr 1979	20.0	9.0
		May–June 1979	18.0	6.0
		Aug 1979	9.0	2.4

do females. In the Boston study, males had significantly more single and recurrent (three or more) episodes.[1105] Finnish males had significantly more episodes than did females in eight communities studied in a 1-year period beginning June 1978.[897] Males undergo more myringotomies and tympanoplasties than do females, a fact suggesting that chronic or severe infections of the middle ear are more common among males.[1047]

Race

Selected racial groups, most in developing countries or hostile environments, have an extraordinary incidence of severe episodes of acute otitis media with frequent perforation of the tympanic membrane and persistent suppurative drainage and necrotizing process in the middle ear, including destruction of the ossicles. However, differences among races are not necessarily explained by socioeconomic factors. As an example, in Hong Kong, rates of otitis media with effusion in European 5 to 6 year olds were seven times higher than same-aged Chinese children.[955]

American Indian and Inuit Studies

Americans Indians and Alaskan and Canadian Inuits have a high incidence of severe otitis media. The following examples illustrate the extent and severity of ear disease in these populations. In a prevalence study of an Apache community of 500 people of all ages, evidence of present or past ear infection was found in 23% (draining ear, 5.6%; perforation, 2.8%; healed perforation or tympanosclerosis or both, 13.1%).[1227] Arctic Health Research inves-

tigators found a high rate of otorrhea in Alaskan Inuit children: by 1 year of age, 38% had at least one episode, and 20% of all children had two or more episodes; by 4 years of age, 62% of children had one or more episodes of otorrhea, and 40% of the children had two or more episodes.[915] Ling et al[651] found that 31% of Canadian Inuit children 10 years of age or younger living on Baffin Island had draining ears at the time of examination. None of the children was febrile or had evidence of acute otitis media.[651] Chronic suppurative otitis media was present in 6% of 142 3- to 8-year-old Inuit children living in Greenland.[850]

Children in Developing Areas

Children in developing areas are also afflicted by severe and disabling suppurative episodes of otitis media. Chronic suppurative otitis media and sensorineural hearing loss (likely as a sequela of the chronic infection) are frequent. Perforation and mastoiditis are relatively frequent in children presenting to ear, nose, and throat clinics, and severe complications are seen, including subperiosteal abscess, labyrinthitis, facial palsy, meningitis, and brain abscess.[93]

Lack of access to medical care and local environmental factors are some of the causes of these severe sequelae of acute infection of the middle ear. Use of herbal remedies and poultices placed in the ear canal may alter the course of infection and influence the microbiologic flora (personal communication, L. Haller). An increase in rates of otitis media with effusion in 8- to 10-year old Vietnamese children was thought to be due to beginning work in the rice fields.[1048] Chronic suppurative otitis media was more frequent among rural school children (9.4%) than among urban school children (1.3%) in Tanzania.[746] In addition, the rural children had higher rates of sensorineural hearing impairment (14.1%) than did urban children (7.7%). The prevalence of perforated eardrums in an aboriginal settlement in Queensland was 25% of children 4 to 12 months of age and approximately 10% of children 6 to 12 years of age.[320] Wet or dry perforation was observed in 4.2% of 170 children younger than 15 years living in a Nigerian village.[745] In a prevalence study of children and adults in Micronesia, approximately half of Micronesian infants younger than 1 year had otitis media with effusion, and 4% of ears examined of persons aged 2 months to 25 years had a perforation.[281]

The "Safe Ear"

A form of middle-ear infection, termed *necrotizing otitis media*, is seen in children living in developing countries that is rarely seen in children living in developed areas. An episode of acute middle-ear infection progresses to perforation of the tympanic membrane with profuse discharge. Necrosis of the tympanic membrane follows, leaving a large central perforation that may persist for many years. This ear is called a "safe ear" because the perforation allows drainage of the middle-ear infection, and intracranial complications rarely occur, even without use of antimicrobial agents. However, there may be destruction of the ossicular chain, and deafness may result.[234, 319, 869] Parents in these areas accept otorrhea as a way of life.

Chronic Granulomatous Otitis Media

Timmermans and Gerson[1123] described a more indolent form of otitis media in Inuit children that they termed *chronic granulomatous otitis media*. After one or more episodes of acute otitis media (usually treated with antimicrobial agents), there is a sudden onset of otorrhea without pain or fever. The discharge may persist for years, interspersed with periods of variable length in which the ear is dry. A large central perforation of the tympanic membrane is present, and granulomatous tissue fills the middle-ear cavity. Resolution occurs with a scarred tympanic membrane and a mild to moderate hearing deficit.

African-American Children

Early surveys of African-American children indicated that they had a lower incidence of otitis media than did white children. The incidence of pathologic ear disorders and hearing impairment was higher in white children than in black American children aged 6 months through 11 years who lived in Washington, D.C.[582] Ear disease was noted in 35% of 112 white children and 18% of 2031 black children. Hearing was tested in children 4 to 11 years of age; 20% of 82 white children and 6% of 1545 black children had significant impairment of hearing. The predominance of ear disease in white children was not readily explained. The results may be related to the relatively small size of the sample of white children or to socioeconomic factors unique to the white children living in a predominantly African-American community.

In a second study in the Washington, D.C. area, investigators observed a 10-fold difference in the incidence of acute otitis media in white and black children. The disease rate in children younger than 15 years with at least one encounter for acute otitis media was 155 per 1000 children attending a clinic in an affluent, predominantly white suburb; it was 15 per 1000 children attending a clinic in a blue-collar area of northeast Washington, D.C., in which nearly all of the patients were African-American.

The results of the interracial Washington studies are corroborated by studies from Cleveland and Boston and by the recent CDC survey. Acute otitis media during the first year of life occurred in significantly more white (38 of 44, 86%) than black (16 of 26, 62%) Cleveland children.[696] In Boston children, Pelton and coworkers[851–854] noted a higher incidence of persistent effusions in white children (51% of 51 children) than in black children (21% of 42 children).

The CDC surveillance of office practice in the United States noted that visits for otitis media were significantly higher for white persons younger than 15 years of age than for black persons in the same age group for 1980, 1985, and 1990. White persons younger than 15 years made about 25.5 visits per 100 in 1980, compared with 7.2 visits per 100 black persons in the same age group. The comparable figures in 1990 were 38.8 and 16.1, respectively, with both groups showing an increase in the time period.[979] The higher incidence of ear disease in white children (or lower incidence in black children) is not readily explained, although the number of all visits for medical attention may be lower in the African-American community and explain in part the smaller number of diagnoses of otitis media in black children contrasted with diagnoses in white children. Results of a study of black and white Pittsburgh children observed from birth at monthly intervals and whenever an upper respiratory infection or ear signs occurred indicate no racial differences.[211] The cumulative incidence of acute otitis media was 60% for black children and 56% for white children. If these data are corroborated by other studies of similar design, the differences in incidence of ear infections in black and white children may best be explained by fewer health care visits and observations for ear disease in the African-American children.

Anthropologic, Physiologic, and Socioeconomic Factors

Doyle[299] demonstrated differences in the position of the bony eustachian tube in skulls of African-Americans, Americans of European ancestry, and Americans Indians. Significant differences among the racial groups were present in the length, width, and angle of the tube, implicating an anatomic basis for racial predisposition to, or protection from, otitis media.

Further information about possible mechanisms was provided by Beery et al,[77] who studied eustachian tube

function in Apaches living in Arizona. The results of inflation-deflation tests indicated that Americans Indians had
lower forced opening pressures than had been measured
previously in a group of whites (with perforations secondary to chronic otitis media). The eustachian tube of the
American Indian was functionally different from that of
the whites previously studied and was characterized by
comparatively abnormal, low passive tubal resistance,
which may be considered to facilitate ventilatory activity
but to impair the protective function of the tube. The
authors speculated that the difference may account for
the high prevalence of otitis media with perforation (and
the low incidence of cholesteatoma) in this population.
Todd and Bowman[1129] studied Apaches in Arizona at two
periods, 16 years apart, and arrived at similar conclusions.

Few interracial studies have been done, and therefore
we cannot fully evaluate the significance of the extent and
severity of ear disease in different racial groups. Poverty
is a common factor among many of the nonwhite populations that have been studied. Other variables include extremes of climate (temperature, humidity, altitude),
crowding in the homes, inadequate hygiene, poor sanitation, and lack of medical care. Although the difference in
disease incidence for different racial groups may be real,
other explanations must be considered, including differences in the perception of signs of ear infection by parents, the basis for visits to the physician, the basis of
payment for medical services, and the diagnostic acumen
or style of the clinic physicians.[183]

Social and Economic Conditions

Poverty has been considered an important risk factor for
the rate and severity of otitis media. A study of Pittsburgh children found an inverse relationship during the
first 2 years of life between the total number of days with
middle-ear effusion and a socioeconomic index based on
type of health insurance and level of maternal education.[841] Children in suburban practices (likely to be affluent) had a mean percentage of days with middle ear
effusion of 15.4 and 13.9 in the first and second years of
life, respectively, compared with 27.7 and 20.8 in the first
and second years of life of children from urban practices
(more likely to include parents with low incomes).

Cambon et al[191] noted a strong relationship between
middle-ear disease and poor social conditions among native Americans of British Columbia. The specific reasons
for the high incidence and severity of disease were not
identified. The factors suggested include crowded living
conditions, poor sanitation, and inadequate medical care.
"The running ear is the heritage of the poor"[181] may be
true today as in the past, but we still do not understand
the reasons for the high incidence and marked severity of
disease among the underprivileged.

Children living in households with many members are
more likely to have otitis media than are children living
in smaller households. Canadian Inuit children living in
camps have less disease than do children living in villages
and towns.[978] Finnish children living in rural areas have
fewer episodes of acute otitis media than do children
living in towns,[899] and Finnish children in the lowest
socioeconomic classes had more acute otitis media during

the first year of life than did infants in the highest socioeconomic class.[581]

Paradoxically, recent data from the 1988 National
Health Interview Survey on Child Health indicated an
increased incidence of recurrent ear infections in children
in higher socioeconomic groups[461]; the diagnosis of "repeated ear infection" occurred in 28.8% of children
whose parents had family income in excess of $35,000 in
1988, whereas 21.5% of children whose parents had family income less than $10,000 had this diagnosis. These
data may reflect access to medical facilities with increased
number of office visits among the children in more affluent households.

Day Care Centers

The setting for child day care in the preschool years
(child's home, other home, family-based care, or large
center facility) is an important factor in the incidence of
otitis media. The more children in the day care group,
the more exposure to respiratory pathogens, the higher
the rate of respiratory tract infections, including otitis
media. Early placement of the child in out-of-home
group day care may discourage breast feeding, with a
decrease in the benefit of breast feeding in reducing the
incidence of otitis media in the first year of life. Use of
group day care in various countries is associated with
maternal leave policies. In the United States, children
may be placed in day care in the first months of life,
whereas children in Norway typically enter day care at
about 1 year of age, and placement of the infant in day
care is socially unacceptable in Germany (personal communication, Franz E. Babl).

The number of American children who receive some
form of day care is large and growing. Current estimates
are that more than 11 million children receive full- or
part-time day care. More than 50% of mothers who have
children younger than 6 years of age work outside the
home. Day care centers vary in size from small groups in
the responsibility of one or two adults to large, organized
group centers. Similarly, some facilities have adequate
room and ventilation, whereas others are crowded and
poorly ventilated. In the day care setting, coughing and
sneezing at close range are common. Rhinovirus and respiratory syncytial virus (RSV) can remain infective for
hours to days in moist or dried secretions on nonporous
materials such as toys, and the organisms can survive for
more than 30 minutes on cloth or paper tissues saturated
with secretions. Epidemics of disease due to respiratory
viruses are common. Thus, there is ample opportunity for
spread of respiratory infections among children in day
care and for a higher incidence of infection in children
attending day care than in children who receive care at
home. Day care attendance has increased substantially in
the last 25 years (Table 25–9).

In urban areas of Finland, community day care centers
are common; children in day care have a higher incidence
of otitis media than do children living in the Finnish
countryside, who are more likely to be cared for in their
homes.[900] Alho et al[9] in Oulu, Finland, identified day care
in a local authority nursery as the major risk factor for
acute otitis media. Danish children cared for outside the

TABLE 25–9. Changing Patterns of Care of Preschool Children in the United States*

Type of Care	Percentage of Children	
	1965	*1990*
Daycare center	6	28
Parent	29	28
Relative	33	19
In-home care	15	3
Family day care	16	20

* Based on surveys of employed mothers.
From New York Times, January 28, 1993. Copyright, 1993 by The New York Times Company. Reprinted by permission.

home have shown a history of otitis media that is 25% higher than that for children cared for in the home; in addition, effusion, identified by tympanometry, occurred more frequently in children cared for outside the home than at home.[1165] Three or more episodes of otitis media occurred in 10% of 150 Swedish children aged 6 to 24 months in family day care[55] or in day care centers[123] and in none of 57 children who received care at home.[1074] Pittsburgh children observed from birth who were in group day care (seven children or more) had many more episodes of otitis media than did children in home care. Myringotomy and ventilating tube placements were performed by the second year of life in 21% of children in group day care and only 3% of children in home care.[1172] The frequency and severity of infections diminished in time, with fewer days of respiratory illness in year 3 compared with years 1 and 2.[1173] Other studies that have identified the increased incidence of otitis media in children attending day care centers include studies from Norway,[779] Minnesota,[266] and the metropolitan Boston area.[214]

Parental Paid Leave

The placement of infants in day care is usually necessitated by the professional needs of one or both parents. The inevitability of multiple respiratory infections, including otitis media, in the first years of life for infants placed in large group day care suggests that any measures to delay placement in day care would be a worthy step in prevention of otitis media. Paid parental leave is available in many countries but is only now reaching a stage of discussion and experimental programs in the United States. The Federal Family and Medical Leave Act now guarantees only 6 weeks of unpaid leave. On December 1, 1999, the Clinton administration presented an experimental program that would allow states to expand unemployment compensation.[639]

Pacifier Use

Niemela et al[798] suggested that pacifier use was a significant risk factor for recurrent acute otitis media in chil-

dren attending day care centers. Of children younger than 2 years of age who used a pacifier, 29.5% had more than three episodes of acute otitis media, contrasted with 20.6% of children who did not use a pacifier. In children 2 to 3 years of age, the rates of recurrent acute otitis media were 30.6% and 13.2% for children who did and did not use pacifiers. A meta-analysis of risk factors for acute otitis media by Uhari et al[1147] revealed that pacifier use increased the risk (relative risk, 1.66). A study of bacterial cultures of pacifiers of children with acute otitis media indicated that pacifiers did not carry large numbers of organisms and therefore were unlikely to be a cause of transmission of microbial pathogens.[168] Niemela et al[796] evaluated a randomized controlled trial of parental counseling in day care centers to limit pacifier use. After the intervention, a 21% decrease was achieved in continuous pacifier use at 7 to 18 months, and the occurrence of acute otitis media per person-months at risk was 29% lower in children attending day care where interventions took place.

Sleep Position

A longitudinal study of 13,000 infants from the MRC Institute of Hearing Research in Nottingham indicated that sleep position was a determinant of middle ear history. Children who slept in the prone position were at increased risk for otitis media, contrasted with children who slept in the supine position. The authors suggested that front-lying infants had higher airway temperature, favoring bacterial colonization.[394]

Season

The seasonal incidence of infections of the middle ear parallels the seasonal variations of upper respiratory tract infections. Acute episodes peak during the winter but are also frequent in the fall and spring; they are least frequent in the summer. In observations during 3 years in the Boston study, 27% of children had an episode of otitis in the summer, compared with 48% in the spring and fall and 51% in the winter.[1109] The incidence of episodes of otitis media also increases during outbreaks of viral infections of the respiratory tract in children; these are most likely to occur in the winter and spring seasons.[484]

Four- to 5-year-old children in New Orleans had different prevalences of middle-ear effusion in winter and fall: 29% of children tested in February and 6% of those tested in September had effusion.[1044] Examination of Pittsburgh preschool-age children attending a day care center identified a prevalence of 0% for otitis media with effusion in August, 7% in September, and 25% in January and February.[212] A 1-year study of 389 7-year-old Danish schoolchildren used tympanometry on eight to 10 occasions during the year to test for the presence of middle-ear effusions. Twenty-six percent of the children had evidence of middle-ear effusion on one or more tests during the year. The prevalence varied from 5.7% in August 1978 to 9% in November through April and returned to 2.4% in August 1979. Middle-ear effusion occurring in the winter months persisted longer than effusion occurring in the summer months.[663]

Smoking and Ambient Air Pollution

Passive smoking and environmental pollutants have come under increased scrutiny as agents responsible for structural and physiologic changes in the respiratory tree. Smoke exposure can result in goblet cell hyperplasia and mucus hypersecretion in the respiratory tract[1150] and ciliostasis and decreased mucociliary transport[1176]; it may play a role in altering immune defenses of the respiratory tract. The availability of a biochemical marker—salivary, serum, or urinary cotinine—has made documentation of passive exposure to tobacco smoke more reliable than that provided by history alone. Cotinine concentrations were related to the number of smokers in the household.[1073] Concentrations of cotinine in urine were directly associated with exacerbations of asthma in children.[250]

Results of early studies of the effect of household cigarette smoke exposure on the incidence of otitis media were inconclusive because investigators depended on history provided by the parents and had difficulty measuring the amount, intensity, and proximity of the exposure.[618, 1106, 1165a] Etzel et al[342] demonstrated that high concentrations of serum cotinine were associated with increased incidence of acute otitis media and increased duration of middle-ear effusion after an acute episode. Heavy maternal smoking (>20 cigarettes per day) was a significant risk factor for three or more episodes of acute otitis media (but not for any acute otitis media) in the first year of life. The rate of recurrent infections (32%) was higher in those infants whose mothers were heavy smokers during pregnancy and since delivery than among infants whose mothers were heavy smokers after delivery only (19%). The smoking effect was stronger among infants of lower birth weight.[344]

Intense investigation of the effects of environmental pollutants such as ozone, carbon monoxide, airborne particulate matter, and acidic aerosols with various human diseases are underway. Kim et al,[587] in Houston, documented the association of invasive pneumococcal infections in children and adults with levels of sulfur dioxide (a marker for air pollution) and higher ragweed pollen counts. Epidemiologic studies identify increased ozone concentrations with exacerbations of asthmatic symptoms and changes in pulmonary function in children. Although there are no data relevant to eustachian tube function or middle-ear disease, it appears likely that structural or physiologic changes due to a toxin that is identified in one area of the lower respiratory tract will have a reflection in the upper respiratory tract. The current status of respiratory hazards to children of ambient air pollution is discussed in a statement of the American Academy of Pediatrics.[244]

Genetic Factors

Genetic predisposition to middle-ear infection is suggested by the aggregation of cases in families, by the association of severe and recurrent disease with genetically determined features such as skull configuration and subtle immunologic defects, and by results of studies in twins. A genetic influence may be based on anatomic differences of the skull, nasopharynx, and eustachian tube; physiologic differences in eustachian tube function; or impairment of the immune response predisposition.

Familial predisposition to recurrent and severe disease has been identified in multiple studies. A meta-analysis by Uhari et al[1147] identified an increase in risk (relative risk, 2.63) if any other member of the family had had acute otitis media. Children enrolled in the Boston study who had single or recurrent episodes of otitis media were more likely to have siblings with histories of significant middle-ear infections than were children who had no episodes of otitis media.[1054] Adopted Apache children had more episodes of acute otitis media than did their non-Apache siblings and had an illness rate similar to that of Apache children who remained on the reservation.[895]

Studies of the incidence of otitis media in twins indicate that there is a strong genetic component to the amount of time with middle-ear effusion and the episodes of acute otitis media in children. Casselbrant et al[210] prospectively studied 168 same-sex twin sets and 7 triplet sets in Pittsburgh: the estimate of heritability of middle ear-effusion was 0.73 and there was a strong correlation between members of monozygotic twins or triplet sets compared with dizygotic sets. Kwaerner et al[623] obtained retrospective histories of the occurrence of recurrent ear infections among 2750 pairs of Norwegian twins; heritability of ear infections was higher in females than males (74% vs 45%).

Low responses to pneumococcal polysaccharides were associated in some adults with lack of certain genetic markers of immunoglobulins.[18, 19] Immunoglobulin allotypes were investigated in children with recurrent episodes of acute otitis media and in their parents by Prellner et al[885]; the results did not identify differences among children with recurrent otitis media and control subjects for markers of genetic loci involved in antibody responses to pneumococcal polysaccharide antigens. The epidemiologic data suggest that genetic susceptibility to middle-ear disease does exist and that further investigation of genetic markers is likely to yield useful information.

The genetic basis for anatomical differences that predispose to severe and recurrent otitis media is suggested in several studies. As noted in the section on Race, Doyle[299] demonstrated differences in the morphology of the eustachian tube, tensor veli palatini, and cranial base relations of Eskimos and American Indians as contrasted with African-Americans and whites; the shorter, straighter tube found in American Indians is associated with a higher incidence of chronic middle-ear disease.[77] Lateral cephalometric analysis of children with secretory otitis media revealed a significant reduction in certain skeletal and soft tissue dimensions in the nasopharynx.[712] The degree of pneumatization of the mastoid process (possibly associated with predisposition to otitis media) was more similar in monozygotic than in dizygotic twins.[1065] Down syndrome and cleft palate, which predispose to persistent middle-ear disease, may occur on a genetic basis. Todd and Todd[1127, 1128] described an association of recurrent otitis media and children with congenital cardiac outflow tract anomalies. The investigators hypothesized that a neural crest–determined branchial field defect influences development of the cardiac outflow tract and that children with this congenital cardiotruncal anomaly are otitis-prone.

Breast Feeding

Breast feeding has been identified as an important factor in the prevention of respiratory and gastrointestinal infections in infancy. Breast feeding diminished nasopharyngeal colonization.[349] Does breast feeding prevent otitis media? Various investigators have attempted to answer that question in different geographic areas and different cultural populations. Schaefer[978] surveyed Canadian Inuit children in five areas, including an urban center (Frobisher Bay), village settlements, and hunting camps. There was an increase in the incidence of middle-ear disease in children who lived in urban centers compared with those living in villages or camps, but in each area there was an inverse relationship of incidence of middle-ear disease and duration of breast feeding. Children who were breast fed for 12 or more months had significantly less ear disease related to otitis media than did infants who were bottle fed at birth or within the first month. Timmermans and Gerson[1123] conducted a prevalence study of ear disease in a small Inuit community in Labrador. The number of children with evidence of otitis media (defined as acute otitis media, or wet or dry perforation) was inversely related to the age at onset of bottle feeding. History of the infant's feeding was obtained by interview of the mother at the time of the prevalence study. Children who were bottle fed at or soon after birth had significantly more disease (67 of 160 children, 42%) than did children who had been bottle fed only after 6 months of breast feeding (0 of 21 children).

Chandra[222] reported a significant decrease in episodes of otorrhea (observed or recorded by a nurse midwife) among 35 infants who lived in a rural community in India and were breast fed for at least 2 months, when they were compared with 35 bottle-fed infants matched for socioeconomic status and family size. Cunningham[259] reviewed the medical records of infants who were born at the Mary Imogene Bassett Hospital in Cooperstown, New York, and who were seen regularly in the pediatric clinic in the first year of life. A significant difference in acute lower respiratory tract infections occurred in infants who were breast fed for at least 4½ months, compared with infants who were bottle fed. The incidence of otitis media was lower in the breast fed infants, but the difference was not statistically significant.

Saarinen[958] observed 256 healthy term infants from birth through the first 3 years of life. Breast feeding was categorized as long (only source of milk until 6 months or more), intermediate (2 to 6 months), and little or none (2 months). The incidence of otitis media was inversely associated with the duration of breast feeding. The differences persisted to age 3 years. No differences were associated with other respiratory infections.

In the Boston study,[1106] children were observed from birth, with frequent examinations and assessments of the mode of feeding. A large number of children were studied,[855] and multivariable analysis was performed; 31.2% of children were breast fed at some time. Breast feeding was strongly associated with a decreased risk for acute otitis media during the first year of life. Analysis of duration of feeding indicated that breast feeding for 3 months was associated with decreased risk for acute otitis media or recurrent episodes of acute otitis media in the first year of life.

Infants in two suburban Buffalo pediatric practices were observed to assess the relationship of exclusive breast feeding and episodes of acute otitis media and otitis media with effusion.[318] Between 6 and 12 months, the cumulative incidence of first acute otitis media episodes increased from 25% to 51% in infants exclusively breast fed and from 54% to 76% in infants formula fed from birth. A twofold elevated risk of first episodes of acute otitis media or otitis media with effusion was observed in exclusively formula fed infants compared with infants exclusively breast fed for 6 months. In the logistic regression analysis, formula feeding was the most significant predictor of acute otitis media and otitis media with effusion episodes.

Other studies that show a lower rate of otitis media in breast fed versus bottle fed infants include Duncan et al,[321] Wright et al,[1199] and Daly et al.[266] A meta-analysis of 22 studies of risk factors for acute otitis media identified the protective effect of breast feeding for at least 3 months.[1147]

Duncan et al[321] confirmed that exclusive breast feeding of 4 months or more protected infants from single and recurrent episodes of otitis media during the first year of life. Thus, some factor in breast milk of durable quality protects against middle-ear infection.

These studies do not provide reasons for the protective effect of breast feeding for otitis media. Is breast feeding beneficial or is bottle feeding harmful? A number of hypotheses have been suggested:

1. Immunologic factors of value are provided in breast milk, and these prevent various bacterial and viral infections. Breast milk contains important anti-infective agents, including immunoglobulins (secretory IgA and IgG), various leukocytes (B cells, T cells, macrophages, and neutrophils), and components of complement. Colostrum and, to a lesser extent, breast milk have neutralizing activity to respiratory syncytial virus.[297] However, Rosen et al[937] found that antipneumococcal antibodies in breast milk did not prevent nasopharyngeal carriage of pneumococci or subsequent acute otitis media.

2. Nonimmune protective factors include interferon, glycoproteins, lactadherin, glycolipids, glycosaminoglycans, oligosaccharides, monoglycerides, and unsaturated fatty acids. Human milk contained both specific antibodies and free oligosaccharides that corresponded to the pneumococcal carbohydrate receptor,[26, 457] suggesting that milk may protect against otitis media by blocking attachment of bacterial pathogens to respiratory mucosa. However, studies by Faden et al[348] indicated that adherence of nontypeable *Haemophilus influenzae* to respira-

tory epithelium was not influenced by breast feeding.

3. Anti-inflammatory factors in breast milk that may limit the infection include antioxidants (ascorbic acid, cysteine, and alpha-tocopherol), lactoferrin, tumor necrosis factor-alpha soluble receptors, and interleukin-1 and -10.

4. Allergy to one or more components in cow or formula milk may result in alteration of the mucosa of the eustachian tube and middle ear.

5. The facial musculature of breast fed infants develops differently from that of bottle fed infants. The muscles may affect eustachian tube function and assist in promoting the drainage of middle-ear fluids.

6. Aspiration of fluids into the middle ear occurs during bottle feeding, because the bottle fed infant is required to produce high negative intraoral pressure, whereas breast feeding involves nipple massage and reflex "let-down" of milk.

7. The breast fed infant is maintained in a vertical or semivertical reclining position, whereas the bottle-fed infant is placed in a reclining or horizontal position. The horizontal position may result in reflux of milk through the wide and horizontal eustachian tube. The practice of propping a bottle in bed has been criticized because fluids are forced under pressure into the oral cavity, with possible reflux into the middle ear. Tully et al[1141] demonstrated that a higher proportion of infants fed in the supine position had abnormal postfeeding tympanographic results compared with infants fed in the semi-upright position.

The results of a study of children with cleft palate appear to diminish the importance of the positional advantage of breast feeding.[837] None of the 222 infants fed formula only was free of ear effusion at any examination during the first 18 months of life, whereas in 11 of 30 infants fed breast milk, one or both ears were free of effusion at one or more examinations. The results suggest that breast milk protected infants in spite of the severe anatomic disability. Since all feedings, of breast milk or formula, were given via an artificial feeder, the protection afforded the infants was more likely to be in the quality of the milk rather than the mode of feeding.

Although of uncertain importance for the development of otitis media, breast milk may play a role in transmission of bacterial and viral pathogens. Bacterial pathogens include *Staphylococcus aureus*, *Listeria monocytogenes*, and *Salmonella* species. Viruses transmitted by breast milk include cytomegalovirus, human immunodeficiency virus, herpes simplex virus, and human T-lymphotropic virus 1.[603]

Altered Host Defenses and Underlying Disease

Although most children have no obvious defect responsible for chronic otitis media with effusion, a small number may have altered host defenses, including anatomic changes (cleft palate, cleft uvula, submucous cleft), alter-

ation of normal physiologic defenses (patulous eustachian tube or barotrauma), congenital or acquired immunologic deficiencies (immunoglobulin deficiencies, chronic granulomatous disease), presence of malignant neoplasms, or use of drugs that suppress immune processes. Active middle-ear disease is almost a constant event in children with cleft palate (see later section on management).

Some patients may have disease states, such as nasopharyngeal tumors or connective tissue disorders, that lead to otitis media. An increased incidence of otitis media occurs in children with Down syndrome.[984] These conditions are too infrequent to affect epidemiologic studies but should be considered in the management of individual patients.

Local and systemic bacterial infections, including otitis media, are early manifestations of acquired immunodeficiency syndrome (AIDS) in infants. Children with AIDS had a higher age-specific incidence of otitis media, beginning at 6 months of age, compared with uninfected children or children who initially had the antibody for human immunodeficiency virus (HIV) but seroreverted[58] (Fig. 25–3).

Various procedures in the nose, throat, or airway may increase susceptibility to infection in the middle ear. Nasotracheal intubation was identified as a factor in the development of middle-ear effusion in neonates.[85] A similar observation was made in children 2 days to 5 years of age in an intensive care unit; nasotracheal, but not nasogastric, intubation was associated with the development of middle-ear effusion. Effusion was identified within 4 days of intubation and appeared earlier in the ear on the side of intubation than in the contralateral ear.[859] Derkay et al[279] noted that otitis media was common in the pediatric intensive care unit and was probably caused by prolonged dysfunction of the eustachian tube associated with orally and nasally placed tubes. The bacteriology of the otitis reflected nosocomial infection (including *Pseudomonas aeruginosa* and *Staphylococcus epidermidis*) rather than the usual pathogens of community-acquired disease.

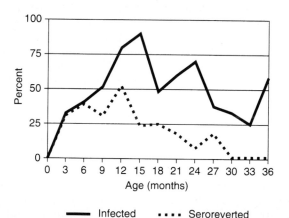

FIGURE 25–3. Age-specific incidence of otitis media from birth to 3 years of age in children infected with the human immunodeficiency virus and in children who seroreverted. (From Barnett ED, Klein JO, Pelton SI, Luginbuhl LM. Otitis media in children born to human immunodeficiency virus-infected mother. Pediatr Infect Dis J 11:460, 1992.)

TABLE 25–10. Composition of the Eustachian Tube as an Organ

Lumen-mucosa
Osseous portion
Lateral membranous wall
Extraluminal soft tissue
Cartilage
Ostmann fat pad
Muscles
   Tensor veli palatini (and tensor tympani)
   Levator veli palatini
   Salpingopharyngeus
Innervation
Blood supply
Lymphatics
Osseous support
   Sphenoid sulcus
   Medial pterygoid plate

Cost Analyses

Various analyses of cost of management of otitis media for the health care payer as well as the societal perspective have provided additional insights into the epidemiology of otitis media.[16, 201, 329, 1070] Direct costs of an episode of otitis media include health care visits and consultations, cost of drugs (antibiotics, decongestants), surgical procedures, audiometry and remedial speech and language visits, and hospitalizations related to otitis media or its complications. Indirect costs include transportation, baby sitter, and lost time from work. Usually not calculated are the loss of intellectual potential and contributions to the family and community. The average total cost of treating an episode of otitis media has been estimated to be between $116[567] and $131.[201] Antibiotics account for a relatively small proportion of these costs of acute care. In 1996, the combined cost of acute otitis media with its sequela was estimated to be more than $5 billion every year.[399]

Anatomy of Nasopharynx–Eustachian Tube–Middle Ear System

Even though the etiology and pathogenesis of otitis media is multifactorial, including genetic, immunologic, and environmental factors, the structure and function of the eustachian tube is recognized as a key component. In this section we describe the anatomy of the eustachian tube in relation to the organs to which it connects. We also explain why the infant eustachian tube is developmentally immature and contributes to the prevalence of otitis media in this highly susceptible age group.

Eustachian Tube as an Organ Within a System

Contrary to current concepts, the eustachian tube is not just a tube but is an *organ* consisting of a lumen with its mucosa, cartilage, surrounding soft tissue, paratubal muscles (i.e., tensor veli palatini, tensor tympani, levator veli palatini, and salpingopharyngeus), and its bony support (sphenoid sulcus and medial pterygoid plate). The term *middle-ear cleft* is often used to describe the eustachian tube, middle ear, and mastoid gas cells (Table 25–10). The larynx, another organ in the airway, has many similarities to the eustachian tube in that both have comparable (1) anatomy, including a lumen that is covered by mucosa, cartilage support, and a muscular opening mechanism; (2) physiologic functions, e.g., ventilation, protection, and clearance; and (3) pathophysiology, i.e., the lumen can be too open, too closed, or experience a failure of the opening or closing mechanism.

The eustachian tube is part of a *system* of contiguous organs including the nasal cavity, palate, and pharynx at its proximal end, and the middle ear and mastoid gas cells at its distal end (Fig. 25–4).

Structure of the Eustachian Tube

The eustachian tube can be divided into three continuous portions: *cartilaginous, junctional,* and *osseous.* The cartilaginous portion is proximal and opens into the nasopharynx. The osseous portion is distal and opens into the anterior middle ear. The junctional portion is the part of the tube where the cartilaginous and osseous portions connect and was previously thought to be the narrowest part of the tubal lumen, the isthmus. A recent three-dimensional study of nine human temporal bone specimens by Sudo et al[1078] demonstrated the isthmus portion of the lumen to be near the distal end of the cartilaginous portion and not at the junction of the cartilaginous and osseous portions (see later). Respiratory mucosa lines the entire tubal lumen. Figure 25–5 shows the anatomy of the tube and its muscles.

It is important to describe the growth and development of the tube to understand why infants and young children have more middle-ear infections than older children and adults.

Developmental Anatomy

The structure of the adult eustachian tube is the culmination of 18 years of development and growth. Thus, we can best appreciate the eustachian tube's structure and function in the context of these processes. Further, identifying abnormalities and their consequences depends on a knowledge of normal anatomy.

Prenatal Growth

The eustachian tube lumen develops from persistence of the first pharyngeal pouch in the embryo. The entodermal lining of the first pharyngeal pouch extends laterally, making contact with the ectoderm of the bottom of the first gill furrow on either side of the gill plate. The distal pouch becomes elongated and expanded to form the tubotympanic recess, the primordium of the middle-ear cavity. The proximal portion then becomes narrowed to form the eustachian tube. The lumen at this stage has a smooth margin with unciliated low columnar epithelium.[845] The structures associated with this lumen develop

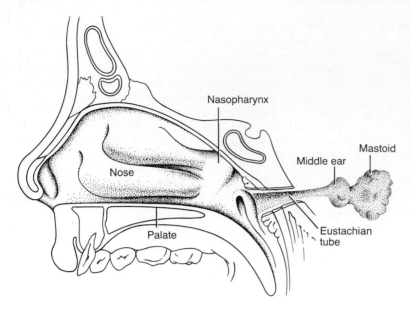

FIGURE 25–4. The eustachian tube is part of a system; the pharynx, palate, and nasal cavities are at its proximal end and the middle ear and mastoid gas cells are at its distal end. (From Bluestone CD, Klein JO. Otitis media in Infants and Children, 3rd ed. Philadelphia, WB Saunders, 2001.)

from the surrounding mesenchyme in a predictable sequence.

Swarts et al[1091] studied tubal development in 20 human fetuses between 7 and 38 weeks postconception. Their results confirm and extend those of Wolff[1196] and Tos.[1135] Before 10 weeks postconception, only the epithelial lining of the lumen has differentiated. Between 10 and 12 weeks after conception, the levator veli palatini and tensor veli palatini muscles develop. The first evidence of the third muscle, the tensor tympani muscle, is apparent approximately 2 weeks later. At about the same time (14 weeks postconception), the initial differentiation of the cartilage begins. Also at this time, the lumen begins to show folding of the epithelium into the rugae characteristic of the eustachian tube after birth.

Accompanying these changes, glandular tissue appears in the pharyngeal wall, medial to the cartilage and between it and the more lateral lumen. By 20 weeks after conception, the initial center of chondrification has increased in size and a perichondrium is clearly differentiated in the anteromedial portions of the tube. By parturition, these processes yield a eustachian tube structure very similar to that of an adult eustachian tube. The cartilage is clearly delimited by a perichondrium throughout its length and shows the classic J-shaped form. The muscles are well circumscribed and, relative to the cartilage, are positioned similarly to those of the adult. Glandular tissue has proliferated and now occupies the regions between the cartilage and nasopharynx, between the cartilage and the lumen, and between the lumen and the tensor veli palatini muscle.

As ontogeny proceeds, morphometric changes occur among the eustachian tube structures and with respect to the rest of the head. The most pronounced change is the increase in tubal length from 1 mm at 10 weeks to 13 mm at birth. Most of this increase occurs in the cartilaginous portion of the tube. Since the fetal cranial base is relatively flat, the tube deviates from the horizontal plane only minimally, a condition that persists into early childhood. During postnatal development, the cranial base angle and the vertical dimensions of the skull increase. The

hard palate drops away from the skull base. As this occurs, the angle between the cartilaginous tube and the skull base increases.

Postnatal Growth

After birth, the eustachian tube in the infant and young child is immature in structure and function compared with that in the older child and adult. There are at least eight major anatomic differences, which are summarized in Table 25–11 and discussed subsequently.

Length of Tube. Sadler-Kimes et al[964] used a three-dimensional computer graphic technique to analyze the size, shape, and positional association of the eustachian tube cartilage, lumen, and paratubal muscles. They compared temporal bone histopathologic specimens from children younger than 7 years of age with those from children 7 years of age and older. In infants, the eustachian tube is about one half as long as in the adult; it averages about 18 mm. The tube lengthens rapidly during early childhood, and by 7 years of age it is approximately as long as an adult's.[1022, 1023] Ishijima et al[529] found the length of the lumen of the infant tube to be 21 mm, as compared with the 37 mm average length of an adult's. The cartilaginous tube represents somewhat less than two thirds of this distance. In contrast, the osseous portion is relatively longer and wider in diameter than it is in the adult. The increase in length from infancy to adult is primarily due to elongation of the bony portion of the eustachian tube.[529] The shorter tube in the infant and young child (i.e., the tube is "too short" compared to adult tubal length) is most likely related to an impaired protective function, e.g., nasopharyngeal secretions can reflux or insufflate into the middle ear (see next section, Physiology, Pathophysiology, and Pathogenesis).

The cartilage, lumen, and levator veli palatini muscle all increase in cross-sectional area and volume after age 7. Also in older children, the tube's cartilage and lumen are more elongated and the distance from the levator veli palatini muscle to the other structures of the tube is

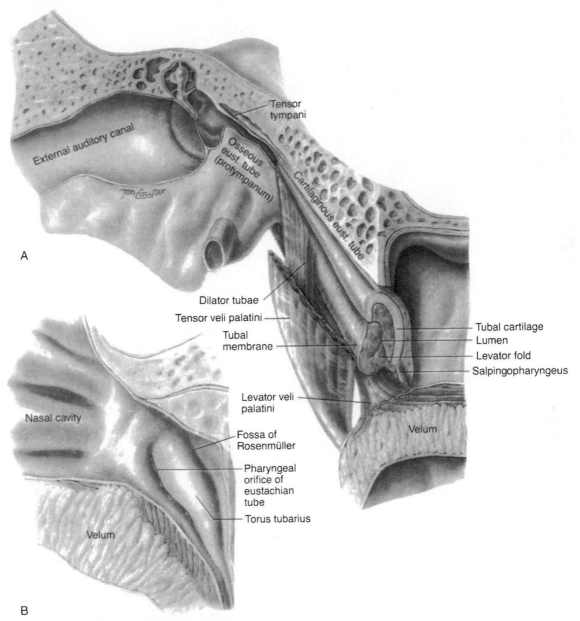

FIGURE 25–5. Anatomy of the eustachian tube. *A*, Complete dissection of the eustachian tube and middle ear. The relationship of the eustachian tube, paratubal muscles, cranial base, and the positioning of the juncture between the osseous portion of the eustachian tube and the middle ear, i.e., the aural orifice of the tube, are evident. *B*, Appearance of the nasopharyngeal orifice of the eustachian tube. Note the large torus tubarius and its inferior continuation at the salpingopharyngeus muscle.

TABLE 25–11. Developmental Differences of Eustachian Tube Between Infants and Adults

Anatomic Features of the Eustachian Tube	Difference Compared with the Adult	Study
Length of tube	Shorter	Sadler-Kimes et al[964]
Angle of tube to horizontal plane	10- vs 45-degree angle	Proctor[894]
Angle of tensor veli palatini muscle to cartilage	Variable vs stable	Swarts and Rood[1093]
Cartilage cell density	Greater	Yamaguchi et al[1205]
Elastin at hinge portion of cartilage	Less	Matsune et al[705]
Lumen	Smaller area	Kitajiri et al[592], Suzuki et al[1086]
Ostmann fat pad	Relatively wider	Aoki et al[30]
Mucosal folds	Greater	Sudo and Sando[1077]
Cartilage volume	Less	Takasaki et al[1101]

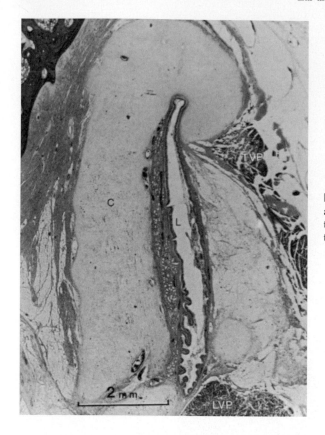

FIGURE 25–6. Midcartilaginous portion of the normal eustachian tube of a 1-day-old girl. Note the size of the cartilage (C) compared with that of the adult in Figure 25–9. L, tubal lumen; LVP, levator veli palatini; TVP, tensor veli palatini. (Courtesy of I. Sando, M.D.)

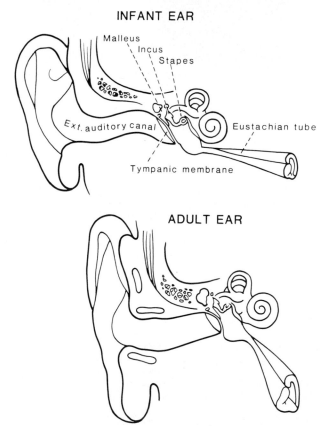

FIGURE 25–7. The difference in the angle of the eustachian tube in the infant and the adult. This most likely adversely affects the function of the infant tensor veli palatini muscle.

significantly longer. The distances from the tensor veli palatini muscle to the lumen and to the levator palatini muscle are also larger in individuals over the age of 6. Holborow[497] demonstrated that in infants, the medial cartilaginous lamina is relatively shorter. Cartilage mass also increases from birth to puberty (Fig. 25–6).[1101]

Angle of Tube. In the infant, the direction of the tube varies from horizontal to an angle of about 10 degrees to the horizontal, and the tube is not angulated at the junctional portion but merely narrows.[436] In the adult, the tube is approximately 45 degrees related to the horizontal plane.[894] This difference in angles between infants and adults has been thought to impair clearance of the eustachian tube–middle ear in the infant, but it is most likely the muscle vector of the tensor veli palatini that is adversely affected in this age group (Fig. 25–7).

Angle Between Tensor Muscle and Tube. The angle that the tensor veli palatini muscle makes with the lumen is almost identical in children and adults. However, the angle between the tensor veli palatini muscle and the cartilage is different. In the child, the angle between the muscle and the cartilage is larger in the nasopharyngeal portion of the tube and decreases posteriorly toward the middle-ear end of the tube. In the adult, this angular relationship is stable throughout the length of the tube.[1092] This angular difference between children and adults may be related to the known inefficient tubal function (i.e., the tube "won't open") in children compared with adults and the increased incidence of otitis media in children.[185, 186]

Cartilage Cell Density. Yamaguchi et al[1205] studied the cartilage cell density in the eustachian tube of temporal bone histopathologic specimens from humans ranging in age from 26 weeks' gestation to 85 years (24 were under 3 years of age). The cartilage cell density was statistically greater in specimens from children younger than 7 years compared to specimens from older children and adults. This variation may be related to (1) the observations that infants and young children have increased compliance of the eustachian tube (i.e., the tube is "too floppy"), contributing to their inability to effectively open or dilate the tubal lumen when the tensor veli palatini muscle contracts (i.e., functional obstruction); and (2) increased distensibility of the tube, which can promote insufflation of nasopharyngeal secretions into the middle ear during crying, closed-nose swallowing (i.e., Toynbee phenomenon), and blowing the nose.[121, 124]

Elastin in the Cartilage. Matsune et al[705] assessed the amount of elastin in the hinge portion of the cartilage of the eustachian tube (i.e., the intermediate portion between the lateral and medial laminae) in temporal bone histopathologic specimens from infants and adults. They found that elastin was statistically less dense in the infant specimens and postulated that this may be related to the hypothesis of functional obstruction in children (i.e., failure of the tubal opening mechanism, or the tube "won't open"). The relatively less dense elastin in the hinge portion in the infant could also result in inadequate passive tubal closure and a lumen more distensible to nasopharyngeal positive pressures. Both possibilities would impair the eustachian tube's protective function.

Tubal Lumen Area. Kitajiri et al[592] studied the postnatal development of the eustachian tube lumen and found that the area of the lumen increased almost fivefold from the newborn to age 20 years; the midcartilaginous portion increased most dramatically. The cross-sectional length of the lumen significantly increased during development, especially in the pharyngeal area of the tube. There appeared to be little growth in the width of the lumen from the newborn to the adult. A larger luminal area of the eustachian tube in the adult would promote more effective pressure regulation of the tube compared with the infant's tube. Suzuki et al[1086] recently confirmed these early findings.

Ostmann Fat Pad. Aoki et al[30] measured the amount of the Ostmann fat pad from temporal bone specimens ranging from neonates to adults. They found an increase in volume with advancing age until adulthood, primarily in height, but little growth in width. Since the fat pad is positioned in the inferolateral aspect of the eustachian tube, it may prevent excessive dilatation of the tubal lumen. On the other hand, the relatively greater mass of the fat pad in the infant could contribute to less effective opening of the lumen of the tube.

Mucosal Folds. Sando et al[971] found the inferior portion of the lumen of the eustachian tube to contain numerous mucosal folds, which increase the surface area. In contrast, the superior portion of the tubal lumen has rela-tively no folds, and these folds progressively decrease until age 20.[1077] The significance of this developmental change is currently uncertain but may be related to the growth of the tubal luminal area.

Significance of Developmental Differences

The observed differences in the anatomy of the eustachian tube as an organ in the infant, young child, and adult provide convincing evidence to explain some of the major functional differences also identified in these age groups. This helps our understanding of the increased incidence of middle-ear disease in the pediatric population. Pressure regulation function is less efficient in the young, most likely due to the tubal lumen's ineffective active opening (i.e., the tube "won't open") by contraction of the tensor veli palatini muscle. This is probably due to either the difference in the muscle vector or the highly compliant tubal cartilage (i.e., the tube is "too floppy"), or both. Inefficient ventilatory function of the tube (i.e., the tube is "too closed") results in middle-ear underpressures—especially during periods of upper respiratory infections—which, if prolonged, can progress into middle-ear effusion.

Since infants and young children have eustachian tubes that are "too short" and "too floppy" compared with those of older children and adults, nasopharyngeal secretions can reflux or be insufflated more readily into the middle ear and result in middle-ear infection (see next section, Physiology, Pathophysiology, and Pathogenesis).

Adult Anatomy

The length of the adult eustachian tube has been reported to be as short as 30 mm[1052] and as long as 40 mm,[46] but the usual range of length reported in the literature is 31 to 38 mm.[28, 299, 894] In a more recent study, Sudo et al[1078] found the average length of the cartilaginous, junctional, and osseous portions from temporal bone specimens to be 24 mm, 3.0 mm, and 6 mm, respectively (i.e., total length of 33 mm) and forming a 42-degree angle with a parasagittal plane through the medial pterygoid plate.

In the adult, the eustachian tube begins in the nasopharynx and passes posteriorly and laterally through the petrous temporal bone. The tube does not take a straight course from the nasopharynx to the middle ear but rather a slowly curving inverted S course. Spilberg[1052] found that in adults the tube makes two curves from the tympanic cavity, arching downward and forward across the space between the anterior canal wall and the bony external auditory meatus in the condyle of the mandible. Before the pharyngeal orifice, it makes another slight curve downward and forward. Additional observations[1091] support Spilberg's data, although variability is great.

The nasopharyngeal end of the eustachian tube lies about 20 mm above the plane of the hard palate.[436] The cartilage protrudes into the nasopharynx and is known as the *torus tubarius* (see Fig. 25–5B). A thick layer of epithelium continuous with the soft tissue lining of the nasopharynx covers it.

Lumen of Tube

The osseous and cartilaginous portions of the eustachian tube lumen resemble two truncated cones attached at a *junctional* area. Their broadest ends represent the nasopharyngeal and tympanic orifices. The nasal orifice is 8.5 mm in height. This dimension decreases steadily to a minimum of 3.5 mm after the eustachian tube enters the petrous portion of the temporal bone. A 20-degree angle exists between the roof of the lumen and its floor. The sum of this angle with that formed by the cranial base and roof of the lumen accounts for the approximately 45-degree ascent the eustachian tube makes in its course from the nasopharynx to the middle ear (see Fig. 25–7).

The narrowest segment of the lumen of the tube is the *isthmus*. The isthmus is not at the junctional portion (i.e., where the cartilaginous and osseous portions meet) as formerly thought; it is within the cartilaginous part.[749, 1078] Three-dimensional measurements of the tube in temporal bone specimens by Sudo et al[1078] revealed the isthmus to be 21 mm from the pharyngeal orifice and 3 mm from the pharyngeal margin of the junctional portion, i.e., the most anterior margin of bone surrounding the tubal lumen. The reduced caliber of the lumen at the isthmus is a critical component of the physiologic protective function of the eustachian tube, i.e., the flask effect, in preventing nasopharyngeal secretions from entering the middle ear (see next section on Physiology, Pathophysiology, and Pathogenesis). However, any increase in the lumen at the isthmus impairs the protection of the middle ear due to *reflux*, *aspiration*, or *insufflation* of nasopharyngeal secretions into the middle ear. Sadé[960] found no difference in the calibers of the isthmus when comparing children with otitis media and those without. This finding lends support to the hypothesis that *functional* obstruction of the eustachian tube (i.e., failure of the opening mechanism) as opposed to anatomic (mechanical) obstruction of the tube is a cause of otitis media.[122]

Mucous Membrane of Tubal Lumen

The tubal lumen is lined with pseudostratified, columnar epithelium of the ciliated type, which sweeps material from the middle ear to the nasopharynx (Fig. 25–8). The mucosa is continuous with the lining of the tympanic cavity at its distal end and with the nasopharynx at its proximal end. Goblet cells are associated with these ciliated epithelial cells and account for about 20% of the cell population.[648] Tos and Bak-Pedersen[1133] studied temporal bones from premature and newborn infants, children, and adults who were free of signs of otitis media and made counts of 30,000 to 60,000 goblet cells in different portions of the eustachian tube, e.g., pharyngeal to tympanic ends and the lateral, medial, floor, and roof of the mucosa of the lumen. They found very low densities in all parts of the tube in premature infants, gradually increasing densities in the pharyngeal portions through childhood, and very high densities in the adult. Similar densi-

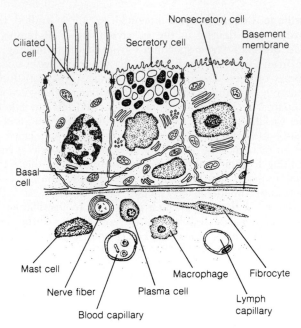

FIGURE 25–8. Mucosa of the middle ear. (Adapted from Klein JO, Daum RS. The Diagnosis and Management of the Patient with Otitis Media. Copyright Biomedical Information Corporation, New York, 1985.)

ties were reported between the lateral and medial walls and in the floor of the tube, but lower in the roof.

This is consistent with the findings reported by Sando et al,[971] who described more mucosal folds in the inferior half than in the superior half of all portions of the tube (i.e., pharyngeal, cartilaginous, isthmus, and osseous), a finding that statistically increased the mucosal margin in the floor compared to the roof. Copious ciliated cells, glands, and goblet cells were within the mucosa of the floor. From these findings they postulated that the superior portion of the lumen in the cartilaginous portion of the tube is probably involved in *ventilation* of the tube (i.e., pressure regulation) and the lower portion is related to the *clearance* function of the tube. These mucosal folds progressively decrease in the first 20 years of life.[1077]

Matsune et al[707] identified mucosa-associated lymphoid tissue (MALT) within the mucous membrane of the cartilaginous portion of the eustachian tube in human temporal bone specimens from adults with no evidence of middle-ear disease. These lymphoid follicles develop by extravasation of lymphocytes from the postcapillary high endothelial venule into mucosal inflammatory sites. They are more abundant in the osseous portion of the eustachian tube and middle ear when middle-ear infection has been present.

Cartilaginous Portion of Tube

The cartilaginous portion of the tube is angled in most cases 30 to 40 degrees to the transverse plane and 45 degrees to the sagittal plane.[436] The tube is closely attached to the base of the skull and is fitted to a sulcus tubae (i.e., sphenoid sulcus) between the greater wing of the sphenoid bone and the petrous portion of the tempo-

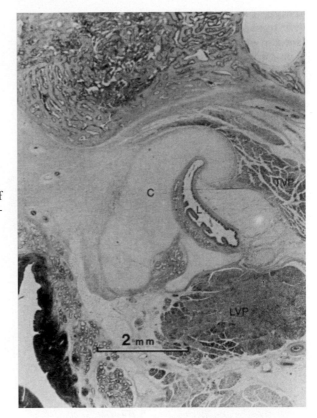

FIGURE 25–9. Midcartilaginous portion of the normal eustachian tube of an adult (vertical section). C, tubal cartilage; L, tubal lumen; LVP, levator veli palatini; TVP, tensor veli palatini. (Courtesy of I. Sando, M.D.)

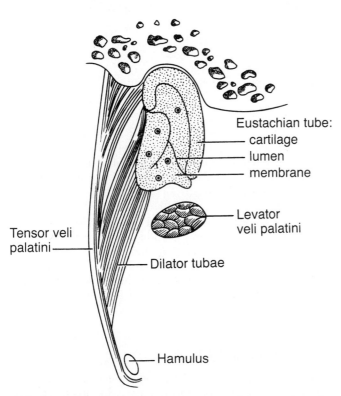

FIGURE 25–10. Schematic representation of a coronal section through the eustachian tube and its related musculature. Note that this section is from the posterior third of the cartilaginous portion of the tube and that the position of the hamulus is highly schematized to illustrate its relationship to the tensor veli palatini muscle. (From Bluestone CD, Klein JO. Otitis Media in Infants and Children, 3rd ed. Philadelphia, WB Saunders, 2001.)

ral bone (see Fig 25–5A). The cartilaginous part of the tube is firmly attached at its posterior end to the osseous orifice by fibrous bands and usually extends some distance (3 mm) into the osseous portion of the tube. At its inferomedial end, it is attached to a tubercle on the posterior edge of the medial pterygoid lamina.[28, 299, 436, 894, 934, 1093]

Cartilage Structure and Composition. The cartilage of the eustachian tube is intimately related to its functioning. Thus, function depends on cartilage structure, composition, and attachment to the cranial base and paratubal muscles (Fig. 25–9). The cartilage of the tube is shaped like an inverted J in cross section (Fig. 25–10). The cartilage has been described as being composed of a short lateral lamina and an elongated medial lamina. Some investigators describe two laminae, the medial and lateral,[704] but the cartilage is actually a dome-shaped structure with arms of different lengths. The lateral arm has a constant height. The medial arm, however, starts as a short structure and increases rapidly in height just posterior and lateral to where the cartilage attaches to the medial pterygoid plate.

Elastic fibers are in the cartilaginous portion of the tube. Guild[446] described a radial organization of elastic fibers around the dome of the cartilage, which suggests that motion of the lateral arm relative to the medial arm is possible. Matsune et al[705] found a rich, meshlike distribution of elastin along the luminal side of the intermediate portion (also called the *hinge* portion) between the medial and lateral laminae of the tubal cartilage. They later speculated that this acted to return the lateral lamina to its original position at rest following contraction of

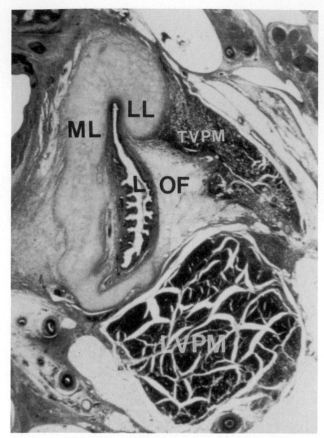
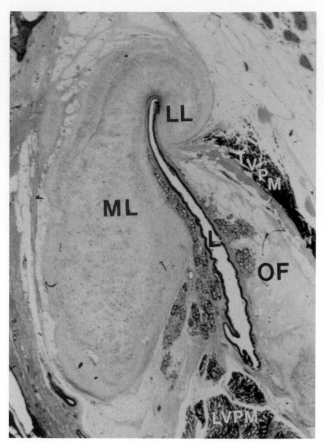

FIGURE 25–11. Photomicrographs of cross sections through the midcartilaginous portion of the eustachian tube of a 3-month-old girl (*left*) and a 34-year-old man (*right*) showing the developmental difference of Ostmann fat pad (OF) and size of the eustachian tube. L, lumen; LL, lateral lamina of the eustachian tube cartilage; LVPM, levator veli palatini muscle; ML, medial lamina of the eustachian tube cartilage; TVPM, tensor veli palatini muscle. (Courtesy of I. Sando, M.D.)

the tensor veli palatini muscle and dilatation of the upper half of the tube.[971] Also, as stated earlier, the elastin in the cartilage is less dense in the infant than in the adult.[705]

Cartilage mass increases from birth to puberty, and cartilage cell density is greater in infants.[1205] These differences may be related to the tube's relatively ineffective opening by the tensor veli palatini muscle in infants and young children compared with older children and adults. In the young, the cartilage likely does not provide adequate support during attempts at opening and may buckle (see next section, Physiology, Pathophysiology, and Pathogenesis).

Lateral Membranous Wall. The lateral membranous wall is closely associated with the eustachian tube lumen. This structure is not clearly delineated but is invoked in many descriptions of eustachian tube function. It is most clearly defined in the middle portion of the cartilaginous portion of the tube (see Fig. 25–9). Its medial boundary is the submucosa of the lumen. Laterally, a robust connective tissue layer is the insertion of the tensor veli palatini muscle. This fibrous lateral membrane is anchored superiorly to the inferior curvature of the lateral arm of the eustachian tube cartilage. The region between these two

boundaries is occupied by glandular tissue anteriorly and adipose tissue posteriorly. Most likely, forces from the tensor veli palatini muscle during contraction are passed to the lateral arm of the cartilage and not to the lateral submucosa of the lumen.

Ostmann Fat Pad. The Ostmann fat pad is the fat tissue located in the inferolateral portion of the eustachian tube and most likely aids in closing the tube.[621] As described before, the fat pad increases in volume after birth, primarily in height (associated with an increase in tubal height) but not in width, and thus makes a greater mass in the child (Fig. 25–11).[30]

Junctional Portion of Tube

Sudo et al[1078] have named the segment where the cartilaginous and osseous portions connect the *junctional* portion. They determined the length of this segment to be 3 mm. However, there is a gradual transition from the cartilaginous portion to the osseous portion; the lumen in the junctional portion increases from the proximal end (i.e., pharyngeal margin) to the distal end (i.e., the tympanic margin).

Osseous Portion of Tube

The osseous portion of the eustachian tube—also called the protympanic, aural, bony, or middle-ear portion—is patent at all times when the middle ear is healthy. In contrast, the cartilaginous portion is closed at rest and opens only during swallowing or when forced open, such as during the Valsalva maneuver. This segment of the tube lies completely within the petrous portion of the temporal bone and is directly continuous with the anterior wall of the superior portion of the middle ear. The juncture of the osseous portion of the tube and the epitympanum is 4 mm above the floor of the tympanic cavity (Fig. 25–12A).[436] This relationship is misrepresented in the more popular descriptions and depictions of the eustachian tube–middle ear juncture (too low in the mesotympanum) and is important in the functional clearance of middle-ear fluids.

The course of the osseous portion of the tube is linear anteromedially. It follows the petrous apex and deviates little from the horizontal plane. The lumen is roughly triangular and measures 2 to 3 mm vertically and 3 to 4 mm horizontally. The medial wall of the bony portion of the eustachian tube consists of two parts: posterolateral (labyrinthine) and anteromedial (carotid), whose size, shape, and relations depend on the position of the internal carotid artery.[975] The average thickness of the anteromedial portion is 1.5 to 3 mm and is absent in 2% of individuals, exposing the carotid artery. The aural orifice, an oval structure, lies above the floor of the middle-ear space and measures about 5 mm by 2 mm.[436] The medial wall of the osseous portion of the tube lies close to the carotid canal and the labyrinth. Savic and Djeric[975] found that in about two thirds of the specimens they examined, the carotid canal noticeably impinged on the osseous portion of the eustachian tube.

The mucosal lining of this portion of the eustachian tube is similar to that of the middle ear and includes both mucus-producing and ciliated cells.

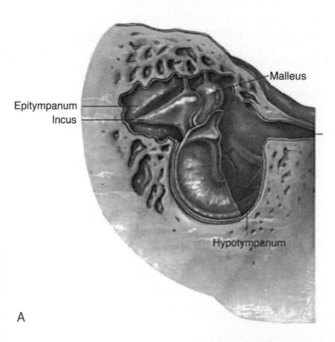

FIGURE 25–12. *A*, Anatomy of the osseous (i.e., protympanic, middle-ear end, aural) portion of the eustachian tube as viewed from the external auditory canal. Note that the orifice of the eustachian tube is relatively high in the middle ear. *B*, Sagitally rotated coronal view of the middle ear, the ossicles, and relationship to the inner ear. (From Bluestone CD, Klein JO. Otitis Media in Infants and Children, 3rd ed. Philadelphia, WB Saunders, 2001.)

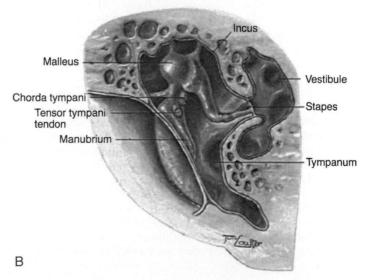

Muscles of the Tube

Four muscles are associated with the eustachian tube: the tensor veli palatini, the tensor tympani, the levator veli palatini, and the salpingopharyngeus. At one time or another, each has been directly or indirectly implicated in tubal function.[28, 430, 935]

The eustachian tube is passively closed at rest. It opens during swallowing, yawning, or sneezing, permitting equalization of middle-ear and atmospheric pressures. Most anatomic and physiologic evidence supports active dilatation induced either solely by the tensor veli palatini muscle[198, 502, 920] or with help from the levator veli palatini muscle.[892, 1093] Tubal closure has been attributed to passive reapproximation of the tube's walls by extrinsic forces that surrounding deformed tissues exert, by the recoil of elastic fibers within the tubal cartilage, or by both mechanisms. More recent experimental and clinical data suggest that, at least for certain abnormal populations, the closely applied internal pterygoid muscle may assist tubal closure by an increase in its mass within the pterygoid fossa. This increase applies medial pressure to the tensor veli palatini muscle and consequently to the lateral membranous wall of the eustachian tube[198, 303, 944] (see next section, Physiology, Pathophysiology, and Pathogenesis).

Tensor Veli Palatini. The tensor veli palatini muscle is composed of two fairly distinct bundles of muscle fibers, the tensor veli palatini and the *dilator tubae*, divided by a layer of fibroelastic tissue (see Fig. 25–10). The bundles lie mediolateral to the tube. The more lateral bundle (the tensor veli palatini proper) is of an inverted triangular design. Its origin is from the scaphoid fossa and from the greater wing of the sphenoid bone superior to the eustachian tube. The force the muscle exerts on this origin creates the lateral osseous ridge of the sulcus tubarius. The muscle descends anteriorly, laterally, and inferiorly to converge in a tendon that rounds the hamular process of the medial pterygoid lamina about an interposed bursa. This fiber group then inserts into the posterior border of the horizontal process of the palatine bone and into the palatine aponeurosis of the anterior portion of the velum (Fig. 25–13).

The dilator tubae is the medial bundle of the tensor veli palatini muscle and lies immediately adjacent to the lateral membranous wall of the eustachian tube. It was first described by Valsalva and subsequently confirmed by other anatomic dissections.[192, 430, 934] Its superior origin is in the posterior half of the fibrous lateral membranous wall of the cartilaginous eustachian tube. The fibers descend sharply to enter and blend with the fibers of the lateral bundle of the tensor veli palatini muscle. This inner bundle is primarily responsible for active dilatation of the tube. The angular relationship between the tensor veli palatini muscle and the cartilage varies in the infant but is relatively stable in the adult.[1092]

The dilator tubae of the tensor veli palatini muscle only inserts into the cartilaginous portion of the eustachian tube. (see Fig. 25–10) It is important for dilatation of the tube to equilibrate middle-ear pressure during swallowing. It is apparent that an inefficient tensor veli

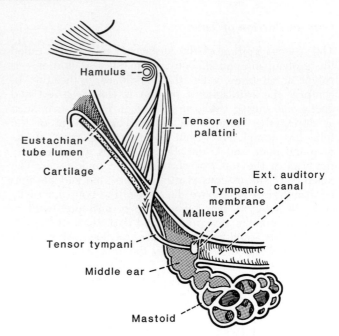

FIGURE 25–13. Diagrammatic representation of the tensor veli palatini muscle attachment along the lateral wall of the eustachian tube, its course around the hamulus of the pterygoid bone, and its attachment into the posterior margin of the hard palate.

palatini muscle will not effectively open the tube (i.e., the tube "won't open") (see next section, Physiology, Pathophysiology, and Pathogenesis).

Tensor Tympani. The more posterosuperior muscle fibers of the tensor veli palatini muscle lack an osseous origin and instead extend into the semicanal of the tensor tympani muscle. Here they receive a second muscle slip, which originates from the tubal cartilage and sphenoid bone. These muscle fibers converge in a tendon that rounds the cochleariform process and inserts into the manubrium of the malleus (Fig. 25–14). This arrangement gives a bipennate form to the tensor tympani muscle (see Fig. 25–13).[65, 672, 933] The tensor tympani muscle does not appear to be involved in active dilatation of the eustachian tube.[503] However, stretch receptors in the tympanic membrane may be related to modulation of the middle-ear pressure through the tensor tympani muscle, thereby affecting the tensor veli palatini in opening the eustachian tube (see later).[324, 747, 930]

Levator Veli Palatini. The levator veli palatini muscle arises from the inferior aspect of the petrous apex of the temporal bone. The fibers pass inferomedially, paralleling and lying beneath the tubal cartilage and luminal floor (see Fig. 25–5A and Fig. 25–11). In most instances, the interaction between the levator veli palatini muscle and the posterior half of the cartilaginous eustachian tube lumen is precluded by an extension of the medial arm of the cartilage. Near the nasopharyngeal end of the eustachian tube, where the cartilage is at its maximum height, the levator veli palatini lies lateral to its medial arm. The fibers of this muscle insert by fanning out and blending

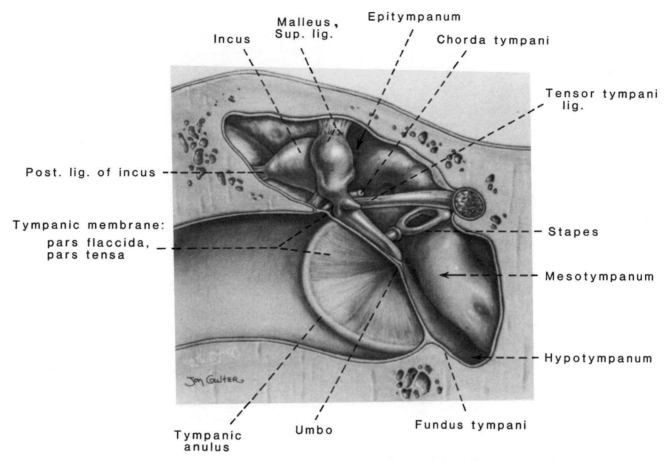

FIGURE 25–14. The tensor tympani inserts into the manubrium of the malleus as viewed from anterior to posterior in the middle ear.

with the dorsal surface of the soft palate.[436, 935] Most investigators deny a tubal origin for this muscle and believe that it is related to the tube only by loose connective tissue.[732, 1028] We assessed eustachian tube ventilatory function both before and after bilateral excision of the levator palatini muscle within the palate and found no change in any parameter of the testing.[196] The levator is not the primary dilator of the tube but probably adds to its support and contributes to its function by elevating the medial arm of the cartilage at the nasopharyngeal end of the eustachian tube.[1079, 1093]

Salpingopharyngeus. The salpingopharyngeus muscle arises from the medial and inferior borders of the tubal cartilage via muscular and tendinous fibers (see Fig. 25–5A). The muscle then courses inferoposteriorly to blend with the palatopharyngeal muscle.[436, 732] Rosen[938] examined 10 hemisected human heads and identified the muscle in 9 specimens. In all cases, there were few muscle fibers and they appeared to lack any ability to perform physiologically.

Innervation of Tube

The pharyngeal orifice of the eustachian tube is innervated by branches from the otic ganglion, the sphenopala-

tine nerve, and the pharyngeal plexus. The remainder of the tube receives its sensory innervation from the tympanic and the pharyngeal plexuses. The glossopharyngeal nerve probably plays the predominant role in tubal innervation. Sympathetic innervation of the tube depends on the sphenopalatine ganglion, the otic ganglion, paired glossopharyngeal nerves, the petrosal nerves, and the caroticotympanic nerve.[894] Mitchell[748] suggested that the parasympathetic nerve supply is derived from the tympanic branch of the glossopharyngeal nerve. Nathanson and Jackson[783] provided experimental evidence for a secondary parasympathetic innervation via the vidian nerve from the sphenopalatine ganglion. Innervation of the tensor veli palatini and tensor tympani muscles is from the ventromedial part of the ipsilateral trigeminal motor nucleus through the trigeminal nerve (mandibular division). The levator veli palatini muscle receives its innervation from the nucleus ambiguus through the vagus nerve.[324, 478, 531]

Blood Supply of Tube

Five arteries constitute the blood supply to the eustachian tube: the ascending palatine artery, the pharyngeal branch of the internal maxillary artery, the artery of the pterygoid canal, the ascending pharyngeal artery, and the middle meningeal artery. Venous drainage is via the pterygoid venous plexus.[436]

Lymphatics of Tube

An extensive lymph network is in the tunica propria of the submucosa of the eustachian tube, and it is more abundant in the cartilaginous portion than in the osseous portion. This network drains into either the retropharyngeal nodes medially or the deep cervical nodes laterally.[436] Early investigators[894] described a lymphoid mass within the tube of a 6-month-old infant. However, Wolff,[1196] in an examination of 250 subjects, and Aschan,[39] in a histologic study of 39 eustachian tubes, failed to find such a structure. Further, in a study of the developmental anatomy of the tubal system, Rood and Doyle[934] failed to find this lymphoid mass and concluded, with Wolff and Aschan, that this tubal tonsil was a rare pathologic abnormality.

Organs at the Proximal and Distal Ends of the Eustachian Tube

At its proximal end, the eustachian tube system consists of the nose, pharynx, and palate. At its distal end, it consists of the tube, middle ear, and mastoid gas cells (see Fig. 25–4).

Nose

The physiologic functions of the nose are an important part of a healthy eustachian tube system. Functions include humidifying, warming, and filtering gas—initially atmospheric air and then end-expiratory gas in the nasopharynx—supplied to the eustachian tube and then to the middle ear–mastoid. Patent nasal cavities are also important for physiologic functioning of the eustachian tube, since nasal obstruction may result in abnormal nasopharyngeal pressures during swallowing, i.e., Toynbee phenomenon. Unfortunately, little information is available concerning nasopharyngeal pressures in the infant (see next section, Physiology, Pathophysiology, and Pathogenesis). However, it is possible in infants, with their relatively small nasal cavities, that nasopharyngeal (and meso- and hypopharyngeal) pressures may be abnormal during certain activities, e.g., sucking on the nipple or pacifier, even when the nose is open.

Pharynx

The nasopharynx is involved in the eustachian tube system, and the meso- and hypopharynx may also be involved if there is abnormal anatomy or pathophysiology in this region. This is because pressures inferior to the palate can affect nasopharyngeal pressures during swallowing when nasal obstruction is present, as with the Toynbee phenomenon.[147] Also, when there is an overt cleft of the palate, or any velopharyngeal insufficiency, pressures in the entire pharynx may affect the eustachian tube (and middle ear–mastoid). In the adult, when nasal obstruction is absent and velopharyngeal closure is adequate, the

nasopharynx is the key part of the proximal end of the system. Pressures during swallowing should approximate ambient pressures.

Nasopharynx

The torus tubarius is a prominence on the lateral wall of the nasopharynx that protrudes into the nasopharynx (see Fig. 25–5B). Abundant soft tissue overlying the cartilage of the eustachian tube forms this prominence. Anterior to this is the triangularly shaped nasopharyngeal orifice of the tube. From the torus tubarius a raised ridge of mucous membrane descends vertically. This is the salpingopharyngeal fold. The adenoids, or pharyngeal tonsils, lie on the posterior wall and are composed of abundant lymphoid tissue. A variable depression within the mucous membrane, the pharyngeal bursa, is above the tonsils. Behind the torus tubarius is a deep pocket that extends the nasopharynx posteriorly along the medial border of the eustachian tube. This pocket, the fossa of Rosenmüller (see Fig. 25–5B), varies from 8 to 10 mm in height and from 3 to 10 mm in depth.[894] Adenoid tissue usually extends into this pocket and gives soft tissue support to the tube. Niemela et al[797] studied the dimensions of the nasopharynx in 238 school-aged children using radiographs and found that children with a relatively small nasopharynx had a higher incidence of recurrent otitis media than children with larger dimensions. The findings of this study were similar to one reported earlier by Maw et al.[712]

Palate

The structure and function of the palate should be normal within the eustachian tube system. Competent velopharyngeal closure during swallowing is important in maintaining the physiologic functions of the eustachian tube. The integrity of the tensor veli palatini muscle within the palate is important for efficient active opening of the tube during swallowing, since it is the only active dilator of the eustachian tube.

Fibers from the levator veli palatini muscle pass inferomedially, paralleling the tubal cartilage and lying within the vault of the tubal floor (see Fig. 25–5A). They fan out and blend with the dorsal surface of the soft palate. Loss of function of the levator veli palatini muscle does not impair normal function of the active opening mechanism of the eustachian tube.[196]

Middle Ear and Mastoid Gas Cells

The eustachian tube's primary physiologic function is to equilibrate gas pressure in the middle ear with ambient pressure to maintain normal compliance of the middle-ear structures for optimal hearing. Middle-ear abnormalities can affect the eustachian tube system. For example, a nonintact tympanic membrane can enhance liquid flow from the nasopharynx through a patent eustachian tube into the middle ear, i.e., reflux (see next section, Physiology, Pathophysiology, and Pathogenesis).

The middle ear and the eustachian tube are connected

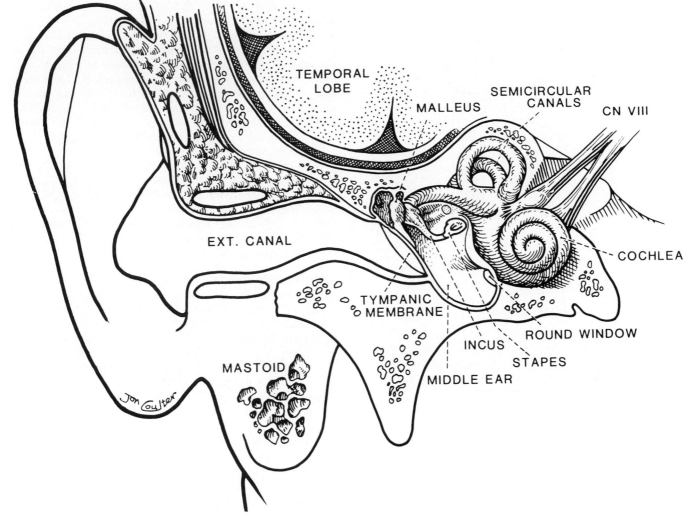

FIGURE 25–15. Illustration of the relationship of the middle ear to the external auditory canal and inner ear. (From Bluestone CD, Klein JO. Otitis Media in Infants and Children, 3rd ed. Philadelphia, WB Saunders, 2001.)

anatomically and are intimately associated in function. The promontory of the middle ear has a neural gas-regulating reflex arc with the function of the eustachian tube (see later discussion). The mastoid, with its system of interconnected cells, is also an important part of the eustachian tube–middle-ear system. No consensus exists concerning the function of these gas-filled cells. The most

likely possibility is that they provide a "surge tank" of gas to maintain a normally pressurized middle ear; or, the mastoid's mucosa provides transfer of gases between the mastoid gas cells and the middle ear and mucosal blood vessels, or both functions co-exist.

Middle Ear

The middle ear is an irregular, laterally compressed, gas-filled space lying within the petrous portion of the temporal bone between the external auditory canal and the inner ear (Fig. 25–15). This cavity can be considered to be divided into three parts superoinferiorly in relation to the tympanic membrane. The epitympanum, or attic, refers to that space lying above the superior border of the tympanic membrane. The mesotympanum lies opposite the membrane. The hypotympanum lies below the membrane. Within the middle ear are the ossicles, the stapes, the incus, and the malleus (Fig. 25–16). The volume of the middle ear is 1.5 times larger in the adult than in the infant, which is primarily due to progressive increase in

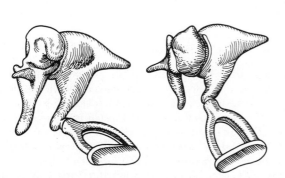

FIGURE 25–16. Middle-ear ossicles viewed from medial to lateral (*left*) and from above (*right*).

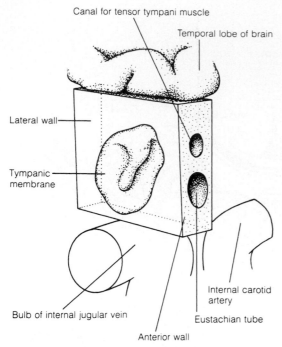

Canal for tensor tympani muscle

Temporal lobe of brain

Lateral wall

Tympanic membrane

Bulb of internal jugular vein

Anterior wall

Internal carotid artery

Eustachian tube

FIGURE 25–17. Relation of the middle ear to surrounding structures. (From Klein JO, Daum RS. The Diagnosis and Management of the Patient with Otitis Media. Copyright Biomedical Information Corporation, New York, 1985.)

height; the hypotympanum increases the most and the mesotympanum the least.[524] The vertical and anteroposterior diameters measure about 15 mm. The transverse diameter measures 4 mm at the epitympanum, 2 mm at the mesotympanum, and 6 mm at the hypotympanum.[430] Because of these dimensions, the middle ear has been termed a *cleft*, or *narrow box*.

Superiorly, the cavity is bounded by a thin plate of bone, the tegmen tympani. It extends forward to cover the semicanal of the tensor tympani muscle and posteriorly to cover the attic, thus isolating the middle ear from the middle cranial fossa (Fig. 25–17). Anteriorly, the floor of the middle-ear cavity is raised to become continuous with that of the bony portion of the eustachian tube. Superiorly and beneath the tegmen tympani is the cylindric semicanal for the tensor tympani muscle (see Fig. 25–14). It is separated from the eustachian tube by an upwardly concave thin bony septum, the cochleariform process. This process enters the middle ear along its superomedial margin to end just above the oval window. There, it flares laterally. This termination of the cochleariform process serves as a pulley about which the tendon of the tensor tympani muscle makes a right-angled turn to proceed laterally to its insertion on the muscular process of the malleus.

The middle ear is bounded medially by the lateral surface of the bone covering the labyrinth of the inner ear. A bulbous, hollowed prominence formed by the outward projection of the basal turn of the cochlea occupies the position between the oval and round windows. This structure, the promontory, is cross-hatched by the various branches of the tympanic plexus of nerves. The Jacobson nerve, a branch of the glossopharyngeal nerve, enters the

cavity through its floor, divides, and ramifies about the promontory to contribute to the plexus (Fig. 25–18). The tympanic plexus has connections to the ventral subnucleus of the ipsilateral nucleus of the solitary tract within the brain stem. This has been postulated to provide sensory input from middle-ear chemoreceptors, baroreceptors, or both, and is thus related to middle-ear ventilation.[324] It has also been postulated recently that middle-ear baroreceptors may be stimulated by stretch receptors in the tympanic membrane that respond to alterations in external ear canal pressure.[930]

The lateral wall of the middle ear is formed by the tympanic membrane, the tympanic ring, and a portion of the squamous temporal bone called the septum. The posterior border of the middle ear is demarcated by the anterior wall of the mastoid cavity and the pyramidal prominence and is connected to the mastoid antrum by the aditus-ad-antrum (see Fig. 25–4).

Tympanic Membrane. The tympanic membrane is the lateral wall of the mesotympanum. Its integrity is essential to a healthy eustachian tube–middle ear; for instance, a nonintact tympanic membrane can impair the tube's protective function, resulting in reflux of nasopharyngeal secretions. Conversely, abnormal function of the eustachian tube can adversely affect the tympanic membrane and cause, for example, atelectasis of the tympanic membrane–middle ear (see Chap. 26).

The tympanic membrane has areas with relatively high compliance, i.e., a lack of stiffness. This is related to the pathogenesis of retraction pockets and acquired cholesteatoma. Khanna and Tonndorf[584] used holography to show that the pars flaccida and the posterosuperior quadrant of the pars tensa are the most compliant areas (Fig. 25–19). Thus, extreme underpressures within the middle ear can cause these portions of the tympanic membrane to retract. This is the first stage of the development of a retraction pocket/cholesteatoma. The pars flaccida has high compliance due to its relatively thin medial fibrous layer and lack of an annulus. The posterosuperior portion is the most "floppy" quadrant of the pars tensa, since it has a relatively large surface area. When the middle ear is full of effusion, these two areas will become full, will eventually bulge laterally, and can rupture. The anterosuperior and anteroinferior quadrants of the tympanic membrane are relatively stiff and can also rupture.[537] The posterior portions are floppy and can either distend or retract with positive or negative middle-ear pressure, respectively.

Mastoid Gas-Cell System

The mastoid is that portion of the petrous temporal bone that lies posterior to the middle-ear cavity. In the adult, it extends exteriorly and interiorly, forming a process to which the sternocleidomastoid muscle is attached superficially. The mastoid is filled with a system of interconnected cells. The mastoid antrum is posterior, continuous with the epitympanum, and the largest of these gas-filled spaces (see Fig. 25–4). The antrum serves as a patent communication between the middle ear and the mastoid gas cells. In the infant, the mastoid process is small and

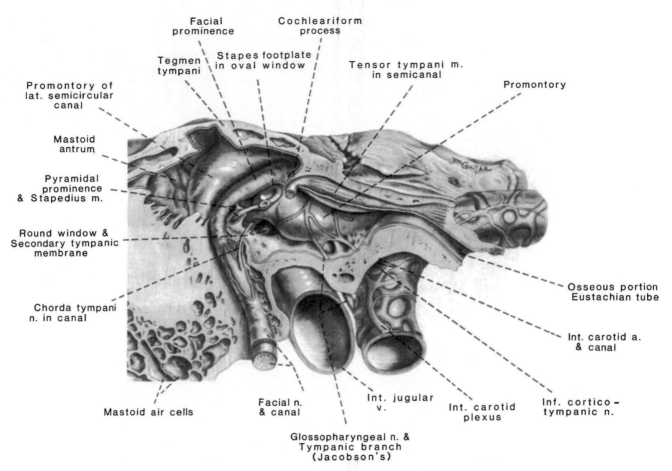

FIGURE 25–18. The innervation of the middle ear, as depicted from lateral to medial aspect.

the degree of pneumatization low. This small gas-cell system may be partly related to the susceptibility of infants to high negative middle-ear pressure and subsequently otitis media. Between 5 and 10 years of age, pneumatization is for the most part complete. It is estimated that mean volume of the mastoid gas cell system in the adult is 10.43 cm^3 (range, 6.24–20.52 cm^3).[846] Incomplete development of the mastoid gas-cell system has also been associated with frequent bouts of otitis media in infants and young children.

Mucous Membrane

The middle-ear and mastoid mucous membrane is continuous with that of the nasopharynx through the eustachian tube (see Fig. 25–8). This membrane covers all structures in the middle ear, including the ossicles, vessels, and nerves. Examining cells of the mucous membrane within the tympanic cavity reveals a gradual change from tall, columnar cells with interspersed goblet cells to shorter cuboidal cells at the posterior portion of the promontory and aditus-ad-antrum, antrum, and mastoid cells.

Innervation

Innervation of the tympanic cavity and its structures comes from the branches of the tympanic plexus of nerves. As described before, the Jacobson nerve, a branch of the glossopharyngeal nerve, enters the cavity through its floor, divides, and ramifies about the promontory to contribute to the plexus (see Fig. 25–17). Eden et al[324] have described the tympanic plexus as having neural connections to the ventral subnucleus of the ipsilateral nucleus of the solitary tract within the brain stem. This has been postulated to provide sensory input from middle-ear chemoreceptors, baroreceptors, or both and is thus related to middle-ear ventilation. In a later report from the same laboratory, a twofold increase in the average myelin thickness, and a greater than threefold increase in the ratio of myelinated to unmyelinated fibers of the tympanic nerve (the afferent limb of the neural circuit), was observed from the newborn to the adult cynomolgus monkey.[325]

Experiments in the same animal species have provided physiologic evidence that a neural arc exists between the middle ear and the eustachian tube.[1013] The investigators reported differences in eustachian tube ventilatory function when the middle-ear gas composition was altered. This can be explained by the presence of baroreceptors or chemoreceptors, or both, in the middle ear (see Physiology, Pathophysiology, and Pathogenesis). The finding of a feedback modulation of middle-ear pressure regulation and the possible immaturity of the mechanism in young animal models, if confirmed to be present in the human, might be able to explain the relatively inefficient tubal

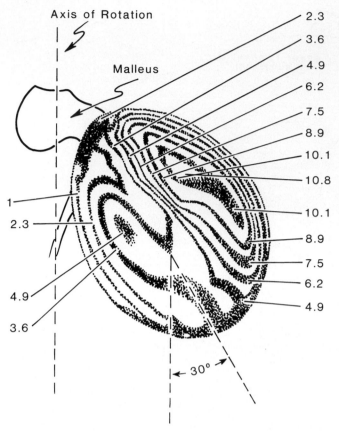

Axis of Rotation

Malleus

2.3
3.6
4.9
6.2
7.5
8.9
10.1
10.8
10.1
8.9
7.5
6.2
4.9

1
2.3
4.9
3.6

← 30° →

FIGURE 25–19. Time-averaged hologram of the tympanic membrane of a human cadaver taken at frequencies between 500 and 5000 Hz. The displacement pattern of the tympanic membrane starts to become more complex at about 3000 Hz posteriorly and at about 4000 Hz anteriorly as well. At 5000 Hz, the characteristic and relatively simple pattern of low-frequency response is almost lost. (From Tonndorf J, Khanna SM. Tympanic membrane vibrations in human cadaver ears studied by time-averaged holography. J Acoust Soc Am 52:1221, 1972.)

membrane that respond to alterations in external ear canal pressure.[930]

Sympathetic innervation to the plexus is provided by the superior and inferior caroticotympanic nerves and parasympathetic fibers by the smaller superficial petrosal nerve. Oyagi et al[820] described sympathetic innervation of the middle-ear mucosa as arising from the ipsilateral superior cervical ganglion and not the stellar ganglion. They also showed that parasympathetic fibers probably arise from the ipsilateral pterygopalatine ganglion.

Physiology, Pathophysiology, and Pathogenesis

Even though the etiology and pathogenesis of otitis media are multifactorial and include genetic, infectious, immunologic, allergic, environmental, and social factors (as discussed in other sections of this chapter), dysfunction of the eustachian tube plays an important role (Fig. 25–20). A functionally and structurally immature eustachian tube and an immature immune system are probably the most important factors related to the increased incidence of otitis media in infants and young children. A genetic predisposition is also critical in many infants and children.[210, 623] When they are exposed to upper respiratory tract infections, otitis media is a common complication.

The pathogenesis of otitis media is likely to have the following sequence of events in most children: The patient has an antecedent event (usually an upper respiratory tract viral infection) resulting in congestion of the respiratory mucosa of the nose, nasopharynx, and eustachian tube. Congestion of the mucosa in the eustachian tube obstructs the narrowest portion of the tube, the isthmus. This obstruction causes negative middle-ear pressure followed by a middle-ear effusion.[314, 761] The mucosal secretions of the middle ear have no way out and accumulate there. If the effusion is relatively asymptomatic, i.e., without the signs and symptoms of acute infection, it is termed *otitis media with effusion.*

Most patients with otitis media and related conditions have (or have had in the past) abnormal function of the eustachian tube that may cause secondary mucosal disease of the middle ear, such as inflammation.[146] Infection

ventilatory function in infants and young children. It was also postulated recently that middle-ear baroreceptors may be stimulated by stretch receptors in the tympanic

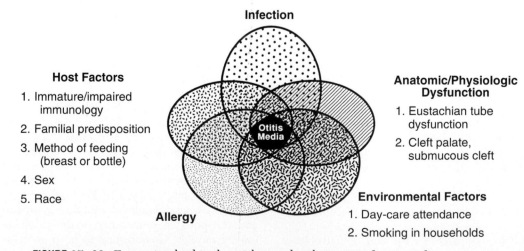

Infection

Host Factors

1. Immature/impaired immunology
2. Familial predisposition
3. Method of feeding (breast or bottle)
4. Sex
5. Race

Anatomic/Physiologic Dysfunction

1. Eustachian tube dysfunction
2. Cleft palate, submucous cleft

Otitis Media

Environmental Factors

1. Day-care attendance
2. Smoking in households

Allergy

FIGURE 25–20. Factors involved in the etiology and pathogenesis of otitis media.

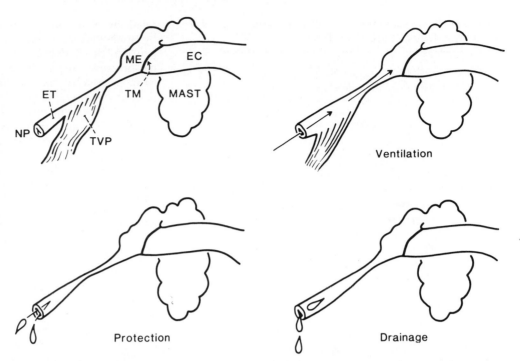

FIGURE 25–21. The eustachian tube–middle ear system. Note the three physiologic functions of the eustachian tube related to the middle ear. Note also that active dilation of the tube is by contraction of the tensor veli palatini muscle. EC, external canal; ET, eustachian tube; MAST, mastoid air cells; ME, middle ear; NP, nasopharynx; TM, tympanic membrane; TVP, tensor veli palatini muscle. (From Bluestone CD, Klein JO: Otitis Media in Infants and Children, 3rd ed. Philadelphia, WB Saunders, 2001, p 35.)

results from *reflux, aspiration,* or *insufflation* of nasopharyngeal bacteria up the eustachian tube and into the middle ear.[122] *Acute otitis media* is characterized by the signs and symptoms of acute infection—fever and otalgia.[177] Inflammation due to infection or allergy may also cause intrinsic mechanical obstruction of the eustachian tube.[2, 125, 178, 314, 390, 719] A much smaller number of patients may have primary mucosal disease of the middle ear as a result of allergy[305, 742] or, more rarely, an abnormality of cilia, such as in Kartagener syndrome.[378]

For children with recurrent episodes of acute otitis media or otitis media with effusion, anatomic or physiologic abnormality of the eustachian tube appears to be one of the most important factors. The child with such an underlying abnormality of the eustachian tube may be subject to recurrent episodes of otitis media or persistent fluid in the middle ear.

The hypothesis that abnormal function of the eustachian tube is the most important factor in the pathogenesis of middle-ear disease was first suggested more than 100 years ago by Politzer.[877] Later studies,[961, 999, 1080, 1226] however, suggested that otitis media was a disease primarily of the middle-ear mucous membrane and was caused by infection or allergic reactions in this tissue, rather than by dysfunction of the eustachian tube. Related to this hypothesis is the concept that nasopharyngeal infection spreads up the mucosa of the eustachian tube. Studies conducted at the Children's Hospital of Pittsburgh, which involved humans as well as animals, in turn have shown that the "hydrops ex vacuo" theory originally proposed by Politzer most likely represents the primary pathogenic mechanism.[15, 178, 208, 311]

In this section, we review our current understanding of the physiology (function) of the middle-ear system, including the nasal cavities, eustachian tube, middle ear, and mastoid gas cells. We also present a new, simplified, and evidence-based classification of the pathophysiology

(dysfunction) of the eustachian tube. Finally, we describe our current understanding of the pathogenesis of acute otitis media and otitis media with effusion.[132a] Other features of physiology, pathophysiology, and pathogenesis are discussed in sections on Anatomy of the Eustachian Tube System, Epidemiology, Microbiology, and Immunology.

Physiology of Eustachian Tube within Its System

As shown in the previous section on Anatomy, the eustachian tube is not just a tube but an organ that is part of a system of organs. The nasal cavities, palate, and pharynx are at the proximal end of the eustachian tube, and the middle ear and mastoid gas cell system are at its distal end. Thus, the functions of the eustachian tube must be assessed within this system, since the normal eustachian tube functions most effectively when the system at either end is also normal.

Three physiologic functions are attributed to the eustachian tube: (1) *pressure regulation* (ventilation) of the middle ear that equilibrates gas pressure in the middle ear with atmospheric pressure; (2) *protection* of the middle ear from nasopharyngeal sound pressure and secretions; and (3) *clearance* (drainage) of secretions produced within the middle ear into the nasopharynx (Fig. 25–21). In this section the pathophysiology of the eustachian tube within its system is presented. Table 25–12 shows a classification of the physiology and pathophysiology of the eustachian tube system.

Pressure Regulation (Ventilation) Function

Of the three physiologic functions of the eustachian tube, the most important is *regulation of pressure* (ventilation) within the middle ear, since hearing is optimal when middle-ear gas pressure is relatively the same as air pressure in the external auditory canal, i.e., tympanic mem-

TABLE 25–12. Classification of Physiology and Pathophysiology of Eustachian Tube

Physiology (Functions)

Pressure regulation (ventilatory function)
Protection
  Anatomic
  Immunologic and mucociliary defense
Clearance
  Mucociliary clearance
  Muscular clearance (pumping action)
Surface tension factors

Pathophysiology (Dysfunctions)

Impairment of pressure regulation
  Anatomic obstruction
    Intraluminal
    Periluminal
    Peritubal
  Failure of opening mechanism (functional obstruction)
Loss of protective function
  Abnormal patency
  Short tube
  Abnormal gas pressures
    Intratympanic
    Nasopharyngeal
  Nonintact middle ear and mastoid
Impairment of clearance
  Mucociliary
  Muscular

brane and middle-ear compliance is optimal. Normally, the intermittent active opening of the eustachian tube, which happens when the tensor veli palatini muscle contracts during swallowing, maintains nearly ambient pressures in the middle ear (see section on Anatomy).[198, 208, 502, 920] The gas in the nasopharynx that ventilates the middle ear is 79.2% nitrogen, 14.7% oxygen, 1% argon, and 5.1% carbon dioxide. This is the same composition as that of the expiratory phase of the respiratory cycle (Table 25–13).[489]

Under physiologic conditions, fluctuations in ambient pressure are bidirectional (i.e., either to or from the middle ear), relatively small, and not readily appreciated.[306, 313] These fluctuations reflect the rise and fall in barometric pressures associated with changing weather conditions and elevation, or both. However, changes in middle-ear pressure show mass directionality, can achieve appreciable magnitudes, and can result in pathologic changes. This is because the middle-ear and mastoid gas cell system is a relatively rigid (i.e., noncollapsible) gas pocket surrounded by a mucous membrane in which gases are exchanged between the middle-ear space and the mucosa. Differential pressure exceeds 54 mm Hg between the middle-ear space at atmospheric pressure and the microcirculation in the mucous membrane. This represents a diffusion-driven gradient from the middle-ear cavity to the mucosa that can produce an underpressure (relative to ambient pressure) in the middle ear of more than 600 mm H_2O during equilibration.

Some investigators have postulated that gases can pass to and from the middle ear through the tympanic membrane. Doyle et al[301] recently reported experiments revealing that there is no O_2 and CO_2 transtympanic membrane exchange from the external ear canal into the middle ear. There is an exchange of N_2, although not at physiologic rates.

In an effort to describe normal eustachian tube function by using the microflow technique inside a pressure chamber, Elner et al,[333] in a classic study, evaluated 102 adults with intact tympanic membranes and no apparent history of otologic disorders (Table 25–14). Patients were divided into four groups according to their abilities to equilibrate static relative positive and negative pressures of 100 mm H_2O in the middle ear. Patients in group 1 were able to completely equilibrate pressure differences across the tympanic membrane. Those in group 2 equilibrated positive pressure, but a small residual negative pressure remained in the middle ear. Subjects in group 3 equilibrated only relative positive pressure with a small residual remaining, but no negative pressure. Those in group 4 were incapable of equilibrating any pressure. These data probably indicate decreased stiffness (increased compliance) of the eustachian tube in the subjects in groups 2, 3, and 4 compared with those in group 1. This study also showed that 95% of normal adults could equilibrate an applied positive pressure and that 93% could equilibrate applied negative pressure to some extent by active swallowing. However, 28% of the subjects could not completely equilibrate either applied positive pressure or applied negative pressure, or both.

Children have less efficient eustachian tube function than adults. Using a pressure chamber, children and adults who were considered otologically normal were evaluated in Sweden. The study revealed that 35.8% of the children could not equilibrate applied negative intratympanic pressure by swallowing, and only 5% of the

TABLE 25–13. Gas Composition and Pressure in the Nasopharynx, Middle Ear, and Microcirculation of the Middle-Ear Mucosa Compared with Air (mmHg)

	Air	Nasopharynx (Mixed Expiratory Air)	Middle-Ear Cavity	Microcirculation of Middle-Ear Cavity
P_{N_2}	596	Lower (566)	Higher (621)	Lower (573)
P_{O_2}	158	Low (120)	Lower (46)	Lowest (40)
P_{CO_2}	0.3	High (27)	Higher (46)	Higher (46)
P_{H_2O}	5.7	Higher (47)	Higher (47)	Higher (47)

Adapted from Ostfeld EJ, Silberberg A. Gas composition and pressure in the middle ear: a model for the physiological steady state. Laryngoscope 101:297, 1991; and Felding JU, Rasmussen JB, Lildholdt T. Gas composition of the normal and the ventilated middle ear cavity. Scand J Clin Lab Invest 47(Suppl 186):31, 1987. Published by Blackwell Science Ltd., Oxford, United Kingdom.

TABLE 25–14. Eustachian Tube Function Test Results of 102 Otologically Normal Adults with Intact Tympanic Membranes

Tubal Function Group	Number of Subjects (%)	Equilibration		Toynbee-Positive, n/n (%)	Valsalva-Positive, n/n (%)
		Pressure + 100 mm H₂O	Pressure − 100 mm H₂O		
1	74 (72)	Yes	Yes	67/69 (97)	63/73 (86)
2	21 (21)	Yes	Residual	7/18 (39)	16/21 (76)
3	2 (2)	Residual	No	0/2 (0)	2/2 (100)
4	5 (5)	No	No	0/5 (0)	5/5 (85)
Total				74/94 (79)	86/101 (85)

Adapted from Elner A, Ingelstedt S, Ivarsson A. The normal function of the eustachian tube: a study of 102 cases. Acta Otolaryngol (Stockh) 72:320, 1971.

adults were unable to perform this function.[184] Children between 3 and 6 years of age had worse function than those 7 to 12 years of age. In this study and a subsequent one reported by the same research team, children who had middle-ear negative pressure evaluated by tympanometry had poor function.[186]

These studies show that even in apparently otologically healthy children, eustachian tube function is not as good as in adults. However, eustachian tube function does improve with advancing age, consistent with the decreasing incidence of otitis media from infancy to adolescence.[185] Since there are several differences in the anatomy of the child and adult eustachian tube, we also find functional differences in the ability to open the eustachian tube during swallowing activity to equilibrate pressure differences between the middle ear and the nasopharynx (see previous section, Anatomy).

Another explanation for finding high negative middle-ear pressure in children is the possibility that some individuals who are habitual "sniffers" actually create underpressure within the middle ear by this act.[356] However, this mechanism is uncommon in children.

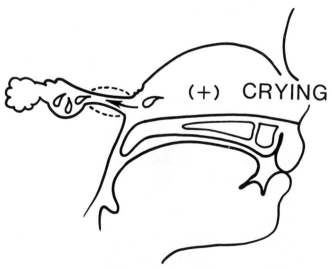

FIGURE 25–22. Since the eustachian tube is short and floppy in infants, crying most likely insufflates nasopharyngeal gas into the middle ear to compensate for their inefficient tubal opening mechanism. During periods of upper respiratory tract infection, however, nasopharyngeal secretions as well as viruses and bacteria may also be insufflated into the middle ear. (From Bluestone CD, Klein JO. Otitis Media in Infants and Children, 3rd ed. Philadelphia, WB Saunders, 2001, p 37.)

Otoscopy and tympanometry have shown that many children with no apparent middle-ear disease have high negative middle-ear pressure. An inefficient active opening of the tube in children probably explains this frequent finding.[75] Brooks[173] studied the parameters of middle-ear pressure using tympanometry and determined that the resting middle-ear pressure in a large group of apparently normal children was between 0 and −175 mm H₂O. However, pressures outside this range have been reported as normal for large populations of apparently asymptomatic children.[539] High negative middle-ear pressure does not necessarily indicate disease; it may indicate only physiologic obstruction of the eustachian tube. Ventilation occurs, but only after the nasopharynx–middle-ear pressure gradient reaches an opening pressure. It has been suggested that these children probably should be considered at risk for middle-ear problems until more is learned about the normal and abnormal physiology of the eustachian tube.[123] In normal adults, Alberti and Kristensen[6] obtained resting middle-ear pressures of between 50 and −50 mm H₂O. Again, a pressure outside this range does not necessarily mean the patient has ear disease.

Because infants have an inefficient active opening mechanism, they most likely compensate in some way to regulate pressure within the middle ear. One possible compensatory mechanism is crying, and high positive pressure is apparent when some infants with no middle-ear effusion cry during otoscopy and tympanometry. This mechanism could also explain why infants cry when they are descending in an airplane; they are most likely *insufflating* air into their middle ears (Fig. 25–22).

The physiologic role of the *mastoid air cell system* in relation to the middle ear is not fully understood. However, the current thinking is that either it acts as a surge tank of gas (air) available to the relatively smaller middle-ear cavity, or the mucosa lining the mastoid gas cells are the primary area for the transfer of gases between the middle ear and mastoid gas cells and the microcirculation, or both functions coexist. During intervals of eustachian tube dysfunction, compliance of the tympanic membrane and ossicular chain (which would affect hearing) would not be decreased due to reduced middle-ear gas pressure, as there is a reservoir of gas in the mastoid air cells. If this thinking is correct, then a small mastoid air cell system could be detrimental to the middle ear if the eustachian tube is dysfunctional. Likewise, a small mastoid cellular system would allow for a less efficient gas exchange between the middle-ear cleft and the microcirculation of the mucosa.[72] But, Doyle,[306] based on experimental results, rejects the hypothesis that the mastoid gas cell system has a pressure-regulating system, arguing rather that it is a gas reserve.

Posture appears to have an effect on eustachian tube function. The mean volume of air passing through the eustachian tube was found to be reduced by one third when the body was elevated 20 degrees to the horizontal, and by two thirds when in the horizontal position.[526] This reduced function with change in body position was found to be the result of venous engorgement of the eustachian tube.[546]

A *seasonal variation* in eustachian tube function occurs in children.[76] Children who had tympanostomy tubes inserted for recurrent or chronic otitis media with effusion and were evaluated using serial inflation-deflation studies had better eustachian tube function in the summer and fall than in the winter and spring.

Protective Function

The eustachian tube system's protective function is what helps maintain a healthy middle ear. The eustachian tube system helps protect the middle ear and mastoid gas cell system in two ways: (1) through its functional anatomy and (2) through the immunologic and mucociliary defense of its mucous membrane lining.[560] Protection of the middle ear from abnormal nasopharyngeal sound pressures and secretions depends on the normal structure and function of the eustachian tube and the ability of the middle-ear and mastoid gas cell system to maintain a *gas cushion*. In addition, the proximal end of the system (nasal cavities, palate, and pharynx) should have normal anatomy and physiologic gas pressures. The middle-ear-mastoid is also protected by the respiratory epithelium of the eustachian tube lumen through its local immunologic defense and its mucociliary defense, i.e., clearance. An immunoreactive pulmonary surfactant protein that is thought to facilitate the clearance of microbial pathogens from the alveolus of the lung has been isolated from the middle ears of animals and humans and is hypothesized to have the same function in the ear.[323, 611, 1211]

Studies using radiographic techniques have been used to determine the protective function of the tube.[136, 146, 154, 1194] In these studies, radiopaque material was instilled into the nose and nasopharynx of children who had otitis media then compared to those who were otologically healthy (see later). In the physiologic state, radiopaque material entered the nasopharyngeal end of the eustachian tube during swallowing activity but did not enter the middle ear. By contrast, the dye did reflux into the middle ear in some patients who had middle-ear disease, especially during closed-nose swallowing.

These radiographic studies in children revealed the following sequence of events: At rest, the normal eustachian tube is collapsed and the tubal lumen is closed. This prevents liquid—and abnormal nasopharyngeal sound pressures—from entering the nasopharyngeal end of the tube. During swallowing, when the proximal end (i.e., the cartilaginous portion) opens, liquid can enter this part of the tube, but does not go into the middle ear because of the tube's narrow midportion, the isthmus.

Flask Model of Protective Function

To better understand this anatomic concept, think of the entire eustachian tube–middle-ear system as a flask with a long, narrow neck. The mouth of the flask represents the nasopharyngeal end, the narrow neck represents the isthmus, and the bulbous portion represents the middle ear and mastoid gas cell system (Fig. 25–23).[122, 146] Fluid flow through the neck depends on the pressure at either end, the radius and length of the neck, and the viscosity of the liquid. When a small amount of liquid is instilled into the mouth of the flask, the liquid flow stops somewhere in the narrow neck owing to capillarity within the neck and the relative positive air pressure that develops in the chamber of the flask. This basic geometric design is considered critical for the protective function of the eustachian tube–middle-ear system.

Clearance Function

Clearance (drainage) of secretions from the middle ear into the nasopharynx is provided by two physiologic methods: (1) *mucociliary clearance* and (2) *muscular clearance*. The mucociliary system of the eustachian tube and some areas of the middle-ear mucous membrane clear secretions from the middle ear, and the pumping action of the eustachian tube during closing provides the other method.

Investigators have studied mucociliary clearance by instilling radiopaque material into the middle ear of children with nonintact tympanic membranes, when the material entered the middle ear (intact tympanic membrane) from the nasopharynx, and following insertion of foreign material into the middle ear of animal models.[8, 146, 154, 1061] Such material flows toward the middle-ear portion of the eustachian tube and out of the tube. This movement is related to ciliary activity in the eustachian tube and parts of the middle ear. Ciliated cells in the middle ear are increasingly more active as they become more distal to the opening of the tube.[810]

The *pumping action* of the eustachian tube to drain

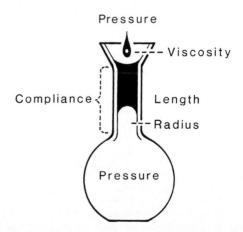

FIGURE 25–23. Flask model of the eustachian tube–middle ear–mastoid air cell system. The mouth of the flask represents the nasopharyngeal end of the eustachian tube, the neck is the cartilaginous portion of the tube, and the bulbous portion represents the middle ear and mastoid air cells (see text).

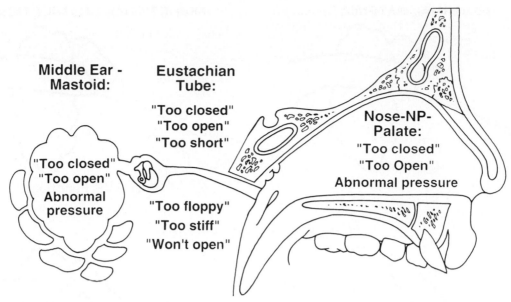

Middle Ear - Mastoid:

Eustachian Tube:
"Too closed"
"Too open"
"Too short"

"Too closed"
"Too open"
Abnormal pressure

"Too floppy"
"Too stiff"
"Won't open"

Nose-NP-Palate:
"Too closed"
"Too Open"
Abnormal pressure

FIGURE 25–24. Evidence-based, simplified classification of eustachian tube dysfunction. The eustachian tube system can be either "too closed" or "too open," or there is "too much" or "too little" pressure at either end. (From Bluestone CD, Klein JO. Otitis Media in Infants and Children, 3rd ed. Philadelphia, WB Saunders, 2001, p 40.)

middle-ear fluid was first reported by Honjo and colleagues.[501, 505] In experiments in both animal models and humans, the eustachian tube was shown during closing to "pump" radiographic contrast material that had been instilled into the middle ear out of the middle ear and into the nasopharynx. The passive closing process of the eustachian tube begins at the middle-ear end of the tube and progresses toward the nasopharyngeal end, thus pumping out secretions.

Surface Tension Factors

Other factors may be involved in maintaining normal eustachian tube function. One of these factors may involve the surface tension within the lumen of the eustachian tube. Birkin and Brookler[116] isolated surface tension–lowering substances from the washings of eustachian tubes of dogs. They postulated that these substances could enhance eustachian tube functions, similar to surfactant in the lung. Rapport et al[912] described a similar substance and demonstrated the effect that washing out the eustachian tube had on the opening pressure in the experimental animal. Other investigators have also demonstrated a surfactant-like phospholipid in the middle ear and eustachian tube of animals and humans.[451, 568, 1189] In a recent study in gerbils, Fornadley and Burns[380] produced middle-ear effusions by injecting killed *Streptococcus pneumoniae* into the middle ear through the tympanic membrane to increase the opening pressure of the eustachian tube. When the investigators introduced exogenous surfactant, the opening pressure dropped. Ramet et al[909] recently reported a surfactant protein-A gene locus associated with recurrent otitis media.

Pathophysiology of Eustachian Tube within Its System

The dysfunctional eustachian tube can be described as follows: *"too closed," "won't open," "too floppy," "too open," "too short," "too stiff."* Or, the system can be described as *"too closed"* or *"too open,"* or as having *"too much" or "too little"* pressure at either end of the system (Fig. 25–24).[132] More precisely, the pathophysiology can be classified into (1) impairment of pressure regulation; (2) loss of protective function; and (3) impairment of clearance. Figure 25–25 depicts some of the types of eustachian tube dysfunction, which are described in more detail in the following sections.

Impairment of Pressure Regulation

Impairment of pressure regulation within the middle ear (and mastoid) can be due to either anatomic obstruction of the eustachian tube (the tube is "too closed") or failure of the opening mechanism of the eustachian tube (the tube "won't open").

Anatomic Obstruction

Anatomic (i.e., mechanical) obstruction of the eustachian tube can occur in the cartilaginous or osseous portion of the tube or at either end of the system, regardless of the status of the structure and function of the eustachian tube itself. When an anatomic obstruction involves the tube it can be intraluminal, periluminal, or peritubal (the eustachian tube is "too closed"). Obstruction of the lumen or within the periluminal tissues (i.e., intrinsic obstruction) can be due to inflammation secondary to infection

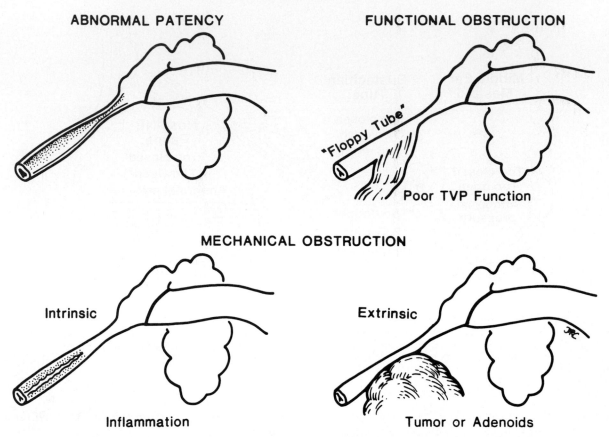

FIGURE 25–25. Some of the dysfunctions of the eustachian tube. The tube can be either abnormally patent or obstructed. When obstruction is present, it may be due to either failure of the opening mechanism (functional) or anatomic (mechanical); the latter condition may be due to either intrinsic or extrinsic causes. (From Bluestone CD, Klein JO. Otitis Media in Infants and Children, 3rd ed. Philadelphia, WB Saunders, 2001, p 40.)

or allergy.[125, 178, 390, 719] Congenital or acquired stenosis of the eustachian tube has also been diagnosed in adults but is a rare finding in children.[564] Peritubal obstruction of the cartilaginous portion of the tube (i.e., *extrinsic* obstruction) could be the result of compression caused by a tumor or an adenoid mass.[124, 154, 180, 583, 1199]

Anatomic obstruction may be present at the middle-ear end of the tube (the system at the distal end of the eustachian tube is "too closed"). This type of obstruction is usually due to acute or chronic inflammation of the mucosal lining and may also be associated with polyps or a cholesteatoma due to middle-ear disease. Likewise, at the proximal end of the system—in the nasopharynx—the tubal orifice can be anatomically obstructed even when the eustachian tube itself is patent and functions normally. Such an obstruction can be caused by a variety of factors, including adenoids, a foreign body (e.g., packing), or a tumor; the nasopharynx is "too closed."

Failure of Opening Mechanism ("Functional Obstruction")

One of the most common types of eustachian tube dysfunction is when the lumen of the cartilaginous portion of the eustachian tube fails to open during swallowing activity (the eustachian tube "won't open"). This may be caused by (1) persistent collapse of the eustachian tube due to increased tubal compliance (i.e., lack of stiffness, or the tube is "too floppy"); (2) an inefficient active opening mechanism; or (3) both defects coexist. This condition has also been termed *functional obstruction* of the eustachian tube: The tube is not anatomically (i.e., mechanically) obstructed, but it is functionally obstructed. This type of obstruction was first described in infants with unrepaired palatal clefts who had had chronic otitis media with effusion.[136] Failure of the opening mechanism of the eustachian tube is common in infants and younger children without cleft palate or history of middle-ear disease but is more common in children with middle-ear disease.[121, 127, 146, 186, 1063]

The eustachian tube's failure to open can be attributable to persistent collapse of the tubal cartilage, since there is less cartilage in infants than in older children and adults. Cartilage cell density also decreases with advancing age and can affect the stiffness of the tubal cartilage in the infant and young child.[964, 1205] If the tubal cartilage lacks stiffness (the tube is "too floppy") the lumen may not open when the tensor veli palatini muscle contracts. Also, the density of elastin in the cartilage is less in the infant, and the Ostmann fat pad is smaller in volume in

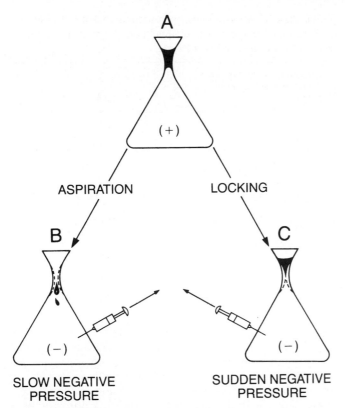

FIGURE 25–26. The flask model of the middle-ear system for fluid flow through a flask with a compliant neck. *A*, Fluid stopped in the neck of the flask. *B*, Effect of negative pressure applied slowly to the bottom of the flask. *C*, Effect of negative pressure applied suddenly to the bottom of the flask. (From Bluestone CD, Klein JO. Otitis Media in Infants and Children, 3rd ed. Philadelphia, WB Saunders, 2001, p 42.)

the infant than in the adult (see previous section, Anatomy).[30, 705]

Failure of the eustachian tube's opening mechanism may also be due to an inefficient tensor veli palatini muscle, which is related to the effect of age on the craniofacial base. The angle of a child's tube is different from the angle of the adult's tube. In the adult, the tube is inclined approximately 45 degrees related to the horizontal plane. In infants, this inclination is only 10 degrees.[894] Some investigators think that this difference in the angle is related to possible clearance problems in children, but this hypothesis has not been confirmed. What is more likely is that this difference in angulation affects the function of the active opening mechanism (i.e., tensor veli palatini muscle contraction). Swarts and Rood[1092] found that the angular relationship between the tensor veli palatini muscle and the cartilage varies in the infant but is relatively stable in the adult (see previous section, Anatomy).

One way the eustachian tube becomes *functionally* obstructed is when sudden high negative pressure develops at either end of the eustachian tube system. This is graphically demonstrated by the flask model (see Fig. 25–23). One of the major differences between a flask with a rigid neck and a biologic tube, such as the eustachian tube, is that the isthmus (neck) of the human tube is

compliant. The effect of applied negative pressure in a flask with a compliant neck is shown in Figure 25–26. Flow of fluid—shown as a liquid for graphic purposes—through the neck does not occur until negative pressure is slowly applied to the bottom of the flask. However, if the negative pressure is applied suddenly, temporary locking of the compliant neck prevents the liquid from flowing. This is called the *locking phenomenon* of the eustachian tube. Therefore, the speed with which the negative pressure is applied and the compliance in such a system is a critical factor in whether the tube becomes functionally obstructed. Clinically, gas may be aspirated into the middle ear, since negative middle-ear pressure develops slowly as gas is absorbed by the middle-ear mucous membrane. If negative middle-ear pressure is applied suddenly (during rapid alternations in atmospheric pressure, such as when an airplane descends, with diving in water, especially scuba diving, or during an attempt to test the ventilatory function of the eustachian tube), the tube can lock, preventing the flow of air (see later in this section).

Loss of Protective Function

The eustachian tube system can lose its protective function for the following reasons: (1) because the lumen of the tube is abnormally patent (the tube is "too open"); (2) because the tube is relatively short (the tube is "too short"); (3) because abnormal gas pressures develop at either end of the tubal system; or (4) because there is a nonintact middle ear, e.g., perforation (or tympanostomy tube) of the tympanic membrane resulting in a loss of the middle-ear gas cushion (the tube is "too open" at the middle-ear end of the eustachian tube system).

Abnormal Patency

The eustachian tube lumen may be abnormally open, and, in the extreme, it is open even at rest. This is called an abnormally patent, or *patulous*, eustachian tube; it is "too open." Lesser degrees of abnormal patency result in a *semipatulous* tube that is closed at rest but has a lumen that has low resistance to the flow of gas or liquids compared to the normal tube.[144] Increased patency of the tube may be due to abnormal tube geometry or to a decrease in the peritubal pressure that can occur after weight loss or as a result of periluminal factors.[1207]

The flask model is illustrative when the eustachian tube lumen is too open. When compared to a flask with a narrow neck, reflux of liquid into the body of the flask occurs if the neck is excessively wide. Increasing the radius of the flask neck increases fluid flow. This is analogous to an abnormally patent human eustachian tube in which there is free flow of air and nasopharyngeal secretions from the nasopharynx into the middle ear. The result is *reflux otitis media*.

The eustachian tube may be abnormally patent even when the caliber of the lumen appears normal when collapsed at rest. It can also be functionally hyperpatent, making it less protective of the middle ear. Because the cartilaginous portion of the eustachian tube is *distensible* (compliant), fluid (gas or liquid) can be forced into the middle ear by abnormally high positive nasopharyngeal pressure, which can occur during nose blowing, with the Valsalva maneuver, or during closed-nose swallowing, i.e., the *Toynbee phenomenon* (see later). The ability to insufflate the middle ear during these activities depends on the amount of positive pressure developed in the nasopharynx and the degree of compliance (lack of stiffness) of the tube. Since the eustachian tube has been found to be highly compliant (the tube is "too floppy") in infants and young children, this increase in distensibility of the tube may result in abnormal patency, especially when there is high nasopharyngeal pressure, possibly during crying (see Fig. 25–22). A highly distensible tube can easily permit nasopharyngeal secretions to be *insufflated* into the middle ear, as radiographic studies in infants with middle-ear disease have demonstrated.[136, 146]

We can use the flask model to illustrate this phenomenon if the narrow portion of the flask's neck is compliant, making it more consistent with the human eustachian tube. Applying positive pressure at the mouth of a flask with a compliant neck will distend the neck and enhance fluid—gas and liquid—flow into the vessel. Thus, less positive pressure is needed to insufflate liquid into the vessel. In humans, insufflating nasopharyngeal secretions into the middle ear occurs more readily if the eustachian tube is abnormally distensible (has increased compliance).

In teenagers and adults, the patulous tube has been found to be "too stiff," compared with normal tubal compliance,[967] which recently has been shown to be associated with chronic middle-ear inflammation.[1140] A patulous eustachian tube usually permits gas to flow readily from the nasopharynx into the middle ear, effectively regulating middle-ear pressure. However, unwanted secretions from the nasopharynx can more readily gain access, i.e., *reflux*, into the middle ear when the tube is abnormally patent. Certain special populations have been found to have patulous or semipatulous eustachian tubes, including American Indians and patients who have Down syndrome and middle-ear disease.[77, 1188] Chronic suppurative otitis media is a common disease in certain special populations around the world, including the Australian Aborigines, North American Inuits, and American Indians.[133]

Failure of the eustachian tube's passive closing mechanism (the tube is "too open") has been postulated to be related to sniff-induced middle-ear disease (see later).[356]

Short Tube

One of the most important structural differences of the eustachian tube between infants or young children and older children or adults is the length of the tube. The tube is shorter in children younger than 7 years of age (the tube is "too short") (see previous section, Anatomy).[964] Certain special populations may also have shorter tubes. Infants and young children with cleft palate have eustachian tubes that are statistically shorter than the tubes of age-matched control subjects younger than 6 years (Table 25–15). The tube is also shorter in children with Down syndrome.[964] The shorter the tube, the more likely it is that secretions can reflux into the middle ear.

TABLE 25–15. Abnormalities of Eustachian Tube Anatomy in Extended Temporal Bone Specimens from Infants and Young Children with Cleft Palate

Abnormality Compared with Specimens without Cleft Palate	Study
Length of tube shorter	Sadler-Kimes et al[964] Siegel et al[1022]
Angle between cartilage and TVP larger	Sadler-Kimes et al[964]
Cartilage cell density greater	Shibahara and Sando[1009]
Ratio of lateral and medial laminae area of cartilage smaller	Matsune et al[704] Takasaki et al[1101]
Curvature of lumen less	Matsune et al[704]
Elastin at hinge portion of cartilage less	Matsune et al[705]
Insertion ratio of TVP to cartilage less	Matsune et al[706]

TVP, tensor veli palatini.

(An analogy can be made to the length of the urethra: females of all ages have more urinary tract infections than males, since the urethra is shorter in the female.) This may be one explanation for the frequent occurrence of troublesome otorrhea in infants and young children, especially those with a cleft palate, Down syndrome, or a nonintact tympanic membrane (there is a perforation or a tympanostomy tube is in place). Cranial anatomy may also play a role in the length of the eustachian tube. Todd[1130] has postulated from studies in cadavers that the longer the cranial base, the longer the eustachian tube, resulting in less middle-ear disease.

The effect of a short eustachian tube is graphically illustrated in Figure 25–27. A flask with a short neck would not be as protective as a flask with a long neck. Accordingly, the tube that is "too short" is more likely to reflux secretions from the nasopharynx into the middle ear than a tube that is longer. Since infants have a

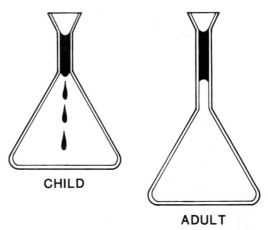

FIGURE 25–27. Flask model used to show how the shorter length of the eustachian tube can adversely affect the protective function in the child, as compared with the case in the adult. (From Bluestone CD, Klein JO. Otitis Media in Infants and Children, 3rd ed. Philadelphia, WB Saunders, 2001, p 43.)

shorter eustachian tube than adults, reflux is more likely in the baby. A tube that is "too short" can be included in the classification of being "too open," since secretions from the nasopharynx can more easily enter the middle ear than when a tube is of normal length.

Abnormal Gas Pressures

Loss of the tube's protective function can also occur when unphysiologic pressures develop at either end of the eustachian tube system. At the distal end of the system, high negative middle-ear pressure, secondary to obstruction of the eustachian tube that is anatomic (common during a viral upper respiratory tract infection) or due to a failure of the active opening, or both, may develop and result in aspiration of nasopharyngeal secretions into the middle ear. A chinchilla model of this process has been established (W.J. Doyle, Ph.D., unpublished data, 1989).

Loss of the tube's protective function can also occur when high positive nasopharyngeal pressures develop at the proximal end of the eustachian tube system. This abnormally high pressure, from blowing the nose, crying in the infant, or when nasal/nasopharyngeal obstruction is present, can cause nasopharyngeal secretions to be insufflated into the middle ear. An animal model has been developed in which high positive nasopharyngeal pressure produced by Politzer's technique can insufflate nasopharyngeal liquids into the middle ear (W.J. Doyle, Ph.D., unpublished data, 1990). Also, middle-ear underpressures have been recorded in infants during bottle feeding, with conventional nonventilated bottles, which was presumable due to high negative nasopharyngeal pressures generated during the feeding.[174]

Swallowing when the nasal cavities, nasopharynx, or both, are obstructed (due to inflammation or enlarged adenoids) results in an initial positive nasopharyngeal gas pressure followed by a negative pressure phase (Fig. 25–28). These pressures are produced in the meso- and hypopharynx during swallowing activity and are reflected in the nasopharynx during closed-nose swallowing. When the tube is pliant, positive nasopharyngeal pressure might insufflate infected secretions into the middle ear, especially when the middle ear has high negative pressure. With negative nasopharyngeal pressure, a pliant tube could be prevented from opening and could be further obstructed functionally. The effect of closed-nose swallowing has been termed the *Toynbee phenomenon*.[121] Other investigators have reported this phenomenon in the human,[549, 1115] and a ferret animal model of complete nasal obstruction resulted in persistent high positive middle-ear pressure, most likely secondary to insufflation of air into the middle ear during swallowing activity.[179] Rapid alterations in ambient pressures, which can occur during swimming, diving, airplane flying, and hypobaric pressure treatments, can also result in aspiration or insufflation of nasopharyngeal secretions.

Figure 25–29 uses the flask model to show the effect of these unphysiologic pressures at either end of the eustachian tube system. When negative pressure ("too little" pressure) is applied to the bottom of the flask, liquid is aspirated into the vessel. In the clinical situation, high negative middle-ear air pressure can cause nasopharyngeal secretions to be aspirated into the middle ear. When positive pressure ("too much" pressure) is applied to the mouth of the flask, liquid is insufflated into the vessel. Nose blowing, crying, closed-nose swallowing, ascent in an airplane, or scuba diving could create high positive nasopharyngeal pressure related to middle-ear pressure and result in a similar condition in the human system.

Nonintact Middle Ear and Mastoid

Nasopharyngeal secretions cannot enter the middle ear when the structure of the eustachian tube is normal because of the cushion of gas within an intact middle-ear and mastoid gas cell system. When there is a perforation of the tympanic membrane (or a tympanostomy tube is in place) or, in the extreme condition, when a radical mastoidectomy is present (the eardrum is absent and the middle ear, mastoid, and ear canal communicate, forming a single cavity), the gas pocket (cushion) is lost, allowing secretions from the nasopharynx to reflux into the middle ear.[127, 146] Thus, even though the anatomy and function of the tube itself is normal, the system at its distal end is defective (the tube is "too open"). This concept is important when the surgeon is considering repairing a perforation of the tympanic membrane or removing a retained tympanostomy tube (see section on Management).

Using the flask model, Figure 25–29 illustrates how liquid can reflux into the vessel if there is a hole in the bulbous portion of the flask. This prevents the creation of the slight positive pressure in the bottom of the flask that deters reflux and thus the middle ear and mastoid physiologic gas cushion is lost. This hole is analogous to a perforation of the tympanic membrane or the presence of

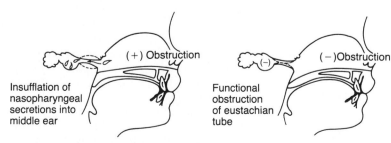

FIGURE 25–28. When the nose or nasopharynx is obstructed, unphysiologic pressures can develop in the nasopharynx and adversely affect the eustachian tube and middle ear, which is termed the *Toynbee phenomenon*. (From Bluestone CD, Klein JO. Otitis Media in Infants and Children, 3rd ed. Philadelphia, WB Saunders, 2001, p 44.)

POSITIVE PHASE   NEGATIVE PHASE

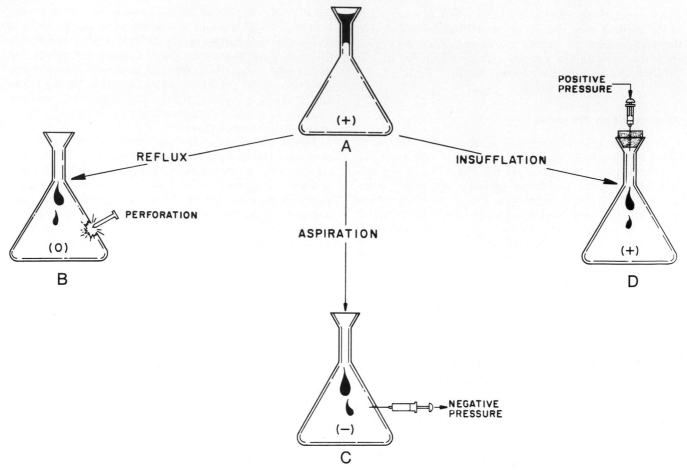

FIGURE 25–29. The flask model of the middle-ear system for fluid flow. *A*, Model of normal function. *B*, Effect of perforation. *C*, Effect of negative pressure on the bottom of the flask. *D*, Effect of positive pressure on the mouth of the flask (see text). (From Bluestone CD, Klein JO. Otitis Media in Infants and Children, 3rd ed. Philadelphia, WB Saunders, 2001, p 45.)

a tympanostomy tube, both of which can allow reflux of nasopharyngeal secretions because the middle ear and mastoid air cushion is lost. Similarly, following a radical mastoidectomy, a patent eustachian tube could cause troublesome otorrhea.[127]

Impairment of Clearance Function

Clearance (drainage) of secretions from the middle ear and eustachian tube can be adversely affected in several ways. Ohashi et al[809] conducted studies in guinea pigs and demonstrated that bacteria, their toxins, and irradiation can impair ciliary function. Park et al[844] demonstrated that influenza A virus alters the ciliary activity and dye transport function in the eustachian tube of the chinchilla. Rhee et al[919] reported that platelet-activating factor, an inflammatory mediator induced by infection, impairs ciliary clearance in the eustachian tube. Allergic response probably does not impair ciliary motility but may alter the mucus blanket in the eustachian tube.[811] Most investigators consider an impaired clearance function to be related to failure to resolve middle-ear effusions and not the primary cause of the disease.[757] How-

ever, patients with ciliary dysmotility in their upper respiratory tract mucous membrane have been observed to have chronic middle-ear effusions.[1012] Also, the tube's pumping action is most likely ineffective when its opening mechanism is inadequate, and this function has been demonstrated to be impaired when negative pressure is in the middle ear.[801, 1098]

If the physiologic clearance system—mucociliary and pumping action—is impaired, retained liquid is not likely to come out because of the negative pressure that develops within the middle ear and mastoid gas cell system. This is because the liquid moves even by gravity toward the eustachian tube and into the nasopharynx. This movement can be shown graphically using the flask model. Figure 25–30 shows certain aspects of fluid flow from the middle ear and eustachian tube into the nasopharynx by inverting the flask of the model. In this case, the liquid trapped in the bulbous portion of the flask does not flow out of the vessel because of the relative negative pressure that develops inside the chamber. However, if a hole is made in the vessel, the liquid drains out of the flask because the suction is broken. Clinically, these conditions occur in cases of middle-ear effusion, i.e., pressure

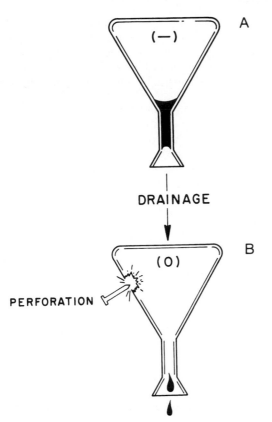

FIGURE 25–30. The flask model of the middle-ear system for fluid flow from an inverted flask. *A,* Fluid trapped by relative negative pressure in the chamber. *B,* Effect of perforation of the chamber. (From Bluestone CD, Klein JO. Otitis Media in Infants and Children, 3rd ed. Philadelphia, WB Saunders, 2001, p 46.)

is relieved when the tympanic membrane ruptures spontaneously or by myringotomy. Inflating air into the flask could also relieve the pressure, possibly explaining the frequent success of the Politzer or Valsalva method in clearing a middle-ear effusion (see section on Management).

Even though there are several known mechanisms of impairment of the clearance function, in general this dysfunction can be included in the simplified classification as being related to the tube being "too closed."

Dysfunction Related to Cleft Palate

Otitis media is universally present in infants with an unrepaired cleft palate.[835, 1071] Palate repair appears to improve middle-ear status, but middle-ear disease nonetheless often continues or recurs even afterwards.[304, 834] Studies suggest failure of the tube's opening mechanism in the infants with an unrepaired cleft palate as the primary cause of dysfunction.[136, 147, 304] As described earlier, histopathologic temporal bone studies have confirmed that the eustachian tube of cleft palate patients is not anatomically obstructed, giving credence to a failure of the opening mechanism as the underlying defect, i.e., functional as opposed to anatomic obstruction. Other anatomic findings, such as the abnormal cartilage and lumen, insertion

ratio of the tensor veli palatini muscle into the cartilage, deficient attachment of the tensor veli palatini muscle into the lateral lamina of the cartilage, and deficient elastin at the hinge portion of the cartilage, most likely explains the functional obstruction identified by radiographic and manometric eustachian tube function tests (see Table 25–15).[591, 704, 706, 1009, 1101] Also, the craniofacial skeleton is abnormal in children with cleft palate, which may influence eustachian tube function, development of otitis media with effusion, and the hearing loss that is associated with the middle-ear effusion.[205, 575] Animals whose palates had been surgically split also developed middle-ear effusion.[304, 308, 804]

From these studies in humans and animals, it appears that the high incidence of otitis media in children with cleft palate is related to a failure of the tube's opening mechanism and that the tube is functionally obstructed (the tube "won't open"). It may also be related to the deficient length of the eustachian tube, as a short tube may permit nasopharyngeal secretions to enter the middle ear, causing troublesome otorrhea. If infants with an intact palate are able to inflate their middle ears during crying as a physiologic compensatory mechanism for their ineffective active tubal opening, then infants with an unrepaired cleft palate have an additional handicap (the proximal end of the eustachian tube system is "too open").

Children with cleft palate have middle-ear disease characterized by either persistent or recurrent high negative middle-ear pressure, effusion, or both. Cholesteatoma is a frequent sequela. However, this is not the case in American Indians, in whom the eustachian tube has been shown to be hyperpatent (i.e., to have low tubal resistance).

Patients with a submucous cleft of the palate appear to have the same risk of developing middle-ear disease as those with an overt cleft. In addition, a bifid uvula has been associated with a high incidence of otitis media.[1103] Both conditions are probably associated with the same pathogenic mechanism for otitis media that is found in patients with overt cleft palates (i.e., functional obstruction of the eustachian tube).

Dysfunction Related to Allergy

Allergy is thought to be one of the etiologic factors in otitis media because otitis media occurs frequently in allergic individuals.[316] The mechanism by which allergy might cause otitis media is hypothetical and controversial.[104, 756] Figure 25–31 illustrates allergy's role in the etiology and pathogenesis of otitis media by one or more of the following mechanisms: (1) the middle-ear mucosa functioning as a "shock (target) organ"; (2) inflammatory swelling of the eustachian tube mucosa; (3) inflammatory obstruction of the nose; (4) aspiration of bacteria-laden allergic nasopharyngeal secretions into the middle-ear cavity.[134] Doyle[311] has also proposed another possible mechanism. This hypothesis is based on the possible increase in circulating inflammatory mediators from local allergic reactions in the mucosa of the nose or stomach, which in turn could alter the middle-ear mucosal perme-

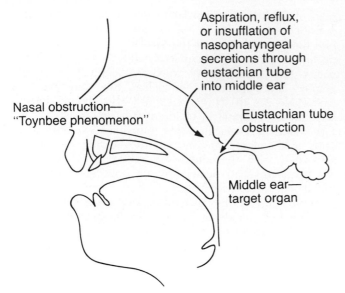

Nasal obstruction—
"Toynbee phenomenon"

Aspiration, reflux,
or insufflation of
nasopharyngeal
secretions through
eustachian tube
into middle ear

Eustachian tube
obstruction

Middle ear—
target organ

FIGURE 25–31. Allergy may affect the eustachian tube and middle ear by four hypothetical mechanisms, which could result in middle-ear disease. (From Bluestone CD, Klein JO. Otitis Media in Infants and Children, 3rd ed. Philadelphia, WB Saunders, 2001, p 47.)

inflammatory response by eosinophils, neutrophils, and mast cells in the middle ear and found a difference between atopic and nonatopic individuals, which led to their conclusion that the middle-ear mucosa is capable of an allergic response, similar to other portions of the respiratory tract.

Studies at the Children's Hospital of Pittsburgh involving adult volunteers demonstrated a relationship between intranasal antigen challenge, allergic rhinitis, and eustachian tube obstruction.[2, 307, 390] Table 25–17 summarizes studies that demonstrated a relationship among intranasal challenge with allergens, virus, and mediators in volunteers who did and did not have allergic rhinitis, and the effect on their nasal and eustachian tube function.[2, 307, 390, 1035, 1036, 1068] None of these studies produced otitis media in the volunteers and none of the subjects had preexisting eustachian tube dysfunction. It is possible that repeated challenge with antigen over a prolonged period of time would cause individuals who are hypersensitive to the specific antigen and who also have poor eustachian tube function to develop middle-ear effusion. It seems reasonable that children with signs and symptoms of upper respiratory allergy may have otitis media as a result of the allergic condition.

ability and result in altered gas exchange. Ohashi et al[811] found that allergic responses did not impair mucociliary activity but could adversely affect the structure of the eustachian tube's mucus blanket. More recently, investigators from Finland reported a higher incidence of recurrent otitis media in children who experienced cow's milk allergy in infancy.[554]

Bernstein et al[104] provided evidence that the eustachian tube may be adversely affected by allergy, as opposed to the middle ear as a target organ. They investigated the role of IgE-mediated hypersensitivity in 100 children with recurrent otitis media. The children were divided into nonallergic and allergic groups based on their history and physical examination findings, prick testing results for selected antigens, total IgE, and specific IgE radioallergosorbent testing. Following aspiration of the children's middle ears and testing for IgE, the authors concluded that 35% of the 100 children may have had IgE-mediated allergy as a cause of their effusion, and in 8% of the children the middle ear was a possible target organ. In the other 27%, they postulated that the eustachian tube might have been the target organ (Table 25–16). More recently, Hurst and Venge[518] assessed the

Other Causes of Eustachian Tube Dysfunction

Eustachian tube dysfunction has also been associated with deviation of the nasal septum (the tube is "too closed" at the proximal end of the system); trauma induced by nasogastric and nasal endotracheal tubes (the tube is "too closed"); trauma to the palate, pterygoid bone, or tensor veli palatini muscle (the tube "won't open"); injury to the mandibular branch of the trigeminal nerve (the tube "won't open"); and trauma associated with surgical procedures, such as palatal or maxillary resection for tumor (the tube "won't open" or is "too open" at the proximal end of the system).[733, 734, 777, 856, 1134, 1171] Benign or malignant neoplastic disease that invades the palate, pterygoid bone, or tensor veli palatini muscle can also cause the opening mechanism of the tube to fail (the tube "won't open"), causing otitis media.[777, 1095, 1183, 1206]

Since a cleft of the palate can functionally obstruct the eustachian tube, any child with a craniofacial malformation that has an associated cleft of the palate will have recurrent and persistent otitis media. A common example is Robin sequence. However, children with craniofacial anomalies that do not include an overt cleft of the palate

TABLE 25–16. Summary of 100 Allergic and Nonallergic Children with Recurrent Otitis Media

Group	Possible Target Organ		Probably Not Target Organs
	Middle Ear	*Eustachian Tube*	
Allergic	8	27	0
Nonallergic	0	0	65
Total	8	27	65

Adapted from Bernstein, JM, Lee, J, Conboy, K, et al.: Further observations on the role of IgE-mediated hypersensitivity in recurrent otitis media with effusion. Otolaryngol. Head Neck Surg. 93:611–615, 1985.

TABLE 25–17. Effect of Nasal Challenge on Nasal and Eustachian Tube Function*

Nasal Provocation	Nasal Function		Eustachian Tube Function	
	Normal	*Allergic*	*Normal*	*Allergic*
Allergens (pollens, mite)	0	+	0	+
Virus	+	+	+	+
Mediators				
Histamine	+	+	0	+
Prostaglandin	+	+	0	+
Methacholine	+	+	0	0

+, adverse effect; 0, little effect.
* Results of studies at the Children's Hospital of Pittsburgh.

also have an increased incidence of middle-ear disease. Eustachian tube dysfunction has been described in children with Down syndrome and otitis media.[1188] Even though there have been no reports of formal eustachian tube function studies in individuals with other disorders, such as Turner's or Apert's syndrome or Crouzon's disease, eustachian tube dysfunction is the most likely cause of ear disease in these patients. Indeed, patients with chromosomal aberrations have abnormal eustachian tube anatomy,[750, 752] as well as those who have oculoauriculovertebral spectrum.[750, 752] Also, presumably, a defect related to the abnormal craniofacial complex, most often at the base of the skull, influences the relationship between the eustachian tube and its associated anatomy.[576] Other syndromes associated with a high rate of otitis media and hearing loss, such as has been recently observed in the velocardiofacial syndrome,[918] may also have abnormal function of the eustachian tube as the origin of the middle-ear disease.

Patients with dentofacial abnormalities often have otitis media or develop middle-ear disease as a result of these abnormalities. Recently, dental overbite has been associated with otitis media in children.[723] Correction of the defect to relieve the eustachian tube dysfunction is indicated.

Some individuals, but rarely children, are habitual "sniffers" and actually create underpressure within the middle ear by this act.[356] In a study from Japan, Sakakihara et al[967] evaluated 17 subjects, with a mean age of 16 years, who had sniff-induced otitis media and found that their eustachian tubes were excessively patent (the tube is "too open") with poor active opening mechanisms (the tube "won't open").

Evidence-Based, Simplified Classification of Eustachian Tube Dysfunction

As described earlier, we now have enough evidence from assessments of human temporal bones, experiments in animals, and clinical studies to simplify the classification of the pathophysiology of the eustachian tube system. This classification can be helpful in describing these abnormalities to patients and parents. Simply stated, dysfunction of the eustachian tube within its system can be summarized as follows: the tubal system is either "too closed" or "too open," or "too much" or "too little pressure" is present at either end (see Fig. 25–24).

Eustachian Tube Function Testing

Before the section on the Role of Eustachian Tube in Pathogenesis of Otitis Media is presented, the methods of testing the eustachian tube are described so that the studies that provide the evidence can be better understood.

Methods to assess the ventilatory function of the system are readily available to the clinician and should be performed when indicated (described later). The ventilatory function is the most important of the three functions, since adequate hearing depends on equal air pressure on both sides of the tympanic membrane being maintained. In addition, impairment of the ventilatory function can result not only in hearing loss but also in otitis media.

Before the patient is examined, the presence of certain signs and symptoms may indicate whether eustachian tube dysfunction is present. Conductive hearing loss, otalgia, otorrhea, tinnitus, or vertigo may be present with this disorder.

Otoscopy

Visually inspecting the tympanic membrane is one of the simplest and oldest ways to assess how the eustachian tube functions. The appearance of a middle-ear effusion or the presence of high negative middle-ear pressure, or both, determined by a pneumatic otoscope,[150] is presumptive evidence of eustachian tube dysfunction, but the type of impairment, such as functional or mechanical obstruction, and the degree of abnormality cannot be determined by this method. Moreover, a normal-appearing tympanic membrane is not evidence of a normally functioning eustachian tube. For example, a patulous or semipatulous eustachian tube may be present when the tympanic membrane appears to be normal. In addition, the presence of one or more of the complications or sequelae of otitis media (such as a perforation or atelectasis that can be seen through an otoscope) may not correlate with dysfunction of the eustachian tube at the time of the examination, since eustachian tube function may improve with growth and development.

Nasopharyngoscopy and Endoscopy of the Eustachian Tube

Indirect mirror examination of the nasopharyngeal end of the eustachian tube is also an old but still important part of the clinical assessment of a patient with middle-ear disease. For instance, a neoplasm in the fossa of Rosenmüller may be diagnosed by this simple technique. The development of endoscopic instruments has greatly improved the accuracy of this type of examination. Not only can certain aspects of the structure of the eustachian tube be determined with the aid of currently available instruments, but some investigators have been able to assess eustachian tube function.[330, 875, 1076, 1099]

Tympanometry

Using an admittance instrument to obtain a tympanogram is an excellent way of determining the status of the tympanic membrane–middle-ear system, and it can be helpful in assessing eustachian tube function.[120] The presence of a middle-ear effusion or high negative middle-ear pressure determined by this method usually indicates impaired eustachian tube function. However, unlike the otoscopic evaluation, tympanometry is an objective way of determining the degree of middle-ear negative pressure. Unfortunately, assessing the abnormality of values of negative pressure is not so simple: high negative pressure may be present in some patients, especially children, who are asymptomatic and who have relatively good hearing. In others, symptoms such as hearing loss, otalgia, vertigo, and tinnitus may be associated with modest degrees of negative pressure or even with normal middle-ear pressures. The middle-ear air pressure may depend on the time of day, season of the year, or condition of the other parts of the system, such as the presence of an upper respiratory tract infection. For instance, a young child with a common cold may have transitory high negative middle-ear pressure while he or she has the cold but may be otherwise otologically normal.[207] The clinician making the decision as to whether high negative pressure is abnormal or is only a physiologic variation should take into consideration the presence or absence of signs and symptoms of middle-ear disease. If severe atelectasis or adhesive otitis media of the tympanic membrane–middle-ear system is present, the tympanogram may not be a reliable indicator of the actual pressure within the middle ear.

Therefore, a resting pressure that is highly negative is associated with some degree of eustachian tube obstruction, but the presence of normal middle-ear pressure does not necessarily indicate normal eustachian tube function; a normal tympanogram is obtained when the eustachian tube is patulous.

Manometry

The pump-manometer system of the electroacoustic impedance bridge is usually adequate to assess eustachian tube function clinically when the tympanic membrane is not intact. However, owing to the limitations of the manometric systems of all of the commercially available instruments, a controlled syringe and manometer (a water manometer will suffice) should be available when these limitations are exceeded (e.g., when eustachian tube opening pressure exceeds +400 to +600 mm H_2O).

Methods of Assessing Eustachian Tube Function in the Clinical Setting

Classical Tests of Tubal Patency

Valsalva and Politzer developed methods to assess eustachian tube patency (see also section on Management). When the tympanic membrane is intact and the middle ear inflates following the execution of one of these techniques, then the tube is not totally mechanically obstructed. Likewise, if the tympanic membrane is not intact, passage of air into the middle ear indicates patency of the tube. When the tympanic membrane is intact, the assessment is more objective with a tympanogram. When the tympanic membrane is not intact, the assessment is more objective with a manometric observation on the impedance instrument. However, inflation of the eustachian tube and middle ear from the nasopharynx end of the system by one of these classic methods is an assessment only of tubal patency, not of function, and failure to inflate the middle ear does not necessarily indicate a lack of patency of the eustachian tube.

Elner et al[333] reported that 86% of 100 otologically normal adults could perform the Valsalva test. In young children, the Valsalva test is usually more difficult to perform than the Politzer test. However, in a study by Bluestone et al,[129] six of seven children who had a traumatic perforation but who were otherwise otologically "normal" could perform the Valsalva test, but only 11 of 28 children who had a retraction pocket or a cholesteatoma could do so. The Valsalva and Politzer tests may be more beneficial as management options in selected patients than they are as methods to assess tubal function, although there is controversy about the efficacy of this procedure for treatment of middle-ear effusion.[219, 1057]

Toynbee Test

One of the oldest and still one of the best tests of eustachian tube function is the Toynbee test (Fig. 25–32). Test results are usually considered positive when an alteration in middle-ear pressure results. More specifically, if negative pressure (even transitory in the absence of a patulous tube) develops in the middle ear during closed-nose swallowing, the eustachian tube function can most likely be considered normal. When the tympanic membrane is intact, the presence of negative middle-ear pressure must be determined by pneumatic otoscopy or, more accurately, by obtaining a tympanogram before and immediately following the test (Fig. 25–33). When the tympanic membrane is not intact, the manometer of the impedance bridge can be observed to determine middle-ear pressure. In the study by Elner et al,[333] results of the Toynbee test were positive in 79% of normal adults. Can-

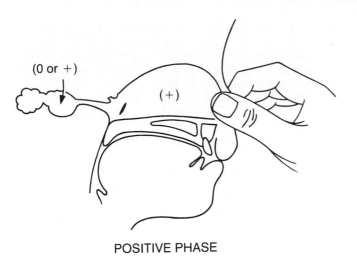

POSITIVE PHASE

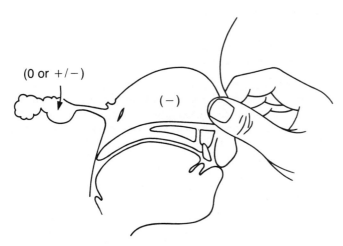

NEGATIVE PHASE

FIGURE 25–32. The Toynbee test of eustachian tube function. Closed-nose swallowing results first in positive pressure in the nose and nasopharynx, followed by a negative pressure phase. When positive pressure is in the nasopharynx, air may enter the middle ear, creating positive pressure. During or after the negative pressure phase, negative pressure may develop in the middle ear, or positive pressure may still be in the middle ear (no change in middle-ear pressure during negative phase), or positive pressure may be followed by negative middle-ear pressure, or ambient pressure will be present if equilibration takes place before the tube closes. If the tube does not open during either the positive or negative phase, no change in middle-ear pressure will occur. (From Bluestone CD, Klein JO. Otitis Media in Infants and Children, 3rd ed. Philadelphia, WB Saunders, 2001, p 167.)

tekin et al[193] reported that only 7 of 106 ears (6.6%) of subjects (mostly children) who had had tympanostomy tubes inserted for otitis media could show positive results when given a modification of the Toynbee test (closed-nose equilibration attempt with applied negative middle-ear pressure of 100 or 200 mm H_2O). Likewise, in a series of patients, most of whom were older children and adults with chronic perforations of the tympanic membrane, only 3 of 21 (14.3%) passed the test. However, in children with a traumatic perforation of the tympanic membrane who otherwise had a negative otologic history,

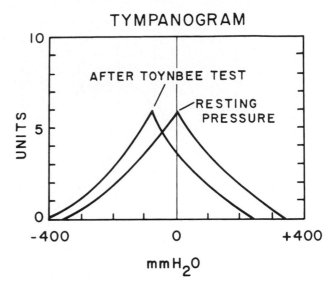

FIGURE 25–33. Tympanograms obtained before and after the Toynbee test. Negative middle-ear pressure is objectively demonstrated in the middle ear; this is considered to be associated with good eustachian tube function. (From Bluestone CD, Klein JO. Otitis Media in Infants and Children, 3rd ed. Philadelphia, WB Saunders, 2001, p 167.)

3 of 10 (30%) could pass the test. In the study by Bluestone and Cantekin[129] of "normal" children with traumatic perforations, six of seven children could change the middle-ear pressure, but *none* of the 21 ears of children who had a retraction pocket or a cholesteatoma showed pressure change.

The test is of greater value in determining normal or abnormal eustachian tube function in adults than it is in children. The test is still of considerable value since, regardless of age, if negative pressure develops in the middle ear during or following the test, the eustachian tube function is most likely normal, because the eustachian tube actively opens and is sufficiently stiff to withstand nasopharyngeal negative pressure (i.e., it does not "lock"). If positive pressure is noted or no change in pressure occurs, the function of the eustachian tube may still be normal, and other tests of eustachian tube function should be performed.

Patulous Eustachian Tube Test

If a patulous eustachian tube is suspected, the diagnosis can be confirmed by otoscopy or objectively by tympanometry when the tympanic membrane is intact.[120] One tympanogram is obtained while the patient is breathing normally, and a second is obtained while the patient is holding his or her breath. Fluctuation of the tympanometric trace that coincides with breathing confirms the diagnosis of a patulous tube (Fig. 25–34). The examiner can elicit an exaggeration in fluctuation by asking the patient to occlude one nostril with the mouth closed during forced inspiration and expiration or perform the Toynbee maneuver. When the tympanic membrane is not intact, a patulous eustachian tube can be identified by the free flow of air into and out of the eustachian tube using the pump-manometer portion of the electroacoustic imped-

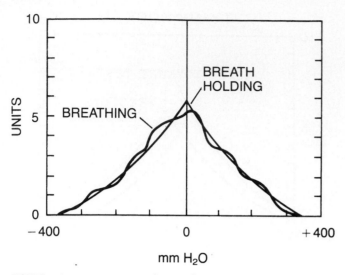

FIGURE 25–34. Diagnosis of a patulous eustachian tube by employing the tympanogram. (From Bluestone CD, Klein JO. Otitis Media in Infants and Children, 3rd ed. Philadelphia, WB Saunders, 2001, p 168.)

ance bridge. These tests should not be performed while the patient is in a reclining position, since the patulous eustachian tube will close.[144]

Nine-Step Inflation-Deflation Tympanometric Test

Another method of assessing eustachian tube function when the tympanic membrane is intact, developed by Bluestone et al,[124] is called the nine-step inflation-deflation tympanometric test, although the applied middle-ear pressures are very limited in magnitude. The middle ear must be free of effusion. The nine-step tympanometry procedure can be summarized as follows (Fig. 25–35):

1. The tympanogram records resting middle-ear pressure.
2. Ear canal pressure is increased to +200 mm H_2O with medial deflection of the tympanic membrane and a corresponding increase in middle-ear pressure. The subject swallows to equilibrate middle-ear overpressure.
3. While the subject refrains from swallowing, ear canal pressure is returned to normal, thus establishing a slight negative middle-ear pressure (as the tympanic membrane moves outward). The tympanogram documents the established middle-ear underpressure.
4. The subject swallows in an attempt to equilibrate negative middle-ear pressure. If equilibration is successful, airflow is from the nasopharynx to the middle ear.
5. The tympanogram records the extent of equilibration.
6. Ear canal pressure is decreased to −200 mm H_2O, causing a lateral deflection of the tympanic membrane and a corresponding decrease in middle-ear pressure. The subject swallows to equilibrate negative middle-ear pressure; airflow is from the nasopharynx to the middle ear.

7. The subject refrains from swallowing while external ear canal pressure is returned to normal, thus establishing a slight positive pressure in the middle ear as the tympanic membrane moves medially. The tympanogram records the overpressure established.
8. The subject swallows to reduce overpressure. If equilibration is successful, airflow is from the middle ear to the nasopharynx.
9. The final tympanogram documents the extent of equilibration.

The test is simple to perform, can give useful information regarding eustachian tube function, and should be part of the clinical evaluation of patients with suspected eustachian tube dysfunction. In general, most normal adults can perform all or some parts of this test,[719a, 1151] but even normal children have difficulty performing it. However, if a child can pass some or all of the steps, eustachian tube function is considered good.

Modified Inflation-Deflation Test (Nonintact Tympanic Membrane)

When the tympanic membrane is not intact, the pump-manometer system of the immittance instrument can be used to perform the modified inflation-deflation eustachian tube function test, which assesses passive as well as active functioning of the eustachian tube.[193, 525] With this test, the middle ear should be free of any drainage for an accurate assessment of eustachian tube function. The middle ear is inflated (i.e., positive pressure is applied) until the eustachian tube spontaneously opens (Fig. 25–36). At this time, the pump is manually stopped and air is discharged through the eustachian tube until the tube closes passively. The pressure at which the eustachian tube is passively forced open is called the *opening pressure*, and the pressure at which it closes passively is called the *closing pressure*.[146, 532] The patient is then instructed to equilibrate the middle-ear pressure actively by swallowing. The residual pressure remaining in the middle ear after the patient swallows is recorded. The active function is also recorded by applying over- and underpressure to the middle ear, which the patient then attempts to equilibrate by swallowing. The residual negative pressure that remains in the middle ear after the attempt to equilibrate applied negative pressure of -200 mm H_2O is also noted (Fig. 25–37).

This procedure is not performed in patients who cannot equilibrate applied overpressure. If the eustachian tube does not open following application of positive pressure using the electroacoustic impedance bridge, and if no reduction in positive pressure occurs during swallowing, then the eustachian tube must be assessed using a manometric system other than that available with the electroacoustic impedance audiometer. The opening pressure may be higher than 400 to 600 mm H_2O pressure or not present at all (severe mechanical obstruction). Example A in Figure 25–38 shows that, following passive opening and closing of the eustachian tube during the inflation phase of the study, the patient was able to completely equilibrate the remaining positive pressure. Active swallowing also completely equilibrated applied negative pressure (deflation). This is considered to be characteris-

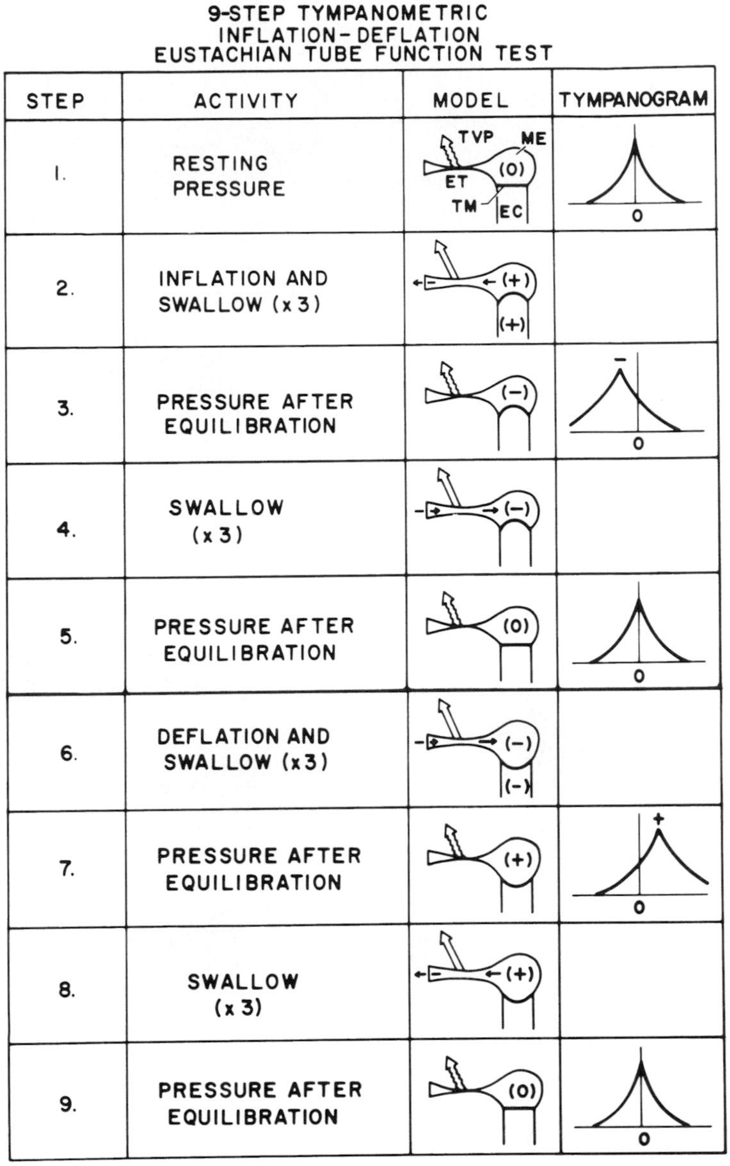

9-STEP TYMPANOMETRIC
INFLATION-DEFLATION
EUSTACHIAN TUBE FUNCTION TEST

STEP	ACTIVITY	MODEL	TYMPANOGRAM
1.	RESTING PRESSURE		
2.	INFLATION AND SWALLOW (x 3)		
3.	PRESSURE AFTER EQUILIBRATION		
4.	SWALLOW (x 3)		
5.	PRESSURE AFTER EQUILIBRATION		
6.	DEFLATION AND SWALLOW (x 3)		
7.	PRESSURE AFTER EQUILIBRATION		
8.	SWALLOW (x 3)		
9.	PRESSURE AFTER EQUILIBRATION		

FIGURE 25–35. Nine-step inflation-deflation tympanometric test. EC, ear canal; ET, eustachian tube; ME, middle ear; TM, tympanic membrane; TVP, tensor veli palatini muscle. (From Bluestone CD, Klein JO. Otitis Media in Infants and Children, 3rd ed. Philadelphia, WB Saunders, 2001, p 169.)

tic of normal eustachian tube function. Example B shows the eustachian tube passively opened and closed following inflation, but subsequent swallowing failed to equilibrate the residual positive pressure. In the deflation phase of the study, the patient was unable to equilibrate negative pressure. Inflation to a pressure below the opening pressure but above the closing pressure could not be equilibrated by active swallowing. This type of result is considered to be abnormal but may be found in a few subjects who do not have any obvious otologic disease.

Failure to equilibrate the applied negative pressure during the test may indicate locking of the eustachian tube. This type of tube is considered to have increased compliance or to be "floppy" in comparison with a tube with perfect function.[154, 967] The tensor veli palatini muscle is unable to open (dilate) the tube.

Even though the inflation-deflation test of eustachian tube function does not strictly duplicate physiologic functions of the tube, the results are helpful in differentiating normal from abnormal function. The mean opening pres-

sure for apparently normal subjects with a traumatic perforation and negative otologic history reported by Cantekin et al[195] was 330 mm H_2O (+70 mm H_2O). If the test results reveal passive opening and closing within the normal range, residual positive pressure can be equilibrated by swallowing, and applied negative pressure can also be equilibrated completely, then the eustachian tube can be considered to have normal function. However, if the tube does not open to a pressure of 1000 mm H_2O, one can assume that total mechanical obstruction is present. This pressure is not hazardous to the middle ear or inner ear windows if the pressure is applied slowly. An extremely high opening pressure (e.g., greater than 500 to 600 mm H_2O) may indicate partial obstruction, whereas a very low opening pressure (e.g., less than 100 mm H_2O) would indicate a semipatulous eustachian tube. Inability to maintain even a modest positive pressure within the middle ear would be consistent with a patulous tube (i.e., one that is open at rest). Complete equilibration of applied negative pressure by swallowing is usually associated

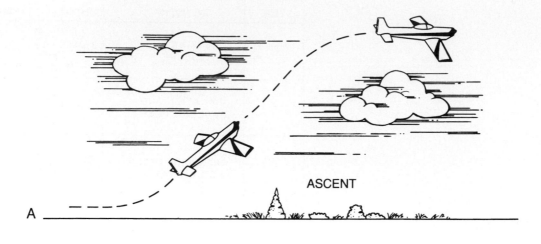

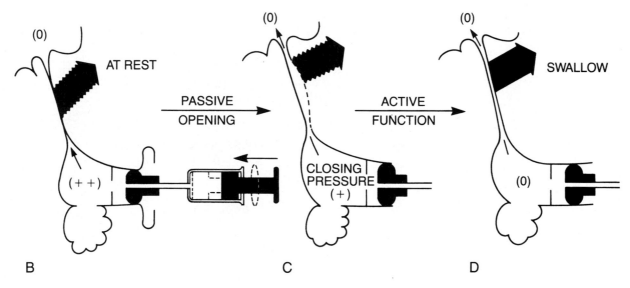

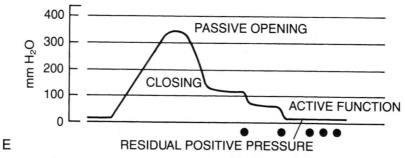

FIGURE 25–36. Test of passive and active function of the eustachian tube following application of positive middle-ear pressure. *A,* Analogous ascent in an airplane. *B,* Assessment of passive function. *C,* Closing pressure. *D,* Assessment of active function (swallowing). *E,* Strip chart recording showing an example of normal pressure tracing. *Black circles* represent swallows. (From Bluestone CD, Klein JO. Otitis Media in Infants and Children, 3rd ed. Philadelphia, WB Saunders, 2001, p 170.)

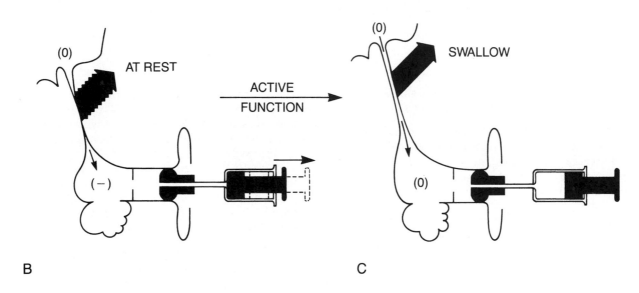

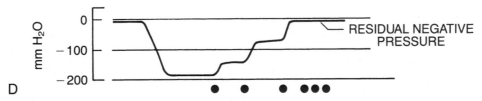

FIGURE 25–37. Deflation phase of eustachian tube testing. *A,* Analogous descent in an airplane. *B,* Application of low negative pressure to the middle ear. *C,* Equilibration by active tubal opening. *D,* Strip chart recording showing an example of a normal tracing. *Black circles* represent swallows. (From Bluestone CD, Klein JO. Otitis Media in Infants and Children, 3rd ed. Philadelphia, WB Saunders, 2001, p 171.)

with normal function, but partial equilibration or even failure to reduce any applied negative pressure may or may not be considered abnormal, since even a normal eustachian tube will lock when negative pressure is rapidly applied. Therefore, inability to equilibrate applied negative pressure may not indicate poor eustachian tube function, especially when it is the only abnormal result of testing. Serial testing is advised, since test results can vary with time in children who had had otitis media in the past and have functioning tympanostomy tubes in place at the time of testing.[182]

Other Methods Available for Investigational Studies

Other methods are available to test the functioning of the eustachian tube, but they are currently limited to use in the laboratory for investigational purposes.

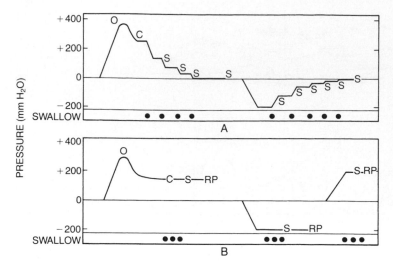

FIGURE 25–38. Examples of results of inflation-deflation ventilation studies that employed a strip chart recorder. *A,* Normal adult with a traumatic perforation. *B,* A 4-year-old boy with a functioning tympanostomy tube who had a persistent otitis media with effusion. *Black circles* represent swallows. C, closing pressure; O, opening pressure; RP, residual pressure; S, pressure after swallow. (From Bluestone CD, Klein JO. Otitis Media in Infants and Children, 3rd ed. Philadelphia, WB Saunders, 2001, p 172.)

Radiographic Studies of Protective and Clearance Functions and Dysfunctions

Even though the ventilatory function is the most important of the functions of the eustachian tube, the protective and clearance functions are also important in maintaining the physiologic state. The clearance and drainage functions of the eustachian tube have been assessed by a variety of methods in the past. By means of radiographic techniques, the flow of contrast media from the middle ear (tympanic membrane not intact) into the nasopharynx has been assessed by Welin,[1184] Aschan,[38, 39] Compere,[247, 248] Parisier and Khilnani,[843] Bluestone,[136] Bluestone et al,[147, 154] Ferber and Holmquist,[364] and Honjo et al.[505] Rogers et al[932] instilled a solution of fluorescein into the middle ear and assessed the clearance function by subsequently examining the pharynx with an ultraviolet light. LaFaye et al[628] used a radioisotope technique to monitor the flow of saline solution down the eustachian tube. Bauer et al[70] assessed clearance by observing methylene blue in the pharynx after it had been instilled into the middle ear. Elbrond and Larsen[328] assessed middle-ear–eustachian tube mucociliary flow by determining the time that elapsed after saccharin had been placed on the mucous membrane of the middle ear until the subject reported tasting it. Unfortunately, all of these methods are qualitative and actually test eustachian tube patency rather than measure the clearance function of the tube quantitatively.

Even though abnormalities of the protective function are directly related to the pathogenesis of otitis media, this function has been assessed only by radiographic techniques[136, 147, 154] by a test that was a modification of a tubal patency test described by Wittenborg and Neuhauser.[1194]

The protective and clearance functions of the eustachian tube have been assessed by a combined radiographic technique.[147, 154] Radiopaque material was instilled through the nose of patients so that the retrograde flow of the medium from the nasopharynx into the eustachian tube could be observed (Fig. 25–39). Patients were considered to have normal protective function when radiopaque material entered only the nasopharyngeal or isthmic portion of the tube and did not enter the bony portion of the tube or middle-ear cavity during swallowing. The normal eustachian tube protected the middle ear from the contrast material even when the liquid was under increased nasopharyngeal pressure during closed-nose swallowing (Fig. 25–40). If, during the retrograde study, contrast material traversed the entire eustachian tube and refluxed into the middle ear during swallowing, the tube was considered to have increased distensibility and poor protective function (Fig. 25–41).

The effectiveness of the eustachian tube in clearing the radiopaque medium instilled into the middle ear was taken as an indication of the effectiveness of the eustachian tube in the clearance of secretions. Rapid and complete clearance of the medium into the nasopharynx was considered to indicate normal drainage function, whereas failure of the contrast material to drain from the middle ear into the nasopharynx indicated mechanical obstruction of the eustachian tube (Fig. 25–42), especially when contrast material also failed to enter the nasopharyngeal portion of the tube during the retrograde study (Fig. 25–43). These abnormal functions of the tube were found in patients with otitis media and were not found in a small group of normal subjects.

Tests of Ventilatory Functions

When the tympanic membrane is intact, the microflow technique[526] or an impedance method[184] (both of which require a pressure chamber), sonotubometry,[719a, 774, 812, 826, 1167a] sequential scintigraphy,[823] microendoscopy,[1076] or directly inserting a balloon catheter into the cartilagenous eustachian tube[564, 763] can be used. When the tympanic membrane is not intact, the forced-response test[198] can be used. Sonotubometry is currently in use in routine research studies but is not yet available for clinical use.[180, 312, 719] A new measurement of eustachian tube mechanical properties using a modified forced response test is currently being tested in animals and humans.[406]

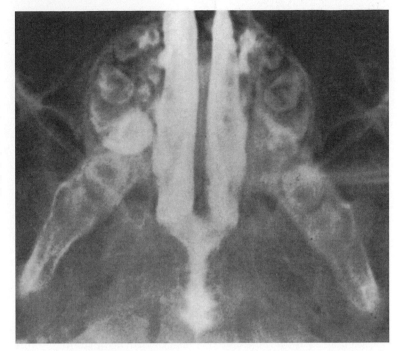

FIGURE 25–39. Submentovertex radiograph of a child without middle-ear disease. Radiopaque contrast material instilled into the nose and nasopharynx did not enter the eustachian tube when the subject did not swallow.

Clinical Indications for Testing Eustachian Tube Function

Diagnosis

One of the most important reasons for assessing eustachian tube function is the need to make a differential diagnosis in a patient who has an intact tympanic membrane without evidence of otitis media but who has symptoms that might be related to eustachian tube dysfunction (such as otalgia, snapping or popping in the ear, fluctuating hearing loss, tinnitus, or vertigo). An example of such a case would be a child or adolescent who complains of fullness in the ear without hearing loss at the time of the examination, a symptom that could be related to abnormal functioning of the eustachian tube or due to an inner ear disorder. A tympanogram that reveals high negative pressure (-50 mm H_2O or less) is strong evidence of eustachian tube obstruction, whereas normal resting middle-ear pressure is not diagnostically significant. However, when the resting intratympanic pressure is within normal limits and the patient can develop negative middle-ear pressure following the Toynbee test or can perform all or some of the functions in the nine-step inflation-deflation tympanometric test, the eustachian tube is probably functioning normally. Unfortunately, failure to develop negative middle-ear pressure during the Toynbee test or an inability to pass the nine-step test does not necessarily indicate poor eustachian tube function, since many children who are otologically normal cannot actively open their tubes during these tests. Tympanometry not only is of value in determining whether eustachian tube obstruction is present, but it can also identify abnormality

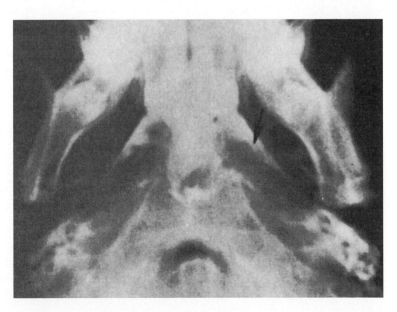

FIGURE 25–40. Normal retrograde function. During both open-nose and closed-nose swallowing, radiopaque contrast material filled the nasopharyngeal portion of the eustachian tube (*arrow*) of a child with normal tympanic membranes and a negative otologic history.

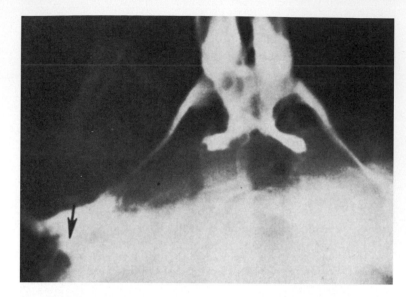

FIGURE 25–41. Retrograde reflux. Radiograph of a 6-year-old boy with recurrent otitis media with effusion. On open-nose swallowing, contrast material traversed the entire eustachian tube and refluxed into the middle ear and mastoid (*arrow*).

at the other end of the spectrum of eustachian tube dysfunction, and the presence of an abnormally patent eustachian tube can be confirmed by the results of the tympanometric patulous tube test.

Screening for the presence of high negative pressure in certain high-risk populations (i.e., children with known sensorineural hearing losses, developmentally delayed and mentally impaired children, children with cleft palates or other craniofacial anomalies, American Indian and Eskimo children, and children with Down syndrome) appears to be helpful in identifying those individuals who may need to be monitored closely for the occurrence of otitis media.[462]

Tympanometry appears to be a reliable method for detecting the presence of high negative pressure as well as otitis media with effusion in children.[75, 172] The identification of high negative pressure without effusion in children indicates some degree of eustachian tube obstruction. These children and those with middle-ear effusions should have follow-up serial tympanograms, since they may be at risk of developing otitis media with effusion.

However, the best methods available to the clinician today for testing eustachian tube function are the nine-step test when the eardrum is intact, or, when the eardrum is not intact, the inflation-deflation test. A perfora-tion of the tympanic membrane or a tympanostomy tube must be present for the latter test to be performed. The test uses the simple apparatus described earlier, with or without the impedance audiometer pump-manometer system. This test will aid in determining the presence or absence of a dysfunction, and the type of dysfunction (obstruction vs. abnormal patency) and its severity when one is present. No other test procedures may be needed if the patient has either functional obstruction of the eustachian tube or an abnormally patent tube. However, if there is a mechanical obstruction, especially if the tube appears to be totally blocked anatomically, then further testing may be indicated. In such cases, computed tomography of the nasopharynx–eustachian tube–middle-ear region can be performed to determine the site and cause of the blockage, such as a cholesteatoma or tumor. In most cases in which mechanical obstruction of the tube is found, inflammation is present at the middle-ear end of the eustachian tube (osseous portion), and this usually resolves with medical management or middle-ear surgery, or both. Serial inflation-deflation studies should show resolution of the mechanical obstruction. However, if no middle-ear cause is obvious, other studies should be performed to rule out the possibility of a neoplasm in the nasopharynx.

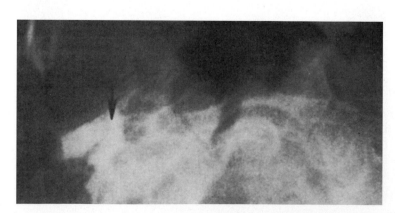

FIGURE 25–42. Radiograph showing prograde obstruction at the middle-ear end of the isthmus of the eustachian tube (*arrow*). Radiopaque contrast material failed to flow from the middle ear into the nasopharynx.

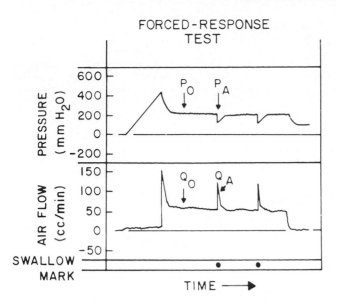

FORCED-RESPONSE TEST

FIGURE 25–43. Retrograde obstruction. Radiograph of a 5-year-old boy with otitis media. Radiopaque material failed to enter the nasopharyngeal portion of the eustachian tube during both open-nose and closed-nose swallowing. Note the enlarged adenoids (*arrow*).

Eustachian Tube Function Tests Related to Management

Ideally, patients with recurrent acute otitis media or chronic otitis media with effusion, or both, should have eustachian tube function studies as part of their otolaryngologic work-up. But for most children with these conditions, one can assume eustachian tube function to be poor. However, patients in whom tympanostomy tubes have been inserted may benefit from serial eustachian tube function studies.[1204] Improvement in function as indicated by inflation-deflation tests might help the clinician determine the proper time to remove the tubes. Cleft palate repair,[154, 834] adenoidectomy,[124, 147] elimination of nasal and nasopharyngeal inflammation,[125] treatment of a nasopharyngeal tumor, or growth and development of a child[497] may be associated with improvement in eustachian tube function.

Studies of the eustachian tube function of the patient with a chronic perforation of the tympanic membrane may be helpful preoperatively in determining the potential results of tympanoplastic surgery. Holmquist[498] studied eustachian tube function in adults before and after tympanoplasty and reported that the operation had a high rate of success in patients with good eustachian tube function (i.e., those who could equilibrate applied negative pressure), but that in patients without good tubal function, surgery frequently failed to close the perforation. These results were corroborated,[742a, 1020] but other investigators[241, 327, 632, 1168] found no correlation between the results of the inflation-deflation tests and success or failure of tympanoplasty. Most of these studies failed to define the criteria for "success," and the postoperative follow-up period was too short. Bluestone et al[128] assessed children before tympanoplasty and found that of 51 ears of 45 children, 8 ears could equilibrate an applied negative pressure (-200 mm H_2O) to some degree. In 7 of these ears, the graft took, no middle-ear effusion occurred, and no recurrence of the perforation developed during a follow-up period of 1 to 2 years. A subsequent study by Manning et al[694] had a similar outcome. However, as in the studies in adults, failure to equilibrate an applied negative pressure did not predict failure of the tympanoplasty.

The conclusion to be drawn from these studies is that if the patient is able to equilibrate an applied negative pressure, regardless of age, the success of tympanoplasty is likely, but failure to perform this difficult test will not help the clinician in deciding not to operate. However, the value of testing a patient's ability to equilibrate negative pressure lies in the possibility of determining from the test results whether a young child is a candidate for tympanoplasty, when one might decide on the basis of other findings alone to withhold surgery until the child is older (see Chap. 26).

In children who have unilateral perforation of the tympanic membrane or a tympanostomy tube in place and a contralateral tympanic membrane that is intact, the status of the intact side, observed for at least 1 year, can aid in determining whether tympanoplasty should be performed or a tube should be removed. Repair of the eardrum or removal of the tube is usually successful if the contralateral intact side has remained normal (i.e., no middle-ear effusion or high negative pressure). Conversely, if the opposite ear has developed middle-ear disease during the previous year, tympanoplasty should be postponed, or, if a tympanostomy tube is in place, it should not be removed.[152]

Role of Eustachian Tube in Pathogenesis of Otitis Media

Experiments on animal models and clinical studies involving adult volunteers have proven that eustachian tube dysfunction is involved in the pathogenesis of certain types of middle-ear disease. Several clinical studies in which adult volunteers had an intranasal virus challenge have convincingly demonstrated the sequence of events from a viral upper respiratory tract infection, to eustachian tube obstruction, to negative middle-ear pressure, to otitis media. The following sections detail these animal and clinical studies.

Experiments in Animals

Both underpressures and middle-ear effusion have been successfully produced in animal models using several methods. These studies are summarized in Table 25–18.

When the tensor veli palatini muscle is experimentally impaired (altered or inactivated) in animal models, the active opening of the eustachian tube is impaired. This results in negative middle-ear pressure followed by middle-ear effusion. In one experiment, excision of a portion of the tensor veli palatini muscle at the pterygoid hamulus in the palate resulted in negative pressure in the middle ear followed by an effusion.[195] A similar experiment in which the muscle was completely excised or the superficial muscle bundle was transected, or the tendon

TABLE 25–18. Animal Models of High Negative Middle-Ear Pressure and Middle-Ear Effusion

| (Study) | Animal | Diagnostic | Method | Outcomes | | Resolved Long-Term |
				HNP	MEE	
Cantekin et al[195]	Monkey	Otomicroscopy and tympanometry	TVP excised	Yes	Yes	No
Cantekin et al[197]	Monkey	Otomicroscopy and tympanometry	TVP			
			1. excised	Yes	Yes	No
			2. transected	Yes	Yes	No/yes
			3. transposed	Yes	Yes	Yes
Casselbrant et al[208]	Monkey	Otomicroscopy and tympanometry	Botulinum into TVP	Yes	Yes	Yes
Buchman et al[177]	Ferret	Otomicroscopy and tympanometry	Influenza A nasal inoculation	Yes	No	Yes
Swarts et al[1090]	Monkey	MRI	CO_2 insufflation into middle ear	Yes	Yes	NA
Alper et al[14]	Monkey	MRI	Botulinum into TVP	Yes	Yes	Yes

HNP, high negative middle-ear pressure; MEE, middle-ear effusion; MRI, magnetic resonance imaging; NA, not applicable (acute experiment); TVP, tensor veli palatini muscle.

medial to the hamular process was transposed, had comparable outcomes.[200] Complete excision resulted in middle-ear underpressures followed by persistent effusion. Transecting the muscle resulted in negative middle-ear pressure, or effusion, or both (and in some animals the middle ear returned to normal after the muscle healed). When the tendon was transposed, outcomes were similar to those of surgical alteration, but the middle ear rapidly returned to normal. Using a noninvasive method, Casselbrant et al[208] injected botulinum toxin into the tensor muscle, which resulted in negative pressure and then effusion. When the effect of the botulinum toxin resolved, the middle-ear status returned to normal.

In these earlier studies, middle-ear status was diagnosed with otomicroscopy and tympanometry. More recently, Alper et al[14] used magnetic resonance imaging and tympanometry to identify middle-ear and mastoid effusion. These investigators also injected botulinum toxin into the tensor veli palatini muscle of monkeys, resulting in a eustachian tube that failed to open, middle-ear underpressure, and effusion. In ears that developed underpressure within the middle ear, increased vascular permeability was observed on the magnetic resonance imaging scan. These experiments created a functional obstruction of the eustachian tube (i.e., an impairment of the active opening of the tube), impeding pressure regulation of the middle ear and resulting in an effusion. As in the earlier study, when the effect of the botulinum toxin resolved, the middle-ear status returned to normal.

Buchman et al,[177] using a ferret model, evaluated the effect of influenza A virus nasal challenge on the function of the eustachian tube. Results were assessed by forced-response and inflation-deflation tests, and middle-ear status was evaluated by otomicroscopy and tympanometry. All 10 animals in the experiment became infected and all had eustachian tube dysfunction associated with middle-ear underpressures, although no middle-ear effusion developed in any of the ferrets. The investigation also showed that even though the eustachian tube did not become totally obstructed, abnormally high negative pressures developed in the middle ear.

Using a different approach, Swarts et al[1090] were also able to produce unilateral middle-ear effusion in the monkey shortly after inducing middle-ear negative pressure by inflating the middle ear with CO_2. Increased vascular permeability was identified on the magnetic resonance imaging scan using a contrast agent. None of these changes were found in the contralateral control ear. When the middle-ear cleft was flushed with oxygen, lesser middle-ear underpressures developed, but no middle-ear effusion or other changes on the magnetic resonance imaging scan developed. Even though the eustachian tube was not altered in this experiment, the study showed the effect of middle-ear negative pressure in the development of middle-ear effusion.

These six experiments show that the eustachian tube has an important role in the development of otitis media in animal models. There is now equally convincing evidence from studies in adult volunteers that the eustachian tube is involved in the pathogenesis of otitis media.

Studies in Humans

Several studies of adult volunteers assessed nasal function, eustachian tube function, and the status of the middle-ear following the intranasal challenge of viruses. These studies demonstrate the role the eustachian tube plays in the pathogenesis of middle-ear underpressures, otitis media with effusion, and acute otitis media; the studies are summarized on Table 25–19.

Doyle et al[310] determined the effect of an upper respiratory tract infection (i.e., a cold) on eustachian tube function and the status of the middle ear after intranasal challenge of rhinovirus in a group of 40 adult volunteers. After rhinovirus was inoculated into the nose, all subjects were found to be infected, but only 80% developed the signs and symptoms of a clinical illness. Before and periodically after this nasal challenge, assessments were made of eustachian tube function (using sonotubometry and the nine-step test), middle-ear pressure (using tympanometry), and nasal patency (using active posterior rhinometry). All subjects with a cold had decreased nasal patency, 50% had eustachian tube obstruction, and 30% had ab-

TABLE 25–19. Effect of Nasal Virus Challenge on Eustachian Tube and Middle-Ear Status in Human Volunteers

Study	Number of Subjects	Virus	Outcomes (%)			
			ET OBS	HNP	MEE	AOM
Doyle et al[310]	40	Rhinovirus	50	30	0	0
McBride et al[719]	32	Rhinovirus	80	50	0	0
Buchman et al[178]	60	Rhinovirus	NT	39	3	0
Doyle et al[314]	33	Influenza A	80	80	23	0
Buchman et al[177]	27	Influenza A	NT	59	25	4

AOM, acute otitis media; ET OBS, eustachian tube obstruction; HNP, high negative pressure; MEE, middle-ear effusion; NT, not tested.

normal negative middle-ear pressure for approximately 1 week after the inoculation. All outcomes completely resolved within 16 days, and none of the volunteers developed a middle-ear effusion.

Using similar methods and design as those described in the Doyle et al[310] study, McBride et al[719] recruited 32 adult volunteers. After the challenge with rhinovirus, abnormal findings were limited to the 24 (75%) subjects who developed clinical signs and symptoms of infection. After 2 days, 80% had eustachian tube obstruction, 50% had high negative middle-ear pressure, and 46% had decreased nasal patency. Again, none of the subjects developed a middle-ear effusion. These abnormal findings resolved 6 to 10 days after the challenge.

In yet another similar study, Buchman et al[178] evaluated 60 adult volunteers. After nasal inoculation with rhinovirus, 95% of the subjects became infected and 60% had a clinical cold. Before the nasal challenge, 3 volunteers (5%) had abnormal middle-ear pressure and in 2 of these subjects a middle-ear effusion developed. Of the 60 subjects, 22 (39%) had high negative middle-ear pressure. None of the subjects who had normal middle-ear pressure before the challenge developed an effusion, indicating that a rhinovirus infection may result in a middle-ear effusion if the patient has a preexisting dysfunction of the eustachian tube. Doyle et al[314] also reported that intranasal challenge with influenza A virus in 33 healthy adult volunteers resulted in 80% demonstrating eustachian tube obstruction and 80% having negative middle-ear pressure. With this virus, however, 5 (23%) of 21 infected subjects also developed a middle-ear effusion. Most likely, influenza A virus is more virulent than rhinovirus in the pathogenesis of eustachian tube and middle-ear abnormalities.

In an important study, Buchman et al[177] demonstrated the events leading to the development of acute otitis media in the human. Using a design similar to the previous studies, they recruited 27 adult volunteers, in whom influenza A was inoculated into the nose. All subjects developed a nasal infection and 16 (59%) subsequently developed high negative middle-ear pressure. In one subject, acute otitis media was present. Using polymerase chain reaction, a middle-ear aspirate revealed the virus and *S. pneumoniae*; traditional viral and bacterial culture methods failed to grow these organisms from the middle-ear effusion. It is possible that these microorganisms were aspirated from the nasopharynx into the middle-ear cavity due to the high negative middle-ear pressure.

A recent informative clinical investigation by Moody et al[761] also demonstrated this sequence of events in children. In this study, the parents of 20 children between the ages of 2 and 6 monitored the middle-ear status of their children every day using a tympanometer. They reported that when an upper respiratory tract infection developed in the children, many soon also developed middle-ear underpressures, and some then developed a middle-ear effusion.

In a more recent study, Doyle et al[312] infected 18 adult subjects with influenza A and showed that those individuals who had preexisting good eustachian tube function reduced the otologic complications of the viral upper respiratory tract infection.

These studies in both humans and animal models support the causal relationship between a viral upper respiratory tract infection, partial eustachian tube obstruction, abnormal middle-ear underpressures, and otitis media.

Pathogenesis of Otitis Media and Related Conditions

Acute otitis media, otitis media with effusion, eustachian tube dysfunction, and chronic suppurative otitis media are the most frequent middle-ear diseases clinicians encounter. Following the onset of either acute otitis media or otitis media with effusion, persistent middle-ear effusion may develop.

Acute Otitis Media

The pathogenesis of acute otitis media usually occurs with the following pattern in most children: the patient has an antecedent event (usually an upper respiratory viral infection) that results in congestion of the respiratory mucosa of the upper respiratory tract, including the nasopharynx and eustachian tube. Congestion of the mucosa in the eustachian tube obstructs the eustachian tube, negative middle-ear pressure develops, and, if prolonged, potential pathogens (viruses and bacteria) are *aspirated* from the nasopharynx into the middle ear. Since the eustachian tube is obstructed, the middle-ear effusion, due to the infection, accumulates in the middle ear. Microbial pathogens proliferate in the secretions, resulting in a suppurative and symptomatic otitis media.

For children with recurrent acute otitis media, an anatomic or physiologic abnormality of the eustachian tube appears to be an important factor, if not the most important factor. In Sweden, Stenstrom et al[1063] studied the pathogenesis of recurrent acute otitis media in 50 otitis-prone children (defined as more than 11 episodes of acute otitis media). Using the pressure chamber to test eustachian tube function, they found the otitis-prone children to have significantly poorer active tubal function than 49 normal (control) children who had no history of acute otitis media. This finding indicates that the pathogenesis of recurrent acute otitis media is the result of functional obstruction of the eustachian tube, as opposed to mechanical obstruction. However, it is likely that infants and young children with their "short, floppy" eustachian tubes can reflux or insufflate nasopharyngeal secretions into the middle ear during a viral upper respiratory tract infection. Another possible mechanism is an infection that progressively ascends from the nasopharynx into the mucosa of the eustachian tube. This most likely occurs when an indwelling obstructing foreign object is in the nasopharynx, such as a nasogastric or nasotracheal tube.

Otitis Media with Effusion

The acute onset of otitis media with effusion is relatively asymptomatic in children but usually has a similar sequence of events as that described for acute otitis media. Bacteria can be isolated from middle-ear effusions of patients with otitis media with effusion,[152, 881, 914] but prolonged negative pressure within the middle ear can cause a sterile middle-ear effusion. As described earlier, otitis media with effusion has been produced in the monkey animal model following excision of[195] and injection of[14, 208] botulinum toxin into the tensor veli palatini muscle, which resulted in the eustachian tube failing to open, middle-ear underpressures, and effusion. These experiments confirm the *hydrops ex vacuo* theory of the pathogenesis of middle-ear effusion. This theory postulates that when the eustachian tube does not open, the gas exchange from the middle ear into the microcirculation of the mucous membrane causes a middle-ear underpressure, followed by transudation of effusion. Swarts et al[1090] were also able to produce middle-ear effusion in the monkey by flushing the middle ear with CO_2 shortly after inducing middle-ear negative pressure. In the studies by McBride et al[719] and by Buchman et al[178] that involved adult volunteers, nasal challenge with rhinovirus resulted in eustachian tube obstruction, negative middle-ear pressure, and, in two subjects, middle-ear effusion. Doyle et al[314] also demonstrated that intranasal challenge of influenza A virus in adult volunteers resulted in eustachian tube obstruction, negative middle-ear pressure, and, in infected subjects, middle-ear effusion. Most likely, influenza A virus is more virulent than rhinovirus. Also, preexisting poor eustachian tube function predisposes to obstruction of the tube and middle-ear abnormalities.[179, 312]

Periods of upper respiratory tract infection can then result in atelectasis of the tympanic membrane-middle ear (i.e., high negative middle-ear pressure), sterile otitis media with effusion, or acute bacterial otitis media. Because the tube can open in a middle ear with an effusion, nasopharyngeal secretions can be aspirated, creating the clinical condition in which otitis media with effusion and

recurrent acute bacterial otitis media occur together. The most dramatic example of the ex vacuo cause of acute middle-ear effusion is following barotrauma, e.g., descent during scuba diving or airplane flying.

In a study of eustachian tube function in 163 ears of Japanese children and adults who had otitis media with effusion and chronic otitis media, Iwano et al[532] found an impaired active opening function of the tube in children and adults. They concluded the tube was functionally obstructed. Organic (i.e., mechanical or anatomic) obstruction was also considered to be involved in the pathogenesis in adults.

Persistent Middle-Ear Effusion

There are probably similarities in the pathogenesis of persistent middle-ear effusion after the initial stage of a viral or bacterial infection in the middle ear or following transudation of effusion when high negative pressure is in the middle ear. Cytokines are stimulated, such as interleukins 1, 2, and 6, tumor necrosis factor, interferon-gamma from inflammatory cells of the middle-ear mucous membrane, and growth factors,[251, 493, 552, 814, 1192, 1213, 1215] followed by two pathways of inflammation: (1) upregulation of submucosal receptors, primarily selectins and integrins that trap lymphocytes into the mucosa, which also produce cytokines and inflammatory mediators; and (2) stimulation of inflammatory mediators, such as leukotrienes, prostaglandins, thromboxane, prostacyclin, and platelet-activating factor,[800, 919] which in turn can promote fluid leakage from the mucous membrane. Nitric oxide[94] and free radicals[450, 1010] have also been implicated in the pathogenesis of persistent middle-ear effusion. At this stage, there is probably an increase in blood flow within the mucous membrane, due to engorgement of blood vessels and angioneogenesis. This then results in further negative pressure within the middle ear due to an increase of N_2 into the microcirculation of the mucosa.[313] There is some evidence that infection caused by *Haemophilus influenzae* predisposes the middle-ear cleft to persistent effusion.[213] In addition, the effusion that is produced is trapped in the middle ear due to the anatomy of the system, i.e., a closed space with a narrow outlet, the eustachian tube. Also, the mucociliary system and the pumping action of the tube are most likely impaired, causing persistent middle-ear effusion.

Eustachian Tube Dysfunction

Eustachian tube dysfunction can be due to either an obstruction of the tube or a patulous tube. These will cause signs and symptoms referable to the ear, despite the lack of a middle-ear effusion. Obstruction of the tube can cause middle-ear negative pressure, retraction of the tympanic membrane, hearing loss, and, in its severe form, atelectasis of the middle ear, i.e., loss of the middle-ear space. Obstruction can be due to inflammation or failure of the opening mechanism. Obstruction can be acute or chronic, but infrequent periodic tubal opening probably occurs to prevent the accumulation of an effusion. A patulous tube can cause the patient to complain of autophony and hearing his or her own breathing. Both conditions have been documented during the last trimester of pregnancy.[280] Eustachian tube obstruction is common in girls during puberty and may be related to hormonal changes, but we do not know the underlying cause of this problem.

Chronic Suppurative Otitis Media

Chronic suppurative otitis media (without cholesteatoma) is the chronic stage following an attack of acute otitis media in which there is a perforation of the tympanic membrane (or a tympanostomy tube is present) and there is continuous discharge. From our studies of the pathogenesis of chronic suppurative otitis media,[578, 579] it appears that the sequence of events may be in one of two ways. In one way, the tympanic membrane is not intact, and bacteria from the nasopharynx gain access to the middle ear due to reflux of nasopharyngeal secretions. This is especially true when there is inflammation (secondary to infection or possibly allergy) of the nose, nasopharynx, or paranasal sinuses, and reflux occurs through the eustachian tube, since the middle-ear gas cushion is lost. In most instances, these bacteria are initially the same as those isolated when acute otitis media occurs behind an intact tympanic membrane, such as *S. pneumoniae* and *H. influenzae*, and when acute otorrhea develops when tympanostomy tubes are in place.[683] Following the acute otorrhea, *Pseudomonas aeruginosa*, *Staphylococcus aureus*, and other organisms from the external ear canal enter the middle ear through the nonintact tympanic membrane, resulting in the chronic infection. The second common way in which chronic suppurative otitis media occurs is when organisms (e.g., *P. aeruginosa*) present in water enters through the nonintact eardrum during bathing and swimming and contaminates the middle-ear cleft (see Chap. 26).

Conclusions and Treatment Implications

The etiology and pathogenesis of otitis media is multifactorial, but abnormalities of the structure and function of the eustachian tube appear to be the most important. Eustachian tube dysfunction can cause otitis media and related conditions because of (1) impairment of pressure regulation as the result of anatomic obstruction of the tube (the tube is "too closed") or failure of the tubal opening mechanism (the tube "won't open"), i.e., functional obstruction; (2) loss of protective function due to abnormal patency of the tube (the tube is "too open"), a tube that is "too short," abnormal gas pressures within the middle ear or nasopharynx, or a nonintact middle ear and mastoid; or (3) impairment of clearance function. These abnormalities can be simply described as the eustachian tube system is either "too closed" or "too open," or either end of the system is "too open" or "too closed," or "too much" or "too little" pressure is present.

With this better understanding of the physiology and pathophysiology of eustachian tube function, and recent studies that have demonstrated the effect of intranasal challenge with virus, allergens, and mediators in adult volunteers on nasal and eustachian tube function, our knowledge of the pathogenesis of otitis media has greatly increased. This should lead to improved management methods.

Nonspecific Factors and Materials Present in the Middle Ear That May Contribute to or Protect Against Infections

Tissue Factors

A variety of nonspecific factors are present in the middle ear that may play roles in the defense against infection. The epithelium of the eustachian tube and middle ear is ciliated with mucus-producing cells that are equipped to trap and expel inhaled particles. The network of fibrin that is present in middle-ear effusions, particularly in mucoid and purulent effusions, restricts movement of organisms and facilitates phagocytosis. Destruction of white blood cells and cells lining the mucosa produces lactic acid and a decrease in pH sufficient to kill or inhibit growth of many bacteria.

Oxidative and Hydrolytic Enzymes

Biochemical studies of middle-ear fluids reveal the presence of a variety of oxidative and hydrolytic enzymes. Oxidative enzymes include lactate, malate, and succinate dehydrogenases. Hydrolytic enzymes include lysozyme, acid and alkaline phosphatases, nonspecific esterase, and leucine and alanine aminopeptidases. The enzymes in the middle-ear effusion may have a host cell origin derived from the blood or the inflamed mucosa. In some studies, concentrations of specific enzymes differed, depending on the quality (mucoid or serous) of the fluid. At present, most of the information about enzymes in middle-ear effusions is descriptive, but the increasing data may lead to hypotheses about the role of tissue and cell products in initiation and maintenance of the middle-ear effusion.

Lysozyme is a hydrolytic enzyme with bacteriolytic activity that is present in blood, urine, tears, middle-ear effusions, and other body fluids. Lysozyme is found in the lysosomes of neutrophils, monocytes, and phagocytic cells of the reticuloendothelial system. The bacteriolytic activity of lysozyme is the result of its ability to solubilize the rigid cell wall common to all bacteria. Lysozyme acts synergistically with complement and specific antibodies to achieve its antibacterial effect. High levels of lysozyme have been found in the middle-ear effusions of patients with otitis media with effusion.[551, 653, 1163] Lysozyme concentrations in middle-ear effusions are higher than those in serum and are higher in mucoid than in serous effusions.[629] The high concentration of this antimicrobial substance may explain the bactericidal and virucidal effects of middle-ear effusion identified by Siirala and colleagues.[1025, 1026]

Significant concentrations in middle-ear effusions of lactate dehydrogenase, malate dehydrogenase, leucine aminopeptidase, and alkaline phosphatase were identified by Juhn and Huff.[551] Lactate dehydrogenase is an intracellular enzyme liberated during the destruction of tissue. Malate dehydrogenase and the other dehydrogenases of the tricarboxylic acid (Krebs) cycle are believed to be bound to the inner mitochondrial membrane. In otitis media, proliferation of ciliated cells in the middle-ear mucosa occurs. The increase in number of cells and increase in mitochondria may result in higher activity of the enzyme in the middle-ear fluid than in serum.[551] Leucine aminopeptidase is a proteolytic enzyme that is present in various tissues and is concentrated in leukocytes. Histochemical studies of the location of the enzyme in the middle-ear mucosa show increased activity throughout the mucoperiosteum. The concentrations of all enzymes are higher in middle-ear effusions than they are in simultaneously obtained serum, and they are higher in mucoid than in serous middle-ear effusions. Glew et al[412] also found that there were higher concentrations of selected hydrolytic and oxidative enzymes in mucoid middle-ear fluids than there were in serous ones. The specific activity of alpha-glucosidase, alpha-mannosidase, beta-glucuronidase, hexosaminidase, acid phosphatase, beta-galactosidase, alkaline phosphatase, and lactate dehydrogenase was 3 to 10 times greater in the mucoid effusions.

Collagenase activity was identified in middle-ear effusions by Ganstrom et al.[395] The enzyme had characteristics similar to those of granulocyte-derived collagenase. The authors hypothesized a role for the enzyme in tissue destruction and development of fluid in the middle ear.

Granulocyte proteases and protease inhibitors have been identified in middle-ear effusions.[204] The proteases may play a role in enhancing the inflammatory response. Protease inhibitors alpha$_1$-antitrypsin, alpha$_1$-antichymotrypsin, and alpha$_2$-macroglobulin, alone or in complex with proteases, were identified in middle-ear effusions of patients with acute otitis media and otitis media with effusion.[204] The relative importance of the proteases and the inhibitors in the evolution and resolution of middle-ear effusion is uncertain.

Recently Described Factors with Possible Roles in Pathogenesis

The pathogenesis of acute otitis media and otitis media with effusion is not yet understood. The limited insight into modes of pathogenesis restricts rational and appropriate therapy. Therapy is now based on pragmatic responses; acute infection is treated with antimicrobial agents; persistent fluid is drained. Further understanding of the pathogenesis of middle-ear infection and its sequelae should yield more effective therapy.

In addition to the issues related to physiology, anatomy (defects in the integrity of the middle-ear system), epidemiology (genetic susceptibility), microbiology (products of microorganisms that elicit inflammation), and immunology (response to various antigens that lead to tissue injury), the following factors may play roles in the pathogenesis of middle-ear infection and its sequelae.

Mucosal Damage

Damage to the epithelium of the upper respiratory tract, including nasal cavity, eustachian tube, and middle ear, may subject the individual to further damage from infectious or environmental agents. This theory suggests that early infection results in more disease because of damage caused by the agent, instead of genetic predisposition to disease that is identified by early infection.

Ciliary Dyskinesia

Intact mechanical processes of the mucosa of the respiratory tract prevent particulate antigens from reaching immunocompetent cells in the middle ear. Coordinated function of ciliated and secretory cells entraps and clears the airways of excess secretions, foreign particles, and cellular debris. A defect in ciliary activity may result in impairment of these functions. The ciliary defect may be genetic or may be due to acquired infectious or environmental factors. Children with the immotile cilia syndrome have recurrent pulmonary disease but also have chronic sinusitis and otitis media with effusion.[778] Infections by respiratory viruses are associated with transient abnormalities of cilia in nasal epithelium.[206] Thus, antecedent viral infection may lead to compromise in mucociliary clearance, producing pooling of secretions in the middle ear and multiplication of bacteria and resulting in acute suppurative infection in the middle ear.

Bacterial Adherence

Bacterial pathogens attach to respiratory mucosa by means of specific cell surface components. To attach to mucosal surfaces, the bacteria express adhesive structures, or adhesins, that bind the organism to complementary molecular structures or receptors of epithelial cells. The bacterial adhesins may be part of fimbriae or pili, fibrillae, cell walls, or other peripheral structures.

The special role in acute otitis media of the predominant bacterial pathogens, *H. influenzae* and *S. pneumoniae,* is suggested in studies of abundant attachment of these bacteria to nasopharyngeal epithelium in otitis-prone children.[1011, 1062] In addition, these bacteria have a greater affinity for nasopharyngeal epithelial cells of children than for those of adults, and adherence is greater in children with otitis media than in healthy children.[1011] However, Porras et al[879] found a lack of correlation between patterns of adherence and frequency of acute otitis media due to nontypeable *H. influenzae.* Andersson and co-workers[25] found that adherence was a frequent property of pneumococci, but adherence did not distinguish between strains that colonized the nasal epithelium and those that caused acute otitis media.

Blocking bacterial adhesion is a new approach to prevention of infection. Strategies to prevent bacterial infections by inhibiting adhesion of the organisms to mucosal surfaces include passive or active immunization with adhesin, use of receptor analogues, metabolic inhibitors, and dietary inhibitors.[805] Secretory IgA in nasopharyngeal secretions can inhibit adherence of *S. pneumoniae* and *H. influenzae.*[1011] As an example of dietary inhibitors, cranberry juice, which has been used to treat urinary tract infections, was found to contain inhibitors of adhesion of *Escherichia coli* to epithelial cells.[1220] More pertinent to otitis media are studies of Andersson and colleagues[26] that found that attachment of *S. pneumoniae* and *H. influenzae* to human pharyngeal and buccal epithelial cells was inhibited by human milk. In contrast, infant formulas and cow's milk showed less inhibitory activity against adhesion of pneumococci and enhanced adhesion of *H. influenzae*.

Biochemical factors of the mucosal membrane may inhibit or promote attachment of bacteria to respiratory mucosa. Preliminary studies of Jorgensen and Holmquist[549] identified increased receptivity for bacteria to nasopharyngeal epithelial cells in patients with acute otitis media, compared with healthy control subjects.

Drug Factors

Drugs used for general or specific signs or symptoms may alter defense mechanisms and make the patient more or less susceptible to infection. Prostaglandins increase bronchial fluid secretions, whereas prostaglandin inhibitors decrease the output of serous and mucous cells. Salicylates, however, may also decrease lung mucociliary clearance and tracheal mucociliary transport rate.[405] Similar mechanisms may occur in the eustachian tube and may result in development and persistence of effusion in the middle ear.

These factors are of speculative interest in developing pathogenic models for middle-ear infection. Future investigations will identify whether they are important.

Surfactant

Pulmonary alveoli are lined with surface-active material, pulmonary surfactant, that stabilizes the alveoli by decreasing surface tension on expiration and preventing alveolar collapse. The major constituents of surfactant are dipalmitoylphosphatidylcholine (lecithin) and phosphatidylglycerol, two apoproteins, and cholesterol. The phospholipids are synthesized and stored in type II alveolar cells. Surfactant is released into the alveoli, reducing the surface tension and maintaining alveolar stability by preventing collapse of air spaces during expiration. Surface tension-lowering substances have been reported to be present in the eustachian tube[116, 451] and in middle-ear effusion.[433, 492] Yamanaka et al[1211] demonstrated surfactant apoprotein in middle-ear effusion and concluded that the surfactant was locally produced in the middle-ear mucosa or eustachian tube. The role of surfactant or lack of the substance in children with recurrent and severe otitis media is unknown. The availability of bovine and synthetic surfactant for therapy of hyaline membrane disease in neonates suggests need for further investigation to determine whether such substances might be of value for maintaining optimal function of the eustachian tube and middle ear in the management of otitis media with effusion.

Inflammation

Investigations of the inflammatory response have led to elucidation of the pathogenesis of various infectious diseases, most notably sepsis and meningitis, and to the introduction of drugs to decrease inflammation, reduce tissue damage, and limit mortality. We now recognize that damage to tissues due to acute infection is only in part from the direct action of the microorganism and its products (endotoxin of gram-negative bacteria or lipoteichoic acid-peptidoglycan complex of gram-positive bacteria); an interaction of inflammatory cytokines is also activated in response to the presence of components of the bacterial pathogens. Some of the information about the inflammatory cascade resulting from research of sepsis and meningitis may be applicable to the pathogenesis of acute otitis media and to the persistent middle-ear effusion that follows every episode of acute infection. As a corollary, some of the therapies used for various stages of inflammation may be of value for management of children with acute otitis media and may reduce the duration of middle-ear effusion.

Infection stimulates macrophages and lymphocytes to produce and release polypeptides, the cytokines. Cytokines are not stored preformed within cells; production requires new protein and in most cases new mRNA synthesis. The three most prominent cytokines are produced by macrophages: monocytes and endothelial cells–tumor necrosis factor alpha (TNF), interleukin-1 (IL-1), and interleukin-6. Other inflammatory mediators include IL-8, platelet-activating factor, interferon-gamma, macrophage-derived proteins, and arachidonic acid metabolites. These mediators activate and arm neutrophils, increasing their adherence to endothelium and stimulating them to produce more superoxide and other active oxygen forms, provoking the release of the intracellular granular contents. Inflammatory cytokines and thrombin stimulate the release of plasminogen-activator inhibitor from platelets and the endothelium. The end results of the host response to infection may be diffuse endovascular injury, microvascular thrombosis, activation of coagulation, and inhibition of fibrinolysis.

Some data are available about inflammation in the middle ear, but much more information is available about the role of inflammation in sepsis and meningitis. A brief review of results of studies of the role of inflammatory reactants and management strategies for sepsis and meningitis is of value because of possible extrapolation to the role of infection and inflammation in the middle ear.

Inflammation and Gram-Negative Sepsis

The following stages are a composite from various studies of the role of inflammatory reactants in gram-negative sepsis.[966]

1. Gram-negative bacteria invade the bloodstream and release endotoxin (lipopolysaccharide).
2. Lipopolysaccharide complexes with lipopolysaccharide-binding protein, which attaches to CD14 receptors on white blood cells, monocytes, and endothelial cells and causes kinase activation of proteins within the cells.
3. The activated cells release tumor necrosis factor (TNF)-alpha, IL-1, platelet-activating factor, and other inflammatory cytokines and release granules

containing proteases and oxygen free radicals, which damage tissue.

4. Within blood vessels, the cytokines increase vascular permeability and stimulate endothelial cells to produce adhesion molecules to which macrophages and other phagocytic cells bind.
5. The cytokines induce phagocytes to migrate to the vascular wall, where they attach and migrate into surrounding tissue.

A rapid drop in blood pressure, tissue damage, failure of vital organs, shock, and death may follow.

Inflammation and Gram-Negative or Gram-Positive Meningitis

The pathophysiology of bacterial meningitis has been extensively studied by various investigators and reviewed in recent publications.[360, 904]

1. Attachment: Organisms attach to cell surface receptors on the mucosa of the nasopharynx with components on the microbial cell surface, such as the pili of *Neisseria meningitidis*; mucosal colonization is enhanced by phenotypic expression of binding adhesins and bacterial secretion of IgA proteases that split secretory IgA on the mucosal surface.
2. Invasion: The microorganisms are transported across specialized cells of the mucosa into the bloodstream within phagocytic vacuoles.
3. Transport across blood-brain barrier: Organisms traverse the blood-brain barrier through interaction of microbial surface proteins that serve to facilitate attachment and affect endothelial cells and stimulate cytokine production.
4. Bacterial products: Within the cerebrospinal fluid, organisms multiply and liberate cell wall– or membrane-active components such as endotoxin from gram-negative organisms or teichoic acid from gram-positive organisms. The bacterial products stimulate release of inflammatory mediators and cytokines, including TNF, IL-1, arachidonic acid metabolites, platelet-activating factor, interferons, and other interleukins. The cytokines activate adhesion-promoting receptors on leukocytes and complementary ligands on vascular endothelia, resulting in attraction and attachment of leukocytes at the site. Other activities of the cytokines include endothelial injury with increase in blood-brain barrier permeability and vasogenic edema; activation of leukocytes with cytotoxic and interstitial edema; and a coagulation cascade with injury to blood vessels and thrombosis.

Current Studies of Management of Inflammation

The new data about the inflammatory response suggest that antimicrobial agents alone are inadequate to resolve some infections and that adjunctive measures to decrease the effects of inflammatory reactants are needed. Paradoxically, bactericidal antibiotics sterilize the infected fluid or tissue but lyse the bacteria and release large amounts of bacterial products, which in turn stimulate local pro-

duction of inflammatory cytokines.[388] In theory, bacteriostatic drugs may be less likely to reduce bacterial products. Erythromycin inhibited lipopolysaccharide-stimulated TNF-alpha by human monocytes,[523] and lower levels of TNF were found in chloramphenicol-treated animals in experimental *Escherichia coli* meningitis.[388]

To combat this cascade, various products have been evaluated or considered.

1. Corticosteroids prevent the production of inflammatory cytokines by macrophages incubated with endotoxin but only if the corticosteroids are present before endotoxin comes in contact with the macrophages.
2. Monoclonal antibodies against CD18 adhesion-promoting receptors block migration of white blood cells. Expression of functional CD18 molecules was essential for migration of white blood cells in the inflammatory reaction and necessary for the initial binding of leukocytes to endothelium. Tuomanen et al[1142] demonstrated reduction of inflammation, tissue damage, and mortality in the rabbit model of bacterial meningitis by use of monoclonal antibodies against adhesion-promoting receptors on white blood cells.
3. Hyperimmune serum, vaccines, or monoclonal antibodies against lipopolysaccharide are designed to bind and neutralize the endotoxin before it can bind to the CD14 receptor or can disrupt the lipopolysaccharide–protein binding complex.
4. IL-1 receptor antagonists can be produced by monocytes and by recombinant technology.
5. Monoclonal antibodies against TNF and soluble receptors and receptor antagonists may be of value in preventing TNF-alpha and platelet-activating factor from reaching the cellular receptor specific for each.
6. Pentoxifylline is a methylxanthine derivative that lowers blood viscosity, has fibrinolytic activity, inhibits platelet aggregation, increases tissue oxygen levels, and inhibits cytokine activation of neutrophils and prevents their adherence to endothelium and release of toxic products on degranulation. The drug also inhibits production of TNF by endotoxin-stimulated monocytes.
7. Activated protein C is an endogenous protein that promotes fibrinolysis and inhibits thrombosis and inflammation. A recombinant human activated protein C was evaluated in patients with severe sepsis. A significant reduction in mortality rate was associated with administration of activated protein C (24.7%), as compared with control patients (30.8%).[96]

Inflammation in the Middle Ear

Specific information about the role of inflammatory reactants within the middle ear is limited. Endotoxin has been identified in middle-ear effusions obtained from patients with otitis media with effusion.[276, 968] In addition, various cytokines have been identified in middle-ear effusions of patients with otitis media with effusion, including

TNF,[814, 1213] IL-1, IL-2,[1215] IL-6,[1216] and interferon-gamma.[1215] Leukotrienes and prostaglandins have also been identified in middle-ear effusions.[165] IL-1 was present in higher concentrations in purulent than in serous and mucoid effusion.[493] IL-1 levels were higher in younger children, and TNF concentrations were higher in older children and in children with more prolonged disease.[493, 552, 1216]

Medical management of persistent middle-ear effusion has been evaluated most extensively for corticosteroids (see Chap. 11). Studies of other anti-inflammatory therapies, including the prostaglandin inhibitors ibuprofen[553] and naproxen,[1161] have been limited and the results negative.

At present, the studies of the inflammatory reaction after acute otitis media and otitis media with effusion are preliminary and descriptive. A likely hypothesis is that bacteria and other microbes incite an inflammatory reaction and that inflammatory mediators play a role in damage to the middle-ear mucosa, leading to development of chronic pathologic changes and persistence of fluid in the middle ear. Candidate therapies for optimal medical management of persistent middle-ear effusion may be suggested by the results of studies to regulate and modify release of cytokines in the models of sepsis and meningitis.

Pathology

In the initial stages of classic acute otitis media, the mucoperiosteum of the middle ear and mastoid air cells is hyperemic and edematous. This is followed by an exudation of polymorphonuclear leukocytes and serofibrinous fluid into the middle ear. The quantity of fluid increases until the middle ear is filled and pressure is exerted against the tympanic membrane (Fig. 25–44). If the disease progresses, the bulging tympanic membrane may rupture spontaneously. The resultant discharge is at first serosanguineous but then becomes mucopurulent. Throughout the middle ear and mastoid, the mucosa becomes markedly thickened by a mixture of inflammatory cells, new capillaries, and young fibrous tissue. This process may become associated with blockage of the aditus ad antrum, resulting in inadequate drainage of the mastoid air cells and a consequent mastoiditis. Extension beyond the mucoperiosteum may lead to intratemporal complications, such as facial paralysis, labyrinthitis, and petrositis, or intracranial complications, which may include lateral sinus thrombophlebitis, meningitis, otitic hydrocephalus, subdural abscess, epidural abscess, and brain abscess.

The pathologic findings associated with the serous (Fig. 25–45) and mucoid types of chronic middle-ear effusion are similar. There is an increase in the number of secretory cells, including glands and ciliated cells. The lamina propria or connective tissue layer becomes thickened by edema and infiltration of numerous inflammatory cells consisting of lymphocytes, plasma cells, macrophages, and polymorphonuclear leukocytes. These changes are more striking in the presence of a mucoid effusion than for a pure serous effusion, in which tissue edema is the predominant finding in addition to the presence of chronic inflammatory cells (Fig. 25–46). It is generally believed that mucoid effusions are mainly the result of secretion, whereas serous effusions are mostly transudates. Recent histopathologic studies of temporal bones of individuals who had cystic fibrosis revealed low densities of goblet cells, which may contribute to reduced amounts of viscous mucus, which in turn may be related to the low incidence of otitis media in this population.[1217] Persistent atelectasis of the middle ear, chronic middle-ear effusions, or both are associated with a number of intratemporal complications and sequelae, including hearing loss, tympanosclerosis, adhesive otitis media, perforation with discharge, chronic mastoiditis, and cholesteatoma.

Microbiology of Otitis Media

The microbiologic causes of otitis media have been documented by appropriate cultures of middle-ear effusions obtained by needle aspiration. Many bacteriologic studies of acute otitis media have been performed, and the results are remarkably consistent in demonstrating the importance of S. pneumoniae and H. influenzae. Investigations have identified an increased incidence of infection due to Moraxella catarrhalis. Studies of asymptomatic children with middle-ear effusion indicate that bacterial pathogens are also present in these fluids, suggesting that bacteria may be a factor in the development and persistence of the effusion. Epidemiologic evidence associates viral infection with otitis media, but viruses have been isolated or identified by detection of antigen in relatively few episodes of acute otitis media. Chlamydia trachomatis is responsible for some episodes of otitis media in infants 6 months of age and younger. Use of new techniques such as polymerase chain reaction (PCR) are expanding our knowledge of the microbiology of otitis media. The results of these microbiologic studies are reviewed, and various aspects of the infectious process in the middle ear are considered. The microbiology of complications of otitis media is discussed in Chapters 26 and 27.

Bacteriology

Geographic and Temporal Surveys in Children

The results of bacteriologic studies of acute otitis media in children from Sweden, Finland, and the United States during the periods 1952 to 1981 and 1985 to 1992 are similar from country to country (Table 25–20). The largest series of published data on the bacteriology of otitis media is from the Pittsburgh Otitis Media Study Group[151]; the results of bacterial cultures of middle-ear fluids from 2807 patients with acute otitis media and of fluids from 4589 patients with otitis media with effusion are displayed in Figure 25–47 and are similar to the results of the 12 studies identified in Table 25–20. Temporal changes, most notably an increase in the incidence of disease due to S. pneumoniae, are identified in the Pittsburgh data for 1980 through 1989 (Fig. 25–48). In summary, S. pneumoniae and H. influenzae remain the

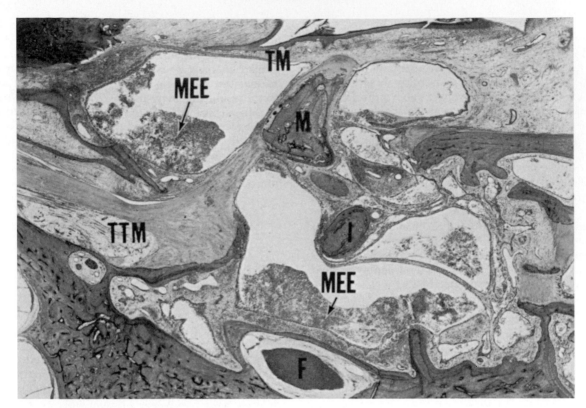

FIGURE 25–44. Acute otitis media (Hematoxylin & eosin, ×15). F, facial nerve; I, incus; M, malleus; MEE, middle-ear effusion; TM, tympanic membrane; TTM, tensor tympani muscle. (Courtesy of H. F. Schuknecht, M.D.)

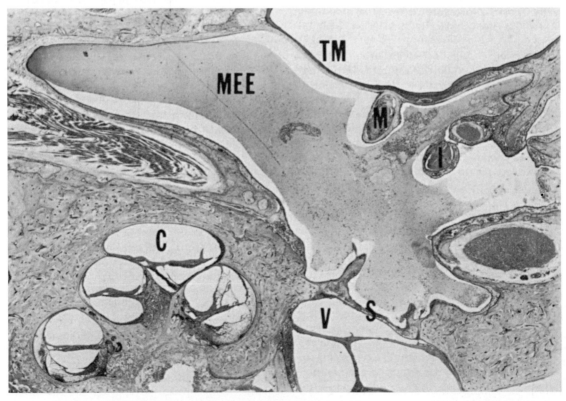

FIGURE 25–45. Otitis media with serous effusion (Hematoxylin & eosin, ×11). C, cochlea; I, incus; M, malleus; MEE, middle-ear effusion; TM, tympanic membrane; S, stapes; V, vestibule. (Courtesy of H. F. Schuknecht, M.D.)

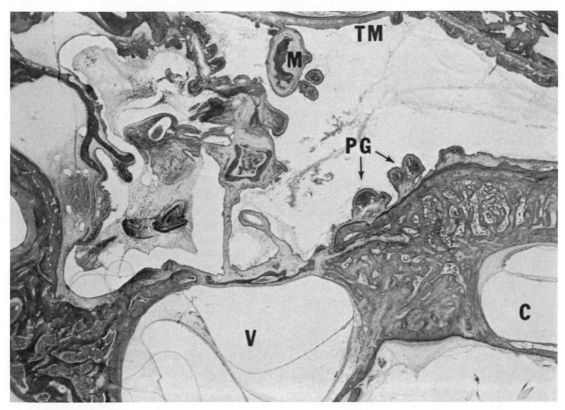

FIGURE 25–46. Chronic otitis media (Hematoxylin & eosin, ×15). C, cochlea; M, malleus; PG, polypoid granulation tissue; TM, tympanic membrane; V, vestibule. (Courtesy of I. Sando, M.D.)

most frequent bacterial pathogens, followed by *M. catarrhalis*. Group A streptococcus, *Staphylococcus aureus*, and gram-negative enteric bacilli are infrequent causes of otitis. No growth (or isolation of an organism considered to be a contaminant, such as *S. epidermidis* or diphtheroids) occurs in approximately one quarter to one third of effusions obtained from patients with acute otitis media; however, some patients have pathogens identified by PCR that are negative by usual bacterial culture.

Surveys in Older Children and Adults

The bacteriology of otitis media is similar in all age groups after the newborn period. Data from school-age children and adolescents[988, 989] and adults[219, 488, 986, 1081] identify similar patterns of dominance by *S. pneumoniae* and nontypeable *H. influenzae*. The corollary to these microbiologic results is that initial therapy for acute otitis media is the same in all age groups.

Sites of Culture

Aspiration of middle-ear fluids by tympanocentesis provides the most valid identification of organisms associated with otitis media. Bacteremia is infrequent. Nasopharyngeal and throat cultures are sufficiently insensitive and nonspecific as to be inadequate to assess efficacy of antimicrobial agents and vaccines. Viruses are present in the nasopharynx, but fewer than half are identified in the

same infants with acute otitis media (see later). Techniques for culture vary, and some, such as use of broth subculture, may increase the yield of bacterial pathogens.[272]

Although the bacteriologic techniques of isolation and identification are standardized, the use of broth subculture increases yield and decreases the number of patients identified with bacterial pathogens.[272] In addition, studies of bacterial antigens in middle-ear fluids may identify bacteria not grown by usual culture techniques.

Nasopharyngeal Cultures

Bacteria with potential to cause acute otitis media are frequent colonizers of the nasopharynx but are responsible for acute infection infrequently. The circumstances that are necessary for an organism colonizing the nasopharynx to gain access to the middle ear and cause inflammatory disease are uncertain but are likely to include coinfection with viruses or strain virulence. Faden et al[353] prospectively assessed children for nasopharyngeal carriage and for middle-ear isolates during episodes of acute otitis media. Respiratory pathogens were usually present in the nasopharynx during an acute episode of otitis media due to the homologous strain; thus, of cases of otitis media due to nontypeable *H. influenzae*, the homologous strain was present in the nasopharynx in 95% of cases, as were 91% of *S. pneumoniae* strains and 86% of *M. catarrhalis* strains. However, 62.9% of the nasopharyngeal cul-

TABLE 25–20. Bacterial Pathogens Isolated from Middle-Ear Aspirates in Infants and Children with Acute Otitis Media

| | Percentage of Children with Pathogen | | | |
| | 1952–1981* | | 1985–1992† | |
Bacterial Pathogen	Mean	Range	Mean	Range
Streptococcus pneumoniae	33	26–53	38	27–52
Haemophilus influenzae	21	14–31	27	16–52
Moraxella catarrhalis	3	0–4	10	2–15
Streptococcus, group A	8	0.3–24	3	0–11
Staphylococcus aureus	2	0–3	2	0–16
Miscellaneous bacteria	1	0–2	8	0–24
None or nonpathogens	31	2–47	28	12–35

* Based on year of publication; 12 reports from centers in the United States, Finland, and Sweden, 1952 to 1981: Bjuggren and Tunevall, 1952; Lahikainen,[624] Mortimer and Watterson,[765] Gronroos et al,[441] Coffey, 1966; Feingold et al,[362] Halstead et al,[453] Nilson et al., 1969; Howie et al., 1970; Kamme et al,[561] Howard et al,[507] Schwartz, 1981.

† Twelve reports from the United States, Canada, Columbia, and Finland, 1985 to 1992: Harrison et al,[465] Odoi et al,[803] Rodriguez et al., 1985; Kaleida et al., 1986, 1987; Karma et al., 1986; Marchant et al., 1986; Bergeron et al., 1987; Carlin et al., 1987; Kenna et al., 1987; Trujillo et al., 1989; Del Beccaro et al.[272]

Total percentages are greater than 100% because of multiple pathogens per middle-ear effusion.

tures concurrently yielded a second middle-ear pathogen. The absence of a middle-ear pathogen in the nasopharyngeal culture strongly suggested that the pathogen was not present in the middle-ear space (Table 25–21). Similar results were obtained in a study of nasopharyngeal secretions and middle-ear aspirates in 354 children with acute otitis media.[403]

During acute infections, the proportion of nasopharyngeal cultures with organisms not considered pathogens (viridans streptococci, diphtheroids, *Neisseria* species, and nonhemolytic streptococci) declined significantly, as compared with cultures from the healthy control subjects. Groothuis et al[442] confirmed that nasopharyngeal cultures had a significant predictive clinical value only when they were negative in identifying children likely to have sterile middle-ear effusion. In summary, although nasopharyngeal cultures may provide useful information about the presence of a pathogen in the middle ear, the cultures are inadequate to provide the degree of specificity needed for investigative purposes or for care of the patient.

Bacteremia with Otitis Media

Bacteremia is uncommon in children with diagnoses of otitis media. Teele et al[1110] reported that 1.5% of children younger than 2 years with temperatures greater than 38.9°C were bacteremic. In an office practice, Schwartz and Wientzen[993] found that 5.8% of febrile infants with otitis media had bacteremia, and McCarthy et al[720] noted a similar incidence in a study of bacteremia in children managed in the outpatient setting. Schutzman et al[983] reviewed 2982 patients managed as outpatients and concluded that 3% of children with otitis media had bacteremia, a rate comparable to that reported in children with

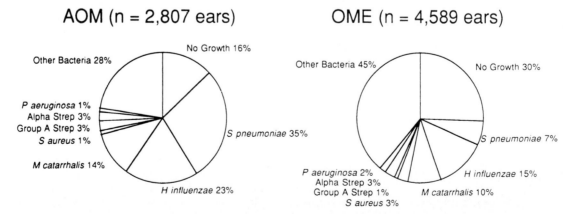

FIGURE 25–47. Comparison of distribution of isolates in 2807 effusions from patients with acute otitis media and 4589 effusions from patients with otitis media with effusion at the Pittsburgh Otitis Media Research Center between 1980 and 1989. (Total percentages are greater than 100% because of multiple organisms.) AOM, acute otitis media; OME, otitis media with effusion. (Modified from Bluestone CD, Stephenson JS, Martin LM. Ten-year review of otitis media pathogens. Pediatr Infect Dis J 11:S7, 1992.)

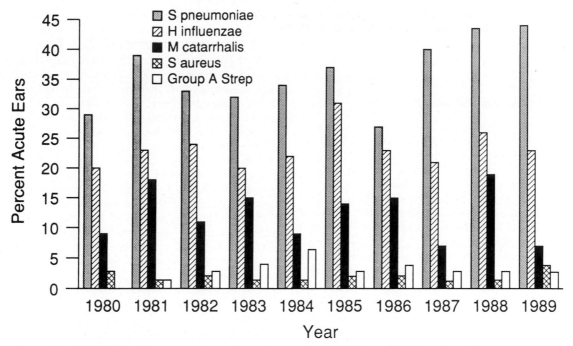

FIGURE 25–48. Prevalence of *Streptococcus pneumoniae, Haemophilus influenzae, Moraxella catarrhalis, Staphylococcus aureus,* and group A beta-hemolytic streptococci in 2807 effusions from patients with acute otitis media at the Pittsburgh Otitis Media Research Center, 1980 to 1989. (Redrawn from Bluestone CD, Stephenson JS, Martin LM. Ten-year review of otitis media pathogens. Pediatr Infect Dis J 11:S7, 1992.)

no focus of infection. As is the case with other bacteremia studies, the incidence of bacteremia increases with higher temperatures.

Bacterial Quantification in Middle-Ear Fluids

Although animal experiments permit quantification of middle-ear fluids, few studies of bacterial colony counts in suppurative middle-ear fluids obtained from patients with acute otitis media have revealed information of value to direct management. Raisanen and Stenfors[907] did colony counts on middle-ear fluids obtained from children with acute otitis media, otitis media with effusion, and chronic suppurative otitis media. Fluids from children with acute otitis media contained bacteria with median counts of 107; fluids from mucoid effusion in otitis media with effusion had median counts of 104; and fluids from children with chronic suppurative otitis media had me-

dian colony counts of 108. Homogenization of thick mucoid or purulent materials presents technical problems and may not allow adequate sampling to provide valid colony counts.

Streptococcus pneumoniae Infection

Streptococcus pneumoniae is the most frequent bacterial agent associated with acute otitis media and the most frequent cause of severe disease and suppurative complications. The increasing incidence of multidrug-resistant strains and the introduction of safe and effective conjugate polysaccharide vaccines have focused interest in the role of the pneumococcus in systemic and local diseases including acute otitis media. Pneumococcal otitis media was first described in 1888, and much of the microbiology, pathogenicity, and immunology was already known at the beginning of the antimicrobial era in the 1930s. Inter-

TABLE 25–21. Correlation of Nasopharyngeal Colonization and Concurrent Pathogens Isolated from Middle-Ear Fluids in Children with Acute Otitis Media

	Nasopharyngeal Colonization, %		
Cause of Acute Otitis Media	*Nontypeable* Haemophilus influenzae	Streptococcus pneumoniae	Moraxella catarrhalis
Nontypeable *H. influenzae* (n = 43)	95	44	40
S. pneumoniae (n = 21)	43	91	48
M. catarrhalis (n = 28)	50	43	86

Modified from Faden, H., Stanievich, J., Brodsky, L., et al.: Changes in nasopharyngeal flora during otitis media of childhood. Pediatr Infect Dis J 9:623–626, 1990.

ested readers should refer to the classic text *The Biology of Pneumococcus* written by Benjamin White and published in 1938[1187] for a comprehensive understanding of the history and microbiology of this organism.

Serotypes Responsible for Acute Otitis Media

There are now 90 antigenically distinct serotypes of *S. pneumoniae*.[486] Because of the potential value of a multitype vaccine, investigators have carefully studied the types responsible for infections of the middle ear. The results of aspirates of middle-ear fluids in children with acute otitis media in the United States, Western Europe, and Israel in the past 25 years have indicated that relatively few types are responsible for most disease.[43, 437, 561, 817, 1051] The most common types responsible for acute otitis media in order of decreasing frequency were 19, 23, 6, 14, 3, and 18 (Table 25–22). In developing countries, the type distribution may be different. Serotypes isolated from Pakistani children during the winters of 1986 to 1989 were, in decreasing order, types 19F, 31, 16, 18A, 9V, 6A, and 15C.[703] Similar to local disease represented by acute otitis media, six to eight serogroups are responsible for 75% of pneumococcal isolates recovered from blood and cerebrospinal fluid.[469]

The serotypes responsible for sequential episodes of acute otitis media were described by Austrian et al.[43] Of interest is the relative constancy of the four most frequently isolated types—19, 23, 6, and 14. The implications of these data are that children have recurrent disease due to the most common types. Other features of these studies included (1) simultaneous infection of the middle-ear fluid by two pneumococcal types, (2) isolation of the same type in consecutive episodes of acute otitis media, and (3) isolation of the same type after an intercurrent episode of acute otitis media due to another type.

The vast majority of isolates of *S. pneumoniae* from middle-ear fluids were included in the currently available 23-type pneumococcal polysaccharide vaccine. Because the polysaccharide antigens have limited immunogenicity in infants, the vaccine was not useful for prevention of acute otitis media. New conjugate pneumococcal vaccines contain seven types but are immunogenic in infants as young as 2 months of age and are likely to provide type-specific protection for infants with acute otitis media. The immunogenicity of the pneumococcal vaccines is described in the next section of this chapter, and the types present in the polysaccharide and conjugate vaccines are listed in Table 25–27. The results of clinical trials reported in 1999 are summarized later in this chapter under Management.

Pneumococci are frequent colonizers of infants and children (see Table 25–21), and the organisms present in the nasopharynx are frequently the types that result in acute otitis media. The pneumococcal polysaccharide vaccines did diminish colonization due to types present in the vaccine and one of the endpoints that will be closely watched in the studies of the pneumococcal conjugate vaccines will be the ability to decrease colonization. Data from South Africa[718] and Israel[263] indicate that colonization due to types present in the vaccine decrease but are replaced by nonvaccine types. Whether or not these nonvaccine types will be responsible for acute otitis media, diminishing the efficacy of the conjugate pneumococcal vaccine, will be closely observed.

TABLE 25–22. Distribution of Major Serotypes of *Streptococcus pneumoniae* in Patients with Acute Otitis Media

	Percentage of Strains		
Serotype	Middle-Ear Fluids: Acute Otitis Media, 1970, 1977, 1979* (1837 strains)	Normally Sterile Sites Including Middle-Ear Fluids, 1979–1987† (5469 strains)	Middle-Ear Fluids: Acute Otitis Media, 1985–1989‡ (228 strains)
1	2.1	2.8	1.8
3	8.5	4.7	6.1
4	3.4	8.0	0.9
6	12.0	—	14.0
6A	—	3.6	—
6B	—	8.9	—
7	2.3	2.3	0.4
8	1.5	2.3	—
9	2.9	—	4.4
9A	—	0.9	—
9N	—	2.0	—
9V	—	5.7	—
11	—	—	3.1
14	10.3	15.8	10.9
18	5.8	5.5	2.2
19	23.0	—	33.2
19A	—	3.5	—
19F	—	7.1	—
23	12.5	7.7	14.0

* Year of publication: Austrian et al[43]; Gray et al[437]; Kamme et al.[561]
† Years of survey: Spika et al.[1051]
‡ Years of survey: Orange and Gray.[817]

Capsular polysaccharide antigens have been identified in most middle-ear fluids from which pneumococci can be cultured and also in some fluids that are sterile.[826] Detection of bacterial antigens is discussed later.

Adherence of Pneumococci to Respiratory Mucosa

Microbial adherence identifies the binding of bacteria to components of the mucosal cell surface. Selective adherence to receptors on the mucosa of the nasopharynx and middle ear may contribute to the pathogenesis of acute otitis media.[1089] Studies of adherence of pneumococci to mucosal surfaces suggest mechanisms of pathogenicity for respiratory infections. Pneumococci isolated from patients with recurrent episodes of acute otitis media adhered in larger numbers to epithelial cells from the nasopharynx than did strains from cases of bacteremia or meningitis.[24] More bacteria attached to epithelial cells from patients with recurrent episodes of acute otitis media than to cells obtained from control subjects.[548] The availability of oligosaccharides that block the carbohydrate receptors on cells of the mucosa suggest an important mode of prevention of pneumococcal disease.[1228] However, the results of a randomized double-blind trial with one oligosaccharide (NE-1530) administered as an intranasal spray to 507 healthy children did not document any effect in prevention of acute otitis media or nasopharyngeal carriage of bacterial pathogens.[1148]

Susceptibility of Pneumococci to Antimicrobial Agents

Increased resistance to available antimicrobial agents of bacterial pathogens has been a constant concern since the introduction of antimicrobial agents: within a few years after introduction of the sulfonamides, previously susceptible group A streptococci and pneumococci became resistant; multidrug-resistant S. aureus was a cause of pandemic disease in the 1950s and 1960s; gram-negative enteric bacteria that developed resistance to available antibiotics became a concern, particularly in hospitals during the 1960s and 1970s; beta-lactamase-producing H. influenzae and M. catarrhalis were identified in the 1970s; and multidrug-resistant pneumococci were first identified in the 1970s but are now a major clinical concern throughout the world.

Resistance is based on alteration in the penicillin-binding proteins in the cell wall. Change in susceptibility is reflected in an increase in the minimum inhibitory concentration, or MIC (least amount of drug required to inhibit growth of the organism), of the drug required to inhibit or kill the organism. Pneumococcal strains are designated *susceptible* or *nonsusceptible*. Susceptible pneumococci have a MIC of less than 0.12 μg/mL; nonsusceptible strains are intermediate, defined as having an MIC of 0.12 to 1.0 μg/mL, and resistant strains have an MIC of 2 μg/mL or more. In contrast with the absolute resistance of organisms that produce beta-lactamase (including H. influenzae and M. catarrhalis), which cleave the beta-lactam ring of penicillins and result in inactive drug, pneumococcal resistance to penicillins and cephalo-

sporins can be overcome by achieving concentrations of drug at the site of infection higher than the MIC of the organism. Emergence of penicillin resistance in a community usually begins with identification of intermediate strains, which increase and are followed by resistant strains.

The clinical relevance of these numbers lies in comparing the MIC of the strain of bacteria with levels of antibiotic achieved at the site of infection. Because pneumococci show incremental levels of resistance, most infections caused by intermediate strains of pneumococci may be treated adequately with usual doses of penicillins, and even some resistant strains may be inhibited. As an example, a usual oral dose of the penicillin or amoxicillin will achieve peak concentrations of approximately 2 μg/mL in middle-ear fluids of patients with otitis media, but doubling the dose will achieve approximately twice these concentrations at the site of infection,[996] with resultant inhibition of an increased number of resistant strains of pneumococci.

Clinical failure due to multidrug-resistant strains of S. pneumoniae that were highly resistant to penicillin G (MIC >4 mg/mL) were first noted in South Africa in 1977.[31] These strains were then identified in western Europe. In Spain, the incidence of penicillin-resistant pneumococci rose from 6% in 1979 to 44% in 1989[363]; approximately half the nonsusceptible strains had MICs of equal to or greater than 2 μg/mL. Multidrug-resistant pneumococci have now been reported from all continents but with variability by region and by country: the highest rates of nonsusceptible pneumococci (in excess of 80%) have been reported from Korea, Thailand, and other Asian countries where antibiotics are freely available; the lowest rates have been reported from countries that have restrictive policies for antibiotic usage, such as The Netherlands (rates reported <1%).[278] Recent data from the United States indicate that penicillin resistance has been increasing each year since the 1980s. The incidence of penicillin-nonsusceptible strains varies from hospital to hospital and by state and region. A seven-state survey for 1997 by the Centers for Disease Control and Prevention identified an incidence of nonsusceptible invasive strains of S. pneumoniae that varied from 15% in Maryland to 38% in Tennessee with 50% or more in each state being resistant.[217] Jacobs et al[533] reported data on pneumococcal isolates by region in the United States: the incidence of penicillin nonsusceptible strains varied between 35.8% and 62.4%; 17.9% were intermediate and 32.5% were highly resistant; resistance was highest in the southern half of the United States.

The increase in resistance to penicillin has been accompanied by increased resistance to other antimicrobial agents. The proportion of resistant strains is usually lower for oral cephalosporins compared with penicillin resistance,[1119] and resistance to macrolides (erythromycin, azithromycin, and clarithromycin) and to clindamycin is lower than resistance to the beta-lactam drugs and sulfonamides. In a national survey of approximately 1500 strains of S. pneumoniae obtained from patients in the United States in 1997, the percentage of susceptible strains was 49.6% penicillin, 63.5% amoxicillin, 68% ceftriaxone, and 69.8% azithromycin and clarithromycin.[533] Of particular concern are reports of resistance to trimethoprim-sulfamethoxazole (TMP-SMX). This antimicrobial agent is inexpensive and is the most frequently used drug for presumed bacterial acute respiratory infections in developing countries. A study of pneumococci obtained from the lower respiratory tract of Pakistani children during the winters of 1986 to 1989 identified 31% of pneumococci resistant to TMP-SMX.[703]

Factors associated with the incidence of multidrug-resistant pneumococci include source (a higher proportion of middle-ear isolates are resistant than blood and cerebrospinal fluid isolates); age (a higher proportion of infants and young children have isolates with multi-drug resistance than adults); prior use of an antimicrobial agent in the patient (within 30 days); volume of antimicrobial drug use in the community, region, or country; and out-of-home day care, which serves to expose many infants and children to respiratory pathogens, including multidrug-resistant bacteria.[33] No clinical features distinguish infections by resistant organisms from infection by susceptible organisms, and there does not appear to be increased virulence of the disease caused by the former. The clinical implications of pneumococcal resistance and strategies to decrease the incidence of resistant strains are discussed later.

Haemophilus influenzae

Nontypeable strains of H. influenzae are commonly found in the nasopharynx of infants. Faden et al[350] studied the epidemiology of nasopharyngeal colonization in the first 2 years of life: 44% of children were colonized on one or more occasions; colonization with the initial strain persisted for 1 to 5 months (median, 2 months); and children carried one predominant strain at a time but were colonized with up to seven different strains. Otitis media due to H. influenzae is associated with nontypeable strains in the vast majority of patients. When type b strains were prevalent, prior to the introduction of the polysaccharide vaccine, approximately 10% of the cases were type b; and about one quarter of the cases of type b acute otitis media had concomitant bacteremia or meningitis.[460] Cases of otitis media due to types a, e, and f have been reported but are infrequent.

Studies by St. Geme et al[1056] suggest that nontypeable strains of H. influenzae evolved from encapsulated organisms. The nonencapsulated types are heterogeneous and can be classified by biochemical and antigenic markers. The majority of strains of nontypeable H. influenzae isolated from middle-ear fluids belong to two biotypes based on assays of indole, urease, and ornithine decarboxylase.[274] Current studies of outer membrane proteins also aim at a means of classifying the nonencapsulated strains.[658] A serotyping system based on antigenic patterns of outer membranes has been suggested.[767] The outer membrane protein profiles of paired nasopharyngeal and middle-ear isolates in children with acute otitis media are similar.[1164] In addition, bacterial chromosomal DNA has been used to determine the epidemiology and transmission of nontypeable H. influenzae.[661]

Haemophilus influenzae was considered to be restricted in importance to otitis media occurring in pre-school children; however, the organism is a significant cause of otitis media in older children, adolescents, and adults. H. influenzae was isolated from middle-ear fluids of 36% of children, aged 5 to 9 years, with acute otitis media.[990] H. influenzae was the cause of otitis media in 33% of 18 children aged 8 through 17 years[988] and was also isolated from 15 of 45 patients older than 16 years of age.[488] In a survey of patients with cases of acute otitis seen in primary care hospitals in metropolitan Tokyo for the year beginning July 1979, 28% of 31 bacteria isolated from middle-ear effusions of patients 10 to 15 years of age and 15% of 76 bacteria found in patients 16 to 70 years of age were H. influenzae.[1081] Thus, the proportion of acute otitis media due to H. influenzae is approximately the same in all age groups.

Haemophilus influenzae appears to be the primary pathogen of the conjunctivitis-otitis media syndrome. Bodor et al[157] obtained H. influenzae from simultaneous cultures of conjunctivae and middle ear fluids in 18 of 20 episodes of the syndrome. Biotyping and outer membrane protein analysis identified that isolates obtained from the conjunctivae and middle ear were concordant.

Fifteen to 30% of nontypeable strains of H. influenzae isolated from middle ear effusions of children with acute otitis media produce a beta-lactamase that hydrolyzes ampicillin, amoxicillin, and penicillins G and V. The incidence of beta-lactamase-producing strains has varied between 20% and 45% in Pittsburgh between 1981 and 1989[151] and was 41.6% in a 1997 United States surveillance study.[533] Virtually all H. influenzae strains were susceptible to amoxicillin-clavulanate and cefixime; other cephalosporins had lower proportions of susceptible organisms (cefuroxime 78%; cefprozil 14%; loracarbef 9%).

Moraxella catarrhalis

Nasopharyngeal colonization with M. catarrhalis is common throughout infancy; by 2 years of age, three quarters of children have been colonized.[351] In a study of children in the Buffalo, New York area, colonization was more frequent in otitis-prone children than in children who did not have otitis media. Children tended to acquire and lose a number of different strains. Prior to the 1980s, M. catarrhalis was isolated infrequently from purulent middle-ear fluids,[238] and many practitioners considered the organism a commensal with limited potential for causing disease. In 1983, reports from Pittsburgh[617] and Cleveland[1015] noted a marked increase in incidence; the organism was isolated from middle ear fluids of 22% and 27%, respectively, of a consecutive series of children enrolled in studies of acute otitis media. In Dallas, during a similar time period, the incidence of M. catarrhalis in middle-ear fluids was lower: 6% of 150 children.[803] The mean of the 12 recent studies identified in Table 25–20 indicates that the proportion of acute otitis media caused by M. catarrhalis is 10%. The clinical course and epidemiology of acute otitis media due to M. catarrhalis were described by Van Hare et al.[1159] The pattern of outer membrane proteins appears to be homogeneous, including eight proteins with minimal variability among strains.[66]

Prior to 1970, almost all strains of M. catarrhalis were

sensitive to penicillin and ampicillin. Today, a majority of strains of *M. catarrhalis* isolated from middle ear fluids produce beta-lactamase, and many of the patients fail to improve if treated with a beta-lactamase-susceptible drug.[1159] The data from Pittsburgh are similar to those from other centers in the United States and Scandinavia[666] and identify approximately 80% resistance in strains obtained from children with acute otitis media and close to 100% in fluids obtained from children with otitis media with effusion.[151]

Leinonen et al[635] provided serologic evidence for a pathogenic role of *M. catarrhalis* in children with acute otitis media. The presence of IgG and IgA antibodies to *M. catarrhalis* in serum or middle-ear fluid, or both, was correlated with isolation of the organism from the middle ear. An increase in titer of antibodies to the organism was found between acute and convalescent serums in 10 of 19 children with acute otitis media whose middle-ear fluid yielded *M. catarrhalis* alone, and no increase was seen in 14 children with acute otitis media whose middle-ear fluids yielded other pathogens.

Groups A and B Streptococci

During the preantibiotic era, otitis due to group A streptococcus infection was frequently associated with scarlet fever and was often of a destructive form.[231] *Streptococcus hemolyticus* (presumably group A streptococcus) was the most prevalent organism in cultures taken at myringotomy for acute otitis media and the most frequent cause of mastoid infection in patients undergoing mastoidectomy during 1934.[822] More recently, group A streptococcus has been a significant pathogen in some studies of otitis media from Scandinavia, but this has not been the case in most studies from the United States. Otitis media due to group A streptococcus now seems to be less frequent and less virulent.

Milder forms of acute otitis media may occur with signs of common cold or pharyngitis in children younger than 3 years of age with culture and serologic evidence of streptococcal infection.[636] In addition, Combs[243] demonstrated that eustachian tube dysfunction was common in children with pharyngitis due to group A *Streptococcus*. However, acute necrotizing otitis media caused by this streptococcus still occurs: rapid destruction of the tympanic membrane may be followed by mastoiditis and intracranial complications.[1053]

Group B streptococci have been isolated from various body fluids, including middle-ear fluid in neonates with otitis media. Bacteremia is frequently associated with otitis media in these infants.[700]

Staphylococcus aureus

Staphylococcus aureus is an uncommon cause of acute otitis media; the organism was isolated in less than 3% of samples of middle-ear fluids from children with acute infection (Table 25–23). Studies from Japan indicate a higher incidence of middle-ear infection, approximately 10%, due to *S. aureus*,[45] and a study of Italian children with HIV infection found a higher proportion of *S. au-* *reus* in middle-ear fluids of HIV-infected children (10%) contrasted with non–HIV-infected children (2.5%).[683] *S. aureus* was found in acute otorrhea that follows tympanostomy tube insertion.[683]

Staphylococcus epidermidis and Diphtheroids

The roles of coagulase-negative staphylococci[361] and diphtheroids in acute otitis media are uncertain. These organisms are considered commensals and are part of the skin flora of the external-ear canal. Isolation of pure cultures of coagulase-negative staphylococci from cases of purulent middle-ear effusions after adequate cleansing of the external canal suggests a pathogenic role in a limited number of cases. Nine different species of coagulase-negative staphylococci have been isolated from middle-ear fluids; *S. epidermidis* is the most common.[100]

Specific antibody to diphtheroids was identified in middle-ear effusions and sera of children undergoing myringotomy for chronic otitis media with effusion.[640] Bernstein et al[105] found antibody-coated *S. epidermidis* and diphtheroids in the middle ears of children with otitis media with effusion. The fluids contained specific antibody, and, in several cases of otitis due to *S. epidermidis*, antibody was present in middle-ear fluid but absent from serum. These data indicate that diphtheroids and *S. epidermidis* may elicit an immune response in the middle ear. The role of these organisms in middle-ear disease, however, remains uncertain. It is possible that they are opportunistic bacteria that invade the middle ear only under certain circumstances, such as persistent effusion.

Gram-Negative Bacilli

Gram-negative bacilli are responsible for about 20% of cases of otitis media in young infants, but these organisms are rarely present in the middle-ear effusions of older children with acute otitis media (see Table 25–23).

TABLE 25–23. Bacterial Pathogens Isolated from 169 Infants with Otitis Media During the First 6 Weeks of Life

Microorganism	Percentage of Infants with Pathogen
Respiratory Bacteria	
Streptococcus pneumoniae	18.3
Haemophilus influenzae	12.4
S. pneumoniae and *H. influenzae*	3.0
Staphylococcus aureus	7.7
Streptococcus, groups A and B	3.0
Moraxella catarrhalis	5.3
Enteric Bacteria	
Escherichia coli	5.9
Klebsiella and *Enterobacter* species	5.3
Pseudomonas aeruginosa	1.8
Miscellaneous	5.3
None or nonpathogens	32.0

Data from Berman et al.,[85] Bland,[118] Shurin et al.[1014] Tetzlaff et al.[1113]

A report from Israel described 33 patients of varying ages with acute otitis media caused by gram-negative bacilli.[818] *P. aeruginosa* was isolated from middle-ear fluids of 23 patients, and an indole-positive *Proteus* species was isolated from the fluids in 6 patients. Seven of the patients were 3 months of age or younger, 16 were 4 to 24 months of age, and 10 were 2 to 80 years of age. Four adult patients had diabetes mellitus, but there were no other patients with significant underlying diseases. The patients had a high rate of other disease manifestations due to the organism isolated from the middle-ear effusion; of these patients, five had acute mastoiditis, three had accompanying bacteremia, and four adult patients showed extensive osteomyelitis of the base of the skull. Culture material was obtained from purulent drainage from the middle ear in patients with perforated tympanic membranes, and the bacteriologic results may represent contaminants from the external ear. In addition, some patients had prolonged courses that might be better described as chronic suppurative otitis media. Nevertheless, this series indicates a potential danger of acute middle-ear infection due to gram-negative bacilli.

Pseudomonas aeruginosa has a special role in chronic suppurative otitis media (see Chap. 26). The organism acts as an opportunistic pathogen, flourishes in moist environments such as the external ear canal, and may cause suppurative disease in contiguous sites. *P. aeruginosa* was the most frequent bacterial pathogen and was isolated from 38 of 40 Pittsburgh infants and children with chronic suppurative otitis media.[580] The organism may also be found in the acute otorrhea that follows tympanostomy tube insertion.[683]

Anaerobic Bacteria

Recent improvements in techniques for isolation and identification of anaerobic bacteria have provided a better understanding of the anaerobic flora of humans and the roles of these organisms in disease. A workshop on the role of anaerobic bacteria in infections of the upper respiratory tract provided current information about the role of these organisms in acute otitis media and otitis media with effusion.[139] The consensus of the conference was that aerobic bacteria played a minor role in acute and chronic otitis media and were not significant pathogens in intracranial complications. Of the studies that demonstrated a limited role for anaerobic bacteria in acute otitis media,[170] *Peptostreptococcus* species were the most frequent pathogen. *Fusobacterium* species and *Bacteroides* species in addition to *Peptostreptococcus* species have been implicated in chronic otitis media.[167]

Mixed and Disparate Cultures

Disparate results of cultures of middle-ear fluids occur when cultures of the two ears in bilateral disease yield different information: effusion from one ear is sterile but a bacterial pathogen is isolated from the other ear, or a different bacterial pathogen is isolated from each of the two ears. Mixed cultures may also occur: two types or two species of bacteria are found in the same middle-ear

fluid. Gronroos et al[441] reported 31.6% disparate results of cultures from children with bilateral otitis media. All children had *S. pneumoniae*, *H. influenzae*, or group A streptococci in fluid from one middle ear and sterile fluid in the other. Van Dishoeck et al[1157] found that 19% of cultures from children with bilateral otitis media yielded different results. The majority of children had a pathogen recovered from one ear and sterile fluid in the other. Also included were six cases in which cultures of one middle-ear fluid sample yielded a single pathogen, but in the opposite middle-ear fluid sample, two pathogens were found. Austrian et al[43] recovered different serotypes of *S. pneumoniae* from middle-ear fluids in 18 children, which represented 1.5% of the cases of bilateral pneumococcal otitis media. Pelton et al[854] cultured middle-ear fluid from both ears of 122 children with bilateral acute otitis media. Disparate results were found in 31 (25%) of the children: in 25 children, a pathogen was present in one ear and the fluid from the other ear was sterile or yielded a nonpathogen; in six children, different pathogens (*H. influenzae* and *S. pneumoniae* in each case) were isolated from the two fluids. Howard et al[507] noted *S. pneumoniae* and *H. influenzae* together in 20 effusions (5% of those studied).

These data indicate that investigative microbiologic studies of bilateral otitis media must include aspiration of both ears to determine the efficacy of methods of treatment (i.e., trials of antimicrobial agents) or prevention (i.e., evaluation of vaccines or drugs). In addition, the complete bacteriologic assessment of the middle ear for a child undergoing tympanocentesis for diagnostic purposes can only be accomplished by aspirating both middle-ear effusions when the disease is bilateral.

Identification of Bacterial Antigens and DNA in Middle Ear Fluids

Results of studies using techniques for identification of bacterial antigens provide new insights into the infectious process and add to the number of cases of otitis media due to a bacterial pathogen. Countercurrent immunoelectrophoresis, latex agglutination, and enzyme-linked immunosorbent assay have been used to detect bacterial antigens such as capsular polysaccharides of *S. pneumoniae*, *H. influenzae* type b, *Neisseria meningitidis*, and group B streptococci in blood, urine, cerebrospinal fluid, and other body fluids. These methods are advantageous because of their ease of performance, rapidity, specificity, sensitivity (as little as 0.2 ng of polysaccharide capsular antigens can be detected), and ability to identify bacteria that do not grow in culture media.

Streptococcus pneumoniae is identified by countercurrent immunoelectrophoresis in most middle-ear fluids in which the organism is cultured and in many specimens that have no bacterial growth. Luotonen and colleagues identified pneumococcal capsular polysaccharide in 83% of middle-ear fluids from which *S. pneumoniae* was cultured and in about one third of middle-ear effusions from which no bacteria were grown.[635, 671] Type-specific pneumococcal antigens may persist for periods in excess of 6 months.[573] Palva and Lehtinen[826] found pneumococcus capsular polysaccharide antigen in 16% of 108 middle-ear effusions from children who had otitis media with effusion; pneumococcus was isolated in only 1% of these samples. Different serotypes have differing sensitivity of antigen detection. Thus, sensitivity for detection in culture-positive samples of types 1, 15, and 19 was high, whereas sensitivity for type 23 was low; the sensitivity for type 6A was higher than that for 6B.[490] These methods used to detect bacterial antigen add information about the large number of patients who have negative results of bacterial cultures.

Use of PCR for bacterial and viral genome sequences adds another technique for identification of the role of microorganisms in acute otitis media and otitis media with effusion. Post et al[881] identified DNA of *S. pneumoniae, H. influenzae,* and *M. catarrhalis* in 97 middle ear fluids of patients with otitis media with effusion: 28.9% were both culture- and PCR-positive, but an additional 48% were PCR-positive and culture-negative for these bacterial species (Fig. 25–49). Subsequent studies by the same group identified evidence of bacterial messenger RNA for *H. influenzae* in 11.8% of 93 specimens that were positive by culture and in 31.2% of specimens that were negative by culture.[914] Middle-ear effusions from HIV-positive subjects were PCR-positive for HIV.[642]

Beswick et al[112] used a technique for extraction of DNA from middle ear effusions of patients with otitis media with effusion and noted mixed bacterial populations, including organisms usually considered contaminants (*Staphylococcus* spp and *Propionibacterium acnes*) or not previously identified with otitis media (*Shigella flexneri, Alloiococcus otitis*). The use of techniques that are far more sensitive than prior modes of microbiologic diagnosis raises questions about the importance of the new information in gaining insight into the role of various organisms in acute and chronic middle ear infections.

Sterile Cultures

In all studies of acute otitis media, a significant proportion (approximately one third) of middle-ear fluids are sterile after appropriate and usual cultures for bacteria have been made. The cause of these cases of otitis media may be one or more of the following:

1. A nonbacterial organism, such as a virus, chlamydia, or mycoplasma
2. A fastidious bacterial organism, such as an anaerobic bacterium, that is not isolated by usual laboratory techniques
3. The presence of bacterial antigens in the absence of viable organisms, indicating past or present bacterial infection and suppression of growth of the organism
4. An immune response to a noninfectious agent, such as pollen or other antigen
5. Prior administration of an antimicrobial agent that would suppress growth of bacteria
6. The presence of antimicrobial enzymes, such as lysozymes, alone or in combination with immunoglobulins in middle-ear fluid, that would suppress growth of bacteria
7. An acute illness in a child who has persistent middle-ear effusion from an episode of otitis media

some time in the past. Because children may have middle-ear effusion for weeks to months after the onset of acute otitis media,[1105] an illness due to a subsequent infectious episode that occurs during the time spent with middle-ear effusion persisting from a prior episode of otitis might be assumed by the physician to be a recurrence of acute otitis media.

Evidence of current or prior infection can be detected by use of Gram stain, PCR, antigen detection, and culture for L-forms; this can increase the number of specific microbiologic diagnoses for acute otitis media and otitis media with effusion. Use of the Gram stain is of value in identification of fastidious bacterial organisms and may provide evidence of bacterial infection in spite of antibiotics or antimicrobial substances that inhibit the growth of bacteria. Use of PCR and antigen detection increases the sensitivity for identification of bacteria and viruses in various body fluids, including middle-ear fluids. L-forms are atypical morphologic forms of bacteria that have lost their rigidity because of defective cell walls. The L-forms require hypertonic media such as hypertonic thioglycollate broth and hypertonic soft agar and are undetectable by conventional culture methods. Ataoglu et al[41] identified L-forms in 6 of 40 specimens of middle-ear effusion obtained at the time of placement of tympanostomy tubes.

In summary, recent techniques for identification of bacterial and viral antigens and PCR are also likely to decrease the number of episodes of otitis that are now categorized as no growth.

Viruses

The clinical history suggests that viral infection is an initiating event of acute otitis media by producing congestion of the mucosa of the upper respiratory tract, which may progress to obstruction of the eustachian tube with pooling of middle-ear secretions behind the obstruction. Abnormalities of middle-ear pressure have been demonstrated during rhinovirus colds[332] and following experimental rhinovirus[178] and influenza virus infections[177] in adult volunteers. Epidemiologic data support the concept that viral infection is frequently an antecedent of acute otitis media. In a longitudinal study of respiratory illnesses and complications in children 6 weeks to 6 years of age attending a day care and school program, Henderson et al[484] demonstrated a correlation between isolation of viruses from the upper respiratory tract and clinical diagnosis of otitis media. Concurrent or antecedent (within 14 days) viral infection was identified in 26.3% of episodes of otitis media in children younger than 3 years of age. Viral outbreaks coincided with epidemics of otitis media. Otitis media was increased in the 14 days after isolation from the upper respiratory tract of respiratory syncytial viruses (RSV), adenoviruses (usually types 1, 2, and 5), influenza virus types A and B, parainfluenza and mumps viruses, and enteroviruses.

Further evidence for the role of viruses in the etiology of acute otitis media has been obtained by isolation of viruses or viral antigens from middle ear fluids. The re-

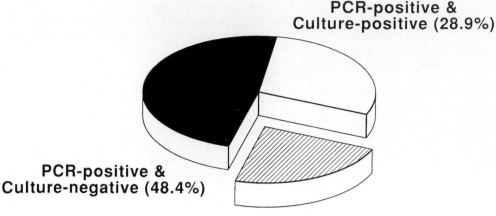

PCR-positive (77.3%)

**PCR-positive &
Culture-positive (28.9%)**

**PCR-positive &
Culture-negative (48.4%)**

**PCR-negative &
Culture-negative (22.7%)**

FIGURE 25–49. In a study of 100 middle-ear aspirates from children with chronic middle-ear effusions, polymerase chain reaction identified bacterial pathogens in 77.3%, in contrast to only 28.9% isolated by culture. (Modified from Post JC, Preston RA, Aul JJ, et al. Molecular analysis of bacterial pathogens in otitis media with effusion. JAMA 273:1598, 1995. Copyright 1995, American Medical Association.)

sults of early studies indicated that virus isolation from middle-ear fluids of children with acute otitis media was infrequent; a survey published in 1976 indicated that virus was isolated from only 4.4% of 663 patients.[606] The yield of virus in middle-ear fluids has increased in recent years with the use of more sophisticated techniques for virus isolation and identification of viral antigens. Ruuskanen et al[956] summarized eight studies published between 1982 and 1990 of the virology of acute otitis media in 944 patients using immunoassay or isolation or both: the middle-ear fluid was positive for virus in 17% of samples and was identified as a single agent in middle-ear fluid in 6%; virus was found in combination with a bacterial pathogen in 11% of samples; nasopharyngeal aspirates were positive in 39% of the patients; and RSV, rhinovirus, and adenovirus were most frequently isolated. Similar data were presented by Heikkinen et al[481] in a study of middle-ear fluids of 456 children studied between 1989 and 1993 (Table 25–24): respiratory syncytial virus was the dominant viral agent and was identified in 48 children (10.5%), followed by parainfluenza virus (3.3%), and influenza viruses (2.2%).

Use of reverse-transcriptase PCR provides a more sen-

sitive tool than virus culture for identification of viruses in middle-ear fluids. Pitkaranta and colleagues studied Finnish children with acute otitis media and otitis media with effusion[870, 871]: evidence of rhinovirus RNA was found in 22% and 19%, respiratory syncytial virus in 18% and 8%, and coronavirus in 7% and 3% in the acute and chronic infections, respectively. Pass[848] noted that none of the studies for detection of virus included a control group of well children.

Most patients with coexisting viral and bacterial infections respond well to appropriate antibacterial agents, but persisting symptoms may be due to underlying virus infection.[34] Chonmaitree et al[226] noted that a higher proportion of patients with viruses and bacteria in middle-ear fluids failed to clear the bacteria 2 to 4 days following initiation of therapy compared with the group who had bacteria alone. Rhinovirus was associated with a higher rate of bacteriologic failure than other respiratory viruses, including RSV, parainfluenza virus, and influenza viruses.[1084] The data suggest that the presence of virus in the middle-ear infection may interfere with bacteriologic and clinical responses to antimicrobial agents.

Otitis media may accompany exanthematous viral infections, such as measles and infectious mononucleosis caused by Epstein-Barr virus.[1082] The isolation of cytomegalovirus and herpes simplex virus in middle-ear fluids from 10 of 271 (4%) children with acute otitis media by Chonmaitree et al[227] raised questions about the role of the organism in the clinical course of the disease. Eight of the children with cytomegalovirus infection were 14 months of age or younger, which raised the possibility of persistent congenital infection. Cytomegalovirus and herpes simplex virus were present in the middle-ear fluids alone or in combination with bacteria or other viruses. Among other rare causes of viral otitis media, smallpox virus has been demonstrated by the presence of Guarnieri bodies in the tympanic membrane of a fatal case in a 3-month-old Indian child who died of smallpox.[158]

TABLE 25–24. Identification of Viruses in Middle-Ear Fluids and the Nasopharynx of Children with Otitis Media

Virus	Middle-Ear Fluid, % (n = 5810)	Nasopharyngeal, % (n = 773)
Respiratory syncytial virus	7	15
Rhinovirus	3	14
Influenza virus	2	2
Adenovirus	2	5
Parainfluenza viruses	1	2
Enteroviruses	1	1
Total	16	39

Modified from Ruuskanen O, Arola M, Heikkinen T, Ziegler T. Virus in acute otitis media: increasing evidence for clinical significance. Pediatr Infect Dis J 10: 425, 1991.

penicillin, for infection caused by beta-lactamase-producing organisms. Which host defense mechanism is responsible for ridding the middle ear of bacterial pathogens? What are the roles of specific antibody and complement? Are the bacteria opsonized, phagocytosed by neutrophils, and killed intracellularly? The introduction of effective vaccines may decrease the incidence of the disease but may also provide insight into the immune defenses of the middle ear. The interested reader is referred to a contemporary review of topics about immunology and immunologic diseases of the ear by Bernstein et al[102] and the proceedings of a symposium, Otitis Media: A Preventable Disease?[265]

Methodology in Studies of Immune Reactions in the Middle Ear

Immunologic studies of otitis media in the human are based on assays of serum, middle-ear effusion (obtained by needle aspiration through the tympanic membrane), and middle-ear mucosa (obtained by biopsy). Problems in methodology and limitations of data from human materials must be considered in evaluating results of these studies, as follows:

1. Middle-ear effusion or mucosa is most readily obtained at operation. Therefore, most reports include patients with chronic disease who required an operative procedure. Only a few reports of materials obtained from patients with acute otitis media are available.
2. Without information gathered prospectively, the investigator cannot identify the stage of disease when material is obtained. In most reports, the stage of otitis media is identified grossly as acute or chronic by the characteristics of the middle-ear effusion (serous, mucoid, purulent, or hemorrhagic). Few studies have results from more than one specimen or one observation. Thus, there is a paucity of information on the sequence of immune events.
3. Techniques for assay of the same function vary in sensitivity and specificity. Newer techniques may provide results at variance with those of previously used methods.
4. The quality and quantity of middle-ear fluid obtained by tympanocentesis is limited. The volume of most aspirates is 0.3 mL or less. Only a few studies can be performed with each sample. In addition, the liquid may be fibrinous or mucoid or filled with cellular debris, making homogenization difficult.
5. Materials are not usually available from "normal" patients, and control subjects are difficult to define.
6. The investigator may not be able to identify the origin of the substance in the effusion. Trauma may occur during the course of aspiration and contaminate the effusion with products of blood and tissue. The liquid represents the sum of substances derived from serum, inflamed middle-ear mucosa, degenerating white blood cells, or other cellular elements.

Experiments in animal models have provided important new information and stimulated new concepts. However, significant differences exist between species, and data derived from studies in animals must be viewed with caution. For the purposes of this discussion, only data derived from studies of humans are presented.

Immunology of the Pharynx

Immunocompetent lymphoid tissue is present in the mucosa of the upper respiratory tract, the site of initial exposure for ingested and inhaled antigens. The lymphoid tissue of the pharynx includes the palatine tonsils and adenoids, the lymphoid tissue at the base of the tongue (lingual tonsil), the lymphoid tissue on the posterior wall of the pharynx (pharyngeal tonsil), and a circular ring of lymphoid tissue (Waldeyer ring). Plasma cells capable of producing all the major classes of immunoglobulins have been identified in the tonsils. The immunologic aspects of the tonsils have been reviewed by Wong and Ogra.[1197]

The specific immunologic relationship of the tonsils and adenoids with the middle ear is unknown. The immunocompetent cells in the tonsils and adenoids are an important defense in excluding microbial and environmental antigens from the systemic lymphoid system, thus performing a "gatekeeper" function. Because microbial organisms responsible for infection of the middle ear proliferate first in the throat or nasopharynx, the tonsils may play a significant immunologic role in the host's defense against otitis media.

Humoral Factors

Immunoglobulin A and Secretory Immunoglobulin A

Immunoglobulin A is secreted by plasma cells in lymphoid tissues lining the gastrointestinal, genitourinary, and respiratory tracts. Secretory component IgA is a nonimmune glycoprotein, formed by local epithelial cells, that exists either in a bound state with IgA or in a free state in effusion fluids. Two IgA molecules combine with secretory component in the epithelium, and the complex (SIgA) is transported through the cell and into the lumen. The production of SIgA begins when antigen is presented to immunocompetent cells in the mucosa.

Immunoglobulin A is the predominant immunoglobulin in middle-ear effusions. The ratio of IgA to IgG is higher in middle-ear effusion than in serum in most patients, and some patients have IgA in middle-ear fluid but not in serum. IgA is also found in nasopharyngeal secretions of patients with recent infection. Fluorescent antibody staining of middle-ear mucosa demonstrates SIgA in the epithelium. Small amounts of free SIgA are present, but most secretory component in middle-ear effusions is bound to IgA.[759] IgA subclasses differ in the amino acid sequence of the hinge region; both IgA1 and IgA2 have been identified in middle-ear effusions,[540] but the functional significance of the subclasses in the middle ear is uncertain.

A specific IgA or SIgA response takes place in the middle-ear mucosa after exposure to antigen. IgA and SIgA specific for adenovirus, RSV, and parainfluenza viruses have been identified in middle-ear fluids of children with otitis media with effusion.[741, 1208] The presence of specific IgA antibody for measles, mumps, and rubella viruses and poliovirus in middle-ear fluid and its absence in some specimens of simultaneously obtained serum indicate that local antibody production takes place.[1041]

Specific IgA can interfere with adhesion of bacteria to mucous membrane and can neutralize viruses. In the intestine, IgA prevents absorption of toxic proteins and antigens. Which, if any, of these functions applies to IgA and SIgA in the middle ear is unknown.

Immunoglobulin G

Immunoglobulin G is present in the effusions of patients with both acute and chronic otitis media in concentrations suggesting that local development of IgG occurs in the middle ear. IgG is divided into subclasses IgG1, IgG2, IgG3, and IgG4 on the basis of differences in structure of the gamma heavy polypeptide chain. Data presented by Freijd et al[385] suggest an association between plasma IgG2 concentrations and susceptibility to otitis media in children. Otitis-prone children (eight to 17 episodes by 30 months of age) had significantly lower plasma concentrations of IgG2 than did children who were not otitis-prone (fewer than two episodes by 30 months of age) at ages 12 and 32 months. Concentrations of IgG1, IgG3, and IgG4 were similar in the two groups.

Immunoglobulin M

Immunoglobulin M is produced in response to primary exposure to a microbial antigen; it is an effective mediator of complement fixation and regulates B-cell function. IgM is present in the middle-ear effusions of patients with both acute and chronic otitis media with effusion; but concentrations are lower than in serum, and studies of middle-ear mucosa obtained by biopsy in patients with chronic otitis media with effusion suggest that local synthesis of IgM does not occur.

Immunoglobulin D

Immunoglobulin D has been identified in middle-ear effusions of patients with otitis media with effusion in excess of concentrations found in serum.[1163] Immunoglobulin D has no identifiable function.[647]

Immunoglobulin E

Immunoglobulin E is part of the external secretory system of antibody produced in the lymphoid tissue of the respiratory and gastrointestinal tracts. Increased concentration of IgE has been found in serum and secretions of patients with various atopic diseases. IgE antibody, when combined with appropriate antigen, causes release of histamine, slow-reacting substance, and chemotactic substance from mast cells and basophilic granulocytes.

Immunoglobulin E–producing plasma cells have been identified in biopsy specimens of mucosa of the middle ear, and IgE has been found in the middle-ear effusions of patients with both acute and chronic otitis media. The source of IgE in the middle-ear fluid of patients with otitis media with effusion may be middle-ear mucosa in some patients[106, 864] and a transudate of serum in others.[522, 624]

Complement

Complement represents a system that includes 11 discrete but interacting proteins and possesses a wide variety of activities, such as viral neutralization, phagocytosis, immune adherence, chemotaxis, anaphylatoxin activities on smooth muscle and blood vessels, and a cytotoxic effect that may serve a protective function leading to destruction of foreign cells.[1177] Activation of complement occurs by the classic or alternative pathways. The classic pathway is usually activated by antigen-antibody complexes and proceeds in sequence from C1 to C9. The alternative pathways do not require immune complex for activation but use materials such as endotoxin or bacterial polysaccharide. The early factors of the classic pathway (C1, C2, C4) are not required, but properdin and C3 are involved in activation.

Evidence for activation of complement in the middle-ear effusions of patients with acute and chronic otitis media has been reviewed by Bernstein et al[109] and Prellner et al.[888] Studies of middle-ear effusion indicate that levels of C2, C3, C4, and C5 are significantly depressed compared with corresponding levels in serum and that the amounts of C3 breakdown products are significantly elevated in the middle-ear fluid of children with otitis media with effusion,[740] indicating use of complement in the middle ear during the course of the disease. Meri et al[740] suggested that activation of complement in middle-ear fluid may play a significant role in the pathogenesis of otitis media with effusion either by decreasing local defenses against bacterial infection or by generating breakdown products that maintain and prolong the inflammatory process.

Rheumatoid Factor

Rheumatoid factor, an IgM that has the capacity to react with IgG in vitro, has been identified in the serum of patients with rheumatoid arthritis and other chronic inflammatory diseases. Rheumatoid factors may participate in the inflammatory process stimulated by immune complexes. DeMaria et al[275] demonstrated rheumatoid factor in 85% of 156 middle-ear fluids obtained from patients with otitis media with effusion; the factor was found in only 8% of serum samples from the same patients. The investigators suggested that rheumatoid factor is produced in the middle ear and may participate in the pathogenesis of middle-ear effusion. These results were not corroborated by Bernstein[106]; none of 21 middle-ear fluids tested showed positive results for rheumatoid factor.

Products of Immune Reactions

A variety of other substances that take part in immune or inflammatory reactions have been identified in the middle-ear effusions of patients with chronic otitis media with effusion.

1. A chemotactic factor for neutrophils and a macro-

phage factor have been found.[98] Chemotactic substances alter the pattern of movement of neutrophils so that cells, which otherwise would migrate randomly, are directed to the vicinity of the chemotactic substance.

2. Macrophage inhibitory factor inhibits the migration of macrophages in vitro; in vivo, it serves to contain macrophages at the site of injury or inflammation.[98] Macrophage inhibitory factor augments the capacity of the macrophage to kill certain bacteria.

3. Lactoferrin inhibits growth of iron-dependent bacteria by competing for elemental iron. Bernstein et al[102a] identified lactoferrin in mucoid but not serous effusions.

4. Prostaglandins have a wide range of biologic activities, including increasing capillary permeability, contraction of smooth muscles, and release of lysosomal enzymes. Bernstein et al[107] found prostaglandins E and F in middle-ear fluids; in some patients, the concentration in the fluid was higher than it was in serum. The effect of prostaglandins on capillary permeability may play a role in development and persistence of middle-ear effusion.

5. Histamine was identified in 104 of 131 middle-ear fluid samples of patients with otitis media with effusion at time of placement of tympanostomy tubes. Berger et al[83] postulated that mast cells in the middle-ear mucosa were triggered to degranulate and release histamine by a product derived from activation of the complement system.

6. Products derived from microorganisms that participate in immune or inflammatory responses (endotoxins, interferon, neuraminidase) are discussed in the section on microbiology.

Cytology of the Middle Ear and Middle-Ear Effusions

Neutrophils, macrophages, and lymphocytes are the predominant cell types in middle-ear effusions.[1031, 1209] The proportion of B- and T-lymphocytes varies widely in published reports. Bernstein et al[110] found that mucoid middle-ear effusions contained many B-cells but few T-cells, whereas serous effusions contained mainly T-cells but no B-cells. Monocytes and phagocytes are present, but they occur in small numbers in most specimens. Giant phagocytes with ingested cells, cell debris, and bacteria are occasionally seen. Eosinophils, mast cells, basophils, and plasma cells are rare. Epithelial cells include numerous flat endothelial cells and few ciliated and goblet cells.

After onset of acute otitis media, the middle-ear effusion contains large numbers of neutrophils and few lymphocytes, monocytes, and phagocytes. Initially, polymorphonuclear leukocytes may defend the middle ear from bacterial infection as well as contribute to the middle-ear effusion by release of enzymes that stimulate an inflammatory response. After several weeks, the proportion of cells is reversed, and lymphocytes, monocytes, and phagocytes predominate.[903]

Similar cell types are found in middle-ear mucosa obtained by biopsy of patients with otitis media with effu-

sion. Inflammatory cells in the submucosa are predominantly of the mononuclear type. Plasma cells and small lymphocytes predominate. The presence of IgA and IgG was demonstrated by use of an immunofluorescent stain of mononuclear cells from middle-ear effusions; IgM and IgE were infrequently detected.[825]

Immunology of Acute Otitis Media

Role of Serum Antibody

An immune response reflected in a rise in specific serum antibody occurs in some children after acute infection of the middle ear. The response is age dependent, with youngest children less likely to respond, and is also dependent on the antigenic stimulus of the organism. The antibodies may be evident in middle-ear fluids as well as serum early in the course of the disease.[511, 569] The evidence indicates that serum antibody plays an important role in protection of the middle ear from bacterial infection. The infant is protected by passively transferred antibody from the mother; antibody concentrations to *S. pneumoniae* in cord blood correlate with the development of pneumococcal otitis media in the first months of life.[969] Passive or active immunization protects against acute otitis media: the efficacy of enriched immune globulin for respiratory syncytial virus and the conjugate pneumococcal vaccine is presumed to be based on the presence of protective serum and local antibodies.

Otitis Media Due to Streptococcus pneumoniae

The number of infants who develop protective antibodies following pneumococcal otitis media is variable and dependent on the age of the patient and the pneumococcal serotype. Infants respond to acute pneumococcal infection with low levels of serum antibody. Eighteen percent of Finnish children younger than 1 year of age, 48% of 1-year-olds, and 39% of children 2 to 7 years old had a significant increase in type-specific antibody following pneumococcal otitis media. Types 3 and 18 induced the highest concentrations of antibody irrespective of age; types 4, 7, 8, and 9 were intermediate; and types 6, 19, and 23 were poor antigens, even in older children.[615] Age-specific responses were also found in Alabama children who had acute otitis media due to *Streptococcus pneumoniae;* only 12% of children younger than 1 year of age had a significant rise in type-specific antibody in the convalescent serum, whereas 48% of the children 2 years of age or older responded.[1042]

In contrast to the type specificity of the capsular polysaccharide, the cell wall (C) polysaccharide is common to all pneumococcal strains. Following acute pneumococcal otitis media or immunization with the polysaccharide vaccine, children developed antibody to pneumococcal C polysaccharide, the species-specific cell wall antigen,[616] but the protective role of antibody to the C polysaccharide against subsequent infection is uncertain.[775]

Pneumolysin is a species-specific protein toxin produced intracellularly by pneumococci. Virolainen et al[1166] demonstrated serum antibodies to pneumolysin in infants following pneumococcal otitis media but less frequently

(7%) than antibodies to pooled capsular polysaccharides (27%). Antibodies to the protein antigen pneumolysin developed at an earlier age than antibodies to the capsular polysaccharides. Since seroconversion is uncommon, the value of pneumolysin as a diagnostic test for pneumococcal infection is limited.

Nasopharyngeal antibodies to pneumococcal capsular polysaccharides were detected in children with acute otitis media. Local production of IgA but not IgM or IgG class antibody was detected in infants as young as 6 months of age.[1167] The role of mucosal antibody in decreasing carriage or protecting against subsequent infection is unknown.

Otitis Media Due to Haemophilus influenzae

The antigens of nontypeable H. influenzae are enclosed in an outer membrane of approximately 20 proteins and a lipoligosaccharide. Antibody to some of the outer membrane proteins is bactericidal. Specific serum and middle-ear fluid antibodies develop after episodes of acute otitis media due to nontypeable H. influenzae.[55, 346, 347, 1017, 1039] Susceptibility to Haemophilus otitis correlates with the absence of bactericidal antibody in acute serum samples.[1017] Recurrent episodes of acute otitis media due to various strains of nontypeable H. influenzae indicate lack of cross-protection; an immune response to one strain does not protect against another and argues for multiple and different antigenic types.

A majority of Alabama children 2 years of age or younger with H. influenzae infection had specific antibody in convalescent serum.[1039] Shurin et al[1017] found similar immune responses in children 2 months to 12 years of age with acute otitis media due to nontypeable strains of H. influenzae: 11% of the children had homotypic antibody in the acute serum, but 78% had antibody in the convalescent specimen. Barenkamp and Bodor[55] identified homotypic bactericidal antibody in convalescent sera of each of eight children with acute otitis media due to nontypeable H. influenzae; antibody was absent in the acute serum samples.

Harabuchi et al[458] demonstrated the presence of nasopharyngeal secretory IgA antibodies reactive with the P6 outer membrane protein in colonized children. The results suggested that elimination of the organism from the nasopharynx was associated with a mucosal immune response.

Otitis Media Due to Moraxella catarrhalis

The antigens of M. catarrhalis are found in the outer membrane; eight proteins have been identified. Leinonen et al[635] identified an antibody rise to a pool of M. catarrhalis antigens in 50% of children with acute middle ear infections due to this organism. Faden et al[352] found antibody to homologous outer membrane proteins in the middle ear and serum of patients with acute M. catarrhalis infections. The role of antibody in elimination of the organism from the middle ear or protection from subsequent infection is unknown.

Recurrent Episodes of Acute Otitis Media

Children with recurrent episodes of otitis media have new middle-ear infections due to the same spectrum of organisms that was responsible for the first episode. S. pneumoniae and nontypeable H. influenzae are the most common bacteria in recurrent infections, but the new episodes are rarely due to the same serotype that infected the child in a prior episode. Austrian et al[43] found that approximately 1% of isolates of S. pneumoniae in recurrent episodes of pneumococcal otitis media were due to the same serotype responsible for a prior episode. Recurrent episodes of otitis media due to nontypeable H. influenzae are also associated with new types. Using outer membrane protein gel analysis and biotyping, Barenkamp et al[56] determined that episodes of early recurrence of otitis due to nontypeable H. influenzae (less than 30 days after initial H. influenzae infection) had first and second isolates that were identical. In contrast, children with late recurrences of nontypeable H. influenzae (more than 30 days after initial infection) had disease due to a different strain. These data suggest that infections due to S. pneumoniae or nontypeable H. influenzae produce an immune response that protects the child against subsequent infection due to the same type.

Role of Antibody in Clearance of Middle-Ear Effusion

Specific antibody to homotypic strains is present in middle-ear effusions as well as in serum after episodes of acute otitis media. Type-specific IgG predominates in the middle-ear fluid; IgM- or IgA-specific antibodies are present in a small proportion of children with acute infections.[346] In response to acute otitis media due to nontypeable H. influenzae, IgG titers increased in serum in a period of 2 months, whereas middle-ear fluid titers initially increased, then decreased and disappeared at 3 months. Specific IgG antibody was present in both ears in bilateral and unilateral otitis media, although in lower titers in the unaffected ear.[346]

Clearance of fluid from the middle ear in patients with acute otitis media due to S. pneumoniae and H. influenzae was significantly associated with the presence and concentration of specific antibody to the infecting strain in the middle-ear fluid at the time of diagnosis.[1040] Clearing of the effusion by the second visit (2 to 7 days after diagnosis) was associated with specific antibody in the middle-ear effusion obtained at first visit and was directly associated with the concentration of specific antibody. Effusion was cleared rapidly in more children with infection due to H. influenzae (45.3%) than in those with infection due to S. pneumoniae (13.6%), whether or not antibody was present. The source for the antibody in the effusion at the time of presentation of acute otitis media is uncertain; antibody may have developed after a prior infection, may have developed rapidly after a current infection, or may indicate a delay of presentation until the time when the specimen of middle-ear fluid was obtained. If type-specific antibody was present from a prior infection, it did not protect the patient from a recurrent episode of acute otitis media but did reduce the duration of effusion.

Polymorphonuclear Leukocyte Response

Although recurrent acute otitis media is a frequent early sign of children with significant defects in white blood cell response to infection (see Children with Defects of the Immune System), there are patients who appear to be immunologically competent but have subtle changes in polymorphonuclear leukocyte response.

Hill et al[491] identified defective chemotactic response in selected patients with recurrent episodes of otitis media and diarrhea. Ichimura[520] identified defective neutrophil chemotaxis in 20 children who had had recurrent episodes of otitis media (four or more episodes during the preceding year) but were well at the time of examination.

Immunology of Otitis Media with Effusion

Role of Antibody in Middle-Ear Fluid

All the major classes of immunoglobulins (IgA, IgG, IgM, IgD, and IgE) have been identified in the middle-ear fluids of patients with chronic otitis media with effusion. SIgA, IgA, and IgG are synthesized by the mucosa of the middle ear; synthesis of other immunoglobulins in the middle ear is less certain.[108] Both IgA and IgG are present in middle-ear effusions in concentrations higher than those found in simultaneously obtained serum, whereas IgM and IgE are present in equivalent or lower concentrations in effusion than in serum. The highest concentrations of each of the major classes of immunoglobulins are present in mucoid effusions; the lowest are found in serous effusions, and intermediate values occur in leukocytic middle-ear effusions.

Polymorphonuclear Leukocyte Response

Giebink and colleagues[407] studied the polymorphonuclear leukocyte response in children with chronic otitis media with effusion at the time of myringotomy or placement of ventilating tubes and, in a few cases, 2 to 8 weeks later. In some children, there were transient abnormalities of polymorphonuclear leukocyte motility (depressed chemotactic responsiveness), phagocytosis (depressed polymorphonuclear leukocyte bactericidal activity), or intracellular oxidation (depressed polymorphonuclear leukocyte chemoluminescence). Repeated studies performed after surgery found these indexes to be normal in the majority of children, suggesting that leukocyte dysfunction was transient and probably associated with the inflammatory reaction that elicited the middle-ear fluid.

Viruses may depress neutrophil function, but the role of this result of antecedent viral infection and bacterial otitis media is uncertain.[1]

Immune Complexes

Some investigators suggest that chronic otitis media with effusion may be an immune complex disease. Antigen (microbial agents or allergens) may combine with antibody (locally produced or derived from serum) to form an immune complex, which activates the complement sequence through the classic or alternative pathways. Polymorphonuclear leukocytes and monocytes are attracted to the site. With the death of these cells, intracellular enzymes are released, producing local tissue damage and stimulating effusion. Maxim et al[717] identified immune complexes in middle-ear fluids by use of the fluorescent Raji cell assay. Other investigators have not been able to corroborate the results.[99] Yamanaka et al[1212] concluded, after a study of 245 patients with otitis media with effusion, that immune complexes formed in the middle ear might prolong the inflammatory process through complement activation after chemotaxis of neutrophils. If immune complexes do occur in middle-ear fluid, they may represent microbial antigen-antibody complexes as a part of the normal process of elimination of infectious product through phagocytosis.

Children with Defects of the Immune System

Most children with recurrent episodes of acute otitis media have no apparent systemic or local immune defect and do not suffer from infections at other sites. These children have normal serum concentrations of IgG, IgM, and IgA,[90] normal systemic cell-mediated responses, and normal phagocytic and bactericidal capacity of neutrophils in peripheral blood.[410] Available data about the immune system of the middle ear in children with recurrent otitis media with effusion indicate that most children with recurrent disease have the essential elements for immunologic resistance, including T- and B-cell responses that are fully operative, macrophages that are available for engulfing and ingesting antigenic material, and appropriate antibody response by middle-ear mucosa.[824]

Children with congenital or acquired immunodeficiency may have defects of phagocyte function or humoral systems. Infections of the respiratory tract, including otitis media, are associated with defects of chemotaxis, phagocytosis (neutropenia or intrinsic cellular defects), or killing (chronic granulomatous disease); problems with the humoral system include deficiency of circulating antibody (hypo- or agammaglobulinemia), mucosal antibody (IgA deficiency), or complement. Multiple infections in the same system (respiratory tract, urinary tract, or central nervous system) suggest a local anatomic or physiologic defect. Most children with recurrent episodes of otitis media as the sole form of recurrent infectious disease probably have an underlying defect that is not immunologically mediated, e.g., eustachian tube dysfunction. A few children have recurrent respiratory infections, including recurrent otitis media and pyogenic infections in other systems, as part of an immunodeficiency syndrome.[82, 448, 542]

Multiple serious pyogenic skin infections (furunculosis, subcutaneous abscess, or cellulitis), accompanied by pneumonia or recurrent otitis media, suggest neutropenia, defective chemotaxis, or problems with phagocytosis. A pattern of subcutaneous abscesses or furunculosis, accompanied by abscess formation in lymph nodes, liver, or lung, and recurrent acute otitis media suggests chronic granulomatous disease. Meningitis, osteomyelitis, septic arthritis with recurrent acute otitis media, or pneumonia raises concern for a deficiency of antibody or C3. Protracted diarrhea, when accompanied by recurrent episodes of otitis media, sinusitis, or pneumonia, suggests IgA deficiency (although many children with deficiencies of IgA are otherwise normal without undue susceptibility to infection). Children with selective IgG2 or IgG3 subclass deficiency had recurrent sinopulmonary infections and otitis media (more than six episodes per year).[1149] The bacterial pathogens of acute otitis media in children with primary immunodeficiencies are likely to be the same as those in normal hosts, including S. pneumoniae, H. influenzae, and M. catarrhalis but also S. aureus.[448]

Patients with defects in splenic function are susceptible to overwhelming infection due to encapsulated organisms such as S. pneumoniae or H. influenzae type b. Such patients, including those with congenital or acquired asplenia and those with sickle cell disease, have not been identified as groups with unusual susceptibility to infections at local sites, such as the skin and soft tissues or middle ear.

Human immunodeficiency virus, the organism responsible for AIDS, is highly tropic for T-lymphocytes. Children with AIDS have abnormalities of T-cell, B-cell, and complement functions and phagocytosis. The children are susceptible to local and systemic pyogenic infections, and otitis media is only one of the many bacterial diseases that may occur. In a study of Boston children observed from infancy, otitis media was as frequent in infants with AIDS as in infants who were initially HIV-positive because of maternal antibody and seroverted to normal. After age 2 years, however, the children with AIDS continued to have recurrent episodes of acute otitis media, whereas the children who now were seronegative had the expected lower age-specific incidence.[58] Although microbiologic data were not available for these children with HIV infection, they responded to usual antibacterial therapy and probably had the usual bacterial pathogens of acute otitis media. The prevalence of S. pneumoniae, H. influenzae, and group A Streptococcus isolated from middle-ear fluids of children with acute otitis media was similar in HIV-infected and in normal children.[698] HIV-infected children younger than 2 years of age were able to respond to a five-valent pneumococcal conjugate vaccine, which suggests that the vaccine may be useful for reducing both local and invasive pneumococcal disease in HIV-infected infants.[588]

Children with recurrent and severe acute otitis media may have subtle immune deficits that are elicited only by indirect techniques, such as response to infection and immunization. Prellner et al[887] demonstrated that children with recurrent acute otitis media had IgG antibody concentrations to pneumococcus types 6A and 19F, but not against type 3, throughout the first 3 years of life that were lower than those of age-matched healthy children. The antibody response to rubella vaccine was significantly lower in children with recurrent otitis media, but the response to diphtheria and tetanus toxoids was similar to that of children without experience with recurrent acute otitis media.[886] Similarly, Yamanaka and Faden[1210] noted that otitis-prone children had poor responses to the outer membrane protein P6 of nontypeable H. influenzae; otitis-prone children observed longitudinally had lower concentrations of antibody to P6 than did normal children. Pelton et al[853] identified impaired response to Haemophilus capsular polysaccharide protein conjugate vaccine in children with recurrent otitis media. These data suggest that some children who have recurrent middle-ear infections are immunologically different from children without recurrent ear infections and may benefit from the use of bacterial polysaccharide immune globulin.[1018]

The evaluation of a child with recurrent acute otitis media for possible immune deficiencies was reviewed by Adamkeicwicz and Quie.[3]

The Role of Allergy in Otitis Media

The role of allergy in the etiology of otitis media with effusion is uncertain. The role of allergy in eustachian tube function was considered earlier (Physiology, Pathophysiology, and Pathogenesis). Few critical studies of appropriate design are available to clarify the relationship of allergy and otitis media. Available studies are often biased (enrollees include children referred for allergy evaluation) and do not include appropriate control patients. However, the association of reaginic antibody with IgE provides a specific measure for precise definition of allergy and has already provided some significant information about the primary or secondary role of allergy in otitis media with effusion. Mogi and Suzuki[758] summarized current information about the evidence for IgE-mediated allergic reactions in the pathogenesis of otitis media with effusion.

The evidence for a role of allergy in recurrent otitis media with effusion in some children was presented by Siegel[1024] and Bernstein[103]:

1. Many patients with recurrent otitis media with effusion have concomitant allergic respiratory disease.
2. A history of one or more major allergic illnesses in parents is usually present.
3. Nasal or peripheral eosinophils are often present in increased numbers.
4. Positive skin test reactions to allergens or positive results of a radioallergosorbent test are present in many patients.
5. Elevated IgE levels in the middle-ear effusions and serum of some children have been identified.
6. Mast cells (some that are degranulating) are found frequently throughout the middle-ear mucosa.
7. An elimination diet led to improvement in serous otitis media in infants identified as having food allergy by means of skin prick testing, specific IgE tests, and food challenge.[802]

Evidence against a major role of allergy in otitis media with effusion was summarized by Bernstein[103]:

1. In unselected series of cases of otitis media with effusion, fewer than one third of patients are atopic. Allergic airway disease was sought and found not to be a predisposing factor for Arizona native American children with recurrent otitis media.[1131] In these children, other factors are probably responsible for the susceptibility to middle-ear infection.
2. The seasonal incidence of otitis media with effusion (winter to spring) is contrary to the season when

grasses, trees, and pollens cause acute nasal allergy (late spring and early fall).

3. Most studies indicate an absence of eosinophils and absence of, or only small numbers of, IgE-producing cells in middle-ear fluids and middle-ear mucosa.

4. A failure to improve with aggressive allergic treatment, including hyposensitization and use of antihistamines, in spite of improvement in nasal symptoms, is seen in most patients.

The role of allergy in the etiology of otitis media continues to be hypothetical and controversial.[111, 756] Four possible mechanisms have been postulated: (1) middle-ear mucosa functioning as a shock (target) organ; (2) inflammatory swelling of the mucosa of the eustachian tube; (3) inflammatory obstruction of the nose; or (4) aspiration of bacteria-laden allergic nasopharyngeal secretions into the middle-ear cavity.[134] In an investigation by Bernstein et al,[104] the role of IgE-mediated hypersensitivity in the etiology of recurrent otitis media was studied. Children were divided into nonallergic and allergic groups on the basis of their history and physical examination findings, prick testing responses for selected antigens, and total IgE and specific IgE radioallergosorbent test results. After aspiration of the middle ears and testing for IgE, the authors concluded that 35% of the 100 children may have had IgE-mediated allergy as a cause of their effusion and that the middle ear was a possible target organ in 8% of the children. In the other 27%, they postulated that the eustachian tube might have been the target organ. Indeed, in a series of studies involving adult volunteers, a relationship among intranasal antigen challenge, allergic rhinitis, and eustachian tube obstruction was demonstrated.[2, 307, 390] These studies demonstrated a relationship among intranasal challenge with allergens, virus, and mediators, in volunteers who did and did not have allergic rhinitis, and the effect on nasal and eustachian tube function.[2, 302, 307, 390, 1035, 1036, 1068]

Thus, many patients may be allergic and many children have recurrent otitis media, but there is no conclusive evidence correlating the two conditions. However, as described before, there is some evidence now from studies in children and adult volunteers that it is likely that the allergic response plays a role in some children with otitis media or in some episodes of otitis media. The presence of specific IgE on mast cells in middle-ear mucosa could result in release of mediators of inflammation, with the mucosa functioning as a shock organ similar to respiratory mucosa in other areas. Alternatively, the allergic reaction might be a predisposing factor producing congestion of the mucosa of the nose and eustachian tube, leading to obstruction of the tube with retention of fluid in the middle ear. Microbial and environmental antigens may act in a similar pattern to injure middle-ear mucosa or elicit a similar response from cells with immune function in the mucosa.

Vaccines and Immunoglobulins for Prevention of Otitis Media

If type-specific serum antibody is correlated with protection from homotypic infection, bacterial vaccines may be an effective mode of prevention of type-specific otitis media. The conjugate polysaccharide vaccine for *H. influenzae* type b has been successful in reducing the incidence of invasive disease caused by this organism in immunized infants but is of limited interest in prevention of acute otitis media because the type b organisms cause only about 2% of acute otitis media. A vaccine for nontypeable *H. influenzae* is not available, but current investigations focus on the use of outer membrane antigens for the development of a vaccine (see later, Nontypeable *Haemophilus influenzae* Vaccines).

A 23-type pneumococcal polysaccharide vaccine is available, but few of the types in the vaccine are sufficiently immunogenic in infants to provide protection against otitis media. More promising are results of recent studies of conjugate pneumococcal vaccines indicating immunogenicity in infants as young as 2 months of age. The results of use of a seven-type pneumococcal conjugate vaccine in Northern California indicated efficacy in reducing the incidence of clinically diagnosed acute otitis media.[117] The apparent increase in *M. catarrhalis* as a pathogen for acute otitis media suggests that this organism may also need to be included in an "otitis media vaccine." Influenza virus vaccines and vaccines and immunoglobulins for protection against infection due to respiratory syncytial virus (RSV) have been effective in reducing the number of episodes of acute otitis media in infants and will need to be included in the overall immunization strategy to reduce otitis media.

In addition to immunization of the infant, protection during the first months of life can be provided by passively transferred antibody from the mother. In developing countries, tetanus toxoid immunization of the mother has been successful in the prevention of almost all neonatal tetanus deaths. Immunization with respiratory vaccines would provide passively transferred antibody that could protect from acute otitis media during the first months of life until the infant is able to respond to active immunization. Salazar and colleagues[969] found that low cord blood immunoglobulin G antibodies predicted early onset acute otitis media in Minnesota infants. Shahid et al[1004] immunized healthy pregnant women in Bangladesh with pneumococcal polysaccharide vaccine and found antibody concentrations of 6.8 and 7.5 μg/mL to types 6B and 19F in cord blood. The median half-life of the passively transferred antibody was about 35 days. The Minnesota group is now studying the efficacy of maternal immunization with pneumococcal vaccine for prevention of acute otitis media in their infants (Giebink, personal communication).

Prevention of acute otitis media by viral vaccines including influenzavirus vaccines[413] and RSV vaccines[23] is likely to be of increasing importance as investigators seek to interrupt the initial stages in the pathogenesis of acute otitis media. The potential value of bacterial and virus vaccines was extensively discussed at two symposia: Pittsburgh in 1989[148] and Annecy, France in 2000.[265]

Pneumococcal Polysaccharide Vaccines

Streptococcus pneumoniae is responsible for about 40% of episodes of acute otitis media; in theory, a pneumococcal vaccine that included 80% of the types responsible for otitis media and was 80% effective could reduce the overall incidence of otitis media by about 25%. Even if we assume a small excess in cases associated with nonvaccine serotypes, the reduction is likely to be between 15% and 20%. The experience with polysaccharide vaccines was disappointing; only a limited decrease in the number of cases of type-specific otitis media occurred. In contrast, the preliminary data about the efficacy of conjugate pneumococcal vaccines suggest that a substantial reduction in the incidence of acute otitis media can be achieved.

Although there are 90 antigenically separable types, relatively few serotypes are responsible for most infections. A 14-type pneumococcal polysaccharide vaccine was licensed for use in the United States in 1978 and was replaced by a 23-valent vaccine licensed in 1983. As new vaccines (both polysaccharide and conjugate polysaccharide) are formulated, it is likely that they will include most of the types in the 23-valent vaccine. The vaccine contains purified polysaccharide antigens of types associated with otitis media in children. Each polysaccharide is extracted, separated, and combined into the final vaccine. A 0.5 mL dose contains 25 μg of each polysaccharide type dissolved in isotonic saline solution containing 0.25% phenol or 0.01% thimerosal as a preservative; it is administered subcutaneously or intramuscularly. The vaccine is well tolerated, and no significant reactions have been noted in children.

Each pneumococcal type polysaccharide antigen produces an independent antibody response. In older children (older than 2 years of age) and adults, antibody develops in about 2 weeks. In general, children younger than 2 years of age exhibit unsatisfactory serologic responses to most polysaccharide types following a single dose. *S. pneumoniae* type 3 evokes a significant antibody response in infants as young as 6 months of age,[679] suggesting that some polysaccharides are adequate immunogens in children of all ages. In contrast, the conjugated pneumococcal polysaccharide vaccines provide enhanced immunogenicity in infants as young as 2 months of age.

Investigations of 8- or 14-type polysaccharide pneumococcal vaccines for prevention of recurrent episodes of acute otitis media were initiated in 1975 in Boston, Massachusetts, and Huntsville, Alabama, and in 1977 in Oulu and Tampere, Finland; the investigations were completed in 1980.[570, 679, 1043, 1105] Types of *S. pneumoniae* present in the vaccine were isolated less frequently from middle-ear fluid samples of children in the vaccine group with acute episodes of otitis media following immunization than from children in the control group in each of the three studies. The number of episodes of otitis media due to types not present in the vaccine and due to other pathogens (predominantly *H. influenzae*) was similar in the vaccine and control groups. In a Swedish study of older children (2 to 5 years of age), clinically diagnosed episodes of acute otitis media were reduced in the children who received the 14-type vaccine.[936]

In spite of the decrease in middle-ear infections due to some of the pneumococcal types present in the vaccine, the clinical experience of children younger than 2 years of age in the vaccine groups was similar to that of children in the control groups; the number of children who had one or more episodes of otitis media and the mean number of episodes of acute otitis media after immunization were similar in the vaccine and control groups. There were differences in some subsets; Huntsville children, 6 to 12 months of age, in the vaccine group had fewer episodes of otitis media than did children in the control group. The pneumococcal vaccine was effective in the prevention of new clinical episodes of otitis media in black children 6 to 11 months of age in Huntsville, but the vaccine was ineffective in preventing otitis media in white infants of the same age.[510] These data suggest racial differences in terms of preventing disease; prior studies had suggested a genetic difference in response to polysaccharide vaccines.[18, 435] The duration of middle-ear effusion following an episode of pneumococcal otitis media was similar for the vaccine and the control groups.[1105]

These data about lack of efficacy in diminishing the burden of otitis media in children younger than 2 years of age dampened enthusiasm for the use of the polysaccharide pneumococcal vaccines. The vaccines were considered, however, for older children at risk for recurrent acute otitis media.

Pneumococcal Polysaccharide Conjugate Vaccines

Polysaccharide antigens are processed as non-T-lymphocyte-dependent antigens, and the immune system of infants younger than 2 years of age does not respond adequately to such antigens with a strong, durable response that could be boosted with subsequent administration. Protein antigens are processed by T-lymphocytes, and young infants can mount an adequate antibody response. The conjugate *H. influenzae* type b vaccine linked saccharides to a protein carrier that could be processed by T-lymphocytes, resulting in a protective antibody response and immunologic memory in infants as young as 2 months of age. The success of the *H. influenzae* conjugate vaccine in eliciting protective antibody in infants as young as 2 months of age led to the use of similar technologies for the development of type-specific pneumococcal vaccine. For the *Haemophilus* vaccines, capsular polysaccharides were combined with proteins that included diphtheria toxoid, tetanus toxoid, a diphtheria mutant toxin protein (CRM 197), and an outer membrane protein of meningococcus group B. The same proteins have been used for preparation of conjugate pneumococcal vaccines.

Because each type of pneumococcus elicits a separate immune response, it is necessary to develop a conjugate vaccine for each type and to combine the most common types in a single product. The amount of capsular antigen and the amount of carrier protein must be evaluated to determine the optimal composition for each serotype. Different combinations of serotypes have been proposed based on the surveillance of strains in local areas. The most common types of *S. pneumoniae* in children admitted to 10 Connecticut hospitals were 14, 6B, 19F, 4, 18C, 9V, and 23F.[1005] In contrast, the most common types in Israeli children were types 1, 5, 14, 6B, 7F, and 23.[261]

Finnish children had disease due to types 14, 6, 19, 7, 18, 23, 9d, and 4.[341] Thus, there may be need for different vaccines based on dominant types in a geographic region. The conjugate pneumococcal vaccines will contain fewer serotypes than the polysaccharide vaccines because of a limit on the amount of protein that can be administered and the expense of preparing separate type combinations. Conjugate vaccines of 7 to 10 types are likely to be the first products introduced for infant immunization.

Conjugate pneumococcal polysaccharide vaccines were found to be safe and effective in infants. The vaccines have been immunogenic in infants beginning at 2 months of age and included studies of conjugates with outer membrane protein complex of *Neisseria meningitidis* four-valent[574] or seven-valent[22]; conjugates with diphtheria toxin mutant protein CRM 197 five-valent[5, 631] or seven-valent[916]; and conjugate vaccines with antigen conjugated to meningococcal outer membrane protein. The CRM 197 conjugate vaccine was equally effective in otitis-prone and otitis-free children,[61, 1050] and as immunogenic among infants with sickle cell disease as in control subjects without disease.[821]

A seven-type pneumococcal conjugate vaccine (polysaccharide types 4, 6B, 9V, 14, 19F, 23F and oligosaccharide serotype 18C conjugated to CRM 197) was effective in preventing invasive disease in a study of 37,830 children in Northern California. Infants were randomized at 2 months of age to receive either the pneumococcal conjugate vaccine ($n = 18,999$) or meningococcus group C conjugate vaccine ($n = 18,930$) at 2, 4, and 6 months of age, with a booster at 12 to 15 months. The results of the final intent-to-treat analysis for invasive disease (sepsis and/or meningitis) was 93.7% (3 cases in children receiving pneumococcal vaccine, only one because of a serotype in the vaccine, and 49 in the children receiving the control vaccine). An analysis of the effect of the vaccine for prevention of acute otitis media included only clinical data based on office and emergency room visits; there was an 8.9% decrease in all visits for otitis media, a 22.8% decrease in children with recurrent otitis media (defined as five episodes in 6 months or six episodes in 12 months) and a 20.1% decrease in placement in ventilating tubes in the vaccinated children.[117]

Eskola et al[340] completed a blinded, randomized trial using the same vaccines and schedule of administration as was used in the Northern California study. In contrast to the California study design, myringotomy was performed when acute otitis media was diagnosed and the middle-ear fluid was aspirated for bacterial culture. The investigators enrolled 1662 children: half received the conjugate vaccine; half received hepatitis B vaccine. Efficacy of the pneumococcal vaccine was indicated by a 57% reduction for serotype-specific acute otitis media, 34% reduction for any pneumococcal serotype, and 6% reduction for acute otitis media of any origin. Among vaccine serotypes, vaccine efficacy was lowest for 19F and highest for 6B. Of particular interest was the 51% decrease in episodes of otitis due to cross-reactive serotypes, including 6A and 19A. Of concern was an increased number of episodes due to nonvaccine serotypes (33%) and an increase in episodes of otitis due to nontypeable *H. influenzae* (11%) in recipients of the pneumococcal conjugate vaccine.

Pneumococcal C Polysaccharide

The ideal vaccine for protection against pneumococcal infection would include an antigen common to all types of pneumococci. The C polysaccharide is a cell wall component common to all known types of pneumococci. Unfortunately, antibodies against the C polysaccharide do not protect against infection in humans.[1094] Henrichsen and Sorensen[487] suggest that the reason for lack of immunogenicity of the C polysaccharide is that the capsular polysaccharides of growing pneumococci conceal the cell wall and prevent binding of anti−C polysaccharide antibodies to the bacterial cells. The anti−C polysaccharide antibodies do bind to nonencapsulated or only partly encapsulated pneumococci and promote phagocytosis of such bacterial cells. Koskela[616] demonstrated serum antibodies to pneumococcal C polysaccharide in children after acute pneumococcal otitis media or vaccination with polysaccharide vaccine. Henrichsen and Sorensen[487] demonstrated anti−C polysaccharide immune globulin in nasopharyngeal secretions of children with recurrent otitis media. The role of antibody response to the C polysaccharide is controversial; protection against subsequent infection is unproven, and Henrichsen and Sorensen[487] suggest that prompt production of these antibodies may lead to immune complex formation and continuous local inflammation before the infant is capable of mounting protective type-specific antibodies to combat the infection.

Nontypeable *Haemophilus influenzae* Vaccines

Current investigations of antigens of nontypeable *H. influenzae* that elicit protective antibodies against middle-ear infections include outer membrane proteins, pilus surface proteins, and oligosaccharides. Twenty outer membrane proteins, with six predominant proteins, have been identified among strains of nontypeable *H. influenzae*. Children have recurrent infections with reinfection by different strains rather than persistence of the same strain. Thus, the available data suggest that there is no cross-protection and that multiple infections with nontypeable *H. influenzae* occur with different antigenic determinants.[347, 771] The goal of identifying an antigen common to nontypeable strains of *H. influenzae* that will elicit protective antibody and could be incorporated into an otitis media vaccine remains elusive.

Studies by Murphy and colleagues[768, 769] have identified a number of outer membrane proteins that are immunogenic in infants. Current studies are directed to determine the variety of outer membrane proteins of *H. influenzae* and the antigen characterization of selected proteins that make up large proportions of the outer membrane, including P6[768] and P2.[769] Failure of infants with acute otitis media due to nontypeable *H. influenzae* to mount an antibody response to P6 raises doubts about its efficacy as a vaccine candidate.[1210]

Blocking attachment of the organism to receptors on respiratory mucosa would be another approach to prevention of infection by *H. influenzae*. High molecular weight proteins and pili or fimbriae play roles in attachment. St. Geme et al[1055] identified high molecular weight proteins of nontypeable *H. influenzae* that mediated attachment to human epithelial cells. Their findings suggest potential vaccine candidates that would elicit antibodies to prevent attachment. Brinton et al[162] have studied the roles of pili as vaccine candidates for nontypeable *H. influenzae*. Pili are filamentous appendages on the bacterial cell surface that may be responsible for adhesion of the bacteria to mucosal cells and may be a virulence factor for some pathogens. A family of pili have been identified as occurring on the surface of nontypeable *H. influenzae*. Antibodies directed against the pili may protect against disease that is pilus-specific. A preliminary study by Bakaletz et al[48] suggests that there is antigenic heterogeneity among pili of nontypeable strains of *H. influenzae*, requiring inclusion of multiple antigens in an effective vaccine. Sirakova et al[1032] found antigenic heterogeneity among pili of nontypeable strains of *H. influenzae*, indicating the need for inclusion of multiple antigens in an effective vaccine.

Lipo-oligosaccharides are present in the outer membrane of nontypeable *H. influenzae*. Patrick et al[849] used monoclonal antibodies to characterize the antigenic properties of lipo-oligosaccharides and identified common lipo-oligosaccharide antigens among nontypeable and type b strains; but diversity existed among the lipo-oligosaccharide antigens of nontypeable strains. A review of the various candidate vaccines for nontypeable *H. influenzae* was presented by Poolman et al.[878]

Moraxella catarrhalis Vaccines

Moraxella catarrhalis has been isolated from the middle-ear fluids of approximately 10% of children with acute otitis media, but data are sparse about the role of antibody in protection against subsequent infection. Efforts to develop a vaccine using surface antigens of the organism are in progress. Eight outer membrane proteins have been identified.[770] In addition, Murphy[772] is investigating the potential value of lipo-oligosaccharides and fimbriae as antigens for vaccines. Since *M. catarrhalis* organisms have surface fimbriae, antibodies to fimbriae could block attachment of the organism to respiratory mucosa. A review of the various candidate vaccines for *M. catarrhalis* was presented by McMichael.[731]

Viral Vaccines

Viral infection is the likely antecedent of many episodes of acute otitis media. Effective vaccines for the major respiratory viral infections could prevent many episodes of acute otitis media. Influenza A vaccine administered to Finnish infants attending day care in anticipation of epidemic influenzal disease reduced the incidence of upper respiratory tract infections, including acute otitis media, in the vaccine.[479] Influenza A vaccine reduced the incidence of acute otitis media in 6- to 30-month-old North Carolina children in day care during the influenza season.[233] A trivalent live attenuated intranasal influenza vaccine administered as a nasal spray was effective in reducing the incidence of type-specific influenzal disease and febrile otitis media.[78] The potential value of influenzavirus

vaccines for prevention of otitis media was recently reviewed by Glezen.[413]

The ease of administration should enhance the acceptability of influenza virus vaccines, which in the past required one or two parenteral administrations for efficacy. Other viral vaccines that might limit the incidence of acute episodes of otitis media are in various investigational phases, including vaccines for respiratory syncytial viruses[23] and adenoviruses.

Immunoglobulins

A specific serum antibody is correlated with protection from homotypic infection, and prevention of disease may be achieved (albeit for a limited time) by the administration of immunoglobulins. Since infants who have recurrent episodes of acute otitis media usually improve with age, it is possible that a program of passive immunization might be effective in early infancy.

Diamant et al[282] suggested that patients with recurrent episodes of acute otitis media associated with hypogammaglobulinemia or agammaglobulinemia benefit from frequent administration of gammaglobulin. Children 1 to 7 years of age were enrolled after the first visit to the Ear, Nose, and Throat Department in Halmstad, Sweden. Children born on an odd date were given gammaglobulin at their first visit and then once a month for 6 months. Children born on an even date received no gammaglobulin. Of the 113 children treated, 10 had one or more episodes of acute otitis media during the months of administration of the gammaglobulin; of 118 untreated children, 25 had one or more episodes of the disease during the same period. The protective effect of the gammaglobulin persisted during the 8 months after cessation of administration; 25 episodes occurred in the treated group and 53 in the untreated group. In the untreated group, some patients had up to five episodes, whereas no patient in the treated group had more than two bouts of acute otitis media.

Use of intravenous immunoglobulin for prevention of recurrent episodes of acute otitis media indicated lack of efficacy in pooled human immunoglobulin but efficacy of a bacterial polysaccharide immunoglobulin (BPIG). Jorgensen et al[547] noted no benefit from intramuscular administration of human pooled gammaglobulin every 3 weeks for 6 months to otitis-prone children (three or more episodes in the prior year). Kalm et al[559] evaluated the efficacy of immunoglobulin infusions administered at 3 to 4 weeks to children with recurrent acute otitis media (defined as six or more episodes of acute infection during the preceding 12 months); there was no difference in the number of episodes of acute otitis media in the children who received the immunoglobulin or in the control subjects during a 7-month period of observation.

The use of a bacterial polysaccharide immunoglobulin for prophylaxis of acute otitis media was investigated by Shurin et al.[1018] An immunoglobulin was prepared from subjects who had recently been immunized with 14-valent pneumococcal vaccine. Children with previous episodes of acute otitis media were enrolled in the first 24 months of life and randomized to a double-blind, placebo-controlled

TABLE 25–27. Bacterial Pathogens* Causing Acute Otitis Media in Infants Treated with Bacterial Polysaccharide Immunoglobulin or Placebo

Bacteria	Episodes	Number of Patients
S. pneumonia	7	17
Nonpneumococci	28	21†

* Isolates from middle ear during 120-day study period.
† *P* = .038.
From Shurin PA, Rehmus JM, Johnson CE, et al. Bacterial polysaccharide immune globulin for prophylaxis of acute otitis media in high-risk children. J Pediatr 123:801, 1993.

trial using the intramuscularly administered hyperimmunoglobulin preparation. Significantly fewer episodes of acute otitis media caused by the pneumococcus occurred in the group who received the globulin (Table 25–27) during the 120-day observation period. The authors noted that colonization was not reduced in the vaccinated group; thus, the effect of the immunoglobulin was directed to protection of the middle ear from infection. The results also indicated that circulating antibody was effective in prevention of acute otitis media without stimulation of specific local immunity. Since systemic administration of polysaccharide vaccines may stimulate both systemic and local antibody responses, use of the immunoglobulin for protection suggests that systemic antibody alone is protective against middle-ear infection.

An intravenously administered RSV-enriched hyperimmunoglobulin administered monthly was effective in reducing the incidence of RSV respiratory infections and the overall incidence of acute otitis media.[1029] The difficulty of monthly intravenous infusions, concerns about interference with the immune response to live attenuated vaccines, and an unexpected increase in adverse events in children with cyanotic heart disease undergoing surgery[1030] have limited the use of the hyperimmunoglobulin. The RSV-specific hyperimmunoglobulin has been replaced by a humanized monoclonal antibody directed against a surface protein (the F glycoprotein of RSV).

Reduction of Colonization by Vaccines

Since colonization of the nasopharynx may be the point of initiation and the reservoir for infection of the middle ear, the ability of a vaccine or immunoglobulin to reduce nasopharyngeal carriage may be important in reducing the incidence of otitis media. Although not significant for acute otitis media, the conjugate *H. influenzae* type b vaccine was effective in reducing implantation and carriage of type b organisms. The 14-valent pneumococcal polysaccharide vaccine failed to reduce carriage in healthy children.[291] Preliminary data about pneumococcal carriage following administration of conjugate pneumococcal vaccines suggest that carriage of types present in the vaccine are reduced but may be replaced in the nasopharynx by nonvaccine types.[264, 718] Since carriage is important in both the pathogenesis and the communicability of respiratory infections, this outcome will be closely monitored as each immunizing product is developed.

Diagnosis

The methods of examination of a child with ear disease (including pneumatic otoscopy) were extensively described in Chapter 10; the specific diagnostic features that characterize the various forms of otitis media and certain related conditions are presented here.

Clinical Description

For the clinician, the diagnosis of otitis media usually depends on a high index of suspicion and the presence of symptoms, but primarily on the pneumatic otoscopic findings.

Acute Otitis Media

The usual picture of acute otitis media is seen in a child who has an upper respiratory tract infection for several days and in whom otalgia, fever, and hearing loss suddenly develop. Examination with the pneumatic otoscope reveals a hyperemic, opaque, bulging tympanic membrane that has poor mobility. Purulent otorrhea is usually also a reliable sign. In addition to fever, other systemic signs and symptoms may include irritability, lethargy, anorexia, vomiting, and diarrhea. However, all of these may be absent, and even earache and fever are unreliable guides and may frequently be absent.[474, 797, 992a] Likewise, otoscopic findings may consist only of a bulging or full, opaque, poorly mobile eardrum without evidence of erythema. Hearing loss will not be a complaint of the very young or even noted by the parents.

Tympanometry usually reveals an effusion pattern (flat) or a high positive-pressure pattern but may show a pattern that is not classically associated with an effusion; therefore, it is not as sensitive and specific a method for diagnosis of acute otitis media as it is when otitis media with effusion is present.

When performed, tympanocentesis is usually productive of a purulent middle-ear aspirate, but a serous or mucoid effusion is present in approximately 20 per cent.[127a] Because of the variability of symptoms, infants and young children with diminished or absent mobility and opacification of the tympanic membrane should be suspected of having acute otitis media.

Otitis Media with Effusion

Most children with chronic middle-ear effusions are asymptomatic. Some may complain of hearing loss and, less commonly, tinnitus and vertigo. In children, the attention of an alert parent or teacher may be drawn to a suspected hearing loss. Sometimes the child has a behavioral disorder because of the hearing deficit and consequent inability to communicate adequately. More often, the reason for referral is the detection of hearing loss during a school hearing screening test or when acute otitis media fails to resolve completely. Occasionally, the first evidence of the disease is discovered during a routine examination or in evaluation of high-risk cases, such as children with a cleft palate.

Older children will describe a frank hearing loss or, more commonly, a "plugged" feeling or "popping" in their ears. The symptoms are usually bilateral. Unilateral signs and symptoms of chronic middle-ear effusion may result from a nasopharyngeal neoplasm, such as an angiofibroma or even a malignant neoplasm.

Pneumatic otoscopy frequently reveals either a retracted or full tympanic membrane that is usually opaque; but when it is translucent, an air-fluid level or air bubbles may be visualized, and a blue or amber color is noted. The mobility of the eardrum is almost always altered.

It is evident from the preceding clinical description of acute otitis media and chronic otitis media with effusion that there is considerable overlap; hence, it is often difficult for the clinician to distinguish between acute and chronic forms unless the child has been observed for a period before the onset of disease or there are associated specific (otalgia) or systemic (fever) symptoms. It may not be possible to distinguish between the two even when the middle-ear effusion is aspirated (tympanocentesis) because the effusion may be serous, mucoid, or purulent in both acute and chronic otitis. In approximately half of chronic effusions, bacteria have been cultured that are frequently found in ears of children with classic signs and symptoms of acute otitis media.[922]

Eustachian Tube Dysfunction

Some children, especially older ones, will complain of a periodic popping or snapping sound in the ear, which may be preceded or accompanied by a feeling of fullness in the ear, hearing loss, tinnitus, or vertigo. The condition appears to be more common in girls during puberty than in boys of the same age. Otoscopic examination may reveal a normal tympanic membrane or possibly slight retraction of the eardrum, but the middle-ear pressure may be within normal limits, or periodic negative middle-ear pressure may be present. These children have obstruction of the eustachian tube that is not severe enough to cause chronic middle-ear negative pressure, atelectasis, or a middle-ear effusion but nevertheless may be disconcerting. When it is troublesome, the child should be managed in the same manner as children who have middle-ear effusion.

On occasion, older children may complain of autophony (hearing one's own voice in the ear) and hearing their own breathing. The eustachian tube is most likely patulous (abnormally patent), in which case the tympanic membrane appears normal when visualized through the otoscope. Middle-ear pressure is normal; however, if the child is asked to breathe forcefully through one nasal cavity, the opposite being occluded with a finger, the posterosuperior portion of the tympanic membrane is observed to move in and out with respiration, which confirms the diagnosis. Tympanometry may also aid in diagnosis (see earlier description of patulous tube test).

When eustachian tube dysfunction is chronic, and middle-ear pressure remains negative for prolonged periods, atelectasis of the middle ear can occur, which is a sequela of eustachian tube dysfunction and is described in detail in Chapter 26.

Microbiologic Diagnosis

The correlation between bacterial cultures of the nasopharynx or the oropharynx and those of middle-ear fluids is poor (see section on Microbiology). The poor correlation occurs because of the frequency of colonization of the upper respiratory tract with organisms of known pathogenicity for the middle ear and, less commonly, because of absence in cultures of the oropharynx or nasopharynx of the pathogen responsible for infection of the middle ear. Thus, cultures of the upper respiratory tract are of limited value in specific bacteriologic diagnosis of otitis media. Specific microbiologic diagnosis is achieved by culture of middle-ear fluid obtained by needle aspiration through the intact tympanic membrane. If the patient has toxic signs or symptoms or has a localized infection elsewhere, culture of the blood or the focus of infection should be performed. Bacteremia is rarely associated with otitis media due to nontypeable strains of *H. influenzae*, uncommonly associated with otitis media due to *S. pneumoniae*, but frequently associated with otitis media due to type b strains of *H. influenzae*.[460]

The consistent results of microbiologic studies of middle-ear fluid of children with acute otitis media provide an accurate guide to the most likely pathogens. Thus, initial therapy in the uncomplicated case does not require specimens to be obtained for bacterial diagnosis. If the patient is critically ill when first seen, has altered host defenses (as is the case with the newborn infant, the patient with malignant neoplasm, or the patient with immunologic disease), or fails to respond appropriately to initial therapy for acute otitis media and has toxic signs or symptoms, culture of the middle-ear fluid is indicated. In addition, culture of the blood is warranted for critically ill children and those with altered defenses.

Diagnostic Aspiration of Middle Ear: Tympanocentesis

When the diagnosis of acute otitis media is in doubt or when determination of the causative agent is desirable, aspiration of the middle ear should be performed (Fig. 25–50). Indications for tympanocentesis or myringotomy include the following:

1. Otitis media in patients who are toxic or have signs of invasive bacterial disease
2. Unsatisfactory response to antimicrobial therapy; because of the increasing incidence of multidrug-resistant pneumococci, identification of the etiologic agent is required to identify appropriate therapy for the child who did not respond to the initial drug and is toxic[152]
3. Onset of otitis media in a patient who is receiving antimicrobial agents
4. Presence of suppurative complications
5. Otitis media in the newborn, the very young infant, or the immunologically deficient patient, in each of whom an unusual organism may be suspected

An example of how valuable tympanocentesis can be in the management of children with middle-ear infection is when an infant is encountered who has suspected sepsis

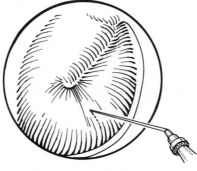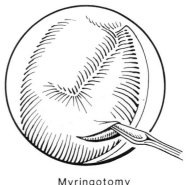

Tympanocentesis   Myringotomy

FIGURE 25–50. Tympanocentesis, a needle aspiration of a middle-ear effusion, is used primarily for diagnosis of the presence or absence of an effusion and for microbiologic study (*left panel*). Myringotomy is an incision in the tympanic membrane used primarily for therapeutic drainage (*right panel*).

and in whom the middle ear may be the source. Arriaga et al[36] reviewed the charts of 40 such infants at the Children's Hospital of Pittsburgh and reported that, in 80%, the clinical management of these babies was directly affected by the results of the tympanocentesis. Infants and children who are in intensive care units have a high frequency of otitis media, and tympanocentesis has been shown to be a valuable aid in diagnosis as well as in identifying the causative organisms.[279]

Both of these procedures can usually be performed without general anesthesia. In certain instances, premedication with a combination of a short-acting barbiturate and either morphine or meperidine, or even a general anesthetic, is advisable. The procedures can be carried out with an otoscope with a surgical head or with the otomicroscope. Adequate immobilization of the patient is essential when a general anesthetic is not used.

One can perform diagnostic aspiration through the inferior portion of the tympanic membrane by employing an 18-gauge spinal needle attached to a syringe or collection trap (Fig. 25–51). Culture of the ear canal and

cleansing of the canal with alcohol should precede the procedure (Fig. 25–52). The canal culture is helpful in determining whether organisms cultured are contaminants from the exterior canal or pathogens from the middle ear. When therapeutic drainage is required, a myringotomy knife should be employed and the incision should be large enough to allow adequate drainage and aeration of the middle ear (see later discussion of myringotomy).

After tympanocentesis, the effusion caught in the syringe or collection trap is sent to the laboratory for culture. A gram-stained smear may provide immediate information about the bacterial pathogens.

The external ear swab and the fluid aspirated from the middle ear are inoculated onto appropriate solid media and into broth to isolate the likely organisms. Sensitivities of organisms isolated should be tested by the standard method described by Bauer et al.[70]

Nasopharyngeal Culture

In an attempt to identify the causative organism in a child with acute otitis media, obtaining a nasopharyngeal specimen for culture would be less traumatic than tympanocentesis or myringotomy. Bacteria found in middle-ear aspirates are usually present in the nasopharynx of children with acute otitis media, but multiple pathogens may be present in the nasopharynx that are not present in the middle ear. Nasopharyngeal cultures for bacterial pathogens are sensitive but not specific for the organism responsible for acute otitis media (see section on Microbiology). Although not useful for microbiologic diagnosis of acute otitis media, nasopharyngeal cultures are of value for monitoring antibiotic susceptibility patterns of bacterial pathogens associated with acute otitis media. Schwartz et al[990a] and Long et al[660] reported a technique that improved the correlation of organisms isolated by the nasopharyngeal culture with bacteria identified by culture of middle-ear fluid. The method involved immediate plating of the nasopharyngeal swab on solid media and a semiquantitative estimation of colonies growing on culture plates.

Fluorescence Emission Spectrophotometry

Fluorescence emission spectrophotometry is an exciting new method that has been reported to have the capability of detecting the four common pathogens that cause acute

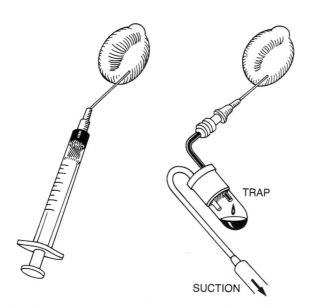

TRAP

SUCTION

FIGURE 25–51. Tympanocentesis can be performed by employing a needle attached to a tuberculin syringe (*left*) or by using an Alden-Senturia trap (Storz Instrument Co., St. Louis, MO) with a needle attached (*right*). (From Bluestone CD, Klein JO. Otitis Media in Infants and Children. Philadelphia, WB Saunders, 1988.)

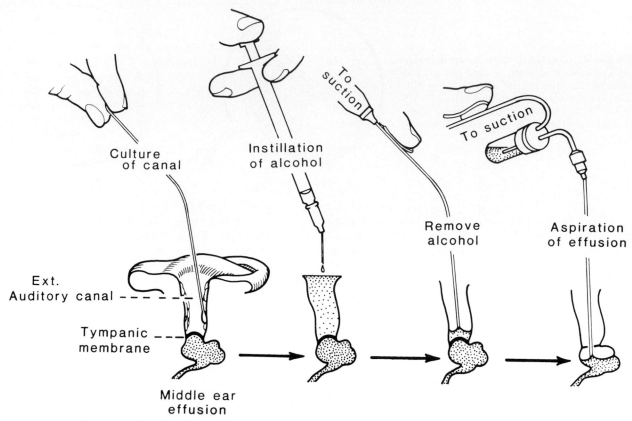

FIGURE 25–52. Method recommended for tympanocentesis and aspiration of a middle-ear effusion for microbiologic assessment. A culture of the external auditory canal is obtained with a Calgiswab (Falton, Oxford, CA), which has been moistened with soy broth. The canal is then filled with 70% ethyl alcohol for 1 minute, after which as much as possible of the alcohol is removed from the ear canal by aspiration. Tympanocentesis is performed in the inferior portion of the tympanic membrane with an Alden-Senturia trap (Storz Instrument Co., St. Louis, MO), with a needle attached. Care is taken not to close the suction hole in the trap before entering the middle ear.

otitis media by noninvasively determining the optical fluorescence through the tympanic membrane.[1185] The technology and clinical applicability will require more research, but this type of advance may replace the need for invasive procedures.

Blood Culture

Blood samples for culture were obtained from 600 consecutive children 1 to 24 months of age coming to a Boston hospital walk-in clinic with fever: 166 children had a diagnosis of otitis; only 2 (1.2%) had concomitant bacteremia.[1111] Studies of young infants include information that is selected because those who had cultures of blood showed toxic symptoms or were hospitalized. In four series of infants 8 weeks of age or younger[256, 440, 928, 1014] and in two series of patients 3 months of age or younger,[980, 1113] 5 of 136 infants (3.7%) with otitis media had positive blood cultures (two group B *Streptococcus*, one *S. pneumoniae*, one *P. aeruginosa*, and one enterococcus). The yield of cultures of blood is low in children with uncomplicated otitis media, but it is likely to be higher in chil-

dren who have toxic symptoms, high fever, or concurrent infection at other foci (pneumonia, meningitis).

White Blood Cell Count

Although white blood cell counts are too variable to be helpful in distinguishing the child with otitis media due to a bacterial pathogen from the child with otitis media and a sterile effusion, data suggest that the mean white blood cell count of children with bacterial otitis media is higher than that of children with sterile middle-ear effusion. Lahikainen[624] noted that the mean white blood cell count (per cubic millimeter) of children with otitis due to *Streptococcus pyogenes* was 13,400; due to *S. pneumoniae*, 10,500; and due to *H. influenzae*, 11,500. Of children with sterile middle-ear effusion, the mean white blood cell count was 8700. Mortimer and Watterson[765] found similar results in children who had a bacterial pathogen in the middle-ear effusion, the mean white blood cell count being 10,300. The mean white blood cell count was 6700 in children with sterile effusions. Feingold et al[362] found an association of higher white blood cell counts with isolation of a bacterial pathogen from the middle-ear effusion; of 35 children with white blood cell counts of 15,000 or more, 27 (77%) had a bacterial pathogen grown from the middle-ear effusion. Of children with a white blood cell count of 9000 or less, 8 of 20 (40%) had a bacterial pathogen grown from the middle-ear effusion.

C-Reactive Protein

Several investigators have shown that elevation of C-reactive proteins can be related to bacterial acute otitis media caused by S. pneumoniae and H. influenzae; but when M. catarrhalis was isolated from middle-ear aspirates, the serum C-reactive protein levels were comparable to those of patients with sterile effusions.[572, 613] Therefore, this test is not reliable in detecting bacterial acute otitis media.

Sedimentation Rate

Lahikainen[624] found increases in sedimentation rate in children with otitis media and differences among the bacterial pathogens isolated from the middle-ear effusion. The mean sedimentation rate for 104 children with otitis media due to S. pyogenes was 43.7; for 171 children with otitis media due to S. pneumoniae, 30.2; for 43 children with otitis media due to H. influenzae, 17.3; and for 85 children with sterile effusion, 21.3.

Allergy Testing

Allergy testing is indicated in patients who have recurrent acute or chronic middle-ear effusions in association with signs and symptoms of allergy of the upper respiratory tract or a family history of nasal allergy. Methods are discussed in Chapter 49.

Radiologic Imaging

For the uncomplicated case of acute otitis media, imaging of the temporal bones is not indicated. However, when recurrent acute or chronic otitis media with effusion is present, radiographic evaluation of the paranasal sinuses may be helpful in identifying sinusitis that can be related causally to the otitis media. When signs and symptoms of sinusitis are present (e.g., purulent nasal discharge, cough, and fetor oris), conventional radiographic examination of the paranasal sinuses (i.e., occipitomental [Waters], frontal [Caldwell], basal [submentovertical], and lateral erect views) may be helpful, but CT scans are more sensitive and specific; in many institutions, CT scans are about the same cost as four-view radiographs of the paranasal sinuses. The lateral soft tissue radiograph of the nasopharynx can be beneficial in assessing the adenoid size in relation to the nasopharynx. However, if coronal and axial CT views of the paranasal sinuses and nasopharynx are obtained, the adenoids can be evaluated more effectively than by traditional radiographs. If a tumor of the nasopharynx or skull base is suspected as the cause of obstruction (functional or mechanical) of the eustachian tube and otitis media with effusion, CT scans are indicated. Chronic nasal obstruction, with or without epistaxis or cervical lymphadenopathy, in association with otitis media, should prompt the clinician to suspect a nasopharyngeal tumor. CT and nuclear magnetic resonance imaging are described in detail in Chapter 36.

When certain complications or sequelae of otitis media are suspected or present, radiologic evaluation of the temporal bones is indicated. Plain radiographs (Towne, Laws, Stenvers) may be helpful in the diagnosis of osteitis of the mastoid or a cholesteatoma but are rarely obtained today. CT is more precise, and scans should be obtained if a suppurative intratemporal or intracranial complication is suspected (Chaps. 26 and 27). In addition, CT can be an aid in visualizing the eustachian tube[781] (see Chap. 12).

Endoscopy of the Nasopharynx

When infants or children have the possibility of a nasal or nasopharyngeal pathologic state contributing to their middle-ear disease, transnasal endoscopy can be helpful if other diagnostic methods are not definitive. Nasopharyngeal disease, such as choanal polyps, and neoplasms can cause dysfunction of the eustachian tube[504] (see Chaps. 35 and 48).

Biopsy of the Nasopharynx

When nasopharyngeal tumor is suspected as the cause of the otitis media, a biopsy of the nasopharynx is indicated. Progressive nasal obstruction in conjunction with cervical adenopathy would lead the clinician to suspect a tumor in this area. Also, the onset of a cranial nerve deficit, such as facial paralysis, in association with otitis media would prompt a thorough examination for tumor to be the cause of the middle-ear disease (see Chap. 48).

Vestibular Testing

Otitis media with effusion and eustachian tube dysfunction are the most common causes of dysequilibrium (e.g., vertigo, falling, and "clumsiness") in infants and children. The dysequilibrium is frequently resolved when the middle-ear effusion is absent or the child no longer has fluctuating middle-ear pressures. Frequently, the parents report a dramatic disappearance of dysequilibrium immediately after insertion of tympanostomy tubes for recurrent acute or chronic otitis media with effusion or eustachian tube obstruction (fluctuating high negative pressure). Jones et al,[544] in a study from England, evaluated vestibular function by use of a fixed force plate body sway platform in 34 children with chronic otitis media with effusion who were between the ages of 3 and 5 years and compared them with 34 children without effusions matched for age and sex. Compared with the control group, the children with effusions had significantly worse balance, which was resolved after tympanostomy tube insertion. In a later study from Pittsburgh, Casselbrant et al[208a] assessed 41 children who had middle-ear effusion with use of the moving platform posturography both before and after tympanostomy tube insertion and compared their results with those of a group of 50 children without middle-ear disease. Children with effusions had higher velocity, which resolved after tympanostomy tube insertion. Two studies from Israel by Golz et al[422] and by Ben-David et al[79] also demonstrated balance disorders in children with middle-ear effusions.

For most infants and children with otitis media and signs and symptoms of dysequilibrium, sophisticated vestibular testing is not indicated, as nonsurgical or surgical management of the eustachian tube–middle-ear disorder will resolve the problem. In addition, currently available tests are not usually feasible in children, especially infants. However, when the dysequilibrium persists despite the resolution of the middle-ear effusion and the presence of normal middle-ear pressures, the child should undergo assessment of vestibular function to rule out the possibility of another cause of imbalance (see Chap. 17). Also, children who have frequent attacks of vertigo, with or without fluctuating or progressive sensorineural hearing loss, in association with otitis should be suspected of having a labyrinthine fistula.

The tests that can assess vestibular function in infants and children were described in Chapter 13. Rotational tests and gross caloric testing can be performed in the infant and young child, and electronystagmography is feasible in the older child.

NOTE: Other diagnostic tests, such as aural acoustic immittance measurements (including tympanometry), and measurements of hearing are described in detail elsewhere in the book. Also, acoustic reflectometry instruments are now available both for the clinician and for use in the home to diagnose middle-ear effusion, which are described in detail in Chapter 10, under Diagnosis. Tests of eustachian tube function are described in detail earlier in the section on Physiology, Pathophysiology, and Pathogenesis.

High-Risk Populations

Patients with Cleft Palate

In patients with cleft palate, ear disease and hearing loss have long been recognized as common problems. This association was first reported in 1878 by Alt,[17] who noted hearing improvement after treatment of otorrhea associated with cleft palate. Thorington[1118] reported increased hearing in a patient after artificial correction of a destroyed palate. In 1893, Gutzmann[447] noted hearing loss in half of his patients with cleft palate. Lannois[630] reported the association of middle-ear disease and hearing loss in patients with cleft palate. In 1906, the need for otologic examination of patients with cleft palate was stressed by Brunck.[176] Since these early descriptions, many reports have appeared in the literature related to the incidence, nature, and degree of hearing loss in patients with cleft palate.

Hearing Loss

The prevalence of hearing loss in the cleft palate population, as reported in the literature, varies considerably. Findings range from no hearing loss[415] to 90% prevalence[974]; but among all the studies, the average prevalence is approximately 50%. Even though the criteria of hearing loss were not generally agreed on, it has been identified as conductive and usually bilateral. Halfond and Ballenger[452] found that of the 69 patients tested, 37 (54%) had a hearing loss of 20 dB or greater. Miller[744] reported that 19 (54%) of 35 children with cleft palate had a hearing loss greater than 30 dB. That the prevalence may be even greater is suggested by Walton,[1175] who studied 93 school-age children with cleft palate: one half of those who would have passed conventional audiometric screening at the 20 dB level were found to have air-bone gaps indicative of conductive hearing loss. This contention is supported by the study of Bluestone et al,[123] who found high-viscosity middle-ear effusions in children, including those with cleft palate, who would have passed a 25 dB screening audiogram. Even though a conductive hearing impairment would be expected, Bennett[80] reported that 30% of 100 adults with cleft palate had either sensorineural or mixed hearing loss. This finding might be explained by the work of Paparella et al,[828] who found sensorineural hearing loss in some patients with otitis media and ascribed this to directly associated pathologic changes in the inner ear, presumably mediated by the round window. The hearing in the infant with an unrepaired cleft palate has been tested using auditory brain stem response by Fria et al[386] and found to be abnormal and associated with the chronic otitis media with effusion present in these infants' middle ears. Anteunis et al[29] have suggested using otoacoustic emissions as a feasible method to screen children with cleft lip and palate for hearing loss.

Aural Pathology

Infants. Variot,[1160] in 1904, was the first to report ear disease in an infant with cleft palate. In 1936, Beatty[74] described "acute tubotympanic congestion frequently found between the ages of 3 months and 2 years." Sataloff and Fraser[974] reported that, in their experience, "examination of the ears of very young children with cleft palate reveals a high incidence of pathologic changes, despite the absence of subjective symptoms of otitis media." In 1958, Skolnick[1034] reported that only 6% of cleft palate patients younger than 1 year, and only 27% of those between the ages of 1 and 4 years, had aural pathologic changes. Linthicum et al,[652] however, discovered ear pathologic findings in 77% of a group of 100 infants and children with cleft palate. In 1967, Stool and Randall[1071] reported that middle-ear effusion was present at myringotomy in 94% of 25 cleft palate infants. Paradise et al,[835] employing standard office otoscopy, diagnosed middle-ear disease in 49 of 50 infants with cleft palate. Most had full or bulging, opaque, immobile tympanic membranes, although spontaneous perforations and otorrhea were observed. Subsequent studies by the same team indicate that throughout the first 2 years of life in infants with unrepaired cleft palate, otitis media is a virtually constant complication.[136, 834] The otitis is usually characterized by an inflammatory effusion of variable viscosity; suppuration also occurs occasionally.[136, 840]

Older Children and Adults. Although the criteria of an aural pathologic state in older children and adults with cleft palate vary considerably, its prevalence appears to be high. Meissner[738a] examined 213 such patients between the ages of 10 and 35 years and found that 83% had abnormal tympanic membranes. Skolnick[1034] found that the prevalence of aural pathologic changes was 67% in patients older than 5 years. Graham and Lierle[434] found ear pathologic changes in 44% of 29 patients with cleft palate and in 55% of 146 patients with a cleft of both palate and lip. In a group of 82 patients, Aschan[37] found that 78% had aural abnormalities. In a retrospective, longitudinal study of 191 patients with cleft palate between 5 and 27 years of age, Severeid[1000] reported that 83% had a middle-ear effusion confirmed by myringotomy. In Bennett's study[80] of 100 adults with cleft palate, 30% had aural pathologic findings consisting of signs of eustachian tube obstruction (13%), chronic suppurative otitis media with or without mastoiditis (8%), dry tympanic membrane perforation (6%), and chronic adhesive otitis media (3%).

Schools and Programs for the Deaf

Severely to profoundly deaf children (primarily those whose hearing loss is sensorineural), whether they are enrolled in a special class, in a regular school (mainstreamed), or in a residential school for the deaf, are of particular concern. Should a conductive hearing loss due to chronic or recurrent otitis media with effusion or high negative pressure, or both, be superimposed on the preexisting hearing loss, auditory input may be severely affected. This may critically interfere with the education of such children.[949]

The incidence of middle-ear problems in deaf children has not been studied systematically, but the few studies that have been reported indicate the incidence to be equal to or possibly higher than that in nondeaf children. Porter[880] found that 25% of 79 deaf children aged 6 to 10 years had abnormal tympanograms. Brooks[173] reported that 5-year-old children in a residential school for the deaf in England had a higher incidence of abnormal tympanograms than did nondeaf children. Mehta and Erlich[738] found a high incidence of otitis media with effusion in children in a school for the deaf. Rubin[951] reported the incidence of middle-ear effusion in children 3 to 6 years of age to be 30%. In a period of 1 year, Stool et al[1069a] conducted otoscopic, tympanometric, and audiometric evaluations on 446 students at a school for the deaf and reported that the incidence of middle-ear effusions was 8%, whereas that of high negative middle-ear pressure was 21%. However, the incidence of otitis media with effusion in this study was 26% in the 2- to 5-year age group. In addition, they found that 79% of the students who initially were identified as having high negative middle-ear pressure consistently had abnormal negative pressures during the 1-year observation period.

From these few studies, it is apparent that continuous surveillance for middle-ear disease and early treatment should be part of every program or school for deaf children. This is especially critical for those children with some residual hearing who benefit from amplification, because even the slightest conductive hearing loss may decrease or eliminate the efficacy of amplification. It is recommended that every school for deaf children be afforded appropriate health care professionals who are competent in otoscopy, tympanometry, audiometry, and treatment of otologic disorders to carry out this program. Most schools for the deaf do not have sufficient provisions for such care of the child.

Because the external canals of deaf children are frequently obstructed with cerumen, frequent examination and removal of the cerumen may be extremely beneficial, especially for those children who wear a hearing aid.[922] This finding alone is reason enough for frequent periodic otologic examination; however, a schedule for screening for otitis media with effusion and high negative pressure should be established. Until a formal long-term study has been completed that will offer recommendations for a screening program in schools for the deaf, the following schedule of examinations of such children is proposed on the basis of preliminary findings.[253, 370, 922, 1069a] All children should have an otoscopic, tympanometric, and audiometric examination on entering the school and periodically during the first school year. Because infants and young children are at highest risk, they should be examined once a month by otoscopy (and tympanometry when indicated) during this first year. Older children and adolescents can probably be evaluated on entry and every 3 months during the first year, as the incidence of middle-ear disease in this age group is less than in the younger age group. All students should be examined during periods of upper respiratory tract infection and whenever there are signs or symptoms related to the ear, such as otalgia or otorrhea. In addition, a child should be examined if the teacher or parent suspects a middle-ear problem owing to a noticeable lack of attention, sudden or gradual failure to benefit from amplification, or overt and progressive loss of hearing.

After the first year of follow-up, the children usually separate into one of four groups, based on the occurrence of otitis media with effusion, high negative pressure, or both: (1) no disease, (2) infrequent disease of short duration, (3) frequently recurrent disease, and (4) chronic disease. Infants and young children who fit into either of the first two categories based on examinations during the first year may be examined at less frequent intervals, such as every 2 to 3 months during the second year. Older children who have no evidence of disease during the first year can probably be examined once a year, either on entering school in the fall or, more ideally, during the winter months. Older children with infrequent problems during the first year should probably be examined every 3 months during the second year. All infants and children who have frequently recurrent or chronic middle-ear disease during the first year must be examined every month and with each upper respiratory tract infection until they, too, have a year without significant problems. Screening during the succeeding years should be related to the middle-ear disease experience in the preceding year. Children who have multiple handicaps, in addition to deafness, are considered to be at high risk for middle-ear disease, which can significantly compound their handicap owing to the attendant conductive hearing loss. Therefore, screening for all such students during the first year should be the program recommended for infants and young children.

Ideally, every examination should be conducted by a physician who is expert in the diseases of the middle ear, but this is not always feasible. Therefore, a nurse should be trained to perform routine otoscopy, examination of the nose and throat, and removal of cerumen from the external canal when present. Tympanometry can be performed by the nurse, a technician, or, if available, an audiologist. Even though an otologist cannot examine every child with the frequency recommended, every school for the deaf must have a physician, preferably an otologist, assigned to the school for diagnosis and treatment of those children found to have middle-ear disease.

It is important that all children with severe or profound deafness be considered at risk for the development of middle-ear disease. Therefore, they should have regular periodic examinations of the ear by competent health care professionals and appropriate early management instituted so that their educational handicap is not further compromised by a condition that is amenable to medical or surgical management.

Other Possible High-Risk Populations

Infants and children who have parents or siblings with otitis media with effusion appear to have a greater risk for development of otitis media with effusion than do those whose parents or siblings have no evidence of disease. Teele et al[1107] studied 2565 infants from birth to their third birthdays. They found that children who had single or recurrent episodes of otitis media were more likely to have parents or siblings with histories of significant middle-ear infections than were children who had no episodes of otitis media. Therefore, children whose siblings have had otitis media are at higher risk and should have more frequent otologic examinations than children whose siblings have not had the disease.

Upper respiratory tract allergy is thought to be involved in the etiology of otitis media and therefore requires close surveillance. Even though there is no proof that children who have an upper respiratory tract allergy have a higher incidence of otitis media than do children without such an allergy, they should be examined frequently for possible occurrence of otitis media.

Other possible risk factors, such as prematurity or some other reason for placing the infant in a neonatal intensive care unit,[85] first episode of otitis media during early infancy,[509] malnutrition, and child abuse,[298] are not proven but warrant consideration for close surveillance until these factors are disproved by further studies.

Management

This section on management is organized so that the reader can first have our recommendations for strategies to manage the most common stages of otitis media and related conditions, which is then followed by an in-depth discussion of the specific management options. Table 25–28 provides a detailed table of contents or "road map" for

TABLE 25–28. Road Map for the Section on Management

this section so that the reader can readily find a specific topic without having to search the entire chapter.

First we provide strategies for management of acute otitis media and otitis media with effusion, which are the most frequently encountered diseases that are treated by physicians who provide health care to infants and children. Also included are strategies for the prevention of otitis media. Even though less common than otitis media, also included are strategies for management of the various types of eustachian tube dysfunction, such as obstruction, abnormal patency, and otitic barotrauma, which can cause symptoms similar to those associated with otitis media, but there is usually little or no effusion present in

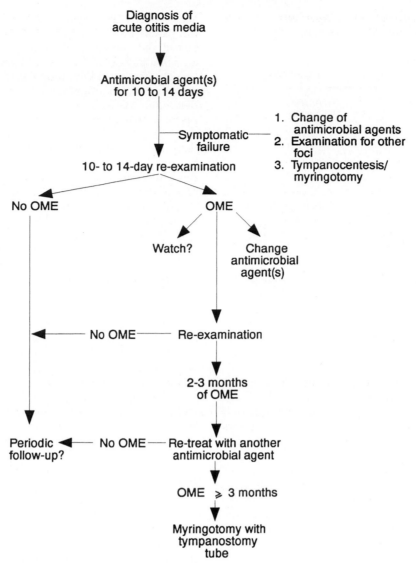

FIGURE 25–53. Recommended algorithm for management of acute otitis media (see text). OME, otitis media with effusion. (From Bluestone CD, Klein JO. Otitis Media in Infants and Children, 3rd ed. Philadelphia, WB Saunders, 2001.)

the middle ear. We then provide a detailed presentation of our state of knowledge of the specific medical and surgical methods of treatment and prevention of these diseases and disorders of the middle ear. We have included in this section medical options, such as antibiotics, decongestants, antihistamines, corticosteroids, immuno-prophylaxis and immunotherapy, and hyposensitization and the surgical and mechanical options, such as middle-ear inflation, myringotomy, tympanostomy tube insertion, adenoidectomy with or without tonsillectomy, tympano-plasty, tympanomastoidectomy, watchful waiting, and hearing aids.

Strategies for Management

We have categorized our strategies for management of the various stages of inflammation and related conditions of the middle ear into (1) treatment of acute otitis media; (2) treatment of otitis media with effusion; (3) prevention

of recurrent episodes of otitis media; and (4) treatment and prevention of eustachian tube dysfunction.

Strategies for Treating Acute Otitis Media

Figure 25–53 is our algorithm for treatment of acute otitis media and for effusion that persists following treatment. Infants and children who have signs and symptoms of acute otitis media should receive an antimicrobial agent with efficacy against the three major bacterial path-ogens, *S. pneumoniae, H. influenzae,* and *M. catarrhalis.*

Selection of drugs is based on clinical and microbio-logic efficacy, acceptability (taste, texture, etc.) of the oral preparation, absence of side effects and toxicity, conve-nience of dosing schedule, and cost. As of this writing, 18 drugs are approved by the Food and Drug Administration (FDA) and commonly used for treatment of acute otitis media (Table 25–29). Ofloxacin otic is approved for acute

TABLE 25–29. Antimicrobial Agents Approved for Therapy of Acute Otitis Media: United States, 2000

Drug	Trade Name
Amoxicillin	Amoxil
Amoxicillin-clavulanate	Augmentin
Cephalexin	Keflex
Cefaclor	Ceclor
Loracarbef	Lorabid
Cefixime	Suprax
Ceftibuten	Cedax
Cefprozil	Cefzil
Cefpodoxime	Vantin
Cefuroxime axetil	Ceftin
Cefdinir	Omnicef
Ceftriaxone IM	Rocephin
Erythromycin + sulfisoxazole	Pediazole
Azithromycin	Zithromax
Clarithromycin	Biaxin
Trimethoprim-sulfamethoxazole	Bactrim, Septra
Ofloxacin otic	Floxin Otic

From Bluestone CD, Klein JO. Otitis Media in Infants and Children, 3rd ed, Philadelphia, WB Saunders, 2001.

otorrhea in children who have tympanostomy tubes in place. Amoxicillin remains the current drug of choice because it continues to be effective, safe, and relatively inexpensive.[293] Doubling the dosage schedule provides increased concentrations of drug in the middle ear.[996] The increased concentrations provide activity against most intermediate nonsusceptible strains of S. pneumoniae and many of the resistant strains. Although most experts agree on the continued use of amoxicillin as the drug of choice for initial therapy of acute otitis media, there is less consensus on the appropriate drug to use when amoxicillin fails. A Centers for Disease Control and Prevention (CDC) consensus report suggested amoxicillin-clavulanate, cefuroxime axetil, and intramuscular ceftriaxone.[293] A macrolide (erythromycin + sulfisoxazole, azithromycin, or clarithromycin) is the preferred drug for acute otitis media for children who are allergic to beta-lactam antimicrobial agents, but trimethoprim-sulfamethoxazole may still be useful in regions where pneumococcal resistance to this combination is not a concern.[604]

Duration of therapy is based on clinical trials and tradition. Most clinical trials and standard pediatric practice include a 10-day course of an oral antimicrobial agent. Other dosage schedules, longer or shorter than the traditional 10-day course, have been investigated.[842, 866] Azithromycin and cefpodoxime are now approved for 5-day courses. A single dose of intramuscular ceftriaxone was found to be as effective as 10-day courses of amoxicillin or trimethoprim-sulfamethoxazole.[62, 439] For other oral drugs, including amoxicillin/clavulanate, 10 days is preferable to a shorter course for infants (<2 years of age), children with severe acute disease (including otorrhea), children with histories of severe and recurrent acute otitis media, and children with some defect in immune response.

The clinical course of a child who receives appropriate antimicrobial therapy includes significant resolution of acute signs within 48 to 72 hours. Initial instructions to the parent should indicate the need to contact the physician if the signs or symptoms are worse at any time or are unimproved at 72 hours. Persistent ear pain or systemic signs including fever would signal the need for reevaluation, to examine for other foci of infection, to determine the need for another antimicrobial agent, or to perform tympanocentesis or myringotomy to incise and drain the middle ear abscess and culture the fluid to determine the pathogen. If surgery is not necessary or is not feasible (the parents or child might refuse surgery, or the physician is not accustomed to performing this type of surgery, in which case an otolaryngologist should be consulted), then a new antibiotic that includes activity against beta-lactamase-producing strains and possible penicillin-resistant pneumococci should be administered.

Incision and drainage is of value initially for patients with unusually severe earache or systemic toxicity; myringotomy provides immediate relief by draining the abscess. Tympanocentesis or needle aspiration of the middle ear fluid prior to therapy is of value in identifying the microbial pathogen. Tympanocentesis for microbial diagnosis should be considered in children who are toxic, have severe suppurative or nonsuppurative complications (i.e., mastoiditis, facial nerve palsy), or who have underlying conditions that compromise immune functions.

Follow-up visits should be made to determine that the child has recovered from the acute infection and to diagnose persistent middle ear effusion if present. A visit at 10 to 14 days is useful to determine which children need longer therapy only if the caregiver reports that the illness has not resolved.[468] Most children will still have fluid present in the middle ear at the 10- to 14-day visit, but persistent signs of illness such as an inflamed tympanic membrane or mild to moderate systemic signs or symptoms would warrant prolonging therapy to 21 days. A subsequent visit at 2 to 3 months is of value in determining the duration of middle-ear effusion after the acute episode and identifying children who may be candidates for placement of tympanostomy tubes.

Symptomatic therapy, including analgesics, antipyretics, and local heat, will usually be helpful. An oral decongestant, such as pseudoephedrine hydrochloride, may relieve nasal congestion, and antihistamines may help patients with known or suspected nasal allergy. The efficacy of antihistamines and decongestants in the treatment of acute otitis media has not been proved, however (see Strategies for Antibiotic Treatment of Acute Otitis Media).

Persistent Middle-Ear Effusion

Following antibiotic treatment for an episode of acute otitis media, 30% to 70% of infants and children will have a persistent middle-ear effusion 10 to 14 days later that can last for weeks to months; without further treatment, only 6% to 26% will have an effusion remaining in the middle ear 3 months after the onset of the acute episode.[557, 558, 685, 803, 943a, 1104] The mean duration of persistent middle-ear effusion is approximately 23 days. Since most effusions resolve spontaneously without further treatment and most of the patients are relatively asymptomatic, non-surgical or surgical treatment for this stage of acute otitis media, such as another course of an antimicrobial agent is not usually recommended. Indeed, the CDC and the American Academy of Pediatrics (AAP) specifically advise against re-treating asymptomatic infants and children with an antimicrobial agent when persistent middle-ear effusion occurs following an initial course of antibiotic for an attack of acute otitis media, since this perceived widespread practice is thought to be contributing to the ever-increasing rate of antibiotic-resistant otitic bacteria.[294] Thus, watchful waiting is advised.

Some children may require treatment, especially when the effusion persists for 3 or more months, as in chronic otitis media with effusion. Management of persistent middle-ear effusion is similar to management of otitis media with effusion, which is described in the section Strategies for Treatment of Otitis Media with Effusion. (See also Plan for Medical Therapy of the Child with Persistent Middle Ear Effusion later in this chapter.)

Strategies for Preventing Otitis Media

The physician should design a strategy to manage the child with severe and recurrent acute otitis media. The strategy should include parent education, chemoprophylaxis, immunoprophylaxis, and a consideration of surgery. Selected children may require diagnostic tests for host problems, including immune and anatomic defects.

Parents should be informed about the risk factors for acute otitis media. Although host features are not subject to change, parents may be empowered to change environmental risk features, including eliminating cigarette smoking from the household, reducing use of a pacifier, and encouraging home or family day care or small group out-of-home care (see Epidemiology earlier in this chapter).

Chemoprophylaxis has proven to be successful in the prevention of new symptomatic episodes of middle-ear infections. However, the use of a modified and prolonged course of an antimicrobial agent may result in selection of resistant bacteria in the nasopharynx. Breakthrough episodes are likely to occur and may be due to multidrug-resistant pneumococci or beta-lactamase-resistant *H. influenzae*. Because of concern for the development of resistant strains, chemoprophylaxis should be reserved for patients who have three or more documented episodes of acute otitis media in 6 months or four or more episodes in 12 months.

The seven-valent conjugate pneumococcal vaccine has been documented to benefit children with severe and recurrent acute otitis media, including a 57% decrease in vaccine-type pneumococcal disease.[117, 339] Parenterally and intranasally administered influenza virus vaccine resulted in a decreased number of cases of acute otitis media, as contrasted with control findings.[78, 233, 479] Influenza virus vaccine should be administered in the fall to children who have had recurrent episodes of acute otitis media the prior winter. Compliance with influenza immunization programs will likely increase when the intranasal influenza virus vaccine becomes available.

If the child continues to suffer from recurrent episodes of acute otitis media after the prior steps have been taken, myringotomy with insertion of tympanostomy tubes is valuable in the prevention of recurrent episodes of acute otitis media.[209] Tympanostomy tubes provide ventilation to the middle ear and thus prevent the development of middle-ear negative pressure during an upper respiratory tract infection as well as providing drainage of middle-ear effusion from the middle ear down the eustachian tube into the nasopharynx. Although children may still develop inflammation of the mucosa of the middle ear due to viruses or bacteria, the number of symptomatic episodes of acute otitis media decreases. Adenoidectomy, irrespective of the size of the adenoids, has been demonstrated to reduce the rate of recurrent episodes of acute otitis media in children who had one or more insertions of tympanostomy tubes in the past,[836] but adenoidectomy was not shown to be effective for the long term in those children who had not received tympanostomy tubes in the past.[832] Nevertheless, adenoidectomy may be indicated as an adjunct to initial tympanostomy tube insertion, if they are the cause of chronic upper airway obstruction due to hypertrophy.

Tonsillectomy is withheld at any stage unless there are other compelling indications for the removal of the tonsils, such as for those children who have had recurrent pharyngotonsillitis[831] or moderate to severe chronic airway obstruction due to hypertrophy of the tonsils. When recurrent episodes of acute otitis media are superimposed on chronic otitis media with effusion, then the child should receive management consistent with the chronic effusion, such as myringotomy and tympanostomy tube placement and not prophylactic antibiotics.

Diagnostic tests should be considered for selected children who suffer recurrent episodes of acute otitis media to identify underlying host features that predispose to infection, including the following:

1. Examination for anatomic defects such as submucous cleft palate or obstruction of the upper airway by tumor
2. A search for respiratory allergy
3. Radiographs to define the presence of paranasal sinusitis
4. Immunologic studies to identify defects in cellular or humoral immunity

(See also Specific Medical Options for Prevention of Recurrent Otitis Media and Specific Surgical and Mechanical Therapies, later in this chapter.)

Strategies for Treating Otitis Media with Effusion

Management of patients with otitis media with effusion is currently the subject of considerable debate. However, we now have enough evidence-based information to make some of the important decisions regarding treatment or no treatment, and which therapeutic options are effective and which ones are not.[940]

Otitis media with effusion in most children will resolve without active treatment in two or three months,[207] but treatment may be indicated in some children, because there are possible complications and sequelae associated with this condition. Since impairment of hearing of some degree usually accompanies a middle-ear effusion,[386] treatment may be warranted when long-standing hearing loss is present. Although the significance of this hearing loss is still uncertain, such a loss may impair cognitive and language function and result in disturbances in psychosocial adjustment.[1106] Important factors that should be considered when deciding to treat (and which treatment) or not to treat are the following:

1. Significant associated conductive hearing loss
2. Occurrence in young infants, since they are unable to communicate about their symptoms and may have suppurative disease
3. An associated acute suppurative upper respiratory tract infection
4. Concurrent permanent conductive or sensorineural hearing loss
5. Presence of speech or language delay associated with effusion and hearing loss
6. Alterations of tympanic membrane, such as a retraction pocket
7. Middle-ear changes, such as adhesive otitis media or ossicular involvement
8. Previous surgery for otitis media, e.g., tympanostomy tube placement or adenoidectomy
9. When episodes recur frequently
10. When the effusion persists for 3 months or longer in both ears or 6 or more months when the effusion is only in one ear, i.e., chronic otitis media with effusion, prior to consideration for tympanostomy tube placement

The most compelling indications would be progression of the disease into the chronic stage.[295, 1069]

Similar to a patient who has had recurrent acute otitis media, before initiating a nonsurgical or surgical method of management of patients with frequently recurrent or chronic effusions, a thorough search for an underlying cause should be attempted, as described earlier.

Nonsurgical Treatment Options

If active treatment is elected, options are limited. Even though a combination of an oral decongestant and antihistamine was thought to be effective—and widely used—in the past, two Pittsburgh studies that involved more than 1000 infants and children failed to demonstrate its efficacy in eliminating middle-ear effusion.[196, 688] Despite the apparent efficacy of systemic corticosteroid therapy in clinical trials,[942] an official government guideline found the risks of this option in children to outweigh its possible benefits.[1069] As of yet, clinical trials have not been reported that have tested the efficacy of topical nasal corticosteroid treatment, immunotherapy, and control of allergy in children who have nasal allergy and middle-ear disease. Nevertheless, this method of management seems reasonable in children who have frequently recurrent or chronic otitis media with effusion and evidence of upper respiratory allergy. Inflation of the eustachian tube-middle ear using Politzer's method or the Valsalva maneuver has been advocated for more than a century for this condition. However, a randomized controlled trial by Chan and

Bluestone[219] found a lack of efficacy of middle-ear inflation for chronic effusion, and, therefore, it is not recommended in children; efficacy in adults remains uncertain. Inflation may be effective for all age groups for the management of middle-ear effusion that follows barotrauma (e.g., after air travel or scuba diving).

Of all the medical treatments that have been advocated, a trial of an antimicrobial agent would appear to be most appropriate in those children who have not received an antibiotic recently. A meta-analysis of the effect of antimicrobial agents in the treatment of otitis media with effusion was reported by Rosenfeld and Post,[943] which confirmed their efficacy, particularly when the effusion is chronic. Two other meta-analyses also verified their short-term effect, but, as expected, there was no long term efficacy.[1069, 1193] Other strategies, such as antimicrobial prophylaxis[684] or surgery, are required for long-term control, since the disease frequently recurs because of repeated exposure to upper respiratory tract infections.

As in acute otitis media, amoxicillin is a reasonable choice for treating otitis media with effusion, since one clinical trial conducted in Pittsburgh demonstrated its efficacy, albeit limited, in the 518 infants and children who participated in the study.[688] Other antimicrobial agents have also been recommended, but none have been reported to be more effective than amoxicillin at this time; cefaclor, erythromycin-sulfisoxazole, and ceftibuten have been shown to be equal or inferior to amoxicillin.[684, 691] A 10-day course of amoxicillin is recommended, but a longer duration of therapy with this or any other antimicrobial agent is not recommended at this time. A recently reported clinical trial compared the efficacy of a 10-day course of amoxicillin with a 20-day regimen and found that the longer therapy provided no advantage over the shorter duration of therapy.[686] Prolonging antimicrobial treatment for longer than 10 days is excessive and is not recommended, especially with our current antibiotic-resistance problem.

When the effusion is chronic, surgical intervention should be considered, especially when antimicrobial therapy fails. Even though the recent guideline from the government has recommended either antimicrobial therapy or tympanostomy tube insertion for bilateral chronic effusions (i.e., 3–4 months' duration) associated with hearing loss,[1069] we recommend a trial of amoxicillin therapy, irrespective of the level of hearing, prior to consideration for surgical intervention.[140] Indeed, a trial of antibiotic therapy for children who had chronic otitis media with effusion conducted in the Netherlands by primary care physicians, who normally reserve these drugs for only severe acute otitis media, was found to be so effective they recommended a course prior to referral of the patient to an otolaryngologist for possible surgery.[1154] (See also Effect of Antimicrobial Therapy on Otitis Media with Effusion, later in this chapter.)

Surgical Treatment Options

Myringotomy with tympanostomy tube placement, or adenoidectomy and myringotomy, with and without tube insertion, have been demonstrated to be effective in children with chronic effusions who are unresponsive to a trial of antibiotics. Two Pittsburgh clinical trials showed that tympanostomy tube insertion was more effective than myringotomy without tube insertion or no surgery (i.e., controls) for chronic effusions.[689, 690]

Adenoidectomy, in conjunction with myringotomy with and without tympanostomy tube placement, has been shown to be effective for chronic effusions in two large, well-controlled clinical trials in children.[397, 836] Our preference is to recommend only tympanostomy tube insertion if the child has not had them inserted in the past and does not have nasal obstruction caused by adenoid hypertrophy, since the two Pittsburgh studies[689, 690] showed that about half of the subjects did not require another operation. If obstructive adenoids are present, we recommend their removal at the initial procedure. For those children who have recurrence of chronic effusion following extrusion of the tubes and who need a second surgical procedure, we advise an adenoidectomy, irrespective of adenoid size, with myringotomy; the decision to place tympanostomy tubes at this operation is made on an individualized basis. Even though the recent guideline panel recommended against adenoidectomy (in the absence of adenoid pathologic lesions) for this indication in children younger than the age of 4 years,[1069] a Pittsburgh trial showed that the procedure was also effective for subjects in this age group.[836] We have discussed this difference of opinion in detail elsewhere.[138]

Tonsillectomy in conjunction with adenoidectomy for chronic effusions was shown in a clinical trial in Great Britain to provide no significant benefit over adenoidectomy alone,[711] and we do not recommend the removal of tonsils unless there are other compelling indications, such as frequently recurrent throat infections,[831] or severe airway obstruction secondary to grossly enlarged tonsils. (See also Specific Surgical and Mechanical Therapies, later in this chapter.)

Strategies for Management of Eustachian Tube Dysfunction

Eustachian tube dysfunction can occur in the absence of a middle-ear effusion. Abnormal function of the eustachian tube can cause otologic symptoms despite the lack of otitis media. The symptoms can be intermittent or persistent, and the severity of the complaints can be mild, moderate, or severe. At the time of the examination, the tympanic membrane may have a normal appearance and its mobility may or may not be impaired when tested with a pneumatic otoscope or by tympanometry. The tympanic membrane may or may not be retracted. The condition can be either of short duration (acute) or longstanding (chronic). The child commonly will have a past history of episodes of acute otitis media, otitis media with effusion, or both. Two types of eustachian tube dysfunction can be present: obstruction or abnormal patency (see also Physiology, Pathophysiology, and Pathogenesis, earlier in this chapter). Also, rapid alterations in barometric pressure, such as when flying in an airplane or scuba diving, can cause obstruction of the eustachian tube, which can result in otologic symptoms, i.e., otitic baro-

trauma, especially in children who have an underlying eustachian tube dysfunction.

Eustachian Tube Obstruction

When the eustachian tube is obstructed, but no middle-ear effusion is present, the tube periodically opens to regulate the gas pressure (ventilate) within the middle-ear cavity but at less frequent intervals than normal; in this case, high negative intratympanic pressure may be present for transient or prolonged periods, i.e., acute or chronic. The obstruction of the tube can be either anatomic (mechanical) or functional (failure of the opening of the tube), or both. Anatomic obstruction may be due to infection or allergy, or possibly adenoids, whereas functional obstruction is idiopathic. This type of intermittent middle-ear ventilation can cause periods of otalgia, a feeling of fullness or pressure, hearing loss, popping and snapping noises, tinnitus, dysequilibrium, or even vertigo. These symptoms are more commonly encountered in older children and teenagers than young children. Most likely infants and young children have these symptoms but rarely complain. Frequently, patients will have otologic symptoms upon awakening and then periodically during the rest of the day. When symptomatic, the child will commonly have a retracted tympanic membrane, which will have limited or no mobility to applied negative pressure, and no mobility when positive pressure is applied during pneumatic otoscopy, which indicates the presence of negative pressure in the middle-ear cavity.

Tympanometry can be helpful in confirming and documenting the high middle-ear negative pressure (see also Diagnosis, earlier in this chapter). But a child may have no evidence of middle-ear negative pressure at the time of the examination, since the pressure can fluctuate during the course of the day. Audiometric testing will frequently reveal normal hearing, but, if high negative middle-ear pressure is present, there may be a mild conductive hearing loss, which is due to the impaired compliance of the middle ear. This disorder is relatively common in children during puberty, especially girls, and can be present even when a past history of middle-ear infection is absent.

Management of a child who has eustachian tube obstruction is related to the frequency, severity, and duration of the symptoms and to the underlying cause. If the condition is present only during episodes of an acute upper respiratory tract infection, medical treatment should be directed toward relief of the nasal congestion and counseling the patient and parent that the disorder will resolve spontaneously. A systemic decongestant may be helpful. Inflation of the middle ear can be tried (see later in this chapter, Inflation of Eustachian Tube–Middle Ear). But if the symptoms are extremely troublesome and are interfering with concentration, then a myringotomy may be required; this surgical intervention is rarely necessary, however.

When symptoms are of a chronic nature, a search for an underlying cause (e.g., paranasal sinusitis, nasal allergy, or hypertrophy of the adenoids) should be attempted, and, if found, appropriate management should be instituted. Frequently, there is a strong family history of middle-ear disease, which implies a hereditary factor in children who not only have otitis media but also eustachian tube obstruction (see Epidemiology, earlier in this chapter). If no underlying cause is uncovered, then a trial with a systemic decongestant may be helpful or inflation of the eustachian tube–middle ear may be tried, but there is no evidence that these treatment options are effective for the long term. If the nonsurgical methods are not successful and the symptoms are troublesome to the child, then myringotomy and insertion of a tympanostomy tube may be necessary, which will alleviate the symptoms while the tubes are functioning. The condition, even though chronic, will usually resolve with advancing age, but some children, especially adolescents, may need to have the tympanostomy tubes replaced several times, and some may even need a "permanent" tympanostomy tube (see Myringotomy and Tympanostomy Tube, later in this chapter).

When eustachian tube obstruction is chronic, sequelae are possible, such as atelectasis of the middle ear (and tympanic membrane), that can progress into a retraction pocket and then a cholesteatoma; ossicular damage can also occur that can result in permanent conductive hearing loss (see Chap. 26).

Abnormally Patent (Patulous) Eustachian Tube

At the other end of the spectrum of eustachian tube dysfunction is abnormal patency. In its extreme form, the hyperpatent eustachian tube is open even at rest (i.e., patulous). Lesser degrees of abnormal patency result in a semipatulous eustachian tube that is closed at rest but has low tubal resistance to airflow in comparison with the normal tube. A patulous eustachian tube may be caused by abnormal tube geometry or a decrease in extramural pressure, such as occurs as a result of weight loss or, possibly, mural or intraluminal changes. These last conditions may be seen when the extracellular fluid is altered by medical treatment of another unrelated condition. Interruption of the innervation of the tensor veli palatini muscle has also been shown to be a cause of a hyperpatent eustachian tube.[857]

Clinically, the presence of a patulous eustachian tube is a relatively uncommon finding in adolescents and adults but is even less commonly encountered in young children. When present, however, this disorder can be misdiagnosed as eustachian tube obstruction and inappropriately treated. The patient frequently complains of hearing his or her own breathing or voice (autophony), or both, in the ear. Otoscopic examination reveals a tympanic membrane that moves medially on inspiration and laterally on expiration; the movement can be exaggerated with forced respiration. The condition is relieved when the patient is recumbent, since extramural pressure in the eustachian tube is increased by paratubal venous engorgement in this position. The patient should therefore be examined in the sitting position. The diagnosis can also be made by measuring the impedance of the middle ear.[120] A tympanogram is obtained while the patient is breathing normally, and a second one is obtained while the patient holds his or her breath. Fluctuation in the tympanometric line should coincide with breathing. The fluctuation can be exaggerated by asking the patient to occlude one nostril and close the mouth during forced inspiration and expiration, or by performing the Toynbee or Valsalva maneuver (see Physiology, Pathophysiology and Pathogenesis, and Diagnosis, earlier in this chapter).

Management of a patulous eustachian tube depends on first determining the cause of the problem. If the symptoms are of relatively short duration, the condition may subside without any active treatment. In children and teenagers, this condition is usually self-limited and probably related to changes in the structure and function of the eustachian tube and adjacent areas secondary to rapid growth and development. Interruption of the neuromuscular component of the eustachian tube, such as from trauma or surgery, may be the cause; more commonly, rapid loss of weight is the underlying pathogenesis. In adults, a neurologic disorder may be present, but in children the condition is most commonly idiopathic. When the symptoms are disturbing and the condition is chronic, active treatment is indicated. Myringotomy with insertion of a tympanostomy tube may be helpful in some patients, probably because of the coexistence of obstruction and abnormal patency. But tympanostomy tube placement make exaggerate the symptoms if the tube is consistently hyperpatent.

Insufflation of powders into the eustachian tube and instillation of 2% iodine or 5% trichloroacetic acid solution have also been advocated.[715] Infusion of an absorbable gelatin sponge solution has also been suggested,[808] as has injection of polytetrafluoroethylene (Teflon) into the paratubal area,[901] but all of these methods have major disadvantages. They are, for the most part, irreversible and may not improve the condition or may provide only temporary relief. Total obstruction of the eustachian tube can also be a complication. Stroud et al[1075] have suggested the transposition of the tensor veli palatini through a palatal incision, but the procedure has not been shown to be safe and effective in a large number of patients by other investigators. DiBartolomeo and Henry[283] reported initial success in treating 8 of 10 patients who had patulous tubes with a new intranasal medication composed of diluted hydrochloric acid, chlorobutanol, and benzyl alcohol. The safety and long-term efficacy of this experimental treatment has not been confirmed.[144]

At present, the most logical choice for relief when the discomfort becomes severe is a procedure that would alleviate the symptoms simply, reversibly, and without untoward reactions. A technique described by Bluestone and Cantekin[129] has been used successfully in adults but is rarely indicated or necessary in children, since the patulous tube condition is usually self-limited in this population. The procedure involves placement of a plastic catheter into the middle-ear end of the eustachian tube (Fig. 25–54).[143]

Otitic Barotrauma

Many parents and children, as well as their attending physicians, are concerned about flying in airplanes when

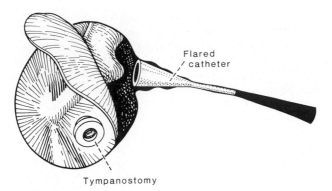

FIGURE 25–54. Placement of an indwelling catheter used to obstruct a patulous eustachian tube.

the child has otitis media. Barotitis usually occurs in individuals who have eustachian tube obstruction, either functional or mechanical. On ascent, the normal eustachian tube opens spontaneously, that is, there is forced opening, and the relative positive middle-ear gas pressure is equilibrated with the cabin pressure. Most commercial aircraft are pressurized to an equivalent altitude of 7000 feet. On descent, however, the eustachian tube does not open spontaneously; rather, the tube opens by actively swallowing, that is, contraction of the tensor veli palatini muscle, to equilibrate the relative negative middle-ear pressure. If the eustachian tube is totally mechanically obstructed, which is extremely rare in children and adults, then the patient will have otalgia and barotitis on both ascent and descent. Since functional eustachian tube obstruction is the most common type of dysfunction of the tube, the child will have difficulty only on descent, since the tube can easily open spontaneously during ascent, but not on descent; infants and children even without a history of middle-ear disease frequently have trouble on descent, since their ability to actively open the tube by swallowing is inefficient compared to that of most adults (see Physiology, Pathophysiology and Pathogenesis, earlier in this chapter).

The child may have little or no symptoms during flying in an airplane until he or she develops an upper respiratory tract infection or during a period in which his or her allergic rhinitis is present (i.e., inflammation of the tube is superimposed on a pre-existing functional obstruction). Evidence that infants have relatively inefficient active tubal opening is their crying during descent, which probably inflates their middle ears, a physiologic compensatory mechanism.

Barotitis that is symptomatic and persistent is the result of the eustachian tube being persistently closed, or even "locked," after descent (see Physiology, Pathophysiology and Pathogenesis). The tympanic membrane movement is retracted and high middle-ear pressure is present. The middle-ear mucous membrane can actually tear, which can result in bleeding in the middle ear (hemotympanum) secondary to the alterations in middle-ear gas pressure and the pressure in the cabin of the airplane. A middle-ear effusion can be present and is secondary to the negative middle-ear pressure. If the child has a preexisting middle-ear effusion, then there is little or no movement of the tympanic membrane, and thus no otalgia on

descent. If the child has had recurrent otitis media and has eustachian tube dysfunction, however, but has no effusion, then otalgia and barotitis is possible; symptoms are similar to those described when eustachian tube obstruction is present. Indeed, Weiss and Frost[1182] evaluated 14 children whose ages ranged from 3 to 11 years and who had middle-ear effusion in one or both ears before an air flight. None of the children experienced difficulty in the ears with effusion, but two of the children had symptoms attributable to barotitis in a contralateral effusion-free ear.

We recommend that children who have middle-ear effusion present in both ears may fly in commercial aircraft without any preventative medication. If the child has had recurrent otitis media, however, or signs and symptoms of eustachian tube dysfunction and has no middle-ear effusion in either ear, then prevention is advisable. We recommend an oral decongestant, such as pseudoephedrine hydrochloride, prior to the flight, and a topical nasal decongestant, such as oxymetazoline, immediately before descent; two sprays are administered in each nostril and then two more sprays are administered after about 5 minutes. Most patients have little or no difficulty with this method of prevention.

Scuba diving is not a common recreational activity in young children but it can be common in older children and adolescents. The pathophysiology during descent and ascent is similar to that described above during flying in an airplane, and the methods of prevention and treatment are also similar. However, we do not recommend scuba diving for children who have recurrent or chronic otitis media, or eustachian tube obstruction, since an adverse outcome may occur and may even be life-threatening if severe vertigo develops.

Scuba diving is not a physiologic activity that evolved in humans, and when this activity is associated with possible severe ear complications, it should be avoided. But, flying in airplanes is part of our current culture and therefore should not be withheld from children who have middle-ear problems. Fortunately, infants and children who have tympanostomy tubes in place have no difficulty during flying, since their middle-ear pressure is always equilibrated with the ambient pressure.

Specific Medical Treatment Options

Antimicrobial Agents

Decisions about optimal chemotherapy for otitis media are based on information about (1) the pathogens isolated from middle ear fluids; (2) the in vitro activity of antimicrobial agents against these pathogens; (3) the clinical pharmacologic action of antimicrobial agents of value, including concentrations of drug achieved in middle ear fluid; and (4) the results of clinical and microbiologic studies. The effective antimicrobial agent sterilizes the middle ear infection, produces resolution of acute signs and symptoms within 72 hours, decreases the duration of middle-ear effusion, and prevents suppurative complications.

Development of resistance to antimicrobial agents has been a constant feature of antimicrobial drug therapy since the introduction of the sulfonamides in the mid-1930s. Identification of beta-lactamase-producing strains of *H. influenzae* and *M. catarrhalis* in the 1970s and the increased incidence of multidrug-resistant pneumococci in the 1980s are important factors in deciding whether to treat acute otitis media and, if the decision is made to treat, which antimicrobial agent to choose. Clinicians should be aware of data for drug resistance in their community, risk features associated with increased resistance, and the clinical implications for use and selection of antimicrobial agents.

Microbiology of Otitis Media: Therapeutic Implications

The preferred antimicrobial agent for treatment of the patient with otitis media must be active against *S. pneumoniae, H. influenzae,* and *M. catarrhalis,* the three most important bacterial pathogens in all age groups. Group A *Streptococcus* and *S. aureus* are less frequent causes of acute otitis media. Gram-negative enteric bacilli must be considered when otitis media occurs in the newborn infant and other hosts with immune defects. Anaerobic bacteria appear to have a limited role in chronic otitis media and a minimal role in acute otitis media. The bacterial pathogens are discussed further under Microbiology, in this chapter.

Streptococcus pneumoniae. *S. pneumoniae* is susceptible to penicillins, cephalosporins, macrolides, clindamycin,

and the combination of trimethoprim-sulfamethoxazole (TMP-SMX). Chloramphenicol and sulfonamides have moderate activity. Aminoglycosides are relatively ineffective.

With the introduction of the penicillins more than 40 years ago, *S. pneumoniae* was uniformly and markedly sensitive to penicillin G and other penicillins. Clinical and microbiologic resistance of pneumococci to penicillin was identified in South Africa in the 1970s[31] and is now a worldwide problem. Pneumococcal strains are designated *susceptible* and *nonsusceptible*. The latter are termed *intermediate* or *resistant* according to the minimum inhibitory concentration (MIC) of penicillin required to inhibit growth of the organism. Increments of drug needed to inhibit the organism are exhibited by nonsusceptible strains: susceptible strains are inhibited by MICs of less than 0.12 μg/mL; among nonsusceptible strains, intermediate strains are inhibited by 0.12 to 1.0 μg/mL and resistant strains require 2 μg/mL or more for inhibition.

The clinical relevance of these numbers lies in comparing the MIC of the strain of bacteria with levels of antibiotic achievable at the site of infection. Most infections caused by intermediate strains can be treated adequately with usual doses of penicillins, and even some resistant strains may be inhibited. For example, the usual dosage schedules of amoxicillin achieves peak concentrations of approximately 2 μg/mL in middle-ear fluid (Table 25–30); most of the intermediate strains and some resistant strains are likely to be inhibited by concentrations of amoxicillin in middle-ear fluids. Doubling the dose of

TABLE 25–30. Concentration of Antimicrobial Agents in Serum (S) and Middle-Ear Fluids (MEF)

Agent	Dosage (mg/kg)	Concentration (μg/mL)			Study
		S	**MEF**	**MEF/S**	
Penicillin V	13 PO	8.1	1.8	0.22	Kamme et al[562]
	26 PO	15.5	6.3	0.41	
Ampicillin	10 PO	4.3	1.2	0.28	Lahikainen et al[626]
Amoxicillin	10 PO	4.8	2.2	0.46	Howard et al[507]
	13.3 PO	11.2	2.8	0.25	Krause et al[620]
	15 PO	13.6	5.6	0.41	Klimek et al[609]
Bacampicillin	800 total IM	7.7	2.4	0.31	Virtanen and Lahikainen[1169]
Cefaclor	10 PO	7.0	1.3	0.19	Ginsburg et al[411]
	13 PO	3.6	0.96	0.30	Barr et al[63]
Cefuroxime	250 total PO	5.4	1.2	0.22	Haddad et al[449]
Cefixime	8 PO	2.5	1.3	0.52	Harrison et al. (1997)
	8 PO	4.2	1.5	0.36	Kafetzis et al[555]
Cefpodoxime	5 PO	NA	0.2	NA	Nelson et al[786]
	10 PO	NA	0.24	NA	
Cefprozil	15 PO	5.5	2.0	0.36	Kafetzis et al[555]
Ceftibuten	9 PO	5.9	4.03	0.80	Barr et al[63]
Loracarbef	7.5 PO	4.2	2.0	0.48	Kusmiesz et al[622]
	15 PO	9.3	3.9	0.42	
Cefotaxime	25 IM/IV	5.8	2.1	0.36	Danon[270]
Ceftriaxone	50 IM	NA	35	NA	Gudnasson et al[445]
Erythromycin	15 PO	3.6	1.7	0.49	Ginsburg et al[411]
Estolate	15 PO	1.2	0.5	0.42	
Clarithromycin	7.5 PO	1.7	2.5	1.47	Guay and Kraft[444]
14-hydroxy metabolite	—	0.8	1.3	1.62	
Azithromycin	10 PO	0.07	2.32	33.14	Dagan et al[265]
Sulfonamide (trisulfapyrimidine)	30 PO	13.4	8.3	0.62	Howard et al[507]

From Bluestone CD, Klein JO. Otitis Media in Infants and Children, 3rd ed, Philadelphia, WB Saunders, 2001.

amoxicillin achieves approximately twice these concentrations at the site of infection,[996] with resultant inhibition of an increased number of resistant strains of pneumococci (see Table 25–30).

Penicillin resistance in pneumococci is caused by changes in penicillin-binding proteins in the cell wall, resulting in reduced affinity for beta-lactam drugs. Emergence of penicillin resistance in a community usually begins with identification of intermediate strains, which increase and are followed by resistant strains. Penicillin resistance is usually accompanied by resistance to other antimicrobial agents whose mode of resistance differs from that of penicillin and the beta-lactam drugs.

Surveys of susceptibilities of S. pneumoniae in the United States are uniform in indicating increasing rates of resistance each year throughout the country. A survey of 51 medical centers for the winter 1996–1997 was conducted by Thornsberry et al[1120]: 17% of strains were intermediate and 19% were highly resistant to penicillin. The prevalence of resistance varied by region, with rates highest in the East South Central region (56% of strains nonsusceptible) and lowest in the Pacific region (25% of strains nonsusceptible). Additional U.S. survey data for 1997 were reported by Jacobs et al[533]: nonsusceptible strains varied by region between 35.8% and 62.4%; 17.9% of all strains showed intermediate and 32.5% were highly resistant. As in the Thornsberry et al study, resistance was highest in the southern half of the United States.

Pneumococcal resistance is universal and found in varying incidence in all countries. Rates of penicillin resistance of pneumococci have been increasing over the past 20 years: Spain, France, Hungary, and Israel reported rates in excess of 40%; Korea and the Far East have the highest reported to date, exceeding 80%; The Netherlands, in contrast, reports less than 1%.[278] In Spain, the incidence of penicillin-resistant pneumococci rose from 6% in 1979 to 44% in 1989[363]; approximately half the nonsusceptible strains had MICs of greater than 2 μg/mL.

The increase in resistance to penicillin has been accompanied by increased resistance to other antimicrobial agents. The proportion of resistant strains is usually lower for oral cephalosporins than for penicillin,[1120] and resistance to macrolides (erythromycin, clarithromycin, and azithromycin) and to clindamycin is lower than resistance to the beta-lactam drugs. Few strains of S. pneumoniae are resistant to the newer fluoroquinolones, but these drugs are still proscribed for use in children because of the occurrence of arthropathies following administration to juvenile animals. Of particular concern are reports of resistance to TMP-SMZ. This antimicrobial agent is inexpensive and is the most frequently used drug for respiratory infections in developing countries. A study of pneumococci obtained from the lower respiratory tract of Pakistani children during the winters of 1986 to 1989 identified 31% resistant to TMP-SMZ.[703] In the survey of U.S. medical centers, 11.9% of pneumococcal strains were resistant to TMP-SMZ.[1120]

Risk features for multidrug-resistant pneumococci include use of an antimicrobial agent in the prior 28 days, hospitalization, and out-of-home day care. Isolates from mucosal surfaces such as the throat and nasopharynx yield higher rates of resistance than do isolates from body fluids such as blood and cerebrospinal fluid. Isolates from children have higher rates of resistance than isolates from adults, probably because prior antibiotic use is more likely in children.[1120]

No clinical features distinguish infection with resistant organisms from infection by susceptible organisms, and there does appear to be increased virulence of the disease caused by resistant strains. The proportion of cases of pneumococcal otitis media that fail treatment because of resistance to penicillin or amoxicillin is uncertain, but well-documented cases of clinical and microbiologic failure have occurred in meningitis because of moderately resistant strains.[675, 1180] Pneumococcal meningitis due to strains resistant to ceftriaxone or cefotaxime has also been reported.[160, 388, 1038] At present, susceptibility testing should be considered for strains of S. pneumoniae causing cases of otitis media that do not respond to an appropriate course of a usually effective antimicrobial agent. No change in use of amoxicillin as the drug of choice for acute otitis media[293] is necessary now, but physicians need to be alert for unexpected clinical or microbiologic failures that may herald an increasing problem with pneumococcal resistance.

Haemophilus influenzae. Strains of H. influenzae responsible for otitis media can be subdivided on the basis of production of beta-lactamase and susceptibility to amoxicillin. Almost all amoxicillin-resistant strains of H. influenzae produce the enzyme, beta-lactamase, which breaks open the beta-lactam ring, rendering the drug ineffective. Amoxicillin- or ampicillin-sensitive strains are only slightly less susceptible to penicillin G than they are to ampicillin, but they are much less susceptible to penicillin V and the penicillinase-resistant penicillins. Addition of a beta-lactamase inhibitor, clavulanic acid, to oral amoxicillin provides activity against H. influenzae without regard to production of the enzyme. Oral and parenteral second- and third-generation agents (Table 25–31) are active against H. influenzae and are effective against ampicillin-sensitive and -resistant strains. Erythromycin is relatively inactive against H. influenzae, but the new macrolides (azithromycin and clarithromycin) have improved activity.

Amoxicillin-resistant strains of both nontypeable and type b H. influenzae have been reported throughout the United States. The resistance appears to be a recent phenomenon; few resistant strains were detected before 1972. Since the resistance to ampicillin is based on production of a beta-lactamase that hydrolyzes the penicillin nucleus, all penicillins that are susceptible to beta-lactamase, including penicillin G, penicillin V, ampicillin, amoxicillin, carbenicillin, ticarcillin, and piperacillin, are likely to be ineffective against these strains. The incidence of beta-lactamase-producing strains varied between 20% and 45% in Pittsburgh between 1981 and 1989[151] and was 41.6% and 33.5% in two 1997 U.S. surveys.[533, 1120]

Strains of H. influenzae that were beta-lactamase negative but resistant to amoxicillin and amoxicillin-clavulanate have been identified. A multicenter survey of antibiotic resistance among clinical isolates of H. influenzae in the United States in 1994 and 1995 identified 38.9% resistant

TABLE 25–31. The Cephalosporins: 2000

Generic Name	Trade Name	Route
First Generation		
Cephalothin	Keflin	IM, IV
Cefazolin	Ancef, Kefzol	IM, IV
Cephapirin	Cefadyl	IM, IV
Cephalexin	Keflex	PO
Cephradine	Velosef, Anspor	PO, IM, IV
Cefadroxil	Ultracef, Duricef	PO
Second Generation		
Cefamandole	Mandol	IM, IV
Cefoxitin	Mefoxin	IM, IV
Cefaclor	Ceclor	PO
Cefuroxime	Zinacef, Kefurox	IM, IV
Cefuroxime axetil	Ceftin	PO
Cefixime	Suprax	PO
Ceftibuten	Cedax	PO
Ceforanide°	Precef	IM, IV
Cefonicid°	Monocid	IM, IV
Cefotetan°	Cefotan	IM, IV
Cefprozil	Cefzil	PO
Cefpodoxime	Vantin	PO
Cefdinir	Omnicef	PO
Loracarbef	Lorabid	PO
Cefmetazole°	Zefazone	IV
Third Generation		
Moxalactam	Moxam	IM, IV
Cefoperazone°	Cefobid	IM, IV
Cefotaxime	Claforan	IM, IV
Ceftizoxime	Cefizox	IM, IV
Ceftriaxone	Rocephin	IM, IV
Ceftazidime	Fortax, Tazidime, Tazicef	IM, IV
Cefepime°	Maxipime	IM, IV

° Not available for children
From Bluestone CD, Klein JO. Otitis Media in Infants and Children, 3rd ed, Philadelphia, WB Saunders, 2001.

to amoxicillin, including 4.5% of strains resistant to amoxicillin-clavulanate (presumably resistant on the basis of a mechanism other than production of beta-lactamase).[286] Thornsberry et al[1120] found only one of 672 strains of *H. influenzae* that was beta-lactamase negative but resistant to amoxicillin-clavulanate.

Drug-resistant strains of *H. influenzae* have also been documented for other antimicrobial agents commonly used for treatment of otitis media. Some cephalosporins (cefaclor, loracarbef, and cefprozil) have overall rates of resistant *H. influenzae* of 5% to 12% overall and 13% to 32% for beta-lactamase-producing strains; resistance has been less than 1% for others (cefixime, ceftibuten, and cefuroxime). TMP-SMX–resistant strains were identified in Boston (12.3%) in the period of 1987 to 1989[852] and in the multihospital survey in the United States (10.2%) in the period of 1996 to 1997.[1120] Although few strains of *H. influenzae* are resistant in vitro to the new macrolides (azithromycin and clarithromycin),[1120] clinical studies indicate frequent microbiologic failures based on middle-ear aspirates of patients with acute otitis media.[262] No fluoroquinolone-resistant strains were identified among 1029 strains tested in the multihospital survey.[1120]

Moraxella catarrhalis. Most current strains of *M. catarrhalis* produce beta-lactamase and are resistant to ampi-

cillin, amoxicillin, and other beta-lactamase–susceptible penicillins. But they are susceptible to the combination of amoxicillin-clavulanate, cephalosporins, macrolides, chloramphenicol, and TMP-SMX.[286] A survey of 444 strains of *M. catarrhalis* obtained from 51 medical centers in the United States found that 93% were beta-lactamase producers.[1120]

As is the case with *H. influenzae*, the isolation of beta-lactamase-producing strains of *M. catarrhalis* is a relatively new phenomenon. In 1970, Kamme[563] reported that all 108 strains of *M. catarrhalis* isolated in the Department of Clinical Bacteriology in Lund, Sweden, were highly susceptible to penicillin G and ampicillin. In 1980, 15% of strains of *M. catarrhalis* isolated in the same laboratory produced beta-lactamase. A similar experience was described in nearby Finland: the proportion of strains of *M. catarrhalis*–producing beta-lactamase increased from 0% to 60% in 1978 to 1983 and from 60% to 80% in 1988 to 1990.[799]

Shurin et al[1015] and Kovatch et al,[617] from Cleveland and Pittsburgh, respectively, reported that more than 20% of isolates from acute middle-ear effusions had *M. catarrhalis* and that three fourths of those isolates produced beta-lactamase. The temporal changes of the incidence of beta-lactamase–producing strains of *M. catarrhalis* in Pittsburgh was documented by Bluestone et al.[151]

M. catarrhalis resistance to selected cephalosporins is increased for beta-lactamase–producing strains. Almost all *M. catarrhalis* are susceptible in vitro to the macrolides, quinolones, and trimethoprim-sulfamethoxazole.[1120]

Groups A and B Streptococci. There are no known strains of groups A and B streptococci that are resistant to the penicillins. These streptococci are markedly sensitive to the penicillins, cephalosporins, chloramphenicol, and clindamycin. Resistance to erythromycin and the newer macrolides has increased in the past years but remains low in the United States at 2% to 4%.[1195] They are relatively resistant to aminoglycosides and to sulfonamides. TMP-SMX in combination is more active than either component alone, but clinical efficacy is uncertain against group A streptococci. The current increase in invasive and toxin-producing strains of group A streptococcus causing toxic shock syndromes and tissue necrosis is not associated with a change in the antimicrobial susceptibility pattern of the streptococci.

Staphylococcus aureus **and** ***Staphylococcus epidermidis.*** Most strains of hospital-acquired *S. aureus* produce beta-lactamase and are resistant to penicillin G and amoxicillin; the number of strains of resistant staphylococci in patients who have community-acquired disease is lower but significant. The penicillinase-resistant penicillins are the drugs of choice for initial management of the patient with suspected or documented staphylococcal otitis media. Most cephalosporins, macrolides, and clindamycin are also effective against penicillinase-producing strains.

Disease due to methicillin-resistant staphylococci was reported shortly after the introduction of the drug. The strains are usually resistant to penicillinase-resistant penicillins and to most cephalosporins. Bacterial resistance must be considered as a possible cause of therapeutic failure whenever a patient with staphylococcal disease who is on an adequate dosage schedule of a penicillinase-resistant penicillin does not respond favorably. Vancomycin is usually effective for these strains.

Most strains of *S. epidermidis* produce beta-lactamase and are also more resistant than *S. aureus* to the penicillinase-resistant penicillins, cephalosporins, macrolides, and clindamycin. Vancomycin is usually effective against methicillin-resistant *S. epidermidis*.

Gram-Negative Enteric Bacilli. The choice of antibiotics for infections due to gram-negative bacteria depends on the particular pattern of susceptibility in the hospital or community. These patterns vary in different hospitals or communities, and from time to time within the same institution. In most areas, the most effective agents for *E. coli*, *Proteus* (indole-positive and -negative) species, *Klebsiella* and *Enterobacter* species, and *P. aeruginosa* are the aminoglycosides tobramycin, gentamicin, netilmicin, and amikacin. Some of the new oral cephalosporins (i.e., cefixime and ceftibuten) and some parenteral cephalosporins (cefoxitin, moxalactam, cefoperazone, cefotaxime, cefixime, ceftriaxone, and ceftazidime) have activity against most gram-negative bacilli; ceftazidime alone among the parenteral cephalosporins has significant activity against *P. aeruginosa*. Since the susceptibility of gram-negative enteric bacilli is variable and unpredictable, isolates should be tested to determine the optimal choice of antimicrobial agents.

Anaerobic Bacteria. Most anaerobic bacteria responsible for infection and disease in the upper respiratory tract, including anaerobic cocci, gram-positive nonsporulating anaerobic bacilli, and anaerobic gram-negative bacilli, are susceptible to penicillin G.[371] Some strains of anaerobic gram-negative bacilli, such as *Bacteroides melaninogenicus*, are resistant to penicillin G. *Bacteroides fragilis* is an uncommon pathogen in the respiratory tract; most strains are resistant to penicillin G but susceptible to clindamycin, chloramphenicol, and metronidazole. The role of anaerobic bacteria in otitis media and infections of the head and neck was reviewed at a symposium held in Pittsburgh in 1989.[139]

***Chlamydia trachomatis* and *Chlamydia pneumoniae*.** *C. trachomatis* and *C. pneumoniae* are susceptible to macrolides, sulfonamides, tetracyclines, and chloramphenicol. *C. trachomatis* may be associated with infection of the respiratory tract, including otitis media, in young infants; a macrolide or sulfonamide has been recommended for documented or suspected infection. Although controlled trials of efficacy of these drugs in young infants with respiratory infection have not been performed, results of uncontrolled studies suggest that either drug shortens the course of the illness. No data are available about the efficacy of any antimicrobial drugs for otitis media due to *Chlamydia* species.

***Mycoplasma pneumoniae*.** Otitis media may accompany respiratory infection due to *M. pneumoniae*. The organisms are susceptible to macrolides and tetracyclines. Controlled trials indicate that the duration of signs of lower respiratory tract infection, such as cough, rales, and fever, is less in patients receiving one of these drugs, but there are no data about the efficacy of antibiotics for otitis media due to *M. pneumoniae*.

Clinical Pharmacology of Antimicrobial Agents of Value in Therapy of Otitis Media and its Suppurative Complications

The clinical pharmacologic effects of orally administered antimicrobial agents of value in otitis media are discussed below. Parenterally administered drugs of value for suppurative complications of otitis media are also discussed in this chapter.

The Penicillins (Table 25–32)

Penicillin G and Penicillin V. Oral preparations of buffered penicillin G and phenoxymethyl penicillin (penicillin V) are absorbed well from the gastrointestinal tract. The peak level of serum activity of penicillin V is approximately 40% and that of buffered penicillin G is approximately 20% of the level achieved by the same dose of

TABLE 25–32. The Penicillins: 2000

Generic Name	Trade Name	Route
Traditional		
Penicillin G	Many	PO
Aqueous	Many	IM, IV
Procaine	Many	IM
Benzathine	Cicillin, Permapen	IM
Penicillin V	Many	PO
Penicillinase Resistant		
Methicillin	Staphcillin, Celbenin	IM, IV
Oxacillin	Prostaphlin, Bactocill	PO, IM, IV
Nafcillin	Unipen, Nafcil	PO, IM, IV
Cloxacillin	Tegopen, Cloxapen	PO
Dicloxacillin	Dynapen, Pathocil, Veracillin	PO
Broad Spectrum		
Ampicillin	Omnipen	PO, IM, IV
Ampicillin-sulbactam	Unasyn	IM, IV
Amoxicillin	Amoxil, Wymox	PO
Amoxicillin-clavulanate	Augmentin	PO
Bacampicillin	Spectrobid	PO
Cyclacillin	Cyclapen	PO
Extended Spectrum		
Carbenicillin	Geopen, Pyopen	IM, IV
	Geocillin	PO
Ticarcillin	Ticar	IM, IV
Ticarcillin-clavulanate°	Timentin	IM, IV
Azlocillin	Azlin	IM, IV
Mezlocillin	Mezlin	IM, IV
Piperacillin°	Pipracil	IM, IV
Piperacillin-tazobactam°	Zosyn	IM, IV
Carbapenem		
Imipenem°	Primaxin	IM, IV
Meropenem	Merem	IM, IV

° Not available for infants or children younger than 12 years of age.
From Bluestone CD, Klein JO. Otitis Media in Infants and Children, 3rd ed, Philadelphia, WB Saunders, 2001.

aqueous penicillin G administered intramuscularly. Oral penicillins are satisfactory for the treatment of mild to moderately severe infections due to susceptible organisms. Group A streptococci remain uniformly susceptible to all penicillins and cephalosporins. Penicillin V and penicillin G are of approximately equivalent efficacy in vitro against gram-positive cocci, but penicillin V is less effective than penicillin G against *H. influenzae*. The efficacy of penicillin G against *H. influenzae* in vitro is only two times less than that of amoxicillin.

Parenteral Preparations of Penicillin G.

Parenteral penicillin G preparations include the potassium or sodium salts of aqueous penicillin and procaine and benzathine penicillin G, which modify absorption and thereby produce different patterns of peak and duration of antibacterial activity in serum and tissues. Aqueous penicillin G produces high peak levels of antibacterial activity in serum within 30 minutes of intramuscular administration but is rapidly excreted; thus, the concentration in serum is low within 2 to 4 hours after administration. If aqueous penicillin G is given by the intravenous route, the peak is higher and earlier, and the duration of antibacterial activity in serum is shorter (approximately 2 hours). Aqueous penicillin G, given intramuscularly or intravenously, is used for severe disease, including suspected sepsis and meningitis.

Procaine penicillin G given intramuscularly produces lower levels of serum antibacterial activity (approximately 10–30% of the peak level) than the same dose of the aqueous form, but activity persists in serum for as long as 12 hours. Intramuscular administration of procaine penicillin G should be reserved for the patient with mild to moderate disease who cannot tolerate oral penicillins (patients who are vomiting or have diarrhea, or the comatose patient) or the patient who requires the reliability of parenteral administration, although the disease is not severe enough to warrant frequent intramuscular or intravenous doses of aqueous penicillin G.

Benzathine penicillin G given intramuscularly is a repository preparation providing low levels of serum activity (approximately 1–2% of the peak level achieved by the same dose of the aqueous form). After administration of this drug, low concentrations of penicillin activity are measurable in serum for 14 days or more, and in urine for several months. Significant pain at the site of injection is the major deterrent to widespread usage of this unique antibiotic. Combination of the benzathine and procaine salts (900,000 and 300,000 units, respectively) is less painful and is comparable in efficacy to benzathine alone (1,200,000 units) for treatment of streptococcal pharyngitis.[68] Benzathine penicillin G is appropriate only for highly sensitive organisms present in tissues that are well vascularized, so that the drug can diffuse readily to the site of infection. Although little used today, benzathine penicillin G has been effective for treatment of children with otitis media due to sensitive *S. pneumoniae*[513]; but it would likely fail if pneumococcal strains were nonsusceptible or disease was due to *H. influenzae*. The current place of intramuscular benzathine penicillin G in treatment and prevention of infections in infants and children was reviewed at a 1985 symposium, the proceedings of which were published in *The Pediatric Infectious Disease Journal*.[598]

Penicillinase-Resistant Penicillins.

Methicillin was the first penicillinase-resistant penicillin to be introduced and is available in parenteral form only. Oxacillin and nafcillin are available in both parenteral and oral preparations and have greater in vitro activity against gram-positive cocci. Cloxacillin and dicloxacillin are available in oral forms only and are absorbed more efficiently from the gastrointestinal tract than are the other oral drugs. Differences among these five penicillins include degree of binding to proteins, degree of degradation by beta-lactamases, and in vitro level of susceptibility. All are effective for the treatment of staphylococcal disease, however, and clinical studies have shown them to be comparable when used according to appropriate dosage schedules. In addition, all but methicillin have proved to be effective against infections due to *S. pneumoniae* and group A streptococci. The penicillinase-resistant penicillins are of value when otitis media or a complication is suspected to be due to *S. aureus*.

Broad-Spectrum Penicillins

Ampicillin and Amoxicillin.

Ampicillin and amoxicillin are effective in vitro against a wide spectrum of bacteria, including gram-positive cocci (*S. pneumoniae*, group A streptococci, non-penicillinase–producing strains of *S. aureus*, and oropharyngeal strains of anaerobic bacteria), gram-negative cocci (*M. catarrhalis*), gram-negative coccobacilli (non-penicillinase-producing strains of *H. influenzae*), and some gram-negative enteric bacilli (*E. coli* and *Proteus mirabilis*). Both drugs are susceptible to beta-lactamase-producing organisms. The beta-lactam ring is cleaved, rendering the drugs inactive. Both drugs are available for oral administration; ampicillin alone is available in a parenteral form.

Amoxicillin provides levels of activity in serum that are higher and more prolonged than those achieved with equivalent doses of ampicillin. An additional advantage of amoxicillin is that absorption is not altered when the antibiotic is administered with food, whereas absorption of ampicillin is decreased significantly when it is given with food. Because of its long record of safety and efficacy, amoxicillin is now the preferred oral drug for the treatment of acute otitis media, but, because of concern for nonsusceptible strains of *S. pneumoniae*, the dosage has been increased to 70 to 90 mg/kg/day in two or three doses.[293]

Cyclacillin and Bacampicillin.

These oral drugs are analogues to ampicillin, with a similar spectrum of activity and some administrative advantages. At present, neither has achieved any significant use for otitis media in the United States.

Peak serum concentrations of cyclacillin are three to four times greater than equivalent doses of ampicillin, but in vitro activity is 25% to 50% less than that of ampicillin. Patients who received cyclacillin had fewer side effects, including diarrhea and rash, than did patients who received ampicillin in a double-blind clinical trial involving 2581 patients.[729]

Bacampicillin is a semisynthetic ester of ampicillin that is hydrolyzed to yield ampicillin after oral administration. The drug is rapidly and completely absorbed after oral administration and achieves peak serum levels that are more than twice as high as those of ampicillin and approximately 30% greater than those of amoxicillin. As a result of the more prolonged activity, dosage schedules require only two doses per day. Clinical experience with bacampicillin was summarized in a series of articles published in 1981.[255]

Amoxicillin-Clavulanate. Amoxicillin in combination with clavulanate potassium (Augmentin) was introduced in 1984 for oral administration. Clavulanate potassium is the salt of clavulanic acid, a beta-lactam antibiotic, with poor in vitro activity against pathogenic bacteria but potent activity as an inhibitor of beta-lactamase enzymes. The addition of clavulanic acid restores the original spectrum of amoxicillin, preventing its destruction by the beta-lactamases of S. aureus (but not methicillin-resistant strains), H. influenzae, M. catarrhalis, Neisseria gonorrhoea, E. coli, Proteus species, and anaerobic bacteria, including Bacteroides fragilis. The pharmacokinetics of amoxicillin and clavulanic acid are similar; both are rapidly absorbed and are not affected when taken with food. The drug is now available for twice-a-day dosing. Diarrhea, abdominal pain, and nausea are more frequent with the combination than with amoxicillin alone. Loose stools and diarrhea may be explained in part by clavulanate-related increased small bowel peristalsis. Because bowel peristalsis is inhibited after ingestion of food, administration of amoxicillin-clavulanate at mealtimes reduces the rate of diarrhea.[463]

Amoxicillin-clavulanate may be of value if a beta-lactamase–producing organism is known or suspected to be the cause of otitis media. The combination may be of importance if the proportion of beta-lactamase–producing strains of H. influenzae increases or if these strains or those of M. catarrhalis (the majority of which are beta-lactamase producers), or both, are identified more frequently as pathogens in otitis media, sinusitis, and other respiratory tract infections. Because of the protection by clavulanic acid of the activity of amoxicillin against beta-lactamase enzyme, the combination with the enzyme-binding clavulanate is considered one of the options for children who fail initial therapy with amoxicillin. The higher dosage of the amoxicillin component should be used to include activity against nonsusceptible S. pneumoniae as well as beta-lactamase–producing M. catarrhalis and H. influenzae.

Ampicillin-Sulbactam. Sulbactam is a semisynthetic beta-lactam antibiotic that is an irreversible inhibitor of various beta-lactamases. When combined with ampicillin, sulbactam efficiently protects ampicillin from degradation by beta-lactamases. The inherent activity of ampicillin against beta-lactamase-producing strains of H. influenzae, S. aureus, and N. gonorrhoeae is expressed without inactivation of the antibiotic by the enzyme. Ampicillin-sulbactam at a 2:1 ratio is approved by the FDA for parenteral use only

in patients 12 years of age or older. The antimicrobial activity, pharmacokinetics, and clinical efficacy and safety are discussed in the proceedings of a symposium held in 1985 and published in *Review of Infectious Diseases*.[657]

Carbenicillin, Ticarcillin, and Ticarcillin-Clavulanate. Carbenicillin and ticarcillin have a broader spectrum of activity than previously available penicillins, including P. aeruginosa. The drugs are also effective against gram-positive cocci, H. influenzae, anaerobic bacteria, including Bacteroides species, and gram-negative enteric bacilli, including Enterobacter species, indole-positive organisms, and Proteus species. High concentrations are required to inhibit the gram-negative organisms, but this disadvantage is overcome in part by the low toxicity of the drugs, even when they are given in large intravenous doses. Combination of carbenicillin or ticarcillin with an aminoglycoside such as gentamicin or tobramycin produces synergistic activity against many gram-negative enteric bacilli, and such a combination has been used effectively in initial therapy of sepsis of unknown origin or suspected to be due to gram-negative enteric bacilli in patients with malignancy or immunosuppressive disease.[590] An oral form of carbenicillin produces very low concentrations of drug in serum and should be restricted to therapy of infections of the urinary tract.

Ticarcillin is similar to carbenicillin, but it is more active against some strains of P. aeruginosa and less active against gram-positive cocci. Because of the increased activity, smaller dosages of ticarcillin than of carbenicillin may be used for treatment of disease due to gram-negative organisms.[391]

Ticarcillin in combination with potassium clavulanate extends the antibacterial activity of ticarcillin to include beta-lactamase–producing strains of S. aureus, Klebsiella pneumoniae, and B. fragilis. At present, the combination drug is not approved for children younger than 12 years of age.

Although ticarcillin and carbenicillin have no dose-related toxicity, both drugs are disodium salts; the large amounts in which they are given include significant quantities of sodium: 1 g of carbenicillin contains 4.7 mEq, or 108 mg, of sodium; 1 g of ticarcillin contains 5.2 mEq, or 120 mg, of sodium. The amount of sodium administered may be of concern in the treatment of certain patients with renal or cardiac disease.

For otitis media, the primary uses of carbenicillin, ticarcillin, or ticarcillin-clavulanate are in cases of chronic suppurative otitis media with perforation and discharge due to P. aeruginosa or Proteus species that are unresponsive to other forms of medical treatment, such as ototopical drops.

Piperacillin, Mezlocillin, and Azlocillin. These parenteral penicillins have a spectrum of activity similar to that of carbenicillin and ticarcillin but show greater activity in vitro against some gram-negative bacilli and anaerobic bacteria. Piperacillin and azlocillin are more active than carbenicillin, ticarcillin, or mezlocillin against P. aeruginosa. Piperacillin and mezlocillin are more active in vitro than carbenicillin or ticarcillin against susceptible strains of E. coli and Klebsiella, Enterobacter, and Serratia species. Each of these penicillins is inactivated by beta-lactamases. Piperacillin combined with a beta-lactamase inhibitor, tazobactam, is a new preparation that preserves the activity of piperacillin against beta-lactamase–producing staphylococci, *Enterobacteriaceae*, anaerobes, *H. influenzae, M. catarrhalis,* and *P. aeruginosa.* Combination with an aminoglycoside results in synergy against some gram-negative enteric bacilli.

Clinical experience with these drugs in infants and children is limited. The available data from children and adults indicate that each penicillin is effective against susceptible organisms, but the evidence is inadequate to demonstrate a significant advantage of any single drug (carbenicillin, ticarcillin, piperacillin, mezlocillin, or azlocillin). The last three drugs have half the sodium content per gram of carbenicillin or ticarcillin, a factor of some importance in patients who require large amounts of the penicillin and have cardiac or renal disease. Bluestone and colleagues used azlocillin and other antipseudomonal agents for treatment of chronic suppurative otitis media due to *P. aeruginosa.*[579] A significant proportion of children were cured and did not require surgery. The results of this study suggest that use of a broad-spectrum penicillin may be effective alone for children with chronic suppurative middle-ear infections.

Imipenem. Imipenem was introduced in 1985 as the first carbapenem antibiotic. Carbapenems have the same ring structure as the penicillins, with substitution of carbon for sulphur in the five-member ring. Imipenem has the broadest antimicrobial spectrum available among beta-lactam antibiotics, including gram-positive cocci, gram-negative cocci, gram-negative bacilli, and anaerobic bacteria. Its uses include single-drug therapy for the immunocompromised patient with suspected sepsis, as an alternative to combination therapy for serious intra-abdominal infections, and for serious, hospital-acquired infections. The drug is not approved for use in children younger than 12 years old. Whether the drug at present has a special role in therapy for infections of the head and neck is unclear.

Meropenem. Meropenem is a carbapenem antibiotic that was approved in 1996 for intravenous therapy of complicated intra-abdominal infections and bacterial meningitis in children 3 months of age and older. The drug has a broad spectrum of antibacterial activity similar to that of imipenem, including gram-positive and gram-negative aerobes and anaerobes. Meropenem is effective for bacterial meningitis, but the data are insufficient to compare its efficacy to that of ceftriaxone or cefotaxime for infections caused by penicillin-resistant pneumococci. The broad spectrum of activity suggests a possible role in the treatment of complicated infections of the head and neck.

Toxicity and Sensitization

The penicillins have minimal dose-related toxicity but may produce allergic reactions. Because most allergic reactions are believed to be due to a metabolic breakdown product of the penicillin nucleus, allergy to any one penicillin implies allergy to all.

Seizures may occur under circumstances that result in extraordinarily high concentrations of penicillin in nervous tissues: rapid intravenous infusion of single large doses, large dosage schedules for prolonged periods in patients with impaired renal function, high concentrations given by the intrathecal route, or direct application of penicillin to brain tissue (as might occur inadvertently during a neurosurgical procedure).

Nephritis has followed administration of some penicillins, most frequently methicillin. The mechanism of the nephrotoxicity is uncertain, but recent data suggest that the renal injury is probably an immunologic reaction and not a direct toxic effect.[67]

Thrombocytopenia with purpura due to drug-induced platelet aggregation has been noted as a rare event after the use of carbenicillin and penicillin G. Penicillin-induced hemolytic anemia is associated with high and sustained levels of penicillin in the blood. Circulating red blood cells are coated with a penicillin hapten, the patient makes antibody to the penicillin antigen, the antibody binds to the altered red cell surface, and the cell undergoes lysis or sequestration.[862]

Other uncommon adverse events include neutropenia, which may occur following use of any penicillin (white blood cell counts return to normal after the drug is discontinued); platelet dysfunction following use of carbenicillin and ticarcillin; and hepatic dysfunction reflected in elevated serum aspartate transaminase, which has been identified following the use of oxacillin, nafcillin, and carbenicillin.

If toxicity is not a significant concern with the penicillins, sensitization is a most important factor. Four types of reactions may occur after administration of a penicillin (or any drug or antigen):

1. Immediate or anaphylactic reactions occur within 30 minutes after administration and are life-threatening events. Clinical signs include hypotension or shock, urticaria, laryngeal edema, and bronchospasm. Acute anaphylaxis is rare after administration of penicillin (approximately one case per 20,000 courses of treatment in adults), but a significant number of fatalities occur each year because of the extensive use of these drugs. Children are believed to have fewer systemic reactions than adults, presumably because of less previous exposure to penicillin antigens. Oral preparations are less likely to result in an immediate reaction than are parenteral forms, perhaps because antigens are altered in the gastrointestinal tract or because of slower absorption.

2. Accelerated reactions occur from 1 to 72 hours after administration. The signs are similar to those of the immediate reaction but occur in a less severe form.

3. Late allergic reactions usually occur after 3 days. The major sign is skin rash. This is the most perplexing reaction to penicillin because it is nonspecific, and the rash may be due to other drugs given at the same time or may be a sign of the infectious, usually viral, disease. Skin rash is associated with approximately 4% of courses of penicillins (up to 7% in the case of ampicillin).

4. Immune-complex reactions include serum sickness, hemolytic anemia, and drug fever.

Identification of the patient who will have a significant reaction if penicillin is administered is still difficult. Serologic assays for detection of antibodies to penicillin have been considered; however, such assays lack specificity. Since the immediate reaction is largely mediated by IgE reagin or skin-sensitizing antibody, the patient who may subsequently respond with a life-threatening reaction could be identified by use of intradermal tests with appropriate antigens. Selection of the antigens to be used for skin testing, however, is an uncertain procedure because many different antigens play roles in the allergic reaction. At least 10 metabolic breakdown products of the penicillin nucleus have been identified; macromolecular impurities are present in solutions of the drug and high molecular weight penicillin polymers can be found in poorly buffered penicillin solutions standing for prolonged periods; side chains of the various penicillins may be responsible for reactions; and, finally, bacterial enzymes (amidases) used to prepare semisynthetic penicillins may cause an allergic reaction.[847] Thus, investigators have had difficulty in choosing sensitive and specific antigens to use for skin testing.

The most promising studies of skin-test antigens have come from the laboratories of Levine et al[638] at New York University and of Parker[847] in St. Louis. Levine and colleagues identified two materials for use in skin testing, penicilloyl polylysine (Pre-pen, Kremers-Urban Co., Milwaukee, WI) and a "minor determinant mixture," a preparation of a dilute solution of aqueous crystalline penicillin G that includes metabolic breakdown products. In contrast, Parker used four skin-test antigens associated with penicillin and its products. A positive result is indicated by a wheal and flare reaction in 10 to 15 minutes and suggests a significant chance of reaction on subsequent administration of a penicillin; a negative result suggests that a significant allergic reaction will not take place. Although much effort has gone into clinical tests of these antigens, their prognostic value in children is still uncertain.[438, 638]

At present, the physician must rely on the patient's history of an adverse reaction after administration of a penicillin to identify the patient who is likely to be allergic. If the reaction appears to be related to the administration of penicillin, the drug should be avoided for minor infections. If a life-threatening infection should occur and penicillin is clearly the drug of choice, as in the case of overwhelming disease due to S. pneumoniae, the physician may choose to administer the drug under carefully controlled conditions. A small dose can be injected initially in an extremity and can be followed by increasingly larger doses given every 30 minutes. Epinephrine, a tourniquet, and a tracheotomy set should be available in the event of a severe reaction during the testing period.

The Cephalosporins

At present there are 28 parenteral and oral cephalosporins (see Table 25–31). Eight oral cephalosporins (cefaclor, cefixime, cefuroxime axetil, cefprozil, cefpodoxime, ceftibuten, cefdinir, and loracarbef), and one parenteral cephalosporin (ceftriaxone) have been evaluated in clinical trials for therapy of acute otitis media. With some differences, all are approximately of equal clinical efficacy. Cephalexin was approved for the indication of acute otitis media by the FDA but is little used (and usually is omitted from lists of drugs approved for acute otitis media) because of limited activity against H. influenzae. Parenteral ceftazidime with activity against S. aureus and P. aeruginosa is of particular importance for the treatment of chronic suppurative otitis media. The cephalosporins have been categorized as first-, second-, and third-generation (see Table 25–31), based on time of introduction and, to a lesser extent, similar in vitro activity.

First-Generation Cephalosporins. The first-generation cephalosporins are effective against gram-positive cocci, including beta-lactamase–producing S. aureus, and have variable activity against gram-negative enteric bacilli. Six first-generation cephalosporins are currently available for use in infants and children: the parenteral drugs cephalothin, cefazolin, and cephapirin; the oral products cephalexin and cefadroxil; and cephradine, which is available in both oral and parenteral forms. Cefazolin produces higher concentrations in blood than the other parenteral first-generation drugs. The three oral preparations have comparable in vitro activity.[753] Only cephalexin has been approved by the FDA for treatment of acute otitis media, but the drug is little used because of limited activity against H. influenzae.

The first-generation cephalosporins are alternatives to penicillin for disease caused by S. aureus, S. pneumoniae, group A streptococcus, and susceptible gram-negative enteric bacilli that are resistant to other drugs. Activity against H. influenzae is limited. First-generation cephalosporins are not the drug of choice for any pediatric infection but are of value for children with disease due to susceptible organisms who have an ambiguous history of allergic reaction to a penicillin. Cefadroxil is of value for treatment of streptococcal pharyngitis because it can be administered once a day. Cephalexin may be used for mild to moderately severe staphylococcal infections of the skin and soft tissues. Cefazolin is extensively used for perioperative prophylaxis.

Second-Generation Cephalosporins. The second-generation cephalosporins consist of seven parenteral drugs (cefamandole, cefoxitin, cefuroxime, ceforanide, cefonicid, cefotetan, and cefmetazole) and eight oral preparations (cefaclor, cefuroxime axetil, cefprozil, cefpodoxime, ceftibuten, cefixime, cefdinir, and loracarbef). Each of the oral preparations is of value for the treatment of acute otitis media with activity against pneumococci, H. influenzae, and M. catarrhalis, including beta-lactamase–producing strains. Among the parenteral preparations, cefotetan, ceforanide, cefonicid, and cefmetazole are not approved for use in infants and children.

Cefoxitin has excellent activity against anaerobic organisms, particularly B. fragilis, and selective activity against gram-negative enteric bacilli, and has been effective for therapy of intra-abdominal, gynecologic, and respiratory infections due to mixed bacterial pathogens, including anaerobic bacteria. Cefotetan was introduced in 1986 with an in vitro spectrum of activity and clinical usage similar to that of cefoxitin but is not approved for use in children.

Cefamandole is active against gram-positive cocci, including *S. aureus,* and was the first cephalosporin to be effective for infections due to *H. influenzae* (including beta-lactamase–producing strains). Reports of clinical and microbiologic failure in a small number of cases of meningitis due to *H. influenzae* (presumably due to inadequate concentrations of drug in cerebrospinal fluid) indicate limited use of cefamandole for disease in which sepsis is not a concern.

Cefuroxime is available in oral and parenteral forms and is of value in the treatment of diseases in which gram-positive cocci, particularly *S. aureus* as well as *H. influenzae,* are the likely pathogens, as occurs in upper respiratory tract infections, including otitis media and sinusitis, orbital cellulitis, and severe pneumonias. The oral preparation, cefuroxime axetil, is considered an alternative for patients who fail initial therapy with amoxicillin. The oral suspension has a bitter taste, which limits its use in infants and young children.

Cefprozil is an oral cephalosporin with in vitro activity against gram-positive cocci, certain *Enterobacteriaceae,* and gram-negative respiratory pathogens. Clinical trials indicate efficacy comparable to amoxicillin-clavulanate for acute otitis media. The drug is well absorbed from the gastrointestinal tract, has a twice-a-day dosing schedule, and has a paucity of side effects or dose-related toxicity. The clinical experience with cefprozil was reviewed at a recent symposium.[601]

Cefaclor is an oral preparation that is effective in vitro against gram-positive cocci and *H. influenzae,* including beta-lactamase–producing strains. Extensive experience in clinical trials indicates efficacy in therapy of otitis media, sinusitis, and mild to moderate cases of pneumonia. An unusual serum-sickness reaction has been associated with administration of cefaclor in some patients (see Sensitization and Toxicity).

Cefixime is an oral preparation that has been identified as a third-generation drug because of increased activity for gram-negative organisms but is included here for comparison with the other oral cephalosporins of value for acute otitis media. Decreased activity against some gram-positive strains, including nonsusceptible *S. pneumoniae,* has led to some clinical failures in children with pneumococcal otitis media. *S. aureus* and coagulase-negative staphylococci are relatively resistant. Administrative advantages have made the drug popular with patients: The strawberry taste is well accepted by young patients; the half-life is sufficiently long to justify usage in a once-a-day dosage schedule; and the suspension does not need refrigeration, which is of value when families travel.[149, 659, 794]

Ceftibuten is an oral preparation with a spectrum of activity similar to that of cefixime and a stability to common plasmid- or chromosomal-mediated beta-lactamases, including some enzymes that hydrolyze parenteral third-generation cephalosporins. The half-life of 2 to 3 hours permits once-a-day dosing. Mean peak plasma and middle-ear fluid concentrations are comparable; after a dose

of 9 mg/kg once daily for 3 days, the peak was 14 μg/mL at 2 hours in plasma and 4 hours in the middle ear.[649] Recent clinical trials indicate clinical efficacy comparable to amoxicillin/clavulanate[730] and cefaclor.[155]

Cefpodoxime proxetil is an oral preparation with in vitro activity against both gram-negative and gram-positive organisms of importance in otitis media. The drug has a half-life of 2.1 to 2.8 hours, which permits maintenance of therapeutic levels in a twice-daily oral dosage schedule. The in vitro activity, pharmacokinetics, and clinical experience are provided in the proceedings of a recent symposium.[762] The drug is now approved for treatment of acute otitis media with a dosage schedule of once a day for 5 days.

Cefdinir is active against the bacterial pathogens of importance in acute otitis media. Peak concentrations achieved in serum following single doses of 14 mg/kg were 3.86 μg/mL. Mean middle-ear concentrations were approximately 15% of corresponding plasma concentrations. The 14 mg/kg dosage can be administered once a day. A single randomized trial showed comparability of cefdinir in a once-a-day dosage schedule vs. amoxicillin/clavulanate in a three times a day dosage schedule for treatment of acute otitis media.[4] A recent symposium on the role of cefdinir for pediatric infectious diseases provides a comprehensive review of pharmacokinetics, pharmacodynamics, and safety and clinical information from various trials, including efficacy for infants and children with acute otitis media.[867]

Loracarbef is an oral preparation that is chemically identical to cefaclor, except that the sulfur atom in the dihydrothiazine ring has been replaced by a methylene group. The new drug is termed a *carbacephem* rather than a cephalosporin. Loracarbef is similar in antibacterial activity to cefaclor, with in vitro activity against most gram-positive cocci and *H. influenzae* and *M. catarrhalis.* The serum-sickness–like reaction with rash, arthritis, and fever that has been reported with cefaclor has not been identified with loracarbef. Clinical studies identify efficacy in a twice-daily regimen.[326]

Third-Generation Cephalosporins. Cefoperazone, cefotaxime, moxalactam, ceftriaxone, ceftizoxime, and ceftazidime are parenteral products with efficacy in vitro against gram-positive cocci, gram-negative enteric bacilli, and *H. influenzae.* Of interest is marked increased activity against gram-negative bacilli when compared with the activity of first- and second-generation cephalosporins and lesser activity against gram-positive cocci. For example, activity against *H. influenzae* is excellent but activity against *S. aureus* is limited, requiring caution in usage for serious staphylococcal infections. Cefoperazone has not been approved for use in children younger than 12 years of age.

Moxalactam was equivalent to ampicillin or chloramphenicol for treatment of meningitis in children due to *H. influenzae*[566] and equivalent (when each was used in combination with ampicillin) to amikacin for treatment of meningitis in neonates that was caused by gram-negative enteric bacilli.[722] Moxalactam alone was successful in curing cases of chronic suppurative otitis media and malignant external otitis due to *P. aeruginosa.*[470]

Ceftriaxone is effective against gram-positive cocci, including *S. aureus,* group A streptococci, *S. pneumoniae,* and *H. influenzae,* and selected gram-negative enteric bacilli. The unique quality of ceftriaxone is the long duration of effective concentrations of drug in blood and tissues; the serum half-life is approximately 6.5 hours. Serum concentrations are significantly higher for more than 24 hours than minimum inhibitory concentrations of bacteria causing acute otitis media and infections of the head and neck. High concentrations are achieved in the middle ear that persist for more than 48 hours after a single intramuscular dose.[445] For diseases requiring prolonged therapy, ceftriaxone may be of value for use outside the hospital in single daily intramuscular doses or for intravenous administration in children with venous access. A single dose of intramuscular ceftriaxone was equivalent in clinical efficacy to 10 days of amoxicillin,[439] trimethoprim-sulfamethoxazole,[62] or amoxicillin-clavulanate.[240] The single intramuscular dose was favored by parents when compared with the traditional 10 days of oral drug.[71] For children who have failed amoxicillin and other oral therapies for acute otitis media, ceftriaxone was clinically and microbiologically effective when administered in three consecutive daily intramuscular doses.[402, 404, 634] An alternative regimen for children who have failed initial therapy with amoxicillin is a single dose of ceftriaxone and observation for 48 hours. If clinical signs resolve, no further therapy is necessary. If clinical signs persist, a second dose is administered, and if necessary, a third dose.[604]

Ceftizoxime has a spectrum of activity similar to that of cefotaxime and moxalactam. Clinical experience with the drug in children is limited. Although ceftizoxime has been approved for treatment of meningitis due to *H. influenzae* and *S. pneumoniae,* its role in pediatric infectious diseases is uncertain.

Ceftazidime was introduced for clinical use in the United States in 1985. The drug is highly resistant to inactivation by a broad spectrum of beta-lactamases and has excellent activity in vitro against *P. aeruginosa,* including strains resistant to antipseudomonal penicillins. Its use in middle-ear infections in children is likely to focus on chronic suppurative otitis media or other infections in which *P. aeruginosa* plays an important role.

Cefepime is a parenteral cephalosporin with excellent activity against gram-positive organisms and enhanced gram-negative activity including *P. aeruginosa* and has been demonstrated to have efficacy equivalent to other third-generation cephalosporins such as cefotaxime, ceftazidime, and ceftriaxone. It is not approved for use in infants and children as of this writing.

Role of the Cephalosporins in Infants and Children. Although many cephalosporins are available, there are only a few infectious diseases in children for which one of these drugs offers a unique advantage over previously available antimicrobial agents. Some of the cephalosporins are appropriate alternatives when a previously available drug cannot be used (e.g., penicillin allergy), and some have potential advantages that have not been adequately studied in children. For treatment of otitis media and its complications, cephalosporins may be considered in the following circumstances:

1. Disease caused by *S. aureus,* group A streptococcus, and *S. pneumoniae* in children with known or suspected allergy to penicillin: oral or parenteral first-generation cephalosporin.
2. Otitis media, sinusitis, and mild lower respiratory infections including cases in children who may have failed on amoxicillin because of beta-lactamase–producing strains of *H. influenzae* or *M. catarrhalis*: cefaclor, cefixime, cefuroxime axetil, cefprozil, cefpodoxime, ceftibuten, cefdinir, and loracarbef.
3. Mixed infections, including anaerobic bacteria: cefoxitin, cefotetan.
4. Orbital cellulitis: cefuroxime or ceftriaxone.
5. Severe complications due to gram-negative enteric bacilli: cefotaxime, ceftriaxone, or ceftazidime.
6. Ambulatory therapy for patients requiring high and sustained concentrations of drug in the blood and tissues: ceftriaxone.
7. Infections due to or suspected to be due to *P. aeruginosa*: ceftazidime.

Toxicity and Sensitization. The cephalosporins, like the penicillins, are safe for children and have almost no dose-related toxicity. Physicians should be alert for the uncommon reactions, including kidney problems, alcohol intolerance, serum-sickness–like reactions, and bleeding. Nephrotoxicity has been reported in adults who received cephalothin in combination with gentamicin.[67] Bleeding problems due to hypoprothrombinemia, thrombocytopenia, or platelet dysfunction have been associated with several cephalosporins, in particular moxalactam. If due to hypoprothrombinemia, bleeding was reversed by the administration of vitamin K.

The cephalosporins may produce allergic reactions similar to those caused by the penicillins. There is cross-sensitization among the cephalosporins, and allergy to one implies (as is the case with the penicillins) allergy to all. Various degrees of immunologic cross-reaction of penicillins and cephalosporins have been demonstrated in vitro and in animal models.[863] Patients with a history of penicillin allergy have shown increased reactivity to cephalosporins. Some patients who are allergic to penicillin, however, have an increased incidence of hypersensitivity to unrelated drugs, and it is still uncertain whether the penicillin-allergic patient reacts to a cephalosporin because of cross-allergenicity. Most patients who are believed to be allergic can may be given cephalosporins without an adverse reaction occurring. Although a cephalosporin can be used with caution as an alternative to penicillin in children who have an ambiguous history of skin rash, these cephalosporins should be avoided for the patient with a known immediate or accelerated reaction to a penicillin.

An unusual serum-sickness–like reaction has been reported in children who received cefaclor.[773] The children developed a generalized pruritic rash, similar to erythema multiforme; in some cases it was accompanied by purpura and arthritis, with pain and swelling in the knees and ankles. The signs appeared 5 to 19 days after the start of therapy with cefaclor and generally disappeared within 4 to 5 days after the drug was discontinued. The children had no prior history of allergy to a penicillin or a cepha-

TABLE 25–33. Pharmacokinetics of Macrolides

Drug (Trade Name)	Dosage Schedule (hr)	Peak Serum Concentration (mg/mL)	Concentration PMN/serum	Half-life (hr)
Erythromycin (many)	3–4	4–8	1.5–3.0	6
Azithromycin (Zithromax)	0.4	25–50	11–14	24
Clarithromycin (Biaxin)	1.5–3.0	>15	3.8	1

PMN, polymorphonuclear leukocytes.
From Bluestone CD, Klein JO. Otitis Media in Infants and Children, 3rd ed, Philadelphia, WB Saunders, 2001.

losporin. Levine[637] compared rates of serum sickness reactions to cefaclor and amoxicillin in 2026 children who received 4871 courses of the antibiotics. Serum sickness (defined as arthritis/arthralgia plus a rash or urticaria) or erythema multiforme occurred in 11 children who received cefaclor (1.1%) and in no children given amoxicillin.

The Macrolides

The macrolides possess a many-membered lactone ring attached to one or more deoxy sugars. The first macrolide, erythromycin, was introduced in the 1950s as the drug of choice for penicillin-allergic patients. Two newer oral macrolide antibiotics, clarithromycin and azithromycin, were introduced for use in infants and children in the period of 1994 through 1996. Azithromycin differs from erythromycin in having a methyl-substituted nitrogen in its 15-member lactone ring. Clarithromycin has a 14-member ring structure with a methoxy group in the position C6 of the lactone ring of erythromycin. The two new macrolides, when compared with erythromycin, have prolonged half-lives; high and prolonged concentrations in cells and tissues; increased in vitro activity against selected organisms; and, possibly, less gastrointestinal distress. Pharmacologic and clinical data about the new macrolides are reviewed in the proceedings of a symposium on the macrolides and like compounds,[795, 1225] the proceedings of a symposium about the use of clarithromycin in pediatric infections,[788] and the proceedings of two symposia about the use of azithromycin in childhood infections published in the *Pediatric Infectious Diseases Journal* (*New Approaches to the Treatment of Pediatric Respiratory Tract Infections: Focus on Azithromycin* [April 1995] and Clinical and *Bacteriologic Profile of Azithromycin Childhood Infections* [September 1996]) (Table 25–33).

In Vitro Activity. All the macrolides are effective against gram-positive coccal infections, group A streptococci, pneumococci, susceptible *S. aureus*, and *M. catarrhalis*. Clarithromycin and azithromycin have greater activity against *H. influenzae* than does erythromycin. Other organisms of importance in respiratory infections that are susceptible to the macrolides include *M. pneumoniae*, *Legionella* species, *Chlamydia* species, *Bordetella pertussis*, and *Corynebacterium diphtheriae*. The new drugs are also active against *Chlamydia pneumoniae* and *Mycobacterium avium* complex. The macrolides are likely to have variable efficacy against moderately or highly penicillin-resistant pneumococci and are likely to be ineffective against erythromycin-resistant staphylococci and streptococci.

Clinical Pharmacology. Erythromycin, azithromycin, and clarithromycin are well absorbed from the gastrointestinal tract.[596] Because food decreases absorption of azithromycin, the drug should be administered 1 hour before or 2 hours after meals. Food does not affect the bioavailability of erythromycin or clarithromycin; hence, the drugs may be given without regard to meals.

Biliary excretion is the major route of elimination of the macrolides. The prolonged half-lives permit a once-a-day dosage schedule for azithromycin and a twice-a-day schedule for clarithromycin, in contrast to the four times a day schedule of erythromycin.

Concentration in cells and tissues occurs with each macrolide but most prominently with azithromycin and, to a lesser degree, with clarithromycin. High concentrations of drug have been identified in polymorphonuclear leukocytes, fibroblasts, alveolar macrophages, tonsils, sinus and middle-ear fluids, and middle-ear mucosa.[571]

Clinical Efficacy. Erythromycin can be considered for treatment of otitis media that is known to be due to *S. pneumoniae*, group A streptococcus, and *S. aureus* (mild to moderate disease), but the drug has variable activity against *H. influenzae* and thus should not be relied on as the single antibiotic for treatment of acute otitis media. *C. trachomatis* is a cause of otitis media in young infants (2 weeks to 6 months of age); this disease appears to respond to therapy with either sulfonamides or erythromycin.

A fixed combination of erythromycin ethylsuccinate and sulfisoxazole (Pediazole) is available and effective for treatment of acute otitis media. Each 5 mL contains 200 mg of erythromycin activity and the equivalent of 600 mg of the sulfonamide. The combination provides activity against the pneumococcus and ampicillin-sensitive and -resistant strains of *H. influenzae*. The combination drug is of value for children who are allergic to penicillin or who fail initially when treated with amoxicillin and may have infection due to an ampicillin-resistant strain of *H. influenzae*.

Azithromycin is approved for treatment of acute otitis media in a one dose per day, 5-day regimen. Higher concentrations are achieved in cells and tissues than in serum. Thus, high concentrations are achieved in white blood cells and lung tissue concurrent with very low serum concentrations. Dagan et al[262] compared serum and middle-ear concentrations in 14 patients: serum concentrations varied between 0.01 μg/mL and 3.2 μg/mL, whereas middle-ear fluid concentrations varied between 0.24 μg/mL and 13 μg/mL. However, if cells are removed from the middle-ear specimen prior to the assay and only cell-free middle-ear fluid is tested, the concentrations are comparable to those in serum.

Clinical trials comparing the efficacy of a single dose per day, 5-day course of azithromycin and three times per day, 10-day course of amoxicillin-clavulanate indicate comparability of the two regimens.[35, 585, 727] However, a concern about the efficacy of azithromycin for acute otitis media due to H. influenzae has been raised by microbiologic studies of fluids before and after therapy. Dagan et al[262] compared the bacteriologic efficacy or azithromycin and cefaclor for treatment of acute otitis media and found a high incidence of bacteriologic failure in both arms of the study. Tympanocenteses were performed on entry into the study and 3 to 4 days after onset of treatment. Microbiologic failure was correlated with the susceptibility of the organism. Treatment failure was frequent in children with acute otitis media due to H. influenzae in the cefaclor group (53%) and the azithromycin group (52%). The failure to eradicate the organism in the azithromycin patients was puzzling, because most had high concentrations of drug in the middle ear (varying between 0.5 and 13 μg/mL). Animal studies suggest that the failure to clear H. influenzae at day 3 to 4 in the azithromycin arm may be due to a slower rate of eradication and that sterilization does occur but later in the course of therapy.[221]

Clarithromycin has a spectrum of activity similar to erythromycin but has increased activity against H. influenzae as a result of its active metabolite, 14-hydroxyclarithromycin.[597] Concentrations of clarithromycin and the active metabolite in middle-ear fluid exceed concentrations in serum; serum concentrations of clarithromycin and metabolite were 1.73 μg/mL and 0.82 μg/mL, respectively, and middle-ear fluid concentrations were 2.53 μg/mL and 1.27 μg/mL.[444] Clinical trials of children with acute otitis media document comparability of clarithromycin with cefaclor,[426] amoxicillin,[897] and amoxicillin clavulanate.[721]

Toxicity and Side Effects. The estolate of erythromycin may give rise to a cholestatic jaundice, which is believed to be due to a hypersensitivity reaction. The jaundice has been reported to occur almost exclusively in adults who receive the estolate for more than 14 days and usually resolves when administration of the drug is stopped. Few cases of jaundice in children have been reported, but physicians should consider a limit of therapy to 10 days and be alert for signs of liver toxicity.[161]

Concurrent use of erythromycin and theophylline in patients with asthma has been a concern because of the effect of the antibiotic on the pharmacokinetics of theophylline. Increases in serum theophylline concentrations have been demonstrated with erythromycin and clarithromycin but not azithromycin.

Clindamycin and Lincomycin

Clindamycin and lincomycin are effective in vitro against gram-positive cocci, including S. pneumoniae. Many penicillin-resistant strains of S. pneumoniae are susceptible to clindamycin; a multihospital study of 1275 isolates of S. pneumoniae identified only 6.3% that were resistant to clindamycin.[1120] Clindamycin is also active against a wide range of anaerobic bacteria, including penicillin-resistant Bacteroides species. Clindamycin provides higher levels of activity in serum than does lincomycin, and, in contrast to lincomycin, oral absorption is not decreased when the drug is taken with food. Because of its limited activity against H. influenzae, clindamycin can be used as initial therapy for otitis media only when the pathogen is identified as a susceptible gram-positive coccus or, when the organism is not known, when clindamycin is combined with a drug, such as a sulfonamide, that is active against Haemophilus species.

Clindamycin is well tolerated in children; diarrhea is a common side effect, but enterocolitis, of concern in adults, is rare in children. Antibiotic-associated colitis has been reported in as many as 10% of adult patients after treatment with clindamycin. The epithelium of the colon undergoes necrosis, the mucous glands dilate, and an inflammatory plaque forms and adheres loosely to the underlying epithelium. This disease has been associated with other antibiotics that alter intestinal flora, including ampicillin,[42] tetracycline, chloramphenicol, and lincomycin. Overgrowth of toxin-producing strains of Clostridium difficile is responsible for most cases of antibiotic-associated colitis. The antibiotic suppresses the normal flora in the colon, and the C. difficile organisms proliferate and produce an enterotoxin that is responsible for the disease. Most of these reactions have occurred in elderly patients, those with severe illness, or those receiving multiple antimicrobial agents[429]; concern for enterocolitis should not limit the use of clindamycin for children.

The Sulfonamides and Trimethoprim-Sulfamethoxazole

The first sulfonamide (and the first drug of the modern antimicrobial era), Prontosil, was reported in 1935 by Domagk[289] to be effective against infections due to beta-hemolytic streptococci. Sulfapyridine was introduced in 1938 and was the first antimicrobial agent effective for pneumococcal pneumonia. Soon after the introduction of these drugs, however, both streptococci and pneumococci developed resistance to the sulfonamides. Today, sulfonamides are used in the treatment of a wide variety of infections in children, including otitis media due to nontypeable strains of H. influenzae, usually in combination with a penicillin or erythromycin to provide coverage for S. pneumoniae. Sulfisoxazole was used by Perrin et al[858] for prophylaxis in children with recurrent episodes of acute otitis media.

Trimethoprim-sulfamethoxazole is an antimicrobial combination with significant activity against a broad spectrum of gram-positive cocci and gram-negative enteric pathogens. Trimethoprim is more active than the sulfonamide, but the mixture is significantly more effective than either drug alone. The drugs act in synergy by blocking the sequence of steps by which folic acid is metabolized: The sulfonamide competes with and displaces para-aminobenzoic acid in the synthesis of dihydrofolate; trimethoprim binds dihydrofolate reductase, inhibiting conversion of dihydrofolate to tetrahydrofolate. The effect of sulfonamide in bacteria is circumvented in the mammal, which obtains folates from food sources. The reaction inhibited by trimethoprim is similar in bacteria and mammals but differs quantitatively in the extent of binding of the drug to the enzyme. Mammalian dihydrofolate reductase is 60,000 times less sensitive to trimethoprim than is the enzyme from *E. coli*.

Sulfamethoxazole was chosen as the sulfonamide to use in combination with trimethoprim because the drugs have similar patterns of absorption and excretion. Both are well absorbed from the gastrointestinal tract, and food does not affect absorption. A parenteral preparation is available. Rapid absorption and peak serum activity occur between 1 and 4 hours after oral administration; serum activity persists for more than 12 hours, but there is no significant accumulation after repeated doses given at 12-hour intervals.

Adverse reactions to the combination include rashes similar to those previously associated with sulfonamides (maculopapular or urticarial rashes, purpura, photosensitivity reactions, and erythema multiforme bullosum) and gastrointestinal symptoms, primarily nausea and vomiting. Hematologic indices have been carefully evaluated because of the antifolate activity of trimethoprim. Leukopenia, thrombocytopenia, agranulocytosis, and aplastic anemia have been associated with administration of trimethoprim-sulfamethoxazole, but the incidence of these adverse reactions is low. Hemolysis may occur in patients with erythrocyte deficiency of glucose-6-phosphate dehydrogenase. According to Choo,[228] "In spite of the low incidence of blood dyscrasias and generalized skin disorders, the Committee on Safety of Medicine of the United Kingdom limited the indications for trimethoprim-sulfamethoxazole including use for acute otitis media in children only when there is good reason to prefer the combination."

The combination of trimethoprim-sulfamethoxazole (TMP-SMX) in children has been effective in the treatment of acute otitis media due to *S. pneumoniae* or *H. influenzae* (including beta-lactamase–producing strains). An increasing proportion of strains of *S. pneumoniae* are resistant to TMP-SMX; 21% of nasopharyngeal isolates obtained from Boston children with acute otitis media had MICs greater than or equal to 0.05 mg/mL for the combination drug.[60] The drug is not effective when group A streptococci or *S. aureus* is the causative organism of acute otitis media. It also is not recommended for pharyngitis due to group A streptococcus. The combination has been used with success for children who are allergic to penicillins or who fail after an initial course of ampicillin due to beta-lactamase–producing strains of *H. influenzae*.[992, 1105]

Vancomycin

Vancomycin is a parenterally administered antimicrobial agent with a spectrum of activity limited to gram-positive organisms. It is usually administered by the intravenous route because intramuscular injection causes pain and tissue necrosis. Ototoxicity and nephrotoxicity resulted from high concentrations in serum of early preparations, but improvements in the manufacturing process have resulted in a product that is believed to have lower toxicity. The principal uses in children are treatment of serious staphylococcal disease caused by *S. aureus* or *S. epidermidis* resistant to the penicillinase-resistant penicillins (methicillin-resistant staphylococci) and of sepsis caused by enterococci in the patient who has a significant history of allergy to penicillin.

Vancomycin is one of the few drugs (rifampin, fusidic acid, and bacitracin are others) that are effective in vitro against penicillin-resistant strains of *S. pneumoniae*.[534] In areas with high rates of pneumococcal resistance to penicillins and cephalosporins, the Centers for Disease Control and Prevention[216] suggests empirical therapy with vancomycin in addition to an extended-spectrum cephalosporin for cases of meningitis potentially caused by *S. pneumoniae* until results of culture and susceptibility testing are available. The value of vancomycin for otitis media would be restricted to cases due to penicillin- or cephalosporin-resistant gram-positive cocci.

The Tetracyclines

Tetracyclines are effective against a broad range of microorganisms, including gram-positive cocci and some gram-negative enteric bacilli. Tetracycline should not be considered to be a substitute for penicillin for patients with otitis media due to, or suspected to be due to, gram-positive cocci, because a significant proportion of group A streptococci and some strains of *S. pneumoniae* are resistant. Possible uses of the tetracyclines for otitis media include treatment of uncommon infections in children older than 8 years of age due to *C. pneumoniae* or *M. pneumoniae*.

Seven tetracycline compounds are available for oral administration in the United States: tetracycline, chlortetracycline, oxytetracycline, demeclocycline (Declomycin), methacycline, doxycycline, and minocycline. Tetracycline, chlortetracycline, doxycycline, and minocycline are also available for intravenous administration. With few exceptions, there are only minor differences in the in vitro activity of the different preparations. Minocycline, however, may be effective against some strains of *S. aureus*, and doxycycline may inhibit strains of *B. fragilis* that are resistant to the other tetracyclines.[793]

Tetracyclines are deposited in teeth during the early stages of calcification and cause dental staining. A relationship between the total dose and the degree of visible staining has been established. Tetracyclines cross the placenta, and discoloration of teeth has been seen in babies of mothers who received tetracycline or its analogues after the sixth month of pregnancy. The permanent teeth are stained if the drug is administered after 6 months and before 6 years of age. Other adverse effects include phototoxicity (particularly with Declomycin), nephrotoxicity (with tetracycline hydrochloride, oxytetracycline, and declomycin), and vestibular toxicity (with minocycline).

There are few indications for administering a tetracycline to a young child with infection of the respiratory tract, including otitis media; other effective drugs are available for almost all infections for which tetracycline might be considered. For the child 8 years of age and older, a tetracycline may be considered as an alternative to erythromycin for disease due to *M. pneumoniae* or chlamydial infections (psittacosis, trachoma, and inclusion conjunctivitis) and rickettsial diseases, including Rocky Mountain spotted fever.

The Aminoglycosides

Aminoglycosides provide broad coverage against gram-negative enteric bacilli and some gram-positive organisms (such as *S. aureus*), are rapidly bactericidal, and are readily absorbed after administration. The major concerns in their use are nephrotoxicity, ototoxicity, and poor diffusion across biologic membranes, including passage into cerebrospinal fluid. The aminoglycosides of current importance include streptomycin, kanamycin, gentamicin, tobramycin, netilmicin, and amikacin. Major usage for otitis media would be for chronic suppurative otitis media, which is frequently due to *P. aeruginosa* and other gram-negative bacilli. Although not covered in this monograph, the aminoglycosides are of value for suppurative and malignant otitis externa.

The in vitro activity of these antibiotics against gram-negative enteric bacilli varies and must be defined for each institution on the basis of current sensitivity tests. Streptomycin is not included in routine disk sensitivity tests nowadays because results for many years indicated that it is ineffective against a significant proportion of gram-negative enteric bacilli. The other aminoglycosides are active against most isolates of *E. coli* and *Enterobacter*, *Klebsiella*, and *Proteus* species. At present, gentamicin, tobramycin, netilmicin, and amikacin are the most active of the aminoglycosides against these organisms and against *P. aeruginosa*. The spectra of activity of gentamicin, netilmicin, and tobramycin are similar, and strains resistant to one are usually resistant to the other. The major advantage of tobramycin is its activity against some strains of *P. aeruginosa* that are resistant to gentamicin. The spectrum of activity of amikacin is similar to that of gentamicin, netilmicin, and tobramycin, but there is little cross-resistance, and some gram-negative organisms resistant to these aminoglycosides are sensitive to amikacin.

The aminoglycosides have significant in vitro activity against *S. aureus* but are less effective for group A and B streptococci and *S. pneumoniae*. A combination of a penicillin and an aminoglycoside results in more rapid killing and lower concentration of drug required to inhibit selected strains of gram-negative enteric bacilli and enterococci.

After parenteral administration, the aminoglycosides distribute rapidly in extracellular body water, with slow accumulation in tissues. Peak levels occur in serum 1 to 2 hours after administration, and significant activity persists for 6 to 8 hours. Penetration across biologic membranes is variable, and diffusion into cerebrospinal fluid is limited (the concentration in cerebrospinal fluid is approximately 10% of the peak serum concentration).

All aminoglycosides may produce renal injury and ototoxicity. In general, gentamicin and tobramycin are more likely to affect vestibular function, and amikacin and kanamycin are more likely to damage the cochlear apparatus, but both functions may be affected by each drug. The cochlear effect may present as a high-frequency hearing loss or tinnitus; vestibular disturbances include vertigo, nystagmus, and ataxia. Some of the effects may be reversible, but permanent damage is frequent. Nephrotoxicity may present as albuminuria, the presence of white and red blood cells and casts in the urine sediment, or elevation of blood urea nitrogen or serum creatinine. Toxicity appears to be dose related, although eighth nerve damage has followed the use of relatively small doses in patients with renal failure. Toxicity has not been a significant problem in children with normal kidney function who were treated with aminoglycosides according to currently recommended dosage schedules. Toxicity has usually been associated with administration of high doses for a long time, previous therapy with other aminoglycosides, administration of drugs to patients with impaired kidney function, or concurrent administration of other agents that are potentially nephrotoxic (e.g., the diuretics furosemide and ethacrynic acid).

Concentrations of aminoglycosides in serum are variable and unpredictable. Patients who receive a prolonged course of aminoglycosides or who have impaired renal function require careful monitoring to determine safety as well as efficacy of the aminoglycoside. Blood should be obtained to determine the drug concentration at the expected peak (1 to 2 hours after parenteral administration) or trough (before the next dose, i.e., 8 or 12 hours after last administration). Specimens of blood should be obtained early in the course of therapy (within the first 3 days) to be certain that effective levels in serum are achieved and at subsequent intervals (every 3 to 4 days) to determine that the concentration of aminoglycoside in serum is below the level of toxicity.[3443] The desired peaks for the aminoglycosides are gentamicin and tobramycin, 5 to 10 mg/mL, and kanamycin and amikacin, 15 to 25 mg/mL. The trough should not exceed 2 mg/mL for gentamicin and tobramycin and 10 mg/mL for kanamycin and amikacin. The toxic ranges are considered to be 14 mg/mL for gentamicin and tobramycin and 40 mg/mL for kanamycin and amikacin. Dosage schedules should be modified if concentrations in serum are either too low, and therefore inadequate for optimal therapy, or too high and potentially toxic.

The major use of aminoglycosides for otitis media in children is for serious disease that is due to, or suspected to be due to, gram-negative enteric bacilli; these include infections of the neonate and suppurative complications of acute otitis media in the child with malignancy or immunologic defect. Aminoglycosides may be of value alone or in combination with a broad-spectrum penicillin for chronic suppurative otitis media due to *P. aeruginosa*. The aminoglycosides can be administered intramuscularly or intravenously (by slow drip over 1 to 2 hours). Oral preparations are not absorbed.

Published proceedings of symposia should be consulted for more specific information about the pharmacologic actions and clinical uses of gentamicin,[374] tobramycin,[375] and amikacin.[373]

Chloramphenicol

Chloramphenicol is active against many gram-positive and gram-negative bacteria and chlamydiae. Oral preparations are well absorbed. The intravenous route is preferred for parenteral administration, since lower levels of serum activity follow intramuscular use. The drug diffuses well across biologic membranes, even in the absence of inflammatory reaction. Approximately 70% of the concentration of chloramphenicol in serum is present in the cerebrospinal fluid of patients with meningitis, and similar high concentrations would be expected in the middle ear. Chloramphenicol may be of value for selected cases of otitis media due to organisms, particularly gram-negative enteric bacilli, resistant to other drugs and uniquely susceptible to chloramphenicol.

The major limiting factor in the use of chloramphenicol is its toxic effect on bone marrow.[917] A dose-related anemia occurs in most patients receiving high-dosage schedules for more than a few days. The anemia is concurrent with therapy, ceases when the drug is discontinued, and is characterized by decreased reticulocyte count, increased concentration of serum iron, and cytoplasmic vacuolization of early erythroid and myeloid precursors in bone marrow.[995]

Aplastic anemia is a rare (approximately 1 case per 20,000 to 40,000 courses of treatment) idiosyncratic reaction that is usually fatal. Most cases of aplastic anemia follow use of the oral preparation of chloramphenicol; few reports have been published of aplastic anemia that followed parenteral administration alone.[1174] In some of these cases, other drugs or the patient's disease could have been responsible for the aplastic anemia. Since very few patients receive chloramphenicol by the parenteral route only, as compared with the extensive worldwide oral usage of chloramphenicol (particularly in the many countries of Central and South America and Africa, where the oral drug is available without a prescription), and since the incidence of aplastic anemia is so low, we cannot be certain that aplastic anemia occurring almost exclusively after oral usage, rather than after parenteral administration, is a true event or one of statistical chance. Since cases of aplastic anemia following parenteral administration are extraordinarily rare, clinicians should not avoid the use of intravenous chloramphenicol when it is indicated.

Wide variability occurs in concentrations of chloramphenicol in serum of infants and children, requiring monitoring serum concentrations two or three times a week during therapy. Peak serum concentrations should be 15 to 25 mg/mL to be safe and effective.[389]

Metronidazole

Although introduced in 1959 for treatment of *Trichomonas vaginalis* infections, metronidazole is now more widely used for infections due to anaerobic bacteria. The drug diffuses well into all tissues in both oral and parenteral forms. Anaerobic bacteria may play a role in chronic otitis media and complications that follow including chronic sinusitis and brain abscesses. Metronidazole should be included in the regimen for treatment of abscesses that may include anaerobic bacteria.

The Polymyxins

Polymyxin and colistin are highly effective in vitro against a broad spectrum of gram-negative enteric bacilli, including *P. aeruginosa*. These drugs do not diffuse well across biologic membranes, however, and are usually effective only when they are applied topically, as would be the case for external otitis media.

Fluoroquinolones

The fluoroquinolones have a broad spectrum of activity, good oral absorption, and good tolerability but are proscribed for use in pediatrics because of arthropathies in juvenile animals. Nevertheless, because the quinolones are the only oral drugs with activity against *P. aeruginosa*, they have been extensively used in pediatric patients with pseudomonal infections, particularly children with cystic fibrosis, as well as children with chronic suppurative otitis media, malignant external otitis, pseudomonal osteomyelitis, and febrile neutropenia.[230]

The history of use of quinolones in pediatrics begins with the introduction of nalidixic acid in 1962, used mostly for infections of the urinary tract. The arthropathy and osteochondrosis was first described in weight-bearing joints in juvenile animals in 1972. Although there is no evidence that quinolones cause joint manifestations in children, the family of drugs has caused arthropathies in every juvenile animal species tested, which led to a restriction of the use of quinolones in children and adolescents younger than 18 years of age.

A number of products with a broad spectrum of activity have become popular oral agents in adults, including ciprofloxacin, norfloxacin, enoxacin, ofloxacin, levofloxacin, and others. Although the use of quinolones in pediatrics has been a subject for frequent discussion, the FDA has not permitted an indication for this class of drugs for children younger than 18 years of age. Because new fluoroquinolones such as gemifloxacin and clinafloxacin[550] have increased activity against levofloxacin-resistant pneumococci and administrative advantages such as once-a-day therapy, the question about broader use in pediatrics, including use for acute otitis media, is being considered again.

Antiviral Agents

A broad array of antiviral agents is now available for treatment of herpes simplex virus and varicella-zoster viruses (acyclovir, famciclovir, valacyclovir), HIV (multiple), cytomegalovirus infections (ganciclovir, foscarnet, cidofovir, fomiversen), hepatitis B and C viruses (lamivudine and alpha-interferon, alone or in combination with ribavirin for the C virus), enterovirus infections (pleconaril), RSV infections (ribavirin), and influenzavirus infections (amantadine, rimantadine, zanamivir, and oseltamivir) (Drugs for Non-HIV Viral Infections, 1999). Of these agents, only drugs active against influenzavirus and RSV infections are of interest for the management of otitis media. New agents directed against viruses responsible for respiratory tract infection will undoubtedly be introduced over the next few years and alter the management of otitis media. The availability of agents with activity against specific viruses will hasten the introduction of new diagnostic techniques for isolation and identification of viral infections.

Amantadine (Symmetrel), 1-adamantanamine hydrochloride, is active against influenzavirus A. A syrup is available for use in infants and young children, and the drug is well absorbed. When started before the person's exposure to influenza A, amantadine is 70% to 90% effective in preventing illness. Treatment begun within 48 hours after the onset of illness decreases the duration of fever and symptoms by 1 to 2 days. The drug has little or no activity against influenza B, and higher concentrations that can be safely achieved in humans are required to inhibit rubella, parainfluenza, and RSVs. Although the precise mode of action is unknown, antiviral activity appears to be due to interference with virus uncoating rather than direct inactivation of infectious virus. Rimantadine (Flumadine) is 4- to 10-fold more active than amantadine and has a similar mechanism of activity but is, in general, better tolerated than amantadine. Neither drug is approved for children younger than 1 year of age. There are no data specific to prevention of acute otitis media, but it is likely that prevention of influenza virus A infection also decreases otitis media due to this infection.

Zanamivir (Relenza) and oseltamivir (Tamiflu) are inhibitors of influenza A and B virus neuraminidases and effective for infection due to both influenzaviruses (whereas amantadine and rimantadine are active only against influenza A). Zanamivir administered by nasal spray or inhalation was effective in shortening the duration and severity of symptoms of influenza A and B virus infections in adults if administered within 30 hours of onset of symptoms.[473] Prophylactic usage was 84% effective in preventing febrile influenza.[760]

Oseltamivir was effective in adults for both prevention and treatment of influenza A and B virus infections.[472] If the drug is started within 36 hours of onset of symptoms, it can decrease the severity and duration of symptoms as well as the incidence of upper respiratory complications. Prophylactic administration was 87% effective in preventing culture-proven influenzavirus infection. At this time, no data are available about its use in pediatric age groups.

Ribavirin (Virazole) is a synthetic nucleoside that inhibits a wide variety of DNA and RNA viruses. Infants with bronchiolitis or pneumonia due to respiratory syncytial virus improved with aerosolized ribavirin, and the drug is now approved for treatment of hospitalized infants. Ribavirin is teratogenic in animals and is contraindicated in pregnancy. Because the aerosol is dispersed in the patient's environment, it is recommended that a hood or other entrapment device be used and that pregnant health care workers not be involved in the care of patients receiving the drug. Ribavirin is rapidly transported into cells, where it is converted by cellular enzymes to monophosphate, diphosphate, and triphosphate derivates that then inhibit viral or virally induced enzymes involved in viral nucleic acid synthesis.

Interferons are proteins that are released by cells in response to infection or other stimuli and induce a temporary antiviral state in uninfected cells. The interferon genes have been cloned into bacterial and yeast plasmids, and large quantities of interferon are available. Alpha-2-interferon has been administered as an intranasal spray against infection due to rhinoviruses and coronaviruses, causes of the common cold. Alpha-interferon was administered as a nasal spray for short-term prophylaxis against the common cold in the household. Almost all the effect was against rhinovirus infections, with no preventive benefit for colds due to other agents.[292, 471] At present, the only approved uses of alpha-interferon are for chronic hepatitis due to hepatitis B and C viruses and papillomavirus infections; uses for respiratory tract infections have not been exploited.

Selected Aspects of Administration of Antimicrobial Agents

Dosage Schedules for Infants and Children

Dosage schedules of antimicrobial agents useful in otitis media are listed for infants (beyond the newborn period) and children in Table 25–34. Parenteral administration should be considered for severe infections due to less susceptible organisms and when sepsis or suppurative complications are present or imminent (Table 25–35).

The clinical pharmacologic action of antimicrobial agents administered to the newborn infant is unique and cannot be extrapolated from the results of studies done in older children or adults. Physiologic and metabolic processes that affect the distribution, metabolism, and excretion of drugs undergo rapid changes during the first few weeks of life. The increased efficiency of kidney function after the first 7 days of life requires a decrease in the interval between doses of penicillins and aminoglycosides to maintain high concentrations of drug in blood and tissues. Thus, different dosage schedules are provided for the first week of life and for subsequent weeks of the neonatal period.[965] Otitis media in the neonate (to 20 days old) may occur alone or be accompanied by signs of sepsis and usually warrants parenteral therapy.[1016, 1113]

Food Interference with Absorption

The absorption of some oral antimicrobial agents is significantly decreased when the drug is taken with food or near mealtime. These drugs include unbuffered penicillin G, penicillinase-resistant penicillins (nafcillin, oxacillin, cloxacillin, and dicloxacillin), ampicillin, azithromycin, and lincomycin. Milk, milk products, and other foods or medications containing calcium or magnesium salts interfere with absorption of the tetracyclines. Absorption of penicillin V, buffered penicillin G, amoxicillin, oral cephalosporins currently available, chloramphenicol, erythromycin, clarithromycin, and clindamycin is only slightly affected by food. Antibiotics whose absorption is affected by con-

TABLE 25–34. Antimicrobial Agents for Otitis Media: Dosage Schedules

Drug (Trade Name)	Number of Doses × Days	Dosage (per kg/day)
Amoxicillin (Amoxil)	2–3/day × 10	40–80 mg
Amoxicillin-clavulanate (Augmentin)	2/day × 10	40–80 mg
Azithromycin (Zithromax)	1/day × 5	10 mg day 1; 5 mg days 2–5
Clarithromycin (Biaxin)	2/day × 10	40 mg
Erythromycin + sulfisoxazole (Pediazole)	4/day × 10	40 mg
Ceftriaxone (Rocephin)	1/day × 1	50 mg
Ceftibuten (Cedax)	1/day × 10	9 mg
Loracarbef (Lorabid)	2/day × 10	30 mg
Cefprozil (Cefzil)	2/day × 10	30 mg
Cefpodoxime (Vantin)	2/day × 10	10 mg
Cefuroxime axetil (Ceftin)	2/day × 10	30 mg
Cefaclor (Ceclor)	2–3/day × 10	40 mg
Cefdinir (Omnicef)	1–2/day × 10	14 mg
Cefixime (Suprax)	1/day × 10	8 mg
Trimethoprim-sulfamethoxazole (Bactrim, Septra)	2/day × 10	8 mg/40 mg

From Bluestone CD, Klein JO. Otitis Media in Infants and Children, 3rd ed, Philadelphia, WB Saunders, 2001.

current administration of food should be taken 1 or more hours before or 2 or more hours after meals.

Intravenous and Intramuscular Administration

After intravenous administration of most antimicrobial agents, there is a period when the concentration of drug in the serum is higher than it is following intramuscular administration. No therapeutic advantage of intravenous administration of antibiotics over intramuscular administration has been demonstrated, however. Intravenous ad-

TABLE 25–35. Daily Dosage Schedules for Parenteral Antimicrobial Agents of Value in Infants (Other than Neonates) and Children with Sepsis or Suppurative Complications of Otitis Media

Drug	Route	Dosage (per kg/24 hr*)
Penicillin G, crystalline	IV, IM	100,000–400,000 U in 4–6 doses
Methicillin	IV, IM	200 mg in 4–6 doses
Oxacillin	IV, IM	200 mg in 4–6 doses
Nafcillin	IV, IM	200 mg in 4–6 doses
Ampicillin	IV, IM	200–300 mg in 4–6 doses
Carbenicillin	IV, IM	400–600 mg in 4–6 doses
Ticarcillin	IV, IM	200–300 mg in 4–6 doses
Mezlocillin	IV	200–300 mg in 4–6 doses
Azlocillin	IV	200–300 mg in 4–6 doses
Cephalothin	IV, IM	100–150 mg in 4–6 doses
Cefazolin	IV, IM	50–150 mg in 4 doses†
Cefoxitin	IV, IM	80–160 mg in 4–6 doses
Ceftizoxime	IV, IM	150–200 mg in 3 doses
Cefuroxime	IV, IM	175–240 mg in 3 doses
Moxalactam	IV	150–200 mg in 4 doses
Cefamandole	IV, IM	100–150 mg in 4–6 doses
Cefotaxime	IV, IM	150–200 mg in 4 doses
Ceftriaxone	IV, IM	50–100 mg in 2 doses
Ceftazidime	IV	125–150 mg in 3 doses
Erythromycin	IV	50 mg in 4 doses†
Clindamycin	IV, IM	25–40 mg in 3–4 doses
Vancomycin	IV	40–60 mg in 4 doses
Chloramphenicol	IV	50–100 mg in 4 doses

* Use high-dosage schedule if meningitis is diagnosed or suspected.
† Administer in continuous drip or by slow infusion over 30–60 minutes or more.
From Bluestone CD, Klein JO. Otitis Media in Infants and Children, 3rd ed, Philadelphia, WB Saunders, 2001.

ministration should be used if the patient is in shock or suffers from a bleeding diathesis. If prolonged parenteral therapy is anticipated, the pain on injection and the small muscle mass of the young child preclude the intramuscular route and make intravenous therapy preferable. Although intramuscular benzathine penicillin has been used in combination with a sulfonamide for therapy of acute otitis media, single-dose intramuscular ceftriaxone is the only parenteral agent to be evaluated in recent clinical trials. One-dose ceftriaxone was equivalent to 10 days of oral amoxicillin[439] or trimethoprim-sulfamethoxazole.[62]

Antibacterial concentrations in blood are similar after oral and intravenous administration of chloramphenicol and trimethoprim-sulfamethoxazole. Parenteral administration may be preferred because of hypothesized lesser bone marrow toxicity of chloramphenicol and ease of administration for the patient unable to take oral trimethoprim-sulfamethoxazole.

Chloramphenicol, the tetracyclines, and erythromycin should be administered parenterally by the intravenous, rather than the intramuscular, route. Chloramphenicol has variable absorption from intramuscular sites. The intramuscular injection of parenteral tetracyclines and erythromycin causes local irritation and pain.

The physician must be alert for thrombophlebitis that may result from prolonged intravenous administration and sterile abscesses that may follow intramuscular administration. The technique and complications of intramuscular injections were reviewed by Bergeson et al.[84] In general, the site of injection in young infants is the upper lateral thigh, in children older than 2 years of age it is the gluteal area, and for older children it is the deltoid muscle. After selection of the proper site and insertion of the needle into the muscle, one applies negative pressure by pulling back on the plunger to be certain that the needle is not in a blood vessel.

Use of Drugs for Children in School or Group Day Care Centers

Infants and children may return to school or a day care center during a course of antimicrobial therapy. Because

TABLE 25–36. Antimicrobial Suspensions Taste Scores for Selected Antimicrobial Agents of Value for Therapy of Acute Otitis Media

Generic (Trade) Name	Overall Rank*
Loracarbef (Lorabid)	1
Cephalexin (Keflex)	2
Cefixime (Suprax)	3
Cefaclor (Ceclor)	4
Cefazolin (Cefzil)	5
Amoxicillin-clavulanate (Augmentin)	6
Penicillin V	
(V-cillin-K)	7
(VeeTids)	8
Cefpodoxime (Vantin)	9
Trimethoprim-sulfamethoxazole (Sulfatrim)	10
Erythromycin + sulfisoxazole (Pediazole)	11
Dicloxacillin (Dynapen)	12

* Based on smell, texture, and taste.

Modified from Demers DM, Chan CD, Bass JW. Antimicrobial drug suspensions: a blinded comparison of taste of twelve common pediatric drugs including cefixime, cefpodoxime, cefprozil, and loracarbef. Pediatr Infect Dis J 13:87, 1994.

of the problems with administration of drugs outside the home, physicians should use medications that are given infrequently and need only simple directions. Drugs that are administered once or twice a day are preferred. Use of chewable tablets, when available, may be of value in reducing the need for the school or day care provider to measure specific amounts of liquid suspension. Single-dosage regimens, such as intramuscular benzathine penicillin G for group A streptococcal infections, may be advantageous. Guidelines for administration of medications in school were prepared by the Committee on School Health of the American Academy of Pediatrics and may also serve as a model for the physician who is prescribing drugs to be administered in a day care center.[1222] Administration of medications during day care is addressed in a monograph, *Infectious Diseases in Child Day Care* by Smith and Aaronson.[1045]

Compliance

The most frequent drug-related factor in failure of antibiotic therapy is inadequate compliance. Frequency of dosing is important. If possible, administration of a dose during day care is to be avoided because of the uncertainty of compliance by caretakers. Once or twice a day is now the rule for new antimicrobial agents for infants and young children. Schedules that are shorter have an administrative advantage: azithromycin given once a day for 5 days is optimal. Cefpodoxime may be administered in a twice-a-day schedule for 5 days. A single dose of intramuscular ceftriaxone ensures compliance but may not be acceptable to all parents (or children). Current clinical trials include shorter courses of oral antimicrobial agents for management of acute otitis media, but there is concern about shorter than recommended courses of oral drugs in infants younger than 2 years of age.[842]

Unacceptable taste or odor of drugs may result in poor compliance. Demers et al[277] performed a blinded comparison of taste for 14 commonly prescribed pediatric suspensions. The study participants (pediatric staff and house staff and other health care workers) compared the drugs in a manner similar to that used in wine tasting, including texture, smell, taste, and aftertaste. The results for eight drugs used for therapy of acute otitis media are given in Table 25–36. The cephalosporins, including cefixime, cephalexin, and cefaclor, had the highest overall scores. Dicloxacillin and penicillin V were the least acceptable. Other investigators have noted similar results.[789, 992] In a recent study by Steele et al,[1060] suspension of cefuroxime, cefpodoxime, and erythromycin plus sulfisoxazole were "judged to be so unpalatable as to potentially jeopardize compliance." The analysis of antibiotic suspensions for palatability was further adjusted for cost, duration of therapy, and dosing intervals: overall taste and cost ratings adjusted for duration and dosing interval identified azithromycin, cefdinir, loracarbef, and cefixime as the best choices and amoxicillin-clavulanate, cefuroxime, ciprofloxacin, and clarithromycin as the least favorable.[1059] Administration of the initial dose of a new antimicrobial agent has the advantage of determining whether the product is acceptable to the patient (in addition, this practice provides immediate therapy rather than waiting for a prescription to be filled).

Among other features that lead to problems with compliance are side effects such as diarrhea. Diarrhea leads to discontinuance of courses more frequently with amoxicillin/clavulanate and ampicillin than with amoxicillin or TMP-SMX.[358]

Mattar et al[709] evaluated treatment given at home for children with otitis media. Full compliance with prescribed medications occurred in only 5 of 100 patients. Factors limiting compliance included incorrect dosage schedules (36%), early termination (37%), inadequate dispensing of medication at drugstores (15%), spilled medicine (7%), and a series of other errors by physician, pharmacist, and parent (Table 25–37). Compliance improved

TABLE 25–37. Factors in Failure of Patients to Comply with Prescribed Medication

Physician Errors

Action of drugs and possible side effects not explained to parent
Dosage schedule ambiguous or incorrect; instructions absent or incomplete
Multiple drug prescribed, resulting in confusion
Cost of expensive trade brand used exceeds Medicaid reimbursement rate

Pharmacist Errors

Misleading or incorrect labels
Underfilling of prescriptions
Drugstores not open at time of day when parents seek medication

Parent and Home Factors

Difficulty in giving medication; two people often necessary to administer drug
Use of household teaspoon unsatisfactory; bottles broken or spilled
Schedule of administration unrealistic for parent; babysitter inadequate to dispense medication

Modified from Mattar ME, Markello J, Yaffe SJ. Pharmaceutic factors affecting pediatric compliance. Pediatrics 55:101, 1975. Reproduced by permission of Pediatrics.

to more than half when hospital pharmacy personnel gave patients and parents verbal and written instructions for administration of medications that were dispensed with a calibrated measuring device and a calendar to record doses taken. Single-dose intramuscular ceftriaxone would be of value for families that have difficulty maintaining a multidose, 10-day oral schedule in infants and young children. A survey of parents indicated a preference for single dose intramuscular therapy for acute otitis media over standard 10-day oral therapy.[71]

Other drug-related factors that play roles in the failure of compliance include inappropriate dosage schedule and inadequate duration of therapy. Some antimicrobial agents deteriorate with prolonged storage. Adherence to expiration dates recommended by the manufacturer safeguards against inadequate potency of the drug.

Cost of Therapy for the Consumer and the Health Care System

The office visit and prescription for the antimicrobial agent are the most obvious costs to the consumer. It is axiomatic that recently introduced trade preparations will cost more than older drugs available in generic form.[736] The National Center for Health Statistics[979] estimated that 20.6 million antibiotic prescriptions for the treatment of otitis media in children were written in 1990. One third of these prescriptions were for amoxicillin. The increased cost is evident if, for reasons of decreased efficacy or consumer acceptance, trade drugs are substituted for generic preparations such as amoxicillin or TMP-SMX.

Analyses of cost indicate that there are other aspects of the total cost of the disease to be considered.[190, 201, 1181] The office visits include the initial visit and at least one additional ear check. At each visit, there are expenses for time lost for the working parent (a minimum of 2 hours), transportation costs to and from the physician's office, and baby sitting for the children who remain at home. If there are side effects or clinical failure, an additional visit and change in prescription adds to the expense. For the child with severe and recurrent disease, costs expand to include visits to specialists, including otolaryngologists, audiologists, and speech and language therapists, and fees for the tests and therapy provided by these professionals. Capra et al[201] calculated costs of otitis media in a managed care population: medical costs for a simple episode were $131, but work-loss cost for one or both parents was almost equivalent, $114; if the patient relapsed, the costs of the episode for medical care was $327 and work-loss cost was $404.

Pharmacologic Interactions

Concurrent administration of an antimicrobial agent and a second drug may result in altered pharmacokinetics of either drug. The tubular secretion of penicillins and most cephalosporins is blocked by probenecid. This effect can be exploited by coadministration of probenecid (in a dosage of 10 mg/kg four times a day in children to a maximum dosage of 500 mg/kg four times a day) to produce a higher peak and more sustained level of antimicrobial activity.

Administration of chloramphenicol succinate with the anticonvulsant drugs phenobarbital and phenytoin leads to significant changes in concentrations of the antibiotic in serum: lower serum concentrations of chloramphenicol resulted when phenobarbital was coadministered, whereas higher serum concentrations of chloramphenicol were detected when phenytoin was coadministered. Phenobarbital may have induced the activity of hepatic endoplasmic reticulum, thereby increasing the metabolism of chloramphenicol, resulting in decreased concentrations of active antibiotic in serum and tissues. Phenytoin may cause induction of hepatic microsomal enzymes and compete with chloramphenicol for binding sites, resulting in elevated serum concentration of one or both drugs, possibly to toxic levels. Patients who receive chloramphenicol and anticonvulsant therapy require monitoring of serum concentrations to be certain of the safety and efficacy of the antibiotic.[619]

Erythromycin and clarithromycin interfere with the hepatic metabolization of theophylline, resulting in increased serum concentrations of theophylline, which may produce nausea, vomiting, and other signs of toxicity. Coadministration of the two drugs is frequent in children with asthma. An alternative antibiotic should be considered, and, if a suitable alternative is not optimal therapy, the dosage schedule of theophylline should be reduced and serum levels monitored.[891]

Ototopical Use of Antimicrobial Agents

Use of ototopical preparations has been described in the literature since 1500 BC. A multitude of therapeutic options have been described, including use of astringents, antiseptics, alcohol, benzoin, and various powders. Myer[776] has related the use of various potions including red lead and resin, frankincense and goose grease, cream from cow's milk, vermilion, olive oil, and many others. By 1900, we had progressed to use of "rattlesnake oil"—ear drops that contained turpentine, camphor, menthol, and sassafras. Antimicrobial agents for ototopical use were stimulated by trials of various sulfonamides for otorrhea and otitis externa.

Currently available antimicrobial suspensions that are used extensively as ototopical drugs include colistin, neomycin and hydrocortisone (Cortisporin TC Otic Suspension); polymyxin, neomycin, and hydrocortisone (Coly-Mycin S Otic); tobramycin and dexamethasone (Tobradex); gentamicin (Garamycin ophthalmic); ciprofloxacin and hydrocortisone (Cipro HC Otic); and ofloxacin (Floxin Otic). Antiseptic ototopical drops such as acetic acid are commonly used in developing countries and are believed to be effective. The use of ototopical agents for treatment of chronic suppurative otitis media is reviewed by Bluestone and Klein.[137] The papers in proceedings on the use of topical ofloxacin for otic diseases in infants and children include reviews of various ototopical preparations for otitis externa, chronic suppurative otitis media, and acute otitis media (otorrhea) in children with tympanostomy tubes.[599]

Only ofloxacin otic solution is indicated for treatment of acute otitis media in patients with tympanostomy tubes and chronic suppurative otitis media in patients with perforated tympanic membranes. The gentamicin and tobramycin solutions were prepared for ophthalmic use. Cortisporin and Cipro HC Otic are approved only for acute otitis externa. Colymycin S Otic is approved for acute otitis externa and for treatment of infections of mastoidectomy and fenestration cavities. Although several of the preparations include a corticosteroid, there are no data that document more rapid resolution of the inflammation with addition of a steroid. The aminoglycosides neomycin, gentamicin, and tobramycin may be ototoxic, but there is a paucity of human data to indicate adverse effects from instillation of the suspension as ear drops. Nevertheless, the package inserts for Colymycin and Cortisporin carry a precautionary statement that the drug should be used with care in cases of perforated tympanic membranes and in long-standing cases of chronic otitis media because of the possibility of ototoxicity caused by neomycin. Sensitization does not appear to be an important problem with topical antibiotics, although some patients with chronic dermatoses may react to certain agents such as neomycin.

Ofloxacin otic was evaluated in children with tympanostomy tubes who presented with acute otorrhea reflecting an acute otitis media.[417] The study compared the efficacy of 10 days' administration of ofloxacin otic solution twice a day or amoxicillin-clavulanate orally three times a day; the cure rate was 76% for ofloxacin vs. 69% for amoxicillin-clavulanate. The eradication rates were similar for *S. pneumoniae*, *H. influenzae*, and *M. catarrhalis*, but ofloxacin had superior cure rates for *S. aureus* and *P. aeruginosa*. To our knowledge, this is the only study that evaluated a topical antibiotic otic preparation with a systemic antibiotic for acute otitis media in patients with tympanostomy tubes. The efficacy of the otic suspension for acute otitis media indicates that high concentrations of drug reach the mucosa of the middle ear through the tube resulting in high clinical and microbiologic cure rates.

Diffusion of Antimicrobial Agents into Middle Ear Fluids

Although studies of concentrations of various drugs in serum and middle-ear fluid, cited in Tables 25–30 and 25–33, differ in dosage schedules, time of collection, and methods of assay, the results indicate that most antimicrobial agents of value for the treatment of acute otitis media achieve significant concentrations in middle-ear fluid. Because the middle ear is embryologically, morphologically, and physiologically part of the respiratory tract, penetration of systemically administered antibiotics into middle-ear mucosa and middle-ear fluid provides a model for the dynamics of diffusion of antibiotics in other areas of the respiratory tract.

The interested reader will find data about diffusion of the listed antimicrobial agent into the middle-ear fluid of patients with acute or chronic middle-ear infection in two review articles[254, 786] and the following references:

Penicillin G: Lahikainen,[625] Silverstein et al[1027]

Penicillin V: Howard et al[507], Kamme et al,[562] Ingvarsson et al,[527] Lundgren et al,[668] Nelson et al[787]

Ampicillin: Coffey,[237] Klimek et al,[609] Lahikainen et al[626]

Amoxicillin: Howard et al,[507] Klimek et al,[609] Nelson et al,[787] Krause et al[620]

High-dose formulations: Seikel et al[996]

Bacampicillin: Virtanen and Lahikainen[1169]

Erythromycin estolate, ethyl succinate: Bass et al,[69] Ginsburg et al,[411] Nelson et al,[787] Sundberg et al[1083]

Clarithromycin: Guay and Craft,[444] Gan et al[393]

Azithromycin: Dagan et al[262]

Trimethoprim-sulfamethoxazole: Klimek et al,[608] Nelson et al[787]

Cefaclor: Ginsburg et al,[411] Lildholdt et al,[644] Nelson et al,[787] Ernstson et al,[338] Barr et al[63]

Cefuroxime axetil: Haddad et al,[449] Thoroddsen et al[1121]

Cefotaxime: Danon[270]

Loracarbef: Kusmiesz et al[622]

Ceftibuten: Barr,[63] Lin et al[649]

Cefprozil: Shyu et al,[1019] Kafetzis et al[555]

Cefixime: Harrison et al,[464] Kafetzis et al[555]

Cefpodoxime: van Dyck et al[1158]

Ceftriaxone: Gudnason et al[445]

Ceftibuten: Barr et al[63]

Oxytetracycline: Silverstein et al[1027]

Metronidazole: Jokipii et al[543]

These studies of penetration of systemically administered antibiotics have the following limitations in design that need to be considered in interpreting the results:

1. Most include specimens obtained after a single dose, whereas Sundberg et al[1083] showed that concentrations of erythromycin increased in middle-ear fluids when specimens were obtained after multiple doses. The increment with successive doses may be applicable to some or all antimicrobial agents.

2. Standard curves of antibiotics are prepared in buffered solutions, which may not represent an adequate control for middle-ear fluid.

3. Results of assays of materials obtained at various intervals after administration of drug give different concentrations in middle-ear fluids and different ratios of middle-ear fluid with simultaneously obtained serum. Peak values occur at different times for different drugs. Therefore, values taken at one sample time may not provide an adequate indication of penetration into middle-ear fluid.

4. Homogenization of mucoid or purulent middle-ear fluid is difficult.

5. Specimens containing blood are not always excluded. Cefixime penetration into middle-ear fluid of children with acute otitis media was limited; only specimens contaminated with blood had any entry into the middle ear.[1191] Thus, blood-contaminated specimens should be identified or deleted from reported results.

6. The condition of the mucosa is not accurately portrayed. Differences in penetration may vary, depending on the degree of inflammation of the mucosa, and this may not be identified or known by the investigator.

7. Binding of antimicrobial agents to protein may pro-

TABLE 25–38. Concentrations of Ceftibuten and Cefaclor in Serum (S) and Middle-Ear Fluids (MEF) of Children with Acute Otitis Media over Time

Antibiotic (Dose)	Sample Type	Concentration				
		2 hrs	4 hrs	6 hrs	8 hrs	12 hrs
Ceftibuten (9 mg/kg)	S	6.73	5.93	3.15	1.56	0.80
	MEF	0.85	4.03	1.28	0.62	0.52
	MEF/S	0.13	0.68	0.41	0.40	0.65
Cefaclor (13.3 mg/kg)	S	3.63	0.69	ND	ND	NA
	MEF	0.96	0.49	ND	ND	NA
	MEF/S	0.26	0.71			

ND, not detectable; *NA*, not available.
From Barr WH, Affrime M, Lin CC, Batra V. Pharmacokinetics of ceftibuten in children. Pediatr Infect Dis J 14:S93, 1995.

vide a prolonged duration of activity in the middle ear but low concentrations at any point in time.

In spite of these limitations, data from assays of concentrations of drug in middle-ear fluid provide useful information, which, along with in vitro susceptibility data, guide the choice of antimicrobial agents for otitis media. Harrison[466] correlated the susceptibility of the bacterial pathogens and the antibiotic concentrations in middle-ear fluid to predict potential clinical efficacy.

Significant concentrations of most of the drugs tested appeared promptly in middle-ear fluid. The concentrations of drug in the middle-ear fluid were, in general, parallel though lower than concentrations of drug in serum. The peak activity in middle-ear fluid was delayed when compared with peak activity achieved in serum, but duration of activity was similar in both serum and middle-ear fluid. Concentrations of penicillin V and ampicillin in middle-ear fluid of patients with chronic otitis media were lower than concentrations of fluid of patients with acute disease, but concentrations of amoxicillin, erythromycins, and cefaclor were similar in acute and chronic effusions. The concentrations in middle-ear fluid and serum of ceftibuten and cefaclor over time are provided in Table 25–38.

Purulent fluids had higher concentrations of drug than did mucoid or serous fluids, and concentrations were similar to those found in purulent fluids of children with acute otitis media.[787]

Penicillins and cephalosporins achieved concentrations in middle-ear fluids that were approximately one fifth to one third the levels present in serum. Sulfonamides and erythromycin achieved middle ear concentrations that were approximately 50% of serum concentrations. Concentrations of the macrolides, azithromycin and clarithromycin, in middle-ear effusions were far higher than in serum, reflecting the intracellular concentration of the drugs.[262, 393, 444]

Sterilization of Middle-Ear Fluids by Antimicrobial Agents

To determine the ability of antimicrobial agents to eradicate bacterial pathogens from middle-ear fluids of children with acute otitis media, investigators have used serial aspirates of the infected fluids to determine the drug's microbiologic efficacy. The initial aspirate identifies the bacterial pathogen of the acute middle-ear infection; the second aspirate, days after initiation of therapy, defines the ability of the drug to eradicate the infection. Drs. Virgil Howie and John Ploussard, pediatricians in practice in Huntsville, Alabama, published in 1969 results of their dual aspirates, termed by the authors the "in vivo sensitivity test." Since then, Howie, at the University of Texas School of Medicine in Galveston, and other investigators have used similar techniques to document the microbiologic efficacy of new antibacterial drugs and to correlate clinical and microbiologic results (Table 25–39). The microbiologic efficacy of antibacterial drugs for acute otitis media defined by the in vivo efficacy test is summarized in a recent review.[602]

The placebo effect is instructive in identifying resolution of acute middle-ear infection without antimicrobial agents.[508] Whereas pneumococci resolved without antimicrobial agents in 20% of cases, approximately one half of the infections due to nontypeable *H. influenzae* were sterile at the time of the second aspirate. Although no placebo studies are available when *M. catarrhalis* is the pathogen, a spontaneous clearance rate may be assumed for the beta-lactamase–producing organisms when a beta-lactamase–susceptible penicillin was used; most infections cleared in the absence of an effective antimicrobial agent. The differential clearing of the bacteria with relative persistence of pneumococci but substantial resolution of infection due to nontypeable *H. influenzae*, and possibly *M. catarrhalis*, is likely to be associated with some immune or bacteriostatic factor in the middle-ear fluid that acts to sterilize the middle-ear fluid of these organisms.

The results of the in vivo susceptibility test are generally consistent with data available from in vitro assays of the drugs against the major bacterial pathogens and the concentrations of drug achieved in the middle-ear fluids. Most of the double tap studies were performed before the increase in resistant pneumococci, and there is a paucity of data relating to sterilization of middle-ear fluids of multidrug-resistant strains. Susceptible pneumococcal infections were efficiently sterilized by most penicillins, cephalosporins, and macrolides. Sulfonamides alone were ineffective but TMP-SMX sterilized the middle-ear fluid of pneumococci. When infection due to *H. influenzae* was present, penicillin V (phenoxymethyl penicillin) usually failed, and failure rates in excess of 20% were evident for the cephalosporins, cefaclor and cefprozil, and the

TABLE 25–39. Persistence of Bacterial Pathogens in Middle-Ear Fluids after Therapy for Acute Otitis Media

Study	Drug	Days after Therapy	No. of Patients from Whom Organism Was Recovered During Therapy/No. of Patients with Bacterial Otitis Media (%)		
			Streptococcus Pneumoniae	Haemophilus Influenzae	Moraxella Catarrhalis
Howie[508]	Placebo	2–7	46/57 (81)	13/57 (52)	NA
Howie and Ploussard[513]	Phenoxymethyl penicillin	2–10	0/2	7/7	NA
	Phenoxymethyl penicillin with triple sulfonamides	2–10	0/17	2/6	NA
	Benzathine penicillin G	2–10	1/9	7/7	NA
	Benzathine with trimetho-prim-sulfamethoxazole	2–4	0/17	4/18	1/15
McLinn[728]	Amoxicillin	2	4/37	3/14	0/6
McLinn and Serlin (1983)		2–3	0/35	0/23	0/4
Howie and Owen (1987); Howie[508]		3–5; 2–7	1/18	5/8° 0/13†	3/12°
Johnson et al (1991)		3–5	1/15	2/3° 3/10†	1/7°
Owen et al (1993)		4–6	2/31	9/35	5/13
	Total amoxicillin		8/136 (5)	6/50† (12)	0/10† (0)
Howie[508]	Amoxicillin-clavulanate	2–7	2/42	10/43	2/23
Marchant et al (1986)		3–6	0/21	1/15†	0/4°
	Total amoxicillin-clavulanate		2/63 (3)	11/58 (19)	2/30 (7)
Marchant et al[696]	TMP-SMZ	3–6	0/19	1/14	0/9
Johnson et al (1991)		3–5	6/32	14/46	NA
	Total TMP-SMZ		6/51 (12)	15/61 (25)	0/9 (0) 4
Marchant et al[696]	Cefaclor 3 × daily	3–6	1/37	3/20	0/2
Marchant et al (1986)	3 × daily	3–6	2/14	4/14	2/7
Marchant et al[696]	2 × daily	3–6	4/20	8/18	0/8
Howie et al (1985)	4 × daily	3–6	9/17	12/30	NA
Dagan et al[265]	4 × daily	4–5	10/27	13/25	NA
	Total cefaclor		26/115 (23)	40/107 (37)	2/17 (12)
Howie and Owen (1987)	Cefixime	3–5	7/19	1/22	2/14
Owen et al (1993)		4–6	5/26	3/34	0/10
Johnson et al (1991)		3–5	4/16	0/10	1/6
	Total cefixime		16/61 (26)	4/66 (0)	3/30 (10)
Howie and Ploussard[513]	Erythromycin ethylsuccin-ate	2–10	1/15	17/20	NA
	Erythromycin ethylsuccin-ate plus triple sulfona-mides		3/8	2/7	NA
McLinn[728]	Cyclacillin		0/40	0/18	1/5
Howie[508]	Cefprozil		1/13	8/14	1/4
	Cefuroxime		0/11	1/5	0/3
	Cefpodoxime		4/24	1/22	6/15
Howie (1993)	Ceftriaxone		0/24	0/30‡	3/20
Howie[508]	Clarithromycin		0/12	12/15	1/5
Dagan et al[265]	Azithromycin		5/17	16/30	NA

° Beta-lactamase positive
† Beta-lactamase negative
‡ Two patients had positive cultures at 10 days
NA, not available
From Bluestone CD, Klein JO. Otitis Media in Infants and Children, 3rd ed, Philadelphia, WB Saunders, 2001.

macrolides, erythromycin, azithromycin, and clarithromy-cin. Single-dose intramuscular ceftriaxone uniformly steri-lized middle-ear fluids infected with pneumococci or *H. influenzae.*

The correlation of bacteriologic efficacy and clinical results was discussed by Marchant et al[695] (Table 25–40). Clinical success by days 3 to 6 was usually achieved (93% of cases) when the bacterial pathogen was eradicated from the middle ear. When the drug was ineffective and failed to sterilize the middle-ear infection, clinical success was still evident in a majority of patients (62%) probably owing to the placebo effect for *Haemophilus* and *Morax-ella* infections or other reasons noted earlier. When a bacterial pathogen was not isolated from the middle-ear fluids, clinical success occurred in 80% of the patients.

Dagan et al[263] have suggested that the dual aspirate studies be the gold standard for assessment of microbio-logic efficacy of drugs used for acute otitis media. In the United States, the guidelines for evaluation of anti-infec-tive drugs prepared by the members of the Infectious Diseases Society of America and funded by the FDA[73] do not require repeated aspirates to define microbiologic ef-

TABLE 25–40. Comparative Efficacy of Antibacterial Agents for Acute Otitis Media*

Microbiologic Efficacy	Clinical Success, %
Success in eradicating bacteria	93.2
Failure to eradicate bacteria	62.5
Nonbacterial otitis media	80.0

* Tympanocentesis and clinical evaluation 3 to 6 days after onset of therapy
From Marchant CD, Carlin SA, Johnson CE, et al. Measuring the comparative efficacy of antibacterial agents for acute otitis media: the "Pollyanna phenomenon." J Pediatr 120:72, 1992.

ficacy of the test drugs and note a "second aspiration of middle ear effusion cannot be recommended for children who are clinically cured or improved." The guidelines accept microbiologic response as presumptive eradication based on the initial aspirate to identify the pathogen and clinical results. Nevertheless, the results of the dual aspirates provide information of importance about the efficacy of the various drugs that are approved for use in acute otitis media, and Dagan et al[262] in Beersheva continue to perform studies of value.

Efficacy of Antimicrobial Agents

Poultices, purgatives, and ear drops were the treatments of choice for acute otitis media in the 19th century.[454] Physicians who cared for children with severe acute otitis media had available only the surgical techniques of incision and drainage of the middle-ear abscess. Most physicians were accomplished in performing myringotomy, and the myringotomy knife was standard equipment. If otorrhea was noted, according to Hamilton,[454] "some warm milk and water ought to be carefully injected by a syringe three or four times a day, in order to wash out the matter." Removal of secretions from the nasopharynx with a warm spray of salt and water was advocated by Wurdemann in 1892.[1202] In the pre-antibiotic era, beta-hemolytic streptococci and *S. aureus* accounted for 25% and 11% of middle-ear isolates, respectively (pneumococci accounted for 27% and "influenza" for 2% of isolates).[921] The introduction of the sulfonamides, then the penicillins and broad-spectrum antibiotics, led to a variety of effective regimens for acute otitis media and chronic suppurative otitis media. The microbiology of acute otitis media changed during the early years of the antibiotic era, with pneumococci and *H. influenzae* emerging as the major pathogens and beta-hemolytic streptococci and *S. aureus* relegated to minor roles. At first, penicillin G or V alone was used extensively, but Mortimer and Watterson,[765] in 1956, pointed out that penicillin was inadequate for infection due to *H. influenzae* and that the addition of a sulfonamide should be considered for mild to moderate infections and chloramphenicol for severe disease. The introduction of ampicillin in 1962 and amoxicillin approximately 10 years later permitted single-drug therapy for coverage of the important pathogens of acute otitis media. Current concern about changing susceptibility patterns of the bacterial pathogens warrants consideration of new antimicrobial agents.

Antibiotic Resistance and the Need for Judicious Use of Antimicrobial Agents for Acute Otitis Media

The increasing incidence of multidrug-resistant *S. pneumoniae* and *H. influenzae* has raised concerns about the continued efficacy of antimicrobial agents. Antibiotic resistance has been, is now, and will be a problem in the management of infectious diseases.

Development of resistance was evident from the first experiences with chemotherapy. Sulfonamides were initially effective against group A streptococci and pneumococci, but within 10 years after introduction, these streptococcal species had developed modes of resistance. Each subsequent decade brought new challenges in the form of development of resistance of important bacterial pathogens to available antimicrobial agents. In the past, the response of industry and research laboratories has been the introduction of new drugs effective against the resistant strains. But it is possible that resistant strains will emerge that will be unaffected by available or investigational drugs.

Selection of resistance bacteria is promoted in the patient by the current or prior use of antimicrobial agents and in the community by the amount of drug used (see prior section on *S. pneumoniae*). Because of the need to restrict the use of antimicrobial drugs to thwart the further development of resistant bacteria, national organizations have developed protocols for the judicious use of antimicrobial agents. The CDC and the AAP have developed guidelines for the appropriate use of antimicrobial agents for pediatric upper respiratory tract infections, including acute otitis media.[295] The CDC and AAP guidelines support the prevalent American view that antimicrobial agents *are* indicated for treatment of acute otitis media. The guidelines emphasize the need to distinguish acute otitis media as a treatable disease from persistent middle-ear effusion without acute signs of illness. In addition, the guidelines call attention to concern for overdiagnosis of acute otitis media. It is likely that many physicians who find ambiguous signs of acute otitis media on examination choose to treat with antimicrobial agents rather than observe the patient for evolution or resolution of the disease. It is too early to determine whether these guidelines have had the desired effect of promoting judicious use of antimicrobial agents. The antimicrobial choices of a consensus panel convened by the CDC in April, 1997,[217] to discuss management of acute otitis media are listed in Table 25–41.

Assessment of Efficacy of Antimicrobial Agents

The efficacy of antimicrobial agents for otitis media can be assessed in terms of clinical, microbiologic, and immunologic results. Clinically, we expect effective drugs to produce a significant decrease in signs and symptoms of disease in 48 to 72 hours, to limit the duration of time of middle-ear effusion, and to prevent complications of disease that occur by extension to adjacent tissues.

The major microbiologic criterion for efficacy of antimicrobial drugs is sterilization of the middle-ear infection. Recent studies indicate that bacterial antigens persist in middle-ear fluid, although the antibiotic may have rid the

TABLE 25–41. Evaluation of New Antimicrobial Agents for Otitis Media: Infectious Diseases Society of America, 1992

1. In vitro activity of test drug
   Effective for major pathogens
2. In vivo efficacy in animal model
3. Selection of comparison drug
   Current standard therapy or known effective agent
4. Enrollment criteria for patients
   Definition of disease: middle-ear effusion plus a sign of acute illness
   Exclusions: antimicrobial agents for 7 days or fewer
5. Microbiologic study
   Use of tympanocentesis to define microbiology (approx. 100 patients)
6. Clinical study
   Clinical criteria alone
   Sufficient sample size to identify differences in study and comparison drugs
7. Times for evaluation after onset of therapy (for a 10-day course of oral drug)
   3–5 days to define initial cure/failure
   10–14 days to identify relapse
   15–28 days to identify recurrence

From Chow AW, Hall CB, Klein JO, et al. Evaluation of new anti-infective drugs for the treatment of respiratory tract infections. Clin Infect Dis 15(Suppl. 1): S62, 1992. With permission from the University of Chicago Press.

ear of viable organisms. Pneumococcal polysaccharide has been identified in the vast majority of fluids in which the organism is isolated and in many specimens that have no bacterial growth. The role of these bacterial products in diseases and the effect of antibacterial drugs in processing and eliminating the antigens are unknown but may be important in dealing with the problem of effusion that persists after acute infection.

The immunologic process of otitis media is incompletely understood, and little information is available about the effect of antimicrobial agents on the development of local and systemic immunity after acute or chronic otitis media. Do antibiotics limit the immune response to infection in the middle ear? Do antibiotics differ in their effect on local or systemic immunity of the middle ear? How will these features of the immune response affect the duration of fluid in the middle ear? How will these features affect type-specific protection against the same bacteria? Antimicrobial agents undoubtedly play a role in modulating the immune response of the mucosa of the middle ear, but little is known about that role.

History of Clinical Trials

The design of clinical trials for evaluation of efficacy of antimicrobial agents in children with acute otitis media has undergone significant changes in the past 30 years. Prior to 1960, most American studies were performed without tympanocentesis and, thus, without a specific microbiologic diagnosis. Children were enrolled to evaluate two or more drugs; the definition of otitis media was broadly stated and included such signs as inflammation of the tympanic membrane (which most experts now do not accept as a suitable sole criterion for otitis media with effusion); the drugs were assigned by some random method; and results of therapy were presented in general terms such as *good response* or *therapeutic failure*. The results were usually ambiguous and demonstrated only minimal differences between the drugs studied.[1066] Although it is possible to design a study without microbiologic diagnosis, the early studies lacked sufficient sample size of enrolled patients to identify differences of the new drug when compared with the standard preparation.

Tympanocentesis to define the etiologic agent in the middle-ear fluid of children with otitis media with effusion had been common to clinical trials by Scandinavian investigators, but it became customary in American studies only in the 1960s. About this time, more investigators, both in the private practice of pediatrics and in academic centers, became interested in various aspects of infection of the middle ear, including evaluation of antimicrobial agents. The study designs were more precise; many studies were double-blinded; sterilization was defined in some studies by reaspiration of persisting middle-ear fluid; compliance was evaluated by assessment of use of the drug (weighing returned bottles of medication or assay of urine for antimicrobial activity); the clinical course was followed with precise end-points; and side effects and toxicity of the antimicrobial agents were carefully assessed by clinical evaluation and laboratory tests. Dual aspirate studies to define microbiologic efficacy were used extensively in the past, as indicated by the results of such studies as those listed in Table 25–39 and have provided important data about the biology of the disease.[263] In recent years, many investigators have limited dual aspirate studies to children who fail initial therapy to provide a basis for appropriate choice of drug and give insight into the reasons for drug failure.[605]

Guidelines for Evaluation of Antimicrobial Agents for Acute Otitis Media: Infectious Diseases Society of America

Guidelines for the evaluation of anti-infective drugs for infectious diseases, including otitis media, were developed by the Infectious Diseases Society of America for the United States FDA in 1992.[73] The purpose of the guidelines was to provide a basis for a study design of protocols for assessing the clinical and microbiologic efficacy of antimicrobial agents. The guidelines for otitis media[229] are summarized in Table 25–41.

1. *Clinical criteria:* Acute otitis media is defined as inflammation of the middle ear evidenced by the presence of fluid and accompanied by specific signs or symptoms such as ear pain, ear drainage, or hearing loss, or nonspecific findings such as fever, lethargy, irritability, anorexia, vomiting, or diarrhea. The presence of middle-ear effusion is defined by pneumatic otoscopy with or without the use of tympanometry or acoustic reflectometry.
2. *Microbiologic criteria:* Determined by aspiration of middle ear fluids. Both ears should be aspirated when the patient has bilateral disease.
3. *Activity of the test drug:* The drug under consideration should have proven in vitro activity against S.

pneumoniae, H. influenzae, and *M. catarrhalis.* In vivo evidence of sterilization of bacterial pathogens can be obtained with use of an appropriate dosage schedule in an animal model of acute otitis media (such as the chinchilla).

4. *Demographic characteristics of study population:* Clinical studies should be conducted with patients of different age groups and racial backgrounds. Children should be excluded if they have focal anatomic, physiologic, or systemic immune defects; if they received a systemic antimicrobial agent within the past 7 days; and if they are 12 weeks of age or younger.

5. *Selection of the comparison drug:* The control agent should be selected on the basis of expected patterns of in vitro susceptibility of the common bacterial pathogens and/or should be considered the current standard in the community for treatment of otitis media.

6. *Initial study with documentation of microbiology:* A small trial (approximately 100 patients with a minimum of 20 cases due to each of the three major bacterial pathogens) should be conducted in which middle ear aspiration and culture is performed for all patients to document the unique microbiology of the population to be studied. Repeat aspiration of middle-ear fluid is required only if there is evidence of clinical failure. Because the number of centers that perform tympanocenteses is currently limited and a second aspiration of middle-ear effusion cannot be recommended for children who are clinically cured or improved, the microbiologic response is correctly termed *presumptive eradication.*

7. *Clinical evaluation without documentation of microbiology:* If the presumed microbiologic response rate is favorable, 80% or larger, a comparative trial with an active control should be conducted. A double-blind study design is desirable whenever feasible, or at a minimum the evaluator should be blinded.

8. *Statistical significance and power:* The sample size should be determined to provide significance with sufficient power (0.80 is appropriate for most studies) to determine an expected difference between the test drug and the standard. As an example, a sample size of 440 evaluable patients would be required to identify a significant difference with a power of 0.80, with an expected cure rate of 80% to 90%.

9. *Evaluability:* After enrollment, observations should be made 3 to 5 days after initiation of therapy and at least 2 and 4 to 6 weeks later. The precise period of post-treatment evaluation will vary according to knowledge of the anticipated duration of anti-infective activity of the test drugs. At each visit, an interval medical history, otoscopic examination, and objective measurements, such as tympanometry or acoustic reflectometry, should be performed. Children should be assessed at each visit for other foci of infection and for adverse effects of the test drug.

10. *Criteria for clinical efficacy: Cure* is defined as resolution of signs and symptoms exclusive of middle-ear effusion within 72 hours of onset of therapy. *Relapse* is defined as reappearance of signs and symptoms after initial response during or within 4 days after conclusion of therapy. *Recurrence* is defined as reappearance of signs and symptoms of acute otitis media 5 to 14 days after conclusion of therapy.

Are Antimicrobial Agents Indicated for All Children with Acute Otitis Media?

Before the introduction of sulfonamides in 1936, management of acute otitis media included watchful waiting or, when the suppurative process produced severe clinical signs or complications, use of myringotomy to drain the middle-ear abscess. Spread of infection to the mastoid, meninges, or other intracranial foci was a feared complication of otitis media.

Early therapeutic trials identified the value of the new drugs for early resolution of clinical signs and decreased incidence of mastoiditis and other complications. In 1938, the frequency of mastoidectomy associated with acute otitis media was 20%; by 1948, it was 2.5%[1049] and in some studies dropped to 0%.[488] Today, suppurative complications of acute otitis media are prevalent only in regions with limited access to medical care, and the severity of complications is similar to the severity of complications identified in the pre-antibiotic era. The effective antimicrobial agent sterilizes the middle-ear abscess and results in resolution of acute signs and symptoms in more than 90% of children by day 3. The duration of middle-ear effusion is shorter in treated than in untreated children.[558]

The majority of children with acute otitis media respond clinically without the use of antimicrobial agents. Those who improve without such drugs include the one third of children with acute otitis media who have a sterile effusion and are presumed to have a viral infection. The microbiologic data (see Sterilization of Middle Ear Fluids by Antimicrobial Agents, and Table 25–39) indicate that about 20% of children with pneumococcal otitis media, one half of children with initial aspirates that grow *H. influenzae,* and about 75% of children with otitis due to *M. catarrhalis* clear the organism from the middle ear and have resolution of acute signs of illness without use of an appropriate antibacterial drug.[602] In addition, some children will have a sterile effusion from a prior episode of acute otitis media with persistent effusion and have an intercurrent illness, not acute otitis media.

Based on studies by van Buchem and colleagues,[1155, 1156] and others, many physicians in western Europe manage acute otitis media by symptomatic treatment and observation and use antimicrobial agents only if the illness persists for 3 or more days. The Dutch guidelines for the management of acute otitis media are listed in Table 25–42.[322] There is increased interest in this management plan because of concern for increased resistance of the bacterial pathogens of acute otitis media. Surveillance of pneumococcal resistance suggests that one factor in the inci-

TABLE 25–42. Guidelines for Management of Acute Otitis Media: Dutch College of General Practitioners

Patients 2 years of age and older:
Analgesia; perhaps decongestive nose drops
Parent instructions:
    Recovery within 3 days: no follow-up
    Return if symptoms persist or worsen (pain +/− fever +/−
        sickness)
    If drum perforates, follow up 2 weeks after onset of running ear
If earache +/− fever persists, amoxicillin (if contraindicated, eryth-
    romycin) for 7 days
Parent instructions:
    Re-evaluate if no improvement after 48 hours of drug
    If no improvement in ear signs, referral
Patients 6 months to 2 years:
*Act as for older children, but more active attitude related to higher
    probability of deterioration.*
Visit or phone contact person 24 hours after initial examination
    If no improvement, another 24 hours of observation or amoxicil-
        lin (if contraindicated, erythromycin) for 7 days
Contact 24 hours later; examination if necessary
    If no improvement, referral
Special patients
*Younger than 6 months of age, recurrent episodes (three or more
    within a year), immunocompromised hosts*
Start amoxicillin (or erythromycin) for 7 days
Re-evaluate at 24 hours
    Refer if patient deteriorates
Follow-up 2 weeks after evaluation

From Dutch College of General Practitioners. NGH Standard Acute Otitis Media, June 1993.

dence of resistant strains is the volume of antimicrobial drugs used in the community. Studies from The Netherlands indicate a rate of resistance that is among the lowest from reporting countries.[278] Since the low incidence of resistance is probably associated with the decreased volume of antimicrobial agent used in the community, and since otitis media is the most frequent reason for the use of antimicrobial drugs in children, the practice of observation alone for initial management of children should be carefully analyzed for applicability in other countries.

There is a paucity of data about initial management of acute otitis media with observation alone in children younger than 2 years of age. The van Buchem studies that form the basis for the Dutch practice of initial observation did not include children younger than 2 years of age. Since the disease is more prevalent, more severe, and more likely to be associated with morbidity in the infant age group, observation alone may not be optimal management at this time for these children. A joint statement of the CDC and the AAP supported the prevalent American view that antimicrobial agents are indicated for treatment of appropriately diagnosed acute otitis media.[295]

To adopt the policy of initial observation of children with acute otitis media, more data are needed to permit physicians to establish criteria for using or withholding antimicrobial drugs. Can the degree of fever, the range of otalgia, the extent of inflammation of the tympanic membrane, or the presence or absence of pus in the middle ear distinguish the child who benefits from immediate antimicrobial therapy from the child who can be initially observed? Until these data are available, children younger

than 2 years of age should be treated with antimicrobial agents. At this time, physicians may consider observation alone for children older than 2 years with mild to moderate disease: those who are afebrile, without notable ear pain, or signs of middle-ear inflammation or pus in the middle ear and carefully monitor the clinical course.

Results of Therapeutic Trials Including Children Who Received Placebo

The use of a placebo group in a comparative trial with one or more antimicrobial agents has been studied by many investigators in the past 30 years. These studies have provided important insights into the pathogenesis of middle ear infections and provide a context for assessing the efficacy of antimicrobial agents. The results do not describe the natural course of otitis media, because most include a drainage procedure, either tympanocentesis (aspiration) or myringotomy (incision and drainage). Only studies that used a method of aspiration of middle-ear fluid to define the microbiologic agents are cited.

1. Rudberg[952] evaluated 1365 patients with acute, uncomplicated otitis media treated as inpatients or outpatients at the Ear, Nose, and Throat Department of Sahlgrensk Sjukhuset, Gothenberg, between January 1951 and May 1952. All patients were confined to bed and had their ears drained daily by syringe, as long as discharge was present. If spontaneous perforation did not occur, myringotomy was performed. Four regimens of antimicrobial agents were used: penicillin G tablets or a triple sulfonamide preparation alone or in combination, or an IM injection of a combination of benzathine and procaine penicillin G. A fifth group received none of the drug regimens. The criteria for efficacy included the duration of discharge and incidence of complications. Between 236 and 333 cases were included in each group.

    Duration of ear discharge was significantly shortened in infections due to the pneumococcus and *H. influenzae* in patients who received penicillin or sulfonamide preparations, when compared with those who received placebo. Infections due to *S. aureus* and beta-hemolytic streptococcus were favorably altered by use of penicillin. Complications, including exacerbation of clinical signs, mastoiditis, and failure of the infection to subside, occurred significantly more often in the placebo group than in the groups receiving penicillin, but the complications in patients receiving a sulfonamide were not significantly different from those of the placebo group. Mastoiditis occurred in 44 of 254 patients (17%) receiving placebo, in 4 of 267 patients treated with sulfonamides, and in none of 844 patients managed with one of the penicillin regimens. The highest incidence of complications occurred in patients with disease due to beta-hemolytic streptococcus and *H. influenzae*.

2. In 1953, Lahikainen[624] reported a study of children who were managed by use of myringotomy alone or in combination with penicillin G. The duration

of discharge was significantly decreased in the group who received the antibiotic. No complications occurred in the penicillin-treated group, but 9 of 153 patients who had myringotomy alone developed complications, including seven cases of mastoiditis, one case of meningitis, and one case of sinus thrombosis and brain abscess that resulted in death.

3. Van Dishoeck et al[1157] reported that 50% of 400 children treated with eardrops alone recovered in 7 to 17 days, but 13 children developed mastoiditis.

4. Halstead et al,[453] in 1968, identified clinical improvement in a majority of untreated patients with suppurative otitis (almost all had cultures that were positive for S. pneumoniae or H. influenzae), but two thirds of the children (13 of 19) continued to be ill.

5. Lorentzen and Haugsten[662] evaluated 505 children and from these defined three treatment groups: myringotomy, penicillin V, and penicillin V in combination with myringotomy. Significantly more failures occurred in the myringotomy group (15%) than in the penicillin group (4%) or the penicillin plus myringotomy group (5%). Thus, penicillin V was more efficacious than myringotomy alone, but myringotomy did not add to the effectiveness of the drug.

6. Van Buchem et al[1156] reported that antimicrobial therapy had no effect on the outcome of children with acute otitis media. The investigators enrolled 171 children in a double-blind study of four regimens: amoxicillin alone, amoxicillin plus myringotomy, myringotomy alone, and neither drug nor surgery. Children aged 2 to 12 years were enrolled by 12 general practitioners in or near Tilburg, The Netherlands. The results suggested that the clinical course (pain, temperature, otoscopic appearances, and recurrence rate) were not different in any of the groups, although ears had discharge for a longer time and eardrums took longer to heal (neither difference was significant) in the children treated without antibiotics. The authors concluded that "symptomatic therapy with nosedrops and analgesics seems a reasonable initial approach to acute otitis media in children."[1155]

Critics of the study[957] identify flaws in the study design and analysis of results and question the validity of the conclusions. The criticisms focus on the age of the patients (excluding infants, who have the highest age-specific incidence of disease), the small number of patients in each treatment group, the methods of statistical analysis, the absence of microbiologic data, the absence of definition of disease, the failure to assess observer reliability for the many participating physicians, and the failure to consider important variables of disease in randomization for therapy.

Van Buchem et al[1156] performed a second trial in which 4860 children 2 years of age or older with acute otitis media were treated with nose drops and analgesics alone for the first 3 or 4 days. Children whose condition took "an unsatisfactory course" (high temperature, otalgia, or persistent discharge) were treated with antimicrobial drug alone or in combination with myringotomy. More than 90% of the children recovered within a few days using this regimen, but two developed mastoiditis. Group A streptococci were cultured from ear fluids of 39% of the children with the "unsatisfactory course" who underwent myringotomy; S. pneumoniae was cultured from 17%, but H. influenzae was cultured from only one child (1.4%). Again, the most important criticism of this study by van Buchem and colleagues is the absence of children younger than 2 years of age. Because acute otitis media is more severe in children younger than 2 years, the failure of the two studies by van Buchem and colleagues to include children from this age group compromises the importance of the results. The Dutch protocols include management of infants younger than 2 years but the data supporting such recommendations are unclear, since data are not available from the van Buchem et al studies.

7. Engelhard et al[335] randomly assigned 105 Israeli infants, aged 3 to 12 months, with acute otitis media to either an antimicrobial agent or myringotomy, or both. At the end of treatment, 60% of both the antibiotic-treated groups (with and without myringotomy) recovered, as compared with only 23% of those in the myringotomy (without antibiotic) group. The investigators concluded that myringotomy alone is inadequate therapy for treatment of acute otitis media in infants, and that the addition of myringotomy to antibiotic treatment will not shorten the recovery period.

8. Kaleida et al[558] from the Otitis Media Research Center in Pittsburgh evaluated amoxicillin or placebo for management of nonsevere otitis media. Enrollment criteria were based on an otalgia scoring system that took into account estimated parental anxiety and reliability, and assigned points for each hour of earache or apparent discomfort and also included temperatures less than 39.5°C rectally. Initial treatment failure occurred in 7.7% of 492 episodes managed with placebo and 3.9% of 488 episodes managed with amoxicillin (Table 25–43). Children with severe disease were randomized to receive amoxicillin, amoxicillin and myringotomy, or placebo and myringotomy. Initial treatment failure occurred in 9.6% of 156 episodes treated with amoxicillin alone, 11.5% of 96 episodes managed with amoxicillin and myringotomy, and 23.5% of 34 episodes managed with placebo and myringotomy. The authors concluded that amoxicillin is warranted for both nonsevere and severe acute otitis media, but routine use of myringotomy, either alone or in combination with an antimicrobial agent, did not benefit the patient.

9. Howie[508] reviewed studies of microbiologic efficacy with various therapeutic regimens including a pla-

TABLE 25–43. Amoxicillin or Myringotomy or Both for Acute Otitis Media

Amoxicillin vs. Placebo for Nonsevere Acute Otitis Media

Outcome	Amoxicillin, % (522 Episodes)	Placebo, % (527 Episodes)	P Value
Initial treatment failure	3.9	7/7	<.009
Effusion at 2 weeks	46.9	62.5	<.001
Effusion at 6 weeks	45.9	51.5	NS
Recurrence at 2–6 weeks	27.9	27.6	NS

Amoxicillin vs. Amoxicillin + Myringotomy vs. Placebo and Myringotomy for Severe Acute Otitis Media

Outcome	Amoxicillin, % (167 Episodes)	Amoxicillin + Myringotomy, % (104 Episodes)	Placebo + Myringotomy, % (35 Episodes)
Initial treatment failure	9.6	11.5	23/5
Effusion at 2 weeks	60.6	56.4	52.2
Effusion at 6 weeks	55.7	51.6	35.0
Recurrence at 2–6 weeks	40.9	35.2	17.2

° NS, not significant; none of the differences were statistically significant except for placebo + myringotomy vs. drug groups in children older than 2 years.
From Kaleida PH, Casselbrant ML, Rockette HE, et al. Amoxicillin or myringotomy or both for acute otitis media: results of a randomized clinical trial. Pediatrics 87:466, 1991. Reprinted by permission of Pediatrics.

cebo group. Pneumococci persisted in most untreated patients (81%), whereas one half of patients with initial aspirates of nontypeable *H. influenzae* had sterile aspirates on second culture. These studies suggest that many cases of infection of the middle ear resolve spontaneously or with the assistance of surgical drainage. The data indicate that pneumococcal otitis media is unlikely to resolve clinically or microbiologically, whereas infection due to *H. influenzae* and possibly *M. catarrhalis* clears without antibiotics in about one half of cases.

10. Damoiseaux et al[269] performed a randomized double-blind trial of amoxicillin versus placebo for acute otitis media in children younger than 2 years of age. Two hundred forty children 6 months to 2 years of age were enrolled in 53 general practices in The Netherlands. Persistent symptoms at day 4 were less common in the amoxicillin group; the median duration of fever was 2 days in the amoxicillin group vs. 3 in the placebo group; mean duration of pain and crying was 6 days in the amoxicillin group and 9 days in the placebo group; and mean consumption of analgesia in first 10 days (doses) was 2.3 in the amoxicillin group and 4.1 in the placebo group. One child in the placebo group developed meningitis on day 3. The authors concluded that the antibiotic resulted in a "modest effect that does not justify prescribing of antibiotics at the first visit."

The reasons for resolution of acute otitis media without use of antimicrobial agents are the following:

- The condition was caused by a nonbacterial organism
- The condition was caused by a noninfectious process
- Middle-ear effusion is present from a prior episode of otitis media

- Middle-ear fluid drained through perforation of the tympanic membrane
- The acute otitis media was sterilized by immune factors in the middle-ear fluid and/or mucosa

Many cases improve because the contents of the middle-ear infection are discharged through the eustachian tube or after spontaneous perforation of the tympanic membrane. However, these features of drainage would not explain the differential of failure to spontaneously resolve pneumococcal otitis and the frequent resolution of acute otitis media due to *H. influenzae* and *M. catarrhalis*. Presumably, resolution is due to nonspecific factors in the middle-ear effusion that inhibit or kill selectively the bacterial pathogens of otitis media. In addition, many children have acute otitis media due to viruses or other microorganisms that are not affected by antibacterial therapy.

In summary, we treat all patients with acute otitis media because we cannot distinguish the patients who will resolve spontaneously. If we consider the number of patients with nonbacterial infections unaffected by antibacterial therapy and the one third to one half of those with bacterial otitis who respond spontaneously, we are providing antibacterial therapy for about one third of all patients with acute otitis media. Other benefits of antimicrobial agents are (1) the duration of drainage and other signs of clinical disease are decreased, and (2) the incidence of complications, though low, is significantly decreased.

Recent Clinical Trials. A list of selected clinical trials of various antimicrobial agents in children with acute otitis media between 1965 and 2001 is given in Table 25–44. The list includes only studies that identified the bacterial cause by aspiration of middle-ear fluid. The clinical results were consistent with the results that would be expected based on in vitro studies of the activity of

TABLE 25–44. Selected Trials of Antimicrobial Agents for Acute Otitis Media: Microbiology Defined by Initial Aspirate

Study	Drugs
Nilson et al. (1969)	Penicillin V
	Penicillin V trisulfapyrimidines
	Ampicillin
Howie and Ploussard[513]	Placebo
	Ampicillin
	Erythromycin estolate (E) trisulfa-pyrimidines (S)E&S
Feigin et al[359]	Ampicillin
	Clindamycin
Howie et al. (1974)	Ampicillin
	Amoxicillin
Howard et al[507]	Amoxicillin
	Penicillin
	Erythromycin estolate E&S
Stechenberg et al. (1976)	Ampicillin
	Cephalexin
Shurin et al[1017]	Ampicillin
	Trimethoprim-sulfamethoxazole
Mandel et al[681]	Amoxicillin
	Cefaclor
Berman and Laver (1983)	Cefaclor
	Amoxicillin
Blumer et al. (1984)	Trimethoprim-sulfamethoxazole
	Cefaclor
Marchant et al[696]	Trimethoprim-sulfamethoxazole
	Cefaclor
Odoi et al[803]	Amoxicillin-clavulanate
	Cefaclor
Rodriguez et al. (1985)	Erythromycin-sulfisoxazole
	Amoxicillin
Marchant et al. (1986)	Amoxicillin-clavulanate
	Cefaclor
Bergeron et al. (1987)	Erythromycin-sulfisoxazole
	Cefaclor
Kaleida et al[557]	Amoxicillin-clavulanate
	Cefaclor
Kenna et al. (1987)	Cefixime
	Cefaclor
Johnson et al. (1991)	Cefixime
	Amoxicillin
Gan et al. (1991)	Loracarbef
	Amoxicillin-clavulanate
Foshee (1992)	Loracarbef
	Amoxicillin-clavulanate
Mendelman et al. (1992)	Cefpodoxime
	Amoxicillin-clavulanate
Chan et al. (1993)	Sultamicillin
	Amoxicillin-clavulanate
Green and Rothrock[439]	Ceftriaxone
	Amoxicillin
Harrison et al. (1993)	Cefixime
	Cefaclor
Owen et al. (1993)	Cefixime
	Amoxicillin
	Clarithromycin
Gooch et al[426]	Cefaclor
	Clarithromycin
Pukander et al[897]	Amoxicillin
	Clarithromycin
McLinn et al. (1994)	Cefuroxime axetil
	Amoxicillin-clavulanate
Blumer et al. (1995)	Ceftibuten
	Cefaclor
Aronowitz[35]	Azithromycin
	Amoxicillin-clavulanate
Goldblatt et al[417]	Ofloxacin otic
	Amoxicillin-clavulanate
Dagan et al[262]	Azithromycin
	Cefaclor

From Bluestone CD, Klein JO. Otitis Media in Infants and Children, 3rd ed. Philadelphia, WB Saunders, 2001.

antimicrobial agents and data about concentrations of drug achieved in middle-ear fluid.

Clinical Failure, Relapse, and Recurrence

Clinical *cure* is defined as resolution of signs and symptoms (exclusive of middle-ear effusion) within 72 hours of onset of therapy in a child who remains well through the period of observation. *Failure* is defined as persistent signs or symptoms or clinical deterioration or new foci within 72 hours of onset of therapy. Failure may be due to ineffective drug or an organism that is not susceptible to appropriate antibacterial therapy (virus infection) or serious disease with multiple foci. *Relapse* is defined as reappearance of signs and symptoms of acute otitis media after initial response or within 4 days of conclusion of therapy and should be considered a failure of therapy or a new infection. *Recurrence* is defined as reappearance of signs and symptoms of acute otitis media 5 to 14 days after the conclusion of therapy and may not be due to a fault in the therapeutic regimen but may be associated with a new infection and is likely to occur in children who are exposed to viral or bacterial pathogens in day care or school.

Factors influencing outcome of treatment of acute otitis media include the following:

- Age—children younger than 18 months of age had higher rates of failure than children who were older
- History of prior ear infections—children with recurrent otitis media were more likely to fail
- Winter respiratory season
- Concurrent virus infection and occurrence in the winter respiratory season
- Failure of the parents to comply with the prescribed regimen[94, 203]

Knowledge of the risk factors for possible failure of the antimicrobial agents to achieve a clinical cure should promote closer observation of children at risk.

Microbiology of Relapse and Recurrence

Microbiologic features of children who do not have clinical cure after complete courses of therapy were investigated in two studies. Schwartz et al[991] evaluated children whose clinical disease did not respond after a 10-day course of ampicillin, amoxicillin, or erythromycin-sulfonamide mixture. Middle-ear fluid was aspirated and cultured for bacteria: Ampicillin-resistant *H. influenzae* was found in about one third (31%) of samples, ampicillin-susceptible strains of *S. pneumoniae* or *H. influenzae* were identified in about one half (51%) of samples, and no bacterial growth was found in the other fluid samples. Boston children who failed to respond to therapy were studied in a similar fashion with the following results: Nineteen percent had organisms resistant to initial therapy and 57% had no bacteria isolated from the middle-ear fluids.[1105] Pichichero and Pichichero[868] evaluated the microbiology of patients who failed initial therapy. Tympanocenteses provided middle-ear fluid samples of 83 patients who had initially been treated with amoxicillin: 44 patients had no growth; *S. pneumoniae* was isolated from

TABLE 25–45. Choice of Antimicrobial Agents for Management of Acute Otitis Media: Recommendations of the Centers for Disease Control and Prevention Drug-Resistant *Streptococcus Pneumoniae* Therapeutic Working Group

	No Antibiotics in Prior Month	Antibiotics in Prior Month
Initial Therapy	Usual dose amoxicillin High-dose amoxicillin	High-dose amoxicillin High-dose amoxicillin-clavulanate Cefuroxime axetil
Clinical Failure on Day 3	High-dose amoxicillin-clavulanate Cefuroxime axetil IM ceftriaxone	IM ceftriaxone Clindamycin Tympanocentesis
Clinical Failure on Days 10–28	Same as day 3	High-dose amoxicillin-clavulanate Cefuroxime axetil IM ceftriaxone Tympanocentesis

Dowell SF, Butler JC, Giebink GS, et al. Acute otitis media: management and surveillance in an era of pneumococcal resistance—a report from the Drug-Resistant *Streptococcus pneumoniae* Therapeutic Working Group. Pediatr Infect Dis J 18:1–9, 1999.

18 (though only 2 were found to be nonsusceptible, of 11 tested); *H. influenzae* was isolated from 7 (5 were beta-lactamase-positive); and *M. catarrhalis* was isolated from 7 (all beta-lactamase–positive).

These data indicate that some children who fail clinically do so because of a bacterial pathogen resistant to initial therapy, but many children have bacteria that are susceptible to the drug, and some have negative bacterial cultures and presumably have a nonbacterial microorganism as the cause of otitis media or some other reason for the persistent fever. The child who fails to respond to therapy in 48 to 72 hours, or later relapses, should receive a new antimicrobial regimen that provides effective activity against organisms that might be resistant to the initial therapy (i.e., beta-lactamase–producing organisms that would inactivate ampicillin).

The bacteriologic features of middle-ear infection in children who have recurrent episodes of acute otitis media are, in general, similar to those found in first episodes: The predominant pathogens are *S. pneumoniae* (though of different serotypes) and nontypeable strains of *H. influenzae*. Because antibiotics administered in the prior 30 days may result in selection in resistant strains, consideration should be given to the choice of an antimicrobial agent effective against pathogens resistant to the previously administered antibiotic. The CDC recommendations for treatment of relapses and recurrences are provided in Table 25–45.

Effect of Antimicrobial Agents on Duration of Middle-Ear Effusion after Acute Otitis Media

The primary role of antimicrobial agents is to eradicate the local infection and to prevent spread to continuous and distant tissues. Recent studies demonstrating the persistence of middle ear effusions after acute infection suggest a need to consider duration of fluid in the middle ear among the criteria for efficacy of an antimicrobial agent. The clinical trial by Kaleida et al,[558] in which amoxicillin was compared to placebo in infants and children who had "nonsevere" acute otitis media, showed that amoxicillin was associated with a statistically shorter duration of middle-ear effusion, as compared with placebo, at the completion of treatment of each episode during the 1 year the subjects were in the study. Since middle-ear effusion is associated with hearing loss,[386] this finding lends further support to our recommendation of treating all children who have acute otitis media with an antimicrobial agent.

Most therapeutic trials show similar durations of middle-ear effusions for the drugs evaluated, including drugs of different families such as penicillins, cephalosporins, sulfonamides, and macrolides. One of the few studies to demonstrate a difference in duration of effusion examined the efficacy of cefaclor and amoxicillin in children with acute otitis media.[681] Fourteen days after the onset of therapy, more children who received cefaclor had aeration of the middle ear (59 of 106, 55.7%) than did children who received amoxicillin (40 of 97, 41.2%; $P = .05$). On day 42, the proportion of children with normal aerated ears was the same: 68.9% for cefaclor and 67.5% for amoxicillin. It is possible that the differences on day 14 were related to differing effects of the antimicrobial drugs on the inflammatory response in the middle ear, whereas by day 42 host factors were dominant and little difference would be expected, irrespective of the antibiotic used.

The pathogenesis of prolonged duration of middle-ear effusion after middle-ear infection remains obscure, and the failure of different types of antimicrobial agents to effectively alter the duration in spite of the use of drugs that achieve high concentrations in tissue (macrolides) or very high concentrations in serum, and presumably middle-ear fluids (ceftriaxone), means that the drugs are inadequate as probes to provide insights into the pathogenesis of middle-ear effusion.

Effect of Antimicrobial Agents on Otitis Media with Effusion

Bacterial pathogens are identified in about one third of children with chronic otitis media with effusion based on culture of middle-ear fluids at the time of placement of tympanostomy tubes[477, 922, 1058] (see Microbiology of Otitis

Media earlier in this chapter). The role of the bacteria in the persistence of fluid in the middle ear is uncertain. One hypothesis is that the bacteria, their antigens, or their products are a factor in the continued secretion of fluids by the mucosa. Would a course of an appropriate antimicrobial agent assist in ridding the ear of fluid?

A number of investigators have considered courses of 10 days to 6 months of different antimicrobial agents for children with persistent middle-ear effusion.

Trimethoprim-sulfamethoxazole (8 mg trimethoprim and 40 mg sulfamethoxazole per kg per day in two doses) was administered for 4 weeks to 200 children in greater Boston who were 2 to 5 years of age and had middle-ear effusion present for longer than 12 weeks. The proportion of children who were free of effusion at the 4-week observation was significantly higher for the antibiotic-treated group (58%), as compared with the observation group (6%).[475]

Cefaclor was given to children for the treatment of otitis media with effusion by Ernston et al.[338] Children were randomized to receive cefaclor (20 mg/kg twice daily) or no antimicrobial therapy during the 10 days preceding the day appointed for surgery. On the day scheduled for surgery, in 24 of 46 treated children the middle-ear effusion had resolved, compared with 5 of 45 untreated children ($P < .001$). Eighteen of the 24 primarily healed children remained unoperated upon at a follow-up examination, which was made at a median of 20 months.

Amoxicillin-clavulanate administered for 1 month was compared with placebo in a randomized, double-blind study of Danish children with otitis media with effusion.[1117] The incidence of effusion was significantly reduced at the end of the treatment period (61% resolution in children who received amoxicillin-clavulanate contrasted with 30% in children in the placebo group), and the difference remained significant at 3 and 5 months but not at 10 months. Van Balen et al[1154] evaluated the efficacy of amoxicillin/clavulanate for children who had been observed to have bilateral middle-ear effusions for 3 months. A total of 433 children, aged 6 months to 6 years, were randomized to receive amoxicillin/clavulanate (20 mg/kg amoxicillin) or placebo three times a day for 14 days. At the 2-week follow-up, the antibiotic-treated group had significantly lower rates of effusion in one or both ears (77% vs. 93%).

Amoxicillin was evaluated in 488 children with persistent middle-ear effusion in the greater Pittsburgh area. Mandel et al[688] reported that those treated with amoxicillin for 2 weeks had higher rates of resolution of the effusion at 2 and 4 weeks after initiation of treatment than did placebo-treated control subjects.

Erythromycin-sulfisoxazole, cefaclor, amoxicillin, or placebo was administered in a sequel by the same investigators.[691] The study reaffirmed that amoxicillin was effective in some children in resolving the middle-ear effusion; significantly more children in the amoxicillin group than the placebo group had resolution of the effusion after 2 weeks of therapy (31.6% vs. 14.1%). The sample size was insufficient to identify the benefit of erythromycin-sulfisoxazole or cefaclor compared with placebo.

Sulfisoxazole in a therapeutic dosage schedule of 75 mg/kg per day in two daily doses for 6 months was administered to Ottawa children who were candidates for placement of tympanostomy tubes.[97] The children were randomly assigned to the medical or surgical groups. Failures were defined as persistent middle-ear effusion with hearing loss greater than 25 dB or allergic reaction to the drug or three or more episodes of acute otitis media. At the conclusion of the 6-month period of medical therapy and 6 months after the operative procedure, 34% of the medically treated patients failed to clear the effusion, contrasted with 20% of the surgically treated children. Although the results were better in the children who received tympanostomy tubes, the success in two thirds of children treated medically indicated the value of the course of antimicrobial agent.

In addition to the above studies, other investigators have used a variety of study designs to evaluate medical therapies for persistent middle-ear effusion: erythromycin-sulfisoxazole in combination with a decongestant[400]; erythromycin ethylsuccinate or sulfisoxazole[252]; TMP-SMX combined with prednisone[89, 267]; and cefaclor.[290] In general, the regimens demonstrated short-term benefits. Where observations were of sufficient duration, long-term benefits were usually absent. Once antimicrobial treatment ended in the two trials evaluating the efficacy of amoxicillin[688, 691] and amoxicillin-clavulanate,[1117] the likelihood of recurrence of the middle-ear effusion was high, indicating that the benefit of the medical therapy was temporary. These data suggest that antibiotic therapy may not alter the underlying pathologic condition, and observation is necessary for the child who cleared the middle-ear effusion initially with medical therapy but may subsequently have a recurrence. In addition, three meta-analyses have been published during the last few years that addressed the efficacy of antimicrobial treatment of otitis media with effusion, and all three showed efficacy.[943, 1069, 1193]

Plan for Medical Therapy of the Child with Persistent Middle-Ear Effusion

Although the data remain incomplete about medical therapy of the child with persistent middle-ear effusion, the available information is sufficiently consistent and compelling to warrant considering a plan for use of a prior antimicrobial agent for children who are candidates for placement of ventilating tubes. The interested reader should review the referenced articles. There are a number of variables among the investigations, including different enrollment criteria (age, duration of effusion, laterality of effusion), varying antimicrobial agents alone or combined with adjunctive therapy, duration of therapy, length of follow-up, and criteria for diagnosis, that the results of the studies have to be considered individually rather than cumulatively. The authors believe that the risk of a course of antimicrobial agent is limited and that the gain in time and avoidance of surgery is of sufficient importance to warrant a trial of medical therapy prior to placement of tympanostomy tubes. A recently published Guideline addressed these management options.

Guideline for Management of Otitis Media with Effusion

The *Clinical Practice Guideline, Otitis Media with Effusion in Young Children*, by Stool et al[1069] was an attempt by the Agency for Health Care Policy and Research, which is part of the Public Health Service, U.S. Department of Health and Human Services, to provide health care providers, policy makers, and the public a guideline for management; the focus of the report was on children 1 to 3 years of age. The *Guideline* panel of experts concluded the following regarding management of otitis media with effusion in this age group:

1. Environmental Risk Factor Control was recommended, such as avoidance of exposure to tobacco smoke, child day care, and bottle feeding (as opposed to breast feeding).
2. Antimicrobial treatment is effective and was recommended as an alternative to "observation" when the duration of the effusion is less than 3 months, or as an alternative to myringotomy and tympanostomy tube placement, if the effusion persists for longer than 3 months, is bilateral, and is associated with a hearing deficit (defined as 20 dB hearing threshold level or worse in the better hearing ear). Tympanostomy tube placement is recommended when the effusion meets the above criteria and persists for longer than 4 months.
3. Systemic decongestants/antihistamines are ineffective and were not recommended for any age group.
4. Steroid therapy was not recommended for any age group.
5. Adenoidectomy was not recommended for this age group (1 to 3 years).
6. Tonsillectomy was not recommended for any age group.
7. With regard to allergy management and other therapies, such as chiropractic, holistic, naturopathic, traditional or indigenous, and homeopathic, no recommendations were made.

We have published our opinion as to the strengths and weaknesses of this *Guideline*.[138] The *Guideline* recommends either observation or active treatment with an oral antimicrobial agent as options when the duration of effusion is less than 3 months. We agree with this recommendation not only for children in the 1- to 3-year-old age group, but also for children who are older than 3 years of age.

There are many factors that should enter into management decisions. One important factor is the status of the child's hearing. The recommendation in the *Guideline* is to test a child's hearing when the effusion persists for 3 months or longer; if there is bilateral effusion and hearing loss of 20 dB or worse, treatment should be instituted. We are concerned about this recommendation for the following reasons: (1) hearing loss is not the only factor that should enter into the clinician's decision-making process; (2) the availability and feasibility of testing infants and children in the usual primary-care setting is uncertain; and (3) the level of hearing loss selected is arbitrary and not based on data that established that a chosen level is more or less deleterious than another. More importantly, two clinical trials, in which hearing was tested monthly for up to 3 years in children who had persistent otitis media with effusion, revealed that hearing fluctuated over the period.[689, 690] In the first trial, subjects who had normal or only mild hearing loss were randomly assigned to be observed (i.e., control group), and half of these children subsequently developed "significant" hearing loss during the first year of the trial and had tympanostomy tubes inserted, since they were designated as "treatment failures."[690]

We also recommend assessing hearing when the effusion is chronic, but only if such an assessment is practical. Ideally, determination of the level of hearing would be helpful prior to consideration for tympanostomy tube insertion.[153] However, if the child is found to have relatively normal hearing at one time and is to be observed and not actively treated, we advise serial evaluations to determine whether the hearing has deteriorated. Formal audiometric testing is not necessarily needed at these intervals, since gross evaluation of the hearing is often sufficient. Development of hearing loss or delay or alteration in the child's speech and language would prompt the clinician to actively treat, rather than continue to observe, the child.

In addition to the problem of hearing fluctuation associated with middle-ear effusion, structural changes, such as cholesteatoma, ossicular dislocation, and adhesive otitis media, can develop within the middle ear (although the incidence is probably low) secondary to persistent inflammation, irrespective of the level of hearing in that ear. Numerous reports describe long-term sequelae in children who had cleft palate and chronic otitis media with effusion and who where evaluated before tympanostomy tubes were employed as often as they are today; these sequelae included relatively high rates of permanent conductive/sensorineural hearing loss as well as development of cholesteatoma in an unacceptable number of patients[1001] (see Management of Special Populations: Infants and Children with Cleft Palate, later in this chapter).

Factors other than hearing loss that we consider important in making the decision to initiate medical treatment include (1) presence of bilateral effusion in contrast to disease in only one ear; (2) pneumatic otoscopic examination that reveals complete opacification, and limited or no mobility of the tympanic membrane, as opposed to a tympanic membrane that has good mobility and is translucent, in which only bubbles of air or an air-fluid level is present; (3) occurrence in young infants, because it is difficult to assess hearing in the usual clinical setting in this age group, and because they are unable to communicate about their symptoms and may have suppurative disease; (4) one or more insertions of tympanostomy tubes in a single patient or an adenoidectomy in the past, because these factors put the child at higher risk for persistent and recurrent disease than those children who have had no prior surgery for otitis; (5) presence of cleft palate or other craniofacial abnormalities, upper respiratory allergy, or a deficiency or impairment of immunologic status; (6) an associated acute purulent upper respiratory tract infection; (7) concurrent permanent conductive or sensorineural hearing loss, especially in children who rely on a hearing aid; (8) presence of dysequilibrium, vertigo, or tinnitus; (9) alterations of the tympanic membrane, such as severe atelectasis, especially a deep retraction pocket in the posterosuperior quadrant or the pars flaccida, or both; (10) middle-ear changes, such as adhesive otitis or ossicular involvement; (11) effusion that persists for 3 months or longer, i.e., chronic otitis media with effusion; or (12) when the episodes recur frequently, such as in 6 or more of the preceding 12 months.

We recommend amoxicillin for first-line therapy, when antibiotic treatment is elected, since the clinical trials by Mandel et al[687, 688] demonstrated efficacy, and no other microbial agent has been more effective than amoxicillin. Mandel et al[687] showed that cefaclor and erythromycin-sulfisoxazole are not as effective. However, other antimicrobial agents that are beta-lactamase–stable drugs, such as amoxicillin-clavulanate, or an oral cephalosporin (other than cefaclor) in therapeutic doses may be effective, since they provide more complete coverage. The dosage schedule is a therapeutic dosage for 2 weeks; to date, there are no published clinical trials that have shown that therapy longer than 2 weeks is effective. If children clear the effusion, they should be reevaluated at monthly intervals because of the high rate of recurrence of effusion. If children fail to clear the effusion and were candidates for placement of tympanostomy tubes, then the procedure is performed.

The efficacy of medical treatment, such as decongestants, antihistamines, and steroids for decreasing the duration of middle-ear effusions, as well as the role of tympanostomy tube insertion and adenoidectomy, is discussed subsequently in this chapter.

Strategies for Antibiotic Treatment of Acute Otitis Media

Amoxicillin has been the drug of choice for initial therapy of acute otitis media since its introduction in the early 1970s because of its spectrum of activity against the major bacterial pathogens, its low cost, and the infrequency of side effects. There are, however, an increasing proportion of nonsusceptible pneumococci and beta-lactamase–producing H. influenzae and M. catarrhalis organisms causing acute otitis media that require an answer to the question: Is amoxicillin still the drug of choice for initial therapy of acute otitis media?

The conclusion of the Drug Resistant S. pneumoniae Therapeutic Working Group,[293] convened by the CDC, was that amoxicillin remains the antimicrobial drug of first choice for treatment of uncomplicated acute otitis media (see Table 25–45). The bases for the recommendation were the following: (1) amoxicillin displays the best pharmacodynamic profile (longest time above MIC 90) against drug-resistant pneumococci of any of the commonly available oral agents; (2) it has a long record of safety and clinical efficacy in treating otitis media; (3) it has a narrower spectrum of activity than many of the alternative agents; and (4) low cost. The recommendation recognized that beta-lactamase production that would in-

activate amoxicillin was identified in about 35% of strains of H. influenzae and 90% of strains of M. catarrhalis, but that otitis media due to these two pathogens was more likely to resolve spontaneously.

Administration of amoxicillin in standard doses achieves peak middle-ear fluid concentrations of 1 to 6 μg/mL,[411, 609, 620, 786] which would be expected to inhibit susceptible and most intermediate strains of pneumococci. Higher doses of amoxicillin (70–90 mg/kg per day) in two doses would achieve concentrations in the middle ear of 3 to 8 μg/mL for 3 or more hours after the dose.[996] These concentrations would be likely to inhibit most of the nonsusceptible strains of pneumococci. The CDC working group suggested the use of the higher dosage as initial therapy for high-risk patients whereas patients at low risk for infection with resistant strains may continue to be treated with the standard dose of 40 to 45 mg/kg per day. Parents should be counseled to bring the child to the physician if there is no resolution of signs or symptoms within 48 hours, at which time the patient can be reevaluated and an alternative medication prescribed.

The recommendations for the continued use of amoxicillin (particularly in the higher dosage) are appropriate because of the expected low failure rates for children with acute otitis media treated with amoxicillin. Based on the following calculations, the current expected clinical failure rate for children with acute otitis media treated with amoxicillin would be 6% or less:

- S. pneumoniae is responsible for about 40% of cases of acute otitis media. If 25% are highly resistant to penicillin, about 8% of acute otitis media cases would be due to a penicillin-resistant pneumococcus. But, about 20% of these cases would be expected to resolve spontaneously. Therefore, the likely clinical failure rate for a child with pneumococcal acute otitis media treated with amoxicillin would be about 6%.
- H. influenzae is responsible for about 25% of cases of acute otitis media. If 30% are beta-lactamase–producing strains, about 8% of all cases of acute otitis media would be due to a beta-lactamase–producing strain of H. influenzae. But, about 50% of these cases would be expected to resolve spontaneously. Therefore, the likely clinical failure rate for a child with H. influenzae acute otitis media treated with amoxicillin would be about 4%.

Because rates of resistance vary by region in the United States, physicians can calculate the likely chances of clinical failure in acute otitis media due to either of the two major pathogens and consider whether or not amoxicillin continues to be the drug of choice in their community.

Alternatives to Amoxicillin for Therapy of Acute Otitis Media. Eighteen drugs are approved for treatment of acute otitis media by the FDA, including the following (see Table 25–29):

- Amoxicillin and amoxicillin-clavulanate
- Nine oral cephalosporins—cefaclor, loracarbef, cefixime, ceftibuten, cefpodoxime, cefprozil, cefuroxime axetil, cefdinir, and cephalexin

- One parenteral cephalosporin—ceftriaxone
- Three macrolides—erythromycin combined with sulfisoxazole, azithromycin, and clarithromycin
- One sulfonamide combination—trimethoprim-sulfamethoxazole
- One trimethoprim
- One ofloxacin otic for children with tympanostomy tubes

Although there are varying qualities among these drugs, including in vitro activity, acceptability, and cost, all have been found by the FDA to be safe and effective.

If amoxicillin remains the drug of choice for therapy of uncomplicated acute otitis media, which drug or drugs should be considered when amoxicillin fails? There is no one ideal agent for treatment of acute otitis media—amoxicillin is susceptible to inactivation by beta-lactamase–producing organisms and each of the other drugs approved for acute otitis has some limitation. Although experts agree about the use of amoxicillin, the choice of an alternative agent is more controversial. The CDC Working group listed choices (see Table 25–45) based on whether or not the child had received an antimicrobial agent in the prior 30 days. If no therapy had been received, the recommendations included high-dose amoxicillin-clavulanate, cefuroxime axetil, or three daily doses of intramuscular ceftriaxone. If the child had received antibiotics during the prior 30 days, the group recommended initial therapy with high-dose amoxicillin, high-dose amoxicillin-clavulanate, or cefuroxime axetil. If treatment failure followed use of one of these regimens, the recommendations included three daily doses of intramuscular ceftriaxone, clindamycin, or tympanocentesis.

Each of the recommended alternatives to amoxicillin for treatment of otitis media is reasonable, but each has some limiting feature:

- High-dose amoxicillin-clavulanate responds to concern about failure of amoxicillin due to beta-lactamase–producing organisms but would not provide an advantage if failure was due to high-level resistant pneumococci.
- Cefuroxime axetil has an excellent in vitro profile against S. pneumoniae and H. influenzae but has a bitter taste and is not well accepted by young patients. Cefdinir has a similar in vitro profile, demonstrated clinical efficacy, and is well accepted by infants and children. For these reasons, cefdinir may be preferable to cefuroxime axetil as the oral cephalosporin that is an alternative to amoxicillin.[867, 1059]
- Intramuscular ceftriaxone in a schedule of three daily doses was recommended based on limited information about the efficacy of three doses.[402, 634] Although one dose has been found to be effective for treatment of acute otitis media,[62] the Working Group chose three doses as more likely to provide efficacy for amoxicillin failures. Parents would be discouraged by the regimen of three intramuscular doses.
- Clindamycin has a low rate of pneumococcal resistance but has minimal activity against H. influenzae and M. catarrhalis. The physician would need to know that the episode was due to S. pneumoniae (presumably on the basis of a positive culture of middle-ear fluid). Because this circumstance is likely to be uncommon, the recommendation of clindamycin has limited utility.

All of these choices of alternatives to amoxicillin are likely to be effective in the majority of children with acute otitis media, but some choices may be better than others for a particular patient. The physician responsible for the care of the child with acute otitis media benefits from the recommendations of consensus panels, such as the Working Group, but must tailor the recommendations to the needs of the patient.

Management of the Child Who is Allergic to Beta-Lactam Drugs

Because of a history of allergic reaction to one or more beta-lactam drugs, some children require an alternative antimicrobial agent. TMP-SMZ and the macrolides are the only currently available products for the beta-lactam–allergic child with acute otitis media. Because the resistance of pneumococci to TMP-SMZ is high in many regions of the United States, and in some areas more frequent than penicillin resistance, the combination drug must be used only in communities where it is known to still be effective. Among the macrolides, erythromycin plus sulfisoxazole is effective, but some children will refuse the agent because of taste[1060] or gastrointestinal upset. A 5-day regimen of azithromycin or a 10-day course of clarithromycin may be preferred.

Taste. A number of investigators have used novel techniques in adults to assess the taste of suspensions to be administered to children. Several studies used a blinded taste test (see Table 25–36). Loracarbef, cephalexin, cefixime, and cefaclor came out as best in taste in a comparison of antimicrobial suspensions.[277, 954] Some antimicrobial agents have a bitter taste that raises concern about compliance in infants and children. In a recent examination by Steele et al[1060] of the palatability of antimicrobial suspensions, cefuroxime axetil, cefpodoxime, and erythromycin plus sulfisoxazole were judged "so unpalatable as to potentially jeopardize compliance." For further information, see the section on Compliance.

Side Effects. Diarrhea is more frequent in patients who receive amoxicillin-clavulanate than in those who receive therapeutic doses of the new cephalosporins.

Administrative Advantages. Once-a-day preparations such as cefixime, ceftibuten, and azithromycin have advantages in achieving compliance, but twice-a-day preparations such as cefuroxime axetil, cefprozil, cefpodoxime, and clarithromycin can be administered in the morning and evening at home without concern for administration at day care or in school. Cefixime does not require refrigeration—an advantage for parents who are traveling with their children.

Cost. New trade preparations are likely to be much more expensive than drugs that are available in generic form, such as amoxicillin and TMP-SMX.

Dosage Schedules and Duration of Therapy. Dosage schedules have been determined on the basis of studies of clinical pharmacology and results of clinical trials. For many years, the standard duration of oral therapy was 10 to 14 days, although it is uncertain how that course was decided. Results of studies that addressed the issue of duration of therapy suggest that many children improve with shorter courses of therapy, but some may require longer treatment.[47, 224, 239, 425, 485, 487, 528, 739, 893] Five days of a single dose per day of azithromycin was found to provide clinical results equivalent to 10 days of amoxicillin/clavulanate.[35] A 5-day course of oral cefpodoxime is also approved by the Food and Drug Administration (FDA). A single dose of intramuscular ceftriaxone, which provides concentrations of active drug in the middle ear for 48 hours or longer, was clinically equivalent to 10 days of amoxicillin[439] or TMP-SMX.[62]

Some patients may require a longer duration of therapy. Infants younger than 2 years of age have higher rates of success with 10 than with 5 days of amoxicillin/clavulanate.[239] The success rate in children younger than 2 years who received amoxicillin/clavulanate in a twice-a-day dosage schedule for 10 days was twice that of children who received the drug for 5 days.[494] Children 6 to 12 years of age had equivalent clinical success with the 5- or 10-day regimens; children 2 to 5 years of age were benefited by 10-day rather than 5-day regimens. The study by Hendrickse et al[485] suggested that patients with acute otitis media with intact tympanic membranes were satisfactorily treated with a 5-day course, but children with spontaneous purulent drainage required longer therapy. Paradise[842] reviewed current studies of short-course antimicrobial therapy for acute otitis media and concluded that the short course was inadequate for infants and young children.

A consensus panel of experts from the CDC and the AAP suggested that many children could be treated satisfactorily with a duration of therapy of 5 to 7 days.[295] The recommendation was based on the desire to reduce the selective pressure of antibiotics in the community and in the individual patient. The recommendations include important exclusions to using a 5- to 7-day course: most importantly excluded are children younger than 2 years of age who are at increased risk for treatment failure even with traditional dosage schedules, children with severe or complicated acute otitis media including perforation of the tympanic membrane, and children with histories of severe and recurrent acute otitis media. Other than the 5-day courses of azithromycin and cefpodoxime and single-dose intramuscular ceftriaxone, the short-course therapeutic regimens should be reserved for children 2 years of age and older with uncomplicated disease.

Failure to Respond to Initial Therapy. With appropriate antimicrobial therapy, most children with acute bacterial otitis media are significantly improved within 48 to 72 hours. The physician should be in contact with the patient to ascertain that improvement has occurred. If the patient does not respond to initial therapy with ampicillin or amoxicillin, infection with a resistant strain of *H. influenzae* or *S. pneumoniae* should be considered. Toxicity with persistent or recurrent fever or otalgia should prompt the clinician to recommend tympanocentesis or myringotomy, or both, to identify the causative organism; a specific antimicrobial agent may then be chosen on the basis of the results of the culture of the middle-ear effusion and sensitivity testing. If signs persist but the child has no toxic symptoms and aspiration to culture the middle-ear effusion is not performed, the initial antimicrobial agent should be changed to a regimen to which most uncommon organisms, such as a beta-lactamase–producing *H. influenzae* or *M. catarrhalis,* would be sensitive. If amoxicillin was initially given, then the amoxicillin-clavulanate, a cephalosporin, or a sulfa-containing drug should be administered. If *S. pneumoniae* resistant to penicillin is isolated, results of antimicrobial agents will be needed to guide optimal therapy. Failure may also occur owing to failure of patients to comply with prescribed medication (see Table 25–37).

Decongestants and Antihistamines

Nasal and oral decongestants, administered either alone or in combination with an antihistamine, are currently among the most popular medications for the treatment of otitis media with effusion. The common concept is that these drugs reduce congestion of the mucosa of the eustachian tube; however, the efficacy of this mode of therapy for otitis media with effusion has not been demonstrated.

A number of investigators have evaluated decongestants with or without antihistamines, but the quality of design of the programs has varied and therefore the results are difficult to interpret.

1. Collipp[242] evaluated the use of phenylephrine hydrochloride nose drops in treating acute purulent otitis media with effusion in 180 children aged 2 to 14 years. Half of the children were treated with nasal spray by their parents four times per day; the other half received no decongestant. All subjects were given an initial injection of procaine penicillin G and a 10-day course of sulfisoxazole, chlorpheniramine maleate, and phenylephrine hydrochloride. No statistical differences were noted between the otologic status of the children who received the nasal spray and the otologic status of those who did not.

2. Rubenstein et al[950] treated 462 episodes of otitis media with effusion using several antimicrobial agents and the decongestant pseudoephedrine. Although some improvement was noted to be the result of treatment with the antimicrobial agents, the addition of pseudoephedrine to the medication regimen did not appear to improve treatment results significantly.

3. Miller[743] evaluated the effect of a decongestant mixture containing carbinoxamine maleate and pseudoephedrine hydrochloride on 13 children with tympanostomy tubes that had been inserted to treat recurrent otitis media with effusion. The study used drug or placebo in a limited double-blind crossover design. The success of the placebo or drug was determined by the results of eustachian tube function tests that measured the ability to equilibrate applied negative middle-ear pressures. An almost equal number of patients demonstrated "suggestive" positive response or no re-

sponse to the drug, whereas none of the children showed any response to the placebo.

4. Stickler et al,[1067] in a follow-up to Rubenstein's study,[950] evaluated the effects of penicillin and antihistamine (chlorpheniramine maleate), of penicillin alone, and of penicillin with sulfonamides on otitis media with effusion. Although sulfonamides did not improve the effects of the penicillin, the addition of the antihistaminic agent to penicillin did produce better results.

5. Holmquist[499] reported the effect of a combination of ephedrine and antihistamine compared with that of a placebo in a double-blind study on eustachian tube function in 58 patients (62 ears). The eustachian tube function was evaluated by means of air pressure equalization and tympanometry. In the 28 ears of patients who received the drug, a "positive effect" was noted in 16 (57%), whereas of the 34 ears of subjects who received the placebo, a "positive effect" was reported in only six (18%); the difference was statistically significant at the 95% confidence level.

6. Olson et al[813] evaluated the efficacy of pseudoephedrine hydrochloride by studying the response to treatment of 96 children who had had acute otitis media with effusion that had not responded to treatment for 2 weeks. Following a double-blind protocol that compared the effects of the drug with those of the placebo, the children were treated for 4 or more weeks and were re-examined by pneumatic otoscopy and tympanometry. No significant differences between the treatment groups were found. Although the findings were not statistically significant, these researchers did note that males and children with an allergic history did worse on the decongestant.

7. In children with otitis media with effusion, Fraser et al[384] compared ephedrine nosedrops; a combination of brompheniramine maleate, phenylephrine hydrochloride, and phenylpropanolamine hydrochloride; autoinflation; and no treatment and found no difference in tympanic membrane compliance, middle ear pressure, or audiometric findings among the treatment groups. In addition to problems associated with documentation of otitis media with effusion, the investigators had eight treatment regimens with only 10 or 11 subjects in each group, which leads one to question the design and statistical analysis of the study.

8. In a double-blind study, Roth et al[945] showed that pseudoephedrine hydrochloride decreased nasal resistance in adults who had an upper respiratory infection. Past studies, employing a modified inflation-deflation manometric technique to assess eustachian tube function in children who had had recurrent or chronic otitis media with effusion, showed that the obstruction of the eustachian tube was functional rather than mechanical.[121, 193] Further studies during periods of upper respiratory infection, however, showed that eustachian tube function was decreased from the baseline measurements at these times.[125] This decrease was at-

tributed to intrinsic mechanical obstruction superimposed on the functional obstruction.

9. In an attempt to determine the effect of an oral decongestant with or without an antihistamine on the ventilatory function of the eustachian tube, two separate studies were conducted in 50 children who had had chronic or recurrent otitis media with effusion and in whom tympanostomy tubes had been inserted previously.[194] The first was a double-blind study that compared the effect of an oral decongestant, pseudoephedrine hydrochloride, with the effect of a placebo in 22 children who developed an upper respiratory infection during an observation period. Certain measures of eustachian tube function were significantly elevated above baseline values during the upper respiratory infection, which was attributed to intrinsic mechanical obstruction of the eustachian tube. It was found that oral decongestants tended to alter these parameters of eustachian tube function in the direction of the baseline (before upper respiratory infection) values. Even though the effect was statistically significant, the favorable changes in measurements of tubal function were only partial and were more prominent on the second day of the trial, after the subjects had received four doses of the decongestant. The administration of a nasal spray of 1% ephedrine, however, had no effect on eustachian tube function in these children.

The second study was a double-blind crossover design. In this study of 28 children who did not have an upper respiratory infection, the effect of a decongestant-antihistamine combination (pseudoephedrine hydrochloride and chlorpheniramine maleate) was compared with that of a placebo. When the subjects were given the decongestant-antihistamine medication, there were favorable changes in certain eustachian tube function measures that were not observed when the children received the placebo. Again, the response differences between the two groups were statistically significant. Even though these two studies indicated that an oral decongestant appeared to favorably affect the eustachian tube function of children who had an upper respiratory infection, and that the combination of an oral decongestant and antihistamine had a similar effect on tubal function in children without an upper respiratory infection, an evaluation of the efficacy of these commonly employed medications must await the results of controlled clinical trials in children with otitis media with effusion.

10. Lildholdt et al[643] evaluated the effect of a topical nasal decongestant spray on eustachian tube function in 40 children with tympanostomy tubes. Five parameters of tubal function were assessed, employing a modified-inflation test and forced-response test before and after spraying of the nose with either oxymetazoline hydrochloride or placebo, according to a double-blind study design. The results showed no significant differences between the two treatment groups of the study in

children who had severe functional tubal dysfunction, as documented by the constrictions of eustachian tube lumen during swallowing.

11. Cantekin et al,[196] in a double-blind, placebo-controlled, randomized clinical trial of an oral decongestant and antihistamine combination in 553 infants and children with otitis media with effusion, showed no efficacy of these drugs. In addition, side effects such as irritability and sleepiness were more common in children in the drug group than in subjects who received placebo.

12. Mandel et al[688] reported that amoxicillin was effective when compared with placebo in the treatment of otitis media with effusion. The addition of a combination of an oral decongestant and antihistamine to amoxicillin, however, provided no additional benefit over amoxicillin alone; more side effects were noted in children who received the decongestant and antihistamine combination.

13. Stillwagon et al[1068] recruited 10 adult volunteers who had ragweed allergic rhinitis and underwent progressive intranasal challenge with ragweed pollen out of the ragweed season. Prior to the challenge, the subjects received either chlorpheniramine maleate and phenylpropanolamine or placebo in a double-blind randomized crossover design. All the subjects had had objective measurements of nasal and eustachian tube function prior to and following the challenge. They found a beneficial effect of the drug therapy on nasal and eustachian tube function as compared with placebo and concluded that there is a role for antihistamine-decongestant treatment of allergic rhinitis as well as potential allergen-induced eustachian tube dysfunction.

14. Turner and Darden[1144] evaluated the effect of intranasal instillation of a topical adrenergic decongestant, phenylephrine nose drops, in decreasing abnormal middle-ear pressures that developed in infants who had a common cold. They found no significant difference in abnormal negative middle-ear pressures between subjects randomized to receive the topical decongestants and those randomized to placebo nose drops 1 hour following installation.

The conclusion from these studies is that topical or systemic decongestants and antihistamines for otitis media with effusion are not warranted but may be effective for less severe conditions such as eustachian tube obstruction.[194] Also, these agents may be effective for those patients who have allergic rhinitis causing their tubal dysfunction.[1068] In children receiving systemic decongestants and antihistamines, however, side effects are common, and some, such as visual hallucinations, are quite disturbing. Even though extended use of the topical nasal decongestant, oxymetazoline, has been reported to not cause rebound nasal swelling in adults, the effect of long-term use in children has not been reported.[1218] Also, in a recent randomized, double-blind, placebo-controlled study by Clemens et al,[232] the combination of an antihistamine-decongestant did not even relieve the symptoms of the

common cold in 59 preschool children but did have a significantly greater sedative effect than placebo.

The guideline *Otitis Media with Effusion in Young Children* concluded that antihistamine/decongestant therapy is ineffective and did not recommend treatment with these agents for this disease for infants and children of any age.[1069]

Corticosteroids

New insights into the pathogenesis of inflammation and the key roles played by inflammatory mediators directed the attention of investigators to the use of anti-inflammatory drugs to prevent central nervous system pathologic conditions and resultant sequelae.[360] The results of animal studies indicated the efficacy of dexamethasone in reducing brain water content, cerebrospinal fluid pressure, cerebrospinal fluid pleocytosis, lactate concentration, tumor necrosis factor (TNF) activity, and other indices of meningeal inflammation. These studies were the basis for a series of investigations in children with meningitis. The results indicated the efficacy of dexamethasone in the prevention of hearing loss and other neurologic sequelae when the drug was administered at the time of or before the use of antimicrobial agents for infants with meningitis due to *H. influenzae* or *S. pneumoniae*.

The role of inflammatory mediators in acute otitis media and otitis media with effusion is still obscure, but current investigations should yield information to provide a basis for the use of corticosteroids in children with middle-ear infection. The administration of corticosteroids in the form of either a topical nasal spray or a systemic preparation has been advocated for the treatment of otitis media with effusion for the past two decades. Heisse[482] reported excellent results with depomethylprednisone in 30 allergic patients who had otitis media with effusion. Oppenheimer[815, 816] recommended a short-term trial of corticosteroids in children. Shea[1008] also reported success in treating allergic children who had middle ear effusions with a 4-day course of prednisone. Persico et al[860] rated one group of 160 children with prednisone and ampicillin and another group of 116 children with ampicillin only. They reported a 53% resolution of the effusion in the group that received the steroid and ampicillin treatment, as compared with 13% in the group that was treated only with the antibiotic. None of these studies, however, was a randomized, controlled trial.

1. Schwartz et al[987] reported 70% success in treating 41 children with a 7-day course of prednisone in a double-blind, placebo-controlled, crossover study. The steroid appeared to be equally effective in those children who did and in those who did not have a history of allergy. Resolution of otitis media with effusion was reported by Podoshin et al[874] in a double-blind, randomized, prospective study comparing a combination of amoxicillin and prednisone with an amoxicillin-treated group and a placebo-treated group.

2. Berman et al[88, 89] have evaluated the use of prednisone and trimethoprim-sulfamethoxazole for children with persistent middle-ear effusion. A suffi-

cient number of children experienced complete resolution with 1 month of therapy to warrant consideration of this approach prior to placement of tympanostomy tubes.

3. Macknin and Jones,[680] however, conducted a controlled trial in children with either otitis media with effusion or persistent middle-ear effusion after acute otitis media who were randomly assigned to enter a course of dexamethasone or placebo. The study was stopped before the trial was completed, since the investigators found no benefit in giving the drug. Daly et al[267] found temporary resolution of effusion in children who received prednisone and TMP-SMX for 2 weeks, but the duration of aerated middle ear was similar in the placebo recipients and the treated patients, indicating that the benefit of steroids was short lived.

Studies have been reported that have evaluated the effects of administering a topical corticosteroid nasal spray. Schwartz et al[987] noted, however, that when beclomethasone dipropionate spray was given to 10 children with otitis media with effusion, it was effective in only 3. Lildholdt et al,[643] in a double-blind study employing beclomethasone nasal spray in children with otitis media with effusion, failed to show efficacy. A study by Shapiro et al[1006] did show some therapeutic effect of 3 weeks of daily administration of nasal dexamethasone (versus placebo) in 45 children 2 to 10 years of age with eustachian tube dysfunction, but the authors also reported "worrisome cortisol changes" in 2 subjects.

1. Rosenfeld et al[942] reported the results of their meta-analysis of the effect of systemic steroids on otitis media with effusion. They included 8 of the 10 published studies in their analysis and found that systemic steroids were beneficial, especially when combined with antimicrobial therapy, but they concluded that the question of safety and efficacy still had not been adequately answered.

2. Berman[91] recommended a regimen of corticosteroid and antibiotic for management of otitis media with effusion persisting for 6 to 9 weeks or longer: prednisone in two divided doses for 7 days combined with a broad-spectrum antibiotic, such as TMP-SMX, for 21 days. He estimated that the probability of cure of the effusion was 15% for observation only, 39% for antibiotic alone, and 64% for antibiotic plus steroid.[95]

3. Hemlin et al,[483] in a randomized, double-blind, placebo-controlled study, evaluated the effect of a combination of cefixime and betamethasone for treatment of chronic otitis media with effusion in 142 children 2 to 12 years of age and found a 24% rate difference between cefixime with betamethasone versus cefixime with placebo, but no long-term effect due to the high relapse rate in both groups. Both treatments were significantly better than no treatment (placebo), but again had no long-term efficacy.

4. Most recently, Mandel et al[686] reported the outcome of a randomized, double-blind, placebo-controlled clinical trial of the effect of the combination of amoxicillin and prednisolone in 144 patients aged 12 months to 9 years who had chronic otitis media with effusion. The rate difference in the proportion effusion-free patients at 2 weeks between the amoxicillin with steroid-placebo group and amoxicillin with active-steroid group was approximately 17%, but this effect was less at 4 weeks and was no longer statistically significant. The investigators concluded that the lack of a dramatic and long-lasting effect precluded a recommendation for use in all children with chronic otitis media with effusion.

If, indeed, adrenocorticosteroid therapy is effective in the treatment of otitis media with effusion, the mode of action remains only speculative at this time but may be related to the anti-inflammatory action of the drug. The most promising area of investigation in the pathogenesis of middle-ear effusion remains the action of microbial organisms and products and the induction of inflammatory mediators. Persico et al[860] postulated that the drug altered the surface tension forces within the lumen of the eustachian tube. Schwartz et al[987] suggested that steroids may shrink the lymphoid tissue around the eustachian tube, acting on mucoproteins to decrease the viscosity of the middle-ear effusion by reducing tubal edema or reversing metaplasia of the middle-ear mucosa.

From these few studies, it appears that a short course of systemic adrenocorticosteroid therapy is of uncertain safety and efficacy in alleviating the problems of otitis media with effusion in children. At this time, the potential adverse side effects associated with the administration of a systemic adrenocorticosteroid for otitis media does not appear to justify its routine use in infants and children. Indeed, the *Guideline, Otitis Media with Effusion in Young Children* concluded that corticosteroid therapy in children is not recommended treatment for infants and children of any age because of its unproven efficacy and potential adverse side effects.[1069]

Allergy Control, Immunotherapy, and Systemic and Topical Medications

Since the precise role of allergy in the development of otitis media with effusion has not been documented, and since at times it is difficult to establish or confirm the diagnosis of allergy with certainty, it is not possible at this time to quantify the relative efficacy of allergic management of otitis media with effusion in children. This topic is discussed further in the section on Physiology, Pathophysiology, and Pathogenesis (Dysfunction Related to Allergy), earlier in this chapter. In spite of this dilemma, owing to a lack of information, there are clinicians who advocate allergy management for infants and children who have recurrent or chronic otitis media with effusion. Other physicians doubt that allergy plays any part in the origin of otitis media with effusion and rarely, if ever, consider directing their treatment of a patient with this problem to a possible underlying allergy. For example, Bluestone and Shurin[150] and Paradise,[840] in extensive reviews of otitis media in infants and children, did not include control of allergy as a management option. On the other hand, there are those who include allergy in the differential diagnosis if there are one or more of the following factors: (1) past or present atopy in the child, (2) family history of allergy, or (3) signs of upper respiratory allergy present at the time of the clinical examination. These investigators have employed various regimens in their management of allergies, but all have reported obtaining good results from such treatment.[315, 316, 367, 594, 864, 911, 1186]

Clemis[236] considers inhalant allergy the easiest to identify and treat and therefore advocates searching for inhalant sensitivities before looking for allergies to foods and chemicals. In his experience, house dust is the most frequent inhalant allergen identified. When house dust is identified as the problem, he advises "dust-proofing" the child's environment (especially the child's bedroom) and using electrostatic air filters. If environmental control measures are not successful in reducing symptoms, then hyposensitization to house dust may be considered. Mold spores are the second most common aeroallergen responsible for nonpollen allergy, for which he advocates environmental control, and, if unsuccessful, hyposensitization. The treatment of choice when an adverse food reactivity is suspected is total dietary elimination of that food. In Clemis' experience,[236] pollinosis plays a much less dominant role than dusts, molds, and foods in causing otitis media, but when pollinosis is present, he recommends hyposensitization. Pets may also be a source of allergy, but in this case, hyposensitization is not as successful as exclusion of the offending pet from the house. In Clemis's view,[236] antihistamines are not of benefit in treating otitis media caused by allergy, and he advises against the use of cortisone, in either the systemic or topical intranasal forms, for therapy. Waickman[1170] agrees with Clemis that house dust is the most common allergic offender in patients who have otitis media with effusion that persists for 2 weeks or longer and has been unresponsive to adequate therapy for infection. Other inhalant antigens are considered to be less common offenders than dust, but for all inhalants, the Rinkel method of immunotherapy is advocated.[925]

In a double-blind, crossover study by Friedman et al[390] that involved adult volunteers without otitis media, eustachian tubes became obstructed when the subjects were challenged intranasally with the antigen to which they were sensitive but not when they were challenged with a placebo (i.e., an antigen to which they were not sensitive). In a subsequent study, Skoner et al[1037] showed that nasal and eustachian tube function was altered during natural pollen exposure.

In animal studies from Japan, Mogi and coworkers[754, 756] concluded that IgE-mediated immune reaction in the middle ear is a causative factor in the production of middle ear effusion, and that the eustachian tube is anatomically and functionally altered in type I allergic reactions of the nose, but tubal dysfunction is transient and does not result in a middle-ear effusion. They concluded, however, that this dysfunction does interfere with middle-ear and tubal clearance. To date, there is no animal model that verifies that allergic nasal and tubal disease causes a middle-ear effusion. In the human, the allergic condition is prolonged, which then could result in an effusion, and an animal model that corresponds to the pathogenesis in the human has just not been developed.

Hurst and Venge[519] and Hurst[517] demonstrated an elevated level of eosinophil cationic protein in the middle-ear effusion and the mucosa of patients with allergies and otitis media, which suggests that type I allergy has a role in the pathogenesis of otitis media.

Bernstein[111] suggests that there is some supporting evidence that food immune complexes, mainly dairy products, may be an important etiologic factor in infants who are otitis-prone. There is no study reported, however, that has shown that elimination of dairy products in otitis-prone infants is effective.

Unfortunately, none of these studies was based on randomized, controlled trials in children with otitis media. Nevertheless, there does appear to be some evidence that chronic and recurrent otitis media with effusion may be associated with upper respiratory tract allergy. Therefore, until our knowledge of the origin, method of diagnosis, and management of allergy in relation to otitis media with effusion increases, when a child has recurrent or chronic middle-ear disease and evidence of upper respiratory tract allergy, management of the allergy should be considered as a treatment option. A history of itching of the eyes, nose, or throat; of paroxysms of sneezing; and of chronic or frequently recurrent watery rhinorrhea in the presence or absence of the classic signs of nasal allergy should prompt the clinician to evaluate further the possibility that the child has an upper respiratory tract allergy. Since no convincing clinical trials of the treatment options have been reported, however, no single method of treatment can be recommended. Currently, we recommend allergy control and, in selected children, immunotherapy.

Even though clinical trials that evaluated the safety and efficacy of the newer topical nasal steroids (e.g., beclomethasone aqueous) have not been reported, we do recommend their use in the hope that improved nasal function will improve eustachian tube function, and subsequently prevent and even treat middle-ear effusion. The use of intranasal cromolyn sodium may also be beneficial, but again there are no data to support its use, and most children have difficulty with compliance, since it must be used frequently during the day. Again, even though there are no data to support the use of the antihistamine-decongestant combinations in allergic children who have otitis media, there is some evidence from the study by Stillwagon et al[1068] that these agents may be of benefit in adults. Also, a recently reported study in an animal model of otitis media and nasal allergy by Suzuki et al[1087] showed a beneficial effect of the antiallergic drug azelastine hydrochloride in promoting clearance of middle-ear effusion.

It does not seem favorable at present to treat for allergy those children who have recurrent or chronic or both types of middle-ear effusion and who lack the signs and symptoms of upper respiratory tract allergy. This could change, however, in the event that convincing data were presented to establish that the middle ear is a shock organ. The *Guideline, Otitis Media with Effusion in Young Children* had no recommendation regarding allergy management of otitis media with effusion in an otherwise healthy child aged 1 through 3 years, based on insufficient evidence clarifying the relationship between allergy and otitis media with effusion.[1069]

Other Medical Therapies

Since there is some evidence that surfactant may play a role in eustachian tube function,[116, 433, 492] there may be a role for treatment of eustachian tube dysfunction and otitis media with nebulized surfactant. Indeed, studies in animal models have demonstrated some beneficial effect of this therapy,[380, 792] but clinical studies with nebulized surfactant have not been reported.

Alternative and Complementary Therapies

Various alternative and complementary therapies, including osteopathic and chiropractic manipulation, use of herbal remedies, and homeopathic medicine are used in the management of otitis media. The scientific base for evaluating these therapies is almost nonexistent, but some investigators are framing questions for appropriate study to identify safety as well as efficacy.

Garlic extract has activity against multidrug-resistant pneumococci, beta-lactamase–producing *H. influenzae*, and methicillin-resistant *S. aureus*[357] and had a synergistic effect with vancomycin against vancomycin-resistant enterococci.[545] Unfortunately, the anti-bacterial activity of garlic disappears when the extract is heated and does not survive the acid pH of gastric juice.[357]

Herbal and homeopathic remedies are used extensively for treatment of acute and chronic otitis media. Claims for various herbs include the decongestant effect of ephedra leaves and stalks, the anti-inflammatory effects of chamomile, and the immune-stimulating effect of echinacea leaves, stalks, and roots.[577] Barnett et al[59] evaluated homeopathic treatment of acute otitis media in a pilot study of 24 children. Although only 2 children required treatment with antibiotic therapy, this result may be no more than expected for resolution of acute otitis media without use of antimicrobial agents. The authors indicate the challenges of evaluating homeopathic therapy for acute and chronic otitis media, including demographic differences in families who seek homeopathic vs. allopathic care, the large number of homeopathic remedies used (10 different medications were used for the initial therapy in the 24 patients), the possible differences in outcome measures (failure of one homeopathic medicine to cure the disease is not viewed as a failure of therapy if a subsequent homeopathic medicine cures the patient).

Chiropractic manipulation is used for children with acute and chronic otitis media. Two studies of appropriate design have evaluated the efficacy of such treatment, but Sawyer et al[976] conducted a pilot study in 20 patients 6 months to 6 years of age with otitis media with effusion. The investigators concluded that a randomized controlled trial would be feasible.

Specific Medical Options for Prevention of Recurrent Otitis Media

Prevention of new episodes of acute otitis media in children who are "otitis-prone" may be achieved by a variety of surgical and medical procedures and alteration of the environment. Chemoprophylaxis with the use of modified courses of antimicrobial agents for prolonged periods of time has been studied extensively and found to be successful. New products with anti-infective qualities are in the early stages of investigation for prevention of recurrent acute otitis media: Xylitol was demonstrated in two studies to reduce the incidence of acute otitis media in Finnish children; oligosaccharides prevent adhesion of microbial pathogens to carbohydrate receptors on mucosal cell surfaces and is currently under study in Finland for the prevention of otitis media. Immunization with the new seven-valent pneumococcal vaccine and various virus vaccines suggest promise in limiting the impact of infectious agents in causing acute infections. Placement of tympanostomy tubes and adenoidectomy have been effective in reducing the incidence of acute middle-ear infections. Finally, parents of children with problems of middle-ear infections can be empowered to limit the risks for acute infection in their child (see also section on Epidemiology, earlier in this chapter).

Antimicrobial Chemoprophylaxis

The rationale for the use of chemoprophylaxis for the prevention of acute otitis media is that a modified dose of antimicrobial agents administered over a prolonged period of time will decrease the rate or intensity of upper respiratory tract colonization by bacterial pathogens. Once the bacterial load is reduced, even though the child is still vulnerable to viral respiratory infections or allergic reactions that can obstruct the eustachian tube, the proliferation of bacteria that produces acute otitis media is less likely to occur.

Since prolonged courses of any drug may have harmful effects, the physician must be assured that the benefits of decreased risk of infection outweigh the risks of prolonged usage of the drug. For any form of chemoprophylaxis, the following criteria should be considered:

1. The patient is at risk if infection occurs.
2. The microorganisms are known and are consistent causes of disease.
3. The microorganisms are unlikely to develop resistance to the drug used for a prolonged course.
4. The drug is well tolerated and can be administered in a convenient dosage and form.
5. The drug has limited side effects or toxicity.

Recurrent episodes of otitis media are of sufficient importance to warrant consideration of chemoprophylaxis. The bacteriology of otitis media is well documented and consistent: *S. pneumoniae, M. catarrhalis,* and nontypeable strains of *H. influenzae* are the major bacterial pathogens. The sulfonamides and penicillins are available in a variety of convenient forms that are well tolerated in infants and older children. Drug toxicity is minimal with these two families of drugs, but allergic reactions are to be expected. The most important concern, at present, is the risk of selective pressure of the drug for emergence of resistant organisms. The concern for the development of resistance warrants careful selection of children who would, on balance, benefit from a chemoprophylactic regimen.

Children are at risk for recurrent episodes of acute otitis media during a relatively short period of life: most episodes occur between 6 and 24 months of age. If the child who is susceptible to recurrent otitis media could be protected from infection during this period, the morbidity of middle ear disease in infancy might be limited.

Risks of Chemoprophylaxis

The major concerns with the use of chemoprophylaxis for prolonged periods of time are that resistant strains of bacteria will develop and be responsible for episodes of acute infection, and that the toxicity or side effects of the drug may increase with prolonged use.

There is a paucity of data about the bacteriology and antimicrobial susceptibility of bacteria responsible for breakthrough episodes during chemoprophylaxis. The few studies of middle-ear aspirates of episodes of acute otitis media during chemoprophylaxis suggest that the same species of bacteria are responsible—pneumococcus, H. influenzae, and M. catarrhalis—but there may be selection of resistant strains. In their study of amoxicillin prophylaxis versus placebo, Casselbrant et al[209] found the same proportion of bacterial species responsible for breakthrough episodes, including pneumococci and beta-lactamase–producing H. influenzae and M. catarrhalis; no unusual pathogens emerged to colonize the infants or cause acute otitis media; no susceptibility assays were done. An increase was identified in the number of penicillin-resistant bacteria in the oropharynx of 20 children receiving amoxicillin for prophylaxis for otitis media studied by Brook and Gober.[169]

None of the investigators of published reports of the use of chemoprophylaxis noted an increase in side effects or toxicity in the children who received prolonged modified courses of chemoprophylaxis. The incidence of side effects was no greater than would be expected from using the same drugs to treat acute infections.

Published Reports

Chemoprophylaxis is extensively used for the management of recurrent episodes of acute otitis media. A survey of children who had at least one episode of acute otitis media during the year and were cared for in a large health insurance plan in New England in 1994 and 1995 identified the use of chemoprophylaxis in 9% of the children for a mean duration of about 60 days.[1116] The drugs used for prophylaxis were amoxicillin, TMP-SMX, and sulfisoxazole, with about one third of patients on chemoprophylaxis receiving each drug. Breakthrough episodes were most frequent in the children receiving sulfisoxazole (20.4%) and least frequent in children receiving amoxicillin (13.2%) and TMP-SMX (15.5%). There are data from

subsequent years of analysis that the percentage of children who received chemoprophylaxis declined between the period of 1994 through 1995 (9%) and the period of 1997 through 1998 (5.6%) (Thompson et al, unpublished data).

Many reports of controlled clinical trials of modified courses of antimicrobial agents compared with placebo, surgery or historical controls have been published (Table 25–46). The majority of studies used a sulfonamide or ampicillin or amoxicillin, a few evaluated penicillin V or a macrolide (erythromycin or azithromycin), and some studies included a group with placement of tympanostomy tubes. Most of the reports indicated benefit to the enrollees: Amoxicillin efficacy varied from 44% to 67%; sulfonamides (including TMP-SMX) efficacy was 40% to 88%, with one low value of 8%. An exception to the experience of benefit to those who received chemoprophylaxis is a recent study by Roark and Berman[926]; no benefit was identified for children who received amoxicillin in a dosage of 20 mg/kg per day administered once or twice a day. The efficacy of intermittent use of the prophylactic agent with first signs of upper respiratory tract infection was variable.[114, 480, 884] Because the signs of upper respiratory tract infection and acute otitis media may be concurrent, intermittent use appears less likely to succeed than continuous use of chemoprophylaxis. A meta-analysis summarizing results of studies of chemoprophylaxis concluded that the benefit to treated children was an average decrease in the number of episodes of acute otitis media of 0.11 episodes per patient per month or about 1 episode per year. Children who were most likely to be benefited by chemoprophylaxis were younger than 2 years of age and in out-of-home child care.[1193]

Few of the studies evaluated middle-ear effusion or asymptomatic middle-ear effusion. Mandel et al[684] identified the efficacy of amoxicillin in the prevention of recurrent episodes of otitis media with effusion and a decreased percentage of time with middle-ear effusion as well as a decreased incidence of acute otitis media. The rates per person-year of new episodes of disease in the amoxicillin and placebo groups were as follows: acute otitis media, 0.28 vs. 1.04; and otitis media with effusion, 1.53 vs. 2.15.

The results of the various studies of chemoprophylaxis should be evaluated separately rather than cumulatively because of the variations in criteria for enrollees, differences in number of patients evaluated, different durations of drug use, and varying periods of observation. Nevertheless, the pattern of a decreased number of episodes in children who receive prolonged courses of appropriate antimicrobial agents is consistent.

Among the first and most influential investigations of chemoprophylaxis for children with recurrent acute otitis media was the study of Perrin et al[858] (Table 25–47). Sulfisoxazole or a placebo was administered to 54 children aged 11 months to 8 years who had three or more episodes in the previous 18 months or a total of five episodes. In the double-blind trial, children received a placebo or 500 mg of sulfisoxazole twice a day for 3 months. They were then switched to the alternate regimen for another 3-month period. A significant decrease in new episodes of acute otitis media occurred in the

TABLE 25–46. Selected Controlled Trials of Chemoprophylaxis in Children for Prevention of Acute Otitis Media (AOM)

Investigator	Study Design	Drugs and Daily Dosage
Maynard et al (1972) Alaska	Double-blind, placebo	Ampicillin 125–250 mg × 1
Perrin et al (1974) New York	Double-blind, placebo, crossover	Sulfisoxazole 500 mg × 2
Hughes et al (1977) Tennessee	Double-blind, placebo	TMP-SMX 75/375 mg × 2
Biedel (1978) Washington	Decongestant control	Sulfisoxazole 100–130 mg/kg°
Gray (1981) Alabama	Double-blind	TMP-SMX 4 mg/20 mg/kg × 1
Schwartz et al (1982) Washington, DC	Double-blind Placebo Crossover	Sulfamethoxazole 25 mg/kg × 1
Schuller (1983) Pennsylvania	No comparison drug	
Liston et al (1983) Texas	Double-blind Placebo Crossover	Sulfisoxazole 500 mg × 2
Varsano et al (1985) Israel	Double-blind Placebo Crossover	Sulfisoxazole 250–500 mg × 2
Persico et al (1978) Israel	Unblinded No prophylaxis	Penicillin V 25 mg/kg × 1
Lampe and Weir (1986) Texas	Historical control	Erythromycin ethylsuccinate 10 mg/kg dose × 2 Sulfisoxazole 500 mg × 2
Gonzalez et al (1986) Colorado/Washington	Double-blind Placebo	Sulfisoxazole 500 mg × 2 Ventilating tubes
Principi et al (1989) Milan	Single-blind Placebo	Amoxicillin 20 mg/kg × 1 TMP-SMX 12 mg/kg × 1
Casselbrant et al (1992) Pennsylvania	Placebo	Amoxicillin Ventilating tubes
Berman et al (1992) Colorado	Continuous vs. intermittent therapy	Amoxicillin 10 mg/kg × 2
Prellner et al (1994) Copenhagen	Intermittent vs. double-blind	Penicillin V Placebo
Heikinnen et al (1995) Turku, Tampere	Intermittent, double-blind Double-blind	Amoxicillin-clavulanate 40 mg/kg × 2
Marchisio et al (1996) Milan	Continuous, single-blind	Azithromycin 5–10 mg/kg (1 ×/week) Amoxicillin 20 mg/kg × 1
Roark and Berman (1997) Denver	Continuous, double-blind	Amoxicillin 20 mg/kg × 1–2 Placebo
Thompson et al (1999) Boston	Survey of insurance data	Amoxicillin Sulfisoxazole TMP-SMX

TMP-SMX, trimethoprim-sulfamethoxazole
° Also trisulfapyrimidine 100–300 mg/kg or sulfamethoxazole 55 mg/kg
From Bluestone CD, Klein JO. Otitis Media in Infants and Children, 3rd ed, Philadelphia, WB Saunders, 2001.

group of children receiving the antimicrobial agent. The older children, 6 to 8 years of age, showed a minimal or insignificant decrease in the incidence of otitis media when on the prophylactic regimen.

TABLE 25–47. Effects of Chemoprophylaxis with Sulfisoxazole on Recurrence of Acute Otitis Media

Drug	Number of Children (n = 54)	Number of Episodes	
		None	One or More
First Trial (12/72 to 2/73)			
Sulfisoxazole	28	25	3
Placebo	26	14	12
Second Trial (3/73 to 5/73)			
Sulfisoxazole	26	25	1
Placebo	28	19	9

Reprinted with permission from Perrin JM, Charney E, MacWhinney JB, Jr, et al. Sulfisoxazole as chemoprophylaxis for recurrent otitis media: a double-blind crossover study in pediatric practice. N Engl J Med 291:664, 1974.

Plan for Prophylaxis

We proposed a plan for chemoprophylaxis in the first issue of the *Pediatric Infectious Diseases Journal* in January 1982 that has continued to be of value over the years.[595] The principles have been reaffirmed by the American Academy of Pediatrics Report of the Committee on Infectious Diseases[20] and a consensus statement by members of the AAP and the CDC in 1998.[295]

Who? Children who have had three distinct and well documented episodes of acute otitis media in 6 months or four episodes in 12 months should be considered for the program. Because of the epidemiologic data that children who have episodes of acute infection early in life or have siblings with severe and recurrent ear infections are "otitis-prone," children who have one episode in the first 6 months of life and have a family history of ear infections, or have two episodes in the first year of life should be considered for chemoprophylaxis.

Which Drugs? A sulfonamide or amoxicillin were the agents used most frequently in published studies and provide the advantages of demonstrated efficacy, safety, and low cost. Trimethoprim-sulfamethoxazole is effective and extensively used, but the manufacturer indicates in the package insert that the drug is not indicated for prophylaxis or prolonged administration for otitis media. A recent survey of children in a large-group health insurance program[116] indicated that fewer children on prophylactic regimens had breakthrough episodes with use of amoxicillin (13.2%) and TMP-SMX (15.5%) than with sulfisoxazole (20.4%).

What Dosage? Half the therapeutic dose should be administered once a day (usually bedtime offers maximal compliance, but any consistent time during the day would be satisfactory): amoxicillin, sulfisoxazole. The recent recommendation to double the therapeutic dosage of amoxicillin for acute infection suggests that an increase in the prophylactic dosage may be warranted.[293]

How Long? During the winter and spring period, when respiratory tract infections are most frequent, treatment should be applied for a period up to 6 months.

What Type of Follow-up? Children should be examined at approximately 2-month intervals when they are free of acute signs to determine whether middle-ear effusion is present. Management of prolonged middle-ear effusion should be considered separately from prevention of recurrences of acute infection.

How Should Acute Infections Be Treated? Acute infections are expected to occur, although at a lesser rate, during the course of prophylaxis. The infection should be treated with the alternative regimen. An effective oral cephalosporin or amoxicillin-clavulanate would be a suitable alternative, irrespective of the drug used for prophylaxis.

Xylitol

Finnish investigators demonstrated that xylitol sugar was effective in preventing new episodes of acute otitis media. Xylitol is a five-carbon sugar alcohol that can be produced from birch trees and is found in various fruits such as raspberries and plums. Xylitol is used extensively as a sweetener in toothpaste, chewing gum, and other foods. Because xylitol inhibits the growth of *Streptococcus mutans*, it is used throughout Scandinavia and Great Britain for the prevention of dental caries. Kontiokari et al[614] (1995) demonstrated inhibition of growth of *S. pneumoniae* in vitro, stimulating the investigators to develop protocols for prevention of acute otitis media. Xylitol-induced inhibition of pneumococcal growth is mediated via the fructose phosphotransferase system in a way similar to that in which mutans group streptococcal growth is inhibited.[1102]

Results of two studies have been published that demonstrate the efficacy of xylitol in the prevention of acute otitis media. In the first, xylitol or sucrose (control) chewing gum was administered five times a day to 306 children in out-of-home group day care (mean age, 4.9 years).[1145] During the 2-month period of observation, one or more episodes of acute otitis media were experienced by 20% of children receiving control (sucrose) gum, compared with 12.1% of the children receiving xylitol gum. There was no difference in carriage of pneumococci in the treated and control children. In the second study, 857 healthy children were recruited from day care centers to receive, in a five times a day schedule, control or xylitol syrup, control or xylitol chewing gum, or xylitol lozenge during a 3-month period of observation.[1146] The incidence rates of acute otitis media per patient year were as follows: 3.03 in the control and 2.01 in the xylitol syrup groups ($P = .006$); 1.69 in the control and 1.04 in the xylitol chewing gum groups ($P = .012$); and 1.33 in the lozenge group. The higher rates in the syrup group were due to the younger age of patients who received syrup rather than gum or lozenge.

These results are promising, but corroborative studies need to define optimal use in children who are "otitis-prone," develop data on the pharmacokinetics and mechanism of action of xylitol, and consider different dosage schedules that would increase compliance (contrasted with the five times per day schedule used in the original studies).

Oligosaccharides

Many viral and bacterial respiratory pathogens bind to carbohydrate receptors on the respiratory mucosa. Natural oligosaccharides act as decoys in the mucosa (and in saliva, tears, urine, sweat, and breast milk) to bind to the carbohydrate-binding proteins of the microbial pathogens and prevent attachment. One of the major defenses for the neonate is the ability of oligosaccharides in breast milk to prevent bacterial attachment and protect against respiratory and enteric infections. Anderson et al[21] (1986) showed that a human milk oligosaccharide could inhibit binding of *S. pneumoniae* to desquamated cells of the human naso- and oropharynx. Zopf and Roth[1228] described the potential of large-scale manufacture of human oligosaccharides for use in studies of prevention of various infectious diseases, including acute otitis media.

Oligosaccharides interfere with the establishment and progression of experimental pneumococcal pneumonia. Intratracheal administration of the oligosaccharides together with bacteria decreased pneumococcal load in the lungs of rabbits and protected against bacteremia. Intranasally administered oligosaccharides prevented colonization of the nasopharynx of infant rats.[521] A trial of an oligosaccharides (NE-1530) administered as an intranasal spray twice daily for 3 months did not prevent acute otitis media or diminish the nasopharyngeal carriage of bacteria in 507 healthy children.[1148]

Immunoprophylaxis

(See also section on Immunology, earlier in this chapter.)

Pneumococcal Vaccines

After a century of waiting, physicians who care for children finally have a pneumococcal vaccine that is effective for infants, the group of patients with the highest attack rates for invasive and local pneumococcal diseases. The conjugate pneumococcal vaccine is immunogenic in infants beginning at 2 months of age.[117]

History of the Development of Pneumococcal Vaccines. The first pneumococcal vaccine was a whole-cell, heat-killed product that was found to be effective in reducing mortality from pneumonia in South African mine workers.[1198] The success of the vaccine apparently went unappreciated, and little attention was paid to the development of a vaccine over the next 20 years. In the 1930s, the type specificity and immunogenicity of the pneumococcal capsular polysaccharide was described.[383] Type-specific serum therapy produced from immunization of horses with capsular polysaccharides was effective in reducing the mortality of bacteremic pneumococcal pneumonia.[1122] The first capsular polysaccharide vaccine prepared from four types was evaluated in Air Force recruits during World War II: the vaccine was 87% effective in reducing disease caused by the four vaccine types but had no effect on disease due to other types, which were responsible for most disease among the recruits.[676] Again, there was little follow-up to the initial success of the polysaccharide vaccine, probably because of the dramatic results of treatment with penicillin and the broad-spectrum antimicrobial agents.

Not until the 1970s was a 14- and then a 23-type pneumococcal polysaccharide vaccine introduced and the first evaluations done of the efficacy of a pneumococcal vaccine for prevention of acute otitis media. The results were disappointing for the group in greatest need, those children younger than 2 years of age. Few of the types in the vaccine were sufficiently immunogenic to provide protection against invasive disease or otitis media in infants. The problem of decreased immunogenicity of polysaccharide vaccines for infants was resolved with development of the conjugate technology used successfully in production of the *H. influenzae* type b vaccine. And now we have the development of a multivalent pneumococcal conjugate vaccine and the results of the first large clinical trials of a seven-type vaccine for the prevention of acute otitis media.

Pneumococcal Polysaccharide Vaccines. Although the pneumococcal polysaccharide vaccines are of limited importance in the prevention of otitis media in infants, the experience in otitis media trials with the polysaccharide vaccines is worthy of presentation because of the positive and negative results obtained. In addition, some of the general statements about the polysaccharide vaccine are applicable to the conjugate vaccine.

More than 90% of isolates of *S. pneumoniae* from middle-ear fluids are among the 23 types present in the pneumococcal polysaccharide vaccines.[600] The 14-type pneumococcal polysaccharide vaccine was licensed for use in the United States in 1978 followed by introduction of the 23-valent vaccine in 1983. The vaccine contains purified polysaccharide antigens of types associated with otitis media in children. These types include Danish types 1, 2, 3, 4, 5, 6B, 7F, 8, 9N, 9V, 10A, 11A, 12F, 14, 15B, 17F, 18C, 19A, 19F, 20, 22F, 23F, and 33F. Each polysaccha-

ride is extracted, separated, and combined into the final vaccine. A 0.5 mL dose contains 25 mg of each polysaccharide type dissolved in isotonic saline solution containing 0.25% phenol as a preservative; it is administered subcutaneously or intramuscularly. The vaccine was well tolerated. Children who received the vaccine have some pain, erythema, and induration at the site of injection, and a small number have a minimal elevation in temperature.

Each antigen produces an independent antibody response. In older children (more than 2 years of age) and adults, antibody develops in about 2 weeks. Studies in children indicate that, as with polysaccharide vaccines prepared from capsular materials of *H. influenzae* type b and *N. meningitides* group C, children younger than 2 years of age exhibit unsatisfactory serologic responses to a single-dose regimen. *N. meningitides* group A[416] and *S. pneumoniae* type 3,[679] however, evoke significant antibody responses in infants as young as 6 months, suggesting that some polysaccharides are adequate immunogens in young infants.

Investigations of 8- or 14-type pneumococcal vaccines for the prevention of recurrent episodes of acute otitis media were initiated in 1975 in Boston, Massachusetts, and Huntsville, Alabama, and in 1977 in Oulu and Tampere, Finland. The investigations were completed in 1980.[570, 676, 679, 1043, 1105] Results were evaluated by number of clinical episodes of acute otitis media and by bacteriologic features of the infection, identified by aspiration of middle-ear fluids.

Types of *S. pneumoniae* present in the vaccine were isolated less frequently from middle-ear fluids of children in the vaccine group with acute episodes of otitis media following immunization than from children in the control group in each of the three studies. If the estimates of relative risk for the three studies are combined, the overall risk indicates a significant protective effect in children who received the vaccine.

The number of episodes of otitis media due to types not present in the vaccine and due to other pathogens (predominantly *H. influenzae*) was similar in the vaccine and control groups. Finnish children 2 to 7 years of age who received pneumococcal vaccines had 50% fewer episodes of otitis media caused by the types present in the vaccine. Acute otitis media was also reduced in a Swedish study of children between 2 and 5 years of age. Rosen et al[936] performed a double-blind trial of the 14-type vaccine; in contrast with the other vaccine studies, results were identified only by clinical evaluation.

In spite of the decrease in middle-ear infections due to pneumococcal types present in the vaccine, the clinical experience of children younger than 2 years of age in the vaccine groups was similar to that of children in the control groups. In general, the number of children who had one or more episodes of otitis media and the mean number of episodes of acute otitis media after immunization were similar in the vaccine and control groups. The pneumococcal vaccine was effective in the prevention of new clinical episodes of otitis media in black children 6 to 11 months of age in Huntsville, but the vaccine was ineffective in preventing otitis media in white infants of the same age.[510] These data suggest racial differences in terms of preventing disease; prior studies had suggested a genetic difference in response to polysaccharide vaccines.[18, 435] The duration of middle ear effusion following an episode of pneumococcal otitis media was similar for the vaccine and the control groups (analyzed only by the Boston group).

Conjugate Pneumococcal Polysaccharide Vaccines. Conjugate vaccines combining the polysaccharides of the pneumococcus with a protein carrier such as the diphtheria toxin mutant (CRM 197), meningococcus group B outer membrane protein, or tetanus toxoid have been developed. A heptavalent type conjugate vaccine employing CRM 197 (Prevnar, Wyeth Lederle) was introduced in the United States in early 2000. The vaccine combined pneumococcal serotypes 4, 6B, 9V, 18C, 19F, and 23 F. The vaccine is immunogenic in children as young as 2 months of age[117]; infants responded to each conjugate polysaccharide type with concentrations of antibody believed to be protective against invasive disease. Protective titers were achieved after doses administered at 2, 4, and 6 months of age but waned during the following 6 months, requiring a booster between 12 and 15 months of age. Safety and immunogenicity of the conjugate vaccine was also demonstrated in patients with sickle cell disease who responded with antibody concentrations comparable to infants without the disease.[821] The other conjugate pneumococcal polysaccharide vaccines are still in various stages of development and in clinical trials.

Beginning in October 1995, the seven-type conjugate vaccine was administered to almost 38,000 children in Northern California in a double-blind trial.[117] The children received either the pneumococcal conjugate vaccine or meningococcus type C CRM 197 vaccine. The vaccine was effective in the prevention of vaccine-type invasive disease (97.4% efficacy in fully vaccinated cases) and pneumonia (35% decrease for radiographically identifiable disease). For otitis media, data were available from clinical records of office visits, emergency room visits, and hospitalizations: efficacy against visits, episodes, recurrent disease (five episodes in 6 months or six episodes in 12 months) and tympanostomy tube placement was 8.9%, 7.0%, 22.8%, and 20.1%.

Children who received the conjugate vaccine had 5% fewer oral antibiotic prescriptions during the period of observation than did children who received the placebo (Black SL, personal communication).

The bacteriologic efficacy of the seven-type pneumococcal conjugate vaccine was evaluated in studies in Finnish children.[340] The same schedule was used as for the California studies; the sole difference was the use of hepatitis B vaccine as the control. Bacteriologic diagnosis was based on aspiration of middle-ear fluids in patients with acute otitis media. The reduction in the number of episodes in the per-protocol analysis was 57% against culture-confirmed, serotype-specific acute otitis media, 34% against culture-confirmed pneumococcal acute otitis media (irrespective of the serotype) and 6% against acute otitis media irrespective of etiology. Of particular interest was a 51% protective effect against cross-reactive serotypes of types in the vaccine, most prominently 6A and 19A. Of concern among recipients of the pneumococcal

conjugate vaccine was a 33% increase in episodes of acute otitis media due to pneumococcal serotypes not in the vaccine and not included in the cross-reactive group and an 11% increase in disease due to nontypeable *H. influenzae*. The results of the vaccine trials in Northern California and Finland are summarized in Table 25–48.

With the widespread distribution of the first conjugate pneumococcal vaccine, investigators and clinicians will need to monitor the impact of the vaccine on the incidence of invasive and local disease. Unlike the *H. influenzae* type b conjugate vaccine, pneumococcal disease will not disappear among immunized children. Surveillance will be needed to determine the influence of the vaccine on carriage of pneumococci in the nasopharynx; preliminary data suggest that carriage of pneumococci due to types present in the vaccine is reduced, but there may be an increase in nonvaccine type pneumococci.[718] If the vaccine is effective in the reduction of disease due to pneumococcal types present in the vaccine, will there be an increase in pneumococcal disease due to types not in the vaccine? Will the vaccine blunt the increasing incidence of multidrug-resistant pneumococci? Because the conjugate vaccine appeared to be more effective in the prevention of invasive disease than against the prevention of acute otitis media, investigators need to focus on the reasons for the difference in efficacy. It is possible that more serum or more local antibody is required or a qualitatively different type of antibody is needed to further reduce otitis media due to vaccine type pneumococci.

In August and October, 2000 the American Academy of Pediatrics[245] and the Advisory Committee on Immunization Practices[218] approved universal immunization with the conjugate pneumococcal vaccine for infants 2 years of age and younger. The vaccine was also approved for children at high risk for invasive pneumococcal disease and children with high-risk features for other respiratory infections, including severe and recurrent acute otitis media, who were 2 to 5 years of age.

Nontypeable Haemophilus influenzae

Since nontypeable *H. influenzae* lacks capsular materials, different techniques will be necessary to develop a vaccine. Current investigations focus on the use of outer

TABLE 25–48. Efficacy of Seven-Valent Pneumococcal Conjugate Vaccine for Prevention of Acute Otitis Media (AOM) in California and Finnish Infants

Analysis	Percentage Reduction	
	California	*Finland*
Episodes of AOM	7.0	6.0
Frequent AOM°	22.8	NA
Tympanostomy tube placement	20.1	NA
Serotype specific AOM	NA	57
Any pneumococcal AOM	NA	34

° Five or more episodes in 6 months or six or more episodes in 12 months
Black S, Shinefield H, Fireman B, et al. Efficacy and safety of a heptavalent pneumococcal conjugate vaccine in infancy. Pediatr Infect Dis J *In Press*.
Eskola J, Kilpi T. Potential of bacterial vaccines in the prevention of acute otitis media. Pediatr Infect Dis J *In Press*.

membrane proteins as candidate antigens for development of a vaccine[414] and antibodies that would alter the antigens that are critical for adherence of the organism to epithelial cells. Areas of current investigation are discussed in the section on Immunology, earlier in this chapter.

Immunoprophylaxis against Respiratory Viruses

The development of an influenzavirus vaccine resulted in a reduction in cases of influenza A as well as a 36% decline in otitis media in children attending a day care center.[233] A similar reduction (30%) in episodes of febrile otitis media was also reported in children after administration of live-attenuated, cold-adapted intranasal influenza vaccine.[78] Use of currently available influenzavirus vaccine should be part of the strategy for reducing the incidence of acute otitis media for children with recurrent and severe disease.

Respiratory syncytial virus (RSV) is the viral pathogen most closely associated with acute otitis media. Immunoprophylaxis against RSV disease has progressed with the use of high-titered RSV immunoglobulin[1029] and the introduction of palivizumab, a high-titer RSV monoclonal antibody immunoglobulin with high titers of neutralizing RSV antibody (Impact-RSV Study Group, 1998). The RSV immunoglobulin but not the monoclonal antibody was effective in reducing the number of episodes of acute otitis media.

Protective Effect of Immunoglobulins

Specific serum antibody is correlated with protection from homotypic infection, and prevention of disease can be achieved (albeit for limited duration) by administration of immunoglobulins. Since infants who have recurrent episodes of acute otitis media usually improve with age, it is possible that a program of passive immunization might be effective.

Diamant et al[282] suggested that patients with recurrent episodes of acute otitis media associated with hypogammaglobulinemia or agammaglobulinemia are benefited by frequent administration of gammaglobulin. Children aged 1 to 7 years were enrolled after the first visit to the Ear, Nose, and Throat Department in Halmstad, Sweden. Children born on an odd date were given gammaglobulin at their first visit and then once a month for 6 months. Children born on an even date received no gammaglobulin. Of the 113 children treated, 10 had one or more episodes of acute otitis media during the months of administration of the gammaglobulin; of 118 untreated children, 25 had one or more episodes of the disease during the same period of time. The protective effect of the gammaglobulin persisted during the 8 months following cessation of administration; 25 episodes occurred in the treated group and 53 in the untreated group. In the untreated group, some patients had up to five episodes, whereas no patient in the treated group had more than two bouts of acute otitis media.[282]

Empowering Parents

Parents should be informed about the risk features for otitis media (see also section on Epidemiology, earlier in this chapter). Although little can be done about host features, other than to suggest prognosis for severe and recurrent disease, some environmental factors can be altered to provide more protection for the infant. Education of the parents should focus on the following before or after the birth of the infant:

1. Breast feeding should be encouraged.
2. The home should be made a smoke-free environment.
3. Crowded living conditions, poor sanitation, and episodic and inadequate medical care should be alleviated with cooperation of social services and guidance of the health care provider.
4. Pacifier use should be discouraged.
5. Family or small group out of home day care should be encouraged.
6. The day care facility should be inspected by parents for adequate room and ventilation and adherence of caretakers to hand washing and other infection precautions.

Specific Surgical and Mechanical Management Options

Inflation of the Eustachian Tube – Middle Ear

Procedures that force air through the eustachian tube and into the middle ear and mastoid cavities have been employed for more than 100 years in an effort to normalize negative intratympanic pressure and to eliminate middle-ear effusion. The methods of Valsalva and Politzer are the most commonly used in children.[876, 1153] Catheterization of the eustachian tube has also been utilized but is of limited usefulness in children, since the procedure can be frightening and is technically difficult to perform in young patients. All three of these methods are also crude tests of eustachian tube patency and were described in detail earlier in the section on Physiology, Pathophysiology, and Pathogenesis.

From a physiologic standpoint, inflation of the eustachian tube, middle ear, and mastoid has merit. Figure 25–55 shows the flask model of the nasopharynx-eustachian tube-middle ear system: Liquid is shown in the body and narrow neck of an inverted flask. Relative negative pressure inside the body of the flask prevents the flow of the liquid out of the flask. This is analogous to an effusion in a middle ear that has abnormally high negative pressure. If air is insufflated up into the liquid, through the neck and into the body of the flask, the negative pressure is converted to ambient or positive pressure and the liquid will flow out of the flask. If the liquid is of high viscosity, however, the likelihood of air being forced through the liquid into the body of the flask is remote, especially if the thick liquid completely fills the chamber. Therefore, in the human system, a thin, or serous, effusion would be more likely to flow out of the middle ear and down the eustachian tube than would a thick, mucoid effusion that fills the middle-ear and mas-

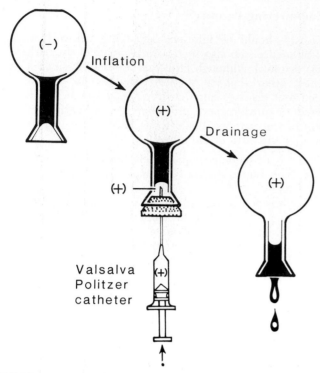

FIGURE 25–55. Flask model showing the rationale of how inflation of the middle ear promotes drainage down the eustachian tube. The eustachian tube–middle ear–mastoid air cell system can be likened to an inverted flask with a long, narrow neck (see text).

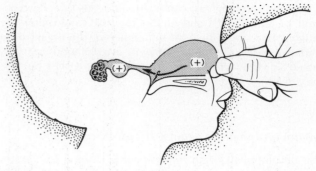

FIGURE 25–56. Self-inflation of the eustachian tube-middle ear by the method of Valsalva.

toid cavities. The method probably is not effective in maintaining normal middle-ear pressure in children who have atelectasis caused by eustachian tube obstruction (i.e., high negative pressure), since experiments in animals have shown inflation of the middle ear not to be effective.[197]

Theoretically, then, inflation of the eustachian tube and middle ear should be an effective treatment option for children with certain types of otitis media with effusion or atelectasis, or both; however, in reality, there are several problems with this method of management. The self-inflation method of Valsalva is somewhat difficult for children to learn, since it is a technique involving forced nasal expiration with the nose and lips closed. Cantekin et al[193] tested 66 children between the ages of 2 and 6 years who had had chronic or recurrent otitis media with effusion and who had functioning tympanostomy tubes in place. They asked each subject to try to blow his or her nose with the glottis closed (Fig. 25–56). None of these children could passively open their eustachian tubes and force air into the middle ear by the Valsalva method, even though they developed a maximum nasopharyngeal pressure of 538.8 ± 237.0 mm H_2O. It was concluded that the Valsalva method of opening the eustachian tube in this age group was not successful owing to possible tubal compliance problems. Unfortunately, children in this age group have a high incidence of otitis media; for infants, who have the highest incidence of otitis media, the procedure cannot be used at all.

Politzer's method of opening the eustachian tube in-

volves inserting the tip of a rubber air bulb into one nostril while the other nostril is compressed by finger pressure (Fig. 25–57) and then asking the child to swallow while the rubber bulb is compressed. Some children complain of a sudden "pop" in the ear as the positive pressure is forced up the eustachian tube and have discomfort with the procedure. This method, however, is also extremely difficult to perform in infants.

The major difficulty with both methods is determining whether the middle ear is actually inflated by the procedure. If a child hears a "pop" or has a pressure sensation in the ear, there is only presumptive evidence of passage of air into the middle ear. Auscultation of the ear (listening for the sound of air entering the middle ear during the procedure) is helpful in determining whether or not the procedure is successful, but a sound may be heard even when air does not enter the middle ear. Objective otoscopic evidence that the middle ear is actually inflated would be constituted by the presence of bubbles or a fluid level behind the tympanic membrane when these findings were not present prior to inflation. Another excellent method for determining objectively whether the inflation is successful is to obtain a tympanogram before and after the procedure: The compliance peak should shift toward or be in the positive pressure zone after inflation (Fig. 25–58). If none of the results of these presumptive or objective methods of determining the success of inflation is definitive, then the clinician cannot be certain that the procedure has been therapeutic. Failure

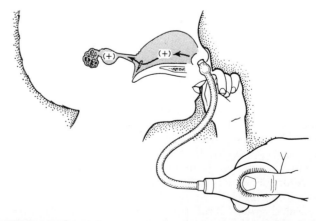

FIGURE 25–57. Politzer method of inflation of the eustachian tube–middle ear.

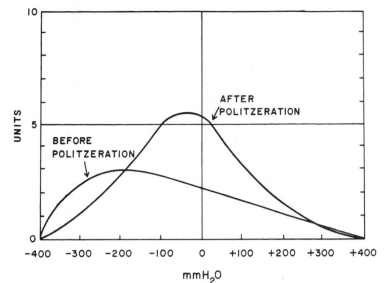

FIGURE 25–58. Tympanogram demonstrating objective evidence that inflation of the middle ear is successful. Before inflation, the compliance peak is in the negative-pressure zone (an effusion pattern), whereas after inflation, the peak is shifted toward the positive-pressure zone.

to achieve a successful result may be related to (1) inability of the patient to learn the method; (2) insufficient nasopharyngeal overpressure to open the eustachian tube passively; (3) eustachian tube abnormality; or (4) a middle ear filled with a very thick, mucoid effusion.

Unfortunately, the beneficial effect of the Valsalva and Politzer methods of inflation for treatment of otitis media with effusion or atelectasis has been subjected to only a limited number of randomized, controlled trials. Most of the evidence has been anecdotal until recently. Gottschalk[431, 432] described remarkable success with a modification of the Politzer method in more than 12,000 patients; the average course of treatment was a minimum of 12 inflations in the office on three separate days. Schwartz et al[985] have shown that it is possible to inflate the middle ears of children at home by the Politzer method; they documented the results of the method by tympanometry but did not test its efficacy. Kaneko et al[564] inflated the ears of 149 children who were 3 to 9 years of age and reported success related to season, but this trial did not include a control group.

One of the first controlled trials of this method was reported by Fraser et al,[384] and they were not able to demonstrate that it was efficacious. Chan and Bluestone[219] also conducted a randomized clinical trial in 40 Pittsburgh children, most of whom had chronic otitis media with effusion that was unresponsive to antimicrobial treatment. All the children were taught how to use the specially developed system, which consisted of a flowmeter attached to a disposable anesthesia mask, based on a modified Valsalva technique.[220] The children were stratified according to their ability to achieve eustachian tube opening as determined by tympanometry. Subjects were randomly assigned to either autoinflation three times each day for 2 weeks, or to no inflation (i.e., control). Of the 19 children who autoinflated their ears, only 1 patient (5%) was effusion-free at the end of the trial. This result was comparable to the control group, in which only 2 (10%) of 21 subjects were without middle-ear effusion (Table 25–49). The investigators concluded that autoinflation as conducted in the trial was ineffective for treatment of otitis media with effusion.

In a later clinical trial from Denmark by Strangerup et al,[1057] however, autoinflation was considered to be effective using a new device that consists of a balloon attached to a nasal tube (Otovent, Technilab, Montreal, Canada).

TABLE 25–49. Status (Percentage) of Middle-Ear Effusion after 2 Weeks of Autoinflation vs. Control in 40 Pittsburgh Children with Otitis Media with Effusion

Entry Status and Treatment Group	No Effusion, %	Unilateral Effusion, %	Bilateral Effusion, %	Total Subjects, n
Unilateral Effusion				
Inflation	0	60	40	5
Control	11	78	11	9
Bilateral Effusion				
Inflation	7	7	86	14
Control	8	17	75	12
Total Subjects				
Inflation	5	21	74	19
Control	10	43	48	21

Modified from Chan KH, Bluestone CD. Lack of efficacy of middle-ear inflation: treatment of otitis media with effusion in children. Otolaryngol Head Neck Surg 100:317, 1989.

The child inserts the device into one nostril and blows up the balloon through one side of the nose while the other side is closed with the child's finger pressure. The technique could only be taught to children who were 3 years of age and older, and during the trial many of the children failed to use the instrument the prescribed three times daily during the 2-week regimen. In those children who had type B tympanograms on entry, the investigators concluded that the tympanometric conditions were "better" in the treated group than in the untreated children at the end of the 2 weeks, but there were no statistically significant differences after 2 or 3 months between the two groups. Because the effect was "short-lasting," they advocated repeated use. Since this study had several shortcomings—for example, tympanometry only to identify middle ear effusion, analysis by ear and not by subject—the safety and efficacy of this device awaits further study, especially when used repeatedly by children who have chronic and recurrent disease.

In a series of recently reported studies in monkeys, inflation of the middle ears was not effective in preventing the occurrence of middle-ear effusion even when repeated over days using the inert gas argon[11] and may be related to timing of the inflations to be potentially successful.[12, 300] A more recent study in the monkey model by Alper et al[13] revealed that inflation merely displaces the middle-ear effusion to other portions of the middle-ear cleft, which appears to be clear in the middle ear.

At present, it would appear reasonable to recommend autoinflation of middle ears for the following conditions. Barotrauma (following flying or swimming) should respond ideally to autoinflation if atelectasis with high negative pressure or otitis media with effusion or both are present. Although not confirmed in clinical trials, inflation of the middle ear should be helpful under these circumstances, since this condition is usually not due to chronic eustachian tube dysfunction, and inflation may resolve the acute, subacute, or chronic disorder rapidly. When a middle ear effusion not due to barotrauma is found in a patient who only occasionally has a problem and in whom frequently recurrent or chronic disease is not suspected, then the procedure may also be successful, especially if a small amount of serous effusion is visible behind a translucent tympanic membrane. It is unlikely, however, that a mucoid or purulent effusion could be evacuated by this technique, and if it could be, it would probably recur immediately after the procedure. Atelectasis of the tympanic membrane and middle ear, with or without high negative pressure, can also be treated by repeated autoinflation (Valsalva) or the Politzer method, but even if the middle ear is successfully inflated, the benefit is usually only of short duration and the procedure must be repeated frequently.

Therefore, it is unlikely that inflation will be successful in alleviating for any length of time frequently recurrent or chronic eustachian tube dysfunction. There is also a remote possibility that bacteria can be forced into the middle ear from the nasopharynx during this procedure, and the possibility that repeated autoinflation could cause the tympanic membrane to lose its stiffness, that is, to become hypercompliant.

In conclusion, these procedures may be worthwhile for children with barotitis and for children who have an occasional episode of otitis media with effusion or eustachian tube dysfunction, but they are probably not helpful in children who have chronic or frequently recurrent middle-ear effusion or atelectasis, or both. (see Chap. 26, section on Atelectasis of the Middle Ear). But, laboratory and clinical studies are continuing in more than one center in an effort to resolve the ongoing controversy regarding the efficacy of inflation of the eustachian tube and middle ears of children in preventing eustachian tube dysfunction or otitis media, especially when a common cold is present, and treatment of these conditions when they are present.

Myringotomy and Tympanocentesis

Myringotomy, or the incision of the tympanic membrane for acute otitis media, was first described by Sir Ashley Cooper in 1802.[7] This procedure became increasingly popular until the 1940s, when antimicrobial agents came into wide use. Nowadays, myringotomy is reserved only for selected cases and performed primarily by otolaryngologists and a handful of primary care physicians; the indications are usually limited to those children who have severe otalgia or suppurative complications, or both. Facing an apparent recent increase in the prevalence and incidence of acute and chronic otitis media with effusion, however, there has been considerably more effort to study the efficacy of myringotomy in the management of this disease. The potential benefit from more liberal use of the procedure in cases of acute otitis media might be relief of otalgia and a decrease in persistence and recurrence rates. When chronic otitis media with effusion is present, myringotomy may be as effective in eliminating the middle-ear effusion as when the procedure is followed with the insertion of a tympanostomy tube, with its attendant complications and sequelae (assuming a surgical procedure is indicated at all).

The results of studies conducted in the past to determine the efficacy of myringotomy for acute otitis media are shown in Table 25–50. In the study by Roddey et al,[931] all 181 children received an antimicrobial agent, and in approximately half of the subjects myringotomy was performed as well. The only significant difference between the two groups—judged by otoscopy at 2, 10, 30, and 60 days and by audiometry at 3 to 6 months—was more rapid pain relief among a small group who had severe otalgia initially. Fewer children who had the myringotomy and antimicrobial therapy had middle ear effusion at the end of 6 weeks than did those who received antimicrobials alone, but the difference was not statistically significant. If a larger number of children had been involved in the study, however, the difference might have achieved statistical significance. Herberts et al[488] found no difference in the percentages of children with persistent effusion 10 days after either myringotomy and antimicrobial therapy or antimicrobial therapy alone. Lorentzen and Haughsten[662] found the "myringotomy only" group to have the same recovery rate (88%) as both the group treated with penicillin V alone and the group treated with penicillin V and myringotomy. Puhakka et al[896] repeated the same study with 158 children and found that 4

TABLE 25–50. Percentage of Patients with Persistent Middle-Ear Effusion Following Initial Myringotomy and Antimicrobial Therapy Compared with Those Receiving Antimicrobial Therapy Alone for Acute Otitis Media

| Investigator | Procedure | Number of Subjects | Percentage with Persistent Effusion | | | Statistical Significance Achieved |
			10 to 14 Days	4 Weeks	6 Weeks	
Roddey et al[931]	AB	121	35	7	2	No
	AB&M	94	24	9	1	
Herberts et al[488]	AB	81	10	—	—	No
	AB&M	91	18	—	—	
Lorentzen and Haugsten[662]	AB	190	16	6	—	No
	AB&M	164	20	6	—	
Puhakka et al[896]	AB	90	78	29	—	Yes
	AB&M	68	29	10		
Qvarnberg and Palva[905]	AB	151	50	—	—	Yes
	AB&M	97	28	—	—	
Schwartz et al[988]	AB	361	47	—	—	No
	AB&M	415	51			
Engelhard et al[335]	AB	55	40	—	—	No
	AB&M	53	40	—	—	
Kaleida et al[558]	AB	167*	61	—	56	No
	AB&M	104	56	—	52	

AB, antibiotic; AB&M, antibiotic and myringotomy.
* Episodes of acute otitis media for infants and children.
From Bluestone CD, Klein JO. Otitis Media in Infants and Children, 3rd ed. Philadelphia, WB Saunders, 2001.

weeks after the onset of acute otitis media, 71% of the children who did not undergo myringotomy but were treated with penicillin V were cured, whereas 90% of the group that had myringotomy and penicillin V treatment had the same outcome, indicating that "myringotomy clearly accelerates the recovery rate from acute otitis media." Qvarnberg and Palva[905] reported results of their study of 248 children in which they compared the efficacy of penicillin V and myringotomy, penicillin V alone, and amoxicillin and concluded that if the first attack of acute otitis media is treated with myringotomy and antibiotics (penicillin V or amoxicillin), cure is the rule, but that if antibiotics alone (either one) are used, 10% of the patients will run a prolonged course. Schwartz et al[991] treated 776 children with a variety of antimicrobial agents, half of whom also had myringotomy (without aspiration), and found no difference in the relief of pain or in the percentage with persistent effusion 10 days after myringotomy therapy.

Unfortunately, all of these studies had design and methodologic flaws that make interpreting their results and answering the question of the value of myringotomy for acute otitis media difficult. For example, in the study conducted by Puhakka et al,[896] myringotomy was performed along with aspiration of the middle-ear effusion, but it was a nonrandomized trial. Children who received a myringotomy, however, had a significantly shorter course of their disease than those who did not have a myringotomy. On the other hand, Schwartz et al[991] failed to find a difference between those children who did and those who did not receive a myringotomy. There was no attempt to aspirate the middle-ear effusion, and the children were not randomly assigned into the two treatment groups.

In an excellent study from Israel, Engelhard et al[335] randomly assigned 105 infants who had acute otitis media to one of three treatment options: (1) amoxicillin-clavulanate, (2) myringotomy plus placebo (for amoxicillin-clavulanate), and (3) amoxicillin-clavulanate and myringotomy. The two myringotomy groups were double-blinded. Using otoscopy as an outcome measure, 60% of the infants receiving the antibiotic, with or without myringotomy, recovered, whereas only 23% of subjects who received myringotomy and placebo recovered. The authors concluded that the addition of myringotomy to the amoxicillin-clavulanate did not appear to affect either the persistence of infection after treatment or the residual middle-ear effusion (Table 25–51).

In Pittsburgh, Kaleida et al[558] randomly assigned children who had "severe" acute otitis media to receive either 10 days of amoxicillin, myringotomy with placebo (for amoxicillin), or both amoxicillin and myringotomy; infants in the trial received only amoxicillin with or without myringotomy. Outcome included an algorithm that included otoscopy (by a validated otoscopist, i.e., against myringotomy findings), tympanometry, and acoustic reflex testing. There were statistically more initial treatment failures in those children who received myringotomy alone, as compared with those who received amoxicillin, with or without the myringotomy. Subjects assigned to receive amoxicillin alone and those assigned to receive amoxicillin and myringotomy had similar outcomes (Table 25–52). The investigators concluded that amoxicillin (or an equivalent antimicrobial agent) is indicated for treatment of acute otitis media, and that the data did not support the routine use of myringotomy, either alone or in combination with amoxicillin. The authors did recommend myringotomy for selected infants and children, however, such as those with severe otalgia, antimicrobial treatment failures, and when a suppurative complication is present.

TABLE 25–51. Otoscopic Findings Following Randomized Trial of Amoxicillin-Clavulanate, Myringotomy, or Both, in 105 Israeli Infants

	Group 1 (Amoxicillin-Clavulanate)	Group 2 (Myringotomy and Amoxicillin-Clavulanate)	Group 3 (Myringotomy and Placebo)	P Value
Subjects recovered, %	60	60	23	<.01°
Persistent infection, %	7	17	70	<.001°
Ears recovered, %	64	65	31	<.001°
Persistent infection, %	4	13	64	<.001°
Middle-ear effusion, %	31	23	6	
Nonclosure of myringotomy, %	—	6	21	<.04†
Otorrhea at myringotomy site, %	—	4	17	<.04†

° For group 3 vs. 2, and group 3 vs. 1.
† For group 3 vs. 2.
Modified from Engelhard D, Cohen D, Strauss N, et al. Randomized study of myringotomy, amoxicillin-clavulanate, or both, for acute otitis media in infants. Lancet 2: 141, 1989.

Indications

There is now ample evidence that the routine use of myringotomy for all children with acute otitis media is not necessary, but there are certain indications for which there is consensus at present.

Suppurative Complications. Whenever a child has acute mastoiditis, labyrinthitis, facial paralysis, or one or more of the intracranial suppurative complications, such as meningitis, myringotomy and aspiration should be performed as an emergency procedure. Tympanocentesis should precede myringotomy to identify the causative organism. In addition, in such cases the insertion of a tympanostomy tube should be attempted to provide prolonged drainage.

Severe Otalgia Requiring Immediate Relief. Even though some studies have failed to show that myringotomy alleviated earache,[991] Roddey et al[931] did show that acute pain was relieved in those children who received myringotomy. Culture of the effusion is reasonable, since the middle ear is being opened, but it is not absolutely necessary if there is no reason to suspect the presence of an unusual organism.

Tympanocentesis. Although not as compelling as the other indications, whenever diagnostic tympanocentesis is indicated, myringotomy for drainage may follow the needle aspiration, especially when a copious amount of middle ear effusion is identified by the tympanocentesis. Myringotomy may then reasonably follow tympanocentesis

when acute otitis media is present and (1) when the child is critically ill[36, 279]; (2) when there is persistent or recurrent otalgia or fever, or both, in spite of adequate and appropriate antimicrobial therapy; (3) when acute otitis media occurs during the course of antimicrobial therapy given for another infection, and when the agent should be effective against the most common organisms causing otitis (for example, amoxicillin or ampicillin); (4) when otitis media occurs in the neonatal period; and (5) when it occurs in the immunologically compromised host. (The specific indications and techniques for tympanocentesis are discussed completely earlier in this chapter, under Diagnosis.)

The benefit of performing myringotomy on all infants and children with acute otitis media is uncertain at present, but it is a reasonable procedure, especially if otalgia is present. If a middle-ear effusion persists after 10 to 14 days of antimicrobial therapy, myringotomy may also be appropriate if the child is still symptomatic, but if the child is relatively asymptomatic, the indications for the procedure would be less valid, because most effusions at this stage would be expected to clear spontaneously during the next several weeks. If the middle-ear effusion persists for longer than 3 months, surgical drainage would appear to be a reasonable choice. If the procedure can be performed without the need of a general anesthetic, myringotomy alone would seem appropriate, with the physician reserving the insertion of a tympanostomy tube in case the effusion recurs soon after the myringotomy incision heals. If a general anesthetic is required to perform the surgical drainage of chronic otitis media with effusion,

TABLE 25–52. Outcomes After Episodes of Severe Acute Otitis Media in Pittsburgh Children 2 Years of Age and Older

	Amoxicillin (52 Episodes)	Amoxicillin + Myringotomy (35 Episodes)	Placebo + Myringotomy (35 Episodes)	P Value
Initial Treatment Failure, %	4.1	3.1	23.5	.006
Effusion at 2 Weeks, %	53.7	54.2	52.2	.37
Effusion at 6 Weeks, %	63.0	54.5	35.0	.15
Recurrence 2–6 Weeks, %	31.8	31.0	17.2	.30

Adapted with permission from Kaleida PH, Casselbrant ML, Rockette HE, et al. Amoxicillin or myringotomy or both for acute otitis media: results of a randomized clinical trial. Pediatrics 87:466, 1991.

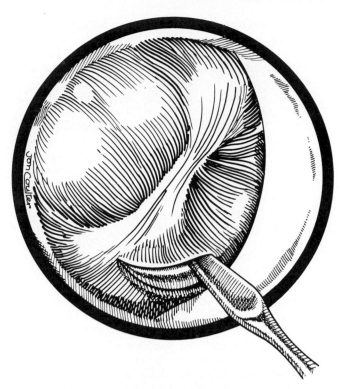

FIGURE 25–59. Myringotomy incision through the tympanic membrane for drainage of the middle ear. (From Bluestone CD, Klein JO. Otitis Media in Infants and Children, 3rd ed., Philadelphia, WB Saunders, 2001, p 255.)

however, myringotomy and tympanostomy tube insertion is the preferred procedure. This recommendation is appropriate, because Gates et al[397] and Mandel et al[689] have shown that myringotomy with insertion of a tympanostomy tube was more effective than myringotomy alone in children who have chronic otitis media with effusion that is unresponsive to antimicrobial therapy (see section on Tympanostomy Tubes for details of these clinical trials).

Performance of the Procedure

Tympanocentesis is a needle aspiration of the middle ear contents for diagnostic purposes, but myringotomy is a procedure in which an incision of the tympanic membrane by a myringotomy knife is made to provide adequate drainage (Fig. 25–59). To accomplish this goal, the incision should be large enough to provide not only adequate and prolonged drainage into the external auditory canal but also aeration of the middle ear to enhance drainage down the eustachian tube. When acute otitis media is present in the infant or young child, adequate restraint employing a sheet or board especially designed for restraining children may be all that is needed; sedation is not necessary. For older children, however, sedation or even general anesthesia may be required. Iontophoresis does not effectively provide anesthesia of the tympanic membrane when acute otitis media is present. When myringotomy is to be performed for a middle-ear effusion when acute disease is not present, however, iontophoresis may be a satisfactory method. The use of a topical solution of phenol gently applied to the exact spot

on the tympanic membrane to be opened may be all that is necessary in older children and teenagers. The myringotomy incision should be a wide circumferential incision encompassing both inferior quadrants of the tympanic membrane in order to provide adequate drainage, and an attempt should be made to aspirate as much of the middle-ear effusion as possible. Frequently, insertion of the suction tip through the incision on the tympanic membrane will enhance removal of the effusion and provide a larger opening, which, it is hoped, will remain open longer than just an incision alone.

The procedure can be performed through an otoscope with a surgical head attached, or, for better magnification and binocular vision, the otomicroscope is desirable. For the routine case, the otoscope is quite adequate and makes the procedure readily available to the clinician in settings other than an operating room or otologic outpatient area, where an otomicroscope would be available. By becoming proficient with the otoscope in performing myringotomy, the physician can perform the procedure in emergency rooms, inpatient pediatric floors, the child's home, or any other setting in which a child is examined and is in need of myringotomy.

In almost all conditions in which myringotomy is performed, diagnostic tympanocentesis may precede it. In such instances, the procedure should be performed as described earlier in this chapter, Diagnosis.

Complications and Sequelae

The complications of performing a myringotomy properly are few. The persistent otorrhea that follows the procedure and is the most common finding after myringotomy can hardly be considered a complication, since it is the desired outcome; however, the discharge may become profuse and cause an eczematoid external otitis. If this occurs, meticulous cleaning of the external auditory canal with a cotton-tipped applicator; instillation of otic drops containing hydrocortisone, neomycin, and polymyxin; and insertion of a small piece of cotton (which should be changed frequently) in the outer canal will usually eliminate the problem. Dislocation of the incudostapedial joint, severing of the facial nerve, and puncturing of an exposed jugular bulb are dreaded complications but are so rare in experienced hands that they should not deter the trained practitioner from employing the procedure when indicated. The most common sequelae of the procedure are persistent perforation, atrophic scar, and tympanocentesis at the site of the incision. Even though the incidence of these conditions has not been systematically studied in a prospective manner, the risk of any or all occurring should not outweigh the benefits of myringotomy when indicated. The incidence of these sequelae occurring would rise in children who require repeated myringotomy, and in these patients a tympanostomy tube should be considered, even though this is not without complications and sequelae. The evidence-based studies that have evaluated the benefits and risks of myringotomy have also been recently reviewed by Bluestone and Lee.[142]

It has been suggested by some investigators[164, 249, 427,]

[1021] that the myringotomy incision be created with a laser when middle-ear effusion is present in an effort to prolong the duration of the opening in hopes of preventing tympanostomy tube placement, but to date randomized clinical trials that have compared the short- and long-term efficacy and complications of laser myringotomy to myringotomy with insertion of tympanostomy tube are lacking, and thus this procedure should be considered experimental and of uncertain benefit. But, there may be atypical indications for using the laser to perform a myringotomy, such as in a child who has hemophilia.[81] Clearly, myringotomy alone provides no long-term advantage for prevention of recurrent acute otitis media (see next section, Myringotomy and Tympanostomy Tube Placement).

Myringotomy and Tympanostomy Tube Placement

Myringotomy with insertion of tympanostomy tubes is currently the most common surgical procedure performed in children that requires general anesthesia. The use of tympanostomy tubes was first suggested by Politzer more than 100 years ago (1862),[877] but they did not become readily available until they were reintroduced by Armstrong in 1954. Since then, they have become increasingly popular. It has been estimated that 2 million tubes are manufactured yearly and, presumably, inserted through the tympanic membranes of probably more than 1 million patients.[839]

Even though there remains uncertainty among many clinicians and investigators regarding the safety and efficacy of tympanostomy tube placement,[156, 865] we now have the results of clinical trials to arrive at reasonable criteria for insertion of tubes.

Clinical Trials

Otitis Media with Effusion. Several studies have addressed the question of the efficacy of myringotomy and the insertion of tympanostomy tubes for the treatment of otitis media with effusion.

1. Shah[1003] performed a myringotomy and aspiration in one ear and a myringotomy and aspiration with tympanostomy tube insertion on the opposite ear of children with bilateral mucoid otitis media with effusion. Adenoidectomies were performed on all of these children at the time that ear surgery was performed. Shah found that the hearing in the ears into which the tympanostomy tubes had been inserted was better than the hearing in the other ears 6 to 12 months after the procedures.
2. Kilby et al[586] also performed bilateral myringotomies (and inserted a tympanostomy tube into only one ear) in a series of children but did not perform an adenoidectomy at the same time. These investigators found no difference in the hearing in the two ears of these children 2 years after surgery, when all the tubes had been extruded.
3. Kokko[612] compared findings in the ears of children who had undergone adenoidectomy, myringotomy,

and tympanostomy tube insertion with the findings in the ears of those who had undergone adenoidectomy and myringotomy without insertion of tubes. He found, 4½ half years after the procedures, no differences in the pathologic conditions of the tympanic membranes or in the degree of hearing loss in the two groups.
4. Yagi[1203] compared 100 children who underwent an adenoidectomy, myringotomy, and tympanostomy tube insertion with 100 children who underwent only adenoidectomy. There were no significant differences between the two groups in (1) the number of children whose hearing problems were "cured" without further surgery, (2) the number of children requiring insertion of tubes due to recurrence of problems after initial treatment, (3) the number of patients having abnormal tympanic membranes, and (4) the number of patients with more than a 20 dB hearing loss 18 months after treatment.
5. Mawson and Fagan[714] performed adenoidectomy, myringotomy, and tympanostomy tube insertion on a number of children and found that the degree of hearing loss and the number of tympanic membrane abnormalities (such as tympanosclerosis) increased the longer the children were followed. The authors reported that 76% of the children in their study required insertion of another tympanostomy tube within 4 years of initial treatment.
6. Tos and Poulsen[1137] performed adenoidectomy, myringotomy, and tympanostomy tube insertion on 108 children. During a 5- to 8-year follow-up period, the authors reported that only 2.5% of the children into whose ears tympanostomy tubes had been placed had hearing losses, but that scarring was a frequently observed abnormality.
7. Marshak and Neriah[702] did a retrospective study on 58 children, half of whom had undergone adenoidectomy and myringotomy for chronic otitis media with effusion and the other half of whom had only had tympanostomy tubes inserted. Only 20.7% of the adenoidectomized children had normal hearing and aerated middle ears during a 2-year follow-up, whereas 59% of the children who had had tympanostomy tubes inserted had normal hearing and aerated middle ears for the same period.
8. Gates et al[397] evaluated 578 Texas children in a trial that randomly assigned children 4 to 8 years of age, who had chronic otitis media with effusion that was unresponsive to antimicrobial therapy, into one of four surgical treatment groups: myringotomy, myringotomy and tympanostomy tube insertion, adenoidectomy and myringotomy, and adenoidectomy and myringotomy and tube insertion. The study did not include a control group of no surgery, but all three of the other treatments had statistically better results did than myringotomy without tube placement. (For details of this trial, see next section, Tonsillectomy and Adenoidectomy.)
9. Mandel et al[690] conducted a study in 109 children who had chronic otitis media with effusion that had been unresponsive to antimicrobial therapy and randomly assigned subjects to receive (1) myringotomy,

TABLE 25–53. Morbidity for First Year of Randomized Trial of Myringotomy, Myringotomy and Tympanostomy Tube, and No Surgery (Control) in 109 Pittsburgh Infants and Children with Chronic Otitis Media with Effusion

	Treatment Groups			
Outcome Measure	1: No Surgery (n = 35)	2: Myringotomy (n = 38)	3: Myringotomy and Tympanostomy Tube (n = 36)	Statistically Significant Difference
Treatment failure (proportion of subjects)	0.56	0.70	0.06	Yes°
Acute otitis media (episodes/person-year)	0.95	0.81	0.23	<.001†
Middle-ear effusion (proportion of time)	0.64	0.61	0.17	<.001†

° Actuarial rate: 90% confidence intervals for group 3 vs. groups 1 and 2.
† For group 1 vs. 3.
From Mandel EM, Rockette HE, Bluestone CD, et al. Efficacy of myringotomy with and without tympanostomy tubes for chronic otitis media with effusion. Pediatr Infect Dis J 11:270, 1992.

(2) myringotomy and tube insertion, or (3) no surgery (control). During this 3-year trial, in which subjects were evaluated monthly and whenever an ear, nose, and throat illness supervened, patients who had tympanostomy tubes inserted had less middle-ear disease and better hearing than either children who had only myringotomy or those subjects in whom no surgery had been performed. In addition, half of the subjects in the myringotomy group had to have tympanostomy tubes inserted during the first year of the trial, owing to an excessive number of myringotomies to control their disease. Likewise, half of the subjects in the control group required tympanostomy tube insertion during the course of the year because of development of "significant" hearing loss associated with their chronic middle-ear effusion, even though none of the children had this degree of hearing loss when they entered the trial.

About half of the children, however, had at least one bout of otorrhea when the tubes were in place, but these episodes were usually easily treated and short-lasting, although two children did develop chronic otorrhea that required intravenous antimicrobial therapy to eliminate the drainage. In addition, one subject who had tubes inserted eventually had to have bilateral tympanoplasties to repair chronic tympanic membrane perforations that persisted after the tubes spontaneously extruded. Myringotomy (without tube) provided no major advantage over no surgery (i.e., control) regarding percentage of time with middle-ear effusion, number of bouts of acute otitis media, and the number of subsequent surgical procedures. The investigators concluded that myringotomy and tube placement provided more effusion-free time and better hearing than either myringotomy without tube insertion or no surgery, but some patients who received tubes did develop otorrhea, and perforation was a problem in one of the children. Since the researchers considered the interpretation of this trial's results to be difficult, owing to the complexities of the design, the protocol was revised and a second clinical trial was conducted.

In the second trial, 111 children were randomized into the same three groups as in the first study: myringotomy, myringotomy and tympanostomy tube insertion, and no surgery control. As in the first trial, subjects were re-examined at least every month for 3 years. Similar outcomes were observed in this trial as were reported in the first study. Again, subjects in the myringotomy and tube placement group had less time with middle-ear effusion and better hearing than either those children who had only a myringotomy performed or those who had no surgery (Table 25–53). Similar to the initial trial, otorrhea occurred in 41% of those who were randomized to the tube insertion group, and three subjects developed chronic perforations after the tubes extruded; two of these children eventually required a tympanoplasty when the perforation failed to spontaneously heal after 2 years.

The investigators recommended, based on these two randomized clinical trials that evaluated a total of 220 subjects, that for children who have otitis media with effusion that is unresponsive to nonsurgical treatment and is persistent for 4 months or longer, myringotomy and tympanostomy tube insertion would be the first surgical procedure to perform, as opposed to myringotomy alone. Even though Gates et al[397] recommended an adenoidectomy and myringotomy (without tympanostomy tube insertion) as "the initial surgical procedure," Mandel and coworkers[689, 690] recommended reserving adenoidectomy for those children who required another surgical procedure if otitis media recurred following extrusion of the initial tube. This recommendation was made because the study by Gates and colleagues in 1987 showed that adenoidectomy in their population was only a little better than myringotomy and tube, and because in the two studies by Mandel and coworkers[689, 690] about 50% of the subjects required only one myringotomy and tube insertion during the 3-year trial. If the child has significant nasal obstruction due to obstructive adenoids, however, then adenoidectomy and myringotomy (with or without tube insertion) as an initial procedure is a reasonable option.

Recurrent Acute Otitis Media. Three randomized clinical trials have tested the efficacy of tympanostomy tube insertion for the prevention of recurrent acute otitis media.

1. Gebhart[401] in Columbus, Ohio, evaluated otitis-prone infants in whom half had tubes inserted and half had no surgery. Efficacy was demonstrated, but infants with middle-ear effusion were also enrolled and follow-up was limited to 6 months.

TABLE 25–54. Outcome of Randomized 2-Year Clinical Trial of Amoxicillin Prophylaxis and of Tympanostomy Tube Insertion vs. Placebo for Prevention of Recurrent Acute Otitis Media in 264 Pittsburgh Children, Ages 7–35 Months

Outcome Measure	Treatment Groups			P Value Groups		
	1: Amoxicillin	2: Placebo	3: Tympanostomy Tube	1 vs. 2	3 vs. 2	1 vs. 3
Rates of AOM AOM/otorrhea (child years)	0.60	1.08	1.02	<.001	NS	.001
Mean percentage Time with OM	10.0	15.0	6.6	.03	<.001	NS
Median time to first episode of AOM/otorrhea (mos.)	22.1	8.2	11.2	.002	NS	NS

AOM, acute otitis media; *OM*, otitis media; *NS*, not significant.

Modified from Casselbrant ML, Kaleida PH, Rockette HE, et al. Efficacy of antimicrobial prophylaxis and of tympanostomy tube insertion for prevention of recurrent otitis media: results of a randomized clinical trial. Pediatr Infect Dis J 11:278, 1992.

2. Gonzalez et al,[423] in a multicenter study conducted in the United States Army, enrolled 65 otitis-prone infants into a trial that randomly assigned subjects into three groups: sulfisoxazole prophylaxis, tympanostomy tubes, and placebo. Similar to the Gebhart trial,[401] infants were entered with and without middle-ear effusion, they were not stratified, and they were followed for only 6 months. Infants in the tympanostomy group did significantly better if they had middle-ear effusion at entry, but the attack rates of acute otitis media were not reduced significantly in those subjects who were effusion-free at the time of random assignment.

3. Casselbrant et al[209] randomly assigned 264 Pittsburgh children 7 to 35 months of age to one of three groups: amoxicillin prophylaxis, myringotomy and tube insertion, and placebo. Unlike the two previously reported trials, this one entered only patients who had no middle-ear effusion and followed the children monthly, and whenever an ear, nose, and throat illness supervened, for 2 years. The average rate of new bouts of acute otitis media was significantly reduced in those subjects who were in the amoxicillin prophylaxis group compared with the tube insertion or placebo groups (Table 25–54). There was no significant difference between the tube insertion and the placebo group for this outcome measure. Postoperative otorrhea through a tympanostomy tube was considered to be an episode of acute otitis media, which occurred at about the same rate as the number of episodes of acute otitis media in the placebo group, but the bouts of otorrhea were usually asymptomatic and less troublesome than when acute middle-ear infection developed in the placebo or amoxicillin prophylaxis groups. When the average portion of time with otitis media of any type (i.e., acute otitis media, otorrhea, or otitis media with effusion) was evaluated, only 6.6% of the tube placement group had bouts of otitis media, compared with 10.0% for the amoxicillin group and 15.0% for subjects who received placebo. The amoxicillin group had adverse side effects in 7.0%, primarily urticaria and vaginitis, and 3.9% of the tube placement group developed persistent perforation of the tympanic membrane; all of these eventually healed spontaneously. Since relatively long-term antimicrobial prophylaxis may be related to the development of resistant bacteria, this question was addressed in the trial, but there were no consistent differences in percentages of beta-lactamase-positive *H. influenzae* or *M. catarrhalis* found in the serial nasopharyngeal cultures between patients who received amoxicillin prophylaxis and those who were in the placebo group. During the 2-year trial, 70% of the subjects who were randomly assigned to the tube group required only one procedure, whereas 26% had to have a second set of tubes inserted; only one child (1%) had to have three sets of tubes.

The investigators recommended that in infants and young children, the age group included in the trial, amoxicillin prophylaxis would be the first method used to prevent the recurrent episodes, and, if this failed, then tympanostomy tube placement would be the next option. They also recommended that children who are placed on prophylaxis should be re-evaluated periodically, even though they are symptom-free, since asymptomatic middle-ear effusion may develop.

Rationale for the Use of Tympanostomy Tubes

Results of controlled clinical trials have now been reported that show that tympanostomy tube insertion can be beneficial in selected infants and children, since middle-ear disease is reduced and hearing is restored, although there are known complications and sequelae associated with the surgery. The rationale for the procedure can be found in certain physiologic and pathophysiologic aspects of the nasopharynx, eustachian tube, middle ear, and mastoid air cell system that are related to the pathogenesis of otitis media. The eustachian tube has three important physiologic functions in relation to the middle ear (Fig. 25–60): (1) middle-ear pressure regulation, (2) drainage of secretions down the eustachian tube, and (3) protection of the middle ear from the entrance of unwanted nasopharyngeal secretions.[122]

A functioning tympanostomy tube would maintain ambient pressure within the middle ear and mastoid and

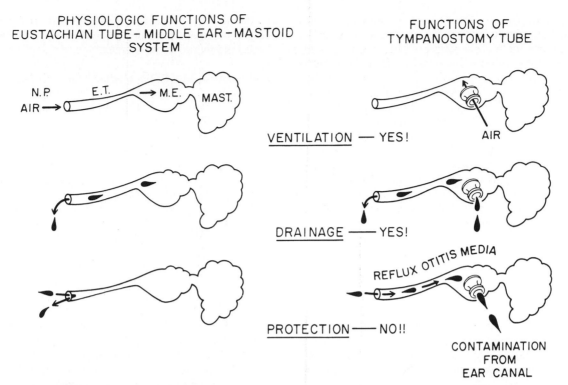

PHYSIOLOGIC FUNCTIONS OF
EUSTACHIAN TUBE – MIDDLE EAR – MASTOID
SYSTEM

FUNCTIONS OF
TYMPANOSTOMY TUBE

VENTILATION — YES!

DRAINAGE — YES!

PROTECTION — NO!!

CONTAMINATION
FROM
EAR CANAL

FIGURE 25–60. Physiologic functions of the eustachian tube that are related to the middle ear (see text). ET, eustachian tube; MAST, mastoid; ME, middle ear; NP, nasopharynx. (From Bluestone CD, Klein JO. Otitis Media in Infants and Children, 3rd ed. Philadelphia, WB Saunders, 2001, p 260.)

provide adequate drainage down the eustachian tube and through the tympanostomy tube. Therefore, two physiologic functions of the eustachian tube are fulfilled by the tympanostomy tube. The protective function of the eustachian tube may be impaired by tympanostomy tube insertion, since all of the conventional tympanostomy tubes leave an opening in the tympanic membrane, and the physiologic middle-ear air cushion is not present if the tympanic membrane is open. Therefore, reflux of nasopharyngeal secretions into the middle ear may be enhanced when a tympanostomy tube eliminates the middle-ear air cushion, a situation that can result in "reflux otitis media" and otorrhea.

The ideal eustachian tube prosthesis would be a transtympanic tube that fulfills all three of the important physiologic functions of the eustachian tube: pressure regulation, drainage, and protection.

Recommended Indications for Insertion of Tympanostomy Tubes

Chronic Otitis Media with Effusion. We now have the results of clinical trials that addressed the efficacy of tympanostomy tube insertion for chronic otitis media with effusion.[397, 689, 690]

Patients who have had bilateral otitis media with effusion that has been unresponsive to nonsurgical treatment, which should include a course of an antimicrobial agent, and has been present for at least 3 months, are reasonable candidates for the insertion of tympanostomy tubes.

For children who have unilateral effusion, the duration can probably be extended to 6 months prior to consideration for tube placement, since hearing is assumed to be good in the unaffected ear. Factors to be taken into account in the decision-making process to insert tubes for chronic effusion, in addition to the duration, would be the degree of hearing loss, the type and amount of effusion thought to be within the middle-ear cleft (e.g., observed small amount of serous effusion with air/fluid level and bubbles versus a completely opaque, immobile tympanic membrane), and the presence of a retraction pocket. Attendance in child day care has been shown to increase the frequency of tympanostomy tube insertion. In a study by Postma et al,[882] 31% of 346 children who attended day care had tympanostomy tubes in place, as compared with only 11% of 63 age- and sex-matched children who were in home care; also, the reintubation rate of tubes was 36% in the day care children as compared with only 11% in those who were in home care.

Even though myringotomy alone did not prove to be effective compared to myringotomy with tube insertion in the trials conducted by Mandel et al[689, 690] and Gates et al,[397] it would seem reasonable to attempt a myringotomy and aspiration of the middle-ear effusion prior to insertion of a tympanostomy tube in both older children and adults who are cooperative and who do not require general anesthesia. If the effusion rapidly recurs, then a tympanostomy tube can usually be inserted, again without the need for a general anesthetic. If general anesthesia is necessary to perform a myringotomy in infants and children who have chronic effusion (as is invariably the case in this age group), insertion of a tympanostomy tube at the time of the myringotomy is the preferred treatment.

Removal of a middle-ear effusion that is asymptomatic, especially when significant hearing loss is not present, is questionable. All children with such a condition have some degree of conductive hearing loss if followed closely, however, and the short- and long-term effects of even modest degrees of hearing loss may have an impact on certain aspects of child development. Indeed, in the first clinical trial conducted by Mandel et al,[690] patients with "significant" hearing loss were not randomized into the no surgery (control) group; however, half of these subjects developed "significant" hearing loss at the end of the first year, and became treatment failures. In addition, it is not known what chronic irreversible changes, such as adhesive otitis media, tympanosclerosis, ossicular disconti-nuity, or cholesteatoma, might occur in the middle-ear space if such an effusion is not treated. Therefore, the ultimate decision for the use of tympanostomy tubes for chronic otitis media with effusion must be based on many factors, most of which remain arbitrary. At present, how-ever, it seems to be reasonable to insert tympanostomy tubes in selected children to remove the effusion, to re-store hearing, and to prevent possible complications and sequelae of recurrent and chronic otitis media with effu-sion.

Stool et al[1069] concluded that myringotomy and tube placement is an option to antimicrobial treatment when the duration of otitis media with effusion persists for longer than 3 months, is bilateral, and is associated with a hearing deficit (defined as 20 dB hearing threshold level or worse in the better hearing ear). Tympanostomy tube placement is recommended when the effusion meets these criteria and persists for longer than 4 months. In contradistinction to the recommendations of the *Guide-line* that limits tube insertion to those children who have bilateral chronic effusion and a bilateral hearing loss (greater than 20 dB), we recommend the procedure irre-spective of the child's hearing assessed at one point in time.[138] Assessment of hearing at one point in the time course of chronic otitis media is more reliable than par-ent rating of hearing,[166, 941] but the clinical trial by Man-del et al[690] demonstrated the fluctuation in hearing over time associated with this disease.

Although not addressed in the *Guideline*, we recom-mend tube placement when a unilateral otitis media with effusion persists for 6 or more months, and we reserve placement of tubes for only those patients with chronic effusion that is unresponsive to a trial of appropriate antimicrobial agent. Despite the widespread dissemination of these guidelines in 1994, there is some evidence that they are not being followed by many clinicians. Hsu et al[515] examined the medical care of 59 patients with chronic otitis media with effusion and reported that the adherence rate to the *Guideline* was 0%. Delayed referral occurred in 34% of children and 25% were referred pre-maturely. The authors of this study recommended more timely referral to otolaryngologists.

Apparently, the *Guideline* is not perceived as being very helpful to pediatricians in clinical practice.[257] A re-cent review of physician adherence to clinical practice guidelines is not only a problem with the otitis media *Guideline*; there is also poor adherence with other pub-lished guidelines in medicine.[188]

Recurrent Acute Otitis Media. Many children, especially infants, have recurrent episodes of acute otitis media that respond to medical therapy or resolve spontaneously, and in these children the middle-ear effusion does not be-come chronic. However, it would still be desirable to prevent these episodes when they occur frequently over a relatively short period of time, since hearing is affected when the middle-ear effusion is present and the child may be uncomfortable because of accompanying otalgia and fever. At present, there are three popular methods of prevention for such episodes: (1) antimicrobial prophy-laxis[114, 209, 336, 423, 716]; (2) myringotomy with insertion of tympanostomy tubes[209, 401, 423]; and (3) adenoidectomy[836] (see next section on Tonsillectomy and Adenoidectomy). A fourth method, pneumococcal vaccine in children, is another possible option (see earlier section on Immuno-prophylaxis in this chapter).

We now have the outcomes of clinical trials that have demonstrated that tympanostomy tubes prevent recurrent acute otitis media, to some degree; acute otorrhea still may develop after tube insertion. Presumably, the tube prevents aspiration of infected nasopharyngeal secretions into the middle ear, since ambient, rather than negative, middle ear pressure would be present. Absence of nega-tive middle ear pressure could also prevent accumulation of a noninfected middle-ear effusion. In addition, a non-intact tympanic membrane would allow for excellent drainage down the eustachian tube of any secretions en-tering the middle ear. In children with semipatulous eu-stachian tubes, however, reflux of nasopharyngeal secre-tions can be enhanced when the tympanic membrane is not intact, resulting in otorrhea secondary to reflux otitis media.

Myringotomy with insertion of a tympanostomy tube is helpful for children who suffer frequent, recurrent attacks of acute otitis media. Three or more episodes during the preceding 6 months, or at least four episodes during the preceding year (with the last episode occurring during the preceding 6 months), would be indications for performing this procedure; these were the entry criteria for the study by Casselbrant et al.[209] For such children, however, a trial of antimicrobial prophylaxis would be an acceptable alter-native management option, and myringotomy with inser-tion of tympanostomy tubes reserved for those children in whom chemoprophylaxis has failed. Antimicrobial prophy-laxis should be considered only in those children who have no evidence of a middle-ear effusion between the acute attacks.

But, since there has been an increasing rate of multi-drug-resistant pneumococcus, experts and official organi-zations, such as the CDC and the AAP, now recommend antimicrobial prophylaxis for prevention of recurrent acute otitis media only in selected children.[294, 295] In this era of concern about the overuse of antimicrobial agents, tympanostomy tube placement is a more rational ap-proach to prevention than long-term, low-dose antibiotic prophylaxis.[152] For those children who have recurrent acute episodes superimposed on a chronic otitis media with effusion that is unresponsive to medical treatment, tympanostomy tubes should be considered.

Despite the recommendation by one utilization review corporation to place infants and children who have recurrent acute otitis media on antimicrobial prophylaxis and not insert tympanostomy tube,[607] our rebuttal to restricting options for prevention to only prophylaxis is a matter of record.[140]

(See also previous section on Specific Medical Options for Preventing Recurrent Acute Otitis Media, Antimicrobial Chemoprophylaxis.)

Eustachian Tube Dysfunction. Tympanostomy tubes may restore normal middle-ear pressure in patients who have eustachian tube dysfunction but who do not have a middle-ear effusion when one or more of the following conditions is present: (1) otalgia, (2) significant and symptomatic conductive hearing loss, (3) vertigo, or (4) tinnitus. If these signs and symptoms are believed to be due to eustachian tube obstruction and not related to a condition that can be improved by medical treatment (e.g., sinusitis), then tympanostomy tubes often provide relief. This is not usually the case in patients with a patulous or semipatulous eustachian tube. When an abnormally patent eustachian tube is suspected, a trial with just myringotomy should first be attempted. If the patient is symptom free when the tympanic membrane is not intact, a tympanostomy tube can then be inserted. Chen and Luxford[225] found that insertion of tympanostomy tubes in 46 patients with patulous tubes was helpful in relief of their symptoms in about half the patients and should be tried as initial treatment.

If the symptoms are not eliminated or become worse, a tympanostomy tube should not be inserted. While the tympanic membrane is open, a test of eustachian tube function should be performed in an effort to determine the specific type of dysfunction present. If the function of the eustachian tube is normal, another cause of the symptoms (e.g., inner ear disease) should be sought.

Symptoms of eustachian tube dysfunction may be present in children during puberty, usually in girls, even when they have had little or no past history of middle-ear disease. In these children, tympanostomy tube insertion is frequently successful in eliminating their complaints, for example, popping and snapping sounds in the ear, fluctuating hearing loss, and a sense of fullness in the ear.

Although the need for hyperbaric oxygen therapy is not as common in children as in adults, tympanostomy tube insertion is frequently required to prevent middle-ear barotrauma.[368] One of the indications to place tympanostomy tubes prior to this treatment is a history or presence of otitis media or eustachian tube dysfunction, or both.[889] Since many children have had middle-ear disease, insertion of tympanostomy tubes in this population is recommended. Even if children have not had a history of middle-ear problems in the past, their eustachian tube function is still not likely to be mature enough to equilibrate the two atmospheres of pressure developed in the chamber during the therapy, especially in patients who must be taught to equilibrate middle-ear pressures by autoinflation. Despite the complications that can occur

with the use of tympanostomy tubes for this indication,[235] placement is recommended.

Atelectasis of the Tympanic Membrane and Retraction Pocket. Atelectasis of the middle ear may be the result either of passive collapse of the tympanic membrane, due to lack of stiffness of the drum, or of active retraction of the tympanic membrane secondary to high negative middle-ear pressure. Atelectasis may either be generalized or localized, or both, and may be accompanied by a retraction pocket in the pars flaccida or posterosuperior portion of the tympanic membrane. These two portions of the tympanic membrane are the most compliant areas of the drum.[584] A severe retraction pocket in the posterosuperior portion of the tympanic membrane may cause irreversible destruction of the incus, with resultant conductive hearing loss. Progression of such a retraction pocket may also result in a cholesteatoma. This sequence of events has been shown to be associated with eustachian tube dysfunction[126] and can be reversed by insertion of a tympanostomy tube. If the retraction pocket is associated with adhesive otitis media in which the tympanic membrane is adherent to the incudostapedial joint and the surrounding area, restoration of normal intratympanic pressure with a tympanostomy tube may not be successful in returning the tympanic membrane to its neutral position. Following tympanostomy tube insertion, persistence of such a retraction pocket in the attic or in the posterosuperior quadrant, or in both, may require a tympanoplastic procedure in an effort to prevent progressive disease.

Suppurative Complications of Otitis Media. Whenever a child has an intratemporal or intracranial suppurative complication present, one is suspected to be present, or one is even considered to be developing, myringotomy and tympanocentesis is required to identify the causative organism and to provide drainage. In an effort to provide adequate drainage, insertion of a tympanostomy tube is desirable (see Chaps. 26 and 27).

Tympanoplasty. When tympanoplasty is performed for retraction pocket or acquired cholesteatoma, or both, in which case eustachian tube function is usually abnormal, insertion of a tympanostomy tube at the time of surgery should be considered to maintain normal middle-ear regulation of pressure postoperatively, which should prevent recurrence of the retraction pocket and possibly the development of a cholesteatoma (see Chap. 26, section on Cholesteatoma).[127, 128]

Surgical Technique and Type of Tube Employed

Insertion of a tympanostomy tube into the posterosuperior quadrant of the tympanic membrane is not advised, since this is the most compliant part of the pars tensa and insertion here may result in a permanent perforation or an atrophic scar with subsequent retraction pocket. A retraction pocket could lead to necrosis of the incus or formation of a cholesteatoma, or both. Insertion of a tympanostomy tube under the annulus also may result in a cholesteatoma. It seems more appropriate to insert the tube into the anterior portion of the pars tensa. In fact,

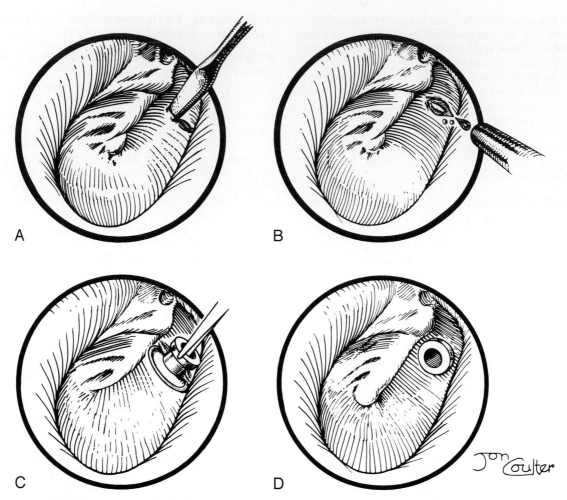

FIGURE 25–61. Method of insertion of a tympanostomy tube. *A,* Radial incision in the tympanic membrane. *B,* Middle-ear effusion aspirated. *C,* Short, biflanged tympanostomy tube (Armstrong-type) inserted by use of alligator forceps. *D,* Tube position in anterosuperior portion of the tympanic membrane. (From Bluestone CD, Klein JO. Otitis Media in Infants and Children, 3rd ed. Philadelphia, WB Saunders, 2001, p 264.)

when there is severe generalized atelectasis, the anterosuperior portion may be the only area into which a tympanostomy tube can be inserted (Fig. 25–61).

A pre- and postoperative evaluation of hearing, commonly made by obtaining a behavioral audiogram, has been advocated,[153, 693, 1162] but owing to concerns over costs in this era of managed care we usually now only obtain a postoperative audiogram to ensure that hearing is normal following the elimination of the middle-ear effusion. In addition, there is a 1% rate of a preexisting sensorineural hearing loss identified in this population.[334, 693]

The type of tube employed varies with the surgeon. The short, double-flanged tubes appear to provide adequate middle ear aeration without a high incidence of obstruction of the lumen by mucus or cerumen, but water can more readily enter the ear through a short tube. When the longer type of tube is used, however, there is a greater chance of obstruction of the lumen. The size of the lumen of the tube is quite variable, but, again, if the lumen is too small, obstruction is a problem, and if the lumen is too large, removal or spontaneous extrusion of

the tube could result in a persistent perforation. Tubes are made of various materials, but no data are available to show the superiority of one type of biocompatible material over another. We prefer the Armstrong type tube that is biflanged. The average life of this tube is approximately 1 year.[209, 689, 690]

Much controversy exists concerning the indications for insertion of tympanostomy tubes that are more or less "permanent." Insertion of such tubes may be warranted in selected patients: those in whom tympanostomy tubes have frequently been tried and in whom eustachian tube dysfunction appears to be not only chronic but also not likely to improve in the near future, such as in children who have had skull fracture, skull-base surgery, or another cause of permanent anatomic (i.e., mechanical) obstruction of the eustachian tube.[145] "Permanent" tubes can also be used in adults with long-standing chronic otitis media with effusion or severe atelectasis. The Per-Lee[113] and Goode T tubes [181, 421, 692, 708, 1126] are associated with a high likelihood of development of a chronic perforation following either spontaneous extrusion or removal. Although rarely encountered, stenosis of the external auditory canal can occur when the Goode T tube remains in place for an excessively long period.[1214] Therefore, these more lasting tubes are indicated when a permanent perforation is desirable.

"Permanent" tubes should rarely be used in children, since the incidence of otitis media with effusion and atelectasis of the tympanic membrane progressively decreases with advancing age during childhood. This is true even for children with cleft palates who have had repeated myringotomies. On the infrequent occasions when permanent tympanostomy tubes are used in children, the function of the eustachian tube should be tested periodically to determine when or if there is evidence of improvement so that the tube may be removed.

Even though many ways to assess eustachian tube function have been tried, there is currently no known method that surpasses observation of the middle ear when the tympanic membrane is intact. Therefore, the best way to determine whether a patient needs another tympanostomy tube after the tube extrudes spontaneously is to examine the ears frequently.

Postoperative Follow-up and Hearing Testing

In this age of managed care[607, 1069] and concern about the cost for the otolaryngologist who inserted the tympanostomy tubes to periodically observe children during the postoperative period, the responsibility for this surgical procedure rests with that surgeon.[528a] For most children, a postoperative visit to the otolaryngologist approximately 2 weeks after the procedure is appropriate. At that time, the tubes are evaluated to determine patency. If a tympanostomy tube is obstructed, ototopical antibiotic and corticosteroid medication is prescribed; if this treatment fails to open the tube, then a small stylet is used to open the tympanostomy tube with the aid of the otomicroscope. If otorrhea is present, an aspirate is obtained for Gram stain and culture, and the children are treated accordingly. When the tubes are patent and without drainage, a postoperative audiogram is obtained; ideally, hearing should be evaluated both before and after the procedure.[152, 693]

If the child's hearing has returned to the expected level, another visit to the surgeon is appropriate 6 months after the procedure; the three studies from Pittsburgh showed that the biflanged tympanostomy tubes used in those studies began to spontaneously extrude after about 6 months.[209, 689, 690] The child is re-evaluated at 3- or 4-month intervals after the 6-month visit. Uncomplicated otorrhea in the interval can usually be evaluated and treated by the patient's primary physician. If the child has persistent otorrhea despite the primary physician's management, the patient should be evaluated and treated by the surgeon. Also, the otolaryngologist should re-evaluate the child if recurrent otorrhea develops (e.g., three episodes within a 3- or 4-month period); at this stage, antimicrobial prophylaxis is an option until the tubes spontaneously extrude.

After either spontaneous extrusion or removal, the patient should be periodically observed (e.g., every 3 or 4 months) for about four seasons to determine whether there is recurrence of the disease or a sequela of the

tube, such as persistent perforation, retraction pocket, or, on a rare occasion, post-tympanostomy tube cholesteatoma.

Protection of the Ears When Tubes Are in Place

Despite a recent meta-analysis by Lee et al[633] that showed no increase in the otorrhea rate when ears of children were left unprotected when exposed to water, water from bathing or swimming should not be allowed to enter the middle ear through the tympanostomy tube, since contamination frequently results in otitis media and discharge. Protection of the ears during swimming is a minor nuisance and may prevent otorrhea. During bathing or hair washing, a wad of either lamb's wool or cotton covered with petroleum jelly should be inserted into the external auditory meatus. Doc's Proplugs (International Aquatic Trades, Inc., Santa Cruz, CA) are usually effective in protecting the middle ear and can be used to permit the patient to swim; surface swimming is recommended only, as diving or swimming deeply under water may lead to contamination of the middle ear.

When Should Tympanostomy Tubes Be Removed?

In general, once tubes have been inserted, they should be permitted to extrude spontaneously into the external auditory canal and not be removed too early. The rationale for such management is based on experience rather than on any controlled clinical trials: In children with tympanostomy tubes in place, eustachian tube function has not been shown to change significantly, even after several years.[76]

There are indications to remove tubes in selected children.[260] Tympanostomy tubes can be removed as an office procedure without the aid of either local or general anesthesia, especially when the tube is partially extruded or there is chronic infection involving the tympanic membrane. In children, however, tympanostomy tubes are frequently removed under general anesthesia in the operating room, since the procedure is usually painful, and since the rim of the perforation can be denuded of epithelium and the defect closed, that is, "paper patch" myringoplasty, following removal of the tube; we prefer to use Steri-Strip to close the defect. This method appears to result in a higher rate of closure of the perforation than when the tube is just removed with no attempt to close the defect.[145, 890]

Most tympanostomy tubes remain in the tympanic membrane for 6 to 12 months, although some have been known to have remained in place for years. In the three Pittsburgh studies that evaluated the Armstrong-type tube for treatment of chronic otitis media with effusion[689, 690] and for prevention of recurrent acute otitis media,[209] the tube life was approximately 1 year; 50% of tubes were extruded in 12 months and 75% in 18 months. In children in whom tympanostomy tubes have been inserted bilaterally and in whom one tube subsequently extrudes but the other remains in place for a prolonged period, the remaining tube can usually be removed if the opposite middle ear remains free of high negative middle-ear pressure or middle-ear effusion, or both, for at least 1 year after the spontaneous extrusion of the opposite tube. This method of management is based on the observation that eustachian tube function is usually about the same in both ears in children. If high negative middle-ear pressure or otitis media with effusion, or both, occur during the observation period, the tube in the opposite ear should not be removed. Unfortunately, this method of management cannot be employed in adults, because eustachian tube function may not be symmetrical.

Removal of tympanostomy tubes depends upon several factors, such as the following:

1. Age of the child
2. Duration of time the tube has remained in place
3. Unilateral versus bilateral tubes
4. Status of the contralateral ear when that tympanic membrane is intact
5. Eustachian tube function
6. Presence or absence of recurrent or chronic otorrhea (and frequency, severity, and duration of otorrhea)
7. Patency of the tube
8. Season of the year

The age of the child is one of the most important factors, since most studies of the epidemiology of otitis media show that the disease has a peak in infancy and declines rapidly after about the age of 6. In addition, the structure and function of the eustachian tube and the child's immunity are usually more mature after 6 years of age. Therefore, removal of tubes in children who are 6 years of age and older is more desirable than in children who are younger. Removing the tube in selected children who are younger, however, may be of benefit, such as when there is unilateral recurrent otorrhea through a tube—apparently due to reflux of nasopharyngeal secretions into the middle ear—that is not controlled medically and the contralateral tympanic membrane is intact (no tube is present) and that ear has been free of middle-ear disease for 1 year or longer.

The indications for removing tubes are as follows:

1. Presence of a retained unilateral tympanostomy tube in children who are 6 years of age or older, when the contralateral tympanic membrane is intact and the middle ear has been free of disease for 1 year or longer.
2. Selected similar children younger than 6 years of age may also be candidates in whom the decision is based on the factors listed above.
3. Presence of retained bilateral tympanostomy tubes in children in whom eustachian tube function is now considered within normal limits due to growth and development, or when a nonsurgical (e.g., allergy control/treatment) or surgical (e.g., adenoidectomy, repair of cleft palate) management may have improved eustachian tube function.
4. Presence of frequently recurrent otorrhea through a tympanostomy tube that is not prevented by antimicrobial prophylaxis. Frequency, severity, and duration of the episodes; age of the patient; and length of time the tube has been in place are important in decision-making.

5. Following chronic otorrhea, especially when the criteria described in the first two points are met.
6. When the tympanostomy tube is imbedded in granulation tissue, which is unresponsive to medical treatment.

Complications and Sequelae

One of the major concerns that patients, parents, and physicians have when tympanostomy tube insertion is being considered is the safety of the general anesthetic. In a study from Buffalo, Markowitz-Spence et al[699] evaluated 510 children who had tubes placed for possible complications of the general anesthetic. No complications were identified in 83%, and in 12% there was a minor degree of airway obstruction. In the remaining patients, only 1.4% had severe airway obstruction during the procedure; there were no serious complications or deaths. The authors concluded that the procedure is relatively safe, especially when the anesthesia is delivered by a pediatric anesthesiologist.

Intraoperative complications from the procedure are rare, but Brodish and Wooley[163] recently encountered two children who had vascular injuries due to the myringotomy incision; one child had an abnormally high-positioned jugular bulb and the other had an exposed carotid artery in the middle ear; both children were successfully treated for these congenital malformations. These cases emphasize the unique role of the otolaryngologist in performing this surgical procedure, since they are fully aware of these rare complications and can appropriately respond when such an emergency occurs.

There are less severe and more commonly known complications and sequelae related to the tympanostomy tube insertion, which include scarring of the tympanic membrane (tympanosclerosis) and localized or diffuse membrane atrophy, with or without retraction pockets, or atelectasis, or both.[612, 644, 924, 1100] Most likely the scarring is of the tympanic membrane, which is said to occur in approximately 50% more tympanic membranes after tube insertion than if the tube was not inserted, but in most instances this degree of scarring of the tympanic membrane is a cosmetic issue, since tympanosclerosis is rarely identified within the middle ear in infants and children, and the hearing is uninvolved.[924]

Less commonly, a perforation may remain at the insertion site following extrusion of the tube. The rate of perforation varies from 0.5% to 25%, depending on the type of tube and the number of tubes inserted into the same tympanic membrane over time; permanent tubes have the highest rate, and the more conventional ones have a low frequency of perforation.[476, 726, 855, 1125] In the Pittsburgh clinical trials that evaluated the safety and efficacy of tympanostomy tube insertion for chronic otitis media with effusion,[689, 690] and for prevention of recurrent acute otitis media,[209] a total of 215 infants and children were prospectively followed for at least 2 to 3 years following entry, and 32 (14.8%) developed a perforation at the tube site following spontaneous extubation; however, almost all of these perforations eventually closed; three children (1.4%) did have to have a tympanoplasty after the perforations failed to close after 2 years, and another child had a persistent perforation that lasted 4 years. A recent review from Israel of 2604 tympanostomy tube placements revealed a rate of 3.06% perforation; perforations occurred more frequently in children younger than 5 years of age, when the indication for placement was for prevention of acute otitis media, with the use of Goode T tubes, and in patients who required reinsertion of tubes.[421]

On rare occasions, a cholesteatoma may develop, usually at the site of the tube insertion, either by invagination of squamous epithelium or from a retraction pocket that develops because of persistent eustachian tube dysfunction and the subsequent middle-ear pressure. Golz et al[420] reported the rate of cholesteatoma to be 1.1% and attributed this relatively high rate to the use of Goode T tubes, when repeat tubes were needed. Other complications include secondary infection accompanied by otorrhea through the tube and dislocation of the tube into the middle-ear cavity.

The most common complication of tympanostomy tube insertion is otorrhea through the lumen of the tube. Otorrhea commonly occurs immediately following tube insertion, especially when a mucoid or purulent effusion is aspirated at the time of the myringotomy; the rate is approximately 12%[49, 51, 337, 408, 908, 994, 1219] but has been reported by some investigators to be over 30%.[57, 610] Garcia et al,[396] in a recently reported meta-analysis, concluded that the use of ototopical drops at the time of surgery was effective in reducing this rate, especially when the middle ear contained mucoid or purulent effusion. The authors did caution the clinician in using the currently available medications indiscriminately, because of possible ototoxicity. Most otolaryngologists, however, commonly prescribe these agents for otorrhea, despite the perceived risk.[670]

After insertion of tympanostomy tubes, otorrhea can occur at any time while the tubes remain in place and patent. This otorrhea that occurs after the postoperative period is usually the result of reflux of nasopharyngeal secretions into the middle ear or from contamination from the external canal. Otorrhea occurs in two thirds of infants with unrepaired cleft palates who have had tympanostomy tubes inserted to treat chronic otitis media with effusion and who are followed during the first 2 years of life.[834] Otorrhea may also occur in children without cleft palates in whom tubes have been inserted. In the three Pittsburgh clinical trials, otorrhea occurred at least once in about half the subjects during the course of the 2- and 3-year studies.[209, 689, 690] This rate is higher than reported in the past, probably because the subjects were re-evaluated every month and whenever they had an ear, nose, or throat illness, and some of the episodes were not evident to the parents. Valtonen et al[1152] followed 281 children prospectively for 5 years following tympanostomy tube placement and reported that otorrhea was more common when the indication for tube placement was otitis media with effusion than prevention of recurrent acute otitis media; extrusion of the tube was more common following post-tube otorrhea and required reinsertion.

When otorrhea occurs, a culture sample should be taken from the middle ear by aspiration through the tym-

panostomy tube. A preliminary culture of the ear canal and meticulous cleaning of the ear canal should precede the aspiration of the middle ear. Oral systemic antimicrobial therapy should be guided by the results of the middle ear culture and susceptibility studies; the same pathogens that cause acute otitis media in the community are usually isolated. In a study reported by Mandel et al,[683] the common causative organisms were isolated from infants and young children, primarily during the winter months, but during the summer months, especially in older children, *P. aeruginosa* was cultured (Fig. 25–62).

Schneider[981] found similar results in smaller numbers of patients; children younger than the age of 3 years had the usual bacterial pathogens that cause acute otitis media, but in children older than that age, he cultured flora that were consistent with the flora of the external canal. A recent study by Brook et al[171] of 55 ear aspirates of 34 children with spontaneous otorrhea also cultured *Pseudomonas* in most of the isolates. A more recent study of post-tympanostomy tube otorrhea in 283 children, 1 to 12 years of age, by Dohar et al,[288] revealed that the most frequently isolated pathogens were *S. pneumoniae* and *H. influenzae*, but *P. aeruginosa* was also cultured. Also, on rare occasions, post-tympanostomy tube otorrhea can be caused by methicillin-resistant *Staphylococcus aureus*.[467]

Treatment in the absence of results from a culture would be the same as recommended when the tympanic membrane is intact, for example, amoxicillin. Topical antimicrobials and irrigation of the middle ear with a variety of agents have been advocated, but the ototoxic effect of these medications must be considered.[69a] Fortunately, we now have an FDA-approved ototopical agent, ofloxacin otic solution 0.3%, that is both safe and effective for treatment of post-tympanostomy acute otorrhea, which, in most instances, is effective without the addition of an orally administered antimicrobial agent.[287] When the otorrhea is unresponsive to oral systemic antimicrobial agents and aural ototopical medications, a more intensive workup and treatment is indicated, which usually includes the use of intravenous antimicrobials.[578] Despite a recent report that mastoidectomy is needed in 1.1% of children with recurrent or chronic otorrhea,[1152] intravenous therapy is highly effective in eliminating the chronic otorrhea without the need to resort to mastoidectomy. Children with Down syndrome tend to have recurrent otorrhea that may be difficult to control,[522] but the alternative is to leave chronic otitis media with effusion untreated, with its attendant hearing loss in these already handicapped children.

For a more complete discussion of the etiology, pathogenesis, and management of acute and chronic otorrhea, see Chapter 26 (sections on acute and chronic perforation), since these aspects of otorrhea through a perforation are similar to otorrhea through a tympanostomy tube. In both instances, the tympanic membrane is not intact, which makes the middle ear susceptible to contamination of bacteria from the external ear canal and reflux of nasopharyngeal secretions.

When frequently recurrent episodes of acute otitis media occur despite the presence of a functioning tympanostomy tube, antimicrobial prophylaxis should be given to prevent the recurrent middle-ear infection and otor-

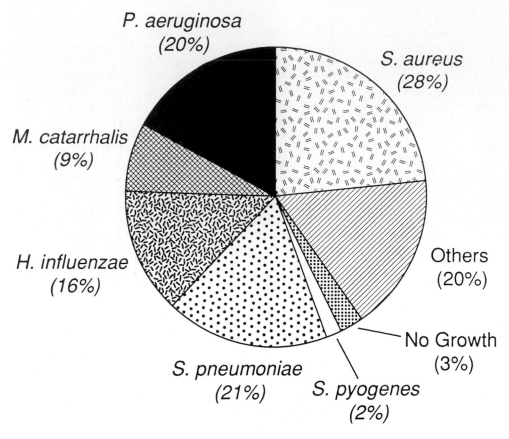

P. aeruginosa
(20%)

S. aureus
(28%)

M. catarrhalis
(9%)

Others
(20%)

H. influenzae
(16%)

No Growth
(3%)

S. pneumoniae
(21%)

S. pyogenes
(2%)

FIGURE 25–62. Bacteriology of 178 episodes of otorrhea from 109 children (194 ears) who had patent tympanostomy tubes. (From Mandel EM, Casselbrant ML, Kurs-Lasky M. Acute otorrhea: bacteriology of a common complication of tympanostomy tubes. Ann Otol Rhinol Laryngol 103: 713, 1994.)

rhea.[716] The selection of antibiotic and dose would be the same as recommended for antimicrobial prophylaxis alone. (See earlier in this chapter Recurrent Acute Otitis Media.)

Conclusions

The efficacy of insertion of tympanostomy tubes in patients with recurrent acute and chronic otitis media with effusion has now been demonstrated in randomized clinical trials.[142] Tubes may also be of benefit in certain related conditions, such as atelectasis and retraction pocket of the tympanic membrane. The beneficial outcomes obtained by this surgical procedure appear to outweigh their known complications and sequelae in selected patients, which warrant their continued use. It does not seem that the insertion of tympanostomy tubes is a modern fad that will become obsolete in the near future. Recurrent acute otitis media and chronic otitis media with effusion are extremely prevalent in infants and young children but are conditions that are highly age related. Since hearing loss secondary to otitis media during infancy and early childhood may impair language or cognitive development, and since insertion of tympanostomy tubes permits hearing preservation and probably prevents many of the complications and sequelae of otitis media while the tubes are in place, their use is advocated despite the fact that otitis media usually improves with increasing age.

Even though some have questioned the existing practice of tympanostomy tube insertion (e.g., indications and timing),[86] a study of 248 children who had tympanostomy tubes placed and were assessed both before and after surgery by Rosenfeld et al[939] showed that tympanostomy tubes produce a large short-term improvement in quality of life for most of the children; outcome was best in the absence of postoperative otorrhea.

Tympanostomy tubes are indicated in the following types of cases: (1) chronic otitis media with effusion that has been present for at least 3 months and is unresponsive to or not improving progressively with nonsurgical methods of management (e.g., antimicrobial therapy), and whose duration is either documented or evident from the history; (2) at least three episodes of recurrent acute otitis media within the preceding 6 months, the frequency documented or evident from the history, especially when antimicrobial prophylaxis has failed or is not deemed feasible or desirable; (3) eustachian tube dysfunction resulting in one or more of the following: significant and symptomatic hearing loss, otalgia, vertigo, tinnitus, or severe atelectasis, especially in those ears in which a deep retraction pocket is present in the posterosuperior quadrant or pars flaccida, or both; (4) following tympanoplasty, when eustachian tube function is known to be poor; and (5) when a suppurative complication is present, such as facial paralysis, since tympanostomy tubes can provide drainage of the middle ear.

Tonsillectomy and Adenoidectomy

Adenoidectomy performed either separately or in combination with tonsillectomy is the most common major surgical procedure employed to prevent otitis media; myringotomy with tympanostomy tube insertion is the most common minor surgical procedure for otitis media with effusion.[839]

Tonsillectomy and adenoidectomy are the most common major operations performed in the United States; it is estimated that one fourth of all children have a tonsillectomy and adenoidectomy during childhood. Such operations account for about one half of all major surgical operations performed on children, one fourth of all hospital admissions of children, and 10% of hospital bed-days utilized by children. In 1996 in the United States, about 287,000 procedures on the tonsils and adenoids were performed in children who were younger than 15 years of age,[819] which represents a substantial reduction from the more than 1 million such operations performed a few decades earlier.

This decrease in the total number of tonsil and adenoid operations may be related to a change in demography, however, since the total reduction during the same period in the number of children in the age group concerned was approximately 20%. Although the number of adenoidectomies without tonsillectomy remained relatively small in comparison with the number of tonsillectomies performed either separately or in combination with adenoidectomy, there was more than a twofold increase in the performance of adenoidectomy without tonsillectomy. Also, there appears to be a wide variation in the rate of performance of these operations by region of the country; the rates for adenoidectomy vary the most widely.[784] There are no data available related to the indications for which these operations were performed. Certainly, for many clinicians, otitis media was one of the indications, and in many instances the only indication, for adenoidectomy either with or without tonsillectomy. The question is whether the potential benefits of adenoidectomy, with or without tonsillectomy, for prevention of otitis media outweigh the known risks of these operations.[910]

Clinical Trials

In the past, there was a great deal of uncertainty and skepticism concerning the efficacy of adenoidectomy in the treatment and prevention of otitis media. In 1930, Kaiser[556] reported the results of following 4400 children, one half of whom underwent tonsillectomy and adenoidectomy (the indications for surgery were not reported) (Table 25–55). Even though there was no difference in

TABLE 25–55. Prevalence of Purulent Otorrhea in 220 Children Who Received Tonsillectomy with Adenoidectomy and 2200 "Comparable" Children Who Did Not

	T&A (%)	No T&A (%)
Before Operation	15	12
10 Years After Operation	5	6

° T&A, tonsillectomy and adenoidectomy.

From Kaiser AD. Results of tonsillectomy: a comparative study of 2,200 tonsillectomized children with an equal number of controls three and ten years after operation. JAMA 95:837, 1930. Copyright 1930, American Medical Association.

TABLE 25–56. Mean Incidence of Otitis Media in Children Aged 2 to 15 Years Receiving Tonsillectomy with Adenoidectomy Compared with Control Group

	Control	T&A	t
First Year	0.33 (154)	0.17 (222)	2.52°
Second Year	0.17 (139)	0.14 (213)	0.54

° Significant change, $P < .01$.

T&A, tonsillectomy and adenoidectomy.

From McKee WJ. A controlled study of the effects of tonsillectomy and adenoidectomy in children. Br J Prev Soc Med 17:46, 1963.

incidence of purulent otorrhea in the children who had been operated on and those who had not, the study cannot be considered to indicate conclusively the lack of efficacy of tonsillectomy and adenoidectomy in preventing otitis media since (1) the two groups may not have been similar at the outset, (2) they were not randomized, (3) the analysis was retrospective, and (4) only purulent otorrhea was considered as a measurement of the effectiveness of tonsillectomy and adenoidectomy. There are now data, however, to support the recommendation for adenoidectomy in selected children that has been established through controlled clinical trials. The following is a summary of the results of these studies as they relate to the efficacy of adenoidectomy (with and without tonsillectomy) for prevention of otitis media.

1. The first truly prospective clinical trial of tonsillectomy and adenoidectomy was reported by McKee[724] and was conducted in Great Britain. The criterion for entry into the study was a history of at least three episodes of "throat infection" or of acute upper respiratory tract infection with cervical adenitis during the preceding year.

    The mean incidence of otitis media among control subjects was twice as high as among children undergoing the tonsillectomy and adenoidectomy during the first year of the trial, but during the second year there was no difference in incidence of otitis media in the group that had been operated on and the control group (Table 25–56). This study was based on the occurrence of sore throats, however, and not on the presence of middle-ear disease in the year preceding the study. In fact, subjects were initially excluded from the study if they had "marked deafness, or recurrent or chronic otitis media." In addition, the follow-up evaluation was based solely on interview data, with no objective examinations being made, and no attempt was made to detect asymptomatic otitis media with effusion or impairment of hearing.

    In a second study, McKee[725] attempted to distinguish the effects of tonsillectomy from those of adenoidectomy. The criterion for entry into the study was the same as in the first study and, again, children with deafness and otitis media were excluded. Two hundred children were randomly assigned to undergo either tonsillectomy and adenoidectomy or adenoidectomy only. The mean incidence of otitis

TABLE 25–57. Relative Frequency of Earache and Otitis Media in 404 Children Receiving Tonsillectomy and Adenoidectomy Compared with Control Group

| Number of Episodes | Relative Frequency (%) | | | | | |
	Year Prior to Trial, Study Group	Control	First Year of Trial, Study Group	Control	Second Year of Trial, Study Group	Control
0	63	65	59	57	58.5	57.5
1	5	4.5	7.5	15	7	9.5
2–3	19	22.5	15.5	18	9	11
4–6	6	3	3.5	2	1	1.5
>7	5	4	—	2.5	—	1

From Mawson SR, Adlington R, Evans M. A controlled study evaluation of adenotonsillectomy in children. J Laryngol Otol 81:777, 1967.

media in each of the two surgical groups was approximately the same.

Therefore, McKee concluded from the two studies that otitis media was infrequent after adenoidectomy or tonsillectomy and adenoidectomy and that the combined operation did not offer any particular advantages in the prevention of the disease. Even though the studies did not select children with a high morbidity of otitis media, McKee stated that it was reasonable to infer that adenoidectomy without tonsillectomy was indicated for the prevention of otitis media with effusion.

2. Mawson et al[713] reported their prospective study of tonsillectomy and adenoidectomy, which was also performed in Great Britain. The design of their experiment was similar to that of the first McKee study in that an unspecified number of children who were severely affected were excluded and operated upon. Minimal criteria for entry were not described. Table 25–57 shows the relative incidence of earache and otitis media before and 1 and 2 years after randomization of 404 children into either the tonsillectomy and adenoidectomy group or the control group. There was no apparent difference at any age between the two groups. As can be seen from Table 25–57, however, more than one half of the children did not have otitis media prior to entry, and the occurrence of asymptomatic otitis media with effusion or the incidence of hearing loss was not reported.

3. In a study from New Zealand, using an experimental design similar to McKee's, Roydhouse[946] reported his findings in 1970. In addition to the group of children who were referred for tonsillectomy and adenoidectomy and who were randomized

into surgery and no-surgery groups, a third matched group of children who were presumably healthy were followed during the trial. Table 25–58 shows the mean incidence of otitis media in the three groups: tonsillectomy and adenoidectomy, tonsillectomy and adenoidectomy withheld, and controls. The results were similar to those reported by McKee, in that there was a reduction in the incidence of otitis media in the first year after tonsillectomy and adenoidectomy, but this difference was not maintained into the second year. In the second year of the trial, however, the total duration of episodes of otitis media in the tonsillectomy and adenoidectomy group lasted less than 60% as long as those that occurred before surgery.

Roydhouse concluded that the operation not only reduced the incidence of otitis media quickly in the first year but also reduced the severity in both years. Like the previous studies, however, patients whose main symptoms were aural were excluded, and no attempt was made to detect asymptomatic otitis media with effusion or impairment in hearing. In a second clinical trial, Roydhouse[947] randomly divided 100 children with persistent otitis media into two groups, adenoidectomy with tympanostomy tube insertion and tympanostomy tube insertion alone. All patients had failed a nonsurgical treatment regimen. He compared these two groups with a third group of 69 other children who had had otitis media but had all been found to be free of middle-ear effusion following the nonsurgical management and received no surgical treatment.

The cure rate was similar in each of the operative groups, with a greater relapse rate in the non-adenoidectomy group, who required 9% more tym-

TABLE 25–58. Mean Incidence Per Year of Otitis Media in Children Receiving Tonsillectomy and Adenoidectomy Compared with 2 Control Groups

| | Tonsillectomy and Adenoidectomy | | Adenoidectomy Withheld | | Control | |
	Mean Incidence	Number of Children	Mean Incidence	Number of Children	Mean Incidence	Number of Children
First Year	0.19	251	0.29	175	0.12	173
Second Year	0.09	204	0.07	122	0.08	173

Adapted from Roydhouse N. A controlled study of adenotonsillectomy. Arch Otolaryngol 92:611, 1970. Copyright 1970, American Medical Association.

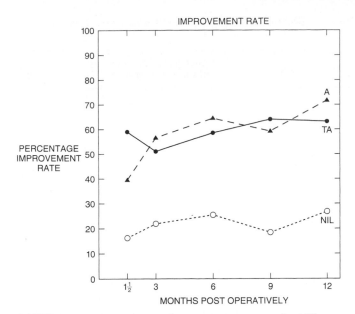

IMPROVEMENT RATE

MONTHS POST OPERATIVELY

FIGURE 25–63. Percentage of improvement rate of middle-ear effusion after adenoidectomy (A), tonsillectomy and adenoidectomy (TA), and no surgery (NIL). (From Maw AR. Chronic otitis media with effusion and adenotonsillectomy: a prospective randomized controlled study. In Lim DJ, Bluestone CD, Klein JO, Nelson JD (eds). Recent Advances in Otitis Media with Effusion. Toronto, BC Decker, 1984, p 301.)

panostomy tube insertions. An estimation from radiographs of the size of the adenoids showed that the group cured without surgery had somewhat smaller adenoids. The relapse rate in the group who received tympanostomy tubes only was independent of the size of the adenoids. The study failed to show a favorable outcome following adenoidectomy.

4. In a study conducted in Bristol, England, of children with bilateral chronic otitis media with effusion, Maw[710] randomly assigned subjects into (1) adenoidectomy, (2) adenoidectomy and tonsillectomy, and (3) nonsurgical control. Tympanostomy tubes were inserted into only one ear of each child; the contralateral ear was not operated upon and was observed for 1 year. One third of the children in the nonsurgical control group had resolution of their middle ear effusion during the year, and one third of the two surgical groups had persistent or

recurrent disease following adenoidectomy with or without tonsillectomy (Fig. 25–63). Maw concluded that adenoidectomy conferred benefit in about one third of the subjects, but those children likely to benefit from the operation could not be identified prior to surgery. In addition, he reported that the addition of tonsillectomy to the adenoidectomy procedure had no more beneficial effect than adenoidectomy alone.

Unfortunately, all of these prospective controlled studies had one or more of the following limitations in experimental design: (1) Entry into the study was based on the occurrence of a sore throat and not on the presence of otitis media; (2) objective evidence of otitis media was not documented by tympanometry or audiometry; (3) other surgical procedures that may have been performed (myringotomy or tympanostomy tube insertions, for example) were not reported; (4) the technique of adenoidectomy (e.g., "midline sweep" or thorough removal of adenoid tissue from the fossa of Rosenmüller) was not described, nor was evidence of complete removal of the adenoids documented; and (5) nasal and eustachian tube function were not assessed objectively. We now have the benefit of two reports of randomized clinical trials, however, that can be used by the clinician when considering the advisability of recommending adenoidectomy for treatment and prevention of otitis media.

5. Gates et al[397] randomly assigned 578 4- to 8-year-old Texas children, who had chronic otitis media with effusion that was unresponsive to antimicrobial therapy, to one of four surgical procedures: (1) myringotomy, (2) myringotomy and tympanostomy tube insertion, (3) adenoidectomy and myringotomy, and (4) adenoidectomy, myringotomy, and tympanostomy tube insertion. Table 25–59 shows a summary of the outcome of this trial. Patients in the myringotomy group had a greater percentage of time with middle-ear effusion, a greater percentage of time with hearing loss, the shortest time to first recurrence, and more repeat surgical procedures over the 2-year follow-up period than did patients in the other three groups. Adenoidectomy and myringotomy, with and without tympanostomy tube insertion, was more effective than myringotomy and

TABLE 25–59. Effectiveness of Various Treatments in 578 Children with Chronic Otitis Media with Effusion*

	Myringotomy	Myringotomy and Tube Insertion	Adenoidectomy and Myringotomy	Adenoidectomy, Myringotomy, and Tube Insertion
Percentage of Time with Effusion	49.1	34.9	30.2	25.8
Percentage of Time with Hearing Loss†	37.5	30.4	22.0	2.4
Median Time to First Recurrence (Days)	54	222	92	240
Number of surgical retreatments	66	36	17	17

* During 2-year follow-up.
† Hearing loss equal to or greater than 20 dB.
Adapted from Gates GA, et al. Effectiveness of adenoidectomy and tympanostomy tubes in treatment of chronic otitis media with effusion. N Engl J Med 317:1444, 1987.

TABLE 25–60. Efficacy of Adenoidectomy for Recurrent Otitis Media in Children Previously Treated with Tympanostomy Placement

Treatment Group	Number of Subjects	Mean Number of Otitis Media Episodes	P Value	Proportion of Days with Otitis Media Present	P Value*
First Year					
Adenoidectomy	48	1.06		15.0	
Control	38	1.45	.51	28.5	.04
Second Year					
Adenoidectomy	45	1.09		17.8	
Control	27	1.67	.01	28.4	.005

* P values by χ-square test.

Adapted from Paradise JL, et al. Efficacy of adenoidectomy for recurrent otitis media in children previously treated with tympanostomy tube placement; results of parallel, randomized and nonrandomized trials. JAMA 263:2066, 1990. Copyright 1990, American Medical Association.

tube insertion; however, the mean time to first recurrence was longer in both groups that included tympanostomy tube insertion.

Gates et al[397] concluded that adenoidectomy, irrespective of adenoid size, should be considered when surgical therapy is indicated in children (of the age group studied) who are severely affected by chronic otitis media with effusion; their recommendation is for adenoidectomy and myringotomy, without tympanostomy tube insertion, because purulent otorrhea through the tube was a problem in their study. When otitis media recurred after adenoidectomy and myringotomy, however, it occurred earlier than when a tube was inserted at the time of the myringotomy.

6. At the Children's Hospital of Pittsburgh, Paradise et al[836] entered 213 children into their study. The criteria for entry into the study were documented episodes of recurrent acute otitis media or chronic otitis media with effusion in a child who had had a myringotomy and insertion of a tympanostomy tube at least once previously. Of the 213 subjects, 99 (46%) were randomly assigned to either the adenoidectomy or the control group; tympanostomy tubes were inserted into patients in both groups if they met criteria for duration and frequency of middle-ear disease. In the other 114 children (54%), their parents declined to participate in the random assignment but agreed to remain in the study. The decision to permit an adenoidectomy or not was left to parental preference. After initial examination, each patient was examined every 6 weeks and at the time of any respiratory illness. Pneumatic otoscopy was performed at every visit. A trained interviewer telephoned each home every 2 weeks to determine whether there had been apparent or suspected illness, to make sure that any ill child was brought in promptly for examination, and to obtain routine information on school attendance, medication usage, and a number of minor symptoms.

Allergy screening was part of every child's workup. A nasal smear was examined for eosinophils, and a battery of skin tests using common inhalant allergens was applied. Other regularly performed studies included lateral soft tissue radiographs of the nasopharynx, to assess adenoid size; sinus radiographs, when sinusitis was suspected; and audiometry and tympanometry, to evaluate hearing and middle-ear status and tympanic membrane compliance.

The degree of middle ear disease developing in the adenoidectomy and nonadenoidectomy groups, respectively, was measured on the basis of three main parameters: (1) number of episodes per year of otitis media with effusion, (2) months of middle-ear effusion, and (3) frequency with which myringotomy is carried out subsequent to the child's entering the clinical trial.

Data concerning subjects assigned randomly either to receive adenoidectomy or to enter the nonadenoidectomy control group were maintained separately from data concerning subjects whose parents decline randomization and opt for or against adenoidectomy.

In both trials, the randomly assigned clinical trial and the nonrandom one, outcomes favored adenoidectomy as compared to no adenoidectomy. In both trials, the control group outcomes were biased, since some subjects who were in the control and nonadenoidectomy groups and had persistent middle-ear disease crossed over into the adenoidectomy group; if such severely affected children had remained in the control and nonadenoidectomy groups, the outcomes most likely would have favored the adenoidectomy groups even more than was found. The most statistically significant differences were detected in the randomized clinical trial. The adenoidectomy group had 47% less time with otitis media than the control group during the first year of the trial, and 37% less disease in the second year. The number of episodes of acute otitis media were also less in the adenoidectomy group; 28% in subjects who received adenoidectomy and 35% in those who did not (Table 25–60). The investigators concluded that adenoidectomy is indicated on an individualized basis for those children who have recurrence of their middle-ear disease after tympanostomy tubes extrude.

7. Most recently, a clinical trial, that was also conducted at the Children's Hospital of Pittsburgh, evaluated the efficacy of adenoidectomy or adenotonsillectomy for prevention of recurrent acute otitis media in children who had not received tympanostomy tube placement in the past.[832] The design and methods were similar as described for the previous trial conducted by the same research team, except that none of the subjects had been previously treated with tympanostomy tubes, and the children were randomly assigned to not only adenoidectomy and control groups (i.e., no surgery), but also to an adenotonsillectomy group.

A total of 461 children (410 followed), aged 3 to 15 years, were enrolled in two parallel trials: 305 subjects enrolled (266 followed) without recurrent throat infection or tonsillar hypertrophy (i.e., three-way trial), and 157 subjects enrolled (144 followed) who had such conditions were randomized to either adenotonsillectomy or control groups (i.e., two-way trial). All subjects had had a history of three or more attacks of acute otitis media in the previous 6 months, or four or more episodes within the previous 12 months, with at least one attack being of recent onset. Table 25–61 shows the mean number of episodes during each of the 3 years of the trial. The efficacy of surgery was modest and limited to the first year of the trial. Since there was only short-term efficacy of both adenoidectomy and adenotonsillectomy, and given the risks of these operations, neither is recommended as a first surgical procedure for children who have not received a previous tube insertion and whose only indication for either operation is recurrent acute otitis media.

Adenoidectomy, as shown in the previously conducted clinical trial, is effective when the child has had previous tube placement, and it is recommended.[836] Since the benefit of adenoidectomy at this stage is effective for the long-term, but not as effective for the short-term, bilateral tympanostomy tube placement at the time of adenoidectomy should provide short-term relief.

Effect of Adenoidectomy on Eustachian Tube Function

In an attempt to improve criteria for the preoperative selection of patients for adenoidectomy, radiographic studies of the nasopharynx and eustachian tube prior to surgery and after adenoidectomy were reported.[154] Of 27 patients who had preoperative obstruction of the nasopharyngeal end of the eustachian tube, adenoidectomy appeared to be helpful in 19 (70%). Results appeared to be quite poor in children with nasal allergy: Only 2 of 10 had good results. Furthermore, children who preoperatively showed reflux of contrast medium from the nasopharynx into the middle ear did not benefit from adenoidectomy. In this study, 20 of 33 children (60%) seemed to have a favorable response to adenoidectomy, but eight had worse middle-ear disease after the operation than before. For example, a few of the children who had asymptomatic otitis media with effusion prior to adenoidectomy developed recurrent acute symptomatic otitis media with effusion following the procedure.

The ventilatory function of the eustachian tube has been studied using the inflation-deflation manometric technique both before and after adenoidectomy in a group of children with otitis media with effusion in whom a tympanostomy tube had been inserted.[124] Inflation-deflation studies of the eustachian tube were obtained in ears that remained intubated, aerated, and dry both before and 8 weeks after adenoidectomy. Nasal pressures during swallowing were also determined in some. The results of this study indicated that, following adenoidectomy, eustachian tube ventilatory function improved in some, remained the same in others, and appeared to have been made worse in a few children. Improvement was related to a reduction of extrinsic mechanical obstruction of the eustachian tube (Fig. 25–64) or to nasal obstruction due to the adenoids (Fig. 25–65), whereas in those patients in whom the function was judged to be worse, the tube was considered to be more pliant after the adenoidectomy than before. This increase in compliance was at-

TABLE 25–61. Mean Number of Episodes of Acute Otitis Media (AOM) in Two Parallel Trials of Efficacy of Adenoidectomy (A) vs. Adenotonsillectomy (T&A) vs. Control (C) for Prevention of Recurrent AOM in 410 Children (3–15 years) Not Treated Previously with Tympanostomy Tubes.

Year	Three-Way Trial (n = 266)			Two-way Trial (n = 144)	
	T&A	*A*	*C*	*T&A*	*C*
1	2.4°	1.8	2.1	1.7	2.2
2	1.3	1.7†	1.2	0.9	0.9
3	1.2	1.3	1.5	0.5	0.9

° $P < .001$; † $P < .04$

Adapted from Paradise JL, Bluestone CD, Colborn DK, et al. Adenoidectomy and adenotonsillectomy for recurrent acute otitis media. Parallel randomized clinical trials in children not previously treated with tympanostomy-tube placement. JAMA 282:945, 1999. Copyright 1999, American Medical Association.

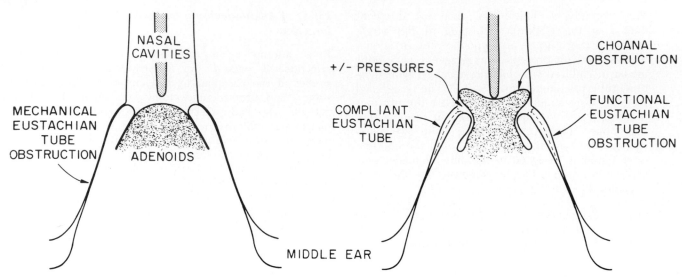

FIGURE 25–64. Two proposed mechanisms by which obstructive adenoids could alter eustachian tube function. The adenoids can cause extrinsic mechanical compression of the eustachian tube in the fossa of Rosenmüller (*left*). Obstruction of the posterior nasal choanae may result in abnormal nasopharyngeal pressures that develop during swallowing (Toynbee phenomenon); it may cause insufflation into the middle ear of nasopharyngeal secretions, prevent the tube from opening, or both (*right*) (see also section on Physiology, Pathophysiology, and Pathogenesis). (From Bluestone CD, Klein JO. Otitis Media in Infants and Children, 3rd ed. Philadelphia, WB Saunders, 2001, p 275.)

tributed to loss of adenoid support of the eustachian tube in the fossa of Rosenmüller (Fig. 25–66). A comparable situation was described in the radiographic study in which several of the children demonstrated reflux of radiopaque liquid medium from the nasopharynx into the middle ear after the adenoidectomy but not before (Fig. 25–67).

Neither of these studies included control subjects. In a recently completed clinical trial of adenoidectomy con-

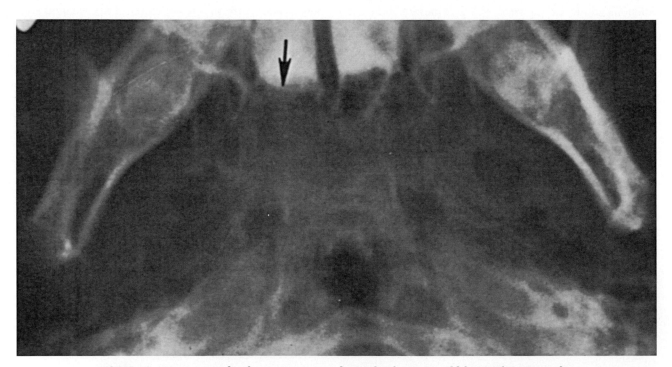

FIGURE 25–65. Retrograde obstruction in a radiograph of a 5-year-old boy with otitis media. Radiopaque medium failed to enter the nasopharyngeal portion of the eustachian tube during both open-nose and closed-nose swallowing. (From Bluestone CD, Klein JO. Otitis Media in Infants and Children, 3rd ed. Philadelphia, WB Saunders, 2001.)

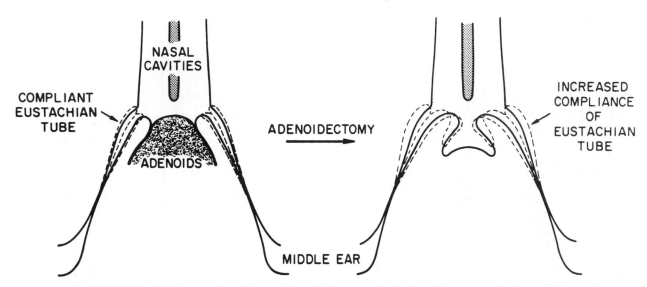

FIGURE 25–66. Proposed mechanism by which removal of adenoids can result in a more pliant eustachian tube after surgery than before. The increase in compliance after the surgery may be due to a decrease in tubal support as a result of the adenoids being removed from the fossa of Rosenmüller. (From Bluestone CD, Klein JO. Otitis Media in Infants and Children, 3rd ed. Philadelphia, WB Saunders, 2001, p 276.)

ducted at the Children's Hospital of Pittsburgh, eustachian tube ventilatory function studies employing the inflation-deflation manometric technique were performed prior to and after randomized selection of children for the study and at any time an upper respiratory tract infection supervened; the degree of nasal obstruction was assessed. Since eustachian tube ventilatory function has been shown to be affected adversely by an upper respiratory tract infection,[125] it is important to assess this function when an upper respiratory tract infection is present as well as when infection is absent in children both be-

fore and after randomization into either the adenoidectomy or the control group. Preliminary outcomes of this study failed to demonstrate any currently measurable effect of adenoidectomy on eustachian tube function, and therefore the hoped for preoperative test to determine ideal candidates for adenoidectomy was not possible.[1098] Owing to methodologic and design problems in the study, however, children with large adenoids that resulted in postnasal obstruction were not entered into the study, since such children had had an adenoidectomy and myringotomy and tympanostomy tube procedure performed

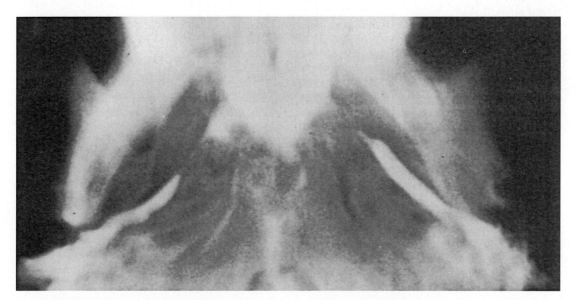

FIGURE 25–67. Postadenoidectomy radiograph of a child who demonstrated reflux of radiopaque material from the nasopharynx into the middle ear. This did not occur during the preadenoidectomy radiographic study. (From Bluestone CD, Klein JO. Otitis Media in Infants and Children, 3rd ed. Philadelphia, WB Saunders, 2001, p 276.)

initially. Therefore, the trial answered the question only for those children who had relatively small adenoids that did not obstruct the nose. It is possible that if such patients were entered, an effect of adenoidectomy on the function of the tube would have been observed. Also, by not entering patients with adenoids that cause nasal obstruction, the hypothetical "Toynbee phenomenon" would not have been present, that is, nasal obstruction affecting the eustachian tube and middle ear during closed-nose swallowing.

More recently, Buchman and Stool[180] demonstrated obstruction of the eustachian tube using manometric testing prior to adenoidectomy, which was relieved following the procedure, but this was an uncontrolled case report. Nevertheless, obstruction of the eustachian tube by the adenoids is one possible cause of middle-ear effusions. The position of the adenoids in the nasopharynx may be a critical factor in the obstruction. Wright et al[1200] visually assessed the position of the adenoids, in patients with and without otitis media, at the time of adenoidectomy, and found that laterally placed hypertrophic adenoids were associated with those children who had otitis media. They postulated that lateral hypertrophy was a possible reason that the recently reported clinical trials showed efficacy of the operation, irrespective of the size of the adenoids. In the trials conducted by Gates et al[397] and Paradise et al,[836] adenoid size was determined by using the lateral soft tissue radiographs in which the adenoidal-nasopharyngeal ratio was used.[392] This ratio has recently been shown to be a somewhat more reliable indicator of clinically significant nasopharyngeal obstruction than just the size of the adenoids alone,[575] but position of the adenoids is probably more important in determining the effect of adenoids on the function of the eustachian tube.

It is possible that a new method to assess the structure and function of the eustachian tube, and size and position of the adenoids will help in preoperative evaluation of patients who would most likely benefit from the surgery. Magnetic resonance imaging and computed tomography are potential candidates for such a test.

Adenoiditis Related to Otitis Media

An alternative explanation for the efficacy of adenoidectomy, irrespective of size, in preventing otitis media in the clinical trials conducted by Maw,[711] Gates et al,[397] and Paradise et al,[837] is that the adenoids in these patients harbored an increased number of pathogenic bacteria, which was eliminated or reduced following the operation. Unfortunately, there is no conclusive evidence to support this hypothesis, but there have been studies that have addressed this possibility. Some have demonstrated that a high percentage of adenoids culture positive for *H. influenzae* in children who had otitis media as compared with those who did not have otitis media,[354, 650] whereas others found no such relationship.[381] Recently, Suzuki et evaluated the clinical, bacteriologic and histologic aspects of the adenoids in children with and without otitis media and found a significantly greater number of cultures of *H. influenzae* in the adenoids of children who had otitis media than those who did not. The authors concluded that

the adenoids may be a reservoir for this bacterium, which is then transmitted to the middle ear through the eustachian tube.

Clinical Practice Guidelines

The *Clinical Practice Guideline, Otitis Media with Effusion in Young Children*, by Stool et al,[1069] recommended that "tonsillectomy should not be performed, either alone or with adenoidectomy, for treatment of otitis media with effusion in a child of any age. [Strong recommendation based on limited scientific evidence and strong Panel consensus.]" Regarding adenoidectomy, the Panel concluded that "adenoidectomy is not recommended for treatment of otitis media with effusion in a child age 1 through 3 years in the absence of specific adenoid pathology. [Based on limited scientific evidence and Panel majority opinion.]" We agree with the *Guideline* Panel that tonsillectomy, without any specific pathologic indication, such as chronic airway obstruction due to hypertrophy or recurrent acute tonsillitis that meets the criteria of Paradise et al,[831] is inappropriate. On the other hand, we disagree with the Panel regarding adenoidectomy. The *Guideline* Panel concluded that adenoidectomy is "not recommended" for children 1 to 3 years of age "when adenoid pathology is not present," since the Panel apparently concluded that there are limited data available from randomized clinical trials to support their recommending the operation for this indication in this age group. The trial conducted by Paradise et al[836] had only about 30 children who were younger than 4 years of age, and the subjects in the study by Gates et al[397] included only those children who were between the ages of 4 and 8 years. (Curiously, the list of references in the *Guideline* does not include either of these two trials.)

We have registered our assessment of the strengths and weaknesses of these Guidelines.[138] We believe that adenoidectomy in younger children may be effective. The phrase "not recommended" is an improper designation, since at this time we do not know whether the procedure is effective or not in young children. We concur with the Panel that the age of the patient may be important, since in the usual operative setting, adenoidectomy is a greater risk in young infants. However, we consider children who are 2 and 3 years of age to be *possible* candidates for adenoidectomy if they meet the relatively stringent criteria used in the two clinical trials described.

A clinical trial is currently underway at the Children's Hospital of Pittsburgh that is addressing the efficacy of adenoidectomy in children 2 and 3 years of age who have chronic otitis media with effusion. It is hoped that this trial will answer the question raised by the *Guideline* Panel.

Conclusions and Recommendations

Prospective studies conducted prior to the 1980s to determine the efficacy of tonsillectomy and adenoidectomy or adenoidectomy alone for otitis media showed a modest reduction in the incidence of ear disease following surgery in some studies[724, 725, 946] but no reduction in others.[556, 713, 836] All of these studies, however, had shortcomings in design and method. Three more recently reported randomized clinical trials,[397, 711, 836] in which most of the problems of the earlier studies were eliminated, have shown a modest but significant reduction in the morbidity of chronic otitis media with effusion following adenoidectomy, which appeared to be independent of adenoid size.[398] A recent analysis employing the evidence-based methodology demonstrated the efficacy of adenoidectomy for otitis media.[142]

Maw[711] failed to show a significant difference between adenoidectomy without tonsillectomy and adenoidectomy with tonsillectomy in children who had chronic otitis media with effusion.

In only two trials, both conducted at the Children's Hospital of Pittsburgh, was the question addressed of the efficacy of adenoidectomy, with or without tonsillectomy, for prevention of recurrent acute otitis media. The outcome of the first trial did demonstrate long-term benefit following adenoidectomy, but all of the subjects had had tympanostomy tubes placed previously.[832] Another recently reported study determined whether adenoidectomy, with or without tonsillectomy, is helpful in decreasing the rate of recurrent acute otitis media in children who had not previously been treated with tympanostomy tube insertion.[832] In that clinical trial, there was no long-term benefit from either operation, and the investigators did not believe the risks of tonsillectomy outweighed the potential benefits for even patients who had received tympanostomy tube placement in the past.

At present, the clinician who is faced with a child who has recurrent acute otitis media or chronic otitis media must decide whether the potential benefits of these operative procedures outweigh the costs and potential risks following assessment of each child individually. That assessment should include, among others, (1) the type of otitis media (i.e., recurrent or chronic otitis media with effusion or recurrent acute otitis media, or both); (2) the frequency, duration, and severity of the middle-ear disease; (3) the age of the child, since children younger than 3 years of age are at greater risk for complications from adenoid surgery than older children[1190]; (4) the presence of other, coexisting conditions that would make adenoidectomy or tonsillectomy more compelling, such as frequently recurrent pharyngotonsillitis[831] or upper airway obstruction caused by obstructive adenoids or tonsils, which of course includes sleep apnea; (5) the presence or absence of upper respiratory tract allergy or infection, including sinusitis,[1096] or both; and (6) the thoughtful consideration of other management options, such as watchful waiting, antimicrobial prophylaxis, or myringotomy and insertion of tympanostomy tubes. Decisions for or against these options should include the child (if he or she is old enough to comprehend) and the parents.

Recurrent Acute Otitis Media

Currently, we withhold adenoidectomy as an initial procedure when surgery is being considered and opt for myringotomy with insertion of tympanostomy tubes for infants and children who have had three or more episodes of acute otitis media within the previous 6 months, or four or more attacks during the previous 12 months, with at least one episode being of recent onset (see earlier section in this chapter, Myringotomy and Tympanostomy Tube). This procedure has been demonstrated to be effective for these criteria in the clinical trial conducted by Casselbrant et al.[209] Antimicrobial prophylaxis is an alternative management option at this stage, but development of antimicrobial-resistant pneumococcus is a possibility with this approach.[293]

Adenoidectomy at this time is reserved for those children who have hypertrophy of the adenoids that causes a significant degree of nasal airway obstruction. Based on the second clinical trial recently reported by Paradise et al,[832] neither adenoidectomy nor adenotonsillectomy is recommended initially for children who have not previously received tympanostomy tube placement when recurrent acute otitis media is the only indication for their removal. Tonsillectomy may also be initially indicated if the child also meets criteria for recurrent throat infections as defined in the clinical trial by Paradise et al,[831] such as three or more episodes of throat infection per year, for 3 or more years, or five or more episodes for each of the previous 2 years, or seven or more attacks within the previous year. Documentation of one or more of these episodes is recommended to confirm the parents' history, and one or more—but not necessarily all—of the following also should be present during the episode: (1) tonsillar exudate, (2) fever, (3) enlarged and tender cervical lymph nodes, or (4) positive culture for group A beta-hemolytic streptococcus; all episodes do not have to be positive for this organism. But, a recently reported clinical trial also conducted in Pittsburgh failed to show a clinically significant advantage in performing either tonsillectomy or adenotonsillectomy in children who had a history of a less compelling frequency and severity of their throat infections than present in the first trial.[833]

Also, although no clinical trial has demonstrated efficacy, significant pharyngeal airway obstruction caused by hypertrophy of the tonsils may be another indication for their removal at the time of initial tympanostomy tube placement.

If the child continues to have recurrent attacks of acute otitis media after the initial tubes extrude, then adenoidectomy, irrespective of size, is recommended, based on the outcomes of the first clinical trial reported by Paradise et al.[836] But, as noted earlier, this surgery is associated with more risk in infants as compared with older children and therefore reinsertion of the tympanostomy tubes without the addition of adenoidectomy is a more reasonable option for this age group; the trial by Paradise et al[836] did not include infants. Insertion of tympanostomy tubes in addition to adenoidectomy at this stage is optional, but since children may continue to develop recurrent episodes during the first postoperative period, we prefer to also place tympanostomy tubes at the time of this surgery.

To date, no clinical trial or outcomes have been reported for adenotonsillectomy at this stage, when prevention of otitis media is the only indication, but it is unlikely that any potential and most likely modest benefits of this operation would outweigh its known risks. As described earlier, however, the addition of tonsillectomy may be warranted if there are other compelling indications for their removal, such as frequently recurrent attacks of throat infection or upper airway obstruction due to enlarged tonsils.

Chronic Otitis Media with Effusion

Myringotomy and tympanostomy tube placement is also recommended when chronic otitis media with effusion is unresponsive to a course of antibiotic treatment, is bilateral for at least 3 to 4 months or unilateral for 6 or more months, and is not improving. This operation has been demonstrated to be effective for initial surgical treatment for chronic otitis media with effusion in the two clinical trials conducted by Mandel et al[689, 690] (see Myringotomy and Tympanostomy Tube section). Adenoidectomy is withheld, since the clinical trial by Gates et al[397] showed only modest efficacy compared with myringotomy and tympanostomy tube only as the first surgical procedure, but it is considered, along with tympanostomy tube insertion, when the child has a significant degree of nasal obstruction caused by enlarged adenoids.

If the child has recurrence of chronic otitis media with effusion following spontaneous extrusion of the tympanostomy tubes, then adenoidectomy, irrespective of size, is advised in addition to reinsertion of the tubes, with the criteria for duration related to laterality of the middle-ear effusion being similar to those recommended for initial tube placement. The trial by Paradise et al[836] supports the recommendation for adenoidectomy in addition to insertion of tympanostomy tubes at this stage of the disease. Adenoidectomy for children with this stage of the disease has greater efficacy than the subjects studied in the trial by Gates et al,[397] since patients who have had one or more previously inserted tympanostomy tube procedures are more severely affected children.

Since the trial by Maw[711] failed to show any increased benefit by the addition of tonsillectomy to the adenoidectomy in children who had had chronic otitis media with effusion, this procedure is not recommended, at the time of the initial or of any subsequent surgery, when prevention of otitis media is the only indication. But, similar to our recommendations for this operation when adenoidectomy surgery is elected in the attempt prevent recurrent acute otitis media, other compelling indications for tonsillectomy, such as frequently recurrent throat infections, or pharyngeal airway obstruction caused by hypertrophied tonsils, might prompt their removal.

Other Possible Indications for Adenoidectomy for Otitis Media and Related Conditions

Some clinicians advocate removal of the adenoids in children who have either a chronic perforation of the tympanic membrane or a tympanostomy tube in place and develop troublesome recurrent acute otorrhea or chronic suppurative otitis media, or both. But, to date, no rigidly controlled randomized clinical trials have been conducted (and reported) that support adenoidectomy for these children. Nevertheless, since the operation is effective for

recurrent acute otitis media without perforation and for chronic otitis media with effusion, adenoidectomy is a reasonable management option for these patients as well, especially for those children who have nasal obstruction secondary to hypertrophied adenoids.

Also, some clinicians recommend adenoidectomy prior to tympanoplasty (or myringoplasty), in an effort to improve the success rate of this operation, but again, there are no data to support performing an adenoidectomy for this indication. Tympanoplasty enjoys a rather high rate of success even when the adenoids are not removed in children, but when the initial attempt to repair the perforation of the tympanic membrane fails, it seems reasonable to remove the adenoids prior to revision tympanoplasty. Since adenoidectomy during the postoperative period might compromise the function of the eustachian tube, it seems prudent to perform tympanoplasty at a later date (see Chap. 26).

Tympanomastoidectomy for Chronic Otitis Media with Effusion

On very rare occasions, a child will require mastoidectomy and middle-ear surgery to eliminate chronic otitis media with effusion when *all* other nonsurgical and surgical methods of management have failed. The operation, which has been advocated by Proctor[893] and Paparella[830] and described in detail by Proud and Duff[895], should be reserved for only those children in whom a thorough search for an underlying origin of the chronic middle-ear effusion has failed to uncover a cause or, if a cause was found, appropriate management has failed to alleviate the problem (for example, the repair of a cleft palate). In addition, all attempts should have been made to maintain an aerated middle-ear space and the mastoid gas cells by means of myringotomy and insertion of a tympanostomy tube, even though the procedure may have to be repeated many times for several years. If, however, the myringotomy and thorough aspiration of the middle-ear fluid is unsuccessful in eliminating the effusion and the insertion of a tympanostomy tube fails to provide an aerated middle-ear space, the child may be considered a candidate for a mastoidectomy. A CT scan is indicated at this time, which may reveal the underlying pathologic lesion, such as chronic mastoiditis (with osteitis) or a previously unsuspected congenital or acquired cholesteatoma, or both. Also, a cholesterol granuloma may be the cause, but it is possible that treatment with a course of a systemically administered corticosteroid in addition to tympanostomy tube insertion will prove successful and a tympanomastoidectomy can be avoided.[1099] At the time of surgery, the chronic mastoiditis in these children is characterized by a cellular mastoid containing edematous, hyperplastic mucosa, with granulomatous tissue, polypoid tissue, and a very thick mucoid effusion. The condition is usually reversible with mastoid–middle ear surgery, but an aerated middle ear–mastoid air cell system should be maintained by the insertion of a tympanostomy tube at the time of the mastoid surgery; the tube should be reinserted if otitis media with effusion or atelectasis, or both, recurs. Insertion of permanent tympanostomy tube such as Per-Lee or T tube may be more appropriate in these cases than the traditional shorter-duration tubes.

It should be stressed that tympanomastoidectomy is rarely indicated and should be performed only in those few children for whom tympanostomy tube placement and other methods have been unsuccessful.

Hearing Aids

A management option recommended by some clinicians as an alternative to surgical intervention is fitting a hearing aid on a child who has conductive hearing loss due to chronic otitis media with effusion.[379, 536] The rationale is that the hearing loss may interfere with normal development of speech, language, and learning, and the middle-ear condition is self-limited and should improve as the child grows older. It is appropriate to be concerned about the effect of the hearing loss on child development,[1069] but it is not appropriate to continue to watch children with chronic otitis media with effusion when placement of tympanostomy tubes is an effective means of restoring normal hearing.[689, 690] Since we do not know the natural history of chronic middle-ear effusion in the individual child, the fluid—and the associated hearing loss—can last for excessive periods.

Hearing loss is only one of the complications of middle-ear effusion, however. Balance and motor function have also been shown to be affected.[210] In addition, sequelae of long-standing middle-ear effusion can occur, such as severe atelectasis, adhesive otitis, tympanosclerosis, ossicular fixation or disarticulation or cholesteatoma. An excellent example of these consequences of long-standing middle-ear effusion is the population of children who have cleft palate, in whom atelectasis, retraction pocket, and cholesteatoma formation are frequent sequelae of their ever-present chronic middle-ear effusions when tympanostomy tubes are withheld. There is little question that maintaining an effusion-free middle-ear space in these children with placement of tympanostomy tubes, which frequently requires multiple insertions over time, has reduced the incidence of these sequelae. Therefore, the fitting of a hearing aid on such individuals could obscure the pathologic sequelae of otitis media in an effort to promote adequate hearing and avoid placement of tympanostomy tubes.

On the other hand, fitting a hearing aid on selected children should be considered and attempted when the hearing loss is interfering with the child's development and the middle-ear disease cannot be reversed by medical or surgical methods, such as when the sequelae of otitis media are already present. In some ears, especially those with severe atelectasis of the tympanic membrane, a tympanostomy tube either is difficult to insert or remains in place for only a short period. Fluctuating hearing loss in children so affected could be detrimental, and amplification of the hearing may be beneficial. Likewise, a child who already has damage to the ossicular chain and must wait to grow older before reconstructive middle-ear surgery is performed may also be a good candidate for a hearing aid.

Therefore, the fitting of hearing aids should be considered only in selected children, and if this method of rehabilitation is selected, close medical monitoring is mandatory so that sequelae of otitis media, which can permanently damage the middle ear, does not develop. Middle-ear effusion is not only associated with hearing loss but can also cause disturbances in equilibrium, balance, and motor function, as well as possible irreversible structural damage to the middle-ear.

Management of Special Populations

There are certain types of children who are known to be at high risk for developing otitis media and in whom continuing surveillance and more attentive management is necessary to prevent the complications and sequelae of the disease. In addition, children who have handicaps otherwise unrelated to middle ear disease may deserve special attention, since the occurrence of otitis media with its attendant conductive hearing loss may further compromise the preexisting handicap and possibly interfere with the educational and social development of the child.

Infants and Children with Cleft Palate

Since otitis media with effusion is a universal finding in infants with an unrepaired cleft palate,[835, 1071] it seems reasonable to attempt to maintain the middle ears of these children free of effusion and with normal pressures. Because there is always a conductive hearing loss[387] and usually discomfort associated with a middle-ear effusion, prevention of otitis media as early in life as possible should be the goal of management. Medical treatment, such as a trial of antimicrobial therapy in young infants with an unrepaired cleft palate, has not been systematically tested; however, in older infants and children, the nonsurgical methods of management have usually been unsuccessful in eliminating middle-ear effusion and restoring hearing. This failure of nonsurgical methods of management is most likely due to the structural abnormalities that result in a functional obstruction of the eustachian tube in the child who has a cleft palate.[124, 136, 1097] (See also section on Physiology, Pathophysiology, and Pathogenesis, dysfunction related to cleft palate.) Therefore, the most reasonable method of management for young infants with an unrepaired cleft palate would be the insertion of a tympanostomy tube as early in life as feasible.[136, 802a, 834] If a repair of a cleft lip is performed at 2 or 3 months of age, the tympanostomy tubes can be inserted at this time. In any event, a tympanostomy tube should probably be inserted sometime during the first 6 months of life. Infants with Robin sequence appear to have greater levels of hearing loss than those who have an isolated cleft and thus these youngsters should receive tympanostomy tubes as early as possible.[456]

The overall reduction in middle-ear disease that follows palate repair appears to constitute a basis for consideration of earlier repair than might otherwise be undertaken.[834] Paradise et al[835] pointed out that the middle-ear damage and hearing loss prevalent during later life in patients who had cleft palates probably originated with chronic middle-ear effusion in infancy; they further suggest that the restrictions in language skill[735] and the psychological problems that also seem to be prevalent in these patients later in life may have the same origin, since the persistent middle-ear effusion of infants with cleft palates is probably accompanied by variable degrees of hearing loss. When spontaneous extubation occurs in these children, the tubes should be reinserted if otitis media with effusion recurs.

Patients with a cleft palate and otitis media should be considered uncertain candidates for adenoidectomy, since there is a distinct possibility that the operation may worsen velopharyngeal function. In a retrospective study by Severeid,[1000] adenoidectomy was not found to be effective in relieving otitis media in children with cleft palates.

Other Craniofacial Malformations

All children with craniofacial malformations who have an associated cleft palate will have a high incidence of otitis media early in life. Otitis media in these children should be managed as previously outlined for children with only cleft palates. Children in this category include those with Robin sequence (glossoptosis, micrognathia, and cleft of the soft palate) and those with trisomy 21 (Down syndrome).[456, 701, 1188] Children with Down syndrome have an extremely high incidence of otitis media with effusion. Balkany et al[52, 53] have reported that more than 50% of such children will have a middle-ear effusion and that more than three fourths have a conductive hearing loss. Antimicrobial therapy is usually not successful in eliminating the effusion, and most patients will require myringotomy and tympanostomy tube insertion to restore the hearing to normal. If a conductive hearing loss persists after successful placement of a tympanostomy tube (the middle ear appears to be aerated), then an ossicular malformation should be suspected, since this congenital anomaly is commonly found in association with these syndromes.

Even though the incidence of otitis media with effusion in many of the infants and children with craniofacial malformations has not been formally studied, children with some of the following malformations are considered to be at high risk for developing middle-ear effusions: mandibulofacial dysostosis (Treacher-Collins syndrome), craniofacial dysostosis (Crouzon disease), gonadal dysgenesis (Turner syndrome), and mucopolysaccharidosis (Hunter-Hurler syndrome). Other syndromes associated with a high incidence of otitis media with effusion are cleft palate, micrognathia, glossoptosis (Robin sequence), trisomy 21 (Down syndrome), trisomy 13-15 (Patau syndrome), oculoauriculovertebral dysplasia (Goldenhar syndrome), acrocephalosyndactyly (Apert syndrome), craniometaphyseal dysplasia (Pyle disease), and orofacial-digital syndrome (Mohr syndrome). Any child with a congenital craniofacial malformation, however, should be followed to detect the development of otitis media with effusion; a child acquiring this problem might most reasonably be managed by myringotomy with insertion of a tympanostomy tube.

Racial Groups

Certain racial groups are believed to have a high incidence of otitis media with effusion: Native Americans (Indians and Eskimos), the Maori of New Zealand, natives of Guam, Greenland Eskimos, Australian Aborigines, and Laplanders.[133] The prevalence and incidence of otitis media has been studied in these populations, which has shown an extraordinary rate of chronic suppurative otitis media. Early in life, however, the children of these populations appear to develop recurrent acute otitis media, perforation of the tympanic membrane, otorrhea, and a propensity for chronic otitis media with discharge as a later sequela. When infants in these racial groups contract upper respiratory tract infections, which are so frequently associated with the ear disease, they should be aggressively treated by medical means, and antimicrobial therapy should be instituted for otitis media as early as possible. A perforation appears to be part of the natural history of ear disease in these children, and, if it occurs, meticulous cleansing of the purulent material from the canal (aural toilet) should be performed frequently. In addition, an appropriate topical aural antibiotic, selected on the basis of the results of the culture, should be instilled. Antimicrobial prophylaxis is a reasonable treatment option for such children. Ensign et al[336] demonstrated a decreased incidence of otitis media in American Indians when prophylactic doses of a sulfonamide were administered. In a later study, Maynard et al[716] were able to decrease the incidence of otorrhea in about 50% of Alaskan Eskimos who were given a prophylactic daily dose of ampicillin over a 1-year period. For those children in whom compliance was considered best, there was a two thirds reduction in the incidence of ear discharge.

The insertion of tympanostomy tubes into the ears of such children has not been as successful in alleviating the recurrent otitis media as it has in children with cleft palates. This may be due to the basic differences in the origin and pathogenesis of the disease in these two groups of children: Children with cleft palates usually have otitis media with effusion, whereas American Indians more commonly have recurrent otitis media, followed by perforation and discharge.

If a perforation persists in infants and children who have a racial predilection for developing otitis media and tympanoplasty is not performed, a hearing aid should be fitted to help restore the child's hearing (see also Chap. 26, section on Chronic Perforation with Chronic Otitis Media).

Immunocompromised Host

Infants and children who have congenital, acquired, or drug-induced compromise of their immune systems require special consideration when otitis media is present. Children with congenital conditions that compromise their defense systems are more susceptible to infections in general and may be more susceptible to otitis media in particular. When otitis media is present in patients with immune deficiency, the possibility of an unusual organism should be considered. Medications such as corticosteroids, antibiotics, and cytotoxic drugs may compromise the immune system. Lymphoproliferative disease states such as lymphoma or leukemia may also compromise the host.

For such children, the occurrence of acute signs and symptoms of otitis media warrants identification of the causative organism employing tympanocentesis and possibly drainage (i.e., myringotomy). Culture and susceptibility testing of the middle-ear aspirate will be helpful in selecting the appropriate antimicrobial agent effective against the causative organism. In certain children who are immunocompromised, frequently recurrent and chronic otitis media are potentially life-threatening, and more permanent drainage may be required. Myringotomy and insertion of a tympanostomy tube should be considered to eliminate the middle-ear effusion and to prevent recurrence of suppurative disease, so as to prevent intracranial and intratemporal complications such as labyrinthitis and meningitis.

Immotile Cilia Syndrome

Infants and children with chronic otitis media with effusion, paranasal sinusitis, and bronchitis (and bronchiectasis) should be suspected of having a chronic respiratory tract infection secondary to abnormal cilia, which will significantly interfere with the mucociliary transport system.[331] It is now appreciated that Kartagener syndrome (dextrocardia with situs inversus, bronchiectasis, sinusitis, or agenesis of the frontal sinuses) is associated with the immotile cilia syndrome. Patients with this condition should undergo bilateral myringotomy and tympanostomy tube insertion to eliminate the middle-ear effusion, restore the hearing, and prevent the complications and sequelae of otitis media with effusion. Nonsurgical methods of management, such as antimicrobial prophylaxis, may be effective, but when a persistent effusion is present, myringotomy with insertion of a tympanostomy tube is indicated.

Concurrent Permanent Hearing Loss

Infants and children with preexisting hearing losses who subsequently develop otitis media with effusion or abnormal negative middle-ear pressure (atelectasis), or both, are at higher risk for impairment of language acquisition and learning than are those children whose hearing loss is due to the middle-ear effusion and negative pressure alone. Therefore, the former children should be observed at more frequent intervals than children without a concurrent permanent hearing loss and may require more aggressive management for the superimposed conductive hearing loss, since it is amenable to treatment.

The preexisting hearing loss may be conductive, sensorineural, or mixed. The child with a congenital malformation of the middle-ear ossicles who has a conductive hearing loss may develop persistent or recurrent otitis media with effusion or high negative pressure, which would increase his or her hearing handicap. Likewise, children who have a preexisting sensorineural hearing loss of some degree are often severely handicapped socially and educationally if they then acquire a middle-ear effusion. These children should be managed in the same way as those

without a concurrent hearing loss from another cause, but it is even more important to eliminate the middle-ear effusion in these children rapidly and to prevent the development of any further hearing loss, if possible. If medical treatment does not eliminate the superimposed conductive hearing loss within a relatively short time, myringotomy and insertion of a tympanostomy tube should be considered at an earlier time than for children without a concurrent hearing loss. Middle-ear effusion is common in all children but appears to have an even higher incidence in some children with a congenital middle-ear malformation (e.g., Down syndrome) and those who have a sensorineural loss. For this reason, surgical intervention should be considered earlier in children who have recurrent middle-ear effusion and persistent or fluctuating conductive hearing loss to prevent further impairment of hearing and, consequently, of development.

Today many children with moderate to severe permanent hearing losses attend regular schools ("mainstreaming"), and some may not even require a hearing aid. Regardless of their functional level of hearing, however, any child who has such a hearing loss should be evaluated more frequently for possible occurrence of otitis media with effusion than should the child without a permanent hearing loss. Children of all ages are at high risk, but infants, preschoolers, and young school-age children are at particular risk, since the incidence of otitis media is higher in these age groups. Examination of such infants and children twice a year is a reasonable goal if the child had no past history or evidence of the disease, but more frequent evaluation (three or four times per year) is desirable for those children who have had recurrent middle-ear effusions. Since all infants and young children are at high risk for developing otitis media with effusion and high negative pressure, all infants identified as having a sensorineural hearing loss early in life should be more frequently examined for possible recurrence of otitis media. Even if such children show no objective evidence of middle-ear effusion by otoscopy or tympanometry, or both, if there is a history of fluctuating hearing loss the child should be actively treated, since even the presence of transient high negative pressure may lead to a compounding of the educational handicap.

Schools or Programs for the Deaf

Children with severe to profound deafness who are enrolled in schools for the deaf or in special programs in regular schools (mainstreamed) are at high risk for compounding their handicaps if they develop an added conductive hearing loss secondary to otitis media with effusion or high negative pressure, or both. Since the incidence of intercurrent middle ear problems appears to be high in such children, early identification employing a formal screening program, such as the one proposed earlier, is mandatory. Some children develop troublesome cerumen that obstructs the ear canal and may interfere with the function of a hearing aid. Such children should be examined frequently and the cerumen should be periodically removed.

As suggested earlier, otitis media with effusion or high

negative pressure, or both, should be suspected during periods of upper respiratory tract infection, or when the children have signs and symptoms of otologic disease, such as otorrhea and otalgia, or when there has been a noticeable loss of hearing reported by the parents or teachers. Regular periodic screening employing otoscopy or tympanometry, or both, will identify those children with middle-ear problems who might otherwise be overlooked because obvious signs and symptoms associated with hearing loss may be absent.

Treatment of such children would depend on the type, severity, frequency, and duration of the middle-ear problem. More aggressive treatment, however, is indicated for this special population. Myringotomy and tympanostomy tube insertion should be considered earlier in such children when otitis media with effusion is frequently recurrent or chronic. Since sustained or transient high negative middle-ear pressure without a middle ear effusion can cause a persistent or fluctuating conductive hearing loss, the insertion of tympanostomy tubes should also be considered at an earlier time than in nondeaf children. The presence of a hearing aid will not interfere with the function of tympanostomy tubes, since a small bore hole can be placed in the ear mold to provide ventilation. It is important when tympanostomy tubes are inserted in such children that a short tube be used so that the ear mold can be inserted.

Early identification and appropriate management of middle-ear disease in a child with severe to profound deafness, especially those who use their residual hearing, are imperative so that maximum rehabilitation may be accomplished

Guidelines for Audiologic and Otologic Referral

The primary care provider is responsible for management of the child with otitis media, including therapy of acute episodes and determination of when special services should be provided. These services include audiologic assessments and consideration of surgical therapies. We suggest the following guidelines for referral:

Audiologic assessment:

1. Parental concern for decreased hearing
2. Speech and language delay
3. Inattentive behavior
4. Behavior change at home, day care, or school

Otologic referral:

1. An attack of acute otitis media that is unresponsive to appropriate and adequate antimicrobial therapy that may require tympanocentesis/myringotomy to relieve otalgia and fever and to identify the causative organism.
2. Recurrent episodes of acute otitis media, such as three or more episodes within the previous 6 months, or four or more episodes within the previous 12 months, with the last attack being of recent onset, especially when the frequency, severity, and duration are unaffected by antimicrobial prophylaxis.
3. Three or more months of middle-ear effusion in both ears (i.e., chronic) or 6 or months of effusion

in one ear, which has been unresponsive to a course of antibiotic (e.g., 10-day course of amoxicillin).

4. Recurrent otitis media with effusion in which each episode fails to meet criteria for being chronic yet the cumulative duration is excessive, such as 6 of the preceding 12 months.
5. Middle-ear effusion associated with hearing loss of 25 dB or more that is unresponsive to medical treatment.
6. Persistent high negative middle-ear pressure, retraction pocket, or atelectasis of the middle ear.
7. Symptoms associated with eustachian tube dysfunction, such as fluctuating hearing loss, otalgia, or tinnitus, that is chronic or recurrent and causing concern for the child or parent or both.
8. Speech and language delay associated with recurrent otitis media.
9. Persistent otorrhea through a tympanostomy tube that is unresponsive to initial appropriate and adequate medical treatment, e.g., ototopical/oral antimicrobial agents.
10. Acquired anatomic abnormality, such as persistent perforation of the tympanic membrane, with or without chronic suppurative otitis media, or presence (or suspicion) of cholesteatoma.
11. Suppurative complication of acute otitis media present or suspected, such as mastoiditis, labyrinthitis or facial palsy, or any associated central nervous system signs or symptoms, such as severe headache, blurred vision, or ataxia.

Acknowledgments

The authors want to thank Ms. Maria Bonasso Bluestone, M.A. for her patient, diligent, and painstaking editing of this chapter and of Chapters 26 and 27. They would also like to thank Mr. Jon Coulter for design and preparation of the artwork, and William J. Doyle, Ph.D., for assistance in preparation of the sections on anatomy and physiology.

SELECTED REFERENCES

Bluestone CD. Otologic surgical procedures. In Bluestone CD, Stool SE (eds). Atlas of Pediatric Otolaryngology. Philadelphia, WB Saunders, 1995, pp 27–128.

The author of the chapter in this atlas of otologic surgical procedures is the coauthor of this chapter and has described his surgical techniques in more detail than here.

Bluestone CD, Doyle WJ. Eustachian tube function: physiology and role in otitis media. Ann Otol Rhinol Laryngol Suppl 120:94, 1985.

The supplement presents an excellent state of knowledge of the anatomy, pathology, physiology, and pathophysiology of the eustachian tube.

Lim DJ, Bluestone CD, Klein JO, et al. Recent Advances in Otitis Media—Proceedings of the Sixth International Symposium. Toronto, Decker Periodicals, 1996.

This book has the latest research information on many aspects of otitis media that were presented at the Sixth International Symposium on Recent Advances on Otitis Media in Ft. Lauderdale, Florida, 1995.

Mogi G, Honjo I, Ishii T, et al. Recent Advances in Otitis Media. New York, Kugler, 1993.

This supplement contains many excellent extended abstracts on the basic science aspects and management of otitis media of presentations from an international meeting held in Oita, Japan, in 1993.

Rosenfeld RM, Bluestone CD. Evidence-based otitis media. Hamilton, Ontario, B. C. Decker, 1999.

This book provides the first attempt to evaluate the medical and surgical methods of management of otitis media using evidence-based methodology.

Schuknecht HF. Pathology of the Ear, 2nd ed. Philadelphia, Lea & Febiger, 1993, pp 191–234.

This elegant text is the best description of the pathology of various stages of otitis media.

REFERENCES

1. Abramson JS, Mills EL. Depression of neutrophil function induced by viruses and its role in secondary microbial infections. Rev Infect Dis 10:326, 1988.
2. Ackerman MN, Friedman RA, Doyle WJ, et al. Antigen-induced eustachian tube obstruction: an intranasal provocative challenge test. J Allergy Clin Immunol 73:604, 1984.
3. Adamkeicwicz T, Quie PG: When to evaluate a child with recurrent infections for immunodeficiency. Rep Pediatr Infect Dis 2:26, 1992.
4. Adler M, McDonald PJ, Trostmann U, et al. Cefdinir versus amoxicillin/clavulanic acid in the treatment of suppurative acute otitis media in children. Eur J Clin Microbiol Infect Dis 16:214, 1997.
5. Ahman H, Kayhty H, Tamminen P, et al. Pentavalent pneumococcal oligosaccharide conjugate vaccine PncCRM is well-tolerated and able to induce an antibody response in infants. Pediatr Infect Dis J 15:134, 1996.
6. Alberti PR, Kristensen R. The clinical application of impedance audiometer. Laryngoscope 80:735, 1970.
7. Alberti PW. Myringotomy and ventilating tubes in the 19th century. Laryngoscope 84:805, 1974.
8. Albiin N, Hailstorm S, Stenfors LE. Clearance of effusion material from the attic space—an experimental study in the rat. Int J Pediatr Otorhinolaryngol 5:1, 1983.
9. Alho O-P, Koivu M, Sorri M, Rantakallio P. Risk factors for recurrent acute otitis media and respiratory infection in infancy. Int J Pediatr Otorhinolaryngol 19:151, 1990.
10. Alho O-P, Koivu M, Sorri M. What is an "otitis-prone" child? Int J Pediatr Otorhinolaryngol 21:201, 1991.
11. Alper CM, Doyle WJ. Repeated inflation does not prevent otitis media with effusion in a monkey model. Laryngoscope 109:1974, 1999.
12. Alper CM, Swarts JD, Doyle WJ. Middle ear inflation for diagnosis and treatment of otitis media with effusion. Auris Nasus Larynx 26:479, 1999.
13. Alper CM, Swarts JD, Doyle WJ. Prevention of otitis media with effusion by repeated air inflation in a monkey model. Arch Otolaryngol Head Neck Surg 126:609, 2000.
14. Alper CM, Tabari R, Seroky JT, Doyle WJ. Magnetic resonance imaging of the development of middle-ear effusion secondary to experimental paralysis of tensor veli palatini muscle. Otolaryngol Head Neck Surg 111:422, 1997.
15. Alper CM, Tabari R, Seroky JT, Doyle WJ. Effects of dopamine, dobutamine and phentolamine on middle ear pressure and blood flow in cynomolgus monkeys. Acta Otolaryngol 115:55, 1995.
16. Alsarraf R, Jung CJ, Perkins J, et al. Measuring the indirect and direct costs of acute otitis media. Arch Otolaryngol Head Neck Surg 125:12, 1999.
17. Alt A: Heilunger Taubstummheit erzielte durch Beseitigung einer Otorrhoe und einer angebornen Gaumenspalte. Arch Augen Ohrenh 7:211, 1878.
18. Ambrosino DM, Barrus VA, DeLange GG, Siber GR. Correlation of the km(1) immunoglobulin allotypes with human anti-polysaccharide antibody concentrations. J Clin Invest 78:361, 1986.
19. Ambrosino DM, Schiffman G, Gotschlich EC, et al. Correlation between G2m(n) immunoglobulin allotype and human antibody response and susceptibility to polysaccharide encapsulated bacteria. J Clin Invest 75:1935, 1985.
20. American Academy of Pediatrics. Report of the Committee on Infectious Diseases, 24th ed. Elk Grove Village, IL, 1997, p 596.
21. Anderson B, Porras O, Hanson LA, et al. Inhibition of attachment of Streptococcus pneumoniae and Haemophilus influenzae by human milk and receptor oligosaccharides. J Infect Dis 1543:232, 1986.
22. Anderson EL, Kennedy DJ, Geldmacher KM, et al. Immunogenicity of heptavalent pneumococcal conjugate vaccine in infants. J Pediatr 128:649, 1996.
23. Anderson LJ. Respiratory syncytial virus vaccines for otitis media. Vaccine 19:S59, 2000.
24. Andersson B, Eriksson B, Falsen E, et al. Adhesion of Streptococcus pneumoniae to human pharyngeal epithelial cells in vitro: differences in adhesive capacity among strains isolated from subjects with otitis media, septicemia, or meningitis or from healthy carriers. Infect Immun 32:311, 1981.
25. Andersson B, Gray BM, Dillon HC, et al: Role of adherence of Streptococcus pneumoniae and Haemophilus influenzae by human milk and receptor oligosaccharides. J Infect Dis 7:476, 1988.
26. Andersson B, Porras O, Hanson LA, et al. Inhibition of attachment of Streptococcus pneumoniae and Haemophilus influenzae in human milk and receptor oligosaccharides. J Infect Dis 153:232, 1986.
27. Anson B (ed). Morris' Human Anatomy. New York, McGraw-Hill, 1967, pp 1195–1196.
28. Anson B, Donaldson J. The Surgical Anatomy of the Temporal Bone and Ear. Philadelphia, W.B. Saunders, 1967, pp 29–30.
29. Anteunis LJC, Brienesse P, Schrander JJP. Otoacoustic emissions in screening cleft lip and/or palate children for hearing loss: feasibility study. Int J Pediatr Otorhinolaryngol 44:259, 1998.
30. Aoki H, Sando I, Takahashi H. Anatomic relationships between Ostmann's fatty tissue and eustachian tube. Ann Otol Rhinol Laryngol 103:211, 1994.
31. Applebaum PC, Bhamjee A, Scragg JN, et al. Streptococcus pneumoniae resistant to penicillin and chloramphenicol. Lancet 2:995, 1977.
32. Armstrong BW. A new treatment for chronic secretory otitis media. Arch Otolaryngol 69:653, 1954.
33. Arnold KE, Leggiadro RJ, Breiman RF, et al. Risk factors for carriage of drug-resistant Streptococcus pneumoniae among children in Memphis, Tennessee. J Pediatr 128:757, 1996.
34. Arola M, Ruuskanen O, Ziegler T, et al. Clinical role of respiratory virus infection in acute otitis media. Pediatrics 86:848, 1990.
35. Aronowitz G. A multicenter, open label trial of azithromycin vs. amoxicillin/clavulanate for the management of acute otitis media in children. Pediatr Infect Dis J 15:S15, 1996.
36. Arriaga MA, Bluestone CD, Stool SE. The role of tympanocentesis in the management of infants with sepsis. Laryngoscope 99:1048, 1989.
37. Aschan GK: Hearing and nasal function correlated to postoperative speech in cleft palate patients with velopharyngoplasty. Acta Otolaryngol (Stockh) 61:371, 1966.
38. Aschan GK: Observations on the eustachian tube. Acta Soc Med Upsalien 57:1, 1952.
39. Aschan GK. The anatomy of the eustachian tube with regard to its function. Acta Soc Med Upsalien 60:131, 1955.
40. Asiri S, Hasham A, Anazy FA, et al. Tympanosclerosis: review of literature and incidence among patients with middle-ear infection. J Laryngol Otol 113:1076, 1999.
41. Ataoglu H, Goksu N, Kemaloglu YK, et al. Preliminary report on L-forms: possible role in the infectious origin of secretory otitis media. Ann Otol Rhinol Laryngol 103:434, 1994.
42. Auritt WA, Hervada AR, Fendrick G. Fatal pseudomembranous enterocolitis following oral ampicillin therapy. J Pediatr 93:882, 1978.
43. Austrian R, Howie VM, Ploussard JH. The bacteriology of pneumococcal otitis media. Johns Hopkins Med J 141:104, 1977.
44. Avery RK, Eavey RD, Della Torre T, et al. Bilateral otitis media

and mastoiditis caused by a highly resistant strain of *Mycobacterium chelonae*. Pediatr Infect Dis J 15:1037, 1996.

45. Baba S. Recent aspects of clinical bacteriology in otitis media. Presented at Presymposium on Management of Otitis Media, Kyoto, Japan, January 12, 1985.

46. Bacher JA. The applied anatomy of the eustachian tube. Laryngoscope 22:21, 1912.

47. Bain J, Murphy E, Ross F. Acute otitis media: clinical course among children who received a short course of high dose antibiotic. Br Med J 291:1243, 1985.

48. Bakaletz LO, Hoepf T, Hoskins P, et al: Serologic relatedness of fimbriae expressed by NTHi isolates recovered from children with chronic otitis media. In Lim DJ, Bluestone CD, Klein JO, et al (eds). Recent Advances in Otitis Media. Proceedings of the Fifth International Symposium. Burlington, Ontario, Decker Periodicals, 1993, pp 157–161.

49. Baker RS, Chole RA. A randomized clinical trial of topical gentamicin after tympanostomy tube placement. Arch Otolaryngol Head Neck Surg 114:755, 1988.

50. Bakwin H, Jacobinzer H. Prevention of purulent otitis media in infants. J Pediatr 14:730, 1939.

51. Balkany TJ, Barkin RM, Suzuki BH, Watson WJ. A prospective study of infection following tympanostomy and tube insertion. Am J Otol 4:288, 1983.

52. Balkany TJ, Berman SA, Simmons MA, Jafek BW. Middle ear effusions in neonates. Laryngoscope 88:398, 1978.

53. Balkany TM, Downs MP, Jafek BW, et al.: Hearing loss in Down's syndrome: a treatable handicap more common than generally recognized. Clin Pediatr 18:116, 1979.

54. Ball SS, Prasma J, Dais D, et al. Nitric oxide: a mediator of endotoxin-induced middle-ear effusions. Laryngoscope 106:1021, 1996.

55. Barenkamp SJ, Bodor FF. Development of serum bactericidal activity following nontypable *Haemophilus influenzae* acute otitis media. Pediatr Infect Dis J 9:333, 1990.

56. Barenkamp SJ, Shurin PA, Marchant CD, et al. Do children with recurrent *Haemophilus influenzae* otitis media become infected with a new organism or require the original strain? J Pediatr 105:533, 1984.

57. Barfoed C, Rosborg J. Secretory otitis media: long-term observations after treatment with grommets. Arch Otolaryngol Head Neck Surg 106:553, 1980.

58. Barnett ED, Klein JO, Pelton SI, Luginbuhl LM. Otitis media in children born to human immunodeficiency virus-infected mothers. Pediatr Infect Dis J 11:360, 1992.

59. Barnett ED, Levatin JL, Chapman EH, et al. Challenges of evaluating homeopathic treatment of acute otitis media. Pediatr Infect Dis 2000, 19:273.

60. Barnett ED, Pelton SI, Bolduc G, Klein J. Antimicrobial resistance of respiratory isolates of *Streptococcus pneumoniae* in pediatric patients in Boston. Program and Abstracts of the 33rd Interscience Conference on Antimicrobial Agents and Chemotherapy, New Orleans, Abstract No. 1045, 1993.

61. Barnett ED, Pelton SI, Cabral JH, et al. Immune response to pneumococcal conjugate and polysaccharide vaccines in otitis-prone and otitis-free children. Clin Infect Dis 2229:191, 1999.

62. Barnett ED, Teele DW, Klein JO, et al. Comparison of ceftriaxone and trimethoprim-sulfamethoxazole for acute otitis media. Pediatrics 99:23, 1997.

63. Barr WH, Affrime M, Lin C-C, Batra V: Pharmacokinetics of ceftibuten in children. Pediatr Infect Dis J 14:S93, 1995.

64. Barr WH. The pharmacokinetics of ceftibuten. Presented at the Symposium, From Molecules to Medicine, Schering-Plough International, New York, April 14–18, 1993.

65. Barsoumian R, Kuehn DP, Moon JP, Canady JW. An anatomic study of the tensor veli palatini and dilator tubae muscles in relation to eustachian tube and velar function. Cleft Palate Craniofac J 35:101, 1998.

66. Bartos LC, Murphy TF. Comparison of the outer membrane proteins of 50 strains of *Branhamella catarrhalis*. J Infect Dis 158:761, 1988.

67. Barza M. The nephrotoxicity of cephalosporins: an overview. J Infect Dis 137:S60, 1978.

68. Bass JW, Crast FW, Knowles CR, et al. Streptococcal pharyngitis in children: a comparison of four treatment schedules with intramuscular penicillin G benzathine. JAMA 235:1112, 1976.

69. Bass JW, Steele RW, Wiebe RA, Dierdorff EP. Erythromycin concentrations in middle ear exudates. Pediatrics 48:417, 1971.

69a. Bath AP, Walsh RM, Bance ML, Rutka JA. Ototoxicity of topical gentamicin preparations. Laryngoscope 109:1088, 1999.

70. Bauer AW, Kirby WM, Sherris JC, et al: Antibiotic susceptibility testing by a standardized single disk method. Am J Clin Pathol 45:493, 1966.

71. Bauchner H, Adams W, Barnett E, Klein J. Therapy for acute otitis media: preference of parents for oral or parenteral antibiotic. Arch Pediatr Adolesc Med 150:396, 1996.

72. Bayramoglu I, Ardic FN, Kara CO, et al. Importance of mastoid pneumatization on secretory otitis media. Int J Pediatr Otorhinolaryngol 40:6, 1997.

73. Beam TR, Gilbert DN, Kunin CM. Guidelines for the evaluation of anti-infective drug products. Clin Infect Dis 15(Suppl 1):55, 1992.

74. Beatty HG. The care of cleft palate patients. Laryngoscope 46:203, 1936.

75. Beery QC, Bluestone CD, Cantekin EI. Otologic history, audiometry, and tympanometry as a case finding procedure for school screening. Laryngoscope 85:1976, 1975.

76. Beery QC, Doyle WJ, Cantekin EI, Bluestone CD. Longitudinal assessment of ventilatory function of the eustachian tube in children. Laryngoscope 89:1446, 1979.

77. Beery QC, Doyle WJ, Cantekin EI, et al. Eustachian tube function in an American Indian population. Ann Otol Rhinol Laryngol 89:28, 1980.

78. Belshe RB, Mendelman PM, Treanor J, et al. The efficacy of live attenuated, cold-adapted, trivalent, intranasal influenza virus vaccine in children. N Engl J Med 338:1459, 1998.

79. Ben-David J, Podoshin L, Fradis M, Faraggi D. Is the vestibular system affected by middle ear effusion? Otolaryngol Head Neck Surg 109:421, 1993.

80. Bennett M. The older cleft palate patient: a clinical otologic-audiologic study. Laryngoscope 82:1217, 1972.

81. Bent JP, April MM, Ward RF. Atypical indications for OtoScan laser-assisted myringotomy. Laryngoscope 111:87, 2001.

82. Berdal P, Brandtzaeg P, Froland S, et al. Immunodeficiency syndromes with otorhinolaryngological manifestations. Acta Otolaryngol (Stockh) 82:185, 1976.

83. Berger G, Hawke M, Proops DW, et al. Histamine levels in middle ear effusions. Acta Otolaryngol (Stockh) 98:385, 1984.

84. Bergeson PS, Singer SA, Kaplan AM. Intramuscular injections in children. Pediatrics 70:944, 1982.

85. Berman SA, Balkany TJ, Simmons MA. Otitis media in the neonatal intensive care unit. Pediatrics 62:198, 1978.

86. Berman S, Bondy J, Byrns PJ, Lezotte D. Surgical management of uncomplicated otitis media in a pediatric Medicaid population. Ann Otol Rhinol Laryngol 109:623, 2000.

87. Berman S, Byrns PJ, Bondy J, et al. Otitis media-related antibiotic prescribing patterns, outcomes, and expenditures in a pediatric Medicaid population. Pediatrics 100:585, 1997.

88. Berman S, Grose K, Cha PAC, et al. Management of chronic middle ear effusion with prednisone combined with trimethoprim-sulfamethoxazole. Pediatr Infect Dis J 9:533, 1990.

89. Berman S, Grose K, Cha PAC, et al. Medical management of chronic middle ear effusion: results of a clinical trial of prednisone combined with sulfamethoxazole and trimethoprim. Am J Dis Child 141:690, 1987.

90. Berman S, Lee B, Nuss R, et al. Immunoglobulin G, total subclass in children with or without recurrent otitis media. J Pediatr 121:249, 1992.

91. Berman S. Medical management of children with otitis media with effusion. Rep Pediatr Infect Dis 3:37, 1993.

92. Berman S, Nuss R, Roark R, et al. Effectiveness of continuous vs. intermittent amoxicillin to prevent episodes of otitis media. Pediatr Infect Dis J 11:63, 1992.

93. Berman S. Otitis media in developing countries. Pediatrics 96:126, 1995.

94. Berman S, Roark R. Factors influencing outcome in children treated with antibiotics for acute otitis media. Pediatr Infect Dis J 12:20, 1993.

95. Berman S, Roark R, Luckey D. Theoretical cost effectiveness of

management options for children with persisting middle ear effusions. Pediatrics 93:353, 1994.

96. Bernard GR, Vincent J-L, Laterre P-F, et al. Efficacy and safety of recombinant human activated protein C for severe sepsis. N Engl J Med 344:699, 2001.

97. Bernard PAM, Stenstrom RJ, Feldman W, et al. Randomized, controlled trial comparing long-term sulfonamide therapy to ventilation tubes for otitis media with effusion. Pediatrics 88:215, 1991.

98. Bernstein JM. Biological mediators of inflammation in middle ear effusions. Ann Otol Rhinol Laryngol 85:90, 1976.

99. Bernstein JM, Brentjens J, Vladutziu A. Immune complex determination in otitis media with effusion. Presented at the ARO Midwinter Meeting, January, 1981, St. Petersburg, Florida.

100. Bernstein JM, Dryja D, Neter E. The clinical significance of coagulase negative staphylococci in otitis media with effusion. In Lim DJ, Bluestone CD, Klein JO, Nelson JD (eds). Recent Advances in Otitis Media with Effusion. Burlington, Ontario, B.C. Decker, 1984, pp 114–116.

101. Bernstein JM, Faden HF, Dryja DM, et al: Micro-ecology of the nasopharyngeal bacterial flora in otitis-prone and non-otitis-prone children. Acta Otolaryngol (Stockh) 113:88, 1993.

102. Bernstein JM, Faden HS, Henderson D, et al (eds). Immunologic diseases of the ear. Ann N Y Acad Sci 830:19, 1997.

102a. Bernstein JM, Haynes ER, Ishikawa T, et al. Secretory otitis media: a histopathologic and immunochemical report. TAAOO 76: 1305, 1972.

103. Bernstein JM. Immunological reactivity in otitis media with effusion. In Oehling A, Mathov E, Glazer I, Arbesman C (eds). Advances in Allergology and Immunology. Oxford, Pergamon Press, 1980, pp 139–146.

104. Bernstein JM, Lee J, Conboy K, et al. Further observations on the role of IgE-mediated hypersensitivity in recurrent otitis media with effusion. Otolaryngol Head Neck Surg 93:611, 1985.

105. Bernstein JM, Myers D, Kosinski D, et al. Antibody coated bacteria in otitis media with effusion. Ann Otol Rhinol Laryngol 89: 104, 1980.

106. Bernstein JM. Observations on immune mechanisms in otitis media with effusion. Int J Pediatr Otorhinolaryngol 8:125, 1984.

107. Bernstein JM, Okazaki T, Reisman RE. Prostaglandins in middle ear effusions. Arch Otolaryngol Head Neck Surg 102:257, 1976.

108. Bernstein JM, Reisman R. The role of acute hypersensitivity in secretory otitis media. Trans Am Acad Ophthalmol Otolaryngol 78:120, 1974.

109. Bernstein JM, Schenkein HA, Genco RJ, Bartholomew W. Complement activity in middle ear effusions. Clin Exp Immunol 33: 340, 1978.

110. Bernstein JM, Szymanski C, Albini B, et al. Lymphocyte subpopulations in otitis media with effusion. Pediatr Res 12:786, 1978.

111. Bernstein JM. The role of IgE-mediated hypersensitivity in the development of otitis media with effusion: a review. Otolaryngol Head Neck Surg 109:611, 1993.

112. Beswick AJ, Lawley B, Fraise AP, et al. Detection of *Alloiococcus otitis* in mixed bacterial populations from middle ear effusions of patients with otitis media. Lancet 354:386, 1999.

113. Bhatnagar RK. Critical evaluation of Per-Lee tubes in children. J Laryngol Otol 104:112, 1990.

114. Biedel CW. Modification of recurrent otitis media by short-term sulfonamide therapy. Am J Dis Child 132:681, 1978.

115. Birch L, Elbrond O. Daily impedance audiometric screening of children in a day-care institution: changes through one month. Scand Audiol 14:5, 1985.

116. Birkin EA, Brookler KH. Surface tension lowering substance of the canine eustachian tube. Ann Otol Rhinol Laryngol 81:268, 1972.

117. Black S, Shinefield H, Fireman B, et al. Efficacy, safety, and immunogenicity of a heptavalent pneumococcal conjugate vaccine in children. Pediatr Infect Dis J 19:187, 2000.

118. Bland RD. Otitis media in the first six weeks of life: diagnosis, bacteriology, and management. Pediatrics 49:187, 1972.

119. Bluestone CD. Acute and chronic mastoiditis and chronic suppurative otitis media. Semin Pediatr Infect Dis 9:12, 1998.

120. Bluestone CD. Assessment of eustachian tube function. In Jerger J, Northern J (eds). Clinical Impedance Audiometry. Acton, MA, American Electromedics Corporation, 1980, pp 83–108.

121. Bluestone CD, Beery QC, Andrus WS. Mechanics of the eustachian tube as it influences susceptibility to and persistence of middle ear effusions in children. Ann Otol Rhinol Laryngol 83(Suppl 11):27, 1974.

122. Bluestone CD, Beery QC. Concepts on the pathogenesis of middle-ear effusions. Ann Otol Rhinol Laryngol 85:182, 1976.

123. Bluestone CD, Beery QC, Paradise JL. Audiometry and tympanometry in relation to middle-ear effusions in children. Laryngoscope 83:594, 1973.

124. Bluestone CD, Cantekin EI, Beery QC. Certain effects of adenoidectomy on eustachian tube ventilatory function. Laryngoscope 85:113, 1975.

125. Bluestone CD, Cantekin EI, Beery QC. Effect of inflammation on the ventilatory function of the eustachian tube. Laryngoscope 87:493, 1977.

126. Bluestone CD, Cantekin EI, Beery QC, et al. Functional eustachian tube obstruction in acquired cholesteatoma and related conditions. In McCabe BF, Sade J, Abramson M (eds). Cholesteatoma: First International Congress. Birmingham, AL, Aesculapius Publishing, 1977, pp 325–335.

127. Bluestone CD, Cantekin EI, Beery QC, Stool SE. Function of the eustachian tube related to surgical management of acquired aural cholesteatoma in children. Laryngoscope 88:1155, 1978.

127a. Bluestone CD, Cantekin EI. Design factors in the characterization and identification of otitis media and certain related conditions. Ann Otol Rhinol Laryngol 88:13, 1979.

128. Bluestone CD, Cantekin EI, Douglas GS: Eustachian tube function related to the results of tympanoplasty in children. Laryngoscope 89:450, 1979.

129. Bluestone CD, Cantekin EI. Management of the patulous eustachian tube. Laryngoscope 91:149, 1981.

130. Bluestone CD. Definitions and classifications: state of the art. In Lim DJ, Bluestone CD, Klein JO, Nelson JD (eds). Recent advances in otitis media with effusion. In Proceedings of the Third International Symposium. Philadelphia, B.C. Decker, 1984, pp 1–4.

131. Bluestone CD, et al. Definitions, terminology, and classification. In Lim D, Bluestone CD, Klein JO, et al (eds). 7th International Symposium on Recent Advances on Otitis Media: Proceedings of the Post-Symposium Research Meeting. Ann Otol Rhinol Laryngol Suppl 2001.

132. Bluestone CD. Definitions, terminology, and classification. In Rosenfeld RM, Bluestone CD (eds). Evidence-Based Otitis Media. Hamiliton, Ontario, B.C. Decker, 1999, pp 85–104.

132a. Bluestone CD, Doyle WJ (eds). Eustachian tube function: physiology and role in otitis media—workshop report. Ann Otol Rhinol Laryngol Suppl 120:1, 1985.

133. Bluestone CD. Epidemiology and pathogenesis of chronic suppurative otitis media: implications for prevention and treatment. Int J Pediatr. Otorhinolaryngol 42:207, 1998.

134. Bluestone CD. Eustachian tube function and allergy in otitis media. Pediatrics 61:753, 1978.

135. Bluestone CD. Eustachian tube function and dysfunction. In Rosenfeld RM, Bluestone CD (eds). Evidence-Based Otitis Media. Hamiliton, Ontario, B.C. Decker, 1999, pp 137–156.

136. Bluestone CD. Eustachian tube obstruction in the infant with cleft palate. Ann Otol Rhinol Laryngol 80:1, 1971.

137. Bluestone CD, Klein JO. Chronic suppurative otitis media. Pediatr Rev 20:277, 1999.

138. Bluestone CD, Klein JO: Clinical practice guideline on otitis media with effusion in young children: strengths and weaknesses. Otolaryngol Head Neck Surg 112:507, 1995.

139. Bluestone CD, Klein JO (eds). Workshop on the role of anaerobic bacteria in infections of the upper respiratory tract: head and neck. Ann Otol Rhinol Laryngol 100(Suppl. 154):1, 1991.

140. Bluestone CD, Klein JO, Gates GA. "Appropriateness" of tympanostomy tubes: setting the record straight. Arch Otolaryngol Head Neck Surg 120:1051, 1994.

141. Bluestone CD, Klein JO. Otitis Media in Infants and Children, 3rd ed. Philadelphia, WB Saunders, 2001.

142. Bluestone CD, Lee D. What to expect from surgical therapy. In Rosenfeld RM, Bluestone CD (eds). Evidence-Based Otitis Media. Hamilton, Ontario, B.C. Decker, 1999, pp 207–222.

143. Bluestone CD, Magit AE. The abnormally patulous eustachian

tube. In Brackmann DE, Shelton C, Arriaga MA (eds). Otologic Surgery. Philadelphia, WB Saunders, 1994, pp 103–109.

144. Bluestone CD. Management of the abnormally patulous eustachian tube. In Myers EN, Bluestone CD, Brackmann DE, Krause CJ (eds). Advances in Otolaryngology-Head and Neck Surgery. St. Louis, Mosby, 1998, pp 205–234.

145. Bluestone CD. Otologic surgical procedures. In Bluestone CD, Stool SE (eds). Atlas of Pediatric Otolaryngology. Philadelphia, WB Saunders, 1995, pp 27–128.

146. Bluestone CD, Paradise JL, Beery QC. Physiology of the eustachian tube in the pathogenesis and management of middle-ear effusions. Laryngoscope 82:1654, 1972.

147. Bluestone CD, Paradise JL, Beery QC, Wittel R. Certain effects of cleft palate repair on eustachian tube function. Cleft Palate J 9:183, 1972.

148. Bluestone CD (ed). Proceedings of a workshop on vaccines for otitis media. Pediatr Infect Dis J 8(Suppl. 1):S1, 1989.

149. Bluestone CD.: Review of cefixime in the treatment of otitis media in infants and children. Pediatr Infect Dis J 12:75, 1993.

150. Bluestone CD, Shurin PA. Middle ear disease in children. Pediatr Clin North Am 21:379, 1974.

151. Bluestone CD, Stephenson JS, Martin LM. Ten-year review of otitis media pathogens. Pediatr Infect Dis J 11:S7, 1992.

152. Bluestone CD. Surgical management of otitis media: current indications and role related to increasing bacterial resistance. Pediatr Infect Dis J 13:1058, 1994.

153. Bluestone CD. Tympanostomy tubes and audiograms (American Society of Pediatric Otolaryngology News). Arch Otolaryngol Head Neck Surg 119:370, 1993.

154. Bluestone CD, Wittel R, Paradise JL, Felder H.: Eustachian tube function as related to adenoidectomy for otitis media. Trans Am Acad Ophthalmol Otolaryngol 76:1325, 1972.

155. Blumer JL, McLinn SE, Deabate CA, et al. Multinational multicenter controlled trial comparing ceftibuten with cefaclor for the treatment of acute otitis media. Pediatr Infect Dis J 12:S77, 1993.

156. Bodner EE, Browning GG, Chalmers FT, Chalmers TC. Can meta-analysis help uncertainty in surgery for otitis media in children? J Laryngol Otol 105:812, 1991.

157. Bodor FF, Marchant CD, Shurin PA, Barenkamp SJ. Bacterial etiology of conjunctivitis-otitis media syndrome. Pediatrics 76:26, 1985.

158. Bordley JE, Kapur YP. The histopathological changes in the temporal bone resulting from acute smallpox and chickenpox infection. Laryngoscope 82:1477, 1972.

159. Boswell JB, Nienhuys TG. Patterns of persistent otitis media in the first year of life in Aboriginal and non-Aboriginal infants. Ann Otol Rhinol Laryngol 105:893, 1996.

160. Bradley JS, Connor JD. Ceftriaxone failure in meningitis caused by Streptococcus pneumoniae with reduced susceptibility to beta-lactam antibiotics. Pediatr Infect Dis J 10:871, 1991.

161. Braun P. Hepatotoxicity of erythromycin. J Infect Dis 119:300, 1969.

162. Brinton CC, Carter MJ, Derber DB, et al. Design and development of pilus vaccines for Haemophilus influenzae diseases. Pediatr Infect Dis J 8:S54, 1989.

163. Brodish BN, Woolley AL. Major vascular injuries in children undergoing myringotomy for tube placement. Am J Otolaryngol 20:46, 1999.

164. Brodsky L, Brookhauser P, Chait D, et al. Office-based insertion of pressure equalization tubes: role of laser-assisted tympanic membrane fenestration. Laryngoscope 109:2009, 1999.

165. Brodsky L, Faden H, Bernstein J, et al: Arachidonic acid metabolites in middle ear effusions of children. Ann Otol Rhinol Laryngol 100:589, 1991.

166. Brody R, Rosenfeld RM, Goldsmith AJ, et al. Parents cannot detect mild hearing loss in children. Otolaryngol Head Neck Surg 121:681, 1999.

167. Brook I. Bacteriology and treatment of chronic otitis media. Laryngoscope 89:1129, 1979.

168. Brook I, Gober AE. Bacterial colonization of pacifiers of infants with acute otitis media. J Larngol Otol 111:614, 1997.

169. Brook I, Gober AE. Prophylaxis with amoxicillin or sulfisoxazole for otitis media: effect on the recovery of penicillin-resistant bacteria from children. Clin Infect Dis 22:143, 1996.

170. Brook I, Schwartz R. Anaerobic bacteria in acute otitis media. Acta Otolaryngol (Stockh) 91:111, 1981.

171. Brook I, Yocum P, Shah K. Aerobic and anaerobic bacteriology of otorrhea associated with tympanostomy tubes in children. Acta Otolaryngol (Stockh) 118:206, 1998.

172. Brooks DN. An objective method of detecting fluid in the middle ear. Int Audiol 7:280, 1968.

173. Brooks D. The use of the electroacoustic impedance bridge in the assessment of middle-ear function. Int J Audiol 8:563, 1969.

174. Brown CE, Magnuson B. On the physics of the infant feeding bottle and middle ear sequela: ear disease in infants can be associated with bottle feeding. Int J Pediatr Otorhinolaryngol 54:13, 2000.

175. Browning GG, Gatehouse D. The prevalence of middle-ear disease in the adult British population. Clin Otolaryngol 17:317, 1992.

176. Brunck W. Die Systematische Untersuchung des Sprachorganes bei Angeborenen Gaumendefekte in Ihrer Beziehung zur Prognose und Therapie. Leipzig, B Angestein, 1906.

177. Buchman CA, Doyle WJ, Skoner DP, et al. Influenza A virus–induced acute otitis media. J Infect Dis 171:1348, 1995.

178. Buchman CA, Doyle WJ, Skoner D, et al. Otologic manifestations of experimental rhinovirus infection. Laryngoscope 104:1295, 1994.

179. Buchman CA, Doyle WJ, Swarts JD, Bluestone CD. Effects of nasal obstruction on eustachian tube function and ear pressure. Acta Otolaryngol (Stockh) 119:351, 1999.

180. Buchman CA, Stool SE. Functional-anatomic correlation of eustachian tube obstruction related to the adenoid in a patient with otitis media with effusion: a case report. Ear Nose Throat J 73:835, 1994.

181. Bulkley WJ, Bowes AK, Marlowe JF. Complications following ventilation of the middle ear using Goode T tubes. Arch Otolaryngol Head Neck Surg 117:895, 1991.

182. Bunne M, Magnuson B, Falk B, Hellstrom S. Eustachian tube function varies over time in children with secretory otitis media. Acta Otolaryngol 120:716, 2000.

183. Bush PJ, Rabin DL. Racial differences in encounter rate for otitis media. Pediatr Res 14:1115, 1980.

184. Bylander A. Comparison of eustachian tube function in children and adults with normal ears. Ann Otol Rhinol Laryngol 89:20, 1980.

185. Bylander A, Tjernström O. Changes in eustachian tube function with age in children with normal ears: a longitudinal study. Acta Otolaryngol (Stockh) 96:467, 1983.

186. Bylander A, Tjernstrom O, Ivarsson A. Pressure opening and closing functions of the eustachian tube by inflation and deflation in children and adults with normal ears. Acta Otolaryngol (Stockh) 96:255, 1983.

187. Byrns PJ, Bondy J, Glazner JE, Berman S. Utilization of services for otitis media by children enrolled in Medicaid. Arch Pediatr Adolesc Med 151:407, 1997.

188. Cabana MD, Rand CS, Powe NR, et al. Why don't physicians follow clinical practice guidelines? A framework for improvement. JAMA 282:1458, 1999.

189. Calhoun KH, Norris WB, Hokanson JA, et al. Bacteriology of middle ear effusions. South Med J 81:332, 1988.

190. Callahan CW. Cost effectiveness of antibiotic therapy for otitis media in a military pediatric clinic. Pediatr Infect Dis J 7:622, 1988.

191. Cambon K, Galbraith JD, Kong G. Middle-ear disease in Indians of the Mount Currie reservation, British Columbia. Can Med Assoc J 93:1301, 1965.

192. Canalis RF. Valsalva's contribution to otology. Am J Otolaryngol 11:420, 1990.

193. Cantekin EI, Bluestone CD, Parkin LP. Eustachian tube ventilatory function in children. Ann Otol Rhinol Laryngol 85:171, 1976.

194. Cantekin EI, Bluestone CD, Rockette HE, Beery QC. Effect of oral decongestant with and without antihistamine on eustachian tube function. Ann Otol Rhinol Laryngol 89(Suppl 68):290, 1980.

195. Cantekin EI, Bluestone CD, Saez CA, et al. Normal and abnormal middle-ear ventilation. Ann Otol Rhinol Laryngol 86:1, 1977.

196. Cantekin EI, Doyle WJ, Bluestone CD. Effect of levator veli palatini muscle excision on eustachian tube function. Arch Otolaryngol 109:281, 1983.

197. Cantekin EI, Doyle WJ, Phillips DC, Bluestone CD. Gas absorption in the middle ear. Ann Otol Rhinol Laryngol 68:71, 1980.

198. Cantekin EI, Doyle WJ, Reichert TJ, et al. Dilation of the eustachian tube by electrical stimulation of the mandibular nerve. Ann Otol Rhinol Laryngol 88:40, 1979.

199. Cantekin EI, Mandel EM, Bluestone CD, et al. Lack of efficacy of a decongestant-antihistamine combination for otitis media with effusion ("secretory" otitis media) in children. N Engl J Med 308:297, 1983.

200. Cantekin EI, Phillips DC, Doyle WJ, et al. Effect of surgical alterations of the tensor veli palatini muscle on eustachian tube function. Ann Otol Rhinol Laryngol 89(Suppl 68):47, 1980.

201. Capra AM, Lieu TA, Black SB, et al. Costs of otitis media in a managed care population. Pediatr Infect Dis J 19:354, 2001.

202. Carlin SA, Marchant CD, Shurin PA, et al. Early recurrences of otitis media: reinfection or relapse? J Pediatr 110:20, 1987.

203. Carlin SA, Marchant CD, Shurin PA, et al. Host factors and early therapeutic response in acute otitis media. J Pediatr 118:178, 1991.

204. Carlsson B, Lundberg C, Ohlsson K: Granulocyte protease inhibition in acute and chronic middle ear effusion. Acta Otolaryngol (Stockh) 95:341, 1983.

205. Carrie S, Sprigg A, Parker AJ. Skull base factors in relation to hearing impairment in cleft palate children. Cleft Palate Craniofac J 37:166, 2000.

206. Carson JL, Collier AM, Hu SS. Acquired ciliary defects in nasal epithelium of children with acute viral upper respiratory infections. N Engl J Med 312:463, 1985.

207. Casselbrant ML, Brostoff LM, Cantekin EI, et al. Otitis media with effusion in preschool children. Laryngoscope 95:428, 1985.

208. Casselbrant ML, Cantekin EI, Dirkmaat DC, et al. Experimental paralysis of tensor veli palatini muscle. Acta Otolaryngol (Stockh) 106:178, 1988.

208a. Casselbrant ML, Furman JM, Rubenstein E, Mandel EM. The effect of otitis media on the vestibular system in children. Ann Otol Rhinol Laryngol 104:620, 1995.

209. Casselbrant ML, Kaleida PH, Rockette HE, et al. Efficacy of antimicrobial prophylaxis and of tympanostomy tube insertion for prevention of recurrent acute otitis media: results of a randomized clinical trial. Pediatr Infect Dis J 11:278, 1992.

210. Casselbrant ML, Mandel EM, Fall PA, et al. The heritability of otitis media: a twin and triplet study. JAMA 202:2125, 1999.

211. Casselbrant ML, Mandel EM, Kurs-Lasky M, et al. Otitis media in a population of black American and white American infants, 0–2 years of age. Int J Pediatr Otorhinolaryngol 33:11, 1995.

212. Casselbrant ML, Okeowo PA, Flaherty MR, et al. Prevalence and incidence of otitis media in a group of preschool children in the United States. In Lim DJ, Bluestone CD, Klein JO, Nelson JD (eds). Recent Advances in Otitis Media with Effusion. Burlington, Ontario, B. C. Decker, 1984, pp 16–19.

213. Caye-Thomasen P, Hermansson A, Tos M, Prellner K. Changes in mucosal goblet cell density in acute otitis media caused by non-typeable Haemophilus influenzae. Acta Otolaryngol (Stockh) 118:211, 1998.

214. Celedon JC, Litonjua AA, Weiss ST, Gold DR. Day care attendance in the first year of life and illnesses of the upper and lower respiratory tract in children with a familial history of atopy. Pediatrics 104:495, 1999.

215. Celin SE, Bluestone CD, Stephenson J, et al. Bacteriology of acute otitis media in adults. JAMA 266:2249, 1991.

216. Centers for Disease Control and Prevention. Drug-resistant Streptococcus pneumoniae: Kentucky and Tennessee, 1993. Morbid Mortal Wkly Rep 43:23, 1994.

217. Centers for Disease Control and Prevention. Geographic variation in penicillin resistance in Streptococcus pneumoniae: selected site, United States, 1997. Morbid Mortal Wkly Rep 48:656, 1999.

218. Centers for Disease Control and Prevention. Preventing pneumococcal disease among infants and young children: recommendations of the Advisory Committee on Immunization Practices. Morbid Mortal Wkly Rep 49:1, 2000.

219. Chan KH, Bluestone CD. Lack of efficacy of middle-ear inflation: treatment of otitis media with effusion in children. Otolaryngol Head Neck Surg 100:317, 1989.

220. Chan KH, Cantekin EI, Karnavas WJ, Bluestone CD. Autoinfla-

tion of eustachian tube in young children. Laryngoscope 97:668, 1987.

221. Chan KH, Swarts JD, Doyle WJ, et al. Efficacy of a new macrolide (azithromycin) for acute otitis media in the chinchilla model. Arch Otolaryngol Head Neck Surg 114:1266, 1988.

222. Chandra RK. Prospective studies of the effect of breast feeding on incidence of infection and allergy. Acta Paediatr Scand 68:691, 1979.

223. Chang MJ, Rodriguez WJ, Mohla C. Chlamydia trachomatis in otitis media in children. Pediatr Infect Dis J 1:95, 1982.

224. Chaput de Saintonge DM, Levine DF, Templae Savage I, et al. Trial of three-day and ten-day courses of amoxycillin in otitis media. Br Med J. 284:1078, 1982.

225. Chen DA, Luxford WM. Myringotomy and tube for relief of patulous eustachian tube symptoms. Am J Otol 11:272, 1990.

226. Chonmaitree T, Owen MJ, Howie VM. Respiratory viruses interfere with bacteriologic response to antibiotic in children with acute otitis media. J Infect Dis 162:546, 1990.

227. Chonmaitree T, Owen MJ, Patel JA, et al. Presence of cytomegalovirus and herpes simplex virus in middle ear fluids from children with acute otitis media. Clin Infect Dis 15:650, 1992.

228. Choo V. UK revises indications for co-trimoxazole. Lancet 346:175, 1995.

229. Chow AW, Hall CB, Klein JO, et al. Evaluation of new anti-infective drugs for the treatment of respiratory tract infections. Clin Infect Dis 15(suppl 1):S62, 1992.

230. Church DA, Echols RM. Ciprofloxacin use in pediatric and cystic fibrosis patients. Pediatr Inf Dis J 16:89, 1997.

231. Clarke TA. Deafness in children: otitis media and other causes; a selective survey of prevention and treatment and of educational problems. Proc R Soc Med 55:61, 1962.

232. Clemens CJ, Taylor JA, Almquist JR, et al. Is an antihistamine-decongestant combination effective in temporarily relieving symptoms of the common cold in preschool children? J Pediatr 130:463, 1997.

233. Clements DA, Langdon L, Bland C, Walter E. Influenza A vaccine decreases the incidence of otitis media in 6- to 30-month old children in day care. Arch Pediatr Adolesc Med 149:1113, 1995.

234. Clements DA. Otitis media and hearing loss in a small aboriginal community. Med J Aust 1:665, 1968.

235. Clements KS, Vrabec JT, Mader JT. Complications of tympanostomy tubes inserted for facilitation of hyperbaric oxygen therapy. Arch Otolaryngol Head Neck Surg 124:278, 1998.

236. Clemis JD. Allergic factors in management of middle ear effusions: recent advances in middle ear effusions. Ann Otol Rhinol Laryngol 85(Suppl 25):259, 1976.

237. Coffey JD Jr. Concentration of ampicillin in exudate from acute otitis media. J Pediatr 72:693, 1968.

238. Coffey JD Jr, Martin AD, Booth HN. Neisseria catarrhalis in exudative otitis media. Arch Otolaryngol Head Neck Surg 86:403, 1967.

239. Cohen R, Levy C, Boucherat M, et al. A multicenter, randomized, double-blind trial of 5 versus 10 days of antibiotic therapy for acute otitis media in young children. J Pediatr 133:634, 1998.

240. Cohen R, Navel M, Grunberg J, et al. One dose ceftriaxone vs. ten days of amoxicilliin/clavulanate therapy for acute otitis media: clinical efficacy and change in nasopharyngeal flora. Pediatr Infect Dis J 18:403, 1999.

241. Cohn AM, Schwaber MK, Anthony LS, et al. Eustachian tube function and tympanoplasty. Ann Otol Rhinol Laryngol 88:339, 1979.

242. Collipp PJ. Evaluation of nose drops for otitis media in children. Northwest Med 60:999, 1961.

243. Combs JT. Eustachian tube dysfunction in children with streptococcal pharyngitis. Pediatr Infect Dis J 9:590, 1990.

244. Committee on Environmental Health. Ambient air pollution: respiratory hazards to children. Pediatrics 91:1210, 1993.

245. Committee on Infectious Diseases, American Academy of Pediatrics. Recommendations for the prevention of pneumococcal infections, including use of pneumococcal conjugate vaccine (Prevnar), pneumococcal polysaccharide vaccine, and antibiotic prophylaxis. Pediatrics 106:362, 2000.

246. Committee on Infectious Diseases, American Academy of Pediatrics. Therapy for children with invasive pneumococcal infections. Pediatrics 99:289, 1997.

247. Compere WE Jr. Radiologic evaluation of the eustachian tube. Otolaryngol Clin North Am 3:45, 1970.

248. Compere WE Jr. The radiologic evaluation of eustachian tube function. Arch Otolaryngol Head Neck Surg 71:386, 1960.

249. Cook SP, Brodsky L, Reilly JS, et al. Effectiveness of adenoidectomy and laser tympanic membrane fenestration. Laryngoscope 111:251, 2001.

250. Coopman SA, Johnson RA, Platt R, Stern RS. Cutaneous disease and drug reactions in HIV infection. N Engl J Med 328:1670, 1993.

251. Cooter MS, Eisma RJ, Burleson JA, et al. Transforming growth factor: expression in otitis media with effusion. Laryngoscope 108:1066, 1998.

252. Corwin MJ, Weiner LB, Daniels D. Efficacy of oral antibiotics for the treatment of persistent otitis media with effusion. Int J Pediatr Otorhinolaryngol 11:109, 1986.

253. Craig HB, Stool SE, Laird MA: "Project Ears": Otologic maintenance in a school for the deaf. Am Ann Deaf 124:458, 1979.

254. Craig WA, Andes D. Pharmacokinetics and pharmacodynamics of antibiotics in otitis media. Pediatr Infect Dis J 15:255, 1996.

255. Craig WA, Kirby WMM. Pulse dosing of antimicrobial drugs with special reference to bacampicillin. Rev Infect Dis 3:1, 1981.

256. Crain EF, Shelov SP: Febrile infants: predictors of bacteremia. J Pediatr 101:686, 1982.

257. Christakis DA, Rivara FP. Pediatricians' awareness of and attitudes about four clinical practice guidelines. Pediatrics 101:825, 1998.

258. Croteau N, Hai V, Pless B, Infante-Rivard C. Trends in medical visits and surgery for otitis media among children. Am J Dis Child 144:535, 1990.

259. Cunningham AS. Morbidity in breast-fed and artificially fed infants. J Pediatr 90:726, 1977.

260. Cunningham MJ, Eavey RD, Krouse JH, Kiskaddon RM. Tympanostomy tubes: experience with removal. Laryngoscope 103:659, 1993.

261. Dagan R, Englehard D, Piccard E, et al. Epidemiology of invasive childhood pneumococcal infections in Israel. JAMA 268:3328, 1992.

262. Dagan R, Leibovitz E, Fliss DM, et al. Bacteriologic efficacies of oral azithromycin and oral cefaclor in treatment of acute otitis media in infants and young children. Antimicrob Agents Chemother 44:43, 2000.

263. Dagan R, Leibovitz E, Greenberg D, et al. Early eradication of pathogens from middle ear fluid during antibiotic treatment of acute otitis media is associated with improved clinical outcome. Pediatr Infect Dis J 17:767, 1998.

264. Dagan R, Givon N, Yagupsky P, et al. Effect of a 9-valent pneumococcal vaccine conjugated to CRM 197 on nasopharyngeal carriage of vaccine type and non-vaccine type S. pneumoniae strains among day care center attendees. Abstracts of the 38th ICAAC, September, 1998, San Diego, California.

265. Dagan R, Klein JO, Chonmaitree T, et al. Otitis media: a preventable disease? Vaccine 19:S1, 2000.

266. Daly KA, Brown JE, Lindgren BR, et al. Epidemiology of otitis media onset by six months of age. Pediatrics 103:1158, 1999.

267. Daly K, Giebink GS, Batalden PB, et al. Resolution of otitis media with effusion with the use of a stepped treatment regimen of trimethoprim-sulfamethoxazole and prednisone. Pediatr Infect Dis J 10:500, 1991.

268. Daly K, Giebink GS, Le CT, et al. Determining the risk for chronic otitis media with effusion. Pediatr Infect Dis J 7:471, 1988.

269. Damoiseaux RAMJ, Van Balen FAM, Hoes AW, et al. Primary care based randomized, double-blind trial of amoxicillin versus placebo for acute otitis media in children under 2 years. BMJ 320:350, 2000.

270. Danon J. Cefotaxime concentrations in otitis media with effusion. J Antimicrob Chemother 6(Suppl A):131, 1980.

271. Deinard AS, Dassenko D, Kloster B, et al. Otogenous tetanus. JAMA 243:2156, 1980.

272. Del Beccaro MA, Mendelman PM, Inglis AF, et al. Bacteriology of acute otitis media: a new perspective. J Pediatr 120:81, 1992.

273. DeMaria TF, Briggs BR, Okazaki N, Lim DJ. Experimental otitis media with effusion following middle ear inoculation of nonviable H. influenzae. Ann Otol Rhinol Laryngol 93:52, 1984.

274. DeMaria TF, Lim DJ, Barnishan J, et al. Biotypes of serologically nontypable Hemophilus influenzae isolated from the middle ears and nasopharynges of patients with otitis media with effusion. J Clin Microbiol 20:1102, 1984.

275. DeMaria TF, McGhee RB Jr, Lim DJ. Rheumatoid factor in otitis media with effusion. Arch Otolaryngol Head Neck Surg 110:279, 1984.

276. DeMaria TF, Prior RB, Briggs BR, et al. Endotoxin in middle ear effusions from patients with chronic otitis media with effusion. In Lim DJ, Bluestone CD, Klein JO, Nelson JD (eds). Recent Advances in Otitis Media with Effusion. Burlington, Ontario, B.C. Decker, 1984, pp 123–124.

277. Demers DM, Chan DS, Bass JW. Antimicrobial drug suspensions: a blinded comparison of taste of twelve common pediatric drugs including cefixime, cefpodoxime, cefprozil and loracarbef. Pediatr Infect Dis J 13:87, 1994.

278. DeNeeling AJ, Van Leeuwen WJ, Van Klingeren B, et al. Epidemiology of resistance of Streptococcus pneumoniae in The Netherlands. Abstracts of the 36th Interscience Conference on Antimicrobial Agents and Chemotherapy, September, 1996, New Orleans, LA, Abstract no. C57, p 44.

279. Derkay CS, Bluestone CD, Thompson AE, Kardatske D. Otitis media in the pediatric intensive care unit: a prospective study. Otolaryngol Head Neck Surg 100:292, 1989.

280. Derkay CS. Eustachian tube and nasal function during pregnancy: a prospective study. Otolaryngol Head Neck Surg 99:558, 1988.

281. Dever GJ, Stewart JL, Davis A. Prevalence of otitis media in selected populations on Pohnpei: a preliminary study. Int J Pediatr Otorhinolaryngol 10:143, 1985.

282. Diamant M, Ek S, Kallos P, Rubensohn G. Gammaglobulin treatment and protection against infections. Acta Otolaryngol 53:317, 1961.

283. DiBartolomeo JR, Henry DF. A new medication to control patulous eustachian tube disorders. Am J Otol 13:323, 1992.

284. Doege TC, Heath CW Jr, Sherman IL: Diphtheria in the United States 1959–1960. Pediatrics 30:194, 1962.

285. Doern GV, Brueggemann AB, Pierce G, et al. Antibiotic resistance among clinical isolates of Haemophilus influenzae in the United States in 1994 and 1995 and detection of beta-lactamase-positive strains resistant to amoxicillin-clavulanate: results of a national multicenter surveillance study. Antimicrob Agents Chemother 41:292, 1997.

286. Doern GV, Tubert TA. In vitro activities of 39 antimicrobial agents for Branhamella catarrhalis and comparison of results with different quantitative susceptibility test methods. Antimicrob Agents Chemother 32:259, 1988.

287. Dohar JE, Garner ET, Nielson RW, et al. Topical ofloxacin treatment of otorrhea in children with tympanostomy tubes. Arch Otolaryngol Head Neck Surg 125:537, 1999.

288. Dohar JE, Seidlin M, Hardiman ST. Microbiology of otorrhea in children with tympanostomy tubes: implications for therapy. Pediatric Infect Dis J (in press).

289. Domagk G. Ein Beitrag zur Chemotherapie der bakteriellen Infektionen. Dtsch Med Wochenschr 61:250, 1935.

290. Donaldson JD, Martin GF, Maltby CC, et al. The efficacy of pulse-dosed antibiotic therapy in the management of persistent otitis media with effusion. J Otolaryngol 19:3, 1990.

291. Douglas RM, Hansman D, Miles HB, Paton JC. Pneumococcal carriage and type-specific antibody: failure of a 14-valent vaccine to reduce carriage in healthy children. Am J Dis Child 140:1183, 1986.

292. Douglas RM, Moore BW, Miles HB, et al. Prophylactic efficacy of intranasal alpha 2-interferon against rhinovirus infections in the family setting. N Engl J Med 314:65, 1986.

293. Dowell SF, Butler JC, Giebink GS, et al. Acute otitis media: management and surveillance in an era of pneumococcal resistance—a report from the Drug-Resistant Streptococcus pneumoniae Therapeutic Working Group. Pediatr Infect Dis J 18:1, 1999.

294. Dowell SF (ed). Principles of judicious use of antimicrobial agents for pediatric upper respiratory tract infections. Pediatrics 101(Suppl 1):163, 1998.

295. Dowell SF, Marcy SM, Phillips WR, et al. Otitis media: principles of judicious use of antimicrobial agents. Pediatrics 101(suppl 2):165, 1998.

296. Downes JJ. Primary diphtheritic otitis media. Arch Otolaryngol Head Neck Surg 70:27, 1959.

297. Downham MA, Scott R, Sims DG, et al. Breast-feeding protects against respiratory syncytial virus infections. Br Med J 2:274, 1976.

298. Downs MP. Identification of children at risk for middle ear effusion problems. Ann Otol Rhinol Laryngol 89:168, 1980.

299. Doyle WJ. A functiono-anatomic description of eustachian tube vector relations in four ethnic populations: an osteologic study. Ph.D. dissertation, University of Pittsburgh, Pittsburgh, PA, 1977.

300. Doyle WJ, Alper CM. A model to explain the rapid pressure decrease after air-inflation of diseased middle ears. Laryngoscope 109:70, 1999.

301. Doyle WJ, Alper CM, Seroky JT, Karnavas WJ. Exchange rates of gases across the tympanic membrane in rhesus monkeys. Acta Otolaryngol (Stockh) 118:567, 1998.

302. Doyle WJ, Boehm S, Skoner DP. Physiologic responses to intranasal dose-response challenges with histamine, methacholine, bradykinin, and prostaglandin in adult volunteers with and without nasal allergy. J Allergy Clin Immunol 86:924, 1990.

303. Doyle WJ, Cantekin EI, Bluestone CD, et al. A nonhuman primate model of cleft palate and its implications for middle-ear pathology. Ann Otol Rhinol Laryngol 89:41, 1980.

304. Doyle WJ, Cantekin EI, Bluestone CD. Eustachian tube function in cleft palate children. Ann Otol Rhinol Laryngol 89:34, 1980.

305. Doyle WJ. Eustachian tube function in special populations: cleft palate children. Ann Otol Rhinol Laryngol 94:39, 1985.

306. Doyle WJ. Experimental results do not support a gas reserve function for the mastoid. Int J Pediatr Otorhinolaryngol 52:229, 2000.

307. Doyle WJ, Friedman R, Fireman P, Bluestone CD. Eustachian tube obstruction after provocative nasal antigen challenge. Arch Otolaryngol Head Neck Surg 110:508, 1984.

308. Doyle WJ, Ingraham AS, Saad M, et al. A primate model of cleft palate and middle-ear disease: results of a one-year postcleft follow-up. In Lim DJ, Bluestone CD, Klein JO, et al (eds). Recent Advances in Otitis Media with Effusion—Proceedings of the Third International Symposium. Philadelphia, B.C. Decker, 1984, pp 215–218.

309. Doyle WJ. Mathematical model explaining the sources of error in certain estimates of the gas exchange constants for the middle ear. Ann Otol Rhinol 109:533, 2000.

310. Doyle WJ, McBride TP, Swarts JD, et al. The response of the nasal airway, middle ear and eustachian tube to provocative rhinovirus challenge. Am J Rhinol 2:149, 1988.

311. Doyle WJ. Panel on etiology of otitis media with effusion: role of allergy and tubal function. In Mogi G (ed). Recent Advances in Otitis Media—Proceedings of the Second Extraordinary International Symposium. Amsterdam, Kugler Publications, 1994, pp 53–60.

312. Doyle WJ, Seroky JT, Angelini BL, et al. Abnormal middle ear pressures during experimental influenza A virus infection: role of eustachian tube function. Auris Nasus Larynx 27:323, 2000.

313. Doyle WJ, Seroky JT. Middle-ear gas exchange in rhesus monkeys. Ann Otol Rhinol Laryngol 103:636, 1994.

314. Doyle WJ, Skoner DP, Hayden F, et al. Nasal and otologic effects of experimental influenza A virus infection. Ann Otol Rhinol Laryngol 103:59, 1994.

315. Draper WL. Allergy in relationship to the eustachian tube and middle ear. Otolaryngol Clin North Am 7:749, 1974.

316. Draper WL. Secretory otitis media in children: a study of 540 children. Laryngoscope 77:636, 1967.

317. Drury DW. Diphtheria of the ear. Arch Otolaryngol Head Neck Surg 1:221, 1925.

318. Duffy LC, Faden H, Wasielewski R, et al. Exlusive breastfeeding protects against bacterial colonization and day care exposure to otitis media. Pediatrics 100:717, 1997.

319. Dugdale AE, Canty A, Lewis AJ, Lovell S. The natural history of chronic middle ear disease in Australian aboriginals: a cross-sectional study. Med J Aust Spec Suppl 1:6, 1978.

320. Dugdale AE, Lewis AN, Canty AA. The natural history of chronic otitis media. N Engl J Med 307:1459, 1982.

321. Duncan B, Ey J, Holberg CJ, et al. Exclusive breast-feeding for at least 4 months protects against otitis media. Pediatrics 91:867, 1993.

322. Dutch College of General Practitioners. NHG Standard Acute Otitis Media. 1993.

323. Dutton JM, Goss K, Khubchandani KR, et al. Surfactant protein A in rabbit sinus and middle ear mucosa. Ann Otol Rhinol Laryngol 108:915, 1999.

324. Eden A, Gannon PI. Neural control of middle-ear aeration. Arch Otol Head Neck Surg 113:133, 1987.

325. Eden AR, Laitman JT, Gannon PJ. Mechanisms of middle ear aeration: anatomic and physiologic evidence in primates. Laryngoscope 100:67, 1990.

326. Eichenwald HF (ed). New directions in antimicrobial therapy: Loracarbef. Pediatr Infect Dis J 11(Suppl. 8):S5, 1992.

327. Ekvall L. Eustachian tube function in tympanoplasty. Acta Otolaryngol Suppl (Stockh) 263:33, 1970.

328. Elbrond O, Larsen E. Mucociliary function of the eustachian tube. Arch Otolaryngol 102:539, 1976.

329. Elden LM, Coyte PC. Socioeconomic impact of otitis media in North America. J Otolaryngol 27(Suppl 2):9, 1998.

330. El-Guindy A. A correlative manometric and endoscopic study of tubal function in chronic otitis media with effusion. Acta Otolaryngol (Stockh) 118:692, 1998.

331. Eliasson R, Mossberg B, Camner P, Afzelius BA. The immotile cilia syndrome: a congenital ciliary abnormality as an etiologic factor in chronic airway infections and male sterility. N Engl J Med 297:1, 1977.

332. Elkhatieb A, Hipskind G, Woerner D, Hayden FG. Middle ear abnormalities during natural rhinovirus colds in adults. J Infect Dis 168:618, 1993.

333. Elner A, Ingelstedt S, Ivarsson A. The normal function of the eustachian tube. Acta Otolaryngol (Stockh) 72:320, 1971.

334. Emery M, Weber PC. Hearing loss due to myringotomy and tube placement and the role of preoperative audiograms. Arch Otolaryngol Head Neck Surg 124:421, 1998.

335. Englehard D, Cohen D, Strauss N, et al. Randomized study of myringotomy, amoxicillin/clavulanate, or both for acute otitis media in infants. Lancet 2:141, 1989.

336. Ensign RR, Ubanich EM, Moran J. Prophylaxis for otitis media in an Indian population. Am J Public Health 50:195, 1960.

337. Epstein JS, Beane J, Hubbell R. Prevention of early otorrhea in ventilation tubes. Otolaryngol Head Neck Surg 107:758, 1992.

338. Ernstson S, Anari M, Cederberg A, et al. Cefaclor in otitis media with effusion: penetration antibacterial effect clinical implications. Acta Otolaryngol (Stockh) Suppl 424:7, 1985.

339. Eskola et al. In press.

340. Eskola J, Kilpi T, Palmu A, et al. Efficacy of a pneumococcal conjugate vaccine against acute otitis media. N Engl J Med 344:403, 2001.

341. Eskola JK, Takala AK, Kela E, et al. Epidemiology of invasive pneumococcal infections in children in Finland. JAMA 268:3323, 1992.

342. Etzel RA, Pattishall EN, Haley NJ, et al. Passive smoking and middle ear effusion among children in day care. Pediatrics 90:228, 1992.

343. Evans WE, Feldman S, Barker LF, et al. Use of gentamicin serum levels to individualize therapy in children. J Pediatr 93:133, 1978.

344. Ey JL, Holberg CJ, Aldous MB, et al. Passive smoke exposure and otitis media in the first year of life. Pediatrics 95:670, 1995.

345. Faden H, Bernstein JM, Brodsky L, et al. Otitis media in children. I. The systemic immune response to nontypable Hemophilus influenzae. J Infect Dis 160:999, 1989.

346. Faden H, Brodsky L, Bernstein J, et al. Otitis media in children: local immune response to non-typeable Haemophilus influenzae. Infect Immun 57:3555, 1989.

347. Faden H, Dryja D. Recovery of a unique bacterial organism in human middle ear fluid and its possible role in chronic otitis media. J Clin Microbiol 27:2488, 1989.

348. Faden H, Duffy L, Hong JJ, et al. Adherence of nontypable Haemophilus influenzae to respiratory epithelium of otitis prone and normal children. Acta Otolaryngol (Stockh) Suppl 523:142, 1996.

349. Faden H, Duffy L, Wasielewski R, et al. Relationship between nasopharyngeal colonization and the development of otitis media in children. J Infect Dis 175:1440, 1997.

350. Faden H, Duffy L, Williams A, et al. Epidemiology of nasopha-

ryngeal colonization with nontypeable *Haemophilus influenzae* in the first 2 years of life. J Infect Dis 177:132, 1995.

351. Faden H, Harabuchi Y, Hong JJ, Tonawanda/Williamsville Pediatrics. Epidemiology of *Moraxella catarrhalis* in children during the first 2 years of life: relationship to otitis media. J Infect Dis 169:1312, 1994.

352. Faden H, Hong J, Murphy T. Immune response to outer membrane antigens of *Moraxella catarrhalis* in children with otitis media. Infect Immun 60:3824, 1992.

353. Faden H, Stanievich J, Brodsky L, et al. Changes in nasopharyngeal flora during otitis media of childhood. Pediatr Infect Dis J 9:623, 1990.

354. Faden H, Waz MJ, Bernstein JM, et al. Nasopharyngeal flora in the first three years of life in normal and otitis prone children. Ann Otol Rhinol Laryngol 100:612, 1991.

355. Falck G, Gnarpe J, Gnarpe H. Prevalence of *Chlamydia pneumoniae* in healthy children and in children with respiratory tract infections. Pediatr Infect Dis J 16:549, 1997.

356. Falk B, Magnuson B. Eustachian tube closing failure in children with persistent middle-ear effusion. Int J Pediatr Otorhinolaryngol 7:97, 1984.

357. Farbman KS, Barnett ED, Bolduc CR, Klein J. Antibacterial activity of garlic and onions: a historical perspective. Pediatr Infect Dis J 126:613, 1993.

358. Feder HM Jr. Comparative tolerability of ampicillin, amoxicillin, and trimethoprim-sulfamethoxazole suspension in children with otitis media. Antimicrob Agents Chemother 121:426, 1982.

359. Feigin RD, Kenney RE, Nusrala J, et al. Efficacy of clindamycin therapy for otitis media. Arch Otolaryngol Head Neck Surg 98:27, 1973.

360. Feigin RD, McCracken GH, Klein JO. Diagnosis and management of meningitis. Pediatr Infect Dis J 11:785, 1992.

361. Feigin RD, Shackelford PG, Campbell J, et al. Assessment of the role of *Staphylococcus epidermidis* as a cause of otitis media. Pediatrics 52:569, 1973.

362. Feingold M, Klein JO, Haslan GE, et al. Acute otitis media in children: bacteriological findings in middle ear fluid obtained by needle aspiration. Am J Dis Child 111:361, 1966.

363. Fenoll A, Bourgon CM, Munoz R, et al. Serotype distribution and antimicrobial resistance of *Streptococcus pneumoniae* isolates causing systemic infections in Spain, 1979–1989. Rev Infect Dis 13:56, 1991.

364. Ferber A, Holmquist J. Roentgenographic demonstration of the eustachian tube in chronic otitis media. Acta Radiol (Diagn) (Stockh) 14:667, 1973.

365. Ferguson PJ, Saulsbury FT. Successful treatment of chronic *Mycobacterium abscessus* otitis media with clarithromycin. Pediatr Infect Dis J 15:384–385, 1996.

366. Ferlito A. A review of the definition, terminology, and pathology or aural cholesteatoma. J Laryngol Otol 107:483, 1993.

367. Fernandez AA, McGovern JP. Secretory otitis media in allergic infants and children. South Med J 58:581, 1965.

368. Fernau JL, Hirsch BE, Derkay C, et al. Hyperbaric oxygen therapy: effect on middle-ear and eustachian tube function. Laryngoscope 102:48, 1992.

369. Fiellau-Nikolajsen M, Lous J, Vang Pedersen S, Schousboe HH. Tympanometry in three-year-old children. I. A regional prevalence study on the distribution of tympanometric results in a nonselected population of three-year-old children. Scand Audiol 6:99, 1977.

370. Findlay RC, Stool SE, Svitko CA. Tympanometric and otoscopic evaluations of a school-age deaf population: a longitudinal study. Am Ann Deaf 122:407, 1977.

371. Finegold SM. Anaerobic infections in otolaryngology. Ann Otol Rhinol Laryngol 90:13, 1981.

372. Finkelstein Y, Zohar Y, Talmi YP, et al. Effects of acute negative middle-ear pressure on hearing. Acta Otolaryngol (Stockh) 112:88, 1992.

373. Finland M, Brumfitt W, Kass EH. (guest eds). Advances in aminoglycoside therapy: amikacin. J Infect Dis 134:S235, 1976.

374. Finland M, Hewitt WL (guest eds). Second International Symposium on Gentamicin, an Aminoglycoside Antibiotic. J Infect Dis 124:S1, 1971.

375. Finland M, Neu HC (guest eds). Tobramycin. Symposium of the

376. Fisch U. Tympanoplasty and Mastoidectomy. New York, Theime, 1994.

377. Fischer GW, Sunakorn P, Duangman C. Otogenous tetanus: a sequela of chronic ear infections. Am J Dis Child 131:445, 1977.

378. Fisher R, McManus J, Entis G, et al: Middle ear ciliary defect in Kartagener's syndrome. Pediatrics 62:443, 1978.

379. Flannagan PM, Knight LC, Thomas A, et al. Hearing aids and glue ear. Clin Otolaryngol 21:297, 1996.

380. Fornadley JA, Burns JK. The effect of surfactant on eustachian tube function in a gerbil model of otitis media with effusion. Otolaryngol Head Neck Surg 110:110, 1994.

381. Forsgren TE, Samuelson A, Lindberg A, et al. Quantitative bacterial culture from adenoid lymphatic tissue with special reference to *Haemophilus influenzae*: age-related associated changes. Acta Otolaryngol (Stockh) 113:668, 1993.

382. Fosarelli P, Wilson M, De Angelis C. Prescription medications in infancy and early childhood. Am J Dis Child 414:772, 1987.

383. Francis T Jr, Tillett WS. Cutaneous reactions in pneumonia: the development of antibodies following the intradermal injection of type-specific polysaccharide. J Exp Med 52:573, 1930.

384. Fraser JG, Mehta M, Fraser PM. The medical treatment of secretory otitis media: a clinical trial of three commonly used regimens. J Laryngol Otol 91:757, 1977.

385. Freijd A, Oxelius V-A, Rynnel-Dagoo B. A prospective study demonstrating an association between plasma IgG2 concentrations and susceptibility to otitis media in children. Scand J Infect Dis 17:115, 1985.

386. Fria TH, Cantekin EI, Eichler JA. Hearing acuity of children with otitis media with effusion. Arch Otolaryngol 111:10, 1985.

387. Fria TJ, Sabo DL. Auditory brainstem responses in children with otitis media with effusion. Ann Otol Rhinol Laryngol 89:200, 1980.

388. Friedland IR, Shelton S, Paris M, et al. Dilemmas in diagnosis and management of cephalosporin-resistant *Streptococcus pneumoniae* meningitis. Pediatr Infect Dis J 12:196, 1993.

389. Friedman CA, Lovejoy FC, Smith AL. Chloramphenicol disposition in infants and children. J Pediatr 95:1071, 1979.

390. Friedman PA, Doyle WJ, Casselbrant ML, et al. Immunologic-mediated eustachian tube obstruction: a double-blind crossover study. J Allergy Clin Immunol 71:442, 1983.

391. Fuchs PC, Gavan TL, Gerlach EH, et al. Ticarcillin: a collaborative *in vitro* comparison with carbenicillin against over 9,000 clinical bacterial isolates. Am J Med Sci 274:255, 1977.

392. Fujioka M, Young LW, Girdany BR. Radiographic evaluation of adenoidal size in children: adenoidal-nasopharyngeal ratio. Am J Radiol 133:401, 1979.

393. Gan VN, McCarthy JM, Chu S-Y, Carr R. Penetration of clarithromycin into middle ear fluid of children with acute otitis media. Pediatr Infect Dis J 8:39, 1997.

394. Gannon MM, Goncalves M, Haggard MP, Golding J. Multiple replication of infant sleeping position as a strong otitis media risk factor. (in press.)

395. Ganstrom G, Holmquist J, Jarlstedt J, et al. Collagenase activity in middle ear effusion. Acta Otolaryngol (Stockh) 100:405, 1985.

396. Garcia P, Gates GA, Schechtman KB. Does topical antibiotic prophylaxis reduce post-tympanostomy tube otorrhea? A meta-analysis. Ann Otol Rhinol Laryngol 103:54, 1994.

397. Gates GA, Avery CA, Prihoda TJ, et al. Effectiveness of adenoidectomy and tympanostomy tubes in the treatment of chronic otitis media with effusion. N Engl J Med 317:1444, 1987.

398. Gates GA, Avery CA, Prihoda TJ. Effect of adenoidectomy upon children with chronic otitis media with effusion. Laryngoscope 98:58, 1988.

399. Gates GA. Cost-effectiveness considerations in otitis media treatment. Otolaryngol Head Neck Surg 114:525, 1996.

400. Gates GA, Wachtendorf C, Holt R, et al. Medical treatment of chronic otitis media with effusion (secretory otitis media). Otolaryngol Head Neck Surg 94:350, 1986.

401. Gebhart DE. Tympanostomy tubes in the otitis media-prone child. Laryngoscope 91:849, 1981.

402. Gehanno P, Berche P, Nguyen L, et al. Resolution of clinical failure in acute otitis media confirmed by in vivo bacterial eradication—efficacy and safety of ceftriaxone injected once daily for 3

days. Abstracts of the 37th Interscience Conference on Antimicrobial Agents and Chemotherapy, Toronto, September 28–October 1, 1997.

403. Gehanno P, Lenoir G, Barry B, et al. Evaluation of nasopharyngeal cultures for bacteriologic assessment of acute otitis media in children. Pediatr Infect Dis J 15:329, 1996.

404. Gehanno P, Nguyen L, Barrie B, et al. Eradication by ceftriaxone of *Streptococcus pneumoniae* isolates with increased resistance to penicillin in cases of acute otitis media. Antimicrob Agents Chemother 43:16, 1999.

405. Gerrity TR, Cotromanes E, Garrard CS, et al: The effect of aspirin on lung mucociliary clearance. N Engl J Med 308:139, 1983.

406. Ghadiali SN, Federspiel WJ, Swarts JD, Doyle WJ. Measurement of eustachian tube mechanical properties using a modified forced response test. BED–Vol. 50, 2001, Bioengineering Conference, ASME, 2001.

407. Giebink GS, Berzins IK, Cates KL, et al. Polymorphonuclear leukocyte function during otitis media. Ann Otol Rhinol Laryngol 89:138, 1980.

408. Giebink GS, Daly K, Buran DJ, et al. Predictors for postoperative otorrhea following tympanostomy tube insertion. Arch Otolaryngol Head Neck Surg 118:491, 1992.

409. Giebink GS, Mills EL, Huff JS, et al. The microbiology of serous and mucoid otitis media. Pediatrics 63:915, 1979.

410. Giebink GS, Quie PG. Otitis media: the spectrum of middle ear inflammation. Ann Rev Med 29:285, 1978.

411. Ginsburg CM, McCracken GH, Nelson JD. Pharmacology of oral antibiotics used for treatment of otitis media and tonsillopharyngitis in infants and children. Ann Otol Rhinol Laryngol 90:37, 1981.

412. Glew RH, Diven WF, Bluestone CD: Lysosomal hydrolases in middle ear effusions. Ann Otol Rhinol Laryngol 90:148, 1981.

413. Glezen WP. Prevention of acute otitis media by prophylaxis and treatment of influenza virus infections. Vaccine 19:S56, 2000.

414. Gnehm HE, Pelton SI, Gulati S, Rice PA. Characterization of antigens from nontypable *Haemophilus influenzae* recognized by human bactericidal antibodies: role of *Haemophilus* outer membrane proteins. J Clin Invest 75:1645, 1985.

415. Goetzinger CP, Embrey JE, Brooks R, et al: Auditory assessment of cleft palate adults. Acta Otolaryngol (Stockh) 52:551, 1960.

416. Gold R, Lepow ML, Goldschneider I, et al. Antibody responses of human infants to three doses of group A *Neisseria meningitidis* polysaccharide vaccine administered at two, four, and six months of age. J Infect Dis 138:731, 1978.

417. Goldblatt EL, Dohar J, Nozza RJ, et al. Topical ofloxacin versus systemic amoxicillin/clavulanate in purulent otorrhea in children with tympanostomy tubes. Int J Pediatr Otorhinolaryngol 46:91, 1998.

418. Goldblatt EL. Efficacy of ofloxacin and other otic preparations for acute otitis media in patients with tympanostomy tubes. Pediatr Infect Dis J 20:116, 2001.

419. Goldstein NA, Casselbrant ML, Bluestone CD, Kurs-Lasky M. Intratemporal complications of acute otitis media in infants and children. Otolaryngol Head Neck Surg 119:444, 1998.

420. Golz A, Goldenberg D, Netzer A, et al. Cholesteatomas associated with ventilation tube insertion. Arch Otolaryngol Head Neck Surg 125:754, 1999.

421. Golz A, Netzer A, Joachims HZ, et al. Ventilation tubes and persisting tympanic membrane perforations. Otolaryngol Head Neck Surg 120:524, 1999.

422. Golz A, Westerman ST, Gilbert LM, et al. Effect of middle ear effusion on the vestibular labyrinth. J Laryngol Otol 105:987, 1991.

423. Gonzalez C, Arnold JE, Woody EA, et al. Prevention of recurrent acute otitis media: chemoprophylaxis versus tympanostomy tubes. Laryngoscope 96:1330, 1986.

424. Goo YA, Hori MK, Voorhies JH Jr, Kuo C-C, et al. Failure to detect *Chlamydia pneumoniae* in ear fluids from children with otitis media. Pediatr Infect Dis J 11:1000, 1995.

425. Gooch WM III, Blair E, Puopolo A, et al. Effectiveness of five days of therapy with cefuroxime axetil suspension for treatment of acute otitis media. Pediatr Infect Dis J 15:157, 1996.

426. Gooch WM. Clarithromycin and cefaclor suspensions in the treatment of acute otitis media in children. Pediatr Infect Dis J 12:S122, 1993.

427. Goode R. CO$_2$ laser myringotomy. Laryngoscope 92:420, 1982.

428. Goodhill V. Ear Diseases, Deafness, and Dizziness. Hagerstown, MD, Harper & Row, 1979, pp 356–379.

429. Gorbach SL, Bartlett JG. Pseudomembranous enterocolitis: a review of its diverse forms. J Infect Dis 135:S89, 1977.

430. Goss C (ed). Gray's Anatomy of the Human Body. Philadelphia, Lea & Febiger, 1967, p 1087.

431. Gottschalk HG. Further experience with controlled middle ear inflation in treatment of serous otitis. EENT Monthly 45:49, 1966.

432. Gottschalk HG. Nonsurgical management of otitis media with effusion. Ann Otol Rhinol Laryngol 89:301, 1980.

433. Grace A, Kwok P, Hawke M. Surfactant in middle ear effusions. Otol Head Neck Surg 96:335, 1987.

434. Graham MD, Lierle DM. Posterior pharyngeal flap palatoplasty and its relation to ear disease and hearing loss: a preliminary report. Laryngoscope 72:1750, 1962.

435. Granoff DM, Squires JE, Munson RS Jr, et al. Siblings of patients with *Haemophilus* meningitis have impaired anticapsular antibody responses to *Haemophilus* vaccine. J Pediatr 103:185, 1983.

436. Graves GO, Edwards LF. The eustachian tube: review of its descriptive, microscopic, topographic, and clinical anatomy. Arch Otolaryngol 39:359, 1944.

437. Gray BM, Converse GM, Dillon HC Jr. Serotypes of *Streptococcus pneumoniae* causing disease. J Infect Dis 140:979, 1979.

438. Green GR, Rosenblum AH, Sweet LC. Evaluation of penicillin hypersensitivity: value of clinical history and skin testing with penicilloylpolysine and penicillin G. A cooperative prospective study of the Penicillin Study Group of the American Academy of Allergy. J Allergy Clin Immunol 60:339, 1977.

439. Green SM, Rothrock SG. Single-dose intramuscular ceftriaxone for acute otitis media in children. Pediatrics 91:23, 1993.

440. Greene JW, Hara C, O'Connor S, et al. Management of febrile outpatient neonates. Clin Pediatr 20:375, 1981.

441. Gronroos JA, Kortekangas AE, Ojala L, Vuori M. The aetiology of acute middle ear infection. Acta Otolaryngol (Stockh) 58:149, 1964.

442. Groothuis JR, Thompson J, Wright PF. Correlation of nasopharyngeal and conjunctival cultures with middle ear fluid cultures in otitis media. Clin Pediatr 25:85, 1986.

443. Grundfast KM, Bluestone CD. Sudden or fluctuating hearing loss and vertigo in children due to perilymph fistula. Ann Otol Rhinol Laryngol 87:761, 1978.

444. Guay DRP, Craft JC. Overview of the pharmacology of clarithromycin suspension in children and a comparison with that in adults. Pediatr Infect Dis J 12:S106, 1993.

445. Gudnasson T, Gudbrandsson F, Barsanti F, Kristinsson KG. Penetration of ceftriaxone into the middle ear fluid of children. Pediatr Infect Dis J 17:258, 1998.

446. Guild SR. Elastic tissue of the eustachian tube. Ann Otol Rhinol Laryngol 64:537, 1955.

447. Gutzmann H. Zur Prognose und Behandlung der angeborenen Gaumendefekte. Mschr Sprachheilk, 1893.

448. Haddad J Jr, Brager R, Bluestone CD. Infections of the ears, nose and throat in children with primary immunodeficiencies. Arch Otolaryngol Head Neck Surg 118:138, 1992.

449. Haddad J, Isaacson G, Respler DS, et al. Concentrations of cefuroxime in serum and middle ear effusion after single dose treatment with cefuroxime axetil. Pediatr Infect Dis J 10:294, 1991.

450. Haddad J. Lipoperoxidation as a measure of free radical injury in otitis media. Laryngoscope 108:524, 1998.

451. Hagan WE. Surface tension lowering substance in eustachian tube function. Laryngoscope 87:1033, 1977.

452. Halfond MM, Ballenger JJ. An audiologic and otorhinologic study of cleft lip and cleft palate cases. Arch Otolaryngol Head Neck Surg 64:58, 1956.

453. Halstead C, Lepow ML, Balassanian N, et al. Otitis media: clinical observations, microbiology, evaluation of therapy. Am J Dis Child 115:542, 1968.

454. Hamilton J. Management of Infants and Children, 4th ed. Edinburgh, Bell & Bradfute, 1824, pp 102–103.

455. Hammerschlag MR, Hammerschlag PE, Alexander ER. The role of *Chlamydia trachomatis* in middle-ear effusion in children. Pediatrics 66:615, 1980.

456. Handzic-Cuk J, Cuk V, Risavi R, et al. Pierre Robin syndrome: characteristics of hearing loss, effect of age on hearing level and possibilities in therapy planning. J Laryngol Otol 110:830, 1996.

457. Hanson LA, Andersson B, Carlsson B, et al. Defense of mucous membranes by antibodies, receptor analogues and nonspecific host factors. Infection 13(Suppl 2):S166, 1985.

458. Harabuchi Y, Faden H, Yamanaka N, et al. Nasopharyngeal colonization with nontypeable *Haemophilus influenzae* and recurrent otitis media. J Infect Dis 170:862, 1994.

459. Harcourt FL, Brown AK. Hydrotympanum (secretory otitis media). Arch Otolaryngol Head Neck Surg 57:12, 1953.

460. Harding AL, Anderson P, Howie VM, et al. *Haemophilus influenzae* isolated from children with otitis media. In Sell SH, Karzon DT (eds). *Haemophilus influenzae.* Nashville, TN, Vanderbilt University Press, 1973, pp 21–28.

461. Hardy AM. Incidence and impact of selected infectious diseases in childhood. Data from the National Health Interview Survey. National Center for Health Statistics Series 10 (no. 180), 1991.

462. Harford ER, Bess FH, Bluestone CD, et al (eds). Impedance Screening for Middle Ear Disease in Children. New York, Grune & Stratton, 1978.

463. Harrison CJ. Amoxicillin-clavulanate (Augmentin): an update. Rep Pediatr Infect Dis 2:26, 1992.

464. Harrison CJ, Chartrand SA, Rodriguez W, et al. Middle ear effusion concentrations of cefixime during acute otitis media with effusion and otitis media with effusion. Pediatr Infect Dis J 16:816, 1997.

465. Harrison CJ, Marks MI, Welch DF. Microbiology of recently treated acute otitis media compared with previously untreated acute otitis media. Pediatr Infect Dis 4:641, 1985.

466. Harrison CJ. Using antibiotic concentrations in middle ear fluid to predict potential clinical efficacy. Pediatr Infect Dis J 16:S12, 1997.

467. Hartnick CJ, Shott S, Willging JP, Myer CM. Methicillin-resistant *Staphylococcus aureus* otorrhea after tympanostomy tube placement. Arch Otolaryngol Head Neck Surg 126:1440, 2000.

468. Hathaway TJ, Katz HP, Dershewitz RA, Marx TJ. Acute otitis media: who needs posttreatment follow-up? Pediatrics 94:143, 1994.

469. Hausdorff WP, Kloek C, Bryant J. The relative importance of specific pneumococcal serogroups as causes of disease, analyzed by geographical setting, age group, disease state and clinical site of isolation. Presented at Pneumococcal Vaccines for the World 1998 Conference, October 12–14, 1998, Washington, DC.

470. Haverkos HW, Caparosa R, Ya VL, Kamerer D. Moxalactam therapy: its use in chronic suppurative otitis media and malignant external otitis. Arch Otolaryngol Head Neck Surg 108:329, 1982.

471. Hayden FG, Albrecht JK, Kaiser DL, Gwaltney JM Jr. Prevention of natural colds by contact prophylaxis with intranasal alpha 2-interferon. N Engl J Med 314:71, 1986.

472. Hayden FG, Atmar RL, Schilling M, et al. Use of the selective oral neuraminidase inhibitor oseltamivir to prevent influenza. N Engl J Med 341:1336, 1999.

473. Hayden FG, Osterhaus ADME, Treanor JJ, et al. Efficacy and safety of the neuraminidase inhibitor zanamivir in the treatment of influenzavirus infections. N Engl J Med 337:874, 1997.

474. Hayden GF, Schwartz RH: 5 characteristics of earache among children with acute otitis media. Am J Dis Child 139:721, 1985.

475. Healy GB. Antimicrobial therapy of chronic otitis media with effusion. Int J Pediatr Otorhinolaryngol 8:13, 1984.

476. Healy GB, McGill TJ, Sullivan KF, et al. Outcome factors in ventilation tube insertion: a prospective monitoring program. In Lim DJ, Bluestone CD, Klein JO, et al (eds). Recent Advances in Otitis Media. Burlington, Ontario, B.C. Decker, 1993, pp 301–304.

477. Healy GB, Teele DW. The microbiology of chronic middle ear effusions in young children. Laryngoscope 87:1472, 1977.

478. Hecht CS, Gannon PJ, Eden AR. Motor innervation of the eustachian tube muscles in the guinea pig. Laryngoscope 103:1218, 1993.

479. Heikkinen T, Ruuskanen O, Waris M, et al. Influenza vaccination in the prevention of acute otitis media in children. Am J Dis Child 145:445, 1991.

480. Heikkinen T, Ruuskanen O, Ziegler T, et al. Short-term use of amoxicillin-clavulanate during upper respiratory tract infection for prevention of acute otitis media. J Pediatr 126:313, 1995.

481. Heikkinen T, Thint M, Chonmaitree T. Prevalence of various respiratory viruses in the middle ear during acute otitis media. N Engl J Med 340:260, 1999.

482. Heisse JW. Secretory otitis media: treatment with depomethylprednisone. Laryngoscope 73:54, 1963.

483. Hemlin C, Carenfelt C, Papatziamos G. Single dose of betamethasone in combined medical treatment of secretory otitis media. Ann Otol Rhinol Laryngol 106:359, 1997.

484. Henderson FW, Collier AM, Sanyal MA, et al. A longitudinal study of respiratory viruses and bacteria in the etiology of acute otitis media with effusion. N Engl J Med 306:1377, 1982.

485. Hendrickse WA, Kusmiesz H, Shelton S, et al. Five vs. ten days of therapy for acute otitis media. Pediatr Infect Dis J 7:14, 1988.

486. Henrichsen J. Six newly recognized types of *Streptococcus pneumoniae.* J Clin Micro 33:2759, 1995.

487. Henrichsen J, Sorensen CH. The role of antibodies of pneumococcal C polysaccharide in otitis media. Pediatr Infect Dis J 8:S26, 1989.

488. Herberts G, Jeppson PH, Nylen O, Branefors-Helander P. Acute otitis media: etiological and therapeutical aspects of acute otitis media. Pract Otorhinolaryngol 33:191, 1971.

489. Hergils L, Magnuson B. Nasal gas composition in humans and its implication of middle-ear pressure. Acta Otolaryngol (Stockh) 118:697, 1998.

490. Herva E, Haiva VM, Koskela M, et al. Pneumococci and their capsular polysaccharide antigens in middle ear effusion in acute otitis media. In Lim DJ, Bluestone CD, Klein JO, Nelson JD (eds). Recent Advances in Otitis Media with Effusion. Burlington, Ontario, B.C. Decker, 1984, pp 120–122.

491. Hill HR, Book LS, Hemming VG, Herbst JJ. Defective neutrophil chemotactic responses in patients with recurrent episodes of otitis media and chronic diarrhea. Am J Dis Child 131:433, 1977.

492. Hills BA. Analysis of eustachian surfactant and its function as a release agent. Arch Otolaryngol Head Neck Surg 110:3, 1984.

493. Himi T, Suzuki T, Takezawa H, et al. Immunologic characteristics of cytokines in otitis media with effusion. Ann Otol Rhinol Laryngol 101:21, 1992.

494. Hobernman A, Paradise JL, Burch DJ, et al. Equivalent efficacy and reduced occurrence of diarrhea from a new formulation of amoxicillin/clavulanate potassium (Augmentin) for treatment of acute otitis media in children. Pediatr Infect Dis J 16:463, 1997.

495. Hoekelman RA. Infectious illness during the first year of life. Pediatrics 59:119, 1977.

496. Hogan SC, Stratford KH, Moore DR. Duration and recurrence of otitis media with effusion in children from birth to 3 years: prospective study using monthly otoscopy and tympanometry. BMJ 314:350, 1997.

497. Holborow C. Eustachian tube function: changes throughout childhood and neuromuscular control. J Laryngol Otol 89:47, 1975.

498. Holmquist J. Eustachian tube function in patients with eardrum perforations following chronic otitis media. Acta Otolaryngol (Stockh) 68:391, 1969.

499. Holmquist J. Medical treatment in ears with eustachian tube dysfunction. Presented at the Symposium on Physiology and Pathophysiology of the Eustachian Tube and Middle Ear, September 28, 1977, Freiburg, West Germany.

500. Homoe P, Christensen RB, Bretlau P. Acute otitis media and age at onset among children in Greenland. Acta Otolaryngol (Stockh) 119:65, 1999.

501. Honjo I, Hayashi M, Ito S, Takahashi H. Pumping and clearance function of the eustachian tube. Am J Otolaryngol 6:241, 1985.

502. Honjo I, Okazaki N, Kumazawa T. Experimental study of the eustachian tube function with regard to its related muscles. Acta Otolaryngol (Stockh) 87:84, 1979.

503. Honjo I, Ushiro K, Hajo I, et al. Role of tensor tympani muscle in eustachian tube function. Acta Otolaryngol (Stockh) 95:329, 1983.

504. Honjo I, Ushiro K, Mitoma T, et al: Eustachian function of children with secretory otitis media. Pract Otol (Kyoto) 77:1111, 1984.

505. Honjo I, Ushiro K, Okazaki N, Kumazawa T. Evaluation of eustachian tube function by contrast roentgenography. Arch Otolaryngol Head Neck Surg 107:350, 1981.

506. House JW, Brackmann DE. Facial nerve grading system. Otolaryngol Head Neck Surg 93:146, 1985.

507. Howard JE, Nelson JD, Clashen J, Jackson LH. Otitis media of infancy and early childhood: a double-blind study of four treatment regimens. Am J Dis Child 130:965, 1976.

508. Howie VM. Eradication of bacterial pathogens from middle ear infections. Clin Infect Dis 14(Suppl 2):209, 1992.

509. Howie VM. Natural history of otitis media. Ann Otol Rhinol Laryngol 84:67, 1975.

510. Howie VM, Ploussard J, Sloyer JL, Hill JC. Use of pneumococcal polysaccharide vaccine in preventing otitis media in infants: different results between racial groups. Pediatrics 73:79, 1984.

511. Howie VM, Ploussard JH, Sloyer JL, Johnston RB Jr. Immunoglobulins of the middle ear fluid in acute otitis media: relationship to serum immunoglobulin concentrations and bacterial cultures. Infect Immun 7:589, 1973.

512. Howie VM, Ploussard JH, Sloyer J. The "otitis-prone" condition. Am J Dis Child 129:676, 1975.

513. Howie VM, Ploussard JH. The "in vivo sensitivity test": bacteriology of middle ear exudate during antimicrobial therapy in otitis media. Pediatrics 44:940, 1969.

514. Howie VM, Pollard RB, Kleyn K, et al. Presence of interferon during bacterial otitis media. J Infect Dis 145:811, 1982.

515. Hsu GS, Levine SC, Giebink GS. Management of otitis media using Agency for Health Care Policy and Research guidelines. The Agency for Health Care Policy and Research. Otolaryngol Head Neck Surg 118:437, 1998.

516. Hughes WT, Kuhn S, Chaudhary S, et al. Successful chemoprophylaxis for Pneumocystis carinii pneumonitis. N Engl J Med 297: 1419, 1977.

517. Hurst DS. Association of otitis media with effusion and allergy as demonstrated by intradermal skin testing and eosinophil cationic protein levels in both middle-ear effusions and mucosal biopsies. Laryngoscope 106:1128, 1996.

518. Hurst DS, Venge P. Evidence of eosinophil, neutrophil, and mast-cell mediators in the effusion of OME patients with and without atopy. Allergy 55:435, 2000.

519. Hurst DS, Venge P. Levels of eosinophil cationic protein and myeloperoxidase from chronic middle-ear effusion in patients with allergy and/or acute infection. Otolaryngol. Head Neck Surg 114: 531, 1996.

520. Ichimura K. Neutrophil chemotaxis in children with recurrent otitis media. Int J Pediatr Otorhinolaryngol 4:47, 1982.

521. Idanpaan-Heikkila I, Simon PM, Zopf D, et al. Oligosaccharides interfere with the establishment and progression of experimental pneumococcal pneumonia. J Infect Dis 176:704, 1997.

522. Iino Y, Imamura Y, Harigai S, Tanaka Y. Efficacy of tympanostomy tube insertion for otitis media with effusion in children with Down syndrome. Int J Pediatr Otorhinolaryngol 49:143, 1999.

523. Iino Y, Toriyama M, Natori Y, et al. Erythromycin inhibition of lipopolysaccharide-stimulated tumor necrosis factor alpha production by human monocytes in vitro. Ann Otol Rhinol Laryngol 101: 16, 1992.

524. Ikui A, Sando I, Haginomori S, Sudo M. Postnatal development of the tympanic cavity: a computer-aided reconstruction and measurement study. Acta Otolaryngol 120:375, 2000.

525. Ingelstedt S, Flisberg K, Ortegren U. On the function of middle ear and eustachian tube. Acta Otolaryngol Suppl (Stockh) 182, 1963.

526. Ingelstedt S, Ivarsson A, Jonson B. Mechanics of the human middle ear: pressure regulation in aviation and diving, a nontraumatic method. Acta Otolaryngol (Stockh) Suppl 228:1, 1967.

527. Ingvarsson L, Kamme C, Lundgren K. Concentration of penicillin V in serum and middle ear exudate during treatment of acute otitis media. Ann Otol Rhinol Laryngol 89(Suppl 68):275, 1980.

528. Ingvarsson L, Lundgren K. The duration of penicillin treatment of acute otitis media children. Acta Otolaryngol (Stockh) 94(Suppl 386):112, 1982.

528a. Isaacson G, Rosenfeld RM. Care of the child with tympanostomy tubes: a visual guide for the pediatrician. Pediatrics 93:924, 1994.

529. Ishijima K, Sando I, Balaban C, et al. Length of eustachian tube and its postnatal development: a computer-aided three-dimensional reconstruction and measurement study. Ann Otol Rhinol Laryngol 109:542, 2000.

530. Istorico LJ, Sanders M, Jacobs RF, et al. Otitis media due to blastomycosis: report of two cases. Clin Infect Dis 14:355, 1992.

531. Ito J, Oyagi S, Honjo I. Localization of motoneurons innervating the eustachian tube muscles in cat. Acta Otolaryngol (Stockh) Suppl 386:108, 1987.

532. Iwano T, Hamada E, Kinoshita T, et al. Passive opening pressure of the eustachian tube. In Lim DJ, Bluestone CD, Klein JO, et al (eds). Recent Advances in Otitis Media—Proceedings of the Fifth International Symposium. Burlington, Ontario, B.C. Decker, 1993, pp 76–78.

533. Jacobs MR, Bajaksouzian S, Zilles A, et al. Susceptibilities of Streptococcus pneumoniae and Haemophilus influenzae to 10 oral antimicrobial agents based on pharmacodynamic parameters: 1997 US surveillance study. Antimicrob Agents Chemother 43:1901, 1999.

534. Jacobs MR, Koornhof HJ, Robins-Browne RM, et al. Emergence of multiple resistant pneumococci. N Engl J Med 299:735, 1978.

535. Jaffe BF, Hurtado F, Hurtado E. Tympanic membrane mobility in the newborn (with seven months' follow-up). Laryngoscope 80: 36, 1970.

536. Jardine AH, Griffiths MV, Midgley E. The acceptance of hearing aids for children with otitis media with effusion. J Laryngol Otol 113:314, 1999.

537. Jensen JH, Bonding P. Experimental pressure induced rupture of the tympanic membrane in man. Acta Otolaryngol (Stockh) 113: 62, 1993.

538. Jensen KJ, Senterfit LB, Scully WE, et al. Mycoplasma pneumoniae infections in children: an epidemiologic appraisal in families treated with oxytetracycline. Am J Epidemiol 86:419, 1967.

539. Jerger J. Clinical experience with impedance audiometry. Arch Otolaryngol Head Neck Surg 92:311, 1970.

540. Jinnin T. IgA subclasses in middle ear effusions and the pharyngeal tonsils. In Lim DJ, Bluestone CD, Klein JO, et al (eds). Recent Advances in Otitis Media. Proceedings of the Fifth International Symposium. Burlington, Ontario, B.C. Decker, 1993, pp 172–174.

541. Johansson U, Hellstrom S, Anniko M. Round window membrane in serous and purulent otitis media: structural study in the rat. Ann Otol Rhinol Laryngol 102:227, 1993.

542. Johnston RB Jr. Recurrent bacterial infections in children. N Engl J Med 310:1237, 1984.

543. Jokipii L, Karma P, Jokipii AM. Access of metronidazole into the chronically inflamed middle ear with reference to anaerobic bacterial infection. Arch Otolaryngol Head Neck Surg 220:167, 1978.

544. Jones NS, Radomskij P, Prichard AJN, Snashall SE. Imbalance and chronic secretory otitis media in children: effect of myringotomy and insertion of ventilation tubes on body sway. Ann Otol Rhinol Laryngol 99:477, 1990.

545. Jonkers D, Sluimer J, Stobberingh E. Effect of garlic on vancomycin-resistant enterococci. Antimicrob Agents Chemother 43: 3045, 1999.

546. Jonson B, Rundcrantz H. Posture and pressure within the internal jugular vein. Acta Otolaryngol (Stockh) 68:271, 1969.

547. Jörgensen F, Andersson B, Hanson LA, et al. Gamma-globulin treatment of recurrent acute otitis media in children. Pediatr Infect Dis J 9:389, 1990.

548. Jorgensen F, Andersson B, Larsson SH, et al. Children with frequent attacks of acute otitis media: a re-examination after eight years concerning middle ear changes, hearing, tubal function, and bacterial adhesion to pharyngeal epithelial cells. In Lim DJ, Bluestone CD, Klein JO, Nelson JD (eds). Recent Advances in Otitis Media with Effusion. Burlington, Ontario, B.C. Decker, 1984, pp 141–144.

549. Jorgensen F, Holmquist J. Toynbee phenomenon and middle-ear disease. Am J Otolaryngol 4:291, 1984.

550. Jorgenssen JH, Weigel LM, Swenson JM, et al. Activity of clinafloxacin, gatifloxacin, gemifloxacin, and trovafloxacin against recent clinical isolates of levofloxacin-resistant Streptococcus pneumoniae. Antimicrob Agent Chemother 44:2962, 2000.

551. Juhn SK, Huff JS: Biochemical characteristics of middle ear effusions. Ann Otol Rhinol Laryngol 85:110, 1976.

552. Juhn SK, Lees C, Amesara R, et al.: Role of cytokines in the pathogenesis of otitis media. In Lim DJ, Bluestone CD, Klein JO, et al (eds). Recent Advances in Otitis Media—Proceedings of the

Fifth International Symposium. Burlington, Ontario, B.C. Decker, 1993, pp 431–434.

553. Juhn SK, Sipila P, Jung TT, Edlin J. Biochemical pathology of otitis media with effusion. Acta Otolaryngol 441:45, 1984.

554. Juntti H, Tikkanen S, Kokkonen J, et al. Cow's milk allergy is associated with recurrent otitis media during childhood. Acta Otolaryngol (Stockh) 119:867, 1999.

555. Kafetzis DA, Carabinos C, Bairamis T, et al. Diffusion of four oral cephalosporins into the middle ear exudate of children suffering from acute otitis media (Abstract 941). Presented at the 33rd Interscience Conference on Antimicrobial Agents and Chemotherapy, New Orleans, LA, October, 1993

556. Kaiser AD. Results of tonsillectomy: a comparative study of 2,200 tonsillectomized children with an equal number of controls three and ten years after operation. JAMA 95:837, 1930.

557. Kaleida PH, Bluestone CD, Rockette HE, et al. Amoxicillin-clavulanate potassium compared with cefaclor for acute otitis media in infants and children. Pediatr Infect Dis J 6:265, 1987.

558. Kaleida PH, Casselbrant ML, Rockette HE, et al. Amoxicillin or myringotomy or both for acute otitis media: results of a randomized clinical trial. Pediatrics 87:466, 1991.

559. Kalm O, Prellner K, Christensen P. The effect of intravenous immunoglobulin treatment in recurrent acute otitis media. Int J Pediatr Otolaryngol 11:237, 1986.

560. Kamimura M, Balaban CD, Sando I, et al. Cellular distribution of mucosa-associated lymphoid tissue with otitis media in children. Ann Otol Rhinol Laryngol 109:467, 2000.

561. Kamme C. Evaluation of the in vitro sensitivity of Neisseria catarrhalis to antibiotics with respect to acute otitis media. Scand J Infect Dis 2:117, 1970.

562. Kamme C, Lundgren K, Rundkrantz H. The concentration of penicillin V in serum and middle ear exudate in acute otitis media in children. Scand J Infect Dis 1:77, 1969.

563. Kamme C. Penicillin-resistant Branhamella catarrhalis. Lakartidningen 77:4858, 1980.

564. Kaneko A, Hosoda Y, Iwano T, et al. Tubal compliance of the patulous and stenotic eustachian tube in the elderly. In Lim DJ, Bluestone CD, Casselbrant ML, et al (eds). Recent Advances in Otitis Media—Proceedings of the Sixth International Symposium. Hamilton, Ontario, B.C. Decker, 1996, pp 90–92.

565. Kaplan GJ, Fleshman JK, Bender TR, et al. Long-term effects of otitis media: a ten-year cohort study of Alaskan Eskimo children. Pediatrics 52:577, 1973.

566. Kaplan SL, Mason EO Jr, Mason SK, et al. Prospective comparative trial of moxalactam versus ampicillin or chloramphenicol for treatment of Haemophilus influenzae type b meningitis in children. J Pediatr 104:447, 1984.

567. Kaplan B, Wandstrat TL, Cunningham JR. Overall cost in the treatment of otitis media. Pediatr Infect Dis J 16:S9, 1997.

568. Karchev T, Watanabe N, Fujiyoshi T, et al. Surfactant-producing epithelium in the dorsal part of the cartilaginous eustachian tube of mice. Acta Otolaryngol (Stockh) 114:64, 1994.

569. Karjalainen H, Koskela M, Luotonen J, et al. Antibodies against Streptococcus pneumoniae, Haemophilus influenzae and Branhamella catarrhalis in middle ear effusion during early phase of acute otitis media. Int J Pediatr Otorhinolaryngol 19:311, 1990.

570. Karma P, Luotonen J, Timonen M, et al. Efficacy of pneumococcal vaccination against recurrent otitis media: preliminary results of a field trial in Finland. Ann Otol Rhinol Laryngol 89:357, 1980.

571. Karma P, Pukander J, Penttila M. Azithromycin concentrations in sinus fluid and mucosa after oral administration. Eur J Clin Microb Infect Dis 10:856, 1991.

572. Karma P, Pukander J, Sipilä M, et al: Middle ear fluid bacteriology or acute otitis media in neonates and very young infants. Int J Pediatr Otorhinolaryngol 14:141, 1987.

573. Karma P, Sipila P, Virtanen T, et al. Pneumococcal bacteriology after pneumococcal otitis media with special reference to pneumococcal antigens. Int J Pediatr Otorhinolaryngol 10:181, 1985.

574. Kayhty H, Ahman H, Ronnberg PR. Pneumococcal polysaccharide: meningococcal outer membrane protein complex conjugate vaccine is immunogenic in infants and children. J Infect Dis 172:1273, 1995.

575. Kemaloglu YK, Goksu N, Inal E, Akyildiz N. Radiographic evaluation of children with nasopharyngeal obstruction due to the adenoids. Ann Otol Rhinol Laryngol 108:67, 1999.

576. Kemaloglu YK, Kobayashi T, Nakajima T. Associations between the eustachian tube and craniofacial skeleton. Int J Pediatr Otorhinolaryngol 53:195, 2000.

577. Kemper KH. Seven herbs every pediatrician should know. Contemp Pediatr 13:79, 1996.

578. Kenna MA, Bluestone CD, Reilly JS, Lusk RP. Medical management of chronic suppurative otitis media without cholesteatoma in children: update 1992. Am J Otol 14:469, 1993.

579. Kenna MA, Rosane BA, Bluestone CD. Medical management of chronic suppurative otitis media without cholesteatoma in children. Laryngoscope 96:146, 1986.

580. Kenna MA. Treatment of chronic suppurative otitis media. Otolaryngol Clin North Am 27:457, 1994.

581. Kero P, Piekkala P. Factors affecting the occurrence of acute otitis media during the first year of life. Acta Pediatr Scand 76:618, 1987.

582. Kessner DM, Snow CK, Singer J. Assessment of Medical Care for Children, Vol. 3. Washington, D.C., Institute of Medicine, National Academy of Sciences, 1974.

583. Kew J, King AD, Leung SF, et al. Middle ear effusions after radiotherapy: correlation with pre-radiotherapy nasophayngeal tumor patterns. Am J Otol 21:782, 2000.

584. Khanna SM, Tonndorf J. Tympanic membrane vibrations in cats studied by time-averaged holography. J Acoust Soc Am 51:1904, 1972.

585. Khurana CM. A multicenter, randomized, open label comparison of azithromycin and amoxicillin/clavulanate in acute otitis media among children attending day care or school. Pediatr Infect Dis J 15:S24, 1996.

586. Kilby D, Richards SH, Hart G. Grommets and glue ears. Two year results. J Laryngol Otol 86:881, 1972.

587. Kim PE, Musher DM, Glezen WP, et al. Association of invasive pneumococcal disease with season, atmospheric conditions, air pollution and the isolation of respiratory viruses. Clin Infect Dis 22:100, 1996.

588. King JC Jr, Vink PE, Farley JJ, et al. Safety and immunogenicity of three doses of a five-valent pneumococcal conjugate vaccine in children younger than two years with and without human immunodeficiency virus infection. Pediatrics 99:575, 1997.

589. Kinsella JP, Grossman M, Black S. Otomastoiditis caused by Mycobacterium avium-intracellulare. Pediatr Infect Dis J 5:704, 1986.

590. Kirby WMM. Symposium on carbenicillin: a clinical profile. J Infect Dis 122:S1, 1970.

591. Kitajiri M, Sando I, Hashida Y, Doyle W. Histopathology of otitis media in infants with cleft and high arched palates. In Lim DJ, Bluestone CD, Klein JO, Nelson JD (eds). Recent Advances in Otitis Media with Effusion—Proceedings of the Third International Symposium. Burlington, Ontario, B.C. Decker, 1984, pp 195–198.

592. Kitajiri M, Sando I, Takahara T. Postnatal development of the eustachian tube and its surrounding structures. Ann Otol Rhinol Laryngol 96:191, 1987.

593. Kitchen WH, Ford GW, Doyle LW, et al. Health and hospital readmissions of very-low-birth-weight and normal-birth-weight children. Am J Dis Child 144:2213, 1990.

594. Kjellman NI, Synnerstad B, Hansson LO. Atopic allergy and immunoglobulins in children with adenoids and recurrent otitis media. Acta Paediatr Scand 65:593, 1976.

595. Klein JO, Bluestone CD. Acute otitis media. Pediatr Infect Dis 1:66, 1982.

596. Klein JO. Clarithromycin and azithromycin. Rep Pediatr Infect Dis 3:1, 1993.

597. Klein JO. Clarithromycin: where do we go from here? Pediatr Infect Dis J 12:S148, 1993.

598. Klein JO (ed). Symposium on long-acting penicillins. Pediatr Infect Dis J 4:569, 1985.

599. Klein JO (ed). The use of topical ofloxacin for otic diseases in infants and children: summary and conclusions. Pediatr Infect Dis J 20:123, 2001.

600. Klein JO. Epidemiology of pneumococcal disorders in infants and children. Rev Infect Dis 3:246, 1981.

601. Klein JO (guest ed). Evaluation of new oral antimicrobial agents and the experience with cefprozil: a broad-spectrum oral cephalosporin. Clin Infect Dis 14(Suppl 2):S183, 1992.

602. Klein JO. Microbiologic efficacy of antibacterial drugs for acute otitis media. Pediatr Infect Dis J 12:973, 1993.

603. Klein JO, Remington JS. Current concepts of infections of the fetus and newborn infant. In Remington JS, Klein JO (eds). Infectious Diseases of the Fetus and Newborn Infant, 4th ed. Philadelphia, WB Saunders, 1995, pp 15–16.

604. Klein JO. Review of consensus reports on management of acute otitis media. Pediatr Infect Dis J 18:1152, 1999.

605. Klein JO. The "in vivo sensitivity test" for acute otitis media revisited. Pediatr Infect Dis J 17: 943–971, 1998

606. Klein JO, Teele DW. Isolation of viruses and mycoplasmas from middle ear effusions: a review. Ann Otol Rhinol Laryngol 85:140, 1976.

607. Kleinman LC, Kosecoff J, Dubois RW, Brook RH. The medical appropriateness of tympanostomy tubes proposed for children younger than 16 years in the United States. JAMA 271:1250, 1994.

608. Klimek JJ, Bates TR, Nightingale C, et al. Penetration characteristics of trimethoprim-sulfamethoxole in middle ear fluid of patients with chronic serous otitis media. J Pediatr 96:1087, 1980.

609. Klimek JJ, Nightingale C, Lehmann WB, Quintiliani R. Comparison of concentrations of amoxicillin and ampicillin in serum and middle ear fluid of children with chronic otitis media. J Infect Dis 135:999, 1977.

610. Klingensmith MR, Strauss M, Conner GH. A comparison of retention and complication rates of large-bore (Paparella II) and small-bore middle ear ventilating tubes. Otolaryngol Head Neck Surg 93:322, 1985.

611. Kobayashi K, Yamanaka N, Kataura A, et al. Presence of an 80 kilodalton protein, cross-reacted with monoclonal antibodies to pulmonary surfactant protein A, in the human middle ear. Ann Otol Rhinol Laryngol 101:491, 1992.

612. Kokko E. Chronic secretory otitis media in children: a clinical study. Acta Otolaryngol (Stockh) 327(Suppl):1, 1974.

613. Komoroski EM, Van Hare G, Shurin PA, et al. Quantitative measurement of C-reactive protein in acute otitis media. J Pediatr 111:81, 1987.

614. Kontiokari T, Uhari M, Koskela M. Effect of xylitol on growth of nasopharyngeal bacteria in vitro. Antimicrobial Agents Chemotherapy 39:1820, 1995.

615. Koskela M, Leinonen M, Luotonen J. Serum antibody response to pneumococcal otitis media. Pediatr Infect Dis J 1:245, 1982.

616. Koskela M. Serum antibodies to pneumococcal C-polysaccharide in children: response to acute pneumococcal otitis media or to vaccination. Pediatr. Infect Dis J 6:519, 1987.

617. Kovatch AL, Wald ER, Michaels RH. β-Lactamase-producing Branhamella catarrhalis causing otitis media in children. J Pediatr 102:261, 1983.

618. Kraemer MJ, Richardson MA, Weiss NS, et al. Risk factors for persistent middle ear effusions. JAMA 249:1022, 1983.

619. Krasinski K, Kusmeisz H, Nelson JD. Pharmacologic interactions among chloramphenicol, phenytoin and phenobarbital. Pediatr Infect Dis J 1:232, 1982.

620. Krause PJ, Owens NG, Nightingale CH, et al. Penetration of amoxicillin, cefaclor, erythromycin-sulfisoxazole, and trimethoprim-sulfamethoxazole into the middle ear fluid of patients with chronic serous otitis media. J Infect Dis 145:815, 1982.

621. Kumazawa T. Objective tubal function test. In Kumazawa T (ed). A Basic and Clinical Study on the Eustachian Tube. Osaka, Japan, Kansai Medical University, 1980, pp 4–29.

622. Kusmiesz H, Shelton S, Brown O, et al. Loracarbef concentrations in middle ear fluid. Antimicrob Agents Chemother 34:2030, 1990.

623. Kvaerner KJ, Harris JR, Tambs K, Magnus P. Distribution and hereditability of recurrent ear infections. Ann Otol Rhinol Laryngol 106:624, 1997.

624. Lahikainen EA. Clinico-bacteriologic studies on acute otitis media: aspiration of tympanum as diagnostic and therapeutic method. Acta Otolaryngol (Stockh) 107(Suppl):1, 1953.

625. Lahikainen EA. Penicillin concentration in middle ear secretion in otitis. Acta Otolaryngol (Stockh) 70:358, 1970.

626. Lahikainen EA, Vuori M, Virtanen S. Azidocillin and ampicillin concentrations in middle ear effusion. Acta Otolaryngol (Stockh) 84:227, 1977.

627. LaMarco KL, Diven WF, Glew RH, et al. Neuraminidase activity in middle ear effusion. Ann Otol Rhinol Laryngol 93:76, 1984.

628. LaFaye M, Gaillard de Collogny L, Jourde H, et al. Etude de la permeabilité de la trompe d'Eustache par les radioisotopes. Ann Otolaryngol Chir Cervicofac 91:665, 1974.

629. Lang RW, Liu YS, Lim DJ, et al: Antimicrobial factors and bacterial correlation in chronic otitis media with effusion. Ann Otol Rhinol Laryngol 85:145, 1976.

630. Lannois M. De l'état de l'oreille moyenne dans les fissures congenitales du palais. Rev Hebd Laryngol 21:177, 1901.

631. Leach A, Ceesay SJ, Banya WAS, Greenwood BM. Pilot trial of a pentavalent pneumococcal polsyacchride/protein conjugate vaccine in Gambian infants. Pediatr Infect Dis J 15:333, 1996.

632. Lee K, Schuknecht HF. Results of tympanoplasty and mastoidectomy at the Massachusetts Eye and Ear Infirmary. Laryngoscope 81:529, 1971.

633. Lee D, Youk A, Goldstein NA. A meta-analysis of swimming and water precautions. Laryngoscope 109:536, 1999.

634. Leibovitz E, Piglansky L, Raiz S, et al. The bacteriologic efficacy of 1-day versus 3-day intramuscular ceftriaxone in the treatment of non-responsive acute otitis media. Abstracts of the 38th Interscience Conference on Antimicrobial Agents and Chemotherapy, San Diego, September 24 to September 27, 1998.

635. Leinonen M, Luotonen J, Herva E, et al. Preliminary serologic evidence for a pathogenic role of Branhamella catarrhalis. J Infect Dis 144:570, 1981.

636. Levin RM, Grossman M, Jordan C, et al. Group A streptococcal infection in children younger than three years of age. Pediatr Infect Dis J 7:581, 1988.

637. Levine LR. Quantitative comparison of adverse reactions to cefaclor vs. amoxicillin in a surveillance study. Pediatr Infect Dis J 4: 358, 1985.

638. Levine BB, Redmond AP, Fellner MJ, et al. Penicillin allergy and the heterogeneous immune responses of man to benzylpenicillin. J Clin Invest 45:1895, 1966.

639. Lewis DE. Clinton starts program for parental paid leave. Boston Globe 12/1/99, pp 1, C-6.

640. Lewis DM, Schram JL, Birck HG, Lim DJ. Antibody activity in otitis media with effusion. Ann Otol Rhinol Laryngol 88:392, 1979.

641. Lewis DM, Schram JL, Lim DJ, et al. Immunoglobulin E in chronic middle ear effusions: comparison of RIST, PRIST, and RIA techniques. Ann Otol Rhinol Laryngol 87:197, 1978.

642. Liederman EM, Post JC, Aul JJ, et al. Analysis of adult otitis media: polymerase chain reaction versus culture for bacteria and viruses. Ann Otol Rhinol Laryngol 107:10, 1998.

643. Lildholdt T, Cantekin EI, Bluestone CD, Rockette HE. Effect of topical nasal decongestant on eustachian tube function in children with tympanostomy tubes. Acta Otolaryngol (Stockh) 94:93, 1982.

644. Lildholdt T, Cantekin EI, Marshak G, et al. Pharmacokinetics of cefaclor in chronic middle ear effusions. Ann Otol Rhinol Laryngol 90:44, 1981.

645. Lim DL, Bluestone CD, Casselbrant ML, et al (eds). Recent Advances in Otitis Media—Proceedings of the Sixth International Symposium. Hamilton, Ontario, B.C. Decker, 1996.

646. Lim DJ, Bluestone CD, Klein JO, et al (eds). Recent Advances in Otitis Media—Proceedings of the Fifth International Symposium. Hamilton, Ontario, B.C. Decker, 1993.

647. Lim DJ, DeMaria TF. Immunobarriers of the tubotympanum. Acta Otolaryngol (Stockh) 103:355, 1987.

648. Lim DJ. Functional morphology of the tubotympanum. Acta Otolaryngol (Stockh) Suppl 414:13, 1984.

649. Lin C, Kumari P, Perrotta RJ, Reidenberg BE. Penetration of ceftibuten into middle ear fluid. Antimicrob Agents Chemother 40:1394, 1996.

650. Linder TE, Marder HP, Munzinger J. Role of adenoids in the pathogenesis of otitis media: a bacteriologic and immunochemical analysis. Ann Otol Rhinol Laryngol 106:619, 1997.

651. Ling D, McCoy RH, Levinson ED. The incidence of middle ear disease and its educational implications among Baffin Island Eskimo children. Can J Public Health 60:385, 1969.

652. Linthicum FH, Body H, Keaster J: Incidence of middle ear disease in children with cleft palate. Cleft Palate Bull 9:23, 1959.

653. Liu YS, Lim DJ, Lang RW, Birck HG. Chronic middle ear effu-

sions: immunochemical and bacteriological investigations. Arch Otolaryngol Head Neck Surg 101:278, 1975.

654. Liu YS, Lim DJ, Lang R, Birck HG. Microorganisms in chronic otitis media with effusion. Ann Otol Rhinol Laryngol 85:245, 1976.

655. Liu YS, Lim DS, Lang RW. Chronic middle ear effusions: immunological and bacteriological investigations. Arch Otolaryngol Head Neck Surg 101:278, 1975.

656. Loda FA, Glezen WP, Clyde WA. Respiratory disease in group day care. Pediatrics 49:428, 1972.

657. Lode H, Kass EH (eds). Enzyme-mediated resistance to b-lactam antibiotics: a symposium on sulbactam/ampicillin. Rev Infect Dis 8(Suppl 5):S465, 1986.

658. Loeb MR, Smith DH. Outer membrane protein composition in disease isolates of *Haemophilus influenzae*: pathogenic and epidemiological implications. Infect Immun 30:710, 1980.

659. Long SS. Cefixime. Rep Pediatr Infect Dis 2:5, 1992.

660. Long SS, Henretig FM, Teter MJ, McGowan KL. Nasopharyngeal flora and acute otitis media. Infect Immun 41:987, 1983.

661. Loos BG, Bernstein JM, Dryja DM, et al. Determination of the epidemiology and transmission of nontypeable *Haemophilus influenzae* in children with otitis media by comparison of total genomic DNA restriction fingerprints. Infect Immun 9:2751, 1989.

662. Lorentzen P, Haugsten P. Treatment of acute suppurative otitis media. J Laryngol Otol 91:331, 1977.

663. Lous J, Fiellau-Nikolajsen M. Epidemiology of middle ear effusion and tubal dysfunction: a one-year prospective study comprising monthly tympanometry in 387 nonselected seven-year-old children. Int J Pediatr Otorhinolaryngol 3:303, 1981.

664. Lowry PW, Jarvis WR, Oberle AD, et al. *Mycobacterium chelonae* causing otitis media in an ear-nose-and-throat practice. N Engl J Med 319:978, 1988.

665. Lucente FE, Lawson W, Novick NL. The External Ear. Philadelphia, WB Saunders, 1995.

666. Lundgren K, Ingvarsson L. Acute otitis media in Sweden: role of *Branhamella catarrhalis* and the rationale for choice of antimicrobial therapy. Drugs 31:125, 1986.

667. Lundgren K, Ingvarsson L, Olofsson B. Epidemiologic aspects in children with recurrent otitis media. In Lim DJ, Bluestone CD, Klein JO, Nelson JD (eds). Recent Advances in Otitis Media with Effusion. Burlington, Ontario, B.C. Decker, 1984, pp 22–25.

668. Lundgren K, Ingvarsson L, Rudcrantz H. The concentration of penicillin V in middle ear exudate. Int J Pediatr Otorhinolaryngol 1:93, 1979.

669. Lundman L, Juhn SK, Bagger-Sjoback D, Svanborg C. Permeability of the normal round window membrane to *Haemophilus influenzae* type b endotoxin. Acta Otolaryngol (Stockh) 112:524, 1992.

670. Lundy LB, Graham MD. Ototoxicity and ototopical medications: a survey of otolaryngologists. Am J Otol 14:141, 1993.

671. Luotonen J, Herva E, Karma P, et al. The bacteriology of acute otitis media in children with special reference to *Streptococcus pneumoniae* as studied by bacteriological and antigen detection methods. Scand J Infect Dis 13:177, 1981.

672. Lupin AJ. The relationship of the tensor tympani and tensor palatini muscles. Ann Otol Rhinol Laryngol 78:792, 1969.

673. Lynn GE, Benitez JT. Temporal bone preservation in a 2600-year-old Egyptian mummy. Science 183:200, 1974.

674. MacAdam AM, Rubio T. Tuberculosis otomastoiditis in children. Am J Dis Child 131:152, 1977.

675. Mace JW, Janik DS, Sauer RL, Quilligan JJ. Penicillin-resistant pneumococcal meningitis in an immunocompromised infant. J Pediatr 91:506, 1977.

676. Macleod CM, Hodges RG, Heidelberger M, Berhard WG. Prevention of pneumococcal pneumonia by immunization with specific capsular polysaccharides. J Exp Med 82:445, 1945.

677. Makela PH, Leinonen M, Tukander J, et al: A study of the polyvaccine in prevention of clinically acute attacks of recurrent otitis media. Rev Infect Dis 3:S124, 1981.

678. Makela PH, Leinonen M, Tukander J, Karma P. A study of the pneumococcal vaccine in prevention of clinically acute attacks of recurrent otitis media. Rev Infect Dis 3:S124, 1981.

679. Makela PH, Sibakov M, Herva E, Henricksen J. Pneumococcal vaccine and otitis media. Lancet 2:547, 1980.

680. Maknin ML, Jones PK. Oral dexamethasone for treatment of persistent middle ear effusion. Pediatrics 75:329, 1985.

681. Mandel EM, Bluestone CD, Rockette HE, et al. Duration of effusion after antibiotic treatment for acute otitis media: comparison of cefaclor and amoxicillin. Pediatr Infect Dis J 1:310, 1982.

682. Mandel EM, Bluestone CD, Takahashi H, Casselbrant ML. Effect of adenoidectomy on eustachian tube function: preliminary results of a randomized clinical trial. In Pfaltz CD (ed). Advances in Otorhinolaryngology, Vol. 47. Basel, Switzerland, Karger Publishing, 1992, pp 227–231.

683. Mandel EM, Casselbrant ML, Kurs-Lasky M. Acute otorrhea: Bacteriology of a common complication of tympanostomy tubes. Ann Otol Rhinol Laryngol 103:713, 1994.

684. Mandel EM, Casselbrant ML, Rockette HE, et al. Efficacy of antimicrobial prophylaxis for recurrent middle ear effusion. Pediatr Infect Dis J 15:1074, 1996.

685. Mandel EM, Casselbrant ML, Rockette HE, et al. Efficacy of 20- versus 10-day antimicrobial treatment for acute otitis media. Pediatrics 96:5, 1995.

686. Mandel EN, Casselbrant ML, Rockette HE, et al. Efficacy of systemic corticosteroid for chronic otitis media with effusion in children. In Lim DJ, Bluestone CD, Klein JO, et al. Recent Advances in Otitis Media: Proceedings of the 7th International Symposium on Recent Advances in Otitis Media. In press.

687. Mandel EM, Kardatzke D, Bluestone CD, Rockette HE. A comparative evaluation of cefaclor and amoxicillin in the treatment of acute otitis media. Pediatr Infect Dis J 12:726, 1993.

688. Mandel EM, Rockette HE, Bluestone CD, et al. Efficacy of amoxicillin with and without decongestant-antihistamine for otitis media with effusion in children: results of a double-blind, randomized trial. N Engl J Med 316:432, 1987.

689. Mandel EM, Rockette HE, Bluestone CD, et al. Efficacy of myringotomy with and without tympanostomy tubes for chronic otitis media with effusion. Pediatr Infect Dis J 11:270, 1992.

690. Mandel EM, Rockette HE, Bluestone CD, et al. Myringotomy with and without tympanostomy tubes for chronic otitis media with effusion. Arch Otolaryngol Head Neck Surg 115:1217, 1989.

691. Mandel EM, Rockette HE, Paradise JL, et al. Comparative efficacy of erythromycin-sulfisoxazole, cefaclor, amoxicillin or placebo for otitis media with effusion in children. Pediatr Infect Dis J 10:899, 1991.

692. Mangat KS, Morrison GAJ, Ganniwalla TM. T-tubes: a retrospective review of 1274 insertions over a 4-year period. Int J Pediatr Otorhinolaryngol 25:119, 1993.

693. Manning SC, Brown OE, Roland PS, Phillips DZ. Incidence of sensorineural hearing loss in patients evaluated for tympanostomy tubes. Arch Otolaryngol Head Neck Surg 120:881, 1994.

694. Manning SC, Cantekin EI, Kenna MA, et al. Prognostic value of eustachian tube function in pediatric tympanoplasty. Laryngoscope 97:1012, 1987.

695. Marchant CD, Carlin SA, Johnson CE, et al. Measuring the comparative efficacy of antibacterial agents for acute otitis media: the "Pollyanna phenomenon." J Pediatr 120:72, 1992.

696. Marchant CD, Shurin PA, Turcyzk VA, et al. Course and outcome of otitis media in early infancy: a prospective study. J Pediatr 104:826, 1984.

697. Marchisio P, Principi N, Sala E, et al. Comparative study of once-weekly azithromycin and once-daily amoxicillin treatments in prevention of recurrent acute otitis media in children. Antimicrob Agents Chemother 40:2732, 1996.

698. Marchisio P, Principi N, Sorella S, et al. Etiology of acute otitis media in human immunodeficiency virus-infected children. Pediatr Infect Dis J 15:58, 1996.

699. Markowitz-Spence L, Brodsky L, Syed N, et al. Anesthetic complications of tympanotomy tube placement in children. Arch Otolaryngol Head Neck Surg 116:809, 1990.

700. Marks MI, Klein JO. Bacterial infections of the respiratory tract. In Remington JS and Klein JO (eds). Infectious Diseases of the Fetus and Newborn Infant. Philadelphia, WB Saunders, 1995, pp 894–898.

701. Maroudias N, Economides J, Christodoulou P, Helidonis E. A study on the otoscopical and audiological findings in patients with Down's syndrome in Greece. Int J Pediatr Otorhinolaryngol 29:43, 1994.

702. Marshak G, Neriah ZB. Adenoidectomy vs. tympanostomy in

chronic secretory otitis media. Ann Otol Rhinol Laryngol 89(Suppl 68):316, 1981.

703. Mastro TD, Ghafoor A, Nomani NK, et al. Antimicrobial resistance of pneumococci in children with acute lower respiratory tract infection in Pakistan. Lancet 337:156, 1991.

704. Matsune S, Sando I, Takahashi H. Abnormalities of lateral cartilaginous lamina and lumen of eustachian tube in cases of cleft palate. Ann Otol Rhinol Laryngol 100:909, 1991.

705. Matsune S, Sando I, Takahashi H. Comparative study of elastic at the hinge portion of eustachian tube cartilage in normal and cleft palate individuals. In Lim DJ, Bluestone CD, Klein JO, et al (eds). Recent Advances in Otitis Media—Proceedings of the Fifth International Symposium. Burlington, Ontario, B.C. Decker, 1993, pp 4–6.

706. Matsune S, Sando I, Takahashi H. Insertion of the tensor veli palatini muscle into the eustachian tube cartilage in cleft palate cases. Ann Otol Rhinol Laryngol 100:439, 1991.

707. Matsune S, Takahashi H, Sando I. Mucosa-associated lymphoid tissue in middle ear and eustachian tube in children. Int J Pediatr Otorhinolaryngol 34:229, 1996.

708. Matt BH, Miller RP, Meyers RM, et al. Incidence of perforation with Goode T-tube. Int J Pediatr Otorhinolaryngol 21:1, 1991.

709. Mattar ME, Markello J, Yaffe SJ. Pharmaceutic factors affecting pediatric compliance. Pediatrics 55:101, 1975.

710. Maw AR. Chronic otitis media with effusion and adenotonsillectomy: a prospective randomized controlled study. In Lim DJ, Bluestone CD, Klein JO, Nelson JD (eds). Recent Advances in Otitis Media with Effusion. Toronto, Ontario, B.C. Decker, 1984, pp 299–302.

711. Maw AR. Chronic otitis media with effusion (glue ear) and adenotonsillectomy: prospective randomised controlled study. Br Med J (Clin Res) 287:1586, 1983.

712. Maw AR, Smith IM, Lance GN. Lateral cephalometric analysis of children with otitis media with effusion: a comparison with age and sex matched controls. J Laryngol Otol 105:71, 1991.

713. Mawson SR, Adlington R, Evans M. A controlled study evaluation of adeno-tonsillectomy in children. J Laryngol Otol 81:777, 1967.

714. Mawson SR, Fagan P. Tympanic effusions in children: long-term results of treatment by myringotomy, aspiration and indwelling tubes (grommets). J Laryngol Otol 86:105, 1972.

715. Mawson SR. The eustachian tube. In Mawson SR (ed). Disease of the Ear. Baltimore, Williams & Wilkins, 1974.

716. Maynard JE, Fleshman JK, Tschopp CF. Otitis media in Alaskan Eskimo children: prospective evaluation of chemoprophylaxis. JAMA 219:597, 1972.

717. Maxim PE, Veltri RW, Sprinkle PM, Pusateri RJ. Chronic serous otitis media: an immune complex disease. Trans Am Acad Ophthalmol Otolaryngol 84:234, 1977.

718. Mbelle N, Wasas A, Huebner R, et al. Immunogenicity and impact on carriage of a 9-valent pneumococal conjugate vaccine given to infants in Soweto, South Africa. J Infect Dis 180:1171, 1999.

719. McBride TP, Doyle WJ, Hayden FG, Gwaltney JM. Alterations of the eustachian tube, middle ear, and nose in rhinovirus infection. Arch Otolaryngol 115:1054, 1989.

719a. McBride TP, Derkay CS, Cunningham MJ, et al. Evaluation of noninvasive eustachian tube function tests in normal adults. Laryngoscope 98:655, 1988.

720. McCarthy PL, Grundy GW, Spiesel SZ, et al. Bacteremia in children: an outpatient clinical review. Pediatrics 57:861, 1976.

721. McCarty JM, Phillips A, Wiisanen R. Comparative safety and efficacy of clarithromycin and amoxicillin/clavulanate in the treatment of acute otitis media in children. Pediatr Infect Dis J 12:S122, 1993

722. McCracken GH Jr, Threlkeld N, Mize S, et al. Moxalactam therapy for neonatal meningitis due to gram-negative enteric bacilli: a prospective controlled evaluation. JAMA 252:1427, 1984.

723. McDonnell JP, Needleman HL, Charchut S, et al. The relationship between dental overbite and eustachian tube dysfunction. Laryngoscope 111:310, 2001.

724. McKee WJE. A controlled study of the effects of tonsillectomy and adenoidectomy in children. Br J Prev Soc Med 17:46, 1963.

725. McKee WJE. The part played by adenoidectomy in the combined operation of tonsillectomy with adenoidectomy: second part of a controlled study in children. Br J Prev Soc Med 17:133, 1963.

726. McLelland CA. Incidence of complications from use of tympanostomy tubes. Arch Otolaryngol Head Neck Surg 106:97, 1980.

727. McLinn SE. A multicenter, double blind comparison of azithromycin and amoxicillin/clavulanate for the treatment of acute otitis media in children. Pediatr Infect Dis J 15:S20, 1996.

728. McLinn SE. Cefaclor in treatment of otitis media and pharyngitis in children. Am J Dis Child 134:560, 1980.

729. McLinn SE, Goldberg F, Kramer R, et al. Double-blind multicenter comparison of cyclacillin and amoxicillin for the treatment of acute otitis media. J Pediatr 101:607, 1982.

730. McLinn SE, McCarty JM, Perrotta R, et al. Multicenter controlled trial comparing ceftibuten with amoxicillin/clavulanate in the empiric treatment of acute otitis media. Pediatr Infect Dis J 12:S70, 1993.

731. McMichael JC. Vaccines for Moraxella catarrhalis. Vaccine 19:S101, 2000.

732. McMyn JK. The anatomy of the salpingopharyngeus muscle. J Laryngol Otol 55:1, 1940.

733. McNicoll WD. Remediable eustachian tube dysfunction in diving recruits: assessment, investigation, and management. Undersea Biomed Res 9:37, 1982.

734. McNicoll WD, Scanlon SG. Submucous resection: the treatment of choice in the nose-ear distress syndrome. J Laryngol Otol 93:357, 1979.

735. McWilliams BJ. Speech and hearing problems in children with cleft palate. J Am Med Wom Assoc 21:1005, 1966.

736. Medical Letter. Drugs for treatment of acute otitis media in children. 36:19, 1994.

737. Medical Letter. Drugs for non-HIV viral infections. 41:13, 1999.

738. Mehta D, Erlich M: Serous otitis media in school for the deaf. Volta Rev 80:75, 1978.

738a. Meissner K. Ohrenerkrankungen bei Gaumen-spalten. Hals Nasen Ohrenarzt 30:6, 1939.

739. Meistrup-Larsen K-I, Sorensen H, Johnson NJ, et al. Two versus seven days penicillin treatment for acute otitis media. Acta Otolaryngol (Stockh) 96:99, 1983.

740. Meri S, Lehtinen T, Palva T. Complement in chronic secretory otitis media: C3 breakdown and C3 splitting activity. Arch Otolaryngol Head Neck Surg 110:774, 1984.

741. Meurman OH, Sarkkinen HK, Puhakka HJ, Virolainen ES. Local IgA class antibodies against respiratory viruses in middle ear and nasopharyngeal secretions of children with secretory otitis media. Laryngoscope 90:304, 1980.

742. Miglets A. The experimental production of allergic middle ear effusions. Laryngoscope 83:1355, 1973.

742a. Miller GF, Bilodeau R. Preoperative evaluation of eustachian tubal function in tympanoplasty. South Med J 60:868, 1967.

743. Miller GF. Influence of an oral decongestant on eustachian tube function in children. J Allergy 45:187, 1970.

744. Miller MH. Hearing losses in cleft palate cases: the incidence, type, and significance. Laryngoscope 66:1492, 1956.

745. Miller SA, Omene JA, Bluestone CD, Torkelson DW. A point prevalence of otitis media in a Nigerian village. Int J Pediatr Otorhinolaryngol 5:19, 1983.

746. Minja BM, Machemba A. Prevalence of otitis media, hearing impairment and cerumen impaction among school children in rural and urban Dar es Salaam, Tanzania. Int J Pediatr Otorhinolaryngol 37:29, 1996.

747. Misurya VK. Tensor tympani, a 'tuner' or tensor palatini muscle. Acta Otolaryngol (Stockh) 82:410, 1976.

748. Mitchell GAC. The autonomic nerve supply of the throat, nose, and ear. J Laryngol Otol 68:495, 1954.

749. Miura M, Sando I, Balaban CD. Estimated locations of the narrowest portion of the eustachian tube lumen during closed and open states: a computer-aided three-dimensional reconstruction and measurement study. Ann Otol Rhinol Laryngol (in press).

750. Miura M, Sando I, Balaban CD, Haginomori S-I. Morphometric study on the eustachian tube and its associated structures in patients with chromosomal aberrations. In press.

751. Miura M, Sando I, Orita Y, Hirsch BE. Histopathological study of the temporal bones and eustachian tubes in children with cholesterol granuloma. Ann Otol Rhinol Laryngol (in press).

752. Miura M, Sando I, Takasaki K, et al. Temporal bone histopathological findings in oculoauriculovertebral spectrum. In press.

753. Moellering RC Jr, Swartz MN. Drug therapy: the newer cephalosporins. N Engl J Med 294:24, 1976.

754. Mogi G, Chaen T, Tomonaga K. Influence of nasal allergic reactions on the clearance of middle ear effusion. Arch Otolaryngol Head Neck Surg 116:331, 1990.

755. Mogi G, Honjo S, Maeda S, et al. Immunoglobulin E (IgE) in middle ear effusions. Ann Otol Rhinol Laryngol 83:393, 1974.

756. Mogi G. Immunologic and allergic aspects of otitis media. In Lim DJ, Bluestone CD, Klein JO, et al (eds). Recent Advances in Otitis Media. Burlington, Ontario, B.C. Decker, 1993, pp 145–151.

757. Mogi G, Kawauchi H, Kurono Y. Tubal dysfunction or infection? Role of bacterial infection and immune response. In Mogi G (ed). Recent Advances in Otitis Media—Proceedings of the Second Extraordinary International Symposium. New York, Kugler Publications, 1993, pp 73–77.

758. Mogi G, Suzuki M. The role of IgE-mediated immunity in otitis media: fact or fiction. In Bernstein JM, Faden JS, Henderson D et al (eds). Immunologic Diseases of the Ear. Ann N Y Acad Sci 830:61, 1997.

759. Mogi G, Yoshida T, Honjo S, Maeda S. Middle ear effusions: quantitative analysis of immunoglobulins. Ann Otol Rhinol Laryngol 82:196, 1973.

760. Monto AS, Robinson DP, Herlocher ML, et al. Zanamivir in the prevention of influenza among healthy adults: a randomized controlled trial. JAMA 282:31, 1999.

761. Moody S, Alper CM, Doyle WJ. Daily tympanometry in children during the cold season: association of otitis media with upper respiratory tract infections. Int J Pediatr Otorhinolaryngol 45:143, 1998.

762. Moore EP, Speller DCE, White LO, et al (eds). Cefpodoxime proxetil: a third-generation oral cephalosporin. J Antimicrob Chemother 26(Suppl E):1, 1990.

763. Morita M, Matsunaga T. Sonotubometry with a tubal catheter as an index for the use of a ventilation tube in otitis media with effusion. Acta Otolaryngol Suppl (Stockh) 501:59, 1993.

764. Morizono T, Giebink GS, Paparella MM, et al. Sensorineural hearing loss in experimental purulent otitis media due to Streptococcus pneumoniae. Arch Otolaryngol 111:794, 1985.

765. Mortimer EA, Watterson RL. Bacteriologic investigation of otitis media in infancy. Pediatrics 17:359, 1956.

766. Mumtaz MA, Schwartz RH, Grundfast KM, Baumgartner RC. Tuberculosis of the middle ear and mastoid. Pediatr Infect Dis J 2:234, 1983.

767. Murphy TF, Apicella MA. Antigenic heterogenicity of outer membrane proteins of nontypable Haemophilus influenzae as a basis for serotyping system. Infect Immun 50:15, 1985.

768. Murphy TF, Bartos LC, Campagnari AA, et al. Antigenic characterization of the P6 protein of nontypable Haemophilus influenzae. Infect Immun 54:774, 1986.

769. Murphy TF, Bartos LC. Purification and analysis with monoclonal antibodies of P2, the major outer membrane protein of nontypable Haemophilus influenzae. Infect Immun 56:1084, 1988.

770. Murphy TF, Bartos LC. Surface-exposed and antigenically conserved determinants of outer membrane proteins of Branhamella catarrhalis. Infect Immun 57:2938, 1989.

771. Murphy TF, Bernstein JM, Dryja DM, et al. Outer membrane protein and lipooligosaccharide analysis of paired nasopharyngeal and middle ear isolates in otitis media due to nontypable Haemophilus influenzae: pathogenic and epidemiological observations. J Infect Dis 156:723, 1987.

772. Murphy TF. The surface of Branhamella catarrhalis: a systematic approach to the surface antigens of an emerging pathogen. Pediatr Infect Dis J 8:S75, 1989.

773. Murray DL, Singer DA, Singer AB. Cefaclor: a cluster of adverse reactions. N Engl J Med 303:1003, 1980.

774. Murti KG, Stern RM, Cantekin EI, et al: Sonometric evaluation of eustachian tube function using broadband stimuli. Ann Otol Rhinol Laryngol 89:178, 1980.

775. Musher DM, Watson DA, RE Baughn. Does naturally acquired IgG antibody to cell wall polysaccharide protect human subjects against pneumococcal infection? J Infect Dis 161:736, 1990.

776. Myer CM III. Historical perspective on the use of otic antimicrobial agents. Pediatr Infect Dis J 20:98, 2001.

777. Myers EN, Beery QC, Bluestone CD, et al. Effect of certain head and neck tumors and their management on the ventilatory function of the eustachian tube. Ann Otol Rhinol Laryngol 93(Suppl 114):3, 1984.

778. Mygind N, Pedersen M: Nose, sinus and ear symptoms in 27 patients with primary ciliary dyskinesia. Eur J Respir Dis 64(Suppl 127):96, 1983.

779. Nafstad P, Hagen JA, Oie L, et al. Day care centers and respiratory health. Pediatrics 103:753, 1999.

780. Naiditch MJ, Bower AG. Diphtheria: a study of 1,433 cases observed during a ten-year period at Los Angeles County Hospital. Am J Med 17:229, 1954.

781. Naito Y, Hrono Y, Honjo I, et al: Magnetic resonance imaging of the eustachian tube. Arch Otolaryngol Head Neck Surg 113:1281, 1987.

782. Nalluswami K, Ko CW, Hou JR, Hoffman JH. Very low birth weight infants are at risk for frequent ear infections [abstract]. Am J Epidemiol 147:S16, 1998.

783. Nathanson SE, Jackson RT. Vidian nerve and the eustachian tube. Ann Otol Rhinol Laryngol 85:83, 1976.

784. National Center for Health Statistics. Surgical Operations In Short—Stay Hospitals: United States—1971. (DHEW Publication No. HRAu1769) Rockville, MD, United States Department of Health, Education and Welfare, 1974.

785. NDTI Review: Leading diagnoses and reasons for patient visits. 1:18, 1970.

786. Nelson CT, Mason EO Jr, Kaplan SL. Activity of oral antibiotics in middle ear and sinus infections caused by penicillin-resistant Streptococcus pneumoniae: implications for treatment. Pediatr Infect Dis J 13:585, 1994.

787. Nelson JD, Ginsburg CM, McLeland O, et al. Concentrations of antimicrobial agents in middle ear fluid, saliva, and tears. Int J Pediatr Otorhinolaryngol 3:327, 1981.

788. Nelson JD, McCracken GH (eds). Clinical perspectives on clarithromycin in pediatric infectious diseases. Pediatr Infect Dis J 12:S98, 1993.

789. Nelson JD, McCracken GH. The drug of choice for otitis media? J Pediatr Infect Dis 6:5, 1980.

790. Nelson WL, Kennedy DL, Lao CS, Kuritsky JN. Outpatient systemic anti-infective use by children in the United States, 1977 to 1986. Pediatr Infect Dis J 7:505, 1988.

791. Nelson WL, Kuritsky JN, Kennedy DL, et al. Outpatient pediatric antibiotic use in the US: trends and therapy for otitis media, 1977–1986. In Program and Abstracts of the 27th Interscience Conference on Antimicrobial Agents and Chemotherapy. Washington, D.C., American Society for Microbiology, 1987.

792. Nemechek AJ, Pahlavan N, Cote DN. Nebulized surfactant for experimentally induced otitis media with effusion. Otolaryngol Head Neck Surg 117:475, 1997.

793. Neu HC. A symposium on the tetracyclines: a major appraisal: introduction. Bull N Y Acad Med 54:141, 1978.

794. Neu HC, McCracken GH Jr. Proceedings of a conference: clinical pharmacology and efficacy of cefixime. Pediatr Infect Dis J 6:951, 1987.

795. Neu HC, Young LS, Zinner SH (eds). The New Macrolides, Azalides, and Streptogramins: Pharmacology and Clinical Applications. New York, Marcel Dekker, 1993.

796. Niemela M, Pihakari O, Pokka T, Uhari M. Pacifier as a risk factor for acute otitis media: a randomized, controlled trial of parental counseling. Pediatrics 106:483, 2000.

797. Niemela M, Uhari M, Lautala P, Huggare J. Association of recurrent acute otitis media with nasopharynx dimensions in children. J Laryngol Otol 108:299, 1994.

798. Niemela M, Uhari M, Mottonen M. Otitis media in day care: are pacifiers to blame? Pediatrics 96:884, 1995.

799. Nissinen A, Gronroos P, Huovinen P, et al. Development of β-lactamase-mediated resistance to pencillin in middle-ear isolates of Moraxella catarrhalis in Finnish children, 1978–1993. Clin Infect Dis 21:1193, 1995.

800. Nonomura N, Giebink GS, Zelterman D, et al. Early biochemical events in pneumococcal otitis media: arachidonic acid metabolites in middle-ear fluid. Ann Otol Rhinol Laryngol 100:385, 1991.

801. Nozoe T, Okazaki N, Koda Y, et al. Fluid clearance of the eustachian tube. In Lim DJ, Bluestone CD, Klein JO, et al (eds). Recent Advances in Otitis Media with Effusion: Proccedings of

the Third International Symposium. Philadelphia, B.C. Decker, 1984, pp 66–68.

802. Nsouli TM, Nsouli SM, Linde RE, et al. Role of food allergy in serous otitis media. Ann Allergy 73:215, 1994.

802a. Nunn DR, Derkay CS, Darrow DH, et al. The effect of very early cleft palate closure on the need for ventilation tubes in the first years of life. Laryngoscope 105:905, 1995.

803. Odoi CM, Kusmiesz H, Shelton D, Nelson JD. Comparative treatment trial of Augmentin versus cefaclor for acute otitis media with effusion. Pediatrics 75:819, 1985.

804. Odoi H, Proud GO, Toledo PS. Effects of pterygoid hamulotomy upon eustachian tube function. Laryngoscope 81:1242, 1971.

805. Ofek I: Special lecture. Blocking bacterial adhesion: a new approach to prevention of infection. In Lim DJ, Bluestone CD, Klein JO, Nelson JD (eds). Recent Advances in Otitis Media—Proceedings of the Fifth International Symposium. Burlington, Ontario, Decker Periodicals, 1993, pp 215–221.

806. Ogawa H, Fujisawa T, Kazuyama Y: Isolation of *Chlamydia pneumoniae* from middle ear aspirates of otitis media with effusion: a case report. J Infect Dis 162:1000, 1990.

807. Ogawa H, Hashiguchi K, Kazuyama Y. Recovery of *Chlamydia pneumoniae* in six patients with otitis media with effusion. J Laryngol Otol 106:490, 1992.

808. Ogawa S, Satoh I, Tanaka H. Patulous eustachian tube: a new treatment with infusion of absorbable gelatin sponge solution. Arch Otolaryngol Head Neck Surg 102:276, 1976.

809. Ohashi Y, Nakai Y, Furuya H, et al. Mucociliary diseases of the middle ear during experimental otitis media with effusion induced by bacterial endotoxin. Ann Otol Rhinol Laryngol 98:479, 1989.

810. Ohashi Y, Nakai Y, Koshimo H, et al. Ciliary activity in the in vitro tubotympanum. Arch Otorhinolaryngol 243:317, 1986.

811. Ohashi Y, Ohno Y, Sugiura Y, et al. Allergic response and mucociliary function in the eustachian tube. In Lim DJ, Bluestone CD, Casselbrant ML, et al (eds). Recent Advances in Otitis Media—Proceedings of the Sixth International Symposium. Hamilton, Ontario, B.C. Decker, 1996, pp 95–97.

812. Okubo J, Watanabe I, Shibusawa M, et al. Sonotubometric measurement of the eustachian tube function by means of band noise. ORL 49:242, 1987.

813. Olson AL, Klein SW, Charney E, et al. Prevention and therapy of serous otitis media by oral decongestant: a double-blind study in pediatric practice. Pediatrics 61:679, 1978.

814. Ophir D, Hahn T, Schattner A, et al. Tumor necrosis factor in middle-ear effusions. Arch Otolaryngol 114:1256, 1988.

815. Oppenheimer P. Short-term steroid therapy: treatment of serous otitis media in children. Arch Otolaryngol Head Neck Surg 88:38, 1968.

816. Oppenheimer RP. Serous otitis: review of 992 patients. EENT Mthly 54:37, 1975.

817. Orange M, Gray BM. Pneumococcal serotypes causing disease in children in Alabama. Pediatr Infect Dis 12:244, 1993.

818. Ostfeld E, Rubinstein E. Acute gram-negative bacillary infections of middle ear and mastoid. Ann Otol Rhinol Laryngol 89:33, 1980.

819. Owings MF, Kozak LJ. Ambulatory and impatient procedures in the United States, 1996. Vital Health Stat 13 (139). Hyattsville, MD: National Center for Health Statistics, 1998, p 13.

820. Oyagi S, Ito J, Honjo I. The origin of autonomic nerves of the middle ear as studied by horseradish peroxidase tracer method. Acta Otolaryngol (Stockh) 104:463, 1987.

821. O'Brien KL, Swift AJ, Winkelstein JA, et al. Safety and immunogenicity of heptavalent pneumococcal vaccine conjugated to CRM197 among infants with sickle cell disease. Pediatrics 2000, 106:965.

822. Page JR. Report of acute infections of middle ear and mastoid process at Manhattan Eye, Ear, and Throat Hospital during 1934: their prevalance and virulence. Laryngoscope 45:839, 1935.

823. Paludetti G, Di Nardo W, Galli J, et al. Functional study of the eustachian tube with sequential scintigraphy. ORL 54:76, 1992.

824. Palva T, Hayry P, Ylikoski J. Lymphocyte morphology in middle ear effusions. Ann Otol Rhinol Laryngol 89:143, 1980.

825. Palva T, Holopainen E, Karma P. Protein and cellular protein of glue ear secretions. Ann Otol Rhinol Laryngol 85:103, 1976.

826. Palva T, Lehtinen T. Pneumococcal antigens and endotoxin in effusions from patients with secretory otitis media. Int J Pediatr Otorhinolaryngol 14:123, 1987.

827. Paparella MM, Goycoolea MV, Meyerhoff WL. Inner ear pathology and otitis media: a review. Ann Otol Rhinol Laryngol 89:249, 1980.

828. Paparella MM, Oda M, Hiraide F, Brady D. Pathology of sensorineural hearing loss in otitis media. Ann Otol Rhinol Laryngol 81:632, 1972.

829. Paparella MM, Schachern P, daCosta SS, et al. Clinical and pathologic correlates of silent (subclinical) otitis media. In Lim DJ, Bluestone CD, Klein JO, Nelson JD, et al (eds). Recent Advances in Otitis Media. Proceedings from the Fifth International Symposium. Hamilton, Ontario, B.C. Decker, 1993, pp 319–322.

830. Paparella MM. The middle ear effusions. In Paparella MM, Shumrick DA (eds). Otolaryngology, Vol. 1. Philadelphia, W.B. Saunders, 1973, pp 93–112.

831. Paradise JL, Bluestone CD, Bachman RZ, et al. Efficacy of tonsillectomy for recurrent throat infection in severely affected children: results of parallel randomized and non-randomized clinical trials. N Engl J Med 310:674, 1984.

832. Paradise JL, Bluestone CD, Colborn DK, et al. Adenoidectomy and adentonsillectomy for recurrent acute otitis media. Parallel randomized clinical trials in children not previously treated with tympanostomy-tube placement. JAMA 282:945, 1999.

833. Paradise JL, Bluestone CD, Colborn DK, et al. Tonsillectomy and adenotonsillectomy for recurrent throat infection in moderately affected children. In press.

834. Paradise JL, Bluestone CD. Early treatment of the universal otitis media in infants with cleft palate. Pediatrics 53:48, 1974.

835. Paradise JL, Bluestone CD, Felder H. The universality of otitis media in fifty infants with cleft palate. Pediatrics 44:35, 1969.

836. Paradise JL, Bluestone CD, Rogers KD, et al. Efficacy of adenoidectomy for recurrent otitis media in children previously treated with tympanostomy-tube placement: results of parallel randomized and nonrandomized trials. JAMA 263:2066, 1990.

837. Paradise JL, Elster BA. Breast milk protects against otitis media with effusion. Pediatrics 94:853, 1994.

838. Paradise JL. Long-term effects of short-term hearing loss: menace or myth? Pediatrics 71:647, 1983.

839. Paradise JL. On tympanostomy tubes, rationale, results, reservations, and recommendations. Pediatrics 60:86, 1977.

840. Paradise JL. Otitis media in infants and children: review article. Pediatrics 65:917, 1980.

841. Paradise JL, Rockette JE, Colborn K, et al. Otitis media in 2253 Pittsburgh-area infants: prevalence and risk factors during the first two years of life. Pediatrics 99:318, 1997.

842. Paradise JL. Short-course antimicrobial treatment for acute otitis media: not best for infants and young children. JAMA 278:1640, 1997.

843. Parisier SC, Khilnani MT. The roentgenographic evaluation of eustachian tubal function. Laryngoscope 80:1201, 1970.

844. Park K, Bakaletz LO, Coticchia JM, Lim DJ. Effect of influenza A virus on ciliary activity and dye transport function in the chinchilla eustachian tube. Ann Otol Rhinol Laryngol 102:551, 1993.

845. Park K, Lim DJ. Luminal development of the eustachian tube and middle ear: murine model. Yonsei Med J 33:159, 1992.

846. Park MS, Yoo SH, Lee DH. Measurement of surface area in human mastoid air cell system. J Laryngol Otol 114:93, 2000.

847. Parker CW. Allergic drug responses: mechanisms and unsolved problems. CRC Crit Rev Toxicol 1:261, 1972.

848. Pass RF. Respiratory virus infection and otitis media. Pediatrics 102:400, 1998.

849. Patrick CC, Kimura A, Jackson MA, et al. Antigenic characterization of the oligosaccharide portion of the lipooligosaccharide of nontypable *Haemophilus influenzae*. Infect Immun 55:2902, 1987.

850. Pedersen CB, Zachau-Christiansen B. Otitis media in Greenland children: acute, chronic and secretory otitis media in three to eight year olds. J Otolaryngol 15:332, 1986.

851. Pelton SI, Shurin PA, Klein JO. Persistence of middle ear effusion after otitis media. Pediatr Res 11:504, 1977.

852. Pelton SI, Teele DW, Bolduc G, et al. Trimethoprim/sulfamethoxazole-resistant nontypable *Haemophilus influenzae*. Pediatr Infect Dis J 10:873, 1991.

853. Pelton SI, Teele DW, Earle R Jr, et al. Impaired response to *Haemophilus* capsular polysaccharide-protein conjugate vaccine in

children with otitis media. In Lim DJ, Bluestone CD, Klein JO, et al (eds). Recent Advances in Otitis Media. Proceedings of the Fifth International Symposium. Burlington, Ontario, B.C. Decker, 1993, pp 167–168.

854. Pelton SI, Teele DW, Shurin PA, Klein JO. Disparate cultures of middle ear fluids. Am J Dis Child 134:951, 1980.

855. Per-Lee JH. Long-term middle ear ventilation. Laryngoscope 91:1063, 1981.

856. Perlman HB. Observations on the eustachian tube. Arch Otolaryngol 53:370, 1951.

857. Perlman HB. The eustachian tube: abnormal patency and normal physiologic state. Arch Otolaryngol Head Neck Surg 30:212, 1939.

858. Perrin JM, Charney E, MacWhinney JB Jr, et al. Sulfisoxazole as chemoprophylaxis for recurrent otitis media: a double-blind cross-over study in pediatric practice. N Engl J Med 291:664, 1974.

859. Persico M, Barker GA, Mitchell DP. Purulent otitis media: a "silent" source of sepsis in the pediatric intensive care unit. Otolaryngol Head Neck Surg 93:330, 1985.

860. Persico M, Podoshin L, Fradis M. Otitis media with effusion. Ann Otol Rhinol Laryngol 87:191, 1978.

861. Pestalozza G. Otitis media in newborn infants. Int J Pediatr Otorhinolaryngol 8:109, 1984.

862. Petz LD, Fudenberg HH. Coombs-positive hemolytic anemia caused by penicillin administration. N Engl J Med 274:171, 1966.

863. Petz LD. Immunologic cross-reactivity between penicillins and cephalosporins: a review. J Infect Dis 137:S74, 1978.

864. Phillips MJ, Knight NJ, Manning H, et al. IgE and secretory otitis media. Lancet 2:1176, 1974.

865. Pichichero ME, Berghash LR, Hengerer AS. Anatomic and audiologic sequelae after tympanostomy tube insertion or prolonged antibiotic therapy for otitis media. Pediatr Infect Dis J 8:780, 1989.

866. Pichichero ME, Cohen R. Shortened course of antibiotic therapy for acute otitis media, sinusitis and tonsillopharyngitis. Pediatr Infect Dis 16:680, 1997.

867. Pichichero ME, Klein JO, McCracken GH Jr. Cefdinir: role of a new cephalosprin for pediatric infectious diseases. Pediatr Infect Dis J 19:S131, 2000.

868. Pichichero ME, Pichichero CL. Persistent acute otitis media: I. Causative pathogens. Pediatr Infect Dis J 14:178, 1995.

869. Pisacane A, Ruas I. Bacteriology of otitis media in Mozambique. Lancet 1:1305, 1982.

870. Pitkaranta A, Jero J, Arruda E, et al. Polymerase chain reaction-based detection of rhinovirus, respiratory syncytial virus and coronavirus in otitis media with effusion. J Pediatr 133:390, 1998.

871. Pitkaranta A, Virolainen A, Jero J, et al. Detection of rhinovirus, respiratory syncytial virus, and coronavirus infections in acute otitis media by reverse transcriptase polymerase chain reaction. Pediatrics 102:291, 1998.

872. Plemmons RM, McAllister K, Liening DA, Garces MC. Otitis media and mastoiditis due to Mycobacterium fortuitum: case report, review of four cases, and a cautionary note. Clin Infect Dis 22:1105, 1996.

873. Ploussard JH. Evaluation of five days of cefaclor vs. ten days of amoxicillin therapy in acute otitis media. Curr Ther. Res 36:641, 1984.

874. Podoshin L, Fradis M, Ben-David Y, Faraggi D. The efficacy of oral steroids in the treatment of persistent otitis media with effusion. Arch Otolaryngol Head Neck Surg 116:1404, 1990.

875. Poe DS, Pyykko I, Valtonen H, Silvola J. Analysis of eustachian tube function by video endoscopy. Am J Otol 21:602, 2000.

876. Politzer A. Disease of the Ear. Philadelphia, Lea & Febiger, 1909.

877. Politzer A. Ueber die willkurlichen Bewegungen des Trommelfells. Weiner Med Halle Nr 18:103, 1862.

878. Poolman JT, Bakaletz L, Cripps A, et al. Developing a nontypeable Haemophilus influenzae vaccine. Vaccine 19:S108, 2000.

879. Porras O, Dillon HC, Gray BM, Svanborg-Eden C. Lack of correlation of in vitro adherence of Haemophilus influenzae to epithelial cells with frequent occurrence of otitis media. Pediatr Infect Dis J 6:41, 1987.

880. Porter TA. Otoadmittance measurements in a residential deaf population. Am Ann Deaf 119:47, 1974.

881. Post JC, Preston RA, Aul JJ, et al. Molecular analysis of bacterial pathogens in otitis media with effusion. JAMA 273:1598, 1995.

882. Postma DS, Poole MD, Wu SM, Tober R. The impact of day care on ventilation tube insertion. Int J Pediatr Otorhinolaryngol 41:253, 1997.

883. Poulsen G, Tos M. Screening tympanometry in newborn infants and during the first six months of life. Scand Audiol 7:159, 1978.

884. Prellner K, Fogle-Hansson M, Jorgensen F, et al. Prevention of recurrent acute otitis media in otitis-prone children by intermittent prophylaxis with penicillin. Acta Otolaryngol 114:182, 1994.

885. Prellner K, Hallberg T, Kalm O, Mansson B. Recurrent otitis media: genetic immunoglobulin markers in children and their parents. Int J Pediatr Otorhinolaryngol 9:219, 1985.

886. Prellner K, Harsten G, Christenson B, et al. Responses to rubella, tetanus, and diphtheria vaccines in otitis-prone and non-otitis-prone children. Ann Otol Rhinol Laryngol 99:628, 1990.

887. Prellner K, Kalm O, Hartsen G, et al. Pneumococcal serum antibody concentrations during the first three years of life: a study of otitis-prone and non-otitis-prone children. Int J Pediatr Otorhinolaryngol 17:267, 1989.

888. Prellner K, Nilsson NI, Johnson U, Laurell AB. Complement and Clq binding substances in otitis media. Ann Otol Rhinol Laryngol 89:129, 1980.

889. Presswood G, Zamboni WA, Stephenson LL, Santos PM. Effect of artificial airway on ear complications from hyperbaric oxygen. Laryngoscope 104:1383, 1994.

890. Pribitkin EA, Handler SD, Tom LWC, et al. Ventilation tube removal: indications for paper patch myringoplasty. Arch Otolaryngol Head Neck Surg 118:495, 1992.

891. Prince RA, Wing DS, Weinberger MM, et al. Effect of erythromycin on theophylline kinetics. J Allergy Clin Immunol 68:427, 1981.

892. Proctor B. Anatomy of the eustachian tube. Arch Otolaryngol 97:2, 1973.

893. Proctor B. Attic-aditus block and the tympanic diaphragm. Ann Otol Rhinol Laryngol 80:371, 1971.

894. Proctor B. Embryology and anatomy of the eustachian tube. Arch Otolaryngol 86:503, 1967.

895. Proud GO, Duff WE. Mastoidectomy and epitympanotomy. Ann Otol Rhinol Laryngol 85:289, 1976.

896. Puhakka H, Virolainen E, Aantaa E, et al. Myringotomy in the treatment of acute otitis media in children. Acta Otolaryngol (Stockh) 88:122, 1979.

897. Pukander JS, Jero JP, Kaprio EA, Sorri MJ. Clarithromycin vs. amoxicillin suspensions in the treatment of pediatric patients with acute otitis media. Pediatr Infect Dis J 12:S118, 1993.

898. Pukander J, Luotonen J, Sipila M, Karma P. Incidence of acute otitis media. Acta Otolaryngol (Stockh) 93:447, 1982.

899. Pukander J. Occurrence of acute otitis media. Academic Dissertation. Acta Universitatis Tamperensis, Series A, Vol. 135, 1982.

900. Pukander J, Sipila M, Karma P. Occurrence of and risk factors in acute otitis media. In Lim DJ, Bluestone CD, Klein JO, Nelson JD (eds). Recent Advances in Otitis Media with Effusion. Burlington, Ontario, B.C. Decker, 1984, pp 9–13.

901. Pulec JL. Abnormally patent eustachian tubes: treatment with injection of polytetrafluoroethylene (Teflon) paste. Laryngoscope 77:1543, 1967.

902. Quagliarello VJ, Scheld WM. New perspectives on bacterial meningitis. Clin Infect Dis 17:603, 1993.

903. Qvarnberg Y, Holopainen E, Palva T. Aspiration cytology in acute otitis media. Acta Otolaryngol (Stockh) 97:443, 1984.

904. Qvarnberg Y, Kantola O, Valtonen H, et al. Bacterial findings in middle ear effusion in children. Otolaryngol Head Neck Surg 102:118, 1990.

905. Qvarnberg Y, Palva T. Active and conservative treatment of acute otitis media: prospective studies. Ann Otol Rhinol Laryngol 89:269, 1980.

906. Raikundalia KB. Analysis of suppurative otitis media in children: aetiology of nonsuppurative otitis media. Med J Aust 1:749, 1975.

907. Raisanen S, Stenfors LE. Bacterial quantification: a necessary complement for the comprehension of middle ear inflammations. Int J Pediatr Otorhinolaryngol 23:117, 1992.

908. Ramadan HH, Tarazi T, Zaytoun GM. Use of prophylactic otic drops after tympanostomy tube insertion. Arch Otolaryngol Head Neck Surg 117:537, 1991.

909. Ramet M, Lofgren J, Alho O-P, Hallman M. Surfactant protein: a

locus associated with recurrent otitis media. J Pediatr 138:266, 2001.

910. Randall DA, Hoffer ME. Complications of tonsillectomy and adenoidectomy. Otolaryngol Head Neck Surg 118:61, 1998.

911. Rapp DJ, Fahey D. Review of chronic secretory otitis and allergy. J Asthma Res 10:193, 1973.

912. Rapport PN, Lim DJ, Weiss HJ. Surface active agent in eustachian tube function. Arch Otolaryngol 101:305, 1975.

913. Rathbun TA, Mallin R. Middle ear disease in a prehistoric Iranian population. Bull N Y Acad Med 53:901, 1977.

914. Rayner MG, Zhang Y, Gorry MC, et al. Evidence of bacterial metabolic activity in culture-negative otitis media with effusion. JAMA 279:296, 1998.

915. Reed D, Struve S, Maynard JE. Otitis media and hearing deficiency among Eskimo children: a cohort study. Am J Public Health 57:1657, 1967.

916. Rennels MB, Edwards KM, Keyserling HL, et al. Safety and immunogenicity of heptavalent pneumococcal vaccine conjugated to CRM 197 in United States infants. Pediatrics 101:604, 1998.

917. Restrepo MA, Zambrano F II. Late onset aplastic anemia secondary to chloramphenicol. Report of ten cases. Antioquia Medica 18:593, 1968.

918. Reyes MRT, LeBlanc EM, Bassila MK. Hearing loss and otitis media in velo-cardio-facial syndrome. Int J Pediatr Otorhinolaryngol 47:227, 1999.

919. Rhee C, Jeong P, Kim Y, et al. Effect of platelet-activating factor on the mucociliary function of the eustachian tube in guinea pigs. In Lim DJ, Bluestone CD, Casselbrant ML, et al (eds). Recent Advances in Otitis Media—Proceedings of the Sixth International Symposium. Hamilton, Ontario, B.C. Decker, 1996, pp 97–100.

920. Rich AR. A physiological study of the eustachian tube and its related muscles. Bull Johns Hopkins Hosp 31:3005, 1920.

921. Richardson JR. Observations in acute otitis meda. Ann Otol Rhinol Laryngol 51:804, 1942.

922. Riding KH, Bluestone CD, Michaels RH, et al. Microbiology of recurrent and chronic otitis media with effusion. J Pediatr 93:739, 1978.

923. Rifkind DR, Chanock RM, Kravetz H, et al. Ear involvement (myringitis) and primary atypical pneumonia following inoculation of volunteers with Eaton agent. Am Rev Respir Dis 85:479, 1962.

924. Riley DN, Herberger S, McBride G, Law K. Myringotomy and ventilation tube insertion: a ten-year follow-up. J Laryngol Otol 111:257, 1997.

925. Rinkel HJ. The management of clinical allergy: parts I, II, III, and IV. Arch Otolaryngol 76:491, 1962; 77:42, 1963; 77:205, 1963; 77:302, 1963.

926. Roark R, Berman S. Continuous twice daily or once daily amoxicillin prophylaxis compared with placebo for children with recurrent acute otitis media. Pediatr Infect Dis J 16:376, 1997.

927. Roberts DB. The etiology of bullous myringitis and the role of mycoplasmas in ear disease: a review. Pediatrics 65:761, 1980.

928. Roberts KB, Borzy MS. Fever in the first eight weeks of life. Johns Hopkins Med J 11:9, 1977.

929. Robinson JM, Nicholas HO. Catarrhal otitis media with effusion: a disease of a retropharyngeal and lymphatic system. South Med J 44:777, 1951.

930. Rockley TJ, Hawke WM. The middle ear as a baroreceptor. Acta Otolaryngol (Stockh) 112:816, 1992.

931. Roddey OF Jr, Earle R Jr, Haggerty R. Myringotomy in acute otitis media: a controlled study. JAMA 197:849, 1966.

932. Rogers RL, Kirchner FR, Proud GO. The evaluation of eustachian tubal function by fluorescent dye studies. Laryngoscope 72:456, 1962.

933. Rood SR, Doyle WJ. Morphology of tensor veli palatini, tensor tympani, and dilator tubae muscles. Ann Otol Rhinol Laryngol 87:202, 1978.

934. Rood SR, Doyle WJ. The nasopharyngeal orifice of the auditory tube: implications for tubal dynamics anatomy. Cleft Palate J 19:119, 1982.

935. Rood SR. Morphology of M. tensor veli palatini in the five-month human fetus. Am J Anat 138:191, 1973.

936. Rosen C, Christensen P, Hovelius B, et al. Effect of pneumococcal vaccination on upper respiratory tract infections in children: design of a follow-up study. Scand J Infect Dis 39(Suppl):3944, 1983.

937. Rosen IA, Hakansson A, Aniansson G, et al. Antibodies to pneumococcal polysaccharides in human milk: lack of relationship to colonization and acute otitis media. Pediatr Infect Dis J 15:498, 1995.

938. Rosen LM. The morphology of the salpingopharyngeus muscle. Master's thesis, University of Pittsburgh, 1970.

939. Rosenfeld RM, Bhaya MH, Bower CM, et al. Impact of tympanostomy tubes on child quality of life. Arch Otolaryngol Head Neck Surg 126:585, 2000.

940. Rosenfeld RM, Bluestone CD (eds). Evidence-Based Otitis Media. Hamilton, Ontario, B. C. Decker, 1999.

941. Rosenfeld RM, Goldsmith AJ, Madell JR. How accurate is parent rating of hearing for children with otitis media? Arch Otolaryngol Head Neck Surg 124:989, 1998.

942. Rosenfeld RM, Mandel EM, Bluestone CD. Systemic steroids for otitis media with effusion in children. Arch Otolaryngol Head Neck Surg 117:984, 1991.

943. Rosenfeld RM, Post JC. Meta-analysis of antibiotics for the treatment of otitis media with effusion. Otolaryngol Head Neck Surg 106:378, 1992.

943a. Rosenfeld RM. Natural history of untreated otitis media. In Rosenfeld RM, Bluestone CD (eds). Evidence-Based Otitis Media. Hamilton, Ontario, B.C. Decker, 1999, pp 157–177.

944. Ross M. Functional anatomy of the tensor palatini: its relevance in cleft palate surgery. Arch Otolaryngol 93:1, 1971.

945. Roth RP, Cantekin EI, Bluestone DC, et al. Nasal decongestant activity of pseudoephedrine. Ann Otol Rhinol Laryngol 86:235, 1977.

946. Roydhouse N. A controlled study of adenotonsillectomy. Arch Otolaryngol Head Neck Surg 92:611, 1970.

947. Roydhouse N. Adenoidectomy for otitis media with effusion. Ann Otol Rhinol Laryngol 89(Suppl 68):312, 1980.

948. Ruben RJ. Efficacy of ofloxacin and other otic preparations for otitis externa. Pediatr Infect Dis J 20:108, 2001.

949. Ruben RJ, Math R. Serous otitis media associated with sensorineural hearing loss in children. Laryngoscope 88:1139, 1978.

950. Rubenstein MM, McBean JB, Hedgecock LD, et al. The treatment of acute otitis media in children: III. A third clinical trial. Am J Dis Child 109:308, 1965.

951. Rubin M. Serous otitis media in severely to profoundly hearing impaired children, ages 0 to 6. Volta Rev 80:81, 1978.

952. Rudberg RD. Acute otitis media: comparative therapeutic results of sulfonamide and penicillin administered in various forms. Acta Otolaryngol (Stockh) 113:1, 1954.

953. Rudin R, Welin L, Svardsudd K, Tibblin G. Middle ear disease in samples from the general population. II. History of otitis and otorrhea in relation to tympanic membrane pathology, the study of men born in 1913 and 1923. Acta Otolaryngol (Stockh) 99:53, 1985.

954. Ruff ME, Schotik DA, Bass JW, et al. Antimicrobial drug suspensions: a blind comparison of taste of fourteen common pediatric drugs. Pediatr Infect Dis J 10:30, 1991.

955. Rushton HC, Tong MC, Yue V, et al. Prevalence of otitis media with effusion in multicultural schools in Hong Kong. J Laryngol Otol 111:804, 1997.

956. Ruuskanen O, Arola M, Heikkinen T, Ziegler T. Viruses in acute otitis media: increasing evidence for clinical significance. Pediatr Infect Dis J 10:425, 1991.

957. Saah AJ, Blackwelder WC, Kaslow RA. Commentary: Treatment of acute otitis media. JAMA 248:1071, 1982.

958. Saarinen UM. Prolonged breast feeding as prophylaxis for recurrent otitis media. Acta Pediatr Scand 71:567, 1982.

959. Sadé J, Halevy A, Klajman A, Mualem T. Cholesterol granuloma. Acta Otolaryngol (Stockh) 89:233, 1980.

960. Sadé J, Luntz M. Eustachian tube lumen: a comparison between normal and inflamed specimens. Ann Otol Rhinol Laryngol 98:630, 1989.

961. Sadé J. Pathology and pathogenesis of serous otitis media. Arch Otolaryngol Head Neck Surg 84:297, 1966.

962. Sade J. The buffering effect of middle ear negative pressure by retraction of the pars tensa. Am J Otol 21:20, 2000.

963. Sadé J. Treatment of cholesteatoma and retraction pockets. Eur Arch Otorhinolaryngol 250:193, 1993.

964. Sadler-Kimes D, Siegel MI, Todhunter JS. Age-related morpho-

logical differences in the components of the eustachian tube-middle-ear system. Ann Otol Rhinol Laryngol 98:854, 1989.

965. Saez-Llorens X, McCracken GH III. Clinicial pharmacology of antimicrobial agents. In Remington JD, Klein JO (eds). Infectious Diseases of the Fetus and Newborn Infant, 5th ed. Philadelphia, WB Saunders, 2001, pp 1419–1467.

966. Saez-Llorens X, McCracken GH Jr. Sepsis syndrome and septic shock in pediatrics: current concepts of terminology, pathophysiology, and management. J Pediatr 123:497, 1993.

967. Sakakihara J, Honjo I, Fujita A, et al. Compliance of the patulous eustachian tube. Ann Otol Rhinol Laryngol 102:110, 1993.

968. Sakakura K, Hamaguchi Y, Harada T. Endotoxin and lysosomal protease activity in acute and chronic otitis media with effusion. Ann Otol Rhinol Laryngol 99:379, 1990.

969. Salazar JC, Daly KA, Giebink GS, et al. Low cord blood pneumococcal immunoglobulin G (IgG) antibodies predict early onset acute otitis media in infancy. Am J Epidemiol 145:1048, 1997.

970. Salonen R, Sarkkinen H, Ruuskanen O. Presence of interferon in middle ear fluid during acute otitis media. J Infect Dis 19:480, 1984.

971. Sando I, Takahashi H, Aoki H, Matsune S. Mucosal folds in human eustachian tube: a hypothesis regarding functional localization in the tube. Ann Otol Rhinol Laryngol 102:47, 1993.

972. Sanyal MA, Henderson FW, Stempel EC, et al. Effect of upper respiratory tract infection on eustachian tube ventilatory function in the preschool child. J Pediatr 97:11, 1980.

973. Sarkkinen H, Meurman O, Puhakka H, et al. Failure to detect viral antigens in the middle ear secretions of patients with secretory otitis media. Acta Otolaryngol (Stockh) 386:106, 1982.

974. Sataloff J, Fraser M. Hearing loss in children with cleft palates. Arch Otolaryngol Head Neck Surg 55:61, 1952.

975. Savic D, Djeric D. Anatomical variations and relations of the bony portion of the eustachian tube. Acta Otolaryngol (Stockh) 99:551, 1985.

976. Sawyer CE, Evans RL, Boline PD, et al. A feasibility study of chiropractic spinal manipulation versus sham spinal manipulation for chronic otitis media with effusion in children. J Manipulative Physiol Therapeutics 22:292, 1999.

977. Schachter J, Grossman M, Holt J, et al. Prospective study of chlamydial infection in neonates. Lancet 2:377, 1979.

978. Schaefer O. Otitis media and bottle-feeding: an epidemiological study of infant feeding habits and incidence of recurrent and chronic middle ear disease in Canadian Eskimos. Can J Public Health 62:478, 1971.

979. Schappert SM. Office visits for otitis media, United States 1975–90. From Vital and Health Statistics of the Centers for Disease Control/National Center for Health Statistics 214:1, 1992.

980. Schlesinger PC. The significance of fever in infants less than three months old: a retrospective review of one year's experience at Boston City Hospital's pediatric walk-in clinic. Thesis submitted to the Yale University School of Medicine, 1982.

981. Schneider ML. Bacteriology of otorrhea from tympanostomy tubes. Arch Otolaryngol Head Neck Surg 115:1225, 1989.

982. Schuknecht HF. Pathology of the Ear, 2nd ed. Philadelphia, Lea & Febiger, 1993, pp 191–234.

982a. Schuknecht HF. Pathology of the Ear. Cambridge, MA, Harvard University Press, 1974.

983. Schutzman SA, Petrycki S, Fleisher GR. Bacteremia with otitis media. Pediatrics 87:48, 1991.

984. Schwartz DM, Schwartz RH. Acoustic impedance and otoscopic findings in young children with Down's syndrome. Arch Otolaryngol Head Neck Surg 104:652, 1978.

985. Schwartz DM, Schwartz RH, Redfield NP. Treatment of negative middle ear pressure and serous otitis media with Politzer's technique: an old procedure revised. Arch Otolaryngol Head Neck Surg 104:487, 1978.

986. Schwartz LE, Brown RB. Purulent otitis media in adults. Arch Intern Med 152:2301, 1992.

987. Schwartz RH, Puglese J, Schwartz DM. Use of a short course of prednisone for treating middle ear effusion: a double-blind crossover study. Ann Otol Rhinol Laryngol 89(Suppl 68):296, 1980.

988. Schwartz RH, Rodriguez WJ. Acute otitis media in children eight years old and older: a reappraisal of the role of Haemophilus influenzae. Am J Otolaryngol 2:19, 1981.

989. Schwartz RH, Rodriguez WJ, Khan WN, et al. Acute purulent

otitis media in children older than five years: incidence of Haemophilus as a causative organism. JAMA 238:1032, 1977.

990. Schwartz RH, Rodriguez WJ, Khan WN, Ross S. Acute purulent otitis media in children older than five years: incidence of Haemophilus as a causative organism. JAMA 238:1032, 1977.

990a. Schwartz RH, Rodriguez WJ, Mann R, et al. The nasopharyngeal culture in acute otitis media: a reappraisal of its usefulness. JAMA 241:2170, 1979.

991. Schwartz RH, Rodriguez WG, Schwartz DM. Office myringotomy for acute otitis media: its value in preventing middle ear effusion. Laryngoscope 91:616, 1981.

992. Schwartz RH, Schwartz DM. Acute otitis media: diagnosis and drug therapy. Drugs 19:107, 1980.

992a. Schwartz RH, Stool SE, Rodriguez WJ, et al. Acute otitis media: toward a more precise diagnosis. Clin Pediatr 20:549, 1982.

993. Schwartz RH, Wientzen RL. Occult bacteremia in toxic-appearing febrile infants. Clin Pediatr 21:659, 1982.

994. Scott BA, Strunk CL Jr. Post-tympanostomy otorrhea: a randomized clinical trial of topical prophylaxis. Otolaryngol Head Neck Surg 106:34, 1992.

995. Scott JL, Finegold SM, Belkin GA, et al. A controlled double-blind study of the hematologic toxicity of chloramphenicol. N Engl J Med 272:1137, 1965.

996. Seikel K, Shelton S, McCracken GH Jr. Middle ear fluid concentrations of amoxicillin after large dosages in children with acute otitis media. Pediatr Infect Dis J 16:710, 1997.

997. Sellars SL, Seid AB. Aural tuberculosis in childhood. S Afr Med J 47:216, 1973.

998. Senturia BH, Bluestone CD, Klein JO, et al. Report of the ad hoc committee on definition and classification of otitis media with effusion. Ann Otol Rhinol Laryngol 89:3, 1980.

999. Senturia BH, Gessert CF, Carr CD, Bauman ES. Studies concerned with tubotympanitis. Ann Otol Rhinol Laryngol 67:440, 1958.

1000. Severeid L. A longitudinal study of the efficacy of adenoidectomy in children with cleft palate and secondary otitis media. Trans Am Acad Ophthalmol Otolaryngol 876:13194, 1972.

1001. Severeid LR. Development of cholesteatoma in children with cleft palate: a longitudinal study. In McCabe BF, Sade J, Abramson M (eds). Cholesteatoma: First International Conference. Birmingham, Alabama, Aesculapius Publishing, 1977, pp 287–292.

1002. Shah KN, Desai MP. Ascaris lumbricoides from the right ear. Indian Pediatr 6:92, 1969.

1003. Shah N. Use of grommets in "glue" ears. J Laryngol Otol 85:283, 1971.

1004. Shahid NS, Steinhoff MC, Hoque SS, et al. Serum, breast milk, and antibody after maternal immunization with pneumococcal vaccine. Lancet 346:1252, 1995.

1005. Shapiro ED, Austrian R. Bacteremic pneumococcal infections in Connecticut children from 1984–92. Pediatr Res 33:182A, 1993.

1006. Shapiro GG, Bierman CW, Furukawa CT, et al. Treatment of persistent eustachian tube dysfunction in children with aerosolized nasal dexamethasone phosphate versus placebo. Ann Allergy 49:81, 1982.

1007. Shapiro NM, Schaitken BM, May M. Facial paralysis in children. In Bluestone CD, Stool SE, Kenna MA (eds). Pediatric Otolaryngology, 3rd ed. Philadelphia, W.B. Saunders, 1996, pp 325–326.

1008. Shea JJ. Autoinflation treatment of serous otitis media in children. J Laryngol Otol 85:1254, 1971.

1009. Shibahara Y, Sando I. Histopathologic study of eustachian tube in cleft palate patients. Ann Otol Rhinol Laryngol 97:403, 1988.

1010. Shigemi H, Kurono Y, Egashira T, Mogi G. Role of superoxide dismutase in otitis media with effusion. Ann Otol Rhinol Laryngol 107:327, 1998.

1011. Shigemi H, Kurono Y, Shimamura K, Mogi G. Role of secretory immunoglobulin A in nasopharyngeal bacterial adherence. In Lim DJ, Bluestone CD, Klein JO, et al (eds). Recent Advances in Otitis Media. Proceedings of the Fifth International Symposium. Burlington, Ontario, B. C. Decker, 1993, pp 182–184.

1012. Shikowitz MJ, Ilardi CF, Gero M. Immotile cilia syndrome associated with otitis media with effusion: a case report. In Lim DJ, Bluestone CD, Klein JO, Nelson JD (eds). Recent Advances in Otitis Media—Proceedings of the Fourth International Symposium. Philadelphia, B.C. Decker, 1988, pp 304–307.

1013. Shupak A, Seroky JT, Tabari R, et al. Effects of middle-ear oxygen and carbon dioxide tensions on eustachian tube ventilatory function. In Lim DJ, Bluestone CD, Casselbrant ML (eds). Recent Advances in Otitis Media—Proceedings of the Sixth International Symposium. Hamilton, Ontario, B.C. Decker, 1996, pp 109–111.

1014. Shurin PA, Howie VM, Pelton SI, et al. Bacterial etiology of otitis media during the first six weeks of life. J Pediatr 92:893, 1978.

1015. Shurin PA, Marchant CD, Kim CH, et al. Emergence of beta-lactamase-producing strains of Branhamella catarrhalis as important agents of acute otitis media. Pediatr Infect Dis J 2:34, 1983.

1016. Shurin PA, Pelton SI, Klein JO. Otitis media in the newborn infant. Ann Otol Rhinol Laryngol 85:216, 1976.

1017. Shurin PA, Pelton SI, Tager IB, Kasper DL. Bactericidal antibody and susceptibility to otitis media caused by nontypable strains of Haemophilus influenzae. J Pediatr 97:364, 1980.

1018. Shurin PA, Rehmus JM, Johnson CE, et al. Bacterial polysaccharide immune globulin for prophylaxis of acute otitis media in high-risk children. J Pediatr 123:801, 1993.

1019. Shyu WC, Haddad J, Reilly J, et al. Penetration of cefprozil into middle ear fluid of patients with otitis media. Antimicrobial Agents Chemotherapy 38:2210, 1994.

1020. Siedentop KH. Eustachian tube dynamics, size of the mastoid air cell system, and results with tympanoplasty. Otolaryngol Clin North Am 5:33, 1972.

1021. Siegel G, Brodsky L, Waner M, Shaha S. Office-based laser assisted tympanic membrane fenestration in adults and children: pilot data to support an alternative to traditional approaches to otitis media. Int J Pediatr Otorhinolaryngol 53:111, 2000.

1022. Siegel MI, Cantekin EI, Todhunter JS, Sadler-Kimes D. Aspect ratio as a descriptor of eustachian tube cartilage shape. Ann Otol Rhinol Laryngol 97(Suppl 133):16, 1988.

1023. Siegel MI, Sadler-Kimes D, Todhunter JS. ET cartilage shape as a factor in the epidemiology of otitis media. In Lim DJ, Bluestone CD, Klein JO, Nelson JD (eds). Recent Advances in Otitis Media—Proceedings of the Fourth International Symposium. Burlington, Ontario, B.C. Decker, 1988, pp 114–117.

1024. Siegel SC. Allergy as it relates to otitis media. In Wiet RJ, Coulthard SW (eds). Proceedings of the Second National Conference on Otitis Media. Columbus, Ohio, Ross Laboratories, 1979, pp 25–29.

1025. Siirala U, Lahikainen EA. Some observations on the bacteriostatic effect of the exudate in otitis media. Acta Otolaryngol (Stockh) 100:20, 1952.

1026. Siirala U, Vuori M. The problem of sterile otitis media. Pract Otorhinolaryngol 19:159, 1956.

1027. Silverstein H, Bernstein JM, Lerner PI. Antibiotic concentrations in middle ear effusion. Pediatrics 38:33, 1966.

1028. Simkins C. Functional anatomy of the eustachian tube. Arch Otolaryngol 38:476, 1943.

1029. Simoes EA, Groothuis JR, Tristram DA, et al. Respiratory syncytial virus-enriched globulin for the prevention of acute otitis media in high risk children. J Pediatr 129:214, 1996.

1030. Simoes EAF, Sondheimer HM, Top FH Jr, et al. Respiratory syncytial virus immune globulin for prophylaxis against respiratory syncytial virus disease in infants and children with congenital heart disease. J Pediatr 133:492, 1998.

1031. Sipila P, Karma P. Inflammatory cells in mucoid effusion of secretory otitis media. Acta Otolaryngol (Stockh) 94:467, 1982.

1032. Sirakova T, Kolattukudy D, Murwin J, et al. Role of fimbriae expressed by nontypeable Haemophilus influenzae in pathogenesis of and protection against otitis media and relatedness of the fimbria subunit to outer membrane protein A. Infect Immun 62:2002, 1994.

1033. Skolnik PR, Nadol JB Jr, Baker AS. Tuberculosis of the middle ear: review of the literature with an instructive case report. Rev Infect Dis 8:403, 1986.

1034. Skolnick EM. Otologic evaluation in cleft palate patients. Laryngoscope 68:1908, 1958.

1035. Skoner DP, Doyle WJ, Chamovitz AH, Fireman P. Eustachian tube obstruction after intranasal challenge with house dust mite. Arch Otolaryngol 112:840, 1986.

1036. Skoner DP, Doyle WJ, Fireman P. Eustachian tube obstruction (ETO) after histamine nasal provocation: a double-blind dose-response study. J Allergy Clin Immunol 79:27, 1987.

1037. Skoner DP, Lee L, Doyle WJ, et al. Nasal physiology and inflammatory mediators during natural pollen exposure. Ann Allergy 65:206, 1990.

1038. Sloas MM, Barrett FF, Chesney PJ, et al. Cephalosporin treatment failure in penicillin- and cephalosporin-resistant Streptococcus pneumoniae meningitis. Pediatr Infect Dis J 11:662, 1992.

1039. Sloyer JL Jr, Cate CD, Howie VM, et al. The immune response to acute otitis media in children. II. Serum and middle ear antibody in otitis media due to Haemophilus influenzae. J Infect Dis 132:685, 1975.

1040. Sloyer JL, Howie VM, Ploussard JH, et al. Immune response to acute otitis media: association between middle ear antibody and the clearing of clinical infection. J Clin Microbiol 4:306, 1976.

1041. Sloyer JL Jr, Howie VM, Ploussard JH, et al. Immune response to acute otitis media in children. III. Implications of viral antibody in middle ear fluid. J Immunol 118:248, 1977.

1042. Sloyer JL Jr, Howie VM, Ploussard JH, et al. Immune response to acute otitis media in children. I. Serotypes isolated in serum and middle ear fluid antibody in pneumococcal otitis media. Infect Immun 9:1028, 1974.

1043. Sloyer JL Jr, Ploussard JH, Howie VM. Efficacy of pneumococcal polysaccharide vaccine in preventing acute otitis media in infants in Huntsville, Alabama. Rev Infect Dis 3:S119, 1981.

1044. Sly RM, Zambie MF, Fernandes DA, Fraser M. Tympanometry in kindergarten children. Ann Allergy 44:1, 1980.

1045. Smith H, Aronson SS. Organizational approach to medication administration in day care. Rev Infect Dis 8:657, 1986.

1046. Sobeslavsky O, Syrucek L, Bruckoya M, Abrahamovic M. The etiological role of Mycoplasma pneumoniae in otitis media in children. Pediatrics 35:652, 1965.

1047. Solomon NE, Harris LJ. Otitis Media in Children. Assessing the Quality of Medical Care Using Short-Term Outcome Measures. Quality of Medical Care Assessment Using Outcome Measures: Eight Disease-Specific Applications. Santa Monica, CA, Rand Corp, 1976.

1048. Son DH, Son NT, Tri L, et al. Point prevalence of secretory otitis media in children in southern Vietnam. Ann Otol Rhinol Laryngol 107:406, 1998.

1049. Sorenson H. Antibiotics in suppurative otitis media. Otolaryngol Clin North Am 10:45, 1977.

1050. Sorensen RU, Leiva LE, Giangrosso PA, et al. Response to a heptavalent conjugate Streptococcus pneumoniae vaccine in children with recurrent infections who are unresponsive to the polysaccharide vaccine. Pediatr Infect Dis J 17:685, 1998.

1051. Spika JS, Facklam RR, Plikaytis BD, et al. Antimicrobial resistance of Streptococcus pneumoniae in the United States, 1979–1987. J Infect Dis 163:1273, 1991.

1052. Spilberg W. Visualization of the eustachian tube by roentgen ray. Arch Otolaryngol 5:334, 1927.

1053. Spingarn AT, Isaacs RS, Levenson MJ. Complications of acute streptococcal otitis media: a resurgence. Otolaryngol Head Neck Surg 111:644, 1994.

1054. Spivey GH, Hirschhorn N. A migrant study of adopted Apache children. Johns Hopkins Med J 140:43, 1977.

1055. St. Geme JW III, Falkow S, Barenkamp SJ. High-molecular weight proteins of nontypeable Haemophilus influenzae mediate attachment to human epithelial cells. Proc Natl Acad Science U S A 90:2875, 1993.

1056. St. Geme J III, Takala A, Esko E, Falkow S. Evidence for capsule gene sequences from pharyngeal isolates of nontypeable Haemophilus influenzae. J Infect Dis 169:337, 1994.

1057. Stangerup SE, Sederberg-Olsen J, Balle V. Autoinflation as a treatment of secretory otitis media. Arch Otolaryngol Head Neck Surg 118:149, 1992.

1058. Stanievich JF, Bluestone CD, Lima JA, et al. Microbiology of chronic and recurrent otitis media with effusion in young infants. Int J Pediatr Otorhinolaryngol 3:137, 1981.

1059. Steele RW, Thomas MP, Begue RE. Compliance issues related to the selection of antibiotic suspensions for children. Pediatr Infect Dis J 20:1, 2001.

1060. Steele RW, Thomas MP, Begue RE, Despinasse BP. Selection of pediatric antibiotic suspensions: taste and cost factors. Infect Medicine 16:197, 1999.

1061. Stenfors LE, Hellstrom S, Albiin N. Middle-ear clearance in eustachian tube function: physiology and role in otitis media. Ann Otol Rhinol Laryngol 94:30, 1985.

1062. Stenfors L-E, Raisanen S. Abundant attachment of bacteria to nasopharyngeal epithelium in otitis-prone children. J Infect Dis 165:1148, 1992.

1063. Stenstrom C, Bylander-Groth A, Ingvarsson L. Eustachian tube function in otitis-prone and healthy children. Int J Pediatr Otorhinolaryngol 21:127, 1991.

1064. Stenstrom C, Ingvarsson L. General illness and need of medical care in otitis prone children. Int J Pediatr Otorhinolaryngol 29:23, 1994.

1065. Stenstrom C, Ingvarsson L. Otitis-prone children and controls: a study of possible predisposing factors. 2. Physical findings, frequency of illness, allergy, day care and parental smoking. Acta Otolaryngol 117:696, 1997.

1066. Stickler GB, McBean JB. The treatment of acute otitis media in children: a second clinical trial. JAMA 187:85, 1964.

1067. Stickler GB, Rubenstein MM, McBean JB, et al. Treatment of acute otitis media in children: IV. A fourth clinical trial. Am J Dis Child 114:123, 1967.

1068. Stillwagon PK, Doyle WJ, Fireman P. Effect of an antihistamine/decongestant on nasal and eustachian tube function following intranasal pollen challenge. Ann Allergy 58:442, 1987.

1069. Stool SE, Berg AO, Carney CJ, et al. Managing otitis media with effusion in young children. Quick Reference Guide for Clinicians. AHCPR Publication No. 94-0623. Rockville, MD, Agency for Health Care Policy and Research, Public Health Service, U.S. Department of Health and Human Services, July 1994.

1069a. Stool SE, Craig HB, Laird MA. Screening for middle ear disease in a school for the deaf. Ann Otol Rhinol Laryngol 89:172, 1980.

1070. Stool SE, Field MJ. The impact of otitis media. Pediatr Infect Dis J 8:S11, 1989.

1071. Stool SE, Randall P. Unexpected ear disease in infants with cleft palate. Cleft Palate J 4:99, 1967.

1072. Storgaard M, Ostergaard L, Jensen JS, et al. *Chlamydia pneumoniae* in children with otitis media. Clin Infect Dis 25:1090, 1997.

1073. Strachan DP, Jarvis MJ, Feyerabend C. Passive smoking, salivary cotinine concentrations, and middle ear effusion in 7 year old children. Br Med J 298:1549, 1989.

1074. Strangert K. Otitis media in young children in different types of day-care. Scand J Infect Dis 9:119, 1977.

1075. Stroud MH, Spector GJ, Maisel RH. Patulous eustachian tube syndrome: a preliminary report of the use of the tensor veli palatini transposition procedure. Arch Otolaryngol Head Neck Surg 99:419, 1974.

1076. Su C. Microendoscopic findings of the eustachian tube in patients with otitis media. In Lim DJ, Bluestone CD, Casselbrant ML, et al (eds). Recent Advances in Otitis Media—Proceedings of the Sixth International Symposium. Hamilton, Ontario, B.C. Decker, 1996, pp 88–89.

1077. Sudo M, Sando I. Developmental changes in folding of the human eustachian tube. Acta Otolaryngol (Stockh) 116:307, 1996.

1078. Sudo M, Sando I, Ikui A. Narrowest (isthmus) portion of eustachian tube: a computer-aided 3-D reconstruction and measurement study. Ann Otol Rhinol Laryngol 106:583, 1997.

1079. Sudo M, Sando I, Suzuki C. Three-dimensional reconstruction and measurement study of human eustachian tube structures: a hypothesis of eustachian tube function. Ann Otol Rhinol Laryngol 107:547, 1998.

1080. Suehs OW. Secretory otitis media. Laryngoscope 62:998, 1952.

1081. Sugita R, Kawamura S, Ichikawa G, et al. Bacteriology of acute otitis media in Japan and chemotherapy, with special reference to *Haemophilus influenzae*. Int J Pediatr Otorhinolaryngol 6:135, 1983.

1082. Sumaya CV, Ench Y. Epstein-Barr virus infectious mononucleosis in children. I. Clinical and general laboratory findings. Pediatrics 75:1003, 1985.

1083. Sundberg L, Eden T, Ernstson S, et al. Penetration of erythromycin through respiratory mucosa. Acta Otolaryngol (Stockh) 88(Suppl 365):1, 1979.

1084. Sung BS, Chonmaitree T, Broemeling LD, et al. Association of rhinovirus infection with poor bacteriologic outcome of bacterial-viral otitis media. Clin Infect Dis 17:38, 1993.

1085. Supance JS, Bluestone CD. Perilymph fistulas in infants and children. Otolaryngol Head Neck Surg 91:663, 1983.

1086. Suzuki C, Balaban C, Sando I, et al. Postnatal development of eustachian tube: a computer-aided 3-d reconstruction and measurement study. Acta Otolaryngol (Stockh) 118:837, 1998.

1087. Suzuki M, Kerakawauchi H, Kawauchi H, Mogi G. Efficacy of an antiallergic drug on otitis media with effusion in association with allergic rhinitis: an experimental study. Ann Otol Rhinol Laryngol 108:554, 1999.

1088. Suzuki M, Watanabe T, Mogi G. Clinical, bacteriological, and histological study of adenoids in children. Am J Otolaryngol 20:85, 1999.

1089. Swanborg C, Andersson B, Andersson von Rosen I, et al. Bacterial adherence and acute otitis media. In Recent Advances in Otitis Media. Proceedings of the Fifth International Symposium May 20–24, 1991. Fort Lauderdale, Decker Periodicals, 1993, pp 367–373.

1090. Swarts JD, Alper CM, Seroky JT, et al. In vivo observation with magnetic resonance imaging of middle-ear effusion in response to experimental underpressures. Ann Otol Rhinol Laryngol 104:522, 1995.

1091. Swarts JD, Rood SR, Doyle WJ. The fetal development of the auditory tube and paratubal musculature. Cleft Palate J 23:289, 1986.

1092. Swarts JD, Rood SR. Preliminary analysis of the morphometry of the infant eustachian tube. In Lim DJ, Bluestone CD, Klein JO, et al (eds). Recent Advances in Otitis Media—Proceedings of the Fifth International Symposium. Toronto, B.C. Decker, 1993, pp 111–113.

1093. Swarts JD, Rood SR. The morphometry and 3-dimensional structure of the adult eustachian tube: implications for function. Cleft Palate J 27:374, 1990.

1094. Szu SC, Schneerson R, Robbin JB. Rabbit antibodies to the cell wall polysaccharide of *Streptococcus pneumoniae* fail to protect mice from lethal challenge with encapsulated pneumococci. Infect Immun S4:448, 1986.

1095. Takahara T, Sando I, Bluestone CD, et al. Lymphoma invading the anterior eustachian tube: temporal bone histopathology of functional tubal obstruction. Ann Otol Rhinol Laryngol 95:101, 1986.

1096. Takahashi H, Fujita A, Honjo I. Effect of adenoidectomy on otitis media with effusion, tubal function, and sinusitis. Am J Otolaryngol 10:208, 1989.

1097. Takahashi H, Honjo I, Fujita A. Eustachian tube compliance in cleft palate: a preliminary study. Laryngoscope 104:83, 1994.

1098. Takahashi H, Honjo I, Hayashi M, Fujita A. Clearance function of eustachian tube and negative middle-ear pressure. Ann Otol Rhinol Laryngol 101:759, 1992.

1099. Takahashi H, Honjo I, Kurata K, Sugimaru T. Steroid and tube insertion for cholesterol granuloma: a preliminary study. In Lim DJ, Bluestone CD, Casselbrant ML, et al (eds). Recent Advances in Otitis Media: Proceedings of the Sixth International Symposium. Hamiliton, Ontario, B.C. Decker, 1996, pp 414–416.

1100. Takahashi H, Sando I. Histopathology of tubotympanum of children with otitis media treated with ventilation tubes. Ann Otol Rhinol Laryngol 101:841, 1992.

1101. Takasaki K, Sando I, Balaban CD, Ishijima K. Postnatal development of eustachian tube cartilage. A study of normal and cleft palate cases. Int J Pediatr Otorhinolaryngol 52:31, 2000.

1102. Tapianinen T, Kontiokari T, Sammalkivi L, et al. Effect of xylitol on growth of *Streptococcus pneumoniae* in the presence of fructose and sorbital. Antimicrob Agents Chemother 45:166, 2001.

1103. Taylor GD. The bifid uvula. Laryngoscope 82:771, 1972.

1104. Teele DW, Healy GB, Tally FP. Persistent effusions of the middle ear: cultures for anaerobic bacteria. Ann Otol Rhinol Laryngol 89:102, 1980.

1105. Teele DW, Klein JO, and the Greater Boston Collaborative Otitis Media Group: Use of pneumococcal vaccine for prevention of recurrent acute otitis media in infants in Boston. Rev Infect Dis 3(Suppl):S113, 1981.

1106. Teele DW, Klein JO, Rosner BA, and The Greater Boston Otitis Media Study Group: Epidemiology of otitis media during the first seven years of life in children in Greater Boston: a prospective, cohort study. J Infect Dis 160:83, 1989.

1107. Teele DW, Klein JO, Rosner BA. Epidemiology of otitis media in children. Ann Otol Rhinol Laryngol 89:5, 1980.

1108. Teele DW, Klein JO, Rosner B, et al. Middle-ear disease and the practice of pediatrics: burden during the first five years of life. JAMA 249:1026, 1983.

1109. Teele DW, Klein JO, Rosner B. Otitis media with effusion during the first three years of life and development of speech and language. Pediatrics 74:282, 1984.

1110. Teele DW, Marshall R, Klein JO. Unsuspected bacteremia in young children. Pediatr Clin North Am 26:773, 1979.

1111. Teele DW, Pelton SI, Grant MJA, et al. Bacteremia in febrile children under 2 years of age: results of cultures of blood of 600 consecutive febrile children seen in a walk-in clinic. J Pediatr 87:227, 1975.

1112. Teele DW, Pelton SI, Klein JO. Bacteriology of acute otitis media unresponsive to initial antimicrobial therapy. J Pediatr 98:537, 1981.

1113. Tetzlaff TR, Ashworth C, Nelson JD. Otitis media in children less than 12 weeks of age. Pediatrics 59:827, 1977.

1114. The Impact-RSV Study Group. Palivizumab, a humanized respiratory syncytial virus monoclonal antibody, reduces hospitalization from respiratory syncytial virus infection in high-risk infants. Pediatrics 102:531, 1998.

1115. Thompson AC, Crowther JA. Effect of nasal packing on eustachian tube function. J Laryngol Otol 105:539, 1991.

1116. Thompson D, Oster G, McGarry LJ, Klein JO. Management of otitis media among children in a large health insurance plan. Pediatr Infect Dis J 18:239, 1999.

1117. Thomsen J, Sederberg-Olsen J, Balle V, et al. Antibiotic treatment of children with secretory otitis media. Arch Otolaryngol Head Neck Surg 115:447, 1989.

1118. Thorington J. Almost total destruction of the velum palati corrected by an artificial soft palate, producing not only greatly improved speech, but an immediate increase of audition. Med News 61:269, 1892.

1119. Thornsberry C, Brown SD, Yee C, et al. Increasing penicillin resistance in streptococcus pneumoniae in the U.S.: effect on susceptibility to oral cephalosporins. Infect Med 1993, pp 15–24.

1120. Thornsberry C, Ogilvie PT, Holley HP Jr, Sahm DF. Survey of susceptibilities of Streptococcus pneumoniae, Haemophilus influenzae and Moraxella catarrhalis: isolates to 26 antimicrobial agents—a prospective study. Antimicrob Agents Chemother 43:2612, 1999.

1121. Thorroddsen E, Marr C, Efthymiopoulos C, Thorarinsson J. Concentraton of cefuroxime in middle ear effusion of children with acute otitis media. Pediatr Infect Dis J 18:959, 1997.

1122. Tilghman RC, Finland M. Clinical significance of bacteremia in penumococcal pneumonia. Arch Intern Med 59:602, 1937.

1123. Timmermans FJ, Gerson S. Chronic granulomatous otitis media in bottle-fed Inuit children. Can Med Assoc J 122:545, 1980.

1124. Tipple MA, Beem MO, Saxon EM. Clinical characteristics of the afebrile pneumonia associated with Chlamydia trachomatis infection in infants less than six months of age. Pediatrics 63:192, 1979.

1125. Todd GB. Audit of the incidence of persistent perforation of the tympanic membrane following grommet removal or extrusion. J Laryngol Otol 107:593, 1993.

1126. Todd GB. Audit of the incidence of persistent perforation of the tympanic membrane following T-tube removal or extrusion. J Laryngol Otol 107:590, 1993.

1127. Todd JL, Todd NW. Congenital cardiac outflow tract anomalies and otitis media. Int J Pediatr Otorhinolaryngol 16:183, 1988.

1128. Todd JL, Todd NW. Conotruncal cardiac anomalies and otitis media. J Pediatr 131:215, 1997.

1129. Todd NW, Bowman CA. Otitis media at Canyon Day, Arizona. A 16-year follow-up in Apache Indians. Arch Otolaryngol Head Neck Surg 111:606, 1985.

1130. Todd NW. Cranial anatomy and otitis media. Am J Otol 19:558, 1998.

1131. Todd NW, Feldman CM. Allergic airway disease and otitis media in children. Int J Pediatr Otorhinolaryngol 10:27, 1985.

1132. Tos M. A new pathogenesis of mesotympanic (congenital) cholesteatoma. Laryngoscope 110:1890, 2000.

1133. Tos M, Bak-Pedersen K. Goblet cell population in the normal middle ear and eustachian tube of children and adults. Ann Otol Rhinol Laryngol 85(Suppl 25):44, 1976.

1134. Tos M, Bonding P. Middle-ear pressure during and after pro-longed nasotracheal and/or nasogastric intubation. Acta Otolaryngol (Stockh) 83:353, 1977.

1135. Tos M. Growth of the fetal eustachian tube and its dimensions. Arch Klin Exp Ohr Nas Kehlk 198:177, 1971.

1136. Tos M, Poulsen G, Borch J. Tympanometry in two-year-old children. ORL 40:77, 1978.

1137. Tos M, Poulsen G. Secretory otitis media: late results of treatment with grommets. Arch Otolaryngol Head Neck Surg 102:672, 1976.

1138. Tos M, Poulsen G. Tympanometry in two-year-old children: seasonal influence on frequency of secretory otitis and tubal function. ORL 41:1, 1979.

1139. Tos M. Spontaneous improvement of secretory otitis and impedance screening. Arch Otolaryngol Head Neck Surg 106:345, 1980.

1140. Tsui T, Yamaguchi N, Aoki K, et al. Mastoid pneumatization of the patulous eustachian tube. Ann Otol Rhinol Laryngol 109:1028, 2000.

1141. Tully SB, Bar-Haim Y, Bradley RL. Abnormal tympanography after supine bottle feeding. J Pediatr 126:S105, 1995.

1142. Tuomanen EI, Saukkonen K, Sande S, et al. Reduction of inflammation, tissue damage, and mortality in bacterial meningitis in rabbits treated with monoclonal antibodies against adhesion-promoting receptors of leukocytes. J Exp Med 170:959, 1989.

1143. Turner AL, Fraser JS. Tuberculosis of the middle ear cleft in children: a clinical and pathological study. J Laryngol Rhinol Otol 30:209, 1915.

1144. Turner RB, Darden PM. Effect of topical adrenergic decongestants on middle-ear pressure in infants with common colds. Pediatr Infect Dis J 15:621, 1996.

1145. Uhari M, Kontiokari T, Koskela M, Niemela M. Xylitol chewing gum in prevention of acute otitis media: double blind randomized trial. Br Med J 313:1180, 1996.

1146. Uhari M, Kontiokari T, Niemala M. A novel use of xylitol sugar in preventing acute otitis media. Pediatrics 102:879, 1998.

1147. Uhari M, Mantysaari K, Niemela M. A meta-analytic review of the risk factors for acute otitis media. Clin Infect Dis 22:1079, 1996.

1148. Ukkonen P, Varis K, Jernfors M, et al. Treatment of acute otitis media with an antiadhesive oligosaccharide: a randomized, double-blind, placebo-controlled trial. Lancet 356:1398, 2000.

1149. Umetsu DT, Ambrosino DM, Quinti I, et al. Recurrent sinopulmonary infection and impaired antibody response to bacterial capsular polysaccharide antigen in children with selective IgG-subclass deficiency. N Engl J Med 313:1247, 1985.

1150. U.S. Department of Health and Human Services: The health consequences of smoking: a report from the Surgeon General. Department of Health and Human Services publication (DHS)84-50205. Rockville, MD, Office on Smoking and Health, 1984, p 292.

1151. Uzun C, Adali MK, Tas A, et al. Use of the nine-step inflation-deflation test as predictor of middle ear barotrauma in sports scuba divers. Br J Audiol 34:153, 2000.

1152. Valtonen H, Qvarnberg Y, Nuutinen J. Tympanostomy in young children with recurrent otitis media: a long-term follow-up study. J Laryngol Otol 113:207, 1999.

1153. Valsalva A. Tractus de aure humana. In Stevenson RS, Guthrie D (eds). A History of Otolaryngology. Edinburgh, E. and S. Livingstone, 1949.

1154. Van Balen FAM, de Melker RA, Touw-Otten FWMM. Double-blind randomized trial of co-amoxiclav versus placebo for persistent otitis media with effusion in general practice. Lancet 348:713, 1996.

1155. van Buchem FL, Dunk JHM, van't Hof MA. Therapy of acute otitis media: myringotomy, antibiotics, or neither? A double-blind study in children. Lancet 2:883, 1981.

1156. van Buchem FL, Peeters MF, van't Hof MA. Acute otitis media: a new treatment strategy. Br Med J 290:1033, 1985.

1157. Van Dishoeck HAE, Derks ACW, Voorhorst R. Bacteriology and treatment of acute otitis media in children. Acta Otolaryngol (Stockh) 50:250, 1959.

1158. Van Dyck J, Terespolsky S, Meyer CS, et al. Penetration of cefpodoxime into middle ear fluid in pediatric patients with acute otitis media. Pediatr Infect Dis J 16:79, 1997.

1159. Van Hare GF, Shurin PA, Marchant CD, et al. Acute otitis media caused by *Branhamella catarrhalis*: biology and therapy. Rev Infect Dis 9:16, 1987.

1160. Variot G. Ecoulement de lait par l'oreille d'un mourisson atteint de division congenitale du voile du palais. Bull Soc Pediatr Paris 6:387, 1904.

1161. Varsano IB, Volvitz BM, Grossman JE. Effect of naproxen, prostaglandin inhibitor, on acute otitis media and persistence of middle ear effusion in children. Ann Otol Rhinol Laryngol 98:389, 1989.

1162. Vartiainen E. Otitis media with effusion in children with congenital or early-onset hearing impairment. J Otolaryngol 29:221, 2000.

1163. Veltri RW, Sprinkle PM. Serous otitis media: immunoglobulin and lysozyme levels in middle ear fluids and serum. Ann Otol Rhinol Laryngol 82:297, 1973.

1164. Villasenor-Sierra A, Santos JI. Outer membrane protein profiles of paired nasopharyngeal and middle ear isolates of nontypable *Haemophilus influenzae* from Mexican children with acute otitis media. Clin Infect Dis 28:267, 1999.

1165. Vinther B, Elbrond O, Pedersen CB. Otitis media in childhood, socio-medical aspects with special reference to day-care and housing conditions. Acta Otolaryngol (Stockh) 386:121, 1982.

1165a. Vinther B, Elbrond O, Pederson CB. A population study of otitis media in childhood. Acta Otolargyngol (Stockh) 360:135, 1979.

1166. Virolainen A, Jero J, Chattopadhyay P, et al. Comparison of serum antibodies to pneumolysin with those to pneumococcal capsular polysaccharides in children with acute otitis media. Pediatr Infect Dis J 15:128, 1996.

1167. Virolainen A, Jero J, Kayhty H, et al. Nasopharyngeal antibodies to pneumococcal capsular polysaccharides in children with acute otitis media. J Infect dis 172:1115, 1995.

1167a. Virtanen H. Sonotubometry: an acoustical method for objective measurement of auditory tubal opening. Acta Otolaryngol (Stockh) 96:93, 1978.

1168. Virtanen H, Palva T, Jauhiainen T. The prognostic value of eustachian tube function measurements in tympanoplastic surgery. Acta Otolaryngol (Stockh) 90:317, 1980.

1169. Virtanen S, Lahikainen EA. Ampicillin concentrations in middle ear effusions in acute otitis media after administration of bacampicillin. Infection 7:472, 1979.

1170. Waickman FJ. Allergic Management of Otitis Media. Transactions of the Second National Conference on Otitis Media. Columbus, OH, Ross Laboratories, 1979, pp 109–114.

1171. Wake M, McCullough DE, Binnington JD. Effect of nasogastric tubes on eustachian tube function. J Laryngol Otol 104:17, 1990.

1172. Wald ER, Dashefsky B, Byers C, et al. Frequency and severity of infections in day care. J Pediatr 112:540, 1988.

1173. Wald ER, Guerra N, Byers C. Frequency and severity of infections in day care: three-year follow up. J Pediatr 118:509, 1991.

1174. Wallerstein RO, Condit PK, Kasper CK, et al. Statewide study of chloramphenicol therapy and fetal aplastic anemia. JAMA 208:2045, 1969.

1175. Walton WK. Audiometrically normal conductive hearing losses among the cleft palate. Cleft Palate J 10:99, 1973.

1176. Wanner A. Clinical aspects of mucociliary transport. Am Rev Resp Dis 116:73, 1977.

1177. Ward PA, McLean R. Complement activity. In Bellanti JA (ed). Immunology H. Philadelphia, W.B. Saunders, 1978, pp 138–150.

1178. Warren WS, Stool SE. Otitis media in lowbirth-weight infants. J Pediatr 79:740, 1971.

1179. Weber PC, Perez BA, Bluestone CD. Congenital perilymphatic fistula and associated middle-ear abnormalities. Laryngoscope 103:160, 1993.

1180. Weingarten RD, Markiewicz Z, Gilbert DN. Meningitis due to penicillin-resistant *Streptococcus pneumoniae* in adults. Rev Infect Dis 12:118, 1990.

1181. Weiss JC, Melman ST. Cost effectiveness in the choice of antibiotics for the initial treatment of otitis media in children: a decision analysis approach. Pediatr Infect Dis J 7:23, 1988.

1182. Weiss MH, Frost JO. May children with otitis media with effusion safely fly? Clin Pediatrics 26:567, 1987.

1183. Weiss MH, Liberatore LA, Kraus DH, Budnick AS. Otitis media with effusion in head and neck cancer patients. Laryngoscope 104:5, 1994.

1184. Welin S. On the radiologic examination of the eustachian tube in cases of chronic otitis. Acta Radiol (Stockh) 28:95, 1947.

1185. Werkhaven JA, Reinisch L, Sorrell BS, et al. Noninvasive optical diagnosis of bacteria causing otitis media Laryngoscope 104:264, 1994.

1186. Whitcomb NJ. Allergy therapy in serous otitis media associated with allergic rhinitis. Clin Allergy 23:232, 1965.

1187. White B. The Biology of Pneumococcus. The Commonwealth Fund 1938. Cambridge, MA, Harvard University Press, 1979.

1188. White BL, Doyle WJ, Bluestone CD. Eustachian tube function in infants and children with Down's syndrome. In Lim DJ, Bluestone CD, Klein JO, et al (eds). Recent Advances in Otitis Media with Effusion—Proceedings of the Third International Symposium. Philadelphia, B.C. Decker, 1984, pp 62–66.

1189. White P. Effect of exogenous surfactant on eustachian tube function in the rat. Am J Otolaryngol 10:301, 1989.

1190. Wiatrak BJ, Myer CM III, Andrews TM. Complications of adeno-tonsillectomy in children under 3 years of age. Am J Otolaryngol 12:170, 1991.

1191. Wiedermann BL, Schwartz RH. Effect of blood contamination on the interpretation of antibiotic concentrations in middle ear fluid. Pediatr Infect Dis J 11:244, 1992.

1192. Willett DN, Rezaee RP, Billy JM, et al. Relationship of endotoxin to tumor necrosis factor: α and interleukin-1β in children with otitis media with effusion. Ann Otol Rhinol Laryngol 107:28, 1998.

1193. Williams RL, Chalmers TC, Stange KC, et al. Use of antibiotics in preventing recurrent acute otitis media and in treating otitis media with effusion: a meta-analytic attempt to resolve the brouhaha. JAMA 270:1344, 1993.

1194. Wittenborg MH, Neuhauser EB. Simple roentgenographic demonstration of eustachian tubes and abnormalities. Am J Roentgenol Radium Ther Nucl Med 89:1194, 1963.

1195. Wittler RR, Yamada SM, Bass JW, et al. Penicillin tolerance and erythromycin resistance of group A beta-hemolytic streptococci in Hawaii and the Phillippines. Am J Dis Child 144:587, 1990.

1196. Wolff D. The microscopic anatomy of the eustachian tube. Ann Otol Rhinol Laryngol 43:483, 1934.

1197. Wong DT, Ogra PL. Immunology of tonsils and adenoids: an update. Int J Pediatr Otorhinolaryngol 2:181, 1980.

1198. Wright AE, Morgan WP, Colebrook L, Dodgson RW. Observations on prophylactic inoculation against pneumococcus infections, and on the results which have been achieved by it. Lancet 1:87, 1914.

1199. Wright AL, Bauer M, Naylor A, et al. Increasing breastfeeding rates to reduce infant illness at the community level. Pediatrics 101:837, 1998.

1200. Wright ED, Pearl AJ, Manoukian JJ. Laterally hypertropic adenoids as a contributing factor in otitis media. Int J Pediatr Otorhinolaryngol 45:207, 1998.

1201. Wright PF, McConnell KB, Thompson JM, et al. A longitudinal study of the detection of otitis media in the first two years of life. Int J Pediatr Otorhinolaryngol 10:245, 1985.

1202. Wurdemann HV. The influence of the reclining posture in fevers upon the production of otitis media. JAMA 18:77, 1892.

1203. Yagi HIA. The surgical treatment of secretory otitis media in children. J Laryngol Otol 91:267, 1977.

1204. Yamaguchi N, Mizorogi N, Okihisa M, et al. Eustachian tube function and prognosis of otitis media with effusion after removal of ventilatory tube. In Lim DJ, Bluestone CD, Klein JO, et al (eds). Recent Advances in Otitis Media—Proceedings of the Fifth International Symposium. Burlington, Ontario, B.C. Decker, 1993, pp 25–27.

1205. Yamaguchi N, Sando I, Hashida Y, et al. Histologic study of eustachian tube cartilage with and without congenital anomalies: a preliminary study. Ann Otol Rhinol Laryngol 99:984, 1990.

1206. Yamaguchi N, Sando I, Hashida Y, et al. Histopathologic study of otitis media in individuals with head and neck tumors. Ann Otol Rhinol Laryngol 99:827, 1990.

1207. Yamaguchi N, Tsuji T, Moriyama H. Patulous eustachian tube: the types of pharyngeal orifice and etiology. In Lim DJ, Bluestone CD, Casselbrant ML, et al (eds). Recent Advances in Otitis Media—Proceedings of the Sixth International Symposium. Hamilton, Ontario, B.C. Decker, 1996, pp 93–94.

1208. Yamaguchi T, Urasawa T, Kataura A. Secretory immunoglobulin A antibodies to respiratory viruses in middle ear effusion of chronic otitis media with effusion. Ann Otol Rhinol Laryngol 93: 73, 1984.

1209. Yamanaka T, Bernstein JB, Cumella J, et al. Immunologic aspects of otitis media with effusion: characteristics of lymphocyte and macrophage reactivity. J Infect Dis 145:804, 1982.

1210. Yamanaka N, Faden H. Antibody response to outer membrane protein of nontypeable *Haemophilus influenzae* in otitis-prone children. J Pediatr 122:212, 1993.

1211. Yamanaka N, Kobayashi K, Kataura A, et al. Implication of surfactant apoprotein in otitis media with effusion. Ann Otol Rhinol Laryngol 100:835, 1991.

1212. Yamanaka N, Somekawa Y, Suzuki T, et al. Immunologic and cytologic studies in otitis media with effusion. Acta Otolaryngol (Stockh) 104:481, 1987.

1213. Yan S, Huang C. Tumor necrosis factor alpha in middle-ear cholesteatoma and its effect on keratinocytes in vitro. Ann Otol Rhinol Laryngol 100:157, 1991.

1214. Yanta MJ, Brown OE, Fancher JR. Bilateral ear canal stenosis from retained Goode T-tubes. Int J Pediatr Otorhinolaryngol 37: 173, 1996.

1215. Yellon RF, Leonard G, Marucha P, et al. Characterization of cytokines present in middle-ear effusions. Laryngoscope 101:165, 1991.

1216. Yellon RF, Leonard G, Marucha P, et al. Demonstration of interleukin 6 in middle ear effusions. Arch Otolaryngol Head Neck Surg 118:745, 1992.

1217. Yildirim N, Sone M, Mutlu C, et al. Histopathologic features of the temporal bone in patients with cystic fibrosis. Arch Otolaryngol Head Neck Surg 126:75, 2000.

1218. Yoo JK, Seikaly H, Calhoun KH. Extended use of topical nasal decongestants. Laryngoscope 107:40, 1997.

1219. Younis RT, Lazar RH, Long TE. Ventilation tubes and prophylactic antibiotic eardrops. Otolaryngol Head Neck Surg 106:193, 1992.

1220. Zafriri D, Ofek I, Adar R, et al. Inhibitory activity of cranberry juice on adherence of type 1 and type P fimbriated *Escherichia coli* to eucaryotic cells. Antimicrob Agents Chemother 33:92, 1989.

1221. Zahraa J, Johnson D, Lim-Dunham JE, Herold BC. Unusual features of osteoarticular tuberculosis in children. J Pediatr 129: 597, 1996.

1222. Zanga J, Donland MA, Newton J, et al. Administration of medication in school. Pediatrics 74:433, 1984.

1223. Zeisel SA, Roberts JE, Gunn EB, et al. Prospective surveillance for otitis media with effusion among black infants in group child care. J Pediatr 127:875, 1995.

1224. Zeisel SA, Roberts JE, Neebe EC, et al. A longitudinal study of otitis media with effusion among 2 to 5 year old African-American children in child care. Pediatrics 103:15, 1999.

1225. Zinner SH, Young LS, Acar JF, Ortiz-Neu C (eds). New Considerations for Macrolides, Azalides, Streptogramins, and Ketolides. New York, Marcel Dekker, 2000.

1226. Zollner R. Anatomie, Physiologie und Klinik der Ohrtrompete. Berlin, Springer-Verlag, 1942.

1227. Zonis RD. Chronic otitis media in the southwestern American Indian. Arch Otolaryngol Head Neck Surg 88:360, 1968.

1228. Zopf D, Roth S. Oligosaccharide anti-infective agents. Lancet 347: 1017, 1996.

26

Intratemporal Complications and Sequelae of Otitis Media

Charles D. Bluestone, M.D. and Jerome O. Klein, M.D.

Whereas intracranial suppurative complications of otitis media, including meningitis, brain abscess, and lateral sinus thrombosis, are relatively uncommon today, the clinician frequently encounters the intratemporal (extracranial) complications and sequelae—those that occur within the middle-ear cleft and adjacent structures of the temporal bone. Acute mastoid osteitis can also spread into the neck and cause an abscess (Bezold abscess). A new classification of complications and sequelae of otitis media and related conditions has been reported.[57] The intratemporal complications of otitis media are hearing loss; vestibular, balance, and motor dysfunctions; perforation of the tympanic membrane (with and without acute otitis media or chronic suppurative otitis media); mastoiditis; petrositis; labyrinthitis, facial paralysis; and external otitis. The following are the intratemporal sequelae of otitis media: atelectasis of the middle ear; adhesive otitis media; cholesteatoma; cholesterol granuloma; tympanosclerosis; and ossicular discontinuity and fixation (Fig. 26–1). The most frequent complication or sequela of otitis media is hearing loss that accompanies most episodes of otitis media.[64] Studies indicate that children who had recurrent episodes of otitis media or persistent middle-ear effusion perform less well on tests of speech and language than do their disease-free peers. These data suggest that delay or impairment of development may be an important sequela of otitis media. In this chapter, we discuss the epidemiology, pathogenesis, microbiology, and management of intratemporal complications and sequelae of otitis media. Chapter 27 presents similar information for intracranial complications.

In developing countries of the world, the burden of otitis media in infants and children is particularly heavy since many are untreated, leading to chronic perforation of the tympanic membrane and disarticulation of the ossicles and causing permanent conductive hearing loss. Indeed, Berman reviewed reports from developing countries that indicated high rates of tympanic membrane perforation, persistent otorrhea (consistent with chronic suppurative otitis media), and mastoiditis.[41] Hearing loss associated with otitis media is a particular concern in developing countries because of the importance of comprehension of normal speech for illiterate persons. The epidemiology of otitis media leading to permanent perforation of the tympanic membrane and other complications are also discussed in Chapter 25.

Surgery may be indicated for many of the aural and intratemporal complications and sequelae of otitis media, but this chapter emphasizes concepts of surgical management as they relate to infants and children rather than explicitly describing surgical techniques. For details of such surgical techniques, the reader is referred to current texts and atlases.[69, 187, 198, 352]

Hearing Loss

Hearing loss that is persistent or fluctuating is present in most children who have middle-ear effusion; impairment of hearing is the most prevalent complication of otitis media. The conductive hearing impairment associated with effusion within the middle ear can remain stable, fluctuate, or alternate with periods of normal hearing, but sensorineural hearing loss can also be a consequence. Even though the hearing loss is characterized as "mild" and self-limited when otitis media is present, the loss can be substantial in some children, especially when associated with a complication or sequela of otitis media.

Conductive Hearing Loss

Audiograms in children with middle-ear effusion usually reveal a mild to moderate conductive loss in the range of 20 and 30 dB, but hearing range is 0 to 60 dB. With such deficits, the softer speech sounds and voiceless consonants may be missed (Fig. 26–1). The average hearing loss in that study was 27 dB HL at 500, 1000, and 4000 Hz; at 2000 Hz the loss was only 24.5 dB, which probably accounts for a better three-frequency (500, 1000, 2000 dB) pure-tone average than is actually present. Other studies have reported similar losses, although with differing criteria.[15, 234] The hearing loss is influenced by the quantity of fluid in the middle ear; ears with thin fluids are not as impaired as ears with fluids of gluelike consistency.[81, 515] Ears that are partially filled with fluid (identified otoscopically by the presence of bubbles or an air-fluid level) have less hearing impairment than ears

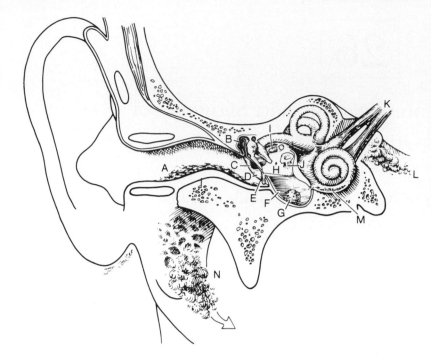

FIGURE 26–1. Intratemporal complications and sequelae of otitis media include (*A*) infectious eczematoid dermatitis, (*B*) cholesteatoma, (*C*) retraction pocket of the tympanic membrane, (*D*) tympanosclerosis, (*E*) perforation of the tympanic membrane, (*F*) chronic suppurative otitis media, (*G*) cholesterol granuloma, (*H*) ossicular discontinuity, (*I*) facial paralysis, (*J*) adhesive otitis media with fixation of the ossicles, (*K*) hearing loss, (*L*) petrositis, (*M*) labyrinthitis, (*N*) mastoiditis with extension into the neck (Bezold abscess).

that are completely filled with fluid.[173] The hearing impairment is usually reversed with resolution of the effusion.[200, 398] On occasion, permanent conductive hearing loss occurs owing to irreversible changes that result from recurrent acute or chronic inflammation (e.g., adhesive otitis media or ossicular discontinuity). High negative pressure in the ear, or *atelectasis*, in the absence of effusion is another cause of conductive hearing loss.[164]

In children with chronic suppurative otitis media, hearing is usually worse than when otitis media with effusion is present. One study from Sierra Leone evaluated the hearing in children who had perforation with and without suppuration. Of the 37 ears that had dry perforations, 33 (89%) had a pure-tone average of 26 dB or greater; of the 100 ears that had chronic suppurative otitis media, 96 (96%) also had this degree of hearing loss.[435]

Sensorineural Hearing Loss

Otitis media and its complications and sequelae can cause sensorineural hearing loss. When a middle-ear effusion is present, a reversible hearing impairment is generally attributed to the effect of increased tension and stiffness of the round window membrane. A permanent sensorineural loss may occur, presumably because of the spread of infection or products of inflammation through the round window membrane,[249, 303, 304, 345, 373, 374, 509] the occurrence of a perilymph fistula in the oval or round window in association with otitis media,[203, 476, 513] or a suppurative complication such as labyrinthitis (see Labyrinthitis). Frequently, sensorineural hearing loss and middle-ear disease coexist. Brookhouser et al[80] evaluated 437 children who had bilateral sensorineural hearing loss and found a sufficient degree of otitis media to warrant tympanostomy tubes in 35%. In Finland, Rahko et al[399] tested 359 children who had a known history of otitis media and found no sensorineural hearing loss. However, Margolis et al[320] reported that extended high-frequency hearing was affected by otitis media, which was not evident when the conventional frequency range was tested.

Chronic suppurative otitis media or cholesteatoma, or both, can be associated with sensorineural hearing loss.[45] Frequently, sensorineural hearing loss and middle-ear dis-

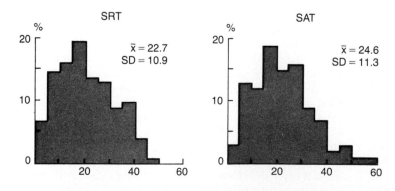

FIGURE 26–2. Frequency distribution of thresholds for speech stimuli associated with otitis media with effusion. *Left,* Speech reception threshold (SRT) of 540 children; *right,* speech awareness threshold (SAT) of 222 infants. x, mean; SD, standard deviation. (From Fria TJ, Cantekin EI, Eichler JA. Hearing acuity of children with otitis media with effusion. Arch Otolaryngol 111:10, 1985. © 1985, American Medical Association.)

ease coexist. As previously mentioned, Brookhouser et al evaluated 437 children with bilateral sensorineural hearing loss and found a sufficient degree of otitis media to warrant tympanostomy tubes in 35%.[80] In Finland, Rahko and co-workers tested 359 individuals who had a known history of otitis media and failed to detect sensorineural hearing loss.[399] However, Mutlu et al reviewed the audiograms of 71 children (119 ears) who had otitis media with effusion and found that 9% had either temporary sensorineural involvement (temporary threshold shift) that improved when the effusion resolved or possibly permanent sensorineural loss, which the authors attributed to the effusion.[350] Also, ultra high-frequency hearing (9000 to 20,000 Hz) can be affected in children with otitis media, which would not be detected in routine audiometric testing[235, 320] and may be important in the long term.[249] It is most likely that otitis media with the presence of bacteria, viruses, inflammatory mediators, enzymes, and possibly even a neurotoxin such as quinolinic acid[528] can affect the inner ear in some children.

Studies of Hearing Loss with Acute Otitis Media

Few studies of hearing have been performed during acute episodes of otitis media.[177] Olmstead et al studied children aged 2½ to 12 years with a diagnosis of acute otitis media who were seen in the outpatient department of St. Christopher's Hospital in Philadelphia.[361] Of 82 children enrolled in the study, 33% had no loss of hearing on the initial audiometric test after acute infection; 40% had loss of hearing (up to 15 dB) initially, which disappeared in 1 to 6 months; 12% had loss of hearing throughout the 6-month period of observation; and 15% had hearing loss initially but were lost to the study between 1 and 4 months after the acute episode of otitis media. The children had no prior history of hearing difficulty or chronic ear infection. Otoscopic examinations were not performed after initial diagnosis, and data concerning duration of fluid in the middle ear were not presented. These data indicate that after a single episode of acute otitis media, many children have prolonged impairment of hearing.

Hearing loss has also been identified in children who have apparently recovered from acute otitis media. A longitudinal study of Alaskan Eskimo children showed a statistically significant association between the frequency of episodes of otitis media and hearing loss of greater than 26 dB. Of children who had one or more attacks of otitis media per year, 49% had hearing loss; hearing loss was evident in 15% of children with no diagnosed episodes of otitis media.[404] Other studies with differing criteria have found the frequency of hearing loss associated with acute otitis media to vary between 6% and 30%.[300, 356]

Studies of Hearing Loss with Otitis Media with Effusion

Conductive hearing loss is a frequent accompaniment of persistent middle-ear effusion (documented at the time of surgery).[52, 274, 515] Fria et al evaluated hearing in 222 infants (aged 7 to 24 months) and 540 older children (aged 2 to 12 years).[173] In both the younger and the older children, average thresholds for speech reception and speech awareness were 24.6 dB and 22.7 dB, respectively (see Fig. 26–2). Not all children with middle-ear effusion have apparent hearing impairment. About one third of the children had air-conduction thresholds of 15 dB, but approximately 25% of children with middle-ear effusion had thresholds of up to 30 dB. The cumulative frequency curves were similar for children of various ages and for duration of effusion. This large study provides a complete picture of the number of children affected and the extent of the hearing loss when middle-ear effusion is present.

Audiometric techniques for children of various ages are discussed in Chapter 11.

Effects of Otitis Media on Development of the Child

Do recurrent episodes of acute otitis media or persistent middle-ear effusions cause any long-term sequelae in children because of impaired hearing? Much has been written about the handicap imposed on the severely hearing-impaired child, but less is known about the effects of the mild and fluctuating hearing loss associated with otitis media on the young child.[160, 270, 335, 336, 382, 524, 534]

The results of many studies of the association of otitis media and development of speech, language, and cognitive abilities have been reviewed by the Agency for Health Care Policy and Research[470] and by Vernon-Feagans.[505] Some studies have identified associations of recurrent otitis media with effusion and lower scores on tests of vocabulary, auditory comprehension, and language skills. Other studies failed to find significant differences among children with and without histories of prolonged middle-ear effusion. The variables in these studies are many: the type of test administered, the socioeconomic class of the parents, the quality and quantity of language in the home and in out-of-home day care, the child's temperament, and the child's and parents' IQ. The variability of the results of these studies suggests that the effects of otitis media may be more substantial in some children than in others. Current studies focus on developing criteria for those children who are most likely to be affected by the hearing loss accompanying otitis media.

It has been established that severe to profound sensorineural hearing loss is associated with impairment of the cognitive, language, and emotional development of children. Compared with peers who have normal hearing, children with sensorineural hearing impairment are significantly retarded in development of vocabulary,[531] are placed below their grade level in school,[273] have poorer articulation and auditory discriminatory abilities,[190] and have a high rate of maladjusted behavior patterns[166] and disturbances in psychosocial adjustment.[384]

The acquisition of language is important even during the first few months of life. The infant is capable of speech sound discrimination as early as age 1 month age. By age 6 weeks, the infant is attracted to human voices more than to environmental sounds and to female more than to male voices. At 5 to 6 months, the infant enters the babble phase and plays with sound making. The child

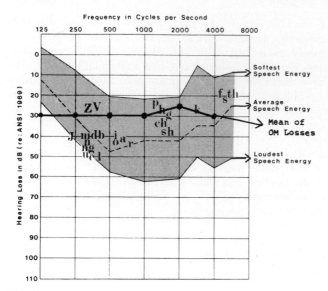

FIGURE 26–3. Range of speech energy related to a standard audiogram. The *shaded area* shows the range of sound energy present in normal speech; the *dashed line* indicates the average of speech energy (adapted from Skinner, 1978). The line connected by *solid circles* shows the mean of hearing losses from otitis media. It can be seen that softer speech sounds may not be heard when otitis media is present.

is putting words together in sentences by 18 months of age, and all the basic syntactic structures that the child will ever use are produced by 4 years.[335]

Since so much progress in language acquisition is made during infancy, any problems in receiving or interpreting sound signals might significantly affect development of speech and language. In particular, softer speech sounds and voiceless consonants may be missed or confused when effusion is present in the middle ear (Fig. 26–3).[138, 139] Important differences have been identified in the early patterns of vocalization of the hearing-impaired infant compared with those of hearing infants. How these data about differences in infant babble relate to ultimate development of speech and language when the hearing impairment is mild and fluctuating is unknown.

The current hypothesis regarding the effects of otitis media on development of the child is presented in Figure 26–4. Children with severe or recurrent otitis media have prolonged episodes of middle-ear effusion. Hearing impairment (average loss, approximately 25 dB) accompanies the effusion in most children. If the hearing impairment occurs at a time of rapid intellectual growth, the result may be impaired development of speech, language, and cognitive abilities.

Studies

The results of more than a dozen studies suggest that children with a history of recurrent episodes of acute otitis media score lower in tests of speech and language than do disease-free peers. A brief résumé of the results of selected studies follows.

One of the earliest and most widely cited studies is

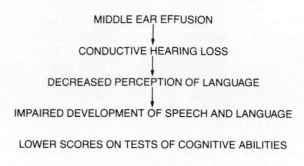

FIGURE 26–4. Long-term sequelae of middle-ear effusion.

that of Holm and Kunze of Seattle.[225] Children aged 5 to 9 years who had a history of chronic otitis media with onset before age 2 years were compared with children in a control group matched for age, sex, and socioeconomic background. Children with a history of ear disease were delayed in all language skills requiring the receiving or processing of auditory stimuli, but responses of the groups were similar in tests measuring visual and motor skills (Fig. 26–5). Diagnosis of otitis media was based on the history. Otoscopic and audiometric examinations were not performed, and the sample size was small (16 children in each group).

Eskimo children were observed prospectively during the first 4 years of life and underwent tests of hearing, intelligence, and assessment of school performance at age 10 years.[257] Children with recurrent episodes of otitis me-

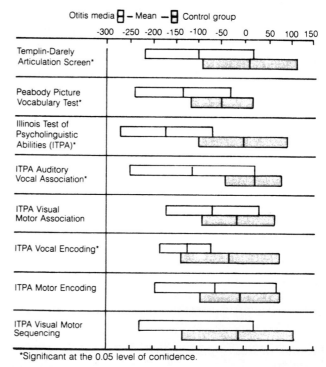

FIGURE 26–5. Results of language tests in children with and without otitis media (standard score mean and standard deviation). (From Holm VA, Kunze LH. Effects of chronic otitis media on language and speech development. Pediatrics 43:833, 1969. Reproduced by permission of Pediatrics, ©1969.)

TABLE 26–1. Otitis Media with Effusion and Scores of Tests of Speech and Language at Age 3 Years: Peabody Picture Vocabulary Test°

Time with Middle-Ear Effusion	All Children	High Socioeconomic Status	Low Socioeconomic Status
<30 days	101.4	104.8	96.6
>130 days	96.4	99.6	92.5
	$p = .002$	$p = .0001$	$p =$ nonsignificant

° Total sample, 190 children; 106, high socioeconomic status; 84, low socioeconomic status.

From Bluestone CD, Klein JO. Otitis Media in Infants and Children. Philadelphia, WB Saunders, 1988.

dia (defined as the presence of a draining ear) during the first 2 years of life and with loss of hearing of 26 dB or more had lower scores in tests of reading, mathematics, and language than did children who had little or no disease in infancy. Otorrhea was the sole criterion for otitis media; data were not available about the presence or duration of middle-ear effusions or episodes of acute otitis media that did not result in otorrhea.

Aboriginal children from Brisbane, Australia, were studied by Lewis.[292] Children aged 7 to 9 years who "failed otoscopic examinations" and had hearing deficits measured by audiometry or tympanometry in a 4-year period were compared with age-matched control children who had consistently passed the audiometric tests and were assumed to be disease-free. Mean scores for speech and language development were significantly lower in children with ear disease than in children without ear disease. The sample size was small (14 children with disease and 18 control subjects).

Needleman evaluated 20 children aged 3 to 8 years with a history of recurrent otitis media and a first episode before age 18 months.[355] Twenty control subjects who had no history of hearing problems or recurrent ear infections were matched with the patients for age, grade, and socioeconomic status. The children were evaluated for their ability to use speech sounds expressively and receptively. Children with a history of ear disease had poorer phonologic abilities than did matched control children. Diagnosis of ear disease was based on history alone.

Sak and Ruben used a sibling control for children with histories of otitis media.[425] Children received tests of speech and language between ages 8 and 11 years. One sibling of each pair had a documented history of persistent otitis media beginning before age 5 years, whereas the other sibling had no middle-ear problem. The children who had otitis media showed a lower verbal IQ, poorer auditory reception, and lower spelling achievement than their matched sibling controls. More of the siblings with otitis media were boys, and more minor abnormalities of the middle ear identified by audiometry or tympanometry were prevalent among the otitis media siblings than among the control siblings. This suggests that deficits were associated with recent, rather than earlier, disease of the middle ear.

Friel-Patti et al examined the association of otitis media early in life with language development at 12, 18, and

24 months.[176] The infants had been selected from intensive care units of low–birth-weight nurseries and were predominantly from low socioeconomic groups. Frequent episodes of otitis media were correlated with a higher prevalence of language delay, but no correlation was found between hearing impairment measured by auditory brain stem response testing and language delay.

To determine the association between time spent with middle-ear effusion and development of speech, language, and cognitive abilities, Teele et al studied 190 white children of varying socioeconomic strata from greater Boston.[481] The children were selected from a cohort of children in five health centers who were observed from birth with regular examinations of the middle ear at each visit to office or clinic, whether for illness or for routine care. The study was prospective, used uniform criteria for diagnosis of acute otitis media and middle-ear effusion, and tested children from all socioeconomic strata.

Tests of speech and language administered at the third birthday included the Peabody Picture Vocabulary Test (a test of both early receptive and expressive language), the Fisher-Logemann and Goldman-Fristoe Tests of Articulation (tests of production of speech sound), and other measurements of complexity of language structure and estimates of intelligibility.

Children who had spent fewer than 30 days with middle-ear effusion during the first 3 years of life were compared with those who had spent 30 to 129 days with middle-ear effusion during the first 3 years of life and with those who had spent 130 or more days with middle-ear effusion from birth to age 3 years. In summary, the results identified lower scores on tests for the total number of children tested, but significant differences were present only in the scores of children from the high socioeconomic group. No significant differences were found for children from low socioeconomic groups (Tables 26–1 and 26–2). The basis for the difference in results for children in lower and upper socioeconomic strata is unclear but might be accounted for by the lower scores of children in the low socioeconomic group. The

TABLE 26–2. Aerobic and Anaerobic Bacterial Isolates from Middle-Ear Aspirates from 61 Ears of 50 Infants and Children Who Had Acute Otitis Media and Developed an Acute Perforation with Otorrhea

Bacteria	Total No. of Isolates	% of Ears
Streptococcus pneumoniae	27	44
Haemophilus influenzae (nontypable)	9	15
Group A β-hemolytic *Streptococcus*	7	11
Moraxella catarrhalis	5	8
Staphylococcus aureus	4	7
Other aerobic bacteria°	5	8
Anaerobic bacteria†	4	6
Total no. organisms	61	

° α-Hemolytic *Streptococcus* (two isolates); *Staphylococcus epidermidis* (two isolates); *Proteus* species (one isolate).

† *Peptostreptococcus* spp. (two isolates); *Proprionibacterium acnes* (two isolates).

Modified from Brook I, Gober AE. Reliability of the microbiology of spontaneously draining acute otitis media in children. Pediatr Infect Dis J 19:571–573, 2000.

tests used may have been insensitive to differences in performance by these children at age 3 years. Increased time with middle-ear effusion during the first year of life was most significantly associated with lower scores in children tested at age 3 years. Confounding variables, such as race and birth order, were either controlled for or excluded.

From the cohort of greater Boston children observed from birth, 196 children were selected for testing within 3 months of their seventh birthday. Time spent with middle-ear effusion during the first 3 years of life and especially during the first year was associated with significantly lower scores in many aspects of cognitive ability, speech, and language at age 7 years. Time spent with middle-ear effusion during the first 3 years of life was also associated with significantly lower scores in mathematics and in reading.[271]

Hubbard et al in Pittsburgh evaluated two matched pairs of children with repaired palatal clefts.[232] The treatment of the children had been equivalent, with the exception that one group had undergone early myringotomy with placement of tympanostomy tubes (mean age, 3 months) and the other group had undergone initial myringotomy later (mean age, 30.8 months) or not at all. Hearing acuity and consonant articulation were significantly less impaired in the group undergoing early myringotomy. Mean verbal performance and full-scale IQs and scores on psychosocial indices were normal in both groups and did not differ significantly between the groups.

Watanabe et al studied total speaking time in infants and children with and without middle-ear effusion.[510] To support the premise that improvements in the child's performance occurred when hearing improved with resolution of middle-ear effusion, the authors developed a technique to identify time of vibration of the vocal cords. Duration of speaking time was measured in children with otitis media with effusion before and after placement of tympanostomy tubes. Preoperative speaking time was found to be 8 minutes and 2 seconds per measured hour when middle-ear effusion was present and 10 minutes per hour when the effusion cleared after placement of tympanostomy tubes. The implications of this innovative study are uncertain but suggest that hearing improvement increases speaking time and causes the child's ordinary behavior to be more animate.

Chase et al studied early development of children with and without experience with otitis media in the first year of life (one episode within 6 months or two episodes in the first year).[106] There were no differences in overall mental and motor development. However, there were clear behavioral differences between 1-year-old children who experienced recurrent otitis media in the first year and those who did not. Children who experienced otitis media were rated as less attentive and less persistent by the examiner during testing and more irregular in their patterns of sleeping, eating, and elimination by their parents. In addition, children who had experienced otitis media were less responsive and less attentive when working with their mothers in a learning situation. These findings suggest that a child who has experienced ear infection and mild hearing loss may show signs of attentional difficulty early in life.

Other studies of otitis media and language performance include:

- A study of Montreal children, aged 3 to 5 years, that identified significant differences among the children with histories of otitis media and matched control subjects[429]
- A study of Danish children aged 3 to 9 years that did not show an effect of otitis media with effusion early in life on reading achievement[298]
- A study by one of the authors that demonstrated a small but significant correlation between flat tympanograms (type B) in first-grade children and silent work reading at the beginning of the second grade[299]
- An evaluation of Apache Indian children aged 6 to 8 years who had contrasting histories of otitis media but no significant difference in language performance[165]
- A retrospective study suggesting that middle-ear disease in school-age children was associated with hyperactivity or inattention, independent of learning ability[5]

Roberts et al examined 61 socioeconomically disadvantaged children during the first years of life and administered standardized tests of intelligence and academic performance at age 3½ to 6 years.[409] These investigators found no relationship between number of days with otitis media and later performance on verbal components of the intelligence tests or later academic achievement. A more recent report by the same team found that among black children, there was no significant relationship between children's early otitis media history or hearing loss and language skills during the preschool year, but the authors did find that children with more frequent otitis media had lower scores on school readiness measures; also, home environment was more strongly related to academic outcomes than otitis media or hearing loss.

The clinical practice guideline for otitis media with effusion in young children[470] also cited studies that identified a significant effect of otitis media with effusion on the development of receptive speech,[199] demonstrated the absence of a significant effect on the development of receptive language,[397, 527] and identified a significant effect on expressive language.[161]

These reports are disturbing, but most have one or more flaws in design: (1) reliance on retrospective history of acute otitis media, (2) uncertain validity of diagnosis of otitis media, (3) lack of information about middle-ear effusion, (4) significant hearing impairment in subjects at the time of tests of speech and language, (5) small numbers of subjects, (6) special populations tested (e.g., Australian aborigines, Alaskan Eskimos, or children with cleft palate), and (7) inadequate criteria for selection of children without disease used for comparison. Hignett summarized the study design issues and evaluated the effectiveness of 10 early studies of otitis media and speech, language, and behavior.[222] The studies of Teele et al[481] and Hubbard et al[232] represent significant advances in study design compared with prior investigations, but each of these studies has been subject to criticism[290, 383] because of perceived limitations and deficiencies. These inadequacies of study design prevent general application of these results to planning care for young children, but they do not prevent concern that many children may suffer from the sequelae of otitis media with persistent middle-ear effusion in infancy.

Paradise et al reported the language, speech sound production, and cognition outcomes related to otitis media in children during their first 3 years of life.[378] This team enrolled 6350 healthy infants by age 2 months and followed them prospectively. From a sample of 241 children, who represented a spectrum of middle-ear effusion, the investigators concluded that either persistent early-life middle-ear effusion actually causes later "small, circumscribed impairments of receptive language and verbal aspects of cognition" in children or other confounding factors were the cause. In a later report from the same group,[379] 429 children with the most persistent middle-ear effusion, of the 6350 initially enrolled, were randomized into two groups: early placement of a tympanostomy tube versus late placement. Formal tests and conversational samples were used to assess development at 3 years of age and suggested that early tympanostomy tube insertion did not benefit developmental outcomes and chronic middle-ear effusion had not adversely affected developmental outcomes. These children are still being followed and will no doubt be reevaluated when they are older.

It is possible that the difference in the duration of middle-ear effusion between early versus late tympanostomy tube placement was not long enough to demonstrate any adverse effect in the trial by Paradise et al.[378] Employing a similar design but a longer duration between early and late tympanostomy tube insertion, Maw et al randomized 182 children who had chronic otitis media with effusion and hearing loss (25 to 70 dB) into 92 subjects assigned to early tympanostomy tube placement versus a group of 90 children who were assigned to watchful waiting for 9 months.[325] Hearing loss, expressive language, and verbal comprehension were assessed at 9 and 18 months. At 9 months, verbal comprehension and expressive language skills in the watchful-waiting group were 3.24 months behind those in the early tube placement group; the watchful-waiting group showed delays with these two measures compared with their age-expected levels. At 18 months, 85% of the watchful-waiting group had received tube placement, at which time the groups did not differ significantly. The investigators concluded that tube placement does benefit verbal comprehension and expressive language, but the timing of the surgery is not critical. These children also underwent measures of behavioral problems, employing the Richman Behavior Checklist: the early surgical group had a significant (17%) reduction in behavioral problems at 9 months compared with the watchful-waiting group; again, both groups were similar at 18 months after tube placement in the watchful-waiting group.[523]

Factors of Importance in Analysis of Studies of Otitis Media and Development of Speech, Language, and Cognitive Abilities

Parents Also Suffer

The working parent who has spent a sleepless night attending a child who is fretful because of ear pain experiences work- and home-related stress. Chase noted that parents of 1-year-old infants who had experienced otitis media were less effective teachers in structured interactive tasks.[106] They were less effective in gaining the child's attention, less able to respond effectively when the child was distracted from the task, and less able to help the child understand and perform the task. The parent must contend with the child's acute pain, persistent irritability and inattentiveness, and the expense and inconvenience of frequent visits to the physician. Although some families can accept and cope with the stress of a child's recurrent illnesses, other families cannot. A constellation of disturbances in psychosocial development may result. Paradise et al noted that stress ratings were highest among those parents whose baseline stress scores were the highest.[380]

Focus groups of parents described chronic middle-ear disease as a condition that affects not only the child who is ill but the entire family. These findings were reported by the Functional Outcomes Project of the American Academy of Pediatrics,[23] whose goals were to assess various aspects of physical, social, and emotional well-being among children with chronic illnesses and their families. Parents reported influence of the disease on the child's behavior, such as aggressiveness, whining, or excessive clinging. Parents worried about the cost of visits to the physician, prescription medication, and tests, and they expressed frustration over the inconsistently effective medications. Siblings often demanded more attention when another was ill, and parents expressed feelings of guilt over spending so much time with one child to the exclusion of siblings. The implications for the practitioner include providing support groups and teaching materials or information sessions for parents and encouraging office-based research in the area of child and family well-being to better understand the family impact of chronic illnesses such as otitis media.

Recurrent and Persistent Otitis Media as a Chronic Disease

The systemic effects of illness, including irritability, malaise, lethargy, and local or generalized pain, may be distracting enough to affect development. These effects of a chronic illness must be distinguished from the specific effects of otitis media (i.e., hearing loss) in the interpretation of the sequelae of the disease. Is the child treated differently by the parents, siblings, peers, or teachers because of the recurrent illnesses? Is the child vulnerable to effects unassociated with the specific morbidity of the disease (kept indoors, away from peers, or out of exercise and athletic programs)?

Critical Ages for Effects of Otitis Media

Otitis media of similar duration may affect children differently at different ages. There may be critical periods of language perception when the child is most vulnerable to mild, fluctuating, or persistent hearing loss. The results of the Boston study suggest that the children were most affected by middle-ear effusion when disease occurred during the first year of life.[481] During early stages of language development, the child learns the sounds of the language; different or changing auditory signals resulting from persistent or fluctuating hearing deficits may impede the child's abilities to form linguistic categories.[40]

Auditory Deprivation

Studies in birds and rodents indicate that deprivation of sound early in life leads to identifiable changes in auditory sectors of the brain. A decrease in the size and the number of neurons in the auditory nuclei of mice occurred when the animals were deprived of auditory stimuli during early development.[514] In normal postnatal development of the mouse, the neurons of the auditory brain stem reach adult size by age 12 days, the time of onset of hearing. Mice that underwent auditory deprivation by experimentally produced conductive hearing loss from 4 to 45 days after birth had auditory brain stem neurons that were significantly smaller than normal. If the mice who underwent induced hearing loss early in life were returned to normal hearing after 45 days, the smaller-than-normal neurons were retained. The size of the neurons was not altered in mice raised in a normal sound environment until 45 days and then deprived of sound until age 90 days.

These data demonstrate a period in the development of mice during which adequate sound stimulation is needed to establish the normal size of neuronal cells in the auditory brain stem. These experimental data in animals raise concerns about irreparable damage from temporary conductive hearing loss in infants. However, Webster points out that the factors in the experimental model differ from the mild to moderate hearing losses of otitis media with effusion in humans; in the experimental model, the conductive loss is approximately 50 dB, greater than the loss in most cases of otitis media with effusion.[514] The loss is persistent rather than fluctuating, and the impairment starts at the inception of hearing in the mouse, whereas inception of sound occurs prenatally in the human. Webster concludes that although the restrictions of the animal model must be kept in mind, "the fact that early auditory restriction has a profound effect on the central nervous system in one mammal must arouse concern about possible related effects in humans."[514]

Unilateral Hearing Loss

Unilateral hearing loss has not been considered a handicap for children. However, data indicate that children with unilateral hearing impairment score less well on auditory, linguistic, and behavioral tests than do children without hearing impairment.[42] Although the children studied had sensorineural hearing deficits, the data suggest that we should no longer consider a unilateral hearing loss benign. Children with unilateral conductive loss may also suffer during critical periods of language perception by confused speech signals.

Effects of Group Day Care

Respiratory infections are readily spread among children in day care, and children in day care are likely to have more episodes of otitis media than children in home care. In relation to development of language, the quantity and quality of the speech sounds around the infants in group care differ from those presented to the child in home care. The factors of increased number of infections and differences in the speech environment in group day care need to be considered in future studies.

Child Behavior and Quality-of-Life Outcomes

Disturbances in children's behavior associated with otitis media have been reported to include restlessness, frequent disobedience, impaired task orientation in the classroom, inattention, short attention span and distractibility, and restricted social interaction. Indeed, the randomized clinical trial conducted by Wilks et al showed a significant reduction in behavioral problems in children who underwent early tympanostomy tube insertion for chronic otitis media with effusion compared with children in whom tympanostomy tubes were inserted approximately 9 months later.[523] Only selected children may be most affected, although this was not specifically addressed in this trial. Paradise et al found that the parent–child stress and behavior problems were highest among children from the most socioeconomically disadvantaged homes.[380] Gray suggested that inconsistencies in the child's ability to hear may have a lasting effect on the child's motivation to achieve and may cause strain in relationships with teachers and parents.[201]

Other Primary Variables that May Relate to Early Childhood Language Development

Future study designs must also consider these additional factors: visual status, physical and motor development, social and emotional development, nutritional status and history of medications, dialect exposure, birth order, and number of siblings.

Test Results and Functional Significance

Do a few percentage points of one or more standard tests of speech, language, or cognitive abilities affect the child's ability to function in the school, play, and home settings? Some investigators question the importance of these statistical differences in terms of child development, but there are reasons for concern. Since the data are expressed here in terms of mean differences, the scores of some children are close to or better than the norm, but others have scores that are much lower. Otitis media is so common in early childhood that even if a small percentage of children are adversely affected in terms of development, the number of children who suffer is large. Of the 4.1 million children born in the United States each year, more than one third will have recurrent episodes of otitis media (three or more) by age 3 years. If only 10% of the children with recurrent episodes are affected adversely, the national impact is greater: more than 100,000 of each year's newborn infants would be involved.

Since the tests measure potential for achievement, it is possible that the loss suffered by children with frequent and recurrent episodes of otitis media accompanied by hearing loss in early infancy is never perceived by parents, teachers, or physicians. These children are not obviously slow or behind peers. The failure of children to reach their potential is a loss for children and families, and because the number of affected children is large each year, this matter is one of national concern.

Summary: Role of Otitis Media in Infant Development

The accumulated results of the various studies of otitis media and development of speech, language, and cognitive abilities suggest that children do suffer long-term effects from otitis media experienced early in life. The clinical practice guideline prepared for the Agency for Health Care Policy and Research concluded that "otitis media with effusion and its related hearing loss have been associated with delayed language development, particularly if the disease is recurrent or of long duration, although available data are insufficient to establish a causal linkage."[470] Some experts are skeptical about available data.[381] In 1982, Ventry concluded that no causal link had been established between early recurrent middle-ear effusion and language delay or learning problems.[504] Rapin noted that no studies published by 1979 "met the standards of rigor needed to provide a definitive answer to this question, although the burden of the evidence is that a persistent and mild hearing loss, especially if present since infancy, probably has a measurably deleterious effect on the language of most, but not all, children."[402] We think that Dr. Rapin's statement is as applicable today as it was in 1979.

The difficulties in study design needed to resolve the issues and to account for many of the variables are formidable. The optimal design needs to include frequent otoscopic observations beginning soon after birth to develop a chronology of the time a child is affected by middle-ear effusion. The intervals between otoscopic examinations need to be short so that persistence or recurrence of middle-ear effusion can be documented. Hearing needs to be assessed when infants have effusion and are free of effusion to measure the duration and severity of hearing deficits. All this needs to be undertaken in the first years of life, when hearing assessments are more difficult and less precise than in the older child. The study needs to be cross-sectional and prospective from birth, and it should be performed by validated otoscopists. Tests of speech, language, and cognitive abilities need to be accurate and standardized for the populations to be tested. The tests should be performed at least annually to define the time of onset or the effect of otitis media on development. The previous discussion identified the other variables that need to be considered, including the quality of parenting, the effect of siblings, and the time spent in group day care. The analyses need to be structured so

that data will be available for selected children within the cohort. The mean and median values may obscure an effect of severe and recurrent acute otitis media and otitis media with effusion for a subset of children in the sample.

A policy statement of the American Academy of Pediatrics expressed concern about the association of disease of the middle ear and development of speech and language. Although recognizing the validity of criticism of published studies, the Committee on Early Childhood, Adoption, and Dependent Care concluded that "there is growing evidence demonstrating a correlation between middle-ear disease with hearing impairment and delays in the development of speech, language, and cognitive skills. When a child has frequently recurring acute otitis media and/or middle-ear effusion persisting for longer than 3 months, hearing should be assessed and the development of communicative skills must be monitored."[15] Until definitive answers are available from studies of appropriate design to evaluate the sequelae of otitis media in early infancy, physicians must decide, for each child under their care, the optimal management of persistent middle-ear effusion. Chapter 25 provides guidelines for such care.

Relevant to these issues of speech, language, and otitis media, the words of the Chilean poet Gabriela Mistral seem appropriate: "Many of the things we need can wait. The child cannot. Right now is the time his bones are being formed, his blood is being made, and his senses are being developed. To him we cannot answer tomorrow. His name is today."

Vestibular, Balance, and Motor Dysfunctions

The most common cause of vestibular disturbance in children is otitis media.[89] Many parents of infants and children report balance problems, such as clumsiness, when a middle-ear effusion is present. We now have evidence from studies of labyrinthine function in children with and without middle-ear effusion to confirm that the vestibular system is adversely affected, and that after tympanostomy tubes are placed, these dysfunctions return to normal.[96, 97, 194] Also, results of motor proficiency tests are abnormal in children when middle-ear effusion is present.[112, 193, 214] Most recently, a study revealed that children with a past history of otitis media, but with no middle-ear effusion at the time of the vestibular testing, also had abnormal function, which indicates some residual effect of otitis media on the labyrinth.[93]

Perforation of the Tympanic Membrane

Tympanic membrane perforations that are secondary to otitis media (and certain related conditions, such as those following extrusion of tympanostomy tubes) can be either *acute* or *chronic*. Otitis media may or may not be present, and when otitis media is present, *otorrhea* may or may not be evident.

The perforation can be classified according to:

Site: pars tensa (anterosuperior, anteroinferior, posterosuperior, or posteroinferior quadrants) or pars flaccida

Extent: limited to one quadrant (<25%); involving two or more quadrants, but not total; or total perforation (all quadrants)

Duration: acute or chronic

A perforation may also be due to a complication of a surgical procedure to manage otitis media, such as myringotomy, tympanostomy tube insertion, or tympanoplasty (i.e., an iatrogenic complication). An acute perforation is most frequently secondary to an episode of acute otitis media; if it persists for more than 3 months, it is considered chronic. The defect may involve almost the entire pars tensa or be so small as to be detectable only when visualized with the otomicroscope or when the immittance testing measures a volume larger than the expected ear canal volume (see Chapter 23). Otitis media (with or without discharge) may be present or absent; when chronic otitis media is present, the condition is called *chronic suppurative otitis media*, which is described in detail in the next discussion. Likewise, a perforation may be associated with some of the other complications and sequelae described in this chapter. In the past, perforations have been classified into *central* and *marginal* types. Regardless of size, if there is a rim of tympanic membrane remaining at all borders, the perforation has been classified as *central*. When any part of the perforation extends to the annulus, it has been called *marginal*.

A defect in the pars flaccida has been commonly called an *attic perforation*. This defect and the so-called marginal perforation of the pars tensa, which usually occurs in the posterosuperior portion, in reality are either a deep retraction pocket or a cholesteatoma, which are described later in this chapter (Fig. 26–6). An *attic perforation* and a *marginal perforation* usually have no continuity between the defect in the membrane and the middle-ear cavity until late in the disease process, when infection erodes the membrane of the pocket or the matrix of the cholesteatoma. Therefore, the terms *marginal perforation* and *attic perforation* are misnomers; they were applied on the basis of observations made before the availability of the otomicroscope, modern middle-ear surgery, advances in temporal bone histopathological techniques, the use of immittance testing, and a better understanding of the pathogenesis of a retraction pocket and cholesteatoma.[59]

Acute Perforation

An acute perforation of the tympanic membrane is usually caused by an episode of acute otitis media that is complicated by rupture of the eardrum. However, an acute perforation can be present in which otitis media is absent, such as when the perforation is secondary to trauma or as a complication of ear surgery (e.g., after tympanotomy tube insertion).

Classification

Acute perforations can be classified into acute perforation without otitis media or acute perforation with otitis me-

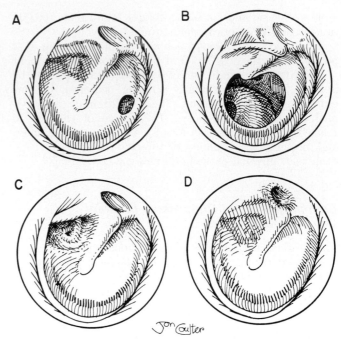

FIGURE 26–6. Examples of defects in the tympanic membrane. *A*, "Small central" perforation in the anteroinferior portion of the pars tensa of the tympanic membrane. *B*, "Central" perforation that involves approximately half of the pars tensa. *C*, Deep retraction pocket in the posterosuperior portion of the pars tensa that has been incorrectly called a marginal perforation. *D*, Deep retraction pocket in the pars flaccida that has been inappropriately called an attic perforation.

dia, with or without otorrhea (acute otitis media with perforation).

Acute Perforation without Otitis Media

An acute perforation of the tympanic membrane can be a complication of an attack of acute otitis media, which is discussed later, but if the perforation persists and the otitis media resolves, the perforation is considered to be an acute perforation without otitis media; if the perforation persists for 3 or more months and otitis media remains absent, it is chronic perforation of the tympanic membrane without otitis media, which is also described later.[60] An acute perforation (without otitis media) may not be a complication of otitis media but can be the result of treatment of otitis media, such as occurs after myringotomy or after spontaneous extrusion or removal of a tympanostomy tube; a perforation can also result from trauma to the tympanic membrane. Management of such perforations consists of "watchful waiting" since most heal within 2 to 3 months. In the two clinical trials conducted in Pittsburgh that evaluated the efficacy of tympanostomy tube placement for chronic otitis media with effusion in 215 children who were followed for 2 to 3 years after the tubes were inserted, 32 (14.8%) had a perforation at the tube site following extrusion, but only 3 children (1.4%) experienced a chronic perforation requiring tympanoplasty.[315, 316] Not only can an acute perforation persist into a chronic perforation, but a child with an acute perforation may experience acute otitis media,[60] both of which are discussed below.

Acute Perforation with Otitis Media

When an acute perforation (not due to trauma) occurs, it is usually secondary to acute otitis media, but a perforation can also occur during the course of chronic otitis media with effusion. Boswell and Nienhuys described spontaneous perforations developing in Australian aborigines who had chronic middle-ear effusions.[71] Since a spontaneous perforation commonly accompanies an episode of acute middle-ear infection, the perforation may be considered part of the disease process rather than a complication. Because such a perforation allows purulent material to drain into the external canal and enhances drainage of pus down the eustachian tube (owing to the effects of an opening in the eardrum), a perforation of the eardrum may prevent further spread of infection within the temporal bone or, more importantly, into the intracranial cavity. Infants and children of certain racial groups, such as Alaskan natives (Eskimos) and some Native American tribes, have a high incidence of spontaneous perforation with discharge: the eardrum is perforated spontaneously with almost every episode of acute otitis media.[60] The disease runs a similar course in certain other children not belonging to these high-risk populations (discussed later under Chronic Perforation).

Pathogenesis

The perforation may occur in high-risk populations such as the White River Apache American Indian tribe because of the presence of a patulous or semipatulous eustachian tube.[38] A eustachian tube with low resistance permits a larger bolus of bacteria-laden purulent material from the nasopharynx to enter (by *reflux, aspiration,* or *insufflation*) the middle ear, causing a more fulminating infection than would occur if the eustachian tube had either normal or high resistance. An alternative explanation of why some children seem to suffer a perforated eardrum with each episode of acute otitis media while others do not could be that there are differences in the virulence of the bacteria (or virus) or decreased resistance of the host. Factors that predispose to acute perforation are most likely similar to those described later under Chronic Perforation, especially in high-risk populations.

The four possible outcomes with an acute perforation associated with an episode of acute otitis media are (Fig. 26–7)

- Complete resolution of the otitis media and otorrhea and healing of the tympanic membrane perforation
- Complete resolution of the otitis media and otorrhea, but the perforation persists and becomes chronic
- Persistence of otitis media and perforation into the chronic stage, which is called *chronic suppurative otitis media*
- A suppurative complication

Microbiology

The organisms most frequently cultured from an aural discharge when acute otitis media is present are the same as those that have been cultured from acute middle-ear effusions when tympanocentesis has been performed, such as *Streptococcus pneumoniae, Haemophilus influenzae, Moraxella catarrhalis,* and *Streptococcus pyogenes.* Brook and Gober reported on the microbiology of spontaneously draining ears in 50 infants and children who had acute otitis media.[78] The authors stressed the need to attempt to aspirate the middle ear as opposed to obtaining the specimen from the otorrhea in the ear canal. Table 26–2 shows that of the middle-ear aspirates of the 61 ears of the 50 patients, *S. pneumoniae, H. influenzae, S. pyogenes,* and *M. catarrhalis* were the most common. It would appear that group A β-hemolytic *Streptococcus* still shows a relatively high rate of perforation, as had been noted in the pre-antibiotic era, since the 11% rate reported by Brook and Gober is higher than the 3% that is isolated from ears with intact tympanic membranes of children who have acute otitis media.[68] A recent study from Japan reported that three patients experienced multiple acute perforations of the tympanic membrane due to *S. pyogenes* and also had a labyrinthine complication.[25]

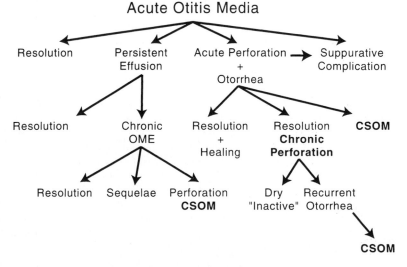

FIGURE 26–7. Possible outcomes after an episode of acute otitis media. (From Bluestone CD. Epidemiology and pathogenesis of chronic suppurative otitis media: implications for prevention and treatment. Int J Pediatr Otorhinolaryngol 42:207, 1998.)

The four most common bacteria isolated from acute otorrhea have also been cultured from infants and young children who have tympanostomy tubes in place and experience an episode of acute otitis media with otorrhea.[314]

Management

Antimicrobial therapy (e.g., amoxicillin) for children with acutely perforated eardrums should be the same as that recommended for those with acute otitis media when a perforation is not present (see Chapter 25). When an aural discharge is present, however, it may be desirable to culture the drainage. The antimicrobial regimen can then be adjusted according to the results of the Gram stain, culture, and susceptibility testing. The most effective method of obtaining a sample of the discharge is to remove as much of the purulent material as possible from the external canal by suction or cotton-tipped applicator and then aspirating pus directly at or through the perforation using a spinal needle attached to a tuberculin syringe or an Alden-Senturia trap (Storz Instrument, St. Louis, MO) and suction.[77]

Some experts argue against using ototopical medication when a perforation is present because of potential ototoxicity. Some children, however, benefit when otic drops are instilled into the external canal. Ototopical medication usually is beneficial when external otitis complicates the picture (see later in this chapter, External Otitis). Many clinicians advocate applying an antibiotic-cortisone otic medication whenever a discharge is present despite the possibility of ototoxicity since the topical medication may treat or prevent an external canal infection and hasten the resolution of the middle-ear infection. Also, ototopical treatment may prevent a secondary middle-ear infection caused by organisms that are in the external ear canal (e.g., *P. aeruginosa*, *S. aureus*, *Proteus* spp., and anaerobic bacteria) from entering the middle ear and mastoid, which can progress to the chronic stage (see later, Chronic Perforation). Even though the new ototopical antimicrobial agent ofloxacin (Floxin Otic) is only approved for treating acute otitis media and otorrhea in children when a tympanostomy tube is in place, this medication should be equally effective when a perforation is present. This agent is currently the only ototopical medication that has been demonstrated to be safe and effective and that has been approved for use when a tympanostomy tube is present.[13] The most common bacterium cultured from the middle ear in chronic suppurative otitis media that develops after acute otorrhea is *P. aeruginosa* and not the common bacteria isolated initially (e.g., *S. pneumoniae* and *H. influenzae*). Therefore, applying an ototopical antibiotic medication during the acute episode likely prevents the secondary chronic infection.

The discharge, especially when profuse, should be prevented from draining onto the pinna and adjacent areas as this usually results in dermatitis. The parent should be instructed to keep cotton in the external auditory meatus and change it as often as necessary to keep the canal dry. Cotton-tipped applicators should not be used by the child or parent.

The tympanic membrane frequently heals after the suppurative process in the middle ear ends. The defect usually closes within a week after onset of infection. When persistent discharge lasts longer than the initial 10-day course of antibiotic treatment, the child requires more intensive evaluation and aggressive management. In addition to obtaining a culture of the purulent material from the middle ear and adjusting antimicrobial agents, frequent cleaning of the canal, followed by instillation of ototopical drops, may also be required.

Acute mastoiditis with periosteitis or acute mastoid osteitis should be suspected if the child has persistent otalgia, tenderness of the ear to touch, erythema, and swelling in the postauricular area (see later, Mastoiditis). Computed tomography (CT) of the mastoids may be helpful but is not always diagnostic of mastoid osteitis. CT can also help diagnose spread of infection outside the middle ear and mastoid. Even if an intratemporal (or intracranial) complication is not readily apparent, if the aural discharge persists 2 or 3 weeks after onset of acute otitis media that has been treated with appropriately administered oral antibiotics, the patient should be hospitalized. The child should be evaluated again thoroughly in a search for an underlying illness that would interfere with resolution of the infection. The otologic assessment should include an examination of the entire external canal and tympanic membrane, using the otomicroscope to determine whether another otologic condition, such as a cholesteatoma or neoplasm, is present. If an adequate examination cannot be performed with the child awake, it should be carried out under general anesthesia, at which time a culture can be obtained directly from the middle ear. If no condition other than the perforation and subacute otitis media is found, parenteral antimicrobial agents should be administered. The selection of both systemic and topical antimicrobial agents should be based on the results of cultures. Frequently, if a gram-negative organism (e.g., *P. aeruginosa*) is present at this stage, management is essentially as recommended later under Chronic Suppurative Otitis Media.

With this method of management, the infection usually subsides. If the discharge persists, an exploratory tympanotomy and complete simple mastoidectomy is indicated even if there are no signs and symptoms of mastoid osteitis and CT fails to show osteitis (i.e., coalescence). During surgery on the middle ear and mastoid, another cause of the persistent infection must be thoroughly searched for. On occasion, a cholesteatoma that could not be visualized through the otomicroscope is found. Resolution of infection in the middle ear and mastoid invariably follows the surgery since mastoid osteitis is the usual cause of this complication of acute otitis media.

Fortunately, such cases are now uncommon and the perforation usually heals rapidly. However, the defect frequently remains open without evidence of otitis media (with or without discharge). If the perforation remains free of infection, it frequently closes in a few months. At this stage, no attempt at surgical closure of an uncomplicated perforation is indicated. If there is no sign of progressive healing after 3 or more months, management should be as described later under Chronic Perforation.

Prevention

In patients who are prone to recurrent acute otitis media and who perforate their tympanic membrane, prevention is desirable (described in detail in Chapter 25). In certain populations at high risk for acute otitis media and perforation that subsequently progresses to chronic suppurative otitis media, the most effective method of prevention of the chronic infection is to prevent an acute perforated tympanic membrane during an attack of acute otitis media. This is most effectively accomplished by treating the child early, appropriately, and adequately with an antimicrobial agent at the onset of the episode of acute otitis media (see the next discussion, Chronic Perforation).[49]

Chronic Perforation

A perforation of the tympanic membrane may remain open after an episode of acute otitis media or spontaneous extrusion (or removal) of a tympanostomy tube. When an acute perforation is present with no signs of healing and there are no signs of otitis media for 3 or more months, the perforation is considered *chronic* and possibly *permanent*. If chronic suppurative otitis media is present, the perforation may close spontaneously after appropriate treatment if the infection resolves. However, the perforation may not heal for the same reason that chronic perforations, without chronic infection, fail to heal: squamous epithelium at the edges of the perforation prevents spontaneous repair. The effect of a small chronic perforation on hearing is not significant, regardless of its location and in the absence of other middle-ear abnormalities. A large perforation, however, can be associated with an appreciable conductive hearing loss (e.g., 20 to 30 dB).

Classification

Chronic perforation of the tympanic membrane can be classified as *chronic perforation without otitis media* or *chronic perforation with otitis media*. Chronic perforation with otitis media can be further classified into *chronic perforation with acute otitis media, with or without otorrhea* or *chronic perforation with chronic otitis media (chronic suppurative otitis media), with or without otorrhea*. The latter disease stage is invariably associated with chronic mastoiditis (see Chapter 25).

Chronic Perforation without Otitis Media

Chronic perforation without otitis media has been inappropriately called chronic otitis media *inactive*. This terminology is confusing and often incorrect.[59] The patient may never experience an attack of acute otitis media—other than possibly the one that originated the perforation—or an episode of chronic suppurative otitis media (see Chapter 25).

Epidemiology

The incidence of chronic perforation in the pediatric population has not been formally studied, but chronic perforation is a common reason for referral to an otolaryngologist. In a study of tympanoplasty for chronic perforation—not associated with infection, cholesteatoma, or ossicular involvement—in children from Finland, Vartiainen and Vartiainen operated on 60 children during a 15-year period.[503] Caylan et al reported on a similar number of children who underwent surgical repair of a chronic perforation in an Italian center during a 10-year period.[100] They also reviewed the literature from 1974 to 1991 and found that 640 children had tympanoplasty as reported in 12 studies. Another review of the literature from 1979 to 1995 reported 870 children with tympanoplasty,[28] and another later review found 1741 cases reported between 1985 and 1998.[123] A more recent report by Tos et al reviewed the long-term outcomes of 116 children who underwent surgery between 1968 and 1980.[492] However, many reports combine children and adults, often preventing assessment of the number of children included. Also, many reports in the literature combine children who have chronic perforation without active infection with patients who have chronic suppurative otitis media (see later under Chronic Perforation with Chronic Otitis Media [Chronic Suppurative Otitis Media]). In addition, the incidence of tympanoplasty performed in children does not accurately reflect the true incidence of chronic perforation since many physicians elect to withhold surgery until later in the child's life. More importantly, most otolaryngologists do not report the results of tympanoplasty in children. Thus, the number of children undergoing surgery for repair of a chronic perforation is a great deal larger than is reported in the literature. Next to myringotomy, with or without tympanostomy tube insertion, tympanoplasty is the most common ear operation performed in children.[25]

Chronic perforation, as a complication of otitis media, is more prevalent in certain racial groups that also have a high prevalence and incidence of perforations associated with acute middle-ear infection. In 1970, new cases of chronic perforation (with or without chronic suppurative otitis media) were reported in 8% of the native population of Alaska, although this rate appears to be dropping.[521] Similar rates have been reported in Native American populations. Zonis reported that in 207 Apache Indian children examined in Canyon Day, Arizona, chronic perforations was the only sign of otitis media in 17 (8%),[536] whereas Todd returned to the same village 16 years later in 1983, examined 145 Indian children, and found only 1 child who had a perforation of the tympanic membrane but 12 (8%) children who had other evidence of otitis media.[486] In remote regions of Australia, where the Aboriginal population is especially prone to chronic perforations, Mak et al reviewed 273 Aboriginal patients who underwent tympanoplasty surgery from 1986 to 1995.[313] Since many of these chronic perforations are associated with chronic middle-ear and mastoid infection, the epidemiology of this complication of otitis media is presented in more detail under Chronic Perforation with Chronic Otitis Media (Chronic Suppurative Otitis Media).

Chronic perforation of the tympanic membrane is a recognized complication of tympanostomy tube insertion. Of the 1062 ears of children who received tympanostomy tubes in a study reported from Germany, 26 ears (2.5%) had a persistent perforation.[347] This figure, however, depends on the site of the tube placement and the type of tube used. The rate of chronic perforation as a complication of tube placement has been reported to be as low as 0.5% and as high as 25%. The conventional tubes are associated with the lowest rate and the permanent tubes with the highest rate. Of the 215 children prospectively followed for at least 2 to 3 years in the prospective clinical trials of efficacy and safety of tympanostomy tube insertion conducted in Pittsburgh, 2.4% had to eventually undergo tympanoplasty for chronic perforation (see Chapter 25).[95, 315, 316]

Management

The management of so-called *dry* chronic perforation (more appropriately called *chronic perforation without otitis media*) in children is both difficult and controversial. On one hand, the perforation provides ventilation and drainage of the middle ear. On the other hand, the physiologic protective function of the eustachian tube/middle-ear system is impaired; the middle ear is *too open*. The middle ear and mastoid gas cells no longer have a gas cushion to prevent nasopharyngeal secretions from entering the ear, which can then result in *reflux otitis media* (Figs. 26–8 and 26–9). In addition, the open tympanic membrane can permit contaminated water to enter the middle ear during bathing and swimming. Therefore, the dilemma of when to close such a perforation is comparable to that regarding the most appropriate time to remove a tympanostomy tube: a small, uncomplicated chronic perforation and a tympanostomy tube have similar benefits and risks. Like a tympanostomy tube, a perforation may be beneficial for a child who had experienced recurrent acute otitis media or chronic otitis media with effusion before the perforation developed, but recurrent acute *reflux otitis media* with discharge, which can progress into chronic suppurative otitis media, may become a problem, making repair of the eardrum defect a consideration. However, recurrent acute otitis media that results

FIGURE 26–8. A perforation of the tympanic membrane may promote the reflux of secretions into the middle ear from the nasopharynx since the middle-ear gas cushion is not present (see also Fig. 26–9).

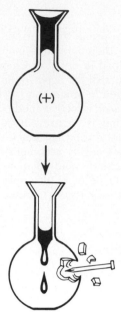

FIGURE 26–9. Flask model showing how a perforation of the tympanic membrane may result in reflux of nasopharyngeal secretions into the middle ear. The nasopharynx/eustachian tube/middle ear/mastoid air-cell system is likened to a flask with a narrow neck. When the system is intact, liquid is prevented from entering the body of the flask, but when the body of the flask is not intact (i.e., when a perforation is present), liquid can readily flow through the system.

in otorrhea through a chronic perforation can be effectively treated and even prevented without repair of the tympanic membrane (or removal of a tympanostomy tube).

When the episodes are infrequent, the treatment of each bout should be the same as recommended for an acute perforation associated with acute otitis media. If the episodes of acute infection are frequent and the interval between bouts short, preventive measures are recommended. Appropriate options are the same as recommended for infants and children whose tympanic membranes are intact but have frequently recurrent acute otitis media (see Chapter 25). Reducing the risk of exposure to viral infections (e.g., eliminating day care or choosing a day-care setting with as few children as possible) may prove helpful. The currently available pneumococcal vaccine and the influenza vaccine can be administered. Also, a search for an underlying problem, such as an immune disorder, adenoid hypertrophy, paranasal sinusitis, or allergy, may help. If none of these recommendations proves beneficial and an underlying problem is not uncovered, prophylaxis with an antimicrobial agent during the risk months for infections of the upper respiratory tract (late fall, winter, and spring) can be initiated. This method was demonstrated to be effective in reducing recurrent otorrhea in Alaskan Natives.[323] A prolonged course of a prophylactic antimicrobial agent—for example, amoxicillin given in one dose before bedtime—may be considered to prevent recurrent middle-ear infection and discharge.

The selection of the agent should be based on the results of the cultures obtained from previous episodes of discharge. Dosage and duration of treatment should be the same as those recommended for children who have experienced frequently recurrent acute otitis media without a perforation. Today, however, with the ever-increasing rate of antibiotic-resistant otogenic bacteria (which has been attributed to the overuse of antibiotics for treatment and prolonged low-dose prophylaxis), other preventive measures should be attempted before antimicrobial prophylaxis. Also, further consideration should be given to repairing the perforation. Children in whom an attack of acute middle-ear infection and discharge persists despite adequate medical treatment and in whom the infection is thought to be chronic should be evaluated and managed as described in the later discussion, Chronic Perforation with Chronic Otitis Media (Chronic Suppurative Otitis Media.)

Indications for Repair of Chronic Perforation

Even though the indications for repair of chronic perforations in the adult population have been defined by many surgeons, the indications for tympanoplasty in children remain controversial. Some surgeons have reported that pediatric tympanoplasty is as successful as that in adults,[7, 39, 87, 174, 223, 265, 282, 284, 400] but others have had the opposite experience.[20, 196, 326] When criteria for a successful tympanoplasty include outcome measures other than just healing of the graft, the success rate is frequently lower in children compared with adults. Even though Lau and Tos reported that 92% of the grafts healed, the success of the procedure later fell to 64%.[282] During the follow-up period, 14% required tympanostomy tube insertion, 5% had persistent middle-ear effusion, and 9% had postoperative atelectasis. Similar outcomes were reported by Manning et al in a study of 56 children (63 ears).[318] Even though 78% of the grafts healed, only 52% of the children had a healed graft and adequate middle-ear function during the postoperative follow-up period.

Some surgeons attribute these differences between adult and pediatric tympanoplasty to the higher frequency of infection of the upper respiratory tract leading to otitis media in children and the unpredictability of their eustachian tube function. Optimal ages at which to perform tympanoplastic surgery have variously been stated to range from age 2 or 3 years to puberty.[27, 121, 188, 265, 326, 472] Paparella states that tympanoplasty can be performed in children of almost any age.[370] However, Sheehy and Anderson do not recommend elective tympanic membrane grafting in children younger than 7 years because of the possibility of postoperative otitis media.[440] More recently, other surgeons[272, 309, 447] have reported tympanoplasty outcomes that agree with the recommendation of Sheehy and Anderson[440] and not Tos and Lau.[491] However, in a more recent review of the long-term outcomes of tympanoplasty by Tos et al, the success rate was 86% after 15 to 27 years.[492] Table 26–3 lists the studies reported from 1979 to 2000, which generally show relatively high success rates. Vrabec et al's meta-analysis of tympano-

TABLE 26–3. Outcome of Myringoplasty and Tympanoplasty in Children Who Had Chronic Perforation of the Tympanic Membrane as Reported from 18 Centers from 1979–2000

Author	No. of Ears	Success Rate (%)
Bluestone et al., 1978[54]	51	35
Cohn et al., 1979[115]	21	81
Raine and Singh, 1983[400]	114	81
Adkins and White, 1984[7]	30	87
Francois et al., 1985	150	81
Lau and Tos, 1986[282]	155	92
Ophir et al., 1987[363]	172	79
Koch et al., 1990[272]	64	73
Prescott and Robartes, 1991	114	84
Kessler et al., 1994[265]	209	92
Black et al., 1995	100	75
Chandrasekhar et al., 1995	268	81
Mitchell et al., 1997	342	80
Vartiainen and Vartiainen, 1997[503]	60	90
Caylan et al., 1998[100]	51	82
Bajaj et al., 1998[28]	45	91
Denoyelle et al., 1999[123]	231	83
Tos et al., 2000[492]	116	86

plasty in children from 1966 to 1997 revealed that the success rate increased with advancing age and that none of the other parameters studied was a significant predictor of success.[508]

In general, infants and children younger than 7 years have less favorable outcomes after tympanoplasty than do older children and adults. The controversy over which age is most appropriate is due to definitions of failure and the duration of follow-up as well as the intervals between observations. Graft take should not be the only outcome measure. Recurrence of middle-ear effusion, high negative middle-ear pressure, atelectasis, subsequent reperforation, and the need for tympanostomy tube placement, in addition to serial assessment of hearing for a long period, should also be included as outcomes. When children at least 7 years old undergo surgery, their outcomes are relatively good.[46] The level of experience of the surgeon has also been questioned,[491] which is reasonable, but a teaching institution has a responsibility to train young surgeons, which is not the case with the private practitioner or in areas where only the attending surgeon performs the surgery. This factor is probably also related to the variation in postoperative outcomes as reported in the literature.

The observation that infants and young children have less favorable outcomes is most likely related to recent epidemiologic studies of otitis media in children and is consistent with the maturation of the structure and function of the eustachian tube (see Chapter 25). However, on occasion, the surgeon must operate on an infant or a young child, such as when cholesteatoma is present.

The following factors are important in the decision-making process when a chronic perforation is present and repair is contemplated: (1) age of the child, (2) duration of the perforation, (3) unilateral versus bilateral perforations, (4) status of the contralateral ear when that tympanic membrane is intact, (5) eustachian-tube function, (6) presence or absence of recurrent/chronic otorrhea (and frequency, severity, and duration of otorrhea), (7) presence or absence of cholesteatoma, and (8) season of the year.

In general, the following are guidelines for repair of a chronic perforation:

- Presence of a unilateral perforation in children who are at least 6 years old when the contralateral tympanic membrane is intact and the middle ear has been free of disease for 1 year or longer
- Selected similar children younger than 6 years may also be candidates (the decision is based on the factors listed earlier)
- Presence of bilateral perforations in children in whom eustachian-tube function is now considered to be within normal limits as a result of growth and development, or when nonsurgical (e.g., allergy control and treatment) or surgical (e.g., adenoidectomy, repair of cleft palate) management may have improved eustachian-tube function

Recurrent otorrhea through a chronic perforation is not a contraindication to repair of a chronic perforation if the child meets the criteria stated, since reflux of nasopharyngeal secretions may be enhanced by the nonintact tympanic membrane; the middle-ear air cushion is lost. Closure of the defect could potentially prevent reflux.

Evaluation of eustachian-tube function before the patient with a chronic perforation of the tympanic membrane undergoes surgery may help determine the potential results of tympanoplasty surgery. Holmquist studied eustachian-tube function in adults before and after tympanoplasty and reported that the operation had a high rate of success when function of the eustachian tube was good (i.e., those who could equilibrate applied negative pressure); however, in patients without good tube function, surgery frequently failed to close the perforation.[26] Miller and Bilodeau[338] and Siedentop[448] reported similar findings, but Ekvall,[154] Lee and Schuknecht,[284] Andreasson and Harris,[16] Cohn et al,[115] and Virtanen et al[506] found no correlation between the results of the inflation-deflation tests and success or failure of tympanoplasty. Most of these studies failed to define the criteria for success, and the postoperative follow-up period was too short. Bluestone et al assessed children before tympanoplasty and found that of 51 ears of 45 children, 8 ears could equilibrate an applied negative pressure (200 mm H$_2$O) to some degree; in seven of these ears, the graft healed, no middle-ear effusion occurred, and no other perforation developed during a follow-up period of 1 to 2 years.[55] However, as was found in studies in adults, failure to equilibrate an applied negative pressure did not predict failure of the tympanoplasty.

In a subsequent study from the same institution, Manning et al reported that good eustachian-tube function was predictive of a good outcome but that poor tube function was not helpful in predicting a poor outcome.[318] In this study, the forced-response test was also used to gauge eustachian-tube function in conjunction with the inflation-deflation test that was used in the first study. The forced-response test showed a significant association

between outcome and preoperative tube function as determined by a combination of active and passive function parameters. In addition, these investigators reported that other factors, such as graft placement (medial or lateral), contralateral middle-ear status, and age of the child, were not associated with outcome. Kumazawa et al consider preoperative evaluation using eustachian-tube function tests to be helpful in prognosis.[277] There is still controversy regarding the value of preoperatively testing the function of the eustachian tube (see Chapter 25).[333]

These studies show that if the child has good tube function, regardless of age, the success of tympanoplasty is probable; if function is poor, these tests will not help the clinician in deciding not to operate. However, the value of testing a patient's tube function lies in the possibility of determining whether a young child is a candidate for tympanoplasty when one would otherwise base the decision to withhold surgery until the child is older on other findings alone. These tests are also of value in the diagnosis of severe or total mechanical obstruction, conditions that contraindicate a simple myringoplasty rather than a tympanoplasty; further evaluation and medical or surgical management of such patients may be indicated, depending on the condition of the ear. The child should be examined for a nasopharyngeal tumor; if none is found, the cause of obstruction could be mucosal swelling of the middle-ear end of the eustachian tube, which may respond to a medical treatment such as ototopical medication. If the obstruction persists despite medical treatment and if the perforation is to be repaired, the examination should include exploration of the middle ear and bony (protympanic) portion of the eustachian tube. An unsuspected cholesteatoma might be found to be the cause of the obstruction.

Some surgeons consider otoscopic and tympanometric assessment of the contralateral ear, if the tympanic membrane is intact, to be helpful in predicting the success of tympanoplasty[55, 363]; however, the study by Manning et al did not support this practice.[318]

A later review of 209 tympanoplasties in 183 children by Kessler et al found that otitis media in the contralateral ear was significantly associated with reperforation.[265] Since eustachian-tube function is best determined by observing the status of the middle ear for at least 1 year (i.e., four seasons) and since eustachian-tube function is usually the same bilaterally in children, the status of the contralateral ear with an intact tympanic membrane may be a good indicator of the expected functioning of the middle ear with a perforated eardrum after repair of the eardrum. If recurrent or persistent high negative pressure or effusion, or both, are present within the middle ear or if there is a cholesteatoma or a retraction pocket in the posterosuperior quadrant of the pars tensa or in the pars flaccida, tympanoplasty is usually unsuccessful. Figure 26–10 illustrates test results of an ideal case for tympanoplasty; Figure 26–11 is an example of results that indicate that the child is an uncertain candidate for surgical repair of the tympanic membrane.

When a unilateral perforation is present and if insertion of a tympanostomy tube is indicated in the opposite, intact side to (1) prevent recurrent otitis media with effusion, (2) eliminate a chronic middle-ear effusion, or (3)

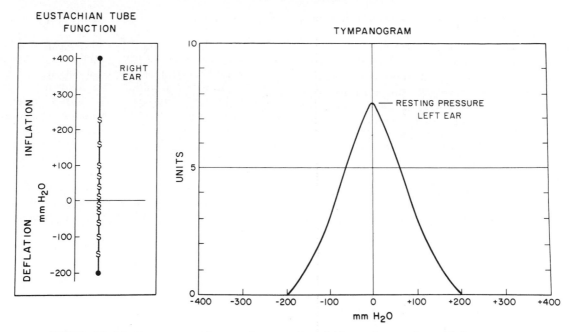

FIGURE 26–10. Pre-tympanoplasty evaluation of a child in whom inflation-deflation eustachian-tube function test results were normal in the perforated ear and resting pressure was normal in the contralateral ear with an intact tympanic membrane. S, swallow.

ventilate a severely atelectatic tympanic membrane (with or without a retraction pocket), tympanoplasty for an uncomplicated chronic perforation is contraindicated until these conditions are absent and a tympanostomy tube is no longer required. Again, an observation period of at least 1 year is required. If the child must undergo mid-

dle-ear surgery and tube function is known to be or is suspected of being poor (because of age, usually less than age 6 years), such as would be the case when the child has a perforation and a cholesteatoma, then either repair of the tympanic membrane can be delayed or the more preferred method of management can be employed, pro-

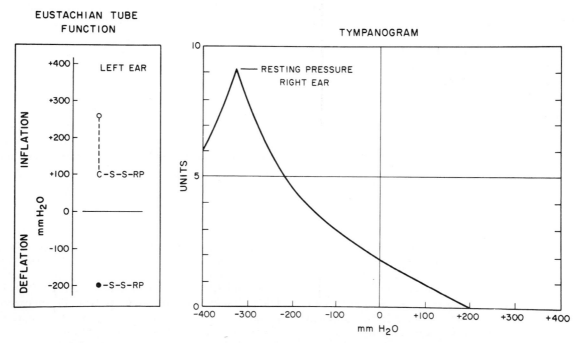

FIGURE 26–11. Results of pre-tympanoplasty evaluation of a child who could not equilibrate applied positive or negative pressure during the inflation-deflation eustachian-tube test in the ear with the perforation. A tympanogram of the contralateral ear with an intact tympanic membrane revealed high negative pressure. O, opening pressure; C, closing pressure; S, swallow; RP, residual pressure.

ceeding with a tympanoplasty followed by insertion of a tympanostomy tube.

Some surgeons recommend adenoidectomy, with and without tonsillectomy, to improve the success rate of tympanoplasty; however, no clinical trials support this contention. Until such studies are available, surgical removal of these structures for the ear condition alone should be considered of uncertain benefit; adenoidectomy for other compelling indications, such as airway obstruction, would be indicated. Three retrospective studies in children failed to show that adenoidectomy had any effect on the outcome of tympanoplasty.[55, 83, 363] However, an argument can be made that adenoidectomy may be beneficial since at least three studies have shown that adenoidectomy for treatment and prevention of recurrent acute otitis media and chronic otitis media with effusion is effective.[179, 324, 377] A possible indication for adenoidectomy might be in a child, older than 6 years, in whom one or more attempts to repair the perforation failed because of recurrent middle-ear disease. However, Vartiainen and Vartiainen reported that their graft failures occurred in patients who had already undergone adenoidectomy.[503] These authors suggest that children who had undergone adenoidectomy in the past most likely had more middle-ear disease and were more likely to experience failed tympanoplasty. Obviously, a randomized clinical trial that addresses this problem is needed.

Most surgeons agree that there should be no signs of otitis media in the ear before a tympanoplasty—that is, the ear should be dry since the presence of discharge is associated with failure of the tympanoplasty.[20] When an acquired cholesteatoma is found in the ear undergoing surgery, tympanoplasty is most likely to be less than optimal.[61] When tympanoplasty is withheld in a child who has significant hearing loss, a hearing aid should be considered until the procedure is performed and hearing improvement is achieved.

In children who have bilateral perforations and in whom tests of eustachian-tube function show no active function when negative pressure is applied, it is uncertain whether tympanoplasty would be successful. A better test of tube function must be devised and the results correlated with the results of the surgery before it will be possible to determine the probable success of tympanoplasty in these cases. When tympanoplasty must be performed and the function of the eustachian tube is thought to be poor, a tympanostomy tube should be inserted.

Surgical Techniques

If a chronic perforation of the tympanic membrane is to be surgically repaired, the chosen technique should have the greatest chance of success while posing the least risk. Most surgical procedures to repair a perforation in children require a general anesthetic; in adults, especially when the perforation is small, local anesthesia is adequate. Therefore, the benefits of surgery in a child must outweigh the risks of general anesthesia. The surgical techniques that we use to repair chronic perforations are described in the *Atlas of Pediatric Otolaryngology*.[65]

Myringoplasty

Myringoplasty is repair of the tympanic membrane defect without exploration of the middle ear. The procedure may be performed in selected patients who have no other abnormalities of the middle ear. A small perforation may heal if the epithelium is removed from its edges and if the circumference of the perforation is cauterized with trichloroacetic acid or, more effectively, with a pick and cup-biting forceps. A micropore strip tape adhesive patch (Steri-Strip) can then be placed over the defect. Saito et al reported a 99.1% success rate with this patch in 108 patients, 2 to 68 years old.[424] This simple technique can be done as an outpatient procedure with local anesthesia in older children and adolescents, but general anesthesia is usually necessary in children. An alternative to this technique is to insert a plug of fat, taken from the earlobe, through the perforation.[121] The procedure should be performed only if the hearing is normal or only slightly impaired and if the remaining portion of the tympanic membrane is translucent; these two criteria must be met to avoid the possibility that the ossicles are involved or that a tympanic membrane–middle ear cholesteatoma (i.e., migration of squamous epithelium through the perforation into the middle ear) is present.

Tympanoplasty

When the defect is large or the middle ear must be explored, such as when there is a significant conductive hearing loss, the defect should be repaired with a fresh autograft, such as temporalis fascia or tragal perichondrium. The middle ear (including the medial side of the tympanic membrane remnant to determine whether cholesteatoma is present) must be inspected during tympanoplasty to rule out another pathologic condition that may require more extensive surgery.

The techniques of tympanoplasty that one of us (CDB) currently employs are specifically designed for children.[65] In general, the surgical techniques for children are similar to those for adults; however, tympanoplasty in children requires certain considerations. Since the external canal is frequently smaller in children than in adults, a postauricular (or endaural) approach may be required to achieve adequate visualization of the tympanic membrane and the middle ear. A transcanal approach should be reserved for children whose ear canals are large enough to provide proper exposure of the entire operative field. Autografts are preferred to homografts and heterografts since we do not know the long-term effects of homografts. For the same reason, when an ossicular chain abnormality is present, a type II or III tympanoplasty (Fig. 26–12), or an autograft ossicle, should be used for the ossiculoplasty rather than inert material (see Ossicular Discontinuity and Fixation). A type IV tympanoplasty is usually unsuccessful in children because of their eustachian tube dysfunction. The preference for a technique that involves placing the graft lateral to the tympanic membrane has some merit since laterally placed grafts have been shown to have a higher initial "take rate" in children.[55] The failure of medially placed grafts may be

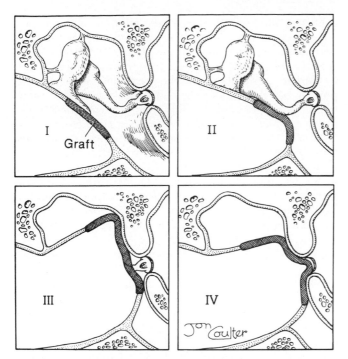

FIGURE 26–12. Tympanoplasty surgical procedures. Type I, ossicular chain intact; type II, the graft lays on the incus; type III, the graft is on the stapes superstructure; type IV, the graft is on the stapes footplate.

related to the fluctuating negative pressure that is so common in the middle ears of children and that could enhance the take of a lateral graft but tends to pull a medial graft away from the tympanic membrane. For smaller perforations, a medial graft may be satisfactory; for a large perforation, the laterally placed fascia graft appears to give better results and, when performed properly, should not lead to the postoperative complication of "blunting" in the anterior sulcus or lateral healing of the graft.[440]

Some surgeons routinely add an extensive simple mastoidectomy to a tympanoplasty in children who show no evidence of disease in the mastoid. The risk of prolonging the general anesthesia does not outweigh the remote possibility of finding occult disease; nor is the risk justified by the possible advantage of increasing the middle ear–mastoid gas volume, which has been purported to enhance the success rate of tympanoplasty. In addition, the potential hazards of radiation appear to outweigh any advantage of routine preoperative radiography of the mastoid when there is no evidence of disease in the area. However, Ruhl and Pensak recommend mastoidectomy when previous tympanoplasty has failed in the hope of improving aeration of the middle-ear cleft.[417]

Postoperative care in children is often more of a problem than when the procedure is performed in adults, especially if the patient is a young child. Such patients are frequently less cooperative when packing, blood clot, or other debris must be removed from the ear canal or when granulation tissue is present. These problems must be considered before a decision to perform elective tympanic grafting in children is made.

Outcome

Unfortunately, regardless of technique and despite adequate follow-up, tympanoplasty is not as successful in children, especially young children, as it is in adults, which is probably why many surgeons delay surgery until a child grows older. In children, the criteria for success for tympanoplasty should include not only initial take of the graft (the tympanic membrane remains intact) but absence of another perforation, persistent high negative middle-ear pressure, atelectasis, retraction pocket, otitis media with effusion, or cholesteatoma for a follow-up period of at least 2 years. The procedure becomes a failure when a tympanostomy tube must be inserted into a tympanic membrane that has undergone tympanoplasty for a central perforation because of subsequent development of chronic or recurrent middle-ear disease. Improvement in hearing is also an important goal. In two studies of children in which the preceding criteria were used to evaluate the outcome of tympanoplasty, about half of the tympanoplasties observed for 1 to 2 years were successful.[55, 318] However, some of these patients initially had cholesteatoma.

Conclusions

Currently, children are candidates for tympanoplastic surgery (especially children at least 6 years old), but the outcome may not be as successful as in adults since eustachian-tube function and the immune system are relatively poor in children. However, the procedure can be successful in selected cases. Tympanoplasty appears to be contraindicated in some cases (e.g., otitis media in the contralateral ear, recent recurrent perforation due to otitis media during the postoperative period following repair of the perforation), whereas the outcome of the operation is less certain in others, such as infants and young children. The clinician's problem is deciding which child should undergo perforation repair. An improved method of testing the eustachian tube, a method that better indicates the actual function available for clinical use, could aid such decisions. A controlled study of the indications for tympanoplasty and the most effective technique of repair (e.g., medial versus lateral graft) in a large group of children is needed. However, when the procedure is indicated and the child and parents are adequately informed about the potential risks and costs, as well as the benefits, the procedure should be successful in the majority of cases.

Chronic Perforation with Otitis Media

When an acute perforation of the tympanic membrane is associated with acute otitis media, the infection can progress into a chronic perforation and chronic otitis media. This is called *chronic suppurative otitis media*. A chronic perforation may also be present with no middle-ear infection but is susceptible to an episode of otitis media. This is initially acute otitis media, which can progress to the chronic stage, i.e., *chronic suppurative otitis media*.

Classification

Chronic perforation with otitis media can be classified as *chronic perforation with acute otitis media, with or without otorrhea* or *chronic perforation with chronic otitis media, with or without otorrhea.*

The term *chronic suppurative otitis media* implies that a chronic perforation of the tympanic membrane is present, as in chronic mastoiditis, but otorrhea may or may not be present.[59]

Chronic Perforation with Acute Otitis Media

A chronic perforation of the tympanic membrane can develop into acute otitis media, which can then have the following possible outcomes:

- Complete resolution of the acute otitis media (and otorrhea) and healing of the chronic perforation
- Complete resolution of the acute otitis media (and otorrhea) but persistence of the chronic perforation
- Acute otitis media persists into the chronic stage, i.e., *chronic suppurative otitis media*
- A suppurative complication, such as acute mastoiditis

The presumed reason that a chronic perforation occasionally heals after an episode of acute otitis media is that the rim (margin) of the perforation is denuded of the epithelium by the infection; the epithelium at the margins prevented healing prior to the infection.

When acute otitis media develops in a child who has a chronic perforation of the tympanic membrane, initial management should be similar to that described earlier for acute perforation during an attack of acute otitis media. If the acute otitis media resolves but the chronic perforation persists, the decision as to whether to close the perforation is the same as described earlier for a chronic perforation without otitis media.

Chronic Perforation with Chronic Otitis Media (Chronic Suppurative Otitis Media)

Chronic suppurative otitis media is the stage of ear disease in which there is chronic inflammation of the middle ear and mastoid and in which a nonintact tympanic membrane (chronic perforation or tympanostomy tube) is present. *Otorrhea* may or may not be evident; a discharge may be present in the middle ear or mastoid, or both, but otorrhea is not evident through the perforation—or tympanostomy tube—or in the external auditory canal. There is no consensus regarding the duration of otitis media to be designated *chronic suppurative otitis media.* Even though 3 or more months appears appropriate, some clinicians consider a shorter duration of otitis media as constituting chronic disease, especially when the causative organism is *Pseudomonas.*

Terminology. *Chronic suppurative otitis media* is the commonly used term when a chronic perforation is associated with chronic otitis media. Mastoiditis is invariably a part of the pathologic process. The condition has also been called *chronic otitis media,* but this term can be confused with *chronic otitis media with effusion,* which is not a complication of otitis media and does not involve perforation of the tympanic membrane.[59] Also, the term *chronic otitis media* has been inappropriately used when a chronic perforation of the tympanic membrane is present but the middle ear and mastoid is free of infection. The proper term for this condition is *chronic perforation without otitis media* or, more simply, *chronic perforation.* Also, some clinicians inappropriately use the terms *chronic otitis media inactive* or *active*; chronic perforation associated with infection is *active,* and when infection is absent it is *inactive.*[83] Other terms for chronic suppurative otitis media are *chronic suppurative otitis media and mastoiditis, chronic purulent otitis media,* and *chronic otomastoiditis.* The most descriptive term is *chronic otitis media with perforation, discharge, and mastoiditis,*[436] but this is not commonly used. When a cholesteatoma is also present, the term *cholesteatoma with chronic suppurative otitis media* is appropriate. However, because an acquired aural cholesteatoma does not have to be associated with chronic suppurative otitis media, cholesteatoma is not part of the pathologic features of the type of ear disease described in this discussion and is presented as a separate entity in this chapter.

Despite this strict definition of chronic suppurative otitis media, a review of the literature reveals that many reports describing various aspects of chronic suppurative otitis media, such as epidemiology and pathogenesis, improperly include chronic perforation without otitis media in this disease entity.

Epidemiology. Chronic suppurative otitis media is a major health problem in many populations around the world, affecting diverse racial and cultural groups living not only in temperate climates but in climate extremes ranging from the Arctic Circle to the equator. From a review of approximately 50 reports published in the past few decades, there appear to be several groups of populations based on the prevalence of the disease (Table 26–4).[60] The populations in which the prevalence of chronic otitis media (defined here as chronic perforation with and without suppuration) has been reported to be the highest are:

- Inuits of Alaska (30% to 46%), Canada (7% to 31%), and Greenland (7% to 12%)[32, 34, 35, 75, 227, 229, 257, 385, 427, 485, 496]
- Australian Aborigines (12% to 25%)[71, 143, 169, 233, 283, 291, 327, 328, 344, 473]
- Certain Native Americans, e.g., Apache and Navajo tribes (4% to 8%).[243, 246, 346, 466, 486, 520, 536] Apparently these North American Indian tribes have higher rates than others.[466] One study from the Eastern Canadian Arctic compared the rates in Cree Indian school children with those in Inuit children living in the same area: the rate was 22% in the Inuit but only 1% in the Cree.[32]
- Populations with moderately high rates are certain natives of the South Pacific islands, such as the Solomon Islands (4% to 6%),[144] New Zealand Maori (4%),[182, 488] Malaysia (4%),[149] and Micronesia (4%)[104, 126, 127] (in contrast with these high rates in some islands of the South

TABLE 26-4. Prevalence of Chronic Suppurative Otitis Media°

Population	Prevalence (%)	References
Alaskan Inuits	30–46	Brody et al, 1965; Kaplan et al, 1973; Tschop, 1977
Canadian Inuits	7–31	Ling et al, 1969; Schaefer, 1971; Baxter & Ling, 1974; Timmermans & Gerson, 1980; Baxter, 1982; Baxter et al, 1986, 1992
Greenland Inuits	7–12	Pederson, 1986; Homoe & Bretlau, 1994; Homoe et al, 1996
Australian Aborigines	12–25	Stuart et al, 1972; Mc-Cafferty et al, 1977; Lewis et al, 1977; Moran et al, 1979; Dugdale et al, 1982; Hudson & Rockette, 1984; McCafferty et al, 1985; Foreman, 1987; Leach et al, 1994; Boswell & Neinhuys, 1996
Apache, Navajo	4–8	Jaffe, 1969; Zonis, 1968; Johnson, 1967; Mortimer, 1973; Wiet, 1979; Todd & Bowman, 1985
Solomon Islands	4–6	Eason et al, 1986
New Zealand Maori	4	Tonkin, 1970; Giles & O'Brien, 1991
Malaysia	4	Elango et al, 1991
Micronesia	4	Dever et al, 1985, 1990; Chan et al, 1993
Sierra Leone	6	Seely et al, 1995
Gambia	4	McPherson & Holborow, 1985
Kenya	4	Hatcher et al, 1995
Nigeria	4	Miller et al, 1983; Okeowa, 1985
Tanzania	2–3	Manni & Lema, 1987; Bastos et al, 1995; Minja & Machemba, 1996
Korea	2	Kim et al, 1993
India	2	Kapur, 1965
Saudi Arabia	1.4	Muhameid et al, 1993
United States	<1	Casselbrant et al, 1985, 1995; Zeisel et al, 1995
United Kingdom	<1	Mawson & Ludman, 1979; Williamson et al, 1994
Denmark	<1	Fiellau-Nikolajsen, 1983
Finland	<1	Marttila, 1986

° Some reports included patients who had chronic perforation but without otitis media. Table proceeds from highest prevalence to lowest prevalence.

Pacific, natives of Melanesia have an extremely low rate [<1%]).[467]

■ Some African populations, such as Sierra Leone [6%], Gambia (4%),[435] Kenya (4%),[332] and Tanzania (2% to 3%).[31, 217, 317] However, not all reports from Africa have documented these relatively high rates. One study from Nigeria reported a rate of less than 1%[339]; another

study found a 4% rate.[360] One study of South African rural blacks also found a rate of less than 1%.[360] A recent study from South India reported a rate of 6% in rural children.[418]

Populations with relatively low rates of chronic otitis media are Korea (2%),[267] India (2%),[258] and Saudi Arabia (1.4%).[348] Studies from highly industrialized nations have reported the lowest rates (zero or <1%), such as the United States,[92, 94, 533] Finland,[321] the United Kingdom[326, 522] (although in one adult population, the rate has been reported to be 3.1%[83]), and Denmark.[163] However, with the widespread use of tympanostomy tubes in these countries, chronic suppurative otitis media is not an uncommon complication in infants and children in whom these tubes have been inserted.[132]

Risk factors that have been attributed to the high rates of chronic suppurative otitis media in these populations are lack of breast feeding, overcrowding, poor hygiene, poor nutrition, passive smoking, high rates of nasopharyngeal colonization with potentially pathogenic bacteria, and inadequate and unavailable health care.[32, 283, 427, 521]

Pathogenesis. The cause and pathogenesis of chronic suppurative otitis media is multifactorial, involving one or more of the risk factors just noted. However, chronic suppurative otitis media begins with an episode of acute otitis media. Thus, the factors that have been associated with acute otitis media may be initially involved, such as infection of the upper respiratory tract; anatomic factors, such as eustachian-tube dysfunction; host factors, such as young age; immature or impaired immunologic status; presence of upper-respiratory allergy; familial predisposition; presence of older siblings in the household; male sex; race; method of feeding (bottle vs. breast); and environmental (e.g., smoking in the household) and social factors. Probably the most important factors related to the onset of acute otitis media in infants and young children are immaturity of the structure and function of the eustachian tube and immaturity of the immune system.[66]

Acute otitis media with perforation (or when a tympanostomy tube is present) usually *precedes* chronic suppurative otitis media, but in certain high-risk populations, such as the Australian Aborigines, chronic otitis media with effusion is initially present.[71] Factors most likely related to the progression of acute otitis media into the chronic stage have been noted, but when long-standing the process usually results in *chronic osteitis* of the middle-ear cleft.[262] Figure 26–7 shows the possible outcomes of an episode of acute otitis media that may result in chronic suppurative otitis media. Since a spontaneous perforation commonly accompanies an episode of acute otitis media that is untreated with an antimicrobial agent, and less commonly despite adequate treatment, the perforation may be part of the natural history of the disease process rather than a complication. Figure 26–13 also shows the sequence of events after an attack of acute otitis media that can lead to a chronic perforation or chronic suppurative otitis media.

When a chronic perforation or tympanostomy tube is present and there is no evidence of infection, reinfection probably occurs in one of two ways.

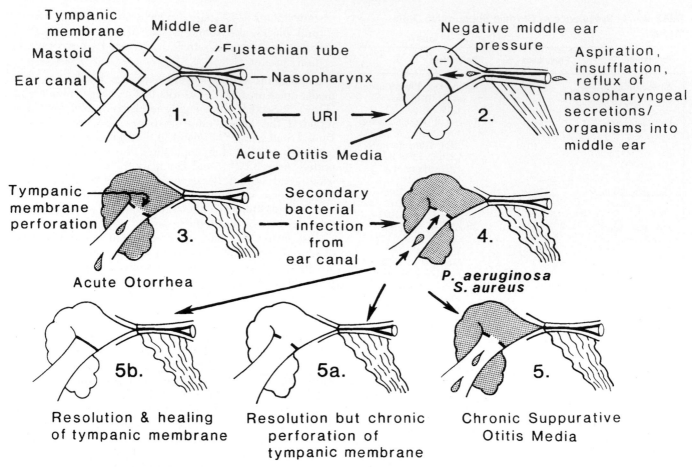

FIGURE 26–13. One possible sequence of events after an episode of acute otitis media that can result in a chronic perforation of the tympanic membrane or chronic suppurative otitis media in a right ear *(1)*. During an infection of the upper respiratory tract (URI), nasopharyngeal secretions with viruses and bacteria can enter the middle ear *(2)* causing acute otitis media, perforation of the tympanic membrane, and otorrhea *(3)*, after which bacteria from the ear canal can enter the middle ear *(4)*, resulting in chronic suppurative otitis media *(5)*; the infection resolves but the perforation persists and becomes chronic *(5a)*, or there is both resolution and healing of the perforation *(5b)*.

Bacteria from the nasopharynx gain access to the middle ear because of *reflux* or *insufflation* of nasopharyngeal secretions (due to crying in the infant, nose blowing, or swallowing when nasal obstruction is present, i.e., the *Toynbee phenomenon*[50]), through the eustachian tube since the middle-ear *air cushion* is lost; an episode usually occurs with an infection of the upper respiratory tract. In most instances, these bacteria are initially the same as those isolated when acute otitis media occurs behind an intact tympanic membrane, such as with *S. pneumoniae* and *H. influenzae* infection.[314] After the acute otorrhea, *P. aeruginosa, Staphylococcus aureus,* and other organisms from the external ear canal enter the middle ear through the nonintact tympanic membrane, which results in *secondary* infection and acute otorrhea and chronic suppurative otitis media (Fig. 26–14).

Chronic suppurative otitis media also occurs when the middle-ear cleft is contaminated by organisms (e.g., *P. aeruginosa*) in water that enters the nonintact eardrum during bathing and swimming (Fig. 26–15).[49]

As has been described, certain populations are at high risk for chronic perforation of the tympanic membrane with and without chronic suppurative otitis media. Because these groups live in diverse geographic regions (see Table 26–4), climate is an unlikely explanation. In these racial groups, it is likely that the pathogenesis is due to genetic differences in eustachian-tube function. Nevertheless, environmental and behavioral factors and the availability of adequate health care are also important in these racial groups. Thus, these other factors (i.e., other than abnormalities of the eustachian tube) would make other populations also at risk.

What other host factors contribute to the high rate of disease in these groups? One possible explanation is that these groups have eustachian tubes that make them more prone to middle-ear infection than others. Indeed, one study identified anatomic differences in the bony segment of the eustachian tube in the bony craniofacial structures of Eskimo, American Indian, Caucasian, and Negro craniums.[140] Also, in a clinical study, White Mountain Apache

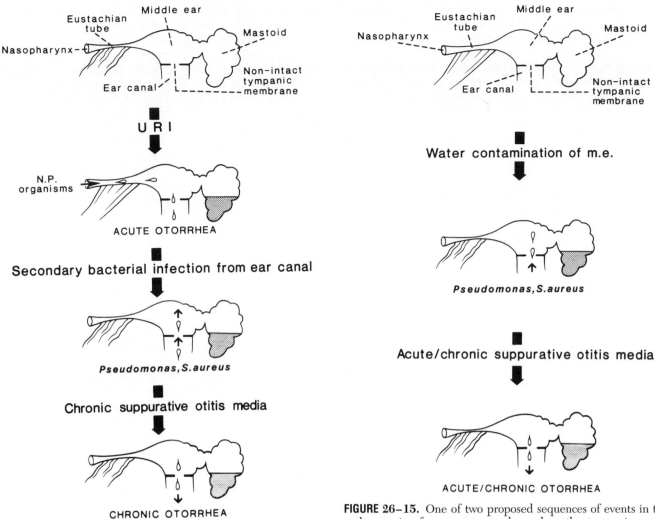

FIGURE 26–14. One of two proposed sequences of events in the pathogenesis of recurrent otorrhea when the tympanic membrane is not intact and active infection is absent in a right ear (1). After an infection of the upper respiratory tract (URI), nasopharyngeal organisms are *refluxed* or *insufflated* into the middle ear (2), which results in acute otitis media and otorrhea (3). Organisms from the external canal can then enter the middle ear (4), which can result in chronic suppurative otitis media (5). TVP, tensor veli palatini muscle (see Fig. 26–15).

FIGURE 26–15. One of two proposed sequences of events in the pathogenesis of recurrent otorrhea when the tympanic membrane is not intact and active infection is absent in a right ear (1). The middle ear is contaminated by organisms in water that enter the middle ear through the perforation (2), which can result in acute otitis media and otorrhea (3) and, if persistent, chronic suppurative otitis media (4). TVP, tensor veli palatini muscle (see Fig. 26–14).

Indians were found to have eustachian tubes that were semipatulous (of low resistance) compared with those of a group of Caucasians.[38] Similar findings have been reported in Canadian Inuits. Ratnesar calibrated the eustachian tube with ureteric catheters in Canadian Inuits and Caucasians and found the tube to be larger in Inuits than in Caucasians.[403]

(Histopathologic studies of temporal bones of young persons who had cleft palate and those who had Down syndrome—both conditions are at high risk for otitis media—had statistically shorter eustachian tubes than age-matched specimens from persons without these disorders.[449]) One study reported that environment plays a role in one high-risk population but that genetic differences are probably more important. Adopted Apache children had more episodes of acute otitis media than did their non-Apache siblings, and the illness rate in adopted Apache children was similar to that of Apache children who remained on the reservation.[457] In a recent study from Greenland of 591 children who were ages 3, 4, 5, and 8 years, 9% had chronic perforation, with and without chronic suppurative otitis media, which was statistically most common in children who had both parents who were native Greenlanders.[228]

Eustachian-tube dysfunction may be involved in the process even in persons who are not members of high-risk populations or who have an obvious craniofacial abnormality. In a study of eustachian-tube function in the ears of Japanese children and adults who had chronic perforations, Iwano et al found impaired active opening function of the tube.[242] They concluded that the tube was functionally obstructed; however, *organic* (i.e., mechanical or anatomic) obstruction was also considered to be involved in the pathogenesis in adults.

Microbiology. The bacteria that cause the initial episode of acute otitis media and perforation or acute otorrhea through a tympanostomy tube are usually not those isolated from cases of chronic suppurative otitis media.[314] The most common organism isolated from around the world is *P. aeruginosa*; *S. aureus* is also found, but less commonly.[168, 239, 263, 375, 502, 529] Table 26–5 shows the frequency of bacteria isolated from children with chronic suppurative otitis media at the Children's Hospital of Pittsburgh.[264] Anaerobic bacteria were isolated infrequently in this study. Anaerobic bacteria have been isolated from ears with chronic suppurative otitis media, but whether they are true pathogens remains to be demonstrated. Brook isolated *Bacteroides melaninogenicus* in 40% and *Peptococcus* species in 35% of middle-ear exudates; the exudate was collected through the perforation in the tympanic membrane using an 18-gauge needle covered by a plastic cannula.[76]

There have also been reports of unusual organisms, such as *Mycobacterium tuberculosis, Mycobacterium chelonae, Mycobacterium avium-intracellulare, Blastomycosis dermatitidis, Actinomyces* species, *Alcaligenes piechaudii,* and *Candida* species.[114, 241, 248, 269, 301, 362, 386]

Pathology. It is important to understand the pathologic process of chronic suppurative otitis media since the decision for or against surgical intervention may depend on the pathologic changes in the middle ear and mastoid.

TABLE 26–5. Bacteriology of Otorrhea in 51 Children (80 Ears) with Chronic Suppurative Otitis Media

Bacteria Isolated	Number of Isolates° (n = 118)
Pseudomonas aeruginosa	56
Staphylococcus aureus	18
Diphtheroids	8
Streptococcus pneumoniae	7
Haemophilus influenzae (non-typable)	6
Bacteroides spp	3
Candida albicans	2
Candida parapsilosis	2
Enterococcus	2
Acinetobacter	2
Staphylococcus epidermidis	1
Morganella morgagni	1
Providencia stuartii	1
Klebsiella spp	1
Proteus spp	1
Serratia marcescens	1
Moraxella	1
Pseudomonas cepacia	1
Providencia rettgeri	1
Pseudomonas maltophilia	1
Achromobacter xylosoxidans	1
Eikenella	1

° Number exceeds 80 because more than one organism was isolated in 38 ears.
From Kenna MA, Rosane BA, Bluestone CD. Medical management of chronic suppurative otitis media without cholesteatoma in children—update 1992. Am J Otolaryngol 14:469–473, 1993.

These changes include edema, submucosal fibrosis, and infiltration with chronic inflammatory cells, which together cause thickening of the mucous membrane.[432] Polyps may result from excessive mucosal edema; in the more advanced stage, there may be polypoid tissue and granulation tissue and osteitis of the mastoid bone, ossicles, and labyrinth. Adhesive otitis media and sclerosis of bone may occur with healing. Tympanosclerosis may also be present and is commonly associated with this disease in Alaskan (Eskimo) natives.[521] If intensive medical treatment is instituted early, these pathologic changes may be reversible without surgery. When long-standing chronic disease has led to irreversible changes, however, middle-ear and mastoid surgery is usually indicated to eradicate the infection.

Diagnosis. A purulent, mucoid, or serous discharge through a "central" perforation of the tympanic membrane for at least 2 or 3 months is evidence of chronic suppurative otitis media. Frequently, a polyp emerges through the perforation or tympanostomy tube (Fig. 26–16). The size of the perforation has no relation to the duration or severity of the disease, but the defect often involves most of the pars tensa. There is no otalgia, mastoid or pinna tenderness, vertigo, or fever. When any of these signs or symptoms are present, the examiner should look for a possible suppurative intratemporal complication, such as mastoiditis or labyrinthitis, or an intracranial complication (see Chap. 27). A search for the underlying cause of the infection may reveal the presence of paranasal sinusitis, which must be actively treated since the ear infection may not respond to medical treatment until the sinusitis resolves. An upper-respiratory allergy or a nasopharyngeal tumor may also contribute to the pathogenesis of chronic suppurative otitis media and must be managed appropriately. The discharge should be appropriately examined by a Gram-stained smear and cultured as described earlier (see Acute Perforation with Otitis Media).

One of the most important parts of the evaluation is a complete examination of the ear canal, tympanic membrane, and, if the perforation is large enough, middle ear. The otomicroscope should be used. If a satisfactory examination cannot be performed with the child awake, general anesthesia is necessary. At this time, the discharge can be aspirated and a culture from the middle ear can be obtained. A search for a polyp or unsuspected cholesteatoma or neoplasm should also be conducted.

A conductive hearing loss usually accompanies chronic suppurative otitis media. If the hearing loss is greater than 20 to 30 dB, the ossicles may be involved. However, the patient may also have a sensorineural component, which is most likely due to serous labyrinthitis.[374] Impedance testing may be helpful if purulent material in the ear canal obscures visualization of the eardrum such that a possible perforation cannot be seen. If perforation is present, the measured volume of the external canal will be larger than expected. However, the tympanometric pattern may be flat, despite the presence of a perforation, if the volume of air in the middle ear and mastoid is small. When this situation is suspected, the pressure on the pump-manometer of the impedance bridge can be increased in an attempt to force open the eustachian

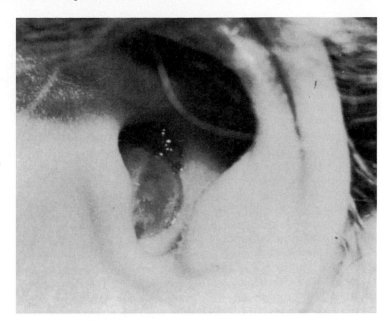

FIGURE 26–16. Aural polyp in the external auditory meatus. The polyp came through a large perforation of an ear with chronic suppurative otitis media.

tube. If the tube can be opened with positive air pressure from the pump-manometer, a perforation must be present.

CT of the middle ear and mastoid should be obtained when intensive medical treatment (including intravenous antimicrobial therapy) fails, the child has an early recurrence, or initially if cholesteatoma is suspected. In the typical case, the sclerotic or undeveloped mastoid will appear cloudy. If there is a defect in the bone due to osteitis, however, CT reveals the area. Discontinuity of the ossicular chain, if present, may be visualized on CT.

Unusual causes of a chronic draining ear, including neoplasms and eosinophilic granuloma, must be considered in the differential diagnosis of chronic suppurative otitis media. In such cases, CT should be obtained initially. Erosion of portions of the temporal bone, especially the labyrinth, suggest a tumor. Also, the tympanic membrane may temporarily heal, but the middle ear and mastoid may still be chronically infected[244] or the tympanic membrane appears to have chronic myringitis,[48, 526] which would signal the need to obtain CT of the temporal bones to determine the status of the middle-ear cleft.

Management. Treatment of chronic suppurative otitis media is initially medical and directed toward eliminating the infection from the middle ear and mastoid. Since the bacteria most frequently cultured are gram-negative, antimicrobial agents should be selected to be effective against these organisms. Some experts currently advocate the use of ototopical agents as first-line treatment.[209]

Ototopical Medications. A suspension containing polymyxin B, neomycin sulfates, and hydrocortisone (Pediotic) and one that has neomycin, polymyxin E, and hydrocortisone (Coly-Mycin) have been used in the past but are no longer available in the United States. Also, caution is advised owing to the concern over the potential ototoxicity of these agents.[388, 392, 411, 518] In addition, a recent in vitro susceptibility study showed that only 18% of middle-ear isolates were sensitive to topical neomycin.[132] Some

clinicians use topical tobramycin with dexamethasone (TobraDex) or gentamicin (Garamycin) ophthalmic drops instilled into the ear when *Pseudomonas* is isolated, but again, these agents are aminoglycosides and may therefore be ototoxic.[82, 85, 205, 238, 337] More importantly, none of these popular medications is approved for use when the tympanic membrane is not intact. Nevertheless, these ototopical agents are used widely and appear to be effective with chronic suppurative otitis media.[452] Clinicians who have employed them with apparent success think that if the infection is not eliminated, it too may cause damage to the inner ear. The bacteria, or their by-products, may enter the inner ear through the round window during a middle-ear infection.[249, 304]

The FDA has recently approved ofloxacin (Floxin Otic), an ototopical agent, for use in children when acute otitis media with otorrhea occurs when a tympanostomy tube is in place. At present, ofloxacin is the only topical antimicrobial agent that has been demonstrated to be safe and effective[131, 191] and approved for this indication in children. It is also approved for adults who have chronic suppurative otitis media, but ofloxacin is currently not approved for this indication in children,[8] even though it has been reported to be effective in this age group.[252] Topical ofloxacin has been shown to be more effective than the combination of neomycin/polymyxin B/hydrocortisone otic drops in adults with chronic suppurative otitis media.[487] Thus, the lack of reported clinical trials in children notwithstanding, it seems reasonable today to use ofloxacin initially in children who have uncomplicated chronic suppurative otitis media.

Ciprofloxacin with hydrocortisone (Cipro HC) has also been approved to treat external otitis in both children and adults. Even though ciprofloxacin is not approved for chronic suppurative otitis media, it appears to be effective.[22, 130, 155, 156] One study showed that topical ciprofloxacin was more effective than topical gentamicin for chronic suppurative otitis media in adults[498]; another showed that this antibiotic was as effective as tobramycin in adults with this infection.[172] No apparent ototoxicity has occurred after using this ototopical agent in patients with chronic suppurative otitis media.[366] In addition, topical ciprofloxacin did not cause ototoxicity in the monkey model of chronic suppurative otitis media.[13] There is still no consensus about the potential efficacy of adding a corticosteroid component to the antimicrobial agent, but steroids may hasten resolution of the inflammation.[116] Alper et al reported that the combination of tobramycin and dexamethasone was more effective than tobramycin alone in the monkey model of chronic suppurative otitis media; tobramycin with and without dexamethasone was not only effective but also safe, i.e., there was no cochlear damage.[12]

As an alternative to an antibiotic topical agent, some clinicians recommend antiseptic drops. An antiseptic ototopical agent (aluminum acetate) was found to be as effective as topical gentamicin sulfate for otorrhea in a randomized clinical trial reported from the United Kingdom.[110] Thorp et al evaluated the in vitro activity of acetic acid and aluminum subacetate (Burow's solution) and found both to be effective against the major pathogens causing chronic suppurative otitis media.[484] Burow's solution was somewhat more effective than acetic acid. Antiseptic drops (e.g., acetic acid) are commonly used in underdeveloped countries and are reputed to be effective. Because of cost and availability, antibiotic ototopical agents are used when antiseptic drops are ineffective.

Table 26–6 provides a list of ototopical agents approved by the FDA for ear infections. As stated earlier, only ofloxacin otic solution is approved for children when the tympanic membrane is nonintact and then only when a tympanostomy tube is present. Nevertheless, other agents, such as ciprofloxacin with hydrocortisone, may be beneficial for use in children with this middle-ear and mastoid infection. The advantage of quinolone topical agents is that there is no evidence of ototoxicity in animal models, which had been reported with aminoglycoside use. Also, with the growing concern over the emergence of multidrug-resistant bacterial otic pathogens, an ototopical agent is desirable since a high concentration of the drug directed at the site of infection should prevent emergence of resistant organisms.

If topical antibiotic medication is elected, the child should ideally return to the outpatient facility daily to have the discharge thoroughly aspirated or swabbed (i.e., *aural toilet, ear mopping*) and to have the ototopical medication directly instilled into the middle ear through the perforation or tympanostomy tube via an otoscope or otomicroscope. Frequently, the discharge improves rapidly (within a week) with this type of treatment, after which the ear drops may be administered at home until the middle-ear/mastoid inflammation resolves completely. When daily administration by the physician is not feasible, the parent or caregiver can administer the drops.

Oral Antimicrobial Agents. Oral antibiotics that are approved to treat acute otitis media may be effective if the bacterium is susceptible, but since the organism is usually *P. aeruginosa*, agents that are currently approved for children usually are not effective; approximately 40% of *Pseudomonas* infections are susceptible in vitro to trimethroprim-sulfamethoxazole.[133] Despite these potential drawbacks, and the recommendation by an expert panel that ototopical medications should be the initial treatment,[209] many clinicians administer a broad-spectrum oral antibiotic hoping that the underlying infection is caused by the usual bacteria that are isolated from ears with acute otitis media. In a recent report of a randomized clinical trial conducted in Kenya, Smith et al compared (1) oral amoxicillin-clavulanate, *dry mopping* of the ear, and ototopical antibiotic-cortisone drops, (2) dry mopping alone, and (3) no treatment; they found that the combination of oral antibiotic and topical agents was statistically more effective than dry mopping alone or no treatment.[452] However, one randomized clinical trial found that topical ofloxacin was more effective than systemic amoxicillin-clavulanate (without ear drops) in adults with chronic suppurative otitis media.[530]

Orally administered ciprofloxacin has been shown to be effective in adults and Israeli children who had chronic suppurative otitis media, but this agent is currently not approved for patients under age 17 years in the United States.[280, 285, 375, 390]

When ototopical agents or oral antimicrobial agents, or both, are used, the child should be reexamined in about 1 week, during which the microbiologic studies can be used to make any needed adjustments in the medications. After approximately 1 week, the discharge should cease or markedly improve. If indeed the otorrhea is improving, the child is reexamined periodically thereafter until resolution occurs. If there is no improvement after 1 to 2 weeks, other treatment options should be considered, such as parenteral antimicrobial therapy.

Parenteral Antimicrobial Agents. If the child experiences treatment failure after the administration of ototopical agents, with or without an oral antimicrobial agent, the patient should receive a parenteral β-lactam antipseudo-

TABLE 26–6. Ototopical Agents Used in the Treatment of Chronic Suppurative Otitis Media°

Generic Name	Trade Name (Company)
Acetic acid (2%) otic solution	Vosol (Wallace Laboratories)
Acetic acid (2%) and hydrocortisone (1%) otic solution	Vosol HC (Wallace Laboratories)
Acetic acid 2% in aqueous aluminum acetate otic solution	Otic Domeboro (Bayer Corporation, West Haven, CT)
Ciprofloxacin hydrochloride and hydrocortisone otic suspension	Ciprofloxin HC Suspension (Alcon, Humacao, P.R.)
Colistin sulfate-neomycin sulfate-thonzonium bromide-hydrocortisone acetate otic suspension	Cortisone-TC Otic Suspension (Monarch Pharmaceuticals, Bristol, TN)
Neomycin, polymycin B sulfate, and hydrocortisone otic suspension	Pediotic Suspension (Monarch Pharmaceuticals, Bristol, TN)
Ofloxacin otic solution 0.3%	Floxin Otic (Daiichi Pharmaceutical Corp. Montvale, NJ)

° Agents listed are commonly used in children and adults; only Floxin Otic has U.S. FDA approval for this indication, but only for adults.

monal drug, such as ticarcillin, piperacillin, or ceftazidime. Empirically, ticarcillin-clavulanate is usually selected since *Pseudomonas,* with and without *S. aureus,* is frequently isolated; the results of the culture and susceptibility studies dictate the antimicrobial agent ultimately chosen (see Chapter 25).[263, 264] Dagan et al in Israel[117] and Arguedas et al in Costa Rica[19] reported excellent results using ceftazidime. In Finland, Vartiainen and Kansanen also recommend a trial of intravenous antimicrobial therapy before considering mastoid surgery.[501] The regimen can be altered when results of culture and susceptibility tests are available. Also, the purulent material and debris in the external canal (and middle ear, if possible) are aspirated and the ototopical medication instilled daily. This method of treatment can be administered with the child hospitalized but is more cost-effective and probably just as effective on an outpatient basis.[117, 157]

In about 90% of children, the middle ear is free of discharge and the signs of chronic suppurative otitis media greatly improved or absent within 5 to 7 days. Kenna et al conducted a study of 36 pediatric patients with chronic suppurative otitis media in which all children received parenteral antimicrobial therapy and daily aural toilet.[263] Medical therapy alone resolved the infection in 32 patients (89%); 4 children required tympanomastoidectomy. The investigators later increased the study group to 66 children and reported similar short-term results; 89% had dry ears after intravenous antibiotic therapy.[262] In a follow-up of that study, 51 of the original 66 were evaluated for their long-term outcomes.[264] With these 51 children, medical treatment resolved initial or recurrent infection in 40 (78%) and mastoid surgery eventually was required in 11 (22%). Failure was associated with older children and with early recurrence. Englender et al performed serotyping and pyocin typing of *P. aeruginosa* organisms from 142 patients, including children, and found that if the patient had a recurrence with a different type, medical treatment was frequently successful.[153] If the recurrence involved the same type, medical therapy usually failed and the patient required mastoid surgery. Leiberman et al found that when recurrence was early, children were less likely to benefit from either medical treatment, including intravenous antibiotics, or surgery.[286] (For details of the surgical technique of mastoidectomy for chronic suppurative otitis media, see Bluestone.[65])

If resolution does not occur and hospitalization is required, the child can be discharged and receive the parenteral antibiotic and eardrops (given by the parent or caregiver) for 10 to 14 days at home. The patient should be followed periodically to watch for signs of spontaneous closure of the perforation, which frequently appear after the middle ear and mastoid are no longer infected. Appropriate intensive medical treatment should be attempted before major ear surgery is recommended since the outcome of surgery is not as favorable when medical treatment is withheld.[502]

Surgery. When chronic suppurative otitis media fails to respond to intensive medical therapy (i.e., intravenous antibiotics, aural toilet, and ototopical medications) within several days, surgery on the middle ear and mastoid, i.e.,

tympanomastoidectomy, may be required to eradicate the infection. CT should be performed. Failures usually occur when there is:

- An underlying blockage of the communication between the middle ear and mastoid (i.e., *aditus-ad-antrum*)
- Irreversible chronic osteitis
- Cholesteatoma (or tumor)
- An early recurrence with the same causative organism[264]

A tympanostomy tube can be helpful if the chronic suppurative otitis media is associated with a perforation that is too small to permit adequate drainage or the perforation frequently closes, only to reopen with episodic drainage. On the other hand, if the chronic infection is related to a tympanostomy tube (i.e., the middle-ear gas cushion is absent), some clinicians advocate removal of the tube, hoping that the infection will subsequently subside. However, the recurrent or chronic ear infections for which the tube was inserted originally frequently recur. This approach may have some merit in a child with a long-standing retained tube.

Prevention of Recurrence. With an understanding of the pathogenesis of chronic suppurative otitis media (i.e., chronic otorrhea is preceded by acute otorrhea), the most effective way to prevent recurrence of otorrhea when the tympanic membrane is intact and an attack of acute otitis media occurs is to promptly, appropriately, and adequately treat the infection with the usual oral antimicrobial agents recommended for acute otitis media. If the tympanic membrane is not intact (i.e., perforation or a tympanostomy tube is present without evidence of infection), early treatment of acute otorrhea (i.e., acute otitis media) should likewise be effective. Treatment with an oral antimicrobial agent may be enhanced by adding an ototopical agent or agents to prevent a secondary infection with external ear-canal organisms such as *Pseudomonas.*

When a perforation (or tympanostomy tube) is present in the absence of middle-ear/mastoid infection, and when it is desirable to maintain middle-ear ventilation through a nonintact eardrum, recurrent episodes of otorrhea can usually be prevented with antimicrobial prophylaxis, e.g., amoxicillin.[323] If a tympanostomy tube is present and the middle ear is now disease-free, its removal may restore the physiology of the middle ear and eustachian tube (i.e., prevent reflux or insufflation of nasopharyngeal secretions). However, removal of tympanostomy tubes may not be desirable, especially in infants and young children; in these cases, antimicrobial prophylaxis should also be considered until the tubes spontaneously extrude.

If the child has a chronic perforation that is now dry, tympanoplastic surgery should be considered. The same factors should be considered when deciding to repair an eardrum perforation in children (as described earlier in terms of removing a tympanostomy tube).[65]

Complications and Sequelae. The most common sequela of chronic suppurative otitis media is chronic hearing loss and the potential deficits related to this disability. The chronic infection may result in permanent conductive hearing loss due to damage to the ossicles; sensorineural loss may also occur. Chronic suppurative otitis media can also progress into one or more of the intratemporal (extracranial) suppurative complications described in this chapter, such as acute mastoiditis, acute labyrinthitis, facial paralysis, or an intracranial suppurative complication that requires immediate surgical intervention. Intracranial complications caused by chronic suppurative otitis media occur with equal or greater frequency as those due to cholesteatoma.[364] This finding is not only important in underdeveloped countries where chronic suppurative otitis media is common but has been reported from industrialized nations (see Chapter 27).[84]

A child who has a chronic suppurative aural discharge and who experiences one or more of the intratemporal suppurative complications, such as acute mastoid osteitis, labyrinthitis, facial paralysis, or an intracranial suppurative complication, requires immediate surgical intervention.[236] A cholesteatoma is not uncommon when an ear with chronic suppurative otitis media fails to respond to intensive medical treatment, even though otomicroscopy or imaging revealed no preoperative evidence of cholesteatoma. The cholesteatoma is usually found in the middle ear (and mastoid) after migration of the squamous epithelium through the perforation in the tympanic membrane. When a cholesteatoma is found, surgical removal is indicated as outlined later in this chapter.

Conclusions. Many children who have chronic suppurative otitis media improve with the administration of ototopical medications or, in some cases, the addition of an orally administered antimicrobial agent if the bacterial organism is susceptible to the antibiotics that are recommended for use in children. Unfortunately, the most common etiologic agent is *Pseudomonas*, for which there is no currently approved antibiotic in children. Children whose infection is refractory to ototopical medication (with or without an orally administered antimicrobial agents) require (1) a thorough examination of the external canal and tympanic membrane with the otomicroscope (under general anesthesia, if necessary), (2) a Gram-stained culture obtained directly from the middle ear, (3) thorough aspiration of the ear canal and, if possible, the middle ear (i.e., aural toilet) and, ideally, direct instillation of the appropriate ototopical medication into the middle ear daily, using the otomicroscope to visualize the middle ear, and (4) parenteral administration of an antimicrobial agent. The ototopical medication and the systemic antimicrobial therapy should be selected after microbiologic assessment of the middle-ear discharge.

If the infection can be eliminated using the methods previously described, recurrence can be prevented with the following options: (1) early and appropriate antimicrobial therapy for acute otitis media in an attempt to prevent bacteria from the external canal from entering the middle ear, (2) prophylactic antimicrobial therapy, (3) removal of the tympanostomy tube, or (4) surgical repair of the tympanic membrane defect. The choice depends on the age of the child and the status of the function of the eustachian tube. Middle-ear and mastoid surgery should be reserved for the children in whom intensive medical therapy fails.

Mastoiditis

In the pre-antibiotic era, acute mastoiditis was the most common infection for which infants and children were hospitalized. Since the widespread use of antimicrobial agents, the incidence has dramatically fallen, but the clinician should always be aware that acute mastoiditis remains the most common suppurative complication of acute otitis media.[57, 128, 192] In addition, there is some evidence that the incidence of acute mastoiditis has recently increased in geographic areas in which antimicrobial agents are withheld in children who have acute otitis media[231] as well as in countries in which antibiotics are employed routinely.[461]

Chronic mastoiditis that develops after an episode of acute mastoiditis has also decreased since the mid-20th century for similar reasons. But chronic mastoiditis is still a major problem when chronic suppurative otitis media is present, especially in racial groups and geographic areas in which this disease is common.[60] Also, both acute and chronic mastoiditis can occur in the presence of cholesteatoma.[364] Thus, both acute and chronic mastoiditis still occur and may be responsible for significant morbidity and life-threatening infection, especially from intracranial extension of the disease.[287]

Anatomy, Pathogenesis, and Pathology

At birth, the mastoid consists of a single cell, the *antrum*, connected to the middle ear by a small channel, the *aditus-ad-antrum*. Pneumatization of the mastoid bone takes place soon after birth and is usually extensive by age 2. The process may continue throughout life. The clinical importance of the mastoid is related to contiguous structures, including the posterior cranial fossa, the middle cranial fossa, the sigmoid and lateral sinuses, the canal of the facial nerve, the semicircular canals, and the petrous tip of the temporal bone. The mastoid air cells are lined with modified respiratory mucosa, and all are interconnected with the antrum (Fig. 26–17).

Infection in the mastoid proceeds after middle-ear infection through the following stages:

1. Hyperemia and edema of the mucosal lining of the pneumatized cells
2. Accumulation of serous and then purulent exudates in the cells
3. Demineralization of the cellular walls and necrosis of bone due to pressure of the purulent exudate on the thin bony septa and ischemia of the septa, caused by decrease in blood flow
4. Formation of abscess cavities due to coalescence of adjacent cells after destruction of cell walls
5. Escape of pus into contiguous areas

This process may halt at any stage, with subsequent resolution. However, when infection persists for more than a week or 10 days, inflammatory granulation tissue forms in the pneumatic cavity. Hypertrophic osteitis develops and results in thickening and sclerosis of cellular walls and reduced cellular space. There may be repeated cycles of absorption and deposition of bone. If the infection remains chronic but low-grade, there is thickening of

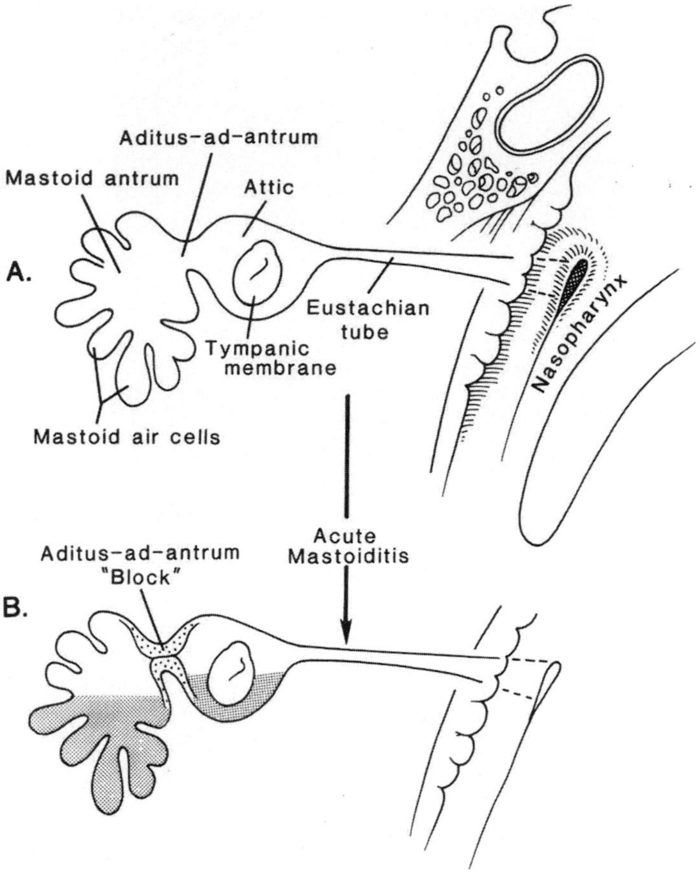

FIGURE 26–17. Schematic depiction of the anatomy of the right eustachian tube, middle ear, and mastoid air cell. The middle ear is normally connected to the mastoid air cells through the narrow aditus-ad-antrum *(A)*. When the middle ear and mastoid are infected, the aditus-ad-antrum can become obstructed because of mucosal edema and granulation tissue, which has been called *aditus block* or *bottleneck (B)*.

the mucosa caused by a fibrinous exudate, which may become organized and lead to permanent adhesions. Columnar metaplasia with new gland formation may result in extensive production of mucus in the former cells.

Mastoiditis can be classified into acute and chronic types. Acute mastoiditis is further subdivided according to the pathologic stage present, which has clinical significance because management depends on the stage of the disease. Unfortunately, because of failure to appreciate the natural history and pathologic features of acute mastoiditis, clinicians and authors are confused about the most appropriate management of each stage. The following classification is most consistent with the current understanding of the stages of acute and chronic mastoiditis and has been reported previously.[59]

Mastoiditis without Periosteitis/Osteitis

Since the mastoid gas cell system is connected to the distal end of the middle ear, all episodes of otitis media are probably associated with some inflammation of the mastoid. Thus, mastoiditis can be a natural extension and part of the pathologic process of middle-ear inflammation; the mastoid may be involved in acute otitis media or otitis media with effusion (of any duration).

Diagnosis

The diagnosis is commonly made after CT or magnetic resonance imaging (MRI) is obtained for another problem

(e.g., sinusitis, head trauma) in a child who has no signs or symptoms referable to the ears, in which case mastoiditis is an incidental finding. No specific signs or symptoms of mastoid infection, e.g., protrusion of the pinna, postauricular swelling, tenderness, pain and erythema, are present in this most common stage of mastoiditis. Imaging of the mastoid area frequently reveals cloudy mastoids, which indicates inflammation, but no mastoid osteitis (i.e., bony erosion of the mastoid air cells) is evident (Fig. 26–18).

Management and Outcome

The process is usually reversible as the middle-ear/mastoid infection resolves, either as a natural process or because of medical management, e.g., antimicrobial therapy. Thus, with no periosteal involvement of the postauricular region, osteitis of the mastoid, or subperiosteal abscess, this stage of mastoiditis is *not* a suppurative complication of otitis media.

When this stage of mastoiditis is diagnosed, such as by CT, in a child who has an episode of acute otitis media, the management is the same as recommended for acute otitis media since the involvement of the mastoid is a natural extension of the middle-ear infection (see Chapter 25). Indications for tympanocentesis (diagnostic aspiration of the middle ear) are the same as when acute otitis media is diagnosed, and the status of the mastoid is undetermined (by CT or MRI), such as when the patient:

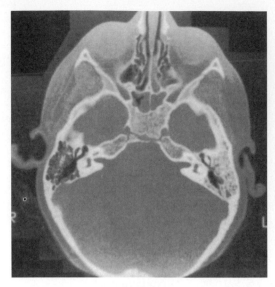

FIGURE 26–18. Mastoiditis without periosteitis/osteitis. Computed tomogram of the left temporal bone of a child with acute otitis media in which the mastoid air cells show signs of inflammation without osteitis; the pinna was not displaced, and the periosteum was not involved. The diagnosis was acute mastoiditis without periosteitis/osteitis, which is common during an episode of acute otitis media and usually resolves when the middle-ear infection is eliminated.

- Is severely ill or toxic
- Fails to improve rapidly while on appropriate and adequate antibiotic treatment
- Experiences otitis media while receiving antimicrobial agents
- Experiences otitis media in the newborn period
- Is immunologically deficient
- Has a suppurative complication (myringotomy is indicated when drainage of the middle ear is desirable, such as when the child has severe otalgia or when a suppurative complication is suspected or is present— see Chapter 23)

When acute infection in the mastoid (and usually middle ear) does not resolve at this stage, the disease can rapidly progress to *acute mastoiditis with periosteitis*, with the next stage being *acute mastoid osteitis*, which can occur with or without the presence of a subperiosteal abscess.

When imaging of the head reveals the incidental finding of inflammation of the mastoid gas cells in a child who has an episode of otitis media with effusion (regardless of the duration of the effusion), management is the same as recommended for this middle-ear inflammation when the status of the mastoid is unknown, i.e., CT or MRI is not obtained (see Chapter 25).

Acute Mastoiditis with Periosteitis

When infection within the mastoid spreads to the periosteum covering the mastoid process, periosteitis can develop. The route of infection from the mastoid cells to the periosteum is by venous channels, usually the mastoid

emissary vein. The condition should not be confused with a subperiosteal abscess since management of the latter condition usually requires a mastoidectomy whereas the former frequently responds to medical treatment and tympanocentesis/myringotomy.

Epidemiology

Before the antibiotic era, the incidence of acute mastoiditis as a complication of acute otitis media was high. In 1938, the rate was 20%, whereas it was 2.8% 10 years later (with an almost 90% reduction in the mortality rate during that period) and in some studies it dropped to almost zero.[221, 369, 460] At the Children's Hospital of Pittsburgh between 1980 and 1995, 72 infants and children had acute mastoiditis but only 18 (25%) required mastoidectomy; the remaining 54 (75%) did not.[192] Most likely, the majority of children who experience acute mastoiditis today have acute mastoiditis with periosteitis. The growing enthusiasm for withholding antimicrobial therapy today in some countries will most likely result in an increase in this suppurative complication.[231] However, in several recent reviews acute mastoiditis developed in infants and children who did and who did not receive antimicrobial agents for the preceding acute otitis media.[128, 294, 305]

Pathogenesis

Infection in the mastoid air cells, which is frequently part of an episode of acute otitis media, usually resolves spontaneously or after effective antimicrobial treatment. The effusion within the mastoid air cells drains into the middle ear, which in turn drains down the eustachian tube, i.e., the clearance function of the tube. The narrow communication between the middle ear and the mastoid air cells is the aditus-ad-antrum (see Fig. 26–17A). Physiologically, the mastoid air-cell system is most likely a reservoir of gas for the middle ear, and this narrow passage makes it more difficult for middle-ear infection to enter the mastoid. However, when infection is in the mastoid, the aditus-ad-antrum can become obstructed from edema and granulation tissue (see Fig. 26–17B). This obstruction has been called the *bottleneck* and has been implicated in the pathogenesis of acute mastoiditis. If the obstruction persists, acute mastoiditis with periosteitis can then develop, which can progress into acute mastoid osteitis (with and without subperiosteal abscess) and further progress into another suppurative complication in the temporal bone or the intracranial cavity.

Clinical Presentation and Diagnosis

Clinically, the child has the classic signs and symptoms of acute otitis media, such as fever and otalgia, but also has postauricular erythema; mild tenderness and some edema may also be present in the postauricular area (Fig. 26–19). The pinna may or may not be displaced inferiorly and anteriorly, with loss of the postauricular crease. Subperiosteal abscess is absent. Examination of the eardrum

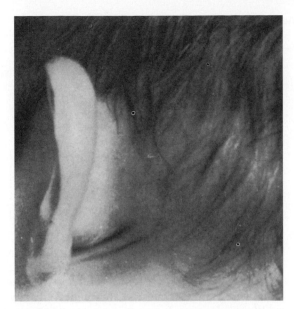

FIGURE 26–19. Example of postauricular periosteitis. This 2-year-old boy had acute otitis media and mastoiditis. In addition to fever and otalgia, there was postauricular swelling, erythema, tenderness to touch, and loss of the postauricular crease but no evidence of a subperiosteal abscess or radiographic evidence of mastoid osteitis. Management consisted of tympanocentesis/myringotomy (and tympanostomy tube insertion) and parenteral antimicrobial therapy, which resulted in complete resolution of the postauricular involvement 24 hours after the beginning of treatment.

typically reveals evidence of acute otitis media. However, the middle ear may be effusion-free in the presence of acute mastoiditis if there is an obstruction of the aditus-ad-antrum. The middle-ear effusion drains down the eustachian tube, but the infection in the mastoid cannot drain into the middle ear. Table 26–7 shows the age and frequency of the presenting signs and symptoms in 72 infants and children who had acute mastoiditis at the Children's Hospital of Pittsburgh from 1980 to 1995 (some of these patients had acute mastoid osteitis with and without subperiosteal abscess). In this series, one half were age 3 or younger; two thirds were younger than 7. Also, only 28% of these cases were diagnosed as middle-ear effusion, which is clinically important since this finding emphasizes how mastoiditis can be present despite the lack of otitis media; the middle-ear effusion resolves but the infection in the mastoid persists.

Table 26–8 shows the hearing status of 41 of these patients who underwent audiometric testing.[192] About half of these 41 children had hearing in the normal range and half had abnormal hearing levels, but most of the severely ill children did not undergo hearing evaluation prior to management, which usually included mastoidectomy.

For this stage of acute mastoiditis, CT of the temporal bones (and intracranial cavity) should be obtained to detect any osteitis of the mastoid. However, CT is not mandatory if the infection is limited to the middle ear and mastoid, the child is not severely ill or toxic, and the child rapidly improves after tympanocentesis/myringotomy and parenterally administered antimicrobial therapy.

TABLE 26–7. Age, Presenting Symptoms, and Signs of 72 Infants and Children with Acute Mastoiditis

	Patients (%)
Age (years)	
0–3	36 (50.0)
4–6	12 (16.7)
7–12	17 (23.6)
13–18	7 (9.7)
Symptoms	
Otalgia	62 (86.1)
Postauricular pain	58 (80.6)
Fever	51 (70.8)
Otorrhea	29 (40.3)
Upper-respiratory infection	17 (23.6)
Irritability	16 (22.2)
Hearing loss	6 (8.3)
Signs	
Postauricular tenderness	58 (80.6)
Pinna protrusion	51 (70.8)
Postauricular erythema	51 (70.8)
Middle-ear effusion	48 (66.7)
Tympanic membrane erythema	42 (58.3)
Contralateral middle-ear abnormalities	35 (48.6)
Middle-ear effusion	20 (27.8)
Tympanic membrane bulging	8 (11.1)
Tympanic membrane erythema	6 (8.3)
Tympanic membrane perforation	1 (1.4)
Tympanic membrane bulging	34 (47.2)
Otorrhea	24 (33.3)
Fever ≥38.3°C	24 (33.3)
Tympanic membrane perforation	13 (18.1)
Postauricular mass	13 (18.1)
Cervical adenopathy	12 (16.7)
Postauricular abscess	9 (12.5)
Sagging of posterior auditory canal wall	2 (2.8)

From Goldstein NA, Casselbrant ML, Bluestone CD, Kurs-Lasky M. Intratemporal complications of acute otitis media in infants and children. Otolaryngol Head Neck Surg 119:444–454, 1998.

Differential Diagnosis

The differential diagnosis of childhood acute mastoiditis with periosteitis includes perichondritis of the pinna and external otitis. The typical presentation of a child with

TABLE 26–8. Hearing Status in 41 Infants and Children with Acute Mastoiditis

Audiologic Findings	Patient (%)
Normal range	21 (51)
Abnormal	20 (49)
Conductive loss (dB)	
30–39	4 (10)
40–49	8 (20)
50–59	2 (5)
Mixed loss (dB)	
60–79	2 (5)
80–99	2 (5)
Sensorineural loss (dB)	
40–49	1 (2)
Profound	1 (2)

From Goldstein NA, Casselbrant ML, Bluestone CD, Kurs-Lasky M. Intratemporal complications of acute otitis media in infants and children. Otolaryngol Head Neck Surg 119:444–454, 1998.

TABLE 26–9. Differential Diagnosis of Postauricular Involvement of Acute Mastoiditis and Periosteitis/Abscess

Disease	Postauricular Signs and Symptoms				External Canal Infection	Middle-Ear Effusion
	Crease°	Erythema	Mass	Tenderness		
Acute mastoiditis with periosteitis	May be absent	Yes	No	Usually	No	Usually
Acute mastoiditis with subperiosteal abscess	Absent	Maybe	Yes	Yes	No	Usually
Periosteitis of pinna with postauricular extension	Intact	Yes	No	Usually	No	No
External otitis with postauricular extension	Intact	Yes	No	Usually	Yes	No
Postauricular lymphadenitis	Intact	No	Yes	Maybe (Circumscribed)	No	No

° Crease, postauricular crease (fold) between pinna and postauricular area.

perichondritis of the pinna is swelling and erythema of the outer ear, which may spread to the periosteum of the postauricular area, but the postauricular crease is usually obliterated and external otitis and middle-ear effusion are absent (unless concurrent, unrelated otitis media is present). External otitis can also spread to the postauricular area, which, like perichondritis, obliterates the postauricular crease. In contrast with these two infections, the postauricular crease is still evident when the perichondritis is an extension of acute mastoiditis, and middle-ear effusion is usually—but not always—present. When the acute mastoiditis has progressed to a subperiosteal abscess, the postauricular swelling may be misdiagnosed as an enlarged lymph node. Typically, lymph-node enlargement in the postauricular area is due to a scalp infection, dermatitis, or an insect bite above the affected ear, and middle-ear effusion is absent. The lymph node is well circumscribed, usually freely movable in all four directions, and is most often not tender to touch. On the other hand, a subperiosteal abscess secondary to acute mastoiditis does not move readily, is not well circumscribed, and is tender to touch (Table 26–9).

Microbiology

Middle-ear aspirates reveal similar bacterial pathogens isolated from children's ears that have uncomplicated acute middle-ear infection, such as *S. pneumoniae*, *S. pyogenes*, or *H. influenzae*,[294, 305, 461] but there may be an unusual organism, such as *Pseudomonas aeruginosa*, if there has been otorrhea.[212, 351] Table 26–10 shows the type and frequency of bacteria isolated from 65 infants and children who had acute mastoiditis (acute mastoiditis with periosteitis and acute mastoid osteitis) at the Children's Hospital of Pittsburgh between 1980 and 1995.[192] Cultures were obtained from one or more of the following sites: the external auditory canal when otorrhea was present, the middle ear by tympanocentesis, or from the middle ear or mastoid, or both, at the time of mastoidectomy. The most common pathogenic bacteria were *S. pneumoniae*, *P. aeruginosa*, and *S. pyogenes*. Most reviews of the microbiology of acute mastoiditis have demonstrated that *S. pneumoniae* is the most commonly isolated pathogen. With the rising rate of antibiotic-resistant pneumococci, acute mastoiditis may become more preva-

lent.[17] Hopefully, with the advent of the new conjugated pneumococcal vaccine being administered to all infants and many young children, the rate of pneumococcal acute mastoiditis will decrease,[57] but in those countries in which this new vaccine is not available the rate will remain high.

Management

The patient may be treated on an ambulatory basis if the infection is not severe. However, hospitalization is usually necessary since parenteral antimicrobial therapy is frequently needed and most patients require an immediate tympanocentesis (for aspiration and microbiologic assessment of the middle-ear/mastoid effusion) and myringotomy to drain the middle ear. In the absence of an aditus-ad-antrum "block," myringotomy should also drain the mastoid. If the child has had recurrent attacks of acute otitis media or if the current episode of acute otitis media is superimposed on chronic otitis media with effusion, a tympanostomy tube is indicated. A tympanostomy tube enhances drainage over a longer period than myringotomy alone. Although there are reports of successful antibiotic treatment without the benefit of tympanocentesis

TABLE 26–10. Bacteriology of Effusions, Otorrhea, and Mastoids in 65 Infants and Children with Acute Mastoiditis

Organism	Number of Isolates (%)
Streptococcus pneumoniae	21 (32.3)
Pseudomonas aeruginosa	19 (29.2)
Streptococcus pyogenes	12 (18.5)
Diphtheroids	9 (13.9)
Anaerobes	7 (10.8)
Others°	39 (60.0)
No Growth	6 (9.2)
Total†	113

° *Staphylococcus* coagulase negative (23), ∝-hemolytic *Streptococcus* (4), *Haemophilus influenzae* (3), *Micrococcus* species (2), *Moraxella catarrhalis* (1), *Staphylococcus aureus* (1), *Staphylococcus* species (1), *Enterobacter cloacae* (1), *Neisseria* species (1), *Enterococcus* species (1), *Citrobacter diversus* (1).

† Total isolates exceed 100% since some cultures were polymicrobial.

From Goldstein NA, Casselbrant ML, Bluestone CD, Kurs-Lasky M. Intratemporal complications of acute otitis media in infants and children. Otolaryngol Head Neck Surg 119:444–454, 1998.

or myringotomy, aspirating the middle ear is an important diagnostic (and therapeutic) procedure today. This is because an antibiotic-resistant bacterial pathogen such as multidrug-resistant pneumococcus may be the causative organism, which may require an antimicrobial agent (e.g., vancomycin) not frequently used for acute otitis media/mastoiditis.[17, 73, 192, 212, 351, 517]

Cultures from the middle ear are required to identify the causative organisms. Antimicrobial susceptibility studies are important to select the most effective antibiotic agent. For empirical parenteral antimicrobial therapy, cefuroxime sodium, ticarcillin disodium with clavulanate potassium, or ampicillin-sulbactam can be initiated until the Gram stain, culture, and susceptibility studies of the middle-ear aspirates are available. When penicillin-resistant *S. pneumoniae* is the possible pathogen, some clinicians also add vancomycin while awaiting the culture and susceptibly report.

The periosteal involvement should resolve within 24 to 48 hours after the tympanic membrane has been opened for drainage and adequate and appropriate antimicrobial therapy has begun. A mastoidectomy should be performed if:

- The symptoms of the acute infection, such as fever and otalgia, persist
- The postauricular involvement does not progressively improve
- A subperiosteal abscess develops

CT can aid the decision as to whether surgery is needed. A mastoidectomy is also indicated if another intratemporal (extracranial) suppurative complication of otitis media is present, such as facial paralysis, labyrinthitis, petrous apicitis, or an intracranial complication (e.g., meningitis, lateral sinus thrombosis, or abscess of the epidural or subdural space or brain).

Outcome

Of the 72 infants and children with acute mastoiditis at the Children's Hospital of Pittsburgh, 54 (75%) were treated conservatively with broad-spectrum intravenous antibiotics and myringotomy, with and without tympanostomy tube insertion.[192] The other 18 (25%) required mastoidectomy. Of these 18 children, 14 (78%) had one or more of the following: mastoid osteitis, subperiosteal abscess, cholesteatoma, or another suppurative complication, e.g., facial paralysis. In Australia, Harley et al had approximately the same experience as in Pittsburgh.[192] Between 1982 and 1993, 58 infants and children were admitted to the Royal Children's Hospital of Melbourne; of these, 45 (78%) were treated conservatively with intravenous antimicrobial therapy, with and without tympanostomy tube insertion. The remaining 13 patients required mastoidectomy. Other centers have recently reported treating most children conservatively and not requiring mastoidectomy.[113, 278, 305] However, other centers have reported that most of their patients require a mastoidectomy.[189, 218, 306, 351, 357, 389, 412, 414] The reasons for these conflicting reports are probably the lack of uniform definition of the disease, dissimilarity in presentation of the cases, and variation in management. Our opinion is that most patients with

acute mastoiditis with only periosteitis recover without the need for mastoidectomy.

Immediate treatment at this stage of acute mastoiditis is mandatory since no treatment may result in acute mastoid osteitis (with or without a subperiosteal abscess) or a potentially more life-threatening condition (e.g., a suppurative complication such as meningitis or brain abscess).[128]

In the absence of mastoid osteitis (with or without subperiosteal abscess), the primary care physician or pediatric infectious disease specialist can provide the initial medical care for patients with acute mastoiditis with periosteitis. However, tympanocentesis/myringotomy is required and an otolaryngologist will be needed if the medical specialists are untrained in this procedure. Referral to an otolaryngologist is appropriate if a mastoidectomy is indicated, as described earlier. Also, immediate referral for surgical evaluation and management is indicated when acute mastoid infection develops in a child with chronic suppurative otitis media or cholesteatoma, or both.

Acute Mastoiditis with Osteitis (with and without Subperiosteal Abscess)

Acute mastoiditis with osteitis has also been called *acute coalescent mastoiditis* or *acute surgical mastoiditis*, but the pathologic process is really *acute mastoid osteitis*. A subperiosteal abscess may or may not be present.[59]

Epidemiology

A recent review over a 20-year period (1977 to 1996) in one Danish county revealed that 79 children underwent mastoidectomy for acute mastoiditis; a subperiosteal abscess was present in 66%.[389] In a review over a 15-year period (1980 to 1995) of 72 children who had acute mastoiditis by Goldstein et al, 31% had either a postauricular mass or a subperiosteal abscess.[192] In a report from Rome, in which 39 children had mastoidectomy for acute mastoiditis, all had a subperiosteal abscess.[310]

Pathogenesis and Pathology

When infection within the mastoid progresses, rarefying osteitis can cause destruction of the bony trabeculae that separate the mastoid cells so that the cells "coalescence." At this stage, a mastoid empyema is present. The pus may spread in one or more of the following directions:

- Anterior to the middle ear through the aditus-ad-antrum, in which case spontaneous resolution usually occurs
- Lateral to the surface of the mastoid process, resulting in a postauricular subperiosteal abscess (Fig. 26–20)
- Anterior into the zygomatic cells, developing into an abscess in the anterior and superior portion of the pinna and preauricular area
- Inferior through the tip of the mastoid and burrowing beneath the skin to form a soft tissue abscess below the pinna or behind the attachment of the sternocleidomastoid muscle in the neck, which is known as a *Bezold abscess*[44, 454] (Figs. 26–21 and 26–22)
- Medial to the petrous air cells, resulting in petrositis

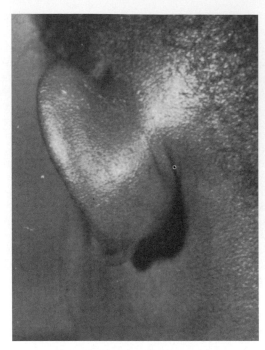

FIGURE 26–20. An example of a subperiosteal abscess in a child who had acute mastoid osteitis. Note that the pinna is displaced inferiorly and anteriorly, with obliteration of the postauricular crease due to the abscess.

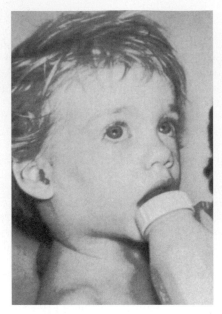

FIGURE 26–21. An abscess in the neck (Bezold abscess) in a child who has a draining ear owing to acute otitis media. The pus has extended from acute mastoid osteitis and empyema into the neck. (From Bluestone CD, Klein JD. Otitis Media in Infants and Children. Philadelphia, WB Saunders, 1988.)

- Posterior to the occipital bone, which can result in osteomyelitis of the calvarium or a *Citelli abscess*

The acute mastoid infection may be associated with an episode of acute otitis media, cholesteatoma, or chronic suppurative otitis media. In the review of 39 Italian children who had this complication, 23 (59%) had acute otitis media; most of the remaining 16 had an associated cholesteatoma.[310]

Infection may also spread medial to the labyrinth, involve the facial nerve,[192] or extend into the intracranial cavity, causing one or more suppurative complications such as dural sinus thrombosis.[128, 305, 469]

Clinical Presentation

The child usually has the same signs and symptoms as those associated with acute otitis media, such as fever and otalgia, although the fever may be low-grade with occasional temperature spikes. Some patients may have toxic symptoms. The signs and symptoms referable to the mastoid infection are:

- Swelling, erythema, and tenderness to touch over the mastoid bone
- Displacement of the pinna outward and downward (Fig. 26–23)
- Swelling or sagging of the posterosuperior external auditory canal wall (see Table 26–9)

A fluctuant subperiosteal abscess or even a draining fistula from the mastoid to the postauricular area may be present (Fig. 26–24). The subperiosteal abscess can be in any of the anatomic sites described earlier.

Examination of the tympanic membrane usually reveals

middle-ear effusion, or there may be a purulent discharge and a perforation. In the 20-year review of 79 Danish children who experienced acute mastoiditis and underwent mastoidectomy, 92% had a purulent middle-ear effusion.[389] Conversely, the tympanic membrane and middle ear may appear almost normal when mastoiditis with periosteitis occurs for the reasons described earlier. Acute mastoid osteitis (without otitis media) may also be the focus of infection when a child has a fever of unknown origin, in which case the disease in the mastoid is *occult* or, as described later, *subacute* or *masked*.

Diagnosis

Clinical signs and symptoms give rise to suspicion of acute mastoiditis with osteitis. CT of the mastoid area usually reveals one or more of the following:

- Haziness, distortion, or destruction of the mastoid outline
- Loss of sharpness of the shadows of cellular walls due to demineralization, atrophy, and ischemia of the bony septa (Fig. 26–25)
- Decrease in density and cloudiness of the areas of pneumatization due to inflammatory swelling of the air cells
- In long-standing cases, a chronic osteoblastic inflammatory reaction that may obliterate the cellular structure (small abscess cavities in sclerotic bone may be confused with pneumatic cells)

Antonelli et al reviewed CT scans of 21 patients with acute coalescent mastoiditis (with osteitis) or acute noncoalescent mastoiditis (without osteitis) and 12 patients with chronic mastoiditis.[18] They found that erosion of the cortical plate overlying the sigmoid sinus was the most sensi-

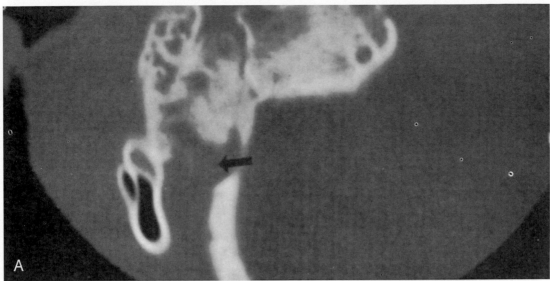

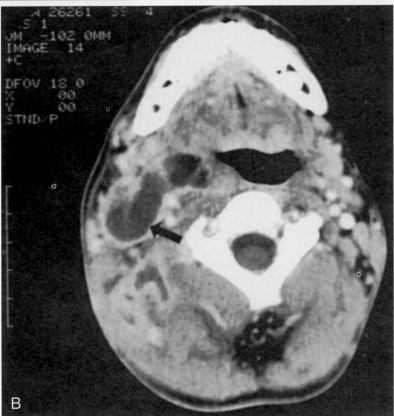

FIGURE 26–22. Computed tomogram of a child with acute mastoiditis and a Bezold abscess. A, Erosion of the mastoid apex is evident *(arrow)*. B, Abscess in the neck is noted by the ring-enhancing defect on the scan *(arrow)*.

tive and specific CT finding to distinguish osteitis from non-osteitis acute disease.

As part of the diagnostic work-up, cultures to determine the causative bacterial organisms should be obtained, either before or at the time of mastoid surgery. When otorrhea is present, cultures for bacteria from the ear drainage must be taken with care to discern fresh drainage from debris in the external canal. As described in detail earlier (see Chronic Perforation with Chronic

Otitis Media [Chronic Suppurative Otitis Media]), the canal must be initially cleaned. Then, if fresh pus is exuding through a perforation in the tympanic membrane, the discharge is cultured at the point of exit from the tympanic membrane with a cotton-tipped wire swab or, preferably, a needle and syringe under direct view. A Gram stain of the pus provides immediate information about the responsible organisms. When the mastoidectomy is performed, portions of mucosa and bone of the mastoid

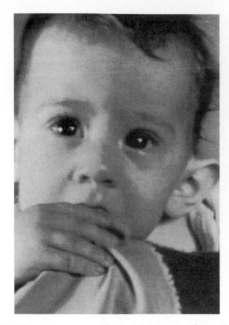

FIGURE 26–23. Acute mastoid osteitis in an infant, showing the outward displacement of the pinna.

should be sent for Gram stain, culture, and antibiotic susceptibility testing.

The differential diagnosis between this stage of mastoiditis and other disease entities (e.g., acute external otitis with postauricular periosteitis or postauricular lymphadenitis) that involve the postauricular area is described earlier under Acute Mastoiditis with Periosteitis (see Table 26–9).

Microbiology

The microbiology of mastoid osteitis is the same as with acute mastoiditis with periosteitis, as described earlier (see Table 26–10). In a review of children who underwent mastoidectomy for acute mastoiditis, Petersen et al found that *S. pneumoniae, S. pyogenes,* and *H. influenzae* were the most common organisms isolated.[389] Unusual organisms, such as *M. avium*[468] and *M. chelonae,*[26] have also been reported.

Management

An otolaryngologist should be consulted whenever acute mastoid osteitis is diagnosed in a child. Parenteral antimicrobial therapy should be instituted as described earlier for acute mastoiditis with periosteitis. To ensure that drainage of the middle ear and mastoid is adequate in the absence of a large perforation and otorrhea, a wide-field large myringotomy should be performed immediately. Insertion of a tympanostomy tube, in addition to a large myringotomy incision, can provide more prolonged drainage from the middle-ear-mastoid than myringotomy alone. Also, the tympanostomy tube placement helps prevent acute otitis media (and mastoiditis) from recurring.

A cortical (simple) mastoidectomy usually is required when acute mastoid osteitis is evident, especially when

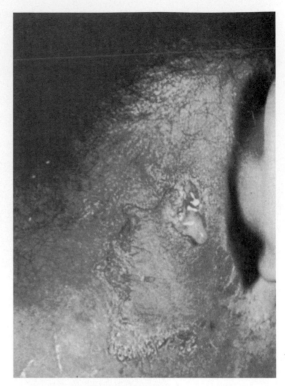

FIGURE 26–24. An example of a postauricular fistula with purulent discharge in a child who had acute mastoid osteitis.

the mastoid empyema has extended outside the mastoid bone and a subperiosteal abscess is present. The procedure should be considered an emergency, but the timing of the operation depends on the status of the child. Ideally, sepsis should be under control, and the patient must be able to tolerate a general anesthetic. The principle is to clean out the mastoid infection, to drain the mastoid air-cell system into the middle ear by eliminating any obstruction caused by edema or granulation tissue in the

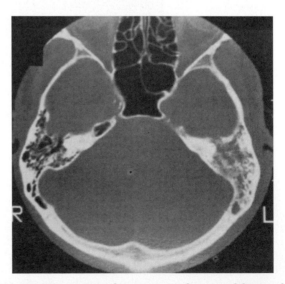

FIGURE 26–25. Computed tomogram of temporal bones showing left acute osteitis with loss of septa between the mastoid air cells, which has been called acute *coalescent mastoiditis;* the right mastoid is normal. Mastoid surgery was performed.

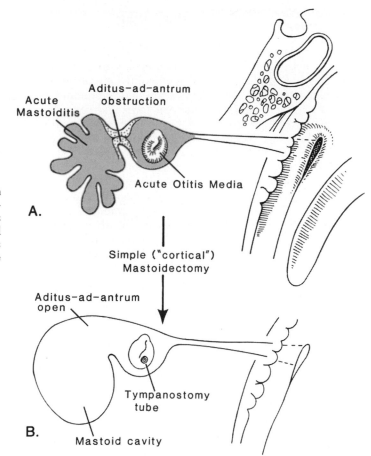

FIGURE 26–26. Schematic depiction of aditus-ad-antrum "block" (A) and the principles of a cortical (*simple*) mastoidectomy (B) in a right ear. The infected mastoid air-cell walls are removed using a surgical drill to form one large mastoid cavity, and the granulation tissue in the aditus-ad-antrum is excised to promote drainage from the mastoid to the middle ear.

aditus ad antrum, and to provide external drainage (Fig. 26–26).[65] Any other suppurative intratemporal or intracranial complications may also require surgical intervention.

Summary of Recommended Treatment Plan Related to the Stage of Acute Mastoiditis

Table 26–11 shows the presenting clinical features of acute mastoiditis and CT findings as related to our recommended management. We recommend consultation with an otolaryngologist for possible tympanocentesis and myringotomy (and tympanostomy tube insertion) when-

ever the primary physician lacks the expertise (or qualifications for tympanostomy tube placement) to perform these procedures. Also, consultation with the otolaryngologist is indicated for possible mastoidectomy whenever a child has acute mastoiditis with subperiosteal abscess, regardless of the CT findings, and when CT reveals osteitis, regardless of the other clinical features.

An otolaryngologist should be immediately consulted whenever acute mastoiditis is associated with another possible suppurative complication of otitis media and mastoiditis and when acute mastoiditis develops in a child who has chronic suppurative otitis media or cholesteatoma, or both.

TABLE 26–11. Features of Acute Mastoiditis Related to Recommended Management

Features				Management			
				Antibiotics			
Pinna Protrusion	*Postauricular Periosteitis*	*Subperiosteal Abscess (on CT)*	*Osteitis*	Oral	Parenteral	*Tympanocentesis ± Myringotomy*	*Mastoidectomy*
No	No	No	No	Yes	No	Opt°	No
No	No	No	Yes	No	Yes	Yes	Yes
Yes	Yes	No	No	No	Yes	Yes	No†
Yes	Yes	No	Yes	No	Yes	Yes	Yes
Yes	No	No	Yes	No	Yes	Yes	Yes
Yes	Yes	Yes	No	No	Yes	Yes	Yes
Yes	Yes	Yes	Yes	No	Yes	Yes	Yes

° Optional; indications same as for acute otitis media since disease in mastoid is mastoiditis without periosteitis/osteitis.
† Yes, if treatment fails after myringotomy and parenteral antibiotics.

Subacute Mastoiditis (Masked Mastoiditis, Occult Mastoiditis)

Complete simple mastoidectomy has been advocated for subacute mastoiditis.[326] The disease appears to be a subacute stage of otitis media and mastoiditis (without osteitis) characterized by the same signs and symptoms as acute otitis media (such as persistent fever and ear pain), except that they are persistent and less severe. Progression to this stage is attributed to failure of the initial antimicrobial agent to resolve the middle-ear and mastoid infection within a short period. Persistent otalgia and fever in a patient receiving an antimicrobial agent is an indication for tympanocentesis and myringotomy to identify the causative organism and promote drainage. In selected children, especially those with frequently recurrent acute otitis media, inserting a tympanostomy tube (in addition to the appropriate antimicrobial therapy) resolves the problem. Mastoid surgery is not indicated unless inserting the tympanostomy tube and intravenous antimicrobial therapy are ineffective.

In France, Denoyelle et al reported 165 children with subacute mastoiditis, identified over 2 years, which was defined as an attack of acute otitis media that did not resolve with 10 days of antibiotic treatment despite intravenous therapy.[122] Middle-ear aspiration (or cultures of otorrhea) revealed *H. influenzae* (28%), *P. aeruginosa* (23%), and *S. pneumoniae* (16%). Of these 165 children, 31 (19%) underwent mastoidectomy. Tympanostomy tubes probably would have prevented mastoidectomy in most, if not all, of these children.

In contrast with the condition just described—which usually results from a failure of initial antimicrobial treatment that frequently resolves after adequate middle-ear drainage and identification of the causative organism followed by administration of a culture-directed antibiotic—infants and children may have a suppurative process in the mastoid that is not clinically obvious, i.e., occult. This mastoid infection may even result in an intratemporal or intracranial complication, in which the middle ear may not appear to be diseased and the patient lacks the classic signs and symptoms of otitis media and mastoiditis. This condition can be called *masked mastoiditis*. The diagnosis is usually made by CT or bone scan.[495] Children who have intracranial suppurative disease or disease of the temporal bone that could possibly be due to mastoid infection should undergo CT of the temporal bones even though there is no otoscopic evidence of middle-ear disease. Although rare, children who have fever of unknown origin may have masked mastoiditis.

On occasion, older children or adolescents complain of persistent or recurrent postauricular pain but the middle ear appears to be free of disease. The communication between the middle ear and the mastoid air cells (i.e., the aditus-ad-antrum) may be blocked, causing mastoiditis. These children usually have had a history of recurrent acute otitis media, recurrent/chronic otitis media with effusion, or chronic suppurative otitis media, and CT reveals mastoiditis. Medical treatment (e.g., antimicrobial therapy) is indicated, but if the symptoms are severe or a trial of medical management fails, a mastoidectomy is indicated to relieve blockage of the aditus-ad-antrum and eliminate the infected cells. More rarely, a child with these symptoms may have relatively normal-appearing mastoid cellular architecture on CT, in which case the patient could have negative pressure within the mastoid due to obstruction of the aditus-ad-antrum. Again, mastoidectomy may be the only method of eliminating the blockage and relieving the symptoms.

Chronic Mastoiditis (with and without Chronic Suppurative Otitis Media/Cholesteatoma)

Today, chronic mastoiditis is most commonly associated with chronic suppurative otitis media (see earlier). However, children occasionally experience acute mastoiditis, which is either untreated, inappropriately treated, or neglected, causing the infection to progress to a chronic stage in which no perforation (or tympanostomy tube) is present in the tympanic membrane. No chronic suppurative otitis media, with or without otorrhea, is present. Nevertheless, the disease in the mastoid progresses to the chronic stage, and otitis media may or may not be present. These children can present with a fever of unknown origin or chronic/recurrent otalgia and tenderness over the mastoid process. Similar to a child who has subacute, or masked, mastoiditis, patients with chronic mastoiditis may have another intratemporal or intracranial complication. A child with an intracranial infectious process, such as a brain abscess, who has no clinical evidence of otitis media or mastoiditis may have chronic mastoiditis as the focus of the intracranial infection.

Diagnosis

Examination of the tympanic membrane shows evidence of middle-ear effusion, but the eardrum may appear normal if the chronic infection is localized only to the mastoid. Mastoid involvement is determined by CT. The mastoid may be poorly pneumatized, sclerotic, or show evidence of bone destruction, with opacification of the mastoid.

Management

The chronic infection, if reversible, may be controlled by medical treatment with antimicrobial agents (similar to those recommended for acute mastoiditis without periosteitis or osteitis). Tympanocentesis (for Gram stain, culture, and susceptibility studies) and myringotomy (for drainage) should be performed. However, when there are extensive amounts of granulation tissue and osteitis in the mastoid (i.e., irreversible mastoid disease) or the condition fails to improve with medical therapy, referral to an otolaryngologist is needed since a tympanomastoidectomy is required to eliminate the chronic mastoid osteitis. When another suppurative complication is present in addition to the chronic mastoiditis, such as a brain abscess, dural sinus thrombosis, or otitic hydrocephalus, mastoidectomy is indicated.

Chronic mastoiditis can also be caused by a cholesteatoma, which is usually manifested by chronic otorrhea through a defect in the tympanic membrane. A cholesteatoma requires definitive surgical treatment.

Petrositis

Petrositis is a relatively rare suppurative complication secondary to an extension of infection from the middle ear and mastoid into the petrous portion of the temporal bone. All the inflammatory and cellular changes that can occur in the mastoid can also occur in the pneumatized petrous pyramid. Only about 30% of persons have well-pneumatized petrous bones.[401] Petrositis may be more frequent than is appreciated by clinical and radiographic signs since the petrosal air cells communicate with the mastoid/middle-ear system. Pneumatization usually does not occur before age 3.

Petrositis may be acute or chronic. In the acute form, acute otitis media and mastoiditis extend into the pneumatized petrous air cells. The condition, like acute mastoiditis, is usually self-limited by resolution of the acute middle-ear and mastoid infection, but occasionally the infection in the petrous portion of the temporal bone does not drain because of mucosal swelling or because granulation is obstructing the passage from the petrous air cells to the mastoid and middle ear. This results in acute petrous osteomyelitis.[107] The widespread use of antimicrobial agents has made this complication rare. Chronic petrous osteomyelitis, however, can be a complication of chronic suppurative otitis media or cholesteatoma, or both, and it is much more common than the acute type. Pneumatization of the petrous portion of the temporal bone does not have to be present since the infection can invade the area by thrombophlebitis, by osteitis, or along fascial planes.[10] The infection may persist for months or years with mild and intermittent signs and symptoms or may spread to the intracranial cavity and result in one or more of the suppurative complications of ear disease, such as an extradural abscess or meningitis.

At the Children's Hospital of Pittsburgh from 1980 to 1995, only four children were admitted with this diagnosis, and three of these patients had simultaneous intracranial suppurative complications such as dural sinus thrombosis.[192] In all of these children, this complication resulted from spread of an attack of acute otitis media.

Microbiology

The organisms that cause acute petrositis are the same as those that cause acute mastoid osteitis: *S. pneumoniae*, *H. influenzae*, and β-hemolytic streptococci. Chronic petrous osteomyelitis, however, may be caused by the bacteria associated with chronic suppurative otitis media and cholesteatoma, such as *P. aeruginosa* or *Proteus* species.

Diagnosis

The disease is characterized by pain behind the eye, deep ear pain, persistent ear discharge, and sixth nerve palsy. However, in the four patients who were admitted to Chil-

dren's Hospital of Pittsburgh with this complication of otitis media, neither eye pain, nor deep ear pain, nor persistent otorrhea were all consistently present,[192] which has been the experience in other reviews. Eye pain is due to irritation of the ophthalmic branch of the fifth cranial nerve. On occasion, the maxillary and mandibular divisions of the fifth nerve are involved and pain occurs in the teeth and jaw. A discharge from the ear is common with acute petrositis but may not be present with chronic disease. Paralysis of the sixth cranial nerve leading to diplopia is a late complication.[184] Acute petrous osteomyelitis should be suspected when persistent purulent discharge follows a complete simple mastoidectomy for mastoid osteitis. The triad of pain behind the eye, aural discharge, and sixth nerve palsy is known as *Gradenigo syndrome*.

The diagnosis of acute petrous osteomyelitis is suggested by the unique clinical signs. Standard radiographs of the temporal bones may show clouding with loss of trabeculation of the petrous bone. The visualization is uncertain, however, because of normal variation in pneumatization (including asymmetry) and the obscuring of the petrous pyramids by superimposed shadows of other portions of the skull. CT of the temporal bones can lead to diagnosis and should be obtained whenever extension of infection into the cranial cavity is possible (Fig. 26–27). This complication must be distinguished from destructive lesions of the petrous apex due to such conditions as cholesteatoma, cholesterol granuloma, and arach-

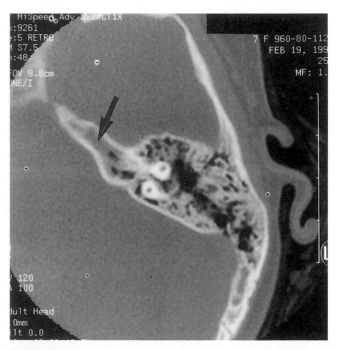

FIGURE 26–27. Computed tomogram of left temporal bone of 6-year-old female who experienced acute mastoiditis and petrositis *(arrow)* after an attack of acute otitis media. She had otalgia, sixth nerve palsy, and face pain. In addition to tympanostomy tube placement, systemic antimicrobial therapy, and cortical mastoidectomy, she underwent lumbar drainage since she also had otitic hydrocephalus. She recovered completely.

noid cysts; CT and MRI can distinguish among these diseases.[105]

Management

Management of acute petrositis is similar to that described for acute mastoiditis with osteitis since, at this stage, acute petrositis can be considered as further spread of the mastoid infection into the pneumatized petrous portions of the temporal bone. All four of the patients with this diagnosis at the Children's Hospital of Pittsburgh were successfully treated with high-dose broad-spectrum intravenous antibiotic therapy and cortical (simple) mastoidectomy without entry into the petrous apex; the petrous apex disease most likely drained into the mastoid cavity in the postoperative period. The three patients with intracranial complications also underwent specific management for the complication.[192] In more severe cases of acute petrous osteomyelitis and acute mastoid osteitis, a more aggressive surgical approach may be required.

Labyrinthitis

A complication of otitis media, labyrinthitis occurs when infection spreads into the cochlear and vestibular apparatus. The usual portal of entry is the round window and, less commonly, the oval window, but invasion may take place from an infectious focus in an adjacent area, such as the mastoid antrum, the petrous bone, or the meninges, or it may result from bacteremia. Schuknecht[432] has reclassified labyrinthitis into three types:

- *Serous (toxic)* labyrinthitis, in which there may be bacterial toxins or biochemical involvement but no bacteria are present
- *Suppurative (acute and chronic otogenic suppurative)* labyrinthitis, in which bacteria have invaded the otic capsule
- *Meningogenic suppurative* labyrinthitis, the result of invasion of bacteria from the subarachnoid space into the labyrinth (labyrinthitis ossificans [labyrinthine sclerosis], in which the normal labyrinthine structures are replaced by fibrous tissue and bone, is the end stage of this complication, if not arrested)

An acceptable classification of labyrinthitis today is the following[59]:

- Acute labyrinthitis
- Subacute labyrinthitis
- Chronic labyrinthitis
- Labyrinthitis ossificans

Acute Labyrinthitis

Acute labyrinthitis can be classified as being either serous or suppurative, and each of these entities can be either localized or generalized.

Acute Serous Labyrinthitis (with or without Perilymphatic Fistula)

The acute serous (toxic) type of labyrinthitis is considered to be one of the most common suppurative complications of otitis media. Paparella et al described the histopathologic evidence of serous labyrinthitis in most of the temporal bone specimens from patients who had otitis media.[374] Bacterial toxins from the infection in the middle ear may enter the inner ear, primarily through an intact round window or through a congenital defect between the middle ear and inner ear. The portal of entry may also be through an acquired defect of the labyrinth, such as from head trauma or previous middle-ear or mastoid surgery.

Biochemical changes within the labyrinth have also been found. The cochlea is usually more severely involved than the vestibular system. Paparella et al reviewed the audiograms of 232 patients who underwent surgery for chronic otitis media and found a significant degree of bone-conduction loss in the younger groups.[371] In addition, there was a marked difference in the presence and degree of sensorineural hearing loss in the affected ear compared with the normal ear in patients of all age groups who had unilateral disease. The authors postulated that the high-frequency sensorineural hearing loss that frequently accompanies this disease is due to a pathologic insult to the basal turn of the cochlea. In the review of intratemporal complications of otitis media from the Children's Hospital of Pittsburgh between 1980 and 1995, three children were admitted with acute serous labyrinthitis representing complications of an attack of acute otitis media.[192]

Fluctuating sensorineural hearing loss has been described in patients with otitis media and has been thought to be due to either endolymphatic hydrops or to a perilymphatic fistula.[203, 476, 513] However, fluctuating/progressive sensorineural hearing loss can be due to variety of other hereditary and acquired etiologies.[79]

Clinical Presentation

The signs and symptoms of serous labyrinthitis (especially when a perilymphatic fistula is present) are a sudden, progressive, or fluctuating sensorineural hearing loss or vertigo, or both, associated with otitis media or one or more of its complications or sequelae, such as mastoid osteitis. The loss of hearing is usually mixed—that is, there are both conductive and sensorineural components when serous labyrinthitis is a complication of otitis media. In some children who have recurrent middle-ear infections, the hearing may be normal between episodes. In other children, only a mild or moderate sensorineural hearing loss is always present. The presence of vertigo may not be obvious in children, especially infants. Older children may describe a feeling of spinning or turning; younger children may not be able to verbalize the symptoms but manifest the dysequilibrium by falling, stumbling, or being clumsy. The vertigo may be mild and momentary, and it may tend to recur over months or years. Onset of vertigo or progressive sensorineural hearing loss, or both, in a patient with preexisting hearing loss is frequently due to a fistula.[167] Spontaneous nystagmus may also be present, but the signs and symptoms of acute suppurative labyrinthitis, such as nausea, vomiting, and deep-seated pain, are usually absent. Fever, if present, is usually due to a concurrent infection of the upper respiratory tract or acute otitis media.

If congenital perilymphatic fistula is present, nystagmus may be present during the course of the episode of acute otitis media in addition to the mixed hearing loss. In a review of 47 infants and children who underwent exploratory tympanotomy for possible fistula at the Children's Hospital of Pittsburgh, 30 children (64%) had a past history of otitis media, and of these 30 patients, a fistula was diagnosed at surgery in 28 (93%) (Table 26–12).[58]

Diagnosis

A labyrinthine fistula may be identified via a fistula test employing a Siegle pneumatic otoscope or by applying positive and negative external-canal pressure using the pump-manometer system of an impedance bridge. The fistula test result is considered positive if these pressures produce nystagmus or vertigo. Electronystagmography is an objective way of documenting the presence or absence of the nystagmus as the findings of the fistula test may be false-positive or false-negative. Electronystagmography can be done in the presence of a perforation of the tympanic membrane or a tympanostomy tube. Fistulas are frequently associated with congenital or acquired defects in the temporal bone such as the Mondini malformation (Fig. 26–28). CT may be helpful in identifying such defects, such as a dilated vestibular aqueduct as shown in Figure 26–29. Weissman et al assessed the CT scans of 10 children (15 ears) with fistula, confirmed at surgery, and identified an abnormality of the inner ear or middle ear, or both, in 53% of the ears.[516] Also, electrocochleography has been advocated to diagnose a fistula,[182] but this method has not been proven to be sensitive and specific enough. Currently, the most effective method to diagnose a perilymphatic fistula is to perform exploratory middle-ear surgery.[67]

Weber et al have proposed a relatively new test for the

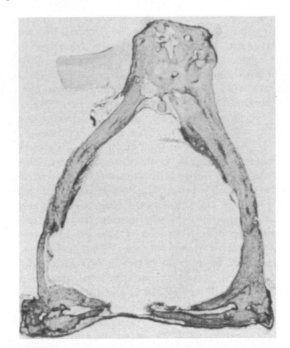

FIGURE 26–28. Congenital defect in the footplate of the stapes removed from an infant who had a Mondini malformation.

presence of perilymph in the middle ear as a way to confirm a perilymphatic fistula.[511, 512] A sample of the suspect fluid in the middle ear must be obtained at the time of exploratory surgery and then is assessed by an immunopathologic assay. The test appears specific but not sensitive.[288] A study by Buchman et al found that the test did not identify perilymph, but results were considered positive when cerebrospinal fluid was present.[86] Thus, positive results most likely confirm the presence of a cerebrospinal fluid leak from the inner to the middle ear; a more appropriate term for these malformations of labyrinthine windows is *congenital perilymphatic/cerebrospinal fistula* since the fluid emanating from the defect may be cerebrospinal fluid.[62]

Management

When this complication occurs during an attack of acute otitis media, tympanocentesis and myringotomy should be performed for microbiologic assessment of the middle-ear effusion and drainage. If possible, a tympanostomy tube should also be inserted for more prolonged drainage and in an attempt to ventilate the middle ear. Antimicrobial agents with efficacy against *S. pneumoniae, H. influenzae,* and *M. catarrhalis,* such as amoxicillin, should be administered; other organisms, such as *S. aureus* and *Pseudomonas,* have also been isolated from middle ears of children with acute labyrinthitis.[192] After resolution of the otitis media with effusion, the signs and symptoms of the labyrinthitis should rapidly disappear; however, sensorineural hearing loss may persist. If the diagnostic assessment indicates a possible congenital or acquired defect of the labyrinth, exploratory tympanotomy should be performed as soon as the middle ear is free of infection. The

TABLE 26–12. Number and Percentage of 47 Infants and Children Who Did and Did Not Have Congenital Perilymph Fistula Confirmed at Surgery (Tympanotomy) Related to History of Otitis Media

Presence of Otitis Media in Past	Perilymph Fistula Present		Total Patients
	Yes	*No*	
Yes	28 (76%)	2 (20%)	30
No	9 (24%)	8 (80%)	17
Total patients	37	10	47

Modified from Bluestone CD. Otitis media and congenital perilymphatic fistula as a cause of sensorineural hearing loss in children. Pediatr Infect Dis J 7: S141, 1988.

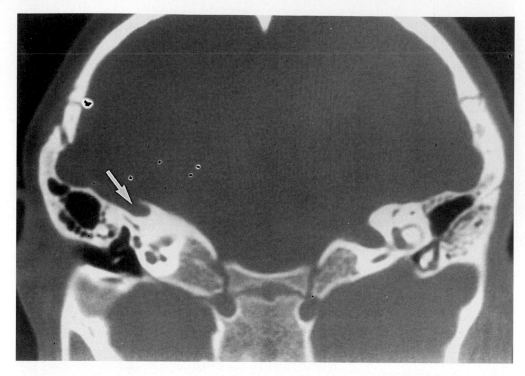

FIGURE 26–29. Computed tomogram of left temporal bone showing a dilated vestibular aqueduct *(arrow).*

most common malformations are abnormal round window and niche (such as a laterally facing round window), deformities of the stapes superstructure and footplate, a deformed long process of the incus, or some combination of these congenital defects (Fig. 26–30). More rarely, a congenital fissure between the round and oval windows is present.[476, 513] If a perilymphatic fistula is found, it should be repaired with temporalis muscle grafts. Even when no defect of the oval or round window is identified, but a fistula is still suspected, the stapes footplate and round window should be covered with connective tissue since a leak may not be present at the time of the tympanotomy but may recur.[203, 476] A tympanostomy tube should be reinserted if recurrent otitis media persists.

When acute mastoid osteitis, chronic suppurative otitis media, or cholesteatoma is present, definitive medical and surgical management of these conditions is essential in eliminating the labyrinthine involvement. A careful search for a labyrinthine fistula is necessary when mastoid surgery is indicated. However, labyrinthectomy is not indicated for serous labyrinthitis. Bluestone describes repair of a perilymphatic/cerebrospinal fluid fistula in detail.[65]

Conclusions

Any child with sensorineural hearing loss (with or without vertigo) who also has recurrent acute or chronic otitis media with effusion should be carefully evaluated for possible serous labyrinthitis, which can be secondary to a perilymphatic fistula. This combination appears to be common, and failure to identify this complication can result in irreversible severe to profound hearing loss, making early diagnosis and prevention imperative. Since prevention of sensorineural hearing loss due to other causes (such as congenital or viral causes) is not yet possible, our goal should be to prevent this loss of function in those children in whom it can be prevented. In addition, serous labyrinthitis may develop into acute suppurative labyrinthitis.

Acute Suppurative Labyrinthitis

Suppurative (purulent) labyrinthitis may develop as a complication of otitis media or may be one of the complications and sequelae of bacterial migration from the middle ear into the perilymphatic fluid through the oval or round window, a preexisting temporal bone fracture, an area in which bone has been eroded by cholesteatoma or chronic infection, or a congenital defect such as a congenital perilymphatic (cerebrospinal) fistula as described earlier. The most common way that bacteria enter the

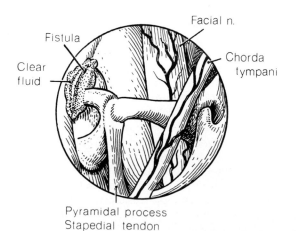

FIGURE 26–30. Abnormal stapes in the left ear. The anterior crus is straight rather than curved, and it joins the central portion rather than the anterior edge of the footplate.

labyrinth is from the meninges, but migration by this route is usually not a complication of otitis media.

Epidemiology and Pathogenesis

The incidence of suppurative labyrinthitis as a complication of otitis media is unknown, but it is rare because of the widespread use of antibiotics. In a series of 96 cases of suppurative intratemporal and intracranial complications of acute and chronic otitis media that were managed from 1956 to 1971, there were only five cases of suppurative labyrinthitis and all were secondary to cholesteatoma that had caused a labyrinthine fistula.[251]

Nonetheless, suppurative labyrinthitis still occurs. When it occurs in children with acute otitis media who are apparently being treated appropriately and adequately, a congenital (or acquired) perilymphatic fistula must be ruled out to prevent further hearing loss and recurrence, which can be life-threatening because of meningitis. Conversely, when a child experiences bacterial meningitis, especially recurrent episodes, a congenital defect of the inner and middle ear must be ruled out. Rupa et al reported on two children who had recurrent meningitis and a congenital perilymph fistula (discovered when their middle ears were explored).[418] A congenital or acquired defect between the paranasal sinuses and the anterior cranial cavity can also cause meningitis. In a review of children who had intratemporal complications of otitis media, Goldstein et al found two patients with suppurative labyrinthitis during a recent 15-year period; 1 child had a congenital defect of the labyrinthine windows that was considered a perilymphatic/cerebrospinal fluid fistula (Fig. 26–31).[192]

Clinical Presentation and Diagnosis

The sudden onset of vertigo, dysequilibrium, deep-seated pain, nausea and vomiting, and sensorineural hearing loss during an episode of acute otitis media or an exacerbation of chronic suppurative otitis media indicates labyrinthitis. The hearing loss is severe, the child cannot repeat words shouted into the affected ear, and sound is masked in the opposite ear. Often, spontaneous nystagmus and past pointing can be observed. Initially, the quick component of the nystagmus is toward the involved ear, and there is a tendency to fall toward the opposite side. However, when there is complete loss of vestibular function, the quick component is toward the normal ear.

Today, radiography can be an invaluable diagnostic aid. MRI can be diagnostic of the labyrinthitis, and CT can identify congenital or acquired defects of the inner and middle ear that may have predisposed the child to spread of the infection from the middle ear to the labyrinth (and subarachnoid space). In the absence of associated meningitis, the cerebrospinal fluid pressure and cell count are normal.

Frequently, the onset of suppurative labyrinthitis may be followed by facial paralysis or meningitis, or both. In later stages, cerebellar abscess can develop. Thus, suppurative labyrinthitis is a serious complication of otitis media. The development of purulent labyrinthitis means that

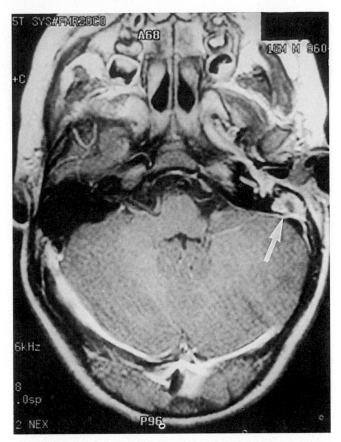

FIGURE 26–31. Magnetic resonance image (axial view) of left acute suppurative (generalized) labyrinthitis *(arrow)* as a complication of the first attack of acute otitis media in a 18-month-old male who had a preexisting congenital perilymphatic/cerebrospinal fluid fistula of the labyrinthine windows. The child presented with left otorrhea, fever, vertigo, and dehydration 5 days after the onset of the acute otitis media; the causative organism was *Pseudomonas aeruginosa*. Labyrinthectomy of the left ear was performed as an emergency procedure, with no further progression of the infection. Since the contralateral (right) ear was found to have a mild sensorineural hearing loss, an exploratory tympanotomy was performed at a later date, at which time an identical middle-ear malformation was diagnosed; the β_2-transferrin test result was positive in this ear. The middle-ear defects were patched at the time of each of the surgical procedures with grafts from the temporalis muscle. The child had no further hearing loss or suppurative complication over the ensuing 3-year follow-up period.

infection has spread to the fluid of the inner ear, and infection can then spread to the subarachnoid space through the cochlear aqueduct, the vestibular aqueduct, or the internal auditory canal. Figure 26–32 shows the radiographic image of a child with acute suppurative labyrinthitis due to otitis media that spread to the labyrinth through a congenital perilymphatic fistula and spread to the meninges, resulting in death.

Management

The management of suppurative labyrinthitis in the absence of meningitis consists of otologic surgery combined with intensive antimicrobial therapy. If this complication

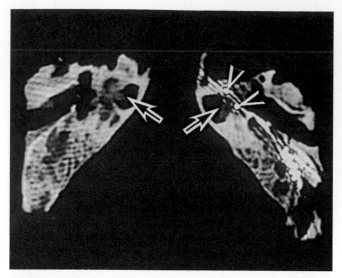

FIGURE 26–32. Computed tomogram of temporal bones showing bilateral Mondini malformation of the inner ears, cochlear implant in left ear, and effusion in right middle ear and mastoid of a 6-year-old male. The child experienced progressive severe headache, photophobia, vomiting, and seizures over a 24-hour period and died of pneumococcal meningitis secondary to otitis media and suppurative labyrinthitis, which in turn spread to the meninges. The infection spread from the middle ear to the labyrinth through a congenital perilymphatic fistula (Suzuki et al., 1998).

is due to acute otitis media, immediate tympanocentesis and myringotomy with tympanostomy tube insertion are indicated, as described for serous labyrinthitis. If acute mastoid osteitis is present, cortical (simple) mastoidectomy should be performed. However, because this complication can be secondary to cholesteatoma, radical mastoidectomy or modified radical mastoidectomy may be required. Modified radical mastoidectomy may also be required when chronic suppurative otitis media is present without cholesteatoma.

If meningitis has also occurred in association with suppurative labyrinthitis, otologic surgery other than a diagnostic and therapeutic tympanocentesis/myringotomy may have to be delayed until the meningitis is under control and the child can tolerate a general anesthetic. However, it is important to control the source of the infection in the middle ear and labyrinth as soon as possible. Labyrinthectomy should be performed only if there is complete loss of labyrinthine function or if the infection has spread to the meninges in spite of adequate antimicrobial therapy. Initially, parenteral antimicrobial agents appropriate to manage the primary middle-ear and mastoid disease should be administered. However, because cholesteatoma and chronic suppurative otitis media are frequent causes of suppurative labyrinthitis, antimicrobials effective for the gram-negative organisms (*P. aeruginosa* and *Proteus*) are frequently required. Culture results of the middle-ear effusion, purulent discharge, or the cerebrospinal fluid may alter the selection of the antibiotics.

Subacute labyrinthitis is the stage between acute and chronic labyrinthitis.

Chronic Labyrinthitis

The most common cause of chronic labyrinthitis as a complication of middle-ear disease is a cholesteatoma that has eroded the labyrinth, resulting in a fistula.[245] Osteitis may also cause bone erosion of the otic capsule. The fistula most commonly occurs in the lateral semicircular canal and is filled by squamous epithelium of a cholesteatoma, granulation tissue, or fibrous tissue entering the labyrinth. The middle ear and mastoid are usually separated from the inner ear by the soft tissue at the site of the fistula, but when there is continuity, acute suppurative labyrinthitis may develop. However, chronic labyrinthitis may be caused by chronic suppurative otitis media or even chronic otitis media with effusion, especially if the child has a congenital defect between the middle and inner ear (congenital perilymphatic fistula).

Clinical Presentation and Diagnosis

The signs and symptoms of chronic labyrinthitis are similar to those of the acute forms of the disease (e.g., sensorineural hearing loss and vertigo) except that their onset is more subtle. The disease is characterized by slowly progressive loss of cochlear and vestibular function over a prolonged period. The fistula test may be helpful in diagnosing a labyrinthine fistula, MRI may reveal labyrinthitis, and CT may reveal a bony defect. When loss of function is complete, signs and symptoms of labyrinthine dysfunction may be absent.

Management

Since a cholesteatoma is the most common cause of this type of labyrinthitis, middle-ear and mastoid surgery must be performed. For children with a labyrinthine fistula due to a cholesteatoma, modified radical mastoidectomy may be required. When labyrinthine function is still present, the cholesteatoma matrix overlying the fistula should be left undisturbed since removal can result in total loss of function. Even though there are advocates of an intact canal-wall procedure and surgeons who prefer to remove the cholesteatoma matrix, either during the initial surgery or in a second-stage procedure, the safest approach is recommended when a cholesteatoma has caused a labyrinthine fistula in a child.

Failure to diagnose this complication and perform the surgery as soon as possible may result in complete loss of cochlear and vestibular function, with possible development of labyrinthine sclerosis or an acute suppurative labyrinthitis. The latter entity can cause a life-threatening intracranial complication such as meningitis.

Labyrinthitis Ossificans (Labyrinthine Sclerosis)

Labyrinthitis ossificans is caused by fibrous replacement or new bone formation (labyrinthitis ossificans) in part or all of the labyrinth, with resulting loss of labyrinthine function. Today, this end stage of labyrinthitis usually results from meningitis, not otitis media. However, a review of CT scans by Weber et al showed that one child had labyrinthitis ossificans associated with a congenital perilymphatic fistula, presumably secondary to otitis media since meningitis had not occurred.[513] Because this condition is the end stage of healing after acute or chronic labyrinthitis, prevention of disease of the middle ear is the most effective way to prevent this complication. Hartnick et al reported that steroids may prevent this unfortunate sequela following pneumococcal meningitis.[215]

Facial Paralysis

Facial paralysis most commonly occurs in children during an episode of acute otitis media because of exposure of the facial nerve from a congenital bony dehiscence in its tympanic portion within the middle ear (Fig. 26–33). Facial paralysis can also be a complication of acute mastoiditis with osteitis[192] or chronic suppurative otitis media.[14] When facial paralysis occurs as a complication of chronic suppurative otitis media, a cholesteatoma is also frequently present (Fig. 26–34). On rare occasions, it can occur in children as a complication of otitis media with effusion.[396] Also rarely, facial paralysis can be bilateral after the onset of acute otitis media[146, 453] or as a complication of acute mastoiditis.[178] Not infrequently, when facial paralysis develops during an attack of otitis media, an underlying disease such as leukemia may be present.[11, 192]

Facial paralysis is a relatively frequent complication of acute otitis media in infants and children. In the pre-antibiotic era, facial paralysis was estimated to occur in 0.5% of patients with acute otitis media, whereas the current rate is 0.005% as reported in a study from Denmark.[150] A review by Goldstein et al of 22 infants and children who had facial paralysis associated with otitis media or related infections at the Children's Hospital of Pittsburgh between 1980 and 1995 revealed that paralysis occurred most frequently in children age 6 years old and younger; 50% of such patients were younger than 4 years

(Table 26–13).[192] Facial weakness, otalgia, otorrhea, concomitant symptoms of infection of the upper respiratory tract, and fever were the most common symptoms. The mean duration of ear symptoms and duration of facial weakness upon presentation to the Hospital was 6 and 4 days, respectively. Two children had acute mastoiditis with periosteitis, and one patient had acute mastoiditis with osteitis and subperiosteal abscess. In 18 patients (80%), initial treatment consisted of antimicrobial therapy, and in all but one of these children, a myringotomy, with or without tympanostomy tube placement, was also performed. However, of these 22 children, 4 patients (18%) underwent further surgery: 2 patients underwent cortical (simple) mastoidectomy for acute mastoiditis; 1 child who had lymphoblastic leukemia underwent facial nerve decompression, radical mastoidectomy, and labyrinthectomy; and 1 who had previously undergone mastoidectomy for cholesteatoma later experienced acute mastoiditis with subperiosteal abscess and facial paralysis and underwent revision tympanomastoidectomy.

In a smaller series of 10 patients who experienced facial paralysis after the onset of acute otitis media in Washington, D.C., Elliott et al reported that 8 had incomplete paralysis, which resolved with only myringotomy and intravenous antibiotics.[151] Two children who had complete paralysis and persistent fever and otorrhea, despite antibiotic treatment, underwent mastoidectomy. None required decompression of the facial nerve.

Management

Most children with facial paralysis that is not associated with acute mastoiditis or a concomitant underlying disease can be treated successfully with parenteral antimicrobial therapy, tympanocentesis, and myringotomy with or without myringotomy tube insertion. When facial paralysis occurs as an isolated complication, tympanocentesis

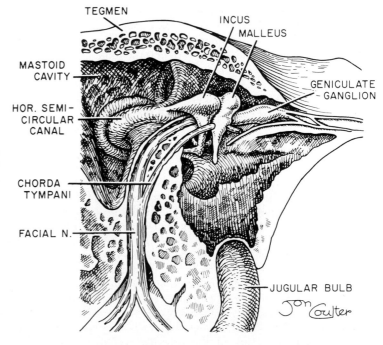

FIGURE 26–33. Course of the facial nerve shown in the middle ear and mastoid. The nerve can be affected by infection in these areas, which can result in facial paralysis.

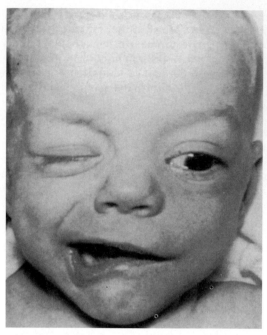

FIGURE 26–34. Infant in whom left facial paralysis developed a day after the onset of acute otitis media.

TABLE 26–13. Age, Presenting Symptoms, and Signs in 22 Infants and Children Who Experienced Acute Facial Paralysis as a Complication of Otitis Media and Related Infection: Children's Hospital of Pittsburgh, 1980–1995

Characteristic	Number of Patients (%)
Age (yr)	
0–3	11 (50)
4–6	6 (27)
7–12	3 (14%)
13–18	2 (9%)
Signs and symptoms	
Facial weakness	22 (100)
Middle-ear effusion	16 (73)
Otalgia	15 (62)
Otorrhea	8 (36)
Perforation of tympanic membrane	8 (36)
Upper-respiratory-tract infection	8 (36)
Fever	7 (32)
Hearing loss	2 (9)
Irritability	2 (9)
Postauricular cellulitis/mass	2 (9)

Modified from Goldstein NA, Casselbrant ML, Bluestone CD, Kurs-Lasky M. Intratemporal complications of acute otitis media in infants and children. Otolaryngol Head Neck Surg 119:444–454, 1998.

and a myringotomy should be performed and parenteral antibiotics effective for *S. pneumoniae* and *H. influenzae* should be administered. A tympanostomy tube is indicated when the child has had recurrent episodes of acute otitis media, when the attack of acute otitis media is superimposed on preexisting chronic otitis media with effusion, and whenever prolonged drainage of the middle ear and mastoid is desirable. The paralysis usually improves rapidly without requiring further surgery (e.g., mastoidectomy or facial nerve decompression). Mastoidectomy is not indicated unless acute mastoiditis with osteitis (*acute "coalescent" mastoiditis*), chronic suppurative otitis media, or cholesteatoma is present. However, if there is complete loss of facial function and electrophysiologic testing indicates degeneration or progressive deterioration of the nerve, facial nerve decompression may be necessary to achieve complete return of function.

Immediate surgical intervention is indicated when facial paralysis develops in a child who has chronic suppurative otitis media or cholesteatoma, or both.

External Otitis

Otitis media with perforation (also a patent tympanostomy tube) can be associated with an infection of the external auditory canal secondary to a discharge from the middle ear and mastoid. This is called *external otitis*; *acute diffuse external otitis* and *acute infectious eczematoid dermatitis* are alternative terms. The infection can be acute or chronic. When acute, it usually follows an episode of acute otitis media in which either the tympanic membrane perforates or a chronic perforation (without otitis media) is present and an episode of acute otitis media occurs. The otorrhea that follows is then complicated by acute infection of the external auditory canal.

Similarly, when a tympanostomy tube is in place, acute otitis media develops with otorrhea, followed by infection of the external canal. An infection in the mastoid may also erode the bone of the ear canal or the postauricular area, resulting in a dermatitis.

Diagnosis

The ear canal skin is erythematous, edematous, and filled with purulent drainage and yellow-crusted plaques, and a perforation of the eardrum (or tympanostomy tube) is present. The clinician often finds it difficult to distinguish among external otitis caused by otitis media, otorrhea secondary to a perforation or tympanostomy tube, and acute diffuse external otitis in which middle-ear disease is absent. However, severe inflammatory stenosis of the external auditory meatus is uncommon when due to middle-ear infection and otorrhea, and therefore the stenosis can be differentiated from the extreme tenderness and pain that are so common in acute external otitis not secondary to middle-ear infection.

When the differential diagnosis is in doubt, the most effective way to make the distinction is to clean the products of the infection from the external auditory canal with a suction or cotton-tipped applicator to determine the status of the tympanic membrane. However, the external auditory canal may be too edematous and tender to allow adequate cleaning of the canal and visualization of the entire drum. In such cases, the immediate past history (e.g., recent episode of acute otitis media) may be valuable. Also, if a significant hearing loss is present and extreme canal stenosis is absent, the patient probably has otitis media associated with the external otitis. A tympanogram can also be helpful if the canal is not too tender to allow insertion of the probe tip of the instrument since a large volume would indicate a nonintact tympanic membrane. Also, the presence of a tympanometric peak in the normal pressure zone, even though somewhat lower than normal, suggests a normal middle ear; a flat pattern (with normal canal volume) suggests a middle-ear effusion without a perforation or patent tympanostomy tube. Also included in the differential diagnosis are impetigo contagiosa and a secondary infection associated with contact, or seborrheic, dermatitis.

When the external otitis due to otitis media involves the pinna and postauricular area, the condition may be misdiagnosed as acute mastoiditis with periosteitis.[230] However, the postauricular crease is commonly obliterated when the swelling is secondary to external otitis, whereas the crease is maintained when acute mastoiditis with periosteitis is present.

Microbiology

The organisms involved are usually the same as those found in the middle-ear/mastoid infection, but the flora of the external canal may contribute to the infectious process. *P. aeruginosa*, *S. aureus*, and *Proteus* organisms are frequently present (Fig. 26–35). Fungi may also be found in chronic cases—usually *Aspergillus niger* or *A. alba*. These bacteria are similar to those isolated from the external canals of patients who have acute external otitis in which the tympanic membrane is intact.[109]

The external auditory canal should be cultured and the results compared with those of a needle aspiration of the middle-ear discharge through the tympanic membrane perforation or the tympanostomy tube. Such culturing helps determine the offending organisms. Antimicrobial therapy can then be selected according to the results of the culture and susceptibility testing. The infection may spread to the auricle, periauricular area, or other parts of the body, possibly because of direct implantation of the organisms or as an autosensitivity phenomenon. Coagulase-positive *S. aureus* is the most frequently involved bacterium in this type of reaction.[302]

Management

Management should be directed toward resolving the middle-ear/mastoid infection, which may require medical treatment or surgery, or both. If the skin of the ear canal is the only area of involvement, the ototopical medications listed in Table 26–6 may be beneficial. However, ofloxacin-otic solution is currently the only ototopical agent approved by the FDA for use in children who have a tympanostomy tube in place and who experience otorrhea. Ofloxacin is safe, effective, and approved for children (and adults) with external otitis.[250] This topical eardrop is probably equally effective when a perforation is present and a episode of acute otitis occurs. The drop is also approved for use in adults who have chronic suppurative otitis media.[209] Other combinations of an antibiotic with hydrocortisone otic drops, such as ciprofloxacin hydrochloride with hydrocortisone, may be effective when external otitis is present and are approved for children when the tympanic membrane is intact and external otitis is present.[204]

Analgesics usually are required to manage the otalgia until the infection is under control. When canal stenosis is present and too severe to permit adequate application of ototopical medications, a cotton or Mericel Pope Ear Wick (Xomed Surgical Products, Jacksonville, FL) may have to be inserted into the ear canal to enhance treatment. When the infection is severe, such as when the patient has a high fever or is "toxic," or when the

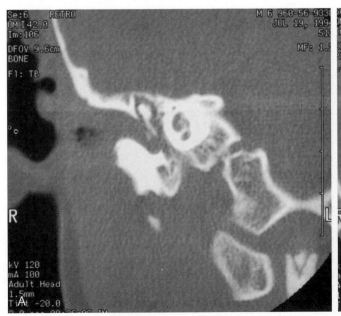
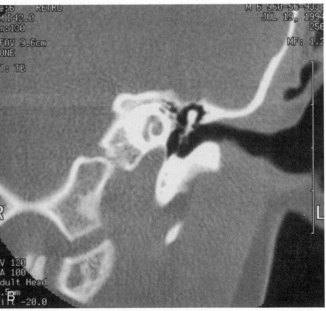

FIGURE 26–35. Coronal CT scan of the temporal bone of a 5-week-old boy with left chronic external otitis associated with chronic suppurative otitis media and mastoiditis (without cholesteatoma) (*A*). The child underwent intravenous antimicrobial therapy for *Pseudomonas aeruginosa* infection and tympanomastoidectomy, with subsequent resolution. *B*, The uninvolved right side.

infection spreads to the pinna, periauricular areas, or cervical lymph nodes, intravenous antimicrobial therapy effective against the offending bacterial organism is required. Even though the oral quinolones are a reasonable initial treatment alternative to parenteral antibiotics at this stage, these agents are not approved for children under age 18.

If a fungal infection is present, M-cresyl acetate eardrops (Cresylate) may be needed. Irrigation of the ear canal with 2% acetic acid or frequent suctioning of the ear canal may also hasten resolution.

When the adjacent skin around the auricle or other parts of the body is involved, the skin should be cleansed with saline solution or aluminum acetate and treated with a local antibiotic-corticosteroid cream. Children should be cautioned about spread of the infection from the ear canal to other parts of the body and should refrain from putting fingers in the ear or scratching the infected skin. Cotton in the external ear canal can be helpful if profuse drainage is present but should be changed as frequently as necessary.

Strategies to prevent recurrence of this complication of otitis media are similar to those described for when acute otitis media or chronic suppurative otitis media occurs in the presence of a perforation of the eardrum or tympanostomy tube (see earlier in this chapter, Perforation of the Tympanic Membrane).

Atelectasis of the Middle ear (with and without Retraction Pocket)

Atelectasis of the middle ear—which includes the tympanic membrane—is a sequela of eustachian tube dysfunction (see "Eustachian Tube Dysfunction" in Chapter 25). As the term implies, the condition occurs when there is recurrent/chronic underpressures in the middle ear that result in *retraction* or *collapse* of the tympanic membrane. Retraction of the tympanic membrane may be attributed to the presence of high negative middle-ear pressure; retraction of the tympanic membrane can also occur in the absence of middle-ear negative pressure. A flaccid, atelectatic tympanic membrane may or may not be associated with high negative intratympanic pressure: the abnormal negative pressure may have been the original cause of such a condition of the membrane but may no longer be present. Also, a middle-ear effusion may or may not be present. The term *atelectasis* has been borrowed from the pulmonary disorder atelectasis of the lung.

Unfortunately, there have been no reports of studies of the incidence of atelectasis and retraction pockets. However, a retraction pocket is a common sequela of atelectasis of the tympanic membrane with or without otitis media with effusion.[419] As a sequela of tympanostomy tube insertion, retraction pockets at the site of the extruded tube are common and are more prevalent as a long-term consequence of tubes in older children, adolescents, and adults than in young children.[118] The incidence of cleft palate must be greater than that of cholesteatoma in this population (7.1%) since a retraction pocket precedes the development of a cholesteatoma in children with cleft palate.[56]

Pathogenesis

Atelectasis of the middle ear results from transient or chronic underpressures within the middle ear, which in turn is caused by eustachian-tube dysfunction. The dysfunction most commonly involves failure of opening of the eustachian tube or anatomic obstruction, or both; the dysfunction is sometimes secondary to habitual sniffing in the presence of a tube that fails to close.[159] Since the eustachian tubes of patients with chronic atelectatic middle ears can be successfully inflated, the tube is not anatomically obstructed.[308] Thus, the tube is more likely functionally obstructed, i.e., the opening mechanism fails.[56, 103] An alternative, but less convincing, hypothesis for the pathogenesis is related to persistence of mesenchyme or an inflammatory reaction, secondary to otitis media, in the middle ear, especially in the posterosuperior quadrant of the pars tensa and the pars flaccida, two sites that commonly develop partial atelectasis with a retraction pocket.[415] However, these two portions of the tympanic membrane are the most compliant areas of the eardrum[266] and thus most likely to retract when there is significant underpressure within the middle ear.

Palva et al attribute poor aeration of the attic to development of a retraction pocket in Prussak's space, which can develop into a cholesteatoma if it is progressive.[368] Hasebe et al found more residual soft tissue density in the mastoid on CT in patients who had severe attic retraction.[216] Also, retraction pockets are not an uncommon sequela after extrusion of tympanostomy tubes. The pocket occurs when the tympanic membrane has a dimeric membrane at the tube site, and if eustachian-tube dysfunction persists, the membrane retracts since it is more compliant than it was before the tube was inserted. Thus, retraction pockets occur at naturally floppy portions of the tympanic membrane (posterosuperior quadrant and pars flaccida) or at the site of an acquired defect, such as a dimeric membrane from a previously inserted tube or the site of a healed spontaneous perforation.

In studies of children with retraction pockets, the opening mechanism of the eustachian tube was determined to have failed, i.e., functional obstruction[54] (see "Physiology, Pathophysiology, and Pathogenesis" in Chapter 25). This sequela of eustachian-tube dysfunction/otitis media increases with advancing age.[118, 493] If the atelectasis is persistent and progressive, it can lead to sequelae such as hearing loss, ossicular chain discontinuity, and cholesteatoma. All are described in this chapter.

Diagnosis and Classification

Atelectasis is diagnosed only by visual inspection with the aid of an otoscope or otomicroscope; tympanometry is not diagnostic. The tympanic membrane is deformed. Atelectasis of the middle ear can be acute or chronic; *partial* (localized), which may or may not be a retraction pocket, or *total* (generalized); and mild, moderate, or severe. Partial atelectasis, with or without a retraction pocket, may also be visualized in an area of a healed perforation or at the site where a tympanostomy tube had been inserted ("atrophic scar" or dimeric membrane). A retraction pocket in the posterosuperior quadrant of the pars tensa or a pars flaccida retraction pocket is more frequently associated with more serious sequelae (ossicular discontinuity or cholesteatoma, or both) than is a retraction pocket in other areas of the tympanic membrane. As described later, these variations should be kept in mind when deciding how to manage atelectasis.

It is appropriate to classify, grade, and stage atelectasis of the middle ear, as visualized by the clinician, according to its extent, severity, and duration since these factors are related to management decisions. The following is a proposed classification.[59]

Partial atelectasis is a localized area of the tympanic membrane that is atelectatic, which may or may not be a retraction pocket since the depth of the retraction can be mild, moderate, or severe. When partial, in the absence of a retraction pocket, it may be in one or more of the four quadrants of the pars tensa (i.e., anterosuperior, anteroinferior, posterosuperior, posteroinferior), in the pars flaccida, or in both the pars tensa and the pars flaccida.

A *retraction pocket* is characterized by a partial area of atelectasis of the tympanic membrane in which there is indrawing of the membrane forming *borders* (i.e., an edge or margin), most frequently at the site of an osseous anatomic structure (e.g., notch of Rivinus or scutum) or the malleus. A retraction pocket can be in one or more of the four quadrants of the pars tensa or in the pars flaccida, or both, and can be either *acute* or *chronic*, or *reversible* or *irreversible*. Sadé has proposed a classification of a posterosuperior retraction pocket that is helpful but does not include duration; include the presence or absence of adhesive changes, which relates to reversibility; or include other sites.[423] Tos and Poulsen classified attic retraction pockets related to their extent and severity.[493]

The stages of retraction pockets are divided into *acute* (<3 months' duration) and *chronic* (3 months or longer in duration).[59] Key factors that affect the progression of the stages of a retraction pocket are:

1. *Relation to middle-ear structures:* does or does not *approximate* (touch) or is or is not *adherent* (i.e., adhesive otitis media) to an ossicle or to ossicles (i.e., incus, incudostapedial joint, stapes, head of malleus, or incudomalleolar joint) or other middle-ear structure, such as promontory of the cochlea
2. *Expands with pressure:* entire pocket does or does not easily expand to the normal position when negative pressure is applied with a pneumatic otoscope or with the Bruening otoscope with a nonmagnifying lens under the otomicroscope, or with positive pressure when the patient is anesthetized with nitrous oxide
3. *Extent visualized:* the entire pocket is visualized or parts are not seen even after applied pressure because the pocket extends beyond the visible portion of the middle-ear space, e.g., sinus tympani, facial recess, epitympanum, or medial to other parts of the tympanic membrane
4. *Self-cleansing and free of infection:* epithelial debris, crusting, or purulent material is or is not within the pocket

Total atelectasis can be acute (<3 months' duration) or chronic (3 months or longer in duration), which involves all four quadrants of the pars tensa, with or without involvement of the pars flaccida, and can be staged as follows:

- **Stage 1$_a$.** *Acute total mild atelectasis*; middle ear aerated
- **Stage 1$_c$.** *Chronic total mild atelectasis*; same as stage 1$_a$ but chronic
- **Stage 2$_a$.** *Acute total severe atelectasis*; middle ear not aerated, i.e., no apparent middle-ear space
- **Stage 2$_c$.** *Chronic total severe atelectasis*; same as stage 2$_a$ but chronic

Management

When atelectasis of the tympanic membrane is of relatively recent onset, a middle-ear effusion is or is not present, and a retraction pocket is absent, current management options are of uncertain benefit and are controversial. No reported clinical trials have addressed the efficacy of the various treatments compared with no treatment. (For decisions related to actively treat or not treat an effusion that is of short duration and treatment options, see Chapter 25, "Management.") Total atelectasis, or even a partial area that is retracted for only a short time (acute retraction), is usually caused by transient high negative middle-ear pressure associated with an acute infection of the upper respiratory tract or barotrauma. This condition is common in children and adolescents and is usually self-limited. No specific treatment should be directed toward the middle ear unless the child complains of severe otalgia, hearing loss, tinnitus, or vertigo. The atelectasis (and high negative intratympanic pressure) and associated symptoms, if present, usually subside when infection of the acute upper respiratory tract disappears. Treatment at this time should be directed toward relief of the nasal symptoms. Topical or systemic nasal decongestants may relieve these symptoms and may also relieve congestion of the eustachian tube, although their effectiveness in this latter area has not been demonstrated. If the symptoms become severe enough, myringotomy may be necessary to provide relief by returning middle-ear pressure to ambient levels, such as when the atelectasis is secondary to barotrauma (see Chapter 25). Middle-ear inflation through the eustachian tube has been advocated, but as described later, this method of management is of uncertain benefit when atelectasis progresses to the chronic stage. Thus, watchful waiting is appropriate.

When the atelectasis is chronic (with or without chronic otitis media with effusion) and there is no evidence of a deep retraction pocket in the posterosuperior quadrant or pars flaccida, a thorough search should be made for an underlying origin, such as hypertrophied adenoids, nasal allergy, or paranasal sinusitis. If none is found, the management options are either watchful waiting or active treatment. (Also, see Chapter 25 concerning chronic otitis media with effusion.) The decision for or against treatment should rest on the presence or absence of other associated symptoms and on whether the middle ear has abnormal negative pressure. The presence of persistent or transient otalgia, hearing loss, vertigo, or tinnitus that is troublesome to the patient warrants active treatment. For chronic atelectasis in this case, a trial with a topical or systemic nasal decongestant with or without an antihistamine may be helpful. However, this type of treatment is often disappointing.

Inflation of the eustachian-tube/middle-ear system using the Valsalva or Politzer methods has been advocated when middle-ear effusion is present.[463] However, studies in animals indicate that these methods do not return the middle-ear pressure to normal for a sustained period when the eustachian tube is functionally obstructed.[13] Also, a clinical trial conducted by Chan and Bluestone[101] failed to show efficacy of middle-ear inflation using a specially designed inflation device in 41 children who had chronic middle-ear effusion.[102] Kaneko et al also failed to show consistent and sustained improvement after inflation in children who had middle-ear effusion.[256]

Inflation of the eustachian tube and middle ear may provide temporary relief of atelectasis in which no effusion is present, but inflation must usually be repeated for permanent control of the symptoms and to maintain the tympanic membrane in a more normal position. However, Luntz and Sade inflated the middle ears of patients with chronic atelectasis with either air or nitrogen for up to 5 consecutive days, and they found that the eardrum returned to its former atelectatic position within 15 minutes to 5 hours following the inflation.[307] More recently, Yung used nasal continuous positive airway pressure in patients with atelectasis and reported a short-term benefit but did not study the long-term effect.[532] Doyle and Alper have explained this phenomenon using a mathematical model.[141]

When a chronic retraction pocket or total atelectasis is present, and when nonsurgical methods of management have failed, myringotomy and insertion of a tympanostomy tube should be performed to prevent possible irreversible changes in the middle ear. After a tympanostomy tube is inserted, the tympanic membrane in the area of the retraction pocket should return to a more neutral position within several weeks or months. If the retraction area remains adherent to the ossicles or middle ear, or both (Fig. 23–36), adhesive otitis media is present (see the next discussion, Adhesive Otitis Media) and tympanoplasty should be considered to prevent further progression of the disease process (such as ossicular discontinuity or cholesteatoma formation, or both). To prevent recurrence of the retraction pocket (or total atelectasis), a portion of cartilage (from the pinna) placed over the affected area is effective (in addition to tympanostomy tube insertion).[136, 180] This method of management appears to be reasonable although it has not been tested in appropriately controlled clinical trials and the natural history of retraction pockets in these areas has not been adequately studied.[53, 65] However, Blaney et al have reported success in surgically managing retraction pockets in children after only excising the pocket and placement of a tympanostomy tube.[47]

When a flaccid tympanic membrane is passively collapsed on the ossicles and middle ear and high negative middle-ear pressure is not present, the nonsurgical and surgical management options described earlier may not effectively restore the tympanic membrane to a more

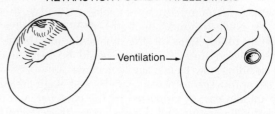

RETRACTION POCKET—ATELECTASIS

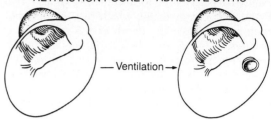

RETRACTION POCKET—ADHESIVE OTITIS

FIGURE 26–36. When a retraction pocket is in the posterosuperior portion of the pars tensa of the tympanic membrane and adhesive otitis media is not present between the tympanic membrane and ossicles, a tympanostomy tube may return the eardrum to the neutral position (*upper frames*). However, if adhesive otitis media is present, the retraction pocket will persist in spite of a tympanostomy tube and an aerated middle ear (*lower frames*). (From Bluestone CD, Klein JD. Otitis Media in Infants and Children. Philadelphia, WB Saunders, 1988.)

normal position. Fortunately, symptoms of high negative middle-ear pressure and eustachian-tube obstruction are frequently absent, so no treatment may be necessary. Even myringotomy and tympanostomy-tube insertion may not be beneficial as the tympanic membrane is no longer actively being retracted by high negative middle-ear pressure. In addition, at this stage, adhesive otitis media may also be present, and portions of the tympanic membrane may be adherent to the middle ear. The posterior or epitympanic (attic) portions of the middle ear may become separated from the anterior portion by adhesions, and, subsequently, ventilation from the eustachian tube or a tympanostomy tube does not aerate the affected area. In such cases, there are two management options: tympanoplasty or periodic observation (once or twice a year).

Tympanoplasty

In selected cases in which severe atelectasis is present, a tympanoplastic procedure may be indicated. The most compelling indication for such a procedure would be the presence of a deep retraction pocket in the posterosuperior portion of the pars tensa that is unresponsive to nonsurgical and other surgical methods of management previously described for this defect. For example, if a tympanostomy tube had been inserted previously but the retraction pocket did not return to the neutral position after several months of equalization of the intratympanic pressure, tympanoplasty should be considered since adhesive otitis media is most likely binding the drum to the ossicles and surrounding structures within the middle ear. Even though the natural history of such deep retraction pockets has not been formally studied, the risk of erosion necrosis of the incus or formation of a cholesteatoma, or both, appears to be high. It is frequently difficult to determine whether there is only a retraction pocket or if a cholesteatoma has already developed; therefore, a thorough examination of the entire external canal and tympanic membrane should be performed with the otomicroscope.

An examination under general anesthesia is required for all infants and children in whom the examination is unsatisfactory without general anesthesia. At the time of the examination under anesthesia, a thorough examination of the retraction pocket, employing a curved blunt probe, should be performed to determine the extent of the pocket. In addition, the continuity of the incus and stapes should be assessed since erosion of the long process of the incus may require surgical correction. Frequently, when nitrous oxide is employed as one of the anesthetic agents, the retraction pocket balloons laterally as visualized through the otomicroscope. When this occurs, insertion of the tympanostomy tube usually is sufficient to prevent recurrence of the retraction pocket. However, reinsertion of the tube may be needed if the retraction pocket recurs after spontaneous extubation.

Many techniques are advocated for repair of a severely atelectatic tympanic membrane, many of which have been shown to be successful.[197, 441] The surgeon should be cautioned, however, that even though the graft "takes" the child will most likely have persistent eustachian-tube dysfunction with sustained fluctuating or negative intratympanic pressure after the procedure, which could result in recurrence of the retraction pocket months or years later. Therefore, a tympanostomy tube should be inserted at the time of the tympanoplastic surgery and reinserted if atelectasis begins to recur after the tympanostomy tube is spontaneously extruded. Some surgeons prefer tragal or conchal cartilage attached to its perichondrium to cover the area of the retraction pocket so as to prevent recurrence of an attic or posterosuperior retraction pocket.[65, 183, 219]

All children who require tympanoplasty for severe atelectasis must be followed at relatively frequent intervals for the first year after the procedure and at appropriate intervals for several succeeding years since recurrence of the atelectasis should always be anticipated.

Adhesive Otitis Media

Adhesive otitis media is a sequela of recurrent and chronic inflammation of the middle ear and mastoid and is a result of the healing process. The mucous membrane is thickened by proliferation of fibrous tissue, which frequently impairs (binds) the movement of the ossicles, resulting in a conductive hearing loss.

Adhesive otitis media can be classified into three stages related to severity, extent, and presence or absence of functional impairment[59]:

- *Stage 1.* Adhesive otitis media within the middle ear or mastoid, or both, in which there is no functional deficit secondary to the adhesive changes, i.e., hearing loss, and the middle ear remains aerated

- *Stage 2.* Adhesive otitis media within the middle ear (with or without mastoid involvement) in which there is mild hearing loss secondary to adhesive pathology, such as involvement of the ossicular chain (fixation or discontinuity, or both—see Ossicular Discontinuity and Ossicular Fixation), or limitation of tympanic membrane compliance, or both, but the middle ear remains aerated

- *Stage 3.* Similar to stage 2, but there is maximum conductive hearing loss (secondary to ossicular pathology) and no middle-ear space, both of which are due to the extensive adhesive otitis media

Pathology and Pathogenesis

Schuknecht described this pathologic condition as a proliferation of fibrous tissue within the middle ear and mastoid and called it *fibrous sclerosis*.[432] When cystic spaces are present, it is called *fibrocystic sclerosis*, and when there is new bone growth in the mastoid, it is called *fibro-osseous sclerosis*.

The etiology and pathogenesis have not been extensively studied. However, using animal experiments, Caye-Thomasen et al proposed that adhesive otitis media is a pathologic phenomenon caused by infection in six pathogenic stages[99]:

1. Localized epithelial rupture
2. Prolapse of subepithelial tissue
3. Epithelialization of the prolapse, resulting in a polypoid, foldlike prominence
4. Growth and elongation of the prominence
5. Fusion of the end-tip of the prominence with another part of the mucosa
6. Formation of an adhesion

Management

Currently, no data are available on the prevalence of adhesive otitis media in children, but the condition is commonly encountered in the pediatric age group when recurrent or chronic middle-ear disease has been a longstanding problem. Unfortunately, we likewise have no data from which to establish the probability of adhesive otitis media developing in a child with recurrent/chronic disease of the middle ear. However, the possibility of adhesive changes when recurrent or chronic inflammation—including atelectasis of the middle ear—is present in the middle ear and mastoid must be seriously considered when selecting the most appropriate medical or surgical treatment of children who have recurrent acute and chronic middle-ear disease.

In addition to fixation of the ossicles, adhesive otitis media may result in ossicular discontinuity and conductive hearing loss due to rarefying osteitis, especially of the long process of the incus. When there is a retraction pocket (severe partial atelectasis) in the posterosuperior portion of the pars tensa of the tympanic membrane, adhesive changes may bind the eardrum to the incus, stapes, and other surrounding middle-ear structures and cause resorption of the ossicles. Once adhesive changes bind the tympanic membrane in this area, a cholesteatoma may also develop. Timely ventilation of the middle ear and mastoid before the adhesive changes may return the tympanic membrane to the normal position, thus preventing ossicular damage. If medical treatment fails, a myringotomy should be performed and a tympanostomy tube should be inserted in an attempt to reverse the potentially progressive pathologic condition. If the tympanic membrane is still attached to the ossicles after tympanostomy tube insertion, adhesive otitis media is present. In children, tympanoplasty should be considered to prevent further structural damage since the process may progress because of persistent eustachian-tube obstruction.

When ossicular fixation occurs, ossiculoplasty may be performed to restore function, but this procedure is not always successful. When the middle ear and mastoid are bound by adhesive otitis media, the results of ossiculoplasty are frequently not permanent because the adhesive process recurs. However, surgery should be considered.

The best method to manage adhesive otitis media is prevention. This involves treating its precursors, recurrent acute otitis media, chronic otitis media with effusion (see Chap. 25), and atelectasis (discussed earlier).

Cholesteatoma

Cholesteatoma is keratinizing stratified squamous epithelium and an accumulation of desquamating epithelium of keratin within the middle ear or other pneumatized portions of the temporal bone. This disease has also been called a *keratoma*, but *cholesteatoma* is the more commonly used term.[162] Histologically, cholesteatoma is similar to epithelium of the skin of the external auditory canal.

Classification

Aural cholesteatoma can be classified as *congenital* and *acquired*. Acquired cholesteatomas can be either a sequela of middle-ear disease or of implantation, which can be due to trauma or related surgery of the middle ear (including the tympanic membrane), external auditory canal, or mastoid (i.e., iatrogenic).

A congenital cholesteatoma has been defined as a congenital rest of epithelial tissue and appears as a white, cystlike structure within the middle ear (intratympanic) or temporal bone. The tympanic membrane is intact, and it is apparently not a sequela of otitis media or eustachian-tube dysfunction.[98, 124] Rosenfeld et al reviewed the records of 232 Pittsburgh children who had cholesteatoma and identified 43 patients (18%) in whom the cholesteatoma was thought to be congenital.[413] It is possible that more cases would have been diagnosed as congenital, but in 46% of the children the advanced stage of the disease prevented the distinction between acquired and congenital origin.

Acquired cholesteatoma may be secondary to implantation or may be a sequela of otitis media or a retraction pocket, or both. Implantation cholesteatoma may develop either from epithelium that has migrated through a traumatic perforation of the tympanic membrane (or the site of a tympanostomy tube) or from epithelium that has been inadvertently overlooked in the middle ear or mastoid during surgery of the ear (iatrogenic).[72] Iatrogenic cholesteatoma can develop in the ear canal after middle-ear and mastoid surgery at the site of the incisions made in the canal and can occur following any of the various incisions.

The most common cholesteatoma is the acquired type, which is a sequela of middle-ear disease. In a study of 1024 patients (adults and children), a cholesteatoma was found in the attic in 42% and in the posterosuperior quadrant in 31%; a cholesteatoma was present in 18% when there was a "total" perforation, in 6% when there was a "central" perforation, and in 3% when there was no perforation.[441] However, it is possible that the posterosuperior portion of the pars tensa was originally involved when the cholesteatoma was associated with a *total* perforation. In children, the most common defect in the tympanic membrane begins developing in the posterosuperior quadrant of the pars tensa or, somewhat less commonly, in the pars flaccida. The term *marginal perforation* has been used to describe the defect in the posterosuperior quadrant, and the defect in the pars flaccida has been called an *attic perforation*; in reality, however, these cases are most frequently not perforations but are either retraction pockets or cholesteatomas that appear otoscopically to be perforations (Fig. 26–37). No continuity between the defect and the middle ear occurs until later in the disease process.

Staging of Acquired Cholesteatoma

It is appropriate to stage cholesteatomas for management, reporting, and research.[59] When staging cholesteatoma, the presence or absence of infection should be noted as should the duration of the otitis media (if present) as follows:

- *Cholesteatoma without infection* is a cholesteatoma that is not associated with infection, either within the cholesteatoma itself, or in any other portion of the middle-ear cleft.
- *Cholesteatoma with infection* is a cholesteatoma that is associated with infection, which can be either acute (with or without otorrhea) or chronic. The most common infection associated with cholesteatoma is chronic suppurative otitis media.

Cholesteatoma can be further classified as to its site and extent:

- *Stage 1.* Cholesteatoma confined to the middle ear (hypo- and mesoepitympanum), without erosion of ossicular chain
- *Stage 2.* Same as stage 1 but there is erosion of one or more ossicles
- *Stage 3.* Involvement of the middle ear and mastoid gas-cell system without erosion of ossicles
- *Stage 4.* Same as stage 3 but there is erosion of one or more ossicles
- *Stage 5.* Extensive cholesteatoma of the middle ear, mastoid, and other portions of the temporal bone, the extent of which is not totally accessible to surgical re-

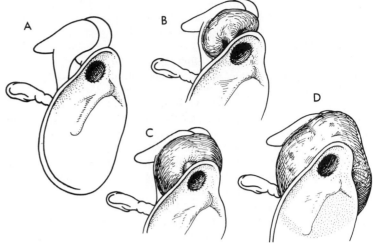

FIGURE 26–37. Evolution of acquired attic cholesteatoma. *A,* Attic retraction pocket (i.e., a defect) that appears on otoscopic examination to be a perforation. *B,* A narrow neck sac developing. *C,* Enlargement of the sac with erosion of the ossicles. *D,* A large cholesteatoma sac, a portion of which can be seen through the eardrum.

moval (e.g., medial to labyrinth), and involvement of one or more ossicles; a fistula of the labyrinth may or may not be present
- *Stage 6.* Same as stage 5 but the cholesteatoma extends beyond the temporal bone

Epidemiology, Complications, and Sequelae

Cholesteatoma has persisted as a sequela of middle-ear disease in adults and children despite the widespread use of antimicrobial agents and tympanostomy tubes since the mid-20th century. However, the mortality associated with cholesteatoma has dramatically fallen during this period in the developed countries of the world.

In an epidemiologic study from Michigan, Ritter compared 152 adults and children who had cholesteatoma identified from 1965 to 1970 to a similar study from Massachusetts of 303 cases that were identified before the use of antimicrobial agents (1925 to 1936).[407] In both series, he found that about 45% of cases of cholesteatoma were operated on before the patient was 20 years old, that the aural discharge had begun by age 11 years in approximately 65% of patients, and that the distribution of sites on the tympanic membrane where the defect was located were about the same. He concluded that antimicrobial agents had not altered the incidence and natural history of cholesteatoma during the 40 years between the two studies. However, Rigner et al concluded that in the Gothenburg area of Sweden, the incidence declined over a 10-year period, between 1977 and 1986; these authors attributed the fall in cases to better accessibility to specialists and improved methods to diagnose middle-ear disease earlier in that community as compared with other parts of the country.[406]

The epidemiology of cholesteatoma in children has been reported by several investigators in recent decades. Harker and Koontz, in a study of the general population in Iowa, reported the overall incidence of cholesteatoma to be 6 per 100,000; in children up to 9 years old, the incidence was 4.7 per 100,000; in children 10 to 19 years old, the incidence of 9.2 per 100,000 was the highest for all age groups.[210] Karma et al in Finland[260] and Tos in Denmark[490] estimated the annual incidence of cholestea-

toma to be 4.5 and 15 per 100,000 children, respectively. In a more recent report from Finland, the mean annual incidence of cholesteatoma during the period 1982 to 1991 in one region for all age groups was 9.2 per 100,000 inhabitants (range, 3.7 to 13.9).[261]

Cholesteatoma is a common sequela in children with cleft palate. Severeid reviewed the records of 160 children and young adults with cleft palates (70% were aged 10 to 16 years), all of whom had had a history of ear disease, and found the incidence of cholesteatoma to be 7.1%.[437] The posterosuperior portion of the pars tensa was the most common site. A later report from the same institution reported that almost 10% of children with cleft palate experienced cholesteatoma.[211] During a recent 10-year period in Finland, 8% of 500 patients who had cholesteatoma also had a cleft palate.[261]

In contrast with this high incidence of cholesteatoma in the population affected by cleft palate is the rare occurrence of cholesteatoma in Alaskan (Eskimo) natives, American Indians,[224] and Australian aboriginal children,[327] in whom other middle-ear disease is very common. This remarkable difference in the incidence of cholesteatoma in children with cleft palates and in certain racial groups, both of which have a high prevalence and incidence of otitis media, is most probably related to differences in the pathogenesis and natural history of the respective middle-ear disease processes (see Chap. 25).

Before the widespread use of antimicrobial agents and modern otologic surgery, complications of cholesteatoma were common. For many children, the result was death when infection involved the intracranial cavity. Serious complications of cholesteatoma in children are now uncommon in developed countries. In a study of 181 children who had cholesteatoma, 8 (4.4%) experienced a labyrinthine fistula and one suffered facial paralysis, but none had intracranial complications.[441] However, in the same study, which also included 843 adults, the incidence of both intratemporal and intracranial complications increased the longer the cholesteatoma was present. Because most of the adults could date the onset of their disease to childhood and because diagnosis and surgery for cholesteatoma is the best way of preventing serious complications, physicians dealing with ear problems in children should treat suspected cholesteatoma early and aggressively. Nevertheless, intratemporal complications and sequelae are still a problem in even the highly industrialized nations of the world.

The rate of cholesteatoma, and especially its complications, in developing countries is relatively high compared with industrialized nations. Prescott recently reported on his experience in treating 81 children who had cholesteatoma from 1988 to 1996; 24 (30%) presented with mastoiditis and 7 (9%) had an intracranial complication.[395] In that study, 56 (70%) of the cholesteatomas were from a retraction pocket, and 21 (25%) were from a central perforation or total atelectasis; 3 were congenital (see Chapter 27).

Sequelae such as ossicular involvement, which not only contribute to the associated conductive hearing loss but are related to the residual and recurrence rates, are common.[413] Also, cholesteatoma with chronic suppurative otitis media has been associated with sensorineural hearing loss.[148]

Pathogenesis

The pathogenesis of acquired middle-ear cholesteatoma is a subject of continuing controversy, but most likely there is more than one pathogenetic mechanism. Of the many hypotheses proposed to explain the pathogenesis of cholesteatoma, the following are the most popular:

- Metaplasia of the middle ear and attic due to infection[497, 519]
- Invasive hyperplasia of the basal layers of the meatal skin adjoining the upper margin of the tympanic membrane[220, 281, 353, 359, 416]
- Invasive hyperkeratosis of the deep external auditory canal[329]
- Retraction or collapse of the tympanic membrane with invagination secondary to eustachian-tube dysfunction[43, 207, 525]

In addition, some authors consider the condition not to be acquired at all but to be an embryonic epidermal rest occurring in the attic.[129, 331, 480] Sudhoff and Tos propose the following sequence of events in the pathogenesis of an attic cholesteatoma[475]: (1) the retraction pocket stage, (2) the proliferation stage of the retraction pocket, subdivided into cone formation and cone fusion, (3) the expansion stage of attic cholesteatoma, and (4) bone resorption. Even though this sequence appears reasonable, it is apparent that cholesteatoma can develop in several ways.[434]

In a study from Pittsburgh, varying degrees of functional rather than mechanical (anatomic) obstruction of the eustachian tube were found in 13 children and adults who had a retraction pocket or an acquired cholesteatoma.[53] Subsequently, the same group reported the findings in 12 children with acquired cholesteatoma, all of whom had functional obstruction of the eustachian tube, in the same center.[60] Children were specifically studied since the acquired cholesteatoma, with its attendant irreversible changes, was thought to develop early in life and since the function of the eustachian tube might improve with growth and development. In these children, the

function of the eustachian tube was assessed by the modified inflation-deflation technique (after Ingelstedt et al[240]).

Bluestone et al[56] and Chan et al[103] performed two other studies to further clarify the cause of this functional obstruction by employing a new test of eustachian-tube function, the forced-response test,[90] and to evaluate a larger group of children who had either a cholesteatoma or a retraction pocket. In addition, children with an apparent congenital cholesteatoma were also studied, and the results obtained in both groups were then compared with the results of children who had traumatic perforation of the tympanic membrane but who were otherwise considered otologically normal. Another goal of the study was to determine whether there were any differences in eustachian-tube function among ears with a posterosuperior or pars flaccida retraction pocket or cholesteatoma, ears with a central perforation and a cholesteatoma, and ears with congenital cholesteatoma.

In a study from Sweden, Lindeman and Holmquist showed similar findings in adults with acquired cholesteatoma.[293] Compared with adults with traumatic perforations (i.e., control subjects), 20 adults with cholesteatoma had poor eustachian-tube test results and smaller mastoid air-cell areas as measured radiographically.

It appears from these studies that the basic problem in children with acquired cholesteatoma is a failure of the opening mechanism of the eustachian tube. This results in a functional obstruction of the tube during swallowing rather than normal dilatation of the tube. (This type of functional obstruction of the eustachian tube was present in subjects with a retraction pocket or cholesteatoma irrespective of the site.) In the absence of cholesteatoma obstructing the middle-ear end of the tube, anatomic (mechanical) obstruction is not involved in the pathogenesis. Abnormal functioning of the tube then results in impaired ventilation of the middle-ear/mastoid air-cell system, which in turn results in fluctuating or sustained high negative middle-ear pressure. Periodic, rather than regular, ventilation could result in wide variations in middle-ear pressures that would produce greater-than-normal excursions of the tympanic membrane. The membrane would then lose elasticity and become flaccid and, eventually, atelectatic. The most flaccid parts of the tympanic membrane are the posterosuperior and pars flaccida areas.[266] When the atelectasis becomes severe and localized in these sites, a retraction pocket forms. Inflammation between the medial portion of the retracted or collapsed tympanic membrane could then result in adhesive changes and could fix the pocket to the ossicles or surrounding structures, or both. The next stage in this series of events would be discontinuity of the ossicles or cholesteatoma formation, or both. Figure 26–38 shows the progression from the stage of a retraction pocket with atelectasis to adhesive otitis media and, finally, to cholesteatoma in the posterosuperior quadrant of the pars tensa and pars flaccida, respectively.

Even with the aid of the otomicroscope, it is frequently difficult to distinguish between a deep retraction pocket and a cholesteatoma in either the posterosuperior quadrant of the pars tensa or the pars flaccida (Fig. 26–39). The transition between the two conditions usually follows a progressive change from a retraction pocket to

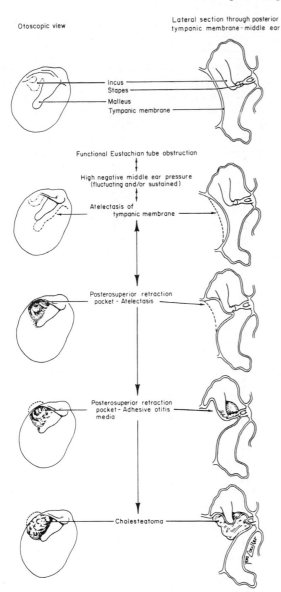

FIGURE 26–38. Chain of events in the pathogenesis of acquired aural cholesteatoma in the posterosuperior portion of the pars tensa or the tympanic membrane.

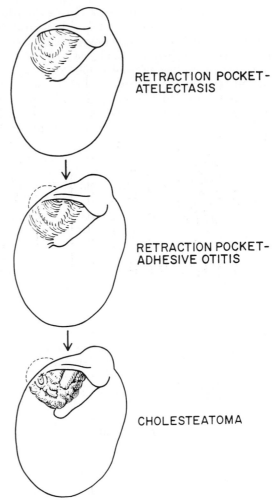

FIGURE 26–39. Sequence of events leading from a localized area of atelectasis (retraction pocket) in the posterosuperior portion of the pars tensa of the tympanic membrane to a cholesteatoma and ossicular discontinuity. Adhesive otitis media in this area is shown as the stage between atelectasis and the development of a cholesteatoma.

cholesteatoma; however, the factors involved in this transition are currently obscure, although infection within the retraction pocket-sac appears to be important.

A cholesteatoma can also develop at the site of a central perforation. This probably is due to migration of epithelium from the tympanic membrane through the perforation and into the middle ear. However, it must be stressed that, in children, this type of acquired cholesteatoma is less common than the posterosuperior or attic type.

There is some uncertainty as to the origin of congenital cholesteatomas. Some authorities consider them to be truly congenital. But children who have an intratympanic cholesteatoma may have had otitis media. On one hand, it could be argued that intratympanic cholesteatoma is the result of metaplasia secondary to middle-ear inflammation and that it is not congenital.[421] On the other hand, otitis media, when present, may be unrelated to a congenital

rest. The fact that children who have congenital cholesteatomas tend to be younger than those who present with a retraction pocket or acquired cholesteatoma supports the idea that a cholesteatoma originating medial to an intact tympanic membrane is congenital.[413] In any event, most acquired cholesteatomas not due to implantation are secondary to otitis media or a retraction pocket, or both, and the disease may have developed in the same way in some children who have an apparently congenital cholesteatoma.[458] Levenson et al think that the pathogenesis of congenital cholesteatoma is an epithelial rest, which is stimulated to grow by otitis media.[288] Tos has proposed that a "congenital" cholesteatoma may, in fact, be acquired and due to otitis media.[489]

Recent studies reveal that inflammatory factors, such as cytokines, adhesion molecules, tumor necrosis factor-α, nuclear phosphoprotein p53 tumor suppressor gene, and angiogenesis and angiogenic growth factors may play a role in invasion, migration, and proliferation of congenital and acquired cholesteatoma.[9, 108, 254, 365, 474, 478]

A common sequela of middle-ear disease in patients with cleft palate is cholesteatoma.[211, 437] It has been shown that all infants with an unrepaired cleft palate have otitis media with effusion[376, 471] and that they have functional obstruction of the eustachian tube due to impairment of the tubal opening mechanism.[51, 61, 70] Studies of infants, children, and adolescents with cleft palate demonstrate constriction of the eustachian tube during the forced-response test.[142] Cholesteatoma is a common sequela of middle-ear disease in patients with cleft palate.[437] Therefore, childhood cleft palate represents an in vivo model of the type of functional eustachian-tube obstruction that can result in an acquired cholesteatoma. Because this type of dysfunction is also common in whites who have otitis media or atelectasis but who do not have cleft palate,[90] such persons are also at risk for cholesteatoma.

In contrast with the frequency of cholesteatoma in the population with cleft palate, cholesteatoma is uncommon in American Indian populations.[521] Jaffe reported that attic perforations are rarely found in Navajo children; in over 200 tympanoplasties performed to repair central perforations, no cholesteatoma was found.[243] Wiet, in a study of 600 White Mountain Apache Indians, also reported a low incidence of cholesteatoma; the few cases he found were mostly of the attic type.[520] In a subsequent study by Beery et al, otoscopic examination of 25 Apache Indians revealed no cholesteatomas.[38] The inflation-deflation and forced-response tests were used to test eustachian-tube function in these Indians and revealed a eustachian tube that had low resistance to airflow (was semipatulous) but had active muscle function. This type of tube would probably preclude high negative middle-ear pressure, a retraction pocket, or cholesteatoma. The Apache Indian appears to have a eustachian tube that allows for easier passage of gas and liquid than does the white person with or without cleft palate. The middle ear of the Apache is easily ventilated and, consequently, is not protected from unwanted secretions from the nasopharynx. It appears that the structure of the eustachian tube of the Apache Indian of the White Mountain Reservation is conducive to the development of reflux otitis media, perforation, and discharge.

Some American Indian tribes would appear to be in vivo models of the semipatulous eustachian tube that actively dilates during swallowing. Cholesteatoma formation is rare in such ears since the middle ear is aerated by the eustachian tube or by a central perforation, or both. By studying these in vivo models, we can gain a clearer perspective of the whole spectrum of eustachian-tube dysfunction (see Chapter 25).

Microbiology

Cholesteatomas may or may not be associated with infection; when infection is present, it can be acute or chronic. Also, an acute infection can be superimposed on a preexisting chronic infection. Frequently, a cholesteatoma is present in the middle ear (and mastoid) without any signs of acute or chronic infection. However, when infection is present, it can involve the entire middle-ear cleft (i.e.,

eustachian tube, middle ear, and mastoid), or only the cholesteatoma is infected and the rest of the middle-ear cleft is apparently free of infection.

When infection is present, the organisms cultured from the discharge are similar to those identified from ears with chronic suppurative otitis media: *P. aeruginosa* and *Proteus* species are the most commonly identified aerobic bacteria, and *Bacteroides* and *Peptococcus-Peptostreptococcus* are the most commonly found anaerobic organisms. Harker and Koontz cultured multiple bacteria from the discharges of over half of 30 patients with cholesteatomas (Table 26–14).[210] Karma et al reported that when they cultured 18 infected cholesteatomas, they found both aerobic and anaerobic bacteria in half.[259] These results suggest that the most appropriate ototopical medication and systemic antimicrobial therapy for patients with an infected cholesteatoma consists of agents that are effective against gram-negative organisms and anaerobic bacteria; however, the results of culturing the discharge aid in selecting the proper antimicrobial therapy. These considerations may be life-saving when an intratemporal or intracranial complication of cholesteatoma is present. In addition, preoperative and postoperative antimicrobial therapy for patients with profuse otorrhea may also be necessary to prevent a postoperative infection.

Pathology

Cholesteatoma is characterized by keratinizing stratified squamous epithelium, with accumulation of desquamating epithelium or keratin within the middle-ear cleft or other pneumatized portions of the temporal bone. Usually, a cystlike structure is produced by the keratinizing squamous epithelium. Laminated keratin from its inverted

TABLE 26–14. Bacteriology of Infected Cholesteatomas in 30 Children and Adults

Organism	Number of Cases
Aerobes	
Pseudomonas aeruginosa	11
Pseudomonas fluorescens	2
Proteus	4
Escherichia coli	4
Klebsiella-Enterobacter-Serratia	4
Streptococcus	8
Alcaligenes-Achromobacter	3
Staphylococcus aureus	1
Staphylococcus epidermidis	2
CBC Group F	2
Anaerobes	
Bacteroides	13
Peptococcus-Peptostreptococcus	11
Propionibacterium acnes	8
Fusobacterium	4
Bifidobacterium	3
Clostridium	3
Eubacterium	2

Adapted from Harker LA, Koontz FP. The bacteriology of cholesteatoma. In McCabe BF, Sadé J, Abramson M (eds). Cholesteatoma: First International Conference. New York, Aesculapius, 1977, pp 264–267.

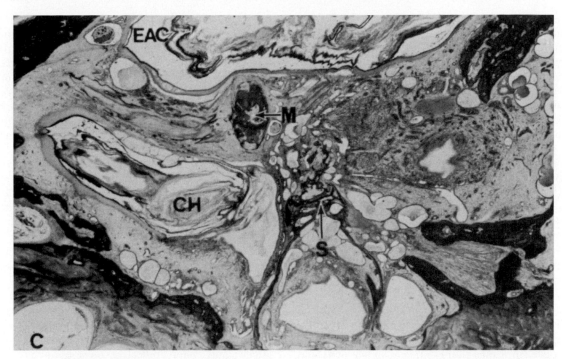

FIGURE 26–40. Cholesteatoma (H&E, ×16). CH, cholesteatoma; EAC, external auditory canal; M, malleus; S, stapes; C, cochlea. (Courtesy of I. Sando, M.D.)

surface accumulates within the cavity, which may also contain necrotic tissue and purulent material (Fig. 26–40). If the pocket is dry, the rate of exfoliation may be slow.[432] A cholesteatoma may or may not be infected or associated with chronic suppurative otitis media. Sheehy et al reported that of 1024 children and adults with cholesteatoma, 26% had no history of aural discharge in the past; in 53% it had been intermittent, and in only 21% was it continuous.[441] When these patients underwent surgery, almost half had no evidence of discharge.

Cholesteatoma usually causes bone resorption, which is thought to be secondary to pressure erosion as the mass enlarges or possibly due to the activity of collagenase.[1] Erosion of bone can occur anywhere in the temporal bone, although the ossicles are commonly involved.[134, 410, 413] Ossicular erosion can result in discontinuity (usually erosion of the long process of the incus) and a conductive hearing loss or fistulization of the labyrinth. (The lateral semicircular canal is the most common site of erosion.)

Alternatively, the epidermis may invade the aerated space of the temporal bone and form an incomplete surface lining into which the desquamated keratin debris overflows. This process may give the impression that the mucous membrane is converted by metaplasia to keratinizing squamous epithelium.[421] However, there is no histopathologic support for this hypothesis.[431]

Cholesteatoma in children is considered to be a more aggressive (invasive) disease than that occurring in adults for two reasons[30, 125, 432]:

- Very extensive disease is found at the time of surgery more frequently in children than in adults.
- Rates of residual (persistent) and recurrent cholesteatoma after surgery have been higher in children than in adults.[158]

Palva et al compared 65 children with cholesteatomas with 65 adults with the same disease and found that whereas 22% of the children had extensive disease that filled the middle ear and mastoid, only 6% of adults had such extensive disease.[367] Cholesteatoma in children frequently extends into the cell tracts of the temporal bone since pneumatization is usually more extensive in children than in adults.[432] This is not the case with adults. However, despite the finding that cholesteatomas tend to be more extensive in children than in adults, childhood cholesteatoma may still be confined to the mesotympanum or epitympanum. Schuring et al compared the extent and outcomes of surgery for cholesteatoma in 228 adults and teenagers to the experience in 38 children and concluded that children had more recurrent disease, greater ossicular necrosis, and poorer hearing postoperatively.[433] Despite the finding that cholesteatomas tend to be more extensive in children than in adults, childhood cholesteatoma may still be confined to the middle ear.

Diagnosis

Since the signs and symptoms of ear disease may be lacking, cholesteatoma may go undetected for many years in children and adults. In children, this is an even greater problem since they are frequently unaware of slowly developing subtle ear problems. Most adults have a history of hearing loss, which is usually progressive and associated with recurrent ear discharge. However, children rarely complain of hearing loss, especially if the disease is unilateral. Frequently, there is no discharge, and otalgia may be absent in most children and adults. In addition, children are usually unaware of the more subtle symptoms associated with the disease, such as fullness in the ear, tinnitus, mild vertigo, and the foul smell of the discharge, when present. Fever is not a sign of cholesteatoma; when it accompanies this disease, and especially when otalgia is also present, an intratemporal or intracranial complication must be sought.

Other signs and symptoms, such as facial paralysis, severe vertigo, vomiting, and headache, should also alert the physician to the presence of a suppurative complication. In children, the attic type of cholesteatoma appears to be less symptomatic than a cholesteatoma in the posterosuperior quadrant since the latter type is frequently preceded by symptomatic recurrent or chronic otitis media with effusion and an early onset of ossicular discontinuity with significant hearing loss. However, in both types, the preceding atelectasis and retraction pocket may not be associated with significant symptoms in children. The intratympanic *congenital* cholesteatoma, which may be secondary to otitis media, is even more obscure since hearing loss may be a late sequela and discharge is not present.

The diagnosis of cholesteatoma is most effectively made with an otoscope or, more accurately, with the otomicroscope. However, otoscopy may be equivocal or difficult to perform if infection is present in the ear canal, or the child may be uncooperative. If otoscopy is not successful and a cholesteatoma is suspected, the child may have to be examined using a general anesthetic. Also, CT may be diagnostic. Recurrent or chronic otorrhea that is unresponsive to medical management can be a sign that a cholesteatoma is the underlying pathology.

In a defect in the posterosuperior portion of the pars tensa or the attic or through a large perforation, otoscopy usually reveals white, shiny, greasy flakes of debris, which may or may not be associated with a foul-smelling discharge. A polyp may emerge through the defect, which, like a crust, can prevent adequate visualization of the tympanic membrane. A crust overlying the area of the posterosuperior quadrant or the pars flaccida must be removed since a retraction pocket or cholesteatoma may be present. The size of the defect in the tympanic membrane may not indicate the extent of the cholesteatoma since a small defect, especially in the attic, may be associated with extensive cholesteatoma. On the other hand, the cholesteatoma may be confined only to the attic or middle ear despite the presence of a large defect. If adequate examination of the child's ear is not possible with the child awake, an examination with the patient under anesthesia is indicated. In every child who must be given a general anesthetic for myringotomy (with or without tympanostomy tube insertion), the entire tympanic membrane should be examined to identify a possible cholesteatoma or its precursor, a retraction pocket. In addition, an intratympanic cholesteatoma may be visualized through the tympanic membrane or through the incision after myringotomy.

It is frequently difficult to determine whether the defect is a retraction pocket or a "dry" cholesteatoma. However, even when this distinction is impossible, the management of the defect is usually the same (see earlier in this chapter, Atelectasis of the Middle Ear).

Unfortunately, there is no tympanometric pattern to diagnose a cholesteatoma. An abnormal-appearing tympanogram should alert the clinician to the presence of middle-ear disease, but the tympanogram may appear normal even when a cholesteatoma is present. Impedance testing may reveal a perforation of the tympanic membrane, but in children this occurs less commonly than in adults. Likewise, audiometric testing may reveal a conductive hearing impairment or possibly a mixed conductive and sensorineural deficit, but a cholesteatoma may be present without loss of hearing. A sensorineural hearing loss is presumably due to serous labyrinthitis[374] or possibly to a labyrinthine fistula.

CT of the temporal bone aids diagnosis and management when a cholesteatoma is suspected.[275] The CT scans should be studied carefully to identify the extent of the cholesteatoma, possible ossicular involvement, and any complications such as a labyrinthine fistula. CT scans should be restudied preoperatively during planning of the surgical procedure; CT can aid decisions concerning the surgical approach and the extent of surgery.[63]

When aural discharge associated with a cholesteatoma is profuse, microbiologic assessment of the discharge is indicated so the infection can be controlled by administering the most appropriate antimicrobial agents preoperatively, and, when indicated, intraoperatively and postoperatively (see Chap. 25).

Management

Management of cholesteatoma and conditions that may be causally related to this disease should be based on an understanding of its pathogenesis. The presence of a deep retraction pocket in the posterosuperior or pars flaccida area of the tympanic membrane, if persistent, should be managed promptly by inserting a tympanostomy tube in an effort to return the tympanic membrane to the neutral position and to prevent adhesions from forming between the tympanic membrane and the middle-ear structures (see Fig. 26–36).[88] If the pocket is not treated, a cholesteatoma may develop. In children, the retraction pocket may be seen to distend during inhalation anesthesia with nitrous oxide (as seen through the otomicroscope); this is a promising sign that the tympanic membrane will return to the normal position after the insertion of a tympanostomy tube. On the other hand, if the retraction pocket does not distend during anesthesia, the surgeon should carefully examine the depth and extent of the pocket, probing gently with a blunt right-angled hook. Mirrors may also help to visualize the extent of the pocket. We prefer a Hopkins rod-lens telescope to determine the exact borders of the pocket (Fig. 26–41).[195]

A retraction pocket can extend into any area of the middle ear, but most frequently it extends into the epitympanum, facial recess, and sinus tympani. If the retraction pocket persists after the middle ear has been ventilated by a tympanostomy tube that has been in place for several weeks, a tympanoplasty to prevent ossicular discontinuity or the development of a cholesteatoma, or both, should be recommended.[65] Heermann et al advocate the use of cartilage to support the tympanic membrane graft to prevent recurrence of the retraction

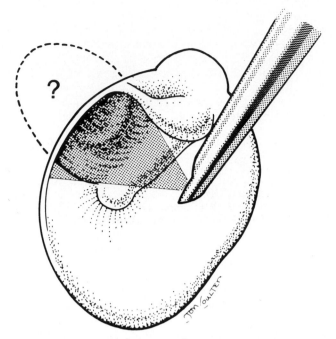

FIGURE 26–41. The extent of the retraction pocket can best be visualized with the 90-degree needle telescope (Olympus Co., Japan). The retraction pocket in this artist's drawing is in the posterosuperior quadrant of a right tympanic membrane.

pocket.[219] Other surgeons have reported good results using cartilage to prevent postoperative retraction.[6, 289, 393, 422] Simple excision of the retraction pocket has also been advocated,[47, 439] but this technique is not as effective as reconstruction of the defect and reinforcing the tympanic membrane with cartilage. In children, a tympanostomy tube should be inserted into the tympanic membrane remnant since eustachian-tube function will most probably remain poor postoperatively.

Surgical Procedures

Surgical intervention is indicated when a cholesteatoma is present. The only exceptions to this form of management are unusual cases (just described) in which simple debridement and insertion of a tympanostomy tube are successful and when a concomitant disease would make surgery under general anesthesia a hazard to the child's health. The surgical procedures currently employed to eradicate a cholesteatoma are briefly described next. These procedures may also be performed for other conditions described in this chapter; however, for detailed descriptions of the surgical techniques, the reader is referred to Chapter 3, Otologic Surgical Procedures, in the *Atlas of Pediatric Otolaryngology*.[69]

Procedures for surgical management of cholesteatoma can be divided into those that provide exposure and removal of disease from the middle ear and mastoid and those designed to reconstruct the middle ear to preserve or restore hearing.

Tympanotomy is a surgical procedure that opens the middle-ear space. In *exploratory tympanotomy*, a tympanomeatal flap is elevated so that the middle ear and its structures can be viewed directly. An exploratory tympan-

otomy is indicated when an abnormality, such as intratympanic cholesteatoma or ossicular chain abnormality, is suspected or as a planned second-stage procedure after a tympanoplasty with or without a mastoidectomy has been performed to manage cholesteatoma.

Myringoplasty is the surgical repair of a defect in the tympanic membrane with no attempt to explore the middle ear. A perforation (or retraction pocket) is commonly repaired by using autogenous connective tissue graft (temporalis fascia or compressed adipose tissue from the earlobe) as a lattice onto which epithelial cells can migrate from the edges of the existing perforation. The procedure is employed to manage a simple uncomplicated tympanic membrane perforation without cholesteatoma.

Tympanoplasty is the surgical reconstruction of the tympanic membrane/ossicle transformer mechanism. If a perforation is present, it is repaired with a connective tissue graft, but unlike the case with myringoplasty, the middle ear is explored. Ossicles can be repositioned (ossiculoplasty) to restore ossicular chain continuity. Traditionally, tympanoplasty operations are characterized according to the degree to which the reconstructed ossicular chain approximates the anatomic juxtaposition of ossicles in the normal middle ear (see the earlier discussion, Perforation of the Tympanic Membrane, and the later discussion, Ossicular Chain Discontinuity and Fixation).

Mastoidectomy involves the surgical exposure and removal of mastoid air cells. There are several types of mastoidectomy (Fig. 26–42). In a *complete simple "cortical" mastoidectomy* (Fig. 26–42A), the mastoid air-cell system is exenterated, including the epitympanum, but the canal wall is left intact. The operation is performed when acute or chronic mastoid osteitis is present and is frequently part of the surgical procedure advocated by some surgeons for cholesteatoma.

A *posterior tympanotomy* or *facial recess tympanotomy* (Fig. 26–42B) involves exenteration of mastoid air cells followed by formation of an opening between the mastoid and middle ear created in the posterior wall of the middle ear lateral to the facial nerve and medial to the chorda tympani. This procedure is an extension of the complete simple mastoidectomy that allows better visualization of the facial recess without removing the canal wall and is primarily advocated for ears in which a cholesteatoma is present.

A *modified radical mastoidectomy* (Fig. 26–42C) is an operation in which a portion of the posterior ear canal wall is removed and a permanent mastoidectomy cavity is created, but the tympanic membrane and some or all of the ossicles are left. The procedure is usually performed when a cholesteatoma cannot be removed without removing the canal wall; some function may be preserved.

Radical mastoidectomy (Fig. 26–42D) involves exenteration of all mastoid air cells, opening of the epitympanum, and removal of the posterior ear-canal wall along with the tympanic membrane, the malleus, and the incus. Only the stapes, or the footplate of the stapes, remains. No attempt is made to preserve or improve function. Removal of the posterior ear-canal wall allows communication among the exenterated mastoid cellular area, middle ear, and external auditory canal, which form a common single cavity. The procedure is indicated when there

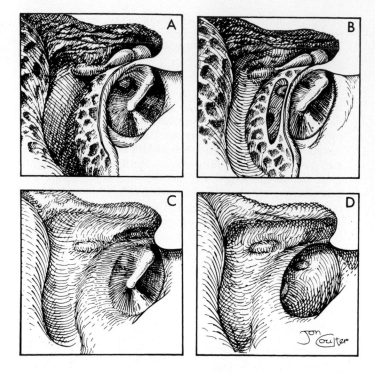

FIGURE 26–42. Four types of mastoid surgery. *A,* Complete simple ("cortical") mastoidectomy in which the canal wall has been left intact. However, the exposure of the epitympanum is an important part of the surgical procedure. *B,* A posterior tympanotomy/facial recess access to the middle ear has been added to the complete simple mastoidectomy. *C,* Modified radical mastoidectomy. *D,* Radical mastoidectomy.

is extensive cholesteatoma in the middle ear and mastoid that cannot be removed by a less radical procedure. In addition, the operation may be indicated for a suppurative complication of otitis media.

Tympanomastoidectomy with tympanoplasty is the term used when a tympanoplasty operation is performed in conjunction with a mastoidectomy. Mastoidectomy operations that leave the posterior ear-canal wall intact are called *closed cavity, canal wall up,* or *intact canal wall* procedures, whereas those in which the posterior canal is partially removed are called *open cavity* or *canal wall down* procedures. For more complete details of the surgical procedures, the reader is referred to Bluestone.[65]

Type of Surgical Procedure Related to Outcome

Controversy exists concerning the best surgical methods to eradicate cholesteatoma from the middle ear and mastoid in all age groups. Some surgeons prefer mastoidectomy and surgery of the middle ear, i.e., canal-wall-up procedures, in which the cholesteatoma is removed without leaving a mastoid cavity and in which function is preserved or restored by tympanoplasty (with or without ossiculoplasty).[24, 119, 186, 247, 341, 426, 442, 444–456] Most of the surgeons who advocate the intact-canal-wall procedure perform a planned second-stage exploratory tympanotomy, at which time cholesteatoma (that had been left either purposefully in a critical area, such as over a labyrinthine fistula, or inadvertently) can be removed.[446] However, opponents to this approach prefer either a modified radical mastoidectomy or, when the cholesteatoma is extensive, a radical mastoidectomy, since they consider the rate of persistence (residual) or recurrence of cholesteatoma after the intact-canal-wall procedures to be unacceptably high.[2, 3] The advocates of the canal-wall-down approach would rather sacrifice the potential pres-

ervation or restoration of function (in some procedures leaving the patient with a mastoid "bowl") for a better chance at total removal of the cholesteatoma—that is, a low rate of residual and recurrent disease.

Palva et al advocate modified radical mastoidectomy in which the mastoidectomy cavity is obliterated with subcutaneous tissue (i.e., a Palva flap) to eliminate the mastoid bowl, and an attempt is made to improve or preserve hearing.[367] However, when they compared 65 children and 65 adults who underwent the procedure to remove a cholesteatoma, the three patients in whom a postoperative residual cholesteatoma occurred were children. Tos advocates fitting the procedure to the pathologic condition found at surgery.[494] Some surgeons now perform mastoidectomy, removing a portion of the posterior ear canal for better visualization to excise the cholesteatoma, but then replace that portion of the canal that was temporarily removed.[134]

The type of surgery to manage cholesteatoma in children should be based on the site and extent of the cholesteatoma and on other factors such as patient age, presence or absence of otitis media, eustachian-tube function, and availability of health care. The operation must be tailored to each child. Today, every effort should be made to maintain the posterior ear canal in children, as opposed to performing canal-wall-down procedures, i.e., modified or radical mastoidectomy. However, when the tympanic membrane is preserved or reconstructed (tympanoplasty), a second operative procedure is indicated in most children, usually 6 months later, to determine whether residual cholesteatoma has been left behind.[410, 413] Unfortunately, CT and MRI are not sensitive enough to replace exploratory surgery; the disease must be far advanced for these scans to be an effective diagnostic tool.[500] Some authors have advocated using a telescope, via a transcanal approach, to detect residual cholestea-

TABLE 26–15. Cause of Cholesteatoma Related to Type of Ear Surgery in 232 Pittsburgh Children (244 Ears)

Cause of Cholesteatoma	Middle-Ear Surgery Only (%)	Type of Mastoidectomy (%)		
Total Procedures (%)		*Canal Wall-up*	*Modified Radical*	*Standard Radical*
Congenital	26 (56)	6 (13)	4 (9)	9 (20)	45 (18)
Acquired	24 (28)	16 (18)	23 (26)	24 (28)	87 (36)
Unknown	31 (28)	24 (21)	26 (23)	31 (28)	112 (46)
Total	81 (33)	46 (19)	53 (22)	64 (26)	244

Modified from Rosenfeld RM, Moura RL, Bluestone CD. Predictors of residual-recurrent cholesteatoma in children. Arch Otolaryngol Head Neck Surg 118:384, 1992. ©1992, American Medical Association.

toma in an effort to avoid the traditional exploratory tympanotomy (and possible mastoidotomy),[206, 479] but we prefer a transcanal tympanotomy, with or without exploration of the mastoid, depending on the extent of the initial disease; a telescope can enhance the procedure.

Rosenfeld et al reviewed the medical records of 232 children (244 ears) who underwent surgery for cholesteatoma at the Children's Hospital of Pittsburgh between 1973 and 1990; 427 surgical procedures were performed in these patients.[413] Of the 232 patients, 43 (18%) had congenital cholesteatoma and 83 (36%) had an acquired type; in 106 (46%) of the children, the type of cholesteatoma could not be classified (i.e., unknown) (Table 26–15). Of the 199 procedures performed for acquired (or of unknown cause) cholesteatoma, 28% required only a middle-ear procedure, 21% involved canal-wall-up mastoidectomy, 25% involved modified mastoidectomy, and 28% required radical mastoidectomy. Of the 170 procedures that did not require an initial standard radical mastoidectomy, only 20 (12%) eventually required a more extensive operation (e.g., modified or standard radical mastoidectomy) because of subsequent residual or recurrent cholesteatoma (Table 26–16).

Current Recommendations

At either end of the spectrum of the disease, the decision as to the most appropriate surgical management of cholesteatoma is relatively straightforward. For children who have a small cystlike cholesteatoma that is localized to the mesotympanum or epitympanum and that can be removed easily, a tympanoplasty can be successful; an atticotomy may be required to remove the cholesteatoma. A second-stage exploratory tympanotomy should be considered 6 months after the initial procedure to uncover residual or recurrent disease. This interval is somewhat shorter than that advocated for adults, but residual cholesteatoma grows more rapidly in children than in adults.

Rosenfeld et al reported that unsuspected residual or recurrent cholesteatoma was identified during 21 (39%) of 54 second-look procedures in our review of 426 procedures (Table 26–17).[413] We reported that ossicular erosion due to the cholesteatoma, and disease in the sinus tympani, were associated with residual or recurrent disease, whereas the type of procedure performed (i.e., canal-wall-up or canal-wall-down) was not related to the rate of residual or recurrent disease. In a smaller study, Stern and Fazekas-May evaluated 53 children with cholesteatoma and also found that disease in the sinus tympani identified at the initial procedure predicted failure in controlling the disease in a significant number of children.[465]

A second-stage procedure may not be necessary if the surgeon is convinced the disease was totally removed at the initial procedure, if the tympanic membrane is translucent without evidence of progressive disease medial to the drum after the surgery, and if the hearing is stable during the postoperative follow-up period (and no second-stage ossiculoplasty is planned). In these cases, the child may be observed. However, a second look should be performed if the tympanic membrane is opaque or if a

TABLE 26–16. Initial Ear Surgical Procedure Related to Most Extensive Procedure Eventually Required to Eradicate Disease in 232 Pittsburgh Children (244 Ears)

Initial Procedure	Procedure Eventually Required°			
	Middle-Ear Surgery Only	Mastoidectomy		
		Canal Wall-Up	*Modified Radical*	*Standard Radical*
Middle-ear surgery only (74)	0	6	1	81 (33)
Mastoidectomy				
Canal wall-up	38	4	4	46 (19)
Modified radical	—	48	5	53 (22)
Standard radical	—	—	64	64 (26)
Total (%) 74 (30)	38 (16)	58 (24)	74 (30)	244

° Total procedures (%).

Modified from Rosenfeld RM, Moura RL, Bluestone CD. Predictors of residual-recurrent cholesteatoma in children. Arch Otolaryngol Head Neck Surg 118:384, 1992. ©1992, American Medical Association.

TABLE 26–17. Type of Ear Surgery in 232 Pittsburgh Children (244 Ears)

Indication for Surgery	Total Procedures (%)
Initial procedure	244 (57)
Second-look procedure	54 (13)
Third-look procedure	2 (<1)
Fourth-look procedure	1 (<1)
Residual or recurrent disease	108 (25)
Reconstruction	17 (4)
Total	426

Modified from Rosenfeld RM, Moura RL, Bluestone CD. Predictors of residual-recurrent cholesteatoma in children. Arch Otolaryngol Head Neck Surg 118: 384, 1992. © 1992, American Medical Association.

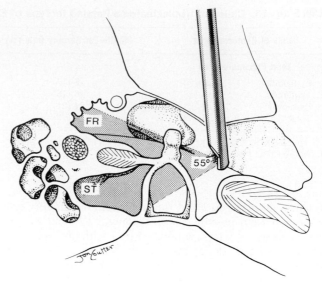

FIGURE 26–43. How the needle telescope can be used during the operation to visualize the sinus tympani (ST) and facial recess (FR) areas to determine whether there is residual cholesteatoma.

progressive loss of hearing develops. If residual cholesteatoma is found during this second procedure and if it is extensive, a canal-wall-down procedure (modified radical mastoidectomy or radical mastoidectomy) may be needed to control the disease.

The 70-degree telescope can be helpful in determining whether cholesteatoma is in the sinus tympani and facial recess during the initial operative procedure and at the time of the second-look exploratory tympanotomy (Fig. 26–43).[195] Other surgeons are also now using telescopes to enhance the removal of cholesteatoma.[145, 330, 394, 483] One of us (CDB) thinks that use of the telescope to aid in removal of the cholesteatoma may allow a less radical procedure, especially since the facial recess, sinus tympani, bony portion of the eustachian tube, hypotympanum, and lateral attic can be better visualized than with only the otomicroscope. On rare occasions, only a small remnant of the original cholesteatoma is found at this second exploration (with no other apparent spread of cholesteatoma); this remnant should be removed, but a third-stage procedure should be planned (see Table 26–17). On the other hand, if no cholesteatoma is found at the planned second-stage procedure, the child is most likely free of the original cholesteatoma. These children must nevertheless be examined periodically for 5 to 7 years.[413] In their review of the medical records of 232 children who underwent surgery for cholesteatoma, Rosenfeld et al[413] recommend at least a 5-year follow-up since more than 50% of patients experienced recurrence during this interval in their series. If severe atelectasis or a retraction pocket develops—which is not unusual in children—prompt myringotomy and insertion of a tympanostomy tube are indicated.[451] An alternative approach for a small attic cholesteatoma is *atticotomy*, that is, exteriorization, especially when a second-stage procedure is not feasible.

At the other end of the spectrum is the extensive cholesteatoma that requires a middle fossa approach.[202] However, the problem for the surgeon is deciding how to manage the majority of cholesteatomas in children that are neither small and easily removed nor so extensive that only radical surgery is indicated.[319, 430] Some experts recommend that only the most experienced surgeons perform these procedures on children.[451, 459] Since the review by Rosenfeld et al,[413] one of us (CDB) now rarely performs a modified or radical mastoidectomy in children

with cholesteatoma, preferring to reoperate at 6-month intervals rather than to leave the child with an open mastoid cavity. In most instances, the endoscope enhances removal of the cholesteatoma, making the removal of the posterior canal unnecessary.

When tympanoplasty is performed in children at the same time that mastoidectomy is performed to eradicate a cholesteatoma, the results of the tympanoplasty may have a poor outcome.[55] Failure of the tympanoplasty is associated with one or more of the following conditions: sloughing of the graft, recurrence of high negative middle-ear pressure and a retraction pocket, recurrent or chronic otitis media with effusion, or recurrence of cholesteatoma. Another study of a large number of adults and children who underwent tympanoplasty at the time of surgery to remove cholesteatoma also showed that tympanoplasties in such patients are not successful[111]; other studies have reported more favorable outcomes.[185, 426, 442] When chronic suppurative otitis media (uncontrolled) is present in addition to the cholesteatoma, a tympanoplasty may have to be withheld and performed as a second-stage procedure when the middle ear is free of infection (see Chronic Suppurative Otitis Media). When a cholesteatoma is infected, with or without the presence of chronic suppurative otitis media (and mastoiditis), preoperative control of the infection with antimicrobial agents is desirable since the presence of infection may affect the outcome of the tympanoplasty as well as increase the risk of a postoperative wound infection. When a tympanoplasty for cholesteatoma is performed, the middle ear must also be artificially ventilated by a tympanostomy tube. However, in older children, eustachian-tube function may be adequate to ventilate the middle ear and tympanoplasty can be performed without tympanostomy tube insertion. When tympanoplasty is performed in children who have a defect in the posterosuperior quadrant of the pars tensa or the pars flaccida, or both, cartilage should be placed to

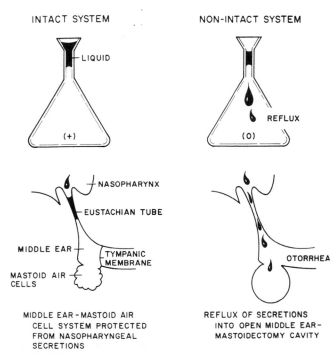

FIGURE 26–44. Liquid flow through a flask is compared with the nasopharynx/eustachian tube/middle ear/mastoid air-cell system. When the system is intact, liquid is prevented from flowing into the body of the flask (middle ear/mastoid air cells). By contrast, the nonintact system permits liquid to reflux into the flask. This condition is analogous to a perforation of the tympanic membrane in which reflux of nasopharyngeal secretions could occur since the middle ear/mastoid air cushion is lost. Similarly, after a radical mastoidectomy, the presence of a patent eustachian tube could cause troublesome otorrhea (see text).

support the grafted tympanic membrane and thus prevent recurrence of cholesteatoma.[219]

When the cholesteatoma is extensive and a radical mastoidectomy is necessary to control the disease, the middle-ear end of the poorly functioning eustachian tube may have to be closed surgically if troublesome postoperative otorrhea occurs since the middle ear–mastoidectomy cavity is then an open system.[53] Nasopharyngeal secretions could reflux into the middle ear–mastoidectomy cavity, resulting in inflammation and otorrhea (Fig. 26–44). The patient who has poorly controlled chronic/recurrent otorrhea in a nonhearing ear is the most ideal candidate. The most effective way to obliterate the bony portion of the eustachian tube is with bone paté.[65] Closure of the eustachian tube at the time of radical mastoidectomy, although not universally performed by modern otologic surgeons, is not a new addition to the procedure but has been advocated for many years. Tests of eustachian-tube function to assess tube patency can be helpful. If the tube is found to be patent, revision middle-ear/mastoid surgery should be performed, and surgical closure of the eustachian tube should be undertaken if a tympanoplasty is not going to be performed at the time of the revision surgery or planned in the future.

Intraoperative monitoring of the facial nerve during surgery to remove cholesteatoma has been advocated to reduce the chance of injury to the nerve.[213, 387] The deci-

sion to monitor the surgical procedure should be based on the preoperative assessment of the extent of the disease (e.g., proximity to the nerve) and the experience of the surgeon. In a teaching institution, intraoperative monitoring can be a valuable aid, and one of us (CDB) advocates its use in this environment.

There is no current consensus on the most appropriate time to perform ossiculoplasty in children who have cholesteatoma. One of us (CDB) prefers to perform ossiculoplasty when there is no evidence of cholesteatoma in the middle ear and the child is free of otitis media for 1 year or longer.

Preventing recurrence of cholesteatoma in these children is important since the same underlying pathogenetic conditions may still be present. Thus, effective management of medical conditions that may interfere with adequate eustachian-tube function, such as adenoids, allergy, or chronic sinusitis, may prove to be beneficial. However, since many of these children have a basic eustachian-tube dysfunction, placement of cartilage grafts or tympanostomy tubes, or both, usually is required to prevent a new cholesteatoma from recurring. Long-term follow-up, e.g., 5 to 7 years, following initial control of cholesteatoma in children is required since recurrence has been reported to be as high as 50% to 70%.[413, 450, 462]

Conclusions

In children with a retraction pocket or acquired cholesteatoma in the posterosuperior or pars flaccida portion of the tympanic membrane, active function of the eustachian tube is abnormal. Acquired cholesteatoma not secondary to implantation is a sequela of otitis media or a retraction pocket, or both. The type of surgery chosen to manage these conditions in children should be based not only on the site and extent of the cholesteatoma but also on other factors, such as the patient's age, presence or absence of otitis media, eustachian-tube function, and availability of health care. The operation must be tailored for each child. Prevention of the pathologic conditions that predispose to this type of cholesteatoma is the most effective method of management.

Cholesterol Granuloma

Cholesterol granuloma is a sequela of chronic otitis media with effusion. It has been described as *idiopathic hemotympanum* since clinically the tympanic membrane appears to be dark blue, a so-called *blue eardrum*. However, this term is a misnomer since there is no evidence that bleeding within the middle ear or the presence of fresh blood or microscopic amounts of old blood are related to the cause of this disease.[420] The condition is rare in all age groups but does occur in children and is most likely due to long-standing changes associated with chronic otitis media with effusion.[372, 443] In a series of 17 cases, cholesterol granuloma of the petrous apex reported by Brodkey et al, 3 (18%) involved adolescents and the rest were adults.[74]

The blue color of the tympanic membrane as visualized through the otoscope is probably due to the reflection of light from the thick liquid (granuloma) within the middle ear. The condition must be differentiated from an uncovered high jugular bulb and a glomus tumor, either tympanicus or jugulare[499] and, more commonly, chronic otitis media with effusion or barotitis. Since cholesterol granuloma is relatively rare in children, the presence of a blue color of the tympanic membrane, as visualized by otoscopy or otomicroscopy, is most commonly middle-ear effusion, and the blue appearance is related to how the light is reflected off the drum.

Chronic granulations, with foreign-body giant cells and foam cells within the middle ear or mastoid, or both, are characteristic of the tissue. Cholesterol crystals are usually present. The condition is similar to a chronic middle-ear effusion except that a soft brownish material that contains shining golden-yellow specks is present. The pathologic process with cholesterol granuloma should not be confused with that of a cholesteatoma.[432] Similar granulomas have been described in other parts of the body: atheromatous and dermoid cysts, periapical and follicular cysts of the jaw, old infarcts, and hematomas.[276] When the granulomas are stained, prominent iron deposits or hemosiderin may be found,[29, 354] but not in quantities sufficient to account for the otoscopic appearance of the blue tympanic membrane.

Miura et al histopathologically evaluated temporal bones from 6 children, 6 months to 15 years old, who had cholesterol granuloma and found that all had large amount of mesenchyme that was in continuity with the hematopoietic bone marrow in the location of the granuloma.[342] All specimens had a middle-ear effusion and inflammation of the eustachian tube; in three of the six specimens the eustachian tube was structurally abnormal. These investigators concluded that eustachian-tube dysfunction was involved in the pathogenesis of the disease.

The condition has been reproduced in experimental animals by injecting foreign material into the middle ears of guinea pigs[175] and rabbits,[137] by obstructing the long bones of birds,[36, 37, 358] and after chronic obstruction of the eustachian tube in monkeys.[315] The pathogenesis described in the latter experimental model is similar to that known to occur in humans when the eustachian tube was obstructed by a muscle pedicle flap[297] or by a tumor.[443] In addition to occurring as an isolated pathologic entity, cholesterol granuloma can be associated with chronic suppurative otitis media with or without cholesteatoma or any inflammation that may obstruct portions of the middle ear or mastoid, or both.

CT may be helpful in the diagnosis and extent of the disease, but MRI is probably more specific as a diagnostic aid.[482]

Management

Cholesterol granuloma does not respond to medical treatment, middle-ear inflation, or myringotomy with tympanostomy tube insertion. However, when a child has a tympanic membrane that has a dark-blue appearance and is unresponsive to nonsurgical management, myringotomy under general anesthesia should be performed since, on occasion, chronic otitis media with effusion may also be

associated with a blue tympanic membrane (again, probably as the result of the way light from the otoscope is reflected from the middle-ear effusion). However, if a thick brown liquid is found during the procedure, successful aspiration of the material is not possible, and if a tympanostomy tube is inserted, it will become occluded immediately. Takahashi et al reported success in treating five patients, ages 6 to 19 years, with a short course of oral prednisone over 10 to 14 days and tympanostomy tube insertion.[477] Despite the small number of patients evaluated, this method of treatment may be helpful since the traditional method of management has been middle-ear and mastoid surgery.

When tympanostomy tube insertion, and possibly a trial of cortisone, fail, the treatment is middle ear and mastoid surgery. The granuloma in the mastoid can be removed by complete simple mastoidectomy, and the middle-ear portion can be removed by using a tympanomeatal approach. There is no reason to remove the canal wall unless a cholesteatoma is present. A tympanostomy tube should be inserted into the tympanic membrane at the time of the procedure and reinserted as often as needed—that is, until the middle ear remains normally aerated after spontaneous extubation.

When cholesterol granuloma involves the petrous apex, conservative management is recommended unless the patient has severe symptoms, such as vertigo and otalgia. When surgery is indicated, a transmastoid drainage procedure is recommended as opposed to resection of the petrous apex.[74] However, recurrence rates have been as high as 60% after a drainage procedure and require an extended middle-fossa approach or petrosal approach.[147]

It would appear from what is known of the pathogenesis and pathology of cholesterol granuloma that the best management is prevention, which should consist of active treatment and prevention of chronic otitis media with effusion.

Tympanosclerosis

Tympanosclerosis may be a sequela of chronic middle-ear inflammation or the result of trauma. This condition is characterized by the presence of whitish plaques in the tympanic membrane and nodular deposits in the submucosal layers of the middle ear.[237] When the disease is limited to the tympanic membrane, it is called *myringosclerosis*. Conductive hearing loss may occur if the ossicles become embedded in the deposits.

Tympanosclerosis was first described by von Troltsch,[507] who called it *sclerosis*, but it was Zollner[535] who called the disorder *tympanosclerosis* and differentiated it from otosclerosis. Schuknecht preferred the term *hyalinization* rather than tympanosclerosis since the histopathologic condition is that of hyalin degeneration, which is the result of a healing reaction characterized by fibroblastic invasion of the submucosa, followed by thickening and fusion of collagenous fibers into a homogeneous mass.[432] He also described the hyalinized collagen around the ossicles. The pathologic condition in the tympanic membrane occurs in the lamina propria, while within the middle ear, the pathologic condition is in the basement membrane; in both sites, there is hyalinization followed by deposition of calcium and phosphate crystals.

Epidemiology and Pathogenesis

Tympanosclerosis (myringosclerosis) of the tympanic membrane is a common sequela in children who have or have had recurrent acute otitis media or chronic otitis media with effusion. It is also common at the site of a healed spontaneous perforation or after myringotomy and tympanostomy tube placement. In children who undergo tympanostomy tube insertion for otitis media, tympanosclerosis increases with advancing age as the incidence of otitis media with effusion declines.[118] The middle ear may have tympanosclerosis without the presence of clinically evident myringosclerosis.[244] Tympanosclerosis is not commonly a sequela of myringotomy, and when due to the aftermath of tympanostomy tube insertion, it is not linked to hearing loss.[405] The chalky patch in the tympanic membrane of children may be due to inflammation or trauma, or both. However, in the pediatric age group as a whole, the condition is not common in the middle ear, especially in infants and young children. In particular, ossicular involvement is rare in very young children. Of 311 cases of tympanosclerosis studied by Kinney, only 20% occurred in patients 30 years old or younger.[268] This implies that the condition in the middle ear may take many years to develop. In a more recent study, Asiri et al reviewed 775 patients with chronic suppurative otitis media and tympanosclerosis in Saudi Arabia, and found only 11% were 15 years old or younger.[21]

Expression of macrophages is an early event.[170] In experiments in rats, Mattsson et al reported that the formation of oxygen-free radicals contributes significantly to the development of myringosclerosis.[322] This finding supported their hypothesis that the condition is secondary to a hyperoxic condition of the middle ear, such as when the tympanic membrane is not intact (e.g., perforation or tympanostomy tube). Also, in experiments in rats, nitrous oxide was found to be involved in this pathologic condition.[171]

Schiff et al hypothesize that tympanosclerosis has an immune component that occurs in the middle ear after an insult or mucosal disruption.[428] They also suggest a genetic component, which would explain the low incidence of the condition in children who have such a high prevalence and incidence of middle-ear inflammation. This hypothesis may explain the relatively high rate of tympanosclerosis among children who are Alaskan natives (Eskimos) and American Indians.[120, 243, 520]

Other factors may predispose these children to the disease, such as differences in eustachian-tube function. Wiet et al reported that tympanosclerosis affected a higher percentage of Alaskan native children than children of a similar age in his New Hampshire private practice; tympanosclerosis of the tympanic membrane or the ossicles, or both, was found in 78 (68%) of 114 Alaskan native children who underwent tympanoplasty, whereas only 7 such cases were diagnosed in 377 consecutive tympanoplasties performed in children in his practice.[521] He also found that far advanced tympanosclerosis that resulted in fixation of the ossicular chain occurred at an early age in the Alaskan native children but not in children in his practice.

Management

Currently, no surgical correction, such as tympanoplasty, is indicated when tympanosclerosis of the tympanic membrane, even though extensive, is the only abnormality of the middle ear. If a middle-ear effusion is present and a myringotomy, with or without a tympanostomy tube insertion, is indicated, the incision should be placed, if possible, in an area without involvement, leaving the affected area untouched. Removal of large tympanosclerotic plaques may result in a permanent perforation of the tympanic membrane. When an incision must be made in an area of tympanosclerosis, only the amount necessary to perform the procedure should be removed. When a tympanoplasty is being performed to repair a perforation of the tympanic membrane and tympanosclerosis is present in the drum remnant, removing the plaque is optional: the plaque may remain if the area of tympanosclerosis does not interfere with the surgical procedure and is not impeding function. When tympanosclerosis is the cause of ossicular fixation and a tympanoplasty procedure is elected, the methods of removing the plaques and ossiculoplasty described by Glasscock and Shambaugh are appropriate for the rare child with this advanced stage of tympanosclerosis.[187] A two-stage stapedectomy has been advocated to correct the conductive hearing loss with some success.[253] However, refixation of the ossicles is not uncommon even after apparently adequate surgical removal of the plaques and ossiculoplasty. A hearing aid should be considered if surgery is not performed or is not successful in restoring the hearing loss.

Even though the pathogenesis of tympanosclerosis is not completely understood, it seems most probable that appropriate management of recurrent and chronic middle-ear inflammation in infants and children is the best method of prevention. Since it also occurs after trauma to the tympanic membrane, myringotomy with tympanostomy tube placement should be performed as tympanosclerosis is one of the potential complications. In general, tympanosclerosis involving the tympanic membrane does not appreciably affect function, although when the ossicles are involved, conductive hearing loss may be significant. Thus, tympanostomy tubes may increase the incidence of tympanosclerosis of the tympanic membrane, but their placement may decrease the frequency of ossicular fixation due to this disease later in life.

Some clinicians think that tympanosclerosis, as a sequelae of tympanostomy tube insertion, causes conductive hearing loss.[391] For the great majority of children who have tympanosclerosis that affects the tympanic membrane secondary to recurrent or chronic otitis media, or tympanostomy tube placement, or both, the condition is cosmetic and does not affect the hearing. Stenstrom and Ingvarsson followed 88 otitis-prone children for up to 8 years and concluded that the level of hearing, as assessed by audiometry, was a poor indicator of tympanic membrane pathology.[464] Of course, more ear disease and increased surgical procedures can eventually lead to in-volvement of the conductive hearing mechanism (see also Chapter 25).

Ossicular Discontinuity and Fixation

Discontinuity and fixation of the ossicles are possible se-quelae of recurrent acute and chronic middle-ear disease and are rare complications of surgery.

Pathology and Pathogenesis

Ossicular interruption results from rarefying osteitis sec-ondary to chronic inflammation of the middle ear. A re-traction pocket or cholesteatoma may also cause resorp-tion of the ossicles. The long process of the incus is most commonly involved, which results in incudostapedial dis-articulation. The commonly accepted reason given for this portion of the incus being eroded is its poor blood sup-ply. However, since the tympanic membrane frequently becomes attached to this part of the incus when a poster-osuperior retraction pocket is present, adhesive otitis me-dia may be the cause of the osteitis and subsequent ero-sion. Also, cholesteatoma in the same area is common.[53] The second most commonly involved ossicle is the stapes, or more specifically its crural arches. The cause of erosion of the stapes is more likely to be associated with presence of a retraction pocket or cholesteatoma rather than with decreased vascular supply. Less commonly, the body of the incus and the manubrium of the malleus may also be eroded. The ossicles may become fixed by fibrous tissue secondary to adhesive otitis media or, more rarely in children, secondary to tympanosclerosis. Neither the inci-dence of ossicular discontinuity and fixation nor the natu-ral history of the pathologic conditions that precede these abnormalities has been formally studied in children. How-ever, ossicular discontinuity is commonly associated with a deep retraction pocket or cholesteatoma in the posterosu-perior portion of the tympanic membrane. Disarticulation or fixation of the ossicles may also occur when there is a central perforation of the tympanic membrane with or without the presence of chronic suppurative otitis media and, more rarely, when the tympanic membrane is intact.

Diagnosis

Ossicular chain abnormalities that are secondary to otitis media and its related conditions are frequently diagnosed by visualization of the defect through the otoscope or, more accurately, the otomicroscope. Erosion of the long process of the incus can usually be seen when a deep posterosuperior retraction pocket is present. A significant conductive hearing loss (e.g., >30 dB) when a perforation of the tympanic membrane is present constitutes evi-dence of ossicular involvement. However, when the tym-panic membrane is normal, a significant conductive loss may be due to prior inflammatory ossicular involvement. However, congenital ossicular abnormalities and otoscle-rosis must be part of the differential diagnosis.

In addition to the history, otoscopic examination, and conventional audiometric testing, immittance audiometry

may aid the diagnosis. A tympanogram showing high compliance is evidence of ossicular chain discontinuity when conductive hearing loss is significant. If the compli-ance is low, ossicular fixation would be more probable. However, the accuracy with which tympanometry can dif-ferentiate between ossicular discontinuity and fixation is not high since several other parameters in the middle ear affect the shape of the tympanogram, such as mobility of the tympanic membrane. CT may also aid in identifying ossicular discontinuity but is usually of diagnostic benefit only when a large defect is present. Linstrom et al re-ported that an endoscope introduced through the naso-pharyngeal end of the eustachian tube helped with assess-ment of the status of the middle ear in determining the timing of ossiculoplasty in adults.[296] However, the most accurate way of diagnosing these defects is exploration of the middle ear—either during exploratory tympanotomy, when the tympanic membrane is intact, or by inspecting the entire ossicular chain when surgery of the middle ear and mastoid is indicated, such as tympanoplasty.

Conductive hearing loss is usually present when the ossicular chain is affected, and the degree depends on the site and the degree of involvement of the ossicles and on the presence or absence of associated conditions such as a perforation of the tympanic membrane. When there is a discontinuity of the incudostapedial joint and the tym-panic membrane is intact, a maximal conductive hearing loss may be present—that is, 50 to 60 dB. However, when both the same ossicular pathologic condition and a perforation are present, the hearing loss may be less se-vere. Erosion of the manubrium of the malleus is usually associated with a perforation of the tympanic membrane but does not contribute to the hearing loss. However, erosion of the ossicles may not be associated with signifi-cant hearing loss if the defect is partial and the continuity of the ossicular chain is present, or if the tympanic mem-brane, retraction pocket, or cholesteatoma connects a dis-articulation. When a cholesteatoma creates this artificial connection, this phenomenon is commonly called *hearing through cholesteatoma.*

Management

The management of ossicular deformities in children is similar to that described for adults, with some notable exceptions. Most adults who have ossicular discontinuity or fixation are no longer at risk for otitis media with effusion or high negative pressure within the middle ear due to eustachian-tube dysfunction, but many children still have or will have these conditions. These conditions could interfere with the success of reconstructive middle-ear surgery generally and ossiculoplasty specifically. Therefore, the indications for timing and the type of middle-ear surgery may be different for children.

When an ossicular deformity is suspected and the tym-panic membrane is intact, such as when the child has a conductive hearing loss, and there is no evidence of otitis media or any of its other complications or sequelae, e.g., retraction pocket or cholesteatoma, the decision to per-form an exploratory tympanotomy to diagnose and possi-bly repair the ossicular deformity depends on several considerations. First, and most importantly, is the child still at risk for a middle-ear effusion or atelectasis (retraction pocket), or both? As a general rule, if neither condition has occurred in either ear for 1 year or longer, the risk is low. However, the younger the child, the higher the risk. If further middle-ear disease may still occur, the operation should be delayed.

The second consideration is the degree of hearing loss and whether or not the defect is unilateral or bilateral. A child who has a maximum conductive hearing loss in both ears is a probable candidate for surgical intervention, while the child who only has a unilateral mild conductive loss is not. Another important consideration is the need for general anesthesia to perform the surgery in all children. The benefit of surgery must be weighed against the risk of general anesthesia. For the child who has a bilateral maximum conductive hearing loss, the benefit of hearing improvement may outweigh the risk of general anesthesia, whereas the risk of anesthesia may not override the potential chance of improving the hearing in a child with only a unilateral mild to moderate hearing loss. Withholding the reconstructive surgery until the child can tolerate a local anesthetic (adolescence) is a preferred option when the hearing loss is unilateral and mild to moderate. Whenever surgical intervention is not planned or the decision to operate is delayed until the child is older, a hearing aid evaluation should be considered, even when the hearing loss is unilateral.

When surgery of the middle ear is indicated because a perforation of the tympanic membrane is present, with or without chronic suppurative otitis media, a cholesteatoma, or a retraction pocket, the very fact that the patient is a child still affects the decision as to whether or not to perform ossiculoplasty. This is because children are at increased risk for future episodes of otitis media and atelectasis or adhesive otitis media. When these conditions are possible, the surgeon should consider staging the surgery and performing the ossiculoplasty when the child is older. If the patient has a cholesteatoma, and a canal-wall-up procedure followed by a planned "second-look" tympanotomy is elected to determine whether residual cholesteatoma is present, the ossiculoplasty can be performed when the middle-ear cleft is free of disease.

The various ways in which ossicles that are either eroded or fixed may be reconstructed have been adequately described elsewhere. However, it is important to reiterate that the type of ossiculoplasty chosen for a child may be different from that performed in an adult. We think—and most experts agree—that in general, middle-ear ossicular implants should only be used in selected children who have ossicular defects as result of middle-ear disease since neither the long-term safety nor the efficacy of these prostheses has been proven. Likewise, the use of tissue adhesives has not been proven to be safe and effective, despite an occasional report of success.[4] However, if the child's middle ear is free of disease and the patient is unlikely to have future middle-ear problems, inserting a prosthesis is an option, although the hearing outcomes will not be as good as they are in adults.[349]

Some surgeons advocate homograft ossicles in children. Whenever possible, only the child's own tissue

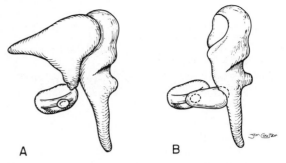

FIGURE 26–45. The most common ossicular discontinuity in children is at the incudostapedial joint and is due to erosion of the long process of the incus (*A*). An autograft-fitted incus is the recommended procedure for children (*B*).

should be used to reconstruct the ossicular chain. For the most common discontinuity encountered, that of the incudostapedial joint, an incus transposition or inserting a fitted incus is the ideal procedure (Fig. 26–45). When the stapes crura are missing, the shaped incus can usually be inserted between the mobile footplate of the stapes and the malleus handle. For all age groups, whenever the stapes is fixed, a stapedectomy should not be performed unless the tympanic membrane is intact; in children who have recently had otitis media, stapedectomy should rarely, if ever, be performed, even when the tympanic membrane is intact since a recurrence of otitis media with suppurative labyrinthitis as a complication is an ever-present risk. Freeing other fixed ossicles can be attempted in children, but refixation often occurs since adhesive otitis media, which is the most frequent cause of fixation, commonly leads to further fibrosis. For further details of surgical techniques, see Bluestone.[65]

SELECTED READINGS

Bluestone CD. Otologic procedures. In Bluestone CD, Rosenfeld RM (eds). Surgical Atlas of Pediatric Otolaryngology, 2nd ed. Hamilton, Ontario, BC Decker, 2002, 1–136.

  The author of the chapter on otologic surgical procedures in this second edition of the Atlas of Pediatric Otolaryngology *is the coauthor of this chapter and has described his surgical techniques in detail.*

Brackmann DE, Shelton C, Arriaga MA. Otologic Surgery. Philadelphia, 2nd ed. WB Saunders, 2001.

  This text provides the details of many of the procedures recommended in this chapter.

Glasscock ME, Shambaugh GE. Surgery of the Ear, 4th ed. Philadelphia, WB Saunders, 1990.

  The indications for surgery and the techniques for the procedures recommended in this chapter are described in detail.

Goycoolea MV, Paparella MM, Nissen RL (eds). Atlas of Otologic Surgery. Philadelphia, WB Saunders, 1989.

  The current techniques for surgery of the middle ear and mastoid are illustrated and described in detail.

Paparella MD, Shumrick DA, Gluckman JL, Meyerhoff WL. Otolaryngology. Philadelphia, WB Saunders, 1991, pp 1381–1404, 1601–1618.

  These chapters provide additional information on intratemporal complications of otitis media.

Schuknecht HF. Pathology of the Ear, 2nd ed. Philadelphia, Lea & Febiger, 1993, pp 191–234.

This is the best description of the pathology of the intratemporal complications and sequelae of otitis media.

Tos M, Thomsen J, Peitersen E (eds). Proceedings of the Third International Conference on Cholesteatoma and Mastoid Surgery. Amsterdam, Kugler & Ghedini, 1989.

This is the state of knowledge of the epidemiology, pathogenesis, management, and complications of cholesteatoma.

REFERENCES

1. Abramson M. Collagenolytic activity in middle ear cholesteatoma. Ann Otol Rhinol Laryngol 78:112, 1969.
2. Abramson M. Open or closed tympanomastoidectomy for cholesteatoma in children. Am J Otol 6:167, 1985.
3. Abramson M, Lachenbruch PA, Press BHJ, et al. Results of conservative surgery for middle ear cholesteatoma. Laryngoscope 87:1281, 1977.
4. Adamson RM, Jeannon JP, Stafford F. A traumatic ossicular disruption successfully repaired with *n*-butyl cyanoacrylate tissue adhesive. J Laryngol Otol 114:130, 2000.
5. Adesman AR, Altshuler LA, Lipkin PH, Walco GA. Otitis media in children with learning disabilities and in children with attention deficit disorder with hyperactivity. Pediatrics 85:442, 1990.
6. Adkins WY. Composite autograft for tympanoplasty and tympanomastoid surgery. Laryngoscope 100:244, 1990.
7. Adkins WY, White B. Type I tympanoplasty: influencing factors. Laryngoscope 94:916, 1984.
8. Agro AS, Garner ET, Wright JW III, et al. Clinical trial of ototopical ofloxacin for treatment of chronic suppurative otitis media. Clin Ther 20:744, 1998.
9. Albino AP, Reed JA, Bogdany JK, et al. Expression of p53 protein in human middle-ear cholesteatomas: pathogenetic implications. Am J Otol 19:30, 1998.
10. Allam AF, Schuknecht HF. Pathology of petrositis. Laryngoscope 78:1813, 1968.
11. Almadori G, Del Ninno M, Cadoni G, et al. Facial nerve paralysis in acute otomastoiditis as presenting symptom of FAB M2, T8;21 leukemic relapse. Case report and review of the literature. Int J Pediatr Otorhinolaryngol 36:45, 1996.
12. Alper CM, Dohar JE, Gulhan M, et al. Treatment of chronic suppurative otitis media with topical tobramycin and dexamethasone. Arch Otolaryngol Head Neck Surg 126:165, 2000.
13. Alper CM, Doyle WJ. Repeated inflation does not prevent otitis media with effusion in a monkey model. Laryngoscope 109:1074, 1999.
14. Altuntas A, Unal A, Aslan A, et al. Facial nerve paralysis in chronic suppurative otitis media: Ankara Numune Hospital experience. Auris Nasus Larynx 25:169, 1998.
15. American Academy of Pediatrics. Committee on Early Childhood, Adoption and Dependent Care. News Comment Pediatr 35:9, 1984.
16. Andreasson L, Harris S. Middle ear mechanics and eustachian tube function in tympanoplasty. Acta Otolaryngol Suppl (Stockh) 360:141, 1979.
17. Antonelli PJ, Dhanani N, Giannoni C. Impact of resistant pneumococcus on rates of acute mastoiditis. Otolaryngol Head Neck Surg 120:190, 1999.
18. Antonelli PJ, Garside JA, Mancuso AA, et al. Computed tomography and the diagnosis of coalescent mastoiditis. Otolaryngol Head Neck Surg 120:350, 1999.
19. Arguedas AG, Herrera JF, Faingezicht I, et al. Ceftazidime for therapy of children with chronic suppurative otitis media without cholesteatoma. Pediatr Infect Dis J 12:246, 1993.
20. Armstrong BW. Tympanoplasty in children. Laryngoscope 75:1062, 1965.
21. Asiri S, Hasham A, Anazy FA, et al. Tympanosclerosis: review of literature and incidence among patients with middle-ear effusion. J Laryngol Otol 113:1076, 1999.
22. Aslan A, Altuntas A, Titiz A, et al. A new dosage regimen for topical application of ciprofloxacin in the management of chronic suppurative otitis media. Otolaryngol Head Neck Surg 118:883, 1998.
23. Asmussen L, Olson LM, Grant EN, et al. Reliability and validity of the Children's Health Survey for Asthma. Pediatrics 104:e71, 1999.
24. Austin DF. The retraction pocket in the treatment of cholesteatoma. Arch Otolaryngol 102:741, 1976.
25. Avery AD, et al. Quality of Medical Care Assessment Using Outcome Measures: Eight Disease-Specific Applications. Prepared for the Health Resources Administration, Department of Health, Education and Welfare by the Rand Corp, Santa Monica, CA, 1976.
26. Avery RK, Eavey RD, Della Torre T, et al. Bilateral otitis media and mastoiditis caused by a highly resistant strain of *Mycobacterium chelonae*. Pediatr Infect Dis J 15:1037, 1996.
27. Bailey TH Jr. Absolute and relative contraindications to tympanoplasty. Laryngoscope 86:67, 1976.
28. Bajaj Y, Bais A, Mukherjee B. Tympanoplasty in children—a prospective study. J Laryngol Otol 112:1147, 1998.
29. Bak-Pederson K, Tos M. The pathogenesis of idiopathic haemotympanum. J Laryngol Otol 86:473, 1972.
30. Baron SH. Management of aural cholesteatoma in children. Otolaryngol Clin North Am 2:71, 1969.
31. Bastos I, Mallya J, Ingvarsson L, et al. Middle-ear disease and hearing impairment in northern Tanzania. A prevalence study of schoolchildren in the Moshi and Monduli districts. Int J Pediatr Otorhinolaryngol 32:1, 1995.
32. Baxter JD, Julien G, Tewfik TL, et al. Observations on the prevalence of ear disease in the Inuit and Cree Indian school population of Kuujjuaraapik. J Otolaryngol 15:25, 1986.
33. Baxter JD, Ling D. Ear disease and hearing loss among the Eskimo population of the Baffin zone. Can J Otolaryngol 3:110, 1974.
34. Baxter JD. Observations on the evolution of chronic otitis media in the Inuit of the Baffin Zone. N W T J Otolaryngol 11:161, 1982.
35. Baxter JD, Stubbing P, Goodbody L, Terraza O. The light at the end of the tunnel associated with the high prevalence of chronic otitis media among Inuit elementary school children in the eastern Canadian Arctic is now visible. Arct Med Res 51:29, 1992.
36. Beaumont GD. The effects of exclusion of air from pneumatized bones. J Laryngol Otol 80:236, 1966.
37. Beaumont GD. Cholesterol granuloma. J Laryngol Soc Aust 2:28, 1967.
38. Beery QC, Doyle WJ, Cantekin EI, et al. Eustachian tube function in an American Indian population. Ann Otol Rhinol Laryngol 89:28, 1980.
39. Bergen G, Shapira A, Marshak G. Myringoplasty in children. J Otolaryngol 12:228, 1983.
40. Berko-Gleason J. Otitis media and language development (workshop on effects of otitis media on the child). Pediatrics 71:639, 1983.
41. Berman S. Otitis media in developing countries. Pediatrics 96:126, 1995.
42. Bess FH, Tharpe AM. Unilateral hearing impairment in children. Pediatrics 74:206, 1984.
43. Bezold F. Cholesteatom, Perforation der Membrana Flaccida Shrapnelli und Tubenverschluss, eine Atiologische Studie. Ohrenheilk 20:5, 1889.
44. Bezold K, Siebenman. Textbook of Otology for Physicians and Students. Chicago, EH Colgrove, 1908, p 141.
45. Blakley BW, Kim S. Does chronic otitis media cause sensorineural hearing loss? J Otolaryngol 27:17, 1998.
46. Blanchard JD, Robson AK, Smith I, et al. A long term view of myringoplasty in children. J Laryngol Otol 104:758, 1990.
47. Blaney SPA, Tierney P, Bowdler DA. The surgical management of the pars tensa retraction pocket in the child—results following simple excision and ventilation tube insertion. Int J Pediatr Otorhinolaryngol 50:133, 1999.
48. Blevins NH, Karmody CS. Chronic myringitis: prevalence, presentation, and natural history. Otol Neurotol 22:3, 2001.
49. Bluestone CD. Acute and chronic mastoiditis and chronic suppurative otitis media. Semin Pediatr Infect Dis 9:12, 1998.
50. Bluestone CD, Beery QC, Andrus S. Mechanics of the Eustachian tube as it influences susceptibility to and persistence of middle-ear effusions in children. Ann Otol Rhinol Laryngol 83:27, 1974.
51. Bluestone CD, Beery QC, Cantekin EI, et al. Eustachian tube ventilatory function in relation to cleft palate. Ann Otol Rhinol Laryngol 84:333, 1975.
52. Bluestone CD, Beery QC, Paradise JL. Audiometry and tympa-

nometry in relation to middle ear effusions in children. Laryngoscope 83:594, 1973.

53. Bluestone CD, Cantekin EI, Beery QC, et al. Functional eustachian tube obstruction in acquired cholesteatoma and related conditions. In McCabe BF, Sadé J, Abramson M (eds). Cholesteatoma: First International Conference. New York, Aesculapius, 1977, pp 325–335.
54. Bluestone CD, Cantekin EI, Beery QC, et al. Function of the eustachian tube related to surgical management of acquired aural cholesteatoma in children. Laryngoscope 88:1155, 1978.
55. Bluestone CD, Cantekin EI, Douglas GS. Eustachian tube function related to the results of tympanoplasty in children. Laryngoscope 89:450, 1979.
56. Bluestone CD, Casselbrant ML, Cantekin EI. Functional obstruction of the eustachian tube in the pathogenesis of aural cholesteatoma in children. In Sadé J (ed). Cholesteatoma and Mastoid Surgery. Proceedings of the Second International Conference on Cholesteatoma and Mastoid Surgery. Amsterdam, Kugler, 1982, pp 211–224.
57. Bluestone CD. Clinical course, complications and sequelae of acute otitis media. Pediatr Infect Dis J 19:S37, 2000.
58. Bluestone CD. Current management of chronic suppurative otitis media in infants and children. Pediatr Infect Dis J 7:S137, 1988.
59. Bluestone CD. Definitions, terminology, and classification. In Rosenfeld RM, Bluestone CD (eds). Evidence-Based Otitis Media. Hamilton, Ontario, BC Decker, 1999, pp 85–104.
60. Bluestone CD. Epidemiology and pathogenesis of chronic suppurative otitis media: implications for prevention and treatment. Int J Pediatr Otol 42:207, 1998.
61. Bluestone CD. Eustachian tube obstruction in the infant with cleft palate. Ann Otol Rhinol Laryngol 80:1, 1971.
62. Bluestone CD. Implications of beta-2 transferrin assay as a marker for perilymphatic versus cerebrospinal fluid labyrinthine fistula. Am J Otol 20:701, 1999.
63. Bluestone CD. Invited comments: clinical forum—routine preoperative imaging in chronic ear surgery. Am J Otol 19:536, 1998.
64. Bluestone CD, Klein JO, Paradise JL, et al. Workshop on effects of otitis media on the child. Pediatrics 71:639, 1983.
65. Bluestone CD. Otologic procedures. In Bluestone CD, Stool SE (eds). Atlas of Pediatric Otolaryngology. Philadelphia, WB Saunders, 1995, pp 27–128.
66. Bluestone CD. Pathogenesis of otitis media: role of eustachian tube. Pediatr Infect Dis J 14:281, 1996.
67. Bluestone CD: Perilymphatic fistula in children. In Gates GA (ed). Current Therapy in Otolaryngology Head Neck Surgery. St Louis, Mosby-Year Book, 1998, pp 67–71.
68. Bluestone CD, Stephenson JS, Martin LM. Ten-year review of otitis media pathogens. Pediatr Infect Dis J 11:S7, 1992.
69. Bluestone CD, Stool SE (eds). Atlas of Pediatric Otolaryngology. Philadelphia, WB Saunders, 1994.
70. Bluestone CD, Wittel RA, Paradise JL. Roentgenographic evaluation of the eustachian tube function in infants with cleft and normal palates. Cleft Palate J 9:93, 1972.
71. Boswell JB, Nienhuys TG. Patterns of persistent otitis media in the first year of life in Aboriginal and non-Aboriginal infants. Ann Otol Rhinol Laryngol 105:893, 1996.
72. Brandow EC Jr. Implant cholesteatoma in the mastoid. In McCabe BF, Sadé J, Abramson M (eds). Cholesteatoma: First International Conference. New York, Aesculapius, 1977, pp 253–256.
73. Breiman RF, Butler JC, Tenover FC, et al. Emergence of drug-resistant pneumococcal infections in the United States. JAMA 271:1831, 1994.
74. Brodkey JA, Robertson JH, Shea JJ III, Gardner G. Cholesterol granulomas of the petrous apex: combined neurosurgical and otological management. J Neurosurg 85:625, 1996.
75. Brody JA, Overfield T, McAlister R. Draining ears and deafness among Alaskan Eskimos. Arch Otolaryngol 81:29, 1965.
76. Brook I. Prevalence of beta-lactamase-producing bacteria in chronic suppurative otitis media. Am J Dis Child 139:280, 1985.
77. Brook I, Gober AE. Bacterial interference in the nasopharynx following antimicrobial therapy of acute otitis media. J Antimicrob Chemother 41:489, 1998.
78. Brook I, Gober AE. Reliability of the microbiology of spontaneously draining acute otitis media in children. Pediatr Infect Dis J 19:571, 2000.

79. Brookhouser PE, Worthington DW, Kelly WJ. Fluctuating and/or progressive sensorineural hearing loss in children. Laryngoscope 104:958, 1994.
80. Brookhouser PE, Worthington DW, Kelly WJ. Middle ear disease in young children with sensorineural hearing loss. Laryngoscope 103:371, 1993.
81. Brown DT, Marsh RR, Potsic WP. Hearing loss induced by viscous fluids in the middle ear. Int J Pediatr Otorhinolaryngol 5:39, 1983.
82. Browning GG, Gatehouse S, Calder IT. Medical management of active chronic otitis media: a controlled study. J Laryngol Otol 102:491, 1988.
83. Browning GG, Gatehouse D. The prevalence of middle ear disease in the adult British population. Clin Otolaryngol 17:317, 1992.
84. Browning GG. The unsafeness of "safe" ears. J Laryngol Otol 98:23, 1984.
85. Brummet RE, Harris RF, Lindgren JA. Detection of ototoxicity from drugs applied topically to the middle ear space. Laryngoscope 86:1177, 1976.
86. Buchman CA, Luxford WM, Hirsch BE, et al. Beta-2 transferrin assay in the identification of perilymph. Am J Otol 20:174, 1999.
87. Buchwach KA, Birck HG. Serous otitis media and type I tympanoplasties in children. Ann Otol Rhinol Laryngol 89:324, 1980.
88. Buckingham RA, Ferrer JL. Reversibility of chronic adhesive otitis with polyethylene tube. Laryngoscope 76:993, 1966.
89. Busis SN. Vertigo. In Bluestone CD, Kenna MA (eds). Pediatric Otolaryngology, 3rd ed. Philadelphia: WB Saunders, 1996, pp 285–301.
90. Cantekin EI, Saez CA, Bluestone CD, et al. Airflow through the eustachian tube. Ann Otol Rhinol Laryngol 88:603, 1979.
91. Casselbrant ML, Black FO, Nashner L, et al. Vestibular function assessment in children with otitis media with effusion. Ann Otol Rhinol Laryngol 107:46, 1983.
92. Casselbrant ML, Brostoff LM, Cantekin EI, et al. Otitis media with effusion in preschool children. Laryngoscope 95:428, 1985.
93. Casselbrant ML, Furman JM, Mandel EM, et al. Past history of otitis media and balance in four-year old children. Laryngoscope 110:773, 2000.
94. Casselbrant ML, Furman JM, Rubenstein E, Mandel EM. Effect of otitis media on the vestibular system in children. Ann Otol Rhinol Laryngol 104:620, 1995.
95. Casselbrant ML, Kaleida PH, Rockette HE, et al. Efficacy of antimicrobial prophylaxis and of tympanostomy tube insertion for prevention of recurrent acute otitis media: results of a randomized clinical trial. Pediatr Infect Dis J 11:278, 1992.
96. Casselbrant ML, Mandel EM, Kurs-Lasky M, et al. Otitis media in a population of black American and white American infants, 0–2 years of age. Int J Pediatr Otorhinolaryngol 33:1, 1995.
97. Casselbrant ML, Redfern MS, Furman JM, et al. Visual-induced postural sway in children with and without otitis media. Ann Otol Rhinol Laryngol 107:401, 1998.
98. Cawthorne T, Griffith A. Primary cholesteatoma of the temporal bone. Arch Otolaryngol 73:252, 1961.
99. Caye-Thomasen P, Hermansson A, Tos M, Prellner K. Pathogenesis of middle-ear adhesions. Laryngoscope 106:463, 1996.
100. Caylan R, Titiz A, Falcioni M, et al. Myringoplasty in children: factors influencing surgical outcome. Otolaryngol Head Neck Surg 118:709, 1998.
101. Chan KH, Bluestone CD. Lack of efficacy of middle-ear inflation: treatment of otitis media with effusion in children. Otolaryngol Head Neck Surg 100:317, 1989.
102. Chan KH, Cantekin EI, Karnavas WJ, Bluestone CD. Autoinflation of eustachian tube in young children. Laryngoscope 97:668, 1987.
103. Chan KC, Sculerati N, Casselbrant ML, et al. Comparison of eustachian tube function tests between children with cholesteatoma/retraction pocket and those with chronic otitis media with effusion. In Tos M, Thomsen J, Peitersen E (eds). Proceedings of the Third International Conference on Cholesteatoma and Mastoid Surgery. Amsterdam, Kugler & Ghedini, 1989, pp 485–487.
104. Chan KH, Swarts JD, Rudoy R, et al. Otitis media in the Republic of Palau. Arch Otolaryngol Head Neck Surg 119:425, 1993.
105. Chang P, Fagan PA, Atlas MD, Roche J. Imaging destructive lesions of the petrous apex. Laryngoscope 108:599, 1998.
106. Chase C. Hearing loss and development: a neuropsychologic perspective. In Eavey RD, Klein JO (eds). Hearing Loss in Childhood:

A Primer. Report of the 102nd Ross Conference on Pediatric Research, Columbus, OH, 1992, pp 88–94.

107. Chole RA, Donald PJ. Petrous apicitis: clinical considerations. Ann Otol Rhinol Laryngol 92:544, 1983.

108. Cinnamon U, Kronenberg J, Benayahu D. Structural changes and protein expression in the mastoid bone adjacent to cholesteatoma. Laryngoscope 110:1198, 2000.

109. Clark WB, Brook I, Bianki D, Thompson DH. Microbiology of otitis externa. Otolaryngol Head Neck Surg 116:23, 1997.

110. Clayton MI, Osborne JE, Rutherford D, Rivron RP. A double-blind, randomized, prospective trial of a topical antiseptic versus a topical antibiotic in the treatment of otorrhea. J Otolaryngol 15:7, 1990.

111. Cody DT. The definition of cholesteatoma. In McCabe BF, Sadé J, Abramson M (eds). Cholesteatoma: First International Conference. New York, Aesculapius, 1977, pp 6–9.

112. Cohen H, Friedman EM, Lai D, et al. Balance in children with otitis media with effusion. Int J Pediatr Otorhinolaryngol 42:107, 1997.

113. Cohen-Kerem R, Uri N, Rennert H, et al. Acute mastoiditis in children: is surgical treatment necessary? J Laryngol Otol 113:1081, 1999.

114. Cohen SR, Thompson JW. Otitic candidiasis in children: an evaluation of the problem and effectiveness of ketoconazole in 10 patients. Ann Otol Rhinol Laryngol 99:427, 1990.

115. Cohn AM, Schwaber MK, Anthony LS, et al. Eustachian tube function and tympanoplasty. Ann Otol Rhinol Laryngol 88:339, 1979.

116. Crowther JA, Simpson D. Medical treatment of chronic otitis media: steroid or antibiotic with steroid ear-drops? Clin Otolaryngol 16:142, 1991.

117. Dagan R, Fliss DM, Einhorn M, et al. Outpatient management of chronic suppurative otitis media without cholesteatoma in children. Pediatr Infect Dis J 11:542, 1992.

118. Daly KA, Hunter LL, Levine SC, et al. Relationships between otitis media sequelae and age. Laryngoscope 108:1306, 1998.

119. Darrouzet V, Duclos J-Y, Portmann D, Bebear J-P. Preference for the closed technique in the management of cholesteatoma of the middle ear in children: a retrospective study of 215 consecutive patients treated over 10 years. Am J Otol 21:474, 2000.

120. DeBlanc GB. Otologic problems in Navajo Indians of the Southwestern United States. Hear Instrum 26:15, 1975.

121. Deddens AE, Muntz HR, Lusk RP. Adipose myringoplasty in children. Laryngoscope 103:216, 1993.

122. Denoyelle F, Garabedian FN, Roelly P, et al. Protracted acute otitis media and subacute mastoiditis: a prospective study of 165 cases. In Lim DJ (ed). Recent Advances in Otitis Media. Burlington, Ontario, Decker Periodicals, 1993, pp 264–267.

123. Denoyelle F, Roger G, Chauvin P, Garabedia EN. Myringoplasty in children: predictive factors of outcome. Laryngoscope 109:47, 1999.

124. Derlacki EL, Clemis JD. Congenital cholesteatoma of the middle ear and mastoid. Ann Otol Rhinol Laryngol 74:706, 1965.

125. Derlacki EL. Congenital cholesteatoma of the middle ear and mastoid. A third report. Arch Otolaryngol 97:177, 1973.

126. Dever GJ, Stewart JL, David A. Prevalence of otitis media in selected populations on Pohnpei: a preliminary study. Int J Pediatr Otorhinolaryngol 10:143, 1985.

127. Dever GJ, Stool SE, Manning S, Stewart J. Otitis Oceania: middle-ear disease in the Pacific basin. Ann Otol Rhinol Laryngol 99:25, 1990.

128. Dhooge IJM, Albers FWJ, Van Cauwenberge PB. Intratemporal and intracranial complications of acute suppurative otitis media in children: renewed interest. Int J Pediatr Otorhinolaryngol 49(Suppl 1):S109, 1999.

129. Diamant M. Chronic Otitis. A Critical Analysis. New York, S Karger, 1952.

130. Dohar JE, Alper CM, Bluestone CD, et al. Treatment of chronic suppurative otitis media with topical ciprofloxacin. In Lim DJ, Bluestone CD, Casselbrant ML, et al (eds). Recent Advances in Otitis Media—Proceedings of the Sixth International Symposium. Hamilton, Ontario, BC Decker, 1996, pp 525–528.

131. Dohar JE, Garner ET, Nielsen RW, et al. Topic ofloxacin treatment of otorrhea in children with tympanostomy tubes. Arch Otolaryngol Head Neck Surg 125:537, 1999.

132. Dohar JE, Kenna MA, Wadowsky RM. In vitro susceptibility of aural isolates of *P. aeruginosa* to commonly used ototopical antibiotics. Am J Otol 17:207, 1996.

133. Dohar JE, Kenna MA, Wadowsky RM. Therapeutic implications in the treatment of aural *Pseudomonas* infections based on in vitro susceptibility patterns. Arch Otolaryngol Head Neck Surg 121:1022, 1995.

134. Dornhoffer JL, Colvin GB, North P. Evidence of residual disease in ossicles of patients undergoing cholesteatoma removal. Acta Otolaryngol (Stockh) 119:89, 1999.

135. Dornhoffer JL. Retrograde mastoidectomy with canal wall reconstruction: a single-stage technique for cholesteatoma removal. Ann Otol Rhinol Laryngol 109:1033, 2000.

136. Dornfoffer JL. Surgical management of the atelectactic ear. Am J Otol 21:315, 2000.

137. Dota T, Nakamura K, Saheki M, et al. Cholesterol granuloma: experimental observations. Ann Otol Rhinol Laryngol 72:346, 1963.

138. Downs MP. Audiologist's overview of sequelae of early otitis media. Pediatrics 71:643, 1983.

139. Downs MP. Hearing loss: definition, epidemiology and prevention. Public Health Rev 4:255, 1975.

140. Doyle WJ. A functiono-anatomic description of eustachian tube vector relations in four ethnic populations: an osteologic study. Microfilm. Ann Arbor, University of Michigan, 1977.

141. Doyle WJ, Alper CM. A model to explain the rapid pressure decrease after air-inflation of diseased middle ears. Laryngoscope 109:70, 1999.

142. Doyle WJ, Cantekin EI, Bluestone CD. Eustachian tube function in cleft palate children. Ann Otol Rhinol Laryngol 89:34, 1980.

143. Dugdale AE, Lewis AN, Canty AA. The natural history of otitis media [letter]. N Engl J Med 307:1459, 1982.

144. Eason RJ, Harding E, Nicholson R, et al. Chronic suppurative otitis media in the Solomon Islands: a prospective, microbiological, audiometric and therapeutic survey. N Z Med J 99:812, 1986.

145. Edelstein DR, Magnan J, Parisier SC, et al. Microfiberoptic evaluation of the middle ear cavity. Am J Otol 15:50, 1994.

146. Edmond CV, Antoine G, Yim D, et al. A case of facial diplegia associated with acute bilateral otitis media. Int J Pediatr Otorhinolaryngol 18:257, 1990.

147. Eisenberg MB, Haddad G, Al-Mefty O. Petrous apex cholesterol granulomas: evolution and management. J Neurosurg 86:822, 1997.

148. Eisenman DJ, Parisier SC. Is chronic otitis media with cholesteatoma associated with neurosensory hearing loss? Am J Otol 19:20, 1998.

149. Elango S, Purohit GN, Hashim M, Hilmi R. Hearing loss and ear disorders in Malaysian school children. Int J Pediatr Otorhinolaryngol 22:75, 1991.

150. Ellefsen B, Bonding P. Facial palsy in acute otitis media. Clin Otolaryngol 21:393, 1996.

151. Elliott CA, Zalzal GH, Gottlieb WR. Acute otitis media and facial paralysis in children. Ann Otol Rhinol Laryngol 105:58, 1996.

152. Ellis MA, Lee WW, Wallace IF, Gravel JS. Hearing sensitivity and otitis media in one-year old infants: a preliminary report. In Lim DJ, Bluestone CD, Casselbrant M, et al (eds). Recent Advances in Otitis Media—Proceedings of the Sixth International Symposium. Hamilton, Ontario, BC Decker, 1995, p 396.

153. Englender M, Harell M, Guttman R, et al. Typing of *Pseudomonas aeruginosa* ear infections related to outcome of treatment. J Laryngol Otol 104:678, 1990.

154. Ekvall L. Eustachian tube function in tympanoplasty. Acta Otolaryngol Suppl (Stockh) 263:33, 1970.

155. Esposito S, D'Errico G, Montanaro C. Topical and oral treatment of chronic otitis media with ciprofloxacin. Arch Otolaryngol Head Neck Surg 116:557, 1990.

156. Esposito S, Noviello S, D'Errico G, Montanaro C. Topical ciprofloxacin vs. intramuscular gentamicin for chronic otitis media. Arch Otolaryngol Head Neck Surg 118:842, 1992.

157. Esposito S. Outpatient parenteral treatment of bacterial infections: the Italian model as an international trend? J Antimicrob Chemother 45:724, 2000.

158. Fageeh NA, Schloss MD, Elahi ME, et al. Surgical treatment of cholesteatoma in children. J Otolaryngol 28:309, 1999.

159. Falk B, Magnuson B. Eustachian tube closing failure in children with persistent middle ear effusion. Int J Pediatr Otorhinolaryngol 7:97, 1984.

160. Feagans L. Otitis media: a model for long-term effects with implications for intervention. In Kavanagh J (ed). Otitis Media and Child Development. Parkton, MD, York Press, 1986, pp 192–208.

161. Feagans L, Sanyal FM, Henderson F, et al. J Pediatr Psychol 12: 581, 1987.

162. Ferlito A. A review of the definition, terminology and pathology of aural cholesteatoma. J Laryngol Otol 107:483, 1993.

163. Fiellau-Nikolajsen M. Tympanometry and secretory otitis media: observations on diagnosis, epidemiology, treatment, and prevention in prospective cohort studies of three-year old children. Acta Otolaryngol (Stockh) 394:62, 1983.

164. Finkelstein Y, Zohar Y, Talmi YP, et al. Effects of acute negative middle ear pressure on hearing. Acta Otolaryngol (Stockh) 112:88, 1992.

165. Fischler RS, Todd NW, Feldman CM. Otitis media and language performance in a cohort of Apache Indian children. Am J Dis Child 139:355, 1985.

166. Fisher B. The social and emotional adjustment of children with impaired hearing attending ordinary classes. Br J Educ Psychol 36: 319, 1966.

167. Fitzgerald DC. Perilymphatic fistula in teens and young adults: emphasis on preexisting sensorineural hearing loss. Am J Otol 17: 397, 1996.

168. Fliss DM, Meidan N, Dagan R, et al. Aerobic bacteriology of chronic suppurative otitis media without cholesteatoma in children. Ann Otol Rhinol Laryngol 101:866, 1992.

169. Foreman AEW. Thesis: The aetiology and prevention of otitis media in aborginal children in the Northern Territory, Australia. Sydney, Australia, University of Sydney, 1987.

170. Forseni M, Eriksson A, Bagger-Sjoback D, et al. Development of tympanosclerosis: can predicting factors be identified? Am J Otol 18:298, 1997.

171. Forseni M, Hansson GK, Bagger-Sjoback D, Hultcrantz M. An immunohistochemical study of inducible nitric oxide synthase in the rat middle ear, with reference to tympanosclerosis. Acta Otolaryngol 119:577, 1999.

172. Fradis M, Brodsky A, Ben-David J, et al. Chronic otitis media treated topically with ciprofloxacin or tobramycin. Arch Otolaryngol Head Neck Surg 123:1057, 1997.

173. Fria TJ, Cantekin EI, Eichler JA. Hearing acuity of children with otitis media with effusion. Arch Otolaryngol 111:10, 1985.

174. Friedberg J, Gillis T. Tympanoplasty in childhood. J Otolaryngol 9: 165, 1980.

175. Friedmann I. Epidermoid cholesteatoma and cholesterol granuloma: experimental and human. Ann Otol Rhinol Laryngol 68:57, 1959.

176. Friel-Patti S, Finitzo-Hieber T, Conti G, et al. Language delay in infants associated with middle-ear disease and mild fluctuating hearing impairment. Pediatr Infect Dis J 1:104, 1982.

177. Fry J, Dillane JB, McNab Jones RF, et al. The outcome of acute otitis media. (A report to the Medical Research Council.) Br J Prev Soc Med 23:205, 1969.

178. Fukuda T, Sugie H, Ito M, Kikawada T. Bilateral facial palsy caused by bilateral masked mastoiditis. Pediatr Neurol 18:351, 1998.

179. Gates GA, Avery CA, Prihoda TJ, et al. Effectiveness of adenoidectomy and tympanostomy tubes in the treatment of chronic otitis media with effusion. N Engl J Med 317:1444, 1987.

180. Gerber MJ, Mason JC, Lambert PR. Hearing results after primary cartilage tympanoplasty. Laryngoscope 110:1994, 2000.

181. Gibson WP. Electrocochleography in the diagnosis of perilymphatic fistula: intraoperative observations and assessment of a new diagnostic office procedure. Am J Otol 13:146, 1992.

182. Giles M, O'Brien P. The prevalence of hearing impairment amongst Maori schoolchildren. Clin Otolaryngol 16:174, 1991.

183. Glasscock ME, Strasnick B. Tympanoplasty: the undersurface graft technique—postauricular approach. In Brachmann DE, Shelton C, Arriaga MA (eds). Otologic Surgery. Philadelphia, WB Saunders, 1994, pp 141–152.

184. Glasscock ME. Chronic petrositis: diagnosis and treatment. Ann Otol Rhinol Laryngol 81:677, 1972.

185. Glasscock ME, Dickins JRE, Wiet R. Cholesteatoma in children. Laryngoscope 91:1743, 1981.

186. Glasscock ME. Results in cholesteatoma surgery. In McCabe BF, Sadé J, Abramson M (eds). Cholesteatoma: First International Conference. New York, Aesculapius, 1977, pp 401–403.

187. Glasscock ME, Shambaugh GE. Surgery of the Ear, 4th ed. Philadelphia, WB Saunders, 1990.

188. Glasscock ME. Symposium: contraindications to tympanoplasty: II. An exercise in clinical judgment. Laryngoscope 86:70, 1976.

189. Gliklich RE, Eavey RD, Iannuzzi RA, Camacho AE. A comtemporary analysis of acute mastoiditis. Arch Otolaryngol Head Neck Surg 122:135, 1996.

190. Goetzinger CP, Harrison C, Baer CJ. Small perceptive hearing loss: its effect in school-age children. Volta Rev 66:124, 1964.

191. Goldblatt EL, Dohar J, Nozza RJ, et al. Topic ofloxacin versus systemic amoxicillin/clavulanate in purulent otorrhea in children with tympanostomy tubes. Int J Pediatr Otorhinolaryngol 46:91, 1998.

192. Goldstein NA, Casselbrant ML, Bluestone CD, Kurs-Lasky M. Intratemporal complications of acute otitis media in infants and children. Otolaryngol Head Neck Surg 119:444, 1998.

193. Golz A, Angel-Yeger B, Parush S. Evaluation of balance disturbances in children with middle-ear effusion. Int J Pediatr Otorhinolaryngol 43:21, 1998.

194. Golz A, Westerman ST, Gilbert LM, et al. Effect of middle ear effusion on the vestibular labyrinth. J Laryngol Otol 105:987, 1991.

195. Gonzalez C, Bluestone CD. Visualization of a retraction pocket/ cholesteatoma: indications for use of the middle-ear telescope in children. Laryngoscope 96:109, 1986.

196. Goodey RJ, Smyth GD. Combined approach tympanoplasty in children. Laryngoscope 82:166, 1972.

197. Goodhill V. Ear Diseases, Deafness, and Dizziness. Hagerstown, MD, Harper & Row, 1979, p 356.

198. Goycoolea MV, Paparella MM, Nissen RL (eds). Atlas of Otologic Surgery. Philadelphia, WB Saunders, 1989.

199. Gravel JS, Wallace IF. Listening and language at 4 years of age. Effects of early otitis media. J Speech Hear Res 35:588, 1992.

200. Gravel JS, Wallace IF, Ruben RJ. Early otitis media and later educational risk. Acta Otolaryngol (Stockh) 115:279, 1995.

201. Gray SW. Cognitive development in relation to otitis media. Pediatrics 71:645, 1983.

202. Grayeli AB, Mosnier I, Garem HE, Bouccara D, Sterkers O. Extensive intratemporal cholesteatoma: surgical strategy. Am J Otol 21:774, 2000.

203. Grundfast KM, Bluestone CD. Sudden or fluctuating hearing loss and vertigo in children due to perilymph fistula. Ann Otol Rhinol Laryngol 87:761, 1978.

204. Guthrie RM, Bailey BJ, Baroody FM, et al. Diagnosis and treatment of acute otitis externa: an interdisciplinary update. Ann Otol Rhinol Laryngol 108(Suppl 176), 1999.

205. Gyde MC. When the weeping stopped: an otologist views otorrhea and gentamicin. Arch Otolaryngol 102:542, 1976.

206. Haberkamp TJ, Tanyeri H. Surgical techniques to facilitate endoscopic second-look mastoidectomy. Laryngoscope 109:1023, 1999.

207. Habermann J. Zur Entstehung des Cholesteatoms des Mittelohrs (Cysten in der Schleimhaut der Paukenhohle, Atrophie der Nerven in der Schnecke). Arch Ohrenheilk (Leipz) 27:42, 1888.

208. Halama AR, Boogt GR, Musgrave GM. Prevalence of otitis media in children in a black rural community in Venda (South Africa). Int J Pediatr Otorhinolaryngol 11:73, 1986.

209. Hannley MT, Denneny JC, Holzer SS. Use of ototopical antibiotics in treating 3 common ear diseases. Otolaryngol Head Neck Surg 122:934, 2000.

210. Harker LA, Koontz FP. The bacteriology of cholesteatoma. In McCabe BF, Sadé J, Abramson M (eds). Cholesteatoma: First International Conference. New York, Aesculapius, 1977, pp 264–267.

211. Harker LA, Severeid LR. Cholesteatoma in the cleft palate patient. In Sadé J (ed). Cholesteatoma and Mastoid Surgery. Amsterdam, Kugler, 1982, pp 32–40.

212. Harley EH, Sdralis T, Berkowitz RG. Acute mastoiditis in children: a 12-year retrospective study. Otolaryngol Head Neck Surg 116:26, 1997.

213. Harner SG, Daube JR, Beatty CW, Ebersold MJ. Intraoperative monitoring of the facial nerve. Laryngoscope 98:209, 1988.

214. Hart MC. Childhood imbalance and chronic otitis media with effusion: effect of tympanostomy tube insertion on standardized tests of balance and locomotion. Laryngoscope 108:665, 1998.

215. Hartnick CJ, Kim HY, Chute PM, Parisier SC. Preventing labyrinthitis ossificans. Arch Otolaryngol Head Neck Surg 127:180, 2001.

216. Hasebe S, Takahashi H, Honjo I, Sudo M. Organic change of effusion in the mastoid in otitis media with effusion and its relation to attic retraction. Int J Pediatr Otorhinolaryngol 53:17, 2000.

217. Hatcher J, Smith A, Mackenzie I, et al. A prevalence study of ear problems in school children in Kiambu district, Kenya, May 1992. Int J Pediatr Otorhinolaryngol 33:197, 1995.

218. Hawkins DB, Dru D, House JW, Clark RW. Acute mastoiditis in children: a review of 54 cases. Laryngoscope 93:568, 1983.

219. Heermann J Jr, Heermann H, Kopstein E. Fascia and cartilage palisade tympanoplasty. Arch Otolaryngol 91:228, 1970.

220. Hellman K. Studien über das Sekundare Cholesteatom des Felsenbeins. Z Hals Nas Ohrenheilk 11:406, 1925.

221. Herberts G, Jeppson PH, Nylen O, Branesfors-Helander P. Acute otitis media: etiological aspects of acute otitis media. Prac Otol Rhinol Laryngol 33:191, 1971.

222. Hignett W. Effect of otitis media on speech, language, and behavior. Ann Otol Rhinol Laryngol 92:47, 1983.

223. Hildmann H, Scheerer WD, Meertens HJ. Tympanoplasty in children and anatomical variations of the epipharynx. Am J Otol 6:225, 1985.

224. Hinchcliffe R. Cholesteatoma: epidemiological and quantitative aspects. In McCabe BF, Sadé J, Abramson M (eds). Cholesteatoma: First International Conference. New York, Aesculapius, 1977, pp 277–286.

225. Holm VA, Kunze LH. Effects of chronic otitis media on language and speech development. Pediatrics 43:833, 1969.

226. Holmquist J. The role of the eustachian tube in myringoplasty. Acta Otolaryngol (Stockh) 66:289, 1968.

227. Homoe P, Bretlau P. Cholesteatomas in Greenlandic Inuit. A retrospective study and follow-up of treated cases from 1976–1991. Arct Med Res 53:86, 1994.

228. Homoe P, Christensen RB, Bretlau P. Acute otitis media and age at onset among children in Greenland. Acta Otolaryngol (Stockh) 119:65, 1999.

229. Homoe P, Christensen RB, Bretlau P. Prevalence of otitis media in a survey of 591 unselected Greenlandic children. Int J Pediatr Otorhinolaryngol 36:215, 1996.

230. Hopkins RJ, Bergeson PS. Otitis externa posing as mastoiditis. Arch Pediatr Adolesc Med 148:1346, 1994.

231. Hoppe JE, Koster S, Bootz F, Niethammer D. Acute mastoiditis—relevant once again. Infection 22:178, 1994.

232. Hubbard TW, Paradise JL, McWilliams BJ, et al. Consequences of unremitting middle-ear disease in early life: otologic, audiologic and developmental findings in children with cleft palate. N Engl J Med 312:1529, 1985.

233. Hudson HM, Rockette IR. An environmental and demographic analysis of otitis media in rural Australian Aborigines. Int J Epidemiol 13:73, 1984.

234. Hunter LL, Margolis RH, Giebink CS, et al. Long-term prospective study of hearing loss in children after tympanostomy tube treatment of chronic otitis media with effusion. In Lim DJ, Bluestone CD, Casselbrant M, et al (eds). Recent Advances in Otitis Media—Proceedings of the Sixth International Symposium. Hamilton, Ontario, BC Decker, 1995, p 383.

235. Hunter LL, Margolis RH, Rykken JR, et al. High frequency hearing loss associated with otitis media. Ear Hear 17:1, 1996.

236. Ibekwe AO, Okoye BCC. Subperiosteal mastoid abscesses in chronic suppurative otitis media. Ann Otol Rhinol Laryngol 97:373, 1988.

237. Igarashi M, Konishi S, Alford BR, et al. The pathology of tympanosclerosis. Laryngoscope 80:233, 1970.

238. Ikeda K, Morizono T. Effect of ototopic application of a corticosteroid preparation on cochlear function. Am J Otolaryngol 12:150, 1991.

239. Indudharan R, Haq JA, Aiyar S. Antibiotics in chronic suppurative otitis media: a bacteriologic study. Ann Otol Rhinol Laryngol 108:440, 1999.

240. Ingelstedt S, Flisberg K, Ortegren U. On the function of middle ear and eustachian tube. Acta Otolaryngol Suppl (Stockh) 182, 1963.

241. Istorico LJ, Sanders M, Jacobs RF, et al. Otitis media due to blastomycosis: report of two cases. Clin Infect Dis 14:355, 1992.

242. Iwano T, Hamada E, Kinoshita T, et al. Passive opening pressure

243. Jaffe BF. The incidence of ear disease in the Navajo Indians. Laryngoscope 79:2126, 1969.

244. Jaisinghani VJ, Paparella MM, Schachern PA, Le CT. Tympanic membrane/middle ear pathologic correlates in chronic otitis media. Laryngoscope 109:712, 1999.

245. Jang CH, Merchant SN. Histopathology of labyrinthine fistulae in chronic otitis media with clinical implication. Am J Otol 18:15, 1997.

246. Johnson RL. Chronic otitis media in school age Navajo Indians. Laryngoscope 77:1901, 1967.

247. Jansen C. Cartilage-tympanoplasty. Laryngoscope 73:1288, 1963.

248. Jeang MK, Fletcher EC. Tuberculous otitis media. JAMA 249:2231, 1983.

249. Johansson U, Hellstrom S, Anniko M. Round window membrane in serous and purulent otitis media. Structural study in the rat. Ann Otol Rhinol Laryngol 102:227, 1993.

250. Jones RN, Milazzo J, Seidlin M. Ofloxacin otic solution for treatment of otitis externa in children and adults. Arch Otolaryngol Head Neck Surg 123:1193, 1997.

251. Juselius H, Kaltiokallio K. Complications of acute and chronic otitis media in the antibiotic era. Acta Otolaryngol (Stockh) 74:445, 1972.

252. Kaga K, Ichimura K. A preliminary report: clinical effects of otic solution of ofloxacin in infantile myringitis and chronic otitis media. Int J Pediatr Otorhinolaryngol 42:199, 1998.

253. Kamal SA. Surgery of tympanosclerosis. Laryngol Otol 111:917, 1997.

254. Kambhampati VSS, Sastry R, Sharma SC, et al. Aural cholesteatoma: role of tumor necrosis factor-alpha in bone destruction. Am J Otol 20:158, 1999.

255. Kanazawa T, Hagiwara H, Kitamura K. Labyrinthine involvement and multiple perforations of the tympanic membrane in acute otitis media due to group A streptococci. J Laryngol Otol 114:47, 2000.

256. Kaneko Y, Takasaka T, Sakuma M, et al. Middle-ear inflation as a treatment for secretory otitis media in children. Acta Otolaryngol (Stockh) 117:564, 1997.

257. Kaplan GJ, Fleshman JK, Bender TR, et al. Long-term effects of otitis media: a ten-year cohort study of Alaskan Eskimo children. Pediatrics 52:577, 1973.

258. Kapur YP. A study of hearing loss in school children in India. J Speech Hear Dis 30:225, 1965.

259. Karma P, Jokipii L, Ojala K, et al. Bacteriology of the chronically discharging middle ear. Acta Otolaryngol (Stockh) 86:110, 1978.

260. Karma P, Sipila M, Pukander J, Parala M. Occurrence of cholesteatoma and secretory otitis media in children. In Tos M, Thomsen J, Peitersen E (eds). Cholesteatoma and Mastoid Surgery. Amsterdam, Kugler, 1989, pp 335–338.

261. Kemppainen HO, Puhakka HJ, Laippala PJ, et al. Epidemiology and aetiology of middle-ear cholesteatoma. Acta Otolaryngol 119:568, 1999.

262. Kenna MA, Bluestone CD. Medical management of chronic suppurative otitis media without cholesteatoma. In Lim DJ, Bluestone CD, Klein JO, Nelson JD (eds). Proceedings of the Fourth International Symposium on Otitis Media. Burlington, Ontario, BC Decker, 1988, pp 222–226.

263. Kenna MA, Bluestone CD, Reilly J. Medical management of chronic suppurative otitis media without cholesteatoma in children. Laryngoscope 96:146, 1986.

264. Kenna MA, Rosane BA, Bluestone CD. Medical management of chronic suppurative otitis media without cholesteatoma in children—update 1992. Am J Otolaryngol 14:469, 1993.

265. Kessler A, Potsic WP, Marsh RR. Type I tympanoplasty in children. Arch Otolaryngol Head Neck Surg 120:487, 1994.

266. Khanna SM, Tonndorf J. Tympanic membrane vibrations in cats studied by time-averaged holography. J Acoust Soc Am 51:1904, 1972.

267. Kim CS, Jung HW, Yoo KY. Prevalence of otitis media and allied diseases in Korea. J Kor Med Sci 8:34, 1993.

268. Kinney SE. Postinflammatory ossicular fixation in tympanoplasty. Laryngoscope 88:821, 1978.

269. Kinsella JP, Grosman M, Black S. Otomastoiditis caused by *Mycobacterium avium-intracellulare*. Pediatr Infect Dis J 5:704, 1986.
270. Klein JO, Chase C, Teele DW, et al. Otitis media and the development of speech, language, and cognitive abilities at seven years of age. In Lim DJ, Bluestone CD, Klein JO, et al (eds). Recent Advances in Otitis Media. Toronto, BC Decker, 1988, pp 396–397.
271. Klein JO, Teele DW, Chase C, et al. Otitis media and the development of speech, language and cognitive abilities. In Nelson JD (ed). Update on Otitis Media. Royal Society of Medicine: International Congress and Symposium Series, 1990, pp 75–78.
272. Koch WM, Friedman EM, McGill TJI, et al. Tympanoplasty in children. The Boston Children's Hospital Experience. Arch Otolaryngol Head Neck Surg 116:35, 1990.
273. Kodman F. Educational status of hard of hearing children in the classroom. J Speech Hear Disord 28:297, 1963.
274. Kokko E. Chronic secretory otitis media in children. Acta Otolaryngol Suppl (Stockh) 327:7, 1974.
275. Koltai PJ, Eames FA, Parnes SM. Comparison of computed tomography and magnetic resonance imaging in chronic otitis media with cholesteatoma. Arch Otolaryngol Head Neck Surg 115:1231, 1989.
276. Korthals Altes AJ. Cholesterol granuloma in the tympanic cavity. J Laryngol Otol 80:691, 1966.
277. Kumazawa T, Iwan T, Ushiro K, et al. Tubotympanoplasty. Acta Otolaryngol Suppl (Stockh) 500:14, 1993.
278. Kvestad E, Kvaerner KJ, Mair IWS. Acute mastoiditis: predictors for surgery. Int J Pediatr Otorhinolaryngol 52:149, 2000.
279. Laitila P, Karma P, Sipila M, et al. Extended high frequency hearing and history of acute otitis media in 14-year-old children in Finland. Acta Otolaryngol Suppl (Stockh) 529:27, 1997.
280. Lang R, Goshen S, Raas-Rothschild A, et al. Oral ciprofloxacin in the management of chronic suppurative otitis media without cholesteatoma in children: preliminary experience in 21 children. Pediatr Infect Dis J 11:925, 1992.
281. Lange W. Tief Eingezogene Membrana Flaccida und Cholesteatom. Z Hals Nas Ohrenheilk 30:575, 1932.
282. Lau T, Tos M. Tympanoplasty in children: an analysis of late results. Am J Otol 7:55, 1986.
283. Leach AJ, Boswell JB, Asche V, et al. Bacterial colonization of the nasopharynx predicts very early onset and persistence of otitis media in Australian Aboriginal infants. Pediatr Infect Dis J 13:983, 1994.
284. Lee K, Schuknecht HF. Results of tympanoplasty and mastoidectomy at the Massachusetts Eye and Ear Infirmary. Laryngoscope 81:529, 1971.
285. Legent F, Bordure P, Beauvillain C, Berche P. Controlled prospective study of oral ciprofloxacin versus amoxicillin/clavulanic acid in chronic suppurative otitis media in adults. Chemotherapy 40(suppl 1):16, 1994.
286. Leiberman A, Fliss DM, Dagan R. Medical treatment of chronic suppurative otitis media without cholesteatoma in children: two-year follow-up. Int J Pediatr Otorhinolaryngol 24:25, 1992.
287. Leiberman A, Lupu L, Landsberg R, Fliss DM. Unusual complications of otitis media. Am J Otolaryngol 15:444, 1994.
288. Levenson MJ, Parisier SC, Chute P, et al. A review of twenty congenital cholesteatomas of the middle ear in children. Otolaryngol Head Neck Surg 94:560, 1986.
289. Levinson RM. Cartilage perichondrial composite graft tympanoplasty in the treatment of posterior marginal and attic retraction pockets. Laryngoscope 97:1069, 1987.
290. Leviton A, Bellinger D. Consequences of unremitting middle-ear infection in early life. N Engl J Med 313:1352, 1985.
291. Lewis AN, Coman W, McCafferty G, Shaw E. The prevalence of ear disease in Queensland Aboriginals. J Otolaryngol Soc Aust 4:112, 1977.
292. Lewis N. Otitis media and linguistic incompetence. Arch Otolaryngol 102:387, 1976.
293. Lindeman P, Holmquist J. Mastoid volume and eustachian tube function in ears with cholesteatoma. Am J Otol 8:5, 1987.
294. Linder TE, Briner HR, Bischoff T. Prevention of acute mastoiditis: fact or fiction? Int J Pediatr Otorhinolaryngol 56:129, 2000.
295. Ling D, McCoy RH, Levinson ED. The incidence of middle-ear disease and its educational implications among Baffin Island Eskimo children. Can J Public Health 60:385, 1969.
296. Linstrom CJ, Silverman CA, Rosen A, Meiteles LZ. Eustachian tube endoscopy in patients with chronic ear disease. Laryngoscope 110:1884, 2000.
297. Linthieum FH Jr. Cholesterol granuloma (iatrogenic), further evidence of etiology, a case report. Ann Otol Rhinol Laryngol 80:207, 1971.
298. Lous J, Fiellau-Nikolajsen M. A 5-year prospective case-control study of the influence of early otitis media with effusion on reading achievement. Int J Pediatr Otorhinolaryngol 8:19, 1984.
299. Lous J. Silent reading and secretory otitis media in school children. Int J Pediatr Otorhinolaryngol 25:25, 1993.
300. Lowe JF, Bamforth JS, Pracy R. Acute otitis media: one year in a general practice. Lancet 2:1129, 1963.
301. Lowry PW, Jarvis WR, Oberle AD, et al. *Mycobacterium chelonae* causing otitis media in an ear-nose-and-throat practice. N Engl J Med 319:978, 1988.
302. Lucente F, Lawson W, Novick N (eds). The External Ear: Diagnosis and Management of Diseases of the Auricle, 3rd ed. Philadelphia, WB Saunders, 1987.
303. Lundman L, Juhn SK, Bagger-Sjoback D, et al. Permeability of the normal round window membrane to *Haemophilus influenzae* type b endotoxin. Acta Otolaryngol (Stockh) 112:524, 1992.
304. Lundman L, Santi PA, Morizono T, et al. Inner ear damage and passage through the round window membrane of *Pseudomonas aeruginosa* exotoxin in a chinchilla model. Ann Otol Rhinol Laryngol 101:437, 1992.
305. Luntz M, Brodsky A, Nusem S, et al. Acute mastoiditis—the antibiotic era: a multicenter study. Int J Pediatr Otorhinolaryngol 57:1, 2001.
306. Luntz M, Keren G, Nusem S, Kronenberg J. Acute mastoiditis—revisited. Ear Nose Throat J 73:648, 1994.
307. Luntz M, Sade J. The value of politzerization in the treatment of atelectatic ears. J Laryngol Otol 102:779, 1988.
308. Luntz M, Sade J. Value of middle ear inflation as a diagnostic indicator of eustachian tube patency. J Laryngol Otol 104:134, 1990.
309. MacDonald RR, Lusk RP, Muntz HR. Fasciaform myringoplasty in children. Arch Otolaryngol Head Neck Surg 120:138, 1994.
310. Magliulo G, Vingolo GM, Petti R, et al. Acute mastoiditis in pediatric age. Int J Pediatr Otorhinolaryngol 31:147, 1995.
311. Maharaj D, Jadwat A, Fernandez CM, et al. Bacteriology in acute mastoiditis. Arch Otolaryngol Head Neck Surg 113:514, 1987.
312. Main TS, Shimada T, Lim DJ. Experimental cholesterol granuloma. Arch Otolaryngol 91:356, 1970.
313. Mak D, MacKendrick A, Weeks S, Plant AJ. Middle-ear disease in remote Aboriginal Australia: a field assessment of surgical outcomes. J Laryngol Otol 114:26, 2000.
314. Mandel EM, Casselbrant ML, Kurs-Lasky M. Acute otorrhea: bacteriology of a common complication of tympanostomy tubes. Ann Otol Rhinol Laryngol 103:713, 1994.
315. Mandel EM, Rockette HE, Bluestone CD, et al. Efficacy of myringotomy with and without tympanostomy tubes for chronic otitis media with effusion. Pediatr Infect Dis J 11:270, 1992.
316. Mandel EM, Rockette HE, Bluestone CD, et al. Myringotomy with and without tympanostomy tubes for chronic otitis media with effusion. Arch Otolaryngol Head Neck Surg 115:1217, 1989.
317. Manni JJ, Lema PN. Otitis media in Dar es Salaam, Tanzania. J Laryngol Otol 101:222, 1987.
318. Manning SC, Cantekin EI, Kenna MA, et al. Prognostic value of eustachian tube function in pediatric tympanoplasty. Laryngoscope 97:1012, 1987.
319. Marco-Algara J, Gimenez F, Mallea I, et al. Cholesteatoma in children: results in open versus closed techniques. J Laryngol Otol 105:820, 1991.
320. Margolis RH, Hunter LL, Rykken JR, et al. Effects of otitis media on extended high-frequency hearing in children. Ann Otol Rhinol Laryngol 102:1, 1993.
321. Marttila TI. Results of audiometrial screening in Finnish school-children. Int J Pediatr Otorhinolaryngol 11:39, 1986.
322. Mattsson C, Marklund SL, Hellstrom S. Application of oxygen free radical scavengers to diminish the occurrence of myringosclerosis. Ann Otol Rhinol Laryngol 106:513, 1997.
323. Maynard JE, Fleshman JK, Tschopp CF. Otitis media in Alaskan Eskimo children: prospective evaluation of chemoprophylaxis. JAMA 219:597, 1972.
324. Maw AR. Chronic otitis media with effusion (glue ear) and adeno-

tonsillectomy: prospective randomised controlled study. Br Med J Clin Res 287:1586, 1983.

325. Maw R, Wilks J, Harvey I, et al. Early surgery compared with watchful waiting for glue ear and effect on language development in preschool children: a randomized trial. Lancet 353:960, 1999.

326. Mawson SR, Ludman H. Diseases of the Ear: A Textbook of Otology. Chicago, Year Book, 1979, pp 378–380.

327. McCafferty GJ, Coman WB, Shaw E, et al. Cholesteatoma in Australian aboriginal children. In McCabe BJ, Sadé J, Abramson M (eds). Cholesteatoma: First International Conference. New York, Aesculapius, 1977, pp 293–301.

328. McCafferty GJ, Lewis AN, Coman WB, Mills C. A nine-year study of ear disease in Australian Aboriginal children. J Laryngol Otol 99: 117, 1985.

329. McGuckin F. Concerning the pathogenesis of destructive ear disease. J Laryngol Otol 75:949, 1961.

330. McKennan KX. Endoscopic "second look" mastoidoscopy to rule out residual epitympanic/mastoid cholesteatoma. Laryngoscope 103: 810, 1993.

331. McKenzie D. The pathogeny of aural cholesteatoma. J Laryngol Otol 46:163, 1931.

332. McPherson B, Holborow CA. A study of deafness in West Africa: the Gambian hearing health project. Int J Pediatr Otorhinolaryngol 10:115, 1985.

333. Megerian CA. Pediatric tympanoplasty and the role of preoperative eustachian tube evaluation. Arch Otolaryngol Head Neck Surg 126: 1039, 2000.

334. Menyuk P. Effect of persistent otitis media on language development. Ann Otol Rhinol Laryngol 89:257, 1980.

335. Menyuk P. Effects of hearing loss on language acquisition in the babbling stage. In Jaffee BF (ed). Hearing Loss in Children. Baltimore, University Park Press, 1977, pp 621–629.

336. Menyuk P. Predicting speech and language problems with persistent otitis media. In Kavanaugh J (ed). Otitis Media and Child Development. Parkton, MD, York Press, 1986, pp 83–96.

337. Meyerhoff WL, Morizono T, Shaddock LC, et al. Tympanostomy tubes and otic drops. Laryngoscope 93:1022, 1983.

338. Miller GF Jr, Bilodeau R. Preoperative evaluation of eustachian tube function in tympanoplasty. South Med J 60:868, 1967.

339. Miller SA, Omene JA, Bluestone CD, et al. A point prevalence of otitis media in a Nigerian village. Int J Pediatr Otorhinolaryngol 5: 19, 1983.

340. Minja BM, Machemba A. Prevalence of otitis media, hearing impairment and cerumen impaction among school children in rural and urban Dar es Salaam, Tanzania. Int J Pediatr Otorhinolaryngol 37:29, 1996.

341. Mishiro Y, Sakagami M, Okumura S-I, et al. Postoperative results of cholesteatoma in children. Auri Naris Larynx 27:223, 2000.

342. Miura M, Sando I, Orita Y, Hirsch BE. Histopathological study of the temporal bones and eustachian tubes in children with cholesterol granuloma. In press.

343. Monsell EM (ed). Ossiculoplasty. Otolaryngol Clin North Am 27: 641, 1994.

344. Moran DJ, Waterford JE, Hollows F, Jones DL. Ear disease in rural Australia. Med J Aust 2:210, 1979.

345. Morizono T, Giebink GS, Paparella MM, et al. Sensorineural hearing loss in experimental purulent otitis media due to Streptococcus pneumoniae. Arch Otolaryngol 111:794, 1985.

346. Mortimer EA. Indian health: an unmet problem. Pediatrics 51: 1065, 1973.

347. Muenker G. Results after treatment of otitis media with effusion. Ann Otol Rhinol Laryngol 89:308, 1980.

348. Muhaimeid H, Zakzouk S, Bafaqueeh S. Epidemiology of chronic suppurative otitis media in Saudi children. Int J Pediatr Otorhinolaryngol 26:101, 1993.

349. Murphy TP. Hearing results in pediatric patients with chronic otitis media after ossicular reconstruction with partial ossicular replacement prostheses and total ossicular replacement prostheses. Laryngoscope 110:536, 2000.

350. Mutlu C, Odabasi O, Metin K, et al. Sensorineural hearing loss associated with otitis media with effusion in children. Int J Pediatr Otorhinolaryngol 46:179, 1998.

351. Nadol D, Herrmann P, Baumann A, Fanconi A. Acute mastoiditis: clinical, microbiological, and therapeutic aspects. Eur J Pediatr 149:560, 1990.

352. Nadol JB, Schuknecht HF. Surgery of the Ear and the Temporal Bone. New York, Raven Press, 1993.

353. Nager F. The cholesteatoma of the middle ear. Ann Otol Rhinol Laryngol 34:1249, 1925.

354. Nager GT, Vanderveen TS. Cholesterol granuloma involving the temporal bone. Ann Otol Rhinol Laryngol 85:204, 1976.

355. Needleman H. Effects of hearing loss from early recurrent otitis media on speech and language development. In Jaffe BF (ed). Hearing Loss in Children. Baltimore, University Park Press, 1977, pp 640–649.

356. Neil JF, Harrison SH, Morbry RD, et al. Deafness in acute otitis media. Br Med J 1:75, 1966.

357. Ogle JW, Lauer BA. Acute mastoiditis. Diagnosis and complications. Am J Dis Child 140:1178, 1986.

358. Ojala L. Pneumatization of the bone and environmental factors: experimental studies on chick humerus. Acta Otolaryngol Suppl (Stockh) 133, 1957.

359. Ojala L, Saxen A. Pathogenesis of middle ear cholesteatoma arising from Shrapnell's membrane (attic cholesteatoma). Acta Otolaryngol Suppl (Stockh) 100:33, 1952.

360. Okeowa PA. Observations on the incidence of secretory otitis media in Nigerian children. J Trop Pediatr 31:295, 1985.

361. Olmstead RW, Alvarez MC, Moroney JD, et al. The pattern of hearing following acute otitis media. J Pediatr 65:252, 1964.

362. Olson TS, Seid AB, Pransky SM. Actinomycosis of the middle ear. Int J Pediatr Otorhinolaryngol 17:51, 1989.

363. Ophir D, Porat M, Marshak G. Myringoplasty in the pediatric population. Arch Otolaryngol Head Neck Surg 113:1288, 1987.

364. Osma U, Cureoglu S, Hosoglu S. The complications of chronic otitis media: report of 93 cases. J Laryngol Otol 114:97, 2000.

365. Ottaviani F, Neglia CB, Berti E. Cytokines and adhesion molecules in middle-ear cholesteatoma. A role in epithelial growth? Acta Otolaryngol 119:462, 1999.

366. Ozagar A, Koc A, Ciprut A, et al. Effects of topical otic preparation on hearing in chronic otitis media. Otolaryngol Head Neck Surg 117:405, 1997.

367. Palva A, Karma P, Karja J. Cholesteatoma in children. Arch Otolaryngol 103:74, 1977.

368. Palva T, Johnson L-G, Ramsey H. Attic aeration in temporal bones from children with recurring otitis media: tympanostomy tubes did not cure disease in Prussak's space. Am J Otol 21:485, 2000.

369. Palva T, Virtanen H, Mckinen J. Acute and latent mastoiditis in children. J Laryngol Otol 99:127, 1985.

370. Paparella MM. Otologic surgery in children. Otolaryngol Clin North Am 10:145, 1977.

371. Paparella MM, Goycoolea MV, Meyerhoff WL. Inner ear pathology and otitis media: a review. Ann Otol Rhinol Laryngol 89:249, 1980.

372. Paparella MM, Lim DJ. Pathogenesis and pathology of the "idiopathic" blue eardrum. Arch Otolaryngol 85:249, 1967.

373. Paparella MM, Morizono T, Le CT, et al. Sensorineural hearing loss in otitis media. Ann Otol Rhinol Laryngol 93:623, 1984.

374. Paparella MM, Oda M, Hiraide F, et al. Pathology of sensorineural hearing loss in otitis media. Ann Otol Rhinol Laryngol 81:632, 1972.

375. Papastavros T, Giamarellou H, Varlejides S. Preoperative therapeutic considerations in chronic suppurative otitis media. Laryngoscope 99:655, 1989.

376. Paradise JL, Bluestone CD, Felder H. The universality of otitis media in fifty infants with cleft palate. Pediatrics 44:35, 1969.

377. Paradise JL, Bluestone CD, Rogers KD, et al. Efficacy of adenoidectomy for recurrent otitis media in children previously treated with tympanostomy-tube and non-randomized clinical trials. N Engl J Med 310:674, 1984.

378. Paradise JL, Dollighan CA, Campbell TF, et al. Language, speech sound production, and cognition in three-year-old children in relation to otitis media in their first three years of life. Pediatrics 105: 1119, 2000.

379. Paradise JL, Feldman HM, Campbell TF, et al. Early vs late tube placement of persistent middle-ear effusion (MEE) in the first 3 years of life: effects on language, speech sound production, and cognition at age 3 years [abstract 1273]. Pediatr Res 47:216A, 2000.

380. Paradise JL, Feldman HM, Colborn DK, et al. Parental stress and

parent-rated child behavior in relation to otitis media in the first three years of life. Pediatrics 104:1264, 1999.

381. Paradise JL. Long-term effects of short-term hearing loss—menace or myth? Pediatrics 71:647, 1983.

382. Paradise JL. On tympanostomy tubes and rationale, results, reservations, and recommendations. Pediatrics 60:86, 1977.

383. Paradise JL, Rogers KD. On otitis media, child development, and tympanostomy tubes: new answers or old questions. Pediatrics 77:88, 1986.

384. Peckham CS, Sheridan M, Butler NR. School attainment of seven-year-old children with hearing difficulties. Dev Med Child Neurol 14:592, 1972.

385. Pedersen CB, Zachau-Christiansen B. Otitis media in Greenland children: acute, chronic, and secretory otitis media in three- to eight-year-olds. J Otolaryngol 15:332, 1986.

386. Peel MM, Hibberd AJ, King BM, et al. *Alcaligenes piechaudii* from chronic ear discharge. J Clin Microbiol 26:1580, 1988.

387. Pensak ML, Willging JP, Keith RW. Intraoperative facial nerve monitoring in chronic ear surgery: a resident training experience. Am J Otol 15:108, 1994.

388. Perry BP, Smith DW. Effect of cortisporin otic suspension on cochlear function and efferent activity in the guinea pig. Laryngoscope 106:1557, 1996.

389. Petersen CG, Ovesen T, Pedersen CB. Acute mastoidectomy in a Danish county from 1977 to 1997—operative findings and long-term results. Int J Pediatr Otolaryngol 45:21, 1998.

390. Piccirillo JF, Parnes SM. Ciprofloxacin for the treatment of chronic ear disease. Laryngoscope 99:510, 1989.

391. Pichichero ME, Berghash LR, Hengerer AS. Anatomic and audiologic sequelae after tympanostomy tube insertion or prolonged antibiotic therapy for otitis media. Pediatr Infect Dis J 8:780, 1989.

392. Podoshin L, Fradis M, David B. Ototoxicity of ear drops in patients suffering from chronic otitis media. J Laryngol Otol 103:46, 1989.

393. Poe DS, Gadre AK. Cartilage tympanoplasty for management of retraction pockets and cholesteatomas. Laryngoscope 103:614, 1993.

394. Poe DS, Rebeiz EE, Pankratov MM, et al. Transtympanic endoscopy of the middle ear. Laryngoscope 102:993, 1992.

395. Prescott CAJ. Cholesteatoma in children—the experience at the Red Cross War Memorial children's Hospital in South Africa 1988–1996. Int J Pediatr Otorhinolaryngol 49:15, 1999.

396. Prior AJ. Facial palsy caused by otitis media with effusion: the pathophysiology discussed. ORL J Otorhinolaryngol Relat Spec 57:348, 1995.

397. Rach GH, Zielhuis GA, van Baarle PW, van den Broek P. The effect of treatment with ventilating tubes on language development in preschool children with otitis media with effusion. Clin Otolaryngol 16:128, 1991.

398. Rahko T, Laitila P, Sipila M, et al. Hearing and acute otitis media in 13-year-old children. Acta Otolaryngol (Stockh) 115:190, 1995.

399. Rahko T, Karma P, Sipila M. Sensorineural hearing loss and acute otitis media in children. Acta Otolaryngol (Stockh) 108:107, 1989.

400. Raine CH, Singh SD. Tympanoplasty in children: a review of 114 cases. J Laryngol Otol 97:217, 1983.

401. Ranier A. Development and construction of the pyramidal cells. Arch Ohren Nasen Khelkopfh 145:3, 1938.

402. Rapin I. Conductive hearing loss effects on children's language and scholastic skills: a review of the literature. Ann Otol Rhinol Laryngol 88:3, 1979.

403. Ratnesar P. Aeration: a factor in the sequelae of chronic ear disease along the Labrador and Northern Newfoundland coast. In McCabe BF, Sadé J, Abramson M (eds). Cholesteatoma: First International Conference. New York, Aesculapius, 1977, pp 302–307.

404. Reed D, Struve S, Maynard JE. Otitis media and hearing deficiency among Eskimo children. A cohort study. Am J Public Health 57:1657, 1967.

405. Riley DN, Herberger S, McBride G, Law K. Myringotomy and ventilation tube insertion: a ten-year follow-up. J Laryngol Otol 111:257, 1997.

406. Rigner P, Renvall U, Tjellstrom A. Late results after cholesteatoma surgery in early childhood. Int J Pediatr Otorhinolaryngol 22:213, 1991.

407. Ritter FN. Complications of cholesteatoma. In McCabe BF, Sadé J, Abramson M (eds). Cholesteatoma: First International Conference. New York, Aesculapius, 1977, pp 430–437.

408. Roberts JE, Burchinal MR, Jackson SC, et al. Otitis media in early childhood in relation to preschool language and school readiness skills among Black children. Pediatrics 196:725, 2000.

409. Roberts JE, Sanyal MA, Burchinal MR, et al. Otitis media in early childhood and its relationship to later verbal and academic performance. Pediatrics 78:423, 1986.

410. Roger G, Denoyelle F, Chauvin P, et al. Predictive risk factors of residual cholesteatoma in children: a study of 256 cases. Am J Otol 18:550, 1997.

411. Roland PS. Clinical ototoxicity of topical antibiotic drops. Otolaryngol Head Neck Surg 110:598, 1994.

412. Rosen A, Ophir D, Marshak G. Acute mastoiditis: a review of 69 cases. Ann Otol Rhinol Laryngol 95:222, 1986.

413. Rosenfeld RM, Moura RL, Bluestone CD. Predictors of residual-recurrent cholesteatoma in children. Arch Otolaryngol Head Neck Surg 118:384, 1992.

414. Rubin JS, Wei WI. Acute mastoiditis: a review of 34 patients. Laryngoscope 95:963, 1985.

415. Ruah CB, Schachern PA, Paparella MM, Zederman D. Mechanisms of retraction pocket formation in the pediatric tympanic membrane. Arch Otolaryngol Head Neck Surg 118:1298, 1992.

416. Ruedi L. Cholesteatosis of the attic. J Laryngol Otol 72:593, 1958.

417. Ruhl CM, Pensak ML. Role of aerating mastoidectomy in noncholesteatomatous chronic otitis media. Laryngoscope 109:1924, 1999.

418. Rupa V, Rajshekhar V, Weider DJ. Syndrome of recurrent meningitis due to congenital perilymph fistula with two different clinical presentations. Int J Pediatr Otorhinolaryngol 54:173, 2000.

419. Sadé J, Avraham S, Brown M. Dynamics of atelectasis and retraction pockets. In Sadé J (ed). Cholesteatoma and Mastoid Surgery. Amsterdam, Kugler, 1982, pp 267–281.

420. Sadé J, Halevy A, Klajman A, et al. Cholesterol granuloma. Acta Otolaryngol (Stockh) 89:233, 1980.

421. Sadé J. Pathogenesis of attic cholesteatoma: the metaplasia theory. In McCabe BF, Sadé J, Abramson M (eds). Cholesteatoma: First International Conference. New York, Aesculapius, 1977, pp 212–232.

422. Sadé J. Treatment of cholesteatoma. Am J Otolaryngol 8:524, 1987.

423. Sadé J. Treatment of cholesteatoma and retraction pockets. Eur Arch Otorhinolaryngol 250:193, 1993.

424. Saito H, Kazama Y, Yazawa Y. Simple maneuver for closing traumatic eardrum perforation by micropore strip tape patching. Am J Otol 11:427, 1990.

425. Sak RJ, Ruben RJ. Recurrent middle-ear effusion in childhood: implications of temporary auditory deprivation for language and learning. Ann Otol Rhinol Laryngol 90:546, 1982.

426. Sanna M, Zini C, Gamoletti R, et al. The surgical management of childhood cholesteatoma. J Laryngol Otol 101:1221, 1987.

427. Schaefer O. Otitis media and bottle-feeding: an epidemiological study of infant feeding habits and incidence of recurrent and chronic middle-ear disease in Canadian Eskimos. Can J Public Health 62:478, 1971.

428. Schiff M, Poliquin JF, Catanzaro A, et al. Tympanosclerosis: a theory of pathogenesis. Ann Otol Rhinol Laryngol 89:1, 1980.

429. Schlieper A, Kisilevsky H, Mattingly H, et al. Mild conductive hearing loss and language development: a one-year follow-up study. Dev Behav Pediatr 6:65, 1985.

430. Schmid H, Dort JC, Fisch U. Long-term results of treatment for children's cholesteatoma. Am J Otol 12:83, 1991.

431. Schuknecht HF. Pathology of the Ear. Cambridge, MA, Harvard University Press, 1974, pp 227–233.

432. Schuknecht HF. Pathology of the Ear, 2nd ed. Philadelphia, Lea & Febiger, 1993, pp 191–234.

433. Schuring AG, Lippy WH, Rizer FM, et al. Staging for cholesteatoma in the child, adolescent, and adult. Ann Otol Rhinol Laryngol 99:256, 1990.

434. Sculerati N, Bluestone CD. Pathogenesis of cholesteatoma. Otolaryngol Clin North Am 22:859, 1989.

435. Seely DR, Gloyd SS, Omope AD, Norton SJ. Hearing loss prevalence and risk factors among Sierra Leonean children. Arch Otolaryngol Head Neck Surg 121:853, 1995.

436. Senturia BH, Bluestone CD, Lim DJ, et al. Recent advances in otitis media with effusion. Ann Otol Rhinol Laryngol 89(Suppl 68), 1980.

437. Severeid LR. Development of cholesteatoma in children with cleft palate: a longitudinal study. In McCabe BF, Sadé J, Abramson M (eds). Cholesteatoma: First International Conference. New York, Aesculapius, 1977, pp 287–292.

438. Shambaugh GE, Glasscock ME. Surgery of the Ear, 3rd ed. Philadelphia, WB Saunders, 1980, pp 432–436.

439. Sharp JF, Robinson JM. Treatment of tympanic membrane retraction pockets by excision. A prospective study. J Laryngol Otol 106:882, 1992.

440. Sheehy JL, Anderson RG. Myringoplasty: a review of 472 cases. Ann Otol Rhinol Laryngol 89:331, 1980.

441. Sheehy JL, Brachman DE, Graham MD. Complications of cholesteatoma: a report on 1024 cases. In McCabe BF, Sadé J, Abramson M (eds). Cholesteatoma: First International Conference. New York, Aesculapius, 1977, pp 420–429.

442. Sheehy JL. Cholesteatoma surgery in children. Am J Otol 6:170, 1985.

443. Sheehy JL, Linthicum FH Jr, Greenfield EC. Chronic serous mastoiditis, idiopathic hemotympanum and cholesterol granuloma of the mastoid. Laryngoscope 79:1189, 1969.

444. Sheehy JL, Patterson ME. Intact canal wall tympanoplasty with mastoidectomy: a review of 8 years' experience. Laryngoscope 77:1502, 1967.

445. Sheehy JL, Shelton C. Tympanoplasty: to stage or not to stage. Otolaryngol Head Neck Surg 104:399, 1991.

446. Shelton C, Sheehy JL. Tympanoplasty: review of 400 staged cases. Laryngoscope 100:679, 1990.

447. Shih L, de Tar T, Crabtree JA. Myringoplasty in children. Otolaryngol Head Neck Surg 105:74, 1991.

448. Siedentop KH. Eustachian tube dynamics, size of the mastoid air cell system, and results with tympanoplasty. Otolaryngol Clin North Am 1:33, 1968.

449. Siegel MI, Sadler-Kimes D, Todhunter JS. Eustachian tube cartilage shape as a factor in the epidemiology of otitis media. In Lim DJ, Bluestone CD, Klein JO, Nelson JD (eds). Recent Advances in Otitis Media. Proceedings of the Fourth International Symposium. Philadelphia, BC Decker, 1988, pp 114–117.

450. Silvola J, Palva T. Long-term results of pediatric primary one-stage cholesteatoma surgery. Int J Pediatr Otorhinolaryngol 48:101, 1999.

451. Silvola J, Palva T. One-stage revision surgery for pediatric cholesteatoma: long-term results and comparison with primary surgery. Int J Pediatr Otorhinolaryngol 56:135, 2000.

452. Smith AW, Hatcher J, Mackenzie IJ, et al. Randomised controlled trial of treatment of chronic suppurative otitis media in Kenyan schoolchildren. Lancet 348:1128, 1996.

453. Smith V, Traquina DN. Pediatric bilateral facial paralysis. Laryngoscope 108:519, 1998.

454. Smouha EE, Levenson MJ, Anand VK, Parisier SC. Modern presentations of Bezold's abscess. Arch Otolaryngol Head Neck Surg 115:1126, 1989.

455. Smyth GD. Tympanic reconstruction. Otolaryngol Clin North Am 5:111, 1972.

456. Smyth GDL, Hassard TH. Tympanoplasty in children. Am J Otol 1:119, 1980.

457. Spivey GH, Hirschhorn N. A migrant study of adopted Apache children. Johns Hopkins Med J 140:43, 1977.

458. Sobol SM, Reichert TJ, Faw KD, et al. Intramembranous and mesotympanic cholesteatomas associated with an intact tympanic membrane in children. Ann Otol Rhinol Laryngol 89:312, 1980.

459. Soldati D, Mudry A. Cholesteatoma in children: techniques and results. Int J Pediatr Otorhinolaryngol 52:269, 2000.

460. Sorensen H. Antibiotics in suppurative otitis media. Otolaryngol Clin North Am 10:45, 1977.

461. Spratley J, Silveira H, Alverez I, Pais-Clemente M. Acute mastoiditis in children: review of the current status. Int J Pediatr Otorhinolaryngol 56:33, 2000.

462. Stangerup SE, Drozdziewicz D, Tos M, Trabalzini F. Surgery for acquired cholesteatoma in children: long-term results and recurrence of cholesteatoma. J Laryngol Otol 112:742, 1998.

463. Stangerup S-E, Sederberg-Olsen J, Balle V. Autoinflation as a treatment of secretory otitis media: a randomized controlled study. Arch Otolaryngol 118:149, 1992.

464. Stenstrom C, Ingvarsson L. Late effects on ear disease in otitis-prone children: a long-term follow-up study. Acta Otolaryngol (Stockh) 115:658, 1995.

465. Stern SJ, Fazekas-May M. Cholesteatoma in the pediatric population: prognostic indicators for surgical decision making. Laryngoscope 102:1349, 1992.

466. Stewart JL. Current status of otitis media in the American Indian population. In Bluestone CD, Casselbrant ML (eds). Workshop on Epidemiology of Otitis Media. Ann Otol Rhinol Laryngol 99(suppl 149):20–22, 1990.

467. Stewart IA, Byrne W. Discharging ears in Melanesian children [letter]. N Z Med J 287, 1976.

468. Stewart MG, Troendle-Atkins J, Starke JR, Coker NJ. Nontuberculous mycobacterial mastoiditis. Arch Otolaryngol Head Neck Surg 121:225, 1995.

469. Stokroos R, Manni JJ, de Kruijk JR, Soudijn ER. Lemierre syndrome and acute mastoiditis. Arch Otolaryngol Head Neck Surg 125:589, 1999.

470. Stool SE, Berg AO, Berman S, et al. Otitis media and effusion in young children. Clinical Practice Guideline No. 12. AHCPR Publication No. 94-0622. Agency for Health Care Policy and Research, Public Health Service, U.S. Dept. of Health and Human Services, July 1994, Rockville, MD.

471. Stool SE, Randall P. Unexpected ear disease in infants with cleft palate. Cleft Palate J 4:99, 1967.

472. Storrs LA. Contraindications to tympanoplasty. Laryngoscope 86:79, 1976.

473. Stuart JE, Quayle CJ, Lewis AN, Harper J. Health, hearing and ear disease in Aboriginal school children. Med J Aust 1:855, 1972.

474. Sudhoff H, Dazert S, Gonzales AM, et al. Angiogenesis and angiogenic growth factors in middle ear cholesteatoma. Am J Otol 21:793, 2000.

475. Sudhoff H, Tos M. Pathogenesis of attic cholesteatoma: clinical and immunochemical support for combination of retraction theory and proliferation theory. Am J Otol 21:786, 2000.

476. Supance JS, Bluestone CD. Perilymph fistulas in infants and children. Otolaryngol Head Neck Surg 91:663, 1983.

477. Takahashi H, Honjo W, Kurata K, Sugimaru T. Steroid and tube insertion for cholesterol granuloma: a preliminary study. In Lim DJ, Bluestone CD, Casselbrant ML, et al (eds). Recent Advances in Otitis Media—Proceedings fo the Sixth International Symposium. Hamilton, Ontario, BC Decker, 1995, pp 414–416.

478. Tanaka Y, Kojima H, Miyazaki H, et al. Roles of cytokines and cell cycle regulating substances in proliferation of cholesteatoma epithelium. Laryngoscope 109:1102, 1999.

479. Tarabichi M. Endoscopic management of cholesteatoma: long-term results. Otolaryngol Head Neck Surg 122:874, 2000.

480. Teed RW. Cholesteatoma verum tympani. Its relationship to first epibranchial placode. Arch Otolaryngol 24:455, 1936.

481. Teele DW, Klein JO, Rosner BA, and the Greater Boston Otitis Media Study Group. Otitis media with effusion during the first three years of life and development of speech and language. Pediatrics 74:282, 1984.

482. Thedinger BA, Nadol JB, Montgomery WW, et al. Radiographic diagnosis, surgical treatment, and long-term follow-up of cholesterol granulomas of the petrous apex. Laryngoscope 99:896, 1989.

483. Thomassin JM, Korchia D, Doris JMD. Endoscopic-guided otosurgery in the prevention of residual cholesteatomas. Laryngoscope 103:939, 1993.

484. Thorp MA, Kruger J, Oliver S, et al. The antibacterial activity of acetic acid and Burrow's solution as topical otological preparations. J Laryngol Otol 112:925, 1998.

485. Timmermans FJ, Gerson S. Chronic granulomatous otitis media in bottle-fed Inuit children. Can Med Assoc J 122:545, 1980.

486. Todd NW, Bowman CA. Otitis media at Canyon Day, Arizona: a 16-year follow-up in Apache Indians. Arch Otolaryngol 111:606, 1985.

487. Tong MCF, Woo JKS, van Hasslet CA. A double-blind comparative study of ofloxicin otic drops versus neomycin-polymyxin B-hydrocortisone otic drops in the medical treatment of chronic suppurative otitis media. J Laryngol Otol 110:309, 1996.

488. Tonkin S. Maori infant health: study of morbidity and medicosocial aspects. N Z Med J 72:229, 1970.

489. Tos M. A new pathogenesis of mesotympanic (congenital) cholesteatoma. Laryngoscope 110:1890, 2000.

490. Tos M. Incidence, etiology and pathogenesis of cholesteatoma in children. Adv Otorhinolaryngol 40:110, 1988.

491. Tos M, Lau T. Stability of tympanoplasty in children. Otolaryngol Clin North Am 22:15, 1989.

492. Tos M, Orntoft S, Stangerup SE. Results of tympanoplasy in children after 15 to 27 years. Ann Otol Rhinol Laryngol 109:17, 2000.

493. Tos M, Poulsen G. Attic retractions following secretory otitis. Acta Otolaryngol 89:479, 1980.

494. Tos M. Treatment of cholesteatoma in children. A long-term study of results. Am J Otol 4:189, 1983.

495. Tovi F, Gatot A. Bone scan diagnosis of masked mastoiditis. Ann Otol Rhinol Laryngol 101:707, 1992.

496. Tschopp CF. Chronic otitis media and cholesteatoma in Alaskan native children. In McCabe BF, Sadé J, Abramson M (eds). Cholesteatoma: First International Conference. New York, Aesculapius, 1977, pp 290–292.

497. Tumarkin A. A contribution to the study of middle ear suppuration with special reference to the pathogeny and treatment of cholesteatoma. J Laryngol Otol 53:685, 1938.

498. Tutkun A, Ozagar A, Koc A, et al. Treatment of chronic ear disease: topical ciprofloxacin vs. topical gentamicin. Arch Otolaryngol Head Neck Surg 121:1414, 1995.

499. Valvassori GE, Buckingham RA. Middle ear masses mimicking glomus tumors: radiographic and otoscopic recognition. Ann Otol Rhinol Laryngol 83:606, 1974.

500. Vanden Abeele D, Coen E, Parizel PM, Van de Heyning P. Can MRI replace a second look operation in cholesteatoma surgery? Acta Otolaryngol 119:555, 1999.

501. Vartiainen E, Kansanen M. Tympanomastoidectomy for chronic otitis media without cholesteatoma. Otolaryngol Head Neck Surg 106:230, 1992.

502. Vartiainen E, Vartiainen J. Effect of aerobic bacteriology on the clinical presentation and treatment results of chronic suppurative otitis media. J Laryngol Otol 110:315, 1996.

503. Vartiainen E, Vartiainen J. Tympanoplasty in young patients: the role of adenoidectomy. Otolaryngol Head Neck Surg 117:583, 1997.

504. Ventry IM. Research design issues in studies of effects of middle-ear effusion. Pediatrics 71:644, 1983.

505. Vernon-Feagans. Impact of otitis media on child quality of life. In Rosenfeld RM, Bluestone CD (eds). Evidence-Based Otitis Media. Hamilton, Ontario, BC Decker, 1999, pp 353–373.

506. Virtanen H, Palva T, Jauhiainen T. The prognostic value of eustachian tube function measurements in tympanoplastic surgery. Acta Otolaryngol (Stockh) 90:317, 1980.

507. von Troltsch AF. Handbuch der Ohrenheilkunde. Leipzig, W Engelmann, 1869.

508. Vrabec JT, Deskin RW, Grady JJ. Meta-analysis of pediatric tympanoplasty. Arch Otolaryngol Head Neck Surg 125:530, 1999.

509. Walby AP, Barrera A, Schuknecht HF. Cochlear pathology in chronic suppurative otitis media. Ann Otol Rhinol Laryngol 92(suppl 103):1–19, 1983.

510. Watanabe H, Shin T, Fukaura J, et al. Total actual speaking time in infants and children with otitis media with effusion. Int J Pediatr Otorhinolaryngol 10:171, 1985.

511. Weber PC, Bluestone CD, Kenna MA, Kelly RH. Correlation of beta$_2$-transferrin and middle-ear abnormalities in congenital perilymphatic fistula. Am J Otol 16:277, 1995.

512. Weber PC, Kelly RH, Bluestone CD, et al. β_2-Transferrin confirms perilymphatic fistula in children. Otolaryngol Head Neck Surg 110:381, 1994.

513. Weber PC, Perez BA, Bluestone CD. Congenital perilymphatic fistula and associated middle ear abnormalities. Laryngoscope 103:160, 1993.

514. Webster DB. Conductive loss affects auditory neural soma size only during a sensitive postnatal period. In Lim DJ, Bluestone CD, Klein JO, et al (eds). Recent Advances in Otitis Media with Effusion. Burlington, Ontario, BC Decker, 1983, pp 344–346.

515. Weiderhold ML, Zajtchuk JT, Vap JG, et al. Hearing loss in relation to physical properties of middle-ear effusions. Ann Otol Rhinol Laryngol 89:185, 1980.

516. Weissman JL, Weber PC, Bluestone CD. Congenital perilymphatic fistula: CT appearance of middle ear and inner ear anomalies. Otolaryngol Head Neck Surg 111:243, 1994.

517. Welby PL, Keller DS, Cromien JL, et al. Resistance to penicillin and no-beta-lactam antibiotics of Streptococcus pneumoniae at a children's hospital. Pediatr Infect Dis J 13:281, 1994.

518. Welling DB, Forrest LA, Goll F. Safety of ototopical antibiotics. Laryngoscope 105:472, 1995.

519. Wendt H. Desquamative Entzundung des Mittelohrs (Cholesteatom des Felsenbeins). Arch Ohrenheilk (Leipz) 14:428, 1873.

520. Wiet RJ. Patterns of ear disease in the Southwestern American Indian. Arch Otolaryngol 105:381, 1979.

521. Wiet RJ, DeBlanc GB, Stewart J, et al. Natural history of otitis media in the American native. Ann Otol Rhinol Laryngol 89:14, 1980.

522. Williamson IG, Dunleavey J, Bain J, Robinson D. The natural history of otitis media with effusion: three-year study of the incidence and prevalence of abnormal tympanograms in four South West Hampshire infant and first schools. J Laryngol Otol 108:930, 1994.

523. Wilks J, Maw R, Peters TJ, et al. Randomized controlled trial of early surgery versus watchful waiting for glue ear: the effect on behavioral problems in pre-school children. Clin Otolaryngol 25:209, 2000.

524. Wishik SM, Kramm ER, Koch EM. Audiometric testing of school children. Public Health Rep 73:265, 1958.

525. Wittmaack K. Wie ensteht ein genuines Cholesteatom? Arch Ohren Nasen Kehlkopfh 137:306, 1933.

526. Wolf M, Primov-Fever A, Barshack I, Kronenberg J. Granular myringitis in children. Int J Pediatr Otorhinolaryngol 57:17, 2001.

527. Wright PF, Sell SH, McConnell KB, et al. Impact of recurrent otitis media on middle-ear function, hearing and language. J Pediatr 118:581, 1988.

528. Yellon RF, Rose E, Kenna MA, et al. Sensorineural hearing loss from quinolinic acid: a neurotoxin in middle ear effusions. Laryngoscope 104:176, 1994.

529. Yuen APW, Chau PY, Wei WI. Bacteriology of chronic suppurative otitis media: ofloxacin susceptibility. J Otolaryngol 24:206, 1995.

530. Yuen PW, Lau SK, Chau PY, et al. Ofloxacin eardrop treatment for active chronic suppurative otitis media: prospective randomized study. Am J Otol 15:670, 1994.

531. Young C, McConnell F. Retardation of vocabulary development in hard of hearing children. Except Child Ann 368, 1957.

532. Yung MW. The effect of nasal continuous positive airway pressure on normal ears and on ears with atelectasis. Am J Otol 20:568, 1999.

533. Zeisel SA, Roberts JE, Gunn EB, et al. Prospective surveillance for otitis media with effusion among black infants in group child care. J Pediatr 127:875, 1995.

534. Zinkus PW, Gottlieb MI, Schapiro M. Developmental and psychoeducational sequelae of chronic otitis media. Am J Dis Child 132:1100, 1978.

535. Zollner F. Tympanosclerosis. J Laryngol Otol 70:77, 1956.

536. Zonis RD. Chronic otitis media in the southwestern American Indians: prevalence. Arch Otolaryngol Head Neck Surg 88:360, 1968.

27

Intracranial Complications of Otitis Media and Mastoiditis

Charles D. Bluestone, M.D., and Jerome O. Klein, M.D.

There has been an overall decline in the incidence of suppurative intracranial complications of otitis media and mastoiditis since the advent of antimicrobial agents. Today, these complications occur more often in association with chronic suppurative otitis media and mastoiditis, with or without cholesteatoma, than in association with acute otitis media.[43]

The middle ear and mastoid air cells are adjacent to important structures, including the dura of the posterior and middle cranial fossa, the sigmoid venous sinus of the brain, and the inner ear. Suppuration in the middle ear or mastoid, or both, may spread to these structures, producing the following suppurative intracranial complications: meningitis, extradural abscess, subdural empyema, focal encephalitis, brain abscess, lateral (sigmoid) sinus thrombosis, and otitic hydrocephalus (Fig. 27–1).

Having more than one intracranial complication occur is common and frequently depends on the route of infection. Thus, a patient may have meningitis, lateral sinus thrombosis, and cerebellar abscess, or other combinations of suppurative disease involving adjacent areas.[50] In a review from Thailand of 43 children and adults in whom intracranial complications from otitis media developed, 44% had two or more complications, and meningitis was the most common co-disease.[45] A more recent report from India of 45 patients reported that 24% had more than one intracranial complication.[66] Also, multiple complications have occurred in highly industrialized nations as recently reported by Go and associates[25] in which they encountered three patients who had sigmoid sinus thrombosis in association with either an epidural abscess or meningitis.

Any child with acute or chronic otitis media in whom one or more of the following signs or symptoms develop, especially while receiving medical treatment, should be suspected of having a suppurative intracranial complication: persistent headache, lethargy, malaise, irritability, severe otalgia, onset of fever, nausea, and vomiting. The following are definitive signs and symptoms necessitating an intensive search for an intracranial complication: stiff neck, focal seizures, ataxia, blurred vision, papilledema, diplopia, hemiplegia, aphasia, dysdiadochokinesia, intention tremor, dysmetria, and hemianopia. Conversely, children with intracranial infection, such as meningitis or a brain abscess, must have middle-ear mastoid disease ruled out as the origin of, or concomitant with, the central nervous system (CNS) disease.

In children who have acute otitis media or chronic middle-ear and mastoid disease (e.g., chronic suppurative otitis media, cholesteatoma), the presence of headache, even though this is a nonspecific symptom, should indicate a potential complication. Irritability, lethargy, or other changes in personality may be secondary to intracranial spread of the infection. Even though fever is common with an acute infection of the ear, persistent or recurrent fever may be a potentially dangerous sign. Fever is rarely present in children with chronic suppurative otitis media and, when found, may be a hallmark of an impending intracranial complication. The presence of both persisting fever and headache should alert the clinician. Albers[1] recently confirmed the association of persistent fever and headache as the most common early symptoms of an intracranial complication and stressed the need to make an early diagnosis to reduce the risk of morbidity and mortality. Schwaber and colleagues[81] reviewed 12 cases of neurotologic complications of chronic suppurative otitis media, which included epidural abscess, meningitis, petrous apicitis, and lateral sinus thrombosis, and concluded that purulent malodorous otorrhea, headache, and fever were the most significant early findings. An altered mental status was a late finding. In a study from India, Rupa and Raman[76] compared a large group of patients with intracranial complications of otitis media and mastoiditis with patients who had had a mastoidectomy but without a complication. They found that those who had a complication were younger, had a shorter duration of ear discharge, and had had a perforation of the pars tensa.

The diagnosis of intracranial complications has been greatly improved since the advent and widespread availability of computed tomography (CT) and magnetic resonance imaging (MRI); if these are not available, arteriography should be used. CT can frequently identify extradural, subdural, and brain abscess, but the addition of contrast material enhances the diagnosis, especially when lateral sinus thrombosis is suspected.[38, 91] MRI pro-

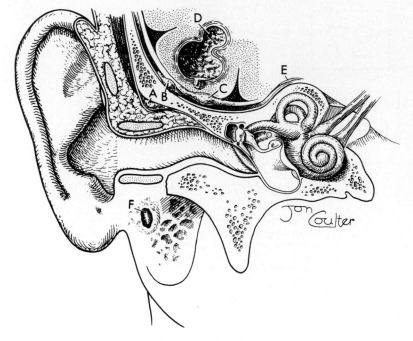

FIGURE 27–1. Suppurative complications of otitis media and mastoiditis. *A,* Subperiosteal abscess; *B,* extradural abscess; *C,* subdural empyema; *D,* brain abscess; *E,* meningitis; *F,* lateral sinus thrombosis.

vides excellent resolution of intracranial suppuration and its consequences (edema, thrombosis, and hydrocephalus) (see Chap. 12).

Intracranial extension of infection may be due to any of the following: (1) progressive thrombophlebitis, permitting the inflammatory process to spread through the intact bone (osteothrombophlebitis), (2) erosion of the bony walls of the middle ear or mastoid (osteitis), and (3) extension along preformed pathways—the round window, dehiscent sutures, skull fracture, or congenital or surgically acquired bony dehiscences (mastoidectomy with dura exposure).

This section presents the incidence, pathogenesis, etiology, diagnosis, management, and outcome of suppurative intracranial complications as they relate to infants and children. After a description of the specific complications, there is a section on the timing and type of otologic surgery appropriate for children. However, a detailed description of the operative procedures has not been included; the latest otologic and neurologic surgical techniques are adequately described and illustrated in currently available texts listed at the end of the chapter.

Incidence

Before the introduction of antimicrobial agents, intracranial complications developed in 2.3% of all patients with acute and chronic suppurative otitis media, and two thirds of these cases were due to chronic disease of the middle ear.[97] The rate was even higher in patients with mastoiditis. In 1935, Kafka[44] reported that an intracranial complication developed in 6.4% of 3225 patients with mastoiditis and, of these patients, 76.4% died as result of their infection. The effect of antibiotics for treating otitis media and thus reducing these potentially life-threatening complications was dramatic. Lund[55] reported the mortality rate from intracranial complications decreased from 36% from 1939 to 1949 (pre- and early antibiotic era) to

6% between 1950 and 1960, to 0% from 1961 to 1971. A report from Finland in 1953 provided evidence that the dramatic decrease of these complications was due to the use of antibiotics. In this report, in which 629 patients with acute otitis media were studied, 176 patients were given penicillin and 453 received no antimicrobial agent.[52] There were no complications in the penicillin-treated group, but complications developed in nine patients in the untreated group: seven had mastoiditis, one had meningitis, and one patient died as the result of otogenic sinus thrombosis and brain abscess.

In the antibiotic era, intracranial complications are uncommon, but nearly two thirds of such complications are still caused by chronic ear disease.[41] Panda and colleagues[66] recently reported from India that, between 1992 and 1995, chronic otitis media was responsible for suppurative complications in children, even when ear drainage was of short duration. However, Dawes[13] reported that most intracranial complications in children were secondary to acute otitis media. In a study from Boston, Friedman and co-workers[21] reviewed the hospital charts of 259 children who had CNS infection between 1981 and 1984 and reported that 92 patients (36%) had associated acute middle-ear disease. It is uncertain, however, whether the middle ear was the actual source of the intracranial infection. Ritter[73] reviewed 152 cases of cholesteatoma, about one half of which were present in patients younger than 20 years. The study represented cases between 1965 and 1970 and included four cases with suppurative intracranial complications: two patients with sigmoid sinus thrombosis and one patient each with extradural abscess and brain abscess. In a review by Sheehy et al[86] of 1024 operations for cholesteatoma performed from 1965 through 1974 in 949 patients, 17.7% of whom were 15 years old or younger, only one patient had meningitis and in only two patients was there an extradural abscess. However, neither of these complications occurred in children. In a recent study of suppurative intracranial complications of

TABLE 27–1. Distribution of 48 Suppurative Intracranial Complications of Otitis Media* in 37 Children—Children's Hospital of Pittsburgh, 1980–1997

	Number of Patients
Meningitis	20
Epidural abscess	7
Brain abscess	1
Lateral sinus thrombosis	9
Otitic hydrocephalus	9
Cavernous sinus thrombosis	1
Carotid artery thrombosis	1
Total	48†

* Acute otitis media and chronic suppurative otitis media.
† 9 (24.3%) patients had coexisting complications.
From Don DM, Goldstein NA, Alper CM, et al. Intracranial complications of acute and chronic suppurative otitis media in children [abstract]. Presented at the American Society of Pediatric Otolaryngology, Palm Desert, Calif, April 1999.

acute otitis media and chronic suppurative otitis media in 37 consecutive children undergoing treatment at the Children's Hospital of Pittsburgh from January 1980 through June 1997, meningitis was the most common complication[17] (Table 27–1). This has also been the case in other reports in the antibiotic era.[43, 49, 69] In a report from South Africa, Singh and Maharaj[87a] found that, of 181 patients with intracranial complications (74% of whom were 20 years old or younger), 51% had a brain abscess and only 12% had meningitis. Cholesteatoma caused 57% of the complications.

These complications are still associated with relatively high mortality rates in developing nations. Indeed, in a recent report from Turkey, Osma and associates[65] reviewed cases of 39 children and adults in whom intracranial complications developed between 1990 and 1999, resulting in a 26% mortality rate. Intracranial complications of otitis media and mastoiditis are most common in developing countries, such as South Africa and India, but still occur in highly industrialized nations in both children and adults.[2] Indeed, in a recent review from the Netherlands, Dhooge and colleagues[15] reported that, between 1993 and 1996, 21 children had an intracranial complication from otitis media.

Meningitis

Meningitis may be associated with infections of the middle ear in three circumstances: (1) direct invasion, in which a suppurative focus in the middle ear or mastoid spreads through the dura and extends to the pia-arachnoid, causing generalized meningitis, (2) inflammation in an adjacent area, in which the meninges may become inflamed if there is suppuration in an adjacent area such as a subdural abscess, a brain abscess, or lateral sinus thrombophlebitis, and (3) concurrent infection, in which otitis media arises by contiguous spread from an infectious focus in the upper respiratory tract, and meningitis results from invasion of the blood from the upper respiratory focus. The infections are simultaneous, but meningitis does not arise from the middle-ear infection.

Hematogenous spread is the most common route. Less common is direct invasion through congenital preformed pathways or through thrombophlebitis, which usually extends to the middle cranial fossa through the petrosquamous suture or to the posterior cranial fossa through the subarcuate fossa (i.e., the first route). In the preantibiotic era, Lindsay[53] examined the histopathology of temporal bones of patients who had acute otitis media and meningitis and found that most of the specimens had evidence of direct spread of the infection through the petrous apex. However, since the advent of the widespread use of antimicrobial agents, extension of the infection has been thought to be along preformed pathways or by direct extension through the dura. Spread of infection from the middle ear and mastoid through the inner ear to the meninges is another pathway, but this is thought to be rare compared with the other pathogenic mechanisms.[80] In a review of 39 Israeli children with intracranial complications of ear and sinus disease, 25 (64%) had meningitis, and in 21 of these, otitis media was the purported source of the infection.[50] However, Eavey and co-workers[19] examined 16 temporal bones from children who had died of meningitis, finding otitis media in 14 bones, but could find no evidence that the middle-ear infection had spread to the meninges. Richardson and co-workers[72] recently provided support for this finding. They could not find any evidence that either acute otitis media or otitis media with effusion was the cause of meningitis that developed in 124 children in Great Britain, especially since 92 (74%) had meningococcal meningitis, which is not a otitic bacterial pathogen. However, meningitis is still a complication of otitis media in developing countries. From South Africa, Singh and Maharaj[87a] reported that, of 181 patients with intracranial complications, 22 (12%) had meningitis (Table 27–2). As shown in Table 27–3, a more recent review from Thailand by Kangsanarak and co-workers[45]

TABLE 27–2. Intracranial Complications of Otitis Media and Mastoiditis in 181 Patients in South Africa, 1985–1990

	Intracranial Complications					
Cholesteatoma	Brain Abscess	Subdural Empyema	Lateral Sinus Thrombosis	Meningitis	Extradural Empyema	Total Complications
Yes	54	25	19	9	11	118 (57)†
No	39	11	17	13	8	88 (43)
Total complications	93 (51)*	36 (20)	36 (20)	22 (12)	19 (10)	206

* Percentage with complications of 181 patients.
† Percentage with and without cholesteatoma of 206 complications.
Modified from Singh B, Maharaj TJ. Radical mastoidectomy: its place in otitic intracranial complications. J Laryngol Otol 107:1113, 1993.

TABLE 27-3. Intracranial Complications of Otitis Media in 43 Patients from Thailand between 1983 and 1990

	Number of Cases*	Percentage
Meningitis	22	51
Brain abscess	18	42
Lateral sinus thrombosis	8	19
Extradural abscess	7	16
Perisinus abscess	5	12
Cerebellitis	2	5
Internal jugular vein thrombosis	2	5
Otitic hydrocephalus	2	5
Encephalitis	1	2
Cavernous sinus thrombosis	1	2

* Some patients had more than one complication.
From Kangsanarak J, Fooanant S, Ruckphaopunt K, et al. Extracranial and intracranial complications of suppurative otitis media. Report of 102 cases. J Laryngol Otol 107:999, 1993.

TABLE 27-4. Age of Infants and Children with Meningitic Complications Related to Stage of Ear Disease Treated at the Wake Forest University Medical Center, 1963-1982

Age	Acute Ear Disease	Chronic Ear Disease	Total
12 mo	38	1	39
13-24 mo	15	2	17
2-5 yr	4	0	4
6-10 yr	1	0	1
11-20 yr	0	4	4
Total	58	7	65

Adapted from Gower DJ, McQuirt WF, Kelly DL. Intracranial complications of ear disease in a pediatric population with special emphasis on subdural effusion and empyema. South Med J 78:429, 1985.

reported that meningitis was the most common intracranial complication, either as the only complication or in combination with another one; 51% of 43 children and adults had meningitis.

Clinical Presentation

The symptoms of meningitis caused by any of the three mechanisms include fever, headache, neck stiffness, and altered consciousness. A CT scan should be considered before lumbar puncture if there are signs of increased intracranial pressure, to define the presence of abscess or mass effect. Examination of cerebrospinal fluid (CSF) reveals pleocytosis and elevation of protein concentration in all routes of infection, but depression of sugar levels is common in only the first and third routes. Polymorphonuclear leukocytes are the predominant cell type in the early phase of meningitis caused by the first and third mechanisms. When infection occurs by the second mechanism, it is likely to be more chronic; therefore, lymphocytes usually predominate. Organisms are usually isolated from the spinal fluid when meningitis is caused by the first and third mechanisms, but not when the second one is the cause. Thus, meningitis from the second mechanism may be defined as an aseptic meningitis (clinical signs of meningitis associated with cells in the CSF but without bacteria isolated by usual laboratory techniques). Gower and colleagues[26] provide information about 65 children and adults with suppurative intracranial complications of acute or chronic otitis media (Table 27-4).

Microbiology

The bacteria responsible for meningitis are associated with acute otitis media, and the common agents of meningitis are *Streptococcus pneumoniae* and *Haemophilus influenzae* type b. About 20% of all cases of acute otitis media are due to *H. influenzae,* but fewer than 10% of these are type b.[32] Feigin[20] reported that 14% of children with *H. influenzae* type b otitis media also had meningitis. Invasive disease resulting from *H. influenzae* type b has been markedly reduced since the introduction in 1990 of the conjugate polysaccharide vaccine for infants, begin-

ning at 2 months of age. In the review of 20 infants and children at the Children's Hospital of Pittsburgh in whom meningitis developed as a complication of otitis media and mastoiditis between 1980 and 1997, *H. influenzae* and *Pneumococcus* were the most common pathogens isolated from the middle ear, mastoid, or both. *H. influenzae* was isolated in 12 children (60%), of which cases, 11 were type b and one could not be typed; 11 cases (55%) were *S. pneumoniae* infections, of which one was penicillin-resistant. *H. influenzae* and *S. pneumoniae* were also the most frequently isolated bacteria from the CSF.[6]

Management

Meningitis should be treated initially with high doses of antimicrobial agents. If the causative agent is unknown, a third-generation cephalosporin (ceftriaxone or cefotaxime) or a combination of ampicillin and chloramphenicol is administered. Because of concern for multidrug-resistant *S. pneumoniae*, vancomycin (with uniform efficacy for *Pneumococcus*) should be added to the cephalosporin regimen in communities where resistant strains are prevalent. The regimen may be modified after results of CSF cultures are known. If cultures are negative and there is concern that the aseptic process may be caused by a suppurative focus, diagnostic tests should be performed to identify the focus, obtain material for culture, and clear the local infection, usually by incision and drainage. If an acute otitis media or otitis media with effusion is present, tympanocentesis and myringotomy (for drainage) should be performed immediately to identify the causative organism within the middle ear. If otorrhea is present, a culture should be obtained from the middle ear, if possible. Likewise, if chronic suppurative otitis media is present, the purulent material from the middle ear should be aspirated and sent for Gram stain, culture, and susceptibility tests (see Chap. 10).

If an acute mastoiditis with osteitis is present, a complete simple mastoidectomy is indicated as soon as the child can tolerate a general anesthetic. If chronic suppurative otitis media or cholesteatoma, or both, is present, then tympanomastoidectomy is frequently required and should be performed when the patient is stable. If there is bilateral middle-ear disease and the offending side is uncertain, then bilateral tympanomastoidectomy is a reasonable procedure.[42] Most otologic surgeons attempt to perform hearing preservation surgery for these patients, instead of the radical or modified radical mastoidectomy recommended in the past. However, appropriate management of any of the suppurative intratemporal complications (e.g., petrositis, labyrinthitis) or intracranial complications (e.g., extradural abscess) may require surgical management and consultation with a neurologist or a neurologic surgeon, or both.

Occasionally, after trauma to the temporal bone, an acute otitis media develops that is complicated by meningitis. Tympanocentesis and myringotomy should be performed immediately for culture and drainage and any otorrhea should be cultured. However, exploration of the middle ear and mastoid may be necessary later to search for and repair possible defects in the dura, especially if otorrhea or CSF is present.

Prognosis

When management is appropriate for both the meningitis and the suppurative focus within the temporal bone, the outcome should be favorable, although some studies report high mortality rates despite the use of antimicrobial agents. Kessler and co-workers[47] reported a mortality rate of 33% in their series of 51 cases of otitic meningitis. In the study by Gower and associates,[26] a 7% mortality rate was reported in 58 patients (mostly infants), but the rate was 43% in the seven patients in whom meningitis developed secondary to chronic ear disease. Overall mortality rate was 10.7%.

Extradural Abscess

Extradural (epidural) abscess usually results from the destruction of bone adjacent to dura by cholesteatoma or infection, or both. This occurs when granulation tissue and purulent material collect between the lateral aspect of the dura and adjacent temporal bone. Dural granulation tissue within a bony defect is much more common than an actual accumulation of pus. When an abscess is present, there may also be a dural sinus thrombosis or, less commonly, a subdural or brain abscess. If extensive bone destruction has occurred in the presence of acute mastoid osteitis (acute "coalescent" mastoiditis), an extradural abscess may develop in the area of the sigmoid dural sinus.

Symptoms can include severe earache, low-grade fever, and headache in the temporal region with deep local throbbing pain, but the more common extradural abscess encountered today may produce no signs or symptoms. Frequently, an asymptomatic extradural abscess is found in patients undergoing elective mastoidectomy for cholesteatoma.

Otorrhea may be present when an extradural abscess is diagnosed and is characteristically profuse, creamy, and pulsatile. Compression of the ipsilateral jugular vein may increase the rate of discharge and the degree of pulsation. There is usually no accompanying fever, but malaise and anorexia may be observed. Generally, there are no neurologic signs, intracranial pressure is normal, and it is difficult to detect any displacement of the brain. CSF cell

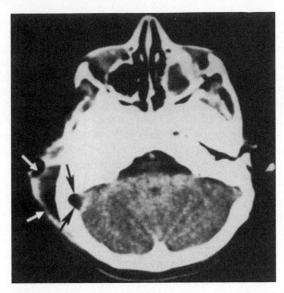

FIGURE 27–2. Computed tomogram (CT) of a 9-year-old girl showing a right perisinus extradural abscess (*black arrows*) as a complication of acute mastoiditis with osteitis and a subperiosteal abscess (*white arrows*). There had been a 1-week history of hearing loss, otalgia, and profuse, foul-smelling otorrhea, and a 3-day history of high fever, postauricular swelling, disorientation, and irritability, which persisted in spite of parenterally administered antimicrobial agents. A complete simple mastoidectomy and drainage of the extradural abscess resulted in a favorable outcome.

count and pressure are normal unless meningitis is also present. CT may demonstrate a sizable extradural abscess (Fig. 27–2).

Even though identification of the infecting organism and appropriate antimicrobial therapy can help prevent the development of an intradural complication from an extradural abscess, the treatment of extradural abscess itself consists of surgical drainage. A mastoidectomy is performed, enough bone is removed so that the dura of the middle and posterior fossae may be inspected directly, the extradural abscess is identified and removed (in some instances a drain is also inserted), and the otologic procedure that will provide optimal exteriorization of the diseased area is completed by removing all the granulation tissue until normal dura is found.

Subdural Empyema

Subdural empyema is a collection of purulent material within the potential space between the dura externally and arachnoid membrane internally. Since the pus collects in a preformed space, it is correctly termed empyema rather than abscess. Subdural empyema may develop as a direct extension of infection or, more rarely, by thrombophlebitis through venous channels. Today, it is one of the rarer complications of otitis media and mastoiditis in highly developed nations, and when subdural empyema is diagnosed, sinusitis is usually the origin. In a review of 19 patients with this diagnosis at Duke University Hospital from 1979 to 1988, Hoyt and Fisher[37] reported that sinusitis was the cause in nine patients (53%) and otitis media in only two, both of whom were infants.

However, in underdeveloped and developing countries, otitis media is still a relatively frequent cause of this suppurative complication. In a study from India, Pathak and colleagues[68] reported on the 41 cases they treated from 1977 to 1988. Otitis media was the cause in 15 (37%) and there were 22 children in this series, including 11 infants. A similar experience was reported from South Africa by Bok and Peter.[7] They reviewed 90 patients with this diagnosis from 1979 to 1991 and found 14 children in whom the cause was otitis media. Subdural empyema is not as common a complication of otitis media as it is when paranasal sinusitis is the cause.[16]

Clinical Presentation and Diagnosis

A child who has a subdural empyema is extremely toxic and febrile. There are usually the signs and symptoms of a locally expanding intracranial mass along with severe headache in the temporoparietal area. CNS findings may include seizures, hemiplegia, dysmetria, belligerent behavior, somnolence, stupor, deviation of the eyes, dysphagia, sensory deficits, stiff neck, and a positive Kernig sign. Hemiplegia and jacksonian epilepsy in a child with suppurative disease of the middle ear and mastoid are usually indicative of a subdural empyema. CT scan with contrast enhancement is often diagnostic of the process.[7] The peripheral white blood cell count is high, and there is a predominance of polymorphonuclear leukocyte. The CSF glucose concentration is normal, and no microorganisms are seen on smear or culture of the CSF.

Management and Outcome

Management of subdural empyema includes intensive intravenous antimicrobial therapy, anticonvulsants, and neurosurgical drainage of the empyema through bur holes or craniotomies. Percutaneous needle aspiration in infants has also been successful.[14, 68] Corticosteroids are occasionally needed to diminish severe edema despite their effects on the inflammatory response. Mastoid surgery to locate and drain the source of infection is usually delayed until after neurosurgical intervention has yielded some improvement in neurologic status. The condition still carries a mortality rate of 13% to 55%,[89] and more than half of those children who recover have some neurologic deficit.

Focal Otitic Encephalitis

Focal otitic encephalitis is a localized area of the brain that becomes edematous and inflamed as a sequela of acute or chronic otitis media or of one or more of the suppurative complications of these disorders, such as extradural abscess or dural sinus thrombophlebitis. The signs and symptoms may be similar to those that are characteristic of a brain abscess, except that there is no suppuration within the brain. Ataxia, nystagmus, vomiting, and giddiness indicate a possible focus within the cerebellum; drowsiness, disorientation, restlessness, seizures, and coma may indicate a cerebral focus. In both sites, headache may be present. However, since these signs and symptoms are also commonly associated with a brain abscess or subdural empyema, needle aspiration may be necessary to rule out an abscess. CT or MRI can help make this distinction. If an abscess is not thought to be present, the focal encephalitis should be treated by administering therapeutic doses of antimicrobial agents and by an appropriate otologic surgical procedure to remove the infection. This should be performed as soon as possible, since failure to control the source of the infection within the temporal bone, as well as the focal encephalitis, may result in the development of a brain abscess. Anticonvulsive medication is given when there is cerebral involvement.

Brain Abscess

Infants and children have the highest incidence of brain abscess.[9] However, the incidence of brain abscess associated with suppurative infection originating in the middle ear has decreased significantly in the antibiotic era. From 1930 to 1960, there were 89 cases of otogenic brain abscess at the Otolaryngological Hospital of the University of Helsinki; between 1961 and 1969, there were only three cases.[95] Several studies have reported that infection of the middle ear and mastoid was the predominant source of infection when abscess in the brain occurred in children.[3, 54, 60] However, Jadavji and co-workers[40] reviewed 74 cases of brain abscess diagnosed at Toronto Hospital for Sick Children between 1960 and 1984 and found cyanotic congenital heart disease (24%) to be the most common cause; 10 children (14%) had chronic otitis media with or without mastoiditis. Nalbone and co-workers[62] reviewed the records of 45 consecutive patients admitted to their hospital in Syracuse from 1975 to 1990 and found only five cases that had an otogenic origin; three adults had an associated cholesteatoma, and only two infants had an abscess. In both infants, the cause was acute otitis media. Chronic suppurative otitis media with cholesteatoma is thought to be more commonly the cause when brain abscess is present, but Browning[11] found that 10 of 26 consecutive patients with brain abscess had chronic ear disease without cholesteatoma.

Currently, South Africa appears to have the highest incidence of reported cases of otogenic brain abscess in the world. A total of 173 cases have been reported during the 1980s from three centers,[57, 79, 99] which has been attributed to the relative lack of primary health care in certain regions in that country.[88]

Otogenic abscess of the brain may follow directly from acute or chronic middle-ear and mastoid infection or may follow the development of an adjacent infection, such as lateral sinus thrombophlebitis, petrositis, or meningitis. The dura overlying the infected mastoid is invaded either along vascular pathways or by adherence of the dura to underlying infected bone. Chronic otitis media or mastoiditis with or without cholesteatoma may lead to erosion of the tegmen tympani by pressure necrosis and perforation of the bone, with resultant inflammation of the dura and invasion by pathogenic organisms. An extradural abscess occurs with subsequent infiltration of the dura and spreads to the subdural space. A localized subdural abscess or leptomeningitis ensues. Invasion of brain tissue follows, and the various stages of abscess formation take place: inflammatory reaction, suppuration, necrosis and liquefaction, and development of a fibrinous capsule. If delimitation of the abscess does not occur, infection may rarely extend to the meninges or rupture into the ventricles.

A brain abscess that is due to otitis media and mastoiditis is in an area closest to the primary source of infection. Thus, temporal lobe abscesses occur after invasion through the tegmen tympani or petrous bone. Cerebellar abscesses occur when the infectious focus is the posterior surface of the petrous bone or thrombophlebitis of the lateral sinus. An abscess occurs more commonly in the temporal lobe than in the cerebellum, and multiple abscesses are not uncommon.

The natural history of brain abscesses if left untreated includes resorption and healing through gliosis and calcification, spontaneous rupture through a fistulous tract, or spillage into the ventricles or subarachnoid space, producing encephalitis or meningitis.

Microbiology

The bacterial pathogens responsible for brain abscesses include the virulent invasive strains associated with acute disease of the middle ear or the more indolent strains associated with chronic disease.[9] These include (1) gram-positive cocci—group A *Streptococcus*, *S. pneumoniae*, *Streptococcus viridans*, and *Staphylococcus aureus*; (2) gram-negative coccobacilli—*H. influenzae* and *Haemophilus aphrophilus*; (3) gram-negative enteric bacilli—*Escherichia coli*, *Proteus*, *Enterobacter aerogenes*, *Enterobacter cloacae*, and *Pseudomonas aeruginosa*; (4) anaerobic bacteria—*Eubacterium*, *Bacteroides*, *Peptostreptococcus*, and *Propionibacterium acnes*.[35] In the review of the 101 children from Costa Rica and Dallas who had brain abscess, *S. aureus* was the most common causative organism overall, but in the 22 who had an otogenic brain abscess, anaerobes such as *Bacteroides* sp. and *Bacteroides fragilis* were most commonly isolated.[77] In 1992, Brook[10] reported on 23 California children with intracranial abscess, four of whom had chronic otitis media and two of whom also had mastoiditis. The most common organisms were anaerobic; gram-positive cocci and gram-negative bacilli predominated. In a study from Greece, anaerobic bacteria were also the predominant bacterial pathogens in 21 patients with brain abscess.[90] But, the common bacterial pathogens that cause acute otitis media may also be isolated from a brain abscess. Grigoriadis and Gold[30] reported a case from Toronto and found 23 other case reports in the literature of pneumococcal pathogen as the bacterial etiology of brain abscess.

Clinical Presentation

Signs and symptoms of CNS invasion usually occur about 1 month after an episode of acute otitis media or an acute exacerbation of chronic otitis media. Most children are febrile, although systemic signs, including fever and chills, are variable and may be absent. Signs of a general-

ized CNS infection include severe headache, vomiting, drowsiness, seizures, irritability, personality changes, altered levels of consciousness, anorexia and weight loss, and meningismus. In addition to these signs of an expanding intracranial lesion, there may be specific signs of involvement of the temporal or cerebellar lobes. Temporal lobe abscesses are associated with seizures in some children and may be associated with visual field deficits (optic radiation involvement) or may be silent. Cerebellar abscesses cause vertigo, nystagmus, ataxia, dysmetria, and symptoms of hydrocephalus. There may be persistent purulent ear drainage, suggesting the primary site of infection. Terminal signs include coma, papilledema, and cardiovascular changes.

Diagnostic Procedures

Diagnosis is based on the development of clinical signs and the results of imaging of the brain by either CT or MRI, which can be invaluable diagnostic aids (Fig. 27–3).[18, 61, 91] Radionuclide brain scans can be abnormal when focal encephalitis or a brain abscess is present. Of particular concern is the sudden appearance of signs of acute disease—fever and headache—in a patient with chronic disease of the middle ear.

Lumbar puncture is not recommended owing to the possibility of herniation of the brain and death, and should be performed only after a CT scan shows no mass effect. However, when lumbar puncture is performed, the CSF may be normal if the abscess is deep in the tissue and does not produce inflammation of the meninges; if it does, there may be an increased number of cells, initially a predominance of polymorphonuclear leukocytes, and then lymphocytes. The concentration of protein may be high, but the sugar level is not usually reduced unless there is bacterial invasion of the meninges. Cultures of the spinal fluid are usually negative in the absence of suppurative meningitis.

Management

Treatment includes use of antimicrobial agents, drainage or resection of the brain abscess, as well as surgical debridement of the primary focus, the mastoid, or adjacent infected tissues such as in thrombophlebitis of the lateral sinus. Aspiration of the abscess to define the cause is most helpful.[23] The decision to either excise the lesion or perform stereotactic aspiration may depend on the depth of the abscess,[75] but some centers have reported more sequelae, primarily epilepsy, after partial or total removal.[56, 75] The choice of the most appropriate antimicrobial regimen is difficult because of the varied bacteriology of otogenic brain abscesses. Initial therapy should include administration of a penicillin for gram-positive cocci, an aminoglycoside for gram-negative enteric pathogens, and chloramphenicol to combat gram-negative organisms and, more important, anaerobic bacteria. A penicillinase-resistant penicillin should be substituted as the penicillin if Gram stain suggests a staphylococcal infection. The use of a beta-lactam agent in combination with chloramphenicol or metronidazole for 2 months has also been recom-

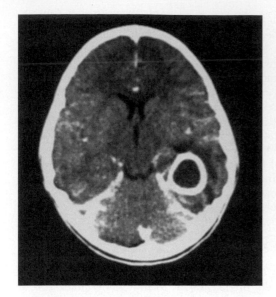

FIGURE 27–3. Computed tomographic scan of a 10-year-old male showing a right cerebellar brain abscess as a complication of right acute mastoiditis with osteitis. The child had a 3-week history of headache and vertigo 1 day following the onset of fever, and presented with increasing lethargy, vertigo, slurred speech, nausea, and head-tilting to the left. Examination revealed ataxia, nystagmus, slow speech, mild confusion, and right-sided weakness, but no otalgia or otorrhea. Otoscopic examination revealed left middle-ear effusion which was confirmed by tympanocentesis. The brain abscess was drained and cortical mastoidectomy (and tympanostomy tube insertion) was performed. Purulent material was found within the mastoid at the time of mastoid surgery and culture of the abscess revealed *S. pneumoniae*, susceptible to penicillin. The child made a complete recovery, without any sequelae, following the brain and mastoid surgery, and 6 weeks of intravenous penicillin therapy.

mended; the parenteral route of administration for the first 2 weeks is usually advised. Some centers recommend the addition of dexamethasone to the antimicrobial treatment, since this drug may potentially decrease cerebral edema, lower intracranial pressure, restore capillary permeability, stabilize cellular membranes, and have a regulatory effect on the blood-brain barrier.[67] However, in the 39 cases reported from Switzerland by Seydoux and Francioli,[84] 28 (72%) received corticosteroids, but these authors could not detect any difference in outcome between patients who were given the drug and those who were not. The authors recommended the drug only for cases of massive cerebral edema. Several reports have described successful medical treatment of brain abscess without neurosurgical intervention.[4, 48, 71] Mastoid surgery, when indicated, is usually withheld until the patient's status improves,[62] but initial tympanocentesis to identify the causative organisms should be performed on admission.

Outcome

Even with the administration of antimicrobial agents, the mortality rate of patients with brain abscess has been approximately 30%;[58, 60] rates in more recent reports were 4% to 20%.[46, 56, 84] Yildizhan and colleagues[101] reported 41 patients in Turkey with brain abscess; more than 50% were 20 years of age or younger, and in 59% the middle ear and mastoid were the origin. The mortality rate was 44%, but this was before the availability of CT scanning. In a review of 122 patients in Taiwan in whom brain abscess developed from several sources, the mortality rate was 3.8% when the infection was caused by an otolaryngologic focus compared with 24% when the abscess was from other sources.[101] The best results, a zero mortality rate, were reported for brain abscesses in children who underwent catheter drainage.[83] The level of consciousness[101] and severely impaired mental and neurologic status on admission have been associated with poor outcomes related to mortality and sequelae.[84]

Lateral Sinus Thrombosis

Lateral and sigmoid sinus thrombosis or thrombophlebitis arises from inflammation in the adjacent mastoid. The superior and petrosal dural sinuses are also intimately associated with the temporal bone but are rarely affected. The mastoid infection in contact with the sinus walls produces inflammation of the adventitia, followed by penetration of the venous wall. Formation of a thrombus occurs after the infection has spread to the intima. The mural thrombus may become infected and may propagate, occluding the lumen. Embolization of septic thrombi or extension of infection into the tributary vessels may produce further disease.

Incidence and Pathogenesis

Lateral sinus thrombosis is still a relatively common suppurative complication of otitis media and mastoiditis in children even in developed countries,[22, 64] but it is more frequently encountered in developing nations (see Table 27–3). Of 13 patients who had otogenic lateral sinus disease at the Groote Schuur Hospital in South Africa from 1967 to 1970, nine were younger than 20 years old, three children had acute ear infection, and six had chronic ear infection.[82] In a review from Iran, 13 children had a diagnosis of sigmoid sinus involvement secondary to chronic mastoid infection from 1978 to 1985. From 1972 to 1990, 39 Israeli children had intracranial infection secondary to either ear or sinus disease and, of these, 10 (26%) had a lateral sinus thrombosis from acute or chronic otitis media.[50] In a more recent study from Israel, 13 cases of otogenic lateral sinus thrombosis were diagnosed in children during the 15-year period 1982 to 1997; five (38%) were complications of acute otitis media, whereas the remaining eight (62%) were due to chronic otitis media.[46]

Garcia and colleagues[22] reviewed the world literature from 1960 to 1995 and found 58 children having lateral sinus thrombosis as a complication of ear disease; 57%

had middle-ear and mastoid infection and 43% had only otitis media. Many patients with this suppurative complication of otitis media have one or more other intracranial complications, such as brain abscess, otitic hydrocephalus, or epidural abscess.[95]

Clinical Presentation

The clinical signs of lateral sinus thrombosis may be grouped as follows:

1. General: fever, headache, and malaise. With the formation of the infectious mural thrombus, the patient may have spiking fever and chills.
2. CNS: headache, papilledema, signs of increased intracranial pressure, altered states of consciousness, and seizures.
3. Metastatic disease caused by infected thrombi: pneumonia, septic infarcts, empyema, bone and joint infection, and (less commonly) thyroiditis, endocarditis, ophthalmitis, and abscess of the kidney.[74]
4. Spread to skin and soft tissues: cellulitis or abscess.
5. Signs of intracranial complications, including meningitis, cavernous sinus thrombosis, and brain abscess.

Today, however, the classic presentation of sinus thrombosis may be altered by treatment with antimicrobial agents, especially when the drugs are not the best choice for treatment of acute and chronic otitis media.[64, 96]

Microbiology

In Rosenwasser's series of 100 patients with lateral sinus thrombosis,[74] the specific years of coverage are not mentioned. However, only 19 patients received sulfonamides, so presumably most were evaluated before 1935. Bacteremia was frequent. In 80 patients, presurgical cultures of the blood were positive. Eight patients whose cultures had been negative preoperatively had positive cultures postoperatively. Bacteremia persisted after the operation in 36 patients for a median of 4 to 5 days and a range of 1 to 24 days. The predominant organisms were beta-hemolytic streptococci (68 patients); S. pneumoniae type 3 (three patients), Proteus sp. (two patients), S. aureus (one patient), and P. aeruginosa (one patient) were also found.

In the antibiotic era, Singh[87] reported 36 patients receiving treatment between 1985 and 1990. Similar organisms were isolated from the blood, but Proteus mirabilis and Enterobacter sp. were found to be resistant to ampicillin and penicillin. In a more recent report, Syms and colleagues[94] isolated several bacteria from the ears of six patients with this complication, such as B. fragilis, Peptostreptococcus sp., Proteus sp., and Pseudomonas sp.

Diagnosis

MRI and magnetic resonance angiography are recommended diagnostic procedures and should precede a lumbar puncture[12] (Fig. 27–4). Contrast-enhanced CT that shows the "empty triangle" or "delta" sign is suggestive of

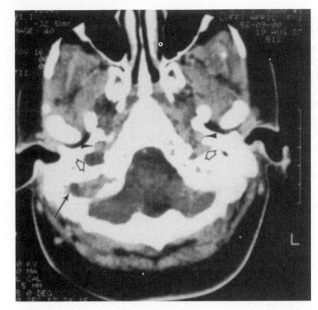

FIGURE 27–4. CT showing a right lateral sinus thrombosis. The bolus of intravenous contrast material shows good opacification of the carotid arteries (arrowheads), but the jugulars (open arrows) are asymmetric. The left side enhances normally; the right shows no enhancement, again suggesting thrombosis. The sigmoid sinus (arrow) also shows no opacification.

the diagnosis, and MRI scan with gadolinium enhancement may reveal lack of flow and an abnormal signal from the sinus that is diagnostic.[39, 96] An MRI scan that reveals high-signal intensity on T_1- and T_2-weighted images and absence of flow within thrombosed sinuses on gradient echo images indicate this complication.[22] A negative CT or MRI scan does not rule out the presence of lateral sinus thrombosis.[64] Holzman and colleagues[36] preferred contrast-enhanced CT scanning in their review of six children who had lateral sinus thrombosis as a complication of otitis media and mastoiditis. The Queckenstedt test, which measures changes in CSF pressure with compression and release of the jugular vein, can show variations in CSF pressure. If the sinus is occluded, there is no elevation in pressure when the jugular vein of the affected side is compressed, whereas compressing the contralateral jugular vein results in a brisk increase and decrease in pressure. However, if the intracranial pressure is increased, the brain may herniate. In addition to this potential danger, the Queckenstedt test may give falsely negative or inconclusive results.[43] There are usually no other abnormalities in the CSF, although in some cases, leakage of red cells and subsequent xanthochromia may occur.[29]

Management

Management includes using appropriate antimicrobial agents—penicillin, an aminoglycoside, and clindamycin (or metronidazole) are recommended to manage brain abscess. Some clinicians advocate using anticoagulant medication, but there is no consensus on this treatment.[22, 34] Those who advise against anticoagulation medication cite the fear that septic emboli could be released from a lateral sinus that has septic thrombophlebitis.[78] Deciding to perform middle-ear and mastoid surgery depends upon the disease status in these anatomic sites. If only otitis media is present, myringotomy and tympanostomy tube insertion may be effective without the need for mastoid surgery.[22] If acute mastoid osteitis, chronic suppurative otitis media, cholesteatoma, or a combination of these conditions exist, tympanomastoidectomy is usually indicated. When mastoidectomy is required, the sinus should be uncovered and any perisinuous abscess drained. Some surgeons recommend opening the lateral sinus and removing any thrombus. Others recommend only needle aspiration, and still others recommend neither procedure.[22, 88] Today, the internal jugular vein rarely requires ligation. For a complete description of the surgical technique, see the discussions by Glasscock and Shambaugh,[24] Harris and Darrow,[33] and Brackmann et al.[8]

Outcome

In Rosenwasser's series, the mortality rate was 27%, with an increased risk in patients older than 30 years of age,[74] and the rate was reported to still be high in the postantibiotic era.

In the review of the world literature of the 58 children by Garcia and colleagues[22] in the antibiotic era (1960 to 1995), only three patients died (5%), all of whom were reported from South Africa and had other intracranial complications, such as brain abscess, sepsis, and cavernous sinus thrombosis. In the recent report from Israel in which 13 children had a thrombosis, only one child died who also had a brain abscess.[46] Today, with appropriate and adequate management, children with lateral sinus thrombosis should have a favorable outcome. Approximately 25% to 33% of patients with lateral sinus thrombosis will have otitic hydrocephalus.[22, 95]

Otitic Hydrocephalus

Otitic hydrocephalus was a term introduced by Symonds in 1931 to describe a syndrome of increased intracranial pressure but with no abnormalities of the CSF complicating acute otitis media.[94] The pathogenesis of the syndrome is unknown, but since the ventricles are not dilated, the term *benign intracranial hypertension* also seems appropriate. The disease is frequently associated with lateral sinus thrombosis that can be diagnosed with MRI.[97]

Symptoms include a headache that is often intractable, blurring of vision, nausea, vomiting, and diplopia. Signs include a draining ear, abducens paralysis of one or both lateral rectus muscles, and papilledema.

CSF pressure is high, sometimes greater than 300 mm H_2O, but protein, cells, and sugar concentrations are normal, and the ventricles are of normal or small size. Although thought of as benign, otitic hydrocephalus in some cases has proceeded to loss of vision secondary to optic atrophy.

Management is similar to that recommended earlier for lateral sinus thrombosis, e.g., antimicrobial agents, myringotomy and tympanostomy tube insertion, possible tympanomastoid surgery, medication (acetazolamide or furosemide), repeated lumbar punctures, or a lumboperitoneal shunt to normalize intracranial pressure. An aggressive surgical approach is warranted because of the possibility of optic atrophy.

Type and Timing of Otologic Surgical Intervention

In general, an aggressive approach to surgical management should be taken when a suppurative intracranial complication of otitis media and mastoiditis is present. If an acute or chronic middle-ear effusion is present, immediate tympanocentesis for culture of the middle-ear effusion and myringotomy for drainage are mandatory. A tympanostomy tube should also be inserted to promote continued drainage of the middle ear and mastoid. The tympanostomy tube can be inserted even though a purulent middle-ear effusion is present. If the tube is subsequently extruded spontaneously owing to profuse otorrhea, it can be replaced if the perforation closes. However, the insertion of a tympanostomy tube that remains in place eliminates the need for subsequent myringotomies if the myringotomy incision heals during the course of the illness (when a tube is not inserted). There is no reason to withhold this procedure even in the critically ill child, since a tympanocentesis/myringotomy can be invaluable for the diagnosis and management of the infection. If the child is toxic, the procedure can be performed without general anesthesia. The technique should include a culture of the ear canal followed by sterilization of the external ear canal before the tympanocentesis, since an unusual organism may be present (see Chap. 25, section on Tympanocentesis and Myringotomy).

When more extensive otologic surgery is required to eliminate the infection within the temporal bone, the timing of the surgical intervention depends on the status of the child. Ideally, the otologic surgery should be performed as soon as the diagnosis of an intracranial complication is confirmed, and it should be performed concurrently with the neurosurgical procedure.[51] However, this is frequently not possible, since the neurologic status of the patient or the presence of sepsis, or both, may make the child an anesthesia risk. For such patients, otologic surgical intervention may not be possible until their condition has stabilized. If immediate neurosurgical intervention is required, as when a brain abscess or subdural empyema is present, the otologic surgery can be performed at the same time if the child's condition is stable at the end of the neurosurgical procedure. However, if the patient's condition does not warrant prolonging the anesthesia, the otologic surgery should be performed as soon as the child is able to tolerate a second surgical procedure, usually within a few days or a week. However, the surgery should not be delayed so long that the primary source of the infection is not controlled, because lack of control of the primary source of infection can interfere with the resolution of the intracranial infection or can even result in another intracranial complication.

The type of otologic surgical procedure chosen depends on the type of pathologic process.[27, 28, 59, 63, 85] If there is acute mastoid osteitis, a complete simple (cortical) mastoidectomy should be performed and a drain inserted into the mastoid cavity. The middle ear must also be drained, which may be accomplished by inserting a tympanostomy tube if there is no perforation. If a subperiosteal abscess is present, a drain should also be used. If a child has an ear infection that has resulted in a suppurative intracranial complication, drainage of the mastoid may not be achieved by a myringotomy alone because of an aditus ad antrum obstruction; a mastoidectomy to drain the infection should therefore be considered. In these cases, the mastoidectomy is performed as an emergency procedure. Occasionally, when such an obstruction exists between the middle-ear and mastoid air cell system, the middle ear is found to be free of effusion (as confirmed by a myringotomy), but the mastoid is infected. In such cases, the mastoid infection must be drained as soon as possible.

When the suppurative intracranial infection is secondary to cholesteatoma with or without chronic suppurative otitis media, a radical mastoidectomy or, when possible, a modified radical mastoidectomy is invariably indicated. However, when cholesteatoma is absent, a less radical procedure may be effective. Singh and Maharaj[88] reported relative success with this approach in 181 patients with intracranial complications; 74% of these patients were 20 years of age or younger. A possible exception to these guidelines is the incidental finding of extradural granulation tissue or an abscess during mastoid surgery to remove cholesteatoma. If there is an intratemporal complication, such as petrositis or labyrinthitis, definitive surgery must be performed. A search for a labyrinthine fistula, an extradural abscess, or extension of infection into the sigmoid sinus should always be part of the surgical procedure.

Prevention

The life-threatening complications of middle-ear disease in children are relatively uncommon. Our goal should be to reduce the incidence of these complications still further by effective management of acute otitis media and chronic otitis media with effusion and by prevention of chronic suppurative otitis media and cholesteatoma. Several factors may influence the extension of infection from the middle ear and mastoid to the intracranial cavity, such as the virulence of the bacteria, the efficacy of antimicrobial therapy, defects in anatomy, altered host immunity, and surgical drainage. An impending complication may be prevented from developing into a life-threatening condition if tympanocentesis and myringotomy are performed to identify the causative organism and to provide adequate drainage when children with acute otitis media have persistent or recurrent fever, otalgia, or other signs and symptoms of toxicity that are not responding to medical management. This aggressive management is especially important with the relatively high incidence of multidrug-resistant otitic bacterial pathogens. In such patients, the results of the culture from the middle-ear effusion should guide the clinician in the selection of the appropriate

antimicrobial agent. If there is persistent or recurrent discharge through a perforation, a culture should be obtained by needle aspiration of the purulent material within the middle-ear cavity. The antimicrobial agent chosen should be administered in a dosage that is adequate by the route appropriate to prevent a suppurative complication.

In children who have had an episode of meningitis as a complication of acute otitis media, a perilymphatic (CSF) fistula must be ruled out, especially if more than one episode of meningitis has occurred. The fistula may be in the area of the oval or round window, or both, and may be of congenital origin or due to an acquired defect.[31, 92, 98] Suppurative labyrinthitis is usually present, and the fistula must be repaired to prevent recurrence of the intracranial complication. Acute mastoid osteitis and petrositis are other possible intratemporal complications of acute otitis media in which the infection may spread to the intracranial cavity. Early diagnosis and appropriate management of these conditions can prevent intracranial complications.

A suppurative complication should be suspected in children who have the signs and symptoms of acute infection or when preexisting chronic suppurative otitis media is present with or without a cholesteatoma. An acute exacerbation in a chronically infected ear may destroy bone and permit bacteria to enter the intracranial cavity. A persistent aural discharge may indicate this type of pathologic process.

In children who have chronic suppurative otitis media and in whom the discharge from the ear is persistent despite medical treatment, such as ototopical medication and orally administered antimicrobial agents, hospitalization may be required to provide more aggressive therapy. A parenterally administered antimicrobial agent may be necessary, depending on the results of the culture of the discharge, and direct instillation through the tympanic membrane perforation of appropriate ototopical medication, after thorough aspiration of the middle ear, may be warranted. This procedure is best performed with the otomicroscope. If the suppurative process continues despite this type of medical management, surgical intervention is indicated. Frequently, a cholesteatoma that could not be identified by inspection of the tympanic membrane even with the aid of the otomicroscope is found in the middle ear and possibly in the mastoid. Even if a cholesteatoma is not present, middle-ear and mastoid surgery is still indicated in such cases to drain the ear and decrease the possibility of further complications. Tympanoplasty surgery, which may be performed at the time of the initial procedure or as a second-stage operation, may be required to prevent subsequent episodes of discharge. (See also reference 5.)

When a cholesteatoma is present, the diagnosis should be made as soon as possible, and surgery is indicated, since structural damage to the middle ear and mastoid is usually progressive and suppurative complications are an ever-present danger. The most important goals of surgery in such ears are complete eradication of the cholesteatoma (or its exteriorization), elimination of the infection, and prevention of potential intratemporal or intracranial complications. If these goals are met, the ear is "safe."

Prolonged follow-up of children who have had cholesteatoma is mandatory, since recurrence is common. In patients who have undergone middle-ear and mastoid surgery and in whom infection in the middle-ear or mastoid cavity, or both, persists despite medical management, surgical intervention may again be necessary. In cases in which a radical mastoidectomy has been performed, the middle ear and mastoid discharge may be the result of reflux of nasopharyngeal secretions through a patent eustachian tube into the middle ear. Surgical closure of the middle-ear end of the eustachian tube may be required to eliminate the reflux and chronic infection.[93] Likewise, identification of an extradural abscess can prevent spread of the infection further into the intracranial cavity. During surgery, a thorough examination of the tegmen tympani should be performed, since such an abscess may be present as a result of cholesteatoma or infection, or both, in the area. If the cholesteatoma is in the area of the lateral semicircular canal, the possibility of a labyrinthine fistula must be ruled out. Juselius and Kaltiokallio[43] reported that, of 42 patients with labyrinthine fistulas, five had suppurative labyrinthitis and meningitis.

Antimicrobial agents have greatly reduced the incidence of intracranial complications of infections of the middle ear and mastoid, but the physician must remain alert to the possibility of an unusual event. In less developed areas of the world, where the availability of medical facilities is still limited, complications occur and carry significant morbidity and mortality rates.[70]

SELECTED REFERENCES

Bluestone CD. Otologic procedures. In Bluestone CD, Stool SE, eds. Atlas of Pediatric Otolaryngology. Philadelphia, WB Saunders, 1995, pp 27–128.

This atlas provides a detailed description of the otologic surgical procedures that may be needed to eliminate and prevent complications and sequelae of otitis media and mastoiditis.

Brackmann DE, Shelton C, Arriaga MA. Otologic Surgery. Philadelphia, WB Saunders, 1994, pp 202–210, 257–276.

This atlas provides clear illustrations of otologic surgical procedures.

Glasscock ME III, Shambaugh GE. Surgery of the Ear, 4th ed. Philadelphia, WB Saunders, 1990.

The description in this text of the otologic surgical techniques employed for patients with suppurative disease in the intracranial cavity is excellent.

Goycoolea MV, Jung TTK. Complications of suppurative otitis media. In Paparella MM, Shumrick DA, Gluckman JL, Meyerhoff WL, eds. Otolaryngology, vol. II, 3rd ed. Philadelphia, WB Saunders, 1991, pp 1381–1403.

The intracranial suppurative complications of otitis media are described in a clear and concise manner.

Goycoolea MV, Jung TTK. Surgical procedures in different forms of otitis media. In Goycoolea MV, Paparella MM, Nissen RL, eds. Atlas of Otologic Surgery. Philadelphia, WB Saunders, 1989, pp 164–209.

This atlas includes descriptions of surgical procedures for the middle ear and mastoid when intracranial complications of otitis media are present.

Harris JP, Darrow DH. Complications of chronic otitis media. In Nadol JB, Schuknecht HF, eds. Surgery of the Ear and Temporal Bone. New York, Raven Press, 1993, pp 171–193.

An up-to-date description of the methods of surgical management of complications of otitis media.

Neely JG. Intratemporal and intracranial complications of otitis media. In Bailey BJ, ed. Head and Neck Surgery—Otolaryngology. Philadelphia, JB Lippincott, 1993, pp 1607–1622.

A detailed description of the intracranial complications of otitis media by a clinician with extensive experience.

Schuknecht HF. Pathology of the Ear, 2nd ed. Philadelphia, Lea & Febiger, 1993, pp 223–230.

This text has the best description of the pathology of intracranial suppurative complications of otitis media written for the otolaryngologist.

REFERENCES

1. Albers FWJ. Complications of otitis media: the importance of early recognition. Am J Otol 20:9, 1999.
2. Barry B, Delattre J, Vie F, Bedos J-P, Gehanno P. Otogenic intracranial infections in adults. Laryngoscope 109:483, 1999.
3. Beller AJ, Sahar A, Praiss I. Brain abscess: review of 89 cases over a period of 30 years. J Neurol Neurosurg Psychiatry 36:757, 1973.
4. Berg B, Franklin G, Cuneo R, et al. Nonsurgical care of brain abscess: early diagnosis and follow-up with computerized tomography. Ann Neurol 3:474, 1978.
5. Bluestone CD. Otologic procedures. In Bluestone CD, Stool SE, eds. Atlas of Pediatric Otolaryngology. Philadelphia, WB Saunders, 1994, pp 27–128.
6. Bluestone CD. Clinical course, complications and sequelae of acute otitis media. Pediatr Infect Dis J 19:S37, 2000.
7. Bok APL, Peter JC. Subdural empyema: burr holes or craniotomy? J Neurosurg 78:574, 1993.
8. Brackmann DE, Shelton C, Arriaga MA. Otologic Surgery. Philadelphia, WB Saunders, 1994, pp 202–210, 257–276.
9. Brewer NS, MacCarty CS, Wellman WE. Brain abscess: a review of recent experience. Ann Intern Med 82:571, 1975.
10. Brook I. Aerobic and anaerobic bacteriology of intracranial abscesses. Pediatr Neurol 8:210, 1992.
11. Browning GG. The unsafeness of "safe" ears. J Laryngol Otol 98:23, 1984.
12. Davison SP, Facer GW, McGough PF, et al. Use of magnetic resonance imaging and magnetic resonance angiography in diagnosis of sigmoid sinus thrombosis. Ear Nose Throat J 76:436, 1997.
13. Dawes JDK. Complications of infections of the middle ear. In Ballantyne J, Groves J, eds. Scott Brown's Diseases of the Ear, Nose, and Throat, vol. II, 4th ed. London, Butterworth, 1979, pp 305–384.
14. de Falco R, Scarano E, Cigliano A, et al. Surgical treatment of subdural empyema: a critical review. J Neurosurg Sci 40:53, 1996.
15. Dhooge IJM, Albers FWJ, Van Cauwenberge PB. Intratemporal and intracranial complications of acute suppurative otitis media in children: renewed interest. Int J Pediatr Otorhinol 49(Suppl 1):S109, 1999.
16. Dill SR, Cobbs CG, McDonald CK. Subdural empyema: analysis of 32 cases and review. Clin Infect Dis 20:372, 1995.
17. Don DM, Goldstein NA, Alper CM, et al. Intracranial complications of acute and chronic suppurative otitis media in children [abstract]. Presented at the American Society of Pediatric Otolaryngology, Palm Desert, Calif, April 1999.
18. du Boulay GH. Current practice in neurosurgical radiology. In Symon L, ed. Neurosurgery. In: Rob C, Smith R, eds. Operative Surgery Series, 3rd ed. London, Butterworth, 1979, pp 13–45.
19. Eavey RD, Gao YZ, Schuknecht HF, et al. Otologic features of bacterial meningitis of childhood. J Pediatr 106:402, 1985.
20. Feigin RD. Bacterial meningitis beyond the neonatal period. In: Feigin RD, Cherry JD, eds. Textbook of Pediatric Infectious Diseases, vol. I, 3rd ed. Philadelphia, WB Saunders, 1992, pp 401–428.
21. Friedman EM, McGill TJI, Healy GB. Central nervous system complications associated with acute otitis media in children. Laryngoscope 100:149, 1990.
22. Garcia RDJ, Baker AS, Cunningham MJ, Weber AL. Lateral sinus thrombosis associated with otitis media and mastoiditis in children. Pediatr Infect Dis J 14:617, 1995.
23. Garfield J. Intracranial abscess. In Symon L, ed. Neurosurgery. In

Rob C, Smith R, eds. Operative Surgery Series, 3rd ed. London, Butterworth, 1979, p 335.

24. Glasscock ME III, Shambaugh GE. Surgery of the Ear, 4th ed. Philadelphia, WB Saunders, 1990.

25. Go C, Bernstein JM, de Long AL, et al. Intracranial complications of acute mastoiditis. Int J Pediatr Otorhinolaryngol 52:143, 2000.

26. Gower DJ, McQuirt WF, Kelly DL. Intracranial complications of ear disease in a pediatric population with special emphasis on subdural effusion and empyema. South Med J 78:429, 1985.

27. Goycoolea MV, Jung TTK. Complications of suppurative otitis media. In Paparella MM, Shumrick DA, Gluckman JL, Meyerhoff WL, eds. Otolaryngology, vol. II, 3rd ed. Philadelphia, WB Saunders, 1991, pp 1381–1403.

28. Goycoolea MV, Jung TTK. Surgical procedures in different forms of otitis media. In Goycoolea MV, Paparella MM, Nissen RL, eds. Atlas of Otologic Surgery. Philadelphia, WB Saunders, 1989, pp 164–209.

29. Greer M, Berk MS. Lateral sinus obstruction and mastoiditis. Pediatrics 31:840, 1963.

30. Grigoriadis E, Gold WL. Pyogenic brain abscess caused by *Streptococcus pneumoniae*: case report and review. Clin Infect Dis 25: 1108, 1997.

31. Grundfast KM, Bluestone CD. Sudden or fluctuating hearing loss and vertigo in children due to perilymph fistula. Ann Otol Rhinol Laryngol 87:761, 1978.

32. Harding AL, Anderson P, Howie VM, et al. *Haemophilus influenzae* isolated from children with otitis media. In Sell SH, Karzon DT, eds. *Haemophilus influenzae*. Nashville, Tenn, Vanderbilt University Press, 1973, pp 21–28.

33. Harris JP, Darrow DH. Complications of chronic otitis media. In Nadol JB, Schuknecht HF, eds. Surgery of the Ear and Temporal Bone. New York, Raven Press, 1993, pp 171–193.

34. Hawkins DB. Lateral sinus thrombosis: a sometimes unexpected diagnosis. Laryngoscope 95:674, 1985.

35. Heineman HS, Braude AI. Anaerobic infection of the brain: observations on 18 consecutive cases of brain abscess. Am J Med 35: 682, 1963.

36. Holzman D, Huisman TAGM, Linder TE. Lateral dural sinus thrombosis in childhood. Laryngoscope 109:645, 1999.

37. Hoyt DJ, Fisher SR. Otolaryngologic management of patients with subdural empyema. Laryngoscope 101:20, 1991.

38. Hulcelle PJ, Dooms GC, Mathurin P, Cornelis G. MRI assessment of unsuspected dural sinus thrombosis. Neuroradiology 31:217, 1989.

39. Irving RM, Jones NS, Hall-Craggs MA, Kendall B. View from within: radiology in focus. CT and MR imaging in lateral sinus thrombosis. J Laryngol Otol 105:693, 1991.

40. Jadavji T, Humphreys RP, Prober CG. Brain abscess in infants and children. Pediatr Infect Dis J 4:394, 1985.

41. Jeanes A. Otogenic intracranial suppuration. J Laryngol Otol 76: 388, 1962.

42. Job A, Kurien K, Jacob A, Mathew J. Bilateral simultaneous hearing preservation mastoidectomy in otogenic meningitis. Ann Otol Rhinol Laryngol 107:872, 1998.

43. Juselius H, Kaltiokallio K. Complications of acute and chronic otitis media in the antibiotic era. Acta Otolaryngol (Stockh) 74:445, 1972.

44. Kafka MM. Mortality of mastoiditis and cerebral complications with review of 3225 cases of mastoiditis with complications. Laryngoscope 45:790, 1935.

45. Kangsanarak J, Fooanant S, Ruckphaopunt K, et al. Extracranial and intracranial complications of suppurative otitis media. Report of 102 cases. J Laryngol Otol 107:999, 1993.

46. Kaplan K. Brain abscess. Med Clin North Am 69:345, 1985.

47. Kessler L, Dietzmann K, Krish A. Beitrag zur otogenen Meningitis. Z Laryngol Rhinol Otol 49:93, 1970.

48. Keven G, Tyrell LJ. Nonsurgical treatment of brain abscess: report of two cases. Pediatr Infect Dis J 3:331, 1984.

49. Krajina Z. Observations on endocranial complications of the ear and sinuses in the era of antibiotics. Pract Otorhinolaryngol (Basel) 18:1, 1956.

50. Kraus M, Tovi F. Central nervous system complications secondary to otorhinologic infections. An analysis of 39 pediatric cases. Int J Pediatr Otorhinolaryngol 24:217, 1992.

51. Kurien M, Job A, Mathew J, Chandry M. Otogenic intracranial abscess: concurrent craniotomy and mastoidectomy—changing trends in a developing country. Arch Otolaryngol Head Neck Surg 124:1353, 1998.

52. Lahikainen EA. Clinico-bacteriologic studies on acute otitis media: aspiration of the tympanum as a diagnostic and therapeutic method. Acta Otolaryngol (Stockh) Suppl 107:1, 1953.

53. Lindsay JR. Suppuration in the petrous pyramid. Ann Otol Rhinol Laryngol 47:3, 1938.

54. Liske E, Weikers NJ. Changing aspects of brain abscesses: review of cases in Wisconsin 1940 through 1962. Neurology 14:294, 1964.

55. Lund WS. A review of 50 cases of intracranial complications from otogenic infection between 1961 and 1977. Clin Otolaryngol 3:494, 1978.

56. Mampalam TJ, Rosenblum ML. Trends in the management of bacterial brain abscesses: a review of 102 cases over 17 years. Neurosurgery 23:451, 1988.

57. Mathews TJ, Marus G. Otogenic intradural complications. A review of 37 patients. J Laryngol Otol 102:121, 1988.

58. McGreal DA. Brain abscess in children. Can Med Assoc J 86:261, 1962.

59. Miglets AW, Paparella MM, Saunders WH. Atlas of Ear Surgery, 4th ed. St Louis, CV Mosby, 1986, pp 71–77, 157–227, 261–415.

60. Morgan H, Wood MW, Murphey F. Experience with 88 consecutive cases of brain abscess. J Neurosurg 38:698, 1973.

61. Munz M, Farmer JP, Auger L, et al. Otitis media and CNS complications. J Otolaryngol 21:224, 1992.

62. Nalbone VP, Kuruvilla A, Gacek RR. Otogenic brain abscess: the Syracuse experience. Ear Nose Throat J 71:238, 1992.

63. Neely JG. Intratemporal and intracranial complications of otitis media. In Bailey BJ, ed. Head and Neck Surgery—Otolaryngology. Philadelphia, JB Lippincott, 1993, pp 1607–1622.

64. O'Connell JE. Lateral sinus thrombosis: a problem still with us. J Laryngol Otol 104:949, 1990.

65. Osma U, Cureoglu S, Hosoglu S. The complications of chronic otitis media: report of 93 cases. J Laryngol Otol 114:97, 2000.

66. Panda NK, Sreedharan S, Mann MS, Sharma SC. Prognostic factors in complicated and uncomplicated chronic otitis media. Am J Otolaryngol 17:391, 1996.

67. Pasaoglu A, Yildizhan A, Kandemir B. Treatment of experimental brain abscess. Acta Neurochir 100:79, 1989.

68. Pathak A, Sharma BS, Mathuriya SN, et al. Controversies in the management of subdural empyema. A study of 41 cases with review of literature. Acta Neurochir (Wien) 102:25, 1990.

69. Proctor CA. Intracranial complications of otitic origin. Laryngoscope 76:288, 1966.

70. Raikundalia KB. Analysis of suppurative otitis media in children: aetiology of nonsuppurative otitis media. Med J Aust 1:749, 1975.

71. Rennels MB, Woodward CL, Robinson WL, et al. Medical cure of apparent brain abscesses. Pediatrics 72:220, 1983.

72. Richardson MP, Reid A, Williamson TJ, Chir B, et al. Acute otitis media and otitis media with effusion in children with bacterial meningitis. J Laryngol Otol 111:913, 1997.

73. Ritter N. Complications of cholesteatoma. In: McCabe BF, Sade J, Abramson M, eds. Cholesteatoma: First International Conference. New York, Aesculapius, 1977, pp 430–437.

74. Rosenwasser H. Thrombophlebitis of the lateral sinus. Arch Otolaryngol 41:117, 1945.

75. Rousseaux M, Lesoin F, Destee A, et al. Long term sequelae of hemispheric abscesses as a function of the treatment. Acta Neurochir 74:61, 1985.

76. Rupa V, Ramon R. Chronic suppurative otitis media: Complicated versus uncomplicated disease. Acta Otolaryngol (Stockh) 111:530, 1991.

77. Saez-Llorens XJ, Umana MA, Odio CM, et al. Brain abscess in infants and children. Pediatr Infect Dis J 8:449, 1989.

78. Samuel J, Fernandes CMC. Lateral sinus thrombosis: a review of 45 cases. J Laryngol Otol 101:1227, 1987.

79. Samuel J, Fernandes CMC, Steinberg JL. Intracranial otogenic complications: a persisting problem. Laryngoscope 96:272, 1986.

80. Schuknecht HF. Pathology of the Ear, 2nd ed. Philadelphia, Lea & Febiger, 1993, pp 223–230.

81. Schwaber MK, Pensak ML, Bartels LJ. The early signs of neurotologic complications of chronic suppurative otitis media. Laryngoscope 99:373, 1989.

82. Seid AB, Sellars SL. The management of otogenic lateral sinus disease at Groote Schuur Hospital. Laryngoscope 83:397, 1973.

83. Selker RG. Intracranial abscess: treatment by continuous catheter drainage. Childs Brain 1:368, 1975.

84. Seydoux CH, Francioli P. Bacterial brain abscesses: factors influencing mortality and sequelae. Clin Infect Dis 15:394, 1992.

85. Shambaugh GE, Glasscock ME. Surgery of the Ear, 3rd ed. Philadelphia, WB Saunders, 1980, pp 302–312.

86. Sheehy JL, Brackmann DE, Graham MD. Complications of cholesteatoma: a report on 1024 cases. In McCabe BF, Sadé J, Abramson M, eds. Cholesteatoma: First International Conference. New York, Aesculapius, 1977, pp 420–429.

87. Singh B. The management of lateral sinus thrombosis. J Laryngol Otol 107:803, 1993.

87a. Singh B, Maharaj TJ. Radical mastoidectomy: its place in otitic intracranial complications. J Laryngol Otol 107:1113, 1993.

88. Smith HP, Hendrick EB. Subdural empyema and epidural abscess in children. J Neurosurg 58:392, 1983.

89. Sofianou D, Selviarides P, Sofianos E, et al. Etiological agents and predisposing factors of intracranial abscesses in a Greek university hospital. Infection 24:144, 1996.

90. Stein EH, Cunningham MJ, Weber AL. Noninvasive radiologic options in evaluating intracranial complications of otitis media. Ann Otol Rhinol Laryngol 101:363, 1992.

91. Supance JS, Bluestone CD. Perilymph fistulas in infants and children. Otolaryngol Head Neck Surg 91:663, 1983.

92. Supance JS, Bluestone CD. "How I do it"—Medical management of the chronic draining ear. Laryngoscope 93:661, 1983.

93. Symonds CP. Otitic hydrocephalus. Brain 54:55, 1931.

94. Syms MJ, Tsai PD, Holtel MR. Management of lateral sinus thrombosis. Laryngoscope 109:1616, 1999.

95. Tarkkanen J, Kohonen A. Otogenic brain abscess. Arch Otolaryngol 91:91, 1970.

96. Tovi F, Hirsch M. Computed tomographic diagnosis of septic lateral sinus thrombosis. Ann Otol Rhinol Laryngol 100:79, 1991.

97. Turner AL, Reynolds EE. Intracranial Pyogenic Diseases. Edinburgh, Oliver & Boyd, 1931.

98. Weber PC, Perez BA, Bluestone CD. Congenital perilymphatic fistula and associated middle ear abnormalities. Laryngoscope 103:160, 1993.

99. Yaniv E, Pocock R. Complications of ear disease. Clin Otolaryngol 13:357, 1988.

100. Yen PT, Chan ST, Huang TS. Brain abscess: with special reference to otolaryngologic sources of infection. Otolaryngol Head Neck Surg 113:15, 1995.

101. Yildizhan A, Pasaoglu A, Ozkul MH, et al. Clinical analysis and results of operative treatment of 41 brain abscesses. Neurosurg Rev 14:279, 1991.

28

Diseases of the Inner Ear and Sensorineural Hearing Loss

Patrick E. Brookhouser, M.D., F.A.C.S.

The detection of congenital and early-onset hearing loss by the age of 1 year has been a long-standing but elusive public health goal. Past initiatives, including public awareness campaigns, high-risk questionnaires for completion at the time of delivery, and various types of mass neonatal hearing screening techniques, proved to be either clinically unworkable or prohibitively expensive. The 1982 statement of the Joint Committee on Infant Hearing[79] promulgated a list of specific risk factors (e.g., congenital/neonatal infections, ear deformities) to identify infants at risk for hearing impairment for careful follow-up assessment. This risk indicator list was augmented in the Committee's 1990 statement[80] to include factors that become manifest after the neonatal period. A major deficiency of early identification programs targeted at only high-risk infants was their propensity to miss up to 50% of children who subsequently present with a sensorineural hearing loss (SNHL) during elementary school.

A reawakening of interest in universal newborn hearing screening was spawned by the introduction of simplified screening technologies such as evoked otoacoustic emission testing (EOAE) and automated auditory brain stem response (ABR) systems. The widely publicized national health objectives embodied in the document Healthy People 2000[166] and, more recently, in Healthy People 2010 include early identification of hearing loss coupled with early intervention. The 1993 National Institutes of Health Consensus Statement on "Early Identification of Hearing Impairment in Infants and Young Children"[120] recommended that all infants admitted to a neonatal intensive care unit be screened and that universal screening of all other infants be accomplished within the first 3 months of life. The Consensus Panel believe that EOAEs should be used for the initial screening of all babies and that rescreening of EOAE failures should be accomplished with ABR. Failure of the ABR screening would trigger referral for definitive evaluation.

The vexing problem posed by SNHL with an onset after 3 months of age, which is characteristic of such disorders as congenital cytomegalovirus infection, was addressed by the Joint Committee on Infant Hearing 1994 Position Statement[81] and further amplified in the 2000 Statement.[187]

In its 2000 Position Statement, the Joint Committee on Infant Hearing endorses "early detection of, and intervention for, infants with hearing loss (early hearing detection and intervention) through integrated, interdisciplinary state and national systems of universal newborn hearing screening, evaluation, and family-centered intervention." The statement notes that, denied opportunities to learn language, "children who are hard of hearing or deaf will fall behind their hearing peers in language, cognition, and social-emotional development," impairing educational and employment levels in adulthood.[59] In addition to recommending screening of all newborns' hearing using objective, physiologic measures, the Joint Committee on Infant Hearing states that infants who are referred for definitive audiologic evaluation and medical evaluations should be seen before 3 months of age. Intervention before 6 months of age should be initiated for infants with confirmed hearing loss by health care professionals and educators having expertise in hearing loss and deafness in infants and young children. The Statement further recommends that "regardless of prior hearing screening outcomes, all infants who demonstrate risk indicators for delayed onset or progressive hearing loss should receive ongoing audiologic and medical monitoring for 3 years and at appropriate intervals thereafter to ensure prompt identification and intervention."[4] Appropriate early intervention programs should be "family-centered, interdisciplinary, culturally competent, and build on informed choice for families."[7]

This Statement recommends either ABR or EOAE as the procedure of choice for newborn screening. An expanded list of "Indicators Associated with Sensorineural and/or Conductive Hearing Loss" was recommended for use with neonates in environments where universal screening capability is not available and for use with all infants who require rescreening or periodic monitoring of hearing, as follows:

A. For use with neonates (birth to 28 days) when universal screening is not available.
  1. An illness or condition requiring admission of 48 hours or greater to a neonatal intensive care unit.
  2. Stigmata or other findings associated with a syn-

drome known to include a sensorineural or conductive hearing loss, or both.

3. Family history of permanent childhood sensorineural hearing loss.
4. Craniofacial anomalies, including morphologic abnormalities of the pinna and ear canal.
5. In utero infection such as cytomegalovirus infection, herpes, toxoplasmosis, or rubella.

B. For use with infants (29 days to 2 years) when certain health conditions develop that require rescreening.

1. Parental or caregiver concern regarding hearing, speech, language, or developmental delay.
2. Family history of permanent childhood hearing loss.
3. Stigmata or other findings associated with a syndrome known to include a sensorineural or conductive hearing loss or eustachian tube dysfunction.
4. Postnatal infection associated with sensorineural hearing loss, including bacterial meningitis.
5. In utero infections such as cytomegalovirus infection, herpes, rubella, syphilis, and toxoplasmosis.
6. Neonatal indicators, specifically hyperbilirubinemia at a serum level requiring exchange transfusion, persistent pulmonary hypertension of the newborn associated with mechanical ventilation, and conditions requiring the use of extracorporeal membrane oxygenation.
7. Syndromes associated with progressive hearing loss, such as neurofibromatosis, osteopetrosis, and Usher syndrome.
8. Neurodegenerative disorders, such as Hunter syndrome, or sensory motor neuropathies, such as Friedreich ataxia and Charcot-Marie-Tooth syndrome.
9. Head trauma.
10. Recurrent or persistent otitis media with effusion for at least 3 months.

Patterns of Sensorineural Hearing Loss Etiology

Each year, more than 250,000 children with mental and physical defects are born in the United States.[162] Consisting of inborn anomalies affecting structure, function, or biochemical processes, these birth defects constitute the leading cause of death during the first year of life. A continuum of abnormal events leading to congenital defects can involve numerical or structural alterations of chromosomes, structural defects within individual genes, a breakdown in normal genetic regulation, or disturbances of finely tuned interactions of genes with the embryonic or fetal environment during development. Environmental factors may perturb expression of the phenotype, and complex inheritance patterns can result from variable penetrance and segregation of multiple single gene traits, which interact with one another. More than 200 mutations have been identified in the X-chromosome alone. Notable advances have been made in identifying a number of genes responsible for both syndromic and nonsyndromic hereditary hearing losses, and the prospect of genetic testing of deaf and hard-of-hearing infants and children looms on the horizon, raising both cultural and ethical concerns, particularly among the adult Deaf community. Developments in the field of microchip technology should allow clinicians to test infants with newly identified hearing loss for an array of the most common genetic mutations known to be responsible for genetic SNHL.

In addition to genetic and chromosomal abnormalities, congenital defects can be attributable to environmental teratogens,[24] including physical factors (e.g., hyperthermia, exposure to radiation), intrauterine infections (e.g., with cytomegalovirus, herpes simplex virus, human immunodeficiency virus, and *Toxoplasma*), maternal metabolic disturbances such as diabetes and hypothyroidism,[113] alcohol intake, use of illicit drugs (e.g., cocaine), exposure to industrial chemicals (e.g., solvents, pesticides, maternal cigarette smoking, pharmacologic agents), exposure to synthetic retinoids (e.g., isotretinoin), and exposure to chemotherapeutic agents.

Historical epidemiologic studies of hearing-impaired school-age populations attribute approximately 50% of childhood hearing impairment to genetic factors.[55] Of the remainder, about 20% to 25% are typically assigned to prenatal, perinatal, or postnasal environmental causes and 25% to 30% comprise sporadic cases of unknown cause. Advances in preventive intervention, particularly conjugate vaccine technology, are producing a major shift in the mix of causes responsible for each succeeding age cohort of children with SNHL. Widespread immunization against mumps, measles, and rubella has all but eradicated these formerly significant nongenetic causes of childhood deafness. The conjugate vaccine against *Haemophilus influenzae* type B administered during the first year of life reduces the incidence among infants and children of invasive *H. influenzae* disease, including meningitis, by as much as 90%.[54] Conjugate vaccines against meningococcal, *Escherichia coli*, and pneumococcal disease promise further reduction in bacterial meningitis cases. Strategies for immunization against cytomegalovirus are moving away from the attenuated live-virus Towne vaccine toward the development of a safer subunit conjugate vaccine.[108] Molecular biology and genetics have yielded advanced diagnostic methods, such as the polymerase chain reaction, which promise rapid and precise detection of congenital infections due to agents such as cytomegalovirus and *Toxoplasma*, even during the prenatal period. Mitochondrial inheritance has been implicated as a mechanism to explain enhanced familial susceptibility to ototoxic drugs and chemicals, raising the possibility of preexposure identification of at-risk individuals.[68] As the major causative factors responsible for nongenetic SNHL are negated through effective preventive and therapeutic measures, genetic causes will assume even greater importance in the differential diagnosis of newly identified SNHL in children.

Genetic hearing loss may be congenital or delayed in onset, variable in severity and audiometric configuration, progressive or nonprogressive, unilateral or bilateral, and syndromic (involving other identifiable physical characteristics) or nonsyndromic.[48, 88, 89, 112] Hearing loss is a component in more than 100 identifiable syndromes, although a relatively small number of these are responsible for the majority of syndromic hearing impairment. Classifications of syndromic deafness are usually based on other involved organ systems: craniofacial/cervical, skeletal, integumentary, ocular, neurologic, renal, cardiovascular, or metabolic, for example. Nonsyndromic genetic hearing disorders (i.e., isolated hearing loss) are described in terms of audiologic characteristics, age of onset, presence or absence of progression, associated vestibular deficit, if any, and mode of inheritance.

Dominant inheritance accounts for approximately 18% to 20% of genetic hearing loss in surveys of schools for the deaf and for an even higher percentage of cases referred to large centers for medical and audiologic evaluation.[11] Dominant hearing loss syndromes are often characterized by structural organ system abnormalities, as well as variable penetrance and expressivity, which further complicate diagnostic efforts. By virtue of variable expressivity, each affected family member can exhibit a different array of phenotypic characteristics, while decreased penetrance may produce an absence of detectable phenotypic features in an obligate gene carrier.

Recessive inheritance is implicated in about 80% of genetic childhood hearing loss, with about one half of these cases involving recognizable syndromes. Heterozygotic (one abnormal allele) carriers for autosomal recessive genes generally do not manifest any phenotypic characteristics, and there is only a 25% risk of recurrence among the offspring of two heterozygotic parents, minimizing the likelihood of multiple affected siblings in a single family. A unique diagnostic challenge is presented by a hearing-impaired child with a negative history for nongenetic hearing risk factors and no family history of hearing loss. A significant percentage of hearing losses of uncertain cause are thought to be singleton cases of autosomal recessive nonsyndromic hearing impairment. Although as many as 200 genes may be implicated in recessive nonsyndromic hearing losses, the surprisingly high frequency of mutations in the connexin 26 gene in a substantial number of these cases should provide a powerful new diagnostic tool in further reducing the number of children with hearing losses of uncertain cause. As researchers identify genes for nonsyndromic deafness, it is evident that the genes are widely distributed among the body's organ systems, raising the specter of heretofore unappreciated systemic effects of abnormal "nonsyndromic" deafness genes. Until more is known about the function of these abnormal genes outside the auditory system, these concerns should dictate caution when one counsels parents of an infant with newly identified hearing loss that is attributable to a nonsyndromic deafness gene.

Sex-linked genetic inheritance is involved in only 1% to 2% of all cases of hereditary hearing losses but may be responsible for about 6% of cases of nonsyndromic profound hearing impairment in males. Linkage studies with sex-linked disorders are generally easier than with autosomal disorders, and consequently the X-chromosome has been extensively mapped. The Alport syndrome gene on the X-chromosome has already been identified as coding for 4A5 collagen,[9] but the exact pathophysiologic mechanism by which inner ear function is compromised is unclear. Some genetic hearing disorders appear to result from a combination of genetic factors interacting with environmental influences, so-called multifactorial inheritance. Examples of this type of inheritance include clefting (i.e., cleft lip/palate) syndromes, conditions involving conductive hearing loss, and the microtia/hemifacial microsomia/Goldenhar spectrum.

Multidisciplinary Team Evaluation

The diagnostic protocol to be followed when evaluating infants and children with newly identified SNHL is in a state of flux, with the prospect of genetic testing on the horizon. The availability of definitive genetic diagnoses will obviate the need for a more exhaustive and multifaceted etiologic search. At present, it would seem logical to continue a systematic approach to evaluation and diagnosis, with a particular emphasis on identification of syndromic components that could be debilitating, if not life threatening (e.g., Jervell and Lange-Nielsen syndrome), as the basis for meaningful genetic counseling and planning of a habilitation program.

The coordinated efforts of a multispecialty team are necessary to provide comprehensive evaluation, treatment, and rehabilitative services to infants and children with hearing loss and their families. A prototypical team would include an otologist or otolaryngologist with pediatric expertise, a pediatric audiologic team able to perform both behavioral and electrophysiologic hearing evaluation, an aural rehabilitation specialist competent to determine amplification needs, a clinician skilled in pediatric vestibular evaluation, a pediatrician attuned to subtle dysmorphic features and other components of deafness syndromes, a geneticist or genetic counselor, a pediatric ophthalmologist with skill in electroretinography, a psychologist able to evaluate both cognitive and behavioral dimensions in a hearing-impaired child, a deaf education and early intervention specialist, and a speech and language pathologist to assess oral motor function and linguistic development as well as develop an individualized intervention plan. The consulting services of such related specialists as a pediatric neurologist and a radiologist should also be accessible.

The starting point in evaluating a child with SNHL must be a comprehensive case history exploring prenatal, perinatal, and postnatal factors that have been etiologically implicated in hearing loss. Diagnostic clues should be sought for both syndromic and nonsyndromic genetic hearing loss disorders, as well as an array of nongenetic causes. A careful family history should explore the possibility of consanguineous relationships involving parents, grandparents, or earlier ancestors on either the paternal or maternal side. Genealogic records including birth certificates may be of help in identifying previously unsuspected blood relationships. Because mental retardation and early childhood deafness were often confused diagnostically until recent decades, institutionalization of an ancestor early in life may be a clue to possible familial hearing loss. A history of multiple miscarriages or stillbirths could indicate a genetic disorder. Any history of hearing loss in a blood relative who wore a hearing aid or required special schooling (e.g., school for the deaf) should be carefully explored. If a family history of hearing loss is elicited, an extensive pedigree, including three or more generations, should be constructed. Specific questions should address the age of onset, bilaterality versus unilaterality, and stability versus progression of the hearing loss.

A diligent search for organ system anomalies and disorders associated with genetic hearing loss involves a careful physical examination. Clinically significant findings include the presence of holes, pits, or skin tags in or near the ear (branchio-otorenal, or BOR, disorder); external ear deformity (e.g., microtia), displacement of the auricles, or stenosis or atresia of the external ear canal (bilateral, Treacher Collins syndrome; unilateral, Goldenhar syndrome); a history of ear surgery other than tympanostomy tube placement (middle-ear anomalies, otosclerosis); or history of a "brain" tumor involving the hearing or balance nerve (neurofibromatosis). Evidence of delay in developmental motor milestones such as sitting unsupported, standing, or walking, a persistent broad-based gait, spatial disorientation in dark environments, or difficulty standing on one foot or riding a bicycle should prompt consideration of a vestibular deficit (e.g., Usher syndrome type I).

Visual problems should alert the examiner to several disorders. For example, myopia requiring corrective lenses early in life, retinal detachment, and cataracts are associated with Stickler syndrome; congenital blindness or microphthalmia with Norrie syndrome; night blindness and retinitis pigmentosa with Usher syndrome types 1 and 2; "widely spaced" eyes (dystopia canthorum) and heterochromia iridis with Waardenburg syndrome; lid abnormalities, including coloboma and palpebral fissures, with Treacher Collins syndrome; blue sclerae with osteogenesis imperfecta; and optic atrophy with Cockayne syndrome.

Musculoskeletal disorders of interest would be recurrent fractures (osteogenesis imperfecta)[106]; abnormal fingers or toes, including web-type deformity or abnormal nails (otopalatodigital disorder); vertebral deformities (Wildervanck and Goldenhar syndromes); early arthritis or enlarged or hyperextensible joints (Stickler syndrome); and short stature, webbed neck, and shield chest deformity (Turner syndrome).

Syndromic findings that affect the integumentary system are white forelock (Waardenburg syndrome); café au lait spots and peripheral neurofibromas (von Recklinghausen syndrome); and cervical cysts or fistulae (BOR disorder). Cleft lip or palate, as well as micrognathia, is associated with Stickler syndrome and the Robin sequence (aka Pierre Robin syndrome), and facial asymmetry characterizes Goldenhar syndrome. Lip pits or mounds may also be linked with deafness, as may other patterns of nasal and facial deformities (Treacher Collins syndrome). A history of hearing loss coupled with renal deformities or disorders, in some instances necessitating renal dialysis or transplant, would point toward BOR or Alport syndrome. A euthyroid goiter usually apparent during the first decade of life is a component of Pendred syndrome, and syncopal, or fainting, episodes during childhood, adoles-

cence, or early adulthood, particularly a history of unexplained sudden death at a young age, point to Jervell and Lange-Nielsen syndrome.

In addition to otolaryngologic and pediatric examinations, evaluation of a hearing-impaired child by an ophthalmologist is essential because of the heightened neurosensory role demanded of the visual system. Detection of coexisting ocular disorders such as retinitis pigmentosa by means of electroretinography is important from both a prognostic and a rehabilitative point of view.

Currently, selected laboratory studies could include complete blood count with differential and sickle cell test, if appropriate; routine blood chemistry, lipid, blood sugar, creatinine, blood urea nitrogen, and thyroid function tests; and urinalysis. More sophisticated renal studies (e.g., ultrasonography) should be ordered if evidence of kidney disease (e.g., hematuria, or "red diaper") is present. Both congenital toxoplasmosis and syphilis are potentially treatable and, if suspected, should be ruled out by laboratory tests (e.g., fluorescent treponemal antibody absorption test). Most women of childbearing age in the United States should have received the rubella vaccine, but children born in other countries may present with congenital rubella infection identifiable by serologic or viral isolation techniques. While congenital cytomegalovirus infection may be etiologically implicated in a significant percentage of cases of nongenetic congenital or early-onset hearing loss, definitive diagnosis is challenging. If laboratory confirmation of congenital cytomegalovirus infection is not obtained within the first month of life, antibodies resulting from perinatal acquisition of the virus can obscure the diagnosis. Immune-mediated systemic disorders that have been linked to SNHL in adults include Cogan syndrome[29] (nonsyphilitic interstitial keratitis with hearing loss and vestibular dysfunction), polyarteritis nodosa,[131] systemic lupus erythematosus,[26] relapsing polychondritis,[31, 72] Behçet disease,[17] and giant cell arteritis.[58] The role that autoimmune disorders play in the etiology of SNHL in children is currently unclear, and judgments regarding the cost-effectiveness of studies aimed at detecting such disease processes must await evidence regarding their prevalence.[148] Immunoassays (e.g., Western blot) designed to detect certain antibodies against cochlear tissues can be obtained by special arrangement with the research laboratories of scientists studying immune-mediated inner ear disease.

The pediatric audiologic team is charged with characterizing the type of hearing loss (conductive, sensorineural, or mixed), the degree of loss (mild, moderate, severe, profound, or anacoustic), the audiometric configuration and symmetry, and, finally, the stability or progression of the loss, or the serial assessment. Age-appropriate evaluation techniques should be selected from the range of available options, including electrophysiologic measures such as ABR for very young and hard to test infants, and behavioral methods involving conditioning paradigms such as visual reinforcement audiometry, conditioned play audiometry, and tangible reinforcement operant conditioning audiometry. Because broad-band click stimuli used in most ABR protocols present a much more accurate assessment of auditory acuity for test frequencies above

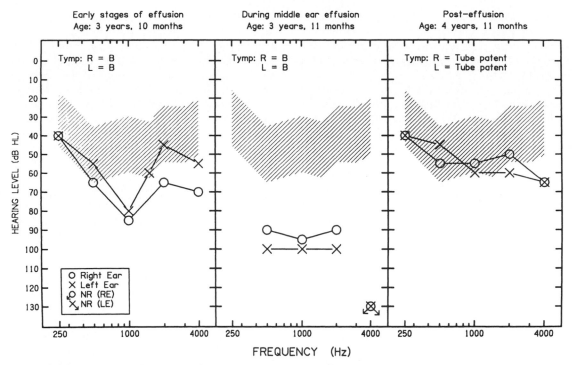

FIGURE 28-1. Effect of middle-ear effusion in a patient with moderate sensorineural hearing loss. (From Brookhauser PE, et al. Middle ear disease in children with a sensorineural hearing loss. Laryngoscope 103:371, 1993.)

2000 Hz, final rehabilitative decisions should be based on definitive behavioral audiologic data across a broad range of frequencies.

To avoid the compounding variable posed by differences in audiologic technique, the same audiologic team should be assigned to the child for successive evaluation sessions. Clinician flexibility and a willingness to assess the difficult-to-evaluate child over the course of multiple test sessions are essential ingredients for success. When possible, auditory discrimination measures, using age- and language-appropriate materials, should be obtained. Prelingual children can often identify environmental sounds or favorite toys as a gauge of auditory discrimination. Immittance audiometry is essential because coexisting middle-ear disease can produce significant decrements in auditory acuity (Fig. 28–1). Because bone conduction vibrators cannot transmit an undistorted signal above approximately 70 dB, an inaccurate picture of the degree and configuration of a child's residual hearing may be drawn. Definitive characterization of a SNHL must be accomplished in an effusion-free condition.

A subset of infants and children will demonstrate intact otoacoustic emissions, indicating functional cochlear elements, particularly outer hair cells, but a significantly abnormal or absent auditory brain stem response. These patients have been classified as having auditory neuropathy, and they pose a special habilitative challenge. Conventional amplification may not be appropriate or beneficial for these children, and some reports regarding the efficacy of cochlear implants in ears with auditory neuropathy are encouraging. It is important to note that newborn screening programs that rely exclusively on EOAEs may fail to identify cases with isolated auditory neuropathy, which reinforces the requirement for continued vigilance by parents and clinicians regarding the communicative development of infants who have ostensibly passed newborn hearing screening.

Vestibular symptoms may coexist with hearing loss in children with genetic deafness (e.g., Usher syndrome type I) and hearing loss resulting from such nongenetic causes as bacterial meningitis.[124] Clinical studies of children and adolescents with severe to profound SNHL revealed vestibular deficits in 20% or more.[23] Standard electronystagmography procedures using caloric irrigation may not be suitable for young children, and various useful modifications have been suggested.[37, 38] Computerized rotational testing has proven useful in pediatric vestibular evaluation, particularly for longitudinal assessment of vestibular function in children receiving potentially vestibulotoxic medications.

Progressive and fluctuating SNHL, with or without vertigo, in children raises the specter of possible perilymphatic fistula (PLF).[63, 67] A history of mechanical stress factors such as head or ear trauma or exertional activity such as gymnastics may point to this diagnosis. While preoperative confirmation of PLF remains elusive, a monitored fistula test seems a reasonable course in these cases. A positive fistula test result may be helpful, while a negative result must be considered inconclusive on the basis of reported series. Temporal bone imaging techniques are helpful in identifying middle-ear anomalies in children with conductive or mixed losses, as well as inner ear or internal auditory canal anomalies or lesions, in cases of SNHL. The relatively low yield and high cost of such studies make their uniform application questionable. The utility of computed tomography (CT) scans for assessing profoundly deaf children for cochlear implant candidacy has resulted in the increased use of this diagnostic modality in recent years.

In the past, a diligent search for the cause of SNHL in a child, using state-of-the-art techniques, proved inconclusive in 30% to 40% of cases. With the declining incidence of nongenetic causes, such as prenatal rubella, measles, mumps, and *H. influenzae* meningitis, an increasing percentage of newly identified cases will be attributable to genetic factors. Parents are anxious to determine the cause of their child's loss for prognostic and family planning considerations. Clinicians serving the needs of these families must be prepared to address their concerns regarding the lack of a definitive diagnosis.

Several detailed etiologic classifications of SNHL in children have been published, but terminology such as *genetic* versus *acquired* and *congenital* versus *acquired* can be confusing. It seems most helpful to envision SNHL cases in terms of a three-dimensional matrix as either genetic or nongenetic with onset being either congenital or delayed (i.e., postnatal). Although genetic factors ultimately responsible for a hearing loss are present at birth, many genetic hearing losses are not congenital. A number of nongenetic hearing impairments (e.g., rubella deafness) are present at birth while others occur later in life. Expanding knowledge regarding genetics should lead to techniques for the prenatal or early postnatal diagnosis of these genetic hearing loss disorders, even in the absence of detectable hearing impairment.

Genetic Principles

It has been estimated that the human genome contains 3 billion base pairs of DNA per diploid cell arrayed along 47 chromosomes (i.e., 22 pairs of autosomes, two sex chromosomes, and the mitochondrial chromosome). Sequence data obtained from the Human Genome Project indicate that humans may have a substantially smaller number of actual genes (estimated at 30,000 to 40,000) than previously supposed. Information in each gene is stored in the form of triplets, or codons, which encode for specific amino acids during translation of messenger RNA (mRNA) as part of the process of transcription. After the mRNA reaches the cytoplasm, it is translated into protein synthesis. Exons, the segments of genes containing codons, are separated by noncoding sequences called *intervening sequences* or *interons*. Each chromosome pair carries a specific set of gene loci, which may accommodate several alternative codes or alleles. If the genotype consists of two identical alleles, it is said to be homozygous, while a genotype composed of two disparate alleles is heterozygous. The term *phenotype* denotes the physical expression of the genetic trait in a specific individual. An autosomal allele is termed *dominant* if it is expressed in either a homozygous or a heterozygous state, while a recessive allele is manifest only when present in a homozygous condition. An X-linked recessive allele will be expressed in a hemizygous condition in a carrier male because the Y-chromosome does not carry a complemen-

tary allele. Attempts to account for the vast differences among humans and between humans and lower animals has focused attention on the emerging field of proteomics, which is the study of the variability of protein forms that can result from the actions of the same gene.

Genetic linkage analysis is used to determine the precise chromosomal location of a specific gene. Through a process known as crossover, genetic material can be randomly exchanged between the two chromosomes in a pair during cell mitosis. Two genetic loci are said to be linked when they are sufficiently close on the same chromosome to be transmitted together more often than is expected by chance. Once a gene has been mapped to a specific chromosome, sophisticated molecular genetic techniques can be used to identify, clone, and sequence the gene, preparing the way for the development of animal models and eventually effective treatment or preventive strategies. The vast amount of nucleotide sequence data that is being generated by the Human Genome Project has provided a new pathway for identifying candidate genes through the use of computer analysis of existing databases. This approach can substantially reduce the time required to move from initial gene localization to positive gene identification for a particular disorder. A wide range of different mutations can occur in a single gene, and the DNA of different individuals with a particular syndrome, who are phenotypically indistinguishable, may harbor different mutations in the same gene. Certain gene mutations may yield a syndromic deafness phenotype while other mutations in the same gene may produce nonsyndromic hearing loss. Individuals with recessive disorders may carry two copies of an abnormal gene, each copy harboring a different mutation that could alter the gene's function in a distinct manner.

Structural Malformations of the Inner Ear

The cochlea achieves full growth by the ninth gestational week. Deformity of inner ear structures involving hearing impairment can result from either an arrested normal developmental process (agenesis) or an aberrant development (dysgenesis).[77] The most commonly observed minor anomalies involve the vestibular portion of the labyrinth, specifically the horizontal semicircular canal (Fig. 28–2).

In Michel aplasia, complete agenesis of the temporal bone is observed, including absence of the sensory and neural structures of the inner ear. The anomaly is readily detectable by CT imaging; only labyrinthitis ossificans, a sequela of meningitis, presents similar radiographic findings. Usually inherited in an autosomal dominant fashion, Michel aplasia has been observed in patients with Klippel-Feil syndrome and thalidomide embryopathy. Affected ears are anacoustic and not suitable for insertion of a cochlear implant.

Mondini aplasia is characterized by a decreased number of cochlear turns, with only the basal coil being identifiable in many cases. Modiolar hypoplasia and absence of the interscalar septum can cause the remaining cochlear coils to assume a cloacal form. Recent histopathologic reports of temporal bones having Mondini aplasia have also identified dilatation of the endolymphatic sac

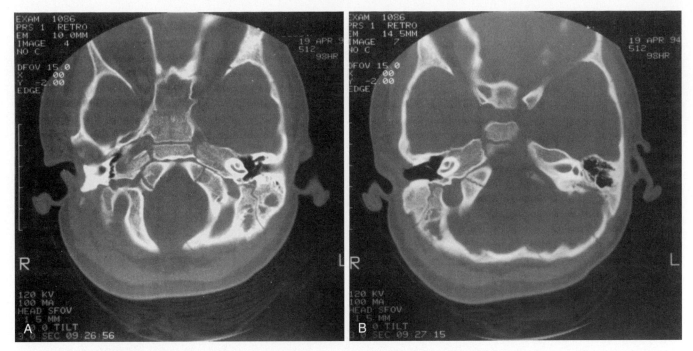

FIGURE 28–2. A and B, Computed tomographic scans showing total bilateral absence of semicircular canals.

and duct with attendant endolymphatic hydrops. Stapedial footplate anomalies including bony discontinuities, observed in some cases, predispose these patients to perilymphatic fistula formation and otogenic meningitis. As an isolated trait, the Mondini malformation is inherited in an autosomal dominant pattern, but it has also been described with other disorders, including Pendred, Waardenburg, Treacher Collins, Wildervanck, Klippel-Feil, trisomy 13, trisomy 18, and DiGeorge syndromes.

In ears with Bing-Siebenmann aplasia, both the cochlear and the vestibular components of the membranous labyrinth are malformed while the bony labyrinth is normal, thus precluding radiographic detection of the anomaly. Abnormal intracochlear anatomy generally includes a rudimentary mound of undifferentiated cells replacing the organ of Corti against which the Reissner membrane is collapsed. This anomaly may be associated with retinitis pigmentosa and mental retardation.

With cochleosaccular or Scheibe aplasia, the entire bony labyrinth is normally differentiated, as is the superior portion of the membranous labyrinth, including the utricle and semicircular canals. Abnormalities, limited to the saccule and cochlea, tend to be more severe in the basal turn than apically. Microscopic findings generally include stria vascularis atrophy, a deformed tectorial membrane, and a poorly differentiated organ of Corti, against which the Reissner membrane is collapsed. Scheibe aplasia, not detectable radiologically, is the most commonly observed temporal bone abnormality in cases of profound congenital SNHL. Inherited as an autosomal recessive trait, this aplasia has also been observed with Jervell and Lange-Nielsen, Refsum, Usher, Waardenburg, and trisomy 18 syndromes. Viral disorders such as congenital rubella infection can also give rise to Scheibe aplasia.

Alexander aplasia is characterized by incomplete differentiation of the cochlear duct in the basal turn with attendant changes in the organ of Corti and ganglion cells. These patients have high-frequency hearing loss with enough residual low-frequency hearing to benefit from amplification.

Apart from horizontal semicircular canal abnormalities, the more common developmental anomalies of the inner ear detectable radiographically include shortened cochlea, a widely patent cochlear aqueduct, and an enlarged vestibule. An enlarged vestibular aqueduct has been observed in temporal bone imaging studies of patients with early-onset SNHL, which is usually bilateral and often fluctuating and may be associated with vertigo. Correlational studies have related the degree of deformity with severity of the hearing loss, which may be exacerbated by factors such as minor head trauma.[123] Endolymphatic sac surgery, initially advocated for these patients, is not beneficial and may lead to additional hearing loss.

Autosomal Dominant Disorders

The clinical features of BOR, or Melnick-Fraser, syndrome, which is transmitted as an autosomal dominant disorder, include malformations of the external, middle, or inner ear with associated conductive, sensorineural, or mixed hearing loss; branchial cleft sinuses; cervical fistulas; and renal anomalies, which range from mild hypoplasia to bilateral renal agenesis. The phenotypic expression can vary significantly between and within affected families, and renal ultrasonography or intravenous pyelography is essential to determine the extent of renal involvement. Branchial anomalies, preauricular pits, and hearing loss have been described in the absence of renal dysplasia as branchio-oto syndrome, which may constitute a distinct entity. Older reports indicate that BOR has a prevalence of 1 in 40,000 people and is responsible for about 2% of profound childhood deafness. Some cases of BOR syndrome are caused by mutations in EYA1 on chromosome 8q, while other cases have been linked to an as yet unidentified gene on 1q31.[1, 93]

Waardenburg syndrome, which may demonstrate variable expressivity, is characterized by pigmentary abnormalities such as white forelock (20% to 30%); premature graying or vitiligo and heterochromic irides; craniofacial anomalies such as dystopia canthorum, broadened nasal root, and synophrys; and unilateral or bilateral SNHL in about 20% of affected individuals.[125] Two clinical subtypes are distinguished by the presence (WSI) or absence (WSII) of dystopia canthorum. Sensorineural hearing impairment is more prevalent with the WSII subgroup. A combination of WS type I characteristics with upper limb abnormalities is called Klein-Waardenburg syndrome or WS type III, while recessively inherited WS type II characteristics paired with Hirschsprung disease has been called Waardenburg-Shah syndrome or WS type IV. Genetic mapping has identified the Waardenburg gene as a homeobox gene PAX3 on chromosome 2, and molecular techniques have been used to detect several mutations within the involved homeodomain, including a point mutation in the human gene.[96]

Stickler syndrome stigmata may include a small jaw with or without a cleft palate (Robin sequence); myopia, which may occur in conjunction with retinal detachment or cataracts; and joint hypermobility or enlargement progressing to arthritis in early adulthood and spondyloepiphyseal dysplasia in some cases. Hearing impairment, occurring in approximately 15% of affected individuals, may be either a sensorineural or a mixed loss. Phenotypic characteristics of Stickler syndrome have been observed with mutations in COL2A1, COL11A2, or COL11A1. Classic Stickler (STL1) is associated with mutations in COL2A1, a fibrillar collagen. Mutations in COL11A2 cause STL2, a disorder pairing the typical facial features of STL1 with hearing impairment. Cleft palate and mild arthropathy can be present, but typical ocular findings (high myopia, vitreoretinal degeneration, and retinal detachment) are absent. STL3 is caused by mutations in COL11A1, and the associated phenotypic findings are identical to those of STL1. The phenotypic differences between STL2 and STL1/STL3 can be explained by the absence of COL11A2 in the vitreous, where it is replaced by COLV.[170]

Otologic findings in Treacher Collins syndrome (mandibulofacial dysostosis) may include microtia and aural meatal atresia with associated conductive hearing loss (30% of cases), SNHL, and a vestibular deficit. Typical facial characteristics are malar hypoplasia associated with underdeveloped zygomatic arches, mandibular hypoplasia, palpebral fissures that slant downward, and lower eyelid coloboma. Goldenhar syndrome and other oculoauricular vertebral syndromes (ocular-auricular-vertebral spectrum) may have similar features, but they occur unilaterally, in contrast with the bilateral presentation in Treacher Collins patients, and the coloboma typically involves the upper rather than the lower eyelid. In addition, Treacher Collins syndrome is inherited as an autosomal dominant trait, while ocular-auricular-vertebral spectrum appears to be a multifactorial trait. The gene responsible for Treacher Collins, TCOF1, encodes a protein (TREACLE) that is thought to play a role in nucleolar-cytoplasmic transport.

Clinical components of neurofibromatosis may be café au lait spots (variably sized light brown pigmented skin areas) and multiple fibromatous tumors that can involve cutaneous structures, peripheral nerves, the central nervous system, and viscera. In affected individuals, the lesions may lead to mental retardation, blindness, and SNHL. Phenotypically, two forms of the disorder have been identified, of which the more prevalent is classic neurofibromatosis (von Recklinghausen syndrome) with multiple café au lait spots and cutaneous neurofibromas and only a small incidence (5%) of acoustic neuromas, which are typically unilateral. The other genetically distinct type, central neurofibromatosis (NF-2), is characterized by bilateral acoustic neuromas in as many as 95% of affected individuals that may not become clinically apparent until early adulthood. Fewer café au lait spots and cutaneous neurofibromas are found in NF-2 patients than in patients with NF-1. The gene for NF-1 is a nerve growth factor gene on chromosome 17, while NF-2 results from mutation of a tumor suppressor gene on chromosome 22.[143] Both types of neurofibromatosis are transmitted as autosomal dominant disorders with a high degree of penetrance but variable expressivity and high mutation rates.

Osteogenesis imperfecta is inherited as an autosomal dominant disorder with variable expressivity and incomplete penetrance. Classic clinical features include fragile bones subject to multiple fractures, blue (clear) sclerae, hearing loss (conductive, mixed, or sensorineural), and hyperelasticity of joints and ligaments. The most common, tarda type of osteogenesis imperfecta can initially become clinically evident at variable ages, but a severe congenital form can lead to intrauterine fractures severe enough to threaten fetal viability. Progressive hearing loss begins early in childhood in an osteogenesis imperfecta subtype called van der Hoeve syndrome. Histopathologic studies of stapedial footplates in osteogenesis imperfecta patients with conductive hearing loss generally reveal a marked central thickening with minimal peripheral fixation in contrast to the pattern usually found in otosclerosis.

Autosomal Recessive Disorders

Usher syndrome, characterized by SNHL and retinitis pigmentosa, is responsible for at least 50% of combined deafness and blindness cases in the United States.[154] The frequency of the disorder approximates 4.4 per 100,000 in the total population. Based on clinical phenotype, two distinct types, USH1 and USH2, can be distinguished by the degree of hearing loss and vestibular function deficit. Patients with USH1 are born with a profound bilateral sensorineural hearing impairment accompanied by essentially a complete loss of measurable vestibular function. In USH1, the retinitis pigmentosa is generally diagnosed before puberty because visual fields are significantly restricted early in life, although the visual deficit tends to progress slowly, and few individuals with this form of the disorder ever become totally blind.

Patients with USH2 demonstrate a bilaterally symmetrical severe to profound SNHL, which shows little or no progression over time, and normal vestibular function. Visual symptoms in USH2 cases may present as early as 6 or 7 years of age, but they are milder than observed with USH1 so that definitive diagnosis of retinitis pigmentosa is usually made after puberty. Additional loss of vision may occur more rapidly with USH2 than USH1, and the type 2 patients are likely to have more restricted visual fields and cataracts with advancing age.[115] A third clinical type, USH3, is characterized by a hearing loss similar to that of USH2, in childhood, that progressively deteriorates, together with an apparent decrease in vestibular function over time.[14, 51] Ophthalmologic evaluation is an essential part of the diagnostic work-up of suspected Usher syndrome patients, and subnormal electroretinographic patterns have been observed in affected children as young as 2 to 3 years of age, before retinal changes are evident funduscopically. Young hearing-impaired children who are slow to sit unsupported, stand, or walk should be suspected of having a vestibular deficit, and the diagnosis of USH1 should at least be entertained.

As many as 10 distinct genes may be responsible for various types of Usher syndrome. Two USH-causing genes have been cloned. The first, *MYO7A* (*USH1B*), is an unconventional myosin; mutations in this gene have also been linked etiologically with DFNB2 and DFNA11 loci.[178] The second, *USH2A*, encodes a novel, tissue-specific, extracellular matrix protein or cell adhesion molecule (usherin).[86] Extracellular matrix proteins are known to be highly expressed in both connective tissue elements and specific cells, including inner hair cells, of the membranous labyrinth. Within the retina, both the Bruch membrane and the interphotoreceptor cell matrix contain extracellular matrix proteins.

Pendred syndrome, initially reported in 1896,[132] is an autosomal recessive disorder in which affected individuals have an SNHL associated with a defect in iodine metabolism, producing a euthyroid goiter. The goiter becomes clinically apparent at about 8 years of age, although earlier detection, even in infancy, is possible in some cases. Inner ear deformities, particularly Mondini malformation, have an increased prevalence among Pendred syndrome patients. The perchlorate discharge test provides definitive evidence of abnormal organification of nonorganic iodine. Exogenous thyroid hormone is a preferred treatment, while surgical thyroidectomy has proven ineffective. The *PDS* gene is part of a gene family encoding highly hydrophobic proteins that function in sulfate transport. The *PDS* gene product, called pendrin, contains 11 transmembrane proteins. Two mutations in the *PDS* gene have been reported in the single consanguineous family with *DFNB4*.[105]

Jervell and Lange-Nielsen (1957)[78] described a recessively inherited syndrome in which a congenital severe SNHL is associated with a cardiac conduction defect (torsades de pointes arrhythmias), which can lead to syncopal episodes early in life and, in some cases, sudden death. An electrocardiogram of affected individuals reveals enlarged T-waves with prolongation of the Q-T interval.

Beta-adrenergic blocking agents (e.g., propanolol) have proven effective in treating this disorder. Because Pendred syndrome is potentially fatal, an electrocardiogram should be obtained from children with SNHL of uncertain origin, particularly if the child has experienced syncopal episodes or there is a history of sudden unexplained death involving child or adolescent blood relatives. Within the inner ear, a delayed rectifier potassium channel involving proteins encoded by the *KVLQT1* and *KCNE1* genes plays a role in endolymph homeostasis, which affects children who are homozygous-by-descent for a mutation in *KCNE1*. The phenotypes associated with mutations in the genes are the same. Heterozygotes for the genes have Romano-Ward syndrome, which does not include severe-to-profound hearing loss in the phenotype.

Sex-Linked Disorders

Norrie syndrome is a sex-linked disorder with an array of features such as congenital or rapidly progressive blindness and pseudogliomas, as well as ocular opacification and degeneration leading to microphthalmia. Approximately one third of affected persons experience progressive SNHL with onset in the second or third decade. The Norrie gene (*Norrin*) is thought to be involved in neuroectodermal cell-cell interaction.

The components of otopalatodigital syndrome consist of craniofacial anomalies, including supraorbital deformity, hypertelorism, flat midface, nasal hypoplasia, and cleft palate; short stature; and variable digital length and thickness, as well as widened interdigital spaces. Ossicular malformation in these individuals leads to a conductive hearing impairment.

Clinical features of Wildervanck syndrome include Klippel-Feil malformation with fixed cervical vertebrae, sensorineural or mixed hearing loss,[56] and Duane syndrome involving sixth cranial nerve paralysis with resultant ocular retraction on lateral gaze. Wildervanck syndrome affects primarily females because the X-linked dominant form is almost universally fatal. Hearing loss can also be observed with isolated Klippel-Feil sequence or Duane syndrome in a small percentage of cases.

Children with Alport syndrome present clinically with SNHL and renal disease of varying severity. The hearing loss is generally progressive, but it may not become evident until the second decade of life. Hematuria may be present in infancy (e.g., "red diaper"), but the renal disease may remain asymptomatic during the first decade of life and then progress to renal insufficiency. Renal involvement is more severe in affected males, and death from uremia prior to 30 years of age was typical before the availability of kidney dialysis and renal transplantation. Familial studies of Alport syndrome indicate that most cases are inherited as X-linked traits, although an autosomal dominant inheritance pattern with decreased expression in females has been described. Molecular genetic studies confirm that the defect responsible for the X-linked disorder may be any of a heterogeneous group of mutations in the collagen 4A5 gene on the X-chromosome.[9] The pathologic and physiologic defect in these cases clearly involves the basement membrane, but the

TABLE 28–1. Genes Responsible for Nonsyndromic Hearing Impairment

Locus	Gene	Study
Autosomal Recessive Loci		
DFNB1	GJB2 (Cx26)	Kelsell et al[85]
DFNB2	MYO7A	Li et al[105]; Weil et al[179]
DFNB3	MYO15	Probst et al[137]
DFNB4	PDS	Li et al[105]
DFNB8/DFNB10	TMPRSS3	Scott et al[151]
DFNB9	OTOF	Yasunaga et al[186]
DFNB12	CDH23	Bork et al[16]
DFNB21	TECTA	Mustafa et al[118]
DFNB29	CLDN14	Wilcox et al[183]
Autosomal Dominant Loci		
DFNA1	DIAPH1	Lynch et al[107]
DFNA2	GJB3 (Cx31)	Xia et al[185]
DFNA2	KCNQ4	Kubisch et al[92]
DFNA3	GJB2 (Cx26)	Kelsell et al[85]
DFNA3	GJB6 (Cx30)	Grifa et al[62]
DFNA5	DFNA5	Van Laer et al[169]
DFNA8/DFNA12	TECTA	Verhoeven et al[171]
DFNA9	COCH	Robertson et al[141]
DFNA10	EYA4	Wayne et al[177]
DFNA11	MYO7A	Liu et al[106]
DFNA13	COL11A2	McGuirt et al[111]
DFNA15	POU4F3	Vahava et al[167]
DFNA17	MYH9	Lalwani et al[95]
X-linked Loci		
DFN3	POU3F4	de Kok et al[43]

Adapted from Van Camp G, Smith RJH. Hereditary Hearing Loss Homepage. Available at *http://dnalab-www.uia.ac.be.dnalab/hhh/* (retrieved 7/2001).

exact mechanism by which this defect leads to hearing loss is currently unclear.

Alport syndrome is attributable to mutations in COL4A3, COL4A4, or COL4A5. These collagens have a more restricted tissue distribution than either COL4A1 or COL4A2, the most prevalent forms of basement membrane collagens. COL4A3, COL4A4, and COL4A5 are found in the basilar membrane, parts of the spiral ligament, and the stria vascularis.[33] The mechanism of hearing loss in Alport syndrome is unknown, but the pathophysiologic findings may mirror changes in the glomerulus, where focal thinning and thickening with eventual basement membrane splitting have been observed.

Nonsyndromic Genetic Hearing Loss

Autosomal dominant progressive SNHL can be variable in age of onset and rate of progression. This type of loss eventually progresses to a severe or profound degree of impairment and is distinguishable from otosclerosis by lack of ossicular and otic capsule involvement and presentation at an earlier age than presbycusis. Konigsmark and colleagues[90] recognized four types of dominant progressive hearing loss based on age of onset and initial frequencies involved: early-onset, high-frequency, mid-frequency, and low-frequency. Linkage studies involving a large Costa Rican family with dominant progressive hearing loss have assigned the gene for at least one form of the disorder to chromosome 5q31.[101]

It is likely that the nonsyndromic recessively inherited

SNHL is the most pervasive cause of severe hereditary hearing impairment in children. Early efforts at mapping genes responsible for this type of inherited deafness have been frustrated by the extreme heterogeneity observed among affected families. It is estimated that 200 or more genes may be responsible for nonsyndromic hearing impairment, necessitating single-family linkage studies in kindreds with large numbers of affected members. Epidemiologic studies have defined at least two broad categories of nonsyndromic recessive loss: early-onset rapidly progressive (i.e., profound loss by 6 years of age) and moderate slowly progressive. The surprising frequency of mutations in the connexin 26 gene among children with nonsyndromic hearing loss has raised hope that a relatively small number of genes may account for a substantial percentage of these cases, paving the way for definitive genetic diagnoses early in life.[46, 60, 100]

About 6% of cases of nonsyndromic profound hearing loss in males may be inherited as sex-linked traits. Nonsyndromic X-linked mixed hearing loss with stapes fixation and perilymphatic gusher has been mapped to the Xq13-q21.1 region, and X-linked congenital profound SNHL has been localized to the Xq13-q21.1 area. Linkage to Xp has been reported for a variety of X-linked dominant SNHLs, which demonstrates incomplete and variable penetrance in carrier females, who usually present with mild to moderate high-frequency SNHL with onset in the second decade of life. Affected males manifest congenital, profound SNHL, which is bilateral and not associated with structural temporal bone anomalies.[94]

Localization and identification of genes responsible for nonsyndromic hearing loss has proceeded at a rapid pace. For ease of identification, a nomenclature system has been developed in which DFN connotes nonsyndromic X-linked loci, DFNA signifies autosomal dominant loci, and DFNB signifies autosomal recessive loci. Each locus is numbered sequentially as reported (e.g., DFNB1,2 and so on). Because any published material is likely to be quickly outdated, the reader should become acquainted with various World Wide Web sites that contain the most up-to-date information regarding the identification of hearing loss genes. Selected examples of genes identified to date are listed in Tables 28–1 and 28–2.

DFNB1 and DFNA3

Gene: Gap Junction Protein, Beta-2 (GJB2), Also Called Connexin 26 (Cx26)

Gap junctions are plasma membrane channels consisting of connexins, which facilitate exchange of molecules between cells.[85] GJB2 is expressed in the stria vascularis, the basement membrane, the limbus, and the spiral prominence of the cochlea. The most common mutation is 35delG (also called 30delG), which is found in more than two thirds of persons with DFNB1. A second mutation, 167delT, primarily affects Ashkenazi Jews but has recently been found in some Palestinians.[116] In some series, Cx26 mutations have been identified in nearly half of infants with congenital nonsyndromic SNHL, and the gene contains one or more sites with a high probability of mutation.

TABLE 28–2. Genes Responsible for Syndromic Hearing Impairment

Locus Name	Location	Gene	Most Important Study
Alport Syndrome			
	Xq22	*COL4A5*	Barker et al[9]
	2q36-q37	*COL4A3,* *COL4A4*	Mochizuki et al[114]
Branchio-Otorenal Syndrome			
BOR	8q13.3	*EYA1*	Abdelhak et al[1]
BOR2?	1q31	unknown	Kumar et al[93]
Jervell and Lange-Nielsen Syndrome			
JLNS1	11p15.5	*KVLQT1*	Neyroud et al[122]
JLNS2	21q22.1-q22.2	*KCNE1 (IsK)*	Tyson et al[165]; Schulze-Bahr et al[149]
Norrie Disease			
ND	Xp11.3	*Norrin*	Berger et al[10]; Chen et al[28]
Pendred Syndrome			
PDS	7q21-34	*PDS*	Everett et al[49]
Stickler Syndrome			
STL1	12q13.11-q13.2	*COL2A1*	Williamson et al[181]
STL2	6p21.3	*COL11A2*	Vikkula et al[175]
STL3	1p21	*COL11A1*	Richards et al[139]
Treacher Collins Syndrome			
TCOF1	5q32-q33.1	*TCOF1*	Dixon et al[135]
Usher Syndrome: Molecular Classification			
USH1A	14q32	unknown	Kaplan et al[82]
USH1B	11q13.5	*MYO7A*	Weil et al[179]
USH1C	11p15.1	*USH1C*	Smith et al[154]; Verpy et al[174]; Bitner-Glindzicz et al[13]
USH1D	10q	*CDH23*	Wayne et al[177]; Bork et al[16]; Bolz et al[14]
USH1E	21q	unknown	Chaib et al[27]
USH1F	10q21-22	*PCDH15*	Ahmed et al[3]
USH2A	1q41	*USH2A*	Kimberling et al[86]; Eudy et al[47]
USH2B	3p23-24.2	unknown	Hmani et al[69]
USH2C	5q14.3-q21.3	unknown	Pieke-Dahl et al[133]
USH3	3q21-q25	unknown	Sankila et al[145]
Waardenburg Syndrome: Molecular Classification			
WS type I (WS1)	2q35	*PAX3*	Tassabehji et al[161]
WS type II (WS2)	3p14.1-p12.3	*MITF*	Tassabehji et al[160]
WS type III	2q35	*PAX3*	Hoth et al[70]
WS type IV	13q22	*EDNRB*	Attie et al[5]
WS type IV	20q13.2-q13.3	*EDN3*	Edery et al[45]
WS type IV	22q13	*SOX10*	Pingault et al[134]

Adapted from Van Camp G, Smith RJH. Hereditary Hearing Loss Homepage. Available at *http://dnalab-www.uia.ac.be/dnalab/hhh/* (retrieved 7/2001).

DFNA1

Gene: *DIAPH1*

The human DFNA1 protein product is *DIAPH1*. The gene is from the forming gene family that are involved in cytokinesis and the establishment of cell polarity. *DIAPH1* is expressed in multiple tissues.[107]

DFNB2, DFNA11, USH1B

Gene: Myosin 7 (*MYO7A*)

The heads of unconventional myosins, such as myosin VIIA, move along actin filaments using actin-activated adenosine triphosphatase activity. In the ear, myosin VIIA is found in both inner and outer hair cells. In the eye, it can be found in microvilli projections in retinal pigmentary epithelial cells and photoreceptor cells. Mutations in myosin VIIA have been identified in both Usher syndrome type 1b, and nonsyndromic deafness (DFNB2).[106, 178]

DFN3

Gene: *POU3F4*

POU is an acronym for the pituitary-specific transcription factor (Pit-1), B-cell specific transcription factor (Oct-1), ubiquitous binding protein (Oct-2), and *Caenorhabditis elegans*. These genes are developmental regulators that determine cell phenotypes. *POU3F4* (class 3, transcription factor 4) mutations produce X-linked congenital mixed conductive and sensorineural hearing loss with stapedial fixation and a risk of perilymphatic gusher.[76, 142]

DFNA15

Gene: POU4F3

POU4F3 is required for high-affinity binding to DNA target sites. Targeted mutagenesis of both POU4F3 alleles leads to profound deafness and vestibular dysfunction in "knock-out" mice.

A mutation was found in a family with autosomal dominant nonsyndromic hearing loss.[167]

DFNB4

Gene: Pendred Syndrome (PDS)

Numerous different mutations in the PDS gene have been reported to cause Pendred syndrome. Four mutations account for 67% of cases of Pendred disease. Two mutations in the PDS gene have been identified in a family with DFNB4.[35, 168]

DFNA8, DFNA12, DFNB21

Gene: Alpha-Tectorin (TECTA)

TECTA encodes a protein, 95% identical to mouse alpha-tectorin, that interacts with beta-tectorin to form the non-collagenous tectoral membrane matrix. Three different missense mutations in this gene have been found in families with autosomal dominant hearing impairment.[172]

DFNB3

Gene: Myosin 15 (MYO15)

Myosin subclasses include class I and other unconventional myosins (XIII to XIV). In the shaker-2 mouse, hair cells with very short stereocilia and a long actin-containing bundle that protrudes from the basal end are demonstrated, suggesting that myosin 15 facilitates actin organization in hair cells.[137]

DFNA9

Gene: COCH

The COCH gene is expressed at very high levels in the cochlear and vestibular systems. In situ hybridization shows localization of Coch mRNA in the supporting structures and neural channels within these labyrinths[141] and corresponds to human inner ear structure histopathologic findings of homogeneous acidophilic deposits in DFNA9 patients. DFNA9 is the only type of autosomal dominant nonsyndromic deafness reported to involve vestibular symptoms.

DFNA5

Gene: DFNA5

The DFNA5 gene is expressed in the cochlea. It shows no significant homology to any other known gene and gives no clues to its function. The DFNA5 gene appears to be the same as the ICERE1 gene.[163]

DFNA2

Gene: Gap Junction Protein, Beta-3 (GJB3), Also Called Connexin 31 (Cx31)

Two Chinese families with nonsyndromic autosomal dominant hearing loss have demonstrated missense and nonsense mutations in GJB3.[185] The mutations were also present in normally hearing family members, indicating reduced penetrance. Mutations in Cx31 and Cx26 result in nonsyndromic hearing impairment, together with hyperkeratosis syndromes.

DFNA2

Gene: KCNQ4

A potassium channel gene (KCNQ4) encodes a protein that has been detected in heart, brain, and skeletal muscle by Northern blot assay and in mouse cochlear and vestibular cells by reverse transcriptase polymerase chain reaction.[92] Hybridization studies demonstrated gene activity only in outer hair cells of the organ of Corti, indicating a possible role in the recycling of potassium ions to the endolymph after hair cell stimulation. Potassium channels have been implicated previously in syndromic hearing loss (see discussion of Jervell and Lange-Nielsen syndrome).

DFNB9

Gene: Otoferlin (OTOF)

The gene OTOF is homologous to the C. elegans FER-1, which encodes a cytosolic protein involved in the movement of membrane vessicles.[186] OTOF is mainly expressed in the inner hair cells of the organ of Corti and the vestibular type I sensory hair cells. A mutation was found in families with nonsyndromic sensorineural severe-to-profound prelingual deafness.

DFNA3

Gene: Gap Junction Protein, Beta-6 (GJB6, Also Called Cx30)

Some families with disorders linked to the DFNA3 locus proved negative for GJB2 (Cx26) mutations. Grifa et al[62] cloned the human homologue of mouse GJB6, and mutations in this gene were detected in three patients from a single family. They found a missense mutation in three patients from a single family. Electrophysiologic measurements on Xenopus oocytes expressing the mutant connexin indicated that the mutation has a dominant negative effect on wild-type channels.

DFNA13

Gene: COL11A2

Mutations in COL11A2 cause autosomal dominant and autosomal recessive OSMED syndrome, a combination of osteochondrodysplasia and hearing impairment. Mutations in COL11A2 have been linked to nonsyndromic hearing impairment, which is nonprogressive and mostly affects the middle frequencies.[110] Electron micrographs of the cochlea in COL11A2 knockout mice revealed an abnormal tectorial membrane.

Mitochondrial Hearing Impairment

Mitochondria contain small pieces of non-nuclear DNA in a ring form. Each mitochondrion contains two, one, or zero copies of the mitochondrial genome, each of which comprises about 16 kilobases containing the genes for messenger, ribosomal, and transfer RNAs required for synthesis of mitochondrial proteins. These proteins interact with proteins encoded by the nuclear chromosomes and facilitate energy production through adenosine triphosphate synthesis and oxidative phosphorylation. The mutation rate of mitochondrial DNA exceeds that observed with nuclear DNA, whereas DNA repair mechanisms in the mitochondria are less effective. There are hundreds of mitochondria in each cell, only some fraction of which may contain a specific mutation (a condition known as heteroplasmy), and different percentages of mutated mitochondria may be present in different tissues. Typically, mitochondrial diseases involve progressive neuromuscular degeneration with ataxia, ophthalmoplegia, and progressive hearing loss. Disorders such as Kearns-Sayre, MELAS (mitochondrial encephalopathy, lactic acidosis, and stroke), MERRF (myoclonic epilepsy with ragged red fibers), and Leber hereditary optic neuropathy are all mitochondrial disorders. Recently, mutations involving hearing loss were discovered.

Mitochondrial inheritance is different from inheritance patterns seen with nuclear genes. Because sperm transmit few if any mitochondria, nearly the entire contribution is from the egg, producing a matrilineal inheritance that affects male and female offspring equally. If the mother is homoplasmic for a mitochondrial mutation, all the offspring will be affected. A condition involving diabetes, progressive hearing loss, and stroke has been attributed to a mitochondrial deletion. A few families have been described with nonsyndromic hearing loss that is due to the combination of a mitochondrial mutation along with a recessive mutation in a nuclear gene. One such mutation involving nucleotide 1555 was found in a large Arabic kindred. This mutation as well as several other mitochondrial mutations produces enhanced sensitivity to the ototoxic effects of aminoglycosides, such as streptomycin. Milder hearing loss may be expressed in family members who have these mutations but have not yet been exposed to aminoglycosides. Screening for these mutations would be indicated in maternal relatives of persons showing hearing loss in response to normal therapeutic doses of aminoglycosides. Because the gradual accumulation of mitochondrial mutations in affected tissues results in worsening of the phenotype over time, a mitochondrial role in presbycusis has been postulated, although definitive evidence is lacking at this time.

Chromosomal Abnormalities

Augmentation or deletion of autosomal chromosomal material in each cell generally produces multiple severe anomalies, which are often fatal. Sex chromosome abnormalities are usually expressed as less severe phenotypic traits. Trisomy connotes the presence of three copies of a given chromosome in each cell, as observed in trisomy 21 (Down syndrome) or, less commonly, in the more severe trisomy 13 (Patau syndrome) or trisomy 18 (Edward syndrome). Most other trisomies and essentially all monosomies (i.e., absence of one chromosome in a pair) are lethal. Variable phenotypes result from chromosome segment deletions or duplications.

Multifactorial Genetic Disorders

The interaction of genetic factors with environmental influences appears to be operative in the elaboration of multifactorial disorders. Those disorders associated with hearing loss include primarily clefting syndromes (conductive hearing loss) and the microtia/hemifacial microsomia/Goldenhar spectrum. The range of anomalies in patients with these disorders includes preauricular tags or pits, vertebral anomalies such as cervical hypoplastic or hemivertebrae, epibulbar dermoids, and coloboma of the upper lid. Some reports of Goldenhar syndrome (oculoauriculovertebral dysplasia) describe an autosomal dominant inheritance pattern in some families.

Infectious Etiologies

Tinghitella's excellent review[164] reiterates the diverse mechanisms operative in the replication and spread of viral infections in humans. Specific viruses often exhibit a tendency to invade specific cell types, such as neurons or lymphocytes. The viral/host immune response interaction can span the gamut from total elimination of the virus to fulminant infection, chronic infection, or latent (i.e., nonactive) infection. Host response to infection itself, including the attendant inflammatory reaction, can sometimes enhance the extent of tissue damage, thus dictating development of clinical methods for downward modulation of the host immune response. Viral isolation by means of tissue culture techniques has been the standard, albeit time-consuming and expensive, method for documenting infection by a virus.[42] Diagnostic innovations involving DNA or RNA hybridization and the polymerase chain reaction permit detection of small amounts of viral material and allow greater specificity in identifying cellular loci where viruses reside during latent infection. More rapid and accurate prenatal and neonatal diagnosis of congenital infections such as cytomegalovirus infection and toxoplasmosis is becoming possible with polymerase chain reaction and virus-specific monoclonal antibody methodologies.

Agents that have been documented as infecting the human labyrinth include cytomegalovirus, rubella, mumps, and rubeola (measles). Achieving a definitive diagnosis can be challenging. Serologic detection and virus isolation from nonlabyrinthine tissues confirm a virus' presence in the body, but documentation of labyrinthine infection requires viral isolation from perilymph, endolymph, or postmortem inner ear specimens; localization of viral antigen in labyrinthine tissues by immunohistochemical techniques; or identification of virus-specific histopathologic changes, such as inclusion bodies or giant cells.

Experimental viral labyrinthitis models developed by Davis and Johnson[41] and others demonstrated that the mumps virus has a predilection to infect non-neuroepithelial cells as found in the Reissner membrane, the stria vascularis, Henson and Claudius supporting cell layers, and the walls of the utricle and saccule. A less common neurotropic strain of mumps virus invades neurons of the spiral and vestibular ganglia without directly entering hair cells. Human temporal bone studies of patients with SNHL following mumps reveal similar changes in the stria vascularis, together with organ of Corti atrophy and partial collapse of the Reissner membrane. The most likely mode of entry into the inner ear is through viremia or direct extension from infected cerebrospinal fluid, accounting for the observed emergence of mumps-associated deafness toward the end of the first week of parotitis.

Rubeola (measles) virus, on the other hand, generally invades the neuroepithelial structures of the cochlea, utricle, saccule, and semicircular canals. Human temporal bone specimens from cases of measles-related SNHL reveal sensorineural degeneration in both the cochlea and vestibular organs, thickened tectorial membrane, stria vascularis atrophy, and saccular/utricular collapse. Herpes simplex virus types 1 and 2 are generally demonstrable in neuroepithelial components of the cochlea, utricle, saccule, and semicircular canals, together with spiral and vestibular ganglia neurons. Although herpesvirus is suspected to cause human labyrinthine damage, definitive evidence is currently lacking.

Mouse and guinea pig cytomegalovirus strains seek out primarily cochlear and vestibular perilymphatic elements, as well as neurons in the spiral and vestibular ganglia. Labyrinthine involvement with cytomegalovirus can follow intravenous cytomegalovirus inoculation, and transplacental cytomegalovirus transmission has been documented. It appears from human temporal bone studies that the human strain of cytomegalovirus has a predilection to invade endolymphatic rather than perilymphatic cells. Intralabyrinthine human cytomegalovirus can persist for some time, leading to delayed-onset hearing loss after a period of quiescence. Harris et al[66] observed that ganciclovir protected cytomegalovirus-susceptible adult guinea pigs from labyrinthine invasion by the virus. Cyclophosphamide treatment to produce immunosuppression before intracochlear cytomegalovirus inoculation ameliorated cellular infiltration in the scala media and the resultant hearing loss. Classic cytomegaloviral inclusion bodies have

been observed in both cochlear and vestibular endolymphatic ducts in the temporal bones of infants with documented congenital cytomegalovirus infection. Stagno et al[155] believe that the immune response may have an equally important parallel role to viral cytopathology in producing the neurosensory deficit.

Congenital Cytomegalovirus Infection

Cytomegaloviruses are pervasive and species-specific members of the herpesvirus family. Human cytomegalovirus infection is the most important cause of congenital infection, affecting 1% of live newborns in the United States, and is undoubtedly the most common nongenetic cause of early-onset SNHL in infants and children. In immunocompetent children and adults, cytomegalovirus infection may be essentially asymptomatic, but the developing fetus and individuals with suppressed immunity related to pharmacologic immunosuppression or disorders (e.g., acquired immunodeficiency syndrome [AIDS]) are at risk for serious sequelae. Premortem cytomegaloviremia occurs in nearly all AIDS patients, and cytomegalovirus is the most common cause of fatal opportunistic infection in both pediatric and adult AIDS patients.[108]

Approximately 30,000 to 40,0000 infants with congenital cytomegalovirus are born excreting the virus each year; reported rates range from 0.5% to 1.2% of all live births.[182] Although the risk of fetal infection increases if maternal infection occurs later in gestation (i.e., first trimester, 20%; second trimester, 30%; third trimester, 40%),[162] the likelihood of severe sequelae appears to be greater for infants infected during the first or second trimester. An additional 4% to 10% of infants acquire cytomegalovirus infection perinatally or postnatally through virus in cervical secretions, in breast milk, or through blood transfusions.

The earliest clinical reports detailing signs and symptoms of congenital cytomegalovirus infection were based on observations of neonates who are symptomatic at birth. This subgroup of infants, accounting for about 10% of all newborns with congenital cytomegalovirus, manifest classic cytomegalic inclusion disease, which may include mental retardation, severe to profound hearing loss (30% to 50%), ocular problems (e.g., chorioretinitis with optic atrophy), language or learning difficulties, cerebral palsy, hepatosplenomegaly, petechiae, jaundice, microcephaly, and growth retardation or prematurity.[48, 53] Severe mental and perceptual deficits are generally evident in these children by 2 years of age, and mortality rates in large clinical series range up to 30%. Of the remaining 90% of congenitally infected infants who are initially asymptomatic, some have low birth weights or below normal head size at birth, and about 15% will go on to develop significant disabilities such as SNHL, which may be progressive after initially being delayed in onset beyond the first year of life. Generally accepted predictors of which cytomegalovirus-infected neonates will suffer hearing loss are not currently available, although one study reported significantly increased risk of SNHL in neonates who had periventricular radiolucencies or calcifications on CT scan.[182] Congenital cytomegaloviral SNHL occurs bilaterally in about 50% of cases, varying in magnitude from 50 to 110 dB.

Transplacental passage of cytomegalovirus to the developing fetus can occur not only during primary (i.e., initial) maternal infection but also as a result of reactivated infection in pregnant women who demonstrated preconceptual natural immunity. Shedding of more than one strain of cytomegalovirus has been documented in some cases, confirming that exogenous viral strains can infect persons with preexisting natural immunity to another strain. While the largest percentage of congenital infection occurs following recurrent maternal infection, the concurrent transplacental passage of maternal anti-cytomegalovirus antibodies appears to exert a protective effect, and these infants are seldom, if ever, severely affected. Essentially all infants with symptomatic congenital cytomegalovirus are products of pregnancies during which primary maternal infection has occurred.

Diagnosis of primary maternal cytomegalovirus infection during pregnancy, which may be largely asymptomatic, can be challenging. A higher percentage of women of lower socioeconomic status demonstrate preconceptual immunity, placing women of higher socioeconomic status at greater risk for primary infection during pregnancy. Epidemiologically, children's day care facilities can serve as reservoirs for cytomegalovirus through which young children acquire the virus, suffering a relatively asymptomatic infection, but then proceed to transmit the virus to their pregnant mother and prospective sibling. There has been a 20-fold increase of parental infections noted in families in whom a child is excreting the virus and a 10-fold increase among day care workers.[162] The most definitive evidence for primary maternal cytomegalovirus infection would be seroconversion during pregnancy, as documented by a first-trimester serum sample negative for cytomegalovirus immunoglobulin (Ig) G and a later sample containing the antibody. Because cytomegalovirus IgM antibody usually persists no longer than 3 to 6 months following primary infection, the presence of both cytomegalovirus IgM and IgG in the third-trimester or immediate postpartum maternal serum sample can provide credible evidence of primary infection during pregnancy. If maternal serum is positive for cytomegalovirus IgG before and during pregnancy, with no cytomegalovirus IgM detectable during the first trimester, a congenitally infected neonate must be the product of a reactivated maternal infection or reinfection with a second cytomegalovirus strain. To simplify determination of cytomegalovirus immune status in large populations of expectant mothers, a skin test using antigen derived from a heat-inactivated Towne strain of human cytomegalovirus is being tested.[64]

Isolation of cytomegalovirus from a newborn's urine is the gold standard for confirming congenital infection. Distinguishing prenatally infected infants who are at definite risk for sequelae from those who acquire the infection during or soon after birth is complicated because perinatally infected infants can commence excreting virus between 3 and 12 weeks of age. Effective programs for mass screening of newborns shortly after birth could re-solve this dilemma but have been implemented only in research environments, for a variety of reasons. Traditional cytomegalovirus isolation techniques involve incubation of urine samples from at-risk patients with human fibroblasts in tissue culture, a process that is not only labor intensive but also requires about 4 weeks before a definitive result is forthcoming. Recent methodologic advances have reduced turnaround time to 24 hours by means of a microtiter plate fluorescent antibody assay using monoclonal antibodies incubated with urine samples previously enhanced by ultracentrifugation.[8]

Widespread application of this technique is confounded by practical difficulties in obtaining satisfactory urine samples from as many as 25% of neonates before hospital discharge. An alternative strategy, using the microtiter technique, employs neonatal saliva samples obtained by swabbing of the oral cavity with a cotton-tipped applicator. About 10% of infected mothers shed virus in cervical mucus and vaginal secretions, posing a risk of potential contamination immediately after birth, and nearly 30% of these mothers will have virus-positive breast milk. Colostrum, on the other hand, is virus-positive in only up to 5% of cases. Weighing these factors, proponents of the saliva screening technique recommend that samples be collected from neonates on the second day of life. It is quite likely that a universal cytomegalovirus screening protocol will be advocated for general implementation in the near future, raising the possibility of preventive intervention in those congenitally infected infants with normal hearing in the neonatal period.

The high prevalence of opportunistic cytomegalovirus infection associated with AIDS has stimulated clinical trials of alternative therapeutic agents, particularly for cytomegalovirus retinitis, which affects as many as 25% of these patients. Standard intravenous therapy with ganciclovir or foscarnet sodium risks side effects, primarily renal and hematologic, and is extremely costly. While this regimen is initially effective, reactivation of the infection occurs in nearly 75% of cases within 4 months. Recent clinical trials involved localized ocular therapy delivered through a device surgically affixed to the sclera, which is capable of delivering a constant dose of ganciclovir through a semipermeable membrane for up to 4 months.[84] The safety and efficacy of low-dose, sustained-release systems for treating chronic infections of the inner ear have not been demonstrated but remain an intriguing possibility. Lower dose systemic therapy, preferably by an oral route, might be coupled with targeted local drug delivery to reduce the likelihood of systemic side effects.

Although human cytomegalovirus was isolated more than 30 years ago, a comprehensive program for prevention of the infection, particularly among women of childbearing age, has been slow to develop. An attenuated live cytomegalovirus vaccine, the Towne vaccine, which is both immunogenic and ostensibly safe, has been available since 1975. Clinical application of the Towne vaccine has been delayed by residual safety concerns. Transforming elements, identified in the cytomegalovirus genome, could have oncogenic properties, as have been documented with other herpesviruses. The cytomegalovirus has also demonstrated the ability to establish latent infection, leading to periodic reactivation and the risk of reversion of an attenuated strain to a more virulent strain in immunosuppressed individuals. Finally, cytomegalovirus has been postulated to have a possible role in atherosclerosis. To address these concerns, recent vaccine development efforts have been directed toward the identification of noninfectious immunogenic cytomegalovirus derivates or constituents that do not contain viral DNA. A subunit viral vaccine based on a recombinant envelope glycoprotein B with an adjuvant is undergoing clinical trials.

Congenital Toxoplasmosis

Toxoplasma gondii is a protozoan that may infect humans and a number of other warm-blooded species. The primary reservoirs of infection are members of the cat family, which harbor the sexual stages of the protozoa's life cycle and excrete oocyst-containing sporozoites in their feces. Initially, cats are infected through carnivorism, minimizing the risk posed by domestic house cats that remain indoors. One strategy to interrupt this avenue of spread has been the recent development of a antitoxoplasma vaccine for kittens, which has proven 84% effective at preventing oocyst excretion in animals challenged with *Toxoplasma* organisms.[57] Human infection may occur via several routes, including ingestion of *Toxoplasma* cysts in undercooked meat or oocysts in food contaminated with cat feces, receipt of an infected transplanted organ, or transplacental transmission to a developing fetus. One can render *Toxoplasma*-contaminated food safe by heating it to at least 70°C for 10 minutes.

Because French cultural traditions involve eating relatively undercooked meat, seroprevalence in childbearing women in France approaches 85%. The figure is much lower for the United States, approximately 20% to 30% in coastal regions and less in dry, mountainous climates. The overall prevalence of seronegativity among U.S. women of childbearing age approaches 85% to 90%, placing large numbers of women at risk for primary *Toxoplasma* infection during pregnancy. Immunocompetent older children and adults may experience a subclinical primary infection, or the disorder may present as a mild flu-like illness with fatigue, muscle spasms, and lymphadenopathy in about 10% to 20% of cases. The organism generally enters via the intestinal epithelium and is disseminated to cells throughout the body, where intracellular multiplication occurs. The immune response of the host factors conversion of the *Toxoplasma* to cyst-forming bradyzoite forms, which most commonly reside in skeletal muscle, myocardium, and brain. Suppression of the host immune system secondary to immunosuppressive medications or diseases, especially AIDS, permits reactivation of the infection with diffuse organ system involvement, including life-threatening *Toxoplasma* encephalitis.

The overall likelihood of transplacental transmission in untreated mothers with primary infection is about 50%, increasing to 90% if infection occurs in the third trimester.[138] Estimates indicate that 3000 infants with congenital toxoplasmosis are born in the United States annually, with about 5% to 10% displaying severe involvement at birth.

Others may be asymptomatic initially, with signs of chronic infection such as retinal and central nervous system signs and symptoms gradually emerging. In untreated congenitally infected individuals, sight-threatening bilateral chorioretinitis caused by intraocular cyst rupture often becomes manifest in adolescence or early adulthood. Hearing loss occurs in about 25% of these untreated patients, with educationally significant bilateral SNHL present in about 10% to 15%. *Toxoplasma* tachyzoites have been observed histopathologically in the middle ears of congenitally infected infants, and calcifications similar to those observed in the central nervous system have been seen in the cochlear spiral ligament. Central nervous system involvement may also play a role in the pathogenesis of the SNHL.

Standard techniques for confirming the diagnosis of toxoplasmosis are aimed at identifying antibodies in serum, plasma, cerebrospinal fluid, and intraocular fluid. Anti-*Toxoplasma* IgG antibodies generally appear 6 to 8 weeks after the infection and decline slowly over several years. The methylene blue dye test of Sabin and Feldman has been the routine antibody identification methodology, supplemented recently by an indirect fluorescent antibody test, an enzyme immunoassay, and an enzyme-linked immunosorbent assay.[184] Acute infection can be distinguished from chronic infection by the presence of IgM antibodies, which appear 1 week after the infection and disappear over a 6- to 9-month period.

Negative methylene blue dye test, indirect fluorescent antibody test IgG, or enzyme immunoassay IgG findings effectively rule out acquired toxoplasmosis in an immunocompetent individual. Confirmatory evidence of acute infection can be provided by seroconversion, including a fourfold rise in antibody titer, in serial specimens over several weeks. Definitive diagnosis of a congenital *Toxoplasma* infection rests on documentation of an acute maternal infection during pregnancy, coupled with detection of infection in the fetus prenatally or in the neonate. A multifaceted strategy must be employed in many cases. The *Toxoplasma* organism may be cultured from amniotic fluid or fetal blood and *Toxoplasma*-specific IgM antibodies. It can be detected in fetal serum. Diagnostic ultrasonographic techniques can detect cerebral calcification in the developing fetus. Newer diagnostic methods, using the polymerase chain reaction, have the potential to detect a single organism by targeting a *Toxoplasma*-specific rDNA repetitive gene. Pathognomonic cerebral calcifications can also be demonstrated by a CT head scan during early infancy.

When acute maternal *Toxoplasma* infection is suspected, spiramycin therapy is recommended until a definitive diagnosis has been made. Spiramycin is safe, concentrates in the placenta, and appears to reduce the risk of transplacental transmission by nearly 60%.[157] If fetal infection is confirmed, a protocol using pyrimethamine/sulfonamide combination therapy that minimizes fetal damage should be followed during the remainder of the pregnancy. It has been recommended that infected neonates be treated for 1 year with a pyrimethamine/sulfadiazine combination alternating with spiramycin therapy.[39] Several longitudinal studies have provided some evidence supporting the efficacy of this treatment strategy in preventing the early emergence of sensory deficits such as SNHL.[34, 144, 157] Results from French studies involving prenatal treatment of infected mothers reveal a 0.6% fetal infection rate with maternal infection preconception or in early pregnancy, a 3.7% infection rate from maternal infection during the sixth to the 16th week of gestation, and a 20% rate following maternal infection during the 16th through the 25th week. The incidence of fetal infection among the 16- to 25-week group was 70% below that observed in previous studies, confirming the efficacy of aggressive treatment of primary maternal infection during pregnancy. Infants with confirmed maternal infection should be treated for up to 1 year with alternating courses of pyrimethamine and sulfonamide (sulfadiazine), coupled with folinic acid to prevent pyrimethamine complications. Careful follow-up should include CT scans to assess central nervous system status, ophthalmologic examination for chorioretinitis, and audiologic evaluation to detect delayed-onset hearing loss. Outcome studies indicate that treatment of congenitally infected infants, begun at birth, can reduce the frequency of chorioretinitis from 60% to 10%. A Chicago-based study of treated infants with longitudinal ABR and behavioral audiologic tests found no hearing loss among 57 infected infants.[31] Temporal bone histopathology from two infected infants revealed calcified scars, predominantly in the stria vascularis, comparable to those observed in the central nervous system. Experience with serious ocular *Toxoplasma* infections in AIDS patients has demonstrated the efficacy of quadruple therapy with pyrimethamine, trisulfapyrimidines, prednisone, and clindamycin, which concentrates in the ocular choroid.[97] Because clindamycin does not penetrate the central nervous system well, it is not indicated for treatment of active central nervous system disease in infants and children.

Congenital Syphilis

If the *Treponema pallidum* organism passes transplacentally after the fourth month of gestation, the developing fetus may become infected. The sequelae of such an infection may be evident at birth or appear later in life. The classic clinical picture associated with congenital syphilitic infection includes hearing loss (SNHL), interstitial keratitis, Hutchinson teeth (notched incisors), and nasal septal perforation. Prevalence estimates for SNHL in these patients varies from 3% to 38%, with 37% of affected children presenting before the age of 10 years.[40, 75, 83] Other cases may remain clinically inapparent until much later in life. In children, otosyphilis has been associated with varying degrees of hearing loss, a common pattern being a bilateral flat configuration, which may be sudden in onset. In late congenital syphilis, the hearing loss can mimic other disorders by fluctuating and progressing in an asymmetrical fashion with accompanying vertigo and tinnitus. Speech discrimination scores tend to be worse than predicted by the pure tone average, and loudness recruitment is often severe. Other findings can include a positive fistula test result (Hennebert sign) and disequilibrium in the presence of loud sounds (Tullio phenomenon).

The fluorescent treponema antibody absorption test

has a high degree of specificity with low false-positive rates during all stages of syphilis. The microhemagglutination assay for *T. pallidum* and the *T. pallidum* inhibition test represent highly specific but costly alternatives for confirmatory use in questionable cases. Because *Treponema*-specific tests may still yield positive after an adequate course of treatment has been administered, a Western blot assay has been developed to detect *Treponema* antibody isotypes.[12] Both IgM and IgG antibodies are known to be present during active infection, while only the IgG type persists after successful treatment. Parenteral penicillin at adequate dosage levels to overcome diffusion limitations posed by the blood–cerebrospinal fluid and blood-perilymph barriers remains the recommended treatment in patients not allergic to penicillin. Current treatment recommendations from the Centers for Disease Control and Prevention should be consulted before therapy is initiated; desensitization to penicillin, rather than alternative therapy in penicillin-allergic patients, may be indicated in some instances.

The interval between successive replications of *T. pallidum* in patients with late congenital syphilis may be as long as 90 days, dictating the need for extended treatment regimens. Systemic corticosteroids used in conjunction with antibiotic therapy have proven effective in stabilizing or improving auditory acuity, particularly speech discrimination, in approximately 50% of otosyphilitic patients.[188] Relative contraindications to steroid administration include no previous history of or recent exposure to varicella in susceptible individuals, recent immunization against varicella, hypertension, diabetes mellitus, glaucoma, pregnancy, and peptic ulcers.

Congenital Rubella

Australian investigators[61, 159, 164] initially recognized the teratogenic potential of prenatal maternal rubella, particularly during the first trimester, to produce a triad of congenital hearing loss, cataracts, and heart defects in the congenitally infected infant. The rubella epidemic that swept the United States in the mid-1960s occurred shortly after the rubella myxovirus had been isolated in 1962. The resultant availability of laboratory-based viral isolation and serologic techniques for confirming even subclinical infection allowed for elaboration of an expanded rubella syndrome, including hearing loss, congenital heart defects, ocular defects, microcephaly, hepatosplenomegaly, thrombocytopenia, mental or motor retardation, long bone radiolucencies, interstitial pneumonitis, encephalitis, and low birth weight.[65] Nearly half of the cases in one study of 165 laboratory-documented cases of maternal infection were subclinical (49%) versus clinically apparent (51%).[15]

While first trimester infection proved most hazardous to the fetus, laboratory-confirmed second trimester rubella resulted in deafness, microcephaly, cataracts, and mental or motor retardation. The most commonly observed defect in infants with congenital rubella was a midfrequency SNHL, ranging from moderate to severe, occurring as an isolated finding in 22% of cases. Nearly 30% of babies born to mothers with subclinical but laboratory-confirmed infection had a hearing loss. About 25% of infants with hearing loss resulting from congenital rubella demonstrated a progressive loss of auditory acuity over time. Temporal bones from congenital rubella infants with documented hearing loss revealed Scheibe-type cochleosaccular changes, with the utricle, semicircular canals, and spiral ganglion remaining unaffected. Reissner membrane collapse with adherence to the stria vascularis and organ of Corti was also observed, and the tectorial membrane was rolled into the internal sulcus in some sections. Until the introduction of a safe and effective rubella vaccine, rubella epidemics occurred at intervals of 6 to 9 years, accounting for nearly 60% of newly identified cases of childhood SNHL during these epidemic periods. Widespread administration of the vaccine has all but eradicated the disease from most developed countries, but newly arrived immigrants to the United States may deliver congenitally infected babies.

Measles and Mumps

In addition to the rubella vaccine, safe and effective vaccines for mumps and measles have decreased the incidence of these infections in the United States by nearly 95%. Mumps was commonly associated with a unilateral profound SNHL occurring without vestibular symptoms. In patients without accompanying meningoencephalitis, these two viruses apparently gain access to the inner ear through the stria vascularis during the viremia stage of the disease. Injury to the stria has been postulated to alter the volume and composition of endolymph, leading to collapse of the Reissner membrane and degeneration of the organ of Corti, the tectorial membrane, and peripheral cochlear neurons, with the earliest damage detectable in the basal coil. This mode of spread tends to spare the perilymphatic system, vestibular sensory organs, and cochleovestibular nerves.

Meningoencephalitis caused by mumps and measles produces inner ear histopathologic changes similar to those observed following meningogenic bacterial labyrinthitis. Spread in these cases proceeds along the vessels and nerves of the internal auditory canal, leading to severe neural degeneration in the absence of strial degeneration in some instances. Postrecovery intralabyrinthine fibrosis and osteoneurogenesis may be found in perilymphatic spaces.

Herpes Simplex Encephalitis

About 25% to 30% of cases of herpes simplex encephalitis occur in children, and a rise in the neonatal infection rate has paralleled the increased number of cases of genital herpes among women of childbearing age.[162] A primary genital infection during pregnancy with herpes simplex (HSV) type I or II may be responsible for spontaneous abortion, premature labor, central nervous system damage to the fetus, or intrauterine growth retardation. The developing fetus can acquire the infection either by transplacental transmission or through an ascending route from infected genitalia. Approximately 75%

of congenital HSV infections are attributable to HSV II, with the remainder being HSV I infections. Approximately 1 in 2000 newborns acquires HSV infection perinatally, with fatality rates approaching 10%. Another 60% of infected newborns suffer severe central nervous system sequelae.

Neonatal HSV infection may be limited to mucocutaneous involvement or may present as a disseminated infection. In infants with the disseminated type of infection, there is about a 25% to 30% incidence of meningoencephalitis. Suggestions regarding the route of spread of the virus to the central nervous system include hematogenous dissemination, direct ingress through the cribriform plate from nasopharyngeal mucosa, and retrograde entry through infected ganglia. Temporal and frontal lobe areas are most often involved. The meningoencephalitis is likely to occur in the second or third week of life, and the absence of a definite maternal or paternal history of HSV does not effectively exclude the diagnosis. Abnormal cerebrospinal fluid findings are present in about 90% of cases and may be accompanied by fever and altered mental state. Focal meningoencephalitis can be detected by electroencephalography and brain imaging studies (e.g., CT scan and magnetic resonance imaging), with results of the diagnostic gold standard, brain biopsy, being positive in about 33% to 50% of patients. A 10- to 14-day course of acyclovir has been recommended for treatment. SNHL associated with herpes simplex encephalitis has been postulated to involve central nervous system mechanisms.

Bacterial Meningitis

The introduction of effective antimicrobial agents reduced the mortality rate for bacterial meningitis in young children from over 90% to 2% to 3% for patients older than 1 month of age.[36, 44, 87] Among neonates, *Escherichia coli* and group B beta-hemolytic streptococci are the most common bacterial causes of meningitis, while *Haemophilus influenzae*, *Neisseria meningitidis*, and *Streptococcus pneumoniae* had historically been responsible for about 84% of cases in children 6 to 9 months of age. In previous studies, *H. influenzae* was the most commonly isolated bacterium, but recent introduction of a safe and effective protein conjugate *H. influenzae* B vaccine for infants and children older than 2 months of age has markedly reduced this pathogen's role in meningitis.

Immediate and long-term meningitic sequelae have not been eliminated by antibiotic treatment. Immediate sequelae include seizures in 28% to 40% of meningitis patients prior to or during their hospital stay. Follow-up CT scans reveal findings compatible with brain infarction, arterial occlusion, and brain or spinal cord necrosis in meningitis patients with long-term sequelae. Approximately 57% of pneumococcal meningitis survivors and 14.5% of those with *H. influenzae* meningitis have at least one detectable handicap 12 months later. The multiplicity of postmeningitic disabilities, which can diminish a hearing-impaired child's level of cooperation with diagnostic and rehabilitative procedures, can include, in addition to SNHL, seizure disorders, motor abnormalities (e.g., cerebral palsy, hemiparesis, diplegia, quadriplegia), hydro-cephalus, vestibular deficits, speech and language disorders, attention deficit disorder, visual impairment, and learning disabilities.

Most reports estimate the incidence of postmeningitic SNHL at 15% to 20%, the majority being permanent, bilateral, severe to profound losses. In a series of 64 postmeningitic children with hearing loss evaluated by the author and coworkers, 38% had bilateral asymmetrical SNHL and 11% exhibited unilateral losses.[18] Meningitis-related hearing loss has its onset early in the course of the disease, and the incidence has not been decreased by any specific antibiotic regimen. Although otitis media with direct spread through labyrinthine windows may precede onset of the disease in some cases, a more likely route is penetration of bacteria and bacterial toxins via cochlear aqueduct or internal auditory canal contents, resulting in perineuritis or neuritis of the cochleovestibular nerve and/or suppurative labyrinthitis. Other pathophysiologic mechanisms operative in producing hearing loss may include serous or toxic labyrinthitis, thrombophlebitis or embolization of labyrinthine vessels, and hypoxia or anoxia of the eighth nerve and central auditory pathways.[119]

If a child with meningitis exhibits a normal ABR after the first few days of inpatient antibiotic therapy, it is unlikely that SNHL will develop later, and some youngsters with an initially abnormal ABR may revert to normal by discharge or shortly thereafter, suggesting a resolving serous labyrinthitis. A few individuals with documented mild to moderate losses after discharge have shown some improvement over time, while more severe losses, in some children, have fluctuated for as long as a year after hospital discharge. Well-documented late progression of postmeningitic SNHL after years of stability has been reported in a few cases.

Both direct bacterial action on nervous tissue and the host's inflammatory response may be operative in producing postmeningitic sequelae.[117] Significant tissue damage has been demonstrated experimentally during the initial hours of antibiotic therapy, probably secondary to the inflammatory response evoked by bacterial disintegration products resulting from antibiotic action. Bacterial surface components, including endotoxin and cell wall constituents, can produce symptoms and signs of meningitis in experimental animals, even in the absence of viable bacteria. Studies of *H. influenzae* meningitis in animal models revealed that *H. influenzae* type B lipo-oligosaccharide is solely responsible for the induction of meningeal inflammation, brain edema, and elevated intracranial pressure.[162] At the molecular level, interleukin-1-beta and tumor necrosis factor emanating from astroglia trigger the inflammatory response, which is inhibited in experimental animal models by the administration of dexamethasone, which decreases cerebrospinal fluid pressure and brain edema. Strategies aimed at down-modulating host inflammatory response with corticosteroids (i.e., dexamethasone) in clinical studies have led to promising results, including a decrease in indices of meningeal inflammation at 24 hours and fewer neurologic sequelae in dexamethasone-treated patients compared with placebo controls.[74, 99, 146] The effectiveness of this regimen in decreasing the inci-

dence of postmeningitic hearing loss has not been conclusively demonstrated, but additional large clinical studies are underway.

Prevention of Bacterial Meningitis

Three pathogens have historically been responsible for about 80% of bacterial meningitis cases around the world: *H. influenzae* type B, *N. meningitidis*, and *S. pneumoniae*.[104] They all colonize the respiratory tract and are encapsulated bacteria that can cause both bacteremia and invasive disease. Efforts to prevent bacterial meningitis have proceeded along three vectors[104]: first, the use of hyperimmune globulins for passive immunization during epidemic periods, which has been effective but quite expensive; second, treatment of high-risk patients or their contacts with prophylactic antibiotics, which has proven effective for limited periods of time; and finally, active immunization with vaccines such as the recently introduced *H. influenzae* type B protein conjugate vaccine.

Reports of *H. influenzae* meningitis from 20 states in the United States documented a decrease of 82% from 1985 through 1991.[2] From 1989 to 1991, a decrease of 71% in the incidence of *H. influenzae* type B infections was observed in children younger than 5 years of age. In addition to meningitis, *H. influenzae* type B can cause pneumonia, bacteremia, epiglottitis, septic arthritis, cellulitis, and pericarditis. The peak incidence of *H. influenzae* type B disease is between 6 and 12 months of age, with 85% of all invasive infections affecting children younger than 5 years of age. Overall, 1 in 250 children develops invasive *H. influenzae* type B disease, with nearly 50% of these representing cases of meningitis.

The presence or absence of a polysaccharide capsule is the general criterion for distinguishing *H. influenzae* strains, and the encapsulated group is further subdivided into six serotypes (A, B, C, D, E, and F) distinguishable both antigenically and biochemically. Unencapsulated strains are etiologically involved in mucosal infections such as otitis media and sinusitis. About 95% of infections attributable to encapsulated *H. influenzae* strains are caused by type B serotype organisms. The specific antigenic component of the capsule that elicits a host immune response is a polysaccharide, a heteropolymer of polyribosyl ribitol phosphate (PRP). Early *H. influenzae* type B vaccines, based on the PRP moiety, were not sufficiently immunogenic in children younger than 2 years of age, necessitating development of a conjugated vaccine in which a protein carrier is covalently linked with the PRP component to elicit a long-lasting T-cell-based immune response, even in young patients. The PRP vaccine was originally licensed in 1985 for use with children older than 29 months, but in October 1990, a conjugate vaccine was licensed for use with infants older than 2 months of age.

Typically, *Neisseria meningitidis* has accounted for about 20% of all cases of meningitis reported annually to the Centers for Disease Control and Prevention's National Bacterial Meningitis Reporting System.[147] Infants in the first year of life have the greatest susceptibility, and the mortality rate across all age groups hovers around 10%. Of the 12 meningococcal serotypes (A, B, C, H, I, K, L, X, Y, Z, 29E, and W135) characterized by capsular saccharide antigens, types B (50%) and C (20%) account for most meningococcal meningitis cases in the United States.[104] Polysaccharide-based vaccines against group A pathogens have demonstrated efficacy in children as young as 3 months of age, but the effectiveness declines impressively over several years, particularly in children younger than 4 years of age. Similar group C vaccines proved even less immunogenic in young infants. A recently developed polyvalent protein conjugate vaccine evokes antibodies against both group B and C meningococci and *E. coli* type K1. Recommendations regarding potential application of the vaccine to young children must await the results of large clinical trials, some of which are currently underway in the United Kingdom.

The third leading cause of bacterial meningitis in the United States, accounting for 13% of cases, is *S. pneumoniae* infection, with an incidence of 1.2 to 2.8 per 100,000 annually. Children younger than 2 years of age have greater susceptibility to the infection. The overall mortality rate associated with pneumonococcal meningitis is the highest of all of the three leading pathogens, being approximately 26%. In some studies, a higher incidence of morbidity has been noted, particularly as regards sensorineural hearing loss. The pneumococcus is also an important etiologic agent in otitis media and pneumonia. *S. pneumoniae* serotypes are defined on the basis of antigenic specificity of capsular polysaccharides, which evoke type-specific protective antibodies in adults and children older than 2 years of age. The immune systems of children younger than 2 years process polysaccharide antigens as immunogens that are non–T-lymphocyte dependent, and the resultant antibodies are weak and short-lived. If conjugate vaccine techniques are used to link the capsular polysaccharide to protein carriers, a much stronger and long-lasting immune response can be evoked, even in infants.

Of the 84 known pneumococcal serotypes, types 4, 6, 14, 18, 19, and 23 most commonly affect children in the United States. All but type 6D are contained in a currently available 23-valent nonconjugated vaccine. A conjugate vaccine that links pneumococcal polysaccharide with tetanus toxoid and provides increased immunogenicity in children 2 to 5 years of age has recently been developed. Unfortunately, each serotype must be conjugated individually, limiting the number that can be included in a single vaccine. In February 2000, a 7-valent pneumococcal polysaccharide–protein conjugate vaccine was approved for use in infants and young children. The Centers for Disease Control and Prevention recommend use of the vaccine with all children aged 2 to 23 months and with children aged 24 to 59 months who are at increased risk for pneumococcal disease.

Ototoxic Drugs and Chemicals

Aminoglycosides

Aminoglycosides are bactericidal antibiotics used primarily for the treatment of tuberculosis and aerobic gram-nega-

tive bacterial infections. Known side effects of these medications include nephrotoxicity, which is often reversible, and ototoxicity, which is usually irreversible.[102, 103, 153] The aminoglycoside class includes streptomycin, neomycin, kanamycin, gentamicin, tobramycin, sisomycin, amikacin, lividomycin, and netilmicin. Excreted fairly rapidly by patients with normal renal function, these drugs can accumulate in the serum if renal status is compromised. Streptomycin and gentamicin are predominantly vestibulotoxic, while amikacin, kanamycin, and neomycin are primarily cochleotoxic.

It has been demonstrated that the toxic actions of these medications are mediated through a metabolite rather than the drug per se.[136] In the cochlea, polyphosphoinositides in hair cell membranes are affected by aminoglycosides (i.e., toxic metabolites), resulting in altered permeability and a magnesium ion loss, which impairs magnesium-dependent metabolic processes, leading to cell death. Histopathologically, aminoglycosides have been observed to cause outer hair cell degeneration initially followed by inner hair cell damage, usually beginning at the basal cochlear coil and proceeding apically. The stria vascularis can be affected, but ganglion cells usually remain intact. Although aminoglycoside ototoxicity can be reversible in some instances, it may also worsen after cessation of therapy. A known synergism exists between aminoglycosides and loop diuretics, but the order in which the medications are administered affects the outcome. If a loop diuretic is administered first, followed by an aminoglycoside, the synergism is minimal, whereas aminoglycosides administered initially followed by a loop diuretic produce a significant synergistic effect. This phenomenon is thought to be related to permeability alterations occurring during the administration of an aminoglycoside enhancing the loop diuretic's toxicity.

Transplacental passage of aminoglycosides has been observed in animal studies, while clinical monitoring of pregnant women treated for tuberculosis with streptomycin demonstrated the drug in the human fetus and amniotic fluid at approximately 50% of maternal blood levels. Fetal susceptibility to ototoxicity appears somewhat less than that observed in the mother, and, in general, the overall risk of severe fetal cochlear or vestibular damage is considered slight. Factors that could protect the fetus from labyrinthine damage are the placental barrier, which lowers the relative concentration in the fetal blood, the duration of treatment, and the stage of auditory and cochlear nerve development at the time the medication is administered.

In studies of relative aminoglycoside ototoxicity, gentamicin was found to be ototoxic in 5% to 8.6% of cases, amikacin in 7.5% to 13.9%, tobramycin in 6.1%, and netilmicin in 2.4%.[51, 109] Neomycin and kanamycin are highly toxic when administered parenterally and are effectively limited to topical use. Kanamycin and amikacin are more cochleotoxic than gentamicin and tobramycin. Gentamicin is vestibulotoxic in approximately two thirds of affected patients and cochleotoxic in the remaining one third, the cochlear toxicity being reversible in about 50% of cases over a time frame varying from 1 week to 6 months.

Apparent decreased risk of ototoxicity in neonates and

children compared with adults remains a matter of debate. The increased elimination capacity of the infant could result in more rapid clearance of the drug, but results of animal studies suggest that premature infants may actually be more sensitive than full-term infants and adults to the ototoxic effects of these medications. Among preterm infants, those with a complicated perinatal course and prolonged or high-dose aminoglycoside treatment demonstrated the highest incidence of ototoxicity. Studies have shown that the incidence of ototoxic effects varies from 0% to 36%, depending on the age, the patient population, the dose duration, and the specific aminoglycoside antibiotic employed. Eviatar and Eviatar[50] performed longitudinal studies of vestibular function in infants treated in the perinatal period with kanamycin and gentamicin. They reported a 7% incidence of SNHL and laboratory evidence of vestibular function and delayed head and posture control in 18.6% of patients. They advised that dosage regimens of aminoglycosides be based on body surface rather than weight because of the larger volume of distribution and the faster clearance rate. Finitzo-Hieber et al[52] longitudinally followed a group of neonates, gestational age 27 to 42 weeks, who were given amikacin and netilmicin in standard therapeutic dosages. They did observe some transient auditory impairment, which improved following cessation of treatment. It is also reported that kanamycin, when used in proper therapeutic doses and serum concentrations, poses little risk to the neonate of irreversible effects. Several investigators have indicated the possibility of a genetic predisposition to aminoglycoside toxicity. In some families, it appears to follow an autosomal dominant inheritance pattern, and in one Chinese study, the possibility of mitochondrial inheritance was postulated.[71]

Loop Diuretics

The loop diuretics furosemide (which is widely used to treat bronchopulmonary dysplasia) and ethacrynic acid have been observed to cause ototoxic effects. Furosemide rapidly crosses the placenta, and drug levels in the fetus may actually exceed maternal levels after multiple doses. SNHL, reversible in most cases, has been associated with higher doses, longer duration of treatment, and concomitant administration of ostensibly safe doses of aminoglycosides with loop diuretics. Animal studies suggest a critical age period of enhanced susceptibility to loop diuretics. The drugs appear to have a prolonged effect in low–birth-weight, premature infants, the standard every-12-hours dose leading to potentially toxic plasma levels. Ethacrynic acid decreases the potassium gradient between the endolymph and perilymph, probably by inhibiting the potassium pump in the stria vascularis. The drug may also inhibit the adenylate cyclase system in the stria vascularis and could have a direct effect on the outer hair cells and stereocilia. The ototoxic effects of furosemide are generally rapid in onset and quickly reversible, whereas the ethacrynic acid ototoxicity may be more gradual in onset, with a longer period of recovery. The ototoxic effects of ethacrynic acid may involve a different mechanism than is operative with furosemide, because pretreatment with organic acid ameliorates furosemide effects but not those produced by ethacrynic acid.

Retinoids

Retinoids are either natural or synthetic derivatives of vitamin A, which plays an integral part in normal growth and development. The role of retinoic acid appears to involve pattern formation within developing limbs and central nervous system structure. A significant teratogenic risk is associated with recently developed synthetic retinoids used for treating dermatologic and oncologic conditions.[101] Isotretinoin (Accutane), which is administered systemically for severe recalcitrant cystic acne, can produce either spontaneous abortion or severe malformations if administered to a pregnant woman during embryonic development. In addition to central nervous system, cardiovascular, and respiratory anomalies, associated craniofacial deformities may include cleft lip, cleft palate, and defects of the external ears, with or without ear canal agenesis.

Erythromycin

Erythromycin is a macrolide antibiotic, the ototoxic effects of which were initially observed with high parenteral doses used for treatment of Legionnaire disease.[150] Initially, a reversible hearing loss occurs, except in rare cases in which a permanent defect may result. The ototoxic mechanism is not known, but the initial effect in animal and human studies was noted in the auditory brain stem response, suggesting a central nervous system site of the lesion. Erythromycin ototoxicity appears to be dose related and more severe in the presence of impaired hepatic or renal function.[91] The loss typically occurs in the speech frequencies, so that the patient experiences symptoms earlier than is usual with aminoglycoside ototoxicity, which initially affects higher frequencies.

Vancomycin

Despite sporadic reports in the literature regarding vancomycin ototoxicity, the ototoxic potential of this medication is still unclear. A thorough review by Brummett[25] reveals that most individuals in whom vancomycin ototoxicity was reported were also treated with aminoglycosides, thus complicating interpretation of results.

Chemotherapeutic Agents

The tumoricidal mechanism of action for these drugs is not clear in all cases, but there is an inherent risk of ototoxicity compounded by the concomitant administration of aminoglycosides, diuretics, and other chemotherapeutic agents. Cisplatin, a first-generation platinum coordination complex, is a divalent platinum compound that is associated with a dose-limiting high-frequency SNHL, peripheral neuropathy, and dose-related cumulative renal insufficiency with tubular necrosis and interstitial nephritis. Tinnitus is also observed with cisplatin ototoxicity in about 7% of cases, although it may be a reversible phenomenon. The degree of SNHL associated with cisplatin is dependent on the mode of administration, tumor site, patient's age, renal function, prior cranial irradiation, possible synergistic interaction with noise, interaction between cisplatin and concomitantly administered aminoglycosides and diuretics, the cumulative dose, and the total dose per treatment.[156] Strategies to minimize cisplatin's nephrotoxic effects by predose hydration with hypertonic saline and mannitol diuresis have been effective in protecting renal function but not in ameliorating cochlear neurotoxicity.

Cisplatin ototoxicity may be a twofold phenomenon in the inner ear, involving injury to both the stria vascularis, where enzymatic activity is blocked, and the organ of Corti. Cisplatin is known to inhibit adenylate cyclase activity in the lateral wall of the stria vascularis in guinea pigs. There are a few reports of confirmed cisplatin vestibulotoxicity. The mechanisms of platinum-induced ototoxicity are probably distinct from those involved in nephrotoxicity, because the coadministration of inhibitory agents having a protective effect on renal function has failed to ameliorate ototoxic effects. Suggested mechanisms of cisplatin ototoxicity are multifactorial, with multifocal sites being involved, including possible inhibition of DNA, RNA, and protein synthesis.

There is significant individual variability in susceptibility to cisplatin, and, in some cases, a severe hearing deterioration can occur after a single dose. Early studies indicated that approximately 62% of patients experience some degree of ototoxicity with cisplatin administration, the incidence ranging from 11% to 97%. The observed SNHL is generally bilateral, but in some cases can be asymmetrical and involve 4000 and 8000 Hz initially. As early as 3 to 4 days after initial cisplatin administration, auditory impairment can be observed, and losses have ranged from 15 to 65 dB, primarily involving frequencies above the speech range. The incidence of clinically apparent hearing loss in these studies ranged from 0% to 25% (average 7%). Children appear to be at considerable risk for cisplatin SNHL because of the increasingly widespread use of the drug in the management of pediatric solid tumors such as osteogenic sarcoma and neuroblastomas. Some studies indicate that cisplatin-induced ototoxicity is more severe in the pediatric population, ranging from 84% to 100%, and may be enhanced by concurrent or pretreatment cranial irradiation. Cisplatin-induced high-frequency hearing loss (40 dB or greater at 1000 Hz and above) occurs in up to one half of all children treated with a standard dose of cisplatin (60 to 100 mg/m² per course). About one third of the affected children have severe enough losses to require amplification. Treatment protocols distributing a specific cisplatin dosage over 6 months produced less ototoxicity than 1-month and 3-month protocols. Unilateral hearing loss appears to be more common with low-dose regimens. Careful audiologic monitoring should be carried out in children when dosage levels of 400 mg/m² or greater are reached.[129] Particular attention should be paid to thresholds at 6000 and 8000 Hz.

Anoxia and Hypoxia

Increased risk for SNHL has been described among infants who experienced hypoxia or anoxia during the perinatal period, resulting from factors such as placental insufficiency, mechanical compression of the umbilical cord, or neonatal seizures. Objective indicators of oxygen deprivation or fetal distress in the history or physical findings might include neonatal acidosis, meconium staining, primary apnea (e.g., low Apgar score at 1 and 5 minutes), resuscitation at birth, or a history of prolonged ventilatory assistance. The precise pathophysiologic mechanism by which oxygen deprivation produces SNHL is unclear, but studies of neonates with chronic hypoxemia secondary to persistent fetal circulation revealed a 20% incidence of SNHL, 75% of the losses being moderate to severe and 25% profound.

Hyperbilirubinemia

Elevated serum bilirubin during the neonatal period with associated kernicterus has been etiologically tied to SNHL for decades. Insufficient conjugation of bilirubin, impaired serum albumin binding, or enhanced production of unconjugated bilirubin can elevate serum levels sufficiently to permit passage through the blood-brain barrier, with resulting bilirubin deposition in the basal ganglia, including the ventrocochlear nucleus, leading to neurologic sequelae such as SNHL. There are conflicting opinions regarding the magnitude of SNHL risk posed by varying serum bilirubin levels. Some authors suggest that "bili lights" and exchange transfusions should be used more aggressively, while recent longitudinal follow-up studies from a very large collaborative perinatal project conducted in the 1960s tend to minimize the risk of transient neonatal hyperbilirubinemia.[121]

Neonatal Intensive Care

Many of the factors that prompt admission of a neonate to an intensive care unit, such as anoxia or hypoxia, sepsis, hyperbilirubinemia, low birth weight, dysmaturity, and orofacial anomalies, constitute, in themselves, high-risk indicators for SNHL. It is estimated that premature infants (birth weight less than 2500 g) experience a 20-fold increase in risk for SNHL as compared with full-term, normal control subjects.[173] Admission to the neonatal intensive care unit is a reliable indicator for identifying those infants in need of auditory screening and careful follow-up if results are equivocal.

Recurrent Otitis Media and Mastoid Disease

Apart from the associated conductive hearing loss, studies by Paparella and others suggest that otitis-prone children have a predilection, over an extended period of middle-ear and mastoid disease, to develop a coexisting SNHL.[126, 127] Pathogenic mechanisms might include penetration of the labyrinthine windows (e.g., round window membrane) by infectious by-products or toxins, topical medications with ototoxic potential, or a combination thereof. Animal studies of round window membrane permeability demonstrate a greater degree of penetration of middle-ear contents into the inner ear than observed empirically in humans. Treatment of otitis media in patients with a nonintact tympanic membrane barrier (e.g., patent tympanostomy tubes) with otic drops containing potentially ototoxic drugs and chemicals has been a widespread practice among clinicians with scarcely any demonstrable risk of SNHL. Mucosal edema and granulation tissue in the middle ear, which generally accompany otitis media, have been postulated to play a protective role in helping prevent transmission of undesirable substances through the round window membrane.

Ear and Temporal Bone Trauma

Penetrating or blunt trauma to the ear and temporal bone can produce conductive, sensorineural, or mixed hearing loss. Transcanal injury with objects such as cotton swabs can perforate the tympanic membrane and disrupt the ossicular chain. Skull trauma may lead to skull fractures involving the temporal bone, which are classified as either longitudinal or transverse in relation to the long axis of the temporal bone. The longitudinal variety accounts for about 70% to 80% of temporal bone fractures, and patients with such an injury usually present with pain, tympanic membrane perforation, bloody otorrhea, and conductive hearing loss. The transverse type may transect the inner ear and internal auditory canal, resulting in SNHL, vertigo, and often facial paralysis. Even in the absence of detectable fractures, closed head trauma can damage delicate intralabyrinthine structures, producing tinnitus, vertigo, and SNHL, usually involving the high frequencies, which may also accompany disruption of the normal membranous barrier between the middle ear and labyrinth (i.e., perilymphatic fistula). One retrospective study of children admitted to the hospital following head trauma revealed a 7% incidence of temporal bone fracture, while 13% had SNHL.[22, 110] Among 324 children and adolescents with unilateral SNHL in a second study, 10.8% of the losses were attributed to head trauma, 35% of which occurred prior to the age of 8 years.[22]

Perilymphatic Fistula

A perilymphatic fistula results from an abnormal discontinuity in the bony/membranous enclosure that normally surrounds the perilymphatic spaces and prevents leakage of perilymph. The majority of PLFs occur in or near the oval and round windows, although bony erosion secondary to cholesteatoma or fractures of the temporal bone can produce dehiscences in other sites. Conditions and precipitating events associated with PLF may include ear surgery (stapes or chronic ear procedures), head or ear trauma, noise trauma, barotrauma, significant physical exertion, cranial or inner ear anomalies, and ossicular or middle-ear deformities, particularly involving the stapes or round window. The potential for a spontaneous PLF serving as a contributing cause of sudden, fluctuating, and progressive SNHL in children has been mentioned by several authors.[63, 128, 158] Ingress of air into the labyrinth may play as important a pathophysiologic role as leakage of perilymph in producing the symptoms associated with PLF.

An array of signs and symptoms have been reported by patients with surgically confirmed PLF, including aural fullness, sudden, fluctuating, or progressive SNHL, fluctuating speech discrimination scores, tinnitus (i.e., roaring), and balance disturbances (unsteadiness rather than true vertigo).[18] Relatively symptom-free intervals may be followed by an exacerbation of symptoms triggered by nose blowing, straining, Valsalva maneuver, eustachian tube dysfunction, or physical exertion. Young children may not be linguistically competent to describe their symptoms, so parental diaries regarding the child's auditory responsiveness, clumsiness, or ear-related symptoms are helpful. Standard fistula test procedures using pneumatic otoscopy or tympanometry with or without concurrent posture platform testing are helpful if results are positive but not exclusionary if results are negative. Absence of a pathognomonic symptom complex or a reliable noninvasive technique for identifying the presence of a PLF leaves direct inspection of the middle ear through a tympanotomy approach or a myringotomy (e.g., with otologic endoscopes) as the definitive approach to diagnosis. Even at surgery, using Trendelenburg position, venous compression, and ossicular chain palpation, definitive demonstration of a PLF may not be possible. Recent studies have been directed toward identifying a specific chemical or immunologic marker to distinguish perilymph from other fluids present in the middle ear at surgery, such as mucus or local anesthetic solution.[130] Beta-2 transferrin has been advocated as a marker unique to perilymph and cerebrospinal fluid, and it could thus be useful in demonstrating a PLF at surgery. Rapid analysis techniques potentially acceptable for intraoperative use are being developed currently.[152] The availability of a sensitive and specific indicator for perilymph will allow an accurate assessment of the prevalence of PLF among children with sudden, fluctuating, or progressive SNHL.

Noise-Induced Hearing Loss

Sounds of sufficient intensity and duration will damage the human ear, producing temporary or permanent hearing loss, often accompanied by tinnitus. Sound overstimulation can produce irreversible inner ear damage at any age, including early infancy. A typical noise-induced hearing loss (NIHL) can impair speech discrimination enough to affect performance in the classroom. With adequate ear protection, NIHL is entirely preventable, except in cases of accidental exposure.

More than 20 million Americans, including children and adolescents, are exposed on a regular basis to hazardous sound levels that could result in hearing loss. While a significant percentage of hazardous noise exposure occurs in the work environment, the proliferation of potentially harmful noise sources at home, on the farm, and in recreational environments places increasing numbers of unsuspecting people at risk. A 1990 National Institutes of Health Consensus Statement on Noise and Hearing Loss, together with recent congressional hearings on the topic of NIHL in children and youth, has heightened interest in this issue.[32]

Regulations issued by the U.S. Department of Labor

Loud Noises Signal Danger

(dB)		
D	140	Firecrackers, Gunshot Blast, Jet Engine
A	130	"Boom" Cars, Jack Hammer
N	120	Rock Concerts, Band Practice, Headphones
G	110	Shouting in Ear, Disco, Chain Saw
E	100	Snowmobile, Subway, Woodworking Shop
R	90	Traffic, Lawn Mower, Motorcycle, Orchestra

85 dB ▬▬▬▬▬▬▬▬▬▬▬▬▬▬▬▬▬▬

	80	Alarm Clock, Hair Dryer, Assembly Line
	70	Restaurant, Vacuum Cleaner, Sewing Machine
	60	Conversation, Air Conditioner
	50	Average Home, Refrigerator
	40	Principal's Office
	30	Quiet Library, Soft Whisper

FIGURE 28–3. List of typical noise exposures and their decibel levels, indicating danger-level noise exposure over 85 dB. (From Brookhauser PE. Evaluation of sensorineural hearing loss in infants and children. Adv Otolaryngol Head Neck Surg 7:187, 1993.)

currently set the boundary between acceptable and damaging noise in the workplace at 85 dB(A) for continuous exposure during a full workday. The "A" refers to a type of sound filter used in a sound level meter when measuring potentially damaging sounds. These devices can measure both continuous loud noise, as produced by heavy machinery, and intermittent, short-duration noises with very loud peak components, as exemplified by gunfire. Damage risk criteria are based on the average responses of large numbers of people (Fig. 28–3).[20] Because the decibel scale is exponential, a change of a few decibels represents a significant change in loudness. Ear damage from hazardous noise exposure may be classified as either acoustic trauma or NIHL. The pattern of damage resulting from a specific exposure to a sound source depends on the frequency content, intensity (i.e., loudness), duration, and scheduling (i.e., continuous or intermittent) of

the noise, as well as susceptibility of the ear involved. Exposure to very intense sounds (greater than 140 dB[A]) of short duration, such as gunfire or an explosion, can produce immediate, severe, and permanent hearing loss, designated as acoustic trauma. Moderate exposure to less intense but potentially damaging sounds may cause a temporary threshold shift. With additional exposure, NIHL gradually becomes permanent, initially involving frequencies in the 3000 to 6000 Hz range, resulting in a characteristic "notch" configuration in the audiogram (Fig. 28–4). Prolonged exposure will lead to additional loss first in higher and then in lower frequencies. Temporal bone histopathologic studies in NIHL patients reveal the hair cells themselves to be most vulnerable to structural damage. Hair cell degeneration can lead to eventual loss of auditory nerve fibers, which can further damage hearing.

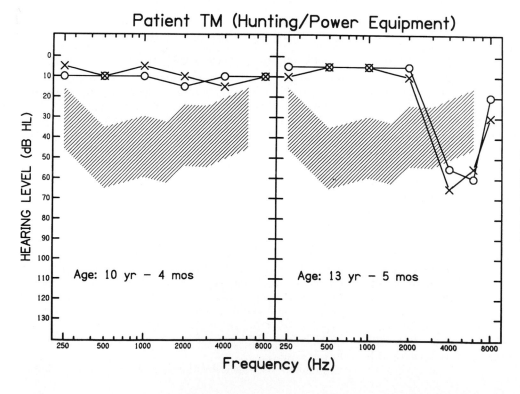

FIGURE 28–4. A patient's audiologic results after noise exposure by hunting and power equipment. (From Brookhauser PE, Worthington DW, Kelly WJ. Noise-induced hearing loss in children. Laryngoscope 102:645, 1992.)

Impulse noises, such as gunfire or a firecracker, are characterized by short duration and very high sound intensity levels, 132 to 170 dB(A). Large-caliber rifles and shotguns are particularly hazardous. Parents and public policy makers have expressed concern about hearing risks posed by exposure to rock music, "boom" cars, motorcycles, and personal cassette players (e.g., Walkman). Sound levels in a typical discotheque approximate 95 dB(A), but at rock concerts it is common to experience amplified sound as loud as 105 to 115 dB(A).[30] Not only the audience but especially the rock musicians, stage hands, ushers, and concessionaires are at risk for acquiring NIHL after prolonged exposure. Most people can experience short periods of exposure during a typical concert without suffering a permanent hearing loss, but practically everyone will experience a temporary loss (temporary threshold shift) and often tinnitus. Personal cassette players are capable of producing sound levels in excess of 100 to 115 dB(A) at the ear, and exposure time can be lengthy. Surveys have found that 80% of children in the middle elementary school age group own or use personal cassette players and 5% to 10% listen for extended periods at potentially dangerous volume settings.[6, 30] Sound levels attained in many so-called boom cars, which contain very powerful stereo amplifiers and speakers, may exceed 120 dB(A). All individuals exposed to such high ambient sound levels for prolonged periods risk permanent NIHL.

Outdoor lawn care tools, such as gasoline-powered leaf blowers, can produce sound levels of 110 to 112 dB(A) at the operator's ear level. Sound levels approaching 116 dB(A) emanate from a typical chain saw. Hearing protection is recommended for anyone using such loud devices as chain saws, unmuffled lawn mowers, leaf blowers, power saws, heavy duty vacuums, and rug cleaning machines. Recreational vehicles that produce potentially damaging noise include all-terrain vehicles, snowmobiles, go-carts, some model airplanes, and motocross bikes. Although most casual users will not exceed allowable exposure periods, differences in individual susceptibility to damage warrant caution. Persons living in rural settings may be exposed to many noisy devices on a daily basis and appear to be particularly at risk for NIHL.

In a recent study of NIHL in 114 children and adolescents, males accounted for 90.3% of the study population, which is consistent with previous findings regarding gender-specific incidence.[23] The average male child or adolescent is assumed to participate in more leisuretime activities involving potentially hazardous noise exposure. Fireworks or firearms were identified as the sole noise source in 36% of cases of children with bilateral NIHL and 67% of cases of youngsters with unilateral impairments. Including children exposed to multiple noise sources, 46% of all the study children had histories of exposure to live or amplified music, and live or amplified music was identified in 12% of the cases as the principal source of noise exposure. Noise exposure histories often included descriptions of children riding with a parent on a recreational vehicle (e.g., motorcycle, snowmobile), assisting in a home workshop, or accompanying an adult on a hunting trip or a visit to a target range. Well-child visits to health providers, school or sports physicals, kindergarten round-up, school health or science curricula, music

instruction, automotive repair training, woodworking courses, vocational agriculture programs, and firearm safety classes all present opportunities to instruct young people and their parents about hazardous noise. Public and private educational initiatives have been undertaken to address this need, including "Quiet Pleases" by Sertoma International and "I Love What I Hear" by the National Institute of Deafness and Other Communication Disorders.

Conclusion

The gradual introduction of mandatory newborn hearing screening, coupled with advances in genetics, vaccine development, hearing aid technology, and cochlear implants, will markedly alter the etiologic mix and prospects for treatment and habilitation of future generations of children who are deaf and hard of hearing. Otolaryngologists who aspire to serve the needs of these children and their families must rapidly expand their scope of knowledge, particularly in the field of genetics, to provide the expected standard of care.

REFERENCES

1. Abdelhak S, Kalatzis V, Heilig R, et al. A human homologue of the Drosophilia eyes absent gene underlies branchio-oto-renal (BOR) syndrome and identifies a novel gene family. Nat Genet 15:157, 1997.
2. Adams WG, Deaver KA, Cochi SL, et al. Decline of childhood haemophilus influenzae type b (Hib) disease in the Hib vaccine era. JAMA 269:221, 1993.
3. Ahmed ZM, Tiazuddin S, Bernstein SL, et al. Mutations of the protocadherin gene pcdh15 cause usher syndrome type 1f. Am J Hum Genet 69:25, 2001.
4. American Speech-Language-Hearing Association, American Academy of Audiology & Alexander Graham Bell Association for the Deaf. A model universal newborn/infant hearing screening, tracking and intervention bill. Rockville, MD, ASHA, 1997.
5. Attie T, Till M, Pelet A, et al. Mutation of the endothelin-receptor B gene in Waardenburg-Hirschsprung disease. Hum Mol Genet 4:2407, 1995.
6. Axelsson A. Noise exposure in adolescents and young adults [abstract]. NIH Consensus Development Conference, January 22–24, 1990, pp 77–82.
7. Baker-Hawkins S, Easterbrooks S (eds). Deaf and hard of hearing students: education service delivery guidelines. Alexandria, VA, National Association of State Directors of Special Education, 1994.
8. Balcarek KB, Warren W, Smith RJ, et al. Neonatal screening for congenital cytomegalovirus infection by detection of virus in saliva. J Infect Dis 167:1433, 1993.
9. Barker DF, Hostikka SL, Zhous J, et al. Identification of mutations in the COL4A5 collagen gene in Alport syndrome. Science 248:1224, 1990.
10. Berger W, Meindl A, van de Pol TJ, et al. Isolation of a candidate gene for Norrie disease by positional cloning. Nat Genet 1:199, 1992.
11. Bergstrom LB. Pathology of congenital deafness: present status and future priorities. Ann Otol Rhinol Laryngol 89(suppl 74):31, 1980.
12. Birdsall HH, Baugh RE, Jenkins HA. The diagnostic dilemma of otosyphilis: a new western blot assay. Arch Otolaryngol Head Neck Surg 116:617, 1990.
13. Bitner-Goindziicz M, Lindley KJ, Rutland P, et al. A recessive contiguous gene deletion causing infantile hyperinsulinism, enteropathy and deafness identifies the Usher type 1C gene. Nat Genet 26:56, 2000.
14. Bolz H, Von Brederlow B, Ramierz A, et al. Mutation of CDH23,

encoding a new member of the cadherin gene family, causes Usher syndrome type 1D. Nat Genet 27:108, 2001.

15. Bordley JE, Brookhouser PE, Hardy WG. Prenatal rubella. Acta Otolaryngol 66:1, 1968.

16. Bork JM, Peters LM, Riazuddin S, et al. Usher syndrome 1D and nonsyndromic autosomal recessive deafness DFNB12 are caused by allelic mutations of the novel cadherin-like gene CDH23. Am J Hum Genet 68:26, 2001.

17. Brama I, Fainaru M: Inner ear involvement in Behçet's disease. Arch Otolaryngol 106:215, 1980.

18. Brookhouser PE. Perilymphatic fistula in children. In Healy GB (ed). Common Problems in Pediatric Otolaryngology. Chicago, Year Book Medical Publishers, 1990.

19. Brookhouser PE. Evaluation of sensorineural hearing loss in infants and children. In Advances in Otolaryngology—Head and Neck Surgery, vol. 7. Philadelphia, Mosby–Year Book, 1993, pp 159–191.

20. Brookhouser PE, Auslander MC, Meskan ME. The pattern and stability of postmeningitic hearing loss in children. Laryngoscope 98:940, 1988.

21. Brookhouser PE, Cyr DG, Beauchaine K. Vestibular findings in the deaf and hard of hearing. Otolaryngol Head Neck Surg 90:773, 1982.

22. Brookhouser PE, Worthington DW, Kelly WJ. Unilateral hearing loss in children. Laryngoscope 101:1264, 1991.

23. Brookhouser PE, Worthington DW, Kelly WJ. Noise-induced hearing loss in children. Laryngoscope 102:645, 1992.

24. Brown KS. Genetic and environmental factors in profound prelingual deafness. Med Clin North Am 53:741, 1969.

25. Brummett RE. Ototoxicity of vancomycin and analogues. Otolaryngol Clin North Am 24:821, 1993.

26. Calderelli DD, Rejowski JE, Corey JP. Sensorineural hearing loss in lupus erythematosus. Am J Otol 7:210, 1986.

27. Chaib H, Kaplan J, Gerber S, et al. A newly identified locus for Usher syndrome type I, USH1E, maps to chromosome 21q21. Hum Mol Genet 6:27, 1997.

28. Chen ZY, Hendriks RW, Jobling MA, et al. Isolation and characterization of a candidate gene for Norrie disease. Nat Genet 1:204, 1992.

29. Cheson BD, Bluming AZ, Alroy J. Cogan's syndrome: a systemic vasculitis. Am J Med 60:549, 1976.

30. Clark WW. Noise exposure and hearing loss from leisure activities [abstract]. NIH Consensus Development Conference, 1990, pp 55–58.

31. Cody DT, Sones DA. Relapsing polychondritis: audiovestibular manifestations. Laryngoscope 81:1208, 1971.

32. Consensus Conference. Noise and hearing loss. JAMA 263:3185, 1990.

33. Cosgrove D, Samuelson G, Pint J. Immunohistochemical localization of basement membrane collagens and associate proteins in the murine cochlea. Hear Res 97:54, 1996.

34. Couvreur J, Thulliez P, Daffos F, et al. In utero treatment of otoxoplasmic fetopathy with the combination pyrimethamine-sulfadiazine. Fetal Diagn Ther 8:45, 1993.

35. Coyle B, Reardon W, Herbrick JA, et al. Molecular analysis of the PDS gene in Pendred syndrome. Hum Mol Genet 7:1105, 1998.

36. Crook WG, Clanton BR, Hodes HL. Hemophilus influenzae meningitis: observations on the treatment of 110 cases. Pediatrics 4:643, 1949.

37. Cyr DG. Vestibular testing in children. Ann Otol Rhinol Laryngol 89:63, 1980.

38. Cyr DG, Brookhouser PE, Valente MA, Grossman A. Vestibular evaluation of infants and preschool children. Otolaryngol Head Neck Surg 93:463, 1985.

39. Daffos F, Forestier F, Capella-Pavlovsky M, et al. Prenatal management of 746 pregnancies at risk for congenital toxoplasmosis. N Engl J Med 318:271, 1988.

40. Darmstadt GL, Harris JP. Leutic hearing loss: clinical presentation, diagnosis and treatment. Am J Otolaryngol 10:410, 1989.

41. Davis LE, Johnson LG. Viral infections of the inner ear: clinical, virologic, and pathologic studies of humans and animals. Am J Otolaryngol 4:347, 1983.

42. Davis LE. Comparative experimental viral labyrinthitis. Am J Otolaryngol 1:382, 1990.

43. de Kok YJ, van der Maarel SM, Bitner-Glindicz M, et al. Associa-

tion between X-linked mixed deafness and mutations in the POU domain gene POU3F4. Science 267:685, 1995.

44. Dodge PR. Sequelae of bacterial meningitis. Pediatr Infect Dis 5:618, 1986.

45. Edery P, Attie T, Amiel J, et al. Mutation of the endothelin-3 gene in the Waardenburg-Hirschsprung disease (Shah-Waardenburg syndrome). Nat Genet 12:442, 1996.

46. Estivill X, Fortina P, Surrey S, et al. Connexin-26 mutations in sporadic and inherited sensorineural deafness. Lancet 351:394, 1998.

47. Eudy JD, Weston MD, Yao S, et al. Mutation of a gene encoding a protein with extracellular matrix motifs in Usher syndrome type IIa. Science 280:1753, 1998.

48. Everberg G. Further studies on hereditary unilateral deafness. Acta Otolaryngol (Stockh) 51:615, 1960.

49. Everett LA, Glaser B, Beck JC, et al. Pendred syndrome is caused by mutations in a putative sulphate transporter gene (PDS). Nat Genet 17:411, 1997.

50. Eviatar L, Eviatar A. Development of head control and vestibular responses in infants treated with aminoglycosides. Devel Med Child Neurol 24:372, 1982.

51. Federspil P, Schatzle W, Tiesler E. Pharmacokinetics and ototoxicity of gentamicin, tobramycin and amikacin. J Infect Dis 134:S200, 1976.

52. Finitzo-Hieber T, McCracken GH Jr, Brown KC. Prospective controlled evaluation of auditory function in neonates given netilmicin or amikacin. J Pediatr 106:129, 1985.

53. Fisch L. Deafness in cerebral-palsied school-children. Lancet 2:370, 1955.

54. Fraser GR. The causes of profound deafness in childhood. Baltimore, Johns Hopkins University Press, 1976.

55. Fraser GT. Profound childhood deafness. J Med Genet 1:118, 1984.

56. Fraser WI, MacGillivary RC. Cervico-oculo-acoustic dysplasia: "the syndrome of Wildervanck". J Ment Defic Res 12:322, 1968.

57. Frenkel JK, Pfefferkorn ER, Smith DD, Fisback JL. Prospective vaccine prepared from a new mutant of Toxoplasma gondii for use in cats. Am J Vet Res 52:759, 1991.

58. Friedmann I, Bauer F. Wegener's granulomatosis causing deafness. J Laryngol Otol 87:449, 1973.

59. Gallaudet University Center for Assessment and Demographic Study. Thirty years of the annual survey of deaf and hard of hearing children and youth: a glance over the decades. Am Ann Deaf 142:72, 1998.

60. Gasparini P, Rabionet R, Barbujani G, et al. High carrier frequency of the 35delG deafness mutation in European populations. Genetic Analysis Consortium of GJB2 35delG. Eur J Hum Genet 8:19, 2000.

61. Gregg NM. Congenital cataract following German measles in the mother. Ophthal Cos Aust 3:35, 1941.

62. Grifa A, Wagner CA, D'Ambrosio L, et al. Mutations in GJB6 cause nonsyndromic autosomal dominant deafness at DFNA3 locus. Nat Genet 23:16, 1999.

63. Grundfast KM, Bluestone CD. Sudden or fluctuating hearing loss and vertigo in children due to perilymph fistula. Ann Otol Rhinol Laryngol 87:761, 1978.

64. Gupta R, Gonczol E, Manning ML, et al. Delayed type hypersensitivity to human cytomegalovirus. J Med Virol 39:109, 1993.

65. Hardy JB. Clinical and developmental aspects of congenital rubella. Arch Otolaryngol 98:230, 1973.

66. Harris JP, Fran JT, Keithley EM. Immunologic responses in experimental cytomegalovirus labyrinthitis. Am J Otolaryngol 11:304, 1990.

67. Healy LA, Wilske KR. The systemic manifestation of temporal arteritis. New York, Grune & Stratton, 1978.

68. Henley CM, Rybak LP. Developmental ototoxicity. Otolaryngol Clin North Am 26:857, 1993.

69. Hmani M, Ghorbel A, Boulila-Elgaied A, et al. A novel locus for Usher syndrome type II, USH2B, maps to chromosome 3 at p23–24.2. Eur J Hum Genet 7:363, 1999.

70. Hoth CF, Milunsky A, Lipsky N, et al. Mutations in the paired domain of the human PAX3 gene cause Klein-Waardenburg syndrome (WS-III) as well as Waardenburg syndrome type I (WS-I). Am J Hum Genet 52:455, 1993.

71. Hu D-N, Qui W-Q, Wut B-T, et al. Genetic aspects of antibiotic

induced deafness: mitochondrial inheritance. J Med Genet 27:79, 1991.

72. Hughes GB, Barna BP, Kinney SE, et al. Clinical diagnosis of immune inner-ear disease. Laryngoscope 98:251, 1988.

73. Hughes GB, Kinney SE, Barna BP, Calabrese LH. Rh factor and deafness: the problem, its psychological, physical and educational manifestations. Except Child 34:5, 1967.

74. Hughes GB, Kinney SE, Barna BP, Calabrese LH. Practical versus theoretical management of autoimmune inner ear disease. Laryngoscope 98:758, 1984.

75. Hughes GB, Rutherford I. Predictive value of serologic tests for syphilis in otology. Ann Otol Rhinol Laryngol 95:250, 1986.

76. Ingraham HA, Albert VR, Chen RP, et al. A family of POU-domain and Pit-1 tissue-specific transcription factors in pituitary and neuroendocrine development. Annu Rev Physiol 52:773, 1990.

77. Jackler RK, Luxford WM, House WF. Congenital malformations of the inner ear: a classification based on embryogenesis. Laryngoscope 97:2, 1987.

78. Jervell A, Lange-Nielsen F. Congenital deaf-mutism, functional heart disease with prolongation of the QT interval, and sudden death. Am Heart J 54:59, 1957.

79. Joint Committee on Infant Hearing. Position statement. ASHA 24:1017, 1982.

80. Joint Committee on Infant Hearing. 1990 Position statement. ASHA 33:3, 1991.

81. Joint Committee on Infant Hearing 1994 Position statement. American Academy of Pediatrics Joint Committee on Infant Hearing. Pediatrics 95:152, 1995.

82. Kaplan J, Gerber S, Bonneau D, et al. A gene for Usher syndrome type I (USH1A) maps to chromosome 14q. Genomics 14:979, 1992.

83. Karmody CS, Schunecht HF. Deafness in congenital syphilis. Arch Otolaryngol 83:18, 1966.

84. Keijer WJ, Burger DM, Neuteboom GH, et al. Ocular complications of the acquired immunodeficiency syndrome. Focus on the treatment of cytomegalovirus retinitis with ganciclovir and foscarnet. Pharm World Sci 15:56, 1993.

85. Kelsell DP, Dunlop J, Stevens HP, et al. Connexin 26 mutations in hereditary non-syndromic sensorineural deafness. Nature 387:80, 1997.

86. Kimberling WJ, Weston MD, Moller C, et al. Localization of Usher syndrome type II to chromosome 1q. Genomics 7:245, 1990.

87. Koch R, Carson MJ. Management of Hemophilus influenzae, type B meningitis: analysis of 128 cases. J Pediatr 46:18, 1955.

88. Konigsmark BW. Hereditary deafness in man. N Engl J Med 281:712, 1969.

89. Konigsmark BW, Gorlin RJ (eds). Genetic and Metabolic Deafness. Philadelphia, WB Saunders, 1976.

90. Konigsmark BW, Mengel M, Berlin CI. Familial low frequency hearing loss. Laryngoscope 81:759, 1971.

91. Kroboth PD, McNeil MA, Kreeger A, et al. Hearing loss and erythromycin pharmacokinetics in a patient receiving hemodialysis. Arch Intern Med 143:1263, 1983.

92. Kubisch C, Schroeder BC, Friedrich T, et al. KCNQ4, a novel potassium channel expressed in sensory outer hair cells, is mutated in dominant deafness. Cell 96:437, 1999.

93. Kumar S, Deffenbacher K, Marres HA, et al. Genomewide search and genetic localization of a second gene associated with autosomal dominant-branchio-oto-renal syndrome: clinical and genetic implications. Am J Hum Genet 66:1715, 2000.

94. Lalwani AK, Brister R, Fex J, et al. A new nonsyndromic x-linked sensorineural hearing loss linked to Xp21.2 [abstract]. ARO 402, 1994.

95. Lalwani AK, Goldstein JA, Kelley MJ, et al. Human nonsyndromic hereditary deafness DFNA17 is due to a mutation in nonmuscle myosin MYH9. Am J Hum Genet 67:1121, 2000.

96. Lalwani AK, Grundfast K, Fex J, et al. Identification of a point mutation in the homeobox of PAX3 gene causing type I Waardenburg syndrome [abstract]. ARO 409, 1994.

97. Lam S, Tessler HH. Quadruple therapy for ocular toxoplasmosis. Can J Ophthalmol 28:58, 1993.

98. Lammer EJ, Chen DT, Har RM, et al. Retinoic acid embryopathy. N Engl J Med 313:837, 1985.

99. Lebel MH, Freij BJ, Syrogiannopoulos GA, et al. Dexamethasone therapy for bacterial meningitis: results of two double-blind, placebo-controlled trials. N Engl J Med 319:964, 1988.

100. Lench NJ, Markham AF, Mueller RF, et al. A Moroccan family with autosomal recessive sensorineural hearing loss caused by a mutation in the gap junction protein gene connexin 26 (GJB2). J Med Genet 35:151, 1998.

101. Leon PE, et al. The gene for an inherited form of deafness maps to chromosome 5q31. Proc Nat Acad Sci 89:5181, 1992.

102. Lerner SA, Matz GJ. Aminoglycoside ototoxicity. Am J Otolaryngol 1:169, 1980.

103. Lerner SA, Matz GJ, Hawkins JE Jr (eds). Aminoglycoside ototoxicity. Boston, Little, Brown, 1981.

104. Lieberman JM, Greenberg DP, Ward JI. Prevention of bacterial meningitis: vaccines and chemoprophylaxis. Infect Dis Clin North Am 4:703, 1990.

105. Li XC, Everett LA, Lalwani AK, et al. A mutation in PDS causes non-syndromic recessive deafness. Nat Genet 18:215, 1998.

106. Liu XZ, Walsh J, Mburu P, et al. Mutations in the myosin VIIA gene cause non-syndromic recessive deafness. Nat Genet 16:188, 1997.

107. Lynch ED, Lee MK, Morrow JE, et al. Nonsyndromic deafness DFNA1 associated with mutation of a human homolog of the Drosophilia gene diaphanous. Science 278:1315, 1997.

108. Marshall GS, Plotkin SA. Progress toward developing a cytomegalovirus vaccine. Infect Dis Clin North Am 4:283, 1990.

109. Matz GJ. Aminoglycoside cochlear ototoxicity. Otolaryngol Clin North Am 26:705, 1993.

110. McGuirt WF, Stool SE. Temporal bone fractures in children: a review with emphasis on long-term sequelae. Clin Pediatr 31:12, 1992.

111. McGuirt WT, Prasad SD, Griffith AJ, et al. Mutations in COL11A2 cause non-syndromic hearing loss (DFNA13). Nat Genet 23:413, 1999.

112. McKusick VA. Mendelian Inheritance in Man, 7th ed. Baltimore, Johns Hopkins University Press, 1986.

113. Meyerhoff WL. Hypothyroidism and the ear: electrophysiological, morphological, and chemical considerations. Laryngoscope 89:1, 1979.

114. Mochizuki T, Lemmink HH, Mariyama M, et al. Identification of mutations in the alpha 3(IV) and alpha 4(IV) collagen genes in autosomal recessive Alport syndrome. Nat Genet 8:77, 1994.

115. Moller CG, Kimberling WJ. Clinical studies of Usher syndrome [abstract]. ARO 404, 1994.

116. Morell RJ, Kim HJ, Hood LJ, et al. N Engl J Med 339:1500, 1998.

117. Mustafa MM, Ramilo O, Saez-Llorens X, et al. Cerebrospinal fluid prostaglandins, interleukin 1B and tumor necrosis factor in bacterial meningitis. AJDC 144:833, 1990.

118. Mustafa M, Weil D, Chardenoux S, et al. Hum Mol Genet 8:409, 1999.

119. Nadol JB Jr. Medical progress: hearing loss [review]. N Engl J Med 329:1092, 1993.

120. National Institutes of Health. Early identification of hearing impairment in infants and young children. Consensus Development Conference on Early Identification of Hearing Impairment in Infants and Young Children, 1993.

121. Newman TB, Klebanoff MA. Neonatal hyperbilirubinemia and long-term outcome: another look at the collaborative perinatal project. Pediatrics 92:651, 1993.

122. Neyroud N, Tesson F, Denjoy I, et al. A novel mutation in the potassium channel gene KVLQT1 causes the Jervell and Lange-Nielsen cardioauditory syndrome. Nat Genet 15:113, 1997.

123. Okumura T, Takahashi H, Honjo I, Takagi A. Sensorineural hearing loss in patients with large vestibular aqueduct [abstract]. ARO 154, 1994.

124. Olsson JE. Neurotologic findings in basilar migraine. Laryngoscope 101:1, 1991.

125. Pantke OA, Cohen MMJ. The Waardenburg syndrome. Birth Defects 7:147, 1971.

126. Paparella MM, Brady DR, Hoell R. Sensorineural hearing loss in chronic otitis media and mastoiditis. Trans Am Acad Ophthalmol Otolaryngol 74:108, 1970.

127. Paparella MM, Morizono T, Le CT, et al. Sensorineural hearing loss in otitis media. Ann Otol Rhinol Laryngol 93:623, 1984.

128. Parnes LS, McCabe BF. Perilymph fistula: an important cause of deafness and dizziness in children. Pediatrics 80:524, 1987.

129. Pasic TR, Dobie RA. Cis-platinum ototoxicity in children. Laryngoscope 101:985, 1991.

130. Paugh DR, Telian SA, Disher JJ. Identification of perilymph proteins by two-dimensional gel electrophoresis. Otolaryngol Head Neck Surg 104:517, 1991.

131. Peitersen E, Carlsen BH. Hearing impairment as the initial sign of polyarteritis nodosa. Acta Otolaryngol (Stockh) 61:189, 1966.

132. Pendred V. Deaf mutism and goiter. Lancet 2:532, 1896.

133. Pieke-Dahl S, Moller CG, Kelley PM, et al. Genetic heterogeneity of Usher syndrome type II: localization to chromosome 5q. J Med Genet 37:256, 2000.

134. Pingault V, Bondurand N, Kuhlbrodt K, et al. SOX10 mutations in patients with Waardenburg-Hirschsprung disease. Nat Genet 18:171, 1998.

135. The Treacher Collins Syndrome Collaborative Group. Positional cloning of a gene involved in the pathogenesis of Treacher Collins syndrome. Nat Genet 12:130, 1996.

136. Priuska EM, Crann SA, Schacht J. Forays into the uncharged biochemical regions of gentamicin ototoxicity [abstract]. ARO 258, 1994.

137. Probst FJ, Fridell RA, Raphael Y, et al. Correction of deafness in shaker-2 mice by an unconventional myosin in a BAC transgene. Science 280:1444, 1998.

138. Remington JS. The tragedy of toxoplasmosis. Pediatr Infect Dis J 9:762, 1990.

139. Richards AJ, Yates JR, Williams R, et al. A family with Stickler syndrome type 2 has a mutation in the COL11A1 gene resulting in the substitution of glycine 97 by valine in alpha 1 (XI) collagen. Hum Mol Genet 5:1339, 1996.

140. Robertson MS, Gregory J. Deafness, blue sclerotics, and fragilitis ossium. J Laryngol Otol 76:655, 1962.

141. Robertson NG, Lu L, Heller S, et al. Mutations in a novel cochlear gene cause DFNA9, a human nonsyndromic deafness with vestibular dysfunction. Nat Genet 20:299, 1998.

142. Rosenfeld MG. POU-domain transcription factors: powerful developmental regulators. Genes Dev 5:897, 1991.

143. Rouleau GA, Merel P, Lutchman M, et al. Alteration in a new gene encoding a putative membrane-organizing protein causes neurofibromatosis type 2. Nature 363:515, 1993.

144. Sande MA, Whitley RJ, McCracken GH, et al. Evaluation of new anti-infective drugs for the treatment of toxoplasma encephalitis. Clin Infect Dis 15:S200, 1992.

145. Sankila EM, Pakarinen L, Kaariainen H, et al. Assignment of an Usher syndrome type III (USH3) gene to chromosome 3q. Hum Mol Genet 4:93, 1995.

146. Schaad UB, Lips U, Gnehm HE, et al. Dexamethasone therapy for bacterial meningitis in children. Swiss Meningitis Study Group. Lancet 342:457, 1993.

147. Schlech WF, Ward JI, Band JD, et al. Bacterial meningitis in the United States, 1978 through 1981: the National Bacterial Meningitis Surveillance Study. JAMA 253:1749, 1985.

148. Schuknecht HF. Ear pathology in autoimmune disease. Adv Otorhinolaryngol 88:585, 1979.

149. Schulze-Bahr E, Wang Q, Wedekind H, et al. KCNE1 mutations cause Jervell and Lange-Nielsen syndrome. Nat Genet 17:267, 1997.

150. Schweitzer VG, Olson N. Ototoxic effect of erythromycin therapy. Arch Otolaryngol 110:258, 1984.

151. Scott HS, Kudoh J, Wattenhofer M, et al. Insertion of beta-satellite repeats identifies a transmembrane protease causing both congenital and childhood onset autosomal recessive deafness. Nat Genet 27:59, 2001.

152. Skedros DG, Cass SP, Hirsch BE, Kelly RH. Sources of error in use of beta-2 transferrin analysis for diagnosis perilymphatic and cerebral spinal fluid leaks. Otolaryngol Head Neck Surg 109:861, 1993.

153. Smith CR, Lipsky JJ, Laskin OL, et al. Double-blind comparison of the nephrotoxicity and auditory toxicity of gentamicin and tobramycin. N Engl J Med 302:1106, 1980.

154. Smith RJH, Lee EC, Kimberling WJ, et al. Localization of two genes for Usher syndrome type I to chromosome 11. Genomics 14:995, 1992.

155. Stagno S, Pass RF, Dworsky ME, et al. Congenital cytomegalovirus infection: the relative importance of primary and recurrent maternal infection. N Engl J Med 306:945, 1982.

156. Strauss M, Towfighi J, Lipton A, et al. Cisplatinum ototoxicity: clinical experience and temporal bone histopathology. Laryngoscope 93:1544, 1983.

157. Stray-Pedersen B. Treatment of toxoplasmosis in the pregnant mother and newborn child. Scand J Infect Dis 84:23, 1992.

158. Supance JS, Bluestone CD. Perilymph fistulas in infants and children. Otolaryngol Head Neck Surg 91:663, 1983.

159. Swan S, Tostevin AL, Moore B, et al. Congenital defects in infants following infectious diseases during pregnancy. With special reference to the relationship between German measles and cataract, deaf-mutism, heart disease and microcephaly and to the period of pregnancy in which the occurrence of rubella is followed by congenital abnormalities. Med J Aust 2:201, 1943.

160. Tassabehji M, Newton VE, Read AP. Waardenburg syndrome type 2 caused by mutations in the human microphthalmia (MITF) gene. Nat Genet 8:251, 1994.

161. Tassabehji M, Read AP, Newton VE, et al. Waardenburg's syndrome patients have mutations in the human homologue of the Pax-3 paired box gene. Nature 355:635, 1992.

162. The Development Biology, Genetics and Teratology Branch Report to the National Advisory Child Health and Human Development Council, January, 1994, The Program of the Developmental Biology, Genetics and Teratology Branch of the Center for Research for Mothers and Children.

163. Thompson DA, Weigel RJ. Characterization of a gene that is inversely correlated with estrogen receptor expression (ICERE-1) in breast carcinomas. Eur J Biochem 252:169, 1998.

164. Tinghitella TJ. Pathogenesis of viral infections: the role of the immune response. Am J Otolaryngol 11:309, 1990.

165. Tyson J, Tranebjaerg L, Bellman S, et al. IsK and KvLQT1: mutation in either of the two subunits of the slow component of the delayed rectifier potassium channel can cause Jervell and Lange-Nielsen syndrome. Hum Mol Genet 6:2179, 1997.

166. U.S. Department of Health and Human Services, Public Health Service. Healthy People 2000: National Health Promotion and Disease Prevention Objectives. Washington, D.C., U.S. Government Printing Office, 1990.

167. Vahava O, Morell R, Lunch ED, et al. Mutation in transcription factor POU4FC associated with inherited progressive hearing loss in humans. Science 279:1950, 1998.

168. Van Hauwe P, Everett LA, Coucke P, et al. Two frequent missense mutations in Pendred syndrome. Hum Mol Genet 7:1099, 1998.

169. Van Laer L, Huizing EH, Verstreken M, et al. Nonsyndromic hearing impairment is associated with a mutation in DFNA5. Nat Genet 20:194, 1998.

170. Van Steensel MA, Buma P, de Waal Malefijt MC, et al. Otospondylo-megaepiphyseal dysplasia (OSMED): clinical description of three patients homozygous for a missense mutation in the COL11A2 gene. Am J Med Genet 70:315, 1997.

171. Verhoeven K, Van Laer L, Kirschofer K, et al. Nat Genet 19:60, 1998.

172. Verhoeven K, Van Laer L, Kirschofer K, et al. Mutations in the human alpha-tectorin gene cause autosomal dominant non-syndromic hearing impairment. Nat Genet 21:449, 1999.

173. Vernon M. Prematurity and deafness: the magnitude and nature of the problem among deaf children. Except Child 33:289, 1967.

174. Verpy E, Leibovici M, Zwaenepoel I, et al. A defect in harmonin, a PDZ domain-containing protein expressed in the inner ear sensory hair cells, underlies Usher syndrome type 1C. Nat Genet 26:51, 2000.

175. Vikkula M, Mariman EC, Lui VC, et al. Autosomal dominant and recessive osteochondrodysplasias associated with the COL11A2 locus. Cell 80:431, 1995.

176. Wayne S, Der Kaloustain VM, Schloss M, et al. Localization of the Usher syndrome type ID gene (Ush1D) to chromosome 10. Hum Mol Genet 5:1689, 1996.

177. Wayne S, Robertson NG, DeClau F, et al. Hum Mol Genet 10:195, 2001.

178. Weil D, Blanchard S, Kaplan J, et al. Defective myosin VIIA gene responsible for Usher syndrome type 1B. Nature 374:60, 1995.

179. Weil D, Kussel P, Blanchard S, et al. The autosomal recessive isolated deafness, DFNB2, and the Usher 1B syndrome are allelic defects of the myosin-VIIA gene. Nat Genet 16:191, 1997.

180. Williams CJ, Ganguly A, Considine E, et al. A-200>G transition at the 3′ acceptor splice site of IVS17 characterizes the COL2A1 gene mutation in the original Stickler syndrome kindred. Am J Med Genet 63:461, 1996.

181. Williamson WD, Demmler GJ, Percy AK, Catlin FI. Progressive hearing loss in infants with asymptomatic congenital cytomegalovirus infection. Pediatrics 90:862, 1992.

182. Williamson WD, Percy AK, Yow MD, et al. Asymptomatic congenital cytomegalovirus infection: audiologic, neuroradiologic, and neurodevelopmental abnormalities during the first year. Am J Dis Child 144:1365, 1990.

183. Wilcox ER, Burton QL, Naz S, et al. Mutations in the gene encoding tight junction claudin-14 cause autosomal recessive deafness DFNB29. Cell 104:165, 2001.

184. Wilson M, McAuley JB. Laboratory diagnosis of toxoplasmosis. Clin Lab Med 11:923, 1991.

185. Xia JH, Liu CY, Tang BS, et al. Mutations in the gene encoding gap junction protein beta-3 associated with autosomal dominant hearing impairment. Nat Genet 20:370, 1998.

186. Yasunaga S, Grati M, Cohen-Salmon M, et al. A mutation in OTOF, encoding otoferlin, a FER-1-like protein, causes DFNB9, a nonsyndromic form of deafness. Nat Genet 21:363, 1999.

187. Joint Committee on Infant Hearing, American Academy of Audiology, American Academy of Pediatrics, American Speech-Language-Hearing Association, and Directors of Speech and Hearing Programs in State Health and Welfare Agencies. Year 2000 position statement: principles and guidelines for early hearing detection and intervention programs. Pediatrics 106:798, 2000.

188. Zoller M, Wilson WR, Nadol JB Jr. Treatment of syphilitic hearing loss: combined penicillin and steroid therapy in 29 patients. Ann Otol Rhinol Laryngol 88:160, 1988.

29

Cochlear Implants in Children

Richard T. Miyamoto, M.D., and Karen Iler Kirk, M.D.

Cochlear implantation has been an approved therapeutic option for selected deaf children since the early 1980s. Cochlear implants are used to replace a nonfunctional inner-ear hair-cell transducer system by converting mechanical sound energy into electrical signals that can be delivered to the cochlear nerve in profoundly deaf patients. In this way, damaged or missing hair cells of the cochlea are bypassed.

Despite differences in design, all multichannel cochlear implant systems have several essential components in common.[57] These include:

- A surgically implanted electrode array that is in the cochlea near the auditory nerve
- An external microphone, which picks up acoustic information and converts it to electrical signals
- An externally worn speech processor that processes the signal according to a predefined strategy and produces stimuli for the electrode array
- A transmission link between the external components and the surgically implanted array

The processed speech signal is amplified and compressed to match the narrow electrical dynamic range of the ear. The typical response range of a deaf ear to electrical stimulation is on the order of only 10 to 20 dB, even less in the high frequencies. Transmission of the electrical signal across the skin from the external unit to the implanted electrode array usually is accomplished with electromagnetic induction or radio frequency transmission. The spiral ganglion cells or axons appear to be the critical residual neural elements that are stimulated.

Cochlear Implant Systems

Multichannel, multielectrode cochlear implant systems are designed to take advantage of the tonotopic organization of the cochlea. The incoming speech signal is filtered into a number of frequency bands, each corresponding to a given electrode in the array. Thus, multichannel cochlear implant systems use place coding to transfer spectral information in the speech signal as well as encode the durational and intensity cues of speech.

Nucleus Cochlear Implant Systems

The Nucleus 22-channel cochlear implant[4] was the first multichannel cochlear implant to receive FDA approval for use in adults and children. This device has been used in more patients than any other cochlear implant system worldwide. The Nucleus CI24M cochlear implant (Fig. 29–1) received FDA approval for adults and children in 1998.

Early speech-processing strategies (F0F2 and F0F1F2) used with the Nucleus 22-channel cochlear implant involved feature extraction, which conveyed information about key speech features such as the amplitude and frequency of vowel formants and the fundamental frequency of voiced sounds. The third-generation speech-processing strategy, MPEAK, encoded additional high-frequency information by stimulating two of three more basal fixed electrodes; the goal was to provide additional information that would yield improved consonant recognition scores.

Three processing strategies are currently available for use with the Nucleus cochlear implants. Two of the strategies utilize the *n-of-m* approach, in which the speech signal is filtered into *m* bandpass channels and the *n* highest envelope signals are selected for each cycle of stimulation.[58] The spectral peak, or SPEAK, strategy is the most widely used with the Nucleus 22-channel cochlear implant and is available to users of either the Nucleus 22-channel or the Nucleus CI24M system. This strategy filters the incoming speech signal into 20 frequency bands; on each stimulation cycle, an average of six electrodes are stimulated at a rate that varies adaptively between 180 and 300 pulses per second. An n-of-m strategy using much higher rates of stimulation, known as Advanced Combined Encoder (ACE) strategy, can be implemented in the new Nucleus CI24M device. The third processing strategy available with the Nucleus CI24M system is the Continuous Interleaved Sampling (CIS) strategy.[59] The CIS strategy filters the speech signal into a fixed number of bands, obtains the speech envelope, and then compresses the signal for each channel. On each cycle of stimulation, a series of interleaved digital pulses rapidly stimulates consecutive electrodes in the array. The

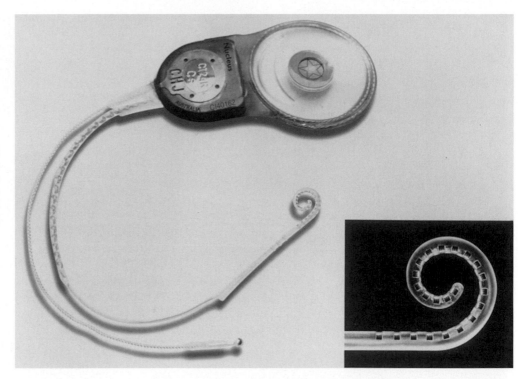

FIGURE 29–1. Nucleus 24 Contour implant. The active intracochlear electrode array is precurved to wrap around the modiolus. A stylus is used to straighten the electrode during insertion.

CIS strategy is designed to preserve fine temporal details in the speech signal by using high-rate, pulsatile stimuli.

Two different speech processors are available for new Nucleus cochlear implant recipients. The body-worn SPRINT processor can implement any of the three current speech processing strategies. The ear-level ESPRIT speech processor currently can implement only the SPEAK processing strategy.

Clarion Cochlear Implant Systems

The Clarion "multistrategy" cochlear implant system[19, 44, 45] is manufactured by the Advanced Bionics Corporation. The Clarion device has been approved by the FDA for use in adults (1996) and children (1997). The earliest-generation Clarion employs a perimodiolar (spiraled) electrode developed at UCSF. Eight independent current output sources allow for nonsimultaneous (sequential) as well as partially and fully simultaneous stimulation in three sound-processing strategies: (1) CIS (described earlier) stimulates up to eight monopolar electrodes sequentially at an overall rate of 6700 biphasic pulses per second, (2) Simultaneous Analog Stimulation (SAS) filters and then compresses the incoming speech signal for simultaneous presentation to the corresponding eight bipolar or seven "enhanced" bipolar electrode pairs, and (3) the relative amplitudes and temporal details of the incoming speech signal are conveyed at a rate of 13,000 digital updates per second on each channel; Paired Pulsatile Sampler (PPS) stimulates two electrodes (either monopolar or bipolar) simultaneously, thereby increasing the stimulation rate compared with the nonsimultaneous CIS strategy.

A new-generation Clarion, the CII Bionic Ear System (CII), introduced in early 2001, can be programmed to emulate the eight-channel CIS, PPS, and SAS strategies of the earlier Clarion technology. Applied in Emulation Mode, the CII has FDA market approval for use in adults and children. All advanced new features of the CII system must be enabled through FDA-monitored clinical trials, which are in progress in postlingually deafened adults.

The Bionic Ear has 16 independent output circuits, each of which serves one of the 16 planar HiFocus electrodes. The electrode contacts are oriented medially near the modiolar wall with placement of a soft, silastic "Positioner." Each electrode can be coupled in monopolar, bipolar, or multipolar combinations to yield as many as 31 stimulation channels. In the CII's High Resolution Mode, patient-specific program instructions are downloaded into the memory of the internal circuitry. This frees the RF transmission link to sample and deliver more of the fine acoustic details of sound input to the user. The CII can produce more than 250,000 biphasic pulses per second (sequential stimulation) and 1,000,000 digital updates per second (simultaneous stimulation).

The most recent Clarion body-worn processor is the Platinum Series Sound Processor (PSP), commercially released in the spring of 2000. Presently, behind-the-ear versions of the PSP and the CII Bionic Ear processor are undergoing field trials in North America.

Medical Electronic (Med-El) Cochlear Implant System

The Combi 40+ cochlear implant system (Fig. 29–2) manufactured by the Med-El Corporation in Innsbruck, Austria is currently undergoing clinical trials in the United States. The Med-El cochlear implant has 12 elec-

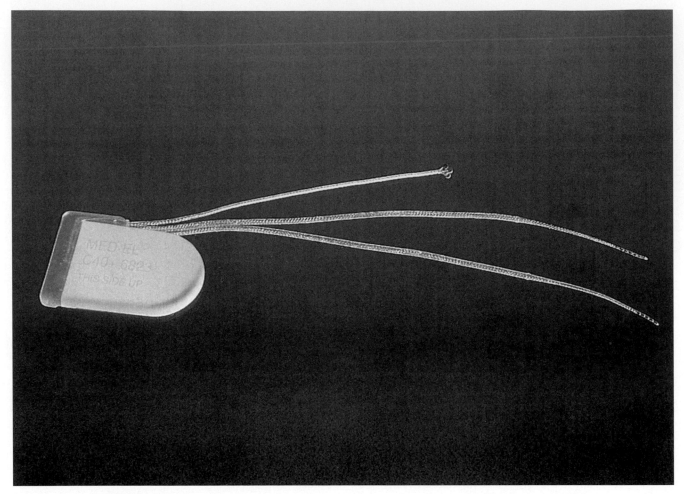

FIGURE 29–2. Med-El split electrode. One electrode is placed in a tunnel drilled into the basal turn, and the second electrode is inserted into a second cochleostomy created just anterior to the oval window.

trode pairs and has the capability of deep electrode insertion into the apical regions of the cochlea.[11] This device uses the CIS processing strategy and can provide the most rapid stimulation rate of any of the cochlear implant systems currently available. Both body-worn and ear-level speech processors (the CIS Pro+ and Tempo+, respectively) are available for the Med-El cochlear implant.

New Developments in Cochlear Implant Electrode Design

New designs of the internal electrode array have been introduced for the Nucleus and Clarion cochlear implants. The Nucleus Contour electrode array is a curved electrode that is straightened by a stylet for insertion purposes. After surgical placement into the scala tympani, the stylet is withdrawn. The electrode then assumes its preformed shape, more closely approximating the modiolar wall of the cochlea. The Clarion HiFocus electrode is positioned closer to the modiolar wall via insertion of a separate positioner into the scala tympani. Because the spiral ganglion cells are thought to be the sites stimulated

by cochlear implants, directing the electrodes toward the modiolus and further positioning the array may improve spatial specificity of stimulation and reduce the current needed to drive the electrodes.[57]

Selection of Patients

The selection of cochlear implant candidates is a complex and ever-evolving process that requires careful consideration of many factors. Candidacy criteria have successively expanded since the technology became available. The first patients to undergo implantation were postlingually deafened adults with no hearing and absolutely no benefit from amplification. These patients were deemed suitable candidates as there was little likelihood that their hearing could worsen with cochlear implantation. As clinicians and researchers learned more about the benefits of cochlear implantation, candidacy criteria were broadened to include prelingually deafened children and patients with some minimal residual hearing. Current candidacy criteria differ according to the age of the patients being considered. The current criteria are listed in Table 29–1.

TABLE 29-1. Pediatric Candidacy Criteria for Cochlear Implantation

Children Aged 12 Mos to 24 Mos	Children Aged 25 Mos to 17 Yrs, 11 Mos
Bilateral profound hearing loss	Bilateral severe-to-profound hearing loss
Lack of auditory skills development and minimal hearing aid benefit (documented by parent questionnaire)	Lack of auditory skills development and minimal hearing aid benefit (word recognition scores <30% correct)
No medical contraindications	No medical contraindications
Enrollment in a therapy of education program emphasizing auditory development	Enrollment in a therapy of education program emphasizing auditory development

Implantation of Very Young Children

As noted earlier, current FDA guidelines permit the implantation of children as young as 12 months. In fact, a number of infants younger than 1 year have received cochlear implants in the United States. This has occurred for a couple of reasons. First, with the advent of Universal Newborn Hearing Screening, children with profound hearing loss are being identified and fitted with hearing aids at very young ages. If children have completed an adequate trial of hearing aid use prior to their first birthday, and if they do not demonstrate benefit from the hearing aids, many clinicians see little need to delay cochlear implant surgery. Second, early implantation may be particularly important when the cause of deafness is meningitis as progressive intracochlear ossification can occur and preclude standard electrode insertion. The window of time during which this advancing process can be circumvented is relatively short. Thus, infants with deafness secondary to meningitis may undergo implantation before the age of 1 year if they have completed a brief hearing aid trial with no evident benefit.

This trend toward earlier cochlear implantation in children is due to an attempt to ameliorate the devastating effects of early auditory deprivation. Electrical stimulation appears to be capable of preventing at least some of the degenerative changes in the central auditory pathways.[25] Furthermore, implantation in very young congenitally or neonatally deafened children may have substantial advantages because the development of speech perception, speech production, and language competence normally begins at a very early age.

Although implantation in very young children has become more routine for experienced cochlear implant teams, it remains somewhat controversial because the audiologic assessment, surgical intervention, and postimplant management in this population are challenging. Profound deafness must be substantiated and the inability to benefit from conventional hearing aids demonstrated. These criteria can be difficult to satisfy in young children with limited language abilities. For very young children, parental questionnaires are commonly used to assess the potential of amplification.

With very young children, special consideration must be given to the small dimensions of the temporal bone and to potential problems from postoperative temporal bone growth. In addition, the high incidence of otitis media in children younger than 2 years might compromise the biosafety of cochlear implants. Nonetheless, extension of implant candidacy to children who are 6 to 12 months old is anatomically justified. The cochlea is adult-sized at birth; by age 1 year, the facial recess and mastoid antrum, which provide access to the middle ear for electrode placement, are adequately developed.[22]

Previous Auditory Experience

Children who become deaf at or after age 5 years generally are classified as postlingually deafened. These patients have developed many or all aspects of spoken language before the onset of their deafness. However, once they lose access to auditory input and feedback, they frequently demonstrate rapid deterioration in the intelligibility of their speech. Implantation soon after the onset of deafness potentially can ameliorate this rapid deterioration in speech production and perception abilities.[10] Cochlear implantation may be less successful in postlingually deafened children if there is a long delay between the onset of deafness and implantation. For example, Gordon et al[10] reported the case of a child deafened at age 5 years who underwent subsequent implantation 10 years later. This child never achieved the ability to understand speech through listening alone.

A postlingual onset of deafness is an infrequent occurrence in the pediatric population. If this were to be the only category for which cochlear implants positively affected deaf children, this technology would have limited applicability in children.

Implantation of Congenitally or Early-Deafened Adolescents

Congenitally or early-deafened adolescents who wish to pursue a cochlear implant present a special challenge for any cochlear implant team. In the past, electrical stimulation of the auditory system has not led to high levels of success in this patient group. Adolescents with profound hearing loss who have a history of consistent hearing aid use and who communicate primarily through audition and spoken language are among the best candidates in this age group. Conversely, adolescents with little previous auditory experience and those who rely primarily on sign language for communication may have difficulty learning to use the sound provided by an implant and may find it disruptive. Such adolescents are at high risk for nonuse of a cochlear implant. With both groups, implantation can be successful if time is spent counseling about potential outcomes and ensuring that both patients and their families have realistic expectations for postimplant benefit.

Determining Cochlear Implant Candidacy

Audiologic Assessment

The audiologic evaluation is the primary means of determining suitability for cochlear implantation. Audiologic evaluations should be conducted in both an unaided condition and with appropriately fit conventional amplification. Thus, all potential candidates must have completed a period with a properly fit hearing aid, preferably coupled with training in an appropriate aural rehabilitation program. The audiologic evaluation includes measurement of pure-tone thresholds along with tests of word and sentence recognition. Aided speech recognition scores are the primary audiologic determinant of cochlear implant candidacy. For very young children or those with limited language abilities, parent questionnaires are used to determine hearing aid benefit.

Medical Assessment

The medical assessment includes the otologic history and physical examination. Radiologic evaluation of the cochlea determines whether the cochlea is present and patent and identifies congenital deformities of the cochlea. High-resolution, thin-section computed tomography (CT) of the cochlea remains the imaging technique of choice.[61] Intracochlear bone formation resulting from labyrinthitis ossificans usually can be demonstrated by CT; however, when soft tissue obliteration occurs after sclerosing labyrinthitis, CT may not detect the obstruction. In these cases, T_2-weighted magnetic resonance imaging (MRI) is an effective adjunctive procedure providing additional information regarding cochlear patency. The endolymph/perilymph signal may be lost in sclerosing labyrinthitis. Intracochlear ossification is not a contraindication to cochlear implantation but can limit the type and insertion depth of the electrode array that can be introduced into the cochlea. Congenital malformations of the cochlea are likewise not contraindications to cochlear implantation. Cochlear dysplasia has been reported to occur in approximately 20% of children with congenital sensorineural hearing loss.[17] Several reports of successful implantations in children with inner-ear malformations have been published.[16, 24, 29, 46, 53] A thin cribriform area between the modiolus and a widened internal auditory canal is often observed[47] and is thought to be the route of egress of cerebrospinal fluid (CSF) during surgery or postoperatively. A CSF gusher was reported in several cases. Temporal-bone dysplasia also may be associated with an anomalous facial nerve, which may increase the surgical risk.

The precise cause of deafness cannot always be determined but is identified whenever possible; however, stimulable auditory neural elements are nearly always present regardless of cause.[12] Two exceptions are the *Michel deformity*, which involves congenital agenesis of the cochlea, and the *small internal auditory canal syndrome*, in which the cochlear nerve may be congenitally absent.

Routine otoscopic evaluation of the tympanic membrane is performed. The otologic condition should be stable before implantation is considered. The ear proposed for cochlear implantation must be free of infection, and the tympanic membrane should be intact. If these conditions are not met, medical or surgical treatment is required before implantation. The management of middle-ear effusions in children who are under consideration for cochlear implantation or who already have a cochlear implant deserves special consideration. Conventional antibiotic treatment usually accomplishes this goal, but when it does not, myringotomy and insertion of tympanostomy tubes may be required. Removal of the tube several weeks before cochlear implantation usually results in a healed, intact tympanic membrane. When an effusion occurs in an ear with a cochlear implant, no treatment is required as long as the effusion remains uninfected. Chronic otitis media, with or without cholesteatoma, must be resolved before implantation; this is accomplished with conventional otologic treatments. Prior ear surgery that has resulted in a mastoid cavity does not contraindicate cochlear implantation, but this situation may require mastoid obliteration with closure of the external auditory canal or reconstruction of the posterior bony ear canal.

Psychological Assessment

Psychological testing is performed for exclusionary reasons to identify subjects who have organic brain dysfunction, mental retardation, undetected psychosis, or unrealistic expectations. Valuable information related to the family dynamics and other factors in the patient's milieu that may affect implant acceptance and performance are assessed.

Surgical Implantation

Cochlear implantation in both children and adults requires meticulous attention to the delicate tissues and small dimensions. Skin incisions are designed to provide access to the mastoid process and coverage of the external portion of the implant package while preserving the blood supply of the postauricular skin. The incision used at the Indiana University Medical Center has eliminated the need for a large postauricular flap. The inferior extent of the incision is made well posterior to the mastoid tip to preserve the branches of the postauricular artery. From here the incision is directed posterosuperiorly and then directed superiorly without a superoanterior limb. In children, the incision incorporates the temporalis muscle to give added thickness. A subperiosteal pocket is created for positioning the implant induction coil. A bone well tailored to the device being implanted is created, and the induction coil is fixed to the cortex with a fixation suture or periosteal flaps.

After the skin is incised, mastoidectomy is performed. The horizontal semicircular canal is identified in the depths of the mastoid antrum, and the short process of the incus is identified in the fossa incudis. The facial recess is opened using the fossa incudis as an initial landmark. The facial recess is a triangular area bound by (1) the fossa incudis superiorly, (2) the chorda tympani nerve laterally and anteriorly, and (3) the facial nerve medially and posteriorly. The facial nerve usually can be visualized through the bone without exposing it. The round window niche is visualized through the facial recess about 2 mm inferior to the stapes. Occasionally, the round window niche is posteriorly positioned and is not well visualized through the facial recess or is obscured by ossification.

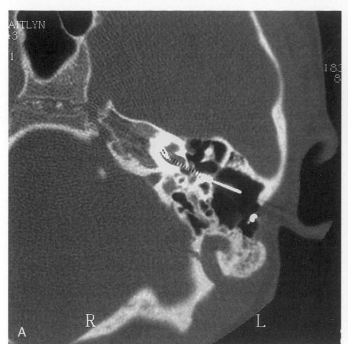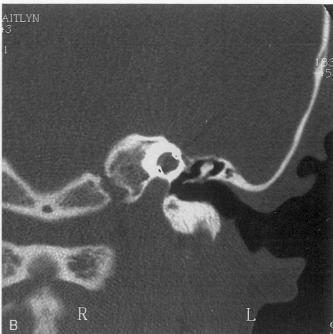

FIGURE 29–3. *A,* Active electrode in the initial segment of the basal turn of a deformed cochlea. The electrode is introduced into the basal end of the cochlea. *B,* Active electrode positioned to outer wall of common cavity deformity.

Particularly in these situations, it is important not to be misdirected by hypotympanic air cells. Entry into the scala tympani is accomplished best through a cochleostomy created anterior and inferior to the annulus of the round window membrane. A small fenestra slightly larger than the electrode to be implanted (usually 0.5 mm) is developed. A small diamond burr is used to "blue line" the endosteum of the scala tympani, and the endosteal membrane is removed with small picks. This approach bypasses the hook area of the scala tympani, allowing direct insertion of the active electrode array. After insertion of the active electrode array, the cochleostomy area is sealed with small pieces of fascia (Fig. 29–3).

Unusual Surgical Considerations

Cochlear Dysplasia

In cases of cochlear dysplasia, a CSF gusher may be encountered upon fenestration of the cochlea during cochleostomy. The flow of CSF has been successfully controlled by entry of the cochlea through a small fenestra, allowing the CSF reservoir to drain off, insertion of the electrode into the cochleostomy, and tight packing of the electrode with fascia at the cochleostomy. It is postulated that the source of the leak is through the lateral end of the internal auditory canal. Supplementally, a lumbar drain can be placed to reduce the spinal fluid reservoir until tissue is satisfactorily sealed. In severe dyplasia with a common cavity deformity, the electrode array may be inserted directly by a transmastoid labyrinthotomy approach. The otic capsule is opened posterosuperior to the second genu of the facial nerve, and the common cavity

is entered. Several patients have been treated in this way with no vestibular side effects.[26]

Aberrant Facial Nerve

In patients who have malformations of the labyrinth, and occasionally in patients with otherwise normal anatomy, the facial nerve may follow an aberrant course. Although not all aberrant facial nerves affect cochlear implant surgery, those that do must be recognized and dealt with effectively. Two anomalous courses of the facial nerve that place it at risk are the laterally and anteriorly displaced vertical portion of the facial nerve and a facial nerve that courses over the promontory over or anterior to the round window.[27]

Intracochlear Ossification

Ossification at the round window is common in postmeningitic patients and has been encountered in approximately half of the children whose cause of deafness was meningitis and who have received a cochlear implant at our center. In these patients, a cochleostomy is developed anterior to the round window and the new bone is drilled until an open scala is entered. A full electrode insertion can then be accomplished. Less frequently, labyrinthitis ossificans with extensive intracochlear bone formation may occur with complete obliteration of the scala tympani. In these cases, our preference has been to drill open the basal turn of the cochlea and create a tunnel approximately 6 mm deep and to partially insert a Nucleus electrode. This allows implantation of 10 to 12 active electrodes, which has yielded very satisfactory results.

More recently, a specially designed split electrode developed by the Med-El Corporation has been used wherein one branch of the electrode array is placed in the tunnel described earlier and the second active electrode is inserted into an additional cochleostomy developed just anterior to the oval window. Gantz et al[9] described an extensive drill-out procedure to gain access to the upper basal turn. Steenerson et al[49] described insertion of the active electrode into the scala vestibuli in cases of cochlear ossification. Although this procedure has merit, the scala vestibuli is frequently ossified when the scala tympani is completely obliterated.

Complications

Complications have been infrequent with cochlear implant surgery and can be largely avoided by careful preoperative planning and meticulous surgical technique. Among the most commonly encountered problems are those associated with the incision and postauricular flap and facial-nerve injury.[14] Using the incision we describe, we have experienced only one flap breakdown in our pediatric cochlear implant population. (This occurred several years postoperatively after head trauma.) We experienced one transient delayed facial paresis and one CSF gusher in a child with a Mondini deformity.[32] Gushers have also occurred in several patients with the large vestibular aqueduct syndrome.

Because children are more susceptible to otitis media than adults, justifiable concern has been expressed that a middle-ear infection could cause an implanted device to become an infected foreign body, requiring its removal. Two children in our series experienced delayed mastoiditis (several years after the implant surgery) resulting in a postauricular abscess. These cases were treated by incision and drainage and intravenous antibiotics without the need to remove the implant. An even greater concern is that infection might extend along the electrode into the inner ear, resulting in a serious otogenic complication, such as meningitis or further degeneration of the central auditory system. Although the incidence of otitis media in children who have received cochlear implants parallels that in the general pediatric population, no serious complications related to otitis media have occurred in our patients.

Clinical Results

Although cochlear implants are now an established therapeutic option for selected deaf children, the range of performance with current implant systems remains wide. Some cochlear implant recipients can communicate without the benefit of lip reading and are able to communicate on the telephone without a telephone code; others use their implants primarily to reestablish environmental contact and enhance their speech-reading abilities. This variation in performance levels is thought to relate to biologic and cognitive factors. It would be expected that poor auditory nerve survival or atrophic central auditory systems would correlate with poor performance, whereas a more intact auditory nervous system should permit better results, given a well-designed and fitted cochlear prosthesis.[18]

Postlingually deafened children use the information transmitted by a cochlear implant to make comparisons to previously stored representations of spoken language. However, the majority of children who receive cochlear implants have congenital or prelingually acquired hearing loss. These children must use the sound provided by a cochlear implant to acquire speech perception, speech production, and spoken language skills. Furthermore, because young children have limited linguistic skills and attention spans, the assessment of performance in this population can be challenging. To effectively evaluate the communication benefits of cochlear implant use in children, a battery of tests that are developmentally and linguistically appropriate should be employed. (See references 20 and 21 for a review of these issues.)

Speech Perception Outcomes

In early investigations, children who used the Nucleus cochlear implant with a feature extraction strategy demonstrated significant improvement in closed-set word identification (i.e., the ability to identify words from a limited set of alternatives) but very limited open-set word recognition.[30, 48] The introduction of newer processing strategies yielded greater speech perception benefits in children, just as in adults. Many children with current cochlear implant devices achieve at least moderate levels of open-set word recognition. For example, Cohen et al[5] reported word recognition scores for a group of 19 children that ranged from 4% to 76% words correct with a mean of 44% words correct. Similarly, Osberger et al[40] reported average scores of approximately 30% correct on a more difficult measure of isolated word recognition in children with the Clarion cochlear implant. The development rate of postimplant auditory skills seems to be increasing as cochlear implant technology improves and as children undergo implantation at a younger age.[5, 40, 60] Furthermore, it appears that pediatric cochlear implant recipients continue to make communication gains long after they have been implanted. For example, O'Donoghue et al reported that children who received cochlear implants prior to age 7 years were still demonstrating improvements at 5 years post implant, with no evidence of a plateau.[37] Finally, comparison studies have shown that the speech perception abilities of pediatric cochlear implant recipients meet or exceed those of their peers who use hearing aids, with unaided pure-tone average thresholds of greater than 90 dB HL.[33, 51]

Factors Influencing Speech Perception Outcomes

A number of demographic factors have been shown to influence performance results in children with cochlear implants. Early results suggested better speech perception performance in children deafened at an older age with a corresponding shorter period of deafness.[7, 39, 48] However, when only children with prelingual deafness (i.e., <3 years) were considered, age at onset of hearing loss was no longer significant.[31] It is clear that earlier implantation yields superior cochlear implant performance in children.[8, 15, 23, 28, 35, 36] Although the critical period for implantation of congenitally or prelingually deafened children has not been determined,[3] preliminary evidence suggests that implantation prior to age 3 years may yield improved results.[54–56]

The variables of communication mode and unaided residual hearing also influence speech perception performance.[6, 13, 38, 62] Oral children, and those who have more residual hearing prior to implantation, typically demonstrate superior speech understanding. This has led to some controversy over whether to implant the better- or poorer-hearing ear.[43, 62]

Postimplant factors also have been shown to affect outcomes in children. One such factor is the adequacy of the speech processor fitting, or *map*.[10] As age at implantation drops, it becomes more difficult to obtain reliable behavioral responses from children during mapping. Recently developed objective measures of auditory responses to electrical stimulation, such as Neural Response Telemetry (or NRT), can aid the fitting process.[1] A second postimplant factor that influences outcome is the (re)habilitation program. Outcome is typically better in children who participate in regular therapy sessions than in those who do not.[10] Furthermore, children in oral programs typically develop better speech perception abilities than children who are in programs that advocate the combined use of signed and spoken English.[13] Finally, it has been reported that children with motor or cognitive delays prior to implantation demonstrate significant delays in developing speech perception abilities after implantation.[42]

Speech Intelligibility and Language

Improvements in speech perception are the most direct benefit of cochlear implantation. However, if children with cochlear implants are to succeed in the hearing world, they must also acquire intelligible speech and their surrounding linguistic system. The speech intelligibility and language abilities of children with cochlear implants improve significantly over time[2, 3, 34, 50, 52] and, on average, exceed those of their age- and hearing-matched peers with hearing aids.[50, 52] Speech intelligibility and spoken language acquisition are significantly correlated with the development of auditory skills.[34, 41] Although variability is wide, the best pediatric cochlear implant users demonstrate highly intelligible speech and age-appropriate language skills. These superior performers usually undergo implantation at a young age and are educated in an oral/aural modality.[34]

Conclusions

Cochlear implants are an appropriate sensory aid for selected deaf children who receive minimal benefit from conventional amplification. Improvements in technology and refinements in candidacy criteria have secured a permanent role for cochlear implantation. With improved postoperative performance, implantation is clearly justified not only in patients with bilateral profound sensorineural hearing loss but also in patients with severe sensorineural hearing loss. Patients as young as 12 months may undergo implantation under current FDA guidelines, and experience with even younger children is accumulating.

Intersubject performance variability continues to be wide. However, most postlingually deafened adults with current cochlear implants achieve auditory-only word recognition and communicate very effectively when auditory cues are combined with lip reading. The best adult recipients can converse fluently without lip-reading cues. Children using cochlear implants have acquired speaking and listening skills and have developed a spoken language system that is beyond what previously could be achieved with hearing aids. Children who undergo implantation at a young age and use oral communication have the best prognosis for developing intelligible speech and age-appropriate language abilities.

Challenges remain in effectively assessing peripheral auditory neuronal survival and matching electrically transmitted signals to the future potential of the central auditory system in deaf subjects.

Acknowledgments

This work was supported in part by NIH NIDCD grants RO1 DC00064, RO1 DC00423, and K23 DC00126 and by Psi Iota Xi.

REFERENCES

1. Abbas PJ, Brown CJ, Shallop JK, et al. Summary of results using the Nucleus CI24M implant to record the electronically evoked compound action potential. Ear Hear 20:45, 1999.
2. Allen MC, Nikolopoulos TP, O'Donoghue GM. Speech intelligibility in children after cochlear implantation. Am J Otol 19:742, 1998.
3. Brackett D, Zara CV. Communication outcomes related to early implantation. Am J Otol 19:453, 1998.
4. Clark GM, Tong YC, Dowell RC, et al. A multiple-channel cochlear implant: an evaluation using nonsense syllables. Ann Otol Rhinol Laryngol 90:227, 1981.
5. Cohen MH. Early results using the Nucleus C124M in children. Am J Otol 20:198, 1999.
6. Cowan RS, DelDot J, Barker EJ, et al. Speech perception results for children with implants with different levels of preoperative residual hearing. Am J Otol 18(Suppl):125, 1997.
7. Fryauf-Bertschy H, Tyler RS, Kelsay DM, Gantz BJ. Performance over time of congenitally deaf and postlingually deafened children using a multichannel cochlear implant. J Speech Lang Hear Res 35:913, 1992.
8. Fryauf-Bertschy H, Tyler RS, Kelsay DM, et al. Cochlear implant use by prelingually deafened children: the influences of age at implant and length of device use. J Speech Lang Hear Res 40:183, 1997.
9. Gantz BJ, McCabe BF, Tyler RS. Use of multichannel cochlear implants in obstructed and obliterated cochleas. Otolaryngol Head Neck Surg 98:72, 1988.
10. Gordon KA, Daya H, Harrison RV, Papsin BC. Factors contributing to limited open-set speech perception in children who use a cochlear implant. Int J Pediatr Otorhinolaryngol 56:101, 2000.
11. Gstoettner WK, Baumgartner WD, Franz P, Hamzari J. Cochlear implant deep insertion surgery. Laryngoscope 107:544, 1997.
12. Hinojosa R, Marion M. Histopathology of profound sensorineural deafness. Ann N Y Acad Sci 405:459, 1983.
13. Hodges AV, Ash MD, Balkany TJ, et al. Speech perception results in children with cochlear implants: contributing factors. Otolaryngol Head Neck Surg 121:31, 1999.

14. Hoffman RA, Cohen NL. Complications of cochlear implant surgery. Ann Otol Rhinol Laryngol 104(Suppl 166):420, 1995.
15. Illg A, Lesinki-Schiedat A, von der Haar-Heise S, et al. Speech perception results for children implanted with the Clarion cochlear implant at the Medical University of Hannover. Ann Otol Rhinol Laryngol 108:93, 1999.
16. Jackler RK, Luxford WM, House WF. Sound detection with the cochlear implant in five ears of four children with congenital malformations of the cochlea. Laryngoscope 97(Suppl 40):15, 1987.
17. Jensen J. Tomography of the inner ear in deaf children. Radiological demonstration of two cases with the Mondini malformation. J Laryngol Otol 81:27, 1967.
18. Kessler DK, Loeb GE, Barker MJ. Distribution of speech recognition results with the Clarion cochlear prosthesis. Ann Otol Rhinol Laryngol 104(Suppl 166):283, 1995.
19. Kessler DK, Schindler RA. Progress with a multistrategy cochlear system: the Clarion. In: Hochmair-Desoyer IJ, Hochmair ES (eds). Advances in Cochlear Implants. Wein, Manz, 1994, pp 354–362.
20. Kirk KI. Challenges in the clinical investigation of cochlear implant outcomes. In: Niparko JK, Kirk KI, Mellon NK, et al (eds). Cochlear Implants: Principles and Practices. Philadelphia, Lippincott Williams & Wilkins, 2000, pp 225–259.
21. Kirk KI, Diefendorf AO, Pisoni DB, Robbins AM. Assessing speech perception in children. In: Mendel L, Danhauer J (eds). Audiological Evaluation and Management and Speech Perception Training. San Diego, Singular, 1997, pp 101–132.
22. Lenarz T. Cochlear implantations in children under the age of two years. In: Honjo I, Takahashi H (eds). Otorhinolaryngology. 1997, pp 204–210.
23. Lenarz T, Illg A, Lesinki-Schiedat A, et al. Cochlear implantation in children under the age of two: the MHH experience with the Clarion cochlear implant. Ann Otol Rhinol Laryngol 108:44, 1999.
24. Mangabeira-Albernaz PL. The Mondini dysplasia: from early diagnosis to cochlear implant. Acta Otolaryngol 95:627, 1983.
25. Matsushima JI, Shepard RK, Seldon HL, et al. Electrical stimulation of the auditory nerve in deaf kittens: effects on cochlear nucleus morphology. Hear Res 56:133, 1991.
26. McElveen JT, Carrasco VN, Miyamoto RT, et al. Surgical approaches for cochlear implantation in patients with cochlear malformations. Paper presented at the Vth International Cochlear Implant Conference, New York, 1997.
27. Miyamoto RT, Kaiser AR. Facial nerve anomalies in cochlear implantation. In: Kim CS, Chang SO, Lim D (eds). Updates in Cochlear Implantation. Advances in Oto-Rhino-Laryngology. Basel, Karger, 2000, pp 131–133.
28. Miyamoto RT, Kirk KI, Robbins AM, et al. Speech perception and speech intelligibility in children with multichannel cochlear implants. In: Honjo I, Takahashi H (eds). Advances in Oto-Rhino-Laryngology. Basel, Karger, 1997, pp 198–203.
29. Miyamoto RT, McConkey AJ, Myres WA, Pope ML. Cochlear implantation in the Mondini inner ear malformation. Am J Otol 7:258, 1986.
30. Miyamoto RT, Osberger MJ, Myers WA, et al. Comparison of sensory aids in deaf children. Ann Otol Rhinol Laryngol 98(Suppl 8 Part 2):2, 1989.
31. Miyamoto RT, Osberger MJ, Robbins AM, et al. Prelingually deafened children's performance with the nucleus multichannel cochlear implant. Am J Otol 14:437, 1993.
32. Miyamoto RT, Young M, Myres WA, et al. Complications of pediatric cochlear implantation. Eur Arch Otolaryngol 253:1, 1996.
33. Meyer TA, Svirsky MA, Kirk KI, Miyamoto RT. Improvements in speech perception by children with profound prelingual hearing loss: effects of device, communication mode, and chronological age. J Speech Lang Hear Res 41:846, 1998.
34. Moog JS, Geers A. Speech and language acquisition in young children after cochlear implantation. Otolaryngol Clin North Am 32:1127, 1999.
35. Nikolopoulos TP, O'Donoghue GM, Archbold SM. Age at implantation: its importance in pediatric cochlear implantation. Laryngoscope 109:595, 1999.
36. O'Donoghue GM, Nikolopoulos TP. Speech perception in children after cochlear implantation. Am J Otol 19:762, 1999.
37. O'Donoghue GM, Nikolopoulos TP, Archbold SM, Tait M. Speech perception in children after cochlear implantation. Am J Otol 19:762, 1998.
38. Osberger MJ, Fisher LM. Preoperative predictors of postoperative implant performance in children. Paper presented at the 7th Symposium on Cochlear Implants in Children, Iowa City, 1998.
39. Osberger MJ, Todd SL, Berry SW, et al. Effect of age at onset of deafness on children's speech perception abilities with a cochlear implant. Ann Otol Rhinol Laryngol 100:883, 1991.
40. Osberger MJ, Zimmerman-Phillips S, Geier LL, Barker M. Clinical trials of the Clarion cochlear implant in children. Ann Otol Rhinol Laryngol 108:88, 1999.
41. Pisoni DB, Svirsky MA, Kirk KI, Miyamoto RT. Looking at the "Stars": a first report on the intercorrelations among measures of speech perception, intelligibility and language development in pediatric cochlear implant users. Bloomington, Indiana, Indiana University, 1997, pp 51–91.
42. Pyman BC, Blamey PJ, Lacey P, et al. The development of speech perception in children using cochlear implants: effects of etiologic factors and delayed milestones. Am J Otol 21:57, 2000.
43. Rubenstein JT, Miller CA. How do cochlear prostheses work? Curr Opin Neurobiol 9:399, 1999.
44. Schindler RA, Kessler DK. The UCSF/Storz cochlear implant: patient performance. Am J Otol 8:247, 1987.
45. Schindler RA, Kessler DK. Clarion cochlear implant: phase I investigational results. Am J Otol 14:263, 1993.
46. Silverstein H, Smouha E, Morgan N. Multichannel cochlear implantation in a patient with bilateral Mondini deformities. Am J Otol 9:451, 1988.
47. Schuknecht HF. Mondini dysplasia: a clinical and pathological study. Ann Otol Rhinol Laryngol 89(Suppl 65):1, 1980.
48. Staller SJ, Beiter AL, Brimacombe J, et al. Pediatric performance with the Nucleus 22-channel cochlear implant system. Am J Otol 12(Suppl):126, 1991.
49. Steenerson RL, Gary LB, Wynens MS. Scala vestibuli cochlear implantations for labyrinthine ossification. Am J Otol 11:360, 1990.
50. Svirsky MA. Speech intelligibility of pediatric cochlear implant users and hearing aid users. In: Waltzman SB, Cohen NL (eds). Cochlear Implants. New York, Thieme, 2000, pp 312–314.
51. Svirsky MA, Meyer TA. Comparison of speech perception in pediatric Clarion cochlear implant and hearing aid users. Ann Otol Rhinol Laryngol 108(Supp 177):104, 1999.
52. Svirsky MA, Robbins AM, Kirk KI, et al. Language development in profoundly deaf children with cochlear implants. Psych Sci 11:153, 2000.
53. Tucci DL, Telian SA. Cochlear implantation in patients with cochlear malformations. Arch Otolaryngol Head Neck Surg 121:833, 1995.
54. Waltzman SB, Cohen NL. Cochlear implantation in children younger than 2 years old. Am J Otol 19:158, 1998.
55. Waltzman S, Cohen NL, Gomolin R, et al. Perception and production results in children implanted between two and five years of age. In: Hongo I, Takahashi H (eds). Advances in Oto-Rhino-Laryngology. Basel, Karger, 1997, pp 177–180.
56. Waltzman S, Cohen N, Shapiro W. Effects of cochlear implantation on the young deaf child. In: Uziel A, Mondain M (eds). Advances in Otorhinolaryngology. Basel, Karger, 1995, pp 125–128.
57. Wilson BS. Cochlear implant technology. In: Niparko JK, Kirk KI, Mellon NK et al (eds). Cochlear Implants: Principles and Practices. Philadelphia, Lippincott Williams & Wilkins, 2000, pp 109–127.
58. Wilson BS. Strategies for representing speech information with cochlear implants. In: Niparko JK, Kirk KI, Mellon NK et al (eds). Cochlear Implants: Principles and Practices. Philadelphia, Lippincott Williams & Wilkins, 2000, pp 129–170.
59. Wilson BS, Lawson DT, Finley CC, Wolford RD. Coding strategies for multichannel cochlear prostheses. Am J Otol 12(Suppl 1):56, 1991.
60. Young NM, Carrasco VN, Grohne KM, Brown C. Speech perception of young children using Nucleus 22-channel or Clarion cochlear implants. Ann Otol Rhinol Laryngol 108:99, 1999.
61. Yune HY, Miyamoto RT. Medical imaging in cochlear implant candidates. Am J Otol 12(Suppl):11, 1991.
62. Zwolan TA, Zimmerman-Phillips S, Ashbaugh CJ, et al. Cochlear implantation of children with minimal open-set speech recognition skills. Ear Hear 18:240, 1997.

30

Diseases of the Labyrinthine Capsule

Richard J. H. Smith, M.D., Chantal M. Giguère, M.D., and Nancy M. Bauman, M.D.

The delicate membranous labyrinth of the inner ear is surrounded and protected by a bony labyrinth known as the otic capsule. This structure develops from a cartilaginous precursor that begins to ossify during the second trimester of gestation. Further bone deposition produces a trilaminar structure of inner and outer periosteal layers and a middle endosteal layer. The otic capsule has become the densest bone in the body by the time development is complete.[38]

With the exception of otosclerosis, most diseases of the otic capsule also manifest in other bony and soft tissue sites. Signs and symptoms of otic capsule disease include sensorineural hearing loss (SNHL), conductive hearing loss (CHL), facial nerve paralysis, tinnitus, and vertigo.

Otosclerosis

Otosclerosis is a disease limited to the otic capsule characterized by abnormal destruction and redeposition of bone leading to hearing loss.[52, 145] Although multiple factors such as autoimmunity, vascular changes, viral infections, genetic abnormalities, and hormonal mechanisms have been proposed in its pathogenesis,[84, 112, 132, 148] most studies indicate that it is an autosomal dominant disorder of variable penetrance.[52, 132, 148] A recent study localizing a gene for otosclerosis to chromosome 15q25-q26 supports this hypothesis.[138]

Although the prevalence of clinical otosclerosis approaches 1% in white populations,[50, 108, 132] the disease is seldom seen in persons of African or Asian descent.[50, 108, 132] Age at presentation typically ranges from the teenage years to the late forties, with individuals younger than 18 years accounting for only 15% of cases.[79, 108, 111] Females are affected more frequently than males and during pregnancy or estrogen administration may experience rapid progression of hearing loss.[51, 111, 112, 132]

The hearing loss is typically conductive in nature, insidious in onset, and slowly progressive. Between ears, the losses are usually asymmetric, reflecting disproportionate degrees of stapedial footplate fixation. The most common site of involvement is anterior to the oval window near the fissula ante fenestram.[77] At this site, histiocytic lysosomes laden with hydrolytic enzymes dissolve the dense organized bone of the labyrinthine capsule.[23]

Subclinical otosclerosis identified by histologic examination is common. Foci of disease may be identified in 4% of temporal bones from patients between 5 and 19 years of age and in 10% of adult bones;[54] however, fewer than 10% of persons with histologic otosclerosis have clinical signs of stapedial fixation. Foci of active or immature disease often are vascular and on clinical examination impart to the promontory a bright red hue known as Schwartze sign.[41] As the extent of disease expands, the annular ligament of the stapes footplate can become involved. When the vascular spongiotic bone mineralizes, the stapedial footplate becomes fixed, causing the characteristic CHL. In the presence of estrogen, the histiocytic lysosomal membranes are more fragile, which may account for the accelerated hearing loss associated with pregnancy or hormone replacement therapy.[23, 132]

The diagnosis of otosclerosis is suggested by history, physical examination, audiologic evaluation, and radiographic studies. Affected persons often complain of a "hollowness" in their hearing and may describe "paracusis of Willi" (improved hearing in background noise), both findings associated with CHL. Occasionally, tinnitus and vestibular symptoms may accompany the hearing loss. These symptoms seldom appear prior to 9 years of age, and there is a family history of otosclerosis in half of these persons.[37, 108, 132]

Clinically, the course of otosclerosis is more aggressive when it manifests in childhood; many studies report a higher incidence of bilaterality, as well as obliterative disease, when compared to adult studies.[37, 78, 79, 108, 132] Physical examination must exclude other more common pediatric causes of CHL, such as middle-ear effusion, tympanosclerosis, or fixation of the malleus handle. Features characteristic of syndromic forms of congenital hearing impairment also should be excluded.

The conductive hearing loss of otosclerosis can range from 0 to 50 dB.[25] The air-bone gap usually begins in the low frequencies and slowly widens, with the initial stiffness tilt due to ossicular chain fixation disappearing as the disease progresses.[56] There also may be a decrease in bone conduction at 2000 Hz. This finding, known as Carhart's notch, is highly suggestive of otosclerosis.[21, 52] Although an air-bone gap of greater than 30 dB is expected with bony ankylosis of the footplate, the extent of footplate involvement cannot be predicted by the size of the air-bone gap.[25]

Mixed or pure SNHL occurs less commonly in patients with otosclerosis.[37, 108] Theories proposed to explain SNHL include the toxic effects of osteolytic enzymes in the perilymph, expansion of the otosclerotic focus into the endosteal layer, changes in the spiral ligament and stria vascularis, and vascular shunts.[3, 23, 77, 92, 109] Tympanograms are normal (type A) or stiff (type As), depending on the degree of ossicular fixation. Acoustic reflexes are characteristically absent once fixation occurs but may show a pathognomonic diphasic shape early in the disease process before an air-bone gap is present.

High-resolution computed tomography can be used to detect vascular spongiotic and otosclerotic foci of the temporal bone (Fig. 30–1). Between 20% and 50% reduction in cortical bone can be measured in otospongiotic lesions,[57] and although it may be possible to appreciate the extent of oval window and footplate pathology by CT scan,[140] definitive diagnosis requires exploratory tympanotomy. Careful palpation of the ossicular chain excludes the more common congenital ossicular anomalies in pediatric patients.

Treatment options include observation, hearing amplification, and stapedectomy.[89] Although all choices must be discussed with the patient and family, observation is not desirable in school-age children due to possible impairment of language skills, social development, and academic performance.[132] Hearing aids should be used as soon as the loss is detected. Amplification is the preferred option of rehabilitation when bilateral impairment is present. Stapedectomy has proven to be a safe and effective treatment for otosclerosis in pediatric patients.[79, 89] Although age is seldom a contraindication to stapedectomy, most authors advise delaying surgical intervention in young children until the risk of otitis media is negligible.[79, 132] Numerous stapedectomy techniques are available, including the recently popularized use of the laser-assisted small-fenestra stapedotomy.[37, 80, 117, 119]

Complications of stapedectomy include oval window fistula, granuloma formation, suppurative labyrinthitis, and SNHL.[50] Because of the small but serious risk of total SNHL, some otologists prefer to delay surgery until the patient is old enough to participate in the decision-making process.[37, 79, 89] Although complications do not occur more commonly in pediatric patients, drill-out procedures

for biscuit footplate obliterative otosclerosis are required four times more frequently in children than adults.[30, 37, 61, 108] This fact should not be seen as a contraindication to operating because deferring surgery will only lead to worsening of the footplate pathology.[37, 108]

In adult patients with SNHL, sodium fluoride is recommended to prevent further progression of hearing impairment.[22, 120] This treatment reduces bone remodeling activity in active otospongiotic foci, increases antitrypsin levels to offset the toxic effect of trypsin on hair cells, and promotes calcification to make active foci inactive. In children, data on the efficacy of sodium fluoride are inconclusive; however, moderate daily doses of 1.5 to 10 mg may be beneficial.[22, 30] Consultation with an endocrinologist before initiation of therapy is advisable, and serial bone scans should be obtained to detect early signs of reversible fluorosis.

Osteogenesis Imperfecta

Osteogenesis imperfecta (OI), also known as "brittle bone disease," is one of the more common heritable connective tissue disorders. The overall incidence is .5 per 10,000 births and the sex ratio is 1:1.[15, 137] Studies have shown that all forms of OI are caused by molecular defects of type I collagen, the major structural component of the extracellular matrix of bone, tendon, and dermis. Most mutations have been linked to the COL1A1 and, to a lesser extent, the COL1A2 genes.[1, 32, 81, 137]

As classified by the Sillence scheme, four types of OI are recognized by mode of inheritance and severity of disease.[32, 123, 137] Type I (van der Hoeve syndrome) is the mildest form of OI and is characterized by autosomal dominant inheritance, nondeforming fractures during childhood, ligamentous laxity, normal stature, blue sclerae, and CHL. Type II, the most severe form of OI, is usually lethal in utero or shortly thereafter. Transmitted in an autosomal dominant fashion, affected fetuses can be recognized by ultrasound or radiologic studies examination as early as in the first trimester.[1, 15] Radiographic features include generalized osteopenia, beaded ribs and long bones, platyspondylisis, and calvarial demineralization[32] (Fig. 30–2). OI type III is characterized by progressive growth failure, frequent fractures, severe deformity, severe osteoporosis, extreme short stature, and dentinogenesis imperfecta. It is generally autosomal recessive except in rare instances of autosomal dominant inheritance. OI type IV is intermediate in severity between OI types I and III. There is mild-to-moderate bone deformity and short stature. Inheritance is autosomal dominant, although rare recessive transmission has been documented.[1, 32, 81, 137] Hearing impairment is frequently associated with OI and affects 20% of 5-year-old children and 90% of adults with the disease.[19, 104] It is most common in OI type I patients,[137] and usually conductive, reflecting middle ear disease.[16] The ossicular chain may be fractured at the crura of the stapes or the handle of the malleus, the head of the malleus may be ankylosed to the lateral wall of the scutum, or the stapedial footplate may be markedly thickened and mildly ankylosed.[8] The stapes is the most frequently affected ossi-

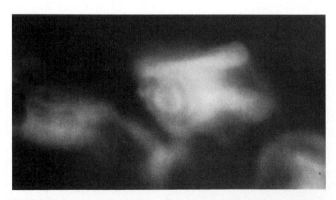

FIGURE 30–1. Polytomogram of a patient with cochlear otosclerosis. The dense bone deposition creates the impression of a cochlea within a cochlea.

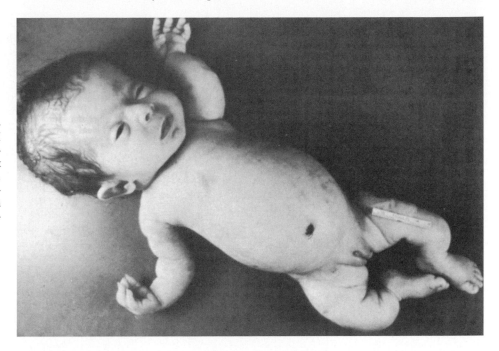

FIGURE 30–2. Neonate who has osteogenesis imperfecta (OI) Type II and died shortly after birth of respiratory complications. (From Black FO, Bergstrom L, Downs MP, et al. Congenital Deafness: A New Approach to Diagnosis Using a High Risk Register. Boulder, CO, Associated University Press, 1971.)

cle.[137] Footplate involvement is characteristically thick, soft, and chalky, unlike the hard anterior fixation of otosclerosis[8, 19, 45] (Fig. 30–3). OI and otosclerosis can occur concomitantly and display similar clinical and histopathologic manifestations. There may be an association between otosclerosis and mild OI through mutations within the *COL1A1* gene.[32, 83]

Computed tomography of mild forms of OI with temporal bone involvement shows extensive thickening of the otic capsule and narrowing of the middle-ear space with under-mineralized bone.[133] Histologic examination demonstrates widespread deficiency of ossification of the ossicles and bony labyrinth.[16, 19, 91, 137, 149] Large remnants of persistent cartilage attest to incomplete ossification. Insufficient perichondrial bone deposition in the internal auditory canal gives it a wide appearance, and the mastoid air cells appear unusually well pneumatized. Densitometry studies may predict disease activity and cochlear

involvement, information that is helpful in surgical planning.[140]

Less commonly recognized otolaryngologic manifestations of OI include lopped pinnae, notched or folded helices, mandibular prognathism, and maxillary hypoplasia.[19, 137] Defective dentin formation in deciduous and permanent teeth causes a blue-to-brown color with a distinctive translucence of dentinogenesis imperfecta.[94] In addition to being discolored, teeth are often small, misshapen, and constricted at the base. Blue sclerae, a hallmark of OI, may be present in 95% of affected persons with CHL. The color is imparted by the choroid, visible through the abnormally translucent sclera.[8, 102]

The natural history of OI is highly variable, although affected members of the same family share similar clinical features. Life expectancy in types I and IV OI is only modestly reduced when compared to the general population. Type II is perinatally lethal and type III carries a decreased life expectancy.[101]

Although the clinical history, radiographic features, and physical examination may suggest the diagnosis of OI, confirmation requires identification of abnormal procollagen from cultured fibroblasts or demonstration of specific genomic mutations.[1] Gene mutations within a family are homogeneous, and intrafamilial screening is possible once the inherited mutation is identified.[104]

Treatment of OI is symptomatic.[32, 81] Skeletal fractures occur with little associated soft tissue swelling, are relatively painless, and heal without delay after immobilization.[29, 104] CHL requires preferential classroom seating, hearing amplification, or ossiculoplasty. Stapedectomy may be performed with the same expected degree of success as in otosclerosis, but extra care is required in elevating the thin skin of the external auditory canal and separating the incudostapedial joint because of the marked brittle and fragile nature of the ossicles.[8, 29, 102] Some surgeons also report poorer long-term results due to the progressive nature of the disease process.

FIGURE 30–3. Polytomogram of a patient with osteogenesis imperfecta Type I. The disease process has created a cochlea within a cochlea similar to that seen in Figure 30–1 (*arrow*). (Courtesy of W. Hanafee, M.D.)

Osteopetrosis

Osteopetrosis (OP, marble bone disease) is a rare hereditary skeletal dysplasia characterized by a marked increase in bone density resulting from an imbalance in bone remodeling.[9, 27, 95] Dysfunctional osteoclasts are unable to resorb bone and calcified cartilage.[43, 71, 82, 121] Osteoblast function proceeds unchecked, with excessive deposition of new, often immature osteoid. Excessive osteoid leads to dense and sclerotic but paradoxically fragile bones that fracture with minimal trauma.[9, 43, 71]

In general, osteopetrosis is divided into three types.[9, 142] One type is malignant infantile OP, which is autosomal recessive. It affects neonates and, if untreated, survival beyond adolescence is rare.[128] A second type is inherited in an autosomal dominant fashion and is referred to as benign adult OP. This form is often detected incidentally and does not compromise lifespan.[127] The third type is intermediate OP and, like infantile OP, is an autosomal recessive disease. Usually, it is diagnosed late in infancy or early childhood and follows a course of moderate severity between the two aforementioned types[9, 142] (Fig. 30–4).

In the malignant recessive form of OP, deposits of immature woven bone obliterate bone marrow and unresorbed islands of calcified cartilage.[58] With obliteration of marrow, life-threatening anemia, thrombocytopenia, and leukemia develop, with compensatory extramedullary he-

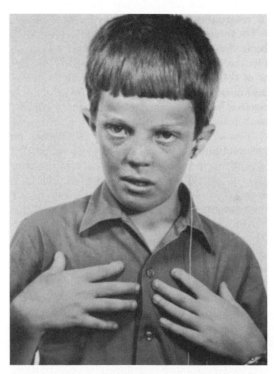

FIGURE 30–4. Twelve-year-old boy with the benign form of osteopetrosis. He had several episodes of facial palsy and underwent facial nerve decompression at age 6 years. Note his relatively expressionless face. He also required canaloplasty to widen the external auditory canals and an exploratory tympanotomy for incudomalleolar fixation. Ultimately, stapedial fixation developed. Other features of osteopetrosis in this boy include absent fingernails, syndactyly, and skull enlargement. (Courtesy of H. Hammersma, M.D.)

matopoiesis and hepatosplenomegaly. In addition, proptosis, blindness, papilledema, nystagmus, hydrocephalus, ocular paresis, deafness, obstructive sleep apnea, pathologic fractures, and osteomyelitis have been reported.[9, 43, 95, 128] The diagnosis of the malignant form of OP is generally apparent early in childhood.[73] Radiographically, horizontal bands of alternating density can be observed in the shafts of long bones and in the vertebrae.[43]

In the less severe autosomal dominant form of OP, bone marrow is largely uncompromised and anemia and hepatosplenomegaly are not typically seen.[9, 95] The diagnosis of benign OP is suggested by clinical symptoms and confirmed by roentgenographic findings. Cortical and medullary components of long bones appear densely homogeneous, cranial foramina are narrowed by insufficient bone remodeling, and skull thickness may reach an impressive 3 cm.[55] On histologic examination, dense sclerotic bone is seen in the periosteal and endochondral layers of the otic capsule, sparing the endosteal layer.[130] A subtype of the benign dominant form, Albers-Schönberg disease, is further characterized radiographically by the sandwich-like appearance of the spine and by endobones—a "bone-within-a-bone" phenomenon.[14, 142] Recently, a gene for Albers-Schönberg was localized to a region on chromosome 1p21.[142]

In the intermediate type of OP, signs and symptoms are similar to the malignant variant; however, they are less severe. A particular subtype of intermediate OP manifests as cerebral calcification and renal tubular acidosis, and results from a deficiency of carbonic anhydrase II.[9, 43, 142]

Otolaryngologic manifestations in symptomatic patients with any form of OP include hearing loss, facial nerve paralysis, and osteomyelitis of the mandible and maxilla. Hearing loss is almost always conductive and is due to excessive bony deposition in the walls of the tympanic cavity, ossicles, or external auditory canal.[58, 64] Because of defective resorption and remodeling of the ossicles, particularly the stapes, a fetal configuration of these bones is not unusual[90] (Fig. 30–5). Factors such as fibrous layer thickening of the tympanic membrane as well as recurrent otitis media have been described in OP and may cause CHL. The SNHL associated with OP is thought to be due to cochlear nerve compression secondary to abnormal bone growth in the internal auditory canal.[128]

Stenosis of neural foramina in the skull base occurs in patients with OP. Nerve tracts become compressed as they exit the cranial vault. The optic nerve is most frequently involved, followed by the facial nerve.[9, 43, 95, 128] When facial paralysis becomes bilateral, affected persons ultimately portray a blunted, unemotional facial expression.

Osteomyelitis of the mandible is a well-documented complication of OP.[9] Eruption of teeth, infection following tooth extraction, and mild trauma are the usual contributing factors.[9, 95, 128] Possible facial findings resulting from osteomyelitis include hyperplasia of facial bones, square jaw, soft tissue swelling, skin erythema, and multiple persistent draining fistulae.[128]

Recently, numerous treatment modalities have been proposed in the management of OP, including high-dose glucocorticoids, low-calcium diets and high-dose Calcitrol,

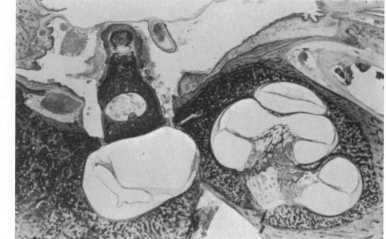

FIGURE 30–5. Horizontal temporal bone section from a young deaf-blind child with the malignant form of osteopetrosis. Lack of resorption of stapedial cartilage has prevented bony remodeling of the ossicle into its adult form. (Courtesy of S. E. Stool, M.D.)

monocyte-macrophage colony-stimulating factor, interferon gamma-1b therapy, and bone marrow transplantation.[9, 43, 128] Certain authors claim that bone marrow transplantation is the treatment of choice for malignant infantile OP;[128] however, further studies are required to evaluate these therapies since they have been used in only a small number of patients and long-term follow-up is generally not available. Antibiotics and surgery often are required to treat complications of OP. Supportive measures such as transfusions also have been shown to be beneficial.[9, 95, 128]

Langerhans Cell Histiocytosis

In 1953, Lichtenstein recognized the histologic similarities of eosinophilic granuloma, Hand-Schüller-Christian disease, and Letterer-Siwe disease, and collectively referred to these diseases as types of histiocytosis X.[75] In spite of their similar histologic appearance, the systemic manifestations and prognosis of these conditions are different. In 1985, the Writing Group of the Histiocyte Society recommended the designation Langerhans cell histiocytosis (LCH) to describe the spectrum of diseases characterized by proliferation of Langerhans cells with local or systemic effects.[26, 44, 97, 131] Authors who have reviewed patients with head and neck manifestations of LCH have classified this disease into three groups: LCH with only a single focus; LCH with multiple nonvital organ foci; and LCH with vital organ disease.[4]

The pathogenesis of LCH remains unknown.[20, 105] Although the disease can present at any age, the peak incidence is between 1 and 3 years of age[143] and most affected persons are under the age of 10.[6] The annual incidence in children has been estimated at 3 per million, with a male to female ratio of 2:1.[63, 98] Although the disease course is highly variable, significant predictive factors are age at diagnosis and organ involvement.[4, 69] Patients presenting before the age of 2 years are more susceptible to widely disseminated disease that carries a 25% mortality rate.[125]

The most frequent clinical presentation of LCH is localized bone pain with an associated soft tissue mass.[11] More than 60% of persons present with head and neck

involvement.[63, 105] Otolaryngologic sites of manifestation include the skull vault, external auditory canal, cervical lymph nodes, temporal bone, maxilla, and mandible.[11, 63] Bone disease is the single most common disease manifestation, occurring in about 80% of patients.[125] Flat bones are frequently involved, and lesions in the cranium appear as radiolucent areas with scalloped edges. Temporal bone involvement is seen in approximately 20% of affected children and frequently is heralded by chronic foul-smelling otorrhea, postauricular swelling, and aural polyps[11, 44, 63] (Fig. 30–6). Posterior external auditory canal granulation tissue in the presence of an intact tympanic membrane is nearly pathognomonic for temporal bone LCH.[6, 116] The granulation tissue usually covers a fistula between the external auditory canal and mastoid air cells. If postauricular swelling is present, it can mimic acute mastoiditis but lacks the associated pain, fever, and systemic symptoms.[122] Intractable "otomastoiditis," despite conventional management, should prompt consideration of LCH[44] (Fig. 30–7). A recent study on a limited number of patients has suggested that LCH with ear involvement carries an unfavorable outcome.[131] CHL can arise from occlusion of the external auditory canal, soft tissue in the middle-ear space, or destruction of the ossicles.[44] Less commonly, SNHL occurs and may represent erosion of the bony labyrinth.[63, 129, 139] Facial paralysis is reported in 2.8% to 5% of cases and is attributed to erosion-induced vascular compromise of the horizontal and vertical segments of the fallopian canal.[11, 34, 63, 139]

Radiographs in persons with temporal bone involvement demonstrate lytic lesions.[4] High-resolution computed tomography displays "punched-out" osteolytic lesions or a soft tissue mass in the mastoid air cells[35] (Fig. 30–8). Generally, the lesions have indistinct margins and the ossicles, as well as the bony labyrinth, may show erosion.[44] On magnetic resonance imaging, soft tissue masses appear hyperintense on T_2-weighted images, appear hypointense on T_1-weighted images, and show marked enhancement after administration with gadolinium.[4, 44]

Although clinical and radiographic signs may be suggestive of LCH, definitive diagnosis requires histologic confirmation of the disease process. The Writing Group

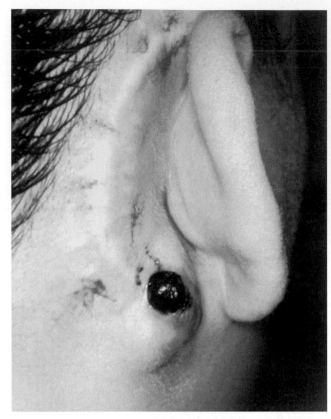

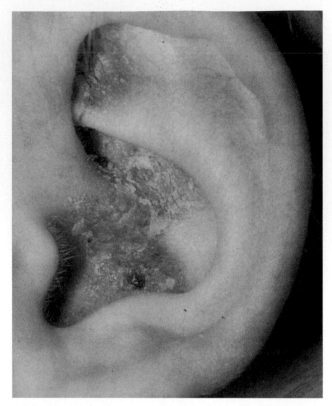

FIGURE 30–6. Postauricular skin breakdown over a focus of Langerhans cell histiocytosis in a young boy. The mastoid cavity has been cleaned of disease, but subsequent recurrence approximately 8 months later was heralded by breakdown of the inferior aspect of the surgical incision.

FIGURE 30–7. Scaling lesion of the conchal bowl and fossa triangularis in a young boy. Biopsy findings are consistent with Langerhans cell histiocytosis.

of the Histiocyte Society recommends the designation "presumptive diagnosis" when biopsy findings are consistent with LCH by conventional staining methods.[26] A higher level of diagnostic certainty, termed "diagnosis," requires special stains for ATPase, S-100 protein, alpha-D-mannosidase, or characteristic binding of peanut lectin. Definitive diagnosis requires electron microscopic confirmation of Birbeck granules or positive immunostaining for CD1a on lesional cells.[42] These last two studies require fresh, nonfixed tissue for diagnosis.[63]

Management of LCH is highly controversial. The natural course of the disease is studded with recurrences sometimes followed by spontaneous remissions. Lack of controlled studies demonstrating the efficacy of one therapeutic approach over another complicates disease management.[143]

In general, isolated bony lesions do not require treatment other than biopsy with or without curettage.[4, 11] Further local therapies such as surgery or intralesional steroid injection may be indicated if the lesions are symptomatic. If these therapies are not feasible, low-dose radiation (6-10 Gy) remains an option.[143] Intervention with chemotherapy is reserved for lesions located near vital structures or in patients with multifocal or disseminated disease.[105]

In cases of temporal bone disease, central nervous sys-

tem involvement, hearing loss, vertigo, facial nerve paralysis, or fistula of the external auditory canal can occur. For these reasons, treatment is warranted. Local treatment of LCH of the temporal bone classically has included mas-

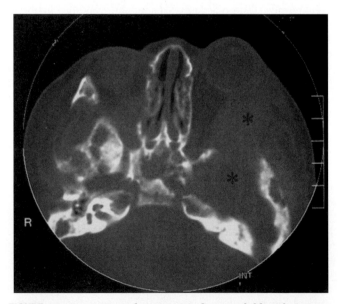

FIGURE 30–8. Computed tomogram from a child with Langerhans cell histiocytosis (LCH). A large soft tissue mass is seen on the left with destruction of the lateral orbital wall, temporal bone, and sphenoid bone.

FIGURE 30–9. Lateral skull film of a young boy with fibrous dysplasia. The sphenoid and temporal bones appear densely sclerotic. Depending of the degree of fibrous tissue, a pagetoid or cystic appearance can also be produced.

toidectomy and radiotherapy. More recently, excellent local control with the use of intralesional steroids has been demonstrated.[11, 44, 63]

Fibrous Dysplasia

Fibrous dysplasia (FD) is a slowly progressing, benign fibro-osseous lesion in which normal lamellar bone is replaced by the proliferation of fibrous connective tissue interspersed with irregular trabeculae of woven bone.[85, 100, 147] Three variants of FD have been described: monostotic, polyostotic, and McCune-Albright syndrome. The latter syndrome is a variant of polyostotic FD that is also accompanied by abnormal skin pigmentation, endocrinopathies, and precocious sexual development.[88] The male to female ratio of FD is 2:1 with a notable race predilection—whites comprise 80% of all cases, blacks 2%, and Asians 1%.[100] Mechanisms have been proposed to explain the occurrence of FD, including abnormal enzymatic activity in bone-forming mesenchyme, disrupted calcium and phosphorus metabolism, and hyperplasia of osteoblasts; however, the exact etiology is unclear.[85]

Most affected individuals have monostotic or limited polyostotic FD and present between 11 and 14 years of age, although symptoms can be absent until adulthood.[76, 126, 141] Craniofacial involvement is more common in polyostotic FD, with the frontal and sphenoid bones being most often involved.[67, 93] Temporal bone FD is uncommon, tends to be unilateral, and occurs in approximately 18% of cases where there is craniofacial involvement.[88] The most common clinical features of FD of the temporal bone are progressive stenosis of the external auditory canal and CHL, swelling, and entrapment of cholesteatoma. Although rare, SNHL has been attributed to this lesion—resulting from either cochlear destruction, internal auditory canal stenosis, or vestibular

fistulization.[88, 100] Facial nerve paralyses and invasion of the posterior cranial fossa can occur.[28]

There have been reported cases of craniofacial FD undergoing spontaneous malignant transformation;[110] however, none of these malignant cases have been associated with temporal bone FD.[88, 100] The overall rate of spontaneous transformation to malignancy has been estimated at .4% of cases.[85]

On radiographs, FD appears sclerotic (23%), cystic (21%), or pagetoid with intermediate lucency (56%), depending on the ratio of fibrous and osseous components[48] (Fig. 30–9). Temporal bone lesions display a sclerotic pattern in two-thirds of cases.[88, 100] The mixture of fibrous and bony elements produces the classic but not pathognomonic ground-glass appearance on computed tomography[85, 126] (Fig. 30–10).

The differential diagnosis of FD includes Paget's disease, ossifying and nonossifying fibroma, eosinophilic granuloma, osteochondroma, aneurysmal bone cyst, and giant cell reparative granuloma.

Definitive diagnosis of FD requires the correlation of radiographic findings with histopathologic features.[85] The microscopic features of FD consist of irregularly shaped trabeculae of immature bone in a loosely arranged fibrous stroma. The curvilinear shapes of these different trabeculae take on a characteristic jigsaw puzzle or "Chinese alphabet" pattern.[96, 124, 134] Although the lesions are not contained within a specific capsule, the demarcation between normal bone and FD is readily identified.[100]

Asymptomatic lesions do not require surgical intervention. The indications for surgical treatment of FD include CHL; management of complications from cholesteatoma

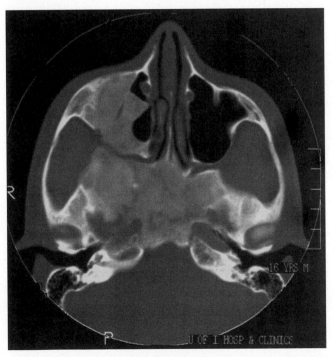

FIGURE 30–10. Computed tomogram from an adolescent male with fibrous dysplasia. The scan demonstrates extensive bony involvement of the skull base with a characteristic ground-glass appearance.

that may interfere with cranial nerve (VII, VIII) function; and cosmetic deformity.[85, 100, 118, 147] Radiation therapy is not recommended due to the risk of sarcomatous transformation.[88, 118]

Lysosomal Storage Diseases

Lysosomal storage diseases (LSD) are a heterogeneous group of over 40 distinct disorders, each consisting of a specific deficiency in the lysosomal system. Collectively, LSD have an incidence of approximately one in 7000 to 8000 live births,[146] encompassing a variety of conditions, including mucopolysaccharidoses, mucolipidoses, lipid storage diseases, and glycoprotein storage diseases. Inheritance is usually autosomal recessive with the exceptions of Hunter syndrome and Fabry disease, which are cross-linked.[12] Generally, the course of LSD is progressive and often fatal in childhood and adolescence. The inappropriate accumulation of macromolecules leads to visceromegaly, macroglossia, macrocephaly, progressive neurologic dysfunction, and skeletal dysostosis. Affected children often do not achieve normal childhood developmental milestones at expected times and attained milestones can be lost. With disease progression, coarse facies, corneal clouding, an exaggerated startle response, abdominal distention, joint pain, stiffness, hernias, and recurrent infections develop. The diagnosis of LSD consists of recognition of clinical symptoms and identification of the specific enzyme deficiency.[146]

Hurler syndrome, a specific type of mucopolysaccharidosis, is caused by a deficiency of alpha-L-iduronidase. The accumulated stored material in this syndrome is heparan sulfate and dermatan sulfate.[12] Affected children experience excessive growth in the first year of life but eventually are of short stature. Hearing loss is very common and is usually a combination of CHL and SNHL. In addition, the presence of eustachian tube obstruction in these persons leads to a greater likelihood of middle-ear infections. Death, usually in the first decade, is due to hydrocephalus, occlusion of the coronary arteries, pneumonia, and obstructive airway disease.[136]

Hunter syndrome bears some similarity to Hurler syndrome, but is distinguished by cross-linked recessive inheritance, absence of corneal clouding, and less severe neurologic impairment. It is due to a deficiency in iduronosulfate sulfatase enzyme activity. Mixed hearing loss is a frequent component of Hunter syndrome, including the index cases reported by Hunter in 1917[62, 103] (Fig. 30–11).

Histologic temporal bone features of the mucopolysaccharidoses include mucopurulent hemorrhagic effusions, basophilic excretions within the stria vascularis, occlusion of the middle-ear cavity with residual mesenchyme, and replacement of mastoid air cells with vacuolated foam cells.[47, 66, 86, 114, 115] The vacuolated foam cells, also referred to as Hurler, balloon, or gargoyle cells, can infiltrate the spiral ganglion in large numbers to produce SNHL.

Fabry disease is a rare cross-linked LSD that develops due to deficiency of alpha-galactosidase A, resulting in the

FIGURE 30–11. Young man with Hunter syndrome. Note coarse facial features including broad nasal bridge, broad nasal tip, increased interpupillary distance, and enlarged lips. Patient is wearing a hearing aid on the left.

accumulation of trihexosylceramide (galactosyl-galactosyl-glucosyl-ceramide), painful neuropathy, angiokeratoma, hypohidrosis, corneal opacification, cardiomyopathy, and progressive renal impairment. Histologic examination of the temporal bone demonstrates hyperplastic the middle ear mucosa, seropurulent effusions, atrophy of the stria vascularis and spiral ligament, decreased ganglion cells in the basal turn of the cochlea, and accumulated glycosphingolipids in the vascular endothelium and ganglion cells. SNHL, vertigo, and tinnitus ensue.[113]

Craniometaphyseal Dysplasia

Craniometaphyseal dysplasia (CMD) is a rare syndrome involving abnormal modeling of the long bones and sclerosis of the cranium.[43, 46] It can present as a mild autosomal dominant form or as a more severe autosomal recessive form. To date, about 10 cases of autosomal recessive CMD and 100 cases of autosomal dominant CMD have been reported.[13, 99] The exact pathogenesis of CMD is unknown. Decreased osteoclastic activity in the periosteal and endosteal layers resulting in poor reabsorption and remodeling of spongy tissue of long bones has been suggested as a possible etiology.[46]

Affected persons have frontal and paranasal bossing, broad flat nasal bridge with saddle deformity, mandibular

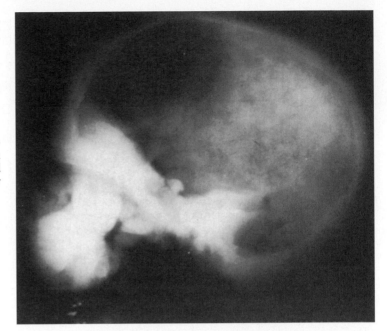

FIGURE 30–12. Lateral skull film of a patient with craniometaphyseal dysplasia. Dense sclerotic bony overgrowth has changed the normal facial appearance and extended posteriorly to the temporal bones to obliterate the bony labyrinth. (Courtesy of Lorraine Smith, M.D.)

prognathism, dental malocclusion, hypertelorism, narrow external auditory canals with progressive CHL or SNHL, facial paralysis, other cranial nerve palsies, raised intracranial pressure, cerebellar tonsil compression with resultant nystagmus, and brain stem compression due to constriction of the foramen magnum.[13, 18, 106] CHL is caused by fixation of middle ear structures, obliteration of the oval window, and hyperostosis. SNHL may result from stenosis of the internal auditory meatus.[46] Bone overgrowth also causes narrowing of the eustachian tube, paranasal sinus ostia, nasal lacrimal ducts, and nares. There is more marked cranial nerve palsy and facial distortion in the autosomal recessive type.[13] Without a family history, distinguishing between the two types of CMD is difficult in infancy and early childhood; however, in later childhood, clinical and radiographic signs improve in the dominant form, while there is continued overgrowth and craniofacial deformity in the recessive form.[40]

Radiographic features include hyperostosis of the skull and facial bones, poor pneumatization or obliteration of the paranasal sinuses and mastoid antrum, and flaring and decreased density of the metaphyses of long bones (which takes on a distinctive Erlenmeyer flask configuration in childhood and club shape in adulthood).[13] Computed tomography of the temporal bone shows diffuse bone thickening and sclerosis with reduced mastoid air cell development[40] (Fig. 30–12). The internal and external auditory canals, jugular foramina, and internal carotid artery canals become progressively narrowed.[70]

Temporal bone histologic examination shows increased amounts of subperiosteal and subendosteal compact laminar bone, dilated haversian canals with osteoblasts and osteocytes but no osteoclasts, and increased amounts of intracellular ground substance.[68]

CMD must be differentiated from Pyle disease, a distinctive autosomal recessive condition with gross metaphyseal expansion but without cranial sclerosis.[13]

Frontometaphyseal Dysplasia

Frontometaphyseal dysplasia is a rare congenital syndrome similar to CMD. It also results from failure of absorption of secondary spongiosa bone.[53, 60] The likely inheritance pattern is cross-linked, and prominent features include patchy sclerosis and disfiguring overgrowth or exostoses of the supraorbital ridges to produce horn-like projections, atrophy of the temporalis muscles, agenesis of the frontal sinuses, microcephaly, micrognathia, high-arched palate, limited joint mobility (particularly of the elbow), undermodeled and disproportionately long limbs, poor muscle development, hirsutism, low-set ears, strabismus, decreased vision, subglottic stenosis, and progressive mixed hearing loss.[39, 135, 144] Intelligence is generally normal, although cases of mental handicap associated with frontometaphyseal dysplasia have been reported.[144]

CT studies of frontometaphyseal dysplasia display marked craniofacial deformity; with prominent bulging of the temporoparietal layer and forehead, thickened cortical bone, missing or underdeveloped paranasal sinuses, and notably short internal auditory channel.[39]

The conductive component of the hearing loss in frontometaphyseal dysplasia is due to fusion of the malleus and incus with malformation of the stapes.[7] SNHL can occur secondary to abnormal endosteal bone metabolism. Abnormal metabolism results in irregular thickening of the otic capsule.

Other Dysplasias

Hearing loss of varying degrees and types has been reported in other bone disorders including craniofacial dysostosis, diastrophic dwarfism, Larsen syndrome, Paget disease, Engelmann disease (progressive diaphyseal dysplasia), and an unclassified bone dysplasia associated with retinal detachment and deafness.[10, 17, 59, 63, 87, 107]

Neoplasms

Primary and metastatic tumors that invade the otic capsule and labyrinth are rare in children, but temporal bone involvement with rhabdomyosarcoma, myofibromatosis, osteosarcoma, Ewing sarcoma, osteoblastoma, osteoma, ossifying fibroma, neurofibromatosis, chondrosarcoma, hemangiopericytoma, leukemia, hemangioma, paraganglioma, and chloroma has been reported.[2, 24, 35, 36, 72, 74, 150] Disseminated fungal infections also may invade the temporal bone.[5]

REFERENCES

1. Ablin DS. Osteogenesis imperfecta: a review. Can Assoc Radiol J 49:110, 1998.
2. Aikawa T, Ohtani I. Temporal bone findings in central nervous system leukemia. Am J Otolaryngol 12:320, 1991.
3. Altmann F, Kornfeld M, Shea JJ. Inner ear changes in otosclerosis. Ann Otol Rhinol Laryngol 75:5, 1966.
4. Angeli SI, Alcalde J, Hoffman HT, Smith RJH. Langerhans cell histiocytosis of the head and neck in children. Ann Otol Rhinol Laryngol 104:173, 1995.
5. Angtuaco EEC, Angtuaco EJC, Glasier CM, Benitez CM. Nasopharyngeal and temporal bone blastomycosis: CT and MR findings. AJNR 12:725, 1991.
6. Appling D, Jenkins HA, Patton GA. Eosinophilic granuloma in the temporal bone and skull. Otolaryngol Head Neck Surg 91:358, 1983.
7. Arenberg IK, Shambaugh GE, Valvassori GE. Otolaryngologic manifestations of frontometaphyseal dysplasia. The Gorlin-Holt syndrome. Arch Otolaryngol 199:52, 1974.
8. Armstrong BW. Stapes surgery in patients with osteogenesis imperfecta. Ann Otol Rhinol Laryngol 93:634, 1984.
9. Bakeman RJ, Abdelsayed RA, Sutley SH, Newhouse RF. Osteopetrosis: a review of the literature and report of a case complicated by osteomyelitis of the mandible. J Oral Maxillofac Surg 56:1209, 1998.
10. Baldwin JL. Dysostosis craniofacialis of Crouzon. Laryngoscope 78:1660, 1968.
11. Bauer PW, MacDonald CB, Domanowski GF, Fuleihan NS. Pathologic quiz case 2: Langerhans cell histiocytosis (LCH) of the temporal bone. Arch Otolaryngol Head Neck Surg 124:1395, 1998.
12. Beaudet AL. Lysosomal storage diseases. In Wilson JD, Branowald E, Isselbacher KJ, et al (eds). Harrison's Principles of Internal Medicine. New York, McGraw-Hill, 1991, pp 1845–1854.
13. Beighton P. Craniometaphyseal dysplasia (CMD), autosomal dominant form. J Med Genet 32:370, 1995.
14. Benichou OD, Laredo JD, de Vernejoul MC. Type II autosomal osteopetrosis (Albers-Schönberg disease): clinical and radiological manifestations in 42 patients. Bone 26:87, 2000.
15. Berge LN, Marton V, Tranebjaerg L, et al. Prenatal diagnosis of osteogenesis imperfecta. Acta Obstet Gynecol Scand 74:321, 1995.
16. Berger G, Hawke M, Johnson A. Histopathology of the temporal bone in osteogenesis imperfecta congenita: a report of 5 cases. Laryngoscope 95:193, 1985.
17. Bergstrom L. A high risk registry to find congenital deafness. Otolaryngol Clin North Am 4:369, 1971.
18. Bergstrom L. Diseases of the labyrinthine capsule. In: Bluestone CD, Stool SE (eds). Pediatric Otolaryngology. Philadelphia, WB Saunders, 1990, pp 571–577.
19. Bergstrom L. Osteogenesis imperfecta: otologic and maxillofacial aspects. Laryngoscope 87:1, 1977.
20. Calming U, Henter J-I. Elevated erythrocyte sedimentation rate and thrombocytosis as possible indicators of active disease in Langerhans' cell histiocytosis. Acta Paediatr 87:1085, 1998.
21. Carhart R. Clinical application of bone conduction audiometry. Arch Otolaryngol Head Neck Surg 51:798, 1950.
22. Causse J, Chavance LG, Shambaugh GE. Clinical experience and experimental findings with sodium fluoride in otosclerosis (otospongiosis). Ann Otol Rhinol Laryngol 83:643, 1974.
23. Causse JR, Shambaugh GE, Causse JB, Bretlau P. Enzymology of otospongiosis and NaF therapy. Am J Otol 1:206, 1980.
24. Cemiloglu R, Tekalan SA, Patiroglu, Unlu Y. Rhabdomyosarcoma of the temporal bone: clinical report. Arch Otorhinolaryngol 244:195, 1987.
25. Cherukupally SR, Merchant SN, Rosowski JJ. Correlations between pathologic changes in the stapes and conductive hearing loss in otosclerosis. Ann Otol Rhinol Laryngol 107:319, 1998.
26. Chu T, D'Angio GJ, Favara B, et al. Histiocytosis syndromes in children. Lancet 1:208, 1987.
27. Coccia PF, Krivit W, Cervenka J, et al. Successful bone marrow transplantation for infantile malignant osteopetrosis. N Engl J Med 302:701, 1980.
28. Cohen A, Rossenwasser I. Fibrous dysplasia of the temporal bone. Arch Otolaryngol 89:31, 1969.
29. Cohen BJ. Osteogenesis imperfecta and hearing loss. Ear Nose Throat J 63:55, 1984.
30. Cole JM. Surgery for otosclerosis in children. Laryngoscope 92:859, 1982.
31. Cole WG. The molecular pathology of osteogenesis imperfecta. Clin Orthop 343:235, 1997.
32. Cole WG, Dalgleish R. Perinatal lethal osteogenesis imperfecta. J Med Genet 32:284, 1995.
33. Cunningham MJ, Curtin HD, Butkiewicz BL. Histiocytosis X of the temporal bone: CT findings. J Comput Assist Tomogr 12:70, 1988.
34. Cunningham MJ, Curtin HD, Jaffe R, Stool S. Otologic manifestations of Langerhans cell histiocytosis. Arch Otolaryngol Head Neck Surg 115:807, 1989.
35. Cunningham MJ, Myers EN. Tumors and tumorlike lesions of the ear and temporal bone in children. Ear Nose Throat J 67:726, 1988.
36. Davidson MJC. Ewing's sarcoma of the temporal bone, a case report. Oral Surg Oral Med Oral Pathol 72:534, 1991.
37. de la Cruz A, Angeli S, Slattery WH. Stapedectomy in children. Otolaryngol Head Neck Surg 120:487, 1999.
38. Donaldson JA. The ear: developmental anatomy. In: Donaldson JA, Duckert LG, Lambert PM, Rubel EW (eds). Surgical Anatomy of the Temporal Bone. New York, Raven Press, 1992, pp 31–43.
39. Ehrenstein T, Maurer J, Liokumowitsch M, et al. CT and MR findings in frontometaphyseal dysplasia. J Comput Assist Tomogr 21:218, 1997.
40. Elcioglu N, Hall CM. Temporal aspects in craniometaphyseal dysplasia: autosomal recessive type. Am J Med Genet 76:245, 1998.
41. Emmett JR. Physical examination and clinical evaluation of the patient with otosclerosis. Otolaryngol Clin North Am 26:353, 1993.
42. Favara BE, Jaffe R. The histopathology of Langerhans cell histiocytosis. Br J Cancer Suppl 23:S17, 1994.
43. Felix R, Hofstetter W, Cecchini MG. Recent developments in the understanding of the pathophysiology of osteopetrosis. Eur J Endocrin 134:143, 1996.
44. Fernandez-Latorre F, Menor-Serrano F, Alonso-Charterina S, et al. Langerhans cell histiocytosis of the temporal bone in pediatric patients: imaging and follow-up. AJR 174:217, 2000.
45. Flintoff WM, Karmody CS, Rabuzzi DD. Osteogenesis imperfecta of the stapes: a histological study. J Otolaryngol 5:37, 1976.
46. Franz DC, Horn KL, Aase J. Craniometaphyseal dysplasia: operative findings and treatment. Am J Otol 17:283, 1996.
47. Friedmann I, Spellacy E, Crow J, Watts RWE. Histopathological studies of the temporal bones in Hurler's disease (mucopolysaccharidosis [MPS] IH). J Laryngol Otol 99:29, 1985.
48. Fries JW. The roentgen features of fibrous dysplasia of the skull and facial bones. Am J Roentgenol 77:71, 1957.
49. Glasscock ME, Shambaugh GE. Diagnosis, indications for surgery, and medical therapy of otospongiosis. In Glasscock ME, Shambaugh GE (eds). Surgery of the Ear. Philadelphia, WB Saunders, 1990, pp 376–378.
50. Glasscock ME, Shambaugh GE. Operations for otospongiosis (otosclerosis). In Glasscock ME, Shambaugh GE (eds). Surgery of the Ear. Philadelphia, WB Saunders, 1990, pp 401–408.
51. Gordon MA. The genetics of otosclerosis: a review. Am J Otol 10:426, 1989.

52. Gordon MA, McPhee J, et al. Aberration of the tissue collagenase system in association with otosclerosis. Am J Otol 13:398, 1992.

53. Gorlin RJ, Cohen MM. Frontometaphyseal dysplasia: a new syndrome. Am J Dis Child 118:487, 1969.

54. Guild SR. Histologic otosclerosis. Ann Otol Rhinol Laryngol 53:246, 1944.

55. Hammersma H. Osteopetrosis (marble bone disease) of the temporal bone. Laryngoscope 80:1518, 1970.

56. Hannley MT. Audiologic characteristics of the patient with otosclerosis. Otolaryngol Clin North Am 26:381, 1993.

57. Havriliak D, Parisier SC. Cochlear otosclerosis presenting in children: a case report. Am J Otol 12:61, 1991.

58. Hawke M, Jahn AF, Bailey D. Osteopetrosis of the temporal bone. Arch Otolaryngol 107:278, 1981.

59. Higashi K, Matsuki C. Hearing impairment in Engelmann disease. Am J Otol 17:26, 1996.

60. Holt JF, Thomson GR, Arenberg IK. Frontometaphyseal dysplasia. Radiol Clin North Am 10:225, 1972.

61. House JW, Sheehy JL, Antunez JC. Stapedectomy in children. Laryngoscope 90:1804, 1980.

62. Hunter C. Hunter: a rare disease in two brothers. Proc R Soc Med 10:104, 1917.

63. Irving RM, Broadbent V, Jones NS. Langerhans cell histiocytosis in childhood: management of head and neck manifestations. Laryngoscope 104:64, 1994.

64. Jones MD, Mulcahy ND. Osteopathia striata, osteopetrosis and impaired hearing. Arch Otolaryngol 87:116, 1968.

65. Kaga K, Suzuki J, Kimizuka M. Temporal bone pathology of two infants with Larsen's syndrome. Int J Pediatr Otorhinolaryngol 22:257, 1991.

66. Keleman G. Hurler's syndrome and the hearing organ. J Laryngol Otol 80:791, 1966.

67. Kessler A, Wolf M, Ben-Shoshan J. Fibrous dysplasia of the temporal bone presenting as an osteoma of the external auditory canal. Ear Nose Throat J 69:197, 1990.

68. Kietzer G, Paparella MM. Otolaryngologic disorders in craniometaphyseal dysplasia. Laryngoscope 79:921, 1969.

69. Kilpatrick SE, Wenger DE, Gilchrist GS, et al. Langerhans cell histiocytosis (histiocytosis X) of bone. A clinicopathologic analysis of 263 pediatric and adult cases. Cancer 76:2471, 1995.

70. Kim BH. Roentgenography of the ear and eye in Pyle disease. Arch Otolaryngol 99:458, 1974.

71. Kovanlikaya A, Loro ML, Gilsanz V. Pathogenesis of osteosclerosis in autosomal dominant osteopetrosis. AJR 168:929, 1997.

72. Lee YY, Tassel PV, Nauert C, et al. Craniofacial osteosarcomas: plain film, CT and MR findings in 46 cases. AJNR 9:379, 1988.

73. Lehman RA, Reeves JD, Wilson WB, Wesenberg RL. Neurological complications of infantile osteopetrosis. Ann Neurol 2:378, 1977.

74. Levy R, Shvero J, Sandbank J. Granulocytic sarcoma (chloroma) of the temporal bone. Int J Pediatr Otorhinolaryngol 18:163, 1989.

75. Lichtenstein L. Histiocytosis X. Arch Pathol 56:84, 1953.

76. Lichtenstein L, Jaffe HL. Fibrous dysplasia of bone. Arch Pathol 33:777, 1942.

77. Linthicum FH Jr. Histopathology of otosclerosis. Otolaryngol Clin North Am 26:335, 1993.

78. Lippy WH, Berenholz LP, Burkey JM. Otosclerosis in the 1960s, 1970s, 1980s, and 1990s. Laryngoscope 109:1307, 1999.

79. Lippy WH, Burkey JM, et al. Short- and long-term results of stapedectomy in children. Laryngoscope 108:569, 1998.

80. Lundy LB. Otosclerosis update. Otolaryngol Clin North Am 29:257, 1996.

81. Marini JC, Gerber NL. Osteogenesis imperfecta—rehabilitation and prospects for gene therapy. JAMA 277:746, 1997.

82. Marks SC Jr. Pathogenesis of osteopetrosis in the ia rat: reduced bone resorption due to reduced osteoclast function. Am J Anat 138:165, 1973.

83. McKenna MJ, Kristiansen AG, Bartley ML, et al. Association of COL1A1 and Otosclerosis—evidence for a shared genetic etiology with mild osteogenesis imperfecta. Am J Otol 19:604, 1998.

84. McKenna MJ, Mills BG. Immunohistochemical evidence of measles virus antigens in active otosclerosis. Otolaryngol Head Neck Surg 101:415, 1989.

85. Megerian CA, Sofferman RA, McKenna MJ, et al. Fibrous dysplasia of the temporal bone: ten new cases demonstrating the spectrum of otologic sequelae. Am J Otol 16:408, 1995.

86. Meyerhoff WL, Liston S. Metabolism and hearing loss. In: Paparella MM, Shumrick DA (eds). The Ear, 3rd ed. Philadelphia, WB Saunders, 1980, pp 1828–1845.

87. Monsell EM, Bone HG, Cody DD. Hearing loss in Paget's disease of bone: evidence of auditory nerve integrity. Am J Otol 16:27–33, 1995.

88. Morrisey DD, Talbot JM, Schleuning AJ II. Fibrous dysplasia of the temporal bone: reversal of sensorineural hearing loss after decompression of the internal auditory canal. Laryngoscope 107:1336, 1997.

89. Murphy TP, Wallis DL. Stapedectomy in the pediatric patient. Laryngoscope 106:1415, 1996.

90. Myers EN, Stool SE. The temporal bone in osteopetrosis. Arch Otolaryngol 89:460, 1969.

91. Nager GT. Osteogenesis imperfecta of the temporal bone and its relation to otosclerosis. Ann Otol Rhinol Laryngol 97:585, 1988.

92. Nager GT. Sensorineural deafness and otosclerosis. Ann Otol Rhinol Laryngol 75:481, 1966.

93. Nager GT, Holliday MJ. Fibrous dysplasia of the temporal bone: update with case reports. Ann Otol Rhinol Laryngol 93:630, 1984.

94. Neville BW, Damm DD, Allen CM, et al. Abnormalities of teeth. In: Neville BW, et al. Oral and Maxillofacial Pathology. Philadelphia, WB Saunders, 1995, pp 84–85.

95. Neville BW, Damm DD, Allen CM, et al. Abnormalities of teeth. In: Neville BW, et al. Oral and Maxillofacial Pathology. Philadelphia, WB Saunders, 1995, pp 444–445.

96. Neville BW, Damm DD, Allen CM, et al. Abnormalities of teeth. In: Neville BW, et al. Oral and Maxillofacial Pathology. Philadelphia, WB Saunders, 1995, pp 461–464.

97. Nezelof C, Basset F. Langerhans cell histiocytosis research—past, present, and future. Hematol Oncol Clin North Am 12:385, 1998.

98. Nicholson HS, Egeler RM, Nesbit ME. The epidemiology of Langerhans cell histiocytosis. Hematol Oncol Clin North Am 12:379, 1998.

99. Nurnberg P, Tinschert S, Mrug M, et al. The gene for autosomal dominant craniometaphyseal dysplasia maps to chromosome 5p and is distinct from the growth hormone-receptor gene. Am J Hum Genet 61:918, 1997.

100. Papadakis CE, Skoulakis CE, Prokopakis EP, et al. Fibrous dysplasia of the temporal bone: report of a case and a review of its characteristics. Ear Nose Throat J 79:52, 2000.

101. Paterson CR, Ogston SA, Henry RM. Life expectancy in osteogenesis imperfecta. BMJ 312:351, 1996.

102. Patterson CN, Stone HB III. Stapedectomy in van der Hoeve's syndrome. Laryngoscope 50:544, 1970.

103. Peck JE. Hearing loss in Hunter's syndrome—mucopolysaccharidoses II. Ear Hear 5:243, 1984.

104. Prokop DJ. Heritable disorders of connective tissue. In: Wilson JD, Brauowald E, Isselbacher KJ, et al (eds). Harrison's Principles of Internal Medicine. New York, McGraw-Hill, 1991, pp 1860–1865.

105. Quraishi MS, Blayney AW, Walker D, et al. Langerhans cell histiocytosis: head and neck manifestations in children. Head Neck 17:226, 1995.

106. Richards A, Brain C, Dillon MJ, Bailey CM. Craniometaphyseal and craniodiaphyseal dysplasia, head and neck manifestations and management. J Laryngol Otol 110:328, 1996.

107. Roaf R, Longmore JB, Forrester RM. A childhood syndrome of bone dysplasia, retinal detachment and deafness. Dev Med Child Neurol 9:464, 1967.

108. Robinson M. Juvenile otosclerosis: a 20-year study. Ann Otol Rhinol Laryngol 92:561, 1983.

109. Ruedi L, Spooendlin H. Pathogenesis of sensorineural deafness in otosclerosis. Ann Otol Rhinol Laryngol 75:525, 1966.

110. Ruggieri P, Sim FH, Bond JR, Unni KK. Malignancies in fibrous dysplasia. Cancer 73:1411, 1994.

111. Sabitha R, Ramalingham R, et al. Genetics of otosclerosis. J Laryngol Otol 111:109, 1997.

112. Sakihari Y, Parving A. Clinical otosclerosis, prevalence estimates and spontaneous progress. Acta Otolaryngol 119:468, 1999.

113. Schachern PA, Paparella MM, Shea DA, Yoon TH. Otologic histopathology of Fabry's disease. Ann Otol Rhinol Laryngol 98:359, 1989.

114. Schachern PA, Shea DA, Paparella MM. Mucopolysaccharidoses I-H (Hurler's syndrome) and human temporal bone histopathology. Ann Otol Rhinol Laryngol 93:65, 1984.

115. Schuknecht HF. Developmental defects. In: Pathology of the Ear. Cambridge, Mass, Harvard University Press, 1974, pp 115–190.

116. Schuknecht HF, Papapyrou S. Histiocytosis X. Otolaryngol Head Neck Surg 88:544, 1980.

117. Sedwick JD, Louden CL, Shelton C. Stapedectomy vs. Stapedotomy—do you really need a laser? Arch Otolaryngol Head Neck Surg 123:177–180, 1997.

118. Selesnick SH. Diseases of the external auditory canal. The Otolaryngol Clin North Am 29:813, 1996.

119. Shabana YK, Allam H, Pedersen CB. Laser stapedotomy. J Laryngol Otol 113:413, 1999.

120. Shambaugh GE, Causse J. Ten years experience with fluoride in otosclerotic (otospongiotic) patients. Ann Otol Rhinol Laryngol 83:635, 1974.

121. Shapiro F, Glimcher MJ, Holtrop ME, et al. Human osteopetrosis. A histological and ultrastructural, and biochemical study. J Bone Joint Surg Am 62A:384, 1980.

122. Shelby JH, Sweet RM. Eosinophilic granuloma of the temporal bone: medical and surgical management in the pediatric patient. South Med J 76:65, 1983.

123. Sillence DO, Rimoin DL. Classification of osteogenesis imperfecta. Lancet 1:1041, 1978.

124. Smith JF. Fibrous dysplasia of the jaws. Arch Otolaryngol 81:592, 1965.

125. Smith RJH, Evans JNG. Head and neck manifestations of histiocytosis X. Laryngoscope 94:395, 1984.

126. Smouha EE, Edelstein DR, Parisier SC. Fibrous dysplasia involving the temporal bone: report of three new cases. Am J Otol 8:103, 1987.

127. Sofferman RA, Smith RO, English GM. Albers-Schönberg disease (osteopetrosis). Laryngoscope 82:41, 1971.

128. Stocks RMS, Wang WC, Thompson JW, et al. Malignant infantile osteopetrosis—otolaryngological complications and management. Arch Otolaryngol Head Neck Surg 124:689, 1998.

129. Straka JA, Caparosa RJ. Eosinophilic granuloma of the temporal bone. Laryngoscope 82:41, 1972.

130. Suga F, Lindsay JR. Temporal bone histopathology of osteopetrosis. Ann Otol Rhinol Laryngol 85:15, 1976.

131. Surico G, Muggeo P, Muggeo V, et al. Ear involvement in childhood Langerhans cell histiocytosis. Head Neck 22:42, 2000.

132. Syms CA, de la Cruz A. Pediatric otology. Otolaryngol Clin North Am 29:411, 1996.

133. Tabor EK, Curtin HD, Hirsch BE, May M. Osteogenesis imperfecta tarda: appearance of the temporal bones at CT. Radiology 175:181, 1990.

134. Talbot IC, Keith DA, Lord IJ. Fibrous dysplasia of the cranio-facial bones, a clinico-pathological survey of seven cases. J Laryngol Otol 88:429, 1974.

135. Tewfik TL, Teebi AS, Der Kaloustian VM. Syndromes and conditions associated with genetic diseases. In: Tewfik TL, Der Kaloustian VM. Congenital Anomalies of the Ear, Nose, and Throat. New York, Oxford University Press, 1997, pp 145–180.

136. Tewfik TL, Teebi AS, Der Kaloustian VM. Selected syndromes and conditions. In: Tewfik TL, Der Kaloustian VM. Congenital Anomalies of the Ear, Nose, and Throat. New York, Oxford University Press, 1997, pp 490–494.

137. Tewfik TL, Teebi AS, Der Kaloustian VM. Selected syndromes and conditions. In: Tewfik TL, Der Kaloustian VM. Congenital Anomalies of the Ear, Nose, and Throat. New York, Oxford University Press, 1997, pp 505–507.

138. Tomek MS, Brown MR, Mani SR, et al. Localization of a gene for otosclerosis to chromosome 15q25-q26. Hum Mol Genet 7:285, 1998.

139. Tos M. A survey of Hand-Schueller-Christian disease in otolaryngology. Acta Otolaryngol (Stockh) 62:217, 1966.

140. Valvassori GE. Imaging of otosclerosis. Otolaryngol Clin North Am 26:359, 1993.

141. Van Horn PE Jr, Dahlin DC, Bickel WH. Fibrous dysplasia: a clinical pathologic study of orthopaedic surgical cases. Mayo Clin Proc 38:175, 1963.

142. Van Hul W, Bollerslev J, Gram J, et al. Localization of a gene for autosomal dominant osteopetrosis (Albers-Schönberg Disease) to chromosome 1p21. Am J Hum Genet 61:363–369, 1997.

143. Velez-Yanguas MC, Warrier RP. Langerhans cell histiocytosis. Orthop Clin North Am 27:615–623, 1996.

144. Verloes A, Lesenfants S, Barr M, et al. Fronto-otopalatodigital osteodyplasia: clinical evidence for a single entity encompassing Melnick-Needles syndrome, otopalatodigital syndrome types 1 and 2, and frontometaphyseal dysplasia. Am J Med Genet 90:407, 2000.

145. Wang PC, Merchant SN, McKenna MJ, et al. Does otosclerosis occur only in the temporal bone? Am J Otol 20:162, 1999.

146. Winchester B, Vellodi A, Young E. The molecular basis of lysosomal storage diseases and their treatment. Biochem Soc Trans 28:150, 2000.

147. Xenellis J, Bibas A, Savy L, et al. Monostotic fibrous dysplasia of the temporal bone. J Laryngol Otol 113:772, 1999.

148. Yoo TJ. Etiopathogenesis of otosclerosis: a hypothesis. Ann Otol Rhinol Laryngol 93:28, 1984.

149. Zajtchuk JT, Lindsay JR. Osteogenesis imperfecta congenita and tarda: a temporal bone report. Ann Otol Rhinol Laryngol 84:350, 1975.

150. Zappia JJ, LaRoure MJ, Telian SA. Massive ossifying fibroma of the temporal bone. Otolaryngology 103:480, 1990.

31

Injuries of the Ear and Temporal Bone

Simon C. Parisier, M.D., Jose N. Fayad, M.D., and William F. McGuirt, Jr., M.D.

Accidental injuries have become a major problem in modern mechanized society. Vehicular and pedestrian accidents account for more than 25% of the deaths of persons in the first two decades of life.[90] Falls continue to be a leading cause of injuries of children younger than 5 years.[33, 56] Moreover, the head injuries that commonly occur in such accidents are often accompanied by damage to the ear.[36, 65] The popularity of scuba diving, water skiing, and other sports has exposed an additional number of young people to possible ear injuries. When these hazards are added to the fetish of cleaning wax from the ear canals of infants, or the apparent sensual satisfaction that young children experience when playing with their ears, the extent of the problem becomes apparent. This chapter reviews the variety of injuries that involve the ear and temporal bone.

The Physician and the Injured Child

Traumatic injuries to the ear and temporal bone are more common in children and adolescents than in adults.[36, 89] In dealing with children, the physician must establish himself or herself as a gentle, concerned person. Any examination, no matter how routine, should be explained or demonstrated beforehand so that it can be understood, thus eliminating fear of the unknown. For example, the otoscope or ear speculum can be introduced to the child by examining the child's hand with it before placing it in the ear. The examiner can familiarize the patient with the wax curette by first tickling a hand with it, then touching the auditory meatus, before using the metal instrument to clean the canal. The child can be prepared for the loud noise of the suction aspirator by a demonstration of its function with a cup of water. When a procedure is expected to be painful, a general anesthetic is recommended, even in small infants who can be restrained effectively. The child who is confident that the physician will not cause unnecessary pain is usually a cooperative patient.

Trauma to the ear, even a minor scratch that causes bleeding from the external canal, generally seems catastrophic to the injured patient and the parents. The physician treating the child must enroll the family's full cooperation by explaining the problem in terms the family understands. The attitude of the parent toward the physician is transmitted to the injured child.

Sharp and Blunt Trauma of the Pinna

In evaluating lacerations and blunt trauma of the pinna, the presence of contusions, hematomas, and exposed cartilage becomes important. Each of these conditions must be carefully assessed and treated for prevention of further tissue loss or perichondritis. A detailed and comprehensive review of the reconstructive techniques for evaluating and repairing the injured pinna is beyond the scope of this chapter; however, excellent reviews are available.[7, 44, 66, 85] Basic principles of management are reviewed here.

The most common potential complications of blunt trauma to the ear are contusions and hematomas. Contusions may lead to perichondritis and thus loss of cartilage support. The formation of a hematoma between the perichondrium and cartilage may result in infection, loss of cartilage, or fibrous organization of the clot ("cauliflower ear"). In treating a hematoma, prompt aspiration of the blood with the application of a pressure dressing may be successful, but often incision and drainage must be performed to evacuate the clot or to prevent its reaccumulation[60, 62] (Fig. 31–1).

Laceration or avulsion injuries to the pinna require early treatment begun in the emergency room to allow the best possible cosmetic results. Pinnae that have been partially or totally avulsed can be reattached. Because of their rich blood supply, pinnae frequently heal with minimal deformity. Initially, they should be copiously irrigated. However, debridement should be judicious and minimal. Local flaps and skin grafts should be used to preserve and cover perichondrium and exposed cartilage. Initial efforts should be aimed at reconstruction of the external auditory canal and meatus. Accurate reapproximation of the helical rim and tragus is also important. Partial or incomplete avulsions are treated conservatively to preserve tissue (Fig. 31–2). Complete avulsions have been treated successfully by immediate reanastomosis. Iced saline and the avoidance of pressure dressings on the pinna have been used as adjunctive measures to decrease the metabolic needs of the implant, the formation of free radicals, and further hypoxic injury. Dextran, heparin, leeches, and antibiotics have been used to prevent

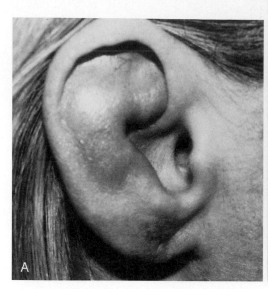 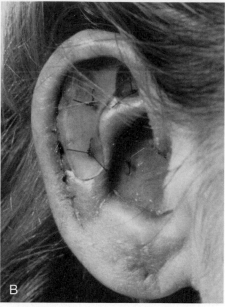

FIGURE 31–1. *A*, Patient with auricular hematoma after blunt trauma. *B*, Same patient as in *A* after incision and drainage of hematoma and placement of Silastic stents with sutures through the auricle to provide coaptation.

intravascular coagulation, venous insufficiency, and infection.[44, 66] If contamination or other reconstructive limitations prevent immediate reanastomosis, large pieces of cartilage or the entire pinna may be denuded of skin and buried in the postauricular area. Diseases and injuries of the external ear are discussed further in Chapters 22 and 45.

Injuries and Foreign Bodies of the External Auditory Canal

The cleaning of cerumen from the ears seems to be a cultural phenomenon. To gain access to the ear canal, a variety of objects, ranging from bobby pins to matchsticks, are used. It is not uncommon for a new mother in the United States to be given free samples of products for her newborn. Included in the gift package may be cotton-tipped applicators, which are often used to clean the baby's ear canals. Thus, from infancy, we are taught that the ever-present cerumen is a form of dirt and must be removed regularly.

During the ear-cleansing ritual, the mother's manipulations may be painful, causing the child to jerk the head, and the ear may be injured. Only a minor laceration of the ear canal ordinarily results. Although the bleeding may be profuse at the onset, it usually stops spontaneously, forming a clot that may obstruct the external canal. To determine whether the tympanic membrane has been damaged, the debris should be removed gently. It may not be possible to clean the canal if a child is unable to cooperate adequately or if the blood has formed a tenacious crust that is firmly attached to the skin of the canal wall or to the drum. In such instances, rather than risk inflicting further damage by traumatic manipulations, the physician should observe the child's progress. To prevent infection, the ear must be kept dry. When bathing the child, parents are instructed to prevent water from getting into the external auditory canal by occluding the

meatus with a nonabsorbent cotton (lamb's wool) impregnated with petroleum jelly.

During play, young children frequently place small beads, paper, peanuts, or other foreign bodies into their external ear canals. Even an older child may innocently put something into a friend's ear canal. If the child does not complain, a foreign body may not be detected until later, during a routine examination or because the ear has become secondarily infected.

Removal of these foreign bodies can be both technically difficult for the physician and painful to the child, especially when the foreign body is wedged in the ear canal. The problem may be compounded if an unskilled person has unsuccessfully attempted to remove the material, thereby producing local trauma and edema within the ear canal. Should a secondary infection be present, the problem is complicated by inflammatory changes characterized by edema of the canal wall skin, otorrhea, and, if the inflammation is severe, granulation tissue. These findings, which can mimic a chronic mastoid infection, do not generally respond to local or systemic antibiotics and completely resolve only after the offending object is removed. When introduced as a foreign body, button batteries have been documented to cause early injury to ear tissue.[10, 55] Button batteries contain an anode and a cathode attached to current collectors that lead outside the cell. A cumulative electrical burn may arise by the passage of low-voltage direct current between cathode and anode. Moisture, which may result from this electrical burn, causes leakage of a button battery's alkaline electrolyte solution. Alkaline burns result in liquefactive necrosis and extensive tissue damage. Health care personnel must recognize the potential dangers and urgency for removal of button batteries as foreign bodies. Furthermore, the use of irrigation to remove the battery should be strictly discouraged.

As a rule, the removal of a foreign body requires that the patient be extremely cooperative; an inappropriate movement can result in further injury, with damage to

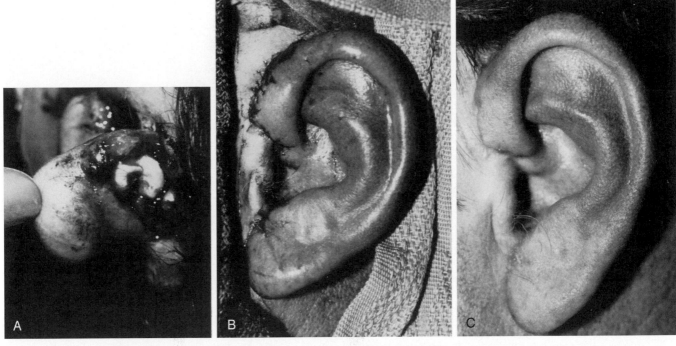

FIGURE 31–2. *A*, Patient with partial avulsion injury of the auricle. *B*, Same patient as in *A* after reanastomosis of the auricle. *C*, After the ear has healed.

the eardrum and the ossicular chain. Therefore, the use of a general anesthetic for removal of the foreign body should be considered if the physician anticipates that the process may be technically difficult and painful or if the child is not able to hold still without being restrained.

Traumatic Middle-Ear Injuries

Trauma to the delicate tympanic membrane resulting in a tympanic membrane perforation occurs often and may be caused by a variety of injuries.[82, 96] An explosive blast, such as a firecracker going off near an ear, produces a violent shock wave capable of rupturing the drum.[83, 87] A damaging shock wave can be produced if a child is slapped with an open hand across the ear (e.g., by an angry parent or when fighting with another child). If the blow occludes the external auditory meatus, the resulting inward displacement of the air column contained in the external canal causes a rupture of the membrane. A similar type of injury can occur during dives or falls into swimming pools, during water skiing, while surfboarding, or while tumbling in a rough surf. A perforation may occur if the ear hits the water in such a way that the column of air contained within the external canal is forcibly displaced or if the water strikes the ear with considerable impact.

Tympanic membrane lacerations frequently occur when a cotton-tipped applicator or other object being used to relieve an itch or clean out cerumen is accidentally pushed through the drum. Iatrogenic tears of the drum have occurred in the process of removing foreign bodies from the ear of a struggling child. In addition, the tympanic membrane can be perforated by use of an ear syringe to remove cerumen. Occasionally, the pressure of

the water being instilled into the external canal is enough to drive a hard waxy pellet through the drum.

After an uncomplicated tympanic membrane perforation, audiometric testing shows a mild conductive hearing loss (10 to 35 dB). Although small children rarely complain of loss of hearing acuity, a tympanic membrane laceration occasionally occurs in a child who has an unrecognized preexisting hearing loss in the opposite ear, thus causing a bilateral loss. In such cases, behavioral changes may reveal the change in hearing.

When a traumatic tympanic membrane perforation occurs, there is generally considerable pain accompanied by bleeding from the ear that stops spontaneously. If water gets into the ear, a secondary infection may occur that should be treated with systemic antibiotics (e.g., ampicillin) and local nonirritating acidified eardrops.

Injuries severe enough to rupture the tympanic membrane may also damage the ossicular chain.[82, 96] A dislocation of the incus is the most common injury. Usually, the incudostapedial joint is separated or the stapes arch is fractured,[73] or both. This trauma may cause a transient subluxation of the stapes into the inner-ear vestibule, resulting in a tear of the annular ligament and a perilymphatic fluid leak into the middle-ear space.[21, 82] This fluid leak generally produces a significant sensory hearing loss or severe vertigo, or both (Fig. 31–3).

Traumatic perilymphatic fistulas can also occur without ossicular involvement. An injury forceful enough to cause perforation of the tympanic membrane may result in an accompanying rupture of the round window membrane. Such a defect allows leakage of perilymph into the middle ear, producing the characteristic symptoms of sensory hearing loss and vertigo (Fig. 31–4).

Ear injuries that result in the production of excessive

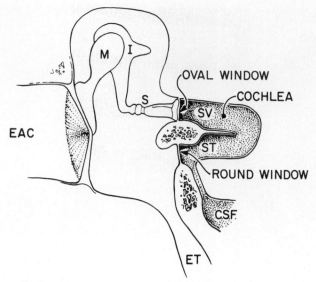

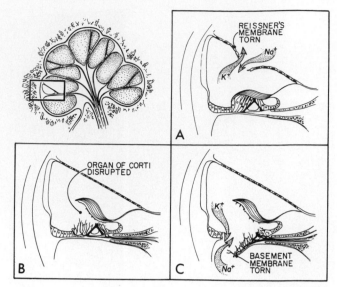

FIGURE 31–3. Diagram of the ear. Movement of the stapes (S) in the oval window produces a perilymphatic fluid wave that travels from the scala vestibuli (SV) through the scala tympani (ST) and causes a displacement of the round window membrane. The perilymph communicates with the cerebrospinal fluid (CSF) through the cochlear aqueduct. EAC, external auditory canal; M, malleus; I, incus; ET, eustachian tube.

FIGURE 31–5. Excessive vibrations of the stapes can produce a forceful perilymphatic fluid wave that may result in intracochlear damage. *A,* Reissner's membrane, which normally separates the endolymph (high potassium-low sodium) from the perilymph (low potassium-high sodium), may be torn. The resulting changes in the K^+-Na^+ concentration damage the affected hair cells, producing a sensory hearing loss. *B,* Excessive vibrations of the basilar membrane may produce a disruption of the organ of Corti. *C,* Tears of the basilar membrane are associated with severe injuries to the organ of Corti and a profound hearing loss.

stapedial vibrations can also produce intracochlear damage.[37] Such trauma may be caused by a sudden explosive noise, an excessive excursion of the intact tympanic membrane, or a direct force applied to the stapes. These injuries cause a damaging piston-like movement of the stapes that produces a forceful perilymphatic fluid wave. This movement results in traumatic excursions of the basilar membrane that can lead to a loss of hair cells and even avulsion of the organ of Corti (Fig. 31–5).

Treatment of Middle-Ear Injuries

Most traumatic tympanic membrane perforations heal spontaneously. Small perforations may repair themselves within a few weeks. Occasionally, however, a large perforation persists. In such cases, the lacerated epithelial margins of the defect do not grow across the drum defect to bridge the existing gap. Instead, the edges curl under the remaining drum remnant, forming a healed epithelial rim; thus, the perforation becomes permanent.

If a tympanic membrane perforation is recent, an attempt can be made to realign the torn edges. The procedure can be performed either with use of general anesthesia or, in a cooperative child, under local anesthesia. The edges of the perforation, which frequently become inverted below the residual drum remnant, should be approximated and the fragments supported by absorbable gelatin sponge (Gelfoam) placed in the middle ear.

A persistent tympanic membrane perforation can often be encouraged to heal. The epithelialized edge of the drum remnant can be debrided chemically by cauterization, with use of minute quantities of 50% trichloroacetic acid. A mildly irritating topical medication is prescribed to stimulate spontaneous reparative processes.[15, 39] The treatment generally has to be repeated several times; it is somewhat painful and therefore may not be well tolerated by young children.

Although most traumatic tympanic membrane perforations heal spontaneously, immediate surgery is necessary in certain instances.[82] If, after a middle-ear injury, the patient suffers a sensorineural hearing loss and vertigo,

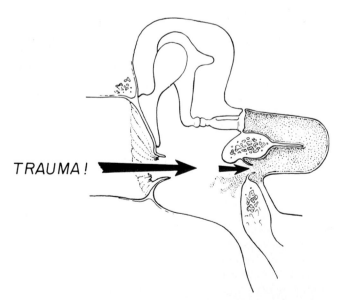

FIGURE 31–4. Trauma *(large arrow)* sufficient to rupture the tympanic membrane may also cause a round window membrane rupture *(small arrow)* with a resulting leak of perilymph *(stippling)* into the middle ear.

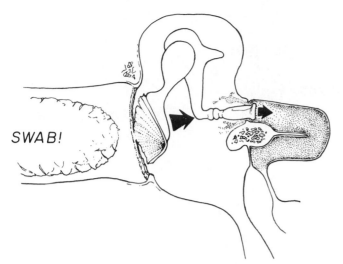

FIGURE 31–6. An injury to the middle ear, caused by a cotton-tipped swab accidentally pushed through the drum, displaced the stapes (*larger arrow*) into the vestibule and produced an oval window perilymphatic fluid leak (*stippled area, smaller arrow*).

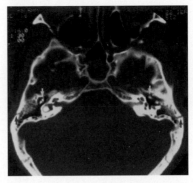

FIGURE 31–7. CT of a patient with bilateral longitudinal temporal bone fractures (*black arrows* point to fracture line) and left-sided ossicular discontinuity with intact right-sided ossicular chain (*white arrows* point to intact chain on the right and dislocation on the left).

the middle ear should be explored for a possible perilymph leak (Fig. 31–6). A stapedial subluxation should be corrected by a return of the stapes to its original position. Additionally, the oval window area should be sealed with a tissue graft (e.g., muscle, vein, fat, or fascia). The possibility of round window membrane rupture should be explored; the presence of this condition is confirmed by the observation of clear fluid welling up from the round window niche or by visualization of an actual tear in the round window membrane. In such cases, the area should be packed with a tissue graft. Another indication for immediate surgery is complete facial paralysis, the onset of which is noted immediately after the middle-ear trauma. This problem is taken up in the later discussion of temporal bone fractures.

If ossicular chain involvement is suspected after injury to the middle ear, elective surgery to correct the hearing mechanism may be advantageous.[3] Patients with a tympanic membrane perforation generally have a 20- to 40-dB conductive hearing loss. In these situations, a patch test may be useful in determining whether the hearing loss is due to the existing tympanic membrane perforation. This test is performed by first documenting the existing hearing loss with a preliminary audiogram. Next, a patch made of cigarette paper is placed over the entire drum defect. If the perforation is large, it may not be possible to cover it entirely; moreover, the anterior edge of the defect is sometimes obscured by a prominent overhang of the canal wall. After the patch is applied, a repeated audiogram is obtained. A significant improvement in hearing indicates that the ossicular chain is intact and that the hearing loss is due to the perforation. However, when the hearing acuity is unchanged or is worse, a coexisting ossicular discontinuity should be suspected.

Examination of the ossicular chain by computed tomography (CT) has superseded polytomography in evaluating patients with trauma to the middle ear.[11, 96] CT reveals a dislocated incus or malleus 90% of the time.

However, the delicately structured stapes may not be adequately visualized (Fig. 31–7).

When the ossicular chain is disrupted, elective surgical correction may be considered. The immediate repair of traumatic injuries to the ossicular chain allows the surgeon to reduce an existing dislocation and to restore an essentially normal condition before fibrotic adhesions form. In addition, at the time of the ossicular repair, the tympanic membrane perforation may be grafted to restore hearing to a normal level.

Before undertaking elective repair of a traumatic middle-ear defect, one must carefully evaluate the child's ability to cooperate with the surgeon who will care for the ear postoperatively. In younger children particularly, the past medical background must be reviewed for problems suggestive of underlying eustachian-tube dysfunction that would jeopardize the chances for successful otologic surgery. A history of recurrent serous or purulent otitis media, an allergic background, symptoms suggestive of chronic nasal congestion, and a history of frequent infections of the upper respiratory tract with otalgia indicate that the child is not a suitable candidate for elective middle-ear reconstructive surgery (see Chapter 24). In such children, especially if they are very young, the most suitable therapeutic alternative may be to temporize and accept the presence of a chronic tympanic membrane perforation. One must not overlook the clinical reality that the treatment for many children with eustachian-tube dysfunction and serous otitis media is myringotomy (i.e., creation of a perforation) that is kept open by insertion of a tube that ventilates the middle ear.

When a child has a tympanic membrane perforation, water must be prevented from entering the ear. Water irritates the exposed middle-ear mucosa, producing a profuse seromucinous otorrhea. When infection supervenes, acute bacterial otitis media occurs. Fungi, whose growth is stimulated by the moist environment of these draining ears, are a common cause of superficial infections. These problems can be avoided by occluding the external ear canal with either lamb's wool and petroleum jelly or wax-like commercially available plugs when there is any chance that water may get into the ear. When swimming, the child should wear a bathing cap to ensure that the

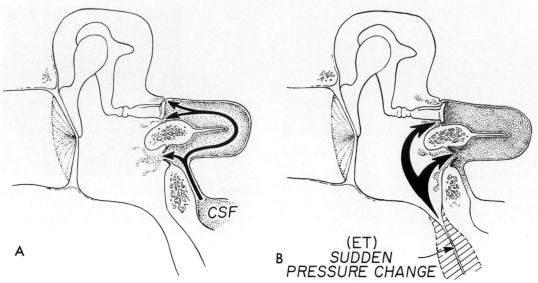

FIGURE 31–8. Perilymph leaks due to round or oval window ruptures. *A,* Sudden increases in cerebrospinal fluid (CSF) pressures *(arrows)* occur during such vigorous physical activities as sneezing. The cerebrospinal and perilymph fluid spaces communicate through the cochlear aqueduct. Abrupt increases in CSF pressure may be transmitted to the labyrinth, producing ruptures and leakage of perilymph into the middle ear (explosive route). *B,* Sudden air pressure changes transmitted through the eustachian tube (ET, *arrows*) into the middle-ear space can produce ruptures of the round window membrane or of the annular ligament in the oval window and leakage of perilymph into the middle ear (implosive route). (From Goodhill V. Sudden deafness and round window rupture. Laryngoscope 81:1462, 1974.)

plug sealing the ear canal is not displaced. Definitive surgery to close the tympanic membrane perforation may be performed when the child has "outgrown" the frequent ear problems associated with respiratory tract infections.

Surgical Repair of Middle-Ear Injuries

Fracture of the ossicles can be corrected by tympanoplastic surgery in which the conductive mechanism is reconstructed, often dramatically improving the hearing level. Thus, when the long process of the incus has been fractured, the continuity of the ossicular chain can be restored by appropriately reshaping the incus and interposing it between the malleus handle and the stapes capitulum.[64] An alternative technique uses a stainless steel wire to connect these two structures.[6] When both the stapes superstructure and the long process of the incus are fractured, the body of the incus can be sculptured to extend from the malleus handle to the stapes footplate. Fractures of the malleus are usually associated with fracture or dislocation of the incus. In such cases, the sound-conducting mechanism can be reconstituted by placing a strut of cartilage onto the stapes capitulum or the footplate, thereby enabling it to make contact with the tympanic membrane.

In comminuted temporal bone fractures, the patient's incus may have been shattered and therefore may not be available for ossicular reconstruction. In such cases, a hydroxyapatite prosthesis[93] and cartilage autografts have been used. The use of cortical bone for ossicular replacement in children is discouraged because there is a tendency for a bony ankylosis to form, with fixation to adja-

cent bony structures that results in recurrence of the conductive hearing loss.

Tympanic membrane defects can be repaired by grafting. The most common type of tissue used is the fascia that covers the temporalis muscle. The perichondrium obtained from the tragal cartilage is also a useful material for closing small defects or for reconstructing the ossicular mechanism when cartilage is required.

Otitic Barotrauma

As previously noted, snorkeling and scuba diving have become popular, with many adolescents participating in underwater diving as a recreational activity. Even more common is travel by airplane. These activities, however, require a person to adapt to rapid changes in pressures.[18, 26] The use of hyperbaric oxygen treatments for carbon monoxide poisoning and other injuries may also result in barotrauma.[38] Boyle's law states that at a constant temperature, the volume of a gas varies inversely with the pressure. As the atmospheric pressure increases, the volume decreases. Barotrauma may result in pain, hearing loss, tympanic membrane ruptures, and vestibular injury. Trauma may occur in the ear canal, middle ear, or inner ear.

In the ear canal, barotrauma occurs only if there is a blocked ear canal and thus trapped air. Pain is the most common symptom, and examination may reveal blebs and petechial hemorrhages. Middle-ear barotrauma is most common. During ascent in an airplane, the pressure in the middle ear increases until it reaches a point at which the eustachian tube is forced open. On descent, as the plane prepares to land, a negative middle-ear pressure builds. Because the eustachian tube is normally closed while at rest, this pressure difference persists until the person swallows. With the muscle activity of swallowing, the tensor veli palatini muscle contracts, the tubal lumen is opened, and the tympanic pressure is equalized. The same pathophysiologic events occur in barotrauma from scuba diving.

If the eustachian tube fails to open, the resulting negative middle-ear pressure causes a retraction of the tympanic membrane. To equilibrate the induced negative pressure, a transudation of serous fluid from the mucosal surface fills the middle ear.[22] If the pressure changes are sudden, bleeding into the middle-ear space may result or the tympanic membrane may rupture.[76] In adults, these pressure changes have been known to produce traumatic perilymph leaks owing to round or oval window ruptures, or both[24, 25, 70] (Fig. 31–8).

Inner-ear barotrauma is related to middle-ear clearing difficulties and results in damage to the hydrodynamics of the inner-ear fluids. The symptoms of inner-ear barotrauma include sensorineural hearing loss, tinnitus, and vertigo. These injuries are much less frequent than middle-ear barotrauma; however, they may result in permanent cochleovestibular damage. Sudden pressure changes from the Valsalva maneuver or sudden changes in cerebrospinal fluid (CSF) pressure have been postulated to cause this effect.[23, 81] The primary treatment is complete bed rest with the head elevated. Most investigators think that once the diagnosis of a fistula is suspected or the patient's condition deteriorates during bed rest, immediate exploration should be performed to offer the best opportunity for recovery.[5, 81]

Eustachian-tube function is generally compromised when a person has a disorder of the upper respiratory tract. Thus, diving or flying—both of which require good eustachian-tube function to equilibrate the middle-ear pressure—may cause certain persons to experience the difficulties described before. Many young children have borderline eustachian-tube function and should not fly when they have an upper respiratory infection. Even on commercial airlines, as descent takes place, negative middle-ear pressure may produce severe pain and hearing loss. These problems can be minimized by oral and topical nasal decongestants to shrink the nasal and the eustachian-tube mucosal linings before the plane begins to descend. Encouraging a child to swallow repeatedly, giving a child chewing gum, or giving an infant a bottle keeps the normal forces that are necessary to open the eustachian tube. In addition, the child should be kept in an erect position with the head elevated to decrease the passive venous mucosal congestion that tends to further compromise eustachian-tube patency.[72]

Temporal Bone Fractures

Evaluation of the Accident Victim

Head trauma is frequently associated with a simultaneous injury to the ear. A temporal bone fracture is associated with 30% to 75% of cases of blunt head trauma.[32, 94] When the patient with multiple injuries is evaluated, primary consideration must be given to ensuring an adequate airway, preventing shock due to blood loss, controlling bleeding, and maintaining a stable neurologic state.

After adequate ventilation is ensured, the patient should be evaluated for bleeding. Hypotensive shock is rarely caused by a head injury alone. The common signs and symptoms of acute blood loss are a rising pulse rate and falling blood pressure. The opposite findings occur with increased intracranial pressure: the pulse rate slows and the blood pressure rises.

After the patient's respiratory and circulatory systems are stabilized, neurologic status should be evaluated. The possibility of spinal column injury must be considered in the initial evaluation of the accident victim. The high frequency of cervical spine injuries with head injuries mandates immobilization of the patient, including a cervical collar, until radiographs are obtained to rule out spinal column injury. The patient's level of consciousness must be explicitly documented. The fundi should be evaluated for papilledema as an indication of increased intracranial pressure. Pupil size, equality, and reactivity and corneal reflexes should be recorded. Spontaneous or induced extraocular movements and the presence of nystagmus should be noted. Facial movements, either spontaneous or provoked by painful stimuli, should be documented. Moreover, symmetry of limb movements, muscle tone, and reflexes must be evaluated.

The initial neurologic evaluation establishes a baseline. The patient's clinical status is determined by any changes in these primary observations. Thus, an improving level of consciousness and the absence of asymmetric lateralizing findings are positive signs. Increasing coma, dilatation of a pupil, and hemiparesis suggest a deteriorating condition that may be caused by cerebral edema or an expanding intracranial hematoma that may require neurosurgical intervention.

Once the patient is stabilized, a careful neuro-otologic examination should be performed. If the patient's condition allows, questions regarding disequilibrium, vertigo, hearing loss, and prior otologic history are pursued. The direction and site of impact of the head trauma are determined. The external ear is examined for evidence of lacerations, hematomas, bone deformity, or bleeding from the ear canal. Otoscopic examination, including use of the binocular operating microscope when appropriate, is performed as aseptically as possible. The ear should not be flushed or irrigated to cleanse the canal because this may introduce contaminated debris to the cranium. The external ear canal is examined for lacerations, a bony step deformity, or bleeding from a ruptured tympanic membrane. An intact tympanic membrane is examined for evidence of hemotympanum or fluid collection in the middle-ear space. Cranial nerve examination should include a gross assessment of hearing when appropriate, either with tuning forks or by repetition of words whispered in both ears. The observation and characterization of drainage in the ear canal are discussed subsequently.

The care of a patient with multiple injuries requires the specialized attention of physicians from various disciplines who must work cooperatively as a team. The otolaryngologist generally has the dual responsibilities of (1) establishing and maintaining a proper airway and (2) evaluating otoneurologic status.

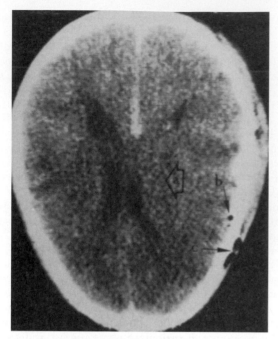

FIGURE 31–9. Computed tomography performed because of a head injury. Intracerebral edema with compression of the lateral ventricle (a) *(arrowhead)*, pneumocephalus (b) *(arrow)*, and subcutaneous emphysema (c) *(arrow)*.

The radiologic examination of a patient with head injury should be performed only after the patient's acute problems have been stabilized. Magnetic resonance imaging and CT of the head are useful for demonstrating intracranial damage, such as an intracerebral or subdural hematoma and pneumocephalus (Fig. 31–9). The scans may also demonstrate a fracture of the skull or temporal bone. High-resolution CT used in the axial plane and consisting of 1.5-mm-thick slices with 1-mm increments from the tegmen to the base of the skull is the preferred method to evaluate suspected temporal bone fractures (Fig. 31–10).[94] Skull radiographs should be obtained to observe for sutural splitting, a linear or depressed skull fracture, and the existence of pneumocephalus.

Classification of Temporal Bone Fractures

The diagnosis of a temporal bone fracture depends on a history of antecedent trauma combined with a constellation of clinical findings and must be supported radiographically. The clinical findings may include bleeding from the ear, hemotympanum, tympanic membrane perforation, hearing loss, CSF leak, facial paralysis, and vestibular symptoms. If one understands the mechanism of injury, the diagnosis, treatment, and prognosis can be better appreciated. Temporal bone fractures are traditionally classified as longitudinal or transverse fractures according to their course relative to the long axis of the temporal bone.[28, 31, 69, 92] However, the use of three-dimensional reconstruction of high-resolution CT has shown the majority of injuries to be either a combination of the two classic forms or an oblique fracture.[2, 95] This new understanding allows the clinician to incorporate the varied clinical findings in the patient with a temporal bone fracture. On the other hand, the traditional classification provides an accepted format to discuss and under-

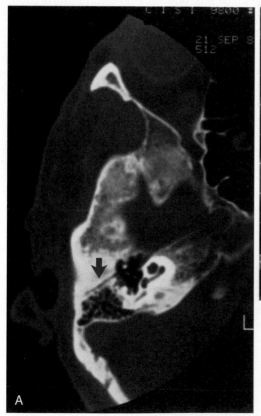

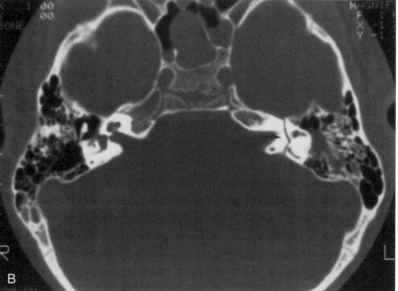

FIGURE 31–10. *A*, CT of a patient with longitudinal temporal bone fracture *(arrow)*. *B*, CT of a patient with transverse temporal bone fracture *(arrow)*.

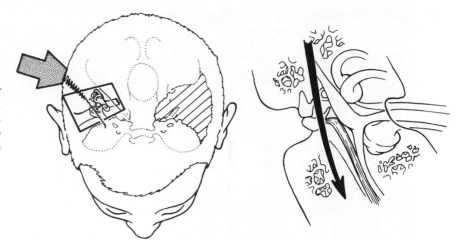

FIGURE 31–11. Longitudinal fractures of the temporal bone usually result from a circumscribed blow delivered to the temporoparietal area *(shaded arrow)*. The fracture line follows a course parallel to the long axis of the petrous apex *(solid arrow)*.

stand the pathophysiologic mechanism of temporal bone fractures.

The longitudinal fracture that follows a course parallel to the long axis of the petrous apex is the most common; such fractures account for 80% of temporal bone fractures (Fig. 31–11). Clinically, this type of fracture occurs after a circumscribed blow to the temporoparietal region. The patient may not be knocked unconscious. However, the injury causes a bending inward of the skull and results in a fracture that follows a characteristic pathway. The separation extends from the squama to involve the posterosuperior bony canal wall, lacerating the attached skin and causing bleeding from the ear. Evidence of the defect can sometimes be seen otoscopically, appearing as a steplike deformity with notching of the tympanic ring. The fracture continues anteriorly through the area of the tegmen. The fracture line that involves the roof of the middle ear causes mucosal bleeding that produces hemotympanum.

When the force of the impact is sufficient to cause a separation of the bony segments, significant middle-ear injuries can result. In such a case, the tympanic membrane may be torn and the ossicles may be dislocated or

fractured, or both. Injury to the facial nerve generally occurs in the horizontal portion at or distal to the geniculate ganglion. The facial nerve is involved in 5% to 30% of patients with longitudinal fractures. In reviews restricted to pediatric patients, the frequency of facial paralysis appears to be lower, and this is thought to be due to the decreased ossification of the pediatric skull.[45, 52] The fracture line continues anteriorly and parallel to the eustachian tube toward the foramen lacerum.

Transverse fractures, which run perpendicular to the long axis of the temporal bone, are much less common (Fig. 31–12). They result from forceful blows that usually produce serious head injury and loss of consciousness. Such blows may be fatal. In general, the impact is exerted over the occipital or frontal area, which causes anteroposterior compression of the calvarium. This results in a fracture wherein the skull is structurally weakest (i.e., in the area of the foramen magnum and at the base of the petrous bone, where it is perforated by many canals and foramina). The resulting bony rent characteristically crosses the pyramid at a right angle, extending into the area of the internal auditory canal, the cochlea, and the vestibule. This injury to the auditory and vestibular sys-

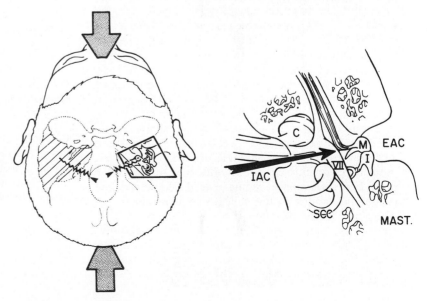

FIGURE 31–12. Transverse fractures of the temporal bone usually result from a forceful blow, the impact of which is exerted over the frontal or occipital area *(shaded arrows)*. This compresses the calvarium in an anteroposterior direction with a fracture where the skull is weakest, i.e., the foramen magnum and the foramen within the petrous bone. The fracture line crosses the long axis *(zigzag line and arrowheads)* of the petrous apex at right angles and may be bilateral *(solid arrow)*. C, cochlea; M, malleus; I, incus; IAC, internal auditory canal; EAC, external auditory canal; MAST, mastoid; SCC, superior semicircular canal.

TABLE 31–1. Classification of Temporal Bone Fractures

	Longitudinal Fractures	Transverse Fractures
Percentage of temporal bone fractures	80%	20%
Point of impact	Temporoparietal area	Frontal or occipital area
Force of impact	Moderate to severe	Severe
Loss of consciousness	Not always present	Present
Associated Otologic Findings		
Ear canal bleeding	Frequent	Infrequent
Tympanic membrane perforation	Frequent	Infrequent
Hemotympanum	Common	Less common
Hearing loss	Variable: conductive, mixed, and sensorineural	Profound sensorineural loss
Vertigo	Variable frequency and severity	Frequent; severe
Facial nerve		
Injury	Variable severity	Severe
Frequency	25%	50%
Paralysis	May be incomplete; onset may be delayed	Immediate onset; complete paralysis

tem immediately produces profound sensorineural hearing loss and vertigo. In 50% of these cases, a severe facial nerve injury occurs that results in an immediate facial paralysis. The fracture may or may not extend into the middle ear. If the promontory surface is involved, rupture of the round and oval windows may occur, accompanied by dislodgment of the stapes. Because the tympanic membrane generally remains intact, hemotympanum may also be observed. Moreover, the fracture can extend to involve the jugular bulb area and other structures of the base of the skull.

The classification of temporal bone fractures into longitudinal and transverse is useful in that it emphasizes the various important anatomic structures likely to be injured (Table 31–1). However, on radiographic examinations, the fracture may not fall into either classification.[97] The small child's skull is elastic, and after significant head trauma, inward compression of the convex surface can result in extensive lines of fracture. This may produce a comminuted type of fracture having both a longitudinal temporoparietal component and a transverse base-of-skull component[31, 67] (Fig. 31–13).

Additionally, in spite of the presence of CSF otorrhea, a temporal bone fracture may not be apparent radiographically.[31, 68] High-resolution CT with multiplanar reconstruction allows visualization of the majority of these complex fractures. However, even with CT, when the fragments are not greatly displaced, not all fractures may be visualized despite strong clinical evidence supporting a temporal bone fracture[58, 95] (see Chapter 12 for a complete discussion of temporal bone radiography). Therefore, serious damage can occur to the tympanic membrane, ossicular chain, and cochleovestibular systems without radiographic documentation of either a skull or a temporal bone fracture. Furthermore, radiographs of the temporal bones frequently require anesthesia or sedation for proper positioning of the child to be maintained. Radiographs are indicated when there is evidence of CSF otorrhea, CSF rhinorrhea, hearing loss, or facial nerve paralysis. Documentation of a temporal bone fracture is important for medicolegal as well as therapeutic reasons. In an existing facial paralysis or CSF leak, visualization of

the existing fracture may determine the operative approach and predict the complexity of the injury. Radiographs may also reveal an ossicular disruption. However, the inability to demonstrate a fracture radiographically does not exclude injury, nor does the demonstration of a fracture necessarily warrant intervention.

Treatment of Temporal Bone Fractures

Comprehensive care of the accident victim has been discussed. However, depending on the severity of any coexisting trauma, it may be necessary to postpone such diagnostic procedures as audiometric evaluation, caloric tests, radiography, and facial nerve testing. Even minor operative procedures may have to be deferred until the patient's condition is stable, especially with small children who require general anesthesia. On occasion, when a serious concomitant condition requires operative intervention with general anesthesia, it may be possible to evaluate and treat existing otologic problems at the same time. For example, while the child is under general anesthesia, the external ear canal can be cleaned of blood clots and ceruminous debris and the tympanic membrane can be examined. If there has been a perforation, the edges can be reapproximated and the drum defect repaired. At the same time, minor ossicular defects can be corrected.

Evaluation and Management of Signs and Symptoms Associated with Temporal Bone Injuries

In considering the management of temporal bone fractures, the saying, "It's what's inside that counts" is appropriate. Therapy is aimed at restoring the function of the injured structures. Therefore, treatment must be guided by the victim's signs and symptoms.

Bleeding

Bleeding from the ear is common after acute trauma to the temporal area.[28, 58, 69, 71] To determine the significance

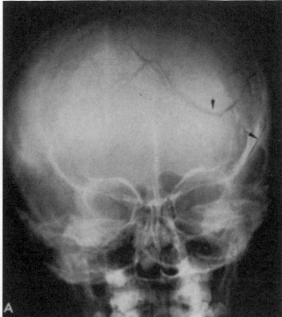

FIGURE 31-13. Frontal (A) and lateral (B) views of a 9-year-old boy involved in a bicycle/automobile accident; he suffered a head injury with a period of unconsciousness. An extensive comminuted skull fracture that involves the temporal bone is present (arrows).

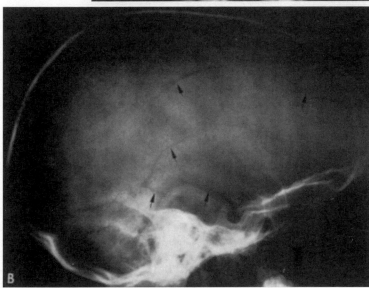

of bleeding, the exact source of the hemorrhage must be identified. Glancing blows that displace the pinna from its soft tissue attachments to the scalp can produce a shearing effect that may lacerate the skin of the bony external canal and produce bleeding even with an intact tympanic membrane. Injuries violent enough to produce a temporal bone fracture are frequently associated with a tear of the external canal that extends to and perforates the adjacent drum. Finally, severe trauma to the chin can cause the mandibular condyle to fracture through the anterior wall of the external auditory canal, causing bleeding from the ear, malocclusion, trismus, and severe otalgia when the mouth is opened. Generally, the bleeding is self-limiting and requires no active therapy. Instilling a few drops of a sterile vasoconstrictor (1:100,000 epinephrine, 1% phenylephrine [Neo-Synephrine]) can usually control the bleeding. Only rarely does significant hemorrhage result, with

bleeding coming from the ear as well as going through the eustachian tube into the nose and pharynx. In such cases, packing for hemostasis is required.

After an ear injury, the external ear canal should be cleansed of ceruminous debris and blood clots. As soon as the more pressing injuries have been treated and the child is stable, the extent of injury to the ossicles and tympanic membrane should be assessed. Admittedly, this task may be extremely difficult when dealing with a frightened child who is unable to cooperate. As discussed before, if an associated injury has required general anesthesia, the ear can be evaluated and treated efficiently while the child is asleep.

It is not unusual for an ecchymotic area to appear in the area of the mastoid process (Battle's sign) 4 or 5 days after a fracture of the base of the skull. This is caused by the extravasation of blood pigments into the area and is

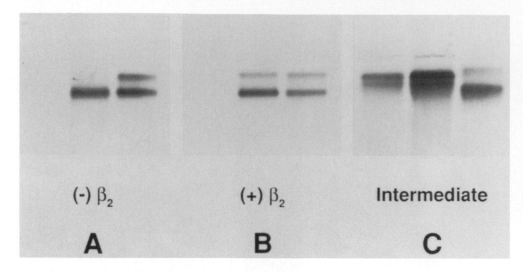

FIGURE 31–14. Zone electrophoresis on samples being tested for β_2-transferrin. *A,* Negative assay. The right column is a control specimen of cerebrospinal fluid (lower band, β_1; upper band, β_2). The left column is from the patient. *B,* Positive assay. Left column shows both a β_1 and a β_2 band. *C,* Intermediate assay. Right column is control; specimen in middle column is undiluted specimen; left column is specimen diluted 1:100. This pattern suggests a drug interaction.

evidence of an existing fracture but, in itself, is not an indication for any therapy.

Cerebrospinal Fluid Otorrhea

CSF otorrhea noted after head trauma is a definite sign that the skull has been fractured and a meningeal tear has occurred. This traumatic communication can be the pathway for bacterial contamination and the cause of meningitis. In the pediatric population with head trauma, the frequency of post-traumatic CSF leakage is low and thought to be due to the resilience of children's skulls as well as the underdevelopment of the mastoid and sinus air cells.[9] However, several large series have examined temporal bone fractures in children specifically and report a frequency of CSF fistula (20% to 26%) similar to that in adult series (16% to 32%).[31, 52, 58, 79] This high frequency of CSF fistula in temporal bone fractures may be related to the severity of head injury in temporal bone fractures as well as to the early ossification of the petrous bone.

The identification of traumatic CSF leakage is based on the physical examination, determination of the fluid as CSF, and temporal relation to the antecedent trauma. A CSF leak may be obscured by active bleeding from the injured ear. When a CSF leak is suspected, the bloody material from the ear should be collected and a sample placed on a filter paper. If CSF is present, it separates from the blood, forming a clear ring around the central hemorrhagic spot ("halo" sign). The halo, or double-ring, sign suggests but is not diagnostic of a CSF leak. As the coexisting bleeding ceases, the character of the otorrhea changes. Moreover, as the fluid becomes more watery and clearer, the CSF leak becomes more obvious. In cases in which the tympanic membrane has remained intact, the presence of CSF behind the drum mimics the otoscopic findings observed in serous otitis media (i.e., a dull, immobile drum). In such cases, if the patient is instructed to bend over or is held upside-down, clear fluid may pass down the eustachian tube and drip out the nose. An alternative way of obtaining a sample of the fluid is to perform a myringotomy and to collect the fluid directly from the middle ear. Biochemical testing is indicated when the true nature of the drainage is in question.

The determination of the glucose or protein content of the fluid has been used to differentiate CSF from nasal or middle-ear secretions. Glucose concentration of greater than 40 mg/100 mL or protein concentration from 100 mg/100 mL to a maximum of 200 mg/100 mL suggests a CSF leak. However, normal nasal drainage has been shown to be falsely positive in 45% to 75% of cases, and bedside testing with glucose oxidase sticks is unreliable.[98] β_2-Transferrin has been identified as a noninvasive, reliable chemical marker of CSF leakage.[53, 59] β_2-Transferrin is a protein found in CSF and perilymph, but not in serum, nasal drainage, or middle-ear secretions. β_2-Transferrin analysis is based on standard, reproducible principles of protein electrophoresis and immunofixation (Fig. 31–14). The major advantages of this technique are the small amount of fluid necessary for study ($>1.5\ \mu L$), the high sensitivity and specificity, and the insignificance of contamination by other body fluids.[53, 59]

In most cases, traumatic CSF otorrhea stops spontaneously within 2 weeks and rarely requires surgical intervention. The use of prophylactic antibiotics to prevent meningitis is controversial.[41, 46] Initial management of CSF fistula is aimed at decreasing intracranial CSF pressure and includes bed rest, head elevation of 15 to 25 degrees, and avoidance of activity or straining.

A persistent or recurrent CSF leak is a common cause of recurrent meningitis. The bony labyrinth heals by fibrous union and thus provides a pathway of least resistance for recurrent meningitis. When this possibility is suspected, the presence of the leak should be documented and its exact location identified. The area from which the contrast material extravasates into the temporal bone may be pinpointed by a posterior fossa contrast-dye study.[40, 78] The presence of a CSF leak may also be detected by using radioisotopes.[63] Indium-111 diethylenetriamine penta-acetic acid is injected into the CSF spaces; if a tympanic membrane perforation is present, a pledget is placed adjacent to the drum opening. Additional pledgets are inserted intranasally to absorb any CSF leaking down the eustachian tube. Fluorescein (5% fluorescein injected intrathecally) may also be used with a similar

TABLE 31-2. Frequency of Traumatic Neurosensory Hearing Loss

Reference	Fracture of Temporal Bone (%)	Head Injury (%)
Hough and Stuart[36]	62	
Barber[4]	63	46
Proctor et al[69]	56	83
Tos[89]	27	
Røhrt[71]	14	
Mitchell and Stone[58]°	13	
McGuirt and Stool[53]°	26	
Grove[28]	63	24–45
Podoshin and Fradis[65]		19

° Pediatric series.

technique.[59] High-resolution CT in conjunction with metrizamide cisternography has been documented to be reliable, safe, and sensitive. Thus, this method has gained widespread acceptance.[12]

Indwelling spinal catheters are an effective treatment for CSF leaks that are persistent or associated with increased intracranial pressure.[80] If the CSF leak persists for more than 2 weeks or with evidence of a large petrous bone defect, late-onset CSF leak, brain herniation, or recurrent episodes of meningitis, surgery should be considered. The two main approaches for repair are intracranial/extradural through a subtemporal approach and transmastoid/middle ear. The benefits of a subtemporal approach include preservation of hearing, better direct access to the dural tear, more reliable results, and treatment of associated intracranial injury.[9] The otologic repair of CSF otorrhea avoids the morbidity of craniotomy, affords inspection of middle-ear structures, and allows easier identification of the fistula.[91] This repair is performed with free temporalis fascia and muscle or pedicled local flaps.

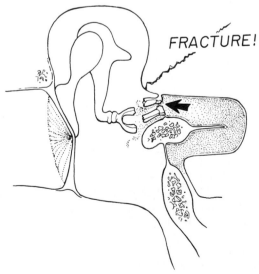

FIGURE 31-15. Temporal bone fracture with disruption of the stapes and a perilymph leak (*arrow*) producing a sensory hearing loss.

Hearing Loss

After a significant head injury, medical attention is focused on controlling life-threatening problems and closely monitoring the patient's neurologic status. When there is no bleeding from the ear and the tympanic membrane is intact, it may be erroneously concluded that no significant ear damage has occurred. Indeed, infants and young children generally do not complain of a hearing loss. As a result, traumatic hearing losses may not be detected at the time of the injury, especially when they are unilateral and the child suffers no functional impairment. Thus, it is common for the effect of the trauma not to be recognized until much later. For example, it may first be detected when the child's hearing acuity is screened in school, or even later during a military preinduction or an employment physical examination when the person is noted to have an unusual hearing loss of undetermined origin. Therefore, after significant head injury, an attempt should be made to establish accurate auditory thresholds. In infants, this may require repeated evaluations performed over many months until reliable thresholds can be obtained (see the discussion of audiologic assessment in Chapter 11).

The hearing losses that result from head trauma vary considerably. The type and severity of the hearing loss depend on the force of the injury and the location of the fracture. The most common type of hearing impairment after head and temporal bone trauma is sensorineural hearing loss (Table 31-2), which has been reported in 13% to 83% of patients with these injuries.[4, 29, 36, 52, 58, 65, 71, 89] Audiometric analysis of the hearing loss by complete site-of-lesion tests has demonstrated that some patients have a cochlear loss, whereas others exhibit a retrocochlear loss. Even when a conductive hearing disorder is present, a coexisting sensorineural type of loss is common.

Pathogenesis of Cochlear Hearing Loss

When trauma to the head is significant, with or without fracture, the force of the impact momentarily compresses the child's relatively elastic skull, which rapidly regains its original configuration. The pressure wave involves the encased cochlear structures and is thought to cause an excessive displacement of the basilar membrane.[37, 74, 75] This displacement produces a hearing loss similar to that caused by intense acoustic stimulation (i.e., a discreet drop in acuity in the range of 4000 to 8000 Hz). The discrimination scores are good, recruitment may be present, and there is no abnormal tone decay. Similar hearing losses have been produced experimentally in animals.[77] A powerful blow to a cat's head held in a fixed position produced a loss of acuity confined to 3000 to 8000 Hz. The pathologic findings observed in these temporal bones resembled those of patients with a history of head trauma. Histologic examination showed varying degrees of damage to the organ of Corti. This damage was most marked in the midbasal cochlear turn.

A traumatic cochlear-type hearing loss may result from leakage of perilymph from the inner-ear vestibule[21] (Fig. 31-15). A blow to the skull may produce a shock wave that distorts the area of the round window niche and disrupts the attachment of the round window membrane, thereby causing it to tear. After a significant head injury, the stapes, which is suspended within the air-containing middle-ear cleft, is exposed to a compressional force different from that surrounding temporal bone. Moreover, the trauma may stimulate the simultaneous contraction of the stapedius muscle, which acts to rotate the stapes posteriorly and laterally out of the oval window. As a result of these forces, a subluxation of the stapes occurs that produces a tear of the annular ligament. After either of these injuries involving the round or oval window, there is a resulting perilymph leak that is associated with a hearing loss of varying severity. Furthermore, the traumatic distortion of the cochlear configuration after a blow to the head can produce a rupture of the relatively delicate basilar or Reissner's membrane. This results in a disruption of the partition between the cochlear duct and the scala tympani or vestibuli. As a consequence, the potassium-rich endolymph mixes with the sodium-rich perilymph, producing biochemical changes that cause a significant labyrinthine disorder (see Fig. 31–5).

Symptomatically, vertigo usually occurs after cochlear membrane tears or the perilymph leaks, or both. The spinning and accompanying nausea with vomiting may be so unpleasant that the patient is not immediately aware of the associated hearing loss. The treatment of traumatic perilymph leaks is discussed in the consideration of treatment of middle-ear injuries.

Pathogenesis of a Traumatic Retrocochlear Hearing Loss

After a head injury, the patient may have a hearing loss characterized audiometrically by a discrimination score that is surprisingly low and the presence of pathologic tone decay. These findings indicate a retrocochlear process. Brain stem evoked responses may be used to confirm this finding. Animal experiments have demonstrated that after trauma to the freely mobile head, a retrocochlear or central auditory loss occurs.[47–49] At the moment of impact, the brain, which is suspended in CSF, moves independently within the rigid skull, causing a substantial amount of swirling. This rotational displacement of the brain around the brain stem frequently results in a contrecoup cerebral injury. Moreover, this movement can severely stretch the cranial nerves where they leave the brain to enter their respective foramina.[86] The abducens and the auditory-vestibular nerves seem to be particularly susceptible to this type of shearing force. As a result of this type of injury, multiple unilateral or bilateral cranial nerve deficits may occur even without skull fractures.

Pathologic examination of temporal bones obtained from persons who died from head trauma has shown hemorrhages of the eighth cranial nerve at the fundi of the internal auditory canal.[27, 47] Animal experiments were performed that were designed to simulate the kind of injury that occurs to humans[47, 49]; guinea pigs with freely mobile heads were shaken within a padded cell. None of the experimental animals suffered a skull fracture. Nevertheless, the experiments did produce retrocochlear, cen-

tral, or both types of hearing losses. The pathologic findings were similar to those observed in human temporal bones. Areas of hemorrhage were present in the cerebrum, cerebellum, brain stem, eighth nerve, and seventh nerve.

The extent of the sensorineural hearing loss that occurs after head trauma is not always consistent with the severity of the blow or with the extent of the resulting neurologic trauma. A patient who has had mild head injury occasionally has a surprisingly severe sensorineural hearing loss, whereas the victim with a serious concussion may not experience a significant loss of acuity. In addition, the sensorineural hearing loss observed after trauma is not always permanent. Frequently, there is some return of hearing acuity. Low-frequency losses, for instance, have a greater tendency to resolve than do higher-frequency losses. Indeed, depending on the mechanism of the injury, hearing may improve spontaneously. The hemorrhage and edema within a nerve caused by stretching may also resolve, leaving little permanent damage. Finally, the healing of intracochlear membrane tears and the sealing off of traumatic oval or round window leaks may be accompanied by the recovery of hearing.

Conductive Hearing Loss

A longitudinal fracture of the temporal bone is often associated with middle-ear injuries because bleeding into the middle-ear space frequently results from the trauma. When the drum remains intact, hemotympanum results.[33, 65] This has been estimated to occur in 3% to 5% of patients with skull fractures and in 20% to 65% of patients with temporal bone fractures.[52, 58] The condition is usually temporary, improving spontaneously when the blood is either resorbed from the tympanic cavity or evacuated from the area through the eustachian tube into the nasopharynx. Occasionally, the fluid collection persists for many weeks. In these cases, when myringotomy is performed, the aspirated fluid resembles serum. In such cases, a tube should be inserted to ventilate the middle-ear cleft.

When the force of an injury fractures the temporal bone, a gap results between the fragments as they momentarily separate. This rent characteristically extends through the posterosuperior canal wall and produces a rupture of the tympanic membrane, with bleeding from the ear canal. Tympanic membrane perforations occur in about 20% to 50% of patients with temporal bone fractures.[28, 52, 58] Often, the traumatic drum defect heals spontaneously. In some cases, the traumatic fragmentation of the temporal bone can damage the contained ossicles[14, 17, 35, 36, 84, 96] (Table 31–3; Fig. 31–16). This type of injury usually occurs with head trauma intense enough to cause unconsciousness. The most common type of ossicular injury associated with temporal bone fractures is a separation of the incudostapedial joint (Fig. 31–17). Dislocation of the incus occurs almost as often. In fact, it is not unusual for these two types of injuries to occur simultaneously. Stapedial crural fractures are less common (Fig. 31–18), with the malleus being the ossicle least likely to be injured (Fig. 31–19).

32

Tumors of the Ear and Temporal Bone

Ryan L. Van De Graaff, M.D., and Stephen P. Cass, M.D., M.P.H.

Tumors related to the temporal bone are relatively uncommon; with an estimated incidence of approximately 6 per million in adults.[11] Such tumors are even rarer in the pediatric population and also constitute only a very small percentage of head and neck tumors in children. In a review of 241 children with malignancy of the head and neck, the temporal bone was the primary site in only 1.5% of cases.[17] Moreover, of 25,000 pediatric neoplasms on file at the Armed Forces Institute of Pathology, only 100 are primary neoplasms of the ear. In addition to being rare, pediatric temporal bone lesions demonstrate two important attributes: an often-insidious clinical presentation and great variability of histologic type.

Neoplastic and paraneoplastic lesions of the temporal bone are often overlooked at the time of initial clinical presentation. Children who have temporal bone lesions most commonly present with signs and symptoms of acute otitis media, chronic otitis media, or external otitis. Aural polyps are commonly found and may initially be assumed to be of inflammatory nature, since most are the result of acute or chronic inflammatory disease of the middle ear. Physicians need to have a very high degree of suspicion for neoplastic lesions whenever a child does not improve after treatment, or has ear pain out of proportion or unrelated to infection. In addition, associated facial paralysis, sensorineural hearing loss, or vertigo should immediately alert the physician to the possibility of a neoplastic process. A tissue evaluation is critical for making the correct diagnosis. Unfortunately, a delay in diagnosis is common.

An incredibly wide spectrum of lesions have been reported to occasionally involve the ear and temporal bone in children (Table 32–1).[9, 16] Most of these lesions are rare in both adults and children; only a few affect children more commonly than adults. This chapter focuses on a few of the most common lesions affecting the ear and temporal bone in children: rhabdomyosarcoma, the most common malignancy of the ear in children; Langerhans cell histiocytosis; congenital cholesteatoma; fibrous dysplasia; and metastatic involvement of the temporal bone due to leukemia.

Rhabdomyosarcoma

Introduction

Rhabdomyosarcoma is the most common soft tissue sarcoma in infants and children, making up 5% to 15% of all neoplasms in children and 4% to 8% of all malignancies in children under 15 years old.[14] The peak incidence is between ages 2 and 5, with a second peak occurring between ages 15 and 19.[4] The head and neck are the most common sites of involvement, giving rise to approximately 50% of cases of pediatric rhabdomyosarcoma. Less than 10% of these tumors begin in the temporal bone, yet rhabdomyosarcoma is the most common pediatric malignancy of the temporal bone.[47]

Rhabdomyosarcoma has four histologic subtypes: embryonal, botryoid, alveolar, and pleomorphic; the embryonal form is the most common histologic subtype found in the head and neck. It is believed to arise from undifferentiated mesenchymal tissue rather than immature striated muscle tissue.[55] This explains why rhabdomyosarcoma may arise from areas where striated muscle is scant or absent such as in the middle ear, paranasal sinuses, or mastoid. Cross striations typical of muscle are uncommon, making the histologic diagnosis difficult. Up to 50% of proved cases of rhabdomyosarcoma are incorrectly diagnosed on the initial biopsy.

The natural history of rhabdomyosarcoma of the ear and temporal bone is of a highly aggressive, locally destructive, and invasive lesion with a high propensity for central nervous system involvement and distant metastatic spread by both lymphatic and hematogenous routes. Approximately 15% of patients with rhabdomyosarcoma involving the temporal bone have distant metastasis at the time of diagnosis. The lungs are the most common sites of metastasis, but the skeletal system, brain, breast, and intestines may be involved also. Regional lymph node spread occurs in approximately 5% to 20% of patients.[14]

Rhabdomyosarcoma involving the middle ear may spread by invasion and destruction of the fallopian canal. The latter is apparently a vulnerable area on the medial wall of the ear that, once penetrated, provides a direct

TABLE 32–1. Neoplastic and Paraneoplastic Lesions Reported Involving the Temporal Bone in Children

Benign Tumors	Malignant Tumors	Congenital and Paraneoplastic Conditions
Adenoma	Adenocarcinoma	Bone cyst, aneurysmal and unicameral
Carcinoid tumor	Adenoid cystic carcinoma	Carotid artery, aberrant and aneurysmal
Chondroblastoma	Squamous cell carcinoma	Choristoma, neural and salivary
Chondromyxoid fibroma	Rhabdomyosarcoma	Congenital and acquired cholesteatoma
Endodermal sinus tumor	Chondrosarcoma	Dermoid reparative granuloma
Ossifying fibroma	Ewing sarcoma	Fibrous dysplasia
Giant cell tumor	Fibrosarcoma	Langerhans cell histiocytosis
Glomus tumor	Desmoid tumor	Wegener granulomatosis
Granular cell tumor	Juvenile fibromatosis	
Hamartoma	Fibrous histiocytoma	
Hemangioma	Ganglioneuroblastoma	
Hemangiopericytoma	Granulocytic sarcoma	
Lipoma	Hemangiosarcoma	
Lymph angiomatosis	Liposarcoma	
Melanotic neuroectodermal tumor of infancy	Burkitt lymphoma	
Meningioma	Lymphosarcoma	
Neurofibroma	Metastatic neuroblastoma of adrenal gland origin	
Osteoblastoma		
Osteoma		
Acoustic schwannoma		
Chorda tympani schwannoma		
Facial nerve schwannoma		
Jugular foramen schwannoma		
Trigeminal schwannoma		
Teratoma		

Data from Bellet et al.[9]

channel for extension to the internal auditory canal and posterior fossa.[4, 36] Other potential routes of extension from the temporal bone include first, extension into the middle cranial fossa through the mastoid and tympanic tegmen to involve the temporal lobe. Second, after invasion of the labyrinth, the vestibular and cochlear aqueducts may provide pathways to the posterior fossa. Third, invasion may proceed inferiorly to involve the jugular bulb and carotid artery. Fourth, direct extension into the infratemporal fossa or nasopharynx may occur.

Clinical Presentation

Rhabdomyosarcoma of the temporal bone usually presents with insidious middle-ear involvement that mimics chronic otitis media with otorrhea, otalgia, seemingly innocuous-appearing inflammatory granulation tissue or aural polyp, or occasionally presumptive idiopathic Bell palsy. Prat and Gray[41] reviewed symptoms in 50 well-documented cases of temporal bone rhabdomyosarcoma reported in the literature. Patients' ages ranged from 2 to 12 years with an average of 4.4 years and a peak incidence at 3 years. The initial clinical findings in the 50 patients included a mass in the region of the ear (56%), polyp in the ear canal (54%), discharge from the ear (40%), bleeding from the ear (30%), earache (22%), hearing loss (14%), and seventh nerve palsy (14%). Because treatment is usually first directed at chronic otitis media, the interval of symptom onset to diagnosis averages almost 8 weeks and may be delayed for up to 6 months.[4, 53]

Thus, in a child, a history of otitis media with a polyp presenting in the ear canal that is unresponsive to antibiotics should raise the suspicion of tumor. Inflammatory granulation tissue in the external auditory canal (EAC) should never be thought of as innocuous. Aggressive treatment, including deep biopsy and close follow-up, is required in children.

Cranial nerve paralysis, especially facial nerve paralysis, should always be investigated for the possibility of an underlying neoplasm. In fact, about 30% of cases of temporal bone rhabdomyosarcoma are discovered from neurologic findings, notably facial nerve palsy.[41, 47] Rhabdomyosarcoma has been described as arising from the pneumatized air cells of the petrous ridge, giving rise to multiple cranial nerve palsies.[55]

Evaluation

In children with a suspected neoplasm of the middle ear and temporal bone, a tissue biopsy is the key to the diagnosis of rhabdomyosarcoma. The diagnostic evaluation should include a complete history, physical examination, neuro-otologic examination, complete blood cell count, chest radiograph, urinalysis, and blood chemistry profile, including liver enzymes. Computed tomographic (CT) scans should be obtained of the chest and any other suspected extrapulmonary metastatic site. Bone scan, liver spleen scan, bone marrow aspirate, and lumbar puncture may be necessary also to rule out metastatic disease.[41]

Proper evaluation of rhabdomyosarcoma of the ear and temporal bone truly requires both CT and magnetic resonance imaging (MRI).[31] CT provides the necessary bone detail to show the extent of the lesion and bone destruction within the temporal bone. The forte of MRI lies in its ability to delineate precisely the extent of rhabdomyosarcoma, guide fine-needle biopsy, and help plan radiation therapy. MRI is essential to demonstrate intracranial extension, especially in lesions in parameningeal regions.[27, 54]

CT evaluation of patients with suspected temporal bone rhabdomyosarcoma is usually performed with thin, 1.5-mm images. Bone and soft tissue algorithms with contrast material are used to detect bone destruction and enhance the image of possibly involved meninges. In general, rhabdomyosarcoma of the ear and temporal bone appears as a soft tissue mass within the middle ear and mastoid. The lesion is often poorly defined and homogeneous but distorts soft tissue planes and destroys bone. Intravenous contrast generally enhances rhabdomyosarcoma to the same degree as adjacent muscle.[27]

The most common MR appearance of rhabdomyosarcoma is that of a homogeneous mass, hyperintense to both muscle and fat on long TR/long TE (T_2-weighted) images and isointense or minimally hyperintense to muscle on short TR/short TE (T_1-weighted) images.[54] Rhabdomyosarcoma enhances markedly with gadolinium.

Rhabdomyosarcoma should be differentiated easily from benign lesions in the head and neck in children (e.g., brachial cleft cysts and thyroglossal duct cysts), since these lesions are usually of lower intensity than muscle on T_1-weighted images and high in intensity on T_2-weighted images.[27, 54]

Unfortunately, other relatively common tumors of the head and neck such as lymphoma or nasopharyngeal carcinoma often have the same signal characteristics as rhabdomyosarcomas. Lymphomas are usually homogeneous in signal intensity, and a heterogeneous signal would more likely suggest either nasopharyngeal carcinoma or rhabdomyosarcoma. High-grade malignancies of the paranasal sinuses or salivary glands often have lower signal intensity on T_2-weighted images. Liposarcomas usually have imaging characteristics similar to those of fat, with high intensity in T_1-weighted images and lower intensity on T_2-weighted images. The presence of areas of calcification seen as signal voids may suggest the diagnosis of chordoma, chondrosarcoma, chondroma, or osteosarcoma.[54]

Classification

The International Rhabdomyosarcoma Study Group system differs from other standard staging systems in that it is based on the extent of disease as defined by surgical resectability of the gross detectable tumor (whether or not resection was deemed feasible) and, if surgery was performed, on the extent of surgical resection[14]; therefore, this scheme relies partly on the surgical skills and disposition of the physician. It should be recognized that technical advances over time could alter the limits of surgical resectability and in turn change the stage of otherwise similar tumors.

In the International Rhabdomyosarcoma Study classification system, clinical group I includes patients with localized disease that is completely resected. Clinical group II includes patients who have regional disease that is grossly resected with or without involvement of local nodes, or grossly resected tumors with microscopic resid-

ual. Clinical group III includes patients with incomplete (partial) resection or in whom biopsy has shown gross residual disease. Clinical group IV includes patients with distant metastasis present at the outset of treatment. Data on rhabdomyosarcoma are also commonly stratified by site. Rhabdomyosarcoma of the temporal bone is included in the parameningeal site, which also includes the nasopharynx and paranasal sinuses. It has been consistently shown that the clinical group and primary site are the two most important predictors of survival.[14]

Treatment

Rhabdomyosarcoma should be treated aggressively because of its propensity to be locally invasive and to metastasize at a high rate. An attempt should be made to control the local tumor with surgery and/or radiotherapy; the risk of distant metastasis is controlled with chemotherapy. Treatment guidelines for these rare tumors have emerged largely from the International Rhabdomyosarcoma Study group protocols and have been based on the collective experience since 1972.

The role of surgery, which was once the only form of treatment before effective chemotherapeutic agents were discovered, has changed over time. Before the 1960s, surgery and radiotherapy often had dismal results for two reasons: distant failure due to metastases, and local failure due to the technical inability to completely resect the tumor, especially at the skull base. During the 1960s and 1970s, surgery for advanced head and neck rhabdomyosarcoma was rarely used; protocol-driven application of combined radiation therapy and chemotherapy alone has dramatically improved survival rates for children with rhabdomyosarcoma.

Because of the combined efforts of medical oncologists, radiotherapists, and surgeons, rhabdomyosarcoma continues to be an increasingly treatable lesion. Improved chemotherapeutic agents are better able to treat systemic micrometastases, thus leading to increased long-term survival. The 1980s and 1990s also brought the possibility of applying advanced surgical techniques, including craniofacial, skull base, and infratemporal fossa surgical approaches, to these tumors.[21, 31] Advanced surgical techniques should allow more cases to be staged as group I or II lesions, since complete resection of these tumors is now possible. The ability to move lesions from clinical stage III to clinical stages I and II should translate to improved survival.

The overall role of surgery is still controversial; however, the long-term effects of high-dose radiation to children, including arrested growth in the cranial facial skeleton and the appearance of new tumors within the field of radiation over time, are forcing oncologists to evaluate more carefully each individual patient in terms of the most appropriate treatment.[21, 31]

It is generally agreed that if the tumor is localized and can be excised completely or with only microscopic residual, without untoward disability or mutilation, such surgery should be performed.[4] This would place the patient in clinical group I or II with a good prognosis. Patients should also receive chemotherapy to control distant metastasis. In these patients, radiation therapy could be reserved for the possibility of future local recurrence. Extensive surgery should not be performed initially if vital structures need to be sacrificed. More aggressive surgical approaches with sacrifice of vital structures such as the facial nerve or the globe may be required to treat recurrent or residual disease after completion of combination therapy.[21, 31]

Patients whose tumors are not resectable (group III) or disseminated (group IV) should begin intense chemotherapy as soon as the diagnostic evaluation is completed. It may be possible to excise a tumor that, after chemotherapy, has become more amenable to surgery. Radiation therapy is also added to the protocol.

Prognosis

The long-term survival rates of patients with middle-ear or temporal bone rhabdomyosarcoma remain poor because of the anatomic location, proximity to the central nervous system, and delay in arriving at the correct diagnosis.[53] Children with rhabdomyosarcoma affecting the temporal bone fall into the parameningeal group of patients, and three-fourths of all patients with parameningeal involvement have clinical group III disease. There is a strong relationship between clinical group and survival, with decreasing survival from clinical group I to IV. Survival at 5 years decreases from approximately 82% in patients with localized group I tumors to approximately 24% in patients with metastatic disease (group IV).[14] These results re-emphasize the crucial role of postsurgically defined extent of disease (clinical group) in predicting survival. A primary parameningeal site also has a significantly poorer prognosis than other sites. The overall survival rate for clinical group III patients with parameningeal involvement is 45% to 66%.[14]

In the past, rhabdomyosarcoma of the temporal bone was thought to be seldom amenable to gross total surgical removal (clinical group I or II) because of its location. However, after central nervous system involvement has been ruled out by high resolution imaging and a spinal tap, the recent advances in cranial base surgery should allow for more aggressive surgical treatment of these lesions.[47]

It is interesting to note that, because of the high local relapse rate in the International Rhabdomyosarcoma Study I series of patients with parameningeal primary sites, the protocol was modified in the International Rhabdomyosarcoma Study II series. These protocol changes did not involve more aggressive surgery but introduced more aggressive multidrug chemotherapy.

Langerhans Cell Histiocytosis

Introduction

Langerhans cell histiocytosis is a more descriptive term now used to describe the disease commonly referred to as histiocytosis X, or more specifically the triad of eosinophilic granuloma, Hand-Schüller-Christian disease, and Letterer-Siwe disease.[6] The proliferating cell in all three disorders is the Langerhans cell, yet the clinical course ranges from benign to aggressive and lethal disease. The pathologic diagnosis of Langerhans cell histiocytosis requires the appearance of histiocytes or Langerhans cells under electron microscopy. Langerhans cells can be identified by the presence of Birbeck granules, which are laminar rod-shaped organelles present within the nuclear cytoplasm. A Langerhans cell is a histiocyte that normally acts as a tissue macrophage in the dermis and also interacts with lymphocytes in T-cell–dependent areas of lymph nodes. In the characteristic lesions of Langerhans cell histiocytosis, these cells appear to be responsible for both the release of osteoclastic activating factor and the eosinophilic infiltration. It is currently unknown whether Langerhans cell histiocytosis involves the proliferation of normal or pathologic Langerhans cells. The stimulus for proliferation is also unknown but may involve malignant transformation or possibly a metabolic, genetic, infectious, or immunologic etiology.

The term *eosinophilic granuloma* has been used to refer to the rather benign form of Langerhans cell histiocytosis characterized by unifocal or multifocal osseous lesions. The most common site of osseous involvement is the skull, but additional sites may involve the long bones, extremities, pelvis, ribs, mandible, maxilla, and vertebrae. Localized bone pain, often accompanied by a soft tissue mass, is a frequent presentation. Eosinophilic granuloma can occur at any age, but about one-half of patients are diagnosed before age 5, and most before age 20. The clinical course is typically benign, with an excellent prognosis.[3, 6, 15]

Hand-Schüller-Christian disease represents a more severe, systemic form of Langerhans cell histiocytosis. It classically involves the triad of diabetes insipidus, proptosis, and bone disease and is characterized by multifocal osseous lesions with limited extraskeletal involvement of skin, lymph nodes, and viscera. Children between the ages of 1 and 5 are typically afflicted, but the disease can present in young adulthood also. Hand-Schüller-Christian disease usually follows a chronic course with significant secondary morbidity.

Letterer-Siwe disease is a disseminated form of Langerhans cell histiocytosis with multiorgan involvement that characteristically presents with fever, rash, lymphadenopathy, hepatosplenomegaly, dyspnea, and blood dyscrasias in infants and children under age 3 years. Historically, the disease course is rapidly progressive, with a high mortality rate.

The overall incidence of Langerhans cell histiocytosis in the United States ranges from .05 to .5 cases per 100,000 children per year.[22] The reported incidence of temporal bone involvement in Langerhans cell histiocytosis ranges from 15% to 61% of cases, with an initial otologic presentation in as many as 25% (Table 32–2). Temporal bone involvement is more common in the more advanced forms of disease. In one clinical series,[15] 60% of the children presented with unifocal or multifocal osseous disease consistent with the diagnosis of classic eosinophilic granuloma, and 10% of these children presented with temporal bone involvement. Twenty percent of children presented with multifocal disease but without vital organ dysfunction (Hand-Schüller-Christian disease),

TABLE 32–2. Reported Incidence of Temporal Bone Involvement in Langerhans Cell Histiocytosis

Source	Incidence (%)	Initial Otologic Presentation (%)
Tos (1966)	61	25
McCaffrey (1979)	15	5
Schloss (1981)	40	—
Coutte (1984)	—	15
Anonsen (1987)	25	20
Cunningham (1989)	29	10
Alessi (1992)	28	9

and 75% of these manifested temporal bone involvement. Ten percent of the children had multifocal disease with vital organ dysfunction (Letterer-Siwe disease), and 40% of these had temporal bone involvement.

Clinical Presentation

Temporal bone involvement can be mistaken easily for more common conditions such as otitis externa, recurrent otitis media, chronic suppurative otitis media, or cholesteatoma. Common aural symptoms include otorrhea unresponsive to medical therapy, postauricular swelling, conductive hearing loss, and aural polyp or granulation tissue. The polyps associated with Langerhans cell histiocytosis generally can be differentiated from those arising in the setting of mastoiditis because they tend to arise in the mastoid and erode the posterosuperior canal wall. In addition, they often spare the middle ear and ossicles, leaving a normal tympanic membrane in place.[22]

Other symptoms such as facial nerve paralysis, vertigo, or sensorineural loss are rare.[6] These complications are usually due to disruption of vascular supply and not direct invasion of the otic capsule, which is resistant to destruction by granulomatous tissue even in the face of gross surrounding bony erosion. Direct labyrinthine invasion thus is rare, but should be suspected in children with known Langerhans cell histiocytosis and sensorineural hearing loss, nystagmus, vertigo, or behavior change.[38]

In a review by Coutte and associates[13] of 65 children with Langerhans cell histiocytosis, 10 presented with symptoms of recurrent otitis media. All children in this series were under the age of 3 on presentation. Aural granulation tissue or polyps are common findings in chronic otitis media regardless of the underlying cause, and in this clinical series a polyp was present in the middle ear or EAC in 50% of children. Biopsy of this tissue sometimes can be diagnostic, but the inflammatory changes in the middle ear also can be secondary and nonspecific, and in Langerhans cell histiocytosis the diagnosis may only be made from biopsy of the bony lesion. Interestingly, an elevated erythrocyte sedimentation rate was consistently seen in these children, a feature not usually seen in children presenting with aural polyps and cholesteatoma.

The radiologic findings in these children included decreased pneumatization and sclerosis of the mastoid, soft tissue in the middle ear, and blurring of the ossicles.

These nonspecific findings in combination with bone erosion often were regarded as suggestive of cholesteatoma; however, the additional presence of lytic bone lesions should be regarded as suggestive of Langerhans cell histiocytosis. MR imaging or these lesions demonstrates a mass isointense with brain on T_1-weighted images that enhances with contrast. A cystic component is often seen. These cysts give rounded, low T_1-weighted signals with peripheral postcontrast enhancement. The tumor usually also demonstrates an intermediate and heterogeneous T_2-weighted signal.[5]

Evaluation

Physicians not only should be aware of the ways in which Langerhans cell histiocytosis can present, but also realize the need for timely work-ups to expedite treatment. Even disease presenting as a unifocal condition should receive a complete evaluation, including general pediatric examination, hematologic evaluation, erythrocyte sedimentation rate, liver function test, urinalysis, chest radiography, and bone marrow biopsy. A skeletal survey or radionucleotide study to detect skeletal lesions should be included in the initial evaluation. It has been estimated that 30% of patients with unilateral temporal bone involvement will eventually have progressive osseous or nonosseous disease; therefore, follow-up is critical.[6]

As the mortality rate for Langerhans cell histiocytosis approaches 10%, it is important to recognize the prognostic indicators related to this disease. Poor prognosis is generally associated with age less than 1 year at presentation; systemic involvement, especially of the liver and bone marrow; and immune deficiency. A congenital form of this disease exists that can be rapidly fatal in intrauterine life or shortly after birth. Patients with ear involvement from this disease generally have a younger age at diagnosis and near totality of multisystem involvement (93%), which portends a poorer overall prognosis generally.[1, 50]

Treatment

There is a consensus in the literature that localized osseous lesions do not require vigorous therapy and can be managed with surgical curettage or low-dose radiation therapy. Because a biopsy specimen should be obtained for diagnosis, biopsy can be followed by curettage in most cases. Lesions limited to the mastoid cortex may be treated by cortical mastoidectomy. Some authors recommend observation for nondestructive lesions, because some were noted to remit spontaneously. Others have treated temporal bone lesions with intralesional steroids with good results.[22, 42] Large, destructive lesions with both middle-ear and mastoid involvement; smaller lesions arising within the petrous or tympanic bone; and recurrent residual temporal bone disease all warrant radiotherapy. Radiotherapy may be used alone or in combination with surgical curettage to treat all symptomatic temporal bone lesions regardless of size. Otorrhea, postauricular swelling, and conductive hearing loss typically clear or considerably improve after radiotherapy. A treatment course of 600 to

1000 cGy is recommended, dosages that appear to be clinically therapeutic while still being low enough to avoid the complications of radiation. Cure rates for unifocal osseous disease are greater than 90% regardless of the therapy chosen.[13] When the temporal bone is one of the multiple sites involved in multifocal osseous disease without visceral involvement, radiotherapy may be used as a single therapeutic tool also.

Because the late effects of radiotherapy in small children need to be considered, some advocate the use of chemotherapy first for the treatment of multifocal or surgically inaccessible disease. The most effective chemotherapeutic agent combinations are still being investigated in the current international trial of the Histiocytosis Society. For this reason, consultation with a pediatric oncologist is recommended for treatment of these patients.[7, 10]

The more common scenario of temporal bone involvement in the presence of multisystemic disease is more controversial. When otologic symptoms are severe or hearing is significantly compromised, local treatment may proceed as previously outlined. Multiorgan or systemic disease requires chemotherapy.

A significant response to initial therapy even in unifocal osseous Langerhans cell histiocytosis does not ensure a cure; long-term follow-up of these children is necessary. Monthly or bimonthly examinations for the first year are suggested, and a follow-up CT scan 1 year after therapy is recommended in the absence of clinical symptoms for children with temporal bone involvement.

Congenital Cholesteatoma

Congenital Middle-Ear Cholesteatoma

Congenital cholesteatoma of the middle ear is an uncommon clinical entity that classically presents as an asymptomatic white mass situated behind an intact tympanic membrane in the anterosuperior quadrant of the middle ear (Fig. 32–1). Congenital cholesteatomas are presumably present since birth and thus may be discovered any time during childhood. The most common age at diagnosis is 4 years old but ranges from infancy to the teens. Males are affected more often than females in a 3:1 ratio.[33] Often the diagnosis is made initially by a pediatrician on routine otoscopy of an asymptomatic child, or in a child with a history of unilateral or bilateral otitis media or hearing loss. Occasionally an otolaryngologist discovers congenital cholesteatoma on evaluation of a chronic middle-ear effusion that does not resolve after normal management, or at the time of insertion of ventilation tubes. The importance of early diagnosis of congenital cholesteatoma cannot be overemphasized. When the cholesteatoma is encapsulated and localized in the middle ear, a relatively simple procedure can be performed to remove it without affecting hearing or risking residual or recurrent cholesteatoma (Chap. 20).

A number of theories have been put forward regarding the origin of congenital cholesteatoma, including: (1) squamous epithelium from the external auditory meatus entering the middle ear by evasion through a pre-existing marginal perforation or retraction pocket,[44] (2) squamous

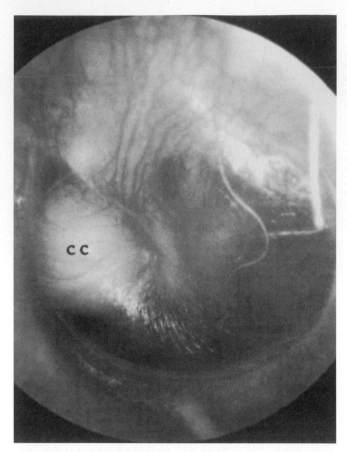

FIGURE 32–1. Otoscopic view of the left ear in a child showing an asymptomatic white mass (cc) situated behind an intact membrane in the anterosuperior quadrant of the middle ear. (From Levenson MJ, Michaels L, Parisier SC, Juarbe C. Congenital cholesteatomas in children: an embryologic correlation. Laryngoscope 98:953, 1988.)

metaplasia of the middle ear,[45] (3) ectodermal implants in the fusion planes of the first and second brachial arches,[39] and (4) amniotic fluid squamous debris developing into a primary cholesteatoma. However, the most likely theory is that congenital middle-ear cholesteatomas arise from the continued growth instead of regression of the epidermoid formation.[34, 35] The epidermoid formation is a normally occurring epidermoid cell rest at the junction of the eustachian tube with the middle ear near the anterior tympanic annulus. The origin of the epidermal rest can be traced to early fetal life and the ectoderm of the first brachial groove. In embryonic and early fetal life the epidermoid formation may act to organize the development of the tympanic membrane and middle ear.[28] After 33 weeks of gestation the epidermoid formation normally disappears. Wang and colleagues independently confirmed the existence of the epidermoid formation, which has also been observed in fetal ears in the collection at the Massachusetts Eye and Ear Infirmary.[33, 52]

Recently, epidermoid rests have been documented in fetuses older than 33 weeks gestation as well as in children up to the age of 10. In one study, 25 epidermoid rests were noted in 226 middle ears from fetuses and children, for an incidence of 11%. The clinical significance of these rests is unknown because they did not contain keratinizing epithelium.[25, 26, 29]

Presentation

Congenital middle-ear cholesteatoma usually originates anterior to the handle of the malleus in the anterior mesotympanum and, when small, usually consists of "closed" unilocular cysts surrounded by normal mucosa (Fig. 32–2). Although generally described as originating in the anterior mesotympanum, they can occur in the posterior quadrant.[24] Over time, the cholesteatoma enlarges as keratin debris accumulates within the cyst. The orifice of the eustachian tube can become obstructed, with resultant formation of middle-ear effusion and recurrent otitis media. There may be further growth with extension medial to the ossicles into the epitympanum and posterior mesotympanum, with erosion of the middle-ear ossicles. If the cyst-like structure of the congenital cholesteatoma ruptures, keratin is set free and may extend throughout the entire middle ear and temporal bone air

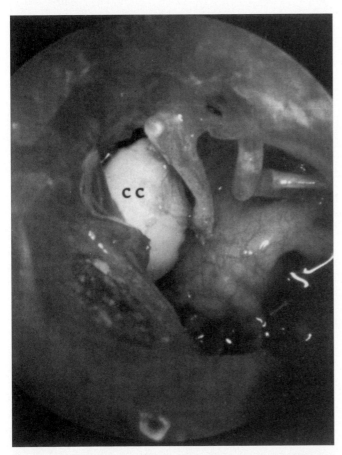

FIGURE 32–2. Surgical view of a congenital middle-ear cholesteatoma (cc). The congenital cholesteatoma is in the anterior mesotympanum and consists of a unilocular cyst. This surgical view corresponds to the otoscopic view shown in Figure 32–1. (From Levenson MJ, Michaels L, Parisier SC, Juarbe C. Congenital cholesteatomas in children: an embryologic correlation. Laryngoscope 98:953, 1988.)

cell system. This "open" congenital cholesteatoma is far more destructive and difficult to eradicate than the earlier stage of a closed cholesteatoma. After repeated infection and subsequent tympanic membrane perforation, it may be difficult to clearly differentiate an advanced open congenital cholesteatoma from an acquired cholesteatoma.

Treatment

Its site of origin, whether it is closed or open, and its size and degree of extension largely dictate the surgical approach for congenital cholesteatoma. CT is valuable in determining the exact position and extent of the cholesteatoma within the middle ear. If it is visualized during otoscopy and clearly localized to the anterosuperior quadrant, a CT scan may not be necessary, but CT is advisable when the superior or posterior limit of the cholesteatoma cannot be visualized by otoscopy.

Surgical removal can be performed using an extended tympanotomy for localized middle-ear disease, and a tympanoplasty and mastoidectomy for disease that has extended into the attic and mastoid. If the cholesteatoma is localized to the anterosuperior quadrant, a tympanomeatal flap may be elevated in such a way that the anterior and superior mesotympanum is exposed (Fig. 32–3). If there is limited extension of the cholesteatoma into the attic, a small atticotomy may be performed anteriorly (Fig. 32–4). Endoscopic surgical resection is another option.[51] If the congenital cholesteatoma is found to be rounded and closed, then this can usually be removed intact, and a second-look operation is not necessary. However, if the cholesteatoma has broken free from its cyst and there appears to be extension medial to the heads of the malleus or incus, a complete tympanoplasty and mastoidectomy is required for total excision, and a second-look operation may be required.

A study from the House Institute reviewed their experience treating 60 patients with congenital cholesteatoma. Of these patients, 24 had disease limited to the mesotympanum, whereas 18 had cholesteatoma in both the mesotympanum and epitympanum, two in the epitympanum alone, and 16 in the mesotympanum, epitympanum, and mastoid. Twenty percent of patients were treated with single-stage lateral graft tympanoplasty, whereas the remainder required multiple surgeries. Based on their experience with these extensive cholesteatomas, they recommend near total removal of the tympanic membrane to improve visualization and reduce the chance of residual disease involving the tympanic membrane.[18]

Congenital Petrous Apex Cholesteatoma

Less commonly, congenital cholesteatoma may occur in other regions of the temporal bone, most often involving the petrous apex. The cause of congenital cholesteatoma of the petrous apex is unknown. Gacek has suggested that it may arise from epithelial remnants trapped in the region of the foramen lacerum.[20] Because the petrous apex is a relatively silent region, the cholesteatoma may grow

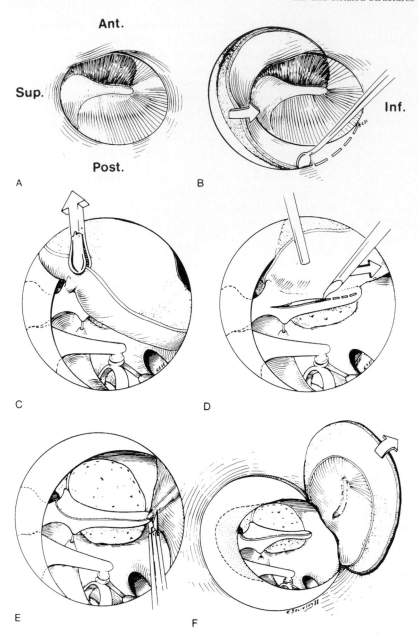

FIGURE 32–3. Surgical steps for exposure of a congenital middle-ear cholesteatoma. (From Levenson MJ, Michaels L, Parisier SC. Congenital cholesteatomas of the middle ear in children. Otolaryngol Clin North Am 22:950, 1989.)

to a rather large size before symptoms are noted. Initial symptoms are often associated with headache, but hearing loss and facial nerve spasms or paralysis are also common findings of congenital cholesteatoma of the petrous apex. Patients with this condition present at a later age than those with the middle-ear variety, often in the teens or twenties.

Congenital petrous apex cholesteatoma is only one of a number of abnormalities that may be found in the petrous apex. Others include cholesterol granuloma and cyst; mucous cyst; normal bone marrow; and neoplasms such as chondroma, chondrosarcoma, or chordoma.

Evaluation

CT and MRI are the most valuable diagnostic tests for detecting and evaluating petrous apex congenital choleste-

atoma.[23] CT is able to provide superior bone information regarding lesions of the petrous apex. The pattern of bone destruction and remodeling and the presence of contrast enhancement are characteristics that help differentiate lesions of this region. Benign lesions often reveal remodeling of cortical bone with dense hyperostotic or sclerotic margins reflecting their slow expansive growth. Contrast enhancement provides additional information for distinguishing neoplasms such as neuromas and meningiomas from nonenhancing cholesteatomas, cholesterol granulomas, mucoceles, and dermoids. Cholesterol granuloma is frequently isodense with brain, whereas cholesteatoma is hypodense with brain and isodense to cerebrospinal fluid. Mucoceles may be hypodense to brain unless infected and may be distinguished from cholesterol granuloma. Table 32–3 provides a summary of the CT and MRI characteristics that may help determine the nature of the lesion (Chap. 12).

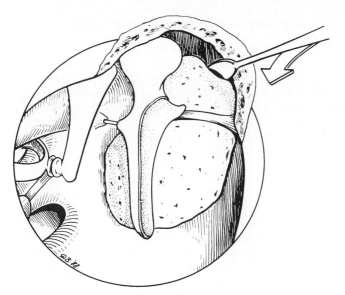

FIGURE 32–4. If the middle-ear cholesteatoma shows limited extension into an attic, the small atticotomy may be performed as shown. (From Levenson MJ, Michaels L, Parisier SC. Congenital cholesteatomas of the middle ear in children. Otolaryngol Clin North Am 22:951, 1989.)

Treatment

Treatment of petrous apex cholesteatoma is a surgical challenge.[8] Total resection of the cholesteatoma is generally recommended. This may be performed via a transcochlear approach if hearing is lost, or a middle fossa approach if hearing is present. If complete removal of the cholesteatoma matrix is not possible, the cholesteatoma should be widely exteriorized to the EAC.

Fibrous Dysplasia

Overview of Fibrous Dysplasia

Fibrous dysplasia is a congenital, nonfamilial, benign disorder of undetermined cause that accounts for 2.5% of all bony tumors and over 7% of all nonmalignant tumors of bone.[19] Liechtenstein first used the term *fibrous dysplasia* in 1938 but was not the first to report on this condition.[30]

In 1861 von Recklinghausen described a number of patients with the condition now called neurofibromatosis, but also included were some patients with striking bone lesions that we now call fibrous dysplasia. Albright in 1937 also described a group of patients with fibrous dysplasia, pigmented areas in related distributions of the skin, and precocious puberty in females. This triad has now become known as Albright syndrome and represents a subset of fibrous dysplasia.[2]

Histologically, fibrous dysplasia represents a locally circumscribed area of bone that displays an arrest of bone maturation in an immature stage of woven bone. The cause of this arrested bone maturation may be a disturbance of cancellous bone metabolism or possibly a misdifferentiation of the bone-forming mesenchyme.[43, 46] The abnormal tissue in fibrous dysplasia consists mostly of cells that are forming collagen with very little production of cancellous tissue. A more accurate term to describe fibrous dysplasia is fibro-osseous dysplasia or fibrous osteodysplasia; however, custom and usage dictate that the term fibrous dysplasia be retained. It is a proliferative process that sooner or later may extend beyond normal boundaries and produce bony expansion, distortion, compression, and structural weakness. Since fibrous dysplasia involves primarily cancellous but not cortical bone formation, the lesion replaces the normal cortex by erosion from within, leaving a surrounding shell of thin, normal cortical bone.

Fibrous dysplasia usually appears in late childhood, with an average age of onset of 10 years. It may begin with painless swellings, and about one third of children with bony lesions have café au lait or chestnut-colored nevi distributed in various areas of the body. Fibrous dysplasia can occur either in a single bone (monostotic) or in multiple bones (polyostotic). Both forms share an identical histologic appearance but distinguish themselves in their clinical course.[19, 30, 37, 46] The monostotic form of fibrous dysplasia is about four times more common than the polyostotic variety and 30 times more common than the complete Albright syndrome. The skin and endocrine changes described by Albright are extremely rare in the monostotic form of fibrous dysplasia. The monostotic form often comes to an arrest during puberty, whereas the polyostotic form is more likely to progress beyond the third decade and even later.

TABLE 32–3. CT/MR Imaging of the Petrous Apex

	CT Scan	Magnetic Resonance Imaging		Gadolinium Enhancement	Comments
		T_1	T_2		
Bone marrow	Dense	High intensity	Low intensity	Negative	
Cholesteatoma	Bone erosion, clearly defined punched-out region of bone destruction	Low intensity	High intensity	Negative	Contralateral petrous apex is often sclerotic
Mucous cyst	Dense without evidence of bone erosion	Decreased intensity	Increased intensity	Negative	
Cholesterol granuloma or cyst	Cystic dilatation	Increased intensity	Increased intensity	Negative	Contralateral apex is usually extensively pneumatized
Neoplasm	Shows evidence of irregular bone erosion	Decreased intensity	Decreased intensity	Increased intensity	

The incidence of craniofacial involvement by fibrous dysplasia is about 10% in monostotic disease and about 50% in polyostotic disease with moderate skeletal involvement, but reaches 100% in polyostotic disease with extensive skeletal involvement. Monostotic lesions tend to involve most commonly the ribs, femur, tibias, cranium, maxillas, and mandible. The cranial bones most frequently involved include the frontal and sphenoid bones, followed by the ethmoid, parietal, and occipital bones. The temporal bones are involved in about one-fifth of cases with cranial bone involvement; this is more often a manifestation of monostotic than polyostotic disease, with a ratio of about 2:1.[37] All four portions of the temporal bone (mastoid, tympanic, petrous, and squama) can be affected by fibrous dysplasia.

Radiographs characteristically demonstrate bony enlargement associated with sclerosis or a uniform ground-glass appearance of the augmented bone. Occasionally, areas of radiolucency and cortical thickening may be observed. CT imaging is most valuable for the diagnosis and delineation of temporal bone lesions; expansile growth, thinning of the surrounding cortical bone, and displacement rather than destruction of adjacent structures are characteristic features. The otic capsule is usually spared and may appear to float within the lesion.[49]

On MRI, fibrous dysplasia displays a low to intermediate signal on T_1-weighted and T_2-weighted images.[12] The lesions enhance with gadolinium but are only isointense or mildly hyperintense compared with fat. High clinical and pathologic activity appears to correlate with higher signal intensity on both T_1-weighted and T_2-weighted sequences and with stronger enhancement with gadolinium. MRI is more capable of sharply delineating the margins of the lesion than CT and thus may be used as an adjunct to better determine the true extent of the lesion once the diagnosis has been made.

Physicians should not depend solely on radiographic interpretations for the diagnosis of fibrous dysplasia but should also obtain histologic confirmation. Other lesions that may be similar in appearance to fibrous dysplasia on radiologic imaging include Paget's disease of bone, hemangiomas of bone, giant cell tumors, aneurysmal bone cysts, ossifying fibroma, and (especially in the temporal bone) eosinophilic granuloma and plasma cell myeloma.

Malignant degeneration has been reported to occur in some patients with fibrous dysplasia and appears to be greatest in males with polyostotic fibrous dysplasia. Among patients with the monostotic form the incidence of malignant degeneration is reported to be highest in the craniofacial region. The clinical signs of developing malignancy are pain, rapid swelling, and elevation of alkaline phosphatase levels. Significantly, half of all patients developing malignancy have received earlier treatment with radiotherapy. The incidence of sarcoma is increased 400 times above the spontaneous rate in patients who have received irradiation. Thus, radiation therapy should never be used to treat fibrous dysplasia. The overall risk of malignant change is estimated to be approximately one in 200 cases of fibrous dysplasia that are left untreated.[19]

Fibrous Dysplasia of the Temporal Bone

In a review of 69 patients with fibrous dysplasia of the temporal bone, there was a male to female ratio of about 2:1, 26 had the monostotic form, and 15 had the polyostotic form; in 28 patients the form of dysplasia was not specified.[37] The most common presenting symptoms in descending order of frequency were: (1) increase in size of the temporal bone, (2) progressive hearing loss, (3) progressive bony occlusion of the EAC, and (4) facial nerve paralysis.

Another study reviewed 43 patients with fibrous dysplasia of the temporal bone. They found that monostotic fibrous dysplasia accounted for 69.8%, polyostotic fibrous dysplasia 23.7%, and Albright syndrome 7% of these patients. The mean age of the patients presenting was 19.6 years and 60.4% of the patients were male. The presenting symptoms were hearing loss (79.1%), temporal bone mass (25.6%), unilateral otorrhea (13.9%), otalgia (6.9%), facial nerve paralysis (9.3%), and trismus (2.3%). The majority of patients with hearing loss were noted to have a conductive etiology, but 14% suffered from sensorineural hearing loss.[32]

Painless, slowly progressive deformity of the temporal bone is a pathognomonic feature of fibrous dysplasia. The increase in size of the temporal bone is often postauricular but may also be periauricular, preauricular, or supra-auricular. Hearing loss is most commonly conductive in nature, but sensorineural hearing loss may occur also. Stenosis of the ear canal is common and may give rise to a canal cholesteatoma and secondary complications such as abscess, labyrinthitis, or facial nerve paralysis. Trismus may occur, reflecting involvement of the temporomandibular joint. Otorrhea or symptoms of external otitis are rarely observed unless there is stenosis of the EAC.

Since this condition is a dysplasia but not a neoplasm, the presence of a histologically confirmed lesion does not necessarily justify immediate surgical intervention. Radical resection of the lesion is unnecessary for this benign disease, and radiation therapy is contraindicated because of its potential for inducing malignant transformation. Instead, fibrous dysplasia of the temporal bone or cranial base should be followed carefully at regular intervals. Conservative surgery should be performed when important function is threatened or deformity becomes substantial.

Deformities related to the expanding mass can be eliminated or minimized by surgery. Simply recontouring the expanded bone back to normal dimensions may be effective; however, approximately 25% of patients so treated show some recurrence of bony enlargement. Narrowing of the internal auditory meatus or fallopian canal may be associated with impairment of cranial nerve function, and in selected cases it may be necessary to perform surgical decompression.

Progressive stenosis of the EAC producing secondary cholesteatoma or hearing loss is an indication for reconstruction of the canal. Several technical factors may make the operation difficult.[49] These include diffuse bleeding from the dysplastic bone and the loss of normal surgical landmarks. The normal architecture of the mastoid is usually replaced by a solid mass of soft, spongy, crumbly, or gritty proliferative bone. Vital structures such as the facial nerve and inner ear may be encased by the dysplastic bone and thus may be more vulnerable to injury.

In the previously mentioned series of 43 patients, 86% of patients underwent at least one surgical procedure for canal stenosis. Restenosis occurred in 48.6% of these patients. Of those patents who underwent a transcanal or endaural canaloplasty, 88.9% restenosed. In those patients who received a postauricular canaloplasty combined with a mastoidectomy, usually canal wall down, the restenosis rate was 0% with at least 6-month follow-up. Thus, they recommend this approach for the management of canal stenosis in the presence of fibrous dysplasia.[32]

In cases of EAC occlusion, restenosis is common; in Nager and colleagues' review, 50% of patients were operated on only once, 25% twice, 15% three times, and almost 10% four times.[37] Three surgical principles appear to be helpful in the management of EAC stenosis. First, sufficient diseased bone must be removed to create an oversized ear canal. Second, denuded bone areas should be resurfaced with split-thickness skin grafts to prevent secondary soft tissue contractions. Third, a meatoplasty that will allow the widened canal to be examined and cleaned postoperatively is helpful.[49]

In summary, fibrous dysplasia may involve the temporal bone and commonly causes deformity of the temporal bone, progressive hearing loss, and progressive stenosis of the EAC. Serious secondary complications include formation of an EAC cholesteatoma with erosion of middle-ear ossicles, the inner ear, and the fallopian canal; blockage of the eustachian tube leading to recurrent serous otitis media; and cranial nerve neuropathy.

Leukemic Involvement of the Temporal Bone

Acute lymphocytic or lymphoblastic leukemia is the most common malignancy of childhood. Involvement of the temporal bone occurs in approximately 20% of leukemic patients, with a reported range of 16% to 35%.[40, 48, 57] Although unusual, the temporal bone manifestation may be the initial or presenting symptom or sign of leukemia.

Leukemic involvement of the temporal bone may present in a variety of ways, including auricular or external canal skin lesions, a red or thickened membrane, middle-ear effusions, otitis media, hearing loss or mastoiditis, and (very rarely) facial nerve paralysis.[56]

The histopathologic findings in temporal bones from patients with leukemia may be classified into three main categories: leukemic infiltration, hemorrhage, and infection.[40] There may be thickening and infiltration of the tympanic membrane, middle-ear, and mastoid mucosa. Infiltration of the bone marrow spaces of the petrous apex is very common. Perineural leukemic infiltration of the seventh and eighth cranial nerves has been observed; however, leukemic infiltration within the membranous labyrinth of the inner ear is rare. Hemorrhage is also commonly seen in patients with leukemia in the middle ear, mastoid, and eustachian tube; it was observed in the inner ear in only one case.[40]

Treatment is usually conservative, directed at any secondary infection. The temporal bone manifestations generally improve with treatment of the underlying leukemia.

SELECTED REFERENCES

Alessi DM, Maceri D. Histiocytosis X of the head and neck in a pediatric population. Arch Otolaryngol Head Neck Surg 118:945, 1992.

A contemporary review of the literature of histiocytosis X and review of 28 cases treated at the Children's Hospital of Los Angeles, California. Diagnostic criteria, prognostic factors, and treatment options are clearly outlined.

Bellet PS, Benton C, Matt BH, Myer CM. Evaluation of the ear canal, middle ear, temporal bone and cerebellopontine angle masses in infants, children and adolescents. Adv Pediatr 39:167, 1992.

A concisely written and comprehensive review of the wide variety of rarely reported neoplastic lesions affecting the temporal bone in children. This short article includes 158 references and thus can serve as a useful resource guide.

Crist WM, Garnsey L, Beltangady MS, et al. Prognosis in children with rhabdomyosarcoma: a report of the Intergroup Rhabdomyosarcoma Studies I and II. J Clin Oncol 8:442, 1990.

A comprehensive review of the previous rhabdomyosarcoma studies. Survival statistics and patient prognostic factors are outlined; summary data are presented in table form, and previous schemata of treatment, schedules, drugs, doses, and length of therapy are provided.

MacArthur CJ, McGill TJI, Healy GB. Pediatric head and neck rhabdomyosarcoma. Clin Pediatr (Phila) 31:66, 1992.

A concise and clearly written review of rhabdomyosarcoma.

Nager GT, Kennedy DW, Kopstein E. Fibrous dysplasia: a review of the disease and its manifestations in the temporal bone. Ann Otol Rhinol Laryngol 91:1, 1982.

A comprehensive, "must read" review of fibrous dysplasia and its manifestations in the temporal bone.

REFERENCES

1. Al-Ammar AY, Tewfik TL, Bond M, Schloss MD. Langerhans cell histiocytosis: pediatric head and neck study. J Otolaryngol 28:266, 1999.
2. Albright F, Butler AM, Hampton AO, Smith PH. Syndrome characterized by otitis fibrosa disseminata, areas of pigmentation and endocrine dysfunction, with precocious puberty in females: report of five cases. N Engl J Med 216:727, 1937.
3. Alessi DM, Maceri D. Histiocytosis X of the head and neck in a pediatric population. Arch Otolaryngol Head Neck Surg 118:945, 1992.
4. Anderson GJ, Tom LWC, Womer RB, et al. Rhabdomyosarcoma of the head and neck in children. Arch Otolaryngol Head Neck Surg 116:428, 1990.
5. Angeli SI, Luxford WM, Lo WW. Magnetic resonance imaging in the evaluation of Langerhans cell histiocytosis of the temporal bone: case report. Otolaryngol Head Neck Surg 114:120, 1996.
6. Anonsen CK, Donaldson SS. Langerhans cell histiocytosis of the head and neck. Laryngoscope 97:537, 1987.
7. Arceci RJ, Brenner MK, Pritchard J. Controversies and new approaches to treatment of Langerhans cell histiocytosis. Hem/Onc Clin North Am 12:339, 1998.
8. Atlas MD, Moffat DA, Hardy DG. Petrous apex cholesteatoma: diagnostic and treatment dilemmas. Laryngoscope 102:1363, 1992.
9. Bellet PS, Benton C, Matt BH, Myer CM. Evaluation of the ear canal, middle ear, temporal bone and cerebellopontine angle masses in infants, children and adolescents. Adv Pediatr 39:167, 1992.
10. Broadbent V, Gadner H. Current therapy for Langerhans' cell histiocytosis. Hem/Onc Clin North Am 12:339, 1998.
11. Brugler G. Case report: tumors presenting as aural polyps: a report of four cases. Pathology 24:315, 1992.

12. Casselman JW, DeJonge I, Neyt L, et al. MRI in craniofacial fibrous dysplasia. Neuroradiology 35:234, 1993.
13. Coutte A, Pedersen C, Bartholdy N, Thommesen P. Histiocytosis X: recurrent otitis media as a presenting symptom in children, with special references to cholesteatoma. Clin Otolaryngol 9:111, 1984.
14. Crist WM, Garnsey L, Beltangady MS, et al. Prognosis in children with rhabdomyosarcoma: a report of the Intergroup Rhabdomyosarcoma Studies I and II. J Clin Oncol 8:443, 1990.
15. Cunningham MJ, Curtin HD, Jaffe R, Stool SE. Otologic manifestations of Langerhans cell histiocytosis. Arch Otolaryngol Head Neck Surg 115:807, 1989.
16. Cunningham MJ, Myers EN. Tumors and tumorlike lesions of the ear and temporal bone in children. Ear Nose Throat J 67:726, 1988.
17. Cunningham MJ, Myers EN, Bluestone CD. Malignant tumors of the head and neck in children: a twenty year review. Int J Pediatr Otorhinolaryngol 13:279, 1987.
18. Doyle KJ, Luxford WM. Congenital aural cholesteatoma: Results of surgery in 60 cases. Laryngoscope 105:263, 1995.
19. Edgerton MT, Persing JA, Jane JA. The surgical treatment of fibrous dysplasia. Ann Surg 202:459, 1985.
20. Gacek RR. Diagnosis and management of primary tumors of the petrous apex. Ann Otol Rhinol Laryngol 84:1, 1975.
21. Healy GB, Upton J, Black P, Ferraro N. The role of surgery in rhabdomyosarcoma of the head and neck in children. Arch Otolaryngol Head Neck Surg 117:1185, 1991.
22. Irving RM, Broadbent V, Jones NS. Langerhans cell histiocytosis in childhood: management of head and neck manifestations. Laryngoscope 104:64, 1994.
23. Jackler RK, Parker DA. Radiographic differential diagnosis of petrous apex lesions. Am J Otol 13:561, 1992.
24. Karmarkar S, Bhatia S, Khashaba A, et al. Congenital cholesteatomas of the middle ear: a different experience. Am J Otol 17:288, 1996.
25. Karmody CS, Byahatti SV, Blevins N, et al. The origin of congenital cholesteatoma. Am J Otol 19:292, 1998.
26. Kayhan FT, Mutlu C, Schachern PA, et al. Significance of epidermoid formations in the middle ear in fetuses and children. Arch Otolaryngol Head Neck Surg 123:1293, 1997.
27. Latack JT, Hutchinson RJ, Heyn RM. Imaging of rhabdomyosarcoma of the head and neck. Am J Neuroradiol 8:353, 1987.
28. Levenson MJ, Michaels L, Parisier SC, Juarbe C. Congenital cholesteatomas in children: an embryologic correlation. Laryngoscope 98:949, 1988.
29. Levine JL, Wright CG, Pawlowski KS, Meyerhoff WL. Postnatal persistence of epidermoid rests in the human middle ear. Laryngoscope 108:70, 1998.
30. Liechtenstein L. Polyostotic fibrous dysplasia. Arch Surg 36:874, 1938.
31. MacArthur CJ, McGill TJI, Healy GB. Pediatric head and neck rhabdomyosarcoma. Clin Pediatr (Phila) 31:66, 1992.
32. Megerian CA, Sofferman RA, McKenna MJ, et al. Fibrous dysplasia of the temporal bone: ten new cases demonstrating the spectrum of otologic sequelae. Am J Otol 16:408, 1995.
33. McGill TJ, Merchant S, Healy GB, Friedman EM. Congenital cholesteatoma of the middle ear in children: a clinical and histopathological report. Laryngoscope 101:606, 1991.
34. Michaels L. An epidermoid formation in the developing middle ear: possible source of cholesteatoma. J Otolaryngol 15:69, 1986.
35. Michaels L. Origin of congenital cholesteatoma from a normally occurring epidermoid rest in the developing middle ear. Int J Pediatr Otorhinolaryngol 15:51, 1988.
36. Myers EN, Stool SE, Weltschew A. Rhabdomyosarcoma of the middle ear. Ann Otol Rhinol Laryngol 77:949, 1968.
37. Nager GT, Kennedy DW, Kopstein E. Fibrous dysplasia: a review of the disease and its manifestations in the temporal bone. Ann Otol Rhinol Laryngol 91:1, 1982.
38. Nanduri VR, Pritchard J, Chong WK, et al. Labyrinthine involvement in Langerhans cell histiocytosis. Int J Ped Otorhinolaryngol 46:109, 1998.
39. Paparella M, Rybak L. Congenital cholesteatoma. Otolaryngol Clin North Am 11:113, 1978.
40. Paparella MM, Berlinger NT, Oda M, et al. Otologic manifestations of leukemia. Laryngoscope 83:1510, 1973.
41. Prat J, Gray GF. Massive neuraxial spread of aural rhabdomyosarcoma. Arch Otolaryngol 103:301, 1977.
42. Quraishi MS, Blayney AW, Breatnach F. Aural symptoms as primary presentation of Langerhans cell histiocytosis. Clin Otolaryngol 18:317, 1993.
43. Reed RJ. Fibrous dysplasia of bone. Arch Pathol 75:480, 1963.
44. Rudei L. Cholesteatoma forming in the middle ear in animal experiments. Acta Otolaryngol (Stockh) 50:233, 1959.
45. Sade J, Babiacki A, Pinkus G. The metaplastic and congenital origin of cholesteatoma. Acta Otolaryngol (Stockh) 96:119, 1983.
46. Schlumberger HG. Fibrous dysplasia of single bones (monostotic fibrous dysplasia). Milit Surg 99:504, 1946.
47. Schwartz RH, Movassaghi N, Marion ED. Rhabdomyosarcoma of the middle ear: a wolf in sheep's clothing. Pediatrics 65:1131, 1980.
48. Shambron E, Finch SC. The auditory manifestations of leukemia. Yale J Biol Med 31:144, 1958.
49. Smouha EE, Edelstein DR, Parisier SC. Fibrous dysplasia involving the temporal bone: report of three new cases. Am J Otol 8:103, 1987.
50. Surico G, Muggeo P, Muggeo V, et al. Ear involvement in childhood Langerhans cell histiocytosis. Head Neck 22:42, 2000.
51. Tarabichi M. Endoscopic middle ear surgery. Ann Otol Rhinol Laryngol 108:39, 1999.
52. Wang RG, Hawke M, Kwok P. The epidermoid formation (Michael's structure) in the developing ear. J Otolaryngol 16:327, 1987.
53. Wiatrak BJ, Pensak ML. Rhabdomyosarcoma of the ear and temporal bone. Laryngoscope 99:1188, 1989.
54. Yousem DM, Lesa FJ, Bilaniuk LT, Zimmerman RI. Rhabdomyosarcoma in the head and neck: MR imaging evaluation. Radiology 177:683, 1990.
55. Zampa V, Mascalchi M, Giordaro GP, et al. Rhabdomyosarcoma of the petrous ridge: CT and MR imaging in an atypical case with multiple cranial nerve palsies. Acta Radiol 33:76, 1992.
56. Zappia JJ, Bunge FA, Koopmann CF Jr, McClatchy KD. Facial nerve paresis as the presenting symptom of leukemia. Int J Pediatr Otorhinolaryngol 19:259, 1990.
57. Zechner G, Altman F. Histological studies of the temporal bone in leukemia. Ann Otol Rhinol Laryngol 78:375, 1969.

Index

Note: Page numbers followed by b refer to boxes; page numbers followed by f refer to figures; page numbers followed by t refer to tables.

Aarskog syndrome
  characteristics of, 54
  ear anomalies in, 401
Abacavir, for HIV infection, 126
Abbé flap, for lip avulsion repair, 1340
Abdominal abnormalities, hearing impairment
    associated with, 312t
Aborigines. See Australian Aborigines.
ABR. See Auditory brain stem response (ABR).
Abrasion, definition of, 1752
Abscess
  apical, of teeth, 1693
  Bezold, 1681, 1682f
  Citelli (osteomyelitis of calvaria), 720
  epidural, computed tomography of, 235,
    236f
  extradural
    as complication of otitis media, 769,
      769f
    definition of, 483
  in head and neck spaces, differential diagno-
    sis of, computed tomography in, 1684
  intracerebral, due to sinusitis, 1028
  of brain. See Brain, abscess(es) of.
  of canine space, 1693
  of lung, 1493–1494
  of nasal septum, 1021–1022
  of neck
    computed tomography of, 1633–1634,
      1635f
    in bacterial cervical adenitis, needle aspira-
      tion of, 1669, 1669f
    ultrasonography of, 1633
  of parotid space, 1693
  peritonsillar, 1688–1689
  Pott, 1681
  retropharyngeal
    epiglottitis vs., 1488
    incision and drainage of, 1690–1691
    radiography of, 1683, 1684f
  subperiosteal. See Subperiosteal abscess.
Accutane (isotretinoin)
  ear anomalies associated with, 406
  sensorineural hearing loss associated with,
    799
Acetic acid
  for chronic suppurative otitis media, 712
  for external otitis, 467, 467t, 734
Acetyl-L-cysteine, N-. See N-acetyl-L-cysteine.
Acetylcholine, in vasomotor reaction, 909
Achalasia
  cricopharyngeal
    causes of, 1354, 1354t
    dysphagia in, 1295, 1354
    myotomy for, 1354

Achalasia (Continued)
    diagnosis of, 1296
    dysphagia associated with, 1135
    treatment of, 1296
Achondroplasia
  bone abnormalities in, 26–27, 26f
  ear anomalies in, 396
  hearing impairment associated with, 325t
Acids
  esophageal effects of, 1314. See also Esopha-
    gus, burns of.
  oropharyngeal effects of, 1347
Acinar cell carcinoma, of salivary glands, 1263
Acoustic damping, 1812
Acoustic immitance measurement, 195–202
  ear-canal volume estimates by, 202
  impedance vs. admittance in, 195–196
  in hearing aid selection, 1802
  in middle-ear effusion diagnosis, 200–202,
    221
  instrumentation for, 196
  probe-tone effects in, 196
  tympanometry in, 196–199, 69f, 198t
Acoustic middle-ear muscle reflex. See Acoustic
    reflex.
Acoustic nerve, action potential of, 163, 162f
Acoustic neurilemoma, sensorineural tinnitus
    due to, 363
Acoustic neurinoma, dizziness associated with,
    356
Acoustic neuroma, magnetic resonance imaging
    of, 237, 247f–248f
Acoustic reflectometry
  for otalgia, 294
  in middle ear effusion diagnosis, 201–202,
    204
Acoustic reflex, 203–205
  contralateral (crossed), 203
  functions of, 150
  immittance measured by, 195
  interpretation of, 204–205
  ipsilateral (uncrossed), 203
  middle ear impairment and, 204
  threshold of, 204
  type of hearing impairment and, 204
Acoustic rhinometry, 894–895
Acoustic trauma. See also Noise.
  definition of, 147
  hearing loss due to, 846
  types of, 846
Acousticofacial ganglion, 135
Acquired immunodeficiency syndrome (AIDS).
    See also Human immunodeficiency virus
    (HIV) infection.
  criteria for case definition of,
    clinical categories in, 114

Acquired immunodeficiency syndrome (AIDS)
    (Continued)
    expanded surveillance case definitions for,
      114
    indicator diseases for, 113–114
  Kaposi sarcoma in. See Kaposi sarcoma.
Acrocephalosyndactyly type I. See Apert syn-
    drome.
Acrocephalosyndactyly type II (Carpenter syn-
    drome), 87
Acrocephalosyndactyly type III. See Saethre-
    Chotzen syndrome.
Acrocephalosyndactyly type V. See Pfeiffer syn-
    drome.
Acrofacial dysostosis. See Nager syndrome.
Actin, in hair cell structure, 154
Actinomyces species
  cervical adenopathy associated with, 1673
  chronic otitis media due to, tympanic mem-
    brane perforation in, 710
Actinomycosis
  mouth ulcers associated with, 1356
  oropharyngeal, 1205
Action potential
  compound, 163
  whole nerve, 163, 162f
Acyclovir
  for facial paralysis, 385
  for pneumonia, in immunocompromised
    child, 1493
  for viral stomatitis, 1202
"Adam's apple," formation of, 1423
Adenitis, cervical. See Cervical adenitis.
Adenoid(s). See also Adenotonsillar hypertro-
    phy.
  atrophy of, velopharyngeal insufficiency asso-
    ciated with, 1793
  blood supply to, 1096
  development of, 1096
  hyperplasia of, nasal obstruction due to, 916
  hypertrophy of
    nasal obstruction due to, 916
    obstructive sleep apnea due to, 1224
    radiography of, 1113f
  immune functions of, 559
  innervation of, 1096
  location of, in nasopharynx, 1094
  radiography of, in newborn, 1097
Adenoid cystic carcinoma, bronchial, 1569
Adenoid facies, 1191
Adenoidectomy
  adverse effects of, 1219
  clinical studies of, 1213–1216
    Children's Hospital of Pittsburgh Tonsil
      and Adenoid Study in, 1213–1215
    efficacy of, 1214–1215

Education *(Continued)*
  bilingual bicultural education in, 1830
  deaf culture and, 335
  individualized program for, 1831, 1831t
  infants, 330
  laws for assurance of, 334
  models of, 1831–1832
  options for, 334
  preschool-age child, 334–335
  support services for, 1832
Edwards syndrome (trisomy 18)
  characteristics of, 38t
  ear anomalies in, 395
Efferent pathway, in coughing, 1395, 1396f
EGFR gene, Greig cephalopolysyndactyly, 16
Ekman syndrome. *See* Osteogenesis imperfecta.
Electrical burns. *See* Burns, electrical.
Electrocardiography, in evaluation of hearing
  loss, 318
Electrocochleography
  components of, 161–163, 162f
  in hearing assessment, 161–163, 162f, 212,
    214
Electromyography
  evoked, in facial paralysis, 377
  in facial paralysis, 377
  of esophageal disorders, 1294
  of vocal cords, 1387
Electronystagmography (ENG)
  caloric testing in, 282–283, 282f
  for dizziness, 281–283
  in acute labyrinthitis, 727
  ocular motor testing in, 281–282, 280f–281f
  positional testing in, 282
Electro-oculogram, in sleep apnea, 1229,
  1229f
ELISA (enzyme-linked immunosorbent assay)
  for allergic rhinitis, 1072
  in diagnosis of HIV infection, 119
Ellis–van Creveld syndrome, autosomal recessive inheritance in, 46t
Embolism
  air, due to vascular injuries, 1751
  pulmonary, 1501
Embolization
  arterial, for epistaxis, 930
  for arteriovenous malformations, 969
  for venous malformations, 968
  preoperative, for juvenile nasopharyngeal an-
    giofibroma, 1061
Embryo
  differential growth of, 3, 4f, 5
  esophageal development in, 1361–1365,
    1362f–1365f
  laryngeal development in, 1361–1365,
    1362f–1365f
  period of growth of, 3, 4f
  tracheal development in, 1361–1365, 1362f–
    1365f
Embryogenesis, schema for, 1083, 1084f
Embryology. *See under specific anatomic part.*
Embryoma, of salivary gland, 1645
Emphysema
  congenital lobar, 1456, 1456f
  obstructive, due to foreign body, 1548, 1549,
    1549f
  pulmonary interstitial
    due to alveolar rupture, 1502
    in acute respiratory distress syndrome,
      1450, 1450f
  subcutaneous
    associated with pneumomediastinum and
      pneumothorax, 1502
    due to tracheotomy, 1589, 1590, 1590f
    in laryngotracheal reconstruction, 1539
    palpation of, 1381

Empyema
  fungal, in pleural effusions, 1492
  subdural, as complication of otitis media,
    769–770
    clinical presentation and diagnosis of, 770
    definition of, 483
    management and outcome of, 770
Encephalitis
  due to rubeola, 1236
  focal otitic, as complication of otitis media,
    770
    definition of, 483
Encephalocele(s)
  basal
    diagnosis of, 980–981
    presentation of, 979
    types of, 983
  in orbital malformations, 944
  nasal, 979–984
    assessment of, 983, 983f
    diagnosis of, 980–982, 982f
    embryology of, 980, 981f–982f
    nasal glioma vs., 979
    occurrence of, 979
    skull base surgery and, 979
    treatment of, 983–984
  nasofrontal, in cleft palate, 1358, 1358f
  occipital, 979
  sincipital
    classification of, 982
    diagnosis of, 980–981
    presentation of, 979
    surgical treatment of, 982–983
Endochondral ossification, 24, 25f
Endocrine disorders
  due to glandular injuries, in neck, 1748
  dysphagia related to, 1134
  hearing impairment associated with, 313t
  oropharyngeal manifestation of, 1240
  salivary gland involvement in, 1261–1262
Endolymphatic duct, developmental anatomy
  of, 138
Endolymphatic potential (EP), in hair cell
  transduction, 152
Endolymphatic sac
  developmental anatomy of, 138
  tumor of, computed tomography of, 241,
    254f
Endoscopic surgery
  for juvenile nasopharyngeal angiofibroma,
    1061
  for nasal polyps, 1055
  for rhinosinusitis, 1014–1018
  for subperiosteal abscess, of orbit, 1027
Endoscopy. *See also* Bronchoscopy; Esophagos-
    copy; Laryngoscopy.
  cranial vault procedures via, 92
  fiberoptic
    for dysphagia evaluation, 1130
    of pharyngeal phase of swallowing, 1114
  flexible, for stridor evaluation, 1442–1443,
    1444t
  for aspiration, 1408
  for dysphagia evaluation, 1130
  for esophageal lacerations, 1342
  for eustachian tube function testing, 526
  for foreign body removal, 1550–1555
    analysis of problem in, 1550
    anesthesia for, 1328, 1552–1553
    esophagoscopes for, 1329
    in peripheral and upper lobes, 1554
    instrument selection for, 1550–1551,
      1551t, 1552f
    medical evaluation for, 1328
    medical history and physical examination
      before, 1550

Endoscopy *(Continued)*
  of coins, 1326, 1444f, 1445
  parent education for, 1328
  parental consultation in, 1550
  planning for, 1550–1552
  pointed objects in, 1554, 1554f
  practice extraction before, 1328
  rigid endoscopy in, 1444f, 1445
  stripping of object in, 1553
  technique of, 1553–1554
  unsuccessful, 1554
  for sleep apnea, 1230
  history of, 64
  in airway examination, 1385–1393
    bronchoscopy in, 1387–1393
    direct laryngoscopy in, 1385–1387, 1386f
    electromyography in, 1387
    in office examination, 1383–1384
    photographic documentation in, 1384
  in choanal atresia repair, 992
  in epistaxis, 929
  in nasal obstruction, 909
  in subglottic stenosis, 1521–1522
  injuries due to, 1342
  nasopharyngeal
    in nasal examination, 888, 888f
    in otitis media, 573
  rigid
    for foreign body removal, 1444f, 1445
    for stridor evaluation, 1445–1446
      estimation of subglottic size for, 1445f,
        1445t, 1446
      indications for, 1444t, 1445
    in airway examination, for neck injury,
      1749, 1749f
    in subglottic stenosis, 1467
Endothelins, 879
Endotoxin, in middle-ear fluids, 556
Endotracheal intubation. *See also* Intubation.
  flexible bronchoscopy through, 1393,
    1393f
  for acute croup, 1601
  for chronic ventilation, tracheotomy vs.,
    1584–1585
  for diaphragmatic hernia, 1453
  in laryngotracheal trauma, 1516
Endotracheal tube
  as stent, in anterior laryngotracheal decom-
    pression, 1524
  flexible bronchoscopy through, 1393, 1393f
  laser surgery and, 1577
  sizing of
    for acute croup, 1601
    for estimation of tracheostomy tube size,
      1586, 1586t–1587t
    for subglottic stenosis, 1467, 1468t, 1520,
      1522
  trauma from, chronic respiratory distress syn-
    drome due to, 1451
Enophthalmos, in orbital fractures, 1049
Enteric cysts, 1481
Enteric cytopathogenic human orphan (ECHO)
  virus, pharyngitis related to, 1120
Enterobacter aerogenes, brain abscess due to,
  771
Enterobacter cloacae, brain abscess due to, 771
Enterobacteriaceae, in pneumonia, 1491
Enuresis, nocturnal, in sleep apnea, 1227
Environment
  control of, for allergen avoidance, 1074–1075
  endemic cretinism associated with, 406
  evaluation of, in large airway disease, 1497
  nasal obstruction and rhinorrhea related to,
    911
  pollen persistence in, 1071–1072
  sound in, and hearing aid systems, 1803

Infant(s) *(Continued)*
   causes of, 328–330
     characterization of, 328
     confirmation of, 327–328
     evaluation of, 327–330
   illness of, developmental effects of, 1835
   laryngeal development in, 1366–1369,
     1367f–1368f
   positioning of, for otoscopy, 173, 174f
   risk of otitis media in, 489
   screening for hearing loss in
     indicators for, 219–220, 219t
     referral for auditory brain stem response
      testing, 217
   sleep apnea in, 1226
   tracheal development in, 1366–1369, 1367f–
     1368f
   tympanometry in, 202, 203f
Infection(s)
   acute, imaging studies of, 233–237, 234f–
     236f, 238f–239f
   after microtia reconstruction, 432
   bacterial. *See* Bacterial infection(s).
   dysphagia related to, 1131t, 1133–1134
   facial paralysis due to, 381–382
   fungal. *See* Fungal infection(s).
   genetic susceptibility to, 75
   in day care centers
     epidemiology of otitis media related to,
      492–493, 493t
     otitis media related to, 694
   in epistaxis, 925, 927f
   in reconstructive surgery, 99
     intracranial, 98
   molecular biologic diagnosis of, 74–75
   opportunistic, associated with AIDS and HIV
     infection, 113, 114t, 121
   orbital swelling due to, 944–945, 944f, 944t
   oropharyngeal manifestation of, 1234–1237,
     1235t
   prenatal, diseases associated with, 405
   susceptibility to, in otitis-prone children,
     487
   tracheal, after tracheotomy, 1591
   upper respiratory tract. *See* Upper respiratory
     tract infection(s).
   viral. *See* Viral infection(s).
Infectious Diseases Society of America, protocols of, for judicious use of antimicrobials,
   607, 607t
Infectious mononucleosis. *See* Mononucleosis,
   infectious.
Inflammation
   gram-negative sepsis and, 541–542
   in bacterial meningitis, 797
   in epistaxis, 925, 927f, 927t
   in middle ear, 542–543
   in pathogenesis of otitis media, 541–543
   management of, current studies of, 542
   mediators of, in allergic rhinitis, 1069, 1069t,
     1070
   meningitis and, 541–542
Inflammatory disorder(s)
   cervical adenopathy associated with, 1667–
     1674, 1667t
   chronic, computed tomography of, 237,
     244f–245f
   dysphagia related to, 1131t, 1133–1134
   nasal obstruction and rhinorrhea in, 912t,
     914–917
   neck masses due to, 1638, 1639f, 1640
   of larynx, hoarseness associated with, 1416
   of salivary glands, 1256–1262, 1257t
   orbital swelling due to, 944–945, 944f, 944t
   oropharyngeal manifestation of, 1235t, 1238–
     1239

Inflammatory pseudotumor
   bronchial, 1568
   subglottic, 1567
Inflation, of eustachian tube. *See* Eustachian
   tube, inflation of.
Inflation-deflation tympanometric test
   modified, 528–531, 530f–532f
   nine-step, 528, 529f
Influenza virus
   pharyngitis due to, 1120, 1199
   type A
     identification of, in middle ear and naso-
      pharynx, 553, 554t
     in lower respiratory tract infections, 1485t
     in pneumonia, 1490t
   type B
     in lower respiratory tract infections, 1485t
     in pneumonia, 1490t
Infrabullar cells, development of, 867
Infrahyoid muscles, development of, 1609
Infrared group amplification system, 1818
Infratemporal fossa tumors, otalgia referred
   from, 291
Infundibulum
   anterior, development of, 865
   development of, 864
Inhalant allergen(s), 1067
Inhalation burns, 1345–1347, 1754
Inheritance
   anticipation in, 50, 51f
   autosomal dominant. *See* Autosomal domi-
     nant inheritance.
   autosomal recessive. *See* Autosomal recessive
     inheritance.
   dynamic mutations in, 50, 51f, 52t
   imprinting in, 49, 49f, 50t
   in hereditary hearing impairment, 339–340,
     345–346, 346t
   mendelian
     diseases associated with, 42, 396–405
     principles of, 42, 42f
   mitochondrial, 48–49, 49f, 50t
   pedigree construction and analysis of, 43,
     44f–45f, 45
   phenocopy in, 50
   terminology of, 42–43
   uniparental disomy in, 49–50, 49t
   variations and exceptions to traditional men-
     delian inheritance, 48–50
   X-linked. *See* X-linked inheritance.
   Y-linked, 48, 48f, 49t
Injury(ies). *See* Trauma.
Inner ear. *See also* Ear(s); Middle ear.
   anatomy of, developmental, 137–141
   congenital anomaly(ies) of, 441–453
     classification of, 319, 319t
      history of, 441–442, 442f–443f, 443t
     cochlear implantation and, 452–453, 452f
     diagnosis of, 451–452
     enlarged cochlear aqueduct as, 450
     internal auditory canal anomalies in, 450–
      451
     large vestibular aqueduct as. *See* Vestibular
      aqueduct syndrome, large (LVAS).
     membranous labyrinth malformations in,
      443–446
     middle-ear anomalies associated with, 451,
      451f
     osseous labyrinth malformations in, 444–
      446
     perilymphatic fistula associated with, 458,
      459, 461f
     sensorineural hearing loss associated with,
      784–785, 785f
     structural, 143, 143t

Inner ear *(Continued)*
     vestibular labyrinth malformations in, 445–
      446
Innominate artery
   aberrant, tracheal compression by, 1473–
     1474, 1475f, 1651
     surgical treatment of, 1651, 1651f–1652f
   erosion of, after tracheotomy, 1590
   injury of
     during tracheotomy, 1589, 1589f
     evaluation and management of, 1750–1751
Insertions, chromosomal, 39
Inspection
   of airways, 1380–1381
   of neck, 1621
   of oropharynx, 1109–1110, 1110f–1111f
   of thorax, 1380
Inspiration, physiology of, 1373, 1373f
Institutions, for pediatric otolaryngology, 64–
   65, 65f
Insurance data, incidence of otitis media indicated by, 486, 486t
Integrin(s), in control of neural crest migration,
   15
Intensity, of sound
   difference limen for, 147
   neural encoding of, 156–157, 157f
Intercom, for monitoring of tracheotomy, 1595
Interferon(s)
   alpha, as antiviral agent, 599
   alpha-2a
     for hemangioma, 967
      of neck, 1643
      of subglottis or trachea, 1471
     for rhinitis prevention, 997
   as antiviral agents, 599
   for recurrent respiratory papillomatosis,
     1561–1562
   for subglottic hemangioma, 1564
   in middle-ear fluids, due to viral or bacterial
     infections, 556
Intergroup Rhabdomyosarcoma Study
   staging system of, 1714, 1714t
   treatment guidelines of, 1714
Interleukin(s), genes encoding, allergy related
   to, 1067
Internal auditory canal (IAC)
   abnormal, hearing loss related to
     radiographic findings in, 322
     size of IAC and, 450–451
   aplasia of, on computed tomography, 241,
     251f
   facial nerve in, 369–370, 370f, 371t
   thin bony plate of, on radiography, 321
   X-linked sensorineural hearing loss associated
     with, 241
International Liaison Committee on Resuscitation, policy statement of, on first aid for
   choking, 1545, 1545b
International Neuroblastoma Staging System
   Committee, 1725, 1725t
International Rhabdomyosarcoma Study classification system, 851
Interstitial lung disease, 1503
Intracranial complications of sinusitis, 1027–
   1029
Intramembranous ossification, 24, 25f
Intratympanic muscle(s)
   congenital anomalies of, 409–410
   tinnitus associated with, 364–365
Intraventricular hemorrhage, in acute respira-
   tory distress syndrome, 1450–1451
Intron, definition of, 79
Intubation. *See also* Extubation.
   during mandibular distraction procedure, 105
   endotracheal. *See* Endotracheal intubation.

Labyrinthitis (*Continued*)
  chronic
    clinical presentation and diagnosis of, 730
      management of, 730
    classification of, 480, 726
    vertigo due to, 353
Labyrinthitis ossificans, 730–731
  causes of, 730
  cochlear implantation and, 813–814
  computed tomography of, 237, 245f
  prevention of, 731
Laceration, definition of, 1749
Lacrimal sac, infection of, orbital swelling due
    to, 945
Lacrimoauriculodentodigital syndrome, ear
    anomalies in, 401–402
β-Lactam antibiotics, for brain abscess, 771
Lactamase. *See* Beta-lactamase production.
Lactate dehydrogenase, in middle ear infection,
    539
Lactoferrin, as product of immune reactions,
    561
Lambdoidal suture
  early or asymmetrical closure of
    cloverleaf skull due to, 85–86
    plagiocephaly due to, 84
  unilateral synostosis, characteristics of, 84
Lamellae, of lateral nasal wall, 864
Lamina papyracea, in endoscopic surgery, for
    rhinosinusitis, 1017
Lamina propria, developmental anatomy of,
    1421–1422, 1424f
Lamivudine, for HIV infection, 126
Langer-Giedion syndrome. *See* Tricho-rhino-
    phalangeal syndrome.
Langerhans cell histiocytosis, 821–823, 852–
    854
  cervical adenopathy associated with, 1675
  clinical presentation of, 821, 822f, 853
  computed tomography of, 237, 239, 241,
    249f
  diagnosis of, 821–822
  evaluation of, 853
  forms of, 852
  incidence of, 821, 852–853, 853t
  management of, 822–823
  neck manifestation of, 1645
  orbital swelling due to, 947
  oropharyngeal manifestation of, 1237
  treatment of, 853–854
Language. *See also* Speech.
  acquisition of, in hearing-impaired children,
    1828–1829
    instruction for, 1830
  cochlear implantation and, 815
  comprehension of
    evaluation of, 1775
    in language disorders, 1774
  development of
    chronic illness effects on, 1838
    delay of, in hearing-impaired infant, 329,
      330, 1825, 1828–1829
    otitis media effects on, 659, 689–695
  disorders of, 1773–1776
    causal factors in, 1774
    definition of, 1773–1774
    evaluation of, components of, 1775
    expressive, 1774
    prevalence of, 1774
    prognosis in, 1775–1776
    referral indicators for, 1774–1775
    treatment of, 1775
  production of, evaluation of, 1775
Language Development Survey, 1774–1775
Large vestibular aqueduct. *See* Vestibular aque-
    duct syndrome, large (LVAS).

Larsen syndrome
  characteristics of, 55
  ear anomalies in, 402
Laryngeal mirror, in airway examination, 1383
Laryngeal nerve
  recurrent
    anatomy of, 1737
    disorders of, hoarseness associated with,
      1416
    injury of
      birth trauma in, 1372, 1507
      causes of, 1507–1508
      surgical, hoarseness associated with,
        1417
    stretching of, in cardiovascular anomalies,
      1507
  superior, anatomy of, 1737
Laryngeal primordium, 1361, 1363f
Laryngitis
  characteristics of, 1487
  fungal, hoarseness associated with, 1416
  reflux, 1429–1430
  treatment of, 1487
Laryngocele(s)
  combined, 1463, 1464f
  definition of, 1363, 1463
  diagnosis of, 1463, 1465
  external, 1463, 1464f
  internal, 1463, 1464f
  pathogenesis of, 1463
  saccular cyst vs., 1463
  symptoms of, 1463
  treatment of, 1465
Laryngomalacia, 1460–1463
  causes of, developmental, 1368–1369
  complications of, 1463
  cough associated with, 1399–1400
  diagnosis of, 1461–1462
  hoarseness associated with, 1414
  in gastroesophageal reflux disease, 1304–
    1305
  pathophysiology of, 1461, 1461f
  physiology of, 1372
  stridor in
    bronchoscopy for, 1305
    characteristics of, 1460
    esophageal biopsy for, 1305
  symptoms of, 1460–1461
  terminology related to, 1460
  treatment of, 1462–1463, 1462f
Laryngopharyngoscope, flexible, in airway ex-
    amination, 1383
Laryngoplastic phonosurgery, 1509
Laryngopyocele, 1463
Laryngoscope
  flexible fiberoptic, types of, 1385, 1386f
  Jackson, in esophagoscopy, 1117
  Parsons, in foreign body removal, 1551
  size of, for foreign body removal, 1551,
    1551t
  Tucker side-slide, in foreign body removal,
    1551
Laryngoscopy
  direct
    for gastroesophageal reflux disease, 1295
    for hoarseness, 1418–1420
    for laryngomalacia, 1461, 1461f
    for oropharyngeal chemical injuries, 1347
    in airway examination, 1385–1387, 1386f
    in laryngotracheal trauma, 1514
    of hypopharynx, 1114
  flexible fiberoptic
    for voice disorders, 1428
    in laryngotracheal trauma, 1514
    in vocal cord paralysis, 1508
    of hypopharynx, 1112

Laryngoscopy (*Continued*)
  of nasopharynx, 1111, 1112f
  indirect, for hoarseness, 1418
  rigid telescope with, in vocal cord paralysis,
    1508
Laryngospasm
  in sudden infant death syndrome, 1368
  physiology of, 1368
Laryngostroboscopy, 1428
Laryngotracheal decompression, for subglottic
    stenosis. *See also* Cricoid cartilage grafting.
  goal of, 1468
  indications for, 1468
  procedure for, 1523–1524, 1525f
Laryngotracheal reconstruction (LTR)
  cartilage grafts in, voice effects of, 1431,
    1432
  for subglottic stenosis
    complications of, 1539–1540
    follow-up for, 1540
    revision of, 1537
    single-stage reconstruction in, 1529–1530
  voice disorders due to, 1431–1432, 1432t
Laryngotracheal trauma, 1511–1518
  adult injuries vs., 1511, 1512f
  blunt injuries in, 1511, 1512f–1513f, 1513
  complications of, 1517
  diagnosis of, 1514–1515
    endoscopy in, 1514
    history and physical examination in, 1514
    imaging in, 1514–1515, 1515f
  incidence of, 1511
  laryngotracheal separation in, 1511
  penetrating injuries in, 1513–1514
  tracheobronchial rupture in, 1511
  treatment of, 1515–1517, 1516f–1517f
Laryngotracheobronchitis. *See* Croup.
Laryngotracheoesophageal clefts, 1468–1469
  classification of, 1365, 1365f
  hoarseness associated with, 1415
  mortality in, 1469
  symptoms and diagnosis of, 1469
  treatment of, 1469, 1470f
Larynx. *See also* Vocal cord(s).
  aditus of, 1361, 1363
  anatomy of, developmental
    endolaryngeal/histologic studies of, 1421–
      1423, 1422f–1424f
    in adolescent, 1369–1370
    in child, 1369
    in embryo, 1361–1365, 1362f–1365f
    in fetus, 1365–1366, 1366f
    in infant, 1366–1369, 1367f–1368f
  atresia of
    complete, 1466
    types of, 1363, 1365
  clefts of, 1468–1469
  congenital defects of, dysphagia related to,
    1131t, 1132–1133
  cysts of, hoarseness associated with, 1414
  diversion/separation of, for chronic aspiration,
    1409–1410, 1410f
  edema of, subglottic and supraglottic, 1372
  eustachian tube compared with, 497
  evaluation of, in voice disorders, 1783
  foreign bodies of. *See also* Airway, foreign
    bodies of.
    location of, 1546
    signs and symptoms of, 1547, 1548f
    stridor associated with, 1442
  fractures of
    causes of, 1381
    in neck injury, 1749, 1749f
  functions of, 1371–1372, 1460
  growth of
    in adolescence, 1369

Larynx (*Continued*)
    relation of, to crown–heel length, 1423
    in cough reflex, 1371–1372
    inflammatory disorders of, hoarseness associated with, 1416
    innervation of, 1371
    musculature of, intrinsic, 1371
    nodule of, hoarseness due to, 1415–1416
    obstruction of, pathophysiology of, 1372
    otalgia referred from, 292
    palpation of, 1381
    papillomas of, dysphagia related to, 1134
    paralysis of. *See* Vocal cord(s), paralysis of.
    phonatory, development of, 1421–1425
    physiology of, 1371–1372, 1437
    reflexes of, 1371
    stents of, dysphagia related to, 1133
    structure of, 1371
    trauma to. *See also* Laryngotracheal trauma.
      crush injury of, repair of, 1516
      hoarseness associated with, 1416–1417
      in neck injuries, 1746
      postoperative, hoarseness associated with, 1417
    tumor(s) of, 1558–1567
      benign, 1559t, 1566–1567
      hoarseness due to, 1416
      malignant, 1559t, 1567
      neurogenic, 1566
      recurrent respiratory papillomatosis as, 1558–1563
      subglottic hemangioma as, 1563–1566
    vascular anomalies of, 1469–1471, 1471f
    webs of, 1465–1467
      hoarseness associated with, 1414–1415
      symptoms of, 1466, 1466f
      treatment of, 1466–1467
      velocardiofacial syndrome associated with, 1528
Laser beam, definition of, 1574
Laser(s), 1573–1581
    anesthesia with, 1577
    argon
      applications of, 1575
      for epistaxis, 930
      tissue effects of, 1575
    argon pump dye, applications of, 1576
    carbon dioxide (CO_2)
      applications of, 1576
      for choanal atresia, 992
      for hemangioma
        subglottic, 1565
        subglottic or tracheal, 1471
      for recurrent respiratory papillomatosis, 1561
      for subglottic stenosis, 1467–1468, 1526
      failure of, 1526, 1526t
    control of, by operator, 1574
    flashlamp-excited dye
      applications of, 1576
      for hemangiomas and vascular malformations, 1580–1581
      tissue effects of, 1575
    history of, 1573
    holmium:YAG, in rhinologic applications, 1578
    midline glossectomy via, for obstructive sleep apnea, 1232
    neodymium:yttrium-aluminum-garnet (Nd:YAG)
      applications of, 1576
      for choanal atresia, 992
      for hemangioma, 967, 1054
      for nasal papilloma, 1055
      tissue effects of, 1575
    physics of, 1573–1574

Laser(s) (*Continued*)
    potassium titanyl phosphate (KTP)
      applications of, 1575
      for hemangioma, 967
        subglottic, 1565
      for subglottic stenosis, 1467–1468
      for venous malformations, 968
      tissue effects of, 1575
    safety of, 1576–1577
    smoke plume from, protection against, 1577
    surgery with, 1575–1576
      cutaneous applications of, 1580–1581
      for port-wine stain, 967–968
      glottic applications of, 1580
      oral/oropharyngeal applications of, 1579
      otologic applications of, 1577–1578
      rhinologic applications of, 1578–1579
      tonsillectomy as, 1579–1580
      tracheal applications of, 1580
      tissue effects of, 1574–1575
LASHAL classification, of clefts, 950
Lasix (furosemide)
    for bronchopulmonary dysplasia, 1457
    sensorineural hearing loss associated with, 799
Lateral sinus
    development of, 866–867, 867f
    thrombosis of. *See* Thrombosis, of lateral sinus.
Lateralization, binaural, 159
    Weber test of, 160, 160f
Lathyrogens, for esophageal burns, 1317
Laurence-Moon-Biedl-Bardet syndrome, hearing impairment associated with, 326t
Lavage
    antral, for rhinosinusitis, 1013
    bronchoalveolar
      for gastroesophageal reflux disease, 1302
      for pneumonia, in immunocompromised child, 1493
    pulmonary, for pulmonary alveolar proteinosis, 1502
Le Fort I procedure, in midface distraction procedure, 106
Le Fort III procedure
    early advancement with, 100
    extracranial, 95, 97f
    in midface distraction procedure, 106
Lead
    from foreign bodies, 1034
    mouth ulcers associated with, 1356
Leber hereditary optic neuropathy
    as mitochondrial inheritance disorder, 50t
    as Y-linked syndrome, 49t
Leg(s), abnormalities of, hearing impairment associated with, 312t
Legionella pneumophila, in pneumonia, 1491
Leiomyoma, of tongue, 1274
Lentigines, multiple (in leopard syndrome), pterygium colli in, 1650
Lenz microphthalmia, ear anomalies in, 402
Leopard syndrome, pterygium colli in, 1650
Léri-Weill syndrome, ear anomalies in, 400
Lesch-Nyhan syndrome, dental dysplasia in, 1358
Letterer-Siwe disease, 852
Leucine aminopeptidase, in middle ear infection, 540
Leukemia
    lymphoid, orbital swelling due to, 948
    myeloid, orbital swelling due to, 948
    nasal lesions in, 1057
    oropharyngeal manifestation of, 1237
    temporal bone involvement by, 859
Leukoencephalopathy, dysphagia associated with, 1351, 1352

Leukoplakia, oral hairy, in HIV infection, 124–125, 1234–1235
    candidiasis vs., 122
Leukotriene(s), in allergic rhinitis, 1069, 1069t, 1070
Leukotriene receptor antagonist(s)
    for allergic rhinitis, 1078
    for asthma, 1499
Levator labii superioris alaeque nasi muscle, 876
Levator veli palatini muscle
    anatomy of, 506–507, 504f
      in newborn, 1088t, 1089
      of nasopharynx, 1094
      of palate, 1150, 1151t
      of velopharyngeal sphincter, 1789, 1790f–1791f
Levocabastine (Livostin), 1076
Levy-Hollister syndrome, ear anomalies in, 401–402
Lichen planus, 1247–1248, 1248f
Lifestyle changes, for gastroesophageal reflux disease, 1307
Lincomycin, pharmacology of, 595
Linear IgA disease, 1247
Lingual thyroid
    embryology of, 1154–1155, 1609
    functional tissue in, 1738
    management of, 1155
    size of, 1155, 1156f
Lingual tonsil(s)
    development of, 1096
    laser surgical removal of, 1579
Lip(s)
    anatomy of, in newborn, 1088
    electrical burns of
      mechanisms of, 1343, 1343f–1344f
      prevention of, 1345
      splinting for, 1344–1345, 1345f–1346f
      surgical reconstruction of, 964–965, 965f, 1344
    hemangioma of, inspection of, 1109, 1110f
    injuries of
      animal or human bites in, 1342–1343
      lacerations and avulsions in, 1339–1341
        surgical repair of
          full-thickness flaps in, 1340
          local and regional flaps in, 1340–1341
          wedge excision in, 1339–1340, 1340f
    lower, palsy of
      in acute otitis media, 381, 381f
      in congenital facial paralysis, 380
    neuromas of, 1273–1274
    position of, in orthodontic analysis, 1188–1189, 1189f
Lipopolysaccharide, monoclonal antibodies against, 542
Listening, off-frequency, 157
Listeria monocytogenes, in pneumonia, 1490t
Literacy development, in hearing-impaired children, 1831–1832
Livostin (levocabastine), 1076
Lobar emphysema, congenital, 1456, 1456f
Lobule
    anatomy of, developmental, 129, 130f
    congenital anomalies of, 407
    reconstruction of, in microtia, 427, 428f, 429
    thickened, with incudostapedial malunion, 404
Localization, monaural, 160–161
Locus heterogeneity, 43
London Dysmorphology Database, 324
Loop diuretics
    sensorineural hearing loss associated with, 799
    synergism of, with aminoglycosides, 798

Muscle(s). *See also specific muscle.*
  craniofacial, development of, 8, 11f
  disorders of, dysphagia related to, 1351t
  facial, distribution of, 33–34, 33f
  free transfer of, in rehabilitation of facial paralysis, 386
  intratympanic, congenital anomalies of, 409–410
  masseter or temporal, pedicled transposition of, in rehabilitation of facial paralysis, 386
  neck
    anomalies of, 1649–1650
    developmental anatomy of, 1609
Muscularis mucosae, esophageal, 1097
Musculoskeletal disorder(s), sensorineural hearing loss associated with, 782
Musculus uvulae
  absence of, velopharyngeal incompetence due to, 1150
  of velopharyngeal sphincter, 1789–1790, 1790f–1791f
Mutation(s)
  dynamic, 50, 52t
  hearing impairment associated with, screening for, 333
  of fibroblast growth factor (FGF) receptors, 16–17
  of homeobox (*HOX*) gene(s), 13
  of mitochondrial genes, 73
  of paired box (*PAX*) genes, 13–14, 13t
Myasthenia, neonatal
  hoarseness associated with, 1415
  transient, 1354
Myasthenia gravis
  characteristics of, 1353–1354
  vocal cord paralysis due to, 1507
Myasthenic syndromes, neurologic effects of, 1353
Mycobacterial cervical adenitis, 1670–1671
  diagnosis of, 1670–1671, 1671t
  nontuberculous
    clinical manifestations of, 1671, 1671f
    mycobacterial adenitis vs., 1670, 1671t
    treatment of, 1638, 1671
  tuberculous, 1670, 1672
Mycobacterial disease(s)
  chronic otitis media due to, tympanic membrane perforation in, 710
  in HIV infection, 122–123
  in immunodeficient states, 1493t
  otitis media associated with, 556
Mycobacterium avium-intracellulare, cervical adenopathy due to, 1638, 1670
Mycobacterium cheilonei, in otitis media, with effusion, 557
Mycobacterium scrofulaceum, in cervical adenitis, 1670
Mycobacterium tuberculosis. See also Tuberculosis.
  in head and neck space infections, 1683
  in otitis media, 555–556
Mycoplasma pneumoniae
  antimicrobial therapy for, 587
  cervical adenopathy associated with, 1672
  cough associated with, 1403
  in acute bronchitis, 1488
  otitis media and, 555
  pneumonia due to, 1490t, 1491
Myeloid leukemia, orbital swelling due to, 948
Myenteric plexus of Auerbach, 1290
MYH9 gene, in Usher syndrome, 72
MYO7A gene
  hereditary hearing impairment associated with, 341t, 789t
  in Usher syndrome, 72

MYO7A gene (*Continued*)
  nonsyndromic hereditary hearing impairment associated with, 788t, 789
    autosomal-recessive, 344t
  sensorineural hearing loss associated with, 787
MYO15 gene, nonsyndromic hereditary hearing impairment associated with, 788t, 790
  autosomal-recessive, 344t
Myoclonic epilepsy with ragged red fibers
  as mitochondrial inheritance disorder, 50t
  as Y-linked syndrome, 49t
Myoclonus, palatal
  in dysarthria, 1355
  tinnitus associated with, 364, 365t
Myopathy, hearing impairment associated with, 313t
Myosin genes, hereditary hearing impairment associated with, 343
Myositis ossificans, hearing impairment associated with, 325t
Myotomy, esophageal, for achalasia, 1296, 1409
Myotonic dystrophy
  as trinucleotide repeat disorder, 52t
  dysphagia associated with, 1354, 1354f
  facial paralysis due to, 384
Myringitis
  bullous, 467
  otalgia due to, 288
Myringoplasty
  for cholesteatoma, 745
  in tympanic membrane perforation repair, 701t, 704
Myringosclerosis, 750. *See also* Tympanosclerosis.
Myringotomy, 632–636
  complications and sequelae of, 635–636
  for facial paralysis, in otitis media, 732
  for labyrinthine fistula, 727
  for mastoiditis
    with osteitis, acute, 722, 723, 723t
    with periosteitis, 718
  for otitis media
    adhesive, 738
    indications for, 634–635
    intracranial complications of, 774
    studies of efficacy of, 632–633, 633t–634t
    tympanocentesis with, 634–635
    with effusion, 580–581
  for tympanic membrane atelectasis, 735
  laser surgery in, 1578
  procedure for, 635, 635f
  tympanostomy tube placement via. *See* Tympanostomy tube(s), insertion of.
  with amoxicillin, clinical trial of, 610, 611t
Myriodontium keratinophilum, allergic sinusitis due to, 1009
Myxofibroma(s), of sinuses, 1060
Myxoma, of jaw, 1277

N-acetyl-L-cysteine
  as mucolytic, pooling of secretions due to, 1377
  for esophageal burns, 1317
Nafcillin, with metronidazole, for complications of rhinosinusitis, 1029
Nager syndrome, 56, 88, 1159
Nares, primitive, 1085
Nasacort (triamcinolone acetonide), 1077t
Nasal ala, formation of, 1085
Nasal breathing, obligatory, in infants
  nasal obstruction and, 911–913
  reasons for, 912–913
  switching to mouth breathing from, 1095
Nasal capsule, chondrification and ossification of, 867–870, 869f

Nasal cavity
  cartilaginous cupular recess of, 899
  dimensions of, 878
  fetal
    primary, 862
    secondary, 862, 863f–864f
Nasal cycle
  in nasal obstruction, 911
  physiology of, 878
Nasal fin, replacement by mesenchyme, 1085
Nasal gland(s), types of, 879
Nasal glioma. *See* Glioma(s), nasal.
Nasal obstruction, 908–921. *See also* Airway obstruction.
  adenoidectomy for, clinical trial of, 1215
  airflow physiology and, 909–910
    as normal physiologic state, 910–911, 910t
  dysphagia related to, 1132
  endoscopy of, 909
  environmental stimuli in, 911
  evaluation of, 909
    algorithm for, 920–921, 920f
  from adenotonsillitis, intensive care management of, 1599
  in immunocompromised child, 1604
  historical perspective on, 908
  imaging of, 910
  in allergic rhinitis, 1071, 1073
  in disease, 911–921
    classification of, 911, 912t
    congenital, 912t, 913–914
    idiopathic, 912t, 919–920
    inflammatory, 912t, 914–917
    metabolic, 912t, 918–919
    neoplastic, 912t, 918
    traumatic, 912t, 917–918
  nasal cycle and, 911
  nasopulmonary reflex in, 911
  paradoxic, 911
  psychosomatic factors in, 911
  puberty and menstruation in, 911
  signs and symptoms of, 908
  vasomotor reaction in, 908–909
  without choanal atresia, 992
Nasal packing, for epistaxis, 929, 930f
Nasal pits, 861, 863f, 1085, 1085f
Nasal placode, 861, 862f, 1085
Nasal prominences
  lateral, fusion of, 1085
  midline, fusion of, 1085
Nasal provocation test, for allergic rhinitis, 1073
Nasal resonance. *See* Hypernasal resonance.
Nasal septum
  abscess of, 1021–1022
  development of, 869
  deviated, congenital, 993
  epistaxis and, 928
  examination of, 887–888
  hemangioma of, 1054
  hematoma of, 1021–1022
    cartilage necrosis due to, 1022
    in nasal fractures, evaluation of, 1046
    nasal obstruction due to, 917
    treatment of, 1022
  physiologic anatomy of, 878
  postnatal growth of, 31
  reconstructive surgery of, future growth concerns in, 974
Nasal valve
  airflow in, 876–878, 877f
  alterations in, 878
  in nasal obstruction, 909
Nasal wall, lateral, 862
  lamellae of, 864
Nasalis muscle, 876
Nasarel (flunisolide), 1077t

Neck (*Continued*)
parotid, 1618–1619
peritonsillar, 1619
pharyngomaxillary, 1617–1618, 1619f
potential, 1615–1616
retropharyngeal, 1617, 1616f–1617f
submandibular, 1617, 1618f
suprahyoid, 1617–1619
vascular, 1617
surface anatomy of, 1611–1612
triangles of
anterior, 1612, 1613f
posterior, 1612, 1613f
tumors of
cervical adenopathy associated with, 1674–1675
diagnosis of, 1644–1645, 1644f
malignant, 1703–1728
age distribution of, 1703, 1705t
anatomic locations of, 1703, 1706t
evaluation of, 1703–1705
histopathologic features of, 1703, 1704t
survival rate in, 1703, 1705t
treatment of, 1705
veins of, developmental anatomy of, 1606–1608
zones of, evaluation of, in penetrating injury, 1749, 1749t
Neck dissection
in melanoma, 1727
in salivary gland cancer, 1723
in thyroid carcinoma, 1743
modified, for thyroid carcinoma, 1720
Necrotizing (malignant) external otitis, 468–470
Necrotizing sialometaplasia, 1207
Necrotizing ulcerative gingivitis. *See* Gingivitis, acute necrotizing ulcerative (ANUG).
Needle(s)
large-bore, for emergency resuscitation, 1588, 1588f
tympanocentesis via, 571, 571f
Needle aspiration. *See also* Fine-needle aspiration (FNA).
in tympanocentesis, 571, 571f
of deep neck abscess, 1669, 1669f
of head and neck space masses, 1683, 1699
of peritonsillar abscess, 1689
Neisseria gonorrhoeae
in odontogenic cellulitis, 1179
pharyngitis due to, 1122, 1124
Neisseria meningitidis, 797–798
Neodymium:yttrium-aluminum-garnet (Nd:YAG) lasers. *See* Laser(s), neodymium:yttrium-aluminum-garnet (Nd:YAG).
Neomycin
allergic sensitization to, 302, 467
combined with other ototopical antibiotics, 301
for otitis externa, 467, 467t
ototoxicity of, 798
Neonatal intensive care
hearing impairment associated with, 324
sensorineural hearing loss associated with, 800
Neonate(s). *See* Newborn(s).
Neoplasms. *See* Tumor(s).
Nephritis, due to penicillin, 590
Nerve(s). *See also specific nerve.*
afferent pathway of, in coughing, 1395, 1396f
congenital anomalies of, 409, 410f
craniofacial, development of, 8, 9
efferent pathway of, in coughing, 1395, 1396f
injuries of
blunt, 1752–1753
initial evaluation of, 1748
penetrating, 1751

Nervous system. *See* Central nervous system.
Nervus intermedius, 135
Neural crest cells
abnormality due to failed migration of, 5, 6f
development of, 5, 6f
migration of, 5, 6f
in nasal development, 979, 980f
integrins in control of, 15
Neuralgia
glossopharyngeal, 1353
otalgia referred from, 293
rarity of, in children, 936
trigeminal
in children, 1353
otalgia referred from, 293
Neuraminidase, bacterial, in middle-ear fluids, 556
Neurapraxia, of facial nerve, 374
Neurilemoma, laryngeal, 1566
Neurinoma, acoustic, dizziness associated with, 356–357
Neuritis
retrobulbar, headache associated with, 937
vestibular, vertigo due to, 353
Neuroblastoma
of head and neck, 1724–1725
evaluation of, 1724
metastasis of, 1724, 1724f
prognosis in, 1725
staging of, 1725, 1725t
survival rate in, 1725
treatment of, 1724–1725
olfactory
nasal obstruction and rhinorrhea due to, 918
skull base surgery for, 1758–1759, 1759t
case example of, 1765–1766, 1769f
orbital swelling due to, 948
Neurocranium, 5
Neuroectodermal tumor of infancy, melanotic, 1276
Neurofibroma
laryngeal, 1566
of head and neck (malignant Schwannoma), 1716–1717
Neurofibromatosis
laryngeal neurofibroma associated with, 1566
malignant neurofibrosarcoma related to, 1716
oropharyngeal manifestation of, 1237, 1358
Neurofibromatosis 1
molecular advances in, 74
sensorineural hearing loss associated with, 786
Neurofibromatosis 2
acoustic neurinoma associated with, 356
molecular advances in, 74
sensorineural hearing loss associated with, 786
Neurologic defense mechanisms, pulmonary, 1377
Neurologic disorders, oropharyngeal, 1349–1359
clinical manifestations of, 1349–1350
dysarthria in, 1354–1355, 1355t
dysphagia in, 1351–1354, 1351t, 1353f–1354f, 1354t
examination of, 1349–1350
structural changes associated with, 1355–1359
Neurologic manifestations, of HIV infection, 125
Neuroma(s), of lips, 1273–1274
Neuromuscular junction disorders
dysarthria related to, 1355t
dysphagia related to, 1351t

Neuromuscular system
disorders of, dysphagia due to, 1131t, 1134–1135
postnatal growth of, 34
Neuropathy
auditory, screening for, 219
cranial, due to diphtheria, 1353
due to chemotherapy, 1353
hereditary, as microdeletion syndrome, 40t
Leber hereditary optic, 49t, 50t
motor, hearing impairment associated with, 313t
sensory, hearing impairment associated with, 313t
with ataxia and retinitis pigmentosa
as Y-linked syndrome, 49t
with ragged red fibers, as mitochondrial inheritance disorder, 50t
Neurotoxins, dysphagia associated with, 1136
Neurotransmitters
in lower esophageal sphincter relaxation, 1291
of nonadrenergic, noncholinergic (NANC) system, 882
Neutropenia
cyclic, oropharyngeal manifestation of, 1238
susceptibility to fungal infection in, 1492
Neutrophil(s)
chemotactic factor for, as product of immune reactions, 560
in middle ear effusions, 561
response of, in otitis media, 563
Neutrophilic dermatosis, acute febrile (Sweet syndrome), 1243
Nevus(i)
acquired, classification of, 971
congenital, 971
giant congenital, transformation to melanoma, 1727
melanocytic, plastic surgery for, 971
melanoma vs., 1727
white sponge, of mouth, 1272–1273
Nevus of Ota, 971
Newborn(s). *See also* Infant(s).
facial paralysis in, intrapartum, 845–846
hearing impairment in
drug-dependence in, 324–326
fetal alcohol syndrome in, 326–327
hereditary congenital, 324, 325t–601
nonhereditary congenital, 324–327
premature birth and neonatal intensive care in, 324
hearing loss in. *See also* Hearing loss.
care of, 327
cause of, 324–327
characterization of, 323–324
confirmation of, 322–323
evaluation of, 322–327
habilitation programs for, 323
hoarseness of, evaluation of, 1414–1415
lips of, anatomy of, 1088
nasal obstruction and rhinorrhea in, algorithm for evaluation of, 920–921, 920f
otoscopic examination of, 181, 183f–184f
palate of, anatomy of, 1088–1089, 1088f
pharynx of, anatomy of, 1094–1095, 1094f
pulmonary hypertension of, 1453–1454
respiratory disorders of, 1448–1458
risk of otitis media in, 488–489
screening for hearing loss in. *See also* Hearing, screening of.
for early identification and interventions, 217
otoacoustic emission testing in, 167
universal screening in, 217–218, 322–323
sleep apnea in, 1226

QT interval, prolonged, in Jervell and Lange-Nielsen syndrome, 318
Quinine, ototoxicity of, 309
Quinolone(s). *See* Fluoroquinolone(s).
Quinsy, tonsillectomy in, 1688–1689, 1689t

Rabies prophylaxis, for animal bites, 1343
"Raccoon eyes" (periorbital ecchymosis), 1042
Racial groups. *See also* Africans; Australian Aborigines; Inuit people; Native Americans.
    encephalocele occurrence in, 979
    otitis media in
        anthropologic, physiologic, and socioeconomic factors in, 491–492
        epidemiology of, 490–492
        management of, 658
Radiation
    exposure to
        salivary gland cancer related to, 1722
        squamous cell carcinoma related to, 1727
        thyroid carcinoma associated with, 1645, 1718, 1739–1740
    low-dose, for keloids, 966, 967f
Radiation therapy
    adverse effects of, dental care for, 1181
    for hemangiopericytoma, 1717
    for Hodgkin disease, 1708
    for nasopharyngeal carcinoma, 1726
    for neuroblastoma, 1725
    for rhabdomyosarcoma, 1714–1715
    for salivary gland cancer, 1723
    for subglottic hemangioma, 1564
    implications of, for skull base surgery, 1761
    of rhabdomyosarcoma, oral, 1274–1275
    oropharyngeal manifestation of, 1237
    thyroid carcinoma associated with, 1645
    xerostomia due to, 1181, 1253
Radioactive iodine (^{131}I), in ablation therapy, for thyroid carcinoma, 1720, 1740
Radioallergosorbent test (RAST), for allergic rhinitis, 1072
Radiography. *See also* Computed tomography (CT); Magnetic resonance imaging (MRI).
    Caldwell view in, 892, 889f
    cephalometric, of craniofacial complex, 31
    in airway examination, 1384–1385
    in cochlear implantation evaluation, 812
    in hearing loss evaluation, 319–322, 319t
    in nasal examination, 891–892, 889f–892f
    lateral view in, 892, 891f
    of airway, for stridor, 1443–1444, 1442f–1443f
    of airway obstruction, in sleep apnea, 1228
    of bronchiectasis, 1494
    of bronchopulmonary dysplasia, 1457, 1457f
    of cervical adenopathy, 1676–1677, 1676t
    of chest
        for hoarseness, 1418
        in pneumonia, 1491
        in subglottic stenosis, 1521
    of craniometaphyseal dysplasia, 825, 825f
    of esophagus
        contrast studies in, 1292
        in newborn, 1099
        plain chest radiograph in, 1292
        views in, 1114–1115, 1114f
    of eustachian tube, 516, 532, 533f–535f
    of foreign bodies
        in airway, 1440f–1441f, 1548–1550, 1549f
            diagnostic accuracy of, 1549–1550
        in esophagus, 1325
        in nose, 1033, 1033f
    of head and neck space infections, 1683
    of hypopharynx, 1114
    of laryngotracheal trauma, 1514

Radiography (*Continued*)
    of lungs, in respiratory distress syndrome, 1449, 1449f
    of maxillofacial trauma, 1043
    of nasopharynx, 1111–1112, 1113f
    of neck
        lateral, for aspiration, 1407
        plain films in, 1625, 1626f
    of neck masses, 1631–1633, 1632f
    of orbital swelling, 942–943, 943f
    of otitis media, 573
    of paranasal sinuses, 901–902
        computed tomography vs., 902
    of pharynx, in newborn, 1097
    of pneumothorax, in acute respiratory distress syndrome, 1450, 1451f
    of salivary glands, 1255
    of sinusitis, 1001–1002, 1002f–1003f
        recommendations on, 1001
    of subglottic stenosis, 1521
    of swallowing, 1130
    of temporal bone fracture, 836
    of tongue base, 1111
    of vocal cord paralysis, 1508–1509
    plain film, uses for, 230
    submentovertical view in, 892, 892f
    Waters view in, 892, 890f
Radionuclide scanning
    for cerebrospinal fluid leak, 840
    gastroesophageal (milk scan)
        for aspiration, 1407–1408
        for gastroesophageal reflux, 1294, 1302–1303
    of brain abscess, 771
    of neck masses, 1634–1635
    of neck structures, 1627–1628
    of necrotizing (malignant) external otitis, 469
    of salivary glands, 1628
    of thyroid carcinoma, 1719, 1740–1741
    of thyroid gland, 1627–1628
Rales, auscultation of, 1382
Ramsay Hunt syndrome, facial paralysis due to, 382
Ranula(s)
    after submandibular duct relocation, 1145, 1147f
    dysphagia related to, 1134
    laser surgery of, 1579
    of mouth, 1272, 1272f
    of salivary glands, 1261, 1261f
Rapid plasma reagin (RPR) test, for congenital syphilis, 998
Rapidly adapting receptor(s), in coughing, 1395
RAST (radioallergosorbent test), for allergic rhinitis, 1072
Reactance
    compliant, 195–196
    in impedance, 195
    mass, 195–196
    negative, 195
    positive, 195
Reading, in hearing-impaired children, 1831–1832
REAL classification, of Hodgkin disease, 1707, 1707t
Real-ear verification, of hearing aid selection, 1815–1816, 1816f
Recessive inheritance, 43. *See also* Autosomal recessive inheritance.
Recombinant DNA Advisory Committee, 76
Recombinant DNA technology, 70
Recombination, chromosomal, 69
Recurrent laryngeal nerve. *See* Laryngeal nerve, recurrent.
Recurrent respiratory papillomatosis. *See* Papillomatosis, recurrent respiratory.

Reed-Sternberg cells, in Hodgkin disease, 1705–1706
Reflex(es)
    as pulmonary defense mechanism, 1377–1378
    vestibulo-ocular, 273–274, 274f–275f
Reflux
    after esophageal atresia/tracheoesophageal fistula repair, antireflux procedure for, 1285–1286, 1286f
    gastroesophageal. *See* Gastroesophageal reflux (GER).
Reflux laryngitis, 1429–1430
Refsum syndrome, hearing impairment associated with, 326t
Reglan (metoclopramide), for gastroesophageal reflux disease, 1308, 1408
Rehabilitation, for facial paralysis, 385–386
Reissner membrane
    collapse of, in congenital rubella, 796
    of cochlear duct, 140
Reiter syndrome, oral effects of, 1207
Relapsing polychondritis, of external ear, 471–472
Relenza (zanamivir)
    efficacy of, 599
    for pneumonia, 1490
    for rhinitis, 996
Remodeling
    of bone, 24–27, 26f
    orbital, 30–31
Renal agenesis, bilateral, ear anomalies in, 404
Rendu-Osler-Weber disease, neurologic manifestation of, 1356
Replication, definition of, 79
Resistance
    in impedance, 195
    to antimicrobials. *See* Antimicrobial agent(s), resistance to.
Respiration. *See* Breathing.
Respiratory arrest, after tracheotomy, 1589–1590
Respiratory disorder(s). *See* Airway, disorders of.
Respiratory distress syndrome, 1449–1452
    clinical presentation of, 1449
    complications of, 1450–1451
        acute, 1450–1451
        chronic, 1451
    history of, in airway examination, 1379–1380
    pathophysiology of, 1449
    prevention of, 1451
    radiographic findings in, 1449, 1449f
    surfactant deficiency in. *See* Surfactant, deficiency of.
    treatment of, 1449–1450
Respiratory papillomatosis, recurrent. *See* Papillomatosis, recurrent respiratory.
Respiratory rate
    observation of, 1380–1381
    regulation of, components in, 1376–1377
Respiratory rhythm, observation of, 1381
Respiratory syncytial virus (RSV)
    antiviral agents for, in rhinitis, 996
    identification in middle ear and nasopharynx, 553, 554, 554t
    immunization for, 569
    in bronchiolitis, 1489
    in bronchopulmonary dysplasia, 1500
    in lower respiratory tract infections, 1485t
    in pneumonia, 1490t
    nasal obstruction due to, 915
    passive immunization for, 1490
Respiratory tract. *See* Airway; Lower respiratory tract; Upper respiratory tract infection(s).
Restriction enzyme, definition of, 79